WEST'S BUSINESS LAW

TEXT
CASES
LEGAL, ETHICAL, INTERNATIONAL, AND E-COMMERCE ENVIRONMENT
EIGHTH EDITION

Kenneth W. Clarkson

University of Miami

Roger LeRoy Miller

Institute for University Studies
Arlington, Texas

Gaylord A. Jentz

Herbert D. Kelleher Emeritus Professor in Business Law
University of Texas at Austin

Frank B. Cross

Herbert D. Kelleher Centennial Professor in Business Law
University of Texas at Austin

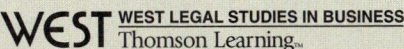

WEST LEGAL STUDIES IN BUSINESS
Thomson Learning™

Australia • Canada • Denmark • Japan • Mexico • New Zealand • Philippines
Puerto Rico • Singapore • South Africa • Spain • United Kingdom • United States

Vice President/Team Director: Jack Calhoun
Senior Acquisitions Editor: Rob Dewey
Senior Developmental Editor: Jan Lamar
Marketing Manager: Mike Worls
Production Editor: Bill Stryker
Manufacturing Coordinator: Charlene Taylor
Internal Design: Bill Stryker
Copy Editor: Suzie DeFazio
Compositor: Parkwood Composition Service
Printer: RR Donnelley & Sons Company
        Willard Manufacturing Division

Library of Congress Cataloging-in-Publication Data
West's business law: text, cases, legal, ethical, international, and e-commerce environment
/Kenneth W. Clarkson. . .[et al.].—8th ed.
    p. cm
Includes bibliographic references and index.

ISBN 0–324–01661–1 (package)   (alk. paper)
ISBN 0–324–07064–0 (text)

    1. Commercial law—United States—Cases. 2. Business law—United States—Cases.
    3. Trade regulation—United States—Cases. I. Clarkson, Kenneth W.

KF888.C55 2000
346.7307—dc21   00–035932

This book is printed on acid-free paper.

Contents in Brief

Contents

UNIT FIVE
Creditors' Rights and Bankruptcy 503

Chapter 28 ■ Secured Transactions 504

Chapter 29 ■ Other Creditors' Remedies and Suretyship 531

Chapter 30 ■ Bankruptcy Law 544

UNIT SIX
Agency 571

UNIT SEVEN
Business Organizations 615

UNIT NINE
Government Regulation 803

UNIT TEN
Property 865

CONCEPT SUMMARIES LIST

EXHIBITS LIST

EMERGING TRENDS IN TECHNOLOGY

EMERGING TRENDS IN BUSINESS LAW

Preface to the Instructor

Business law and, more generally, the legal environment of business have universal applicability. A student entering virtually any field of business must have at least a passing understanding of business law in order to function in the real world. Additionally, students preparing for a career in accounting, government and political science, economics, and even medicine can fruitfully use much of the information they learn in a business law and legal environment course. In fact, every individual throughout a lifetime can use a knowledge of contracts, real property law, landlord-tenant relationships, and the like. Consequently, we have fashioned this text as a useful "tool for living" for all students (including those taking the CPA exam).

Key Areas of Emphasis

To make sure that instructors and students alike can rely on the coverage, accuracy, and applicability of *West's Business Law*, Eighth Edition, we emphasize the following throughout the text:

- **Cyberlaw and E-Commerce**—Technology is affecting not only the world around us but also business law and the legal environment. We are proud to include a trend-setting chapter on cyberlaw and e-commerce (Chapter 9). In addition, throughout the text there are special features entitled *Emerging*

Trends in Technology. These features examine, for the most part, how the Internet has affected the law. Cyberlaw issues are also addressed in the CNN Update Video (discussed later in this Preface).

- **Access to Technology**—Just as the content of *West's Business Law* is up to date, so, too, is the manner in which the content can be accessed. Your students can use *West's Business Law* Interactive CD-ROM Edition (discussed below) to complement the printed text. Additionally, every chapter ends with a feature entitled *Law on the Web*, in which students are directed to useful online resources as well as Internet activities that they can perform to explore specific legal sources on the Web. Also, every *Focus on Legal Reasoning* (described below) and *Emerging Trends in Technology* presented in this text concludes with a brief section that refers students to relevant Web sites. Whenever possible, the citations to cases presented in the text are followed by a URL that students can use to access the case on an online database. Moreover, whenever a *Company Profile* is included in a case, the URL of the company's home page is indicated. To facilitate online research efforts by students, each student is provided with a complimentary booklet entitled *Online Legal Research*. As always, adopters of this book have free access to Westlaw®, which now includes two significant new features:

KeyCite and *Court Link*. The latter allows access to the dockets of more than 180 federal courts and 250 state courts. Westlaw® is now also available on the Internet at http:// www.westlaw.com. Finally, extensive online legal resources keyed to the text are found at the *West's Business Law* Web site at http://wbl.westbuslaw. com (discussed below).

■ **Limited Liability Companies and Limited Liability Partnerships**—Because these new forms of business organization are becoming increasingly important, we have included an entire chapter (Chapter 38) on their uses and restrictions.

■ **Entrepreneurship**—Chapter 53, entitled "Law for Entrepreneurs," allows your students to see how various elements of the book apply to small-business enterprises in a real-world context. This chapter has been thoroughly revised to reflect the changing legal environment for small-business owners.

■ **Comprehensiveness**—Virtually every important topic in business law and the legal environment is covered in this book. Our comprehensive coverage gives instructors complete flexibility in choosing those areas of the law and legal environment that they wish to emphasize.

■ **Authoritativeness**—We have fully researched every aspect of business law and the legal environment included in this text. Instructors can rely on its accuracy and can find references to case and statutory law, as needed, for any authority. Complete parallel citations are given throughout the text. An extensive set of appendices includes the Uniform Commercial Code and other uniform codes and statutes. Accuracy is the watchword of *West's Business Law*.

■ **Ethics**—In addition to the discussion of business ethics in Chapter 40 ("Ethics and Business Decision Making"), every unit ends with a *Focus on Ethics*. Additionally, selected cases within the text end with *Ethical Considerations*, and one chapter in every unit includes A *Question of Ethics* at the end of the *Questions and Case Problems* section.

■ **Critical Thinking and Legal Reasoning**—Your students' critical-thinking and legal-reasoning skills will be increased as they work through the numerous pedagogical devices within the book and its *Study Guide*. Questions concluding the *Emerging Trends* features and *Focus on Ethics* sections encourage critical thinking about the topics covered in those features. We have added two new features to the Eighth Edition, entitled *In Your Court* and

Focus on Legal Reasoning, that will help your students develop skills in the areas of legal reasoning and analysis, as well as critical thinking. (These features will be described in more detail later in the Preface.) Finally, each unit also concludes with a *Cumulative Business Hypothetical*—a set of questions relating to topics covered throughout the unit.

■ **International and Comparative Law**—Chapter 52 ("International and Comparative Law") helps your students gain a background in the international and comparative aspects of the law, an increasingly important subject. Additionally, selected cases in the text end with *International Considerations*. Finally, the entire unit on the law of sales and lease contracts integrates the United Nations Convention on Contracts for the International Sale of Goods (CISG).

■ **AACSB Curriculum Requirements**—This text explicitly addresses the AACSB's broad array of curriculum requirements by focusing on the global, political, ethical, social, environmental, technological, and cultural context of many of the cases presented. Specifically, selected cases are preceded by a *Historical and [Social, Economic, Political, Technological, Environmental, or International] Setting*, which places the case in a particular political, ethical, social, or other setting. Additionally, *Company Profiles* precede many of the cases in this edition. Finally, the materials in Unit One (Chapters 1 through 9) explore virtually every facet of the AACSB's curriculum requirements. The AACSB's emphasis on the global and ethical context of the law is addressed throughout the rest of the text in features already mentioned: the *International* and *Ethical Considerations* that follow selected cases and the *Focus on Ethics* section found at the end of each unit.

West's Business Law on the Web

When you visit our Web site at http://wbl.westbuslaw. com, you will find a broad array of teaching/learning resources, including the following:

■ A continually updated set of new cases, specifically keyed to each chapter in the text.

■ Current legal events updated regularly and keyed to chapters in this text.

■ Professors' Exchange: You will be able to e-mail your questions about *West's Business Law* to Frank Cross.

■ A variety of classroom materials.

- Internet Applications, which include at least one Internet activity for every chapter in the text.
- Online quizzes.
- Other contents will be added as we continue to improve our Web site to make it more useful for you and your students.

The *West's Business Law* Interactive CD–ROM Edition

Those of you who have used the CD-ROM edition of *West's Business Law* in the past will be impressed with the new edition. Instead of just placing the entire text on the CD-ROM, we have gone several steps further. While this edition of the CD-ROM retains the video segments, audio segments, and the like from the Seventh Edition, it organizes the information in a more appropriate, pedagogically sound manner. Your students will find sections on *Content, Chapters*, and *Applications*. No other business law and legal environment text offers such advanced learning capacity.

THE LATEST UCC REVISIONS

For this edition, we have included in the Uniform Commercial Code (UCC)—see Appendix C—the 1999 revision of Article 9 (Secured Transactions), which some states have already adopted. We have also retained the unrevised Article 9 so that users of this text can have the relevant law at hand for all states. Additionally, Appendix C includes all other revisions of the UCC that were completed prior to 1999, including the revised Article 5 and the revised Article 8.

An Effective Case Format

To ensure that *West's Business Law*, Eighth Edition, meets the needs of instructors and students alike, we have devoted significant efforts to finding cases that not only provide on-point illustrations of the principles of law discussed in the text but also are of high interest to students. Our selection includes classic, landmark cases as well as some of the most modern examples of business law. For those instructors who like to see the entire court opinions for cases presented in the text, we also offer a supplement called *Case Printouts to Accompany West's Business Law, Eighth Edition*. This supplement contains the output from Westlaw® (without headnotes) for virtually every case that is included in each chapter. If the instructor wishes, the full court opinions may be copied and handed out to students.

BASIC CASE FORMAT

Each case in *West's Business Law* is presented in the following basic format:

- *Case Title and Full Case Citation*—The case title and full case citation (including all parallel citations) are presented at the beginning of each case. When available, a URL for a Web site that includes the case is given.
- *Background and Facts*—This section contains a summary, in the authors' own words, of the events leading up to the lawsuit.
- *In the Language of the Court*—Following the summary of the background of the case, an excerpt from the actual court opinion is presented—in a contrasting type to differentiate it from the surrounding textual material. Whenever the court opinion contains a term or phrase that may be difficult for the student to understand, we provide a brief explanation of the term in brackets. When important phrases and sentences are italicized, bracketed notes clearly indicate that the emphasis was added by the authors, not by the court.
- *Decision and Remedy*—In this section, the authors summarize, in their own words, the outcome of the case.

ADDITIONAL SECTIONS IN THE CASES

Many cases include one of the following sections, which have already been described.

- *Company Profiles*—Numerous companies are profiled before appropriate cases. Each profile, which describes the history of the company involved in a particular case, is designed to give your students the real-world context of the case before the court. When available, the URL for the profiled company's Web site is given.
- *Historical and [Social or Other] Settings*—When appropriate, the global, political, ethical, social, environmental, technological, or cultural context of a case is presented in one of these settings.
- *Ethical Considerations*—These sections, as mentioned previously, discuss ethical aspects of the law or laws under consideration.
- *International Considerations*—As explained above,

these sections let your students know how the particular issue at bar is treated in other countries.

Other Special Features of this Text

We have included in *West's Business Law*, Eighth Edition, a number of additional pedagogical devices and special features, including those discussed here.

EMERGING TRENDS

Presented throughout this text are over two dozen features entitled *Emerging Trends in Technology*. These new features examine the effect of the Internet on business law and the legal environment. There are also features entitled *Emerging Trends in Business Law*, which focus on other types of emerging developments in business law and the legal environment. Here are some examples of these features:

Emerging Trends in Technology

- Taxation Issues in Cyberspace (Chapter 4).
- Electronic Monitoring in the Workplace (Chapter 41).

Emerging Trends in Business Law

- The Enforcement of Preliminary Agreements (Chapter 11).
- Employee Rights for Contingent Workers (Chapter 31).

CONCEPT SUMMARIES

Whenever key areas of the law need additional emphasis, we provide a *Concept Summary*. These summaries have always been a popular pedagogical tool in this text. There are now more than fifty of these summaries, including the following:

- Types of Crimes (Chapter 8).
- Violations of Virtual Property Rights (Chapter 9).
- Equitable Remedies (Chapter 18).
- Valid Defenses against Holders of Negotiable Instruments (Chapter 26).

EXHIBITS

When appropriate, we have illustrated important aspects of the law in graphic or summary form in exhibits. In all, over ninety exhibits are featured in

West's Business Law, Eighth Edition, including the following:

- Areas of the Law That May Affect Business Decision Making (Exhibit 1–6).
- Forms of Intellectual Property (Exhibit 7–1).
- Major Changes in Revised Article 9 (Exhibit 28–6).
- Major Forms of Business Compared (Exhibit 38–2).

VOCABULARY STRESSED

In addition to including bracketed explanations of difficult terms and phrases within the court opinions presented in the text, we also boldface and fully define every important legal term when it is first introduced. Additionally, at the end of each chapter, all terms that were boldfaced within the chapter are listed in alphabetical order under the heading *Terms and Concepts to Review*. The page on which the term is defined is given after each term. For selected terms, particularly those of Latin origin, a special pronunciation guide has been included in footnotes within the chapters as well as in the Glossary at the end of the text.

QUESTIONS AND CASE PROBLEMS

Every chapter in this text ends with nine or ten questions and case problems. Normally, the first three to five of these are hypothetical questions. The remainder are actual case problems, many of which are from the late 1990s. Concluding each *Questions and Case Problems* section is a special problem entitled *In Your Court*. The problem poses a hypothetical situation and then asks a series of questions that require the student to engage in legal reasoning and analysis. In selected chapters, *A Question of Ethics* is also included at the end of the *Questions and Case Problems* section. Complete answers are given in a separate manual for all questions and case problems in the text.

ALTERNATE PROBLEM SETS WITH ANSWERS

To expand the number of case problems available to instructors, for each chapter of *West's Business Law*, Eighth Edition, we have created a set of five or more alternate case problems. These alternate case problems, along with their answers, are included at the end of the manual accompanying this text entitled *Answers to Questions and Case Problems and*

Alternate Problem Sets with Answers. The alternate case problems and their answers are presented on perforated pages for easy removal and copying.

SPECIAL UNIT-ENDING MATERIALS

Each of the eleven units in this text concludes with the following special features:

- **Cumulative Business Hypothetical**—In addition to the hypotheticals in the *Questions and Case Problems* section, we include at the end of each unit a *Cumulative Business Hypothetical.* This feature first posits a scenario—such as a small business just getting under way—and then poses a series of questions for the student to answer. The questions provide an excellent means of reviewing legal concepts covered throughout the unit. Suggested answers for these hypotheticals are also included in the *Answers to Questions and Case Problems.*

- **Extended Case Studies and Case Briefing Assignments**—Just following the *Cumulative Business Hypothetical* we present an extended case study entitled *Focus on Legal Reasoning.* The subtitle of each *Focus* gives the full case title of the case being studied. The feature then opens with an *Introduction* followed by a *Case Background.* We then present excerpts from court's majority and dissenting opinions (including legal sources cited by the justices). Following the excerpts, a series of questions ask the student to perform tasks involving legal research, legal analysis, critical thinking, and case briefing. The feature concludes with a *Going Online* section, in which students are referred to one or more Web sites for further study of the case or the issue it addresses.

- **Focus on Ethics**—The unit-ending materials conclude with a *Focus on Ethics.* These sections address ethical aspects of the law discussed in the preceding unit. Each section is designed to elicit comments and discussion from the student-readers on ethical issues. For this reason, each *Focus* ends with a set of discussion questions.

APPENDICES

Because the majority of students keep their business law texts as a reference source, we have included a full set of appendices. In all, the following appendices are included in *West's Business Law,* Eighth Edition:

A How to Brief Cases and Analyze Case Problems.
B The Constitution of the United States.
C The Uniform Commercial Code—including the revised Article 9.
D The United Nations Convention on Contracts for the International Sale of Goods (Excerpts).
E The Uniform Partnership Act.
F The Revised Uniform Partnership Act (Excerpts).
G The Revised Uniform Limited Partnership Act.
H The Revised Model Business Corporation Act (Excerpts).
I The Uniform Limited Liability Company Act (Excerpts).
J The Securities Act of 1933 (Excerpts).
K The Securities Exchange Act of 1934 (Excerpts).
L Title VII of the Civil Rights Act of 1964 (Excerpts).
M The Americans with Disabilities Act of 1990 (Excerpts).
N The Civil Rights Act of 1991 (Excerpts).
O The Administrative Procedure Act of 1946 (Excerpts).
P The General Agreement on Tariffs and Trade (Excerpts).
Q The North American Free Trade Agreement (Excerpts).
R Spanish Equivalents for Important Legal Terms in English.

Revised Appendix A. We have included in Appendix A a new section entitled "Analyzing Case Problems." This section contains tips for students on how they can "get started" when they are assigned to work on case problems. Included in the section is a discussion of the IRAC method of case analysis and an example of how students can apply this method when analyzing case problems.

Revised Appendix C. As mentioned earlier, this edition includes the 1999 version of the Uniform Commercial Code, including both the revised and unrevised versions of Article 9 (Secured Transactions). For clarity and easy reference, the pages containing the revised version are color tabbed on the edges.

The Most Complete Supplements Package Available Today

This edition of *West's Business Law* is accompanied by an expansive number of teaching and learning supplements. We have already mentioned one of them—

the CD-ROM Edition. In addition, there are numerous other supplements, including those listed below, that make up the complete teaching/learning package for the Eighth Edition. For further information on the *West's Business Law* teaching/learning package, contact your local West sales representative. An additional source of information is our *West's Business Law* Web site at http://wbl.westbuslaw.com.

PRINTED SUPPLEMENTS

- *Online Legal Research* (free with every new copy of the text).
- *Instructor's Course Planning Guide and Media Handbook.*
- *Instructor's Manual* (also available in computerized form).
- *Study Guide* by William Eric Hollowell and text author Roger LeRoy Miller, including essay questions and sample CPA exam questions.
- A comprehensive *Test Bank* (co-written by text author Roger LeRoy Miller)—Contains approximately 2,500 multiple-choice questions with answers, over 1,600 true-false questions with answers, and short essay questions. Also available on software.
- *Answers to Questions and Case Problems and Alternate Problem Sets with Answers.*
- *Case Printouts.*
- *Handbook of Landmark Cases and Statutes in Business Law and the Legal Environment.*
- *Business Law and the CPA Exam.*
- *Advanced Topics and Contemporary Issues: Expanded Coverage,* Third Edition, by Frank B. Cross.
- *Handbook on Critical Thinking and Writing in Business Law and the Legal Environment.*
- *A Guide to Personal Law.*
- *Law and Women's Issues.*
- *Instructor's Manual* for the *Drama of the Law* video series.
- *Quicken® Business Law Partner® CD-ROM and Applications.*

SOFTWARE AND VIDEO SUPPLEMENTS

- *Quicken® Business Law Partner® CD-ROM.*
- Computerized *Instructor's Manual.*
- ExamView Testing Software.
- Web Tutor on WebCT.
- *Lecture Outline System.*
- PowerPoint slides.
- Transparency Acetates.

- "The Legal Tutor on Contracts" software.
- "The Legal Tutor on Sales" software.
- Interactive Software—Contracts.
- Interactive Software—Sales.
- "You Be the Judge" software.
- Case-Problem Cases on Diskette.
- Westlaw®.
- West's Business Law and Legal Environment Audiocassette Library.
- Videocassettes, including those discussed next.

CNN LEGAL ISSUES Update Video

You can update your coverage of legal issues and cyberlaw, as well as spark a lively classroom discussion and foster a deeper understanding of business law, by using the *CNN Legal Issues* update video. This video is produced by Turner Learning, Inc., using the resources of CNN, the world's first twenty-four-hour, all-news network.

With the introduction of the *CNN Legal Issues* update video, West Legal Studies in Business is proud to be the educational partner of CNN for textbook/video integration for legal issues. By making use of the *CNN Legal Issues* update video, you can bring the power of CNN, the network known for providing live, in-depth coverage and analysis of breaking news events, to your classroom.

ADDITIONAL VIDEOS

South-Western's *Business Law* video series, a set of situational videos, covers a range of topics for the full business law course, including the Uniform Commercial Code, employment law, and the business law portion of the CPA exam.

THE NEW YORK TIMES GUIDE TO LEGAL STUDIES IN BUSINESS

The New York Times Guide to Legal Studies in Business, by Marianne Jennings and Jamie Murphy, is more than just a printed collection of articles. The guide gives you access, via password, to an online collection of the most current and relevant *New York Times* articles that are continually posted as news breaks. Also included are articles from *CyberTimes,* the online technology section of the *New York Times* on the Web. Correlation guides for all South-Western legal studies in business texts are available on the South-Western *New York Times* Web site at http://nytimes.swcollege.com. Ask your West sales representative about this great new supplement for your students.

For Users of the Seventh Edition

First of all, we want to thank you for helping make *West's Business Law* the best-selling business law text in the United States today. Second, we want to make you aware of the numerous additions and changes that we have made in this edition. The major additions and changes are summarized below.

A NEW CHAPTER ON CYBERLAW AND E-COMMERCE

As discussed earlier in this Preface, this chapter ensures that your students will stay abreast of the important elements of the law that have been affected by the Internet, e-commerce, and technology in general. This chapter is guaranteed to make business law and the legal environment come alive for your students.

A NEW CHAPTER ON LIMITED LIABILITY COMPANIES AND LIMITED LIABILITY PARTNERSHIPS

As discussed earlier in this Preface, these new forms of business organization have taken on increasing importance. This chapter outlines their major characteristics and uses.

SIGNIFICANTLY REVISED CHAPTERS

—*Ethics:* The chapter on ethics was moved to the end of the Business Organizations unit (Unit Seven) and now appears as Chapter 40 ("Ethics and Business Decision Making").

—*Comparative Law:* The chapter on comparative law was moved to the final unit of the text (Unit Eleven—Special Topics) and combined with the chapter on international law. The combined chapter appears in the Eighth Edition as Chapter 52 ("International and Comparative Law").

—*Torts:* Chapters 6 and 7 of the Seventh Edition ("Torts and Strict Liability" and "Basic Business Torts," respectively) were combined into one chapter for the Eighth Edition (Chapter 5, enti-tled "Torts"). The discussion of strict liability, formerly in Chapter 6, is now included in Eighth Edition Chapter 6 ("Strict Liability and Product Liability").

—*Contracts:* We combined the coverage of capacity (formerly covered in Chapter 15, entitled "Capacity") and legality (formerly covered in Chapter 17, entitled "Legality and the Statute of Frauds") into one chapter for the Eighth Edition (Chapter 13, entitled "Capacity and Legality").

—*Negotiable Instruments:* We divided Seventh Edition Chapter 26 ("Basic Concepts, Negotiability, and Transferability") into two chapters, incorporating the discussion of the HDC doctrine into the second chapter in this unit. The new unit on negotiable instruments still has the same number of chapters, but the coverage is now as follows:

- Chapter 24: The Function and Creation of Negotiable Instruments.
- Chapter 25: Transferability and Holder in Due Course.
- Chapter 26: Liability, Defenses, and Discharge.
- Chapter 27: Checks and Electronic Fund Transfers.

—*Employment Unit:* This unit now appears between the unit on Business Organizations and the unit on Government Regulation, instead of appearing before the Business Organizations unit as it did in the Seventh Edition.

—*Business Organizations Unit:* Adding a new chapter on limited liability companies and partnerships necessitated some reorganization of this unit (Unit Seven):

- The materials in the unit-opening chapter summarizing the major forms business organization were integrated into the subsequent chapters, as appropriate. The remainder of the chapter materials now appear in a later chapter of the unit, Chapter 39 ("Special Business Forms and Private Franchises").
- The partnerships chapters were combined into one chapter (Chapter 33), which also includes, in the opening pages, a discussion of sole proprietorships. The materials on limited partnerships and limited liability partnerships were moved to the new chapter on limited liability companies and partnerships (Chapter 38).
- The corporations chapters (Chapters 34 through 37 in the Eighth Edition) remain largely the same.
- The unit now concludes with Chapter 40 ("Ethics and Business Decision Making").

—*Consumer and Environmental Law:* These topics (formerly covered in Chapters 45 and 46) were combined into one chapter for this edition (Chapter 44, entitled "Consumer and Environmental Law").

—*Personal Property and Bailments:* These topics (formerly covered in Chapters 48 and 49) were combined into one chapter for this edition (Chapter 46, entitled "Personal Property and Bailments").

WHAT ELSE IS NEW?

In addition to the changes already noted, we have included in the Eighth Edition a number of new pedagogical features and have added some new supplements. The new features and elements are listed below.

New Features. We have added the following new features to the Eighth Edition, each of which has been described earlier in this Preface:

- *In Your Court.*
- *Focus on Legal Reasoning.*
- *Law on the Web.*

New *Emerging Trends*. All of the *Emerging Trends in Technology* and the *Emerging Trends in Business Law* are new to this edition.

New *Concept Summaries*. A number of new *Concept Summaries* have been added for this edition, including those listed earlier in the Preface.

New Exhibits. Several of the more than ninety exhibits in this edition are new, including those listed earlier in the Preface.

New Cases. In all, over 70 percent of the cases in Eighth Edition are from the late 1990s. Many classic cases have been included also.

New Case Problems. Of the over 250 case problems in this text, more than 100 are new to the Eighth Edition. The majority of these new case problems are from 1998 and 1999.

Revised Appendices. Appendix A and Appendix C have been revised, as explained earlier.

NEW SUPPLEMENTS AND SPECIAL RESOURCES

- *Online Legal Research.*
- Web Tutor on WebCT.
- *Internet Activities* (on the *West's Business Law* Web site).
- A *Guide to Personal Law* as a separate paperback supplement.
- *The New York Times Guide to Legal Studies in Business.*

Acknowledgments for Previous Editions

Since we began this project a number of years ago, a sizable number of business law professors and others have helped us in various phases of the undertaking. The following reviewers offered numerous constructive criticisms, comments, and suggestions during the preparation of all previous editions.

Jeffrey E. Allen
University of Miami

Judith Anshin
Sacramento City College

Thomas M. Apke
California State University, Fullerton

Raymond August
Washington State University

William Auslen
San Francisco City College

John J. Balek
Morton College, Illinois

David L. Baumer
North Carolina State University

Barbara E. Behr
Bloomsburg University of
Pennsylvania

Heidi Boerstler
University of Colorado at Denver

Lawrence J. Bradley
University of Notre Dame

Doug Brown
Montana State University

Kristi K. Brown
University of Texas at Austin

William J. Burke
University of Massachusetts, Lowell

Kenneth Burns
University of Miami

Joseph E. Cantrell
DeAnza College, California

Donald Cantwell
University of Texas at Arlington

Robert Chatov
State University of New York, Buffalo

Robert J. Cox
Salt Lake Community College

Thomas Crane
University of Miami

Kenneth S. Culott
University of Texas at Austin

Larry R. Curtis
Iowa State University

Richard Dalebout
Brigham Young University

Michele A. Dunkerley
University of Texas at Austin

O. E. Elmore
Texas A&M University

Robert J. Enders
California State Polytechnic
University, Pomona

Michael Engber
Ball State University

David A. Escamilla
University of Texas at Austin

Frank S. Forbes
University of Nebraska, Omaha

Joe W. Fowler
Oklahoma State University

Stanley G. Freeman
University of South Carolina

Bob Garrett
American River College, California

Gary L. Giese
University of Colorado at Denver

Thomas Gossman
Western Michigan University

Patrick O. Gudridge
University of Miami School of Law

James M. Haine
University of Wisconsin, Stevens Point

Gerard Halpern
University of Arkansas

Christopher L. Hamilton
Golden West College, California

JoAnn W. Hammer
University of Texas at Austin

Charles Hartman
Wright State University, Ohio

Richard A. Hausler
University of Miami School of Law

Harry E. Hicks
Butler University, Indianapolis

Janine S. Hiller
Virginia Polytechnic Institute and
State University

Rebecca L. Hillyer
Chemeketa Community College

E. Clayton Hipp, Jr.
Clemson University

Anthony H. Holliday, Jr.
Howard University

Telford Hollman
University of Northern Iowa

June A. Horrigan
California State University,
Sacramento

John P. Huggard
North Carolina State University

Terry Hutchins
Pembroke State University,
North Carolina

Robert Jesperson
University of Houston

Bryce J. Jones
Northeast Missouri State University

Margaret Jones
Southwest Missouri State College

Peter A. Karl III
SUNY Institute of Technology at Utica

Jack E. Karns
East Carolina University

Tamra Kempf
University of Miami

Judith Kenney
University of Miami

Carey Kirk
University of Northern Iowa

Nancy P. Klintworth
University of Central Florida

Kathleen M. Knutson
College of St. Catherine, St. Paul,
Minnesota

Susan Liebeler
Loyola University

Thomas E. Maher
California State University, Fullerton

Sal Marchionna
Triton College

Gene A. Marsh
University of Alabama

Karen Kay Matson
University of Texas at Austin

Woodrow J. Maxwell
Hudson Valley Community College,
New York

Bruce E. May
University of South Dakota

John W. McGee
Southwest Texas State University

Cotton Meagher
University of Nevada, Las Vegas

Roger E. Meiners
University of Texas at Arlington

Gerald S. Meisel
Bergen Community College,
New Jersey

Richard Mills
Cypress College

David Minars
City University of New York, Brooklyn

Alan Moggio
Illinois Central College

Violet E. Molnar
Riverside City College

James E. Moon
Meyer, Johnson & Moon,
Minneapolis

Melinda Ann Mora
University of Texas at Austin

Bob Morgan
Eastern Michigan University

Joan Ann Mrava
Los Angeles Southwest College

Dwight D. Murphey
Wichita State University

Daniel E. Murray
University of Miami School of Law

Paula C. Murray
University of Texas

George A. Nation III
Lehigh University

Caleb L. Nichols
Western Connecticut State University

John M. Norwood
University of Arkansas

Michael J. O'Hara
University of Nebraska, Omaha

Rick F. Orsinger
College of DuPage, Illinois

Daniel J. O'Shea
Hillsborough Community College

Thomas L. Palmer
Northern Arizona University

Charles M. Patten
University of Wisconsin, Oshkosh

Peyton J. Paxson
University of Texas at Austin

Ralph L. Quinones
University of Wisconsin, Oshkosh

Carol D. Rasnic
Virginia Commonwealth University

Marvin H. Robertson
Harding University

Gary K. Sambol
Rutgers State University

Rudy Sandoval
University of Texas, San Antonio

Martha Sartoris
North Hennepin Community College

Barbara P. Scheller
Temple University

S. Alan Schlact
Kennesaw College, Georgia

Lorne H. Seidman
University of Nevada, Las Vegas

Roscoe B. Shain
Austin Peay University

Bennett D. Shulman
Lansing Community College,
Michigan

Dana Blair Smith
University of Texas at Austin

Arthur Southwick
University of Michigan

Sylvia A. Spade
University of Texas at Austin

John A. Sparks

Grove City College

Brenda Steuer
North Harris College, Houston

Irwin Stotsky
University of Miami School of Law

Larry Strate
University of Nevada at Las Vegas

Raymond Mason Taylor
North Carolina State University

H. Allan Tolbert
Central Texas College

Jesse C. Trentadue
University of North Dakota

Edwin Tucker
University of Connecticut

Gary Victor
Eastern Michigan University

David Vyncke
Scott Community College, Iowa

Robert J. Walter
University of Texas at El Paso

William H. Walker,

Indiana University–Purdue University,
Fort Wayne

Gary Watson
California State University, Los
Angeles

John L. Weimer
Nicholls State University, Louisiana

Marshall Wilkerson
University of Texas at Austin

Arthur D. Wolfe
Michigan State University

Elizabeth A. Wolfe
University of Texas at Austin

Daniel R. Wrentmore
Santa Barbara City College

Norman Gregory Young
California State Polytechnic
University, Pomona

Ronald C. Young
Kalamazoo Valley Community
College, Michigan

Acknowledgments for the Eighth Edition

In preparing the Eighth Edition of *West's Business Law*, we worked closely with the following reviewers, each of whom offered us valuable suggestions for how to improve the text:

Mary B. Bader
Moorhead State University

Frank Bagan
County College of Morris

Michael G. Barth
University of Phoenix

Jeanne A. Calderon
New York University

William H. Daughtrey, Jr.
Virginia Commonwealth University

Gregory T. Hinton
Fairmont State College

James E. Holloway
East Carolina University

Barbara Kincaid
Southern Methodist University

Kurtis P. Klumb
University of Wisconsin at Milwaukee

M. Alan Lawson
Mt. San Antonio College

Michael J. O'Hara
University of Nebraska at Omaha

Gregory J. Naples
Marquette University

S. Jay Sklar
Temple University

Michael Smydra
Oakland Community College,
Michigan

As in all past editions, we owe a debt of extreme gratitude to the numerous individuals who worked directly with us or at West. We especially wish to thank Lavina Leed Miller for her management of the entire project, as well as for the application of her superb editorial skills. William Eric Hollowell, who also co-authored the *Instructor's Manual, Study Guide*, and *Test Bank*, helped with much of the research. We were fortunate to have the copyediting services of Suzie Franklin DeFazio. Literally dozens of individu-

als helped proofread the galleys and pages of this edition over many, many months. They include Lavina Leed Miller, William Eric Hollowell, Suzie Franklin DeFazio, Pat Lewis, and Roxanna Lee.

We continue to be the fortunate recipients of an incredibly skilled and dedicated editorial, production, and printing and manufacturing team at West. In particular, we wish to thank Rob Dewey and Jan Lamar for their helpful advice and guidance during all of the stages of this new edition. Jan Lamar also assisted us in making sure we addressed all reviewers' criticisms and suggestions, and she was instrumental in ensuring that the supplements came out on time. Kurt Gerdenich deserves a special note of appreciation for his incredibly masterful work on the *West's Business Law* home page, the *West's Business Law* Interactive CD-ROM Edition, and just about everything else relating to technology for this text. Shawn Geoffroy Miller coordinated the CD-ROM with the text, *Study Guide,* and other supplements. We thank him also.

Our long-time textbook designer and production manager at West, Bill Stryker, came through again.

He provided us with a visually stunning new edition and an error-free printing. His ability to turn around our materials quickly continues to amaze us. We thank him more than he can ever imagine.

Through the years, we have enjoyed a continuing correspondence with many of you who have found points on which you wish to comment. We continue to welcome all comments and promise to respond promptly. By incorporating your ideas, we can continue to write a business law text that is best for you and best for your students.

DEDICATION

To Robert L. Birnbaum, Esquire, with
whom I spent years in the distant
past. What a treat to meet again! It will
only get better.

R.L.M.

To my wife, JoAnn; my children, Kathy,
Gary, Lori, and Rory; and my grandchildren,
Erin, Megan, Eric, Emily, Michelle, Javier,
Carmen, and Steve.

G.A.J.

To my parents and sisters.

F.B.C.

UNIT ONE

The Legal Environment of Business

CONTENTS

Introduction to Law and Legal Reasoning

O NE OF THE IMPORTANT FUNCTIONS OF LAW in any society is to provide stability, predictability, and continuity so that people can be sure of how to order their affairs. If any society is to survive, its citizens must be able to determine what is legally right and legally wrong. They must know what sanctions will be imposed on them if they commit wrongful acts. If they suffer harm as a result of others' wrongful acts, they need to know how they can seek redress. By setting forth the rights, obligations, and privileges of citizens, the law enables individuals to go about their business with confidence and a certain degree of predictability. The stability and predictability created by the law provide an essential framework for all civilized activities, including business activities.

In this introductory chapter, we first look at the nature of law and then examine the foundation and fundamental characteristics of the American legal system. We next describe the basic sources of American law and some general classifications of law. We conclude with sections offering practical guidance on several topics, including how to find the sources of law discussed in this chapter (and referred to throughout the text), how to read and understand court opinions, and why a basic knowledge of the law is important for those who contemplate a career in business.

Section 1

What Is Law?

There have been and will continue to be different definitions of law. Although the definitions of law vary in their particulars, they all are based on the general observation that, at a minimum, **law** consists of *enforceable rules governing relationships among individuals and between individuals and their society.* These "enforceable rules" may consist of unwritten principles of behavior established by a nomadic tribe. They may be set forth in a law code, such as the Code of Hammurabi in ancient Babylon or the law code of one of today's European nations. They may consist of written laws and court decisions created by modern legislative and judicial bodies, as in the United States. Regardless of how such rules are created, they all have one thing in common: they establish rights, duties, and privileges that are consistent with the values and beliefs of their society or its ruling group.

While few legal philosophers and scholars would disagree with these general observations about the law, those who embark on a study of law will find that these broad statements leave unanswered some important questions concerning the nature of law. Part of the study of law, often referred to as **jurisprudence,** involves learning about different schools of jurisprudential thought and discovering how the approaches to law characteristic of each school can affect judicial decision making.

SCHOOLS OF JURISPRUDENTIAL THOUGHT

You may think that legal philosophy is far removed from the practical study of business law and the legal environment. In fact, it is not. As you will learn in the chapters of this text, how judges apply the law to specific disputes, including disputes relating to the business world, depends in part on their philosophical approaches to law. We look now at some of the significant schools of legal, or jurisprudential, thought that have evolved over time.

The Natural Law School. An age-old question about the nature of law has to do with the finality of a nation's laws, such as the laws of the United States at the present time. For example, what if a particular law is deemed to be a "bad" law by a substantial number of that nation's citizens? Must a citizen obey the law if it goes against his or her conscience to do so? Is there a higher or universal law to which individuals can appeal? One who adheres to the natural law tradition would answer this question in the affirmative. **Natural law** denotes a system of moral and ethical principles that are inherent in human nature and that people can discover through the use of their natural intelligence.

The natural law tradition is one of the oldest and most significant schools of jurisprudence. It dates back to the days of the Greek philosopher Aristotle (384–322 B.C.E.), who distinguished between natural law and the laws governing a particular nation. According to Aristotle, natural law applies universally to all humankind.

The notion that people have "natural rights" stems from the natural law tradition. Those who claim that a specific foreign government is depriving certain citizens of their human rights implicitly are appealing to a higher law that has universal applicability. The question of the universality of basic human rights also comes into play in the context of international business operations. Should rights extended to workers in this country, such as the right to be free of discrimination in the workplace, be applied to a U.S. firm doing business in another country that does not pro-

vide for such rights? This question is rooted implicitly in a concept of universal rights that has its origins in the natural law tradition.

The Positivist School. In contrast, **positive law,** or national law (the written law of a given society at a particular point in time), applies only to the citizens of that nation or society. Those who adhere to the **positivist school** believe that there can be no higher law than a nation's positive law. According to the positivist school, there is no such thing as "natural rights." Rather, human rights exist solely because of laws. If the laws are not enforced, anarchy will result. Thus, whether a law is "bad" or "good" is irrelevant. The law is the law and must be obeyed until it is changed—in an orderly manner through a legitimate lawmaking process. A judge with positivist leanings probably would be more inclined to defer to an existing law than would a judge who adheres to the natural law tradition.

The Historical School. The **historical school** of legal thought emphasizes the evolutionary process of law by concentrating on the origin and history of the legal system. Thus, this school looks to the past to discover what the principles of contemporary law should be. The legal doctrines that have withstood the passage of time—those that have worked in the past—are deemed best suited for shaping present laws. Hence, law derives its legitimacy and authority from adhering to the standards that historical development has shown to be workable. Adherents of the historical school are more likely than those of other schools to strictly follow decisions made in past cases.

Legal Realism. In the 1920s and 1930s, a number of jurists and scholars, known as legal realists, rebelled against the historical approach to law. **Legal realism** is based on the idea that law is just one of many institutions in society and that it is shaped by social forces and needs. The law is a human enterprise, and judges should take social and economic realities into account when deciding cases. Legal realists also believe that the law can never be applied with total uniformity. Given that judges are human beings with unique personalities, value systems, and intellects, obviously different judges will bring different reasoning processes to the same case.

Legal realism strongly influenced the growth of what is sometimes called the **sociological school** of jurisprudence. This school views law as a tool for promoting justice in society. In the 1960s, for example, the justices of the United States Supreme Court played a leading role in the civil rights movement by upholding long-neglected laws calling for equal treatment for all Americans, including African Americans and other minorities. Generally, jurists who adhere to this philosophy of law are more likely to depart from past decisions than are those jurists who adhere to the other schools of legal thought.

JUDICIAL INTERPRETATION OF THE LAW

Because of our common law tradition (which will be discussed shortly), the courts—and thus the personal views and philosophies of judges—play a paramount role in the American legal system. This is particularly true of the United States Supreme Court, which has the final say on how a particular law or legal principle should be interpreted and applied. Indeed, Oliver Wendell Holmes, Jr., once stated that law was a set of rules that allowed one to predict how a court would resolve a particular dispute—"the prophecies [predictions] of what the courts will do in fact, and nothing more pretentious, are what I mean by the law."

Clearly, judges are not free to decide cases solely on the basis of their personal philosophical views or their opinions on the issues before the court. A judge's function is not to make the laws—that is the function of the legislative branch of government—but to interpret and apply them. From a practical point of view, however, the courts play a significant role in defining what the law is. This is because laws enacted by legislative bodies tend to be expressed in general terms. Judges thus have some flexibility in interpreting and applying the law. It is because of this flexibility that different courts can, and often do, arrive at different conclusions in cases that involve nearly identical issues, facts, and applicable laws. This flexibility also means that each judge's unique personality, legal philosophy, set of values, and intellectual attributes necessarily frame the judicial decision-making process to some extent.

SECTION 2

The Common Law Tradition

Because of our colonial heritage, much of American law is based on the English legal system, which originated in medieval England and continued to evolve in the following centuries. A knowledge of this system

is necessary to an understanding of the American legal system today.

EARLY ENGLISH COURTS

The origins of the English legal system—and thus the U.S. legal system as well—date back to 1066, when the Normans conquered England. William the Conqueror and his successors began the process of unifying the country under their rule. One of the means they used to this end was the establishment of the king's courts, or *curiae regis*. Before the Norman Conquest, disputes had been settled according to the local legal customs and traditions in various regions of the country. The king's courts sought to establish a uniform set of customs for the country as a whole. What evolved in these courts was the beginning of the **common law**—a body of general rules that prescribed social conduct and applied throughout the entire English realm.

Courts of Law and Remedies at Law. In the early English king's courts, the kinds of **remedies** (the legal means to recover a right or redress a wrong) that could be granted were severely restricted. If one person wronged another in some way, the king's courts could award as compensation one or more of the following: (1) land, (2) items of value, or (3) money. The courts that awarded this compensation became known as **courts of law,** and the three remedies were called **remedies at law.** (Today, the remedy at law normally takes the form of money **damages**—money given to a party whose legal interests have been injured.) Even though the system introduced uniformity in the settling of disputes, when a complaining party wanted a remedy other than economic compensation, the courts of law could do nothing, so "no remedy, no right."

Courts of Equity and Remedies in Equity. Equity is a branch of law, founded on what might be described as notions of justice and fair dealing, that seeks to supply a remedy when no adequate remedy at law is available. When individuals could not obtain an adequate remedy in a court of law because of strict technicalities, they petitioned the king for relief. Most of these petitions were decided by an adviser to the king, called a **chancellor,** who was said to be the "keeper of the king's conscience." When the chancellor thought that the claims were fair, new and unique remedies were granted. Eventually, formal chancery courts, or **courts of equity,** were established.

The remedies granted by equity courts became known as **remedies in equity,** or equitable remedies. These remedies include *specific performance* (ordering a party to perform an agreement as promised), an *injunction* (ordering a party to cease engaging in a specific activity or to undo some wrong or injury), and *rescission* (the cancellation of a contractual obligation). We discuss these and other equitable remedies in more detail at appropriate points in the chapters that follow. As a general rule, today's courts, like the early English courts, will not grant equitable remedies unless the remedy at law—money damages—is inadequate.

In fashioning appropriate remedies, judges often were (and continue to be) guided by so-called **equitable maxims**—propositions or general statements of equitable rules. Exhibit 1–1 lists some important equitable maxims. The last maxim listed in that exhibit—"Equity aids the vigilant, not those who rest on their rights"—merits special attention. It has become known as the equitable doctrine of **laches** (a term derived from the Latin *laxus*, meaning "lax" or "negligent"), and it can be used as a defense. A **defense** is an argument raised by the **defendant** (the party being sued) indicating why the **plaintiff** (the suing party) should not obtain the remedy sought. (Note that in equity proceedings, the party bringing a lawsuit is called the **petitioner,** and the party being sued is referred to as the **respondent.**)

EXHIBIT 1–1   EQUITABLE MAXIMS

1. *Whoever seeks equity must do equity.* (Anyone who wishes to be treated fairly must treat others fairly.)

2. *Where there is equal equity, the law must prevail.* (The law will determine the outcome of a controversy in which the merits of both sides are equal.)

3. *One seeking the aid of an equity court must come to the court with clean hands.* (Plaintiffs must have acted fairly and honestly.)

4. *Equity will not suffer a wrong to be without a remedy.* (Equitable relief will be awarded when there is a right to relief and there is no adequate remedy at law.)

5. *Equity regards substance rather than form.* (Equity is more concerned with fairness and justice than with legal technicalities.)

6. *Equity aids the vigilant, not those who rest on their rights.* (Equity will not help those who neglect their rights for an unreasonable period of time.)

The doctrine of laches arose to encourage people to bring lawsuits while the evidence was fresh. What constitutes a reasonable time, of course, varies according to the circumstances of the case. Time periods for different types of cases are now usually fixed by **statutes of limitations.** After the time allowed under a statute of limitations has expired, no action can be brought, no matter how strong the case was originally.

LEGAL AND EQUITABLE REMEDIES TODAY

The establishment of courts of equity in medieval England resulted in two distinct court systems: courts of law and courts of equity. The systems had different sets of judges and granted different types of remedies. Parties who sought legal remedies, or remedies at law, would bring their claims before courts of law. Parties seeking equitable relief, or remedies in equity, would bring their claims before courts of equity. During the nineteenth century, however, most states in the United States adopted rules of procedure that resulted in combined courts of law and equity—although some states, such as Arkansas, still retain the distinction. A party now may request both legal and equitable remedies in the same action, and the trial court judge may grant either or both forms of relief.

The distinction between legal and equitable remedies remains relevant to students of business law, however, because these remedies differ. To seek the proper remedy for a wrong, one must know what remedies are available. Additionally, certain vestiges of the procedures used when there were separate courts of law and equity still exist. For example, a party has the right to demand a jury trial in an action at law, but not in an action in equity. In the old courts of equity, the chancellor heard both sides of an issue and decided what should be done. Juries were considered inappropriate. In actions at law, however, juries participated in determining the outcome of cases, including the amount of damages to be awarded. Exhibit 1–2 on the next page summarizes the procedural differences (applicable in most states) between an action at law and an action in equity.

THE DOCTRINE OF *STARE DECISIS*

One of the unique features of the common law is that it is *judge-made* law. The body of principles and doctrines that form the common law emerged over time as judges decided actual legal controversies.

EXHIBIT 1–2   PROCEDURAL DIFFERENCES BETWEEN AN ACTION AT LAW AND AN ACTION IN EQUITY

PROCEDURE	ACTION AT LAW	ACTION IN EQUITY
Initiation of lawsuit	By filing a complaint	By filing a petition
Parties	Plaintiff and defendant	Petitioner and respondent
Decision	By jury or judge	By judge (no jury)
Result	Judgment	Decree
Remedy	Monetary damages	Injunction, specific performance, or rescission

Case Precedents and Case Reporters. When possible, judges attempted to be consistent and to base their decisions on the principles suggested by earlier cases. They sought to decide similar cases in a similar way and considered new cases with care, because they knew that their decisions would make new law. Each interpretation became part of the law on the subject and served as a legal **precedent**—that is, a decision that furnished an example or authority for deciding subsequent cases involving similar legal principles or facts.

By the early fourteenth century, portions of the most important decisions of each year were being gathered together and recorded in *Year Books*, which became useful references for lawyers and judges. In the sixteenth century, the *Year Books* were discontinued, and other forms of case publication became available. Today, cases are published, or "reported," in volumes called **reporters**, or *reports*. We describe today's case reporting system in detail later in this chapter.

Stare Decisis and the Common Law Tradition. The practice of deciding new cases with reference to former decisions, or precedents, became a cornerstone of the English and American judicial systems. The practice forms a doctrine called *stare decisis*[1] (a Latin phrase meaning "to stand on decided cases"). Under this doctrine, judges are obligated to follow the precedents established within their jurisdictions.

For example, suppose that the lower state courts in California have reached conflicting conclusions on whether drivers are liable for accidents they cause while merging into freeway traffic, even though the drivers looked and did not see any oncoming traffic and even though witnesses (passengers in their cars) testified to that effect. To settle the law on this issue, the California Supreme Court decides to review a case involving this fact pattern. The court rules that in such a situation, the driver who is merging into traffic is liable for any accidents caused by the driver's failure to yield to freeway traffic—regardless of whether the driver looked carefully and did not see an approaching vehicle.

The California Supreme Court's decision on this matter will influence the outcome of all future cases on this issue brought before the California state courts. Similarly, a decision on a given question by the United States Supreme Court (the nation's highest court) is binding on all courts. Case precedents, as well as statutes and other laws that must be followed, are referred to as **binding authorities.** (Nonbinding legal authorities on which judges may rely for guidance, such as precedents established in other jurisdictions, are referred to as *persuasive authorities*.)

The doctrine of *stare decisis* helps the courts to be more efficient, because if other courts have carefully analyzed a similar case, their legal reasoning and opinions can serve as guides. *Stare decisis* also makes the law more stable and predictable. If the law on a given subject is well settled, someone bringing a case to court can usually rely on the court to make a decision based on what the law has been in the past.

Departures from Precedent. Although courts are obligated to follow precedents, sometimes a court will depart from the rule of precedent if it decides that the precedent should no longer be followed. If a court decides that a ruling precedent is simply incorrect or that technological or social changes have rendered the precedent inapplicable, the court might rule contrary to the precedent. Cases that overturn precedent often receive a great deal of publicity.[2]

---

1. Pronounced *ster*-ay dih-*si*-ses.

2. For example, when the United States Supreme Court held in the 1950s that racial segregation in the public schools was unconstitutional, it expressly overturned a Supreme Court precedent upholding the constitutionality of "separate-but-equal" segregation. The Supreme Court's departure from precedent received a tremendous amount of publicity as people began to realize the ramifications of this change in the law. See *Brown v. Board of Education of Topeka*, 347 U.S. 483, 74 S.Ct. 6896, 98 L.Ed. 873 (1954). (Legal citations are explained later in this chapter.)

Note that judges have some flexibility in applying precedents. For example, a trial court may avoid applying a Supreme Court precedent by arguing that the facts of the case before the court are distinguishable from the facts in the Supreme Court case. Therefore, the Supreme Court's ruling on the issue does not apply to the case before the court.

When There Is No Precedent. Occasionally, cases come before the courts for which no precedents exist. Such cases, called *cases of first impression*, often result when new practices or technological developments in society create new types of legal disputes. In the last several years, for example, the courts have had to deal with disputes involving transactions conducted via the Internet. When existing laws governing free speech, pornography, fraud, jurisdiction, and other areas were drafted, cyberspace did not exist. Although new laws are being created to govern such disputes, in the meantime the courts have to decide, on a case-by-case basis, what rules should be applied.

Generally, in deciding cases of first impression, courts may consider a number of factors, including persuasive authorities (such as cases from other jurisdictions, if there are any), legal principles and policies underlying previous court decisions or existing statutes, fairness, social values and customs, **public policy** (governmental policy based on widely held societal values), and data and concepts drawn from the social sciences. Which of these sources is chosen or receives the greatest emphasis depends on the nature of the case being considered and the particular judge or judges hearing the case. As mentioned previously, judges are not free to decide cases on the basis of their own personal views. In cases of first impression, as in all cases, judges must have legal reasons for ruling as they do on particular issues. When a court issues a written opinion on a case (we discuss court opinions later in this chapter), the opinion normally contains a carefully reasoned argument justifying the decision.

STARE DECISIS AND LEGAL REASONING

Legal reasoning is the reasoning process used by judges in deciding what law applies to a given dispute and then applying that law to the specific facts or circumstances of the case. Through the use of legal reasoning, judges harmonize their decisions with those that have been made before—which the doctrine of *stare decisis* requires.

Students of business law also engage in legal reasoning. For example, you may be asked to provide answers for some of the case problems that appear at the end of every chapter in this text. Each problem describes the facts of a particular dispute and the legal question at issue. If you are assigned a case problem, you will be asked to determine how a court would answer that question and why. In other words, you will need to give legal reasons for whatever conclusion you reach.[3] We look here at the basic steps involved in legal reasoning and then describe some forms of reasoning commonly used by the courts in making their decisions.

Basic Steps in Legal Reasoning. At times, the legal arguments set forth in court opinions are relatively simple and brief. At other times, the arguments are complex and lengthy. Regardless of the brevity or length of a legal argument, however, the basic steps of the legal reasoning process remain the same in all cases. These steps, which you also can follow when analyzing cases and case problems, form what is commonly referred to as the *IRAC method* of legal reasoning. IRAC is an acronym comprising the first letters of the following words: Issue, Rule, Application, and Conclusion. To apply the IRAC method, you would ask the following questions:

1. *What are the key facts and issues?* For example, suppose that a plaintiff comes before the court claiming *assault* (a wrongful and intentional action, or tort, in which one person makes another fearful of immediate physical harm). The plaintiff claims that the defendant threatened her while she was sleeping. Although the plaintiff was unaware that she was being threatened, her roommate heard the defendant make the threat. The legal issue, or question, raised by these facts is whether the defendant's actions constitute the tort of assault, given that the plaintiff was not aware of those actions at the time they occurred.

2. *What rules of law apply to the case?* A rule of law may be a rule stated by the courts in previous decisions, a state or federal statute, or a state or federal administrative agency regulation. In our hypothetical case, the plaintiff **alleges** (claims) that the defendant committed a tort. Therefore, the applicable law is the common law of torts—specifically, tort law governing assault (see Chapter 5 for more detail on torts). Case

---

3. See Appendix A for further instructions on how to analyze case problems.

precedents involving similar facts and issues thus would be relevant. Often, more than one rule of law will be applicable to a case.

3. *How do the rules of law apply to the particular facts and circumstances of this case?* This step is often the most difficult one, because each case presents a unique set of facts, circumstances, and parties. Although there may be similar cases, no two cases are ever identical in all respects. Normally, judges (and lawyers and law students) try to find **cases on point**—previously decided cases that are as similar as possible to the one under consideration. (Because of the difficulty—and importance—of this step in the legal reasoning process, we discuss it in more detail in the next subsection.)

4. *What conclusion should be drawn?* This step normally presents few problems. Usually, the conclusion is evident if the previous three steps have been followed carefully.

Forms of Legal Reasoning.　Judges use many types of reasoning when following the third step of the legal reasoning process—applying the law to the facts of a particular case. Three common forms of reasoning are deductive reasoning, linear reasoning, and reasoning by analogy.

Deductive Reasoning.　Deductive reasoning is sometimes called syllogistic reasoning because it employs a **syllogism**—a logical relationship involving a major premise, a minor premise, and a conclusion. For example, consider the hypothetical case presented earlier, in which the plaintiff alleged that the defendant committed assault by threatening her while she was sleeping. The judge might point out that "under the common law of torts, an individual must be *aware* of a threat of danger for the threat to constitute civil assault" (major premise); "the plaintiff in this case was unaware of the threat at the time it occurred" (minor premise); and "therefore, the circumstances do not amount to a civil assault" (conclusion).

Linear Reasoning.　A second important form of legal reasoning that is commonly employed might be thought of as "linear" reasoning, because it proceeds from one point to another, with the final point being the conclusion. An analogy will help make this form of reasoning clear. Imagine a knotted rope, with each knot tying together separate pieces of rope to form a tight length. As a whole, the rope represents a linear progression of thought logically connecting various points, with the last point, or knot, representing the

conclusion. For example, suppose that a tenant in an apartment building sues the landlord for damages for an injury resulting from an allegedly dimly lit stairway. The court may engage in a reasoning process involving the following "pieces of rope":

1. The landlord, who was on the premises the evening the injury occurred, testifies that none of the other nine tenants who used the stairway that night complained about the lights.
2. The fact that none of the tenants complained is the same as if they had said the lighting was sufficient.
3. That there were no complaints does not prove that the lighting was sufficient but proves that the landlord had no reason to believe that it was not.
4. The landlord's belief was reasonable, because no one complained.
5. Therefore, the landlord acted reasonably and was not negligent in respect to the lighting in the stairway.

On the basis of this reasoning, the court concludes that the tenant is not entitled to compensation on the basis of the stairway's lighting.

Reasoning by Analogy.　Another important type of reasoning that judges use in deciding cases is reasoning by *analogy*. To reason by **analogy** is to compare the facts in the case at hand to the facts in other cases and, to the extent that the patterns are similar, to apply the same rule of law to the present case. To the extent that the facts are unique, or "distinguishable," different rules may apply. For example, in case A, it is held that a driver who crosses a highway's center line is negligent. In case B, a driver crosses the line to avoid hitting a child. In determining whether case A's rule applies in case B, a judge would consider what the reasons were for the decision in A and whether B is sufficiently similar for those reasons to apply. If the judge holds that B's driver is not liable, that judge must indicate why case A's rule does not apply to the facts presented in case B.

THERE IS NO ONE "RIGHT" ANSWER

Many persons believe that there is one "right" answer to every legal question. In most situations involving a legal controversy, however, there is no single correct result. Good arguments can often be made to support either side of a legal controversy. Quite often, a case does not present the situation of a "good" person suing a "bad" person. In many cases, both parties have acted in good faith in some measure or have acted in bad faith to some degree.

Additionally, as already mentioned, each judge has his or her own personal beliefs and philosophy, which shape, at least to some extent, the process of legal reasoning. What this means is that the outcome of a particular lawsuit before a court can never be predicted with absolute certainty. In fact, in some cases, even though the weight of the law would seem to favor one party's position, judges, through creative legal reasoning, have found ways to rule in favor of the other party in the interests of preventing injustice.

CONCEPT SUMMARY 1.1 — THE COMMON LAW TRADITION

SOURCE	DESCRIPTION
Origins of the Common Law	The American legal system is based on the common law tradition, which originated in medieval England. Following the conquest of England in 1066 by William the Conqueror, king's courts were established throughout England, and the common law was developed in these courts.
Legal and Equitable Remedies	The distinction between remedies at law (money or items of value, such as land) and remedies in equity (including specific performance, injunction, and rescission of a contractual obligation) originated in the early English courts of law and courts of equity, respectively.
Case Precedents and the Doctrine of *Stare Decisis*	In the king's courts, judges attempted to make their decisions consistent with previous decisions, called precedents. This practice gave rise to the doctrine of *stare decisis*. This doctrine, which became a cornerstone of the common law tradition, obligates judges to abide by precedents established in their jurisdictions.
Stare Decisis and Legal Reasoning	Legal reasoning refers to the reasoning process used by judges in applying the law to the facts and issues of specific cases. Legal reasoning involves becoming familiar with the key facts of a case, identifying the relevant legal rules, linking those rules to the facts, and forming a conclusion. In linking the legal rules to the facts of a case, judges may use deductive reasoning, linear reasoning, or reasoning by analogy.

SECTION 3

Sources of American Law

There are numerous sources of American law. *Primary sources of law*, or sources that establish the law, include the following:

1. The U.S. Constitution and the constitutions of the various states.
2. Statutory law—including laws passed by Congress, state legislatures, or local governing bodies.
3. Regulations created by administrative agencies, such as the Food and Drug Administration.
4. Case law and common law doctrines.

We describe each of these important sources of law in the following pages.

Secondary sources of law are books and articles that summarize and clarify the primary sources of law. Examples are legal encyclopedias, treatises, articles in law reviews, and compilations of law, such as the *Restatements of the Law* (which will be discussed shortly). Courts often refer to secondary sources of law for guidance in interpreting and applying the primary sources of law discussed here.

CONSTITUTIONAL LAW

The federal government and the states have separate written constitutions that set forth the general organization, powers, and limits of their respective governments. **Constitutional law** is the law as expressed in these constitutions.

According to Article VI of the U.S. Constitution, the Constitution is the supreme law of the land. As such, it is the basis of all law in the United States. A law in violation of the Constitution, if challenged, will be declared unconstitutional and will not be enforced, no matter what its source. Because of its importance in the American legal system, we present the complete text of the U.S. Constitution in Appendix B.

The Tenth Amendment to the U.S. Constitution reserves all powers not granted to the federal government to the states. Each state in the union has its own constitution. Unless it conflicts with the U.S. Constitution or a federal law, a state constitution is supreme within the state's borders.

STATUTORY LAW

Laws enacted by legislative bodies at any level of government, such as the statutes passed by Congress or by state legislatures, make up the body of law generally referred to as **statutory law.** When a legislature passes a statute, that statute ultimately is included in the federal code of laws or the relevant state code of laws (these codes are discussed later in this chapter).

Statutory law also includes local **ordinances**—statutes (laws, rules, or orders) passed by municipal or county governing units to govern matters not covered by federal or state law. Ordinances commonly have to do with city or county land use (zoning ordinances), building and safety codes, and other matters affecting the local unit.

A federal statute, of course, applies to all states. A state statute, in contrast, applies only within the state's borders. State laws thus may vary from state to state. No federal statute may violate the U.S. Constitution, and no state statute or local ordinance may violate the U.S. Constitution or the relevant state constitution.

Uniform Laws. The differences among state laws were particularly notable in the 1800s, when conflicting state statutes frequently made trade and commerce among the states very difficult. To counter these problems, in 1892 a group of legal scholars and lawyers formed the National Conference of Commissioners (NCC) on Uniform State Laws to draft **uniform laws,** or model laws, for the states to consider adopting. The NCC still exists today and continues to issue uniform laws.

Each state has the option of adopting or rejecting a uniform law. *Only if a state legislature adopts a uniform law does that law become part of the statutory law of that state.* Note that a state legislature may adopt all or part of a uniform law as it is written, or the legislature may rewrite the law however the legislature wishes. Hence, even when a uniform law is said to have been adopted in many states, those states' laws may not be entirely "uniform."

The earliest uniform law, the Uniform Negotiable Instruments Law, had been completed by 1896 and adopted in every state by the early 1920s (although not all states used exactly the same wording). Over the following decades, other acts were drawn up in a similar manner. In all, over two hundred uniform acts have been issued by the NCC since its inception. The most ambitious uniform act of all, however, was the Uniform Commercial Code.

The Uniform Commercial Code. The Uniform Commercial Code (UCC), which was created through the joint efforts of the NCC and the American Law Institute,[4] was first issued in 1952. The UCC has been adopted in all fifty states,[5] the District of Columbia, and the Virgin Islands. The UCC facilitates commerce among the states by providing a uniform, yet flexible, set of rules governing commercial transactions. The UCC assures businesspersons that their contracts, if validly entered into, normally will be enforced.

As you will read in later chapters, from time to time the NCC revises the articles contained in the UCC and submits the revised versions to the states for adoption. During the 1990s, for example, four articles were revised (Articles 3, 4, 5, and 9). Additionally, new articles were added (Articles 2A and 4A). Because of its importance in the area of commercial law, we cite the UCC frequently in this text. We also present the UCC in Appendix C.

ADMINISTRATIVE LAW

An important source of American law is **administrative law**—which consists of the rules, orders, and decisions of administrative agencies. An **administrative agency** is a federal, state, or local government agency estab-

---

4. This institute was formed in the 1920s and consists of practicing attorneys, legal scholars, and judges.
5. Louisiana has not adopted Articles 2 and 2A (covering contracts for the sale and lease of goods), however.

lished to perform a specific function. Administrative law and procedures, which will be examined in detail in Chapter 43, constitute a dominant element in the regulatory environment of business. Rules issued by various administrative agencies now affect virtually every aspect of a business's operation, including the firm's capital structure and financing, its hiring and firing procedures, its relations with employees and unions, and the way it manufactures and markets its products.

At the national level, numerous **executive agencies** exist within the cabinet departments of the executive branch. The Food and Drug Administration, for example, is an agency within the Department of Health and Human Services. Executive agencies are subject to the authority of the president, who has the power to appoint and remove officers of federal agencies. There are also major **independent regulatory agencies** at the federal level, such as the Federal Trade Commission, the Securities and Exchange Commission, and the Federal Communications Commission. The president's power is less pronounced in regard to independent agencies, whose officers serve for fixed terms and cannot be removed without just cause.

There are administrative agencies at the state and local levels as well. Commonly, a state agency (such as a state pollution-control agency) is created as a parallel to a federal agency (such as the Environmental Protection Agency). Just as federal statutes take precedence over conflicting state statutes, so federal agency regulations take precedence over conflicting state regulations.

CASE LAW AND COMMON LAW DOCTRINES

As is evident from the earlier discussion of the common law tradition, another basic source of American law comprises the rules of law announced in court decisions. These rules of law include interpretations of constitutional provisions, of statutes enacted by legislatures, and of regulations created by administrative agencies. Today, this body of law is referred to variously as the common law, judge-made law, or **case law.**

The Relationship between the Common Law and Statutory Law.   Common law doctrines and principles govern all areas not covered by statutory or ad-

ministrative law. In a dispute concerning a particular employment practice, for example, if a statute regulates that practice, the statute will apply rather than the common law doctrine that applied prior to the enactment of the statute.

Even though the body of statutory law has expanded greatly since the beginning of this nation, thus narrowing the applicability of common law doctrines, there is a significant overlap between statutory law and the common law. For example, many statutes essentially codify existing common law rules, and thus the courts, in interpreting the statutes, often rely on the common law as a guide to what the legislators intended.

Additionally, how the courts interpret a particular statute determines how that statute will be applied. If you wanted to learn about the coverage and applicability of a particular statute, for example, you would, of course, need to locate the statute and study it. You would also need to see how the courts in your jurisdiction have interpreted the statute—in other words, what precedents have been established in regard to that statute. Often, the applicability of a newly enacted statute does not become clear until a body of case law develops to clarify how, when, and to whom the statute applies.

Restatements of the Law.   The American Law Institute (ALI) has drafted and published compilations of the common law called *Restatements of the Law*, which generally summarize the common law rules followed by most states. There are *Restatements of the Law* in the areas of contracts, torts, agency, trusts, property, restitution, security, judgments, and conflict of laws. The *Restatements*, like other secondary sources of law, do not in themselves have the force of law but are an important source of legal analysis and opinion on which judges often rely in making their decisions.

Many of the *Restatements* are now in their second or third editions. For example, as you will read in Chapter 6, the ALI has recently published the first volume of the third edition of the *Restatement of the Law of Torts*. We refer to the *Restatements* frequently in subsequent chapters of this text, indicating in parentheses the edition to which we are referring. For example, we refer to the second edition of the *Restatement of the Law of Contracts* simply as the *Restatement (Second) of Contracts*.

CONCEPT SUMMARY 1.2 — SOURCES OF AMERICAN LAW

SOURCE	DESCRIPTION
Constitutional Law	The law as expressed in the U.S. Constitution and the state constitutions. The U.S. Constitution is the supreme law of the land. State constitutions are supreme within state borders to the extent that they do not violate a clause of the U.S. Constitution or a federal law.
Statutory Law	Laws (statutes and ordinances) created by federal, state, and local legislatures and governing bodies. None of these laws may violate the U.S. Constitution or the relevant state constitution. Uniform statutes, when adopted by a state, become statutory law in that state.
Administrative Law	The rules, orders, and decisions of federal or state government administrative agencies.
Case Law and Common Law Doctrines	Judge-made law, including interpretations of constitutional provisions, of statutes enacted by legislatures, and of regulations created by administrative agencies. The common law—the doctrines and principles embodied in case law—governs all areas not covered by statutory or administrative law.

SECTION 4

Classifications of Law

Because the body of law is so large, one must break it down by some means of classification. A number of classification systems have been devised. For example, one classification system divides law into substantive law and procedural law. **Substantive law** consists of all laws that define, describe, regulate, and create legal rights and obligations. **Procedural law** consists of all laws that establish the methods of enforcing the rights established by substantive law.

Another classification system divides law into civil law and criminal law. **Civil law** is concerned with the duties that exist between persons or between citizens and their governments, excluding the duty not to commit crimes. Typically, in a civil case, a private party sues another private party (although the government can also sue a party for a civil law violation) to make that other party comply with a duty or pay for the damage caused by failure to comply with a duty. Much of the law that we discuss in this text is civil law. Contract law, for example, covered in Chapters 10 through 18, is civil law. The whole body of tort law (see Chapters 5 and 6) is civil law.

Criminal law, in contrast, is concerned with wrongs committed *against the public as a whole.* Criminal acts are defined and prohibited by local,

state, or federal government statutes and prosecuted by public officials, such as a district attorney (D.A.), on behalf of the state, not by their victims or other private parties. (See Chapter 8 for a further discussion of the distinction between civil law and criminal law.)

Other classification systems divide law into federal law and state law, private law (dealing with relationships between private entities) and public law (addressing the relationship between persons and their governments), national law and international law, and so on.

SECTION 5

How to Find Primary Sources of Law

This text includes numerous citations to primary sources of law—federal and state statutes, regulations issued by administrative agencies, and court cases. (A **citation** is a reference to a publication in which a legal authority—such as a statute or a court decision or other source—can be found.) In this section, we explain how you can use citations to find primary sources of law.

FINDING STATUTORY LAW

When Congress passes laws, they are collected in a publication titled *United States Statutes at Large.*

When state legislatures pass laws, they are collected in similar state publications. Most frequently, however, laws are referred to in their codified form—that is, the form in which they appear in the federal and state codes.

In these codes, laws are compiled by subject. The *United States Code* (U.S.C.) arranges all existing federal laws of a public and permanent nature by subject. Each of the fifty subjects into which the U.S.C. arranges the laws is given a title and a title number. For example, laws relating to commerce and trade are collected in Title 15, "Commerce and Trade." Titles are subdivided by sections. A citation to the U.S.C. includes title and section numbers. Thus, a reference to "15 U.S.C. Section 1" means that the statute can be found in Section 1 of Title 15. ("Section" may also be designated by the symbol §, and "Sections," by §§.) Sometimes a citation includes the abbreviation *et seq.*, as in "15 U.S.C. Sections 1 *et seq.*" The term is an abbreviated form of *et sequitur*, which in Latin means "and the following"; when used in a citation, it refers to sections that concern the same subject as the numbered section and follow it in sequence.

State codes follow the U.S.C. pattern of arranging law by subject. They may be called codes, revisions, compilations, consolidations, general statutes, or statutes, depending on the preferences of the states. In some codes, subjects are designated by number. In others, they are designated by name. For example, "13 Pennsylvania Consolidated Statutes Section 1101" means that the statute can be found in Title 13, Section 1101, of the Pennsylvania code. "California Commercial Code Section 1101" means the statute can be found under the subject heading "Commercial Code" of the California code in Section 1101. Abbreviations may be used. For example, "13 Pennsylvania Consolidated Statutes Section 1101" may be abbreviated "13 Pa. C.S. §1101," and "California Commercial Code Section 1101" may be abbreviated "Cal. Com. Code §1101."

Commercial publications of these laws and regulations are available and are widely used. For example, West Group publishes the *United States Code Annotated* (U.S.C.A.). The U.S.C.A. contains the complete text of laws included in the U.S.C., plus notes on court decisions that interpret and apply specific sections of the statutes, as well as the text of presidential proclamations and executive orders. The U.S.C.A. also includes research aids, such as cross-references to related statutes, historical notes, and library references. A citation to the U.S.C.A. is similar to a citation to the U.S.C.: "15 U.S.C.A. Section 1."

FINDING ADMINISTRATIVE LAW

Rules and regulations adopted by federal administrative agencies are initially published in the *Federal Register*, a daily publication of the U.S. government. Later, they are incorporated into the *Code of Federal Regulations* (C.F.R.). Like the U.S.C., the C.F.R. is divided into fifty titles. Rules within each title are assigned section numbers. A full citation to the C.F.R. includes title and section numbers. For example, a reference to "17 C.F.R. Section 230.504" means that the rule can be found in Section 230.504 of Title 17.

FINDING CASE LAW

To understand how to read citations to court cases, we need first to look briefly at the court system. As will be discussed in Chapter 2, there are two types of courts in the United States, federal courts and state courts. Both the federal and state court systems consist of several levels, or tiers, of courts.

Trial courts, in which evidence is presented and testimony given, are on the bottom tier (which also includes lower courts handling specialized issues). Decisions from a trial court can be appealed to a higher court, commonly an intermediate *court of appeals*, or an *appellate court*. Decisions from these intermediate courts of appeals may be appealed to an even higher court, such as a state supreme court or the United States Supreme Court.

When reading the cases presented in this text, you will note that most of the state court cases are from state appellate courts. This is because most state trial court opinions are not published. Except in New York and a few other states that publish selected opinions of their trial courts, decisions from the state trial courts are merely filed in the office of the clerk of the court, where they are available for public inspection. Many of the federal trial (district) courts do publish their opinions, however, and you will find that several of the cases set forth in this book are from these courts, as well as the federal appellate courts.

State Court Decisions. Written decisions of the state appellate, or reviewing, courts are published and distributed in volumes called *Reports*, which are numbered consecutively.

Reporters Containing State Court Decisions.

Decisions of the appellate courts of a particular state are found in the reporters of that state. A few states—including those with intermediate appellate courts, such as California, Illinois, and New York—have more than one reporter for opinions given by their courts.

Additionally, state court opinions appear in regional units of the National Reporter System, published by West Group. Most lawyers and libraries have the West reporters because they report cases more quickly, and are distributed more widely, than the state-published reporters. In fact, many states have eliminated their own reporters in favor of West's National Reporter System. The National Reporter System divides the states into the following geographical areas: *Atlantic* (A. or A.2d), *South Eastern* (S.E. or S.E.2d), *South Western* (S.W. or S.W.2d), *North Western* (N.W. or N.W.2d), *North Eastern* (N.E. or N.E.2d), *Southern* (So. or So.2d), and *Pacific* (P. or P.2d). (The *2d* in the preceding abbreviations refers to *Second Series*. In the near future, the designation *3d*, for *Third Series*, will be used for some of the regional reporters.) The states included in each of these regional divisions are indicated in Exhibit 1–3, which illustrates West's National Reporter System.

Case Citations.

After an appellate decision has been published, it is normally referred to (cited) by the name of the case (called the *style* of the case); the volume, name, and page of the state's official reporter (if different from West's National Reporter System); the volume, unit, and page number of the National Reporter; and the volume, name, and page number of any other selected reporter. (Citing a reporter by volume number, name, and page number, in that order, is common to all citations; often, as in this book, the year the decision was made will be included in parentheses, just following the citations to reporters.) When more than one reporter is cited for the same case, each reference is called a *parallel citation*.[6]

---

6. Note that Wisconsin recently adopted a "public domain citation system" in which the format is somewhat different. For example, a Wisconsin Supreme Court decision might be designated "2000 WI 40," meaning that the case was decided in the year 2000 by the Wisconsin Supreme Court and was the fortieth decision issued by that court during that year. (Parallel citations to the *Wisconsin Reports* and West's *North Western Reporter* are still required when citing Wisconsin cases, but they must follow the public domain citation.)

For example, consider the following case citation: *Crews v. Hollenbach*, 126 Md.App. 609, 730 A.2d 742 (1999). We see that the opinion in this case may be found in Volume 126 of the official *Maryland Appellate Reports*, on page 609. The parallel citation is to Volume 730 of the *Atlantic Reporter, Second Series*, page 742. In reprinting appellate opinions in this text, in addition to the reporter, we give the name of the court hearing the case and the year of the court's decision.

Sample citations to state court decisions are explained in Exhibit 1–4, beginning on page 16.

Federal Court Decisions.

Federal district (trial) court decisions are published unofficially in West's *Federal Supplement* (F.Supp. or F.Supp.2d), and opinions from the circuit courts of appeals are reported unofficially in West's *Federal Reporter* (F., F.2d, or F.3d). Cases concerning federal bankruptcy law are published unofficially in West's *Bankruptcy Reporter* (Bankr.).

The official edition of all decisions of the United States Supreme Court for which there are written opinions is the *United States Reports* (U.S.), which is published by the federal government. The series includes reports of Supreme Court cases dating from the August term of 1791, although many of the Supreme Court's decisions were not reported in the early volumes.

Unofficial editions of Supreme Court cases include West's *Supreme Court Reporter* (S.Ct.), which includes cases dating from the Court's term in October 1882; and the *Lawyers' Edition of the Supreme Court Reports* (L.Ed. or L.Ed.2d), published by the Lawyers Cooperative Publishing Company (now a part of West Group). The latter contains many of the decisions not reported in the early volumes of the *United States Reports*.

Sample citations for federal court decisions are also listed and explained in Exhibit 1–4.

Old Case Law.

On a few occasions, this text cites opinions from old, classic cases dating to the nineteenth century or earlier; some of these are from the English courts. The citations to these cases appear not to conform to the descriptions given above, because the reporters in which they were published were often known by the name of the person who compiled the reporter and have since been replaced.

Case Digests and Legal Encyclopedias.

The body of American case law consists of over five million

EXHIBIT 1–3 NATIONAL REPORTER SYSTEM—REGIONAL/FEDERAL

Regional Reporters	Coverage Beginning	Coverage
Atlantic Reporter (A. or A.2d)	1885	Connecticut, Delaware, Maine, Maryland, New Hampshire, New Jersey, Pennsylvania, Rhode Island, Vermont, and District of Columbia.
North Eastern Reporter (N.E. or N.E.2d)	1885	Illinois, Indiana, Massachusetts, New York, and Ohio.
North Western Reporter (N.W. or N.W.2d)	1879	Iowa, Michigan, Minnesota, Nebraska, North Dakota, South Dakota, and Wisconsin.
Pacific Reporter (P. or P.2d)	1883	Alaska, Arizona, California, Colorado, Hawaii, Idaho, Kansas, Montana, Nevada, New Mexico, Oklahoma, Oregon, Utah, Washington, and Wyoming.
South Eastern Reporter (S.E. or S.E.2d)	1887	Georgia, North Carolina, South Carolina, Virginia, and West Virginia.
South Western Reporter (S.W. or S.W.2d)	1886	Arkansas, Kentucky, Missouri, Tennessee, and Texas.
Southern Reporter (So. or So.2d)	1887	Alabama, Florida, Louisiana, and Mississippi.

Federal Reporters		
Federal Reporter (F., F.2d, or F.3d)	1880	U.S. Circuit Court from 1880 to 1912; U.S. Commerce Court from 1911 to 1913; U.S. District Courts from 1880 to 1932; U.S. Court of Claims (now called U.S. Court of Federal Claims) from 1929 to 1932 and since 1960; U.S. Court of Appeals since 1891; U.S. Court of Customs and Patent Appeals since 1929; and U.S. Emergency Court of Appeals since 1943.
Federal Supplement (F.Supp. or F.Supp.2d)	1932	U.S. Court of Claims from 1932 to 1960; U.S. District Courts since 1932; and U.S. Customs Court since 1956.
Federal Rules Decisions (F.R.D.)	1939	U.S. District Courts involving the Federal Rules of Civil Procedure since 1939 and Federal Rules of Criminal Procedure since 1946.
Supreme Court Reporter (S.Ct.)	1882	U.S. Supreme Court since the October term of 1882.
Bankruptcy Reporter (Bankr.)	1980	Bankruptcy decisions of U.S. Bankruptcy Courts, U.S. District Courts, U.S. Courts of Appeals, and U.S. Supreme Court.
Military Justice Reporter (M.J.)	1978	U.S. Court of Military Appeals and Courts of Military Review for the Army, Navy, Air Force, and Coast Guard.

NATIONAL REPORTER SYSTEM MAP

EXHIBIT 1–4   HOW TO READ CITATIONS

State Courts

256 Neb. 170, 589 N.W.2d 318 (1999)[a]

N.W. is the abbreviation for West's publication of state court decisions rendered in the *North Western Reporter* of the National Reporter System. *2d* indicates that this case was included in the *Second Series* of that reporter. The number 589 refers to the volume number of the reporter; the number 318 refers to the first page in that volume on which this case can be found.

Neb. is an abbreviation for *Nebraska Reports,* Nebraska's official reports of the decisions of its highest court, the Nebraska Supreme Court.

75 Cal.App.4th 500, 89 Cal.Rptr.2d 146 (1999)

Cal.Rptr. is the abbreviation for West's unofficial reports—titled *California Reporter*—of the decisions of California courts.

85 N.Y.2d 549, 650 N.E.2d 829, 626 N.Y.S.2d 982 (1995)

N.Y.S. is the abbreviation for West's unofficial reports—titled *New York Supplement*—of the decisions of New York courts.

N.Y. is the abbreviation for *New York Reports,* New York's official reports of the decisions of its court of appeals. The New York Court of Appeals is the state's highest court, analogous to other states' supreme courts. In New York, a supreme court is a trial court.

236 Ga.App. 582, 512 S.E.2d 27 (1999)

Ga.App. is the abbreviation for *Georgia Appeals Reports,* Georgia's official reports of the decisions of its court of appeals.

Federal Courts

___ U.S. ___, 119 S.Ct. 1961, 144 L.Ed.2d 319 (1999)

L.Ed. is an abbreviation for *Lawyers' Edition of the Supreme Court Reports,* an unofficial edition of decisions of the United States Supreme Court.

S.Ct. is the abbreviation for West's unofficial reports—titled *Supreme Court Reporter*—of decisions of the United States Supreme Court.

U.S. is the abbreviation for *United States Reports,* the official edition of the decisions of the United States Supreme Court. Volume and page numbers are not included in this citation because they have not yet been assigned.

a. The case names have been deleted from these citations to emphasize the publications. It should be kept in mind, however that the name of a case is as important as the specific numbers of the volumes in which it is found. If a citation is incorrect, the correct citation may be found in a publication's index of case names. The date of a case is also important because, in addition to providing a check on error in citations, the value of a recent case as an authority is likely to be greater than that of an earlier case.

EXHIBIT 1–4 HOW TO READ CITATIONS (CONTINUED)

Federal Courts (continued)

177 F.3d 114 (2d Cir. 1999)

> *2d Cir.* is an abbreviation denoting that this case was decided in the United States Court of Appeals for the Second Circuit.

38 F.Supp.2d 1233 (D.Colo. 1999)

> *D.Colo.* is an abbreviation indicating that the United States District Court for the District of Colorado decided this case.

English Courts

9 Exch. 341, 156 Eng.Rep. 145 (1854)

> *Eng.Rep.* is an abbreviation for *English Reports, Full Reprint*, a series of reports containing selected decisions made in English courts between 1378 and 1865.

> *Exch.* is an abbreviation for *English Exchequer Reports*, which included the original reports of cases decided in England's Court of Exchequer.

Statutory and Other Citations

18 U.S.C. Section 1961(1)(A)

> *U.S.C.* denotes *United States Code*, the codification of *United States Statutes at Large.* The number 18 refers to the statute's U.S.C. title number and 1961 to its section number within that title. The number 1 refers to a subsection within the section and the letter A to a subdivision within the subsection.

UCC 2–206(1)(b)

> *UCC* is an abbreviation for *Uniform Commercial Code*. The first number 2 is a reference to an article of the UCC and 206 to a section within that article. The number 1 refers to a subsection within the section and the letter b to a subdivision within the subsection.

Restatement (Second) of Contracts, Section 162

> *Restatement (Second) of Contracts* refers to the second edition of the American Law Institute's *Restatement of the Law of Contracts.* The number 162 refers to a specific section.

17 C.F.R. Section 230.505

> *C.F.R.* is an abbreviation for *Code of Federal Regulations,* a compilation of federal administrative regulations. The number 17 designates the regulation's title number, and 230.505 designates to a specific section within that title.

EXHIBIT 1–4   HOW TO READ CITATIONS (CONTINUED)

Westlaw® Citations[b]

2000 WL 12345

WL is an abbreviation for Westlaw®. The number 2000 is the year of the document that can be found with this citation in the Westlaw® database. The number 12345 is a number assigned to a specific document. A higher number indicates that a document was added to the Westlaw® database later in the year.

Uniform Resource Locators[c]

www.westlaw.com

The suffix *com* is the top-level domain (TLD) for this Web site. The TLD *com* is an abbreviation for "commercial," which means that a for-profit entity hosts (maintains or supports) this Web site.

westlaw is the host name—the part of the domain name selected by the organization that registered the name. In this case, West Group registered the name. This Internet site is the Westlaw database on the Web.

www is an abbreviation for "World Wide Web." The Web is a system of Internet servers that support documents formatted in *HTML* (hypertext markup language). HTML supports links to text, graphics, and audio and video files.

www.uscourts.gov

This is "The Federal Judiciary Home Page." The host is the Administrative Office of the U.S. Courts. The TLD *gov* is an abbreviation for "government." This Web site includes information and links from, and about, the federal courts.

www.law.cornell.edu/index.html

This part of an URL points to a Web page or file at a specific location within the host's domain. This page, at this Web site, is a menu with links to documents within the domain and to other Internet resources.

This is the host name for a Web site that contains the Internet publications of the Legal Information Institute (LII), which is a part of Cornell Law School. The LII site includes a variety of legal materials and links to other legal resources on the Internet. The TLD *edu* is an abbreviation for "educational institution" (a school or a university).

www.ipl.org.ref/RR

RR is an abbreviation for this Web site's "Ready Reference Collection," which contains links to a variety of Internet resources.

ref is an abbreviation for "Internet Public Library Reference Center," which is a map of the topics into which the links at this Web site have been categorized.

ipl is an abbreviation for Internet Public Library, which is an online service that provides reference resources and links to other information services on the Web. The IPL is supported chiefly by the School of Information at the University of Michigan. The TLD *org* is an abbreviation for "organization (nonprofit)."

---

b. Many court decisions that are not yet published or that are not intended for publication can be accessed through Westlaw®, an online legal database.

c. The basic form for a URL is "service://hostname/path." The Internet service for all of the URLs in this text is *http* (hypertext transfer protocol). Most Web browsers will add this prefix automatically when a user enters a host name or a hostname/path.

decisions, to which more than forty thousand decisions are added each year. Because judicial decisions are published in chronological order, finding relevant precedents would be a Herculean task if it were not for secondary sources of law that classify decisions according to subject. Two important "finding tools" that are helpful when researching case law are case digests, such as West's *American Digest System*; and legal encyclopedias, such as *American Jurisprudence, Second Edition*, and *Corpus Juris Secundum*, both published by West Group.

SECTION 6

How to Read and Understand Case Law

The decisions made by the courts establish the boundaries of the law as it applies to business firms and business relationships. It thus is essential that businesspersons know how to read and understand case law. The cases that we present in this text have been condensed from the full text of the courts' opinions—that is, in each case we have summarized the background and facts, as well as the court's decision and remedy, in our own words and have included only selected portions of the court's opinion ("in the language of the court"). For those who wish to review court cases to perform research projects or to gain additional legal information, however, the following sections will provide useful insights into how to read and understand case law.

CASE TITLES

The title of a case, such as *Adams v. Jones*, indicates the names of the parties to the lawsuit. The *v.* in the case title stands for *versus*, which means "against." In the trial court, Adams was the plaintiff—the person who filed the suit. Jones was the defendant. If the case is appealed, however, the appellate court will sometimes place the name of the party appealing the decision first, so that the case may be called *Jones v. Adams* if Jones is appealing. Because some appellate courts retain the trial court order of names, it is often impossible to distinguish the plaintiff from the defendant in the title of a reported appellate court decision. You must carefully read the facts of each case to identify the parties. Otherwise, the discussion by the appellate court will be difficult to understand.

TERMINOLOGY

The following terms, phrases, and abbreviations are frequently encountered in court opinions and legal publications. Because it is important to understand what is meant by these terms, phrases, and abbreviations, we define and discuss them here.

Parties to Lawsuits.   As mentioned previously, the party initiating a lawsuit is referred to as the *plaintiff* or *petitioner*, depending on the nature of the action, and the party against whom a lawsuit is brought is the *defendant* or *respondent*. Lawsuits frequently involve more than one plaintiff and/or defendant. When a case is appealed from the original court or jurisdiction to another court or jurisdiction, the party appealing the case is called the **appellant**. The **appellee** is the party against whom the appeal is taken. (In some appellate courts, the party appealing a case is referred to as the petitioner, and the party against whom the suit is brought or appealed is called the respondent.)

Judges and Justices.   The terms *judge* and *justice* are usually synonymous and represent two designations given to judges in various courts. All members of the United States Supreme Court, for example, are referred to as justices, and justice is the formal title usually given to judges of appellate courts, although this is not always the case. In New York, a *justice* is a judge of the trial court (which is called the Supreme Court), and a member of the Court of Appeals (the state's highest court) is called a *judge*. The term *justice* is commonly abbreviated to J., and *justices*, to JJ. A Supreme Court case might refer to Justice Kennedy as Kennedy, J., or to Chief Justice Rehnquist as Rehnquist, C.J.

Decisions and Opinions.   Most decisions reached by reviewing, or appellate, courts are explained in written **opinions.** The opinion contains the court's reasons for its decision, the rules of law that apply, and the judgment.

When all judges or justices unanimously agree on an opinion, the opinion is written for the entire court and can be deemed a *unanimous opinion*. When there is not a unanimous opinion, a *majority opinion* is written; it outlines the views of the majority of the judges or justices deciding the case. If a judge agrees, or concurs, with the majority's decision, but for different reasons, that judge may write a *concurring opinion*. A *dissenting opinion* is written by one or more judges who disagree with the majority's decision. The dissenting opinion is important because it may form the basis of the arguments used years later in overruling the precedential majority opinion.

Occasionally, a court issues a *per curiam* opinion. *Per curiam* is a Latin phrase meaning "of the court." In *per curiam* opinions, there is no indication of which judge or justice authored the opinion. This term may also be used for an announcement of a court's disposition of a case that is not accompanied by a written opinion. Sometimes, the cases presented in this text are *en banc* decisions. When an appellate court reviews a case *en banc*, which is a French term (derived from a Latin term) for "in the bench," generally all of the judges sitting on the bench of that court review the case.

A SAMPLE COURT CASE

To illustrate the various elements contained in a court opinion, we present in Exhibit 1–5 an annotated court opinion. The opinion is from an actual case that the U.S. Court of Appeals for the Second Circuit decided in 2000. Federal Express Corporation initiated the lawsuit against Federal Espresso, Inc., and others, claiming in part that the name "Federal Espresso" infringed on the Federal Express trademark. The court denied the plaintiff's request for a *preliminary injunction* (an injunction granted at the beginning of a suit to restrain the defendant from doing some act, the right to which is in dispute). Thus, the issue before the appellate court was whether the trial court erred in refusing to grant the injunction.

You will note that triple asterisks (*   *   *) and quadruple asterisks (*   *   *   *) frequently appear in the opinion. The triple asterisks indicate that we have deleted a few words or sentences from the opinion for the sake of readability or brevity. Quadruple asterisks mean that an entire paragraph (or more) has been omitted. Additionally, when the opinion cites another case or legal source, the citation to the case or other source has been omitted to save space and to improve the flow of the text. These editorial practices are continued in the other court opinions presented in this text.[7] In addition, whenever we present a court opinion that includes a term or phrase that may not be readily understandable, a bracketed definition or paraphrase has been added.

Knowing how to read and understand court opinions and the legal reasoning used by the courts is an essential step in undertaking accurate legal research. Yet a further step is "briefing," or summarizing, the case. Legal researchers routinely brief cases by reducing the texts of the opinions to their essential elements. Instructions on how to brief a case are given in Appendix A, which also includes a briefed version of the sample court case presented in Exhibit 1–5.

SECTION 7

Businesspersons and the Law

Those entering into the world of business will find that laws and government regulations affect virtually all business activities—from hiring and firing decisions, to the manufacturing and marketing of products, to financing matters, and so on. To make good business decisions, a basic knowledge of the laws and regulations governing these activities is beneficial—if not essential. The study of business law is thus a sound investment for anyone who wishes to succeed in today's business arena.

As you will note, each of the chapters in this text covers a specific area of the law and shows how the legal rules in that area of law affect businesses. While compartmentalizing the law in this fashion promotes conceptual clarity, it does not indicate the extent to which one area of law overlaps with another.

Consider an example. Net Systems, Inc., creates and maintains computer network systems for its clients, including business firms. Net Systems also markets software for customers who need an internal computer network but cannot afford an individually designed intranet. Mark is the president of Net Systems. Janet, an operations officer for Southwest Distribution Corporation (SDC), contacts Mark by e-mail about a possible contract concerning SDC's computer network. In deciding whether to enter into a contract with SDC, Mark needs to consider, among other things, the legal requirements for an enforceable contract. Are there different requirements for a contract for services and a contract for products? What are the options if SDC **breaches** (breaks, or fails to perform) the contract? The answers to these questions are part of contract law and sales law.

Other questions might concern payment under the contract. How can Net Systems guarantee that it will be paid? If a payment is made with, for example, a check that is returned for insufficient funds, what are Net Systems's options? Answers to these questions can be found in the laws that relate to negotiable instruments (such as checks) and creditors' rights. Also,

---

7. We make an exception in the *Focus on Legal Reasoning* sections, however, in which we retain the court's citations to facilitate student research.

EXHIBIT 1–5   A SAMPLE COURT CASE

FEDERAL EXPRESS CORP. v. FEDERAL ESPRESSO, INC.

United States Court of Appeals, Second Circuit, 2000.
201 F.3d 168.

> This line gives the name of the judge who authored the opinion of the court.

KEARSE, Circuit Judge.

* * * *

> The court divides the opinion into three parts, headed by roman numerals. The first part of the opinion summarizes the factual background of the case.

I. BACKGROUND

* * * Federal Express, incorporated in 1972, invented the overnight shipping business. It has used the name "Federal Express" since 1973. * * * Federal Express currently has 140,000 employees, ships 2.9 million packages per day, and has annual revenues of more than $11 billion.

Federal Express provides service in at least 210 countries * * *.

* * * *

In March 1994, defendants Anna Dobbs ("Dobbs") and David J. Ruston, her brother, formed a business called New York Espresso in Syracuse, New York, for the wholesale distribution of commercial espresso machines. In April 1994, Dobbs, her husband defendant John Dobbs, and Ruston decided to change the name of the business from New York Espresso to "Federal Espresso." * * *

* * * [I]n November 1995, Dobbs opened a coffee shop, called "Federal Espresso," [in] Syracuse * * *.

* * * *

> The unauthorized use or imitation of another's trademark.

Defendants opened a second store * * * in August 1997. * * *

* * * Federal Express commenced the present action in August 1997. It principally asserted claims of * * * **trademark infringement**

> A doctrine that protects a trademark from infringement by another party even when there is no competition or likelihood of confusion, such as when products are dissimilar.

* * * and claims of **dilution** of the distinctive quality of its famous mark * * *; and it moved for a preliminary injunction.

> A federal trial court in which a lawsuit is initiated.

* * * [T]he **district court denied the motion** * * *.

* * * *

> The decision of the trial court, from which the appeal was taken.

II. DISCUSSION

> The second major section of the opinion analyzes the issue before the court.

* * * [A] party seeking a preliminary injunction must demonstrate (1) the likelihood of **irreparable injury** in the absence of such an injunction, and (2) * * * likelihood of success on the **merits** * * *.

> A wrong of a repeated and continuing nature for which damages are difficult to estimate.

* * * *

* * * The hallmark of [trademark] infringement * * * is **likelihood of confusion.**

> The substance, elements, or grounds of a cause of action.

> *Likelihood of confusion* occurs when a substantial number of ordinarily prudent purchasers are likely to be misled or confused as to the source of a product.

EXHIBIT 1–5   A SAMPLE COURT CASE (CONTINUED)

A **presumption** is an assumption of fact that the law requires to be made from another fact.

To make apparent or clear, by evidence; to prove.

To justify or call for; to deserve.

Impending; near at hand; on the point of happening.

The final section of the opinion, in which the court gives its order.

* * * [P]roof of a likelihood of confusion would create a **presumption** of irreparable harm, and thus a plaintiff would not need to prove such harm independently. By the same token, however, if the plaintiff does not **show** likelihood of success on the merits, it cannot obtain a preliminary injunction without making an independent showing of likely irreparable harm.

As to Federal Express's claims of trademark infringement, we have no difficulty with the district court's ruling that Federal Express did not show likelihood of confusion and hence did not show that it was likely to succeed on the merits of those claims. * * * Accordingly, since Federal Express did not make any independent showing of likelihood of irreparable harm, the trademark infringement claims did not **warrant** the granting of a preliminary injunction.

* * * *

The type of dilution pertinent to the present case is "blurring," a process that may occur where the defendant uses or modifies the plaintiff's trademark to identify the defendant's goods and services, raising the possibility that the mark will lose its ability to serve as a unique identifier of the plaintiff's product. * * *

* * * *

* * * Here, * * * the principal products—coffee and overnight delivery service—are dissimilar; there would seem to be little likelihood of confusion; and while Federal Express is a vast organization, operating in 210 countries, employing 140,000 persons., and grossing more than $11 billion annually, defendants are three individuals with two stores in Syracuse. * * * The court was entitled to conclude, given these facts and the tiny extent of the overlap among customers of Federal Express and Federal Espresso, that dilution was not **imminent** and that a preliminary injunction was not needed.

* * * *

III. CONCLUSION

* * * The order of the district court denying a preliminary injunction is affirmed.

a dispute may occur over the rights to Net Systems's software, or there may be a question of liability if the software is defective. There may be an issue as to the authority of Mark or Janet to make a deal. A disagreement may arise from such circumstances as an accountant's evaluation of the contract. Resolutions of these questions may be found in areas of the law that relate to intellectual property, e-commerce, torts, product liability, agency, business organizations, or professional liability.

Finally, if any dispute cannot be resolved amicably, then the laws and the rules concerning courts and court procedures spell out the steps of a lawsuit. Exhibit 1–6 illustrates the various areas of law that may influence business decision making.

EXHIBIT 1–6   AREAS OF THE LAW THAT MAY AFFECT BUSINESS DECISION MAKING

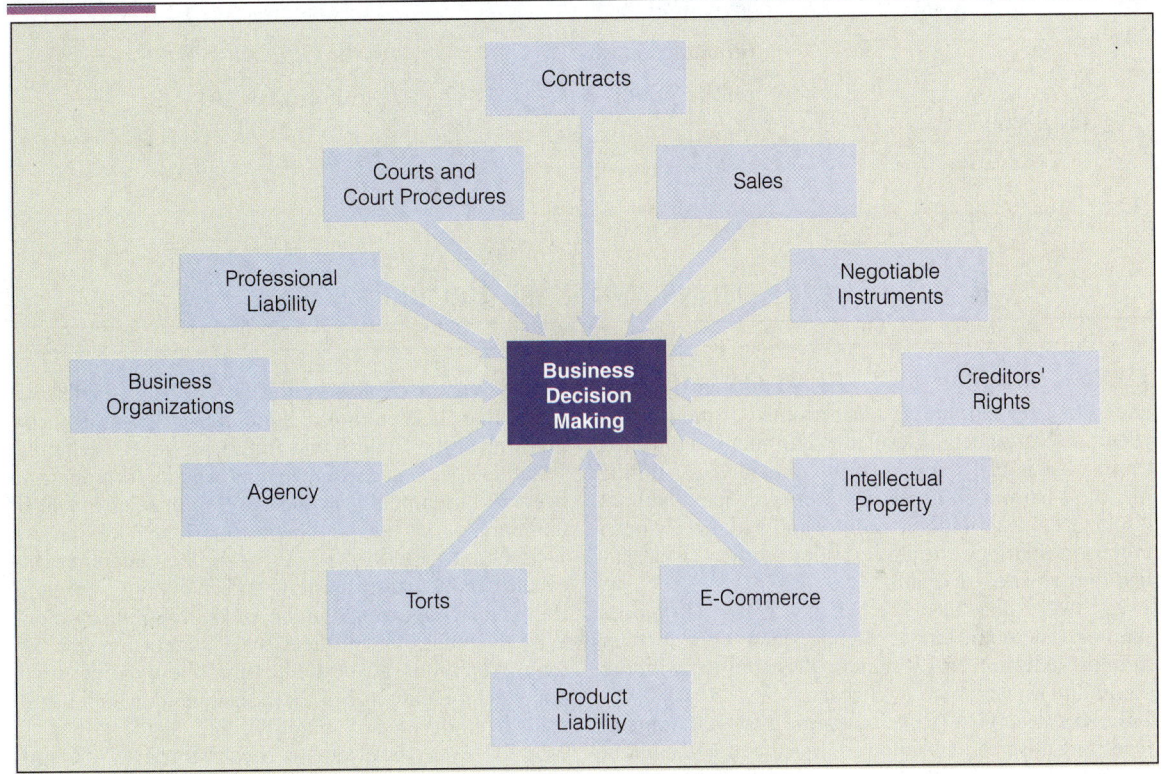

TERMS AND CONCEPTS TO REVIEW

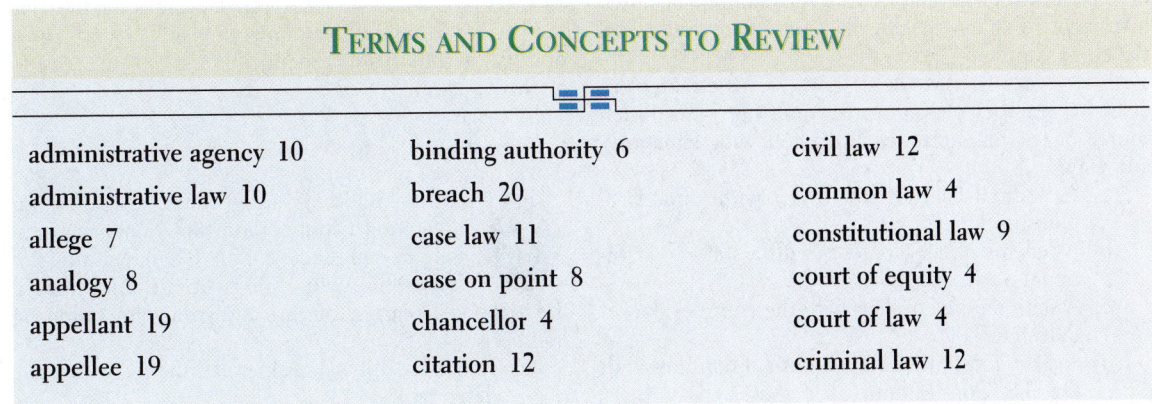

administrative agency 10	binding authority 6	civil law 12
administrative law 10	breach 20	common law 4
allege 7	case law 11	constitutional law 9
analogy 8	case on point 8	court of equity 4
appellant 19	chancellor 4	court of law 4
appellee 19	citation 12	criminal law 12

damages 4	legal reasoning 7	remedy at law 4
defendant 5	natural law 3	remedy in equity 5
defense 5	opinion 19	reporter 6
equitable maxims 5	ordinance 10	respondent 5
executive agency 11	petitioner 5	sociological school 3
historical school 3	plaintiff 5	*stare decisis* 6
independent regulatory agency 11	positive law 3	statute of limitations 5
jurisprudence 3	positivist school 3	statutory law 10
laches 5	precedent 6	substantive law 12
law 2	procedural law 12	syllogism 8
legal realism 3	public policy 7	uniform law 10
	remedy 4	

QUESTIONS AND CASE PROBLEMS

1–1. PHILOSOPHY OF LAW. After World War II, which ended in 1945, an international tribunal of judges convened at Nuremberg, Germany. The judges convicted several Nazis of "crimes against humanity." Assuming that the Nazi war criminals who were convicted had not disobeyed any law of their country and had merely been following their government's (Hitler's) orders, what law had they violated? Explain.

1–2. STATUTORY VERSUS COMMON LAW. How does statutory law come into existence? How does it differ from the common law? If statutory law conflicts with the common law, which law will govern?

1–3. READING CITATIONS. Assume that you want to read the entire court opinion in the case of *Millennium Enterprises, Inc. v. Millennium Music, LP,* 33 F.Supp.2d 907 (D.Or. 1999). The case considers whether a South Carolina business firm could be sued in Oregon based on the circumstance that its Web site could be accessed in Oregon. Explain specifically where you would find the court's opinion.

1–4. SOURCES OF AMERICAN LAW. This chapter discussed a number of sources of American law. Which source of law takes priority in the following situations, and why?
(a) A federal statute conflicts with the U.S. Constitution.
(b) A federal statute conflicts with a state constitutional provision.
(c) A state statute conflicts with the common law of that state.
(d) A state constitutional amendment conflicts with the U.S. Constitution.

1–5. STARE DECISIS. In the text of this chapter, we stated that the doctrine of *stare decisis* "became a cornerstone of the English and American judicial systems." What does *stare decisis* mean, and why has this doctrine been so fundamental to the development of our legal tradition?

1–6. COURT OPINIONS. What is the difference between a concurring opinion and a majority opinion? Between a concurring opinion and a dissenting opinion? Why do judges and justices write concurring and dissenting opinions, given the fact that these opinions will not affect the outcome of the case at hand, which has already been decided by majority vote?

1–7. COMMON LAW VERSUS STATUTORY LAW. Courts can overturn precedents and thus change the common law. Should judges have the same authority to overrule statutory law? Explain.

1–8. STARE DECISIS. "The judge's role is not to make the law but to uphold and apply the law." Do you agree or disagree with this statement? Discuss fully the reasons for your answer.

1–9. IN YOUR COURT

Arthur Rabe is suing Xavier Sanchez for breaching a contract in which Sanchez promised to sell Rabe a Van Gogh painting for $150,000. Assume that you are the judge in the trial court hearing the case and answer the following questions:
(a) In this lawsuit, who is the plaintiff and who is the defendant?

(b) Rabe wants Sanchez to perform the contract as promised. If you agree to Rabe's request, what remedy will you grant?

(c) Suppose that Rabe wants to cancel the contract because Sanchez fraudulently misrepresented the painting as an original Van Gogh when in fact it is a copy. If you agree to this request, what remedy will you grant?

(d) Will the remedy Rabe seeks in either situation be a remedy at law or a remedy in equity?

(e) Suppose that you find in Rabe's favor and grant one of these remedies. Sanchez then appeals the decision to a higher court. On appeal, which party will be the appellant (or petitioner), and which party will be the appellee (or respondent)?

LAW ON THE WEB

Today, business law professors and students can go online to access information on virtually every topic covered in this text. A good point of departure for online legal research is the Web site for *West's Business Law*, Eighth Edition, at http://wbl.westbuslaw.com. There you will find numerous materials relevant to this text and to business law generally, including links to various legal resources on the Web. Additionally, every chapter in this text ends with a *Law on the Web* feature that contains selected Web addresses.

You can access many of the sources of law discussed in Chapter 1 at the FindLaw Web site, which is probably the most comprehensive source of free legal information on the Internet. Go to

http://www.findlaw.com

The Legal Information Institute (LII) at Cornell Law School, which offers extensive information about U.S. law, is also a good starting point for legal research. The URL for this site is

http://www.law.cornell.edu

The Library of Congress offers extensive links to state and federal government resources at

http://www.loc.gov

Villanova University's Center for Information Law and Policy provides access to numerous legal resources, including opinions from the federal appellate courts. Go to

http://www.law.vill.edu

The Virtual Law Library Index, created and maintained by the Indiana University School of Law, provides an index of legal sources categorized by subject at

http://www.law.indiana.edu

LEGAL RESEARCH EXERCISES ON THE WEB

The text's Web site also offers online research exercises. These exercises will help you find and analyze specific types of legal information available at specific Web sites. There is at least one of these exercises for each chapter in *West's Business Law*, Eighth Edition. To access these exercises, go to this book's Web site at http://wbl.westbuslaw.com and click on "Internet Applications." When that page opens, select the relevant chapter to find the exercise or exercises relating to topics in that chapter. The following activity will direct you to some of the important sources of law discussed in Chapter 1:

Activity 1–1: Internet Sources of Law

Courts and
Alternative Dispute Resolution

TODAY IN THE UNITED STATES there are fifty-two court systems—one for each of the fifty states, one for the District of Columbia, and a federal system. Keep in mind that the federal courts are not superior to the state courts; they are simply an independent system of courts, which derives its authority from Article III, Section 2, of the U.S. Constitution. By the power given to it under Article I of the U.S. Constitution, Congress has extended the federal court system beyond the boundaries of the United States to U.S. territories such as Guam, the Virgin Islands, and Puerto Rico.[1] As we shall see, the United States Supreme Court is the final controlling voice over all of these fifty-two systems, at least when questions of federal law are involved.

Every businessperson will likely face a lawsuit at some time in his or her career. It is thus important for anyone involved in business to have an understanding of the American court systems, as well as the various methods of dispute resolution that can be pursued outside the courts. In this chapter, after examining the judiciary's general role in the American governmental scheme, we discuss some basic requirements

that must be met before a party may bring a lawsuit before a particular court. We then look at the court systems of the United States in some detail. We conclude the chapter with an overview of some alternative methods of settling disputes.

SECTION 1

The Judiciary's Role in American Government

As you learned in Chapter 1, the body of American law includes the federal and state constitutions, statutes passed by legislative bodies, administrative law, and the case decisions and legal principles that form the common law. These laws would be meaningless, however, without the courts to interpret and apply them. This is the essential role of the judiciary—the courts—in the American governmental system: to interpret the laws and apply them to specific situations.

As the branch of government entrusted with interpreting the laws, the judiciary can decide, among other things, whether the laws or actions of the other two branches are constitutional. The process for mak-

---

1. In Guam and the Virgin Islands, territorial courts serve as both federal courts and state courts; in Puerto Rico, they serve only as federal courts.

ing such a determination is known as **judicial review.** The power of judicial review enables the judicial branch to act as a check on the other two branches of government, in line with the checks and balances system established by the U.S. Constitution.[2]

The power of judicial review is not mentioned in the Constitution (although many constitutional scholars conclude that the founders intended the judiciary to have this power). Rather, this power was established by the United States Supreme Court in 1803 by its decision in *Marbury v. Madison,*[3] in which the Supreme Court stated, "It is emphatically the province and duty of the Judicial Department to say what the law is. . . . If two laws conflict with each other, the courts must decide on the operation of each. . . . So if the law be in opposition to the Constitution . . . [t]he Court must determine which of these conflicting rules governs the case. This is the very essence of judicial duty." Since the *Marbury v. Madison* decision, the power of judicial review has remained unchallenged. Today, this power is exercised by both federal and state courts.

SECTION 2

Basic Judicial Requirements

Before a lawsuit can be brought before a court, certain requirements must be met. These requirements relate to jurisdiction, venue, and standing to sue. We examine each of these important concepts here.

JURISDICTION

In Latin, *juris* means "law," and *diction* means "to speak." Thus, "the power to speak the law" is the literal meaning of the term **jurisdiction.** Before any court can hear a case, it must have jurisdiction over the person against whom the suit is brought or jurisdiction over the property involved in a lawsuit. The court must also have jurisdiction over the subject matter. Keep in mind throughout this discussion of jurisdiction that we are talking about jurisdiction over the *defendant* in a lawsuit.

Jurisdiction over Persons. Generally, a particular court can exercise *in personam* **jurisdiction** (personal jurisdiction) over residents of a certain geographical area. A state trial court, for example, normally has jurisdictional authority over residents of a particular area of the state, such as a county or district. A state's highest court (often called the state supreme court)[4] has jurisdictional authority over all residents within the state.

In some cases, under the authority of a state **long arm statute,** a court can exercise personal jurisdiction over nonresident defendants as well. Before a court can exercise jurisdiction over a nonresident defendant under a long arm statute, though, it must be demonstrated that the defendant had sufficient contacts, or *minimum contacts,* with the state to justify the jurisdiction.[5] For example, if an individual has committed a wrong within the state, such as injuring someone in an automobile accident or selling defective goods, a court can usually exercise jurisdiction even if the person causing the harm is located in another state. Similarly, a state may exercise personal jurisdiction over a nonresident defendant who is sued for breaching a contract that was formed within the state.

In regard to corporations,[6] the minimum-contacts requirement is usually met if the corporation does business within the state, advertises or sells its products within the state, or places its goods into the "stream of commerce" with the intent that the goods be sold in the state. Suppose that a business incorporated under the laws of Maine and headquartered in that state has a branch office or manufacturing plant in Georgia. Does this corporation have sufficient contacts with the state of Georgia to allow a Georgia court to exercise jurisdiction over the corporation? Yes, it does. If the Maine corporation advertises and sells its products in Georgia, or places goods within the stream of commerce with the expectation that the goods will be purchased by Georgia residents, those activities may also suffice to meet the minimum-contacts requirement.

In the following case, the issue was whether phone calls and letters constituted sufficient minimum contacts to give a court jurisdiction over a nonresident defendant.

2. In a broad sense, judicial review occurs whenever a court "reviews" a case or legal proceeding—as when an appellate court reviews a lower court's decision. When referring to the judiciary's role in American government, however, the term *judicial review* is used to indicate the power of the judiciary to decide whether the actions of the other two branches of government do or do not violate the Constitution.
3. 5 U.S. (1 Cranch) 137, 2 L.Ed. 60 (1803).
4. As will be discussed shortly, a state's highest court is often referred to as the state supreme court, but there are exceptions. For example, in New York the supreme court is a trial court.
5. The minimum-contacts standard was established in *International Shoe Co. v. State of Washington,* 326 U.S. 310, 66 S.Ct. 154, 90 L.Ed. 95 (1945).
6. In the eyes of the law, corporations are "legal persons"—entities that can sue and be sued. See Chapter 34.

CASE 2.1   Cole v. Mileti

United States
Court of Appeals,
Sixth Circuit, 1998.
133 F.3d 433.
http://www.law.emory.
edu/6circuit/jan98/
index.html[a]

HISTORICAL AND ECONOMIC SETTING   *A movie production company is expensive to operate. Over the two to five years it can take to produce a film, there are many expenses, including maintaining an office and hiring professionals of all kinds. Newcomers to the industry make many of the same mistakes that are the pitfalls of all businesses. For a novice producer or investor, there is the uncertainty of not knowing what you are doing and the danger of being outnegotiated by those who prey on a novice's ignorance. Finally, once a film is made, there is the audience, which may not choose to see it.*

BACKGROUND AND FACTS   *Nick Mileti, a resident of California, co-produced a movie called* Streamers *and organized a corporation, Streamers International Distributors, Inc., to distribute the film. Joseph Cole, a resident of Ohio, bought two hundred shares of Streamers stock. Cole also lent the firm $475,000, which he borrowed from Equitable Bank of Baltimore. The film was unsuccessful. Mileti agreed to repay Cole's loan in a contract arranged through phone calls and correspondence between California and Ohio. When Mileti did not repay the loan, the bank sued Cole, who in turn filed a suit against Mileti in a federal district court in Ohio. The court entered a judgment against Mileti. He appealed to the U.S. Court of Appeals for the Sixth Circuit, arguing in part that the district court's exercise of jurisdiction over him was unfair.[b]*

IN THE LANGUAGE OF THE COURT   *MERRITT*, Circuit Judge.

*   *   *   *

*   *   * [There is] a three-part test to determine whether specific jurisdiction exists over a nonresident defendant like Mileti. First, the defendant must purposefully avail himself of the privilege of conducting activities within the forum state [the state in which the court sits]; second, the cause of action must arise from the defendant's activities there; and third, the acts of the defendant or consequences caused by the defendant must have a substantial enough connection with the forum state to make its exercise of jurisdiction over the defendant fundamentally fair.

If, as here, a nonresident defendant transacts business by negotiating and executing a contract via telephone calls and letters to an Ohio resident, then the defendant has purposefully availed himself of the forum by creating a continuing obligation in Ohio. Furthermore, if the cause of action is for breach of that contract, as it is here, then the cause of action naturally arises from the defendant's activities in Ohio. Finally, when we find that a defendant like Mileti purposefully availed himself of the forum and that the cause of action arose directly from that contact, we presume the specific assertion of personal jurisdiction was proper.

DECISION AND REMEDY   *The U.S. Court of Appeals for the Sixth Circuit held that the district court could exercise personal jurisdiction over Mileti. The appellate court reasoned that a federal district court in Ohio can exercise personal jurisdiction over a resident of California who does business in Ohio via phone calls and letters.*

---

a. This page, which is part of the Web site of the Emory University School of Law, lists the published opinions of the U.S. Court of Appeals for the Sixth Circuit for January 1998. Scroll down the list of cases to the *Cole* case. To access the opinion, click on the case name.

b. As will be discussed shortly, federal courts can exercise jurisdiction over disputes between parties living in different states. This is called *diversity-of-citizenship* jurisdiction. When a federal court exercises diversity jurisdiction, the court normally applies the law of the state in which the court sits—in this case, the law of Ohio.

Jurisdiction over Property. A court can also exercise jurisdiction over property that is located within its boundaries. This kind of jurisdiction is known as *in rem* **jurisdiction,** or "jurisdiction over the thing." For example, suppose a dispute arises over the ownership of a boat in dry dock in Fort Lauderdale, Florida. The boat is owned by an Ohio resident, over whom a Florida court normally cannot exercise personal jurisdiction. The other party to the dispute is a resident of Nebraska. In this situation, a lawsuit concerning the boat could be brought in a Florida state court on the basis of the court's *in rem* jurisdiction.

Jurisdiction over Subject Matter. Jurisdiction over subject matter is a limitation on the types of cases a court can hear. In both the federal and state court systems, there are courts of *general* (unlimited) *jurisdiction* and courts of *limited jurisdiction.* A court of general jurisdiction can decide cases involving a broad array of issues. An example of a court of general jurisdiction is a state trial court or federal district court. An example of a state court of limited jurisdiction is a probate court. **Probate courts** are state courts that handle only matters relating to the transfer of a person's assets and obligations after that person's death, including issues relating to the custody and guardianship of children. An example of a federal court of limited subject-matter jurisdiction is a bankruptcy court. **Bankruptcy courts** handle only bankruptcy proceedings, which are governed by federal bankruptcy law (discussed in Chapter 30).

A court's jurisdiction over subject matter is usually defined in the statute or constitution creating the court. In both the federal and state court systems, a court's subject-matter jurisdiction can be limited not only by the subject of the lawsuit but also by how much money is in controversy, whether the case is a felony (a more serious type of crime) or a misdemeanor (a less serious type of crime), or whether the proceeding is a trial or an appeal.

Original and Appellate Jurisdiction. The distinction between courts of original jurisdiction and courts of appellate jurisdiction normally lies in whether the case is being heard for the first time. Courts having original jurisdiction are courts of the first instance, or trial courts—that is, courts in which lawsuits begin, trials take place, and evidence is presented. In the federal court system, the *district courts* are trial courts. In the various state court systems, the trial courts are known by different names, as will be discussed shortly.

The key point here is that normally, any court having original jurisdiction is known as a trial court. Courts having appellate jurisdiction act as reviewing courts, or appellate courts. In general, cases can be brought before appellate courts only on appeal from an order or a judgment of a trial court or other lower court.

Jurisdiction of the Federal Courts. Because the federal government is a government of limited powers, the jurisdiction of the federal courts is limited. Article III of the U.S. Constitution establishes the boundaries of federal judicial power. Section 2 of Article III states that "[t]he judicial Power shall extend to all Cases, in Law and Equity, arising under this Constitution, the Laws of the United States, and Treaties made, or which shall be made, under their Authority." In effect, this clause means that whenever a plaintiff's cause of action is based—at least in part—on the U.S. Constitution, a treaty, or a federal law, a **federal question** arises, and the case comes under the judicial authority of the federal courts. Any lawsuit involving a federal question can originate in a federal court. People who claim that their constitutional rights have been violated can begin their suits in a federal court.

Federal district courts can also exercise original jurisdiction over cases involving **diversity of citizenship.** This term applies whenever a federal court has jurisdiction over a case that does not involve a question of federal law. The most common type of diversity jurisdiction has two requirements:[7] (1) the plaintiff and defendant must be residents of different states, and (2) the dollar amount in controversy must exceed $75,000. For purposes of diversity jurisdiction, a corporation is a citizen of both the state in which it is incorporated and the state in which its principal place of business is located. A case involving diversity of citizenship can be filed in the appropriate federal district court. If the case starts in a state court, it can sometimes be transferred, or "removed," to a federal court. A large percentage of the cases filed in federal courts each year are based on diversity of citizenship.

Note that in a case based on a federal question, a federal court will apply federal law. In a case based on diversity of citizenship, however, a federal court will

---

7. Diversity jurisdiction also exists in cases between (1) a foreign country and citizens of a state or of different states and (2) citizens of a state and citizens or subjects of a foreign country. These bases for diversity jurisdiction are less commonly used.

apply the relevant state law (which is often the law of the state in which the court sits).

Exclusive versus Concurrent Jurisdiction.   When both federal and state courts have the power to hear a case, as is true in suits involving diversity of citizenship, **concurrent jurisdiction** exists. When cases can be tried only in federal courts or only in state courts,

exclusive jurisdiction exists. Federal courts have exclusive jurisdiction in cases involving federal crimes, bankruptcy, patents, and copyrights; in suits against the United States; and in some areas of admiralty law (law governing transportation on the seas and ocean waters). The states also have exclusive jurisdiction in certain subject matters—for example, divorce and adoption.

CONCEPT SUMMARY 2.1   JURISDICTION

TYPE OF JURISDICTION	DESCRIPTION
Personal/Property	Exists when a defendant or a defendant's property is located within the territorial boundaries within which a court has the right and power to decide cases. Jurisdiction may be exercised over out-of-state defendants under state long arm statutes.
Subject Matter	Limits the court's jurisdictional authority to particular types of cases. 1. *Limited jurisdiction*—Exists when a court is limited to a specific subject matter, such as probate or divorce. 2. *General jurisdiction*—Exists when a court can hear cases involving a broad array of issues.
Original	Exists with courts that have the authority to hear a case for the first time (trial courts).
Appellate	Exists with courts of appeal and review; generally, appellate courts do not have original jurisdiction.
Federal	Arises in the following situations: 1. When a federal question is involved (when the plaintiff's cause of action is based at least in part on the U.S. Constitution, a treaty, or a federal law). 2. In diversity-of-citizenship cases between citizens of different states when the amount in controversy exceeds $75,000. (Diversity jurisdiction also exists in cases between a foreign country and citizens of a state or of different states and in cases between citizens of a state and citizens or subjects of a foreign country.)
Concurrent	Exists when both federal and state courts have authority to hear the same case.
Exclusive	Exists when only state courts or only federal courts have authority to hear a case.

VENUE

Jurisdiction has to do with whether a court has authority to hear a case involving specific persons, property, or subject matter. **Venue**[8] is concerned with the most appropriate location for a trial. For example, two

state courts (or two federal courts) may have the authority to exercise jurisdiction over a case, but it may be more appropriate or convenient to hear the case in one court than in the other.

Basically, the concept of venue reflects the policy that a court trying a suit should be in the geographical neighborhood (usually the county) in which the incident leading to the lawsuit occurred or in which

---

8. Pronounced *ven-yoo*.

the parties involved in the lawsuit reside. Pretrial publicity or other factors, though, may require a change of venue to another community, especially in criminal cases in which the defendant's right to a fair and impartial jury has been impaired.

For example, a change of venue from Oklahoma City to Denver, Colorado, was ordered for the trials of Timothy McVeigh and Terry Nichols after they had been indicted in connection with the 1995 bombing of the federal building in Oklahoma City. As a result of the bombing, more than 160 persons were killed, and hundreds of others were wounded. In view of these circumstances, it was felt that to hold the trial in Oklahoma City could prejudice the rights of the defendants to a fair trial.

STANDING TO SUE

In order to bring a lawsuit before a court, a party must have **standing to sue,** or a sufficient "stake" in a matter to justify seeking relief through the court system. In other words, a party must have a legally protected and tangible interest at stake in the litigation in order to have standing. The party bringing the lawsuit must have suffered a harm or been threatened with a harm by the action about which he or she has complained. In some circumstances, a person can have standing to sue on be-

half of another person. For example, suppose that a child suffers serious injuries as a result of a defectively manufactured toy. Because the child is a minor, a lawsuit can be brought on his or her behalf by another person, such as the child's parent or legal guardian.

Standing to sue also requires that the controversy at issue be a **justiciable[9] controversy**—a controversy that is real and substantial, as opposed to hypothetical or academic. For instance, in the above example, the child's parent could not sue the toy manufacturer merely on the ground that the toy was defective. The issue would become justiciable only if the child had actually been injured due to the defect in the toy as marketed. In other words, the parent normally could not ask the court to determine what damages might be obtained if the child had been injured, because this would be merely a hypothetical question.

Meeting standing requirements is not always easy. In the following case, for example, an environmental organization sued a company for allegedly discharging pollutants into waterways beyond the amount allowed by the Environmental Protection Agency. At issue in the case was whether the organization had standing to sue under federal environmental laws.

---

9. Pronounced jus-*tish*-a-bul.

CASE 2.2

Friends of the Earth, Inc. v. Crown Central Petroleum Corp.

United States
Court of Appeals,
Fifth Circuit, 1996.
95 F.3d 358.
http://www.ca5.
uscourts.gov/oparchdt.
cfm?Year-1996[a]

BACKGROUND AND FACTS   *Crown Central Petroleum Corporation does business as La Gloria Oil & Gas Company. Under a permit issued by the Environmental Protection Agency (EPA), La Gloria's oil refinery discharges storm-water run-off into Black Fork Creek. Black Fork Creek flows into Prairie Creek, which flows into the Neches River, which flows into Lake Palestine eighteen miles downstream. Friends of the Earth, Inc. (FOE), is a not-for-profit corporation dedicated to the protection of the environment. FOE filed a suit in a federal district court against La Gloria under the Federal Water Pollution Control Act.[b] FOE claimed that La Gloria had violated its EPA permit and that this conduct had directly affected "the health, economic, recreational, aesthetic and environmental interests of FOE's members" who used the lake. La Gloria filed a motion for summary judgment, arguing that FOE lacked standing to bring the suit. The court granted the motion, and FOE appealed.*

IN THE LANGUAGE OF THE COURT

PATRICK E. HIGGINBOTHAM, Circuit Judge:

    *   *   *   *

---

a. This is a page within the Web site of the U.S. Courts of the Fifth Judicial Circuit. Click on "1996." When the link opens, click on "September." When that link opens, click on "September 3." From the list of cases that appears, click on the the case name to access the opinion.
b. 33 U.S.C. Sections 1251–1387.

> To demonstrate that FOE's members have standing, FOE must show that *   *   * the injury is "fairly traceable" to the defendant's actions *   *   * .
>
> *   *   *   *   *
>
> *   *   * FOE offered no competent evidence that La Gloria's discharges have made their way to Lake Palestine or would otherwise affect Lake Palestine. *   *   * FOE and its members relied solely on the truism that water flows downstream and inferred therefrom that any injury suffered downstream is "fairly traceable" to unlawful discharges upstream. At some point this common sense observation becomes little more than surmise. At that point certainly the requirements [for standing] are not met.

DECISION AND REMEDY   *The U.S. Court of Appeals for the Fifth Circuit affirmed the lower court's decision. FOE lacked standing to bring a suit against La Gloria.*

SECTION 3

The State and Federal Court Systems

As mentioned earlier in this chapter, each state has its own court system. Additionally, there is a system of federal courts. Although no two state court systems are exactly the same, the left-hand side of Exhibit 2–1 illustrates the basic organizational framework characteristic of the court systems in many states. The exhibit also shows how the federal court system is structured. We turn now to an examination of these court systems, beginning with the state courts.

STATE COURT SYSTEMS

Typically a state court system includes several levels, or tiers, of courts. As indicated in Exhibit 2–1, state courts may include (1) trial courts of limited jurisdiction, (2) trial courts of general jurisdiction, (3) intermediate appellate courts, and (4) the state's highest court (often called the state supreme court). Judges in the state court system are usually elected by the voters for specified terms.

Generally, any person who is a party to a lawsuit has the opportunity to plead the case before a trial court and then, if he or she loses, before at least one

EXHIBIT 2–1   THE STATE AND FEDERAL COURT SYSTEMS

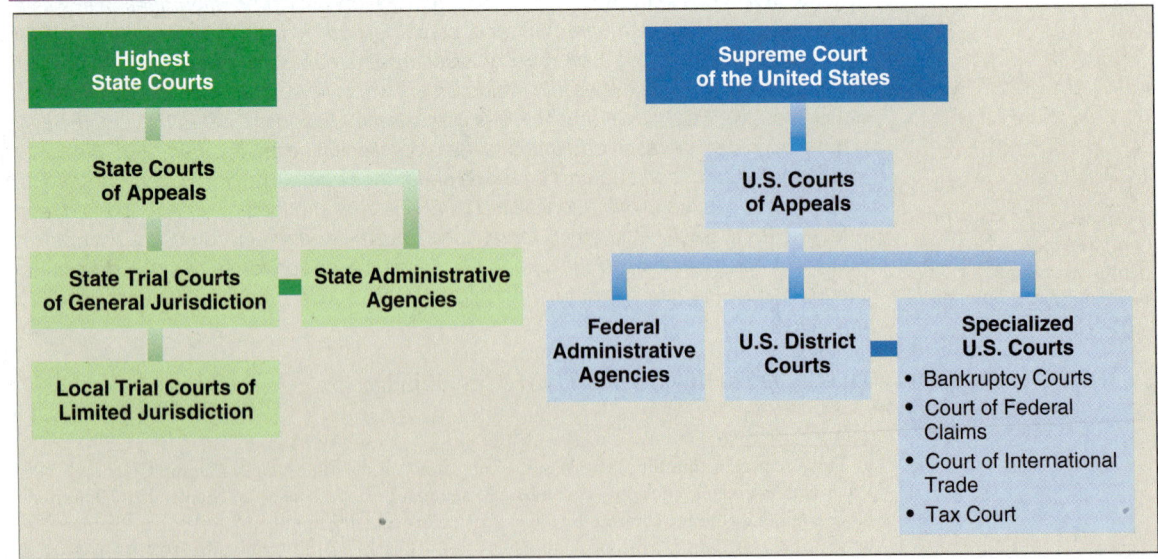

level of appellate court. Finally, if a federal statute or federal constitutional issue is involved in the decision of a state supreme court, that decision may be further appealed to the United States Supreme Court.

Trial Courts. Trial courts are exactly what their name implies—courts in which trials are held and testimony taken. State trial courts have either general or limited jurisdiction. Trial courts that have general jurisdiction as to subject matter may be called county, district, superior, or circuit courts.[10] State trial courts of general jurisdiction have jurisdiction over a wide variety of subjects, including both civil disputes and criminal prosecutions. In some states, trial courts of general jurisdiction may hear appeals from courts of limited jurisdiction.

Courts of limited jurisdiction as to subject matter are often called special inferior trial courts or minor judiciary courts. **Small claims courts** are inferior trial courts that hear only civil cases involving claims of less than a certain amount, such as $2,500 (the amount varies from state to state). Suits brought in small claims courts are generally conducted informally, and lawyers are not required. In a minority of states, lawyers are not even allowed to represent people in small claims courts for most purposes. Decisions of small claims courts may be appealed to a state trial court of general jurisdiction.

Other courts of limited jurisdiction include domestic relations courts, which handle only divorce actions and child custody cases; local municipal courts, which mainly handle traffic cases; and probate courts, as mentioned earlier.

Courts of Appeals. Every state has at least one court of appeals (appellate court, or reviewing court). A court of appeals may be an intermediate appellate court or the state's highest court. About three-fourths of the states have intermediate appellate courts. Generally, courts of appeals do not conduct new trials, in which evidence is submitted to the court and witnesses are examined. Rather, an appellate court panel of three or more judges reviews the record of the case on appeal, which includes a transcript of the trial proceedings, and then determines whether the trial court committed an error.

Appellate courts look at questions of law and procedure. Usually, they do not look at questions of fact.

A **question of law** is a question concerning the application or interpretation of the law, on which only a judge, not a jury, can rule. A **question of fact** is a question about what really happened in regard to the dispute being tried. Questions of fact are decided by a trial judge (in a nonjury trial) or by a jury (in a jury trial) based on the evidence presented. Normally, an appellate court will defer to the trial court's judgment on questions of fact because the trial court judge and jury were in a better position to evaluate testimony. They directly observed witnesses' gestures, demeanor, and other nonverbal behavior during the trial. At the appellate level, the judges review the written transcript of the trial, which does not include these nonverbal elements.

An appellate court will tamper with a trial court's finding of fact only when the finding is clearly erroneous (that is, when it is contrary to the evidence presented at trial) or when there is no evidence to support the finding. For example, if at trial a jury concluded that a manufacturer's product had harmed the plaintiff but no evidence was submitted to the court to support that conclusion, the appellate court would hold that the trial court's decision was erroneous. The options exercised by appellate courts will be further discussed in Chapter 3.

State Supreme (Highest) Courts. The highest state courts usually are called simply supreme courts, but they may be designated by other names. For example, in both New York and Maryland, the highest state court is called the court of appeals. In Maine and Massachusetts, the highest court is labeled the supreme judicial court. In West Virginia, the highest state court is the supreme court of appeals. The decisions of each state's highest court on all questions of state law are final. Only when issues of federal law are involved can a decision made by a state's highest court be overruled by the United States Supreme Court.

THE FEDERAL COURT SYSTEM

The federal court system is basically a three-tiered model consisting of (1) U.S. district courts (trial courts of general jurisdiction) and various courts of limited jurisdiction, (2) U.S. courts of appeals (intermediate courts of appeals), and (3) the United States Supreme Court.

Unlike state court judges, who are usually elected, federal court judges—including the justices of the Supreme Court—are appointed by the president of

---

10. The name in Ohio and Pennsylvania is Court of Common Pleas; the name in New York is Supreme Court, Trial Division.

the United States, subject to confirmation by the U.S. Senate. Article III of the Constitution states that federal judges "hold their offices during good Behaviour." In effect, this means that federal judges have lifetime appointments. Although they can be impeached (removed from office) for misconduct, this is rarely done. In the entire history of the United States, only seven federal judges have been removed from office through impeachment proceedings.

U.S. District Courts. At the federal level, the equivalent of a state trial court of general jurisdiction is the district court. U.S. district courts have original jurisdiction in federal matters, and federal cases typically originate in district courts. There are other federal courts with original, but special (or limited), jurisdiction, such as the federal bankruptcy courts and others shown earlier in Exhibit 2–1.

There is at least one federal district court in every state. The number of judicial districts can vary over time, primarily owing to population changes and corresponding changes in caseloads. Currently, there are ninety-four federal judicial districts. Exhibit 2–2 on page 36 shows the boundaries of U.S. district courts, as well as the U.S. courts of appeals (discussed next).

U.S. Courts of Appeals. In the federal court system, there are thirteen U.S. courts of appeals—referred to as U.S. circuit courts of appeals. Twelve of the federal courts of appeals (including the Court of Appeals for the D.C. Circuit) hear appeals from the federal district courts located within their respective judicial "circuits," or geographical boundaries (shown in Exhibit 2–2). The court of appeals for the thirteenth circuit, called the Federal Circuit, has national appellate jurisdiction over certain types of cases, such as cases involving patent law and cases in which the U.S. government is a defendant. The decisions of a circuit court of appeals are binding on all courts within the circuit court's jurisdiction and are final in most cases, but appeal to the United States Supreme Court is possible.

United States Supreme Court. At the highest level in the three-tiered federal court system is the United States Supreme Court. According to the language of Article III of the U.S. Constitution, there is only one national Supreme Court. All other courts in the federal system are considered "inferior." Congress is empowered to create other inferior courts as it deems necessary. The inferior courts that Congress has created include the second tier in our model—the U.S.

circuit courts of appeals—as well as the district courts and the various federal courts of limited, or specialized, jurisdiction.

The United States Supreme Court consists of nine justices. Although the Supreme Court has original, or trial, jurisdiction in rare instances (set forth in Article III, Section 2), most of its work is as an appeals court. The Supreme Court can review any case decided by any of the federal courts of appeals, and it also has appellate authority over cases involving federal questions that have been decided in the state courts. The Supreme Court is the final arbiter of the Constitution and federal law.

How Cases Reach the Supreme Court. To bring a case before the Supreme Court, a party requests the Court to issue a writ of *certiorari*. A **writ of *certiorari***[11] is an order issued by the Supreme Court to a lower court requiring the latter to send it the record of the case for review. The Court will not issue a writ unless at least four of the nine justices approve of it. This is called the **rule of four.**

Whether the Court will issue a writ of *certiorari* is entirely within its discretion. The Court is not required to issue one, and most petitions for writs are denied. (Thousands of cases are filed with the Supreme Court each year, yet it hears, on average, less than one hundred of these cases.[12]) A denial is not a decision on the merits of a case, nor does it indicate agreement with the lower court's opinion. Furthermore, denial of the writ has no value as a precedent. A denial of the writ simply means that the decision of the lower court remains the law within that court's jurisdiction.

Typically, the petitions granted by the Court involve cases that raise important constitutional questions or cases that conflict with other state or federal court decisions. For example, if federal appellate courts are rendering conflicting or inconsistent opinions on an important issue, such as how a particular federal statute should be applied to a specific factual situation, the Supreme Court may agree to review a case involving that issue. The Court can then render a definitive opinion on the matter, thus clarifying the law for the lower courts.

---

11. Pronounced sur-shee-uh-*rah*-ree.
12. From the mid-1950s through the early 1990s, the Supreme Court reviewed more cases per year than it has in the last few years. In the Court's 1982–1983 term, for example, the Court issued written opinions in 151 cases. In contrast, during the Court's 1998–1999 term, the Court issued written opinions in only 75 cases.

CONCEPT SUMMARY 2.2

TYPES OF COURTS

COURT	DESCRIPTION
Trial Courts	Trial courts are courts of original jurisdiction in which actions are initiated. 1. *State courts*—Courts of general jurisdiction can hear any case that has not been specifically designated for another court; courts of limited jurisdiction include domestic relations courts, probate courts, municipal courts, small claims courts, and others. 2. *Federal courts*—The federal district court is the equivalent of the state trial court. Federal courts of limited jurisdiction include the bankruptcy court and others shown in Exhibit 2–1.
Intermediate Appellate Courts	Courts of appeals are reviewing courts; generally, appellate courts do not have original jurisdiction. About three-fourths of the states have intermediate appellate courts; in the federal court system, the U.S. circuit courts of appeals are the intermediate appellate courts.
Supreme Court	The highest state court is that state's supreme court, although it may be called by some other name. Appeal from state supreme courts to the United States Supreme Court is possible only if a federal question is involved. The United States Supreme Court is the highest court in the federal court system and the final arbiter of the Constitution and federal law.

SECTION 4

Alternative Dispute Resolution

Alternative dispute resolution (ADR) refers to the various methods by which disputes are settled outside the court system. Typically, to save time and money for all parties involved, attorneys advise their clients to attempt a settlement before resorting to **litigation**—the process of resolving a dispute through the court system. Frequently, a settlement is achieved after a lawsuit has been initiated and pretrial investigations undertaken, but before a trial takes place. At this point, the parties and their attorneys have an opportunity to assess the evidence and attempt a settlement based on the relative strengths or weaknesses of their positions. Most civil lawsuits (about 95 percent) are settled before they go to trial.

ADR offers many advantages to disputing parties. Litigating even the simplest complaint is costly, and because of the backlog of cases pending in many courts, it may sometimes be several years before a case is actually tried. ADR, in contrast, usually entails fewer costs and allows disputes to be resolved relatively quickly. ADR also offers the advantage of pri-

vacy. Court proceedings are public, whereas ADR allows the parties to come together privately and work out an agreement. Another advantage of ADR is its flexibility. Normally, the parties themselves can control how the dispute will be settled, what procedures will be used, and whether the decision reached (either by the parties themselves or by a neutral third party) will be legally binding or nonbinding. ADR also offers advantages for the courts. To ease the burden on the courts and reduce costs, both the state and federal court systems have implemented programs that encourage or even require some form of ADR prior to trial.

Methods of ADR range from neighbors sitting down over a cup of coffee in an attempt to work out their differences to huge multinational corporations agreeing to resolve a dispute through a formal hearing before a panel of experts. Some of the most commonly used methods of ADR include negotiation, mediation, and arbitration.

NEGOTIATION

One of the simplest forms of ADR is **negotiation,** a process in which the parties attempt to settle their

EXHIBIT 2–2   U.S. DISTRICT COURTS AND COURTS OF APPEALS

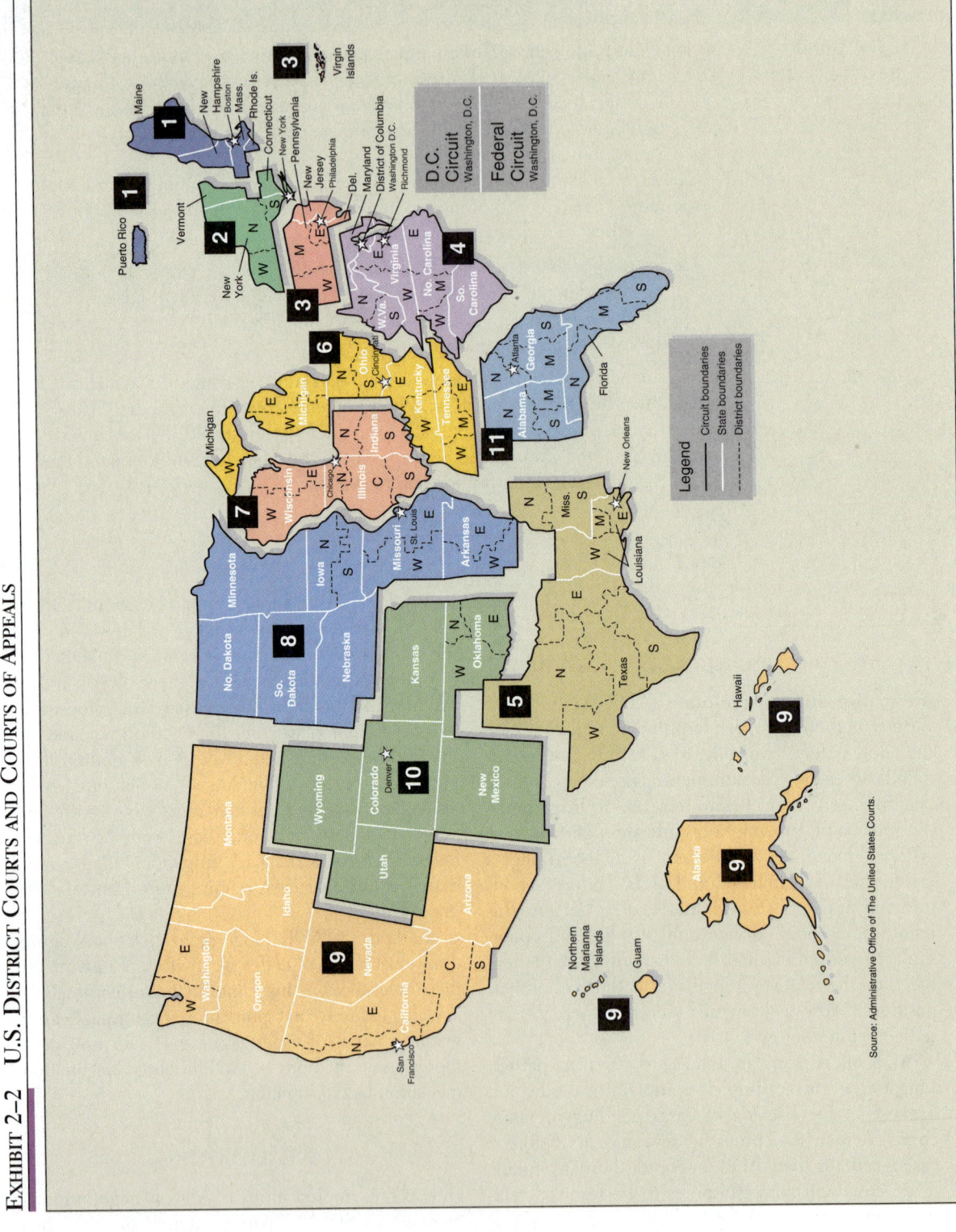

Source: Administrative Office of The United States Courts.

dispute informally, with or without attorneys to represent them. Typically, during the pretrial stages of litigation, the parties and/or their attorneys may meet informally one or more times to see if a mutually satisfactory agreement can be reached. In some courts, pretrial negotiation is mandatory. In these courts, before parties may proceed to trial, they must first meet with each other and attempt to negotiate a settlement. Only if the parties cannot reach an agreement will the court decide the issue. In other courts, negotiation is one of a menu of ADR options that the parties may (or must, in some cases and in some courts) pursue prior to trial.

In working out a mutually satisfactory agreement, disputing parties often find it helpful to have the input of a neutral (unbiased) third party. In the traditional negotiation process, however, attorneys act as advocates for their clients, which means that they put their clients' interests first. In recent years, to facilitate negotiation, various forms of what might be called "assisted negotiation" have been employed. Forms of ADR associated with the negotiation process include mini-trials, early neutral case evaluation, summary jury trials, and conciliation.

Mini-Trials. A **mini-trial** is a private proceeding in which each party's attorney briefly argues the party's case before the other party. Typically, a neutral third party, who acts as an adviser and an expert in the area being disputed, is also present. If the parties fail to reach an agreement, the adviser renders an opinion as to how a court would likely decide the issue. The proceeding assists the parties in determining whether they should negotiate a settlement of the dispute or take it to court.

Early Neutral Case Evaluation. In **early neutral case evaluation,** the parties select a neutral third party (generally an expert in the subject matter of the dispute) to evaluate their respective positions. The parties explain their points of view to the case evaluator however they wish. The case evaluator then assesses the strengths and weaknesses of the parties' positions, and this evaluation forms the basis for negotiating a settlement.

Summary Jury Trials. A form of ADR that has been successfully employed in the federal court system is the **summary jury trial (SJT).** In an SJT, which occurs after a lawsuit has been initiated but before the trial, the litigants present their arguments and evidence to a jury. The jury then renders a verdict. The jury's verdict, however, is not binding. Rather, it serves as a guide to both sides in reaching an agreement during the mandatory negotiations that immediately follow the trial. Because no witnesses are called, the SJT is much speedier than a regular trial, and frequently the parties are able to settle their dispute without resorting to an actual trial. If no settlement is reached, both sides have the right to a full trial later.

Conciliation. Disputes may also be resolved in a friendly, nonadversarial manner through **conciliation,** in which a third party assists parties to a dispute in reconciling their differences. The conciliator helps to schedule negotiating sessions and carries offers back and forth between the parties when they refuse to face each other in direct negotiations. Technically, conciliators are not to recommend solutions. In practice, however, they often do. In contrast, a mediator is expected to propose solutions.

MEDIATION

One of the oldest forms of ADR is mediation. In the **mediation** process, the parties themselves attempt to negotiate an agreement, but with the assistance of a neutral third party, called a mediator. The mediator need not be a lawyer. The mediator may be a single person, such as a paralegal, an attorney, or a volunteer from the community. Alternatively, a panel of mediators may be used. Usually, a mediator charges a fee, which can be split between the parties. Mediation is essentially a form of assisted negotiation, but one in which the mediator plays a more active role than the neutral third parties in negotiation-associated forms of ADR.

As with negotiation, some courts may encourage or require the parties to undertake mediation prior to a trial. Some states offer mediation as the only ADR method that may (or must) be undertaken before proceeding to trial. Florida, for example, has a comprehensive statewide mediation program to facilitate pretrial settlements.

The Mediator's Role. The mediator's role is basically to help the parties evaluate their positions and clarify the issues on which they do and do not agree. A mediator will try to discern what the parties' real interests are, as opposed to the stances that the parties have put forward. This is often done by holding

EMERGING TRENDS IN TECHNOLOGY

ADR Goes Online

Given the increasing use of the World Wide Web for commercial transactions, it should come as no surprise that alternative dispute resolution (ADR) services are now available online as well. For some time, ADR *resources* have been available on the Web. For example, if you go to the Web site of the American Arbitration Association (AAA), you will find information on ADR methods, AAA rules, and sample AAA forms that can be downloaded or printed out for use in submitting a dispute to arbitration before the AAA. You can also find articles on topics ranging from how to draft an arbitration clause to creating a company ADR policy. Today, however, a number of Web sites are going even further: they offer parties to a dispute an opportunity to settle, mediate, or otherwise resolve their dispute using online forums.

ONLINE SETTLEMENTS

Traditionally, the parties to a dispute had a number of options for settling their differences. One option, of course, was coming to an agreement themselves. Another was enlisting the help of their attorneys in trying to work out a reasonable settlement. Still another alternative was to mediate or arbitrate the dispute. Indeed, if

their contract contained an arbitration clause, then the dispute would have to be arbitrated. Finally, the parties could take their dispute to court. Today, various Web sites offer yet another option: settling disputes by the click of a mouse.

Consider the services offered by clickNsettle.com (at **http://www. clickNsettle.com**), a subsidiary of National Arbitration & Mediation. At clickNsettle.com's Web site, disputing parties may be able to settle their dispute for only a small fee (currently ranging from $75 to $275). The settlement process is conducted through a series of confidential "bids," similar to those used in online auctions. First, the claimant submits a claim against the defendant to clickNsettle.com, which then notifies the defendant of the claim via e-mail. The defendant submits three amounts that it is willing to pay to settle the claim, following which the claimant submits an amount that he or she considers reasonable. If the claimant's amount falls within a specified range of one of the three amounts stated by the defendant, the matter is settled. If it does not, the claimant can submit two more amounts, or "bids."

Other online ADR providers use similar processes. For example, cyber$ettle.com (at **http://www. cybersettle.com**) gives disputing parties three opportunities, or "rounds," to settle their dispute. One demand and one offer can be entered for each round. The amount

demanded in a particular round is compared to the amount offered for that round. If an offer is within 30 percent, or $5,000, of the amount demanded, then cyber$ettle lets the parties know that a settlement has been reached, and a written confirmation of the settlement is sent to the parties. If, in all three rounds, the offer differs from a demand by more than 30 percent, or $5,000, no settlement is reached, and the parties are so notified.

One of the appealing aspects of these types of online settlement proceedings is that offers and demands normally are made separately and in confidence, and are never disclosed. Additionally, these sites can be accessed at any time, and little waiting is involved. Once a demand or offer is submitted, the computer program determines if a settlement has—or has not—been reached. If no settlement is reached, the parties can try some other form of ADR, such as mediation, before taking their case to court.

CYBERMEDIATION

People who wish to mediate their disputes can now go online to one of a number of Web sites that offer mediation services. Indeed, cybermediation is becoming an increasingly popular Web business. Through the use of e-mail, "chat rooms," videoconferencing, and other technologies, online mediators assist parties in finding acceptable resolutions to their disputes.

EMERGING TRENDS IN TECHNOLOGY

ADR Goes Online, continued

One of the first Web-based mediation services appeared in 1996, when the Virtual Magistrate (VM) Web page was launched. The aim of VM was to settle disputes, such as domain-name disputes, arising from online activities. This early effort in cybermediation was not very successful, however—the VM handled only one case. The VM project may ultimately succeed in its mission, though. Currently, the American Arbitration Association, one of the sponsors of the VM project, and other organizations are working with this enterprise to update its site.

As with traditional mediation, Web businesses that offer commercial mediation services typically charge the parties a fee. For example, one such service, Internet Neutral (at **http://www. internetneutral.com**), requires each party to pay a minimum fee of $250 when a request to mediate a dispute is submitted to the Internet Neutral Web site. The fee covers approximately two hours of mediation session time and two hours for reading and preparation. If the mediation continues for more than four hours, there is an hourly fee of $125 per hour, which is split by the parties. During a mediation session, the parties sit before their computers and use two "chat conference rooms." One of these

rooms is used for private conversations between the party and the mediator; the other room is used for private conversations involving both parties and the mediator. Videoconferences may also be held.

A well-known nonprofit mediation center on the Web is the Online Ombuds Office, at **http://aaron.sbs.umass.edu/ center/ombuds/default.htm**. This office was established in 1997 as the dispute-resolution arm of the Center for Information Technology and Dispute Resolution at the University of Massachusetts. The Online Ombuds Office offers online mediation services to disputing parties at no cost. Although the office is primarily interested in mediating disputes that arise out of online activities, it will handle other disputes as well. In a pilot project conducted in early 1999, the Online Ombuds Office mediated 175 disputes at a major Internet auction site, eBay. Consumers who had complaints about their purchases could contact the Online Ombuds Office to have their disputes mediated. The parties communicated with a mediator via e-mail to try to resolve the claim.

IMPLICATIONS FOR THE BUSINESSPERSON

1. The proliferation of online ADR forums and online settlement services may lead to significant savings for businesspersons. The low cost of online settlement processes makes them a

particularly attractive option for businesspersons who wish to settle a dispute quickly and confidentially.

2. For those who do business on a global level, online ADR may be particularly beneficial. One of the risks of engaging in any international business transaction is that if a dispute arises, one (and often both) of the parties will be required to travel to a distant forum to have the dispute resolved, either through ADR or in a court. Because the Internet is a global network, parties from different countries can resolve their disputes through online ADR without leaving their offices.

FOR CRITICAL ANALYSIS

1. What might be some disadvantages of online dispute settlement or mediation?

2. In arbitration, and particularly in formal arbitration proceedings, the parties often present various forms of evidence to the arbitrator. Does this mean that online arbitration is not feasible?

RELEVANT WEB SITES

To learn more about online settlement and mediation services, go to any or all of the Web sites mentioned in this feature. If you are interested in seeing a transcript of the mediation of an actual dispute (between a Web site developer and a newspaper), go to **http://aaron.sbs.umass.edu/ center/ombuds/narrative1.html**.

private sessions with each party, in which the mediator learns what information the parties are unwilling to disclose to each other. Through joint and individual sessions with the parties, the mediator obtains information to assess realistically the alternative ways in which the dispute might be resolved. The mediator then proposes a solution, or alternative solutions, including what compromises will be necessary to reach agreement.

The Advantages of Mediation. Unlike litigation (and, to a certain extent, negotiation), mediation is not adversarial in nature. Rather, a mediator tries to find common grounds on which an agreement can be based. Therefore, the process tends to reduce the antagonism between the disputants and to allow them to resume their former relationship. For this reason, mediation is often the preferred form of ADR for business disputes involving parties who either must or would like to continue an ongoing relationship. For example, business partners may be able to work out their differences through mediation more satisfactorily than through other forms of ADR or through litigation. Mediation is also beneficial in settling differences between employers and employees or other parties involved in long-term relationships.

ARBITRATION

A more formal method of alternative dispute resolution is **arbitration,** in which an arbitrator (a neutral third party or a panel of experts) hears a dispute and renders a decision. The key difference between arbitration and the forms of ADR just discussed is that in arbitration, the third party's decision may be legally binding on the parties, depending on the wishes of the parties.

Many courts, in both the federal and state court systems, require the pretrial arbitration of disputes. Often, arbitration is required only in cases in which the dollar amount in controversy is under a specified threshold amount. For example, courts in several federal districts require pretrial arbitration in cases involving less than $100,000. In Hawaii, all disputes involving less than $150,000 must be arbitrated. When pretrial arbitration is mandated by a court, normally the arbitrator's decision is not legally binding. If either of the parties is not satisfied with the decision, the court will try the case.

The Arbitration Process. In some respects, formal arbitration resembles a trial, although usually the procedural rules are much less restrictive than those governing litigation. In the typical hearing format, the parties present opening arguments to the arbitrator and state what remedies should or should not be granted. Next, evidence is presented, and witnesses may be called and examined by both sides. The arbitrator then renders a decision, called an **award.**

An arbitrator's award is usually the final word on the matter. Although the parties may appeal an arbitrator's decision, a court's review of the decision will be much more restricted in scope than an appellate court's review of a trial court's decision. The general view is that because the parties were free to frame the issues and set the powers of the arbitrator at the outset, they cannot complain about the results. The award will only be set aside if the arbitrator's conduct or "bad faith" substantially prejudiced the rights of one of the parties, if the award violates an established public policy, or if the arbitrator exceeded his or her powers (by arbitrating issues that the parties did not agree to submit to arbitration).

Arbitration Clauses and Statutes. Virtually any commercial matter can be submitted to arbitration. Frequently, parties include an **arbitration clause** in a contract specifying that any dispute arising under the contract will be resolved through arbitration rather than through the court system. Parties can also agree to arbitrate a dispute after it arises.

Most states have statutes (often based in part on the Uniform Arbitration Act of 1955) under which arbitration clauses will be enforced, and some state statutes compel arbitration of certain types of disputes, such as those involving public employees. At the federal level, the Federal Arbitration Act (FAA), enacted in 1925, enforces arbitration clauses in contracts involving maritime activity and interstate commerce—activities that the federal government has the authority to regulate through legislation (see Chapter 4).

Arbitrability. When a dispute arises as to whether the parties to a contract with an arbitration clause have agreed to submit a particular matter to arbitration, one party may file suit to compel arbitration. The court before which the suit is brought will not decide the basic controversy but must decide the issue of *arbitrability*—that is, whether the matter is one that must be resolved through arbitration.

Even when a claim involves a violation of a statute passed to protect a certain class of people, a court may determine that the parties must nonetheless abide by their agreement to arbitrate the dispute. Usually, a court will allow the claim to be arbitrated if the court, in interpreting the statute, can find no legislative intent to the contrary.

In one important case, the United States Supreme Court held that a claim brought under the Age Discrimination in Employment Act (ADEA) of 1967 could be subject to compulsory arbitration. The plaintiff in the case, Robert Gilmer, had been discharged from his employment at the age of sixty-two. Gilmer sued his employer, claiming that he was a victim of age discrimination. The employer argued that Gilmer had to submit the dispute to arbitration because he had agreed, as part of a required registra-

tion application to be a securities representative with the New York Stock Exchange, to arbitrate "any dispute, claim, or controversy" relating to his employment. The Supreme Court held that Gilmer, by agreeing to arbitrate any dispute, had waived his right to sue.[13] (For a fuller discussion of the ADEA, see Chapter 42.)

Note that Gilmer had waived his *own* rights in a broadly worded arbitration clause. In the following case, the Supreme Court addressed the question of whether a union, in an equally broadly worded arbitration clause, can waive the rights of the employees whom it represents.

---

13. *Gilmer v. Interstate/Johnson Lane Corp.*, 500 U.S. 20, 111 S.Ct. 1647, 114 L.Ed.2d 26 (1991).

CASE 2.3   Wright v. Universal Maritime Service Corp.

Supreme Court of the
United States, 1998.
525 U.S. 70,
119 S.Ct. 391,
142 L.Ed.2d 361.
http://supct.law.
cornell.edu/supct/html/
97-156.ZS.html[a]

BACKGROUND AND FACTS   *Ceasar Wright was a longshoreman and a member of the International Longshoremen's Association (ILA). The ILA supplies workers to Universal Maritime Service Corporation and other members of the South Carolina Stevedores Association (SCSA). A collective bargaining agreement (CBA) between the ILA and the SCSA provided for the arbitration of "matters under dispute" in one clause and "all matters affecting wages, hours, and other terms and conditions of employment" in another. Still another clause stated that "[a]nything not contained in this Agreement shall not be construed as being part of this Agreement." Wright suffered a job-related injury that resulted in a disability. When a physician approved Wright's return to work, the SCSA members refused to hire him because of the disability. Wright filed a suit in a federal district court against Universal and others, on the ground that they had discriminated against him in violation of the Americans with Disabilities Act (ADA) of 1990 (see Chapter 42). The defendants argued that the suit should be dismissed because Wright had not submitted his claim to arbitration. The district court ruled in the defendants' favor, and the U.S. Court of Appeals for the Fourth Circuit affirmed this ruling. Wright appealed to the United States Supreme Court.*

**IN THE LANGUAGE
OF THE COURT**

Justice *SCALIA* delivered the opinion of the Court.

*   *   *   *

*   *   * In [a previous case] we stated that a union could waive its officers' statutory right *   *   * to be free of antiunion discrimination, but we held that such a waiver must be *clear and unmistakable*. *   *   * [Emphasis added.]

---

a. This page is part of the Supreme Court Collection of cases maintained by the Legal Information Institute, which is part of Cornell Law School. In the right-hand frame, in the "Arranged by party name" list, in the "1998" links, click on "1st party." On that page, scroll down to the case name and click on it to access the case.

* * * [T]he right to a federal judicial forum is of sufficient importance to be protected against a less-than-explicit union waiver in a CBA. The CBA in this case does not meet that standard. Its arbitration clause is very general, providing for arbitration of "[m]atters under dispute"—which could be understood to mean matters in dispute under the contract. And the remainder of the contract contains no explicit incorporation of statutory antidiscrimination requirements. The Fourth Circuit relied upon the fact that the equivalently broad arbitration clause in *Gilmer v. Interstate/Johnson Lane Corp.*—applying to "any dispute, claim or controversy"—was held to embrace federal statutory claims. But *Gilmer* involved an individual's waiver of his own rights, rather than a union's waiver of the rights of represented employees—and hence the "clear and unmistakable" standard was not applicable.

* * * *

We hold that the collective-bargaining agreement in this case does not contain a clear and unmistakable waiver of the covered employees' rights to a judicial forum for federal claims of employment discrimination. We do not reach the question whether such a waiver would be enforceable.

DECISION AND REMEDY *The Supreme Court held that the arbitration clause in the CBA did not clearly waive the union members' right to have a court rule on federal claims of employment discrimination. Thus, Wright was not required to submit his claim to arbitration. The Court did not decide whether such a waiver would be enforceable if it were clear. The Court vacated the judgment of the lower court and remanded the case.*

PROVIDERS OF ADR SERVICES

ADR services are provided by both government agencies and private organizations. A major provider of ADR services is the **American Arbitration Association (AAA).** Most of the largest law firms in the nation are members of this nonprofit association. Founded in 1926, the AAA now handles over ninety thousand claims a year in its numerous offices around the country. Cases brought before the AAA are heard by an expert or a panel of experts in the area relating to the dispute and are usually settled quickly. Generally, about half of the panel members are lawyers. To cover its costs, the AAA charges a fee, paid by the party filing the claim. In addition, each party to the dispute pays a specified amount for each hearing day, as well as a special additional fee in cases involving personal injuries or property loss.

Hundreds of for-profit firms around the country also provide dispute-resolution services. Typically, these firms hire retired judges to conduct arbitration hearings or otherwise assist parties in settling their disputes. The leading firm in this relatively new private system of justice is JAMS/Endispute, which is based in Santa Ana, California. Private ADR firms normally allow the parties to decide on the date of the hearing, the presiding judge, whether the judge's decision will be legally binding, and the site of the hearing—which may be a conference room, a law school office, or a leased courtroom. The judges follow procedures similar to those of the federal courts and use similar rules. Usually, each party to the dispute pays a filing fee and a designated fee for a hearing session or conference.

There are also international organizations, such as the International Chamber of Commerce, that provide forums for the arbitration of disputes between parties to international contracts. These organizations, as well as some of the advantages and disadvantages of arbitrating disputes in the international context, will be discussed in Chapter 52.

Finally, a growing number of firms are offering dispute-resolution services online. See this chapter's *Emerging Trends in Technology* on pages 38 and 39 for a discussion of this latest development in ADR.

CONCEPT SUMMARY 2.3

ALTERNATIVE DISPUTE RESOLUTION (ADR)

TYPE OF ADR	DESCRIPTION
Negotiation	The parties come together, with or without attorneys to represent them, and try to reach a settlement. Traditionally, no third party was involved in the process. Today, several forms of "assisted negotiation"—negotiation involving a neutral (unbiased) third party—are used, including mini-trials, early neutral case evaluation, and (in some federal courts) summary jury trials, or SJTs. The opinion of the third party (or "jury," in an SJT) forms the basis for negotiating a settlement.
Mediation	The parties themselves reach an agreement with the help of a third party, called a mediator, who plays an active role in the dispute settlement. The mediator tries to discover and assess the real causes of the dispute (through discussions with the parties individually and jointly), assists the parties in evaluating their positions, and proposes possible solutions. Mediation is usually the preferred method of ADR in cases involving ongoing or long-term relationships.
Arbitration	In this more formal method of ADR, the parties submit their dispute to a neutral third party, the arbitrator, who renders a decision. The decision is binding unless the parties (or a court, in court-related arbitration) specify otherwise. Arbitration awards may be appealed to a court, but only in special circumstances (such as if the award is contrary to public policy) will a court set aside an arbitrator's award. If there is a question concerning the arbitrability of a certain type of claim, a court must decide the issue.

TERMS AND CONCEPTS TO REVIEW

QUESTIONS AND CASE PROBLEMS

2–1. ARBITRATION. In an arbitration proceeding, the arbitrator need not be a judge or even a lawyer. How, then, can the arbitrator's decision have the force of law and be binding on the parties involved?

2–2. COURTS OF APPEALS. The defendant in a lawsuit is appealing the trial court's decision in favor of the plaintiff. On appeal, the defendant claims that the evidence presented at trial to support the plaintiff's claim was so scanty that no reasonable jury could have found for the plaintiff. Therefore, argues the defendant, the appellate court should reverse the trial court's decision. May an appellate court ever reverse a trial court's findings with respect to questions of fact? Discuss fully.

2–3. COURTS OF APPEALS. Appellate courts normally see only written transcripts of trial proceedings when they are reviewing cases. Today, in some states, videotapes are being used as the official trial reports. If the use of videotapes as official reports continues, will this alter the appellate process? Should it? Discuss fully.

2–4. JURISDICTION. Marya Callais, a citizen of Florida, was walking one day near a busy street in Tallahassee, Florida, when a large crate flew off a passing truck and hit her, resulting in numerous injuries. She incurred a great deal of pain and suffering, plus significant medical expenses, and she could not work for six months. She wants to sue the trucking firm for $300,000 in damages. The firm's headquarters are in Georgia, although the company does business in Florida. In what court might Callais bring suit—a Florida state court, a Georgia state court, or a federal court? What factors might influence her decision?

2–5. ARBITRATION. Randall Fris worked as a seaman on an Exxon Shipping Co. oil tanker for eight years without incident. One night, he boarded the ship for duty while intoxicated, in violation of company policy. This policy also allowed Exxon to discharge employees who were intoxicated and thus unfit for work. Exxon discharged Fris. Under a contract with Fris's union, the discharge was submitted to arbitration. The arbitrators ordered Exxon to reinstate Fris on an oil tanker. Exxon filed a suit against the union, challenging the award as contrary to public policy, which opposes having intoxicated persons operate seagoing vessels. Can a court set aside an arbitration award on the ground (legal basis) that the award violates public policy? Should the court set aside the award in this case? Explain. [*Exxon Shipping Co. v. Exxon Seamen's Union,* 11 F.3d 1189 (3d Cir. 1993)]

2–6. ARBITRATION. Phillip Beaudry, who suffered from mental illness, worked in the Department of Income Maintenance for the state of Connecticut. Beaudry was fired from his job when it was learned that he had misappropriated approximately $1,640 in state funds. Beaudry filed a complaint with his union, Council 4 of the American Federation of State, County, and Municipal Employees (AFSCME), and eventually the dispute was submitted to an arbitrator. The arbitrator concluded that Beaudry had been dismissed without "just cause," because Beaudry's acts were caused by his mental illness and "were not willful or volitional or within his capacity to control." Because Beaudry had a disability, the employer was required, under state law, to transfer him to a position that he was competent to hold. The arbitrator awarded Beaudry reinstatement, back pay, seniority, and other benefits. The state appealed the decision to a court. What public policies must the court weigh in making its decision? How should the court rule? [*State v. Council 4, AFSCME,* 27 Conn.App. 635, 608 A.2d 718 (1992)]

2–7. JURISDICTION. Cal-Ban 3000 is a weight loss drug made by Health Care Products, Inc., a Florida corporation, and marketed through CKI Industries, another Florida corporation. Enticed by North Carolina newspaper ads for Cal-Ban, the wife of Douglas Tart bought the drug at Prescott's Pharmacies, Inc., in North Carolina for her husband. Within a week, Tart suffered a ruptured colon. Alleging that the injury was caused by Cal-Ban, Tart sued Prescott's Pharmacies, CKI, the officers and directors of Health Care, and others in a North Carolina state court. CKI and the Health Care officers and directors argued that North Carolina did not have personal jurisdiction over them because CKI and Health Care were Florida corporations. How will the court rule? Why? [*Tart v. Prescott's Pharmacies, Inc.,* 118 N.C.App. 516, 456 S.E.2d 121 (1995)]

2–8. STANDING. Blue Cross and Blue Shield insurance companies (the Blues) provide 68 million Americans with health-care financing. The Blues have paid billions of dollars for care attributable to illnesses related to tobacco use. In an attempt to recover some of this amount, the Blues filed a suit in a federal district court against tobacco companies and others, alleging fraud, among other things. The Blues claimed that beginning in 1953, the defendants conspired to addict millions of Americans, including members of Blue Cross plans, to cigarettes and other tobacco products. The conspiracy involved misrepresentation about the safety of nicotine and its addictive properties, marketing efforts targeting children, and agreements not to produce or market safer cigarettes. Their success caused lung, throat, and other cancers, as well as heart disease, stroke, emphysema, and other illnesses. The defendants asked the court to dismiss the case on the ground that the plaintiffs did not have standing to sue. Do the Blues have standing in this case? Why or why not? [*Blue Cross and Blue Shield of New Jersey, Inc. v. Philip Morris, Inc.,* 36 F.Supp.2d 560 (E.D.N.Y. 1999)]

2–9. IN YOUR COURT

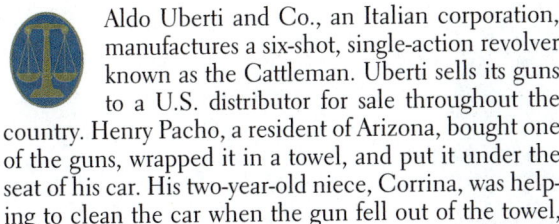

Aldo Uberti and Co., an Italian corporation, manufactures a six-shot, single-action revolver known as the Cattleman. Uberti sells its guns to a U.S. distributor for sale throughout the country. Henry Pacho, a resident of Arizona, bought one of the guns, wrapped it in a towel, and put it under the seat of his car. His two-year-old niece, Corrina, was helping to clean the car when the gun fell out of the towel, hit the pavement, and discharged. The bullet struck Corrina in the head and killed her. Corrina's parents filed a suit in an Arizona state court against Uberti, alleging that the company was liable for the "design, manufacture, sale, and distribution of a defective and unreasonably dangerous product." Uberti asked the court to dismiss the suit on the ground that the court did not have personal jurisdiction over Uberti. Assume that you are the Arizona state judge hearing this case and answer the following questions:

(a) Did Corrina's parents have "standing to sue" in this case? Explain.

(b) Can an Arizona state court exercise jurisdiction over the defendant in this case? Why or why not?

LAW ON THE WEB

For updated links to resources available on the Web, as well as a variety of other materials, visit this text's Web site at http://wbl.westbuslaw.com.

The decisions of the United States Supreme Court and of all of the U.S. courts of appeals are now published online shortly after the decisions are rendered (often within hours). You can find these decisions and obtain information about the federal court system by accessing the Federal Court Locator at

http://www.law.vill.edu

For information on the justices of the United States Supreme Court, links to opinions they have authored, and other information about the Supreme Court, go to

http://oyez.nwu.edu

The Web site for the federal courts offers information on the federal court system and links to all federal courts at

http://www.uscourts.gov

The National Center for State Courts (NCSC) offers links to the Web pages of all state courts. Go to

http://www.ncsc.dni.us/court/sites/courts.htm

For information on alternative dispute resolution, go to the American Arbitration Association's Web site at

http://www.adr.org

LEGAL RESEARCH EXERCISES ON THE WEB

Go to http://wbl.westbuslaw.com, the Web site that accompanies this text. Select "Internet Applications," and then click on "Chapter 2." There you will find the following Internet research exercises that you can perform to learn more about alternative dispute resolution and the judiciary's role in American government:

Activity 2–1: Alternative Dispute Resolution

Activity 2–2: The Judiciary's Role in American Government

Court Procedures

AMERICAN AND ENGLISH COURTS follow the *adversary system of justice.* Although clients are allowed to represent themselves in court (called *pro se* representation),[1] most parties to lawsuits hire attorneys to represent them. Each lawyer acts as his or her client's advocate, presenting the client's version of the facts in such a way as to convince the judge (or the judge and jury, in a jury trial) that this version is correct.

Most of the judicial procedures that you will read about in this chapter are rooted in the adversarial framework of the American legal system. In this chapter, after a brief overview of judicial procedures, we illustrate the steps involved in a lawsuit with a hypothetical civil case (criminal procedures will be discussed in Chapter 8).

SECTION 1

Procedural Rules

The parties to a lawsuit must comply with the procedural rules of the court in which the lawsuit is filed. These rules specify what must be done at each stage of the litigation process. All civil trials held in federal district courts are governed by the **Federal Rules of Civil Procedure (FRCP).**[2] Each state also has rules of civil procedure that apply to all courts within that state. In addition, each court has its own local rules of procedure that supplement the federal or state rules.

Broadly speaking, there are three phases of the litigation process: pretrial, trial, and posttrial. Each phase involves specific procedures. Although civil lawsuits may vary greatly in terms of complexity, cost, and detail, they typically progress through the specific stages charted in Exhibit 3–1.

We now turn to our hypothetical civil case. The case arose from an automobile accident, which occurred when a car driven by Antonio Carvello, a resident of New Jersey, collided with a car driven by Jill Kirby, a resident of New York. The accident took place at an intersection in New York City. Kirby suffered personal injuries, incurring medical and hospital expenses as well as lost wages for four months. In all, she calculated that the cost to her of the accident was $100,000.[3] Carvello and Kirby have been unable to agree on a settlement, and Kirby now must decide whether to sue Carvello for the $100,000 compensation she feels she deserves.

---

2. The United States Supreme Court's authority to promulgate these rules is set forth in 28 U.S.C. Sections 2071–2077.

3. We are ignoring in this example damages for pain and suffering or for permanent disabilities. Often in personal injury cases, plaintiffs seek such damages.

---

1. This right was definitively established in *Faretta v. California,* 422 U.S. 806, 95 S.Ct. 2525, 45 L.Ed.2d 562 (1975).

EXHIBIT 3–1   STAGES IN A TYPICAL LAWSUIT

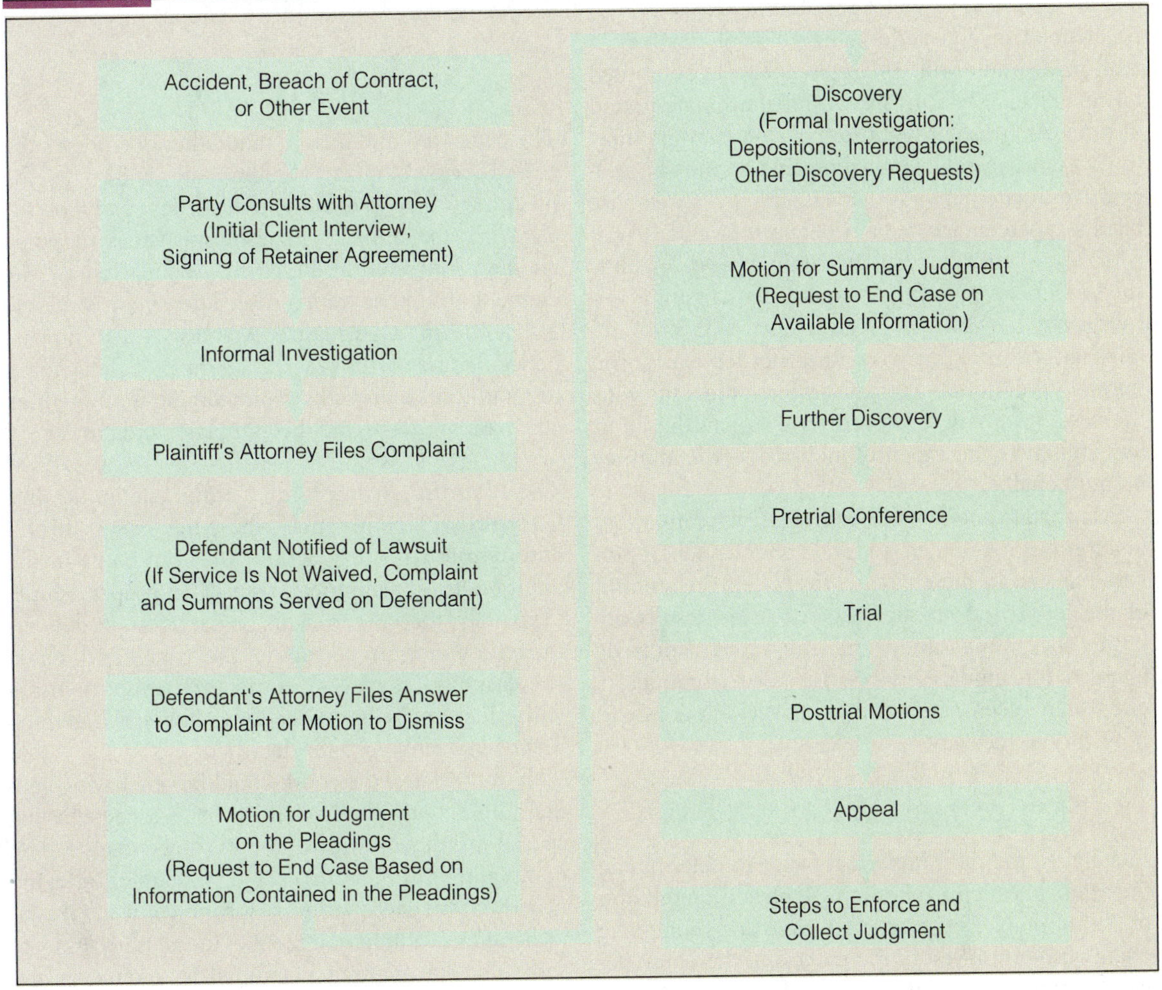

Accident, Breach of Contract,
or Other Event

Party Consults with Attorney
(Initial Client Interview,
Signing of Retainer Agreement)

Informal Investigation

Plaintiff's Attorney Files Complaint

Defendant Notified of Lawsuit
(If Service Is Not Waived, Complaint
and Summons Served on Defendant)

Defendant's Attorney Files Answer
to Complaint or Motion to Dismiss

Motion for Judgment
on the Pleadings
(Request to End Case Based on
Information Contained in the Pleadings)

Discovery
(Formal Investigation:
Depositions, Interrogatories,
Other Discovery Requests)

Motion for Summary Judgment
(Request to End Case on
Available Information)

Further Discovery

Pretrial Conference

Trial

Posttrial Motions

Appeal

Steps to Enforce and
Collect Judgment

SECTION 2

Consulting with an Attorney

The first step taken by virtually anyone contemplating a lawsuit is to obtain the advice of a qualified attorney. In the hypothetical Kirby-Carvello case, Kirby may consult with an attorney, who will advise her as to what she can expect to gain from a lawsuit, her probability of success if she sues, what procedures will be involved, and how long it may take to resolve the issue through the judicial process. Depending on the court hearing the case, the time costs of the litigation may be significant. Personal injury cases may take two to three years to resolve, and this is an important factor for Kirby to consider.

LEGAL FEES

Another crucial factor that Kirby must consider is, of course, the cost of the attorney's time—the legal fees that she will have to pay to collect damages from the defendant, Carvello. Attorneys base their fees on such factors as the difficulty of a matter, the amount of time involved, the experience and skill of the attorney in the particular area of the law, and the cost of doing business. In the United States, legal fees range from $60 per hour to $450 per hour (the average fee per hour is between $140 and $160). Not included in attorneys' fees are various expenses relating to a case, often called "out-of-pocket" costs, that the attorneys must pay. These costs include court filing fees, travel expenses, the cost of expert witnesses and investigators, and so on.

A particular legal matter may include one type or a combination of several types of fees. *Fixed fees* may be charged for the performance of such services as drafting a simple will. *Hourly fees* may be computed for matters that will involve an indeterminate period of time. Any case brought to trial, for example, may involve an expenditure of time that cannot be precisely estimated in advance. *Contingency fees* are fixed as a percentage (usually between 25 and 40 percent) of a client's recovery in certain types of lawsuits, such as a personal injury lawsuit. If the lawsuit is unsuccessful, the attorney receives no fee. If Kirby retains an attorney on a contingency-fee basis, she normally will not have to pay any fees unless she wins the case. (She will, however, have to pay the court fees and any other expenses incurred by the attorney on her behalf.)

Many state and federal statutes allow for an award of attorneys' fees in certain legal actions, such as probate matters. In these cases, a judge sets the amount of the fee, based on such factors as the results obtained by the attorney and the fee customarily charged for similar services. In some situations, a client may receive an award of attorneys' fees as part of his or her recovery.

SETTLEMENT CONSIDERATIONS

Frequently, the most important factor in determining the extent to which an attorney will pursue a resolution of a legal problem is how much time and money the client wishes to invest in the process. If the client decides that he or she can afford a lengthy trial and one or more appeals, the attorney may pursue those actions. Often, once a client learns the extent of the costs involved in litigating a claim, he or she may decide to settle the claim for a lower amount by using one of the methods of alternative dispute resolution discussed in Chapter 2, such as negotiation or mediation.

Another important factor in deciding whether to pursue litigation is the defendant's ability to pay the damages sought. Even if Kirby is awarded damages, it may be difficult to enforce the court's judgment. (We will discuss the problems involved in enforcing a judgment later in this chapter.)

SECTION 3

Pretrial Procedures

The pretrial litigation process involves the filing of the *pleadings*, the gathering of evidence (called

discovery), and possibly other procedures, such as a pretrial conference and jury selection.

THE PLEADINGS

The *complaint* and *answer* (and other documents discussed below), taken together, are known as the **pleadings.** The pleadings notify each party of the claims of the other and specify the issues (disputed questions) involved in the case. Pleadings remove the element of surprise from a case. They allow lawyers to gather the most persuasive evidence and to prepare better arguments, thus increasing the probability that a just and true result will be forthcoming from the trial. The basic pleadings are the complaint and answer.

The Plaintiff's Complaint. Kirby's action against Carvello will commence when her lawyer files a **complaint**[4] with the clerk of the trial court in the appropriate geographical area—the proper venue. (Typically, the lawyer or his or her assistant delivers the complaint in person to the trial court clerk. Increasingly, however, courts are experimenting with electronic filing—see this chapter's *Emerging Trends in Technology* for details.)

In most states, the court would be one having general jurisdiction; in others, it might be a court having special jurisdiction with regard to subject matter. The complaint will contain (1) a statement alleging (asserting) the facts necessary for the court to take jurisdiction, (2) a short statement of the facts necessary to show that the plaintiff is entitled to a remedy, and (3) a statement of the remedy the plaintiff is seeking. A typical complaint is shown in Exhibit 3–2 on page 51.

The complaint will state that Kirby was driving her car through a green light at the specified intersection, exercising good driving habits and reasonable care, when Carvello negligently drove his vehicle through a red light and into the intersection from a cross street, striking Kirby and causing serious personal injury and property damage. The complaint will go on to state that Kirby is seeking $100,000 in damages. (Note that in some state civil actions, the amount of damages sought is not specified.)

Service of Process. Before the court can exercise jurisdiction over the defendant (Carvello)—in effect, before the lawsuit can begin—the court must have proof that the defendant was notified of the

---

4. Sometimes, the document filed with the court is called a petition or a declaration instead of a complaint.

EMERGING TRENDS IN TECHNOLOGY

Filing Court Documents Electronically

In any litigation, a number of documents must be filed with the court. In complex litigation, this number may spiral into the hundreds or even thousands. Complaints and answers, claims and counterclaims, amendments to the pleadings, pretrial motions, discovery requests—all of these documents and more may have to be filed with the court during the pretrial phase of litigation. During and after the trial, other motions may need to be filed. Additionally, these documents must be made available to the other party or parties involved in the lawsuit. At the same time, today's courts are overloaded with work. Court dockets are packed, and record-keeping facilities are bulging.

ENTER TECHNOLOGY

One of the promises of today's communications technology, and particularly the Internet, is that it will help to reduce the mountains of paperwork typically involved in litigation. A number of courts have taken steps to reduce the burden of paperwork by allowing parties to a lawsuit to file court documents electronically. Filing documents with a court by electronic means may involve transferring the documents over the Internet, such as through an

e-mail system, or delivering them to the court on a computer disk or CD-ROM.

The federal court system first experimented with an electronic filing system in January 1996, in an asbestos case heard by the U.S. District Court for the Northern District of Ohio. In the same year, the Federal Rules of Civil Procedure were amended to change the definition of *filing* so that it permits the filing of papers by electronic means—the decision is left up to the individual federal courts. Currently, more than a dozen federal courts permit attorneys to file documents electronically in certain types of cases. At last count, more than 130,000 documents in approximately 10,000 cases had been filed electronically in federal courts.

State and local courts also are setting up electronic court filing systems. Since late 1997, the Pima County, Arizona, court system has been accepting pleadings via e-mail. In 1998, the supreme court of the state of Washington also began to accept online filings of litigation documents. Electronic filing projects are also being developed in other states, including Kansas, Virginia, Utah, and Michigan. Notably, the judicial branch of the state of Colorado recently decided to implement the first statewide court e-filing system in the United States. When implementation is complete, an Internet-based service will allow all Colorado civil courts to accept legal filings electronically. In California,

Florida, and a few other states, some court clerks offer docket information and other searchable databases online.

THERE ARE STILL HURDLES TO OVERCOME

Although electronic filing provides many benefits, there are numerous hurdles to overcome on the road to this "paperless" future. These hurdles involve both technological and human factors. For one thing, electronic filing typically is permissible only in cases specifically approved by the court and (usually) only if all parties involved in the case agree to the procedure. The parties' agreement to electronic filing is important because if certain hardware or software is required, one party may bear more of a burden than the other.

For example, in one case, an appellant filed a brief (an attorney's written argument supporting his or her client's position in a case) on a CD-ROM using an Internet browser interface. Every citation was in the form of a hyperlink. The brief also contained the entire trial record, including a transcript, and an audio-video appendix with deposition testimony. The federal court of appeals refused to accept the brief because the other party to the lawsuit did not have the equipment to "read" it and access the hypertext links included on the CD-ROM. In its written opinion, the court emphasized that although it did not wish to discourage electronic filing, it did not seem fair

EMERGING TRENDS IN TECHNOLOGY

Filing Court Documents Electronically,
continued

to impose such a burden on the other party.[a]

Software and hardware incompatibilities also pose problems. For example, when a state trial court judge in Mississippi was about to try a lawsuit brought by thousands of plaintiffs against twelve corporate defendants, the judge ordered the parties to file their documents electronically. The parties were to use specially designed software called LawPlus. Problems immediately surfaced. First, LawPlus used a proprietary system that relied on Microsoft Word, while practically all of the law firms involved used WordPerfect. As a result, the attorneys encountered constant problems with document conversion. Second, the system was modem based and very slow. Ultimately, LawPlus was abandoned, and the parties went back to using paper.[b]

---

a. *Yukiyo, Ltd. v. Watanabe,* 111 F.3d 883 (Fed.Cir. 1997).
b. For a discussion of this problem and other technological challenges faced by the judge in this case, see Wendy R. Leibowitz, "Courts in Tech Trenches," *The National Law Journal,* April 19, 1999, p. A25.

No doubt, ways to overcome these technological problems will be found in the coming years. Currently, for example, the Administrative Office of the U.S. Courts is looking for a new electronic database management system that will be set up in most federal courts and provide some uniformity. The system will provide electronic filing and document management capabilities, as well as case management features (details about cases that normally would be in paper files, appointment books, accounting systems, and personal computers).

IMPLICATIONS FOR THE BUSINESSPERSON

1. Clearly, the effects of electronic filing will be felt most directly by the legal profession and by the court systems. Nonetheless, businesspersons who are involved in litigation will benefit indirectly, through lower legal costs, by the time and cost savings resulting from electronic filing systems.
2. Businesspersons may also benefit from having pleadings, discovery documents, motions, supporting briefs, and other litigation materials available in electronic format. In an attempt to safeguard their reputations, a number of companies involved in lawsuits, including Microsoft Corporation, have posted such documents on their Web sites to inform the public of their side of the story.
3. The availability of pleadings and discovery materials on the Web may have a significant impact on businesses that are being sued in

similar cases. For example, in its landmark case against the tobacco industry, Minnesota's Blue Cross and Blue Shield put on the Web more than thirty million pages of documents that the state had collected from the tobacco companies during discovery. Shortly after the documents were posted, plaintiffs in other states—and even in other nations—began to use some of the documents to support their claims against tobacco companies.

FOR CRITICAL ANALYSIS

1. Is there any way to guarantee the security of documents that are filed via e-mail with a court? In other words, how can a court be sure of a document's origin or guarantee that a document hasn't been tampered with—by a computer hacker, for example?
2. Should private vendors be in charge of providing electronic filing systems for the courts, or should the government own and control any such systems to protect the integrity of public information?

RELEVANT WEB SITES

You can find a list of the courts that are experimenting with electronic filing at the following Web site, which is sponsored by Maryland Judge Arthur Ahalt: **http://www. mdlaw.net/efile.htm**. For an example of a hyperlinked court opinion, see the decision in *C.L.I.C. Electronics International, Inc. v. Casio, Inc.,* 975 F.Supp. 1343 (M.D.Fla 1997), at **http:// www.fedjudge.org/96-929.htm**.

EXHIBIT 3–2   A TYPICAL COMPLAINT

IN THE UNITED STATES DISTRICT COURT
FOR THE _Southern_ DISTRICT OF _New York_

CIVIL NO. 2-1047

Jill Kirby
_____
                Plaintiff

vs.   COMPLAINT

Antonio Carvello
_____
                Defendant.

The plaintiff brings this cause of action against the defendant, alleging as follows:

1. This action is between the plaintiff, who is a resident of the State of New York, and the defendant, who is a resident of the State of New Jersey. There is diversity of citizenship between the parties.
2. The amount in controversy, exclusive of interest and costs, exceeds the sum of $75,000.
3. On September 10th, 2001, the plaintiff, Jill Kirby, was exercising good driving habits and reasonable care in driving her car through the intersection of Boardwalk and Pennsylvania Avenue, New York City, New York, when the defendant, Antonio Carvello, negligently drove his vehicle through a red light at the intersection and collided with the plaintiff's vehicle.
4. As a result of the collision, the plaintiff suffered severe physical injury, which prevented her from working, and property damage to her car.

WHEREFORE, the plaintiff demands judgment against the defendant for the sum of $100,000 plus interest at the maximum legal rate and the costs of this action.

By _Joseph Roe_
Joseph Roe
Attorney for Plaintiff
100 Main Street
New York, New York

1/2/02

lawsuit. The process of notifying the defendant of a lawsuit is called **service of process.** Service of process involves serving the defendant with a summons and a copy of the complaint—that is, delivering these items to the defendant. The **summons** notifies defendant Carvello that he is required to prepare an answer to the complaint and to file a copy of his answer with both the court and the plaintiff's attorney within a specified time period (twenty days in the federal courts).

The summons also informs Carvello that if he fails to answer or respond to the plaintiff's complaint within the required time period (unless he can provide a convincing reason to the court why he could not do so), the result will be a default judgment for the plaintiff. A **default judgment** in Kirby's favor would mean that she would be awarded the damages alleged in her complaint. A typical summons is shown in Exhibit 3–3.

How service of process occurs depends on the rules of the court or jurisdiction in which the lawsuit is brought. Under the Federal Rules of Civil Procedure (FRCP), service of process in federal court cases may be effected by anyone who is not a party to the lawsuit and who is at least eighteen years of age. In state courts, the process server is often a county sheriff or deputy. Usually, the server effects the service by handing the summons to the defendant personally or by leaving it at the defendant's residence or place of business. In a few states, a summons can be served by mail if the defendant so agrees. When the defendant cannot be reached, special rules sometimes permit serving the summons by leaving it with a designated person, such as the secretary of state.

Serving Corporate Defendants.   In cases involving corporate defendants, the summons and complaint may be served on an officer or *registered agent* (representative) of the corporation. The name of a corporation's registered agent can usually be obtained from the secretary of state's office in the state in which the company incorporated its business (and, usually, from the secretary of state's office in any state in which the corporation does business).

Waiver of Formal Service of Process.   The FRCP allow formal service of process to be waived by defendants in federal cases, providing that certain procedures are followed. Kirby's attorney, for example, could mail to defendant Carvello a copy of the complaint, along with "Waiver of Service of Summons" forms for Carvello to sign. If Carvello signs and returns the forms within thirty days, formal service of process is waived. To encourage defendants to waive formal service of process, the FRCP provide that defendants who sign and return the waiver are not required to respond to the complaint for sixty days after the date on which the request for waiver of service was sent, instead of the twenty days allowed if formal service of process is undertaken.

The Defendant's Response.   The defendant's response to the plaintiff's complaint may take the form of an **answer,** in which the defendant either admits the statements or allegations set out in the complaint or denies them and sets out any defenses that the defendant may have. If Carvello admits to all of Kirby's allegations in his answer, a judgment will be entered for Kirby. If Carvello denies Kirby's allegations, the matter will proceed further.

Carvello can also admit the truth of Kirby's complaint but raise new facts to show that he should not be held liable for Kirby's damages. This is called raising an **affirmative defense.** As will be discussed in subsequent chapters, there are affirmative defenses that can be raised by defendants in both civil and criminal cases. For example, a defendant accused of physically harming another might claim that he or she acted in self-defense. A defendant charged with breach of contract might defend on the ground (legal basis) of mistake or the fact that the contract was oral when it was required by law to be in writing. In the Kirby-Carvello case, assume that Carvello has obtained evidence that Kirby was not exercising good driving habits at the time the accident occurred (she was looking at a child in the back of her car instead of watching the road). Carvello could assert Kirby's own negligence as a defense. In some states, a plaintiff's contributory negligence operates as a complete defense. In most states, however, the plaintiff's own negligence constitutes only a partial defense (see Chapter 5).

Carvello could also deny Kirby's allegations and set forth his own claim that the accident occurred as a result of Kirby's negligence, and therefore Kirby owes Carvello money for damages to his car. This is appropriately called a **counterclaim.** If Carvello files a counterclaim, Kirby will have to submit an answer to the counterclaim.

EXHIBIT 3–3   A TYPICAL SUMMONS

SUMMONS IN A CIVIL ACTION

United States District Court

FOR THE Southern **DISTRICT OF:** New York

CIVIL ACTION FILE No. 2-1047

Jill Kirby

Plaintiff

v.

Antonio Carvello

Defendant

SUMMONS

To the above named Defendant:

You are hereby summoned and required to serve upon

plaintiff's attorney, whose address is

Joseph Roe

100 Main Street

New York, New York

an answer to the complaint which is herewith served upon you, within 20 days after service of this summons upon you, exclusive of the day of service. If you fail to do so, judgment by default will be taken against you for the relief demanded in the complaint.

Samuel Raeburn
_____
Clerk of Court

Mary Doakes
_____
Deputy Clerk.

Date: 1/10/02

[Seal of Court]

NOTE:—This summons is issued pursuant to Rule 4 of the Federal Rules of Civil Procedure.

DISMISSALS AND
JUDGMENTS BEFORE TRIAL

Many actions for which pleadings have been filed never come to trial. The parties may, for example, negotiate a settlement of the dispute at any stage of the litigation process. There are also numerous procedural avenues for disposing of a case without a trial. Many of them involve one or the other party's attempts to get the case dismissed through the use of various motions.

A **motion** is a procedural request submitted to the court by an attorney on behalf of his or her client. When one party files a motion with the court, that party must also send to, or serve on, the opposing party a *notice of motion*. The notice of motion informs the opposing party that the motion has been filed. **Pretrial motions** include the motion to dismiss, the motion for judgment on the pleadings, and the motion for summary judgment.

Motion to Dismiss. If the defendant challenges the sufficiency of the plaintiff's complaint, the defendant can present to the court a **motion to dismiss** for failure to state a claim for which relief (a remedy) can be granted, or a *demurrer*. (The rules of civil procedure in many states do not use the term *demurrer*; they use only *motion to dismiss*.) The motion to dismiss for failure to state a claim for which relief can be granted is an allegation that even if the facts presented in the complaint are true, their legal consequences are such that there is no reason to go further with the suit and no need for the defendant to present an answer. If, for example, Kirby's complaint had alleged facts that excluded the possibility of negligence on Carvello's part, Carvello could move to dismiss the case.

Defendant Carvello could also file a motion to dismiss if he believed that he had not been properly served, that the complaint had been filed in the wrong court (for example, that the court lacked personal or subject-matter jurisdiction or the venue was improper), or for other specific reasons.

A motion to dismiss may be—and often is—filed with the court by a defendant instead of an answer. If the court denies the motion, the defendant generally is given an extension of time to file an answer (or further pleading). If the defendant fails to file the appropriate pleading, a judgment will normally be entered for the plaintiff. If the court grants the motion to dismiss, the defendant is not required to answer the complaint. The plaintiff generally is given time to file an

amended complaint. If the plaintiff does not file this amended complaint, a judgment will be entered against the plaintiff solely on the basis of the pleadings, and the plaintiff will not be allowed to bring suit on the matter again.

If Kirby wishes to discontinue the suit because, for example, an out-of-court settlement has been reached, she can likewise move for dismissal. The court can also dismiss a case on its own motion.

Motion for Judgment on the Pleadings. After the pleadings are closed—after the complaint, answer, and any other pleadings have been filed—either of the parties can file a **motion for judgment on the pleadings.** This motion may be filed when it appears from the pleadings that the plaintiff has failed to state a cause of action for which relief may be granted. The motion may also be filed when the pleadings indicate that no facts are in dispute and the only question is how the law applies to a set of agreed-on facts. For example, assume for a moment that in the Kirby-Carvello case, defendant Carvello admitted to all of Kirby's allegations in his answer and raised no affirmative defenses. In this situation, Kirby would file a motion for judgment on the pleadings in her favor.

The difference between this motion and a motion for summary judgment, discussed next, is that the party requesting the motion may support a motion for summary judgment with sworn statements and other materials that will be admissible as evidence at trial; on a motion for a judgment on the pleadings, however, a court may consider only what is contained in the pleadings.

Motion for Summary Judgment. The **motion for summary judgment** is similar to a motion for judgment on the pleadings in that the party filing the motion is asking the court to grant a judgment in its favor without a trial. As with a motion for judgment on the pleadings, a court will grant a motion for summary judgment only if it determines that no facts are in dispute and the only question is how the law applies to the facts.

To support a motion for summary judgment, one party can submit, prior to trial, sworn evidence obtained at any point prior to trial (including during the discovery stage of litigation—to be discussed shortly) that refutes the other party's factual claim. The evidence may consist of **affidavits** (sworn statements by parties or witnesses), as well as documents, such as a contract. The evidence must be *admissible* evidence—that is, evidence that the court would allow to be presented during the trial. Hearsay, for example, normally would not be admissible. As mentioned, the use of this additional evidence is one of the features that distinguishes the motion for summary judgment from the motion to dismiss and the motion for judgment on the pleadings.

In the Kirby-Carvello accident, whether or not the light was red is a question of fact. Assume that during discovery, Carvello obtained undisputable evidence that the stoplight was not working when he drove through the intersection. Assume further that Carvello has evidence (a witness's testimony) that he

was not exceeding the legal speed limit. Carvello could file a motion for summary judgment on the ground that there was no evidence in the record to support Kirby's claim. The court might grant Carvello's motion, because there would be no genuine factual dispute and Carvello would be entitled to judgment as a matter of law.

A motion for summary judgment can be made before or during a trial, but it will be granted only if, when the evidence is viewed in the light most favorable to the other party, it is clear that there are no factual disputes in contention. The following case illustrates this point.

CASE 3.1   Ausley v. Bishop

Court of Appeals of
North Carolina, 1999.
515 S.E.2d 72.
http://www.aoc.state.
nc.us/www/public/html/
opinions.html [a]

BACKGROUND AND FACTS *In November 1994, Andrew Ausley, a state-certified real estate appraiser, hired Bryan Bishop, who wanted to become a certified appraiser, as an apprentice (a requirement for certification). Between November 1994 and April 1997, Bishop prepared and signed appraisal reports, as required by the North Carolina Appraisal Board. For each report, Bishop also prepared a log sheet. The board required that a supervising appraiser sign the log sheets. Ausley told Bishop to let his log sheets accumulate and he (Ausley) would sign them later. By April 1997, Bishop was qualified to receive an appraiser's license, subject only to Ausley signing the log sheets. Ausley said that before he'd sign them, he wanted Bishop to sign a new employment contract. Bishop agreed. Ausley signed the log sheets, and the state issued Bishop his license. That summer, to buy a house, Bishop applied for a mortgage with Robert Phillips of Southern Fidelity Mortgage, with whom Bishop also hoped to do business as an appraiser. In September, Ausley proposed renegotiating his contract with Bishop under terms that included reduced pay. Bishop refused and, a couple of days later, opened his own appraisal office. Ausley then told Phillips that Bishop had submitted false information to obtain his mortgage. Ausley also told others with whom Bishop had done, or hoped to do, business that Bishop had engaged in unethical behavior. After Bishop was seen leaving his old office at Ausley's place of business with a box, Ausley reported to the police that Bishop had stolen files. Ausley mentioned the police report to a person at Piedmont Home Equity, another of Bishop's potential clients. Finally, Ausley filed a suit in a North Carolina state court against Bishop, alleging, among other things, that Bishop breached (failed to perform) their contract. Bishop filed an answer that included a counterclaim charging Ausley with slander (wrongfully injuring Bishop's good reputation with false statements—see Chapter 5). Ausley filed a motion for summary judgment, which the court granted. Bishop appealed.*

**IN THE LANGUAGE
OF THE COURT**

EDMUNDS, Judge.

     *   *   *   *

A trial court's grant of summary judgment is fully reviewable by this Court. The standard of review for whether summary judgment is proper is whether the trial court

---

a. This is a page within the official Web site of the North Carolina judicial branch. In the "Court of Appeals" column, click on "Reported Decisions© 1999." On that page, scroll down to "18 May 1999" and click on the case name to access the opinion.

properly concluded that there was no genuine issue of material fact and that the moving party [Ausley, in this case] was entitled to judgment as a matter of law. The record is to be viewed in the light most favorable to the non-movant [Bishop, in this case], giving it the benefit of all inferences reasonably arising therefrom. *   *   *

*   *   *   * Defendant [Bishop] alleged in his counterclaim that plaintiff [Ausley] committed slander by communicating to defendant's personal mortgage lender statements to the effect that defendant had committed loan fraud. *   *   *

*   *   * Plaintiff admitted in his deposition that he made statements that impeached [discredited] defendant in his trade. During a line of questions pertaining to a form signed by plaintiff and submitted by defendant to mortgage broker Southern Fidelity to finance defendant's own home, plaintiff was asked, "Did you suggest, infer, or imply to Robert [Phillips] at Southern Fidelity that your signature was procured by fraud or some other unlawful means on that appraisal report?" Plaintiff responded, "Correct." *   *   * [Plaintiff] also admitted telling the same Robert Phillips at Southern Fidelity that "Mr. Bishop had not been truthful about his income in qualifying for the loan that Southern Fidelity brokered, arranged or gave to the Bishops," when there was evidence that plaintiff previously had verified defendant's income to Southern Fidelity. Additionally, defendant stated in his affidavit that "[plaintiff] contacted several of my clients and potential clients and advised them, untruthfully, that I had engaged in various unethical conduct." Because defendant was launching his own business as an appraiser, plaintiff's incorrect statements to defendant's clients and potential clients undoubtedly had the capacity to harm defendant in his trade or profession.

In a second episode, plaintiff admitted reporting to police that defendant had stolen client files. The evidence to support plaintiff's report was that defendant was seen leaving his old office at plaintiff's business with a box, and that later *   *   * files containing defendant's resumes and sample appraisal files were *   *   * missing from a file cabinet. Although the investigation subsequently was dropped without any charges being brought, plaintiff admitted communicating to at least one person at Piedmont Home Equity that he suspected defendant had taken files, and had called the police. Again, this statement to a potential client of defendant was capable of harming him in his trade or profession. We therefore conclude that defendant has forecast sufficient evidence of all essential elements of his claim to make a *prima facie* case[b] at trial to survive plaintiff's motion for summary judgment. We reverse as to this issue and remand for further proceedings.

DECISION AND REMEDY   *The Court of Appeals of North Carolina held that Bishop had enough proof of his claim for it to go to trial. The court reversed the lower court's grant of summary judgment on this issue and remanded the case (sent it back to the trial court) for trial.*

---

b. A *prima facie* case is one in which a party shows sufficient evidence of his or her claim to go to trial. The evidence should be enough to compel a conclusion in the charging party's favor unless the other party has evidence to disprove the claim.

DISCOVERY

Before a trial begins, the parties can use a number of procedural devices to obtain information and gather evidence about the case. Kirby, for example, will want to know how fast Carvello was driving, whether he had been drinking or was under the influence of any medication, whether he was wearing corrective lenses if he was required by law to do so while driving, and so on. The process of obtaining information from the opposing party or from witnesses prior to trial is known as **discovery.**

The Federal Rules of Civil Procedure and similar rules in the states set forth the guidelines for discovery activity. Discovery includes gaining access to witnesses, documents, records, and other types of evidence. The rules governing discovery are designed to make sure that a witness or a party is not unduly harassed, that privileged material is safeguarded, and that only information relevant to the case at hand—or likely to lead to the discovery of relevant information—is discoverable.

Of course, there are limits as to what a party can obtain as part of the discovery process. For example, a business firm in litigation with a competitor normally will not be given unrestricted access to the competitor's trade secrets, customer lists, and other confidential records. A court may order that only the firm's attorneys and certain experts can view such sensitive information.

Discovery prevents surprises by giving both parties access to evidence that might otherwise be hidden. This allows the litigants to learn as much as they can about what to expect at a trial before they reach the courtroom. Discovery also serves to narrow the issues so that trial time is spent on the main questions in the case. Currently, the trend is toward allowing more discovery and thus fewer surprises.[5]

Depositions and Interrogatories. At a minimum, discovery involves the use of depositions, interrogatories, or both. A **deposition** is sworn testimony by a party to the lawsuit or by any witness, recorded by an authorized court official. The person deposed gives testimony and answers questions asked by the attorneys from both sides. The questions and answers are recorded, sworn to, and signed. These answers, of course, will help the attorneys prepare their cases. Depositions also give attorneys the opportunity to evaluate how their witnesses will conduct themselves at trial. In addition, depositions can be employed in court to impeach (challenge the credibility of) a party or a witness who changes testimony at the trial. A deposition can also be used as testimony if the witness is not available at trial.

Interrogatories are written questions for which written answers are prepared and then signed under oath. Interrogatories are addressed only to parties directly involved in a lawsuit (plaintiffs or defendants), not to witnesses, and the parties can prepare their an-

swers with the aid of attorneys. Whereas depositions are useful for eliciting candid responses from a party and answers not prepared in advance, interrogatories are designed to obtain accurate information about specific topics, such as how many contracts were signed, the specific dates on which certain contracts were signed, and so on.

Requests for Admissions. One party can serve a written request to the other party for an admission of the truth of matters relating to the trial. Any fact admitted under such a request is conclusively established as true for the trial. For example, Kirby can ask Carvello to admit that his driver's license was suspended at the time of the accident. A request for admission shortens the trial, because the parties will not have to spend time proving facts on which they already agree.

Requests for Documents, Objects, and Entry upon Land. A party can gain access to documents and other items not in his or her possession in order to inspect and examine them. Likewise, a party can gain "entry upon land" to inspect the premises. Carvello, for example, can gain permission to inspect and copy Kirby's repair bills.

Request for Examinations. When the physical or mental condition of one party is in question, the opposing party can ask the court to order a physical or mental examination by an independent examiner. If the court is willing to make the order, the opposing party can obtain the results of the examination. Note that the court will make such an order only when the need for the information outweighs the right to privacy of the person to be examined.

PRETRIAL CONFERENCE

After discovery has taken place and before the trial begins, the attorneys may meet with the trial judge in a **pretrial conference.** The purpose of this conference is to clarify the issues that remain in dispute after discovery has taken place and to explore the possibility of settling the conflict without a trial. If a settlement is not possible at this time, the parties and the judge discuss the manner in which the trial will be conducted. In particular, the parties may attempt to establish ground rules to restrict such things as the number of expert witnesses or the admissibility of certain types of evidence. Once the pretrial

---

5. This is particularly evident in the 1993 revision of the Federal Rules of Civil Procedure. The revised rules provide that each party must disclose to the other, on an ongoing basis, the types of evidence that will be presented at trial, the names of witnesses that may or will be called, and other relevant information.

conference concludes, both parties will have to turn their attention to the trial itself and, if the trial is to be a jury trial, to the selection of jurors who will hear the case.

THE RIGHT TO A JURY TRIAL

The Seventh Amendment to the U.S. Constitution guarantees the right to a jury trial for cases at law in federal courts when the amount in controversy exceeds $20. Most states have similar guarantees in their own constitutions, although many states restrict the guarantee to a higher minimum amount. For example, Iowa requires the dollar amount of damages to be at least $1,000 before there is a right to a jury trial. The right to a trial by jury does not have to be exercised, and many cases are tried without a jury. If there is no jury, the judge determines the truth of the facts alleged in the case. In most states and in federal courts, one of the parties must request a jury, or the right is presumed to be waived.

JURY SELECTION

Prior to the commencement of any jury trial, a panel of jurors must be assembled. The clerk of the court will usually notify local residents by mail that they have been selected for jury duty. The process of selecting the names of these prospective jurors varies, but often they are randomly chosen by the court clerk from lists of registered voters or those within the state to whom driver's licenses have been issued. These persons then report to the courthouse on the date specified in the notice. There they are gathered into a single pool of jurors, and the process of selecting those jurors who will actually hear the case begins. Although some types of trials require twelve-person juries, most civil matters can be heard by six-person juries.

Voir Dire. The process by which the jury is selected is known as *voir dire.*[6] In most jurisdictions, *voir dire* consists of oral questions that attorneys for the plaintiff and the defendant ask a group of prospective jurors to determine whether a potential

juror is biased or has any connection with a party to the action or with a prospective witness. Usually, jurors are questioned one at a time, although when large numbers of jurors are involved, the attorneys may direct their questions to groups of jurors instead to minimize the amount of time spent in jury selection. Sometimes, jurors are asked to fill out written questionnaires. Some trial attorneys use psychologists and other professionals to help them select jurors.

Challenges during Voir Dire. During *voir dire*, a party may challenge a certain number of prospective jurors *peremptorily*—that is, ask that these individuals not be sworn in as jurors without providing any reason. The total number of peremptory challenges allowed each side is determined by statute or by the court. Furthermore, a party may challenge any juror *for cause*—that is, provide a reason why an individual should not be sworn in as a juror. If the judge grants the challenge, the individual is asked to step down. A prospective juror may not be excluded from participation in the trial process, however, by use of discriminatory challenges, such as those based on racial criteria[7] or gender.[8]

After both sides have completed their challenges, those jurors who have been excused will be permitted to leave. The remaining jurors—those who have been found acceptable by the attorneys for both sides—will be seated in the jury box.

Alternate Jurors. Because unforeseeable circumstances or illness may necessitate that one or more of the sitting jurors be dismissed, the court, depending on the rules of the particular jurisdiction and the expected length of the trial, might choose to have two or three alternate jurors present throughout the trial. If a juror has to be excused in the middle of the trial, then an alternate may take his or her place without disrupting the proceedings. Once the jury members are seated, the judge will swear in the jury members, and the trial itself can begin.

---

6. Pronounced *vwahr deehr.* Literally, these French verbs mean "to see, to speak." During the *voir dire* phase of litigation, attorneys do in fact see the jurors speak. In legal language, however, the phrase refers to the process of interrogating jurors to learn about their backgrounds, attitudes, and so on.

7. *Batson v. Kentucky,* 476 U.S. 79, 106 S.Ct. 1712, 90 L.Ed.2d 69 (1986).

8. *J.E.B. v. Alabama ex rel. T.B.,* 511 U.S. 127, 114 S.Ct. 1419, 128 L.Ed.2d 89 (1994). (*Ex rel.* is an abbreviation of the Latin *ex relatione.* The phrase refers to an action brought on behalf of the state, by the attorney general, at the instigation of an individual who has a private interest in the matter.)

CONCEPT SUMMARY 3.1

PRETRIAL PROCEDURES

PROCEDURE	DESCRIPTION
Pleadings	1. *The plaintiff's complaint*—The plaintiff's statement of the cause of action and the parties involved, filed with the court by the plaintiff's attorney. After the filing, the defendant is notified of the suit through service of process. 2. *The defendant's response*—The defendant's response to the plaintiff's complaint may take the form of an answer, in which the defendant may admit to or deny the plaintiff's allegations. The defendant may raise an affirmative defense and/or assert a counterclaim.
Pretrial Motions	1. *Motion to dismiss*—A motion made by the defendant—often prior to filing an answer to the complaint—requesting the judge to dismiss the case for reasons that are provided in the motion (such as failure to state a claim for which relief can be granted). 2. *Motion for judgment on the pleadings*—May be made by either party; will be granted if no facts are in dispute and only questions of law are at issue. 3. *Motion for summary judgment*—May be made by either party; will be granted if no facts are in dispute and only questions of law are at issue. Unlike the motion for judgment on the pleadings, the motion for summary judgment may be supported by evidence outside the pleadings, such as testimony and other evidence obtained during the discovery phase of litigation.
Discovery	The process of gathering evidence concerning the case; involves (1) *depositions* (sworn testimony by either party or any witness); (2) *interrogatories* (in which parties to the action write answers to questions with the aid of their attorneys); and (3) requests for admissions, documents, examinations, or other information relating to the case.
Pretrial Conference	A pretrial hearing, at the request of either party or the court, to identify the matters in dispute after discovery has taken place and to explore the possibility of settling the dispute without a trial. If no settlement is possible, the parties plan the course of the trial.
Jury Selection	In a jury trial, the selection of members of the jury from a pool of prospective jurors. During a process known as *voir dire*, the attorneys for both sides may challenge prospective jurors either for cause or peremptorily (for no cause).

SECTION 4

The Trial

Various rules and procedures govern the trial phase of the litigation process. There are rules governing what kind of evidence will or will not be admitted during the trial, as well as specific procedures that the participants in the lawsuit must follow.

RULES OF EVIDENCE

Whether evidence will be admitted in court is determined by the **rules of evidence**—a series of rules that have been created by the courts to ensure that any evidence presented during a trial is fair and reliable. The Federal Rules of Evidence govern the admissibility of evidence in federal courts.

Evidence will not be admitted in court unless it is relevant to the matter in question. **Relevant evidence** is evidence that tends to prove or disprove a fact in question or to establish the degree of probability of a fact or action. For example, evidence that a suspect's gun was in the home of another person when a victim was shot would be relevant—because it would tend to prove that the suspect did not shoot the victim.

Even relevant evidence may not be admitted in court if its reliability is questionable or if its probative (proving) value is substantially outweighed by other important considerations of the court. For example, a video or a photograph that shows in detail the severity of a victim's injuries would be relevant evidence, but the court might exclude this evidence on the ground that it would emotionally inflame the jurors.

Generally, hearsay is not admissible as evidence. **Hearsay** is defined as any testimony given in court about a statement made by someone else. Literally, it is what someone heard someone else say. For example, if a witness in the Kirby-Carvello case testified in court concerning what he or she heard another observer say about the accident, that testimony would be hearsay—secondhand knowledge. Admitting hearsay into evidence carries many risks because, even though it may be relevant, there is no way to test its reliability.

OPENING STATEMENTS

At the commencement of the trial, both attorneys are allowed to make **opening statements** concerning the facts that they expect to prove during the trial. The opening statement provides an opportunity for each lawyer to give a brief version of the facts and the supporting evidence that will be used during the trial.

EXAMINATION OF WITNESSES

Because Kirby is the plaintiff, she has the burden of proving that her claim is correct. Kirby's attorney begins the presentation of Kirby's case by calling the first witness for the plaintiff and examining (questioning) the witness. (For both attorneys, the types of questions and the manner of asking them are governed by the rules of evidence.) This questioning is called **direct examination**. After Kirby's attorney is finished, the witness is subject to **cross-examination** by Carvello's attorney. Then Kirby's attorney has another opportunity to question the witness in *redirect examination*, and Carvello's attorney may follow the redirect exam-

ination with a *recross-examination*. When both attorneys have finished with the first witness, Kirby's attorney calls the succeeding witnesses in the plaintiff's case, each of whom is subject to examination by the attorneys in the manner just described.

At the conclusion of the plaintiff's case, the defendant's attorney has the opportunity to ask the judge to direct a verdict for the defendant on the ground that the plaintiff has presented no evidence to support the plaintiff's claim. This is called a **motion for a directed verdict** (federal courts use the term *judgment as a matter of law* instead of *directed verdict*). In considering the motion, the judge looks at the evidence in the light most favorable to the plaintiff and grants the motion only if there is insufficient evidence to raise an issue of fact. (Motions for directed verdicts at this stage of trial are seldom granted.)

The defendant's attorney then presents the evidence and witnesses for the defendant's case. Witnesses are called and examined by the defendant's attorney. The plaintiff's attorney has the right to cross-examine them, and there may be a redirect examination and possibly a recross-examination. At the end of the defendant's case, either attorney can move for a directed verdict, and the test again is whether the jury can, through any reasonable interpretation of the evidence, find for the party against whom the motion has been made. After the defendant's attorney has finished introducing evidence, the plaintiff's attorney can present a **rebuttal,** which includes additional evidence to refute the defendant's case. The defendant's attorney can, in turn, refute that evidence in a **rejoinder.**

CLOSING ARGUMENTS

After both sides have rested their cases, each attorney presents a closing argument. In the **closing argument,** each attorney summarizes the facts and evidence presented during the trial, indicates why the facts and evidence support the client's claim, reveals the shortcomings of the points made by the opposing party during the trial, and generally urges a verdict in favor of the client. Each attorney's comments must be relevant to the issues in dispute.

JURY INSTRUCTIONS

After the closing arguments, the judge instructs the jury (assuming it is a jury trial) in the law that applies to the case. The instructions to the jury are often called *charges*. A charge is a document that includes statements of the applicable laws, as well as a review of the facts as they were presented during the case. Because the jury's role is to serve as the fact finder, the factual account contained in the charge is not binding on them. Indeed, the jurors may disregard the facts as noted in the charge entirely. They are not free to ignore the statements of law, however. The charge will help to channel the jurors' deliberations.

THE JURY'S VERDICT

Following its receipt of instructions, the jury retires to the jury room to deliberate the case. In a civil case, the standard of proof is a *preponderance of the evidence*. That is, the plaintiff (Kirby in our hypothetical case) need not provide indisputable proof that she is entitled to a judgment. She need only show that her factual claim is more likely to be true than the defendant's. (As you will read in Chapter 8, in a criminal trial, the prosecution has a higher standard of proof to meet—it must prove its case *beyond a reasonable doubt*.)

Note that some civil claims must be proved by a "clear and convincing evidence" standard, under which the evidence must show that the truth of the party's claim is highly probable. This standard applies in suits involving charges of fraud, suits to establish the terms of a lost will, some suits relating to oral contracts, and other suits involving circumstances in which there is thought to be a particular danger of deception.

Once the jury has reached a decision, it may issue a **verdict** in favor of one party, which specifies the jury's factual findings and the amount of damages to be paid by the losing party. After the announcement of the verdict, which marks the end of the trial itself, the jurors will be discharged.

CONCEPT SUMMARY 3.2 — TRIAL PROCEDURES

PROCEDURE	DESCRIPTION
Opening Statements	Each party's attorney is allowed to present an opening statement indicating what the attorney will attempt to prove during the course of the trial.
Examination of Witnesses	1. Plaintiff's introduction and direct examination of witnesses, cross-examination by defendant's attorney, possible redirect examination by plaintiff's attorney, and possible recross-examination by defendant's attorney. 2. Defendant's introduction and direct examination of witnesses, cross-examination by plaintiff's attorney, possible redirect examination by defendant's attorney, and possible recross-examination by plaintiff's attorney. 3. Possible rebuttal of defendant's argument by plaintiff's attorney, who presents more evidence. 4. Possible rejoinder by defendant's attorney to meet that evidence.
Closing Arguments	Each party's attorney argues in favor of a verdict for his or her client.
Jury Instructions	The judge instructs the jury as to how the law applies to the issue.
Jury Verdict	The jury renders its verdict, thus bringing the trial to an end.

SECTION 5

Posttrial Motions

After the jury has rendered its verdict, either party may make a posttrial motion. The prevailing party usually files a motion for a judgment in accordance with the verdict. The nonprevailing party frequently files one of the motions discussed next.

MOTION FOR A NEW TRIAL

At the end of the trial, a motion can be made to set aside an adverse verdict and any judgment and to hold a new trial. The **motion for a new trial** will be granted only if the judge (1) is convinced, after looking at all the evidence, that the jury was in error but (2) does not feel it is appropriate to grant judgment for the other side. This will usually occur when the jury verdict is the obvious result of a misapplication of the law or a misunderstanding of the evidence presented at trial.

A new trial can also be granted on the grounds of newly discovered evidence, misconduct by the partic-

ipants (such as the attorneys, the judge, or the jury) during the trial, or error by the judge. If a motion for a new trial is denied, the judge's denial may be appealed to a higher court. In the following case, the defendants filed a motion for a new trial based on the "improper and inflammatory" remarks made by the plaintiff's attorney.

CASE 3.2   LeBlanc v. American Honda Motor Co.

Supreme Court of
New Hampshire, 1997.
141 N.H. 579,
688 A.2d 556.
http://www.state.nh.us/
courts/supreme/
opinions/9701/honda.
htm[a]

HISTORICAL AND SOCIAL SETTING   *One of the principles on which the United States was founded is that all persons are created equal and are entitled to have their individual dignity respected. There have been continual efforts by legislative enactments and judicial decisions to purge our society of racial and other prejudices. Despite these efforts, such biases still appear to influence decisions by many people who would deny equal respect to those of us of a different race, religion, or ethnic origin.*

BACKGROUND AND FACTS   *While riding on a snowmobile, Thomas LeBlanc was injured when the snowmobile collided with an off-road vehicle manufactured by American Honda Motor Company (a subsidiary of a Japanese corporation). LeBlanc sued Honda and the driver in a New Hampshire state court. During the trial, LeBlanc's lawyer, Vincent Martina, asked Honda's expert witness if he had ever wondered why the Honda vehicle was "red, white, and blue, the color of the American flag." During his closing argument, Martina told the jury that the case was not about "Pearl Harbor or the Japanese prime minister saying Americans are lazy and stupid. * * * What this case is about is not American xenophobia; it's about corporate greed." When the jury returned a verdict in favor of LeBlanc, Honda filed a motion for a new trial, which the court denied. Honda appealed to the Supreme Court of New Hampshire, arguing in part that Martina's remarks so tainted the proceedings as to deprive Honda of a fair trial.*

**IN THE LANGUAGE
OF THE COURT**

BROCK, Chief Justice.
     *   *   *   *

     *   *   * To justify a [new trial], remarks or *   *   * conduct must be more than merely inadmissible; they must constitute an irreparable injustice *   *   * .
     *   *   *   *

     *   *   * [A] new trial may be warranted where counsel attempts to appeal to the sympathies, passions, and prejudices of jurors grounded in race or nationality, by reference to the opposing party's religious beliefs or lack thereof, or by reference to a party's social or economic condition or status. Such an appeal was attempted in this case.
     *   *   * It is true that counsel's closing reference was brief. At the same time, when an elephant has passed through the courtroom one does not need a forceful reminder.

**DECISION
AND REMEDY**

The Supreme Court of New Hampshire reversed the decision in favor of LeBlanc and remanded the case for a new trial. The court held that remarks made during a trial to cultivate in the jury a racial and national bias constitute sufficient grounds for a new trial.

---

a. This is a page within the collection of New Hampshire Supreme Court opinions available at the Web site of the New Hampshire state government.

MOTION FOR JUDGMENT N.O.V.

If Kirby wins, and if Carvello's attorney has previously moved for a directed verdict, Carvello's attorney can now make a **motion for judgment *n.o.v.*** (from the Latin *non obstante veredicto*, meaning "notwithstanding the verdict"; federal courts use the term *judgment as a matter of law* instead of judgment *n.o.v.*). The standards for granting a judgment *n.o.v.* often are the same as those for granting a motion to dismiss or a motion for a directed verdict. Carvello can state that even if the evidence is viewed in the light most favorable to Kirby, a reasonable jury should not have found in Kirby's favor. If the judge finds this contention to be correct or decides that the law requires the opposite result, the motion will be granted. If the motion is denied, Carvello may then appeal the case. (Kirby may also appeal the case, even though she won at trial. She might appeal, for example, if she received a smaller money award than she had sought.)

SECTION 6

The Appeal

Either party may appeal not only the jury's verdict but also any pretrial or posttrial motion. Many of the appellate court cases that appear in this text involve appeals of motions to dismiss, motions for summary judgment, or other motions that were denied by trial court judges. Note that few trial court decisions are reversed on appeal. In most appealed cases (approximately 90 percent), the trial court's decision is affirmed and thus becomes final.

FILING THE APPEAL

If Carvello decides to appeal the verdict in Kirby's favor, then his attorney must file a *notice of appeal* with the clerk of the trial court within a prescribed period of time. Carvello then becomes the *appellant*. The clerk of the trial court sends to the reviewing court (usually an intermediate court of appeals) the *record on appeal*, which contains the following: (1) the pleadings, (2) a transcript of the trial testimony and copies of the exhibits, (3) the judge's rulings on motions made by the parties, (4) the arguments of counsel, (5) the instructions to the jury, (6) the verdict, (7) the posttrial motions, and (8) the judgment order from which the appeal is taken.

Carvello's attorney will file a **brief** with the reviewing court. The brief contains (1) a short statement of the facts; (2) a statement of the issues; (3) the rulings by the trial court that Carvello contends are erroneous and prejudicial (biased in favor of one of the parties); (4) the grounds for reversal of the judgment; (5) a statement of the applicable law; and (6) arguments on Carvello's behalf, citing applicable statutes and relevant cases as precedents. The attorney for the *appellee* (Kirby, in our hypothetical case) usually files an answering brief. Carvello's attorney can file a reply, although it is not required. The reviewing court then considers the case.

APPELLATE REVIEW

As mentioned in Chapter 2, a court of appeals does not hear any evidence. Its decision concerning a case is based on the record on appeal and the briefs. The attorneys can present oral arguments, after which the case is taken under advisement. The court then issues a written opinion. In general, the appellate courts do not reverse findings of fact unless the findings are unsupported or contradicted by the evidence.

An appellate court has several options after reviewing a case: it can *affirm* the trial court's decision; it can *reverse* the trial court's judgment if it concludes that the trial court erred or that the jury did not receive proper instructions; or it can *remand* (send back) the case to the trial court for further proceedings consistent with its opinion on the matter. The court might also affirm or reverse a decision *in part*. For example, the court might affirm the jury's finding that Carvello was negligent but remand the case for further proceedings on another issue (such as the extent of Kirby's damages). An appellate court can also *modify* a lower court's decision. If the appellate court decided that the jury awarded an excessive amount in damages, for example, the court might reduce the award to a more appropriate, or fairer, amount.

HIGHER APPELLATE COURTS

If the reviewing court is an intermediate appellate court, the losing party may be allowed by the court to appeal the decision to the state supreme court. Such a petition corresponds to a petition for a writ of *certiorari* in the United States Supreme Court. If the petition is granted, new briefs must be filed before the state supreme court, and the attorneys may be allowed or requested to present oral arguments. Like the intermediate appellate courts, the supreme court may reverse or affirm the appellate court's decision or remand the case.

At this point, unless a federal question is at issue, the case has reached its end. If a federal question is involved, the losing party (or the winning party, if that party is dissatisfied with the relief obtained) may appeal the decision to the United States Supreme Court by petitioning the Court for a writ of *certiorari*. (As discussed in Chapter 2, the Supreme Court may or may not grant the writ, depending on the significance of the issue in dispute.)

CONCEPT SUMMARY 3.3   POSTTRIAL OPTIONS

PROCEDURE	DESCRIPTION
Posttrial Motions	1. *Motion for a new trial*—If the judge is convinced that the jury was in error, the motion will be granted.
	2. *Motion for judgment* n.o.v. (*"notwithstanding the verdict"*)—The party making the motion must have filed a motion for a directed verdict at the close of all the evidence during the trial; the motion will be granted if the judge is convinced that the jury was in error.
Appeal	Either party can appeal the trial court's judgment to an appropriate court of appeals.
	1. *Filing the appeal*—The appealing party must file a notice of appeal with the clerk of the trial court, who forwards to the appellate court the record on appeal. Attorneys' briefs are filed.
	2. *Appellate review*—The appellate court does not hear evidence but bases its opinion, which it issues in writing, on the record on appeal and the attorneys' briefs and oral arguments. The court may affirm or reverse all (or part) of the trial court's judgment and/or remand the case for further proceedings consistent with its opinion. Most decisions are affirmed on appeal.
	3. In some cases, further review may be sought from a higher appellate court, such as a state supreme court. Ultimately, if a federal question is involved, the case may be appealed to the United States Supreme Court.

SECTION 7

Enforcing the Judgment

The uncertainties of the litigation process are compounded by the lack of guarantees that any judgment will be enforceable. Even if the jury awarded Kirby the full amount of damages requested ($100,000), for example, she might not, in fact, "win" anything at all. Carvello's auto insurance coverage might have lapsed, in which event the company would not pay any of the damages. Alternatively, Carvello's insurance policy might be limited to $50,000, meaning that Carvello would have to pay personally the remaining $50,000.

If Carvello did not have that amount of money available, then Kirby would need to go back to court and request that the court issue a *writ of execution*—an order, usually issued by the clerk of the court, directing the sheriff to seize and sell Carvello's nonexempt assets (certain assets are exempted by law from creditors' actions). The proceeds of the sale would then be used to pay the damages owed to Kirby. Any excess proceeds of the sale would be returned to Carvello. Alternatively, the nonexempt property itself could be transferred to Kirby in lieu of an outright payment. (Creditors' remedies, including those of judgment creditors, as well as exempt and nonexempt property, will be discussed in more detail in Chapter 29.)

The problem of collecting a judgment is less pronounced, of course, when a party is seeking to satisfy a judgment against a defendant, such as a major corporation, that has substantial assets that can be easily located. Usually, one of the factors considered before a lawsuit is initiated is whether the defendant has sufficient assets to cover the amount of damages sought, should the plaintiff win the case.

TERMS AND CONCEPTS TO REVIEW

affidavit 54	hearsay 60	pretrial conference 57
affirmative defense 52	interrogatories 57	pretrial motion 54
answer 52	motion 54	rebuttal 60
brief 63	motion for a directed verdict 60	rejoinder 60
closing argument 60	motion for a new trial 62	relevant evidence 60
complaint 48	motion for judgment *n.o.v.* 63	rules of evidence 59
counterclaim 52	motion for judgment on the pleadings 54	service of process 52
cross-examination 60	motion for summary judgment 54	summons 52
default judgment 52	motion to dismiss 54	verdict 61
deposition 57	opening statement 60	*voir dire* 58
direct examination 60	pleadings 48	
discovery 56		
Federal Rules of Civil Procedure (FRCP) 46		

QUESTIONS AND CASE PROBLEMS

3–1. APPELLATE PROCESS. If a judge enters a judgment on the pleadings, the losing party can usually appeal but cannot present evidence to the appellate court. Does this seem fair? Explain.

3–2. ATTORNEYS' FEES. Attorneys in personal injury and other tort lawsuits (see Chapter 5) frequently charge clients on a contingency-fee basis. That is, a lawyer will agree to take on a client's case in return for, say, 30 percent of whatever damages are recovered. What are some of the social benefits and costs of the contingency-fee system? In your opinion, do the benefits of this system outweigh the costs?

3–3. DISCOVERY. In the past, the rules of discovery were very restrictive, and trials often turned on elements of surprise. For example, a plaintiff would not necessarily know until the trial what the defendant's defense was going to be. Within the last twenty-five years, however, new rules of discovery have substantially changed all this. Now each attorney can find out practically all the evidence that the other side will be presenting at trial, with the exception of certain information—namely, the opposing attorney's work product. Work product is not a clear concept. Basically, it includes all the attorney's thoughts on the case. Can you see any reason why such information should not be made available to the opposing attorney? Discuss fully.

3–4. MOTIONS. When and for what purpose are each of the following motions made? Which of them would be appropriate if a defendant claimed that the only issue between the parties was a question of law and that the law was favorable to the defendant's position?

   (a) A motion for judgment on the pleadings.
   (b) A motion for a directed verdict.
   (c) A motion for summary judgment.
   (d) A motion for judgment *n.o.v.*

3–5. PEREMPTORY CHALLENGES. During *voir dire*, the parties or their attorneys select those persons who will serve as jurors during the trial. The parties are prohibited, however, from excluding potential jurors on the basis of race or other discriminatory criteria. One issue concerns whether the prohibition against discrimination extends to potential jurors who have physical or mental disabilities. Federal law prohibits discrimination against an otherwise qualified person with a disability when that person could be accommodated without too much difficulty. Should this law also apply to the jury selection process? For example, should parties be prohibited from excluding blind persons, through either challenges for cause or peremptory challenges, from serving on juries? Discuss fully.

3–6. MOTION TO DISMISS. Martin brought a civil rights action against his employer, the New York Department of Mental Hygiene, when it failed to promote him on several occasions. His complaint stated only that the defendant had discriminated against him on the basis of race by denying him "the authority, salary, and privileges commensurate with this position." The employer made a motion to dismiss the claim for failure to state a cause of action. Discuss whether the employer could be successful. [*Martin v. New York State Department of Mental Hygiene,* 588 F.2d 371 (2d Cir. 1978)]

3–7. JURY TRIALS. On June 16, 1986, the director of the Administrative Office of the U.S. Courts notified all federal district courts that no civil jury trials could be initiated until the end of the fiscal year (September 30) due to lack of funds with which to pay the jurors. Armster and others claimed that the consequent delay (of three and a half months) in scheduling a jury trial violated the Seventh Amendment right to a civil jury trial. The Justice Department maintained that although the Sixth Amendment guarantees a speedy criminal jury trial, the Seventh Amendment does not guarantee a speedy civil jury trial. The Justice Department further noted that district courts have postponed civil jury trials before, although for other reasons—such as court-calendar congestion, the lack of a sufficient number of judges, and the priority accorded to trying criminal cases before civil actions. Discuss whether the suspension of civil jury trials for a period of three and a half months due to lack of funds to pay jurors violates the constitutional right to a trial by jury. Are people always entitled to a jury trial in civil lawsuits? [*Armster v. U.S. District Court for the Central District of California,* 792 F.2d 1423 (9th Cir. 1986)]

3–8. MOTION FOR A NEW TRIAL. Washoe Medical Center, Inc., admitted Shirley Swisher for the treatment of a fractured pelvis. During her stay, Swisher suffered a fatal fall from her hospital bed. Gerald Parodi, the administrator of her estate, and others filed an action against Washoe in which they sought damages for the alleged lack of care in treating Swisher. During *voir dire,* when the plaintiffs' attorney returned a few minutes late from a break, the trial judge led the prospective jurors in a standing ovation. The judge joked with one of the prospective jurors, whom he had known in college, about his fitness to serve as a judge and personally endorsed another prospective juror's business. After the trial, the jury returned a verdict in favor of Washoe. The plaintiffs moved for a new trial, but the judge denied the motion. The plaintiffs then appealed, arguing that the tone set by the judge during *voir dire* prejudiced their right to a fair trial. Should the appellate court agree? Why or why not? [*Parodi v. Washoe Medical Center, Inc.,* 111 Nev. 365, 892 P.2d 588 (1995)]

3–9. DISCOVERY. Advance Technology Consultants, Inc. (ATC), contracted with RoadTrac, L.L.C., to provide software and client software systems for the products for global positioning satellite system (GPS) technology being developed by RoadTrac. RoadTrac agreed to provide ATC hardware with which ATC's software would interface. Problems soon arose, however. ATC claimed that RoadTrac's hardware was defective, making it difficult to develop the software. RoadTrac contended that its hardware was fully functional and that ATC simply failed to provide supporting software. ATC told RoadTrac that it considered their contract terminated. RoadTrac filed a suit in a Georgia state court against ATC, charging, among other things, breach of contract. During discovery, RoadTrac requested ATC's customer lists and marketing procedures. Before producing this material, ATC asked the court to limit RoadTrac's use of the information. Meanwhile, RoadTrac and ATC had become competitors in the GPS industry. How should the court rule regarding RoadTrac's discovery request? [*Advance Technology Consultants, Inc. v. RoadTrac, L.L.C.,* 236 Ga.App. 582, 512 S.E.2d 27 (1999)]

3–10. IN YOUR COURT

Ronald Metzgar placed his fifteen-month-old son Matthew, awake and healthy, in his playpen. Ronald left the room for five minutes and on his return found Matthew lifeless. A purple toy block had lodged in the boy's throat, choking him to death. Ronald called 911, but efforts to revive Matthew were to no avail. There was no warning of a choking hazard on the box containing the block. Matthew's parents sued Playskool, Inc., the manufacturer of the block, and others, alleging, among other things, that the manufacturer had been negligent in failing to warn of the block's hazard. Playskool filed a motion for summary judgment, arguing that the danger of a young child choking on a small block was obvious. Assume that you are the judge in the trial court hearing this case and answer the following questions:

(a) Is the question of whether a child could choke on one of the small blocks a question of fact or a question of law?

(b) Should you grant Playskool's request for summary judgment? Why or why not?

(c) Suppose that Matthew had not choked on the block but his father, concerned that Matthew *could have* choked on the block, filed a lawsuit against Playskool anyway. In the suit, the father asked the court to order Playskool to place a warning on the box as to the choking hazard so that other consumers would not be harmed. In this situation, would the father have standing to sue? [Hint: See the section on basic judicial requirements in Chapter 2.]

LAW ON THE WEB

For updated links to resources available on the Web, as well as a variety of other materials, visit this text's Web site at http://wbl.westbuslaw.com.

If you are interested in learning more about the Federal Rules of Civil Procedure (FRCP) and the Federal Rules of Evidence (FRE), they can now be accessed via the Internet at the following Web site:

http://www.cornell.edu

Procedural rules for several of the state courts are now also online and can be accessed via the courts' Web pages. You can find links to the Web pages for state courts at the Web site of the National Center for State Courts. Go to

http://www.ncsc.dni.us/court/sites/courts.htm

For an example of a typical set of state rules governing attorney conduct, you can access Idaho's Rules of Professional Conduct Governing Lawyers at

http://www.law.cornell.edu:80/lawyers/ruletable.html

LEGAL RESEARCH EXERCISES ON THE WEB

Go to http://wbl.westbuslaw.com, the Web site that accompanies this text. Select "Internet Applications," and then click on "Chapter 3." There you will find the following Internet exercise that you can perform to learn more about the court procedures involved in civil lawsuits and in small claims courts:

Activity 3–1: Civil Procedure

Activity 3–2: Small Claims Courts

Constitutional Authority
to Regulate Business

T HE U.S. CONSTITUTION IS THE SUPREME law in this country.[1] As mentioned in Chapter 1, neither Congress nor any state may pass a law that conflicts with the Constitution. Laws that govern business have their origin in the lawmaking authority granted by this document.

Before the Constitution was written, a *confederal form* of government existed. The Articles of Confederation, which went into effect in 1781, established a confederation of independent states and a central government of very limited powers. The central government could handle only those matters of common concern expressly delegated to it by the member states, and the national congress had no authority to make laws directly applicable to individuals unless the member states explicitly supported such laws. In short, *the sovereign power*[2] to govern rested essentially with the states. The Articles of Confederation clearly reflected the central tenet of the American Revolution—that a national government should not have unlimited power.

After the Revolutionary War, however, the states began to pass laws that hampered national commerce and foreign trade by preventing the free movement of goods and services. Consequently, in 1787, the Constitutional Convention assembled to **amend** (change, alter) the Articles of Confederation. Instead, the delegates to the Convention created the Constitution and a completely new type of federal government, which they believed was much better equipped than its predecessor to resolve the problems of the nation.

S E C T I O N 1

The Constitutional
Powers of Government

The U.S. Constitution established a federal form of government. A **federal form of government** is one in which the states form a union and the sovereign power is divided between a central governing authority and the member states. The Constitution delegates certain powers to the national government, and the states retain all other powers. The relationship be-

---

1. See Appendix B for the full text of the U.S. Constitution.
2. Sovereign power refers to that supreme power to which no other authority is superior or equal.

tween the national government and the state governments is a partnership—neither partner is superior to the other except within the particular area of exclusive authority granted to it under the Constitution.

To prevent the possibility that the national government might use its power arbitrarily, the Constitution provided for three branches of government. The legislative branch makes the laws, the executive branch enforces the laws, and the judicial branch interprets the laws. Each branch performs a separate function, and no branch may exercise the authority of another branch.

Each branch, however, has some power to limit the actions of the other two branches. Congress, for example, can enact legislation relating to spending and commerce, but the president can veto that legislation. The executive branch is responsible for foreign affairs, but treaties with foreign governments require the advice and consent of members of the Senate. Although Congress determines the jurisdiction of the federal courts, the federal courts have the power to hold acts of the other branches of the federal government unconstitutional.[3] Thus, with this system of **checks and balances,** no one branch of government can accumulate too much power.

THE COMMERCE CLAUSE

Article I, Section 8, of the U.S. Constitution expressly permits Congress "[t]o regulate Commerce with foreign Nations, and among the several States, and with the Indian Tribes." This clause, referred to as the **commerce clause,** has had a greater impact on business than any other provision in the Constitution. This power was delegated to the federal government to ensure the uniformity of rules governing the movement of goods through the states.

One of the questions posed for the courts by the commerce clause is whether the word *among* in the phrase "among the several States" meant *between* the states or *between and within* the states. For some time, the federal government's power under the commerce clause was interpreted to apply only to commerce between the states (*interstate* commerce) and not commerce within the states (*intrastate* commerce). In 1824, however, in *Gibbons v. Ogden,*[4] the United

States Supreme Court held that commerce within the states could also be regulated by the national government as long as the commerce concerned more than one state.

The Breadth of the Commerce Clause. As a result of the Supreme Court's interpretation of the commerce clause in *Gibbons v. Ogden,* the national government exercised increasing authority over all areas of economic affairs throughout the land. In a 1942 case,[5] for example, the Court held that wheat production by an individual farmer intended wholly for consumption on his own farm was subject to federal regulation. The Court reasoned that the home consumption of wheat reduced the demand for wheat and thus could have a substantial effect on interstate commerce. In *McLain v. Real Estate Board of New Orleans, Inc.,*[6] a 1980 case, the Supreme Court acknowledged that the commerce clause had "long been interpreted to extend beyond activities actually in interstate commerce to reach other activities, while wholly local in nature, which nevertheless substantially affect interstate commerce."

Today, at least theoretically, the power over commerce authorizes the national government to regulate every commercial enterprise in the United States. The breadth of the commerce clause permits the national government to legislate in areas in which there is no explicit grant of power to Congress. Only rarely has the Supreme Court limited the regulatory reach of the national government under the commerce authority. One of these occasions was in 1995, in *United States v. Lopez.*[7] In that case, the Court held—for the first time in sixty years—that Congress had exceeded its regulatory authority under the commerce power when it passed the Gun-Free School Zones Act in 1990. The Court stated that the act, which banned the possession of guns within one thousand feet of any school, was unconstitutional because it attempted to regulate an area that had "nothing to do with commerce, or any sort of economic enterprise."

Generally, today's Supreme Court has indicated a willingness to rein in the constitutional powers of the national government to a far greater extent than the Court has during the past six decades. In addition to restricting the national government's regulatory reach

---

3. As discussed in Chapter 2, the power of judicial review was established by the United States Supreme Court in *Marbury v. Madison,* 5 U.S. (1 Cranch) 137, 2 L.Ed. 60 (1803).
4. 22 U.S. (9 Wheat.) 1, 6 L.Ed. 23 (1824).

5. *Wickard v. Filburn,* 317 U.S. 111, 63 S.Ct. 82, 87 L.Ed. 122 (1942).
6. 444 U.S. 232, 100 S.Ct. 502, 62 L.Ed.2d 441 (1980).
7. 514 U.S. 549, 115 S.Ct. 1624, 131 L.Ed.2d 626 (1995).

under the commerce clause, the Court issued a number of decisions in the late 1990s that significantly enhanced the sovereign powers of the states within the federal system.[8]

The Regulatory Powers of the States.   A problem that frequently arises under the commerce clause concerns a state's ability to regulate matters within its own borders. The U.S. Constitution does not expressly exclude state regulation of commerce, and there is no doubt that states have a strong interest in regulating activities within their borders. As part of their inherent sovereignty, states possess **police powers.** The term does not relate solely to criminal law enforcement but rather refers to the broad right of state governments to regulate private activities to protect or promote the public order, health, safety, morals, and general welfare. Fire and building codes, antidiscrimination laws, parking regulations, zoning restrictions, licensing requirements, and thousands of other state statutes covering virtually every aspect of life have been enacted pursuant to states' police powers.

When state regulations impinge on interstate commerce, courts must balance the state's interest in the merits and purposes of the regulations against the burden placed by the regulations on interstate commerce. Generally, state laws enacted pursuant to a state's police powers carry a strong presumption of validity. If state laws *substantially* interfere with interstate commerce, however, they will be held to violate the commerce clause of the Constitution.

In *Raymond Motor Transportation, Inc. v. Rice,*[9] for example, the United States Supreme Court invalidated Wisconsin administrative regulations limiting the length of trucks traveling on the state's highways. The Court weighed the burden on interstate commerce against the benefits of the regulations and concluded that the challenged regulations "place a substantial burden on interstate commerce and they cannot be said to make more than the most speculative contribution to highway safety." Because courts balance the interests involved, it is extremely difficult to predict the outcome in a particular case.

The commerce clause also limits the states' ability to impose sales taxes on out-of-state businesses. In today's online world, this limitation has serious implications for state budgets—see this chapter's *Emerging Trends in Technology* on pages 72 and 73 for a discussion of this issue.

THE SUPREMACY CLAUSE AND FEDERAL PREEMPTION

Article VI of the Constitution provides that the Constitution, laws, and treaties of the United States are "the supreme Law of the Land." This article, commonly referred to as the **supremacy clause,** is important in the ordering of state and federal relationships. When there is a direct conflict between a federal law and a state law, the state law is rendered invalid. Because some powers are *concurrent* (shared by the federal government and the states), however, it is necessary to determine which law governs in a particular circumstance.

Federal Preemption.   When Congress chooses to act exclusively in an area in which the federal government and the states have concurrent powers, it is said to have *preempted* the area. When federal **preemption** occurs, a valid federal statute or regulation will take precedence over a conflicting state or local law or regulation on the same general subject.

Whether the federal government has preempted a certain area can have important implications for businesspersons. For example, for some time it was not clear whether tobacco companies that complied with federal cigarette-labeling requirements could be sued under state laws requiring cigarette manufacturers to sufficiently warn consumers of the potential dangers associated with cigarette smoking. In a 1992 case, *Cipollone v. Liggett Group, Inc.,*[10] the United States Supreme Court held that the Federal Cigarette Labeling and Advertising Act of 1965, which requires specific warnings to be included on cigarette packages, preempted the state laws requiring warnings. The Court stated, however, that there was no indication that Congress had intended to preempt state laws that fall *outside* the scope of the federal law, such as laws governing fraudulent misrepresentation.

Determining Congressional Intent.   In *Cipollone* and other cases involving preemption issues, the courts must decide whether Congress, when enacting a particular statute, *intended* to preempt the area and

---

8. See, for example, *Printz v. United States,* 521 U.S. 898, 117 S.Ct. 2365, 138 L.Ed.2d 914 (1997); and *Alden v. Maine,* ___ U.S. ___, 119 S.Ct. 2240, 144 L.Ed.2d 636 (1999).
9. 434 U.S. 429, 98 S.Ct. 787, 54 L.Ed.2d 664 (1978).

10. 505 U.S. 504, 112 S.Ct. 2608, 120 L.Ed.2d 407 (1992).

thus preclude plaintiffs from bringing claims under state law. In determining congressional intent, courts look at the wording of the statute itself, as well as at the legislative history of the statute (such as congressional committee reports on the topic).

For example, in *Tebbetts v. Ford Motor Co.,*[11] a plaintiff alleged that a 1988 Ford Escort was defectively designed because it did not contain an air bag on the driver's side. The defendant-manufacturer contended that it had complied with federal safety regulations authorized by the National Traffic and Motor Vehicle Safety Act (NTMVSA) of 1966 and that those regulations preempted recovery under state product-safety laws. The court interpreted House and Senate reports on the issue, as well as a clause included in the act itself, to mean that not all state law claims were preempted by the federal regulations. (The relevant clause stated that "[c]ompliance with any Federal motor vehicle safety standard issued under this [act] does not exempt any person from any liability under common law.") Thus, the plaintiff in *Tebbetts* was not precluded by the NTMVSA from suing Ford under state product-liability laws (see Chapter 6).

Generally, it is difficult to predict whether a defendant will be subject to liability under state laws notwithstanding the defendant's compliance with federally mandated product-safety standards. Courts differ in their interpretations of congressional intent, and the outcomes in cases involving similar facts can thus also differ.

THE TAXING AND SPENDING POWERS

Article I, Section 8, provides that Congress has the "Power to lay and collect Taxes, Duties, Imposts, and Excises." Section 8 further provides that "all Duties, Imposts and Excises shall be uniform throughout the United States." The requirement of uniformity refers to uniformity among the states, and thus Congress may not tax some states while exempting others.

Traditionally, if Congress attempted to regulate indirectly, by taxation, an area over which it had no authority, the tax would be invalidated by the courts. Today, however, if a tax measure is reasonable, it is generally held to be within the national taxing power. Moreover, the expansive interpretation of the commerce clause almost always provides a basis for sustaining a federal tax.

Under Article I, Section 8, Congress has the power "to pay the Debts and provide for the common Defence and general Welfare of the United States." Through the spending power, Congress disposes of the revenues accumulated from the taxing power. Congress can spend revenues not only to carry out its enumerated powers but also to promote any objective it deems worthwhile, so long as it does not violate the Bill of Rights. For example, Congress could not condition welfare payments on the recipients' agreement not to criticize government policies. The spending power necessarily involves policy choices, with which taxpayers may disagree.

SECTION 2

Business and the Bill of Rights

The importance of a written declaration of the rights of individuals eventually caused the first Congress of the United States to submit twelve amendments to the Constitution to the states for approval. The first ten of these amendments, commonly known as the **Bill of Rights,** were adopted in 1791 and embody a series of protections for the individual against various types of interference by the federal government.[12] The protections guaranteed by these ten amendments are summarized in Exhibit 4–1.[13] Some of these constitutional protections apply to business entities as well. For example, corporations exist as separate legal entities, or *legal persons*, and enjoy many of the same rights and privileges as *natural persons* do.

As originally intended, the Bill of Rights limited only the powers of the national government. Over time, however, the United States Supreme Court "incorporated" most of these rights into the protections against state actions afforded by the Fourteenth Amendment to the Constitution. That amendment, passed in 1868 after the Civil War, provides in part that "[n]o State shall . . . deprive any person of life, liberty, or property, without due process of law." Starting in 1925, the Supreme Court began to define various rights and liberties guaranteed in the national Constitution as constituting "due process of law," which was required of state governments under the

---

11. 665 A.2d 345 (N.H. 1995).

12. Another of these proposed amendments was ratified 203 years later (in 1992) and became the Twenty-seventh Amendment to the Constitution. See Appendix B.
13. See the Constitution in Appendix B for the complete text of each amendment.

EMERGING TRENDS IN TECHNOLOGY

Taxation Issues in Cyberspace

Every year, consumers purchase more goods and services—ranging from automobiles to software to CDs to objects of art—from online merchants. Business-to-business sales are also increasing at a rapid rate. It is estimated that Internet sales will climb from $20 billion today to about $250 billion in 2005.

The potential tax revenues from today's burgeoning e-commerce have not escaped the attention of state governments. In fact, most states have extended their telecommunications tax laws to cover at least some of the components of e-commerce. For example, about a dozen states have imposed some form of access tax on Internet services, such as a fee added to the Internet subscription charge. Some jurisdictions attempt to tax the transfer of data downloaded by users. Some states, including Texas and New York, impose sales taxes on a broad array of e-commerce components, including software that is downloaded electronically and Internet access.

Not surprisingly, Internet companies, various business coalitions, and other groups have resisted such taxation. Some argue that the taxes so far imposed are unfair and discriminatory. Consider that in some places a newspaper customer pays no tax if the paper is physically delivered to the subscriber's doorstep. Yet the same customer must pay a tax if he or she downloads the electronic version of the paper posted on the Web. Others claim that attempts to tax Internet transactions will constrain the growth of e-commerce. Still others believe that if cyberspace is to be subject to taxation, the states must at least develop a more uniform taxation scheme.

THE PROBLEM FACING THE STATES

For most state governments, sales taxes are important sources of income. Typically, between 35 and 40 percent of state revenues are obtained through sales taxes. Today, however, the states are facing declining sales tax revenues. In part, this is because of the growth in direct-marketing sales made via mail order or the Internet. In a direct-marketing transaction, a seller, such as a mail-order house, sells goods directly to consumers located around the country. The problem for the states is that their ability to impose tax obligations on out-of-state sellers is limited.

This limitation was established by the United States Supreme Court long before the rise of the Internet. In 1967, the Court held that it was a violation of the commerce clause for a state to impose tax obligations on a business located outside the state's borders *unless* the business had a "nexus" with—a substantial physical presence in—the taxing state.[a] Generally, the nexus requirement is satisfied if a business has outlets, sales representatives, or other significant property in the taxing state. In a 1992 case, *Quill Corp. v. North Dakota*,[b] the Supreme Court held specifically that mail-order firms that lack this required nexus are exempt from state taxes. The reasoning in the *Quill* case can be extended to online direct marketing, meaning that it is impossible for a state to collect taxes from online merchants who have no physical presence in the state.

Because of these tax rulings, state governments claim that they are losing billions of dollars each year.

---

a. *National Bellas Hess, Inc. v. Department of Revenue of the State of Illinois*, 386 U.S. 753, 87 S.Ct. 1389, 18 L.Ed.2d 505 (1967).
b. 504 U.S. 298, 112 S.Ct. 1904, 119 L.Ed.2d 91 (1992).

Fourteenth Amendment. Today, most of the rights and liberties set forth in the Bill of Rights apply to state governments as well as the national government. In other words, neither the federal government nor state governments can deprive individuals of those rights and liberties.

The rights secured by the Bill of Rights are not absolute. As you can see in Exhibit 4–1, many of the rights guaranteed by the first ten amendments are described in very general terms. For example, the Fourth Amendment prohibits *unreasonable* searches and seizures, but it does not define what constitutes an un-

EMERGING TRENDS IN TECHNOLOGY

Taxation Issues in Cyberspace,

continued

THE INADEQUACY OF EXISTING TAX LAWS

Clearly, the nexus requirements set forth by the Supreme Court have become inadequate in today's electronic age. As a result, the states are proposing new theories of nexus that would enable them to impose taxes on direct-marketing transactions. For example, one proposal is that nexus requirements be changed to require merely an "economic" presence in the state (via the Internet) rather than a "physical presence." At the same time, the Clinton administration favored a tax-free Internet, as have business groups generally.

THE INTERNET TAX FREEDOM ACT

In response to pressure from various groups to take action, Congress passed the Internet Tax Freedom Act of 1998, which President Clinton signed into law on October 21, 1998. The act imposed a three-year moratorium

on all new taxes directed specifically at Web-based activities. (It did not, however, affect any state taxation systems that were already in place by March 1998.) During the three-year moratorium, which will expire on October 21, 2001, the act calls for a study and a report to Congress on various methods of Internet taxation. A central issue to be examined is how taxes might be imposed on Web-based activities without significantly constraining e-commerce.

IMPLICATIONS FOR THE BUSINESSPERSON

1. To date, retailers engaged in e-commerce have held a clear advantage over those who sell their goods through traditional outlets, at least with respect to sales taxes. The moratorium on Internet taxation means that this advantage will continue to exist until October 2001. Additionally, the moratorium offers a window of opportunity for entrepreneurs or existing firms to take advantage of the commercial capabilities of the Internet until that date.
2. It seems unrealistic to assume that online commerce will forever remain largely untaxed, as it is now. Therefore, business representatives and groups should

consider the merits of working in conjunction with tax agencies to help ensure that whatever rules are developed will be fair and consistent.

FOR CRITICAL ANALYSIS

1. Is it unfair for states to impose sales taxes on goods sold through traditional outlets—such as those located in downtown areas or shopping malls—but not on similar goods sold by online direct marketers? Would your answer be the same if you knew that the taxation of goods sold online would stifle the growth of e-commerce?
2. If new tax laws should be applied to e-commerce, what enforcement problems might arise? (Hint: Remember, the Internet is a global network.)

RELEVANT WEB SITES

You can find a "plain English" summary of the Internet Tax Freedom Act at **http://www.house.gov/chriscox/nettax**. For a Web site focusing on Internet taxation issues, go to **http://www.nettaxfairness.org**.

reasonable search or seizure. Similarly, the Eighth Amendment prohibits excessive bail or fines, but no definition of *excessive* is contained in that amendment. Ultimately, it is the United States Supreme Court, as the final interpreter of the Constitution, that defines our rights and determines their boundaries.

FREEDOM OF SPEECH

A democratic form of government cannot survive unless people can freely voice their political opinions and criticize government actions or policies. Freedom of speech, particularly political speech, is

EXHIBIT 4–1   PROTECTIONS GUARANTEED BY THE BILL OF RIGHTS

First Amendment: Guarantees the freedoms of religion, speech, and the press and the rights to assemble peaceably and to petition the government.	**Sixth Amendment:** Guarantees the accused in a criminal case the right to a speedy and public trial by an impartial jury and with counsel. The accused has the right to cross-examine witnesses against him or her and to solicit testimony from witnesses in his or her favor.
Second Amendment: Guarantees the right to keep and bear arms.	
Third Amendment: Prohibits, in peacetime, the lodging of soldiers in any house without the owner's consent.	**Seventh Amendment:** Guarantees the right to a trial by jury in a civil case involving at least twenty dollars.[a]
Fourth Amendment: Prohibits unreasonable searches and seizures of persons or property.	**Eighth Amendment:** Prohibits excessive bail and fines, as well as cruel and unusual punishment.
Fifth Amendment: Guarantees the rights to indictment by grand jury, to due process of law, and to fair payment when private property is taken for public use; prohibits compulsory self-incrimination and double jeopardy (trial for the same crime twice if the first trial ends in acquittal or conviction).	**Ninth Amendment:** Establishes that the people have rights in addition to those specified in the Constitution.
	Tenth Amendment: Establishes that those powers neither delegated to the federal government nor denied to the states are reserved for the states.

a. Twenty dollars was forty days' pay for the average person when the Bill of Rights was written.

thus a prized right, and traditionally the courts have protected this right to the fullest extent possible.

Symbolic speech—gestures, movements, articles of clothing, and other forms of expressive conduct—is also given substantial protection by the courts. For example, in a 1989 case, *Texas v. Johnson*,[14] the United States Supreme Court ruled that state laws that prohibited the burning of the American flag as part of a peaceful protest violated the freedom of expression protected by the First Amendment. Congress responded by passing the Flag Protection Act of 1989, which was ruled unconstitutional by the Supreme Court in 1990.[15] Congress and George Bush, who was then president, pledged immediately to work for a constitutional amendment to "protect our flag"—an effort that has yet to be successful. In a subsequent case, the Supreme Court ruled that a city statute banning bias-motivated disorderly conduct (including, in this case, the placing of a burning cross in another's front yard as a gesture of hate) was an unconstitutional restriction of speech.[16]

Governments can and do place restraints on free speech, of course, but such restraints are permissible only when they are necessary to protect other substantial interests and rights. It is up to the courts—and ultimately, the United States Supreme Court—to determine the point at which laws restricting free speech can be justified by the need to protect other rights.

Commercial Speech.   Speech and communications—primarily advertising—made by business firms are called *commercial speech*. Although commercial speech is protected by the First Amendment, it is not protected as extensively as noncommercial speech. A state may restrict certain kinds of advertising, for example, in the interest of preventing consumers from being misled by the advertising practices. States also have a legitimate interest in the beautification of roadsides, and this interest allows states to place restraints on billboard advertising.

Generally, a restriction on commercial speech will be considered valid as long as it meets the following three criteria: (1) it must seek to implement a substantial government interest, (2) it must directly advance that interest, and (3) it must go no further than necessary to accomplish its objective. At issue in the following case was whether a government agency's decision to prohibit the inclusion of a certain illustration on beer labels unconstitutionally restricted commercial speech.

---

14. 491 U.S. 397, 109 S.Ct. 2533, 105 L.Ed.2d 342 (1989).
15. *United States v. Eichman*, 496 U.S. 310, 110 S.Ct. 2804, 110 L.Ed.2d 287 (1990).
16. *R.A.V. v. City of St. Paul, Minnesota*, 505 U.S. 377, 112 S.Ct. 2538, 120 L.Ed.2d 305 (1992).

CASE 4.1   # Bad Frog Brewery, Inc. v. New York State Liquor Authority

United States
Court of Appeals,
Second Circuit, 1998.
134 F.3d 87.
http://www.tourolaw.
edu/2ndCircuit/
January98/97-79490.
html[a]

HISTORICAL AND CULTURAL SETTING   *Hand gestures signifying insults have been in use throughout the world for centuries. Hand gestures regarded as insults in some countries include an extended right thumb, an extended little finger, raised index and middle fingers, and gestures effected with two hands. A gesture using the extended middle finger of either hand (sometimes referred to as "giving the finger" or "flipping the bird") is generally acknowledged to convey an obscene, offensive message: a suggestion to have intercourse with one's self. This gesture is said to have been used by Diogenes (a Greek philosopher in the fourth century B.C.E. who was known for his disregard of social niceties) to insult Demosthenes (a Greek statesman and contemporary of Diogenes).[b]*

BACKGROUND AND FACTS   *Bad Frog Brewery, Inc., makes and sells alcoholic beverages. Some of the beverages feature labels that display a drawing of a frog making the gesture generally known as "giving the finger." Bad Frog's authorized New York distributor, Renaissance Beer Company, applied to the New York State Liquor Authority (NYSLA) for brand label approval, as required by state law before the beer could be sold in New York. The NYSLA denied the application, in part because "the label could appear in grocery and convenience stores, with obvious exposure on the shelf to children of tender age." Bad Frog filed a suit in a federal district court against the NYSLA, asking for, among other things, an injunction against the denial of Bad Frog's application. The court granted summary judgment in favor of the NYSLA. Bad Frog appealed to the U.S. Court of Appeals for the Second Circuit.*

IN THE LANGUAGE OF THE COURT

JON O. NEWMAN, Circuit Judge:

*   *   *   *

*   *   * [T]o support its asserted power to ban Bad Frog's labels [NYSLA advances] *   *   * the State's interest in "protecting children from vulgar and profane advertising" *   *   * .

[This interest is] substantial *   *   * . States have a compelling interest in protecting the physical and psychological well-being of minors *   *   * .

*   *   *   *

*   *   * NYSLA endeavors to advance the state interest in preventing exposure of children to vulgar displays by taking only the limited step of barring such displays from the labels of alcoholic beverages. In view of the wide currency of vulgar displays throughout contemporary society, including comic books targeted directly at children, barring such displays from labels for alcoholic beverages cannot realistically be expected to reduce children's exposure to such displays to any significant degree.

*   *   * If New York decides to make a substantial effort to insulate children from vulgar displays in some significant sphere of activity, at least with respect to materials likely to be seen by children, NYSLA's label prohibition might well be found to make a justifiable contribution to the material advancement of such an effort, but its currently isolated response to the perceived problem, applicable only to labels on a product that children cannot purchase, does not suffice. *   *   * [A] state must demonstrate that its commercial speech limitation is part of a substantial effort to advance a valid state interest, not merely the removal of a few grains of offensive sand from a beach of vulgarity.

*   *   *   *

---

a. This page is part of a Web site maintained by the Touro College Jacob D. Fuchsberg Law Center in Huntington, New York.
b. Betty J. Bauml and Franz H. Bauml, *Dictionary of Worldwide Gestures*, 2d ed. (Lanham, Md.: Scarecrow Press, 1997), p. 159.

* * * Even if we were to assume that the state materially advances its asserted interest by shielding children from viewing the Bad Frog labels, it is plainly excessive to prohibit the labels from all use, including placement on bottles displayed in bars and taverns where parental supervision of children is to be expected. Moreover, to whatever extent NYSLA is concerned that children will be harmfully exposed to the Bad Frog labels when wandering without parental supervision around grocery and convenience stores where beer is sold, that concern could be less intrusively dealt with by placing restrictions on the permissible locations where the appellant's products may be displayed within such stores.

DECISION AND REMEDY *The U.S. Court of Appeals for the Second Circuit reversed the judgment of the district court and remanded the case for the entry of a judgment in favor of Bad Frog. The NYSLA's ban on the use of the labels lacked a "reasonable fit" with the state's interest in shielding minors from vulgarity, and the NYSLA did not adequately consider alternatives to the ban.*

Corporate Political Speech. Political speech that otherwise would fall within the protection of the First Amendment does not lose that protection simply because its source is a corporation. For example, in *First National Bank of Boston v. Bellotti*,[17] national banking associations and business corporations sought United States Supreme Court review of a Massachusetts statute that prohibited corporations from making political contributions or expenditures that individuals were permitted to make. The Court ruled that the Massachusetts law was unconstitutional because it violated the right of corporations to freedom of speech. Similarly, the Court has held that a law forbidding a corporation from using bill inserts to express its views on controversial issues violates the First Amendment.[18] Although in 1990 a more conservative Supreme Court reversed this trend somewhat,[19] corporate political speech continues to be given significant protection under the First Amendment.

Unprotected Speech. The United States Supreme Court has made it clear that certain types of speech will not be protected under the First Amendment. Speech that harms the good reputation of another, or defamatory speech (see Chapter 5), is not protected under the First Amendment. Speech that violates criminal laws (threatening speech, pornography, and so on) is not constitutionally protected. Other unprotected speech includes "fighting words" (speech that is likely to incite others to respond violently). Many people think that the "hate speech" exchanged between members of different groups on college campuses should be included in the category of "fighting words." Courts, however, have been reluctant to uphold university codes banning hate speech, concluding that the codes go too far in restricting the free speech of students.[20]

Another category of unprotected speech is obscene speech. Numerous state and federal statutes make it a crime to disseminate obscene materials. The United States Supreme Court has grappled from time to time with the problem of trying to establish an operationally effective definition of obscene speech. Frequently, this determination is left to state and local authorities, who customarily base their definitions of obscenity on community standards. Generally, obscenity is still a constitutionally unsettled area. In the interest of preventing the abuse of children, however, the Supreme Court has upheld state laws prohibiting the sale and possession of child pornography.[21] In the interest of protecting women against sexual harassment on the job, at least one court has banned lewd speech and pornographic pinups in the workplace.[22]

17. 435 U.S. 765, 98 S.Ct. 1407, 55 L.Ed.2d 707 (1978).
18. *Consolidated Edison Co. v. Public Service Commission*, 447 U.S. 530, 100 S.Ct. 2326, 65 L.Ed.2d 319 (1980).
19. See *Austin v. Michigan Chamber of Commerce*, 494 U.S. 652, 110 S.Ct. 1391, 108 L.Ed.2d 652 (1990), in which the Court upheld a state law prohibiting corporations from using general corporate funds for independent expenditures in state political campaigns.

20. See, for example, *Doe v. University of Michigan*, 721 F.Supp. 852 (1989); and *The UWM Post v. Board of Regents of the University of Wisconsin System*, 774 F.Supp. 1163 (E.D.Wis. 1991).
21. See *Osborne v. Ohio*, 495 U.S. 103, 110 S.Ct. 1691, 109 L.Ed.2d 98 (1990).
22. *Robinson v. Jacksonville Shipyards, Inc.*, 760 F.Supp. 1486 (M.D.Fla. 1991).

In recent years, obscenity issues have also arisen in relation to television shows, movies, the lyrics and covers of music albums, and the content of monologues by "shock" comedians. In addition, as will be discussed in Chapter 9, a challenging legal issue today is how to regulate the availability of obscene materials on the Internet.

FREEDOM OF RELIGION

The First Amendment states that the government may neither establish any religion nor prohibit the free exercise of religious practices. The first part of this constitutional provision is referred to as the **establishment clause,** which has to do with the separation of church and state. The second part of the provision is known as the **free exercise clause.**

The Establishment Clause. The establishment clause prohibits the government from establishing a state-sponsored religion, as well as from passing laws that promote (aid or endorse) religion or that show a preference for one religion over another. Establishment clause issues often involve such matters as the legality of allowing or requiring school prayers, the teaching of evolutionary versus creationist theory, and state and local government aid to religious organizations and schools.

Federal or state laws that do not promote or place a significant burden on religion are constitutional even if they have some impact on religion. "Sunday closing laws," for example, make the performance of some commercial activities on Sunday illegal. These statutes, also known as "blue laws" (from the color of the paper on which an early Sunday law was written), have been upheld on the ground that it is a legitimate function of government to provide a day of rest. The United States Supreme Court has held that the closing laws, although originally of a religious character, have taken on the secular purpose of promoting the health and welfare of workers.[23] Even though closing laws admittedly make it easier for Christians to attend religious services, the Court has viewed this effect as an incidental, not a primary, purpose of Sunday closing laws.

The First Amendment does not require a complete separation of church and state. On the contrary, it affirmatively mandates accommodation of all reli-

gions and forbids hostility toward any.[24] An ongoing challenge for the courts is determining the extent to which governments can accommodate a religion without appearing to promote that religion, which would violate the establishment clause. For example, in *Lynch v. Donnelly,*[25] the United States Supreme Court held that a municipality could include religious symbols, such as a Nativity scene, or crèche, in its annual holiday display as long as the religious symbols constituted just one part of a display in which other, nonreligious symbols (such as reindeer and candy-striped poles) were also featured. The Court has applied this same reasoning in subsequent cases and continues to face such issues.[26]

The Free Exercise Clause. The free exercise clause guarantees that no person can be compelled to do something that is contrary to his or her religious beliefs. For this reason, if a law or policy is contrary to a person's religious beliefs, exemptions are often made to accommodate those beliefs. When, however, religious practices work against public policy and the public welfare, the government can act. For example, children of Jehovah's Witnesses are not required to say the Pledge of Allegiance at school, but their parents cannot prevent these children from accepting medical treatment (such as blood transfusions) if the children's lives are in danger.

For business firms, an important issue involves the accommodation that businesses must make for the religious beliefs of their employees. For example, if an employee's religion prohibits him or her from working on a certain day of the week or at a certain type of job, the employer must make a reasonable attempt to accommodate these religious requirements. Employers must reasonably accommodate an employee's religious belief even if the belief is not based on the tenets or dogma of a particular church, sect, or denomination. The only requirement is that the belief be religious in nature and sincerely held by the employee.[27] (See Chapter 42 for a further discussion of religious freedom in the employment context.)

23. *McGowan v. Maryland*, 366 U.S. 420, 81 S.Ct. 1101, 6 L.Ed.2d 393 (1961).

24. *Zorach v. Clauson*, 343 U.S. 306, 72 S.Ct. 679, 96 L.Ed. 954 (1952).
25. 465 U.S. 668, 104 S.Ct. 1355, 79 L.Ed.2d 604 (1984).
26. See, for example, *County of Allegheny v. American Civil Liberties Union*, 492 U.S. 573, 109 S.Ct. 3086, 106 L.Ed.2d 472 (1989); and *Capitol Square Review and Advisory Board v. Pinette*, 515 U.S. 753, 115 S.Ct. 2440, 132 L.Ed.2d 650 (1995).
27. *Frazee v. Illinois Department of Employment Security*, 489 U.S. 829, 109 S.Ct. 1514, 103 L.Ed.2d 914 (1989).

SELF-INCRIMINATION

The Fifth Amendment guarantees that no person "shall be compelled in any criminal case to be a witness against himself." Thus, in any federal proceeding, an accused person cannot be compelled to give testimony that might subject him or her to any criminal prosecution. Nor can an accused person be forced to testify against himself or herself in state courts, because the due process clause of the Fourteenth Amendment (discussed later in this chapter) incorporates the Fifth Amendment provision against self-incrimination.

The Fifth Amendment's guarantee against self-incrimination extends only to natural persons. Because a corporation is a legal entity and not a natural person, the privilege against self-incrimination does not apply to it. Similarly, the business records of a partnership do not receive Fifth Amendment protection.[28] When a partnership is required to produce these records, it must give the information even if it incriminates the persons who constitute the business entity. In contrast, sole proprietors and sole practitioners (those who fully own their businesses) who have not incorporated cannot be compelled to produce their business records. These individuals have full protection against self-incrimination, because they function in only one capacity; there is no separate business entity.

In the following case, a state's investigation into the commercial practices of a certain corporation led the state's attorney general to issue a subpoena for the firm's business records. On the basis of the privilege against self-incrimination, the corporation refused to provide the records unless it was guaranteed immunity from prosecution.

---

28. The privilege has been applied to some small family partnerships. See *United States v. Slutsky*, 352 F.Supp. 1005 (S.D.N.Y. 1972).

CASE 4.2   Verniero v. Beverly Hills Ltd., Inc.

Superior Court of New Jersey, Appellate Division, 1998.
316 N.J.Super. 121,
719 A.2d 713.
http://lawlibrary.rutgers.
edu/search.shtml[a]

BACKGROUND AND FACTS   *The New Jersey Division of Consumer Affairs, under the state Consumer Affairs Act, investigated the marketing practices of Beverly Hills Limited, Inc. On the division's behalf, Peter Verniero, the state's attorney general, served a subpoena on Beverly Hills. The subpoena ordered the firm to provide certain business records, including its marketing agreements with other companies and documents relating to the firm's status as a corporation. Beverly Hills and its attorney responded that it was entitled to "exemption from both civil and criminal punishment in the event demanded documents would in any way result in self-incrimination" and demanded a guarantee of immunity before turning over its records. They cited N.J.S.A. [New Jersey Statutes Annotated] 56:8-7, which provides a privilege against self-incrimination for "a person who is entitled by law to, and does assert such privilege," when ordered to produce documents. Verniero filed a suit in a New Jersey state court to enforce the subpoena against Beverly Hills, arguing that the corporation had no privilege against self-incrimination. The court ruled in favor of Beverly Hills. Verniero appealed to a state intermediate appellate court.*

IN THE LANGUAGE OF THE COURT

SKILLMAN, J.A.D. [Judge, Appellate Division]
* * * *

The Fifth Amendment to the United States Constitution provides that "[n]o person * * * shall be compelled to be a witness against himself." Although the New Jersey Constitution does not contain a similar privilege, New Jersey has a common law privi-

---

a. Rutgers University School of Law in Camden, New Jersey, maintains this Web site. On this page, scroll down to the "Find Case by Citation" box. Select "N.J.Super." from the choices on the menu in the "Reporter" box. Enter "316" in the "Volume" box and "121" in the "Page" box. Click on "Submit Form" to access the case.

lege against self-incrimination which is now codified in [N.J.S.A. 2A:84-17 through 2A:84-19]. It is firmly established that a corporation may not invoke either the Fifth Amendment or the New Jersey privilege against self-incrimination. Moreover, a custodian of corporate records may not rely upon his or her personal privilege against self-incrimination as a basis for refusing to produce corporate records.

Beverly Hills is admittedly a corporation, and the subpoena issued by the Division only sought the production of Beverly Hills' records. Therefore, it is clear that neither Beverly Hills nor [its attorney] could invoke the Fifth Amendment or the New Jersey privilege against self-incrimination incorporated in N.J.S.A. 2A:84-17 to 19 as a basis for refusing to produce the records.

*   *   *   *

N.J.S.A. 56:8-7 *   *   * only confers immunity upon a person who is "entitled by law to *   *   * assert [the] privilege" against self-incrimination. Thus, a person claiming immunity under N.J.S.A. 56:8-7 must identify some "law" other than N.J.S.A. 56:8-7 as the source of a privilege against self-incrimination. By construing N.J.S.A. 56:8-7 to provide immunity from prosecution to a party who is not entitled to invoke the privilege against self-incrimination, the trial court effectively read the words "entitled by law to *   *   * assert such privilege" out of the statute. *   *   *

DECISION AND REMEDY   *The state intermediate appellate court held that a corporation could not invoke a privilege against self-incrimination as a basis for refusing to produce documents in response to a subpoena. The court reversed the judgment of the lower court and remanded the case for the entry of an order compelling Beverly Hills to comply with the subpoena.*

SEARCHES AND SEIZURES

The Fourth Amendment protects the "right of the people to be secure in their persons, houses, papers, and effects." Before searching or seizing private property, law enforcement officers must obtain a **search warrant**—an order from a judge or other public official authorizing the search or seizure.

Search Warrants and Probable Cause. To obtain a search warrant, the officers must convince a judge that they have reasonable grounds, or probable cause, to believe a search will reveal a specific illegality. **Probable cause** requires law enforcement officials to have trustworthy evidence that would convince a reasonable person that the proposed search or seizure is more likely justified than not. Furthermore, the Fourth Amendment prohibits *general* warrants. It requires a particular description of that which is to be searched or seized. General searches through a person's belongings are impermissible. The search cannot extend beyond what is described in the warrant.

There are exceptions to the requirement for a search warrant, as when it is likely that the items sought will be removed before a warrant can be obtained. For example, if a police officer has probable cause to believe an automobile contains evidence of a crime and it is likely that the vehicle will be unavailable by the time a warrant is obtained, the officer can search the vehicle without a warrant.

Searches and Seizures in the Business Context. Constitutional protection against unreasonable searches and seizures is important to businesses and professionals. As federal and state regulation of commercial activities increased, frequent and unannounced government inspections were conducted to ensure compliance with the regulations. Such inspections were at times extremely disruptive. In *Marshall v. Barlow's, Inc.,*[29] the United States Supreme Court held that government inspectors do not have the right to enter business premises without a warrant, although the standard of probable cause is not the same as that required in nonbusiness contexts. The existence of a general and neutral enforcement plan will justify issuance of the warrant.

Lawyers and accountants frequently possess the business records of their clients, and inspecting these documents while they are out of the hands of their

---

29. 436 U.S. 307, 98 S.Ct. 1816, 56 L.Ed.2d 305 (1978).

true owners also requires a warrant. A warrant is not required, however, for the seizure of spoiled or contaminated food. In addition, warrants are also not required for searches of businesses in such highly regulated industries as liquor, guns, and strip mining. General manufacturing is not considered to be one of these highly regulated industries, however.

Of increasing concern to many government employers is how to maintain a safe and efficient workplace without jeopardizing the Fourth Amendment rights of employees "to be secure in their persons." Requiring government employees to undergo random drug tests, for example, may be held to violate the Fourth Amendment. In Chapter 41, we will discuss Fourth Amendment issues in the employment context, as well as employee privacy rights in general, in greater detail.

SECTION 3

Other Constitutional Protections

Other constitutional guarantees of great significance to Americans are mandated by the *privileges and immunities clause* and the *full faith and credit clause* of Article IV of the Constitution, the *due process clauses* of the Fifth and Fourteenth Amendments, and the *equal protection clause* of the Fourteenth Amendment.

THE PRIVILEGES AND IMMUNITIES CLAUSE

Article IV, Section 2, of the Constitution provides that the "Citizens of each State shall be entitled to all Privileges and Immunities of Citizens in the several States." This clause is often referred to as the interstate **privileges and immunities clause.**[30] When a citizen of one state engages in basic and essential activities in another state (the "foreign state"), such as transferring property, seeking employment, or accessing the court system, the foreign state must have a *substantial reason* for treating the nonresident differently from its own residents. The foreign state must also establish that its reason for the discrimination is substantially related to the state's ultimate purpose in adopting the legislation or activity.[31]

Charging nonresidents $2,500 for a shrimp-fishing license, for example, while residents are charged only $25 for the same license, may be considered unconstitutional discrimination against nonresidents who are pursuing the essential activity of making a living.[32] Similarly, attempting to limit the practice of law to residents only (on the premise that it would help reduce the state's unemployment rate) may unconstitutionally restrict a nonresident's professional pursuit without substantial justification.[33]

The Fourteenth Amendment provides that "[n]o State shall make or enforce any law which shall abridge the privileges or immunities of citizens of the United States." This clause also protects all individuals, as citizens of the United States, from *state* action that might infringe on their privileges or immunities.[34]

THE FULL FAITH AND CREDIT CLAUSE

Article IV, Section 1, of the Constitution provides that "Full Faith and Credit shall be given in each State to the public Acts, Records, and judicial Proceedings of every other State." This clause, which is referred to as the **full faith and credit clause,** applies only to civil matters. It ensures that rights established under deeds, wills, contracts, and the like in one state will be honored by other states. It also ensures that any judicial decision with respect to such property rights will be honored and enforced in all states.

The full faith and credit clause originally was included in the Articles of Confederation to promote mutual friendship among the people of the various states. In fact, it has contributed to the unity of American citizens, because it protects their legal rights as they move about from state to state. It also protects the rights of those to whom they owe obligations, such as judgment creditors. This is extremely important for the conduct of business in a country with a very mobile citizenry.

---

30. The terms *privilege* and *immunity* are commonly used synonymously with regard to the interpretation of this clause. Generally, the terms refer to certain rights, benefits, or advantages enjoyed by individuals.

31. *Supreme Court of New Hampshire v. Piper*, 470 U.S. 274, 105 S.Ct. 1272, 84 L.Ed.2d 205 (1985).

32. *Toomer v. Witsell*, 334 U.S. 385, 68 S.Ct. 1156, 92 L.Ed. 1460 (1948).

33. *Hicklin v. Orbeck*, 437 U.S. 518, 98 S.Ct. 2482, 57 L.Ed.2d 397 (1978).

34. Unlike the due process and equal protection clauses (to be discussed shortly), the privileges and immunities clause of the Fourteenth Amendment does not apply to the individual rights found in the Bill of Rights.

DUE PROCESS

Both the Fifth and the Fourteenth Amendments provide that no person shall be deprived "of life, liberty, or property, without due process of law." The **due process clause** of these constitutional amendments has two aspects—procedural and substantive. Note that the due process clause applies to "legal persons" (that is, corporations) as well as to individuals.

Procedural Due Process. *Procedural* due process requires that any government decision to take life, liberty, or property must be made equitably. For example, fair procedures must be used in determining whether a person will be subjected to punishment or have some burden imposed on him or her. Fair procedure has been interpreted as requiring that the person have at least an opportunity to object to a proposed action before a fair, neutral decision maker (which need not be a judge). Thus, for example, if a driver's license is construed as a property interest, some sort of opportunity to object to its suspension or termination by the state must be provided.

Substantive Due Process. *Substantive* due process focuses on the content, or substance, of legislation. If a law or other governmental action limits a *fundamental right*, it will be held to violate substantive due process unless it promotes a *compelling* or *overriding state interest*. Fundamental rights include interstate travel, privacy, voting, and all First Amendment rights. Compelling state interests could include, for example, the public's safety. Thus, laws designating speed limits may be upheld even though they affect interstate travel, if they are shown to reduce highway fatalities, because the state has a compelling interest in protecting the lives of its citizens.

In all other situations, a law or action does not violate substantive due process if it rationally relates to any legitimate government purpose. It is almost impossible for a law or action to fail this "rational basis" test. Under this test, virtually any business regulation will be upheld as reasonable—the United States Supreme Court has upheld insurance regulations, price and wage controls, banking controls, and controls of unfair competition and trade practices against substantive due process challenges.

Suppose that a state legislature enacted a law imposing a fifteen-year term of imprisonment without a trial on all businesspersons who appeared in their own television commercials. This law would be unconsti-

tutional on both substantive and procedural grounds. Substantive review would invalidate the legislation because it abridges freedom of speech, a fundamental right. Procedurally, the law is constitutionally invalid because it imposes a penalty without giving the accused a chance to defend his or her actions.

EQUAL PROTECTION

Under the Fourteenth Amendment, a state may not "deny to any person within its jurisdiction the equal protection of the laws." The United States Supreme Court has used the due process clause of the Fifth Amendment to make the **equal protection clause** applicable to the federal government. Equal protection means that the government must treat similarly situated individuals in a similar manner.

Both substantive due process and equal protection require review of the substance of the law or other governmental action rather than review of the procedures used. When a law or action limits the liberty of all persons to do something, it may violate substantive due process; when a law or action limits the liberty of some persons but not others, it may violate the equal protection clause. Thus, for example, if a law prohibits all persons from buying contraceptive devices, it raises a substantive due process question; if it prohibits only unmarried persons from buying the same devices, it raises an equal protection issue.

In an equal protection inquiry, when a law or action distinguishes between or among individuals, the basis for the distinction—that is, the classification—is examined by the courts. The courts may use one of three standards: strict scrutiny, intermediate scrutiny, or the "rational basis" test.

Strict Scrutiny. If a law or action prohibits or inhibits some persons from exercising a fundamental right, the law or action will be subject to "strict scrutiny" by the courts. Under this standard, the classification must be necessary to promote a *compelling state interest*. Also, if the classification is based on a *suspect trait*—such as race, national origin, or citizenship status—the classification must be necessary to promote a compelling state interest. Compelling state interests include remedying past unconstitutional or illegal discrimination but do not include correcting the general effects of "society's" discrimination. Thus, for example, if a city gives preference to minority applicants in awarding construction contracts, the city normally must identify the past unconstitutional or illegal discrimination against minority construction firms that it is attempting to correct. Generally, few laws or actions survive strict-scrutiny analysis by the courts.

Intermediate Scrutiny. Another standard, that of "intermediate scrutiny," is applied in cases involving discrimination based on gender or legitimacy. Laws using these classifications must be *substantially related to important government objectives.*

For example, an important government objective is preventing illegitimate teenage pregnancies. Therefore, because males and females are not similarly situated in this regard—only females can become pregnant—a law that punishes men but not women for statutory rape will be upheld, even though it treats men and women unequally. A state law requiring illegitimate children to bring paternity suits within six years of their births, however, will be struck down if legitimate children are allowed to seek support from their parents at any time. An important objective behind statutes of limitations is to prevent persons from bringing stale or fraudulent claims, but distinguishing between support claims on the basis of legitimacy has no relation to this objective.

The "Rational Basis" Test. In matters of economic or social welfare, the classification will be considered valid if there is any conceivable *rational basis* on which the classification might relate to a legitimate government interest. It is almost impossible for a law or action to fail the rational basis test. Thus, for example, a city ordinance that in effect prohibits all pushcart vendors except a specific few from operating in a particular area of the city will be upheld if the city provides a rational basis—perhaps regulation and reduction of traffic in the particular area—for the ordinance. In contrast, a law that provides unemployment benefits only to people over six feet tall would violate the guarantee of equal protection. There is no rational basis for determining the distribution of unemployment compensation on the basis of height. Such a distinction could not further any legitimate government objective.

Is there a rational basis for a city ordinance that provides free garbage collection for the owners of some residences but requires the owners of other dwellings to pay for the same service? That was the question in the following case.

CASE 4.3   WHS Realty Co. v. Town of Morristown

Superior Court of New Jersey, Appellate Division, 1999. 323 N.J.Super. 553, 733 A.2d 1206.

BACKGROUND AND FACTS   *The Town of Morristown enacted an ordinance that provided for free garbage collection for all residential dwellings with three or fewer units and condominium developments in which no more than 50 percent of the units were owned by one person or entity. Excluded from the ordinance were all multifamily dwellings with four or more units. WHS Realty Company owned an apartment complex that consisted of 140 units and thus did not receive the free service. WHS filed a suit in a New Jersey state court against Morristown, claiming in part that the ordinance violated the Constitution's equal protection clause. Morristown argued, among other things, that the ordinance was rationally related to fostering home ownership. The court determined that the ordinance was unconstitutional, finding it was not rationally related to the fostering of home ownership or any other legitimate state interest. The court ordered Morristown to collect garbage and recyclable materials from WHS's apartment complex according to the terms applied to condominium complexes. Morristown appealed.*

IN THE LANGUAGE OF THE COURT

HAVEY, P.J.A.D. [Presiding Judge, Appellate Division]
*   *   *   *

A municipality is not mandated to provide for municipal garbage removal. *   *   *
However, once the service is provided by a municipality, *   *   * [t]here is a violation of equal protection of the laws unless the service is available to all persons in like circumstances upon the same terms and conditions. Persons situated alike shall be treated alike.
*   *   *   *

*   *   * [T]here is nothing about the mechanics or costs of solid waste collection that justifies differentiating between apartment complexes and other residents within the community. As the trial court observed during an early stage of the proceedings, "people are people," and the type and quality of solid waste generated by all types of residential dwellings is the same. *   *   *

*   *   *   *

The Town defendants nevertheless argue that the *   *   * ordinance is rationally related to fostering home ownership. *   *   *

*   *   *   *

*   *   * Here, *   *   * the facts established that approximately 42% of the dwelling units receiving garbage collection service are not occupied by their owners. Only 27% and 11.7% of the two- and three-family dwelling units are owner-occupied. If the disputed classification in fact promotes home ownership, particularly among the two- and three-family owners, there is no question that the percentages of owner-occupancy would be significantly higher. The low percentages of owner-occupants necessarily indicate that the disputed classification is irrational.

*   *   * [T]he only service involved is collection of solid waste, which, according to the [facts], costs approximately $400 per residential unit per year. *   *   * The Town performed no studies or surveys indicating that people are more inclined to purchase a home if free garbage collection service is provided. No interviews of home-owners were conducted.

*   *   *   *

The Town defendants also advance, as a rational basis for the ordinance, the fact that condominiums are taxed differently than apartment units. *   *   *

*   *   *   *

*   *   * We conclude that the methodology of taxing apartment complexes and condominium units is not a rational basis for upholding the ordinance.

DECISION AND REMEDY *The state intermediate appellate court affirmed the ruling of the lower court. The appellate court held that the ordinance violated the equal protection clause because it was not rationally related to any legitimate governmental interest. The court remanded the case, however, for a determination of the amount of damages, if any, to be paid to WHS.*

PRIVACY RIGHTS

A personal right to privacy is held to be so fundamental as to be applicable at both the state and the federal levels. Although there is no specific guarantee of a right to privacy in the Constitution, such a right has been derived from guarantees found in the First, Third, Fourth, Fifth, and Ninth Amendments. Invasion of another's privacy is also a tort, or civil wrong (see Chapter 5), and over the last several decades legislation has been passed at the federal level to protect the privacy of individuals in numerous areas of concern.

Privacy rights often relate to emotionally charged issues, such as abortion, assisted suicide for terminally ill people, and gay and lesbian relationships. In the business world, issues of privacy often arise in the employment context, a topic we examine in Chapter 41.

TERMS AND CONCEPTS TO REVIEW

amend 68	establishment clause 77	privileges and immunities clause 80
Bill of Rights 71	federal form of government 68	probable cause 79
checks and balances 69	free exercise clause 77	search warrant 79
commerce clause 69	full faith and credit clause 80	supremacy clause 70
due process clause 81	police powers 70	symbolic speech 74
equal protection clause 81	preemption 70	

QUESTIONS AND CASE PROBLEMS

4–1. COMMERCE CLAUSE. A Georgia state law requires the use of contoured rear-fender mudguards on trucks and trailers operating within Georgia state lines. The statute further makes it illegal for trucks and trailers to use straight mudguards. In approximately thirty-five other states, straight mudguards are legal. Moreover, in Florida, straight mudguards are explicitly required by law. There is some evidence that suggests that contoured mudguards might be a little safer than straight mudguards. Discuss whether this Georgia statute violates any constitutional provisions.

4–2. COMMERCIAL SPEECH. A mayoral election is about to be held in a large U.S. city. One of the candidates is Luis Delgado, and his campaign supporters wish to post campaign signs on lampposts and utility posts throughout the city. A city ordinance, however, prohibits the posting of any signs on public property. Delgado's supporters contend that the city ordinance is unconstitutional because it violates their right to free speech. Do you agree? In your answer, discuss what factors a court might consider in determining the constitutionality of the ordinance.

4–3. FREEDOM OF RELIGION. A business has a backlog of orders, and to meet its deadlines, management decides to run the firm seven days a week, eight hours a day. One of the employees, Abe Placer, refuses to work on Saturday on religious grounds. His refusal to work means that the firm may not meet its production deadlines and may therefore suffer a loss of future business. The firm fires Placer and replaces him with an employee who is willing to work seven days a week. Placer claims that his employer, in terminating his employment, has violated his constitutional right to the free exercise of his religion. Do you agree? Why or why not?

4–4. GOVERNMENT POWERS. The framers of the Constitution feared the twin evils of tyranny and anarchy. Discuss how specific provisions of the Constitution and the Bill of Rights reflect these fears and protect against both of these extremes.

4–5. FREEDOM OF RELIGION. Thomas worked in the nonmilitary operations of a large firm that produced both military and nonmilitary goods. When the company discontinued the production of nonmilitary goods, Thomas was transferred to a plant producing war materials. Thomas left his job, claiming that it violated his religious principles to participate in the manufacture of materials to be used in destroying life. In effect, he argued, the transfer to the war-materials plant forced him to quit his job. He was denied unemployment compensation by the state because he had not been effectively "discharged" by the employer but had voluntarily terminated his employment. Did the state's denial of unemployment benefits to Thomas violate the free exercise clause of the First Amendment? Explain. [*Thomas v. Review Board of the Indiana Employment Security*

Division, 450 U.S. 707, 101 S.Ct. 1425, 67 L.Ed.2d 624 (1981)]

4–6. COMMERCE CLAUSE. South Dakota Disposal Systems, Inc. (SDDS), applied to the South Dakota Department of Water and Natural Resources (DWNR) for a permit to operate a solid waste disposal facility (Lonetree). It was estimated that 90 to 95 percent of the waste would come from out of state. The DWNR determined that Lonetree would be environmentally safe and issued a permit. Later, a public referendum was held. The state attorney general issued a pamphlet to accompany the referendum that urged the public to vote against "the out-of-state dump" because "South Dakota is not the nation's dumping grounds." The measure was defeated. SDDS filed a suit against the state, challenging the referendum as a violation of, among other things, the commerce clause. Was the referendum unconstitutional? Why or why not? [*SDDS, Inc. v. State of South Dakota*, 47 F.3d 263 (8th Cir. 1995)]

4–7. EQUAL PROTECTION. With the objectives of preventing crime, maintaining property values, and preserving the quality of urban life, New York City enacted an ordinance to regulate the locations of commercial establishments that featured adult entertainment. The ordinance expressly applied to female, but not male, topless entertainment. Adele Buzzetti owned the Cozy Cabin, a New York City cabaret, that featured female topless dancers. Buzzetti and an anonymous dancer filed a suit in a federal district court against the city, asking the court to block the enforcement of the ordinance. The plaintiffs argued in part that the ordinance violated the equal protection clause. Under the equal protection clause, what standard applies to the court's consideration of this ordinance? Under this test, how should the court rule? Why? [*Buzzetti v. City of New York*, 140 F.3d 134 (2d Cir. 1998)]

4–8. FREEDOM OF SPEECH. The City of Tacoma, Washington, enacted an ordinance that prohibited the playing of car sound systems at a volume that would be "audible" at a distance greater than fifty feet. Dwight Holland was arrested and convicted for violating the ordinance. The conviction was later dismissed, but Holland filed a civil suit in a Washington state court against the city. He claimed in part that the ordinance violated his freedom of speech under the First Amendment. On what basis might the court conclude that this ordinance is constitutional? (Hint: In playing a sound system, was Holland actually expressing himself?) [*Holland v. City of Tacoma*, 90 Wash.App. 533, 954 P.2d 290 (1998)]

4–9. FREEDOM OF SPEECH. The members of Greater New Orleans Broadcasting Association, Inc., operate radio and television stations in New Orleans. They wanted to broadcast ads for private, for-profit casinos that are legal in Louisiana. A federal statute banned casino advertising, but other federal statutes exempted ads for tribal, government, nonprofit, and "occasional and ancillary" commercial casinos. The association filed a suit in a federal district court against the federal government, asking the court to hold that the statute, as it applied to their ads, violated the First Amendment. The government argued that the ban should be upheld, because "[u]nder appropriate conditions, some broadcast signals from Louisiana broadcasting stations may be heard in neighboring states including Texas and Arkansas," where private casino gambling is unlawful. What is the test for whether a regulation of commercial speech violates the First Amendment? How might it apply in this case? How should the court rule? [*Greater New Orleans Broadcasting Association, Inc. v. United States*, 527 U.S. 173, 119 S.Ct. 1923, 144 L.Ed.2d 161 (1999)]

operator, sued the state to block enforcement of the law. Alderman asserted, among other things, that the statute violated the equal protection clause, because it placed requirements on motorcyclists that were not imposed on other motorists. Assume that you are the judge in the trial court hearing this case and answer the following questions:

    (a) What type of government interest must be served in order to justify discriminatory classifications under each of the three standards of scrutiny, or "tests," discussed in this chapter?

    (b) Which standard, or test, applies to this case? Why?

    (c) Applying this standard, or test, is the helmet statute constitutional? Why or why not?

4–10. IN YOUR COURT

A state legislature enacted a statute that required any motorcycle operator or passenger on the state's highways to wear a protective helmet. Jim Alderman, a licensed motorcycle

LAW ON THE WEB

For updated links to resources available on the Web, as well as a variety of other materials, visit this text's Web site at http://wbl.westbuslaw.com.

    For an online version of the Constitution that provides hypertext links to amendments and other changes, go to

http://www.law.cornell.edu/constitution/constitution.overview.html

    An ongoing debate in the United States is whether the national government exercises too much regulatory control over intrastate affairs. To find current articles on this topic, go to

http://www.vote-smart.org/issues/FEDERALISM_STATES_RIGHTS

For discussions of current issues involving the rights and liberties contained in the Bill of Rights, go to the Web site of the American Civil Liberties Union at

http://www.aclu.org

Summaries and the full texts of constitutional law decisions by the United States Supreme Court are included at the following site:

http://oyez.nwu.edu

LEGAL RESEARCH EXERCISES ON THE WEB

Go to http://wbl.westbuslaw.com, the Web site that accompanies this text. Select "Internet Applications," and then click on "Chapter 4." There you will find the following Internet research exercises that you can perform to learn more about free speech issues:

Activity 4–1: Flag Burning

Activity 4–2: Begging and the First Amendment

CHAPTER 5

Torts

P ART OF DOING BUSINESS TODAY—and, indeed, part of everyday life—is the risk of being involved in a lawsuit. The list of circumstances in which businesspersons can be sued is long and varied. An employee injured on the job may attempt to sue the employer because of an unsafe working environment. A consumer who is injured while using a product may attempt to sue the manufacturer because of a defect in the product. At issue in these examples is alleged wrongful conduct by one person that causes injury to another. Such wrongful conduct is covered by the law of **torts** (the word *tort* is French for "wrong").

Of course, a tort is not the only type of wrong that exists in the law. Crimes also involve wrongs. A crime, however, is an act so reprehensible that it is considered a wrong against the state or against society as a whole, as well as against the individual victim. Therefore, the *state* prosecutes and punishes (through fines and/or imprisonment—and possibly death) persons who commit criminal acts. A tort action, in contrast, is a civil action in which one party brings a suit against another to obtain compensation (money damages) or other relief for the harm suffered. Some wrongs, however, provide a basis for both a criminal prosecution and a tort action—see Chapter 8.

As you will see in later chapters of this book, many of the lawsuits brought by or against business firms are based on the tort theories discussed in this chapter. Some of the torts examined here can occur in any con-

text, including the business environment. Others traditionally have been referred to as **business torts,** which are defined as wrongful interferences with the business rights of others. Included in business torts are such vaguely worded concepts as *unfair competition* and *wrongfully interfering with the business relations of others.* Because so many of today's lawsuits against businesses involve product liability (liability for defective products) and strict liability, we devote all of Chapter 6 to a discussion of those tort theories.

SECTION 1

The Basis of Tort Law

The basic purpose of tort law is to provide remedies for the invasion of various *protected interests.* Society recognizes an interest in personal physical safety, and tort law provides remedies for acts that cause physical injury or that interfere with physical security and freedom of movement. Society recognizes an interest in protecting property, and tort law provides remedies for acts that cause destruction or damage to property. Society also recognizes an interest in protecting certain intangible interests, such as personal privacy, family relations, reputation, and dignity, and tort law provides remedies for invasion of these interests.

In the remainder of this chapter, we examine two broad classifications of torts: *intentional torts* and *unintentional torts* (torts involving negligence). The classification of a particular tort depends largely on how the tort occurs (intentionally or negligently) and the surrounding circumstances. (Under the doctrine of strict liability discussed in the following chapter, liability may be imposed regardless of fault.)

SECTION 2

Intentional Torts against Persons and Business Relationships

An **intentional tort,** as the term implies, requires *intent.* The **tortfeasor** (the one committing the tort) must intend to commit an act, the consequences of which interfere with the personal or business interests of another in a way not permitted by law. An evil or harmful motive is not required—in fact, the actor may even have a beneficial motive for committing what turns out to be a tortious act. In tort law, intent only means that the actor intended the consequences of his or her act or knew with substantial certainty that certain consequences would result from the act. The law generally assumes that individuals intend the *normal* consequences of their actions. Thus, forcefully pushing another—even if done in jest and without any evil motive—is an intentional tort (if injury results), because the object of a strong push can ordinarily be expected to go flying.

Intentional torts against persons and business relationships include assault and battery, false imprisonment, infliction of emotional distress, defamation, invasion of the right to privacy, appropriation, misrepresentation, and wrongful interference.

ASSAULT AND BATTERY

Any intentional, unexcused act that creates in another person a reasonable apprehension or fear of immediate harmful or offensive contact is an **assault.** Note that apprehension is not the same as fear. If a contact is such that a reasonable person would want to avoid it, and if there is a reasonable basis for believing that the contact will occur, then the plaintiff suffers apprehension whether or not he or she is afraid. The interest protected by tort law concerning assault is the freedom from having to expect harmful or offensive contact. The arousal of apprehension is enough to justify compensation.

The *completion* of the act that caused the apprehension, if it results in harm to the plaintiff, is a **battery,** which is defined as an unexcused and harmful or offensive physical contact *intentionally* performed. For example, Ivan threatens Jean with a gun, then shoots her. The pointing of the gun at Jean is an assault; the firing of the gun (if the bullet hits Jean) is a battery. The interest protected by tort law concerning battery is the right to personal security and safety.

Essentially, any unpermitted, offensive contact, whether harmful or not, is a battery. The contact may be merely an unwelcome kiss or smoke intentionally blown in one's face. The contact can involve any part of the body or anything attached to it—for example, a hat or other item of clothing, a purse, or a chair or an automobile in which one is sitting. Whether the contact is offensive is determined by the *reasonable person standard.*[1] The contact can be made by the defendant or by some force the defendant sets in motion—for example, a rock thrown, food poisoned, or a stick swung. If the plaintiff shows there was contact, and the jury agrees that the contact was offensive, the plaintiff has a right to compensation. There is no need to establish that the defendant acted out of malice; in fact, proving a motive is never necessary.

A number of legally recognized defenses can be raised by a defendant who is sued for assault, battery, or both:

1. *Consent.* When a person consents to the act that damages him or her, there is generally no liability for the damage done.
2. *Self-defense.* An individual who is defending his or her life or physical well-being can claim self-defense. In a situation of either *real* or *apparent* danger, a person may normally use whatever force is *reasonably* necessary to prevent harmful contact (see Chapter 8 for a more detailed discussion of self-defense).
3. *Defense of others.* An individual can act in a reasonable manner to protect others who are in real or apparent danger.
4. *Defense of property.* Reasonable force may be used in attempting to remove intruders from one's home, although force that is likely to cause death or great bodily injury normally cannot be used just to protect property.

---

1. The reasonable person standard is an objective test of how a reasonable person would have acted under the same circumstances. See the subsection entitled "The Duty of Care and Its Breach" later in this chapter.

FALSE IMPRISONMENT

False imprisonment is defined as the intentional confinement or restraint of another person's activities without justification. It involves interference with the freedom to move without restriction. The confinement can be accomplished through the use of physical barriers, physical restraint, or threats of physical force. Moral pressure does not constitute false imprisonment. Furthermore, it is essential that the person being restrained not comply with the restraint willingly. In other words, the person being restrained must not agree to the restraint.

Businesspersons are often confronted with suits for false imprisonment after they have attempted to confine a suspected shoplifter for questioning. Under the privilege to detain granted to merchants in some states, a merchant can use the defense of *probable cause* to justify delaying a suspected shoplifter. Probable cause exists when the evidence to support the belief that a person is guilty outweighs the evidence against that belief. The detention, however, must be conducted in a *reasonable* manner and for only a *reasonable* length of time.

INTENTIONAL INFLICTION OF EMOTIONAL DISTRESS

The tort of *intentional infliction of emotional distress* can be defined as an intentional act that amounts to extreme and outrageous conduct resulting in severe emotional distress to another. For example, a prankster telephones an individual and says that the individual's spouse has just been in a horrible accident. As a result, the individual suffers intense mental pain or anxiety. The caller's behavior is deemed to be extreme and outrageous conduct that exceeds the bounds of decency accepted by society and is therefore **actionable** (capable of serving as the ground for a lawsuit).

Emotional distress claims pose several problems. One major problem is that such claims must be subject to some limitation, or the courts could be flooded with lawsuits alleging emotional distress. A society in which individuals are rewarded if they are unable to endure the normal emotional stresses of day-to-day living is obviously undesirable. Therefore, the law usually focuses on the nature of the acts that fall under this tort. Indignity or annoyance alone is usually not sufficient to support a lawsuit based on intentional infliction of emotional distress.

Many times, however, repeated annoyances (such as those experienced by a person who is being stalked), coupled with threats, are enough. In a business context, for example, the repeated use of extreme methods to collect an overdue debt may be actionable. Also, an event causing an unusually severe emotional reaction, such as the severe distress of a woman incorrectly informed that her husband and two sons have been killed, may be actionable. Because it is difficult to prove the existence of emotional suffering, a court may require that the emotional distress be evidenced by some physical symptom or illness or a specific emotional disturbance that can be documented by a psychiatric consultant or other medical professional.

In the following case, the court looks at one of the requirements that plaintiffs must meet to establish an emotional distress claim.

CASE 5.1   Roach v. Stern

Supreme Court of
New York,
Appellate Division,
Second Department,
1998.
675 N.Y.S.2d 133.

BACKGROUND AND FACTS *Deborah Roach—known as "Debbie Tay"—was a frequent guest on* The Howard Stern Show, *on which she discussed her purported sexual encounters with female aliens. Tay used her notoriety to launch her own cable television show. After her death from a drug overdose at the age of twenty-seven, her sister Melissa Driscol had the body cremated and gave a portion of the remains to Tay's friend Chaunce Hayden. Shortly afterward, Tay's brother, Jeff Roach, learned that Hayden was to appear on Stern's show and asked the producer to cancel the appearance. Hayden went on as planned, and during his appearance, the participants in the program handled and joked about Tay's remains. For example, Stern held up bone fragments while he guessed whether they came from Tay's skull or ribs. Tay's brother and sister filed a suit in a New York state court against Stern and others, seeking $8 million in damages for, among other things, intentional infliction of emotional distress. The defendants filed a motion to dismiss, contending that the conduct at issue was not particularly shocking, in light* *of Stern's reputation for vulgar humor and Tay's actions during her guest appearances on his show. The court granted the motion, and the plaintiffs appealed.*

IN THE LANGUAGE OF THE COURT

MEMORANDUM BY THE COURT.

*   *   *   *

*   *   * In order to impose liability for this intentional tort, the conduct complained of must be so outrageous in character, and so extreme in degree, as to go beyond all possible bounds of decency, and to be regarded as atrocious, and utterly intolerable in a civilized community. *The element of outrageous conduct is rigorous, and difficult to satisfy, and its purpose is to filter out trivial complaints and assure that the claim of severe emotional distress is genuine.* *   *   * [Emphasis added.]

Upon our review of the allegations in the case at bar, we conclude that the Supreme Court erred in determining that the element of outrageous conduct was not satisfied *   *   * . Although the defendants contend that the conduct at issue was not particularly shocking, in light of Stern's reputation for vulgar humor and Tay's actions during her guest appearances on his program, a jury might reasonably conclude that the manner in which Tay's remains were handled, for entertainment purposes and against the express wishes of her family, went beyond the bounds of decent behavior.

We further conclude that the remaining elements necessary to establish a cause of action to recover damages for the intentional infliction of emotional distress were also sufficiently pleaded in the complaint.

DECISION AND REMEDY

The state intermediate appellate court reversed the decision of the lower court and remanded the case for trial. The court held that a jury could reasonably conclude the manner in which Tay's remains were handled could constitute intentional infliction of emotional distress.

DEFAMATION

As discussed in Chapter 4, the freedom of speech guaranteed by the First Amendment is not absolute. In interpreting the First Amendment, the courts must balance the vital guarantee of free speech against other pervasive and strong social interests, including society's interest in preventing and redressing attacks on reputation.

Defamation of character involves wrongfully hurting a person's good reputation. The law imposes a general duty on all persons to refrain from making false, defamatory statements of fact about others. Breaching this duty orally involves the tort of **slander;** breaching it in writing involves the tort of **libel.** The tort of defamation also arises when a false statement of fact is made about a person's product, business, or title to property. We deal with these torts later in this chapter.

The Publication Requirement. The basis of the tort of defamation is the publication of a statement or statements that hold an individual up to contempt, ridicule, or hatred. *Publication* here means that the defamatory statements are communicated to persons other than the defamed party. If Thompson writes Andrews a private letter falsely accusing him of embezzling funds, the action does not constitute libel. If Peters falsely states that Gordon is dishonest and incompetent when no one else is around, the action does not constitute slander. In neither case was the message communicated to a third party.

The courts have generally held that even dictating a letter to a secretary constitutes publication, although the publication may be privileged (a concept that will be explained shortly). Moreover, if a third party overhears defamatory statements by chance, the courts usually hold that this also constitutes publication. Defamatory statements made via the Internet are actionable as well (see Chapter 9). Note also that any individual who repeats (republishes) defamatory statements normally is liable even if that person reveals the source of the statements.

Damages for Defamation. Once a defendant's liability for libel is established, "general damages" are presumed as a matter of law. General damages are designed to compensate the plaintiff for nonspecific harms such as disgrace or dishonor in the eyes of the community, humiliation, injured reputation, emotional distress, and so on—harms that are difficult to measure. In other words, to recover damages in a libel case, the plaintiff need not prove that he or she was actually injured in any way as a result of the libelous statement.

In a case alleging slander, however, the plaintiff must prove "special damages" to establish the defendant's liability. The plaintiff must show that the slanderous statement caused the plaintiff to suffer actual economic or monetary losses. Unless this initial hurdle of proving special damages is overcome, a plaintiff alleging slander normally cannot go forward with the suit and recover any damages. This requirement is imposed in cases involving slander because slanderous statements have a temporary quality. In contrast, a libelous (written) statement has the quality of permanence, can be circulated widely, and usually results from some degree of deliberation on the part of the author.

Exceptions to the burden of proving special damages in cases alleging slander are made for certain types of slanderous statements. If a false statement constitutes "slander *per se,*" no proof of special damages is required for it to be actionable. The following four types of utterances are considered to be slander *per se:*

1. A statement that another has a loathsome communicable disease.
2. A statement that another has committed improprieties while engaging in a profession or trade.
3. A statement that another has committed or has been imprisoned for a serious crime.
4. A statement that an unmarried woman is unchaste.

Defenses to Defamation.   Truth is almost always a defense against a defamation charge. In other words, if a defendant in a defamation case can prove that the allegedly defamatory statement of fact was actually true, normally no tort has been committed. Other defenses to defamation may exist if the speech is privileged or concerns a public figure.

Privileged Speech.   In some circumstances, a person will not be liable for defamatory statements because he or she enjoys a **privilege,** or immunity. Privileged communications are of two types: absolute and qualified. Only in limited cases, such as in judicial and legislative proceedings, is *absolute* privilege granted. For example, statements made by attorneys and judges in the courtroom during a trial are absolutely privileged.

So are statements made by legislators during congressional floor debate, even if the legislators make such statements maliciously—that is, knowing them to be untrue. An absolute privilege is granted in these situations because judicial and legislative personnel deal with matters that are so much in the public interest that the parties involved should be able to speak out fully and freely and without restriction.

In other situations, a person will not be liable for defamatory statements because he or she has a *qualified,* or conditional, privilege. For example, statements made in written evaluations of employees are qualifiedly privileged. Generally, if the communicated statements are made in good faith and the publication is limited to those who have a legitimate interest in the communication, the statements fall within the area of qualified privilege. The concept of conditional privilege rests on the common law assumption that in some situations, the right to know or speak is equal in importance to the right not to be defamed. If a communication is conditionally privileged, to recover damages, the plaintiff must show that the privilege was abused.

Public Figures.   In general, false and defamatory statements that are made about **public figures** (public officials who exercise substantial governmental power and any persons in the public limelight) and published in the press are privileged if they are made without "actual malice." To be made with **actual malice,** a statement must be made *with either knowledge of falsity or a reckless disregard of the truth.*[2]

Statements made about public figures, especially when they are communicated via a public medium, are usually related to matters of general public interest; they refer to people who substantially affect all of us. Furthermore, public figures generally have some access to a public medium for answering disparaging falsehoods about themselves; private individuals do not. For these reasons, public figures have a greater burden of proof in defamation cases (they must prove actual malice) than do private individuals.

INVASION OF PRIVACY

A person has a right to solitude and freedom from prying public eyes—in other words, to privacy. As mentioned in Chapter 4, the courts have held that certain

---

2. *New York Times Co. v. Sullivan,* 376 U.S. 254, 84 S.Ct. 710, 11 L.Ed.2d 686 (1964).

amendments to the U.S. Constitution imply a right to privacy. Some state constitutions explicitly provide for privacy rights. Additionally, a number of federal and state statutes have been enacted to protect individual privacy rights in specific areas. Tort law also safeguards these rights through the tort of *invasion of privacy*. Four acts qualify as invasion of privacy:

1. *The use of a person's name, picture, or other likeness for commercial purposes without permission.* For example, using without permission someone's picture to advertise a product or someone's name to enhance a company's reputation invades the person's privacy. (This tort, which is usually referred to as the tort of *appropriation*, will be examined shortly.)
2. *Intrusion on an individual's affairs or seclusion.* For example, invading someone's home or illegally searching someone's briefcase is an invasion of privacy. This tort has been held to extend to eavesdropping by wiretap, unauthorized scanning of a bank account, compulsory blood testing, and window peeping.
3. *Publication of information that places a person in a false light.* This could be a story attributing to someone ideas not held or actions not taken by that person. (The publication of such a story could involve the tort of defamation as well.)
4. *Public disclosure of private facts about an individual that an ordinary person would find objectionable.* A newspaper account of a private citizen's sex life or financial affairs could be an actionable invasion of privacy.

A pressing issue in today's online world has to do with the privacy rights of Internet users. For an exploration of this issue, see this chapter's *Emerging Trends in Technology.*

APPROPRIATION

The use of another person's name, likeness, or other identifying characteristic, without permission and for the benefit of the user, constitutes the tort of **appropriation.** Under the law, normally an individual's right to privacy includes the right to the exclusive use of his or her identity. For example, in a case involving a Ford Motor Company television commercial in which a Bette Midler "sound-alike" sang a song that Midler had made famous, the court held that Ford "for their own profit in selling their product did appropriate part of her identity."[3]

A court ruled similarly in a case brought by Vanna White, the hostess of the popular television game show *Wheel of Fortune,* against Samsung Electronics America, Inc. Without White's permission, Samsung included in an advertisement for Samsung videocassette recorders a depiction of a robot dressed in a wig, gown, and jewelry, posed in a setting that resembled the *Wheel of Fortune* set, in a stance for which White is famous. The court held in White's favor, holding that the tort of appropriation does not require the use of a celebrity's name or likeness. The court stated that Samsung's robot ad left "little doubt" as to the identity of the celebrity that the ad was meant to depict.[4]

Cases of wrongful appropriation, or misappropriation, may also involve the rights of those who invest time and money in the creation of a special system, such as a method of broadcasting sports events. Commercial misappropriation may also occur when a person takes and uses the property of another for the sole purpose of capitalizing unfairly on the goodwill or reputation of the property owner.

FRAUDULENT MISREPRESENTATION

A misrepresentation leads another to believe in a condition that is different from the condition that actually exists. This is often accomplished through a false or an incorrect statement. Misrepresentations may be innocently made by someone who is unaware of the facts. The tort of **fraudulent misrepresentation,** or *fraud,* however, involves intentional deceit for personal gain. The tort includes several elements:

1. A misrepresentation of material facts or conditions with knowledge that they are false or with reckless disregard for the truth.
2. An intent to induce another party to rely on the misrepresentation.
3. A justifiable reliance on the misrepresentation by the deceived party.
4. Damages suffered as a result of that reliance.
5. A causal connection between the misrepresentation and the injury suffered.

For fraud to occur, more than mere **puffery,** or *seller's talk,* must be involved. Fraud exists only when a person represents as a fact something he or she knows is untrue. For example, it is fraud to claim that the roof of a building does not leak when one knows

---

3. *Midler v. Ford Motor Co.,* 849 F.2d 460 (9th Cir. 1988).

4. *White v. Samsung Electronics America, Inc.,* 971 F.2d 1395 (1992).

EMERGING TRENDS IN TECHNOLOGY

The Protection of Privacy Rights in Cyberspace

You may not know it, but when you surf the Web you usually do not do so anonymously. When you visit a Web site, the site's owner or operator often knows where you are located, the kind of computer you have, the name of your Internet service provider, and other details. In fact, a 1998 Federal Trade Commission (FTC) survey of 1,400 Web sites found that although more than 85 percent of the sites collected personal information on visitors, only 14 percent of these sites informed visitors of their information-collecting practices.

Ironically, at a time when the value of personal information is higher than ever, the ability of individuals to control how that information is used is at a low

point. A growing concern today is how to protect Internet users' privacy rights without impeding the development of e-commerce and the flow of information online.

THE VALUE OF PERSONAL INFORMATION

In February 1999, Free-PC, a company based in Pasadena, California, announced that it would distribute 10,000 free Compaq computers immediately (and some 90,000 more computers in the future). Within days, the company received more than 1.2 million applications. What did Free-PC expect to get in return? The answer is—information. Those who received the computers had to disclose their ages, incomes, hobbies, and a variety of other details about their lives. They also had to permit their online travels to be tracked.

Online companies realize that profits can be made by gathering and using personal customer information, selling it to third parties, or sharing it with partners.

A user's name and everything connected to it have become valuable commodities to be purchased, sold, and otherwise exchanged for a profit in today's electronic marketplace.

WEB SITE PRIVACY POLICIES AND GUIDELINES

To ward off possible government action, as well as to avoid liability under existing laws, most online businesses are now taking steps to create and implement Web site privacy policies. Web site privacy guidelines are available from a number of online privacy groups and other organizations, including the Online Privacy Alliance, the Internet Alliance, and the Direct Marketing Association. Some organizations, including the Better Business Bureau, have even developed a "seal of approval" that Web-based businesses can display at their sites if they follow the organization's privacy guidelines.

Online privacy guidelines generally recommend that

it does. Facts are objectively ascertainable, whereas seller's talk is not. "I am the best architect in town" is seller's talk. The speaker is not trying to represent something as fact, because the term *best* is a subjective, not an objective, term.

Normally, the tort of fraudulent misrepresentation occurs only when there is reliance on a *statement of fact*. Sometimes, however, reliance on a *statement of opinion* may involve the tort of fraudulent misrepresentation if the individual making the statement of opinion has a superior knowledge of the subject matter. For example, when a lawyer, in a state in which he or she is licensed to practice, makes a statement of opinion about the law, a court would construe re-

liance on such a statement to be equivalent to reliance on a statement of fact.

Fraudulent and nonfraudulent misrepresentation will be examined further in Chapter 14, in the context of contract law. A growing problem in the online era is fraudulent misrepresentation in Internet transactions, a topic we examine in Chapter 44.

WRONGFUL INTERFERENCE

Torts involving wrongful interference with another's business rights generally fall into two categories—interference with a contractual relationship and interference with a business relationship.

EMERGING TRENDS IN TECHNOLOGY

The Protection of Privacy Rights in Cyberspace,

continued

businesses post a notice on their Web sites about the type of information being collected, how it will be used, and the parties to whom it will be disclosed. Other recommendations include allowing Web site visitors to access and correct or remove personal information and giving visitors an "opt-in" or "opt-out" choice. For example, if a user selects an "opt-out" policy, the personal data collected by the site owner would be kept private. Ultimately, new technology may make privacy a structural component of the Internet. For example, software is currently being developed by Microsoft and other firms that

would enable Web browsers to display a warning if a user visits a Web site that does not have a privacy policy or that collects data the user does not wish to disclose.

Because of these and other efforts, the FTC recently proposed to Congress that pending legislative action be postponed for a time to see if the online industry can regulate itself. For self-regulation to be effective, however, online companies and privacy organizations will need to agree on uniform privacy policy standards and devise appropriate enforcement mechanisms. These obstacles may be difficult—if not impossible—to overcome.

IMPLICATIONS FOR THE BUSINESSPERSON

1. Any company involved in e-commerce today should consider creating and implementing a Web site privacy policy to avoid liability for violating the privacy rights of Web site visitors.
2. Online businesses should also consider joining an online privacy

organization, both to obtain guidelines for privacy policies and to promote further self-regulation of e-commerce.

FOR CRITICAL ANALYSIS

1. Is self-regulation by the online industry a realistic option, or will the government inevitably have to step in to further protect online privacy rights?
2. What benefits do Internet users derive from disclosing personal information to Web merchants?

RELEVANT WEB SITES

To obtain a free privacy analysis of your computer (and learn what information you disclose simply by visiting the site), go to **http://www.Privacy.net**. Free-PC describes its business operations at **http://www.free-pc.com/about.tp**. For information on the Online Privacy Alliance, go to **http://www.privacyalliance.org**.

Wrongful Interference with a Contractual Relationship. The body of tort law relating to *wrongful interference with a contractual relationship* has increased greatly in recent years. A landmark case in this area involved an opera singer, Joanna Wagner, who was under contract to sing for a man named Lumley for a specified period of years. A man named Gye, who knew of this contract, nonetheless "enticed" Wagner to refuse to carry out the agreement, and Wagner began to sing for Gye. Gye's action constituted a tort, because it interfered with the contractual relationship between Wagner and Lumley. (Of course, Wagner's refusal to carry out the

agreement also entitled Lumley to sue Wagner for breach of contract.)[5]

In principle, any lawful contract can be the basis for an action of this type. The plaintiff must prove that the defendant actually knew of the contract's existence and *intentionally induced* the breach of the contractual relationship, not merely that the defendant reaped the benefits of a broken contract. For example, suppose that Carlin has a contract with Sutter that calls for Sutter to do gardening work on Carlin's large estate every week for fifty-two weeks at

5. *Lumley v. Gye,* 118 Eng.Rep. 749 (1853).

a specified price per week. Mellon, who needs gardening services, contacts Sutter and offers to pay Sutter a wage that is substantially higher than that offered by Carlin—although Mellon knows nothing about the Sutter-Carlin contract. Sutter breaches his contract with Carlin so that he can work for Mellon. Carlin cannot sue Mellon, because Mellon knew nothing of the Sutter-Carlin contract and was totally unaware that the higher wage he offered induced Sutter to breach that contract.

Three elements are necessary for wrongful interference with a contractual relationship to occur:

1. A valid, enforceable contract must exist between two parties.
2. A third party must know that this contract exists.
3. This third party must *intentionally* cause one of the two parties to the contract to breach the contract, and the interference must be for the purpose of advancing the economic interest of the third party.

The contract may be between a firm and its employees or a firm and its customers, suppliers, competitors, or other parties. Sometimes a competitor of a firm draws away a key employee. If the original employer can show that the competitor induced the

breach of the employment contract—that is, that the employee would not normally have broken the contract—damages can be recovered.

In a famous case in the 1980s, Texaco, Inc., was found to have wrongfully interfered with an agreement between the Pennzoil Company and the Getty Oil Company. After Pennzoil had agreed to purchase a portion of Getty Oil, Texaco made an offer to purchase Getty Oil, and Getty Oil accepted Texaco's offer. Pennzoil then successfully sued Texaco for wrongful interference with Pennzoil's contractual relationship with Getty Oil.[6]

The following case illustrates the elements of the tort of wrongful interference with a contractual relationship in the context of an agreement not to compete (agreements not to compete are discussed in further detail in Chapter 13).

6. *Texaco, Inc. v. Pennzoil Co.*, 725 S.W.2d 768 (Tex.App.—Houston [1st Dist.] 1987, writ ref'd n.r.e.). (Generally, a complete Texas Court of Appeals citation includes a writ-of-error history showing the Texas Supreme Court's disposition of the case. In this case, "writ ref'd n.r.e." is an abbreviation for "writ refused, no reversible error," which means that Texas's highest court refused to grant the appellant's request to review the case, because the court did not consider there to be any reversible error.)

CASE 5.2   Kallok v. Medtronic, Inc.

Supreme Court of Minnesota, 1998. 573 N.W.2d 356. http://www.courts.state.mn.us/library/archive/sctjl.html[a]

COMPANY PROFILE   *Medtronic, Inc. (http://www.medtronic.com), is the world's leading manufacturer of implantable biomedical devices. The company was started in 1949 by Earl Bakken, who was then a graduate student at the University of Minnesota, and Palmer Hermundslie, who worked in a lumberyard. The company's initial focus was the repair of hospital laboratory equipment. Today, Medtronic's most important products relate to cardiovascular and neurological health. Medtronic makes the most often prescribed heart pacemakers, as well as heart valves, implantable neurostimulation and drug-delivery systems, catheters used in angioplasties, and other products. Medtronic sells these products in more than 120 countries.*

BACKGROUND AND FACTS   *Michael Kallok signed a series of noncompete agreements when he worked for Medtronic, Inc., a medical device manufacturer. The agreements restricted his ability to work for Medtronic's competitors, including Angeion Corporation. When Kallok later approached Angeion for a job, he told it about the agreements. Angeion consulted with its attorneys, who advised that Kallok would not breach the agreements by accepting a job with Angeion. Angeion did not tell the attorneys all of the details of the agreements, however. After Kallok resigned from Medtronic to work for*

Angeion, he and Angeion filed a suit in a Minnesota state court against Medtronic, asserting that the noncompete agreements were unenforceable. Medtronic counterclaimed, alleging wrongful interference by Angeion. Angeion argued that its hiring of Kallok was justified because it consulted attorneys first. The court held Angeion liable and, among other things, awarded Medtronic damages. The plaintiffs appealed. The state intermediate appellate court took away the award. Medtronic appealed to the Minnesota Supreme Court.

IN THE LANGUAGE OF THE COURT

ANDERSON, Justice.

*   *   *   *

Medtronic easily established the *   *   * elements [of a cause of action for tortious interference with a contractual relationship]. First, as Kallok signed valid noncompete agreements, it is evident that a contract existed between him and Medtronic. Second, Angeion knew of the existence of Kallok's noncompete agreements before it hired him. *   *   * Third, *   *   * Angeion *   *   * procured the breach of his noncompete agreements by offering him the *   *   * position that he eventually accepted.

*   *   * Angeion, however, asserts that *   *   * its actions were justified because it consulted with its outside legal counsel before hiring Kallok *   *   * . We conclude that Angeion's argument lacks merit.

*   *   * Angeion did not fully inform its outside counsel about Kallok's background at Medtronic or the intricacies of his noncompete agreements. Had Angeion candidly provided its attorneys with all relevant information *   *   * Angeion would have understood that hiring Kallok would cause him to breach his noncompete agreements with Medtronic. *   *   *

*   *   *   *

*   *   * As a result, Medtronic was forced into court to protect the legitimate interest embodied in Kallok's noncompete agreements. *   *   * We hold that the [trial] court *   *   * correctly allowed Medtronic to recover from Angeion the *   *   * expenses it incurred in enforcing its noncompete agreements with Kallok.

DECISION AND REMEDY

The Minnesota Supreme Court reversed the decision of the lower court. The state supreme court reinstated Medtronic's award of damages for Angeion's interference with the noncompete agreements between Medtronic and Kallok.

Wrongful Interference with a Business Relationship. Individuals devise countless schemes to attract business, but they are forbidden by the courts to interfere unreasonably with another's business in their attempts to gain a share of the market. There is a difference between *competitive practices* and *predatory behavior*. The distinction usually depends on whether a business is attempting to attract customers in general or to solicit only those customers who have already shown an interest in the similar product or service of a specific competitor.

For example, if a shopping center contains two shoe stores, an employee of Store A cannot be positioned at the entrance of Store B for the purpose of diverting customers to Store A. This type of activity constitutes the tort of wrongful interference with a business relationship, often referred to as interference with a prospective (economic) advantage, and it is commonly considered to be an unfair trade practice. If this type of activity were permitted, Store A would reap the benefits of Store B's advertising.

Generally, a plaintiff must prove the following elements to recover damages for the tort of wrongful interference with a business relationship:

1. There was an established business relationship.
2. The tortfeasor, by use of predatory methods, *intentionally* caused this business relationship to end.
3. The plaintiff suffered damages as a result of the tortfeasor's actions.

Defenses to Wrongful Interference. A person will not be liable for the tort of wrongful interference with a contractual or business relationship if it can be shown that the interference was justified, or permissible. Bona fide competitive behavior is a permissible interference even if it results in the breaking of a contract.

For example, if Jerrod's Meats advertises so effectively that it induces Sam's Restaurant to break its contract with Burke's Meat Company, Burke's Meat Company will be unable to recover against Jerrod's Meats on a wrongful interference theory. After all, the public policy that favors free competition in advertising definitely outweighs any possible instability that such competitive activity might cause in contractual relations. Therefore, although luring customers away from a competitor through aggressive marketing and advertising strategies obviously interferes with the competitor's relationship with its customers, such activity is permitted by the courts.

SECTION 3

Intentional Torts against Property

Intentional torts against property include trespass to land, trespass to personal property, and conversion. These torts are wrongful actions that interfere with individuals' legally recognized rights with regard to their land or personal property. The law distinguishes real property from personal property (see Chapter 46). *Real property* is land and things permanently attached to the land. *Personal property* consists of all other items, which are basically movable. Thus, a house and lot are real property, whereas the furniture inside a house is personal property. Money and securities are also personal property.

TRESPASS TO LAND

The tort of **trespass to land** occurs any time a person, without permission, enters onto, above, or below the surface of land that is owned by another; causes anything to enter onto the land; or remains on the land or permits anything to remain on it. Note that actual harm to the land is not an essential element of this tort, because the tort is designed to protect the right of an owner to exclusive possession. Common types of trespass to land include walking or driving on the land; shooting a gun over the land; throwing rocks or spraying water on a building that belongs to someone else; building a dam across a river, thus causing water to back up on someone else's land; and placing part of one's building on an adjoining landowner's property.

In the past, the right to land gave exclusive possession of a space that extended from "the center of the

earth to the heavens," but this rule has been relaxed. Today, reasonable intrusions are permitted. Thus, aircraft can normally fly over privately owned land. Society's interest in air transportation preempts the individual's interest in the airspace.

Trespass Criteria, Rights, and Duties. Before a person can be a trespasser, the real property owner (or other person in actual and exclusive possession of the property) must establish that person as a trespasser. For example, "posted" trespass signs expressly establish as a trespasser a person who ignores these signs and enters onto the property. Any person who enters onto another's property to commit an illegal act (such as a thief entering a lumberyard at night to steal lumber) is established impliedly as a trespasser, without posted signs.

A guest in one's home is not a trespasser—unless he or she has been asked to leave but refuses. A *licensee* (a person who has a revocable right to come onto another person's land—see Chapter 47) who is asked to leave and refuses to do so is also a trespasser. For example, one who purchases a ticket to a play has a right to enter the theater, but the theater manager may revoke (take back) that right—if the playgoer becomes rowdy during the play's performance, for instance.

At common law, a trespasser is liable for damages caused to the property and generally cannot hold the owner liable for injuries that the trespasser sustains on the premises. This common law rule is being abandoned in many jurisdictions in favor of a "reasonable duty" rule that varies depending on the status of the parties. For example, a landowner may have a duty to post a notice that the property is patrolled by guard dogs. Also, under the "attractive nuisance" doctrine, a landowner may be held liable for injuries sustained by young children on the landowner's property if the children were attracted to the premises by some object, such as a swimming pool or an abandoned building. Finally, an owner can remove a trespasser from the premises—or detain a trespasser on the premises for a reasonable time—through the use of reasonable force without being liable for assault and battery or false imprisonment.

Defenses against Trespass to Land. Trespass to land involves wrongful interference with another person's real property rights. If it can be shown that the trespass was warranted, however, as when a trespasser enters to assist someone in danger, a defense exists.

TRESPASS TO PERSONAL PROPERTY

Whenever any individual, without consent, harms the personal property of another or otherwise interferes with the personal property owner's right to exclusive possession and enjoyment of that property, **trespass to personal property**—also called *trespass to personalty*—occurs. Trespass to personal property involves intentional meddling. If Kelly takes Ryan's business law book as a practical joke and hides it so that Ryan is unable to find it for several days prior to a final examination, Kelly has engaged in a trespass to personal property.

If it can be shown that trespass to personal property was warranted, then a complete defense exists. Most states, for example, allow automobile repair shops to hold a customer's car (under what is called an *artisan's lien*, discussed in Chapter 29) when the customer refuses to pay for repairs already completed.

CONVERSION

Conversion is defined as any act that deprives an owner of personal property without that owner's permission and without just cause. Conversion is the civil side of crimes related to theft. A store clerk who steals merchandise from the store commits a crime and engages in the tort of conversion at the same time. When conversion occurs, the lesser offense of trespass to personal property usually occurs as well. If the initial taking of the property was a trespass, retention of that property is conversion. If the initial taking of the property was permitted by the owner or for some other reason is not a trespass, failure to return it may still be conversion.

Even if a person mistakenly believed that he or she was entitled to the goods, a tort of conversion may still have occurred. In other words, good intentions are not a defense against conversion; in fact, conversion can be an entirely innocent act. Someone who buys stolen goods, for example, has committed the tort of conversion even if he or she did not know the goods were stolen.

A successful defense against the charge of conversion is that the purported owner does not in fact own the property or does not have a right to possess it that is superior to the right of the holder. Necessity is another possible defense against conversion. If Abrams takes Mendoza's cat, Abrams is guilty of conversion. If Mendoza sues Abrams, Abrams must return the cat or pay damages. If, however, the cat had rabies and Abrams took the cat to protect the public, Abrams has a valid defense—necessity.

CONCEPT SUMMARY 5.1

INTENTIONAL TORTS

CATEGORY	NAME OF TORT
Intentional Torts against Persons and Business Relationships	1. *Assault and battery*—Any unexcused and intentional act that causes another person to be apprehensive of immediate harm is an assault. An assault resulting in physical contact is battery. 2. *False imprisonment*—An intentional confinement or restraint of another person's movement without justification. 3. *Intentional infliction of emotional distress*—An intentional act that amounts to extreme and outrageous conduct resulting in severe emotional distress to another. 4. *Defamation (libel or slander)*—A false statement of fact, not made under privilege, that is communicated to a third person and that causes damage to a person's reputation. For public figures, the plaintiff must also prove that the statement was made with actual malice. 5. *Invasion of privacy*—Publishing or otherwise making known or using information relating to a person's private life and affairs, with which the public had no legitimate concern, without that person's permission or approval.

CONCEPT SUMMARY 5.1  INTENTIONAL TORTS *(continued)*

CATEGORY	NAME OF TORT
Intentional Torts against Persons and Business Relationships (continued)	6. *Appropriation*—The use of another person's name, likeness, or other identifying characteristic, without permission and for the benefit of the user. 7. *Fraudulent misrepresentation (fraud)*—A false representation made by one party, through misstatement of facts or through conduct, with the intention of deceiving another and on which the other reasonably relies to his or her detriment. 8. *Wrongful interference with a contractual or a business relationship*—The knowing, intentional interference by a third party with an enforceable contractual relationship or an established business relationship between other parties for the purpose of advancing the economic interests of the third party.
Intentional Torts against Property	1. *Trespass to land*—The invasion of another's real property without consent or privilege. Specific rights and duties apply once a person is expressly or impliedly established as a trespasser. 2. *Trespass to personal property*—The intentional interference with an owner's right to use, possess, or enjoy his or her personal property without the owner's consent. 3. *Conversion*—The wrongful taking and use of another person's personal property for the benefit of the tortfeasor or another. 4. *Disparagement of property*—Any economically injurious falsehood that is made about another's product or property; an inclusive term for the torts of *slander of quality* and *slander of title*.

DISPARAGEMENT OF PROPERTY

Disparagement of property occurs when economically injurious falsehoods are made not about another's reputation but about another's product or property. *Disparagement of property* is a general term for torts that can be more specifically referred to as *slander of quality* or *slander of title*.

Slander of Quality. Publishing false information about another's product, alleging it is not what its seller claims, constitutes the tort of **slander of quality.** This tort has also been given the name **trade libel.** The plaintiff must prove that actual damages proximately resulted from the slander of quality. That is, it must be shown not only that a third person refrained from dealing with the plaintiff because of the improper publication but also that the plaintiff suffered damages because the third person refrained from

dealing with him or her. The economic calculation of such damages—they are, after all, conjectural—is often extremely difficult.

It is possible for an improper publication to be both a slander of quality and a defamation. For example, a statement that disparages the quality of a product may also, by implication, disparage the character of a person who would sell such a product. In one case, for instance, the claim that a product that was marketed as a sleeping aid contained "habit-forming drugs" was held to constitute defamation.[7]

Slander of Title. When a publication falsely denies or casts doubt on another's legal ownership of property, and when this results in financial loss to the

---

7. *Harwood Pharmacal Co. v. National Broadcasting Co.*, 9 N.Y.2d 460, 174 N.E.2d 602, 214 N.Y.S.2d 725 (1961).

property's owner, the tort of **slander of title** may exist. Usually, this is an intentional tort in which someone knowingly publishes an untrue statement about another's ownership of certain property with the intent of discouraging a third person from dealing with the person slandered. For example, it would be difficult for a car dealer to attract customers after competitors published a notice that the dealer's stock consisted of stolen autos.

SECTION 4

Negligence

In contrast to intentional torts, in torts involving **negligence,** the tortfeasor neither wishes to bring about the consequences of the act nor believes that they will occur. The actor's conduct merely creates a risk of such consequences. If no risk is created, there is no negligence. Moreover, the risk must be foreseeable; that is, it must be such that a reasonable person engaging in the same activity would anticipate the risk and guard against it. In determining what is reasonable conduct, courts consider the nature of the possible harm. A very slight risk of a dangerous explosion might be unreasonable, whereas a distinct possibility of someone's burning his or her fingers on a stove might be reasonable.

To succeed in a negligence action, the plaintiff must prove the following:

1. That the defendant owed a duty of care to the plaintiff.
2. That the defendant breached that duty.
3. That the plaintiff suffered a legally recognizable injury.
4. That the defendant's breach caused the plaintiff's injury.

We discuss here each of these four elements of negligence.

THE DUTY OF CARE AND ITS BREACH

Central to the tort of negligence is the concept of a **duty of care.** This concept arises from the notion that if we are to live in society with other people, some actions can be tolerated and some cannot; some actions are right and some are wrong; and some actions are reasonable and some are not. The basic principle underlying the duty of care is that people are free to act

as they please so long as their actions do not infringe on the interests of others.

The law of torts defines and measures the duty of care by the **reasonable person standard.** In determining whether a duty of care has been breached, for example, the courts ask how a reasonable person would have acted in the same circumstances. The reasonable person standard is said to be (though in an absolute sense it cannot be) objective. It is not necessarily how a particular person would act. It is society's judgment on how an ordinarily prudent person should act. If the so-called reasonable person existed, he or she would be careful, conscientious, prudent, even tempered, and honest. That individuals are required to exercise a reasonable standard of care in their activities is a pervasive concept in business law, and many of the issues dealt with in subsequent chapters of this text have to do with this duty.

In negligence cases, the degree of care to be exercised varies, depending on the defendant's occupation or profession, his or her relationship with the plaintiff, and other factors. Generally, whether an action constitutes a breach of the duty of care is determined on a case-by-case basis. The outcome depends on how the court judge (or jury, if it is a jury trial) decides a reasonable person in the position of the defendant would act in the particular circumstances of the case. In the following subsections, we examine the degree of care typically expected of landowners and professionals.

Duty of Landowners.   Landowners are expected to exercise reasonable care to protect from harm individuals coming onto their property. As mentioned earlier in this chapter, in some jurisdictions, landowners are held to have a duty to protect even trespassers against certain risks. Landowners who rent or lease premises to tenants are expected to exercise reasonable care to ensure that the tenants and their guests are not harmed in common areas, such as stairways, entryways, and laundry rooms (see Chapter 48).

Retailers and other firms that explicitly or implicitly invite persons to come onto their premises are usually charged with a duty to exercise reasonable care to protect these **business invitees.** For example, if you entered a supermarket, slipped on a wet floor, and sustained injuries as a result, the owner of the supermarket would be liable for damages if, when you slipped, there was no sign warning that the floor was wet. A court would hold that the business owner was negligent because the owner failed to exercise a reasonable degree of care in protecting the store's customers against foreseeable risks about which the owner knew or *should have known.* That a patron might slip on the wet floor and be injured as a result was a foreseeable risk, and the owner should have taken care to avoid this risk or warn the customer of it.[8]

Some risks, of course, are so obvious that an owner need not warn of them. For example, a business owner does not need to warn customers to open a

door before attempting to walk through it. Other risks, however, even though they may seem obvious to a business owner, may not be so in the eyes of another, such as a child. For example, a hardware store owner may not think it is necessary to warn customers that, if climbed, a stepladder leaning against the back wall of the store could fall down and harm them. It is possible, though, that a child could tip the ladder over while climbing it and be hurt as a result.

In the following case, the court had to decide whether a store owner should be held liable for a customer's injury on the premises. The question was whether the owner had notice of the condition that led to the customer's injury.

---

8. A business owner can warn of a risk in a number of ways—for example, by placing a sign, traffic cone, sawhorse, board, or the like near a hole in the business's parking lot. See *Hartman v. Walkertown Shopping Center, Inc.,* 113 N.C.App. 632, 439 S.E.2d 787 (1994).

CASE 5.3   Martin v. Wal-Mart Stores, Inc.

United States
Court of Appeals,
Eighth Circuit, 1999.
183 F.3d 770.

BACKGROUND AND FACTS *Harold Martin was shopping in the sporting goods department of a Wal-Mart store. There was one employee in the department at that time. In front of the sporting goods section, in the store's main aisle (which the employees referred to as "action alley"), there was a large display of stacked cases of shotgun shells. On top of the cases were individual boxes of shells. Shortly after the sporting goods employee walked past the display, Martin did so, but Martin slipped on some loose shotgun shell pellets and fell to the floor. He immediately lost feeling in, and control of, his legs. Sensation and control returned, but during the next week, he lost the use of his legs several times for periods of ten to fifteen minutes. Eventually, sensation and control did not return to the front half of his left foot. Doctors diagnosed the condition as permanent. Martin filed a suit against Wal-Mart in a federal district court, seeking damages for his injury. The jury found in his favor, and the court denied Wal-Mart's motion for a directed verdict. Wal-Mart appealed to the U.S. Court of Appeals for the Eighth Circuit.*

**IN THE LANGUAGE
OF THE COURT**

BEAM, Circuit J. [Judge]

*   *   *   *

*   *   * [T]he traditional rule * * * required a plaintiff in a slip and fall case to establish that the defendant store had either actual or constructive notice of the dangerous condition. The defendant store [was] deemed to have actual notice if it [was] shown that an employee created or was aware of the hazard. Constructive notice could be established by showing that the dangerous condition had existed for a sufficient length of time that the defendant should reasonably have known about it.

*   *   *   *

*   *   * [R]etail store operations have evolved since the traditional liability rules were established. In modern self-service stores, customers are invited to traverse the same aisles used by the clerks to replenish stock, they are invited to retrieve merchandise from displays for inspection, and to place it back in the display if the item is not selected for purchase. Further, a customer is enticed to look at the displays, thus reducing the chance that the customer will be watchful of hazards on the floor. * * * [C]ustomers may take merchandise into their hands and may then lay articles that no longer interest them down in the aisle. * * * The risk of items creating dangerous conditions on the floor, previously created by employees, is now created by other customers as a result of the store's decision to employ the self-service mode of operation. * * * Thus, in slip and fall cases in self-service stores, the inquiry of whether the danger existed long enough that the store should have reasonably known of it (constructive notice) is made in light of the fact that the store has notice that certain dangers arising through customer involvement are likely to occur, and the store has a duty to anticipate them.

*   *   *   *

Wal-Mart *   *   * claims that Martin *   *   * failed to establish that Wal-Mart had actual or constructive notice of the pellets in the action aisle. We disagree. We find there is substantial evidence of constructive notice in the record. Martin slipped on shotgun shell pellets on the floor which were next to a large display of shotgun shells immediately abutting the sporting goods department. The chance that merchandise will wind up on the floor (or merchandise will be spilled on the floor) in the department in which that merchandise is sold or displayed is exactly the type of foreseeable risk [that is part of the self-service exception to the traditional rule]. Under [this exception], Wal-Mart has notice that merchandise is likely to find its way to the floor and create a dangerous condition, and *it must exercise due care to discover this hazard and warn customers or protect them from the danger.* *   *   * Even assuming that the hazard was created by a customer, a jury could easily find, given that it had notice that merchandise is often mishandled or mislaid by customers in a manner that can create dangerous conditions, that, had Wal-Mart exercised due care under the circumstances, it would have discovered the shotgun pellets on the floor. [Emphasis added.]

DECISION AND REMEDY   *The U.S. Court of Appeals for the Eighth Circuit affirmed the judgment of the lower court. There was sufficient evidence for a jury to find that Wal-Mart had constructive notice of the pellets on the floor in the main aisle.*

Duty of Professionals. If an individual has knowledge, skill, or intelligence superior to that of an ordinary person, the individual's conduct must be consistent with that status. Professionals—including physicians, dentists, psychiatrists, architects, engineers, accountants, and lawyers, among others—are required to have a standard minimum level of special knowledge and ability. Therefore, in determining what constitutes reasonable care in the case of professionals, the court takes their training and expertise into account. In other words, an accountant cannot defend against a lawsuit for negligence by stating, "But I was not familiar with that general principle of accounting."

If a professional violates his or her duty of care toward a client, the client may bring a **malpractice** suit against the professional. For example, a patient might sue a physician for *medical malpractice*. A client might sue an attorney for *legal malpractice*. The liability of professionals will be examined in further detail in Chapter 51.

No Duty to Rescue. Although the law requires individuals to act reasonably and responsibly in their relations with others, if a person fails to come to the aid of a stranger in peril, that person will not be considered negligent under tort law. For example, assume that you are walking down a city street and notice that

a pedestrian is about to step directly in front of an oncoming bus. You realize that the person has not seen the bus and is unaware of the danger. Do you have a legal duty to warn that individual? No. Although most people would probably concede that in this situation, the observer has an *ethical* or *moral* duty to warn the other, tort law does not impose a general duty to rescue others in peril. Duties may be imposed in regard to certain types of peril, however. For example, most states require a motorist involved in an automobile accident to stop and render aid. Failure to do so is both a tort and a crime.

THE INJURY REQUIREMENT AND DAMAGES

To recover damages (receive compensation), the plaintiff in a tort lawsuit must prove that he or she suffered a *legally recognizable* injury. That is, the plaintiff must have suffered some loss, harm, wrong, or invasion of a protected interest. This is true in lawsuits for intentional torts as well as lawsuits for negligence. Essentially, the purpose of tort law is to compensate for legally recognized harms and injuries resulting from wrongful acts. If no harm or injury results from a given negligent action, there is nothing to compensate—and no tort exists.

For example, if you carelessly bump into a passerby, who stumbles and falls as a result, you may be liable in tort if the passerby is injured in the fall. If the person is unharmed, however, there normally can be no suit for damages, because no injury was suffered. Although the passerby might be angry and suffer emotional distress, few courts recognize negligently inflicted emotional distress as a tort unless it results in some physical disturbance or dysfunction.

As already mentioned, the purpose of tort law is not to punish people for tortious acts but to compensate the injured parties for damages suffered. **Compensatory damages** are intended to compensate, or reimburse, a plaintiff for actual losses—to make the plaintiff whole. Occasionally, however, punitive damages are also awarded in tort lawsuits. **Punitive damages,** or *exemplary damages*, are intended to punish the wrongdoer and deter others from similar wrongdoing. Punitive damages are rarely awarded in lawsuits for ordinary negligence and usually are given only in cases involving intentional torts. They may be awarded, however, in suits involving *gross negligence*, which can be defined as an intentional failure to perform a manifest duty in reckless disregard of the consequences of such a failure for the life or property of another.

CAUSATION

Another element necessary to a tort is *causation*. If a person breaches a duty of care and someone suffers injury, the wrongful activity must have caused the harm for a tort to have been committed.

Causation in Fact and Proximate Cause. In deciding whether the requirement of causation is met, the court must address two questions:

1. *Is there causation in fact?* Did the injury occur because of the defendant's act, or would it have occurred anyway? If an injury would not have occurred without the defendant's act, then there is causation in fact. **Causation in fact** can usually be determined by use of the *but for* test: "but for" the wrongful act, the injury would not have occurred.

2. *Was the act the proximate cause of the injury?* Theoretically, causation in fact is limitless. One could claim, for example, that "but for" the creation of the world, a particular injury would not have occurred. Thus, as a practical matter, the law has to establish limits, and it does so through the concept of proximate cause. **Proximate cause,** or *legal cause*, exists when the connection between an act and an injury is strong enough to justify imposing liability. Consider an example. Ackerman carelessly leaves a campfire burning. The fire not only burns down the forest but also sets off an explosion in a nearby chemical plant that spills chemicals into a river, killing all the fish for a hundred miles downstream and ruining the economy of a tourist resort. Should Ackerman be liable to the resort owners? To the tourists whose vacations were ruined? These are questions of proximate cause that a court must decide.

Foreseeability. Questions of proximate cause are linked to the concept of foreseeability, because it would be unfair to impose liability on a defendant unless the defendant's actions created a foreseeable risk of injury. Probably the most cited case on the concept of foreseeability as a requirement for proximate cause—and as a measure of the extent of the duty of care generally—is the *Palsgraf* case. The question before the court was as follows: Does the defendant's duty of care extend only to those who may be injured as a result of a foreseeable risk, or does it extend also to persons whose injuries could not reasonably be foreseen?

CASE 5.4   Palsgraf v. Long Island Railroad Co.

Court of Appeals of
New York, 1928.
248 N.Y. 339,
162 N.E. 99.

BACKGROUND AND FACTS   *The plaintiff, Palsgraf, was waiting for a train on a station platform. A man carrying a package was rushing to catch a train that was moving away from a platform across the tracks from Palsgraf. As the man attempted to jump aboard the moving train, he seemed unsteady and about to fall. A railroad guard on the car reached forward to grab him, and another guard on the platform pushed him from behind to help him board the train. In the process, the man's package, which (unknown to the railroad guards) contained fireworks, fell on the railroad tracks and exploded. There was nothing about the package to indicate its contents. The repercussions of the explosion caused scales at the other end of the train platform to fall on Palsgraf, causing injuries for which she sued the railroad company. At the trial, the jury found that the railroad* *guards had been negligent in their conduct. The railroad company appealed. The appellate court affirmed the trial court's judgment, and the railroad company appealed to New York's highest state court.*

IN THE LANGUAGE OF THE COURT

CARDOZO, C.J. [Chief Justice].

*   *   *   *

The conduct of the defendant's guard, if a wrong in its relation to the holder of the package, was not a wrong in its relation to the plaintiff, standing far away. Relatively to her it was not negligence at all. *   *   *

*   *   *   *

*   *   * What the plaintiff must show is "a wrong" to herself; i.e., a violation of her own right, and not merely a wrong to someone else[.] *   *   * *The risk reasonably to be perceived defines the duty to be obeyed[.]* *   *   * Here, by concession, there was nothing in the situation to suggest to the most cautious mind that the parcel wrapped in newspaper would spread wreckage through the station. If the guard had thrown it down knowingly and willfully, he would not have threatened the plaintiff's safety, so far as appearances could warn him. His conduct would not have involved, even then, an unreasonable probability of invasion of her bodily security. Liability can be no greater where the act is inadvertent. [Emphasis added.]

*   *   * One who seeks redress at law does not make out a cause of action by showing without more that there has been damage to his person. If the harm was not willful, he must show that the act as to him had possibilities of danger so many and apparent as to entitle him to be protected against the doing of it though the harm was unintended. *   *   * The victim does not sue *   *   * to vindicate an interest invaded in the person of another. *   *   * He sues for breach of a duty owing to himself.

*   *   * [To rule otherwise] would entail liability for any and all consequences, however novel or extraordinary.

DECISION AND REMEDY

Palsgraf's complaint was dismissed. The railroad had not been negligent toward her, because injury to her was not foreseeable. Had the owner of the fireworks been harmed, and had he filed suit, there could well have been a different result.

INTERNATIONAL CONSIDERATIONS

Differing Standards of Proximate Cause *The concept of proximate cause is common among countries around the globe, but its application differs from country to country. French law uses the phrase "adequate cause." An event breaks the chain of adequate cause if the event is both unforeseeable and irresistible. England has a "nearest cause" rule that attributes liability based on which event was nearest in time and space. Mexico bases proximate cause on the foreseeability of the harm but does not require that an event be reasonably foreseeable.*

DEFENSES TO NEGLIGENCE

The basic defenses to liability in negligence cases are (1) assumption of risk, (2) superseding cause, and (3) contributory negligence.

Assumption of Risk. A plaintiff who voluntarily enters into a risky situation, knowing the risk involved, will not be allowed to recover. This is the defense of **assumption of risk.** For example, a driver entering an automobile race knows there is a risk of being injured or killed in a crash. The driver has as-

sumed the risk of injury. The requirements of this defense are (1) knowledge of the risk and (2) voluntary assumption of the risk.

The risk can be assumed by express agreement, or the assumption of risk can be implied by the plaintiff's knowledge of the risk and subsequent conduct. Of course, the plaintiff does not assume a risk different from or greater than the risk normally carried by the activity. In our example, the race driver assumes the risk of being injured in the race but not the risk that the banking in the curves of the racetrack will give way during the race because of a construction defect.

Risks are not deemed to be assumed in situations involving emergencies. Neither are they assumed when a statute protects a class of people from harm and a member of the class is injured by the harm. For example, courts have generally held that an employee cannot assume the risk of an employer's violation of safety statutes passed for the benefit of employees.

In the following case, a gas company worker was severely injured in a natural gas explosion that occured during an attempt to repair a gas leak. The question before the court is whether the worker should be barred from recovering for the injury by the defense of assumption of risk.

CASE 5.5   Crews v. Hollenbach

Court of Special
Appeals of Maryland,
1999.
126 Md.App. 609,
730 A.2d 742.

BACKGROUND AND FACTS   *Maryland Cable Partners, Limited Partnership,*[a] *hired Excalibur Cable Communications, Inc., to install cable lines in Bowie, Maryland. Byers Engineering Company was retained to locate the buried utility lines in the area where the cable lines were to be buried. Excalibur hired Honcho & Sons, Inc., to do the excavation. While Honcho's employee John Hollenbach was digging a hole, he struck a natural gas line owned by Washington Gas Company. Neither the police nor the fire department was promptly notified. Eventually, someone who smelled gas a mile and a half away contacted the fire department. Washington Gas was notified more than two hours later and dispatched a crew to fix the leak. The foreman was Lee James Crews. While Crews and his co-workers were attempting to repair the leak, an explosion occurred, severely injuring Crews. He filed a suit in a Maryland state court against Hollenbach and the others. The defendants filed a motion for summary judgment, claiming that Crews had assumed the risk of a gas explosion by virtue of his occupation. The court granted the motion. Crews appealed to a state intermediate appellate court.*

IN THE LANGUAGE OF THE COURT

HOLLANDER, Judge.

*   *   *   *

Appellant complains that there are issues relevant to whether he *   *   * assumed the risk, which the trial court did not consider and that the record did not address, such as the nature of the risk, whether appellant had a choice to respond to the scene, and whether appellant knew that the gas had been leaking for some two hours when he arrived at the scene. It is clear to us that these matters, including the apparent delay of some two hours in reporting the gas leak, do not defeat the application of the doctrine of *   *   * assumption of risk.

There is no basis to conclude that a gas company is always promptly advised about a possible gas leak. Indeed, it seems just as likely that a gas company would not immediately learn about a gas leak, for any number of reasons. To illustrate, a line could develop a leak in the middle of the night, and no one might realize it until hours later. *   *   * When a gas leak repairman accepts a position with the gas company, he does not assume only those risks associated with the least dangerous gas leak, or one that is reported within minutes of the occurrence. Rather, he assumes the dangers associated with gas leaks generally. *   *   *

*   *   *   *

*   *   * [T]he risk of an explosion from a gas leak is precisely within the scope of dangers intrinsic to the occupation of a gas leak repairman, much like a helicopter crash for a helicopter rescue team, an animal bite for a veterinarian, or a fireman's fall down an elevator shaft [while fighting a fire]. As appellant acknowledged in his deposition, "any type of gas leak or odor is always dangerous," because a fire could always "start behind natural gas." Thus, *   *   * appellant had reason to anticipate the danger. Indeed,

---

a. A limited partnership is a special form of a business organization. See Chapter 38.

Crews admitted that when working on a volatile natural gas leak "anything can set it off, gravels [sic] or rocks that hit together, hitting metal."

Crews "accept[ed] that responsibility when * * * [he] first got hired." Clearly, there was a direct causal relationship between the performance of appellant's duties as a gas leak repairman and the cause of his injury. Because appellant knew that his occupation carried with it certain risks, he may not now be heard to complain when one of those job-related foreseeable risks materialized. Under such circumstances, we agree with the trial court that appellant was barred from recovery.

DECISION AND REMEDY	*The state intermediate appellate court affirmed the ruling of the lower court. The appellate court held that Crews accepted the responsibility as a gas leak repairman to fix leaks in the face of dangers, including an explosion. By virtue of his employment, Crews was thus barred from recovering for his injury by the defense of assumption of risk.*

Superseding Cause. An unforeseeable intervening event may break the causal connection between a wrongful act and an injury to another. If so, it acts as a *superseding cause*—that is, it relieves a defendant of liability for injuries caused by the intervening event. For example, suppose that Derrick, while riding his bicycle, negligently hits Julie, who is walking on a sidewalk. As a result of the impact, Julie falls and fractures her hip. While she is waiting for help to arrive, a small aircraft crashes nearby and explodes, and some of the fiery debris hits her, causing her to sustain severe burns. Derrick will be liable for damages caused by Julie's fractured hip, but normally he will not be liable for the wounds caused by the plane crash—because the risk of a plane crashing nearby and injuring Julie was not foreseeable.

Contributory Negligence. Traditionally, under the common law, if a plaintiff's own negligence contributed to his or her injury, the defendant could raise the defense of **contributory negligence.** Contributory negligence on the part of the plaintiff was a complete defense to liability for negligence. Today, contributory negligence can be used as a defense in only a very few states.

In those jurisdictions that do allow the defense of contributory negligence, the *last clear chance* doctrine can excuse the effect of a plaintiff's negligence. The last clear chance doctrine allows the plaintiff to recover full damages despite his or her failure to exercise care. This rule operates when, through his or her own negligence, the plaintiff is endangered (or his or her property is endangered) by a defendant who has an opportunity to avoid causing damage but fails to take advantage of that opportunity. For example, if

Murphy walks across the street against the light, and Lewis, a motorist, sees her in time to avoid hitting her but hits her anyway, Lewis (the defendant) is not permitted to use Murphy's (the plaintiff's) prior negligence as a defense. The defendant negligently missed the opportunity to avoid injuring the plaintiff.

Neither the complete defense of contributory negligence nor the last clear chance doctrine applies in states that have adopted a comparative negligence standard, as the majority of states have done. Under the doctrine of **comparative negligence,** both the plaintiff's negligence and the defendant's negligence are taken into consideration, and damages are awarded accordingly. Some jurisdictions have adopted a "pure" form of comparative negligence that allows the plaintiff to recover damages even if his or her fault is greater than that of the defendant. For example, if the plaintiff was 80 percent at fault and the defendant was 20 percent at fault, the plaintiff may recover 20 percent of his or her damages. Many states' comparative negligence statutes, however, contain a "50 percent" rule, under which the plaintiff recovers nothing if he or she was more than 50 percent at fault.

SPECIAL NEGLIGENCE DOCTRINES AND STATUTES

There are a number of special doctrines and statutes relating to negligence that are important. We examine a few of them here.

Res Ipsa Loquitur. Generally, in lawsuits involving negligence, the plaintiff has the burden of proving that the defendant was negligent. In certain situations, the courts may presume that negligence has occurred, in which case the burden of proof rests on the defendant—that is, the defendant must prove that he or she was *not* negligent. The presumption of the defendant's negligence is known as the doctrine of *res ipsa loquitur,*[9] which translates as "the facts speak for themselves."

This doctrine is applied only when the event creating the damage or injury is one that ordinarily does not occur in the absence of negligence. For example, if a person undergoes knee surgery and following the surgery has a severed nerve in the knee area, that person can sue the surgeon under a theory of *res ipsa loquitur.* In this case, the injury would not have occurred but for the surgeon's negligence.[10] For the doctrine of *res ipsa loquitur* to apply, the event must have been within the defendant's power to control, and it must not have been due to any voluntary action or contribution on the part of the plaintiff.

Negligence *Per Se.* Certain conduct, whether it consists of an action or a failure to act, may be treated as **negligence *per se*** ("in or of itself"). Negligence *per se* may occur if an individual violates a statute or an ordinance providing for a criminal penalty and that violation causes another to be injured. The injured person must prove (1) that the statute clearly sets out what standard of conduct is expected, when and where it is expected, and of whom it is expected; (2) that he or she is in the class intended to be protected by the statute; and (3) that the statute was designed to prevent the type of injury that he or she suffered. The standard of conduct required by the statute is the duty that the defendant owes to the plaintiff, and a violation of the statute is the breach of that duty.

For example, a statute may require a landowner to keep a building in safe condition and may also subject the landowner to a criminal penalty, such as a fine, if the building is not kept safe. The statute is meant to protect those who are rightfully in the building. Thus, if the owner, without a sufficient excuse, violates the statute and a tenant is thereby injured, then a majority of courts will hold that the owner's unexcused violation of the statute conclusively establishes a breach of a duty of care—that is, that the owner's violation is negligence *per se.*

"Danger Invites Rescue" Doctrine. Under the "danger invites rescue" doctrine, if a person commits an act that endangers another, the person committing the act will be liable for any injuries the other party suffers as well as any injuries suffered by a third person in an attempt to rescue the endangered party. For example, suppose that Ludlam, while driving down a street, fails to see a stop sign because he is trying to stop a squabble between his two young children in the car's back seat. Salter, on the curb near the stop sign, realizes that Ludlam is about to hit a pedestrian walking across the street at the intersection. Salter runs into the street to push the pedestrian out of the way, and Ludlum's vehicle hits Salter instead. In this situation, Ludlam will be liable for Salter's injury, as well as for any injuries the other pedestrian sustained. Rescuers can injure themselves, or the persons rescued, or even bystanders, but the original wrongdoers will still be liable.

Special Negligence Statutes. A number of states have enacted statutes prescribing duties and responsibilities in certain circumstances. For example, most states now have what are called **Good Samaritan statutes.** Under these statutes, persons whom others aid voluntarily cannot turn around and sue the "Good Samaritans" for negligence. These laws were passed largely to protect physicians and medical personnel who voluntarily render their services in emergency situations to those in need, such as individuals hurt in car accidents.

Many states have also passed **dram shop acts,** under which a tavern owner or bartender may be held liable for injuries caused by a person who became intoxicated while drinking at the bar or who was already intoxicated when served by the bartender. Some states have statutes that impose liability on *social hosts* (persons hosting parties) for injuries caused by guests who became intoxicated at the hosts' homes. Under these statutes, it is unnecessary to prove that the tavern owner, bartender, or social host was negligent. Sometimes, the definition of a "social host" is fashioned broadly. For example, in a New York case, the court held that the father of a minor who hosted a "bring your own keg" party could be held liable for injuries caused by an intoxicated guest.[11]

---

9. Pronounced *rihz ihp-*suh *low-*kwuh-duhr.
10. *Edwards v. Boland,* 41 Mass.App.Ct. 375, 670 N.E.2d 404 (1996).

---

11. *Rust v. Reyer,* 693 N.E.2d 1074, 670 N.Y.S.2d 822 (1998).

CONCEPT SUMMARY 5.2

NEGLIGENCE

TERM	DESCRIPTION
Definition of Negligence	The careless performance of a legally required duty or the failure to perform a legally required act.
Elements of Negligence	1. The defendant owed a duty of care to the plaintiff. 2. The defendant breached that duty. 3. The plaintiff suffered a legally recognizable injury. 4. The defendant's breach of the duty of care caused the plaintiff's injury.
Defenses to Negligence	1. Assumption of risk. 2. Superseding cause. 3. Contributory negligence.
Special Negligence Doctrines and Statutes	1. *Res ipsa loquitur*—A doctrine under which a plaintiff need not prove negligence on the part of the defendant because "the facts speak for themselves." 2. *Negligence per se*—A type of negligence that may occur if a person violates a statute or an ordinance providing for a criminal penalty and the violation causes another to be injured. 3. *Special negligence statutes*—State statutes that prescribe duties and responsibilities in certain circumstances, the violation of which will impose civil liability. Good Samaritan statutes and dram shop acts are examples of special negligence statutes.

TERMS AND CONCEPTS TO REVIEW

QUESTIONS AND CASE PROBLEMS

5–1. NEGLIGENCE. In which of the following situations will the acting party be liable for the tort of negligence? Explain fully.

(a) Shannon goes to the golf course on Sunday morning, eager to try out a new set of golf clubs she has just purchased. As she tees off on the first hole, the head of her club flies off and injures a nearby golfer.

(b) Shannon goes to the golf course on Sunday morning. While she is teeing off at the eleventh hole, her golf ball veers off toward a roadway next to the golf course and shatters the windshield of a car.

(c) Shannon's doctor gives her some pain medication and tells her not to drive after she takes it, as the medication induces drowsiness. In spite of the doctor's warning, Shannon decides to drive to the store while on the medication. Owing to her lack of alertness, she fails to stop at a traffic light and crashes into another vehicle, causing a passenger in that vehicle to be injured.

5–2. CAUSATION. Ruth carelessly parks her car on a steep hill, leaving the car in neutral and failing to engage the parking brake. The car rolls down the hill, knocking down an electric line. The sparks from the broken line ignite a grass fire. The fire spreads until it reaches a barn one mile away. The barn houses dynamite, and the burning barn explodes, causing part of the roof to fall on and injure a passing motorist, Jim. Can Jim recover damages from Ruth? Why or why not?

5–3. WRONGFUL INTERFERENCE. Lothar owns a bakery. He has been trying to obtain a long-term contract with the owner of Martha's Tea Salons for some time. Lothar starts a local advertising campaign on radio and television and in the newspaper. This advertising campaign is so persuasive that Martha decides to break the contract she has had with Harley's Bakery so that she can patronize Lothar's bakery. Is Lothar liable to Harley's Bakery for the tort of wrongful interference with a contractual relationship? Is Martha liable for this tort? For anything?

5–4. DUTY OF CARE. As pedestrians exited at the close of an arts and crafts show, Jason Davis, an employee of the show's producer, stood near the exit. Suddenly and without warning, Davis turned around and collided with Yvonne Esposito, an eighty-year-old woman. Esposito was knocked to the ground, fracturing her hip. After hip-replacement surgery, she was left with a permanent physical impairment. Esposito filed a suit in a federal district court against Davis and others, alleging negligence. What are the factors that indicate whether Davis owed Esposito a duty of care? What do those factors indicate in these circumstances? [*Esposito v. Davis*, 47 F.3d 164 (5th Cir. 1995)]

5–5. NEGLIGENCE PER SE. A North Carolina Department of Transportation regulation prohibits the placement of telephone booths within public rights of way. Despite this regulation, GTE South, Inc., placed a booth in the right of way near the intersection of Hillsborough and Sparger Roads in Durham County. Laura Baldwin was using the booth when an accident at the intersection caused a dump truck to cross the right of way and smash into the booth. To recover for her injuries, Baldwin filed a suit in a North Carolina state court against GTE and others. Was Baldwin within the class of persons protected by the regulation? If so, did GTE's placement of the booth constitute negligence *per se*? Explain. [*Baldwin v. GTE South, Inc.*, 335 N.C. 544, 439 S.E.2d 108 (1994)]

5–6. TORT THEORIES. On the morning of October 2, 1989, a fire started by an arsonist broke out in the Red Inn in Provincetown, Massachusetts. The inn had smoke detectors, sprinklers, and an alarm system, all of which alerted the guests, but there were no emergency lights or clear exits. Attempting to escape, Deborah Addis and James Reed, guests at the inn, found the first-floor doors and windows locked. Ultimately, they forced open a second-floor window and jumped out. To recover for their injuries, they filed a suit in a Massachusetts state court against Tamerlane Corp., which operated the inn under a lease, and others (including Duane Steele, who worked for the owner of the inn). Under what tort theory discussed in this chapter might Addis and Reed recover damages from Tamerlane and the others? What must they prove to recover damages under this theory? Discuss fully. [*Addis v. Steele*, 38 Mass.App.Ct. 433, 648 N.E.2d 773 (1995)]

5–7. DUTY OF LANDOWNERS. The Oklahoma State Board of Cosmetology inspected the equipment of the Poteau Beauty College and found it to be in satisfactory condition. A month later, Marilyn Sue Weldon, a student at Poteau, was injured when a salon chair failed to work properly. Weldon had washed the hair of a woman with the chair in a reclining position. The chair did not spring back, and due to a previous injury, the client had to be helped into an upright position. The chair was close to a manicure table, and in maneuvering around the table, Weldon twisted her back. Weldon filed a suit in an Oklahoma state court against Poteau and others, claiming in part that the college was negligent. Assuming that Weldon was an invitee, what duty did Poteau, as the owner of the premises, owe to her? On what basis might the court rule that Poteau was not liable? [*Weldon v. Dunn*, 962 P.2d 1273 (Okla.Sup. 1998)]

5–8. MISAPPROPRIATION. The United States Golf Association (USGA) was founded in 1894. In 1911, the USGA developed the Handicap System, which was designed to enable individual golfers of different abilities to compete fairly with one another. The USGA revised the system and implemented new handicap formulas between 1987 and 1993. The USGA permits any entity to use the system free of charge as long as it complies with the USGA's procedure for peer review through authorized golf associations of the handicaps issued to individual golfers. In 1991, Arroyo Software Corp. began marketing software known as EagleTrak, which incorporated the USGA's system, and used its name in Arroyo's ads without the USGA's permission. Arroyo's EagleTrak did not incorporate any means for obtaining peer review of handicap computations. The USGA filed a suit in a California state court against Arroyo, alleging, among other things, misappropriation. The USGA asked the court to stop Arroyo's use of its system. Should the court grant the injunction? Why or why not? [*United States Golf Association v. Arroyo Software Corp.*, 69 Cal.App.4th 607, 81 Cal.Rptr.2d 708 (1999)]

5–9. IN YOUR COURT

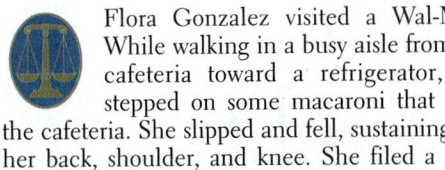

Flora Gonzalez visited a Wal-Mart store. While walking in a busy aisle from the store's cafeteria toward a refrigerator, Gonzalez stepped on some macaroni that came from the cafeteria. She slipped and fell, sustaining injuries to her back, shoulder, and knee. She filed a suit against Wal-Mart, alleging that the store was negligent. She presented evidence that the macaroni had "a lot of dirt" and tracks through it and testified that the macaroni "seemed like it had been there awhile." Assume that you are the judge in the trial court hearing this case and answer the following questions:

(a) What is the nature of the duty owed by businesses, such as Wal-Mart in this case, to their patrons?
(b) Did Wal-Mart breach that duty in this case?
(c) In deciding whether Wal-Mart should be held liable for Gonzalez's injuries, does it matter that she was walking in a busy aisle when she stepped on the macaroni?
(d) Compare the facts in this case to the facts in Case 5.3 (*Martin v. Wal-Mart Stores, Inc.*). What are the similarities and differences between the fact patterns in these two cases? If the facts are quite similar in both cases, are you obligated, under the doctrine of *stare decisis*, to apply the ruling in Case 5.3 to the *Gonzalez* case? Why or why not?

5–10. A QUESTION OF ETHICS

Patsy Slone, while a guest at the Dollar Inn, a hotel, was stabbed in the thumb by a hypodermic needle concealed in the tube of a roll of toilet paper. Slone, fearing that she might have been exposed to the virus that causes acquired immune deficiency syndrome (AIDS), sued the hotel for damages to compensate her for the emotional distress she suffered after the needle stab. An Indiana trial court held for Slone and awarded her $250,000 in damages. The hotel appealed, and one of the issues before the court was whether Slone had to prove that she was actually exposed to AIDS to recover for emotional distress. The appellate court held that she did not and that her fear of getting AIDS was reasonable in these circumstances. [*Slone v. Dollar Inn, Inc.*, 395 N.E.2d 185 (Ind.App. 1998)]

(a) Should the plaintiff in this case have been required to show that she was actually exposed to the AIDS virus in order to recover for emotional distress? Should she have been required to show that she actually acquired the AIDS virus as a result of the needle stab?
(b) In some states, plaintiffs are barred from recovery in emotional distress cases unless the distress is evidenced by some kind of physical illness. Is this fair?

LAW ON THE WEB

For updated links to resources available on the Web, as well as a variety of other materials, visit this text's Web site at http://wbl.westbuslaw.com.

You can find cases and articles on torts, including business torts, in the tort law library at the Internet Law Library's Web site. Go to

http://www.lawguru-com/ilawlib

LEGAL RESEARCH EXERCISES ON THE WEB

Go to http://wbl.westbuslaw.com, the Web site that accompanies this text. Select "Internet Applications," and then click on "Chapter 5." There you will find the following Internet research exercises that you can perform to learn more about privacy rights in an online world and the elements of negligence:

Activity 5–1: Privacy Rights in Cyberspace

Activity 5–2: Negligence and the *Titanic*

CHAPTER 6

Strict Liability
and Product Liability

THE INTENTIONAL TORTS AND TORTS of negligence discussed in Chapter 5 involve acts that depart from a reasonable standard of care and cause injuries. In this chapter, we look at another basis for liability in tort—strict liability. Under the tort doctrine of **strict liability,** liability for injury is imposed for reasons other than fault. We open this chapter with an examination of this doctrine. We then look at an area of tort law of particular importance to businesspersons—product liability. **Product liability** refers to the liability incurred by manufacturers and sellers of products when product defects cause injury or property damage to consumers, users, or **bystanders** (people in the vicinity of the product).

SECTION 1

Strict Liability

The modern concept of strict liability traces its origins, in part, to the 1868 English case of *Rylands v. Fletcher.*[1] In the coal-mining area of Lancashire, England, the Rylands, who were mill owners, had constructed a reservoir on their land. Water from the reservoir broke through a filled-in shaft of an abandoned coal mine

nearby and flooded the connecting passageways in an active coal mine owned by Fletcher. Fletcher sued the Rylands, and the court held that the defendants (the Rylands) were liable, even though the circumstances did not fit within existing tort liability theories.

In justifying its decision, the court compared the situation to the trespass of dangerous animals: "the true rule of law is, that the person who for his own purposes brings on his land and collects and keeps there anything likely to do mischief if it escapes, must keep it at his peril, and, if he does not do so, is *prima facie* [at first sight; on the face of it] answerable for all the damage which is the natural consequence of its escape."

The doctrine that emerged from *Rylands v. Fletcher* was liberally applied by British courts. Initially, few U.S. courts accepted this doctrine, presumably because the courts were worried about its effect on the expansion of American businesses. Today, however, the doctrine of strict liability is the norm rather than the exception.

ABNORMALLY DANGEROUS ACTIVITIES

The influence of *Rylands v. Fletcher* can be seen in the strict liability rule for abnormally dangerous activities, which is one application of the strict liability

---

1. L.R. 3 H.L. 330 (1868).

doctrine. Abnormally dangerous activities have three characteristics:

1. The activity involves potential harm, of a serious nature, to persons or property.
2. The activity involves a high degree of risk that cannot be completely guarded against by the exercise of reasonable care.
3. The activity is not commonly performed in the community or area.

Clearly, the primary basis of liability is the creation of an extraordinary risk. For example, even if blasting with dynamite is performed with all reasonable care, there is still a risk of injury. Balancing that risk against the potential for harm, it seems reasonable to ask the person engaged in the activity to pay for any injury it causes. Although there is no fault, there is still responsibility because of the dangerous nature of the undertaking.

OTHER APPLICATIONS OF STRICT LIABILITY

Persons who keep wild animals are strictly liable for any harm inflicted by the animals. The basis for applying strict liability is the fact that wild animals, should they escape from confinement, pose a serious risk of harm to persons in the vicinity. An owner of domestic animals (such as dogs, cats, cows, or sheep) may be strictly liable for harm caused by those animals if the owner knew, or should have known, that the animals were dangerous or had a propensity to harm others.

A significant application of strict liability is in the area of product liability, which we discuss next. Strict liability is also applied in certain types of *bailments* (a bailment exists when goods are transferred temporarily into the care of another—see Chapter 46).

SECTION 2

Product Liability

Product liability encompasses the tort theories of negligence and misrepresentation, which were discussed in Chapter 5, as well as strict liability. Product liability can also be based on warranty theory, a topic we treat in Chapter 23.

PRODUCT LIABILITY BASED ON NEGLIGENCE

In Chapter 5, *negligence* was defined as the failure to exercise the degree of care that a reasonable, prudent person would have exercised under the circumstances. If a manufacturer fails to exercise "due care" to make a product safe, a person who is injured by the product may sue the manufacturer for negligence.

Due care must be exercised in designing the product, in selecting the materials, in using the appropriate production process, in assembling and testing the product, and in placing adequate warnings on the label informing the user of dangers of which an ordinary person might not be aware. The duty of care also extends to the inspection and testing of any purchased components that are used in the final product sold by the manufacturer. A manufacturer's negligence *per se*—which occurs when a manufacturer violates a duty imposed by statute, such as a labeling statute (see Chapter 5)—may also serve as a ground for a tort action for damages.

A product-liability action based on negligence does not require the injured plaintiff and the negligent defendant-manufacturer to be in **privity of contract.** That is, the plaintiff and the defendant need not be directly involved in a contractual relationship. A manufacturer is liable for its failure to exercise due care to *any person* who sustains an injury proximately caused by a negligently made (defective) product. Relative to the long history of the common law, this exception to the privity requirement is a fairly recent development, dating to the early part of the twentieth century.[2]

PRODUCT LIABILITY BASED ON MISREPRESENTATION

When a fraudulent misrepresentation has been made to a user or consumer and that misrepresentation ultimately results in an injury, the basis of liability may be the tort of fraud. In this situation, the misrepresentation must have been made knowingly or with reckless disregard for the facts. An example is the intentional concealment of a product's defects. In contrast to actions based on negligence and strict liability, in a suit based on fraudulent misrepresentation, the plaintiff does not have to show that the product was defective or that it malfunctioned in any way.[3]

Nonfraudulent misrepresentation, which occurs when a merchant *innocently* misrepresents the character or quality of goods, can also provide a basis of liability. In this situation, the plaintiff does not have to prove that the misrepresentation was made knowingly.

2. A landmark case in this respect is *MacPherson v. Buick Motor Co.*, 217 N.Y. 382, 111 N.E. 1050 (1916).
3. See, for example, *Khan v. Shiley, Inc.*, 217 Cal.App.3d 848, 266 Cal.Rptr. 106 (1990).

A famous example involved a drug manufacturer and a victim of addiction to a prescription medicine called Talwin. The manufacturer, Winthrop Laboratories, a division of Sterling Drug, Inc., innocently indicated to the medical profession that the drug was not physically addictive. Using this information, a physician prescribed the drug for his patient, who developed an addiction that turned out to be fatal. Even though the addiction was a highly uncommon reaction resulting from the victim's unusual susceptibility to this product, the drug company was still held liable.[4]

Whether fraudulent or nonfraudulent, the misrepresentation must be of a material fact (a fact concerning the quality, nature, or appropriate use of the product on which a normal buyer may be expected to rely). There must also have been an intent to induce the buyer's reliance on the misrepresentation. Misrepresentation on a label or advertisement is enough to show an intent to induce the reliance of anyone who may use the product. The buyer also must rely on the misrepresentation. If the buyer is not aware of the misrepresentation or if it does not influence the transaction, there is no liability.

SECTION 3

Strict Product Liability

As explained earlier in this chapter, under the doctrine of strict liability people may be liable for the results of their acts regardless of their intentions or their exercise

---

4. *Crocker v. Winthrop Laboratories, Division of Sterling Drug, Inc.*, 514 S.W.2d 429 (Tex. 1974).

of reasonable care. In several landmark cases involving manufactured goods in the 1960s, courts applied the doctrine of strict liability, and it has since become a common method of holding manufacturers liable. Some states, however, including Massachusetts and Virginia, have refused to recognize strict product liability. Additionally, some courts limit the application of the doctrine only to cases involving personal injuries, not property damage. Until recently, recovery for economic loss was not available in an action based on strict liability; even today, it is rarely available.

STRICT PRODUCT LIABILITY AND PUBLIC POLICY

Strict product liability is imposed by law as a matter of public policy. This public policy rests on the threefold assumption that (1) consumers should be protected against unsafe products; (2) manufacturers and distributors should not escape liability for faulty products simply because they are not in privity of contract with the ultimate user of those products; and (3) manufacturers, sellers, and lessors of products are in a better position to bear the costs associated with injuries caused by their products—costs that they can ultimately pass on to all consumers in the form of higher prices.

California was the first state to impose strict product liability in tort on manufacturers. In the landmark decision that follows, the California Supreme Court sets out the reason for applying tort law rather than contract law (including laws governing warranties—guarantees made by sellers and lessors to those who buy or lease their products) to cases in which consumers are injured by defective products.

CASE 6.1   # Greenman v. Yuba Power Products, Inc.

Supreme Court of
California, 1962.
59 Cal.2d 57,
377 P.2d 897,
27 Cal.Rptr. 697.
http://mcs.newpaltz.
edu/~zuckerma/cases/
green1.htm[a]

BACKGROUND AND FACTS   *The plaintiff, Greenman, wanted a Shopsmith—a combination power tool that could be used as a saw, drill, and wood lathe—after seeing a Shopsmith demonstrated by a retailer and studying a brochure prepared by the manufacturer. The plaintiff's wife bought and gave him one for Christmas. More than a year later, a piece of wood flew out of the lathe attachment of the Shopsmith while the plaintiff was using it, inflicting serious injuries on him. About ten and a half months later, the plaintiff filed suit in a California state court against both the retailer and the manufacturer for breach of warranties and negligence. The trial court jury found for the plaintiff. The case was ultimately appealed to the Supreme Court of California.*

TRAYNOR, Justice.

❋   ❋   ❋   ❋

---

a. This case is included within the Web site for an "Introduction to Law" course taught by Paul Zuckerman, a professor with the State University of New York at New Paltz.

IN THE LANGUAGE
OF THE COURT

Plaintiff introduced substantial evidence that his injuries were caused by defective design and construction of the Shopsmith. * * * The jury could therefore reasonably have concluded that the manufacturer negligently constructed the Shopsmith. The jury could also reasonably have concluded that statements in the manufacturer's brochure were untrue, that they constituted express warranties, and that plaintiff's injuries were caused by their breach.

* * * *

[But] to impose strict liability on the manufacturer under the circumstances of this case, it was not necessary for plaintiff to establish an express warranty * * * . *A manufacturer is strictly liable in tort when an article he places on the market, knowing that it is to be used without inspection for defects, proves to have a defect that causes injury to a human being.* * * * [Emphasis added.]

* * * *

* * * The purpose of such liability is to insure that the costs of injuries resulting from defective products are borne by the manufacturers * * * rather than by the injured persons who are powerless to protect themselves.

DECISION
AND REMEDY

The Supreme Court of California upheld the jury verdict for the plaintiff. The manufacturer was held strictly liable in tort for the harm caused by its unsafe product.

THE REQUIREMENTS FOR STRICT PRODUCT LIABILITY

As mentioned in Chapter 1, the courts often look to the *Restatements of the Law* for guidance, even though the *Restatements* are not binding authorities. Section 402A of the *Restatement (Second) of Torts* indicates how it was envisioned that the doctrine of strict product liability should be applied. This *Restatement* was issued in 1964, and during the decade following its release it became a widely accepted statement of the liabilities of sellers of goods (including manufacturers, processors, assemblers, packagers, bottlers, wholesalers, distributors, retailers, and lessors). Section 402A reads as follows:

(1) One who sells any product in a defective condition unreasonably dangerous to the user or consumer or to his property is subject to liability for physical harm thereby caused to the ultimate user or consumer or to his property, if
    (a) the seller is engaged in the business of selling such a product, and
    (b) it is expected to and does reach the user or consumer without substantial change in the condition in which it is sold.

(2) The rule stated in Subsection (1) applies although
    (a) the seller has exercised all possible care in the preparation and sale of his product, and
    (b) the user or consumer has not bought the product from or entered into any contractual relation with the seller.

The bases for an action in strict liability as set forth in Section 402A of the *Restatement (Second) of Torts*, and as the doctrine came to be commonly applied, can be summarized as a series of six requirements, which are listed here. Depending on the jurisdiction, if these requirements were met, a manufacturer's liability to an injured party could be virtually unlimited.[5]

1. The product must be in a defective condition when the defendant sells it.
2. The defendant must normally be engaged in the business of selling (or otherwise distributing) that product.
3. The product must be unreasonably dangerous to the user or consumer because of its defective condition (in most states).
4. The plaintiff must incur physical harm to self or property by use or consumption of the product.
5. The defective condition must be the proximate cause of the injury or damage.
6. The goods must not have been substantially changed from the time the product was sold to the time the injury was sustained.

Thus, under these requirements, in any action against a manufacturer, seller, or lessor, the plaintiff

---

5. In a number of states, *statutes of repose* (discussed later in this chapter) place a limit on the time period within which product-liability actions may be brought.

does not have to show why or in what manner the product became defective. To recover damages, however, the plaintiff must show that the product was so "defective" as to be "unreasonably dangerous"; that the product caused the plaintiff's injury; and that at the time the injury was sustained, the condition of the product was essentially the same as when it left the hands of the defendant manufacturer, seller, or lessor.

A court could consider a product so defective as to be an **unreasonably dangerous product** if either (1) the product was dangerous beyond the expectation of the ordinary consumer or (2) a less dangerous alternative was economically feasible for the manufacturer, but the manufacturer failed to produce it. As will be discussed later, a product may be unreasonably dangerous due to a flaw in the manufacturing process, a design defect, or an inadequate warning.

MARKET-SHARE LIABILITY

Generally, in cases involving product liability, a plaintiff must prove that the defective product that caused his or her injury was the product of a specific defendant. In recent decades, however, in cases in which plaintiffs could not prove which of many distributors of a harmful product supplied the particular product that caused their injuries, courts have dropped this requirement.

This has occurred, for example, in several cases involving DES (diethylstilbestrol), a drug administered in the past to prevent miscarriages. DES's harmful character was not realized until, a generation later, daughters of the women who had taken DES developed health problems, including vaginal carcinoma, that were linked to the drug. Partly because of the passage of time, a plaintiff-daughter often could not prove which pharmaceutical company—out of as many as three hundred—had marketed the DES her mother had ingested. In these cases, some courts applied **market-share liability,** holding that all firms that manufactured and distributed DES during the period in question were liable for the plaintiffs' injuries in proportion to the firms' respective shares of the market.[6]

Market-share liability has also been applied in other situations.[7] In one case, the New York Court of Appeals (that state's highest court) held that even if a firm can prove that it did not manufacture the particular product that caused injuries to the plaintiff, the firm can be held liable based on the firm's share of the national market.[8]

OTHER APPLICATIONS OF STRICT PRODUCT LIABILITY

Strict product liability also applies to suppliers of component parts. For example, suppose that General Motors buys brake pads from a subcontractor and puts them in Chevrolets without changing their composition. If those pads are defective, both the supplier of the brake pads and General Motors will be held strictly liable for the damages caused by the defects. Under the *Restatement (Third) of Torts: Products Liability*, which will be discussed shortly, a component supplier may be liable if the component is defective "at the time of sale or distribution." A supplier may also be liable if it "substantially participates in the integration of the component into the design of the product," the "integration" causes the product to be defective, and the defect causes harm.[9]

Although the drafters of Section 402A of the *Restatement (Second) of Torts* did not take a position on bystanders, all courts extend the strict liability of manufacturers and other sellers to injured bystanders. For example, in one case, an automobile manufacturer was held liable for injuries caused by the explosion of a car's motor. A cloud of steam that resulted from the explosion caused multiple collisions because other drivers could not see well.[10] In the following classic case, the court indicates some policy reasons for extending the protections of Section 402A to bystanders whose injuries from defective products are reasonably foreseeable.

6. See, for example, *Martin v. Abbott Laboratories,* 102 Wash.2d 581, 689 P.2d 368 (1984).

7. See, for example, *Smith v. Cutter Biological, Inc.,* 72 Haw. 416, 823 P.2d 717 (1991).

8. *Hymowitz v. Eli Lilly and Co.,* 73 N.Y.2d 487, 539 N.E.2d 1069, 541 N.Y.S.2d 941 (1989).

9. *Restatement (Third) of Torts: Products Liability,* Section 5.

10. *Giberson v. Ford Motor Co.,* 504 S.W.2d 8 (Mo. 1974).

CASE 6.2

Embs v. Pepsi-Cola Bottling Co. of Lexington, Kentucky, Inc.

Court of Appeals of
Kentucky, 1975.
528 S.W.2d 703.

**IN THE LANGUAGE
OF THE COURT**

BACKGROUND AND FACTS *Janice Embs was buying some groceries at Stamper's Cash Market. Unnoticed by her, a carton of 7-Up was sitting on the floor at the edge of the produce counter about one foot from where she was standing. Several of the 7-Up bottles exploded. Embs's leg was injured severely enough that Embs had to be taken to the hospital by a managing agent of the store. Embs brought an action in a Kentucky state court against the manufacturer, but the trial court dismissed her claim. Embs appealed.*

JUKOWSKY, Judge.

* * * *

Our expressed public policy will be furthered if we minimize the risk of personal injury and property damage by charging the costs of injuries against the manufacturer who can procure liability insurance and distribute its expense among the public as a cost of doing business; and since the risk of harm from defective products exists for mere bystanders and passersby as well as for the purchaser or user, there is no substantial reason for protecting one class of persons and not the other. The same policy requires us to maximize protection for the injured third party and promote the public interest in discouraging the marketing of products having defects that are a menace to the public by imposing strict liability upon retailers and wholesalers in the distributive chain responsible for marketing the defective product which injures the bystander. *The imposition of strict liability places no unreasonable burden upon sellers because they can adjust the cost of insurance protection among themselves in the course of their continuing business relationship.* [Emphasis added.]

We must not shirk from extending the rule to the manufacturer for fear that the retailer or middleman will be impaled on the sword of liability without regard to fault. Their liability was already established under Section 402A of the *Restatement of Torts 2d.* As a matter of public policy the retailer or middleman as well as the manufacturer should be liable since the loss for injuries resulting from defective products should be placed on those members of the marketing chain best able to pay the loss, who can then distribute such risk among themselves by means of insurance and indemnity agreements. * * *

The result which we reach does not give the bystander a "free ride." When products and consumers are considered in the aggregate, bystanders, as a class, purchase most of the same products to which they are exposed as bystanders. Thus, as a class, they indirectly subsidize the liability of the manufacturer, middleman and retailer and in this sense do pay for the insurance policy tied to the product.

Public policy is adequately served if parameters are placed upon the extension of the rule so that it is limited to bystanders whose injury from the defect is reasonably foreseeable.

For the sake of clarity we restate the extension of the rule. The protections of Section 402A of the *Restatement of Torts 2d* extend to bystanders whose injury from the defective product is reasonably foreseeable.

**DECISION
AND REMEDY**

The appellate court reversed the trial court's dismissal of Embs's claim. The case was remanded to the lower court for a new trial.

SECTION 4

The *Restatement (Third) of Torts*

Because Section 402A of the *Restatement (Second) of Torts* did not clearly define such terms as "defective"

and "unreasonably dangerous," these terms have been subject to different interpretations by different courts. To address these concerns, the American Law Institute (ALI) drafted a new restatement of the principles and policies underlying product-liability law. In particular, the ALI attempted to respond to questions that had not been part of the legal landscape thirty-five years earlier. The result was the *Restatement (Third) of Torts: Products Liability,* which was released in 1997.

Traditionally, the law has categorized product defects into three types: manufacturing defects, design defects, and warning defects—each of which will be discussed shortly. The *Restatement (Third) of Torts: Products Liability* defines the three types of defects and integrates the applicable legal principles into the definitions. By defining defects in this manner, the new *Restatement* does away with some of the hard-to-understand distinctions that developed when different theories of liability were applied to the same defects.

For example, in one case, a court upheld a verdict that found a product "not defective" on a theory of strict liability but its manufacturer liable for harm caused by the product on a theory of breach of warranty.[11] The court based its decision on the various tests that exist under the different legal theories. The new *Restatement* sets out a single test to be applied for each type of defect regardless of the type of legal claim involved.

MANUFACTURING DEFECTS

According to Section 2(a) of the new *Restatement,* a product "contains a manufacturing defect when the product departs from its intended design even though all possible care was exercised in the preparation and marketing of the product." This statement imposes liability on the manufacturer (and on the wholesaler and retailer) whether or not the manufacturer acted "reasonably." This is strict liability, or liability without fault.

DESIGN DEFECTS

A determination that a product has a design defect (or a warning defect, discussed later in this chapter) can affect all of the units of a product. A product "is defective in design when the foreseeable risks of harm

posed by the product could have been reduced or avoided by the adoption of a reasonable alternative design by the seller or other distributor, or a predecessor in the commercial chain of distribution, and the omission of the alternative design renders the product not reasonably safe."[12]

Different states have applied different tests to determine whether a product has a design defect under Section 402A of the *Restatement (Second) of Torts.* There has been much controversy regarding the different tests, particularly about one that focused on the "consumer expectations" concerning a product. The test prescribed by the *Restatement (Third) of Torts: Products Liability* focuses on a product's actual design and the reasonableness of that design.

To succeed in a product-liability suit alleging a design defect, a plaintiff has to show that there is a reasonable alternative design. In other words, a manufacturer or other defendant is liable only when the harm was reasonably preventable. According to the Official Comments accompanying the new *Restatement,* factors that a court may consider on this point include

the magnitude and probability of the foreseeable risks of harm, the instructions and warnings accompanying the product, and the nature and strength of consumer expectations regarding the product, including expectations arising from product portrayal and marketing. The relative advantages and disadvantages of the product as designed and as it alternatively could have been designed may also be considered. Thus, the likely effects of the alternative design on production costs; the effects of the alternative design on product longevity, maintenance, repair, and esthetics; and the range of consumer choice among products are factors that may be taken into account.

Note that the "consumer expectations" element, instead of being the whole test, is only one factor taken into consideration. Another factor is the warning that accompanies a product. Can a warning insulate a manufacturer from liability for the harm caused by a design defect? That was the issue in the following case.

---

11. *Denny v. Ford Motor Co.,* 87 N.Y.2d 248, 662 N.E.2d 730, 639 N.Y.S.2d 250 (1995). The *Restatement* has not eliminated all of these distinctions, however, because in some cases, they may be necessary.

---

12. *Restatement (Third) of Torts: Products Liability,* Section 2(b).

CASE 6.3   Rogers v. Ingersoll-Rand Co.

United States
Court of Appeals,
District of Columbia
Circuit, 1998.
144 F.3d 841.
http://laws.findlaw.com
/DC/977131A.html[a]

COMPANY PROFILE   *Ingersoll-Rand Company (http://www.ingersoll-rand.com) is a manufacturer of air compressors, construction and mining equipment, bearings and precision components, tools, locks and architectural hardware, and industrial machinery. The company also makes Bobcat skid-steer loaders, Blaw-Knox pavers, Club Car golf cars and light utility vehicles, and Thermo King transport temperature control systems. In joint ventures with other firms, Ingersoll-Rand is a supplier of pumps and hydrocarbon processing equipment and services. Ingersoll-Rand distributes its products in more than one hundred countries. Forty percent of its sales are outside the United States.*

BACKGROUND AND FACTS   *Among the equipment that Ingersoll-Rand makes is a milling machine. In the maintenance manual that accompanies the machine are warnings that users should stay ten feet away from the rear of the machine when it is operating, verify that the back-up alarm is working, and check the area for the presence of others. There is also a sign on the machine that tells users to stay ten feet away. While using the machine to strip asphalt from a road being repaved, Terrill Wilson backed up the machine. The alarm did not sound, and Cosandra Rogers, who was standing with her back to the machine, was run over and maimed. Rogers filed a suit in a federal district court against Ingersoll-Rand, alleging in part strict liability on the basis of a design defect. The jury awarded Rogers $10.2 million in compensatory damages and $6.5 million in punitive damages. Ingersoll-Rand appealed to the U.S. Court of Appeals for the District of Columbia, emphasizing the adequacy of its warnings.*

IN THE LANGUAGE OF THE COURT

SENTELLE, Justice.

  *   *   *   *

    *   *   * Under [a risk-utility balancing] test [in a defective design case], a plaintiff must show the risks, costs and benefits of the product in question and alternative designs, and that the magnitude of the danger from the product outweighed the costs of avoiding danger. *   *   *

    [Ingersoll-Rand argues that] the adequacy of its warnings [should be] the sole consideration in the risk-utility analysis. As Ingersoll-Rand would have it, once the jury evaluates the milling machine's warnings and finds them adequate, its job is over; it "should find for [the] defendant." *   *   * [T]he "warnings" defense would have instructed the jury that adequate warnings trump all other factors—including the "magnitude of the danger from the product" *   *   * .

  *   *   *   *

    We do not mean to dispute that warnings may tip the balance in a manufacturer's favor in individual cases. On the other hand, *warnings need not be the [deciding] factor in every case.* Here, for example, it seems reasonably foreseeable that a worker with her back to a milling machine would be in no position to "heed" a sign on the machine instructing her to keep ten feet away. Under these circumstances, a manufacturer may have a heightened responsibility to incorporate additional safety features to guard against foreseeable harm. [Emphasis added.]

DECISION AND REMEDY   *The U.S. Court of Appeals for the District of Columbia Circuit upheld the jury's award. The court held that an adequate warning cannot immunize a manufacturer from any liability caused by a defectively designed product.*

---

a. This is a page within the Web site of FindLaw, a resource for Internet legal sources.

WARNING DEFECTS

A product may also be deemed defective because of inadequate instructions or warnings. Section 2(c) of the *Restatement (Third) of Torts: Products Liability* states that a product "is defective because of inadequate instructions or warnings when the foreseeable risks of harm posed by the product could have been reduced or avoided by the provision of reasonable instructions or warnings by the seller or other distributor, or a predecessor in the commercial chain of distribution, and the omission of the instructions or warnings renders the product not reasonably safe."[13]

Important factors for a court to consider under the *Restatement (Third) of Torts: Products Liability* include the risks of a product, the "content and comprehensibility" and "intensity of expression" of warnings and instructions, and the "characteristics of expected user groups."[14] For example, children would likely respond readily to bright, bold, simple

---

13. *Restatement (Third) of Torts: Products Liability*, Section 2(c).
14. *Restatement (Third) of Torts: Products Liability*, Section 2, Comment h.

warning labels, while educated adults might need more detailed information.

There is no duty to warn about risks that are obvious or commonly known. Warnings about such risks do not add to the safety of a product and could even detract from it by making other warnings seem less significant. The obviousness of a risk and a user's decision to proceed in the face of that risk may be a defense in a product-liability suit based on a warning defect. (Defenses to product liability will be discussed shortly.)

Generally, a seller must warn those who purchase its product of the harm that can result from the foreseeable misuse of the product as well. The key is the foreseeability of the misuse. According to the Official Comments accompanying the new *Restatement*, sellers "are not required to foresee and take precautions against every conceivable mode of use and abuse to which their products might be put."

Is a manufacturer obligated to warn buyers that an alteration to its product (in this case, the removal of the safety guard from a meat grinder) would make the manufacturer's product unsafe? The court addressed this question in the following case.

| CASE 6.4 | **Liriano v. Hobart Corp.** |

United States
Court of Appeals,
Second Circuit, 1999.
170 F.3d 264.
http://www.findlaw.com/
casecode/courts/2nd.
html[a]

BACKGROUND AND FACTS   *Hobart Corporation makes and sells commercial food-handling equipment, including meat grinders. In New York, a Super Associated grocery store bought one of the grinders. The grinder did not include a warning indicating that it should be operated only with the safety guard attached. After Super bought the grinder, the guard was removed. Later, Super hired Luis Liriano, who was seventeen years old and a recent immigrant to the United States. During Liriano's first week on the job, although he was not told how to operate the grinder, he used it two or three times. On his next use, his hand became caught in the grinder by a mechanism that anyone operating the appliance was not able to see. He was severely injured—he lost his hand and part of his forearm. He filed a suit in a federal district court against Hobart, claiming, among other things, that the lack of a warning about the safety guard constituted negligence. The jury returned a verdict for Liriano. Hobart appealed, arguing in part that the danger was so obvious that no warning was needed.*

**IN THE LANGUAGE
OF THE COURT**

CALABRESI, Circuit Judge:
* * * * *

* * * [A] warning can convey at least two types of messages. One states that a particular place, object, or activity is dangerous. Another explains that people need not risk the danger posed by such a place, object, or activity in order to achieve the purpose for which they might have taken that risk. Thus, a highway sign that says "Danger—Steep

---

a. This is a page within the Web site of the "Findlaw Internet Legal Resources" database. In the "1999" row, click on "March." On that page, scroll down to the case name and click on it to access the opinion.

Grade" says less than a sign that says "Steep Grade Ahead — Follow Suggested Detour to Avoid Dangerous Areas."

* * * *

One who grinds meat, like one who drives on a steep road, can benefit not only from being told that his activity is dangerous but from being told of a safer way. * * * [O]ne can argue about whether the risk involved in grinding meat is sufficiently obvious that a responsible person would fail to warn of that risk, believing reasonably that it would convey no helpful information. But if it is also the case — as it is — that the risk posed by meat grinders can feasibly be reduced by attaching a safety guard, we have a different question. Given that attaching guards is feasible, does reasonable care require that meat workers be informed that they need not accept the risks of using unguarded grinders? Even if most ordinary users may * * * know of the risk of using a guardless meat grinder, it does not follow that a sufficient number of them will * * * also know that protective guards are available, that using them is a realistic possibility, and that they may ask that such guards be used. It is precisely these last pieces of information that a reasonable manufacturer may have a duty to convey even if the danger of using a grinder were itself deemed obvious.

* * * A jury could reasonably find that there exist people who are employed as meat grinders and who do not know (a) that it is feasible to reduce the risk with safety guards, (b) that such guards are made available with the grinders, and (c) that the grinders should be used only with the guards. Moreover, a jury can also reasonably find that there are enough such people, and that warning them is sufficiently inexpensive, that a reasonable manufacturer would inform them that safety guards exist and that the grinder is meant to be used only with such guards.

DECISION AND REMEDY — *The U.S. Court of Appeals for the Second Circuit upheld the verdict in Liriano's favor. The court ruled that a manufacturer could be liable for failing to warn about alterations, such as the removal of a safety guard, that would make its product unsafe.*

SECTION 5

Defenses to Product Liability

Defendants in product-liability suits can raise a number of defenses. One defense, of course, is to show that there is no basis for the plaintiff's claim. For example, in a product-liability case based on negligence, if a defendant can show that the plaintiff has not met the requirements (such as causation) for an action in negligence, the defendant will not be liable. In regard to strict product liability, a defendant can claim that the plaintiff failed to meet one of the requirements for an action in strict liability. For example, if the defendant establishes that the goods have been subsequently altered, the defendant will not be held liable.[15] Defendants may also assert the defenses discussed next.

ASSUMPTION OF RISK

Assumption of risk can sometimes be used as a defense in a product-liability action. To establish such a defense, the defendant must show that (1) the plaintiff knew and appreciated the risk created by the product defect, and (2) the plaintiff voluntarily assumed the risk, even though it was unreasonable to do so. For example, if a buyer failed to heed a seller's product recall, the buyer may be deemed to have assumed the risk of the product defect that the seller offered to cure. (See Chapter 5 for a more detailed discussion of assumption of risk.)

PRODUCT MISUSE

Similar to the defense of voluntary assumption of risk is that of **product misuse.** Here, the injured party *does not know that the product is dangerous for a particular use* (contrast this with assumption of risk), but the use is not the one for which the product was designed. The courts have severely limited

---

15. Under some state laws, the failure to properly maintain a product may constitute a subsequent alteration. See, for example, *LaPlante v. American Honda Motor Co.*, 27 F.3d 731 (1st Cir. 1994).

this defense, however. Even if the injured party does not know about the inherent danger of using the product in a wrong way, if the misuse is reasonably foreseeable, the seller must take measures to guard against it.

For example, in one case two men were using a crane to retrieve drilling pipe from beneath power lines when the crane cable touched one of the lines. The cable did not have an insulated link and thus conducted electricity from the line to the pipe, electrocuting one of the men. The man's widow sued the crane manufacturer, alleging that the crane—without the insulated link—was defectively designed and unreasonably dangerous. The manufacturer argued that the men had been using the crane to sideload (a practice that causes the crane's cable to extend its slack in unpredictable ways) and that sideloading was an unreasonable misuse of the product. The court held that although sideloading was a misuse, the misuse was reasonably foreseeable. Because the manufacturer had failed to guard against this foreseeable misuse, it was liable to the widow for damages.[16]

Contributory Negligence

As discussed in Chapter 5, under the doctrine of contributory negligence, a defendant in a negligence suit may avoid liability in whole or in part if the plaintiff's own negligence contributed to the injury for which the plaintiff seeks damages. Whereas earlier the plaintiff's conduct was not a defense to strict liability, today some jurisdictions consider the negligent or intentional actions of both the plaintiff and the defendant in the apportionment of liability and damages. In other words, in those jurisdictions a comparative negligence standard is applied in strict liability cases.

Commonly Known Dangers

The dangers associated with certain products (such as matches and guns) are so commonly known that manufacturers need not warn users of those dangers. If a defendant succeeds in convincing the court that a plaintiff's injury resulted from a *commonly known danger*, the defendant will not be liable.

A classic case on this issue involved a plaintiff who was injured when an elastic exercise rope she had purchased slipped off her foot and struck her in the eye, causing a detachment of the retina. The plaintiff claimed that the manufacturer should be liable because it had failed to warn users that the exerciser might slip off a foot in such a manner. The court stated that to hold the manufacturer liable in these circumstances "would go beyond the reasonable dictates of justice in fixing the liabilities of manufacturers." After all, stated the court, "[a]lmost every physical object can be inherently dangerous or potentially dangerous in a sense. . . . A manufacturer cannot manufacture a knife that will not cut or a hammer that will not mash a thumb or a stove that will not burn a finger. The law does not require [manufacturers] to warn of such common dangers."[17]

A related defense is the *knowledgeable user* defense. If a particular danger is or should be commonly known by particular users of a product, the manufacturer need not warn these users of the danger.

Statutes of Limitations and Repose

As discussed in Chapter 1, *statutes of limitations* restrict the time within which an action may be brought. A typical statute of limitations provides that an action must be brought within a specified period of time after the cause of action accrues. Generally, a cause of action is held to accrue when some damage occurs. Sometimes, the running of the prescribed period is *tolled* (that is, suspended) until the party suffering an injury has discovered it or should have discovered it.

Many states have passed laws placing outer time limits on some claims so that the defendant will not be left vulnerable to lawsuits indefinitely. These **statutes of repose** may limit the time within which a plaintiff can file a product-liability suit. Typically, a statute of repose begins to run at an earlier date and runs for a longer time than a statute of limitations. For example, a statute of repose may require that claims must be brought within twelve years from the date of sale or manufacture of the defective product. It is immaterial that the product is defective or causes an injury if the injury occurs after this statutory period has lapsed. In addition, some of these legislative enactments have limited the application of the doctrine of strict liability to new goods.

---

16. *Lutz v. National Crane Corp.,* 884 P.2d 455 (Mont. 1994).

17. *Jamieson v. Woodward & Lothrop,* 247 F.2d 23 (D.C. 1957).

TERMS AND CONCEPTS TO REVIEW

bystander 110

market-share liability 114

privity of contract 111

product liability 110

product misuse 119

statute of repose 120

strict liability 110

unreasonably dangerous product 114

QUESTIONS AND CASE PROBLEMS

6–1. THEORIES OF LIABILITY. Chen buys a television set manufactured by Quality TV Appliance, Inc. She is going on vacation, so she takes the set to her mother's house for her mother to use. Because the set is defective, it explodes, causing her mother to be seriously injured. Chen's mother sues Quality to obtain compensation for her injury and for the damage to her house. Under what theory or theories discussed in this chapter might Chen's mother recover damages from Quality?

6–2. DEFENSES TO PRODUCT LIABILITY. A water pipe burst, flooding a company's switchboard and tripping the switchboard circuit breakers. Company employees assigned to reactivate the switchboard included an electrical technician with twelve years of on-the-job training, a licensed electrician, and an electrical engineer with twenty years of experience who had studied power engineering in college. The employees attempted to switch one of the circuit breakers back on without testing for short circuits, which they later admitted they knew how to do and should have done. The circuit breaker failed to engage but ignited an explosive fire. The company sued the supplier of the circuit breakers for damages, alleging that the supplier had failed to give adequate warnings and instructions regarding the circuit breakers. How might the supplier defend against this claim? Discuss.

6–3. LIABILITY IN TORT. Colt manufactures a new pistol. The firing of the pistol depends on an enclosed high-pressure device. The pistol has been thoroughly tested in two laboratories in the Midwest, and its design and manufacture are in accord with current technology. Wayne purchases one of the new pistols from Hardy's Gun and Rifle Emporium. When he uses the pistol in the high altitude of the Rockies, the difference in pressure causes the pistol to misfire, resulting in serious injury to Wayne. Colt can prove that all due care was used in the manufacturing process, and it refuses to pay for Wayne's injuries. Discuss Colt's liability in tort.

6–4. LIABILITY TO THIRD PARTIES. Baxter manufactures electric hair dryers. Julie purchases a Baxter dryer from her local Ace Drugstore. Cox, a friend and guest in Julie's home, has taken a shower and wants to dry her hair. Julie tells Cox to use the new Baxter hair dryer that she has just purchased. As Cox plugs in the dryer, sparks fly out from the motor, and sparks continue to fly as she operates it. Despite this, Cox begins drying her hair. Suddenly, the entire dryer ignites into flames, severely burning Cox's scalp. Cox sues Baxter on the basis of negligence and strict liability in tort. Baxter admits the dryer was defective but denies liability, particularly because Cox was not the person who purchased the dryer. In other words, Cox had no contractual relationship with Baxter. Discuss the validity of Baxter's defense. Are there any other defenses that Baxter might assert to avoid liability? Discuss fully.

6–5. STRICT LIABILITY. Gina is standing on a street corner waiting for a ride to work. Gomez has just purchased a new car manufactured by Optimal Motors. Gomez is driving down the street when suddenly the steering mechanism breaks, causing him to run over Gina. Gina suffers permanent injuries. Gomez's total income per year has never exceeded $15,000. Gina files suit against Optimal under the theory of strict liability in tort. Optimal claims that it is not liable because (1) due care was used in the manufacture of the car, (2) Optimal is not the manufacturer of the steering mechanism (Smith is), and (3) strict product liability applies only to users or consumers, and Gina is neither. Discuss the validity of the defenses claimed by Optimal.

6–6. NEGLIGENCE. A two-year-old child lost his leg when he became entangled in a grain auger on his grandfather's farm. The auger had a safety guard that prevented any item larger than 4⅝ inches from coming into contact with the machine's moving parts. The child's foot was smaller than the openings in the safety guard. Was such an injury reasonably foreseeable? Discuss. [*Richelman v. Kewanee Machinery & Conveyor Co.*, 59 Ill.App.3d 578, 375 N.E.2d 885, 16 Ill.Dec. 778 (1978)]

6–7. DEFENSES TO PRODUCT LIABILITY. The Campbell Soup Co. manufactured, sold, and shipped packages of chicken-flavored Campbell's Ramen Noodle Soup to a distributor. The distributor sold and shipped the packages to Associated Grocers. Associated Grocers shipped the packages to Warehouse Foods, a retail grocer. Six weeks after Campbell first shipped the soup to the distributor, Warehouse Foods sold a package of the soup to Kathy Jo Gates. Gates prepared the soup. Halfway through eating her second bowl, she discovered beetle larvae in the noodles. She filed a product-liability suit against Campbell and others. Gates argued, in effect, that the mere presence of the bugs in the soup was sufficient to hold Campbell strictly liable. How might Campbell defend itself? [*Campbell Soup Co. v. Gates*, 319 Ark. 54, 889 S.W.2d 750 (1994)]

6–8. FAILURE TO WARN. When Mary Bresnahan drove her Chrysler LeBaron, she sat very close to the steering wheel—less than a foot away from the steering-wheel enclosure of the driver's-side air bag. At the time, Chrysler did not provide any warning that a driver should not sit close to the air bag. In an accident with another car, Bresnahan's air bag deployed. The bag caused her elbow to strike the windshield pillar and fracture in three places, resulting in repeated surgery and physical therapy. Bresnahan filed a suit in a California state court against Chrysler to recover for her injuries, alleging in part that they were caused by Chrysler's failure to warn consumers about sitting near the air bag. At the trial, an expert testified that the air bag was not intended to prevent arm injuries, which were "a predictable, incidental consequence" of the bag's deploying. Should Chrysler pay for Bresnahan's injuries? Why or why not? [*Bresnahan v. Chrysler Corp.*, 76 Cal.Rptr.2d 804, 65 Cal.App.4th 1149 (1998)]

6–9. PRODUCT LIABILITY. New England Ecological Development, Inc. (NEED), a recycling station in Rhode Island, needed a conveyor belt system and gave the specifications to Colmar Belting Co. Colmar did not design or make belts but distributed the component parts. For this system, Emerson Power Transmission Corp. (EPT) manufactured the wing pulley, a component of the nip point (the point at which a belt moves over the stationary part of the system). Kenneth Butler, a welder, assembled the system with assistance from Colmar. Neither Colmar nor EPT recommended the use of a protective shield to guard the nip point, and as finally built, NEED's system did not have a shield. Later,

as Americo Buonanno, a NEED employee, was clearing debris from the belt, his arm was pulled into the nip point. The arm was severely crushed and later amputated at the elbow. Buonanno filed a suit in a Rhode Island state court against Colmar and EPT, alleging in part strict liability. The defendants filed a motion for summary judgment, arguing that as sellers of component parts, they had no duty to ensure the proper design of the final product. On what grounds might the court deny the motion? [*Buonanno v. Colmar Belting Co.*, 733 A.2d 712 (R.I. 1999)]

6–10. IN YOUR COURT

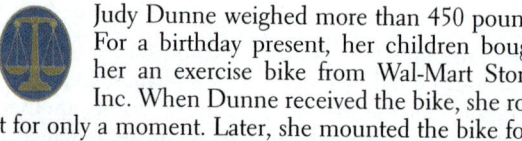

Judy Dunne weighed more than 450 pounds. For a birthday present, her children bought her an exercise bike from Wal-Mart Stores, Inc. When Dunne received the bike, she rode it for only a moment. Later, she mounted the bike for a second time and pedaled for three or four rotations. The bike then collapsed, and Dunne fell off, sustaining numerous injuries. The bike was designed for use by people who weigh under 250 pounds (which is 99 percent of the population) and had been tested up to 440 pounds. The manufacturer did not specify any weight limit in marketing the bike, however, and there was no way that Dunne could have known of this weight limit. Assume that you are the judge in this case and answer the following questions:

(a) Was it reasonably foreseeable that a person who weighed over 450 pounds would use the exercise bike?

(b) Why is the question of foreseeability relevant to this case?

(c) Was the bike "unreasonably dangerous" because an adequate warning was not provided?

(d) Suppose that Wal-Mart argues that the risk of the bike collapsing under a weight of more than 450 pounds was "open and obvious." Would you allow Wal-Mart to avoid liability based on this defense?

LAW ON THE WEB

For updated links to resources available on the Web, as well as a variety of other materials, visit this text's Web site at http://wbl.westbuslaw.com.

For information on the *Restatements of the Law*, including the *Restatement (Second) of Torts* and the *Restatement (Third) of Torts: Products Liability*, go to the Web site of the American Law Institute at

http://www.ali.org

The law firm of Horvitz & Levy offers a review of recent judicial decisions in the area of product liability at

http://www.horvitzlevy.com/yirtoc4b.html

For information on product-liability suits against tobacco companies and recent settlements, go to

http://www.usatoday.com/news/smoke/smoke00.htm

A discussion of the "demise of privity" with respect to product liability in leading cases decided by the New York Court of Appeals can be found at the following Web page within the site offered by the *New York Law Journal*:

http://www.nylj.com/links/150sterk.html

Law Journal EXTRA! has articles on current cases and issues in the area of product liability, as well as proposed legislation, at

www.ljx.com/practice/productliability/index.html

LEGAL RESEARCH EXERCISES ON THE WEB

Go to http://wbl.westbuslaw.com, the Web site that accompanies this text. Select "Internet Applications," and then click on "Chapter 6." There you will find the following Internet research exercise that you can perform to learn more about product-liability litigation.

Activity 6–1: Product-Liability Litigation

CHAPTER 7

Intellectual Property

MOST PEOPLE THINK OF WEALTH in terms of houses, land, cars, stocks, and bonds. Wealth, however, also includes **intellectual property,** which consists of the products that result from intellectual, creative processes. Although it is an abstract term for an abstract concept, intellectual property is nonetheless wholly familiar to virtually everyone. *Trademarks, service marks, copyrights,* and *patents* are all forms of intellectual property. The book you are reading is copyrighted. Undoubtedly, the personal computer you use at home is trademarked. Exhibit 7–1 offers a comprehensive summary of these forms of intellectual property, as well as intellectual property that consists of *trade secrets.* In this chapter, we examine each of these forms in some detail.

The study of intellectual property law is important because intellectual property has taken on increasing significance, not only within the United States but globally as well. Today, ownership rights in intangible intellectual property are more important to the prosperity of many U.S. companies than are their tangible assets. A major challenge to businesspersons today is how to protect these valuable rights in the online world—a topic we treat at some length in Chapter 9. (See also the *Emerging Trends in Technology* feature later in this chapter, which discusses the problem of copyright protection in a digital age.)

The need to protect creative works was voiced by the framers of the U.S. Constitution over two hundred years ago: Article I, Section 8, of the U.S. Constitution authorized Congress "[t]o promote the Progress of Science and useful Arts, by securing for limited Times to Authors and Inventors the exclusive Right to their respective Writings and Discoveries." Laws protecting patents, trademarks, and copyrights are explicitly designed to protect and reward inventive and artistic creativity. Although intellectual property law limits the economic freedom of some individuals, it does so to protect the freedom of others to enjoy the fruits of their labors—in the form of profits.

SECTION 1

Trademarks and Related Property

A **trademark** is a distinctive mark, motto, device, or implement that a manufacturer stamps, prints, or otherwise affixes to the goods it produces so that they may be identified on the market and their origin vouched for. At common law, the person who used a symbol or mark to identify a business or product was protected in the use of that trademark. Clearly, if one used the trademark of another, it would lead consumers to believe that one's goods were made by the

EXHIBIT 7–1   FORMS OF INTELLECTUAL PROPERTY

	PATENT	COPYRIGHT	TRADEMARKS (SERVICE MARKS AND TRADE DRESS)	TRADE SECRETS
Definition	A grant from the government that gives an inventor exclusive rights to an invention.	An intangible property right granted to authors and originators of a literary work or artistic production that falls within specified categories.	Any distinctive word, name, symbol, or device (image or appearance), or combination thereof, that an entity uses to identify and distinguish its goods or services from those of others.	Any information (including formulas, patterns, programs, devices, techniques, and processes) that a business possesses and that gives the business an advantage over competitors who do not know the information or processes.
Requirements	An invention must be: 1. Novel. 2. Not obvious. 3. Useful.	Literary or artistic works must be: 1. Original. 2. Fixed in a durable medium that can be perceived, reproduced, or communicated. 3. Within a copyrightable category.	Trademarks, service marks, and trade dresses must be sufficiently distinctive (or must have acquired a secondary meaning) to enable consumers and others to distinguish the manufacturer's, seller's, or business user's products or services from those of competitors.	Information and processes that have commercial value, that are not known or easily ascertainable by the general public or others, and that are reasonably protected from disclosure.
Types or Categories	1. Utility (general). 2. Design. 3. Plant (flowers, vegetables, and so on).	1. Literary works (including computer programs). 2. Musical works. 3. Dramatic works. 4. Pantomime and choreographic works. 5. Pictorial, graphic, and sculptural works. 6. Films and audiovisual works. 7. Sound recordings.	1. Strong, distinctive marks (such as fanciful, arbitrary, or suggestive marks). 2. Marks that have acquired a secondary meaning by use. 3. Other types of marks, including certification marks and collective marks. 4. Trade dress (such as a distinctive decor, menu, or style or type of service).	1. Customer lists. 2. Research and development. 3. Plans and programs. 4. Pricing information. 5. Production techniques. 6. Marketing techniques. 7. Formulas. 8. Compilations.
How Acquired	By filing a patent application with the U.S. Patent and Trademark Office and receiving that	Automatic (once in tangible form); to recover for infringement, the copyright must be	1. At common law, ownership is created by use of mark. 2. Registration (either with the U.S. Patent and Trademark Office or with the	Through the originality and development of information and processes that are

EXHIBIT 7–1   FORMS OF INTELLECTUAL PROPERTY (CONTINUED)

	PATENT	COPYRIGHT	TRADEMARKS (SERVICE MARKS AND TRADE DRESS)	TRADE SECRETS
How Acquired (continued)	office's approval.	registered with the U.S. Copyright Office.	appropriate state office) gives constructive notice of date of use. 3. Federal registration is permitted if the mark is currently in use *or* if the applicant intends use within six months (period can be extended to three years). 4. Federal registration can be renewed between the fifth and sixth years and, thereafter, every ten years.	unique to a business, that are unknown by others, and that would be valuable to competitors if they knew of the information and processes.
Rights	An inventor has the right to make, use, sell, assign, or license the invention during the duration of the patent's term. The first to invent has patent rights.	The author or originator has the exclusive right to reproduce, distribute, display, license, or transfer a copyrighted work.	The owner has the right to use the mark or trade dress and to exclude others from using it. The right of use can be licensed or sold (assigned) to another.	The owner has the right to sole and exclusive use of the trade secrets and the right to use legal means to protect against misappropriation of the trade secrets by others. The owner can license or assign a trade secret.
Duration	Twenty years from the date of application; for design patents, fourteen years.	1. For authors: the life of the author, plus 70 years. 2. For publishers: 95 years after the date of publication or 120 years after creation.	Unlimited, as long as it is in use. To continue notice by registration, the registration must be renewed by filing.	Unlimited, as long as not revealed to others.
Civil Remedies for Infringement	Monetary damages, which include reasonable royalties and lost profits, *plus* attorneys' fees. (Treble damages are available for intentional infringement.)	Actual damages, plus profits received by the infringer; *or* statutory damages of not less than $500 and not more than $20,000 ($100,000, if infringement is willful); *plus* costs and attorneys' fees.	1. Injunction prohibiting future use of mark. 2. Actual damages, plus profits received by the infringer (can be increased to three times the actual damages under the Lanham Act). 3. Impoundment and destruction of infringing articles. 4. *Plus* costs and attorneys' fees.	Monetary damages for misappropriation (the Uniform Trade Secrets Act permits punitive damages up to twice the amount of actual damages for willful and malicious misappropriation); *plus* costs and attorneys' fees.

other. The law seeks to avoid this kind of confusion. We examine in this section various aspects of the law governing trademarks.

In the following famous case concerning Coca-Cola, the defendants argued that the Coca-Cola trademark was entitled to no protection under the law, because the term did not accurately represent the product.

CASE 7.1 — The Coca-Cola Co. v. The Koke Co. of America

Supreme Court of the
United States, 1920.
254 U.S. 143,
41 S.Ct. 113,
65 L.Ed. 189.
http://www.findlaw.com/
casecode/supreme.
html[a]

COMPANY PROFILE *John Pemberton, an Atlanta pharmacist, invented a caramel-colored, carbonated soft drink in 1886. His bookkeeper, Frank Robinson, named the beverage Coca-Cola after two of the ingredients, coca leaves and kola nuts. Asa Candler bought the Coca-Cola Company (http://www.cocacolacompany.com) in 1891, and within seven years, he made the soft drink available in all of the United States, as well as in parts of Canada and Mexico. Candler continued to sell Coke aggressively and to open up new markets, reaching Europe before 1910. In doing so, however, he attracted numerous competitors, some of whom tried to capitalize directly on the Coke name.*

BACKGROUND AND FACTS *The Coca-Cola Company sought to enjoin (prevent) the Koke Company of America and other beverage companies from, among other things, using the word Koke for their products. The Koke Company of America and other beverage companies contended that the Coca-Cola trademark was a fraudulent representation and that Coca-Cola was therefore not entitled to any help from the courts. The Koke Company and the other defendants alleged that the Coca-Cola Company, by its use of the Coca-Cola name, represented that the beverage contained cocaine (from coca leaves), which it no longer did. The trial court granted the injunction against the Koke Company, but the appellate court reversed the lower court's ruling. Coca-Cola then appealed to the United States Supreme Court.*

IN THE LANGUAGE OF THE COURT

Mr. Justice *HOLMES* delivered the opinion of the Court.
 ＊　＊　＊　＊

 ＊　＊　＊ Before 1900 the beginning of [Coca-Cola's] good will was more or less helped by the presence of cocaine, a drug that, like alcohol or caffeine or opium, may be described as a deadly poison or as a valuable item of the pharmacopoeia according to the rhetorical purposes in view. The amount seems to have been very small,[b] but it may have been enough to begin a bad habit and after the Food and Drug Act of June 30, 1906, if not earlier, long before this suit was brought, it was eliminated from the plaintiff's compound. ＊　＊　＊

 ＊　＊　＊ Since 1900 the sales have increased at a very great rate corresponding to a like increase in advertising. The name now characterizes a beverage to be had at almost any soda fountain. It means a single thing coming from a single source, and well known to the community. It hardly would be too much to say that the drink characterizes the name as much as the name the drink. In other words Coca-Cola probably means to most persons the plaintiff's familiar product to be had everywhere rather than a compound of particular substances. ＊　＊　＊ [B]efore this suit was brought the plaintiff had advertised to the public that it must not expect and would not find cocaine, and had eliminated everything tending to suggest cocaine effects except the name and the picture of [coca] leaves and nuts, which probably conveyed little or nothing to most who saw it. It appears to us that it would be going too far to deny the plaintiff relief against a palpable fraud

---

a. In the "Citation Search" section, enter "254" in the left box and "143" in the right box, and click "Get It" to access the opinion.

b. In reality, until 1903 the amount of active cocaine in each bottle of Coke was equivalent to one "line" of cocaine.

because possibly here and there an ignorant person might call for the drink with the hope for incipient cocaine intoxication. The plaintiff's position must be judged by the facts as they were when the suit was begun, not by the facts of a different condition and an earlier time.

DECISION AND REMEDY   *The district court's injunction was allowed to stand. The competing beverage companies were enjoined from calling their products* Koke.

STATUTORY PROTECTION OF TRADEMARKS

Statutory protection of trademarks and related property is provided at the federal level by the Lanham Trade-Mark Act of 1946.[1] The Lanham Act was enacted in part to protect manufacturers from losing business to rival companies that used confusingly similar trademarks. The Lanham Act incorporates the common law of trademarks and provides remedies for owners of trademarks who wish to enforce their claims in federal court. Many states also have trademark statutes.

In 1995, Congress amended the Lanham Act by passing the Federal Trademark Dilution Act,[2] which extended the protection available to trademark owners by creating a federal cause of action for trademark **dilution.** Until the passage of this amendment, federal trademark law only prohibited the unauthorized use of the same mark on competing—or on noncompeting but "related"—goods or services when such use would likely confuse consumers as to the origin of those goods and services. Trademark dilution laws, which have also been enacted by about half of the states, protect "distinctive" or "famous" trademarks (such as Jergens, McDonald's, RCA, and Macintosh) from certain unauthorized uses of the marks *regardless* of a showing of competition or a likelihood of confusion.

In one of the first cases to be decided under the 1995 act's provisions, a federal court held that a famous mark may be diluted not only by the use of an *identical* mark but also by the use of a *similar* mark. The lawsuit was brought by Ringling Bros.–Barnum & Bailey, Combined Shows, Inc., against the state of Utah. Ringling Bros. claimed that Utah's use of the slogan "The Greatest Snow on Earth"—to attract visitors to the state's recreational and scenic resorts—diluted the dis-

tinctiveness of the circus's famous trademark, "The Greatest Show on Earth." Utah moved to dismiss the suit, arguing that the 1995 provisions only protect owners of famous trademarks against the unauthorized use of identical marks. The court disagreed and refused to grant Utah's motion to dismiss the case.[3]

TRADEMARK REGISTRATION

Trademarks may be registered with the state or with the federal government. To register for protection under federal trademark law, a person must file an application with the U.S. Patent and Trademark Office in Washington, D.C. Under current law, a mark can be registered (1) if it is currently in commerce or (2) if the applicant intends to put it into commerce within six months.

Under extenuating circumstances, the six-month period can be extended by thirty months, giving the applicant a total of three years from the date of notice of trademark approval to make use of the mark and file the required use statement. Registration is postponed until the mark is actually used. Nonetheless, during this waiting period, any applicant can legally protect his or her trademark against a third party who previously has neither used the mark nor filed an application for it. Registration is renewable between the fifth and sixth years after the initial registration and every ten years thereafter (every twenty years for those trademarks registered before 1990).

Registration of a trademark with the U.S. Patent and Trademark Office gives notice on a nationwide basis that the trademark belongs exclusively to the registrant. The registrant is also allowed to use the symbol ® to indicate that the mark has been registered. Whenever that trademark is copied to a substantial degree or used in its entirety by another, intentionally or

---

1. 15 U.S.C. Sections 1051–1127.
2. 15 U.S.C. Section 1125.

3. *Ringling Bros.–Barnum & Bailey, Combined Shows, Inc. v. Utah Division of Travel Development,* 935 F.Supp. 736 (E.D.Va. 1996).

unintentionally, the trademark has been *infringed* (used without authorization). When a trademark has been infringed, the owner of the mark has a cause of action against the infringer. A person need not have registered a trademark in order to sue for trademark infringement, but registration does furnish proof of the date of inception of the trademark's use.

DISTINCTIVENESS OF MARK

A central objective of the Lanham Act is to reduce the likelihood that consumers will be confused by similar marks. For that reason, only those trademarks that are deemed sufficiently distinctive from all competing trademarks will be protected. A trademark must be sufficiently distinct to enable consumers to identify the manufacturer of the goods easily and to distinguish between those goods and competing products.

Strong Marks. Fanciful, arbitrary, or suggestive trademarks are generally considered to be the most distinctive (strongest) trademarks. This is because these types of marks are normally taken from outside the context of the particular product and thus provide the best means of distinguishing one product from another.

Fanciful trademarks include invented words, such as Xerox for one manufacturer's copiers and Kodak for another company's photographic products. Arbitrary trademarks include actual words used with products that have no literal connection to the words, such as English Leather used as a name for an after-shave lotion (and not for leather processed in England). Suggestive trademarks are those that suggest something about a product without describing the product directly. For example, the trademark Dairy Queen suggests an association between the products and milk, but it does not directly describe ice cream.

Secondary Meaning. Descriptive terms, geographic terms, and personal names are not inherently distinctive and do not receive protection under the law until they acquire a secondary meaning. A secondary meaning may arise when customers begin to associate a specific term or phrase (such as London Fog) with specific trademarked items (coats with London Fog labels). Whether a secondary meaning becomes attached to a term or name usually depends on how extensively the product is advertised, the market for the product, the number of sales, and other factors. Once a secondary meaning is attached to a term or name, a trademark is considered distinctive and is protected. Even a shade of color can qualify for trademark protection, once customers associate the color with the product.[4]

Generic Terms. Generic terms, such as *bicycle* and *computer*, receive no protection, even if they acquire secondary meanings. A particularly thorny problem arises when a trademark acquires generic use. For example, *aspirin* and *thermos* were originally the names of trademarked products, but today the words are used generically. Other examples are *escalator, trampoline, raisin bran, dry ice, lanolin, linoleum, nylon,* and *corn flakes*. Even so, the courts will not allow another firm to use those marks in such a way as to deceive a potential consumer. In the following case, the issue before the court was whether the phrase "You Have Mail" is a generic term.

---

4. *Qualitex Co. v. Jacobson Products Co.*, 514 U.S. 159, 115 S.Ct. 1300, 131 L.Ed.2d 248 (1995).

CASE 7.2   America Online, Inc. v. AT&T Corp.

United States
District Court,
Eastern District of
Virginia, 1999.
64 F.Supp.2d 549.
**http://zeus.bna.com/
e-law/cases/aolatt.html**[a]

BACKGROUND AND FACTS   *In the late 1960s and early 1970s, AT&T Corporation developed UNIX, a computer operating system facilitating communications over the Internet. When a user connects to UNIX, if the user has e-mail, the system displays a phrase something like "You Have Mail." In the 1980s, America Online, Inc. (AOL), the world's largest Internet service provider, started using "YOU HAVE MAIL" in its e-mail notification service for its members. AT&T provides Internet access to subscribers through its WorldNet Service. Since 1998, when a member visits the WorldNet home page, a "You Have Mail!" notification window pops up. AOL filed a suit in a federal district court against*

---

a. This is a page in the library of documents at the "Electronic Commerce & Law Report" Web site maintained by the Bureau of National Affairs, Inc.

AT&T, alleging in part trademark infringement of the phrase "YOU HAVE MAIL," which AOL claimed to own. AT&T filed a motion for summary judgment, asking the court to rule that the term was generic.

**IN THE LANGUAGE
OF THE COURT**

HILTON, J. [Judge]

*   *   *   *

*   *   * [A] plaintiff who is seeking to establish a valid trademark must show that the primary significance of the term in the minds of the consuming public is not the product but the producer. *   *   * [T]he following evidence [may] be used to determine the primary significance of a mark: (1) competitors' use of the mark, (2) plaintiff's use of the mark, (3) dictionary definitions, (4) media usage, (5) testimony of persons in the trade, and (6) consumer surveys.

*   *   *   *

*   *   * Under the primary significance test, the "mail" component of YOU HAVE MAIL means "e-mail."

First, the Court notes that even AOL uses the words "mail" and "e-mail" interchangeably. For example, in its *   *   * complaint AOL repeatedly uses the word "mail" as referring to "e-mail." *   *   *

Next, it is undisputed that numerous competitors of AOL use "mail" as a synonym for "e-mail." *   *   *

Regarding media usage and testimony of persons involved in the trade, [there are] numerous examples of the books printed to describe the e-mail notification features used by both UNIX and AOL. All of the authors, without fail, use "mail" and "e-mail" interchangeably. *   *   *

Last, the Court would note that *   *   * consumer surveys [are used] as a means of determining whether the primary significance of a mark is generic. However, when determining whether a mark is generic, the Court is not to consider whether the mark has acquired any secondary meaning, because generic marks with secondary meaning are still not entitled to protection. *   *   *

*   *   *   *

The primary significance of the phrase YOU HAVE MAIL indicates to the public-at-large what the service is, not where it came from. *   *   * Further, this holding does not rest on considering solely the "mail" component of the phrase YOU HAVE MAIL. *   *   * The "you" and the "have" of YOU HAVE MAIL (either separately or together) do not carry with them any especial significance which would change the primary significance of the mark as previously stated. Since the "you," "have," and "mail" of YOU HAVE MAIL are all used for their everyday, common meaning, the phrase as a whole is generic *   *   * .

**DECISION
AND REMEDY**

The court granted a summary judgment in favor of AT&T. The court ruled that "You have mail" is a generic expression and therefore cannot be owned by AOL.

TRADE DRESS

The term **trade dress** refers to the image and overall appearance of a product—for example, the distinctive decor, menu, layout, and style of service of a particular restaurant. Basically, trade dress is subject to the same protection as trademarks. In cases involving trade dress infringement, as in trademark infringement cases, a major consideration is whether con-

sumers are likely to be confused by the allegedly infringing use.

SERVICE, CERTIFICATION, AND COLLECTIVE MARKS

A **service mark** is similar to a trademark but is used to distinguish the services of one person or company from those of another. For example, each airline has a particular mark or symbol associated with its name. Titles and character names used in radio and television are frequently registered as service marks.

Other marks protected by law include certification marks and collective marks. A **certification mark** is used by one or more persons other than the owner to certify the region, materials, mode of manufacture, quality, or accuracy of the owner's goods or services. When used by members of a cooperative, association, or other organization, it is referred to as a **collective mark.** Examples of certification marks are the phrases "Good Housekeeping Seal of Approval" and "UL Tested." Collective marks appear at the ends of motion picture credits to indicate the various associations and organizations that participated in the making of the film. The union marks found on the tags of certain products are also collective marks.

TRADE NAMES

Trademarks apply to *products.* The term **trade name** is used to indicate part or all of a business's name, whether the business is a sole proprietorship, a partnership, or a corporation. Generally, a trade name is directly related to a business and its goodwill. A trade name may be protected as a trademark if the trade name is the same as the name of the company's trademarked product—for example, Coca-Cola. Unless also used as a trademark or service mark, a trade name cannot be registered with the federal government. Trade names are protected under the common law, however. As with trademarks, words must be unusual or fancifully used if they are to be protected as trade names. The word *Safeway,* for example, was held by the courts to be sufficiently fanciful to obtain protection as a trade name for a foodstore chain.[5]

SECTION 2

Patents

A **patent** is a grant from the government that gives an inventor the exclusive right to make, use, and sell an invention for a period of twenty years from the date of filing the application for a patent. Patents for a fourteen-year period are given for designs, as opposed

to inventions. For either a regular patent or a design patent, the applicant must demonstrate to the satisfaction of the U.S. Patent and Trademark Office that the invention, discovery, process, or design is genuine, novel, useful, and not obvious in light of current technology. A patent holder gives notice to all that an article or design is patented by placing on it the word *Patent* or *Pat.* plus the patent number. In contrast to patent law in other countries, in the United States patent protection is given to the first person to invent a product or process, even though someone else may have been the first to file for a patent on that product or process.

PATENT INFRINGEMENT

If a firm makes, uses, or sells another's patented design, product, or process without the patent owner's permission, the tort of patent infringement occurs. Patent infringement may arise even though the patent owner has not put the patented product in commerce. Patent infringement may also occur even though not all features or parts of an invention are copied. (With respect to a patented process, however, all steps or their equivalents must be copied in order for infringement to occur.)

Often, litigation for patent infringement is so costly that the patent holder will instead offer to sell to the infringer a license to use the patented design, product, or process (licensing will be discussed in Chapter 9). Indeed, in many cases, the costs of detection, prosecution, and monitoring are so high that patents are valueless to their owners, because the owners cannot afford to protect them.

In the past, parties involved in patent litigation also faced another problem: it was often hard to predict the outcome of litigation because jurors found it difficult to understand the issues in dispute. This was particularly true when the claims involved patents on complicated products—such as sophisticated technological or biotechnological products. In a significant case decided in 1996, *Markman v. Westview Instruments, Inc.,*[6] the United States Supreme Court held that it is the responsibility of judges, not juries, to interpret the scope and nature of patent claims. In other words, before a case goes to the jury, the judge must interpret the nature of the claim and give the jury instructions based on that interpretation.

---

5. *Safeway Stores v. Suburban Foods,* 130 F.Supp. 249 (E.D.Va. 1955).

6. 517 U.S. 370, 116 S.Ct. 1384, 134 L.Ed.2d 577 (1996).

EMERGING TRENDS IN TECHNOLOGY

Copyright Protection in a Digital Age

Most intellectual property does not sell for the cost of production plus a normal profit. Rather, intellectual property is sold at a price that reflects heavy research costs for ingenious ideas. Any property that involves high development costs and low production costs is vulnerable to "piracy"—the unauthorized copying and use of the property.

In the past, copying intellectual products was time consuming, and the pirated copies were worse than the originals. In today's online world, however, things have changed. Millions of unauthorized copies can now be reproduced simply by clicking a mouse, and pirated duplicates of copyrighted works obtained via the Internet are exactly the same as the originals—after all, they are digitized.

HOW BIG IS THE PROBLEM?

The Business Software Alliance estimates that half of the global market for software is supplied today by pirated products. The International Federation of the phonographic industry believes that 20 percent of recorded music is pirated. Much of the piracy of intellectual property, especially software and music, is deemed "altruistic." People illegally give intellectual property away not to make any money but because they want to be generous. There is also a problem with respect to copyright law, which makes a distinction between reproduction for public use (which requires the copyright holder's permission) and reproduction for private use (which, within limits, does not require such permission). The difficulty here is distinguishing between private and public use.

Additionally, current copyright law is based on national boundaries. The Internet, however, knows no such limits. Despite attempts to increase protection for intellectual property on a global level (see Chapter 9), countries vary widely in their implementation and enforcement of international agreements.

IS THERE ANY SOLUTION TO THE PROBLEM?

Is there any current solution to the increasing problem of the piracy of intellectual property via the Internet? The simple answer is no. Efforts to find partial solutions are being made, nonetheless. One such attempt is to develop pirate-proof ways of transmitting materials. For example, IBM has developed so-called secure "packaging" for sending digital information over the Internet.

New technologies are also simplifying the task of searching online databases for pirated copies of copyrighted materials. Providers of online "business intelligence," such as Cyveillance, Ewatch, and Cybercheck, help companies detect and combat infringing uses of their software, text, music, or other copyrighted works. These "digital detectives" use special search tools, called "spiders" or "robots," to monitor the Web for sites containing copyrighted works, such as music files.

Once an infringing use is detected, the copyright owner has several options. The owner can send a cease-and-desist (warning) letter to the infringer, take the infringer to court, or issue a license to the infringer. Often, the last option is preferred, simply because the other two may be impractical. For one thing, efforts to shut down infringing Web sites have had limited success. In part, this is because of the ease with which a "mirror" site can be created—at a

PATENTS FOR SOFTWARE

At one time, it was difficult for developers and manufacturers of software to obtain patent protection because many software products simply automate procedures that can be performed manually. In other words, the computer programs do not meet the "novel" and "not obvious" requirements previously mentioned. Also, the basis for software is often a mathematical equation or formula, which is not patentable. In 1981, however, the United States Supreme Court held that it is possible to obtain a patent for a process that incorporates a computer program—providing, of course, that the process itself is

EMERGING TRENDS IN TECHNOLOGY

Copyright Protection in a Digital Age,

continued

new location. Initiating a lawsuit against a Web site or user may also be difficult because of jurisdictional problems (see Chapter 9).

GOVERNMENT EFFORTS TO PROTECT COPYRIGHT HOLDERS

The government has also taken action to protect copyright holders. In 1997, Congress passed the No Electronic Theft (NET) Act, which extended criminal liability for the piracy of copyrighted materials to a broader group. Prior to the act, criminal penalties could be imposed only if unauthorized copies were exchanged for financial gain. To combat "altruistic" piracy, the NET imposes criminal penalties on persons who exchange unauthorized copies of copyrighted works, such as software, even though they realize no profit from the exchange. The act also imposes penalties on

those who make unauthorized electronic copies of books, magazines, movies, or music for *personal* use, thus altering the traditional "fair use" doctrine. The criminal penalties for violating the act are steep; they include fines as high as $250,000 and incarceration for up to five years.

More recently, in 1998, Congress passed the Digital Millennium Copyright Act, which allows civil and criminal penalties to be imposed on persons who circumvent encryption software or other technological antipiracy protection. Global efforts are also under way to protect intellectual property, including copyrights. Some of these efforts are mentioned elsewhere in this chapter. (See also Chapter 9, which treats this topic in greater detail.)

IMPLICATIONS FOR THE BUSINESSPERSON

1. Anybody who has ownership rights in intellectual property should be aware that it is increasingly possible for the property to be pirated via the Internet.
2. Businesspersons must weigh potential benefits against potential costs when deciding how many resources can be devoted to

combating the online piracy of their copyrighted works.

FOR CRITICAL ANALYSIS

1. Can the distribution of copyrighted materials via the Internet ever be effectively regulated by copyright laws? Should it?
2. What argument would you present to convince somebody that stealing intellectual property is no different from stealing tangible property?

RELEVANT WEB SITES

For information on the types of services offered by Cyveillance, go to the company's Web site at http://www.cyveillance.com. For articles containing recent facts and figures on software piracy, as well as a summary of applicable U.S. laws (including the No Electronic Theft Act), go to http://www.nopiracy.com.

---

patentable.[7] Subsequently, many patents have been issued for software-related inventions.

Another obstacle to obtaining patent protection for software is the procedure for obtaining patents. The process can be expensive and slow. The time element

is a particularly important consideration for someone wishing to obtain a patent on software. In light of the rapid changes and improvements in computer technology, the delay could undercut the product's success in the marketplace.

Despite these difficulties, patent protection is used in the computer industry. If a patent is infringed, the patent holder may sue for an injunction, damages,

---

7. *Diamond v. Diehr*, 450 U.S. 175, 101 S.Ct. 1048, 67 L.Ed.2d 155 (1981).

and the destruction of all infringing copies, as well as attorneys' fees and court costs.

Section 3

Copyrights

A **copyright** is an intangible property right granted by federal statute to the author or originator of a literary or artistic production of a specified type. Currently, copyrights are governed by the Copyright Act of 1976,[8] as amended. Works created after January 1, 1978, are automatically given statutory copyright protection for the life of the author plus 70 years. For copyrights owned by publishing houses, the copyright expires 95 years from the date of publication or 120 years from the date of creation, whichever is first. For works by more than one author, the copyright expires 70 years after the death of the last surviving author.

Copyrights can be registered with the U.S. Copyright Office in Washington, D.C. A copyright owner no longer needs to place the symbol © or the term *Copr.* or *Copyright* on the work, however, to have the work protected against infringement. Chances are that if somebody created it, somebody owns it.

A major problem facing today's businesspersons is how to protect copyrighted materials, including software, in cyberspace. See this chapter's *Emerging Trends in Technology* feature on pages 132–133 for a discussion of this issue.

What Is Protected Expression?

Works that are copyrightable include books, records, films, artworks, architectural plans, menus, music videos, product packaging, and computer software. To obtain protection under the Copyright Act, a work must be original and fall into one of the following categories: (1) literary works; (2) musical works; (3) dramatic works; (4) pantomimes and choreographic works; (5) pictorial, graphic, and sculptural works; (6) films and other audiovisual works; and (7) sound recordings. To be protected, a work must be "fixed in a durable medium" from which it can be perceived, reproduced, or communicated. Protection is automatic. Registration is not required.

Section 102 of the Copyright Act specifically excludes copyright protection for any "idea, procedure, process, system, method of operation, concept, principle, or discovery, regardless of the form in which it is described, explained, illustrated, or embodied." Note that it is not possible to copyright an *idea*. The underlying ideas embodied in a work may be freely used by others. What is copyrightable is the particular way in which an idea is expressed. Whenever an idea and an expression are inseparable, the expression cannot be copyrighted. Generally, anything that is not an original expression will not qualify for copyright protection. Facts widely known to the public are not copyrightable. Page numbers are not copyrightable, because they follow a sequence known to everyone. Mathematical calculations are not copyrightable.

Compilations of facts, however, are copyrightable. Section 103 of the Copyright Act defines a compilation as "a work formed by the collection and assembling of preexisting materials or data that are selected, coordinated, or arranged in such a way that the resulting work as a whole constitutes an original work of authorship." The key requirement in the copyrightability of a compilation is originality. Therefore, the White Pages of a telephone directory do not qualify for copyright protection when the information that makes up the directory (names, addresses, and telephone numbers) is not selected, coordinated, or arranged in an original way.[9] In one case, even the Yellow Pages of a telephone directory did not qualify for copyright protection.[10]

Copyright Infringement

Whenever the form or expression of an idea is copied, an infringement of copyright has occurred. The reproduction does not have to be exactly the same as the original, nor does it have to reproduce the original in its entirety. If a substantial part of the original is reproduced, there is copyright infringement.

Those who infringe copyrights may be liable for damages or criminal penalties. These range from actual damages or statutory damages, imposed at the court's discretion, to criminal proceedings for willful violations. Actual damages are based on the harm caused to the copyright holder by the infringement, while statutory damages, not to exceed $150,000, are provided for under the Copyright Act. Criminal proceedings may result in fines and/or imprisonment.

---

8. 17 U.S.C. Sections 101 *et seq.*

9. *Feist Publications, Inc. v. Rural Telephone Service Co.*, 499 U.S. 340, 111 S.Ct. 1282, 113 L.Ed.2d 358 (1991).

10. *Bellsouth Advertising & Publishing Corp. v. Donnelley Information Publishing, Inc.*, 999 F.2d 1436 (11th Cir. 1993).

An exception to liability for copyright infringement is made under the "fair use" doctrine. In certain circumstances, a person or organization can reproduce copyrighted material without paying royalties (fees paid to the copyright holder for the privilege of reproducing the copyrighted material). Section 107 of the Copyright Act provides as follows:

[T]he fair use of a copyrighted work, including such use by reproduction in copies or phonorecords or by any other means specified by [Section 106 of the Copyright Act], for purposes such as criticism, comment, news reporting, teaching (including multiple copies for classroom use), scholarship, or research, is not an infringement of copyright. In determining whether the use made of a work in any particular case is a fair use the factors to be considered shall include—

(1) the purpose and character of the use, including whether such use is of a commercial nature or is for nonprofit educational purposes;

(2) the nature of the copyrighted work;
(3) the amount and substantiality of the portion used in relation to the copyrighted work as a whole; and
(4) the effect of the use upon the potential market for or value of the copyrighted work.

Because these guidelines are very broad, the courts determine whether a particular use is fair on a case-by-case basis. Thus, anyone reproducing copyrighted material may still be subject to a violation. In determining whether a use is fair, courts have often considered the fourth factor to be the most important.

The following case indicates what must be proved to win a case involving charges of copyright infringement of a musical work.

CASE 7.3   Repp v. Webber

United States
Court of Appeals,
Second Circuit, 1997.
132 F.3d 882.
http://www.tourolaw.
edu/2ndCircuit/
December97[a]

HISTORICAL AND CULTURAL SETTING *Musical works fall within the category of works of authorship that can be protected by copyright. A protected musical work can consist of lyrics or music alone, or of both lyrics and music, as in a song. A musical work can exist in a number of different forms, including a tape, a compact disk, and sheet music. To determine whether a copyright of a musical work has been infringed, an expert might dissect the works into musical phrases and compare those phrases to other works by the same, or other, composers. Pitch and rhythm—the elements of a melody—might also be dissected and compared. Harmony—the chordal elements that support the melody—can also be an important element in comparing pop compositions.*

BACKGROUND AND FACTS *Over a period of thirty years, Ray Repp wrote and published more than 120 musical compositions, including the song "Till You," which was registered with the U.S. Copyright Office in 1978. Repp included "Till You" on his album "Benedicamus" and in two books of sheet music, and performed the song in over two hundred concerts. Andrew Lloyd Webber, the composer of such musicals as* Cats *and* Evita, *wrote the musical* Phantom of the Opera *in 1983 and 1984. Claiming that "Phantom Song," one of the songs in* Phantom of the Opera, *infringed on the copyright of "Till You," Repp and others filed a suit in a federal district court against Lloyd Webber and others. Lloyd Webber responded that he never heard of Repp or "Till You" and that "Phantom Song" was an "independent creation." Musical experts offered conflicting testimony about the similarity of the songs' melodies, harmonics, and phrases. Despite this conflict, the court stated that "the two songs do not share a striking similarity" and issued a summary judgment for Lloyd Webber. The court added that Repp failed to show "Phantom Song" was not created independently. Repp appealed to the U.S. Court of Appeals for the Second Circuit.*

---

a. This is the "Decisions for December 1997" page within the collection of opinions of the U.S. Court of Appeals for the Second Circuit. Scroll down the list of cases to the entry for the *Repp* case. Click on the case name to read the court's opinion.

IN THE LANGUAGE
OF THE COURT

MINER, Circuit Judge:
    *   *   *   *

    While there was little, if any, evidence demonstrating access, there was considerable evidence that "Phantom Song" is so strikingly similar to "Till You" as to preclude the possibility of independent creation and to allow access to be inferred without direct proof. *   *   * Two highly qualified experts *   *   * gave unequivocal opinions based on musicological analyses. *   *   *
    *   *   * The issue of "striking similarity," by virtue of the supported opinions of the experts *   *   * was shown to be a genuine issue of material fact. Access to the music of Repp being an essential element of his case, it cannot be said that there is an absence of evidence to support proof of that element through the inference generated by the striking similarity of the two pieces.
    *   *   *   *

    *   *   * The plaintiffs here have established a *prima facie* case of access through striking similarity *   *   * . Whether the evidence of independent creation here is sufficient to rebut the *prima facie* case established in this action is a question for the factfinder *   *   * . .

DECISION
AND REMEDY

The U.S. Court of Appeals reversed the decision of the lower court and remanded the case. Because the issues of "striking similarity" and "independent creation" were disputed, there was a genuine disagreement about the material facts and summary judgment was not appropriate.

COPYRIGHT
PROTECTION FOR SOFTWARE

In 1980, Congress passed the Computer Software Copyright Act, which amended the Copyright Act of 1976 to include computer programs in the list of creative works protected by federal copyright law. The 1980 statute, which classifies computer programs as "literary works," defines a computer program as a "set of statements or instructions to be used directly or indirectly in a computer in order to bring about a certain result."

Because of the unique nature of computer programs, the courts have had many difficulties in applying and interpreting the 1980 act. In a series of cases decided in the 1980s, the courts held that copyright protection extended not only to those parts of a computer program that can be read by humans, such as the "high-level" language of a source code, but also to the binary-language object code of a computer program, which is readable only by the computer.[11] Additionally, such elements as the overall structure,

sequence, and organization of a program were deemed copyrightable.[12]

By the early 1990s, the issue had evolved into whether the "look and feel"—the general appearance, command structure, video images, menus, windows, and other screen displays—of computer programs should also be protected by copyright. Although the courts have disagreed on this issue, the tendency has been not to extend copyright protection to look-and-feel aspects of computer programs. For example, in 1995 the Court of Appeals for the First Circuit held that Lotus Development Corporation's menu command hierarchy for its Lotus 1-2-3 spreadsheet was not protectable under the Copyright Act. The court deemed that the menu command hierarchy is a "method of operation," and Section 102 of the Copyright Act specifically excludes methods of operation from copyright protection.[13] The decision was affirmed by the United States Supreme Court in 1996.[14]

---

11. See *Stern Electronics, Inc. v. Kaufman*, 669 F.2d 852 (2d Cir. 1982); and *Apple Computer, Inc. v. Franklin Computer Corp.*, 714 F.2d 1240 (3d Cir. 1983).

12. *Whelan Associates, Inc. v. Jaslow Dental Laboratory, Inc.*, 797 F.2d 1222 (3d Cir. 1986).

13. *Lotus Development Corp. v. Borland International, Inc.*, 49 F.3d 807 (1st Cir. 1995).

14. *Lotus Development Corp. v. Borland International, Inc.*, 517 U.S. 843, 116 S.Ct. 804, 113 L.Ed.2d 610 (1996). This issue may again come before the Supreme Court for a decision, because only eight justices heard the case, and there was a tied vote; the effect of the tie was to affirm the lower court's decision.

SECTION 4

Trade Secrets

Some business processes and information that are not, or cannot be, patented, copyrighted, or trademarked are nevertheless protected against appropriation by competitors as trade secrets. **Trade secrets** consist of customer lists, plans, research and development, pricing information, marketing techniques, production techniques, and generally anything that makes an individual company unique and that would have value to a competitor.

Under Section 757 of the *Restatement of Torts*, "One who discloses or uses another's trade secret, without a privilege to do so, is liable to the other if (1) he discovered the secret by improper means, or (2) his disclosure or use constitutes a breach of confidence reposed in him by the other in disclosing the secret to him." The theft of confidential business data by industrial espionage, as when a business taps into a competitor's computer, is a theft of trade secrets without any contractual violation and is actionable in itself.

One of the problems faced by businesses is that they must share their trade secrets with some persons, particularly key employees. To protect themselves, firms generally have all employees who use the process or information agree in their contracts (in a confidentiality—or nondisclosure—clause) never to divulge it. Thus, if a salesperson tries to solicit the company's customers for noncompany business, or if an employee copies the employer's unique method of manufacture, he or she has appropriated a trade secret and has also broken a contract—two separate wrongs.

Until recently, virtually all law with respect to trade secrets was common law. In an effort to reduce the unpredictability of the common law in this area, a model act, the Uniform Trade Secrets Act, was presented to the states in 1979 for adoption. Parts of the act have been adopted in more than twenty states. Typically, a state that has adopted parts of the act has adopted only those parts that encompass its own existing common law. (In 1996, Congress passed the Economic Espionage Act, which made the theft of trade secrets a federal crime. We examine the provisions and significance of this act in Chapter 8.)

Does a trade secret lose its protection under the Uniform Trade Secrets Act when an employee commits it to memory rather than takes it in written form? That was the question in the following case.

CASE 7.4   # Ed Nowogroski Insurance, Inc. v. Rucker

Supreme Court of
Washington, 1999.
137 Wash.2d 427,
971 P.2d 936.

BACKGROUND AND FACTS   *Jerry Kiser, Darwin Rieck, and Michael Rucker worked for Ed Nowogroski Insurance, Inc., an insurance agency, as sales and service representatives. When friction developed between the agency and Kiser, Rieck, and Rucker, the three quit to go to work for Potter, Leonard and Cahan, Inc., a competing insurance firm. During their employment with Potter, the former Nowogroski employees used Nowogroski customer lists to attract business. Kiser and Rucker used written client information that they had copied from their ex-employer's files. Rieck worked chiefly from memory. The Nowogroski agency filed a suit in a Washington state court against its former employees and their new employer, alleging misappropriation of trade secrets. The court concluded that the client information fit the definition of a trade secret under the Uniform Trade Secrets Act and issued a judgment in the plaintiff's favor. The court decided, however, that only the written information was protected and did not award damages for the use of the memorized data. Nowogroski appealed to an intermediate state appellate court, which held that there is no distinction between written and memorized information and ordered a recalculation of the damages. The defendants appealed to the Washington Supreme Court.*

**IN THE LANGUAGE
OF THE COURT**

HILTON, J. [Judge]
*   *   *   *

The Uniform Trade Secrets Act does not distinguish between written and memorized information. The Act does not require a plaintiff to prove actual theft or conversion of physical documents embodying the trade secret information to prove misappropriation. The Washington Uniform Trade Secrets Act defines a "trade secret" to include compilations of information which have certain characteristics without regard to the form that such information might take. The definition of "misappropriation" includes unauthorized "disclosure or use." *   *   * [T]wo types of information mentioned in the Uniform Trade Secrets Act as examples of trade secrets include "method" and "technique"; these do not imply the requirement of written documents.

*   *   *   *

The form of information, whether written or memorized, is immaterial under the trade secrets statute; the Uniform Trade Secrets Act makes no distinction about the form of trade secrets. Whether the information is on a CD, a blueprint, a film, a recording, a hard paper copy or memorized by the employee, the inquiry is whether it meets the definition of a trade secret under the Act and whether it was misappropriated. Absent a contract to the contrary, an employee is free to compete against his or her former employer, and a former employee may use general knowledge, skills and experience acquired during the prior employment in competing with a former employer. However, an employee may not use or disclose trade secrets belonging to the former employer to actively solicit customers from a confidential customer list. In this case, the former employees actively solicited customers from the employer's customer lists, which the trial court found to be of independent value because unknown and subject to reasonable efforts to keep secret. *   *   * [W]e conclude the Court of Appeals was correct in holding that there is no legal distinction between written and memorized information under the Uniform Trade Secrets Act and in remanding for a recalculation of damages.

DECISION AND REMEDY   *The Washington Supreme Court affirmed the judgment of the state intermediate appellate court. Under the Uniform Trade Secrets Act, there is no legal distinction between written and memorized information.*

SECTION 5

International Protection for Intellectual Property

For many years, the United States has been a party to various international agreements relating to intellectual property rights. For example, the Paris Convention of 1883, to which about ninety countries are signatory, allows parties in one country to file for patent and trademark protection in any of the other member countries. Other international agreements in this area include the Berne Convention and the TRIPS agreement.

THE BERNE CONVENTION

Under the Berne Convention of 1886, an international copyright agreement, if an American writes a book, his or her copyright in the book must be recognized by every country that has signed the convention. Also, if a citizen of a country that has not signed the convention first publishes a book in a country that

has signed, all other countries that have signed the convention must recognize that author's copyright. Copyright notice is not needed to gain protection under the Berne Convention for works published after March 1, 1989.

Currently, the laws of many countries as well as international laws are being updated to reflect changes in technology and the expansion of the Internet. Copyright holders and other owners of intellectual property generally agree that changes in the law are needed to stop the increasing international piracy of their property. The World Intellectual Property Organization (WIPO) Copyright Treaty of 1996, a special agreement under the Berne Convention, attempts to update international law governing copyright protection to include more safeguards against copyright infringement via the Internet. The United States, which signed the WIPO treaty in 1996, implemented its terms in the Digital Millennium Copyright Act of 1998. These developments are covered in more detail in Chapter 9, in the context of international protection for intellectual property rights in cyberspace.

The Berne Convention and other international agreements have given some protection to intellectual property on a global level. Another significant worldwide agreement to increase such protection is the Trade-Related Aspects of Intellectual Property Rights agreement—or, more simply, the TRIPS agreement.

The TRIPS Agreement

The TRIPS agreement was signed by representatives from over one hundred nations in 1994. It was one of several documents that were annexed to the agreement that created the World Trade Organization, or WTO, in 1995. The TRIPS agreement established, for the first time, standards for the international protection of intellectual property rights, including patents, trademarks, and copyrights for movies, computer programs, books, and music.

Prior to the TRIPS agreement, one of the difficulties faced by U.S. sellers of intellectual property in the international market was that another country might either lack laws to protect intellectual property rights or fail to enforce what laws it had. To address this problem, the TRIPS agreement provides that each member country must include in its domestic laws broad intellectual property rights and effective remedies (including civil and criminal penalties) for violations of those rights.

Generally, the TRIPS agreement provides that member nations must not discriminate (in terms of the administration, regulation, or adjudication of intellectual property rights) against foreign owners of such rights. In other words, a member nation cannot give its own nationals (citizens) favorable treatment without offering the same treatment to nationals of all member countries. For example, if a U.S. software manufacturer brings a suit for the infringement of intellectual property rights under Japan's national laws, the U.S. manufacturer is entitled to receive the same treatment as a Japanese domestic manufacturer. Each member nation must also ensure that legal procedures are available for parties who wish to bring actions for infringement of intellectual property rights. Additionally, as part of the agreement creating the WTO, a mechanism for settling disputes among member nations was established.

Particular provisions of the TRIPS agreement refer to patent, trademark, and copyright protection for intellectual property. The agreement specifically provides copyright protection for computer programs by stating that compilations of data, databases, and other materials are "intellectual creations" and are to be protected as copyrightable works. Other provisions relate to trade secrets and the rental of computer programs and cinematographic works.

Terms and Concepts to Review

certification mark 131	intellectual property 124	trade name 131
collective mark 131	patent 131	trade secret 137
copyright 134	service mark 130	trademark 124
dilution 128	trade dress 130	

Questions and Case Problems

7–1. Fair Use Doctrine. Professor Wise is teaching a summer seminar in business torts at State University. Several times during the course, he makes copies of relevant sections from business law texts and distributes them to his students. Wise does not realize that the daughter of one of the textbook authors is a member of his seminar. She tells her father about Wise's copying ac-

tivities, which have taken place without her father's or his publisher's permission. Her father sues Wise for copyright infringement. Wise claims protection under the fair use doctrine. Who will prevail? Explain.

7–2. Copyright Infringement. In which of the following situations would a court likely hold Ursula liable for copyright infringement?

(a) From a scholarly journal at the library, Ursula photocopies ten pages relating to a topic on which she is writing a term paper.

(b) Ursula makes blouses, dresses, and other clothes and sells them in her small shop. She advertises some of the outfits as Guest items, hoping that customers might mistakenly assume that they were made by Guess, the well-known clothing manufacturer.

(c) Ursula teaches Latin American history at a small university. She has a VCR and frequently tapes television programs relating to Latin America. She then takes the videos to her classroom so that her students can watch them.

7–3. COPYRIGHT PROTECTION. One day during algebra class, Diedra, an enterprising fourteen-year-old student, began drawing designs on her shoelaces. By the end of the class, Diedra had decorated her shoelaces with the name of the school, Broadson Junior High, written in blue and red (the school colors) and with pictures of bears, the school's mascot. After class, she showed the designs to her teacher, Mrs. Laxton. When Diedra got home that night, she wrote about her idea in her diary, in which she also drew her shoelace design. Mrs. Laxton had been trying to think of how she could build school spirit. She thought about Diedra's shoelaces and decided to go into business for herself. She called her business Spirited Shoelaces and designed shoelaces for each of the local schools, decorating the shoelaces in each case with the school's name, mascot, and colors. The business became tremendously profitable. Even though Diedra never registered her idea with the patent or copyright office, does she nonetheless have intellectual property rights in the shoelace design? Will her diary account be sufficient proof that she created the idea? Discuss.

7–4. TRADEMARK INFRINGEMENT. In 1987, Quality Inns International, Inc., announced a new chain of economy hotels to be marketed under the name McSleep Inns. McDonald's wrote Quality Inns a letter stating that the use of this name infringed on the McDonald's family of trademarks characterized by the prefix Mc attached to a generic term. Quality Inns claimed that Mc had come into generic use as a prefix and therefore McDonald's had no trademark rights to the prefix itself. Quality Inns filed an action seeking a declaratory judgment from the court that the mark McSleep Inns did not infringe on McDonald's federally registered trademarks or common law rights to its marks and would not constitute an unfair trade practice. What factors must the court consider in deciding this issue? What will be the probable outcome of the case? Explain. [*Quality Inns International, Inc. v. McDonald's Corp.,* 695 F.Supp. 198 (D.Md. 1988)]

7–5. TRADEMARK INFRINGEMENT. CBS, Inc., owns and operates Television City, a television production facility in Los Angeles that is home to many television series. The name Television City is broadcast each week in connection with each show. CBS sells T-shirts, pins, watches, and so on emblazoned with "CBS Television City." CBS registered the name Television City with the U.S. Patent and Trademark Office as a service mark "for television production services." David and William Liederman wished to open a restaurant in New York City using the name Television City. Besides food, the restaurant would sell television memorabilia such as T-shirts, sweatshirts, and posters. When CBS learned of the Liedermans' plans, it asked a federal district court to order them not to use the name Television City in connection with their restaurant. Does CBS's registration of the Television City mark ensure its exclusive use in all markets and for all products? If not, what factors might the court consider to determine whether the Liedermans can use the name Television City in connection with their restaurant? [*CBS, Inc. v. Liederman,* 866 F.Supp. 763 (S.D.N.Y. 1994)]

7–6. TRADE SECRETS. William Redmond, as the general manager for PepsiCo, Inc., in California, had access to the company's inside information and trade secrets. In 1994, Redmond resigned to become chief operating officer for the Gatorade and Snapple Co., which makes and markets Gatorade and Snapple and is a subsidiary of the Quaker Oats Co. PepsiCo brought an action in a federal district court against Redmond and Quaker Oats, seeking to prevent Redmond from disclosing PepsiCo's secrets. The court ordered Redmond not to assume new duties that were likely to trigger disclosure of those secrets. The central issue on appeal was whether a plaintiff can obtain relief for trade secret misappropriation on showing that a former employee's new employment will inevitably lead him or her to rely on the plaintiff's trade secrets. How should the court rule on this issue? Discuss fully. [*PepsiCo v. Redmond,* 54 F.3d 1262 (7th Cir. 1995)]

7–7. COPYRIGHT INFRINGEMENT. James Smith, the owner of Michigan Document Services, Inc. (MDS), a commercial copyshop, concluded that it was unnecessary to obtain the copyright owners' permission to reproduce copyrighted materials in coursepacks. Smith publicized his conclusion, claiming that professors would not have to worry about any delay in production at his shop. MDS then compiled, bound, and sold coursepacks to students at the University of Michigan without obtaining the permission of copyright owners. Princeton University Press and two other publishers filed a suit in a federal district court against MDS, alleging copyright infringement. MDS claimed that its coursepacks were covered under the fair use doctrine. Were they? Explain. [*Princeton University Press v. Michigan Document Services, Inc.,* 99 F.3d 1381 (6th Cir. 1996)]

7–8. TRADEMARK INFRINGEMENT. Elvis Presley Enterprises, Inc. (EPE), owns all of the trademarks of the Elvis Presley estate. None of these marks is registered for use in the restaurant business. Barry Capece registered "The Velvet Elvis" as a service mark for a restaurant and tavern with the U.S. Patent and Trademark Office. Capece opened a nightclub called "The Velvet Elvis" with a menu, décor, advertising, and promotional events that evoked Elvis Presley and his music. EPE filed a suit in a federal district court against Capece and others, claiming, among other things, that "The Velvet Elvis" service mark infringed on EPE's trademarks. During the trial, witnesses testified that they thought the bar was associated with Elvis Presley. Should Capece be ordered to stop using "The Velvet Elvis" mark? Why or why not? [*Elvis Presley Enterprises, Inc. v. Capece,* 141 F.3d 188 (5th Cir. 1998)]

7–9. TRADEMARK INFRINGEMENT. A&H Sportswear Co., a swimsuit maker, obtained a trademark for its MIRACLESUIT in 1992. The MIRACLESUIT design makes the wearer appear slimmer. The MIRACLESUIT, which was widely advertised and discussed in the media, was also sold for a brief time in the Victoria's Secret (VS) catalogue, which is published by Victoria's Secret Catalogue, Inc. In 1993, Victoria's Secret Stores, Inc., began selling a cleavage-enhancing bra, which was named THE MIRACLE BRA and for which a trademark was obtained. The next year, THE MIRACLE BRA swimwear debuted in the VS catalogue and stores. A&H filed a suit in a federal district court against VS Stores and VS Catalogue, alleging in part that THE MIRACLE BRA mark, when applied to swimwear, infringed on the MIRACLESUIT mark. A&H argued that there was a "possibility of confusion" between the marks. The VS entities contended that the appropriate standard was "likelihood of confusion" and that in this case, there was no likelihood of confusion. In whose favor will the court rule, and why? [*A&H Sportswear, Inc. v. Victoria's Secret Stores, Inc.,* 166 F.3d 197 (3d Cir. 1999)]

7-10. IN YOUR COURT

Texaco, Inc., conducts research to develop new products and technology in the petroleum industry. As part of the research, Texaco employees routinely photocopy articles from scientific and medical journals without the permission of the copyright holders. The publishers of the journals brought a copyright infringement action against Texaco in a federal district court. Texaco argued that the copying was a "fair use" of the materials. Assume that you are the judge in the federal court hearing this case and answer the following questions:

(a) Under the "fair use" section of the Copyright Act, what four factors should you consider in determining whether Texaco's actions infringed on the rights of the copyright owners?

(b) How would you characterize the "purpose and character" of Texaco's use of the copyrighted materials? In other words, was the use of a "commercial nature" or was it "for nonprofit educational purposes"? In this respect, is the use of copyrighted materials by Texaco any different from the use of copyrighted materials by the "coursepack" preparer in the case described in Case Problem 7–7?

(c) Generally, what will your opinion be in this case? Will you hold Texaco liable for copyright infringement? Why or why not?

LAW ON THE WEB

For updated links to resources available on the Web, as well as a variety of other materials, visit this text's Web site at http://wbl.westbuslaw.com.

Information on intellectual property law is available at the following site:

http://wbl.legal.net/intellct.htm

You can find answers to frequently asked questions (FAQs) about trademark and patent law—and links to registration forms, statutes, international patent and trademark offices, and numerous other related materials—at the Web site of the U.S. Patent and Trademark Office. Go to

http://www.uspto.gov

To access the federal database of registered trademarks directly, go to

www.uspto.gov/tmdb/index.html

To perform patent searches and to access information on the patenting process, go to

http://www.bustpatents.com

You can also access information on patent law at the following Internet site:

http://www.patents.com

For information on copyrights, go to the U.S. Copyright Office at

lcweb.loc.gov/copyright

You can find extensive information on copyright law—including United States Supreme Court decisions in this area and the texts of the Berne Convention and other international treaties on copyright issues—at the Web site of the Legal Information Institute at Cornell University's School of Law. Go to

http://www.law.cornell.edu/topics/copyright.html

An online magazine that deals, in part, with intellectual property issues is *Law Technology Product News.* The URL for this publication is

http://www.ljextra.com/ltpn

The Cyberspace Law Institute (CLI) offers articles and information on such topics as copyright infringement, privacy, trade secrets, and trademarks. To access the CLI's Web site, go to

http://www.cli.org

LEGAL RESEARCH EXERCISES ON THE WEB

Go to http://wbl.westbuslaw.com, the Web site that accompanies this text. Select "Internet Applications," and then click on "Chapter 7." There you will find the following Internet research exercises that you can perform to learn more about intellectual property rights:

Activity 7–1: The Price of Free Speech

Activity 7–2: Gray-Market Goods

CHAPTER 8

Criminal Law and Procedures

THE LAW IMPOSES VARIOUS sanctions in attempting to ensure that individuals engaging in business in our society can compete and flourish. These sanctions include those imposed by civil law, such as damages for various types of tortious conduct (discussed in Chapters 5 and 6); damages for breach of contract (to be discussed in Chapter 18); and the equitable remedies discussed in Chapter 1. Additional sanctions are imposed under criminal law. Indeed, many statutes regulating business provide for criminal as well as civil penalties. Therefore, criminal law joins civil law as an important element in the legal environment of business.

In this chapter, after examining some essential differences between criminal law and civil law, we look at how crimes are classified, the basic requirements that must be met for criminal liability to be established, the various types of crimes, and the defenses that can be raised to avoid criminal liability. The chapter concludes with a discussion of criminal procedures.

SECTION 1

Civil Law and Criminal Law

Recall from Chapter 1 that *civil law* pertains to the duties that exist between persons or between citizens and their governments. Criminal law, in contrast, has to do with crime. A **crime** can be defined as a wrong

against society proclaimed in a statute and punishable by a fine and/or imprisonment—or, in some cases, death. As mentioned in Chapter 1, because crimes are *offenses against society as a whole,* they are prosecuted by a public official, such as a district attorney (D.A.) or an attorney general (A.G.), not by victims.

MAJOR DIFFERENCES BETWEEN CIVIL LAW AND CRIMINAL LAW

Because the state has extensive resources at its disposal when prosecuting criminal cases, there are numerous procedural safeguards to protect the rights of defendants. One of these safeguards is the higher standard of proof that applies in a criminal case. As you can see in Exhibit 8–1 on the next page, which summarizes some of the key differences between civil law and criminal law, in a civil case the plaintiff usually must prove his or her case by a *preponderance of the evidence.* Under this standard, the plaintiff must convince the court that, based on the evidence presented by both parties, it is more likely than not that the plaintiff's allegation is true.

In a criminal case, in contrast, the state must prove its case **beyond a reasonable doubt.** Every juror in a criminal case must be convinced, beyond a reasonable doubt, of the defendant's guilt. The higher standard of proof in criminal cases reflects a fundamental social value—a belief that it is worse to convict an

EXHIBIT 8–1   CIVIL AND CRIMINAL LAW COMPARED

ISSUE	CIVIL LAW	CRIMINAL LAW
Area of concern	Rights and duties between individuals	Offenses against society as a whole
Wrongful act	Harm to a person or to a person's property	Violation of a statute that prohibits some type of activity
Party who brings suit	Person who suffered harm	The state
Standard of proof	Preponderance of the evidence	Beyond a reasonable doubt
Remedy	Damages to compensate for the harm or an equitable remedy	Punishment (fine and/or imprisonment)

innocent individual than to let a guilty person go free. We will look at other safeguards later in the chapter, in the context of criminal procedure.

The sanctions imposed on criminal wrongdoers are also harsher than those that are applied in civil cases. Remember from Chapter 5 that the purpose of tort law is to allow persons harmed by the wrongful acts of others to obtain compensation, or money damages, from the wrongdoer or to enjoin (prevent) a wrongdoer from undertaking or continuing a wrongful action. Rarely are tortfeasors subject to punitive damages— damages awarded simply to *punish* the wrongdoer. In contrast, criminal sanctions are designed to punish those who commit crimes in order to deter others from committing similar acts in the future.

CIVIL LIABILITY FOR CRIMINAL ACTS

Some torts, such as assault and battery, provide a basis for a criminal prosecution as well as a tort action. For example, Jonas is walking down the street, minding his own business, when suddenly a person attacks him. In the ensuing struggle, the attacker stabs Jonas several times, seriously injuring him. A police officer restrains and arrests the wrongdoer. In this situation, the attacker may be subject both to criminal prosecution by the state and to a tort lawsuit brought by Jonas to compensate Jonas for his injuries. Exhibit 8–2 illustrates how the same wrongful act can result in both a civil (tort) action and a criminal action against the wrongdoer.

S E C T I O N   2

Classification of Crimes

Depending on their degree of seriousness, crimes are classified as felonies or misdemeanors.

FELONIES

Felonies are serious crimes punishable by death or by imprisonment in a federal or state penitentiary for one year or longer.[1] The Model Penal Code[2] provides for four degrees of felony:

1. Capital offenses, for which the maximum penalty is death.
2. First degree felonies, punishable by a maximum penalty of life imprisonment.
3. Second degree felonies, punishable by a maximum of ten years' imprisonment.
4. Third degree felonies, punishable by up to five years' imprisonment.

Although criminal laws vary from state to state, some general rules apply when grading crimes by degree. For example, most jurisdictions punish a burglary that involves a forced entry into a home at night more harshly than a burglary that takes place during the day and involves a nonresidential building or structure. A homicide—the taking of another's life—is classified according to the degree of intent involved.

For example, first degree murder requires that the homicide be premeditated and deliberate, instead of being a spontaneous act of violence. When no premeditation or deliberation is present but the offender

---

1. Some states, such as North Carolina, consider felonies to be punishable by incarceration for at least two years.
2. The American Law Institute issued the Official Draft of the Model Penal Code in 1962. The Model Penal Code is not a uniform code. Uniformity in criminal law among the states is not as important as uniformity in other areas of the law. Crime varies with local circumstances, and it is appropriate that punishments vary accordingly. The Model Penal Code contains four parts: (1) general provisions, (2) definitions of special crimes, (3) provisions concerning treatment and corrections, and (4) provisions on the organization of correction.

EXHIBIT 8–2   TORT LAWSUIT AND CRIMINAL PROSECUTION FOR THE SAME ACT

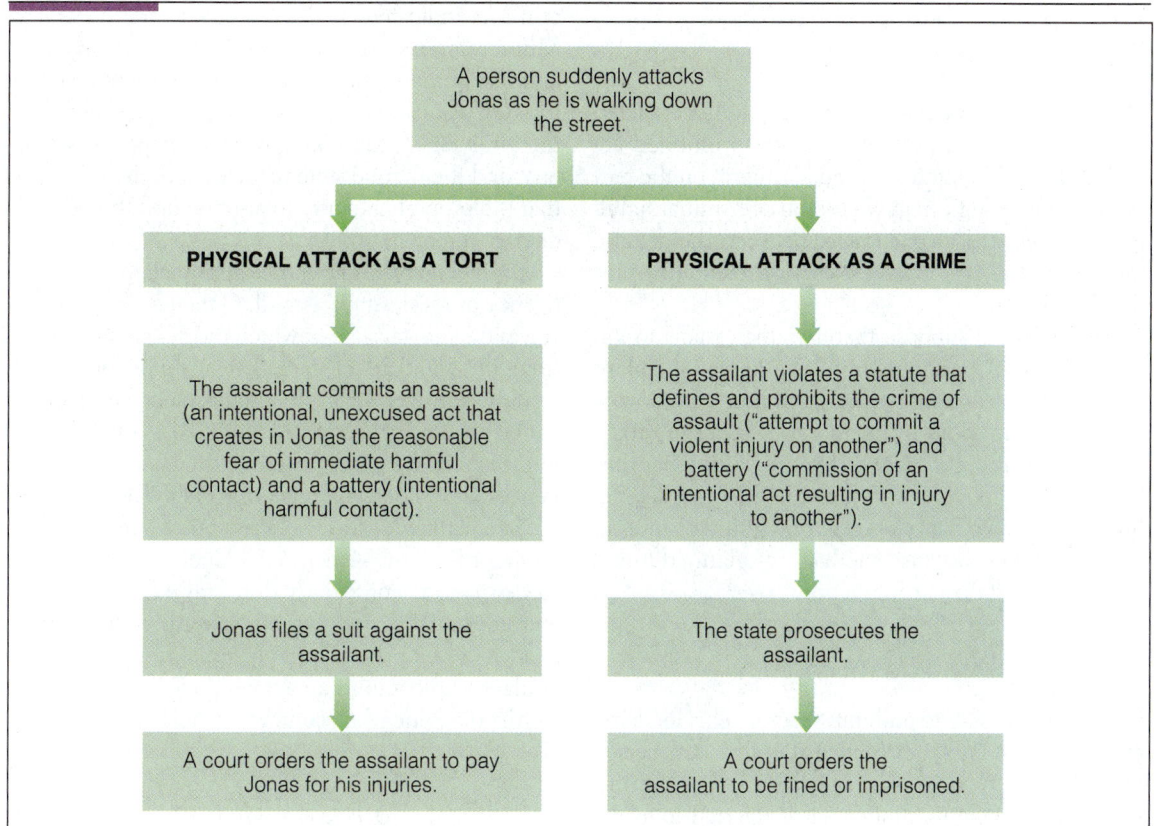

acts with *malice aforethought* (that is, with wanton disregard of the consequences of his or her actions for the victim), the homicide is classified as second degree murder. A homicide that is committed without malice toward the victim is known as *manslaughter*. *Voluntary manslaughter* occurs when the intent to kill may be present, as in a crime committed in the heat of passion, but malice is lacking. A homicide is classified as *involuntary manslaughter* when it results from an act of negligence, such as when a drunk driver causes the death of another person, and there is no intent to kill.

MISDEMEANORS AND PETTY OFFENSES

Under federal law and in most states, any crime that is not a felony is considered a **misdemeanor.** Misdemeanors are crimes punishable by a fine or by incarceration (imprisonment) for up to one year. If confined, the guilty party goes to a local jail instead of a penitentiary. Disorderly conduct and trespass are

common misdemeanors. Some states have several classes of misdemeanors. For example, in Illinois, misdemeanors are either Class A (confinement for up to a year), Class B (not more than six months), or Class C (not more than thirty days). Whether a crime is a felony or a misdemeanor can also determine if the case is tried in a magistrate's court (for example, by a justice of the peace) or a general trial court.

In most jurisdictions, **petty offenses** are considered to be a subset of misdemeanors. Petty offenses are minor violations, such as violations of building codes or driving under the influence of alcohol. Even for petty offenses, however, a guilty party can be put in jail for a few days, fined, or both, depending on state law.

Probation and community service are often imposed on those who commit misdemeanors, especially juveniles. Also, most states have decriminalized all but the most serious traffic offenses. These infractions are treated as civil proceedings, and civil fines are imposed. In many states, "points" are assessed against the violator's driving record.

SECTION 3

The Essentials of Criminal Liability

Two elements must exist for a person to be convicted of a crime: (1) the performance of a prohibited act and (2) a specified state of mind, or intent, on the part of the actor. Additionally, to establish criminal liability, there must be a *concurrence* between the act and the intent. In other words, these two elements must occur together.

For example, suppose that a woman plans to kill her husband by poisoning him. On the day she plans to do so, she is driving her husband home from work and swerves to avoid hitting a cat crossing the road. The car crashes into a tree as a result, killing her husband. Even though she had planned to murder her husband, the woman would not be guilty of murder in this situation because she had not planned to kill him by driving the car into a tree.

THE CRIMINAL ACT

Every criminal statute prohibits certain behavior. Most crimes require an act of *commission*; that is, a person must *do* something in order to be accused of a crime. In criminal law, a prohibited act is referred to as the *actus reus*,[3] or guilty act. In some cases, an act of omission can be a crime, but only when a person has a legal duty to perform the omitted act. Failure to file a tax return is an example of an omission that is a crime.

The *guilty act* requirement is based on one of the premises of criminal law—that a person should be punished for harm done to society. Thus, for a crime to exist, the guilty act must cause some harm to a person or to property. Thinking about killing someone or about stealing a car may be wrong, but the thoughts do no harm until they are translated into action. Of course, a person can be punished for *attempting* murder or robbery, but only if substantial steps toward the criminal objective have been taken. Additionally, the punishment for an attempt to commit a crime is normally less severe than it would be if the act had been completed.

STATE OF MIND

A wrongful mental state (*mens rea*)[4] is as necessary as a wrongful act in establishing guilt. The mental state,

or requisite intent, required to establish guilt of a crime is indicated in the applicable statute or law. Murder, for example, involves the guilty act of killing another human being, and the guilty mental state is the desire, or intent, to take another's life. For theft, the guilty act is the taking of another person's property, and the mental state involves both the awareness that the property belongs to another and the desire to deprive the owner of it.

A guilty mental state can be attributed to acts of negligence or recklessness as well. *Criminal negligence* involves the mental state in which the defendant deviates from the standard of care that a reasonable person would use under the same circumstances. The defendant is accused of taking an unjustified, substantial, and foreseeable risk that resulted in harm. Under the Model Penal Code, a defendant is negligent even if he or she was not actually aware of the risk but *should have been aware* of it.[5] The Model Penal Code defines *criminal recklessness* as "consciously disregard[ing] a substantial and unjustifiable risk."[6] In other words, a defendant is reckless if he or she is *actually aware* of the risk. A defendant who commits an act recklessly is more blameworthy than one who is criminally negligent.

SECTION 4

Corporate Criminal Liability

As will be discussed in Chapter 34, a corporation is a legal entity created under the laws of a state. Both the corporation as an entity and the individual directors and officers of the corporation are potentially subject to liability for criminal acts.

LIABILITY OF THE CORPORATE ENTITY

At one time, it was thought that a corporation could not incur criminal liability because, although a corporation is a legal person, it can act only through its agents (corporate directors, officers, and employees). Therefore, the corporate entity itself could not "intend" to commit a crime. Under modern criminal law, however, a corporation may be held liable for crimes. Obviously, corporations cannot be imprisoned, but they can be fined or denied certain legal privileges (such as a license).

---

3. Pronounced *ak*-tuhs ray-uhs.
4. Pronounced *mehns ray*-uh.

5. Model Penal Code Section 2.02(2)(d).
6. Model Penal Code Section 2.02(2)(c).

The Model Penal Code provides that a corporation may be convicted of a crime in the following situations:

1. The criminal act by the corporation's agent or employee is within the scope of his or her employment, and the purpose of the statute defining the act as a crime is to impose liability on the corporation.
2. The crime consists of a failure to perform a specific affirmative duty imposed on corporations by law.
3. The crime was authorized, requested, commanded, committed, or recklessly tolerated by one of the corporation's high managerial agents.[7]

As implied by the first statement in the above list, corporate criminal liability is vicarious—the corporation as an entity may be liable for the criminal acts of its employees when the acts are committed within the scope of employment. Thus, the corporation that is found to be criminally responsible for an act committed by an employee can be fined for that offense. Through the fine, stockholders and other employees suffer because of the vicarious liability of the corporation. The justification for such criminal liability involves a showing that the corporation could have prevented the act or that there was authorized consent to or knowledge of the act by persons in supervisory positions within the corporation.

LIABILITY OF CORPORATE OFFICERS AND DIRECTORS

Corporate directors and officers are personally liable for the crimes they commit, regardless of whether the crimes were committed for their private benefit or on the corporation's behalf. Additionally, corporate directors and officers may be held liable for the actions of employees under their supervision. Under what has become known as the "responsible corporate officer" doctrine, a court may impose criminal liability on a corporate officer regardless of whether he or she participated in, directed, or even knew about a given criminal violation.

For example, in *United States v. Park*,[8] the chief executive officer of a national supermarket chain was held personally liable for sanitation violations in corporate warehouses, in which the food was exposed to contamination by rodents. The court imposed personal liability on the corporate officer not because he intended the crime or even knew about it. Rather, liability was imposed because the officer was in a "responsible relationship" to the corporation and had the power to prevent the violation. Since the *Park* decision, courts have applied this "responsible corporate officer" doctrine on a number of occasions to hold corporate officers liable for their employees' statutory violations.

The following case illustrates that corporate officers and supervisors who oversee operations causing environmental harm may be held liable under the criminal provisions of environmental statutes. (The statute involved in this case—the federal Clean Water Act—will be discussed at some length in Chapter 44.)

---

7. Model Penal Code Section 2.07.

8. 421 U.S. 658, 95 S.Ct. 1903, 44 L.Ed.2d 489 (1975).

CASE 8.1   United States v. Hanousek

United States
Court of Appeals,
Ninth Circuit, 1999.
176 F.3d 1116.
http://www.ca9.
uscourts.gov[a]

BACKGROUND AND FACTS   *Edward Hanousek worked for Pacific & Arctic Railway and Navigation Company (P&A) as a roadmaster of the White Pass & Yukon Railroad in Alaska. Hanousek was responsible "for every detail of the safe and efficient maintenance and construction of track, structures and marine facilities of the entire railroad," including special projects. One project was a rock quarry, known as "6-mile," above the Skagway River. Next to the quarry, and just beneath the surface, ran a high-pressure oil pipeline owned by Pacific & Arctic Pipeline, Inc., P&A's sister company. When the quarry's*

---

a. The U.S. Court of Appeals for the Ninth Circuit maintains this Web site. Click on the "OPINIONS" oval. From that page, click on the "CLICK HERE: GO TO OPINIONS" box. On the next page, click on the "1999" icon, and when the menu opens, click on "March." Scroll down to "USA V HANOUSEK" and click on the case name to access the case.

backhoe operator punctured the pipeline, an estimated 1,000 to 5,000 gallons of oil were discharged into the river. Hanousek was charged with, among other things, negligently discharging a harmful quantity of oil into a navigable water of the United States in violation of the criminal provisions of the Clean Water Act (CWA). After a trial in a federal district court, a jury convicted Hanousek, and the court imposed a sentence of six months' imprisonment, six months in a halfway house, six months' supervised release, and a fine of $5,000. Hanousek appealed to the U.S. Court of Appeals for the Ninth Circuit, arguing in part that the statute under which he was convicted violated his right to due process because he was not aware of what the CWA required.

In the Language of the Court

DAVID R. THOMPSON, Circuit Judge.

*   *   *   *

The criminal provisions of the CWA [Clean Water Act] constitute public welfare legislation. Public welfare legislation is designed to protect the public from potentially harmful or injurious items and may render criminal a type of conduct that a reasonable person should know is subject to stringent public regulation and may seriously threaten the community's health or safety.

It is well established that a public welfare statute may subject a person to criminal liability for his or her ordinary negligence without violating due process. [Emphasis added.]

*   *   * [W]here *   *   * dangerous or deleterious devices or products or obnoxious waste materials are involved, the probability of regulation is so great that anyone who is aware that he is in possession of them or dealing with them must be presumed to be aware of the regulation.

Hanousek argues that *   *   * he was simply the roadmaster of the White Pass & Yukon railroad charged with overseeing a rock-quarrying project and was not in a position to know what the law required under the CWA. *   *   * In the context of a public welfare statute, as long as a defendant knows he is dealing with a dangerous device of a character that places him in responsible relation to a public danger, he should be alerted to the probability of strict regulation. *   *   * Hanousek *   *   * does not dispute that he was aware that a high-pressure petroleum products pipeline owned by Pacific & Arctic's sister company ran close to the surface next to the railroad tracks at 6-mile, and does not argue that he was unaware of the dangers a break or puncture of the pipeline by a piece of heavy machinery would pose. Therefore, Hanousek should have been alerted to the probability of strict regulation.

In light of [the fact] that the criminal provisions of the CWA constitute public welfare legislation, and the fact that a public welfare statute may impose criminal penalties for ordinary negligent conduct without offending due process, we conclude that [the CWA] does not violate due process by permitting criminal penalties for ordinary negligent conduct.

Decision and Remedy

The U.S. Court of Appeals for the Ninth Circuit affirmed Hanousek's conviction. A corporate manager who has responsibility for operations with the potential to cause harm can be held criminally liable for harm that results even if he or she does not actually know of the specific statute under which liability may be imposed.

SECTION 5

Types of Crimes

The number of actions that are designated as criminal is nearly endless. Federal, state, and local laws provide for the classification and punishment of hundreds of thousands of different criminal acts. Generally, though, criminal acts can be grouped into six broad categories: violent crime (crimes against persons), property crime, public order crime, white-collar crime, organized crime, and computer crime.

VIOLENT CRIME

Some types of crime are called *violent crimes,* or crimes against persons, because they cause others to suffer harm or death. Murder is a violent crime. So is sexual assault, or rape. Assault and battery, which were discussed in Chapter 5, are also classified as violent crimes. **Robbery**—defined as the taking of money, personal property, or any other article of value from a person by means of force or fear—is also a violent crime. Typically, states have more severe penalties for *aggravated robbery*—robbery with the use of a deadly weapon.

Each of these violent crimes is further classified by degree, depending on the circumstances surrounding the criminal act. These circumstances include the intent of the person committing the crime, whether a weapon was used, and (in cases other than murder) the level of pain and suffering experienced by the victim.

PROPERTY CRIME

The most common type of criminal activity is property crime, or those crimes in which the goal of the offender is some form of economic gain or the damaging of property. Robbery is a form of property crime, as well as a violent crime, because the offender seeks to gain the property of another. We look here at a number of other crimes that fall within the general category of property crime.

Burglary. At common law, **burglary** was defined as breaking and entering the dwelling of another at night with the intent to commit a felony. Originally, the definition was aimed at protecting an individual's home and its occupants. Most state statutes have eliminated some of the requirements found in the common law definition. The time at which the breaking and entering occurs, for example, is usually immaterial. State statutes frequently omit the element of breaking, and some states do not require that the building be a dwelling. *Aggravated burglary*—which is defined as burglary with the use of a deadly weapon, burglary of a dwelling, or both—incurs a greater penalty.

Larceny. Any person who wrongfully or fraudulently takes and carries away another person's personal property is guilty of **larceny**. Larceny includes the fraudulent intent to deprive an owner permanently of property. Many business-related larcenies entail fraudulent conduct. Whereas robbery involves force or fear, larceny does not. Therefore, picking pockets is larceny, not robbery.

In most states, the definition of property that is subject to larceny statutes has been expanded to cover relatively new forms of theft. For example, stealing computer programs may constitute larceny even though the "property" consists of magnetic impulses. Stealing computer time may also be considered larceny. So, too, may the theft of natural gas. Trade secrets may be subject to larceny statutes. Intercepting cellular phone calls to obtain another's phone card number—and then using that number to place long-distance calls, often overseas—is a form of property theft. These types of larceny are covered by "theft of services" statutes in many jurisdictions.

The common law makes a distinction between grand and petit larceny based on the value of the property taken. Many states have abolished this distinction, but in those that have not, grand larceny (theft above a certain amount) is a felony and petit larceny, a misdemeanor.

Arson. The willful and malicious burning of a building (and in some states, personal property) owned by another is the crime of **arson**. At common law, arson applied only to burning down another person's house. The law was designed to protect human life. Today, arson statutes have been extended to cover the destruction of any building, regardless of ownership, by fire or explosion.

Every state has a special statute that covers a person's burning a building for the purpose of collecting insurance. If Shaw owns an insured apartment building that is falling apart and sets fire to it himself or pays someone else to do so, he is guilty not only of arson but also of defrauding insurers, which is an attempted larceny. Of course, the insurer need not pay the claim when insurance fraud is proved.

Receiving Stolen Goods. It is a crime to receive stolen goods. The recipient of such goods need not know the true identity of the owner or the thief. All that is necessary is that the recipient knows or should know that the goods are stolen, which implies an intent to deprive the owner of those goods.

Forgery. The fraudulent making or altering of any writing in a way that changes the legal rights and liabilities of another is **forgery**. If, without authorization, Severson signs Bennett's name to the back of a check made out to Bennett, Severson is committing forgery. Forgery also includes changing trademarks, falsifying public records, counterfeiting, and altering a legal document.

Obtaining Goods by False Pretenses. It is a criminal act to obtain goods by false pretenses—for example, to buy groceries with a check, knowing that one has insufficient funds to cover it. Using another's credit-card number to obtain goods is another example of obtaining goods by false pretenses. Statutes dealing with such illegal activities vary widely from state to state. For example, in some states an intent to defraud must be proved before a person is criminally liable for writing a bad check. Some states define the theft and use of another's credit card as a separate crime, while others consider credit-card crime as a form of forgery.

PUBLIC ORDER CRIME

Historically, societies have always outlawed activities that are considered contrary to public values and morals. Today, the most common public order crimes include public drunkenness, prostitution, gambling, and illegal drug use. These crimes are sometimes referred to as *victimless crimes* because they harm only the offender. From a broader perspective, however, they are deemed detrimental to society as a whole because they often create an environment that may give rise to property and violent crimes.

WHITE-COLLAR CRIME

Crimes occurring in the business context are popularly referred to as white-collar crimes. Although there is no official definition of **white-collar crime,** the term is commonly used to mean an illegal act or series of acts committed by an individual or business entity using some nonviolent means to obtain a personal or business advantage. Usually, this kind of crime takes place in the course of a legitimate business occupation. The crimes discussed next normally occur only in the business environment and thus fall into the category of white-collar crimes. Note, though, that certain property crimes, such as larceny and forgery, may also fall into this category if they occur within the business context.

Embezzlement. When a person entrusted with another person's property or funds fraudulently appropriates that property or those funds, **embezzlement** occurs. Typically, embezzlement involves an employee who steals funds from his or her employer. Banks face this problem, and so do a number of businesses in which corporate officers or accountants "doctor" the

books to cover up the fraudulent conversion of funds for their own benefit. Embezzlement is not larceny, because the wrongdoer does not physically take the property from the possession of another, and it is not robbery, because no force or fear is used.

It does not matter whether the accused takes the money from the victim or from a third person. If, as the financial officer of a large corporation, Carlson pockets a certain number of checks from third parties that were given to her to deposit into the corporate account, she is embezzling.

Ordinarily, an embezzler who returns what has been taken will not be prosecuted, because the owner usually will not take the time to make a complaint, give depositions, and appear in court. That the accused intended eventually to return the embezzled property, however, does not constitute a sufficient defense to the crime of embezzlement.

Mail and Wire Fraud. One of the most potent weapons against white-collar criminals is the Mail Fraud Act of 1990.[9] Under this act, it is a federal crime to use the mails to defraud the public. Illegal use of the mails must involve (1) mailing or causing someone else to mail a writing—something written, printed, or photocopied—for the purpose of executing a scheme to defraud and (2) contemplating or organizing a scheme to defraud by false pretenses. If, for example, Johnson advertises by mail the sale of a cure for cancer that he knows to be fraudulent because it has no medical validity, he can be prosecuted for fraudulent use of the mails.

Federal law also makes it a crime (wire fraud) to use wire, radio, or television transmissions to defraud.[10] Violators may be fined up to $1,000, imprisoned for up to five years, or both. If the violation affects a financial institution, the violator may be fined up to $1 million, imprisoned for up to thirty years, or both.

Bribery. Basically, three types of bribery are considered crimes: commercial bribery, bribery of public officials, and bribery of foreign officials. As an element of the crime of bribery, intent must be present and proved. The bribe can be anything the recipient considers to be valuable. Realize that the *crime of bribery occurs when the bribe is offered.* It does not matter whether the person to whom the bribe is offered accepts the bribe or

---

9. 18 U.S.C. Sections 1341–1342.
10. 18 U.S.C. Section 1343.

agrees to perform whatever action is desired by the person offering the bribe. *Accepting a bribe* is a separate crime.

Typically, people make commercial bribes to obtain proprietary information, cover up an inferior product, or secure new business. Industrial espionage sometimes involves commercial bribes. For example, a person in one firm may offer an employee in a competing firm some type of payoff in exchange for trade secrets or pricing schedules. So-called kickbacks, or payoffs for special favors or services, are a form of commercial bribery in some situations.

The attempt to influence a public official to act in a way that serves a private interest is a crime. Bribing foreign officials to obtain favorable business contracts is also a crime. This crime is discussed in detail in Chapter 40, along with the Foreign Corrupt Practices Act of 1977, which was passed to curb the use of bribery by American businesspersons in securing foreign contracts.

Bankruptcy Fraud. Today, federal bankruptcy law (see Chapter 30) allows individuals and businesses to be relieved of oppressive debt through bankruptcy proceedings. Numerous white-collar crimes may be committed during the many phases of a bankruptcy action. A creditor, for example, may file a false claim against the debtor, which is a crime. Also, a debtor may fraudulently transfer assets to favored parties before or after the petition for bankruptcy is filed. For example, a company-owned automobile may be "sold" at a bargain price to a trusted friend or relative. Closely related to the crime of fraudulent transfer of property is the crime of fraudulent concealment of property, such as the hiding of gold coins.

Insider Trading. An individual who obtains "inside information" about the plans of publicly held corporations can often make stock-trading profits by using the information to guide decisions relating to the purchase or sale of corporate securities. *Insider trading* is a violation of securities law and will be considered more fully in Chapter 37. At this point, it may be said that one who possesses inside information and who has a duty not to disclose it to outsiders may not profit from the purchase or sale of securities based on that information until the information is available to the public.

The Theft of Trade Secrets. As discussed in Chapter 7, trade secrets constitute a form of intellectual property that for many businesses can be ex-

tremely valuable. The Economic Espionage Act of 1996[11] makes the theft of trade secrets a federal crime. The act also makes it a federal crime to buy or possess another person's trade secrets, knowing that the trade secrets were stolen or otherwise acquired without the owner's authorization.

Violations of the act can result in steep penalties. The act provides that an individual who violates the act can be imprisoned for up to ten years and fined up to $500,000. If a corporation or other organization violates the act, it can be fined up to $5 million. Additionally, the law provides that any property acquired as a result of the violation and any property used in the commission of the violation is subject to criminal forfeiture—meaning that the government can take the property. A theft of trade secrets conducted via the Internet, for example, could result in the forfeiture of every computer, printer, or other device used to commit or facilitate the violation.

ORGANIZED CRIME

White-collar crime takes place within the confines of the legitimate business world. Organized crime, in contrast, operates *illegitimately* by satisfying the public's demand for illegal goods and services. For organized crime, the traditional preferred markets are gambling, prostitution, illegal narcotics, pornography, and loan sharking (lending money at higher than legal interest rates), along with more recent ventures into counterfeiting and credit-card scams.

Money Laundering. The profits from organized crime and other illegal activities amount to billions of dollars a year, particularly the profits from illegal drug transactions and, to a lesser extent, from racketeering, prostitution, and gambling. Under federal law, banks, savings and loan associations, and other financial institutions are required to report currency transactions of over $10,000. Consequently, those who engage in illegal activities face difficulties in depositing their cash profits from illegal transactions.

As an alternative to simply placing cash from illegal transactions in bank deposits, wrongdoers and racketeers have invented ways to launder "dirty" money to make it "clean." This **money laundering** is done through legitimate businesses. For example, a successful drug dealer might become a partner with a restaurateur. Little by little, the restaurant shows an

---

11. 18 U.S.C. Sections 1831–1839.

increasing profit. As a shareholder or partner in the restaurant, the wrongdoer is able to report the "profits" of the restaurant as legitimate income on which federal and state taxes are paid. The wrongdoer can then spend those monies without worrying about whether his or her lifestyle exceeds the level possible with his or her reported income.

The Federal Bureau of Investigation estimates that organized crime alone has invested tens of billions of dollars in as many as a hundred thousand business establishments in the United States for the purpose of money laundering. Globally, it is estimated that $300 billion in illegal money moves through the world banking system every year.

RICO. In 1970, in an effort to curb the apparently increasing entry of organized crime into the legitimate business world, Congress passed the Racketeer Influenced and Corrupt Organizations Act (RICO).[12] The act, which was enacted as part of the Organized Crime Control Act, makes it a federal crime to (1) use income obtained from racketeering activity to purchase any interest in an enterprise, (2) acquire or maintain an interest in an enterprise through racketeering activity, (3) conduct or participate in the affairs of an enterprise through racketeering activity, or (4) conspire to do any of the preceding activities.

Racketeering activity is not a new type of substantive crime created by RICO; rather, RICO incorporates by reference twenty-six separate types of federal crimes and nine types of state felonies[13] and declares that if a person commits two of these offenses, he or she is guilty of "racketeering activity." The act provides for both civil and criminal liability.

Civil Liability under RICO. The penalties for violations of the RICO statute are harsh. In the event of a violation, the statute permits the government to seek civil penalties, including the divestiture of a defendant's interest in a business (called forfeiture) or the dissolution of the business. Perhaps the most controversial aspect of RICO is that in some cases, private individuals are allowed to recover three times their actual losses (treble damages), plus attorneys' fees, for business injuries caused by a violation of the statute.

The broad language of RICO has allowed it to be applied in cases that have little or nothing to do with organized crime, and an aggressive trial attorney may attempt to show that any business fraud constitutes

"racketeering activity." In its 1985 decision in *Sedima, S.P.R.L. v. Imrex Co.,*[14] the United States Supreme Court interpreted RICO broadly and set a significant precedent for subsequent applications of the act. Plaintiffs have used the RICO statute in numerous commercial fraud cases because of the inviting prospect of being awarded treble damages if they win. The most frequent targets of civil RICO lawsuits are insurance companies, employment agencies, commercial banks, and stockbrokerage firms.

One of the requirements of RICO is that there be more than one offense—there must be a "pattern of racketeering activity." What constitutes a "pattern" has been the subject of much litigation. According to the interpretation of some courts, a pattern must involve, among other things, continued criminal activity. This is known as the "continuity" requirement. Part of this requirement is that the activity occur over a "substantial" period of time.

Criminal Liability under RICO. Many criminal RICO offenses, such as gambling, arson, and extortion, have little, if anything, to do with normal business activities. But securities fraud (involving the sale of stocks and bonds) and mail and wire fraud also may constitute criminal RICO violations, and RICO has become an effective tool in attacking these white-collar crimes in recent years. Under the criminal provisions of RICO, any individual found guilty of a violation is subject to a fine of up to $25,000 per violation, imprisonment for up to twenty years, or both.

COMPUTER CRIME

The American Bar Association defines **computer crime** as any act that is directed against computers and computer parts, that uses computers as instruments of crime, or that involves computers and constitutes abuse. A variety of different types of crime can be committed with or against computers, including the cyber crimes discussed in Chapter 9. The dependence of businesses on computer operations has left firms vulnerable to sabotage, fraud, embezzlement, and the theft of proprietary data, such as trade secrets or other intellectual property (discussed in Chapter 7).

Many computer crimes fall into the broad category of financial crimes. Computer networks provide opportunities for employees and others to commit crimes that can involve serious economic losses. For

---

12. 18 U.S.C. Sections 1961–1968.
13. See 18 U.S.C. Section 1961(1)(A).

14. 473 U.S. 479, 105 S.Ct. 3275, 87 L.Ed.2d 346 (1985).

example, employees of accounting and computer departments can transfer monies among accounts with little effort and often with less risk than that involved in transactions evidenced by paperwork. The potential for crime in the area of financial transactions is great; most monetary losses from computer crime are suffered in this area.

The theft of computer equipment and the theft of goods with the aid of computers (such as by manipulating inventory records to disguise the theft of goods) are subject to the same criminal and tort laws as thefts of other physical property. In many jurisdictions, the unauthorized use of computer data or services is considered larceny. Other computer crimes include vandalism and destructive programming. A knowledgeable individual, such as an angry employee whose job has just been terminated, can do a considerable amount of damage to computer data and files. Destructive programming in the form of "viruses" presents an ongoing problem for businesspersons and other computer users today.

CONCEPT SUMMARY 8.1 — TYPES OF CRIMES

CRIME CATEGORY	DEFINITION AND EXAMPLES
Violent Crime	1. *Definition*—Crimes that cause others to suffer harm or death. 2. *Examples*—Murder, assault and battery, sexual assault (rape), and robbery.
Property Crime	1. *Definition*—Crimes in which the goal of the offender is some form of economic gain or the damaging of property; the most common form of crime. 2. *Examples*—Burglary, larceny, arson, receiving stolen goods, forgery, and obtaining goods by false pretenses.
Public Order Crime	1. *Definition*—Crimes contrary to public values and morals. 2. *Examples*—Public drunkenness, prostitution, gambling, and illegal drug use.
White-Collar Crime	1. *Definition*—An illegal act or series of acts committed by an individual or business entity using some nonviolent means to obtain a personal or business advantage; usually committed in the course of a legitimate occupation. 2. *Examples*—Embezzlement, mail and wire fraud, bribery, bankruptcy fraud, insider trading, and the theft of trade secrets.
Organized Crime	1. *Definition*—A form of crime conducted by groups operating illegitimately to satisfy the public's demand for illegal goods and services (such as narcotics or pornography). 2. *Money laundering*—The establishment of legitimate enterprises through which "dirty" money (obtained through criminal activities, such as organized crime) can be "laundered" (made to appear as legitimate income). 3. *RICO*—The Racketeer Influenced and Corrupt Organizations Act (RICO) of 1970 makes it a federal crime to (a) use income obtained from racketeering activity to purchase any interest in an enterprise, (b) acquire or maintain an interest in an enterprise through racketeering activity, (c) conduct or participate in the affairs of an enterprise through racketeering activity, or (d) conspire to do any of the preceding activities. RICO provides for both civil and criminal liability.
Computer Crime	1. *Definition*—Any act that is directed against computers and computer parts, that uses computers as instruments of crime, or that involves computers and constitutes abuse. 2. *Examples*—Virtually all crimes involving computer use or abuse, including financial crimes (such as embezzlement), the theft of computer equipment, the theft of goods or services with the aid of computers, and destructive programming (such as viruses).

SECTION 6

Defenses to Criminal Liability

In certain circumstances, the law may allow a person to be excused from criminal liability because he or she lacks the required mental state. Criminal defendants may also be relieved of criminal liability if they can show that their criminal actions were justified, given the circumstances. Among the most important defenses to criminal liability are infancy, intoxication, insanity, mistake, consent, duress, justifiable use of force, necessity, entrapment, and the statute of limitations. Also, in some cases, defendants are given *immunity* from prosecution and thus relieved, at least in part, of criminal liability for their actions. We look next at each of these defenses.

Note that procedural violations (such as obtaining evidence without a valid search warrant) may operate as defenses also—because evidence obtained in violation of a defendant's constitutional rights may not be admitted in court. If the evidence is suppressed, then there may be no basis for prosecuting the defendant.

INFANCY

The term *infant*, as used in the law, refers to any person who has not yet reached the age of majority (see Chapter 13). In all states, certain courts handle cases involving children who are alleged to have violated the law. In some states, juvenile courts handle children's cases exclusively. In most states, however, courts that handle children's cases also have jurisdiction over other matters, such as traffic offenses.

Originally, juvenile court hearings were informal, and lawyers were rarely present. Since 1967, however, when the United States Supreme Court ordered that a child charged with delinquency must be allowed to consult with an attorney before being committed to a state institution,[15] juvenile court hearings have become more formal. In some states, a child will be treated as an adult and tried in a regular court if he or she is above a certain age (usually fourteen) and is guilty of a felony, such as rape or murder.

INTOXICATION

The law recognizes two types of intoxication, whether from drugs or from alcohol: involuntary

and voluntary. *Involuntary intoxication* occurs when a person either is physically forced to ingest or inject an intoxicating substance or is unaware that a substance contains drugs or alcohol. Involuntary intoxication is a defense to a crime if its effect was to make a person incapable of understanding that the act committed was wrong or incapable of obeying the law.

Using voluntary drug or alcohol intoxication as a defense is based on the theory that extreme levels of intoxication may negate the state of mind that a crime requires. Many courts are reluctant to allow *voluntary intoxication* as a defense to a crime, however. After all, the defendant, by definition, voluntarily chose to put himself or herself into an intoxicated state.

INSANITY

Just as a child is often judged incapable of the state of mind required to commit a crime, so also may be someone suffering from a mental illness. Thus, insanity may be a defense to a criminal charge. The courts have had difficulty deciding what standards should be used to measure sanity for the purposes of a criminal trial. One of the oldest standards, or tests, for insanity is the *M'Naghten* test,[16] which is still used in about one-third of the states. Under this test, which is sometimes called the "right-wrong" test, a criminal defendant is not responsible if, at the time of the offense, he or she did not know the nature and quality of the act or did not know that the act was wrong.

Several other jurisdictions use the less restrictive irresistible-impulse test to determine sanity. Under this test, a person may be found insane even if he or she was aware that a criminal act was wrong, providing that some "irresistible impulse" resulting from a mental deficiency drove him or her to commit the crime.

Today, almost all federal courts and about half of the states use the relatively liberal standard set forth in the Model Penal Code:

> A person is not responsible for criminal conduct if at the time of such conduct as a result of mental disease or defect he lacks *substantial capacity* either to appreciate the wrongfulness of his conduct or to conform his conduct to the requirements of the law.[17] [Emphasis added.]

---

15. *In re Gault*, 387 U.S. 1, 87 S.Ct. 1428, 18 L.Ed.2d 527 (1967).

16. A rule derived from *M'Naghten's Case*, 8 Eng.Rep. 718 (1843).
17. Model Penal Code Section 4.01.

This "substantial-capacity" standard is considerably easier to meet than the *M'Naghten* test or the irresistible-impulse test.

Under any of these tests, it is extremely difficult to prove insanity. For this reason, the insanity defense is rarely used. It is raised in only about 1 percent of felony cases and is unsuccessful in about three-fourths of those cases.

MISTAKE

Everyone has heard the saying "Ignorance of the law is no excuse." Ordinarily, ignorance of the law or a mistaken idea about what the law requires is not a valid defense. In some states, however, that rule has been modified. People who claim that they honestly did not know that they were breaking a law may have a valid defense if (1) the law was not published or reasonably made known to the public or (2) the people relied on an official statement of the law that was erroneous.

A *mistake of fact*, as opposed to a *mistake of law*, operates as a defense if it negates the mental state necessary to commit a crime. If, for example, Oliver Wheaton mistakenly walks off with Julie Tyson's briefcase because he thinks it is his, there is no theft. Theft requires knowledge that the property belongs to another.

CONSENT

What if a victim consents to a crime or even encourages the person intending a criminal act to commit it? Depending on the circumstances, the law may allow **consent** as a defense. In each case, one question is whether the law forbids an act committed against the victim's will or forbids the act without regard to the victim's wish. The law forbids murder, prostitution, and drug use whether the victim consents or not. Also, if the act causes harm to a third person who has not consented, there is no escape from criminal liability. Consent or forgiveness given after a crime has been committed is not really a defense, although it can affect the likelihood of prosecution. Consent operates as a defense most successfully in crimes against property.

DURESS

Duress exists when the *wrongful threat* of one person induces another person to perform an act that

he or she would not otherwise have performed. In such a situation, duress is said to negate the mental state necessary to commit a crime. For duress to qualify as a defense, the following requirements must be met:

1. The threat must be of serious bodily harm or death.
2. The harm threatened must be greater than the harm caused by the crime.
3. The threat must be immediate and inescapable.
4. The defendant must have been involved in the situation through no fault of his or her own.

One crime that cannot be excused by duress is murder. It is difficult to justify taking a life as a result of duress even if one's own life is threatened.

JUSTIFIABLE USE OF FORCE

Probably the most well-known defense to criminal liability is **self-defense.** Other situations, however, also justify the use of force: the defense of one's dwelling, the defense of other property, and the prevention of a crime. In all of these situations, it is important to distinguish between the use of deadly and nondeadly force. *Deadly force* is likely to result in death or serious bodily harm. *Nondeadly force* is force that reasonably appears necessary to prevent the imminent use of criminal force.

Generally speaking, people can use the amount of nondeadly force that seems necessary to protect themselves, their dwellings, or other property or to prevent the commission of a crime. Deadly force can be used in self-defense if there is a *reasonable belief* that imminent death or grievous bodily harm will otherwise result, if the attacker is using unlawful force (an example of lawful force is that exerted by a police officer), and if the defender has not initiated or provoked the attack. Deadly force can be used to defend a dwelling only if the unlawful entry is violent and the person believes deadly force is necessary to prevent imminent death or great bodily harm or—in some jurisdictions—if the person believes deadly force is necessary to prevent the commission of a felony in the dwelling.

What if deadly force results from a mechanical device, such as a spring gun rigged to go off when a trespasser enters through a doorway? A leading case on this issue is *Katco v. Briney*, presented below.

CASE 8.2   Katco v. Briney

Supreme Court of Iowa,
1971.
183 N.W.2d 657.

BACKGROUND AND FACTS   *In 1957, Bertha Briney inherited her parents' farm. Over the next ten years, the unoccupied farmhouse was broken into a number of times, resulting in the loss of some household items, in broken windows, and in the "messing up of the property in general." In June 1967, the Brineys set a shotgun trap in one of the bedrooms. Wire was rigged from the gun's trigger to the doorknob so that the gun would fire when the door was opened. On the night of July 16, Marvin Katco and Marvin McDonough broke into the house looking for antique bottles and jars. When Katco opened the bedroom door, he detonated the shotgun and was hit in the right leg above the ankle bone. Much of his leg, including part of the tibia, was blown away. He spent forty days in the hospital, a year on crutches, and a year in a special brace. He pleaded guilty to criminal charges of larceny, paid a $50 fine, and was paroled for good behavior from a sixty-day jail sentence. Katco sued the Brineys in an Iowa state court for damages. The trial court instructed the jury that "one may use reasonable force in the protection of his property, but * * * one may not use such means of force as will take human life or inflict great bodily injury." The jury returned a verdict for Katco for $30,000. The Brineys appealed.*

IN THE LANGUAGE OF THE COURT

MOORE, Chief Justice.

*   *   *   *   *

The overwhelming weight of authority, both textbook and case law, supports the trial court's statement of the applicable principles of law.

*   *   *   *   *

Restatement of Torts, [S]ection 85, states: "The value of human life and limb, not only to the individual concerned but also to society, so outweighs the interest of a possessor of land in excluding from it those whom he is not willing to admit thereto that a possessor of land has *   *   * no privilege to use force intended or likely to cause death or serious harm against another whom the possessor sees about to enter his premises or meddle with his [property], unless the intrusion threatens death or serious bodily harm to the occupiers or users of the premises. *   *   * *A possessor of land cannot do indirectly and by a mechanical device that which, were he present, he could not do immediately and in person.* *   *   * " [Emphasis added.]

*   *   *   *   *

In *Hooker v. Miller*, we held [a] defendant vineyard owner liable for damages resulting from a spring gun shot although plaintiff was a trespasser and there to steal grapes. [In the opinion,] this statement is made: "This court has held that a mere trespass against property *   *   * is not a sufficient justification to authorize the use of a deadly weapon by the owner in its defense; and that if death results in such a case it will be murder, though the killing be actually necessary to prevent the trespass." *   *   *

*   *   *   *   *

In addition to civil liability many jurisdictions hold a land owner criminally liable for serious injuries or homicide caused by spring guns or other set devices.

DECISION AND REMEDY   *The Supreme Court of Iowa affirmed the trial court's decision. The Brineys were liable for Katco's injuries.*

NECESSITY

Sometimes criminal defendants can be relieved of liability by showing that a criminal act was necessary to prevent an even greater harm. According to the Model Penal Code, the defense of **necessity** is justiable if "the harm or evil sought to be avoided by such conduct is greater than that sought to be prevented by the law defining the offense charged."[18] For example, in one case a convicted felon was threatened by an acquaintance with a gun. The felon grabbed the gun and fled the scene, but subsequently he was arrested under a statute that prohibits convicted felons from possessing firearms. In this situation, the necessity defense succeeded because the defendant's crime avoided a "greater evil."[19]

ENTRAPMENT

Entrapment is a defense designed to prevent police officers or other government agents from encouraging crimes in order to apprehend persons wanted for criminal acts. In the typical entrapment case, an undercover agent *suggests* that a crime be committed and somehow pressures or induces an individual to commit it. The agent then arrests the individual for the crime. For entrapment to be considered a defense, both the suggestion and the inducement must take place. The defense is intended not to prevent law enforcement agents from setting a trap for an unwary criminal but rather to prevent them from pushing the individual into that trap. The crucial issue is whether a person who committed a crime was predisposed to commit the crime or did so because the agent induced it.

STATUTE OF LIMITATIONS

With some exceptions, such as for the crime of murder, statutes of limitations apply to crimes just as they do to civil wrongs. In other words, criminal cases must be prosecuted within a certain number of years. If a criminal action is brought after the statutory time period has expired, the accused person can raise the statute of limitations as a defense. The running of the time period in a statute of limitations may be tolled— that is, suspended or stopped temporarily—if the defendant is a minor or is not in the jurisdiction. When the defendant reaches the age of majority or returns, the statute revives—that is, its time period begins to run or to run again.

---

18. Model Penal Code Section 3.02.
19. *United States v. Paolello*, 951 F.3d 537 (3d Cir. 1991).

IMMUNITY

At times, the state may wish to obtain information from a person accused of a crime. Accused persons are understandably reluctant to give information if it will be used to prosecute them, and they cannot be forced to do so. The privilege against self-incrimination is granted by the Fifth Amendment to the Constitution, which reads, in part, "nor shall [any person] be compelled in any criminal case to be a witness against himself." In cases in which the state wishes to obtain information from a person accused of a crime, the state can grant *immunity* from prosecution or agree to prosecute for a less serious offense in exchange for the information. Once immunity is given, the person can no longer refuse to testify on Fifth Amendment grounds, because he or she now has an absolute privilege against self-incrimination.

Often a grant of immunity from prosecution for a serious crime is part of the **plea bargaining** between the defending and prosecuting attorneys. The defendant may be convicted of a lesser offense, while the state uses the defendant's testimony to prosecute accomplices for serious crimes carrying heavy penalties.

SECTION 7

Criminal Procedures

Criminal law brings the force of the state, with all of its resources, to bear against the individual. Criminal procedures are designed to protect the constitutional rights of individuals and to prevent the arbitrary use of power on the part of the government.

The U.S. Constitution provides specific safeguards for those accused of crimes. The United States Supreme Court has ruled that most of these safeguards apply not only in federal but also in state courts by virtue of the due process clause of the Fourteenth Amendment. These safeguards include the following:

1. The Fourth Amendment protection from unreasonable searches and seizures.
2. The Fourth Amendment requirement that no

warrant for a search or an arrest be issued without probable cause.

3. The Fifth Amendment requirement that no one be deprived of "life, liberty, or property without due process of law."

4. The Fifth Amendment prohibition against **double jeopardy** (trying someone twice for the same criminal offense).[20]

5. The Fifth Amendment requirement that no person be required to be a witness against (incriminate) himself or herself.

6. The Sixth Amendment guarantees of a speedy trial, a trial by jury, a public trial, the right to confront witnesses, and the right to a lawyer at various stages in some proceedings.

7. The Eighth Amendment prohibitions against excessive bail and fines and cruel and unusual punishment.

THE EXCLUSIONARY RULE

Under what is known as the **exclusionary rule,** all evidence obtained in violation of the constitutional rights spelled out in the Fourth, Fifth, and Sixth Amendments normally is not admissible at trial. All evidence derived from the illegally obtained evidence is known as the "fruit of the poisonous tree," and such evidence normally must also be excluded from the trial proceedings. For example, if a confession is obtained after an illegal arrest, the arrest is the "poisonous tree," and the confession, if "tainted" by the arrest, is the "fruit."

The purpose of the exclusionary rule is to deter police from conducting warrantless searches and from other misconduct. The rule is sometimes criticized because it can lead to injustice. Many a defendant has "gotten off on a technicality" because law enforcement personnel failed to observe procedural

requirements based on the above-mentioned constitutional amendments. Even though a defendant may be obviously guilty, if the evidence of that guilt is obtained improperly (without a valid search warrant, for example), it cannot be used against the defendant in court.

Over the last several decades, however, the United States Supreme Court diminished the scope of the exclusionary rule by creating some exceptions to its applicability. For example, in 1984 the Court held that if illegally obtained evidence would have been "inevitably" discovered and obtained by the police using lawful means, the evidence will be admissible at trial.[21] In another case decided in the same year, the Court held that a police officer who used a technically incorrect search warrant form to obtain evidence had acted in good faith and therefore the evidence was admissible. The Court thus created the "good faith" exception to the exclusionary rule.[22] Additionally, the courts can exercise a certain amount of discretion in determining whether evidence has been obtained improperly, thus somewhat balancing the scales.

THE MIRANDA RULE

In regard to criminal procedure, one of the questions many courts faced in the 1950s and 1960s was not whether suspects had constitutional rights—that was not in doubt—but how and when those rights could be exercised. Could the right to be silent (under the Fifth Amendment's prohibition against self-incrimination) be exercised during pretrial interrogation proceedings, or only during the trial? Were confessions obtained from suspects admissible in court if the suspects had not been advised of their right to remain silent and other constitutional rights?

To clarify these issues, the United States Supreme Court issued a landmark decision in 1966 in *Miranda v. Arizona,* presented on the next page. The procedural rights required by the Court in this case are familiar to virtually every American.

---

20. The prohibition against double jeopardy means that once a criminal defendant is found not guilty of a particular crime, the government may not reindict the person and retry him or her for the same crime. The prohibition against double jeopardy does not preclude a *civil* suit's being brought against the same person by the crime victim to recover damages. For example, a person found not guilty of assault and battery in a criminal case may be sued by the victim in a civil tort case for damages. Additionally, a state's prosecution of a crime will not prevent a separate federal prosecution of the same crime, and vice versa. For example, a defendant found not guilty of violating a state law can be tried in federal court for the same act, if the act is defined as a crime under federal law.

21. *Nix v. Williams,* 467 U.S. 431, 104 S.Ct. 2501, 81 L.Ed. 377 (1984).
22. *Massachusetts v. Sheppard,* 468 U.S. 981, 104 S.Ct. 3424, 82 L.Ed.2d 737 (1984).

CASE 8.3   Miranda v. Arizona

Supreme Court of the
United States, 1966.
384 U.S. 436,
86 S.Ct. 1602,
16 L.Ed.2d 694.

BACKGROUND AND FACTS   *On March 13, 1963, Ernesto Miranda was arrested at his home for the kidnapping and rape of an eighteen-year-old woman. Miranda was taken to a Phoenix, Arizona, police station and questioned by two officers. Two hours later, the officers emerged from the interrogation room with a written confession signed by Miranda. A paragraph at the top of the confession stated that the confession had been made voluntarily, without threats or promises of immunity, and "with full knowledge of my legal rights, understanding any statement I make may be used against me." Miranda was at no time advised that he had a right to remain silent and a right to have a lawyer present. The confession was admitted into evidence at the trial, and Miranda was convicted and sentenced to prison for twenty to thirty years. Miranda appealed the decision, claiming that he had not been informed of his constitutional rights. The Supreme Court of Arizona held that Miranda's constitutional rights had not been violated and affirmed his conviction. The* Miranda *case was subsequently consolidated with three other cases involving similar issues and reviewed by the United States Supreme Court.*

IN THE LANGUAGE OF THE COURT

Mr. Chief Justice WARREN delivered the opinion of the Court.

The cases before us raise questions which go to the roots of our concepts of American criminal jurisprudence; the restraints society must observe consistent with the Federal Constitution in prosecuting individuals for crime. *   *   *
*   *   *   *

At the outset, if a person in custody is to be subjected to interrogation, he must first be informed in clear and unequivocal terms that he has the right to remain silent. *   *   *
*   *   *   *

The warning of the right to remain silent must be accompanied by the explanation that anything said can and will be used against the individual in court. This warning is needed in order to make him aware not only of the privilege, *but also of the consequences of forgoing it.* *   *   . * [Emphasis added.]

The circumstances surrounding in-custody interrogation can operate very quickly to overbear the will of one merely made aware of his privilege by his interrogators. Therefore the right to have counsel present at the interrogation is indispensable to the protection of the Fifth Amendment privilege under the system we delineate today.
*   *   *   *

In order fully to apprise a person interrogated of the extent of his rights under this system then, it is necessary to warn him not only that he has the right to consult with an attorney, but also that if he is indigent [without funds] a lawyer will be appointed to represent him. *   *   * The warning of a right to counsel would be hollow if not couched in terms that would convey to the indigent—the person most often subjected to interrogation—the knowledge that he too has a right to have counsel present.

DECISION AND REMEDY

The Supreme Court held that Miranda could not be convicted of the crime on the basis of his confession because his confession was inadmissible as evidence. For any statement made by a defendant to be admissible, the defendant must be informed of certain constitutional rights prior to police interrogation. If the accused waives his or her rights to remain silent and to have counsel present, the government must demonstrate that the waiver was made knowingly, voluntarily, and intelligently.

INTERNATIONAL CONSIDERATIONS

The Right to Remain Silent in Great Britain *The right to remain silent has long been a legal hallmark in Great Britain as well as in the United States. In 1994, however, the British Parliament passed an act that provides that a criminal defendant's silence may be interpreted as evidence of the defendant's guilt. British police officers are now required, when making arrests, to inform the suspects, "You do not have to say anything. But if you do* *not mention now something which you later use in your defense, the court may decide that your failure to mention it now strengthens the case against you. A record will be made of everything you say, and it may be given in evidence if you are brought to trial."*

Exceptions to the *Miranda* Rule. As part of a continuing attempt to balance the rights of accused persons against the rights of society, the Supreme Court has made a number of exceptions to the *Miranda* ruling. In 1984, for example, the Court recognized a "public safety" exception to the *Miranda* rule. The need to protect the public warranted the admissibility of statements made by the defendant (in this case, indicating where he placed the gun) as evidence in a trial, even when the defendant had not been informed of his *Miranda* rights.[23]

In 1986, the Court further held that a confession need not be excluded even though the police failed to inform a suspect in custody that his attorney had tried to reach him by telephone.[24] In an important 1991 decision, the Court stated that a suspect's conviction will not be automatically overturned if the suspect was coerced into making a confession. If the other evidence admitted at trial was strong enough to justify the conviction without the confession, then the fact that the confession was obtained illegally can be, in effect, ignored.[25] In yet another case, in 1994, the Supreme Court ruled that a suspect must unequivocally and assertively state his right to counsel in order to stop police questioning. Saying, "Maybe I should talk to a lawyer" during an interrogation after being taken into custody is not enough. The Court held that police officers are not required to decipher the suspect's intentions in such situations.[26]

Section 3501 of the Omnibus Crime Control Act of 1968. In 1999, the U.S. Court of Appeals for the Fourth Circuit stunned the nation's legal establishment by enforcing a long-forgotten provision, Section 3501, of the Omnibus Crime Control Act of 1968. Congress passed the act two years after the Supreme Court's *Miranda* decision in an attempt to reinstate a rule that

had been in effect for 180 years before *Miranda*—namely, that statements by defendants can be used against them as long as they are voluntarily made.

The Justice Department immediately disavowed Section 3501 as unconstitutional and continues to hold this position. The Fourth Circuit, however, could see no reason not to enforce the provision. According to that court, Congress has the "unquestioned power to establish the rules of procedure and evidence in federal courts," and there is no explicit constitutional requirement that defendants be told of their rights to counsel and to remain silent.[27] Not surprisingly, the Fourth Circuit's decision has led to substantial controversy, which will likely continue until the Supreme Court (which has agreed to review the case) issues its decision on the matter.

Videotaped Interrogations. There are no guarantees that *Miranda* will survive indefinitely—particularly in view of the numerous exceptions that are made to the rule and the Fourth Circuit's decision on the issue. Additionally, law enforcement personnel are increasingly using videotapes to record interrogations. According to some scholars, the videotaping of *all* custodial interrogations would satisfy the Fifth Amendment's prohibition against coercion and in the process render the *Miranda* warnings unnecessary.

CRIMINAL PROCESS

As mentioned earlier in this chapter, a criminal prosecution differs significantly from a civil case in several respects. These differences reflect the desire to safeguard the rights of the individual against the state. Exhibit 8–3 summarizes the major steps in processing a criminal case. We discuss below in more detail three phases of the criminal process—arrest, indictment or information, and trial.

Arrest. Before a warrant for arrest can be issued, there must be probable cause for believing that the individual in question has committed a crime. As discussed in

---

23. *New York v. Quarles,* 467 U.S. 649, 104 S.Ct. 2626, 81 L.Ed.2d 550 (1984).

24. *Moran v. Burbine,* 475 U.S. 412, 106 S.Ct. 1135, 89 L.Ed.2d 410 (1986).

25. *Arizona v. Fulminante,* 499 U.S. 279, 111 S.Ct. 1246, 113 L.Ed.2d 302 (1991).

26. *Davis v. United States,* 512 U.S. 452, 114 S.Ct. 2350, 129 L.Ed.2d 362 (1994).

27. *United States v. Dickerson,* 97 F.3d 4750 (4th Cir. 1999).

EXHIBIT 8–3   MAJOR STEPS IN PROCESSING A CRIMINAL CASE

BOOKING
After arrest, at the police station, the suspect is searched, photographed, fingerprinted, and allowed at least one telephone call. After the booking, charges are reviewed, and if they are not dropped, a complaint is filed and a judge or magistrate examines the case for probable cause.

INITIAL APPEARANCE
The suspect appears before the judge, who informs the suspect of the charges and of his or her rights. If the suspect requests a lawyer, one is appointed. The judge sets bail (conditions under which a suspect can obtain release pending disposition of the case).

PRELIMINARY HEARING
In a proceeding in which both sides are represented by counsel, the judge determines whether there is probable cause to believe that the suspect committed the crime, based on the evidence.

GRAND JURY REVIEW
The federal government and about half of the states require grand jury indictments for at least some felonies. In those states, a grand jury determines whether the evidence justifies a trial on the charges sought by the prosecutor.

PROSECUTORIAL REVIEW
In jurisdictions that do not require grand jury indictments, a prosecutor issues an information. An information is similar to an indictment: both are charging instruments that replace the complaint.

ARRAIGNMENT
The suspect is brought before the trial court, informed of the charges, and asked to enter a plea.

PLEA BARGAIN
A plea bargain is a prosecutor's promise of concessions (or promise to seek concessions) in return for the defendant's guilty plea. Concessions include a reduced charge and/or a lesser sentence.

GUILTY PLEA
In more jurisdictions, most cases that reach the arraignment stage do not go to trial but are resolved by a guilty plea, often as the result of a plea bargain. The judge sets the case for sentencing.

TRIAL
If the defendant refuses to plead guilty, he or she proceeds to either a jury trial (in most instances) or a bench trial.

Chapter 4, *probable cause* can be defined as a substantial likelihood that the person has committed or is about to commit a crime. Note that probable cause involves a likelihood, not just a possibility. Arrests may sometimes be made without a warrant if there is no time to get one, but the action of the arresting officer is still judged by the standard of probable cause.

Indictment or Information.   Individuals must be formally charged with having committed specific crimes before they can be brought to trial. If issued by a grand jury, such a charge is called an **indictment.**[28] A **grand jury** does not determine the guilt or innocence of an accused party; rather, its function is to determine, after hearing the state's evidence, whether a reasonable basis (probable cause) exists for supposing that a crime has been committed and whether a trial ought to be held.

Usually, grand juries are called in cases involving serious crimes, such as murder. For lesser crimes, an individual may be formally charged with a crime by an **information,** or criminal complaint. An information will be issued by a magistrate (a public official vested with judicial authority) if the magistrate determines that there is sufficient evidence to justify bringing the individual to trial.

Trial.   At a criminal trial, the accused person does not have to prove anything; the entire burden of proof is on the prosecutor (the state). As discussed at the beginning of this chapter, the burden of proof in a criminal case is higher than that in a civil case. The prosecution must show that, based on all the evidence, the defendant's guilt is established *beyond a reasonable doubt*. If there is any reasonable doubt that a criminal defendant did not commit the crime with which he or she has been charged, then the verdict must be "not guilty." Note that giving a verdict of "not guilty" is not the same as stating that the defendant is innocent; it merely means that not enough evidence

was properly presented to the court to prove guilt beyond all reasonable doubt.

Courts have complex rules about what types of evidence may be presented and how the evidence may be brought out in criminal cases, especially in jury trials. These rules are designed to ensure that evidence presented at trials is relevant, reliable, and not prejudicial against the defendant.

FEDERAL SENTENCING GUIDELINES

Traditionally, persons who had committed the same crime might have received very different sentences, depending on the judge hearing the case, the jurisdiction in which it was heard, and many other factors. In 1984, however, Congress passed the Sentencing Reform Act. This act created the U.S. Sentencing Commission, which was charged with the task of standardizing sentences for federal crimes. The commission's guidelines, which became effective in 1987, established a range of possible penalties for each federal crime. Judges must select a sentence from within this range when sentencing criminal defendants, taking into consideration the defendant's criminal record, the seriousness of the offense, and other factors specified in the guidelines.

The commission also created specific guidelines for the punishment of crimes committed by corporate employees (white-collar crimes). These guidelines, which went into effect in 1991, established stiffer penalties for mail and wire fraud, commercial bribery and kickbacks, and money laundering, as well as for criminal violations of securities laws (see Chapter 37), employment laws (see Chapters 41 and 42), and antitrust laws (see Chapter 45). The guidelines allow judges to take into consideration a number of factors when selecting from the range of possible penalties for a specified crime. These factors include the defendant company's history of past violations, the extent of management's cooperation with federal investigators, and the extent to which the firm has undertaken specific programs and procedures to prevent criminal activities by its employees.

---

28. Pronounced in-*dyte*-ment.

TERMS AND CONCEPTS TO REVIEW

actus reus 146	**beyond a reasonable doubt** 143	**computer crime** 152
arson 149	**burglary** 149	**consent** 155

QUESTIONS AND CASE PROBLEMS

8–1. TYPES OF CRIMES. The following situations are similar (in all of them, Juanita's television set is stolen), yet three different crimes are described. Identify the three crimes, noting the differences among them.
  (a) While passing Juanita's house one night, Sarah sees a portable television set left unattended on Juanita's lawn. Sarah takes the television set, carries it home, and tells everyone she owns it.
  (b) While passing Juanita's house one night, Sarah sees Juanita outside with a portable television set. Holding Juanita at gunpoint, Sarah forces her to give up the set. Then Sarah runs away with it.
  (c) While passing Juanita's house one night, Sarah sees a portable television set in a window. Sarah breaks the front-door lock, enters, and leaves with the set.

8–2. TYPES OF CRIMES. Which, if any, of the following crimes necessarily involves illegal activity on the part of more than one person?
  (a) Bribery.
  (b) Forgery.
  (c) Embezzlement.
  (d) Larceny.
  (e) Receiving stolen property.

8–3. DOUBLE JEOPARDY. Armington, while robbing a drugstore, shot and seriously injured a drugstore clerk, Jennings. Armington was subsequently convicted in a criminal trial of armed robbery and assault and battery. Jennings later brought a civil tort suit against Armington for damages. Armington contended that he could not be tried again for the same crime, as that would constitute double jeopardy, which is prohibited by the Fifth Amendment to the Constitution. Is Armington correct? Explain.

8–4. RECEIVING STOLEN PROPERTY. Rafael stops Laura on a busy street and offers to sell her an expensive wristwatch for a fraction of its value. After some questioning by Laura, Rafael admits that the watch is stolen property, although he says he was not the thief. Laura pays for and receives the wristwatch. Has Laura committed any crime? Has Rafael? Explain.

8–5. ENTRAPMENT. Suppose that in the hypothetical situation discussed in Problem 8–4, Rafael is an undercover police officer. As soon as Laura pays for and receives the wristwatch, Rafael arrests her for the crime of receiving stolen property. At trial, Laura contends that she was a victim of entrapment. What should be the result of the trial? Discuss fully.

8–6. EMBEZZLEMENT. Faulkner, a truck driver, was hauling a load of refrigerators from San Diego to New York for the trucking company that employed him. He departed from his assigned route and stopped in Las Vegas, where he attempted to display and sell some of the refrigerators to a firm. Although the refrigerators never left the truck, to display them he had to break the truck's seals, enter the cargo department, and open two refrigerator cartons. The store owner refused to purchase the appliances, and when Faulkner left the store, he was arrested. He was later convicted under federal law for the embezzlement of an interstate shipment. Faulkner appealed, claiming that the charge of embezzlement should not apply because the property had not been physically removed from the owner's possession. Will the appellate court agree with Faulkner? Explain. [*United States v. Faulkner,* 638 F.2d 129 (9th Cir. 1981)]

8–7. CRIMINAL LIABILITY. In January 1988, David Ludvigson was hired as chief executive officer of Leopard Enterprises, a group of companies that owned funeral homes and cemeteries in Iowa and sold "pre-need" funeral contracts. Under Iowa law, 80 percent of the funds obtained under such a contract must be set aside in trust until the death of the person for whose benefit the funds were paid. Shortly after Ludvigson was hired, the firm began having financial difficulties. Ludvigson used money from the funeral contracts to pay operating expenses until the company went bankrupt and was placed in receivership. Ludvigson was charged and found guilty on five counts of second degree theft stemming from the misappropriation of these funds. He appealed, alleging, among other things, that he was not guilty of any crime, because he had not intended to permanently deprive any of the clients of their trust funds. Furthermore, because none of the victims whose trust funds were used to cover operating expenses was denied services, no injury was done. Will the court agree with Ludvigson? Explain. [*State v. Ludvigson*, 482 N.W.2d 419 (Ia. 1992)]

8–8. CRIMINAL LIABILITY. On the grounds of a school, Gavin T., a fifteen-year-old student, was eating lunch. He threw a half-eaten apple toward the outside wall of a classroom some distance away. The apple sailed through a slowly closing door and struck a teacher who was in the room. The teacher was knocked to the floor and lost consciousness for a few minutes. Gavin was charged, in a California state court, with assault by "any means of force likely to produce great bodily injury." The court found that he did not intend to hit the teacher but only intended to see the apple splatter against the outside wall. To send a "message" to his classmates that his actions were wrong, however, the court convicted him of the charge. Should Gavin's conviction be reversed on appeal? Why or why not? [*In re Gavin T.*, 66 Cal.App.4th 238, 77 Cal.Rptr.2d 701 (1998)]

8–9. FIFTH AMENDMENT. The federal government was investigating a corporation and its employees. The alleged criminal wrongdoing, which included the falsification of corporate books and records, occurred between 1993 and 1996 in one division of the corporation. In 1999, the corporation pled guilty and agreed to cooperate in an investigation of the individuals who might have been involved in the improper corporate activities. "Doe I," "Doe II," and "Doe III" were officers of the corporation during the period in which the illegal activities occurred and worked in the division where the wrongdoing took place. They were no longer working for the corporation, however, when, as part of the subsequent investigation, the government asked them to provide specific corporate documents in their possession. All three asserted the Fifth Amendment privilege against self-incrimination. The government asked a federal district court to order the three to produce the records. Corporate employees can be compelled to produce corporate records in a criminal proceeding, because they hold the records as representatives of the corporation, to which the Fifth Amendment privilege against self-incrimination does not apply. Should *former employees* also be compelled to produce corporate records in their possession? Why or why not? [*In re Three Grand Jury Subpoenas* Duces Tecum *Dated January 29, 1999*, 191 F.3d 173 (2d Cir. 1999)]

8–10. IN YOUR COURT

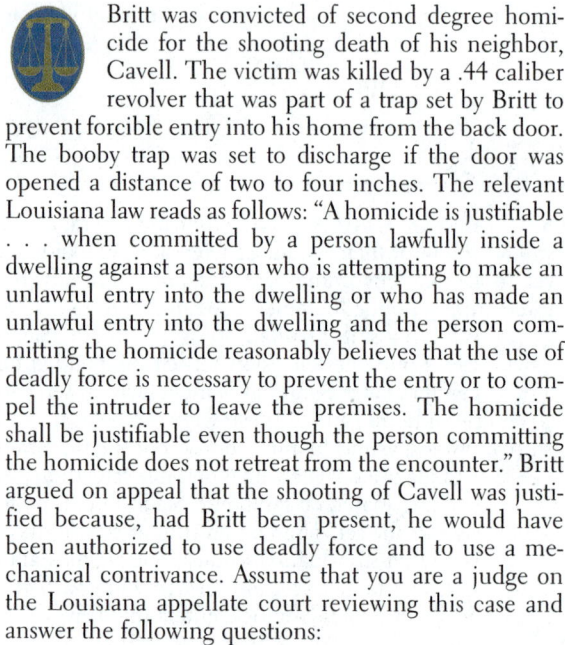

Britt was convicted of second degree homicide for the shooting death of his neighbor, Cavell. The victim was killed by a .44 caliber revolver that was part of a trap set by Britt to prevent forcible entry into his home from the back door. The booby trap was set to discharge if the door was opened a distance of two to four inches. The relevant Louisiana law reads as follows: "A homicide is justifiable . . . when committed by a person lawfully inside a dwelling against a person who is attempting to make an unlawful entry into the dwelling or who has made an unlawful entry into the dwelling and the person committing the homicide reasonably believes that the use of deadly force is necessary to prevent the entry or to compel the intruder to leave the premises. The homicide shall be justifiable even though the person committing the homicide does not retreat from the encounter." Britt argued on appeal that the shooting of Cavell was justified because, had Britt been present, he would have been authorized to use deadly force and to use a mechanical contrivance. Assume that you are a judge on the Louisiana appellate court reviewing this case and answer the following questions:

(a) Applying the statutory language cited above to the facts of this case, what would your decision be on the issue raised by Britt on appeal? Why?

(b) Compare this case to Case 8.2 (*Katco v. Briney*). How are the two cases similar? How do they differ? Would the court's reasoning in the *Katco* case be relevant to your decision in the *Britt* case? Why or why not?

LAW ON THE WEB

For updated links to resources available on the Web, as well as a variety of other materials, visit this text's Web site at <u>http://wbl.westbuslaw.com</u>.

    The Bureau of Justice Statistics in the U.S. Department of Justice offers an impressive collection of statistics on crime at the following Web site:

<u>http://www.ojp.usdoj.gov/bjs</u>

    For summaries of famous criminal cases and documents relating to these trials, go to Court TV's Web site at

<u>http://www.courttv.com/index.html</u>

If you would like to learn more about criminal procedures, the following site offers an "Anatomy of a Murder: A Trip through Our Nation's Legal Justice System":

http://tqd.advanced.org/2760/home.htm

At the above site, you can also find a glossary of terms used in crminal law, view actual forms that are filled out during the course of an arrest, and learn about some controversial issues in criminal law.

Many state criminal codes are now online. To find your state's code, go to

http://www.findlaw.com

and select "State" under the link to "Laws: Cases and Codes."

You can learn about some of the constitutional questions raised by various criminal laws and procedures by going to the Web site of the American Civil Liberties Union at

http://www.aclu.org

The text of the U.S. Sentencing Guidelines Manual is online at

http://www.ussc.gov

LEGAL RESEARCH EXERCISES ON THE WEB

Go to http://wbl.westbuslaw.com, the Web site that accompanies this text. Select "Internet Applications," and then click on "Chapter 8." There you will find the following Internet research exercise that you can perform to learn more about criminal procedures:

Activity 8–1: Revisiting *Miranda*

CHAPTER 9

Cyberlaw and E-Commerce

TECHNOLOGY AFFECTS BUSINESS PRACTICES and, for this reason, can affect business law. Cyberspace, the Internet, and the World Wide Web represent the latest in technological developments. In general, the law is attempting to catch up with the changes in business practices caused by these profoundly different capabilities.

There are three aspects to this new technology that are affecting the law. First, the new technology represents mass communication on an unprecedented scale. Geographic limits do not apply—any person or business with a computer has a potentially worldwide audience. Second, this mass communication does not originate from a few central locations. Physical and political limits are immaterial. Third, information on the Internet is highly changeable. A database can be easily downloaded and its data modified and passed on without detection.

These factors challenge the traditional governmental means for controlling the use and communication of information. In fact, they indicate that complete government monitoring and control of cyberspace would be impractical, unrealistic, and probably impossible. Some observers argue that the law does not, or should not, apply in cyberspace. Others think that the law is responding too slowly to technological developments. Still others contend that it is not necessary to change the law to respond to these developments. How the law is currently dealing with these factors is the subject of this chapter.

SECTION 1

The Courts

Technological developments, including the Internet, promise to relieve the courts of the burden created by overloaded dockets and record-keeping challenges—providing that the courts, the parties, and their attorneys are willing to use technology. Technology can save judges, lawyers, litigants, and court personnel time and overhead. Technology can reduce storage space, paperwork, and drudgery, and it can speed up legal research.

We have already looked at how electronic filing can reduce the paperwork and storage space required during litigation (see Chapter 3's feature entitled *Emerging Trends in Technology* for details). Here we look at how technology is changing other court practices and procedures as well. We also examine some of the jurisdictional issues posed by Internet transactions.

CHANGES IN PRACTICES AND PROCEDURES

Most courts have sites on the Web. Of course, it is up to each court to decide what to make available at its site. Some courts display only the names of court personnel and office phone numbers. Others add court rules and forms. Some include judicial decisions, although generally the sites do not feature archives of old decisions. Instead, the time period within which

166

decisions are available online is limited. For example, California keeps opinions online for only sixty days.[1] The official opening Web page for the opinions of the California state courts at http://www.courtinfo.ca.gov/opinions is illustrated in Exhibit 9–1.

Someday, we may see the use of **virtual courtrooms,** in which judicial proceedings take place only on the Internet. The parties to a case could meet online to make their arguments and present their evidence. This might be done with e-mail submissions, through video cameras, in designated "chat" rooms, at closed sites, or through the use of any other Internet facility. These courtrooms could be efficient and economical. Will we also see the use of virtual lawyers, judges, or juries—computers or software replacing court personnel? How would this affect the application of the law? Would removing the "human" aspect of justice result in radical changes to the legal system as we know it? These are questions for the future.

---

1. Older judicial opinions are available at other sites. As of this writing, however, except for the decisions of the United States Supreme Court and some opinions in classic cases, there are not many court decisions available online that predate the 1990s.

JURISDICTION IN CYBERSPACE

The Internet's capacity to bypass political and geographic boundaries makes it revolutionary. This ability undercuts the traditional basis for a court to assert personal jurisdiction. This basis includes the contacts a party has with a court's geographic jurisdiction. For a court to compel a defendant to come before the court, there must be at least minimum contacts—the presence of a salesperson within the state, for example. Are there sufficient minimum contacts if the only connection to a jurisdiction is an ad on the Web originating from a remote location?

Consider an example. Adam lives in Florida. Carol, who lives in New York and has never been to Florida or done business with anyone in Florida, advertises her business on the Web. Carol's home page has received hundreds of "hits" by residents of Florida. Adam files a suit against Carol in a Florida state court. Can the court compel Carol to appear?

On the one hand, it could be argued that Carol knows (or should know) that her Web site could be accessed by residents of Florida, and by advertising her business on the Web, she should reasonably expect to be called into court there. If this reasoning is

EXHIBIT 9–1 OPENING WEB PAGE FOR CALIFORNIA COURT OPINIONS

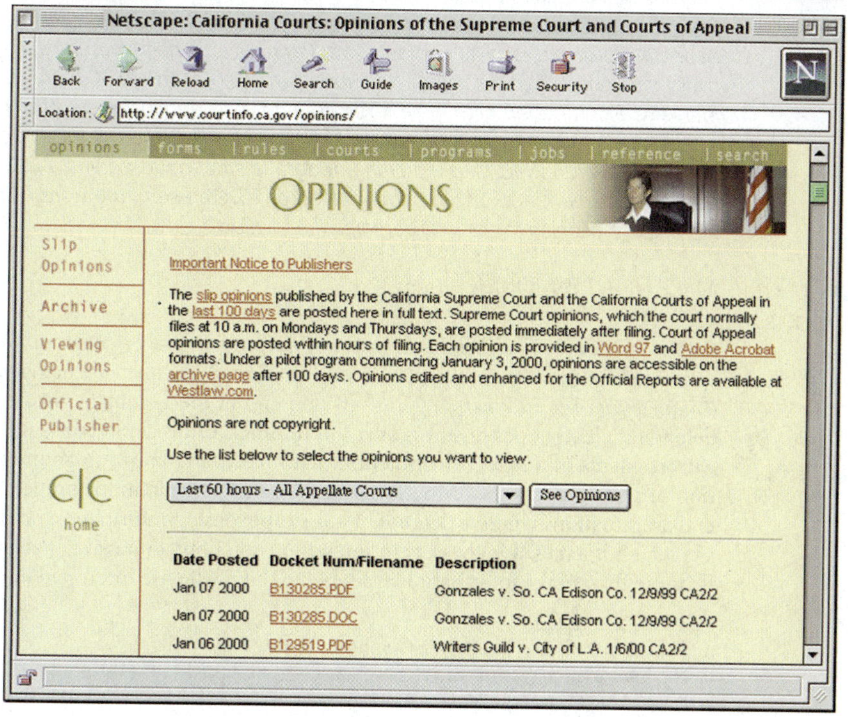

applied, then setting up a Web site could subject the owner to a suit anywhere that the site can be accessed. Some courts have upheld exercises of jurisdiction on the basis of the accessibility of a Web page.[2]

On the other hand, it could be argued that it is not possible for Carol to set up a Web page that excludes residents of Florida (or of any other specific jurisdiction). With this in mind, it would seem unreasonable and unfair to subject Carol to the possible personal jurisdiction of every court in the United States and maybe the world. For this reason, some courts have

concluded that without more, a presence on the Web is not enough to support jurisdiction over nonresident defendants.[3]

Recently, a new standard is becoming generally accepted for evaluating the exercise of jurisdiction based on contacts over the Internet. This standard is a "sliding scale." On this scale, a court's exercise of personal jurisdiction depends on the amount of business that an individual or firm transacts over the Internet. The standard is explained more fully in the following case.

---

2. See, for example, *Minnesota v. Granite Gates Resorts, Inc.*, 568 N.W.2d 715 (Minn.App. 1997), aff'd 576 N.W.2d 747 (Minn. 1998).

3. See, for example, *Weber v. Jolly Hotels*, 977 F.Supp. 327 (D.N.J. 1997).

CASE 9.1   # Zippo Manufacturing Co. v. Zippo Dot Com, Inc.

United States
District Court,
Western District of
Pennsylvania, 1997.
952 F.Supp. 1119.
http://zeus.bna.com/
e-law/cases/zippo.html[a]

HISTORICAL AND TECHNOLOGICAL SETTING   *In a case decided before 1960, the United States Supreme Court noted that "[a]s technological progress has increased the flow of commerce between States, the need for jurisdiction has undergone a similar increase."[b] Twenty-seven years later, the Court observed that jurisdiction could not be avoided "merely because the defendant did not physically enter the forum state. * * * [I]t is an inescapable fact of modern commercial life that a substantial amount of commercial business is transacted solely by mail and wire communications across state lines."[c]*

BACKGROUND AND FACTS   *Zippo Manufacturing Company (ZMC) makes, among other things, "Zippo" lighters. Zippo Dot Com, Inc. (ZDC), operates a Web page and an Internet subscription news service. ZDC has the exclusive right to use the domain names "zippo.com," "zippo.net," and "zipponews.com." ZMC is based in Pennsylvania. ZDC is based in California, and its contacts with Pennsylvania have occurred almost exclusively over the Internet. Two percent of its subscribers (3,000 of 140,000) are Pennsylvania residents who contracted over the Internet to receive its service. Also, ZDC has agreements with seven Internet service providers in Pennsylvania to permit their subscribers to access the service. ZMC filed a suit in a federal district court against ZDC, alleging trademark infringement and other claims, based on ZDC's use of the word "Zippo." ZDC filed a motion to dismiss for lack of personal jurisdiction.*

IN THE LANGUAGE
OF THE COURT

McLAUGHLIN, District Judge.
           *   *   *   *

     *   *   * [T]he likelihood that personal jurisdiction can be constitutionally exercised is directly proportionate to the nature and quality of commercial activity that an entity conducts over the Internet. * * * At one end of the spectrum are situations where a defendant clearly does business over the Internet. If the defendant enters into contracts with residents of a foreign jurisdiction that involve the knowing and repeated transmission of computer files over the Internet, personal jurisdiction is proper. At the opposite end are situations where a defendant has simply posted information on an Internet Web site which is accessible to users in foreign jurisdictions. A passive Web site that does little more than make information available to those who are interested in it is not grounds

---

a. This is a page in the "Electronic Commerce & Law Report" library.
b. *Hanson v. Denckla*, 357 U.S. 235, 78 S.Ct. 1228, 2 L.Ed.2d 1283 (1958).
c. *Burger King Corp. v. Rudzewicz*, 471 U.S. 462, 105 S.Ct. 2174, 85 L.Ed.2d 528 (1985).

for the exercise of personal jurisdiction. The middle ground is occupied by interactive Web sites where a user can exchange information with the host computer. In these cases, the exercise of jurisdiction is determined by examining the level of interactivity and commercial nature of the exchange of information that occurs on the Web site. [Emphasis added.]

* * * *

* * * We are being asked to determine whether [ZDC's] conducting of electronic commerce with Pennsylvania residents constitutes * * * doing business in Pennsylvania. We conclude that it does. [ZDC] has contracted with approximately 3,000 individuals and seven Internet access providers in Pennsylvania. The intended object of these transactions has been the downloading of the electronic messages that form the basis of this suit in Pennsylvania.

DECISION AND REMEDY   *The court held that it has jurisdiction over parties that conduct substantial business in its jurisdiction exclusively over the Internet. The court concluded that ZDC fits this description and denied the motion to dismiss.*

SECTION 2

The Constitution

To date, most of the Internet and new technology issues raised under the Constitution involve regulations of the freedom of speech. Legal challenges to laws that attempt to inhibit speech have generally been most successful when based on the commerce clause or the First Amendment. (For a discussion of the commerce clause, see Chapter 4.)

The problem is related to the unique feature of the Internet—its ability to cross political and geographic borders—and the inability of current technology to effectively filter out what legislators and government regulators might like to block. The issues are not unique to the United States. China and some European countries, among other nations, have attempted, with varying success, to block what their governments believe is bad for their citizens.

One of the basic questions involved in this issue concerns how much freedom of speech we are willing to sacrifice to allow the government to further a particular value, such as shielding children from certain material or preventing terrorism and crime. Phrased another way, how much of any value are we willing to sacrifice to protect our freedom of speech? There is no clear, definite answer to this question. Generally, the courts hold that speech may be restricted to serve a *compelling interest* but only if the restriction is the *least restrictive means* of doing so. (See Chapter 4 for a fuller discussion of freedom of speech.)

ENCRYPTION CODES

Privacy is one of the primary worries of most of those who use the Internet. It is possible to "eavesdrop" on Internet communications. The wrong person might learn your credit-card number when you enter it to make an online purchase. Your Social Security number might be revealed when it is passed through cyberspace. Details of your business transactions or personal specifics of your private life might be revealed to persons to whom you would not otherwise give such information.

Encryption is the process by which a message (plaintext) is transformed into something (ciphertext) that the sender and receiver intend third parties not to understand. Decryption is the process of transforming ciphertext into plaintext. An encryption code is a program used in encryption software to transform plaintext into ciphertext and vice versa. This software includes source codes, object codes, applications software, and system software.

Law enforcement authorities are afraid that the wrong persons, including international terrorists, will take advantage of Internet security to engage in illegal activities. For this reason, the U.S. Department of Commerce has attempted to restrict the export of encryption code. (The export of cryptography is also a violation of a federal criminal statute that is discussed later in this chapter.[4]) These restrictions have been challenged in a few cases on the ground that an

---

4. 15 C.F.R. Part 772.

encryption code is speech and therefore protected by the First Amendment. That would mean that the regulations banning its export are unconstitutional.[5] In a recent case, however, a federal district court held that an encryption code is not speech, because its purpose is to "transfer functions, not to communicate ideas."[6]

THE CONTENTS OF WEB SITES

The Communications Decency Act (CDA) of 1996 sought to protect minors from harmful material on the Internet by taking a broad approach. The CDA made it a crime to make available to minors online any "obscene or indecent" message that "depicts or describes, in terms patently offensive as measured by contemporary community standards, sexual or excretory activities or organs."[7]

The United States Supreme Court disapproved of this approach, and in 1997, in *Reno v. American Civil Liberties Union*,[8] the Court ruled that portions of the act were unconstitutional. The Court said that "[t]he general, undefined terms 'indecent' and 'patently offensive' cover large amounts of nonpornographic material with serious educational or other value. Moreover, the 'community standards' criterion as applied to the Internet means that any communication available to a nationwide audience will be judged by the standards of the community most likely to be offended by the message."

Congress made a further attempt to regulate Internet speech in 1998. Included in the federal budget bill passed in that year was the Child Online Protection Act (COPA). The act imposed criminal penalties on those who distribute material that is "harmful to minors" without using some kind of age-verification system to separate adult and minor users. Like the CDA, the COPA was immediately challenged in court by civil rights groups, Web site operators, and others. In 1999, a federal district court issued an injunction against the COPA's enforcement until the constitutional questions could be decided.[9]

Are there forms of speech that the government can effectively restrict online? On the Internet, extreme hate speech is known as **cyber hate speech.** Racist

materials and Holocaust denials on the Web, for example, are cyber hate speech. Can such online speech be restricted?[10] Should it? Are there other forms of speech that the government should limit?[11] Content restrictions generally amount to censorship and can be difficult to enforce. In cyberspace, they are almost impossible to carry out.

Even if it were possible to enforce content restrictions online, U.S. federal law (or the law of any single nation) is only "local" law in cyberspace—less than half of the users of the Internet are in the United States. This highlights one of the criticisms of restricting online content at its source. Such restrictions are out of step with the revolutionary nature of the Internet. Any source of content may be in a different jurisdiction than those who view it. Information may be legal in some jurisdictions and not in others.

ACCESS TO WEB SITES

An alternative to regulating the content of Web sites is to block access to them. An employer may want to limit what his or her employees can do in cyberspace during working hours. A parent may wish to block what his or her child views on the Internet. **Filtering software,** or filters, can prevent certain persons from viewing certain Web sites at certain times by responding to a site's uniform resource locator (URL), or Internet address, or to its **meta tags,** or key words. This technology is at the core of the current debate on the control and regulation of information on the Internet.

There are concerns about this software and whether it effectively does what it claims to do. There are questions about the tags: What should they consist of, and who should decide which sites have which tags? Using filters to control the accessibility of information on the Internet also raises issues about the relationship of technology to law. Because the First Amendment is aimed at curtailing the government's power to censor speech, the fundamental issue is whether the law should apply in cyberspace, and if so, how it should operate.

---

5. See, for example, *Bernstein v. U.S. Department of Justice,* 176 F.3d 1132 (9th Cir. 1999).

6. *Junger v. Daley,* 8 F.Supp.2d 708 (N.D.Ohio 1998).

7. 47 U.S.C. Section 223(a)(1)(B)(ii).

8. 521 U.S. 844, 117 S.Ct. 2329, 138 L.Ed.2d 874 (1997).

9. *American Civil Liberties Union v. Reno,* 31 F.Supp.2d 473 (E.D.Pa. 1999).

10. In 1999, a jury in Portland, Oregon, ordered antiabortion activists to pay more than $100 million in punitive damages for material posted on a Web site that the jury found violated the federal Racketeer Influenced and Corrupt Organizations Act (RICO). The activists had argued that the material was protected by the First Amendment. For more on RICO, see Chapter 8.

11. The content of some speech is regulated to a certain extent by tort law, copyright law, and other laws. See, for example, the discussions of defamation, cyber fraud, and copyright infringement later in this chapter and in Chapters 5 and 7.

The debate centers on the use of filters by government employers, public schools, and public libraries. In its opinion in the *Reno v. American Civil Liberties Union* case noted above, the United States Supreme Court seemed to approve of the use of filters as a "less restrictive alternative."[12]

SECTION 3

Cyber Crimes

A **cyber crime** is a crime that occurs in the virtual community of the Internet. Some of these crimes are discussed in the following subsections.

The "location" of cyber crime—cyberspace—raises new issues in the investigation of crimes and the prosecution of perpetrators. It is the unique nature of the Internet that causes one of the toughest problems in enforcing laws against cyber crimes: the issue of jurisdiction. A person who commits an act against a business in California, where the act is a cyber crime, might never have set foot in California but instead might reside in New York, or even in Canada, where the act may not be a crime. If the crime were committed via e-mail, would the e-mail constitute sufficient "minimum contacts" for the victim's state to exercise jurisdiction?

Other difficulties include identifying the perpetrators. Cyber criminals do not leave physical traces, such as fingerprints or DNA samples, as evidence of their crimes. Even electronic "footprints" can be hard to find and follow. For example, e-mail may be sent through a remailer, an online service that guarantees that a message cannot be traced to its source.

CYBER STALKING

California enacted the first stalking law in 1990, in response to the contemporary murders of six women—including Rebecca Schaeffer, a television star—by the men who had harassed them. The law made it a crime to harass or follow a person while making a "credible threat" that puts that person in reasonable fear for his or her safety or the safety of the person's immediate family.[13] Most other states have also enacted stalking laws.

Generally speaking, the stalking laws in about half of the states require a physical act (following the victim). **Cyber stalkers**—stalkers who commit their crimes in cyberspace—find their victims through Internet relay chat (or live chat), Usenet newsgroups or other bulletin boards, and e-mail. None of these communications requires that a stalker physically "follow" his or her prey. For this reason, these statutes do not apply in the virtual community. About three-quarters of the stalking laws in the other states *could* apply in cyberspace, because those statutes deem tools of harassment to include written communications (e-mail) or telephones (Internet connections).

As of this writing, seven states have statutes that specifically address stalking by computer, or cyber stalking. It is also a federal crime to harass someone by means of interstate "telecommunications devices."[14] Some of the state statutes are based on California's law and require a "credible threat." Others require only an intention to harass, annoy, or alarm.[15]

CYBER THEFT

In cyberspace, thieves are not subject to the physical limitations of the "real" world. A thief can steal data stored in a networked computer with dial-in access from anywhere on the globe. Only the speed of the connection and the thief's computer equipment limit the quantity of data that can be stolen.

For this reason, laws written to protect physical property are difficult to apply in cyberspace. For example, the federal statute that bans the interstate transportation of stolen property refers to "goods, wares and merchandise."[16] At least one court has held that this does not apply to intangible property such as computer data.[17] Another federal statute makes it illegal to threaten physical violence to property.[18] A threat to delete files may not qualify.

To address abuses that stem from the misuse of new technology, Congress amended the Counterfeit Access Device and Computer Fraud and Abuse Act of

---

12. In 1999, Michigan enacted the Library Privacy Act to permit public libraries to filter their patrons' access to the Internet as long as at least one unfiltered terminal is provided for restricted use by adults and minors accompanied by parents or guardians.
13. Cal. Penal Code Section 646.9.

14. 47 U.S.C. Section 223(1)(A) and (B). See also 18 U.S.C Section 875. Another possibility was indicated in 1998, when a former University of California student was convicted under federal civil rights law for sending hate e-mail to Asian students.
15. See, for example, Conn. General Statutes Sections 53a-182b and 53a-183.
16. 18 U.S.C. Section 2314.
17. *United States v. Brown*, 925 F.2d 1301 (10th Cir. 1991).
18. 18 U.S.C. Section 1951(a).

1984 with the National Information Infrastructure Protection Act of 1996.[19] The 1996 act provides, among other things, that a person who accesses a computer online, without authority, to obtain classified, restricted, or protected data, or attempts to do so, is subject to criminal prosecution. These data could include financial and credit records, medical records, legal files, military and national security files, and other confidential information in government or private computers. The crime has two elements: accessing a computer without authority and taking the data.

This theft is a felony if it is committed for a commercial purpose or for private financial gain, or if the value of the stolen data (or computer time) exceeds $5,000. Penalties include fines and imprisonment for up to twenty years. A victim of computer theft can also bring a civil suit against the violator to obtain damages, an injunction, and other relief.

Persons who use one computer to break into another are sometimes referred to as **hackers.** Hackers who break into computers without authorization commit cyber theft. Often, their principal aim is to prove how smart they are by gaining access to others'

password-protected computers and causing random data errors or making unpaid-for telephone calls.[20] Such crimes should not be taken lightly, but from a larger perspective, they might be considered the equivalent of new-tech car theft.

CYBER TERRORISM

Cyber terrorists are hackers who aim not to gain attention but to remain undetected in order to exploit computers for a more serious impact. Just as a "real" terrorist might explode a bomb to shut down an embassy, a cyber terrorist might explode a "logic bomb" to shut down a central computer. Other goals might include a wholesale theft of data, such as a merchant's customer files, or the monitoring of a computer to discover a business firm's plans and transactions. A cyber terrorist might want to insert false codes or data. For example, the processing control system of a food manufacturer could be changed to alter the levels of ingredients so that consumers of the food would become ill.

---

19. 18 U.S.C. Section 1030.

20. The total cost of crime on the Internet is estimated to be several billion dollars annually, but two-thirds of that total is said to consist of unpaid-for toll calls.

CONCEPT SUMMARY 9.1

CYBER CRIMES

CRIME	DESCRIPTION
Cyber Stalking	Harassing someone by computer.
Cyber Theft	Accessing a computer without authority and taking the data. This is a felony under the National Information Infrastructure Protection Act of 1996.
Cyber Terrorism	Exploiting a computer for a serious impact, such as inserting false codes or data.

SECTION 4

Cyber Torts

In the area of torts, as in other areas of the law affected by the new technology, there are more questions than answers. One of the foremost issues is the question of who should be held liable for a **cyber tort** (a tort committed in cyberspace). For example, who should be held liable when someone in a newsgroup posts a defamatory **flame** (an online message in which one party attacks another in harsh, often personal, terms)?

Should an Internet service provider (ISP) be liable for the remark if the ISP was unaware that it was being made? Who should be held liable for an employee's defamatory remark on a company bulletin board?

Other questions involve issues of proof. How, for example, can it be proved that an online defamatory remark was "published" (which requires that a third party see or hear it)? How can the identity of the person who made the remark be discovered? Can an ISP be forced to reveal the source of an anonymous comment? Answers to some of these questions are explored in the following sections.

DEFAMATION ONLINE

Online forums allow anyone—customers, employees, or crackpots—to complain about a business firm. The complaint could concern the firm's personnel, policies, practices, or products, and it might have an impact on the business of the firm. This is possible regardless of whether the complaint is justified and whether it is true.

If a statement is not true, it may constitute defamation. Defamation is any published or publicly spoken false statement that causes injury to another's good name, reputation, or character. Like other torts, defamation is governed by state law, and the elements of the tort can vary from state to state. As discussed in Chapter 5, generally a plaintiff must show that a statement was false, was not subject to a privilege, was communicated to a third person, and resulted in damage to the plaintiff. A public figure must also show that the statement was made with actual malice.

Newspapers, magazines, and television and radio stations may be held liable for defamatory remarks that they disseminate, even if those remarks are prepared or created by others. Under the Communications Decency Act of 1996, however, Internet service providers (ISPs), or "interactive computer service providers," are not liable with respect to such material.[21] An ISP typically provides access to the Internet through a local phone number and may provide other services, including access to databases available only to the ISP's subscribers.

As of this writing, there is no proved case of an untrue, negative posting on the Internet ruining a business. Defamation suits involving online statements have not yet resulted in decisions in U.S. courts that plaintiffs were defamed and are entitled to a remedy. The courts have focused chiefly on such issues as determining who would be held liable, which was the issue in the following case.

---

21. 47 U.S.C. Section 230.

CASE 9.2   Blumenthal v. Drudge

United States
District Court,
District of Columbia,
1998.
992 F.Supp. 44.
http://www.courttv.com
/legaldocs/cyberlaw/
drudge2.html[a]

COMPANY PROFILE   *Founded in 1985, America Online, Inc. (AOL) (**http://www. aol.com**), operates two global Internet online services: AOL Interactive Services and CompuServe Interactive Services. This makes AOL the world's largest Internet service provider (ISP). AOL also operates AOL Studios, which develops original and local content for AOL's online and Web-based brands, including AOL, AOL.com, CompuServe, and Digital City. As many as fifty million subscribers or other users use AOL as a conduit to receive and disseminate huge quantities of information over its computer network. In 1998, AOL merged with Netscape. In 2000, AOL bought Time Warner.*

BACKGROUND AND FACTS   *Under a licensing agreement with America Online, Inc. (AOL), the* Drudge Report, *an online political publication, was made available free to all AOL subscribers. According to the agreement, AOL could remove content that it determined was in violation of AOL's "standard terms of service." One issue of the* Drudge Report *contained an article charging that Sidney Blumenthal, an assistant to the president of the United States, "has a spousal abuse past that has been effectively covered up." Blumenthal's spouse, Jacqueline Blumenthal, also worked in the White House as the director of a presidential commission. When the* Report's *editor, Matt Drudge, learned that the article was false, he printed a retraction and publicly apologized to the Blumenthals. The Blumenthals filed a suit in a federal district court against Drudge, AOL, and others, alleging in part that the original remarks were defamatory. AOL filed a motion for summary judgment.*

**IN THE LANGUAGE
OF THE COURT**

PAUL L. FRIEDMAN, District Judge.

  *   *   *   *

  *   *   * AOL was nothing more than a provider of an interactive computer service on which the *Drudge Report* was carried, and Congress has said quite clearly [in the

---

a. This site is Court TV Online's "Technology and Computers" section within its "Legal Documents" collection.

Communications Decency Act (CDA) of 1996] that such a provider shall not be treated as a "publisher or speaker" and therefore may not be held liable in tort.

* * * *

Plaintiffs make the additional argument, however, that * * * Drudge was not just an anonymous person who sent a message over the Internet through AOL. He is a person with whom AOL contracted, whom AOL paid * * * and whom AOL promoted to its subscribers and potential subscribers as a reason to subscribe to AOL. * * *

* * * *

If it were writing on a clean slate, this Court would agree with plaintiffs. * * * But Congress has made a different policy choice by providing immunity even where the interactive service provider has an active, even aggressive role in making available content prepared by others. * * * Congress has conferred immunity from tort liability as an incentive to Internet service providers to self-police the Internet for obscenity and other offensive material, even where the self-policing is unsuccessful or not even attempted.

DECISION AND REMEDY   *The court granted AOL's motion for summary judgment. The court held that under the CDA, an Internet service provider is not liable for failing to edit, withhold, or restrict access to defamatory remarks that it disseminates but did not create.*

SPAM

Spam is "junk" e-mail—bulk, unsolicited e-mail—or junk newsgroup postings.[22] Typical spam consists of a product ad sent to all of the users on an e-mailing list or all of the members of a newsgroup.

Because spam can waste user time and network bandwidth (the amount of data that can be transmitted within a certain time), some individuals and organizations are attempting to inhibit its use. The Internet is a public forum, however. Under the First Amendment (see Chapter 4), this limits what can be done to restrict the use of spam.

In California, an unsolicited e-mail ad must state in its subject line that it is an ad ("ADV:"). The ad must also include a toll-free phone number or return e-mail address through which the recipient can contact the sender to request that no more ads be e-mailed.[23] An Internet service provider (ISP) can bring a successful suit in a California state court against a spammer who violates the ISP's policy that prohibits or restricts unsolicited e-mail ads. The court can award damages of up to $25,000 per day.[24]

In the following antispam case, an ISP argued in a federal district court that spamming is trespassing. Would the court accept this argument and block the sending of unsolicited ads to the ISP's subscribers?

---

22. The term *spam* is said to come from a Monty Python song with the lyrics, "Spam spam spam spam, spam spam spam spam, lovely spam, wonderful spam." Like these lyrics, spam online is often considered to be a repetition of worthless text.

23. Ca. Bus. & Prof. Code Section 17538.4.
24. Ca. Bus. & Prof. Code Section 17538.45.

CASE 9.3   CompuServe, Inc. v. Cyber Promotions, Inc.

United States District Court, Southern District of Ohio, 1997.
962 F.Supp. 1015.
http://www.Loundy.com/
Cases/CompuServe_v_
Cyber_Promo.html[a]

BACKGROUND AND FACTS   *Through a nationwide computer network, CompuServe, Inc., operates a communication service that includes e-mail for CompuServe subscribers. E-mail sent to the subscribers is processed and stored on CompuServe's equipment. Cyber Promotions, Inc., is in the business of sending unsolicited e-mail ads, or spam, to Internet users. CompuServe subscribers complained to the service about Cyber Promotions's ads, and many canceled their subscriptions. Handling the ads also placed a tremendous burden on CompuServe's equipment. CompuServe told Cyber Promotions to stop using CompuServe's equipment to process and store the ads—in effect, to stop sending the ads to CompuServe subscribers. Ignoring the demand, Cyber Promotions stepped up the volume of its ads. After CompuServe attempted unsuccessfully to block the flow with screening software, it filed a suit against Cyber Promotions in*

---

a. This page is at the E-LAW Web site, "the home page of David J. Loundy, an attorney and author."

a federal district court, seeking an injunction on the ground that the ads constituted trespass to personal property.

IN THE LANGUAGE OF THE COURT

GRAHAM, District Judge.

* * * *

* * * [An] actor may commit a trespass by an act which brings him [or her] into an intended physical contact with a chattel [property] in the possession of another[.]

* * * It is undisputed that plaintiff has a possessory interest in [a right to possess] its computer systems. Further, defendants' contact with plaintiff's computers is clearly intentional. Although electronic messages may travel through the Internet over various routes, the messages are affirmatively directed to their destination.

* * * *

* * * Harm to the personal property or diminution of its quality, condition, or value as a result of defendants' use can also be the predicate for liability. * * * To the extent that defendants' multitudinous electronic mailings demand the disk space and drain the processing power of plaintiff's computer equipment, those resources are not available to serve CompuServe subscribers. Therefore, the value of that equipment to CompuServe is diminished even though it is not physically damaged by defendants' conduct.

* * * *

Many subscribers have terminated their accounts specifically because of the unwanted receipt of bulk e-mail messages. Defendants' intrusions into CompuServe's computer systems, insofar as they harm plaintiff's business reputation and goodwill with its customers, are actionable.

DECISION AND REMEDY

The court held that spamming is trespassing. The court issued an injunction, ordering Cyber Promotions to stop distributing its ads to e-mail addresses maintained by CompuServe.

SECTION 5

Virtual Property

The legal issues relating to **virtual property**—property in cyberspace—are essentially legal questions involving intellectual property. As discussed in Chapter 7, intellectual property consists of trademarks, patents, copyrights, and trade secrets. Legal protection for these forms of property makes it possible to market goods and services profitably, which provides an incentive to sell competitive goods and services.

In the context of cyberspace, a fundamental issue has to do with the degree of legal protection that should be given to virtual property. If the protection is inadequate, the incentive to make new works available online will be reduced. If the protection is too strict, the free flow and fair use of data will be impaired.

CYBER MARKS

In cyberspace, trademarks are sometimes referred to as **cyber marks.** An early legal issue relating to cyber

marks concerned the rights of a mark's owner to use it as part of a domain name (an Internet address). The question was whether *cybersquatting* (registering another party's mark as a domain name and offering to forfeit it for a sum of money) constituted a commercial use of the mark so as to violate federal law. Generally, the courts have held that cybersquatting does violate the law.[25]

As the dust settles around this once contentious issue, cyber mark issues that courts are more likely to confront in the future revolve around other uses and abuses of those marks. Some of the questions are not new, but the context of cyberspace requires new answers. Some of the questions, however, are as new as the technological ability to create hypertext links and frames and to embed hidden code called meta tags in Web sites.

Domain Names. The Internet Corporation for Assigned Names and Numbers (ICANN) is a non-profit corporation that the federal government

---

25. See, for example, *Panavision International, L.P. v. Toeppen,* 141 F.3d 1316 (9th Cir. 1998).

designated to coordinate certain functions of the Internet. Among other responsibilities, ICANN oversees the Internet domain name system and accredits companies to sell domain name registrations in the .com, .net, and .org domains.

In 1999, ICANN approved a draft of a Uniform Domain Name Dispute Resolution Policy. Generally, under this policy, when a registration company receives a complaint concerning the impact of a domain name on a trademark, the company can act only on instructions from the domain-name holder or an order of a court, arbitrator, or other decision maker deciding the parties' dispute. There is an exception for a dispute involving cybersquatting. In that case, a neutral decision maker selected from a panel set up for this purpose may resolve the dispute online, in less than forty-five days. Of course, the parties may still go to court to contest the outcome.

Meta Tags. Search engines compile their results by looking through a Web site's key words field. Meta tags, or key words, may be inserted in this field to increase a site's appearance in search engine results, even though the site has nothing to do with the inserted words. Using this same technique, one site may appropriate the key words of other sites with more frequent hits, so that the appropriating site appears in the same search engine results as the more popular site. One use of meta tags was at issue in the following case.

CASE 9.4   **Playboy Enterprises, Inc. v. Welles**

United States District Court, Southern District of California, 1998.
7 F.Supp.2d 1098.
http://www.Loundy.com/CASES/Playboy_v_Welles.html[a]

COMPANY PROFILE   *Playboy Enterprises, Inc. (PEI) (**http://www.playboy.com**), is an international publishing and entertainment company. Since 1953, PEI has published* Playboy *magazine, a popular magazine with approximately ten million readers each month. PEI also publishes numerous specialty magazines and other publications. In addition, PEI produces television programming for cable and satellite transmission, and sells and licenses other goods and services. PEI bestows on its models, who appear in the magazine, such titles as "Playmate of the Month" and "Playmate of the Year." PEI encourages its models to identify themselves and to use their titles for their self-promotion and the promotion of its magazines and other goods and services.*

BACKGROUND AND FACTS   *Playboy Enterprises, Inc. (PEI), maintains Web sites to promote* Playboy *magazine and PEI models. PEI's trademarks include the terms "Playboy," "Playmate," and "Playmate of the Year." Terri Welles is a self-employed model and spokesperson, who was featured as the "Playmate of the Year" in June 1981. Welles maintains a Web site titled "Terri Welles—Playmate of the Year 1981." As meta tags, Welles's site uses the terms "Playboy" and "Playmate," among others. PEI asked Welles to stop using these terms, but she refused. PEI filed a suit in a federal district court against Welles, asking the court to order her to, among other things, stop using those terms as meta tags. PEI argued, in part, that this constituted trademark infringement under the Lanham Act (see Chapter 7). Welles responded in part that her use of the terms is a "fair use," because she was and is the "Playmate of the Year 1981."*

IN THE LANGUAGE OF THE COURT

GRAHAM, District Judge.
   *   *   *   *

In a case where the mark is used only to describe the goods or services of [a] party, or their geographic origin, trademark law recognizes a "fair use" defense. *   *   *
   *   *   *   *

It is clear that defendant is selling Terri Welles and only Terri Welles on the website. There is no overt attempt to confuse the websurfer into believing that her site is a Playboy-

---

a. This is a different URL for a page within the E-LAW site described in the footnote to Case 9.3 as "the home page of David J. Loundy, an attorney and author."

related website. In this case, then, defendant's use of the term Playmate of the Year 1981 is descriptive of and used fairly and in good faith only to describe [herself]. *   *   *

With respect to the meta tags, the court finds there to be no trademark infringement where defendant has used plaintiff's trademarks in good faith to index the content of her website. *   *   * *Much like the subject index of a card catalog, the meta tags give the websurfer using a search engine a clearer indication of the content of a website.* The use of the term Playboy is not an infringement because it references not only her identity as a "Playboy Playmate of the Year 1981," but it may also reference the legitimate editorial uses of the term Playboy contained in the text of defendant's website. [Emphasis added.]

DECISION AND REMEDY   *The court held that a party can use another's trademarks as meta tags when those marks describe the party who uses them. The court ruled that Welles was entitled to the "fair use" of the "Playboy" and "Playmate" marks as meta tags.*

Dilution. As discussed in Chapter 7, trademark *dilution* occurs when a trademark is used, without authorization, in a way that diminishes the distinctive quality of the mark. Unlike trademark infringement, a dilution cause of action does not require proof that consumers are likely to be confused by a connection between the unauthorized use and the mark. For this reason, the products involved do not have to be similar. In the first case alleging dilution on the Web, a court precluded the use of "candyland.com" as the URL for an adult site. The suit was brought by the maker of the "Candyland" children's game and owner of the "Candyland" mark.[26]

A dilution case does require, however, that a mark be famous when the dilution occurs. Gateway 2000 has been making personal computers since 1985 and owns the mark "Gateway 2000." In 1988, Gateway.com, Inc., an entirely different company, began to use "gateway.com" as part of its URL and registered it as a domain name in 1990. Gateway 2000 later filed a suit to block the use of "gateway" on the ground of dilution. The court refused to grant the request, concluding that Gateway 2000 could not prove that its name was famous at the time Gateway.com chose "gateway" as a domain name.

In another interesting case, a court issued an injunction on the ground that spamming under another's logo is trademark dilution.[27] In that case, Hotmail, Inc., provided e-mail services and worked to dissociate itself from spam. Van$ Money Pie, Inc., and others spammed thousands of e-mail customers,

using the free e-mail Hotmail as a return address. The court ordered the defendants to stop.

Licensing. One of the ways to make use of another's mark (or another's copyright, patent, or trade secret), while avoiding litigation, is to obtain a license to do so. A license in this context is essentially an agreement to permit the use of a mark for certain purposes. A licensee (the party obtaining the license) might be allowed to use the mark of the licensor (the party issuing the license) as part of the name of its company, or as part of its domain name, without otherwise using the mark on any products or services.

A licensee must not break the terms of the license, however, or litigation could ensue and liability may result. In the first case involving a trademark license in cyberspace, the licensee took advantage of its licensor's increasingly famous mark to make its Web site look more like the licensor's. Alleging a violation of the licensing agreement, the licensor sued. The court granted the licensor's motion for a preliminary injunction, holding that the licensee likely breached the license and infringed the mark.[28]

PATENTS ONLINE

There are four noteworthy aspects to patents and the new technology. First is the rapidly increasing number of patents that the U.S. Patent and Trademark Office (USPTO) has granted in recent years. For example, there are now more than ten thousand applications pending. Software technology has progressed

---

26. *Hasbro, Inc. v. Internet Entertainment Group, Ltd.,* 1996 WL 84853 (W.D.Wash. 1996).

27. *Hotmail Corp. v. Van$ Money Pie, Inc.,* 1998 WL 388389 (N.D.Cal. 1998).

28. *Digital Equipment Corp. v. AltaVista Technology, Inc.,* 960 F.Supp. 456 (D.Mass. 1997).

quickly. This points to another important feature of the new technology that relates to patents.

Software developers use combinations of previous software to create new products and processes. This practice has led to uncertainty and controversy about the ownership and the use of patent rights to the hybrid products. One way to prevent legal problems in this regard is for a software developer or maker to obtain licenses for others' products and to issue licenses for its own.

The third aspect of patents as they relate to the new technology concerns one of the most important reasons that a patent is granted. A developer obtains a patent to prevent others from patenting the same product or process. When more than one party is developing the same product or process, the first party to obtain a patent is the party who gets the protection. Even before a patent is obtained, however, the disclosure of a product or process can block others from obtaining a patent for it. For this reason, those who

reveal their inventions to the public are rewarded. It is a practice in the software industry to keep technology secret, but this is risky. A developer could lose all rights to a product by keeping it secret.

Finally, a significant development relating to patents is the availability online of the world's patent databases. The USPTO provides at its Web site searchable databases covering U.S. patents granted since 1976. This page of the USPTO is illustrated in Exhibit 9–2. The European Patent Office (EPO) maintains at its Web site databases covering all patent documents in sixty-five nations and the legal status of patents in twenty-two of those countries.

COPYRIGHTS IN DIGITAL INFORMATION

Copyright law is probably the most important form of intellectual property protection on the Internet. This is because much of the material on the Internet consists of works of authorship (including multimedia

EXHIBIT 9–2   PATENT DATABASES OF THE
                U.S. PATENT AND TRADEMARK OFFICE

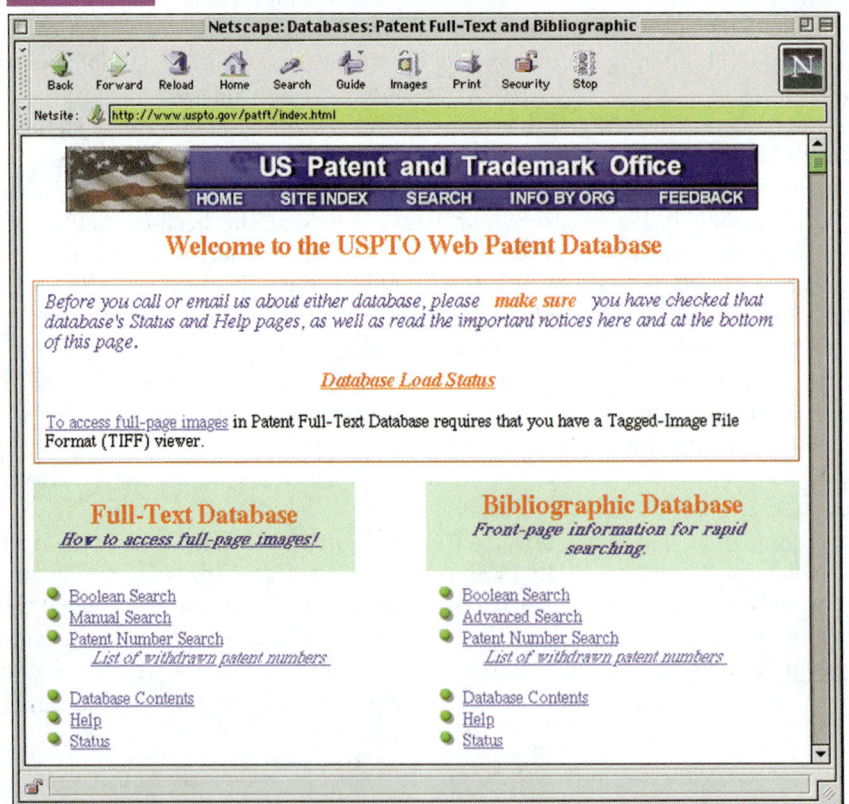

presentations, software, and database information). These works are the traditional focus of copyright law. Copyright law is also important because the nature of the Internet requires that data be "copied" to be transferred online. Copies are a significant part of the traditional controversies arising in this area of the law.

The Copyright Act of 1976. Remember from the discussion of copyright law in Chapter 7 that copyright law is concerned chiefly with the creation, distribution, and sale of protected works of authorship. When Congress drafted the principal U.S. law governing copyrights, the Copyright Act of 1976, cyberspace did not exist for most of us. The threat to copyright owners was posed not by computer technology but by unauthorized tangible copies of works and the sale of rights to movies, television, and other media.

Some of the issues that were unimagined when the Copyright Act was drafted have posed thorny questions for the courts. For example, to sell a copy of a work, permission of the copyright holder is necessary. Because of the nature of cyberspace, however, one of the early controversies was determining at what point an intangible, electronic "copy" of a work has been made. The courts have held that loading a file or pro-

gram into a computer's random access memory, or RAM, constitutes the making of a "copy" for purposes of copyright law.[29] RAM is a portion of a computer's memory into which a file, for example, is loaded so that it can be accessed (read or written over). Thus, a copyright is infringed when a party downloads software into RAM if that party does not own the software or otherwise have a right to download it.[30] (Technology designed to curb unauthorized copying and other aspects of digital copyright protection are discussed in the *Emerging Trends in Technology* feature in Chapter 7.)

Other rights, including those relating to the revision of "collective works" such as magazines, were acknowledged thirty years ago but were considered to have only limited economic value. Today, technology has made some of those rights vastly more significant. How does the old law apply to these rights? That was one of the questions in the following case.

---

29. *MAI Systems Corp. v. Peak Computer, Inc.*, 991 F.2d 511 (9th Cir. 1993).
30. *DSC Communications Corp. v. Pulse Communications, Inc.*, 170 F.3d 1354 (Fed. Cir. 1999).

CASE 9.5   Tasini v. The New York Times Co.

United States
Court of Appeals,
Second Circuit, 1999.
192 F.3d 356.
http://www.findlaw.com/
casecode/courts/
2nd.html[a]

BACKGROUND AND FACTS *Magazines and newspapers, including the* New York Times, *buy and publish articles written by freelance writers. Unless the parties agree otherwise, under Section 201(c) of the Copyright Act the writers retain the copyrights in the separate articles, but the publishers obtain copyrights in the "collective work." Besides circulating hard copies of their periodicals, these publishers sell the contents to e-publishers for inclusion in online and other electronic databases. Jonathan Tasini and five other freelance writers filed a suit in a federal district court against the New York Times Company and other publishers, including the e-publishers, contending that the e-publication of the articles violated the Copyright Act. The publishers responded, among other things, that the Copyright Act gave them a right to produce "revisions" of their publications. The writers argued that articles included in e-databases were not "revisions." The publishers filed a motion for summary judgment, which the court granted. The writers appealed to the U.S. Court of Appeals for the Second Circuit.*

**IN THE LANGUAGE
OF THE COURT**

WINTER, Chief Judge.
    *   *   *   *

    *   *   * [Under Section 201(c) of the Copyright Act] the privilege granted to a collective-work [publisher] to use individually copyrighted contributions is limited to the reproduction and distribution of the individual contribution as part of: (i) "that particular [i.e., the original] collective work"; (ii) "any revision of that collective work"; or

---

a. In the "1999" row, click on "Sept." On that page, scroll down to the case name and click on it to access the opinion.

(iii) "any later collective work in the same series." Because it is undisputed that the electronic databases are neither the original collective work—the particular edition of the periodical—in which the Authors' articles were published nor a later collective work in the same series, appellees [the publishers] rely entirely on the argument that each database constitutes a "revision" of the particular collective work in which each Author's individual contribution first appeared. We reject that argument.

*   *   *   *

The most natural reading of the "revision" of "that collective work" clause is that the Section 201(c) privilege protects only later editions of a particular issue of a periodical, such as the final edition of a newspaper. Because later editions are not identical to earlier editions, use of the individual contributions in the later editions might not be protected under the preceding clause. Given the context provided by the surrounding clauses, this interpretation makes perfect sense. It protects the use of an individual contribution in a collective work that is somewhat altered from the original in which the copyrighted article was first published, but that is not in any ordinary sense of language a "later" work in the "same series."

*   *   *   *

Moreover, *   *   * if the contents of an electronic database are merely a "revision" of a particular "collective work," e.g., the August 16, 1999 edition of *The New York Times,* then the third clause of the privilege sentence—permitting the reproduction and distribution of an individually copyrighted work as part of "a later collective work in the same series"—would be superfluous. An electronic database can contain hundreds or thousands of editions of hundreds or thousands of periodicals, including newspapers, magazines, anthologies, and encyclopedias. To view the contents of databases as revisions would eliminate any need for a privilege for "a later collective work in the same series."

DECISION AND REMEDY   *The U.S. Court of Appeals for the Second Circuit held that the publishers, to put the contents of their periodicals into e-databases and onto CD-ROMs, needed the permission of the writers whose articles were included in the periodicals. The court reversed the lower court's summary judgment and remanded the case with instructions to enter a judgment for the writers.*

The World Intellectual Property Organization (WIPO) Copyright Treaty of 1996. Technology, particularly the Internet, offers new outlets for creative products. It also makes them easier to steal—copyrighted works can be pirated and distributed around the world quickly and efficiently. To curb this crime, in 1996 the World Intellectual Property Organization (WIPO) enacted the WIPO Copyright Treaty, a special agreement under the Berne Convention. (The Berne Convention was discussed in Chapter 7.) The purpose was to upgrade global standards of copyright protection, particularly for the Internet.

Special provisions of the WIPO treaty relate to rights in digital data. The treaty strengthens some rights for copyright owners, in terms of their application in cyberspace, but leaves other questions unresolved. For example, the treaty does not make clear what, for purposes of international law, constitutes the making of a "copy" in electronic form. The United States signed the WIPO treaty in 1996 and implemented its terms in the Digital Millennium Copyright Act of 1998, which is discussed next.

The Digital Millennium Copyright Act of 1998. The Digital Millennium Copyright Act of 1998 created civil and criminal penalties for anyone who circumvents encryption software or other technological antipiracy protection. Also prohibited are the manufacture, import, sale, or distribution of devices or services for circumvention.

There are exceptions to fit the needs of libraries, scientists, universities, and others. In general, the new law does not restrict the "fair use" of circumvention for educational and other noncommercial purposes. For example, circumvention is allowed to test computer security, to conduct encryption research, to protect personal privacy, or to allow parents to monitor their children's use of the Internet. The exceptions are to be reconsidered every three years.

An Internet service provider (ISP) is not liable for any copyright infringement by its customer if the ISP is unaware of the subscriber's violation. An ISP may be held liable only after learning of the violation and failing to take action to shut the subscriber down. A copyright holder has to act promptly, however, by pursuing a claim in court, or the subscriber has the right to be restored to online access.

TRADE SECRETS IN CYBERSPACE

The nature of the new technology—the versatility of e-mail in particular—undercuts a business firm's ability to protect its confidential information, including trade secrets (trade secrets were defined and discussed in more detail in Chapter 7).[31] For example, a dishonest employee could transmit trade secrets in a company's computer to anyone via an e-mail connection on the Internet. "Anyone" could be a thief, a

competitor, or a future employer. If e-mail is not an option, the employee might walk out with the information on a computer disk. Even honest employees can make mistakes, sending confidential data to the wrong e-mail address—a competitor, for example, instead of a client—or losing a disk on a business trip.

An illustration of what a departing employee might do is provided by a criminal case that involved two competing software developers, Borland International, Inc., and Symantec. Eugene Wang, a Borland vice president, expressed dissatisfaction with his job and quit. Other Borland officers reviewed Wang's e-mail files and found messages to Gordon Eubanks, Symantec's president and chief executive officer. Believing that the messages contained trade secrets and other confidential information, Borland filed a civil suit to recover damages and also notified the police. After an investigation, criminal charges, including the theft of trade secrets, were filed against both Wang and Eubanks.[32]

---

31. Note that in a recent case, the court indicated that customers' e-mail addresses may constitute trade secrets. See *T-N-T Motorsports, Inc. v. Hennessey Motorsports, Inc.*, 965 S.W.2d 18 (Tex.App.—Hous. [1 Dist.] 1998), rehearing overruled (1998), petition dismissed (1998).

32. *People v. Eubanks*, 14 Cal.4th 580, 14 Cal.4th 1282D, 927 P.2d 310, 59 Cal.Rptr.2d 200 (1996), as modified on denial of rehearing (1997). The charges were dismissed after Borland paid a substantial part of the cost of the criminal investigation. The California Supreme Court felt that Borland's payment made it unlikely that the defendants would receive fair treatment.

CONCEPT SUMMARY 9.2

VIOLATIONS OF VIRTUAL PROPERTY RIGHTS

VIRTUAL PROPERTY	VIOLATION
Cyber Marks	Trademark infringement may occur in cyberspace if (1) another site's key words are used improperly as meta tags; (2) the quality of another's mark is diluted by improper use; (3) another's mark is used without a license; or (4) a licensing agreement is broken. (Trademark infringement can also occur with certain uses of hypertext links and framing technology.)
Patents	Patent infringement of a cyberspace product or process may occur if a user, including a software developer, fails to obtain a license to use the item.
Copyrights	Loading a computer program or data into the RAM of a computer is making a "copy" and may violate U.S. copyright law if it is done without the permission of the copyright holder. (International law does not clearly resolve this issue.) The Digital Millennium Copyright Act of 1998 created civil and criminal penalties for anyone who circumvents encryption software or other technological antipiracy protection.
Trade Secrets	Communicating trade secrets via new technology without authorization may be a violation of criminal and civil laws.

SECTION 6

E-Commerce

The increasing use of the Internet to do business brings to light at least two important concerns for persons who engage in commerce online, or **e-commerce**, and agree to **e-contracts**. There is some question about the ability of current Internet technology to guarantee the security of e-commerce. There is also concern about whether the legal framework can guarantee the enforcement of e-contracts.

In the following sections, we discuss these concerns in the context of the following types of Internet business transactions: contracting in cyberspace, making payments and investing online, and marketing on the Internet.

CONTRACTING IN CYBERSPACE

Over the last ten years, the new technology has transformed society and is defining new ways of doing business. This revolution in technology has even changed the nature of many of the goods and services that are the subjects of e-commerce and e-contracts. The most important legal questions concern how the law should be altered to accommodate these changes.

Cyberspace Agreements. A significant issue is how the law should be adapted to reflect business practices regarding such cyberspace agreements as Web site click-on agreements, software licenses (some types of licensing agreements were discussed earlier in this chapter), e-data interchange, and online sales. Some aspects of these agreements will be discussed in the *Emerging Trends in Technology* in Chapter 19. Other facets are discussed in this chapter's *Emerging Trends in Technology*.

Electronic Transactions. The National Conference of Commissioners (NCC) on Uniform State Laws has also promulgated the Uniform Electronic Transactions Act (UETA). The goal of the UETA is not to create rules for electronic transactions—for example, the act does not require digital signatures—but to support the enforcement of e-contracts.

Under the UETA, contracts entered into online, as well as other electronic documents, are presumed valid. For instance, the UETA defines *record* as "information that is inscribed on a tangible medium or that is stored in an electronic or other medium and is

retrievable in perceivable form."[33] In other words, a contract would not be unenforceable simply because it is in an electronic form.

The act also defines and supports the validity of electronic signatures. An electronic signature is "an electronic sound, symbol, or process attached to or logically associated with an electronic record and executed or adopted by a person with the intent to sign the electronic record."[34] This includes encrypted digital signatures, names (intended as signatures) at the ends of e-mail messages, and the click on a Web page if the click includes the identification of the person. (For a further discussion of electronic signatures, see the *Emerging Trends in Technology* in Chapter 15.)

The UETA does not apply to transactions governed by the Uniform Commercial Code or the Uniform Computer Information Transactions Act, or to wills or testamentary trusts. (Wills and trusts will be examined in Chapter 50.)

E-Contracts. As already indicated, one of the foremost issues in the area of contract law in cyberspace is the enforceability of an e-contract. Does a business deal agreed to online meet the legal requirements for a contract (see Chapter 10)? For example, does an e-contract fulfill the requirement of a "writing"? How can a party to the agreement verify that the other party "signed" this "writing"? These and other issues are discussed in *Emerging Trends in Technology* features in later chapters, including those presented in Chapters 15 and 19.

A party to a business deal often wants to know that any agreement made online is binding not only in the United States, but in other countries as well. In the United States, as discussed above, the federal government and the National Conference of Commissioners on Uniform State Laws are working on uniform laws to facilitate e-commerce and enforce e-contracts. Internationally, the United Nations Commission on International Trade Law (UNCITRAL) has completed a model law that relates to e-contracts. The International Chamber of Commerce has also issued model e-commerce guidelines.

E-MONEY

The technological revolution is changing the nature of financial services, including banking and investing, in fundamental ways. Traditional concepts of branches, networks, and payment systems do not

---

33. UETA 102(15).
34. UETA 102(8).

apply in cyberspace. A bank or an investment broker with a home office in Kansas, for example, can do business with a customer anywhere in the world. In fact, an online financial institution does not even need a physical office—a Web page is enough.

One of the most important ways in which the new technology is changing the nature of financial services is the method in which payments are made. Electronic money, or **e-money,** includes a number of alternatives to traditional means of payment. From a consumer's point of view, these alternatives include prepaid funds recorded on the consumer's personal computer or on a card.

Card-Based Money.   Card-based e-money is of two types. One type involves recording a balance of funds on a magnetic stripe on a card that is debited by a computer terminal on each use. The second type uses a microprocessor chip embedded in a so-called **smart card.** A smart card is safer and more versatile than a magnetic-stripe card. A smart card can be encrypted to protect the value on the card from theft. Also, a smart card can function simultaneously as a credit card, a debit card, a stored value card, and a personal information card, such as a driver's license.

Payment Information.   Current technology allows e-money to be used in a variety of ways. E-money can be used like cash, in which no personally identifiable records are created. It can also be used as part of a system that identifies and keeps information about every transaction of every consumer. The use and possible misuse of this information are concerns.

Presently, it is not clear which, if any, laws apply to the security of e-money payment information. The Federal Reserve has decided not to impose Regulation E, which governs certain electronic funds transfers, on e-money transactions. (Regulation E is discussed in Chapter 27.) Federal laws prohibiting unauthorized access to electronic communications might apply, however. For example, the Electronic Communications Privacy Act of 1986 prohibits any person from knowingly divulging to any other person the contents of an electronic communication while that communication is in transmission or in electronic storage. (For a discussion of other laws governing the use of e-money, see the *Emerging Trends in Technology* in Chapter 27.)

MARKETING ON THE INTERNET

On the Web, advertising is everywhere. It is a source for the funds that pay the Internet servers and others who maintain the connections in cyberspace. It presents opportunities for consumers and merchants around the world. It also presents a challenge for those charged with protecting consumers from dishonest sellers: How can the law be administered without stifling the potential of the Internet?

Fraud, deception, misleading information—despite new advances, some things never change. Here, we point out three situations in which consumers and businesses need to be careful.

Consumer Data.   Information about consumers can be used to aim advertising at those persons who might be most interested in what is being sold. It is not illegal to attempt to target only those consumers who might buy what a merchant is selling.

Data about users can also be compiled with their awareness and consent. Nearly all commercial Web sites, for example, collect information about their visitors and members, and most do so with those users' knowledge.[35] Few of these sites have a privacy policy, however, and many do not provide details about what they do with the data.

One commercial site that collects information about its members is GeoCities, a provider of free home pages and e-mail addresses. GeoCities has more than one million members and hosts one of the five most frequently visited sites on the Web. At one time, GeoCities told new members that it would not share the information that it collects with anyone without the permission of the persons from whom it was collected but would "use it to gain a better understanding of who is visiting GeoCities."

In 1998, the Federal Trade Commission (FTC) charged that the contrary was taking place. In the first case involving Internet privacy, the FTC claimed that GeoCities "misrepresent[ed] the purposes for which it collect[ed] personal identifying information from children and adults." On its registration form, GeoCities treated the failure of a member or visitor to click on a box that would let the user opt out of marketing offers as "permission" to share the information. Those who did not click on the box were considered to have opted in. The FTC also claimed that GeoCities sold the data to third parties "who used

---

35. Under the Children's Online Privacy Protection Act of 1998 and rules issued by the Federal Trade Commission in 1999, commercial Web sites must normally obtain parents' permission before asking children under the age of thirteen for personal information, and the information cannot be shared with others. See 15 U.S.C. Sections 6501–6506.

EMERGING TRENDS IN TECHNOLOGY

The Uniform Computer Information Transactions Act

To reflect current and future business conditions, the law needs to change to provide a legal framework for e-contracts and contracts related to software, information databases, and other aspects of the new technology.

The National Conference of Commissioners (NCC) on Uniform State Laws is aware of this need. To partially meet it, the NCC promulgated the Uniform Computer Information Transactions Act (UCITA), which governs all contracts for software development, sale, license, maintenance, and support, and contracts for information in digital form. Products, such as computers, that contain software may also be covered.

BEYOND ARTICLE 2 OF THE UCC

UCITA's outline and some of its legal principles parallel those of

Article 2 of the Uniform Commercial Code (UCC) (see Chapters 19 through 23). For example, the terms of an Article 2 sales contract and a UCITA licensing agreement include the express terms, as well as the terms arising from the *course of performance,* the *course of dealing,* and the *usage of trade.* (These italicized legal terms will be defined in Chapter 19.) Both articles give these concepts the same priority: express terms take precedence over the course of performance, followed by the course of dealing and the usage of trade.[a]

The UCITA goes beyond Article 2, however, to define, among other things, an *electronic transaction* as a contract in which humans may not review the messages. An *electronic agent* is "a computer program, electronic or other automated means used to independently initiate an action or to respond to electronic messages or performances without review by an individual."[b] (For more information on electronic agents, see the *Emerging Trends in Technology* in Chapter 32.)

___
a. UCITA 302.
b. UCITA 102(a)(28).

KEY PROVISIONS OF THE UCITA

The UCITA covers electronically disseminated information. Excluded are other types of licenses of information, such as contracts for motion picture exhibition, and the distribution of information in traditional forms, such as books and magazines.

Under the UCITA, the *licensor* (the party who sells the right to use the software) can control how the *licensee* (the party who buys the right to use the software) uses mass-marketed software. Licensees and other consumers are not entirely without protection, however. The UCITA includes provisions that would do the following:

■ Endorse the shrinkwrap licenses that accompany software.
■ Permit software licensors to electronically disable software after the cancellation of a license.
■ Extend the warranty laws that cover other goods to software licenses.
■ Require a cost-free refund from a software seller to a consumer if the terms of the use of the software are not acceptable to the consumer.

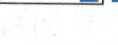

[the information] to target members solicitations beyond those agreed to by the member." Without admitting any wrongdoing, GeoCities agreed to change its policies on disclosing user information.

Web Site Content. In any market, the prices and the availability of products change quickly. This is as true in cyberspace as it is at your local mall. Even

with the global reach of the Internet, what is a glut on a Web market one day can be a scarcity the next. Partly for this reason, one of the most important details to watch for is the date of the content placed on a particular Web site.

It is equally as important for those who host pages on the Web to make sure that their content is current. Merchants should take special care to update their

EMERGING TRENDS IN TECHNOLOGY

The Uniform Computer Information Transactions Act
continued

SUPPORT AND OPPOSITION

Some observers believe that by providing a legal framework for the emerging technological age, the UCITA may become the most significant law of the new century. Our economy is now centered on information products and services. The UCITA would provide uniform legal rules for some of this commerce, which in turn will encourage its further development.

Others, including consumer groups, law professors, librarians, some software developers, and the Federal Trade Commission's Bureau of Consumer Protection, oppose the enactment of the UCITA. It is claimed that among other things, the UCITA would not make current business practices into law but would instead require modifications to those practices.

Critics charge that under the UCITA, software vendors could disclaim all responsibility for their products, even those that are defective or that damage the buyer's hardware (because, for example, the product is infected by a virus). It is also alleged that software vendors could bury the terms of their licenses or sales in "fine print" or in pamphlets inside their products' boxes. Consumers would have little choice as to whether to accept these terms.

IMPLICATIONS FOR THE BUSINESSPERSON

1. Major software makers and marketers might favor the enactment of the UCITA because of its support for shrinkwrap and clickwrap agreements. If widely enacted, it would make the law governing such agreements consistent throughout the United States.
2. Businesses that need a software program's code to make it compatible with other programs may oppose the enactment of the UCITA. Under the act, a shrinkwrap license may prohibit what is known as "reverse engineering." This would mean that a firm could hire only a

representative of the software maker to fix incompatibilities.

FOR CRITICAL ANALYSIS

1. Should the law treat software and electronic information differently than other products?
2. Is it possible to draft a uniform law that both the proponents and the critics of the UCITA would support?

RELEVANT WEB SITES

To learn more about the UCITA, you can go to the Web site of the National Conference of Commissioners on Uniform State Laws (NCCUSL) at **http://www. nccusl.org**. Click on "Questions & Answers about UCITA." For more background and discussion of the UCITA (which was formerly known as Article 2B of the UCC), see **http://www.2bguide.com**. Click on any link. This site is maintained by Carol Kunze, an attorney who participated in the drafting of the UCITA and the Uniform Electronic Transactions Act.

publicized prices to avoid penalties and potential lawsuits. An airline was fined $14,000 for failing to update expired fare information. A bank or other financial institution may be subject to liability if it displays expired interest rate information on its site.

One step to take to guard against liability for outdated information is to include on the site a disclaimer page. Because a visitor may bypass a home page and go directly to an inner page, the disclaimer should be linked to all pages on the site.

Cyber Fraud.   No one knows the full extent of cyber fraud (fraud committed on the Internet). Indications are that cyber fraud is increasing with the rising use of the Internet. Scams that were once conducted solely by mail or phone can now be found online, and new technology is contributing to more creative ways to commit fraud.

Cyber fraud takes many forms. A common form involves the sale of misrepresented or undelivered products and services via the Internet. Cyber fraud also includes bogus bidding in Web auctions, empty promises of huge profits for investing in business "opportunities," schemes in which profits are made from recruiting others instead of from sales of goods or services, and so on.

The unique nature of the Internet makes it easy for cyber wrongdoers to hide their identities and locations. Attractive, impressive Web sites can be set up for a small price. For a similarly low cost, e-mail can be sent to hundreds of thousands of users. Phony tips concerning fraudulent investments can be posted in newsgroups and chat rooms. Return addresses can be falsified or omitted. A wrongdoer can operate from anywhere in the world.

Besides the difficulty of identifying and finding cyber wrongdoers, it can be difficult to bring legal actions against them. When they are located in other states or countries, questions involving jurisdiction may arise (see the discussion of jurisdiction earlier in this chapter). In other places, it can be complicated to obtain search warrants and to seize evidence and the proceeds of criminal activity. Anywhere, it can be expensive to pursue legal proceedings.

Despite these limitations, most state and federal laws that apply to unfair and deceptive acts and practices also apply to cyber fraud. State consumer fraud and false advertising laws are based on Section 5 of the Federal Trade Commission Act, which is discussed in Chapters 44 and 45.

CONCEPT SUMMARY 9.3  LEGAL PROTECTION FOR E-COMMERCE

ASPECT OF E-COMMERCE	LEGAL PROTECTION
Contracts	If the states adopt the Uniform Computer Information Transactions Act and the Uniform Electronic Transactions Act, these model laws may provide the legal framework for an economy centered on the licensing of information products and services.
E-Money	The Electronic Communications Privacy Act, which prohibits a person from revealing the contents of an electronic communication without authority, may protect the security of e-money payment information. Other laws may also cover e-money and e-money transactions (see Chapter 27's *Emerging Trends in Technology* feature).
Marketing	State and federal laws that regulate fraud and deception by other means prohibit those same acts in cyberspace.

TERMS AND CONCEPTS TO REVIEW

cyber crime 171	e-commerce 182	hacker 172
cyber hate speech 170	e-contract 182	meta tags 170
cyber mark 175	e-money 183	smart card 183
cyber stalker 171	encryption 169	spam 174
cyber terrorist 172	filtering software 170	virtual courtroom 167
cyber tort 172	flame 172	virtual property 175

QUESTIONS AND CASE PROBLEMS

9–1. TECHNOLOGY AND THE LAW. Some observers believe that the law should not apply in cyberspace because they think that it inhibits the Internet's development. In what ways is the law facilitating the development of technology in cyberspace?

9–2. FREEDOM OF SPEECH. Jill is a professor who teaches a business law course. Jill maintains a Web site that contains background material for the class sessions. This material includes student research papers, which are submitted in advance of the classes at which they are discussed. In preparation for a class discussion on computers and the law, Mark, one of Jill's students, submits a paper that includes encryption programs he wrote to show how computers work. Jill posts this paper on her Web site. Is this post an "export"? Assuming that it is, what arguments could you make that it is protected by the First Amendment? What arguments could you make that it is not so protected?

9–3. ELECTRONIC FILING. Like other courts, the Washington county courts thoroughly document their proceedings. Even oral proceedings are transcribed so that the written records are complete. The courts make use of copy machines, word processors, and computers (for legal research). The basic functions of filing, storing, locating, updating, searching, and cross-referencing court documents are still done manually, however. What advantages would the Washington county courts realize if they were to switch to an electronic filing system?

9–4. JURISDICTION. Cybersell, Inc., is an Arizona corporation (Cybersell AZ) that provides Internet marketing services. Cybersell AZ applied with the U.S. Patent and Trademark Office (USPTO) to register "Cybersell" as a service mark. Before the application was granted, unrelated parties formed Cybersell, Inc., a Florida corporation (Cybersell FL), to provide consulting services for marketing on the Internet. Cybersell FL put up a Web site using the name "Cybersell," but its interactivity was limited to taking a surfer's name and address. No one in Arizona contacted Cybersell FL, or even hit on its Web page, before the USPTO granted Cybersell AZ's service mark application. Cybersell AZ then told Cybersell FL to stop using "Cybersell" and filed a suit in a federal district court in Arizona against Cybersell FL, alleging, among other things, trademark infringement. Cybersell FL filed a motion to dismiss for lack of jurisdiction. How should the court rule? Why? [*Cybersell, Inc., an Arizona Corporation v. Cybersell, Inc., a Florida Corporation*, 130 F.3d 414 (9th Cir. 1997)]

9–5. FREEDOM OF SPEECH. The Commonwealth (state) of Virginia enacted a statute to restrict the ability of state employees to access sexually explicit material on state-owned or leased computers. Melvin Urofsky and other professors at colleges and universities in Virginia felt that the statute interfered with their teaching. For example, Urofsky was reluctant to have students do certain online research assignments. Urofsky and others filed a suit in a federal district court against Virginia Governor George Allen and others, contending that the statute violated their First Amendment right to free speech. Both sides filed motions for summary judgment. Why would the court grant the professors' motion? Why would the court rule in the Commonwealth's favor? [*Urofsky v. Allen*, 995 F.Supp. 634 (E.D.Va. 1998)]

9–6. DEFAMATION. An unidentified person posted messages on America Online, Inc. (AOL), advertising for sale T-shirts and other items with offensive slogans related to the 1995 bombing of the federal building in Oklahoma City. Buyers were instructed to call the business phone number of Ken Zeran, who knew nothing about the ad. Zeran received a high volume of calls, consisting of derogatory messages and death threats. He called AOL and was assured that the messages would be removed. The postings remained up for five days, however, during which time the angry calls to Zeran intensified. Zeran filed a suit in a federal district court against AOL, arguing in part that AOL was liable for unreasonably delaying the removal of the defamatory messages. Why would the court rule in AOL's favor? [*Zeran v. America Online, Inc.*, 129 F.3d 327 (4th Cir. 1997)]

9–7. CYBER MARKS. Playboy Enterprises, Inc. (PEI), owns the rights to the cyber marks "Playboy," "Playboy magazine," and "Playmate." Without authorization, Calvin Designer Label used the terms as meta tags for its Web sites on the Internet. As tags, the terms were invisible to viewers (in black type on a black background), but they caused the Web sites to be returned at the top of the list of a search engine query for "Playboy" or "Playmate." PEI filed a suit in a federal district court against Calvin Designer Label, alleging, among other things, trademark infringement. Should the court order the defendant to stop using the terms as tags? Why or why not? [*Playboy Enterprises, Inc. v. Calvin Designer Label*, 985 F.Supp. 1220 (N.D.Cal. 1997)]

9–8. COPYRIGHTS. Webbworld operates a Web site called Neptics, Inc. The site accepts downloads of certain images from third parties and makes these images available to any user who accesses the site. Before being allowed to view the images, however, the user must pay a subscription fee of $11.95 per month. Over a period of several months, images were available that were originally created by or for Playboy Enterprises, Inc. (PEI). The images were displayed at Neptics's site without PEI's permission. PEI filed a suit in a federal district court against Webbworld, alleging copyright infringement. Webbworld argued in part that it should not be held liable because, like an Internet service provider that furnishes access to the Internet, it did not create or control the content of the information available to its subscribers. Do you agree with Webbworld? Why or why not? [*Playboy Enterprises, Inc. v. Webbworld,* 968 F.Supp. 1171 (N.D.Tex. 1997)]

9–9. IN YOUR COURT

Storm Impact, Inc., produces software, including the games TaskMaker and MacSki. To market upgraded versions of the games, Storm distributed them as shareware with locks built into the programs. A user could sample the unlocked portions at no charge and then buy a key, in the form of a floppy disk and registration number, to use the whole program. A legend expressly encouraged users to give unaltered copies to others but prohibited users from charging others for the shareware. Software of the Month Club (SOMC) provides collections of new shareware to its members for a $24.95 monthly fee.

When Storm's games were included in one of SOMC's collections, Storm filed a suit against SOMC, alleging, among other things, copyright infringement. Assume that you are the judge in the trial court hearing this case and answer the following questions:

(a) SOMC argued that by endorsing and distributing shareware, it was performing a service for the creators, much like a book reviewer does for a book. Therefore, claimed SOMC, its copying and distribution of the games constituted a "fair use." Was it? (Before you answer this question, you may want to review the "fair use" doctrine discussed in Chapter 7.)

(b) Should the fact that SOMC was charging for something that was otherwise free on the Internet affect your decision in this case? Similarly, should Storm's restriction on charging for its shareware affect your decision?

LAW ON THE WEB

For updated links to resources available on the Web, as well as a variety of other materials, visit this text's Web site at http://wbl.westbuslaw.com.

The Washtenaw County Trial Court in Michigan provides an excellent example of what a court can do at a site on the Web at

http://www.co.washtenaw.mi.us/depts/courts/index.htm

The U.S. Patent and Trademark Office can be accessed at

http://www.uspto.gov

The World Intellectual Property Organization offers information on the background of intellectual property, including copyrights, and its international protection at

http://www.wipo.org/eng/newindex/intellct.htm

The most recent drafts of the Uniform Computer Information Transactions Act and the Uniform Electronic Transactions Act can be found at

http://www.law.upenn.edu/bll/ulc/ulc.htm

LEGAL RESEARCH EXERCISES ON THE WEB

Go to http://wbl.westbuslaw.com, the Web site that accompanies this text. Select "Internet Applications," and then click on "Chapter 9." There you will find the following Internet research exercises that you can perform to learn more about cyber crime and free speech issues in cyberspace:

Activity 9–1: Cyber Crime

Activity 9–2: Cyberspace and Free Speech

UNIT ONE—CUMULATIVE BUSINESS HYPOTHETICAL

MicroWare, Inc., which has its headquarters in Sunnyvale, California, is one of the leading software manufacturers in the United States. The company invests millions of dollars in researching and developing new software applications and games, which are sold worldwide. It also has a large service department and has taken great pains to offer its customers excellent support services.

1. Olway Toy Mart, Inc., a Kansas retailer that sells MicroWare computer games, wants to sue MicroWare for allegedly breaching a contract. If Olway brought suit in a Kansas state court, could that court exercise jurisdiction over MicroWare? Explain.

2. Recently, MicroWare has been losing sales to a new competitor in the field, the Trivan Co. Trivan has launched an advertising campaign in which it claims that MicroWare has its customers test its software, instead of fully testing and debugging the computer programs before they are marketed. MicroWare knows this is not true and that it is unfair of Trivan to make such a claim. Could MicroWare sue Trivan for the harm Trivan is causing to MicroWare's reputation? If so, on what grounds? Explain.

3. MicroWare has just developed a new software application that the company hopes will produce substantial profits. It has taken the company two years and a sizable investment of money to create the program. MicroWare learns that its competitor, Trivan, has already filed for a patent on a nearly identical program and has sold the software to many of its customers. MicroWare learns from a reliable source that Trivan paid one of MicroWare's employees a considerable sum of money to obtain a copy of the program. What legal recourse does MicroWare have against Trivan? Discuss fully.

4. The head of MicroWare's accounting department, Roy Olson, has to pay his daughter's college tuition within a week, or his daughter will not be able to continue taking classes. The payment due is over $20,000. Roy will be able to make the payment in two months but cannot do so until then. The college refuses to wait that long. In desperation, Roy—through a fictitious bank account and some clever accounting—"borrows" funds from MicroWare. Before Roy can pay back the borrowed funds, an auditor discovers what Roy has done. MicroWare's president alleges that Roy has "stolen" company funds and informs the police of the theft. Has Roy committed a crime? If so, what crime? Explain.

5. MicroWare hosts a Web site that advertises its software products, features upgrades and "patches" for its existing software products, and accepts orders for its products from consumers throughout the world. Mary, who owns and operates Business Records, Inc., a small bookkeeping and payroll business in Colorado, orders from the Web site a copy of MicroWare's Office Books software. Office Books is designed to help accountants and bookkeepers maintain accurate business records. When Office Books is found to have a defect in its calculating program, MicroWare offers a patch on its Web site to fix the problem. Mary has already lost several customers because of the miscalculations caused by the defect, however, and files a suit against MicroWare in a Colorado state court. Can the court exercise jurisdiction over MicroWare? Why or why not?

FOCUS ON LEGAL REASONING
Merrill v. Navegar, Inc.

INTRODUCTION

In Chapter 5, we discussed the common law principles of negligence. In this *Focus on Legal Reasoning,* we examine *Merrill v. Navegar, Inc.,*[1] a recent decision involving the application of the principles of negligence in the context of the sale of guns.

CASE BACKGROUND

On July 1, 1993, Gian Luigi Ferri entered 101 California Street, a high-rise office building in San Francisco, California, armed with two semiautomatic assault weapons (TEC-9 and TEC-DC9) manufactured and distributed by Navegar, Inc., 250 rounds of

---

1. 75 Cal.App.4th 500, 75 Cal.App.4th 1037C, 89 Cal.Rptr.2d 146 (1999).

9-millimeter ammunition, and a .45-caliber semiautomatic pistol. On the thirty-second, thirty-third, and thirty-fourth floors, on the premises of a law firm against which he held a grudge, Ferri coldbloodedly opened fire on persons in the offices and hallways, killing eight men and women and wounding six others before fatally shooting himself in a stairwell.

The survivors and representatives of some of those who died filed a suit in a California state court against Navegar, based in part on negligence. They claimed that Navegar had a duty not to create risks to the public beyond those inherent in the lawful use of firearms. They offered evidence that Navegar knew or in the exercise of reasonable care should have known that, among other things, the

TEC-DC9 "ha[s] no legitimate sporting or self-defense purpose and is particularly well adapted to a military-style assault on large numbers of people" and that "the TEC-9 and TEC-DC9 would be used to kill or injure innocent persons in violent criminal acts such as the mass killing committed by Ferri." They also attempted to show that the TEC-DC9 advertising "targets a criminal clientele," further increasing the risk of harm.

Navegar filed a motion for summary judgment, which the court granted. The plaintiffs appealed to a state intermediate appellate court. In the excerpt below, the appellate court responds to Navegar's contentions that it had no duty to protect the plaintiffs and that the plaintiffs' injuries were not foreseeable.

MAJORITY OPINION

KLINE, J. [Judge]
* * * *

It must be acknowledged that the risk of harm from the criminal misuse of firearms is always present in a society such as ours, in which the presence of firearms is fairly widespread and many individuals possess the capacity to criminally misuse them. It follows that the manufacturer and distributor of a legal and nondefective firearm may not be found negligent merely because it manufactured and/or distributed the weapon. This does not mean, however, that those who manufacture, market and sell firearms have no duty to use due care to minimize risks which exceed those necessarily presented by such commercial activities, which can be accomplished without unreasonably depriving responsible citizens of the right to purchase and use firearms.
* * *

* * * *

In another context, such a duty not to increase the risk of harm inherent in an activity has been recognized.

[In] *Knight v. Jewett* (1992) 3 Cal.4th 296, 11 Cal.Rptr.2d 2, 834 P.2d 696, * * * [t]he court concluded: "Although defendants generally have no legal duty to eliminate (or protect a plaintiff against) risks inherent in [a] sport itself, it is well established that defendants generally do have a duty to exercise due care not to increase the risks to a participant over and above those inherent in the sport."

* * * Sporting activities, like handguns, are inherently dangerous in a variety of ways, but they are viewed as socially desirable and useful, and are therefore permitted to be free of the general duty to eliminate all integral risks of harm. * * * Like the provision of certain sporting facilities, making handguns "available to the general public," as alleged by appellants, contains an element of danger that cannot be eliminated without effectively barring the activity. Manufacturers and distributors of firearms, however, can be expected to refrain from affirmatively increasing the inherent risk of danger posed by the furnishing of their product.
* * * *

* * * Not only does the evidence show Navegar had substantial reason to foresee that many of those to whom it made the TEC-DC9 available would criminally misuse it to kill and injure others, but as well that its targeted marketing of the weapon invited or enticed persons likely to so misuse the weapon to acquire it. * * * .

* * * Here, the likelihood that a third person would make use of the TEC-DC9 in the kind of criminal rampage Ferri perpetrated is *precisely* the hazard that would support a determination that Navegar's conduct was negligent.

* * * *

For the foregoing reasons, the grant of summary judgment as to the cause of action for ordinary negligence was error and reversal is warranted.

DISSENTING OPINION

HAERLE, J. [Judge], * * * dissenting: * * *

* * * *

The terrible tragedy of July 1, 1993, in San Francisco will not soon be forgotten, nor should it be. But something else which needs to be kept in mind is the whole issue of responsibility * * * .

Gian Luigi Ferri organized and executed every aspect of the tragedy underlying this litigation. He—and he alone—planned it * * * . Even as a lay value judgment, we should be reluctant to allow understandable bitterness regarding the losses inflicted on so many innocent people and the invidious nature of Navegar's products to combine to divert attention from where the singular responsibility for those losses rests. And we should be even more reluctant to do so via judicial improvisations on such significant legal concepts as duty

* * * .

* * * *

* * * Justice Felix Frankfurter [said]: "It is not easy to stand aloof and allow want of wisdom to prevail, to disregard one's own strongly held view of what is wise in the conduct of affairs. But it is not the business of this Court to pronounce policy. It must observe a fastidious regard for limitations on its own power, and this precludes the Court's giving effect to its own notions of what is wise or politic. That self-restraint is of the essence in the observance of the judicial oath. * * * " (*Trop v. Dulles* (1958) 356 U.S. 86, 120, 78 S.Ct. 590, 2 L.Ed.2d 630 [dis. opn. of Frankfurter, J.].) Several decades earlier, Justice [Louis] Brandeis made the same point when he cautioned that " * * * we must ever be on our guard, lest we erect our prejudices into legal principles." (*New State Ice Co. v. Liebmann* (1932) 285 U.S. 262, 311, 52 S.Ct. 371, 76 L.Ed. 747 [dis. opn. of Brandeis, J.].)

It takes, I submit, no great insight to discern that the TEC-DC9 is far from either a necessary or desirable product in our society. I not only share the majority's obvious distaste for the people who design, manufacture and market such instruments, I am also bewildered regarding the mental processes of those who purchase them. But I am simply not willing to transpose these personal opinions into judicial doctrine. That unwillingness stems both from my understanding that we are not elected policymakers of the State of California and from my respect for the principle summed up so eloquently by Justices Brandeis and Frankfurter, that of judicial restraint. I regretfully conclude that, by its opinion of today, the majority has abandoned that important principle.

LEGAL REASONING AND ANALYSIS

1. **Legal Analysis.** Find the *Knight v. Jewett* case (see the *Law on the Web* feature at the end of Chapter 2 for instructions on how to access state court opinions). Compare the facts and issues in that case to the facts and issues of the *Merrill* case. How are they similar? How are they different? Why did the court refer to this case in its opinion?

2. **Legal Reasoning.** Contrast the conclusion of the majority with that of the dissent. What arguments did the dissent make to support its assertion that the majority's conclusion was incorrect? What legal sources did the dissent cite to justify its position?

3. **Legal Reasoning.** Review the discussion of legal reasoning in Chapter 1. Which, if any, of the forms of legal reasoning described there did the majority use to reach its conclusion?

4. **Implications for the Business Manager.** How is the holding in this case of particular interest to businesses that are currently dealing with, or may in the future deal with, products that can be used to commit crimes?

5. **Case Briefing Assignment.** Using the guidelines for briefing cases given in Appendix A of this text, brief the *Merrill* case.

GOING ONLINE

This text's Web site, at http://wbl.westbuslaw.com, offers links to court cases, as well as to other online research sources. You can also locate court cases at the Web sites listed in the *Law on the Web* section at the end of Chapter 2.

FOCUS ON ETHICS
Ethics and the Legal Environment of Business

As you will learn in Chapter 40, which is devoted entirely to ethics and business decision making, *ethics* can be defined as the study of what constitutes right or wrong behavior. *Business ethics,* as the term implies, focuses on what constitutes right or wrong behavior in the business world.

Business ethics and business law are closely intertwined concepts, because ultimately the law rests on social beliefs about right and wrong behavior in the business world. Thus, businesspersons, merely by complying with the law, are acting ethically. Mere legal compliance (the "moral minimum" in terms of business ethics), however, is often not enough. This is because the law does not—and cannot—provide the answers for all ethical questions. Rather, the law assumes that those in business will behave ethically in their day-to-day dealings. If they do not, the courts will not come to their assistance.

The main question facing many businesspersons is this: How can they know what constitutes ethical conduct in a particular situation? Furthermore, at what point does unethical conduct cross the line separating unethical from illegal conduct? Often, as mentioned, the laws do not make this line clear—this is left for the courts to decide on a case-by-case basis. In other words, in some cases, businesspersons learn too late that they have violated not just business ethical standards but also the law.

In preparing for a career in business, you will find that a background in business ethics and a commitment to ethical behavior are just as important as a knowledge of the specific laws that are covered in this text. No textbook, however, can provide answers for the many ethical questions that arise in the business context. Nor can it anticipate the types of ethical questions that will arise in the future, as technology continues to transform the workplace and business relationships. The most we can do is provide examples of the types of ethical issues that businesspersons have faced in the past and that they are facing today. The *Focus on Ethics* sections in this book survey some of the important ethical issues that arise in various areas of business activity.

In this *Focus,* we look first at some obstacles to ethical behavior in the business context. We then examine a concept that has become a significant element of the legal environment of business: corporate social responsibility.

OBSTACLES TO ETHICAL BUSINESS BEHAVIOR

People sometimes behave unethically in the business context, just as they do in their private lives. Some businesspersons knowingly engage in unethical behavior because they think that they can "get away with it"—that no one will ever learn of their unethical actions. Examples of this kind of unethical behavior include padding expense accounts, casting doubts on the integrity of a rival co-worker to gain a job promotion, stealing company supplies or equipment, and so on. Obviously, these acts are unethical, and many of them are illegal as well. In other situations, businesspersons who would choose to act ethically may be deterred from doing so because of situational circumstances or external pressures.

Ethics and the Corporate Environment

Individuals in their personal lives normally are free to decide ethical issues as they wish and to follow through on those decisions. In the business world, and particularly in the corporate environment, rarely is such a decision made by one person. If you are an officer or a manager of a large company, for example, you will find that the decision as to what is right or wrong for the company is not totally yours to make. Your input may weigh in the decision, but ultimately a corporate decision is a collective undertaking.

Additionally, collective decision making, because it places emphasis on consensus and unity of opinion, tends to hinder individual ethical assertiveness. For example, suppose that a director has ethical misgivings about a planned corporate venture that promises to be highly profitable. If the other directors have no such misgivings, the director who does may be swayed by the enthusiasm of the others for the project and downplay his or her own criticisms.

Furthermore, just as no one person makes a collective decision, so no one person (normally) is held accountable for the decision. The corporate enterprise thus tends to shield corporate personnel from both personal exposure to the consequences of their decisions (such as direct experience with someone who suffers harm from a corporate product) and personal accountability for those decisions.

Ethics and Management

Much unethical business behavior occurs simply because management does not always make it clear what ethical standards and behaviors are expected of the firm's employees. Although most firms now issue ethical policies or codes of conduct, these policies and codes are not always effective in creating an ethical workplace. At times, this is because the firm's ethical policies are not communicated clearly to employees or do not bear on the real ethical issues confronting decision makers. Additionally, particularly in a large corporation, unethical behavior in one corporate department may simply escape the attention of those in control of the corporation or the corporate officials responsible for implementing and monitoring the company's ethics program.

Another deterrent to ethical behavior exists when corporate management, by its own conduct, indicates that ethical considerations take second place. If management makes no attempt to deter unethical behavior—through reprimands or employment terminations, for example—it will be clear to employees that management is not all that serious about ethics. Likewise, if a company gives promotions or salary increases to those who obviously use unethical tactics to increase the firm's profits, then employees who do not resort to such tactics will be at a disadvantage. An employee in this situation may decide that because "everyone else does it," he or she might as well do it too.

Of course, an even stronger deterrent to ethical behavior occurs when employers engage in blatantly unethical or illegal conduct and expect their employees to do so as well. An employee in this situation faces two options, neither of which is satisfactory: participate in the conduct or "blow the whistle" on (inform authorities of) the employer's actions—and, of course, risk being fired. (See Chapter 41 for a more detailed discussion of this ethical dilemma and its consequences for employees.)

CORPORATE SOCIAL RESPONSIBILITY

Perhaps no concept is more riddled with ethical perplexities than that of corporate social responsibility—the idea that corporations can and should act ethically and be accountable to society for their actions. We will discuss some of the ethical (and legal) duties that corporations owe to their employees and to the users of their products in Chapter 40. Here we look at some problematic aspects of a corporation's responsibilities to other groups, including corporate shareholders, other "stakeholders" in the firm, the community in which the corporation operates, and society at large.

Duty to Shareholders

Corporate directors and officers have a duty to act in the shareholders' interest. Because of the nature of the relationship between corporate directors and officers and the shareholder-owners, the law holds directors and officers to a high standard of care in business decision making (see Chapter 35). Traditionally, it was perceived that this duty to shareholders took precedence over all other corporate duties and that the primary goal of corporations

should be profit maximization. Milton Friedman, the Nobel Prize–winning economist and a proponent of the profit-maximization view, saw "one and only one" social responsibility of a corporation: "to use its resources and engage in activities designed to increase its profits, so long as it stays within the rules of the game."[1] The "rules of the game" are the "basic rules of society, both those embodied in law and those embodied in ethical custom."[2]

Those who support the profit-maximization view of social responsibility contend that the duty to maximize profits must outweigh any other duty when obligations conflict—to the extent, of course, that in maximizing shareholders' profits a firm does not violate the "basic rules of society." The question here is, what are these basic rules?

Duty to Stakeholders

Increasingly, the traditional duty to shareholders is being balanced against a corporation's duty to other groups affected by corporate decisions. In the last decade or so, for example, about half of the states have enacted statutes that allow corporate decision makers to take into consideration not only the welfare of shareholders but also the welfare of *stakeholders*— employees, customers, suppliers, communities, and any group that has a stake in the corporation. Some of the statutes, such as those of Indiana and Pennsylvania, allow corporate management to place the interests of stakeholders above those of shareholders.

The reasoning behind these statutes—and behind what has come to be called "the stakeholder

1. *Capitalism and Freedom* (Chicago: University of Chicago Press, 1962), p. 133.
2. Milton Friedman, "Does Business Have Social Responsibility?" *Bank Administration,* April 1971, pp. 13–14.

view of corporate social responsibility"—is that in some circumstances, other groups may have a greater stake in company decisions than the shareholders do. Consider an example. A heavily indebted corporation is facing imminent bankruptcy. The shareholder-investors have little to lose in this situation, because their stock is already next to worthless. The corporation's creditors will be first in line for any corporate assets remaining. Because in this situation it is the creditors who have the greatest "stake" in the corporation, under the stakeholder view, corporate directors and officers should give greater weight to the creditors' interests than to those of the shareholders.

Duty to the Community

In some circumstances, the community in which a business enterprise is located has a substantial stake in the firm. Assume, for example, that a company employs two thousand workers at one of its plants. If the company decides that it would be profitable to close the plant or move it to another location, the employees—and the community—would suffer as a result. Today, to be considered socially responsible (and, in some circumstances, to comply with laws governing plant shutdowns), a corporation must take both employees' needs and community needs into consideration when making such a decision.

Another ethical question sometimes arises when a firm moves into a community. Does the company have an obligation to evaluate first how its presence will affect that community? This question has surfaced in regard to the expansion of Wal-Mart Stores, Inc., into small towns. Generally, most people in such areas welcome the lower prices and wider array of goods that Wal-Mart

offers relative to other, smaller stores in the vicinity. A vocal minority of people in some communities, however, claim that smaller stores often find it impossible to compete with Wal-Mart's prices and thus are forced to go out of business. Many of these smaller stores have existed for years and, according to Wal-Mart's critics, enhance the quality of community life. These critics claim that it is unethical of Wal-Mart to disregard a town's interest in the quality and character of life for its residents.

In the past decade, beginning in Oklahoma, Wal-Mart has been consolidating some of its smaller stores into large "superstores." In the process of this consolidation, Wal-Mart is closing stores in some of the very towns in which it drove its smaller competitors out of business. This development raises yet another ethical question: Does a store such as Wal-Mart have an obligation to continue operations in a community once it has forced its competitors to close their doors?

Duty to Society

Perhaps the most disputed area in the controversy surrounding corporate social responsibility is the nature of a corporation's duty to society at large. Generally, the question turns less on whether corporations owe a duty to society than on how that duty can best be fulfilled.

Those who contend that corporations should first and foremost attend to the goal of profit maximization would argue that it is by generating profits that a firm can best contribute to society. Society benefits by profit-making activities, because profits can only be realized when a firm markets products or services that are desired by society. These products and services enhance the standard of living, and the profits accumulated by successful

business firms generate national wealth. Our laws and court decisions promoting trade and commerce reflect the public policy that the fruits of commerce (wealth) are desirable and good. Because our society values wealth as an ethical goal, corporations, by contributing to that wealth, automatically are acting ethically.

Those arguing for profit maximization as a corporate goal also point out that it would be inappropriate to use the power of the corporate business world to fashion society's goals by promoting social causes. Determinations as to what exactly is in society's best interest involve questions that are essentially political, and therefore the public, through the political process, should have a say in making those determinations. The legislature—not the corporate board room—is thus the appropriate forum for such decisions.

Critics of the profit-maximization view believe that corporations should become actively engaged in seeking and furthering solutions to social problems. Because so much of the wealth and power of this country is controlled by business, business in turn has a responsibility to society to use that wealth and power in socially beneficial ways. Corporations should therefore promote human rights, strive for equal treatment of minorities and women in the workplace, take care to preserve the environment, and generally not profit from activities that society has deemed unethical. The critics also point out that it is ethically irresponsible to leave decisions concerning social welfare up to the government, because many social needs are not being met sufficiently through the political process.

It Pays to Be Ethical

Most corporations today have learned that it pays to be ethically responsible—even if it means less profit in the short run (and it often does). Today's corporations are subject to more intensive scrutiny—by both government agencies and the public—than corporations of the past. If a corporation fails to conduct its operations ethically or to respond quickly to an ethical crisis, its goodwill and reputation (and thus future profits) will likely suffer as a result.

There are other reasons as well for a corporation to behave ethically. For example, companies that demonstrate a commitment to ethical behavior—by implementing ethical programs, complying with environmental regulations, and promptly investigating product complaints, for example—often receive more lenient treatment from government agencies and the courts. We will return to this aspect of corporate governance in Chapter 40.

Additionally, investors may shy away from a corporation's stock if the corporation is perceived to be socially irresponsible. Since the 1970s, certain investment funds have guaranteed to the purchasers of their shares that they will invest only in companies that are ethical. For example, some funds invest money only in corporations that are "environmentally kind."

DISCUSSION QUESTIONS

1. What might be some other deterrents to ethical behavior in the business context, besides those discussed in this *Focus?*

2. Can you think of a situation in which a business firm may be acting ethically but not in a socially responsible manner? Explain.

3. Why are consumers and the public generally more concerned with ethical and socially responsible business behavior today than they were, say, fifty years ago?

4. Suppose that an automobile manufacturing company has to choose between two alternatives: contributing $1 million annually to United Way or reinvesting the $1 million in the company. In terms of ethics and social responsibility, which is the better choice?

5. Using the Internet, a small handful of activists can bring significant pressure to bear on a corporation that, in the opinion of those activists, is acting unethically. What are the implications of this development for corporate ethical decision making?

UNIT TWO

Contents

CHAPTER 10

Nature and Terminology

THE NOTED LEGAL SCHOLAR Roscoe Pound once said that "[t]he social order rests upon the stability and predictability of conduct, of which keeping promises is a large item."[1] A **promise** is an assurance that one will or will not do something in the future. A **contract** is "a promise or a set of promises for the breach of which the law gives a remedy, or the performance of which the law in some way recognizes as a duty."[2] Put simply, a contract is an agreement (based on a promise or an exchange of promises) that can be enforced in court.

Like other types of law, contract law reflects our social values, interests, and expectations at a given point in time. It shows, for example, to what extent our society allows people to make promises or commitments that are legally binding. It distinguishes between promises that create only *moral* obligations (such as a promise to take a friend to lunch) and promises that are legally binding (such as a promise to pay for merchandise purchased). Contract law also demonstrates what excuses our society accepts for

breaking certain types of promises. In addition, it indicates what promises are considered to be contrary to public policy—against the interests of society as a whole—and therefore legally invalid. When a promise is made by a child or a mentally incompetent person, for example, a question will arise as to whether the promise should be enforced. Resolving such questions is the essence of contract law.

The common law governs all contracts except when it has been modified or replaced by statutory law, such as the Uniform Commercial Code (UCC),[3] or by administrative agency regulations. Contracts relating to services, real estate, employment, insurance, and so on generally are governed by the common law of contracts. Contracts for the sale and lease of goods, however, are governed by the UCC—to the extent that the UCC has modified general contract law. The relationship between general contract law and the law governing sales and leases of goods will be explored in detail in Chapter 19. In the discussion of general contract law that follows, we indicate in footnotes the areas in which the UCC has significantly altered common law contract principles.

---

1. R. Pound, *Jurisprudence*, Vol. 3 (St. Paul: West Publishing Co., 1959), p. 162.

2. *Restatement (Second) of Contracts*. The *Restatement of the Law of Contracts* is a nonstatutory, authoritative exposition of the common law of contracts compiled by the American Law Institute in 1932. The *Restatement*, which is now in its second edition (a third edition is being drafted), will be referred to throughout the following chapters on contract law.

3. See Chapter 1 and Chapter 19 for further discussions of the significance and coverage of the Uniform Commercial Code. The UCC is presented in Appendix C at the end of this book.

SECTION 1

The Function of Contract Law

The law encourages competent parties to form contracts for lawful objectives. Indeed, no aspect of modern life is entirely free of contractual relationships. Even the ordinary consumer in his or her daily activities acquires rights and obligations based on contract law. You acquire rights and obligations, for example, when you borrow money to make a purchase or when you buy a DVD or a house. Contract law is designed to provide stability and predictability, as well as certainty, for both buyers and sellers in the marketplace.

Contract law deals with, among other things, the formation and enforcement of agreements between parties (in Latin, *pacta sunt servanda*—"agreements shall be kept"). By supplying procedures for enforcing private contractual agreements, contract law provides an essential condition for the existence of a market economy. Without a legal framework of reasonably assured expectations within which to plan and venture, businesspersons would be able to rely only on the good faith of others. Duty and good faith are usually sufficient, but when price changes or adverse economic factors make it costly to comply with a promise, these elements may not be enough. Contract law is necessary to ensure compliance with a promise or to entitle the innocent party to some form of relief.

SECTION 2

Elements of a Contract

The many topics that will be discussed in the following chapters on contract law require an understanding of the basic elements of a contract and the way in which a contract is created. The following list briefly describes these elements. Each element will be explained more fully in subsequent chapters.

1. *Agreement*. An agreement to form a contract includes an *offer* and an *acceptance*. One party must offer to enter into a legal agreement, and another party must accept the terms of the offer.
2. *Consideration*. Any promises made by the parties to the contract must be supported by legally sufficient and bargained-for *consideration* (something of value received or promised, such as money, to convince a person to make a deal).

3. *Contractual capacity*. Both parties entering into the contract must have the contractual *capacity* to do so; the law must recognize them as possessing characteristics that qualify them as competent parties.
4. *Legality*. The contract's purpose must be to accomplish some goal that is legal and not against public policy.

These four elements constitute what are normally known as the requirements that must be met for a valid contract to exist. If any of these elements is lacking, no contract will have been formed. Even if all of these elements exist, however, a contract may be unenforceable if the following requirements are not met. These requirements typically are raised as *defenses* to the enforceability of an otherwise valid contract.

1. *Genuineness of assent*. The apparent consent of both parties must be genuine. For example, if a contract was formed as a result of fraud, undue influence, mistake, or duress, the contract may not be enforceable.
2. *Form*. The contract must be in whatever form the law requires; for example, some contracts must be in writing to be enforceable.

SECTION 3

The Objective Theory of Contracts

Sometimes, parties claim that they should not be bound in contract because they did not *intend* to form an agreement that would be legally binding. Although the element of intent is of prime importance in determining whether a contract has been formed, it is not the party's *subjective* intent that a court looks to in deciding the issue. In contract law, intent is determined by what is called the objective theory of contracts, not by the personal or subjective intent, or belief, of a party. The theory is that intention to enter into a legally binding agreement, or contract, is judged by outward, objective facts as interpreted by a *reasonable* person, rather than by the party's own secret, subjective intentions. Objective facts include (1) what the party said when entering into the contract, (2) how the party acted or appeared (intent may be manifested by conduct as well as by oral or written words), and (3) the circumstances surrounding the transaction.

Consider an example. Jaffe has just purchased a new car for $28,000. A number of his neighbors are admiring his car, and one neighbor, Logan, states that he would like to own a car exactly like Jaffe's. Jaffe, in front of all of his neighbors, says to Logan, "I'll sell you this car for $20,000 in cash." Logan agrees to buy the car, and they put the agreement in writing and sign it. Jaffe immediately tells everyone that his agreement to sell the car to Logan was only a joke. Is the agreement legally binding? In other words, do Jaffe and Logan have a contract?

The answer depends on whether the circumstances (Jaffe's just having purchased a new car, the price of the new car, and the fact that Jaffe agreed in writing to sell the car) and Jaffe's words would, to a reasonable person, manifest Jaffe's intention to form a contract. It is not Jaffe's inner belief or intent to make a joke that determines the answer. If a person in Logan's position could reasonably believe that Jaffe intended to form the contract with him, Jaffe would be legally required to sell the car to Logan.

SECTION 4

Types of Contracts

There are many types of contracts. The categories into which contracts are placed involve legal distinctions as to formation, enforceability, and performance.

BILATERAL VERSUS UNILATERAL CONTRACTS

Every contract involves at least two parties. The **offeror** is the party making the offer. The **offeree** is the party to whom the offer is made. Whether the contract is classified as *unilateral* or *bilateral* depends on what the offeree must do to accept the offer and to bind the offeror to a contract. If to accept the offer the offeree must only *promise* to perform, the contract is a **bilateral contract.** Hence, a bilateral contract is a "promise for a promise." No performance, such as payment of money or delivery of goods, need take place for a bilateral contract to be formed. The contract comes into existence at the moment the promises are exchanged.

For example, Jeff offers to buy Ann's digital camera for $200. Jeff tells Ann that he will give her the money for the camera next Friday, when he gets paid. Ann accepts Jeff's offer and promises to give him the camera when Jeff pays her on Friday. Jeff and Ann have formed a bilateral contract.

In a **unilateral contract,** in contrast, the offer is phrased so that the offeree can accept the offer only

by completing the contract performance. Hence, a unilateral contract is a "promise for an act."[4] A classic example of a unilateral contract is as follows: O'Malley says to Parker, "If you carry this package across the Brooklyn Bridge, I'll give you $10." Only on Parker's complete crossing with the package does she fully accept O'Malley's offer to pay $10. If she chooses not to undertake the walk, there are no legal consequences. Contests, lotteries, and other competitions involving prizes are examples of offers for unilateral contracts. If a person complies with the rules of the contest—such as by submitting the right lottery number at the right place and time—a unilateral contract is formed, binding the organization offering the prize to a contract to perform as promised in the offer.

A problem arises in unilateral contracts when the **promisor** (the one making the promise) attempts to *revoke* (cancel) the offer after the **promisee** (the one to whom the promise was made) has begun performance but before the act has been completed. The promisee can accept the offer only on full performance, and under traditional contract principles, an offer may be revoked at any time before the offer is accepted. The present-day view, however, is that an offer to form a unilateral contract becomes irrevocable once performance has begun. Thus, even though the offer has not yet been accepted, the offeror is prohibited from revoking it for a reasonable time period.

For instance, in the Brooklyn Bridge example, suppose that Parker is walking across the bridge and has only three yards to go when O'Malley calls out to her, "I revoke my offer." Under traditional contract law, O'Malley's revocation would terminate the offer. Under the modern view of unilateral contracts, however, O'Malley will not be able to revoke his offer because Parker has undertaken performance and walked all but three yards of the bridge. In these circumstances, Parker can finish crossing the bridge and bind O'Malley to the contract.

EXPRESS VERSUS IMPLIED CONTRACTS

An **express contract** is one in which the terms of the agreement are fully and explicitly stated in words, oral

---

4. Clearly, a contract cannot be "one sided," because, by definition, an agreement implies the existence of two or more parties. Therefore, the phrase *unilateral contract*, if read literally, is a contradiction in terms. As traditionally used in contract law, however, the phrase refers to the kind of contract that results when only one promise is being made (the promise made by the offeror in return for the offeree's performance).

or written. A signed lease for an apartment or a house is an express written contract. If a classmate calls you on the phone and agrees to buy your textbooks from last semester for $75, an express oral contract has been made.

A contract that is implied from the conduct of the parties is called an **implied-in-fact contract** or an implied contract. This type of contract differs from an express contract in that the *conduct* of the parties, rather than their words, creates and defines the terms of the contract. (Note that a contract may be a mixture of an express contract and an implied-in-fact contract. In other words, a contract may contain some express terms, while others are implied.) Normally, if the following conditions exist, a court will hold that an implied contract was formed:

1. The plaintiff furnished some service or property.
2. The plaintiff expected to be paid for that service or property, and the defendant knew or should have known that payment was expected.
3. The defendant had a chance to reject the services or property and did not.

For example, suppose that you need an accountant to complete your tax return this year. You look through the Yellow Pages and find an accountant at an office in your neighborhood, so you drop by to see her. You go into the accountant's office and explain your problem, and she tells you what her fees are. The next day you return and give her secretary all the necessary information and documents—canceled checks, W-2 forms, and so on. You say nothing expressly to the secretary; rather, you walk out the door. In this situation, you have entered into an implied-in-fact contract to pay the accountant the usual and reasonable fees for her services. The contract is implied by your conduct and by hers. She expects to be paid for completing your tax return, and by bringing in the records she will need to do the work, you have implied an intent to pay her.

QUASI CONTRACTS— CONTRACTS IMPLIED IN LAW

Quasi contracts, or contracts *implied in law,* are wholly different from actual contracts. Whereas express contracts and implied-in-fact contracts are actual contracts formed by the words or conduct of the parties, quasi contracts are fictional contracts created by courts and imposed on parties in the interests of fairness and justice. Quasi contracts are therefore

equitable, rather than contractual, in nature. Usually, quasi contracts are imposed to avoid the *unjust enrichment* of one party at the expense of another. Under the doctrine of quasi contract, a plaintiff may recover in **quantum meruit,**[5] a Latin phrase meaning "as much as he deserves." *Quantum meruit* essentially describes the extent of compensation owed under a contract implied in law.

For example, suppose that a vacationing doctor is driving down the highway and encounters Potter lying unconscious on the side of the road. The doctor renders medical aid that saves Potter's life. Although the injured, unconscious Potter did not solicit the medical aid and was not aware that the aid had been rendered, Potter received a valuable benefit, and the requirements for a quasi contract were fulfilled. In such a situation, the law will impose a quasi contract, and Potter normally will have to pay the doctor for the reasonable value of the medical services rendered.

A Limitation on Quasi Contracts. Although quasi contracts exist to prevent unjust enrichment, the party obtaining the unjust enrichment is not liable in some situations. Basically, the quasi-contractual principle cannot be invoked by a party who has conferred a benefit on someone else unnecessarily or as a result of misconduct or negligence.

Consider the following example. You take your car to the local car wash and ask to have it run through the washer and to have the gas tank filled. While it is being washed, you go to a nearby shopping center for two hours. In the meantime, one of the workers at the car wash has mistakenly believed that your car is the one that he is supposed to hand wax. When you come back, you are presented with a bill for a full tank of gas, a wash job, and a hand wax. Clearly, a benefit has been conferred on you. But this benefit has been conferred because of a mistake by the car-wash employee. You have not been *unjustly* enriched under these circumstances. People cannot normally be forced to pay for benefits "thrust" on them.

When an Actual Contract Exists. The doctrine of quasi contract generally cannot be used when there is an *actual contract* that covers the area in controversy. For example, Bateman contracts with Cameron to deliver a furnace to a building owned by Jones. Bateman delivers the furnace, but Cameron never pays Bateman.

---

5. Pronounced *kwahn*-tuhm *mehr*-oo-wit.

Jones has been unjustly enriched in this situation, to be sure. Bateman, however, cannot recover from Jones in quasi contract, because Bateman had an actual contract with Cameron. Bateman already has a remedy— he can sue for breach of contract to recover the price of the furnace from Cameron. No quasi contract need be imposed by the court in this instance to achieve justice.

In the following classic case, the court had to decide whether recovery in quasi contract should be allowed in view of the fact that an express contract covered the area in controversy.

CASE 10.1

Industrial Lift Truck Service Corp. v. Mitsubishi International Corp.

Appellate Court of Illinois, First District, Fourth Division, 1982. 104 Ill.App.3d 357, 432 N.E.2d 999, 60 Ill.Dec. 100.

COMPANY PROFILE   *Mitsubishi Group (**http://www.mitsubishi.com**) is one of Japan's leading industrial organizations and the fourth largest diversified service company in the world, with sales of nearly $150 billion. Founded in 1870 by Yataro Iwasaki, Mitsubishi diversified over the next thirty years into mining, banking, shipbuilding, railroads, and Japanese real estate. In 1918, the Mitsubishi conglomerate set up Mitsubishi Trading Corporation as the purchasing, sales, and management arm of the group. Thirty-six years later, Mitsubishi Trading established Mitsubishi International Corporation, which has become the leading exporter of U.S. goods into Japan. Mitsubishi Trading was renamed Mitsubishi Corporation in 1971.*

BACKGROUND AND FACTS   *In 1973 and again in 1976, Industrial Lift Truck Service Corporation (IL) and Mitsubishi International Corporation executed an agreement calling for IL to purchase fork lift trucks from Mitsubishi and to use its best efforts to service and sell the trucks. The agreement also allowed Mitsubishi to terminate the agreement without just cause by giving ninety days' notice. From 1973 to 1977, IL allegedly became the largest dealer of Mitsubishi fork lift trucks in the United States. During this period, IL made design changes in the trucks to better suit the American market, design changes that Mitsubishi did not request but later incorporated into the trucks it sold to other dealers. In 1978, Mitsubishi terminated the agreement. IL sued under quasi-contractual principles to recover the benefits conferred on Mitsubishi by the design changes. The suit was dismissed, and IL appealed.*

IN THE LANGUAGE OF THE COURT

LINN, Justice.
*   *   *   *   *

In the present case, plaintiff obviously made the design changes with a view to being compensated pursuant to the contract terms. By its own admission, the design changes allowed plaintiff to become one of the nation's largest dealers in defendant's product. When the changes were made, plaintiff knew the risk involved. It knew the contract could be terminated as it was terminated, and thus knew when it made the changes that it might not be compensated under the contract to the extent it hoped to be compensated. Now that a situation plaintiff knew could occur has occurred, plaintiff seeks to shift a risk it assumed in light of the contract to defendant. In essence, plaintiff is seeking to use quasi contract as a means to circumvent the realities of a contract freely entered into.
*   *   *   *   *

The contract defined the entire relationship of the parties with respect to its general subject matter—the sale and servicing of defendant's products. Plaintiff's attempt here to bring a quasi-contract action is nothing more than an attempt to unilaterally amend the agreement in a manner prohibited by the agreement. In such circumstances, the benefit received by defendant can hardly be considered unjust. *   *   * Defendant had a right to assume that the contract defined the entire relationship of the parties with respect to all matters related to defendant's product. Defendant had a right to assume, absent a valid amendment to the agreement, that it should not have to compensate plaintiff for any acts done in relation to the subject matter of the contract *except pursuant to the contract terms.* [Emphasis added.]

DECISION AND REMEDY   *The existence of the specific contract barred the plaintiff's action in quasi contract, and the reviewing court held that the plaintiff's action in quasi contract had been properly dismissed.*

FORMAL VERSUS INFORMAL CONTRACTS

Another classification system divides contracts into formal contracts and informal contracts. **Formal contracts** are contracts that require a special form or method of creation (formation) to be enforceable. One type of formal contract is the **contract under seal,** a formalized writing with a special seal attached. The seal may be actual (made of wax or some other durable substance) or impressed on the paper or indicated simply by the word *seal* or the letters *L.S.* at the end of the document. *L.S.* stands for *locus sigilli* and means "the place for the seal."[6]

A written contract may be considered sealed if the promisor *adopts* a seal already on it. A standard-form contract purchased at the local office supply store, for example, may have the word *seal* (or something else that qualifies as a seal) printed next to the blanks intended for the signatures. Unless the parties who sign the form indicate a contrary intention, when they sign the form, they adopt the seal.

Informal contracts include all other contracts. Such contracts are also called *simple contracts.* No special form is required (except for certain types of contracts that must be in writing), as the contracts are usually based on their substance rather than their form. Typically, businesspersons put their contracts in writing to ensure that there is some proof of a contract's existence should problems arise. (Standard contract forms are now available online at numerous Web sites—see this chapter's *Emerging Trends in Technology* for information on some of these sites.)

EXECUTED VERSUS EXECUTORY CONTRACTS

Contracts are also classified according to the degree to which they have been performed. A contract that has been fully performed on both sides is called an **executed contract.** A contract that has not been fully performed on either side is called an **executory contract.** If one party has fully performed but the other has not, the contract is said to be executed on the one side and executory on the other, but the contract is still classified as executory.

For example, assume that you agree to buy ten tons of coal from the Northern Coal Company. Further assume that Northern has delivered the coal to your steel mill, where it is now being burned. At this point, the contract is executed on the part of Northern and executory on your part. After you pay Northern for the coal, the contract will be executed on both sides.

VALID, VOID, VOIDABLE, AND UNENFORCEABLE CONTRACTS

A **valid contract** has the elements necessary to entitle at least one of the parties to enforce it in court. Those elements, as mentioned earlier, consist of (1) an agreement consisting of an offer and an acceptance of that offer, (2) supported by legally sufficient consideration, (3) made by parties who have the legal capacity to enter into the contract, and (4) made for a legal purpose.

A **void contract** is no contract at all. The terms *void* and *contract* are contradictory. A void contract produces no legal obligations on the part of any of the parties. For example, a contract can be void because the purpose of the contract was illegal.

A **voidable contract** is a valid contract but one that can be avoided at the option of one or both of the parties. The party having the option can elect either to avoid any duty to perform or to *ratify* (make valid) the contract. If the contract is avoided, both

---

6. The contract under seal has been almost entirely abolished under such provisions as UCC 2–203 (Section 2–203 of the Uniform Commercial Code). In sales of real estate, however, it is still common to use a seal (or an acceptable substitute).

EMERGING TRENDS IN TECHNOLOGY

Online Contract Forms

Before the printing press, every contract form had to be handwritten. Since the advent of printing, however, most standard contract forms have been readily available at low cost. The introduction of computers into legal practice obviated the need to use preprinted forms and further allowed attorneys to customize contract forms for each given situation. This procedure has been both simplified and expanded by the inclusion of contract forms on simple-to-use CD-ROMs, such as Quicken's *Business Law Partner*. Now the Internet has made available an even larger variety of contract forms, as well as other legal and business forms.

For example, the 'Lectric Law Library has a collection of forms at **www.lectlaw.com/form.html**. In addition to actual forms, there are comments on how the forms should be used and filled out. The site includes forms for the assignment of a contract, a contract for sale of a motor vehicle, and many others. Another excellent online resource for various types of forms is FindForms, at **http://www. findforms.com**.

Other online forms collections can be found at LegalWiz.com (go

to **http://www.legalwiz.com/forms. htm**), a Web site that provides free legal forms, including a form that can be used to sell personal property. At **http://www.legaldocs. com** you will find an electronic forms book that offers hundreds of standardized legal forms, some of which are free. Washburn University School of Law has a Web page containing links to an extensive number of forms archives at **http://www.washlaw. edu/legalformslegalforms.html**. Finally, many law firms post legal forms, including contract forms, on their Web sites as well. For example, see the Web sites of Linsey Law Offices (at **http://www. linseylaw.com**) and Bornstein & Naylor (at **http://www.netset. com/~mb/free.htm**).

IMPLICATIONS FOR THE BUSINESSPERSON

1. Businesspersons should be aware that online contract forms for specific types of contracts are *standardized*—meaning that they contain the terms and conditions that typically appear in such contracts. In other words, such forms should be carefully scrutinized to ensure that they contain terms and conditions specific to the needs of particular contracting parties.
2. The expanding number of forms collections on the Web means that

businesspersons can "shop around" for the forms that most closely meet their needs.
3. Businesspersons who engage in online commerce can post their own customized contract forms on their Web sites for prospective customers or others to review or use. For example, an online merchant may include an offer to purchase or sell certain goods or services and provide a means by which the offer can be accepted—such as by clicking on a box stating "I agree" (see the *Emerging Trends in Technology* in Chapter 19 for further information on online offers).

FOR CRITICAL ANALYSIS

1. Does the availability of contract forms on the Web mean that one need not consult an attorney when forming a contract?
2. Do the downloading and use of contract forms—or any other types of business forms—from Web sites raise any copyright issues?

RELEVANT WEB SITES

In addition to the Web sites mentioned within this feature, FindLaw's forms site, at **http:// www.findlaw.com/16forms/index. html**, provides hyperlinks to a broad array of online collections of contract forms.

parties are released from it. If it is ratified, both parties must fully perform their respective legal obligations.

As a general rule, but subject to exceptions, contracts made by minors are voidable at the option of the minor (see Chapter 13). Contracts entered into under fraudulent conditions are voidable at the option of the defrauded party. In addition, contracts entered into under duress or undue influence are voidable (see Chapter 14).

CONCEPT SUMMARY 10.1  TYPES OF CONTRACTS

CONCEPT	DESCRIPTION
Formation	1. *Bilateral*—A promise for a promise. 2. *Unilateral*—A promise for an act (acceptance is the completed performance of the act). 3. *Express*—Formed by words (oral, written, or a combination). 4. *Implied in fact*—Formed by the conduct of the parties. 5. *Quasi contract* (implied in law)—Imposed by law to prevent unjust enrichment. 6. *Formal*—Requires a special form for creation. 7. *Informal*—Requires no special form for creation.
Performance	1. *Executed*—A fully performed contract. 2. *Executory*—A contract not fully performed.
Enforceability	1. *Valid*—The contract has the necessary contractual elements: agreement (offer and acceptance), consideration, legal capacity of the parties, and legal purpose. 2. *Void*—No contract exists, or there is a contract without legal obligations. 3. *Voidable*—One party has the option of avoiding or enforcing the contractual obligation. 4. *Unenforceable*—A contract exists, but it cannot be enforced because of a legal defense.

An **unenforceable contract** is one that cannot be enforced because of certain legal defenses against it. It is not unenforceable because a party failed to satisfy a legal requirement of the contract; rather, it is a valid contract rendered unenforceable by some statute or law. For example, certain contracts must be in writing (see Chapter 15), and if they are not, they will not be enforceable except in certain exceptional circumstances.

SECTION 5

Interpretation of Contracts

Sometimes parties agree that a contract has been formed but disagree on the meaning or the legal effect of the contract. This may happen if one of the parties is not familiar with the legal terminology used in the contract. To an extent, "plain language" laws have helped to avoid this difficulty. Today, the federal government and a majority of the states have enacted special laws to regulate legal writing. Additionally, however, a dispute over the meaning of a contract may arise simply because the rights or obligations under the contract are not expressed clearly—no matter how "plain" the language used.

In this section, we look at some common law rules of contract interpretation. These rules, which have evolved over time, provide the courts with guidelines for deciding disputes over how contract terms or provisions should be interpreted.

THE PLAIN MEANING RULE

When a contract's writing is clear and unequivocal, a court will enforce it according to its obvious terms. This is sometimes referred to as the *plain meaning rule.* Under this rule, if a contract's words appear to be clear and unambiguous, a court cannot consider *extrinsic evidence,* which is any evidence not contained in the document itself. If a contract's terms are unclear or ambiguous, however, extrinsic evidence may be admissible to clarify the meaning of the contract. The admissibility of such evidence can significantly affect the court's interpretation of ambiguous contractual provisions and thus the outcome of litigation.

The court in the following case applied these principles to a contract's "no-cause termination clause."

CASE 10.2   United Airlines, Inc. v. Good Taste, Inc.

Supreme Court of
Alaska, 1999.
982 P.2d 1259.
http://www.touchngo.
com/sp/spslip99.htm[a]

BACKGROUND AND FACTS *Good Taste, Inc., a food service company located in Anchorage, Alaska, does business under the name Saucy Sisters Catering. Saucy Sisters contracted with United Airlines, Inc., to handle its in-flight catering. The parties' "Catering Agreement" stated that it would run for a period of three years, "provided, however, either party may terminate this Agreement upon ninety (90) days' prior written notice." To fulfill the contract, Saucy Sisters expanded its operation at a cost of nearly $1 million. Just over a year later, United gave Saucy Sisters ninety days' notice, after which their agreement terminated. Saucy Sisters filed a suit in an Alaska state court against United, asserting, among other things, that it had breached their contract. Saucy Sisters argued that the termination clause was ambiguous, alleging that before signing the contract, United had said it had never used the clause and included it only as an "out" if United chose to discontinue its flights to Anchorage. Saucy Sisters filed a motion for summary judgment. The judge ruled that the clause was not ambiguous and that United had not breached the contract, and denied the motion. The jury returned a verdict in favor of the plaintiff on its other claims, however, and the court entered a judgment in favor of Saucy Sisters for more than $3.6 million. Both parties appealed to the Alaska Supreme Court. Saucy Sisters continued to argue that the termination clause was ambiguous and that the trial court should have ruled in its favor on that claim.*

**IN THE LANGUAGE
OF THE COURT**

BRYNER, Justice.
*   *   *   *

The [trial] court found [the termination] provision clear and unambiguous, ruling that it "has only one reasonable interpretation, which is that the contract period is for three years unless one of the parties decides to take affirmative action to end it early." Accordingly, the court determined as a matter of law that United did not breach the express terms of the contract when it terminated the catering contract upon ninety days' written notice.

*   *   * [T]he question of whether a contract is ambiguous is ordinarily one for the court to determine. A disagreement as to contract terms does not in itself create an ambiguity; the reviewing court must initially seek to ascertain the meaning of the contract from the provisions of the contract itself. Contract terms are to be given their plain, ordinary, popular, and natural meaning. And *when the language of a contract is unambiguous, the express provision governs and there is no need for construction or inquiry as to the intention of the parties.* [Emphasis added.]

Here, the meaning of the disputed termination clause is clear and unambiguous on its face when its words are given their plain, ordinary, popular, and natural meaning. This provision clearly fixes the Agreement's term at three years, but allows each party to end it earlier by doing nothing more than giving the other party ninety days' notice. As the [trial] court aptly noted, such termination clauses are hardly uncommon:

> Anyone familiar with real world business practices would instantly recognize this provision as a no-cause termination provision that is often used to limit an otherwise definite term. No-cause termination clauses like the one considered here are widely used, and this one in particular would not cause anyone to second-guess its clear and unambiguous terms.

Because the Agreement's no-cause termination provision was clear and unambiguous on its face, the trial court * * * had no occasion to consider extrinsic evidence supporting Saucy Sisters' assertion that it actually understood the provision to have a different meaning. And because United undisputedly abided by the literal terms of the

---

a. On this page, scroll down to the name of the case, which was issued on July 9, 1999, to access the opinion. This Web site is made available by Touch N' Go Systems, Inc., and the Law Offices of James B. Gottstein, in Anchorage, Alaska.

provision—terminating the Agreement upon ninety days' written notice to Saucy Sisters—the trial court properly concluded that no genuine issue of material fact existed and that United was entitled to summary judgment on Saucy Sisters' breach of contract claim.

DECISION AND REMEDY *The Alaska Supreme Court held that the termination clause was clear and unambiguous and that the contract could be terminated with proper notice by either party. The court also ruled in favor of United on all of the other claims and remanded the case for the entry of a judgment for the airline.*

INTERPRETATION OF AMBIGUOUS TERMS

When the writing contains ambiguous or unclear terms, a court will interpret the language to give effect to the parties' intent as *expressed in their contract*. This is the primary purpose of the rules of interpretation—to determine the parties' intent from the language used in their agreement and to give effect to that intent. Usually, a court will not make or remake a contract, nor will it interpret the language according to what the parties *claim* their intent was when they made it. The following rules are used by the courts in interpreting ambiguous contractual terms:

1. Insofar as possible, a reasonable, lawful, and effective meaning will be given to all of a contract's terms.
2. A contract will be interpreted as a whole; individual, specific clauses will be considered subordinate to the contract's general intent. All writings that are a part of the same transaction will be interpreted together.
3. Terms that were the subject of separate negotiation will be given greater consideration than standardized terms and terms that were not negotiated separately.

4. A word will be given its ordinary, commonly accepted meaning, and a technical word or term will be given its technical meaning, unless the parties clearly intended something else.
5. Specific and exact wording will be given greater consideration than general language.
6. Written or typewritten terms will prevail over preprinted ones.
7. Because a contract should be drafted in clear and unambiguous language, a party who uses ambiguous expressions is held to be responsible for the ambiguities. Thus, when the language has more than one meaning, it will be interpreted against the party who drafted the contract.
8. Evidence of trade usage, prior dealing, and course of performance may be admitted to clarify the meaning of an ambiguously worded contract (these terms are defined and discussed in Chapter 19). When considering custom and usage, a court will look at what is common to the particular business or industry and to the locale in which the contract was made or is to be performed.

TERMS AND CONCEPTS TO REVIEW

bilateral contract 200	informal contract 203	*quantum meruit* 201
contract 198	objective theory of contracts 199	quasi contract 201
contract under seal 203		unenforceable contract 205
executed contract 203	offeree 200	unilateral contract 200
executory contract 203	offeror 200	valid contract 203
express contract 200	promise 198	void contract 203
formal contract 203	promisee 200	voidable contract 203
implied-in-fact contract 201	promisor 200	

QUESTIONS AND CASE PROBLEMS

10–1. TYPES OF CONTRACTS. Suppose that Everett McCleskey, a local businessperson, is a good friend of Al Miller, the owner of a local candy store. Every day on his lunch hour, McCleskey goes into Miller's candy store and spends about five minutes looking at the candy. After examining Miller's candy and talking with Miller, McCleskey usually buys one or two candy bars. One afternoon, McCleskey goes into Miller's candy shop, looks at the candy, and picks up a $1 candy bar. Seeing that Miller is very busy, he waves the candy bar at Miller without saying a word and walks out. Is there a contract? If so, classify it within the categories presented in this chapter.

10–2. TYPES OF CONTRACTS. Janine was hospitalized with severe abdominal pain and placed in an intensive care unit. Her doctor told the hospital personnel to order around-the-clock nursing care for Janine. At the hospital's request, a nursing services firm, Nursing Services Unlimited, provided two weeks of in-hospital care and, after Janine was sent home, an additional two weeks of at-home care. During the at-home period of care, Janine was fully aware that she was receiving the benefit of the nursing services. Nursing Services later billed Janine $4,000 for the nursing care, but Janine refused to pay on the ground that she had never contracted for the services, either orally or in writing. In view of the fact that no express contract was ever formed, can Nursing Services recover the $4,000 from Janine? If so, under what legal theory? Discuss.

10–3. BILATERAL VERSUS UNILATERAL CONTRACTS. Atencio is confined to his bed. He calls a friend who lives across the street and offers to sell her his watch next week for $100. If his friend wishes to accept, she is to put a red piece of paper in her front window. The next morning, she places a red piece of paper in her front window. Is the contract formed bilateral or unilateral? Explain.

10–4. TYPES OF CONTRACTS. Burger Baby restaurants engaged Air Advertising to fly an advertisement above the Connecticut beaches. The advertisement offered $1,000 to any person who could swim from the Connecticut beaches to Long Island across Long Island Sound in less than a day. On Saturday, October 10, at 10:00 A.M., Air Advertising's pilot flew a sign above the Connecticut beaches that read: "Swim across the Sound and Burger Baby pays $1,000." On seeing the sign, Davison dived in. About four hours later, when he was about halfway across the Sound, Air Advertising flew another sign over the Sound that read: "Burger Baby revokes." Davison completed the swim in another six hours. Is there a contract between Davison and Burger Baby? Can Davison recover anything?

10–5. BILATERAL VERSUS UNILATERAL CONTRACTS. Zdanis contacts Joe, who does lawn maintenance work, and makes the following offer: "After my lawn is mowed, I'll pay you $25." Joe responds by saying, "I accept your offer." Is there a contract? Is this an offer to form a bilateral or a unilateral contract? What is the legal significance of the distinction?

10–6. RECOVERY FOR SERVICES RENDERED. Sosa Crisan, an eighty-seven-year-old widow, collapsed while shopping at a local grocery store. The Detroit police took her to the Detroit city hospital by ambulance. She was admitted, and she remained there fourteen days. Then she was transferred to another hospital, at which she died some eleven months later. Crisan had never regained consciousness after her collapse at the grocery store. After she died, the city of Detroit sued her estate to recover the expenses of both the ambulance that took her to the Detroit city hospital and her Detroit city hospital stay. Is there a contract between Sosa Crisan and the Detroit city hospital? If so, how much can the hospital recover? [*In re Estate of Crisan*, 362 Mich. 569, 107 N.W.2d 907 (1961)]

10–7. RECOVERY FOR SERVICES RENDERED. After Walter Washut had suffered a heart attack and could no longer take care of himself, he asked Eleanor Adkins, a friend who had previously refused his proposal of marriage, to move to his ranch. For the next twelve years, Adkins lived with Washut, although she retained ownership of her own house and continued to work full-time at her job. Adkins took care of Washut's personal needs, cooked his meals, cleaned and maintained his house, cared for the livestock, and handled other matters for Washut. According to Adkins, Washut told her on numerous occasions that "everything would be taken care of" and that she would never have to leave the ranch. After Washut's death, Adkins sought to recover in quasi contract for the value of the services she had rendered to Washut. Adkins stated in her deposition that she had performed the services because she loved Washut, not because she had expected to be paid for them. What will the court decide, and why? [*Adkins v. Lawson*, 892 P.2d 128 (Wyo. 1995)]

10–8. INTERPRETATION OF CONTRACTS. Jerilyn Dawson hired Michael Shaw of the law firm of Jones, Waldo, Holbrook, and McDonough to represent her in her divorce. Dawson signed an agreement to pay the attorney's fees. The agreement did not include an estimate of how much the divorce would cost. When Dawson failed to pay, the firm filed a suit in a Utah state court to collect, asking for an award of more than $43,000. During the trial, Shaw testified that he had told Dawson the divorce would cost "something in the nature of $15,000 to $18,000." The court awarded the firm most—but not all—of what it sought. Both parties appealed: Dawson contended that the award was too high, and the firm complained that it was too low. What rule of interpretation discussed in this chapter might the appellate court apply in deciding the appropriate amount of damages in this case? If this rule is applied, what will the court likely decide? Explain. [*Jones, Waldo, Holbrook & McDonough v. Dawson*, 923 P.2d 1366 (Utah 1996)]

10–9. IMPLIED CONTRACT. Thomas Rinks and Joseph Shields developed Psycho Chihuahua, a caricature of a Chihuahua dog with a "do-not-back-down" attitude. They promoted and marketed the character through their company, Wrench, L.L.C. Ed Alfaro and Rudy Pollak, representatives of Taco Bell Corp., learned of Psycho Chihuahua and met with Rinks and Shields to talk about using the character as a Taco Bell "icon." Wrench sent artwork, merchandise, and marketing ideas to Alfaro, who promoted the character within Taco Bell. Alfaro asked Wrench to propose terms for Taco Bell's use of Psycho Chihuahua. Taco Bell did not accept Wrench's terms, but Alfaro continued to promote the character within the company. Meanwhile, Taco Bell hired a new advertising agency, which proposed an advertising campaign involving a Chihuahua. When Alfaro learned of this proposal, he sent the Psycho Chihuahua materials to the agency. Taco Bell made a Chihuahua the focus of its marketing but paid nothing to Wrench. Wrench filed a suit against Taco Bell in a federal district court, claiming in part that it had an implied contract with Taco Bell, which the latter breached. Do these facts satisfy the requirements for an implied contract? Why or why not? [*Wrench L.L.C. v. Taco Bell Corp.*, 51 F.Supp.2d 840 (W.D.Mich. 1999)]

10–10. IN YOUR COURT

Grant Borman, who was engaged in a construction project, leased a crane from Allied Equipment, Inc., and hired Crosstown Trucking Co. to deliver the crane to the construction site. Crosstown, while the crane was in its possession and without permission from either Borman or Allied Equipment, used the crane to install a transformer for a utility company, which paid Crosstown for the job. Crosstown then delivered the crane to Borman's construction site at the appointed time of delivery. When Allied Equipment learned of the unauthorized use of the crane by Crosstown, it sued Crosstown for damages, seeking to recover in quasi contract the rental value of Allied's use of the crane. Assume that you are the judge in the trial court hearing this case and answer the following questions:

(a) Should a quasi contract be imposed on the parties in this situation so that Allied can recover damages from Crosstown?

(b) If so, what amount should Allied be able to recover in *quantum meruit* for Crosstown's unauthorized use of the crane?

(c) How does this case differ from Case 10.1 (*Industrial Lift Truck Service Corp. v. Mitsubishi International Corp.*), which also involved a plaintiff seeking to recover under quasi-contractual principles?

LAW ON THE WEB

For updated links to resources available on the Web, as well as a variety of other materials, visit this text's Web site at http://wbl.westbuslaw.com.

The 'Lectric Law Library provides information on contract law, including a definition of a contract, the elements required for a contract, and so on. Go to

http://www.lectlaw.com

Then go to the Laypeople's Law Lounge, and scroll down to Contracts.

You can keep abreast of recent and planned revisions of the *Restatements of the Law*, including the *Restatement (Second) of Contracts*, by accessing the American Law Institute's Web site at

http://www.ali.org

LEGAL RESEARCH EXERCISES ON THE WEB

Go to http://wbl.westbuslaw.com, the Web site that accompanies this text. Select "Internet Applications," and then click on "Chapter 10." There you will find the following Internet research exercises that you can perform to learn more about contracts and contract provisions:

Activity 10–1: Contracts and Contract Provisions

Activity 10–2: Contracts in Ancient Mesopotamia

CHAPTER 11

Agreement

AN ESSENTIAL ELEMENT for contract formation is **agreement**—the parties must agree on the terms of the contract and manifest to each other their **mutual assent** to the same bargain. Ordinarily, agreement is evidenced by two events: an *offer* and an *acceptance.* One party offers a certain bargain to another party, who then accepts that bargain. The agreement does not necessarily have to be in writing. Both parties, however, must manifest their assent to the same bargain. Once an agreement is reached, if the other elements of a contract are present (consideration, capacity, and legality—discussed in subsequent chapters), a valid contract is formed, generally creating enforceable rights and duties between the parties.

Note that not all agreements are contracts. John and Kevin may agree to play golf on a certain day, but a court would not hold that their agreement is an enforceable contract. A *contractual* agreement only arises when the terms of the agreement impose legally enforceable obligations on the parties.

In today's world, contracts are frequently formed via the Internet. For a discussion of some important factors to be considered in online offers and acceptances, see the *Emerging Trends in Technology* in Chapter 19.

SECTION 1

Requirements of the Offer

As mentioned in Chapter 10, the parties to a contract are the *offeror,* the one who makes an offer or proposal to another party, and the *offeree,* the one to whom the offer or proposal is made. An **offer** is a promise or commitment to do or refrain from doing some specified thing in the future. Under the common law, three elements are necessary for an offer to be effective:

1. The offeror must have a serious intention to become bound by the offer.
2. The terms of the offer must be reasonably certain, or definite, so that the parties and the court can ascertain the terms of the contract.
3. The offer must be communicated by the offeror to the offeree, resulting in the offeree's knowledge of the offer.

Once an effective offer has been made, the offeree has the power to accept the offer. If the offeree accepts, an agreement is formed (and thus a contract, if other essential elements are present).

INTENTION

The first requirement for an effective offer is a serious intent on the part of the offeror. Serious intent is not determined by the *subjective* intentions, beliefs, and assumptions of the offeror. As discussed in Chapter 10, courts generally adhere to the *objective theory of contracts* in determining whether a contract has been formed. Under this theory, a party's words and conduct are held to mean whatever a reasonable person in the offeree's position would think they meant. The court will give words their usual meanings even if "it were proved by twenty bishops that [the] party . . . intended something else."[1]

Offers made in obvious anger, jest, or undue excitement do not meet the intent test, because a reasonable person would realize that a serious offer was not being made. Because these offers are not effective, an offeree's acceptance does not create an agreement. For example, suppose that you and three classmates ride to school each day in Davina's new automobile, which has a market value of $20,000. One cold morn-

ing, the four of you get into the car, but Davina cannot get the car started. She yells in anger, "I'll sell this car to anyone for $500!" You drop $500 in her lap. Given these facts, a reasonable person, taking into consideration Davina's frustration and the obvious difference in worth between the market value of the car and the proposed purchase price, would declare that her offer was not made with serious intent and that you did not have an agreement.

The concept of intention can be further clarified through an examination of the types of expressions and statements that are not offers. We look at these expressions and statements in the subsections that follow.

Lucy v. Zehmer, presented below, is a classic case in the area of contractual agreement. The case involves a business transaction in which boasts, brags, and dares "after a few drinks" resulted in a contract to sell certain property. The sellers claimed that the offer had been made in jest and that, in any event, the contract was voidable at their option because they were intoxicated when the offer was made and thus lacked contractual capacity (see Chapter 13). The court, however, looked to the words and actions of the parties—not their secret intentions—to determine whether a contract had been formed.

---

1. Judge Learned Hand in *Hotchkiss v. National City Bank of New York*, 200 F. 287 (2d Cir. 1911), aff'd 231 U.S. 50, 34 S.Ct. 20, 58 L.Ed. 115 (1913).

CASE 11.1   Lucy v. Zehmer

Supreme Court of
Appeals of Virginia,
1954.
196 Va. 493,
84 S.E.2d 516.

BACKGROUND AND FACTS   *W. O. Lucy and J. C. Lucy, the plaintiffs, filed suit against A. H. Zehmer and Ida Zehmer, the defendants, to compel the Zehmers to transfer title of their property, known as the Ferguson Farm, to the Lucys for $50,000, as allegedly the Zehmers had agreed to do. Lucy had known Zehmer for fifteen or twenty years and for the last eight years or so had been anxious to buy the Ferguson Farm from Zehmer. One night, Lucy stopped in to visit the Zehmers in the combination restaurant, filling station, and motor court they operated. While there, Lucy tried to buy the Ferguson Farm once again. This time he tried a new approach. According to the trial court transcript, Lucy said to Zehmer, "I bet you wouldn't take $50,000 for that place." Zehmer replied, "Yes, I would too; you wouldn't give fifty." Throughout the evening, the conversation returned to the sale of the Ferguson Farm for $50,000. At the same time, the parties continued to drink whiskey and engage in light conversation. Eventually, Lucy enticed Zehmer to write up an agreement to the effect that Zehmer would sell to Lucy the Ferguson Farm for $50,000 complete. Later, Lucy sued Zehmer to go through with the sale. Zehmer argued that he had been drunk and that the offer had been made in jest and hence was unenforceable. The trial court agreed with Zehmer, and Lucy appealed.*

**IN THE LANGUAGE
OF THE COURT**   BUCHANAN, J. [Justice] delivered the opinion of the court.

❋   ❋   ❋   ❋

In his testimony, Zehmer claimed that he "was high as a Georgia pine," and that the transaction "was just a bunch of two doggoned drunks bluffing to see who could talk the biggest and say the most." That claim is inconsistent with his attempt to testify in great detail as to what was said and what was done. *   *   *

*   *   *   *

The appearance of the contract, the fact that it was under discussion for forty minutes or more before it was signed; Lucy's objection to the first draft because it was written in the singular, and he wanted Mrs. Zehmer to sign it also; the rewriting to meet that objection and the signing by Mrs. Zehmer; the discussion of what was to be included in the sale, the provision for the examination of the title, the completeness of the instrument that was executed, the taking possession of it by Lucy with no request or suggestion by either of the defendants that he give it back, are facts which furnish persuasive evidence that the execution of the contract was a serious business transaction rather than a casual, jesting matter as defendants now contend.

*   *   *   *

In the field of contracts, as generally elsewhere, *[w]e must look to the outward expression of a person as manifesting his intention rather than to his secret and unexpressed intention. The law imputes to a person an intention corresponding to the reasonable meaning of his words and acts.* [Emphasis added.]

*   *   *   *

Whether the writing signed by the defendants and now sought to be enforced by the complainants was the result of a serious offer by Lucy and a serious acceptance by the defendants, or was a serious offer by Lucy and an acceptance in secret jest by the defendants, in either event it constituted a binding contract of sale between the parties.

DECISION AND REMEDY   *The Supreme Court of Virginia determined that the writing was an enforceable contract and reversed the ruling of the lower court. The Zehmers were required by court order to carry through with the sale of the Ferguson Farm to the Lucys.*

Expressions of Opinion.   An expression of opinion is not an offer. It does not evidence an intention to enter into a binding agreement. Consider an example. Hawkins took his son to McGee, a doctor, and asked McGee to operate on the son's hand. McGee said that the boy would be in the hospital three or four days and that the hand would *probably* heal a few days later. The son's hand did not heal for a month, but the father did not win a suit for breach of contract. The court held that McGee had not made an offer to heal the son's hand in three or four days. He had merely expressed an opinion as to when the hand would heal.[2]

Statements of Intention.   If Arif says, "I *plan* to sell my stock in Novation, Inc., for $150 per share," a contract is not created if John "accepts" and tenders the $150 per share for the stock. Arif has merely expressed his intention to enter into a future contract for the sale of the stock. If John accepts and tenders the $150 per share, no contract is formed, because a reasonable person would conclude that Arif was only *thinking about* selling his stock, not *promising* to sell it.

Preliminary Negotiations.   A request or invitation to negotiate is not an offer. It only expresses a willingness to discuss the possibility of entering into a contract. Included are statements such as "Will you sell Blythe Estate?" or "I wouldn't sell my car for less than $1,000." A reasonable person in the offeree's position would not conclude that these statements evidenced an intention to enter into a binding obligation. Likewise, when construction work is done for the government and private firms, contractors are invited to submit bids. The *invitation* to submit bids is not an offer, and a contractor does not bind the government or private firm by submitting a bid. (The bids that the contractors submit are offers, however, and the government or private firm can bind the contractor by accepting the bid.)

---

2. *Hawkins v. McGee,* 84 N.H. 114, 146 A. 641 (1929).

Agreements to Agree. During preliminary negotiations, the parties may form an agreement to agree to a material term of a contract at some future date. Traditionally, such "agreements to agree" were not considered to be binding contracts. More recent cases illustrate the view that agreements to agree serve valid commercial purposes and can be enforced if the parties clearly intended to be bound by such agreements.

For example, suppose Zahn Consulting leases office space from Leon Properties, Inc. Their lease agreement includes a clause permitting Zahn to extend the lease at an amount of rent to be agreed on when the lease is extended. Under the traditional rule, because the amount of rent is not specified in the lease clause itself, the clause would be too indefinite in its terms to enforce. Under the current view, a court could hold that the parties intended the future rent to be a reasonable amount and could enforce the clause.[3] In other words, under the current view, the emphasis is on the parties' intent rather than on form. (For a further discussion of this issue, see this chapter's *Emerging Trends in Business Law.*)

Advertisements, Catalogues, Price Lists, and Circulars. In general, advertisements, mail-order catalogues, price lists, and circulars are treated not as offers to contract but as invitations to negotiate. Suppose that Loeser advertises a used paving machine. The ad is mailed to hundreds of firms and reads, "Used Loeser Construction Co. paving machine. Builds curbs and finishes cement work all in one process. Price $42,350." If Star Paving calls Loeser and says, "We accept your offer," no contract is formed. Any reasonable person would conclude that Loeser was not promising to sell the paving machine but rather was soliciting offers to buy it. If such an ad were held to constitute a legal offer, and fifty people accepted the offer, there would be no way for Loeser to perform all fifty of the resulting contracts. He would have to breach forty-nine contracts. Obviously, the law seeks to avoid such unfairness.

Price lists are another form of invitation to negotiate or trade. A seller's price list is not an offer to sell at that price; it merely invites the buyer to offer to buy at that price. In fact, the seller usually puts "prices subject to change" on the price list. Only in rare circum-

stances will a price quotation be construed as an offer.[4]

Although most advertisements and the like are treated as invitations to negotiate, this does not mean that an advertisement can never be an offer. If the advertisement makes a promise so definite in character that it is apparent that the offeror is binding himself or herself to the conditions stated, the advertisement is treated as an offer.[5]

Auctions. Sometimes, what appears to be an offer is not sufficient to serve as the basis for contract formation. Particularly problematic in this respect are "offers" to sell goods at auctions. In an auction, a seller "offers" goods for sale through an auctioneer. This is not, however, a *contractual* offer. Instead, the seller is only expressing a willingness to sell. Unless the terms of the auction are explicitly stated to be *without reserve*, the seller (through the auctioneer) may withdraw the goods at any time before the sale is closed by announcement or by fall of the auctioneer's hammer. The seller's right to withdraw goods characterizes an auction with reserve; all auctions are assumed to be of this type unless a clear statement to the contrary is made.[6] At auctions without reserve, the goods cannot be withdrawn and must be sold to the highest bidder.

In an auction with reserve, there is no obligation to sell, and the seller may refuse the highest bid. The bidder is actually the offeror. Before the auctioneer strikes the hammer, which constitutes acceptance of the bid, a bidder may revoke his or her bid, or the auctioneer may reject that bid or all bids. Typically, an auctioneer will reject a bid that is below the price the seller is willing to accept. When the auctioneer accepts a higher bid, he or she rejects all previous bids. Because rejection terminates an offer (as pointed out later in the chapter), if the highest bidder withdraws his or her bid before the hammer falls, none of the previous bids is reinstated. If the bid is not withdrawn or rejected, the contract is formed when the auctioneer announces, "Going once, going twice, sold" (or something similar) and lets the hammer fall.

In auctions with reserve, the seller may reserve the right to confirm or reject the sale even after the

---

3. *Restatement (Second) of Contracts,* Section 33. See also UCC 2–204, 2–305.

4. See, for example, *Fairmount Glass Works v. Grunden-Martin Woodenware Co.,* 106 Ky. 659, 51 S.W. 196 (1899).
5. See, for example, *Lefkowitz v. Great Minneapolis Surplus Store, Inc.,* 251 Minn. 188, 86 N.W.2d 689 (1957).
6. See UCC 2–328.

EMERGING TRENDS IN BUSINESS LAW

The Enforcement of Preliminary Agreements

Suppose that at some point during protracted contract negotiations, but before a formal contract is drawn up, the parties proclaim that they have "made a deal." Does their agreement mean that an enforceable contract has been formed even though the parties have not signed a formal contract? Or does their agreement simply mean that they have agreed to agree to a contract in the future?

How a court might interpret such a situation can, of course, have significant consequences for the parties—as Texaco Oil Company learned in 1987. When the Pennzoil Company discussed with the Getty Oil Company the possible purchase of Getty's stock, a "memorandum of agreement" was drafted to reflect the terms of the conversations. After more negotiations over the price, both companies issued press releases announcing an agreement in principle on the terms of the memorandum. The next day, Texaco, Inc., offered to buy all of Getty's stock at a higher price.

Getty accepted Texaco's offer, and the two firms signed a merger agreement. When Pennzoil sued Texaco for tortious interference with its "contractual" relationship with Getty, a jury concluded that Getty and Pennzoil had intended a binding contract before Texaco made its offer, with only the details left to be worked out. Texaco was held liable for interfering with this contract and had to pay damages in the millions of dollars.[a]

TYPE I AND TYPE II PRELIMINARY AGREEMENTS

A decision by the U.S. Court of Appeals for the Second Circuit set forth some helpful guidelines for distinguishing between an agreement to agree and an enforceable contract. In doing so, the court distinguished between

---

a. *Texaco, Inc. v. Pennzoil Co.,* 729 S.W.2d 768 (Tex.App—Houston [1st Dist.] 1987, writ ref'd n.r.e.). This case was discussed briefly in Chapter 5. See footnote 6 in that chapter for an explanation of "writ ref'd n.r.e." in Texas citations.

two types of preliminary agreements. A Type I preliminary agreement is one in which all essential terms have been agreed on and no disputed issues remain to be resolved, as in the Getty-Pennzoil memorandum of agreement. The formal contract to follow is simply that—a writing to satisfy formalities. According to the court, in this situation a formal contract is not necessary to create a binding agreement, which has already been created.

Type II preliminary agreements are all other preliminary agreements in which open terms still exist. All that the parties are doing is agreeing to continue negotiations in good faith to work out the remaining terms. Type II preliminary agreements are therefore not binding. The only obligation of the parties is to continue negotiating in good faith in an attempt to resolve open terms, but such a resolution is not legally required.[b]

Important factors in determining whether a Type I or a Type II preliminary agreement has been reached are whether there was a "meeting of the minds" between the parties as to the essential terms of the future contract and whether the parties intended to be

---

b. *Shann v. Dunk,* 84 F.3d 73 (2d Cir. 1996).

"hammer has fallen." In this situation, the seller is obligated to notify those attending the auction that sales of goods made during the auction are not final until confirmed by the seller.

DEFINITENESS OF TERMS

The second requirement for an effective offer involves the definiteness of its terms. An offer must have terms that are reasonably definite so that, if a contract is formed, a court can determine if a breach has occurred and can provide an appropriate remedy. What specific terms are required depends, of course, on the type of contract. Generally, a contract must include the following terms, either expressed in the contract or capable of being reasonably inferred from it:

1. The identification of the parties.
2. The identification of the object or subject matter of

EMERGING TRENDS IN BUSINESS LAW

The Enforcement of Preliminary Agreements,
continued

bound by their agreement. As one court phrased it, "For an enforceable contract to exist there must be both (1) agreement as to all material terms; and (2) intention of the parties to be bound."[c]

AN EXAMPLE OF A TYPE II PRELIMINARY AGREEMENT

The court's evaluation of these factors played a key role in the outcome in a case brought by Fox News Network against Time Warner. A few years prior to the lawsuit, Time Warner and Turner Broadcasting had decided to merge. They knew that the Federal Trade Commission would require them to carry an additional affiliated cable news network in order to receive merger approval. Time Warner started negotiations with

Fox News and MSNBC (a joint venture of Microsoft and NBC), ultimately choosing the latter. Fox sued Time Warner, claiming that such statements as "We are in agreement," "We will certainly reach agreement," and "All the details are set" made by Time Warner during the contract negotiations indicated that the parties agreed on the terms of a contract and intended to be bound by those terms.

A federal district court, however, concluded that the parties had "never reached—or even approached—agreement on the essentials to a contractual relationship." The court stated that Fox should have known better than to rely on statements made by Time Warner during the preliminary negotiations. "These were not Adam-and-Eve-like innocents slipping naked into the cable television and broadcast jungle to negotiate with each other and the serpent," said the court. Rather, "They were hard bitten executives steeled in such hagglings. . . . The 'morals of the marketplace' controlled." The law was not violated.[d]

IMPLICATIONS FOR THE BUSINESSPERSON

1. When engaging in preliminary negotiations, businesspersons should be aware that if all material terms are agreed on, they may be bound in contract even though they have not yet drawn up a formal contract.
2. Businesspersons should always keep in mind that what they say and do during preliminary negotiations—and not their subjective intentions—are the factors that will be considered by the courts in determining contractual intent.

FOR CRITICAL ANALYSIS

1. In deciding whether an agreement to agree or an enforceable contract has been formed, why should it matter whether the parties are "hard bitten executives steeled in such hagglings" or relatively inexperienced businesspersons?
2. Is it fair for a court to hold that parties are bound in contract even though one of the parties claims that it did not intend to form a contract? Generally, should the courts give more weight to subjective intent in determining whether a contract has been formed?

c. *Novecon, Ltd. v. Bulgarian-American Enterprise Fund,* 190 F.3d 556 (D.C. Cir. 1999).

d. *Fox News Network, L.L.C. v. Time Warner, Inc.,* 1997 WL 271720 (E.D.N.Y. 1997).

the contract (also the quantity, when appropriate), including the work to be performed, with specific identification of such items as goods, services, and land.
3. The consideration to be paid.
4. The time of payment, delivery, or performance.

Courts sometimes are willing to supply a missing term in a contract when the parties have clearly manifested an intent to form a contract. If, in contrast, the parties have attempted to deal with a particular term of

the contract but their expression of intent is too vague or uncertain to be given any precise meaning, the court will not supply a "reasonable" term, because to do so might conflict with the intent of the parties. In other words, the court will not rewrite the contract.[7]

7. See Chapter 19 and UCC 2–204. Article 2 of the UCC specifies different rules relating to the definiteness of terms used in a contract for the sale of goods. In essence, Article 2 modifies general contract law by requiring less specificity.

An offer may invite an acceptance to be worded in such specific terms that the contract is made definite. For example, suppose that Marcus Business Machines contacts your corporation and offers to sell "from one to ten MacCool copying machines for $1,600 each; state number desired in acceptance." Your corporation agrees to buy two copiers. Because the quantity is specified in the acceptance, the terms are definite, and the contract is enforceable.

If some terms are not specified in the words of a document, a court may nonetheless find that an enforceable contract exists if the terms can be made definite in light of the surrounding circumstances. The following case illustrates this point.

CASE 11.2   R. K. Chevrolet, Inc. v. Hayden

Supreme Court of Virginia, 1997.
253 Va. 50,
480 S.E.2d 477.
http://www.courts.state.
va.us/opin.htm[a]

HISTORICAL AND SOCIAL SETTING   *Employment contracts are often considered to be a disadvantage to an employer. Such contracts sometimes work to an employer's advantage, however. An employer invests time and money in hiring and training its employees. An employment contract helps to ensure that the employer will get something in return for this investment. An employment contract can also help to ensure that confidential information to which employees are given access will not be disclosed to unauthorized persons.*

BACKGROUND AND FACTS   *R. K. Chevrolet, Inc., an automobile dealership, employed James Hayden as an assistant manager in its used-car department. Hayden's father owned and operated Coastal Chevrolet, one of R. K. Chevrolet's competitors. In May 1992, after Hayden had worked for R. K. Chevrolet for more than a year, he signed the following document:*

> Contract Between James J. Hayden & R. K. Chevrolet, GEO
> May 12, 1992
> I, James J. Hayden, willingly enter into a two year contract of employment with R. K. Chevrolet, Inc., GEO. The only reason allowable for Mr. Hayden to leave in this time frame, under this contract, is the untimely death of his father. Therefore, with the above exception, James J. Hayden agrees to work continuously at R. K. Chevrolet, Inc., GEO for at least two years in good faith.

Nine months later, Hayden quit without notice. After his departure, R. K. Chevrolet did not realize anticipated profits of $348,832 in its used-car department. The dealership filed a suit in a Virginia state court against Hayden, seeking, among other things, damages for breach of contract. Hayden argued that there was no contract because, in part, the terms were too indefinite. The court ruled in Hayden's favor. The dealership appealed.

IN THE LANGUAGE
OF THE COURT

STEPHENSON, Justice.
      *   *   *   *

      *   *   * Even if some terms of a contract are uncertain, it may be read in the light of the surrounding circumstances, and, if from such reading, its meaning may be determined, the contract will be enforced. *   *   *

The trial court concluded that a number of terms were missing from the alleged contract. The court stated that "[t]he document is dated on May the 12th of 1992, but it does not say that it will continue until May the 12th of 1994." The document does state,

---

a. This page, which is part of a Web site maintained by the state of Virginia, includes links to, among other things, some of the "Supreme Court of Virginia Opinions." Under that heading, click on the box for the format in which you want to view the opinion. From that page, scroll down the list of cases to the *R.K. Chevrolet v. Hayden* case and click on the number (960943) to download the opinion.

however, that Hayden agreed to work continuously at R.K. "for at least two years." We think a jury, in the light of the surrounding circumstances, reasonably could conclude that the two-year period commenced on the date the document was executed.

The trial court also stated that there was nothing in the document to indicate what Hayden's position would be. Hayden, however, signed the document as the used car manager, and it is clear from the evidence adduced that he intended to serve in that capacity for the two-year term.

The court further noted that the document did not specify the amount of time Hayden was to work. Again, Hayden was already working as the used car manager when he signed the document, and a jury reasonably could find that he would continue to work the hours in a day and the days in a week that he had been working.

Finally, the trial court stated that the document made no mention of what Hayden's compensation would be. From the surrounding circumstances, however, a jury reasonably could have concluded that Hayden's salary would be that which he was receiving at the time he signed the document.

DECISION AND REMEDY   *The Supreme Court of Virginia held that the terms were sufficiently definite to create an enforceable contract. The court reversed the decision of the lower court and remanded the case for a new trial.*

COMMUNICATION

A third requirement for an effective offer is communication of the offer to the offeree, resulting in the offeree's knowledge of the offer. Ordinarily, one cannot agree to a bargain without knowing that it exists. Suppose that Estrich advertises a reward for the return of his lost dog. Hoban, not knowing of the reward, finds the dog and returns it to Estrich. Hoban cannot recover the reward, because she did not know it had been offered.[8]

SECTION 2

Termination of the Offer

The communication of an effective offer to an offeree gives the offeree the power to transform the offer into a binding, legal obligation (a contract) by an acceptance. This power of acceptance, however, does not continue forever. It can be terminated either by the action of the parties or by operation of law.

---

8. A few states allow recovery of the reward, but not on contract principles. Because Estrich wanted his dog to be returned, and Hoban returned it, these few states would allow Hoban to recover on the basis that it would be unfair to deny her the reward just because she did not know it had been offered.

TERMINATION BY ACTION OF THE PARTIES

An offer can be terminated by the action of the parties in any of three ways: by revocation, by rejection, or by counteroffer.

Revocation of the Offer by the Offeror. The offeror's act of withdrawing an offer is known as **revocation.** Unless an offer is irrevocable, the offeror usually can revoke the offer (even if he or she has promised to keep it open), as long as the revocation is communicated to the offeree before the offeree accepts. Revocation may be accomplished by express repudiation of the offer (for example, with a statement such as "I withdraw my previous offer of October 17") or by performance of acts inconsistent with the existence of the offer, which are made known to the offeree.

The general rule followed by most states is that a revocation becomes effective when the offeree or offeree's agent (a person acting on behalf of the offeree) actually receives it. Therefore, a letter of revocation mailed on April 1 and delivered at the offeree's residence or place of business on April 3 becomes effective on April 3.

An offer made to the general public can be revoked in the same manner the offer was originally communicated. Suppose that a department store offers a

$10,000 reward to anyone giving information leading to the apprehension of the persons who burglarized the store's downtown branch. The offer is published in three local papers and four papers in neighboring communities. To revoke the offer, the store must publish the revocation in all of the seven papers in which it published the offer. The revocation is then accessible to the general public, even if some particular offeree does not know about it.

Irrevocable Offers.　Although most offers are revocable, some can be made irrevocable. One type of irrevocable offer involves the option contract. Increasingly, courts also refuse to allow an offeror to revoke an offer when the offeree has changed position because of justifiable reliance on the offer. (In some circumstances, an offer for the sale of goods made by a merchant may also be considered irrevocable—see the discussion of the "merchant's firm offer" in Chapter 19.)

Option Contract.　**An option contract is created when an offeror promises to hold an offer open for a specified period of time in return for a payment (consideration) given by the offeree.** An option contract takes away the offeror's power to revoke the offer for the period of time specified in the option. If no time is specified, then a reasonable period of time is implied. For example, suppose that you are in the business of writing movie scripts. Your agent contacts the head of development at New Line Cinema and offers to sell New Line your latest movie script. New Line likes your script and agrees to pay you $10,000 for a six-month option. In this situation, you (through your agent) are the offeror, and New Line is the offeree. You cannot revoke your offer to sell New Line your script for the next six months. If after six months no contract has been formed, however, New Line loses the $10,000, and you are free to sell the script to another firm.

Option contracts are also frequently used in conjunction with the sale or lease of real estate. For example, you might agree with a landowner to lease a home and include in the lease contract a clause stating that you will pay $2,000 for an option to purchase the home within a specified period of time. If you decide not to purchase the home after the specified period has lapsed, you forfeit the $2,000, and the landlord is free to sell the property to another buyer.

Additionally, contracts to lease business premises often include options to renew the leases at certain intervals, such as after five years. Typically, a lease contract containing a renewal option requires notification—that is, the person leasing the premises must notify the property owner of his or her intention to exercise the renewal option within a certain number of days or months before the current lease expires.

Detrimental Reliance.　When the offeree justifiably relies on an offer to his or her detriment, the court may hold that this *detrimental reliance* makes the offer irrevocable. For example, assume that Angela has rented commercial property from Jake for the past thirty-three years under a series of five-year leases. Under business conditions existing as their seventh lease nears its end, the rental property market is more favorable for tenants than landlords. Angela tells Jake that she is going to look at other, less expensive properties as possible sites for her business. Wanting Angela to remain a tenant, Jake promises to reduce the rent in their next lease. In reliance on the promise, Angela does not look at other sites but continues to occupy and do business on Jake's property. When they sit down to negotiate a new lease, however, Jake says he has changed his mind and will increase the rent. Can he effectively revoke his promise?

Normally, he cannot, because Angela has been relying on his promise to reduce the rent. Had the promise not been made, she would have relocated her business. This is a case of detrimental reliance on a promise, which therefore cannot be revoked. In this situation, the doctrine of **promissory estoppel** comes into play. To **estop** means to bar, impede, or preclude someone from doing something. Thus, promissory estoppel means that the promisor (the offeror) is barred from revoking the offer, in this case because the offeree has already changed her actions in reliance on the offer. We look again at the doctrine of promissory estoppel in Chapter 12, in the context of consideration.

Detrimental reliance on the part of the offeree can also involve partial performance by the offeree in response to an offer looking toward formulation of a unilateral contract. As discussed in Chapter 10, the offer to form a unilateral contract invites acceptance only by full performance; merely promising to perform does not constitute acceptance. Injustice can result if an offeree expends time and money in partial performance, and then the offeror revokes the offer before performance can be completed. Many courts will not allow the offeror to revoke the offer after the offeree has performed some substantial part of his or her duties.[9] In effect, partial performance renders the offer irrevocable, giving the original offeree reasonable time to complete performance. Of course, once the performance is complete, a unilateral contract exists.

3. **Rejection of the Offer by the Offeree.** The offer may be rejected by the offeree, in which case the offer is terminated. Any subsequent attempt by the offeree to accept will be construed as a new offer, giving the original offeror (now the offeree) the power of acceptance. A rejection is ordinarily accomplished by words or conduct evidencing an intent not to accept the offer. As with revocation, rejection of an offer is effective only when it is actually received by the offeror or the offeror's agent.

Merely inquiring about an offer does not constitute rejection. Suppose that a friend offers to buy your CD-ROM library for $300, and you respond, "Is that your best offer?" or "Will you pay me $375 for it?" A reasonable person would conclude that you had not rejected the offer but had merely made an inquiry for further consideration of the offer. You can still accept and bind your friend to the $300 purchase price. When the offeree merely inquires as to the firmness of the offer, there is no reason to presume that he or she intends to reject it.

Counteroffer by the Offeree. A rejection of the original offer and the simultaneous making of a new offer is called a **counteroffer.** Suppose that Duffy offers to sell her home to Wong for $170,000. Wong responds, "Your price is too high. I'll offer to purchase your house for $160,000." Wong's response is a counteroffer, because it terminates Duffy's offer to sell at $170,000 and creates a new offer by Wong to purchase at $160,000.

At common law, the **mirror image rule** requires the offeree's acceptance to match the offeror's offer exactly—to mirror the offer. Any material change in, or addition to, the terms of the original offer automatically terminates that offer and substitutes the counteroffer. The counteroffer, of course, need not be accepted; but if the original offeror does accept the terms of the counteroffer, a valid contract is created.[10]

TERMINATION BY OPERATION OF LAW

The power of the offeree to transform the offer into a binding, legal obligation can be terminated by operation of law through the occurrence of the following events:

1. Lapse of time.
2. Destruction of the specific subject matter of the offer.
3. Death or incompetence of the offeror or the offeree.
4. Supervening illegality of the proposed contract.

Lapse of Time An offer terminates automatically by law when the period of time specified in the offer has passed. For example, suppose Alejandro offers to sell his camper to Kelly if she accepts within twenty days. Kelly must accept within the twenty-day period, or the offer will lapse (terminate). The time period specified in an offer normally begins to run when the offer is actually received by the offeree, not when it is sent or drawn up. When the offer is delayed (through the misdelivery of mail, for example), the period begins to run from the date the offeree would have received the offer, but only if the offeree knows or should know that the offer is delayed.[11]

If no time for acceptance is specified in the offer, the offer terminates at the end of a *reasonable* period of time. What constitutes a reasonable period of time depends on the subject matter of the contract, business and market conditions, and other relevant circumstances. An offer to sell farm produce, for example, will terminate sooner than an offer to sell farm equipment because farm produce is perishable and subject to greater fluctuations in market value.

Destruction of the Subject Matter. An offer is automatically terminated if the specific subject matter of the offer is destroyed before the offer is accepted.[12] If Johnson offers to sell his prize greyhound to Rizzo, for example, but the dog dies before Rizzo can accept, the offer is automatically terminated. Johnson does not have to tell Rizzo that the animal has died for the offer to terminate.

Death or Incompetence of the Offeror or Offeree. An offeree's power of acceptance is terminated when the offeror or offeree dies or is deprived of legal

---

9. *Restatement (Second) of Contracts*, Section 45.

10. The mirror image rule has been greatly modified in regard to sales contracts. Section 2–207 of the UCC provides that a contract is formed if the offeree makes a definite expression of acceptance (such as signing the form in the appropriate location), even though the terms of the acceptance modify or add to the terms of the original offer (see Chapter 19).

11. *Restatement (Second) of Contracts*, Section 49.

12. *Restatement (Second) of Contracts*, Section 36.

capacity to enter into the proposed contract. If the offer is irrevocable, however, the death of the offeror or offeree does not terminate the offer.[13] A revocable offer is personal to both parties and cannot pass to the heirs, guardian, or estate of either. Furthermore, this rule applies whether or not the other party had notice of the death or incompetence.

Supervening Illegality of the Proposed Contract.
When a statute or court decision makes an offer il-

legal, the offer is automatically terminated.[14] For example, Lee offers to loan Kim $10,000 at an annual interest rate of 12 percent. Before Kim can accept the offer, a law is enacted that prohibits interest rates higher than 10 percent. Lee's offer is automatically terminated. If the law had been passed after Kim accepted the offer, a valid contract would have been formed, because the offer would still have been legal when it was accepted. In some circumstances, such a contract might be unenforceable, however, as when a statute or law is retroactively applied.

---

13. *Restatement (Second) of Contracts*, Section 48. If the offer is such that it can be accepted by the performance of a series of acts, and those acts began before the offeror died, the offeree's power of acceptance is not terminated.

---

14. *Restatement (Second) of Contracts*, Section 36.

CONCEPT SUMMARY 11.1

METHODS BY WHICH AN OFFER CAN BE TERMINATED

METHODS OF TERMINATION	BASIC RULES
BY ACTION OF THE PARTIES	
Revocation	1. An offer can be revoked at any time before acceptance without liability unless the offer is irrevocable.
	2. Option contracts, merchants' firm offers, and, in some circumstances, the promissory estoppel theory render offers irrevocable.
	3. Except for public offers, revocation is not effective until received by the offeree or the offeree's authorized agent.
Rejection	1. Rejection of an offer is accomplished by words or actions that demonstrate a clear intent not to accept the offer or consider the offer further. Inquiries about an offer do not constitute a rejection.
	2. A rejection is not effective until received by the offeror or an authorized agent of the offeror.
Counteroffer	A counteroffer is a rejection of the original offer and the making of a new offer.
BY OPERATION OF LAW	
Lapse of Time	1. If a time period for acceptance is stated in the offer, the offer ends at the stated time.
	2. If no time period for acceptance is stated, the offer terminates at the end of a reasonable period.
Destruction	Destruction of the specific subject matter of the offer terminates the offer.
Death or Incompetence	Death or incompetence of either the offeror or the offeree terminates an offer, unless the offer is irrevocable.
Illegality	Supervening illegality terminates an offer.

SECTION 3

Acceptance

Acceptance is a voluntary act (either words or conduct) by the offeree that shows assent (agreement) to the terms of an offer. The acceptance must be unequivocal and communicated to the offeror.

UNEQUIVOCAL ACCEPTANCE

To exercise the power of acceptance effectively, the offeree must accept unequivocally. This is the *mirror image rule* previously discussed. If the acceptance is subject to new conditions or if the terms of the acceptance materially change the original offer, the acceptance may be deemed a counteroffer that implicitly rejects the original offer. An acceptance may be unequivocal even though the offeree expresses dissatisfaction with the contract. For example, "I accept the offer, but I wish I could have gotten a better price" is an effective acceptance. So, too, is "I accept, but can you shave the price?" In contrast, the statement "I accept the offer but only if I can pay on ninety days' credit" is not an unequivocal acceptance and operates as a counteroffer, rejecting the original offer.

Certain terms when added to an acceptance will not qualify the acceptance sufficiently to constitute rejection of the offer. Suppose that in response to an offer to sell a piano, the offeree replies, "I accept; please send a written contract." The offeree is requesting a written contract but is not making it a condition for acceptance. Therefore, the acceptance is effective without the written contract. If the offeree replies, "I accept if you send a written contract," however, the acceptance is expressly conditioned on the request for a writing, and the statement is not an acceptance but a counteroffer. (Notice how important each word is!)[15]

SILENCE AS ACCEPTANCE

Ordinarily, silence cannot constitute acceptance, even if the offeror states, "By your silence and inaction you will be deemed to have accepted this offer." This general rule applies because an offeree should not be obligated to act affirmatively to reject an offer when no consideration has passed to the offeree to impose such a duty.

In some instances, however, the offeree does have a duty to speak, in which case his or her silence or inaction will operate as an acceptance. For example, silence may be an acceptance when an offeree takes the benefit of offered services even though he or she had an opportunity to reject them and knew that they were offered with the expectation of compensation. Suppose that Sayre watches while a stranger rakes his leaves, even though the stranger has not been asked to rake the yard. Sayre knows the stranger expects to be paid and does nothing to stop her. Here, his silence constitutes an acceptance, and an implied-in-fact contract is created (see Chapter 10). He is bound to pay a reasonable value for the stranger's work. This rule normally applies only when the offeree has received a benefit from the goods or services rendered.

Silence can also operate as acceptance when the offeree has had prior dealings with the offeror. Suppose that a merchant routinely receives shipments from a certain supplier and always notifies the supplier when defective goods are rejected. In this situation, silence regarding a shipment will constitute acceptance. Additionally, if a person solicits an offer specifying that certain terms and conditions are acceptable, and the offeror makes the offer in response to the solicitation, the offeree has a duty to reject—that is, a duty to tell the offeror that the offer is not acceptable. Failure to reject (silence) operates as an acceptance.

COMMUNICATION OF ACCEPTANCE

Whether the offeror must be notified of the acceptance depends on the nature of the contract. In a bilateral contract, communication of acceptance is necessary because acceptance is in the form of a promise (not performance) and the contract is formed when the promise is made (rather than when the act is performed). The offeree must communicate the acceptance to the offeror. Communication of acceptance is not necessary, however, if the offer dispenses with the requirement. Additionally, if the offer can be accepted by silence, no communication is necessary. Because in a unilateral contract the full performance of some act is called for, acceptance is usually evident, and notification is therefore unnecessary. Exceptions do exist, however. When the offeror requests notice of acceptance or has no adequate means

---

15. As noted in footnote 10, in regard to sales contracts the UCC provides that an acceptance may still be valid even if some terms are added. The new terms are simply treated as proposals for addition to the contract.

of determining whether the requested act has been performed, or when the law requires notice of acceptance, then notice is necessary.[16]

MODE AND TIMELINESS OF ACCEPTANCE

Acceptance in bilateral contracts must be timely. The general rule is that acceptance in a bilateral contract is timely if it is made before the offer is terminated. Problems arise, however, when the parties involved are not dealing face to face. In such cases, acceptance takes effect, thus completing formation of the contract, at the time the acceptance is communicated via the mode expressly or impliedly authorized by the offeror. According to the *Restatement (Second) of Contracts*, unless the offeror provides otherwise, "an acceptance made in a manner and by a medium invited by an offer is operative and completes the manifestation of mutual assent as soon as put out of the offeree's possession, without regard to whether it ever reaches the offeror."[17]

This rule traditionally has been referred to as the **mailbox rule,** also called the "deposited acceptance rule," because once an acceptance has been deposited into a mailbox, it is "out of the offeree's possession." Under this rule, if the authorized mode of communication is the mail, then an acceptance becomes valid when it is dispatched by mail (even if it is never received by the offeror). Thus, whereas a revocation becomes effective only when it is received by the offeree, an acceptance becomes effective on *dispatch*, providing that *authorized* means of communication are used.

Authorized Means of Acceptance. An authorized means of communication may be either expressly authorized—that is, expressly stipulated in the offer—or impliedly authorized by the facts and circumstances surrounding the situation or by law. When an offeror specifies how acceptance should be made (for example, by overnight delivery), *express authorization* is said to exist, and the contract is not formed unless the offeree uses that specified mode of acceptance. Moreover, both offeror and offeree are bound in contract the moment this means of acceptance is employed. If overnight delivery is expressly authorized as the only means of acceptance, a contract is created as soon as the offeree delivers the message to the express delivery company. The contract would still exist even if the delivery company failed to deliver the message.

Many offerors, for one reason or another, do not indicate their preferred method of acceptance. When the offeror does not specify expressly that the offeree is to accept by a certain means, or that the acceptance will be effective only when received, acceptance of an offer may be made by any medium that is *reasonable under the circumstances.*[18] When two parties are at a distance, for example, mailing is impliedly authorized because it is a customary mode of dispatch.[19] Several factors determine whether the acceptance was reasonable: the nature of the circumstances as they existed at the time the offer was made, the means used by the offeror to transmit the offer to the offeree, and the reliability of the offer's delivery. If, for example, an offer was sent by FedEx overnight delivery because an acceptance was urgently required, then the offeree's use of first-class mail (which may take three days or more to deliver) might not be deemed reasonable.[20]

An acceptance sent by means not expressly or impliedly authorized is normally not effective until it is received by the offeror. If an acceptance is timely sent and timely received, however, despite the means by which it is transmitted, it is considered to have been effective on its dispatch.[21] If, in the previous example, the acceptance that was sent by first-class mail was actually delivered to the offeror the next day (the same as FedEx overnight delivery), then the court would recognize the acceptance as operative.

These principles are illustrated in the following case in the context of an option to renew a lease.

---

16. Under UCC 2–206(1)(b), an order or other offer to buy goods for prompt shipment may be treated as an offer contemplating either a bilateral or a unilateral contract and may be accepted by either a promise to ship or actual shipment. If the offer is accepted by actual shipment of the goods, the offeror must be notified of the acceptance within a reasonable period of time, or the offeror may treat the offer as having lapsed before acceptance [UCC 2–206(2)]. See also Chapter 19.

17. *Restatement (Second) of Contracts,* Section 63(a).

18. *Restatement (Second) of Contracts,* Section 30. This is also the rule under UCC 2–206(1)(a).

19. *Adams v. Lindsell,* 106 Eng.Rep. 250 (K.B. 1818); *Restatement (Second) of Contracts,* Section 65, Comment c.

20. See, for example, *Defeo v. Amfarms Associates,* 161 A.D.2d 904, 557 N.Y.2d 469 (1990).

21. *Restatement (Second) of Contracts,* Section 67.

CASE 11.3   Osprey L.L.C. v. Kelly-Moore Paint Co.

Supreme Court of
Oklahoma, 1999.
984 P.2d 194.
http://www.oscn.net [a]

BACKGROUND AND FACTS   *Kelly-Moore Paint Company leased a store in Edmond, Oklahoma, from Osprey L.L.C. The parties signed a fifteen-year lease with two five-year renewal options. The lease required Kelly-Moore to give Osprey written notice of the lessee's intent to renew at least six months before the lease expired. The notice "may be delivered either personally or by depositing the same in United States mail, first class postage prepaid, registered or certified mail, return receipt requested." Six months before the end of the fifteen-year term, Kelly-Moore sent the required notice by certified mail. Five years later, however, at the end of the first five-year term, on the last day of the six-month notification deadline, at 5:28 P.M., Kelly-Moore sent the notice by fax. Phone company records indicated that the fax was transmitted correctly, but Osprey denied receiving it. Osprey filed a suit in an Oklahoma state court to evict Kelly-Moore. Osprey argued that the lease specifically prescribed delivery of the notice personally or by mail. Kelly-Moore countered that the lease's use of the word "may" permitted other means of delivery. The court granted a judgment in favor of Kelly-Moore, and Osprey appealed. The state intermediate appellate court reversed this judgment, and Kelly-Moore appealed to the Oklahoma Supreme Court.*

**IN THE LANGUAGE
OF THE COURT**

KAUGER, J. [Justice].

    *   *   *   *

    *   *   * Although the question tendered is novel in Oklahoma, the sufficiency of the notice given when exercising an option contract or an option to renew or extend a lease has been considered by several jurisdictions. A few have found that delivery of notice by means other than hand delivery or by certified or registered mail was insufficient if the terms of the contract specifically referred to the method of delivery. However, the majority have reached the opposite conclusion. These courts generally recognize that, despite the contention that there must be strict compliance with the notice terms of a lease option agreement, *use of an alternative method does not render the notice defective if the substituted method performed the same function or served the same purpose as the authorized method.* [Emphasis added.]

    *   *   *   *

    *   *   * The lease does not appear to be ambiguous. "Shall" is ordinarily construed as mandatory and "may" is ordinarily construed as permissive. *   *   * The provision for delivery, either personally or by certified or registered mail, uses the permissive "may" and it does not bar other modes of transmission which are just as effective.

    *   *   * The purpose of providing notice by personal delivery or registered mail is to insure the delivery of the notice, and to settle any dispute which might arise between the parties concerning whether the notice was received. A substituted method of notice which performs the same function and serves the same purpose as an authorized method of notice is not defective. Here, the contract provided that time was of the essence. Although Osprey denies that it ever received the fax, the fax activity report and telephone company records confirm that the fax was transmitted successfully, and that it was sent to Osprey's correct facsimile number on the last day of the deadline to extend the lease. The fax provided immediate written communication similar to personal delivery and, like a telegram, would be timely if it were properly transmitted before the expiration of the deadline to renew. Kelly-Moore's use of the fax served the same function and the same purpose as the two methods suggested by the lease and it was transmitted before the expiration of the deadline to renew. Under these facts, we hold that the faxed or facsimile delivery of the written notice to renew the commercial lease was sufficient to exercise timely the renewal option of the lease.

---

a. This is the Oklahoma Supreme Court Network Web site, which is part of the Oklahoma Supreme Court Information System. In the box near the top of this page, type "1999 OK 50" and, in the pull-down menu beneath it, select "Retrieve Document." Click "Go" to access the opinion.

DECISION
AND REMEDY

The Oklahoma Supreme Court held that the use of an alternative method to exercise a lease option does not render the notice defective if the substituted notice performs the same function or serves the same purpose as the authorized method. The court vacated the decision of the state intermediate appellate court.

Exceptions. There are three basic exceptions to the rule that a contract is formed when an acceptance is sent by authorized means.

1. If the acceptance is not properly dispatched by the offeree (if it was sent to an incorrect address, for example), in most states it will not be effective until it is received by the offeror.[22] For example, if mail is the authorized means for acceptance, the offeree's letter must be properly addressed and have the correct postage. Nonetheless, if acceptance is timely sent and timely received, despite the offeree's carelessness in sending it, it is still considered to have been effective on dispatch.[23]

2. The offeror can stipulate in the offer that an acceptance will not be effective until it is received by the offeror.

3. Sometimes an offeree sends a rejection first, then later changes his or her mind and sends an acceptance. Obviously, this chain of events could cause confusion and even detriment to the offeror, depending on whether the rejection or the acceptance arrived first. Because of this, the law cancels the rule of acceptance on dispatch in such situations, and the first communication to be received by the offeror determines whether a contract is formed. If the rejection is received first, there is no contract.[24]

---

22. *Restatement (Second) of Contracts,* Section 66.
23. *Restatement (Second) of Contracts,* Section 67.

---

24. *Restatement (Second) of Contracts,* Section 40.

CONCEPT SUMMARY 11.2

EFFECTIVE TIME OF ACCEPTANCE

ACCEPTANCE	TIME EFFECTIVE
By Authorized Means of Communication	Effective at the time communication is sent (deposited in a mailbox or delivered to a courier service) via the mode expressly or impliedly authorized by the offeror (mailbox rule). *Exceptions:* 1. If the acceptance is not properly dispatched, it will not be effective until received by the offeror. 2. If the offeror specifically conditioned the offer on receipt of acceptance, it will not be effective until received by the offeror. 3. If acceptance is sent after rejection, whichever is received first is given effect.
By Unauthorized Means of Communication	Effective on receipt of acceptance by the offeror (if timely received, it is considered to have been effective on dispatch).

TERMS AND CONCEPTS TO REVIEW

QUESTIONS AND CASE PROBLEMS

11–1. OFFER AND ACCEPTANCE. Ball writes Sullivan and inquires how much Sullivan is asking for a specific forty-acre tract of land Sullivan owns. In a letter received by Ball, Sullivan states, "I will not take less than $60,000 for the forty-acre tract as specified." Ball immediately sends Sullivan a telegram stating, "I accept your offer for $60,000 for the forty-acre tract as specified." Discuss whether Ball can hold Sullivan to a contract for sale of the land.

11–2. OFFER. Sachs, operating a sole proprietorship, has a large piece of used farm equipment for sale. He offers to sell the equipment to Barry for $10,000. Discuss the legal effects of the following events on the offer.

(a) Sachs dies prior to Barry's acceptance, and at the time he accepts, Barry is unaware of Sachs's death.

(b) The night before Barry accepts, fire destroys the equipment.

(c) Barry pays $100 for a thirty-day option to purchase the equipment. During this period, Sachs dies, and later Barry accepts the offer, knowing of Sachs's death.

(d) Barry pays $100 for a thirty-day option to purchase the equipment. During this period, Barry dies, and Barry's estate accepts Sachs's offer within the stipulated time period.

11–3. OFFER AND ACCEPTANCE. Perez sees an advertisement in the newspaper that the ABC Corp. has for sale a two-volume set of books, *How to Make Repairs around the House*, for $22.95. All Perez has to do is send in a card requesting delivery of the books for a thirty-day trial period of examination. If he does not ship the books back within thirty days of delivery, ABC will bill him for $22.95. Discuss whether Perez and ABC have a contract under either of the following circumstances.

(a) Perez sends in the card and receives the books in the U.S. mail. He uses the books to make repairs and fails to return them within thirty days.

(b) Perez does not send in the card, but ABC sends him the books anyway through the U.S. mail. Perez uses the books and fails to return them within thirty days.

11–4. ACCEPTANCE. On Thursday, Dennis mailed Tanya a letter offering to sell his car to her for $3,000. On Saturday, having changed his mind, Dennis sent a fax to Tanya's office revoking his offer. Tanya did not go to her office over the weekend and thus did not learn about the revocation until Monday morning, just a few minutes after she had mailed a letter of acceptance to Dennis. When Tanya demanded that Dennis sell his car to her as promised, Dennis claimed that no contract existed because he had revoked his offer prior to Tanya's acceptance. Is Dennis correct? Explain.

11–5. OFFER AND ACCEPTANCE. James sent invitations to a number of potential buyers to submit bids for some timber he wanted to sell. Two bids were received as a result; the higher bid was submitted by Eames. James changed his mind about selling the timber, however, and did not accept Eames's bid. Eames claimed that a contract for sale existed and sued James for breach. Did a contract exist? Discuss. [*Eames v. James*, 452 So.2d 384 (La.App.3d Cir. 1984)]

11–6. AUCTIONS. Ameritrust Co. employed Rosen & Co. to conduct an auction. Included in Rosen's extensive advertisements of the sale was the announcement that the sale was subject to confirmation by Ameritrust. The auctioneer made a similar announcement at the time of the sale. At the auction, the auctioneer first offered the equipment in bulk, but only one bid—from Alpine Co. for $50,000—was received. Then the equipment was offered piecemeal, and total bids of $139,000 were received. Two bids—one from Lawrence Paper Co. and one from American Corrugated Machine Corp. (ACMC)—were accepted, and both companies submitted checks for 25 percent of their bid totals, as requested. Subsequent to the auction, Alpine offered $175,000 for the equipment, and Ameritrust sold the entire lot to Alpine. Lawrence and ACMC sued for breach of contract. Will they succeed in their suit? Why or why not? [*Lawrence Paper Co. v. Rosen & Co.*, 939 F.2d 376 (6th Cir. 1991)]

11–7. INTENTION. Before an employee convention, Nationwide Mutual Insurance Co. created a committee, whose members included Mary Peterson, to select a theme. The committee announced a contest for theme suggestions: "Here's what you could win: His and Hers Mercedes. An all expense paid trip for two around the world. Additional prize to be announced. (All prizes subject to availability.)" David Mears submitted the theme "At the Top and Still Climbing." At a dinner of Nationwide employees, Peterson told Mears that he had won two Mercedes. Mears and others who heard this believed that he had won the cars. Nationwide never gave him the cars, however, and he filed a suit in a federal district court, alleging breach of contract. At the trial, Peterson claimed that she spoke with a facetious tone and, in reality, had no intention of awarding the cars. Is Mears entitled to the cars? Why or why not? [*Mears v. Nationwide Mutual Insurance Co.*, 91 F.3d 1118 (8th Cir. 1996)]

11–8. OFFER. Air Jamaica Vacations (AJV) requested bids from printing firms to produce travel brochures. Moore Graphic Services responded with an offer quoting prices and terms for an agreement to produce between 100,000 and 250,000 brochures. The offer stated that sales tax would be charged and requested that AJV indicate its acceptance by signing and returning the offer. Moore then contacted one of its vendors, Starr Printing Co., about producing the brochures and sent AJV samples of the work to be performed. Meanwhile, AJV returned the offer with some modified terms, including a handwritten notation, "no tax." Moore then told Starr it was putting "the job" on hold and told AJV that it could not perform "the job" because of the dispute about the tax. Starr printed the brochures and demanded payment. AJV refused, claiming in part that the brochures were of "poor quality." Starr filed a suit in a federal district court against AJV. AJV filed a suit against Moore, claiming breach of contract for giving the job to Starr. Moore filed a motion for summary judgment, on the ground that there was no contract. Did Moore and AJV have a contract? Why or why not? [*Starr Printing Co. v. Air Jamaica*, 45 F.Supp.2d 625 (W.D.Tenn. 1999)]

11–9. IN YOUR COURT

Cora Payne was involved in an automobile accident with Don Chappell, an employee of E & B Carpet Cleaning, Inc. E & B's insurance company offered Payne $18,500 to settle her claim against E & B. Payne did not accept the offer at that time but instead filed suit against E & B and its in-surance company (the defendants). Later, Payne offered to settle the case for $50,000, but the defendants refused her offer. Ultimately, Payne told the defendants that she would accept the insurance company's original settlement offer of $18,500, but the insurance company stated that the offer was no longer open for acceptance. When Payne sought to compel the defendants to perform the original settlement offer, the defendants contended that Payne's filing of her lawsuit terminated the insurance company's earlier settlement offer. Assume that you are the judge in the trial court hearing this case and answer the following questions:

(a) What effect did Payne's filing of the lawsuit and later offer to settle the case for $50,000 have on the original offer? Had Payne, by either event, rejected the original offer or made a counteroffer?

(b) If Payne had rejected the original offer or made a counteroffer, did either event terminate the original settlement offer? If so, what will your ruling be? If not, what remedy will you grant to Payne?

LAW ON THE WEB

For updated links to resources available on the Web, as well as a variety of other materials, visit this text's Web site at http://wbl.westbuslaw.com.

You can find articles and information on various areas of law—including contracts—at the Law Office's Web site. Go to

http://lawoffice.com

Select the topic of Business and Commercial Law from the Law Knowledgebase list on the right-hand side of the home page.

To view the terms of a sample contract, go to the "forms" pages of the 'Lectric Law Library at

http://www.lectlaw.com/form

LEGAL RESEARCH EXERCISES ON THE WEB

Go to http://wbl.westbuslaw.com, the Web site that accompanies this text. Select "Internet Applications," and then click on "Chapter 11." There you will find the following Internet research exercise that you can perform to learn more about contract terms:

Activity 11–1: Contract Terms

CHAPTER 12

Consideration

THE FACT THAT A PROMISE has been made does not mean the promise can or will be enforced. Under Roman law, a promise was not enforceable without some sort of *causa*—that is, a reason for making the promise that was also deemed to be a sufficient reason for enforcing it. Since the beginning of the common law tradition in England, good reasons for enforcing informal promises (promises made in contracts that are not under seal) have been held to include something given as an agreed-on exchange, a benefit that the promisor received, and a detriment that the promisee incurred. Over time, these reasons came to be referred to legally as "consideration."

Thus, for centuries, it has been said that no informal promise is enforceable without consideration. **Consideration** is usually defined as the value (such as money) given in return for a promise (such as the promise to sell a stamp collection on receipt of payment). Often, consideration is broken down into two parts: (1) something of *legal value* must be given in exchange for the promise, and (2) there must be a *bargained-for* exchange. The "something of legal value" may consist of a return promise that is bargained for. If it consists of performance, that performance may be (1) an act (other than a promise); (2) a forbearance (a refraining from action); or (3) the creation, modification, or destruction of a legal relation.[1]

For example, Anita says to her son, "When you finish painting the garage, I will pay you $100." Anita's son paints the garage. The act of painting the garage is the consideration that creates Anita's contractual obligation to pay her son $100. Suppose, however, that Anita says to her son, "In consideration of the fact that you are not as wealthy as your brothers, I will pay you $500." This promise is not enforceable, because Anita's son has not given any consideration for the $500 promised.[2] Anita has simply stated her motive for giving her son a gift. The fact that the word *consideration* is used does not, alone, mean that consideration has been given.

SECTION 1

Legal Sufficiency of Consideration

For a binding contract to be created, consideration must be *legally sufficient*. To be legally sufficient, consideration for a promise *must be either legally detrimental to the promisee* (the one receiving the promise) *or legally beneficial to the promisor* (the one making the promise). Recall from Chapter 10 that in a bilateral contract, each party is both a promisor and a promisee. A party can incur legal detriment by

---

1. *Restatement (Second) of Contracts*, Section 71.

2. See *Fink v. Cox*, 18 Johns. 145, 9 Am.Dec. 191 (N.Y. 1820).

either promising to give legal value (such as the payment of money) or by forbearance or a promise of forbearance—that is, by refraining from or promising to refrain from undertaking an action that the party had a legal right to undertake.

Suppose that Sue Ray owns the right to use the name "Sue's Kitchen." Susan Katz (the promisor) offers Ray $5,000 to stop using the name for her restaurant, and Ray (the promisee) agrees. A bilateral contract is formed by this exchange of promises. The consideration flowing from Ray to Katz is Ray's promise to refrain from doing something that she is legally entitled to do—use the name "Sue's Kitchen." The consideration flowing from Katz to Ray is Katz's promise to pay Ray $5,000.

The following case is one of the classics of contract law. The issue before the court was whether refraining from certain behavior at the request of another is sufficient consideration to support a promise to pay a sum of money.

CASE 12.1   Hamer v. Sidway

Court of Appeals
of New York,
Second Division, 1891.
124 N.Y. 538,
27 N.E. 256.

BACKGROUND AND FACTS *William E. Story, Sr., was the uncle of William E. Story II. In the presence of family members and guests invited to a family gathering, the elder Story promised to pay his nephew $5,000 if he would refrain from drinking, using tobacco, swearing, and playing cards or billiards for money until he reached the age of twenty-one. (Note that in 1869, when this contract was formed, it was legal in New York to drink and play cards for money prior to the age of twenty-one.) The nephew agreed and fully performed his part of the bargain. When he reached the age of twenty-one, he wrote and told his uncle that he had kept his part of the agreement and was therefore entitled to $5,000. The uncle replied that he was pleased with his nephew's performance, writing, "I have no doubt but you have, for which you shall have five thousand dollars, as I promised you. I had the money in the bank the day you was twenty-one years old that I intend for you, and you shall have the money certain. . . . P.S. You can consider this money on interest." The nephew received his uncle's letter and thereafter consented that the money should remain with his uncle according to the terms and conditions of the letter. The uncle died about twelve years later without having paid his nephew any part of the $5,000 and interest. The executor of the uncle's estate (Sidway, the defendant in this action) did not want to pay the $5,000 (with interest) to Hamer, a third party to whom the nephew had transferred his rights in the note, claiming that there had been no valid consideration for the promise. The court disagreed with the executor and reviewed the doctrine of detriment and benefit as valid consideration under the law.*

IN THE LANGUAGE OF THE COURT

PARKER, J. [Justice]
          *   *   *   *

          *   *   * Courts will not ask whether the thing which forms the consideration does in fact benefit the promisee or a third party, or is of any substantial value to any one. It is enough that something is promised, done, forborne, or suffered by the party to whom the promise is made as consideration for the promise made to him. *In general a waiver of any legal right at the request of another party is a sufficient consideration for a promise.* Any damage, or suspension, or forbearance of a right will be sufficient to sustain a promise. *   *   * Now, applying this rule to the facts before us, the promisee used tobacco, occasionally drank liquor, and he had a legal right to do so. That right he abandoned for a period of years upon the strength of the promise of the testator that for such forbearance he would give him $5,000. We need not speculate on the effort which may have been required to give up the use of those stimulants. It is sufficient that he restricted his lawful freedom of action within certain prescribed limits upon the faith of his uncle's agreement, and now, having fully performed the conditions imposed, it is of no moment whether such performance actually proved a benefit to the promisor, and the court will not inquire into it; but, were it a proper subject of inquiry, we see nothing in this record that would permit a determination that the uncle was not benefited in a legal sense. [Emphasis added.]

DECISION AND REMEDY *The court ruled that the nephew had provided legally sufficient consideration by giving up smoking, drinking, swearing, and playing cards or billiards for money until he reached the age of twenty-one and was therefore entitled to the money.*

ETHICAL CONSIDERATIONS *The* Hamer v. Sidway *case is a good illustration of the distinction between benefits to the promisor and detriment to the promisee. Here the court did not inquire as to whether a benefit had flowed to the promisor but required only that there had been a legally sufficient detriment to the promisee. The court did note, however, that arguably the promisor had also benefited by the contract—to the extent that the uncle considered it a benefit that his nephew had given up various vices, protected the family's reputation, and so on.*

SECTION 2

Adequacy of Consideration

Adequacy of consideration refers to the fairness of the bargain. In general, a court will not question the adequacy of consideration if the consideration is legally sufficient. Under the "doctrine of freedom of contract," parties are normally free to bargain as they wish. If people could sue merely because they had entered into an unwise contract, the courts would be overloaded with frivolous suits.

In extreme cases, a court may consider the adequacy of consideration in terms of its amount or worth because inadequate consideration may indicate fraud, duress, undue influence, or a lack of bargained-for exchange. It may also reflect a party's incompetence (for example, an individual might have been too intoxicated or simply too young to make a contract). Suppose that Dylan has a house worth $100,000 and he sells it for $50,000. A $50,000 sale could indicate that the buyer unduly pressured Dylan into selling the house at that price or that Dylan was defrauded into selling the house at far below market value. (Of course, it might also indicate that Dylan was in a hurry to sell and that the amount was legally sufficient.)

SECTION 3

Contracts That Lack Consideration

Sometimes, one of the parties (or both parties) to a contract may think that consideration has been exchanged when in fact it has not. Here we look at some situations in which the parties' promises or actions do not qualify as contractual consideration.

PREEXISTING DUTY

Under most circumstances, a promise to do what one already has a legal duty to do does not constitute legally sufficient consideration, because no legal detriment is incurred.[3] The preexisting legal duty may be imposed by law or may arise out of a previous contract. A sheriff, for example, cannot collect a reward for providing information leading to the capture of a criminal if the sheriff already has a legal duty to capture the criminal. Likewise, if a party is already bound by contract to perform a certain duty, that duty cannot serve as consideration for a second contract. To illustrate, suppose that Bauman-Bache, Inc., begins construction on a seven-story office building and after three months demands an extra $75,000 on its contract. If the extra $75,000 is not paid, it will stop working. The owner of the land, having no one else to complete construction, agrees to pay the extra $75,000. The agreement is not enforceable, because it is not supported by legally sufficient consideration; Bauman-Bache was under a preexisting contract to complete the building.

Unforeseen Difficulties. The rule regarding preexisting duty is meant to prevent extortion and the so-called holdup game. What happens, though, when an honest contractor who has contracted with a landowner to construct a building runs into extraordinary difficulties that were totally unforeseen at the time the contract was formed? In the interests of fairness and equity, the courts sometimes allow exceptions to the preexisting duty rule. In the example just mentioned, if the landowner agrees to pay extra compensation to the contractor for overcoming unforeseen difficulties, the court may refrain from applying

---

3. See *Foakes v. Beer*, 9 App.Cas. 605 (1884).

the preexisting duty rule and enforce the agreement. When the "unforeseen difficulties" that give rise to a contract modification involve the types of risks ordinarily assumed in business, however, the courts will usually assert the preexisting duty rule.[4]

Rescission and New Contract. The law recognizes that two parties can mutually agree to rescind their contract, at least to the extent that it is executory (still to be carried out). **Rescission**[5] is defined as the unmaking of a contract so as to return the parties to the positions they occupied before the contract was made. When rescission and the making of a new contract take place at the same time, without a change in the duties of both parties as required in their rescinded contract, the courts frequently are given a choice of applying the preexisting duty rule or allowing rescission and letting the new contract stand.

PAST CONSIDERATION

Promises made in return for actions or events that have already taken place are unenforceable. These promises lack consideration in that the element of bargained-for exchange is missing. In short, you can bargain for something to take place now or in the future but not for something that has already taken place. Therefore, **past consideration** is no consideration.

Suppose, for example, that Elsie, a real estate agent, does her friend Judy a favor by selling Judy's house and not charging any commission. Later, Judy says to Elsie, "In return for your generous act, I will pay you $3,000." This promise is made in return for past consideration and is thus unenforceable; in effect, Judy is stating her intention to give Elsie a gift.

SECTION 4

Problem Areas Concerning Consideration

Problems concerning consideration usually fall into one of the following categories:

1. Promises exchanged when total performance by the parties is uncertain.

2. Settlement of claims.

3. Promises enforceable without consideration.

The courts' solutions to these types of problems give insight into how the law views the complex concept of consideration.

UNCERTAIN PERFORMANCE

If the terms of the contract express such uncertainty of performance that the promisor has not definitely promised to do anything, the promise is said to be *illusory*—without consideration and unenforceable. For example, suppose that the president of Tuscan Corporation says to her employees, "All of you have worked hard, and if profits continue to remain high, a 10 percent bonus at the end of the year will be given—if management thinks it is warranted." The employees continue to work hard, and profits remain high, but no bonus is given. This is an *illusory promise*, or no promise at all, because performance depends solely on the discretion of the president (the management). There is no bargained-for consideration. The statement declares merely that the management may or may not do something in the future. The president is not obligated (incurs no detriment) now or later.

Option-to-cancel clauses in term contracts sometimes present problems in regard to consideration. For example, suppose that I contract to hire you for one year at $5,000 per month, reserving the right to cancel the contract at any time. On close examination of these words, you can see that I have not actually agreed to hire you, as I could cancel without liability before you started performance. I have not given up the opportunity of hiring someone else. This contract is therefore illusory. Suppose, however, that I am required to give you thirty days' notice to exercise the option. The thirty days' notice entitles you to at least one month's salary of $5,000, which is consideration. Thus, until I give you notice, you are entitled to $5,000 per month until the contract is terminated at the end of the year.

There are other types of contracts in which problems with consideration may arise because of uncertainty of performance. Uncertain performance is characteristic of requirements and output contracts, for example. In a *requirements contract*, a buyer and a seller agree that the buyer will purchase from the seller all of the goods of a designated type that the buyer needs, or requires. In an *output contract*, the buyer and seller agree that the buyer will purchase

---

4. Note that under Article 2 of the UCC, an agreement modifying a contract needs no consideration to be binding. See UCC 2–209(1).

5. Pronounced reh-*sih*-zhen.

from the seller all of what the seller produces, or the seller's output. These types of contracts will be discussed further in Chapter 19.

SETTLEMENT OF CLAIMS

Businesspersons or others can settle legal claims in several ways, and it is important to understand the nature of consideration given in these kinds of settlement agreements, or contracts. A common means of settling a claim is through an *accord and satisfaction*, in which a debtor offers to pay a lesser amount than the creditor purports to be owed. Other methods that are commonly used to settle claims include the *release* and the *covenant not to sue*.

Accord and Satisfaction. The concept of **accord and satisfaction** deals with a debtor's offer of payment and a creditor's acceptance of a lesser amount than the creditor originally purported to be owed. The *accord* is defined as the agreement under which one of the parties undertakes to give or perform, and the other to accept, in satisfaction of a claim, something other than that on which the parties originally agreed. *Satisfaction* takes place when the accord is executed. A basic rule is that there can be no satisfaction unless there is first an accord.

For accord and satisfaction to occur, the amount of the debt *must be in dispute*. If a debt is *liquidated*, accord and satisfaction cannot take place. A liquidated debt is one whose amount has been ascertained, fixed, agreed on, settled, or exactly determined. For example, if Baker signs an installment loan contract with her banker in which she agrees to pay a specified rate of interest on a specified sum of borrowed money at monthly intervals for two years, that is a liquidated debt. The total obligation is precisely known to both of the parties, and reasonable persons will not differ over the amount owed.

Suppose that Baker has missed her last two payments on the loan and the creditor demands that she pay the overdue debt. Baker makes a partial payment and states that she believes this payment is all she should have to pay and that, if the creditor accepts the payment, the debt will be satisfied, or discharged. In the majority of states, acceptance of a lesser sum than the entire amount of a liquidated debt is not satisfaction, and the balance of the debt is still legally owed. The rationale for this rule is that no consideration is given by the debtor to satisfy the obligation of paying the balance to the creditor—because the debtor has a preexisting legal obligation to pay the entire debt.

An *unliquidated debt* is the opposite of a liquidated debt. Here, reasonable persons may differ over the amount owed. It is not settled, fixed, agreed on, ascertained, or determined. In these circumstances, acceptance of payment of the lesser sum operates as satisfaction, or discharge, of the debt. For example, suppose that Devereaux goes to the dentist's office. The dentist tells him that he needs three special types of gold inlays. The price is not discussed, and there is no standard fee for this type of work. Devereaux has the work done and leaves the office. At the end of the month, the dentist sends him a bill for $3,000. Devereaux, believing that this amount is grossly out of proportion with what a reasonable person would believe to be the debt owed, sends a check for $2,000. On the back of the check he writes "payment in full for three gold inlays." The dentist cashes the check. Because the situation involves an unliquidated debt—the amount has not been agreed on—payment accepted by the dentist normally will eradicate the debt. One argument to support this rule is that the parties give up a legal right to contest the amount in dispute, and thus consideration is given.

Release. A **release** bars any further recovery beyond the terms stated in the release. Assume that you are involved in an automobile accident caused by Donovan's negligence. Donovan offers to give you $1,000 if you will release him from further liability resulting from the accident. You believe that this amount will cover your damages, so you agree, in writing, to the release. Later you discover that it will cost $1,500 to repair your car. Can you collect the balance from Donovan? The answer is normally no; you are limited to the $1,000 specified in the release because the release represents a valid contract. You and Donovan both assented to the bargain (hence, agreement existed), and sufficient consideration was present. The consideration was the legal detriment you suffered (by releasing Donovan from liability, you forfeited your right to sue to recover damages, should they be more than $1,000).

Clearly, you are better off if you know the extent of your injuries or damages before signing a release. Releases will generally be binding if they are (1) given in good faith, (2) stated in a signed writing (which is required in many states), and (3) accompanied by consideration.[6] The following case illustrates how important it is to understand the effect of a release.

---

6. Under the UCC, a written, signed waiver or renunciation by an aggrieved party discharges any further liability for a breach, even without consideration.

CASE 12.2   Mills v. Berlex Laboratories, Inc.

Court of Appeals of
Georgia, 1999.
235 Ga.App. 873,
510 S.E.2d 621.

BACKGROUND AND FACTS   *William Mills was a pharmaceutical sales representative for Berlex Laboratories, Inc. On February 15, Berlex told Mills that his position was
being eliminated and that he would be terminated effective February 28. Berlex gave
Mills a proposed "Separation Agreement and Release." Mills hired Samuel Cruse, an at-
torney, to review the release. The same week, Mills injured his back while boxing up
Berlex supplies in his home office. Within a few days, Mills signed a revised "Separation
Agreement and Release." This release provided that "as of the day following the
Termination Date, [Mills] will not be eligible to participate in any of Berlex's benefits
plans," and released Berlex from "any claims arising out of or in any way related to
Employee's employment with Berlex and the conclusion thereof." In exchange, Berlex
paid Mills one year's salary as severance pay, a $5,388 bonus, and five days' vacation
pay. Berlex also paid to continue Mills's health insurance for eighteen months and provided him with unlimited outplacement services for one year. On March 3, Mills filed a
disability claim with Berlex for his back injury. Berlex refused to pay. Mills filed a suit in
a Georgia state court against Berlex, seeking disability benefits. When the court ruled in
Berlex's favor, Mills appealed to a state intermediate appellate court.*

**IN THE LANGUAGE
OF THE COURT**

McMURRAY, Presiding Judge.

*   *   *   *

Mills contends the trial court erred when it found his civil action was barred because
the parties did not contemplate that Berlex would deny his short-term disability claim at
the time they entered into the general release. *   *   * The scope of a release is determined by the intention of the parties as expressed in the terms of the particular instrument, considered in the light of all the facts and circumstances. A *general release*, not
restricted by its terms to particular claims or demands, *ordinarily covers all claims and
demands due at the time of its execution and within the contemplation of the parties.*
[Emphasis added.]

We find the evidence authorized the trial court's conclusion that Mills' claim for
short-term disability benefits fell within the scope of the release. By its terms, the release
applies to all claims "arising out of or in any way related to [Mills'] employment with
Berlex and the conclusion thereof *   *   * ." It also specifically provided that Mills
"will not be eligible to participate in any of Berlex's benefit plans" as of the day following his termination date (February 28 *   *   *). This language is sufficient to include
Mills' claim for short-term disability benefits.

Mills' contention that the parties did not contemplate a release of his claim for short-
term disability benefits when they entered into the general release is without merit.
Mills retained counsel to review the release, and the record shows that both Mills and
his attorney were aware of his short-term disability claim before Mills signed the
Separation Agreement and General Release. These facts and circumstances, taken together with the plain language of the release, support the conclusion that Mills' short-
term disability claim was within the contemplation of the parties at the time they
entered into the release.

**DECISION
AND REMEDY**

*The state intermediate appellate court affirmed the judgment of the trial court. The re-
lease barred Mills's claim for short-term disability benefits from Berlex.*

Covenant Not to Sue. A covenant not to sue is
an agreement to substitute a contractual obligation
for some other type of legal action based on a valid
claim. Unlike a release, a covenant not to sue does
not always bar further recovery. Suppose (continuing
the earlier example) that you agree with Donovan
not to sue for damages in a tort action if he will pay
for the damage to your car. If Donovan fails to pay,
you can bring an action against him for breach of
contract.

PROMISES ENFORCEABLE WITHOUT CONSIDERATION

There are some exceptions to the rule that only promises supported by consideration are enforceable. The following types of promises may be enforced despite the lack of consideration:

1. Promises to pay debts that are barred by a statute of limitations.
2. Promises inducing detrimental reliance, under the doctrine of promissory estoppel.
3. Promises to make charitable contributions.

Promises to Pay Debts Barred by a Statute of Limitations. Statutes of limitations in all states require a creditor to sue within a specified period to recover a debt. If the creditor fails to sue in time, recovery of the debt is barred by the statute of limitations. A debtor who promises to pay a previous debt even though recovery is barred by the statute of limitations makes an enforceable promise. *The promise needs no consideration.* (Some states, however, require that it be in writing.) In effect, the promise extends the limitations period, and the creditor can sue to recover the entire debt, or at least the amount promised. The promise can be implied if the debtor acknowledges the barred debt by making a partial payment.

Detrimental Reliance and Promissory Estoppel. As discussed in Chapter 11, under the doctrine of *promissory estoppel,* a person who has reasonably and substantially relied on the promise of another may be able to obtain some measure of recovery. This doctrine is applied in a wide variety of contexts in which a promise is otherwise unenforceable, such as when a promise is not supported by consideration. Under this doctrine, a court may enforce an otherwise unenforceable promise to avoid the injustice that would therefore result. For the doctrine to be applied, the following elements are required:

1. There must be a clear and definite promise.
2. The promisee must justifiably rely on the promise.
3. The reliance normally must be of a substantial and definite character.
4. Justice will be better served by enforcement of the promise.

If these requirements are met, a promise may be enforced even though it is not supported by consideration. In essence, the promisor will be *estopped* (prevented) from asserting the lack of consideration as a defense. For example, suppose that your uncle tells you, "I'll pay you $150 a week so you won't have to work anymore." In reliance on your uncle's promise, you quit your job, but your uncle refuses to pay you. Under the doctrine of promissory estoppel, you may be able to enforce such a promise.[7]

In the following case, an individual sought to recover damages under the doctrine of promissory estoppel from a prospective employer that reneged on its promise of employment.

---

7. *Ricketts v. Scothorn,* 57 Neb. 51, 77 N.W. 365 (1898).

CASE 12.3   Goff-Hamel v. Obstetricians & Gynecologists, P.C.

Supreme Court of
Nebraska, 1999.
256 Neb. 19,
588 N.W.2d 798.
http://www.findlaw.com/
11stategov/ne/neca.
html [a]

BACKGROUND AND FACTS   *Julie Goff-Hamel worked for Hastings Family Planning. After eleven years, Goff-Hamel was earning $24,000, plus benefits: six weeks' paid maternity leave, six weeks' vacation, twelve paid holidays, twelve sick days, educational reimbursement, and medical and dental insurance. In July 1993, representatives of Obstetricians & Gynecologists, P.C.,[b] (Obstetricians)—including part owner Dr. George Adam and personnel consultant Larry Draper—asked Goff-Hamel to work for Obstetricians. Adam told Goff-Hamel that the position was full-time, at a salary of $10 per hour, and included two weeks' paid vacation, three or four paid holidays, uniforms, and an educational stipend. A retirement plan would start after the end of the second year, retroactive to the end of the first year. The job did not include health insurance. Goff-*

---

a. On this page, click on "1999," and on that page, click on "January." Scroll down to the case name, and click on "19990129" to access the opinion.

b. *P.C.* is an abbreviation for "professional corporation," which is a special form for a business entity. Professional corporations are discussed in more detail in Chapter 34.

Hamel agreed to start in October and gave notice to Hastings in August. She was given uniforms for her new job and a copy of her work schedule. The day before she was scheduled to start, Draper told her that she need not report to work and that Janel Foote, the wife of Dr. Terry Foote, a part owner, opposed her hiring. Goff-Hamel filed a suit in a Nebraska state court against Obstetricians, seeking damages in part on the basis of detrimental reliance. The court concluded that because she was to be employed at will,[c] her employment could be terminated at any time—which included before she began working—and issued a summary judgment in favor of Obstetricians. Goff-Hamel appealed to the Nebraska Supreme Court.

IN THE LANGUAGE OF THE COURT

WRIGHT, J. [Justice].

*   *   *   *

Other jurisdictions which have addressed the question of whether a cause of action for promissory estoppel can be stated in the context of a prospective at-will employee are split on the issue. Some have held that an employee can recover damages incurred as a result of resigning from the former at-will employment in reliance on a promise of other at-will employment. They have determined that when a prospective employer knows or should know that a promise of employment will induce an employee to leave his or her current job, such employer shall be liable for the reliant's damages. *   *   * [T]hey have concluded that the employee would have continued to work in his or her prior employment if it were not for the offer by the prospective employer. Although damages have not been allowed for wages lost from the prospective at-will employment, damages have been allowed based upon wages from the prior employment and other damages incurred in reliance on the job offer.

In contrast, other jurisdictions have held as a matter of law that a prospective employee cannot recover damages incurred in reliance on an unfulfilled promise of at-will employment, concluding that reliance on a promise consisting solely of at-will employment is unreasonable as a matter of law because the employee should know that the promised employment could be terminated by the employer at any time for any reason without liability. These courts have stated that an anomalous result occurs when recovery is allowed for an employee who has not begun work, when the same employee's job could be terminated without liability 1 day after beginning work.

*   *   *   *

*   *   * [W]e conclude under the facts of this case that promissory estoppel can be asserted in connection with the offer of at-will employment and that the trial court erred in granting Obstetricians summary judgment. *A cause of action for promissory estoppel is based upon a promise which the promisor should reasonably expect to induce action or forbearance on the part of the promisee [and] which does in fact induce such action or forbearance.* *   *   * [Emphasis added.]

*   *   *   *

The facts are not disputed that Obstetricians offered Goff-Hamel employment. Apparently, at the direction of the spouse of one of the owners, Obstetricians refused to honor its promise of employment. It is also undisputed that Goff-Hamel relied upon Obstetricians' promise of employment to her detriment in that she terminated her employment of 11 years. Therefore, under the facts of this case, the trial court should have granted summary judgment in favor of Goff-Hamel on the issue of liability.

DECISION AND REMEDY

The Nebraska Supreme Court reversed the judgment of the trial court. The state supreme court held that promissory estoppel can be asserted in connection with an offer of at-will employment. The court remanded the case for a determination of the amount of damages to which Goff-Hamel was entitled.

---

c. *Employment at will* is an employment relationship that either party may terminate at any time for any reason. Employment at will is explained in more detail in Chapter 41.

Charitable Subscriptions. Subscriptions to religious, educational, and charitable institutions are promises to make gifts and are unenforceable on traditional contract grounds because they are not supported by legally sufficient consideration. A gift, after all, is the opposite of bargained-for consideration.

There have been cases in which it was held that a promise to give money to a charity was supported by consideration. For example, the promisor may have bargained for and received a promise from the charity that the gift would be used in a specific way or that it would be memorialized with the promisor's name. The modern view, however, is to enforce these promises under the doctrine of promissory estoppel or to find consideration simply as a matter of public policy.

The premise for enforcement is that a promise is made and an institution changes its position because of reliance on that promise. For example, suppose a church solicits and receives pledges (commitments to contribute funds) from church members to erect a new church building. On the basis of these pledges, the church purchases land, employs architects, and makes other contracts that change its position. Courts may enforce the pledges under promissory estoppel. Alternatively, they may find consideration in the fact that each promise was made in reliance on the other promises of support or that the trustees, by accepting the subscriptions, impliedly promised to complete the proposed undertaking.

Such cases represent exceptions to the general rule that consideration must exist for a contract to be formed. These exceptions come about as a result of public policy.

CONCEPT SUMMARY 12.1

CONSIDERATION

CONCEPT	DESCRIPTION
Definition of Consideration	Consideration is the value given in exchange for a promise. A contract cannot be formed without sufficient consideration. Consideration consists of three elements: 1. *Legal value*—Something of legal value must be given in exchange for a promise. In addition to money, value may be an act, a forbearance, a change in a legal relation, or a promise. 2. *Bargained-for exchange*—There must be a bargained-for exchange. 3. *Legal sufficiency*—Consideration must be legally sufficient (see below).
Legal Sufficiency of Consideration	To be legally sufficient, consideration must be either legally detrimental to the promisee (the one to whom the promise is made) or legally beneficial to the promisor (the one making the promise). Doing something, promising to do something, forbearing from doing something, or promising to forbear from doing something that one is otherwise entitled to do is legally sufficient consideration to bind another's promise. The following types of promises normally are not enforceable because they lack sufficient consideration: 1. A promise to perform a preexisting duty. 2. A promise to perform an act that has already been performed (past consideration).
Adequacy of Consideration	Adequacy of consideration relates to how much consideration is given and whether a fair bargain was reached. Courts will inquire into the adequacy of consideration (if the consideration is legally sufficient) only when fraud, undue influence, duress, or unconscionability may be involved.
Problem Areas Concerning Consideration	1. *Uncertain performance*—When the nature or extent of performance is too uncertain, the promise is rendered illusory and unenforceable. 2. *Settlement of claims*—

CONCEPT SUMMARY 12.1

CONSIDERATION *(continued)*

CONCEPT	DESCRIPTION

Problem Areas Concerning Consideration (continued)	a. Accord and satisfaction—A debtor's offer of payment and a creditor's acceptance of a lesser amount than the creditor originally purported to be owed.
	b. Release—An agreement by which, for consideration, a party is barred from further recovery beyond the terms specified in the release.
	c. Covenant not to sue—An agreement not to sue on a present, valid claim.
	3. *Promises enforceable without consideration—*
	   a. Promises to pay debts barred by a statute of limitations.
	   b. Promises inducing detrimental reliance (under the doctrine of promissory estoppel).
	   c. Charitable subscriptions.

TERMS AND CONCEPTS TO REVIEW

accord and satisfaction 231	covenant not to sue 232	release 231
consideration 227	past consideration 230	rescission 230

QUESTIONS AND CASE PROBLEMS

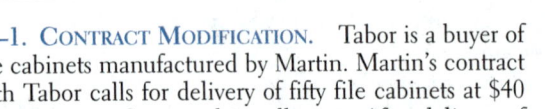

12–1. CONTRACT MODIFICATION. Tabor is a buyer of file cabinets manufactured by Martin. Martin's contract with Tabor calls for delivery of fifty file cabinets at $40 per cabinet in five equal installments. After delivery of two installments (twenty cabinets), Martin informs Tabor that because of inflation, Martin is losing money and will promise to deliver the remaining thirty cabinets only if Tabor will pay $50 per cabinet. Tabor agrees in writing to do so. Discuss whether Martin can legally collect the additional $100 on delivery to Tabor of the next installment of ten cabinets.

12–2. CONTRACT MODIFICATION. Bernstein owns a lot and wants to build a house according to a particular set of plans and specifications. She solicits bids from building contractors and receives three bids: one from Carlton for $60,000, one from Friend for $58,000, and one from Shade for $53,000. She accepts Shade's bid. One month after construction of the house has begun, Shade contacts Bernstein and informs her that because of inflation and a recent price hike in materials, he will not finish the house unless Bernstein agrees to pay an extra $3,000. Bernstein reluctantly agrees to pay the additional sum. After the house is finished, however, Bernstein refuses to pay the extra $3,000. Discuss whether Bernstein is legally required to pay this additional amount.

12–3. PAYMENT FOR SERVICES TO ANOTHER. Daniel, a recent college graduate, is on his way home for the Christmas holidays from his new job. Daniel gets caught in a snowstorm and is taken in by an elderly couple, who provide him with food and shelter. After the snowplows have cleared the road, Daniel proceeds home. Daniel's father, Fred, is most appreciative of the elderly couple's action and in a letter promises to pay them $500. The elderly couple, in need of money, accepts Fred's offer. Then, because of a dispute between Daniel and Fred, Fred refuses to pay the elderly couple the $500. Discuss whether the couple can hold Fred in contract for the services rendered to Daniel.

12–4. CONSIDERATION. Costello hired Sagan to drive his racing car in a race. Sagan's friend Gideon promised to pay Sagan $3,000 if she won the race. Sagan won the race, but Gideon refused to pay the $3,000. Gideon contended that no legally binding contract had been formed because he had received no consideration from Sagan in exchange for his promise to pay the $3,000. Sagan sued Gideon for breach of contract, arguing that winning the race was the consideration given in exchange for Gideon's promise to pay the $3,000. What rule of law discussed in this chapter supports Gideon's claim?

12–5. CONSIDERATION. Martino was a police officer in Atlantic City. Gray, who had lost a significant amount of her jewelry during a burglary of her home, offered a reward for the recovery of the property. Incident to his job, Martino possessed certain knowledge concerning the theft of Gray's jewelry. When Martino informed Gray of his knowledge of the theft, Gray offered Martino $500 to help her recover her jewelry. As a result of Martino's police work, the jewelry was recovered and returned to Gray. Martino sued Gray for the reward he claimed she had promised him. Was there a valid contract between Gray and Martino? [*Gray v. Martino*, 91 N.J.L. 462, 103 A. 24 (1918)]

12–6. ADEQUACY OF CONSIDERATION. In 1972, Thomas L. Weinsaft signed a written agreement with his son, Nicholas L. Weinsaft. Thomas agreed that during his lifetime he would not transfer any interest in his 765 shares of stock of Crane Manufacturing Co. unless he first gave Nicholas an opportunity to purchase it, and on Thomas's death, Nicholas would have the "option and right to purchase all of the stock" from the estate. The agreement stated that it was entered into "In consideration of $10.00 and other good and valuable consideration, including the inducement of Second Party [Nicholas] to remain the chief executive officer of said company." Thomas died in 1980. Nicholas gave notice that he intended to buy the stock, but one of the beneficiaries under Thomas's will objected, contending that there was no consideration for Thomas's promises. Nicholas sued to force the estate to transfer the shares. Discuss whether this contract is supported by consideration. [*In re Estate of Weinsaft*, 647 S.W.2d 179 (Mo.App. 1983)]

12–7. PAST CONSIDERATION. Rivendell Forest Products, Ltd., had a computer program—the *Quote Screen* system—that allowed it to quote prices to its customers many times faster than its competitors. To keep the *Quote Screen* system a secret, Rivendell insisted that all of its employees, including Timothy Cornwell, sign a confidentiality agreement in 1988. Cornwell was employed by Rivendell from 1987 to 1990, when he left Rivendell to work as a marketing manager for the Georgia-Pacific Corp., a competitor. Cornwell introduced Georgia-Pacific to Rivendell's *Quote Screen* system. Rivendell sued Cornwell for, among other things, breach of the confidentiality agreement. The trial court held that the confidentiality agreement was not a valid contract because Rivendell had failed to provide consideration, such as a salary increase or a promotion, in exchange for Cornwell's promise to keep the *Quote Screen* system a secret. If Cornwell had signed the confidentiality agreement when he was first hired, would the result have been the same? Explain. [*Rivendell Forest Products, Ltd. v. Georgia-Pacific Corp.*, 824 F.Supp. 961 (D.Colo. 1993)]

12–8. ACCORD AND SATISFACTION. E. S. Herrick Co. grows and sells blueberries. Maine Wild Blueberry Co. agreed to buy all of Herrick's 1990 crop under a contract that left the price unliquidated. Herrick delivered the berries, but a dispute arose over the price. Maine Wild sent Herrick a check with a letter that stated the check was the "final settlement." Herrick cashed the check but filed a suit in a Maine state court against Maine Wild, on the ground of breach of contract, alleging that the buyer owed more. Given these facts, consider the following questions: What will the court likely decide in this case? Why? [*E. S. Herrick Co. v. Maine Wild Blueberry Co.*, 670 A.2d 944 (Me. 1996)]

12–9. PREEXISTING DUTY. New England Rock Services, Inc., agreed to work as a subcontractor on a sewer project on which Empire Paving, Inc., was the general contractor. For drilling and blasting a certain amount of rock, Rock Services was to be paid $29 per cubic yard or on a time-and-materials basis, whichever was less. From the beginning, Rock Services experienced problems. The primary obstacle was a heavy concentration of water, which, according to the custom in the industry, Empire should have controlled but did not. Rock Services was compelled to use more costly and time-consuming methods than anticipated, and it was unable to complete the work on time. The subcontractor asked Empire to pay for the rest of the project on a time-and-materials basis. Empire signed a modification of the original agreement. On completion of the work, Empire refused to pay Rock Services the balance due under the modification. Rock Services filed a suit in a Connecticut state court against Empire. Empire claimed that the modification lacked consideration and was thus not valid and enforceable. Is Empire right? Why or why not? [*New England Rock Services, Inc. v. Empire Paving, Inc.*, 53 Conn.App. 771, 731 A.2d 784 (1999)]

12–10. IN YOUR COURT

An article written by Claudia Dreifus and published in *Glamour* magazine discussed therapists who sexually exploit their patients. Jill Ruzicka had told Dreifus that she (Ruzicka) was sexually abused as a child by her father and later by her therapist. Dreifus had promised to withhold Ruzicka's identity from the article, and the published article identified Ruzicka by a fictitious name ("Lundquist"). In the article, Dreifus stated that "Lundquist" was an attorney who had served on the Minnesota Task Force against Sexual Abuse. Ruzicka claimed that this detail revealed her true identity because she was, in fact, the only woman on that task force. Ruzicka asserted that she had relied to her detriment on Dreifus's promise and sued Dreifus to recover damages under, among other theories, a theory of promissory estoppel. Assume that you are the judge in the trial court hearing this case and answer the following questions:

(a) What elements are required for the doctrine of promissory estoppel to be applied? Discuss whether each of these elements is (or is not) present in this case and, based on your reasoning, state your decision in the matter.

(b) Would your decision be the same if there had been one other woman, in addition to Ruzicka, on the Minnesota Task Force against Sexual Abuse? Why or why not?

(c) Suppose that Ruzicka had the opportunity to review the final draft of the article before it was published but declined to do so. Would this affect your decision in any way? Explain.

LAW ON THE WEB

For updated links to resources available on the Web, as well as a variety of other materials, visit this text's Web site at http://wbl.westbuslaw.com.

A good way to learn more about how the courts decide such issues as whether consideration was lacking for a particular contract is to look at relevant case law. To find recent cases on contract law decided by the United States Supreme Court and the federal appellate courts, access Cornell University's School of Law site at

http://www.law.cornell.edu/topics/contracts.html

The New Hampshire Consumer's Sourcebook provides information on contract law, including consideration, from a consumer's perspective. You can access this site at

http://www.state.nh.us/oag/cpb.html

LEGAL RESEARCH EXERCISES ON THE WEB

Go to http://wbl.westbuslaw.com, the Web site that accompanies this text. Select "Internet Applications," and then click on "Chapter 12." There you will find the following Internet research exercise that you can perform to learn more about contracts that are enforceable without consideration:

Activity 12–1: Promissory Estoppel

CHAPTER 13

Capacity and Legality

I N ADDITION TO AGREEMENT AND consideration, for a contract to be deemed valid the parties to the contract must have **contractual capacity**—the legal ability to enter into a contractual relationship. Courts generally presume the existence of contractual capacity, but there are some situations in which capacity is lacking or may be questionable. In many situations, a party may have the capacity to enter into a valid contract but also have the right to avoid liability under it. For example, minors usually are not legally bound by contracts. We examine these situations in the first part of this chapter.

We then turn to the topic of legality—another element that is required for a valid contract to exist. The agreement must not call for the performance of an illegal act—that is, any act that is criminal, tortious, or otherwise opposed to public policy. In this section of the chapter, we consider illegal contracts, or contracts that are contrary to state or federal statutes or to public policy, and the effects of an illegal bargain. Such contracts are normally void—that is, they really are not contracts at all.

Realize that capacity and legality are not inherently related other than that they are both contract requirements. We treat these topics in one chapter merely for convenience and reasons of space.

SECTION 1

Contractual Capacity

Historically, the law has given special protection to those who bargain with the inexperience of youth or those who lack the degree of mental competence required by law. *Full competence* exists when both parties have complete legal capacity to enter into a contract and to have the contract enforced against them. *No competence* exists when one or both of the parties have been adjudged by a court to be mentally incompetent and therefore without legal capacity to contract. In this situation, an essential element for a valid contract is missing, and the contract is thus *void*. *Limited competence* exists when one or both of the parties are minors, intoxicated, or mentally incompetent but not yet adjudicated officially as such. These parties have full and legal capacity to enter into a contract; but if they wish, they can normally avoid liability under the contract, which is said to be *voidable*.

MINORS

Today, in virtually all states, the **age of majority** (when a person is no longer a minor) for contractual

239

purposes is eighteen years.[1] In addition, some states provide for the termination of minority on marriage. Minority status may also be terminated by a minor's **emancipation,** which occurs when a child's parent or legal guardian relinquishes the legal right to exercise control over the child. Normally, a minor who leaves home to support himself or herself is considered emancipated. Several jurisdictions permit minors to petition a court for emancipation themselves. For business purposes, a minor may petition a court to be treated as an adult.

The general rule is that a minor can enter into any contract that an adult can, provided that the contract is not one prohibited by law for minors (for example, the sale of tobacco or alcoholic beverages). Indeed, any time a minor purchases goods, such as a car or a video game, he or she is entering into a contract. A contract entered into by a minor, however, is voidable at the option of that minor, subject to certain exceptions. To exercise the option to avoid a contract, a minor need only manifest an intention not to be bound by it. The minor "avoids" the contract by disaffirming it.

Minor's Right to Disaffirm. The technical definition of **disaffirmance** is the legal avoidance, or setting aside, of a contractual obligation. A contract can ordinarily be disaffirmed at any time during minority or for a reasonable period after the minor comes of age. Note that the minor must disaffirm the entire contract, not merely a portion of it. For example, the minor cannot decide to keep part of the goods pur-

chased under a contract and return the remaining goods.

Minor's Obligations on Disaffirmance. Although all state laws permit minors to disaffirm contracts (with certain exceptions), states differ on the extent of a minor's obligations on disaffirmance. Courts in a majority of states hold that the minor need only return the goods (or other consideration) subject to the contract, provided the goods are in the minor's possession or control. For example, suppose that Jim Garrison, a seventeen-year-old, purchases a computer from Radio Shack. While transporting the computer to his home, Garrison negligently drops it, breaking the plastic casing. The next day, he returns the computer to Radio Shack and disaffirms the contract. Under the majority view, this return fulfills Garrison's duty even though the computer is now damaged. Garrison is entitled to receive a refund of the purchase price (if paid in cash) or to be relieved of any further obligations under an agreement to purchase the computer on credit.

An increasing number of states, either by statute or by court decision, place an additional duty on the minor—the duty to restore the adult party to the position he or she held before the contract was made. In the example above, Garrison would be required not only to return the computer but also to pay Radio Shack for the damage to the unit.

In the following case, the Tennessee Supreme Court faced the issue of whether a minor should be held responsible for damage, ordinary wear and tear, and depreciation of goods used by the minor prior to the minor's disaffirmance of the contract. The case illustrates the trend among today's courts in regard to this issue.

---

1. The age of majority may still be twenty-one for other purposes, such as the purchase and consumption of alcohol.

Case 13.1   Dodson v. Shrader

Supreme Court of
Tennessee, 1992.
824 S.W.2d 545.

BACKGROUND AND FACTS   *Joseph Dodson, when he was sixteen years old, bought a used pickup truck for $4,900 from Shrader's Auto, which was owned by Burns and Mary Shrader. Nine months later, the truck developed mechanical problems. A mechanic informed Dodson that the problem might be a burnt valve. Without having the truck repaired, Dodson continued to drive it. One month later, the truck's engine "blew up," and the truck was rendered inoperable. Dodson disaffirmed the contract and sought to return the truck to the Shraders and obtain a full refund of the purchase price. The Shraders refused to refund the purchase price and would not accept possession of the truck. Later, the pickup was hit by an unknown driver while parked in the Dodsons' front yard. Dodson filed suit against the Shraders to compel a refund of the purchase price. Although the Shraders claimed that the truck's value was reduced to $500, the trial court granted* *rescission and ordered the Shraders to refund the full $4,900 purchase price to Dodson on Dodson's delivery of the truck to them. The Shraders appealed.*

IN THE LANGUAGE
OF THE COURT

O'BRIEN, Justice.

*   *   *   *

*   *   * If the minor has not been overreached [taken advantage of] in any way, and there has been no undue influence, and the contract is a fair and reasonable one, and the minor has actually paid money on the purchase price, and taken and used the article purchased, [then] he ought not to be permitted to recover the amount actually paid, without allowing the vendor of the goods reasonable compensation for the use of, depreciation, and willful or negligent damage to the article purchased, while in his hands.

*   *   *

*   *   * Minors are permitted to, and do in fact, transact a great deal of business for themselves, long before they have reached the age of legal majority. *   *   * Further, it does not appear consistent with *   *   * proper moral influence upon young people *   *   * if they are taught that they can make purchases with their own money, for their own benefit, and after paying for them, and using them until they are worn out and destroyed, go back and compel the vendor to return to them what they have paid upon the purchase price. *Such a doctrine can only lead to the corruption of principles and encourage young people in habits of trickery and dishonesty.* [Emphasis added.]

DECISION
AND REMEDY

The Tennessee Supreme Court remanded the case to the trial court for a factual determination of the fairness of the contract and the fair market value of the truck.

Exceptions to the Minor's Right to Disaffirm. State courts and legislatures have carved out several exceptions to the minor's right to disaffirm. Some contracts cannot be avoided simply as a matter of law, on the ground of public policy. For example, marriage contracts and contracts to enlist in the armed services fall into this category. Other contracts may not be disaffirmed for other reasons, including those discussed here.

Misrepresentation of Age. Suppose that a minor tells a seller she is twenty-one years old when she is really seventeen. Ordinarily, the minor can disaffirm the contract even though she has misrepresented her age. Moreover, the minor is not liable in certain jurisdictions for the tort of deceit (fraud) for such misrepresentation, the rationale being that such a tort judgment might indirectly force the minor to perform the contract.

Many jurisdictions, however, find circumstances under which a minor can be bound by a contract when the minor has misrepresented his or her age. First, several states have enacted statutes for precisely this purpose. In these states, misrepresentation of age is enough to prohibit disaffirmance. Other statutes prohibit disaffirmance by a minor who has engaged in business as an adult.

Second, some courts refuse to allow minors to disaffirm executed (fully performed) contracts unless they can return the consideration received. The combination of the minors' misrepresentation and their unjust enrichment has persuaded these courts to *estop* (prevent) minors from asserting contractual incapacity.

Third, some courts allow a misrepresenting minor to disaffirm the contract, but they hold the minor liable for damages in tort. Here, the defrauded party may sue the minor for misrepresentation or fraud. A split in authority exists on this point, because some courts, as previously noted, have recognized that allowing a suit in tort is equivalent to indirectly enforcing the minor's contract.

Contracts for Necessaries. A minor who enters into a contract for necessaries may disaffirm the contract but remains liable for the reasonable value of the goods. Necessaries are basic needs, such as food, clothing, shelter, and medical services, at a level of value required to maintain the minor's standard of living or financial and social status. Thus, what will be considered a necessary for one person may be a luxury for another. For example, if a minor from a low-income family contracts for the purchase of a $2,000 coat, a court may deem the coat a luxury. In this situation, the contract would not be for "necessaries."

Additionally, what is considered a necessary depends on whether the minor is under the care or control of his or her parents, who are required by law to provide necessaries for the minor. If a minor's parents provide him or her with shelter, for example, then a contract to lease shelter (such as an apartment) normally will not be classified as a contract for necessaries.

Generally, then, to qualify as a contract for necessaries, (1) the item contracted for must be necessary to the minor's subsistence, (2) the value of the necessary item must be up to a level required to maintain the minor's standard of living or financial and social status, and (3) the minor must not be under the care of a parent or guardian who is required to supply this item. Unless these three criteria are met, the minor can disaffirm the contract *without* being liable for the reasonable value of the goods used.

Insurance and Loans. Traditionally, insurance has not been viewed as a necessary, so minors can ordinarily disaffirm their insurance contracts and recover all premiums paid. Some jurisdictions, however, prohibit the right to disaffirm insurance contracts—for example, when minors contract for life insurance on their own lives. Financial loans are seldom considered to be necessaries, even if the minor spends the money borrowed on necessaries. If, however, a lender makes a loan to a minor for the express purpose of enabling the minor to purchase necessaries, and the lender personally makes sure the money is so spent, the minor normally is obligated to repay the loan.

Ratification. In contract law, **ratification** is the act of accepting and giving legal force to an obligation that previously was not enforceable. In relation to minors' contracts, ratification may be defined as an expression in words or an act by which a person, *on or after reaching majority,* indicates an *intention* to become bound by a contract made as a minor.

An *express* ratification takes place when the individual, on reaching the age of majority, states orally or in writing that he or she intends to be bound by the contract. For example, if Humphrey enters into a contract to sell his laptop computer to Lombard, a minor, Lombard can avoid her legal duty to pay for the laptop by disaffirming the contract. Suppose, though, that Lombard does not disaffirm the contract and on reaching the age of majority writes a letter to Humphrey stating that she still agrees to buy the laptop. Now

Lombard has ratified the contract and is legally bound by its terms. An *implied* ratification takes place when the minor, on reaching the age of majority, evidences an intent to abide by the contract. For example, if Lombard takes possession of the laptop as a minor and continues to use it after reaching the age of majority, she has impliedly ratified the contract.

If a minor fails to disaffirm a contract within a reasonable time after reaching the age of majority, then the court must determine whether the conduct constitutes ratification or disaffirmance. Generally, a contract that is *executed* (fully performed by both parties) is presumed to be ratified. A contract that is still *executory* (not yet fully performed by both parties) is considered to be disaffirmed.

Parents' Liability for Minor Children's Contracts and Torts. As a general rule, parents are not liable for contracts made by minor children acting on their own. This is why businesses ordinarily require parents to sign any contract made with a minor. The parents then become personally obligated under the contract to perform the conditions of the contract, even if their child avoids liability.

Generally, minors are personally liable for their own torts. In some states, however, a parent may be liable if he or she failed to exercise proper parental control over the minor child and knew or should have known, from the minor's habits and tendencies, that failure to exercise control posed an unreasonable risk of harm to others. Other states have enacted statutes imposing on parents legal responsibility for the consequences of the tortious acts of their children. These statutes vary. For example, in some states, liability will be imposed on parents only for the willful, malicious, or wanton acts of their minor children. In other states, liability will also be imposed on parents for their children's negligent acts that result from the parents' negligence.

INTOXICATION

Intoxication is a condition in which a person's normal capacity to act or think is inhibited by alcohol or some other drug.[2] A contract entered into by an

2. The lack of contractual capacity of a person intoxicated while the contract is being made differs from the contractual capacity of an alcoholic. If an alcoholic makes a contract while sober, there is no lack of capacity. See *Olsen v. Hawkins,* 90 Idaho 28, 408 P.2d 462 (1965).

intoxicated person can be either voidable or valid. If the person was sufficiently intoxicated to lack mental capacity, then the transaction is voidable at the option of the intoxicated person even if the intoxication was purely voluntary. For the contract to be voidable, it must be proved that the intoxicated person's judgment and ability to reason were impaired to such an extent that he or she did not comprehend the legal consequences of entering into the contract. If, despite intoxication, the person understood these legal consequences, the contract will be enforceable.

The fact that the terms of the contract are foolish or obviously favor the other party does not make the contract voidable (unless the other party *fraudulently* induced the person to become intoxicated). Problems often arise in determining whether a party was intoxicated enough to avoid legal duties. Rather than inquire into the intoxicated person's mental state, many courts prefer to look at objective indications to determine whether the contract is voidable owing to intoxication.[3]

If a contract is voidable because of a person's intoxication, that person has the option of disaffirming it—the same option available to a minor. The vast majority of courts, however, require that the intoxicated person make full restitution (fully return any consideration received) as a condition of disaffirmance, except in cases involving necessaries (as explained below). For example, suppose that Briller, who is intoxicated, contracts to purchase a set of encyclopedias from Stevens. If the books are delivered, Briller can disaffirm the executed contract and recover the payment made to Stevens only by returning the encyclopedias.

An intoxicated person, after becoming sober, may ratify a contract expressly or impliedly, just as a minor may do on reaching majority. Implied ratification occurs when a person enters into a contract while intoxicated and fails to disaffirm the contract within a *reasonable* time after becoming sober. Acts or conduct inconsistent with an intent to disaffirm—such as the continued use of property purchased under a voidable contract—will also ratify the contract. In addition, contracts for necessaries are voidable, but the intoxicated person is liable in quasi contract for the reasonable value of the consideration received.

3 MENTALLY INCOMPETENT PERSONS

Contracts made by mentally incompetent persons can be either void, voidable, or valid. If a person has been adjudged mentally incompetent by a court of law and a guardian has been appointed, any contract made by the mentally incompetent person is *void*—no contract exists. Only the guardian can enter into binding legal obligations on the incompetent person's behalf.

If a mentally incompetent person not previously so adjudged by a court enters into a contract, the contract may be *voidable* if the person does not know he or she is entering into the contract or lacks the mental capacity to comprehend its nature, purpose, and consequences. In such a situation, the contract is voidable at the option of the mentally incompetent person but not the other party. The contract may then be disaffirmed or ratified. Like minors and intoxicated persons, mentally incompetent persons are liable (in quasi contract) for the reasonable value of any necessaries they receive.

A contract entered into by a mentally incompetent person not previously so adjudged by a court may also be *valid.* A person may be able to understand the nature and effect of entering into a certain contract yet simultaneously lack capacity to engage in other activities. In such cases, the contract will be valid, because the person is not legally mentally incompetent for contractual purposes.[4] Similarly, an otherwise mentally incompetent person may have a *lucid interval*—a temporary restoration of sufficient intelligence, judgment, and will to enter into contracts without disqualification—during which he or she will be considered to have full legal capacity. (Mental incompetence caused by age or disease, such as Alzheimer's disease, is often a problem facing older persons—see Chapter 50 for a discussion of this difficulty and how individuals can prepare for such a situation.)

3. See, for example, Case 11.1 *(Lucy v. Zehmer)* in Chapter 11.

4. Modern courts no longer require a person to be completely irrational to disaffirm contracts on the basis of mental incompetence. A contract may be voidable if, by reason of a mental illness or defect, an individual was unable to act reasonably with respect to the transaction and the other party had reason to know of the condition. See *Ortelere v. Teachers' Retirement Board,* 25 N.Y.2d 196, 250 N.E.2d 460, 303 N.Y.S.2d 362 (1969).

CONCEPT SUMMARY 13.1

LEGAL EFFECT OF INCAPACITY

	MINORITY	INTOXICATION	MENTAL INCOMPETENCE
General Rule	Contracts entered into by minors are *voidable* at the option of the minor.	If an intoxicated person lacks the mental capacity to comprehend the legal consequences of entering into the contract, the contract is *voidable* at the option of the intoxicated person.	1. Contracts made by a person adjudged to be mentally incompetent by a court of law and for whom a guardian has been appointed are *void*. 2. Contracts made by persons who lack the mental capacity to comprehend the subject matter, nature, and consequences of their actions, but who have not been adjudged by a court to be mentally incompetent, are *voidable*. 3. Contracts made by persons who understand the nature and effect of entering into a contract, even if the persons lack capacity to engage in other activities, are *valid*.
Rules of Disaffirmance	A minor may disaffirm the contract at any time while still a minor and within a reasonable time after reaching the age of majority. Most states do not require restitution.	An intoxicated person may disaffirm the contract at any time while intoxicated and for a reasonable time after becoming sober but must make full restitution.	A mentally incompetent person may disaffirm a voidable contract at any time while mentally incompetent and for a reasonable time after regaining mental competence but must make full restitution.
Exceptions to Basic Rules of Disaffirmance	1. *Necessaries*— Liable for the reasonable value of the necessaries. 2. *Ratification*— After reaching the age of majority, a person can ratify a contract he or she made as a minor, becoming fully liable thereon.	1. *Necessaries*— Liable for the reasonable value of the necessaries. 2. *Ratification*— After becoming sober, a person can ratify a contract he or she made while intoxicated, becoming fully liable thereon.	1. *Necessaries*— Liable for the reasonable value of the necessaries. 2. *Ratification*— After regaining mental competence, an individual can ratify the voidable contract, becoming fully liable thereon.

CONCEPT SUMMARY 13.1  LEGAL EFFECT OF INCAPACITY (*continued*)

	MINORITY	INTOXICATION	MENTAL INCOMPETENCE
Exceptions to Basic Rules of Disaffirmance (continued)	3. *Fraud or misrepresentation—* Misrepresentation of age in many jurisdictions prohibits the right of disaffirmance.		

SECTION 2

Legality

A contract to do something that is prohibited by federal or state statutory law is illegal and, as such, void from the outset and thus unenforceable. Also, a contract that calls for a tortious act or an action contrary to public policy is illegal and unenforceable. It is important to note that a contract or a clause in a contract may be illegal even in the absence of a specific statute prohibiting the action promised by the contract.

CONTRACTS CONTRARY TO STATUTE

Statutes often prescribe the terms of contracts. We now examine several ways in which contracts may be contrary to statute and thus illegal.

Usury. Virtually every state has a statute that sets the maximum rate of interest that can be charged for different types of transactions, including ordinary loans. A lender who makes a loan at an interest rate above the lawful maximum is guilty of **usury.** The maximum rate of interest varies from state to state.

Although usury statutes place a ceiling on allowable rates of interest, exceptions have been made to facilitate business transactions. For example, many states exempt corporate loans from the usury laws. In addition, almost all states have adopted special statutes allowing much higher interest rates on small loans to help those borrowers who are in need of money but simply cannot get loans at interest rates below the normal lawful maximum.

In a few states, a usurious loan is a void transaction, and the lender cannot recover either the principal or the interest. A number of states allow the lender to recover only the principal of a usurious loan along with interest up to the legal maximum. In effect, the lender is denied recovery of the excess interest. In other states, the lender can recover the principal amount of the loan but not the interest.

Gambling. All states have statutes that regulate gambling—defined as any scheme that involves distribution of property by chance among persons who have paid a valuable consideration for the opportunity (chance) to receive the property.[5] Gambling is the creation of risk for the purpose of assuming it. Traditionally, state statutes have deemed gambling contracts to be illegal and thus void.

In several states, however, including Nevada, New Jersey, and Louisiana, casino gambling is now lawful. In other states, certain other forms of gambling are lawful. California, for example, has not defined draw poker as a crime, although criminal statutes prohibit numerous other types of gambling games. Several states allow gambling at horse races, and the majority of the states obtain substantial revenues from legalized state-operated lotteries. Many states also allow gambling on Native American reservations. (For a discussion of some of the legal challenges presented by gambling via the Internet, see this chapter's *Emerging Trends in Technology* on pages 248 and 249.)

Sometimes it is difficult to distinguish a gambling contract from the risk sharing inherent in almost all contracts. Suppose that Isaacson takes out a life insurance policy on Donohue, naming himself as

---

5. See *Wishing Well Club v. Akron*, 66 Ohio Law Abs. 406, 112 N.E.2d 41 (1951).

beneficiary under the policy. At first glance, this may seem entirely legal; but further examination shows that Isaacson is simply gambling on how long Donohue will live. To prevent that type of practice, insurance contracts can be entered into only by someone with an *insurable interest* (see Chapter 49).

The following case illustrates the general problem posed by differences among state statutes on gambling, as well as how people from one state (where gambling debts are not enforceable) can avoid responsibility for gambling debts they incur in another state (where gambling debts are enforceable).

CASE 13.2   Metropolitan Creditors Service of Sacramento v. Sadri

California Court of
Appeal,
First District, 1993.
15 Cal.App.4th 1821,
19 Cal.Rptr.2d 646.

BACKGROUND AND FACTS   *Soheil Sadri, a California resident, incurred debts totaling $22,000 over a two-day period in 1991 while gambling at Caesar's Tahoe casino in Nevada. On January 13 and 14, he wrote the casino two personal checks for $2,000 and $10,000. On January 14, he executed two memoranda of indebtedness for $5,000 each. In exchange for the checks and memoranda, Sadri received chips, which he lost playing the game of baccarat. Sadri subsequently stopped payment on the checks and memoranda, which were drawn on his account at a California bank. Caesar's Tahoe transferred its rights in the checks and memoranda to Metropolitan Creditors Service of Sacramento (MCS) for collection, and MCS sued Sadri in California. The court issued a judgment in favor of Sadri, ruling that his gambling debts were unenforceable in California. MCS appealed.*

IN THE LANGUAGE
OF THE COURT

KING, Associate Justice.
*   *   *   *

California has always had a strong public policy against judicial enforcement of gambling debts, going back virtually to the inception of statehood. *   *   *   *
*   *   *   *

The *   *   * court [in *Hamilton v. Abadjian*, an earlier California case] stated the anti-enforcement rule within a context *   *   * specific to the facts of *   *   * the present case: "The owner of a gambling house who honors a check for the purpose of providing a prospective customer with funds with which to gamble and who then participates in the transaction thus promoted by his act cannot recover on the check."
*   *   *   *

The *Hamilton* rule is on all fours [the facts are similar, and the same questions of law are involved] with the present case. Caesar's Tahoe honored Sadri's checks and memoranda of indebtedness for the purpose of providing him with funds with which to gamble, and then participated in the game. *   *   * [This rule] precludes judicial enforcement of Sadri's gambling debts in California state courts; *   *   * the contracts underlying the debts are against public policy *   *   * and thus the contracts are unlawful and the debts unenforceable.

DECISION
AND REMEDY

The appellate court affirmed the lower court's refusal to enforce the debts, on the ground that the enforcement of gambling debts incurred on credit violates California's public policy.

---

3 **Sabbath (Sunday) Laws.** Statutes that are known as Sabbath (Sunday) laws prohibit the formation or performance of certain contracts on a Sunday. Under the common law, such contracts are legal in the absence of this statutory prohibition. Under a few state statutes, all contracts entered into on a Sunday are illegal. Statutes in other states prohibit only the sale of certain types of merchandise, particularly alcoholic beverages, on a Sunday.

These statutes, which date back to colonial times, are often called blue laws. **Blue laws** get their name from the blue paper on which New Haven, Connecticut, printed its Sabbath law in 1781. The ordinance prohibited all work on Sunday and required all shops to close on the "Lord's Day." A number of states enacted laws forbidding the carrying on of "all secular labor and business on the Lord's Day." Exceptions to Sunday laws permit contracts for necessities (such as food or drugs) and works of charity. A fully performed (executed) contract that was entered into on a Sunday, however, cannot be rescinded (canceled).

Sunday laws are often not enforced, and some of these laws have been held to be unconstitutional on the ground that they are contrary to the freedom of religion. Nonetheless, as a precaution, business owners contemplating doing business in a particular locality should check to see if any Sunday statutes or ordinances will affect their business activities.

Licensing Statutes. All states require that members of certain professions or occupations obtain licenses allowing them to practice. Physicians, lawyers, real estate brokers, architects, electricians, and stockbrokers are but a few of the people who must be licensed. Some licenses are obtained only after extensive schooling and examinations, which indicate to the public that a special skill has been acquired. Others require only that the particular person be of good moral character.

Generally, business licenses provide a means of regulating and taxing certain enterprises and protecting the public against actions that could threaten the general welfare. For example, in nearly all states, a stockbroker must be licensed and must file a bond with the state to protect the public from fraudulent stock transactions. Similarly, a plumber must be licensed and bonded to protect the public against incompetent plumbers and to protect the public health. Only persons or businesses possessing the qualifications and complying with the conditions required by statute are entitled to licenses. Sometimes, for example, an owner of a saloon or tavern is required to sell food as a condition to obtaining a license to sell liquor for consumption on the premises.

When a person enters into a contract with an unlicensed individual, the contract may still be enforceable, depending on the nature of the licensing statute. Some states expressly provide that the lack of a license in certain occupations bars the enforcement of work-related contracts. If the statute does not expressly declare this, one must look to the underlying purpose of the licensing requirements for a particular occupation. If the purpose is to protect the public from unauthorized practitioners, a contract involving an unlicensed individual normally is illegal and unenforceable. If the underlying purpose of the statute is to raise government revenues, however, a contract entered into with an unlicensed practitioner generally is enforceable—although the unlicensed person is usually fined.

Contracts to Commit a Crime. Any contract to commit a crime is a contract in violation of a statute.[6] Thus, a contract to sell an illegal drug (the sale of which is prohibited by statute) is not enforceable. Should the object or performance of the contract be rendered illegal by statute *after* the contract has been entered into, the contract is said to be discharged by law. (See the discussion under "Impossibility or Impracticability of Performance" in Chapter 17.)

CONTRACTS CONTRARY TO PUBLIC POLICY

Although contracts involve private parties, some are not enforceable because of the negative impact they would have on society. We look here at certain types of contracts that are often said to be *contrary to public policy*.

Contracts in Restraint of Trade. Contracts in restraint of trade (anticompetitive agreements) usually adversely affect the public (which favors competition in the economy) and typically violate one or more federal or state statutes.[7] An exception is recognized when the restraint is reasonable and is contained in an ancillary (subordinate) clause in a contract. Many such exceptions involve a type of restraint called a **covenant not to compete,** or a restrictive covenant.

Covenants (promises) not to compete are often contained as ancillary clauses in contracts concerning the sale of an ongoing business. A covenant not to compete is created when a seller agrees not to open a new store in a certain geographic area surrounding the old store. Such agreements enable the seller to sell, and the purchaser to buy, the goodwill and reputation of an ongoing business. If, for example, a well-known merchant sells his or her store and opens a competing business a block away, many of the customers will likely do business at the well-known merchant's new store. This, in turn, renders valueless the good name and reputation purchased by the new

---

6. See, for example, *McConnell v. Commonwealth Pictures Corp.*, 7 N.Y.2d 465, 166 N.E.2d 494, 199 N.Y.S.2d 483 (1960).
7. Such as the Sherman Act, the Clayton Act, and the Federal Trade Commission Act (see Chapter 45).

EMERGING TRENDS IN TECHNOLOGY

Online Gambling

At one time, few states permitted gambling in any form. Even by 1976, only thirteen states had lotteries, two states had approved off-track wagering, and there were no casinos outside Nevada. Today, in contrast, thirty-seven states have lotteries, twenty-eight states have casinos, and twenty-two states allow off-track betting.[a] Moreover, the advent of the Internet has given Americans unprecedented access to gambling facilities.

JURISDICTIONAL CHALLENGES

As noted in Chapter 9, jurisdictional issues become complicated in cases involving Internet transactions. Certainly, this is true with respect to online gambling. For example, in those states that do not allow casino gambling or off-track betting, what can a state government do if residents of the state place bets online? After all, states have no constitutional authority to regulate activities that occur in other states. Complicating

the problem is the fact that many Internet gambling sites are located outside the United States in countries in which Internet gambling is legal, and no state government has jurisdiction over activities that take place in other countries.

Of course, as you learned in Chapter 2, under certain conditions a state court can exercise jurisdiction over an out-of-state party that has a threshold level of contacts ("minimum contacts") with the state. A number of courts have shown a willingness to exercise jurisdiction over gambling sites located out of state—or even out of the country—based on the assumption that Internet advertising of gambling sites constitutes minimum contacts.

For example, in one case the state of Minnesota sued a Nevada corporation that advertised online a sports-betting site called WagerNet. The corporation had no sales force or employees in Minnesota. Under traditional jurisdictional concepts, the Nevada company probably would not have had sufficient contacts (minimum contacts) with the state of Minnesota to allow a Minnesota court to exercise jurisdiction over the Nevada defendant. In this case, however, the court held that the defendant was subject to personal jurisdiction in the state of Minnesota based on its actions of advertising on the Internet the online gambling service and

developing from the Internet a mailing list that included Minnesota residents.[b]

WHERE DOES THE GAMBLING OCCUR?

Another threshold issue in regulating online gambling has to do with determining where the physical act of placing a bet on the Internet occurs. Is it where the gambler is located or where the gambling site is based? For example, suppose that a resident of New York places bets via the Internet at a gambling site located in Antigua. Is the actual act of "gambling" taking place in New York or in Antigua? According to a New York trial court, the act of entering a bet and transmitting information from New York to Antigua via the Internet was adequate to constitute gambling activity within New York. The court held that this determination was consistent with a provision in New York's criminal code, which stated that "if the person engaged in

---

a. Rachel A. Volberg *et al.*, "From Back Room to Living Room: Changing Attitudes toward Gambling," *Public Perspective*, August/September 1999, p. 9.

---

b. *Minnesota v. Granite Gate Resorts, Inc.*, 568 N.W.2d 715 (Minn.App. 1997); aff'd., 576 N.W.2d 747 (Minn. 1998). See also *Thompson v. Handa-Lopez, Inc.*, 998 F.Supp. 738 (W.D.Tex. 1998), in which a Texas court held that Internet advertising by a California company was sufficient to constitute minimum contacts with the state of Texas.

---

owner of the old store for a price. If a covenant not to compete is not ancillary to a sales agreement, however, it is void, because it unreasonably restrains trade and is contrary to public policy.

Agreements not to compete can also be contained in employment contracts. It is common for people in middle-level and upper-level management positions to agree not to work for competitors or not to start compet-

EMERGING TRENDS IN TECHNOLOGY

Online Gambling, continued

gambling is located in New York, then New York is the location where the gambling occurred."[c] How other courts will decide this question, however, is not yet clear.[d]

COLLECTING CREDIT-CARD GAMBLING DEBTS

Many states have laws that bar the collection of illegal gambling debts. Given that nearly 90 percent of Internet gambling is accomplished through the use of credit cards, these laws may have significant implications for credit-card companies, banks, and other issuers of credit cards. Specifically, will credit-card issuers be able to collect debts from cardholders who use their cards to obtain funds for online gambling?

In a series of class-action cases against credit-card companies that

---

c. *People v. World Interactive Gaming Corp.*, No. 404428/98 (N.Y.Sup.Ct. July 29, 1999); unpublished opinion.
d. In a closely watched case, the U.S. Court of Appeals for the Eighth Circuit recently remanded a case to the federal district court for a similar determination. See *Missouri v. Coeur D'Alene Tribe*, 164 F.3d 1102 (8th Cir. 1999).

are currently before the federal courts, the plaintiffs have alleged that they should not have to pay credit-card debts that they incurred for gambling purposes. In addition, they allege that Internet casinos, credit-card companies, and banks have joined together to form an unlawful enterprise to facilitate illegal gambling and to collect gambling debts incurred by cardholders who place bets. These actions, assert the plaintiffs, constitute violations of the Racketeer Influenced and Corrupt Organizations Act, or RICO (discussed in Chapter 8). Still another complaint alleges violations of the federal Wire Communications Act of 1961, which bars the use of wire communication facilities for interstate or foreign gambling purposes.

Clearly, the courts' decisions in these cases will have important consequences for the online gambling industry. In the meantime, opponents of Internet gambling are pressuring Congress to pass legislation that would prohibit the use of the Internet for gambling purposes. Additionally, four states—Illinois, Louisiana, Nevada, and Texas—already have specifically banned Internet gambling.

IMPLICATIONS FOR THE BUSINESSPERSON

1. Clearly, any businessperson who plans to operate an online gambling site should obtain legal

advice before doing so, in order to avoid liability under state or federal laws.
2. Cybermarketers who promote their services or products via online sweepstakes, skill contests, fantasy games, and other devices also need to exercise great caution to make sure that their offerings do not constitute illegal lotteries. Generally, any businessperson contemplating such marketing efforts should check with an attorney before proceeding.

FOR CRITICAL ANALYSIS

1. Should credit-card companies be held responsible for the gambling losses of their cardholders? Why or why not?
2. Would traditional U.S. casino operators likely be for or against Internet gambling? Why?

RELEVANT WEB SITES

You can gain a further understanding of some of these issues by going to the Web sites of the Interactive Gaming Council (which supports Internet gambling) at http://www.igcouncil.org and the American Gaming Association (an organization of land-based casinos that opposes Internet gambling until technology permits adequate regulatory control) at http://www.americangaming.org.

---

ing businesses for a specified period of time after termination of employment. Such agreements are legal so long as the specified period of time (of restraint) is not excessive in duration and the geographic restriction is reasonable.

Basically, a restriction on competition must be reasonable—that is, not any greater than necessary to protect a legitimate business interest. The following case illustrates this point.

CASE 13.3   Brunswick Floors, Inc. v. Guest

Court of Appeals of
Georgia, 1998.
506 S.E.2d 670.

HISTORICAL AND SOCIAL SETTING   *The value of a business frequently depends on the goodwill between key employees and customers. To enhance this value, a business will invest its key employees with training, experience, customer lists, trade secrets, and other valuable information. It can be devastating when a key employee quits, or is fired, and goes into business to compete with his or her former employer. A covenant not to compete can protect goodwill, and other assets, by at least prohibiting an employee from stealing existing customers. A covenant not to compete is enforceable if its provisions are reasonable, if it is part of a valid contract, and if it is related to the protection of a legitimate interest. As much as a business might wish, however, legitimate interests do not include preventing competition.*

BACKGROUND AND FACTS   *Brian Guest was a floor covering installer for Brunswick Floors, Inc. Guest signed a covenant not to compete that prohibited him for two years after termination of employment from engaging in the floor covering business in virtually any way, within an eighty-mile radius of Brunswick's location. After Guest quit Brunswick, he went to work as an independent flooring contractor. Brunswick filed a suit in a Georgia state court against Guest based on the covenant not to compete. The court ruled in part that the covenant unduly restricted Guest's right to earn a living. Brunswick appealed.*

**IN THE LANGUAGE
OF THE COURT**

RUFFIN, Judge.
       *   *   *   *

*   *   * [A]n employer is permitted to include in *   *   * a covenant [not to compete] the territory in which the employee has in fact performed work, thus protecting itself from the unfair appropriation of good will and information acquired in the course of that work. In contrast, [a] restriction relating to the area in which the employer does business is generally unenforceable due to overbreadth, unless the employer can show a legitimate business interest that will be protected by such an expansive geographic description.

In this case, the covenant restricts Guest from working within an 80 mile radius of Brunswick Floors' location *   *   * . The 80 mile radius relates to the area in which the employer, Brunswick Floors, and not the employee, Guest, did business. *   *   *

[Robert] Blake [the president of Brunswick] testified that "if our employees start *   *   * working for our competitors, then certainly our market share would face, you know, diminishing status." *Avoidance of competition, however, is not a legitimate business interest.* [Emphasis added.]

Brunswick Floors contends the training and money expended on Guest legitimizes their interest. *   *   * Here, Guest's minimal training does not outweigh the substantial harm imposed by prohibiting him from installing carpet in an 80 mile radius. Thus, we find this to be an overbroad territorial limitation.

We also find the scope of activity prohibited in the non-compete provision is overbroad. *   *   * This imposes a greater limitation on the employee than is necessary because [Guest] is prohibited from being an officer or director or owning stock in other companies, activities which are very different from [his] work as [a floor covering installer].

**DECISION
AND REMEDY**

The Court of Appeals of Georgia held that a covenant not to compete is unenforceable if it bars an employee from engaging in the employer's business in virtually any way within the area in which the employer does business. The court affirmed the decision of the lower court.

Unconscionable Contracts or Clauses.   Ordinarily, a court does not look at the fairness or equity of a contract. For example, the courts generally do not inquire into the adequacy of consideration (see Chapter 12).

Persons are assumed to be reasonably intelligent, and the courts will not come to their aid just because they have made an unwise or foolish bargain. In certain circumstances, however, bargains are so oppressive that the courts relieve innocent parties of part or all of their duties. Such bargains are called **unconscionable** because they are so unscrupulous or grossly unfair as to be "void of conscience."[8] There are two general types of unconscionability, procedural and substantial.

Procedural Unconscionability. *Procedural* unconscionability has to do with how a term becomes part of a contract and relates to factors that may make it difficult for a party to know or understand the contract terms due to inconspicuous print, unintelligible language ("legalese"), or the lack of an opportunity to read the contract or to ask questions about its meaning. Procedural unconscionability sometimes relates to purported lack of voluntariness due to a disparity in bargaining power between the two parties. Contracts entered into because of one party's vastly superior bargaining power may be deemed unconscionable. These situations usually involve an *adhesion contract,* which, as will be discussed in Chapter 14, is a contract drafted by the dominant party and then presented to the other—the adhering party—on a take-it-or-leave-it basis.[9]

Substantive Unconscionability. *Substantive* unconscionability characterizes those contracts, or portions of contracts, that are oppressive or overly harsh. Courts generally focus on provisions that deprive one party of the benefits of the agreement or leave that party without remedy for nonperformance by the other. For example, suppose that a person with little income and with only a fourth-grade education agrees to purchase a refrigerator for $2,000 and signs a two-year installment contract. The same type of refrigerator usually sells for $400 on the market. Some courts have held this type of contract to be unconscionable, despite the general rule that the courts will not inquire into the adequacy of the consideration, simply because the contract terms are so oppressive as to "shock the conscience" of the court.[10]

Exculpatory Clauses. Closely related to the concept of unconscionability are **exculpatory clauses,** defined as clauses that release a party from liability in the event of monetary or physical injury, no matter who is at fault. Indeed, some courts refer to such clauses in terms of unconscionability. Suppose, for example, that Jones and Laughlin Steel Company hires a laborer and has him sign a contract containing the following clause:

> Said employee hereby agrees with employer, in consideration of such employment, that he will take upon himself all risks incident to his position and will in no case hold the company liable for any injury or damage he may sustain, in his person or otherwise, by accidents or injuries in the factory, or which may result from defective machinery or carelessness or misconduct of himself or any other employee in service of the employer.

This contract provision attempts to remove Jones and Laughlin's potential liability for injuries to the employee, and it would usually be held contrary to public policy.[11] Exculpatory clauses found in rental agreements for commercial property are also frequently held to be contrary to public policy. Additionally, such clauses are almost universally held to be illegal and unenforceable when they are included in residential property leases.

Generally, an exculpatory clause will not be enforced if the party seeking its enforcement is involved in a business that is important to the public interest. These businesses include public utilities, common carriers, and banks. Because of the essential nature of these services, a company offering them has an advantage in bargaining strength and could insist that anyone contracting for its services agree not to hold it liable. As a result, the company would tend to relax its carefulness and the number of injuries would increase. Imagine the results, for example, if all exculpatory clauses in contracts between airlines and their passengers were enforced.

Exculpatory clauses may be enforced, however, when the parties seeking their enforcement are private businesses that are not involved in enterprises considered important to the public interest. These businesses have included health clubs, amusement parks, skiing facilities, horse-rental concessions, golf-cart concessions, and skydiving organizations. Because these services are not essential, the firms offering them are sometimes considered to have no relative advantage in

---

8. The Uniform Commercial Code incorporated the concept of unconscionability in Sections 2–302 and 2A–108. These provisions, which apply to contracts for the sale or lease of goods, will be discussed in Chapter 19.

9. See, for example, *Henningsen v. Bloomfield Motors, Inc.,* 32 N.J. 358, 161 A.2d 69 (1960).

10. See, for example, *Jones v. Star Credit Corp.,* 59 Misc.2d 189, 298 N.Y.S.2d 264 (1969).

11. For a case with similar facts, see *Little Rock & Fort Smith Railway Co. v. Eubanks,* 48 Ark. 460, 3 S.W. 808 (1887). In such a case, the exculpatory clause may also be illegal on the basis of a violation of a state workers' compensation law.

bargaining strength, and anyone contracting for their services is considered to do so voluntarily.

Other Contracts Contrary to Public Policy. Contracts in which a party promises to discriminate on the basis of race, color, national origin, religion, gender, age, or disability are contrary to statute and contrary to public policy.[12] For example, if a property owner promises in a contract not to sell the property to a member of a particular race, the contract is unenforceable. The public policy underlying these prohibitions is very strong, and the courts are quick to invalidate discriminatory contracts.

Contracts that require a party to commit a civil wrong, or tort, have been held to be contrary to public policy. Remember that a tort is an act that is wrongful to another individual in a private sense, even though it may not necessarily be criminal in nature (an act against society).

Contracts that interfere with the duties of a public officer, such as a city commissioner, are contrary to public policy. Agreements that involve a conflict of interest are also often illegal. Public officers cannot enter into contracts that cause conflict between their official duties as representatives of the people and their private interests. Statutes require many public officers to liquidate their interests in private businesses before serving as elected representatives. Other statutes merely require that while they are in office, they take no part in the operation of or decisions concerning any business in which they have an interest, so that private and public responsibilities remain separate.

Any agreement that is intended to delay, prevent, or obstruct the legal process is illegal. For example, an agreement to pay some specified amount if a criminal prosecution is terminated is illegal. Likewise, agreements to suppress evidence in a legal proceeding or to commit fraud on a court are illegal. Tampering with a jury by offering jurors money in exchange for their votes is illegal.

EFFECT OF ILLEGALITY

In general, an illegal contract is void; that is, the contract is deemed never to have existed, and the courts will not aid either party. In most illegal contracts, both parties are considered to be *in pari delicto*[13]

(equally at fault). In such cases, the contract is void. If the contract is executory, neither party can enforce it. If it has been executed, there can be neither contractual nor quasi-contractual recovery.

That one wrongdoer who is a party to an illegal contract is unjustly enriched at the expense of the other is of no concern to the law—except under certain special circumstances that will be discussed below. The major justification for this hands-off attitude is that it is improper to place the machinery of justice at the disposal of a plaintiff who has broken the law by entering into an illegal bargain. Another justification is the hoped-for deterrent effect of this general "hands-off" rule. A plaintiff who suffers loss because of an illegal bargain should presumably be deterred from entering into similar illegal bargains.

Exceptions to the General Rule. There are some exceptions to the general rule that neither party to an illegal bargain can sue for breach and that neither party can recover for performance rendered.

Justifiable Ignorance of the Facts. When one of the parties is relatively innocent, that party can often recover any benefits conferred in a partially executed contract. In this case, the courts will not enforce the contract but will allow the parties to return to their original positions. An innocent party who has fully performed under the contract may sometimes enforce the contract against the guilty party. For example, a trucking company contracts with Gillespie to carry goods to a specific destination for a normal fee of $500. The trucker delivers the goods and later finds out that the contents of the shipped crates were illegal. Although the law specifies that the shipment, use, and sale of the goods were illegal, the trucker, being an innocent party, can still legally collect the $500 from Gillespie.

Members of Protected Classes. When a statute is clearly designed to protect a certain class of people, a member of that class can enforce a contract in violation of the statute even though the other party cannot. For example, flight attendants and pilots are subject to a federal statute that prohibits them from flying more than a certain number of hours every month. If an attendant or a pilot exceeds the maximum, the airline must nonetheless pay for those extra hours of service.

Other examples of statutes designed to protect particular classes of people include *blue sky laws*—state laws that regulate and supervise investment companies for the protection of the public (see Chapter 37)—and state statutes regulating the sale of insurance. If an

---

12. The major federal statute prohibiting discrimination is the Civil Rights Act of 1964, 42 U.S.C. Sections 2000e–2000e-17. For a discussion of this act and other acts prohibiting discrimination in the employment context, see Chapter 42.

13. Pronounced in *paa-ree deh-lick-tow*.

insurance company violates a statute when selling insurance, the purchaser can nevertheless enforce the policy and recover from the insurer.

Withdrawal from an Illegal Agreement. If an agreement has been only partly carried out and the illegal portion of the bargain has not yet been performed, the party rendering performance can withdraw from the contract and recover the performance or its value. For example, Sam and Jim decide to wager (illegally) on the outcome of a boxing match. Each deposits money with a stakeholder, who agrees to pay the winner of the bet. At this point, each party has performed part of the agreement, but the illegal element of the agreement will not occur until the money is paid to the winner. Before such payment occurs, either party is entitled to withdraw from the bargain by giving notice of repudiation to the stakeholder.

Contract Illegal through Fraud, Duress, or Undue Influence. Often, illegal contracts involve two blameworthy parties, but one party is more at fault than the other. When a party has been induced to enter into an illegal bargain by fraud, duress, or undue influence on the part of the other party to the

agreement, that party will be allowed to recover for the performance or its value.

Severable, or Divisible, Contracts. A contract that is *severable*, or divisible, consists of distinct parts that can be performed separately, with separate consideration provided for each part. An *indivisible* contract, in contrast, exists when the parties intended that complete performance by each party would be essential, even if the contract contains a number of seemingly separate provisions.

If a contract is divisible into legal and illegal portions, a court may enforce the legal portion but not the illegal one, so long as the illegal portion does not affect the essence of the bargain. This approach of the courts is consistent with the basic policy of enforcing the legal intentions of the contracting parties whenever possible. For example, if an overly broad and thus illegal covenant not to compete was drafted into an employment contract, the court might allow the employment contract to be enforceable but reform the unreasonably broad covenant by converting its terms into reasonable ones. Alternatively, the court could declare the covenant illegal (and thus void) and enforce the remaining employment terms.

CONCEPT SUMMARY 13.2   LEGALITY

TYPES OF CONTRACTS	APPLICATIONS
Contracts Contrary to Statute	1. *Usury*—The effects of a usurious loan (a loan made for interest rates that exceed the maximum legal rate of interest) vary from state to state. In a few states, the loan is a void transaction; in other states, the lender may recover up to the legal maximum rate of interest; in still other states, the lender cannot recover any interest. 2. *Gambling*—Gambling contracts that contravene (go against) state statutes are deemed illegal and thus are void. 3. *Sabbath (Sunday) laws*—Laws prohibiting the formation or the performance of certain contracts on Sunday vary widely from state to state, and many states do not enforce them. 4. *Licensing statutes*—Contracts entered into by persons who do not have a license, when one is required by state law, may not be enforceable, depending on the purpose of the statute. 5. *Contracts to commit a crime*—All contracts to commit crimes violate statutes and are thus illegal and unenforceable.
Contracts Contrary to Public Policy	1. *Covenants not to compete*—Restrictive covenants may be enforced by the courts if the terms are ancillary to a contract for the sale of a business or to an employment contract and the covenant's terms are reasonable as to time and area of restraint. If the terms are unreasonable as to time and

CONCEPT SUMMARY 13.2

LEGALITY (*continued*)

TYPES OF CONTRACTS	APPLICATIONS
Contracts Contrary to Public Policy (continued)	area of restraint, the court may reform the covenant to make the restraints reasonable or declare the covenant illegal. 2. *Unconscionable contracts and clauses*—When a contract or contract clause is so unfair that it is oppressive to one party or "shocks the conscience" of the court, the court may deem the contract or clause unconscionable; as such, it is illegal and cannot be enforced. 3. *Adhesion contracts*—Contracts that are entered into because of one party's vastly superior bargaining power may be unconscionable and unenforceable. 4. *Exculpatory clauses*—Clauses that exempt one of the parties from all liability for property damage or personal injury arising from the subject matter of the contract are scrutinized closely by the courts and may be deemed unconscionable and thus unenforceable. 5. *Discriminatory contracts*—Contracts in which a party agrees to discriminate against another on the basis of color, race, religion, national origin, or gender are both contrary to public policy and contrary to statute. 6. *Contracts for the commission of a tort*—Contracts that require a party to commit a tort against another are unenforceable. 7. *Contracts conflicting with public service*—Contracts that impede a public official's duties, such as a contract to pay a legislator to vote a certain way, are unenforceable. 8. *Agreements to obstruct the legal process*—Contracts to delay, prevent, or obstruct the legal process are illegal and unenforceable.
Effect of Illegality	1. In general, an illegal contract is void, and the courts will aid neither party when both parties are considered to be equally at fault. If the contract is executory, neither party can enforce it. If the contract is executed, there can be neither contractual nor quasi-contractual recovery. 2. Illegal contracts may be enforced in the following situations: a. When one party to the contract is relatively innocent. b. When one party to the contract is a member of a group of persons protected by statute. c. When one party was induced to enter into an illegal bargain through fraud, duress, or undue influence.

TERMS AND CONCEPTS TO REVIEW

age of majority 239	disaffirmance 240	necessaries 241
blue law 246	emancipation 240	ratification 242
contractual capacity 239	exculpatory clause 251	unconscionable 251
covenant not to compete 247	*in pari delicto* 252	usury 245

QUESTIONS AND CASE PROBLEMS

13–1. INTOXICATION. After Kira had had several drinks one night, she sold Charlotte a diamond necklace worth thousands of dollars for $100. The next day, Kira offered the $100 to Charlotte and requested the return of her necklace. Charlotte refused to accept the $100 or return the necklace, claiming that there was a valid contract of sale. Kira explained that she had been intoxicated at the time the bargain was made and thus the contract was voidable at her option. Was Kira correct? Explain.

13–2. COVENANTS NOT TO COMPETE. A famous New York City hotel, Hotel Lux, is noted for its food as well as its luxury accommodations. Hotel Lux contracts with a famous chef, Chef Perlee, to become its head chef at $6,000 per month. The contract states that should Perlee leave the employment of Hotel Lux for any reason, he will not work as a chef for any hotel or restaurant in New York, New Jersey, or Pennsylvania for a period of one year. During the first six months of the contract, Hotel Lux substantially advertises Perlee as its head chef, and business at the hotel is excellent. Then a dispute arises between the hotel management and Perlee, and Perlee terminates his employment. One month later, he is hired by a famous New Jersey restaurant just across the New York state line. Hotel Lux learns of Perlee's employment through a large advertisement in a New York City newspaper. It seeks to enjoin Perlee from working in that restaurant as a chef for one year. Discuss how successful Hotel Lux will be in its action.

13–3. LICENSING STATUTES. In State X, persons must be at least eighteen years old before they can purchase alcoholic beverages. The state also has passed a law requiring that persons who prepare and serve liquor in the form of drinks in commercial establishments be licensed. The only requirement for obtaining a yearly license is that the person be at least eighteen years old. Moffitt, aged thirty-five, is hired as a bartender for the Lone Star Restaurant. Bekins, a staunch alumnus of a nearby university, brings twenty of his friends to the restaurant to celebrate a football victory. Bekins has ordered four rounds of drinks, and the bar bill exceeds $200. Bekins learns that Moffitt has failed to renew his bartender's license, and Bekins refuses to pay, claiming the contract is unenforceable. Discuss whether Bekins is correct.

13–4. ADHESION CONTRACTS. Patricia Aiken suffered a heart attack and was hospitalized at Phoenix Baptist Hospital and Medical Center, Inc. At the time of her admission, the Aikens told the hospital that they did not have the money to pay for medical care. At the same time, Patricia's husband, Thomas, signed an agreement to pay her medical expenses. He did not read what he signed, no one explained the agreement to him, and he later claimed to have been so upset that he could not remember having signed anything. When the bills were not paid, the hospital filed a suit in an Arizona state court against the Aikens. The court ruled in favor of the hospital, and the Aikens appealed. They argued that the agreement was an adhesion contract obtained under circumstances that made it unenforceable. Were the circumstances such that the agreement may have been unenforceable? Discuss fully. [*Phoenix Baptist Hospital & Medical Center, Inc. v. Aiken,* 179 Ariz. 289, 877 P.2d 1345 (1994)]

13–5. GAMBLING CONTRACTS. No law prohibits citizens in a state that does not sponsor a state-operated lottery from purchasing lottery tickets in a state that does have such a lottery. Because Georgia did not have a state-operated lottery, Talley and several other Georgia residents allegedly agreed to purchase a ticket in a lottery sponsored by Kentucky and to share the proceeds if they won. They did win, but apparently Talley had difficulty collecting his share of the proceeds. In Talley's suit to obtain his portion of the funds, a Georgia trial court held that the "gambling contract" was unenforceable because it was contrary to Georgia's public policy. On appeal, how should the court rule on this issue? Discuss. [*Talley v. Mathis,* 265 Ga. 179, 453 S.E.2d 704 (1995)]

13–6. CONTRACTS BY MINORS. Sergei Samsonov is a Russian and one of the top hockey players in the world. When Samsonov was seventeen years old, he signed a contract to play hockey for two seasons with the Central Sports Army Club, a Russian club known by the abbreviation CSKA. Before the start of the second season, Samsonov learned that because of a dispute between CSKA coaches, he would not be playing in Russia's premier hockey league. Samsonov hired Athletes and Artists, Inc. (A&A), an American sports agency, to make a deal with a U.S. hockey team. Samsonov signed a contract to play for the Detroit Vipers (whose corporate name was, at the time, Arena Associates, Inc.). Neither A&A nor Arena knew about the CSKA contract. CSKA filed a suit in a federal district court against Arena and others, alleging, among other things, wrongful interference with a contractual relationship. What effect will Samsonov's age have on the outcome of this suit? [*Central Sports Army Club v. Arena Associates, Inc.,* 952 F.Supp. 181 (S.D.N.Y. 1997)]

13–7. EXCULPATORY CLAUSE. Norbert Eelbode applied for a job with Travelers Inn in the state of Washington. As part of the application process, Eelbode was sent to Laura Grothe, a physical therapist at Chec Medical Centers, Inc., for a preemployment physical exam. Before the exam, Eelbode signed a document that stated in part, "I hereby release Chec and the Washington Readicare Medical Group and its physicians from all liability arising from any injury to me resulting from my participation in the exam." During the exam, Grothe asked Eelbode to lift an item while bending from the waist using only his back with his knees locked. Eelbode experienced immediate sharp and burning pain in his lower back and down the back of his right leg. Eelbode filed a suit in a Washington state court against Grothe and Chec, claiming that he was injured because of an improperly administered back torso strength test. Grothe and Chec cited the document that Eelbode signed, and filed a motion for summary judgment. Should the court grant the motion? Why or why not? [*Eelbode v. Chec Medical Centers, Inc.*, 984 P.2d 436 (Wash.App. 1999)]

13–8. IN YOUR COURT

Dr. Roger Morris, a research scientist holding a Ph.D. in physical biochemistry, signed an employment contract with Microscan, a company that designed, manufactured, and sold diagnostic equipment for use in microbiological laboratories. The contract indicated that Microscan would be entrusting Morris, as an employee, with confidential information. To protect its trade secrets, Microscan included a covenant not to compete in the contract. The covenant stated that Morris would not "render services, directly or indirectly, for a period of one year after the termination of my employment with Microscan to any competing organization in connection with any competing product within such geographic limits as Microscan and said competing organization are, or would be, in actual competition." A few years later, Morris resigned his employment with Microscan and accepted a position with Vitek, Inc., which was essentially Microscan's only competitor. Microscan brought a suit against Morris to enforce the covenant not to compete. Assume that you are the judge in the trial court hearing this case and answer the following questions:

(a) Given that Vitek was Microscan's only competitor in the market for diagnostic equipment used in microbiological laboratories, is the covenant not to compete overbroad or unreasonably burdensome to Morris? How will you rule on this issue?

(b) Suppose that evidence introduced at trial indicates that Vitek did not intend to elicit trade secrets from Morris and that Vitek has no need for that information. In such circumstances, would it be reasonable to enforce the covenant?

(c) Compare this case to Case 13.3 (*Brunswick Floors, Inc. v. Guest*). Does the court's reasoning in that case influence your decision in the Morris-Microscan case? Should it? Why or why not?

13–9. A QUESTION OF ETHICS

Nancy Levy worked for Health Care Financial Enterprises, Inc., and signed a noncompete agreement in June 1992. When Levy left Health Care and opened up her own similar business in 1993, Health Care brought a court action in a Florida state court to enforce the covenant not to compete. The trial court concluded that the noncompete agreement prevented Levy from working in too broad a geographic area and thus refused to enforce the agreement. A Florida appellate court, however, reversed the trial court's ruling and remanded the case with instructions that the trial court modify the geographic area to make it reasonable and then enforce the covenant. [*Health Care Financial Enterprises, Inc. v. Levy*, 715 So.2d 341 (Fla.App.4th 1998)]

(a) What interests are served by refusing to enforce covenants not to compete? What interests are served by allowing them to be enforced?

(b) What argument could be made in support of reforming (and then enforcing) illegal covenants not to compete? What argument could be made against this practice?

LAW ON THE WEB

For updated links to resources available on the Web, as well as a variety of other materials, visit this text's Web site at http://wbl.westbuslaw.com.

For an example of state statutory provisions governing the emancipation of minors, go to

http://legisweb.state.wy.us/titles/96titles/Title14.htm

If you are interested in reading the first "Sunday law" in colonial America and learning about some of the punishments meted out in those days for failing to obey such laws, go to

http://www.tagnet.org/crsda/first.htm

LEGAL RESEARCH EXERCISES ON THE WEB

Go to http://wbl.westbuslaw.com, the Web site that accompanies this text. Select "Internet Applications," and then click on "Chapter 13." There you will find the following Internet research exercise that you can perform to learn more about the law governing minors:

Activity 13–1: Minors and the Law

CHAPTER 14

Genuineness of Assent

A CONTRACT HAS BEEN ENTERED INTO by two parties, each with full legal capacity and for a legal purpose. The contract is also supported by consideration. The contract thus meets the four requirements for a valid contract that were specified in Chapter 10. Nonetheless, the contract may be unenforceable if the parties have not genuinely assented to its terms. As stated in Chapter 10, lack of **genuineness of assent** can be used as a defense to the contract's enforceability.

Genuineness of assent may be lacking because of a mistake, misrepresentation, undue influence, or duress—in other words, because there is no true "meeting of the minds." In this chapter, we examine problems relating to genuineness of assent.

SECTION 1

Mistakes

We all make mistakes, and it is therefore not surprising that mistakes are made when contracts are formed. It is important to distinguish between *mistakes of fact* and *mistakes of value or quality.* Only a mistake of fact allows a contract to be avoided.

MISTAKES OF FACT

Mistakes of fact occur in two forms—*unilateral* and *mutual (bilateral).* A unilateral mistake is made by only one of the contracting parties; a mutual, or bilateral, mistake is made by both.

Unilateral Mistakes of Fact. A unilateral mistake occurs when one contracting party makes a mistake as to some *material fact*—that is, a fact important to the subject matter of the contract. The general rule is that a unilateral mistake does not afford the mistaken party any right to relief from the contract. For example, DeVinck intends to sell his motor home for $17,500. When he learns that Benson is interested in buying a used motor home, DeVinck faxes Benson an offer to sell the vehicle to him. When typing the fax, however, DeVinck mistakenly keys in the price of $15,700. Benson immediately sends DeVinck a fax, accepting DeVinck's offer. Even though DeVinck intended to sell his motor home for $17,500, his unilateral mistake falls on him. He is bound in contract to sell the motor home to Benson for $15,700.

There are at least two exceptions to this general rule.[1] First, if the *other* party to the contract knows or should have known that a mistake of fact was made, the contract may not be enforceable. In the above example, if Benson knew that DeVinck intended to sell his motor home for $17,500, then DeVinck's unilateral

---

1. The *Restatement (Second) of Contracts*, Section 153, liberalizes the general rule to take into account the modern trend of allowing avoidance even though only one party has been mistaken.

mistake (stating $15,700 in his offer) may render the resulting contract unenforceable. The second exception arises when a unilateral mistake of fact was due to a mathematical mistake in addition, subtraction, division, or multiplication and was made inadvertently and without gross (extreme) negligence. If a contractor's bid was low because he or she made a mistake in addition when totaling the estimated costs, any contract resulting from the bid may be rescinded. Of course, in both situations, the mistake must still involve some *material* fact.

Bilateral Mistakes of Fact. When both parties are mistaken about the same material fact, the contract can be rescinded by either party.[2] To illustrate: Assume that at Umberto's art gallery, Keeley buys a

painting of a landscape. Both Umberto and Keeley believe that the painting is by the artist Van Gogh. Later, Keeley discovers that the painting is a very clever fake. Because neither Umberto nor Keeley was aware of this material fact when they made their deal, Keeley can rescind the contract and recover the purchase price of the painting.

A word or term in a contract may be subject to more than one reasonable interpretation. In that situation, if the parties to the contract attach materially different meanings to the term, their mutual mistake of fact may allow the contract to be rescinded because there has been no "meeting of the minds," or true assent, which is required for a contract to arise. The classic case on mutual mistake involved a ship named *Peerless* that was to sail from Bombay with certain cotton goods on board. More than one ship named *Peerless* sailed from Bombay that winter, however.

---

2. *Restatement (Second) of Contracts*, Section 152.

CASE 14.1   Raffles v. Wichelhaus

Court of Exchequer,
England, 1864.
159 Eng.Rep. 375.

BACKGROUND AND FACTS   *The defendant, Wichelhaus, purchased a shipment of Surat cotton from the plaintiff, Raffles, "to arrive 'Peerless' from Bombay." The defendant expected the goods to be shipped on the* Peerless *sailing from Bombay, India, in October. The plaintiff expected to ship the goods on a different* Peerless, *which sailed from Bombay in December. By the time the goods arrived and the plaintiff tried to deliver them, the defendant was no longer willing to accept them.*

IN THE LANGUAGE OF THE COURT

PER CURIAM [by the whole court].

*   *   *   *

[The defendants asserted that the] ship mentioned in the * * * agreement was meant and intended by the defendants to be the ship called the "Peerless," which sailed from Bombay * * * in October; and that the plaintiff was not ready and willing and did not offer to deliver to the defendants any bales of cotton which arrived by the last mentioned ship, but instead thereof was only ready and willing and offered to deliver to the defendants 125 bales of Surat cotton which arrived by another and different ship, which was also called the "Peerless," and which sailed from Bombay * * * in December.

*   *   *   *

There is nothing on the face of the contract to show that any particular ship called the "Peerless" was meant; but the moment it appears that two ships called the "Peerless" were about to sail from Bombay there is latent ambiguity, and parol evidence[a] may be given for the purpose of shewing [showing] that the defendant meant one "Peerless" and the plaintiff another. That being so, there was no consensus *ad idem* [on the point], and therefore no contract.

DECISION AND REMEDY

The judgment was for the defendant, Wichelhaus. The court held that no mutual assent existed, because the parties had attached materially different meanings to an essential

---

a. With respect to contracts, *parol evidence* is evidence that the document itself does not furnish but that other sources (such as, in this case, oral testimony) provide. See Chapter 15.

term of the written contract (the ship that was to transport the goods). This being so, oral testimony would have been needed to determine whether the parties had actually meant the same ship. If both had meant the same ship, then the contract would have been enforceable.

MISTAKES OF VALUE

If a mistake concerns the future market value or quality of the object of the contract, the mistake is one of *value,* and the contract normally can be enforced by either party. As with mistakes of fact, mistakes of value may be unilateral or bilateral. For example, suppose that Wong Sun plans to buy ten acres of land in Montana, believing that the land is worth $100,000. After he purchases the land, he learns that it is worth only $40,000. Wong Sun's unilateral mistake of value cannot be a basis for avoiding the contract.

Similarly, a bilateral mistake of value or quality will not serve as a basis for avoiding the contract. For example, suppose that Yu Chin, after seeing Bev Weiler's violin, buys it for $250. Although both parties know that it is very old, neither party believes that it is extremely valuable. An antique dealer later informs the parties, however, that old violins in good condition, such as this one, are rare and worth thousands of dollars. Although Weiler may claim that a mutual mistake has been made, the mistake is not a mistake of fact that warrants contract rescission. Both Chin and Weiler mistook the *value* of that particular violin. Therefore, the contract cannot be rescinded.

The reason that mistakes of value or quality have no legal significance is that value is variable. Depending on the time, place, and other circumstances, the same item may be worth considerably different amounts. When parties contract, their agreement establishes the value of the object of their transaction—for the moment. At the next moment, the value may change. Either party may be mistaken as to the shape that change will take, but a mistake as to value will almost never justify voiding a contract. Each party is considered to have assumed the risk that the value will change or prove to be different from what he or she thought. Without this rule, almost any party who did not receive what he or she considered a fair bargain could argue mistake.

Note that in some situations a mistake of value may occur because of a mistake of material fact. As pointed out previously, if the parties are mistaken as to some fact that is material to their transaction, the

transaction may be avoided. This rule applies when the fact affects the value of the subject matter of the parties' deal. For example, an early Michigan case, *Sherwood v. Walker,*[3] involved two farmers who entered into a contract for the purchase of a cow. The owner told the purchaser that the cow was barren (incapable of breeding and producing calves). Based on this belief, the parties negotiated a price several hundred dollars less than it would have been had the cow been capable of breeding. Just before delivery, the owner discovered the cow had conceived a calf, and he refused to deliver the much more valuable cow to the purchaser. In a split decision, the court held that "a barren cow is substantially a different creature than a breeding one," and the transaction was avoided.

SECTION 2

Fraudulent Misrepresentation

Although fraud is a tort (see Chapter 5), it also affects the genuineness of the innocent party's consent to the contract. Thus, the transaction is not voluntary in the sense of involving "mutual assent." When an innocent party is fraudulently induced to enter into a contract, the contract normally can be avoided because that party has not *voluntarily* consented to its terms.[4] Normally, the innocent party can either rescind the contract and be restored to his or her original position or enforce the contract and seek damages for any injuries resulting from the fraud.

The word *fraudulent* means many things in the law. Generally, fraudulent misrepresentation refers only to misrepresentation that is consciously false and is intended to mislead another. The perpetrator of the fraudulent misrepresentation knows or believes that the assertion is false or knows that he or she does not have a basis (stated or implied) for the assertion.[5]

---

3. 66 Mich. 568, 33 N.W. 919 (1887).
4. *Restatement (Second) of Contracts,* Sections 163 and 164.
5. *Restatement (Second) of Contracts,* Section 162.

What is at issue is whether the defendant believed that the plaintiff was substantially certain to be misled as a result of the misrepresentation. Dantzler, for example, makes a statement to the ABC Credit Rating Company about his financial condition that he knows is untrue. Dantzler realizes that ABC will publish this information for its subscribers. Marchetti, a subscriber, receives the published information. Relying on that information, Marchetti is induced to make a contract to lend money to Dantzler. Dantzler's statement is a fraudulent misrepresentation, and the contract is voidable by Marchetti.

Typically, fraudulent misrepresentation consists of the following elements:

1. A misrepresentation of a material fact must occur.
2. There must be an intent to deceive.
3. The innocent party must justifiably rely on the misrepresentation.

To collect damages, a party must also have been injured. To obtain rescission of a contract, or to defend against the enforcement of a contract on the basis of fraudulent misrepresentation, in most states a party need not have suffered an injury.

MISREPRESENTATION HAS OCCURRED

The first element of proving fraud is to show that misrepresentation of a material fact has occurred. This misrepresentation can occur by words or actions. For example, the statement "This sculpture was created by Michelangelo" is an express misrepresentation of fact if the statue was sculpted by another artist. The misrepresentation as to the identity of the artist would certainly be a material fact in the formation of a contract.

Representations of future facts (predictions) and statements of opinion are generally not subject to claims of fraud. Every person is expected to exercise care and judgment when entering into contracts, and the law will not come to the aid of one who simply makes an unwise bargain. Statements such as "This land will be worth twice as much next year" or "This car will last for years and years," for example, are statements of opinion, not fact. Contracting parties should recognize them as such and not rely on them. An opinion is usually subject to contrary or conflicting views; a fact is objective and verifiable. A seller of goods, then, is allowed to use *puffery* to sell his or her wares without liability for fraud.

In certain cases, however, particularly when a naïve purchaser relies on a so-called expert's opinion, the innocent party may be entitled to rescission or reformation. (*Reformation* is an equitable remedy granted by a court in which the terms of a contract are altered to reflect the true intentions of the parties—see Chapter 18.) The issue in the following case was whether the statements made by instructors at a dancing school to one of the school's dance students qualified as statements of opinion or statements of fact.

CASE 14.2   Vokes v. Arthur Murray, Inc.

District Court of Appeal of Florida, Second District, 1968.
212 So.2d 906.

COMPANY PROFILE   *Arthur Murray, Inc. (http://www.arthurmurray.com), began teaching people how to dance in 1919. At the time, dancing was becoming increasingly popular among young people, in part because so many adults were shocked by the new "jazz dancing." Across America, young people wanted to learn the new steps—the turkey trot, the fox trot, the kangaroo dip, the chicken scratch, the bunny hug, the grizzly bear, and others. By the 1930s, Murray's instructors were giving lessons on cruise ships, in tourist hotels, and to the employees of New York stores during the employees' lunch breaks. In 1937, Murray popularized an African American dance known as the Big Apple and, as an offshoot of this success, founded the Arthur Murray Studios, a chain of franchised dance schools. During the 1950s, Murray sponsored a television show—The Arthur Murray Party—to attract students to the schools. Murray retired in 1964, estimating that he had taught more than twenty million people how to dance.*

BACKGROUND AND FACTS   *Audrey E. Vokes, a widow without family, wished to become "an accomplished dancer" and to find "a new interest in life." In 1961, she was invited to attend a "dance party" at J. P. Davenport's "School of Dancing," an Arthur Murray, Inc., franchise. Vokes went to the school and received elaborate praise from her instructor for her grace, poise, and potential as "an excellent dancer." The instructor sold her* *eight half-hour dance lessons for $14.50 each, to be utilized within one calendar month. Subsequently, over a period of less than sixteen months, Vokes bought a total of fourteen dance courses, which amounted to 2,302 hours of dancing lessons, for a total cash outlay of $31,090.45, all at Davenport's school. When it became clear to Vokes that she did not, in fact, have the potential to be an excellent dancer, she filed a suit against the school, alleging fraudulent misrepresentation. When the trial court dismissed her complaint, she appealed.*

IN THE LANGUAGE OF THE COURT

PIERCE, Judge.

*   *   *   *

[The dance contracts] were procured by defendant Davenport and Arthur Murray, Inc., by false representations to her that she was improving in her dancing ability, that she had excellent potential, that she was responding to instructions in dancing grace, and that they were developing her into a beautiful dancer, whereas in truth and in fact she did not develop in her dancing ability, she had no "dance aptitude," and in fact had difficulty in "hearing the musical beat."   *   *   *

*   *   *   *

It is true that generally a misrepresentation, to be actionable, must be one of fact rather than of opinion. *   *   * A statement of a party having *   *   * superior knowledge may be regarded as a statement of fact although it would be considered as opinion if the parties were dealing on equal terms.

It could be reasonably supposed here that defendants had superior knowledge as to whether plaintiff had "dance potential" and as to whether she was noticeably improving in the art of terpsichore [dancing]. And it would be a reasonable inference from the undenied averments [assertions] of the complaint that the flowery eulogiums [praises] heaped upon her by defendants *   *   * proceeded as much or more from the urge to "ring the cash register" as from any honest or realistic appraisal of her dancing prowess or a factual representation of her progress.

*   *   *   *

*   *   * [W]hat is plainly injurious to good faith ought to be considered as a fraud sufficient to impeach a contract, and *   *   * an improvident agreement may be avoided because of surprise, or mistake, *want of freedom, undue influence, the suggestion of falsehood, or the suppression of truth.* [Emphasis added.]

DECISION AND REMEDY

Vokes's complaint was reinstated, and the case was returned to the trial court to allow Vokes to prove her case.

Misrepresentation by Conduct. Misrepresentation can also take place through the conduct of a party, such as concealment. Concealment involves preventing the other party from learning of a material fact.[6] Suppose, for example, that Rakas contracts to buy a new car from Bustamonte, a dealer in new automobiles. The car has been used as a demonstration model for prospective customers to test-drive, but Bustamonte has turned back the odometer. Rakas cannot tell from the odometer reading that the car has been driven nearly five hundred miles, and Bustamonte does not tell Rakas the distance the car has actually been driven. The concealment constitutes fraud because of Bustamonte's conduct.

Misrepresentation of Law. Misrepresentation of law does not *ordinarily* entitle a party to relief from a contract. For example, Camara has a parcel of property that she is trying to sell to Pye. Camara knows that a local ordinance prohibits building anything higher than three stories on the property. Nonetheless, she tells Pye, "You can build a condominium fifty stories high if you want to." Pye buys the land and later discovers that Camara's statement is false. Normally, Pye cannot avoid the contract, because at common law people are assumed to know state and local ordiances.

---

6. *Restatement (Second) of Contracts,* Section 160.

Additionally, a layperson should not rely on a statement made by a nonlawyer about a point of law.

Exceptions to this rule occur, however, when the misrepresenting party is in a profession that is known to require greater knowledge of the law than the average citizen possesses. The courts are recognizing an increasing number of such professions. For example, the courts recognize that real estate brokers are expected by their clients to know the law governing real estate sales, land use, and so on. If Camara, in the preceding example, were a lawyer or a real estate broker, her misrepresentation of the area's zoning status would probably constitute fraud.[7]

Misrepresentation by Silence. Ordinarily, neither party to a contract has a duty to come forward and disclose facts. Therefore, a contract cannot be set aside because certain pertinent information is not volunteered. For example, suppose you have an accident that requires extensive body work on one side of your car. After the repair, the car's appearance and operation are the same as they were before the accident. One year later you decide to sell your car. Do you have a duty to volunteer the information about the accident to the seller? The answer is no. In this case, silence does not constitute misrepresentation. In contrast, if the purchaser asks you if the car has had extensive body work and you lie, you have committed a fraudulent misrepresentation.

Some exceptions to this general rule exist. Generally, if a *serious* defect or a *serious* potential problem is known to the seller but could not reasonably be suspected by the buyer, the seller may have a duty to speak. For example, if a city fails to disclose to bidders subsoil conditions that will cause great expense in constructing a sewer, the city is guilty of fraud.[8] Similarly, if the manufacturer of a mechanical heart valve fails to disclose to a recipient the serious risks attending the use of the valve, of which the manufacturer has knowledge, the recipient has a cause of action for fraud.[9] Other exceptions involve duties imposed on parties involved in certain relationships. An

fiduciary

attorney, for example, has a duty to disclose material facts to a client. Other such relationships include those between physicians and their patients, partners in a partnership, directors of corporations and shareholders, and guardians and wards.[10]

Statutes provide still other exceptions to the general rule of nondisclosure. The Truth-in-Lending Act, for example, requires disclosure of certain facts (see Chapter 44). Statutes may even specify the typeface size to be used in the document providing the information.

INTENT TO DECEIVE

The second element of fraud is knowledge on the part of the misrepresenting party that facts have been falsely represented. This element, normally called *scienter*,[11] or "guilty knowledge," signifies that there was an *intent to deceive*. *Scienter* clearly exists if a party knows a fact is not as stated. *Scienter* also exists if a party makes a statement that he or she believes not to be true or makes a statement recklessly, without regard to whether it is true or false. Finally, this element is met if a party says or implies that a statement is made on some basis such as personal knowledge or personal investigation when it is not.

For example, assume that Meese, a securities broker, offers to sell BIM stock to Packer. Meese assures Packer that BIM shares are blue-chip securities—that is, they are stable, are limited in risk, and yield a high return on investment over time. Meese, however, knows nothing about the quality of BIM stock and does not believe the truth of what he is saying. Meese's statement is a misrepresentation because Meese does not believe the truth of what he has told Packer and because he knows that he does not have any basis for making such a statement. Therefore, if Packer is induced by Meese's intentional misrepresentation of a material fact to enter into a contract to buy the stock, normally he can avoid his obligations under the contract.

In many cases involving a seller's misrepresentation, courts have held that proving fault is unnecessary. That is, a buyer need prove only that the seller's representation was false, without regard to the seller's state of mind. In those cases—often involving sales of land or stock—the courts reason that it is the seller's duty to know the truth of what he or she says.

---

7. *Restatement (Second) of Contracts*, Section 170.
8. *City of Salinas v. Souza & McCue Construction Co.*, 66 Cal.2d 217, 424 P.2d 921, 57 Cal.Rptr. 337 (1967). Normally, the seller must disclose only "latent" defects—that is, defects that would not be readily discovered even by an expert. Thus, termites in a house would not be a latent defect, because an expert could normally discover their presence.
9. *Khan v. Shiley, Inc.*, 217 Cal.App.3d 848, 266 Cal.Rptr. 106 (1990).

10. *Restatement (Second) of Contracts*, Sections 161 and 173.
11. Pronounced sy-*en*-ter.

3 RELIANCE ON THE MISREPRESENTATION

The third element of fraud is reasonably *justifiable reliance* on the misrepresentation of fact. The deceived party must have a justifiable reason for relying on the misrepresentation, and the misrepresentation must be an important factor (but not necessarily the sole factor) in inducing that party to enter into the contract.

Reliance is not justified if the innocent party knows the true facts or relies on obviously extravagant statements. Suppose a used-car dealer tells you, "This old Cadillac will get fifty miles to the gallon." You will not normally be justified in relying on the statement. Or suppose that Kovich, a bank director, induces Mallory, a co-director, to sign a guaranty that the bank's assets will satisfy its liabilities, stating, "We have plenty of assets to satisfy our creditors." If Mallory knows the true facts, he will not be justified

in relying on Kovich's statement. If, however, Mallory does not know the true facts *and has no way of finding them out,* he normally will be justified in relying on the statement.

The same rule applies to defects in property sold. If the defects are of the kind that would be obvious on inspection, the buyer cannot justifiably rely on the seller's representations. If the defects are hidden or latent (that is, not apparent on the surface), the buyer is justified in relying on the seller's statements.

Is a job applicant justified in relying on his or her prospective employer's glowing statements about the future of the employer's business? Would it make any difference if an offered position were "at will"—that is, if the job could be terminated by either employee or employer at any time for any reason? Those were the questions in the following case.

CASE 14.3   Meade v. Cedarapids, Inc.

United States
Court of Appeals,
Ninth Circuit, 1999.
164 F.3d 1218.
http://www.ca9.
uscourts.gov[a]

BACKGROUND AND FACTS   *William Meade, Leland Stewart, Doug Vierkant, and David Girard applied for, and were offered, jobs at the El-Jay Division of Cedarapids, Inc., in Eugene, Oregon. During the interviews, each applicant asked about El-Jay's future. They were told, among other things, that El-Jay was a stable company with few down-sizings and layoffs, sales were up and were expected to increase, and production was expanding. Cedarapids management had already planned to close El-Jay, however. Each applicant signed an at-will employment agreement. To take the job at El-Jay, each new employee either quit his present job or passed up other employment opportunities. Each employee and his family then moved to Eugene. When El-Jay closed soon after they started their new jobs, Meade and the others filed a suit in a federal district court against Cedarapids, alleging, in part, fraudulent misrepresentation, based on the statements made to them during their job interviews. The court granted a summary judgment in favor of Cedarapids. The plaintiffs appealed to the U.S. Court of Appeals for the Ninth Circuit.*

**IN THE LANGUAGE
OF THE COURT**

EZRA, * * * Judge:
    *   *   *   *

The district court held that Plaintiffs were not justified in relying on representations and omissions made during their pre-employment negotiations, as a matter of law, because Plaintiffs each signed an at-will employment agreement. That Plaintiffs' employment with Defendants was at-will does not defeat their justified reliance on Defendants' representations about El-Jay. Even in the presence of language stating "no promises about employment have been made," an action for fraud in the inducement of a contract is possible. The representation Plaintiffs relied upon in this case is that El-Jay was growing and expanding. Plaintiffs were not relying on representations as to the duration of their employment. Plaintiffs accepted at-will employment, but they accepted at-will employment with a company that represented its Eugene facility as growing while failing to disclose and/or concealing that it was closing.

---

a. Click on the "OPINIONS" oval. From that page, click on the "CLICK HERE: GO TO OPINIONS" box. On the next page, click on the "1999" icon, and when the menu opens, click on "January." Scroll down to the case name and click on it to access the case.

Furthermore, Plaintiffs contend that their injuries were suffered as a result of the fraudulent inducement to enter employment, not the premature termination of that employment. The district court apparently treated the claims as breach of contract claims rather than claims of fraudulent inducement to form a contract.

Finally, Plaintiffs maintain that allowing at-will employment to defeat Plaintiffs' reliance would effectively allow employers to make any representations to prospective employees and then not fulfill those representations once employment began. We agree. Although Plaintiffs had no reasonable expectations for employment of any particular duration, they reasonably relied on statements as to the company's future growth, particularly when given in response to Plaintiffs' concerns. If Plaintiffs can prove Defendants' representations were knowingly or recklessly false, then a reasonable trier of fact could find the requisite elements of the tort of fraudulent misrepresentation.

DECISION AND REMEDY *The U.S. Court of Appeals for the Ninth Circuit reversed the lower court's grant of summary judgment in favor of the defendants on the claim of fraudulent misrepresentation and remanded the case for further proceedings. An employer may be held liable for misrepresenting its future business plans to prospective employees.*

4 INJURY TO THE INNOCENT PARTY

Most courts do not require a showing of injury when the action is to *rescind* (cancel) the contract. These courts hold that because rescission returns the parties to the positions they held before the contract was made, a showing of injury to the innocent party is unnecessary.[12]

For a person to recover damages caused by fraud, proof of an injury is universally required. The measure of damages is ordinarily equal to the property's value had it been delivered as represented, less the actual price paid for the property. In actions based on fraud, courts often award *punitive damages*, or *exemplary damages*, which are granted to a plaintiff over and above the proved, actual compensation for the loss. As discussed in Chapter 5, punitive damages are based on the public-policy consideration of punishing the defendant or setting an example to deter similar wrongdoing by others.

SECTION 3

Nonfraudulent Misrepresentation

If a plaintiff seeks to rescind a contract because of *fraudulent* misrepresentation, the plaintiff must prove that the defendant had the intent to deceive.

Most courts also allow rescission in cases involving *nonfraudulent* misrepresentation—that is, innocent or negligent misrepresentation—if all of the other elements of misrepresentation exist.

INNOCENT MISREPRESENTATION

If a person makes a statement that he or she believes to be true but that actually misrepresents material facts, the person is guilty only of an **innocent misrepresentation,** not of fraud. If an innocent misrepresentation occurs, the aggrieved party can rescind the contract but usually cannot seek damages. For example, Parris tells Roberta that a tract contains 250 acres. Parris is mistaken—the tract contains only 215 acres—but Parris does not know that. Roberta is induced by the statement to make a contract to buy the land. Even though the misrepresentation is innocent, Roberta can avoid the contract if the misrepresentation is material.

NEGLIGENT MISREPRESENTATION

Sometimes a party will make a misrepresentation through carelessness, believing the statement is true. This misrepresentation is negligent if he or she fails to exercise reasonable care in uncovering or disclosing the facts or does not use the skill and competence that his or her business or profession requires. For example, an operator of a weight scale certifies the weight of Sneed's commodity, even though the scale's accu-

12. See, for example, *Kaufman v. Jaffe*, 244 App.Div. 344, 279 N.Y.S. 392 (1935).

racy has not been checked in more than a year. In virtually all states, such **negligent misrepresentation** is equal to *scienter*, or to knowingly making a misrepresentation. In effect, negligent misrepresentation is treated as fraudulent misrepresentation, even though the misrepresentation was not purposeful. In negligent misrepresentation, culpable ignorance of the truth supplies the intention to mislead, even if the defendant can claim, "I didn't know."

SECTION 4

Undue Influence

Undue influence arises from special kinds of relationships in which one party can greatly influence another party, thus overcoming that party's free will. Minors and elderly people, for example, are often under the influence of guardians. If the guardian induces a young or elderly ward to enter into a contract that benefits the guardian, undue influence may have been exerted. Undue influence can arise from a number of confidential or fiduciary relationships:[13] attorney-client, physician-patient, guardian-ward, parent-child, husband-wife, or trustee-beneficiary. The essential feature of undue influence is that the party being taken advantage of does not, in reality, exercise free will in entering into a contract. A contract entered into under excessive or undue influence lacks genuine assent and is therefore voidable.[14]

To determine whether undue influence has been exerted, a court must ask, "To what extent was the transaction induced by domination of the mind or emotions of the person in question?" It follows, then, that the mental state of the person in question will often show to what extent the persuasion from the outside influence was "unfair."

When a contract enriches a party at the expense of another who is in a relationship of trust and confidence with, or who is dominated by, the enriched party, the court will often presume that the contract was made under undue influence. For example, if a person challenges a contract made by his or her guardian, the presumption will normally be that the guardian has taken advantage of the ward. To rebut (refute) this presumption successfully, the guardian has to show that full disclosure was made to the ward,

that consideration was adequate, and that the ward received, if available, independent and competent advice before completing the transaction.

In a relationship of trust and confidence, such as between an attorney and a client, the dominant party (the attorney) is held to extreme or utmost good faith in dealing with the other party. Suppose that a long-time attorney for an elderly man induces him to sign a contract for the sale of some of his assets to a friend of the attorney at below-market prices. It is presumed that the attorney has not upheld good faith in dealing with the man. Unless this presumption can be rebutted, the contract will be voidable.

SECTION 5

Duress

Assent to the terms of a contract is not genuine if one of the parties is *forced* into the agreement. Recall from Chapter 8 that forcing a party to do something, including entering into a contract, through fear created by threats is legally defined as *duress*. In addition, blackmail or extortion to induce consent to a contract constitutes duress. Duress is both a defense to the enforcement of a contract and a ground for the rescission of a contract.

Generally, the threatened act must be wrongful or illegal. Threatening to exercise a legal right is not ordinarily illegal and usually does not constitute duress. Suppose that Donovan injures Jaworski in an auto accident. The police are not called. Donovan has no automobile insurance, but she has substantial assets. Jaworski is willing to settle the potential claim out of court for $3,000. Donovan refuses. After much arguing, Jaworski loses her patience and says, "If you don't pay me $3,000 right now, I'm going to sue you for $35,000." Donovan is frightened and gives Jaworski a check for $3,000. Later in the day, she stops payment on the check. Jaworski comes back to sue her for the $3,000. Although Donovan argues that she was the victim of duress, the threat of a civil suit is normally not considered duress.

Economic need is generally not sufficient to constitute duress, even when one party exacts a very high price for an item that the other party needs. If the party exacting the price also creates the need, however, *economic duress* may be found. The Internal Revenue Service, for example, assessed a large tax and penalty against Weller. Weller retained Eyman, the accountant who had filed the tax returns on

---

13. A fiduciary relationship is one involving a high degree of trust and confidence—see Chapter 31.
14. *Restatement (Second) of Contracts*, Section 177.

which the assessment was based, to resist the assessment. Two days before the deadline for filing a reply with the Internal Revenue Service, Eyman declined to represent Weller unless he signed a very high contingency-fee agreement for his services. The agreement was unenforceable.[15] Although Eyman had threatened only to withdraw his services, something that he was legally entitled to do, he was responsible for delaying the withdrawal until the last days. Because it would have been impossible at that late date to obtain adequate representation elsewhere, Weller was forced either to sign the contract or to lose his right to challenge the IRS assessment.

SECTION 6

Adhesion Contracts and Unconscionability

Questions concerning genuineness of assent may arise when the terms of a contract are dictated by a party with overwhelming bargaining power and the signer must agree to those terms or go without the commodity or service in question. As mentioned in Chapter 13, such contracts are often referred to as *adhesion contracts*. An **adhesion contract** is written *exclusively* by one party (the dominant party, usually the seller or the creditor) and presented to the other party (the adhering party, usually the buyer or the

---

15. *Thompson Crane & Trucking Co. v. Eyman*, 123 Cal.App.2d 904, 267 P.2d 1043 (1954).

borrower) on a take-it-or-leave-it basis. In other words, the adhering party has no opportunity to negotiate the terms of the contract.

Standard-form contracts often contain fine-print provisions that shift a risk naturally borne by one party to the other. Such contracts are used by a variety of businesses and include life insurance policies, residential leases, loan agreements, and employment agency contracts. To avoid enforcement of the contract or of a particular clause, the aggrieved party must show that the parties had substantially unequal bargaining positions and that enforcement would be manifestly unfair or oppressive. If the required showing is made, the contract or particular term is deemed *unconscionable* and not enforced. Technically, unconscionability under Section 2–302 of the Uniform Commercial Code (UCC) applies only to contracts for the sale of goods. Many courts, however, have broadened the concept and applied it in other situations.

Although unconscionability was discussed in Chapter 13, it is important to note here that the great degree of discretion permitted a court to invalidate or strike down a contract or clause as being unconscionable has met with resistance. As a result, some states have not adopted Section 2–302 of the UCC. In those states, the legislature and the courts prefer to rely on traditional notions of fraud, undue influence, and duress. On the one hand, this gives certainty to contractual relationships, because parties know they will be held to the exact terms of their contracts. On the other hand, public policy does require that there be some limit on the power of individuals and businesses to dictate the terms of contracts.

CONCEPT SUMMARY 14.1   **GENUINENESS OF ASSENT**

PROBLEMS OF ASSENT	RULE
Mistakes	1. *Unilateral*—Generally, the mistaken party is bound by the contract, *unless* (1) the other party knows or should have known of the mistake or (2) in some states, the mistake is an inadvertent mathematical error in addition, subtraction, and so on, that is committed without gross negligence. 2. *Bilateral (mutual)*—If both parties are mistaken about a material fact, such as the identity of the subject matter, either party can avoid the contract. If the mistake relates to the value or quality of the subject matter, either party can enforce the contract.

CONCEPT SUMMARY 14.1

GENUINENESS OF ASSENT (*continued*)

PROBLEMS OF ASSENT	RULE
Fraudulent Misrepresentation	Three elements are necessary to establish fraudulent misrepresentation: 1. A misrepresentation of a material fact has occurred. 2. There exists an intent to deceive. 3. The innocent party has justifiably relied on the misrepresentation.
Nonfraudulent Misrepresentation	1. *Innocent misrepresentation*—Occurs when a person makes a statement that he or she believes to be true but that actually misrepresents material facts. The aggrieved party can rescind the contract but usually cannot seek damages. 2. *Negligent misrepresentation*—Occurs when a person makes an untrue statement but, through carelessness, believes the statement to be true. Negligent misrepresentation has the same legal effect as fraudulent misrepresentation in virtually all states.
Undue Influence/ Duress	1. *Undue influence*—Arises from special relationships, such as fiduciary relationships, in which one party's free will has been overcome by the undue influence of another. Usually, the contract is avoidable. 2. *Duress*—Defined as forcing a party to enter into a contract under fear of threat—for example, the threat of violence or economic pressure. The party forced to enter into the contract can rescind the contract.
Unconscionability	Concerned with one-sided bargains in which one party has substantially superior bargaining power and can dictate the terms of a contract. Unconscionability typically occurs as a result of the following: 1. "Standard-form" contracts in which a fine-print provision purports to shift a risk normally borne by one party to the other (for example, a liability disclaimer). 2. "Take-it-or-leave-it" adhesion contracts in which the buyer has no choice but to agree to the seller's dictated terms if the buyer is to procure certain goods or services.

TERMS AND CONCEPTS TO REVIEW

QUESTIONS AND CASE PROBLEMS

14–1. ASSENT. Juan is an elderly man who lives with his nephew, Samuel. Juan is totally dependent on Samuel's support. Samuel tells Juan that unless he transfers a tract of land he owns to Samuel for a price 15 percent below market value, Samuel will no longer support and take care of him. Juan enters into the contract. Discuss fully whether Juan can set aside this contract.

14–2. ASSENT. Grano owns a forty-room motel on Highway 100. Tanner is interested in purchasing the motel. During the course of negotiations, Grano tells Tanner that the motel netted $30,000 last year and that it will net at least $45,000 next year. The motel books, which Grano turns over to Tanner before the purchase, clearly show that Grano's motel netted only $15,000 last year. Also, Grano fails to tell Tanner that a bypass to Highway 100 is being planned that will redirect most traffic away from the front of the motel. Tanner purchases the motel. During the first year under Tanner's operation, the motel nets only $18,000. It is at this time that Tanner learns of the previous low profitability of the motel and the planned bypass. Tanner wants his money back from Grano. Discuss fully Tanner's probable success in getting his money back.

14–3. ASSENT. Discuss whether either of the following contracts will be unenforceable on the ground that genuineness of assent is lacking.

(a) Simmons finds a stone in his pasture that he believes to be quartz. Jenson, who also believes that the stone is quartz, contracts to purchase it for $10. Just before delivery, the stone is discovered to be a diamond worth $1,000.

(b) Jacoby's barn is burned to the ground. He accuses Goldman's son of arson and threatens to bring a criminal action unless Goldman agrees to pay him $5,000. Goldman agrees to pay.

14–4. FRAUDULENT MISREPRESENTATION. Lund offered to sell Steck his car and told Steck that the car had been driven only 25,000 miles and had never been in an accident. Steck hired Carvallo, a mechanic, to appraise the condition of the car, and Carvallo said that the car probably had at least 50,000 miles on it and probably had been in an accident. In spite of this information, Steck still thought the car would be a good buy for the price, so he purchased it. Later, when the car developed numerous mechanical problems, Steck sought to rescind the contract on the basis of Lund's fraudulent misrepresentation of the auto's condition. Will Steck be able to rescind his contract? Explain.

14–5. MISTAKE. Steven Lanci was involved in an automobile accident with an uninsured motorist. Lanci was insured with Metropolitan Insurance Co., although he did not have a copy of the insurance policy. Lanci and Metropolitan entered settlement negotiations, during which Lanci told Metropolitan that he did not have a copy of his policy. Ultimately, Lanci agreed to settle all claims for $15,000, noting in a letter to Metropolitan that $15,000 was the "sum you have represented to be the . . . policy limits applicable to this claim." After signing a release, Lanci learned that the policy limits were actually $250,000, and he refused to accept the settlement proceeds. When Metropolitan sued to enforce the settlement agreement, Lanci argued that the release had been signed as the result of a mistake and therefore was unenforceable. Should the court enforce the contract? Explain. [*Lanci v. Metropolitan Insurance Co.*, 388 Pa.Super. 1, 564 A.2d 972 (1989)]

14–6. FRAUDULENT MISREPRESENTATION. Nosrat, a citizen of Iran, owned a hardware store with his brother-in-law, Edwin. Edwin induced Nosrat to sign a promissory note for $11,400, payable to a third party, telling Nosrat that the document was a credit application for the hardware store. Although Nosrat could read and write English, he failed to read the note or to notice that the document was clearly entitled "PROMISSORY NOTE (SECURED) and Security Agreement." The money received from the third party in exchange for the note was spent by Edwin and others. When the third party sued for payment, Nosrat sought to void the note on the basis of Edwin's fraudulent inducement. Will Nosrat succeed in his attempt? Discuss. [*Waldrep v. Nosrat*, 426 So.2d 822 (Ala. 1983)]

14–7. ASSENT. Linda Lorenzo bought Lurlene Noel's home in 1988 without having it inspected. The basement started leaking in 1989. In 1991, Lorenzo had the paneling removed from the basement walls and discovered that the walls were bowed inward and cracked. Lorenzo then had a civil engineer inspect the basement walls, and he found that the cracks had been caulked and painted over before the paneling was installed. He concluded that the "wall failure" had existed "for at least thirty years" and that the basement walls were "structurally unsound." Does Lorenzo have a cause of action against Noel? If so, on what ground? Discuss. [*Lorenzo v. Noel*, 206 Mich.App. 682, 522 N.W.2d 724 (1994)]

14–8. MISREPRESENTATION. W. B. McConkey owned commercial property, including a building that, as McConkey knew, had experienced flooding problems for years. McConkey painted the building, replaced damaged carpeting, and sold the property to M&D, Inc., on an "as is" basis. M&D did not ask whether there were flooding problems, and McConkey said nothing about them. M&D leased the property to Donmar, Inc., to operate a pet supplies store. Two months after the store opened, the building flooded following heavy rain. M&D and Donmar filed a suit in a Michigan state court against McConkey and others, claiming in part that McConkey had committed misrepresentation by silence. Based on this claim, will the court hold McConkey liable? Why or why not? [*M&D, Inc. v. McConkey*, 585 N.W.2d 33 (Mich.App. 1998)]

14–9. FRAUDULENT MISREPRESENTATION. In 1987, United Parcel Service Co. and United Parcel Service of America, Inc. (together known as "UPS"), decided to change its parcel delivery business from relying on contract carriers to establishing its own airline. During the transition, which took sixteen months, UPS hired 811 pilots. At the time, UPS expressed a desire to hire pilots who remained throughout that period with its contract carriers, which included Orion Air. A UPS representative met with more than fifty Orion pilots and made promises of future employment. John Rickert, a captain with Orion, was one of the pilots. Orion ceased operation after the UPS transition, and UPS did not hire Rickert, who obtained employment about six months later as a second officer with American Airlines, but at a lower salary. Rickert filed a suit in a Kentucky state court against UPS, claiming, in part, fraud based on the promises made by the UPS representative. UPS filed a motion for a directed verdict. What are the elements for a cause of action based on fraudulent misrepresentation? In whose favor should the court rule in this case, and why? [*United Parcel Service, Inc. v. Rickert*, 996 S.W.2d 464 (Ky. 1999)]

14–10. IN YOUR COURT

When Michigan Health Care Corp. in Detroit offered Karen Clement-Rowe a position as a nurse, she accepted, sold her home, and moved to Detroit. One month later, in response to a financial crisis, Michigan Health terminated 150 employees, including Clement-Rowe. She filed a suit in a Michigan state court against the employer, claiming in part misrepresentation by silence. She asserted that Michigan Health had a duty to tell her of its financial condition but that the company had told her nothing—even though she had asked—and had intended to induce her to rely on the nondisclosure in accepting the job. Michigan Health responded that it had not been aware of the financial crisis until after Clement-Rowe had been hired. Assume that you are the judge in the Michigan trial court hearing this case and answer the following questions:

(a) Suppose that evidence submitted during the trial shows that Michigan Health *was aware* of its financial difficulties at the time it hired Clement-Rowe. Will you rule that, in this situation, misrepresentation by silence had occurred? How would you justify your conclusion?

(b) Now suppose that evidence submitted during the trial shows that Michigan Health, as it claimed, *was not aware* of its financial difficulties at the time it hired Clement-Rowe. What would your decision be in this situation, and why?

LAW ON THE WEB

For updated links to resources available on the Web, as well as a variety of other materials, visit this text's Web site at http://wbl.westbuslaw.com.

For an article on fraudulent misrepresentation in the context of automobile sales, go to

http://www.carolina-auto.com/ncada/legal/fraud.html

To learn how the Australian government defines unconscionable conduct, go to

http://www.consumer.act.gov.au/CAB/publications/unconscionable.html

LEGAL RESEARCH EXERCISES ON THE WEB

Go to http://wbl.westbuslaw.com, the Web site that accompanies this text. Select "Internet Applications," and then click on "Chapter 14." There you will find the following Internet research exercise that you can perform to learn more about fraud and unconscionability:

Activity 14–1: Fraudulent Misrepresentation

CHAPTER 15

The Statute of Frauds

As discussed in Chapter 14, a contract that is otherwise valid may still be unenforceable if the parties have not genuinely assented to its terms. An otherwise valid contract may also be unenforceable for another reason—because it is not in the proper form. For example, certain types of contracts are required to be in writing. If a contract is required by law to be in writing and there is no written evidence of the contract, it may not be enforceable. In this chapter, we examine the kinds of contracts that require a writing under what is called the **Statute of Frauds.**

The chapter concludes with a discussion of the *parol evidence rule*, under which courts determine the admissibility at trial of evidence that is extraneous, or external, to written contracts. The parol evidence rule is not inherently related to the Statute of Frauds but is a rule that has general application in contract law. We cover these topics within one chapter primarily for reasons of convenience and space.

Prevention of Frauds and Perjuries." The act established that certain types of contracts, to be enforceable, had to be evidenced by a writing and signed by the party against whom enforcement was sought.

Today, almost every state has a statute, modeled after the English act, that stipulates what types of contracts must be in writing. Although the statutes vary slightly from state to state, all states require certain types of contracts to be in writing or evidenced by a written memorandum signed by the party against whom enforcement is sought, unless certain exceptions apply. (These exceptions will be discussed later in this chapter.) In this text, we refer to these statutes collectively as the Statute of Frauds. The actual name of the Statute of Frauds is misleading because it neither applies to fraud nor invalidates any type of contract. Rather, it denies *enforceability* to certain contracts that do not comply with its requirements.

SECTION 1

The Origins of the Statute of Frauds

At early common law, parties to a contract were not allowed to testify. This led to the practice of hiring third party witnesses. As early as the seventeenth century, the English recognized the many problems presented by this practice and enacted a statute to help deal with it. The statute, passed by the English Parliament in 1677, was known as "An Act for the

SECTION 2

Contracts That Fall within the Statute of Frauds

The following types of contracts are said to fall "within" or "under" the Statute of Frauds and therefore require a writing:

1. Contracts involving interests in land.
2. Contracts that cannot by their terms be performed within one year from the date of formation.

3. Collateral, or secondary, contracts, such as promises to answer for the debt or duty of another and promises by the administrator or executor of an estate to pay a debt of the estate personally—that is, out of his or her own pocket.
4. Promises made in consideration of marriage.
5. Under the Uniform Commercial Code (UCC), contracts for the sale of goods priced at $500 or more.

CONTRACTS INVOLVING INTERESTS IN LAND

A contract calling for the sale of land is not enforceable unless it is in writing or evidenced by a written memorandum. Land is real property and includes all physical objects that are permanently attached to the soil, such as buildings, fences, trees, and the soil itself. The Statute of Frauds operates as a *defense* to the enforcement of an oral contract for the sale of land. For example, if Sam contracts orally to sell Blackacre to Betty but later decides not to sell, under most circumstances Betty cannot enforce the contract. The Statute of Frauds also requires all contracts for the transfer of other interests in land, such as mortgages and leases (see Chapters 47 and 48), to be in writing, although most state statutes provide for the enforcement of short-term oral leases.

THE ONE-YEAR RULE

A contract that cannot, *by its own terms,* be performed within one year from the date it was formed must be in writing to be enforceable.[1] The one-year period begins

1. *Restatement (Second) of Contracts*, Section 130.

to run *the day after the contract is made*. Suppose that on June 1 an employer orally contracts to hire you immediately (June 1) for one year at $4,000 per month. This contract is not subject to the Statute of Frauds (and thus need not be in writing to be enforceable) because the one-year period to measure performance begins on June 2. In contrast, if the oral contract is formed on March 1 for one year's work that is to begin on June 1, the contract cannot be performed within one year and thus falls under the Statute of Frauds—that is, it must be in writing to be enforceable.

The test for determining whether an oral contract is enforceable under the one-year rule of the Statute of Frauds is not whether an agreement is *likely* to be performed within a year but whether performance is *possible* within one year. Even if performance takes place more than one year after the date of contract formation, an oral contract is binding as long as performance was possible in less than a year.

For example, suppose that Bankers Life orally contracts to loan $40,000 to Janet Lawrence "as long as Lawrence and Associates operates its financial consulting firm in Omaha, Nebraska." The contract is not within the Statute of Frauds—no writing is required—because Lawrence and Associates could go out of business in one year or less. In this event, the contract would be fully performed within one year.[2] Exhibit 15–1 on page 273 illustrates graphically the application of the one-year rule. In the following case, the question before the court was whether an oral contract for lifetime employment was enforceable.

2. See *Warner v. Texas & Pacific Railroad Co.*, 164 U.S. 418, 17 S.Ct. 147, 41 L.Ed. 195 (1896).

CASE 15.1 — McInerney v. Charter Golf, Inc.

Supreme Court of Illinois, 1997.
176 Ill.2d 482,
680 N.E.2d 1347,
223 Ill.Dec. 911.
http://www.state.il.us/court/supremes/80248.txt[a]

HISTORICAL AND SOCIAL SETTING   *The purpose of the English Statute of Frauds was to prohibit "many fraudulent practices, which are commonly endeavored to be upheld by perjury and subordination of perjury." The statutes of frauds in the United States seek to do the same by barring lawsuits based on nothing more than verbal statements. The one-year provision recognizes that with the passage of time evidence becomes stale and memories fade. This provision functions as an evidentiary safeguard. It protects not just the parties to a contract but also a court from charlatans, liars, and the problems of proof accompanying oral contracts.*

BACKGROUND AND FACTS   *Charter Golf, Inc., manufactures and sells golf apparel and supplies. Dennis McInerney had worked as a Charter sales representative for about*

a. This is a page within a Web site maintained by the state of Illinois that includes some of the recent "Opinions of the Illinois Supreme and Appellate Courts."

a year when he was offered a position with Hickey-Freeman, Inc., one of Charter's competitors. Jerry Montiel, Charter's president, urged McInerney to turn down the offer and promised to guarantee him a 10 percent commission "for the remainder of his life." Montiel also promised McInerney that he would be subject to discharge only for dishonesty or disability. McInerney accepted Montiel's offer. Three years later, Charter fired McInerney. He filed a suit in an Illinois state court against Charter, alleging breach of contract. Charter argued in part that Montiel's oral promises were not enforceable because they were not capable of being performed within one year. The trial court ruled in favor of Charter, and the state intermediate appellate court affirmed. McInerney appealed to the Supreme Court of Illinois.

IN THE LANGUAGE OF THE COURT

Justice *HEIPLE* delivered the opinion of the court:

*   *   *   *

*   *   * A "lifetime" employment contract is, in essence, a permanent employment contract. Inherently, it anticipates a relationship of long duration—certainly longer than one year. In the context of an employment-for-life contract, we believe that the better view is to treat the contract as one not to be performed within the space of one year from the making thereof. To hold otherwise would eviscerate [remove the essence from] the policy underlying the statute of frauds and would invite confusion, uncertainty and outright fraud. Accordingly, we hold that a writing is required for the fair enforcement of lifetime employment contracts.

*   *   *   *

In sum, though an employee's promise to forgo another job opportunity in exchange for a guarantee of lifetime employment is consideration to support the formation of a contract, the statute of frauds requires that contracts for lifetime employment be in writing.

DECISION AND REMEDY

The Supreme Court of Illinois affirmed the lower court's decision. The state supreme court held that an employer's promise of lifetime employment in exchange for an employee's promise to forgo a job opportunity needs to be in writing to satisfy the Statute of Frauds.

3 - COLLATERAL PROMISES

A **collateral promise**, or secondary promise, is one that is ancillary (subsidiary) to a principal transaction or primary contractual relationship. In other words, a collateral promise is one made by a third party to assume the debts or obligations of a primary party to a contract if that party does not perform. Any collateral promise of this nature falls under the Statute of Frauds and therefore must be in writing to be enforceable. To understand this concept, it is important to distinguish between primary and secondary promises and obligations.

Primary versus Secondary Obligations. Suppose that Bancroft forms an oral contract with Harmony's Floral Boutique to send his mother a dozen roses for Mother's Day. Bancroft's oral contract with Harmony's Floral Boutique provides that he will pay for the roses when he receives the bill for the flow-

ers. Bancroft is a direct party to this contract and has incurred a *primary* obligation under the contract. Because he is a party to the contract and has a primary obligation to Harmony's Floral Boutique, this contract does *not* fall under the Statute of Frauds and does not have to be in writing to be enforceable.

Now suppose that Bancroft's mother borrows $1,000 from the International Trust Company on a promissory note payable six months later. Bancroft promises the bank officer handling the loan that he will pay the $1,000 *only if his mother does not pay the loan on time.* Bancroft, in this situation, becomes what is known as a *guarantor* on the loan. That is, he is guaranteeing to the bank that he will pay back the loan if his mother fails to do so. This kind of collateral promise, in which the guarantor states that he or she will become responsible only if the primary party does not perform, must be in writing to be enforceable. Exhibit 15–2 illustrates graphically the concept of a collateral promise. (We will return to the concept of

EXHIBIT 15–1 THE ONE-YEAR RULE

Under the Statute of Frauds, contracts that by their terms are impossible to perform within one year from the date of contract formation must be in writing to be enforceable. Put another way, if it is at all possible to perform an oral contract within one year after the contract is made, the contract will fall outside the Statute of Frauds and be enforceable.

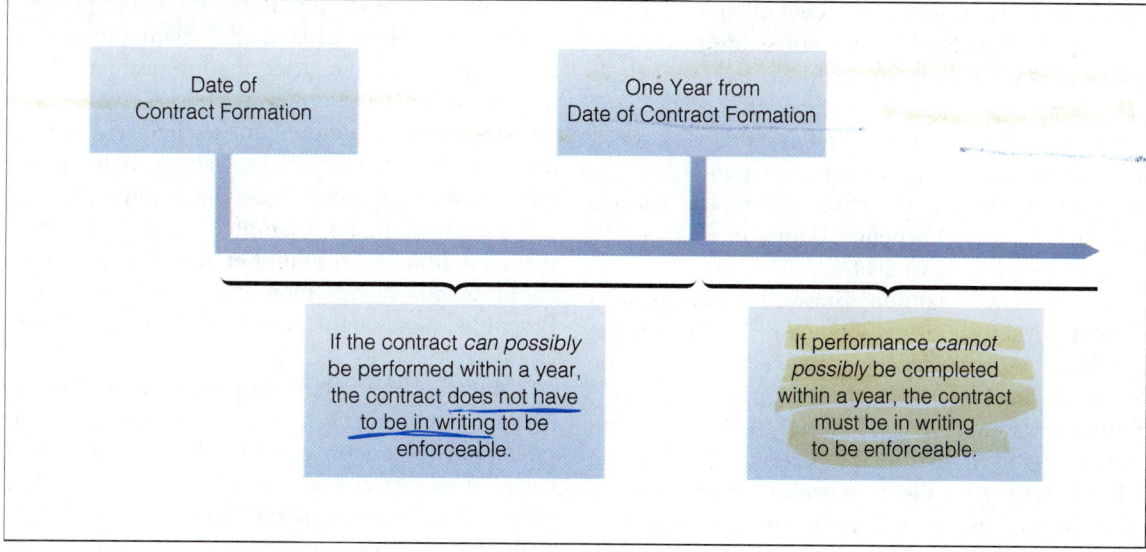

EXHIBIT 15–2 COLLATERAL PROMISES

A collateral (secondary) promise is one made by a third party (C, in this exhibit) to a creditor (B, in this exhibit) to pay the debt of another (A, in this exhibit), who is primarily obligated to pay the debt. Under the Statute of Frauds, collateral promises must be in writing to be enforceable.

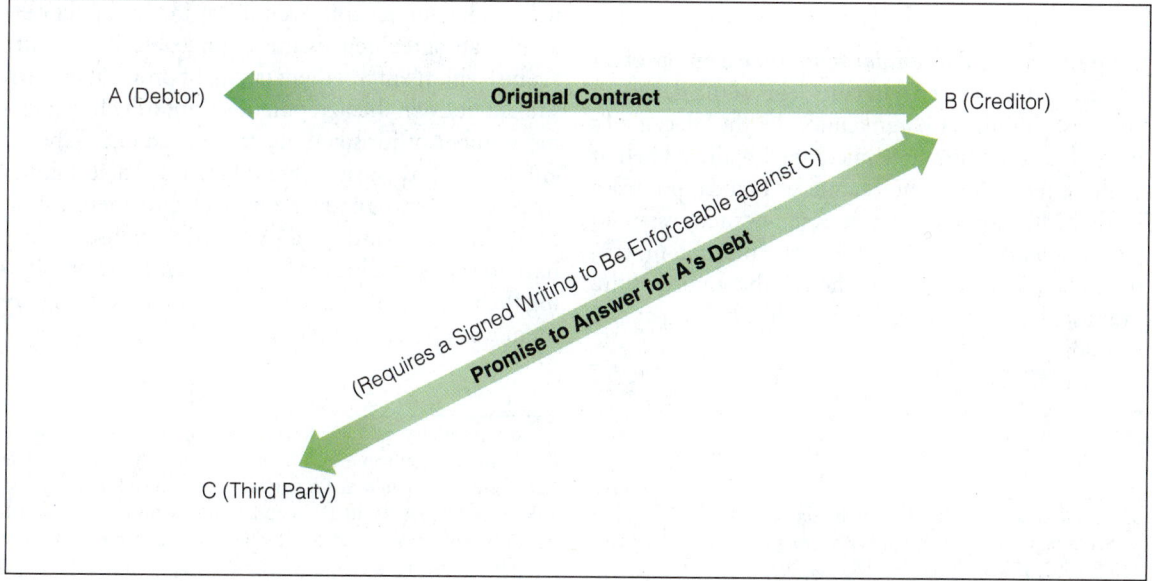

guaranty and the distinction between primary and secondary obligations in Chapter 29, in the context of creditors' rights.)

An Exception—The "Main Purpose Rule." An oral promise to answer for the debt of another is covered by the Statute of Frauds unless the guarantor's main purpose in accepting secondary liability is to secure a personal benefit. This type of contract need not be in writing.[3] The assumption is that a court can infer from the circumstances of a particular case whether the "leading objective" of the promisor was to secure a personal benefit and thus, in effect, to answer for his or her own debt.

Consider an example. Braswell contracts with Custom Manufacturing Company to have some machines custom-made for Braswell's factory. She promises Newform Materials Supply Company, Custom Manufacturing's supplier, that if Newform continues to deliver the materials to Custom Manufacturing for the manufacture of the custom-made machines, she will guarantee payment. This promise need not be in writing, even though the effect may be to pay the debt of another. This is because Braswell's main purpose in forming the contract is to secure a benefit for herself.[4]

Another typical application of the main purpose rule is the situation in which one creditor guarantees the debtor's debt to another creditor to forestall litigation. This allows the debtor to remain in business long enough to generate profits sufficient to pay both creditors.

Estate Debts. The administrator (or executor) of an estate has the duty of paying the debts of the deceased and distributing any remainder to the deceased's heirs. The administrator can contract orally on behalf of the estate. Under the Statute of Frauds, promises made by the administrator or executor of an estate to pay *personally* the debts of the estate must be in writing to be enforceable, even though the nature of the promise is to assume a primary obligation to pay the creditor.

4 ~ PROMISES MADE IN CONSIDERATION OF MARRIAGE

A unilateral promise to pay a sum of money or to give property in consideration of a promise to marry must be in writing. If Mr. Baumann promises to pay Joe Villard $10,000 if Villard promises to marry Baumann's daughter, the promise must be in writing. The same rule applies to **prenuptial agreements**—agreements made before marriage that define each partner's ownership rights in the other partner's property. A couple might make such an agreement if, for example, a prospective wife wished to limit the amount her prospective husband could obtain if the marriage ended in divorce. Prenuptial agreements must be in writing to be enforceable.[5]

Generally, courts tend to give more credence to prenuptial agreements that are accompanied by consideration. For example, assume that Maureen, who has little money, and Kaiser, who has a net worth of $300 million, plan to marry. Kaiser has several children, and he wants them to receive most of his wealth on his death. The couple forms a prenuptial agreement in which Kaiser promises to give Maureen $100,000 a year for the rest of her life should they divorce. Kaiser offers to give Maureen $200,000 if she consents to the agreement. If Maureen consents to the agreement and accepts the $200,000, very likely a court will hold this to be a valid prenuptial agreement should it ever be contested.

In some circumstances, a prenuptial agreement will not be enforceable even if it is in writing. For example, an agreement is not enforceable if the party against whom enforcement is sought proves that he or she did not sign the agreement voluntarily. In a growing number of jurisdictions, the advice of independent counsel is a significant factor in determining whether a party signed a prenuptial agreement voluntarily. In other words, if a prospective spouse did not have the advice of his or her own attorney before signing the agreement, that could indicate that the agreement was not signed voluntarily.

---

3. *Restatement (Second) of Contracts*, Section 116.
4. See *Kampman v. Pittsburgh Contracting and Engineering Co.*, 316 Pa. 502, 175 A. 396 (1934); UCC 2–201(3)(c).

5. To add certainty to the enforceability of prenuptial agreements, the National Conference of Commissioners on Uniform State Laws issued the Uniform Prenuptial Agreements Act (UPAA) in 1983. The act provides that prenuptial agreements must be in writing to be enforceable and that the agreements become effective when the parties marry.

CONTRACTS FOR THE SALE OF GOODS

The UCC generally requires a writing or memorandum for the sale of goods priced at $500 or more. A writing that will satisfy the UCC requirement need only state the quantity term; other terms agreed on can be omitted or even stated imprecisely in the writing, as long as they adequately reflect both parties' intentions. The contract will not be enforceable, however, for any quantity greater than that set forth in the writing. In addition, the writing must have been signed by the person to be charged—that is, by the person who refuses to perform or the one being sued. Beyond these two requirements, the writing need not designate the buyer or the seller, the terms of payment, or the price. Requirements of the Statute of Frauds under the UCC will be discussed in more detail in Chapter 19.

EXCEPTIONS TO THE APPLICABILITY OF THE STATUTE OF FRAUDS

Exceptions to the applicability of the Statute of Frauds are made in certain circumstances. We look here at these exceptions.

Partial Performance. In cases involving contracts relating to the transfer of interests in land, if the purchaser has paid part of the price, taken possession, and made permanent improvements to the property and the parties cannot be returned to their *status quo* before the contract was formed, a court may grant *specific performance* (performance of the contract according to its precise terms). Whether the courts will enforce an oral contract for an interest in land when partial performance has taken place is usually determined by the degree of injury that would be suffered if the court chose not to enforce the oral contract. Under the UCC an oral contract is enforceable to the extent that a seller accepts payment or a buyer accepts delivery of the goods (see Chapter 19 for a fuller discussion of this exception).[6]

Admissions. In some states, if a party against whom enforcement of an oral contract is sought "admits" in pleadings, testimony, or otherwise in court that a contract for sale was made, the contract will be enforceable.[7] Thus, if the president of Ashley Corporation admits under oath that an oral agreement was made

with Com Best, Inc., to sell certain business premises, the agreement will be enforceable in those states. A contract subject to the UCC will be enforceable, but only to the extent of the quantity admitted.[8]

Promissory Estoppel. In some states, an oral contract that would otherwise be unenforceable under the Statute of Frauds may be enforced under the doctrine of promissory estoppel, based on detrimental reliance. Recall from Chapter 12 that if a promisor makes a promise on which the promisee justifiably relies to his or her detriment, a court may *estop* (prevent) the promisor from denying that a contract exists. Section 139 of the *Restatement (Second) of Contracts* provides that in these circumstances, an oral promise can be enforceable notwithstanding the Statute of Frauds if the reliance was foreseeable to the person making the promise and if injustice can be avoided only by enforcing the promise.

Special Exceptions under the UCC. Special exceptions to the applicability of the Statute of Frauds apply to sales contracts. Oral contracts for customized goods may be enforced in certain circumstances. Another exception has to do with oral contracts *between merchants* that have been confirmed in writing. These exceptions and those mentioned above will be examined in greater detail in the discussion of the UCC provisions regarding the Statute of Frauds in Chapter 19.

SECTION 3

Sufficiency of the Writing

The Statute of Frauds and the UCC require either a written contract or a written memorandum evidencing an oral contract signed by the party against whom enforcement is sought, except when there is a legally recognized exception, such as partial performance. The signature need not be placed at the end of the document but can be anywhere in the writing. It can even be an initial rather than the full name. (A significant issue in today's business world has to do with how "signatures" can be created and verified on electronic contracts and other documents. For a discussion of this topic, see this chapter's *Emerging Trends in Technology* beginning on the next page.)

---

6. UCC 2–201(3)(c).
7. *Restatement (Second) of Contracts*, Section 133.

8. UCC 2–201(3)(b).

EMERGING TRENDS IN TECHNOLOGY

E-Signatures

Before the days when most people could write, they signed documents with an "X." Then came the handwritten signature, followed by typed signatures, printed signatures, and, most recently, digital signatures that are transmitted electronically. Throughout the evolution of signature technology, debates over what constitutes a valid signature have occurred, and with good reason: without some consensus on what constitutes a valid signature, little business or legal work could be accomplished. Generally, any written contract or other legally binding document requires the signatures of the parties involved. As discussed elsewhere in this chapter, contracts required to be in writing by the Statute of Frauds also must meet certain signature requirements.

E-SIGNATURE TECHNOLOGIES

Today, there are numerous technologies that allow electronic documents to be signed. The most prevalent e-signature technology is the "asymmetric cryptosystem," which creates a digital signature using two different (asymmetric) cryptographic "keys." In such a system, a person attaches a digital signature to a document using a private key, or code. The key has a publicly available counterpart. Anyone can use it with the appropriate software to verify that the digital signature was made using the private key. A legally recognized certification authority, or "cybernotary," issues the key pair, identifies the owner of the keys, and certifies the validity of the public key. The cybernotary also serves as a repository for public keys. Cybernotaries already exist, but they do not operate within any existing legal framework because they are so new.

One alternative to digital signatures is known as "signature dynamics," which involves capturing a sender's signature using a stylus and an electronic digitizer pad. A computer program takes the signature's measurements, the sender's identity, the time and date of the signature, and the identity of the hardware. This information is then placed in an encrypted "biometric token" attached to the document being transmitted. To verify the authenticity of the signature, the recipient of the document compares the measurements of the signature with the measurements in the token. When this type of e-signature is used, it is not necessary to have a third party verify the signatory's identity. Other e-signature technologies are also being developed.

STATE LAWS GOVERNING E-SIGNATURES

As of 1999, at least forty-four states had passed laws governing e-signatures. The problem is, state e-signature laws are not uniform. For example, some states recognize the validity of only digital signatures, while others permit other types of e-signatures. State laws also vary with respect to the types of documents on which e-signatures can be validly used.

In an attempt to create more uniformity among the states, the National Conference of

---

A memorandum evidencing the oral contract need only contain the essential terms of the contract. Under the UCC, for contracts evidencing sales of goods, the writing need only name the quantity term and be signed by the party to be charged. Any confirmation, invoice, sales slip, check, fax, or e-mail—or such items in combination—can constitute a writing sufficient to satisfy the Statute of Frauds. Under most other provisions of the Statute of Frauds, for contracts evidencing transactions other than sales of goods, the writing must also name the parties, the subject matter, the consideration, and the essential terms with reasonable certainty. In some states, contracts for the sale of land must state the price and describe the property with sufficient clarity to allow them to be determined without reference to outside sources.[9]

---

9. *Rhodes v. Wilkins*, 83 N.M. 782, 498 P.2d 311 (1972).

EMERGING TRENDS IN TECHNOLOGY

E-Signatures, continued

Commissioners (NCC) on Uniform State Laws promulgated the Uniform Electronic Transactions Act (UETA) in 1999. As discussed in Chapter 9, the act defines an electronic signature as "an electronic sound, symbol, or process attached to or logically associated with a record and executed or adopted by a person with the intent to sign the record." The act also states, among other things, that a signature may not be denied legal effect or enforceability solely because it is in electronic form.

Some doubt that the UETA will significantly further the goal of uniformity among the states with respect to e-signatures. For one thing, the act provides that most of its provisions can be varied by agreement and that if UETA provisions conflict with existing laws, the existing law takes precedence. Indeed, the one state, California, that has passed the act to date has made a number of

significant changes in the law. For example, it has curbed the use of digital signatures for many types of financial transactions.

IMPLICATIONS FOR THE BUSINESSPERSON

1. Businesspersons stand to benefit significantly from the use of electronic signatures. Commercial transactions can be completed without the time and expense involved in sending contracts and other documents via regular mail, fax, or courier. Additionally, e-signature technology makes it easier to verify signatures, meaning that signing certain documents before a notary public—to establish proof of identity—will no longer be necessary.
2. Those engaged in Web-based commercial transactions should become familiar with their states' laws governing e-signatures and with the status of proposed congressional legislation.

FOR CRITICAL ANALYSIS

1. Is there any significant difference between a uniform law drafted by the NCC and adopted

by the states, and a uniform law passed by Congress?
2. Should the law require that certain types of records or documents, such as a last will and testament, continue to be created on paper and signed manually (instead of electronically)? Why or why not?

RELEVANT WEB SITES

The Uniform Electronic Transactions Act is online at **http://www.law.upenn.edu/bll/ulc/uecicta/uetast84.htm**. To obtain more information on e-signature bills before Congress, go to **http://thomas.loc.gov** and search for bill "H.R. 1714" and bill "S. 761" to view the versions of the bill introduced into the House of Representatives and the Senate, respectively.

CONCEPT SUMMARY 15.1

THE STATUTE OF FRAUDS

CONCEPT	DESCRIPTION
Applicability of the Statute	The following types of contracts fall under the Statute of Frauds and must be in writing to be enforceable: 1. *Contracts involving interests in land*—The statute applies to any contract for an interest in realty, such as a sale, a lease, or a mortgage.

CONCEPT SUMMARY 15.1   THE STATUTE OF FRAUDS (*continued*)

CONCEPT	DESCRIPTION
Applicability of the Statute (continued)	2. *Contracts whose terms cannot be performed within one year*—The statute applies only to contracts objectively impossible to perform fully within one year from (the day after) the contract's formation. 3. *Collateral promises*—The statute applies only to express contracts made between the guarantor and the creditor whose terms make the guarantor secondarily liable. Exception: main purpose rule. 4. *Promises made in consideration of marriage*—The statute applies to promises to pay money or give property in consideration of a promise to marry and to prenuptial agreements made in consideration of marriage. 5. *Contracts for the sale of goods priced at $500 or more*—Under the UCC's Statute of Frauds provision in UCC 2–201(1).
Exceptions	1. *Partial performance*—Applies to contracts for the sale of land, as well as to contracts for the sale of goods. 2. *Admissions*—Admission under oath, by the party against whom enforcement is being sought, that a contract exists. 3. *Promissory estoppel*—To prevent the injustice that might occur if an oral contract is not enforced.
Sufficiency of the Writing	To constitute an enforceable contract under the Statute of Frauds, a writing must be signed by the party against whom enforcement is sought, must name the parties, must identify the subject matter, and must state with reasonable certainty the essential terms. In a sale of land, the price and a description of the property may need to be stated with sufficient clarity to be determined without reference to outside sources. Under the UCC, a contract for a sale of goods is not enforceable beyond the quantity of goods shown.

SECTION 4

The Parol Evidence Rule

Sometimes, a written contract does not include—or contradicts—an oral understanding reached by the parties before or at the time of contracting. For example, consider the following situation. Laura is about to lease an apartment. As she is signing the lease, she asks the landlord whether cats are allowed in the building. The landlord says that they are and that Laura can keep her cat in the apartment. The lease that Laura actually signs, however, contains a provision prohibiting pets. Later, a dispute arises between Laura and the landlord over whether the landlord agreed that Laura could have a cat in the apartment. Will Laura be able to introduce evidence at trial to show that, at the time the written contract was formed, the landlord orally agreed that she could have a cat, or will the written contract absolutely control?

In determining the outcome of contract disputes such as the one between Laura and her landlord, the courts look to a common law rule governing the admissibility in court of oral evidence, or *parol evidence*. Under the **parol evidence rule,** if a court finds that the parties intended their written contract to be a complete and final embodiment of their agreement, a party cannot introduce in court evidence of any oral agreement or promise made prior to the contract's formation or at the time the contract was created.[10] Because of the rigidity of the parol evidence rule, the courts have created several exceptions:

1. *Contracts subsequently modified.* Evidence of *subsequent modification* (oral or written) of a written contract can be introduced into court. Keep in mind

---

10. *Restatement (Second) of Contracts*, Section 213.

that the oral modifications may not be enforceable if they come under the Statute of Frauds—for example, if they increase the price of the goods for sale to $500 or more or increase the term for performance to more than one year. Also, oral modifications will not be enforceable if the original contract provides that any modification must be in writing.[11]

2. *Voidable or void contracts.* Oral evidence can be introduced in all cases to show that the contract was voidable or void (for example, induced by mistake, fraud, or misrepresentation). In this case, if deception led one of the parties to agree to the terms of a written contract, oral evidence attesting to the fraud should not be excluded. Courts frown on bad faith and are quick to allow such evidence when it establishes fraud.

3. *Contracts containing ambiguous terms.* When the terms of a written contract are ambiguous, evidence is admissible to show the meaning of the terms.

4. *Incomplete contracts.* When the written contract is incomplete in that it lacks one or more of the essential terms, the courts allow evidence to "fill in the gaps."

5. *Prior dealing, course of performance, or usage of trade.* Under the UCC, evidence can be introduced to explain or supplement a written contract by showing a prior dealing, course of performance, or usage of trade.[12] These terms will be discussed in further detail in Chapter 19, in the context of sales contracts. Here, it is sufficient to say that when buyers and sellers deal with each other over extended periods of time, certain customary practices develop. These practices are often overlooked in the writing of the contract, so courts allow the introduction of evidence to show how the parties have acted in the past.

6. *Contracts subject to orally agreed-on conditions.* The parol evidence rule does not apply if the existence of the entire written contract is subject to an orally agreed-on condition. Proof of the condition does not alter or modify the written terms but involves the enforceability of the written contract. A leading case concerning this exception is *Pym v. Campbell,*[13] in which the court stated that "evidence to vary the terms of an agreement in writing is not admissible, but evidence to show that there is not an agreement at all is admissible."

7. *Contracts with an obvious or gross clerical* (or *typographic*) *error that clearly would not represent the agreement of the parties.* Parol evidence is admissible to correct an obvious typographic error.

The key in determining whether evidence will be allowed basically depends on whether the written contract is intended to be a complete and final embodiment of the terms of the agreement. If it is so intended, it is referred to as an **integrated contract,** and extraneous evidence (evidence derived from sources outside the contract itself) is excluded. If it is only partially integrated, evidence of consistent additional terms is admissible to supplement the written agreement.[14]

In the following case, the court applied the parol evidence rule, among other legal principles, in the context of a franchise agreement. (A *franchise* is an arrangement by which the owner of a trademark, trade name, or copyright licenses another to use it, under certain conditions. Franchises are discussed in detail in Chapter 39.)

---

11. UCC 2–209(2), (3).
12. UCC 1–205, 2–202.

13. 6 Ellis and Blackburn Reports 370 (Q.B. [Queen's Bench] 1856).
14. *Restatement (Second) of Contracts,* Section 216.

CASE 15.2   Cousins Subs Systems, Inc. v. McKinney

United States District Court, Eastern District of Wisconsin, 1999. 59 F.Supp.2d 816.

BACKGROUND AND FACTS   *Michael McKinney owns Best Oil Company, which operates a chain of gas station/convenience stores known as The Little Stores in northern Minnesota and Wisconsin. McKinney contracted with Cousins Subs Systems, Inc., to operate Cousins submarine sandwich shops in The Little Stores. McKinney signed an "Area Development Agreement" and a "Franchise Agreement." Each document stated that it constituted the parties' entire agreement, that there were not any other "understandings or agreements," and that McKinney had not been promised any particular level of profits. Within two years, McKinney became disillusioned with the arrangement and told Cousins that he was ending it. Cousins filed a suit in a federal district court against McKinney, charging, among other things, that he wrongfully terminated their agreement. McKinney filed a* *counterclaim against Cousins and others, alleging, in part, breach of contract. McKinney claimed that Daniel Sobiech, a Cousins representative, orally guaranteed, among other things, annual sales at each of McKinney's franchises of "$250,000 to $500,000 per franchise." Cousins filed a motion to dismiss McKinney's counterclaim.*

IN THE LANGUAGE OF THE COURT

ADELMAN, District Judge.
*   *   *   *   *

The main problem with *   *   * McKinney's claims is that the oral promises allegedly made by Cousins are directly contradicted by the written terms of the agreements that he signed *   *   * .

McKinney alleges *   *   * that Cousins through Sobiech orally guaranteed that annual sales at McKinney's franchises would be between $250,000 and $500,000, and that this level of sales was not realized. However, the Area Development Agreement states that McKinney "has not received any warranty or guaranty, express or implied, as to the potential volume, profits, or success of the business venture." The Franchise Agreement contains virtually identical language. Thus, McKinney's claim of guaranteed profits is directly contradicted by the written contracts. *   *   *

McKinney's claims are further undermined by other language in the agreements. The area development and franchise agreements each contain integration clauses which expressly disavow any promises not included in the written agreements between the parties. The Area Development Agreement, for example, states that "this Agreement *   *   * constitutes the entire agreement of the parties, and there are no other oral or written understandings or agreements *   *   * relating to the subject matter of this agreement."

Finally, McKinney's attempt to invoke alleged oral agreements to contradict the terms of the written agreements is barred by the parol evidence rule *   *   * . *The parol evidence rule prohibits the use of oral agreements of the type McKinney relies on to contradict written contracts if the written contract is intended by the parties to be the final expression of their agreement.* The presence of the integration clauses in the written agreements makes clear that the contracts were intended to embody all of the agreed on terms. Thus, the parol evidence rule presents another fundamental bar to all of McKinney's claims. [Emphasis added.]
*   *   *   *   *

In sum, McKinney is an experienced businessman who made a deal which turned out to be less favorable than he anticipated. McKinney expressly acknowledged in detailed written agreements *   *   * that his purchase of a franchise was not a risk-free endeavor. He now makes allegations that are directly contrary to the agreements he signed. For the reasons stated, his claim *   *   * fails.

DECISION AND REMEDY

The court granted Cousins's motion and dismissed McKinney's counterclaim. The court reasoned, among other things, that the parol evidence rule barred McKinney's allegation that oral promises contradicted the terms of his written contract with Cousins.

TERMS AND CONCEPTS TO REVIEW

collateral promise 272	parol evidence rule 278	Statute of Frauds 270
integrated contract 279	prenuptial agreement 274	

QUESTIONS AND CASE PROBLEMS

15–1. THE ONE-YEAR RULE. On May 1, by telephone, Yu offers to hire Benson to perform personal services. On May 5, Benson returns Yu's call and accepts the offer. Discuss fully whether this contract falls under the Statute of Frauds under the following circumstances:

(a) The contract calls for Benson to be employed for one year, with the right to begin performance immediately.

(b) The contract calls for Benson to be employed for nine months, with performance of services to begin on September 1.

(c) The contract calls for Benson to submit a written research report, with a deadline of two years for submission.

15–2. ORAL CONTRACTS. Frances had lived in an apartment for ten years when she decided to buy a house. Her one-year lease would end on May 1. On April 15, she orally contracted to buy Smith's house for $100,000, with the closing (transfer of the deed) to take place on June 1. Smith's lawyer, who was out of town on vacation, would draft a written contract of sale on his return to his office on May 15. Because Frances's lease was terminating, Smith agreed to let her take possession of the house if Frances gave him a "down payment" on the house of $5,000. Frances agreed and gave Smith the $5,000. She moved into the house on May 2, and the following weekend planted trees in the back yard. On May 10, Smith received a written offer from Green to purchase Smith's house for $120,000. Smith accepted Green's offer, asked Frances to move out of the house, and tried to return the $5,000 to Frances. Frances claimed that her oral contract was enforceable. Smith claimed that it was not because the contract was required to be in writing under the Statute of Frauds. Discuss fully who is correct and why.

15–3. COLLATERAL PROMISES. Mallory promises a local hardware store that she will pay for a lawn mower that her brother is purchasing on credit if the brother fails to pay the debt. Must this promise be in writing to be enforceable? Why or why not?

15–4. THE ONE-YEAR RULE. On January 1, Damon, for consideration, orally promised to pay Gary $300 a month for as long as Gary lived, with the payments to be made on the first day of every month. Damon made the payments regularly for nine months and then made no further payments. Gary claimed that Damon had breached the oral contract and sued Damon for damages. Damon contended that the contract was unenforceable because, under the Statute of Frauds, contracts that cannot be performed within one year must be in writing. Discuss whether Damon will succeed in this defense.

15–5. COLLATERAL PROMISES. Jeremy took his mother on a special holiday to Mountain Air Resort.

Jeremy was a frequent patron of the resort and was well known by its manager. The resort required of each of its patrons a large deposit to ensure payment of the room rental. Jeremy asked the manager to waive the requirement for his mother and told the manager that if his mother for any reason failed to pay the resort for her stay there, he would cover the bill. Relying on Jeremy's promise, the manager waived the deposit requirement for Jeremy's mother. After she returned home from her holiday, Jeremy's mother refused to pay the resort bill. The resort manager tried to collect the sum from Jeremy, but Jeremy also refused to pay, stating that his promise was not enforceable under the Statute of Frauds. Is Jeremy correct? Explain.

15–6. THE ONE-YEAR RULE. Fernandez orally promised Pando that if Pando helped her win the New York state lottery, she would share the proceeds equally with him. Pando agreed to purchase the tickets in Fernandez's name, select the lottery numbers, and pray for divine intervention from a saint to help them win. Fernandez won $2.8 million in the lottery, which was to be paid over a ten-year period. When Fernandez failed to share the winnings equally, Pando sued for breach of her contractual obligation. Fernandez countered that the contract was unenforceable under the Statute of Frauds because the contract could not be performed within one year. Could the contract be performed within a year? Explain. [*Pando by Pando v. Fernandez*, 127 Misc.2d 224, 485 N.Y.S.2d 162 (1984)]

15–7. ORAL CONTRACTS. Samuel DaGrossa and others were planning to open a restaurant. At some point prior to August 1985, DaGrossa orally agreed with Philippe LaJaunie that LaJaunie, in exchange for his contribution in designing, renovating, and managing the restaurant, could purchase a one-third interest in the restaurant's stock if the restaurant was profitable in its first year of operations. The restaurant opened in March 1986, and a few weeks later, LaJaunie's employment was terminated. LaJaunie brought an action to enforce the stock-purchase agreement. Is the agreement enforceable? Why or why not? [*LaJaunie v. DaGrossa*, 159 A.D.2d 349, 552 N.Y.S.2d 628 (1990)]

15–8. THE PAROL EVIDENCE RULE. Glenn Grove bought a 1936 Pontiac from Bernard Stanfield. Stanfield signed the certificate of title, which stated that the car was sold for $1,000. No other terms of sale were mentioned in the certificate, and none were incorporated by reference. Three years later, Stanfield filed a suit against Grove in a Missouri state court, claiming that Grove still owed $9,000 on the price of the car. At the trial, Stanfield testified that he and Grove had an oral agreement by which Grove was to pay $1,000 for the "title document" and $9,000 for the actual car. The court entered a judgment in Stanfield's favor. What will happen on appeal? Explain. [*Stanfield v. Grove*, 924 S.W.2d 611 (Mo.App.Div.4 1996)]

15–9. THE PAROL EVIDENCE RULE. Vision Graphics, Inc., provides printing services to customers such as Milton Bradley Co. To perform its services, Vision agreed to buy or lease from E. I. du Pont de Nemours and Co. parts of a computer software system. Vision needed the system to accept files written in "PostScript," a computer language used in the printing industry. Du Pont orally represented to Vision that with three upgrades, its system would be completely "postscriptable." Promises regarding postscriptability were not included in any of the parties' written contracts. Each contract, however, included an integration clause stating that the contract contained the entire agreement of the parties. Before the three upgrades were complete, du Pont determined that for financial reasons, it could no longer support its system and told Vision that the software would not be made postscriptable. Vision lost customers and could not attract new accounts, and its reputation in the industry was damaged. Vision filed a suit in a federal district court against du Pont, alleging, among other things, breach of contract on the basis of the oral promises. Du Pont filed a motion for summary judgment, arguing that whether it breached any oral agreement was "immaterial." Will the court agree? Why or why not? [*Vision Graphics, Inc. v. E. I. du Pont de Nemours & Co.*, 41 F.Supp.2d 93 (D.Mass. 1999)]

15–10. IN YOUR COURT

Wilson Floors contracted to provide flooring materials for a residential and commercial development known as "The Cliffs," which was owned by Sciota Park, Ltd. When the general contractor for Sciota fell behind in payments to Wilson, Wilson stopped work on the project. The bank that was financing the development orally assured Wilson that if Wilson would return to work, the bank would pay it for the work if the general contractor failed to do so. After the project was finished and Wilson submitted its final bill, neither the general contractor nor the bank paid Wilson. Wilson then sued the bank to recover compensation for its work. The bank argued that its promise to Wilson was not enforceable because the Statute of Frauds requires such promises to be in writing. Assume that you are the judge in the trial court hearing this case and answer the following questions:

(a) Did the bank incur a primary or secondary obligation to Wilson when it promised to pay Wilson if the general contractor failed to do so? In either situation, must the contract be in writing to be enforceable?

(b) How will you rule in this case, and why? Explain your reasoning.

LAW ON THE WEB

For updated links to resources available on the Web, as well as a variety of other materials, visit this text's Web site at http://wbl.westbuslaw.com.

The online version of UCC Section 2–201 on the Statute of Frauds includes links to definitions of certain terms used in the section. To access this site, go to

http://www.law.cornell.edu/ucc/2/2-201.html

Professor Eric Talley of the University of Southern California provides an interesting discussion of the history and current applicability of the Statute of Frauds, both internationally and in the United States, at the following Web site:

http://www-bcf.usc.edu/~etalley/frauds.html

LEGAL RESEARCH EXERCISES ON THE WEB

Go to http://wbl.westbuslaw.com, the Web site that accompanies this text. Select "Internet Applications," and then click on "Chapter 15." There you will find the following Internet research exercise that you can perform to learn more about the Statute of Frauds:

Activity 15–1: The Statute of Frauds

CHAPTER 16

Third Party Rights

ONCE IT HAS BEEN DETERMINED that a valid and legally enforceable contract exists, attention can turn to the rights and duties of the parties to the contract. A contract is a private agreement between the parties who have entered into it, and traditionally these parties alone have rights and liabilities under the contract. This principle is referred to as *privity of contract.* A *third party*—one who is not a direct party to a particular contract—normally does not have rights under that contract.

There are exceptions to the rule of privity of contract. As we noted in Chapter 6, privity of contract between a seller and a buyer is no longer a requirement to recover damages under product-liability laws. In this chapter, we look at two other exceptions. One exception allows a party to a contract to transfer the rights or duties arising from the contract to another person through an *assignment* (of rights) or a *delegation* (of duties). The other exception involves a *third party beneficiary contract*—a contract in which the parties to the contract intend that the contract benefit a third party. We look at both of these exceptions to the rule of privity of contract in this chapter, beginning with the law relating to assignments and delegations.

SECTION 1

Assignments and Delegations

In a bilateral contract, the two parties have corresponding rights and duties. One party has a *right* to require the other to perform some task, and the other has a *duty* to perform it. The transfer of contractual *rights* to a third party is known as an **assignment.** The transfer of contractual *duties* to a third party is known as a **delegation.** An assignment or a delegation occurs *after* the original contract was made.

ASSIGNMENTS

When rights under a contract are assigned unconditionally, the rights of the *assignor* (the party making the assignment) are extinguished.[1] The third party (the *assignee,* or party receiving the assignment) has a right to demand performance from the other original party to the contract.

For example, suppose that Brower is obligated by contract to pay Horton $1,000. In this situation, Brower is the *obligor,* because she owes an obligation, or duty, to Horton. Horton is the *obligee,* the one to whom the obligation, or duty, is owed. Now suppose that Horton assigns his right to receive the $1,000 to Kuhn. Horton is the assignor, and Kuhn is the assignee. Kuhn now becomes the obligee, because now Brower owes Kuhn the $1,000. Here, a valid assignment of a debt exists. Kuhn (the assignee-obligee) is entitled to enforce payment in court if Brower (the obligor) does not pay her the $1,000. These concepts are illustrated in Exhibit 16–1 on the next page.

The assignee takes only those rights that the assignor originally had. Furthermore, the assignee's rights are

---
1. *Restatement (Second) of Contracts,* Section 317.

283

EXHIBIT 16–1   ASSIGNMENT RELATIONSHIPS

In the assignment relationship illustrated here, Horton assigns his *rights* under a contract that he made with Brower to a third party, Kuhn. Horton thus becomes the *assignor* and Kuhn the *assignee* of the contractual rights. Brower, the *obligor* (the party owing performance under the contract), now owes performance to Kuhn instead of Horton. Horton's original contract rights are extinguished after assignment.

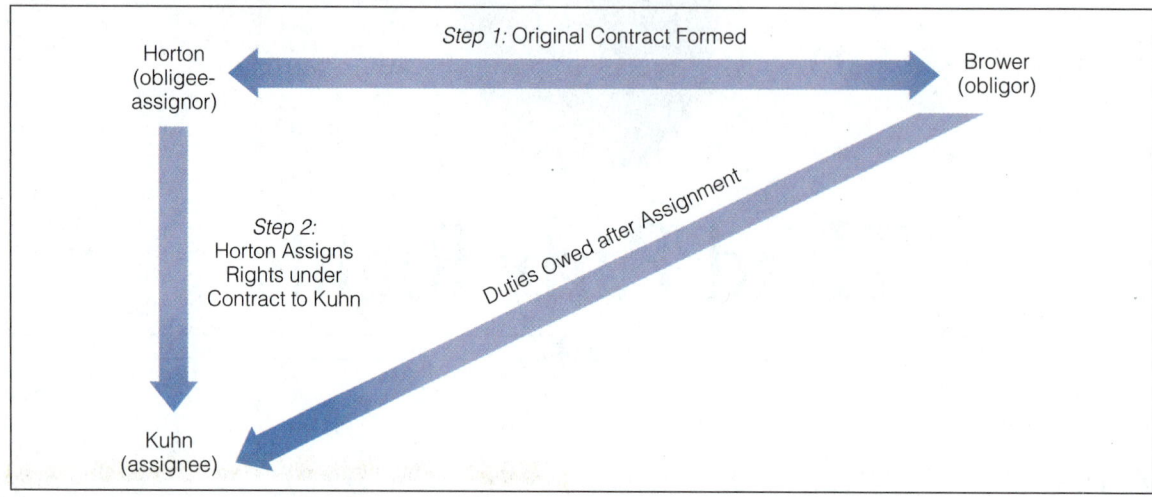

subject to the defenses that the obligor has against the assignor. For example, assume that in the above example, Brower owed Horton the $1,000 under a contract in which Brower agreed to buy Horton's personal computer. Brower, in deciding to purchase the computer, relied on Horton's fraudulent misrepresentation that the computer's hard drive had a storage capacity of 12 gigabytes. When Brower discovered that the computer could store only 6 gigabytes, she told Horton that she was going to return the computer to him and cancel the contract. Even though Horton had assigned his "right" to receive the $1,000 to Kuhn, Brower need not pay Kuhn the $1,000—Brower can raise the defense of Horton's fraudulent misrepresentation to avoid payment.

How Assignments Function.   Assignments are important because they are involved in much business financing. Banks, for example, frequently assign the rights to receive payments under their loan contracts to other firms, which pay for those rights. For example, if you obtain a loan from your local bank to purchase a car, you might later receive in the mail a notice from your bank stating that it has transferred (assigned) its rights to receive payments on the loan to another firm and that, when the time comes to repay your loan, you must make the payments to that other firm.

Banks that make *mortgage loans* (loans to allow prospective home buyers to purchase land or a home)

often assign their rights to collect the mortgage payments to a third party, such as GMAC Mortgage Corporation. Following the assignment, the home buyers are notified that they must make future payments not to the bank that loaned them the funds but to the third party. Millions of dollars change hands daily in the business world in the form of assignments of rights in contracts. If it were not possible to transfer (assign) contractual rights, many businesses could not continue to operate.

Form of the Assignment.   In general, an assignment can take any form, oral or written. Naturally, it is more difficult to prove that an oral assignment occurred, so it is practical to put all assignments in writing. Of course, assignments covered by the Statute of Frauds must be in writing to be enforceable. For example, an assignment of an interest in land must be in writing to be enforceable. In addition, most states require contracts for the assignment of wages to be in writing.[2]

Rights That Cannot Be Assigned.   As a general rule, all rights can be assigned. Exceptions are made, however, in the following circumstances:

1. If a statute expressly prohibits assignment of a particular right, that right cannot be assigned. Suppose

---

2. See, for example, California Labor Code Section 300. There are other assignments that must be in writing as well.

that Quincy is an employee of Specialty Computer, Inc. Specialty Computer is an employer under workers' compensation statutes in this state, and thus Quincy is a covered employee. Quincy is injured on the job and begins to collect monthly workers' compensation checks (see Chapter 41 for a discussion of workers' compensation laws). In need of a loan, Quincy asks Draper to lend her some money and offers to assign to Draper all of her future workers' compensation benefits. The assignment of future workers' compensation benefits is prohibited by state statute, however, and thus such rights cannot be assigned.

2. When a contract is *personal* in nature, the rights under the contract cannot be assigned unless all that remains is a money payment.[3] Suppose that Brower signs a contract to be a tutor for Horton's children. Horton then attempts to assign to Kuhn his right to Brower's services. Kuhn cannot enforce the contract against Brower. Kuhn's children may be more difficult to tutor than Horton's; thus, if Horton could assign his rights to Brower's services to Kuhn, it would change the nature of Brower's obligation. Because personal services are unique to the person rendering them, rights to receive personal services are likewise unique and cannot be assigned.

3. A right cannot be assigned if assignment will materially increase or alter the risk or duties of the obligor.[4] Assume that Horton has a hotel, and to insure it, he takes out a policy with Southeast Insurance. The policy insures against fire, theft, floods, and vandalism. Horton attempts to assign the insurance policy to Kuhn, who also owns a hotel. The assignment is ineffective, because it substantially alters Southeast Insurance's *duty of performance.* An insurance company evaluates the particular risk of a certain party and tailors its policy to

fit that risk. If the policy is assigned to a third party, the insurance risk is materially altered because the insurance company may have no information on the third party. Therefore, the assignment will not operate to give Kuhn any rights against Southeast Insurance.

4. If a contract stipulates that a right cannot be assigned, then *ordinarily* the right cannot be assigned. Whether an antiassignment clause is effective depends in part on how it is phrased. A contract that states that any assignment is "void" effectively prohibits any assignment. Note that restraints on the power to assign operate only against the parties themselves. They do not effectively prohibit an assignment by operation of law, such as an assignment pursuant to bankruptcy or death.

There are several exceptions to the fourth rule. These exceptions are as follows:

1. A contract cannot prevent an assignment of the right to receive money. This exception exists to encourage the free flow of money and credit in modern business settings.

2. The assignment of rights in real estate often cannot be prohibited, because such a prohibition is contrary to public policy. Prohibitions of this kind are called restraints against **alienation** (transfer of land ownership).

3. The assignment of *negotiable instruments* (see Chapter 24) cannot be prohibited.

4. In a contract for the sale of goods, the right to receive damages for breach of contract or for payment of an account owed may be assigned even though the sales contract prohibits such assignment.[5]

In the following case, the central issue was whether a covenant not to compete contained in an employment contract could be assigned.

---

3. *Restatement (Second) of Contracts,* Sections 317 and 318.
4. UCC 2–210(2).

5. UCC 2–210(2).

CASE 16.1 Reynolds and Reynolds Co. v. Hardee

United States District Court, Eastern District of Virginia, 1996. 932 F.Supp. 149.

COMPANY PROFILE   *There is a $23 billion market in North America for business forms and related services. Reynolds and Reynolds Company (**http://www.reynoldsandreynolds.com**) provides business forms and electronic-document management systems for general and specialized business markets. Reynolds's products include traditional business forms, laser-print products, labels, digital printing, and mailers. Reynolds's services include document management, storage, and distribution. These products and services help business firms with accounting, inventory control, and sales. Reynolds's customers include 110 of the "Fortune 500" companies.*

BACKGROUND AND FACTS   *Thomas Hardee worked for Jordan Graphics, Inc., as a sales representative under an employment contract that included a covenant not to* *compete. Reynolds and Reynolds Company contracted to buy most of Jordan's assets. On the day of the sale, Jordan terminated Hardee's employment. Reynolds offered Hardee a new contract that contained a more restrictive covenant not to compete. Hardee rejected the offer and began selling in competition with Reynolds. Reynolds filed a suit in a federal district court against Hardee, seeking, among other things, to enforce the covenant not to compete that was in the contract between Hardee and Jordan. Hardee filed a motion to dismiss the case, asserting that Reynolds was not an assignee of that contract and could not enforce it.*

IN THE LANGUAGE OF THE COURT

REBECCA BEACH SMITH, District Judge.

*   *   *   *

*   *   * [C]ontracts for personal services are not assignable, unless both parties agree to the assignment. Defendant's [Hardee's] Employment Agreement with Jordan [was] clearly a contract for personal services, based on trust and confidence. Defendant's position involved direct sales to clients; he acted as Jordan's agent in its dealings with customers. A person in such a position must necessarily obtain the trust and confidence of his or her employer. Defendant also placed considerable trust in Jordan by even agreeing to the non-compete clause, namely trusting that Jordan would not fire him and then invoke the covenant not to compete.

*   *   *   *

*   *   * Without question, an employment contract of the sort involved in this case is not assignable *   *   * .

DECISION AND REMEDY

The court found that Reynolds was not an assignee of the contract between Hardee and Jordan and thus could not enforce it. The court dismissed this part of Reynolds's claim.

Notice of Assignment. Once a valid assignment of rights has been made, the assignee (the third party to whom the rights have been assigned) should notify the obligor (the one owing performance) of the assignment. For example, when Horton assigns to Kuhn his right to receive the $1,000 from Brower, Kuhn should notify Brower, the obligor, of the assignment. Giving notice is not legally necessary to establish the validity of the assignment, because an assignment is effective immediately, whether or not notice is given. Two major problems arise, however, when notice of the assignment is not given to the obligor.

1. If the assignor assigns the same right to two different persons, the question arises as to which one has priority—that is, which one has the right to the performance by the obligor. Although the rule most often observed in the United States is that the first assignment in time is the first in right, some states follow the English rule, which basically gives priority to the first assignee who gives notice.

2. Until the obligor has notice of assignment, the obligor can discharge his or her obligation by performance to the assignor, and performance by the obligor to the assignor constitutes a discharge to the assignee. Once the obligor receives proper notice, only performance to the assignee can discharge the obligor's obligations. To illustrate: In the Horton-Brower-Kuhn example, assume that Brower, the obligor, is not notified of Horton's assignment of his rights to Kuhn. Brower subsequently pays Horton the $1,000. Although the assignment was valid, Brower's payment to Horton discharges the debt. Kuhn's failure to give notice to Brower of the assignment has caused Kuhn to lose the right to collect the money from Brower. If Kuhn had given Brower notice of the assignment, Brower's payment to Horton would not have discharged the debt, and Kuhn would have had a legal right to require payment from Brower.

DELEGATIONS

Just as a party can transfer rights through an assignment, a party can also transfer duties. Duties are not assigned, however; they are *delegated*. Normally, a delegation of duties does not relieve the party making the delegation (the *delegator*) of the obligation to perform in the event that the party to whom the duty has

EXHIBIT 16–2 DELEGATION RELATIONSHIPS

In the delegation relationship illustrated here, Brower delegates her *duties* under a contract that she made with Horton to a third party, Kuhn. Brower thus becomes the *delegator* and Kuhn the *delegatee* of the contractual duties. Kuhn now owes performance of the contractual duties to Horton. Note that a delegation of duties normally does not relieve the delegator (Brower) of liability if the delegatee (Kuhn) fails to perform the contractual duties.

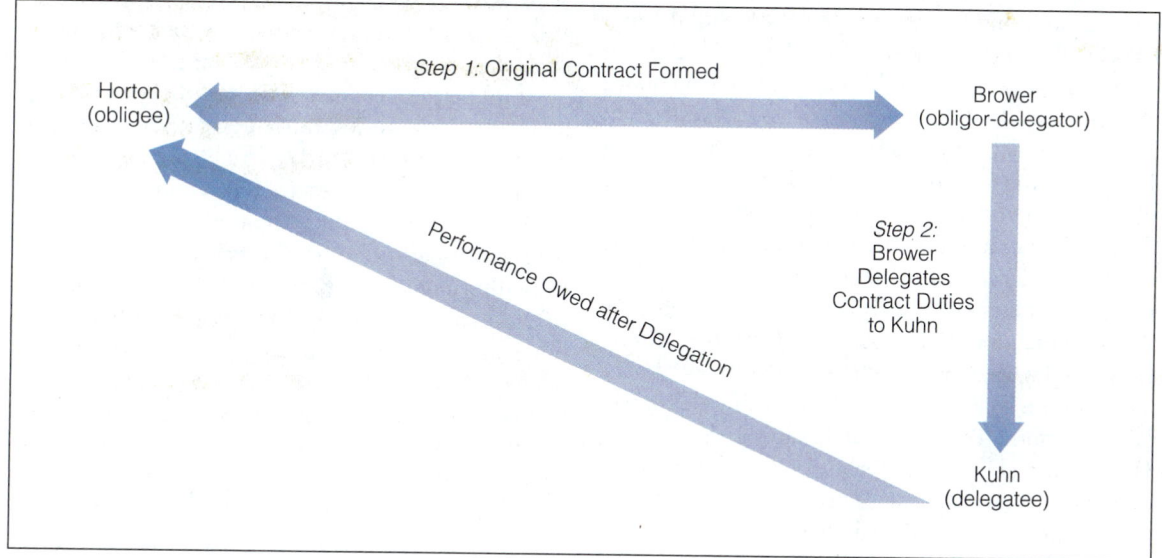

been delegated (the *delegatee*) fails to perform. No special form is required to create a valid delegation of duties. As long as the delegator expresses an intention to make the delegation, it is effective; the delegator need not even use the word *delegate*. Exhibit 16–2 above illustrates delegation relationships.

Duties That Cannot Be Delegated. As a general rule, any duty can be delegated. There are, however, some exceptions to this rule. Delegation is prohibited in the following circumstances:

1. When special trust has been placed in the obligor.
2. When performance depends on the personal skill or talents of the *obligor* (the person contractually obligated to perform).
3. When performance by a third party will vary materially from that expected by the obligee (the one to whom performance is owed) under the contract.
4. When the contract expressly prohibits delegation.

The following examples will help to clarify the kinds of duties that can and cannot be delegated:

1. Suppose that Brower contracts with Horton to tutor Horton in the various aspects of financial underwriting and investment banking. Brower, an experienced businessperson known for her expertise in finance, wants to delegate her duties to a third party, Kuhn. This delegation is ineffective because Brower has contracted to render a service that is founded on her expertise. The delegation would change Horton's expectations under the contract. Therefore, Kuhn cannot perform Brower's duties.

2. Suppose that Horton, who is impressed with Brower's ability to perform veterinary surgery, contracts with Brower to have Brower perform surgery on Horton's prize-winning stallion in July. Brower later decides that she would rather spend the summer at the beach, so she delegates her duties under the contract to Kuhn, who is also a competent veterinary surgeon. The delegation is not effective, no matter how competent Kuhn is, without Horton's consent. The contract is for *personal* performance.

3. Assume that Brower contracts with Horton to pick up and deliver heavy construction machinery to Horton's property. Brower delegates this duty to Kuhn, who is in the business of delivering heavy machinery. This delegation is effective. The performance required is of a *routine* and *nonpersonal* nature,

and the delegation does not change Horton's expectations under the contract.

Effect of a Delegation. If a delegation of duties is enforceable, the obligee (the one to whom performance is owed) must accept performance from the delegatee (the one to whom the duties have been delegated). Consider the third example in the above list, in which Brower delegates to Kuhn the duty to pick up and deliver a heavy construction machine to Horton's property. In that situation, Horton (the obligee) must accept performance from Kuhn (the delegatee), because the delegation was effective. The obligee can legally refuse performance from the delegatee only if the duty is one that cannot be delegated.

As noted, a valid delegation of duties does not relieve the delegator of obligations under the contract.[6] Thus, in the above example, if Kuhn (the delegatee) fails to perform, Brower (the delegator) is still liable to Horton (the obligee). The obligee can also hold the delegatee liable if the delegatee made a promise of performance that will directly benefit the obligee. In this situation, there is an "assumption of duty" on the part of the delegatee, and breach of this duty makes the delegatee liable to the obligee. For example, if Kuhn (the delegatee) promises Brower (the delegator), in a contract, to pick up and deliver the construction equipment to Horton's property but fails to do so, Horton (the obligee) can sue Brower, Kuhn, or both. Although there are many exceptions, the general rule today is that the obligee can sue both the delegatee and the delegator.

ASSIGNMENT OF "ALL RIGHTS"

When a contract provides for an "assignment of all rights," this wording may create both an assignment of rights and a delegation of duties.[7] Therefore, when general words are used (for example, "I assign the contract" or "I assign all my rights under the contract"), the contract normally is construed as implying both an assignment of the assignor's rights and a delegation of any duties of performance owed by the assignor under the contract being assigned. Thus, the assignor remains liable if the assignee fails to perform the contractual obligations.

SECTION 2

Third Party Beneficiaries

Another exception to the doctrine of privity of contract exists when the original parties to the contract intend at the time of contracting that the contract performance directly benefit a third person. In this situation, the third person becomes a **third party beneficiary** of the contract. As an **intended beneficiary** of the contract, the third party has legal rights and can sue the promisor directly for breach of the contract.

Who, though, is the promisor? In bilateral contracts, both parties to the contract are promisors, because they both make promises that can be enforced. In third party beneficiary contracts, courts will determine the identity of the promisor by asking which party made the promise that benefits the third party—that person is the promisor. Allowing a third party to sue the promisor directly in effect circumvents the "middle person" (the promisee) and thus reduces the burden on the courts. Otherwise, a third party would sue the promisee, who would then sue the promisor.

TYPES OF INTENDED BENEFICIARIES

At one time, third party beneficiaries had no legal rights in contracts. Over time, however, the concept developed that a third party for whose benefit a contract was formed could sue the promisor to have the contract enforced. In a classic case decided in 1859, *Lawrence v. Fox*,[8] the court permitted a third party beneficiary to bring suit directly against a promisor. This case established the rule that a *creditor beneficiary* can sue the promisor directly. A creditor beneficiary is one who benefits from a contract in which one party (the promisor) promises another party (the promisee) to pay a debt that party owes to a third party (the creditor beneficiary). The creditor beneficiary, although not a party to the contract between the debtor and the other person, becomes the intended beneficiary and can thus enforce the promisor's promise to pay the debt.

Another type of intended beneficiary is a *donee beneficiary*. When a contract is made for the express purpose of giving a *gift* to a third party, the third party (the donee beneficiary) can sue the promisor directly to enforce the promise.[9] The most common donee

---

6. *Crane Ice Cream Co. v. Terminal Freezing & Heating Co.*, 147 Md. 588, 128 A. 280 (1925).
7. *Restatement (Second) of Contracts*, Section 328; UCC 2–210(1), (4).

8. 20 N.Y. 268 (1859).
9. *Seaver v. Ransom*, 224 N.Y. 233, 120 N.E. 639 (1918).

beneficiary contract is a life insurance contract. Consider the following example of a typical life insurance contract: Akins (the promisee) pays premiums to Standard Life, a life insurance company, and Standard Life (the promisor) promises to pay a certain amount of money on Akins's death to anyone Akins designates as a beneficiary. The designated beneficiary is a donee beneficiary under the life insurance policy and can enforce the promise made by the insurance company to pay him or her on Akins's death.

As the law concerning third party beneficiaries evolved, numerous cases arose in which the third party beneficiary did not fit readily into either category—creditor beneficiary or donee beneficiary. Thus, the modern view, and the one adopted by the *Restatement (Second) of Contracts*, does not draw such clear lines and distinguishes only between intended beneficiaries (who can sue to enforce contracts made for their benefit) and incidental beneficiaries (who cannot sue, as will be discussed shortly).

THE VESTING OF AN INTENDED BENEFICIARY'S RIGHTS

An intended third party beneficiary cannot enforce a contract against the original parties until the rights of the third party have *vested*, which means the rights have taken effect and cannot be taken away. Until these rights have vested, the original parties to the contract—the promisor and the promisee—can modify or rescind the contract without the consent of the third party.

When do the rights of third parties vest? Generally, the rights vest when either of the following occurs:

1. When the third party demonstrates manifest assent to the contract, such as by sending a letter or note acknowledging awareness of and consent to a contract formed for his or her benefit.
2. When the third party materially alters his or her position in detrimental reliance on the contract.

If the contract expressly reserves to the contracting parties the right to cancel, rescind, or modify the contract, the rights of the third party beneficiary are subject to any changes that result. In such a situation, the vesting of the third party's rights does not terminate the power of the original contracting parties to alter their legal relationships.[10] This is particularly true in

most life insurance contracts, in which the right to change the beneficiary is reserved to the policyholder. Exhibit 16–3 on the next page summarizes third party rights in contracts generally, including when the rights of an intended beneficiary vest.

INTENDED VERSUS INCIDENTAL BENEFICIARIES

The benefit that an **incidental beneficiary** receives from a contract between two parties is unintentional. Because the benefit is *unintentional,* an incidental beneficiary cannot sue to enforce the contract. In determining whether a third party beneficiary is an intended or an incidental beneficiary, the courts generally use the *reasonable person* test. That is, a beneficiary will be considered an intended beneficiary if a reasonable person in the position of the beneficiary would believe that the promisee *intended* to confer on the beneficiary the right to bring suit to enforce the contract. The court also looks at a number of other factors. The presence of one or more of the following factors strongly indicates that the third party is an *intended* (rather than an incidental) beneficiary to the contract:

1. Performance is rendered directly to the third party.
2. The third party has the right to control the details of performance.
3. The third party is expressly designated as the beneficiary in the contract.

In contrast, the following are examples of incidental beneficiaries. The third party has no rights in the contract and cannot enforce it against the promisor.

1. Escobedo contracts with Monell to build a cottage on Monell's land. Escobedo's plans specify that All-Weather Insulation Company's insulation materials must be used in constructing the house. All-Weather is an incidental beneficiary and cannot enforce the contract against Escobedo by attempting to require that Escobedo purchase its insulation materials.
2. Bollow contracts with Coolidge to build a recreational facility on Coolidge's land. Once the facility is constructed, it will greatly enhance the property values in the neighborhood. If Bollow subsequently refuses to build the facility, Tran, Coolidge's neighbor, cannot enforce the contract against Bollow because Tran is an incidental beneficiary.

---

10. Defenses against third party beneficiaries are given in the *Restatement (Second) of Contracts*, Section 309.

EXHIBIT 16–3   THIRD PARTY RIGHTS IN CONTRACTS

	ASSIGNMENT	DELEGATION	THIRD PARTY BENEFICIARY CONTRACT
How are third party rights created?	After contract formation, rights are assigned to a third party.	After contract formation, duties are delegated to a third party.	Purpose of original contract is to benefit a third party. If purpose is: 1. To discharge a duty or debt owed, third party is a *creditor* beneficiary. 2. To confer a gift, third party is a *donee* beneficiary.

Is the assignment, delegation, or third party beneficiary contract effective?	To be effective, an assignment cannot involve:
	1. Rights that a statute expressly prohibits from being assigned.
	2. Rights to performance by personal service.
	3. Rights the assignment of which will materially increase or alter the obligor's duties.
	4. Rights that the contract stipulates cannot be assigned, except:
	  a. Rights to receive money.
	  b. Rights in real property (see Chapter 47).
	  c. Rights to negotiable instruments (see Chapter 24).
	  d. Rights to damages for breach of contract or for payment of an account.
		To be effective, a delegation cannot involve:
		1. Duties that involve special trust placed in the obligor.
		2. Duties that depend on the personal skill or talent of the obligor.
		3. Duties the delegation of which will materially increase or alter the performance expected by the obligee.
		4. Duties that the contract stipulates cannot be delegated.
			For a third party beneficiary contract to be effective, rights under the contract must vest by:
			1. Third party's manifesting assent to the contract.
			2. Third party's materially altering position in detrimental reliance on the contract.

Is a party who borrows money to build a house an intended beneficiary of a contract between the lender and a party whom the lender hires to monitor the progress of the home's construction? That was the question in the following case.

CASE 16.2   Vogan v. Hayes Appraisal Associates, Inc.

Supreme Court of Iowa, 1999.
588 N.W.2d 420.
http://www.judicial.
state.ia.us/decisions[a]

BACKGROUND AND FACTS   *Susan and Rollin Vogan wanted to build a home in West Des Moines, Iowa. They met with builder Gary Markley of Char Enterprises, Inc., who agreed to build the home for $169,633.59. The Vogans obtained a $170,000 construction loan from MidAmerica Savings Bank, which hired Hayes Appraisal Associates, Inc., to monitor the progress of the construction. MidAmerica was to disburse payments to Markley based on Hayes's reports. There were cost overruns on the*

a. This Web site is maintained by the state of Iowa. In the left column, under "Decisions and Schedules," click on "Supreme Court." On that page, again in the left column, click on "Opinion Archive." When the archive opens, click on "1999," and in that list, next to "January 21, 1999," click on "Index." Scroll down the list of cases to the *Vogan* case and click on the case name to access the opinion

job, and after three months, there was less than $2,000 remaining of the initial loan. Markley said that it would take another $70,000 to finish the house. The Vogans borrowed $42,050 more, added some of their own money, and gave it to the bank to continue payments to Markley based on Hayes's reports. A few weeks later, Hayes reported that the house was 90 percent complete. Seven months later, with the house unfinished, Markley ceased working on the job. Another contractor estimated that completion would cost an additional $60,000. The Vogans filed a suit in an Iowa state court against Hayes, based in part on Hayes's contract with MidAmerica. Hayes answered in part that the Vogans were not third party beneficiaries of that contract. The court issued a judgment in favor of the Vogans. Hayes appealed to a state intermediate appellate court, which reversed the judgment. The Vogans appealed to the Iowa Supreme Court.

IN THE LANGUAGE OF THE COURT

CARTER, Justice.

*   *   *   *

*   *   * This court has adopted the following principles from the *Restatement (Second) of Contracts* [Section 302] that are applicable to third party beneficiary cases:

> "(1) Unless otherwise agreed between promisor and promisee, a beneficiary of a promise is an intended beneficiary if recognition of a right to performance in the beneficiary is appropriate to [put into effect] the intention of the parties and either
> (a) the performance of the promise will satisfy an obligation of the promisee to pay money to the beneficiary; or
> (b) the circumstances indicate that the promisee intends to give the beneficiary the benefit of the promised performance. *   *   * "

This court has determined that the primary question in a third party beneficiary case is whether the contract manifests an intent to benefit a third party. However, *this intent need not be to benefit a third party directly.* [Emphasis added.]

*   *   * When a contract is made, the two or more contracting parties have separate purposes; each is stimulated by various motives, some of which he may not be acutely conscious. *   *   * A third party who is not a promisee and who gave no consideration has an enforceable right by reason of a contract made by two others *   *   * if the promised performance will be of pecuniary [monetary] benefit to the third party and the contract is so expressed as to give the promisor reason to know that such benefit is contemplated by the promisee as one of the motivating causes of his making the contract. In the present case, MidAmerica is the promisee, who stands to benefit from Hayes Appraisal's performance, and Hayes Appraisal is the promisor, who agreed to provide periodic inspections to the bank.

The promised performance of Hayes Appraisal to MidAmerica will be of pecuniary benefit to the Vogans, and the contract is so expressed as to give Hayes reason to know that such benefit is contemplated by MidAmerica as one of the motivating causes of making the contract. The inspection reports *   *   * that Hayes Appraisal provided MidAmerica contained not only the location of the project, but also the Vogans' name as the home purchasers. This information gave Hayes Appraisal reason to know that the purpose of MidAmerica obtaining the periodic progress reports from Hayes was to provide the Vogans with some protection for the money they had invested in the project. *   *   * [In] these circumstances, the Vogans qualify as [intended] third party beneficiaries of the agreement between MidAmerica and Hayes Appraisal.

DECISION AND REMEDY

The Iowa Supreme Court vacated the decision of the state intermediate appellate court and affirmed the judgment of the trial court. The Vogans were intended third party beneficiaries of the contract between Hayes and MidAmerica, as evidenced by the statements in the contract.

TERMS AND CONCEPTS TO REVIEW

alienation 285

assignment 283

delegation 283

incidental beneficiary 289

intended beneficiary 288

third party beneficiary 288

QUESTIONS AND CASE PROBLEMS

16–1. THIRD PARTY BENEFICIARY. Alexander has been accepted as a freshman at a college two hundred miles from his home for the fall semester. Alexander's rich uncle, Michael, decides to give Alexander a car for Christmas. In November, Michael makes a contract with Jackson Auto Sales to purchase a new car for $10,000 to be delivered to Alexander just before the Christmas holidays, in mid-December. The title to the car is to be in Alexander's name. Michael pays the full purchase price, calls Alexander and tells him about the gift, and takes off for a six-month vacation in Europe. Jackson never delivers the car, and Alexander files an action against Jackson. Discuss fully whether Alexander can recover for Jackson's breach of contract. What if Michael had agreed with Jackson to make installment payments on the car and then failed to make the payments? Could Alexander have sued his uncle for breach of the contract? Discuss.

16–2. ASSIGNMENT. Five years ago, Hensley purchased a house. At that time, being unable to pay the full purchase price, she borrowed money from Thrift Savings and Loan, which in turn took a 9.5 percent mortgage on the house. The mortgage contract did not prohibit the assignment of the mortgage. Then Hensley secured a new job in another city and sold the house to Sylvia. The purchase price included payment to Hensley of the value of her equity and the assumption of the mortgage debt still owed to Thrift. At the time the contract between Hensley and Sylvia was made, Thrift did not know about or consent to the sale. On the basis of these facts, if Sylvia defaults in making the house payments to Thrift, what are Thrift's rights? Discuss.

16–3. ASSIGNMENT. Marsala is a student attending college. He signs a one-year lease agreement that runs from September 1 to August 31. The lease agreement specifies that the lease cannot be assigned without the landlord's consent. In late May, Marsala decides not to go to summer school and assigns the balance of the lease (three months) to a close friend, Fred. The landlord objects to the assignment and denies Fred access to the apartment. Marsala claims Fred is financially sound and should be allowed the full rights and privileges of an assignee. Discuss fully whether the landlord or Marsala is correct.

16–4. DELEGATION. Inez has a specific set of plans to build a sailboat. The plans are detailed in nature, and any boat builder can construct the boat. Inez secures bids, and the low bid is made by the Whale of a Boat Corp. Inez contracts with Whale to build the boat for $4,000. Whale then receives unexpected business from elsewhere. To meet the delivery date in the contract with Inez, Whale delegates its obligation to build the boat, without Inez's consent, to Quick Brothers, a reputable boat builder. When the boat is ready for delivery, Inez learns of the delegation and refuses to accept delivery, even though the boat is built to specifications. Discuss fully whether Inez is obligated to accept and pay for the boat. Would your answer be any different if Inez had not had a specific set of plans but had instead contracted with Whale to design and build a sailboat for $4,000? Explain.

16–5. ASSIGNMENT. Clement was seriously injured in a car accident with King. Clement sued King. King retained Prestwich as her attorney. Because of the alleged negligence of Prestwich, Clement was able to obtain a $21,000 judgment on her claim against King. Clement received from King a purported written assignment of King's malpractice claim against Prestwich as settlement for the judgment against her. Can King assign her cause of action against Prestwich to Clement? Explain. [*Clement v. Prestwich*, 114 Ill.App.3d 479, 448 N.E.2d 1039, 70 Ill.Dec. 161 (1983)]

16–6. ASSIGNMENT. Fox Brothers Enterprises, Inc., agreed to convey to Canfield a lot, Lot 23, in a subdivision known as Fox Estates, together with a one-year option to purchase Lot 24. The agreement did not contain any prohibitions, restrictions, or limitations against assignments. Canfield paid the price of $20,000 and took title to Lot 23. Thereafter, Canfield assigned his option right in Lot 24 to the Scotts. When the Scotts tried to exercise their right to the option, Fox Brothers refused to convey the property to them. The Scotts then brought a suit for specific performance. What was the result? [*Scott v. Fox Brothers Enterprises, Inc.*, 667 P.2d 773 (Colo.App. 1983)]

16–7. ASSIGNMENT. Joseph LeMieux, of Maine, won $373,000 in a lottery operated by the Tri-State Lotto Commission. The lottery is sponsored by the three northern New England states and is administered in Vermont. In accordance with its usual payment plan, Tri-State was to pay the $373,000 to LeMieux in annual installments over a twenty-year period. LeMieux assigned his rights to the lottery installment payments for the years 1996 through 2006 to Singer Freidlander Corp. for the sum of $80,000. LeMieux and Singer Freidlander (the plaintiffs) sought a court judgment authorizing the assignment agreement between them despite Tri-State's regulation barring the assignment of lottery proceeds. The trial court granted Tri-State's motion for summary judgment. On appeal, the plaintiffs argued that Tri-State's regulation was invalid. Is it? Discuss fully. [*LeMieux v. Tri-State Lotto Commission*, 666 A.2d 1170 (Vt. 1995)]

16–8. THIRD PARTY BENEFICIARY. John Castle and Leonard Harlan, who headed Castle Harlan, Inc., an investment firm, entered into an agreement with the federal government to buy Western Empire Federal Savings and Loan. Under the agreement, Castle Harlan was to invest a nominal amount in the bank and arrange for others to invest much more, in exchange for, among other things, a promise that for two years, Western Empire would not be subject to certain restrictions in federal regulations. The government's enforcement of other regulations against Western Empire led to its going out of business. Castle, Harlan, and the other investors filed a suit in the U.S. Court of Federal Claims against the government, alleging breach of contract. The government filed a motion to dismiss all of the plaintiffs except Castle and Harlan, on the ground that the others

did not sign the contract between the government and Castle and Harlan. Is the government correct? Should the court dismiss the claims brought by the other investors? Why or why not? [*Castle v. United States*, 42 Fed.Cl. 859 (1999)]

16–9. IN YOUR COURT

Halston, Inc., operated a store on property owned by the Faragher Corp. The lease required Halston to carry insurance to "protect" and "indemnify" Halston and Faragher against all claims arising out of the use of the property. Halston never obtained the insurance. Lori Duncan, a Halston customer, fell through a trap door inside the entrance to the store. When she learned that there was no insurance, she sued Faragher, arguing that she was an intended third party beneficiary of the insurance provision of the lease and thus could sue Faragher for failing to enforce the provision in the contract requiring Halston to obtain insurance coverage. Assume that you are the judge in the trial court hearing this case and answer the following questions:

(a) Review the court's opinion in Case 16.2 (*Vogan v. Hayes Appraisal Associates, Inc.*). What legal principles did the court apply in that case? Are they applicable to the case now before your court?

(b) How will you rule on Duncan's claim? Explain your reasoning.

LAW ON THE WEB

For updated links to resources available on the Web, as well as a variety of other materials, visit this text's Web site at http://wbl.westbuslaw.com.

You can find a summary of the law governing assignments, as well as "SmartAgreement" forms that you can use for various types of contracts, at

http://www.smartagreements.com/gen1/lp75.htm

A *New York Law Journal* article discussing *Lawrence v. Fox* and other leading decisions from the New York Court of Appeals is online at

http://www.nylj.com/links/150sterk.html

LEGAL RESEARCH EXERCISES ON THE WEB

Go to http://wbl.westbuslaw.com, the Web site that accompanies this text. Select "Internet Applications," and then click on "Chapter 16." There you will find the following Internet research exercise that you can perform to learn more about third party rights in contracts:

Activity 16–1: Third Party Beneficiaries

Performance and Discharge

J UST AS RULES ARE NECESSARY to determine when a legally enforceable contract exists, so also are they required to determine when one of the parties can justifiably say, "I have fully performed, so I am now discharged from my obligations under this contract." The legal environment of business requires the identification of some point at which the parties can reasonably know that their duties are at an end.

The most common way to **discharge,** or terminate, one's contractual duties is by the **performance** of those duties. For example, a buyer and seller have a contract for the sale of a 2000 Buick for $28,000. This contract will be discharged on the performance by the parties of their obligations under the contract— the buyer's payment of $28,000 to the seller and the seller's transfer of possession of the Buick to the buyer.

The duty to perform under a contract may be *conditioned* on the occurrence or nonoccurrence of a certain event, or the duty may be *absolute.* In the first part of this chapter, we look at conditions of performance and the degree of performance required. We then examine some other ways in which a contract can be discharged, including discharge by agreement of the parties and discharge by operation of law.

absolute promises. They must be performed, or the parties promising the acts will be in breach of contract. For example, Jerome contracts to sell Alfonso a painting for $3,000. The parties' promises—Jerome's transfer of the painting to Alfonso and Alfonso's payment of $3,000 to Jerome—are unconditional. The payment does not have to be made if the painting is not transferred.

In some situations, however, performance is contingent on the occurrence or nonoccurrence of a certain event. A **condition** is a possible future event, the occurrence or nonoccurrence of which will trigger the performance of a legal obligation or terminate an existing obligation under a contract.[1] If this condition is not satisfied, the obligations of the parties are discharged. Suppose that Alfonso, in the previous example, offers to purchase Jerome's painting only if an independent appraisal indicates that it is worth at least $3,000. Jerome accepts Alfonso's offer. Their obligations (promises) are conditioned on the outcome of the appraisal. Should the condition not be satisfied (for example, if the appraiser deems the value of the painting to be only $1,500), the parties' obligations to each other are discharged and cannot be enforced.

S E C T I O N   1

Conditions

In most contracts, promises of performance are not expressly conditioned or qualified. Instead, they are

1. The *Restatement (Second) of Contracts,* Section 224, defines a condition as "an event, not certain to occur, which must occur, unless its nonoccurrence is excused, before performance under a contract becomes due."

Three types of conditions can be present in contracts: conditions *precedent*, conditions *subsequent*, and *concurrent* conditions. Conditions are also classified as *express* or *implied*.

CONDITIONS PRECEDENT

A condition that must be fulfilled before a party's performance can be required is called a **condition precedent.** The condition precedes the absolute duty to perform, as in the Jerome-Alfonso example just discussed. Real estate contracts frequently are conditioned on the buyer's ability to obtain financing. For example, Fisher promises to buy Calvin's house if Salvation Bank approves Fisher's mortgage application. The Fisher-Calvin contract is therefore subject to a condition precedent—the bank's approval of Fisher's mortgage application. If the bank does not approve the application, the contract will fail because the condition precedent was not met. Insurance contracts frequently specify that certain conditions must be met before the insurance company will be obligated to perform under the contract.

CONDITIONS SUBSEQUENT

When a condition operates to terminate a party's absolute promise to perform, it is called a **condition subsequent.** The condition follows, or is subsequent to, the arising of an absolute duty to perform. If the condition occurs, the party need not perform any further. For example, imagine that a law firm hires Koker, a recent law school graduate and newly licensed attorney. Their contract provides that the firm's obligation to continue employing Koker is discharged if Koker fails to maintain her license to practice law. This is a condition subsequent, because a failure to maintain the license would discharge a duty that has already arisen.

Generally, conditions precedent are common; conditions subsequent are rare. The *Restatement (Second) of Contracts* does not use the terms *condition subsequent* and *condition precedent* but refers to both simply as conditions.[2]

CONCURRENT CONDITIONS

When each party's absolute duty to perform is conditioned on the other party's absolute duty to perform,

---

2. *Restatement (Second) of Contracts*, Section 224.

there are **concurrent conditions.** Concurrent conditions occur only when the parties expressly or impliedly are to perform their respective duties *simultaneously.* For example, if a buyer promises to pay for goods when they are delivered by the seller, each party's absolute duty to perform is conditioned on the other party's absolute duty to perform. The buyer's duty to pay for the goods does not become absolute until the seller either delivers or tenders the goods. (**Tender** is an unconditional offer to perform by one who is ready, willing, and able to do so.) Likewise, the seller's duty to deliver the goods does not become absolute until the buyer tenders or actually makes payment. Therefore, neither can recover from the other for breach unless he or she first tenders his or her own performance.

EXPRESS AND IMPLIED CONDITIONS

Conditions can also be classified as express or implied in fact. *Express conditions* are provided for by the parties' agreement. An express condition is usually prefaced by the word *if, provided, after,* or *when.*

Conditions *implied in fact* are similar to express conditions because they are understood to be part of the agreement, but they are not found in the express language of the agreement. The court infers them from the promises. For example, Wellbuilt Construction Company builds a house for Kirby, including in the contract a one-year warranty against defects in materials and construction—that is, Wellbuilt promises to fix or replace anything attributable to its work that goes wrong within a year. That Kirby must notify Wellbuilt of any defects is an implied-in-fact condition of Wellbuilt's duty to correct the defects.

SECTION 2

Discharge by Performance

The great majority of contracts are discharged by performance. The contract comes to an end when both parties fulfill their respective duties by performing the acts they have promised. Performance can also be accomplished by *tender.* Therefore, a seller who places goods at the disposal of a buyer has tendered delivery and can demand payment. A buyer who offers to pay for goods has tendered payment and can demand delivery of the goods. Once performance has been tendered, the party making the tender has done everything possible to carry out the terms of the contract. If the other party then refuses to perform, the party making the tender can sue for breach of contract.

TYPES OF PERFORMANCE

There are two basic types of performance—*complete performance* and *substantial performance*. A contract may stipulate that performance must meet the personal satisfaction of either the contracting party or a third party. Such a provision must be considered in determining whether the performance rendered satisfies the contract.

Complete Performance. When a party performs exactly as agreed, there is no question as to whether the contract has been performed. When a party's performance is perfect, it is said to be complete.

Conditions expressly stated in a contract must be fully satisfied for complete performance to take place. For example, most construction contracts require the builder to meet certain specifications. If the specifications are conditions, complete performance is required to avoid material breach. (Material breach will be discussed shortly.) If the conditions are met, the other party to the contract must then fulfill his or her obligation to pay the builder. If the specifications are not conditions and if the builder, without the other party's permission, fails to comply with the standards, performance is not complete. What effect does such a failure have on the other party's obligation to pay? The answer is part of the doctrine of substantial performance.

Substantial Performance. A party who in good faith performs substantially all of the terms of a contract can enforce the contract against the other party under the doctrine of substantial performance. Note that good faith is required, which means that the failure to fully perform must not be willful. Willfully failing to comply with the terms is a breach of the contract. Generally, performance that provides a party with the important and essential benefits of a contract, in spite of any omission or deviation from the terms, is substantial performance.

Determining whether performance has provided the "important and essential benefits" of a contract requires taking into consideration all of the facts. For example, in a construction contract, these facts would include the intended purpose of the structure and the expense required to bring the structure into compliance with the contract. Thus, the exact point at which performance is considered substantial varies from case to case.

Because substantial performance is not perfect, the other party is entitled to damages to compensate for the failure to comply with the contract. The measure of the damages is the cost to bring the object of the contract into compliance with its terms, if that cost is reasonable under the circumstances. If the cost is unreasonable, the measure of damages is the difference in value between the performance that was rendered and the performance that would have been rendered if the contract had been performed completely.

The following classic case on substantial performance emphasizes that there is no exact formula for deciding when a contract has been substantially performed. The case also indicates some of the factors that courts consider in deciding whether a contract has been materially breached or substantially performed.

CASE 17.1   Jacobs & Young, Inc. v. Kent

Court of Appeals of
New York, 1921.
230 N.Y. 239,
129 N.E. 889.

BACKGROUND AND FACTS   *The plaintiff, Jacobs & Young, Inc., was a builder that had contracted with the defendant, George Kent, to construct a country residence for the defendant. A specification in the building contract required that "[a]ll wrought-iron pipe must be well galvanized, lap welded pipe of the grade known as 'standard pipe' of Reading manufacture." The plaintiff installed substantially similar pipe that was not of Reading manufacture. When the defendant became aware of the difference, he ordered the plaintiff to remove all of the plumbing and replace it with the Reading type. To do so would have required removing finished walls that encased the plumbing—an expensive and difficult task. The plaintiff explained that the plumbing was of the same quality, appearance, value, and cost as Reading pipe. When the defendant refused to pay the* *plaintiff the $3,483.46 still owed for the work, the plaintiff sued to compel payment. The trial court ruled in favor of the defendant. The plaintiff appealed, and the appellate court reversed the trial court's decision. The defendant then appealed to the Court of Appeals of New York, the state's highest court.*

IN THE LANGUAGE OF THE COURT

CARDOZO, Justice.

* * * * * * * The courts never say that one who makes a contract fills the measure of his duty by less than full performance. They do say, however, that an omission, both trivial and innocent, will sometimes be atoned for by allowance of the resulting damage, and will not always be the breach of a condition[.] * * *

* * * Where the line is to be drawn between the important and the trivial cannot be settled by a formula. * * * We must weigh the purpose to be served, the desire to be gratified, the excuse for deviation from the letter, [and] the cruelty of enforced adherence. Then only can we tell whether literal fulfillment is to be implied by law as a condition. * * *

* * * [W]e think the measure of the allowance is not the cost of replacement, which would be great, but the difference in value, which would be either nominal or nothing. * * * The owner is entitled to the money which will permit him to complete, unless the cost of completion is grossly and unfairly out of proportion to the good to be attained.

DECISION AND REMEDY

(supreme ct. – highest in NY)

(The Court of Appeals of New York) holding that the plaintiff had substantially performed the contract, affirmed the appellate court's decision. The builder was entitled to the amount owed to it, less the difference in value between the specified and substituted pipe (which the court stated would be "nominal or nothing").

Performance to the Satisfaction of One of the Parties. Contracts often state that completed work must personally satisfy one of the parties. The question then arises whether this satisfaction becomes a condition precedent, requiring actual personal satisfaction or approval for discharge, or whether the test of satisfaction is an absolute promise requiring such performance as would satisfy a "reasonable person" (substantial performance).

When the subject matter of the contract is personal, a contract to be performed to the satisfaction of one of the parties is conditioned, and performance must actually satisfy that party. For example, contracts for portraits, works of art, medical or dental work, and tailoring are considered personal. Therefore, only the personal satisfaction of the party will be sufficient to fulfill the condition. To illustrate: Suppose that Williams agrees to paint a portrait of Hirshon's daughter for $750. The contract provides that Hirshon must be satisfied with the portrait. If Hirshon is not, she will not be required to pay for it. The only requirement imposed on Hirshon is that she act honestly and in good faith. If Hirshon expresses dissatisfaction only to avoid

paying for the portrait, the condition of satisfaction is excused, and her duty to pay becomes absolute. (Of course, the jury, or the judge acting as a jury, will have to decide whether she is acting honestly.)[3]

Contracts that involve mechanical fitness, utility, or marketability need only be performed to the satisfaction of a reasonable person. For example, construction contracts and manufacturing contracts are usually *not* considered to be personal, so the party's personal satisfaction is normally irrelevant. As long as the performance will satisfy a reasonable person, the contract is fulfilled.[4]

Performance to the Satisfaction of a Third Party. At times, contracts may require performance to the satisfaction of a third party (not a party to the contract). To illustrate: Assume that you contract to pave several city streets. The contract provides that the

---

3. For a classic case illustrating this principle, see *Gibson v. Cranage,* 39 Mich. 49 (1878).
4. If, however, the contract specifically states that it is to be fulfilled to the "personal" satisfaction of one or more of the parties, and the parties so intended, the outcome will probably be different.

work will be done "to the satisfaction of Phil Hopper, the supervising engineer." In this situation, the courts are divided. A few courts require the personal satisfaction of the third party—in this example, Phil Hopper. If Hopper is not satisfied, you will not be paid, even if a reasonable person would be satisfied. Again, the personal judgment must be made honestly, or the condition will be excused. A majority of courts require the work to be satisfactory to a reasonable person. Thus, even if Hopper was dissatisfied with the paving work, you would be paid, as long as a qualified supervising engineer would have been satisfied. All of the above examples demonstrate the necessity for *clear, specific wording in contracts.*

MATERIAL BREACH OF CONTRACT

A **breach of contract** is the nonperformance of a contractual duty. The breach is *material*[5] when perform-

5. *Restatement (Second) of Contracts*, Section 241.

ance is not at least substantial—in other words, when there has been a failure of consideration. In such cases, the nonbreaching party is excused from the performance of contractual duties and has a cause of action to sue for damages caused by the breach.

If the breach is *minor* (not material), the nonbreaching party's duty to perform can sometimes be suspended until the breach has been remedied, but the duty to perform is not entirely excused. Once the minor breach has been cured, the nonbreaching party must resume performance of the contractual obligations undertaken. Any breach entitles the nonbreaching party to sue for damages, but only a material breach discharges the nonbreaching party from the contract. The policy underlying these rules allows contracts to go forward when only minor problems occur but allows them to be terminated if major difficulties arise.

Does preventing an employee from working constitute a breach of contract if the employer continues to pay her salary? That was the issue in the following case.

CASE 17.2   Van Steenhouse v. Jacor Broadcasting of Colorado, Inc.

Supreme Court of Colorado, 1998.
958 P.2d 464.
http://www.findlaw.com/11stategov/co/coca.html[a]

BACKGROUND AND FACTS *Jacor Broadcasting of Colorado, Inc., owns and operates Newsradio 85 KOA. In June 1991, Andrea Van Steenhouse signed a three-year agreement to perform as a radio talk-show host for KOA. She was to receive a base salary and a performance bonus, depending on how many people tuned into her show. In January 1994, Jacor replaced her show with Rush Limbaugh's program. Jacor paid Van Steenhouse her base salary for the rest of the term of their agreement but did not employ her as a talk-show host. Van Steenhouse filed a suit in a Colorado state court against Jacor and others, claiming, among other things, breach of contract. The court ruled that Jacor materially breached the contract and awarded Van Steenhouse an amount representing the bonus she could have received if she had not been taken off the air. The state intermediate appellate court affirmed the judgment. Jacor appealed to the Supreme Court of Colorado.*

IN THE LANGUAGE OF THE COURT

Chief Justice VOLLACK delivered the Opinion of the Court.

*   *   *   *

Ordinarily, an employment agreement does not obligate an employer to furnish work for an employee. However, such an obligation may be inferred depending on the circumstances under which the agreement for employment is made or the nature of the employment. In particular, *an obligation to furnish work arises if the employee materially benefits from performing the duties described in the agreement* *   *   * . [W]hen an employer fails to furnish the kind of work specified in an employment agreement, the employee has a cause of action for breach of contract. [Emphasis added.]

*   *   *   *

---

a. In the "Supreme Court" list, in the "1998" row, click on "April." On that page, scroll down the list of cases to the *Van Steenhouse* case, and click on the name to access the opinion.

* * * [I]n this case * * * Jacor breached the Agreement by depriving Van Steenhouse of the opportunity to perform as a talk show host on KOA. * * * As a result, Van Steenhouse lost the opportunity to build and maintain her professional marketability. In addition, Van Steenhouse lost the opportunity to earn a 1994 performance bonus.

Jacor deprived Van Steenhouse of these benefits by refusing to broadcast her show [as] specified by the clear terms of the Agreement. Accordingly, we hold that Van Steenhouse stated a valid claim for breach of contract.

DECISION AND REMEDY   *The Supreme Court of Colorado held that an employee's claim for breach of contract can be based solely on an employer's failure to provide an opportunity to work. The court affirmed this part of the lower court's decision.*

ANTICIPATORY REPUDIATION

Before either party to a contract has a duty to perform, one of the parties may refuse to carry out his or her contractual obligations. This is called **anticipatory repudiation**[6] of the contract and can discharge the nonbreaching party from performance. Until the nonbreaching party treats an early repudiation as a breach, however, the repudiating party can retract his or her anticipatory repudiation by proper notice and restore the parties to their original obligations.[7] There are two reasons for allowing the nonbreaching party to treat an anticipatory repudiation as a present, material breach:

1. The nonbreaching party should not be required to remain ready and willing to perform when the other party has already repudiated the contract.
2. The nonbreaching party should have the opportunity to seek a similar contract elsewhere.[8]

Quite often, anticipatory repudiation occurs when performance of the contract would be extremely unfavorable to one of the parties because of a sharp fluctuation in market prices. For example, Martin Corporation contracts to manufacture and sell ten thousand personal computers to ComAge, a retailer of computer equipment that has five hundred outlet stores. Delivery is to be made six months from the date of the contract. The contract price is based on the seller's present costs of purchasing inventory parts from others. One month later, three inventory suppliers raise their prices to Martin.

Based on these prices, if Martin Corporation manufactures and sells the personal computers to ComAge at the contract price, Martin stands to lose $500,000. Martin immediately writes ComAge that it cannot deliver the ten thousand computers at the contract price. Martin's letter is an anticipatory repudiation of the contract. ComAge has the option of treating the repudiation as a material breach of contract and proceeding immediately to pursue remedies, even though the actual contract delivery date is still five months away.[9]

TIME FOR PERFORMANCE

If no time for performance is stated in the contract, a *reasonable time* is implied.[10] If a specific time is stated, the parties must usually perform by that time. Unless time is expressly stated to be vital, however, a delay in performance will not destroy the performing party's right to payment. When time is expressly stated to be vital, or when it is construed to be "of the essence," the parties normally must perform within the stated time period. The time element becomes a condition.

SECTION 3

Discharge by Agreement

Any contract can be discharged by agreement of the parties. The agreement can be contained in the original

---

6. *Restatement (Second) of Contracts*, Section 253; UCC 2–610.
7. See UCC 2–611.
8. The doctrine of anticipatory repudiation first arose in the landmark case of *Hochster v. De La Tour*, 2 Ellis and Blackburn Reports 678 (1853), when the English court recognized the delay and expense inherent in a rule requiring a nonbreaching party to wait until the time of performance before suing on an anticipatory repudiation.

9. See *Reliance Cooperage Corp. v. Treat*, 195 F.2d 977 (8th Cir. 1952), as a further illustration.
10. See UCC 2–204.

contract, or the parties can form a new contract for the express purpose of discharging the original contract.

DISCHARGE BY RESCISSION

Rescission is the process by which a contract is canceled or terminated and the parties are returned to the positions they occupied prior to forming it. For **mutual rescission** to take place, the parties must make another agreement, which must also satisfy the legal requirements for a contract. There must be an *offer*, an *acceptance*, and *consideration*.

Ordinarily, in an executory contract in which neither party has yet performed, if the parties agree to rescind the original contract, their promises not to perform the acts stipulated in the original contract will be legal consideration for the second contract. The rescission agreement is generally enforceable even if made orally. An exception applies under the Uniform Commercial Code (UCC) to agreements rescinding a contract for the sale of goods regardless of price when the contract requires written rescission.[11]

When one party has fully performed, an agreement to call off the original contract normally will not be enforceable. Because the performing party has received no consideration for the promise to call off the original bargain, additional consideration will be necessary.

In sum, contracts that are *executory on both sides* (contracts on which neither party has performed) can be rescinded solely by agreement.[12] But contracts that are *executed on one side* (contracts on which one party has performed) can be rescinded only if the party who has performed receives consideration for the promise to call off the deal.

DISCHARGE BY NOVATION

A contractual obligation may also be discharged through novation. A **novation** occurs when both of the parties to a contract agree to substitute a third party for one of the original parties. The requirements of a novation are as follows:

1. A previous valid obligation.
2. An agreement of all the parties to a new contract.

3. The extinguishment of the old obligation (discharge of the prior party).
4. A new contract that is valid.

For example, suppose that Union Corporation contracts to sell its pharmaceutical division to British Pharmaceuticals, Ltd. Before the transfer is completed, Union, British Pharmaceuticals, and a third company, Otis Chemicals, execute a new agreement to transfer all of British Pharmaceutical's rights and duties in the transaction to Otis Chemicals. As long as the new contract is supported by consideration, the novation will discharge the original contract (between Union and British Pharmaceuticals) and replace it with the new contract (between Union and Otis Chemicals).

A novation expressly or impliedly revokes and discharges a prior contract.[13] The parties involved may expressly state in the new contract that the old contract is now discharged. If the parties do not expressly discharge the old contract, it will be impliedly discharged because of the change or because of the new contract's different terms, which are inconsistent with the old contract's terms.

DISCHARGE BY SUBSTITUTED AGREEMENT

A *compromise*, or settlement agreement, that arises out of a genuine dispute over the obligations under an existing contract will be recognized at law. Such an agreement will be substituted as a new contract, and it will either expressly or impliedly revoke and discharge the obligations under any prior contract. In contrast to a novation, a substituted agreement does not involve a third party. Rather, the two original parties to the contract form a different agreement to substitute for the original one.

DISCHARGE BY ACCORD AND SATISFACTION

For a contract to be discharged by accord and satisfaction, the parties must agree to accept performance that

---

11. UCC 2–209(2), (4).
12. Certain sales made to a consumer at home can be rescinded by the consumer within three days for no reason at all. This three-day "cooling-off" period is designed to aid consumers who are susceptible to high-pressure door-to-door sales tactics. See Chapter 44 and 15 U.S.C. Section 1635(a).

13. It is this immediate discharge of the prior contract that distinguishes a novation from both an accord and satisfaction, discussed in the next subsection, and an assignment of all rights, discussed in Chapter 16. In an assignment of all rights, the original party to the contract (the assignor) remains liable under the original contract if the assignee fails to perform the contractual obligations. In contrast, in a novation, the original party's obligations are completely discharged.

is different from the performance originally promised. As discussed in Chapter 12, an *accord* is defined as an executory contract to perform some act to satisfy an existing contractual duty.[14] The duty has not yet been discharged. A *satisfaction* is the performance of the accord agreement. An accord and its satisfaction discharge the original contractual obligation.

Once the accord has been made, the original obligation is merely suspended. The obligor (the one owing the obligation) can discharge the obligation by performing the obligation agreed to in the accord or the original obligation. If the obligor refuses to perform the accord, the obligee (the one to whom performance is owed) can bring action on the original obligation or seek a decree compelling specific performance on the accord.

SECTION 4

Discharge by Operation of Law

Under certain circumstances, contractual duties may be discharged by operation of law. These circumstances include material alteration of the contract, the running of the statute of limitations, bankruptcy, and the impossibility or impracticability of performance.

ALTERATION OF THE CONTRACT

To discourage parties from altering written contracts, the law operates to allow an innocent party to be discharged when the other party has materially altered a written contract without consent. For example, contract terms such as quantity or price might be changed without the knowledge or consent of all parties. If so, the party who was unaware of the alteration can treat the contract as discharged or terminated.[15]

STATUTES OF LIMITATIONS

As mentioned earlier in this text, statutes of limitations restrict the period during which a party can sue on a particular cause of action. After the applicable limitations period has passed, a suit can no longer be brought. For example, the limitations period for bringing suits for breach of oral contracts is usually two to three years; for written contracts, four to five years; and for recovery of amounts awarded in judgments, ten to twenty years, depending on state law.

Section 2–725 of the UCC deals with the statute of limitations applicable to contracts for the sale of goods. For purposes of applying this section, the UCC does not distinguish between oral and written contracts. Section 2–725 provides that an action for the breach of any contract for sale must be commenced within four years after the cause of that action has accrued. The cause of action accrues when the breach occurs, regardless of the aggrieved party's lack of knowledge of the breach. By original agreement, the parties can reduce this four-year period to one year. They cannot, however, extend it beyond the four-year limitation period.

Technically, the running of a statute of limitations bars access only to *judicial* remedies; it does not extinguish the debt or the underlying obligation. The statute precludes access to the courts for collection. If, however, the party who owes the debt or obligation agrees to perform (that is, makes a new promise to perform), the cause of action barred by the statute of limitations will be revived. For the old agreement to be restored by a new promise in this manner, many states require that the promise be in writing or that there be evidence of partial performance.

BANKRUPTCY

A proceeding in bankruptcy attempts to allocate the assets the debtor owns to the creditors in a fair and equitable fashion. Once the assets have been allocated, the debtor receives a **discharge in bankruptcy.** A discharge in bankruptcy will ordinarily bar enforcement of most of a debtor's contracts by the creditors. Partial payment of a debt *after* discharge in bankruptcy will not revive the debt. (Bankruptcy will be discussed in detail in Chapter 30.)

IMPOSSIBILITY OR IMPRACTICABILITY OF PERFORMANCE

After a contract has been made, performance may become impossible in an objective sense. This is known as **impossibility of performance** and may discharge a contract.[16]

---

14. *Restatement (Second) of Contracts*, Section 281.
15. The contract is voidable, and the innocent party can also treat the contract as in effect, either on the original terms or on the terms as altered. A buyer who discovers that a seller altered the quantity of goods in a sales contract from 100 to 1,000 by secretly inserting a zero can purchase either 100 or 1,000 of the items.

---

16. *Restatement (Second) of Contracts*, Section 261.

Objective Impossibility of Performance. *Objective impossibility* ("It can't be done") must be distinguished from *subjective impossibility* ("I'm sorry, I simply can't do it"). Examples of subjective impossibility include cases in which goods cannot be delivered on time because of freight car shortages[17] and cases in which money cannot be paid on time because the bank is closed.[18] In effect, the party in each of these cases is saying, "It is impossible for me to perform," not "It is impossible for anyone to perform." Accordingly, such excuses do not discharge a contract, and the nonperforming party is normally held in breach of contract. Three basic types of situations, however, generally qualify as grounds for the discharge of contractual obligations based on impossibility of performance:[19]

1. *When one of the parties to a personal contract dies or becomes incapacitated prior to performance.* For example, Fred, a famous dancer, contracts with Ethereal Dancing Guild to play a leading role in its new ballet. Before the ballet can be performed, Fred becomes ill and dies. His personal performance was essential to the completion of the contract. Thus, his death discharges the contract and his estate's liability for his nonperformance.

2. *When the specific subject matter of the contract is destroyed.* For example, A-1 Farm Equipment agrees to sell Gudgel the green tractor on its lot and prom-

ises to have it ready for Gudgel to pick up on Saturday. On Friday night, however, a truck veers off the nearby highway and smashes into the tractor, destroying it beyond repair. Because the contract was for this specific tractor, A-1's performance is rendered impossible owing to the accident.

3. *When a change in law renders performance illegal.* An example is a contract to build an apartment building, when the zoning laws are changed to prohibit the construction of residential rental property at this location. This change renders the contract impossible to perform.

Commercial Impracticability. Courts may excuse parties from their performance obligations when the performance becomes much more difficult or expensive than originally contemplated at the time the contract was formed. For someone to invoke successfully the doctrine of **commercial impracticability,** however, the anticipated performance must become *extremely* difficult or costly.[20] For example, in one case, a court held that a contract was discharged because a party would have had to pay ten times more than the original estimate to excavate a certain amount of gravel.[21] Caution should be used in invoking commercial impracticability. The added burden of performing must be *extreme* and, more important, *must not have been within the cognizance of the parties when the contract was made.* The element of foreseeability was emphasized in the following case.

---

17. *Minneapolis v. Republic Creosoting Co.,* 161 Minn. 178, 201 N.W. 414 (1924).

18. *Ingham Lumber Co. v. Ingersoll & Co.,* 93 Ark. 447, 125 S.W. 139 (1910).

19. *Restatement (Second) of Contracts,* Sections 262–266; UCC 2–615.

20. *Restatement (Second) of Contracts,* Section 264.

21. *Mineral Park Land Co. v. Howard,* 172 Cal. 289, 156 P. 458 (1916).

CASE 17.3   **Syrovy v. Alpine Resources, Inc.**

Court of Appeals of
Washington, 1992.
841 P.2d 1279.

BACKGROUND AND FACTS *The George Syrovy Trust (Syrovy) agreed to sell Alpine Resources, Inc., all of the timber from Syrovy's property that Alpine could harvest over a two-year period for $140,000. Over the next two years, Alpine harvested some timber and paid Syrovy $50,000. When Syrovy sued for the contract balance of $90,000, Alpine claimed that it should be released from its obligation to pay the remainder of the contract price on the ground of commercial impracticability. Alpine claimed that bad weather conditions during both winters and the fact that Alpine could not engage in logging operations during the hunting season made it impossible to harvest the quantity of timber it had planned on harvesting when the contract was formed. The trial court granted Syrovy's motion for summary judgment, and Alpine appealed.*

IN THE LANGUAGE   SWEENEY, Judge.
OF THE COURT   *   *   *   *

* * * [Under the defense of impracticability] performance is excused if events occur that are not foreseen or anticipated—a "wholly unexpected contingency." *Difficulties that are assumed by a party, at the time of contracting, cannot form the basis of an impracticability defense.* [Emphasis added.]

Alpine argues that the winters of 1988 and 1989 were so severe that harvesting became impossible. However, Mr. Reoh [who negotiated the contract for Alpine] is a logger with considerable experience in purchasing timber. It would be unreasonable to suggest that weather conditions were an unforeseeable event. Also, there is no evidence to support the assertion that the weather was so remarkable that contract performance was impossible.

Alpine also argues that it did not have access to the property during hunting season. * * * Access problems were foreseeable and the risk was allocated in the contract. The problems cannot be asserted as a basis for an impracticability defense.

DECISION AND REMEDY *The trial court's decision was affirmed. Foreseeable problems, such as weather conditions or even more predictable events that may hinder performance, were not sufficient to excuse Alpine's failure to fulfill its part of the contract.*

INTERNATIONAL CONSIDERATION **Impossibility of Performance in Germany** *In the United States, when a party alleges that contract performance is impossible or impracticable because of circumstances unforeseen at the time the contract was formed, a court will either discharge the party's contractual obligations or hold the party to the contract. Under German law, however, a court may adjust the terms of a contract in light of economic developments. If an unforeseen event affects the foundation of the agreement, the court can alter the contract's terms in view of the disruption in expectations, thus making the contract fair to the parties.*

Frustration of Purpose. A theory closely allied with the doctrine of commercial impracticability is the doctrine of **frustration of purpose.** In principle, a contract will be discharged if supervening circumstances make it impossible to attain the purpose both parties had in mind when making the contract. The origins of the doctrine lie in the old English "coronation cases." A coronation procession was planned for Edward VII when he became king of England following the death of his mother, Queen Victoria. Hotel rooms along the coronation route were rented at exorbitant prices for that day. When the king became ill and the procession was canceled, a flurry of lawsuits resulted. Hotel and building owners sought to enforce the room-rent bills against would-be parade observers, and would-be parade observers sought to be reimbursed for rental monies paid in advance on the rooms. Would-be parade observers were excused from their duty of payment because the purpose of the room contracts had been "frustrated."

Temporary Impossibility. An occurrence or event that makes performance temporarily impossible operates to suspend performance until the impossibility ceases. Then, ordinarily, the parties must perform the contract as originally planned. If, however, the lapse of time and the change in circumstances surrounding the contract make it substantially more burdensome for the parties to perform the promised acts, the contract is discharged.

The leading case on the subject, *Autry v. Republic Productions,*[22] involved an actor who was drafted into the army in 1942. Being drafted rendered the actor's contract temporarily impossible to perform, and it was suspended until the end of the war. When the actor got out of the army, the value of the dollar had so changed that performance of the contract would have been substantially burdensome to the actor. Therefore, the contract was discharged.

---

22. 30 Cal.2d 144, 180 P.2d 888 (1947).

CONCEPT SUMMARY 17.1  DISCHARGE OF CONTRACTS

METHOD	BASIC RULES
Discharge by Occurrence or Failure of a Condition	1. *Failure of a condition precedent*—Duty to perform does not become absolute until fulfillment of condition precedent. 2. *Occurrence of a condition subsequent*—A condition subsequent follows an absolute duty to perform and, if it occurs, excuses a party's performance.
Discharge by Performance (or Breach of Contract)	1. *Performance*—Complete or substantial. 2. *Breach*—Material nonperformance discharges the nonbreaching party.
Discharge by Agreement	1. *Mutual rescission*—An enforceable agreement to restore parties to their precontract positions. 2. *Novation*—By valid contract, a new party is substituted for an original party, thereby terminating the old contract. 3. *Accord and satisfaction*—An agreement under which the original contract can be discharged by a different performance.

Discharge by Operation of Law	1. *Alteration*—An innocent party is discharged by material alteration of the contract without consent.
	2. *Statute of limitations*—The plaintiff's delay in filing suit bars the availability of judicial remedies, thus discharging the defendant's duty to perform.
	3. *Bankruptcy*—The decree discharges most of the debtor's contractual obligations.
	4. *Impossibility or impracticability of performance*—
	  a. A person whose performance is essential to completion of the contract dies or is incapacitated.
	  b. The specific subject matter of the contract is destroyed prior to transfer.
	  c. Performance is declared illegal.
	  d. Performance becomes commercially impracticable or is frustrated.
	  e. If performance is temporarily suspended because of events or occurrences (such as war), and subsequent circumstances make the contract substantially more difficult to perform, the parties may be discharged.

TERMS AND CONCEPTS TO REVIEW

QUESTIONS AND CASE PROBLEMS

17–1. PERFORMANCE. The Caplans own a real estate lot, and they contract with Faithful Construction, Inc., to build a house on it for $60,000. The specifications list "all plumbing bowls and fixtures . . . to be Crane brand." The Caplans leave on vacation, and during their absence Faithful is unable to buy and install Crane plumbing fixtures. Instead, Faithful installs Kohler brand fixtures, an equivalent in the industry. On completion of the building contract, the Caplans, on inspection, discover the substitution and refuse to accept the house, claiming Faithful has breached the conditions set forth in the specifications. Discuss fully the Caplans' claim.

17–2. DISCHARGE. Junior owes creditor Iba $1,000, which is due and payable on June 1. Junior has been in a car accident, has missed a great deal of work, and consequently will not have the money on June 1. Junior's father, Fred, offers to pay Iba $1,100 in four equal installments if Iba will discharge Junior from any further liability on the debt. Iba accepts. Discuss the following:

    (a) Is the transaction a novation, or is it an accord and satisfaction? Explain.

    (b) Does the contract between Fred and Iba have to be in writing to be enforceable? (Review the discussion of the Statute of Frauds in Chapter 15.) Explain.

17–3. BREACH. ABC Clothiers, Inc., has a contract with Taylor & Sons, a retailer, to deliver one thousand summer suits to Taylor's place of business on or before May 1. On April 1, Taylor senior receives a letter from ABC informing him that ABC will not be able to make the delivery as scheduled. Taylor is very upset, as he had planned a big ad sale campaign. He wants to file suit against ABC immediately (April 2). Taylor's son, Tom, tells his father that filing a lawsuit is not proper until ABC actually fails to deliver the suits on May 1. Discuss fully who is correct, Taylor or his son, Tom.

17–4. IMPOSSIBILITY OF PERFORMANCE. In the following situations, certain events take place after the formation of contracts. Discuss which of these contracts are discharged because the events render the contracts impossible to perform.

    (a) Jimenez, a famous singer, contracts to perform in your nightclub. He dies prior to performance.

    (b) Raglione contracts to sell you her land. Just before title is to be transferred, she dies.

    (c) Oppenheim contracts to sell you one thousand bushels of apples from her orchard in the state of Washington. Because of a severe frost, she is unable to deliver the apples.

    (d) Maxwell contracts to lease a service station for ten years. His principal income is from the sale of gasoline. Because of an oil embargo by foreign oil-producing nations, gasoline is rationed, cutting sharply into Maxwell's gasoline sales. He cannot make his lease payments.

17–5. TIME FOR PERFORMANCE. Murphy contracts to purchase from Lone Star Liquors six cases of French champagne for $1,200. The contract states that delivery is to be made at the Murphy residence "on or before June 1, to be used for daughter's wedding reception on June 2." The champagne is carried regularly in Lone Star's stock. On June 1, Lone Star's delivery van is involved in an accident, and the champagne is not delivered that day. On the morning of June 2, Murphy discovers the nondelivery. Unable to reach Lone Star because its line is busy, Murphy purchases the champagne from another dealer. That afternoon, just before the wedding reception, Lone Star tenders delivery of the champagne at Murphy's residence. Murphy refuses tender, and Lone Star sues for breach of contract. Discuss fully the result.

17–6. SUBSTANTIAL PERFORMANCE. Grane, a homeowner, contracted with Butkovich & Sons, Inc., to enlarge Grane's basement and build a new room over the remodeled basement area. Butkovich was also to lay a new garage floor and construct a patio. The parties agreed to a price of $19,290 for the work. When the construction was completed, Grane refused to pay the contractor the $9,290 balance he still owed, claiming that Butkovich had failed to install water stops and reinforcing wire in one concrete floor, in accordance with Grane's specifications, and that the main floor of the addition was 8⅞ inches lower than the plans had called for. Butkovich sued Grane for recovery of the $9,290. As a mortgage holder on the property, the State Bank of St. Charles was named co-defendant by Butkovich, because its interests would be affected by a judgment against Grane if the latter could not pay. Butkovich claimed that it had substantially performed the contract. Grane claimed that performance was of poor quality and that failure to follow contract specifications constituted a material breach. Discuss who should win. [*Butkovich & Sons, Inc. v. State Bank of St. Charles*, 62 Ill.App.3d 810, 379 N.E.2d 837, 20 Ill.Dec. 4 (1978)]

17–7. CONDITIONS PRECEDENT. Larry McLanahan's 1985 Lamborghini was stolen, and by the time McLanahan recovered the car, it had been extensively damaged. The car was insured by Farmers Insurance Co. of Washington under a policy providing comprehensive coverage, including coverage for theft. A provision in the policy stated that the coverage for theft damages was subject to certain terms and conditions, including the condition that any person claiming coverage under the policy must allow Farmers "to inspect and appraise the damaged vehicle before its repair or disposal." McLanahan, without notifying Farmers and without giving Farmers an opportunity to inspect the vehicle, sold the car to a wholesale car dealer. Farmers then denied coverage, and McLanahan brought suit to recover for the damages caused to his car by the theft. Did McLanahan have a valid claim against the insurance company? Explain. [*McLanahan v. Farmers Insurance Co. of Washington*, 66 Wash.App. 36, 831 P.2d 160 (1992)]

17–8. CONDITIONS. Heublein, Inc., makes wines and distilled spirits. Tarrant Distributors, Inc., agreed to distribute Heublein brands. When problems arose, the parties entered mediation. Under a settlement agreement, Heublein agreed to pay Tarrant the amount of its "net loss" as determined by Coopers & Lybrand, an accounting firm, according to a specified formula. The parties agreed that Coopers & Lybrand's calculation would be "final and binding." Heublein disagreed with Coopers & Lybrand's calculation, however, and refused to pay. The parties asked a federal district court to rule on the dispute. Heublein argued that the settlement agreement included an implied condition precedent that Coopers & Lybrand would correctly apply the specified formula before Heublein was obligated to pay. Tarrant pointed to the clause that the calculation would be "final and binding." With whom will the court agree, and why? [*Tarrant Distributors, Inc. v. Heublein, Inc.*, 127 F.3d 375 (5th Cir. 1997)]

17–9. PERFORMANCE. Steven McPheters, a house builder and developer, hired Terry Tentinger, who did business as New Horizon Construction, to do some touching up and repainting on one of McPheters's new houses. Tentinger worked two days, billed McPheters $420 (a three-man crew for fourteen hours at $30 per hour), and offered to return to the house to remedy any defects in his workmanship at no cost. McPheters objected to the number of hours on the bill—although he did not express dissatisfaction with the work—and offered Tentinger $250. Tentinger refused to accept this amount and filed a suit in an Idaho state court to collect the full amount. McPheters filed a counterclaim, alleging that Tentinger failed to perform the job in a workmanlike manner, resulting in $2,500 in damages, which it would cost $500 to repair. Tentinger's witnesses testified that although some touch-up work needed to be done, the job had been performed in a workmanlike manner.

McPheters presented testimony indicating that the workmanship was so defective as to render it commercially unreasonable. On what basis could the court rule in Tentinger's favor? Explain fully. [*Tentinger v. McPheters*, 132 Idaho 620, 977 P.2d 234 (Idaho App. 1999)]

17–10. IN YOUR COURT

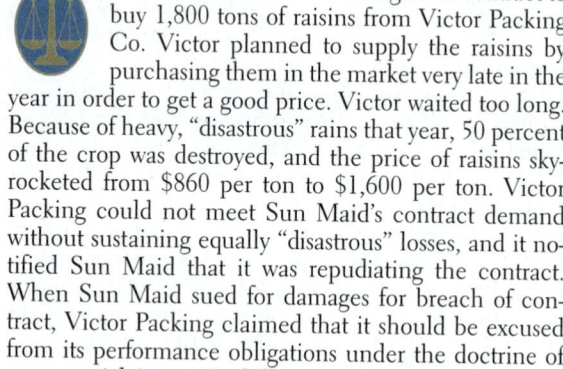 Sun Maid Raisin Growers signed a contract to buy 1,800 tons of raisins from Victor Packing Co. Victor planned to supply the raisins by purchasing them in the market very late in the year in order to get a good price. Victor waited too long. Because of heavy, "disastrous" rains that year, 50 percent of the crop was destroyed, and the price of raisins skyrocketed from $860 per ton to $1,600 per ton. Victor Packing could not meet Sun Maid's contract demand without sustaining equally "disastrous" losses, and it notified Sun Maid that it was repudiating the contract. When Sun Maid sued for damages for breach of contract, Victor Packing claimed that it should be excused from its performance obligations under the doctrine of commercial impracticability. Assume that you are the judge in the trial court hearing this case and answer the following questions:

(a) In forming your decision in this case, you will need to assess whether the heavy rains and subsequent increase in the market price of raisins were "foreseeable" events. How will you decide this question, and why?

(b) Review Case 17.3 (*Syrovy v. Alpine Resources, Inc.*). Should the judge's reasoning and conclusion in that case influence your decision in the case now before your court? Why or why not?

(c) How will you rule in this case? Explain your reasoning.

LAW ON THE WEB

For updated links to resources available on the Web, as well as a variety of other materials, visit this text's Web site at http://wbl.westbuslaw.com.

For a summary of how contracts may be discharged and other principles of contract law, go to

http://www.lawyers.com/site/aboutlaw/contract.html#contract10

Law Guru can lead you to other sources of law relating to contract performance and discharge. Go to

http:lawguru.com/lawlinks.html

LEGAL RESEARCH EXERCISES ON THE WEB

Go to http://wbl.westbuslaw.com, the Web site that accompanies this text. Select "Internet Applications," and then click on "Chapter 17." There you will find the following Internet research exercise that you can perform to learn more about anticipatory repudiation:

Activity 17–1: Anticipatory Repudiation

CHAPTER 18

Breach of Contract and Remedies

WHEN ONE PARTY BREACHES A CONTRACT, the other party—the nonbreaching party—can choose one or more of several remedies. A *remedy* is the relief provided for an innocent party when the other party has breached the contract. It is the means employed to enforce a right or to redress an injury.

The most common remedies available to a non-breaching party include damages, rescission and restitution, specific performance, and reformation. As discussed in Chapter 1, a distinction is made between *remedies at law* and *remedies in equity*. Today, the remedy at law is normally money damages, which are discussed in the first part of this chapter. Equitable remedies include rescission and restitution, specific performance, and reformation, all of which will be examined later in the chapter. Usually, a court will not award an equitable remedy unless the remedy at law is inadequate. Special legal doctrines and concepts relating to remedies will be discussed in the final pages of this chapter.

SECTION 1

Damages

A breach of contract entitles the nonbreaching party to sue for money (damages). As discussed in Chapter

5, damages are designed to compensate a party for harm suffered as a result of another's wrongful act. In the context of contract law, damages compensate the nonbreaching party for the loss of the bargain.[1]

Often, courts say that innocent parties are to be placed in the position they would have occupied had the contract been fully performed.[2] For example, in the famous case of the "hairy hand," a doctor promised to make a boy's scarred hand "a hundred percent perfect." Skin was taken from the boy's chest and grafted onto his thumb and fingers. The hand became infected, and the boy was hospitalized for three months. Use of the hand was greatly restricted, and hair grew out of the grafted skin. In hearing a suit against the doctor, the court explained that the amount of damages was to be determined by the difference between the value to the boy of the "perfect" hand that the doctor had promised and the value of the hand in its condition after the operation.[3]

---

1. Bear in mind that although a nonbreaching party may succeed in obtaining damages from a court from the breaching party, the court's judgment may be difficult to enforce. As discussed in Chapter 3, the breaching party may not have sufficient funds or assets to pay the damages awarded.

2. *Restatement (Second) of Contracts*, Section 347; UCC 1–106(1).

3. *Hawkins v. McGee*, 84 N.H. 114, 146 A. 641 (1929).

307

TYPES OF DAMAGES

There are basically four broad categories of damages:

1. Compensatory (to cover direct losses and costs).
2. Consequential (to cover indirect and foreseeable losses).
3. Punitive (to punish and deter wrongdoing).
4. Nominal (to recognize wrongdoing when no monetary loss is shown).

Compensatory and punitive damages were discussed in Chapter 5 in the context of tort law. Here, we look at these types of damages, as well as consequential and nominal damages, in the context of contract law.

Compensatory Damages. Damages compensating the nonbreaching party for the *loss of the bargain* are known as *compensatory damages.* These damages compensate the injured party only for damages actually sustained and proved to have arisen directly from the loss of the bargain caused by the breach of contract. They simply replace what was lost because of the wrong or damage. To illustrate: Wilcox contracts to perform certain services exclusively for Hernandez during the month of March for $2,000. Hernandez cancels the contract and is in breach. Wilcox is able to find another job during the month of March but can earn only $1,000. He can sue Hernandez for breach and recover $1,000 as compensatory damages. Wilcox can also recover from Hernandez the amount that he spent to find the other job. Expenses that are caused directly by a breach of contract—such as those incurred to obtain performance from another source—are known as *incidental damages.*

The measurement of compensatory damages varies by type of contract. Certain types of contracts deserve special mention. They are contracts for the sale of goods, land contracts, and construction contracts.

Sale of Goods. *(UCC)* In a contract for the sale of goods, the usual measure of compensatory damages is an amount equal to the difference between the contract price and the market price.[4] For example, suppose that Chrysler Corporation contracts to buy ten model UTS 400 network servers from an XEXO Corporation dealer for $8,000 each. The dealer, however, fails to deliver the ten servers to Chrysler. The market price

of the servers at the time the buyer learns of the breach is $8,150. Chrysler's measure of damages is therefore $1,500 (10 × $150) plus any incidental damages (expenses) caused by the breach. In a situation in which the buyer breaches and the seller has not yet produced the goods, compensatory damages normally equal lost profits on the sale, not the difference between the contract price and the market price.

Sale of Land. Ordinarily, because each parcel of land is unique, the remedy for a seller's breach of a contract for a sale of real estate is specific performance—that is, the buyer is awarded the parcel of property for which he or she bargained (specific performance is discussed more fully later in this chapter). When this remedy is unavailable (for example, when the seller has sold the property to someone else), or when the breach is on the part of the buyer, the measure of damages is ordinarily the same as in contracts for the sale of goods—that is, the difference between the contract price and the market price of the land. The majority of states follow this rule.

A minority of states follow a different rule when the seller breaches the contract and the breach is not deliberate:[5] In such a case, these states allow the prospective purchaser to recover any down payment plus any expenses incurred (such as fees for title searches, attorneys, and escrows). This minority rule effectively places purchasers in the position they occupied prior to the sale.

Construction Contracts. The measure of damages in a building or construction contract varies depending on which party breaches and when the breach occurs. The owner can breach at three different stages of the construction:

1. Before performance has begun.
2. During performance.
3. After performance has been completed.

If the owner breaches *before performance has begun,* the contractor can recover only the profits that would have been made on the contract (that is, the total contract price less the cost of materials and labor). If the

---

4. That is, the amount is the difference between the contract price and the market price at the time and place at which the goods were to be delivered or tendered. See UCC 2–708 and UCC 2–713.

5. "Deliberate" breaches include the seller's failure to convey the land because the market price has gone up. "Nondeliberate" breaches include the seller's failure to convey the land because an unknown easement (another's right of use over the property) has rendered title unmarketable. See Chapter 47.

owner breaches *during performance*, the contractor can recover the profits plus the costs incurred in partially constructing the building. If the owner breaches *after the construction has been completed*, the contractor can recover the entire contract price, plus interest.

When the construction contractor breaches the contract by stopping work part way through the project, the measure of damages is the cost of completion, which includes reasonable compensation for any delay in performance. If the contractor finishes late, the measure of damages is the loss of use. If the contractor substantially performs, the courts may use the cost-of-completion formula, but only if there is no substantial economic waste in requiring completion. Economic waste occurs when the cost of additional resources to finish the project exceeds any subjective value placed on the additional work done. For example, if a contractor discovers that it will cost $20,000 to move a large coral rock eleven inches as specified in the contract, and the change in the rock's position will alter the appearance of the project only a trifle, full completion will involve an economic waste. These rules concerning the measurement of damages in breached construction contracts are summarized in Exhibit 18–1 on the next page.

Consequential Damages. Foreseeable damages that result from a party's breach of contract are called **consequential damages,** or *special damages.* They differ from compensatory damages in that they are caused by special circumstances beyond the contract itself. They flow from the consequences, or results, of a breach.

For example, if a seller fails to deliver goods, and the seller knows that a buyer is planning to resell these goods immediately, consequential damages will be awarded for the loss of profit from the planned resale. The buyer will also recover compensatory damages for the difference between the contract price and the market price of the goods.

To recover consequential damages, the breaching party must know (or have reason to know) that special circumstances will cause the nonbreaching party to suffer an additional loss. This rule was enunciated in the classic case of *Hadley v. Baxendale*, which is presented below. This case established the rule that when damages are awarded, compensation is given only for those injuries that the defendant could *reasonably have foreseen* as a probable result of the usual course of events following a breach.

In reading through the following case, realize that in the mid-1800s in England, it was customary for large flour mills to have more than one crankshaft in the event the main one broke and had to be repaired. Also, in those days it was common knowledge that flour mills did indeed have spare crankshafts. It is against this background that the parties in the case presented here argued their respective positions on whether the damages resulting from the loss of profits while the crankshaft was repaired were reasonably foreseeable.

CASE 18.1   Hadley v. Baxendale

Court of Exchequer,
1854.
156 Eng.Rep. 145.

BACKGROUND AND FACTS   *The Hadleys (the plaintiffs) ran a flour mill in Gloucester. The crankshaft attached to the steam engine in the mill broke, causing the mill to shut down. The shaft had to be sent to a foundry located in Greenwich so that the new shaft could be made to fit the other parts of the engine. Baxendale, the defendant, was a common carrier that transported the shaft from Gloucester to Greenwich. The freight charges were collected in advance, and Baxendale promised to deliver the shaft the following day. It was not delivered for a number of days, however. As a consequence, the mill was closed for a number of days. The Hadleys sued to recover the profits lost during that time. Baxendale contended that the loss of profits was "too remote" to be recoverable. The court held for the plaintiffs, and the jury was allowed to take into consideration the lost profits. The defendant appealed.*

IN THE LANGUAGE OF THE COURT

ALDERSON, B.

*   *   *   *

*   *   * Where two parties have made a contract which one of them has broken, the damages which the other party ought to receive in respect of such breach of contract should be such as may fairly and reasonably be considered either arising naturally, i.e., according to the usual course of things, from such breach of contract itself, or such as may reasonably be supposed to have been in the contemplation of both parties, at the time they made the contract, as the probable result of the breach of it. Now, if the special circumstances under which the contract was actually made were communicated by the plaintiffs to the defendants, and thus known to both parties, the damages resulting from the breach of such a contract, *which they would reasonably contemplate*, would be the amount of injury which would ordinarily follow from a breach of contract under these special circumstances so known and communicated. *   *   * Now, in the present case, if we are to apply the principles above laid down, we find that the only circumstances here communicated by the plaintiffs to the defendants at the time the contract was made, were, that the article to be carried was the broken shaft of a mill, and that the plaintiffs were the millers of that mill. *   *   * [S]pecial circumstances were here never communicated by the plaintiffs to the defendants. It follows, therefore, that the loss of profits here cannot reasonably be considered such a consequence of the breach of contract as could have been fairly and reasonably contemplated by both the parties when they made this contract. [Emphasis added.]

DECISION AND REMEDY   *The Court of Exchequer ordered a new trial. According to the court, the plaintiffs would have to have given express notice of the special circumstances that caused the loss of profits to collect consequential damages.*

Punitive Damages. Punitive, or exemplary, damages are generally not awarded in an action for breach of contract. Punitive damages are designed to punish a guilty party and to make an example of the party to deter similar conduct in the future. Such damages have no legitimate place in contract law because they are, in essence, penalties, and a breach of contract is not unlawful in a criminal or societal sense. A contract is simply a civil relationship between the parties. The law may compensate one party for the loss of the bargain, no more and no less.

In a few situations, a person's actions can constitute both a breach of contract and a tort. For example, the parties may establish by contract a certain reasonable standard or duty of care. Failure to live up to that standard is a breach of contract, and the act itself may constitute negligence. Additionally, some intentional torts, such as fraud, may be tied to a breach of the terms of a contract. In such cases, it is possible for the nonbreaching party to recover punitive damages for the commission of the tort, in addition to compensatory and consequential damages for breach of contract.

Nominal Damages. When no actual damages result from a breach of contract and only a technical injury is involved, the court may award **nominal damages** to the innocent party. Awards of nominal damages are often trifling, such as a dollar, but they do establish that the defendant acted wrongfully.

For example, suppose that Jackson contracts to buy potatoes from Stanley at fifty cents a pound. Stanley

EXHIBIT 18–1   MEASUREMENT OF DAMAGES — BREACH OF CONSTRUCTION CONTRACTS

PARTY IN BREACH	TIME OF BREACH	MEASUREMENT OF DAMAGES
Owner	Before construction has begun	Profits (contract price less cost of materials and labor)
Owner	During construction	Profits plus costs incurred up to time of breach
Owner	After construction is completed	Contract price plus interest
Contractor	Before construction is completed	Generally, all costs incurred by owner to complete construction

breaches the contract and does not deliver the potatoes. In the meantime, the price of potatoes has fallen. Jackson is able to buy them in the open market at half the price he contracted for with Stanley. He is clearly better off because of Stanley's breach. Thus, in a suit for breach of contract, Jackson may be awarded only nominal damages for the technical injury he sustained, because no monetary loss was involved. Most lawsuits for nominal damages are brought as a matter of principle under the theory that a breach has occurred and some damages must be imposed regardless of actual loss.

MITIGATION OF DAMAGES

In most situations, when a breach of contract occurs, the innocent injured party is held to a duty to mitigate, or reduce, the damages that he or she suffers. Under this **mitigation of damages** doctrine, the duty owed depends on the nature of the contract.

For example, some states require a landlord to use reasonable means to find a new tenant if a tenant abandons the premises and fails to pay rent. If an acceptable tenant becomes available, the landlord is required to lease the premises to this tenant to mitigate the damages recoverable from the former tenant. The former tenant is still liable for the difference between the amount of the rent under the original lease and the rent received from the new tenant. If the landlord has not used the reasonable means necessary to find a new tenant, presumably a court can reduce the award made by the amount of rent he or she could have received had such reasonable means been used.

In the majority of states, persons whose employment has been wrongfully terminated owe a duty to mitigate damages suffered because of their employers' breach of the employment contract. The damages they receive are their salaries less the incomes they would have received in similar jobs that they could have obtained by reasonable means. The employer must prove both that such a job existed and that the employee could have been hired. As the following case illustrates, however, the employee is under no duty to take a job of a different type and rank.

CASE 18.2   Parker v. Twentieth Century-Fox Film Corp.

Supreme Court of
California, 1970.
3 Cal.3d 176,
474 P.2d 689,
89 Cal.Rptr. 737.

COMPANY PROFILE *Daryl Zanuck and Joseph Schenk formed the Twentieth Century Company in 1933 to make movies. Two years later, they merged with the Fox Film Company, which had been founded by William Fox, and became Twentieth Century-Fox Film Corporation (http://www.fox.com). Today, Twentieth Century-Fox produces movies and television shows as part of the News Corporation Limited, which is headquartered in Australia. The News Corporation also has interests in the production and distribution of newspapers, magazines, books, television programs, and films in Great Britain, Hong Kong, New Zealand, and other countries.*

BACKGROUND AND FACTS *Twentieth Century-Fox Film Corporation planned to produce a musical, Bloomer Girl, and contracted with Shirley MacLaine Parker to play the leading female role. According to the contract, Fox was to pay Parker $53,571.42 per week for fourteen weeks, for a total of $750,000. Fox later decided not to produce Bloomer Girl and tried to substitute for the existing contract another contract under which Parker would play the leading role in Big Country, a Western movie, for the same amount of money guaranteed by the first contract. Fox gave Parker one week in which to accept the new contract. Parker filed suit against Fox to recover the amount of compensation guaranteed in the first contract because, she maintained, the two roles were not at all equivalent. The Bloomer Girl production was a musical, to be filmed in California, and could not be compared with a "Western type" production that was, according to tentative plans, to be produced in Australia. When the trial court held for Parker, Fox appealed.*

IN THE LANGUAGE
OF THE COURT

BURKE, Justice.
*   *   *   *

The general rule is that the measure of recovery by a wrongfully discharged employee is the amount of salary agreed upon for the period of service, less the amount which the employer affirmatively proves the employee has earned or with reasonable effort might have earned from other employment. However, before projected earnings from other employment opportunities not sought or accepted by the discharged employee can be applied in mitigation, the employer must show that the other employment was comparable, or substantially similar, to that of which the employee has been deprived *   *   * .

*   *   *   *

*   *   * The mere circumstance that "Bloomer Girl" was to be a musical review calling upon plaintiff's talents as a dancer as well as an actress, and was to be produced in the City of Los Angeles, whereas "Big Country" was a straight dramatic role in a "Western Type" story taking place in an opal mine in Australia, demonstrates the difference in kind between the two employments; the female lead as a dramatic actress in a western style motion picture can by no stretch of imagination be considered the equivalent of or substantially similar to the lead in a song-and-dance production.

DECISION AND REMEDY   *The Supreme Court of California affirmed the trial court's ruling. Parker could not be required to accept Fox's offer of the Western-movie role to mitigate the damages she had incurred as a result of the breach of contract.*

LIQUIDATED DAMAGES VERSUS PENALTIES

Unliquidated damages are damages that have not been calculated or determined. **Liquidated damages,** in contrast, are damages that are certain in amount. A "liquidated damages provision" in a contract specifies a certain amount to be paid in the event of a *future* default or breach of contract. For example, a provision requiring a construction contractor to pay $300 for every day he or she is late in completing the construction is a liquidated damages provision.

Liquidated damages differ from penalties. **Penalties** specify a certain amount to be paid in the event of a default or breach of contract and are designed to *penalize* the breaching party. Liquidated damages provisions are enforceable; penalty provisions are not.

To determine if a particular provision is for liquidated damages or for a penalty, two questions must be answered:

1. When the contract was entered into, was it apparent that damages would be difficult to estimate in the event of a breach?
2. Was the amount set as damages a reasonable estimate and not excessive?[6]

If the answers to both questions are yes, the provision will be enforced. If either answer is no, the provision will not be enforced. Section 2–718(1) of the Uniform Commercial Code (UCC) specifically permits the inclusion of liquidated damages clauses in contracts for the sale of goods as long as both of these tests are met. In construction contracts, it is difficult to estimate the amount of damages that would be caused by a delay in completing construction, so liquidated damages clauses are often used.

---

6. *Restatement (Second) of Contracts,* Section 356(1).

CONCEPT SUMMARY 18.1   DAMAGES

REMEDY	AVAILABILITY	RESULT
Compensatory Damages	A party sustains and proves an injury arising directly from the loss of the bargain.	The injured party is compensated for the *loss* of the bargain.

CONCEPT SUMMARY 18.1

DAMAGES (continued)

REMEDY	AVAILABILITY	RESULT
Consequential Damages	Special circumstances, of which the breaching party is aware or should be aware, cause the injured party additional loss.	The injured party is given the entire *benefit* of the bargain.
Punitive Damages	Damages are normally available only when a tort is also involved.	The wrongdoer is punished, and others are deterred from committing similar acts.
Nominal Damages	There is no financial loss.	Wrongdoing is established without actual damages being suffered. The plaintiff is awarded a nominal amount (such as $1) in damages.
Liquidated Damages	A contract provides a specific amount to be paid as damages in the event that the contract is later breached.	The nonbreaching party is paid the amount stipulated in the contract for the breach, unless the amount is construed as a penalty.

SECTION 2

Rescission and Restitution

As discussed in Chapter 17, *rescission* is essentially an action to undo, or terminate, a contract—to return the contracting parties to the positions they occupied prior to the transaction. When fraud, a mistake, duress, undue influence, misrepresentation, or lack of capacity to contract is present, unilateral rescission is available.[7] Rescission may also be available by statute.[8] The failure of one party to perform entitles the other party to rescind the contract. The rescinding party must give prompt notice to the breaching party. Generally, to rescind a contract, both parties must make **restitution** to each other by returning goods, property, or money previously conveyed.[9] If the goods

or property received can be restored *in specie*—that is, if the actual goods or property can be returned—they must be. If the goods or property have been consumed, restitution must be made in an equivalent amount of money.

Essentially, *restitution* refers to the plaintiff's recapture of a benefit conferred on the defendant through which the defendant has been unjustly enriched. For example, Katie pays $10,000 to Bob in return for Bob's promise to design a house for her. The next day Bob calls Katie and tells her that he has taken a position with a large architectural firm in another state and cannot design the house. Katie decides to hire another architect that afternoon. Katie can obtain restitution of the $10,000.

Restitution may be appropriate when a contract is rescinded, but the right to restitution is not limited to rescission cases. Restitution may be sought in actions for breach of contract, tort actions, and other actions at law or in equity. Usually, restitution of money or property transferred by mistake or because of fraud can be awarded. An award in a case may include restitution of money or property obtained through embezzlement, conversion, theft, copyright infringement, or misconduct by a party in a confidential or other special relationship.

---

7. In *unilateral* rescission, only one party wants to undo the contract. In *mutual* rescission, the type of recission discussed in Chapter 17, both parties agree to undo the contract. Mutual rescission discharges the contract; unilateral rescission is generally available as a remedy for breach of contract.

8. The Federal Trade Commission and many states have rules or statutes allowing consumers to unilaterally rescind contracts made at home with door-to-door salespersons. Rescission is allowed within three days for any reason or for no reason at all. See, for example, California Civil Code Section 1689.5.

9. *Restatement (Second) of Contracts*, Section 370.

SECTION 3

Specific Performance

The equitable remedy of **specific performance** calls for the performance of the act promised in the contract. This remedy is quite attractive to the non-breaching party for three reasons:

1. The nonbreaching party need not worry about collecting the money damages awarded by a court (see the discussion in Chapter 3 of some of the difficulties that may arise when trying to enforce court judgments).
2. The nonbreaching party need not spend time seeking an alternative contract.
3. The performance is more valuable than the money damages.

Normally, however, specific performance will not be granted unless the party's legal remedy (money damages) is inadequate.[10] For this reason, contracts for the sale of goods rarely qualify for specific performance. The legal remedy, money damages, is ordinarily adequate in such situations, because substantially identical goods can be bought or sold in the market. If the goods are unique, however, a court of equity will decree specific performance. For example, paintings, sculptures, or rare books or coins are so unique that money damages will not enable a buyer to obtain substantially identical substitutes in the market.

SALE OF LAND

Specific performance is granted to a buyer in a contract for the sale of land. The legal remedy for breach of a land sales contract is inadequate, because every parcel of land is considered to be unique. Money damages will not compensate a buyer adequately, because the same land in the same location obviously cannot be obtained elsewhere. Only when specific performance is unavailable (for example, when the seller has sold the property to someone else) will money damages be awarded instead.

CONTRACTS FOR PERSONAL SERVICES

Personal-service contracts require one party to work personally for another party. Courts of equity normally refuse to grant specific performance of personal-service

contracts. If a contract is not deemed personal, the remedy at law may be adequate if substantially identical service (for example, lawn mowing) is available from other persons.

In individually tailored personal-service contracts, courts will not order specific performance by the party who was to be employed because public policy strongly discourages involuntary servitude.[11] Moreover, the courts do not want to have to monitor a continuing service contract if supervision would be difficult—as it would be if the contract required the exercise of personal judgment or talent. For example, if you contracted with a brain surgeon to perform brain surgery on you and the surgeon refused to perform, the court would not compel (and you certainly would not want) the surgeon to perform under those circumstances. A court cannot assure meaningful performance in such a situation.[12]

SECTION 4

Reformation

Reformation is an equitable remedy used when the parties have *imperfectly* expressed their agreement in writing. Reformation allows the contract to be rewritten to reflect the parties' true intentions. It applies most often when fraud or mutual mistake (for example, a clerical error) is present.

Reformation is almost always sought so that some other remedy may then be pursued. For example, if Gregory contracts to buy a certain parcel of land from Cavendish but their contract mistakenly refers to a parcel of land different from the one being sold, the contract does not reflect the parties' intentions. Accordingly, a court can reform the contract so that it conforms to the parties' intentions and accurately refers to the parcel of land being sold. Gregory can then, if necessary, show that Cavendish has breached the contract as reformed. She can at that time request an order for specific performance.

Two other examples deserve mention. The first involves two parties who have made a binding oral con-

---

10. *Restatement (Second) of Contracts*, Section 359.

11. The Thirteenth Amendment to the U.S. Constitution prohibits involuntary servitude, and thus a court will not order a person to perform under a personal-service contract. A court may grant an order (injunction) prohibiting that person from engaging in similar contracts in the future for a period of time, however.
12. Similarly, courts often refuse to order specific performance of construction contracts because courts are not set up to operate as construction supervisors or engineers.

tract. They further agree to put the oral contract in writing, but in doing so, they make an error in stating the terms. Normally, the courts will allow into evidence the correct terms of the oral contract, thereby reforming the written contract. The second example deals with written agreements (covenants) not to compete (see Chapter 13). If the covenant is for a valid and legitimate purpose (such as the sale of a business) but the area or time restraints of the covenant are unreasonable, some courts will reform the restraints by making them reasonable and will enforce the entire contract as reformed. Other courts, however, will throw out the entire restrictive covenant as illegal.

SECTION 5

Recovery Based on Quasi Contract

As stated in Chapter 10, quasi contract is a legal theory under which an obligation is imposed in the absence of an agreement. The courts use this theory to prevent unjust enrichment. Hence, quasi contract provides a basis for relief when no enforceable contract exists. The legal obligation arises because the law considers that a promise to pay for benefits received is implied by the party accepting the benefits. Generally, when one party has conferred a benefit on another party, justice requires the party receiving the benefit to pay the reasonable value for it. The party conferring the benefit can recover in *quantum meruit,* which means "as much as he deserves" (see Chapter 10).

Quasi-contractual recovery is useful when one party has partially performed under a contract that is unenforceable. It can be used as an alternative to a suit for damages and will allow the party to recover the reasonable value of the partial performance, measured in some cases according to the benefit received and in others according to the detriment suffered.

To recover on a quasi contract, the party seeking recovery must show the following:

1. The party conferred a benefit on the other party.
2. The party conferred the benefit with the reasonable expectation of being paid.
3. The party did not act as a volunteer in conferring the benefit.
4. The other party (the party receiving the benefit) would be unjustly enriched by retaining the benefit without making payment.

For example, suppose that Watson contracts to build two oil derricks for Energy Industries. The derricks are to be built over a period of three years, but the parties do not make a written contract. Enforcement of the contract will therefore be barred by the Statute of Frauds.[13] Watson completes one derrick, and then Energy Industries informs him that it will not pay for the derrick. Watson can sue in quasi contract because he conferred a benefit on Energy Industries with the expectation of being paid, and allowing Energy Industries to retain the derrick without paying would enrich the company unjustly. Therefore, Watson should be able to recover in *quantum meruit* the reasonable value of the oil derrick. The reasonable value is ordinarily equal to the fair market value. The following case involved a question of the calculation of the amount of a recovery under the theory of *quantum meruit.*

---

13. Contracts that by their terms cannot be performed within one year must be in writing to be enforceable. See Chapter 15.

CASE 18.3 Maglica v. Maglica

Court of Appeal, Fourth District, Division 3, California, 1998.
66 Cal.App.4th 442,
66 Cal.App.4th 1367C,
78 Cal.Rptr.2d 101.

BACKGROUND AND FACTS *Anthony Maglica founded a machine shop business called Mag Instrument in 1955. In 1971, he and Claire Halasz began to live together, holding themselves out as man and wife, but they never actually married. Claire worked with Anthony to build Mag Instrument, although when it was incorporated in 1974, all shares were issued to Anthony. Anthony, as president, and Claire, as secretary, were paid equal salaries. In 1978, the business began manufacturing flashlights, and thanks to ideas and hard work on Claire's part, the business boomed. The couple separated in 1992, and Claire filed a suit in a California state court against Anthony, seeking a recovery on, among other grounds, the theory of* quantum meruit. *The jury awarded Claire $84 million, based on the business's benefit from her services. Anthony appealed.*

**IN THE LANGUAGE
OF THE COURT**

SILLS, Presiding Justice.

*   *   *   *

*   *   * [T]he threshold requirement [under *quantum meruit*] that there be a benefit from the services can lead to confusion, as it did in the case before us. It is one thing to require that the defendant be benefited by services, it is quite another to measure the reasonable value of those services by the value by which the defendant was "benefited" as a result of them. Contract price and the reasonable value of services rendered are two separate things; sometimes the reasonable value of services exceeds a contract price. And sometimes it does not.

*   *   * Resulting benefit is an open-ended standard, which *   *   * can result in the plaintiff obtaining recovery amounting to *de facto* ownership in a business all out of reasonable relation to the value of services rendered. After all, a particular service timely rendered can have *   *   * disproportionate value to what it would cost on the open market.

*   *   *   *

*   *   * Allowing recovery based on resulting benefit would mean the law imposes an exchange of equity for services, and that can result in a windfall—as in the present case *   *   *. To impose such a measure of recovery would make a deal for the parties that they did not make themselves. *   *   * [Courts cannot] use *quantum meruit* to impose a highly generous and extraordinary contract that the parties did not make.

**DECISION
AND REMEDY**

The state intermediate appellate court reversed the lower court's decision and remanded for a recalculation of the award. The appellate court held that Claire could recover for the value of her services, but she could not recover for the benefit conferred on the business.

CONCEPT
SUMMARY 18.2

EQUITABLE REMEDIES

REMEDY	DESCRIPTION
Rescission and Restitution	1. *Rescission*—A remedy whereby a contract is canceled and the parties are restored to the original positions that they occupied prior to the transaction. When the remedy is available—such as when fraud, a mistake, duress, or failure of consideration is present—the rescinding party must give prompt notice of the rescission to the breaching party. 2. *Restitution*—When a contract is rescinded, both parties must make restitution to each other by returning the goods, property, or money previously conveyed. Restitution prevents the unjust enrichment of the defendant.
Specific Performance	An equitable remedy calling for the performance of the act promised in the contract. Only available in special situations—such as those involving contracts for the sale of unique goods or land—and when monetary damages would be an inadequate remedy. Specific performance is not available as a remedy in breached contracts for personal services.
Reformation	An equitable remedy allowing a contract to be "reformed," or rewritten, to reflect the parties' true intentions. Available when an agreement is imperfectly expressed in writing.

CONCEPT SUMMARY 18.2

EQUITABLE REMEDIES *(continued)*

REMEDY	DESCRIPTION
Recovery Based on Quasi Contract	An equitable theory imposed by the courts to obtain justice and prevent unjust enrichment in a situation in which no enforceable contract exists. The party seeking recovery must show the following: 1. A benefit was conferred on the other party. 2. The party conferring the benefit did so with the reasonable expectation of being paid. 3. The benefit was not volunteered. 4. Retaining the benefit without paying for it would result in the unjust enrichment of the party receiving the benefit.

SECTION 6

Election of Remedies

In many cases, a nonbreaching party has several remedies available. The party must choose which remedy to pursue. The purpose of the doctrine of *election of remedies* is to prevent double recovery.

Suppose that McCarthy agrees in writing to sell his land to Tally. Then McCarthy changes his mind and repudiates the contract. Tally can sue for compensatory damages *or* for specific performance. If Tally could seek compensatory damages in addition to specific performance, she would recover twice for the same breach of contract. The doctrine of election of remedies requires Tally to choose the remedy she wants, and it eliminates any possibility of double recovery. In other words, the election doctrine represents the legal embodiment of the adage "You can't have your cake and eat it, too."

The doctrine has often been applied in a rigid and technical manner, leading to some harsh results. For example, suppose that Wilson is fraudulently induced to buy a parcel of land for $150,000. He spends an additional $10,000 moving onto the land and then discovers the fraud. Instead of suing for damages, Wilson sues to rescind the contract. The court allows Wilson to recover only the purchase price of $150,000. The court denies recovery of the additional $10,000 because the seller, Martin, did not receive the $10,000 and is therefore not required to reimburse Wilson for his moving expenses. So Wilson suffers a net loss of $10,000 on the transaction. If Wilson had elected to sue for damages

instead of seeking the remedy of rescission and restitution, he could have recovered the $10,000 as well as the $150,000.[14]

Because of such problems, the UCC expressly rejects the doctrine of election of remedies.[15] As will be discussed in Chapter 22, remedies under the UCC are not exclusive but cumulative in nature and include all the available remedies for breach of contract.

SECTION 7

Waiver of Breach

Under certain circumstances, a nonbreaching party may be willing to accept a defective performance of the contract. This knowing relinquishment of a legal right (that is, the right to require satisfactory and full performance) is called a **waiver.** When a waiver of a breach of contract occurs, the party waiving the breach cannot take any later action on it. In effect, the waiver erases the past breach; the contract continues as if the breach had never occurred. Of course, the waiver of breach of contract extends only to the matter waived and not to the whole contract.

Businesspersons often waive breaches of contract to get whatever benefit is still possible out of the contract. For example, a seller contracts with a buyer to deliver to the buyer ten thousand tons of coal on or

---

14. See, for example, *Carpenter v. Mason,* 181 Wis. 114, 193 N.W. 973 (1923).
15. See UCC 2–703 and UCC 2–711.

before November 1. The contract calls for the buyer's payment to be made by November 10 for coal delivered. Because of a coal miners' strike, coal is scarce. The seller breaches the contract by not tendering delivery until November 5. The buyer may be well advised to waive the seller's breach, accept delivery of the coal, and pay as contracted.

Ordinarily, the waiver by a contracting party will not operate to waive subsequent, additional, or future breaches of contract. This is always true when the subsequent breaches are unrelated to the first breach. For example, an owner who waives the right to sue for late completion of a stage of construction does not waive the right to sue for failure to comply with engineering specifications on the same job. A waiver will be extended to subsequent defective performance if a reasonable person would conclude that similar defective performance in the future will be acceptable. Therefore, a *pattern of conduct* that waives a number of successive breaches will operate as a continued waiver. To change this result, the nonbreaching party should give notice to the breaching party that full performance will be required in the future.

The party who has rendered defective or less-than-full performance remains liable for the damages caused by the breach of contract. In effect, the waiver operates to keep the contract going. The waiver prevents the nonbreaching party from calling the contract to an end or rescinding the contract. The contract continues, but the nonbreaching party can recover damages caused by defective or less-than-full performance.

SECTION 8

Contract Provisions Limiting Remedies

A contract may include provisions stating that no damages can be recovered for certain types of breaches or that damages must be limited to a maximum amount. The contract may also provide that the only remedy for breach is replacement, repair, or refund of the purchase price. Provisions stating that no damages can be recovered are called *exculpatory clauses* (see Chapter 13). Provisions that affect the availability of certain remedies are called *limitation-of-liability clauses*.

Whether these contract provisions and clauses will be enforced depends on the type of breach that is excused by the provision. For example, a provision excluding liability for fraudulent or intentional injury will not be enforced. Likewise, a clause excluding liability for illegal acts or violations of law will not be enforced. A clause excluding liability for negligence may be enforced in certain cases, however. When an exculpatory clause for negligence is contained in a contract made between parties who have roughly equal bargaining positions, the clause usually will be enforced.

The UCC provides that in a contract for the sale of goods, remedies can be limited. We will examine the UCC provisions on limited remedies in Chapter 22, in the context of the remedies available on the breach of a contract for the sale or lease of goods.

TERMS AND CONCEPTS TO REVIEW

consequential damages 309	nominal damages 310	restitution 313
liquidated damages 312	penalty 312	specific performance 314
mitigation of damages 311	reformation 314	waiver 317

QUESTIONS AND CASE PROBLEMS

18–1. LIQUIDATED DAMAGES. Cohen contracts to sell his house and lot to Windsor for $100,000. The terms of the contract call for Windsor to pay 10 percent of the purchase price as a deposit toward the purchase price, or a down payment. The terms further stipulate that should the buyer breach the contract, the deposit will be retained by Cohen as liquidated damages. Windsor pays the deposit, but because her expected financing of the

$90,000 balance falls through, she breaches the contract. Two weeks later Cohen sells the house and lot to Ballard for $105,000. Windsor demands her $10,000 back, but Cohen refuses, claiming that Windsor's breach and the contract terms entitle him to keep the deposit. Discuss who is correct.

18–2. SPECIFIC PERFORMANCE. In which of the following situations would specific performance be an appropriate remedy? Discuss fully.

(a) Thompson contracts to sell her house and lot to Cousteau. Then, on finding another buyer willing to pay a higher purchase price, she refuses to deed the property to Cousteau.

(b) Amy contracts to sing and dance in Fred's nightclub for one month, beginning May 1. She then refuses to perform.

(c) Hoffman contracts to purchase a rare coin owned by Erikson, as Erikson is breaking up his coin collection. At the last minute, Erikson decides to keep his coin collection intact and refuses to deliver the coin to Hoffman.

(d) There are three shareholders of the ABC Corp.: Panozzo, who owns 48 percent of the stock; Chang, who owns another 48 percent; and Ryan, who owns 4 percent. Ryan contracts to sell her 4 percent to Chang. Later, Ryan refuses to transfer the shares to Chang.

18–3. DAMAGES. Ken owns and operates a famous candy store and makes most of the candy sold in the store. Business is particularly heavy during the Christmas season. Ken contracts with Sweet, Inc., to purchase ten thousand pounds of sugar to be delivered on or before November 15. Ken has informed Sweet that this particular order is to be used for the Christmas season business. Because of production problems, the sugar is not tendered to Ken until December 10, at which time Ken refuses it as being too late. Ken has been unable to purchase the quantity of sugar needed to meet the Christmas orders and has had to turn down numerous regular customers, some of whom have indicated that they will purchase candy elsewhere in the future. What sugar Ken has been able to purchase has cost him 10 cents per pound above the price contracted for with Sweet. Ken sues Sweet for breach of contract, claiming as damages the higher price paid for sugar from others, lost profits from this year's lost Christmas sales, future lost profits from customers who have indicated that they will discontinue doing business with him, and punitive damages for failure to meet the contracted delivery date. Sweet claims Ken is limited to compensatory damages only. Discuss who is correct.

18–4. BREACH. Wallechinsky purchases an automobile from Anderson Motors, paying $1,000 down and agreeing to pay off the balance in thirty-six monthly payments of $200 each. The terms of the agreement call for Wallechinsky to make a payment on or before the first of each month. During the first six months, Anderson receives a $200 payment before the first of each month.

During the next six months, Wallechinsky's payment is never made until the fifth of the month. Anderson accepts and cashes the payment check each time. When Wallechinsky tenders the thirteenth payment on the fifth of the next month, Anderson refuses to accept the check, claiming that Wallechinsky is in breach of contract. Anderson demands the entire balance owed. Wallechinsky claims that Anderson cannot hold her in breach. Discuss the result fully.

18–5. DAMAGES. Kerr Steamship Co. delivered to Radio Corp. of America (RCA) a twenty-nine-word coded message to be sent to Kerr's agent in Manila. The message included instructions on loading cargo onto one of Kerr's vessels. Kerr's profits on the carriage of the cargo were to be about $6,600. RCA mislaid the coded message, and it was never sent. Kerr sued RCA for the $6,600 in profits that it lost because RCA never sent the message. Can Kerr recover? Explain. [*Kerr Steamship Co. v. Radio Corp. of America*, 245 N.Y. 284, 157 N.E. 140 (1927)]

18–6. RESCISSION. Jeffrey Stambovsky was a resident of New York City. While looking at houses in the village of Nyack, New York, Stambovsky came across a riverfront Victorian house that he liked. He purchased it, only to discover later that the house had a local reputation for being haunted. The seller, Helen Ackley, had promoted this reputation herself by reporting to the *Reader's Digest* in 1977 and to the local press in 1982 that the house was haunted. By 1989, the house was included in a five-home walking tour of Nyack because of the purported presence of ghosts in the house. There was even a newspaper article describing it as "a riverfront Victorian (with ghost)." Stambovsky brought an action to rescind the contract, contending that the house's reputation for being haunted impaired the value of the property. What will the court decide? Discuss fully. [*Stambovsky v. Ackley*, 169 A.D.2d 254, 572 N.Y.S.2d 672 (1991)]

18–7. LIQUIDATED DAMAGES VERSUS PENALTIES. The Ivanovs, who were of Russian origin, agreed to purchase the Sobels' home for $300,000. A $30,000 earnest money deposit was placed in the trust account of Kotler Realty, Inc., the broker facilitating the transaction. Tiasia Buliak, one of Kotler's salespersons, negotiated the sale because she spoke fluent Russian. To facilitate the closing without the Ivanovs' having to be present, Buliak suggested they form a Florida corporation, place the cash necessary to close the sale in a corporate account, and give her authority to draw checks against it. The Ivanovs did as Buliak had suggested. Before the closing date of the sale, Buliak absconded with all of the closing money, which caused the transaction to collapse. Subsequently, because the Ivanovs had defaulted, Kotler Realty delivered the $30,000 earnest money deposit in its trust account to the Sobels. The Ivanovs then sued the Sobels, seeking to recover the $30,000. Was the clause providing that the seller could retain the earnest money if the buyer defaulted an enforceable liquidated damages clause or an unenforceable penalty clause? Discuss. [*Ivanov v. Sobel*, 654 So.2d 991 (Fla.App.3d 1995)]

18–8. MITIGATION OF DAMAGES. Patricia Fair worked in a Red Lion restaurant. The employee manual provided that "[d]uring a medical leave of absence, every effort will be made to keep a position available for the employee's return." After sustaining an injury that was unrelated to her work, Fair was given a month's medical leave. On her return, she asked for, and was granted, additional time to submit a physician's release to return to work. She provided the release within the extra time, but before she went back to work she was terminated, effective as of her original return date. When she attempted to resolve the matter, Red Lion offered to reinstate her in her old job. Her response was to set several conditions for a return, including a different job. Red Lion said no, and Fair did not return. Fair filed a suit in a Colorado state court against Red Lion, alleging in part breach of contract. Red Lion argued that by rejecting its offer of reinstatement, Fair failed to mitigate her damages. Assuming that Red Lion was in breach of contract, did Fair fail to mitigate her damages? Explain. [*Fair v. Red Lion Inn, L.P.*, 943 P.2d 431 (Colo. 1997)]

18–9. DAMAGES. In December 1992, Beys Specialty Contracting, Inc., contracted with New York City's Metropolitan Transportation Authority (MTA) for construction work. Beys subcontracted with Hudson Iron Works, Inc., to perform some of the work for $175,000. Under the terms of the subcontract, within seven days after the MTA approved Hudson's work and paid Beys, Beys would pay Hudson. The MTA had not yet approved any of Hudson's work when Beys submitted to the MTA invoices dated May 20 and June 21, 1993. Without proof that the MTA had paid Beys on those invoices, Hudson submitted to Beys an invoice dated September 10, claiming that the May 20 and June 21 invoices incorporated its work. Beys refused to pay, Hudson stopped working, and Beys paid another contractor $25,083 more to complete

the job than if Hudson had completed its subcontract. Hudson filed a suit in a New York state court to collect on its invoice. Beys filed a counterclaim for the additional money spent to complete Hudson's job. In whose favor should the court rule, and why? What might be the measure of damages, if any? [*Hudson Iron Works, Inc. v. Beys Specialty Contracting, Inc.*, 691 N.Y.S.2d 132 (N.Y.A.D., 2 Dept. 1999)]

18–10. IN YOUR COURT

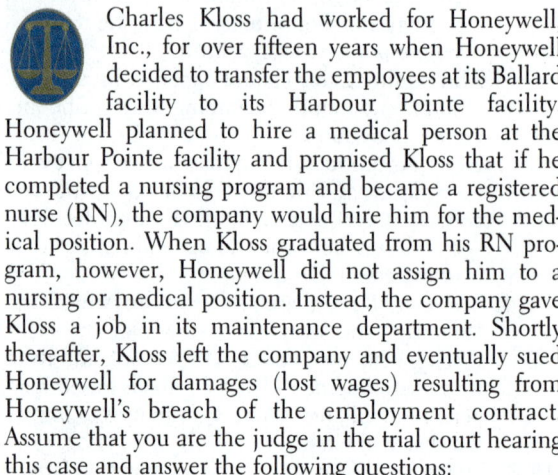

Charles Kloss had worked for Honeywell, Inc., for over fifteen years when Honeywell decided to transfer the employees at its Ballard facility to its Harbour Pointe facility. Honeywell planned to hire a medical person at the Harbour Pointe facility and promised Kloss that if he completed a nursing program and became a registered nurse (RN), the company would hire him for the medical position. When Kloss graduated from his RN program, however, Honeywell did not assign him to a nursing or medical position. Instead, the company gave Kloss a job in its maintenance department. Shortly thereafter, Kloss left the company and eventually sued Honeywell for damages (lost wages) resulting from Honeywell's breach of the employment contract. Assume that you are the judge in the trial court hearing this case and answer the following questions:

(a) One of the issues you will need to decide in this case is whether Kloss, by voluntarily leaving the maintenance job at Honeywell, had failed to mitigate his damages. How will you rule on this issue? Explain your reasoning.

(b) Review Case 18.2 (*Parker v. Twentieth Century-Fox Film Corp.*). Does the court's reasoning in that case on the issue of mitigation of damages apply to Kloss's situation as well? Why or why not?

LAW ON THE WEB

For updated links to resources available on the Web, as well as a variety of other materials, visit this text's Web site at http://wbl.westbuslaw.com.

For a summary of how contracts may be breached and other information on contract law, go to

http://www.lawyers.com/site/aboutlaw/contract.html#contract10

The following sites offer information on contract law, including breach of contract and remedies:

http://www.nolo.com/Chunkcm/CM9.html

http://www.law.cornell.edu/topics/contracts.html

LEGAL RESEARCH EXERCISES ON THE WEB

Go to http://wbl.westbuslaw.com, the Web site that accompanies this text. Select "Internet Applications," and then click on "Chapter 18." There you will find the following Internet research exercise that you can perform to learn more about breach of contract and damages:

Activity 18–1: Contract Damages and Contract Theory

UNIT TWO—CUMULATIVE BUSINESS HYPOTHETICAL

Cooper offers to purchase Brant's coin collection for $5,000, and Brant accepts Cooper's offer. Assuming that their agreement has met all of the requirements for a valid contract, answer the questions raised in each of the following situations:

1. The contract is in writing. Brant is a minor, and Cooper is an adult. Brant gives the coin collection to Cooper and receives the $5,000. Brant then has a change of heart and wants to recover his coin collection from Cooper. Can he do so? Explain. What if Brant was a minor at the time of the sale but did not decide that he wanted the coin collection back until a year after he had turned eighteen?

2. The contract is oral, and both parties are adults. Brant creates a memorandum of the transaction, indicating the names of the parties, the date, and the exact terms of the contract; Brant places the memorandum in his file. Cooper refuses to go through with the agreement. Is the contract enforceable against Cooper? Against Brant?

3. The contract is in writing, and both parties are adults. Although Brant represents to Cooper that the coin collection is worth at least $5,000, in fact, Brant has just had it appraised and knows that it is worth only $2,000. Cooper later learns that the collection is worth only $2,000 and wants to sue Brant. What remedies are available to Cooper?

4. The contract is in writing, and both parties are adults. Cooper pays Brant $5,000, but Brant, having had a change of heart, decides to keep the collection and offers to return the $5,000 to Cooper. Cooper wants the coin collection, not the money. In Cooper's suit against Brant, will the court grant the equitable remedy of specific performance? Explain.

5. The contract is in writing, and both parties are adults. Cooper takes possession of the coin collection and promises to pay Brant the $5,000 in three weeks. Brant, in urgent need of money, borrows $5,000 from his friend Viva and assigns his rights to the $5,000 Cooper owes him to Viva in return for the loan. Viva notifies Cooper of the assignment. Cooper pays Brant the $5,000 on the date stipulated in their contract. Brant refuses to give the money to Viva, and Viva sues Cooper. Is Cooper obligated to pay Viva $5,000 also? Discuss.

FOCUS ON LEGAL REASONING
Demasse v. ITT Corp.

INTRODUCTION

In Chapter 12, we discussed the contract law requirement of consideration. In this *Focus on Legal Reasoning*, we examine *Demasse v. ITT Corp.*,[1] a recent decision involving the application of the elements of consideration in the context of an employment contract and the newest edition of an employee handbook.

CASE BACKGROUND

ITT Cannon (a division of ITT Industries, Inc.) is based in Phoenix, Arizona. ITT issued five editions of its employee handbook, the most recent in 1989. All of the editions stated that layoffs would be made according to

1. 984 P.2d 1138 (Ariz. 1999).

seniority. The 1989 handbook added two new provisions. First, a disclaimer provided that "ITT Cannon does not guarantee continued employment to employees and retains the right to terminate or lay off employees." Second, a new provision read that "ITT Cannon reserves the right to amend, modify or cancel this handbook, as well as any or all of the various policies, rules, procedures and programs outlined in it" through methods other than by issuing a new handbook.

Four years later, ITT notified Roger Demasse and its other hourly employees that effective April 19, 1993, its layoff guidelines would not be based on seniority but on each employee's "abilities and documentation of performance." On April 29, Demasse was laid off, and

over the next nine months, other hourly employees suffered the same fate. All were laid off before less senior employees.

Demasse and the others filed a suit in a federal district court against ITT, alleging the breach of an implied contract created by the pre-1989 handbooks. The court ruled in favor of ITT, and the employees appealed to the U.S. Court of Appeals for the Ninth Circuit. That court asked the Arizona Supreme Court to answer two questions. Most important was whether continued employment alone is sufficient consideration to modify contract terms so that when employees continue to work after a new handbook is distributed, the new edition supersedes prior editions.

MAJORITY OPINION

FELDMAN, Justice.

* * * *

* * * [A]n implied-in-fact employment term [is] governed by the same traditional contract law that governs express promises and must be modified accordingly. See *McIlravy v. Kerr-McGee Corp.*, 119 F.3d 876 (10th Cir.1997) * * * . As a result, to effectively modify a contract, whether implied-in-fact or express, there must be: (1) an offer to modify the contract, (2) assent to or acceptance of that offer, and (3) consideration.

The 1989 handbook, published with terms that purportedly modified or permitted modification of pre-existing contractual provisions, was therefore no more than an offer to modify the existing contract. * * *

* * * *

* * * [C]onsideration necessary to modify an existing contract is any detriment to promisee, or benefit to promisor that supports the new promise. Moreover, legal consideration, like every other part of a contract, must be the result of agreement. The parties must understand

and be influenced to the particular action by something of value * * * that is recognized by all parties * * * as the moving cause. Consideration will be found when an employer and its employees have made a bargained for exchange to support the employees' * * * relinquishment of the protections they are entitled to under the existing contract.

* * * *

The Tenth Circuit Court of Appeals recently dealt with this issue in *McIlravy*. Kerr-McGee issued five handbooks over a twelve-year span. The early handbooks contained a seniority layoff provision. Later handbooks contained disclaimer provisions expressly stating that employment with Kerr-McGee was at will. * * * [T]he Tenth Circuit held that Kerr-McGee failed to show that the disclaimer successfully modified the pre-existing implied-in-fact contract created by the earlier handbooks. * * * [W]e, too, hold that continued employment alone is not sufficient consideration to support a modification to an implied-in-fact contract. Any other result brings us to an absurdity: the employer's threat to breach its promise of job security provides consideration for its rescission of that promise.

* * * *

Continued employment after issuance of a new handbook does not constitute acceptance, otherwise the illusion (and the irony) is apparent: to preserve their right under the existing contract * * * plaintiffs would be forced to quit. It is too much to require an employee to preserve his or her rights under the original employment contract by quitting working. Thus, the employee does not manifest consent to an offer modifying an existing contract without taking affirmative steps, beyond continued performance, to accept. [Emphasis added.]

DISSENTING OPINION

MARTONE, Justice, dissenting * * * .

I disagree with the majority's answer to [the] question [in this case]. The handbook promise here cannot reasonably be construed as a promise that runs in favor of the employee for as long as the employee is employed or else the unilateral promise turns out to be a better deal than a collective bargaining agreement. * * * That the employer could avoid this result by simply laying everyone off (and thus not violate the seniority provision) shows just how untenable the majority approach is. Instead, I believe that the Michigan Supreme Court was correct in concluding that the promise is enforceable against the employer by an individual employee, unless and until the employer changes the promise as to all employees by changing the handbook. See *In re Certified Question (Bankey),* 432 Mich.438, 443 N.W.2d 112 (1989).

This does not make the promise illusory. An employer would have to think long and hard about changing a valuable benefit for 10,000 employees just to disadvantage a single employee. And, unless the employer is willing to pay that price, the employee can enforce the promise against the employer * * * . [T]he promise here was not to provide seniority rights to Demasse for as long as he decided to work for ITT, but was instead a promise to provide seniority rights to him as an individual employee so long as all other ITT employees were also receiving this benefit under the handbook. Demasse's power of acceptance by performance existed only as long as the offer was made.

* * * Both employers and employees will suffer from [the majority's decision in this case]. It will create havoc with employer-employee relations. For example, employers will be subject to different obligations to their many employees depending on the handbook in existence at the time of employment. And, one employee's contract rights may be derived from several different editions of the handbook. Worse, the contract rights of some employees created by one edition of the handbook may conflict with rights provided other employees in other editions. This spells the demise of all such handbooks. No employer will ever issue one for fear of endless obligation * * * .

LEGAL REASONING AND ANALYSIS

1. Legal Analysis. Find the *McIlravy v. Kerr-McGee Corp.* case and the *In re Certified Question (Bankey)* case (see the *Law on the Web* feature at the end of Chapter 2 for instructions on how to access federal court opinions). Compare the facts and issues in those cases to the facts and issues of the *Demasse* case. Do you think that the courts' decisions in the *McIlravy* and *Bankey* cases affected the justices' opinions in this case, or did the justices simply cite those cases to support their opinions? Explain your answer.

2. Legal Reasoning. Contrast the conclusions of the majority and the dissent. What reasons did the dissent give to support its assertion that the majority's conclusion was incorrect? What reasons did the dissent cite to justify its position?

3. Legal Application. An at-will employment agreement is for an indefinite term and can be terminated at any time for good cause or no cause at the will of either party. An at-will employment contract is unilateral and typically starts with an employer's offer of a wage in exchange for work performed. The employee's subsequent performance provides the consideration to create the contract. What is different about the employment contract in the *Demasse* case? Why?

4. Implications for the Employer. Does the decision in this case mean that all employee handbooks create contractual promises? How might an employer avoid creating such promises when issuing a handbook?

5. Case Briefing Assignment. Using the guidelines for briefing cases given in Appendix A of this text, brief the *Demasse* case.

GOING ONLINE

This text's Web site, at http://wbl.westbuslaw.com, offers links to court cases, as well as to other online research sources. You can also locate court cases at the Web sites listed in the *Law on the Web* section at the end of Chapter 2.

Contract Law and the Application of Ethics

As you will learn in Chapter 40, generally a responsible business manager will evaluate a business transaction on the basis of three criteria—legality, profitability, and ethics. But what does acting ethically mean in the area of contracts? If an individual with whom you enter into a contract fails to look after his or her own interests, is that your fault, and should you therefore be doing something about it? If the contract happens to be to your advantage and therefore to the other party's detriment, do you have a responsibility to correct the situation?

For example, assume that a neighbor whom you rarely see places a "for sale" sign on her car, offering to sell it for $3,000. You learn that she is moving to another state and needs the extra cash to help finance the move. You know that she could easily get $6,000 for the car, and you congratulate yourself on your good fortune. Even if you do not need a car, you can purchase it and then sell it at a profit. But you also learn that your neighbor has failed to do the preliminary research—checking *Blue Book* prices on the Web and so on—that most reasonable individuals would undertake when selling a car, and therefore she is unaware that the car is underpriced.

Are you obligated to tell her that she is essentially giving away $3,000 if she sells you the car for only $3,000? Do you have an ethical responsibility toward this woman—whom you will probably never see again—simply because she failed to look after her own

interests? This kind of situation, transplanted into the world of commercial transactions, raises an obvious question: At what point should the savvy businessperson cease looking after his own economic welfare and become "his brother's keeper," so to speak?

FREEDOM OF CONTRACT AND FREEDOM FROM CONTRACT

The answer to the question just raised is not simple. On the one hand, a common ethical assumption in our society is that individuals should be held responsible for the consequences of their own actions, including their contractual promises. This principle is expressed in the legal concept of freedom of contract. Applying this ethical precept to the above example, you could justify not saying anything about the true value of the car to your neighbor by stating that you were upholding the principle of freedom of contract.

On the other hand, another common assumption in our society is that individuals should not harm one another by their actions. This is the basis of both tort law and criminal law. If you applied this ethical yardstick to the example, would you be obligated not to harm your neighbor's interests by taking advantage of her offer? How would you balance these two ethical principles?

In the area of contract law, ethical behavior often involves just such a "balancing act." In the example, if you purchased the car and the neighbor later learned its

true value and sued you for the difference, very likely no court of law would agree that the contract should be rescinded. In other words, the law would not "answer" your ethical question in this case. The court probably would not come to the aid of the neighbor, because she could easily have prevented the injustice by learning, as a "reasonable person" would have, the market value of the car. There are times, however, when courts will hold that the principle of freedom *of* contract should give way to the principle of freedom *from* contract, a principle based on the assumption that people should not be harmed by the actions of others. We look below at some examples of how parties to contracts may be excused from performance under their contracts if that is the only way injustice can be prevented.

Impossibility of Performance

The doctrine of impossibility of performance is based to some extent on the ethical question of whether one party should suffer economic loss when it is impossible to perform a contract. The rule that one is "bound by his or her contracts" is not followed when performance is made impossible. The doctrine of impossibility of performance is applied to relieve a contracting party of liability for failure to perform. This doctrine, however, is applied only when the parties themselves did not consciously assume the risk of the events that rendered performance impossible. Furthermore, this doctrine rests on the assumption that the party claiming the defense of impossibility has acted ethically. In other words, a party cannot arrange events intentionally to make performance impossible.

A contract is discharged, for example, if performance of the contract calls for the delivery of a particular car, and through no fault of either party this car is stolen and completely demolished in an accident. Yet the doctrine of impossibility of performance is not available if the party agreeing to sell his or her car either crashes the car to avoid performance of the contract or causes the car's destruction by his or her negligence. The well-known English case of *Taylor v. Caldwell* [1] is also illustrative of the doctrine of impossibility of performance. In *Taylor,* the plaintiff entered into a contract with the defendant to rent the defendant's music hall for a series of concerts. Before the first concert, but after the contract had been entered into, the music hall was destroyed by fire. The court held that the defendant was discharged from performing. Furthermore, because performance was impossible, his failure to perform was not a breach of contract.

Prior to the late nineteenth century, courts were reluctant to discharge a contract even when it appeared that performance was literally impossible. Just as society's ethics change with the passage of time, however, the law also makes a transition to reflect society's new perceptions of ethical behavior. Today, courts are much more willing to discharge a contract when its performance has become literally impossible. Holding a party in breach of contract, when performance has become literally impossible through no fault of the party claiming the

defense of impossibility, no longer coincides with society's notions of fairness.

Unconscionability

The doctrine of unconscionability represents a good example of how the law attempts to enforce ethical behavior. Under this doctrine, a contract may be deemed to be so unfair to one party as to be unenforceable—even though that party voluntarily agreed to the contract's terms. Unconscionable action, like unethical action, is incapable of precise definition. Information about the particular facts and specific circumstances surrounding the contract is essential. For example, a contract with a marginally literate consumer might be seen as unfair and unenforceable, whereas the same contract with a major business firm would be upheld by the courts.

Section 2–302 of the Uniform Commercial Code, which incorporates the common law concept of unconscionability, similarly does not define the concept with any precision. Rather, it leaves it to the courts to determine when a contract is so one sided and unfair to one party as to be unconscionable and thus unenforceable.

Usually, courts will do all they can to save contracts rather than render them unenforceable. Thus, only in extreme situations, as when a contract or clause is so one sided as to "shock the conscience" of the court, will a court hold a contract or contractual clause unconscionable.

Exculpatory Clauses

In some situations, courts have also refused to enforce exculpatory clauses on the ground that they are unconscionable or that they are contrary to public policy and thus void. An exculpatory clause attempts to excuse a party from liability in the event of monetary or

physical injury, no matter who is at fault. In some situations, such clauses are upheld. For example, assume that a health club requires its members to sign a clause releasing the club from any liability for injuries the members might incur while using the club's equipment and facilities. In essence, the clause requires the members to assume the risks that go along with being a health-club member. The law permits parties to assume, by express agreement, the risks inherent in certain activities.

Nonetheless, the law often takes a dubious view of exculpatory agreements, particularly when the services involved are essential or when there is disparity in bargaining power between the parties. For this reason, such clauses in contracts between employers and employees are almost universally rejected. An exculpatory clause that attempts to exempt an employer from all liability for negligence toward its employees normally is held to be against public policy and thus void. The courts are generally agreed that in such a situation, disparity in bargaining power and economic necessity force the employee to accept the employer's terms. In at least one case, the court extended this "freedom from contract" afforded to employees to an independent contractor (a worker who is hired to undertake a specific function and who is not classified as an employee—see Chapter 31). The court did so largely because it concluded that the disparity in bargaining power between the plaintiff (a newspaper carrier) and the defendant (a major newspaper publisher) was comparable to—if not greater than—that between most employers and employees.[2]

1. 122 Eng.Rep. 309 (K.B. [King's Bench] 1863).

2. *Bunia v. Knight Ridder,* 544 N.W.2d 60 (Minn.App. 1996).

FOCUS ON ETHICS

Covenants Not to Compete

In today's complicated, technological business world, knowledge learned on the job, including trade secrets, has become a valuable commodity. To prevent this knowledge from falling into the hands of competitors, more and more employers are requiring their employees to sign covenants not to compete. The increasing number of lawsuits over noncompete clauses in employment contracts has caused numerous courts to reconsider the reasonableness of these covenants.

For example, in one case all of the workers for the British brokerage firm Exco PLC, located in New Jersey, had to sign noncompete agreements. The agreements stated that Exco employees could not work for one year with any competitors located within one hundred miles of New York City after their employment with Exco terminated. When eight employees quit Exco and joined a rival firm in New York, Exco sued to enforce the noncompete covenants. The state judge hearing the case sided with the employees. The judge held that the covenant not to compete was too broad, because for some highly technical jobs in the brokerage industry (such as trading interest-rate options), New York City is one of the few places the employees could get a job.[3]

Noncompete covenants in employment contracts for Web-based work pose some unique issues with respect to fairness and reasonability. For example, in one case Mark Schlack, who worked as a Web site manager for EarthWeb, Inc., signed a covenant stating that, on termination of his employment, he would not work for any competing company for one year. When the employee later accepted an offer from another company to design a Web site, EarthWeb sued to enforce the covenant not to compete. The court pointed out that the covenant, in effect, prohibited Schlack from working for a competing company located anywhere in the world for one year—because the Internet lacks physical borders. For this reason, and because of the "dynamic nature of this industry," the court held that the one-year time period was excessive in duration and refused to enforce the covenant.[4]

PROBLEMS WITH ORAL CONTRACTS

Oral contracts are made every day. Many—if not most—of them are carried out, and no problems arise. Occasionally, however, oral contracts are not performed, and one party wishes to sue the other. Sometimes, to prevent injustice, the courts will enforce oral contracts under the theory of promissory estoppel if detrimental reliance can be shown. The court may even use this theory to remove a contract from the Statute of Frauds—that is, render the oral contract enforceable.

Promissory Estoppel

Ethical standards certainly underlie the doctrine of promissory estoppel, under which a person who has reasonably relied on the promise of another to his or her detriment can often obtain some measure of recovery. Essentially, promissory estoppel allows a variety of promises to be enforced despite the fact that they lack what is formally regarded as consideration.

An oral promise made by an insurance agent to a business owner, for example, may be binding if the owner relies on that promise to his or her detriment. Employees who rely to their detriment on an employer's promise may be able to recover under the doctrine of promissory estoppel. A contractor who, when bidding for a job, relies on a subcontractor's promise to perform certain construction work at a certain price may be able to recover, on the basis of promissory estoppel, any damages sustained because of the subcontractor's failure to perform. These are but a few of the many examples in which the courts, in the interests of fairness and justice, have estopped a promisor from denying that a contract existed.

The Statute of Frauds

As you learned in Chapter 15, the Statute of Frauds was originally instituted in 1677 in England. The act was intended to prevent harm to innocent parties by requiring written evidence of agreements concerning important transactions. The English act was created specifically to prevent further perpetration of the many frauds occurring when witnesses gave perjured testimony in cases involving breached oral agreements for which no written evidence existed.

The English courts, until the Statute of Frauds was passed, had enforced oral contracts on the strength of oral testimony by witnesses. It was not too difficult, therefore, to evade justice by procuring "convincing" witnesses to support the claim that a contract had been created and then breached. The possibility of fraud in such actions was enhanced by the fact that in seventeenth-century England, courts did not allow oral testimony to be given by the parties to a lawsuit—or by any

---

3. Noam Neusner, "As 'Non-Compete' Clauses Proliferate, So Do Lawsuits over Them," *International Herald Tribune*, May 5, 1997, p. 13.

4. *EarthWeb, Inc. v. Schlack,* 71 F.Supp.2d 299 (S.D.N.Y. 1999).

parties with an interest in the litigation, such as husbands or wives. Defense against actions for breach of contract was thus limited to written evidence or the testimony given by third parties.

Under the Statute of Frauds, if a contract is oral when it is required to be in writing, it will not, as a rule, be enforced by the courts. An exception to this rule is made if a party has reasonably relied, to his or her detriment, on the oral contract. Enforcing an oral contract on the basis of a party's reliance arguably undercuts the essence of the Statute of Frauds. The reason that such an exception is made is to prevent the statute—which was created to avert injustice—from being used to promote injustice. Nevertheless, this use of the doctrine is controversial—as is the Statute of Frauds itself.

Since its inception more than three hundred years ago, the statute has been criticized by some because, although it was created to protect the innocent, it can also be used as a technical defense by a party breaching a genuine, mutually agreed-on oral contract—if the contract falls within the Statute of Frauds. For this reason, some legal scholars believe the act has caused more injustice than it has prevented. Thus, exceptions are sometimes made—such as under the doctrine of promissory estoppel—to prevent unfairness and inequity. Generally, the courts are slow to apply the statute if its application will result in obvious injustice. In some instances, this has required a good deal of inventiveness on the part of the courts.

DISCUSSION QUESTIONS

1. Suppose that you contract to purchase steel at a fixed price per ton. A lengthy steelworkers' strike causes the price of steel to triple from the price specified in the contract. If you demand that the supplier fulfill the contract, the supplier will go out of business. What are your ethical obligations in this situation? What are your legal rights?

2. Many countries have no Statute of Frauds, and even England, the country that created the original Statute of Frauds, has repealed it. Should the United States do likewise? What are some of the costs and benefits to society of the Statute of Frauds?

3. In determining whether an exculpatory clause should be enforced, why does it matter whether the contract containing the clause involves essential services (such as transportation) or nonessential services (such as skiing or other leisure-time activities)?

4. Employers often include covenants not to compete in employment contracts to protect their trade secrets. What effect, if any, will the growth in e-commerce have on the reasonability of covenants not to compete?

UNIT THREE

Domestic and International Sales and Lease Contracts

Contents

CHAPTER 19

The Formation of Sales and Lease Contracts

WHEN WE TURN TO CONTRACTS for the sale and lease of goods, we move away from common law principles and into the area of statutory law. State statutory law governing sales and lease transactions is based on the Uniform Commercial Code (UCC), which, as mentioned in Chapter 1, has been adopted as law by all states.[1] Relevant sections of the UCC are noted in the following discussion of sales and lease contracts. You should refer to Appendix C in the back of the book, which presents the most recent version of the UCC, while examining these notations.

We open this chapter with a discussion of the historical development of sales and lease law and the UCC's significance as a legal landmark. We then look at the scope of the UCC's Article 2 (on sales) and Article 2A (on leases) as a background to the topic of this chapter, which is the formation of contracts for the sale and lease of goods. Because international sales transactions are increasingly commonplace in the business world, the chapter concludes with an examination of the United Nations Convention on Contracts for the International Sale of Goods (CISG), which governs international sales contracts.

---

1. Louisiana has not adopted Articles 2 and 2A, however.

SECTION 1

The Uniform Commercial Code

In the early years of this nation, sales law varied from state to state, and this made multistate sales contracts difficult. The problems became especially troublesome in the late nineteenth century as multistate contracts became the norm. For this reason, numerous attempts were made to produce a uniform body of laws relating to commercial transactions. The National Conference of Commissioners (NCC) on Uniform State Laws drafted two uniform ("model") acts that were widely adopted by the states: the Uniform Negotiable Instruments Law (1896) and the Uniform Sales Act (1906). Several other proposed uniform acts followed, although most were not as widely adopted.

In the 1940s, the need to integrate the half-dozen or so uniform acts covering commercial transactions into a single, comprehensive body of statutory law was recognized. The NCC developed the Uniform Commercial Code (UCC) to serve that purpose. First issued in 1949, the UCC facilitates commercial transactions by making the laws governing sales and lease contracts clearer, simpler, and more readily applicable to the numerous difficulties that can arise during such transactions.

COMPREHENSIVE COVERAGE OF THE UCC

The UCC is the single most comprehensive codification of the broad spectrum of laws involved in a total commercial transaction. The UCC views the entire "commercial transaction for the sale of and payment for goods" as a single legal occurrence having numerous facets.

As an example, first look at the titles of the articles of the UCC in Appendix C. Now consider a consumer who buys a deluxe, side-by-side refrigerator with an icemaker from an appliance store and agrees to pay for it on an installment plan. Several articles of the UCC can be applied to this single commercial transaction. Because there is a contract for the sale of goods, Article 2 will apply. If a check is given as the down payment on the purchase price, it will be negotiated and ultimately passed through one or more banks for collection. This process is the subject matter of Article 3, Negotiable Instruments, and Article 4, Bank Deposits and Collections. If the appliance store extends credit to the consumer through the installment plan, and if it retains a lien on the refrigerator (the collateral), then Article 9, Secured Transactions, will be applicable.

Suppose, in addition, that the appliance company must first obtain the refrigerator from its manufacturer's warehouse, after which it is to be delivered by common carrier to the consumer. The storage and shipment of goods are the subject matter of Article 7, Documents of Title. If the appliance company arranges to pay the manufacturer, located in another state, for the refrigerator supplied, a letter of credit, which is the subject matter of Article 5, may be used. Thus, the UCC attempts to provide a consistent and integrated framework of rules to deal with all the phases *ordinarily arising* in a commercial sales transaction from start to finish.

Two articles of the UCC seem not to apply to the "ordinary" commercial sales transaction. Article 6, Bulk Transfers, involves merchants who sell off the major part of their inventory (sometimes leaving creditors unpaid). Because bulk sales do not ordinarily arise in a commercial sales transaction, most states have repealed Article 6 entirely, although some states have adopted the revised version of Article 6 (see Appendix C). Article 8, Investment Securities, deals with transactions involving certain negotiable securities (stocks and bonds), transactions that do not involve a sale of (or payment for) *goods.* The subject matter of Articles 6 and 8, however, was considered by the UCC's drafters to be related *sufficiently* to commercial transactions to warrant the inclusion of these articles in the UCC.

PERIODIC REVISIONS OF THE UCC

Various articles and sections of the UCC are periodically changed or supplemented to clarify certain rules or to establish new rules when changes in business customs have rendered the existing UCC provisions inapplicable. For example, because of the increasing importance of leases of goods in the commercial context, Article 2A, governing leases, was added to the UCC. To clarify the rights of parties to commercial fund transfers, particularly electronic fund transfers, Article 4A was issued. Articles 3 and 4, covering negotiable instruments and banking, underwent a significant revision in the 1990s, as did Articles 5, 8, and 9. Because of other changes in business and in the law, the NCC has recommended the repeal of Article 6, as mentioned earlier, and has offered a revised Article 6 to those states that prefer not to repeal it. Currently, the NCC is in the process of revising Articles 2 and 2A. When those are complete, Article 1 is scheduled for revision.

SECTION 2

The Scope of Article 2—The Sale of Goods

Article 2 of the UCC governs **sales contracts,** or contracts for the sale of goods. To facilitate commercial transactions, Article 2 modifies some of the common law contract requirements that were discussed in the previous chapters. To the extent that it has not been modified by the UCC, however, the common law of contracts also applies to sales contracts. For example, the common law requirements for a valid contract— agreement (offer and acceptance), consideration, capacity, and legality—that were summarized in Chapter 10 and discussed at length in Chapters 11 through 13 are also applicable to sales contracts. Thus, you should reexamine these common law principles when studying the law of sales.

In general, the rule is that whenever there is a conflict between a common law contract rule and the UCC, the UCC controls. In other words, when a UCC provision addresses a certain issue, the UCC governs; when the UCC is silent, the common law governs. The relationship between general contract law and the law governing sales of goods is illustrated in Exhibit 19–1.

In regard to Article 2, you should keep in mind two things. First, Article 2 deals with the sale of *goods*; it does not deal with real property (real estate), services, or intangible property such as stocks and bonds. Thus, if the subject matter of a dispute is goods, the UCC governs. If it is real estate or services, the common law applies. Second, in some cases, the rules may vary quite a bit, depending on whether the buyer or the seller is a *merchant*. We look now at how the UCC defines a *sale*, *goods*, and *merchant status*.

WHAT IS A SALE?

Section 2–102 of the UCC states that Article 2 "applies to transactions in goods." This implies a broad scope—covering gifts, bailments (temporary deliveries of personal property, discussed in Chapter 46), and purchases of goods. In this chapter, however, we treat Article 2 as being applicable only to an actual sale (as would most authorities and courts). The UCC defines a **sale** as "the passing of title from the seller to the buyer for a price," where *title* refers to the formal right of ownership of property [UCC 2–106(1)]. The price may be payable in money or in other goods, services, or realty (real estate).

WHAT ARE GOODS?

To be characterized as a *good*, an item of property must be *tangible*, and it must be *movable*. **Tangible property** has physical existence—it can be touched or seen. Intangible property—such as corporate stocks and bonds, patents and copyrights, and ordinary contract rights—have only conceptual existence and thus do not come under Article 2. A *movable* item can be carried from place to place. Hence, real estate is excluded from Article 2.

Two areas of dispute arise in determining whether the object of the contract is goods and thus whether Article 2 is applicable. One problem concerns *goods associated with real estate*, such as crops or timber, and the other concerns contracts involving a combination of *goods and services*.

EXHIBIT 19–1   LAW GOVERNING CONTRACTS

This exhibit graphically illustrates the relationship between general contract law and the law governing contracts for the sale of goods. Sales contracts are not governed exclusively by Article 2 of the Uniform Commercial Code but are also governed by general contract law whenever it is relevant and has not been modified by the UCC.

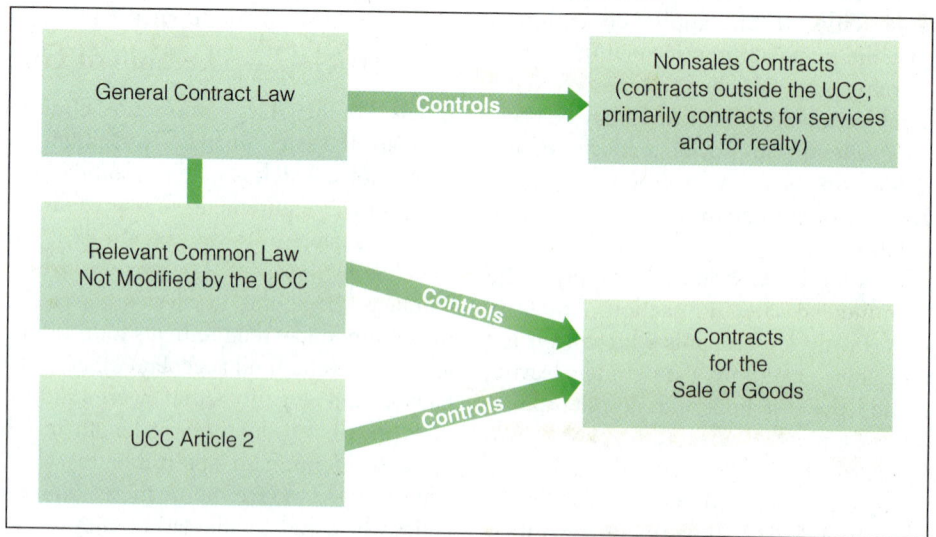

Goods Associated with Real Estate. Goods associated with real estate often fall within the scope of Article 2. Section 2–107 provides the following rules:

1. A contract for the sale of minerals or the like (including oil and gas) or a structure (such as a building) is a contract for the sale of goods if *severance, or separation, is to be made by the seller.* If the *buyer* is to sever (separate) the minerals or structures from the land, the contract is considered to be a sale of real estate governed by the principles of real property law, not the UCC.

2. A sale of growing crops or timber to be cut is a contract for the sale of goods *regardless of who severs them.*

3. Other "things attached" to realty but capable of severance without material harm to the land are considered to be goods *regardless of who severs them.*[2] Examples of "things attached" that are severable without harm to realty are a window air conditioner in a house and tables and stools in a restaurant. Thus, removal of one of these things would be considered a sale of goods. The test is whether removal will cause substantial harm to the real property to which the item is attached.

Goods and Services Combined. In cases in which goods and services are combined, courts disagree. For example, is the furnishing of blood to a patient during an operation a "sale of goods" or the "performance of a medical service"? Some courts say it is a good; others say it is a service. The UCC does stipulate, however, that serving food or drink to be consumed either on or off restaurant premises is a "sale of goods," at least for the purpose of an implied warranty of merchantability (to be explained in Chapter 23) [UCC 2–314(1)]. Other special cases are also explicitly characterized as goods by the UCC, including unborn animals and rare coins.

Whether the transaction in question involves the sale of goods or services is important, because the majority of courts treat services as being excluded by the UCC. If the transaction is not covered by the UCC, then UCC provisions, including those relating to implied warranties, will not apply. The court in the following case considered whether a contract for a sale of customized software was subject to Article 2 of the UCC.

---

2. The UCC avoids the term *fixtures* here because of the numerous definitions of the word. A fixture is anything so firmly or permanently attached to land or to a building as to become a part of it. Once personal property becomes a fixture, it is governed by real estate law. See Chapter 46.

CASE 19.1 Micro Data Base Systems, Inc. v. Dharma Systems, Inc.

United States
Court of Appeals,
Seventh Circuit, 1998.
148 F.3d 649.
http://www.findlaw.
com/casecode/courts/
7th.html[a]

BACKGROUND AND FACTS *Micro Data Base Systems, Inc. (MDBS), an Indiana company, contracted with Dharma Systems, Inc., a New Hampshire firm, to adapt Dharma's software program (known as SQL Access) for use in a system that MDBS was to provide to Unisys Government Systems, Inc. The adapted program was called RDMS (Relational Database Management System) Emulation. MDBS agreed to pay a fee of $125,000 for the use of SQL Access, plus $125,000 for Dharma's adapting the program to MDBS's needs. The fee was to be paid immediately. The rest of the money was to be paid in installments, with the last installment, $25,000, due on "Acceptance by Unisys." Dharma asked MDBS to sign an agreement to limit the distribution of the RDMS Emulation, but MDBS did not sign. After all of the installments except the last one had been paid, Dharma shipped six copies of the RDMS Emulation on disks to MDBS, which sent them to Unisys. When some defects were reported, Dharma refused to fix them until MDBS signed the limited distribution agreement. MDBS filed a suit in a federal district court against Dharma, alleging breach of contract. One of the issues before the court was whether the contract was for services, as the law of Indiana classified it, or a sale of goods, as the law of New Hampshire defined it. The court ruled that the contract was for a sale of goods, and that MDBS had violated it. A jury awarded damages to Dharma, and MDBS appealed to the U.S. Court of Appeals for the Seventh Circuit.*

---

a. In the "1998" row, click on "May." Scroll down the list of cases and click on the case name to access the opinion.

IN THE LANGUAGE
OF THE COURT

POSNER, Chief Judge.

*   *   *   *   *

*   *   * Article 2, the relevant part of the Code, is limited to the sale of "goods." The only Indiana case holds that custom software is a service, while the only New Hampshire case holds that it is a good. *   *   * [Because the New Hampshire case] is consistent with the weight of authority, and reaches the right result—for we can think of no reason why the UCC is not suitable to govern disputes arising from the sale of custom software—we'll follow it.

That cannot be the end of the analysis, however. The contract between MDBS and Dharma was for the sale not only of a good (the RDMS Emulation), as we have just held, but also of a service—the creation of the RDMS Emulation by adaptation of Dharma's preexisting program, the SQL Access program. Under New Hampshire law, to determine whether such a "hybrid" transaction is governed by the Code requires deciding which aspect of the transaction, the sale of goods or the sale of services, predominates (unless, perhaps, the dispute is clearly assignable to either the goods or the services aspect, and it is not here). Here it is the sale of the goods that predominates. Although the contract recites that half the total contract price is for Dharma's "professional services," these were not services to be rendered to MDBS but merely the labor to be expended by Dharma in the "manufacture" of the "good" from existing software. It's no different than if MDBS were buying an automobile from Dharma, and Dharma invoiced MDBS $20,000 for the car and $1,000 for labor involved in customizing it for MDBS's special needs. It would still be the sale of a good within the meaning of the UCC. We doubt that it should even be called a "hybrid" sale, for this would imply that every sale of goods is actually a hybrid sale, since labor is a service and labor is an input into the manufacture of every good.

*   *   *   *

We conclude that the district court's rulings were correct and that the jury's verdict was within the outer bounds of the lawful and the reasonable.

DECISION
AND REMEDY

The U.S. Court of Appeals affirmed the judgment of the lower court. A contract for a sale of customized software is subject to Article 2 of the UCC, because although both goods and services were involved, the goods component predominated.

WHO IS A MERCHANT?

Article 2 governs the sale of goods in general. It applies to sales transactions between all buyers and sellers. In a limited number of instances, however, the UCC presumes that in certain phases of sales transactions involving merchants, special business standards ought to be imposed because of the merchants' relatively high degree of commercial expertise.[3] Such standards do not apply to the casual or inexperienced seller or buyer ("consumer"). Section 2–104 defines three ways in which merchant status can arise:

1. A merchant is a person who *deals in goods of the kind involved in the sales contract.* Thus, a retailer, a wholesaler, or a manufacturer is a merchant of those goods sold in the business. A merchant for one type of goods is not necessarily a merchant for another type. For example, a sporting-equipment retailer is a merchant when selling tennis equipment but not when selling a used computer.
2. A merchant is a person who, by occupation, holds himself or herself out as having knowledge and skill unique to the practices or goods involved in the transaction. This broad definition may include banks or universities as merchants.
3. A person who *employs a merchant as a broker, agent, or other intermediary* has the status of merchant in that transaction. Hence, if a "gentleman farmer" who ordinarily does not run the farm hires a broker to

---

3. The provisions that apply only to merchants deal principally with the Statute of Frauds, firm offers, confirmatory memoranda, warranties, and contract modification. These special rules reflect expedient business practices commonly known to merchants in the commercial setting. They will be discussed later in this chapter.

purchase or sell livestock, the farmer is considered a merchant in the transaction.

In summary, a person is a **merchant** when he or she, acting in a mercantile capacity, possesses or uses an expertise specifically related to the goods being sold. This basic distinction is not always clear-cut. For example, courts in some states have determined that farmers may be merchants, while courts in other states have determined that the drafters of the UCC did not intend to include farmers as merchants.

SECTION 3

The Scope of Article 2A—Leases

In the past few decades, leases of personal property (goods) have become increasingly common. Consumers and business firms lease automobiles, industrial equipment, items for use in the home (such as floor polishers), and many other types of goods. Until Article 2A was added to the UCC, no specific body of law addressed the legal problems that arose when goods were leased, rather than sold. In cases involving leased goods, the courts generally applied a combination of common law rules, real estate law, and principles expressed in Article 2 of the UCC.

Article 2A of the UCC was created to fill the need for uniform guidelines in this area. Article 2A covers any transaction that creates a lease of goods, as well as subleases of goods [UCC 2A–102, 2A–103(k)]. Article 2A is essentially a repetition of Article 2, except that it applies to leases of goods, rather than sales of goods, and thus varies to reflect differences between sales and lease transactions.

DEFINITION OF A LEASE

Article 2A defines a **lease agreement** as the bargain of the lessor and lessee, as found in their language and as implied by other circumstances [UCC 2A–103(k)]. A **lessor** is one who sells the right to the possession and use of goods under a lease [UCC 2A–103(p)]. A **lessee** is one who acquires the right to the possession and use of goods under a lease [UCC 2A–103(o)]. Article 2A applies to all types of leases of goods, including commercial leases and consumer leases. Special rules apply to certain types of leases, however, including consumer leases and finance leases.

CONSUMER LEASES

A *consumer lease* involves three elements: (1) a lessor who regularly engages in the business of leasing or selling, (2) a lessee (except an organization) who leases the goods "primarily for a personal, family, or household purpose," and (3) total lease payments that are less than $25,000 [UCC 2A–103(1)(e)]. In the interest of providing special protection for consumers, certain provisions of Article 2A apply only to consumer leases. For example, one provision states that a consumer may recover attorneys' fees if a court determines that a term in a consumer lease contract is unconscionable [UCC 2A–108(a)].

FINANCE LEASES

A *finance lease* involves a lessor, a lessee, and a supplier. The lessor buys or leases goods from a supplier and leases or subleases them to the lessee [UCC 2A–103(g)]. Typically, in a finance lease, the lessor is simply financing the transaction. For example, suppose that Marlin Corporation wants to lease a crane for use in its construction business. Marlin's bank agrees to purchase the equipment from Jennco, Inc., and lease the equipment to Marlin. In this situation, the bank is the lessor-financer, Marlin is the lessee, and Jennco is the supplier.

Article 2A, unlike ordinary contract law, makes the lessee's obligations under a commercial finance lease irrevocable and independent from the financer's obligations [UCC 2A–407]. That is, the lessee must perform whether or not the financer performs. The lessee also must look almost entirely to the supplier for warranties.

SECTION 4

The Formation of Sales and Lease Contracts

In regard to the formation of sales and lease contracts, the UCC modifies the common law in several ways. We look here at how Article 2 and Article 2A of the UCC modify common law contract rules. (Remember that parties to sales contracts are free to establish whatever terms they wish.) The UCC comes into play when the parties have not, in their contract, provided for a contingency that later gives rise to a dispute. The UCC makes this very clear time and again by its use of such phrases as "unless the parties otherwise agree" and "absent a contrary agreement by the parties."

OFFER

In general contract law, the moment a definite offer is met by an unqualified acceptance, a binding contract is formed. In commercial sales transactions, the verbal exchanges, the correspondence, and the actions of the parties may not reveal exactly when a binding contractual obligation arises. The UCC states that an agreement sufficient to constitute a contract can exist even if the moment of its making is undetermined [UCC 2–204(2), 2A–204(2)].

Open Terms. According to contract law, an offer must be definite enough for the parties (and the courts) to ascertain its essential terms when it is accepted. The UCC states that a sales or lease contract will not fail for indefiniteness even if one or more terms are left open as long as (1) the parties intended to make a contract and (2) there is a reasonably certain basis for the court to grant an appropriate remedy [UCC 2–204(3), 2A–204(3)].

For example, Mike agrees to lease from CompuQuik a highly specialized computer workstation. Mike and one of CompuQuik's sales representatives sign a lease agreement that leaves some of the details blank, to be "worked out" the following week, when the leasing manager will be back from her vacation. In the meantime, CompuQuik obtains the necessary equipment from one of its suppliers and spends several days modifying the equipment to suit Mike's needs. When the leasing manager returns, she calls Mike and tells him that his workstation is ready. Mike says he is no longer interested in the workstation, as he has arranged to lease the same equipment for a lower price from another firm. CompuQuik sues Mike to recover its costs in obtaining and modifying the equipment, and one of the issues before the court is whether the parties had an enforceable contract. The court will likely hold that they did, based on their intent and conduct, despite the blanks in their written agreement.

Although the UCC has radically lessened the requirement of definiteness of terms, keep in mind that if too many terms are left open, a court may find that the parties did not intend to form a contract. (This is also true with respect to online offers—see this chapter's *Emerging Trends in Technology* on pages 338 and 339 for some suggestions on how online sellers can protect themselves against potential problems by including specific terms and provisions in their offers.)

Open Price Term. If the parties have not agreed on a price, the court will determine a "reasonable price at the time for delivery" [UCC 2–305(1)]. If either the buyer or the seller is to determine the price, the price is to be fixed in good faith [UCC 2–305(2)].

Sometimes the price fails to be fixed through the fault of one of the parties. In that case, the other party can treat the contract as canceled or fix a reasonable price. For example, Johnson and Merrick enter into a contract for the sale of goods and agree that Johnson will fix the price. Johnson refuses to fix the price. Merrick can either treat the contract as canceled or set a reasonable price [UCC 2–305(3)].

Open Payment Term. When parties do not specify payment terms, payment is due at the time and place at which the buyer is to receive the goods [UCC 2–310(a)]. The buyer can tender payment using any commercially normal or acceptable means, such as a check or credit card. If the seller demands payment in cash, however, the buyer must be given a reasonable time to obtain it [UCC 2–511(2)]. This is especially important when the contract states a definite and final time for performance.

Open Delivery Term. When no delivery terms are specified, the buyer normally takes delivery at the seller's place of business [UCC 2–308(a)]. If the seller has no place of business, the seller's residence is used. When goods are located in some other place and both parties know it, delivery is made there. If the time for shipment or delivery is not clearly specified in the sales contract, then the court will infer a "reasonable" time for performance [UCC 2–309(1)].

Duration of an Ongoing Contract. A single contract might specify successive performances but not indicate how long the parties are required to deal with each other. Although either party may terminate the ongoing contractual relationship, principles of good faith and sound commercial practice call for reasonable notification before termination so as to give the other party sufficient time to seek a substitute arrangement [UCC 2–309(2), (3)].

Options and Cooperation Regarding Performance. When specific shipping arrangements have not been made but the contract contemplates shipment of the goods, the *seller* has the right to make these arrangements in good faith, using commercial reasonableness in the situation [UCC 2–311]. (The obligations of good faith and commercial reasonableness in sales and lease contracts are discussed in detail in Chapter 21.)

When terms relating to the assortment of goods are omitted from a sales contract, the buyer can specify the assortment. For example, Harley and Babcock contract for the sale of one thousand pens. The pens come in a variety of colors, but the contract is silent on which colors are ordered. Babcock, the buyer, has the right to take whatever colors he wishes. Babcock, however, must make the selection in good faith and must use commercial reasonableness [UCC 2–311].

Open Quantity Term. Normally, if the parties do not specify a quantity, a court will have no basis for determining a remedy. The UCC recognizes two exceptions in requirements and output contracts [UCC 2–306(1)].

In a **requirements contract,** the buyer agrees to purchase and the seller agrees to sell all or up to a stated amount of what the buyer *needs* or *requires.* There is implicit consideration in a requirements contract, for the buyer gives up the right to buy from any other seller, and this forfeited right creates a legal detriment. Requirements contracts are common in the business world and are normally enforceable. If, however, the buyer promises to purchase only if the buyer *wishes* to do so, or if the buyer reserves the right to buy the goods from someone other than the seller, the promise is illusory (without consideration) and unenforceable by either party.

In an **output contract,** the seller agrees to sell and the buyer agrees to buy all or up to a stated amount of what the seller *produces.* Again, because the seller essentially forfeits the right to sell goods to another buyer, there is implicit consideration in an output contract.

The UCC imposes a *good faith limitation* on requirements and output contracts. The quantity under such contracts is the amount of requirements or the amount of output that occurs during a *normal* production year. The actual quantity purchased or sold cannot be unreasonably disproportionate to normal or comparable prior requirements or output [UCC 2–306].

Merchant's Firm Offer. Under regular contract principles, an offer can be revoked at any time before acceptance. The major common law exception is an

option contract (discussed in Chapter 11), in which the offeree pays consideration for the offeror's irrevocable promise to keep the offer open for a stated period. The UCC creates a second exception, which applies only to firm offers for the sale or lease of goods made by a merchant (regardless of whether or not the offeree is a merchant). A **firm offer** arises when a merchant-offeror gives assurances *in a signed writing* that the offer will remain open. The merchant's firm offer is irrevocable without the necessity of consideration[4] for the stated period or, if no definite period is stated, a reasonable period (neither to exceed three months) [UCC 2–205, 2A–205].

To illustrate: Daniels, a used-car dealer, writes a letter to Peters on January 1 stating, "I have a 1996 Pontiac on the lot that I'll sell you for $8,500 any time between now and January 31." By January 18, Daniels has heard nothing from Peters so he sells the Pontiac to another person. On January 23, Peters tenders $8,500 to Daniels and asks for the car. When Daniels tells him the car has already been sold, Peters claims that Daniels has breached a good contract. Peters is right. Daniels is a merchant of used cars and assured Peters in a signed writing that he would keep his offer open until the end of January. Peters's acceptance on January 23 thus created a contract, which Daniels breached.

It is necessary that the offer be both *written* and *signed* by the offeror.[5] When a firm offer is contained in a form contract prepared by the offeree, the offeror must also sign a separate firm-offer assurance. This requirement ensures that the offeror will be made aware of the offer. If the firm offer is buried amid copious language in one of the pages of the offeree's form contract, the offeror may inadvertently sign the contract without realizing that there is a firm offer, thus defeating the purpose of the rule—which is to give effect to a merchant's deliberate intent to be bound to a firm offer.

ACCEPTANCE

The following sections examine the UCC's provisions governing acceptance. As you will see, acceptance of

---

4. If the offeree pays consideration, then an option contract (not a merchant's firm offer) is formed.
5. "Signed" includes any symbol executed or adopted by a party with a present intention to authenticate a writing [UCC 1–201(39)]. A complete signature is not required. Therefore, initials, a thumbprint, a trade name, or any mark used in lieu of a written signature will suffice, regardless of its location on the document.

EMERGING TRENDS IN TECHNOLOGY

Online Offers

Today, numerous sales contracts are being formed online. Consumers purchase books, compact discs, software, airline tickets, clothing, computers, and a host of other goods via the Internet. Although the medium through which sales contracts are generated has changed, the age-old problems attending contract formation have not. Disputes concerning contracts formed online continue to center around contract terms and whether the parties voluntarily assented to those terms. Sellers doing business via the Internet can protect themselves against contract disputes and legal liability by creating offers that clearly spell out the terms that will govern their transactions if the offers are accepted.

DRAFTING AND DISPLAYING THE OFFER

Online offers should not be casually drafted. Rather, they must be carefully constructed and address all key terms and conditions so that, on their acceptance, the resulting contract clearly spells out the obligations of the parties. All important terms should be conspicuous and easily viewed by potential buyers. The seller's Web site should include a hypertext link to a page containing the full contract so that potential buyers are made aware of the terms to which they are assenting. At a minimum, the offer (contract) should include the following provisions:

■ A provision specifying the remedies available to the buyer if the goods turn out to be defective or if the contract is otherwise breached (any limitation of remedies should be clearly spelled out).
■ A forum-selection clause (indicating the forum, or location, for the resolution of any dispute that may arise under the contract). This clause will help to avert future jurisdictional problems, which often arise in online transactions, and help to ensure that the seller will not be required to appear in court in a distant state.
■ The statute of limitations governing the transaction (that is, the time period within which a legal action can be brought over a dispute concerning the contract).
■ A clause that clearly indicates the buyer's agreement to the terms of the offer.

■ A provision specifying how payment for the goods and of any applicable taxes must be made.
■ A statement of the seller's refund and return policies.
■ Disclaimers of liability for certain uses of the goods. For example, an online seller of business forms may add a disclaimer that the seller does not accept responsibility for the buyer's reliance on the forms rather than on an attorney's advice.
■ How the information gathered about the buyer will be used by the seller. (See the *Emerging Trends in Technology* in Chapter 5, concerning privacy rights in cyberspace, for more information on this topic.)

The contract generally must be displayed online in a readable format such as 12-point typeface. All provisions should be reasonably clear. For example, if a seller is offering certain goods priced according to a complex price schedule, that schedule must be fully provided and explained.

ONLINE ACCEPTANCE

An online offer should include some mechanism by which the customer may accept the offer. Typically, online sellers include

an offer to buy, sell, or lease goods generally may be made in any reasonable manner and by any reasonable means.

Methods of Acceptance. The general common law rule is that an offeror can specify, or authorize, a particular means of acceptance, making that means the only one effective for contract formation. Even an unauthorized means of communication is effective, however, as long as the acceptance is received by the specified deadline. For example, suppose that the offer states, "Answer by fax within five days." If the offeree sends a letter, and the offeror receives it within five days, a valid contract is formed. (For a review of the requirements relating to mode and timeliness of acceptance, see Chapter 11.)

Any Reasonable Means. When the offeror does not specify a means of acceptance, the UCC provides that acceptance can be made by any means of communi-

EMERGING TRENDS IN TECHNOLOGY

Online Offers,
continued

boxes containing the words "I agree" or "I accept the terms of the offer" that offerees can click on to indicate acceptance. Electronic "click-on" acceptances have raised several legal issues. One issue is whether the agreement meets the signature requirements of the Statute of Frauds—because a point-and-click agreement is not actually signed by the recipient. A similar issue arises with agreements that are included in virtually all shrink-wrapped software. When the purchaser opens the software package, he or she agrees to abide by the terms of the limited license agreement.

Increasingly, the courts are holding that limited licenses included with shrink-wrapped software, as well as their equivalents on the Internet ("click-on" acceptances), are binding on the buyer. Section 2–204 of the UCC provides that any contract for the sale of goods "may be made in any manner sufficient to show agreement, including conduct by both parties which recognizes the existence of a contract." Thus, a

buyer's failure to object to terms contained within a shrink-wrapped software package (or an online offer) may constitute an acceptance of the terms by conduct.[a]

IMPLICATIONS FOR THE BUSINESSPERSON

1. Online offerors, when drafting their offers, should keep in mind some of the unique issues that can arise in the electronic-contracting environment and include terms and conditions in their offers that specifically address these issues. For example, because the Internet has no physical boundaries, jurisdictional issues often arise in Web-based business dealings. Including a forum-selection clause in the offer can help to prevent such problems.
2. Any businessperson engaging in the online sale of goods should make sure that offerees are instructed, in clear language, that by clicking "I agree" or "I accept" on a computer screen box they are

binding themselves (or their employers) in contract.

FOR CRITICAL ANALYSIS

1. Are there any significant differences between the types of terms and provisions that should be included in online offers as opposed to traditional (offline) offers?
2. What if a Web user claims that he or she clicked on a box stating "I agree" (to the terms and conditions of a contract) by mistake? What steps might online offerors take to reduce the likelihood that such "mistaken" acceptances will occur?

RELEVANT WEB SITES

For an overview of some cases dealing with click-on acceptances, go to **http://www.netlitigation. com/ecommerce.htm**. You can find a more detailed summary of *ProCD, Inc. v. Zeidenberg* (see footnote a in this feature), a landmark case on this issue, at **http://www.ccosta.com/ artprocd.htm**.

---

a. See, for example, *ProCD, Inc. v. Zeidenberg,* 86 F.3d 1447 (7th Cir. 1996); and *Hill v. Gateway 2000, Inc.,* 105 F.3d 1147 (7th Cir. 1997).

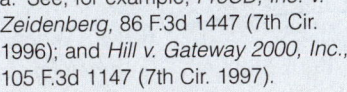

cation that are reasonable under the circumstances [UCC 2–206(1), 2A–206(1)]. This is also the basic rule under the common law of contracts (see Chapter 11).

For example, Anodyne Corporation writes a letter to Bethlehem Industries offering to lease $1,000 worth of goods. The offer states that Anodyne will keep the offer open for only ten days from the date of the letter. Before the ten days have lapsed, Bethlehem sends Anodyne an acceptance by fax. The fax is misdirected by someone at Anodyne's offices and does not reach

the right person at Anodyne until after the ten-day deadline has passed. Is a valid contract formed? The answer is probably yes, because acceptance by fax appears to be a commercially reasonable medium of acceptance under the circumstances. Acceptance would be effective on Bethlehem's transmission of the fax, which occurred before the offer lapsed.

Promise to Ship or Prompt Shipment. The UCC permits acceptance of an offer to buy goods for current or prompt shipment by either a prompt *promise* to ship the goods to the buyer or the prompt shipment of conforming goods (that is, goods that accord with the contract's terms) to the buyer [UCC 2–206(1)(b)]. The prompt shipment of *nonconforming goods* constitutes both an *acceptance* (a contract) and a *breach* of that contract. This rule does not apply if the seller seasonably (within a reasonable amount of time) notifies the buyer that the nonconforming shipment is offered only as an *accommodation,* or as a favor. The notice of accommodation must clearly indicate to the buyer that the shipment does not constitute an acceptance and that, therefore, no contract has been formed.

For example, Barrymore orders one thousand *black* fans from Stroh. Stroh ships one thousand *blue* fans to Barrymore, notifying Barrymore that because Stroh has only blue fans in stock, these are sent as an *accommodation.* The shipment of blue fans is not an acceptance but a counteroffer, and a contract will be formed only if Barrymore accepts the blue fans. If, however, Stroh ships one thousand blue fans instead of black *without* notifying Barrymore that the goods are being shipped as an accommodation, Stroh's shipment acts as both an acceptance of Barrymore's offer and a *breach* of the resulting contract. Barrymore may sue Stroh for any appropriate damages.

Communication of Acceptance. Under the common law, because a unilateral offer invites acceptance by a performance, the offeree need not notify the offeror of performance unless the offeror would not otherwise know about it. The UCC is more stringent than the common law, stating that when the beginning of the requested performance is a reasonable mode of acceptance, an offeror who is not notified of acceptance within a reasonable time may treat the offer as having lapsed before acceptance [UCC 2–206(2), 2A–206(2)].

For example, Lee writes to Pickwick Book Store on Monday, "Please send me a copy of *West's Best Law Text* for $85, C.O.D.," and signs it, "Lee." Pickwick receives the request but does not ship the book for four weeks. When the book arrives, Lee rejects it, claiming that it has arrived too late to be of value. In this situation, because Lee had heard nothing from Pickwick for a month, he was justified in assuming that the store did not intend to deliver the book. Lee could consider that the offer had lapsed because of the length of time Pickwick delayed shipment.

Additional Terms. Under the common law, if Alderman makes an offer to Beale, and Beale in turn

accepts but adds some slight modification, there is no contract. Recall from Chapter 11 that the so-called *mirror image rule* requires that the terms of the acceptance exactly match those of the offer. Beale's modification of the terms of Alderman's offer makes Beale's action a rejection of—and a counteroffer to—the offer. This rule often led to what is known as the *battle of the forms*.

Say, for example, that a buyer contracts with a seller over the phone to purchase a certain piece of equipment. The parties agree to all of the specific terms of the sale—price, quantity, delivery date, and so on. The buyer then enters the terms of the agreement on its standard purchase order form and sends the form to the seller. At the same time, the seller enters the terms on its standard sales form. Because the parties presume that they have reached an oral agreement on the telephone, discrepancies in the terms and conditions contained in their respective forms may go unnoticed. If a dispute arises, however, the discrepancies become significant, and a "battle of the forms" begins, in which each party claims that its form represents the true terms of the agreement.

Under the common law, the courts tended to resolve this difficulty by holding that the last form to be sent was the final counteroffer. To avoid the battle of the forms, the UCC dispenses with the mirror image rule. The UCC generally takes the position that if the offeree's response indicates a *definite* acceptance of the offer, a contract is formed, even if the acceptance includes terms additional to or different from those contained in the offer [UCC 2–207(1)]. What happens to these additional terms? The answer to this question depends, in part, on whether the parties are nonmerchants or merchants.

Rules When One Party or Both Parties Are Nonmerchants. If one (or both) of the parties is a *nonmerchant,* the contract is formed according to the terms of the original offer submitted by the original offeror and not according to the additional terms of the acceptance [UCC 2–207(2)]. For example, Tolsen offers in writing to sell his personal computer to Valdez for $1,500. Valdez faxes a reply to Tolsen in which Valdez states, "I accept your offer to purchase your computer for $1,500. I *would like* a box of computer paper and ten diskettes to be included in the purchase price." Valdez has given Tolsen a definite expression of acceptance (creating a contract), even though Valdez's acceptance also suggests an added term for the offer. Because Tolsen is not a merchant, the additional term is merely a proposal (suggestion), and Tolsen is not legally obligated to comply with that term.

Rules When Both Parties Are Merchants. In contracts *between merchants*, the additional terms automatically become part of the contract unless (1) the original offer expressly limited acceptance to its terms, (2) the new or changed terms materially alter the contract, or (3) the offeror objects to the new or changed terms within a reasonable period of time [UCC 2–207(2)].

What constitutes a material alteration of the contract is frequently a question of fact that only a court can decide. Generally, if the modification involves no unreasonable element of surprise or hardship for the offeror, the court will hold that the modification did not materially alter the contract. The issue in the following case concerns whether an additional term in the acceptance (subjecting any disputes to arbitration) constituted a material alteration of the contract terms.

CASE 19.2   Wilson Fertilizer & Grain, Inc. v. ADM Milling Co.

Court of Appeals of
Indiana, 1995.
654 N.E.2d 848.
**http://www.law.indiana.
edu/law/incourts/1995/
1995.html**[a]

COMPANY PROFILE *Archer-Daniels-Midland Company had its beginnings in 1878 in Minneapolis, Minnesota, when John Daniels started crushing flaxseed to produce linseed oil. Today, Archer-Daniels-Midland, with more processing capacity than any other agricultural enterprise, calls itself the "supermarket to the world." Its customers include virtually every U.S. food company. Archer-Daniels-Midland is the leading global processor and producer of oilseed, ethanol, and soy protein, and it handles nearly 10 percent of the world grain trade. The division of Archer-Daniels-Midland that handles barley, corn, oats, rice, and wheat is ADM Milling Company (**http://www.admworld.com**).*

BACKGROUND AND FACTS *In October 1992, Wilson Fertilizer & Grain, Inc., agreed to sell grain to ADM Milling Company. ADM sent Wilson a confirmation stating that "[t]his contract is also subject to the Trade Rules of the National Grain and Feed Association [NGFA]." The NGFA rules require the arbitration of disputes and limit the time for filing a complaint to one year. Wilson did not respond to the confirmation. A dispute arose under the contract, and Wilson filed suit against ADM in an Indiana state court. ADM moved to dismiss the action, claiming that the Trade Rules of the NGFA require the parties to arbitrate the dispute. Wilson argued that the arbitration provisions were not included in the terms of its agreement with ADM. The trial court granted ADM's motion and ordered the parties to arbitration. By that time, however, the one-year limit had expired. Wilson appealed, arguing in part that ADM's confirmation had materially altered the contract and thus had not become a part of the contract, because the one-year limit imposed a hardship on Wilson.*

**IN THE LANGUAGE
OF THE COURT**

BARTEAU, Judge.
    *   *   *   *

    The test for whether additional terms materially alter an agreement is whether their "incorporation into the contract without express awareness by the other party would result in surprise or hardship." *   *   *

    *   *   * We disagree [with Wilson] for two reasons.

    First of all, *   *   * [the UCC] specifically permits parties to a contract for sale to reduce the time for filing claims to one year *   *   * .

    Second, and even more significantly, we are persuaded by Wilson's apparent ability to have submitted its claim for arbitration within the one-year limit. The contract between Wilson and ADM was formed on October 20, 1992. *   *   * Wilson filed its complaint for damages *   *   * on September 24, 1993 *   *   * . If Wilson was able

---

a. This Web site is maintained by the Indiana University School of Law. In the "Listed by First Party" section, click on "[Indiana Court of Appeals]." Scroll down the list of cases to the *Wilson* case and click on the version in which you'd prefer to read the opinion.

to file its complaint in court within one year after [ADM allegedly breached the contract], we fail to see how a contract provision requiring Wilson to submit its claim for arbitration in the same time period imposes a hardship.

DECISION AND REMEDY *The Court of Appeals of Indiana affirmed the lower court's order that the parties go to arbitration.*

Conditioned on Offeror's Assent. Regardless of merchant status, the UCC provides that the offeree's expression cannot be construed as an acceptance if additional or different terms in the acceptance are expressly *conditioned* on the offeror's assent to the additional or different terms [UCC 2–207(1)]. For example, Philips offers to sell Hundert 650 pounds of turkey thighs at a specified price and with specified delivery terms. Hundert responds, "I accept your offer for 650 pounds of turkey thighs *on the condition that you agree that the weight will be evidenced by a city scale weight certificate.*" Hundert's response will be construed not as an acceptance but as a counteroffer, which Philips may or may not accept.

Additional Terms May Be Stricken. The UCC provides yet another option for dealing with conflicting terms in the parties' writings. Section 2–207(3) states that conduct by both parties that recognizes the existence of a contract is sufficient to establish a contract for sale even though the writings of the parties do not otherwise establish a contract. In this situation, "the terms of the particular contract will consist of those terms on which the writings of the parties agree, together with any supplementary terms incorporated under any other provisions of this Act." In a dispute over contract terms, this provision allows a court simply to strike from the contract those terms on which the parties do not agree.[6]

CONSIDERATION

The common law rule that a contract requires consideration also applies to sales and lease contracts. Unlike the common law, however, the UCC does not require a contract modification to be supported by new consideration. The UCC states that an agreement modifying a contract for the sale or lease of goods "needs no consideration to be binding" [UCC 2–209(1), 2A–208(1)].

Modifications Must Be Made in Good Faith. Of course, any contract modification must be made in good faith [UCC 1–203]. For example, Jim agrees to lease certain goods to Louise for a stated price. Subsequently, a sudden shift in the market makes it difficult for Jim to lease the items to Louise at the given price without suffering a loss. Jim tells Louise of the situation, and Louise agrees to pay an additional sum for the goods. Later, Louise reconsiders and refuses to pay more than the original price. Under the UCC, Louise's promise to modify the contract needs no consideration to be binding. Hence, Louise is bound by the modified contract.

In this example, a shift in the market is a *good faith reason for contract modification.* What if there really was no shift in the market, however, and Jim knew that Louise needed the goods immediately but refused to deliver them unless Louise agreed to pay an additional sum of money? This sort of extortion of a modification without a legitimate commercial reason would be ineffective, because it would violate the duty of good faith. Jim would not be permitted to enforce the higher price.

When Contract Modification without Consideration Requires a Writing. In some situations, modification of a sales or lease contract without consideration must be in writing to be enforceable. For example, if the contract itself prohibits any changes to the contract unless they are in a signed writing, only those changes agreed to in a signed writing are enforceable. If a consumer (nonmerchant buyer) is dealing with a merchant and the merchant supplies the form that contains the prohibition against oral modification, the consumer must sign a separate acknowledgment of the clause [UCC 2–209(2), 2A–208(2)].

---

6. For an application of this solution to the "battle of the forms," see *Ionics, Inc. v. Elmwood Sensors, Inc.,* 896 F.Supp. 66 (D.Mass. 1995).

Also, under Article 2, any modification that brings a sales contract under the Statute of Frauds must usually be in writing to be enforceable. Thus, if an oral contract for the sale of goods priced at $400 is modified so that the contract goods are priced at $600, the modification must be in writing to be enforceable [UCC 2–209(3)]. If, however, the buyer accepts delivery of the goods after the modification, he or she is bound to the $600 price [UCC 2–201(3)(c)]. Although Article 2 contains these provisions to govern modifications of sales contracts, Article 2A does not say whether a lease as modified needs to satisfy the Statute of Frauds.

THE STATUTE OF FRAUDS

The UCC contains Statute of Frauds provisions covering sales and lease contracts. Under these provisions, sales contracts for goods priced at $500 or more and lease contracts requiring payments of $1,000 or more must be in writing to be enforceable [UCC 2–201(1), 2A–201(1)].

Sufficiency of the Writing. The UCC has greatly relaxed the requirements for the sufficiency of a writing to satisfy the Statute of Frauds. A writing or a memorandum will be sufficient as long as it indicates that the parties intended to form a contract and as long as it is signed by the party (or agent of the party) against whom enforcement is sought. The contract normally will not be enforceable beyond the quantity of goods shown in the writing, however. All other terms can be proved in court by oral testimony (For leases, the writing must reasonably identify and describe the goods leased and the lease term.)

Special Rules for Contracts between Merchants. Once again, the UCC provides a special rule for merchants. The rule, however, applies only to sales (under Article 2); there is no corresponding rule that applies to leases (under Article 2A).[7] Merchants can satisfy the requirements of a writing for the Statute of Frauds if, after the parties have agreed orally, one of the merchants sends a signed written confirmation to the other merchant. The communication must indicate the terms of the agreement, and the merchant receiving the confirmation must have reason to know of

its contents. Unless the merchant who receives the confirmation gives written notice of objection to its contents within ten days after receipt, the writing is sufficient against the receiving merchant, even though he or she has not signed anything [UCC 2–201(2)].

For example, Alfonso is a merchant buyer in Cleveland. He contracts over the telephone to purchase $4,000 worth of goods from Goldstein, a New York City merchant seller. Two days later, Goldstein sends written confirmation detailing the terms of the oral contract, and Alfonso subsequently receives it. If Alfonso does not give Goldstein written notice of objection to the contents of the written confirmation within ten days of receipt, Alfonso cannot raise the Statute of Frauds as a defense against the enforcement of the oral contract.

Exceptions. The UCC defines three exceptions to the writing requirements of the Statute of Frauds. An oral contract for the sale of goods priced at $500 or more or the lease of goods involving payments of $1,000 or more will be enforceable despite the absence of a writing in the following circumstances [UCC 2–201(3), 2A–201(4)]. These exceptions and other ways in which sales law differs from general contract law are summarized in Exhibit 19–2 on page 344.

Specially Manufactured Goods. An oral contract is enforceable if (1) it is for goods that are specially manufactured for a particular buyer or specially manufactured or obtained for a particular lessee, (2) these goods are not suitable for resale or lease to others in the ordinary course of the seller's or lessor's business, and (3) the seller or lessor has substantially started to manufacture the goods or has made commitments for the manufacture or procurement of the goods. In these situations, once the seller or lessor has taken action, the buyer or lessee cannot repudiate the agreement claiming the Statute of Frauds as a defense.

For example, suppose Womach orders custom-made draperies for her new boutique. The price is $1,000, and the contract is oral. When the merchant-seller manufactures the draperies and tenders delivery to Womach, Womach refuses to pay for them even though the job has been completed on time. Womach claims that she is not liable because the contract was oral. Clearly, if the unique style and color of the draperies make it improbable that the seller can find another buyer, Womach is liable to the seller. Note that the seller must have made a

---

7. According to the Comments accompanying UCC 2A–201 (Article 2A's Statute of Frauds), the "between merchants" provision was not included because "the number of such transactions involving leases, as opposed to sales, was thought to be modest."

EXHIBIT 19–2   MAJOR DIFFERENCES BETWEEN CONTRACT LAW AND SALES LAW

	CONTRACT LAW	SALES LAW
Contract Terms	Contract must contain all material terms.	Open terms are acceptable, if parties intended to form a contract, but contract is not enforceable beyond quantity term.
Acceptance	Mirror image rule applies. If additional terms are added in acceptance, counteroffer is created.	Additional terms will not negate acceptance unless acceptance is made expressly conditional on assent to the additional terms.
Contract Modification	Modification requires consideration.	Modification does not require consideration.
Irrevocable Offers	Option contracts (with consideration).	Merchants' firm offers (without consideration).
Statute of Frauds Requirements	All material terms must be included in the writing.	Writing is required only for sale of goods of $500 or more, but contract is not enforceable beyond quantity specified. *Exceptions:* 1. Contracts for specially manufactured goods are enforceable. 2. Contracts admitted to under oath by party against whom enforcement is sought are enforceable. 3. Contracts will be enforced to extent goods are delivered or paid for. 4. Confirmatory memorandum (between merchants): Contract is enforceable if merchant fails to object in writing to confirming memorandum within ten days of its receipt.

substantial beginning in manufacturing the specialized item prior to the buyer's repudiation. (Here, the manufacture was completed.) Of course, the court must still be convinced by evidence of the terms of the oral contract.

Admissions.   An oral contract for the sale or lease of goods is enforceable if the party against whom enforcement is sought admits in pleadings, testimony, or other court proceedings that a sales or lease contract was made. In this situation, the contract will be enforceable even though it was oral, but enforceability will be limited to the quantity of goods admitted.

For example, Lane and Sanders negotiate an agreement over the telephone. During the negotiations, Lane requests a delivery price for five hundred gallons of gasoline and a separate price for seven hundred gallons of gasoline. Sanders replies that the price would be the same, $1.10 per gallon. Lane orally orders five hundred gallons. Sanders honestly believes that Lane

ordered seven hundred gallons and tenders that amount. Lane refuses the shipment of seven hundred gallons, and Sanders sues for breach. In his pleadings and testimony, Lane admits that an oral contract was made, but only for five hundred gallons. Because Lane admits the existence of the oral contract, Lane cannot plead the Statute of Frauds as a defense. The contract is enforceable, however, only to the extent of the quantity admitted (five hundred gallons).

Partial Performance.   An oral contract for the sale or lease of goods is enforceable if payment has been made and accepted or goods have been received and accepted. This is the "partial performance" exception. The oral contract will be enforced at least to the extent that performance *actually* took place.

Suppose that Allan orally contracts to lease Opus two thousand chairs at $1 each to be used during a one-day rock concert. Before delivery, Opus sends Allan a check for $500, which Allan cashes. Later, when Allan attempts to deliver the chairs, Opus refuses delivery, claiming the Statute of Frauds as a defense, and demands the return of his $500. Under the UCC's partial performance rule, Allan can enforce the oral contract by tender of delivery of five hundred chairs for the $500 accepted. Similarly, if Opus had made no payment but had accepted the delivery of five hundred chairs from Allan, the oral contract would have been enforceable against Opus for $500, the lease payment due for the five hundred chairs delivered.

PAROL EVIDENCE

If the parties to a contract set forth its terms in a con-firmatory memorandum (a writing expressing offer and acceptance of the deal) or in a writing intended as their final expression, the terms of the contract cannot be contradicted by evidence of any prior agreements or contemporaneous oral agreements. As discussed in Chapter 15, this principle of law is known as the parol evidence rule. The terms of a contract may, however, be explained or supplemented by *consistent additional terms* or by *course of dealing, usage of trade, or course of performance* [UCC 2–202, 2A–202].

Consistent Additional Terms. If the court finds an ambiguity in a writing that is supposed to be a complete and exclusive statement of the agreement between the parties, it may accept evidence of consistent additional terms to clarify or remove the ambiguity. The court will not, however, accept evidence of contradictory terms. This is the rule under both the UCC and the common law of contracts.

Course of Dealing and Usage of Trade. Under the UCC, the meaning of any agreement, evidenced by the language of the parties and by their actions, must be interpreted in light of commercial practices and other surrounding circumstances. In interpreting a commercial agreement, the court will assume that the *course of prior dealing* between the parties and the *usage of trade* were taken into account when the agreement was phrased.

A **course of dealing** is a sequence of previous actions and communications between the parties to a particular transaction that establishes a common basis for their understanding [UCC 1–205(1)]. A course of dealing is restricted to the sequence of actions and communications between the parties that has occurred prior to the agreement in question. The UCC states, "A course of dealing between the parties and any usage of trade in the vocation or trade in which they are engaged or of which they are or should be aware give particular meaning to [the terms of the agreement] and supplement or qualify the terms of [the] agreement" [UCC 1–205(3)].

Usage of trade is defined as any practice or method of dealing having such regularity of observance in a place, vocation, or trade as to justify an expectation that it will be observed with respect to the transaction in question [UCC 1–205(2)]. Further, the express terms of an agreement and an applicable course of dealing or usage of trade will be construed to be consistent with each other whenever reasonable. When such a construction is *unreasonable*, however, the express terms in the agreement will prevail [UCC 1–205(4)]. In the following case, the issue concerned whether evidence of usage of trade could be used to explain the meaning of the quantity figures specified by the parties when a sales contract was formed.

CASE 19.3   ## Heggblade-Marguleas-Tenneco, Inc. v. Sunshine Biscuit, Inc.

Court of Appeal of California, Fifth District, 1976.
59 Cal.App.3d 948, 131 Cal.Rptr. 183.

BACKGROUND AND FACTS   *In 1970, Heggblade-Marguleas-Tenneco, Inc. (HMT), contracted with Sunshine Biscuit, Inc., to supply potatoes to be used in the 1971 production of snack foods. HMT had never marketed processing potatoes before. The quantity mentioned in its contract negotiations was 100,000 sacks of potatoes. The parties agreed that the amount of potatoes to be supplied would vary somewhat with Sunshine Biscuit's needs. Subsequently, a decline in demand for Sunshine Biscuit's products severely reduced its need for potatoes. Sunshine Biscuit was able to take only 60,105 sacks out of the 100,000 previously estimated. HMT filed suit against Sunshine Biscuit in a California state court. Sunshine Biscuit attempted to introduce evidence that it is customary in the potato-processing industry for the number of potatoes specified in sales contracts to be reasonable estimates rather than exact* *numbers that a buyer intends to purchase. The trial court held for Sunshine Biscuit, and HMT appealed.*

IN THE LANGUAGE OF THE COURT

FRANSON, Acting Presiding Justice.

*   *   *   *

[UCC 2–202] states [that evidence of prior agreements or contemporaneous oral agreements that contradict a written contract is inadmissible but] permits a trade usage to be put in evidence "as an instrument of interpretation." The Uniform Commercial Code comment to subdivision (a) of section [2–202] states that evidence of trade usage is admissible " *   *   * in order that the true understanding of the parties as to the agreement may be reached. Such writings are to be read on the assumption that *   *   * the usages of trade were taken for granted when the document was phrased. Unless carefully negated they have become an element of the meaning of the words used. *   *   * "

*   *   *   *

*   *   * Because potatoes are a perishable commodity and their demand is dependent upon a fluctuating market, and because the marketing contracts are signed eight or nine months in advance of the harvest season, common sense dictates that the quantity would be estimated by both the grower and processor. Thus, it cannot be said as a matter of law that HMT was ignorant of the trade custom.

DECISION AND REMEDY

The Court of Appeal of California affirmed the trial court's judgment. Sunshine Biscuit did not have to pay HMT for the difference between the 100,000 sacks of potatoes it estimated it would need and the 60,105 sacks of potatoes it actually purchased.

Course of Performance. The conduct that occurs under the terms of a particular agreement is called a **course of performance.** Presumably, the parties themselves know best what they meant by their words, and the course of performance actually undertaken under their agreement is the best indication of what they meant [UCC 2–208(1), 2A–207(1)].

For example, suppose that Janson's Lumber Company contracts with Barrymore to sell Barrymore a specified number of two-by-fours. The lumber in fact does not measure 2 inches by 4 inches but rather 1⅞ inches by 3¾ inches. Janson's agrees to deliver the lumber in five deliveries, and Barrymore, without objection, accepts the lumber in the first three deliveries. On the fourth delivery, however, Barrymore objects that the two-by-fours do not measure 2 inches by 4 inches.

The course of performance in this transaction— that is, the fact that Barrymore accepted three deliveries without objection under the agreement—is relevant in determining that here a "two-by-four" actually means "1⅞ by 3¾." Janson's can also prove that two-by-fours need not be exactly 2 inches by 4 inches by applying usage of trade, course of dealing, or both.

Janson's can, for example, show that in previous transactions, Barrymore took 1⅞-inch-by-3¾-inch lumber without objection. In addition, Janson's can show that in the trade, two-by-fours are commonly 1⅞ inches by 3¾ inches.

Rules of Construction. The UCC provides *rules of construction* for interpreting contracts. Express terms, course of performance, course of dealing, and usage of trade are to be construed together when they do not contradict one another. When such a construction is unreasonable, however, the following order of priority controls [UCC 1–205(4), 2–208(2), 2A–207(2)]:

1. Express terms.
2. Course of performance.
3. Course of dealing.
4. Usage of trade.

UNCONSCIONABILITY

As discussed in Chapter 13, an unconscionable contract is one that is so unfair and one sided that it would be unreasonable to enforce it. The UCC allows the court to evaluate a contract or any clause in a contract, and if the court deems it to have been unconscionable *at the time it was made*, the court can do any of the following [UCC 2–302, 2A–108]:

1. Refuse to enforce the contract.
2. Enforce the remainder of the contract without the unconscionable clause.
3. Limit the application of the unconscionable clause to avoid an unconscionable result.

The inclusion of Sections 2–302 and 2A–108 in the UCC reflects an increased sensitivity to certain realities of modern commercial activities. Classical contract theory holds that a contract is a bargain in which the terms have been worked out *freely* between parties that are equals. In many modern commercial transactions, this premise is invalid. Standard-form contracts and leases are often signed by consumer-buyers who understand few of the terms used and who often do not even read them. Virtually all of the terms are advantageous to the party supplying the standard-form contract or lease. The UCC's unconscionability provisions give the courts a powerful weapon for policing such transactions, as the next case illustrates.

CASE 19.4   # Jones v. Star Credit Corp.

Supreme Court of New York, Nassau County, 1969.
59 Misc.2d 189,
298 N.Y.S.2d 264.

IN THE LANGUAGE OF THE COURT

BACKGROUND AND FACTS   *The Joneses, the plaintiffs, were welfare recipients who agreed to purchase a freezer for $900 as the result of a salesperson's visit to their home. Tax and financing charges raised the total price to $1,234.80. At trial, the freezer was found to have a maximum retail value of approximately $300. The plaintiffs, who had made payments totaling $619.88, brought a suit in a New York state court to have the purchase contract declared unconscionable under the UCC.*

SOL M. WACHTLER, Justice.
     ❖   ❖   ❖   ❖

Concededly, deciding [this case] is substantially easier than explaining it. No doubt, the mathematical disparity between $300, which presumably includes a reasonable profit margin, and $900, which is exorbitant on its face, carries the greatest weight. Credit charges alone exceed by more than $100 the retail value of the freezer. These alone may be sufficient to sustain the decision. Yet, a caveat is warranted lest we reduce the import of Section 2–302 solely to a mathematical ratio formula. It may, at times, be that; yet it may also be much more. The very limited financial resources of the purchaser, known to the sellers at the time of the sale, is entitled to weight in the balance. Indeed, the value disparity itself leads inevitably to the felt conclusion that knowing advantage was taken of the plaintiffs. In addition, *the meaningfulness of choice essential to the making of a contract, can be negated by a gross inequality of bargaining power.* [Emphasis added.]

There is no question about the necessity and even the desirability of installment sales and the extension of credit. Indeed, there are many, including welfare recipients, who would be deprived of even the most basic conveniences without the use of these devices. Similarly, the retail merchant selling on installment or extending credit is expected to establish a pricing factor which will afford a degree of protection commensurate with the risk of selling to those who might be default prone. However, neither of these accepted premises can clothe the sale of this freezer with respectability.

DECISION AND REMEDY   *Judgment was entered for the plaintiffs. The contract was reformed so that they were required to make no further payments.*

CONCEPT SUMMARY 19.1

THE FORMATION OF SALES AND LEASE CONTRACTS

CONCEPT	DESCRIPTION

Offer and Acceptance	1. *Offer*—
	  a. Not all terms have to be included for a contract to be formed.
	  b. The price does not have to be included for a contract to be formed.
	  c. Particulars of performance can be left open.
	  d. An offer by a merchant in a signed writing with assurances that the offer will not be withdrawn is irrevocable without consideration (for up to three months).
	2. *Acceptance*—
	  a. Acceptance may be made by any reasonable means of communication; it is effective when dispatched.
	  b. The acceptance of a unilateral offer can be made by a promise to ship or by the shipment of conforming goods.
	  c. Acceptance by performance requires notice within a reasonable time; otherwise, the offer can be treated as lapsed.
	  d. A definite expression of acceptance creates a contract even if the terms of the acceptance modify the terms of the offer.

Consideration	A modification of a contract for the sale of goods does not require consideration.

Requirements under the Statute of Frauds	1. All contracts for the sale of goods priced at $500 or more must be in writing. A writing is sufficient so long as it indicates a contract between the parties and is signed by the party against whom enforcement is sought. A contract is not enforceable beyond the quantity shown in the writing.
	2. When written confirmation of an oral contract *between merchants* is not objected to in writing by the receiver within ten days, the oral contract is enforceable.
	3. Exceptions to the requirement of a writing exist in the following situations:
	  a. When the oral contract is for specially manufactured or obtained goods not suitable for resale or lease to others and the seller or lessor has made commitments for the manufacture or procurement of the goods.
	  b. When the defendant admits in pleadings, testimony, or other court proceedings that an oral contract for the sale or lease of goods was made. In this case, the contract will be enforceable to the extent of the quantity of goods admitted.
	  c. The oral agreement will be enforceable to the extent that payment has been received and accepted or to the extent that goods have been received and accepted.

Parol Evidence Rule	1. The terms of a clearly and completely worded written contract cannot be contradicted by evidence of prior agreements or contemporaneous oral agreements.
	2. Evidence is admissible to clarify the terms of a writing in the following situations:
	  a. If the contract terms are ambiguous.
	  b. If evidence of course of dealing, usage of trade, or course of performance is necessary to learn or to clarify the intentions of the parties to the contract.

THE FORMATION OF SALES AND LEASE CONTRACTS (*continued*)

CONCEPT	DESCRIPTION
Unconscionability	An unconscionable contract is one that is so unfair and one sided that it would be unreasonable to enforce it. If the court deems a contract to have been unconscionable at the time it was made, the court can (1) refuse to enforce the contract, (2) refuse to enforce the unconscionable clause of the contract, or (3) limit the application of the unconscionable clause to avoid an unconscionable result.

SECTION 5

Contracts for the International Sale of Goods

International sales contracts between firms or individuals located in different countries are governed by the 1980 United Nations Convention on Contracts for the International Sale of Goods (CISG). The CISG governs international contracts only if the countries of the parties to the contract have ratified the CISG and if the parties have not agreed that some other law will govern their contract. As of 2000, fifty-seven countries had ratified or acceded to the CISG, including the United States, Canada, Mexico, some Central and South American countries, and most of the European nations.

APPLICABILITY OF THE CISG

Essentially, the CISG is to international sales contracts what Article 2 of the UCC is to domestic sales contracts. As discussed in this chapter, in domestic transactions the UCC applies when the parties to a contract for a sale of goods have failed to specify in writing some important term concerning price, delivery, or the like. Similarly, whenever the parties to international transactions have failed to specify in writing the precise terms of a contract, the CISG will be applied. Unlike the UCC, the CISG does not apply to consumer sales, and neither the UCC nor the CISG applies to contracts for services.

Businesspersons must take special care when drafting international sales contracts to avoid problems caused by distance, including language differences and differences in national laws. The fold-out exhibit in this chapter, which shows an actual international sales contract used by Starbucks Coffee Company, illustrates many of the special terms and clauses that are typically contained in international contracts for the sale of goods. Annotations in the exhibit explain the meaning and significance of specific clauses in the contract. (See Chapter 52 for a discussion of other laws that frame global business transactions.)

A COMPARISON OF CISG AND UCC PROVISIONS

The provisions of the CISG, although similar for the most part to those of the UCC, differ from them in some respects. In the event that the CISG and the UCC are in conflict, the CISG applies (because it is a treaty of the national government and therefore is supreme—see the discussion of the supremacy clause of the U.S. Constitution in Chapter 4).

The major differences between the CISG and the UCC in regard to contract formation concern the following:

1. The mirror image rule.
2. Irrevocable offers.
3. The Statute of Frauds.
4. The price term.
5. The time of contract formation.

CISG provisions relating to risk of loss, performance, remedies, and warranties will be discussed in the following chapters as those topics are examined.

The Mirror Image Rule. As discussed earlier in this chapter, the UCC relaxed substantially the rules governing contractual agreement. Under the UCC, a definite expression of acceptance that contains additional terms can still result in the formation of a contract, unless the additional terms are conditioned on the assent of the offeror.

Article 19 of the CISG provides the rules governing additional terms in international sales contracts. Article 19(1) states that if the terms of the acceptance vary from those of the offer, there is no contract: "A reply to an offer which purports to be an acceptance, but contains additions, limitations, or other modifications is a rejection of the offer and constitutes a counter-offer." Article 19(2), though, stipulates that an acceptance containing additional or different terms may still bind the offeror in contract if the additional or different terms do not materially alter the terms of the offer and if the offeror does not object to the discrepancy in a timely manner.

Note that the definition of a "material alteration" under the CISG involves virtually any differences in the terms relating to payment, quality, quantity, price, time and place of delivery, extent of one party's liability to the other, and settlement of disputes under the contract. In effect, then, Article 19 requires that the terms of the acceptance mirror those of the offer. As a practical matter, businesspersons undertaking international sales transactions therefore should not use the sale or purchase forms that they customarily use for transactions within the United States. Rather, such forms need to be specially drafted to suit the needs of the specific transactions.

Irrevocable Offers. UCC 2–205 requires that an irrevocable offer without consideration must be in writing. In contrast, Article 16(2) of the CISG provides that an offer will be irrevocable if the offeror simply states orally that the offer is irrevocable or if the offeree reasonably relies on the offer as being irrevocable. In both of these situations, the offer will be irrevocable even without a writing and without consideration.

Statute of Frauds. As mentioned previously, the UCC states that contracts for the sale of goods priced at $500 or more must be in writing [UCC 2–201]. The writing must be signed by the party against whom enforcement is sought and must be sufficient to show that a contract has been made. Article 11 of the CISG, however, states that a contract of sale "need not be concluded in or evidenced by writing and is not subject to any other requirements as to form. It may be proved by any means, including witnesses."

Article 11 of the CISG accords with the legal customs of most nations, in which contracts no longer need to meet certain formal or writing requirements to be enforceable. Ironically, even England, the nation that created the original Statute of Frauds in 1677, has repealed all of it except the provisions relating to collateral promises and to transfers of interests in land. Many other countries that once had such a statute have also repealed all or parts of it. Civil law countries, such as France, never had a writing requirement.

The Necessity of a Price Term. Under the UCC, if the parties to a contract have not agreed on a price, the contract will not fail if the parties intended to form a contract (had a "meeting of the minds"). If the price term is left open, the court will determine "a reasonable price at the time for delivery" [UCC 2–305(1)]. Under the CISG, however, the price term must be specified, or provisions for its specification must be included in the agreement; otherwise, normally no contract will exist. For example, if the contract states that the price of wheat to be delivered in two months will be its spot price at the Chicago Board of Trade on that day, that is a sufficient price term under the CISG.

Time of Contract Formation. Under the common law of contracts, an acceptance is effective on dispatch, and thus a contract is created when the acceptance is transmitted. The UCC does not alter this so-called mailbox rule. Under the CISG, however, a contract is created not at the time the acceptance is transmitted but only on its *receipt* by the offeror. (The offer becomes *irrevocable*, however, when the acceptance is sent.) Article 18(2) states that an acceptance by return promise "becomes effective at the moment the indication of assent reaches the offeror." Under Article 18(3), the offeree may also bind the offeror by performance even without giving any notice to the offeror. The acceptance becomes effective "at the moment the act is performed." The rule is therefore that it is the offeree's reliance, rather than the communication of acceptance to the offeror, that creates the contract.

SPECIAL PROVISIONS IN INTERNATIONAL CONTRACTS

Language and legal differences among nations can create special problems for parties to international contracts when disputes arise. It is possible to avoid these problems by including in a contract special provisions relating to choice of language, choice of forum, choice of law, and the types of events that may excuse the parties from performance.

Choice of Language.

A deal struck between a U.S. company and a company in another country normally involves two languages. One party may not understand complex contractual terms that are written in the other party's language. Translating the terms poses its own problems, as typically, many phrases are not readily translatable into another language. To make sure that no disputes arise out of this language problem, an international sales contract should have a **choice-of-language clause** designating the official language by which the contract will be interpreted in the event of disagreement.

A choice-of-language clause might state that the agreement is being written in English, which is to be regarded as the authoritative and official language of the contract's text. The clause may further allow that the agreement is to be translated into, say, Spanish; that the translation is to be ratified by both parties; and that the foreign company can rely on the translation. If arbitration is anticipated, an additional clause must be added to indicate that the arbitration will be conducted in, say, English, Spanish, or French—or whatever the case may be.

Choice of Forum.

In international contracts, it is especially important to include a clause designating the **forum** (place, or court) in which any disputes that arise under the contract will be litigated. Including a **forum-selection clause** in an international contract is important because when several countries are involved, litigation may be sought in courts in different nations. There are no universally accepted rules regarding the jurisdiction of a particular court over subject matter or parties to a dispute. As noted in the *Emerging Trends in Technology* presented earlier in this chapter, a forum-selection clause should specifically indicate the court that will have jurisdiction. The forum does not necessarily have to be within the geographic boundaries of either of the parties' nations.

Under certain circumstances, a forum-selection clause will not be valid. Specifically, if the clause denies one party an effective remedy, is the product of fraud or unconscionable conduct, causes substantial inconvenience to one of the parties to the contract, or violates public policy, the clause will not be enforced.

Choice of Law.

A contractual provision designating the applicable law, called a **choice-of-law clause**, is typically included in every international contract. At common law (and in European civil law systems—see Chapter 52), parties are allowed to choose the law that will govern their contractual relationship, provided that the law chosen is the law of a jurisdiction that has a substantial relationship to the parties and to the international business transaction.

Under UCC 1–105, parties may choose the law that will govern the contract as long as the choice is "reasonable." Article 6 of the CISG, however, imposes no limitation on the parties in their choice of what law will govern the contract, and the 1986 Hague Convention on the Law Applicable to Contracts for the International Sale of Goods—often referred to as the Choice-of-Law Convention—allows unlimited autonomy in the choice of law. Whenever a choice of law is not specified in a contract, the Hague Convention indicates that the governing law is that of the country in which the seller's place of business is located.

Force Majeure Clause.

Every contract, and particularly those involving international transactions, should have a *force majeure* **clause**. The definition of the French term *force majeure* is "impossible or irresistible force"—which sometimes is loosely identified as "an act of God." *Force majeure* clauses commonly stipulate that in addition to acts of God, a number of other eventualities (such as governmental orders or regulations, embargoes, or shortages of materials) may excuse a party from liability for nonperformance.

TERMS AND CONCEPTS TO REVIEW

choice-of-language clause 351	course of dealing 345	firm offer 337
choice-of-law clause 351	course of performance 346	*force majeure* clause 351

QUESTIONS AND CASE PROBLEMS

19–1. OFFERS BETWEEN MERCHANTS. A. B. Zook, Inc., is a manufacturer of washing machines. Over the telephone, Zook offers to sell Radar Appliances one hundred model Z washers at a price of $150 per unit. Zook agrees to keep this offer open for ninety days. Radar tells Zook that the offer appears to be a good one and that it will let Zook know of its acceptance within the next two to three weeks. One week later, Zook sends and Radar receives notice that Zook has withdrawn its offer. Radar immediately thereafter telephones Zook and accepts the $150-per-unit offer. Zook claims, first, that no sales contract was ever formed between it and Radar and, second, that if there is a contract, the contract is unenforceable. Discuss Zook's contentions.

19–2. ACCOMMODATION SHIPMENTS. Flint, a retail seller of television sets, orders one hundred Color-X sets from manufacturer Martin. The order specifies the price and that the television sets are to be shipped by Humming Bird Express on or before October 30. The order is received by Martin on October 5. On October 8, Martin writes Flint a letter indicating that the order was received and that the sets will be shipped as directed, at the specified price. This letter is received by Flint on October 10. On October 28, Martin, in preparing the shipment, discovers it has only ninety Color-X sets in stock. Martin ships the ninety Color-X sets and ten television sets of a different model, stating clearly on the invoice that the ten are being shipped only as an accommodation. Flint claims Martin is in breach of contract. Martin claims the shipment was not an acceptance, and therefore no contract was formed. Explain who is correct and why.

19–3. CONTRACT MODIFICATION. Shane has a requirements contract with Sky that obligates Sky to supply Shane with all the gasoline Shane needs for his delivery trucks for one year at $1.10 per gallon. A clause inserted in small print in the contract by Shane, and not noticed by Sky, states, "The buyer reserves the right to reject any shipment for any reason without liability." For six months, Shane orders and Sky delivers under the contract without any controversy. Then, because of a war in the Middle East, the price of gasoline to Sky increases substantially. Sky contacts Shane and tells Shane he cannot possibly fulfill the requirements contract unless Shane agrees to pay $1.30 per gallon. Shane, in need of the gasoline, agrees in writing to modify the contract. Later that month, Shane learns he can buy gasoline at $1.20 per gallon from Collins. Shane refuses delivery of his most recent order from Sky, claiming, first, that the contract allows him to do so without liability and, second, that he is required to pay only $1.10 per gallon if he accepts the delivery. Discuss fully Shane's contentions.

19–4. APPLICABILITY OF THE UCC. Hatter owns 360 acres of land in Bear County. Hatter makes three separate contracts, in writing, with Bean concerning the land. First, Hatter contracts to sell Bean five hundred tons of gravel from a quarry located on the land for a stated price. The contract calls for Bean to remove the gravel. The second contract sells to Bean all the wheat presently growing on a forty-acre tract. Hatter is obligated under the contract to harvest the wheat and deliver it to Bean. The third contract is for the sale of the northeast ninety acres with all corn standing. Discuss fully which of these contracts, if any, fall under the UCC.

19–5. CONTRACT FORMATION. Strike offers to sell Bailey one thousand shirts for a stated price. The offer declares that shipment will be made by the Dependable Truck Line. Bailey replies, "I accept your offer for one thousand shirts at the price quoted. Delivery to be by Yellow Express Truck Line." Both Strike and Bailey are merchants. Three weeks later, Strike ships the shirts by the Dependable Truck Line, and Bailey refuses shipment. Strike sues for breach of contract. Bailey claims, first, that there never was a contract, because the reply, which included a modification of carriers, did not constitute an acceptance, and, second, that even if there had been a contract, Strike would have been in breach owing to having shipped the shirts by Dependable contrary to the contract terms. Discuss fully Bailey's claims.

19–6. STATUTE OF FRAUDS. Peggy Holloway, a real estate broker, guaranteed payment for a shipment of over $11,000 worth of mozzarella cheese sold by Cudahy Foods Co. to Pizza Pride in Jamestown, North Carolina. The entire arrangement was made orally. Cudahy mailed to Holloway an invoice for the order, and Holloway did not object in writing to the invoice within ten days of receipt. Later, when Cudahy demanded payment from Holloway, Holloway denied having guaranteed payment for the cheese and raised the Statute of

Frauds as an affirmative defense. Cudahy claimed that the Statute of Frauds could not be used as a defense, as both Cudahy and Holloway were merchants and Holloway had failed to object in writing within ten days to Cudahy's invoice. Discuss Cudahy's argument. [*Cudahy Foods Co. v. Holloway*, 286 S.E.2d 606 (N.C.App. 1982)]

19–7. CONTRACT MODIFICATION. Ritz-Craft Corp. contracted with the Stanford Management Group (SMG) to "manufacture and install prefabricated multi-family housing units" for SMG. Ritz-Craft was also to set the units on the foundations constructed by SMG, as well as provide some connective work for electricity, plumbing, and so on. The original contract price for forty-nine units was $1,613,500, but a subsequent modification to the contract due to unforeseen circumstances raised the price by $45,000. SMG refused to pay the additional $45,000, arguing that the modification was not enforceable because it had not been accompanied by consideration. Ritz-Craft sued for breach of contract. If no consideration was given, is the agreement to modify the original contract binding? Does the manufacture and installation of modular homes involve goods or services? Discuss fully how the court should rule on each of these issues. [*Ritz-Craft Corp. v. Stanford Management Group*, 800 F.Supp. 1312 (D.Md. 1992)]

19–8. STATUTE OF FRAUDS. SNK, Inc., makes video arcade games and sells them to distributors, including Entertainment Sales, Inc. (ESI). Most sales between SNK and ESI were phone orders. Over one four-month period, ESI phoned in several orders for "Samurai Showdown" games. SNK did not fill the orders. ESI filed a suit against SNK and others, alleging, among other things, breach of contract. There was no written contract covering the orders. ESI claimed that it had faxed purchase orders for the games to SNK but did not offer proof that the faxes had been sent or received. SNK filed a motion for summary judgment. In whose favor will the court rule, and why? [*Entertainment Sales Co. v. SNK, Inc.*, 232 Ga.App. 669, 502 S.E.2d 263 (1998)]

19–9. GOODS AND SERVICES COMBINED. Dennis Dahlmann and Dahlmann Apartments, Ltd., entered into contracts with Sulchus Hospitality Technologies Corp. and Hospitality Management Systems, Inc. (HMS), to buy property management systems. The systems included computer hardware and software, as well

as installation, training, and support services, for the Bell Tower Hotel and the Campus Inn in Ann Arbor, Michigan. The software controlled the central reservations systems at both hotels. When Dahlmann learned that the software was not Y2K compliant—that it could not be used to post reservations beyond December 31, 1999—he filed a suit against Sulchus and HMS, alleging in part breach of contract. The defendants filed a motion for summary judgment. One of the issues was whether the contracts were subject to Article 2 of the UCC. Are they? Why or why not? Explain fully. [*Dahlmann v. Sulchus Hospitality Technologies Corp.*, 63 F.Supp.2d 772 (E.D.Mich. 1999)]

19–10. IN YOUR COURT

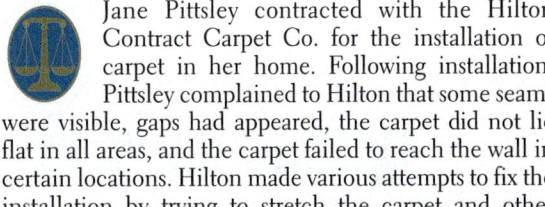

Jane Pittsley contracted with the Hilton Contract Carpet Co. for the installation of carpet in her home. Following installation, Pittsley complained to Hilton that some seams were visible, gaps had appeared, the carpet did not lie flat in all areas, and the carpet failed to reach the wall in certain locations. Hilton made various attempts to fix the installation by trying to stretch the carpet and other methods, but Pittsley was not satisfied with the work. Eventually, Pittsley sued Hilton in an Idaho state court to recover the $3,500 she had paid toward the $4,319.50 contract price for the carpet and its installation. Hilton had paid the installers $700 for the work done in laying Pittsley's carpet. Assume that you are the judge of the trial court hearing this case and answer the following questions:

(a) A threshold issue in this case is whether the contract was a contract for the sale of goods or a contract for the sale of services. How will you rule on this issue? Why?

(b) Review Case 19.1 (*Micro Data Base Systems, Inc. v. Dharma Systems, Inc.*), which presented a similar question to the court with respect to customized software. Are your reasoning and decision in the *Pittsley* case consistent with the court's reasoning and conclusion in Case 19.1? Must they be? [Hint: Before answering the latter question, review the doctrine of *stare decisis* in Chapter 1.]

LAW ON THE WEB

For updated links to resources available on the Web, as well as a variety of other materials, visit this text's Web site at http://wbl.westbuslaw.com.

For information about the National Conference of Commissioners (NCC) on Uniform State Laws and links to online uniform acts, go to

http://www.nccusl.org

The NCC, in association with the University of Pennsylvania Law School, now offers an official site for in-process and final drafts of uniform and model acts. For an index of in-process drafts, go to

http://www.law.upenn.edu/bll/ulc/ulc.htm

For an index of final drafts, go to

http://www.law.upenn.edu/bll/ulc/ulc_final.htm

Cornell University's Legal Information Institute offers online access to the UCC, as well as to UCC articles as enacted by particular states and proposed revisions to articles, at

http://www.law.cornell.edu/ucc/ucc.table.html

The Pace University School of Law's Institute of International Commercial Law maintains a Web site that contains the full text of the CISG, as well as relevant cases and discussions of the law. Go to

http://cisgw3.law.pace.edu

LEGAL RESEARCH EXERCISES ON THE WEB

Go to http://wbl.westbuslaw.com, the Web site that accompanies this text. Select "Internet Applications," and then click on "Chapter 19." There you will find the following Internet research exercises that you can perform to learn more about sales contracts:

Activity 19–1: E-Contracts

Activity 19–2: Is It a Contract?

CHAPTER 20

Title, Risk, and Insurable Interest

BEFORE THE CREATION OF THE Uniform Commercial Code (UCC), *title*—the right of ownership—was the central concept in sales law, controlling all issues of rights and remedies of the parties to a sales contract. There were numerous problems with this concept. For example, frequently it was difficult to determine when title actually passed from seller to buyer, and therefore it was also difficult to predict which party a court would decide had title at the time of a loss. Because of such problems, the UCC divorced the question of title as completely as possible from the question of the rights and obligations of buyers, sellers, and third parties (such as subsequent purchasers, creditors, or the tax collector).

In some situations, title is still relevant under the UCC, and the UCC has special rules for locating title. These rules will be discussed in the sections that follow. In most situations, however, the UCC has replaced the concept of title with three other concepts: (1) identification, (2) risk of loss, and (3) insurable interest.

In lease contracts, of course, title to the goods is retained by the lessor-owner of the goods. Hence, the UCC's provisions relating to passage of title do not apply to leased goods. Other concepts discussed in this chapter, though, including identification, risk of loss, and insurable interest, relate to lease contracts as well as to sales contracts.

SECTION 1

Identification

Before any interest in specific goods can pass from the seller or lessor to the buyer or lessee, two conditions must prevail:

1. The goods must be in existence.
2. They must be identified as the specific goods designated in the contract.

Identification is a designation of goods as the subject matter of a sales or lease contract. Title and risk of loss cannot pass to the buyer from the seller unless the goods are identified to the contract [UCC 2–105(2)]. (As mentioned, title to leased goods remains with the lessor—or, if the owner is a third party, with that party. The lessee does not acquire title to leased goods.) Identification is significant because it gives the buyer or lessee the right to insure (or obtain an insurable interest in) the goods and the right to recover from third parties who damage the goods.

Once the goods are in existence, the parties can agree in their contract on when identification will take place. If they do not so specify, however, the UCC provisions discussed here determine when identification takes place [UCC 2–501(1), 2A–217].

EXISTING GOODS

If the contract calls for the sale or lease of specific and ascertained goods that are already in existence, identification takes place at the time the contract is made. For example, you contract to purchase or lease a fleet of five cars by the serial numbers listed for the cars.

FUTURE GOODS

If a sale involves unborn animals to be born within twelve months after contracting, identification takes place when the animals are conceived. If a lease involves any unborn animals, identification occurs when the animals are conceived. If a sale involves crops that are to be harvested within twelve months (or the next harvest season occurring after contracting, whichever is longer), identification takes place when the crops are planted or begin to grow. In a sale or lease of any other future goods, identification occurs when the goods are shipped, marked, or otherwise designated by the seller or lessor as the goods to which the contract refers.

GOODS THAT ARE PART OF A LARGER MASS

Goods that are part of a larger mass are identified when the goods are marked, shipped, or somehow designated by the seller or lessor as the particular goods to pass under the contract. Suppose that a buyer orders 1,000 cases of beans from a 10,000-case lot. Until the seller separates the 1,000 cases of beans from the 10,000-case lot, title and risk of loss remain with the seller.

A common exception to this rule deals with fungible goods. **Fungible goods** are goods that are alike naturally, by agreement, or by trade usage. Typical examples are specific grades or types of wheat, oil, and wine, usually stored in large containers. If these goods are held or intended to be held by owners in common (owners having shares undivided from the entire mass), a seller-owner can pass title and risk of loss to the buyer without an actual separation. The buyer replaces the seller as an owner in common [UCC 2–105(4)].

For example, Anselm, Braudel, and Carpenter are farmers. They deposit, respectively, 5,000 bushels, 3,000 bushels, and 2,000 bushels of grain of the same grade and quality in a bin. The three become owners in common, with Anselm owning 50 percent of the 10,000 bushels, Braudel 30 percent, and Carpenter 20 percent. Anselm could contract to sell her 5,000 bushels of grain to Tareyton and, because the goods are fungible, pass title and risk of loss to Tareyton without physically separating the 5,000 bushels. Tareyton now becomes an owner in common with Braudel and Carpenter.

SECTION 2

When Title Passes

Once goods exist and are identified, the provisions of UCC 2–401 apply to the passage of title. Unless an agreement is explicitly made,[1] title passes to the buyer at the time and the place the seller performs the *physical delivery* of the goods [UCC 2–401(2)].

SHIPMENT AND DESTINATION CONTRACTS

In the absence of agreement, delivery arrangements can determine when title passes from the seller to the buyer. In a **shipment contract,** the seller is required or authorized to ship goods by carrier, such as a trucking company. Under a shipment contract, the seller is required only to deliver the goods into the hands of a carrier, and title passes to the buyer at the time and place of shipment [UCC 2–401(2)(a)]. *Generally, all contracts are assumed to be shipment contracts if nothing to the contrary is stated in the contract.*

In a **destination contract,** the seller is required to deliver the goods to a particular destination, usually directly to the buyer, although sometimes the buyer designates that the goods should be delivered to another party. Title passes to the buyer when the goods are *tendered* at that destination [UCC 2–401(2)(b)]. A tender of delivery is the seller's placing or holding of conforming goods at the buyer's disposition (with any necessary notice), enabling the buyer to take delivery [UCC 2–503(1)].

---

1. In many sections of the UCC, the words "unless otherwise explicitly agreed" appear, meaning that any explicit agreement between the buyer and the seller determines the rights, duties, and liabilities of the parties, including when title passes.

DELIVERY WITHOUT MOVEMENT OF THE GOODS

When the contract of sale does not call for the seller's shipment or delivery of the goods (when the buyer is to pick up the goods), the passage of title depends on whether the seller must deliver a **document of title,** such as a bill of lading or a warehouse receipt, to the buyer. A *bill of lading* is a receipt for goods that is signed by a carrier and that serves as a contract for the transportation of the goods. A *warehouse receipt* is a receipt issued by a warehouser for goods stored in a warehouse.

When a document of title is required, title passes to the buyer *when and where the document is delivered.* Thus, if the goods are stored in a warehouse, title passes to the buyer when the appropriate documents are delivered to the buyer. The goods never move. In fact, the buyer can choose to leave the goods at the same warehouse for a period of time, and the buyer's title to those goods will be unaffected.

When no documents of title are required, and delivery is made without moving the goods, title passes at the time and place the sales contract is made, if the goods have already been identified. If the goods have not been identified, title does not pass until identification occurs. Consider an example. Rogers sells lumber to Bodan. It is agreed that Bodan will pick up the lumber at the yard. If the lumber has been identified (segregated, marked, or in any other way distinguished from all other lumber), title passes to Bodan when the contract is signed. If the lumber is still in storage bins at the mill, title does not pass to Bodan until the particular pieces of lumber to be sold under this contract are identified [UCC 2–401(3)].

SALES OR LEASES BY NONOWNERS

Problems occur when persons who acquire goods with imperfect titles attempt to sell or lease them. Sections 2–402 and 2–403 of the UCC deal with the rights of two parties who lay claim to the same goods sold with imperfect titles. Generally, a buyer acquires at least whatever title the seller has to the goods sold.

These same UCC sections also protect lessees. Obviously, a lessee does not acquire whatever title the lessor has to the goods; rather, a lessee acquires a right to possess and use the goods—that is, a *leasehold interest.* A lessee acquires whatever leasehold interest the lessor has or has the power to transfer, subject to the lease contract [UCC 2A–303, 2A–304, 2A–305].

Void Title. A buyer may unknowingly purchase goods from a seller who is not the owner of the goods. If the seller is a thief, the seller's title is void—legally, no title exists. Thus, the buyer acquires no title, and the real owner can reclaim the goods from the buyer. The same result would occur if the goods were only leased, because the lessor would have no leasehold interest to transfer.

For example, if Jim steals goods owned by Maren, Jim has a *void title* to those goods. If Jim sells the goods to Shidra, Maren can reclaim them from Shidra even though Shidra acted in good faith and honestly was not aware that the goods were stolen. Article 2A contains similar provisions for leases.

Voidable Title. A seller has a *voidable title* if the goods that he or she is selling were obtained by fraud, paid for with a check that is later dishonored, purchased from a minor, or purchased on credit when the seller was *insolvent.* (Under the UCC, a person is **insolvent** when that person ceases to pay "his debts in the ordinary course of business or cannot pay his debts as they become due or is insolvent within the meaning of federal bankruptcy law" [UCC 1–201(23)].)

In contrast to a seller with void title, a seller with voidable title has the power to transfer a good title to a good faith purchaser for value. A **good faith purchaser** is one who buys without knowledge of circumstances that would make a person of ordinary prudence inquire about the validity of the seller's title to the goods. One who purchases *for value* gives legally sufficient consideration (value) for the goods purchased. The real owner normally cannot recover goods from a good faith purchaser for value [UCC 2–403(1)].[2] If the buyer of the goods is not a good faith purchaser for value, then the actual owner of the goods can reclaim them from the buyer (or from the seller, if the goods are still in the seller's possession).

The same rules apply in circumstances involving leases. A lessor with voidable title has the power to transfer a valid leasehold interest to a good faith lessee for value. The real owner cannot recover the goods, except as permitted by the terms of the lease. The real owner can, however, receive all proceeds arising from the lease, as well as a transfer of all rights, title, and interest as the lessor under the lease, including the lessor's interest in the return of the goods when the lease expires.

Whether the purchaser of a boat was a good faith purchaser for value was at issue in the following case.

---

2. The real owner could, of course, sue the purchaser who initially obtained voidable title to the goods.

Case 20.1   Lane v. Honeycutt

Court of Appeals of
North Carolina, 1972.
14 N.C.App. 436,
188 S.E.2d 604.

BACKGROUND AND FACTS   *Fred H. Lane (the plaintiff) was the owner of Lane's Outboard, and he was engaged in the business of selling boats, motors, and trailers. He sold a new boat, motor, and trailer to a person who called himself John W. Willis. Willis took possession of the goods and paid for them with a check for $6,285. The check was later dishonored. About six months later, the defendant, Jimmy Honeycutt, bought the boat, motor, and trailer for $2,500 from a man identified as "Garrett," who was renting a summer beach house to the defendant that year. The defendant had known Garrett for several years. The plaintiff sought to recover the boat, motor, and trailer from the defendant. The defendant's sole defense was that he was a good faith purchaser and that therefore the plaintiff should not be able to recover from him. The trial court held for the plaintiff, and the defendant appealed.*

**IN THE LANGUAGE
OF THE COURT**

VAUGHN, Judge.
*   *   *   *

Garrett told defendant that he would let defendant have the boat for $2500. Defendant then paid Garrett a deposit of $100. Garrett had nothing to indicate that he was the owner of the boat, motor or trailer. Garrett told defendant he was selling the boat for someone else. "This guy comes down, you know, and does some fishing."

Two weeks later defendant returned to Garden City, South Carolina, with $2400, the balance due (on a boat, and trailer which had been sold new less than six months earlier for $6,285.00). On this occasion,

> "Mr. Garrett had told me *   *   * 'this guy does a lot of fishing around here but I can't seem to get ahold of him.' He said, 'I've called him, but I can't get ahold of him, so since you have the money and you're here after the boat[,] *   *   * I don't believe he would object, so I'll just go ahead and sign this title for you so you can go on and get everything made out to you.' He then signed the purported owner's name on the documents and he signed the title over to me then."

The so-called "document" and "title," introduced as defendant's exhibit No. 8, was nothing more than the "certificate of number" required by G.S. [Section] 75A-5 and issued by the North Carolina Wildlife Resources Commission. This "certificate of number" is not a "certificate of title" to be compared with that required by G.S. [Section] 20-50 for vehicles intended to be operated on the highways of this State. Upon the change of ownership of a motor boat, G.S. [Section] 75A-5(c) authorizes the issuance of a new "certificate of number" to the transferee upon proper application. The application for transfer of the number, among other things, requires the seller's *signature.* A signature is "the name of a person written with his own hand." Defendant observed Garrett counterfeit the signature of the purported owner, John P. Patterson, on the exhibit. Following the falsified signature on defendant's exhibit No. 8, the "date sold" is set out as "June 12, 1970" and the buyer's "signature" is set out as "George (illegible) Williams." There was no testimony as to who affixed the "signature" of the purported buyer, George Williams, and there is no further reference to him in the record.

*   *   * We hold that the evidence was sufficient to support the court's finding that defendant was not a good faith purchaser.

**DECISION
AND REMEDY**

The trial court's ruling was affirmed. The defendant was not a good faith purchaser. The plaintiff was determined to be the owner and to be entitled to immediate possession of the boat, motor, and trailer. The plaintiff was also awarded damages against the defendant for wrongful detention of the property.

The Entrustment Rule. According to UCC 2–403(2), when goods are entrusted to a merchant *who deals in goods of that kind,* and the merchant sells the goods to a *buyer in the ordinary course of business,* that buyer obtains good title to the property. This is known as the entrustment rule. **Entrustment** includes both delivering the goods to the merchant and leaving the purchased goods with the merchant for later delivery or pickup [UCC 2–403(3)]. A buyer in the ordinary course of business is a person who, in good faith and without knowledge that the sale violates the ownership rights or security interest of a third party, buys in ordinary course from a person (other than a pawnbroker) in the business of selling goods of that kind [UCC 1–201(9)].

For example, Jan leaves her watch with a jeweler to be repaired. The jeweler sells both new and used watches. The jeweler sells Jan's watch to Kim, a customer, who does not know that the jeweler has no right to sell it. Kim, as a good faith buyer, gets good title against Jan's claim of ownership.[3] Kim, however, obtains only those rights held by the person entrusting the goods (here, Jan). Suppose that in this example, Jan had stolen the watch from Greg and then left it with the jeweler to be repaired. The jeweler then sold it to Kim. Kim would have obtained good title against Jan, who entrusted the watch to the jeweler, but not against Greg (the real owner), who neither entrusted the watch to Jan nor authorized Jan to entrust it.

Article 2A provides a similar rule for leased goods. If a lessor entrusts goods to a lessee-merchant who deals in goods of that kind, and the lessee-merchant transfers the goods to a buyer or sublessee in the ordinary course of business, the buyer or sublessee acquires all of the rights that the lessor had in the goods [UCC 2A–305(2)].[4]

The following case involved an application of the entrustment doctrine.

---

3. Jan, of course, can sue the jeweler for the tort of conversion (or trespass to personal property) to obtain the equivalent money value of the watch (see Chapter 5).

4. This rule is consistent with the common law of bailments (see Chapter 46).

CASE 20.2   DeWeldon, Ltd. v. McKean

United States Court of Appeals, First Circuit, 1997. 125 F.3d 24. http://www.law.emory. edu/1circuit/2nd-idx. html[a]

HISTORICAL AND SOCIAL SETTING *During World War II, after more than three years of fighting, U.S. forces invaded the island of Iwo Jima in February 1945. In the midst of the costly, month-long battle, five Marines and a Navy corpsman raised a U.S. flag on the peak of Mount Suribachi. A photograph of the flag raising epitomized the valor of the U.S. forces. Within days, work began on a statue to commemorate this courage. The United States Marine Corps Memorial took more than eight years to complete. Today, it is the world's tallest bronze statue. The sculptor was Felix DeWeldon.*

BACKGROUND AND FACTS *Felix DeWeldon, a sculptor and an art collector, owned three paintings valued at $26,000 that were displayed in his home in Rhode Island. When he declared bankruptcy, DeWeldon, Ltd., bought all of his personal property from the bankruptcy trustee (a person appointed by the bankruptcy court to collect and distribute the debtor's assets—see Chapter 30) and entrusted the paintings to Felix. DeWeldon, Ltd., did not put signs on the premises or tags on the paintings to indicate that Felix no longer owned the paintings. Later, Felix paid for an option to repurchase the paintings and the right to retain their possession until the option expired. Within a year, Felix sold the paintings to Robert McKean for $50,000. DeWeldon, Ltd., claiming that Felix DeWeldon had no right to sell the paintings, sued in a federal district court to recover*

---

a. This is a page, within the Web site of the Emory University School of Law, that lists the published opinions of the U.S. Court of Appeals for the First Circuit since November 1995. Scroll down the list of cases to the *DeWeldon* case (included with the cases under the letter "M" for "McKean"). Click on the case name to access the opinion.

them. The court concluded that the entrustment doctrine applied and ruled in favor of McKean. DeWeldon, Ltd., appealed.

IN THE LANGUAGE OF THE COURT

HILL, Senior Circuit Judge.
* * * *

* * * [T]he Uniform Commercial Code (UCC) as adopted by Rhode Island provides that an owner who entrusts items to a merchant who deals in goods of that kind gives him or her power to transfer all rights of the entruster to a buyer in the ordinary course of business. * * *

* * * McKean's purchase of the paintings is protected by the entrustment doctrine. First, DeWeldon, Ltd. entrusted the paintings to Felix DeWeldon. After DeWeldon, Ltd. purchased the paintings, it acquiesced in Felix DeWeldon's retention of them. * * *

Second, McKean was a buyer in the ordinary course of business. * * * McKean gave value for the paintings. * * *

McKean had no actual notice that Felix DeWeldon was no longer the true owner of the paintings. DeWeldon, Ltd. did nothing to shield the paintings in the cloak of its ownership. * * *
* * * *

Third, under the facts of this case, Felix DeWeldon acted as a merchant within the meaning of the [UCC]. * * *
* * * *

* * * Felix DeWeldon was a "well-known" artist whose work was for sale commercially and a "collector." There was artwork all over Felix DeWeldon's home. He had recently sold paintings to a European buyer. By his occupation he held himself out as having knowledge and skill peculiar to art and the art trade.

DECISION AND REMEDY

The U.S. Court of Appeals for the First Circuit affirmed the judgment of the lower court. The appellate court held that the entrustment doctrine protected McKean's purchase of the paintings.

SECTION 3

Risk of Loss

Under the UCC, risk of loss does not necessarily pass with title. When risk of loss passes from a seller or lessor to a buyer or lessee is generally determined by the contract between the parties. Sometimes, the contract states expressly when the risk of loss passes. At other times, it does not, and a court must interpret the existing terms to ascertain whether the risk has passed. When no provision in the contract indicates when risk passes, the UCC provides special rules, based on delivery terms, to guide the courts, as will be discussed shortly.

DELIVERY WITH MOVEMENT OF THE GOODS

When there is no specification in the agreement, the following rules apply to cases involving movement of the goods (carrier cases).

Shipment Contracts. In a shipment contract, if the seller or lessor is required or authorized to ship goods by carrier (but not required to deliver them to a particular destination), risk of loss passes to the buyer or lessee when the goods are duly delivered to the carrier [UCC 2–509(1)(a), 2A–219(2)(a)].

For example, a seller in Texas sells five hundred cases of grapefruit to a buyer in New York, F.O.B. Houston (free on board in Houston—that is, the buyer pays the transportation charges from Houston). The contract authorizes a shipment by carrier; it does not require that the seller tender the grapefruit in New York. Risk passes to the buyer when conforming goods are properly placed in the possession of the carrier. If the goods are damaged in transit, the loss is the buyer's. (Actually, buyers have recourse against carriers, subject to certain limitations, and they may insure the goods from the time the goods leave the seller.) The following case illustrates these principles.

CASE 20.3   Windows, Inc. v. Jordan Panel System Corp.

United States
Court of Appeals,
Second Circuit, 1999.
177 F.3d 114.
**www.law.pace.edu/
lawlib/legal/us-legal/
judiciary/second-
circuit.html**[a]

BACKGROUND AND FACTS *Windows, Inc., is a fabricator and seller of windows, based in South Dakota. Jordan Systems, Inc., is a construction subcontractor, which contracted to install window wall panels at an air cargo facility at John F. Kennedy Airport in New York City. Jordan ordered custom-made windows from Windows. The contract specified that the windows were to be shipped properly packaged for cross-country motor freight transit and "delivered to New York City." Windows built the windows and arranged to ship them to Jordan by Consolidated Freightways Corporation. During the shipment, much of the glass was broken and many of the frames were gouged and twisted. Jordan employees disassembled the window frames to salvage as much of the shipment as possible. Jordan made a claim with Consolidated for the damages, including labor costs from the salvage efforts and other costs from Jordan's inability to perform its contracts on schedule. Jordan also ordered a new shipment from Windows, which was delivered without incident. Jordan did not pay Windows for either shipment. As part of the ensuing litigation, a federal district court heard Jordan's claim against Windows for incidental and consequential damages resulting from the damaged shipment. When the court granted Windows's motion for summary judgment, Jordan appealed to the U.S. Court of Appeals for the Second Circuit.*

**IN THE LANGUAGE
OF THE COURT**

LEVAL, Circuit Judge:

*   *   *   *

*   *   * [A] shipment contract arises [under UCC 2–504] where "the seller is required *   *   * to send the goods to the buyer and the contract does not require him to deliver them at a particular destination." Under a shipment contract, the seller must "put the goods in the possession of such a carrier and make such a contract for their transportation as may be reasonable having regard to the nature of the goods and other circumstances of the case."

Where the terms of an agreement are ambiguous, there is a strong presumption under the U.C.C. favoring shipment contracts. Unless the parties "expressly specify" that the contract requires the seller to deliver to a particular destination, the contract is generally construed as one for shipment. [Emphasis added.]

*   *   *   *

To overcome the presumption favoring shipment contracts, the parties must have explicitly agreed to impose on Windows the obligation to effect delivery at a particular destination. The language of this contract does not do so. Nor did Jordan use any commonly recognized industry term indicating that a seller is obligated to deliver the goods to the buyer's specified destination.

Given the strong presumption favoring shipment contracts, and the absence of explicit terms satisfying both requirements for a destination contract, we conclude that the contract should be deemed a shipment contract.

Under the terms of its contract, Windows thus satisfied its obligations to Jordan when it put the goods, properly packaged, into the possession of the carrier for shipment. Upon Windows' proper delivery to the carrier, Jordan assumed the risk of loss, and cannot recover incidental or consequential damages from the seller caused by the carrier's negligence.

This allocation of risk is confirmed by the terms of [UCC] 2–509(1)(a), entitled "Risk of Loss in the Absence of Breach." It provides that where the contract "does not require [the seller] to deliver [the goods] at a particular destination, the risk of loss passes to the buyer when the goods are duly delivered to the carrier." *   *   * Jordan

---

a. This Web site is a joint project of Touro and Pace University School of Law with the cooperation of the U.S. Court of Appeals for the Second Circuit. In the "1999" column, click on "April." When that page opens, scroll down the list of cases to the case name and click on "Opinion" to access the case.

does not contest the court's finding that Windows duly delivered conforming goods to the carrier. Accordingly, as Windows had already fulfilled its contractual obligations at the time the goods were damaged and Jordan had assumed the risk of loss, there was no "seller's breach" as is required for a buyer to claim incidental and consequential damages * * * . Summary judgment for Windows was therefore proper.

DECISION AND REMEDY *The U.S. Court of Appeals for the Second Circuit affirmed the lower court's decision. The contract was a shipment contract, and thus, when the seller (Windows) put the goods into the hands of the carrier (Consolidated), the risk of loss passed to the buyer (Jordan).*

Destination Contracts. In a destination contract, the risk of loss passes to the buyer or lessee when the goods are tendered to the buyer or lessee at the specified destination [UCC 2–509(1)(b), 2A–219(2)(b)]. In the preceding example, if the contract had been F.O.B. New York, risk of loss during transit to New York would have been the seller's and would not pass to the buyer until the carrier tendered the goods to the buyer in New York.

Contract Terms. Specific terms in the contract help determine when risk of loss passes to the buyer. These terms, which are listed and defined in Exhibit 20–1, relate generally to the determination of which party will bear the costs of delivery, as well as which party will bear the risk of loss.

DELIVERY WITHOUT MOVEMENT OF THE GOODS

The UCC also addresses situations in which the seller or lessor is required neither to ship nor to deliver the goods. Frequently, the buyer or lessee is to pick up the goods from the seller or lessor, or the goods are to be held by a bailee. A *bailment* is a temporary delivery of personal property, without passage of title, into the care of another, called a *bailee*. Under the UCC, a bailee is a party who, by a bill of lading, warehouse receipt, or other document of title, acknowledges possession of goods and contracts to deliver them. A warehousing company, for example, or a trucking company that normally issues documents of title for the goods it receives is a bailee.[5]

Goods Held by the Seller. If the goods are held by the seller, a document of title is usually not used. If the seller is a merchant, risk of loss to goods held by the seller passes to the buyer when the buyer *actually takes physical possession of the goods* [UCC 2–509(3)]. If the seller is not a merchant, the risk of loss to goods held by the seller passes to the buyer on tender of delivery [UCC 2–509(3)].

In respect to leases, the risk of loss passes to the lessee on the lessee's receipt of the goods if the lessor—

---

5. See Chapter 46 for a detailed discussion of the law of bailments.

EXHIBIT 20–1   CONTRACT TERMS—DEFINITIONS

F.O.B. (free on board)—Indicates that the selling price of goods includes transportation costs (and that the seller carries risk of loss) to the specific F.O.B. place named in the contract. The place can be either the place of initial shipment (for example, the seller's city or place of business) or the place of destination (for example, the buyer's city or place of business) [UCC 2–319(1)].

F.A.S. (free alongside)—Requires that the seller, at his or her own expense and risk, deliver the goods alongside the ship before risk passes to the buyer [UCC 2–319(2)].

C.I.F. or C.&F. (cost, insurance, and freight or just cost and freight)—Requires, among other things, that the seller "put the goods in possession of a carrier" before risk passes to the buyer [UCC 2–320(2)]. (These are basically pricing terms, and the contracts remain shipment contracts, not destination contracts.)

Delivery ex-ship (delivery from the carrying vessel)—Means that risk of loss does not pass to the buyer until the goods leave the ship or are otherwise properly unloaded [UCC 2–322].

or supplier, in a finance lease (see Chapter 19)—is a merchant. Otherwise, the risk passes to the lessee on tender of delivery [UCC 2A–219(c)].

Goods Held by a Bailee. When a bailee is holding goods for a person who has contracted to sell them and the goods are to be delivered without being moved, the goods are usually represented by a negotiable or nonnegotiable document of title (a bill of lading or a warehouse receipt). Risk of loss passes to the buyer when (1) the buyer receives a negotiable document of title for the goods, (2) the bailee acknowledges the buyer's right to possess the goods, or (3) the buyer receives a nonnegotiable document of title *and* has had a *reasonable time* to present the document to the bailee and demand the goods. Obviously, if the bailee refuses to honor the document, the risk of loss remains with the seller [UCC 2–503(4)(b), 2–509(2)].

Whether a document of title is negotiable or nonnegotiable may have significant consequences. For example, suppose that Valley Food Products, Inc., delivers five lots of canned goods to a warehouser and receives five warehouse receipts, one for each lot of one hundred cases. The warehouse is open from 8:00 A.M. to 5:00 P.M., Monday through Friday. At 4:00 P.M. on Friday, Valley's sales representative contracts to sell Burdine one of the lots and transfers the warehouse receipt and a bill of sale to Burdine. Burdine does not pick up the cases that afternoon. During the weekend, the warehouse and all of its contents are destroyed by fire. In this situation, who bears the risk of loss, the seller (Valley) or the buyer (Burdine)?

The answer may depend on whether the warehouse receipt is negotiable or nonnegotiable. If the warehouse receipt is *negotiable*, title and risk passed to Burdine when Burdine received the document at 4:00 P.M. on Friday. Therefore, the loss caused by the warehouse fire over the weekend is on Burdine, the buyer. If the document is *nonnegotiable*, the result may be significantly different. Although title passed to Burdine on its receipt of the document, whether risk of loss had passed would depend on whether Burdine had failed to present the document to the bailee so that the bailee could honor it within a "reasonable time" after receipt. The issue here is whether one hour (between 4:00 P.M. and 5:00 P.M. on Friday) is a reasonable time. Very likely, a court would say no, particularly if the warehouse is located in a large city where rush-hour traffic would make it difficult for the buyer to present the document to the bailee within the hour.

With respect to leases, if goods held by a bailee are to be delivered without being moved, the risk of loss passes to the lessee on acknowledgment by the bailee of the lessee's right to possession of the goods [UCC 2A–219(2)(b)].

CONDITIONAL SALES

Buyers and sellers sometimes form sales contracts that are conditioned either on the buyer's approval of the goods or on the buyer's resale of the goods. Under such contracts, the buyer is in possession of the goods. Sometimes, however, problems arise as to whether the buyer or seller should bear the loss if, for example, the goods are damaged or stolen while in the possession of the buyer.

Sale or Return. A **sale or return** (sometimes called a *sale and return*) is a type of contract by which the buyer purchases the goods but has a conditional right to return the goods (undo the sale) within a specified time period. When the buyer receives possession at the time of sale, title and risk of loss pass to the buyer. Title and risk of loss remain with the buyer until the buyer returns the goods to the seller within the time period specified. If the buyer fails to return the goods within this time period, the sale is finalized. The return of the goods is made at the buyer's risk and expense. Goods held under a sale-or-return contract are subject to the claims of the buyer's creditors while they are in the buyer's possession.

The UCC treats a **consignment** as a sale or return. Under a consignment, the owner of goods (the *consignor*) delivers them to another (the *consignee*) for the consignee to sell or to keep. If the consignee sells the goods, the consignee must pay the consignor for them. If the consignee does not sell or keep the goods, they may simply be returned to the consignor. While the goods are in the possession of the consignee, the consignee holds title to them, and creditors of the consignee will prevail over the consignor in any action to repossess the goods [UCC 2–326(3)].

Sale on Approval. Usually, when a seller offers to sell goods to a buyer and permits the buyer to take the goods on a trial basis, a **sale on approval** is made. The term *sale* here is a misnomer, as only an *offer* to sell has been made, along with a bailment created by the buyer's possession.

Therefore, title and risk of loss (from causes beyond the buyer's control) remain with the seller until the buyer accepts (approves) the offer. Acceptance can be made expressly, by any act inconsistent with the *trial* purpose or the seller's ownership, or by the buyer's election not to return the goods within the trial period. If the buyer does not wish to accept, the buyer may notify the seller of that fact within the trial period, and the return is made at the seller's expense and risk [UCC 2–327(1)]. Goods held on approval are not subject to the claims of the buyer's creditors until acceptance.

It is often difficult to determine from a particular transaction which exists—a contract for a sale on approval or a contract for a sale or return. The UCC states that (unless otherwise agreed) "if the goods are delivered primarily for use," the transaction is a sale on approval; "if the goods are delivered primarily for resale," the transaction is a sale or return [UCC 2–326(1)].

RISK OF LOSS WHEN A SALES OR LEASE CONTRACT IS BREACHED

There are many ways to breach a sales or lease contract, and the transfer of risk operates differently depending on which party breaches. Generally, the party in breach bears the risk of loss.

When the Seller or Lessor Breaches.   If the goods are so nonconforming that the buyer has the right to reject them, the risk of loss does not pass to the buyer until the defects are *cured* (that is, until the goods are repaired, replaced, or discounted in price by the seller—see Chapter 21) or until the buyer accepts the goods in spite of their defects (thus waiving the right to reject). For example, a buyer orders blue file cabinets from a seller, F.O.B. seller's plant. The seller ships black file cabinets instead. The black cabinets (nonconforming goods) are damaged in transit. The risk of loss falls on the seller. Had the seller shipped blue cabinets (conforming goods) instead, the risk would have fallen on the buyer [UCC 2–510(2)].

If a buyer accepts a shipment of goods and later discovers a defect, acceptance can be revoked. Revocation allows the buyer to pass the risk of loss back to the seller, at least to the extent that the buyer's insurance does not cover the loss [UCC 2–510(2)].

In regard to leases, Article 2A states a similar rule. If the lessor or supplier tenders goods that are so nonconforming that the lessee has the right to reject them, the risk of loss remains with the lessor or the supplier until cure or acceptance [UCC 2A–220(1)(a)]. If the lessee, after acceptance, revokes his or her acceptance of nonconforming goods, the revocation passes the risk of loss back to the seller or supplier, to the extent that the lessee's insurance does not cover the loss [UCC 2A–220(1)(b)].

When the Buyer or Lessee Breaches.   The general rule is that when a buyer or lessee breaches a contract, the risk of loss *immediately* shifts to the buyer or lessee. There are three important limitations to this rule [UCC 2–510(3), 2A–220(2)]:

1. The seller or lessor must already have identified the contract goods.
2. The buyer or lessee bears the risk for only a *commercially reasonable time* after the seller or lessor has learned of the breach.
3. The buyer or lessee is liable only to the extent of any deficiency in the seller's or lessor's insurance coverage.

CONCEPT SUMMARY 20.1   PASSAGE OF TITLE AND RISK OF LOSS

CONCEPT	DESCRIPTION
Shipment and Destination Contracts	1. *Shipment contracts*—Unless otherwise agreed, title and risk pass on the seller's or lessor's delivery of conforming goods to the carrier [UCC 2–401(2)(a), 2–509(1)(a), 2A–219(2)(a)]. 2. *Destination contracts*—Unless otherwise agreed, title and risk pass on the seller's or lessor's *tender* of delivery of conforming goods to the buyer or lessee at the point of destination [UCC 2–401(2)(b), 2–509(1)(b), 2A–219(2)(b)].
Delivery without Movement of the Goods	1. Unless otherwise agreed, if the goods are not represented by a document of title, title and risk pass as follows: a. Title passes on the formation of the contract [UCC 2–401(3)(b)].

CONCEPT SUMMARY 20.1 **PASSAGE OF TITLE AND RISK OF LOSS** (*continued*)

Delivery without Movement of the Goods (continued)	b. If the seller or lessor (or supplier, in a finance lease) is a merchant, risk passes to the buyer or lessee on the buyer's or lessee's receipt of the goods. If the seller or lessor is a nonmerchant, risk passes to the buyer or lessee on the seller's or lessor's *tender* of delivery of the goods [UCC 2–509(3), 2A–219(c)].
	2. Unless otherwise agreed, if the goods are represented by a document of title, title and risk pass as follows:
	a. If the document is negotiable and the goods are held by a bailee, title and risk pass on the buyer's *receipt* of the document [UCC 2–401(3)(a), 2–509(2)(a)].
	b. If the document is nonnegotiable and the goods are held by a bailee, title passes on the buyer's receipt of the document, but risk does *not* pass until the buyer, after receipt of the document, has had a reasonable time to present the document to demand the goods [UCC 2–401(3)(a), 2–503(4)(b), 2–509(2)(c)].
	3. If the goods are held by a bailee and no document of title is transferred, risk passes to the buyer when the bailee acknowledges the buyer's right to the possession of the goods [UCC 2–509(2)(b)].
	4. In respect to leases, if goods held by a bailee are to be delivered without being moved, the risk of loss passes to the lessee on acknowledgment by the bailee of the lessee's right to possession of the goods [UCC 2A–219(2)(b)].
Sales or Leases by Nonowners	Between the owner and a good faith purchaser or sublessee:
	1. *Void title*—Owner prevails [UCC 2–403(1)].
	2. *Voidable title*—Buyer prevails [UCC 2–403(1)].
	3. *Entrusting to a merchant*—Buyer or sublessee prevails [UCC 2–403(2), (3); 2A–305(2)].
Conditional Sales	1. *Sale-or-return contracts*—When the buyer receives possession of the goods, title and risk of loss pass to the buyer. The buyer has the option of returning the goods to the seller. If the goods are returned to the seller, title and risk pass to the seller as well [UCC 2–327(2)].
	2. *Sale-on-approval contracts*—Title and risk of loss (from causes beyond the buyer's control) remain with the seller until the buyer approves (accepts) the offer [UCC 2–327(1)].
Risk of Loss When a Sales or Lease Contract Is Breached	1. If the seller or lessor breaches by tendering nonconforming goods that are rejected by the buyer or lessee, the risk of loss does not pass to the buyer or lessee until the defects are cured (unless the buyer or lessee accepts the goods in spite of their defects, thus waiving the right to reject) [UCC 2–510(1), 2A–220(1)].
	2. If the buyer or lessee breaches the contract, the risk of loss to identified goods immediately shifts to the buyer or lessee. Limitations to this rule are as follows [UCC 2–510(3), 2A–220(2)]:
	a. The seller or lessor must already have identified the contract goods.
	b. The buyer or lessee bears the risk for only a commercially reasonable time after the seller or lessor has learned of the breach.
	c. The buyer or lessee is liable only to the extent of any deficiency in the seller's or lessor's insurance coverage.

SECTION 4

Insurable Interest

Parties to sales and lease contracts often obtain insurance coverage to protect against damage, loss, or destruction of goods. Any party purchasing insurance, however, must have a sufficient interest in the insured item to obtain a valid policy. Insurance laws—not the UCC—determine sufficiency. The UCC is helpful, however, because it contains certain rules regarding insurable interests in goods.

INSURABLE INTEREST OF THE BUYER OR LESSEE

A buyer or lessee has an **insurable interest** in identified goods. The moment the contract goods are *identified* by the seller or lessor, the buyer or lessee has a special property interest that allows the buyer or lessee to obtain necessary insurance coverage for those goods even before the risk of loss has passed [UCC 2–501(1), 2A–218(1)].

Consider an example. In March, a farmer sells a cotton crop he hopes to harvest in October. The buyer acquires an insurable interest in the crop when it is planted, because those goods (the cotton crop) are identified to the sales contract between the seller and the buyer. The rule stated in UCC 2–501(1)(c) is that such buyers obtain an insurable interest in crops by identification, which occurs when the crops are planted or otherwise become growing crops, providing that the contract is for "the sale of crops to be harvested within twelve months or the next normal harvest season after contracting, whichever is longer."

INSURABLE INTEREST OF THE SELLER OR LESSOR

A seller has an insurable interest in goods as long as he or she retains title to the goods. Even after title passes to a buyer, however, a seller who has a security interest in the goods (a right to secure payment—see Chapter 28) still has an insurable interest and can insure the goods [UCC 2–501(2)]. Hence, both a buyer and a seller can have an insurable interest in identical goods at the same time. Of course, the buyer or seller must sustain an actual loss to have the right to recover from an insurance company. In regard to leases, the lessor retains an insurable interest in leased goods until an option to buy has been exercised by the lessee and the risk of loss has passed to the lessee [UCC 2A–218(3)].

SECTION 5

Bulk Transfers

Article 6 of the UCC covers bulk transfers. A *bulk transfer* is defined as any transfer of a major part of the transferor's material, supplies, merchandise, or other inventory *not made in the ordinary course of the transferor's business* [UCC 6–102(1)]. Article 6 was designed to prevent certain difficulties with such transfers—such as when a business sold a substantial part of its equipment and inventories to a buyer and then failed to pay its creditors. Today, changes in the business and legal contexts in which bulk sales are conducted have largely made their regulation unnecessary. For this reason, the majority of the states have repealed Article 6. Those states that have not repealed the article follow either the original version of Article 6 or its alternative (see Appendix C).

TERMS AND CONCEPTS TO REVIEW

consignment 363	fungible goods 356	insurable interest 366
destination contract 356	good faith purchaser 357	sale on approval 363
document of title 357	identification 355	sale or return 363
entrustment 359	insolvent 357	shipment contract 356

QUESTIONS AND CASE PROBLEMS

20–1. RISK OF LOSS. Mackey orders from Pride one thousand cases of Greenie brand peas from lot A at list price to be shipped F.O.B. Pride's city via Fast Freight Lines. Pride receives the order and immediately sends Mackey an acceptance of the order with a promise to ship promptly. Pride later separates the one thousand cases of Greenie peas and prints Mackey's name and address on each case. The peas are placed on Pride's dock, and Fast Freight is notified to pick up the shipment. The night before the pickup by Fast Freight, through no fault of Pride's, a fire destroys the one thousand cases of peas. Pride claims that title passed to Mackey at the time the contract was made and that risk of loss passed to Mackey when the goods were marked with Mackey's name and address. Discuss Pride's contentions.

20–2. RISK OF LOSS. On May 1, Sikora goes into Carson's retail clothing store to purchase a suit. Sikora finds a suit he likes for $190 and buys it. The suit needs alteration. Sikora is to pick up the altered suit at Carson's store on May 10. Consider the following separate sets of circumstances:

    (a) One of Carson's major creditors obtains a judgment on the debt Carson owes and has the court issue a writ of execution (a court order to seize a debtor's property to satisfy a debt) to collect on that judgment all clothing in Carson's possession. Discuss Sikora's rights in the suit under these circumstances.

    (b) On May 9, through no fault of Carson's, the store burns down, and all contents are a total loss. Between Carson and Sikora, who suffers the loss of the suit destroyed by fire? Explain.

20–3. CONDITIONAL SALES. Zeke, who sells lawn mowers, tells Stasio, a regular customer, about a special promotional campaign. On receipt of a $50 down payment, Zeke will sell Stasio a new Universal lawn mower for $200, even though it normally sells for $350. Zeke further states to Stasio that if Stasio does not like the performance of the lawn mower, he can return it within thirty days, and Zeke will refund the $50 down payment. Stasio pays the $50 and takes the mower. On the tenth day, the lawn mower is stolen through no fault of Stasio's. Stasio calls Zeke and demands the return of his $50. Zeke claims that Stasio should suffer the risk of loss and that he still owes Zeke the remainder of the purchase price, $150. Discuss whether Stasio or Zeke is correct.

20–4. SALES BY NONOWNERS. In the following situations, two parties lay claim to the same goods sold. Discuss which of the parties would prevail in each instance.

    (a) Toscano steals Dean's television set and sells the set to Bosky, an innocent purchaser, for value. Dean learns Bosky has the set and demands its return.

    (b) Kerr takes her television set for repair to Unger, a merchant who sells new and used television sets. By accident, one of Unger's employees sells the set to Gale, an innocent purchaser-customer, who takes possession. Kerr wants her set back from Gale.

20–5. CONDITIONAL SALES. Hargo Woolen Mills had purchased bales of card waste, used in Hargo's manufacture of woolen cloth, from Shabry Trading Co. for many years. On this occasion, however, Shabry shipped twenty-four bales to Hargo without an order. Rather than pay for reshipment, both parties decided that Hargo would retain possession of the bales and pay for what it used. Hargo kept the bales separate inside its warehouse and eventually used, and was billed for, eight bales. The remaining sixteen bales were still kept separate by Hargo. Hargo went bankrupt, and everything in its warehouse was taken by the receiver, Meinhard-Commercial Corp. Shabry claimed that it was the owner and title holder of the bales and requested their return, but Meinhard refused. Discuss fully whether Shabry will be able to retake possession of the bales. [*Meinhard-Commercial Corp. v. Hargo Woolen Mills*, 112 N.H. 500, 300 A.2d 321 (1972)]

20–6. ENTRUSTMENT RULE. Ron Rasmus was a farmer in the business of buying, selling, and raising exotic animals, including ostriches. When Gene Baker began buying flightless birds for investment purposes, he entered into an agreement with Rasmus to board the animals at Rasmus's farm. Mike Pickard bought two pairs of adult breeding ostriches from Rasmus, unaware that they were Baker's. Pickard sold one of the pairs to Gary Prenger. Both Pickard and Prenger arranged to board the ostriches with Rasmus. When Baker removed the birds from Rasmus's farm, Pickard and Prenger filed a suit in an Iowa state court against him, seeking in part to recover the birds. To whom do the birds belong? Discuss fully. [*Prenger v. Baker*, 542 N.W.2d 805 (Iowa 1995)]

20–7. SHIPMENT AND DESTINATION CONTRACTS. Roderick Cardwell owns Ticketworld, which sells tickets (a sale of goods, according to the court) to entertainment and sporting events to be held at locations throughout the United States. Ticketworld's Massachusetts office sold tickets to an event in Connecticut to Mary Lou Lupovitch, a Connecticut resident, for $125 per ticket, although each ticket had a fixed price of $32.50. There was no agreement that Ticketworld would bear the risk of loss until the tickets were delivered to a specific location. Ticketworld gave the tickets to a carrier in Massachusetts who delivered the tickets to Lupovitch in Connecticut. The state of Connecticut brought an action against Cardwell in a Connecticut state court, charging in part a violation of a state statute that prohibited the sale of a ticket for more than $3 over its fixed price. Cardwell contended in part that the statute did not apply because the sale to Lupovitch involved a shipment contract that was formed outside the state. Is Cardwell correct? How will the court rule? Why? [*State v. Cardwell*, 246 Conn. 721, 718 A.2d 954 (1998)]

20–8. RISK OF LOSS. Mark Olmstead sells trailers, doing business as World Cargo in St. Croix Falls, Wisconsin. In 1997, he also sold trailers from a site in Elk River, Minnesota. Gerald McKenzie ordered a custom-made trailer from Olmstead and mailed him a check for $3,620. McKenzie said that he would pick up the trailer at the Elk River site. After the trailer was made, Olmstead shipped it to Elk River and kept it within a locked, fenced area. He told McKenzie that the trailer could be picked up any Tuesday or Thursday before 6:00 P.M. Over Olmstead's protest, McKenzie asked for the trailer to be left outside the fenced area. Olmstead told McKenzie that the area was not secure and that the trailer could not be locked, except to chain the tires. McKenzie insisted, however, and Olmstead complied. When McKenzie arrived to pick up the trailer, it was gone—apparently stolen. McKenzie filed a suit in a Minnesota state court against Olmstead, to recover the amount of the check. Who bore the risk of loss in these circumstances? Why? [*McKenzie v. Olmstead*, 587 N.W.2d 863 (Minn.App. 1999)]

20–9. IN YOUR COURT

Benes contracts to purchase from Glover one hundred cases of Knee High Corn to be shipped F.O.B. Glover's warehouse by Reliant Truck Lines. Glover, by mistake, delivers one hundred cases of Green Valley Corn to Reliant Truck Lines. While in transit, the Green Valley Corn is stolen. Glover demands payment for the corn, but Benes refuses to pay, claiming that Glover should bear the loss. Glover argues that the risk of loss passed to Benes when Glover delivered the corn to Reliant Truck Lines. Assume that you are the judge in the trial court hearing this case and answer the following questions:

(a) A threshold issue in many cases is whether a contract is a shipment contract or a destination contract. Which is it in this case?

(b) Compare this case with Case 20.3 (*Windows, Inc. v. Jordan Panel System Corp.*). Are the facts and issues in both cases similar? Should the court's reasoning in Case 20.3 apply to the Benes-Glover dispute? Why or why not? Would your answer be any different if Glover had shipped Knee High Corn?

(c) How will you rule in the case now before your court? Summarize your reasoning.

20–10. A QUESTION OF ETHICS

Toby and Rita Kahr donated some used clothing to Goodwill Industries, Inc. They were not aware that a small bag containing their sterling silver had been accidentally included within one of the sacks of donated clothing. The silverware, which was valued at over $3,500, had been given to them twenty-seven years earlier by Rita's father as a wedding present and had great sentimental value for them. The Kahrs realized what had happened shortly after Toby returned from Goodwill, but when Toby called Goodwill, he was told that the silver had immediately been sold to a customer, Karon Markland, for $15. Although Goodwill called Markland and asked her to return the silver, Markland refused to return it. The Kahrs then brought an action against Markland to regain the silver, claiming that Markland did not have good title to it. In view of these circumstances, discuss the following issues. [*Kahr v. Markland*, 187 Ill.App.3d 603, 543 N.E.2d 579, 135 Ill.Dec. 196 (1989)]

(a) The basic issue in this case is whether the silver was "lost property" (defined as property unintentionally separated from its owner) or property entrusted to a merchant, Goodwill Industries. If the court decides that the silver was lost, this will mean that the party in possession of the property will have good title against all parties except the true owner—in which case the Kahrs will be able to recover the silver from Markland. If the court decides that the Kahrs entrusted the silver to Goodwill, then the entrustment rule will be applied—in which case the Kahrs will be unable to recover the silver from Markland, a good faith purchaser. If you were the judge, how would you decide the issue? Why?

(b) The entrustment rule can sometimes result in unfair treatment of the entrustor, because the entrustor cannot recover the property from a good faith purchaser (although the entrustor can recover the value of the property from the merchant who wrongfully sold the entrusted property). Given this potential for unfair treatment, how can the entrustment rule be justified from an ethical point of view?

LAW ON THE WEB

For updated links to resources available on the Web, as well as a variety of other materials, visit this text's Web site at http://wbl.westbuslaw.com.

To find information on the UCC, including the UCC provisions discussed in this chapter, refer to the Web sites listed in the *Law on the Web* in Chapter 19.

Information on current commercial law topics, including some of the topics discussed in this chapter, is available at the Web site of the law firm of Hale and Dorr. Go to

http://www.haledorr.com

To review bills of lading, access the following Web site:

http://www.showtrans.com/bl.htm

LEGAL RESEARCH EXERCISES ON THE WEB

Go to http://wbl.westbuslaw.com, the Web site that accompanies this text. Select "Internet Applications," and then click on "Chapter 20." There you will find the following Internet research exercise that you can perform to learn more about passage of title:

Activity 20–1: Passage of Title

CHAPTER 21

Performance of Sales and Lease Contracts

T O UNDERSTAND THE OBLIGATIONS of the parties under a sales or lease contract, it is necessary to know the duties and obligations each party has assumed under the terms of the contract. Keep in mind that "duties and obligations" under the terms of the contract include those specified by the agreement, by custom, and by the UCC.

In the performance of a sales or lease contract, the basic obligation of the seller or lessor is to *transfer and deliver conforming goods.* The basic obligation of the buyer or lessee is to *accept and pay for conforming goods* in accordance with the contract [UCC 2–301, 2A–516(1)]. Overall performance of a sales or lease contract is controlled by the agreement between the parties. When the contract is unclear and disputes arise, the courts look to the UCC. In this chapter, after first scrutinizing the general requirement of good faith, we examine the basic performance obligations of the parties under a sales or lease contract.

SECTION 1

The Good Faith Requirement

The obligations of good faith and commercial reasonableness underlie every sales and lease contract within

the UCC. These obligations can form the basis for a suit for breach of contract later on. The UCC's good faith provision, which can never be disclaimed, reads as follows: "Every contract or duty within this Act imposes an obligation of good faith in its performance or enforcement" [UCC 1–203]. Good faith means honesty in fact. In the case of a merchant, it means honesty in fact and the observance of reasonable commercial standards of fair dealing in the trade [UCC 2–103(1)(b)]. In other words, merchants are held to a higher standard of performance or duty than nonmerchants are.

Good faith can mean that one party must not take advantage of another party by manipulating contract terms. Good faith applies to both parties, even the nonbreaching party. The principle of good faith applies through both the performance and the enforcement of all agreements or duties within a contract. Good faith is a question of fact for the jury.

The standards of good faith and commercial reasonableness provide the framework within which the parties are to specify particulars of performance. If a sales contract leaves open some particulars of performance and permits one of the parties to specify them, "[a]ny such specification must be made in good faith and within limits set by commercial reasonableness"

[UCC 2–311(1)]. Thus, when one party delays specifying particulars of performance for an unreasonable period of time or fails to cooperate with the other party, the innocent party is excused from any resulting delay in performance. In addition, the innocent party can proceed to perform in any reasonable manner.[1]

SECTION 2

Obligations of the Seller or Lessor

The major obligation of the seller or lessor under a sales or lease contract is to tender conforming goods to the buyer or lessee. **Tender of delivery** requires that the seller or lessor have and hold *conforming* goods at the disposal of the buyer or lessee and give the buyer or lessee whatever notification is reasonably necessary to enable the buyer or lessee to take delivery [UCC 2–503(1), 2A–508(1)]. **Conforming goods** are goods that conform exactly to the description of the goods in the contract.

Tender must occur at a *reasonable hour* and in a *reasonable manner*. For example, a seller cannot call the buyer at 2:00 A.M. and say, "The goods are ready. I'll give you twenty minutes to get them." Unless the parties have agreed otherwise, the goods must be tendered for delivery at a reasonable hour and kept available for a reasonable period of time to enable the buyer to take possession of them [UCC 2–503(1)(a)].

All goods called for by a contract must be tendered in a single delivery unless the parties agree otherwise [UCC 2–612, 2A–510] or the circumstances are such that either party can rightfully request delivery in lots [UCC 2–307]. Hence, an order for 1,000 shirts cannot be delivered two shirts at a time. If, however, the seller and the buyer contemplate that the shirts will be delivered in four orders of 250 each, as they are produced (for summer, fall, winter, and spring stock), and the price can be apportioned accordingly, it may be commercially reasonable to deliver the shirts in this way.

PLACE OF DELIVERY

The UCC provides for the place of delivery pursuant to a contract if the contract does not do so. Of course,

the parties may agree on a particular destination, or their contract's terms or the circumstances may indicate the place.

Noncarrier Cases. If the contract does not designate the place of delivery for the goods, and the buyer is expected to pick them up, the place of delivery is the *seller's place of business* or, if the seller has none, the *seller's residence* [UCC 2–308]. If the contract involves the sale of *identified goods*, and the parties know when they enter into the contract that these goods are located somewhere other than at the seller's place of business (such as at a warehouse), then the *location of the goods* is the place for their delivery [UCC 2–308].

For example, Laval and Boyd both live in San Francisco. In San Francisco, Laval contracts to sell Boyd five used trucks, which both parties know are located in a Chicago warehouse. If nothing more is specified in the contract, the place of delivery for the trucks is Chicago. The seller may tender delivery by either giving the buyer a negotiable or nonnegotiable document of title or by obtaining the bailee's (warehouser's) acknowledgment that the buyer is entitled to possession.[2]

Carrier Cases. In many instances, attendant circumstances or delivery terms in the contract make it apparent that the parties intend that a carrier be used to move the goods. There are two ways a seller can complete performance of the obligation to deliver the goods in carrier cases—through a shipment contract and through a destination contract.

Shipment Contracts. Recall from Chapter 20 that a *shipment contract* requires or authorizes the seller to ship goods by a carrier. The contract does not require that the seller deliver the goods at a particular destination [UCC 2–319, 2–509]. Unless otherwise agreed, the seller must do the following:

1. Place the goods into the hands of the carrier.
2. Make a contract for their transportation that is reasonable according to the nature of the goods and their

---

1. See the *Focus on Ethics* following Chapter 23 for a further discussion of the UCC's emphasis on good faith and commercial reasonableness.

2. If the seller delivers a nonnegotiable document of title or merely writes instructions to the bailee to release the goods to the buyer without the bailee's acknowledgment of the buyer's rights, this is also a sufficient tender, unless the buyer objects [UCC 2–503(4)]. Risk of loss, however, does not pass until the buyer has had a reasonable amount of time in which to present the document or the instructions. See Chapter 20.

value. (For example, certain types of goods need refrigeration in transit.)

3. Obtain and promptly deliver or tender to the buyer any documents necessary to enable the buyer to obtain possession of the goods from the carrier.

4. Promptly notify the buyer that shipment has been made [UCC 2–504].

If the seller fails to notify the buyer that shipment has been made or fails to make a proper contract for transportation, and a *material loss* of the goods or a *significant delay* results, the buyer can reject the shipment. Of course, the parties can agree that a lesser amount of loss or any delay will be grounds for rejection.

Destination Contracts. In a *destination contract*, the seller agrees to see that conforming goods will be duly tendered to the buyer at a particular destination. The goods must be tendered at a reasonable hour and held at the buyer's disposal for a reasonable length of time. The seller must also give the buyer appropriate notice. In addition, the seller must provide the buyer with any documents of title necessary to enable the buyer to obtain delivery from the carrier. Sellers often do this by tendering the documents through ordinary banking channels [UCC 2–503].

THE PERFECT TENDER RULE

As previously noted, the seller or lessor has an obligation to ship or tender *conforming goods,* and this entitles the buyer or lessee to accept and pay for the goods according to the terms of the contract. Under the common law, the seller was obligated to deliver goods in conformity with the terms of the contract in every detail. This was called the **perfect tender rule.** The UCC preserves the perfect tender doctrine by stating that if goods or tender of delivery fail *in any respect* to conform to the contract, the buyer or lessee has the right to accept the goods, reject the entire shipment, or accept part and reject part [UCC 2–601, 2A–509].

For example, a lessor contracts to lease fifty Comclear computers to be delivered at the lessee's place of business on or before October 1. On September 28, the lessor discovers that it has only thirty Comclear computers in inventory but will have another twenty Comclear computers within the next two weeks. The lessor tenders delivery of the thirty Comclear computers on October 1, with the promise that the other computers will be delivered within three weeks. Because the lessor has failed to make a

perfect tender of fifty Comclear computers, the lessee has the right to reject the entire shipment and hold the lessor in breach.

EXCEPTIONS TO THE PERFECT TENDER RULE

Because of the rigidity of the perfect tender rule, several exceptions to the rule have been created, some of which we discuss here.

Agreement of the Parties. Exceptions to the perfect tender rule may be established by agreement. If the parties have agreed, for example, that defective goods or parts will not be rejected if the seller or lessor is able to repair or replace them within a reasonable period of time, the perfect tender rule does not apply.

Cure. The UCC does not specifically define the term **cure,** but it refers to the right of the seller or lessor to repair, adjust, or replace defective or nonconforming goods [UCC 2–508, 2A–513]. When any tender of delivery is rejected because of nonconforming goods and the time for performance has not yet expired, the seller or lessor can notify the buyer or lessee promptly of the intention to cure and can then do so *within the contract time for performance* [UCC 2–508(1), 2A–513(1)]. Once the time for performance under the contract has expired, the seller or lessor can still exercise the right to cure if he or she had *reasonable grounds to believe that the nonconforming tender would be acceptable to the buyer or lessee* [UCC 2–508(2), 2A–513(2)].

Sometimes, a seller or lessor will tender nonconforming goods with some type of price allowance, although this is not a requirement under the UCC. The allowance serves as the "reasonable grounds" for the seller or lessor to believe that the nonconforming tender will be acceptable to the buyer or lessee. Other reasons might also serve as the basis for the assumption that a buyer or lessee will accept a nonconforming tender. For example, if in the past a buyer frequently accepted a particular substitute for a good when the good ordered was not available, the seller has reasonable grounds to believe the buyer will again accept such a substitute. Even if the buyer rejects the substitute good on a particular occasion, the seller nonetheless had reasonable grounds to believe that the substitute would be acceptable. Therefore, the seller can cure within a *reasonable time,* even though conforming delivery will occur after the time limit for performance allowed under the contract.

The right to cure substantially restricts the right of the buyer or lessee to reject goods. For example, if a lessee refuses a tender of goods as nonconforming but does not disclose the nature of the defect to the lessor, the lessee cannot later assert the defect as a defense if the defect is one that the lessor could have cured. Generally, buyers and lessees must act in good faith and state specific reasons for refusing to accept goods [UCC 2–605, 2A–514].

Substitution of Carriers.   When an agreed-on manner of delivery (such as the use of a particular carrier to transport the goods) becomes impracticable or unavailable through no fault of either party, but a commercially reasonable substitute is available, this substitute performance is sufficient tender to the buyer and must be used [UCC 2–614(1)]. For example, a sales contract calls for the delivery of a large piece of machinery to be shipped by ABC Truck Lines on or before June 1. The contract terms clearly state the importance of the delivery date. The employees of ABC Truck Lines go on strike. The seller must make a reasonable substitute tender, perhaps by rail, if such is available. Note that the seller here is responsible for any additional shipping costs, unless contrary arrangements have been made in the sales contract.

Installment Contracts.   An **installment contract** is a single contract that requires or authorizes delivery in two or more separate lots to be accepted and paid for separately. In an installment contract, a buyer or lessee can reject an installment *only if the nonconformity substantially impairs the value* of the installment and cannot be cured [UCC 2–307, 2–612(2), 2A–510(1)].

The entire installment contract is breached only when one or more nonconforming installments *substantially* impair the value of *the whole contract*. If the buyer or lessee subsequently accepts a nonconforming installment and fails to notify the seller or lessor of cancellation, however, the contract is reinstated [UCC 2–612(3), 2A–510(2)].

A major issue to be determined is what constitutes substantial impairment of the "value of the whole contract." For example, consider an installment contract for the sale of twenty carloads of plywood. The first carload does not conform to the contract because 9 percent of the plywood deviates from the thickness specifications. The buyer cancels the contract, and immediately thereafter the second and third carloads of plywood arrive at the buyer's place of business. If a lawsuit ensued, the court would have to grapple with the question of whether the nonconforming plywood, comprising 9 percent of one carload, substantially impaired the value of the whole.[3]

A more clear-cut example is an installment contract that involves parts of a machine. Suppose that the first part is delivered and is irreparably defective but is necessary for the operation of the machine. The failure of this first installment will be a breach of the whole contract. Even when the defect in the first shipment is such that it gives the buyer only a "reasonable apprehension" about the ability or willingness of the seller to complete the other installments properly, the breach on the first installment may be regarded as a breach of the whole.

The point to remember is that the UCC significantly alters the right of the buyer or lessee to reject the entire contract if the contract requires delivery to be made in several installments. The UCC strictly limits rejection to cases of *substantial* nonconformity (unless the parties agree that breach of an installment constitutes a breach of the entire contract).

Commercial Impracticability.   As stated in Chapter 17, occurrences unforeseen by either party when a contract was made may make performance commercially impracticable. When this occurs, the rule of perfect tender no longer holds. According to UCC 2–615(a) and 2A–405(a), delay in delivery or nondelivery in whole or in part is not a breach when performance has been made impracticable "by the occurrence of a contingency the nonoccurrence of which was a basic assumption on which the contract was made." The seller or lessor must, however, notify the buyer or lessee as soon as practicable that there will be a delay or nondelivery.

Foreseeable versus Unforeseeable Contingencies. An increase in cost resulting from inflation does not in and of itself excuse performance, as this kind of risk is ordinarily assumed by a seller or lessor conducting business. The unforeseen contingency must be one that would have been impossible to contemplate in a given business situation. For example, a major oil company that receives its supplies from the Middle

---

3. *Continental Forest Products, Inc. v. White Lumber Sales, Inc.,* 256 Or. 466, 474 P.2d 1 (1970). The court held that the deviation did not substantially impair the value of the whole contract. Additionally, the court stated that the nonconformity could be cured by an adjustment in the price.

East has a contract to supply a buyer with 100,000 gallons of oil. Because of an oil embargo by the Organization of Petroleum Exporting Countries (OPEC), the seller is prevented from securing oil supplies to meet the terms of the contract. Because of the same embargo, the seller cannot secure oil from any other source. This situation comes fully under the commercial impracticability exception to the perfect tender doctrine [UCC 2–615, 2A–405].

Can unanticipated increases in a seller's costs, which make performance "impracticable," constitute a valid defense to performance on the basis of commercial impracticability? The court dealt with this question in the following case.

CASE 21.1   Maple Farms, Inc. v. City School District of Elmira

Supreme Court of
New York, 1974.
76 Misc.2d 1080,
352 N.Y.S.2d 784.

BACKGROUND AND FACTS *On June 15, 1973, Maple Farms, Inc., formed an agreement with the city school district of Elmira, New York, to supply the school district with milk for the 1973–1974 school year. The agreement was in the form of a requirements contract, under which Maple Farms would sell to the school district all the milk the district required at a fixed price—which was the June market price of milk. By December 1973, the price of raw milk had increased by 23 percent over the price specified in the contract. This meant that if the terms of the contract were fulfilled, Maple Farms would lose $7,350. Because it had similar contracts with other school districts, Maple Farms stood to lose a great deal if it was held to the price stated in the contracts. When the school district would not agree to release Maple Farms from its contract, Maple Farms brought an action in a New York state court for a declaratory judgment (a determination of the parties' rights under a contract). Maple Farms contended that the substantial increase in the price of raw milk was an event not contemplated by the parties when the contract was formed and that, given the increased price, performance of the contract was commercially impracticable.*

IN THE LANGUAGE OF THE COURT

CHARLES B. SWARTWOOD, Justice.

* * * * *

* * * [The doctrine of commercial impracticability requires that] a contingency— something unexpected—must have occurred. Second, the risk of the unexpected occurrence must not have been allocated either by agreement or by custom. * * *

* * * [H]ere we find that the contingency causing the increase of the price of raw milk was not totally unexpected. The price from the low point in the year 1972 to the price on the date of the award of the contract in June 1973 had risen nearly 10%. And any businessman should have been aware of the general inflation in this country during the previous years * * * .

* * * Here the very purpose of the contract was to guard against fluctuation of price of half pints of milk as a basis for the school budget. Surely had the price of raw milk fallen substantially, the defendant could not be excused from performance. We can reasonably assume that the plaintiff had to be aware of escalating inflation. It is chargeable with knowledge of the substantial increase of the price of raw milk from the previous year's low. * * * It nevertheless entered into this agreement with that knowledge. It did not provide in the contract any exculpatory clause to excuse it from performance in the event of a substantial rise in the price of raw milk. On these facts the risk of a substantial or abnormal increase in the price of raw milk can be allocated to the plaintiff.

DECISION AND REMEDY

The New York trial court ruled that inflation and fluctuating prices did not render performance in this case impracticable and granted summary judgment in favor of the school district.

Partial Performance. Sometimes the unforeseen event only *partially* affects the capacity of the seller or lessor to perform, and the seller or lessor is thus able to fulfill the contract *partially* but cannot tender total performance. In this event, the seller or lessor is required to allocate in a fair and reasonable manner any remaining production and deliveries among its regular customers and those to whom it is contractually obligated to deliver the goods [UCC 2–615(b), 2A–405(b)]. The buyer or lessee must receive notice of the allocation and has the right to accept or reject the allocation [UCC 2–615(c), 2A–405(c)].

For example, a Florida orange grower, Best Citrus, Inc., contracts to sell this season's production to a number of customers, including Martin's grocery chain. Martin's contracts to purchase two thousand crates of oranges. Best Citrus has sprayed *some* of its orange groves with a chemical called Karmoxin. The U.S. Department of Agriculture discovers that persons who eat products sprayed with Karmoxin may develop cancer and issues an order prohibiting the sale of these products. Best Citrus picks all the oranges not sprayed with Karmoxin, but the quantity does not fully meet all the contracted-for deliveries. In this situation, Best Citrus is required to allocate its production, so it notifies Martin's that it cannot deliver the full quantity agreed on in the contract and specifies the amount it will be able to deliver under the circumstances. Martin's can either accept or reject the allocation, but Best Citrus has no further contractual liability.

Destruction of Identified Goods.

Sometimes, an unexpected event, such as a fire, totally destroys goods through no fault of either party and before risk passes to the buyer or lessee. In such a situation, if the *goods were identified at the time the contract was formed*, the parties are excused from performance [UCC 2–613, 2A–221]. If the goods are only partially destroyed, however, the buyer or lessee can inspect them and either treat the contract as void or accept the damaged goods with a reduction of the contract price.

Consider an example. Atlas Sporting Equipment agrees to lease to River Bicycles sixty bicycles of a particular model that has been discontinued. No other bicycles of that model are available. River specifies that it needs the bicycles to rent to tourists. Before Atlas can deliver the bikes, they are destroyed by a fire. In this situation, Atlas is not liable to River for failing to deliver the bikes. The goods were destroyed through no fault of either party, before the risk of loss passed to the lessee. The loss was total, so the contract is avoided. Clearly, Atlas has no obligation to tender the bicycles, and River has no obligation to pay for them.

Assurance and Cooperation.

Two other exceptions to the perfect tender doctrine apply equally to parties to sales and lease contracts: the right of assurance and the duty of cooperation.

The Right of Assurance. The UCC provides that if one of the parties to a contract has "reasonable grounds" to believe that the other party will not perform as contracted, he or she may *in writing* "demand adequate assurance of due performance" from the other party. Until such assurance is received, he or she may "suspend" further performance without liability. What constitutes "reasonable grounds" is determined by commercial standards. If such assurances are not forthcoming within a reasonable time (not to exceed thirty days), the failure to respond may be treated as a *repudiation* of the contract [UCC 2–609, 2A–401].

For example, Zena has contracted to ship Jenkins one hundred shirts on or before October 1, with Jenkins's payment due within thirty days of delivery. Zena has made two previous shipments, neither of which has been paid for by Jenkins. On September 20, Zena demands in writing certain assurances of payment (including payment of the last two orders to bring the account up to date) before she will ship the shirts. If these desired assurances are reasonable, Zena can suspend shipment of the shirts without liability pending Jenkins's compliance. If Jenkins does not provide the assurances within a reasonable time (no longer than thirty days), Zena can hold Jenkins in breach of contract without having made the contracted-for shipment.

The Duty of Cooperation. Sometimes the performance of one party depends on the cooperation of the other. The UCC provides that when such cooperation is not forthcoming, the other party can suspend his or her own performance without liability and hold the uncooperative party in breach or proceed to perform the contract in any reasonable manner [see UCC 2–311(3)(b)].

For example, Amati is required by contract to deliver 1,200 model Z washing machines to locations in the state of California to be specified later by Farrell. Deliveries are to be made on or before October 1. Amati has repeatedly requested the delivery locations, and Farrell has not responded. The 1,200 model Z machines are ready for shipment on October 1, but Farrell still refuses to give Amati delivery locations. Amati does not ship on October 1. Can Amati be held liable? The answer is no. Amati is excused for any resulting delay of performance because of Farrell's failure to cooperate.

SECTION 3

Obligations of the Buyer or Lessee

Once the seller or lessor has adequately tendered delivery, the buyer or lessee is obligated to accept the goods and pay for them according to the terms of the contract.

PAYMENT

In the absence of any specific agreements, the buyer or lessee must make payment at the time and place the buyer or lessee *receives* the goods [UCC 2–310(a), 2A–516(1)]. When a sale is made on credit, the buyer is obliged to pay according to the specified credit terms (for example, 60, 90, or 120 days), not when the goods are received. The credit period usually begins on the *date of shipment* [UCC 2–310(d)]. Under a lease contract, a lessee must make the lease payment specified in the contract [UCC 2A–516(1)].

Payment can be made by any means agreed on between the parties—cash or any other method generally acceptable in the commercial world. If the seller demands cash when the buyer offers a check, credit card, or the like, the seller must permit the buyer reasonable time to obtain legal tender [UCC 2–511].

RIGHT OF INSPECTION

Unless otherwise agreed, or for C.O.D. (collect on delivery) transactions, the buyer or lessee has an absolute right to inspect the goods. This right allows the buyer or lessee to verify, before making payment, that the goods tendered or delivered are what were contracted for or ordered. If the goods are not what the buyer or lessee ordered, the buyer or lessee has no duty to pay. *An opportunity for inspection is therefore a condition precedent to the right of the seller or lessor to enforce payment* [UCC 2–513(1), 2A–515(1)].

Unless otherwise agreed, inspection can take place at any reasonable place and time and in any reasonable manner. Generally, what is reasonable is determined by custom of the trade, past practices of the parties, and the like. Costs of inspecting conforming goods are borne by the buyer unless otherwise agreed [UCC 2–513(2)].

C.O.D. Shipments. If a seller ships goods to a buyer C.O.D. (or under similar terms) and the buyer has not agreed to a C.O.D. shipment in the contract, the buyer can rightfully *reject* the goods. This is because a C.O.D. shipment does not permit inspection before payment, which is a denial of the buyer's right of inspection. When the buyer has agreed to a C.O.D. shipment in the contract, however, or has agreed to pay for the goods on the presentation of a bill of lading, no right of inspection exists, because it was negated by the agreement [UCC 2–513(3)].

Payment Due—Documents of Title. Under certain contracts, payment is due on the receipt of the required documents of title even though the goods themselves may not have arrived at their destination. With C.I.F. and C.&F. contracts,[4] payment is required on receipt of the documents unless the parties have agreed otherwise. Thus, payment is required prior to inspection, and payment must be made unless the buyer knows that the goods are nonconforming [UCC 2–310(b), 2–513(3)].

ACCEPTANCE

A buyer or lessee can manifest assent to the delivered goods in the following ways, each of which constitutes acceptance:

1. There is an acceptance if the buyer or lessee, after having had a reasonable opportunity to inspect the goods, signifies agreement to the seller or lessor that the goods are either conforming or are acceptable in spite of their nonconformity [UCC 2–606(1)(a), 2A–515(1)(a)].
2. Acceptance is presumed if the buyer or lessee has had a reasonable opportunity to inspect the goods and has failed to reject them within a reasonable period of time [UCC 2–602(1), 2–606(1)(b), 2A–515(1)(b)].
3. In sales contracts, the buyer will be deemed to have accepted the goods if he or she performs any act inconsistent with the seller's ownership. For example, any use or resale of the goods generally constitutes an acceptance. Limited use for the sole purpose of testing or inspecting the goods is not an acceptance, however [UCC 2–606(1)(c)].

---

4. See Exhibit 20–1 in Chapter 20 for definitions of *C.I.F.* and *C.&F.*

If some of the goods delivered do not conform to the contract and the seller or lessor has failed to cure, the buyer or lessee can make a *partial* acceptance [UCC 2–601(c), 2A–509(1)]. The same is true if the nonconformity was not reasonably discoverable before acceptance.[5] A buyer or lessee cannot accept less than a single commercial unit, however. A *commercial unit* is defined by the UCC as a unit of goods that, by com- mercial usage, is viewed as a "single whole" for pur- poses of sale, division of which would materially im- pair the character of the unit, its market value, or its use [UCC 2–105(6), 2A–103(c)]. A commercial unit can be a single article (such as a machine), a set of ar- ticles (such as a suite of furniture or an assortment of sizes), a quantity (such as a bale, a gross, or a carload), or any other unit treated in the trade as a single whole.

In the following case, the court considered whether a buyer's actions, in regard to goods shipped to it by the seller, were "inconsistent with the seller's ownership" so as to constitute acceptance under UCC 2–606(1)(c).

---

5. If the nonconformity was not reasonably discoverable before ac- ceptance, the buyer or lessee may be able to revoke the acceptance, as will be discussed in Chapter 22.

CASE 21.2 Industria de Calcados Martini Ltda.[a] v. Maxwell Shoe Co.

Appeals Court of Massachusetts, 1994. 36 Mass.App.Ct. 268, 630 N.E.2d 299.

HISTORICAL AND SOCIAL SETTING   *In the middle of the nineteenth century, New England was the shoe capital of the United States. Except for expensive, custom-made footwear, men's and women's shoes were essentially all the same: black and functional. Near the end of the century, shoemakers in the Midwest began to mass-produce more fashionable dress shoes. The new lines met with instant success. Then, during the 1980s, more casual shoes (tennis shoes and the like), often made out of canvas and other ma- terial, became popular. Indeed, sales of all athletic-type footwear soared. Traditional leather-shoe manufacturing in the United States saw a concomitant decline. Today, most shoes sold in the United States are manufactured elsewhere.*

BACKGROUND AND FACTS   *Maxwell Shoe Company agreed to buy 12,042 pairs of shoes from Industria de Calcados Martini Ltda. (Martini), a Brazilian shoe manufacturer. Maxwell paid part of the price with a check. When the shoes arrived, they were cracked and peeling. Maxwell stopped payment on the check and told Martini that it was reject- ing the shoes. Martini did not respond. Two months later, Maxwell shipped the shoes to Maine to have them refinished, sold the refinished shoes, and kept the money. Martini filed a suit against Maxwell in a Massachusetts state court for, among other things, breach of contract. The court held in part that Maxwell had accepted the shoes when it shipped them to Maine to be refinished, "on the grounds that an alteration or repair of a defect in goods is an act inconsistent with the seller's ownership" under UCC 2–606(1)(c). The court awarded damages to Martini, reduced by the amount that Maxwell had paid for the refinishing. Both parties appealed.*

IN THE LANGUAGE OF THE COURT

PORADA, Justice.

*   *   *   *

*   *   * Maxwell received no *   *   * instructions from Martini. Instead, it acted on its own in sending the shoes for refinishing and then selling them and retaining the proceeds for its own benefit. *   *   * Accordingly, we do not think the judge's ruling *   *   * was clearly erroneous.

DECISION AND REMEDY   *The Court of Appeals of Massachusetts affirmed the lower court's decision. Maxwell was held to have accepted the shoes when it sent them for refinishing.*

---

a. *Ltda.* is an abbreviation for *Limitada*, a business organization form involving limited liability for the owners. (See Chapters 33 through 39 for a discussion of business organization forms.)

CONCEPT SUMMARY 21.1

PERFORMANCE OF SALES AND LEASE CONTRACTS

CONCEPT	DESCRIPTION
Obligations of the Seller or Lessor	1. The seller or lessor must tender *conforming* goods to the buyer or lessee. Tender must take place at a *reasonable hour* and in a *reasonable manner.* Under the perfect tender doctrine, the seller or lessor must tender goods that exactly conform to the terms of the contract [UCC 2–503(1), 2A–508(1)]. 2. If the seller or lessor tenders nonconforming goods and the buyer or lessee rejects them, the seller or lessor may *cure* (repair or replace the goods) within the contract time for performance [UCC 2–508(1), 2A–513(1)]. Even if the time for performance under the contract has expired, the seller or lessor has a reasonable time to substitute conforming goods without liability if the seller or lessor has reasonable grounds to believe the nonconforming tender would be acceptable to the buyer or lessee [UCC 2–508(2), 2A–513(2)]. 3. If the agreed-on means of delivery becomes impracticable or unavailable, the seller must substitute an alternative means (such as a different carrier) if a reasonable one is available [UCC 2–614(1)]. 4. If a seller or lessor tenders nonconforming goods in any one installment under an installment contract, the buyer or lessee may reject the installment only if its value is substantially impaired and cannot be cured. The entire installment contract is breached when one or more installments *substantially* impair the value of the *whole* contract [UCC 2–612, 2A–510]. 5. When performance becomes commercially impracticable owing to circumstances unforeseen when the contract was formed, the perfect tender rule no longer holds [UCC 2–615, 2A–405].
Obligations of the Buyer or Lessee	1. On tender of delivery by the seller or lessor, the buyer or lessee must pay for the goods at the time and place the buyer or lessee *receives* the goods, unless the sale is made on credit. Payment may be made by any method generally acceptable in the commercial world, but the seller can demand cash [UCC 2–310, 2–511]. In a lease contract, the lessee must make lease payments in accordance with the contract [UCC 2A–516(1)]. 2. Unless otherwise agreed, the buyer or lessee has an absolute right to inspect the goods before acceptance, unless the shipment is C.O.D. [UCC 2–513(1), 2A–515(1)]. 3. The buyer or lessee can manifest acceptance of delivered goods expressly in words or by conduct or by failing to reject the goods after a reasonable period of time following inspection or after having had a reasonable opportunity to inspect them. A buyer will be deemed to have accepted goods if he or she performs any act inconsistent with the seller's ownership [UCC 2–606(1), 2A–515(1)].

SECTION 4

Anticipatory Repudiation

What if, before the time for contract performance, one party clearly communicates to the other the intention not to perform? Such an action is a breach of the contract by *anticipatory repudiation.*[6] When anticipatory repudiation occurs, the nonbreaching party has a choice of two responses. He or she can treat the repudiation as a final breach by pursuing a remedy; or

---

6. Refer back to Chapter 17 for a discussion of the common law origins and application of the doctrine of anticipatory repudiation.

he or she can wait, hoping that the repudiating party will decide to honor the obligations required by the contract despite the avowed intention to renege [UCC 2–610, 2A–402]. In either situation, the non-breaching party may suspend performance.

Should the latter course be pursued, the UCC permits the breaching party (subject to some limitations) to "retract" his or her repudiation. This can be done by any method that clearly indicates an intent to perform. Once retraction is made, the rights of the repudiating party under the contract are reinstated [UCC 2–611, 2A–403].

To illustrate: Assume that Cora, who owns a small inn, purchases a suite of furniture from Horton's Furniture Warehouse on April 1. The contract states that "delivery must be made on or before May 1." On April 10, Horton informs Cora that he cannot make delivery until May 10 and asks Cora to consent to the modified delivery date. In this situation, Cora has the option of either treating Horton's notice of late delivery as a final breach of contract and pursuing a remedy or agreeing to the later delivery date. Suppose that Cora does neither for two weeks. On April 24, Horton informs Cora that he will be able to deliver the furniture by May 1, after all. In effect, Horton has retracted his repudiation, reinstating the rights and obligations of the parties under the original contract. The concept of anticipatory repudiation is further illustrated in the following case.

CASE 21.3   Banco International, Inc. v. Goody's Family Clothing

United States District Court, Eastern District of Tennessee, 1999. 54 F.Supp.2d 765.

BACKGROUND AND FACTS *In April 1994, Banco International, Inc., and Goody's Family Clothing contracted for the manufacture of 62,748 custom-made, private-label windsuits (jogging suits) and their delivery in three shipments, for $749,103.60. The first shipment had to be at Goody's distribution center in Knoxville, Tennessee, by September 30 in time for holiday season sales, or the order was subject to cancellation. Banco sent to Goody's what Banco claimed were production samples but which Goody's learned had been produced by another manufacturer. Goody's also learned that a third party had the fabric and other materials that were needed to make the windsuits and would not release them to Banco without payment of a debt. By August 23, Banco had not started production, despite the representations of Muhammed Akhtar, the president and owner of Banco, to the contrary. On that day, Goody's canceled the contract. Akhtar acknowledged that Banco was behind schedule but said it could meet the delivery dates for the first two shipments if it shipped by air and the deadline for the third shipment by shipping by sea. Had Goody's asked how production could be accomplished so quickly, Akhtar later said he would have responded that it was "none of Goody's business." Goody's did not accept Akhtar's assurances. Banco filed a suit in a federal district court against Goody's, alleging breach of contract. Goody's argued that there was an anticipatory repudiation, or breach, of the contract by Banco.*

IN THE LANGUAGE OF THE COURT

MURRIAN, Magistrate J. [Judge]

*   *   *   *

*   *   * *It is not necessary for [anticipatory] repudiation that performance be made literally and utterly impossible.* Repudiation can result from action which reasonably indicates a rejection of the continuing obligation. [Emphasis added.]

Banco's failure to start actual production of the windsuits prior to cancellation of the contract on August 23, 1994, Banco's apparent inability to gain possession and control of the fabric and other raw materials necessary to perform the contract, Banco's false representations about production, and Banco's failure to give Goody's adequate assurances that it could perform the contract in a timely manner during the days following cancellation are the primary actions by Banco which reasonably indicated to Goody's that Banco had rejected its continuing obligation under the contract. These actions justified Goody's suspension of its own performance and cancellation of the contract.

In all contracts governed by Article 2 of the Uniform Commercial Code there is a continuing obligation of good faith and reasonableness. In this case, Goody's came to realize by August 23, 1994, that Mr. Akhtar had not been truthful with Goody's about the status of production of the windsuits; Goody's had reason to believe that the production samples were not production samples at all; Banco did not have possession of the fabric and raw materials to perform the contract; and, as far as Goody's knew, Banco had no prospects of obtaining possession and control of those raw materials. In the days subsequent to the cancellation, Banco's proffered "reasonable assurances" consisted of more promises from Mr. Akhtar (whose credibility had been severely damaged) but without an explanation of just how Banco proposed to perform because Mr. Akhtar believed it was "none of Goody's business."

* * * It was this apparent inability to perform without a substantial breach of the contract that justified Goody's in canceling the contract and in refusing Banco's proffered "reasonable assurances" of performance.

I find that Goody's was justified in reasonably concluding that Banco could not deliver the windsuits to it by the date set in the first purchase order between the parties. Additionally, the failure to deliver the goods by that date would have substantially impaired the value of those goods to Goody's.

DECISION AND REMEDY   *The court entered a judgment in Goody's favor. Goody's was not liable for canceling the purchase orders because of Banco's anticipatory repudiation of their contract. This repudiation was indicated by Banco's failure to start performance within a reasonable time to meet the contract deadlines and by Banco's misrepresentations concerning the status of its performance.*

SECTION 5

Dealing with International Contracts—The Letter of Credit

Because buyers and sellers (or lessees and lessors) engaged in international business transactions may be separated by thousands of miles, special precautions are often taken to ensure performance under international contracts. Sellers and lessors want to avoid delivering goods for which they might not be paid. Buyers and lessees desire the assurance that sellers and lessors will not be paid until there is evidence that the goods have been shipped. Thus, **letters of credit** are frequently used to facilitate international business transactions.

In a simple letter-of-credit transaction, the *issuer* (a bank) agrees to issue a letter of credit and to ascertain whether the *beneficiary* (seller or lessor) performs certain acts. In return, the *account party* (buyer or lessee) promises to reimburse the issuer for the amount paid to the beneficiary. There may also be an *advising bank* that transmits information, and a *paying bank* may be involved to expedite payment under the letter of credit. See Exhibit 21–1 for an illustration of a letter-of-credit transaction.

Under a letter of credit, the issuer is bound to pay the beneficiary (seller or lessor) when the beneficiary has complied with the terms and conditions of the letter of credit. The beneficiary looks to the issuer, not to the account party (buyer or lessee), when it presents the documents required by the letter of credit. Typically, the letter of credit will require that the beneficiary deliver a *bill of lading* to prove that shipment has been made. Letters of credit assure beneficiaries (sellers or lessors) of payment while at the same time assuring account parties (buyers or lessees) that payment will not be made until the beneficiaries have complied with the terms and conditions of the letter of credit.

The basic principle behind letters of credit is that payment is made against the documents presented by the beneficiary and not against the facts that the documents purport to reflect. Thus, in a letter-of-credit transaction, the issuer does not police the underlying contract; a letter of credit is independent of the underlying contract between the buyer and the seller. Eliminating the need for banks (issuers) to inquire into whether or not actual conditions have been satisfied greatly reduces the costs of letters of credit. Moreover, the use of a letter of credit protects all parties to a transaction.

EXHIBIT 21–1   A LETTER-OF-CREDIT TRANSACTION

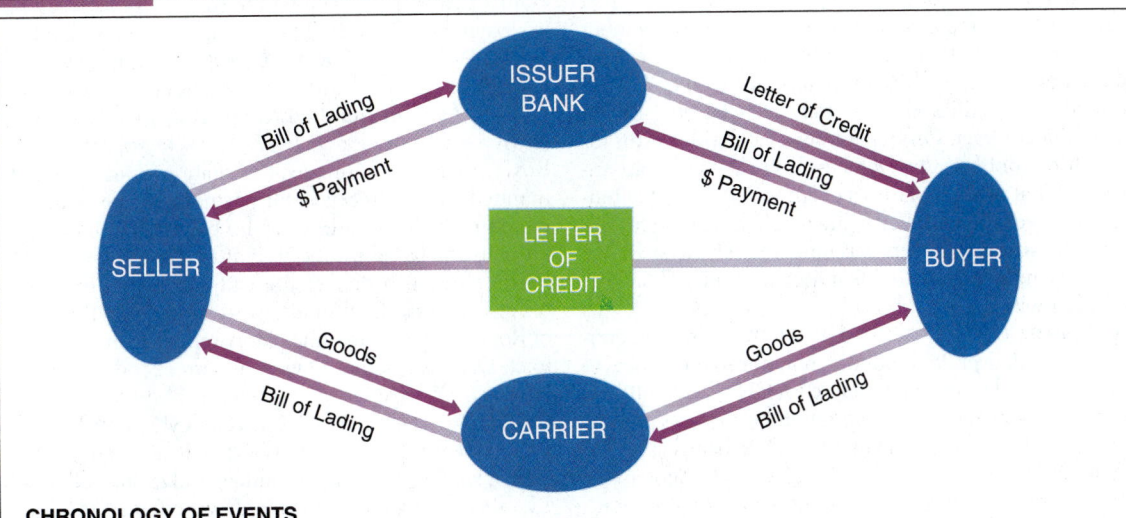

CHRONOLOGY OF EVENTS

1. Buyer contracts with issuer bank to issue a letter of credit; this sets forth the bank's obligation to pay on the letter of credit and buyer's obligation to pay the bank.

2. Letter of credit is sent to seller informing seller that on compliance with the terms of the letter of credit (such as presentment of necessary documents—in this example, a bill of lading), the bank will issue a payment for the goods.

3. Seller delivers goods to carrier and receives a bill of lading.

4. Seller delivers the bill of lading to issuer bank and, if the document is proper, receives payment.

5. Issuer bank delivers the bill of lading to buyer.

6. Buyer delivers the bill of lading to carrier.

7. Carrier delivers the goods to buyer.

8. Buyer settles with issuer bank.

TERMS AND CONCEPTS TO REVIEW

conforming goods 371	installment contract 373	perfect tender rule 372
cure 372	letter of credit 380	tender of delivery 371

QUESTIONS AND CASE PROBLEMS

21–1. NONCONFORMING GOODS. Ames contracts to ship to Curley one hundred model Z television sets. The terms of delivery are F.O.B. Ames's city, by Green Truck Lines, with delivery on or before April 30. On April 15, Ames discovers that because of an error in inventory control, all model Z sets have been sold, and the stock has not been replenished. Ames has model X, a similar but slightly more expensive unit, in stock. On April 16, Ames ships one hundred model X sets, with notice that Curley will be charged the model Z price. Curley (in a proper manner) rejects the model X sets when they are tendered on April 18. Ames does not wish to be held in breach of contract, even though he has tendered nonconforming goods. Discuss Ames's options.

21–2. Nonperformance. Thal contracts to deliver to Hurwitz one thousand bushels of corn at market price. Delivery and payment are to be made on October 1. On September 10, Hurwitz informs Thal that because of financial reverses, she cannot pay on October 1. Thal immediately notifies Hurwitz that he is holding her in breach of contract. On September 15, Thal files suit for breach of contract. On October 3, Hurwitz files an answer to Thal's lawsuit. Hurwitz claims that had Thal tendered delivery on October 1, she would have paid for the corn. Because no delivery was tendered, Hurwitz claims that she cannot be held liable. Discuss whether Thal can hold Hurwitz liable for breach.

21–3. Failure to Tender Delivery. Kirk has contracted to deliver to Doolittle one thousand cases of Wonder brand beans on or before October 1. Doolittle is to specify the means of transportation twenty days prior to the date of shipment. Payment for the beans is to be made by Doolittle on tender of delivery. On September 10, Kirk prepares the one thousand cases for shipment. Kirk asks Doolittle how he would like the goods to be shipped, but Doolittle does not respond. On September 21, Kirk demands in writing assurance that Doolittle will be able to pay on tender of the beans. Kirk's demand is that the money be placed in escrow prior to October 1 in a bank in Doolittle's city named by Kirk. Doolittle does not respond to any of the requests made by Kirk, but on October 5 he wants to file suit against Kirk for breach of contract for failure to deliver the beans as agreed. Discuss Kirk's liability for failure to tender delivery on October 1.

21–4. Anticipatory Repudiation. Moore contracted in writing to sell her 1997 Ford Taurus to Hammer for $8,500. Moore agreed to deliver the car on Wednesday, and Hammer promised to pay the $8,500 on the following Friday. On Tuesday, Hammer informed Moore that he would not be buying the car after all. By Friday, Hammer had changed his mind again and tendered $8,500 to Moore. Moore, although she had not sold the car to another party, refused the tender and refused to deliver. Hammer claimed that Moore had breached their contract. Moore contended that Hammer's repudiation had released her from her duty to perform under the contract. Who is correct, and why?

21–5. Buyer's Obligations. Gibson contracts to deliver one hundred model X color television sets to a new retail customer, Beaver, on May 1, with payment to be made on delivery. Gibson tenders delivery in her own truck. Gibson notices that one or two cartons have scrape marks on them. Beaver inquires of Gibson whether the sets might have been damaged as they were being loaded. Gibson assures Beaver that the sets are in perfect condition. Beaver tenders Gibson a check, but Gibson refuses the check, claiming that the first delivery to new customers is always for cash. Beaver promises to have the cash within two days. Gibson leaves the sets with Beaver, who stores them in a warehouse pending an "opening sale" date. Two days later, Beaver opens some of the cartons and discovers that a number of the televi-

sions are damaged beyond ordinary repair. Gibson claims Beaver has accepted the sets and is in breach by not paying on delivery. Discuss fully Gibson's claims.

21–6. Anticipatory Repudiation. Bryant Lewis contracted to sell Ross Cattle Co. four hundred head of cattle at $47.50 per hundredweight. Ross made an $8,000 down payment. Before delivery, Lewis heard a rumor that Ross was in poor financial condition, and Lewis demanded that he receive full payment before delivering the animals. Ross told Lewis the balance would be paid on delivery, based on the weight of the cattle delivered. Lewis refused to deliver the cattle and sold them to a third party. Ross filed suit. Lewis claimed that the refusal of Ross to pay was an anticipatory repudiation of the contract. Discuss whether Lewis was correct and what action Lewis could have taken on the basis of the rumor. [*Ross Cattle Co. v. Lewis*, 415 So.2d 1029 (Miss. 1982)]

21–7. Tender of Delivery. Rheinberg-Kellerei GMBH, a German wine producer and export seller, sold 1,245 cases of wine to Vineyard Wine Co., a U.S. company. The contract did not specify delivery to any particular destination, and Rheinberg, through its agent, selected the port of Wilmington for the port of entry. Rheinberg delivered the wine to the boat carrier in early December 1978. On or about January 24, 1979, Vineyard learned that the wine had been lost in the North Atlantic sometime between December 12 and December 22, when the boat sank with all hands aboard. Vineyard refused to pay Rheinberg. Rheinberg filed an action for the purchase price, claiming that risk of loss had passed to the buyer, Vineyard, on delivery of the wine to the carrier. Vineyard claimed that because of Rheinberg's failure to give prompt notice of shipment (notice had not been given until after the ship was lost at sea), risk of loss had not passed to the buyer. Discuss fully who is correct. [*Rheinberg-Kellerei GMBH v. Vineyard Wine Co.*, 281 S.E.2d 425 (N.C.App. 1981)]

21–8. Commercial Impracticability. E+E (US) Inc., Manley-Regan Chemicals Division, agreed to sell to Rockland Industries, Inc., three containers of antimony oxide for $1.80 per pound. At the time, both parties knew that there was a global shortage of the chemical, with rising prices, and that Manley-Regan would obtain its supply from GFI Chemicals, Inc. When GFI could not deliver, Manley-Regan told Rockland that it could not fulfill the contract. Rockland bought an equivalent amount of the chemical elsewhere at an increased price and filed a suit in a federal district court against Manley-Regan to recover the difference between the cost of the cover and the contract price. Manley-Regan argued that the failure of delivery by GFI, its sole source for the oxide, excused its failure to perform on the ground of commercial impracticability. Will the court agree? Why or why not? [*Rockland Industries, Inc. v. E+E (US) Inc., Manley-Regan Chemicals Division*, 991 F.Supp. 468 (D.Md. 1998)]

21–9. Acceptance. OSHI Global Co. designs and sells novelty items, including a small children's plastic toy referred to as the "Number 89 Frog," a realistic replica of a frog that squeaks when it is squeezed. At a trade show in Chicago, Michael Osaraprasop, the owner of OSHI, sold a quantity of the frogs to Jay Gilbert, the president of S.A.M. Electronics, Inc. Gilbert asked Osaraprasop to design, make, and sell to S.A.M. a larger version of the frog with a motion sensor that would activate a "ribbit" sound. Osaraprasop agreed. OSHI delivered fourteen containers of the frogs, a number of which S.A.M. resold to its customers. When some of the buyers complained that the frogs were defective, S.A.M. had them repaired. S.A.M. refused to pay OSHI for any of the frogs and wrote a letter claiming to revoke acceptance of them. S.A.M. filed a suit in a federal district court against OSHI and others, alleging in part breach of contract, to which OSHI responded with a similar claim against S.A.M. OSHI argued that by reselling some of the frogs from the fourteen containers, S.A.M. had accepted all of them and must pay. In whose favor will the court rule? Discuss fully. [*S.A.M. Electronics, Inc. v. Osaraprasop*, 39 F.Supp.2d 1074 (N.D.Ill. 1999)]

21–10. IN YOUR COURT

Bobby Murray Chevrolet, Inc., contracted to supply 1,200 school bus chassis to local school boards. The contract stated that "products of any manufacturer may be offered," but Bobby Murray submitted its orders exclusively to General Motors Corp. (GMC). When a shortage of automatic transmissions occurred, GMC informed the dealer that it could not fill the orders. Bobby Murray told the school boards, which bought the chassis from another dealer. The boards filed a suit in a North Carolina state court against Bobby Murray on the ground of breach of contract. The dealer responded that its obligation to perform was excused under the doctrine of commercial impracticability, in part because of GMC's failure to fill its orders. Assume that you are the judge in the North Carolina trial court hearing this case and answer the following questions:

(a) How will you rule in this case? Will you excuse Bobby Murray's failure to perform on the ground of commercial impracticability? Why or why not?

(b) Would your decision be different if the contract stated that only GMC products would be offered? Explain.

(c) Compare this case to Case 21.1 (*Maple Farms, Inc. v. City School District of Elmira*). What are the similarities and differences between the facts and issues in these two cases? How do your decision and legal reasoning in the case before your court compare with the decision and reasoning in Case 21.1?

LAW ON THE WEB

For updated links to resources available on the Web, as well as a variety of other materials, visit this text's Web site at http://wbl.westbuslaw.com.

To find information on the UCC, including the UCC provisions discussed in this chapter, refer to the Web sites listed in the *Law on the Web* in Chapter 19.

The Boeing Company has posted online a summary of the contract rights and duties of parties forming sales contracts with that company. To view the summary, go to

http://www.boeing.com/companyoffices/doingbiz/tcmdhs/sect7_97.htm#c

To obtain information on performance requirements in relation to contracts for the international sale of goods, you can access the Institute of International Commercial Law at Pace University at

http://cisgw3.law.pace.edu

LEGAL RESEARCH EXERCISES ON THE WEB

Go to http://wbl.westbuslaw.com, the Web site that accompanies this text. Select "Internet Applications," and then click on "Chapter 21." There you will find the following Internet research exercise that you can perform to learn more about performance requirements in the international context:

Activity 21–1: International Performance Requirements

CHAPTER 22

Remedies for Breach of Sales and Lease Contracts

BILLIONS OF SALES AND LEASE CONTRACTS are carried out every year in the United States. Most of these contracts involve virtually no problems. This is because most people try to fulfill their contractual obligations. Sometimes, however, circumstances make it difficult for a person to carry out the performance promised in a contract, in which case the contract may be breached. When breach occurs, the aggrieved party looks for remedies. These remedies range from retaining the goods to requiring the breaching party's performance under the contract. The general purpose of these remedies is to put the aggrieved party "in as good a position as if the other party had fully performed."

Recall from Chapter 18 that under the common law of contracts, the doctrine of election of remedies applies. Under this doctrine, a party must elect, or choose, one remedy to pursue. In contrast, remedies under the Uniform Commercial Code (UCC) are *cumulative* in nature. In other words, an innocent party to a breached sales or lease contract is not limited to one, exclusive remedy. (Of course, a party still may not recover twice for the same harm.)

SECTION 1

Remedies of the Seller or Lessor

Numerous remedies are available under the UCC to a seller or lessor when the buyer or lessee is in breach. Generally, the remedies available to the seller or lessor depend on the circumstances existing at the time of the breach, such as which party has possession of the goods, whether the goods are in transit, whether the buyer or lessee has rejected or accepted the goods, and so on.

WHEN THE GOODS ARE IN THE POSSESSION OF THE SELLER OR LESSOR

Under the UCC, if the buyer or lessee breaches the contract before the goods have been delivered to the buyer or lessee, the seller or lessor has the right to pursue the remedies discussed here.

The Right to Cancel the Contract. One of the options available to a seller or lessor when the buyer or lessee breaches the contract is simply to cancel the contract [UCC 2–703(f), 2A–523(1)(a)]. The seller must notify the buyer or lessee of the cancellation, and at that point all remaining obligations of the seller or lessor are discharged. The buyer or lessee is not discharged from all remaining obligations, however; he or she is in breach, and the seller or lessor can pursue remedies available under the UCC for breach.

The Right to Withhold Delivery.

In general, sellers and lessors can withhold or discontinue performance of their obligations under sales or lease contracts when the buyers or lessees are in breach. If a buyer or lessee has wrongfully rejected or revoked acceptance of contract goods (rejection and revocation of acceptance will be discussed later in this chapter), failed to make proper and timely payment, or repudiated a part of the contract, the seller or lessor can withhold delivery of the goods in question [UCC 2–703(a), 2A–523(1)(c)]. If the breach results from the buyer's or the lessee's insolvency (inability to pay debts as they become due), the seller or lessor can refuse to deliver the goods unless the buyer or lessee pays in cash [UCC 2–702(1), 2A–525(1)].

The Right to Resell or Dispose of the Goods.

When a buyer or lessee breaches or repudiates a sales contract while the seller or lessor is still in possession of the goods, the seller or lessor can resell or dispose of the goods, holding the buyer or lessee liable for any loss [UCC 2–703(d), 2–706(1), 2A–523(1)(e), 2A–527(1)].

When the goods contracted for are unfinished at the time of breach, the seller or lessor can do one of two things: (1) cease manufacturing the goods and resell them for scrap or salvage value or (2) complete the manufacture and resell or dispose of the goods, holding the buyer or lessee liable for any deficiency. In choosing between these two alternatives, the seller or lessor must exercise reasonable commercial judgment in order to mitigate the loss and obtain maximum value from the unfinished goods [UCC 2–704(2), 2A–524(2)]. Any resale of the goods must be made in good faith and in a commercially reasonable manner.

In sales transactions, the seller can recover any deficiency between the resale price and the contract price, along with *incidental damages*, defined as those costs to the seller resulting from the breach [UCC 2–706(1), 2–710]. The resale can be private or public, and the goods can be sold as a unit or in parcels. The seller must give the original buyer reasonable notice of the resale, unless the goods are perishable or will rapidly decline in value [UCC 2–706(2), (3)]. A good faith purchaser in a resale takes the goods free of any of the rights of the original buyer, even if the seller fails to comply with these requirements of the UCC [UCC 2–706(5)]. The UCC encourages the resale of the goods because although the buyer is liable for any deficiency, the seller is not accountable to the buyer for any profits made on the resale [UCC 2–706(6)].

In lease transactions, the lessor may lease the goods to another party and recover from the original lessee, as damages, any unpaid lease payments up to the beginning date of the lease term under the new lease. The lessor can also recover any deficiency between the lease payments due under the original lease contract and those under the new lease contract, along with incidental damages [UCC 2A–527(2)].

The Right to Recover the Purchase Price or Lease Payments Due.

Under the UCC, an unpaid seller or lessor who is unable to resell or dispose of the goods can bring an action to recover the purchase price or the payments due under the lease contract, plus incidental damages [UCC 2–709(1), 2A–529(1)]. If a seller or lessor sues under these circumstances, the goods must be held for the buyer or lessee. The seller or lessor can resell or dispose of the goods at any time prior to collection of the judgment from the buyer or lessee, but in that situation the net proceeds from the sale must be credited to the buyer or lessee. This is an example of the duty to mitigate damages.

For example, suppose that Southern Realty contracts with Gem Point, Inc., to purchase one thousand pens with Southern Realty's name inscribed on them. Gem Point delivers the pens, but Southern Realty refuses to pay for them. In this situation, Gem Point has, as a proper remedy, an action for the purchase price. Gem Point has delivered conforming goods, and Southern Realty, because it has failed to pay, is in breach. Gem Point obviously cannot sell to anyone else the pens inscribed with the buyer's business name, so this situation falls under UCC 2–709.

The Right to Recover Damages.

If a buyer or lessee repudiates a contract or wrongfully refuses to accept the goods, a seller or lessor can maintain an action to recover the damages sustained. Ordinarily, the amount of damages equals the difference between the contract price or lease payments and the market price or lease payments at the time and place of tender of the goods, plus incidental damages [UCC 2–708(1), 2A–528(1)]. The time and place of tender are frequently given by such terms as F.O.B., F.A.S., C.I.F.,[1] and the like, which determine whether there is a shipment or destination contract.

If the difference between the contract price or payments due under the lease contract and the market price or payments due under the lease contract is too small to place the seller or lessor in the position that he or she would have been in if the buyer or lessee had fully performed, the proper measure of damages is the lost profits of the seller or lessor, including a reasonable allowance for overhead and other expenses [UCC 2–708(2), 2A–528(2)].

WHEN THE GOODS ARE IN TRANSIT

If the seller or lessor has delivered the goods to a carrier or a bailee but the buyer or lessee has not yet received them, the goods are said to be *in transit*. If, while the goods are in transit, the seller or lessor learns that the buyer or lessee is insolvent, the seller or lessor can stop the carrier or bailee from delivering the goods, regardless of the quantity of goods shipped. If the buyer or lessee is in breach but is not insolvent, the seller or lessor can stop the goods in transit only if the quantity shipped is at least a carload, a truckload, a planeload, or a larger shipment [UCC 2–705(1), 2A–526(1)].

To stop delivery, the seller or lessor must *timely notify* the carrier or other bailee that the goods are to be returned or held for the seller or lessor. If the carrier has sufficient time to stop delivery, the goods must be held and delivered according to the instructions of the seller or lessor, who is liable to the carrier for any additional costs incurred [UCC 2–705(3), 2A–526(3)].

UCC 2–705(2) and 2A–526(2) provide that the right of the seller or lessor to stop delivery of goods in transit is lost when any of the following events occur:

1. The buyer or lessee obtains possession of the goods.
2. The carrier acknowledges the rights of the buyer or lessee by reshipping or storing the goods for the buyer or lessee.

3. A bailee of the goods other than a carrier acknowledges that he or she is holding the goods for the buyer or lessee.

Additionally, in sales transactions, the seller loses the right to stop delivery of goods in transit when a negotiable document of title covering the goods has been properly transferred to the buyer, giving the buyer ownership rights in the goods[2] [UCC 2–705(2)].

WHEN THE GOODS ARE IN THE POSSESSION OF THE BUYER OR LESSEE

When the buyer or lessee breaches a sales or lease contract and the goods are in the buyer's or lessee's possession, the UCC gives the seller or lessor the right to choose among various remedies.

The Right to Recover the Purchase Price or Payments Due under the Lease Contract. If the buyer or lessee has accepted the goods but refuses to pay for them, the seller or lessor can sue for the purchase price of the goods or for the lease payments due, plus incidental damages [UCC 2–709(1), 2A–529(1)].

The Right to Reclaim Goods. In regard to sales contracts, if a seller discovers that the buyer has received goods on credit and is insolvent, the seller can demand return of the goods. Ordinarily, the demand must be made within ten days of the buyer's receipt of the goods; however, the seller can demand and reclaim the goods at any time if the buyer misrepresented his or her solvency in writing within three months prior to the delivery of the goods [UCC 2–702(2)]. The seller's right to reclaim the goods is subject to the rights of a good faith purchaser or other buyer in the ordinary course of business who purchases the goods from the buyer before the seller reclaims.

Under the UCC, a seller seeking to exercise the right to reclaim goods receives preferential treatment over the buyer's other creditors—the seller need only demand the return of the goods within ten days after the buyer has received them.[3] Because of this preferential treatment, the UCC provides that successful reclamation (reclaiming) of

---

1. See Exhibit 20–1 in Chapter 20 for a definition of these contract terms.

2. Negotiable and nonnegotiable documents of title were discussed in Chapter 20.
3. A seller who has delivered goods to an insolvent buyer also receives preferential treatment if the buyer enters into bankruptcy proceedings (discussed in Chapter 30).

goods excludes all other remedies with respect to them [UCC 2–702(3)].

In regard to lease contracts, if the lessee is in default (fails to make payments that are due, for example), the lessor may reclaim the leased goods that are in the lessee's possession [UCC 2A–525(2)].

Section 2

Remedies of the Buyer or Lessee

Under the UCC, numerous remedies are available to the buyer or lessee when the seller or lessor breaches the contract. Like the remedies available to sellers and lessors, the remedies available to buyers and lessees depend on the circumstances existing at the time of the breach.

WHEN THE SELLER OR LESSOR REFUSES TO DELIVER THE GOODS

If the seller or lessor refuses to deliver the goods to the buyer or lessee, the remedies available to the buyer or lessee include those discussed here.

The Right to Cancel the Contract. When a seller or lessor fails to make proper delivery or repudiates the contract, the buyer or lessee can cancel, or rescind, the contract. On giving notice of cancellation, the buyer or lessee is relieved of any further obligations under the contract but retains all rights to other remedies against the seller [UCC 2–711(1), 2A–508(1)(a)]. (The right to cancel the contract is also available to a buyer or lessee who has rightfully rejected goods or revoked acceptance, as will be discussed shortly.)

The Right to Recover the Goods. If a buyer or lessee has made a partial or full payment for goods that remain in the possession of the seller or lessor, the buyer or lessee can recover the goods if the seller or lessor becomes insolvent within ten days after receiving the first payment and if the goods are identified to the contract. To exercise this right, the buyer or lessee must tender to the seller any unpaid balance of the purchase price [UCC 2–502, 2A–522].

The Right to Obtain Specific Performance. A buyer or lessee can obtain specific performance

when the goods are unique or when the remedy at law is inadequate [UCC 2–716(1), 2A–521(1)]. Ordinarily, an award of money damages is sufficient to place a buyer or lessee in the position he or she would have occupied if the seller or lessor had fully performed. When the contract is for the purchase of a particular work of art or a similarly unique item, however, money damages may not be sufficient. Under these circumstances, equity will require that the seller or lessor perform exactly by delivering the particular goods identified to the contract (a remedy of specific performance).

The Right of Cover. In certain situations, buyers and lessees can protect themselves by obtaining cover—that is, by buying or leasing substitute goods for those that were due under the sales contract. This option is available when the seller or lessor repudiates the contract or fails to deliver the goods.[4]

In obtaining cover, the buyer or lessee must act in good faith and without unreasonable delay [UCC 2–712, 2A–518]. After purchasing or leasing substitute goods, the buyer or lessee can recover from the seller or lessor the difference between the cost of cover and the contract price (or lease payments), plus incidental and consequential damages, less the expenses (such as delivery costs) that were saved as a result of the breach [UCC 2–712, 2–715, 2A–518]. Consequential damages are any losses suffered by the buyer or lessee that the seller or lessor could have foreseen (had reason to know about) at the time of contract and any injury to the buyer's or lessee's person or property proximately resulting from the contract's breach [UCC 2–715(2), 2A–520(2)].

Buyers and lessees are not required to cover, and failure to do so will not bar them from using any other remedies available under the UCC. A buyer or lessee who fails to cover, however, risks not being able to collect consequential damages that could have been avoided had he or she purchased or leased substitute goods.

If, by obtaining cover and reselling the substitute goods, a buyer is able to recoup all or most of his or her loss, should the buyer's recovery under UCC 2–712 be reduced? That was the issue confronting the court in the following case.

---

4. The right to obtain cover is also available to a buyer or lessee who has rightfully rejected goods or revoked acceptance. Rejection and revocation of acceptance will be discussed shortly.

CASE 22.1   KGM Harvesting Co. v. Fresh Network

California Court
of Appeal,
Sixth District, 1995.
36 Cal.App.4th 376,
42 Cal.Rptr.2d 286.

BACKGROUND AND FACTS   *McDonald's buys its lettuce from the KGM Harvesting Company, which also sells lettuce to other companies. In 1988, KGM agreed to deliver fourteen loads of lettuce each week to Fresh Network. Fresh Network then sold the lettuce to the Castellini Company, which in turn sold it to Club Chef. Club Chef then chopped and shredded it for Burger King, Taco Bell, and Pizza Hut. In the spring of 1991, the market price of lettuce rose dramatically. KGM chose to sell only to McDonald's and some of its other customers rather than to deliver to Fresh Network the usual fourteen loads at the contract price. Consequently, to fulfill its obligation to Castellini, Fresh Network bought lettuce on the open market at a higher price. Castellini agreed to pay the difference, which it charged to its customer, Club Chef, which in turn passed the higher price on to its customers. In an attempt to recover the extra amount it had to pay for lettuce, Fresh Network refused to pay KGM for previous shipments. KGM filed a suit in a California state court for the balance due. Fresh Network responded with a demand for damages. The court awarded Fresh Network an amount equal to the difference between the contract price and the price it had paid for the substitute lettuce, minus the amount that it owed KGM. KGM appealed, arguing that the court should have taken into consideration the fact that Fresh Network had passed on most of its increased costs to Castellini.*

IN THE LANGUAGE OF THE COURT

COTTLE, Presiding Justice.

*   *   *   *

*   *   * [T]he object of contract damages is to give the aggrieved party as nearly as possible the equivalent of the benefits of performance. *   *   * [P]urchasing replacement lettuce to continue its business did not place buyer in as good a position as if the other party had fully performed. This was because buyer paid more than [the contract price] for the replacement lettuce. Only by reimbursing buyer for the additional costs *   *   * could buyer truly receive the benefit of the bargain. This is the measure of damages set forth in [UCC 2–712].

*   *   *   *

*   *   * What the buyer chooses to do with that bargain is not relevant to the determination of damages under [UCC 2–712].

DECISION AND REMEDY   *The California Court of Appeal affirmed the lower court's award. Fresh Network was entitled to the difference between the contract price and the price it paid for the substitute lettuce, less the amount it owed to KGM, because that would place Fresh Network in as good a position as if KGM had fully performed.*

The Right to Replevy Goods.   Buyers and lessees also have the right to replevy goods. **Replevin**[5] is an action to recover identified goods in the hands of a party who is unlawfully withholding them. Outside the UCC, the term *replevin* refers to a prejudgment process (a proceeding that takes place prior to a court's judgment) involving the seizure of specific personal property in which a party claims a right or an interest. Under the UCC, a buyer or lessee can replevy

goods subject to the contract if the seller or lessor has repudiated or breached the contract. To maintain an action to replevy goods, buyers and lessees must usually show that they were unable to cover for the goods after making a reasonable effort [UCC 2–716(3), 2A–521(3)].

The Right to Recover Damages.   If a seller or lessor repudiates the sales contract or fails to deliver the goods, the buyer or lessee can sue for damages. The measure of recovery is the difference between

---

5. Pronounced ruh-*pleh*-vun.

the contract price (or lease payments) and the market price of the goods (or lease payments that could be obtained for the goods) at the time the buyer (or lessee) *learned* of the breach. The market price or market lease payments are determined at the place where the seller or lessor was supposed to deliver the goods. The buyer or lessee can also recover incidental and consequential damages less the expenses that were saved as a result of the breach [UCC 2–713, 2A–519].

Consider an example. Schilling orders 10,000 bushels of wheat from Valdone for $5.00 a bushel, with delivery due on June 14 and payment due on June 20. Valdone does not deliver on June 14. On June 14, the market price of wheat is $5.50 per bushel. Schilling chooses to do without the wheat. He sues Valdone for damages for nondelivery. Schilling can recover $0.50 × 10,000, or $5,000, plus any expenses the breach has caused him. The measure of damages is the market price on the day Schilling was to have received delivery less the contract price. (Any expenses Schilling saved by the breach would be deducted from the damages.)

WHEN THE SELLER OR LESSOR DELIVERS NONCONFORMING GOODS

When the seller or lessor delivers nonconforming goods, the buyer or lessee has several remedies available under the UCC.

The Right to Reject the Goods. If either the goods or the tender of the goods by the seller or lessor fails to conform to the contract in any respect, the buyer or lessee can reject the goods. If some of the goods conform to the contract, the buyer or lessee can keep the conforming goods and reject the rest [UCC 2–601, 2A–509]. If the buyer or lessee rejects the goods, he or she may then obtain cover or cancel the contract, just as if the seller or lessor had refused to deliver the goods (see the earlier discussion of these remedies).

Timeliness and Reason for Rejection Required. The buyer or lessee must reject the goods within a reasonable amount of time after delivery or tender of delivery, and the seller or lessor must be notified **seasonally**— that is, in a timely fashion or at the proper time [UCC 2–602(1), 2A–509(2)]. Furthermore, the buyer or lessee must designate defects that are ascertainable by reasonable inspection. Failure to do so precludes the buyer or lessee from using such defects to justify rejec-

tion or to establish breach when the seller or lessor could have cured the defects if they had been stated seasonably [UCC 2–605, 2A–514].

Duties of Merchant Buyers and Lessees When Goods Are Rejected. If a *merchant buyer* or *lessee* rightfully rejects goods, and the seller or lessor has no agent or business at the place of rejection, the buyer or lessee is required to follow any reasonable instructions received from the seller or lessor with respect to the goods controlled by the buyer or lessee. The buyer or lessee is entitled to reimbursement for the care and cost entailed in following the instructions [UCC 2–603, 2A–511]. The same requirements hold if the buyer or lessee rightfully revokes his or her acceptance of the goods at some later time [UCC 2–608(3), 2A–517(5)]. (Revocation of acceptance will be discussed shortly.)

If no instructions are forthcoming and the goods are perishable or threaten to decline in value quickly, the buyer or lessee can resell the goods in good faith, taking appropriate reimbursement and a selling commission (not to exceed 10 percent of the gross proceeds) from the proceeds [UCC 2–603(1), (2); 2A–511(1)]. If the goods are not perishable, the buyer or lessee may store them for the seller or lessor or reship them to the seller or lessor [UCC 2–604, 2A–512].

Buyers who rightfully reject goods (or who justifiably revoke acceptance of goods—discussed next) that remain in their possession or control have a *security interest* in the goods (basically, a legal claim to the goods to the extent necessary to recover expenses, costs, and the like—see Chapter 28). The security interest encompasses any payments the buyer has made for the goods, as well as any expenses incurred with regard to inspection, receipt, transportation, care, and custody of the goods [UCC 2–711(3)]. A buyer with a security interest in the goods is a "person in the position of a seller." This gives the buyer the same rights as an unpaid seller. Thus, the buyer can resell, withhold delivery of, or stop delivery of the goods. A buyer who chooses to resell must account to the seller for any amounts received in excess of the security interest [UCC 2–706(6), 2–711].

Revocation of Acceptance. Acceptance of the goods precludes the buyer or lessee from exercising the right of rejection, but it does not necessarily preclude the buyer or lessee from pursuing other remedies (discussed later). Additionally, in certain circumstances, a buyer or lessee is permitted to *revoke* his or her acceptance of the goods. Acceptance of a lot or a commercial unit can be revoked if the nonconformity *substantially* impairs the value of the lot or unit and if one of the following factors is present:

1. Acceptance was predicated on the reasonable assumption that the nonconformity would be cured, and it has not been cured within a reasonable period of time [UCC 2–608(1)(a), 2A–517(1)(a)].
2. The buyer or lessee did not discover the nonconformity before acceptance, either because it was difficult to discover before acceptance or because assurances made by the seller or lessor that the goods were conforming kept the buyer or lessee from inspecting the goods [UCC 2–608(1)(b), 2A–517(1)(b)].

Revocation of acceptance is not effective until notice is given to the seller or lessor. Notice must occur within a reasonable time after the buyer or lessee either discovers or *should have discovered* the grounds for revocation. Additionally, revocation must occur before the goods have undergone any substantial change (such as spoilage) not caused by their own defects [UCC 2–608(2), 2A–517(4)]. Once acceptance is revoked, the buyer or lessee can pursue remedies, just as if the goods had been rejected.

The Right to Recover Damages for Accepted Goods. A buyer or lessee who has accepted nonconforming goods may also keep the goods and recover for any loss "resulting in the ordinary course of events . . . as determined in any manner which is reasonable" [UCC 2–714(1), 2A–519(3)]. The buyer or lessee, however, must notify the seller or lessor of the breach within a reasonable time after the defect was or should have been discovered. Otherwise, the buyer or lessee cannot recover from the seller or lessor damages caused by defects in the goods [UCC 2–607(3), 2A–516(3)]. In addition, the parties to a sales or lease contract can insert a provision requiring that the buyer or lessee give notice of any defects in the goods within a prescribed period.

When the goods delivered are not as warranted, the measure of damages equals the difference between the value of the goods as accepted and their value if they had been delivered as warranted unless special circumstances show proximately caused damages of a different amount [UCC 2–714(2), 2A–519(4)]. For this and other types of breaches in which the buyer or lessee has accepted the goods, the buyer or lessee is entitled to incidental and consequential damages [UCC 2–714(3), 2A–519]. The UCC also permits the buyer or lessee, with proper notice to the seller or lessor, to deduct all or any part of the damages from the price or lease payments still due and payable to the seller or lessor [UCC 2–717, 2A–516(1)].

Who qualifies as a "buyer" under these provisions? Is a party who does not actually purchase a product, but who is injured by its alleged defects, required to give notice of those defects within a reasonable time in order to recover for those injuries? This was an important question in the following case.

CASE 22.2   Yates v. Pitman Manufacturing, Inc.

Supreme Court of
Virginia, 1999.
257 Va. 601,
514 S.E.2d 605.
http://www.courts.state.
va.us/opin.html[a]

BACKGROUND AND FACTS. *In 1982, Pitman Manufacturing, Inc., made and sold a construction crane to Shelton Witt Equipment, a distributor. At the time, Pitman certified that the outrigger on the crane could be seen from its "actuating location." In 1991, Koch Carbon owned the crane and was using it to deliver equipment to Baldwin Coal Corporation. Ira Stiltner, a Koch employee, activated the outrigger from the front of the truck. At the time, he could not see the outrigger or Eddie Yates, a Baldwin employee, who was simultaneously releasing restraining chains from the crane truck's bed. Without warning, the outrigger dropped onto Yates's foot. Yates filed a suit in a Virginia state court against Pitman, seeking $3 million in damages for his injuries on the basis of breach of warranty (see Chapter 23). One of the issues was whether Yates had provided reasonable notice, under UCC 2–607(3), to Pitman of its breach of warranty. Yates argued in part*

---

a. In the "Supreme Court of Virginia" section, click on the version in which you want to read this opinion. To view the opinion in text format, click on "Opinions in Text Format." On that page, scroll down the list of cases to the *Yates* case and click on the docket number ("981474") to access the opinion.

that he did not have to give the notice, because he was not the purchaser of the crane. The court entered a judgment in Pitman's favor. Yates appealed to the Virginia Supreme Court.

IN THE LANGUAGE OF THE COURT

STEPHENSON, Senior Justice.

* * * *

First, we consider whether the trial court erred in holding that Yates was required to provide Pitman with notice of breach of warranty as a prerequisite to recovery therefor. The issue is one of first impression for [an issue never before examined by] this Court.

To resolve the issue, we look to [Virginia] Code [Section] 8.2–607(3) [Virgina's version of UCC 2–607(3)], the only provision of the Sales title of the Uniform Commercial Code (the UCC) that requires notice to be given to a seller of goods. The section provides, in pertinent part, the following:

> Where a tender has been accepted * * * the buyer must within a reasonable time after he discovers or should have discovered any breach notify the seller of breach or be barred from any remedy.

It is firmly established that, when a statute is clear and unambiguous, a court must accept its plain meaning and not resort to extrinsic evidence or rules of construction. The pertinent language in Code [Section] 8.2–607(3) is unambiguous and clearly states that "the buyer must * * * notify the seller of [the] breach." Thus, accepting the statute's plain meaning, it is apparent that the notice of breach is required from the "buyer" of the goods. [Emphasis added.]

In the present case, Yates was not the buyer of the crane unit. Therefore, the notice requirement of Code [Section] 8.2–607(3) does not preclude Yates from maintaining a breach of warranty action.

We hold, therefore, that only buyers, i.e., those who buy or contract to buy goods from a seller, must give notice of breach of warranty to the seller as a prerequisite to recovery. Consequently, the trial court erred in ruling that Yates was required to have given Pitman such notice.

DECISION AND REMEDY

The Virginia Supreme Court reversed the judgment of the lower court and remanded the case for further proceedings consistent with this decision. Yates did not have to give the notice under UCC 2–607(3) to recover for his injuries, because he was not a "buyer."

SECTION 3

Contractual Provisions Affecting Remedies

The parties to a sales or lease contract can vary their respective rights and obligations by contractual agreement. For example, a seller and buyer can expressly provide for remedies in addition to those provided in the UCC. They can also specifiy remedies in lieu of those provided in the UCC, or they can change the measure of damages. The seller can stipulate that the buyer's only remedy on the seller's breach be repair or replacement of the item, or the seller can limit the buyer's remedy to return of the goods and refund of the purchase price. In sales and lease contracts, an agreed-on remedy is in addition to those provided in the UCC unless the parties expressly agree that the remedy is exclusive of all others [UCC 2–719(1), 2A–503(1)].

If the parties state that a remedy is exclusive, then it is the sole remedy. When circumstances cause an exclusive remedy to fail in its essential purpose, however, it is no longer exclusive [UCC 2–719(2), 2A–503(2)]. For example, a sales contract that limits the buyer's remedy to repair or replacement fails in its essential purpose if the item cannot be repaired and no replacements are available.

A contract can limit or exclude consequential damages, provided the limitation is not unconscionable. When the buyer or lessee is a consumer, the limitation of consequential damages for personal injuries resulting from nonconforming goods is *prima facie* unconscionable. The limitation of consequential damages is not necessarily unconscionable when the loss is commercial in nature—for example, lost profits and property damage [UCC 2–719(3), 2A–503(3)]. In the following case, the court had to decide whether a contract clause that excluded liability for consequential damages was unconscionable.

CASE 22.3

Transport Corp. of America, Inc. v. International Business Machines Corp.

United States Court of Appeals, Eighth Circuit, 1994. 30 F.3d 953.

COMPANY PROFILE *Transport Corporation of America, Inc. (TCA), provides a wide range of services to its customers, which include Ford Motor Company, General Mills, 3M Company, and Sears, Roebuck & Company. From ten regional centers, with a fleet of more than 1,100 tractors and 2,600 trailers, TCA provides temperature-controlled trailers, multistop loading and unloading, and time-definite pickup and delivery. In 1994, at a cost of more than $1.5 million, TCA began to develop a more sophisticated computer information system. The system was to combine operational data, through satellite communications, with information on such areas as maintenance, billing, and accounting.*

BACKGROUND AND FACTS *Innovative Computing Corporation (ICC) sold an International Business Machines Corporation (IBM) computer to TCA. As part of the deal, TCA expressly agreed to a disclaimer that stated, in part, "IN NO EVENT SHALL ICC BE LIABLE FOR ANY * * * CONSEQUENTIAL DAMAGES * * * IN CONNECTION WITH * * * THIS AGREEMENT." One year later, the computer failed. The downtime was nearly thirty-four hours. TCA spent more than $4,500 to replace unrecoverable data and lost nearly $470,000 in income while the computer was down. TCA filed a suit in a Minnesota state court against IBM and ICC, alleging, among other things, breach of warranty. The case was moved to a federal district court, and IBM and ICC filed a motion for summary judgment. The court granted the motion, based in part on the disclaimer. TCA appealed, arguing in part that the disclaimer was unconscionable.*

IN THE LANGUAGE OF THE COURT

McMILLIAN, Circuit Judge.
* * * *
* * * The U.C.C. encourages negotiated agreements in commercial transactions, including warranties and limitations. It is at the time of contract formation that experienced parties define the product, identify the risks, and negotiate a price of the goods that reflects the relative benefits and risks to each. An exclusion of consequential damages set forth in advance in a commercial agreement between experienced business parties represents a bargained-for allocation of risk that is consciable as a matter of law.
* * * *
We agree with the district court that the disclaimer of consequential damages was not unconscionable and that the damages claimed by TCA, for business interruption losses and replacement media, were consequential damages. Furthermore, TCA and ICC were sophisticated business entities of relatively equal bargaining power. ICC's disclaimer was not unconscionable and TCA is therefore precluded from recovering consequential damages.

DECISION AND REMEDY *The U.S. Court of Appeals for the Eighth Circuit affirmed the lower court's decision. The clause excluding consequential damages was not unconscionable because it was part of a negotiated agreement between sophisticated business entities of relatively equal bargaining power.*

CONCEPT
SUMMARY 22.1

REMEDIES FOR BREACH OF CONTRACT

CONCEPT	DESCRIPTION

Remedies of the Seller or Lessor	1. *When the goods are in the possession of the seller or lessor*—The seller or lessor may do the following:
	  a. Cancel the contract [UCC 2–703(f), 2A–523(1)(a)].
	  b. Withhold delivery [UCC 2–703(a), 2A–523(1)(c)].
	  c. Resell or dispose of the goods [UCC 2–703(d), 2–706(1), 2A–523(1)(e), 2A–527(1)].
	  d. Sue to recover the purchase price or lease payments due [UCC 2–709(1), 2A–529(1)].
	  e. Sue to recover damages [UCC 2–708, 2A–528].
	2. *When the goods are in transit*—The seller or lessor may stop the carrier or bailee from delivering the goods [UCC 2–705, 2A–526].
	3. *When the goods are in the possession of the buyer or lessee*—The seller or lessor may do the following:
	  a. Sue to recover the purchase price or lease payments due [UCC 2–709(1), 2A–529(1)].
	  b. Reclaim the goods. A seller may reclaim goods received by an insolvent buyer if the demand is made within ten days of receipt (excludes all other remedies on reclamation) [UCC 2–702]; a lessor may repossess goods if the lessee is in default [UCC 2A–525(2)].

Remedies of the Buyer or Lessee	1. *When the seller or lessor refuses to deliver the goods*—The buyer or lessee may do the following:
	  a. Cancel the contract [UCC 2–711(1), 2A–508(1)(a)].
	  b. Recover the goods if the seller or lessor becomes insolvent within ten days after receiving the first payment and the goods are identified to the contract [UCC 2–502, 2A–522].
	  c. Obtain specific performance (when the goods are unique or when the remedy at law is inadequate) [UCC 2–716(1), 2A–521(1)].
	  d. Obtain cover [UCC 2–712, 2A–518].
	  e. Replevy the goods (if cover is unavailable) [UCC 2–716(3), 2A–521(3)].
	  f. Sue to recover damages [UCC 2–713, 2A–519].
	2. *When the seller or lessor delivers nonconforming goods*—The buyer or lessee may do the following:
	  a. Reject the goods [UCC 2–601, 2A–509].
	  b. Revoke acceptance (in certain circumstances) [UCC 2–608, 2A–517].
	  c. Accept the goods and sue to recover ordinary damages, sue for breach of warranty, or deduct the amount of damages from the purchase price [UCC 2–607, 2–714, 2A–519].

Contractual Provisions Affecting Remedies	Remedies may be limited in sales or lease contracts by agreement of the parties. If the contract states that a remedy is exclusive, then that is the sole remedy—unless the remedy fails in its essential purpose. Sellers and lessors can also limit the rights of buyers and lessees to consequential damages—unless the limitation is unconscionable [UCC 2–719, 2A–503].

SECTION 4

Lemon Laws

Some purchasers of defective automobiles—called "lemons"—found that the remedies provided by the UCC, after limitations had been imposed by the seller, were inadequate. In response to the frustration of these buyers, all of the states and the District of Columbia have enacted *lemon laws*. Basically, lemon laws provide that if an automobile under warranty possesses a defect that significantly affects the vehicle's value or use, and the defect has not been remedied by the seller within a specified number of opportunities (usually four), the buyer is entitled to a new car, replacement of defective parts, or return of all consideration paid.

In most states, lemon laws require an aggrieved new-car owner to notify the dealer or manufacturer of the problem and to provide the dealer or manufacturer with an opportunity to solve it. If the problem remains, the owner must then submit complaints to the arbitration program specified in the manufacturer's warranty before taking the case to court. Decisions by arbitration panels are binding on the manufacturer (that is, cannot be appealed by the manufacturer to the courts) but usually are not binding on the purchaser.

Most major automobile companies use their own arbitration panels. Some companies, however, subscribe to independent arbitration services, such as those provided by the Better Business Bureau. Although arbitration boards must meet state and/or federal standards of impartiality, industry-sponsored arbitration boards have been criticized for not being truly impartial in their decisions. In response to this criticism, some states have established mandatory government-sponsored arbitration programs for lemon law disputes.

SECTION 5

Remedies for Breach of International Sales Contracts

The United Nations Convention on Contracts for the International Sale of Goods (CISG) provides international sellers and buyers with remedies very similar to those available under the UCC. Article 74 of the CISG provides for money damages, including foreseeable consequential damages, on a contract's breach. As under the UCC, the measure of damages is normally the difference between the contract price and the market price of the goods. Under Article 49, the buyer is permitted to avoid obligations under the contract if the seller breaches the contract or fails to deliver the goods during the time specified in the agreement or later agreed on by the parties. Similarly, under Article 64, the seller can avoid obligations under the contract if the buyer breaches the contract, fails to accept delivery of the goods, or fails to pay for the goods.

The CISG also allows for specific performance as a remedy under Article 28, which provides that "one party is entitled to require performance of any obligation by the other party." This statement is then qualified, however. Article 28 goes on to state that a court may only grant specific performance as a remedy if it would do so "under its own law in respect of similar contracts of sale not governed by this Convention." As already discussed, in the United States the equitable remedy of specific performance normally will be granted only if no adequate remedy at law (money damages) is available and the goods are unique in nature. In other countries, however, such as Germany, specific performance is a commonly granted remedy for breach of contract.

TERMS AND CONCEPTS TO REVIEW

QUESTIONS AND CASE PROBLEMS

22–1. REMEDIES OF THE SELLER OR LESSOR. Klink contracts to ship Albright via Quickway Truck Line one hundred cases of Knee High brand corn, F.O.B. Albright's city, at $6.50 per case. Albright is to make a 10 percent down payment. The payment is to be received at Klink's place of business before shipment occurs. Klink ships the corn as contracted, although he has not yet received the down payment, and the goods arrive in Albright's city. There they remain in the delivery van. Because Albright has failed to make the down payment, Klink orders Quickway not to make the delivery to Albright's warehouse. Albright claims that the transit has ended and that Klink has no right to stop the delivery of the corn. Discuss the validity of Albright's claim and Klink's action.

22–2. REMEDIES OF THE SELLER OR LESSOR. Topken has contracted to sell Lorwin five hundred washing machines of a certain model at list price. Topken is to ship the goods on or before December 1. Topken produces one thousand washing machines of this model but has not yet prepared Lorwin's shipment. On November 1, Lorwin repudiates the contract. Discuss the remedies available to Topken.

22–3. REMEDIES OF THE BUYER OR LESSEE. Roy has contracted with Schnee for the purchase and delivery of one hundred model Z dryers. At the time for the contracted tender, Schnee does not have a hundred model Z dryers in stock and does not expect to acquire any for at least three months. Schnee tenders eighty model Z dryers and twenty model X dryers. Roy wants one hundred model Z dryers or none at all. Discuss the remedies available to Roy under these circumstances.

22–4. REMEDIES OF THE BUYER OR LESSEE. McDonald has contracted to purchase five hundred pairs of shoes from Vetter. Vetter manufactures the shoes and tenders delivery to McDonald. McDonald accepts the shipment. Later, on inspection, McDonald discovers that ten pairs of the shoes are poorly made and will have to be sold to customers as seconds. If McDonald decides to keep all five hundred pairs of shoes, what remedies are available to her? Discuss.

22–5. REMEDIES OF THE BUYER OR LESSEE. Lehor is an antique car collector. He contracts to purchase spare parts for a 1938 engine from Beem. These parts are not made anymore and are scarce. To get the contract with Beem, Lehor agrees to pay 50 percent of the purchase price in advance. On May 1, Lehor sends the payment, which is received on May 2. On May 3, Beem, having found another buyer willing to pay substantially more for the parts, informs Lehor that he will not deliver as contracted. That same day, Lehor learns that Beem is insolvent. Discuss fully any possible remedies available to Lehor to take possession of these parts.

22–6. REMEDIES OF THE SELLER OR LESSOR. Servbest Foods, Inc., had a contract with Emessee Industries, Inc., under which Emessee was to purchase 200,000 pounds of beef trimmings from Servbest at 52.5 cents per pound. Servbest delivered to Emessee the warehouse receipts and invoices for the beef trimmings. The price of beef trimmings then fell significantly, and Emessee returned the documents to Servbest and canceled the contract. Servbest then sold the beef trimmings for 20.25 cents per pound and sued Emessee for damages (the difference between the contract price and the market price at which it had been forced to sell the trimmings) for breach of contract, plus incidental damages. Discuss whether Servbest Foods exercised a proper remedy and was entitled to the damages alleged in its lawsuit. [*Servbest Foods, Inc. v. Emessee Industries, Inc.*, 82 Ill.App.3d 662, 403 N.E.2d 1, 37 Ill.Dec. 945 (1980)]

22–7. MEASURE OF DAMAGES. Bigelow-Sanford, Inc., entered into a contract to buy 100,000 yards of jute at $0.64 per yard from Gunny Corp. Gunny delivered 22,228 yards to Bigelow but informed the company that no more would be delivered. Several other suppliers to Bigelow defaulted, and Bigelow was forced to go into the market one month later to purchase a total of 164,503 yards of jute for $1.21 per yard. Bigelow sued Gunny for the difference between the market price and the contract price of the amount of jute that Gunny had not delivered. Discuss whether Bigelow could recover this amount from Gunny. [*Bigelow-Sanford, Inc. v. Gunny Corp.*, 649 F.2d 1060 (5th Cir. 1981)]

22–8. LIMITATION OF REMEDIES. Wilk Paving, Inc., bought a street-paving asphalt roller from Southworth-Milton, Inc. In large capital letters, on the front of the contract, was printed, "ADDITIONAL TERMS AND CONDITIONS ON REVERSE SIDE." A clause on the back stated that "under no circumstances shall seller . . . be held liable for any . . . consequential damages." In a hurry to close the deal, Wilk's representative did not notice this clause, and Southworth's representative did not call attention to it. Within sixty days, the roller needed the first of what became continuous repairs for mechanical problems. Wilk asked Southworth for its money back. When Southworth refused, Wilk sued Southworth, seeking the purchase price and consequential damages. Was the clause limiting damages enforceable in these circumstances? Explain. [*Wilk Paving, Inc. v. Southworth-Milton, Inc.*, 649 A.2d 778 (Vt. 1995)]

22–9. LIMITATION OF REMEDIES. Destileria Serralles, Inc., a distributor of rum and other products, operates a rum bottling plant in Puerto Rico. Figgie International, Inc., contracted with Serralles to provide bottle-labeling equipment capable of placing a clear label on a clear bottle of "Cristal" rum within a raised glass oval. The contract stated that Serralles's remedy, in case of a breach of contract, was limited to repair, replacement, or refund. When the equipment was installed in the Serralles plant, problems arose immediately. Figgie attempted to repair the equipment, but when it still did not work properly several months later, Figgie refunded the purchase price and Serralles returned the equipment. Serralles asked Figgie to pay for Serralles's losses caused by the failure of the equipment and by the delay in obtaining alternative machinery. Figgie filed a suit in a federal district court, asserting that it owed nothing to Serralles because its remedy for breach was limited to repair, replacement, or refund. Serralles responded that the limitation "fail[ed] of its essential purpose." In whose favor will the court resolve this dispute? Why? [*Figgie International, Inc. v. Destileria Serralles, Inc.*, 190 F.3d 252 (4th Cir. 1999)]

22–10. IN YOUR COURT

Rachel Hebron bought an Isuzu Trooper four-wheel-drive sports vehicle from American Isuzu Motors, Inc. Their contract required her to give notice of any defects in the car within two years of their discovery. One day, while Hebron was driving the Trooper, another vehicle pulled in front of her. She swerved to avoid hitting it, and the Trooper rolled over, causing her permanent injuries. Hebron waited, for no apparent reason, until two years and one month later to file a suit in a federal district court against American, seeking damages for alleged defects in the car. She had already disposed of the Trooper, without notifying American. American filed a motion for summary judgment based on the contract requirement of notice within two years. Assume that you are the judge in the trial court hearing this case and answer the following questions:

(a) What UCC provision, if any, applies to this dispute?

(b) Case 22.2 (*Yates v. Pitman Manufacturing, Inc.*) also involves the question of notice requirements. How are the facts and issues in that case distinguishable from the case now before your court?

(c) Will you grant American's motion for summary judgment? Why or why not?

LAW ON THE WEB

For updated links to resources available on the Web, as well as a variety of other materials, visit this text's Web site at http://wbl.westbuslaw.com.

To find information on the UCC, including the UCC provisions discussed in this chapter, refer to the Web sites listed in the *Law on the Web* in Chapter 19.

For a discussion of "Lemon Law Basics," go to Car Talk's Web site at

http://www.cartalk.cars.com/Got-A-Car/Lemon/lemon_general.html

For an example of a warranty providing for an exclusive remedy, see the "Warranty and Limited Remedy" of 3M Company, which is online at

http://www.mmm.com/promote/warranty.htm

LEGAL RESEARCH EXERCISES ON THE WEB

Go to http://wbl.westbuslaw.com, the Web site that accompanies this text. Select "Internet Applications," and then click on "Chapter 22." There you will find the following Internet research exercise that you can perform to learn more about lemon laws:

Activity 22–1: Lemon Laws

CHAPTER 23

Sales and Lease Warranties

WARRANTY IS AN AGE-OLD CONCEPT. In sales and lease law, a warranty is an assurance by one party of the existence of a fact on which the other party can rely. Article 2 (on sales) and Article 2A (on leases) of the Uniform Commercial Code (UCC) designate several types of warranties that can arise in a sales or lease contract. These warranties include warranties of title, express warranties, and implied warranties.

Because a warranty imposes a duty on the seller or lessor, a breach of warranty is a breach of the seller's or lessor's promise. If the parties have not agreed to limit or modify the remedies available to the buyer or lessee and if the seller or lessor breaches a warranty, the buyer or lessee can sue to recover damages from the seller or lessor. Under some circumstances, a breach can allow the buyer or lessee to rescind (cancel) the agreement.[1]

Recall from Chapter 6 that product-liability lawsuits include those based on claims for breach of warranty. Warranty law is also part of the broad body of consumer protection law that will be discussed in Chapter 44.

SECTION 1

Warranty of Title

Title warranty arises automatically in most sales contracts. UCC 2–312 imposes the three types of warranties of title discussed here.

GOOD TITLE

In most cases, sellers warrant that they have good and valid title to the goods sold and that transfer of the title is rightful [UCC 2–312(1)(a)]. For example, Alice steals goods from Henry and sells them to Ona, who does not know that they are stolen. If Henry discovers that Ona has the goods, then Henry has the right to reclaim them from Ona. When Alice sold Ona the goods, Alice *automatically* warranted to Ona that the title conveyed was valid and that its transfer was rightful. Because a thief has no title to stolen goods, Alice breached the warranty of title imposed by UCC 2–312(1)(a) and became liable to the buyer for appropriate damages. (See Chapter 20 for a detailed discussion of sales by nonowners.)

NO LIENS

A second warranty of title provided by the UCC protects buyers who are *unaware* of any encumbrances (claims, charges, or liabilities—usually called *liens*[2]) against goods at the time the contract is made [UCC 2–312(1)(b)]. This warranty protects buyers who, for example, unknowingly purchase goods that are subject to a creditor's security interest (see Chapter 28). If a creditor legally repossesses the goods from a buyer *who had no actual knowledge of the security interest,* the buyer can recover from the seller for breach of

---

1. Rescission restores the parties to the positions they were in before the contract was made.

2. Pronounced *leens*. Liens will be discussed in detail in Chapter 29.

warranty. (The buyer who has *actual knowledge of a security interest* has no recourse against a seller.)

To illustrate: Henderson buys a used boat from Loring for cash. A month later, Barish repossesses the boat from Henderson, having proved that she, Barish, has a valid security interest in the boat and that Loring, who has missed five payments, is in default. Henderson demands his money back from Loring. Under Section 2–312(1)(b), Henderson has legal grounds to recover, because the seller of goods warrants that the goods shall be delivered free from any security interest or other lien of which the buyer has no knowledge.

Article 2A affords similar protection for lessees. Section 2A–211(1) provides that during the term of the lease, no claim of any third party will interfere with the lessee's enjoyment of the leasehold interest.

NO INFRINGEMENTS

A merchant seller is also deemed to warrant that the goods delivered are free from any copyright, trademark, or patent claims of a third person[3] [UCC 2–312(3), 2A–211(2)]. If this warranty is breached and the buyer is sued by the party holding copyright, trademark, or patent rights in the goods, the buyer *must notify the seller* of litigation within a reasonable time to enable the seller to decide whether to defend the lawsuit. If the seller states in writing that he or she has decided to defend and agrees to bear all expenses, including that of an adverse judgment, then the buyer must let the seller undertake litigation; otherwise, the buyer loses all rights against the seller if any infringement liability is established [UCC 2–607(3)(b), 2–607(5)(b)].

Article 2A provides for the same notice of litigation in situations that involve leases rather than sales [UCC 2A–516(3)(b), 2A–516(4)(b)]. There is an exception for leases made by individual consumers for personal, family, or household purposes. A consumer who fails to notify the lessor within a reasonable time does not lose his or her remedy against the lessor for any liability established in the litigation [UCC 2A–516(3)(b)].

---

3. Recall from Chapter 19 that a merchant is defined in UCC 2–104(1) as a person who deals in goods of the kind involved in the sales contract or who, by occupation, presents himself or herself as having knowledge or skill peculiar to the goods involved in the transaction.

DISCLAIMER OF TITLE WARRANTY

In an ordinary sales transaction, the title warranty can be disclaimed or modified only by *specific language* in a contract. For example, sellers may assert that they are transferring only such rights, title, and interest as they have in the goods. In a lease transaction, the disclaimer must "be specific, be by a writing, and be conspicuous" [UCC 2A–214(4)].

In certain cases, the circumstances surrounding the sale are sufficient to indicate clearly to a buyer that no assurances as to title are being made. The classic example is a sheriff's sale, when buyers know that the goods have been seized to satisfy debts, and the sheriff cannot guarantee title [UCC 2–312(2)].

SECTION 2

Express Warranties

A seller or lessor can create an **express warranty** by making representations concerning the quality, condition, description, or performance potential of the goods. Under UCC 2–313 and 2A–210, express warranties arise when a seller or lessor indicates any of the following:

1. That the goods conform to any *affirmation or promise* of fact that the seller or lessor makes to the buyer or lessee about the goods. Such affirmations or promises are usually made during the bargaining process. Statements such as "these drill bits will *easily* penetrate stainless steel—and without dulling" are express warranties.

2. That the goods conform to any *description* of them. For example, a label that reads "Crate contains one 150-horsepower diesel engine" or a contract that calls for the delivery of a "wool coat" creates an express warranty that the content of the goods sold conforms to the description.

3. That the goods conform to any *sample or model* of the goods shown to the buyer or lessee.

Express warranties can be found in a seller's or lessor's advertisement, brochure, or promotional materials, in addition to being made orally or in an express warranty provision in a sales or lease contract. To create an express warranty, a seller or lessor does not have to use formal words such as *warrant* or *guarantee*. It is only necessary that a reasonable buyer or lessee would regard the representation as part of the basis of the bargain [UCC 2–313(2), 2A–210(2)].

BASIS OF THE BARGAIN

The UCC requires that for an express warranty to be created, the affirmation, promise, description, or sample must become part of the "basis of the bargain" [UCC 2–313(1), 2A–210(1)]. Just what constitutes the basis of the bargain is hard to say. The UCC does not define the concept, and it is a question of fact in each case whether a representation was made at such a time and in such a way that it induced the buyer or lessee to enter into the contract. Therefore, if an express warranty is not intended, the marketing agent or salesperson should not promise too much. In the following case, the issue was whether statements made by the sellers of a used car to the buyer were part of the basis of the bargain for the purchase of the car.

CASE 23.1   Felley v. Singleton

Appellate Court
of Illinois,
Second District, 1999.
302 Ill.App.3d 248,
705 N.E.2d 930,
235 Ill.Dec. 747.
http://www.state.il.us/
court[a]

BACKGROUND AND FACTS   *Brian Felley went to the home of Thomas and Cheryl Singleton to look at a used car that the Singletons offered for sale. The car was a 1991 Ford Taurus with about 126,000 miles on it. They discussed the car's transmission, tires, brakes, and maintenance. The Singletons told Felley that they had experienced no brake problems and that, except for a bad or missing grommet, the car was in good mechanical condition. After test-driving the car, Felley bought it for $5,800. Two days later, Felley noticed a problem with the clutch. Over the next few days, the clutch problem worsened to the point where Felley was unable to shift the gears, and he paid $942.76 for its repair. The car developed serious brake problems within the same month. Felley paid $1,400.27 for brake work. Robert Hanover, a technician at Car X Muffler, later said that because problems such as those with the car's clutch and brakes take considerable time to develop, they probably existed when Felley bought the car. Felley filed a suit in an Illinois state court against the Singletons, asserting that their telling him that the car was in good mechanical condition was a primary consideration in his decision to buy it. The court concluded that the Singletons' statements were affirmations of fact that constituted an express warranty and became part of the basis of the bargain for Felley's purchase of the car. The Singletons appealed to a state intermediate appellate court.*

IN THE LANGUAGE OF THE COURT

Presiding Justice BOWMAN delivered the opinion of the court:
　　*　　*　　*　　*
　　In defendants' view, their statements to plaintiff cannot fairly be viewed as entering into the bargain. Defendants assert that they are not automobile dealers or mechanics with specialized knowledge of the brake and clutch systems of the car and therefore their statements were merely expressions of a vendor's opinion that did not constitute an express warranty.
　　*　　*　　*　　*

　　*　　*　　* *[A]ffirmations of fact made during a bargaining process regarding the sale of goods are presumed to be part of the basis of the bargain unless clear affirmative proof to the contrary is shown;* *　　*　　* a showing of reliance on the affirmations by the buyer is not necessary for the creation of an express warranty; and *　　*　　* the seller has the burden to establish by clear affirmative proof that the affirmations did not become part of the basis of the bargain. *　　*　　* [T]he seller may be held accountable for breach of warranty where affirmations are a basis of the bargain and the goods fail to conform to the affirmations. [Emphasis added.]
　　*　　*　　* [I]n the context of a used car sale, representations by the seller such as the car is "in good mechanical condition" are presumed to be affirmations of fact that become part of the basis of the bargain. Because they are presumed to be part of the basis of the bargain, such representations constitute express warranties, regardless of the buyer's reliance on them, unless the seller shows by clear affirmative proof that the representations did not become part of the basis of the bargain.

a. This Web site is maintained by the Office of the Reporter of Decisions of the Illinois Judicial System. In the "Appellate Court" section, in the "Second District Opinions" row, click on "1999." When that page opens, in the "January" box, click on the case name to read the opinion.

In this case, it is undisputed that plaintiff asked defendants about the car's mechanical condition and that defendants responded that the car was in good mechanical condition. Under the foregoing principles, defendants' representations are presumed to be affirmations of fact that became a part of the basis of the bargain. Nothing in the record indicates that defendants made a clear and affirmative showing that their representations did not become part of the basis of the bargain. Based on this record, we cannot say that the trial court's findings that defendants' representations were affirmations of fact that became a part of the basis of the bargain and created an express warranty were against the manifest weight of the evidence.

DECISION AND REMEDY   *The state intermediate appellate court affirmed the decision of the lower court. The Singletons' statements to Felley were afffirmations of fact that became part of the basis of the bargain and created an express warranty. Because of the Singletons' breach of that warranty, they were ordered to pay damages in the amount of Felley's paid repair bills.*

STATEMENTS OF OPINION AND VALUE

If the seller or lessor merely makes a statement that relates to the value or worth of the goods, or makes a statement of opinion or recommendation about the goods, the seller or lessor is not creating an express warranty [UCC 2–313(2), 2A–210(2)].

For example, a seller claims that "this is the best used car to come along in years; it has four new tires and a 150-horsepower engine just rebuilt this year." The seller has made several *affirmations of fact* that can create a warranty: the automobile has an engine; it has a 150-horsepower engine; the engine was rebuilt this year; there are four tires on the automobile; and the tires are new. The seller's *opinion* that the vehicle is "the best used car to come along in years," however, is known as "puffing" and creates no warranty. (*Puffing* is an expression of opinion by a seller or lessor that is not made as a representation of fact.) A statement relating to the value of the goods, such as "it's worth a fortune" or "anywhere else you'd pay $10,000 for it," usually does not create a warranty.

Although the ordinary seller or lessor can give an opinion that is not a warranty, if the seller or lessor is an expert and gives an opinion as an expert to a layperson, then a warranty may be created. For example, Saul is an art dealer and an expert in seventeenth-century paintings. If Saul states to Lauren, a purchaser, that in his opinion a particular painting is a Rembrandt, Saul has warranted the accuracy of his opinion.

It is not always easy to determine what constitutes an express warranty and what constitutes puffing. The reasonableness of the buyer's or lessee's reliance appears to be the controlling criterion in many cases. For example, a salesperson's statements that a ladder will "never break" and will "last a lifetime" are so clearly improbable that no reasonable buyer should rely on them. Additionally, the context within which a statement is made might be relevant in determining the reasonableness of a buyer's or lessee's reliance. For example, a reasonable person is more likely to rely on a written statement made in an advertisement than on a statement made orally by a salesperson. The following case illustrates a court's consideration of phrases that were claimed to be express warranties.

CASE 23.2   Martin Rispens & Son v. Hall Farms, Inc.

Supreme Court of Indiana, 1993.
621 N.E.2d 1078.

COMPANY PROFILE   *Among companies that breed and produce hybrid vegetable seeds, Petoseed Company is considered the leader in this country and among the top five in the world. Petoseed has developed a cornucopia of disease-resistant hybrids, including tomato varieties resistant to five major diseases and cucumber hybrids resistant to four major viruses. In the early 1990s, Petoseed established Peto Europe to oversee a network of seed distribution and test stations in Europe, the Middle East, and Africa. Petoseed also has operations in Taiwan, Thailand, Japan, and Indonesia. Currently, Petoseed is marketing seeds or developing new plant varieties in more than one hundred countries.*

BACKGROUND AND FACTS *Hall Farms, Inc., in Knox County, Indiana, produces a variety of crops, including watermelons. In August 1988, Hall Farms ordered forty pounds of the Prince Charles variety of watermelon seeds from Martin Rispens & Son. At the top of Rispens's purchase order was the phrase "strictly high grade seeds." Rispens obtained the seeds from Petoseed and delivered them in February 1989, packaged in sealed one-pound cans. The labels on the cans stated that they contained "top quality seeds." Hall Farms stored the unopened cans until early April, when the seeds were germinated in two greenhouses. On April 25, Mark Hall, the owner of Hall Farms, noted that about fifteen seedlings were spotted with small yellow lesions. The lesions did not affect the plants' growth, however, and no plants died. The seedlings were transplanted to the fields in May. Hall monitored the plants every three or four days for the next several weeks. In early July, Hall spotted a watermelon blemished by a small purple blotch. By mid-July, the blotch had spread to other plants, and by harvest time ten days later, a significant portion of the watermelon crop had been ruined. Hall Farms sued Rispens and Petoseed, arguing, in part, that the phrases on Rispens's purchase order and Petoseed's cans constituted express warranties, which they breached. When Petoseed and Rispens were granted a summary judgment, Hall Farms appealed.*

IN THE LANGUAGE OF THE COURT

KRAHULIK, Justice.

*   *   *   *

*   *   * The label on the Petoseed cans *   *   * is the sole basis for Hall Farms' express warranty claims against Petoseed.

*   *   * The phrase ["top quality seeds"] contains no definitive statement as to how the product is warranted or any assertion of fact concerning the product, but is merely the opinion of Petoseed that the seeds are "top quality." The [lower court] correctly concluded that the statement "top quality seeds" is a classic example of puffery.

*   *   *   *

Hall Farms also argues that the phrase, "strictly high grade seeds," which appeared at the top of the purchase order, created an express warranty. The [lower court] held that this language may have constituted an express warranty, but Hall Farms failed to meet its burden of proof by presenting evidence about the meaning of this phrase, so Rispens was entitled to summary judgment. Whether Rispens gave an express warranty which was breached encompasses a question of fact: in the seed industry, does "high grade" connote some promise that the seeds will be free from disease or is it mere puffing[?] However, it is Rispens' burden *   *   * to show the absence of material fact. Having failed to do so, Rispens is not entitled to summary judgment on the express warranty claim.

DECISION AND REMEDY

On the express warranty claims of Hall Farms, the court upheld part of the summary judgment ("top quality" was not an express warranty), reversed part ("high grade" could be an express warranty in the seed industry, and Rispens failed to show that it was not or that, if it was, the seeds had met that standard), and remanded the case for further proceedings in accordance with its opinion.

SECTION 3

Implied Warranties

An **implied warranty** is one that *the law derives* by inference from the nature of the transaction or the relative situations or circumstances of the parties. Under the UCC, merchants impliedly warrant that the goods they sell or lease are merchantable and, in certain circumstances, fit for a particular purpose. In addition, an implied warranty may arise from a course of dealing or usage of trade. We examine these three types of implied warranties in the following subsections.

IMPLIED WARRANTY OF MERCHANTABILITY

An **implied warranty of merchantability** automatically arises in every sale or lease of goods made *by a merchant* who deals in goods of the kind sold or leased [UCC 2–314, 2A–212]. Thus, a merchant who is in the business of selling ski equipment makes an implied warranty of merchantability every time the merchant sells a pair of skis, but a neighbor selling his or her skis at a garage sale does not.

Merchantable Goods.   To be *merchantable*, goods must be "reasonably fit for the ordinary purposes for which such goods are used." They must be of at least average, fair, or medium-grade quality. The quality must be comparable to quality that will pass without objection in the trade or market for goods of the same description. To be merchantable, the goods must also be adequately packaged and labeled as provided by the agreement, and they must conform to the promises or affirmations of fact made on the container or label, if any.

An implied warranty of merchantability also imposes on the merchant liability for the safe performance of the product. It makes no difference whether the merchant knew of or could have discovered a defect that makes the product unsafe—he or she is liable in either situation. For example, Kaplan buys an ax at Enrique's Hardware Store. No express warranties are made. The first time she chops wood with it, the ax handle breaks, and she is injured. She immediately notifies Enrique. Examination shows that the wood in the handle was rotten but that the rottenness could

not have been noticed by either Enrique or Kaplan. Nonetheless, Kaplan notifies Enrique that she will hold him responsible for her injuries. Enrique is responsible, because a merchant seller of goods warrants that the goods he or she sells are fit for the ordinary purposes for which such goods are used. This ax was obviously not fit for those purposes.

Of course, merchants are not absolute insurers against *all* accidents arising in connection with the goods. For example, a bar of soap is not unmerchantable merely because a user could slip and fall by stepping on it.

Merchantable Food.   The UCC recognizes the serving of food or drink to be consumed on or off the premises as a sale of goods subject to the implied warranty of merchantability [UCC 2–314(1)]. "Merchantable" food is food that is fit to eat on the basis of consumer expectations. For example, the courts assume that consumers should reasonably expect to find on occasion bones in fish fillets, cherry pits in cherry pie, a nutshell in a package of shelled nuts, and so on—because such substances are natural incidents of the food. In contrast, consumers would not reasonably expect to find an inchworm in a can of peas or a piece of glass in a soft drink—because these substances are not natural to the food product.[4] In the following classic case, the court had to determine whether one should reasonably expect to find a fish bone in fish chowder.

---

4. See, for example, *Mexicali Rose v. Superior Court*, 1 Cal.4th 617, 4 Cal.Rptr.2d 145, 822 P.2d 1292 (1992).

CASE 23.3   Webster v. Blue Ship Tea Room, Inc.

Supreme Judicial Court
of Massachusetts, 1964.
347 Mass. 421,
198 N.E.2d 309.

BACKGROUND AND FACTS   *Blue Ship Tea Room, Inc., was located in Boston in an old building overlooking the ocean. Webster, who had been born and raised in New England, went to the restaurant and ordered fish chowder. The chowder was milky in color. After three or four spoonfuls, she felt something lodged in her throat. As a result, she underwent two esophagoscopies; in the second esophagoscopy, a fish bone was found and removed. Webster filed suit against the restaurant in a Massachusetts state court for breach of the implied warranty of merchantability. The jury rendered a verdict for Webster, and the restaurant appealed to the state's highest court.*

REARDON, Justice.

[The plaintiff] ordered a cup of fish chowder. Presently, there was set before her "a small bowl of fish chowder." *   *   * After 3 or 4 [spoonfuls] she was aware that something had lodged in her throat because she "couldn't swallow and couldn't clear her throat by gulping and she could feel it." This misadventure led to two esophagoscopies

IN THE LANGUAGE OF THE COURT

at the Massachusetts General Hospital, in the second of which, on April 27, 1959, a fish bone was found and removed. The sequence of events produced injury to the plaintiff which was not insubstantial.

We must decide whether a fish bone lurking in a fish chowder, about the ingredients of which there is no other complaint, constitutes a breach of implied warranty under applicable provisions of the Uniform Commercial Code * * * . As the judge put it in his charge [jury instruction], "Was the fish chowder fit to be eaten and wholesome? * * * [N]obody is claiming that the fish itself wasn't wholesome. * * * But the bone of contention here—I don't mean that for a pun—but was this fish bone a foreign substance that made the fish chowder unwholesome or not fit to be eaten?"
* * * * *

[We think that it] is not too much to say that a person sitting down in New England to consume a good New England fish chowder embarks on a gustatory [taste-related] adventure which may entail the removal of some fish bones from his bowl as he proceeds. We are not inclined to tamper with age old recipes by any amendment reflecting the plaintiff's view of the effect of the Uniform Commercial Code upon them. We are aware of the heavy body of case law involving foreign substances in food, but we sense a strong distinction between them and those relative to unwholesomeness of the food itself, e.g., tainted mackerel, and a fish bone in a fish chowder. * * * [W]e consider that the joys of life in New England include the ready availability of fresh fish chowder. We should be prepared to cope with the hazards of fish bones, the occasional presence of which in chowders is, it seems to us, to be anticipated, and which, in the light of a hallowed tradition, do not impair their fitness or merchantability.

DECISION AND REMEDY   *The Supreme Judicial Court of Massachusetts "sympathized with a plaintiff who has suffered a peculiarly New England injury" but entered a judgment for the defendant, Blue Ship Tea Room. A fish bone in fish chowder is not a breach of the implied warranty of merchantability.*

IMPLIED WARRANTY OF FITNESS FOR A PARTICULAR PURPOSE

The **implied warranty of fitness for a particular purpose** arises when any *seller or lessor* (merchant or nonmerchant) knows the particular purpose for which a buyer or lessee will use the goods *and* knows that the buyer or lessee is relying on the skill and judgment of the seller or lessor to select suitable goods [UCC 2–315, 2A–213].

A "particular purpose" of the buyer or lessee differs from the "ordinary purpose for which goods are used" (merchantability). Goods can be merchantable but unfit for a particular purpose. For example, suppose that you need a gallon of paint to match the color of your living room walls—a light shade somewhere between coral and peach. You take a sample to your local hardware store and request a gallon of paint of that color. Instead, you are given a gallon of bright blue paint. Here, the salesperson has not breached any warranty of implied merchantability—the bright blue paint is of high quality and suitable for interior

walls—but he or she has breached an implied warranty of fitness for a particular purpose.

A seller or lessor does not need to have actual knowledge of the buyer's or lessee's particular purpose. It is sufficient if a seller or lessor "has reason to know" the purpose. The buyer or lessee, however, must have *relied* on the skill or judgment of the seller or lessor in selecting or furnishing suitable goods for an implied warranty to be created.

For example, Bloomberg leases a computer from Future Tech, a lessor of technical business equipment. Bloomberg tells the clerk that she wants a computer that will run a complicated new engineering graphics program at a realistic speed. Future Tech leases Bloomberg an Architex One computer with a CPU speed of only 233 megahertz, even though a speed of at least 500 megahertz would be required to run Bloomberg's graphics program at a "realistic speed." Bloomberg, after realizing that it takes her forever to run her program, wants her money back. Here, because Future Tech has breached the implied warranty of fitness for a particular purpose,

Bloomberg normally will be able to recover. The clerk knew specifically that Bloomberg wanted a computer with enough speed to run certain software. Furthermore, Bloomberg relied on the clerk to furnish a computer that would fulfill this purpose. Because Future Tech did not do so, the warranty was breached.

IMPLIED WARRANTY ARISING FROM COURSE OF DEALING OR TRADE USAGE

Implied warranties can also arise (or be excluded or modified) as a result of course of dealing, course of performance, or usage of trade [UCC 2–314(3), 2A–212(3)]. In the absence of evidence to the contrary, when both parties to a sales or lease contract have knowledge of a well-recognized trade custom, the courts will infer that both parties intended for that custom to apply to their contract. For example, if it is an industry-wide custom to lubricate a new car before it is delivered and a dealer fails to do so, the dealer can be held liable to a buyer for damages resulting from the breach of an implied warranty. (This, of course, would also be negligence on the part of the dealer.)

SECTION 4

Overlapping Warranties

Sometimes two or more warranties are made in a single transaction. An implied warranty of merchantability, an implied warranty of fitness for a particular purpose, or both, can exist in addition to an express warranty. For example, when a sales contract for a new car states that "this car engine is warranted to be free from defects for 36,000 miles or thirty-six months, whichever occurs first," there is an express warranty against all defects and an implied warranty that the car will be fit for normal use.

The rule under the UCC is that express and implied warranties are construed as *cumulative* if they are consistent with one another [UCC 2–317, 2A–215]. If the warranties are *inconsistent*, the courts usually hold as follows:

1. *Express* warranties displace inconsistent *implied* warranties, except implied warranties of fitness for a particular purpose.
2. Samples take precedence over inconsistent general descriptions.
3. Technical specifications displace inconsistent samples or general descriptions.

In the example described earlier, suppose that when Bloomberg leases the computer at Future Tech, the contract contains an express warranty concerning the speed of the CPU and the application programs that the computer is capable of running. Bloomberg does not realize that the speed expressly warranted in the contract is insufficient for her needs. When she tries to run the software with some engineering plans, the computer slows to a crawl. Bloomberg claims that Future Tech has breached the implied warranty of fitness for a particular purpose. Here, although the express warranty would take precedence over any implied warranty of merchantability, it would not take precedence over an implied warranty of fitness for a particular purpose. Bloomberg therefore has a good claim for the breach of implied warranty of fitness for a particular purpose, because she made it clear that she was leasing the computer to perform certain tasks.

SECTION 5

Warranties and Third Parties

One of the general principles of contract law is that a person who is not one of the parties to a contract has no rights under the contract. As discussed earlier in this text, the connection that exists between the contracting parties is called *privity of contract*. It was established at common law that privity must exist between a plaintiff and a defendant for any action based on a contract to be maintained. Notable exceptions to the rule of privity include product liability (see Chapter 6) and assignments and third party beneficiary contracts (see Chapter 16).

For example, I purchase a ham from retailer Bollinger. I invite you to my house that evening. I prepare the ham properly. You are served first, because you are my guest, and you become severely ill because the ham is spoiled. Can you sue retailer Bollinger for breach of the implied warranty of merchantability? Because warranty is based on a contract for the sale of goods, under the common law you would normally have warranty rights only if you were a party to the purchase of the ham. Therefore, the warranty would extend only to me, the purchaser.

There is sharp disagreement among the states as to how far warranty liability should extend, however. In view of this disagreement, the UCC offers three alternatives for liability to third parties [UCC 2–318, 2A–216]. All three alternatives are intended to eliminate the privity requirement with respect to certain enumerated types of injuries (personal versus property) for certain beneficiaries (for example, household members or bystanders).[5]

S E C T I O N   6

Warranty Disclaimers

Because each type of warranty is created in a special way, the manner in which warranties can be disclaimed or qualified by a seller or lessor varies with the type of warranty.

EXPRESS WARRANTIES

As already stated, any affirmation of fact or promise, description of the goods, or use of samples or models by a seller or lessor creates an express warranty. Obviously, then, express warranties can be excluded if the seller or lessor carefully refrains from making any promise or affirmation of fact relating to the goods, describing the goods, or using a sample or model.

The UCC does permit express warranties to be negated or limited by specific and unambiguous language, provided that this is done in a manner that protects the buyer or lessee from surprise. Therefore, a written disclaimer in language that is clear and conspicuous, and called to a buyer's or lessee's attention, could negate all oral express warranties not included in the written sales or lease contract [UCC 2–316(1), 2A–214(1)]. This allows the seller or lessor to avoid false allegations that oral warranties were made, and it ensures that only representations made by properly authorized individuals are included in the bargain.

Note, however, that a buyer or lessee must be made aware of any warranty disclaimers or modifications *at the time the contract is formed.* In other words, any oral or written warranties—or disclaimers—made during the bargaining process cannot be modified at

a later time by the seller or lessor without the consent of the buyer or lessee.

IMPLIED WARRANTIES

Generally speaking, unless circumstances indicate otherwise, the implied warranties of merchantability and fitness are disclaimed by the expressions "as is," "with all faults," and other similar expressions that in common understanding for *both* parties call the buyer's or lessee's attention to the fact that there are no implied warranties [UCC 2–316(3)(a), 2A–214(3)(a)].

The UCC also permits a seller or lessor to specifically disclaim an implied warranty either of fitness or of merchantability [UCC 2–316(2), 2A–214(2)]. To disclaim an implied warranty of fitness for a particular purpose, the disclaimer must be in writing and be conspicuous. The word *fitness* does not have to be mentioned in the writing; it is sufficient if, for example, the disclaimer states, "THERE ARE NO WARRANTIES THAT EXTEND BEYOND THE DESCRIPTION ON THE FACE HEREOF."

A merchantability disclaimer must be more specific; it must mention *merchantability.* It need not be written; but if it is, the writing must be conspicuous [UCC 2–316(2), 2A–214(4)]. According to UCC 1–201(10),

A term or clause is conspicuous when it is so written that a reasonable person against whom it is to operate ought to have noticed it. A printed heading in capitals . . . is conspicuous. Language in the body of a form is conspicuous if it is in larger or other contrasting type or color.

For example, Forbes, a merchant, sells Maves a particular lawn mower selected by Forbes with the characteristics clearly requested by Maves. At the time of the sale, Forbes orally tells Maves that he does not warrant the merchantability of the mower, as it is last year's model. If the mower proves to be defective and does not work, Maves can hold Forbes liable for breach of the warranty of fitness for a particular purpose but not for breach of the warranty of merchantability. Forbes's oral disclaimer mentioning the word *merchantability* is a proper disclaimer. For Forbes to have disclaimed the implied warranty of fitness for a particular purpose, however, a conspicuous writing would have been required. Because he made no written disclaimer, Forbes can still be held liable.

The conspicuousness of a disclaimer of implied warranties was at issue in the following case.

---

5. For a case illustrating the alternative adopted by North Carolina, see *Crews v. W. A. Brown & Son, Inc.,* 106 N.C.App. 324, 416 S.E.2d 924 (1992). In this case, a teenaged volunteer working on a church's premises sustained severe frostbite while locked in a walk-in freezer with a malfunctioning door-release mechanism. She was unable to recover from the manufacturer of the freezer because she was neither the buyer nor a "family member" of the church.

CASE 23.4   Borden, Inc. v. Advent Ink Co.

Superior Court of
Pennsylvania, 1997.
701 A.2d 255.

BACKGROUND AND FACTS *Borden, Inc., sold Aquablak, a dispersion ingredient used in water-based inks, to Advent Ink Company. On the front of the sales invoice, in red capital letters, was the phrase "SEE REVERSE SIDE." On the reverse side was a list of nineteen conditions of sale, the first of which was a disclaimer of warranties, including the implied warranty of merchantability. On the Aquablak label, beneath Borden's name, phone number, advertising slogan, and other brief statements, was another disclaimer of all warranties. Advent used the Aquablak to make ink that caused problems in the printing equipment of one of its customers. Advent lost the customer's account, which cost the firm over $1 million in profits and caused it to go out of business. When Advent did not pay for the Aquablak, Borden filed a suit in a Pennsylvania state court against Advent to recover the amount. Advent counterclaimed that the Aquablak had not complied with the implied warranties of merchantability and fitness for a particular purpose. Against this claim, Borden filed a motion for summary judgment, pointing to its disclaimers. Advent responded that the disclaimers were not sufficiently conspicuous. The court granted the motion in favor of Borden. Advent appealed.*

IN THE LANGUAGE OF THE COURT

SAYLOR, Judge:

*   *   *   *   *

*   *   * [T]he print on the reverse side of the invoice is no larger than one-sixteenth inch in height. All of the type appears to be bold-faced. Although the disclaimer of warranties is the first of nineteen numbered paragraphs, *   *   * nevertheless there is nothing to indicate that the first paragraph is any more significant than, for example, the seventh ("WEIGHTS") *   *   * .

Even more important, the reference on the front of the invoice to the terms on the reverse side is even less informative *   *   * . The reference *   *   * simply states "SEE REVERSE SIDE"; there is absolutely no indication that among the terms on the reverse side is an exclusion of warranties, including *   *   * the implied warranty of merchantability *   *   * *so commonly taken for granted that its exclusion from a contract is recognized as a matter threatening surprise* *   *   * . [Emphasis added.]

*   *   *   *   *

*   *   * Finally, while the heading "DISCLAIMER" and the disclaimer itself are printed in capitals, so too are the preceding lines of text, and they are printed in larger sizes of type. Taking into account all of these factors, we conclude that this disclaimer, like that on the invoice, is inconspicuous and therefore ineffective.

DECISION AND REMEDY

The Superior Court of Pennsylvania held that the disclaimers were so inconspicuous as to be ineffective. The court affirmed the lower court's decision on other grounds, however.

BUYER'S OR LESSEE'S EXAMINATION OF THE GOODS

If a buyer or lessee actually examines the goods (or a sample or model) as fully as desired before entering into a contract, or, if the buyer or lessee refuses to examine the goods on the seller's or lessor's demand that he or she do so, *there is no implied warranty with respect to defects that a reasonable examination would* reveal or defects that are found on examination [UCC 2–316(3)(b), 2A–214(2)(b)].

For example, suppose that Joplin buys an ax at Gershwin's Hardware Store. No express warranties are made. Joplin, even after Gershwin asks, refuses to inspect the ax before buying it. Had she done so, she would have noticed that the handle of the ax was obviously cracked. If she is later injured by the defective ax, she normally will not be able to hold Gershwin liable for breach of the warranty of merchantability, because she would have spotted the defect during an inspection.

UNCONSCIONABILITY

The UCC sections dealing with warranty disclaimers do not refer specifically to unconscionability as a factor. Ultimately, however, the courts will test warranty disclaimers with reference to the UCC's unconscionability standards [UCC 2–302, 2A–108]. Such things as lack of bargaining position, "take-it-or-leave-it" choices, and a buyer's or lessee's failure to understand or know of a warranty disclaimer will become relevant to the issue of unconscionability.

SECTION 7

Statute of Limitations

An action for breach of contract under the UCC must be commenced *within four years after the cause of action accrues*—that is, within four years after the breach occurs. In addition to filing suit within the four-year period, the aggrieved party usually must notify the breaching party of the breach within a reasonable time, or the aggrieved party is barred from pursuing any remedy [UCC 2–607(3)(a), 2A–516(3)]. By agreement in the contract, the parties can reduce this period to not less than one year, but they *cannot* extend it beyond four years [UCC 2–725(1), 2A–506(1)].

The statute of limitations begins to run when a cause of action accrues (becomes an enforceable right). An action for breach of warranty accrues when the seller or lessor *tenders* delivery. This is the rule even if the aggrieved party is unaware that the cause of action has accrued [UCC 2–725(2), 2A–506(2)]. Remember that tender of delivery takes place under a shipment contract on delivery of the goods to the carrier and under a destination contract on tender of the goods at the specified destination delivery location. The statute of limitations in these cases can have a tremendous impact if the goods purchased are going to be stored primarily for future use. To avoid this effect, the UCC provides that when a warranty explicitly extends to future performance and discovery of its breach must await the time of that performance, the statute of limitations also begins to run at that time [UCC 2–725(2)].

For example, Hoover purchases a central air-conditioning unit for his restaurant. The unit is warranted specifically to keep the temperature below a certain level during the summer months. The unit is installed in the winter, but when summer comes, the restaurant does not stay cool. Because discovery of the warranty's breach is, of necessity, made in the summer and not when the unit is delivered in the winter, the statute of limitations does not begin to run until the summer.

When a buyer or seller brings suit on a legal theory unrelated to the UCC, the limitations periods specified above do not apply, even though the claim relates to goods. For example, Cane buys tires for his automobile. The tires prove to have an inherently dangerous defect. Four years and one month after purchasing the tires, Cane loses control of the car because of a defective tire and injures several passengers, as well as himself. Cane brings a suit against the tire manufacturer based on strict liability in tort (see Chapter 6). In this situation, the suit will not be governed by the UCC's statute of limitations but rather by the state's statute of limitations governing tort cases.

SECTION 8

Magnuson-Moss Warranty Act

The Magnuson-Moss Warranty Act of 1975[6] was designed to prevent deception in warranties by making them easier to understand. The act is enforced primarily by the Federal Trade Commission (FTC). Additionally, the attorney general or a consumer who has been injured can enforce the act if informal procedures for settling disputes prove to be ineffective. The act modifies UCC warranty rules to some extent when *consumer* transactions are involved. The UCC, however, remains the primary codification of warranty rules for industrial and commercial transactions.

No seller is *required* to give a written warranty for consumer goods sold under the Magnuson-Moss Warranty Act. If a seller chooses to make an express written warranty, however, and the cost of the consumer goods is more than $10, the warranty must be labeled as either "full" or "limited." In addition, if the cost of the goods is more than $15, by FTC regulation, the warrantor must make certain disclosures fully and conspicuously in a single document in "readily understood language." This disclosure states the names and addresses of the warrantor(s), what specifically is warranted, procedures for enforcement

---

6. 15 U.S.C. Sections 2301–2312.

of the warranty, any limitations on warranty relief, and that the buyer has legal rights.

FULL WARRANTY

Although a *full warranty* may not cover every aspect of the consumer product sold, what it covers ensures some type of consumer satisfaction in the event that the product is defective. A full warranty requires free repair or replacement of any defective part; if the product cannot be repaired within a reasonable time, the consumer has the choice of either a refund or a replacement without charge. The full warranty frequently does not have a time limit on it. Any limitation on consequential damages must be *conspicuously* stated. Additionally, the warrantor need not perform warranty services if the problem with the product was caused by damage to the product or unreasonable use by the consumer.

LIMITED WARRANTY

A *limited warranty* arises when the written warranty fails to meet one of the minimum requirements of a

full warranty. The fact that only a limited warranty is being given must be conspicuously designated. If it is only a time limitation that distinguishes a limited warranty from a full warranty, the Magnuson-Moss Warranty Act allows the warrantor to identify the warranty as a full warranty by such language as "full twelve-month warranty."

IMPLIED WARRANTIES

Implied warranties are not covered under the Magnuson-Moss Warranty Act; they continue to be created according to UCC provisions. When an express warranty is made, it may not, under the Magnuson-Moss Warranty Act, include disclaimers or modifications of the implied warranties of merchantability and fitness for a particular purpose. A warrantor can impose a time limit on the duration of an implied warranty, but it has to correspond to the duration of the express warranty.[7]

_____

7. This time limit must, of course, be reasonable, conscionable, and set forth in clear and conspicuous language on the face of the warranty.

CONCEPT SUMMARY 23.1   WARRANTIES

CONCEPT	DESCRIPTION
Warranties of Title	The UCC provides for the following warranties of title [UCC 2–312, 2A–211]: 1. *Good title*—A seller warrants that he or she has the right to pass good and rightful title to the goods. 2. *No liens*—A seller warrants that the goods sold are free of any encumbrances (claims, charges, or liabilities—usually called *liens*). A lessor warrants that the lessee will not be disturbed in his or her possession of the goods by the claims of a third party. 3. *No infringements*—A merchant seller warrants that the goods are free of infringement claims (claims that a patent, trademark, or copyright has been infringed) by third parties. Lessors make similar warranties.

Express Warranties	1. *Under the UCC*—An express warranty arises under the UCC when a seller or lessor indicates any of the following as part of the sale or bargain [UCC 2–313, 2A–210]:
	  a. An affirmation or promise of fact.
	  b. A description of the goods.
	  c. A sample or model shown as conforming to the contract goods.
	2. *Under the Magnuson-Moss Warranty Act*—Express written warranties covering consumer goods priced at more than $10, *if made,* must be labeled as one of the following:

CONCEPT SUMMARY 23.1 — WARRANTIES (*continued*)

CONCEPT	DESCRIPTION
Express Warranties (continued)	a. Full warranty—Free repair or replacement of defective parts; refund or replacement for goods if they cannot be repaired in a reasonable time. b. Limited warranty—When less than a full warranty is being offered.
Implied Warranty of Merchantability	When a seller or lessor is a merchant who deals in goods of the kind sold or leased, the seller or lessor warrants that the goods sold or leased are properly packaged and labeled, are of proper quality, and are reasonably fit for the ordinary purposes for which such goods are used [UCC 2–314, 2A–212].
Implied Warranty of Fitness for a Particular Purpose	An implied warranty of fitness for a particular purpose arises when the buyer's or lessee's purpose or use is known by the seller or lessor, and the buyer or lessee purchases or leases the goods in reliance on the seller's or lessor's selection [UCC 2–315, 2A–213].
Implied Warranty Arising from Course of Dealing, Course of Performance, or Trade Usage	Other implied warranties can arise as a result of course of dealing, course of performance, or usage of trade [UCC 2–314(3), 2A–212(3)].

SECTION 9

Warranties under the CISG

The United Nations Convention on Contracts for the International Sale of Goods (CISG) does not use the term *warranty* in regard to the rights and obligations of parties to international sales contracts. Instead, the CISG prefers to phrase the concept of warranty in terms of "conformity of the goods." Although the CISG uses different language, it effectively provides for warranty protection similar to that available under the UCC. Article 35 of the CISG states that the seller "must deliver goods which are of the quantity, quality and description required by the contract and which are contained or packaged in the manner required by the contract." Other provisions of Article 35 are, in effect, equivalent to the UCC express and implied warranties.

TERMS AND CONCEPTS TO REVIEW

express warranty 398	implied warranty of fitness for a particular purpose 403	implied warranty of merchantability 402
implied warranty 401		

QUESTIONS AND CASE PROBLEMS

23–1. EXPRESS WARRANTIES. Shillitani contracted to purchase a used car from Johnson's Quality Used Cars. During the oral negotiations for the sale, Johnson told Shillitani that this used car was in "A-1 condition" and would get sixteen miles to the gallon. Shillitani asked if the car used a lot of oil. Johnson replied that he had personally checked the car, and in his opinion the car did not use a lot of oil. Since delivery, Shillitani has used the car for one month (four hundred miles of driving) and is unhappy with it. The car needs numerous repairs, does not get sixteen miles to the gallon, and has used two quarts of oil. Shillitani claims Johnson is in breach of express warranties as to the condition of the car, gas mileage, and oil use. Johnson claims no express warranties were made. Discuss who is correct.

23–2. IMPLIED WARRANTIES. Moon is a farmer who needs to place a two-thousand-pound piece of equipment in his barn. This will require lifting the equipment thirty feet up into a hayloft. Moon goes to Davidson Hardware and tells Davidson that he needs some heavy-duty rope to be used on his farm. Davidson recommends a one-inch-thick nylon rope, and Moon purchases two hundred feet of it. Moon ties the rope around the piece of equipment; puts it through a pulley; and, with a tractor, lifts the equipment off the ground. Suddenly the rope breaks. In the crash to the ground, the equipment is severely damaged. Moon files suit against Davidson for breach of the implied warranty of fitness for a particular purpose. Discuss how successful Moon will be in his suit.

23–3. WARRANTY DISCLAIMERS. Darrow purchases a new car from Slippery Motors. The retail installment contract states immediately above the buyer's signature in large, bold type: "There are no warranties that extend beyond the description on the face hereof" and "There are no express warranties that accompany this sale unless expressly written in this contract." Before purchasing the car, Darrow specifically informed Slippery's salesperson that he wanted a car that could be driven in a dusty area without needing mechanical repairs. Slippery's salesperson said to Darrow, "Nothing will go wrong with this car, but if it does, return it to us, and we will repair it without cost to you." Neither this statement nor any similar statement appears in the retail sales contract. Darrow drives the car into a dust storm. The air filter gets plugged up, and the car engine overheats, causing motor damage. Slippery Motors refuses to repair the engine under any warranty. Darrow claims that Slippery is liable for breach of the implied warranty of fitness for a particular purpose, that the Magnuson-Moss Warranty Act prohibits disclaiming this implied warranty, and that the salesperson's express warranty has also been breached. Discuss Darrow's claims.

23–4. IMPLIED WARRANTIES. Olivo has a used television set that she wishes to sell. Howard contracts to purchase the set. At the time of the making of the contract, Olivo demands that Howard inspect the set to be sure it is exactly what he wants. Howard tells Olivo that he does not have the time to do so. The set is delivered and paid for. Howard, on using the set, discovers that the picture has a tendency to "jump" and that the vertical control does not always correct that tendency. The cost to repair the set is $50. Howard claims that the set is neither merchantable nor fit for its purpose. Olivo claims she has no liability. Discuss who is correct.

23–5. WARRANTY OF TITLE. Duggin buys a one-carat diamond ring from Shady Sallor for $500. Duggin is assured by Shady that the ring belonged to his deceased mother and that the only reason the price is so low is that he is behind in making payments on his car. Duggin has no reason to believe differently. Bekins, a neighbor, admires the ring and offers to purchase it for $1,000. Duggin agrees to sell the ring to Bekins, stating that he is transferring only such rights as he has in the ring. Two months later, the police confiscate the ring as property stolen in a burglary of Owen's home. Bekins seeks to hold Duggin liable. Discuss Bekins's action under warranty laws.

23–6. EXPRESS WARRANTIES. On March 13, 1980, Judith Roth went to the hairdresser she had been using for the past seven years to have her hair bleached. The hair stylist used a new bleaching product, manufactured by Roux Laboratories, on Roth's hair. Although other Roux products had been used previously with excellent results, the use of the new product resulted in damage to Roth's hair that caused her embarrassment and anguish for the next several months as her hair grew back. The product's label had guaranteed it would not cause damage to a user's hair. Roth sued Ray-Stel's Hair Stylists, Inc., and Roux Laboratories, Inc., alleging, among other claims, breach of express warranty resulting in personal injuries to her. Discuss whether there was a breach of express warranty. [*Roth v. Ray-Stel's Hair Stylists, Inc.*, 18 Mass.App. 975, 470 N.E.2d 137 (1984)]

23–7. WARRANTIES. Prestige Motorcar Imports, Inc., advertised a used 1984 Aston Martin Lagonda for sale for $57,600. The car came with a written warranty that covered specific items. Gary Davenport had the car inspected, then bought it. Over the next couple of days, he had the car inspected further and learned that it needed $13,000 worth of repairs, none of which was covered by the written warranty. He complained to Irvin David, owner of Prestige, who offered to refund Davenport's money or fix the car. Davenport refused both and filed a suit in a Florida state court against David and Prestige, in part for breach of warranty. On what grounds might the court issue a judgment against Davenport? [*David v. Davenport*, 656 So.2d 952 (Fla.App.3d 1995)]

23–8. IMPLIED WARRANTIES. Marilyn Keaton entered an A.B.C. Drug store to buy a half-gallon bottle of liquid bleach. The bottles were stacked at a height above her eye level. She reached up, grasped the handle of one of the bottles, and began pulling it down from the shelf. The cap was loose, however, causing bleach to splash into her face, injuring her eye. Keaton filed a suit in a Georgia state court against A.B.C., alleging, in part, breach of the implied warranty of merchantability. She claimed that the bleach had not been adequately packaged. A.B.C. argued, in part, that Keaton had failed to exercise care for her own safety. Had A.B.C. breached the implied warranty of merchantability? Discuss. [*Keaton v. A.B.C. Drug Co.*, 266 Ga. 385, 467 S.E.2d 558 (1996)]

23–9. EXPRESS WARRANTIES. Ronald Anderson, Jr., a self-employed construction contractor, went to a Home Depot store to buy lumber for a construction project. It was raining, so Anderson bought a tarp to cover the bed of his pickup truck. To secure the tarp, Anderson bought a bag of cords made by Bungee International Manufacturing Corp. The printed material on the Bungee bag included the words "Made in the U.S.A." and "Premium Quality." To secure the tarp at the rear of the passenger's side, Anderson put one hook into the eyelet of the tarp, stretched the cord over the utility box, and hooked the other end in the drainage hole in the bottom of the box. As Anderson stood up, the upper hook dislodged and hit him in the left eye. Anderson filed a suit in a federal district court against Bungee and others, alleging in part breach of express warranty. Anderson alleged that the labeling on the bag of cords was an express warranty that "played some role in [his] decision to purchase this product." Bungee argued that, in regard to the cords' quality, the statements were puffery. Bungee filed a motion for summary judgment on this issue. Will the court grant the motion? Why or why not? [*Anderson v. Bungee International Manufacturing Corp.*, 44 F.Supp.2d 534 (S.D.N.Y. 1999)]

23–10. IN YOUR COURT

Vertis Smith was considering buying a used car from Fitzner Pontiac-Buick-Cadillac, Inc., and test-drove a used Olds Cutlass. Smith told Fitzner's sales representative that if Fitzner would fix a rattle he had heard and paint the car, he would purchase it for $6,000. The salesperson agreed to have these things done and assured Smith that when the car was delivered, it would be "in first class shape." During the first few months after the car was delivered, Smith had to install a new intake gasket, a new transmission, and a new radiator—repairs that were made by others, not Fitzner. Fitzner repaired a broken taillight and adjusted a window mechanism. In addition, Smith claimed that the car stalled frequently in traffic and got only eleven miles per gallon of gas. Nine months after he had purchased the car, Smith sued Fitzner to recover the purchase price of the car plus the cost of the repairs. Smith alleged, among other things, that Fitzner had breached an express warranty. Assume that you are the judge in the trial court hearing this case and answer the following questions:

(a) How will you rule on the issue of whether the phrase "in first class shape" constitutes an express warranty?

(b) Before making your decision, consider the following question: Did the salesperson's remark to Smith that the car would be delivered "in first class shape" go to the basis of the bargain?

(c) Review Case 23.2 (*Martin Rispens & Son v. Hall Farms, Inc.*). Why did the court in Case 23.2 conclude that the phrase "top quality seeds" was mere puffery—a statement of opinion—and not an express warranty? Can you apply the same reasoning to the phrase "in first class shape"? Why or why not?

LAW ON THE WEB

For updated links to resources available on the Web, as well as a variety of other materials, visit this text's Web site at http://wbl.westbuslaw.com.

To find information on the UCC, including the UCC provisions discussed in this chapter, refer to the Web sites listed in the *Law on the Web* in Chapter 19.

For an example of an "as is" clause, see the warranty disclaimer provided by the University of Minnesota for one of its research software products at

http://www.cmrr.drad.umn.edu/stimulate/stimUsersGuide/node7.html

GM's performance parts warranty policies (on automobile parts) are online at

http://www.gmperformanceparts.com/WARRANTY.htm

LEGAL RESEARCH EXERCISES ON THE WEB

Go to http://wbl.westbuslaw.com, the Web site that accompanies this text. Select "Internet Applications," and then click on "Chapter 23." There you will find the following Internet research exercise that you can perform to learn more about warranty law:

Activity 23–1: Warranties

UNIT THREE—CUMULATIVE BUSINESS HYPOTHETICAL

Lesa, who owns a small restaurant on the Oregon coast, orders three new tables and twelve new chairs from Larson's Furniture Plaza, a local furniture store. She gives the store a check for $2,000, the purchase price of the tables and chairs, and Larson, the store's owner, agrees to have the furniture delivered to her restaurant the following week.

1. Larson has only one table-and-chair set in stock. When he calls the manufacturer and orders two more sets, he learns that the manufacturer has increased the price of the furniture. Larson telephones Lesa and informs her of the price increase. Lesa agrees to pay the additional price for the remaining two sets when they are delivered. After the furniture is delivered, however, Lesa refuses to pay the extra amount. She claims that her oral agreement to pay the extra cost is not enforceable because the modification of her contract with Larson was not supported by any new consideration. Is Lesa correct? Why or why not?

2. The manufacturer ships the furniture to Larson via truck, F.O.B. Portland, from its warehouse in Portland, Oregon. If the manufacturer and Larson do not specify when risk of loss will pass from the seller to the buyer, when will risk pass? Explain.

3. Suppose that before the furniture is shipped from the Portland warehouse, the warehouse burns down, destroying all of the furniture it contains. Larson cannot obtain the type of tables specified in the contract with Lesa anywhere else. Lesa sues Larson for breach of contract. How might Larson defend against this suit? Explain fully.

4. Assume that Lesa does receive the furniture. On its arrival, however, she notices a large crack in the top of one of the tables. She tells Larson about the problem and asks him to replace the cracked table with a new, undamaged one. Larson refuses to do so. What remedies might Lesa pursue in this situation?

FOCUS ON LEGAL REASONING
Lickley v. Max Herbold, Inc.

INTRODUCTION

We discussed, in Chapter 19, the principles concerning the formation of a contract for a sale of goods. In Chapter 22, we covered the remedies for a breach of a sales contract. In this *Focus on Legal Reasoning*, we examine *Lickley v. Max Herbold, Inc.*,[1] a recent decision involving the application of these principles to a contract for a sale of potatoes.

CASE BACKGROUND

Under a contract with Max Herbold, Inc., Lonnie Lickley agreed to deliver 12,000 cwt. (hundredweight) of potatoes. The contract, in paragraph C, set a base price of $6.15 per cwt. with, depending on the quality of the potatoes delivered,

---
1. 984 P.2d 687 (Idaho 1999).

price adjustments. The contract set minimum quality standards: "Any load or combination of loads inspecting below fifty percent (50%) well shaped U.S. NO. 1, two inch or 4 ounce minimum will be rejected under the contract." If the inspection of a load was not completed until after it was delivered and commingled, paragraph C(4)e provided that "[t]he price for any load or combination of loads already delivered and placed in Company storage subsequently determined by inspection to be rejectable under this contract will have to be renegotiated between Grower and Company."

Over six days, Lickley delivered twenty-three truckloads, totaling just over 12,000 cwt. of potatoes. Herbold accepted the shipments and mixed the potatoes with deliveries from other growers. Inspections showed

that the combination of loads delivered on each of the first four days failed to meet the minimum standards. Viewing all six days' deliveries as a whole, 85 percent of the potatoes were below standard.

Herbold calculated a net price of $3.22 per cwt. using the formula set out in the contract and notified Lickley. Because a number of the accepted potatoes were "rejectable," Lickley sought to renegotiate the price. Herbold offered to waive the freight charges. Lickley refused, and filed a suit in an Idaho state court against Herbold, alleging breach of contract and asserting more than $80,000 in damages, the market value of the potatoes at the time of delivery. The court ruled in Lickley's favor. Both parties appealed to the Idaho Supreme Court.

MAJORITY OPINION

TROUT, Chief Justice.
* * * *

* * * By commingling and failing to reject any deliveries, Herbold accepted all twenty-three loads. Consequently, it is obligated to pay the contract price. Paragraph C of the contract provided a specific formula to calculate the purchase price. However, under paragraph C(4)e, if Herbold accepted "rejectable" potatoes, the contract required the parties to renegotiate the price. The parties do not dispute that at least Lickley's first four days' deliveries were rejectable, but Lickley contends that all the potatoes were rejectable. Consequently, the parties left the contract price open as to the rejectable potatoes.

So long as the parties intend to enter a contract, their agreement will not fail for indefiniteness where they do not settle the price. It is clear from the record that Herbold and Lickley intended to enter an enforceable agreement. Where the contract leaves the price open for

negotiation and the parties fail to agree, § 28-2-305(1) [Idaho's version of UCC 2–305(1)] provides: "In such a case the price is a reasonable price at the time for delivery * * * ." Lickley and Herbold failed to agree upon a price. Lickley argued * * * that the market price, approximately $7.50 per cwt. at the time for delivery, was the reasonable price. Herbold argued that the market price is not a reasonable price. Instead, a reasonable price could not exceed the price as calculated under paragraph C of the contract. [Emphasis added.]

The district judge determined the market price of $7.55 per cwt. to be a reasonable price at the time for delivery. * * * Without providing an express distinction between the two, the Uniform Commercial Code uses the terms "reasonable price" and "market price" in a number of contexts. As is evident from their use, their meanings are not necessarily interchangeable. The question facing us, however, is whether substantial and competent evidence in the record supports the trial court's finding. Under the limited circumstances

FOCUS ON LEGAL REASONING

presented in this case, we conclude that there is. At the time Lickley delivered potatoes to Herbold, he also sold potatoes from the same field on the open market and received between $7.50 and $8.00 per cwt. Although, as Herbold contends, the intent of the parties as reflected in the contract's pricing structure might lead to a lower price, we cannot, as a matter of law, hold that the trial court erred.

* * * The district judge found that 7,532.30 cwt. or the first four days' loads of the potatoes were rejectable. Lickley cross-appeals arguing that the district judge erred by not finding all twenty-three loads rejectable. The contract provides that "Any load or combination of loads" failing to meet grade will be rejected. Lickley contends that viewing all six days' deliveries in combination, the potatoes inspected well below "fifty percent (50%) well shaped U.S. NO. 1, two inch or 4 ounce minimum." In fact, eighty-five percent of all potatoes failed to meet the standard. Consequently, Lickley argues all six days' shipments were rejectable.

However, a more reasonable interpretation of this provision leads to the ultimate conclusion reached by the trial court. The "combination of loads" language reflects the fact that multiple loads could be and were delivered on a given day. However, the inspection service, as is reflected in the record, sampled each day's deliveries as a whole. The "combination of loads" received on each of the first four days did not conform while the "combination of loads" delivered on the last two did. Therefore, the trial court properly concluded that only the loads delivered on the first four days were rejectable.

DISSENTING OPINION

Justice *Schroeder*, dissenting:
* * * *

The reason buyers and sellers enter contracts such as this is to lock into a predictable price. The potato grower wants to ensure his costs are covered in case of a poor market, and the buyer wants to ensure a supply at a predictable and affordable cost in cases of high demand. By entering pre-season contracts the grower takes the risk that the market price will exceed the contract price. Similarly, the buyer takes the risk that the contract price will exceed the crop's value at the time for delivery. In this case the contract provides a formula to calculate the price for non-rejectable potatoes. Lickley could not reasonably have expected to be paid more for rejectable potatoes than he was for the potatoes meeting the contract's minimum standards, and Herbold could not have expected to pay more for rejectable potatoes than for conforming potatoes. * * * In light of the parties' intentions as reflected in the contract, this Court should conclude that the district court erred in finding the market price to be a reasonable price under the contract. The parties agreed to a specific pricing structure for conforming potatoes. Their intention as to what constitutes a reasonable price for rejectable potatoes can be inferred from that pricing structure.

LEGAL REASONING AND ANALYSIS

1. Ethical Implications. As suggested by the dissent in this case, what are the ethical implications of awarding a seller who delivers "rejectable" goods more than he or she would have been entitled to for delivering "acceptable" goods?

2. Legal Analysis. Contrast the conclusion of the majority with that of the dissent. What arguments did

the majority make to support its assertion that the lower court's judgment was correct? What arguments did the dissent make to justify its position?

3. Legal Reasoning. Which, if any, of the forms of legal reasoning described in Chapter 1 did the majority use to reach its conclusion? Which forms did the dissent use?

4. Implications for Sellers and Buyers. How is the holding in this case of particular interest to businesses that have, are, or may in the future buy or sell goods subject to contractual price adjustments?

5. Case Briefing Assignment. Using the guidelines for briefing cases given in Appendix A of this text, brief the *Lickley* case.

GOING ONLINE

The Legal Information Institute, at http://www.law.cornell.edu/uniform/ucc.html, provides links to state statutes that correspond to UCC articles, including Article 2 and Article 2A. The page includes links to an index of state cases and other material on sales and other legal topics. This Web site is maintained by Cornell Law School in Ithaca, New York.

Domestic and International Sales and Lease Contracts

Transactions involving the sale and lease of goods constitute a major portion of business activity in the commercial and manufacturing sectors of our economy. Since the 1960s, the sale of goods has been governed by the Uniform Commercial Code (UCC) in every state but Louisiana. The UCC now covers leases of goods as well, under Article 2A. Many of the UCC provisions express our ethical standards.

GOOD FAITH AND COMMERCIAL REASONABLENESS

Good faith and commercial reasonableness are two key concepts that permeate the UCC and help to prevent unethical behavior by businesspersons. These two concepts are read into every contract and impose certain duties on all parties. Section 2–311(1) of the UCC indicates that when parties leave the particulars of performance to be specified by one of the parties, "[a]ny such specification must be made in good faith and within limits set by commercial reasonableness."

The requirement of commercial reasonableness means that the term subsequently supplied by one party should not come as a surprise to the other. The party filling in the missing term may not take advantage of the opportunity to add a contractual term that will be beneficial to himself or herself (and detrimental to the other party) and then demand contractual performance of the other party that

was totally unanticipated. Under the UCC, the party filling in the missing term may not deviate from what is commercially reasonable in the context of the transaction. Courts frequently look to course of dealing, usage of trade, and the surrounding circumstances in determining what is commercially reasonable in a given situation.

Good Faith

The obligation of good faith is particularly important in so-called output and requirements contracts. UCC 2–306 states that "quantity" in these contracts "means such actual output or requirements as may occur in good faith." For example, if General Motors contracts with Jalin's Fuel Injectors to purchase all of Jalin's output, Jalin's cannot then increase its production from one eight-hour shift per day to three eight-hour shifts per day to make greater profits under the contract. As another example, assume that Mandrow's Machines has fifty employees assembling IBM clones. Mandrow's has a requirements contract with Advanced Tech Circuit Boards under which Advanced Tech is to supply Mandrow's with all of the circuit boards it needs. If all of a sudden Mandrow's quadruples the size of its business, it cannot insist that Advanced Tech supply it with all of its requirements as specified in the original contract.

In many situations, parties may find it advantageous (profitable) to avoid a legal obligation. Without

the counterobligation of good faith, there exists potential for abuse in the area of sales and lease contracts.

Suppose, for example, that the market price of the goods subject to a requirements contract rises rapidly and dramatically because of a shortage of materials necessary to their production. The buyer could claim that his or her needs are equivalent to the entire output of the seller. Then, after buying all of the seller's output at the contract price, which is substantially below the market price, the buyer could turn around and sell the goods that he or she does not need at the higher market price. Under the UCC, this type of unethical behavior is prohibited—even though the buyer in this instance has not technically breached the contract.

Commercial Reasonableness

Under the UCC, the concept of good faith is closely linked to commercial reasonableness. All commercial actions—including the performance and enforcement of contract obligations—must exhibit commercial reasonableness. A merchant is expected to act in a reasonable manner according to reasonable commercial customs.

The concept of commercial reasonableness is clearly expressed in the doctrine of commercial impracticability. Under this doctrine, which is related to the common law doctrine of impossibility of performance, a party's nonperformance of a contractual obligation may be excused when, because of unforeseen circumstances, performance of the contract becomes impracticable. But the courts make it clear that before performance will be excused under this doctrine, a contractual party must have made every reasonable effort to fulfill performance obligations.

THE CONCEPT OF THE GOOD FAITH PURCHASER

The concept of the good faith purchaser reflects the UCC's emphasis on protecting innocent parties. Suppose, for example, that you innocently and in good faith purchase a boat from someone who appears to have good title and who demands and receives from you a fair market price. The UCC believes that you should be protected from the possibility that the real owner—from whom the seller may have fraudulently obtained the boat—will later appear and demand his or her boat back. (Nothing, however, prevents the true owner from bringing suit against the party who defrauded him or her.)

Ethical questions arise in situations in which the purchaser has reason to suspect that the seller may not have good title to the goods being sold but nonetheless lets the transaction go forward because it is a "good deal." At what point does the buyer, in such a situation, cross over the boundary that separates the good faith purchaser from one who purchases in bad faith? This boundary is a significant one in the law of sales, because the UCC will not be a refuge for those who purchase in bad faith. The term *good faith purchaser* means just that—one who enters into a contract for the purchase of goods without knowing, or having any reason to know, that there is anything shady or illegal about the deal.

UNCONSCIONABILITY

The doctrine of unconscionability represents a good example of how the law attempts to enforce ethical behavior. This doctrine suggests that some contracts may be so unfair to one party as to be unenforceable, even though that party originally agreed to the contract's terms. Section 2–302 of the UCC provides that a court will consider the fairness of contracts and may consider a contract or any clause of a contract to have been unconscionable at the time it was made. If so, the court may refuse to enforce the contract, it may enforce the contract without the unconscionable clause, or it may limit the application of the clause so as to avoid an unconscionable result.

The UCC does not define the term *unconscionability*. The drafters of the UCC, however, have added explanatory comments to the relevant sections of the UCC, and these comments serve as guidelines to the UCC's application. Comment 1 to Section 2–302 suggests that the basic test for unconscionability is whether, under the circumstances existing at the time of the making of the contract, the clause in question was so one sided as to be unconscionable. This test is to be applied against the general commercial background of the contract. For example, a contract with a marginally literate consumer might be seen as unfair and unenforceable, whereas the same contract with a major business firm would be upheld by the courts.

A court may declare an entire contract unconscionable or just one of the clauses in a contract. In a recent application of Section 2–302, a New York appellate court held that an arbitration clause was unconscionable and refused to enforce it. Gateway 2000, Inc., which sells computers and software directly to consumers, included in its retail agreements a clause requiring that any dispute arising out of the contract had to be arbitrated in Chicago, Illinois, in accordance with the arbitration rules of the International Chamber of Commerce (ICC).

A number of consumers who had purchased Gateway products became incensed when they realized that ICC rules governing arbitration required advance fees of $4,000 (more than the cost of most Gateway products), of which the $2,000 registration fee was nonrefundable—even if the consumer prevailed at the arbitration. Additionally, the consumers would have to pay travel expenses to Chicago. In the class-action litigation against Gateway that followed, the New York court agreed with the consumers that the "egregiously oppressive" arbitration clause was unconscionable: "Barred from resorting to the courts by the arbitration clause in the first instance, the designation of a financially prohibitive forum effectively bars consumers from this forum as well; consumers are thus left with no forum at all in which to resolve a dispute."[1]

WARRANTIES

A seller or lessor has not only a legal obligation to provide safe products but also an ethical one. When faced with the possibility of providing additional safety at no extra cost, every ethical businessperson will indeed opt for a safer product. An ethical issue arises, however, when the production of a safer product means higher costs. To some extent, our warranty laws have been deemed necessary to protect consumers from sellers who choose, perhaps, to neglect ethical concerns if what they are doing is both legal and profitable.

---

1. *Brower v. Gateway 2000, Inc.,* 246 A.D.2d 246, 676 N.Y.S.2d 659 (1998).

Express and Implied Warranties

Both express and implied warranties are recognized by the UCC. Under UCC 2–314 and 2A–212, goods sold by a merchant or leased by a lessor must be fit for the ordinary purposes for which such goods are used, be of proper quality, and be properly labeled and packaged. A description of goods is an express warranty, and hence a seller or a lessor of goods may be held to have breached a contract if the goods fail to conform to the seller's or lessor's description. The UCC injects greater fairness into contractual situations by recognizing descriptions as express warranties. The UCC acknowledges the fact that a buyer or lessee may often reasonably believe that a seller or lessor is warranting his or her product, even though the seller or lessor may not use a formal word such as *warrant* or *guarantee*. Thus, the law imposes an ethical obligation on sellers and lessors in a statutory form.

Warranty Disclaimers

The UCC requirement that warranty disclaimers must be sufficiently conspicuous to catch the eye of a reasonable purchaser is based on the ethical premise that sellers of goods should not take advantage of unwary consumers, who may not—in the excitement of making a new purchase—always read the "fine print" on standard purchase order forms. As discussed in Chapter 23, if a seller or lessor, when attempting to disclaim warranties, fails to meet the specific requirements imposed by the UCC, the warranties will not effectively be disclaimed.

The ethical significance of the UCC rules on warranty disclaimers can best be illustrated by looking at the situation that existed prior to the implementation of the UCC. Before the UCC was adopted by the states, purchasers of automobiles,

for example, frequently signed standard-form purchase agreements, drafted by the auto manufacturer, without learning until later what all the fine print meant.

Henningsen v. Bloomfield Motors, Inc.,[2] a case decided in New Jersey before the UCC was in effect in that state, involves just such a situation. Henningsen had purchased a new Chrysler from Bloomfield Motors for his wife. Subsequently, his wife suffered severe injuries as a result of an apparent defect in the steering wheel mechanism. The standard-form purchase order used in the transaction contained an express ninety-day/four-thousand-mile warranty and, in fine print, a disclaimer of any and all other express or implied warranties. Thus, Bloomfield Motors and Chrysler Corporation refused to pay for Mrs. Henningsen's injuries, asserting that the sales contract, which warranted that Bloomfield Motors would repair defects at no charge, disclaimed warranty liabilities for injuries suffered.

The case was eventually heard by the Supreme Court of New Jersey, which expressed outrage at the fact that the automobile manufacturer had used its grossly disproportionate bargaining power, as well as the unfair surprise of fine print, to relieve itself from liability and to impose on the buyer, who in effect had no real freedom of choice, the grave danger of injury that is posed by a defectively made automobile. In a landmark decision, the court held that the disclaimer was unconscionable and allowed the Henningsens to recover from the auto dealer and manufacturer.

Although freedom of contract reflects a basic ethical principle in our society, courts—including the New Jersey court mentioned above—have made it clear that when such freedom leads to gross unfairness, it should be curbed.

2. 32 N.J. 358, 161 A.2d 69 (1960).

ETHICS AND "PUFFING"

As explained in Chapter 23, *puffing* is defined as a salesperson's use of exaggerated claims concerning the quality of goods offered for sale. Puffing is considered a statement of opinion and not a statement of fact, and therefore it does not constitute an express warranty. The law assumes that most buyers or lessees know, or should know, that sellers and lessors traditionally have engaged in "huffing and puffing" their wares, and reasonable buyers and lessees will not be "taken" by this puffery. Nonetheless, in some instances, buyers or lessees may rely on a seller's or lessor's statements of opinion when deciding whether to purchase or lease a particular product.

Consider, for example, what might happen when a salesperson deals with a customer who does not have complete command of the English language. A fast-talking sales representative may engage in a sufficient amount of puffing to convince a customer who does not speak English very well that the product the customer is buying is of much higher quality than it really is.

The line between statements that amount to puffery and statements that constitute express warranties is not always clear. Nor is the line between puffery and fraudulent misrepresentation always readily discernible. For example, in one case, a sales representative for a Mazda dealer was trying to sell a used Mazda to Kevin Garrett. The salesperson said that although the car had nearly 15,000 miles on it, the salesperson himself had used the car as a demonstrator and for his personal use and had "babied it to death." In fact, the car had been stolen from the dealer and driven 10,000 miles, and prior to the theft, the dealer had had to replace the

FOCUS ON ETHICS

engine after the car had been driven only approximately 3,000 miles.

Were the salesperson's statements in this situation mere puffery? Did the salesperson have a duty to disclose the fact that the car had been stolen? When Garrett later experienced numerous problems with the car and eventually sued the dealer, the court held that the theft of the car was a material fact and the salesperson had a duty to disclose this information. In addition, according to the court, the statements made by the salesperson crossed the line between puffing, or "seller's talk," and misrepresentation.[3]

The Battle of the Forms

The drafters of UCC Section 2–207 attempted to avoid the "battle of the forms" by providing that a contract can be entered into even though the acceptance includes additional terms. Nonetheless, the battle continues in earnest because whether a form is defined as an offer or an acceptance can have significant consequences for the parties. Indeed, one of the results of Section 2–207 is that buyers and sellers go to great lengths to draft their responses as "offers" or "counteroffers" (instead of acceptances) so that their terms will control any resulting contracts. Remember that under UCC 2–207(2), as between merchants additional terms in an acceptance, if they materially alter the contract, do not become a part of the contract—the terms of the offer control.

Some courts have taken a different approach in resolving contract disputes when the parties are in fundamental disagreement over a material term. Rather than looking to UCC 2–207(2), they

apply the rule expressed in UCC 2–207(3). This rule provides that when the parties' conduct and communications clearly indicate that a contract was formed, any conflicting material terms may simply be stricken from the contract. This rule is sometimes referred to, aptly enough, as the "knock-out rule."

The Supreme Court of Rhode Island chose to use this approach in a case involving conflicting terms relating to the time for delivery. A number of forms—including purchase orders, amended purchase orders, proposals containing specifications and price quotes, memoranda confirming telephone conversations, and sales orders—were exchanged between the parties. The problem was, although it was clear that the parties had entered into a contract, the forms indicated that they had never mutually agreed on the time for delivery.

In the lawsuit that followed, Rhode Island's highest court concluded that "both prudence and the weight of authority favor adoption of the knock-out rule as the law of this jurisdiction." The court thus struck the delivery term from the contract entirely, stating that the subsequent "gap" in the contract would be filled by the UCC's gap-filling provision concerning the time for delivery—UCC 2–309(1). Under this provision, the time for shipment or delivery, if not agreed on by the parties, "shall be a reasonable time."[4]

One of the goals of the proposed revision of Article 2 of the UCC is to redesign UCC 2–207 so that the battle of the forms can be avoided. Some have suggested that this section should be revised so that it focuses less on contract formation (offer and acceptance) and more on the approach currently provided

under UCC 2–207(3)—that the terms of a contract are only those on which the parties have agreed. To be sure, this could mean that parties may end up with a contract containing a UCC gap-filling term to which neither party agrees. Yet, as the Rhode Island court explained, "the offeror and the offeree both have the power to protect any term they deem critical by expressly making acceptance conditional on assent to that term."

DISCUSSION QUESTIONS

1. Review the UCC provisions applying to the topics discussed in Chapters 19 through 23. Discuss fully how various UCC provisions, excluding the provisions discussed above, reflect social values and ethical standards.
2. How can a court objectively measure good faith and commercial reasonableness?
3. Merchants may "huff and puff" their wares as they traditionally have and still—in most instances—not violate their duty of dealing honestly and in good faith with the buyers of their products. Do you think that the commonplace custom of puffing is a fundamentally dishonest practice that should be abandoned? Is there anything the law can or should do to ensure that buyers and lessees will not be taken in by sellers' and lessors' statements of opinion?
4. Why does the UCC protect innocent persons (good faith purchasers) who buy goods from sellers with voidable title but not innocent persons who buy goods from sellers with void title?

---

3. *Garrett v. Mazda Motors of America*, 844 S.W.2d 178 (Tenn.App. 1992).

4. *Superior Boiler Works, Inc. v. R. J. Sanders, Inc.*, 711 A.2d 625 (R.I. 1998).

UNIT FOUR

Negotiable Instruments

CONTENTS

CHAPTER 24

The Function and Creation of Negotiable Instruments

THE VAST NUMBER OF COMMERCIAL transactions that take place daily in the modern business world would be inconceivable without negotiable instruments. A **negotiable instrument** can be defined as a signed writing that contains an unconditional promise or order to pay an exact sum of money, either when demanded or at a specific future time. The checks you write to pay for groceries and other items are negotiable instruments.

The law governing negotiable instruments grew out of commercial necessity. In the medieval world, merchants dealing in foreign trade used negotiable instruments to finance and conduct their affairs. Problems in transportation and in the safekeeping of gold or coins had prompted this practice. Merchants deposited their precious metals with goldsmiths ("bankers") to avoid the dangers of loss or theft. When they needed funds to pay for the goods they were buying, they gave the seller a written order addressed to the "bank." This authorized the bank to deliver part (or all) of the precious metals to the seller. These orders, called *bills of exchange*, were sometimes used as a substitute for money. Because the English king's courts of those times did not recognize the validity of these bills, the merchants had to develop their own rules governing their use, and these rules were enforced by "fair" or "borough" courts. Eventually, these decisions became a distinct set of laws known as the *Lex Mercatoria* (Law Merchant).

The Law Merchant was codified in England in the Bills of Exchange Act of 1882. In 1896, in the United States, the National Conference of Commissioners on Uniform State Laws drafted the Uniform Negotiable Instruments Law. This law, which by 1920 had been adopted by all of the states, was the forerunner of Article 3 of the Uniform Commercial Code (UCC).

SECTION 1

Article 3 of the UCC

Negotiable instruments must meet special requirements relating to form and content. These requirements, which are imposed by Article 3 of the UCC, will be discussed at length in this chapter. When an instrument is negotiable, its transfer from one person to another is governed by Article 3. Indeed, UCC 3–104(b) defines *instrument* as a "negotiable instrument." For that reason, whenever the term *instrument* is used in this book, it refers to a negotiable instrument.

In 1990, a revised version of Article 3 was issued for adoption by the states. Many of the changes to Article 3 simply clarified old sections; some, however, significantly altered the former UCC Article 3 provisions. As of this writing, almost all of the states have adopted the revised article. Therefore, all references to Article 3 in this chapter and in the following chapters are to the *revised* Article 3. When the revised Article 3 has made important changes in the law, however, we discuss the previous law in footnotes.

Article 4 of the UCC, which governs bank deposits and collections, as well as bank-customer relationships (discussed in Chapter 27), was also revised in 1990. In part, these changes were necessary to reflect changes in Article 3 that affect Article 4 provisions. The revised Articles 3 and 4 are included in their entirety in Appendix C.

S E C T I O N 2

The Function of Instruments

A negotiable instrument can function as a substitute for money or as an extension of credit. For example, when a buyer writes a check to pay for goods, the check serves as a substitute for money. When a buyer gives a seller a promissory note in which the buyer promises to pay the seller the purchase price within sixty days, the seller has essentially extended credit to the buyer for a sixty-day period.

For a negotiable instrument to operate *practically* as either a substitute for money or a credit device, or both, it is essential that the instrument be easily transferable without danger of being uncollectible. This is a fundamental function of negotiable instruments. Each rule described in the following pages can be examined in light of this function.

S E C T I O N 3

Types of Negotiable Instruments

The UCC specifies four types of negotiable instruments: *drafts, checks, notes,* and *certificates of deposit* (*CDs*). These instruments, which are summarized in Exhibit 24–1 on page 422, are frequently divided into the two classifications that we will discuss in the following subsections: *orders to pay* (drafts and checks) and *promises to pay* (promissory notes and CDs).

Negotiable instruments may also be classified as either demand instruments or time instruments. A *demand instrument* is payable on demand. "A promise or order is 'payable on demand' if it (i) states that it is payable on demand or at sight, or otherwise indicates that it is payable at the will of the holder, or (ii) does not state any time of payment" [UCC 3–108(a)]. (The UCC defines a **holder** as "the person in possession if the instrument is payable to bearer or, in the cases of an instrument payable to an identified person, if the identified person is in possession" [UCC 1–201(20)]. The term *bearer* will be explained later in this chapter.)

All checks are demand instruments, because by definition, they must be payable on demand. Therefore, checking accounts are sometimes called **demand deposits.** A demand instrument is payable immediately after it is *issued.* **Issue** is "the first delivery of an instrument by the maker or drawer, whether to a holder or nonholder [usually to the payee], for the purpose of giving rights on the instrument to any person" [UCC 3–105].[1] *Time instruments are payable at a future date.*

DRAFTS AND CHECKS (ORDERS TO PAY)

A **draft** (bill of exchange) is an unconditional written order that involves *three parties.* The party creating the draft (the **drawer**) orders another party (the **drawee**) to pay money, usually to a third party (the **payee**). The most common type of draft is a check.

Time Drafts and Sight Drafts. A *time draft* is payable at a definite future time. A *sight draft* (or demand draft) is payable on sight—that is, when it is presented for payment. A sight draft may be payable on acceptance. **Acceptance** is the drawee's written promise to pay the draft when it comes due. The usual manner of accepting an instrument is by writing the word *accepted* across the face of the instrument, followed by the date of acceptance and the signature of the drawee. A draft can be both a time and a sight draft; such a draft is payable at a stated time after sight. Exhibit 24–2 on the next page shows a typical time draft.

Trade Acceptances. The trade acceptance is a type of draft that is frequently used in the sale of goods. In a **trade acceptance,** the seller of the goods

---

1. Under the unrevised UCC 3–102(1)(a), *issue* was limited to "the first delivery of an instrument to a holder or remitter."

EXHIBIT 24–1   BASIC TYPES OF INSTRUMENTS

INSTRUMENTS	CHARACTERISTICS	PARTIES
Orders to Pay Draft	An order by one person to another person or to bearer [UCC 3–104(e)].	Drawer—The person who signs or makes the order to pay [UCC 3–103(a)(3)].
Check	A draft drawn on a bank and payable on demand [UCC 3–104(f)].ᵃ (With certain types of checks, such as cashier's checks, the bank is both the drawer and the drawee—see Chapter 27 for details.)	Drawee—The person to whom the order to pay is made [UCC 3–103(a)(2)]. Payee—The person to whom payment is ordered.
Promises to Pay Note	A promise by one party to pay money to another party or to bearer [UCC 3–104(e)].	Maker—The person who promises to pay [UCC 3–103(a)(5)].
Certificate of deposit	A note made by a bank acknowledging a deposit of funds made payable to the holder of the note [UCC 3–104(j)].	Payee—The person to whom the promise is made.

a. Under UCC 4–105(1), banks include savings banks, savings and loan associations, credit unions, and trust companies.

is both the drawer and the payee. Essentially, the draft orders the buyer to pay a specified sum of money to the seller, usually at a stated time in the future. For example, Midwestern Style Fabrics sells $50,000 worth of fabric to D & F Clothiers, Inc., each fall on terms requiring payment to be made in ninety days. One year, Midwestern Style needs cash, so it draws a *trade acceptance* that orders D & F to pay $50,000 to the order of Midwestern Style Fabrics ninety days hence. Midwestern Style presents the draft to D & F, which *accepts* the draft by signing and dating the face of the instrument. D & F then returns the draft to Midwestern Style Fabrics. D & F's acceptance creates an enforceable promise to pay

EXHIBIT 24–2   A TYPICAL TIME DRAFT—A BILL OF EXCHANGE

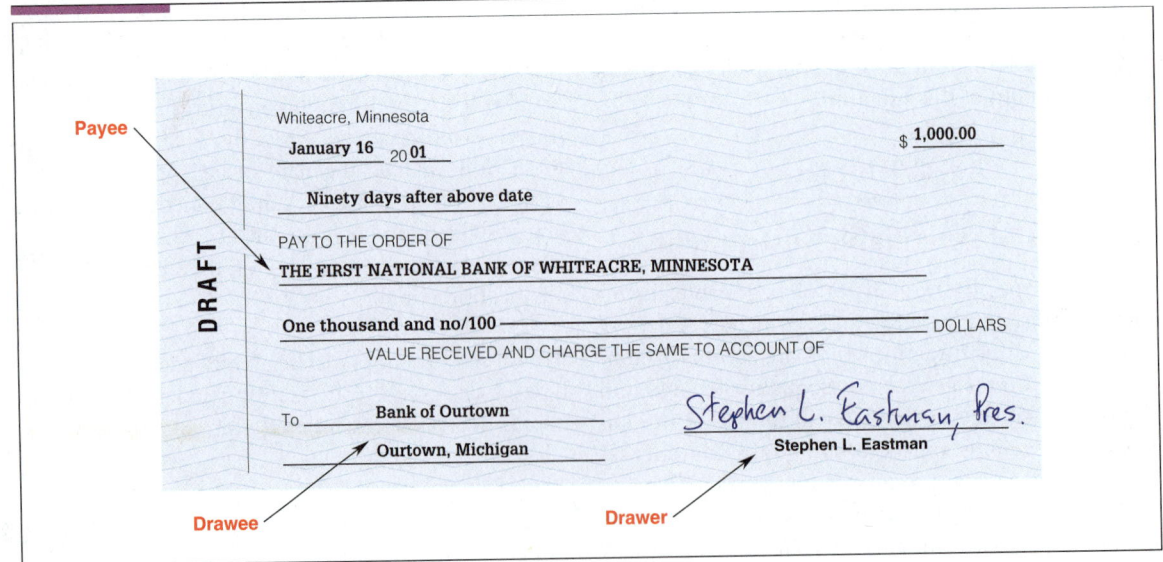

Payee

Whiteacre, Minnesota
January 16   20 01 $ 1,000.00

Ninety days after above date

DRAFT

PAY TO THE ORDER OF
THE FIRST NATIONAL BANK OF WHITEACRE, MINNESOTA

One thousand and no/100 ————————————————————— DOLLARS
VALUE RECEIVED AND CHARGE THE SAME TO ACCOUNT OF

To   Bank of Ourtown   *Stephen L. Eastman, Pres.*
        Ourtown, Michigan   Stephen L. Eastman

Drawee   Drawer

the draft when it comes due in ninety days. Midwestern Style can now sell the trade acceptance in the commercial money market to obtain the cash it needs. Trade acceptances are the standard credit instruments in sales transactions (see Exhibit 24–3).

When the draft is drawn by a seller on the buyer's bank for acceptance, it is called a banker's acceptance. A **banker's acceptance** is commonly used in international trade.

Checks. As mentioned, the most commonly used type of draft is a check. The writer of the **check** is the drawer, the bank on which the check is drawn is the drawee, and the person to whom the check is made payable is the payee. As stated earlier, checks, because they are payable on demand, are demand instruments.

Checks will be discussed more fully in Chapter 27, but it should be noted here that with certain types of checks, such as *cashier's checks*, the bank is both the drawer and the drawee. The bank customer purchases a cashier's check from the bank—that is, pays the bank the amount of the check—and indicates to whom the check should be made payable. The bank, not the customer, is the drawer of the check, as well as the drawee.

PROMISSORY NOTES AND CDs (PROMISES TO PAY)

A **promissory note** is a written promise made by one person (the **maker** of the promise to pay) to another

(usually a payee). A promissory note, which is often referred to simply as a *note*, can be made payable at a definite time or on demand. It can name a specific payee or merely be payable to bearer (bearer instruments are discussed later in this chapter). For example, on April 30, Laurence and Margaret Roberts sign a writing unconditionally promising to pay "to the order of" the First National Bank of Whiteacre $3,000 (with 8 percent interest) on or before June 29. This writing is a promissory note. A typical promissory note is shown in Exhibit 24–4 on the next page.

Notes are used in a variety of credit transactions and often carry the name of the transaction involved. For example, a note that is secured by personal property, such as an automobile, is called a *collateral note*, because the property pledged as security for the satisfaction of the debt is called *collateral*.[2] A note payable in installments, such as installment payments for a large-screen television over a twelve-month period, is called an *installment note*.

A **certificate of deposit (CD)** is a type of note. A CD is issued when a party deposits money with a bank, and the bank promises to repay the money, with

---

2. To minimize the risk of loss when lending money, a creditor often requires the debtor to provide some collateral, or security, beyond a promise that the debt will be repaid. When this security takes the form of personal property (such as a motor vehicle), the creditor has an interest in the property known as a *security interest*. Security interests are discussed in detail in Chapter 28.

EXHIBIT 24–3 A TYPICAL TRADE ACCEPTANCE

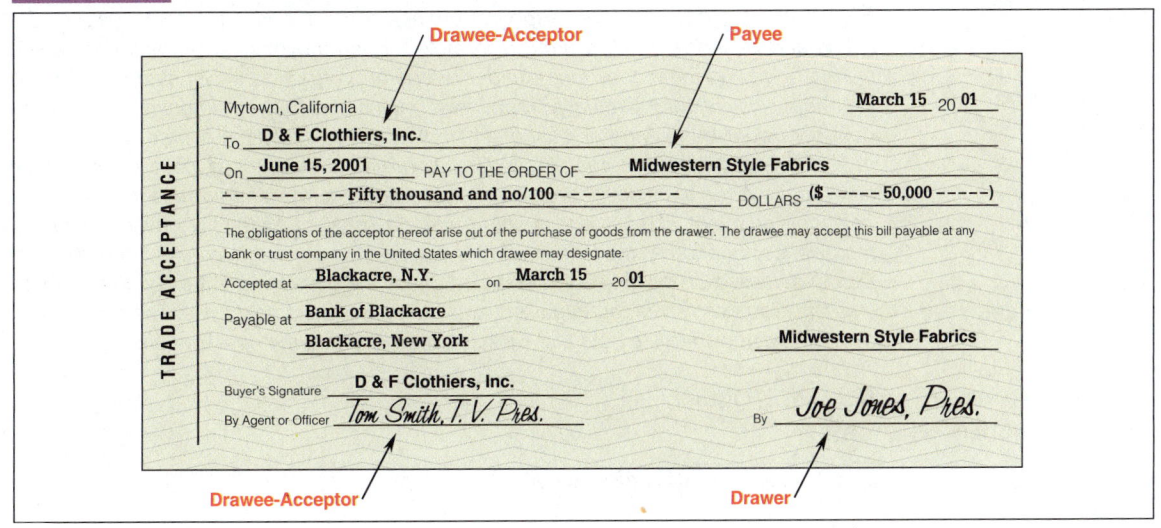

Exhibit 24–4   A Typical Promissory Note

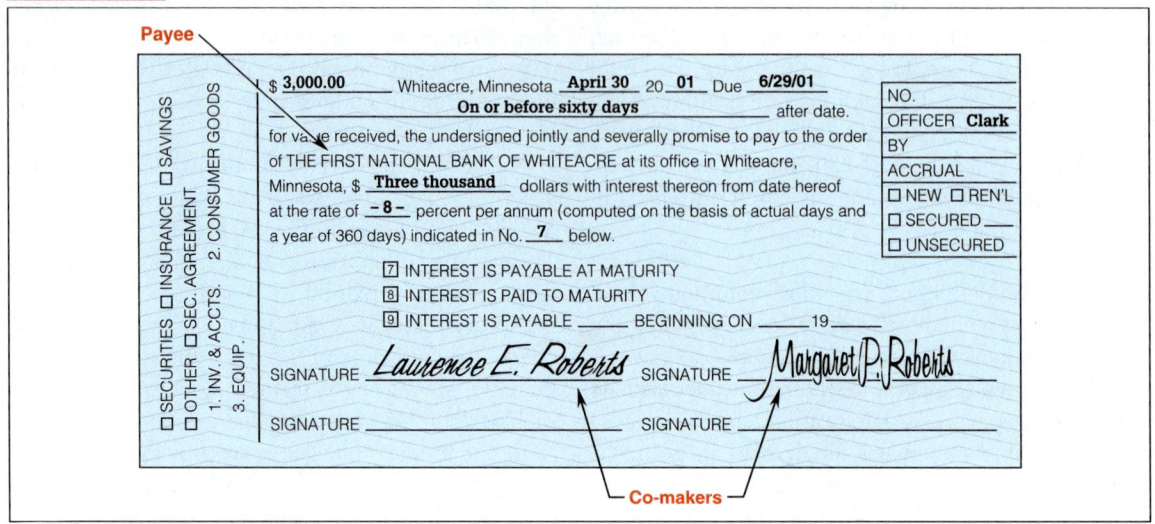

interest, on a certain date [UCC 3–104(j)]. The bank is the maker of the note, and the depositor is the payee. For example, on February 15, Sara Levin deposits $5,000 with the First National Bank of Whiteacre. The bank promises to repay the $5,000, plus 5½ percent interest, on August 15.

Certificates of deposit in small denominations (for amounts up to $100,000) are often sold by savings and loan associations, savings banks, and commercial banks. Certificates of deposit for amounts over $100,000 are called large (or jumbo) CDs. Exhibit 24–5 on page 426 shows a typical small CD.

The following case illustrates how a party can collect on a promissory note—in this case, a note signed by a student to borrow money for his education.

Case 24.1   United States v. Durbin

United States
District Court,
Southern District
of Texas,
Houston Division, 1999.
64 F.Supp.2d 635.

Background and Facts   Robert Durbin, a student, borrowed money for his education and issued (signed) a promissory note for its repayment. The bank from which Durbin borrowed the money lent it under a federal program to assist students at postsecondary institutions.[a] Ordinarily, repayment begins nine to twelve months after the student borrower fails to carry at least one-half of the normal full-time course load at his or her school. Under this program, the federal government guarantees that the note will be fully repaid. When the student defaults on the repayment, the lender presents the current balance—principal, interest, and costs—to the government. When the government pays the balance, it becomes the lender, and the borrower owes the government directly. After Durbin defaulted on his note and also failed to pay the government, the government filed a suit in a federal district court against Durbin to collect the amount due. The government showed that it owned the note that Durbin issued and that the note was unpaid.

In the Language of the Court   HUGHES, District Judge.

*   *   *   *

a. Higher Education Act of 1965, 20 U.S.C. Section 1070.

A note is an unconditional promise to pay. It is an obligation of the borrower to the lender. *The practice and law of notes developed so that people could lend on the credit of a person with confidence that collecting the debt would not be complicated by side issues.* As a result of their unconditional, absolute character, loans are both extended in the first place and traded among lenders with no direct knowledge of the original transaction, reducing their cost to the borrowers. [Emphasis added.]

The government must show three things to win: (1) the defendant is the person who issued the note; (2) the government owns the note; and (3) the note is unpaid. In addition to the unpaid amount, the lender may collect attorney's fees under state and federal law. Federal law also allows reasonable administrative and collection costs.

* * * *

The note may be enforced against the borrower unless he can show that he did not issue it or that he paid it. Unlike many other kinds of cases, the borrower largely has the responsibility to produce evidence. Evidence is not simply saying that something is true; evidence is specific facts of when, who, where, and how much as well as supporting records like canceled checks and tax returns. Under state law, a note is enforceable unless the borrower can show that he paid the note or that the note was forged. * * *

* * * *

Sometimes students would like not to pay the loan because they now feel that the school they attended was not very good or that the education they got was not adequate to get them a good job. Even if these feelings are supported by solid evidence, they do not matter. The bank lent money, and the government promised the bank that the debt would be paid. Neither the bank nor the government guaranteed satisfaction with schools or educations.

Because the choice of institution and curriculum was the student's, the responsibility for a bad choice rests with the student.

* * * *

The government has demonstrated that the defendant issued the promissory note, that the government owns the note, and that the note is in default and unpaid. The law requires that there be a judgment for the government for the principal, interest, costs, and attorney's fees.

DECISION AND REMEDY *The court issued a judgment in favor of the government, holding Durbin liable for the unpaid balance of the note, plus interest, costs, and fees. Durbin issued the note, the government owned it, and it was unpaid.*

SECTION 4

Requirements for Negotiability

For an instrument to be negotiable, it must meet the following requirements:

1. Be in writing.
2. Be signed by the maker or the drawer.
3. Be an unconditional promise or order to pay.
4. State a fixed amount of money.
5. Be payable on demand or at a definite time.
6. Be payable to order or to bearer, unless it is a check.

WRITTEN FORM

Negotiable instruments must be in written form [UCC 3–103(a)(6)].[3] Clearly, an oral promise can create the danger of fraud or make it difficult to determine liability. Negotiable instruments must possess the quality of certainty that only formal, written expression can give. The writing must have the following qualities:

3. The writing requirement comes from the definitions of *order* and *promise* in UCC 3–103(a)(6), (9). In the unrevised Article 3, UCC 3–104(1) refers directly to "[a]ny writing."

EXHIBIT 24–5   A TYPICAL SMALL CD

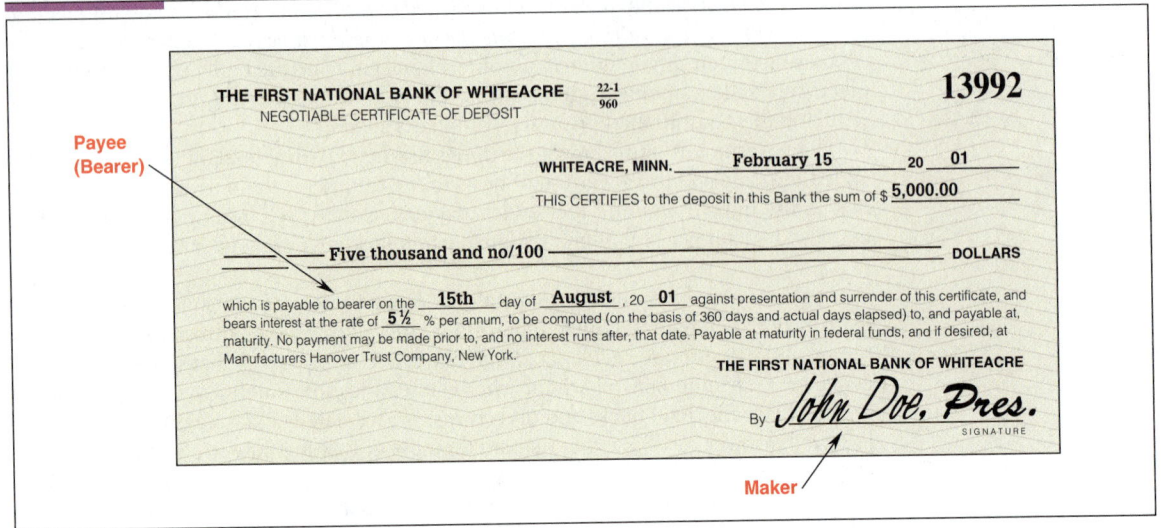

1. The writing must be on material that lends itself to *permanence*. Instruments carved in blocks of ice or recorded on other impermanent surfaces would not qualify as negotiable instruments. Suppose Shanda writes in the sand, "I promise to pay $500 to the order of Jason." This is not a negotiable instrument, because, although it is in writing, it lacks permanence.

2. The writing also must have *portability*. Although this is not a spelled-out legal requirement, if an instrument is not movable, it obviously cannot meet the requirement that it be freely transferable. For example, Cullen writes on the side of a cow, "I, Cullen, promise to pay to Merrill or her order $500 on demand." Technically, this meets the requirements of a negotiable instrument, but as a cow cannot easily be transferred in the ordinary course of business, the "instrument" is nonnegotiable.

2· SIGNATURES

For an instrument to be negotiable, it must be signed by (1) the maker if it is a note or a certificate of deposit or (2) the drawer if it is a draft or a check [UCC 3–103(a)(3), (5)]. If a person signs an instrument as an authorized *agent* for the maker or drawer, the maker or drawer has effectively signed the instrument. (Agents' signatures will be discussed in Chapter 26.)

The UCC grants extreme latitude in regard to what constitutes a signature. UCC 1–201(39) provides that a **signature** may include "any symbol executed or adopted by a party with present intention to authenticate a writing." UCC 3–401(b) expands on this by stating that a "signature may be made (i) manually or by means of a device or machine, and (ii) by the use of any name, including a trade or assumed name, or by a word, mark, or symbol executed or adopted by a person with present intention to authenticate a writing." Thus, initials, an X, or a thumbprint will suffice as a signature. A trade name or an assumed name is also sufficient. Signatures that are placed onto instruments by means of rubber stamps are permitted and frequently used in the business world. If necessary, parol evidence (discussed in Chapter 15) is admissible to identify the signer. When the signer is identified, the signature becomes effective.

The location of the signature on the document is unimportant, though the usual place is the lower right-hand corner. A *handwritten* statement on the body of the instrument, such as "I, Kammie Orlik, promise to pay Janel Tan," is sufficient to act as a signature.

There are virtually no limitations on the manner in which a signature can be made, but one should be careful about receiving an instrument that has been signed in an unusual way. Furthermore, an unusual signature clearly decreases the *marketability* of an instrument, because it creates uncertainty.

3· UNCONDITIONAL PROMISE OR ORDER TO PAY

The terms of the promise or order must be included in the writing on the face of a negotiable instrument. The terms must also be *unconditional*—that is, they cannot be conditioned on the occurrence or nonoccurrence of some other event or agreement [UCC 3–104(a)].

Promise or Order. For an instrument to be negotiable, it must contain an express order or promise to pay. A mere acknowledgment of the debt, which might logically *imply* a promise, is not sufficient under the UCC, because the promise must be an *affirmative* (express) undertaking [UCC 3–103(a)(9)]. For example, the traditional I.O.U. is only an acknowledgment of indebtedness. Although the I.O.U. might logically *imply* a promise, it is not a negotiable instrument, because it does not contain an express promise to repay the debt. If such words as "to be paid on demand" or "due on demand" are added to the I.O.U., however, the need for an express promise is satisfied. Thus, if a buyer executes a promissory note using the words "I promise to pay $1,000 to the order of the seller for the purchase of X goods," then this requirement for a negotiable instrument is satisfied.

A certificate of deposit is exceptional in this respect. No express promise is required in a CD, because the bank's acknowledgment of the deposit and the other terms of the instrument clearly indicate a promise by the bank to repay the sum of money [UCC 3–104(j)].

An *order* is associated with three-party instruments, such as trade acceptances, checks, and drafts. An order directs a third party to pay the instrument as drawn. In the typical check, for example, the word *pay* (to the order of a payee) is a command to the drawee bank to pay the check when presented, and thus it is an order. The order is mandatory even if it is written in a courteous form with such words as "Please pay" or "Kindly pay." Generally, precise language must be used. An order stating "I wish you would pay" does not fulfill the requirement of precision. The order may be addressed to one person or to more than one person, either jointly ("to A *and* B") or alternatively ("to A *or* B") [UCC 3–103(a)(6)].

Unconditionality of Promise or Order. A negotiable instrument's utility as a substitute for money or as a credit device would be dramatically reduced if it had conditional promises attached to it. It would be time consuming and expensive to investigate conditional promises, and therefore the transferability of the negotiable instrument would be greatly restricted. Suppose that Granados promises in a note to pay McGraw $10,000 only if a certain ship reaches port. No one could safely purchase the promissory note without first investigating whether the ship had arrived. Even then, the facts disclosed by the investigation might be incorrect. To avoid such problems, the UCC provides that only instruments with unconditional promises or orders can be negotiable [UCC 3–104(a)].

A promise or order is conditional (and *not* negotiable) if it states any of the following:

1. That there is an express condition to payment.
2. That the promise or order is subject to or governed by another writing.
3. That the rights or obligations with respect to the promise or order are stated in another writing.

A reference to another writing, however, does not of itself make the promise or order conditional [UCC 3–106(a)]. For example, the words "as per contract" or "This debt arises from the sale of goods X and Y" do not render an instrument nonnegotiable.

Similarly, a statement in the instrument that payment can be made only out of a particular fund or source will not render the instrument nonnegotiable [UCC 3–106(b)(ii)].[4] Thus, for example, terms in a note that include the condition that payment will be made out of the proceeds of next year's cotton crop will not make the note nonnegotiable. (The payee of such a note, however, may find the note commercially unacceptable and refuse to take it.)

Finally, a simple statement in an otherwise negotiable note indicating that the note is secured by a mortgage does not destroy its negotiability [UCC 3–106(b)(i)]. Actually, such a statement might even make the note even more acceptable in commerce. Realize, though, that the statement that a note is secured by a mortgage must not stipulate that the maker's promise to pay is *subject to* the terms and conditions of the mortgage [UCC 3–106(a)(ii)].

4· A FIXED AMOUNT OF MONEY

Negotiable instruments must state with certainty a fixed amount of money to be paid at any time the

---

4. Section 3–105(2) of the unrevised Article 3 provided just the opposite: a term providing that payment could be made only out of a particular fund or source rendered the instrument nonnegotiable.

instrument is payable [UCC 3–104(a)]. This require-ment promises clarity and certainty in determining the value of the instrument.

Fixed Amount.

The term *fixed amount* means an amount that is ascertainable from the face of the in-strument. A demand note payable with 10 percent in-terest meets the requirement of a fixed amount because its amount can be determined at the time it is payable [UCC 3–104(a)].

The rate of interest may also be determined with reference to information that is not contained in the instrument if that information is readily ascertainable by reference to a formula or a source described in the instrument [UCC 3–112(b)]. For example, when an instrument is payable at the *legal rate of interest* (a rate of interest fixed by statute), the instrument is ne-gotiable. Mortgage notes tied to a variable rate of in-terest (a rate that fluctuates as a result of market conditions) can also be negotiable.

Payable in Money.

UCC 3–104(a) provides that a fixed amount is to be *payable in money*. The UCC de-fines money as "a medium of exchange authorized or adopted by a domestic or foreign government as a part of its currency" [UCC 1–201(24)].

Suppose that the maker of a note promises "to pay on demand $1,000 in U.S. gold." Because gold is not a medium of exchange adopted by the U.S. government, the note is not payable in money. The same result occurs if the maker promises "to pay $1,000 and fifty liters of 1994 Chateau Lafite-Rothschild wine," be-cause the instrument is not payable *entirely* in money. An instrument payable in government bonds or in shares of IBM stock is not negotiable, because neither is a medium of exchange recognized by the U.S. gov-ernment. The statement "Payable in $1,000 U.S. cur-rency or an equivalent value in gold" would render the instrument nonnegotiable if the maker reserved the op-tion of paying in money *or* gold. If the option were left to the payee, some legal scholars argue that the instru-ment would be negotiable. Any instrument payable in the United States with a face amount stated in a foreign currency can be paid in the foreign money or in the equivalent in U.S. dollars [UCC 3–107].

5 PAYABLE ON DEMAND OR AT A DEFINITE TIME

A negotiable instrument must "be payable on demand or at a definite time" [UCC 3–104(a)(2)]. Clearly, to ascertain the value of a negotiable instrument, it is nec-essary to know when the maker, drawee, or acceptor is required to pay. It is also necessary to know when the obligations of secondary parties, such as *indorsers*[5] (to be discussed in Chapter 25), will arise. Furthermore, it is essential to know when an instrument is due in order to calculate when the statute of limitations may apply [UCC 3–118(a)]. Finally, with an interest-bearing in-strument, it is necessary to know the exact interval dur-ing which the interest will accrue to determine the instrument's value today.

Payable on Demand.

Instruments that are payable on demand include those that contain the words "Payable at sight" or "Payable upon presentment." **Presentment** occurs when a person presents an in-strument to the party liable on the note to collect pay-ment; presentment also occurs when a person presents an instrument to a drawee for acceptance—see the dis-cussion of trade acceptances earlier in this chapter.

The very nature of the instrument may indicate that it is payable on demand. For example, a check, by definition, is payable on demand [UCC 3–104(f)]. If no time for payment is specified and the person re-sponsible for payment must pay on the instrument's presentment, the instrument is payable on demand [UCC 3–108(a)].

Payable at a Definite Time.

If an instrument is not payable on demand, to be negotiable it must be payable at a definite time. An instrument is payable at a definite time if it states that it is payable (1) on a specified date, (2) within a definite period of time (such as thirty days) after sight or acceptance, or (3) on a date or time readily ascertainable at the time the promise or order is issued [UCC 3–108(b)]. The maker or drawee is under no obligation to pay until the specified time.

Suppose that an instrument dated June 1, 2001, states, "One year after the death of my grandfather, Jeremy Adams, I promise to pay to the order of Lucy Harmon $500. [Signed] Jacqueline Wells." This in-strument is nonnegotiable. Because the date of the grandfather's death is uncertain, the instrument is not payable at a definite time, even though the event is bound to occur or has already occurred.

---

5. We should note here that because the UCC uses the spelling *indorse* (*indorsement*, and so on), rather than the more common spelling *endorse* (*endorsement*, and so on), we adopt the UCC's spelling here and in other chapters in the text.

When an instrument is payable on or before a stated date, it is clearly payable at a definite time, although the maker has the option of paying before the stated maturity date. This uncertainty does not violate the definite-time requirement. Suppose that John gives Ernesto an instrument dated May 1, 2001, that indicates on its face that it is payable on or before May 1, 2003. This instrument satisfies the requirement. In contrast, an instrument that is undated and made payable "one month after date" is clearly nonnegotiable. There is no way to determine the maturity date from the face of the instrument.

The issue in the following case was whether a particular promissory note, on which the "date" blanks had not been filled in, was payable at a definite time.

CASE 24.2 Barclays Bank PLC[a] v. Johnson

Court of Appeals of North Carolina, 1998. 129 N.C.App. 370, 499 S.E.2d 768. http://www.aoc.state. nc.us/www/public/html/ opinions.htm[b]

COMPANY PROFILE *Barclays PLC (http://www.barclays.co.uk.) is one of the largest financial services companies in the United Kingdom (UK) and offers banking and investment services in other countries worldwide. Through Barclays Bank PLC and Barclays's other divisions, the company is involved in consumer and business banking (with nearly two thousand branches in the UK and one thousand branches in seventy-six other countries), credit cards, mortgage lending, factoring, leasing services, and travel agency services. Barclays also sells life insurance, manages pensions, and offers private banking services.*

BACKGROUND AND FACTS *Mark Johnson signed a promissory note for $28,979.15 in favor of Healthco International, Inc., as part of Johnson's purchase of supplies from Healthco for his dental practice. The note stated that it was payable as follows:*

> *Payable in ____, Successive Monthly Installments of $ _____ Each, and in 11 Successive Monthly Installments of $2,414.92 Each thereafter, and in a final payment of $2,415.03 thereafter. The first installment being payable on the __ day of _____ 19 __, and the remaining installments on the same date of each month thereafter until paid.*

The blanks were never filled in. Barclays Bank PLC bought the note. When Johnson defaulted on the note, Barclays filed a complaint in a North Carolina state court against Johnson. Johnson responded in part that he had not paid off the note because he had not received all of the supplies. Concluding that the note was not negotiable because it was not payable at a definite time, the court issued a summary judgment in Johnson's favor. Barclays appealed.

IN THE LANGUAGE OF THE COURT

McGEE, Judge.

*   *   *   *

Barclays Bank argues that the note is a negotiable instrument even though it does not state that it is payable on demand or at a definite time. We disagree. Historically, our courts have required strict compliance with the requirements set out under the Uniform Commercial Code defining negotiable instruments. The drafters of the Code encouraged the courts to strictly interpret the definitional requirements to the extent that "in doubtful cases the [court's] decision should be against negotiability." In this case it is undisputed that the note did not state either that it was payable on demand or at a definite time. For this reason, we hold that the note does not meet the requirements of [the UCC] for negotiability.

---

a. *PLC* is an abbreviation for "Public Limited Company," a company in the United Kingdom with more than fifty shareholders that offers its shares for sale to the public but whose shareholders are not liable for company debts beyond the amount of their investments.

b. This page, within the Web site of the North Carolina state courts, contains links to some of the courts' opinions. In the "Court of Appeals Opinions" boxes, click on "1998" and on the page that opens, scroll down the list (or use your browser's "Find" function) to locate this case.

DECISION AND REMEDY   *The Court of Appeals of North Carolina affirmed the judgment of the lower court. The state intermediate appellate court held that to be negotiable, an instrument must state that it is payable on demand or at a definite time.*

Acceleration Clause. An **acceleration clause** allows a payee or other holder of a time instrument to demand payment of the entire amount due, with interest, if a certain event occurs, such as a default in payment of an installment when due.

Assume that Martin lends $1,000 to Ruth. Ruth makes a negotiable note promising to pay $100 per month for eleven months. The note contains an acceleration provision that permits Martin or any holder to demand at once all the payments plus the interest owed to date if Ruth fails to pay an installment in any given month. If, for example, Ruth fails to make the third payment and Martin accelerates the unpaid balance, the note will be due and payable in full. Ruth will owe Martin the remaining principal plus any unpaid interest.

Under the UCC, instruments that include acceleration clauses are negotiable regardless of the reasons for the accelerations, because (1) the exact value of the instrument can be ascertained and (2) the instrument will be payable on a specified date if the event allowing acceleration does not occur [UCC 3–108(b)(ii)]. Thus, the specified date is the outside limit used to determine the value of the instrument.

Extension Clause. The reverse of an acceleration clause is an **extension clause,** which allows the date of maturity to be extended into the future [UCC 3–108(b)(iii), (iv)]. To keep the instrument negotiable, the interval of the extension must be specified if the right to extend is given to the maker or the drawer of the instrument. If, however, the holder of the instrument can extend it, the extended maturity date does not have to be specified.

Suppose that a note reads, "The maker has the right to postpone the time of payment of this note beyond its definite maturity date of January 1, 2003. This extension, however, shall be for no more than a reasonable time." A note with this language is not negotiable, because it does not satisfy the definite-time requirement. The right to extend is the maker's, and the maker has not indicated when the note will become due after the extension.

In contrast, suppose that a note reads, "The holder of this note at the date of maturity, January 1, 2003,

can extend the time of payment until the following June 1 or later, if the holder so wishes." This note is a negotiable instrument. The length of the extension does not have to be specified, because the option to extend is solely that of the holder. After January 1, 2003, the note is, in effect, a demand instrument.

PAYABLE TO ORDER OR TO BEARER

Because one of the functions of a negotiable instrument is to serve as a substitute for money, freedom to transfer is essential. To assure a proper transfer, the instrument must be "payable to order or to bearer" at the time it is issued or first comes into the possession of the holder [UCC 3–104(a)(1)]. An instrument is not negotiable unless it meets this requirement.

Order Instruments. An **order instrument** is an instrument that is payable (1) "to the order of an identified person" or (2) "to an identified person or order" [UCC 3–109(b)]. An identified person is the person "to whom the instrument is initially payable" as determined by the intent of the maker or drawer [UCC 3–110(a)]. The identified person, in turn, may transfer the instrument to whomever he or she wishes. Thus, the maker or drawer is agreeing to pay either the person specified on the instrument or whomever that person might designate. In this way, the instrument retains its transferability. Suppose an instrument states, "Payable to the order of James Jarrot" or "Pay to James Jarrot or order." Clearly, the maker or drawer has indicated that a payment will be made to Jarrot or to whomever Jarrot designates. The instrument is negotiable.

Except for bearer instruments (explained in the following paragraph), the person specified must be named with *certainty*, because the transfer of an order instrument requires an indorsement. (An **indorsement** is a signature placed on an instrument, such as on the back of a check, generally for the purpose of transferring one's ownership rights in the instrument. Indorsements will be discussed at length in Chapter 25.) If an instrument states, "Payable to the order of my kissing cousin," the instrument is nonnegotiable, because a holder could not be sure that the person who indorsed the instrument was actually the "kissing cousin" who was supposed to have indorsed it.

Bearer Instruments. A **bearer instrument** is an instrument that does not designate a specific payee [UCC 3–109(a)]. The term **bearer** refers to a person in possession of an instrument that is payable to bearer or indorsed in blank (with a signature only, as will be discussed in Chapter 25) [UCC 1–201(5), 3–109(a), 3–109(c)]. This means that the maker or drawer agrees to pay anyone who presents the instrument for payment. Any instrument containing one of the following terms is a bearer instrument:

1. "Payable to the order of bearer."
2. "Payable to Rocky Reed or bearer."
3. "Payable to bearer."
4. "Pay cash."
5. "Pay to the order of cash."

In addition, an instrument that "indicates that it is not payable to an identified person" is a bearer instrument [UCC 3–109(a)(3)]. Thus, an instrument that is "payable to X" can be negotiated as a bearer instrument, as though it were payable to cash. An instrument that is "payable to the order of the Camrod Company," however, if no such company exists, is not a bearer instrument, because the UCC does not accept an instrument issued to a nonexistent organization as payable to bearer [UCC 3–109, Comment 2].

CONCEPT SUMMARY 24.1

REQUIREMENTS FOR NEGOTIABILITY

REQUIREMENTS	BASIC RULES
Must Be in Writing UCC 3–103(6), (9)	A writing can be anything that is readily transferable and that has a degree of permanence. [See also UCC 1–201(46).]
Must Be Signed by the Maker or Drawer UCC 1–201(39) UCC 3–103(a)(3), (5) UCC 3–401(b) UCC 3–402	1. The signature can be anyplace on the instrument. 2. It can be in any form (such as a word, mark, or rubber stamp) that purports to be a signature and authenticates the writing. 3. A signature may be made in a representative capacity.
Must Be a Definite Promise or Order UCC 3–103(a)(6), (9) UCC 3–104(a)	1. A promise must be more than a mere acknowledgment of a debt. 2. The words "I/We promise" or "Pay" meet this criterion.
Must Be Unconditional UCC 3–106	1. Payment cannot be expressly conditional on the occurrence of an event. 2. Payment cannot be made subject to or governed by another agreement.
Must Be an Order or Promise to Pay a Fixed Amount UCC 3–104(a) UCC 3–112 (b)	An amount may be considered a fixed sum even if payable in installments, with fixed or variable rates of interest, at a stated discount, or at an exchange rate.
Must Be Payable in Money UCC 3–104(a)(3) UCC 3–107	1. Any medium of exchange recognized as the currency of a government is money. 2. The maker or drawer cannot retain the option to pay the instrument in money *or* something else.

CONCEPT SUMMARY 24.1

REQUIREMENTS FOR NEGOTIABILITY (*continued*)

REQUIREMENTS	BASIC RULES
Must Be Payable on Demand or at a Definite Time UCC 3–104(a)(2) UCC 3–108(a), (b), (c)	1. Any instrument that is payable on sight, presentation, or issue or that does not state any time for payment is a demand instrument. 2. An instrument is still payable at a definite time, even if it is payable on or before a stated date or within a fixed period after sight or if the drawer or maker has an option to extend the time for a definite period. 3. Acceleration clauses do not affect the negotiability of the instrument.
Must Be Payable to Order or Bearer UCC 3–104(a)(1), (c) UCC 3–109 UCC 3–110(a)	1. An order instrument must identify the payee with reasonable certainty. 2. An instrument whose terms intend payment to no particular person is payable to bearer. 3. Checks are not required to be payable to order or bearer.

SECTION 5

Factors Not Affecting Negotiability

Certain ambiguities or omissions will not affect the negotiability of an instrument. Article 3's rules for interpreting ambiguous terms include the following:

1. Unless the date of an instrument is necessary to determine a definite time for payment, the fact that an instrument is undated does not affect its negotiability. A typical example is a check that has no date [UCC 3–113(b)].

2. Postdating or antedating an instrument does not affect negotiability [UCC 3–113(a)].

3. Handwritten terms outweigh typewritten and printed terms (preprinted terms on forms, for example), and typewritten terms outweigh printed terms [UCC 3–114]. For example, if your check is printed, "Pay to the order of," and in handwriting you insert in the blank, "Anita Delgado or bearer," the check is a bearer instrument.

4. Words outweigh figures unless the words are ambiguous [UCC 3–114]. This is important when the numerical amount and written amount on a check differ.

5. When a particular interest rate is not specified but the instrument simply states "with interest," the interest rate is the judgment rate of interest (a rate of interest fixed by statute that is applied to a monetary judgment awarded by a court until the judgment is paid or terminated) [UCC 3–112(b)].

6. A notation on a check that it is "nonnegotiable" or "not governed by Article 3" has no effect on a check's negotiability. Any other instrument, however, even if it meets all of the requirements of negotiability, can be made nonnegotiable by the maker's or drawer's conspicuously noting on it that it is "nonnegotiable" or "not governed by Article 3" [UCC 3–104(d)].[6]

---

6. This is not true under the unrevised Article 3.

TERMS AND CONCEPTS TO REVIEW

acceleration clause 430	bearer instrument 431	draft 421
acceptance 421	certificate of deposit (CD) 424	drawee 421
banker's acceptance 423	check 423	drawer 421
bearer 431	demand deposit 421	extension clause 430

holder 421

indorsement 421

issue 421

maker 423

negotiable instrument 420

order instrument 430

payee 421

presentment 428

promissory note 423

signature 426

trade acceptance 423

QUESTIONS AND CASE PROBLEMS

24–1. PARTIES TO NEGOTIABLE INSTRUMENTS. A college student, Maynard Keynes, wished to purchase a new DVD player from Friedman Electronics, Inc. Because Keynes did not have the cash to pay for the equipment, he offered to sign a note promising to pay $150 per month for the next six months. Friedman Electronics, anxious to sell the player to Keynes, agreed to accept the promissory note, which read, "I, Maynard Keynes, promise to pay to Friedman Electronics or its order the sum of $150 per month for the next six months." The note was signed by Maynard Keynes. About a week later, Friedman Electronics, which was badly in need of cash, signed the back of the note and sold it to the First National Bank of Halston. Give the specific designation of each of the three parties on this note.

24–2. REQUIREMENTS FOR NEGOTIABILITY. The following note is written by Juan Sanchez on the back of an envelope: "I, Juan Sanchez, promise to pay Kathy Martin or bearer $500 on demand." Is this a negotiable instrument? Discuss fully.

24–3. REQUIREMENTS FOR NEGOTIABILITY. The following instrument was written on a sheet of paper by Sabrina Runyan: "I, the undersigned, do hereby acknowledge that I owe Leo Woo one thousand dollars, with interest, payable out of the proceeds of the sale of my horse, Lightning, next month. Payment is to be made on or before six months from date." Discuss specifically why this instrument is nonnegotiable.

24–4. NEGOTIABILITY. Adam's checks are imprinted with the words "Pay to the order of" followed by a blank. Adam fills in an amount on one of the checks and signs it, but he does not write anything in the blank following the "Pay to the order of" language. Adam gives this check to Beth. On another of the checks, Adam writes in the blank "Carl or bearer." Which, if any, of these checks are bearer instruments, and why? Explain.

24–5. NEGOTIABLE VERSUS NONNEGOTIABLE INSTRUMENTS. Briggs signed a note that read in part as follows: "*Ninety days* after date, I, we, or either of us, promise to pay to the order of *Three Thousand Four Hundred Ninety-Eight and 45/100—Dollars.*" The words and symbols in italic were typed, and the remainder of the words in this quotation were preprinted. No blanks had been left on the face of the instrument; any unused space had been filled in with hyphens. The note contained several clauses that permitted acceleration in

the event the holder deemed itself insecure. When the note was not paid at maturity, Broadway Management Corp. brought suit on the note for full payment, claiming that it (Broadway) was a holder. Is this an order or bearer instrument? What changes, if any, would have to be made on the note for it to be a negotiable instrument? [*Broadway Management Corp. v. Briggs*, 30 Ill.App.3d 403, 332 N.E.2d 131 (1975)]

24–6. WORDS VERSUS FIGURES. Eugene Kindy, a seller of diesel engine parts, agreed to buy four diesel engines from Tony Hicks for $13,000. Kindy transferred $6,500 by wire and issued a check for the remainder. Kindy placed two different amounts on the check, because he did not want the check honored until Hicks had delivered the engine parts. Using a check-imprinting machine, Kindy imprinted $5,500 on the check in the space where the dollar amount is normally written in words, but he wrote $6,500 in figures in the box usually reserved for numbers. An employee of Galatia Community State Bank, noticing the discrepancy, altered the figures to read "$5,500," initialed the change, and accepted the check. The check was returned to Galatia by First National Bank at Kindy's request because Hicks had not delivered the engine parts. In the litigation that followed, a key issue was whether the machine-imprinted figure took precedence over the handwritten figure. What should the court decide on this issue? Discuss. [*Galatia Community State Bank v. Kindy*, 807 Ark. 467, 821 S.W.2d 765 (1991)]

24–7. FIXED AMOUNT OF MONEY. William Bailey and William Vaught, as officers for Bailey, Vaught, Robertson, and Co. (BVR), signed a promissory note to borrow $34,000 from the Forestwood National Bank. The interest rate was variable: "the lender's published prime rate" plus 1 percent. Forestwood went out of business, and ultimately, the note was acquired by Remington Investments, Inc. When BVR failed to make payments, Remington filed a suit in a Texas state court against BVR. BVR contended in part that the note was not negotiable because after Forestwood closed, there was no "published lender's prime rate" to use to calculate the interest. Did the note provide for payment of a "fixed amount of money"? Discuss fully. [*Bailey, Vaught, Robertson, and Co. v. Remington Investments, Inc.*, 888 S.W.2d 860 (Tex.App.—Dallas 1994)]

24–8. NEGOTIABILITY. Regent Corp., U.S.A., an import company in New York, contracted with Azmat

Bangladesh, Ltd., a textile company in Bangladesh, for the purchase of bed sheets and pillowcases for import into and resale in the United States. An essential condition of the sale was that the goods be manufactured in Bangladesh. The contract required payment by Regent within ninety days of the date on the bill of lading, and Regent issued promissory notes that indicated this term. After the goods were shipped, Azmat's bank presented drafts drawn against Regent to Regent's banks. Like the notes, each draft indicated that payment was to be made "at 90 days deferred from bill of lading date." The drafts were accompanied by dated bills of lading. On delivery of the goods, U.S. Customs refused to allow their entry because they were partially manufactured in Pakistan. Regent filed a suit in a New York state court against its banks, and Azmat, to stop payment on the drafts. One of the issues was whether the notes and drafts were "payable at a definite time." How should the court rule on this issue? Explain fully. [*Regent Corp., U.S.A. v. Azmat Bangladesh, Ltd.*, 253 A.D.2d 134, 686 N.Y.S.2d 24 (1 Dept. 1999)]

24–9. IN YOUR COURT

Walter Peffer loaned $125,000 to the Pefferoni Pizza Co. The promissory note included a clause that allowed the maker (Pefferoni Pizza) to renegotiate the terms of repayment at any time and then extend the time for repayment by up to eighty-four months. Later, Peffer borrowed money from Northern Bank, using the Pefferoni Pizza note as collateral. When Peffer failed to repay his loan, the bank tried to collect on the collateral note, but the pizza company failed to pay. The bank filed a suit in a Nebraska state court against Pefferoni Pizza to recover on the collateral note. Pefferoni Pizza argued in part that its note was not a negotiable instrument because under the renegotiation clause, it was not payable at a definite time. Assume that you are the judge in the trial court hearing this case and answer the following questions:

(a) In its opinion in Case 24.2 (*Barclays Bank PLC v. Johnson*), the court stated that "in doubtful cases the [court's] decision should be against negotiability." Is the case now before your court a "doubtful" case with respect to the requirements for negotiability? Generally, are the facts in Case 24.2 at all similar to the facts in the case now before your court? Explain.

(b) How will you rule on the issue now before your court? What UCC provision, if any, will you cite to justify your decision?

LAW ON THE WEB

For updated links to resources available on the Web, as well as a variety of other materials, visit this text's Web site at http://wbl.westbuslaw.com.

The National Conference of Commissioners on Uniform State Laws, in association with the University of Pennsylvania Law School, now offers an official site for in-process and final drafts of uniform and model acts. For an index of final acts, including UCC Articles 3 and 4, go to

http://www.law.upenn.edu/bll/ulc/ulc_final.htm

Cornell University's Legal Information Institute offers online access to the UCC, as well as to UCC articles as enacted by particular states and proposed revisions to articles, at

http://www.law.cornell.edu/ucc/ucc.table.html

British author Sir Alan Herbert has some fun with the "written form" requirement for a negotiable instrument in his entertaining (and fictitious) story entitled "The Negotiable Cow," which can be found online at

http://www.kmoser.com/herb04.htm

LEGAL RESEARCH EXERCISES ON THE WEB

Go to http://wbl.westbuslaw.com, the Web site that accompanies this text. Select "Internet Applications," and then click on "Chapter 24." There you will find the following Internet research exercise that you can perform to learn more about negotiable instruments:

Activity 24–1: Overview of Negotiable Instruments

CHAPTER 25

Transferability and Holder in Due Course

O NCE ISSUED, A NEGOTIABLE instrument can be transferred to others by *assignment* or by *negotiation*. Recall from Chapter 16 that an assignment is a transfer of rights under a contract. Under general contract principles, a transfer by assignment to an assignee gives the assignee only those rights that the assignor possessed. Any defenses that can be raised against an assignor can normally be raised against the assignee. This same principle applies when an instrument, such as a promissory note, is transferred by assignment. The transferee is then an *assignee* rather than a *holder*. Sometimes, a transfer fails to qualify as a negotiation because it fails to meet one or more of the requirements of a negotiable instrument, discussed in Chapter 24. A transfer may also fail to qualify as a negotiation if the instrument is transferred by delivery only, without a required indorsement. In either of these situations, the transfer becomes an assignment.

Negotiation is the transfer of an instrument in such form that the transferee (the person to whom the instrument is transferred) becomes a holder [UCC 3–201(a)]. In the first part of this chapter, we look at the requirements for negotiation, which differ depending on whether the instrument is an order instrument or a bearer instrument. We then examine the various types of *indorsements* that are used when order instruments are negotiated.

Under Uniform Commercial Code (UCC) principles, a transfer by negotiation creates a holder who, at the very least, receives the rights of the previous possessor [UCC 3–203(b), 3–305]. Unlike an assignment, a transfer by negotiation can make it possible for a holder to receive *more* rights in the instrument than the prior possessor had [UCC 3–305]. A holder who receives greater rights is known as a *holder in due course*, a concept we discuss in the final pages of the chapter.

SECTION 1

Negotiation

There are two methods of negotiating an instrument so that the receiver becomes a holder. As just mentioned, the method used depends on whether the instrument is an order instrument or a bearer instrument.

NEGOTIATING ORDER INSTRUMENTS

An order instrument contains the name of a payee capable of indorsing, as in "Pay to the order of Elliot Goodseal." If an instrument is an order instrument, it

435

is negotiated by delivery with any necessary indorsements. For example, the Carrington Corporation issues a payroll check "to the order of Elliot Goodseal." Goodseal takes the check to the supermarket, signs his name on the back (an indorsement), gives it to the cashier (a delivery), and receives cash. Goodseal has negotiated the check to the supermarket [UCC 3–201(b)].

NEGOTIATING BEARER INSTRUMENTS

If an instrument is payable to bearer, it is negotiated by delivery—that is, by transfer into another person's possession. Indorsement is not necessary [UCC 3–201(b)]. The use of bearer instruments thus involves more risk through loss or theft than the use of order instruments.

Assume that Alan Tyson writes a check payable to "cash," thus creating a bearer instrument, and hands the check to Blaine Parrington (a delivery). Parrington places the check in his wallet, which is subsequently stolen. The thief has possession of the check. At this point, the thief has no rights in the check. If the thief "delivers" the check to an innocent third person, however, negotiation will be complete. All rights to the check will be passed *absolutely* to that third person, and Parrington will lose all right to recover the proceeds of the check from that person

[UCC 3–306]. Of course, Parrington can recover his money from the thief if the thief can be found.

CONVERTING ORDER INSTRUMENTS TO BEARER INSTRUMENTS AND VICE VERSA

The method used for negotiation depends on the character of the instrument *at the time the negotiation takes place.* For example, a check originally payable to "cash" but subsequently indorsed with the words "Pay to Arnold" must be negotiated as an order instrument (by indorsement and delivery), even though it was previously a bearer instrument [UCC 3–205(a)].

An instrument payable to the order of a named payee and indorsed in blank (by the holder's signature only, as will be discussed shortly) becomes a bearer instrument [UCC 3–205(b)]. For example, a check made payable to the order of Jessie Arnold is issued to Arnold, and Arnold indorses it by signing her name on the back. The instrument, which is now a bearer instrument, can be negotiated by delivery without indorsement. Arnold can negotiate the check to whomever she wishes merely by delivery, and that person can negotiate by delivery without indorsement. If Arnold loses the check after she indorses it, then a finder can negotiate it further. Exhibit 25–1 illustrates how indorsements can convert an order instrument into a bearer instrument and vice versa.

EXHIBIT 25–1   CONVERTING AN ORDER INSTRUMENT TO A BEARER INSTRUMENT AND VICE VERSA

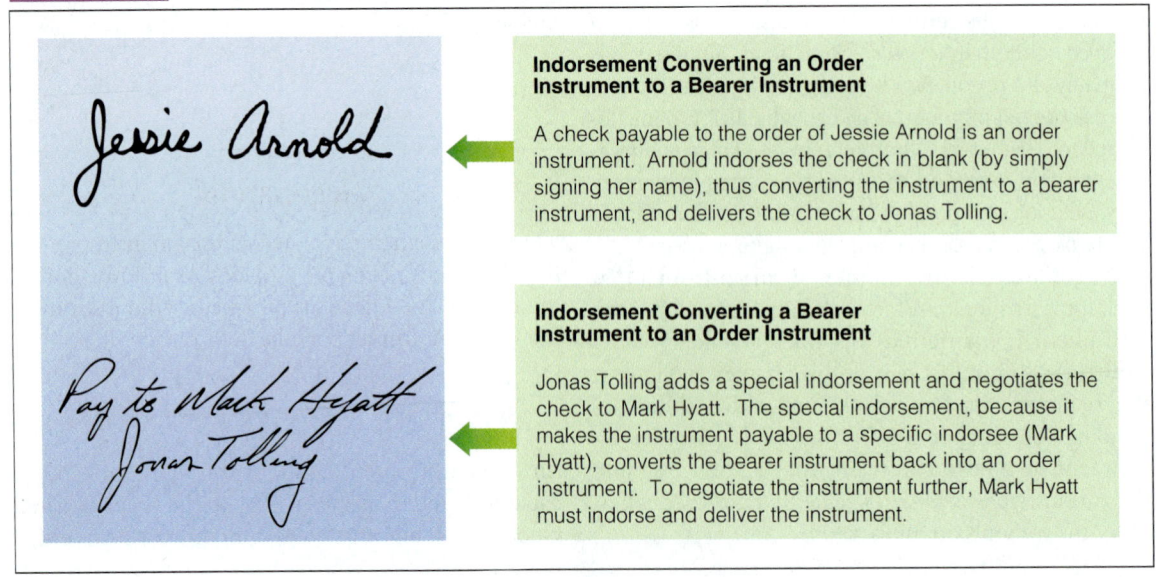

Indorsement Converting an Order Instrument to a Bearer Instrument

A check payable to the order of Jessie Arnold is an order instrument. Arnold indorses the check in blank (by simply signing her name), thus converting the instrument to a bearer instrument, and delivers the check to Jonas Tolling.

Indorsement Converting a Bearer Instrument to an Order Instrument

Jonas Tolling adds a special indorsement and negotiates the check to Mark Hyatt. The special indorsement, because it makes the instrument payable to a specific indorsee (Mark Hyatt), converts the bearer instrument back into an order instrument. To negotiate the instrument further, Mark Hyatt must indorse and deliver the instrument.

SECTION 2

Indorsements

An indorsement is required whenever an instrument being negotiated is classified as an order instrument. An *indorsement* is a signature with or without additional words or statements. It is most often written on the back of the instrument itself. If there is no room on the instrument, indorsements can be written on a separate piece of paper, called an **allonge.**[1] The allonge must be "so firmly affixed [to the instrument] as to become a part thereof" [UCC 3–204(a)]. Pins or paper clips will not suffice. Most courts hold that staples are sufficient.

A person who transfers a note or a draft by signing (indorsing) it and delivering it to another person is an **indorser.** For example, Luisa Parks receives a graduation check for $100. She can transfer the check to her mother (or to anyone) by signing it on the back. Luisa is an indorser. If Luisa indorses the check by writing "Pay to Aretha Parks," Aretha Parks is the **indorsee.**

We examine here four categories of indorsements: blank indorsements, special indorsements, qualified indorsements, and restrictive indorsements.

BLANK INDORSEMENTS

A **blank indorsement** specifies no particular indorsee and can consist of a mere signature [UCC 3–205(b)]. Hence, a check payable "to the order of Mark Deitsch" can be indorsed in blank simply by having Deitsch's signature written on the back of the check. Exhibit 25–2 shows a blank indorsement.

EXHIBIT 25–2   A BLANK INDORSEMENT

Mark Deitsch

An instrument payable to order and indorsed in blank becomes a bearer instrument and can be negotiated by delivery alone [UCC 3–205(b)]. In other words, as discussed earlier, a blank indorsement converts an order instrument to a bearer instrument, which anybody can cash. If Rita Chou indorses in blank a check payable to her order and then loses it on the street,

Coker can find it and sell it to Duncan for value without indorsing it. This constitutes a negotiation, because Coker has made delivery of a bearer instrument (which was an order instrument until it was indorsed in blank).

SPECIAL INDORSEMENTS

A **special indorsement** identifies the person to whom the indorser intends to make the instrument payable; that is, it names the indorsee [UCC 3–205(a)]. For example, words such as "Pay to the order of Clay" or "Pay to Clay," followed by the signature of the indorser, are sufficient. When an instrument is indorsed in this way, it is an order instrument.

To avoid the risk of loss from theft, a holder may convert a blank indorsement to a special indorsement. This changes the bearer instrument back to an order instrument. A holder may "convert a blank indorsement that consists only of a signature into a special indorsement by writing, above the signature of the indorser, words identifying the person to whom the instrument is made payable" [UCC 3–205(c)].

For example, a check is made payable to Hal Jones. He indorses his name by blank indorsement on the back of the check and negotiates the check to William Hunter. Hunter, not wishing to cash the check immediately, wants to avoid any risk should he lose the check. He therefore writes "Pay to William Hunter" above Jones's blank indorsement. In this manner, Hunter has converted Jones's blank indorsement into a special indorsement. Further negotiation now requires William Hunter's indorsement plus delivery. (See Exhibit 25–3.)

EXHIBIT 25–3   A SPECIAL INDORSEMENT

Pay to William Hunter
Hal Jones

QUALIFIED INDORSEMENTS

Generally, an indorser, *merely by indorsing,* impliedly promises to pay the holder, or any subsequent indorser, the amount of the instrument in the event that the drawer or maker defaults on the payment [UCC 3–415(b)]. Usually, then, indorsements are *unqualified indorsements.* That is, the indorser is guaranteeing payment of the instrument in addition to transferring title to it. An indorser who does not wish to be liable on an instrument can use a **qualified indorsement** to

---

1. Pronounced uh-*lohnj.*

disclaim this liability. The notation "without recourse" is commonly used to create a qualified indorsement.

Suppose that a check is made payable to the order of Sarah Jacobs. Sarah wants to negotiate the check to Allison Jong but does not want to assume liability for the check's payment. Sarah could create a qualified indorsement by indorsing the check as follows: "Pay to Allison Jong, without recourse. [Signed] Sarah Jacobs." (See Exhibit 25–4.)

EXHIBIT 25–4   A QUALIFIED INDORSEMENT

Qualified indorsements are often used by persons acting in a representative capacity. For example, insurance agents sometimes receive checks payable to them that are really intended as payment to the insurance company. The agent is merely indorsing the payment through to the insurance company and should not be required to make good on the check if it is later dishonored. The "without recourse" indorsement relieves the agent from any liability on a check. If the instrument is dishonored, the holder cannot obtain recovery from the agent who indorsed "without recourse" unless the indorser has breached one of the transfer warranties discussed in Chapter 26, which relate to good title, authorized signature, no material alteration, and so forth.

A qualified indorsement ("without recourse") can be accompanied by a special indorsement or a blank indorsement. A special qualified indorsement includes the name of the indorsee as well as the words "without recourse," as in Exhibit 25–4. The special indorsement makes the instrument an order instrument, and it requires an indorsement plus delivery for negotiation. A blank qualified indorsement makes the instrument a bearer instrument, and only delivery is required for negotiation. In either situation, the instrument still transfers title to the indorsee and can be further negotiated.

RESTRICTIVE INDORSEMENTS

The **restrictive indorsement** requires indorsees to comply with certain instructions regarding the funds involved. A restrictive indorsement does not prohibit the further negotiation of an instrument [UCC 3–206(a)]. Restrictive indorsements come in many forms, some of which we discuss here.

Indorsements Prohibiting Further Indorsement. An indorsement such as "Pay to Julie Thrush only. [Signed] Thomas Fasulo" does not destroy negotiability. Thrush can negotiate the paper to a holder just as if it had read "Pay to Julie Thrush. [Signed] Thomas Fasulo" [UCC 3–206(a)]. If the holder gives value, this type of restrictive indorsement has the same legal effect as a special indorsement.

Conditional Indorsements. When payment depends on the occurrence of some event specified in the indorsement, the instrument has a conditional indorsement [UCC 3–204(a)]. For example, suppose that Ken Barton indorses a check as follows: "Pay to Lars Johansen if he completes the renovation of my kitchen by June 1, 2002. [Signed] Ken Barton." Article 3 states that an indorsement conditioning the right to receive payment "does not affect the right of the indorsee to enforce the instrument" [UCC 3–206(b)]. A person paying or taking an instrument for value (taking for value will be discussed later in the chapter) can disregard the condition without liability.[2]

A conditional indorsement does not prevent further negotiation of the instrument. If conditional language appears on the *face* of an instrument, however, the instrument is not negotiable, because it does not meet the requirement that a negotiable instrument must contain an unconditional promise to pay.

Indorsements for Deposit or Collection. A common type of restrictive indorsement is one that makes the indorsee (almost always a bank) a collecting agent of the indorser [UCC 3–206(c)]. Exhibit 25–5 illustrates this type of indorsement on a check payable and issued to Aimee St. Amant. In particular, the indorsements "Pay any bank or banker" and "For deposit only" have the effect of locking the instrument into the bank collection process. Only a bank can acquire the rights of a holder following one of the indorsements until the item has been specially indorsed by a bank to a person who is not a bank [UCC 3–206(c), 4–201(b)]. A bank's liability for payment of an instrument with a restrictive indorsement of this kind is discussed in Chapter 27.

---

2. Under Section 3–206(3) of the unrevised Article 3, the indorsement was enforceable (except against intermediary banks, defined in Chapter 27), and neither the indorsee nor any subsequent holder had the right to enforce payment against that indorser on the instrument before the condition was met.

EXHIBIT 25-5 FOR DEPOSIT/FOR COLLECTION INDORSEMENT

> For deposit only
> Aimee St. Amant

or

> For collection only
> Aimee St. Amant

Trust Indorsements. Indorsements to persons who are to hold or use the funds for the benefit of the indorser or a third party are called **trust indorsements** (also known as agency indorsements). For example, assume that Ralph Zimmer asks his accountant, Stephanie Contento, to pay some bills for him while he is out of the country. He indorses a check, drawn by Bill Heise, to Stephanie Contento "as agent for Ralph Zimmer." This agency indorsement obligates Contento to use the funds from the Heise check only for the benefit of Zimmer [UCC 3–206(d), (e)].

The result of a trust indorsement is that legal rights in the instrument are transferred to the original indorsee. To the extent that the original indorsee pays or applies the proceeds consistently with the indorsement (for example, in an indorsement stating "Pay to Ellen Cook in trust for Roger Callahan"), the indorsee is a holder and can become a holder in due course (a status that will be described shortly). Sample trust (agency) indorsements are shown in Exhibit 25–6.

EXHIBIT 25-6 TRUST INDORSEMENTS

> Pay to Stephanie Contento
> as Agent for Ralph Zimmer
>
> Ralph Zimmer

or

> Pay to Ellen Cook
> in trust for Roger Callahan
>
> Roger Callahan

The fiduciary restrictions—restrictions mandated by a relationship involving trust and loyalty—on the instrument do not reach beyond the original indorsee [UCC 3–206(d), (e)]. Any subsequent purchaser can qualify as a holder in due course unless he or she has actual notice that the instrument was negotiated in breach of a fiduciary duty.[3]

SECTION 3

Miscellaneous Indorsement Problems

Of course, a significant problem in relation to indorsements occurs when an indorsement is forged or unauthorized. The UCC rules concerning unauthorized or forged signatures and indorsements will be discussed in Chapter 26 in the context of signature liability and again in Chapter 27 in the context of the bank's liability for payment of an instrument containing an unauthorized signature. Here we look at two other problems that may arise with indorsements.

An indorsement should be identical to the name that appears on the instrument. The payee or indorsee whose name is misspelled can indorse with the misspelled name, the correct name, or both [UCC 3–204(d)]. For example, if Marie Ellison receives a check payable to the order of Mary Ellison, she can indorse the check either "Marie Ellison" or "Mary Ellison." The usual practice is to indorse with the name as it appears on the instrument and follow it by the correct name.

An instrument payable to two or more persons *in the alternative* (for example, "Pay to the order of Ying or Mifflin") requires the indorsement of only one of the payees [UCC 3–110(d)]. If, however, an instrument is made payable to two or more persons *jointly* (for example, "Pay to the order of Bridgette and Tony VanHorn"), all of the payees' indorsements are necessary for negotiation. If an instrument payable to two or more persons does not clearly indicate whether it is payable in the alternative or payable jointly, then "the instrument is payable to the persons alternatively" [UCC 3–110(d)]. The same principles apply to special indorsements that identify more than one person to whom the indorser intends to make the instrument payable [UCC 3–205(a)].

---

3. See *In re Quantum Development Corp.*, 397 F.Supp. 329 (D.Virgin Islands 1975).

A negotiable instrument can be drawn payable to a legal entity such as an estate, a partnership, or an organization. For example, a check may read "Pay to the order of the Red Cross." An authorized representative of the Red Cross can negotiate this check. Similarly, negotiable paper can be payable to a public officer.

For example, checks reading "Pay to the order of the County Tax Collector" or "Pay to the order of Larry White, Receiver of Taxes" can be negotiated by whoever holds the office [UCC 3–110(c)].

The following case raises some interesting questions concerning checks payable to two persons jointly.

CASE 25.1

General Motors Acceptance Corp. v. Abington Casualty Insurance Co.

Supreme Judicial Court of Massachusetts, 1992.
413 Mass. 583,
602 N.E.2d 1085.

COMPANY PROFILE   *One of the major divisions of the General Motors Corporation is the General Motors Acceptance Corporation (GMAC) (**http://www.gmacfs.com**). Created by William Durant, the founder of General Motors (GM) and the president of GM until he resigned in 1920, GMAC originally lent money only to buyers of GM vehicles. Over time, however, GMAC became the second largest mortgage banker in the United States. In the 1980s, GMAC was sometimes more profitable than the GM automotive divisions. In the late 1990s, GMAC held outstanding loans worth more than $100 billion. This was more than was held by any commercial bank in the United States except Citicorp.*

BACKGROUND AND FACTS   *Abington Casualty Insurance Company issued an insurance policy to Robert Azevedo to cover Azevedo's 1984 Jeep. GMAC held a security interest in the vehicle, and the insurance policy named GMAC as the beneficiary. In other words, if the Jeep was damaged and a claim submitted, Abington was to pay GMAC for the amount of appraised damages. The Jeep was later damaged, and Abington appraised the loss and issued a check payable jointly "to the order of Robert A. Azevedo and G.M.A.C." The check was delivered to Azevedo, who then indorsed the check and presented it to the bank. The bank accepted the check, which had not been indorsed by GMAC, and Azevedo received full payment. GMAC never received the funds. GMAC sued the drawer of the check, Abington, to recover the insurance payment it should have received. The trial court dismissed the action, and GMAC appealed.*

IN THE LANGUAGE OF THE COURT

NOLAN, Justice.
        *   *   *   *

Although the issue has never been addressed in Massachusetts, other States have held that the delivery of a negotiable instrument to one joint payee constitutes delivery to all joint payees. *   *   * [S]ince under Massachusetts law a person must seek the endorsements of every payee to negotiate, transfer, or discharge a negotiable instrument, delivery of the instrument to one payee does not jeopardize the rights of other payees. We hold, therefore, that Abington's delivery of the check to only one joint payee, Azevedo, nevertheless constitutes delivery to the remaining joint payee, GMAC.
        *   *   *   *

*   *   * However, *   *   * where there are copayees *   *   *, a negotiable instrument cannot be discharged by the actions of only one payee. [UCC 3–110(d)] expressly prohibits the discharge of an instrument except by all the payees. *   *   * Without this rule, there would be no assurance that all the joint payees would receive payment and that the drawer's underlying obligation would be fully discharged.

DECISION AND REMEDY   *The court held that GMAC had presented a claim on which relief could be granted and reversed the lower court's dismissal of GMAC's complaint. The case was remanded to the trial court. The signature of only one payee on a check made payable to joint payees does not discharge the instrument.*

CONCEPT SUMMARY 25.1

TYPES OF INDORSEMENTS AND THEIR CONSEQUENCES

WORDS CONSTITUTING THE INDORSEMENT	TYPE OF INDORSEMENT	INDORSER'S SIGNATURE LIABILITY[a]
"Mark Deitsch"	Blank	Unqualified signature liability on proper presentment and notice of dishonor.[b]
"Pay to William Hunter, Hal Jones"	Special	Unqualified signature liability on proper presentment and notice of dishonor.
"Without recourse, Sarah Jacobs"	Qualified (blank for further negotiation)	No signature liability. Transfer warranty liability if breach occurs.[c]
"Pay to Allison Jong, without recourse, Sarah Jacobs"	Qualified (special for further negotiation)	No signature liability. Transfer warranty liability if breach occurs.
"Pay to Julie Thrush only, Thomas Fasulo"	Restrictive—prohibitive (special for further negotiation)	Signature liability only on Julie Thrush's receiving payment. If Thrush receives payment, signature liability on proper presentment and notice of dishonor.
"Pay to Lars Johansen if he completes the renovation of my kitchen by June 1, 2001, Ken Barton"	Restrictive—conditional (special for further negotiation)	Signature liability, regardless of whether condition is met, on proper presentment and notice of dishonor.
"For deposit only, Aimee St. Amant"	Restrictive—for deposit (blank for further negotiation)	Signature liability only on St. Amant's having amount deposited in her account. If deposit is made, signature liability on proper presentment and notice of dishonor.
"Pay to Ellen Cook in trust for Roger Callahan, Roger Callahan"	Restrictive—trust (special for further negotiation)	Signature liability to original indorsee only on payment to Ellen Cook for Roger Callahan's benefit. Regardless of whether restriction is met, signature liability to subsequent indorsers on proper presentment and notice of dishonor.

a. Signature liability refers to the liability of a party who signs an instrument. Signature liability is discussed in more detail in Chapter 26.

b. When an instrument is dishonored—that is, when, for example, a drawer's bank refuses to cash the drawer's check on proper presentment—an indorser of the check may be liable on it if he or she is given proper notice of dishonor. Dishonor and notice of dishonor are discussed in Chapter 26.

c. The transferor of an instrument makes certain warranties to the transferee and subsequent holders, and thus, even if the transferor's signature does not render him or her liable on the instrument, he or she may be liable for breach of a transfer warranty. Transfer warranties are discussed in Chapter 26. See also UCC 3–416.

SECTION 4

Holder in Due Course

The body of rules contained in Article 3 of the UCC governs a party's right to payment of a check, draft, note, or certificate of deposit.[4] Problems arise when

4. Other kinds of documents, such as stock certificates and bills of lading, meet the requirements of negotiable instruments, but the rights and liabilities of the parties on these documents are covered by Articles 7 and 8 of the UCC. See Chapter 46 on bailments.

a holder seeking payment of a negotiable instrument learns that a defense to payment exists or that another party has a prior claim to the instrument. In such situations, for the person seeking payment, it becomes important to have the rights of a *holder in due course (HDC)*. An HDC takes a negotiable instrument free of all claims and most defenses of other parties.

SECTION 5

Holder versus Holder in Due Course

As pointed out in Chapter 24, the UCC defines a *holder* as a person in the possession of an instrument "if the instrument is payable to bearer or, in the cases of an instrument payable to an identified person, if the identified person is in possession" [UCC 1–201(20)]. An ordinary holder obtains only those rights that the transferor had in the instrument. In this respect, a holder has the same status as an assignee (see Chapter 16). A holder normally is subject to the same defenses that could be asserted against the transferor, just as an assignee is subject to the defenses that could be asserted against the assignor.

In contrast, a **holder in due course (HDC)** is a holder who, by meeting certain acquisition requirements (to be discussed shortly), takes the instrument free of most of the defenses and claims to which the transferor was subject. Stated another way, an HDC can normally acquire a higher level of immunity than can an ordinary holder in regard to defenses against payment on the instrument or ownership claims to the instrument by other parties.

An example will help to clarify the distinction between the rights of an ordinary holder and the rights of an HDC. Debby Morrison signs a $500 note payable to Alex Jerrod in payment for goods. Jerrod negotiates the note to Beverly Larson, who promises to pay Jerrod for it in thirty days. During the next month, Larson learns that Jerrod has breached his contract with Morrison by delivering defective goods and that, for this reason, Morrison will not honor the $500 note. Whether Larson can hold Morrison liable on the note depends on whether Larson has met the requirements for HDC status. If Larson has met these requirements and thus has HDC status, Larson is entitled to payment on the note. If Larson has not met these requirements, she has the status of an ordinary holder, and Morrison's defense against payment to Jerrod will also be effective against Larson.

SECTION 6

Requirements for HDC Status

The basic requirements for attaining HDC status are set forth in UCC 3–302. An HDC must first be a holder of a negotiable instrument and must have taken the instrument (1) for value; (2) in good faith; and (3) without notice that it is overdue, that it has been dishonored, that any person has a defense against it or a claim to it, or that the instrument contains unauthorized signatures or alterations or is so irregular or incomplete as to call into question its authenticity. We now examine each of these requirements.

TAKING FOR VALUE

An HDC must have given value for the instrument [UCC 3–302(a)(2)(i), 3–303]. A person who receives an instrument as a gift or who inherits it has *not* met the requirement of value. In these situations, the person normally becomes an ordinary holder and does not possess the rights of an HDC.

The concept of value in the law of negotiable instruments is not the same as the concept of consideration in the law of contracts. An executory promise (a promise to give value in the future) is clearly valid consideration to support a contract [UCC 1–201(44)]. It does not, however, normally constitute value sufficient to make one an HDC. UCC 3–303(a)(1) provides that a holder takes the instrument for value only to the extent that the promise has been performed. Therefore, if the holder plans to pay for the instrument later or plans to perform the required services at some future date, the holder has not yet given value. In that situation, the holder is not yet a holder in due course.

In the Larson-Morrison example presented earlier, Larson is not an HDC, because she did not take the instrument (Morrison's note) for value—she had not yet paid Jerrod for the note. Thus, Morrison's defense of breach of contract is valid not only against Jerrod but also against Larson. If Larson had paid Jerrod for the note at the time of transfer (which would mean she had given value for the instrument), she would be an HDC. As an HDC, she could hold Morrison liable on the note even though Morrison has a valid defense against Jerrod on the basis of breach of contract. Exhibit 25–7 illustrates these concepts.

Under UCC 3–303(a), a holder can take an instrument for value in one of five ways:

EXHIBIT 25–7 TAKING FOR VALUE

By exchanging defective goods for the note, Jerrod breached his contract with Morrison. Morrison could assert this defense if Jerrod presented the note to her for payment. Jerrod exchanged the note for Larson's promise to pay in thirty days, however. Because Larson did not take the note for value, she is not a holder in due course. Thus, Morrison can assert against Larson the defense of Jerrod's breach when Larson submits the note to Morrison for payment. If Larson had taken the note for value, Morrison could not assert that defense and would be liable to pay the note.

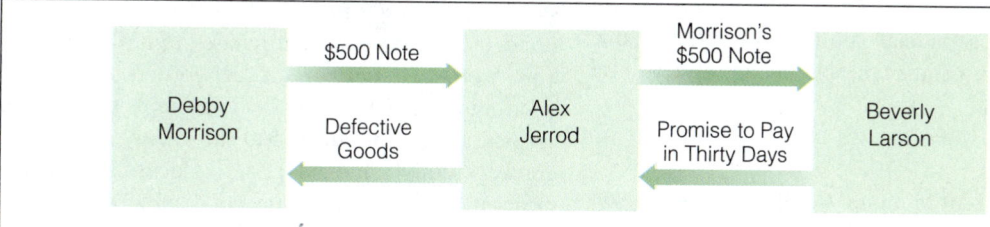

1. By performing the promise for which the instrument was issued or transferred.

2. By acquiring a security interest or other lien in the instrument (other than a lien obtained by a judicial proceeding).[5]

3. By taking an instrument in payment of, or as security for, an antecedent claim.

4. By giving a negotiable instrument as payment.

5. By giving an irrevocable commitment as payment.

Antecedent Claim. When an instrument is given in payment of—or as security for—an **antecedent claim** (a preexisting claim), the value requirement is met [UCC 3–303(a)(3)]. Here again, commercial law and contract law produce different results. An antecedent claim is not valid consideration under general contract law, but it does constitute value sufficient to satisfy the requirement for HDC status in commercial law. To illustrate: Cary owes Dwyer $2,000 on a past-due account. If Cary negotiates a $2,000 note signed by Gordon to Dwyer and Dwyer accepts it to discharge the overdue account balance, Dwyer has given value for the instrument.

Negotiable Instrument as Value. UCC 3–303(a)(4) provides that a holder takes the instrument for value if "the instrument is issued or transferred in exchange for a negotiable instrument." Suppose that Martin has issued a $500 negotiable promissory note to Paula. The note is due six months from the date issued. Paula's financial circumstances are such that she does not want

to wait for the maturity date to collect. Therefore, she negotiates the note to her friend Susan, who pays her $200 in cash and writes her a check—a negotiable instrument—for the balance of $300. Susan has given full value for the note by paying $200 in cash and issuing Paula the check for $300. Note that a negotiable instrument has value when it is issued, not when the underlying obligation is finally paid.

Check Deposits and Withdrawals. Occasionally, a commercial bank can become an HDC when honoring other banks' checks for its own customers. In this situation, the bank becomes an "involuntary" HDC, in that at the time of giving value, the bank has no intention of becoming an HDC.

Assume that on Monday morning at the end of the month, Pat Stevens has $400 in her checking account at the First National Bank. That morning Stevens deposits her payroll check for $300, drawn by her employer on the Second Interstate Bank. During her lunch hour she issues a check to her landlord for $425. The landlord cashes the check at the First National Bank. Later, the Second Interstate Bank returns the payroll check marked "insufficient funds." In most cases, First National would charge this check against Stevens's account. If that cannot be done, however, is the First National Bank an HDC of the employer's check? The answer is yes. According to what is referred to as the *first-money-in, first-money-out rule*, First National Bank has paid to the landlord $25 of its own funds [UCC 4–210(b)]. Therefore, First National is an HDC to the extent it has given value—$25—and the bank can seek recovery of $25 from the employer (the drawer of the check).

---

5. Security interests will be discussed in Chapter 28. Other liens will be discussed in Chapter 29.

Special Situations. In a few exceptional circumstances, a holder can take an instrument for value but still not be accorded HDC status. UCC 3–302(c) specifies that in the following situations, the rights of the holder will be limited to those of an ordinary holder:

1. Purchase at a judicial sale (for example, a bankruptcy sale) or acquisition by taking under legal process.
2. Acquisition when taking over an estate (as an administrator).
3. Purchase as part of a bulk transfer (as when a corporation buys the assets of another corporation).

TAKING IN GOOD FAITH

The second requirement for HDC status is that the holder take the instrument in *good faith* [UCC 3–302(a)(2)(ii)]. Under Article 3, *good faith* is defined as "honesty in fact and the observance of reasonable commercial standards of fair dealing" [UCC 3–103(a)(4)].[6] The good faith requirement applies only to the *holder*. It is immaterial whether the transferor acted in good faith. Thus, a person who in good faith takes a negotiable instrument from a thief may become an HDC.

Because of the good faith requirement, one must ask whether the purchaser, when acquiring the instrument, honestly believed that the instrument was not defective. If a person purchases a $10,000 note for $300 from a stranger on a street corner, the issue of good faith can be raised on the grounds of both the suspicious circumstances and the grossly inadequate consideration (value). The UCC does not provide clear guidelines to determine good faith, so each situation must be examined separately. In the following case, the court considered whether a credit union fulfilled the good faith requirement to qualify as an HDC. Specifically, the issue focused on the component of good faith that requires "the observance of reasonable commercial standards of fair dealing."

---

6. Before the revision of Article 3, the applicable definition of good faith was "honesty in fact in the conduct or transaction concerned" [UCC 1–201(19)].

CASE 25.2   Maine Family Federal Credit Union v. Sun Life Assurance Co. of Canada

Supreme Judicial Court of Maine, 1999.
727 A.2d 335.
http://www.courts.me.us/mescopin.home.html[a]

BACKGROUND AND FACTS   *On the death of Elden Guerrette, Sun Life Assurance Company of Canada issued three checks, each in the amount of $40,759.35, to each of Elden's children, Daniel, Joel, and Claire Guerrette. The checks were drawn on Sun Life's account at Chase Manhattan Bank in Syracuse, New York, and given to Steven Hall, a Sun Life agent, to give to the Guerrettes. Hall and an associate, Paul Richard, fraudulently induced the Guerrettes to indorse the checks in blank and to transfer them to Hall and Richard, purportedly to be invested in "HER, Inc.," a corporation formed by Hall and Richard. Hall took the checks from the Guerrettes and turned them over to Richard, who deposited them into his account at the Maine Family Federal Credit Union (the Credit Union). The Credit Union immediately made the funds available to Richard. The Guerrettes contacted Sun Life the next day to request that Sun Life stop payment on the checks. Sun Life immediately ordered Chase Manhattan to stop payment on the checks. When the checks were presented to Chase Manhattan for payment, Chase refused to pay, and the checks were returned to the Credit Union. By that time, however, Richard had withdrawn from his account all of the funds represented by the checks. The Credit Union was able to recover almost $80,000 from Richard, but there remained an unpaid balance of $42,366.56. The Credit Union filed a suit in a Maine state court against Sun Life, the Guerrettes, and Richard. The court determined that the Credit Union had not acted in good faith and therefore was not a holder in due course, and entered a judgment against it. The Credit Union appealed to the Supreme Judicial Court of Maine, the state's highest court.*

---

a. In the "Chronological Lists of Opinions" click on the appropriate link, which as of this writing, is "Click here for February and March 1999 Opinions." In the "March 1999" section, click on the case name to access the opinion.

IN THE LANGUAGE OF THE COURT

SAUFLEY, J. [Justice]

*   *   *   *

[Under the UCC's definition of "good faith"] the jury's task here was to decide whether the Credit Union observed the banking industries' commercial standards relating to the giving of value on uncollected funds, and, if so, whether those standards are reasonably designed to result in fair dealing.

*   *   *   *

The Credit Union *   *   * asserted that it acted exactly as its policy and the law allowed when it immediately extended provisional credit on these checks *   *   *. Finally, the Credit Union presented expert testimony that most credit unions in Maine follow similar policies.

*   *   * Sun Life and the Guerrettes argued that the Credit Union's conduct did not comport with reasonable commercial standards of fair dealing when it allowed its member access to provisional credit on checks totalling over $120,000 drawn on an out-of-state bank without either: (1) further investigation to assure that the deposited checks would be paid by the bank upon which they were drawn, or (2) holding the instruments to allow any irregularities to come to light.

*   *   *   *

The Credit Union's President admitted the risks inherent in the Credit Union's policy and admitted that it would not have been difficult to place a hold on these funds for the few days that it would normally take for the payor bank to pay the checks. He conceded that the amounts of the checks were relatively large, that they were drawn on an out-of-state bank, and that these circumstances "could have" presented the Credit Union with cause to place a hold on the account. He also testified to his understanding that some commercial banks followed a policy of holding nonlocal checks for three business days before giving provisional credit. Moreover, the Credit Union had no written policy explicitly guiding its staff regarding the placing of a hold on uncollected funds. Rather, the decision on whether to place a temporary hold on an account was left to the "comfort level" of the teller accepting the deposit. There was no dispute that the amount of the three checks far exceeded the $5,000 threshold for a discretionary hold established by the Credit Union's own policy.

On these facts the jury could rationally have concluded that the reasonable commercial standard of fair dealing would require the placing of a hold on the uncollected funds for a reasonable period of time and that, in giving value under these circumstances, the Credit Union did not act according to commercial standards that were reasonably structured to result in fair dealing.

DECISION AND REMEDY

The Supreme Judicial Court of Maine affirmed the judgment of the lower court, as it related to the Guerrettes. In relation to the Guerrettes, the Credit Union was not a holder in due course. The state's highest court vacated that portion of the judgment entered in favor of Sun Life and against the Credit Union, however, on other grounds, and remanded that part of the case for further proceedings.

TAKING WITHOUT NOTICE

The final requirement for HDC status involves notice [UCC 3–302]. A person will not be afforded HDC protection if he or she acquires an instrument and is *on notice* (knows or has reason to know) that it is defective in any one of the following ways [UCC 3–302(a)]:

1. It is overdue.
2. It has been dishonored.
3. There is an uncured (uncorrected) default with respect to another instrument issued as part of the same series.
4. The instrument contains an unauthorized signature or has been altered.

5. There is a defense against the instrument or a claim to the instrument.

6. The instrument is so irregular or incomplete as to call into question its authenticity.[7]

What Constitutes Notice? Notice of a defective instrument is given whenever the holder (1) has actual knowledge of the defect; (2) has received a notice of the defect (such as a bank's receipt of a letter listing the serial numbers of stolen bearer instruments); or (3) has reason to know that a defect exists, given all the facts and circumstances known at the time in question [UCC 1–201(25)]. The holder must also have received the notice "at a time and in a manner that gives a reasonable opportunity to act on it" [UCC 3–302(f)]. A purchaser's knowledge of certain facts, such as insolvency proceedings against the maker or drawer of the instrument, does not constitute notice that the instrument is defective [UCC 3–302(b)].

Overdue Instruments. What constitutes notice that an instrument is overdue depends on whether it is a demand instrument (payable on demand) or a time instrument (payable at a definite time).

Demand Instruments. A purchaser has notice that a *demand instrument* is overdue if he or she either takes the instrument knowing that demand has been made or takes the instrument an unreasonable length of time after its date. A "reasonable time" for the presentment of a check is ninety days after its date, but for other demand instruments, what will be considered a reasonable time depends on the circumstances [UCC 3–304(a)].

Time Instruments. A holder of a *time instrument* who takes the instrument at any time after its expressed due date is on notice that it is overdue [UCC 3–304(b)]. Nonpayment by the due date should indicate to any purchaser that the instrument may be defective. Thus, a promissory note due on May 15 must be acquired before midnight on May 15. If it is purchased on May 16, the purchaser will be an ordinary holder, not an HDC. Sometimes, a time instrument reads, "Payable in thirty days." To count thirty days, you exclude the first day and count the last day. Thus, a note dated December 1 that is payable in

thirty days is due by midnight on December 31. If the payment date falls on a Sunday or holiday, the instrument is payable on the next business day.

If a debt is to be paid in installments or through a series of notes, the maker's default on any one installment or on any one note of the series will constitute notice to the purchaser that the instrument is overdue [UCC 3–304(b)].

An instrument does not become overdue if there is a default on a payment of interest only [UCC 3–304(c)]. Most installment notes provide that any payment by the maker shall be applied first to interest and the balance to the principal. This serves as notice that any installment payment for less than the full amount results in a default on an installment payment toward the principal.

Also, when a series of notes with successive maturity dates is issued at a single time for a single indebtedness, a default on any one note of the series will constitute overdue notice for the entire series. In this way, prospective purchasers know that they cannot qualify as HDCs [UCC 3–302(a)(2)(iii)].

Suppose that a note reads, "Payable May 15, but may be accelerated if the holder feels insecure." A purchaser, unaware that a prior holder has elected to accelerate the due date on the instrument, buys the instrument before May 15. UCC 3–304(b)(3) provides that an instrument becomes overdue on the day after the accelerated due date. The purchaser may still qualify as an HDC, however, because he or she has no reason to know that acceleration has occurred [UCC 3–302(a)(2)(iii)].

Dishonored Instruments. An instrument is *dishonored* when the party to which the instrument is presented refuses to pay it. If a holder has actual knowledge that an instrument has been dishonored or has knowledge of facts that would lead him or her to suspect that an instrument has been dishonored, the holder is on notice [UCC 3–302(a)(2)]. Thus, a person who takes a check clearly stamped "insufficient funds" is put on notice.

For example, Schultz holds a demand note dated September 1 on Apfel, Inc., a local business firm. On September 17, she demands payment, and Apfel refuses (that is, dishonors the instrument). On September 22, Schultz negotiates the note to Brenner, a purchaser who lives in another state. Brenner does not know, and has no reason to know, that the note has been dishonored. Because Brenner is *not* put on notice, Brenner can become an HDC.

---

7. Section 302(1)(c) of the unrevised Article 3 provided that HDC protection is lost if a holder has notice that an instrument is overdue or has been dishonored or if there is a claim to or defense against it.

Notice of Claims or Defenses. A holder cannot become an HDC if he or she has notice of any claim to the instrument or defense against it [UCC 3–302(a)(2)(v), (vi)]. Knowledge of claims or defenses can be imputed to the purchaser if these claims or defenses are apparent on the face of the instrument—if the instrument is incomplete or irregular in any way, for example—or if the purchaser otherwise had reason to know of them from facts surrounding the transaction.[8]

Incomplete Instruments. A purchaser cannot expect to become an HDC of an instrument so incomplete on its face that an element of negotiability is lacking (for example, the amount is not filled in) [UCC 3–302(a)(1)]. Minor omissions (such as the omission of the date—see Chapter 24) are permissible, because these do not call into question the validity of the instrument [UCC 3–113(b)].

Similarly, when a person accepts an instrument that has been completed without knowing that it was incomplete when issued, the person can take it as an HDC [UCC 3–115(b), 3–302(a)(1)]. Even if an instrument is originally incomplete and later completed in an unauthorized manner, the unauthorized completion is not a good defense against an HDC, who can enforce the instrument as completed [UCC 3–407(c)].

To illustrate: Cosford asks Brittany to buy a textbook for him when she goes to the campus bookstore. Cosford writes a check payable to the campus store, leaves the amount blank, and tells Brittany to fill in the price of the textbook. The cost of the textbook is $65. If Brittany fills in the check for $95 before she gets to the bookstore, the bookstore cashier sees only a properly completed instrument. Therefore, the cashier will take the check as an HDC, and the store can enforce it for the full $95. The unauthorized completion is not a sufficient defense against the store in this situation. (Material alterations will be discussed more fully in Chapter 26.)

Irregular Instruments. Any irregularity on the face of an instrument that calls into question its validity or terms of ownership or that creates an ambiguity as to

the party to pay will bar HDC status. A difference between the handwriting used in the body of a check and that used in the signature will not in and of itself make an instrument irregular. Postdating or antedating a check or stating the amount in digits but failing to write out the numbers will not make a check irregular [UCC 3–113(a)]. Visible evidence of forgery of a maker's or drawer's signature, however, or alterations to material elements of negotiable instruments will disqualify a purchaser from HDC status. Conversely, a careful forgery of a maker's or drawer's signature or a careful alteration can go undetected by reasonable examination; therefore, the purchaser can qualify as an HDC [UCC 3–302(a)(1)].

Losses that result from careful forgeries usually fall on the party to whom the forger transferred the instrument (assuming, of course, that the forger cannot be found). Also, a forged indorsement (see Chapter 26) does not transfer title, and thus a person obtaining an instrument that has a forged indorsement of a name necessary to good title cannot normally become a holder or an HDC.

Voidable Obligations. It stands to reason that a purchaser who knows that a party to an instrument has a defense that entitles that party to avoid the obligation cannot be an HDC. At the very least, good faith requires *honesty in fact and the observance of reasonable commercial standards* on the part of the purchaser in a transaction. For example, a potential purchaser who knows that the maker of a note has breached the underlying contract with the payee cannot thereafter purchase the note as an HDC.

Knowledge of one defense precludes a holder from asserting HDC status in regard to all other defenses. For example, Litton, knowing that the note he has taken has a forged indorsement, presents it to the maker for payment. The maker refuses to pay on the grounds of breach of the underlying contract. The maker can assert this defense against Litton even though Litton had no knowledge of the breach, because Litton's knowledge of the forgery alone prevents him from being an HDC in *all* circumstances.

Knowledge that a fiduciary has wrongfully negotiated an instrument is sufficient notice of a claim against the instrument to preclude HDC status. Suppose that O'Banion, a trustee of a university, improperly writes a check on the university trust account to pay a personal debt. Lewis knows that the check has been improperly drawn on university funds, but she accepts it anyway. Lewis cannot claim

---

8. If an instrument contains a statement required by a statute or an administrative rule to the effect that the rights of a holder or transferee are subject to the claims or defenses that the issuer could assert against the original payee, the instrument is negotiable, but there cannot be an HDC of the instrument. See UCC 3–106(d) and the discussion of federal limitations on HDC rights in the next chapter.

to be an HDC. When a purchaser knows that a fiduciary is acting in breach of trust, HDC status is denied [UCC 3–307(b)].

SECTION 7

Holder through an HDC

A person who does not qualify as an HDC but who derives his or her title through an HDC can acquire the rights and privileges of an HDC. According to UCC 3–203(b):

> Transfer of an instrument, whether or not the transfer is a negotiation, vests in the transferee any right of the transferor to enforce the instrument, including any right as a holder in due course, but the transferee cannot acquire rights of a holder in due course by a transfer, directly or indirectly, from a holder in due course if the transferee engaged in fraud or illegality affecting the instrument.

This rule, sometimes called the **shelter principle,** seems counter to the basic HDC philosophy. It is, however, in line with the concept of marketability and free transferability of negotiable instruments, as well as with contract law, which provides that assignees acquire the rights of assignors. The shelter principle extends the HDC benefits, and it is designed to aid the HDC in readily disposing of the

instrument. Anyone, no matter how far removed from an HDC, who can trace his or her title ultimately back to an HDC comes within the shelter principle. Normally, a person who acquires an instrument from an HDC or from someone with HDC rights receives HDC rights on the legal theory that the transferee of an instrument receives at least the rights that the transferor had.

There are some limitations on the shelter principle, however. Certain persons who formerly held instruments cannot improve their positions by later reacquiring them from HDCs [UCC 3–203(b)]. Thus, if a holder was a party to fraud or illegality affecting the instrument or if, as a prior holder, he or she had notice of a claim or defense against the instrument, that holder is not allowed to improve his or her status by repurchasing the instrument from a later HDC.

To illustrate: Matthew and Carla collaborate to defraud Lorena. Lorena is induced to give Carla a negotiable note payable to Carla's order. Carla then specially indorses the note for value to Larry, an HDC. Matthew and Carla split the proceeds. Larry negotiates the note to Stuart, another HDC. Stuart then negotiates the note for value to Matthew. Matthew, even though he obtained the note through an HDC, is not a holder through an HDC, for he participated in the original fraud and can never acquire HDC rights in this note.

CONCEPT SUMMARY 25.2   **RULES AND REQUIREMENTS FOR HDC STATUS**

BASIC REQUIREMENTS	RULES
Must Be a _Holder_	A _holder_ is defined as a person in the possession of an instrument "if the instrument is payable to bearer or, in the cases of an instrument payable to an identified person, if the identified person is in possession" [UCC 1–201(20)].
Must Take _for Value_	A holder gives _value_ by doing any of the following [UCC 3–303]: 1. Performing the promise for which the instrument was issued or transferred. 2. Acquiring a security interest or other lien in the instrument (other than a lien obtained by a judicial proceeding). 3. Taking an instrument in payment of, or as security for, an antecedent debt. 4. Giving a negotiable instrument as payment. 5. Giving an irrevocable commitment as payment.

CONCEPT SUMMARY 25.2

RULES AND REQUIREMENTS FOR HDC STATUS *(continued)*

BASIC REQUIREMENTS	RULES
Must Take *in Good Faith*	*Good faith* is defined for purposes of revised Article 3 as "honesty in fact and the observance of reasonable commercial standards of fair dealing" [UCC 3–103(a)(4)].
Must Take *without Notice*	A holder must not be *on notice* that the instrument is defective in any of the following ways [UCC 3–302, 3–304]: 1. The instrument is overdue. 2. The instrument has been dishonored. 3. There is an uncured (uncorrected) default with respect to another instrument issued as part of the same series. 4. The instrument contains an unauthorized signature or has been altered. 5. There is a defense against the instrument or a claim to the instrument. 6. The instrument is so irregular or incomplete as to call into question its authenticity.
Shelter Principle—Holder through a Holder in Due Course	A holder who cannot qualify as a holder in due course has the rights of a holder in due course if he or she derives title through a holder in due course [UCC 3–203(b)].
Purchasers Who Are Not Holders in Due Course	The following acquisitions cannot result in a holder having HDC status [UCC 3–302(c)]: 1. Purchase at a judicial sale. 2. Acquisition as part of an estate. 3. Purchase as part of a bulk transfer.

TERMS AND CONCEPTS TO REVIEW

QUESTIONS AND CASE PROBLEMS

25–1. INDORSEMENTS. A check drawn by Cullen for $500 is made payable to the order of Jordan and issued to Jordan. Jordan owes his landlord $500 in rent and transfers the check to his landlord with the following indorsement: "For rent paid. [Signed] Jordan." Jordan's landlord has contracted to have Deborah do some land- scaping on the property. When Deborah insists on im- mediate payment, the landlord transfers the check to Deborah without indorsement. Later, to pay for some palm trees purchased from Better-Garden Nursery, Deborah transfers the check with the following indorse- ment: "Pay to Better-Garden Nursery, without recourse.

[Signed] Deborah." Better-Garden Nursery sends the check to its bank indorsed "For deposit only. [Signed] Better-Garden Nursery."

(a) Classify each of these indorsements.
(b) Was the transfer from Jordan's landlord to Deborah, without indorsement, an assignment or a negotiation? Explain.

25–2. REQUIREMENTS FOR HDC STATUS. Celine issues a ninety-day negotiable promissory note payable to the order of Hayden. The amount of the note is left blank, pending a determination of the amount of money Hayden will need to purchase a bull for Celine. Celine authorizes any amount not to exceed $2,000. Hayden, without authority, fills in the note in the amount of $5,000 and thirty days later sells the note to First National Bank of Oklahoma for $4,850. Hayden does not buy the bull and leaves the state. First National Bank has no knowledge that the instrument was incomplete when issued or that Hayden had no authority to complete the instrument in the amount of $5,000.

(a) Does the bank qualify as a holder in due course? If so, for what amount? Explain.
(b) If Hayden had sold the note to a stranger in a bar for $500, would the stranger qualify as a holder in due course? Explain.

25–3. REQUIREMENTS FOR HDC STATUS. Emilio has received from dishonest payees through negotiation two checks with the following histories:

(a) The drawer issued a check to the payee for $9. The payee cleverly altered the numeral on the check from $9 to $90 and the written word from nine to ninety.
(b) The drawer issued a check to the payee without filling in the amount. The drawer authorized the payee to fill in the amount for no more than $90. The payee filled in the amount of $900.

Discuss whether Emilio, by giving value to the payees, can qualify as a holder in due course of these checks.

25–4. REQUIREMENTS FOR NEGOTIATION. Dynamics Corp. and Marine Midland Bank had a long-standing agreement under which Marine Midland received checks payable to Dynamics and indorsed and deposited them into the Dynamics account. Dynamics never saw the checks. They were made out to the order of Dynamics and delivered directly to Marine Midland. Marine Midland stamped the backs of the checks with the Dynamics name and insignia and transferred them. Within the meaning of the UCC, is the act of sending checks to Marine Midland Bank a negotiation? If Marine Midland transfers the checks to other parties, will that be a negotiation? Discuss. [*Marine Midland Bank–New York v. Graybar Electric Co.*, 41 N.Y.2d 703, 363 N.E.2d 1139, 395 N.Y.S.2d 403 (1977)]

25–5. INDORSEMENTS. Universal Premium Acceptance Corp. issued more than $1 million in drafts, intending the payee to be Great American Insurance Co. When the drafts were issued, they were nonnegotiable instruments. Walter Talbot, an insurance agent, intercepted the drafts, forged Great American's indorsements in blank, and deposited the drafts in a phony account at York Bank & Trust Co. After Talbot was caught and convicted, Universal filed a suit in a federal district court against York to recover some of its losses. One of the issues was whether Talbot's indorsements converted the nonnegotiable drafts into negotiable bearer instruments. Did they? Why or why not? [*Universal Premium Acceptance Corp. v. York Bank & Trust Co.*, 69 F.3d 695 (3d Cir. 1995)]

25–6. GOOD FAITH. Stacey Dillabough presented two money orders for payment to Chuckie Enterprises, Inc., a check-cashing service in Philadelphia. Dillabough was known as a previous customer, the orders were presented within thirty days of the date on them, and there was nothing to indicate that they were not valid. Chuckie obtained photo identification from Dillabough, cashed the orders, and submitted them to the issuer, American Express, for payment. American Express recognized the orders as stolen and refused to pay. Chuckie assigned its right to payment to Robert Triffin, who filed a suit against American Express to collect. One of the issues was whether Chuckie was a holder in due course. One of the requirements of HDC status is good faith. Did Chuckie take the money orders in good faith? Discuss. [*Triffin v. Dillabough*, 552 Pa. 550, 716 A.2d 605 (1998)]

25–7. IN YOUR COURT

An employee of Epicycle Corp. cashed a payroll check at Money Mart Check Cashing Center, Inc. Money Mart deposited the check, with others, into its bank account. When the check was returned marked "Payment stopped," Money Mart brought an action against Epicycle to recover the value of the check. Money Mart claimed that it was a holder in due course on the instrument because it had accepted the check for value, in good faith, and without notice that a stop-payment order had been made. Epicycle argued that Money Mart was not a holder in due course because it had failed to verify that the check was good before it cashed the check. Assume that you are the judge in the trial court hearing this case and answer the following questions:

(a) Review the section in this chapter discussing the "taking without notice" requirement for HDC status. In your opinion, did Money Mart meet this requirement?
(b) Do the facts of this case, as summarized above, indicate that Money Mart met the other two requirements for HDC status—taking for value and in good faith?
(c) In view of your answers to the two questions just presented, what should your decision be in this case? Explain your reasoning.

25–8. A QUESTION OF ETHICS

Richard Caliendo, an accountant, prepared tax returns for various clients. To satisfy their tax liabilities, the clients issued checks payable to various state taxing entities and gave them to Caliendo. Between 1977 and 1979, Caliendo forged indorsements on these checks, deposited them in his own bank account, and subsequently withdrew the proceeds. In 1983, after learning of these events and after Caliendo's death, the state brought an action against Barclays Bank of New York, N.A., the successor to Caliendo's bank, to recover the amount of the checks. Barclays moved for dismissal on the ground that because the checks had never been delivered to the state, the state never acquired the status of holder and therefore never acquired any rights in the instruments. The trial court held for the state, but the appellate court reversed. The state then appealed the case to the state's highest court. That court ruled that the state could not recover the amount of the checks from the bank be-

cause, although the state was the named payee on the checks, the checks had never been delivered to the payee. [*State v. Barclays Bank of New York, N.A.*, 561 N.Y.2d 533, 563 N.E.2d 11, 561 N.Y.S.2d 697 (1990)]

(a) If you were deciding this case, would you make an exception to the rule and let the state collect the funds from Barclays Bank? Why or why not? What ethical policies must be balanced in this situation?

(b) Under agency law, which will be discussed in Chapters 31 and 32, delivery to the agent of a given individual or entity constitutes delivery to that person or entity. The court deemed that Caliendo was not an agent of the state but an agent of the taxpayers. Does it matter that the taxpayers may not have known this principle of agency law and might have thought that, by delivering their checks to Caliendo, they were delivering them to the state? Discuss fully.

LAW ON THE WEB

For updated links to resources available on the Web, as well as a variety of other materials, visit this text's Web site at http://wbl.westbuslaw.com.

To find information on the UCC, including the Article 3 provisions discussed in this chapter, refer to the Web sites listed in the *Law on the Web* in Chapter 24.

LEGAL RESEARCH EXERCISES ON THE WEB

Go to http://wbl.westbuslaw.com, the Web site that accompanies this text. Select "Internet Applications," and then click on "Chapter 25." There you will find the following Internet research exercise that you can perform to learn more about concepts in negotiable instruments law:

Activity 25–1: Review of Negotiable Instruments

CHAPTER 26

Liability, Defenses, and Discharge

TWO KINDS OF LIABILITY ARE ASSOCIATED with negotiable instruments: signature liability and warranty liability. *Signature liability* relates to signatures on instruments. Those who sign negotiable instruments are potentially liable for payment of the amount stated on the instrument. *Warranty liability*, in contrast, extends to both signers and nonsigners. A breach of warranty can occur when the instrument is transferred or presented for payment.

Note that the focus is on liability *on the instrument itself or on warranties connected with transfer or presentment of the instrument* as opposed to liability on any underlying contract. Suppose, for example, that Donald agrees to buy one thousand compact discs from Luis and issues a check to Luis in payment. The liability discussed in this chapter does not relate directly to liability arising in connection with the contract (for instance, whether the compact discs are of proper quality or fit for the purpose for which they are intended). The liability discussed here relates to liability arising in connection with the *check* (such as what recourse Luis will have if Donald's bank refuses to pay the check—due to insufficient funds in Donald's account or Donald's order to his bank to stop payment on the check, for example).

The first part of this chapter covers the liability of the parties who sign instruments—for example, drawers of drafts and checks, makers of notes and certificates of deposit, and indorsers. It also covers the liability of accommodation parties and the warranty liability of those who transfer instruments and present instruments for payment. We then examine the defenses that can be raised to avoid liability on an instrument. As you will see, some defenses defeat payments to all holders, including holders in due course (HDCs). Others, however, can be asserted successfully only against ordinary holders. The final section in the chapter looks at some of the ways in which parties can be *discharged* from liability on negotiable instruments.

SECTION 1

Signature Liability

The key to liability on a negotiable instrument is a signature. As discussed in Chapter 24, a signature is "any name, including a trade or assumed name," or "a word, mark, or symbol executed or adopted by a person with present intention to authenticate a writing" [UCC 1–209(39), 3–401(b)]. A signature can be handwritten, typed, or printed; it also can be made by mark, by thumbprint, by machine, or in virtually any other manner. The general rule is as follows: "A person is not liable on an instrument unless (i) the person signed the instrument, or (ii) the person is represented by an agent or representative who signed the instrument and the signature is binding on the represented person" [UCC 3–401(a)].

The requirement of a signature is based on the need to know whose obligation the instrument represents. For example, Lamar writes a check for $1,000 on her account at Universal Bank payable to the order of Carerra. Carerra indorses and delivers the check, for value, to Deere. Deere deposits the check into his account at Universal Bank, but the bank returns the check to Deere marked "insufficient funds." Here the bank has dishonored the check. (**Dishonor** of an instrument occurs when payment or acceptance of the instrument—whichever is required—is refused even though the instrument is presented in a timely and proper manner.) Given the bank's dishonor of the check, does Deere have any recourse against Lamar (the drawer) or Carerra (an indorser)? The UCC provides answers to these and similar questions concerning the liability of those who sign negotiable instruments.

The following subsections discuss the liability of the parties to negotiable instruments and the conditions that must be met before liability can arise. We begin by distinguishing between primary and secondary liability because every party, except a qualified indorser,[1] who signs a negotiable instrument is either primarily or secondarily liable for payment of that instrument when it comes due.

PRIMARY LIABILITY

A person who is primarily liable on a negotiable instrument is absolutely required to pay the instrument—unless, of course, he or she has a valid defense to payment [UCC 3–305]. The primary party's liability is immediate when the instrument is signed or issued and effective when the instrument becomes due. No action by the holder of the instrument is required. *Makers* and *acceptors* are primarily liable [UCC 3–412, 3–413].

The maker of a promissory note promises to pay the note. It is the maker's promise to pay that renders the note a negotiable instrument. The words "I promise to pay" embody the maker's obligation to pay the instrument according to the terms as written at the time of the signing or issue. If the instrument is incomplete when the maker signs it, then the maker's obligation is to pay it according to the terms written when it is completed as authorized (or as completed without authorization if it is later acquired by a holder in due course—see the discussion of defenses later in this chapter) [UCC 3–115, 3–407, 3–412].

An *acceptor* is a drawee that promises to pay an instrument when it is presented later for payment, as discussed in Chapter 24. When a drawee accepts a draft, the drawee becomes primarily liable to all subsequent holders of the instrument. In other words, the drawee's acceptance (promise to pay the instrument when presented for payment) places the drawee in virtually the same position as the maker of a promissory note [UCC 3–413]. A drawee that refuses to accept a draft that requires the drawee's acceptance (such as a trade acceptance—see Chapter 24) has dishonored the instrument. Acceptance of a check is called *certification*, as will be discussed in Chapter 27. Certification is not necessary on checks, and a bank is under no obligation to certify checks. On certification, however, the drawee bank occupies the position of an acceptor and is primarily liable on the check to any holder [UCC 3–409(d)].

The issuer of a cashier's check or other draft drawn on the drawer is also primarily liable on the instrument [UCC 3–412]. (Any "draft drawn on the drawer" is similar to a cashier's check, on which there are really only two parties. The first party is the payee, and the second party is a bank, which is both the drawer and the drawee. Of course, there is a third party—the person who pays the money to the bank for the check—but he or she is not a party to the instrument. Some courts view a bank money order as a "draft drawn on the drawer.")

SECONDARY LIABILITY

Drawers and *indorsers* have secondary liability. Secondary liability on a negotiable instrument is similar to the liability of a guarantor in a simple contract (described in Chapter 29) in the sense that it is *contingent liability*. In other words, a drawer or an indorser will be liable only if the party that is responsible for paying the instrument refuses to do so (dishonors

---

1. A qualified indorser—one who indorses "without recourse"— undertakes no obligation to pay [UCC 3–415(b)]. A qualified indorser merely assumes warranty liability, which is discussed later in this chapter.

the instrument). In regard to drafts and checks, a drawer's secondary liability does not arise until the drawee fails to pay or to accept the instrument, whichever is required. In regard to notes, an indorser's secondary liability does not arise until the maker, who is primarily liable, has defaulted on the instrument [UCC 3–412, 3–415].

Dishonor of an instrument thus triggers the liability of parties who are secondarily liable on the instrument—that is, the drawer and *unqualified* indorsers. In the Lamar-Carerra-Deere hypothetical discussed earlier, for example, the question for Deere is whether the drawer (Lamar) or the indorser (Carerra) can be held liable on the check after the bank has dishonored it. The answer to the question depends on whether certain conditions for secondary liability have been satisfied. According to the UCC, parties that are secondarily liable on a negotiable instrument, such as Lamar and Carerra in our example, promise to pay on that instrument only if the following events occur:[2]

1. The instrument is properly and timely presented.
2. The instrument is dishonored.
3. Timely notice of dishonor is given.[3]

Proper Presentment. The UCC spells out what constitutes a proper presentment. Basically, presentment by a holder must be made to the proper person, must be made in a proper manner, and must be timely [UCC 3–414(f), 3–415(e), 3–501]. The party to whom the instrument must be presented depends on what type of instrument is involved. A note or certificate of deposit (CD) must be presented to the maker for payment. A draft is presented by the holder to the drawee for acceptance, payment, or both, whichever is required. A check is presented to the drawee (bank) for payment [UCC 3–501(a), 3–502(b)].

Presentment can be properly made in any of the following ways, depending on the type of instrument involved [UCC 3–501(b)]:

1. By any commercially reasonable means, including oral, written, or electronic communication (but pre-

sentment is not effective until the demand for payment or acceptance is received).
2. Through a clearinghouse procedure used by banks, such as for deposited checks (discussed in Chapter 27).
3. At the place specified in the instrument for acceptance or payment.

One of the most crucial criteria for proper presentment is timeliness [UCC 3–414(f), 3–415(e), 3–501(b)(4)]. Failure to present on time is the most prevalent reason for improper presentment and consequent discharge of unqualified indorsers from secondary liability. For domestic checks, the holder must present the check for payment or collection within thirty days of its *date* to hold the drawer secondarily liable and within thirty days after an indorsement to hold the indorser secondarily liable [UCC 3–414(f), 3–415(e)].[4] Suppose, for example, that Deere did not deposit Lamar's check into his account until two months after Carerra indorsed it. If the bank dishonored the check, Deere could not hold Carerra liable and risks not being able to hold Lamar liable, because the check was not presented for payment within the time frame specified by the UCC.

Dishonor. As mentioned, an instrument is dishonored when presentment is properly and timely made and required acceptance or payment is refused or cannot be obtained within the prescribed time. An instrument is also dishonored when required presentment is excused (as it would be, for example, if the maker had died) and the instrument is not properly accepted or paid [UCC 3–502(e)].

Note that the postponement of payment or refusal to pay an instrument in certain situations will *not* dishonor the instrument. For example, payment can be postponed without dishonoring the instrument if presentment is made after an established cutoff hour (not earlier than 2:00 P.M.), but payment cannot be postponed beyond the close of the next business day after the day of presentment [UCC 3–501(b)(4)]. Banks frequently establish cutoff hours, after which payment will be postponed to the next business day (see Chapter 27).

In addition, the party to whom presentment is made may refuse payment without dishonoring the

---

2. An instrument can be drafted to provide a waiver of the presentment and notice of dishonor requirements [UCC 3–504]. Presume, for simplicity's sake, that such waivers have *not* been incorporated into the instruments described in this chapter.
3. Note that these requirements are necessary for a secondarily liable party to have *signature* liability on a negotiable instrument, but they are not necessary for a secondarily liable party to have *warranty* liability (to be discussed later in this chapter).

4. Section 3–503(2) of the unrevised UCC *presumes* these periods to be thirty days after the date or issue of the instrument with respect to a drawer's liability and seven days after indorsement for an indorser's liability.

instrument if the holder refuses to exhibit the instrument, to give reasonable identification and/or authority to receive payment, or to sign on the instrument as a receipt for any payment made [UCC 3–501(b)(2)]. For example, suppose that Deere, instead of depositing Lamar's check into his bank account, demands payment from Universal Bank in cash. The bank requests identification, which Deere refuses to provide. In this situation, the bank would be within its rights to refuse payment to Deere, and the bank's refusal to pay would not create a dishonor of the check.

The UCC provides, in accordance with general banking practices, that returning an instrument because it lacks a proper indorsement also is not a dishonor [UCC 3–501(b)(3)(i)]. Assume that Carerra does not indorse Lamar's check before delivering it to Deere. Because at this point the check is an order instrument—payable to Carerra or his order—Carerra's indorsement is required for further negotiation. If Carerra does not indorse the check, and Deere indorses it "For deposit only" into his account, the bank may return the check on the ground that it was not properly indorsed. In this situation, the return of the check is not a dishonor.

Proper Notice. The third requirement to hold secondary parties liable on an instrument is that those parties be properly notified of the dishonor. In our example, Deere would have to notify Carerra or Lamar of the dishonor to hold either party liable for the $1,000 payment. Again, the UCC specifies time frames for proper notice. Any necessary notice must be given by a bank before its midnight deadline (midnight of the next banking day after receipt) [UCC 3–503(c)]. Notice by any party other than a bank, such as Deere, must be given within thirty days following the day on which the person receives notice of dishonor [UCC 3–503(c)].[5]

Except for the dishonor of foreign drafts, notice may be given in any reasonable manner. This includes oral notice, written notice, electronic notice (notice by fax, e-mail, and the like), and notice written or stamped on the instrument itself [UCC 3–503(b)]. To give notice of dishonor of a foreign draft (a draft drawn in one country and payable in another country), a formal notice called a *protest* is required [UCC 3–505(b)]. In our example, Deere

could telephone Lamar and inform her of the dishonor. Lamar, as the drawer, then would become liable for the check's payment. Similarly, Deere could notify Carerra, who indorsed the check, of the dishonor and request payment from Carerra.

Notice operates for the benefit of all parties who have rights in an instrument against the party notified [UCC 3–503(b)]. For example, assume that there are four indorsers on a note that its maker dishonors, and the holder gives timely notice to indorsers 1 and 4. If the holder collects payment from indorser 4, indorser 4 does not have to give notice to indorser 1 again to collect from indorser 1. (Indorsers 2 and 3 are not liable to indorser 4, because they were not given timely notice.) It is important to remember that if more than one indorsement appears on an instrument, each indorser is liable for the full amount to any subsequent indorser or to any holder.

ACCOMMODATION PARTIES

In addition to the parties to instruments already discussed, accommodation parties may also be primarily or secondarily liable on instruments. An **accommodation party** is one who signs an instrument for the purpose of lending his or her name as credit to another party on the instrument [UCC 3–419(a)]. Accommodation parties are one form of security against nonpayment on a negotiable instrument. For example, a bank about to lend money wants some reasonable assurance that the debt will be paid. If the prospective borrower's financial condition is uncertain, the bank may be reluctant to rely solely on the borrower's ability to pay. To reduce the risk of nonpayment, the bank can require the joining of a third person as an accommodation party on the borrower's promissory note. When one person (such as a parent) cosigns a promissory note with the maker (such as the parent's son or daughter), the cosigner is an accommodation party.

If the accommodation party signs on behalf of the *maker*, he or she is an *accommodation maker* and is primarily liable on the instrument. For example, if Abe takes out a loan to purchase a car and has his uncle cosign the note, the uncle becomes primarily liable on the instrument. If, however, the accommodation party signs on behalf of a *payee or other holder* (usually to make the instrument more marketable), he or she is an *accommodation indorser* and, as an indorser, is secondarily liable. For example, if Abe's lender (who has possession of the note) has Mary sign

---

5. Under Section 3–508(2) of the unrevised Article 3, notice by a person other than a bank has to be given "before midnight of the third business day after dishonor or receipt of notice of dishonor."

the note so that Todd will buy it, Mary is an accommodation indorser and her liability is secondary.

Any indorsement not in the ordinary chain of title gives notice of its accommodation character [UCC 3–419(a), (b), (c)]. For example, an indorsement that appears on an instrument above that of the payee, who would normally be the first indorser, is outside the chain of title.

If the accommodation party pays the instrument, he or she has a right of recourse against the party accommodated [UCC 3–419(e)]. If the *accommodated party* pays the instrument, however, does he or she have a right of recourse (contribution) against the *accommodation party?* That was the issue in the following case.

CASE 26.1   Quality Wash Group V, Ltd. v. Shawkat Hallak

California Court of
Appeal, Fourth District,
Division 1, 1996.
58 Cal.Rptr.2d 592.

**IN THE LANGUAGE
OF THE COURT**

BACKGROUND AND FACTS   *Harvey and Patricia Allan built a car wash that was sold to Shawkat and Nahida Hallak. As part of the purchase price, the Hallaks signed a promissory note in favor of the Allans. The Hallaks subsequently sold the car wash to Quality Wash Group V, Ltd. As part of their deal, Quality and the Hallaks signed an amendment to the Allan note under which Quality assumed primary liability on the note. When Quality stopped making payments on the note, the Allans filed a suit in a California state court against Quality and the Hallaks to collect. Quality paid off the note and then filed a claim against the Hallaks. The court ruled in part that the Hallaks were not liable, and Quality appealed.*

PATE, Associate Justice.
    *   *   *   *

   *   *   * [As a result of signing the amendment to the Allan note,] the Hallaks fall within the definition of "accommodation party" under [UCC 3–419(a)], which provides: "If an instrument is issued for value given for the benefit of a party to the instrument ('accommodated party') and another party to the instrument ('accommodation party') signs the instrument for the purpose of incurring liability on the instrument without being a direct beneficiary of the value given for the instrument, the instrument is signed by the accommodation party 'for accommodation.' " Having assumed the Allan note as part of the purchase price of the car wash, Quality was the direct beneficiary of the value given for the note and, therefore, was the "accommodated party."

   [UCC 3–419(e)] provides: " *   *   * An accommodated party who pays the instrument has no right of recourse against, and is not entitled to contribution from, an accommodation party." Accordingly, as an accommodated party to the Allan note who paid the note, Quality has no right of recourse against, and is not entitled to contribution from[,] the Hallaks, who are accommodation parties under the note.

**DECISION
AND REMEDY**

The state appellate court affirmed the part of the judgment that denied Quality the right to recover from the Hallaks. Quality, as the accommodated party, did not have a right of recourse against the accommodation parties.

AUTHORIZED AGENTS' SIGNATURES

Questions often arise as to the liability on an instrument signed by an agent. An **agent** is a person who agrees to represent or act for another, called the **principal.** Agents can sign negotiable instruments, just as they can sign contracts, and thereby bind their principals [UCC 3–401(a)(ii), 3–402(a)]. Without

such a rule, all corporate commercial business would stop—as every corporation can and must act through its agents. (Agency law will be covered in detail in Chapters 31 and 32.) Certain requirements must be met, however, before the principal becomes liable on the instrument. A basic requirement to hold the principal liable on the instrument is that the agent be *authorized* to sign the instrument on the principal's behalf. We will assume here, for purposes of discussion, that such authority exists (unauthorized signatures will be dealt with shortly). Additionally, the UCC imposes certain requirements regarding the way in which the agent signs the instrument.

Liability of the Principal. Generally, an authorized agent binds a principal on an instrument if the agent *clearly names* the principal in his or her signature (by writing, mark, or some symbol). In this situation, the UCC presumes that the signature is authorized and genuine [UCC 3–308(a)]. The agent may or may not add his or her own name, but if the signature shows clearly that it is made on behalf of the principal, the agent is not liable on the instrument [UCC 3–402(b)(1)]. For example, either of the following two signatures by Sandra Binney as agent for Bob Aronson would bind Aronson on the instrument:

1. Aronson, by Binney, agent.
2. Aronson.

Liability of the Agent. What happens if an authorized agent signs just his or her own name on the instrument (such as "Binney") and does not name the principal? In this situation, normally the agent will be *personally* liable to a holder in due course who has no notice that the agent was not intended to be liable. For others, the agent can escape liability if the agent proves that the original parties did not intend the agent to be liable on the instrument [UCC 3–402(a), (b)(2)].[6] In either situation, the principal is bound if the party entitled to enforce the instrument can prove the agency relationship.

There are two other situations in which an authorized agent can be held personally liable on a negotiable instrument. When an instrument is signed in both the agent's name and the principal's name ("Sandra Binney, Bob Aronson" or "Aronson, Binney") but nothing on the instrument indicates the agency relationship (so the agent cannot be distinguished from the principal), the agent may be held personally liable. An agent may also be held personally liable if the agent indicates agency status in signing a negotiable instrument but fails to name the principal ("Sandra Binney, agent") [UCC 3–402(b)(2)]. Because these forms of

signing are ambiguous, however, parol evidence is admissible to prove the agency relationship.

An important exception to the above rules is made for checks that are signed by agents. If an agent signs his or her own name on a check that is payable from the account of the principal, and the principal is identified on the check, the agent will not be personally liable on the check [UCC 3–402(c)]. For example, suppose that Binney, who is authorized to draw checks on Aronson Company's account, signs a check that is preprinted with Aronson Company's name. The signature reads simply "Sandra Binney." In this situation, Binney would not be personally liable on the check.

UNAUTHORIZED SIGNATURES

People normally are not liable to pay on negotiable instruments unless their signatures appear on the instruments. The general rule is that an unauthorized signature is wholly inoperative and will not bind the person whose name is forged. Assume, for example, that Pablo finds Veronica's checkbook lying on the street, writes out a check to himself, and forges Veronica's signature. If a bank negligently fails to ascertain that Veronica's signature is not genuine and cashes the check for Pablo, the bank will generally be liable to Veronica for the amount. (The liability of banks for paying instruments on which there are forged signatures will be discussed further in Chapter 27.)

Similarly, if an agent has no authority to sign the principal's name, the "unauthorized signature is ineffective except as the signature of the unauthorized signer" [UCC 3–403(a)]. Assume that Maya Campbell is the principal and Lena Shem is her agent. Shem, without authority, signs a promissory note as follows: "Maya Campbell, by Lena Shem, agent." Because Maya Campbell's "signature" is unauthorized, Campbell cannot be held liable, but Shem is liable to a holder of the note. This would be true even if Shem had merely signed the note "Maya Campbell," without indicating any agency relationship. In either situation, the unauthorized signer, Shem, is liable on the instrument.

There are two exceptions to the general rule that an unauthorized signature will not bind the person whose name is signed:

1. An exception is made when the person whose name is signed ratifies (affirms) the signature [UCC 3–403(a)]. For example, a principal can ratify an

6. See UCC 3–402, Comment 1. Under Section 3–401(1) of the unrevised UCC, the principal is not liable on an instrument unless his or her signature appears on it, even if the parties are aware of the agency relationship.

unauthorized signature made by an agent, either expressly, by affirming the validity of the signature, or impliedly, by other conduct, such as keeping any benefits received in the transaction or failing to repudiate the signature. The parties involved need not be principal and agent. For example, a mother may ratify her daughter's forgery of the mother's name so that her daughter will not be prosecuted for forgery.

2. Moreover, a person whose name is forged may be precluded from denying the effectiveness of the signature if the person's own negligence substantially contributed to the forgery. For example, Rob leaves his signature stamp and a blank check on an office counter. An employee, using the stamp, fills in and cashes the check. Rob can be estopped (prevented), on the basis of his negligence, from denying liability for payment of the check [UCC 3–115, 3–406, 4–401(d)(2)]. Whatever loss occurs may be allocated, however, between certain parties on the basis of comparative negligence [UCC 3–406(b)].[7] For example, if Rob can demonstrate that the bank was negligent in paying the check, the bank may bear a portion of the loss. The liability of the parties in this type of situation will be discussed further in Chapter 27.

An unauthorized signature operates as the signature of the unauthorized signer in favor of an HDC [UCC 3–403(a)]. For example, if Michel Vuillard signs "Paul Richaud" without Richaud's authorization, Vuillard is personally liable just as if he had signed his own name. Vuillard's liability is limited, however, to persons who take or pay the instrument in good faith. One who knew the signature was unauthorized would not qualify as an HDC and thus could not recover from Vuillard on the instrument. (The defenses that are effective against ordinary holders versus HDCs will be discussed in detail later in this chapter.)

SPECIAL RULES FOR UNAUTHORIZED INDORSEMENTS

Generally, when there is a forged or unauthorized indorsement, the burden of loss falls on the first party to take the instrument with the forged or unauthorized indorsement. This general rule is premised on the concept that the first party to take an instrument is in the best position to prevent the loss.

For example, suppose that a check drawn on Universal Bank and payable to the order of Inga Leed is stolen by Jenny Nilson. Nilson indorses the check "Inga Leed" and presents the check to Universal Bank for payment. The bank, without asking Nilson for identification, pays the check, and Nilson disappears. In this situation, Leed will not be liable on the check, because her indorsement was forged. The bank will bear the loss, which it might have avoided if it had requested identification from Nilson.

There are two important exceptions to this general rule. These exceptions arise when an indorsement is made by an imposter or by a fictitious payee. We look at these two situations here.

Imposters. An **imposter** is one who, by his or her personal appearance or use of the mails, telephone, or other communication, induces a maker or drawer to issue an instrument in the name of an impersonated payee. If the maker or drawer believes the imposter to be the named payee at the time of issue, the indorsement by the imposter is not treated as unauthorized when the instrument is transferred to an innocent party. This is because the maker or drawer *intended* the imposter to receive the instrument. In this situation, under the UCC's *imposter rule*, the imposter's indorsement will be effective—that is, not considered a forgery—insofar as the drawer or maker is concerned [UCC 3–404(a)].

The comparative negligence standard mentioned previously also applies in situations involving imposters [UCC 3–404(d)].[8] If, for example, a bank fails to exercise ordinary care in cashing a check made out to an imposter—for example, if the bank fails to check the identity of the holder-payee and this failure substantially contributes to the drawer's loss—the drawer may have a cause of action against the bank and be able to recover a portion of the loss.

Fictitious Payees. Another situation in which an unauthorized indorsement will be effective occurs when a person causes an instrument to be issued to a payee who will have *no interest* in the instrument [UCC 3–404(b), 3–405]. In this situation, the payee is referred to as a **fictitious payee.** Situations involving fictitious payees most often arise when (1) a dishonest employee deceives the employer into signing an instrument payable to a party with no right to

---

7. Section 3–406 of the unrevised Article 3 does not provide for an allocation of such a loss on a comparative negligence basis.

8. Section 3–405 of the unrevised Article 3 does not provide for an allocation of loss on a comparative negligence basis.

receive payment on the instrument or (2) a dishonest employee or agent has the authority to issue an instrument on behalf of the employer and issues a check to a party who has no interest in the instrument. Under the UCC's *fictitious payee rule*, the payee's indorsement is not treated as a forgery, and the employer can be held liable on the instrument by an innocent holder.

Assume that Goldstar Aviation, Inc., gives its bookkeeper, Leslie Rose, general authority to issue checks in the company name drawn on First State Bank so that Rose can pay employees' wages and other corporate bills. Rose decides to cheat Goldstar out of $10,000 by issuing a check payable to the Del Rey Company, a supplier of aircraft parts. Rose does not intend Del Rey to receive any of the money, nor is Del Rey entitled to the payment. Rose indorses the check in Del Rey's name and deposits the check in an account that she opened in West National Bank in the name "Del Rey Co." West National Bank accepts the check and collects payment from the drawee bank, First State Bank. First State Bank charges Goldstar's account $10,000. Rose transfers $10,000 out of the Del Rey account and closes the account. Goldstar discovers the fraud and demands that the account be recredited.

Who bears the loss? Because Rose's indorsement in the name of a payee with no interest in the instrument is "effective," there is no "forgery" [UCC 3–404(b)(2)]. Under this provision, West National Bank is protected in paying on the check, and the drawee bank is protected in charging Goldstar's account. Thus, it is the employer-drawer, Goldstar, that will bear the loss. Of course, Goldstar has recourse against Rose, if Rose has not absconded with the money. Additionally, if Goldstar can prove that the bank's failure to exercise reasonable care contributed substantially to the loss, the bank may be required to bear a proportionate share of the loss under the UCC's comparative negligence standard [UCC 3–404(d)]. Thus, West National Bank could be liable for a portion of the loss if it failed to exercise ordinary care when it allowed Rose to open an account in the name "Del Rey Co." and to deposit checks and withdraw funds from the account without requiring any proof that she was authorized to act for Del Rey.

Whether a dishonest employee actually signs the check or merely supplies his or her employer with names of fictitious creditors (or with true names of creditors having fictitious debts), the UCC makes no distinction in result. Assume that Dan Symes draws up the payroll list from which employees' salary checks are written. He fraudulently adds the name Penny Trip (a friend not entitled to payment) to the payroll, thus causing checks to be issued to her. Trip cashes the checks and shares the proceeds with Symes. Again, it is the employer-drawer who bears the loss.

CONCEPT SUMMARY 26.1  SIGNATURE LIABILITY

Primary and Secondary Liability	Every party (except a qualified indorser) who signs a negotiable instrument is either primarily or secondarily liable for payment of the instrument when it comes due.
	1. *Primary liability*—Makers and acceptors are primarily liable (an acceptor is a drawee that promises to pay an instrument when it is presented for payment at a later time) [UCC 3–409, 3–412, 3–413].
	2. *Secondary liability*—Drawers and indorsers are secondarily liable [UCC 3–414, 3–415, 3–501, 3–502, 3–503]. Parties who are secondarily liable on an instrument promise to pay on that instrument only if the following events occur:
	  a. The instrument is properly and timely presented.
	  b. The instrument is dishonored.
	  c. Timely notice of dishonor is given to the secondarily liable party.

Accommodation Parties	An accommodation party is one who signs an instrument for the purpose of lending his or her name as credit to another party on the instrument [UCC 3–419]. Accommodation *makers* are primarily liable; accommodation *indorsers* are secondarily liable.

CONCEPT SUMMARY 26.1

SIGNATURE LIABILITY *(continued)*

Agents' Signatures	An *agent* is a person who agrees to represent or act for another, called the *principal*. Agents can sign negotiable instruments and therefore bind their principals. Liability on the instrument depends on whether the agent is authorized and on whether the agent's representative capacity and the principal's identity are both indicated on the instrument [UCC 3–401, 3–402, 3–403]. Agents need not indicate their representative capacity on *checks*—provided the checks clearly identify the principal and are drawn on the principal's account.
Unauthorized Signatures	An unauthorized signature operates as the signature of the unauthorized signer in favor of an HDC but is wholly inoperative as the signature of the person whose name is signed *unless*: 1. The person whose name is signed ratifies (affirms) it [UCC 3–403, 3–406]. 2. The person whose name is signed is precluded from denying it [UCC 3–115, 3–406, 4–401].
Special Rules for Unauthorized Indorsements	An unauthorized indorsement will not bind the maker or drawer of the instrument except in the following circumstances: 1. When an imposter induces the maker or drawer of an instrument to issue it to the imposter (imposter rule) [UCC 3–404(a)]. 2. When a person signs as or on behalf of a maker or drawer, intending that the payee will have no interest in the instrument, or when an agent or employee of the maker or drawer has supplied him or her with the name of the payee, also intending the payee to have no such interest (fictitious payee rule) [UCC 3–404(b), 3–405].

SECTION 2

Warranty Liability

In addition to the signature liability discussed in the preceding section, transferors make certain implied warranties regarding the instruments that they are negotiating. Liability under these warranties is not subject to the conditions of proper presentment, dishonor, and notice of dishonor. These warranties arise even when a transferor does not indorse the instrument (as in delivery of a bearer instrument). Warranty liability is particularly important when a holder cannot hold a party liable on his or her signature.

Warranties fall into two categories: those that arise from the *transfer* of a negotiable instrument and those that arise on *presentment* [UCC 3–416, 3–417]. Both transfer and presentment warranties attempt to shift liability back to a wrongdoer or to the person who dealt face to face with the wrongdoer and thus was in the best position to prevent the wrongdoing.

TRANSFER WARRANTIES

There are five **transfer warranties** [UCC 3–416]. One who transfers an instrument for *consideration* makes the following warranties to all subsequent transferees and holders who take the instrument in good faith (with some exceptions, as will be noted shortly):

1. The transferor is entitled to enforce the instrument.
2. All signatures are authentic and authorized.
3. The instrument has not been altered.
4. The instrument is not subject to a defense or claim of any party that can be asserted against the transferor.[9]
5. The transferor has no knowledge of any insolvency proceedings against the maker, the acceptor, or the drawer of the instrument.

---

9. Under Section 3–417(3) of the unrevised UCC, a qualified indorser who indorses an instrument "without recourse" limits this warranty to a warranty that he or she has "no knowledge" of such a defense rather than that there is no defense. This limitation does not apply under the revised Article 3.

Parties to Whom Warranty Liability Extends. If the person who transfers an instrument receives consideration, the manner of transfer and the negotiation that is used determine how far and to whom a transfer warranty will run. Transfer of an order instrument by indorsement and delivery extends warranty liability to any subsequent holder who takes the instrument in good faith. The warranties of a person who, for consideration, transfers without indorsement (by delivery of bearer paper), however, will extend only to the immediate transferee [UCC 3–416(a)].

Suppose that Wylie forges Kim's name as a maker of a promissory note. The note is made payable to Wylie. Wylie indorses the note in blank, negotiates it for consideration to Bret, and then leaves the country. Bret, without indorsement, delivers the note for consideration to Fern. Fern, in turn without indorsement, delivers the note for consideration to Rick. On Rick's presentment of the note to Kim, the forgery is discovered. Rick can hold Fern (the immediate transferor) liable for breach of the warranty that all signatures are genuine. Rick cannot hold Bret liable, because Bret is not Rick's immediate transferor but is a prior nonindorsing transferor. This example shows the importance of the distinction between transfer by indorsement and delivery (of an order instrument) and transfer by delivery only, without indorsement (of a bearer instrument).

CONCEPT SUMMARY 26.2 — TRANSFER WARRANTY LIABILITY FOR TRANSFERORS WHO RECEIVE CONSIDERATION

TRANSFERORS	TRANSFEREES TO WHOM WARRANTIES EXTEND IF CONSIDERATION IS RECEIVED
Indorsers Who Receive Consideration	Five transfer warranties extend to *all* subsequent holders: 1. The transferor is entitled to enforce the instrument. 2. All signatures are authentic and authorized. 3. The instrument has not been altered. 4. The instrument is not subject to a defense or claim of any party that can be asserted against the transferor. 5. The transferor has no knowledge of insolvency proceedings against the maker, acceptor, or drawer of the instrument.
Nonindorsers Who Receive Consideration	Same as for indorsers, but warranties extend *only* to the *immediate transferee*.

Recovery for Breach of Warranty. A transferee or holder who takes an instrument in good faith can sue on the basis of a breach of a warranty as soon as he or she has reason to know of the breach [UCC 3–416(d)]. Notice of a claim for breach of warranty must be given to the warrantor within thirty days after the transferee or holder has reason to know of the breach and the identity of the warrantor, or the warrantor is not liable for any loss caused by a delay [UCC 3–416(c)]. The transferee or holder can recover damages for the breach in an amount equal to the loss suffered (but not more than the amount of the instrument), plus expenses and any loss of interest caused by the breach [UCC 3–416(b)].

These warranties can be disclaimed with respect to any instrument except a check [UCC 3–416(c)]. In the check-collection process, banks rely on these warranties. For all other instruments, the immediate parties can agree to a disclaimer, and an indorser can disclaim by including in the indorsement such words as "without warranties."

PRESENTMENT WARRANTIES

Any person who presents an instrument for payment or acceptance makes the following presentment warranties to any other person who in good faith pays or accepts the instrument [UCC 3–417(a), 3–417(d)]:

1. The person obtaining payment or acceptance is entitled to enforce the instrument or is authorized to obtain payment or acceptance on behalf of a person who is entitled to enforce the instrument. (This is in

effect a warranty that there are no missing or unauthorized indorsements.)

2. The instrument has not been altered.

3. The person obtaining payment or acceptance has no knowledge that the signature of the drawer of the instrument is unauthorized [UCC 3–417(a), (d)].

These warranties are referred to as **presentment warranties** because they protect the party to whom the instrument is presented. These warranties cannot be disclaimed with respect to checks, and a claim for breach must be given to the warrantor within thirty days after the claimant knows, or has reason to know,

of the breach and the identity of the warrantor, or the warrantor is not liable for any loss caused by a delay [UCC 3–417(e)].

The second and third warranties do not apply in certain cases (to certain parties). It is assumed, for example, that a drawer will recognize his or her own signature and that a maker or an acceptor will recognize whether an instrument has been materially altered.

An important issue in the following case was whether a bank had breached its presentment warranty that there were no unauthorized signatures on an item sent to another bank for payment.

CASE 26.2

First National Bank of Chicago v. MidAmerica Federal Savings Bank

Appellate Court
of Illinois,
First District, Sixth
Division, 1999.
303 Ill.App.3d 176,
707 N.E.2d 673,
236 Ill.Dec. 546.
http://www.state.il.us/
court[a]

COMPANY PROFILE   *In the mid-1990s, First National Bank of Chicago (First Chicago NBD Corporation) was one of the ten largest banks in the United States in terms of assets. In 1998, the merger of First Chicago and Banc One Corporation resulted in the formation of Bank One Corporation (http://www.bankone.com), which then ranked among the top five banks. Bank One operates more than 2,000 banking centers and a national network of automated teller machines (ATMs). Bank One is involved in many types of financial services, including retail banking, commercial banking, and investment management. It is the world's largest Visa credit-card issuer, the third largest bank lender to small businesses, one of the leading managers of mutual funds, and a major lender to purchasers of automobiles and other motor vehicles.*

BACKGROUND AND FACTS   *In 1995, First National Bank of Chicago mailed a notice to its customer Muhamad Mustafa, informing him that his certificate of deposit (CD) was coming to maturity and asking him how he wanted it handled. Instructions, apparently signed by Muhamad, were sent to First Chicago to close the CD account. The bank issued a cashier's check in the amount of $157,611.30, payable to Muhamad, and mailed the check to his address. A few days later, Michael Mustafa, Muhamad's nephew, deposited the check into his account at MidAmerica Federal Savings Bank. When the check was deposited, the purported signature of Muhamad and the signature of Michael were both on it. MidAmerica presented it for payment, First Chicago paid it, and Michael withdrew the funds from his account. Three weeks later, Michael phoned First Chicago and said that he had forged Muhamad's signature, taken the cash, and lost it gambling at a riverboat casino. Muhamad went to First Chicago, stated that he was out of the country when the check was issued, and obtained a replacement check for the full amount of the CD. First Chicago filed a suit in an Illinois state court against MidAmerica, alleging in part that MidAmerica breached the presentment warrranty that there were no unauthorized indorsements on the check. The trial court granted summary judgment in favor of First Chicago. MidAmerica appealed to a state intermediate appellate court.*

**IN THE LANGUAGE
OF THE COURT**   Justice QUINN delivered the opinion of the court:

     *   *   *   *

---

a. In the "Appellate Court" section, in the "First District Opinions" row, click on "1999." On that page, click on "February," or scroll to the list of opinions released in February, and click on the case name to access the opinion.

Under [UCC 3–417(a)], a bank that accepts and pays a check with an unauthorized or forged indorsement warrants to subsequent transferees the validity of that indorsement and may be held liable on that warranty. The purpose of the warranty is to place on the bank taking an instrument from a person making an unauthorized indorsement the responsibility of collecting from that person. As explained in [an earlier case] the reason for imposing the warranty is to:

"speed up the collection and transfer of checks and to take the burden off each bank to meticulously check the endorsements of each item transferred. Following that logic, the first bank taking in the item for collection is primarily responsible for checking the endorsements to make sure that they are proper. Each bank then warrants to each subsequent bank in the collection chain that the endorsements are good. Of course, the original bank has rights over against the person originally presenting the item.

"The rationale suggested puts the burden directly upon the first bank in the collection chain to make sure that the endorsements are valid. This is reasonable because the first bank is in a better position to insure that it is taking the item from someone with good title than are subsequent banks in the chain. If the rationale is to facilitate the speedy transfer and collection of items by removing the burden on each bank to inspect and verify each endorsement, subsequent banks are not negligent if they do not thoroughly inspect each item. In other words, the warranty feature of the statute is designed to remove the duty of each bank to check the endorsements, and, therefore, [the plaintiff bank] would not be negligent to fail to so inspect."

The rule recognizes that, while none of the parties may have had reason to suspect a fraud, *the one who took from the forger was the closest to the person causing the loss and is presumed to have had the best opportunity to have prevented the loss.* [Emphasis added.]

In the instant case, the record establishes that the indorsement on the cashier's check issued to Muhamad Mustafa was unauthorized and ineffective. MidAmerica, as the first bank in the collection chain, had a responsibility to ensure that the indorsement was valid, and through acceptance and payment of the check, MidAmerica warranted that the indorsement was valid. As this indorsement was in fact, invalid, we hold that MidAmerica breached its presentment warranty to First Chicago * * * .

DECISION AND REMEDY *The state intermediate appellate court affirmed the judgment of the lower court and ordered MidAmerica to pay First Chicago the full amount of the check, plus interest and costs. MidAmerica was liable because it breached the presentment warranty that there were no unauthorized signatures on the check.*[b]

b. MidAmerica filed a suit against Michael Mustafa and obtained a judgment against him in the amount of $157,611.30, plus $200,000 in punitive damages and $12,000 in attorneys' fees. Michael also pleaded guilty to a federal crime arising out of this incident.

SECTION 3

Defenses

Depending on whether a holder or an HDC (or a holder through an HDC) makes the demand for payment, certain defenses can bar collection from persons who would otherwise be liable on an instrument. There are two general categories of defenses—*universal defenses* and *personal defenses*.

UNIVERSAL DEFENSES

Universal defenses (also called *real defenses*) are valid against all holders, including HDCs or holders through HDCs. Universal defenses include those described in the following subsections.

Forgery. Forgery of a maker's or drawer's signature cannot bind the person whose name is used unless that person ratifies (approves or validates) the signature or is precluded from denying it (because the forgery was made possible by the maker's or drawer's negligence, for example) [UCC 3–401(a), 3–403(a)]. Thus, when a person forges an instrument, the person whose name is used has no liability to pay any holder or any HDC the value of the forged instrument. In addition, a principal can assert the defense of unauthorized signature against any holder or HDC when an agent exceeds his or her authority to sign negotiable paper on behalf of the principal [UCC 3–403].

Fraud in the Execution.   If a person is deceived into signing a negotiable instrument, believing that he or she is signing something other than a negotiable instrument (such as a receipt), *fraud in the execution*, or inception, is committed against the signer. For example, a consumer unfamiliar with the English language signs a paper presented by a salesperson. The salesperson says the paper is a request for an estimate, but in fact it is a promissory note. Even if the note is negotiated to an HDC, the consumer has a valid defense against payment [UCC 3–305(a)(1)(iii)]. This defense cannot be raised, however, if a reasonable inquiry would have revealed the nature and terms of the instrument.[10] Thus, the signer's age, experience, and intelligence are relevant, because they frequently determine whether the signer should have known the nature of the transaction before signing.

Material Alteration.   An alteration is material if it changes the contract terms between any two parties in any way. Examples of material alterations include completing an instrument, adding words or numbers, or making any other change in an unauthorized manner that relates to the obligation of a party [UCC 3–407(a)]. Thus, cutting off part of the paper of a negotiable instrument, adding a clause, or making any change in the amount, the date, or the rate of interest—even if the change is only one penny, one day, or 1 percent—is material. But it is not a material alteration to correct the maker's address, to have a red line drawn across the instrument to indicate that an auditor has checked it, or to correct the total final payment due when a mathematical error is discovered in the original computation. If the alteration is not material, any holder is entitled to enforce the instrument according to its original terms.

Material alteration is a *complete defense* against an ordinary holder. An ordinary holder can recover nothing on an instrument if it has been materially altered [UCC 3–407(b)]. Material alteration may be at best only a partial defense against an HDC, however. When the holder is an HDC and an original term, such as the monetary amount payable, has been altered, the HDC can enforce the instrument against the maker or drawer according to the original terms but not for the altered amount [UCC 3–407(c)(i)].

If the instrument was originally incomplete and was later completed in an unauthorized manner, alteration can no longer be claimed as a defense against an HDC, and the HDC can enforce the instrument as completed [UCC 3–407(b), (c)]. This is because the drawer or maker of the instrument, as a result of issuing an incomplete instrument, will normally be held responsible for the alteration, which could have been avoided by the exercise of greater care. If the alteration is readily apparent, then obviously the holder has notice of some defect or defense and therefore cannot be an HDC [UCC 3–302(a)(1), (2)(iv)].

Discharge in Bankruptcy.   Discharge in bankruptcy (see Chapter 30) is an absolute defense on any instrument regardless of the status of the holder, because the purpose of bankruptcy is to settle finally all of the insolvent party's debts [UCC 3–305(a)(1)(iv)].

Minority.   Minority, or infancy, is a universal defense only to the extent that state law recognizes it as a defense to a simple contract. Because state laws on minority vary, so do determinations of whether minority is a universal defense against an HDC [UCC 3–305(a)(1)(i)]. See Chapter 13 for a further discussion of the contractual liability of minors.

Illegality.   When the law declares that an instrument is void because it has been executed in connection with illegal conduct, then the defense is universal— that is, absolute against both an ordinary holder and an HDC. If the law merely makes the instrument voidable—as in the personal (rather than the universal) defense of illegality, discussed later—then it is still a defense against a holder, but not against an HDC. The courts are sometimes prone to treat the word *void* in a statute as meaning *voidable* to protect a holder in due course [UCC 3–305(a)(1)(ii)].

---

10. *Burchett v. Allied Concord Financial Corp.*, 74 N.M. 575, 396 P.2d 186 (1964).

Mental Incapacity.   If a person is adjudicated mentally incompetent by state proceedings, then any instrument issued by that person thereafter is null and void. The instrument is void *ab initio* (from the beginning) and unenforceable by any holder or any HDC [UCC 3–305(a)(1)(ii)]. (If a person has not been adjudicated mentally incompetent by state proceedings, mental incapacity is a personal, not a universal, defense.)

Extreme Duress.   When a person signs and issues a negotiable instrument under such extreme duress as an immediate threat of force or violence (for example, at gunpoint), the instrument is void and unenforceable by any holder or HDC [UCC 3–305(a)(1)(ii)]. (Ordinary duress is a personal, not a universal, defense.)

Personal Defenses

Personal defenses, such as those described here, are used to avoid payment to an ordinary holder of a negotiable instrument. Remember that an ordinary holder is a holder that has not met the requirements for HDC status.

Breach of Contract or Breach of Warranty.   When there is a breach of the underlying contract for which the negotiable instrument was issued, the maker of a note can refuse to pay it, or the drawer of a check can stop payment. Breach of warranty can also be claimed as a defense to liability on the instrument.

For example, Elias purchases a dozen pairs of athletic shoes from De Soto. The shoes are to be delivered in six weeks. Elias gives De Soto a promissory note for $1,000, which is the price of the shoes. The shoes arrive, but many of the shoes are stained, and the soles of several pairs are coming apart. Elias has a defense to liability on the note on the basis of breach of contract and breach of warranty. (Under sales law, a seller impliedly promises that the goods are at least merchantable; see Chapter 23.) If, however, the note is no longer in the hands of the payee-seller (De Soto) but is presented for payment by an HDC, the maker-buyer (Elias) will not be able to plead breach of contract or warranty as a defense against liability on the note.

Lack or Failure of Consideration.   The absence of consideration may be a successful defense in in-

stances involving instruments [UCC 3–303(b), 3–305(a)(2)]. For example, Tony gives Cleo, as a gift, a note that states "I promise to pay you $100,000," and Cleo accepts the note. There is no consideration for Tony's promise, and a court will not enforce the promise.

Similarly, if delivery of goods becomes impossible, a party who has issued a draft or note under the contract has a defense for not paying it. Thus, in the hypothetical athletic-shoe transaction described above, if delivery of the shoes became impossible due to their loss in an accident, De Soto could not subsequently sue successfully to enforce Elias's promise to pay the $1,000 promissory note. If the note was in the hands of an HDC, however, Elias's defense would not be available against the HDC.

Fraud in the Inducement (Ordinary Fraud).   A person who issues a negotiable instrument based on false statements by the other party will be able to avoid payment on that instrument, unless the holder is an HDC. To illustrate: Gerhard agrees to purchase Carla's used tractor for $26,500. Carla, knowing her statements to be false, tells Gerhard that the tractor is in good working order and that it has been used for only one harvest. In addition, she tells Gerhard that she owns the tractor free and clear of all claims. Gerhard pays Carla $4,500 in cash and issues a negotiable promissory note for the balance. As it turns out, Carla still owes the original seller $10,000 on the purchase of the tractor, and the tractor is subject to a filed security interest (discussed in Chapter 28). In addition, the tractor is three years old and has been used in three harvests. Gerhard can refuse to pay the note if it is held by an ordinary holder, but if Carla has negotiated the note to an HDC, Gerhard must pay the HDC. Of course, Gerhard can then sue Carla to recover the money.

Illegality.   As mentioned, if a statute provides that an illegal transaction is void, a universal defense exists. If, however, the statute provides that an illegal transaction is voidable, the defense is personal. For example, a state may make gambling contracts illegal and void but be silent on payments of gambling debts. Thus, the payment of a gambling debt becomes voidable and is a personal defense. The effect that a void contract might have on a check issued in payment under it was at issue in the following case.

CASE 26.3   Kedzie and 103rd Street Currency Exchange, Inc. v. Hodge

Supreme Court of
Illinois, 1993.
156 Ill.2d 112,
619 N.E.2d 732,
189 Ill.Dec. 31.

BACKGROUND AND FACTS *Beulah Hodge made out a check to Fred Fentress for $500 as a partial payment in advance for plumbing services at her home. When Fentress failed to appear on the date work was to begin, Hodge ordered her bank to stop payment on the check. Fentress, however, had already cashed the check at Kedzie and 103rd Street Currency Exchange, Inc. When the check was returned to Kedzie marked "Payment stopped," Kedzie filed a suit in an Illinois state court against Hodge to recover the amount of the check. In the meantime, Hodge discovered that Fentress was not a licensed plumber and that under state law, engaging in the plumbing trade without a license was a crime. Hodge filed a motion to dismiss Kedzie's claim on the ground that the plumbing contract was illegal and void. The court granted Hodge's motion, the appellate court affirmed, and Kedzie appealed to the Supreme Court of Illinois.*

IN THE LANGUAGE OF THE COURT

Justice *FREEMAN* delivered the opinion of the court:

*   *   *   *

*   *   * [A] holder in due course is an innocent third party. Such a holder is without knowledge of the circumstances of the contract upon which the instrument was initially exchanged. *   *   *

*   *   *   *

*   *   * Unless the instrument arising from a contract or transaction is, itself, made void by statute, the "illegality" defense under [UCC] 3–305 is not available to bar the claim of a holder in due course.

*   *   *   *

*   *   * It is relevant only to determine whether the Illinois Plumbing License Law provides that any obligation arising from a contract for plumbing services made in violation of its requirements is void. It does not.

DECISION AND REMEDY

The Supreme Court of Illinois reversed the lower court's ruling. Hodge was liable on the check because the statute did not void checks that were issued in payment to unlicensed plumbers.

Mental Incapacity. As mentioned, if a maker or drawer has been declared by a court to be mentally incompetent, any instrument issued by the maker or drawer is void. Hence, mental incapacity can serve as a universal defense [UCC 3–305(a)(1)(ii)]. If a maker or drawer issues a negotiable instrument while mentally incompetent but before a formal court hearing has declared him or her to be so, however, the instrument is voidable. In this situation, mental incapacity can serve only as a personal defense.

Other Personal Defenses. A number of other personal defenses can be used to avoid payment to an ordinary holder, but not an HDC, of a negotiable instrument, including the following:

1. Discharge by payment or cancellation [UCC 3–601(b), 3–602(a), 3–603, 3–604].
2. Unauthorized completion of an incomplete instrument [UCC 3–115, 3–302, 3–407, 4–401(d)(2)].
3. Nondelivery of the instrument [UCC 1–201(14), 3–105(b), 3–305(a)(2)].
4. Ordinary duress or undue influence rendering the contract voidable [UCC 3–305(a)(1)(ii)].

CONCEPT SUMMARY 26.3

VALID DEFENSES AGAINST HOLDERS OF NEGOTIABLE INSTRUMENTS

DEFENSES	TYPES
Universal (Real) Defenses Valid against all holders, including holders in due	1. Forgery. 2. Fraud in the execution.

CONCEPT SUMMARY 26.3

VALID DEFENSES AGAINST HOLDERS OF NEGOTIABLE INSTRUMENTS *(continued)*

DEFENSES	TYPES
course and holders with the rights of holders in due course (through the shelter principle) [UCC 3–305, 3–401, 3–403, 3–407].	3. Material alteration. 4. Discharge in bankruptcy. 5. Minority, if the contract is voidable. 6. Illegality, incapacity, or duress, if the contract is void under state law.
Personal Defenses Valid against ordinary holders but not against holders in due course or holders with the rights of holders in due course [UCC 3–105, 3–115, 3–302, 3–305, 3–306, 3–407, 3–601, 3–602, 3–603, 3–604, 4–401].	1. Breach of contract (including breach of contract warranties). 2. Lack of failure of consideration. 3. Fraud in the inducement. 4. Illegality, incapacity (other than minority), or duress, if the contract is voidable. 5. Previous payment or cancellation of the instrument. 6. Unauthorized completion of an incomplete instrument. 7. Nondelivery of the instrument.

FEDERAL LIMITATIONS ON HDC RIGHTS

Because of the sometimes harsh effects of the HDC doctrine on consumers, the federal government limits HDC rights in certain circumstances. To understand the punitive effects of the doctrine, consider an example. A consumer purchases a used car under express warranty from an automobile dealer. The consumer pays $1,000 down and signs a promissory note to the dealer for the remaining $5,000 due on the car. The dealer sells the bank this promissory note, which is a negotiable instrument, and the bank then becomes the creditor, to whom the consumer makes payments.

The car does not perform as warranted. The consumer returns the car and requests return of the down payment and cancellation of the contract. Even if the dealer refunded the $1,000, however, under the traditional HDC rule, the consumer would normally still owe the remaining $5,000, because the consumer's claim of breach of warranty is a personal defense and the bank is a holder in due course.

Thus, the traditional HDC rule leaves consumers who have purchased defective products liable to HDCs. In order to protect consumers, the Federal

Trade Commission (FTC) in 1976 issued Rule 433,[11] which effectively abolished the HDC doctrine in consumer credit transactions.

Requirements of FTC Rule 433. FTC Rule 433 limits the rights of an HDC in an instrument that evidences a debt arising out of a consumer credit transaction. Rule 433, entitled "Preservation of Consumers' Claims and Defenses," attempts to prevent a situation in which a consumer is required to make payment for a defective product to a third party (the bank, in the previous example) who is an HDC of a promissory note that formed part of the contract with the dealer who sold the defective good.

FTC Rule 433 applies to any seller of goods or services who takes or receives a consumer credit contract. The rule also applies to a seller who accepts as full or partial payment for a sale the proceeds of any purchase-money loan made in connection with any consumer credit contract. Under the rule, these parties must include in the consumer credit contract the following provision:

11. 16 C.F.R. Section 433.2. The rule was enacted in 1976 pursuant to the FTC's authority under the Federal Trade Commission Act, 15 U.S.C. Sections 41–58.

NOTICE

ANY HOLDER OF THIS CONSUMER CREDIT CONTRACT IS SUBJECT TO ALL CLAIMS AND DEFENSES WHICH THE DEBTOR COULD ASSERT AGAINST THE SELLER OF GOODS OR SERVICES OBTAINED PURSUANT HERETO OR WITH THE PROCEEDS HEREOF. RECOVERY HEREUNDER BY THE DEBTOR SHALL NOT EXCEED AMOUNTS PAID BY THE DEBTOR HEREUNDER.

Effect of the Rule. FTC Rule 433 allows a consumer who is party to a consumer credit transaction to bring any defense he or she has against the seller of a product against a subsequent holder as well. In essence, FTC Rule 433 places an HDC of the instrument in the position of a contract assignee. The rule makes the buyer's duty to pay conditional on the seller's full performance of the contract. Both the seller and the creditor are responsible for the seller's misconduct. The rule also clearly reduces the degree of transferability of negotiable instruments resulting from consumer credit contracts. An instrument that contains this notice or a similar statement required by law may remain negotiable, but there cannot be an HDC of such an instrument [UCC 3–106(d)].

What if the seller does not include the notice in a promissory note and then sells the note to a third party, such as a bank? While the seller has violated the rule, the bank has not. Because the FTC rule does not prohibit third parties from purchasing notes or credit contracts that do *not* contain the required rule, the third party does not become subject to the buyer's defenses against the seller. Thus, some consumers remain unprotected by the FTC rule.

S ECTION 4

Discharge

Discharge from liability on an instrument can occur in several ways, including by payment, cancellation, or, as previously discussed, material alteration. Discharge can also occur if a party reacquires an instrument, if a holder impairs another party's right of recourse, or if a holder surrenders collateral without consent.

DISCHARGE BY PAYMENT OR TENDER OF PAYMENT

All parties to a negotiable instrument will be discharged when the party primarily liable on it pays to a holder the amount due in full [UCC 3–602, 3–603].[12] The same is true if the drawee of an unaccepted draft or check makes payment in good faith to the holder. In these situations, all parties on the instruments are usually discharged. In contrast, such payment made by any other party (for example, an indorser) will discharge only the indorser and subsequent parties on the instrument. The party making such a payment still has the right to recover on the instrument from any prior parties.

A party will not be discharged when paying in bad faith to a holder who acquired the instrument by theft or who obtained the instrument from someone else who acquired it by theft (unless, of course, the person has the rights of a holder in due course) [UCC 3–602(b)(2)].

If a tender of payment is made to a person entitled to enforce the instrument and the tender is refused, indorsers and accommodation parties with a right of recourse against the party making the tender are discharged to the extent of the amount of the tender [UCC 3–603(b)]. If a tender of payment of an amount due on an instrument is made to a person entitled to enforce the instrument, the obligor's obligation to pay interest after the due date on the amount tendered is discharged [UCC 3–603(c)].

DISCHARGE BY CANCELLATION OR SURRENDER

Intentional cancellation of an instrument discharges the liability of all parties [UCC 3–604]. Intentionally writing "Paid" across the face of an instrument cancels it. Intentionally tearing up an instrument cancels it. If a holder intentionally crosses out a party's signature, that party's liability and the liability of subsequent indorsers who have already indorsed the instrument are discharged. Materially altering an

---

12. This is true even if the payment is made with knowledge of a claim to the instrument by another person unless the payor knows that "payment is prohibited by injunction or similar process of a court of competent jurisdiction" or, in most cases, "the party making payment accepted, from a person having a claim to the instrument, indemnity against loss resulting from refusal to pay the person entitled to enforce the instrument" [UCC 3–602(a), (b)(1)].

instrument may discharge the liability of all parties, as previously discussed [UCC 3–407(b)]. (An HDC may be able to enforce a materially altered instrument against its maker or drawer according to the instrument's original terms, however.)

Destruction or mutilation of a negotiable instrument is considered cancellation only if it is done with the intention of eliminating obligation on the instrument [UCC 3–604(a)(i)]. Thus, if destruction or mutilation occurs by accident, the instrument is not discharged, and the original terms can be established by parol evidence [UCC 3–309].

A holder of a note may discharge the obligation by surrendering the note to the person to be discharged [UCC 3–604(a)(i)].

DISCHARGE BY REACQUISITION

A person who reacquires an instrument that he or she held previously discharges all intervening indorsers against subsequent holders who do not qualify as holders in due course [UCC 3–207]. Of course, the person reacquiring the instrument may be liable to subsequent holders.

DISCHARGE BY IMPAIRMENT OF RECOURSE OR OF COLLATERAL

Discharge can also occur when a party's right of recourse is impaired [UCC 3–605]. A right of recourse is a right to seek reimbursement. Ordinarily, when a holder collects the amount of an instrument from an indorser, the indorser has a right of recourse against prior indorsers, the maker or drawer, and accommodation parties. If the holder has adversely affected the indorser's right to seek reimbursement from these other parties, however, the indorser is not liable on

the instrument (to the extent that the indorser's right of recourse is impaired). This occurs when, for example, the holder releases or agrees not to sue a party against whom the indorser has a right of recourse. It also occurs when a holder agrees to an extension of the instrument's due date or to some other material modification that results in a loss to the indorser with respect to the right of recourse [UCC 3–605(c), (d)].

Sometimes a party to an instrument gives collateral to secure that his or her performance will occur. When a holder "impairs the value" of that collateral without the consent of the parties who would benefit from the collateral in the event of nonpayment, those parties to the instrument are discharged to the extent of the impairment [UCC 3–605(e), (f)].

For example, suppose that Jerome and Donna sign a note as co-makers, putting up Jerome's property as collateral. The note is payable to Montessa. Montessa is required by law to file a financing statement with the state to put others on notice of Montessa's interest in Jerome's property as collateral for the note. If Montessa fails to file the statement and Jerome goes through bankruptcy—which results in Jerome's property's being sold to pay other debts and leaves him unable to pay anything on the note—Montessa has impaired the value of the collateral to Donna, who is discharged to the extent of that impairment. In other words, Montessa's failure to file the statement prevents Montessa, when Jerome goes through bankruptcy, from taking possession of the collateral, selling it, and crediting the amount owed on the note. Donna, as co-maker, is then responsible only for any remaining indebtedness, instead of the entire unpaid balance. Thus, Donna is discharged to the extent that the proceeds from the sale of the collateral would have discharged her liability on the note.

TERMS AND CONCEPTS TO REVIEW

accommodation party 455	imposter 458	transfer warranties 460
agent 456	personal defense 465	universal defense 463
dishonor 453	presentment warranties 462	
fictitious payee 458	principal 456	

QUESTIONS AND CASE PROBLEMS

26–1. UNAUTHORIZED INDORSEMENTS. What are the exceptions to the rule that a bank will be liable for paying a check over an unauthorized indorsement?

26–2. LIABILITY ON NEGOTIABLE INSTRUMENTS. Waldo makes out a negotiable promissory note payable to the order of Grace. Grace indorses the note by writing "Without recourse, Grace" and transfers the note for value to Adam. Adam, in need of cash, negotiates the note to Keith by indorsing it with the words "Pay to Keith, Adam." On the due date, Keith presents the note to Waldo for payment, only to learn that Waldo has filed for bankruptcy and will have all debts (including the note) discharged in bankruptcy. Discuss fully whether Keith can hold Waldo, Grace, or Adam liable on the note.

26–3. DEFENSES. Niles sold Kennedy a small motorboat for $1,500, maintaining to Kennedy that the boat was in excellent condition. Kennedy gave Niles a check for $1,500, which Niles indorsed and gave to Frazier for value. When Kennedy took the boat for a trial run, she discovered that the boat leaked, needed to be painted, and required a new motor. Kennedy stopped payment on her check, which had not yet been cashed. Niles has disappeared. Can Frazier recover from Kennedy as a holder in due course? Discuss.

26–4. DEFENSES. Williams purchased a used car from Stein for $1,000. Williams paid for the car with a check, written in pencil, payable to Stein for $1,000. Stein, through careful erasures and alterations, changed the amount on the check to read $10,000 and negotiated the check to Boz. Boz took the check for value, in good faith, and without notice of the alteration and thus met the UCC requirements for HDC status. Can Williams successfully raise the universal (real) defense of material alteration to avoid payment on the check? Explain.

26–5. DISCHARGE. Gil makes out a $900 negotiable promissory note payable to Ben. By special indorsement, Ben transfers the note for value to Jess. By blank indorsement, Jess transfers the note for value to Pam. By special indorsement, Pam transfers the note for value to Adrien. In need of cash, Adrien transfers the instrument for value by blank indorsement back to Jess. When told that Ben has left the country, Jess strikes out Ben's indorsement. Later she learns that Ben is a wealthy restaurant owner in Baltimore and that Gil is financially unable to pay the note. Jess contends that, as an HDC, she can hold Ben, Pam, or Adrien liable on the note. Discuss fully Jess's contentions.

26–6. DEFENSES. James Balkus died without leaving a will. A few days later, Ann Vesely, his sister, discovered in his personal effects two promissory notes made payable to her in the amount of $6,000. She presented the notes to the Security First National Bank of Sheboygan Trust Department, the personal representative for the estate of Balkus, for payment. The personal representative refused to pay the notes, claiming that Vesely was not a holder in due course and that nondelivery of the notes to her was a proper defense. The trial court upheld the personal representative's claim, and Vesely appealed. Discuss whether nondelivery is a proper defense against Vesely. [*Vesely v. Security First National Bank of Sheboygan Trust Department,* 128 Wis.2d 246, 381 N.W.2d 593 (1985)]

26–7. DISCHARGE. Richard and Coralea Triplett signed two promissory notes—one for $14,000 and one for $3,500—in favor of FirsTier Bank, N.A. The Tripletts sent the bank a check for $7,200 as payment on the notes. A clerk divided the $7,200 payment to pay the second note in full and to reduce the amount owed on the first note. The clerk then incorrectly stamped the first note "PAID," signed it, and mailed it to the Tripletts. Later, a different clerk stamped the second note "PAID," signed it, and returned it to the Tripletts. When FirsTier sued the Tripletts in a Nebraska state court for the rest of the money due on the first note, the Tripletts asserted that the bank had stamped "PAID" on the note and returned it. The bank contended that it had not intended to release both notes. In deciding whether the first note was discharged, what factors should the court take into consideration? [*FirsTier Bank, N.A. v. Triplett,* 242 Neb. 614, 497 N.W.2d 339 (1993)]

26–8. DISCHARGE. Mary Ann McClusky and her husband Curtis borrowed $75,000 and signed a note payable to Francis and Thomas Gardner. As collateral, Mary Ann gave the Gardners a mortgage on a farm owned in her name only. After the McCluskys divorced, Mary Ann found, in a file in the basement of her house, the note with the word "Paid" written across it. When the Gardners refused to cancel the mortgage, she filed a suit in an Indiana state court against them. During the trial, she testified that she did not know how the note came to be in her basement or who wrote "Paid" across it. The Gardners testified that they had not surrendered it. Should the court presume that the note had been discharged, given that it was in Mary Ann's possession and had the word "Paid" written across it? Discuss. [*Gardner v. McClusky,* 647 N.E.2d 1 (Ind.App. 1995)]

26–9. UNAUTHORIZED INDORSEMENTS. Telemedia Publications, Inc., publishes *Cablecast* magazine, a weekly guide for the listings of the cable television programming in Baton Rouge, Louisiana. Cablecast hired Jennifer Pennington as a temporary employee. Pennington's duties included indorsing subscription checks received in the mail with the Cablecast deposit stamp, preparing the deposit slip, and taking the checks to be deposited to City National Bank. John McGregor, the manager of Cablecast, soon noticed shortages in revenues coming into Cablecast. When he learned that Pennington had taken checks payable to Cablecast and deposited them in her personal account at Premier Bank, N.A., he confronted her. She admitted to taking

$7,913.04 in Cablecast checks. Cablecast filed a suit in a Louisiana state court against Premier Bank. The bank responded in part that Cablecast was solely responsible for losses caused by the fraudulent indorsements of its employees. At trial, Cablecast failed to prove that Premier Bank had not acted in good faith or that it had not exercised ordinary care in its handling of the checks. What rule should the court apply here? Why? [*Cablecast Magazine v. Premier Bank*, N.A., 729 So.2d 1165 (La.App. 1 Cir. 1999)]

26–10. IN YOUR COURT

Nancy Gabbard was the office manager at Golden Years Nursing Home (No. 2), Inc. She was given a signature stamp to issue checks to the nursing home's employees for up to $100 as advances on their pay. The checks were drawn on Golden Years's account at the First National Bank. Over a seven-year period, Gabbard wrote a number of checks to employees exclusively for the purpose of embezzling the money. She forged the employees' indorsements on the checks, signed her name as a second indorser, and deposited the checks in her personal account at Star Bank. The employees whose names were on the checks never actually requested them. When the scheme was uncovered, Golden Years filed a suit against Gabbard, Star Bank, and others to recover the money. Assume that you are the judge in the trial court hearing this case and answer the following questions:

(a) What UCC provision discussed in this chapter will you apply to these facts?

(b) Under this provision, which party, Golden Years or Star Bank, must bear the loss in this situation? Why?

LAW ON THE WEB

For updated links to resources available on the Web, as well as a variety of other materials, visit this text's Web site at http://wbl.westbuslaw.com.

To find information on the UCC, including the Article 3 provisions discussed in this chapter, refer to the Web sites listed in the *Law on the Web* in Chapter 24.

You can find a summary of the most significant changes made to UCC Articles 3 and 4 in the 1991 revision, including changes to the rules governing agents' signatures and a bank's duty of care, at

http://review.law.mercer.edu/48116.htm

LEGAL RESEARCH EXERCISES ON THE WEB

Go to http://wbl.westbuslaw.com, the Web site that accompanies this text. Select "Internet Applications," and then click on "Chapter 26." There you will find the following Internet research exercise that you can perform to learn more about fictitious payees:

Activity 26–1: Fictitious Payees

CHAPTER 27

Checks and Electronic Fund Transfers

CHECKS ARE THE MOST COMMON TYPE of nego-tiable instruments governed by the Uniform Commercial Code (UCC). Issues relating to checks are governed by Article 3 and Article 4 of the UCC. As noted in the preceding chapters, Article 3 establishes the requirements that all negotiable instruments, including checks, must meet. Article 3 also sets forth the rights and responsibilities of parties to negotiable instruments. Article 4 establishes a framework for deposit and checking agreements between a bank and its customers. Article 4 also governs the relationships of banks with one another as they process checks for payment. A check therefore may fall within the scope of Article 3 and yet be subject to the provisions of Article 4 while the check is in the course of collection. If a conflict arises between Article 3 and Article 4, Article 4 controls [UCC 4–102(a)].

In this chapter, we first identify the legal characteristics of checks and the legal duties and liabilities that arise when a check is issued. Then we examine the procedure by which the checks deposited into bank accounts move through banking channels, causing the underlying cash dollars to be shifted from one bank account to another. Increasingly, credit cards, debit cards, and other devices and methods to transfer funds electronically are being used to pay for goods

and services. In the latter part of this chapter, we look at the law governing electronic fund transfers.

SECTION 1

Checks

A **check** is a special type of draft that is drawn on a bank, ordering the bank to pay a fixed amount of money on demand [UCC 3–104(f)]. Article 4 defines a *bank* as "a person engaged in the business of banking, including a savings bank, savings and loan association, credit union or trust company" [UCC 4–105(1)].[1] If any other institution (such as a brokerage firm) handles a check for payment or for collection, the check is not covered by Article 4.

Recall from the preceding chapters that a person who writes a check is called the *drawer*. The drawer is

---

1. Under the unrevised Article 4, the term *bank* is not defined, except to distinguish among banks that deposit, collect, and pay instruments. The term is generally considered to include only commercial banks, which at the time the unrevised Article 4 was written were the only banks that could offer checking accounts. Revised Article 4's definition makes it clear that other depositary institutions now have the authority to issue and otherwise deal with checks.

usually a depositor in the bank on which the check is drawn. The person to whom the check is payable is the *payee*. The bank or financial institution on which the check is drawn is the *drawee*. If Anne Tomas writes a check from her checking account to pay her college tuition, she is the drawer, her bank is the drawee, and her college is the payee.

Between the time a check is drawn and the time it reaches the drawee, the effectiveness of the check may be altered by some event—for example, the drawer may die or order payment not to be made, or the account on which the check is drawn may be depleted. To avoid this problem, a payee may insist on payment by an instrument that has already been accepted by the drawee. Such an instrument may be a cashier's check, a traveler's check, or a certified check.

CASHIER'S CHECKS

Checks are usually three-party instruments, but on certain types of checks, the bank can serve as both the drawer and the drawee. For example, when a bank draws a check on itself, the check is called a **cashier's check** and is a negotiable instrument on issue (see Exhibit 27–1) [UCC 3–104(g)]. Normally, a cashier's check indicates a specific payee. In effect, with a cashier's check, the bank assumes responsibility for paying the check, thus making the check more readily acceptable in commerce.

For example, Blake needs to pay a moving company $7,000 for moving his household goods to a new home in another state. The moving company requests payment in the form of a cashier's check. Blake goes to a bank (he need not have an account at the bank) and purchases a cashier's check, payable to the moving company, in the amount of $7,000. Blake has to pay the bank the $7,000 for the check, plus a small service fee. He then gives the check to the moving company.

Cashier's checks are sometimes used in the business community as nearly the equivalent of cash. Except in very limited circumstances, the issuing bank must honor its cashier's checks when they are presented for payment. If a bank wrongfully dishonors a cashier's check, a holder can recover from the bank all expenses incurred, interest, and consequential damages [UCC 3–411]. This same rule applies if a bank wrongfully dishonors a certified check (to be discussed shortly) or a teller's check. (A **teller's check** is usually drawn by a bank on another bank; when drawn on a nonbank, it is payable at or through a bank [UCC 3–104(h)].)

TRAVELER'S CHECKS

A **traveler's check** has the qualities of a teller's check or a cashier's check. It is an instrument that is payable on demand, drawn on or payable at a bank and designated as a traveler's check. The issuing institution is directly obligated to accept and pay its traveler's check according to the check's terms. The purchaser is required to sign the check at the time it is purchased and again at the time it is used [UCC 3–104(i)]. Most major banks today do not issue traveler's checks; rather, they purchase and issue American Express traveler's checks for their customers (see Exhibit 27–2).

EXHIBIT 27–1 A CASHIER'S CHECK

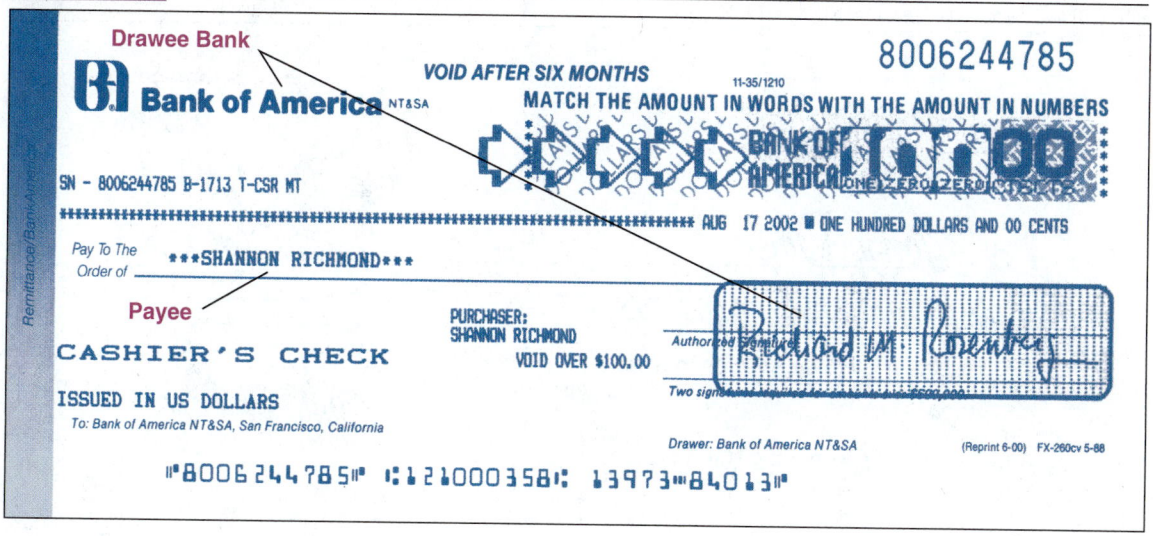

EXHIBIT 27–2   AN AMERICAN EXPRESS TRAVELER'S CHECK

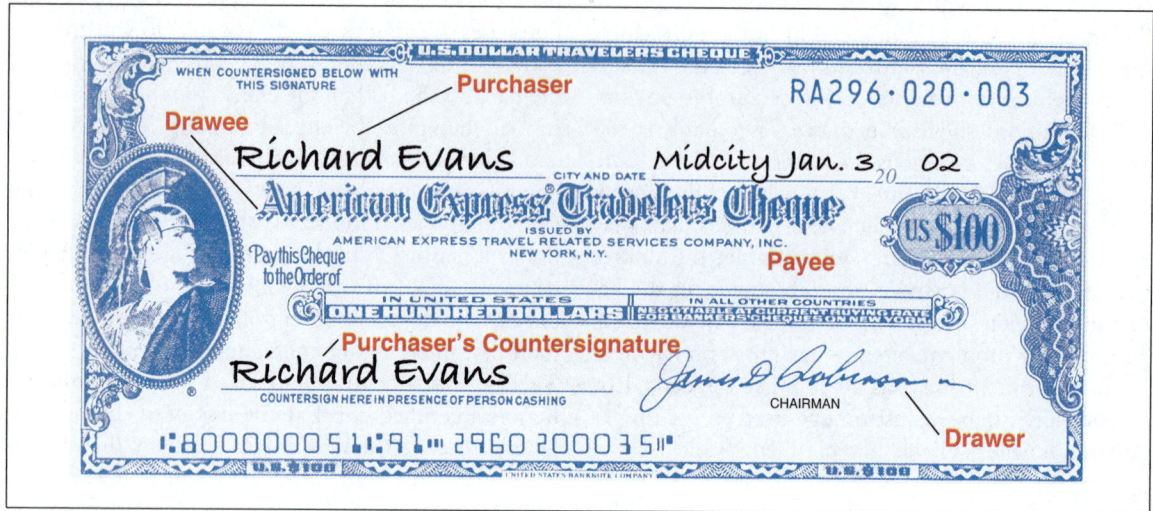

CERTIFIED CHECKS

A **certified check** is a check that has been drawn by a depositor and then *accepted* by the bank on which it is drawn [UCC 3–409(d)]. When a drawee bank agrees to certify a check, it immediately charges the drawer's account with the amount of the check and transfers those funds to its own certified check account. In effect, the bank is agreeing in advance to accept that check when it is presented for payment and to make payment from those funds reserved in the certified check account. Essentially, certification prevents the bank from denying liability. It is a promise that sufficient funds are on deposit and *have been set aside* to cover the check. Exhibit 27–3 illustrates a sample certified check.

A drawee bank is not obligated to certify a check, and failure to do so is not a dishonor of the check [UCC 3–409(d)]. If a bank does certify a check, however, the bank should write on the check the amount that it will pay. If the certification does not state an amount, and the amount is later increased and the instrument negotiated to a holder in due course (HDC),

EXHIBIT 27–3   A CERTIFIED CHECK

the obligation of the certifying bank is the amount of the instrument when it was taken by the HDC [UCC 3–413(b)]. If a certifying bank wrongfully refuses to pay a certified check, "the person asserting the right to enforce the check is entitled to compensation for expenses and loss of interest" and may also recover consequential damages [UCC 3–411(b)].

Certification may be requested by a holder (to ensure that the check will not be dishonored for insufficient funds) or by the drawer. In either circumstance, on certification the drawer and any prior indorsers are completely discharged from liability on the instrument [UCC 3–414(c), 3–415(d)].[2]

LOST, DESTROYED, OR STOLEN CASHIER'S, TELLER'S, AND CERTIFIED CHECKS

What happens if a cashier's, teller's, or certified check is lost? Under UCC 3–312, the **remitter** (the check's purchaser) or the payee of a cashier's check or a teller's check—and the drawer of a certified check—can get a refund of the amount of the check from the bank by asking for it before the check is paid. The bank may require reasonable identification of the claimant.[3]

The claim becomes enforceable ninety days after the date of the check [UCC 3–312(b)(1)]. If a person entitled to enforce the check presents it for payment within that ninety days and the bank pays, the bank is discharged [UCC 3–312(b)(2)]. If the claim becomes enforceable and no one entitled to enforce the check has presented it for payment, the bank's refund to the claimant discharges the bank—even if the claim was false [UCC 3–312(b)(4)]. (This is because a person who asks for a refund warrants to the bank, and to anybody else who might have a right to enforce the check, that the check was in fact lost, stolen, or destroyed. If

it was not lost, stolen, or destroyed, a holder who cannot obtain payment on the check can sue the claimant for breach of warranty.)

SECTION 2

The Bank-Customer Relationship

The bank-customer relationship begins when the customer opens a checking account and deposits money that the bank will use to pay for checks written by the customer. The rights and duties of the bank and the customer are contractual and depend on the nature of the transaction.

A creditor-debtor relationship is created between a customer and a bank when, for example, the customer makes cash deposits into a checking account. When a customer makes a deposit, the customer becomes a creditor, and the bank a debtor, for the amount deposited.

An agency relationship also arises between the customer and the bank when the customer writes a check on his or her account. In effect, the customer is ordering the bank to pay the amount specified on the check to the holder when the holder presents the check to the bank for payment. In this situation, the bank becomes the customer's agent and is obligated to honor the customer's request. Similarly, if the customer deposits a check into his or her account, the bank, as the customer's agent, is obligated to collect payment on the check from the bank on which the check was drawn. To transfer checkbook dollars among different banks, each bank acts as the agent of collection for its customer [UCC 4–201(a)].

Whenever a bank-customer relationship is established, certain contractual rights and duties arise. The respective rights and duties of banks and their customers are discussed in detail in the following pages.

SECTION 3

Honoring Checks

When a banking institution provides checking services, it agrees to honor the checks written by its customers, with the usual stipulation that there be sufficient funds available in the account to pay each check. When a drawee bank *wrongfully* fails to honor a check, it is liable to its customer for damages resulting from its refusal to pay. The UCC does not attempt to specify the

---

2. Under Section 3–411 of the unrevised Article 3, the legal liability of a drawer varies according to whether certification is requested by the drawer or a holder. The drawer who obtains certification remains secondarily liable on the instrument if the certifying bank does not honor the check when it is presented for payment. If the check is certified at the request of a holder, the drawer and anyone who indorses the check before certification are completely discharged.

3. The bank cannot require that the claimant post a bond, which could otherwise be required under UCC 3–309. Requiring that a bond be posted—that funds equal in the amount of the check be deposited with, for example, a court—would give the bank protection against a loss that might occur if there was a claim by another person to enforse the check.

theory under which the customer may recover for wrongful dishonor; it merely states that the drawee is liable. Thus, the customer (drawer) does not have to prove that the drawee (bank) breached its contractual commitment, slandered the customer's credit, or was negligent [UCC 4–402(b)].

The customer's agreement with the bank includes a general obligation to keep sufficient money on deposit to cover all checks written. The customer is liable to the payee or to the holder of a check in a civil suit if a check is not honored. If intent to defraud can be proved, the customer can also be subject to criminal prosecution for writing a bad check.

When the bank properly dishonors a check for insufficient funds, it has no liability to the customer. There are other circumstances as well in which the bank may rightfully refuse payment on a customer's check. We look here at the rights and duties of both the bank and its customers in relation to specific situations.

OVERDRAFTS

When the bank receives an item properly payable from its customer's checking account but there are insufficient funds in the account to cover the amount of the check, the bank has two options. It can either (1) dishonor the item or (2) pay the item and charge the customer's account, thus creating an **overdraft**, providing that the customer has authorized the payment and the payment does not violate any bank-customer agreement [UCC 4–401(a)].[4] The bank can subtract the difference from the customer's next deposit, because the check carries with it an enforceable implied promise to reimburse the bank.

When a check "bounces," a holder can resubmit the check, hoping that at a later date sufficient funds will be available to pay it. The holder must notify any indorsers on the check of the first dishonor, however; otherwise, they will be discharged from their signature liability, as discussed in Chapter 26.

Often, a bank will agree to provide overdraft protection for its customers. If a bank does make a special arrangement with its customer to accept overdrafts on an account, the bank can become liable to the customer for damages proximately caused by its wrongful dishonor of overdrafts [UCC 4–402(a), (b)]. The following classic case illustrates this rule.

---

4. If there is a joint account, the bank cannot hold any joint-account customer liable for payment of an overdraft unless the customer has signed the check or has benefited from the proceeds of the check [UCC 4–401(b)].

CASE 27.1   Kendall Yacht Corp. v. United California Bank

Court of Appeal of California, Fourth District, Division 2, 1975. 50 Cal.App.3d 949, 123 Cal.Rptr. 848.

COMPANY PROFILE   *Amadeo Giannini, the son of an Italian immigrant, had earned enough money by the age of thirty-one to retire. Instead, he dreamed of founding a national bank chain and began the Bank of Italy in San Francisco in 1904. Giannini formed Transamerica in 1928 as an umbrella company over the Bank of Italy and Los Angeles's Bank of America. During the next decade, Transamerica bought other banks in other states. In 1956, however, the federal government forced Transamerica to divorce its California banks (then known as Bank of America) from its other banks, which were organized as Firstamerica. Firstamerica returned to California in 1959, buying California Bank and merging it with the First Western Bank and Trust in 1961 to create United California Bank. Renamed First Interstate Bancorp, the firm was among the top fifteen U.S. banks when it was bought by Wells Fargo & Company (http://www.wellsfargo.com), which some observers consider to be one of the best banks in the world.*

BACKGROUND AND FACTS   *Lawrence and Linda Kendall were officers and the principal shareholders of Kendall Yacht Corporation, a corporation formed to build yachts on special order from customers. The corporation had never issued stock and was in need of operating funds. The corporation had a payroll checking account and a general business checking account with United California Bank. When the corporation ran into financial problems, Mr. Kendall spoke with Ron Lamperts, a loan officer at the bank, in an effort to obtain financing. The bank agreed to honor overdrafts on the corporate account until such time as the corporation was financially more stable. The Kendalls continued to write* *checks for supplies, payroll, and other corporate operating expenses from about mid-October through December. The corporate bank account was by then badly overdrawn, and a number of the checks had been dishonored by the bank. The Kendalls' business failed, and they later brought a lawsuit against United California Bank, charging that its wrongful dishonor of checks that it had initially agreed to accept as overdrafts had damaged the Kendalls' personal and credit reputation. The trial court held for the Kendalls, and the bank appealed.*

IN THE LANGUAGE OF THE COURT

McDANIEL, Associate Justice.

* * * *

The Bank contends first that under [California] Commercial Code section 4402 the wrongful dishonor of a check of a *corporation* does not give a cause of action for damages to individual officers and shareholders of the corporation. [California] Commercial Code section 4402, which represents section 4–402 of the Uniform Commercial Code, reads as follows: "A payor bank is liable to its customer for damages proximately caused by the wrongful dishonor of an item. * * * "

[It] was entirely foreseeable that the dishonoring of the Corporation's checks would reflect directly on the personal credit and reputation of the Kendalls and that they would suffer the adverse personal consequences which resulted when the Bank reneged on its commitments.

DECISION AND REMEDY

The appellate court confirmed the trial court's ruling. The Kendalls were awarded $26,000 each as compensatory damages for the bank's wrongful dishonor of the checks. Once a bank agrees to honor overdrafts, it cannot renege on its agreement without liability to its customers.

POSTDATED CHECKS

A bank may also charge a postdated check against a customer's account, unless the customer notifies the bank of the postdating in time to allow the bank to act on the notice before the bank commits itself to pay on the check [UCC 4–401(c)]. The notice is supposed to be treated like a stop-payment order—to be discussed shortly. If the bank fails to act on the customer's notice and charges the customer's account before the date on the postdated check, the bank may be liable for any damages incurred by the customer. Damages include those that result from the dishonor of checks that are subsequently presented for payment and are dishonored for insufficient funds.

STALE CHECKS

Commercial banking practice regards a check that is presented for payment more than six months from its date as a **stale check.** A bank is not obligated to pay an uncertified check presented more than six months from its date [UCC 4–404]. When receiving a stale check for payment, the bank has the option of paying or not paying the check. If a bank pays a stale check in good faith without consulting the customer, the bank has the right to charge the customer's account for the amount of the check.

DEATH OR INCOMPETENCE OF A CUSTOMER

UCC 4–405 provides that if, at the time a check is issued or its collection has been undertaken, a bank does not know of an adjudication of incompetence against the customer who wrote the check, the item can be paid and the bank will not incur liability. Neither death nor incompetence revokes the bank's authority to pay an item until the bank knows of the situation and has had reasonable time to act on the notice. Even when a bank knows of the death of its customer, for ten days after the *date of death* it can pay or certify checks drawn on or before the date of death—unless a person claiming an interest in that account, such as an heir or an executor of the estate, orders the bank to stop payment. Without this provision, banks would constantly be required to verify the continued life and competence of their drawers.

STOP-PAYMENT ORDERS

A **stop-payment order** is an order by a customer to his or her bank not to pay or certify a certain check. Only a customer or a "person authorized to draw on the account" can order the bank not to pay the check when it is presented for payment [UCC 4–403(a)]. A customer has no right to stop payment on a check that has been certified or accepted by a bank, however. Also, a stop-payment order must be received within a reasonable time and in a reasonable manner to permit the bank to act on it [UCC 4–403(a)]. Although a stop-payment order can be given orally, usually by phone, it is binding on the bank for only fourteen calendar days unless confirmed in writing.[5] A written stop-payment order (see Exhibit 27–4) or an oral order confirmed in writing is effective for six months, at which time it must be renewed in writing [UCC 4–403(b)].

Bank's Liability for Wrongful Payment.

If the bank pays the check over the customer's properly instituted stop-payment order, the bank will be obligated to recredit the customer's account, but only to the extent of the actual loss suffered by the drawer because of the wrongful payment [UCC 4–403(c)].

5. Some states do not recognize oral stop-payment orders; they must be in writing.

Assume that Toshio Murano orders one hundred cellular telephones from Advanced Communications, Inc., at $50 each. Murano pays in advance for the phones with a check for $5,000. Later that day, Advanced Communications tells Murano that it will not deliver the phones as arranged. Murano immediately calls the bank and stops payment on the check. Two days later, in spite of this stop-payment order, the bank inadvertently honors Murano's check to Advanced Communications for the undelivered phones. The bank will be liable to Murano for the full $5,000.

The result would have been different if Advanced Communications had delivered and Murano had accepted ninety-nine phones. Because Murano would have owed Advanced Communications $4,950 for the goods delivered, Murano would probably have been able to establish actual losses of only $50 resulting from the bank's payment over the stop-payment order. Consequently, the bank would have been liable to Murano for only $50.

Customer's Liability for Wrongful Stop-Payment Order.

A stop-payment order has its risks for a customer. The drawer must have a *valid legal ground* for issuing such an order; otherwise, the holder can sue the drawer for payment. Moreover, defenses sufficient to refuse payment against a payee may not be valid grounds to prevent payment against a subsequent

EXHIBIT 27–4 A STOP-PAYMENT ORDER

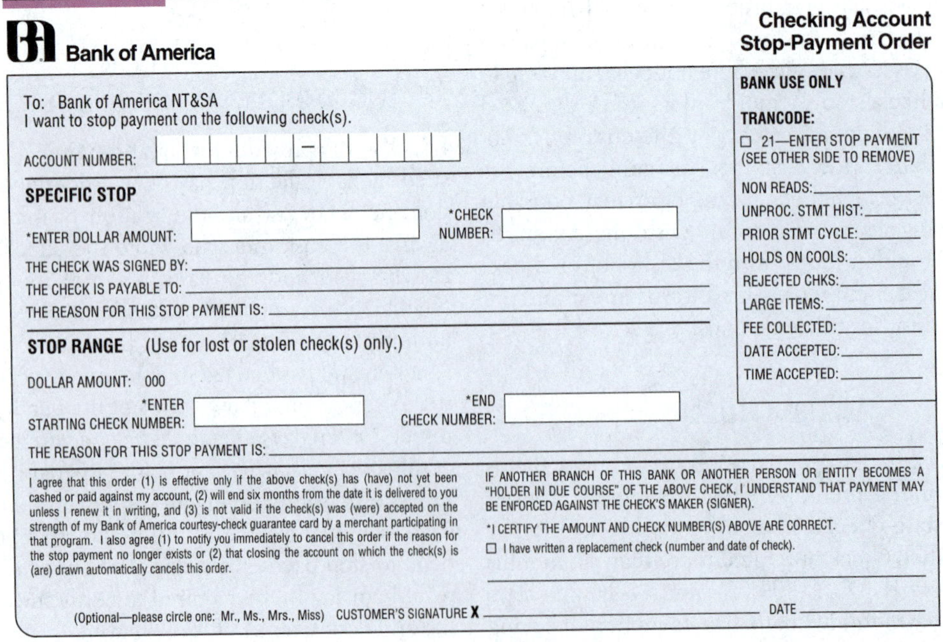
Bank of America

Checking Account Stop-Payment Order

To: Bank of America NT&SA
I want to stop payment on the following check(s).

ACCOUNT NUMBER:

SPECIFIC STOP

*ENTER DOLLAR AMOUNT: *CHECK NUMBER:

THE CHECK WAS SIGNED BY:
THE CHECK IS PAYABLE TO:
THE REASON FOR THIS STOP PAYMENT IS:

STOP RANGE (Use for lost or stolen check(s) only.)

DOLLAR AMOUNT: 000

*ENTER STARTING CHECK NUMBER: *END CHECK NUMBER:

THE REASON FOR THIS STOP PAYMENT IS:

BANK USE ONLY
TRANCODE:
☐ 21—ENTER STOP PAYMENT (SEE OTHER SIDE TO REMOVE)
NON READS:
UNPROC. STMT HIST:
PRIOR STMT CYCLE:
HOLDS ON COOLS:
REJECTED CHKS:
LARGE ITEMS:
FEE COLLECTED:
DATE ACCEPTED:
TIME ACCEPTED:

I agree that this order (1) is effective only if the above check(s) has (have) not yet been cashed or paid against my account, (2) will end six months from the date it is delivered to you unless I renew it in writing, and (3) is not valid if the check(s) was (were) accepted on the strength of my Bank of America courtesy-check guarantee card by a merchant participating in that program. I also agree (1) to notify you immediately to cancel this order if the reason for the stop payment no longer exists or (2) that closing the account on which the check(s) is (are) drawn automatically cancels this order.

IF ANOTHER BRANCH OF THIS BANK OR ANOTHER PERSON OR ENTITY BECOMES A "HOLDER IN DUE COURSE" OF THE ABOVE CHECK, I UNDERSTAND THAT PAYMENT MAY BE ENFORCED AGAINST THE CHECK'S MAKER (SIGNER).

*I CERTIFY THE AMOUNT AND CHECK NUMBER(S) ABOVE ARE CORRECT.

☐ I have written a replacement check (number and date of check).

(Optional—please circle one: Mr., Ms., Mrs., Miss) CUSTOMER'S SIGNATURE X DATE holder in due course [UCC 3–305, 3–306]. A person who wrongfully stops payment on a check not only will be liable to the payee for the amount of the check but also may be liable for consequential damages incurred by the payee as a result of the wrongful stop-payment order.

Cashier's Checks and Teller's Checks. Cashier's checks and teller's checks, both of which were defined earlier in this chapter, are sometimes used in the business community as nearly the equivalent of cash. Except in very limited circumstances, the drawer bank will not stop payment on a cashier's check or a teller's check. Once it has been issued by a bank, the bank must honor it when it is presented for payment. If the bank issuing a cashier's check or a teller's check wrongfully refuses to pay it (whether as an accommodation to its customer or for other reasons), "the person asserting the right to enforce the check is entitled to compensation for expenses and loss of interest" as well as consequential damages [UCC 3–411(b)].

CHECKS BEARING FORGED SIGNATURES

When a bank pays a check on which the drawer's signature is forged, generally the bank suffers the loss.[6] A bank may be able to recover at least some of the amount of the loss, however, from a customer whose negligence substantially contributed to the forgery, from the forger of the check, or from a holder who presented the check for payment (if the holder knew that the signature was forged).

The General Rule. A forged signature on a check has no legal effect as the signature of a drawer [UCC 3–403(a)]. For this reason, banks require a signature card from each customer who opens a checking account so the bank can determine whether the signature on a customer's check is genuine. The general rule is that the bank must recredit the customer's account when it pays on a forged signature.

Customer Negligence. When a customer's negligence substantially contributes to a forgery, the bank normally will not be obliged to recredit the customer's account for the amount of the check [UCC 3–406(a)].

Suppose that CompuNet, Inc., uses a check-writing machine to write its payroll and business checks. A CompuNet employee uses the machine to write himself a check for $10,000, and CompuNet's bank subsequently honors it. CompuNet requests the bank to recredit $10,000 to its account for incorrectly paying on a forged check. If the bank can show that CompuNet failed to take reasonable care in controlling access to the check-writing equipment, CompuNet cannot require the bank to recredit its account for the amount of the forged check.

A customer's liability may be reduced, however, by the amount of a loss caused by negligence on the part of a bank (or other "person") paying the instrument or taking it for value or for collection if the negligence substantially contributes to the loss [UCC 3–406(b)].[7] Thus, in the preceding example, if CompuNet can show that the bank should have been alerted to possible fraud, the loss may be allocated between CompuNet and the bank.

Timely Examination of Bank Statements Required. Banks typically send or make available to their customers monthly statements detailing activity of their checking accounts. Banks are not obligated to include the canceled checks themselves with the statement sent to the customer. If the bank does not send the canceled checks, however, it must provide the customer with information (check number, amount, and date of payment) on the statement that will allow the customer to reasonably identify the checks that the bank has paid [UCC 4–406(a), (b)]. Often, banks send photocopies of the canceled checks with the statement. If the bank retains the canceled checks, it must keep the checks—or legible copies of the checks—for a period of seven years [UCC 4–406(b)]. The customer may obtain a canceled check (or a copy of the check) from the bank during this period of time.

The customer has a duty to examine bank statements (and canceled checks or photocopies, if they are included with the statements) promptly and with reasonable care when the statements are received or made available, and to report any alterations or forged signatures promptly [UCC 4–406(c)]. This includes forged signatures of indorsers, to be discussed later. If the customer fails to fulfill this duty and the bank suffers a loss as a result, the customer will be liable for the loss [UCC 4–406(d)]. Even if the customer can prove

---

6. Each year, check fraud costs banks many billions of dollars—more than the combined losses from credit-card fraud, theft from automated teller machines, and armed robberies.

7. The unrevised Article 3 does not include a similar provision.

that he or she took reasonable care against forgeries, the UCC provides that discovery of such forgeries and notice to the bank must take place within specific time frames in order for the customer to require the bank to recredit his or her account.

Consequences of Failing to Detect Forgeries.　When a series of forgeries by the same wrongdoer has taken place, the UCC provides that the customer, to recover for all the forged items, must have discovered and reported the first forged check to the bank within thirty calendar days of the receipt or availability of the bank statement (and canceled checks or copies, if they are included) [UCC 4–406(d)(2)]. Failure to notify the bank within this period discharges the bank's liability for all forged checks that it pays prior to notification. In the following case, the court was asked to apply the rules set forth in UCC 4–406.

CASE 27.2　　　Marx v. Whitney National Bank

Supreme Court of
Louisiana, 1998.
713 So.2d 1142.

BACKGROUND AND FACTS　*David Marx had a checking account at Whitney National Bank. He did not review the statements for the account for January through April, which showed seventeen forged checks totaling almost $13,000. In April, he added two of his children, Stanley Marx and Maxine Goodman, as joint owners of the account. On the May statement, Stanley discovered five forged checks. David reported the forgeries to the bank and identified the forger as his grandson, Joel Goodman. David admitted that he was negligent for failing to review the January through April statements, but he asked the bank to credit the account for the amount of the forgeries on the May statement. The bank refused. David, Stanley, and Maxine filed a suit in a Louisiana state court, claiming that the bank was obligated to restore the funds. The bank argued that David's failure to discover and report the initial forgeries precluded recovery for the subsequent forgeries. The court issued a summary judgment in David's favor, the state intermediate appellate court affirmed, and the bank appealed to the Louisiana Supreme Court.*

**IN THE LANGUAGE
OF THE COURT**

MARCUS, Justice.
*　*　*　*

*　*　* [UCC 4–406] provides in pertinent part:

(c) If a bank sends or makes available a statement of account *　*　*, the customer must exercise reasonable promptness in examining the statement *　*　* to determine whether any payment was not authorized because *　*　* a purported signature by or on behalf of the customer was not authorized. *　*　* [T]he customer must promptly notify the bank of the relevant facts.

(d) If the bank proves that the customer failed, with respect to an item, to comply with the duties imposed on the customer by Subsection (c), the customer is precluded from asserting against the bank: *　*　* (2) the customer's unauthorized signature *　*　* by the same wrongdoer on any other item paid in good faith by the bank if the payment was made before the bank received notice from the customer of the unauthorized signature *　*　* and after the customer had been afforded a reasonable period of time, not exceeding 30 days, in which to examine the *　*　* statement of account and notify the bank.

The rule stated in Subsection (d)(2) *imposes on the customer the risk of loss on all subsequent forgeries by the same wrongdoer after the customer had a reasonable time to detect an initial forgery if the bank has honored subsequent forgeries prior to notice.* *　*　* [Emphasis added.]
*　*　*　*

In this case, *　*　* David Marx did not review the January *　*　* statement for his account and *　*　* if he had done so the unauthorized signature of his grandson on several checks would have been detected. Since he did not do so, plaintiffs are precluded from asserting against the bank all subsequent forgeries by the same unauthorized signatory.

DECISION AND REMEDY	*The Louisiana Supreme Court reversed the judgment of the lower court. The state supreme court held that David, Stanley, and Maxine could not recover from the bank for any of the forged checks.*

When the Bank Is Also Negligent. There is one situation in which a bank customer can escape liability, at least in part, for failing to notify the bank of forged or altered checks within the required thirty-day period. If the customer can prove that the bank was also negligent—that is, that the bank failed to exercise ordinary care—then the bank will also be liable, and the loss will be allocated between the bank and the customer on the basis of comparative negligence [UCC 4–406(e)]. In other words, even though a customer may have been negligent, the bank may still have to recredit the customer's account for a portion of the loss if the bank failed to exercise ordinary care.

Section 3–103(a)(7) of the UCC defines *ordinary care* to mean the "observance of reasonable commercial standards, prevailing in the area in which [a] person is located, with respect to the business in which that person is engaged." It is customary in the banking industry to manually examine signatures only on checks over a certain amount (such as $1,000, $2,500, or some higher amount). Thus, if a bank, in accordance with prevailing banking standards, fails to examine a signature on a particular check, the bank has not breached its duty to exercise ordinary care.[8]

Regardless of the degree of care exercised by the customer or the bank, the UCC places an absolute time limit on the liability of a bank for paying a check with a forged customer signature. A customer who fails to report his or her forged signature within one year from the date that the statement was made available for inspection loses the legal right to have the bank recredit his or her account [UCC 4–406(f)].

The following case involved a thief who cashed two forged payroll checks. The question before the court was as follows: Who should bear the loss—the bank that cashed the checks, the business that employed the thief, or both parties in proportion to their respective degrees of fault?

---

8. Prior to the 1990 revision of Article 3, courts differed in their interpretation of what constituted ordinary care on the part of a bank. Some courts held that a bank had a duty to examine every signature on the checks it paid; other courts disagreed. The revised Article 3 put an end to the problem by clarifying the meaning of ordinary care in the context of today's banking system.

CASE 27.3   Atlantic Mutual Insurance Co. v. The Provident Bank

Hamilton County
Municipal Court, 1996.
79 Ohio Misc.2d 5,
669 N.E.2d 90.

IN THE LANGUAGE
OF THE COURT

BACKGROUND AND FACTS *Clem Macke Bindery hired Vincent Jones without investigating his background. At Clem Macke, blank checks were kept in a safe that was unlocked during working hours. Jones surreptitiously obtained two checks on which he forged Clem Macke's signature. The checks were made payable to a fictitious "Larry Pope," whose name Jones signed on the back. Jones cashed the checks at The Provident Bank, which did not ask for identification. Clem Macke assigned its claim against the bank for the amount of the checks to Atlantic Mutual Insurance Company, which filed a suit in an Ohio state court against the bank, alleging negligence. The bank responded that the employer had been negligent in hiring and failing to monitor Jones.*

TIMOTHY S. BLACK, Judge.

 *   *   *   *

 *   *   * [T]he failures of the employer to exercise ordinary care in investigating, hiring, and monitoring Jones, accompanied by the failure to keep its blank checks in a locked container, constitute negligence as a matter of law. *   *   *

 *   *   * [T]he bank's failure to exercise ordinary care in determining whether or not to cash the checks, including the bank's failure to require Jones to present any identification as Larry Pope when presenting the checks for payment, constitutes negligence as a matter of law also.

> *   *   * The bank's failure to detect the forgeries at the time of presentment is counterbalanced by the employer's own failure to act in a prudent and safe manner. Accordingly, they shall both wallow equally in the fruits of their failures.

DECISION AND REMEDY   *The court held that because the bank and the employer were equally negligent, the loss would be apportioned equally.*

Other Parties from Whom the Bank May Recover. As noted earlier, a forged signature on a check has no legal effect as the signature of a drawer; a forged signature, however, is effective as the signature of the unauthorized signer [UCC 3–403(a)]. Thus, when a bank pays a check on which the drawer's signature is forged, the bank has a right to recover from the party who forged the signature.

The bank may also have a right to recover from the person (its customer or a collecting bank) who transfers a check bearing a forged drawer's signature and receives a settlement. A customer or collecting bank guarantees that "all signatures on the item are authentic and authorized" [UCC 4–207(a)(2)]. If a drawee bank pays or accepts a check on the mistaken belief that the drawer's signature was authorized, the bank may recover the amount of the check from "the person to whom or for whose benefit payment was made" [UCC 3–418(a)(ii)].

This right is limited, however. A drawee bank cannot recover from "a person who took the instrument in good faith and for value or who in good faith changed position in reliance on the payment or acceptance" [UCC 3–418(c)]. This means that in most cases, a drawee bank will not recover from the person paid, because usually there is a person who took the check in good faith and for value or who in good faith changed position in reliance on the payment or acceptance.

CHECKS BEARING FORGED INDORSEMENTS

A bank that pays a customer's check bearing a forged indorsement must recredit the customer's account or be liable to the customer (drawer) for breach of contract. Suppose that Carlo issues a $500 check "to the order of Sophia." Marcello steals the check, forges Sophia's indorsement, and cashes the check. When the check reaches Carlo's bank, the bank pays it and debits Carlo's account. The bank must recredit Carlo's account $500, because it failed to carry out Carlo's order to pay "to the order of Sophia" [UCC 4–401(a)]. (Carlo's bank will in turn recover—under breach of warranty principles—from the bank that cashed the check [UCC 4–207(a)(2)].)

Eventually, the loss usually falls on the first party to take the instrument bearing the forged indorsement, because, as discussed in Chapter 26, a forged indorsement does not transfer title. Thus, whoever takes an instrument with a forged indorsement cannot become a holder.

The customer, in any case, has a duty to report forged indorsements promptly on discovery or notice. Failure to report forged indorsements within a three-year period after the forged items have been made available to the customer relieves the bank of liability [UCC 4–111].[9]

ALTERED CHECKS

The customer's instruction to the bank is to pay the exact amount on the face of the check to the holder. The bank must examine each check before making final payment. If it fails to detect an alteration, it is liable to its customer for the loss, because it did not pay as the customer ordered. The loss is the difference between the original amount of the check and the amount actually paid. Suppose that a check written for $11 is raised to $111. The customer's account will be charged $11 (the amount the customer ordered the bank to pay). The bank will normally be responsible for the $100 [UCC 4–401(d)(1)].

---

9. The unrevised Article 4 limits this three-year period to the reporting of unauthorized indorsements. The revised Article 4 expands the limitation to cover any "action to enforce an obligation, duty, or right arising under this Article" [UCC 4–111]. In other words, under the revised Article 4, this is a general statute of limitations; it provides that any lawsuit must be begun within three years of the time that the cause of action occurs.

Customer Negligence. As in a case involving a forged drawer's signature, a customer's negligence can shift the loss when payment is made on an altered check. A common example occurs when a person carelessly writes a check, leaving large gaps around the numbers and words so that additional numbers and words can be inserted (see Exhibit 27–5).

Similarly, a person who signs a check and leaves the dollar amount for someone else to fill in is barred from protesting when the bank unknowingly and in good faith pays whatever amount is shown [UCC 4–401(d)(2)]. Finally, if the bank can trace its loss on successive altered checks to the customer's failure to discover the initial alteration, then the bank can reduce its liability for reimbursing the customer's account [UCC 4–406].[10] The law governing the customer's duty to examine monthly statements and canceled checks, and to discover and report alterations to the bank, is the same as that applied to a forged drawer's signature.

In every situation involving a forged drawer's signature or an alteration, a bank must observe reasonable commercial standards of care in paying on a customer's checks [UCC 4–406(e)]. The customer's contributory negligence can be asserted only if the bank has exercised ordinary care.

Other Parties from Whom the Bank May Recover. The bank is entitled to recover the amount of loss (including expenses and any loss of interest) from the transferor who, by presenting the check for payment, warrants that the check has not been altered.[11]

There are two exceptions dealing with accepted drafts, however. If the bank is the drawer (as it is on a cashier's check and a teller's check), it cannot recover on this ground from the presenting party if the party is a holder in due course (HDC) acting in good faith [UCC 3–417(a)(2), 4–208(a)(2)]. The reason is that an instrument's drawer is in a better position than an HDC to know whether the instrument has been altered.

Similarly, an HDC, acting in good faith in presenting a certified check for payment, does not warrant to the check's certifier that the check was not altered before the HDC acquired it [UCC 3–417(a)(2), 4–208(a)(2)]. For

---

10. The bank's defense is the same whether the successive payments were made on a forged drawer's signature or on altered checks. The bank must prove that prompt notice would have prevented its loss. For example, notification might have alerted the bank not to pay further items or might have enabled it to catch the forger.

11. Usually, the party presenting an instrument for payment is the payee, a holder, a bank customer, or a collecting bank. A bank's customers include its account holders, which may include other banks [UCC 4–104(a)(5)]. As will be discussed later in this chapter, a collecting bank is any bank handling an item for collection except the bank on which the check is drawn [UCC 4–105(5)].

EXHIBIT 27–5   A POORLY FILLED-OUT CHECK

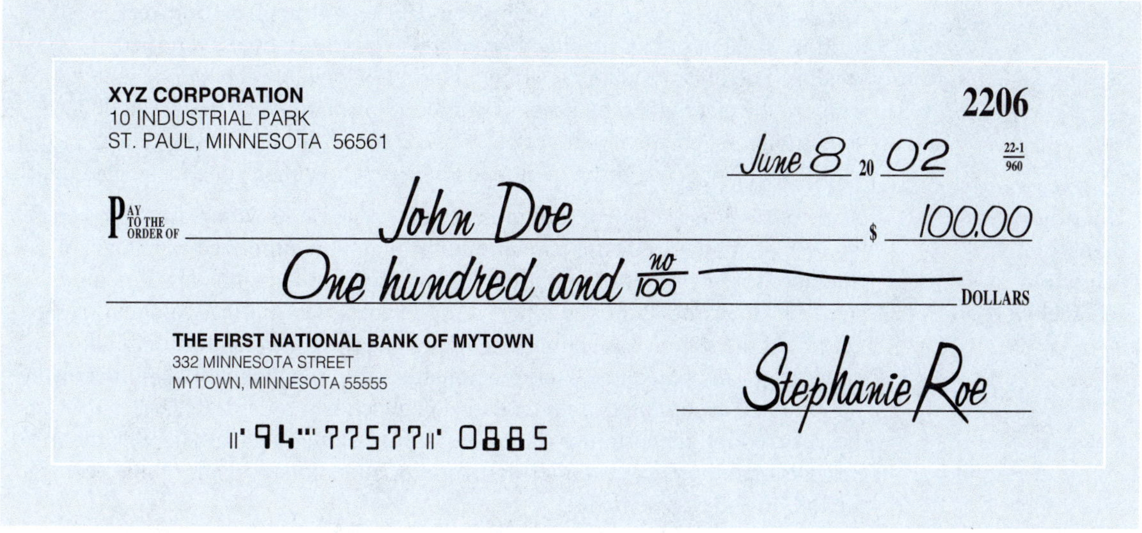

XYZ CORPORATION
10 INDUSTRIAL PARK
ST. PAUL, MINNESOTA 56561

2206

June 8 20 02   22-1/960

PAY TO THE ORDER OF ___ John Doe ___ $ 100.00

One hundred and no/100 ___ DOLLARS

THE FIRST NATIONAL BANK OF MYTOWN
332 MINNESOTA STREET
MYTOWN, MINNESOTA 55555

Stephanie Roe

⑈94⑈77577⑈ 0885

example, Alan, the drawer, draws a check for $500 payable to Pam, the payee. Pam alters the amount to $5,000. The National City Bank, the drawee, certifies the check for $5,000. Pam negotiates the check to Don, an HDC. The drawee bank pays Don $5,000. On discovering the mistake, the bank cannot recover from Don the $4,500 paid by mistake, even though the bank was not in a superior position to detect the alteration. This is in accord with the purpose of certification, which is to obtain the definite obligation of a bank to honor a definite instrument.

CONCEPT SUMMARY 27.1

HONORING CHECKS

SITUATION	BASIC RULES
Wrongful Dishonor [UCC 4–402]	The bank is liable to its customer for wrongful dishonor due to mistake for actual damages proved. Damages can include those proximately caused by subsequent arrest or prosecution of the drawer, as well as other consequential damages.
Overdraft [UCC 4–401]	The bank has a right to charge a customer's account for any item properly payable, even if the charge results in an overdraft.
Postdated Check [UCC 4–401]	A bank may charge a postdated check against a customer's account, unless the customer notifies the bank of the postdating in time to allow the bank to act on the notice before the bank commits itself to pay on the check.
Stale Check [UCC 4–404]	The bank is not obligated to pay an uncertified check presented more than six months after its date, but it may do so in good faith without liability.
Death or Incompetence of a Customer [UCC 4–405]	So long as the bank does not know of the death or incompetence of a customer, the bank can pay an item without liability. Even with knowledge of a customer's death, a bank can honor or certify checks (in the absence of a stop-payment order) for ten days after the date of the customer's death.
Stop-Payment Order [UCC 4–403]	The customer (or a "person authorized to draw on the account") must make a stop-payment order in time for the bank to have a reasonable opportunity to act. Oral orders are binding for only fourteen days unless they are confirmed in writing. Written orders are effective for only six months, unless renewed in writing. The bank is liable for wrongful payment over a timely stop-payment order to the extent that the customer suffers a loss. Except in very limited circumstances, payment will not be stopped on a cashier's check or a teller's check, and payment cannot be stopped on a certified check or an accepted draft.
Unauthorized Signature or Alteration [UCC 4–406]	The customer has a duty to examine account statements with reasonable care on receipt and to notify the bank promptly of any unauthorized signatures or alterations. On a series of unauthorized signatures or alterations by the same wrongdoer, examination and report must be given within thirty calendar days of receipt of the statement. Failure to comply releases the bank from liability unless the bank failed to exercise reasonable care, in which case liability may be apportioned according to a comparative negligence standard. Regardless of care or lack of care, the customer is estopped from holding the bank liable after one year for unauthorized customer signatures or alterations and after three years for unauthorized indorsements.

SECTION 4

Accepting Deposits

A bank has a duty to its customer to accept the customer's deposits of cash and checks. When checks are deposited, the bank must make the funds represented by those checks available within certain time frames. A bank also has a duty to collect payment on any checks payable or indorsed to its customer and deposited by the customer into his or her account. Cash deposits made in U.S. currency are received into the customer's account without being subject to further collection procedures.

AVAILABILITY SCHEDULE FOR DEPOSITED CHECKS

The Expedited Funds Availability Act of 1987[12] and Regulation CC,[13] which was issued by the Federal Reserve Board of Governors (the Federal Reserve System will be discussed shortly) to implement the act, require that any local check deposited must be available for withdrawal by check or as cash within one business day from the date of deposit. A check is classified as a local check if the first bank to receive the check for payment and the bank on which the check is drawn are located in the same check-processing region (check-processing regions are designated by the Federal Reserve Board of Governors). For nonlocal checks, the funds must be available for withdrawal within not more than five business days.

In addition, the act requires the following:

1. That funds be available on the next business day for cash deposits and wire transfers, government checks, the first $100 of a day's check deposits, cashier's checks, certified checks, and checks for which the banks receiving and paying the checks are branches of the same institution.

2. That the first $100 of any deposit be available for cash withdrawal on the opening of the *next business day* after deposit. If a local check is deposited, the next $400 is to be available for withdrawal by no later than 5 P.M. the next business day. If, for example, you deposit a local check for $500 on Monday, you can withdraw $100 in cash at the opening of the business day on Tuesday, and an additional $400 must be available for withdrawal by no later than 5 P.M. on Wednesday.

A different availability schedule applies to deposits made at *nonproprietary* automated teller machines (ATMs). These are ATMs that are not owned or operated by the bank receiving the deposits. Basically, a five-day hold is permitted on all deposits, including cash deposits, that are made at nonproprietary ATMs.

Other exceptions also exist. A banking institution has eight days to make funds available in new accounts (those open less than thirty days). It has an extra four days on deposits over $5,000 (except deposits of government and cashier's checks), on accounts with repeated overdrafts, and on checks of questionable collectibility (if the institution tells the depositor it suspects fraud or insolvency).

INTEREST-BEARING ACCOUNTS

Under the Truth-in-Savings Act (TISA) of 1991[14] and Regulation DD,[15] the act's implementing regulation, banks must pay interest based on the full balance of a customer's interest-bearing account each day. For example, Furman has an interest-bearing checking account with the First National Bank. Furman keeps a $500 balance in the account for most of the month but withdraws all but $50 the day before the bank posts the interest. The bank cannot pay interest on only the $50. The interest must be adjusted to account for all of the days, including those days when Furman's balance was higher.

Before opening a deposit account, new customers must be given certain information in a brochure, pamphlet, or other handout. The information, which must also appear in all advertisements, includes the following:

1. The minimum balance required to open an account and to be paid interest.
2. The interest, stated in terms of the annual percentage yield on the account.
3. How interest is calculated.
4. Any fees, charges, and penalties and how they are calculated. Also, under the TISA and Regulation DD, a customer's monthly statement must declare the interest earned on the account, any fees that were charged, how the fees were calculated, and the number of days that the statement covers.

---

12. 12 U.S.C. Sections 4001–4010.
13. 12 C.F.R. Sections 229.1–229.42.

14. 12 U.S.C. Sections 4301–4313.
15. 12 C.F.R. Sections 230.1–230.9.

THE COLLECTION PROCESS

Usually, deposited checks involve parties who do business at different banks, but sometimes checks are written between customers of the same bank. Either situation brings into play the bank collection process as it operates within the statutory framework of Article 4 of the UCC.

Designations of Banks Involved in the Collection Process. The first bank to receive a check for payment is the **depositary bank.**[16] For example, when a person deposits an IRS tax-refund check into a personal checking account at the local bank, that bank is the depositary bank. The bank on which a check is drawn (the drawee bank) is called the **payor bank.**

Any bank except the payor bank that handles a check during some phase of the collection process is a **collecting bank.** Any bank except the payor bank or the depositary bank to which an item is transferred in the course of this collection process is called an **intermediary bank.**

During the collection process, any bank can take on one or more of the various roles of depositary, payor, collecting, and intermediary bank. To illustrate: A buyer in New York writes a check on her New York bank and sends it to a seller in San Francisco. The seller deposits the check in her San Francisco bank account. The seller's bank is both a *depositary bank* and a *collecting bank.* The buyer's bank in New York is the payor bank. As the check travels from San Francisco to New York, any collecting bank handling the item in the collection process (other than the ones acting as depositary bank and payor bank) is also called an *intermediary bank.* Exhibit 27–6 illustrates how various banks function in the collection process.

---

16. All definitions in this section are found in UCC 4–105. The terms *depositary* and *depository* have different meanings in the banking context. A depository bank refers to a physical place (a bank or other institution) in which deposits or funds are held or stored.

EXHIBIT 27–6   THE CHECK-COLLECTION PROCESS

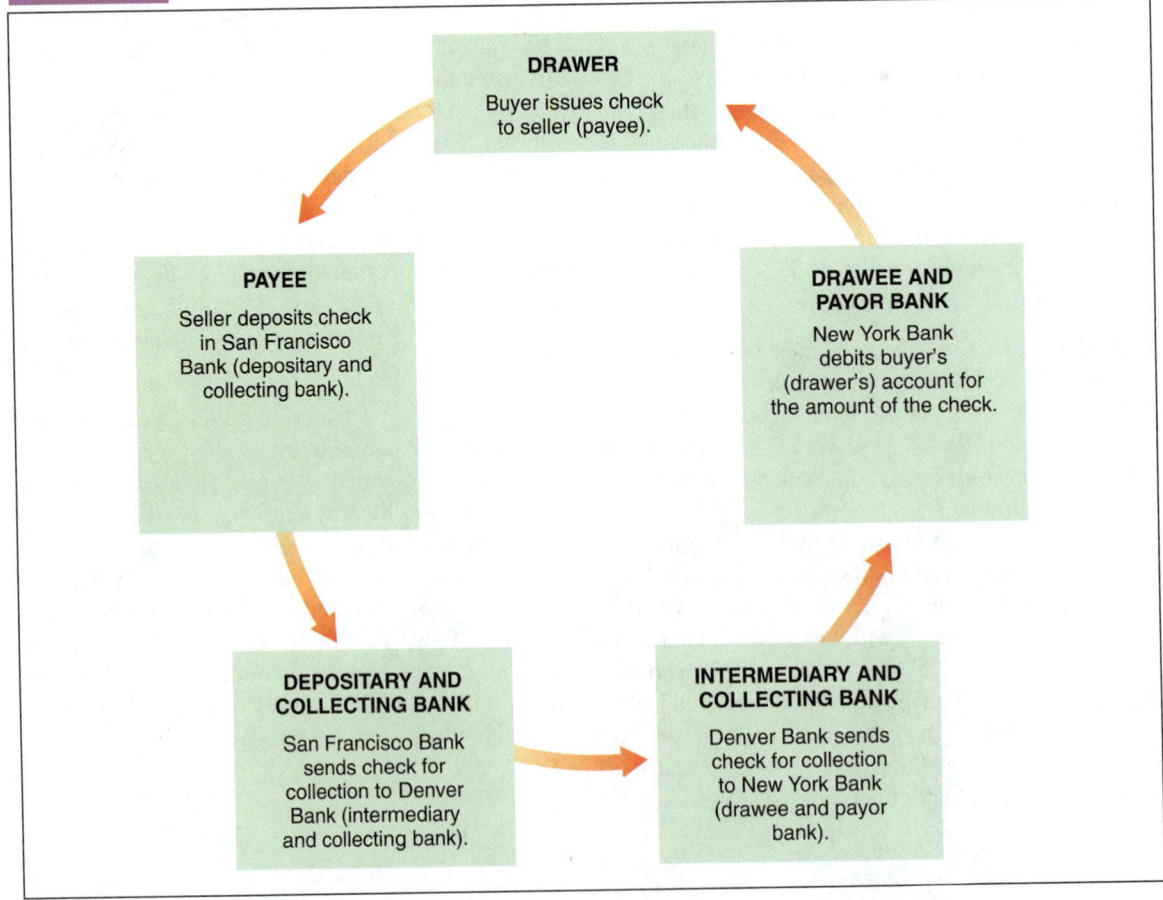

Check Collection between Customers of the Same Bank.

An item that is payable by the depository bank that receives it (which in this case is also the payor bank) is called an "on-us item." If the bank does not dishonor the check by the opening of the second banking day following its receipt, the check is considered paid [UCC 4–215(e)(2)]. For example, Otterley and Martin both have checking accounts at First State Bank. On Monday morning, Martin deposits into his own checking account a $300 check from Otterley. That same day, the bank issues Martin a "provisional credit" for $300. When the bank opens on Wednesday, Otterley's check is considered honored, and Martin's provisional credit becomes a final payment.

Check Collection between Customers of Different Banks.

Once a depositary bank receives a check, it must arrange to present it either directly or through intermediary banks to the appropriate payor bank. Each bank in the collection chain must pass the check on before midnight of the next banking day following its receipt [UCC 4–202(b)].[17] Thus, for example, a collecting bank that receives a check on Monday must forward it to the next collecting bank before midnight on Tuesday. When the check reaches the payor bank, unless the payor bank dishonors the check or returns it by midnight on the next banking day following receipt, the payor bank is accountable for the face amount of the check [UCC 4–302].[18]

Because of this deadline and because banks need to maintain an even work flow in the many items they handle daily, the UCC permits what is called *deferred posting*. According to UCC 4–108, "a bank may fix an afternoon hour of 2 P.M. or later as a cutoff hour for the handling of money and items and the making of entries on its books." Any checks received after that hour "may be treated as being received at the opening of the next banking day." Thus, if a bank's "cutoff hour" is 3 P.M., a check received by a payor bank at 4 P.M. on Monday will be deferred for posting until Tuesday. In this situation, the payor bank's deadline will be midnight Wednesday.

How the Federal Reserve System Clears Checks.

The **Federal Reserve System** is a network of twelve central banks, located around the country and headed by the Federal Reserve Board of Governors. Most banks in the United States have Federal Reserve accounts. The Federal Reserve System has greatly simplified the check-collection process by acting as a **clearinghouse**—a system or a place where banks exchange checks and drafts drawn on each other and settle daily balances. Suppose that Pamela Moy of Philadelphia writes a check to Jeanne Sutton of San Francisco. When Jeanne receives the check in the mail, she deposits it in her bank. Her bank then deposits the check in the Federal Reserve Bank of San Francisco, which transfers it to the Federal Reserve Bank of Philadelphia. That Federal Reserve bank then sends the check to Moy's bank, which deducts the amount of the check from Moy's account. Exhibit 27–7 on page 488 illustrates this process.

Electronic Check Presentment.

In the past, most checks were processed manually—the employees of each bank in the collection chain would physically handle each check that passed through the bank for collection or payment. Today, however, most checks are processed electronically. In contrast to manual check processing, which can take days, *electronic check presentment* can be done on the day of the deposit. With electronic check presentment, items may be encoded with information (such as the amount of the check) that can be read and processed by other banks' computers. In some situations, a check may be retained at its place of deposit, and only its image or information describing it is presented for payment under a Federal Reserve agreement, clearinghouse rule, or *truncation* agreement [UCC 4–110]. (The term *truncation* refers to presentment by notice rather than by delivery.)

Under UCC 4–209, any person who encodes information on an item, or with respect to an item, after the item has been issued warrants to any subsequent bank or payor that the encoded information is correct. This is also true for any person who retains an item while transmitting its image or information describing it as presentation for payment. This person warrants that the retention and presentment of the item comply with the Federal Reserve or other agreement.

---

17. A bank may take a "reasonably longer time," such as when the bank's computer system is down because of a power failure [UCC 4–202(b)].

18. Most checks are cleared by a computerized process, and communication and computer facilities may fail because of weather, equipment malfunction, or other conditions. If such conditions arise and a bank fails to meet its midnight deadline, the bank is "excused" from liability if the bank has exercised "such diligence as the circumstances require" [UCC 4–109(d)].

EXHIBIT 27–7   HOW A CHECK IS CLEARED

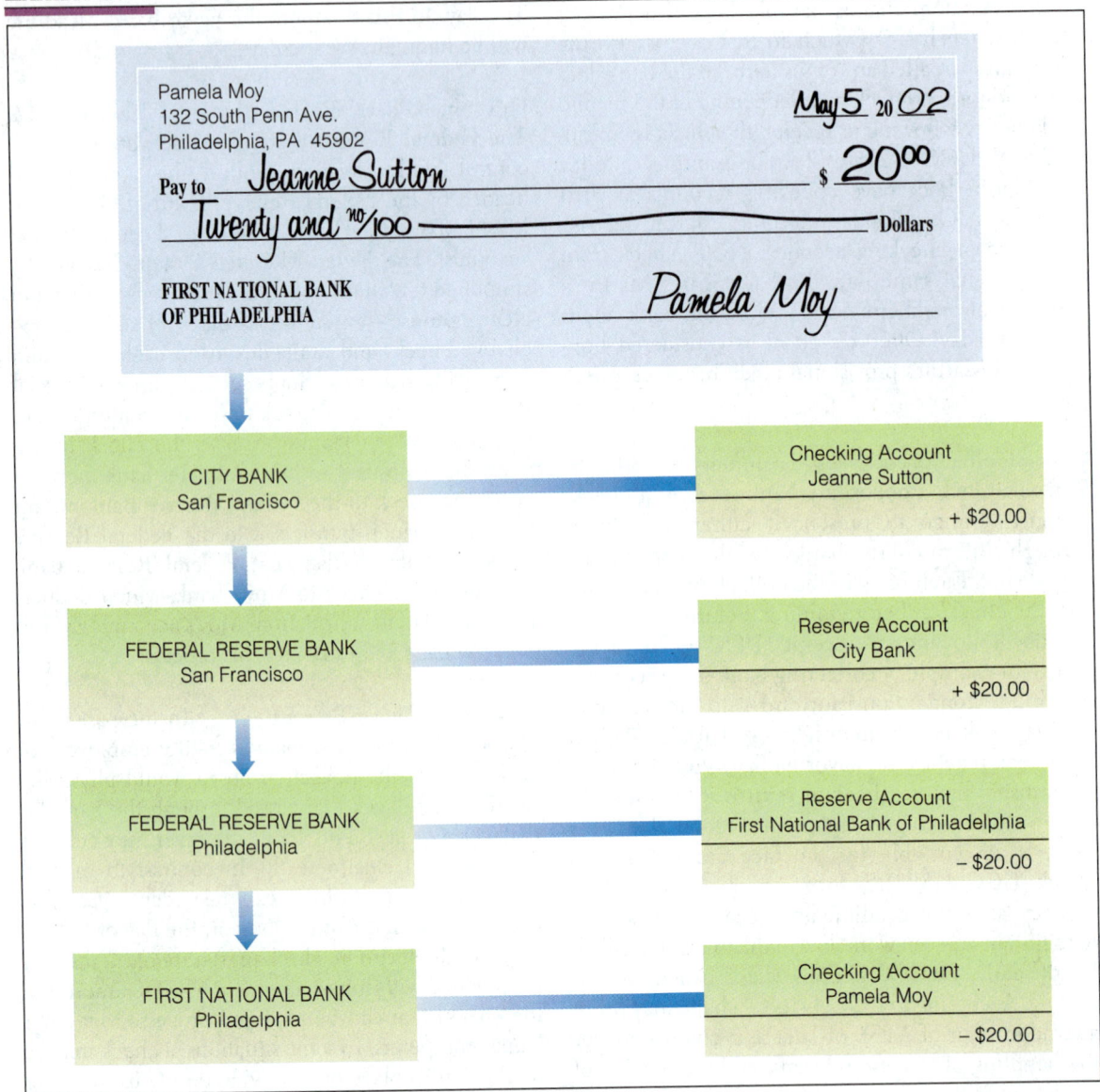

SECTION 5

Electronic Fund Transfers

The application of computer technology to banking, in the form of *electronic fund transfer systems*, has been helping to relieve banking institutions of the burden of having to move mountains of paperwork to process fund transfers. An **electronic fund transfer (EFT)** is a transfer of money made by the use of an electronic ter- minal, a telephone, a computer, or magnetic tape. The law governing EFTs depends on the type of trans- fer involved. Consumer fund transfers are governed by the Electronic Fund Transfer Act (EFTA) of 1978.[19] Commercial fund transfers are governed by Article 4A of the Uniform Commercial Code.

---

19. 15 U.S.C. Sections 1693–1693r. The EFTA is Title IX of the Consumer Credit Protection Act.

TYPES OF EFT SYSTEMS

Most banks today offer EFT services to their customers. We look here at the four most common types of EFT systems used by bank customers. (See this chapter's *Emerging Trends in Technology* on pages 490 and 491 for a discussion of some developing forms of online fund transfers.)

Automated Teller Machines. Automated teller machines (ATMs) are located at banks and at convenient locations such as airports, shopping centers, and supermarkets. ATMs, which are connected online to the bank's computers, receive deposits, dispense funds from checking or savings accounts, make credit-card advances, and accept payments. To access an account through an ATM, the bank customer uses a plastic card (debit card, access card), issued to him or her by the bank, plus a secret *personal identification number (PIN)*.

Point-of-Sale Systems. Point-of-sale systems allow consumers to transfer funds to merchants to pay for purchases. Online terminals are located in, for example, grocery stores. When a purchase is made, the customer's *debit card* (issued by the bank to the customer) is inserted into the terminal, which reads the data encoded on it. The computer at the customer's bank verifies that the card and identification code are valid and that there is enough money in the customer's account to cover the purchase. After the purchase is made, the customer's account is debited for the amount of the purchase.

Direct Deposits and Withdrawals. A direct deposit may be made to a customer's account through an electronic terminal when the customer has authorized the deposit in advance. Social Security payments are often deposited directly into beneficiaries' accounts. Similarly, an employer may agree to make payroll and pension payments directly into an employee's account at specified intervals. A customer may also authorize the bank (or other financial institution at which the customer's funds are on deposit) to make automatic payments at regular, recurrent intervals to a third party. For example, insurance premiums, utility bills, and automobile installment loan payments may often be made automatically.

Pay-by-Telephone Systems. Some financial institutions permit their customers to access the institution's computer system by telephone and direct a transfer of funds. Customers frequently pay utility bills directly using pay-by-telephone systems. Customers may also be permitted to transfer funds between accounts—for example, to withdraw funds from a savings account and make a deposit in a checking account—in this way.

CONSUMER FUND TRANSFERS

The Electronic Fund Transfer Act (EFTA) provided a basic framework for the rights, liabilities, and responsibilities of users of EFT systems. Additionally, the act gave the Federal Reserve Board authority to issue rules and regulations to help implement the act's provisions. The Federal Reserve Board's implemental regulation is called **Regulation E.**

The EFTA governs financial institutions that offer electronic fund transfers involving customer accounts. The types of accounts covered include checking accounts, savings accounts, and any other asset accounts established for personal, family, or household purposes. Note that telephone transfers are covered by the EFTA only if they are made in accordance with a prearranged plan under which periodic or recurring transfers are contemplated. Therefore, if an imposter, posing as an account holder, calls a bank official and requests a transfer of funds, the true account holder cannot hold the bank liable under the EFTA.[20] (The account holder may be able to recover the fraudulently transferred funds in a tort or contract lawsuit, however.)

Disclosure Requirements. The EFTA is essentially a disclosure law benefiting consumers. The act requires financial institutions to inform consumers of their rights and responsibilities, including those listed here, with respect to EFT systems.

1. If a customer's debit card is lost or stolen and used without his or her permission, the customer may be required to pay no more than $50. The customer, however, must notify the bank of the loss or theft within two days of learning about it. Otherwise, the liability increases to $500. The customer may be liable for more than $500 if he or she does not report the unauthorized use within sixty days after it appears on the customer's statement.

2. The customer must discover any error on the monthly statement within sixty days, and he or she must notify the bank. The bank then has ten days to

---

20. *Kashanchi v. Texas Commerce Medical Bank, N.A.*, 703 F.2d 936 (5th Cir. 1983).

EMERGING TRENDS IN TECHNOLOGY

Digital Banking

Within less than half an hour, virtually anybody with the proper software can access his or her account, transfer money, write "checks," pay bills, monitor investments, and often even buy and sell stocks. Much of the online banking software today even talks to you. The benefit of online banking for banks is significant. A paper check costs over a dollar to process. Processing a payment transaction using the Internet costs about one cent.

Online banking that provides for automated bill payment mechanisms is taking off rapidly. Citigroup, First Union Bank, Wells Fargo, and a number of other banks all offer some form of online banking. Consider Securities First Network Bank (SFNB), which allows depositors to open accounts online and to bill payments to those accounts electronically. SFNB is a member of the Federal Deposit Insurance Corporation (FDIC), and thus its accounts are federally insured up to $100,000. Whenever the party receiving an electronic payment is unable to process it, SFNB produces a paper check and sends it.

BEYOND CREDIT CARDS

Until recently, products that are sold online, such as software and videos, were only available to consumers who possessed valid credit cards. Today, improvements in the technology of EFT payment systems have made it possible for consumers to make real-time and secure debit transactions over the Internet.

For example, First Virtual Holdings has developed a payment system that is all completed online. A person who wishes to make a purchase provides his or her First Virtual account number to the seller. The seller then forwards to First Virtual all of the essential information, including the buyer's First Virtual account number, the date and time of the sale, and the dollar value of the purchase. First Virtual then sends an e-mail message to the purchaser asking for confirmation. If a confirming e-mail is returned, First Virtual processes the transaction. Without the confirming e-mail, no purchase will be processed.

In another system, consumers use their checking accounts just like a credit card. The consumer fills out an online form, giving his or her name and address and checking account information, and then clicks on a "submit" button. If there are sufficient funds in the person's checking account, the transaction is approved within a few seconds.

DIGITAL CURRENCY

As discussed in Chapter 9, other forms of "e-money" are also emerging. A number of companies are experimenting with a type of system in which a person who opens an online account can download digital currency to his or her personal computer's hard drive. The company then issues and certifies the value of the currency. Each "customer" must use the company's proprietary software, and so, too, must all retailers who accept its e-money. The customer does not have to open an account with the retailer. Such a system uses an encryption mechanism (discussed in Chapter 9) for security.

A fundamental innovation has been the development of *smart cards,* which, as explained in Chapter 9, have embedded microprocessor chips that store "cash" balances. When the holder of a smart card uses the card to purchase goods from a retailer, the amount of the purchase is deducted from the card and credited to the retailer. The retailer can store its digital cash in special point-of-sale terminals and later transfer accumulated balances to its bank by means of telephone links.

There is no actual "cash," or "legal tender," in a smart card, just as there is no actual currency in a checkbook. Instead, the balance of funds recorded on a smart card represents a balance of funds deposited with a financial institution.

The FDIC insures deposits in most bank accounts, but does e-money qualify as a "deposit"? The FDIC has said that most forms of e-money do not qualify as

investigate and must report its conclusions to the customer in writing. If the bank takes longer than ten days, it must return the disputed amount of money to the customer's account until it finds the error. If there is no error, the customer has to give the money back to the bank.

EMERGING TRENDS IN TECHNOLOGY

Digital Banking, continued

deposits and thus are not covered by deposit insurance. If a bank becomes insolvent, an e-money holder would then be in the position of a general creditor. This means that he or she would be entitled to reimbursement only after nearly everyone else who is owed money is paid (except, of course, for other e-money holders and other general creditors). At that point, there may not be any funds left. (For a further discussion of the priority of creditors when a debtor is insolvent, see Chapter 30.)

LEGAL PROTECTION

There are some existing laws that extend to e-money and e-money transactions. The Federal Trade Commission Act (discussed in Chapter 44) prohibits unfair or deceptive practices in, or affecting, commerce.[a] Under this law, e-money issuers who misrepresent the value of their products, or make other misrepresentations on which e-money consumers rely to their detriment, may be liable for engaging in deceptive practices.

General common law principles also apply. For example, the rights and liabilities of e-money issuers and consumers are subject to the law of contracts (see Chapters 10 through 18). This means that the

---

a. 15 U.S.C. Sections 41–58.

parties' relationships are affected by the terms of the contracts to which they agree. On the whole, however, it is unclear how existing laws will apply to e-money.

Even without legal protection, e-money payment systems could be safer than cash and checks. Encryption (discussed in Chapter 9) may solve some of the problems associated with e-money and with unprotected online exchanges. For example, the theft of encrypted e-money would be a waste of time because without the code a thief could not use the money. The failure of a merchant to give a customer a receipt may not matter if the e-money payment system provides proof of a transaction. Digital signatures could eliminate problems associated with forged and bounced checks. Digital signatures can also increase the enforceability of contracts entered into online.

IMPLICATIONS FOR THE BUSINESSPERSON

1. For businesspersons involved in global transactions, e-money may provide a number of benefits. This is because smart cards and other devices allow payments to travel through cyberspace quickly and without encountering any of the barriers that otherwise could discourage trade across national boundaries.
2. Businesspersons must realize that there are some disadvantages to using e-money. For example, counterfeiting and theft are

potential problems with digital cash, just as they are with physical currency. There is also the potential for monetary breakdowns caused by power outages or hardware malfunctions, as well as security problems, such as the threat of infection by computer viruses.

FOR CRITICAL ANALYSIS

1. The federal government imposes bank-reporting requirements designed to limit money laundering (discussed in Chapter 8). Do smart cards allow persons to avoid these requirements? In other words, will the use of smart cards make it easier to "launder" money obtained through illegal activities?
2. In what ways might bank fraud be easier to perpetrate using online banking methods instead of traditional banking practices?

RELEVANT WEB SITES

You can find links to Internet banks and credit unions at **http://www.netbanker.com**. To find out which banks are having the most success in attracting online banking customers, look at the rankings provided by Electronic Banker at **http://www.electronicbanker.com/fso/rankings.htm**. To learn about the latest developments in smart card technology, go to **http://www.cardshow.com/index.html**.

---

3. The bank must furnish receipts for transactions made through computer terminals, but it is not obligated to do so for telephone transfers.

4. The bank must make a monthly statement for every month in which there is an electronic transfer of funds. Otherwise, the bank must make statements every quarter. The statement must show the amount and date of the transfer, the names of the retailers or other third parties involved, the location or identification of the terminal, and the fees. Additionally, the statement must give an address and a phone number for inquiries and error notices.

5. Any preauthorized payment for utility bills and insurance premiums can be stopped three days before the scheduled transfer. To stop payment of a preauthorized EFT, a customer may notify the financial institution orally or in writing at any time up to three business days before the scheduled date of the transfer. The institution may require the customer to provide written confirmation within fourteen days of an oral notification.

Stopping Payment and Reversibility. As just mentioned, a customer may cancel a preauthorized transfer before the transfer is made, just as a drawer—the person who signs a check—may stop payment on a check before it is paid. For other EFT transactions, however, the EFTA does not provide for the reversal of an electronic transfer of funds once the transfer has occurred. This is because, unlike checks, the instantaneous nature of an EFT provides no "float time" (the time between a check's issuance and final payment) during which an effective reversal of an order to pay can be made.

Unauthorized Transfers. Because of the vulnerability of EFT systems to fraudulent activities, the EFTA of 1978 clearly defined what constitutes an unauthorized transfer. Under the act, a transfer is unauthorized if (1) it is initiated by a person who has no actual authority to initiate the transfer; (2) the consumer receives no benefit from it; and (3) the consumer did not furnish the person "with the card, code, or other means of access" to his or her account. The unauthorized use of EFT system access devices constitutes a federal felony, and unauthorized users of EFT systems are subject to criminal sanctions, including a $10,000 fine and ten years' imprisonment.

Violations and Damages. Banks are held to strict compliance with the terms of the EFTA. If they fail to adhere to the letter of the law of the EFTA, they will be held liable for violation. For a bank's violation of the EFTA, a consumer may recover actual damages, as well as punitive damages of not more than $1,000

or less than $100. (Unlike actual damages, punitive damages are assessed to punish a defendant or to set an example for similar wrongdoers.) In a class-action suit, the punitive-damage limit is the lesser of $500,000 or 1 percent of the institution's net worth. It is a federal misdemeanor to violate the EFTA. Criminal sanctions for violations of the EFTA by banking institutions may subject an institution or its officials to a $5,000 fine and up to one year's imprisonment.

COMMERCIAL FUND TRANSFERS

The transfer of funds "by wire" between commercial parties is another way in which funds are transferred electronically. In fact, the dollar volume of payments made via wire transfers is more than $1 trillion a day—an amount that far exceeds the dollar volume of payments made by other means. The two major wire payment systems are the Federal Reserve wire transfer network (Fedwire) and the New York Clearing House Interbank Payments Systems (CHIPS).

In the past, any disputes arising as a result of unauthorized or incorrectly made transfers were settled by the courts under the common law principles of tort law or contract law. To clarify the rights and liabilities of parties involved in fund transfers not subject to the EFTA or other federal or state statutes, Article 4A of the UCC was issued in 1989. Most states have adopted this article.

The type of fund transfer covered by Article 4A is illustrated in the following example. American Industries, Inc., owes $5 million to Chandler Corporation. Instead of sending Chandler a check or some other instrument that would enable Chandler to obtain payment, American Industries tells its bank, North Bank, to credit $5 million to Chandler's account in South Bank. North Bank instructs South Bank to credit $5 million to Chandler's account. In more complex transactions, additional banks would be involved.

In these and similar circumstances, ordinarily a financial institution's instruction is transmitted electronically. Any means may be used, however, including first-class mail. To reflect this fact, Article 4A uses the term *funds transfer* rather than *wire transfer* to describe the overall payment transaction. The full text of Article 4A is presented in Appendix C, following the revised Article 4 of the Uniform Commercial Code.

TERMS AND CONCEPTS TO REVIEW

cashier's check 473

certified check 474

check 472

clearinghouse 487

collecting bank 486

depository bank 486

electronic fund transfer (EFT) 488

Federal Reserve System 487

intermediary bank 486

overdraft 476

payor bank 486

Regulation E 489

remitter 475

stale check 477

stop-payment order 478

teller's check 473

traveler's check 473

QUESTIONS AND CASE PROBLEMS

27–1. TYPES OF CHECKS. Checks are usually three-party instruments. On what type of check, however, does a bank serve as both the drawer and the drawee? What type of check does a bank agree in advance to accept when the check is presented for payment?

27–2. FORGED SIGNATURES. Gary goes grocery shopping and carelessly leaves his checkbook in his shopping cart. His checkbook, with two blank checks remaining, is stolen by Dolores. On May 5, Dolores forges Gary's name on a check for $10 and cashes the check at Gary's bank, Citizens Bank of Middletown. Gary has not reported the theft of his blank checks to his bank. On June 1, Gary receives his monthly bank statement and canceled checks from Citizens Bank, including the forged check, but he does not examine the canceled checks. On June 20, Dolores forges Gary's last check. This check is for $1,000 and is cashed at Eastern City Bank, a bank with which Dolores has previously done business. Eastern City Bank puts the check through the collection process, and Citizens Bank honors it. On July 1, on receipt of his bank statement and canceled checks covering June transactions, Gary discovers both forgeries and immediately notifies Citizens Bank. Dolores cannot be found. Gary claims that Citizens Bank must recredit his account for both checks, as his signature was forged. Discuss fully Gary's claim.

27–3. DEATH OF BANK CUSTOMER/STALE CHECKS. On January 5, Brian drafts a check for $3,000 drawn on the Southern Marine Bank and payable to his assistant, Shanta. Brian puts last year's date on the check by mistake. On January 7, before Shanta has had a chance to go to the bank, Brian is killed in an automobile accident. The Southern Marine Bank is aware of Brian's death. On January 10, Shanta presents the check to the bank, and the bank honors the check by payment to Shanta. Later, Brian's widow, Joyce, claims that the bank wrongfully paid Shanta, because it knew of Brian's death and also because the check was by date over one year old. Joyce, as executor of Brian's estate and sole heir by his will, demands that Southern Marine Bank recredit Brian's estate for the check paid to Shanta. Discuss fully Southern Marine's liability in light of Joyce's demand.

27–4. ERROR RESOLUTION. Yannuzzi has a checking account at Texas Bank. She frequently uses her access card to obtain money from the automatic teller machines. She always withdraws $50 when she makes a withdrawal, but she never withdraws more than $50 in any one day. When she received the April statement on her account, she noticed that on April 13 two withdrawals for $50 each had been made from the account. Believing this to be a mistake, she went to her bank on May 10 to inform the bank of the error. A bank officer told her that the bank would investigate and inform her of the result. On May 26, the bank officer called her and said that bank personnel were having trouble locating the error but would continue to try to find it. On June 20, the bank sent her a full written report advising her that no error had been made. Yannuzzi, unhappy with the bank's explanation, filed suit against the bank, alleging that it had violated the Electronic Fund Transfer Act. What was the outcome of the suit? Would it matter if the bank could show that on the day in question it deducted $50 from Yannuzzi's account to cover a check that cleared the bank on that day—a check that Yannuzzi had written to a local department store?

27–5. OVERDRAFTS. In September 1976, Edward and Christine McSweeney opened a joint checking account with the United States Trust Co. of New York. Between April 1978 and July 1978, 195 checks totaling $99,063 were written. In July 1978, activity in the account ceased. Ninety-five of the 195 checks, totaling $16,811, were written by Christine, and the rest of the checks were written by Edward. After deposits had been credited for that period, the checks created a cumulative overdraft of $75,983. Can a bank knowingly honor a check when payment creates an overdraft, or must the bank dishonor the check? If the bank pays a check and thereby creates an overdraft, can the bank collect the amount of the overdraft from its customer? [*United States Trust Co. of New York v. McSweeney*, 91 A.D.2d 7, 457 N.Y.S.2d 276 (1982)]

27–6. UNAUTHORIZED TRANSFERS. Parviz Haghighi Abyaneh and Iran Haghighi were co-owners of a savings account at First State Bank. On May 23, 1984, a person identifying himself as Abyaneh entered the Raleigh, North Carolina, office of Citizens Savings and Loan Association of Rocky Mount and opened a savings account. He then called the First State Bank and asked a bank employee to transfer funds from Abyaneh's First State account into the newly created account. As a result, $53,825.66 was transferred to the new account, and subsequently, the funds were withdrawn. When the true owners of the First State Bank account learned of the transfer, they filed suit against Merchants Bank, North, successor by merger to First State Bank, for violating the Electronic Fund Transfer Act. Discuss whether Abyaneh will be able to recover the $53,825.66. [*Abyaneh v. Merchants Bank, North*, 670 F.Supp. 1298 (M.D.Pa. 1987)]

27–7. WIRE TRANSFERS. Dr. As'ad M. Masri and his wife borrowed $150,000 from First Virginia Bank–Colonial (FVBC). Masri then signed a wire transfer request directing FVBC to transfer the funds to the Amro Bank in Amsterdam. The request also stated that the funds were to be deposited to the Lenex Corp.'s account in that bank. FVBC transferred the funds to the Bank of Nova Scotia, an intermediary bank, and sent disbursal instructions directly to Amro. The following day, the funds were credited to the Lenex account at the Amro Bank. They were withdrawn, however, by someone other than the person intended by Masri to withdraw them. When the Masris later defaulted on the loan, FVBC sought full repayment of the funds. The Masris claimed that FVBC had breached the wire transfer agreement. Did FVBC breach the wire transfer agreement? Where did FVBC's responsibility end? Discuss fully. [*First Virginia Bank–Colonial v. Masri, M.D.*, 245 Va. 461, 428 S.E.2d 903 (1993)]

27–8. ARTICLE 3 VERSUS ARTICLE 4. Gary Morgan Chevrolet and Oldsmobile, Inc., issued four checks payable to General Motors Acceptance Corp. (GMAC) on Morgan's account with the Bank of Richmondville. There were insufficient funds in Morgan's account, and the bank gave GMAC oral notice of dishonor. The bank returned the checks two days later. GMAC filed a suit against the bank in a New York state court, claiming that the bank had failed to dishonor the checks before its midnight deadline, because notice of dishonor must be in writing under Article 4. The bank countered that notice of dishonor may be oral under Article 3. Which article controls—Article 3 or Article 4—when there is such a conflict? Explain. [*General Motors Acceptance Corp. v. Bank of Richmondville*, 203 A.D.2d 851, 611 N.Y.S.2d 338 (1994)]

27–9. STALE CHECKS. On July 15, 1986, IBP, Inc., issued to Meyer Land & Cattle Co. a check for $135,234.18 payable to both Meyer and Sylvan State Bank for the purchase of cattle. IBP wrote the check on its account at Mercantile Bank of Topeka. Someone at the Meyer firm misplaced the check. In the fall of 1995, Meyer's president Tim Meyer found the check behind a desk drawer. Jana Huse, Meyer's office manager, presented the check for deposit at Sylvan, which accepted it. After Mercantile received the instrument and its computers noted the absence of any stop-payment order, it paid the check with funds from IBP's checking account. IBP insisted that Mercantile credit IBP's account. Mercantile refused. IBP filed a suit in a federal district court against Mercantile and others, claiming, among other things, that Mercantile had not acted in good faith because it had processed the check by automated means, without examining it manually. Mercantile responded that its check-processing procedures adhered to its own policies, as well as to reasonable commercial standards of fair dealing in the banking industry. Mercantile filed a motion for summary judgment. Should the court grant the motion? Why or why not? [*IBP, Inc. v. Mercantile Bank of Topeka*, 6 F.Supp.2d 1258 (D.Kan. 1999)]

27–10. IN YOUR COURT

 Roy Supply, Inc., had a checking account at Wells Fargo Bank. The account required all checks to carry two signatures—that of Edward Roy and that of Twila June Moore, both of whom were executive officers of the company. Between January 1989 and March 1991, the bank honored hundreds of checks on which Roy's signature was forged by Moore. On January 31, 1992, Roy and the corporation notified the bank of the forgeries and then filed a suit against the bank, alleging that the bank's payment of the checks containing forged signatures constituted negligence. Assume that you are the judge in the trial court hearing this case and answer the following questions:

    (a) Review Case 27.2 (*Marx v. Whitney National Bank*). What UCC provision did the court cite in that case? Is the same provision applicable to the dispute now before your court? Why or why not?

    (b) How will you rule with respect to Roy's claim? How will you justify your decision?

LAW ON THE WEB

For updated links to resources available on the Web, as well as a variety of other materials, visit this text's Web site at http://wbl.westbuslaw.com.

You can obtain an extensive amount of information on banking regulation from the Federal Deposit Insurance Corporation (FDIC) at

http://www.fdic.gov

The American Bankers Association is the largest banking trade association in the United States. To learn more about the banking industry, go to

http://www.aba.com

LEGAL RESEARCH EXERCISES ON THE WEB

Go to http://wbl.westbuslaw.com, the Web site that accompanies this text. Select "Internet Applications," and then click on "Chapter 27." There you will find the following Internet research exercises that you can perform to learn more about check fraud and smart cards:

Activity 27–1: Check Fraud

Activity 27–2:Smart Cards

UNIT FOUR—CUMULATIVE BUSINESS HYPOTHETICAL

Marva Cummings works as a bookkeeper for Standard Printing Corp., a small printing firm. Marva has worked for the firm for years. She is authorized to sign company checks, on which Standard's name and address are printed, and generally handles the firm's accounts. One of her tasks is to reconcile the monthly bank statement from the firm's bank.

1. Standard owes White Paper Co. $350 for paper supplies that Standard ordered and received. Marva, who is distracted by personal problems, writes a check to White Paper but inadvertently fails to add the date. Furthermore, she enters $300 in the box on the check indicating the amount in figures but writes out "Three hundred and fifty and no/100" before the word "Dollars" (which is preprinted on the check). Is this check negotiable? If so, for what amount? If White Paper Co. crosses out the numerical amount $300 and writes "$350" above it, will this constitute a material alteration of the check?

2. Marva writes a check for $250 to Tony Malmo for some repairs Tony performed on the printing press. Tony indorses the check in blank and delivers it to Amber, who qualifies as a holder in due course. Amber loses the check. Felix finds it, indorses the check in blank, and deposits it into his bank account. In the meantime, Marva's employer discovers that Tony did not perform the repairs as promised on the printing press and asks Marva to stop payment on the check, which she does. Describe the rights and liabilities of each of the parties in this situation.

3. Marva writes a check for $3,500 to Latham Manufacturing Co. to pay for new printing equipment ordered and received by Standard. When the check reaches Standard's bank for collection, the bank refuses payment because Standard has insufficient funds in its account to cover the check. Latham learns that Standard is having financial difficulties and decides to sue Marva, claiming that she is personally liable on the check because she signed her name without indicating in her signature that she was acting as an agent for Standard. Will the court hold Marva liable? Why or why not?

4. Business at Standard is booming, and its profits have been increasing each month for over a year. Marva's employer refuses to give her a raise, which she feels she deserves. She decides to pay herself some extra money by engaging in some deception. Each month, she writes a check payable to Ann Barkley for $500, indorses Ann's name on the check, and then deposits the check in her bank account, indorsing the check "For deposit only." Marva assumes that Standard will never learn of her deception, because normally she is the only one who sees the bank statements and copies of the canceled checks. Unfortunately for Marva, after she has written six monthly checks in this way, for a total of $3,000, her employer discovers the scheme. The employer insists that the bank recredit its account for the $3,000 it paid to Marva over the forged indorsements. Must the bank recredit Standard's account? Why or why not?

FOCUS ON LEGAL REASONING
Kolski v. Kolski

INTRODUCTION

In Chapter 24, we discussed the requirements of a negotiable instrument. In this *Focus on Legal Reasoning*, we examine *Kolski v. Kolski*,[1] a recent decision involving a lender's request to a court to "reform" an instrument originally drafted in the form of a check to reflect its intended character as a promissory note.

CASE BACKGROUND

Jennie Kolski loaned $40,000 to her son Alexander and his wife Patricia for them to buy a mortuary business.

---

1. 349 So.2d 169 (Fla.App., 3d Dist. 1999).

The parties agreed orally that the loan was payable on demand, with an interest rate of 10 percent (later reduced to 6 percent) per year payable on a semiannual basis. After Alexander's death, Patricia induced Jennie to forbear collection of the loan by assuming the repayment obligation in full and continuing to make the semiannual interest payments.

Jennie's "Last Will and Testament" set out the terms of the original loan and her agreement that Patricia continue to make the interest payments. Patricia indicated on checks made payable to Jennie that they were for the interest on the loan, and Patricia's tax returns reflected interest deductions that

corresponded to her payments to Jennie. The loan agreement was not otherwise in writing, however.

After Patricia sold the mortuary business, Jennie demanded repayment of the loan. Patricia refused. Jennie filed a suit in a Florida state court against Patricia, seeking restitution. One of the issues was whether one of Patricia's checks could be "reformed" to include the term of the parties' agreement that the loan was payable on demand. (Reformation is discussed in Chapter 18.) The court dismissed the suit, in part for failure to state a claim for reformation. Jennie appealed to a state intermediate appellate court.

MAJORITY OPINION

GREEN, J. [Judge].
* * * *

* * * Jennie seeks a reformation of one of Patricia's canceled checks to reflect the parties' alleged agreement that the $40,000 loan was payable upon demand. * * * Jennie alleges the existence of a "writing which acknowledges a majority of the material terms of an oral demand loan agreement" between the parties and that the subject check is missing the demand payment term as a result of a unilateral mistake on her part and due to Patricia's inequitable conduct. We conclude that these allegations are sufficient to state a cause of action for reformation. Reformation is an equitable remedy, see *Smith v. Royal Automotive Group, Inc.*, 675 So.2d 144 (Fla. 5th DCA 1996), which "acts to correct an error not in the parties' agreement but in the writing which constitutes the embodiment of that agreement." Thus, where the alleged mistake in the writing is the "product of the parties' mutual mistake, or

unilateral mistake on the part of one party and inequitable conduct by the other, the writing should be reformed to accurately reflect the parties' agreement." The underlying rationale is that in reforming the instrument the agreement of the parties is in no way altered but merely corrects the defect in the written document to reflect the true terms of the parties' agreement. We find that the well-pled allegations * * * were sufficient to withstand the motion to dismiss and we reverse the trial court's dismissal * * * .

DISSENTING OPINION

COPE, J. [Judge], * * * dissenting in part.
* * * Reformation is not a proper remedy here.

I agree with the majority that a check may be the subject of reformation action. If a check stated the wrong amount or payee, it could be reformed to correct the error.

The claim in this case is that an already-paid check can be "reformed" so as to change it into a completely different instrument: a promissory note. This is the legal equivalent of turning a frog into a prince. It is not a proper function for a reformation action.

Let us examine the facts. In September 1995, defendant Patricia Kolski wrote a check for $1200 to plaintiff Jennie Kolski. This was an interest payment: the notation on the check indicated "1/2 yr due 10/95 at 6%."

Plaintiff cashed the check. The $1200 has been paid, and the check is defunct.

In her reformation claim, plaintiff asks the trial court to add to the margin of the check the following language: "$40,000 demand obligation." By this technique plaintiff proposes to change an already-paid interest check for $1200 into a promissory note for a principal amount of $40,000. This cannot be done.

The purpose of a reformation action is to correct an error in the original instrument. See *Smith v. Royal Automotive Group, Inc.*, 675 So.2d 144 (Fla. 5th DCA 1996) * * * .

Reformation cannot be used to make a new agreement between the parties. It follows that reformation cannot be employed to transform a dead check for a $1200 interest payment into a live promissory note for $40,000.

LEGAL REASONING AND ANALYSIS

1. **Legal Analysis.** Find the *Smith v. Royal Automotive Group, Inc.*, case (see the *Law on the Web* feature at the end of Chapter 2 for instructions on how to access state court opinions). For what purposes did the majority and the dissent in the *Kolski* case refer to the *Smith* case? Compare the facts, the issues, and the legal principles of the *Smith* case to those of the *Kolski* case. In what ways are they similar? How important are their differences?

2. **Legal Reasoning.** Contrast the conclusions of the majority and the dissent. What reasons did each provide to justify its position?

3. **Legal Application.** One of the reasons that the trial court dismissed this suit was its ruling that the Statute of Frauds barred Jennie's complaint. (The Statute of Frauds is discussed in Chapter 15.) On what basis would the court make this ruling? The state intermediate appellate court reversed the judgment of the trial court on this issue. On what could the appellate court base its decision to reverse the lower court's judgment?

4. **Implications for the Businessperson.** What does the decision in this case indicate for those who wish to lend, or to borrow, money to finance a business?

5. **Case Briefing Assignment.** Using the guidelines for briefing cases given in Appendix A of this text, brief the *Kolski* case.

GOING ONLINE

This text's Web site, at http://wbl.westbuslaw.com, offers links to court cases, as well as to other online research sources. You can also locate court cases at the Web sites listed in the *Law on the Web* feature at the end of Chapter 2. News and recent decisions of the courts on laws affecting negotiable instruments and other subjects can be found at http://www.nlj.com. This Web site is maintained by The National Law Journal, an information service of American Lawyer Media.

FOCUS ON ETHICS
Negotiable Instruments

Articles 3 and 4 of the Uniform Commercial Code (UCC), which deal with negotiable instruments, constitute an important part of the law governing commercial transactions. These articles reflect several fundamental ethical principles. One principle is that individuals should be protected against harm caused by the misuse of negotiable instruments. Another basic principle—and one that underlies the entire concept of negotiable instruments—is that the free flow of commerce should be encouraged by practical and reasonable laws governing the use of negotiable instruments.

In the following pages, we look first at some of the ethical implications of the concept of a holder in due course (HDC). We then examine some other ethical issues that frequently arise in relation to negotiable instruments.

ETHICS AND THE HDC CONCEPT

The drafters of Article 3 did not create the HDC concept out of thin air. Indeed, under the common law, courts had often restricted the extent to which defenses could successfully be raised against a good faith holder of a negotiable instrument. As an example, consider a classic 1884 case, *Ort v. Fowler*.[1]

In this case, Ort, a farmer who was working alone in his field one day, was approached by a

stranger who claimed to be the statewide agent for a manufacturer of iron posts and wire fence. The two men conversed for some time, and eventually the stranger persuaded the farmer to act as an area representative for the manufacturer. The stranger then completed two documents for Ort to sign, telling Ort that they were identical copies of an agreement in which Ort agreed to represent the manufacturer.

Because the farmer did not have his glasses with him and could read only with great difficulty, he asked the stranger to read what the document said. The stranger then purported to read the document to Ort, not mentioning that it was a promissory note. Both men signed each document. The stranger later negotiated the promissory note he had fraudulently obtained from Ort to a party that today we would refer to as an HDC. When this party brought suit against the farmer, the farmer attempted to defend on the basis of fraud in the execution.

The Kansas court deciding the issue entertained three possible views. One was that because Ort never *intended* to execute a note, he should not be held liable for the act. A second view was that the jury should decide, as a question of fact, whether Ort was guilty of negligence under the circumstances. The third view was that because Ort possessed all of his faculties and was able to read the English language, signing a promissory note solely in reliance on a stranger's assurances that it

was a different instrument constituted negligence.

This third view was the one adopted by the court in 1884. The court held that Ort's negligence had contributed to the fraud and that such negligence precluded Ort from raising fraud as a defense against payment on the note. Today, the UCC expresses essentially the same reasoning: fraud is a defense against an HDC only if the injured party signed the instrument "with neither knowledge nor a reasonable opportunity to learn of its character or its essential terms" [UCC 3–305(a)(1)(iii)].

Although it may not seem fair that an innocent victim should have to suffer the consequences of another's fraudulent act, the UCC assumes that it would be even less fair if an HDC could not collect payment. The reasoning behind this assumption is that an HDC, as a third party, is less likely to have been responsible for—or to have had an opportunity to protect against—the fraud in the underlying transaction.

In general, the HDC doctrine, like other sections of the UCC, reflects the philosophy that when two or more innocent parties are at risk, the burden should fall on the party that was in the best position to prevent the loss. For businesspersons, the HDC doctrine means that caution must be exercised in the issuance and acceptance of commercial paper to protect against the risk of loss through fraud.

1. 31 Kan. 478, 2 P. 580 (1884).

GOOD FAITH IN NEGOTIABLE INSTRUMENTS LAW

Clearly, the principle of good faith reflects ethical principles. The most notable application of the good faith requirement in negotiable instruments law, is, of course, the HDC doctrine. From an early time, to acquire the protected status of an HDC, a holder must have acquired an instrument in good faith. Yet other transactions subject to Articles 3 and 4 also require good faith—as, indeed, do all transactions governed by the UCC.

The Importance of Good Faith

A party that acts in bad faith may be precluded from seeking shelter under UCC provisions that would otherwise apply. This point was recently emphasized by a Pennsylvania court with respect to the fictitious payee rule. The bank in this case had accepted 882 payroll checks generated and indorsed by Dorothy Heck, a payroll clerk employed by Pavex, Inc. The checks were made payable to various current and former Pavex employees, indorsed by Heck with the payees' names, and deposited into Heck's personal checking account at her bank.

In spite of its policy that indorsements on checks must match exactly the names of the payees, the bank never refused any of Heck's deposited checks on which the indorsements did not match the payees' names. Furthermore, even though bank personnel discussed Heck's check-depositing activities on more than one occasion, they never contacted her employer to see if Heck was authorized to deposit third party payroll checks.

The court held that to assert the fictitious payee rule, "the bank must have acted in good faith when paying the instrument." In this case, the bank's choice of

ignoring perceived irregularities in Heck's transactions led the court to conclude that the bank had acted in bad faith and was therefore liable for approximately $170,000 of the $250,000 loss suffered by Pavex.[2]

How Should Good Faith Be Tested?

From an early time, there has been a division of opinion with respect to how good faith should be measured, or tested. At one end of the spectrum of views is the position that the test of good faith should be subjective in nature. In other words, as long as a person acts honestly, no matter how negligent or foolish the conduct may be, that person is acting in good faith. At the other end of the spectrum is the "objective" test of good faith. That is, honesty in itself is not enough. A party must also act reasonably under the circumstances. Whereas a fool might pass the subjective test, he or she would not meet the objective test.

Over time, the pendulum seems to have swung from one end of the spectrum to the other. When the UCC was initially drafted, the definition of good faith set forth in UCC 1–201(19) was adopted for use throughout the UCC. That section established a subjective test for good faith by defining good faith as "honesty in fact in the conduct or transaction concerned." The only UCC article that incorporated a more objective test for good faith was Article 2, in which Section 2–103(1)(b) defined good faith as both honesty in fact *and* the observance of reasonable commercial standards of fair dealing in the trade. Under this definition of good faith, a person who acts honestly in fact but does

---

2. *Pavex, Inc. v. York Federal Savings and Loan Association,* 716 A.2d 640 (Pa.Super.Ct. 1998).

not observe reasonable commercial standards of fair dealing will not meet the good faith requirement.

This more objective measure of good faith has since been incorporated into other articles of the UCC, including Articles 3, 4, and 4A. The 1990 revision of Article 3, for example, defines good faith as requiring not only honesty in fact but also "reasonable commercial standards of fair dealing"—see UCC 3–103(a)(4).

EFFICIENCY VERSUS DUE CARE

A major problem faced by today's banking institutions is how to verify customer signatures on the billions of checks that are processed through the banking system each month. If a bank fails to verify a signature on a check it receives for payment and the check turns out to be forged, the bank will normally be held liable to its customer for the amount paid. But how can banks possibly examine, item by item, each signature on every check that they pay?

The banks' solution to this problem is simply not to examine all signatures. Instead, computers are programmed to verify all signatures only on checks exceeding a certain threshold amount, such as $1,000 or $2,500 or perhaps some higher figure. Checks for less than the threshold amount are selected for signature verification only on a random basis. In other words, serious attention is restricted to serious matters. The result is that many checks, if not most, are paid without signature verification. This practice, which has become an acceptable standard within today's banking industry, is economically efficient for banks. Even though liability costs are sometimes incurred—when forged checks are paid—the costs involved in verifying the authenticity of each and every signature would be far higher.

Some people have alleged that banks using such procedures are not exercising due care in the handling of the customers' accounts. Under the UCC, banks are held to a standard of "ordinary care." At one time in the banking industry, ordinary care normally was interpreted to mean that a bank had a duty to inspect *all* signatures on checks. The question is, what constitutes ordinary care in the context of today's world? Does a bank exercise ordinary care if it follows the prevailing industry practice of examining signatures on only a few, randomly selected checks under a certain amount? Or does ordinary care still mean that a bank should examine each signature?

Under the unrevised Article 3, a number of courts have held that banks do not breach their duty of care by establishing and adhering to a practice that is cost effective and customary within the industry. Other courts, however, have reasoned that banks are supposed to verify all signatures on all checks, and thus banks are not exercising ordinary care when they fail to do so. The revised Article 3 specifically addressed this problem in UCC 3–103(a)(7). That section states that "[i]n the case of a bank that takes an instrument for processing for collection or payment by automated means, reasonable commercial standards do not require the bank to examine the instrument if failure to examine does not violate the bank's prescribed procedures and the bank's procedures do not vary unreasonably from the general banking usage."

AGENTS' SIGNATURES ON CHECKS

Fortunately for those who sign corporate checks, the 1990 revision of Article 3 made an exception to the general rules governing agents' signature liability on instruments. Under the revised article, if a corporate agent signs his or her name on a check that clearly indicates the name of the principal (the corporation), the agent will not be held liable even if the agent does not indicate his or her representative capacity. Before Article 3 was revised in 1990, a corporate agent who signed a corporate check without indicating his or her representative status risked being held personally liable on the check. This was true even if the check was clearly imprinted with the name of the corporation.

A classic case in which this provision of the unrevised Article 3 was applied is *Griffin v. Ellinger*.[3] Griffin, the president of Greenway Building Company, issued three checks to Ellinger, drawn on Greenway's account. Griffin signed his name on the checks without revealing his representative capacity. The name of the company was on the face of each check, and Griffin was authorized to sign checks as president of the company. At the time the checks were issued, neither Ellinger (the payee) nor Griffin discussed who was responsible for paying the checks.

The drawee bank refused to honor the checks because of insufficient funds in the Greenway account, and Ellinger sought recovery from Griffin personally. The Texas Supreme Court held that Griffin was personally liable on the three checks because "the burden is on the signer to relieve himself of personal liability by disclosing his agency," and Griffin had failed to meet that burden. One may surmise that many an agent fell into this trap of personal liability by signing imprinted company checks without indicating the agent's representative capacity.

_____
3. 538 S.W.2d 97 (Tex. 1976).

Why did the drafters of the revised Article 3 change this rule? Clearly, it is no less important today than it has been in the past to know who will be liable on an instrument signed by an agent. The reason for the change is given in Official Comment 3 to UCC 3–402(c): "Virtually all checks used today are in personalized form which identify the entity on whose account the check is drawn. In this case, nobody is deceived into thinking that the person signing the check is meant to be liable. The subsection is meant to overrule cases decided under former Article 3 such as *Griffin v. Ellinger*." The revised Article 3's exception for agents who sign imprinted corporate checks reflects the basic principle mentioned in the introduction to this *Focus:* that the free flow of commerce should be encouraged by practical and reasonable laws governing the use of negotiable instruments.

TECHNOLOGY AND BANKING

Electronic banking practices have posed legal—and ethical—issues, just as electronic transactions have created problems in other areas of the law, such as torts and crimes. We look here at some of these issues.

Electronic Fund Transfers

From the time they were first used, electronic fund transfers (EFTs) have given rise to evidentiary issues. In other words, because an EFT leaves no "paper trail," it is difficult for either the customer or the bank to prove what really happened when a dispute arises. For example, if you obtain cash via an automated teller machine (ATM), the only evidence of the transaction is the ATM receipt that you receive and the bank's computerized record of the transaction. There is nothing on the ATM receipt or in the bank's computer files to indicate that you authorized the transaction. If someone else used your personal identification number (PIN) and withdrew the cash from your account—or if a withdrawal from your account was simply due to a computer error—there would be no paper trail, no signatures, and so on that could be used as proof.

Although the Electronic Fund Transfer Act (EFTA) addressed many issues that involve the customer's liability with respect to EFTs and the bank's duty of care to the customer, not all issues have been resolved—particularly those that involve disagreement between the customer and the bank's computer. If the dispute comes before a court, which party should the court believe?[4]

Electronic Check Presentment

The widespread banking practice of presenting checks electronically during the collection process provides an example of how technology has helped to reduce unethical practices. Electronic check presentment means that customers cannot take advantage of float time—the time between the check's issuance and final payment on the check by the bank. In the past, check drawers would often have a float time of several days (depending on where the payee was located). During this time, they could deposit funds to their accounts if they did not have sufficient funds to cover the checks when they wrote them.

---

4. When a similar issue came before a New York court in 1980, the court opted to believe the customer. The court stated, "It is too commonplace in our society that when faced with the choice of man or machine, we readily accept the 'word' of the machine every time. This, despite the tales of computer malfunctions that we hear daily." See *Judd v. Citibank*, 107 Misc.2d 526, 435 N.Y.S.2d 210 (1980).

With electronic banking, this float time is lost.

The lack of float time, though, also has helped to prevent check fraud, particularly in the form of check kiting. *Check kiting* occurs when a person takes advantage of float time to obtain unauthorized credit from a bank during the time it takes checks to clear. For example, Ron writes a check drawn on Bank A for $2,000, knowing there are insufficient funds in that account to cover the check. He then writes a check drawn on an account with Bank B for $2,000, even though he has insufficient money in that account to cover the check, and deposits the check in his account with Bank A—thus covering that check. Then he writes another check on Bank A to cover the check drawn on Bank B, and so on. In other words, Ron is enjoying $2,000 that, in essence, belongs to the bank. In some check-kiting schemes have involved several bank accounts and substantial sums of money.

Technology and Digital Banking

Another technological development with ethical implications is the use of *e-money,* or digital cash. The increasing use of e-money poses many legal (and ethical) problems. For one thing, the traditional definition of money will certainly no longer hold. E-cash moves along completely outside the network of banks, checks, and paper currency. Thus, e-cash—at least as yet—is not subject to government regulation. Furthermore, e-cash may involve difficulties if it is stored in computer systems. What if the systems crash? Additionally, electronic counterfeiting may be a serious problem. Computer hackers who break into an e-cash system might be able to steal money from thousands or even hundreds of thousands of individuals at once. Finally, e-cash

may allow for more tax evasion and money laundering.

DISCUSSION QUESTIONS

1. Because the UCC offers special protection to HDCs, innocent makers of notes or drawers of checks in fraudulent transactions often have no legal recourse. From an ethical standpoint, how could you justify to the "losers" in such situations the provisions of the UCC that fail to protect them? Can you think of a way in which such problems could be handled more fairly or ethically than they are under the UCC?

2. What do you think would result if a change in the law allowed personal defenses to be successfully raised against HDCs? Who would lose, and who would gain? How would such a change in the law affect the flow of commerce in this country?

3. Under Article 4, banks are allowed to send their customers only a monthly itemized checking-account statement containing the check numbers, amounts, dates, and so on. Banks may include the canceled checks, but if the checks are not sent to the customer, the banks must have them available for a period of seven years should a customer wish to examine them [UCC 4–406(a), (b)]. What implications does this provision have for bank customers in terms of liability for unauthorized signatures and indorsements?

4. Do you think that the UCC's provisions are weighted too heavily in favor of banks? How do the revised Articles 3 and 4 compare with the unrevised articles in this respect?

5. What are some of the implications of the growing use of e-money in the marketplace?

UNIT FIVE

Creditors' Rights and Bankruptcy

CONTENTS

CHAPTER 28

Secured Transactions

Whenever the payment of a debt is guaranteed, or secured, by personal property owned by the debtor or in which the debtor has a legal interest, the transaction becomes known as a **secured transaction.** The concept of the secured transaction is as basic to modern business practice as the concept of credit. Logically, sellers and lenders do not want to risk nonpayment, so they will not sell goods or lend money unless the promise of payment is somehow guaranteed. Indeed, business as we know it could not exist without laws permitting and governing secured transactions.

Article 9 of the Uniform Commercial Code (UCC) governs secured transactions. This chapter first presents the basic concept and terminology of the secured transaction and then discusses how the rights and duties of creditors and debtors are created and enforced. Debtor-creditor transactions that are not covered under Article 9 are discussed in the next chapter. As will become evident, the law of secured transactions tends to favor the rights of creditors.

The National Conference of Commissioners (NCC) on Uniform State Laws promulgated a revised version of Article 9 in 1999. As the revised version is adopted by the states, some of the laws you will read about in the following pages will, of course, be modified. This chapter concludes with a summary of the major changes in the law required under the revised Article 9.

SECTION 1

The Terminology of Secured Transactions

The UCC's terminology is now uniformly adopted in all contracts involving secured transactions. Below is a brief summary of the UCC's definitions of terms relating to secured transactions.

1. A **security interest** is any interest "in personal property or fixtures which secures payment or performance of an obligation" [UCC 1–201(37)].

2. A **secured party** is a lender, a seller, or any person in whose favor there is a security interest, including a person to whom accounts or chattel paper have been sold [UCC 9–105(1)(m)]. (**Chattel paper** is any writing evidencing a debt secured by personal property [UCC 9–105(1)(b)].) The terms *secured party* and *secured creditor* are used interchangeably.

3. A **debtor** is the party who owes payment or performance of the secured obligation, whether or not that party actually owns or has rights in the collateral (defined below). When the debtor and the owner of collateral are not the same person, the term *debtor* may refer to the actual owner of the collateral, the person responsible for the obligation, or both, depending on the context in which the term is used [UCC 9–105(1)(d)].

4. A **security agreement** is an agreement that creates or provides for a security interest between the debtor and a secured party [UCC 9–105(1)(l)].

5. **Collateral** is the property subject to a security interest, including accounts and chattel paper that have been sold [UCC 9–105(1)(c)].

These basic definitions form the concept under which a debtor-creditor relationship becomes a secured transaction relationship (see Exhibit 28–1 on page 506).

SECTION 2

Creating Security Interests

Before a creditor can become a secured party, the creditor must have a security interest in the collateral of the debtor. Three requirements must be met for a creditor to have an enforceable security interest:

1. Either (a) the collateral must be in the possession of the secured party pursuant to an agreement, or (b) there must be a written security agreement describing the collateral and signed by the debtor.

2. The secured party must give value.

3. The debtor must have rights in the collateral.

Once these requirements have been met, the creditor's rights are said to attach to the collateral. **Attachment** gives the creditor an enforceable security interest against the debtor [UCC 9–203].

WRITTEN AGREEMENT

When the collateral is not in the possession of the secured party, a security agreement must be in writing to be enforceable. Exhibit 28–2 on page 507 shows a sample security agreement. To be effective, the security agreement must meet the following requirements [UCC 9–110, 9–203(1)]:

1. The security agreement must be signed by the debtor.
2. The agreement must contain a description of the collateral.
3. The description must reasonably identify the collateral.

At issue in the following case was whether two documents, when read together, created an enforceable security interest. The debtor signed one of the documents, but the description of the collateral was in the other.

CASE 28.1   In re Cantu[a]

United States
Bankruptcy Appellate
Panel,
Eighth Circuit, 1999.
238 Bankr. 796.

BACKGROUND AND FACTS   *Under the Hormel Employees Credit Union's loan program, an employee who fills out and signs a general loan agreement is eligible to draw funds. The draws are called "Sub-accounts." The agreement grants a security interest to the credit union but does not describe the property that is to serve as collateral. Instead, the agreement refers to a second document called a "funds advance voucher." This document includes a detailed description of the collateral. The debtor is not required to sign the funds advance voucher. Jesus Cantu bought a truck with financing provided through this program. Cantu signed a loan agreement, and the credit union issued the funds advance voucher, fully describing the collateral by make, model, year, and vehicle identification number. The voucher also provided that all of its terms were incorporated into the loan agreement. Cantu later filed a petition in a federal bankruptcy court to declare bankruptcy. One of the issues was whether the credit union had an enforceable security interest in the truck. Cantu argued that the credit union did not have such an interest because no single document contained his signature, language granting a security interest, and a description of the collateral. The court issued a summary judgment in favor of the credit union. Cantu appealed to the U.S. Bankruptcy Appellate Panel for the Eighth Circuit.*

---

a. The term *in re* means "in the matter of," "concerning," or "regarding." The term is often found in the title of a judicial proceeding on some matter in which judicial action is to be taken, such as a debtor's estate in bankruptcy, but in which there are no adversarial parties. *In re, Matter of, Estate of,* and combinations of these phrases (such as *In re Estate of*) are all commonly used in the titles of cases involving such actions.

IN THE LANGUAGE
OF THE COURT

SCHMERMER, Bankruptcy Judge.

*   *   *   *

*   *   * In this case, both the language used by the parties and their course of conduct demonstrate that the funds advance voucher and the loan agreement together create the security agreement. The loan agreement grants the Credit Union a security interest in property and expressly states that such property will be described in a separate funds advance voucher. The funds advance voucher, when issued thereafter, contains a full description of the collateral and provides that its terms are made part of the loan agreement. By cross-reference, the description of the collateral in the funds advance voucher is made part and parcel of the loan agreement bearing the debtor's signature. Together, these documents constitute the security agreement and satisfy the signed-writing requirement of Minn.Stat. Section 336.9-203(1)(a) [Minnesota's version of UCC 9–203(1)(a)].

The course of conduct of the parties and the purpose of the open-end loan program, also support the conclusion that the loan agreement and funds advance voucher are to be read together as comprising the security agreement. The loan program is designed to operate in such a way that an employee has to sign only one loan agreement, *   *   * and thereafter, the employee may request advances, whether as secured or unsecured Sub-accounts, in person or by telephone. Unless the documents are taken together, the open-end agreement cannot operate as intended. It is the purpose of the Uniform Commercial Code to promote and facilitate commercial transactions *   *   * . To deny enforcement of the security interest in this case would elevate form over substance and negate the underlying principles of the code.

*   *   *   *

The drafters of the Uniform Commercial Code required a signed-writing describing the collateral pledged before a security interest could attach in order to address the very concerns raised by [Cantu]. A signed-writing prevents disputes over precisely which items of property are covered by a security interest. *   *   * *The principal function of a description of the collateral in a security agreement is to enable the parties themselves* *   *   * *to identify it* *   *   * . [Emphasis added.]

*   *   * [T]he court finds no reason to insist that the description of collateral must appear on the very same document which bears the debtor's signature. Provided a writing or writings *   *   * adequately describes the collateral, carries the signature of the debtor, and establishes that in fact a security interest was agreed upon *   *   * the formal requirements of [UCC 9–203] and the policies behind it are satisfied.

DECISION
AND REMEDY

The U.S. Bankruptcy Appellate Panel for the Eighth Circuit affirmed the lower court's judgment. The general loan agreement and the fund advance vouchers, when read together, satisfied the requirements of UCC 9–203(1) to create an enforceable security interest.

EXHIBIT 28–1   SECURED TRANSACTIONS—CONCEPT AND TERMINOLOGY

In a security agreement, a debtor and creditor agree that the creditor will have a security interest in collateral in which the debtor has rights. In essence, the collateral secures the loan and ensures the creditor of payment should the debtor default.

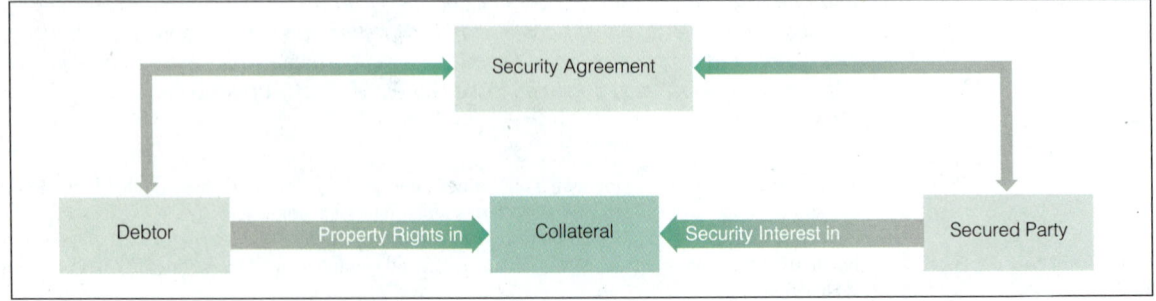

EXHIBIT 28–2   A SAMPLE SECURITY AGREEMENT

_____
Date

_____
Name   No. and Street   City   County   State

(hereinafter called "Debtor") hereby grants to   _____
                                                                      Name

_____
No. and Street   City   County   State

(hereinafter called "Secured Party") a security interest in the following property (hereinafter called the "Collateral"): _____
_____
_____
_____

to secure payment and performance of obligations identified or set out as follows (hereinafter called the "Obligations"): _____
_____
_____
_____

   Default in payment or performance of any of the Obligations or default under any
agreement evidencing any of the Obligations is a default under this agreement. Upon
such default Secured Party may declare all Obligations immediately due and payable
and shall have the remedies of a secured party under the _____ Uniform Commercial Code.
   Signed in (duplicate) triplicate.

_____   _____
Debtor   Secured Party
By_____   By_____

SECURED PARTY MUST GIVE VALUE

The secured party must give value, which, according to UCC 1–201(44), is any consideration that supports a simple contract. In addition, value can be security given for a preexisting (antecedent) obligation or any binding commitment to extend credit. Normally, the value given by a secured party takes the form of a direct loan or involves a commitment to sell goods on credit.

DEBTOR MUST HAVE RIGHTS IN THE COLLATERAL

The debtor must have rights in the collateral; that is, the debtor must have some ownership interest or right

to obtain possession of that collateral. The debtor's rights can represent either a current or a future legal interest in the property. For example, a retail seller-debtor can give a secured party a security interest not only in existing inventory owned by the retailer but also in future inventory to be acquired by the retailer.

SECTION 3

Purchase-Money Security Interest

Often, sellers of consumer durable goods, such as computers and appliances, agree to extend credit for part or all of the purchase price of those goods. Also, lenders not necessarily in the business of selling such goods often agree to lend much of the purchase price for them. There is a special name for the security interest that the seller or the lender obtains when such a transaction occurs. It is called a **purchase-money security interest (PMSI)**. Formally, such an interest exists when one or the other of the following conditions arises:

1. A security interest is retained in, or taken by the seller of, the collateral to secure part or all of its price.
2. A security interest is taken by a person who, by making advances or incurring an obligation, gives something of value that enables the debtor to acquire rights in the collateral or to use it [UCC 9–107].

In either situation, a lender or seller has essentially provided a buyer with the "purchase money" to buy goods. Suppose that Benjamin wants to purchase a new wide-screen television from USA Electronics. The purchase price is $900. Not being able to pay cash, Benjamin signs a purchase agreement to pay $100 down and $50 per month until the balance plus interest is fully paid. USA Electronics is to retain a security interest in the television until full payment has been received. Because the security interest was created as part of the purchase agreement, it is a PMSI.

The same result will occur if Benjamin goes to Statewide Bank and borrows the $900 to buy the television from USA Electronics. Once Benjamin has signed a loan agreement with Statewide Bank, with the to-be-purchased goods as collateral, Statewide Bank has a PMSI the moment the goods are purchased from the appliance store. Obviously, if Benjamin uses the money for other purposes, Statewide Bank will not have a security interest. For this reason, Statewide Bank might arrange to pay the $900 directly to USA Electronics.

Section 4

Perfecting a Security Interest

A creditor has two main concerns if the debtor defaults (fails to pay the debt as promised): (1) satisfaction of the debt through possession of the collateral and (2) priority over any other creditors and purchasers who may have rights in the same collateral. The concept of *attachment*, which establishes the criteria for creating an enforceable security interest, deals with the former concern; the concept of *perfection* deals with the latter.

Even though a security interest has attached, the secured party must nevertheless take steps to protect its claim to the collateral over claims that third parties may have. Third parties may be other secured creditors, nonsecured creditors, trustees in bankruptcy (see Chapter 30), or purchasers of the collateral that is the subject matter of the security agreement. **Perfection** represents the legal process by which secured parties protect themselves against the claims of third parties that may wish to have their debts satisfied out of the same collateral.

Perfection by Filing

The most common method of perfecting a security interest is by the filing of a **financing statement** with the appropriate state or local official. A sample financing statement is shown in Exhibit 28–3. The UCC requires a financing statement to contain the following information [UCC 9–402(1)]:

1. The signature of the debtor.
2. The names and addresses of both the debtor and the creditor.
3. A description of the collateral by type or item.[1]

The Debtor's Name. The UCC requires that a financing statement be filed under the name of the debtor [UCC 9–402(1)]. If the debtor is an individual, the financing statement must be filed in the name of the individual, but if the debtor is a partnership or corporation, the financing statement must be filed under the partnership or corporate name [UCC 9–402(7)]. If a financing statement identifies the debtor by an incorrect name, the statement may be ineffective to perfect a security interest.

What happens to the perfected secured party's interest when the debtor changes its name, as might happen as a result of a business reorganization? In this situation, if the name change causes the financing statement to become *seriously misleading*, "the filing is not effective to perfect a security interest in collateral acquired by the debtor more than four months after the change, unless a new appropriate financing statement is filed before the expiration of that time" [UCC 9–402(7)]. To accomplish the change, the

---

1. Certain types of collateral—crops, timber to be cut, minerals, accounts, or goods that are to become fixtures—require more than mere description; a description of the real estate concerned may also be required [UCC 9–103(5); 9–313; 9–402(1), (5)].

EXHIBIT 28–3   A SAMPLE FINANCING STATEMENT

This FINANCING STATEMENT is presented for filing pursuant to the California Uniform Commercial Code.

1. DEBTOR (LAST NAME FIRST IF AN INDIVIDUAL)	**1A.** SOCIAL SECURITY OR FEDERAL TAX NO.

1B. MAILING ADDRESS	**1C.** CITY, STATE	**1D.** ZIP CODE

2. ADDITIONAL DEBTOR (IF ANY) (LAST NAME FIRST IF AN INDIVIDUAL)	**2A.** SOCIAL SECURITY OR FEDERAL TAX NO.

2B. MAILING ADDRESS	**2C.** CITY, STATE	**2D.** ZIP CODE

3. DEBTOR'S TRADE NAMES OR STYLES (IF ANY)	**3A.** FEDERAL TAX NUMBER

4. SECURED PARTY
  NAME
  MAILING ADDRESS
  CITY   STATE   ZIP CODE
	4A. SOCIAL SECURITY NO., FEDERAL TAX NO.
	OR BANK TRANSIT AND A.B.A. NO.

5. ASSIGNEE OF SECURED PARTY   (IF ANY)
  NAME
  MAILING ADDRESS
  CITY   STATE   ZIP CODE
	5A. SOCIAL SECURITY NO., FEDERAL TAX NO.
	OR BANK TRANSIT AND A.B.A. NO.

6. This FINANCING STATEMENT covers the following types or items of property **(include description of real property on which located and owner of record when required by instruction 4)**.

As security for and in consideration of all present and any future advances or other obligations debtor hereby grants United California Bank a security interest in all of the following types or items of property ("Collateral" herein) in which the debtor now has or hereafter acquires any right, title, or interest, or rights present and future, wheresoever located and whether in the possession of the debtor, a warehouseman, bailee, trustee or any other person, and all increases, therein and replacements, products, and proceeds thereof. Proceeds include but are not limited to inventory, returned merchandise, accounts, chattel paper, general intangibles, insurance proceeds, documents, money, goods, equipment, instruments, and any other tangible or intangible property arising under the sale, lease or other disposition of collateral:

7. CHECK [X] IF APPLICABLE	**7A.** [ ] PRODUCTS OF COLLATERAL ARE ALSO COVERED	**7B.** DEBTOR(S) SIGNATURE NOT REQUIRED IN ACCORDANCE WITH INSTRUCTION 5(c) ITEM: [ ] (1) [ ] (2) [ ] (3) [ ] (4)

8. CHECK [X] IF APPLICABLE   [ ] DEBTOR IS A "TRANSMITTING UTILITY" IN ACCORDANCE WITH UCC/9105 (1) (n)

		C O D E	**10.** THIS SPACE FOR USE OF FILING OFFICER (DATE, TIME, FILE NUMBER AND FILING OFFICER)
9. ▶ SIGNATURE(S) of DEBTOR(S)	DATE:		
TYPE OR PRINT NAME(S) OF DEBTOR(S)		1	
▶		2	
SIGNATURE(S) OF SECURED PARTY(IES)		3	
		4	
TYPE OR PRINT NAME(S) OF SECURED PARTY(IES)		5	
11. *Return copy to:*		6	
NAME		7	
ADDRESS		8	
CITY		9	
STATE		0	
ZIP CODE			

(1) FILING OFFICER COPY	FORM UCC-1 FILING FEE $3.00 *Approved by the Secretary of State*	

MS-336 10-78

secured party merely files a new financing statement, which is signed by the secured party instead of the debtor [UCC 9–402(2)(d)].

Assume that a debtor, Thomas T. Dibello, borrows money from a Pennsylvania bank, which in turn takes a security interest in Dibello's store inventory. The bank properly files a financing statement that lists "Thomas T. Dibello" as the debtor's name. Shortly thereafter, Dibello incorporates his business and changes the name of the business to "Just for Kids, Inc." The bank will continue to be protected as to the existing collateral and as to new collateral acquired by the debtor during the four months following the name change, even if the bank fails to refile. At the end of the four-month period, however, the bank must refile under the new business name of the debtor. Otherwise, its security interest in any collateral acquired after this point will be unperfected.[2]

Description of the Collateral. Both the security agreement and the financing statement must contain a description of the collateral in which the secured party has a security interest. The UCC requires that the security agreement include a description of the collateral, because no security interest in goods can exist unless the parties agree on which goods are subject to the security interest and then describe these goods in writing. The purpose of describing collateral in the financing statement is for the benefit of persons who might later wish to lend to the debtor or purchase the collateral; the description puts these persons on notice that certain goods in the debtor's possession are already subject to a security interest.

Sometimes, the descriptions in the security agreement and the financing statement differ, with the description in the security agreement being more precise and the description in the financing statement more general. For example, a security agreement for a commercial loan to a manufacturer may list all the manufacturer's equipment subject to the loan by serial number, whereas the financing statement may simply state "all equipment owned or hereafter acquired."

To avoid problems arising from such differences, a secured party may repeat exactly the security agreement's description in the financing statement or file the security agreement itself as a financing statement (assuming the security agreement meets the previously discussed criteria). Alternatively, where permitted, the creditor might file a combination security

agreement/financing statement form. If the financing statement is too general or vague, a court may find it insufficient to perfect a security interest.

Where to File. Depending on the classification of collateral, filing is done either centrally with the secretary of state, locally with the county clerk or other official, or both, according to state law. According to UCC 9–401, a state may choose one of three alternatives (see the text of UCC 9–401 in Appendix C for these alternatives).[3] In general, financing statements for consumer goods should be filed with the county clerk.[4] Other kinds of collateral require filing with the secretary of state [UCC 9–401]. An improper filing reduces a secured party's claim in bankruptcy to that of an unsecured creditor.

The classification of collateral is important not only in determining where to file but also in ascertaining whether filing is necessary. Classification is dependent on the use of the collateral to be made by the debtor. Exhibit 28–4 summarizes the various classifications of collateral and the methods of perfecting a security interest in them.

PERFECTION WITHOUT FILING

In two common types of situations, security interests can be perfected without the filing of a financing statement. First, when the collateral is transferred into the possession of the creditor, the creditor's security interest in the collateral is perfected. Second, a PMSI in consumer goods is perfected automatically. These two situations are discussed below. In addition, UCC 9–302(1) mentions other security interests that can be perfected without the filing of a financing statement, including a security interest created by an assignment of a beneficial interest in a trust or a decedent's estate.

Perfection by Possession. Certain items, such as stocks, bonds, and jewelry, are commonly transferred into the creditor's possession when they are used as collateral for loans. This transfer is known as a **pledge.**

---

2. *In re Just for Kids, Inc.*, 150 Bankr. 123 (M.D.Pa. 1992).

3. Approximately half the states have adopted the second alternative. Filing fees range from as low as $3 to as high as $25.

4. In the Food Security Act of 1985 are provisions that protect a purchaser in the ordinary course of business of farm products from a prior perfected security interest, unless the secured party has perfected by filing a special form called an effective financing statement (EFS) centrally or the buyer has received proper notice. Prior to this act, most states required local filing for perfection of security interests in farm-related collateral.

EXHIBIT 28–4   TYPES OF COLLATERAL AND METHODS OF PERFECTION

TYPE OF COLLATERAL	DEFINITION	PERFECTION METHOD	UCC SECTIONS
Tangible	All things that are *movable* at the time the security interest attaches or that are *fixtures* [UCC 9–105(1)(h)]. This includes timber to be cut, growing crops, and unborn animals.		
1. Consumer Goods	Goods used or bought primarily for personal, family, or household purposes—for example, household furniture [UCC 9–109(1)].	For purchase-money security interest, attachment is sufficient; for boats, motor vehicles, and trailers, there is a requirement of filing or compliance with a certificate-of-title statute; for other consumer goods, general rules of filing or possession apply.	9–302(1)(d), (3), (4); 9–305
2. Equipment	Goods bought for or used primarily in business—for example, a delivery truck [UCC 9–109(2)].	Filing or (rarely) possession by secured party.	9–302(1); 9–305
3. Farm Products	Crops, livestock, and supplies used or produced in a farming operation in the possession of a farmer-debtor. This includes products of crops or livestock—for example, milk, eggs, maple syrup, and ginned cotton [UCC 9–109(3)].	Filing or (rarely) possession by secured party.	9–302(1); 9–305
4. Inventory	Goods held for sale or lease and materials used or consumed in the course of business—for example, raw materials or floor stock of a retailer [UCC 9–109(4)].	Filing or (rarely) possession by secured party.	9–302(1); 9–305
5. Fixtures	Goods that become so affixed to realty that an interest in them arises under real estate law—for example, a central air-conditioning unit [UCC 9–313(1)(a)].	Filing only.	9–313(1)
Intangible	Nonphysical property that exists only in connection with something else.		
1. Chattel Paper	Any writing that evidences both a *monetary obligation and a security interest*—for example, a thirty-six-month-payment retail security agreement signed by a buyer to purchase a car [UCC 9–105(1)(b)].	Filing or possession by secured party.	9–304(1), 9–305
2. Documents of Title	Papers that entitle the person in possession to hold, receive, or dispose of the paper or goods the documents cover—for example, bills of lading, warehouse receipts, and dock warrants [UCC 9–105(1)(f), 1–201(15), 7–201].	Filing or possession by secured party.	9–304(1), (3); 9–305
3. Instruments	Any writing that evidences a right to payment of money that is not a security agreement or lease, and	Except for temporary perfected status,	9–304(1), (4), (5); 9–305

EXHIBIT 28–4 TYPES OF COLLATERAL AND METHODS OF PERFECTION (CONTINUED)

TYPE OF COLLATERAL	DEFINITION	PERFECTION METHOD	UCC SECTIONS
3. Instruments (continued)	any negotiable instrument or certificated security that in the ordinary course of business is transferred by delivery with any necessary indorsement or assignment—for example, stock certificates, promissory notes, and certificates of deposit [UCC 9–105(1)(i), 3–104, 8–102(1)(a)].	possession only.	
4. Accounts	Any right to payment for goods sold or leased or for services *rendered* that is not evidenced by an instrument or chattel paper—for example, accounts receivable and contract right payments [UCC 9–106].	Filing required (with exceptions).	9–302(1) (e), (g)
5. General Intangibles	Any personal property other than that defined above—for example, a patent, a copyright, goodwill, or a trademark [UCC 9–106].	Filing only; for copyrights, with the U.S. Copyright Office.	9–302(1)

(When the debt is paid, the collateral is returned to the debtor.) One of the benefits for creditors of having possession of the collateral is that the security agreement is perfected in these circumstances without filing.

For most collateral, however, possession by the secured party is impractical, because it denies the debtor the right to use or derive income from the property to pay off the debt. For example, if a farmer took out a loan to finance the purchase of a piece of heavy farm equipment, using the equipment as collateral, the purpose of the purchase would be defeated if the farmer transferred the collateral into the creditor's possession.

Note that with respect to negotiable instruments, nonnegotiable transferable instruments, and certain securities (such as stocks and bonds), with a few exceptions, the *only* way to perfect a security interest properly is through possession by the secured party [UCC 9–304]. Remember, when the collateral is in the possession of the secured party, a security agreement need not be in writing to create a security interest [UCC 9–203(1)]. Thus, you can create and perfect a security interest at the same time by possession of the collateral.

Purchase-Money Security Interest. In certain circumstances, a security interest in tangible collateral can be perfected automatically at the time of a credit sale—that is, at the time that a PMSI is created under a written security agreement. Note that this automatic-perfection rule with regard to PMSIs applies only when the goods are consumer goods (defined as goods bought or used by the debtor primarily for personal, family, or household purposes). The seller in this situation need do nothing more to perfect his or her interest. There are exceptions to this rule, however, that cover security interests in fixtures and in motor vehicles [UCC 9–302(1)(d)]. In states that have not adopted the 1972 UCC amendments[5] or that have decided to retain certain pre-1972 sections, a PMSI in farm equipment under a specific statutory value is also automatically perfected by attachment.

---

5. Vermont is the only state that has not adopted the 1972 amendments.

CONCEPT SUMMARY 28.1   PERFECTING A SECURITY INTEREST

Perfection by Filing	The most common method of perfection is the filing of a financing statement containing the names and addresses of the secured party and the debtor and describing the collateral by type or item. The financing statement must be signed by the debtor.

CONCEPT SUMMARY 28.1

PERFECTING A SECURITY INTEREST (*continued*)

Perfection by Filing (continued)	1. *Where to file*—State laws determine where the financing statement is to be filed—with the secretary of state, county clerk (or other local official), or both. 2. *Whether to file*—Classification of collateral determines whether filing is necessary (see Exhibit 28–4).
Perfection without Filing	1. *By transfer of collateral*—The debtor can transfer possession of the collateral itself to the secured party. This type of transfer is called a *pledge*. 2. *By attachment of a purchase-money security interest in consumer goods*—If the secured party has a purchase-money security interest in consumer goods (goods bought or used by the debtor for personal, family, or household purposes), the secured party's security interest is perfected automatically. Exceptions: security interests in fixtures or motor vehicles.

PERFECTION OF SECURITY INTERESTS IN MOTOR VEHICLES

Most states require a certificate of title for any motor vehicle, boat, or motor home. The normal methods described above for perfection of a security interest typically do not apply to such vehicles. Rather, perfection of a security interest only occurs when a notation of such an interest appears on the certificate of title that covers the vehicle.

As an example, suppose that your commercial bank lends you 80 percent of the money necessary to purchase a new car. You live in a state that requires certificates of title for all automobiles. If your bank fails to have its security interest noted on the certificate of title, its interest is not perfected. That means that a good faith purchaser of your car would take it free of the bank's interest. In most states, purchasers of motor vehicles can either buy or extend credit on those vehicles with the confidence that no security interest exists that is not disclosed on the certificate of title.[6]

COLLATERAL MOVED TO ANOTHER JURISDICTION

Obviously, collateral may be moved by the debtor from one jurisdiction (state) to another. In general, a properly perfected security interest in collateral moved into a new jurisdiction continues to be perfected in the new jurisdiction for a period of four months from the date on which the collateral was moved into the new jurisdiction or for the period of time remaining under the perfection in the original jurisdiction, whichever expires first [UCC 9–103(1)(d), (3)(e)]. Collateral moved from county to county within a state (if local filing is required), rather than from one state to another, however, may or may not be subject to a four-month limitation [UCC 9–403(3)].

To illustrate, suppose that on January 1, Smith secures a loan from a Nebraska bank by putting up all his wheat-threshing equipment as security. The Nebraska bank files the security interest centrally with the secretary of state. In June, Smith has an opportunity to harvest wheat crops in South Dakota and moves his equipment into that state on June 15. The law just mentioned means that the Nebraska bank's perfection remains effective in South Dakota for a period of four months from June 15. If the Nebraska bank wishes to retain its perfection priority, it must perfect properly in South Dakota, the jurisdiction in which the machine is located, during this four-month period. Should the bank fail to do so, its priority perfection in South Dakota would be lost after four months, and subsequent perfected security interests in the same collateral in South Dakota would prevail.

Among mobile goods, automobiles pose one of the biggest problems. If the original jurisdiction does not require a certificate of title as part of its perfection process for an automobile, perfection automatically ends four months after the automobile is moved into another jurisdiction. When a security interest exists

---

6. In the few states that do not require title registration of motor vehicles, one must examine the appropriate statutes to determine the priority of conflicting security interests.

on an automobile in a state in which title registration is required, and when the security interest is noted on the certificate of title, the perfection of the security interest continues after the automobile is moved to another state requiring a certificate of title until the automobile is registered in the new state [UCC 9–103(2)]. Because each title state requires that the holder surrender the old certificate of title to obtain a new one, and because the secured party typically holds the certificate, the secured party usually is able to ensure that the security interest is noted on the new certificate of title.

EFFECTIVE TIME OF PERFECTION

A financing statement is effective for five years from the date of filing [UCC 9–403(2)]. If a **continuation statement** is filed *within six months* prior to the expiration date, the effectiveness of the original statement is continued for another five years, starting with the expiration date of the first five-year period [UCC 9–403(3)]. The effectiveness of the statement can be continued in the same manner indefinitely.

SECTION 5

The Scope of a Security Interest

A security agreement can cover various types of property in addition to collateral already in the debtor's possession, including the proceeds of the sale of collateral, after-acquired property, and future advances.

PROCEEDS

Proceeds include whatever is received when collateral is sold, exchanged, collected, or disposed of. A secured party has an interest in the proceeds of the sale of collateral. For example, suppose a bank has a perfected security interest in the inventory of a retail seller of heavy farm machinery. The retailer sells a tractor out of this inventory to a farmer, a buyer in the ordinary course of business. The farmer agrees, in a retail security agreement, to pay monthly payments for a period of twenty-four months. If the retailer should go into default on the loan from the bank, the bank is entitled to the remaining payments the farmer owes to the retailer as proceeds.

A security interest in proceeds perfects automatically on perfection of the secured party's security interest and remains perfected for ten days after receipt of the proceeds by the debtor. One way to extend the ten-day automatic period is to provide for such extended coverage in the original security agreement. This is typically done when the collateral is the type that is likely to be sold, such as a retailer's inventory.

The UCC provides that in the following circumstances the security interest in proceeds remains perfected for longer than ten days after the receipt of the proceeds by the debtor:

1. When a filed financing statement covers the original collateral and the proceeds are collateral in which a security interest may be perfected by a filing in the office or offices with which the financing statement has been filed. Furthermore, a secured creditor's interest automatically perfects in property that the debtor acquires with cash proceeds, if the original filing would have been effective as to that property and the financing statement indicates that type of property [UCC 9–306(3)(a)]. Thus, in the farm-equipment example given earlier, if the retailer used the farmer's monthly payments to acquire additional inventory, the bank would be entitled to that inventory, providing that the bank's original filing was effective as to that property and the financing statement indicated that type of property.
2. Whenever there is a filed financing statement that covers the original collateral and the proceeds are identifiable cash proceeds [UCC 9–306(3)(b)].
3. Whenever the security interest in the proceeds is perfected before the expiration of the ten-day period [UCC 9–306(3)(c)].

AFTER-ACQUIRED PROPERTY

After-acquired property is collateral that is acquired by the debtor after the execution of the security agreement. The after-acquired property may consist of inventory, equipment, farm animals, or virtually any other kind of property, including consumer goods acquired within ten days "after the secured party gives value" [UCC 9–204(2)]. The security agreement itself may include a clause to provide for coverage of after-acquired property [UCC 9–204(1)]. This is particularly useful for firms that want to obtain financing for the purchase of inventory (products to be sold in the ordinary course of the firm's business). A secured party whose security interest is in existing inventory knows that the debtor will replace that inventory, thereby reducing the collateral subject to the security interest.

Generally, when the debtor purchases new inventory to replace the inventory that is sold, the secured party wants this newly acquired inventory to be subject to the original security interest. Thus, the after-acquired property clause continues the secured party's claim to any inventory acquired thereafter. This is not to say that such an original security interest will be superior to the rights of all other creditors with regard to this after-acquired inventory, as will be discussed later.

Consider a typical example. Liberta buys factory equipment from Stedler on credit, giving as security an interest in all of her equipment—both what she is buying and what she already owns. The security interest with Stedler contains an after-acquired property clause. Six months later, Liberta pays cash to another seller for additional equipment. Six months after that, Liberta goes out of business before she has paid off her debt to Stedler. Stedler has a security interest in all of Liberta's equipment, even the equipment bought from the other seller.

FUTURE ADVANCES

Often, a debtor will arrange with a bank to have a continuing *line of credit* under which the debtor can borrow funds intermittently. Advances against lines of credit can be subject to a properly perfected security interest in certain collateral. The security agreement may provide that any future advances made against that line of credit are also subject to the security interest in the same collateral.

For example, Holtzman is the owner of a small manufacturing plant with equipment valued at $1 million. He has an immediate need for $50,000 of working capital, so he secures a loan from Northeastern Bank and signs a security agreement, putting up all his equipment as security. The security agreement provides that Holtzman can borrow up to $500,000 in the future, using the same equipment as collateral for any future advances. In such cases, it is not necessary to execute a new security agreement and perfect a security interest in the collateral each time an advance is made to the debtor [UCC 9–204(3)].

THE FLOATING-LIEN CONCEPT

A security agreement may provide for the creation of a security interest in proceeds of the sale of the collateral that was the subject matter of the secured transaction—after-acquired property, future advances, or both. Such an agreement is referred to as a **floating lien.** Floating liens commonly arise in the financing of inventories. A creditor is not interested in specific pieces of inventory, because they are constantly changing, so the lien "floats" from one item to another as the inventory changes.

For example, suppose that Ski Paradise, Inc., a cross-country ski dealer, has a line of credit with New England Community Bank to finance an inventory of cross-country skis. Ski Paradise and New England Community enter into a security agreement that provides for coverage of proceeds, after-acquired inventory, present inventory, and future advances. This security interest in inventory is perfected by a central filing (with the secretary of state). One day, Ski Paradise sells a new pair of the latest cross-country skate skis, for which it receives a used pair in trade. That same day, it purchases two new pairs of skate skis from a local manufacturer with an additional amount of money obtained from New England Community. New England Community gets a perfected security interest in the used pair of skate skis under the proceeds clause, has a perfected security interest in the two new pairs of skate skis purchased from the local manufacturer under the after-acquired property clause, and has a security interest in all of these skis and those in present inventory that were purchased with money advanced to Ski Paradise and secured by the future-advance clause.

All of this is accomplished under the original perfected security agreement. The various items in the inventory have changed, but New England Community still has a perfected security interest in Ski Paradise's inventory, and hence it has a floating lien on the inventory. Exhibit 28–5 on page 516 illustrates graphically the concept of a floating lien.

The concept of the floating lien can also apply to a shifting stock of goods. Under Section 9–205, the lien can start with raw materials and follow them as they become finished goods and inventories and as they are sold, turning into accounts receivable, chattel paper, or cash.

SECTION 6

Resolving Priority Disputes

What happens when several creditors claim a security interest in the same collateral of a debtor? This important issue is addressed by the UCC with a set of rules for determining which of the conflicting security interests has priority—or the best claim to the collateral—when the debtor goes into default. The question

EXHIBIT 28–5   THE FLOATING-LIEN CONCEPT

In this exhibit, a cross-country ski dealer has a line of credit with a bank to finance an inventory of skis. Their security agreement includes clauses that cover proceeds, present inventory, after-acquired inventory, and future advances. Under this agreement, the bank has a security interest in the dealer's present and future inventory of new skis, as well as in whatever cash and trade-ins the dealer receives in doing business.

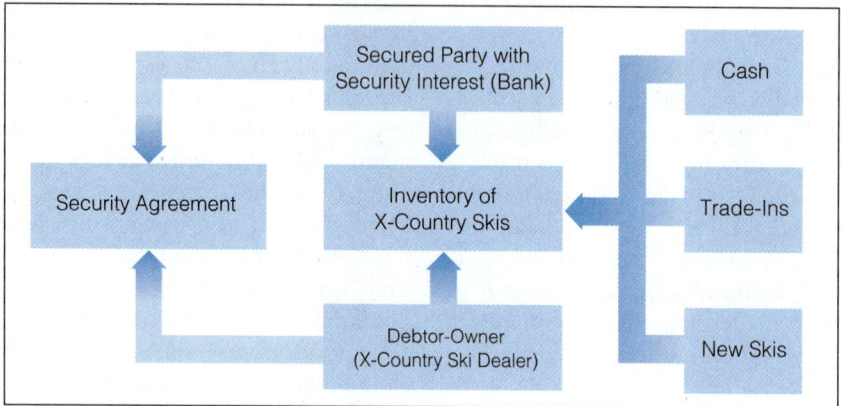

of priority is particularly important when the debtor is in bankruptcy. In this situation, only the perfected secured party will recover, and other creditors may end up with little or nothing.

SECURED VERSUS UNSECURED PARTIES

In general, secured creditors prevail over unsecured creditors and over creditors who have obtained judgments against the debtor but who have not begun the legal process to collect on those judgments [UCC 9–301]. In other words, once a security interest attaches, it has priority over the claims of other creditors who do not have a security interest. This priority does not depend on whether the security interest has been perfected.

SECURED PARTY VERSUS LIEN CREDITOR

A **lien creditor** is one who has a lien on the property because of a judgment.[7] Any security interest that is *perfected* has priority over the claims of lien creditors who acquired their liens after perfection. In contrast, a lien creditor has priority over a party with a security interest that has not yet been perfected. An exception

to this rule, however, provides as follows: if a secured party files with respect to a PMSI during a ten-day period after the debtor receives possession of the collateral, the secured party's claim has priority over the lien creditor's rights that arise between the time the security interest attaches and the time of filing [UCC 9–301(2)]. In many states, this so-called grace period has been extended to twenty days.

WHEN MORE THAN ONE PARTY IS SECURED

When more than one party has a secured interest in the collateral of a defaulting debtor, the issues of perfection and timing become critical, as does the type of collateral involved. There are several general rules and, of course, exceptions to those rules.

The General Rule. Among secured parties, the general rule of priority is as follows: the first security interest to be filed or perfected has priority over other filed or perfected security interests. If, however, none of the conflicting security interests has been perfected, the first security interest to attach has priority [UCC 9–312(5)].

For example, suppose that West Bank filed a financing statement covering Alger's inventory on March 1, and Friendly Savings and Loan filed a financing statement covering the same inventory on

---

7. This definition also includes a receiver in equity, a trustee in bankruptcy, and an assignee for the benefit of creditors.

April 1. West Bank's interest would have priority over Friendly's interest. It would not matter which lender made its loan and attached its security interest first. If West Bank failed to perfect its security interest, however, and Friendly perfected its interest, then Friendly's interest would have priority as the *only* perfected security interest. If both failed to perfect their interests, then the first to attach would have priority. Thus, if West Bank had a security agreement covering Alger's inventory on March 1 and advanced money to Alger on the same day, and Friendly's agreement and advance were made on April 1, West Bank would have priority over Friendly.

An Exception: The PMSI. The general rule, as previously stated, is that the first in time to file or perfect is first in priority rights to the collateral. This rule is always applicable when the first in time to perfect is a purchase-money security interest (PMSI). The UCC provides, however, that under certain conditions a PMSI, properly perfected, will prevail over a non-PMSI in after-acquired collateral, even though the non-PMSI was the first in time to perfect.

If the collateral is *inventory*, a perfected PMSI will prevail over a previously perfected non-PMSI provided that the holder of the PMSI perfects *and* the holder of the non-PMSI security interest receives written notice of his or her interest *before* the debtor takes possession of the newly acquired inventory [UCC 9–312(3)]. If the collateral is other than inventory, a PMSI will have priority over a previously perfected non-PMSI provided that the PMSI is perfected either before or within ten days (in many states, twenty days) *after* the debtor takes possession. No notice is required [UCC 9–312(4)].

To illustrate: Retailer Elena needs a loan of money to be used as working capital. On May 1, she obtains a one-year installment loan from West Bank, signing a security agreement and putting up her present inventory plus any after-acquired inventory as collateral. That same date, West Bank perfects its non-PMSI by filing a financing statement centrally. On August 1, Elena learns that she can purchase directly from Martin, a manufacturer, $10,000 worth of new inventory, which is a bargain. Because she cannot pay this amount in cash, she signs a security agreement with Martin, giving Martin a security interest in the newly purchased inventory. The new inventory is delivered on September 1, as ordered. On September 7, a fire destroys most of Elena's store and warehouse. Only a part of the new inventory remains, and its value is insufficient to cover both debts. Who has priority with regard to the remaining inventory, West Bank or Martin? If Martin perfected by filing *and* gave West Bank written notice of its security interest prior to September 1, the date Elena received possession, Martin prevails. If Martin did not meet these conditions, West Bank prevails.

Suppose that the collateral is equipment, rather than inventory, and Martin perfected on September 8, after the fire. Because Martin properly perfected its PMSI within ten days after Elena received delivery, Martin prevails over West Bank for the remaining after-acquired equipment.

SECURED PARTY VERSUS BUYER

In general, a security interest in collateral continues even after the collateral has been sold unless the secured party has authorized the sale [UCC 9–306(2)]. There are exceptions, however, and they allow the buyers of collateral sold without the secured party's authorization to take that collateral free of the security interest, even in situations when the security interest has been perfected. We examine those situations next.

Buyers in the Ordinary Course of Business. To require buyers to find out if there is an outstanding security interest in, for example, a merchant's inventory would impose a time-consuming restriction and would certainly inhibit commerce. Therefore, the UCC provides that a person who buys goods "in the ordinary course of business" will take the goods free from any security interest attached to those goods, even if the security interest is perfected and even if the buyer knows of its existence [UCC 9–307(1)]. A *buyer in the ordinary course of business* is defined as any person who, in good faith and without knowledge that the sale is *in violation* of the ownership rights or security interest of a third party in the goods, buys in ordinary course from a person in the business of selling goods of that kind [UCC 1–201(9)].[8]

Suppose retail seller Chad secures a loan from West Bank and puts up his existing appliance inventory and any appliance inventory thereafter acquired as collateral. Chad signs a security agreement and a

---

8. Note that a buyer may know of the *existence* of a security interest and still retain the status of a buyer in ordinary course. That status will be lost only if the buyer knows that his or her purchase of goods will *violate* a third party's security interest or other ownership rights.

financing statement, which West Bank properly perfects. Later Chad sells an appliance from inventory covered by the security agreement to Lee, and Lee pays cash. If Chad goes into default on the loan, West Bank's prior perfected security interest has no effect on Lee. Lee took the appliance completely free of West Bank's security interest, even though perfected, and West Bank loses this item of collateral for satisfaction of the debt. (Of course, West Bank has rights in any identifiable cash proceeds.)

Buyers of Farm Products.   Under the UCC, a buyer of farm products takes the products subject to a security interest, even if the buyer knows nothing about the existence of a security agreement [UCC 9–307(1)]. Under the Food Security Act of 1985,[9] this rule was modified, and buyers in the ordinary course of business include buyers of farm products from farmers. Under the Food Security Act, a secured party is not protected against a buyer of farm products from a farmer unless one of the following events occurs:

1. The buyer has received notice of the security interest within one year before the purchase.
2. The buyer fails to register with the secretary of state before the purchase, and the secured party has properly perfected his or her interest centrally.
3. The buyer has received notice from the secretary of state that the farm products being sold are subject to an *effective financing statement (EFS)*. An EFS is a form that a secured party must file in addition to an Article 9 financing statement to protect his or her interest in a farmer's products in those states with EFS filing systems.

Buyers of Consumer Goods from Consumers.
Carla, a consumer, purchases a refrigerator from an appliance store on credit, because she cannot pay the full purchase price. A written security agreement exists in which the seller takes a PMSI in the consumer goods. Further, the seller need not file a financing statement, because, when a PMSI is taken in consumer goods, *perfection occurs automatically* [UCC 9–302(1)(d)]. Later, Carla sells the refrigerator to her next-door neighbor, Nan, who purchases it—as a purchaser not in the ordinary course of business—for home use without any knowledge of the credit arrangements between Carla and the original seller. Subsequently, Carla defaults on the credit payments to the seller. What are the seller's rights? The seller

had a perfected PMSI in the refrigerator when it was held by Carla. Under UCC 9–307(2), however, the perfection is not good against the next-door neighbor.

UCC 9–307(2) requires that a person in the position of this next-door neighbor must purchase (give value for) the goods for personal, family, or household use, and without knowledge of the original seller's security interest, and that the purchase must take place *before* the secured party has filed a financing statement. In this case, recall that the seller took a PMSI, which is perfected automatically. No filing was required. Hence, the next-door neighbor purchased the refrigerator free and clear before the seller had filed a financing statement. The seller could have avoided this possibility simply by *filing* a financing statement, even though a PMSI had been perfected.

Buyers of Chattel Paper and Instruments.   Another purchaser who may not be subject to a secured party's interest despite perfection is the purchaser of chattel paper and instruments. This protection is provided by UCC 9–308. As previously defined, *chattel paper* is a writing, such as a security agreement, that evidences both a monetary obligation and a security interest in specific goods. *Instrument* means a negotiable instrument as defined in UCC 3–104, or a certificated security as defined in UCC 8–102, or basically any other writing that evidences a right to the payment of money and is not itself a security agreement or lease transferred in the ordinary course of business by delivery with any necessary indorsement or assignment [UCC 9–105(1)(i)]. Security interests in instruments can be perfected only by possession.

Chattel paper is a very important class of collateral used in financing arrangements, especially in automobile financing. When chattel paper is sold by a creditor, the creditor can deliver it over to the assignee, who is then responsible for collecting the debt directly from the debtor. This arrangement is known as *notification* or *direct collection*. As an alternative, a creditor can sell chattel paper to an assignee with the understanding that the creditor will retain the chattel paper, make collections from the debtor, and then remit the money to the assignee. This kind of transaction is *nonnotification* or *indirect collection*. The widespread use of both methods of dealing with chattel paper is recognized by the UCC, and hence the UCC permits perfection of a chattel paper security interest either by filing or by taking possession of the chattel paper.

Problems arise when perfection of chattel paper is made by filing only. If the chattel paper is thereafter sold to another purchaser who gives new value and takes possession of the paper in the ordinary course of the purchaser's business, without knowledge that it is subject to a security interest, the new purchaser will have priority over the secured creditor. (Of course, the creditor has rights in the proceeds.)

CONCEPT SUMMARY 28.2

PRIORITY OF CLAIMS TO A DEBTOR'S COLLATERAL

PARTIES	PRIORITY
Unperfected Secured Party	Prevails over unsecured creditors and creditors who have obtained judgments against the debtor but who have not begun the legal process to collect on those judgments [UCC 9–301].
Perfected Secured Parties to Same Collateral	The first to file or perfect is first in right to the collateral [UCC 9–312(5)]. An exception is a purchase-money security interest (PMSI). Even if second in time of perfection, it has priority over a non-PMSI providing: 1. In the case of inventory, that the PMSI is perfected and written notice is given to the holder of the other perfected security interest *on* or *before* the time that the debtor takes possession [UCC 9–312(3)]. 2. In the case of other collateral, that the PMSI has been perfected within ten days after the debtor receives possession [UCC 9–312(4)].
Purchaser of Debtor's Collateral	1. Goods purchased in the ordinary course of the seller's business—purchaser prevails over a perfected secured party even if the purchaser knows of the security interest [UCC 9–307(1)]. 2. Farm products purchased in the ordinary course of business—purchaser prevails unless the purchaser: a. Received notice of the security interest within one year before the purchase. b. Fails to register with the secretary of state before the purchase, and the secured party has properly perfected his or her interest centrally. c. Received notice from the secretary of state that the farm products being sold are subject to an effective financing statement (EFS). 3. Consumer goods purchased out of the ordinary course of business—purchaser prevails over a perfected secured party, providing the purchaser purchased: a. For value. b. Without actual knowledge of the security interest. c. For use as a consumer good. d. Prior to secured party's perfection by *filing* [UCC 9–307(2)]. 4. The chattel paper purchaser prevails over a perfected secured party, providing the purchaser: a. Gave new value. b. Took possession. c. Took in the ordinary course of the purchaser's business. d. Took without *actual* knowledge of the secured party's perfection [UCC 9–308]. 5. The purchaser of negotiable instruments, documents, and securities prevails over a perfected secured party, particularly if the purchaser is the holder in due course, a holder to whom the document has been duly negotiated, or a bona fide purchaser of a security [UCC 9–308, 9–309].

SECTION 7

Other Rights and Duties under Article 9

The security agreement itself determines most of the rights and duties of the debtor and creditor. Article 9 of the UCC, however, imposes some rights and duties that are applicable in the absence of a security agreement to the contrary.

INFORMATION REQUEST BY CREDITORS

Under UCC 9–407(1), a creditor has the option, when making the filing, of asking the filing officer to make a note of the file number, the date, and the hour of the original filing on a copy of the financing statement. The filing officer must send this copy to the person making the request. Under UCC 9–407(2), a filing officer must also give information to a person who is contemplating obtaining a security interest from a prospective debtor. The filing officer must give a certificate that provides information on possible perfected financing statements with respect to the named debtor. The filing officer will charge a fee for the certification and for any information copies provided.

ASSIGNMENT, AMENDMENT, AND RELEASE

A secured party can assign part or all of the security interest to another, called the assignee. That assignee becomes the secured party of record if, for example, he or she either makes a notation of the assignment somewhere on the financing statement or files a written statement of assignment, called a UCC-3 [UCC 9–405(1), (2)]. Whenever desired, a secured party of record also can release part or all of the collateral described in a filed financing statement. This ends his or her security interest in the collateral [UCC 9–406].

It is also possible to amend a financing statement that has already been filed. Note, however, that *the amendment must be signed by both parties*. The debtor signs the security agreement, the original financing statement, and the amendments [UCC 9–402]. All other secured transaction documents (such as releases, assignments, continuations of perfection, perfections of collateral moved into another jurisdiction, and termination statements—all of which are discussed in this chapter) need only be signed by the secured party.

REASONABLE CARE OF COLLATERAL

If a secured party is in possession of the collateral, he or she is a bailee (discussed in Chapter 46) and must use reasonable care in preserving it. Otherwise, the secured party is liable to the debtor [UCC 9–207(1), (3)]. If the collateral increases in value, the secured party can hold this increased value or profit as additional security unless it is in the form of money, which must be remitted to the debtor or applied toward reducing the secured debt [UCC 9–207(2)(c)]. Additionally, the collateral must be kept in identifiable condition unless it consists of fungible goods (goods that are naturally alike, such as wheat or oil) [UCC 9–207(2)(d)]. Finally, the debtor must pay for all reasonable charges incurred by the secured party in preserving, operating, and taking reasonable care of the collateral in possession [UCC 9–207(2)(a)].

THE STATUS OF THE DEBT

During the time that the secured debt is outstanding, the debtor may wish to know the status of the debt. If so, the debtor need only sign a statement that indicates the aggregate amount of the unpaid debt at a specific date (and perhaps a list of the collateral covered by the security agreement). The secured party must then approve or correct this statement in writing. The creditor must comply with the request within two weeks of receipt; otherwise, the creditor is liable for any loss caused to the debtor by the failure to do so [UCC 9–208(2)]. One such request is allowed without charge every six months. For each additional request, the secured party can require a fee not exceeding $10 per request [UCC 9–208(3)].

TERMINATION STATEMENT

When a secured debt is paid, the secured party may send a termination statement to the debtor or file such a statement with the filing officer to whom the original financing statement was given. If the financing statement covers consumer goods, the termination statement *must* be filed by the secured party within one month after the debt is paid, or—if the debtor requests the termination statement in writing—it must be filed within ten days of receipt of the request after the debt is paid, whichever is earlier [UCC 9–404(1)]. In all other cases, the termination statement must be filed or furnished to the debtor within ten days after a written request is made by the debtor.

If the affected secured party fails to file such a termination statement, as required by UCC 9–404(1), or fails to send the termination statement within ten days after proper demand, the secured party will be liable to the debtor for $100. Additionally, the secured party will be liable for any loss caused to the debtor.

SECTION 8

Default

Article 9 of the UCC defines the rights, duties, and remedies of a secured party and of the debtor on the debtor's default. Should the secured party fail to comply with his or her duties, the debtor is afforded particular rights and remedies.

The topic of default is one of great concern to secured lenders and to the lawyers who draft security agreements. What constitutes default is not always clear. In fact, Article 9 does not define the term. Consequently, parties are encouraged in practice and by the UCC to include in their security agreements certain standards to be applied should default occur. In so doing, parties can stipulate the conditions that will constitute a default [UCC 9–501(3)]. Typically, because of the disparity in bargaining position between a debtor and a creditor, these critical terms are shaped by the creditor in an attempt to provide the maximum protection possible. The ultimate terms, however, are not allowed to go beyond the limitations imposed by the good faith requirement of UCC 1–203 and the unconscionability doctrine.

Although any breach of the terms of the security agreement can constitute default, default occurs most commonly when the debtor fails to meet the scheduled payments that the parties have agreed on or when the debtor becomes bankrupt. If the security agreement covers equipment, however, the debtor may have warranted that he or she is the owner of the equipment or that no liens or other security interests are pending on that equipment. Breach of any of these representations can result in default.

BASIC REMEDIES

A secured party's remedies can be divided into two basic categories:

1. A secured party can relinquish a security interest and proceed to judgment on the underlying debt, followed by execution and levy. **Execution** is an action to carry into effect the directions in a court decree or judgment. **Levy** is the obtaining of money by legal process through the seizure and sale of nonexempt property, usually done after an execution has been issued. Execution and levy are rarely done unless the value of the secured collateral has been reduced greatly below the amount of the debt and the debtor has other nonexempt assets available to satisfy the debt.

2. A secured party can take possession of the collateral covered by the security agreement [UCC 9–503]. On taking possession, the secured party can retain the collateral for satisfaction of the debt [UCC 9–505(2)] or can sell the collateral and apply the proceeds toward the debt [UCC 9–504].

The rights and remedies under UCC 9–501(1) are *cumulative*. Therefore, if a creditor is unsuccessful in enforcing rights by one method, another method can be pursued. The UCC does not require election of remedies—that is, the creditor need not choose between an action on the obligation and the repossession of the collateral.

When the Collateral Consists of Both Real and Personal Property. When a security agreement covers both real and personal property, the secured party can proceed against the personal property in accordance with the remedies of Article 9. Alternatively, the secured party can proceed against the entire collateral under procedures set down by local real estate law, in which case the UCC does not apply [UCC 9–501(4)].

For example, this situation occurs when the security interest on a corporate loan applies to the manufacturing plant (real property) and also to the inventory (personal property). Determining whether particular collateral is personal or real property can prove difficult, especially in dealing with *fixtures*— things affixed to real property (see Chapter 46). Under certain circumstances, the UCC allows the removal of fixtures on default; such removal, however, is subject to the provisions of Article 9 [UCC 9–313].

The Soldiers' and Sailors' Relief Act of 1940. The Soldiers' and Sailors' Relief Act of 1940 created an important exception to creditors' rights under Article 9. The act states that if the security interest is created *prior* to the time a person in the military is placed on active duty, the secured party cannot repossess and dispose of the collateral while the person is on active duty and for up to six months after the active duty ends. Furthermore, creditors may not charge more than 6 percent interest on the debt during this period of time unless a higher rate would not impose an undue hardship on the debtor. The provisions of this act do not apply to military personnel whose debts were incurred *while* they were on active duty.

SECURED PARTY'S RIGHT TO TAKE POSSESSION

UCC 9–503 states that "[u]nless otherwise agreed, a secured party has on default the right to take possession of the collateral. In taking possession, a secured party may proceed without judicial process if this can be done without a breach of the peace." The underlying rationale for this "self-help" provision of Article 9 is that it simplifies the process of repossession for creditors and reduces the burden on the courts. Because the UCC does not define *breach of the peace*, how-

ever, it is not always easy to predict what will or will not constitute a breach of the peace.

Generally, the creditor or the creditor's agent cannot enter a debtor's home, garage, or place of business without permission. Consider a situation in which an automobile is collateral. If the repossessing party walks onto the debtor's premises, proceeds up the driveway, enters the vehicle without entering the garage, and drives off, it probably will not amount to a breach of the peace. Normally, if the secured party can take the collateral without committing trespass, breaking or entering, or using force (assault and/or battery), the repossession will be deemed to have been accomplished without a breach of the peace. Whether a creditor's trespass onto a debtor's property was enough to breach the peace is at issue in the following case.

CASE 28.2   Chrysler Credit Corp. v. Koontz

Appellate Court
of Illinois,
Fifth District, 1996.
277 Ill.App.3d 1078,
661 N.E.2d 1171,
214 Ill.Dec. 726.

BACKGROUND AND FACTS   *James Koontz bought a car and financed the purchase with a loan from Chrysler Credit Corporation. When Koontz failed to repay the loan, Chrysler sent M&M Agency to take possession of the vehicle. M&M entered Koontz's yard, where the vehicle was parked in the light of the front porch, to repossess the vehicle. While the repossession was in progress, Koontz, who was in his underwear, rushed outside and shouted, "Don't take it!" The repossessor did not respond and proceeded to take the vehicle. Chrysler sold the car and then filed a suit in an Illinois state court against Koontz to recover the difference between the purchase price and the amount that Koontz owed on the loan. Koontz argued that Chrysler's repossession of the car over his oral protest was a breach of the peace. The court entered a judgment in favor of Chrysler, and Koontz appealed.*

IN THE LANGUAGE OF THE COURT

Justice MAAG delivered the opinion of the court:

*   *   *   *

*   *   * [I]n general, a mere trespass, standing alone, does not automatically constitute a breach of the peace. It is generally held that simply going upon the private driveway of the debtor and taking possession of secured collateral, without more, does not constitute a breach of the peace. The possible factual situations are endless, thus leading to the need for a case-by-case analysis.

In making this analysis, certain principles are clear and must be considered. When the collateral is located inside a fence or is otherwise enclosed, the secured creditor's privilege is considerably abridged. *The creditor's privilege is most severely restricted when repossession can only be accomplished by the actual breaking or destruction of barriers designed to exclude trespassers.* *   *   * [T]he likelihood of a breach of the peace increases in proportion to the efforts of the debtor to prevent unauthorized intrusions and the creditor's conduct in defiance of those efforts. [Emphasis added.]

In this case, Koontz testified that he notified Chrysler prior to the repossession that it was not permitted to enter onto his property. He also testified that he pulled his vehicle into his front yard so that he could see it by the light of the front porch. This testimony was uncontroverted. There was no testimony, however, that Chrysler entered through any barricade or did anything other than simply enter onto the property and drive the car away. Viewing this evidence in the light most favorable to the prevailing party, we believe that Chrysler's entry upon the private real property of Koontz and taking possession of the secured collateral, without more, did not constitute a breach of the peace. Chrysler enjoyed a limited privilege to enter Koontz's property for the sole and exclusive purpose of effecting the repossession. So long as the entry was limited in purpose (repossession), and so long as no gates, barricades, doors, enclosures, buildings, or chains were breached or cut, no breach of the peace occurred by virtue of the entry onto his property.

DECISION AND REMEDY *The Appellate Court of Illinois affirmed the lower court's judgment. The creditor's repossession of the collateral over the debtor's oral protest was not a breach of the peace.*

DISPOSITION OF COLLATERAL

Once default has occurred and the secured party has obtained possession of the collateral, the secured party may sell, lease, or otherwise dispose of the collateral in any commercially reasonable manner [UCC 9–504(1)]. Any sale is always subject to procedures established by state law.

Retention of Collateral by Secured Party. The UCC recognizes that parties are sometimes better off if they do not sell the collateral. Therefore, a secured party can retain collateral in satisfaction of the debt, but this general right is subject to several conditions. The secured party must send written notice of the intention to retain the collateral to the debtor if the debtor has not signed a statement renouncing or modifying his or her rights after default. In the case of consumer goods, no other notice need be given. In all other cases, notice must be sent to any other secured party from whom the secured party in possession of the collateral has received written notice of a claim of interest in the collateral in question.

If within twenty-one days after the notice is sent, the secured party receives an objection in writing from a person entitled to receive notification, then the secured party must sell or otherwise dispose of the collateral in accordance with the provisions of UCC 9–504 (disposition procedures under UCC 9–504 will be discussed shortly). If no such written objection is forthcoming, the secured party can retain the collateral in full satisfaction of the debtor's obligation [UCC 9–505(2)].

Consumer Goods. When the collateral is consumer goods with a PMSI, and the debtor has paid 60 percent or more of the cash price or loan, then the secured party must sell or otherwise dispose of the collateral in accordance with the provisions of UCC

9–504 within ninety days. Failure to comply opens the secured party to an action for conversion (the wrongful taking of another's property—see Chapter 5) or other liability under UCC 9–507(1) unless the consumer-debtor signed a written statement after default renouncing or modifying the right to demand the sale of the goods [UCC 9–505(1)].

Disposition Procedures. A secured party who does not choose to retain the collateral must resort to the disposition procedures prescribed under UCC 9–504. The UCC allows a great deal of flexibility with regard to disposition. The only real limitations are that (1) the sale must be accomplished in a commercially reasonable manner, and (2) normally, the debtor must be notified of the sale.

The Standard of Commercial Reasonableness. A secured party is not compelled to resort to public sale to dispose of the collateral. The party is given latitude under the UCC to seek out the best terms possible in a private, commercially reasonable sale. Generally, no specific time requirements must be met; however, the time must ultimately meet the standard of commercial reasonableness. UCC 9–507(2) supplies some examples of what does or does not meet the standard of commercial reasonableness:

> The fact that a better price could have been obtained by a sale at a different time or in a different method from that selected by the secured party is not of itself sufficient to establish that the sale was not made in a commercially reasonable manner. If the secured party either sells the collateral in the usual manner in any recognized market therefor or if he sells at the price current in such a market at the time of sale or if he has otherwise sold in conformity with reasonable commercial practices among dealers in the type of property sold, he has sold in a commercially reasonable manner.

The secured party should diligently arrange to sell the collateral at the best price possible and avoid self-serving acts that raise suspicions of commercial unreasonableness. Assume that Boender, a secured party, advertises a private sale in a newspaper that is not likely to be read by potential purchasers, requires a minimum deposit of $50,000 with each purchaser's bid (while exempting himself from the deposit requirement), and then purchases the property at the sale for himself, only to resell it shortly thereafter at a substantial profit to a prearranged buyer. Boender's conduct unreasonably diminishes the number of potential purchasers available at the sale. With fewer participants at the sale, the final purchase price is likely to be reduced. When the purchase price is low, the debtor may fail to satisfy its outstanding debt to Boender or to enjoy a surplus from the sale of the collateral (deficiency and surplus are discussed later in this chapter). In such a situation, the debtor may recover any loss caused by Boender's failure to comply with the requirement of commercial reasonableness under the UCC [UCC 9–507].[10]

10. *Boender v. Chicago North Clubhouse Association, Inc.,* 240 Ill.App.3d 622, 608 N.E.2d 207, 181 Ill.Dec. 134 (1992).

Notice to the Debtor. Notice of any sale must be sent by the secured party to the debtor if the debtor has not signed a statement renouncing or modifying the right to notification of sale after default. For consumer goods, no other notification need be sent. In all other cases, notification must be sent to any other secured party from whom the secured party in possession of the collateral has received written notice of a claim of interest in the collateral [UCC 9–504(3)]. Such notice is not necessary, however, when the collateral is perishable or threatens to decline rapidly in value or when it is of a type customarily sold on a recognized market. Generally, proper notice of the place, time, and manner of the sale is required if the sale is to be classified as a sale conducted in a commercially reasonable manner.

How accurate should such a notice be in terms of informing a debtor of the amount owed, the date of the sale, and other details? The court addressed this question in the following case.

CASE 28.3   Fielder v. Credit Acceptance Corp.

United States District Court, Western District of Missouri, 1998. 19 F.Supp.2d 966.

COMPANY PROFILE   *For over twenty-five years, Credit Acceptance Corporation (CAC) (http://www.creditacceptance.com) has helped thousands of auto dealers in the United States, Canada, and the United Kingdom obtain funds for used-car loans to people who have difficulty obtaining credit with other lenders. CAC's services include accounts management, payment collection, and staff training. The firm provides such products as credit life and disability insurance, vehicle protection insurance, and vehicle service contracts. CAC also provides risk assessment and fraud alert services.*

BACKGROUND AND FACTS   *Marvin Fielder and others signed contracts with Northeast Auto Credit, Inc. (NAC), and others to buy used cars. The sellers assigned the contracts to Credit Acceptance Corporation (CAC), which had supplied the contract forms to the sellers. When the buyers defaulted on the loans, CAC repossessed the cars and sent notices that they would be sold. Some of the notices overstated the amounts needed to redeem the vehicles (regain possession of the vehicles by payment of the debt—redemption rights are discussed later in this chapter) without indicating that the figures might be wrong. Others misstated the redemption dates or the dates of the sales. When CAC sold the cars for less than was owed under the contracts, it attempted to collect the difference. Fielder and other buyers filed a suit against CAC and NAC, charging in part that the notices violated UCC 9–504(3). Both sides filed motions for summary judgment in a federal district court.*

IN THE LANGUAGE OF THE COURT   SMITH, District Judge.
                    *   *   *   *
        *   *   * [S]ome of the notices are deficient because the balance figures are overstated and the notices do not discuss [other] charges at all. *   *   * The Court finds that

some of the notices in this case violated the statute because CAC's figures were not only incorrect but were unreasonably misleading as to the principal debt and the notices did not inform the debtors that the stated balance might be inaccurate. * * * Therefore, the debtors did not have reasonable notification of the sale because such notice is designed to ensure the debtors are aware of their rights which include redemption. Plaintiffs are granted summary judgment for those notices that contain inflated figures and no reference to the [other charges] * * * .

                                    * * * *

Lastly, Plaintiffs claim that the pre-sale notices suffer from a host of other defects. Some of the notices contained dates of sale that were prior to the actual date of the notice. One notice was blank as to any date of sale. Another notice shows that payment to redeem must be made three days before the scheduled sale and yet others provide less notice than provided for in the contracts. All of these pre-sale notices violate section [UCC 9–504] and Plaintiffs' motion for summary judgment is granted.

DECISION AND REMEDY *The court issued a summary judgment in the plaintiffs' favor for notices that contained inflated figures, without indicating that possibility, and for notices that misstated the redemption or sale dates. The court reasoned that these notices violated UCC 9–504(3).*

Proceeds from Disposition. Proceeds from the disposition of the collateral must be applied in the following order:

1. Reasonable expenses stemming from the retaking, holding, or preparing for sale are paid first. When authorized by law and if provided for in the agreement, these expenses can include reasonable attorneys' fees and legal expenses.
2. Satisfaction of the balance of the debt owed to the secured party must then be made.
3. Creditors with subordinate security interests whose written demands have been received prior to the completion of distribution of the proceeds are then entitled to receive the remaining proceeds from the sale [UCC 9–504(1)].
4. Any surplus generally goes to the debtor.

Deficiency Judgment. Often, after proper disposition of the collateral, the secured party has not collected all that is still owed by the debtor. Unless otherwise agreed, the creditor is entitled to obtain a

deficiency judgment, which makes the debtor liable for any deficiency. Note, however, that if the underlying transaction was a sale of accounts or of chattel paper, the secured party can collect the deficiency by requesting a court to order a deficiency judgment only if the security agreement so provides [UCC 9–504(2)].

Redemption Rights. Any time before the secured party disposes of the collateral or enters into a contract for its disposition, or before the debtor's obligation has been discharged through the secured party's retention of the collateral, the debtor or any other secured party can exercise the right of *redemption* of the collateral. The debtor or other secured party can do this by (1) tendering performance of all obligations secured by the collateral and (2) paying the expenses reasonably incurred by the secured party in retaking the collateral and maintaining its care and custody, including legal expenses and reasonable attorneys' fees if the security agreement so provides [UCC 9–506].

CONCEPT SUMMARY 28.3  **REMEDIES OF THE SECURED PARTY ON THE DEBTOR'S DEFAULT**

Other Than Provided under the UCC	The secured party may reduce the debt claim to judgment, foreclose, or enforce the security interest by any judicial procedure. For example, the secured party may proceed to a judgment on the underlying debt, followed by execution and levy on the debtor's nonexempt assets.

CONCEPT SUMMARY 28.3

REMEDIES OF THE SECURED PARTY ON THE DEBTOR'S DEFAULT *(continued)*

Repossession of the Collateral

The secured party may take possession (peacefully or by court order) of the collateral covered by the security agreement and then pursue one of two alternatives:

1. Retain the collateral (unless the secured party has a purchase-money security interest in consumer goods and the debtor has paid 60 percent or more of the selling price or loan), in which case:
   a. The creditor must give written notice to the debtor if the debtor has not signed a statement renouncing or modifying his or her rights after default. With consumer goods, no other notice is necessary.
   b. The creditor must send notice to any other secured party with an interest in the same collateral.
   c. If an objection is received from the debtor or any other secured party within twenty-one days, in writing, the creditor must dispose of the collateral according to the requirements of UCC 9–504. Otherwise, the creditor may retain the collateral in full satisfaction of the debt.
2. Sell the collateral, in which case the creditor must do the following:
   a. Notify the debtor and (except in sales of consumer goods) other secured parties having claims to the collateral of the sale (unless the collateral is perishable or will decline rapidly in value).
   b. Sell the goods in a commercially reasonable manner at a public or private sale.
   c. Apply the proceeds in the following order:
      (1) Expenses incurred by the sale (which may include reasonable attorneys' fees and other legal expenses).
      (2) Balance of the debt owed to the secured party. If the proceeds are insufficient to cover the debt, the creditor may obtain a deficiency judgment (unless the collateral consists of chattel paper or accounts).
      (3) Subordinate security interests of creditors whose written demands have been received prior to the completion of the distribution of the proceeds.
      (4) Surplus to the debtor (unless the collateral is chattel paper or accounts).

SECTION 9

Revised Article 9

In 1999, the National Conference of Commissioners (NCC) on Uniform State Laws promulgated a revised version of Article 9 of the UCC. The revised Article 9 will become effective on July 1, 2001. Prior to that time, however, states that adopt the revised article face an unusual problem. Specifically, under the law set forth in the revised Article 9, secured transactions entered into under existing law must be terminated, completed, and enforced under the revised article. In other words, the revision, with some exceptions, applies to transactions or liens within its scope even if the transaction or lien was entered into *before* the revised article becomes effective. Thus, for a period of time there will be some confusion in secured transactions law, particularly with respect to the priority of conflicting claims to collateral.

The revised Article 9 will alter secured transactions law in several ways. Exhibit 28–6 summarizes some of the changes in the law that will be implemented as the revised version of Article 9 is adopted by the states.

Exhibit 28–6   Major Changes in Revised Article 9

Subject	Changes	UCC Revised Article 9 Sections
Scope	The revised Article 9 adds certain types of collateral and kinds of transactions in which a security interest can be perfected. These include electronic chattel paper, deposit accounts, and letter-of-credit rights.	9–102(2), (5), (12), (13), (29), (31), (46), (51), (61); 9–109
Perfection	1. Perfection by "control" is now permitted when collateral consists of electronic chattel paper and is required for deposit accounts and letter-of-credit rights. 2. Possession is no longer the only perfection method for negotiable instruments and transferable nonnegotiable instruments, but it is the only method for a security interest in money. 3. Perfection by attachment now extends to types of collateral that were not covered previously. 4. The time period to perfect a PMSI is increased to twenty days.	9–104; 9–105; 9–309; 9–310(b)(8); 9–312(a), (b)(1), (2), (3); 9–313; 9–317(e)
Choice of Law	Perfection is now generally in the state in which the debtor is located (if the debtor is an entity such as a corporation, this is the state in which the entity is chartered or registered). Exceptions include collateral covered by a certificate of title (the place for perfection is the state that issues the certificate) and fixtures, timber to be cut, and farm products (perfection is possible only in the state in which the collateral is located).	9–301 through 9–307
Perfection by Filing	1. Under the revised Article 9, a central state office is the only place for perfection by filing (except for collateral related to real estate). Filing is possible by electronic means. 2. The revised Article 9 provides for simplified, national financing statements and other forms. Also, many details relating to filing errors and liability are now clearer. 3. The fine for failing to send or file a termination statement is now $500.	9–501(a), (b); 9–502(a); 9–506; 9–507; 9–508; 9–509; 9–513; 9–516(a); 9–517; 9–521; 9–523; 9–625(e)(4)
Default and Enforcement	1. The list of the rights of debtors and the duties of secured parties that cannot be waived has been expanded. 2. Secured parties who sell collateral now impliedly warrant title (unless it is disclaimed) and must give specific notice of sale to certain other creditors and secondary obligors. Also, if the proceeds of the sale are small compared to the market price and the buyer is the secured party or a secondary obligor, the price for determining a debtor's remaining obligation is the market price, not the price paid. 3. Acceptance of collateral in satisfaction of the debt is clarified and encouraged.	9–102(a)(71); 9–602; 9–610; 9–611; 9–612; 9–613; 9–614; 9–615(f); 9–620; 9–624
Effective Date	The effective date of the revised Article 9 is July 1, 2001. All secured transactions (with a few exceptions), however, are subject to the new law even if they were entered into earlier.	9–701 through 9–708

TERMS AND CONCEPTS TO REVIEW

after-acquired property 514	execution 521	purchase-money security interest (PMSI) 508
attachment 505	financing statement 508	secured party 504
chattel paper 504	floating lien 515	secured transaction 504
collateral 505	levy 521	security agreement 505
continuation statement 514	lien creditor 516	security interest 504
debtor 504	perfection 508	
default 508	pledge 510	
deficiency judgment 525	proceeds 514	

QUESTIONS AND CASE PROBLEMS

28–1. PRIORITY DISPUTES. Ray is a seller of electric generators. He purchases a large quantity of generators from manufacturer Martin Corp. by making a down payment and signing a security agreement to make the balance of payments over a period of time. The agreement gives Martin Corp. a security interest in the generators and the proceeds. Martin Corp. files a financing statement on its security interest centrally. Ray receives the generators and immediately sells one of them to Green on an installment contract, with payment to be made in twelve equal installments. At the time of sale, Green knows of Martin's security interest. Two months later, Ray goes into default on his payments to Martin. Discuss Martin's rights against purchaser Green in this situation.

28–2. PERFECTION. Marion has a prize horse named Thunderbolt. Marion is in need of working capital. To secure it, she borrows $5,000 from Rodriguez, and Rodriguez takes possession of Thunderbolt as security for the loan. No written agreement is signed. Discuss whether, in the absence of a written agreement, Rodriguez has a security interest in Thunderbolt and whether Rodriguez can be a perfected secured party without filing a financing statement.

28–3. PERFECTION. Discuss how each secured party would properly perfect his or her security interest in the following situations:

(a) Martin is a manufacturer of refrigerators. Ray, a retailer, buys a number of these refrigerators. Ray signs a security agreement giving Martin a security interest in the refrigerators.

(b) Mary sells a refrigerator to Carla, to be used in Carla's home. Carla signs a security agreement giving Mary a security interest in the refrigerator.

(c) Ray sells a refrigerator to Dr. Dodd, to be used in his office to store medicines. Dr. Dodd signs a security agreement giving Ray a security interest in the refrigerator.

(d) Mary sells a refrigerator to farmer Ames, who needs it to store eggs not sold at market. Ames signs a security agreement giving Mary a security interest in the refrigerator.

28–4. PRIORITY DISPUTES. Martin is a manufacturer of washing machines. On September 1, in need of working capital, Martin's president contacts Smith, a loan officer for the First Bank. The president asks to borrow $200,000 and offers to put up all Martin's equipment as security. Smith agrees to make the loan. In the security agreement signed by Martin's president is a clause stating that this loan is secured not only by the existing equipment presently located at Martin's plant but also by any equipment acquired in the future by Martin. The First Bank files a financing statement centrally on September 5. On November 1, Martin has an opportunity to purchase from Daniel Equipment Corp. some newly manufactured Daniel equipment at a bargain price of $50,000. On that same date, Martin contracts by a security agreement to purchase the equipment from Daniel. The security agreement specifies that Martin will pay $20,000 down, that the balance is to be paid in monthly payments over a three-year period, and that Daniel has a security interest in the purchased equipment. The new equipment is delivered on December 1. On December 7, Daniel perfects its security interest in the newly delivered equipment by filing a financing statement centrally. Later, Martin goes into default to both parties. Discuss whose interest in the new equipment has priority, First Bank's or Daniel's.

28–5. PURCHASE-MONEY SECURITY INTEREST. Ray is a retail seller of television sets. Ray sells a color television set to Clara for her apartment for $600. Clara cannot pay cash and signs a security agreement, paying $100 down and agreeing to pay the balance in twelve equal installments of $50 each. The security agreement gives Ray a security interest in the television set. Clara makes six payments on time; then she goes into default because of unexpected financial problems. Ray repossesses the set and wants to keep it in full satisfaction of the debt. Discuss Ray's rights and duties in this matter.

28–6. ORAL SECURITY AGREEMENTS. John and Melody Fish bought various pieces of expensive jewelry, including a diamond ring, a diamond necklace, and a wedding band, from Odom's Jewelers. The Fishes agreed to make monthly installment payments to Odom's until the purchase price was paid in full. In 1988, the Fishes fell behind in their monthly payments on the account. The Fishes and Odom's orally agreed that the Fishes would return the jewelry to Odom's and that Odom's would hold the items for the Fishes until the account was paid. In 1991, the Fishes filed for bankruptcy protection. The jewelry was still in the possession of Odom's. One of the issues before the bankruptcy court was whether Odom's had a security interest in the jewelry. Did it? Explain. [*In re Fish*, 128 Bankr. 468 (N.D.Okla. 1991)]

28–7. DEBTOR'S NAME. Cambria Fuel Oil Co. sold its business to 306 Fuel Oil Corp. As part of the deal, Cambria Fuel took a security interest in 306 Fuel's assets and filed a financing statement that identified 306 Fuel as the debtor. Six weeks later, 306 Fuel changed its name to Cambria Petroleum Co. Cambria Fuel did not file a new financing statement. Fleet Factors Corp. loaned money to Cambria Petroleum and took a security interest in the same assets as those subject to Cambria Fuel's security interest. When Cambria Petroleum failed to repay the loan, Fleet Factors filed suit in a New York state court to foreclose its security interest. Cambria Fuel claimed that its interest had priority. Whose security interest has priority? Why? [*Fleet Factors Corp. v. Bandolene Industries Corp.*, 86 N.Y.2d 519, 658 N.E.2d 202, 634 N.Y.S.2d 425 (1995)]

28–8. REPOSSESSION. Leroy Headspeth bought a car under an installment sales contract that expressly permitted the creditor to repossess the car if the debtor defaulted on the payments. The seller assigned the contract to Mercedes-Benz Credit Corp. (MBCC). When Headspeth defaulted on the payments, Laurel Adjustment Bureau, Inc. (LAB), repossessed the car on MBCC's behalf. Headspeth filed a suit against MBCC and LAB, contending in part that LAB trespassed onto his property to retake the car and that therefore the repossession was wrongful. Headspeth admitted that the repossession occurred without confrontation. Can a secured creditor legally retake possession of collateral, on the debtor's default, by entering onto the debtor's land, or would that be an illegal breach of the peace? How will the court rule? Explain. [*Headspeth v. Mercedes-Benz Credit Corp.*, 709 A.2d 717 (D.C.App. 1998)]

28–9. FINANCING STATEMENT. In 1994, SouthTrust Bank, N.A., loaned money to Environmental Aspecs,

Inc. (EAI), and its subsidiary EAI of NC, subject to a security interest. SouthTrust perfected its security interest by filing financing statements that listed only EAI as the debtor, described only EAI's assets as collateral, and was signed only on EAI's behalf. SouthTrust believed that both companies were operating as a single business represented by EAI. In 1996, EAI of NC borrowed almost $300,000 from Advanced Analytics Laboratories, Inc. (AAL), using EAI of NC's assets as collateral. AAL filed financing statements that listed the assets of EAI of NC as collateral but identified the debtor as EAI. The statements, however, referred to attached copies of the security agreements, which were signed by the president of EAI of NC and identified the debtor as EAI of NC. One year later, EAI and EAI of NC renegotiated their loan with SouthTrust, and the bank filed financing statements listing both companies as debtors. In 1998, EAI and EAI of NC filed for bankruptcy. One of the issues was the priority of the security interests of SouthTrust and AAL. AAL contended that its failure to identify, on its financing statements, EAI of NC as debtor did not give SouthTrust priority. Is AAL correct? Why or why not? [*In re Environmental Aspecs, Inc.*, 235 Bankr. 378 (E.D.N.C., Raleigh Div. 1999)]

28–10. IN YOUR COURT

To pay for the purchase of several aircraft, Robert Wall borrowed money from the Cessna Finance Corp., using the aircraft as collateral. Wall defaulted on the loans. Cessna took possession of the collateral (the aircraft) and sold it at *Blue Book* value. Cessna then filed a suit against Wall for the difference between the amount due on the loans and the amount received from the sale of the aircraft. Wall claimed that Cessna's sale of the aircraft was not commercially reasonable, because he (Wall) could have obtained a higher price for the aircraft if he had sold them himself. Assume that you are the judge in the trial court hearing this case and answer the following questions:

(a) Suppose that Wall could have obtained a better price for the aircraft. Does this fact, in itself, mean that the sale was not commercially reasonable?

(b) What UCC provision applies to this dispute? How will you rule on this issue, and why?

28–11. A QUESTION OF ETHICS

Raymond and Joan Massengill borrowed money from Indiana National Bank (INB) to purchase a van. Toward the end of the loan period, the Massengills were notified by mail that they were delinquent on their last two loan payments. Joan called INB on a Saturday and said that she did not agree with the amount that INB said was due. It was arranged that the Massengills would go to the bank the following Monday morning and take care of the matter. In the meantime, INB had made arrangements for the van to be repossessed. At 1:30 A.M. Sunday, two men appeared in the Massengills' driveway and began to hook up the van to a tow truck. Raymond, assuming that the van was being stolen, went outside to intervene and did so vociferously. During the course of events, Massengill became entangled in machinery at the rear of the tow truck and was dragged down the street and then run over by his towed van. The "repo men"— those hired by INB to repossess the van—knew of Raymond's plight but sped away. The trial court granted summary judgment for the bank, ruling that the bank was not liable for the injuries caused by the repossession company. On appeal, however, the court ruled that the bank could be liable for the acts of the repossession company and remanded the case for the determination of

damages. [*Massengill v. Indiana National Bank,* 550 N.E.2d 97 (Ind.App.1st Dist. 1990)]

(a) Frequently, courts must decide, as in this case, whether the creditor should be held liable for the wrongful acts of persons hired by the creditor to undertake the actual repossession effort. Is it fair to hold the creditor liable for acts that the creditor did not commit? Why or why not?

(b) Given the potential for violence during repossession efforts, why do you think Article 9 permits creditors to resort to "self-help" repossessions?

(c) Should repossession companies be prohibited from taking collateral from debtors' property during the middle of the night, when debtors are more likely to conclude that the activity is wrongful?

Law on the Web

For updated links to resources available on the Web, as well as a variety of other materials, visit this text's Web site at http://wbl.westbuslaw.com.

The National Conference of Commissioners on Uniform State Laws, in association with the University of Pennsylvania Law School, now offers an official site for UCC articles. To keep abreast of changes in the UCC, including the revisions to Article 9, go to

http://www.law.upenn.edu/bll/ulc/ulc.htm

The Web site of Cornell University's Legal Information Institute offers an overview and menu of sources on legal materials relating to secured transactions at

http://www.law.cornell.edu/topics/secured_transactions.html

Legal Research Exercises on the Web

Go to http://wbl.westbuslaw.com, the Web site that accompanies this text. Select "Internet Applications," and then click on "Chapter 28." There you will find the following Internet research exercise that you can perform to learn more about repossession of collateral under Article 9:

Activity 28–1: Repossession

CHAPTER 29

Other Creditors' Remedies and Suretyship

NORMALLY, CREDITORS HAVE NO PROBLEM collecting the debts owed to them. When disputes arise over the amount owed, however, or when the debtor simply cannot or will not pay, what happens? What remedies are available to creditors when debtors default? We have already discussed, in Chapter 28, the remedies available to secured creditors under Article 9 of the Uniform Commercial Code (UCC). In this chapter, we focus on other laws that assist the debtor and creditor in resolving their disputes without the debtor's having to resort to bankruptcy (discussed in Chapter 30).

SECTION 1

Laws Assisting Creditors

Both the common law and statutory laws other than Article 9 of the UCC create various rights and remedies for creditors. We discuss here some of these rights and remedies, including liens, garnishment, creditors' composition agreements, mortgage foreclosure, and a debtor's assignment of assets for the benefit of creditors.

LIENS

A **lien** is a claim or charge on a debtor's property that must be satisfied before the property (or its proceeds) is available to satisfy the claims of other creditors. As mentioned, liens may arise under the common law or under statutory law. Statutory liens include *mechanic's liens*. Liens created at common law include *artisan's liens* and *innkeeper's liens*. *Judicial liens* include those that represent a creditor's efforts to collect on a debt before or after a judgment is entered by a court.

Generally, a lien creditor has priority over an unperfected secured party but not over a perfected secured party. Thus, a person who becomes a lien creditor before another security interest in the same property is perfected has priority, but one who acquires the lien after perfection does not have priority. Mechanic's and artisan's liens, however, have priority over perfected security interests unless a statute provides otherwise.

Mechanic's Lien. When a person contracts for labor, services, or material to be furnished for the purpose of making improvements on real property but does not immediately pay for the improvements,

531

the creditor can place a **mechanic's lien** on the property. This creates a special type of debtor-creditor relationship in which the real estate itself becomes security for the debt.

For example, a painter agrees to paint a house for a homeowner for an agreed-on price to cover labor and materials. If the homeowner cannot pay or pays only a portion of the charges, a mechanic's lien against the property can be created. The painter is the lienholder, and the real property is encumbered with a mechanic's lien for the amount owed. If the homeowner does not pay the lien, the property can be sold to satisfy the debt. Notice of the *foreclosure* (the enforcement of the lien) must be given to the debtor in advance, however.

The procedures by which a mechanic's lien is created are controlled by state law. Generally, the lien-holder must file a written notice of lien against the particular property involved. The notice of lien must be filed within a specific time period, measured from the last date on which materials or labor were provided (usually within 60 to 120 days). Failure to pay the debt entitles the lienholder to foreclose on the real estate on which the improvements were made and to sell it to satisfy the amount of the debt. Of course, as mentioned, the lienholder is required by statute to give notice to the owner of the property prior to foreclosure and sale. The sale proceeds are used to pay the debt and the costs of the legal proceedings; the surplus, if any, is paid to the former owner.

In the following case, the issue concerned when the time period within which notice of a lien must be filed begins to run.

CASE 29.1　　　Herpel, Inc. v. Straub Capital Corp.

District Court of
Appeal of Florida,
Fourth District, 1996.
682 So.2d 661.

BACKGROUND AND FACTS　*Herpel, Inc., agreed to make a stone fireplace mantel for a house owned by a partnership that included Straub Capital Corporation. The mantel was delivered, but the buyers were not satisfied with its appearance. Herpel took the mantel back for more finishing work and redelivered it five weeks later. The mantel was installed, but the buyers did not pay. Herpel filed a mechanic's lien 113 days after the first delivery but less than 90 days after the redelivery. A state statute limits the time within which notice of a mechanic's lien may be filed to 90 days. Herpel then filed an action against the buyers in a Florida state court to foreclose on the lien. The court granted a summary judgment in the defendants' favor, on the ground that Herpel had filed the notice too late. Herpel appealed.*

**IN THE LANGUAGE
OF THE COURT**

STEVENSON, Judge.
　　　＊　　＊　　＊　　＊

In contracts involving both services and materials, the courts have held that the time limit for filing a lien is not extended by repair, corrective, or warranty work; but that work done in fulfillment of the contract will extend the time for filing of the claim of lien. ＊　＊　＊

＊　＊　＊ *The test to be applied is whether the work was done in good faith, within a reasonable time, in pursuance of the terms of the contract, and whether it was necessary to a "finished job."* [Emphasis added.]

＊　＊　＊ [W]ork done in fulfillment of the contract is contemplated by the contract and extends the time for filing, since the contract is not complete until the work is done. Remedial work in the nature of correction or repair does not extend the time for filing the claim of lien since the contract is already complete, and any additional work performed is merely incidental to the executed contract. ＊　＊　＊ Applying that reasoning, we have little difficulty determining that, as a matter of law, the final furnishing of the materials occurred when the mantel was reinstalled ＊　＊　＊ . The owner rejected the mantel as non-conforming to the contract when it was initially tendered. In response to the owner's objections, Herpel took the mantel back, allowed for further curing, and presented the mantel once again for acceptance. Under the circumstances, it is clear that the additional work on the mantel was performed to complete the job in compliance with the contract.

DECISION AND REMEDY   *The Florida appellate court concluded that Herpel had filed the notice within the required time period, which began after all the work was completed to comply with the contract. The court reversed the decision of the lower court and remanded the case.*

Artisan's Lien. An **artisan's lien** is a security device created at common law through which a creditor can recover payment from a debtor for labor and materials furnished in the repair of personal property. For example, Whitney leaves her diamond ring at the jewelry shop to be repaired and to have her initials engraved on the band. In the absence of an agreement, the jeweler can keep the ring until Whitney pays for the services that the jeweler provides. Should Whitney fail to pay, the jeweler has a lien on Whitney's ring for the amount of the bill and can sell the ring in satisfaction of the lien.

In contrast to a mechanic's lien, an artisan's lien is *possessory.* The lienholder ordinarily must have retained possession of the property and have expressly or impliedly agreed to provide the services on a cash, not a credit, basis. The lien remains in existence as long as the lienholder maintains possession, and the lien is terminated once possession is voluntarily surrendered—unless the surrender is only temporary. With a temporary surrender, there must be an agreement that the property will be returned to the lienholder. Even with such an agreement, if a third party obtains rights in that property while it is out of the possession of the lienholder, the lien is lost.

Modern statutes permit the holder of an artisan's lien to foreclose and sell the property subject to the lien to satisfy payment of the debt. As with the mechanic's lien, the lienholder is required to give notice to the owner of the property prior to foreclosure and sale. In some states, holders of artisan's liens must give notice to title lienholders of automobiles prior to foreclosure. The sale proceeds are used to pay the debt and the costs of the legal proceedings, and the surplus, if any, is paid to the former owner. The artisan's lien has priority over a filed statutory lien (such as a title lien on an automobile or a lien filed under Article 9 of the UCC) as well as priority over a bailee's lien (such as a storage lien).

Innkeeper's Lien. An **innkeeper's lien** is another security device created at common law. An innkeeper's lien is placed on the baggage of guests for any agreed-on hotel charges that remain unpaid. If no express agreement has been made on the amount of those charges, then the lien will be for the reasonable value of the accommodations furnished. The innkeeper's lien is terminated either by the guest's payment of the hotel charges or by the innkeeper's surrender of the baggage to the guest, unless the surrender is temporary. Most state statutes permit the innkeeper to satisfy the debt by means of a public sale of the guest's baggage. Some jurisdictions require that the guest first be given an impartial judicial hearing.[1]

Judicial Liens. A debt must be past due before a creditor can commence legal action against a debtor. Once legal action is brought, the debtor's property may be seized to satisfy the debt. If the property is seized prior to trial proceedings, the seizure is referred to as an *attachment* of the property. The seizure may also occur following a court judgment in the creditor's favor. In that case, the court's order to seize the property is referred to as a *writ of execution.*

Attachment. Under Article 9 of the UCC, as discussed in Chapter 28, *attachment* refers to the process through which a security interest becomes effective and enforceable against a debtor with respect to the debtor's collateral [UCC 9–203]. In the present context, **attachment** refers to a court-ordered seizure and taking into custody of property prior to the securing of a judgment for a past-due debt. Attachment rights are created by state statutes. Normally a *prejudgment* remedy, attachment occurs either at the time of or immediately after the commencement of a lawsuit and before the entry of a final judgment. By statute, the restrictions and requirements for a creditor to attach before judgment are specific and limited. The due process clause of the Fourteenth Amendment to the Constitution limits the courts' power to authorize seizure of a debtor's property without notice to the

---

1. *Klim v. Jones,* 315 F.Supp. 109 (N.D.Cal. 1970).

debtor or a hearing on the facts. In recent years, a number of state attachment laws have been held to be unconstitutional.

To use attachment as a remedy, the creditor must have an enforceable right to payment of the debt under law, and the creditor must follow certain procedures. Otherwise, the creditor can be liable for damages for wrongful attachment. He or she must file with the court an *affidavit* (a written or printed statement, made under oath or sworn to) stating that the debtor is in default and delineating the statutory grounds under which attachment is sought. A bond must be posted by the creditor to cover at least court costs, the value of the loss of use of the good suffered by the debtor, and the value of the property attached. When the court is satisfied that all the requirements have been met, it issues a **writ of attachment,** which is similar to a writ of execution (to be discussed shortly) in that it directs the sheriff or other officer to seize nonexempt property. If the creditor prevails at trial, the seized property can be sold to satisfy the judgment.

Writ of Execution.   If a creditor is successful in a legal action against a debtor, the court awards the creditor a judgment against the debtor (usually for the amount of the debt plus any interest and legal costs incurred in obtaining the judgment). Frequently, the creditor finds it easy to secure a judgment against the debtor but nevertheless fails to collect the awarded amount. If the debtor will not or cannot pay the judgment, the creditor is entitled to go back to the court and obtain a **writ of execution,** which is an order, usually issued by the clerk of the court, directing the sheriff to seize (levy) and sell any of the debtor's nonexempt real or personal property that is within the court's geographic jurisdiction (usually the county in which the courthouse is located). The proceeds of the sale are used to pay off the judgment and the costs of the sale. Any excess is paid to the debtor. The debtor can pay the judgment and redeem the nonexempt property any time before the sale takes place. Because of exemption laws (which cover the debtor's homestead and designated items of personal property) and bankruptcy laws, however, many judgments are virtually uncollectible.

Garnishment.   An order for **garnishment** permits a creditor to collect a debt by seizing property of the debtor (such as wages or money in a bank account) that is being held by a third party (such as an employer or a bank). Typically, a garnishment judgment

is served on a debtor's employer so that part of the debtor's usual paycheck will be paid to the creditor.

The legal proceeding for a garnishment action is governed by state law. As a result of a garnishment proceeding, as noted, a third party (such as the debtor's employer) is ordered by the court to turn over property owned by the debtor (such as wages) to pay the debt. Garnishment can be a prejudgment remedy, requiring a hearing before a court, or a postjudgment remedy. According to the laws in some states, the judgment creditor needs to obtain only one order of garnishment, which will then continuously apply to the judgment debtor's weekly wages until the entire debt is paid. In other states, the judgment creditor must go back to court for a separate order of garnishment for each pay period.

Both federal laws and state laws limit the amount of money that can be taken from a debtor's weekly take-home pay through garnishment proceedings. Federal law provides a minimal framework to protect debtors from losing all their income in order to pay judgment debts.[2] State laws also provide dollar exemptions, and these amounts are often larger than those provided by federal law.[3] State and federal statutes can be applied together to help create a pool of funds sufficient to enable a debtor to continue to provide for family needs while also reducing the amount of the judgment debt in a reasonable way. Under federal law, garnishment of an employee's wages for any one indebtedness cannot be grounds for dismissal of an employee.

One of the questions courts have faced in recent years has to do with whether a debtor's pension fund can be attached by creditors, through garnishment or other proceedings, to satisfy a debt. Under the Employee Retirement Income Security Act (ERISA) of 1974,[4] certain types of pension funds "may not be alienated [transferred]," or attached. The law is less clear, however, on whether pension funds, after they have been received by a retiree, can be subject to attachment by creditors. This issue was before the court in the following case.

---

2. For example, the federal Consumer Credit Protection Act of 1968, 15 U.S.C. Sections 1601–1693r, provides that a debtor can retain either 75 percent of his or her disposable earnings per week or the sum equivalent to thirty hours of work paid at federal minimum wage rates, whichever is greater.
3. A few states (for example, Texas) do not permit garnishment of wages by private parties except under a child-support order.
4. 29 U.S.C. Sections 1001–1461.

CASE 29.2 United States v. Smith

United States
Court of Appeals,
Fourth Circuit, 1995.
47 F.3d 681.
http://www.findlaw.
com/casecode/courts/
4th.html[a]

**IN THE LANGUAGE
OF THE COURT**

BACKGROUND AND FACTS *For nine years, Charles Smith asked his friends and acquaintances to invest their money in his business schemes. Smith used most of the money—estimated to be more than $350,000—for personal expenses. Smith was indicted for criminal fraud and pleaded guilty to that crime in a federal district court. The court imposed a prison sentence and ordered Smith to repay his victims as much as possible by turning over, each month, the entire amount of his pension benefits. Smith appealed the order, claiming that it violated the "anti-alienation" provision of ERISA.*

ERVIN, Chief Judge:
* * * *

This court has long recognized a strong public policy against the alienability of an ERISA plan participant's benefits. The [United States] Supreme Court, as well, has found that it is not "appropriate to approve any generalized equitable exception * * * to ERISA's prohibition on the assignment or alienation of pension benefits."
* * *

* * * The government's position is that once pension funds have been distributed, the anti-alienability statute no longer applies. * * *

* * * The Supreme Court has noted that the purpose of ERISA is to safeguard a stream of income for pensioners. Where an employee elects to draw on her ERISA plan prior to her retirement, she forfeits the protection provided by the Act. Where, however, the funds are paid pursuant to the terms of the plan as income during retirement years, ERISA prohibits their alienation. * * *
* * * *

In the case at hand, the government attempted to require Smith to draw down his benefits due under the plans as a lump sum and turn it over intact as restitution. Upon discovering that Smith was not eligible for lump sum distribution, the government agreed to the recovery of his benefits as they are paid to him. It is clear that the government would not have been successful in requiring Smith to request a lump sum distribution. * * * *[B]enefits in the hands of the fiduciary are beyond the reach of garnishment.* The government should not be allowed to do indirectly what it cannot do directly; it cannot require Smith to turn over his pension benefits in a lump sum, nor can it require him to turn over his benefits as they are paid to him. Understandably, there may be a natural distaste for the result we reach here. The statute, however, is clear. Congress has made a policy decision to protect the ERISA income of retirees, even if that decision prevents others from securing relief for the wrongs done them. [Emphasis added.]

* * * [There is a] danger in eroding through exception the anti-alienation policy of ERISA. That entire legislation was aimed at guaranteeing the security of retirement income for American workers. * * * We decline to participate in the diminution of these safeguards in circumstances which might seem harmless enough in particular instances but which, in the aggregate, might invite creditors to believe that ERISA funds are not, after all, inviolate.

**DECISION
AND REMEDY**

The U.S. Court of Appeals for the Fourth Circuit vacated the lower court's order and remanded the case. The appellate court ordered the lower court to redetermine the amount that Smith was to pay to his victims, based on "a balance of the victims' interest in compensation and Smith's other financial resources."

a. In the "Browsing" section, in the "1995" row, click on "March." When that page opens, scroll down the list to the *Smith* case name and click on it to access the opinion.

CREDITORS' COMPOSITION AGREEMENTS

Creditors may contract with the debtor for discharge of the debtor's liquidated debts (debts that are definite, or fixed, in amount) on payment of a sum less than that owed. These agreements are referred to as *composition agreements* or **creditors' composition agreements** and, unless they are formed under duress, are usually held to be enforceable.

MORTGAGE FORECLOSURE

Mortgage holders have the right to foreclose on mortgaged property in the event of a debtor's default. The usual method of foreclosure is by judicial sale of the property, although the statutory methods of foreclosure vary from state to state. If the proceeds of the foreclosure sale are sufficient to cover both the costs of the foreclosure and the mortgaged debt, any surplus is received by the debtor. If the sale proceeds are insufficient to cover the foreclosure costs and the mortgaged debt, however, the **mortgagee** (the creditor-lender) can seek to recover the difference from the **mortgagor** (the debtor) by obtaining a **deficiency judgment** representing the difference between the mortgaged debt plus foreclosure costs and the amount actually received from the proceeds of the foreclosure sale. A deficiency judgment is obtained in a separate legal action that is pursued subsequent to the foreclosure action. It entitles the creditor to recover from other property owned by the debtor. Some states do not permit deficiency judgments for some types of real estate interests.

Before the foreclosure sale, a defaulting mortgagor can redeem the property by paying the full amount of the debt, plus any interest and costs that have accrued. This right is known as the **equity of redemption.** In some states, a mortgagor may even redeem the property within a certain period of time—called a **statutory period of redemption**—after the sale. In these states, the deed to the property usually is not delivered to the purchaser until the statutory period has expired.

ASSIGNMENT FOR THE BENEFIT OF CREDITORS

Both common law and statutes may provide for a debtor's assignment of assets to a trustee or assignee for the benefit of the debtor's creditors. In these situations, that debtor voluntarily transfers title to assets owned to a trustee or assignee, who in turn sells or liquidates these assets, tendering payment to the debtor's creditors on a pro rata (proportionate) basis. Each creditor may accept the tender (and discharge the debt owed to him or her) or reject it (and attempt to collect the debt in another way).

The flexibility and informality of an assignment for the benefit of creditors may save creditors time and expense and result in better prices when a debtor's property is liquidated. Nevertheless, creditors may decide that this option does not adequately protect their rights. Under the bankruptcy laws, creditors may be able to force the debtor into involuntary bankruptcy, depending on the amount of their claims against the debtor and other factors (see Chapter 30). Thus, a debtor's bankruptcy may supersede assignment for the benefit of creditors—even if the bankruptcy is initiated by creditors.

CONCEPT SUMMARY 29.1
REMEDIES AVAILABLE TO CREDITORS

Liens	1. *Mechanic's lien*—A nonpossessory, filed lien on an owner's real estate for labor, services, or materials furnished to or made on the realty. 2. *Artisan's lien*—A possessory lien on an owner's personal property for labor performed or value added to the personal property. 3. *Innkeeper's lien*—A possessory lien on a hotel guest's baggage for hotel charges that remain unpaid. 4. *Judicial liens*— a. Attachment—A court-ordered seizure of property prior to a court's final determination of the creditor's rights to the property. Attachment is

CONCEPT SUMMARY 29.1

REMEDIES AVAILABLE TO CREDITORS (*continued*)

Liens (continued)	available only on the creditor's posting of a bond and in strict compliance with the applicable state statutes. b. Writ of execution—A court order directing the sheriff to seize (levy) and sell a debtor's nonexempt real or personal property to satisfy a court's judgment in the creditor's favor.
Garnishment	A collection remedy that allows the creditor to attach a debtor's money (such as wages owed or bank accounts) and property that are held by a third person.
Creditors' Composition Agreement	A contract between a debtor and his or her creditors by which the debtor's debts are discharged by payment of a sum less than the sum that is actually owed.
Mortgage Foreclosure	On the debtor's default, the entire mortgage debt is due and payable, allowing the creditor to foreclose on the realty by selling it to satisfy the debt.
Assignment for the Benefit of Creditors	The debtor's assignment of certain assets to a trustee or assignee, who sells or liquidates the assets and tenders payments to creditors on a pro rata basis. Acceptance of the payment by a creditor discharges the debt.

SECTION 2

Suretyship and Guaranty

When a third person promises to pay a debt owed by another in the event the debtor does not pay, either a *suretyship* or a *guaranty* relationship is created. Exhibit 29–1 illustrates these relationships. The third person's credit becomes the security for the debt owed.

SURETYSHIP

A contract of strict **suretyship** is a promise made by a third person to be responsible for the debtor's obligation. It is an express contract between the **surety** and the creditor. The surety in the strictest sense is primarily liable for the debt of the principal. The creditor can demand payment from the surety from the moment that the debt is due. A suretyship contract is not a form of indemnity; that is, it is not merely a promise to make good any loss that a creditor may incur as a result of the debtor's failure to pay. The creditor need not exhaust all legal remedies against the principal debtor before holding the surety responsible for payment. Moreover, a surety agreement does not have to be in writing to be enforceable, although usually such agreements are in writing.

For example, Jason Oller wants to borrow money from the bank to buy a used car. Because Jason is still in college, the bank will not lend him the money unless his father, Stacey Oller, who has dealt with the bank before, will cosign the note (add his signature to the note, thereby becoming jointly liable for payment of the debt). When Mr. Oller cosigns the note, he becomes primarily liable to the bank. On the note's due date, the bank can seek payment from Jason Oller, Stacey Oller, or both jointly.

GUARANTY

A guaranty contract is similar to a suretyship contract in that it includes a promise to answer for the debt or default of another. With a suretyship arrangement, however, the surety is primarily liable for the debtor's obligation. With a guaranty arrangement, the **guarantor**—the third person making the guaranty—is secondarily liable. The guarantor can be required to pay the obligation only after the principal debtor defaults, and usually only after the creditor has made an attempt to collect from the debtor.

For example, a corporation, BX Enterprises, needs to borrow money to meet its payroll. The bank is skeptical about the creditworthiness of BX and requires Dawson, its president, who is a wealthy businessperson and owner of 70 percent of BX Enterprises, to sign an agreement making himself personally liable for payment if BX does not pay off the loan. As a guarantor of the loan, Dawson cannot be held liable until BX Enterprises is in default.

EXHIBIT 29–1   SURETYSHIP AND GUARANTY PARTIES

In a suretyship or guaranty arrangement, a third party promises to be responsible for a debtor's obligations. A third party who agrees to be responsible for the debt even if the primary debtor does not default is known as a surety; a third party who agrees to be *secondarily* responsible for the debt—that is, responsible only if the primary debtor defaults—is known as a guarantor. As noted in Chapter 15, normally a promise of guaranty (a collateral, or secondary, promise) must be in writing to be enforceable.

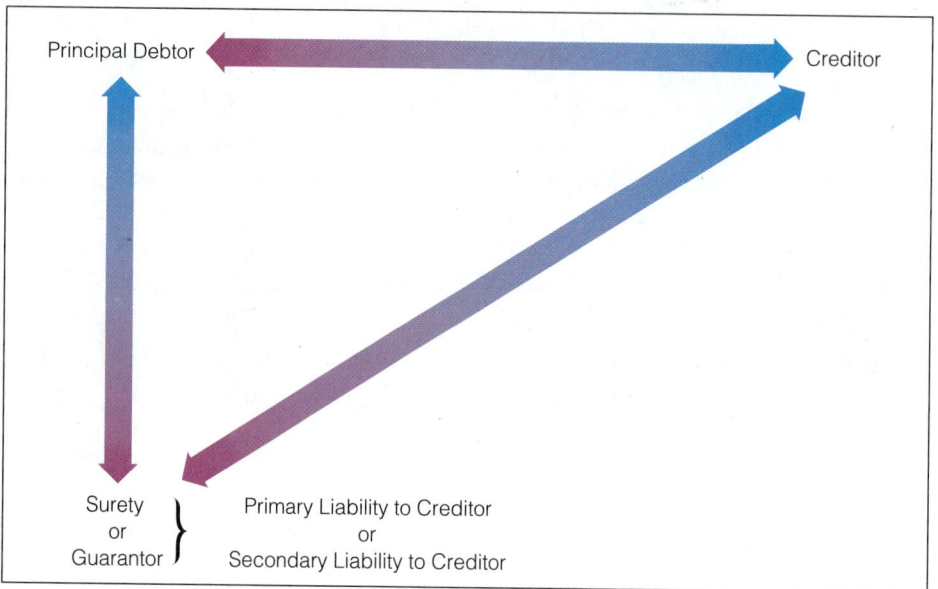

The Statute of Frauds requires that a guaranty contract between the guarantor and the creditor must be in writing to be enforceable unless the *main purpose exception* applies. Briefly, this exception provides that if the main purpose of the guaranty agreement is to benefit the guarantor, then the contract need not be in writing to be enforceable. (See Chapter 15 for a more detailed discussion of this exception.)

The guaranty contract terms determine the extent and time of the guarantor's liability. For example, the guaranty can be *continuing*, designed to cover a series of transactions by the debtor. Also, the guaranty can be *unlimited* or *limited* as to time and amount. In addition, the guaranty can be *absolute*, in which case the guarantor becomes liable immediately on the debtor's default, or *conditional*, in which case the guarantor becomes liable only on the happening of a certain event.

In the following case, the issue was whether a guaranty of a lease signed by the president of a corporation was enforceable against the president personally, although he signed the guaranty as a representative of the corporation.

CASE 29.3   Wilson Court Limited Partnership v. Tony Maroni's, Inc.

Supreme Court of
Washington, 1998.
134 Wash.2d 692,
952 P.2d 590.

COMPANY PROFILE   *Tony Riviera founded Tony Maroni's, Inc., to sell Tony Maroni's Famous Gourmet Pizza in Seattle, Washington, in the late 1980s. Tony Maroni's began by offering pizzas, salads, calzones, and lasagna for delivery only. By 1995, the firm had begun franchising (licensing its brand to investors to operate Tony Maroni's outlets—franchising is discussed in Chapter 39). Two years later, with eleven locations in the Seattle area, including six franchise outlets, and ten more stores in development, the company announced plans to open five hundred locations nationwide before 2002. Despite these plans, by the end of 1997, Tony Maroni's had yet to turn a profit and was nearly $1 million in debt.*

BACKGROUND AND FACTS   *Tony Maroni's, Inc., agreed to lease retail space owned by Wilson Court Limited Partnership. Tony Riviera, Tony Maroni's president, signed the* *lease for 1,676 square feet of space for a sixty-month term. The lease provided for improvements, estimated to be worth $45,520. Initially, Tony Maroni's contributed $5,000 toward the improvements, and was to pay an additional $7,000 over the life of the lease, at $148.73 per month. Wilson contributed the balance of $33,520. When he signed the lease, Riviera also signed a guaranty agreement that was incorporated by reference in the lease. On the signature line of the guaranty, Riviera wrote "President" after his name. The guaranty did not specifically identify who was bound, referring only to "the undersigned" or "Guarantor." Riviera also signed the lease in a representative capacity, but the lease clearly indicated that only Tony Maroni's was bound by its terms. When Tony Maroni's defaulted on the lease, Wilson filed a suit in a Washington state court against Tony Maroni's, Riviera, and others. Riviera asserted in part that he was not personally liable on the guaranty because he signed only in his capacity as a corporate officer. The court issued a summary judgment in favor of Wilson. Riviera appealed to the Washington Supreme Court.*

IN THE LANGUAGE OF THE COURT

TALMADGE, Justice.

* * * *

* * * [The] combination of circumstances [in this case] renders the Guaranty ambiguous.

In construing the Guaranty in light of this ambiguity, we acknowledge contracts to answer for the debt of another must be explicit and are strictly construed, but we must also recognize the commercial context in which this Guaranty was signed. Where two commercial entities sign a commercial agreement, we will give such an agreement a commercially reasonable construction. In this case, such a construction leads us to the conclusion Riviera is personally liable on the Guaranty as a matter of law.

First, any ambiguity in the Guaranty was created by Riviera himself in adding the descriptive language to his signature. *Such ambiguity will be construed against Riviera as the party who drafted this language.* [Emphasis added.]

Second, the language of the Guaranty itself compels the view Riviera is personally liable. We must interpret the Lease and Guaranty as a whole, giving reasonable effect to each of its parts. The plain language of the Guaranty clearly contemplates three separate entities, the Landlord, the Tenant and the Guarantor, and so designates them. It identifies Wilson as the Landlord, Tony Maroni's as the Tenant, and addresses the obligations of a separate third party, referred to interchangeably as the undersigned or Guarantor. * * * The only reasonable interpretation of these provisions is that the Landlord, Tenant and undersigned/Guarantor are three separate and distinct entities. If Riviera signed the Guaranty only in his representative capacity, Tony Maroni's would be both Tenant and Guarantor, rendering the Guaranty provisions absurd. * * *

Moreover, the Guaranty language stands in stark contrast to the language of the Lease where a corporate obligation was unambiguously contemplated. Riviera signed the Lease as president of Tony Maroni's to bind the company. No such intent can be gleaned from the Guaranty. * * *

Third, the very nature of a guaranty is such that Riviera created personal liability by his signature. * * *

* * * *

Riviera is an experienced businessperson with prior experience in commercial leasing who dealt directly with Wilson in securing the Lease. There is no evidence or assertion of any improper conduct by Wilson. Given the commercial sophistication of the parties, the circumstances under which the Guaranty was entered into, and the nature of the Guaranty, a commercially reasonable approach to this case requires us * * * to hold Riviera personally liable under the Guaranty.

DECISION AND REMEDY

The Washington Supreme Court affirmed the judgment of the lower court. The president was personally liable because otherwise the corporation would be the guarantor of its own lease. This would be commercially unreasonable because, as a matter of law, a party cannot be the guarantor of its own contract.

DEFENSES OF THE SURETY AND THE GUARANTOR

The defenses of the surety and the guarantor are basically the same. Therefore, the following discussion applies to both, although it refers only to the surety.

Actions Releasing the Surety. Certain actions will release the surety from the obligation. For example, making any material modification in the terms of the original contract between the principal debtor and the creditor, including the awarding of a binding extension of time for making payment, without first obtaining the consent of the surety will discharge a gratuitous surety (one who receives no consideration in return for acting as a surety) completely and a surety who is compensated to the extent that the surety suffers a loss.

Naturally, if the principal obligation is paid by the debtor or by another person on behalf of the debtor, the surety is discharged from the obligation. Similarly, if valid tender of payment is made, and the creditor for some reason rejects it with knowledge of the surety's existence, then the surety is released from any obligation on the debt.

Defenses of the Principal Debtor. Generally, any defenses available to a principal debtor can be used by the surety to avoid liability on the obligation to the creditor. Defenses available to the principal debtor that the surety *cannot* use include the principal debtor's incapacity or bankruptcy and the statute of limitations. The ability of the surety to assert any defenses the debtor may have against the creditor is the most important concept in suretyship, because most of the defenses available to the surety are also those of the debtor.

Surrender or Impairment of Collateral. In addition, if a creditor surrenders or impairs the debtor's collateral while knowing of the surety and without the surety's consent, the surety is released to the extent of any loss suffered from the creditor's actions. The primary reason for this is to protect the surety who agreed to become obligated only because the debtor's collateral was in the possession of the creditor.

Other Defenses. Obviously, a surety may also have his or her own defenses—for example, incapacity or bankruptcy. If the creditor fraudulently induced the surety to guarantee the debt, the surety can assert fraud as a defense. In most states, the creditor has a legal duty to inform the surety, prior to the formation of the suretyship contract, of material facts known by the creditor that would substantially increase the surety's risk. Failure to so inform is fraud and makes the suretyship obligation voidable.

RIGHTS OF THE SURETY AND THE GUARANTOR

The rights of the surety and the guarantor are basically the same. Therefore, again, the following discussion applies to both.

The Right of Subrogation. When the surety pays the debt owed to the creditor, the surety is entitled to certain rights. First, the surety has the legal **right of subrogation**. Simply stated, this means that any right the creditor had against the debtor now becomes the right of the surety. Included are creditor rights in bankruptcy, rights to collateral possessed by the creditor, and rights to judgments secured by the creditor. In short, the surety now stands in the shoes of the creditor and may pursue any remedies that were available to the creditor against the debtor.

The Right of Reimbursement. Second, the surety has a right to be reimbursed by the debtor. This **right of reimbursement** may stem either from the suretyship contract or from equity. Basically, the surety is entitled to receive from the debtor all outlays made on behalf of the suretyship arrangement. Such outlays can include expenses incurred, as well as the actual amount of the debt paid to the creditor.

The Right of Contribution. Third, in the case of **co-sureties** (two or more sureties on the same obligation owed by the debtor), the **right of contribution** allows a surety who pays more than his or her proportionate share on a debtor's default to recover from the co-sureties the amount paid above the surety's obligation. Generally, a co-surety's liability either is determined by agreement or, in the absence of agreement, is set at the maximum liability under the suretyship contract.

For example, assume that two co-sureties are obligated under a suretyship contract to guarantee the debt of a debtor. Together, the sureties' maximum liability is $25,000. Surety A's maximum liability is $15,000, and surety B's is $10,000. The debtor owes $10,000 and is in default. Surety A pays the creditor the entire $10,000. In the absence of agreement, surety A can recover $4,000 from surety B ($10,000/$25,000 × $10,000 = $4,000, surety B's obligation).

SECTION 3

Protection for Debtors

The law protects debtors, as well as creditors. Certain property of the debtor, for example, is exempt from creditors' actions. Consumer protection statutes also protect debtors' rights. Of course, bankruptcy laws, which will be discussed in the next chapter, are designed specifically to assist debtors in need of help.

EXEMPTIONS

In most states, certain types of real and personal property are exempt from levy of execution or attachment. Probably the most familiar of these exemptions is the **homestead exemption.** Each state permits the debtor to retain the family home, either in its entirety or up to a specified dollar amount, free from the claims of unsecured creditors or trustees in bankruptcy. The purpose is to ensure that the debtor will retain some form of shelter.   *Texas*

Suppose that Beere owes Veltman $40,000. The debt is the subject of a lawsuit, and the court awards Veltman a judgment of $40,000 against Beere. Beere's homestead is valued at $50,000, and the homestead exemption is $25,000. There are no outstanding mortgages or other liens on his homestead. To satisfy the judgment debt, Beere's family home is sold at public auction for $45,000. The proceeds of the sale are distributed as follows:

1. Beere is given $25,000 as his homestead exemption.
2. Veltman is paid $20,000 toward the judgment debt, leaving a $20,000 deficiency judgment (that is, "leftover debt") that can be satisfied from any other nonexempt property (personal or real) that Beere may have, if allowed by state law.

In a few states, statutes permit the homestead exemption only if the judgment debtor has a family. The policy behind this type of statute is to protect the family. If a judgment debtor does not have a family, a creditor may be entitled to collect the full amount realized from the sale of the debtor's home.

State exemption statutes usually include both real and personal property. Personal property that is most often exempt from satisfaction of judgment debts includes the following:

1. Household furniture up to a specified dollar amount.
2. Clothing and certain personal possessions, such as family pictures or a Bible.
3. A vehicle (or vehicles) for transportation (at least up to a specified dollar amount).
4. Certain classified animals, usually livestock but including pets.
5. Equipment that the debtor uses in a business or trade, such as tools or professional instruments, up to a specified dollar amount.

SPECIAL PROTECTION FOR CONSUMER-DEBTORS

Numerous consumer protection statutes and rules apply to debtor-creditor relationships involving **consumer-debtors** (defined as those whose debts are primarily consumer debts). We have already discussed the Federal Trade Commission's rule limiting the rights of a holder in due course (HDC) who holds a negotiable promissory note executed by a debtor-buyer as part of a consumer transaction. This rule, discussed in Chapter 26, provides basically that any personal defenses that the buyer can assert against the seller can also be asserted against an HDC. The seller must disclose this information clearly on the sales agreement.

Other laws regulating debtor-creditor relationships include the Truth-in-Lending Act, which protects consumers by requiring creditors to disclose specific types of information when making loans to consumers. This act, along with other consumer protection statutes, will be discussed in Chapter 44.

TERMS AND CONCEPTS TO REVIEW

artisan's lien 533	consumer-debtor 544	creditors' composition agreement 536
attachment 533	co-surety 540	

QUESTIONS AND CASE PROBLEMS

29–1. LIENS. Sylvia takes her car to Caleb's Auto Repair Shop. A sign in the window states that all repairs must be paid for in cash unless credit is approved in advance. Sylvia and Caleb agree that Caleb will repair Sylvia's car engine and put in a new transmission. No mention is made of credit. Because Caleb is not sure how much engine repair will be necessary, he refuses to give Sylvia an estimate. He repairs the engine and puts in a new transmission. When Sylvia comes to pick up her car, she learns that the bill is $995. Sylvia is furious, refuses to pay Caleb that amount, and demands possession of her car. Caleb demands payment. Discuss the rights of the parties in this matter.

29–2. CREDITORS' REMEDIES. Kanahara is employed by the Cross-Bar Packing Corp. and earns take-home pay of $400 per week. He is $2,000 in debt to the Holiday Department Store for goods purchased on credit over the past eight months. Most of this property is nonexempt and is presently located in Kanahara's apartment. Kanahara is in default on his payments to Holiday. Holiday learns that Kanahara has a girlfriend in another state and that he plans on giving her most of this property for Christmas. Discuss what actions are available and should be taken by Holiday to resolve the debt owed by Kanahara.

29–3. GUARANTY. Natalie is a student at Slippery Stone University. In need of funds to pay for tuition and books, she attempts to secure a short-term loan from West Bank. The bank agrees to make a loan if Natalie will have someone financially responsible guarantee the loan payments. Sheila, a well-known businesswoman and a friend of Natalie's family, calls the bank and agrees to pay the loan if Natalie cannot. Because of Sheila's reputation, the loan is made. Natalie is making the payments, but because of illness she is not able to work for one month. She requests that West Bank extend the loan for three months. West Bank agrees, raising the interest rate for the extended period. Sheila is not notified of the extension (and therefore does not consent to it). One month later Natalie drops out of school. All attempts to collect from Natalie fail. West Bank wants to hold Sheila liable. Discuss West Bank's claim against Sheila.

29–4. CREDITORS' REMEDIES. Grant is the owner of a relatively old home valued at $45,000. He notices that the bathtubs and fixtures in both bathrooms are leaking and need to be replaced. He contracts with Plumber to

replace the bathtubs and fixtures. Plumber replaces them, and on June 1 she submits her bill of $4,000 to Grant. Because of financial difficulties, Grant does not pay the bill. Grant's only asset is his home, which, under state law, is exempt up to $40,000 as a homestead. Discuss fully Plumber's remedies in this situation.

29–5. GARNISHMENT. Harmony Unlimited, Inc., obtained a judgment against John Chivetta and his company, JMC Enterprises. At the time of the judgment, John lacked sufficient funds to pay. Just before Harmony obtained the judgment, John had transferred $126,000 to his mother, Nettie, who had signed a promissory note. The note for $126,000 was payable on demand, carried no interest, and contained a provision that barred John from obtaining a money judgment against his mother. Nettie paid some of John's bills after the transfer of money from her son to her. Harmony served a garnishment summons on Nettie, claiming that she was a party to a fraudulent scheme by her son to conceal his assets and was holding funds that belonged to her son. Nettie argued that Harmony's rights against her could not be any greater than John's rights against her and that because John could not obtain a judgment against her for the money, Harmony could not do so either. Discuss Harmony's right of garnishment against Nettie. [*Harmony Unlimited, Inc. v. Chivetta*, 743 S.W.2d 884 (Mo.App. 1987)]

29–6. RIGHT OF SUBROGATION. Levinson and Johnson, who had both signed a promissory note, did not pay the note when it was due. Instead, American Thermex, Inc., a corporation in which Johnson had a controlling interest, voluntarily paid the note. American Thermex later brought suit against Levinson, seeking reimbursement for the payment. American Thermex argued, among other things, that because it had paid the note, it had the legal right of subrogation against the note's co-maker, Levinson. Will the court agree that American Thermex has a legal right of subrogation? Why or why not? [*Levinson v. American Thermex, Inc.*, 196 Ga.App. 291, 396 S.E.2d 252 (1990)]

29–7. RIGHTS OF THE GUARANTOR. Hallmark Cards, Inc., sued Edward Peevy, who had guaranteed an obligation owed to Hallmark by Garry Peevy. At the time of Edward's guaranty, Hallmark had in its possession property pledged as security by Garry. Before the suit was filed, Hallmark sold the pledged property without notifying Edward and sued Edward for the remaining balance on the debt, seeking a deficiency judgment. Edward contended that because Hallmark had sold the property pledged by Garry as security for the obligation without notifying him (Edward), Hallmark was not entitled to a deficiency judgment against him. Hallmark contended that Edward was not entitled to notice of the sale of the collateral and was not required to give consent. Which party will prevail in court? Discuss. [*Hallmark Cards, Inc. v. Peevy*, 293 Ark. 594, 739 S.W.2d 691 (1987)]

29–8. ARTISAN'S LIEN. Air Ruidoso, Ltd., operated a commuter airline and air charter service between Ruidoso, New Mexico, and airports in Albuquerque and El Paso. Executive Aviation Center, Inc., provided services for airlines at the Albuquerque International Airport. When Air Ruidoso failed to pay more than $10,000 that it owed for fuel, oil, and oxygen, Executive Aviation took possession of Air Ruidoso's plane. Executive Aviation claimed that it had a lien on the plane and filed a suit in a New Mexico state court to foreclose. Do supplies such as fuel, oil, and oxygen qualify as "materials" for the purpose of creating an artisan's lien? Why or why not? [*Air Ruidoso, Ltd. v. Executive Aviation Center, Inc.*, 122 N.M. 71, 920 P.2d 1025 (1996)]

29–9. GUARANTY. In 1988, Jamieson-Chippewa Investment Co. entered into a five-year commercial lease with TDM Pharmacy, Inc., for certain premises in Ellisville, Missouri, on which TDM intended to operate a small drugstore. Dennis and Tereasa McClintock ran the pharmacy business. The lease granted TDM three additional five-year options to renew. The lease was signed by TDM and by the McClintocks individually as guarantors. The lease did not state that the guaranty was continuing. In fact, there were no words of guaranty in the lease other than the single word "Guarantors" on the signature page. In 1993, Dennis McClintock, acting as the president of

TDM, exercised TDM's option to renew the lease for one term. Three years later, when the pharmacy failed, TDM defaulted on the lease. Jamieson-Chippewa filed a suit in a Missouri state court against the McClintocks for the rent for the rest of the term, based on their guaranty. The McClintocks filed a motion for summary judgment, contending that they had not guaranteed any rent payments beyond the initial five-year term. How should the court rule? Why? [*Jamieson-Chippewa Investment Co. v. McClintock*, 996 S.W.2d 84 (Mo.App.E.D. 1999)]

29–10. IN YOUR COURT

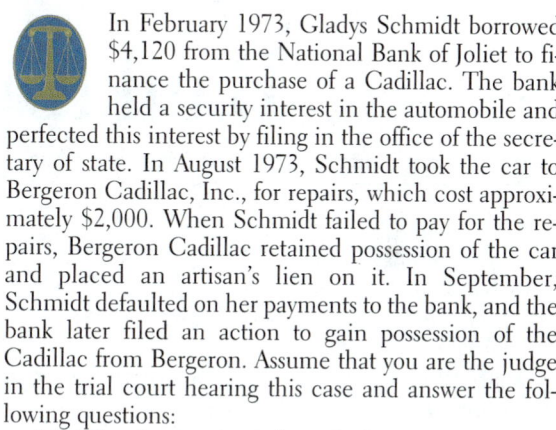

In February 1973, Gladys Schmidt borrowed $4,120 from the National Bank of Joliet to finance the purchase of a Cadillac. The bank held a security interest in the automobile and perfected this interest by filing in the office of the secretary of state. In August 1973, Schmidt took the car to Bergeron Cadillac, Inc., for repairs, which cost approximately $2,000. When Schmidt failed to pay for the repairs, Bergeron Cadillac retained possession of the car and placed an artisan's lien on it. In September, Schmidt defaulted on her payments to the bank, and the bank later filed an action to gain possession of the Cadillac from Bergeron. Assume that you are the judge in the trial court hearing this case and answer the following questions:

(a) What is an artisan's lien? Did Bergeron Cadillac meet the requirements for a valid artisan's lien in this case? Why or why not?

(b) Assuming that Bergeron Cadillac's lien is valid, does it take priority over the bank's title lien on the automobile? What will your ruling be on this issue?

LAW ON THE WEB

For updated links to resources available on the Web, as well as a variety of other materials, visit this text's Web site at http://wbl.westbuslaw.com.

The Legal Information Institute at Cornell University offers a collection of law materials concerning debtor-creditor relationships at

http://www.law.cornell.edu/topics/debtor_creditor.html

For an example of one state's (South Dakota's) laws on garnishment, go to

http://www.state.sd.us/state/legis/lrc/statutes/21/18/211800h.htm

LEGAL RESEARCH EXERCISES ON THE WEB

Go to http://wbl.westbuslaw.com, the Web site that accompanies this text. Select "Internet Applications," and then click on "Chapter 29." There you will find the following Internet research exercise that you can perform to learn more about debtor-creditor relations:

Activity 29–1: Debtor-Creditor Relations

Bankruptcy Law

HISTORICALLY, DEBTORS HAD FEW RIGHTS. Today, in contrast, debtors have numerous rights. Some of these rights were discussed in Chapter 29. In this chapter, we look at another significant right of debtors: the right to petition for bankruptcy relief. This right is established by federal law. Article I, Section 8, of the U.S. Constitution gave Congress the power to establish "uniform Laws on the subject of Bankruptcies throughout the United States."

Bankruptcy law in the United States has two goals to protect a debtor by giving him or her a fresh start, free from creditors' claims, and to ensure equitable treatment to creditors who are competing for a debtor's assets. Federal bankruptcy legislation was first enacted in 1898 and since then has undergone several modifications. Current bankruptcy law is based on the Bankruptcy Reform Act of 1978, as amended—hereinafter called the Bankruptcy Code, or more simply, the Code (not to be confused with the Uniform Commercial Code, which is also sometimes called the Code). Significant changes to the Code were made by the Bankruptcy Reform Act of 1994; we discuss these changes in this chapter. Although bankruptcy law is federal law, state laws on secured transactions, liens, judgments, and exemptions also play a role in federal bankruptcy proceedings.

Bankruptcy proceedings are held in federal bankruptcy courts, which are under the authority of U.S. district courts, and rulings from bankruptcy courts can be appealed to the district courts. Essentially, a bankruptcy court fulfills the role of an administrative court for the federal district court concerning matters in bankruptcy. The bankruptcy court holds proceedings dealing with the procedures required to administer the estate of the debtor in bankruptcy. Bankruptcy court judges are federally appointed. A bankruptcy court can conduct a jury trial if the appropriate district court has authorized it and the parties to the bankruptcy consent.

S E C T I O N   1

Types of Bankruptcy Relief

The Bankruptcy Code is contained in Title 11 of the *United States Code* (U.S.C.) and has eight chapters. Chapters 1, 3, and 5 of the Code include general definitional provisions and provisions governing case administration, creditors, the debtor, and the estate. These three chapters apply generally to all kinds of bankruptcies. The next five chapters of the Code set forth the different types of relief that debtors may seek. Chapter 7 provides for **liquidation** proceedings (the selling of all nonexempt assets and the distribution of the proceeds to the debtor's creditors). Chapter 9 governs the adjustment of debts of a municipality.

Chapter 11 governs reorganizations. Chapters 12 and 13 provide for the adjustment of debts by parties with regular incomes (family farmers under Chapter 12 and individuals under Chapter 13).[1]

To fully inform a consumer-debtor of the various types of relief available, the Code requires that the clerk of the court give all consumer-debtors written notice of each chapter under which they may proceed prior to the commencement of a bankruptcy filing. (Recall from Chapters 28 and 29 that a consumer-debtor is a debtor whose debts result primarily from the purchase of goods for personal, family, or household use.)

In the following sections, we deal first with liquidation proceedings under Chapter 7 of the Code. We then examine the procedures required for Chapter 11 reorganizations and Chapter 12 and 13 plans. The latter three chapters are known as "rehabilitation" chapters.

SECTION 2

Liquidation Proceedings

Liquidation under Chapter 7 of the Bankruptcy Code is generally the most familiar type of bankruptcy proceeding and is often referred to as an *ordinary,* or *straight, bankruptcy*. Put simply, a debtor in a liquidation bankruptcy turns all assets over to a **trustee**. The trustee sells the nonexempt assets and distributes the proceeds to creditors. With certain exceptions, the remaining debts are then **discharged** (extinguished), and the debtors are relieved of their obligation to pay the debts.

Any "person"—defined as including individuals, partnerships, and corporations[2]—may be a debtor in a liquidation proceeding. Railroads, insurance companies, banks, savings and loan associations, investment companies licensed by the Small Business Administration, and credit unions cannot be debtors in a liquidation bankruptcy, however. Rather, other chapters of the Bankruptcy Code or federal or state statutes apply to them.

FILING THE PETITION

A straight bankruptcy may be commenced by the filing of either a voluntary or an involuntary **petition in bankruptcy**—the document that is filed with a bankruptcy court to initiate bankruptcy proceedings.

Voluntary Bankruptcy. When a voluntary petition in bankruptcy is brought by the debtor, he or she files official forms designated for that purpose in the bankruptcy court. The Code requires a consumer-debtor who has opted for liquidation bankruptcy proceedings to state in the petition, at the time of filing, that he or she understands the relief available under other chapters of the Code and has chosen to proceed under Chapter 7. If the consumer-debtor is represented by an attorney, the attorney must file an affidavit stating that he or she has informed the debtor of the relief available under each chapter. A debtor does not have to be insolvent[3] to file for bankruptcy relief. Anyone liable to a creditor can declare bankruptcy.

The voluntary petition contains the following schedules:

1. A list of both secured and unsecured creditors, their addresses, and the amount of debt owed to each.
2. A statement of the financial affairs of the debtor.
3. A list of all property owned by the debtor, including property claimed by the debtor to be exempt.
4. A listing of current income and expenses. (This schedule provides creditors and the court with relevant information on the debtor's ability to pay creditors a reasonable amount from future income. This information could permit a court, on its own motion, to dismiss a debtor's Chapter 7 petition after a hearing and to encourage the filing of a repayment plan under Chapter 13, when that would substantially improve the chances that creditors would be paid.)

The official forms must be completed accurately, sworn to under oath, and signed by the debtor. To conceal assets or knowingly supply false information on these schedules is a crime under the bankruptcy laws. If the voluntary petition for bankruptcy is found to be proper, the filing of the petition will itself constitute an

---

1. There are no Chapters 2, 4, 6, 8, or 10 in Title 11. Such "gaps" are not uncommon in the *United States Code*. This is because chapter numbers (or other subdivisional unit numbers) are sometimes reserved for future use when a statute is enacted. (A gap may also appear if a law has been repealed.)
2. The definition of *corporation* includes unincorporated companies and associations. It also covers labor unions.

3. The inability to pay debts as they become due is known as *equitable* insolvency. A *balance sheet* insolvency, which exists when a debtor's liabilities exceed assets, is not the test. Thus, it is possible for debtors to voluntarily petition for bankruptcy or to be thrown into involuntary bankruptcy even though their assets far exceed their liabilities. This may occur when a debtor's cash flow problems become severe.

order for relief. (An order for relief is a court's grant of assistance to a complainant. In the context of bankruptcy, relief consists of discharging a complainant's debts.) Once a consumer-debtor's voluntary petition has been filed, the clerk of the court or other appointee must give the trustee and creditors mailed notice of the order for relief not more than twenty days after entry of the order. A husband and wife may file jointly for bankruptcy under a single petition.

As mentioned above, debtors do not have to be insolvent to file for voluntary bankruptcy. Debtors do not have unfettered access to bankruptcy proceedings under Chapter 7, however. Section 707(b) of the Bankruptcy Code allows a bankruptcy court to dismiss a petition for relief under Chapter 7 if the granting of relief would constitute "substantial abuse" of Chapter 7. There is no one, uniform standard, or test, for determining what constitutes substantial abuse. In the following case, the court applied the "totality of the circumstances" test to decide whether granting a Chapter 7 discharge to the debtor would constitute substantial abuse.

CASE 30.1   In re Lamanna

United States
Court of Appeals,
First Circuit, 1998.
153 F.3d 1.
http://www.law.emory.
edu/1circuit[a]

BACKGROUND AND FACTS   *In 1996, Richard Lamanna was living with his parents. For this reason, his monthly expenses were only $580. His monthly income was $1,350.96, leaving a difference of $770.96, the amount of his disposable income.[b] He had no plans to move out of his parents' house. During four weeks in October and November, he charged $9,994.45 on credit cards. In February 1997, when his total unsecured debt was $15,911.96, he filed a voluntary petition in a federal bankruptcy court to declare bankruptcy under Chapter 7. The court noted that Lamanna was capable of paying all of his debts under a Chapter 13 repayment plan and dismissed the case. The U.S. Bankruptcy Appellate Panel (BAP) for the First Circuit affirmed the dismissal, and Lamanna appealed to the U.S. Court of Appeals for the First Circuit. Lamanna argued in part that if he did not live with his parents, he would not have as much disposable income, and that thus he was being penalized for living with his parents.*

IN THE LANGUAGE OF THE COURT

LYNCH, Circuit Judge.

* * * * *

The question of whether allowing Lamanna's bankruptcy petition would constitute "substantial abuse" of Chapter 7 under Section 707(b) contains two components: first, the proper test by which "substantial abuse" is measured; second, whether, applying that test, the BAP correctly decided the issue. * * *

* * * * *

* * * Although tests employed by various courts of appeals do not employ precisely the same language, they share common elements. First and foremost, it is agreed that *a consumer debtor's ability to repay his debts out of future disposable income is strong evidence of "substantial abuse."* * * * In determining whether to apply Section 707(b) to an individual debtor, * * * a court should ascertain from the totality of the circumstances whether he is merely seeking an advantage over his creditors, or is "honest," * * * and whether he is "needy" in the sense that his financial predicament warrants the discharge of his debts in exchange for liquidation of his assets. * * * [T]he "totality of the circumstances" test demands a comprehensive review of the debtor's current and potential financial situation. [Emphasis added.]

* * * * *

---

a. This Web site is maintained by Emory University School of Law. In the "Listing by Month of Decision" section, click on "1998 Decisions." On that page, in the "1998 Decisions" list, click on "August." When the list of cases appears, click on the case name to access the opinion.

b. *Disposable income* is income "not reasonably necessary to be expended for the maintenance or support of the debtor or a dependent of the debtor," according to 11 U.S.C. Section 1325(b)(2).

Applying the "totality of the circumstances" test to Lamanna's case results in affirmance of the dismissal of his Chapter 7 petition for "substantial abuse." Lamanna's schedules showed that he has sufficient disposable income to repay his debts under a Chapter 13 repayment plan in three to five years. There is no evidence that Lamanna's living situation was unstable or likely to change in the near future. There is no evidence of other factors that cast doubt on the stability of Lamanna's future income and expenses. Although Lamanna's expenses are particularly low because he lives with his parents, this state of affairs, as the BAP noted, "is not artificial; it is actual." The court properly based its decision on the current and foreseeable facts. If Lamanna's circumstances dramatically change, he is free to seek relief anew.

Lamanna's argument that the court penalized him for living with his parents (and thus having exceptionally low monthly expenses) boils down to the notion that Section 707 requires the bankruptcy court to impute a minimum cost of living to a debtor and then measure the debtor's actual income against the higher of the imputed minimum and the debtor's actual expenses. Section 707 does not contain such an implicit requirement, and this court will not write such a requirement into the statute.

DECISION AND REMEDY	*The U.S. Court of Appeals for the First Circuit affirmed the decision of the lower court and held that granting Lamanna's petition would constitute substantial abuse of Chapter 7. The appellate court looked at the "totality of the circumstances" to reach its conclusion.*

Involuntary Bankruptcy. An involuntary bankruptcy occurs when the debtor's creditors force the debtor into bankruptcy proceedings. An involuntary case cannot be commenced against a farmer[4] or a charitable institution. For an involuntary action to be filed against other debtors, the following requirements must be met: If the debtor has twelve or more creditors, three or more of these creditors having unsecured claims totaling at least $10,775 must join in the petition. If a debtor has fewer than twelve creditors, one or more creditors having a claim of $10,775 may file.

If the debtor challenges the involuntary petition, a hearing will be held, and the bankruptcy court will enter an order for relief if it finds either of the following:

1. The debtor is generally not paying debts as they become due.
2. A general receiver, assignee, or custodian took possession of, or was appointed to take charge of, substantially all of the debtor's property within 120 days before the filing of the petition.

If the court grants an order for relief, the debtor will be required to supply the same information in the bankruptcy schedules as in a voluntary bankruptcy.

An involuntary petition should not be used as an everyday debt-collection device, and the Code provides penalties for the filing of frivolous petitions against debtors. Judgment may be granted against the petitioning creditors for the costs and attorneys' fees incurred by the debtor in defending against an involuntary petition that is dismissed by the court. If the petition is filed in bad faith, damages can be awarded for injury to the debtor's reputation. Punitive damages may also be awarded.

AUTOMATIC STAY

The moment a petition, either voluntary or involuntary, is filed, there exists an **automatic stay,** or suspension, of virtually all litigation and other action by creditors against the debtor or the debtor's property. In other words, once a petition has been filed, creditors cannot commence or continue most legal actions, such as foreclosure of liens, execution on judgments, trials, or any action to repossess property in the hands of the debtor. A secured creditor, however, may petition the bankruptcy court for relief from the automatic stay in certain circumstances. Also, the automatic stay does not apply to paternity,

---

4. The definition of *farmer* includes persons who receive more than 80 percent of their gross income from farming operations, such as tilling the soil, dairy farming, ranching, or the production or raising of crops, poultry, or livestock. Corporations and partnerships may qualify under certain conditions.

alimony, maintenance, and support debts, and to certain other actions, such as criminal proceedings, against the debtor. The Code provides that if a creditor knowingly violates the automatic stay (a willful violation), any party injured, including the debtor, is entitled to recover actual damages, costs, and attorneys' fees and may be entitled to recover punitive damages as well.

Underlying the Code's automatic stay provision for a secured creditor is a concept known as *adequate protection*. The **adequate protection doctrine**, among other things, protects secured creditors from losing their security as a result of the automatic stay. The bankruptcy court can provide adequate protection by requiring the debtor or trustee to make periodic cash payments or a one-time cash payment (or to provide additional collateral or replacement liens) to the extent that the stay may actually cause the value of the property to decrease. Or the court may grant other relief that is the "indubitable equivalent" of (that is, equivalent to, without any doubt) the secured party's interest in the property, such as a guaranty by a solvent third party to cover losses suffered by the secured party as a result of the stay.

PROPERTY OF THE ESTATE

On the commencement of a liquidation proceeding under Chapter 7, an *estate in property* is created. The estate consists of all the debtor's legal and equitable interests in property presently held, wherever located, together with community property, property transferred in a transaction voidable by the trustee, proceeds and profits from the property of the estate, and certain after-acquired property. Interests in certain property—such as gifts, inheritances, property settlements (divorce), and life insurance death proceeds—to which the debtor becomes entitled *within 180 days after filing* may also become part of the estate. Thus, the filing of a bankruptcy petition generally fixes a dividing line: property acquired prior to the filing of the petition becomes property of the estate, and property acquired after the filing of the petition, except as just noted, remains the debtor's.

The issue in the following case was whether payments made under a covenant not to compete should be included in a debtor's estate. The covenant was entered into before the petition was filed, but the payments were due after the filing.

CASE 30.2   In re Andrews

United States
Court of Appeals,
Fourth Circuit, 1996.
80 F.3d 906.
http://www.law.emory.
edu/4circuit/index.
1996.html[a]

COMPANY PROFILE   *John Andrews worked in the ready-mix concrete business most of his life. In 1974, he and various partners formed a ready-mix concrete company in Herndon, Virginia. The company, which ultimately came to be known as AMAX Corporation, grew to be successful, with annual sales of approximately $30 million. By expanding the customer contacts he developed at AMAX, in 1980 Andrews formed a real estate development company, which participated in joint ventures with builders and developers. In 1989, the owners of AMAX began negotiations with Tarmac Acquisition, Inc. (http://www.tarmac.co.uk), for Tarmac's purchase of AMAX. Experts valued the assets at about $9 million. AMAX's customer list, which represented the goodwill of the company, was valued at an additional $1 million.*

BACKGROUND AND FACTS   *Tarmac Acquisition, Inc., bought AMAX Corporation, a ready-mix concrete company. As part of the deal, the AMAX owners, including John Andrews, signed agreements not to compete with Tarmac. Andrews was to receive $1 million, payable in quarterly installments over a five-year period. Three years later, Andrews filed a bankruptcy petition. He asked the federal bankruptcy court not to include, in the property of his estate (which would ultimately be distributed to creditors), any future installments. The court refused, and a federal district court affirmed this decision. Andrews appealed to the U.S. Court of Appeals for the Fourth Circuit.*

a. This Web page, which is part of a Web site maintained by Emory University School of Law, provides access to published opinions of the U.S. Court of Appeals for the Fourth Circuit for 1996. Click on the "April" link. When that page opens, scroll down the list of cases to *Andrews v. Riggs National Bank of Washington*. Click on the case name to access this opinion.

<table>
<tr><td>IN THE LANGUAGE
OF THE COURT</td><td>ELLIS, District Judge:</td></tr>
</table>

IN THE LANGUAGE OF THE COURT

ELLIS, District Judge:

* * * * *

* * * Pre-petition assets, like the NCA [noncompetition agreement] payments, are those assets rooted in the debtor's pre-petition activities, including any proceeds that may flow from those assets in the future. These assets belong to the estate and ultimately to the creditors. Post-petition assets are those that result from the debtor's post-petition activities and are his to keep free and clear of the bankruptcy proceeding. * * * *

Seen in this light, the NCA payments due Andrews fall clearly on the pre-bankruptcy or "past" side of the bright line. These payments are plainly rooted in, and grow out of, Andrews's pre-petition activities. * * * [B]ut for the [AMAX] sale, there would have been no NCA and no quarterly payments to Andrews. * * * Given this close connection between the NCA and the pre-petition sale of the debtor's share in the concrete business, we are persuaded that the payments were well rooted in the pre-bankruptcy past. * * * [T]hey should be included in Andrews's estate.

DECISION AND REMEDY

The U.S. Court of Appeals for the Fourth Circuit affirmed the lower court's decision. Andrews's future installments were to be included in the property of his bankruptcy estate because they were "rooted in the debtor's pre-petition activities."

CREDITORS' MEETING AND CLAIMS

Within a reasonable time after the order for relief has been granted (not less than ten days or more than thirty days), the bankruptcy court must call a meeting of the creditors listed in the schedules filed by the debtor. The bankruptcy judge does not attend this meeting.

The debtor is required to attend the meeting (unless excused by the court) and to submit to examination under oath by the creditors and the trustee. Failing to appear when required or making false statements under oath may result in the debtor's being denied a discharge in bankruptcy. At the meeting, the trustee ensures that the debtor is aware of the potential consequences of bankruptcy and of his or her ability to file for bankruptcy under a different chapter.

To be entitled to receive a portion of the debtor's estate, each creditor must normally file a *proof of claim* with the bankruptcy court clerk within ninety days of the creditors' meeting.[5] The proof of claim lists the creditor's name and address, as well as the amount that the creditor asserts is owed to the creditor by the debtor. If a creditor fails to file a proof of claim, the bankruptcy court or trustee may file the proof of claim on the creditor's behalf but is not obligated to do so.

Generally, any legal obligation of the debtor is a claim. In the case of a disputed, or unliquidated, claim, the bankruptcy court will set the value of the claim. Any creditor holding a debtor's obligation can file a claim against the debtor's estate. These claims are automatically allowed unless contested by the trustee, the debtor, or another creditor. A creditor who files a false claim commits a crime.

The Code, however, does not allow claims for breach of employment contracts or real estate leases for terms longer than one year. Such claims are limited to one year's wages or rent, despite the remaining length of either contract in breach.

EXEMPTIONS

The trustee takes control over the debtor's property, but an individual debtor is entitled to exempt certain property from the bankruptcy. The Bankruptcy Code exempts the following property (the dollar amounts stated in the Bankruptcy Code were adjusted automatically on April 1, 1998, and will be adjusted every three years thereafter based on changes in the Consumer Price Index):[6]

1. Up to $16,150 in equity in the debtor's residence and burial plot (the homestead exemption).

---

5. This ninety-day rule applies in Chapter 12 and Chapter 13 bankruptcies as well.

6. A debtor cannot avoid a judicial lien for paternity, alimony, maintenance, and support debts, however, even if the lien is imposed on exempt property.

2. Interest in a motor vehicle up to $2,575.

3. Interest, up to $425 for a particular item, in household goods and furnishings, wearing apparel, appliances, books, animals, crops, and musical instruments (the aggregate total of all items is limited, however, to $8,625).

4. Interest in jewelry up to $1,750.

5. Interest in any other property up to $850, plus any unused part of the $16,150 homestead exemption up to $8,075.

6. Interest in any tools of the debtor's trade up to $1,625.

7. Any unmatured life insurance contract owned by the debtor.

8. Certain interests in accrued dividends and interest under life insurance contracts owned by the debtor.

9. Professionally prescribed health aids.

10. The right to receive Social Security and certain welfare benefits, alimony and support, and certain pension benefits.

11. The right to receive certain personal injury and other awards up to $16,150.

Individual states have the power to pass legislation precluding debtors from using the federal exemptions within the state; a majority of the states have done this (see Chapter 29). In those states, debtors may use only state, not federal, exemptions. In the rest of the states, an individual debtor (or a husband and wife filing jointly) may choose either the exemptions provided under state law or the federal exemptions.[7] TX

THE TRUSTEE

Promptly after the order for relief in the liquidation proceeding has been entered, an interim, or provisional, trustee is appointed by the **U.S. Trustee** (a government official who performs appointing and other administrative tasks that a bankruptcy judge would otherwise have to perform). The interim, or provisional, trustee presides over the debtor's property until the first meeting of the creditors. At this first meeting, either a permanent trustee is elected or the interim trustee becomes the permanent trustee.

The basic duty of the trustee is to collect the debtor's available estate and reduce it to money for distribution, preserving the interests of both the debtor and unsecured creditors. This requires that the trustee be accountable for administering the debtor's estate. To enable the trustee to accomplish this duty, the Code gives the trustee certain powers, stated in both general and specific terms. These powers must be exercised within two years of the order for relief.

Trustee's Powers. The general powers of the trustee are described by the statement that the trustee occupies a position *equivalent* in rights to that of certain other parties. For example, the trustee has the same rights as a *lien creditor* who could have obtained a judicial lien on the debtor's property or who could have levied execution on the debtor's property. This means that a trustee has priority over an unperfected secured party to the debtor's property. This right of a trustee, equivalent to that of a lien creditor, is known as the *strong-arm power*. A trustee also has power equivalent to that of a *bona fide purchaser* of real property from the debtor.

Nevertheless, in most states a creditor with a purchase-money security interest may prevail against a trustee, if the creditor files within ten days (twenty days, in many states) of the debtor's receipt of the collateral, even if the bankruptcy petition is filed before the creditor perfects. For example, Baker loaned Newbury $20,000 on January 1, taking a security interest in the machinery that Newbury purchased with the $20,000 and that was delivered on that same date. On January 27, before Baker had perfected her security interest, Newbury filed for bankruptcy. The trustee can invalidate Baker's security interest, because it was unperfected when Newbury filed the bankruptcy petition. Baker can only assert a claim as an unsecured creditor. But if Newbury had filed for bankruptcy on January 7, and Baker had perfected her security interest on January 8, she would have prevailed, because she would have perfected her purchase-money security interest within ten days of Newbury's receipt of the machinery.

The trustee has the power to require persons holding the debtor's property at the time the petition is filed to deliver the property to the trustee. (A trustee usually does not take actual possession of a debtor's property. Instead, a trustee's possession is constructive. For example, to obtain control of a debtor's business

---

7. State exemptions may or may not be limited with regard to value. Under state exemption laws, a debtor may enjoy an unlimited value exemption on a motor vehicle, for example, even though the federal bankruptcy scheme exempts a vehicle only up to a value of $2,575. A state's law may also define the property coming within an exemption differently than the federal law or may exclude, or except, specific things from an exemption, making it unavailable to a debtor who fits within the exception.

inventory, a trustee might change the locks on the doors to the business and hire a security guard.) The trustee also has specific powers of *"avoidance"*—that is, the trustee can set aside a sale or other transfer of the debtor's property, taking it back as a part of the debtor's estate. These powers include any voidable rights available to the debtor, preferences, certain statutory liens, and fraudulent transfers by the debtor. Each of these powers is discussed in more detail below.

The debtor shares most of the trustee's avoidance powers. Thus, if the trustee does not take action to enforce one of his or her rights (for example, to recover a preference), the debtor in a liquidation bankruptcy can nevertheless enforce that right.[8]

Voidable Rights. A trustee steps into the shoes of the debtor. Thus, any reason that a debtor can use to obtain the return of his or her property can be used by the trustee as well. These grounds include fraud, duress, incapacity, and mutual mistake.

For example, Ben sells his boat to Tara. Tara gives Ben a check, knowing that there are insufficient funds in her bank account to cover the check. Tara has committed fraud. Ben has the right to avoid that transfer and recover the boat from Tara. Once an order for relief under Chapter 7 of the Code has been entered for Ben, the trustee can exercise the same right to recover the boat from Tara, and the boat becomes a part of the debtor's estate.

Preferences. A debtor is not permitted to transfer property or to make a payment that favors—or gives a preference to—one creditor over others. The trustee is allowed to recover payments made both voluntarily and involuntarily to one creditor in preference over another.

To have made a preferential payment that can be recovered, an *insolvent* debtor generally must have transferred property, for a *preexisting* debt, within *ninety days* of the filing of the petition in bankruptcy. The transfer must give the creditor more than the creditor would have received as a result of the bankruptcy proceedings. The trustee does not have to prove insolvency, as the Code provides that the debtor is presumed to be insolvent during this ninety-day period.

Sometimes the creditor receiving the preference is an **insider**—an individual, a partner, a partnership, a

corporation, or an officer or a director of a corporation (or a relative of one of these) who has a close relationship with the debtor. If this is the situation, the avoidance power of the trustee is extended to transfers made within *one year* before filing; however, the *presumption* of insolvency is confined to the ninety-day period. Therefore, the trustee must prove that the debtor was insolvent at the time of a transfer that occurred prior to the ninety-day period.

Not all transfers are preferences. To be a preference, the transfer must be made for something other than current consideration. Therefore, it is generally assumed by most courts that payment for services rendered within ten to fifteen days prior to the payment of the current consideration is not a preference. If a creditor receives payment in the ordinary course of business, such as payment of last month's telephone bill, the payment cannot be recovered by the trustee in bankruptcy. To be recoverable, a preference must be a transfer for an antecedent (preexisting) debt, such as a year-old printing bill. In addition, the Code permits a consumer-debtor to transfer any property to a creditor up to a total value of $600, without the transfer's constituting a preference. Also, payment of paternity, alimony, maintenance, and support debts is not a preference.

If a preferred creditor has sold the property to an innocent third party, the trustee cannot recover the property from the innocent party. The creditor, however, generally can be held accountable for the value of the property.

Liens on Debtor's Property. The trustee has the power to avoid certain statutory liens against the debtor's property, such as a landlord's lien for unpaid rent. The trustee can avoid statutory liens that first became effective against the debtor when the bankruptcy petition was filed or when the debtor became insolvent. The trustee can also avoid any lien against a bona fide purchaser that was not perfected or enforceable on the date of the bankruptcy filing.

Fraudulent Transfers. The trustee may avoid fraudulent transfers or obligations if they are made within one year of the filing of the petition or if they are made with actual intent to hinder, delay, or defraud a creditor. Transfers made for less than a reasonably equivalent consideration are also vulnerable if by making them, the debtor became insolvent, was left engaged in business with an unreasonably small amount of capital, or intended to incur debts that he

---

8. Under Chapter 11 (to be discussed later), for which no trustee other than the debtor generally exists, the debtor has the same avoidance powers as a trustee under Chapter 7. Under Chapters 12 and 13 (also to be discussed later), a trustee must be appointed.

or she could not pay. When a fraudulent transfer is made outside the Code's one-year limit, creditors may seek alternative relief under state laws. State laws often allow creditors to recover for transfers made up to three years prior to the filing of a petition.

DISTRIBUTION OF PROPERTY

The rights of perfected secured creditors were discussed in Chapter 28. The Code provides that a consumer-debtor, either within thirty days of filing a liquidation petition or before the date of the first meeting of the creditors (whichever is first), must file with the clerk a statement of intention with respect to the secured collateral. The statement must indicate whether the debtor will retain the collateral or surrender it to the secured party.[9] The trustee is obligated to enforce the debtor's statement within forty-five days after it is filed.

If the collateral is surrendered to the perfected secured party, the secured creditor can enforce the security interest either by accepting the property in full satisfaction of the debt or by foreclosing on the collateral and using the proceeds to pay off the debt. Thus, the perfected secured party has priority over unsecured parties as to the proceeds from the disposition of the collateral. Indeed, the Code provides that if the value of the collateral exceeds the perfected secured party's claim and if the security agreement so provides, the secured party also has priority as to the proceeds in an amount that will cover reasonable fees and costs incurred because of the debtor's default. Fees include reasonable attorneys' fees. Any excess over this amount is used by the trustee to satisfy the claims of unsecured creditors. Should the collateral be insufficient to cover the secured debt owed, the secured creditor becomes an unsecured creditor for the difference.

Bankruptcy law establishes an order of priority for classes of debts owed to unsecured creditors, and they are paid in the order of their priority. Each class must be fully paid before the next class is entitled to any of the remaining proceeds. If there are insufficient proceeds to pay fully all the creditors in a class, the proceeds are distributed *proportionately* to the creditors in the class, and classes lower in priority

receive nothing. The order of priority among classes of unsecured creditors is as follows:

1. Administrative expenses—including court costs, trustee fees, and attorneys' fees.
2. In an involuntary bankruptcy, expenses incurred by the debtor in the ordinary course of business from the date of the filing of the petition up to the appointment of the trustee or the issuance by the court of an order for relief.
3. Unpaid wages, salaries, and commissions earned within ninety days of the filing of the petition, limited to $4,300 per claimant. Any claim in excess of $4,300 or earned before the ninety-day period is treated as a claim of a general creditor (listed as item 9 below).
4. Unsecured claims for contributions to be made to employee benefit plans, limited to services performed during 180 days prior to the filing of the bankruptcy petition and $4,300 per employee.
5. Claims by farmers and fishers, up to $4,300, against debtor operators of grain storage or fish storage or processing facilities.
6. Consumer deposits of up to $1,950 given to the debtor before the petition was filed in connection with the purchase, lease, or rental of property or purchase of services that were not received or provided. Any claim in excess of $1,950 is treated as a claim of a general creditor (listed as item 9 below).
7. Paternity, alimony, maintenance, and support debts.
8. Certain taxes and penalties due to government units, such as income and property taxes.
9. Claims of general creditors.

If any amount remains after the priority classes of creditors have been satisfied, it is turned over to the debtor. Exhibit 30–1 illustrates graphically the collection and distribution of property in most voluntary bankruptcies.

In a bankruptcy case in which the debtor has no assets,[10] creditors are notified of the debtor's petition for bankruptcy but are instructed not to file a claim. In such a case, the unsecured creditors will receive no payment, and most, if not all, of these debts will be discharged.

DISCHARGE

From the debtor's point of view, the primary purpose of liquidation is to obtain a fresh start through a discharge

---

9. Also, if applicable, the debtor must specify whether the collateral will be claimed as exempt property and whether the debtor intends to redeem the property or reaffirm the debt secured by the collateral (the reaffirmation of debts will be discussed shortly).

---

10. This type of bankruptcy is called a "no asset" case.

EXHIBIT 30–1 COLLECTION AND DISTRIBUTION OF PROPERTY IN MOST VOLUNTARY BANKRUPTCIES

This exhibit illustrates the property that might be collected in a debtor's voluntary bankruptcy and how it might be distributed to creditors. Involuntary bankrupcies and some voluntary bankruptcies could include additional types of property and other creditors.

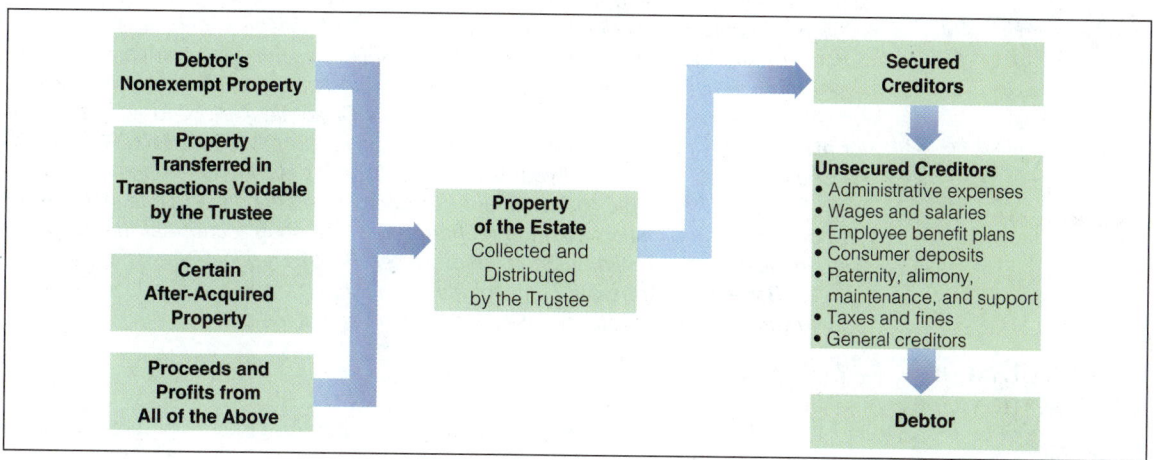

of debts.[11] Certain debts, however, are not dischargeable in bankruptcy. Also, certain debtors may not qualify to have all debts discharged in bankruptcy. These situations are discussed below.

Exceptions to Discharge. Discharge of a debt may be denied because of the nature of the claim or the conduct of the debtor. Claims that are not dischargeable in a liquidation bankruptcy include the following:

1. Claims for back taxes accruing within three years prior to bankruptcy.

2. Claims for amounts borrowed by the debtor to pay federal taxes.

3. Claims against property or money obtained by the debtor under false pretenses or by false representations.

4. Claims by creditors who were not notified and did not know of the bankruptcy; these claims did not appear on the schedules the debtor was required to file.

5. Claims based on fraud or misuse of funds by the debtor while he or she was acting in a fiduciary capacity or claims involving the debtor's embezzlement or larceny.

6. Alimony, child support, and (with certain exceptions) property settlements.

7. Claims based on willful or malicious conduct by the debtor toward another or the property of another.

8. Certain government fines and penalties.

9. Certain student loans, unless payment of the loans imposes an undue hardship on the debtor and the debtor's dependents.

10. Consumer debts of more than $1,075 for luxury goods or services owed to a single creditor incurred within sixty days of the order for relief. This denial of discharge is a rebuttable presumption (that is, the denial may be challenged by the debtor), however, and any debts reasonably incurred to support the debtor or dependents are not classified as luxuries.

11. Cash advances totaling more than $1,075 that are extensions of open-end consumer credit obtained by the debtor within sixty days of the order for relief. A denial of discharge of these debts is also a rebuttable presumption.

12. Judgments or consent decrees against a debtor as a result of the debtor's operation of a motor vehicle while intoxicated.

In the following case, a debtor sought to have his obligation to pay half of the college expenses for his sons discharged in bankruptcy.

---

11. Discharges are granted under Chapter 7 only to individuals, not to corporations or partnerships. The latter may use Chapter 11, or they may terminate their existence under state law.

CASE 30.3   In re Seixas

United States
Bankruptcy Appellate
Panel,
Ninth Circuit, 1999.
239 Bankr. 398.

BACKGROUND AND FACTS   *Michael Seixas and Marsha Booth were married in November 1967 and separated in February 1982. At the time of the separation, they had two boys, ages eight and four. As part of the marital settlement, Seixas agreed, in the "College Education Provision," to pay half of the boys' college expenses. Both parties agreed to carry life insurance with the boys as beneficiaries until they graduated from college or turned twenty-three. Seixas failed to pay his share of the college expenses, so Booth paid the entire cost and then filed a suit in a California state court against Seixas for reimbursement of his half. The court ordered Seixas to pay Booth $10,263.01 of the college expenses. Less than a year later, Seixas filed a petition in a federal bankruptcy court to declare bankruptcy under Chapter 7. Booth asked the court to rule that Seixas's college-expense obligation was nondischargeable. The court found that the obligation was "in the nature of [child] support" and granted Booth's request. Seixas appealed to the U.S. Bankruptcy Appellate Panel for the Ninth Circuit, arguing in part that he had no duty to support his children once they reached the age of majority.*

IN THE LANGUAGE OF THE COURT

RYAN, Bankruptcy Judge.

*   *   *   *

[11 U.S.C.] Section 523(a)(5) excepts from discharge any child support obligation resulting from a separation or divorce agreement. *   *   *

*   *   *   *

*   *   * [A] parent's obligation to pay a child's college education expenses pursuant to a settlement agreement or court order may be nondischargeable under Section 523(a)(5) even though the parent does not have any legal duty to support a child once that child reaches the age of majority under applicable state law. *Because Congress did not limit the word "child" by prefacing it with the word "minor," Section 523(a)(5) allows for the nondischargeability of certain support obligations owed to children even after they have reached the age of majority.* *   *   * [Emphasis added.]

*   *   *   *

The intent of the parties and the substance of the obligation are the touchstone of the Section 523(a)(5) analysis *   *   * . Thus, we look at the surrounding circumstances and all other relevant incidents bearing on the parties' intent to determine whether the parties intended a particular obligation to be in the nature of child support.

*   *   *   *

*   *   * The plain language of the College Education Provision is unambiguous with respect to the parents' contractual obligation to provide for their children's college education expenses and reflects the parties' intent to equally share those expenses. Also, because no money was set aside for their children and the obligation was of limited duration *   *   * , this factor supports a finding that the provision was in the nature of support. Indeed, as is evidenced from the College Education Provision, the parties were concerned enough to provide life insurance for their children's college education in the event that either spouse died. Booth testified that she and Debtor "wanted to make sure *   *   * that there would be money there for their education." This statement is consistent with the plain language of the College Education Provision.

Accordingly, the bankruptcy court's finding that the parties intended the College Education Provision to provide for the educational support of their children was not clearly erroneous. Consequently, the bankruptcy court did not err in determining that Debtor's obligation to pay one half of his children's education expenses was "in the nature of support," and thus, nondischargeable under Section 523(a)(5).

DECISION AND REMEDY   *The U.S. Bankruptcy Appellate Panel for the Ninth Circuit affirmed the judgment of the lower court. The debtor's obligation to pay half of his sons' college expenses was nondischargeable. Support obligations owed to children may include educational expenses if, at the time the obligations are agreed to, the parties intend this.*

Objections to Discharge. In addition to the exceptions to discharge previously listed, a bankruptcy court may also deny the discharge of the *debtor* (as opposed to the debt). In the latter situation, the assets of the debtor are still distributed to the creditors, but the debtor remains liable for the unpaid portion of all claims. Some grounds for the denial of discharge of the debtor are the following:

1. The debtor's concealment or destruction of property with the intent to hinder, delay, or defraud a creditor.
2. The debtor's fraudulent concealment or destruction of financial records.
3. The granting of a discharge to the debtor within six years of the filing of the petition.

Effect of Discharge. The primary effect of a discharge is to void any judgment on a discharged debt and enjoin any action to collect a discharged debt. A discharge does not affect the liability of a co-debtor.

Revocation of Discharge. The Code provides that a debtor may lose his or her bankruptcy discharge by revocation on petition by the trustee or a creditor. The bankruptcy court may, within one year, revoke the discharge decree if it is discovered that the debtor acted fraudulently or dishonestly during the bankruptcy proceedings. The revocation renders the discharge void, allowing creditors not satisfied by the distribution of the debtor's estate to proceed with their claims against the debtor.

REAFFIRMATION OF DEBT

A debtor may wish to pay a debt—such as, for example, a debt owed to a family member, family doctor, bank, or some other creditor—notwithstanding the fact that the debt could be discharged in bankruptcy. An agreement to pay a debt dischargeable in bankruptcy is called a **reaffirmation agreement.** To be enforceable, reaffirmation agreements must be made before the debtor is granted a discharge. The agreement must be filed with the court. Approval by the court is required unless the debtor's attorney files an affidavit stating that the reaffirmation agreement is voluntarily made, that the debtor understands the consequences of the agreement and of a default under the agreement, and that the agreement will not result in an undue hardship on the debtor or the debtor's family. If court approval is required, a separate hearing will be held.

The agreement must contain a clear and conspicuous statement advising the debtor that reaffirmation is not required. The debtor can rescind, or cancel, the agreement at any time prior to discharge or within sixty days of the filing of the agreement, whichever is *later.* This rescission period must be stated *clearly* and *conspicuously* in the reaffirmation agreement.

SECTION 3

Reorganizations

The type of bankruptcy proceeding used most commonly by corporate debtors is the Chapter 11 reorganization. In a reorganization, the creditors and the debtor formulate a plan under which the debtor pays a portion of his or her debts and is discharged of the remainder. The debtor is allowed to continue in business. Although this type of bankruptcy is commonly a corporate reorganization, any debtors (including individuals but excluding stockbrokers and commodities brokers)[12] who are eligible for Chapter 7 relief are eligible for relief under Chapter 11.[13] In 1994, Congress established a "fast track" Chapter 11 for small-business debtors whose liabilities do not exceed $2 million and who do not own or manage real estate. This permits bankruptcy proceedings without the appointment of committees and can save time and costs.

The same principles that govern the filing of a liquidation petition apply to reorganization proceedings. The case may be brought either voluntarily or involuntarily. The same guidelines govern the entry of the order for relief. The automatic stay and adequate protection provisions are applicable in reorganizations as well.

In some instances, creditors may prefer private, negotiated adjustments of creditor-debtor relations, also known as **workouts,** to bankruptcy proceedings. Often, these out-of-court workouts are much more flexible and thus more conducive to a speedy settlement. Speed is critical, because delay is one of the most costly elements in any bankruptcy proceeding. Another advantage of workouts is that they avoid the various administrative costs of bankruptcy proceedings.

Under Section 305(a) of the Bankruptcy Code, a court, after notice and a hearing, may dismiss or suspend all proceedings in a case at any time if dismissal

---

12. In *Toibb v. Radloff,* 501 U.S. 157, 111 S.Ct. 2197, 115 L.Ed.2d 145 (1991), the United States Supreme Court ruled that a non-business debtor may petition for relief under Chapter 11.
13. In addition, railroads are eligible for Chapter 11 relief.

or suspension would better serve the interests of the creditors. Section 1112 also allows a court, after notice and a hearing, to dismiss a case under reorganization "for cause." Cause includes the absence of a reasonable likelihood of rehabilitation, the inability to effect a plan, and an unreasonable delay by the debtor that is prejudicial to (may harm the interests of) creditors.[14]

DEBTOR IN POSSESSION

On entry of the order for relief, the debtor generally continues to operate the business as a **debtor in possession (DIP).** The court, however, may appoint a trustee (often referred to as a *receiver*) to operate the debtor's business if gross mismanagement of the business is shown or if appointing a trustee is in the best interests of the estate.

The DIP's role is similar to that of a trustee in a liquidation. The DIP is entitled to avoid pre-petition preferential payments made to creditors and pre-petition fraudulent transfers of assets. The DIP has the power to decide whether to cancel or assume pre-petition executory contracts (those that are not yet performed) or unexpired leases.

Under the strong-arm clause[15] of the Bankruptcy Code, a DIP can avoid any obligation or any transfer of property of the debtor that could be avoided by certain parties. These parties include (1) a creditor who extended credit to the debtor at the time of bankruptcy (petition) and who consequently obtained a lien on the debtor's property; (2) a creditor who extended credit to the debtor at the time of bankruptcy and who consequently obtained a writ of execution against the debtor that was returned unsatisfied; and (3) a bona fide purchaser of real property from the debtor, if at the time of the bankruptcy the transfer was perfected.

COLLECTIVE BARGAINING AGREEMENTS

Under the Bankruptcy Reform Act of 1978, questions arose as to whether a reorganization debtor could reject a recently negotiated collectively bargained labor contract. In *National Labor Relations Board v. Bildisco and Bildisco*, the United States Supreme Court held that a collective bargaining agreement subject to the National Labor Relations Act of 1935 (see Chapter 41) is an "executory contract" and thus subject to *rejection* by a debtor in possession.[16] The Court emphasized that such a rejection should not be permitted unless there is a finding that the policy of Chapter 11 (successful rehabilitation of debtors) would be served by the action. Hence, when the bankruptcy court determines that rejection of a collective bargaining agreement should be permitted, it must make a reasoned finding *on the record* as to *why* it has determined that a rejection should be permitted.

The Code attempts to reconcile federal policies favoring collective bargaining with the need to allow a debtor company to reject executory labor contracts while trying to reorganize. The Code sets forth standards and procedures under which collective bargaining contracts can be assumed or rejected under a reorganization filing. In general, a collective bargaining contract can be rejected if the debtor has first proposed necessary contractual modifications to the union and the union has failed to adopt them without *good cause*. The company is required (1) to provide the union with the relevant information needed to evaluate this proposal and (2) to confer in *good faith* in attempting to reach a mutually satisfactory agreement on the modifications.

CREDITORS' COMMITTEES

As soon as practicable after the entry of the order for relief, a creditors' committee of unsecured creditors is appointed. The committee may consult with the trustee or the DIP concerning the administration of the case or the formulation of the plan. Additional creditors' committees may be appointed to represent special interest creditors. Orders affecting the estate generally will be entered only with either the consent of the committee or after a hearing in which the judge hears the position of the committee.

Businesses with debts of less than $2 million that do not own or manage real estate can avoid creditors' committees. In these cases, orders can be entered without a committee's consent.

---

14. See 11 U.S.C. Section 1112(b). Debtors are not prohibited from filing successive petitions, however. A debtor whose petition is dismissed, for example, can file a new Chapter 11 petition (which may be granted unless it is filed in bad faith).

15. 11 U.S.C. Section 544(a).

16. 465 U.S. 513, 104 S.Ct. 1188, 79 L.Ed.2d 482 (1984).

THE REORGANIZATION PLAN

A reorganization plan to rehabilitate the debtor is a plan to conserve and administer the debtor's assets in the hope of an eventual return to successful operation and solvency. The plan must be fair and equitable and must do the following:

1. Designate classes of claims and interests.
2. Specify the treatment to be afforded the classes. (The plan must provide the same treatment for all claims in a particular class.)
3. Provide an adequate means for execution.

Only the debtor may file a plan within the first 120 days after the date of the order for relief. If the debtor does not meet the 120-day deadline, however, or if the debtor fails to obtain the required creditor consent (discussed below) within 180 days, any party may propose a plan. If a small-business debtor chooses to avoid creditors' committees, the time for the debtor's filing is shortened to 100 days, and any other party's plan must be filed within 160 days.

Once the plan has been developed, it is submitted to each class of creditors for acceptance. Each class must accept the plan unless the class is not adversely affected by it. A class has accepted the plan when a majority of the creditors, representing two-thirds of the amount of the total claim, vote to approve it.

Even when all classes of claims accept the plan, the court may refuse to confirm it if it is not "in the best interests of the creditors."[17] A spouse or child of the debtor can block the plan if it does not provide for payment of their claims in cash.

The plan is binding on confirmation. The debtor is given a reorganization discharge from all claims not protected under the plan. This discharge does not apply to any claims that would be denied discharge under liquidation.

Even if only one class of claims has accepted the plan, the court may still confirm the plan under the Code's so-called **cram-down provision.** In other words, the court may confirm the plan over the objections of a class of creditors. Before the court can exercise this right of cram-down confirmation, it must be demonstrated that the plan does not discriminate unfairly against any creditors and that the plan is fair and equitable.

Additional Forms of Bankruptcy Relief

In addition to bankruptcy relief through liquidation and reorganization, the Code also provides for individuals' repayment plans (Chapter 13) and family-farmer debt adjustments (Chapter 12).

INDIVIDUALS' REPAYMENT PLAN

Chapter 13 of the Bankruptcy Code provides for "Adjustment of Debts of an Individual with Regular Income." Individuals (not partnerships or corporations) with regular income who owe fixed unsecured debts of less than $269,250 or fixed secured debts of less than $807,750 may take advantage of bankruptcy repayment plans. This includes salaried employees; sole proprietors; and individuals who live on welfare, Social Security, fixed pensions, or investment income. Many small-business debtors have a choice of filing a plan for reorganization or for repayment. There are several advantages, however, with repayment plans. One advantage is that they are less expensive and less complicated than reorganization proceedings or, for that matter, even liquidation proceedings.

Filing the Petition. A repayment plan case can be initiated only by the filing of a voluntary petition by the debtor. Certain liquidation and reorganization cases may be converted to repayment plan cases with the consent of the debtor.[18] A trustee, who will make payments under the plan, must be appointed. On the filing of a repayment plan petition, the automatic stay previously discussed takes effect. Although the stay applies to all or part of a consumer debt, it does not apply to any business debt incurred by the debtor.

The Repayment Plan. A plan of rehabilitation by repayment must provide for the following:

1. The turnover to the trustee of such future earnings or income of the debtor as is necessary for execution of the plan.

---

17. The plan need not provide for full repayment to unsecured creditors. Instead, creditors receive a percentage of each dollar owed to them by the debtor.

18. A Chapter 13 case may be converted to a Chapter 7 case either at the request of the debtor or, under certain circumstances, "for cause" by a creditor. A Chapter 13 case may be converted to a Chapter 11 case after a hearing.

2. Full payment in deferred cash payments of all claims entitled to priority.[19]

3. The same treatment of all claims within a particular class. (The Code permits the debtor to list co-debtors, such as guarantors or sureties, as a separate class.)

Filing the Plan. Only the debtor may file for a repayment plan. This plan may provide either for payment of all obligations in full or for payment of a lesser amount. The time for payment under the plan may not exceed three years unless the court approves an extension. The term, with extension, may not exceed five years.

The Code requires the debtor to make "timely" payments, and the trustee is required to ensure that the debtor commences these payments. (The debtor must begin making payments under the proposed plan within thirty days after the plan has been *filed*.) If the plan has not been confirmed, the trustee is instructed to retain the payments until the plan is confirmed and then distribute them accordingly. If the plan is denied, the trustee will return the payments to the debtor less any costs. Failure of the debtor to make timely payments or to commence payments within the thirty-day period will allow the court to convert the case to a liquidation bankruptcy or to dismiss the petition.

Confirmation of the Plan. After the plan is filed, the court holds a confirmation hearing, at which interested parties may object to the plan. The court will confirm a plan with respect to each claim of a secured creditor under any of the following circumstances:

1. If the secured creditors have accepted the plan.
2. If the plan provides that creditors retain their liens and if the value of the property to be distributed to them under the plan is not less than the secured portion of their claims.
3. If the debtor surrenders the property securing the claims to the creditors.

Objection to the Plan. Unsecured creditors do not have a vote to confirm a repayment plan, but they can object to it. The court can approve a plan over the objection of the trustee or any unsecured creditor only in either of the following situations:

1. When the value of the property to be distributed under the plan is at least equal to the amount of the claims.
2. When all the debtor's projected disposable income to be received during the three-year plan period will be applied to making payments. Disposable income is all income received less amounts needed to support the debtor and dependents and/or amounts needed to meet ordinary expenses to continue the operation of a business.

Modification of the Plan. Prior to completion of payments, the plan may be modified at the request of the debtor, the trustee, or an unsecured creditor. If there is an objection to the modification by any interested party, the court must hold a hearing to determine approval or disapproval of the modified plan.

Discharge. After completion of all payments, the court grants a discharge of all debts provided for by the repayment plan. Except for allowed claims not provided for by the plan, certain long-term debts provided for by the plan, and claims for alimony and child support, all other debts are dischargeable. A discharge of debts under a Chapter 13 repayment plan is sometimes referred to as a "super-discharge." One of the reasons for this is that the law allows a Chapter 13 discharge to include fraudulently incurred debt and claims resulting from malicious or willful injury. Therefore, a discharge under Chapter 13 may be much more beneficial to some debtors than a liquidation discharge under Chapter 7.

Even if the debtor does not complete the plan, a hardship discharge may be granted if failure to complete the plan was due to circumstances beyond the debtor's control and if the value of the property distributed under the plan was greater than would have been paid in a liquidation. A discharge can be revoked within one year if it was obtained by fraud.

FAMILY FARMERS

In 1986, to help relieve economic pressure on small farmers, Congress created Chapter 12 of the Bankruptcy Code. For purposes of Chapter 12, a *family farmer* is one whose gross income is at least 50 percent farm dependent and whose debts are at least 80 percent farm related. The total debt must not exceed $1.5 million. A partnership or closely held corporation (at least 50 percent owned by the farm family) can also take advantage of this law.

---

19. As with a Chapter 11 reorganization plan, full repayment of all claims is not always required.

The procedure for filing a family-farmer bankruptcy plan is very similar to the procedure for filing a repayment plan under Chapter 13. The farmer-debtor must file a plan not later than ninety days after the order for relief. The filing of the petition acts as an automatic stay against creditors' and co-obligors' actions against the estate.

The content of a family-farmer plan is basically the same as that of a Chapter 13 repayment plan. The plan can be modified by the farmer-debtor but, except for cause, must be confirmed or denied within forty-five days of the filing of the plan.

Court confirmation of the plan is the same as for a repayment plan. In summary, the plan must provide for payment of secured debts at the value of the collateral. If the secured debt exceeds the value of the collateral, the remaining debt is unsecured. For unsecured debtors, the plan must be confirmed if either the value of the property to be distributed under the plan equals the amount of the claim or the plan provides that all of the farmer-debtor's disposable income to be received in a three-year period (or longer, by court approval) will be applied to making payments. Disposable income is all income received less amounts needed to support the farmer-debtor and family and to continue the farming operation. Completion of payments under the plan discharges all debts provided for by the plan.

A farmer who has already filed a reorganization or repayment plan may convert the plan to a family-farmer plan. The farmer-debtor may also convert a family-farmer plan to a liquidation plan.

CONCEPT SUMMARY 30.1   FORMS OF BANKRUPTCY RELIEF COMPARED

ISSUE	CHAPTER 7	CHAPTER 11	CHAPTERS 12 AND 13
Purpose	Liquidation.	Reorganization.	Adjustment.
Who Can Petition	Debtor (voluntary) or creditors (involuntary).	Debtor (voluntary) or creditors (involuntary).	Debtor (voluntary) only.
Who Can Be a Debtor	Any "person" (including partnerships, corporations, and municipalities) except railroads, insurance companies, banks, savings and loan institutions, investment companies licensed by the Small Business Administration, and credit unions. Farmers and charitable institutions also cannot be involuntarily petitioned.	Any debtor eligible for Chapter 7 relief; railroads are also eligible.	*Chapter 12*—Any family farmer (one whose gross income is at least 50 percent farm dependent and whose debts are at least 80 percent farm related) or any partnership or closely held corporation at least 50 percent owned by a farm family, when total debt does not exceed $1.5 million. *Chapter 13*—Any individual (not partnerships or corporations) with regular income who owes fixed unsecured debts of less than $269,250 or fixed secured debts of less than $807,750.

CONCEPT SUMMARY 30.1   FORMS OF BANKRUPTCY RELIEF COMPARED (*continued*)

ISSUE	CHAPTER 7	CHAPTER 11	CHAPTERS 12 AND 13
Procedure Leading to Discharge	Nonexempt property is sold with proceeds to be distributed (in order) to priority groups. Dischargeable debts are terminated.	Plan is submitted; if it is approved and followed, debts are discharged.	Plan is submitted and must be approved if the value of the property to be distributed equals the amount of the claims or if the debtor turns over disposable income for a three-year period; if the plan is followed, debts are discharged.
Advantages	On liquidation and distribution, most debts are discharged, and the debtor has an opportunity for a fresh start.	Debtor continues in business. Creditors can either accept the plan, or it can be "crammed down" on them. The plan allows for the reorganization and liquidation of debts over the plan period.	Debtor continues in business or possession of assets. If the plan is approved, most debts are discharged after a three-year period.

TERMS AND CONCEPTS TO REVIEW

adequate protection doctrine 548	discharge 545	preference 551
automatic stay 547	insider 551	reaffirmation agreement 555
cram-down provision 557	liquidation 544	trustee 545
debtor in possession (DIP) 556	order for relief 546	U.S. Trustee 550
	petition in bankruptcy 545	workout 555

QUESTIONS AND CASE PROBLEMS

30–1. VOLUNTARY VERSUS INVOLUNTARY BANKRUPTCY. Burke has been a rancher all her life, raising cattle and crops. Her ranch is valued at $500,000, almost all of which is exempt under state law. Burke has eight creditors and a total indebtedness of $70,000. Two of her largest creditors are Oman ($30,000 owed) and Sneed ($25,000 owed). The other six creditors have claims of less than $5,000 each. A drought has ruined all of Burke's crops and forced her to sell many of her cattle at a loss. She cannot pay off her creditors.

    (a) Under the Bankruptcy Code, can Burke, with a $500,000 ranch, voluntarily petition herself into bankruptcy? Explain.

    (b) Could either Oman or Sneed force Burke into involuntary bankruptcy? Explain.

30–2. PRIORITY OF CREDITORS. Sam is a retail seller of television sets. He sells Gracen a $900 set on a retail installment security agreement in which she pays $100 down and agrees to pay the balance in equal installments. Sam retains a security interest in the set, and he perfects that interest by filing a financing statement locally. Two months later, Gracen is in default on her payments to Sam and is involuntarily petitioned into bankruptcy by her creditors. Sam wants to repossess the television set, as provided for in the security agreement, and he wants to have priority over the trustee in bankruptcy as to any proceeds from the disposal of the set. Discuss fully Sam's right to repossess and whether he has priority over the trustee in bankruptcy as to any proceeds from the disposal of the set.

30–3. PREFERENCES. Peaslee is not known for his business sense. He started a greenhouse and nursery business two years ago, and because of his lack of experience, he soon was in debt to a number of creditors. On February 1, Peaslee borrowed $5,000 from his father to pay some of these creditors. On May 1, Peaslee paid back the $5,000, depleting his entire working capital. One creditor, the Cool Springs Nursery Supply Corp., extended credit to Peaslee on numerous purchases. Cool Springs pressured Peaslee for payment, and on July 1, Peaslee paid Cool Springs half the money owed. On September 1, Peaslee voluntarily petitioned himself into bankruptcy. The trustee in bankruptcy claimed that both Peaslee's father and Cool Springs must turn over to the debtor's estate the amounts Peaslee paid to them. Discuss fully the trustee's claims.

30–4. DISTRIBUTION OF ASSETS. Montoro petitioned himself into voluntary bankruptcy. There were three major claims against his estate. One was made by Carlton, a friend who held Montoro's negotiable promissory note for $2,500; one was made by Elmer, an employee who was owed three months' back wages of $4,500; and one was made by the United Bank of the Rockies on an unsecured loan of $5,000. In addition, Dietrich, an accountant retained by the trustee, was owed $500, and property taxes of $1,000 were owed to Rock County. Montoro's nonexempt property was liquidated, with proceeds of $5,000. Discuss fully what amount each party will receive, and why.

30–5. DISCHARGE IN BANKRUPTCY. East Bank was a secured party on a $5,000 loan it made to Kirksey. Kirksey experienced financial difficulty, and creditors other than East Bank petitioned her into involuntary bankruptcy. The value of the secured collateral had substantially decreased in value. On its sale, the debt to East Bank was reduced to $2,500. Kirksey's estate consisted of $100,000 in exempt assets and $2,000 in nonexempt assets. After the bankruptcy costs and back wages to Kirksey's employees had been paid, nothing was left for unsecured creditors. Kirksey received a discharge in bankruptcy. Later she decided to go back into business. By selling a few exempt assets and getting a small loan, she would be able to buy a small, but profitable, restaurant. She went to East Bank for the loan. East Bank claimed that the balance of its secured debt had not been discharged in bankruptcy. Kirksey signed an agree-

ment to pay East Bank the $2,500, as the bank had not been a party to petitioning her into bankruptcy. Because of this, East Bank made the new unsecured loan to Kirksey.

(a) Discuss East Bank's claim that the balance of its secured debt had not been discharged in bankruptcy.

(b) Discuss the legal effect of Kirksey's agreement to pay East Bank $2,500 after the discharge in bankruptcy.

(c) If one year after buying the restaurant, Kirksey went into voluntary bankruptcy, what effect would the bankruptcy proceedings have on the new unsecured loan?

30–6. REORGANIZATION. Tracey Service Co. filed a petition for a Chapter 11 reorganization. Acar Supply Co., one of Tracey's creditors, filed a motion to convert the case to a Chapter 7 liquidation. The court found that the debtor corporation had no place of business, no inventory, no equipment, no employees, and no business phone. Should Tracey Service be permitted to reorganize under Chapter 11? Explain. [*In re Tracey Service Co.*, 17 Bankr. 405 (Bankr.E.D.Pa. 1982)]

30–7. PREFERENCES. Fred Currey purchased cattle from Itano Farms, Inc. As payment for the cattle, Currey gave Itano Farms worthless checks in the amount of $50,250. Currey was later convicted of passing bad checks, and the state criminal court ordered him to pay Itano Farms restitution in the amount of $50,250. About four months after this court order, Currey and his wife filed for Chapter 7 bankruptcy protection. During the ninety days prior to the filing of the petition, Currey had made three restitution payments to Itano, totaling $14,821. The Curreys sought to recover these payments as preferences. What should the court decide? Explain. [*In re Currey*, 144 Bankr. 490 (D.Ida. 1992)]

30–8. AUTOMATIC STAY. David Sisco had about $600 in an account in Tinker Federal Credit Union. Sisco owed DPW Employees Credit Union a little more than $1,100. To collect on the debt, DPW obtained a garnishment judgment and served it on Tinker. The next day, Sisco filed a bankruptcy petition. Tinker then told DPW that, because of the bankruptcy filing, it could not pay the garnishment. DPW objected, and Tinker asked an Oklahoma state court to resolve the issue. What effect, if any, does Sisco's bankruptcy filing have on DPW's garnishment action? [*DPW Employees Credit Union v. Tinker Federal Credit Union*, 925 P.2d 93 (Okla.App.4th 1996)]

30–9. VOIDABLE PREFERENCE. The Securities and Exchange Commission (SEC) filed a suit in a federal district court against First Jersey Securities, Inc., and others, alleging fraud in First Jersey's sale of securities (stock). The court ordered the defendants to turn over to the SEC $75 million in illegal profits. This order made the SEC the largest unsecured creditor of First Jersey. First Jersey filed a voluntary petition in a federal bankruptcy court to declare bankruptcy under Chapter 11.

On the same day, the debtor transferred 200,001 shares of stock to its law firm, Robinson, St. John, & Wayne (RSW), in payment for services in the SEC suit and the bankruptcy petition. The stock represented essentially all of the debtor's assets. RSW did not find a buyer for the stock for more than two months. The SEC objected to the transfer, contending that it was a voidable preference, and asked that RSW be disqualified from representing the debtor. RSW responded that the transfer was made in the ordinary course of business. Also, asserted RSW, the transfer was not in payment of an "antecedent debt," because the firm had not presented First Jersey with a bill for its services and therefore the debt was not yet past due. Was the stock transfer a voidable preference? Should the court disqualify RSW? Why or why not? [*In re First Jersey Securities, Inc.*, 180 F.3d 504 (3d Cir. 1999)]

30–10. IN YOUR COURT

Ellis and Bonnie Jarrell filed a Chapter 7 petition. The reason for the filing was not calamity, sudden illness, disability, or unemployment—both Jarrells were employed.

Their petition was full of inaccuracies that understated their income and overstated their obligations. For example, they declared as an expense a monthly contribution to an investment plan. The truth was that they had monthly income of $3,197.45 and expenses of $2,159.44. They were attempting to discharge a total of $15,391.64 in unsecured debts. Most of these were credit-card debts, at least half of which had been taken as cash advances. Assume that you are the judge in the bankruptcy court and answer the following questions:

(a) A key question before you is whether the Jarrells have the ability to pay off their debts in three to five years under a Chapter 13 repayment plan. Can they?

(b) Depending on your answer to the above question, would granting the Jarrells' petition constitute "substantial abuse" of Chapter 7? Explain. (Before making your decision, review the court's opinion in Case 30.1, *In re Lamanna*, on how the courts determine when "substantial abuse" occurs.)

LAW ON THE WEB

For updated links to resources available on the Web, as well as a variety of other materials, visit this text's Web site at http://wbl.westbuslaw.com.

The U.S. Bankruptcy Code is online at

http://www.law.cornell.edu:80/uscode/11

You can find links to an extensive number of bankruptcy resources on the Internet by accessing the Bankruptcy Lawfinder at

http://www.agin.com/lawfind

Another good resource for bankruptcy information is the American Bankruptcy Institute (ABI) at

http://www.abiworld.org

LEGAL RESEARCH EXERCISES ON THE WEB

Go to http://wbl.westbuslaw.com, the Web site that accompanies this text. Select "Internet Applications," and then click on "Chapter 30." There you will find the following Internet research exercises that you can perform to learn more about bankruptcy and its alternatives:

Activity 30–1: Bankruptcy

Activity 30–2: Bankruptcy Alternatives

UNIT FIVE—CUMULATIVE BUSINESS HYPOTHETICAL

Dmitri Peter ("Pete") Darin is president of Southside Equipment Corp., a small electronics store. Darin owns 80 percent of the corporation's shares, and Oliver Castle owns the remaining 20 percent. Business is booming, and Darin and Castle decide to expand their business. To do so, they borrow $50,000 from First Bank and Trust. As collateral for the loan, Southside agrees to give the bank a security interest in all of the firm's current and after-acquired inventory. The bank properly perfects its interest in Southside's collateral by filing a financing statement with the appropriate government office.

1. Southside later obtains a loan from Central Bank, using the same inventory as collateral. Central Bank properly perfects its security interest by filing a financing statement. In a priority contest, which bank will have superior rights to the inventory? If First Bank, on its financial statement, identified the debtor only as "Pete Darin," which creditor will have superior rights to the collateral?

2. Southside is experiencing financial setbacks and defaults on its payments to First Bank. Assuming that First Bank's security interest was properly perfected and that no other creditor has rights in the collateral, what basic remedies are available to First Bank?

3. Suppose that Darin has done business with First Bank for years, and First Bank knows that Darin is a good credit risk. The bank also knows that Darin has substantial personal assets. Instead of taking a security interest in Southside's inventory to secure the $50,000 loan, First Bank asks Darin to promise that if Southside defaults, Darin will personally pay the loan. Is Darin a surety or a guarantor in this situation? Is Darin's liability on the loan primary or secondary? Must Darin's promise be in writing to be enforceable? Explain.

4. Darin is experiencing personal financial problems. The amount of income he receives from the corporation is barely sufficient to cover his living expenses, the payments due on his mortgage, various credit-card debts, and some loans that he took out to pay for his son's college tuition. He would like to file for Chapter 7 liquidation to be rid of the debts entirely, but he knows that he could probably pay them off over a four-year period if he really scrimped and used every cent available to pay his creditors. Darin decides to file for bankruptcy relief under Chapter 7. Are all of Darin's debts dischargeable under Chapter 7, including the debts incurred for his son's education? Given the fact that Darin could foreseeably pay off his debts over a four-year period, will the court allow Darin to obtain relief under Chapter 7? Why or why not?

FOCUS ON LEGAL REASONING
Grupo Mexicano de Desarrollo, S.A. v. Alliance Bond Fund, Inc.

INTRODUCTION

From studying the chapters in this unit, it should be clear that a court can issue an order to stop an owner from transferring assets in which a lien, a security interest, or a creditor's claim in bankruptcy exists. In this *Focus on Legal Reasoning*, we examine *Grupo Mexicano de Desarrollo, S.A. v. Alliance Bond Fund, Inc.*,[1] a decision in which the question was whether a court can issue an injunction to stop the transfer of assets in which no lien is claimed. All of the elements of a dispute between a debtor and a creditor were otherwise present: a debt, a missed payment, a belief that the debtor was on the verge of bankruptcy, and a lawsuit.

CASE BACKGROUND

In the early 1990s, the government of Mexico sponsored a road construction program that involved private investors who agreed to build and operate the roads. Grupo

1. 527 U.S. 308, 119 S.Ct. 1961, 144 L.Ed.2d 319 (1999).

Mexicano de Desarrollo, S.A. (GMD), a Mexican company, was one of the contractors hired by the investors to build the roads. Problems in the Mexican economy resulted in losses for the investors, who were then unable to pay GMD and other contractors. In response, in 1997 the Mexican government announced the Toll Road Rescue Program, under which it issued guaranteed "Toll Road Notes" to the investors, in exchange for their ownership interests in the roads. The Toll Road Notes were used to pay the debts of the investors and to pay the contractors. GMD expected to receive approximately $309 million of the Toll Road Notes.

Meanwhile, in February 1994, GMD, to support its various projects, had issued $250 million of *unsecured* promissory notes due in 2001 and guaranteed by four of its subsidiaries. Interest payments were due in February and August of every year. By mid-1997, however, GMD was in serious financial trouble. As a result, neither GMD nor its subsidiaries made the August 1997 interest payment on the notes.

GMD attempted to negotiate repayments of its debts with all of its creditors, but by December the negotiations with the holders of the notes had failed.

Alliance Bond Fund, Inc., and others who had bought approximately $75 million of the GMD notes filed a suit in a federal district court against GMD and its subsidiaries for the amount due.[2] Among other things, the investors asked the court to issue an injunction, before it heard the case, to stop the defendants from transferring their assets, including the Toll Road Notes, to other creditors. The court issued the order. GMD appealed to the U.S. Court of Appeals for the Second Circuit, which affirmed the lower court's order. GMD appealed to the United States Supreme Court. The parties' arguments focused on the power of federal courts to grant remedies in equity. (Equitable remedies were discussed in Chapters 1 and 18.)

2. GMD consented to the court's exercise of personal jurisdiction. Jurisdiction is discussed in Chapter 2.

MAJORITY OPINION

Justice *SCALIA* delivered the opinion of the Court.
* * * *

* * * [It is contended] that the * * * injunction issued in this case is analogous to the relief obtained [at the time of the adoption of the Constitution] in the equitable action known as a "creditor's bill." This remedy was used (among other purposes) to permit a judgment creditor to discover the debtor's assets, to reach equitable interests not subject to execution at law, and

to set aside fraudulent conveyances [transfers of ownership]. It was well established, however, that, as a general rule, a creditor's bill could be brought only by a creditor who had already obtained a judgment establishing the debt. The rule requiring a judgment was a product, not just of the procedural requirement that remedies at law had to be exhausted before equitable remedies could be pursued, but also of the substantive rule that a general creditor (one without a judgment) had no cognizable interest, either at law or in equity, in the property of his debtor, and therefore could not interfere with the debtor's use of that property. * * *

* * * *

* * * [E]quity is flexible; but in the federal system, at least, that flexibility is confined within the broad boundaries of traditional equitable relief. * * * There is absolutely nothing new about debtors' trying to avoid paying their debts, or seeking to favor some creditors over others—or even about their seeking to achieve these ends through "sophisticated * * * strategies." The law of fraudulent conveyances and bankruptcy was developed to prevent such conduct; an equitable power to restrict a debtor's use of his unencumbered property before judgment was not.

* * * *

* * * The requirement that the creditor obtain a prior judgment is a fundamental protection in debtor-creditor law * * * . [B]y adding, through judicial fiat, a new and powerful weapon to the creditor's arsenal, the new rule could radically alter the balance between debtor's and creditor's rights which has been developed over centuries through many laws—including those relating to bankruptcy, fraudulent conveyances, and preferences. Because any rational creditor would want to protect his investment, such a remedy might induce creditors to engage in a "race to the courthouse" in cases involving insolvent or near-insolvent debtors, which might prove financially fatal to the struggling debtor. * * *

* * * *

Because such a remedy was historically unavailable from a court of equity, we hold that the District Court had no authority to issue [an] * * * injunction preventing petitioners from disposing of their assets pending adjudication of respondents' * * * claim * * * .

DISSENTING OPINION

Justice *GINSBURG*, with whom Justice *STEVENS*, Justice *SOUTER*, and Justice *BREYER* join, dissenting:

* * * *

[Equity courts] may have refused to issue injunctions of this sort simply because they were not needed to secure a just result in an age of slow-moving capital and comparatively immobile wealth. * * * But * * * the remedy at law is worthless absent the provisional relief [an injunction] in equity's arsenal. Moreover, increasingly sophisticated foreign-haven judgment proofing strategies, coupled with technology that permits the nearly instantaneous transfer of assets abroad, suggests that defendants may succeed in avoiding meritorious claims in ways unimaginable before the merger of law and equity. * * *

* * * *

* * * Where, as here, legal remedies are not practical and efficient, the federal courts must rely on their flexible jurisdiction in equity * * * to protect all rights and do justice to all concerned.

LEGAL REASONING AND ANALYSIS

1. Legal Reasoning. Contrast the conclusions of the majority and the dissent. What reasons did each provide to justify its position?

2. Legal Analysis. The majority holds that the courts do not have the power to grant the relief requested in this case. The majority states, however, that the courts could be given that power. Who can give the courts this power? What points indicated by the majority or dissent favor giving this power to the courts, and what points argue against it?

3. Legal Application. There have been other cases in which the courts refused to grant the sort of relief sought in this case. (See, for example, *De Beers Consolidated Mines, Ltd. v. United States*, 325 U.S. 212, 65 S.Ct. 1130, 89 L.Ed. 1566 [1945].) There have also been cases in which the courts fashioned remedies that resemble the relief requested in this case. (For example, see the list of cases involving the dissolution of corporations in *United States v. E.I. du Pont de Nemours &*

Co., 366 U.S. 316, 81 S.Ct. 1243, 6 L.Ed.2d 318 [1961].) What do these cases indicate about the U.S. judicial system and the positions taken by the majority and dissent in this case?

4. Implications for the Creditor. What does the decision in this case indicate for those who lend money on an unsecured basis?

5. Case Briefing Assignment. Using the guidelines for briefing cases given in Appendix A of this text, brief the *Grupo* case.

GOING ONLINE

This text's Web site, at http://wbl.westbuslaw.com, offers links to court cases, as well as to other online research sources. You can also locate court cases at the Web sites listed in the *Law on the Web* section at the end of Chapter 2. Hieros Gamos includes links to sources related to credit law at http://www.hg.org/credit.html. The links are to international organizations and national governments, including U.S. resources on federal and state law. Hieros Gamos is maintained by Lex Mundi, an association of independent law firms.

Creditors' Rights and Bankruptcy

We are certainly many years away from that period in our history when debtors' prisons existed. Today, debtors are in a much more favorable position—they can file for protection under bankruptcy law. Indeed, some now say that we have proceeded too far in the direction of protecting debtors and have made it too easy for debtors to avoid paying what they legally owe. Clearly, it is difficult to ensure the rights of both debtors and creditors at the same time, and laws governing debtor-creditor relationships are frequently perceived, by one group or another, as being unfair.

Creditors are given numerous remedies under both the common law and statutory law to protect their legitimate interests. When these rights and remedies are invoked, however, the creditor is often considered by the general public to be employing unfair tactics. For many, the question of fairness revolves around the purpose for which the debt was incurred. If the debt was incurred for a needed item, such as a refrigerator, then common opinion seems to be that the debtor should be dealt with leniently. If, however, the debt was incurred for a trip to the Bahamas, the issue appears to be significantly different.

There is obviously no way in which the law can protect both debtors and creditors at all times under all circumstances. Attempts to balance the rights of both groups necessarily raise questions of fairness and justice. In this *Focus on Ethics,* we look at several aspects of debtor-creditor

relationships that frequently pose ethical problems.

"SELF-HELP" REPOSSESSION

Section 9–503 of the Uniform Commercial Code (UCC) states that "[u]nless otherwise agreed, a secured party has on default the right to take possession of the collateral. In taking possession, a secured party may proceed without judicial process if this can be done without breach of the peace." The underlying rationale for this "self-help" provision of Article 9 is that it simplifies the process of repossession for creditors and reduces the burden on the courts. Because the UCC does not define "breach of the peace," however, it is not always easy to predict what will or will not constitute such a breach.

From the debtor's point of view, it is not always clear what is happening when agents of the creditor appear to repossess collateral. Often, to avoid confrontation with the debtor and any potential violence or breach of the peace, a secured creditor will arrange to have collateral repossessed during the night or in the early-morning hours, when the repossession effort is least likely to be observed. For the debtor, repossession can therefore be very stressful. A debtor may awaken in the night and notice that his or her car is being towed away—without realizing that it is being repossessed.

At the same time, repossession can be risky for the creditor; if the repossession results in a breach of

the peace, the creditor may be liable for substantial damages. Yet there is no way to ensure that such confrontations will not occasionally result from repossession attempts. Indeed, some contend that the self-help provision encourages violence by providing an incentive for debtors to induce creditors to breach the peace, which may entitle the debtors to damages.

GOOD FAITH AND FINANCING STATEMENTS

Having a perfected security interest can be vitally important to a secured creditor if another creditor lays claim to the sale collateral. For this reason, it is important for any creditor, when filing a financing statement, to comply with Article 9 requirements. Additionally, creditors should never lose sight of the good faith requirement set forth in UCC 1–203. This requirement applies to *all* transactions subject to the UCC. Creditors are thus expected to exercise good faith in all transactions falling under Article 9, including the filing of financing statements.

The good faith provision came into play on one occasion when a creditor filed a financing statement that identified the debtors by their individual names even though the creditor knew that the collateral would be transferred immediately to the debtors' newly formed corporation. Later, a second creditor perfected a security interest in the same collateral, and a dispute arose over which creditor's security interest took priority. In the lawsuit that followed, the court held that the first creditor had violated the duty of good faith by including only the debtors' individual names—and not the name of the corporation—on the financing statement. According to the court, the first creditor "had to realize that the financing statement he was filing—while technically correct—contained an imminently misleading debtor designation." As a result of the creditor's "misleading debtor designation," the financing statement was ineffective to perfect the security interest, and the second creditor's perfected security interest prevailed.[1]

THE PROBLEM OF PROCEEDS

One of the ways in which the legal system protects creditors is by making it possible for a creditor to have not only a security interest in collateral but also an interest in the proceeds from the sale of the collateral. Sometimes, though, unfair as it may seem, proceeds have a way of disappearing, and thus the creditor is left empty-handed. For example, when flour is the collateral and it is turned into bread, the flour does not exist anymore, but the bread does, so the security interest persists in the bread. What about cattle or hog feed? If there is a security interest in the feed and it is fed to animals, does the security interest continue in the animals? If we based our logic on the flour example above, the answer would have to be yes. At least one court, however, has come up with the opposite conclusion. Basically, the court reasoned that because the hogs were the same before and after feeding, there were "no traceable proceeds."[2]

As another example, what happens if the collateral is a car, and the car is damaged in an accident? The "proceeds" in this situation consist of the insurance payment made to the debtor. If the debtor fails to pay off the outstanding loan on the car, though, what can the creditor do? If the car has been totaled and turned over to the insurance company in return for the insurance payment, the creditor no longer has any collateral to repossess. In one case, a creditor in this situation sued the debtor's insurance company to recover the insurance payment—the proceeds that were wrongfully (according to the creditor) given to the debtor. The court found, however, that the insurance company's only obligation was to the owner of the insurance policy (the debtor). To make a long story short, the proceeds had simply vanished, and the creditor was left with no collateral to secure the outstanding debt.[3] Other creditors facing similar problems of "disappearing" proceeds are probably also wondering about why they are left with nothing even though they had perfected security interests in the proceeds.

ETHICS AND BANKRUPTCY

The first goal of bankruptcy law is to provide relief and protection to debtors who have "gotten in over their heads." Society has generally concluded that everyone should be given the chance to start over again. But how far should society go in letting debtors avoid obligations that they voluntarily incurred?

Consider the concept of bankruptcy from the point of view of the creditor. The creditor has extended a transfer of purchasing power from himself or herself to the debtor. That transfer of purchasing

power represents a transfer of an asset for an asset. The debtor obtains the asset of money, goods, or services, and the creditor obtains the asset called a *secured* or *unsecured* legal obligation to pay. Once the debtor is in bankruptcy, voluntarily or involuntarily, the asset that the creditor owns most often has a diminished value. Indeed, in many circumstances, that asset has no value. Yet the easier it becomes for debtors to hide behind bankruptcy laws, the greater will be the incentive for debtors to use such laws to avoid payment of legally owed sums of money.

Clearly, bankruptcy law is a balancing act between providing a second chance and ensuring that creditors are given "a fair shake." Understandably, ethical issues arise in the process.

Is Bankruptcy Too Easy?

The total number of bankruptcies has increased dramatically since the Bankruptcy Code was revised in 1978 to make it easier to petition for bankruptcy relief. In 1976, for example, 193,000 debtors petitioned for bankruptcy. By 1999, bankruptcy filings were about 1.4 million per year. Most of those filings (an estimated 97 percent in 1999) were personal bankruptcies. To be sure, bankruptcy filings dropped by 2.6 percent in 1999 over what they had been the year before. But still, overall there has been a staggering rise in bankruptcy filings in the last two decades. In fact, more than half of the 20 million Americans who have filed for personal bankruptcy since the federal bankruptcy laws were created a century ago have done so just since 1985.

Some claim that the law has gone too far in providing relief for debtors and should be changed. Indeed, Congress has been considering proposed legislation that would amend the Bankruptcy

1. *Wollenberg v. Phoenix Leasing, Inc.*, 182 Ariz. 4, 893 P.2d 4 (1994).
2. *Farmers Cooperative Elevator Co. v. Union State Bank*, 409 N.W.2d 178 (Iowa 1987).

3. *Fidelity Financial Services v. Blaser*, 889 P.2d 268 (Okla. 1994).

Code to make it more difficult for some debtors to obtain relief. One proposal, for example, would prevent those earning over $50,000 a year from obtaining relief under Chapter 7; rather, such debtors would have to resort to a Chapter 13 repayment plan, so that creditors would be repaid to the fullest extent possible. Another proposal would make *all* credit-card debt incurred within ninety days of filing for Chapter 7 nondischargeable. The idea behind this proposal is to discourage spending sprees by people who know they will never be able to pay back those debts. (Under current law, credit-card bills up to $1,075 incurred within sixty days of filing for luxury items or cash are nondischargeable.)

Others criticize the credit-card industry for making credit too readily available to consumers. This group would like to see stiffer disclosure requirements imposed on credit-card companies—so that a consumer does not have to rely on the fine print to learn that, say, a "come-on" APR (annual percentage rate) of 2.9 percent will rise to 18 percent four months later. How Congress will ultimately attempt to balance the various interests involved in the bankruptcy reform debate is yet to be seen.

Bankruptcy and Economics

Among other things, the increasing number of bankruptcies means that creditors incur higher risks in making loans, because bankruptcy shifts the cost of the debt from the debtor to the creditor. To compensate for these higher risks, creditors will do one or more of the following: increase the interest rates charged to everyone, require more security (collateral), or be more selective in the granting of credit. Thus, the more lenient bankruptcy laws are, the better off will be those debtors who find themselves in bankruptcy; but

those debtors who will never be in bankruptcy will be worse off. Ethical concerns here must be matched with the economic concerns of other groups of individuals affected by the law.

Consequences for Debtors

Some contend that debtors take unfair advantage of bankruptcy law and see bankruptcy as an easy solution to their financing problems. While it is true that there is less of a stigma attached to bankruptcy today than there once was, bankruptcy is never easy for debtors. Many debtors feel a sense of shame and failure when they petition for bankruptcy. After all, bankruptcy is a matter of public record, and there is no way to avoid this fact. In one case, for example, a couple who filed for Chapter 7 bankruptcy wanted to use their attorney's mailing address in another town on their bankruptcy schedules so that it would be less likely that an elderly parent and one of their employers would learn about the bankruptcy. The court, however, held that debtors are not entitled to be protected from publicity surrounding the filing of their cases.[4]

There are other consequences of bankruptcy for debtors—blemished credit ratings for up to ten years, higher interest charges for new debts, such as those incurred through the purchase of cars or homes, and so on. They may even find it difficult to get jobs. Although a private employer may not fire an employee who has filed for bankruptcy protection, the employer may refuse to hire a job applicant who has done so. The courts provide little relief for job applicants who encounter such an experience.[5]

---

4. *In the Matter of Laws,* 223 Bankr. 714 (D.Neb. 1998).
5. See, for example, *Pastore v. Medford Savings Bank,* 186 Bankr. 553 (D. Mass. 1995).

Clearly, balancing the rights of debtors and creditors is not easy. Because of the consequences of bankruptcy, debtors do not always get the "fresh start" promised by bankruptcy law. At the same time, creditors rarely are able to recover all of the money owed them once a debtor petitions for bankruptcy.

Reaffirmation Agreements

Another ethically problematic aspect of bankruptcy law has to do with reaffirmation agreements. As discussed in Chapter 30, the Bankruptcy Code allows debtors undergoing bankruptcy proceedings to reaffirm certain debts. In other words, a debtor may agree with a particular creditor to go ahead and pay the debt, even though it could have been discharged in bankruptcy. In a sense, reaffirmation agreements conflict with the basic purpose of bankruptcy law, which is to give debtors a fresh start, free from debt. Because of this, the Code imposes special requirements with respect to such agreements—a reaffirmation agreement must be made *before* the debtor is granted a discharge, and the agreement *must* be filed with the court.

Notwithstanding these requirements, some debtors who have had their debts discharged in bankruptcy have fallen victim to creditors through reaffirmations of debt. One of the most notorious examples occurred in the late 1990s, when it was discovered that Sears, Roebuck and Co. had convinced thousands of debtors to reaffirm their credit-card debts to Sears, even though the debts had already been discharged in bankruptcy.

It took years for these practices to come to light because the reaffirmations had not been filed with the court, as required by the Bankruptcy Code. Debtors were enticed to sign the agreements by promises of low monthly payments in return for Sears's promise not to repossess goods purchased on credit. In 1999, following an investigation by the Federal Bureau of Investigation, Sears agreed to plead guilty to a charge of criminal bankruptcy fraud and to pay the government a fine of some $60 million. It also agreed to settle a nationwide class-action suit against the company for $36 million in cash and $118 million in store coupons.[6]

DISCUSSION QUESTIONS

1. How can a creditor who is inexperienced in secured transactions know when he or she is acting in good faith? Should

6. Laurel-Ann Dooley, "Come See the Legal Side of Sears," *The National Law Journal,* October 18, 1999, p. B3.

compliance with the "technical" requirements of Article 9 be sufficient to indicate good faith?

2. Do you think that the law favors debtors at the expense of creditors, or vice versa? Is there any way a better balance between creditors' and debtors' interests could be achieved?

3. So long as a breach of the peace does not result, a lender may repossess goods on the debtor's default under the self-help provision of Article 9. Do you think that debtors have a right to be told in advance about a planned repossession? In determining liability for a breach of the peace under the self-help provision, should the court take into consideration the behavior of the debtor at the time of the repossession?

4. Is it unethical to avoid paying one's debts by going into bankruptcy? Does a person have a moral responsibility to pay his or her debts?

5. Is it ethical for a business to refuse to extend credit to a customer simply because that person once went into bankruptcy, even though that person is now a good credit risk in every other way? Can an employer's discrimination against job applicants on the basis of their history of bankruptcy ever be justified? Is it consistent with bankruptcy law—the whole purpose of which is to rehabilitate debtors—for debtors to be burdened by such consequences? Can they be avoided?

UNIT SIX

Agency

CONTENTS

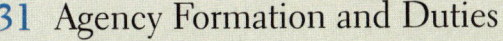

CHAPTER 31

Agency Formation and Duties

ONE OF THE MOST COMMON, important, and pervasive legal relationships is that of **agency**. As discussed in Chapter 26, in an agency relationship between two parties, one of the parties, called the *agent*, agrees to represent or act for the other, called the *principal*. The principal has the right to control the agent's conduct in matters entrusted to the agent. By using agents, a principal can conduct multiple business operations simultaneously in various locations. Thus, for example, contracts that bind the principal can be made at different places with different persons at the same time.

A familiar example of an agent is a corporate officer who serves in a representative capacity for the owners of the corporation. In this capacity, the officer has the authority to bind the principal (the corporation) to a contract. Indeed, agency law is essential to the existence and operation of a corporate entity, because only through its agents can a corporation function and enter into contracts. Because agency relationships permeate the business world, an understanding of the law of agency is crucial to understanding business law.

SECTION 1

Agency Relationships

Section 1(1) of the *Restatement (Second) of Agency*[1] defines *agency* as "the fiduciary relation which results from the manifestation of consent by one person to another that the other shall act in his behalf and subject to his control, and consent by the other so to act." The term **fiduciary** is at the heart of agency law. The term can be used both as a noun and as an adjective. When used as a noun, it refers to a person having a duty created by his or her undertaking to act primarily for another's benefit in matters connected with the undertaking. When used as an adjective, as in the phrase "fiduciary relationship," it means that the relationship involves trust and confidence.

Agency relationships commonly exist between employers and employees. Agency relationships may

---

1. The *Restatement (Second) of Agency* is an authoritative summary of the law of agency and is often referred to by jurists in their decisions and opinions.

sometimes also exist between employers and independent contractors who are hired to perform special tasks or services.

EMPLOYER-EMPLOYEE RELATIONSHIPS

Normally, all employees who deal with third parties are deemed to be agents. All employment laws (state and federal) apply only to the employer-employee relationship. Statutes governing Social Security, withholding taxes, workers' compensation, unemployment compensation, workplace safety laws, employment discrimination, and the like (see Chapters 41 and 42) are applicable only when an employer-employee relationship exists. *These laws do not apply to the independent contractor.*

Because employees may be deemed agents of their employers, agency law and employment law overlap considerably. Agency relationships, though, as will become apparent, can exist outside an employer-employee relationship and thus have a broader reach than employment laws do.

EMPLOYER–INDEPENDENT CONTRACTOR RELATIONSHIPS

Independent contractors are not employees, because by definition, those who hire them have no control over the details of their work performance. Section 2 of the *Restatement (Second) of Agency* defines an **independent contractor** as follows:

> [An independent contractor is] a person who contracts with another to do something for him but who is not controlled by the other nor subject to the other's right to control with respect to his physical conduct in the performance of the undertaking. He may or may not be an agent.

Building contractors and subcontractors are independent contractors, and a property owner does not control the acts of either of these professionals. Truck drivers who own their equipment and hire out on a per-job basis are independent contractors, but truck drivers who drive company trucks on a regular basis are usually employees.

The relationship between a principal and an independent contractor may or may not involve an agency relationship. To illustrate: An owner of real estate who hires a real estate broker to negotiate a sale of his or her property not only has contracted with an independent contractor (the real estate broker) but also

has established an agency relationship for the specific purpose of assisting in the sale of the property. Another example is an insurance agent, who is both an independent contractor and an agent of the insurance company for which he or she sells policies.

CRITERIA FOR ESTABLISHING EMPLOYEE STATUS

A question that frequently comes before the courts is whether a worker should be deemed an employee or an independent contractor. How a court decides this issue can have a significant effect on the rights and liabilities of the parties.

For example, employers normally are held liable as principals for the actions of their employee-agents if those actions are carried out within the scope of employment. Additionally, federal and state statutory laws governing employment discrimination, workplace safety, and compensation for on-the-job injuries normally apply only to employees—not to independent contractors. The tax liability of employers is also affected by the determination of worker status. Whereas employers are responsible for certain taxes, such as Social Security and unemployment taxes, with respect to employees, they are not responsible for these taxes if their workers are classified as independent contractors. (For further examples of the implications of independent contractor versus employee status, see this chapter's *Emerging Trends in Business Law* on pages 574 and 575.)

In deciding whether a worker is categorized as an employee or an independent contractor, courts often consider the following questions:

1. How much control can the employer exercise over the details of the work? (If an employer can exercise considerable control over the details of the work and the day-to-day activities of the worker, this indicates employee status. This is perhaps the most important factor weighed by the courts in determining employee status.)

2. Is the worker engaged in an occupation or business distinct from that of the employer? (If so, this points to independent-contractor status, not employee status.)

3. Is the work usually done under the employer's direction or by a specialist without supervision? (If the work is usually done under the employer's direction, this indicates employee status.)

4. Does the employer supply the tools at the place of work? (If so, this indicates employee status.)

EMERGING TRENDS IN BUSINESS LAW

Employee Rights for Contingent Workers

Not surprisingly, many employers prefer to designate certain workers as independent contractors rather than as employees. After all, if a worker is an independent contractor, the employer is not required to pay the employer's share of Social Security taxes (as is required for employees) or bear the administrative expense of withholding taxes from the worker's paycheck. Furthermore, the employer need not provide employee benefits—such as pension plans, stock option plans, group insurance coverage, and so on—to independent contractors. Finally, the employer is free from many of the obligations imposed on employers under laws protecting employees (see Chapters 41 and 42). As illustrated in Case 31.1, workers also benefit at times from having independent-contractor status.

Another option for employers who wish to save on costs, including the cost of benefits provided to employees, is to hire "temporary" workers through an employment agency. In this situation, the worker is an employee of the agency, rather than an employee of the hiring company, and the agency is responsible for withholding taxes and so on. A number of employers have resorted to hiring "temps" on a long-term basis to avoid having to provide employee benefits to those workers.

Increasingly, though, employers who use independent contractors and temps are finding that their contractual designations of these workers may not hold up under scrutiny. The Internal Revenue Service (IRS) or a court may hold that, despite the agreement between the worker and the employer, the worker is in fact an employee, either under the common law of agency or under a statutory definition of an employee. Under agency law, as stated elsewhere in this chapter, the most important factor in deciding the outcome is the degree of control that the employer exercises over the worker—although the factors in the list beginning on page 573 also bear on the decision.

EMPLOYEE BENEFITS FOR TEMPS

In 1999, the Court of Appeals for the Ninth Circuit handed down a decision in *Vizcaino v. Microsoft* [a] that could have profound implications for employers. The events that led to the lawsuit were set in motion in 1990, when the IRS determined that a number of Microsoft Corporation's independent contractors were actually employees of the company for tax purposes. The IRS arrived at this conclusion based on the significant control that Microsoft exercised over the independent contractors' work performance. As a result of the IRS's findings, Microsoft was ordered to pay back payroll taxes for hundreds of independent contractors who should have been classified as employees. Rather than contest the ruling, Microsoft required most of the workers in question, as well as a number of its other independent contractors, to become associated with employment agencies and work for Microsoft as "temps"—or lose the opportunity to work for Microsoft.

Workers who refused to register with employment agencies, as well as some who did register, sued Microsoft. The workers alleged that they were actually employees of the company and, as such, entitled to participate in Microsoft's stock option plan for employees. Microsoft countered that it need not provide such benefits because each of the workers had signed an independent-contractor agreement specifically stating that the worker

---

a. 173 F.3d 713 (9th Cir. 1999).

---

5. For how long is the person employed? (If the person is employed for a long period of time, this indicates employee status.)

6. What is the method of payment—by time period or at the completion of the job? (Payment by time period, such as once every two weeks or once a month, indicates employee status.)

7. What degree of skill is required of the worker? (If a great degree of skill is required, this may indicate that the person is an independent contractor hired for a specialized job and not an employee.)

Often, the criteria for determining employee status are established by a statute or administrative agency

EMERGING TRENDS IN BUSINESS LAW

Employee Rights for Contingent Workers, continued

was responsible for his or her own benefits. When the case ultimately reached the Court of Appeals for the Ninth Circuit, the court held that the independent contractors were in fact "common law employees" under agency law. Notably, the court held that being an employee of a temporary employment agency did not preclude the employee from having the status of a common law employee of Microsoft at the same time.

EMPLOYMENT DISCRIMINATION AND INDEPENDENT CONTRACTORS

It is often assumed that laws prohibiting employment discrimination apply only to direct (employer-employee) employment relationships. Employers, though, should be wary of making this assumption. For one thing, independent contractors may have a cause of action against their employers under 42 U.S.C. Section 1981, which was enacted as part of the Civil Rights Act of 1866. As will be discussed in Chapter 42, that

section prohibits discrimination on the basis of race in the formation or enforcement of contracts, including contracts between employers and independent contractors.

For another, a number of courts have held that independent contractors have standing to sue their employers under the major federal law prohibiting employment discrimination—Title VII of the Civil Rights Act of 1964. (This law prohibits discrimination in the workplace on the basis of race, color, ethnic origin, religion, or gender—see Chapter 42.)

Moreover, at least one court has held that Title VII's definition of the term *employee* is sufficiently broad that it embraces even an employee of an independent contractor. In *NME Hospitals, Inc. v. Rennels,*[b] an employee who worked for a pathology laboratory that provided services to a hospital sued the hospital for gender discrimination. The hospital argued that the plaintiff did not have standing to sue because she was an employee of an independent contractor and not of the hospital. The court, however, pointed out that Title VII affords relief to any "person claiming to be aggrieved." All the plaintiff need show is that some sort of employment relationship existed between the plaintiff and a third party and that the third party (in this case, the hospital) "controlled access to the plaintiff's

employment opportunities and denied or interfered with the access based on unlawful criteria."

IMPLICATIONS FOR THE BUSINESSPERSON

1. Employers should be wary of trying to cut costs by using independent contractors or temps, because such workers may be deemed employees by a court or under IRS guidelines.
2. Employers should also take steps to avoid discrimination against *any* worker, regardless of whether the worker is an employee, an independent contractor, or even an employee of an independent contractor.

FOR CRITICAL ANALYSIS

1. How can an employer maximize the chances of a quality work product when utilizing independent contractors *without* exercising significant control over those workers?
2. What policy interests are served by allowing employers to hire workers as independent contractors rather than employees? Do you think that these interests should be overridden by the courts or the IRS?

b. 994 S.W.2d 142 (Tex. 1999).

regulation. The Internal Revenue Service (IRS), for example, has guidelines for its auditors to follow in determining whether a worker is an independent contractor or an employee. In the past, auditors were to consider twenty factors in making such a decision. New guidelines effective in 1997, however, encourage IRS examiners to look closely at just one of those factors—the degree of control the business exercises over the worker.

The IRS tends to scrutinize closely a firm's classification of a worker as an independent contractor rather than an employee, because employers can avoid certain tax liabilities by hiring independent contractors instead of employees. Regardless of the firm's classification of a worker's status as an independent contractor, if the IRS decides that the worker should be classified as an employee, then the employer will be responsible for paying any applicable Social Security, withholding, and unemployment taxes.

Sometimes, it is advantageous to have employee status—to take advantage of laws protecting employees, for example. At other times, it may be advantageous to have independent-contractor status—for instance, for tax purposes.

The following case involved a dispute over ownership rights in a computer program. Under the Copyright Act

of 1976, any copyrighted work created by an employee within the scope of his or her employment at the request of the employer is a "work for hire," and the employer owns the copyright to the work. When an employer hires an independent contractor, however, normally the contractor owns the copyright unless the parties agree in writing that the work is a "work for hire." The outcome of the case thus hinged on whether the creator of the program, at the time it was created, was an employee or an independent contractor.

CASE 31.1   Graham v. James

United States
Court of Appeals,
Second Circuit, 1998.
144 F.3d 229.
http://www.findlaw.
com/casecode/courts/
2nd.html[a]

**IN THE LANGUAGE
OF THE COURT**

BACKGROUND AND FACTS *Richard Graham marketed CD-ROM disks containing compilations of shareware, freeware, and public domain software.[b] With five to ten thousand programs per disk, Graham needed a file-retrieval program to allow users to access the software on the disks. Larry James agreed to create the program in exchange for, among other things, credit on the final product. James built into the final version of the program a notice attributing authorship and copyright to himself. Graham removed the notice, claiming that the program was a work for hire and the copyright was his. Graham used the program on several subsequent releases. James sold the program to another CD-ROM publisher. Graham filed a suit in a federal district court against James, alleging, among other things, copyright infringement. The court ruled that James was an independent contractor and that he owned the copyright. Graham appealed the ruling.*

JACOBS, Circuit Judge.

*   *   *   *

The Copyright Act provides, *inter alia* [among other things], that "a work prepared by an employee within the scope of his or her employment" is a work for hire. "[T]he employer or other person for whom the work [for hire] was prepared is considered the author" and the employer owns the copyright *   *   * .

*   *   *   *

*   *   * [In determining whether a hired party is an employee, the important factors are:] (i) the hiring party's right to control the manner and means of creation; (ii) the skill required; (iii) the provision of employee benefits; (iv) the tax treatment of the hired party; and (v) whether the hiring party had the right to assign additional projects to the hired party. *   *   *

We are persuaded by the district court's conclusion that James was an independent contractor. Almost all of the *   *   * factors line up in favor of that conclusion: James is a skilled computer programmer, he was paid no benefits, no payroll taxes were withheld, and his engagement by Graham was project-by-project. The only *   *   * factor arguably favoring Graham is his general control over the work; but the district court has

---

a. This is a page, part of the Findlaw Web site, with links to some of the opinions of the U.S. Court of Appeals for the Second Circuit. In the "1998" row, click on "May." When that page opens, scroll down the list of cases to the *Graham* case and click on the link to access it.

b. *Shareware* is software released to the public to sample, with the understanding that anyone using it will register with the author and pay a fee. *Freeware* is software available for use at no charge. *Public domain software* is software unprotected by copyright.

found, plausibly, that Graham's participation in the development of the [file-retrieval program] was minimal and that his instructions to James were very general.

DECISION AND REMEDY *The U.S. Court of Appeals for the Second Circuit affirmed the lower court's judgment on this issue. The court agreed that James owned the copyright because he was an independent contractor when he developed the program.*

SECTION 2

Formation of the Agency Relationship

Agency relationships are *consensual*; that is to say, they come about by voluntary consent and agreement between the parties. Generally, the agreement need not be in writing,[2] and consideration is not required.

A principal must have contractual capacity. A person who cannot legally enter into contracts directly should not be allowed to do so indirectly through an agent. Because an agent derives the authority to enter into contracts from the principal and because a contract made by an agent is legally viewed as a contract of the principal, it is immaterial whether the agent personally has the legal capacity to make that contract. Thus, a minor can be an agent but in some states cannot be a principal appointing an agent.[3] (When a minor is permitted to be a principal, however, any resulting contracts will be voidable by the minor principal but not by the adult third party.) In sum, any person can be an agent, regardless of whether he or she has the capacity to contract. Even a person who is legally incompetent can be appointed an agent.

An agency relationship can be created for any legal purpose. An agency relationship created for a purpose that is illegal or contrary to public policy is unenforceable. If LaSalle (as principal) contracts with Burke (as agent) to sell illegal narcotics, the agency relationship is unenforceable, because selling illegal narcotics is a felony and is contrary to public policy.

It is also illegal for medical doctors and other licensed professionals to employ unlicensed agents to perform professional actions.

Generally, an agency relationship can arise in four ways: by agreement of the parties, by ratification, by estoppel, and by operation of law. We look here at each of these possibilities.

AGENCY BY AGREEMENT

Because an agency relationship is, by definition, consensual, normally it must be based on an express or implied agreement that the agent will act for the principal and the principal agrees to have the agent so act. An agency agreement can take the form of an express written contract. For example, Arnstein enters into a written agreement with Vogel, a real estate agent, to sell Arnstein's house. An agency relationship exists between Arnstein and Vogel for the sale of the house and is detailed in a document that both parties sign.

Many express agency relationships are created by oral agreement and not based on a contract. If Arnstein asks Grace, a gardener, to contract with others for the care of his lawn on a regular basis, and Grace agrees, an agency relationship exists between Arnstein and Grace for the lawn care.

An agency relationship can also be implied by conduct. For example, a hotel expressly allows only Hans Cooper to park cars, but Hans has no employment contract there. The hotel's manager tells Hans when to work, as well as where and how to park the cars. The hotel's conduct amounts to a manifestation of its willingness to have Hans park its customers' cars, and Hans can infer from the hotel's conduct that he has authority to act as a parking valet. It can be inferred that Hans is an agent for the hotel, his purpose being to provide valet parking services for hotel guests.

AGENCY BY RATIFICATION

On occasion, a person who is in fact not an agent may make a contract on behalf of another (a principal). If

---

2. There are two main exceptions to the statement that agency agreements need not be in writing. An agency agreement must be in writing (1) whenever agency authority empowers the agent to enter into a contract that the Statute of Frauds requires to be in writing (this is called the *equal dignity rule*, to be discussed in the next chapter) and (2) whenever an agent is given power of attorney. 3. Some courts have granted exceptions to allow a minor to appoint an agent for the limited purpose of contracting for the minor's necessities of life. See *Casey v. Kastel,* 237 N.Y. 305, 142 N.E. 671 (1924).

the principal approves or affirms that contract by word or by action, an agency relationship is created by ratification. Ratification involves a question of intent, and intent can be expressed by either words or conduct. The basic requirements for ratification are discussed in Chapter 32.

AGENCY BY ESTOPPEL

When a principal causes a third person to believe that another person is the principal's agent, and the third person acts to his or her detriment in reasonable reliance on that belief, the principal is "estopped to deny" the agency relationship. In such a situation, the principal's actions have created the *appearance* of an agency that does not in fact exist. The third person must prove that he or she *reasonably* believed that an agency relationship existed, however.[4]

Suppose that Jerry accompanies Grant, a seed sales representative, to call on a customer, Palko, the proprietor of the Neighborhood Seed Store. Jerry has per-

formed independent sales work but has never signed an employment agreement with Grant. Grant boasts to Palko that he wishes he had three more assistants "just like Jerry." Palko has reason to believe from Grant's statements that Jerry is an agent for Grant, because Grant's representation to Palko created the impression that Jerry was Grant's agent and had authority to solicit orders. Palko then places seed orders with Jerry.

If Grant does not correct the impression that Jerry is an agent, Grant will be bound to fill the orders just as if Jerry were really Grant's agent. The acts or declarations of a purported agent in and of themselves do not create an agency by estoppel. Rather, it is the deeds or statements of the principal that create an agency by estoppel. If Jerry walked into Palko's store and claimed to be Grant's agent, when in fact he was not, and Grant had no knowledge of Jerry's representations, Grant would not be bound to any deal struck by Jerry and Palko.

The court in the following case considered whether an agency existed by estoppel between the owner of a jewelry cart in a mall and the seller of "The Only Completely Safe, Sterile Ear Piercing Method."

---

4. These concepts also apply when a person who is in fact an agent undertakes an action that is beyond the scope of his or her authority, as will be discussed in Chapter 32.

CASE 31.2   Williams v. Inverness Corp.

Supreme Judicial Court of Maine, 1995. 664 A.2d 1244.

COMPANY PROFILE   *Inverness Corporation is the world's largest maker of body-piercing equipment. Sam Mann founded Inverness in 1975 with a design for piercing equipment that was more sterile and less threatening than the products then in use. The first year, sales totaled more than $750,000. Today, the company makes disposable ear-piercing kits, skin-care products, hair-removal waxes, electrolysis kits, and jewelry dips. Based in Fair Lawn, New Jersey, Inverness sells its products in fifty-two countries. In 1998, Inverness sold the assets of its jewelry components division for more than $38.7 million to Cookson Group (**http://www.cooksongroup.co.uk**), an international industrial materials group based in the United Kingdom.*

BACKGROUND AND FACTS   *Inverness Corporation markets the Inverness Ear Piercing System, which includes a training course, an "eye-catching assortment of selling aids" such as counter displays, and release forms that tout the system as "The Only Completely Safe, Sterile Ear Piercing Method." Margaret Barrera, the owner of a jewelry cart in a mall, bought the system, took the course, and set up the displays. Seventeen-year-old Angela Williams paid Barrera to pierce Williams's ear. The ear became infected, which led to complications. Williams's mother filed a suit on Angela's behalf in a Maine state court against Inverness and Barrera, claiming in part that Inverness was liable on a theory of agency by estoppel. The court issued a judgment in Williams's favor. Inverness appealed to Maine's highest state court.*

IN THE LANGUAGE
OF THE COURT

DANA, Justice.
*   *   *   *
*   *   * There are critical pieces of evidence in the record that can fairly be interpreted as leading to an inference that Inverness did hold Barrera out as its agent. Most important, a jury reasonably could infer that Inverness knew, or should have known, that Barrera distributed Inverness's release forms   *   *   * .

*   *   * A jury reasonably could infer   *   *   * that Inverness knew, or should have known, that Barrera was using the Inverness Ear Piercing System, that she displayed Inverness's "eye-catching assortment of selling aids," and that she used Inverness's training program.

Finally, there was evidence that Angela believed that Barrera was Inverness's agent, that Angela relied on Inverness's manifestations of agency, and that Angela's reliance on Barrera's care and skill was justifiable. *   *   * The release form and display promote the Inverness Ear Piercing System as "The Only Completely Safe, Sterile Ear Piercing Method."

DECISION
AND REMEDY

The Supreme Judicial Court of Maine affirmed the lower court's judgment. Inverness was liable for Williams's injury because Inverness's actions created the appearance of an agency between it and Barrera.

AGENCY BY OPERATION OF LAW

There are also other situations in which the courts will find an agency relationship in the absence of a formal agreement. This may occur in family relationships. For example, suppose one spouse purchases certain basic necessaries (such as food or clothing—see Chapter 13) and charges them to the other spouse's charge account. The courts will often rule that the latter is liable for payment of the necessaries, either because of a social policy of promoting the general welfare of the spouse or because of a legal duty to supply necessaries to family members.

Agency by operation of law may also occur in emergency situations, when the agent's failure to act outside the scope of his or her authority would cause the principal substantial loss. If the agent is unable to contact the principal, the courts will often grant this emergency power. For example, a railroad engineer may contract on behalf of his or her employer for medical care for an injured motorist hit by the train.

CONCEPT SUMMARY 31.1

FORMATION OF PRINCIPAL-AGENT RELATIONSHIP

METHOD OF FORMATION	DESCRIPTION
By Agreement	Agency relationship is formed through express consent (oral or written) or implied by conduct.
By Ratification	Principal either by act or by agreement ratifies conduct of a person who is not in fact an agent.
By Estoppel	Principal causes a third person to believe that another person is the principal's agent, and the third person acts to his or her detriment in reasonable reliance on that belief.
By Operation of Law	Agency relationship is based on a social duty (such as the need to support family members) or formed in emergency situations when the agent is unable to contact the principal.

SECTION 3

Duties of Agents and Principals

Once the principal-agent relationship has been created, both parties have duties that govern their conduct. As discussed previously, the principal-agent relationship is *fiduciary*—one of trust. In a fiduciary relationship, each party owes the other the duty to act with the utmost good faith. In this section, we examine the various duties of agents and principals.

AGENT'S DUTIES TO THE PRINCIPAL

Generally, the agent owes the principal five duties—performance, notification, loyalty, obedience, and accounting.

Performance.   An implied condition in every agency contract is the agent's agreement to use reasonable diligence and skill in performing the work. When an agent fails to perform his or her duties, liability for breach of contract may result. The degree of skill or care required of an agent is usually that expected of a reasonable person under similar circumstances. Generally, this is interpreted to mean ordinary care. An agent may, however, have represented himself or herself as possessing special skills or, by virtue of his or her profession, be expected to exercise certain skills (such as those that an accountant or attorney possesses—see Chapter 51). Similarly, a corporate director, as an agent of the corporation, is expected to exercise a reasonable degree of diligence and oversight in the performance of his or her duties (see Chapter 35). In these situations, the agent is expected to exercise the skill or skills claimed. Failure to do so constitutes a breach of the agent's duty.

Not all agency relationships are based on contract. In some situations, an agent acts gratuitously—that is, without payment. A gratuitous agent cannot be liable for breach of contract, as there is no contract; he or she is subject only to tort liability. Once a gratuitous agent has begun to act in an agency capacity, he or she has the duty to continue to perform in that capacity in an acceptable manner and is subject to the same standards of care and duty to perform as other agents. For example, Bower's friend Alcott is a real estate broker. Alcott offers to sell Bower's farm at no charge. If Alcott never attempts to sell the farm, Bower has no legal cause of action to force Alcott to do so. If Alcott does find a buyer, however, but fails to provide a sales contract within a reasonable period of time, thus causing the buyer to seek other property, then Bower has a cause of action in tort against Alcott for negligence.

Notification.   An agent is required to notify the principal of all matters that come to his or her attention concerning the subject matter of the agency. This is the duty of notification, or the duty to inform. For example, suppose that Lang, an artist, is about to negotiate a contract to sell a series of paintings to Barber's Art Gallery for $15,000. Lang's agent learns that Barber is insolvent and will be unable to pay for the paintings. Lang's agent has a duty to inform Lang of this knowledge because it is relevant to the subject matter of the agency—the sale of Lang's paintings. Generally, the law assumes that the principal knows of any information acquired by the agent that is relevant to the agency—regardless of whether the agent actually passes on this information to the principal.

Loyalty.   Loyalty is one of the most fundamental duties in a fiduciary relationship. Basically stated, the agent has the duty to act solely for the benefit of his or her principal and not in the interest of the agent or a third party. For example, an agent cannot represent two principals in the same transaction unless both know of the dual capacity and consent to it. The duty of loyalty also means that any information or knowledge acquired through the agency relationship is confidential. It would be a breach of loyalty to disclose such information either during the agency relationship or after its termination. Typical examples of confidential information are trade secrets and customer lists compiled by the principal.

In short, the agent's loyalty must be undivided. The agent's actions must be strictly for the benefit of the principal and must not result in any secret profit for the agent. For example, suppose that Remington contracts with Averly, a real estate agent, to sell Remington's property. Averly knows that he can find a buyer who will pay substantially more for the property than Remington is asking. If Averly secretly purchased Remington's property, however, and then sold it at a profit to another buyer, Averly would breach his duty of loyalty as Remington's agent. Averly has a duty to act in Remington's best interests and can only become the purchaser in this situation with Remington's knowledge and approval.

Does an agent breach the duty of loyalty if, while working for a principal, the agent solicits the principal's customers for a new competing business? That was an issue in the following case.

CASE 31.3   American Express Financial Advisors, Inc. v. Topel

United States
District Court,
District of Colorado,
1999.
38 F.Supp.2d 1233.

BACKGROUND AND FACTS *Stephen Topel worked as a financial planner for American Express Financial Advisors, Inc. (AMEX), beginning in April 1992. More than four years later, Topel decided to resign to work for Multi-Financial Securities Corporation, an AMEX competitor. Before resigning, Topel encouraged his customers to liquidate their AMEX holdings and sent them new account forms for Multi-Financial. He ignored the request of customers James and Nancy Hemming to keep their investments with AMEX. In a letter on AMEX letterhead, Topel told Chris and Teresa Mammel to liquidate their AMEX holdings and invest in Multi-Financial's products. Another couple, Mr. and Ms. Rogers, changed their investments on Topel's advice. Before leaving AMEX, Topel sent a letter to all of his clients in which he wrote that he was ending his relationship with AMEX and that their accounts would be assigned to another AMEX adviser. After Topel resigned in May 1997, he solicited the business of Theodore Benavidez, another AMEX customer. AMEX filed a suit in a federal district court against Topel, alleging, among other things, breach of fiduciary duty (duty of loyalty) and seeking damages. AMEX filed a motion for summary judgment on this issue.*

IN THE LANGUAGE OF THE COURT

BABCOCK, District Judge.

*   *   *   *

[The] law provides that unless otherwise agreed, an agent is subject to a duty to his principal to act solely for the benefit of the principal in all matters connected with the agency. While an agent is entitled to make some preparations to compete with his principal after the termination of their relationship, an agent violates his duty of loyalty if he engages in pre-termination solicitation of customers for a new competing business.

As the undisputed facts make clear, Mr. Topel solicited customers for his new venture while he was still affiliated with AMEX. In some instances, there is evidence that Mr. Topel ignored his AMEX customers' requests to keep their investments with AMEX. He also sent correspondence to his AMEX customers to solicit them for his new venture while he was still employed by AMEX and, in at least one instance, on AMEX letterhead. *   *   *

Mr. Topel has not challenged AMEX's statement of the law on this issue; nor has he successfully challenged the facts upon which AMEX relies. *   *   *

*   *   *   *

Nor does Mr. Topel create a genuine issue of material fact by offering the testimony of one customer, Theodore Benavidez, whose unrebutted testimony is that Mr. Topel did not solicit his business until after he left AMEX. Mr. Benavidez' testimony does not negate the testimony of other customers who testified that Mr. Topel solicited their business for Multi-Financial while he was still affiliated with AMEX. Furthermore, even if Mr. Topel sent a neutral letter regarding his resignation to the AMEX clients he serviced on its behalf, it does not follow that no solicitation occurred prior to that letter. In fact, many customers had already signed new account forms with Multi-Financial by the time this neutral letter was purportedly sent. Thus, that it is genuinely disputed whether Mr. Topel solicited improperly some of his customers is irrelevant when [it] is undisputed that he improperly solicited the [Hemmings], [Mr. and] Ms. Rogers, and [the Mammels] before he terminated his employment with AMEX. *   *   * Therefore, I grant AMEX's summary judgment motion on its claim *   *   * for breach of fiduciary duty.

DECISION AND REMEDY *The court granted AMEX's motion for summary judgment on its claim against Topel for breach of fiduciary duty. Topel breached his duty of loyalty, while working for his principal, by soliciting his principal's customers for his new, competing business.*

Obedience. When an agent is acting on behalf of the principal, a duty is imposed on that agent to follow all lawful and clearly stated instructions of the principal. Any deviation from such instructions is a violation of this duty. During emergency situations, however, when the principal cannot be consulted, the agent may deviate from the instructions without violating this duty. Whenever instructions are not clearly stated, the agent can fulfill the duty of obedience by acting in good faith and in a manner reasonable under the circumstances.

Accounting. Unless an agent and a principal agree otherwise, the agent has the duty to keep and make available to the principal an account of all property and money received and paid out on behalf of the principal. The agent has a duty to maintain separate accounts for the principal's funds and the agent's personal funds, and no intermingling of these accounts is allowed. Whenever a licensed professional (such as an attorney) violates this duty to account, he or she may be subject to disciplinary proceedings carried out by the appropriate regulatory institution (such as the state bar association) in addition to being liable to the principal (the professional's client) for failure to account.

PRINCIPAL'S DUTIES TO THE AGENT

The principal also has certain duties to the agent. These duties relate to compensation, reimbursement and indemnification, cooperation, and safe working conditions.

Compensation. In general, when a principal requests certain services from an agent, the agent reasonably expects payment. The principal therefore has a duty to pay the agent for services rendered. For example, when an accountant or an attorney is asked to act as an agent, an agreement to compensate the agent for this service is implied. The principal also has a duty to pay that compensation in a timely manner. Except in a gratuitous agency relationship, in which the agent does not act for money, the principal must pay the agreed-on value for the agent's services. If no amount has been expressly agreed on, then the principal owes the agent the customary compensation for such services.

Reimbursement and Indemnification. Whenever an agent disburses sums of money to fulfill the request of the principal or to pay for necessary expenses in the course of a reasonable performance of his or her agency duties, the principal has the duty to reimburse the agent for these payments.[5] Agents cannot recover

for expenses incurred by their own misconduct or negligence, however.

Subject to the terms of the agency agreement, the principal has the duty to *indemnify* (compensate) an agent for liabilities incurred because of authorized and lawful acts and transactions. For example, if the agent, on the principal's behalf, forms a contract with a third party, and the principal fails to perform the contract, the third party may sue the agent for damages. In this situation, the principal is obligated to compensate the agent for any costs incurred by the agent as a result of the principal's failure to perform the contract. Additionally, the principal must indemnify (pay) the agent for the value of benefits that the agent confers on the principal. The amount of indemnification is usually specified in the agency contract. If it is not, the courts will look to the nature of the business and the type of loss to determine the amount.

Cooperation. A principal has a duty to cooperate with the agent and to assist the agent in performing his or her duties. The principal must do nothing to prevent such performance. For example, when a principal grants an agent an exclusive territory, creating an exclusive agency, the principal cannot compete with the agent or appoint or allow another agent to so compete in violation of the *exclusive agency*. If the principal did so, he or she would be exposed to liability for the agent's lost sales or profits.

Safe Working Conditions. The common law requires the principal to provide safe working premises, equipment, and conditions for all agents and employees. The principal has a duty to inspect working areas and to warn agents and employees about any unsafe situations. When the agency is one of employment, the employer's liability is frequently covered by state workers' compensation insurance, which is the primary remedy for an employee's injury on the job (see Chapter 41).

SECTION 4

Remedies and Rights of Agents and Principals

It is said that every wrong has its remedy. In business situations, disputes between agents and principals may arise out of either contract or tort laws and carry

---

5. This principle applies to acts by gratuitous agents as well. If a finder of a dog that becomes sick takes the dog to a veterinarian and pays the required fees for the veterinarian's services, the agent is entitled to be reimbursed by the owner of the dog for those fees.

corresponding remedies. These remedies include monetary damages, termination of the agency relationship, injunction, and required accountings.

AGENT'S RIGHTS AND REMEDIES AGAINST PRINCIPAL

For every duty of the principal, the agent has a corresponding right. Therefore, the agent has the right to be compensated, reimbursed, and indemnified and to work in a safe environment. An agent also has the right to perform agency duties without interference by the principal.

Remedies of the agent for breach of duty by the principal follow normal contract and tort remedies. For example, suppose that Aaron Hart, a builder who has just completed construction on a new house, contracts with a real estate agent, Fran Boller, to sell the house. The contract calls for the agent to have an exclusive, ninety-day listing and to receive 6 percent of the selling price when the home is sold. Boller holds several open houses and shows the property to a number of potential buyers. One month before the ninety-day listing terminates, Hart agrees to sell the house to another buyer—not one to whom Boller has shown the house—after the ninety-day listing expires. Hart and the buyer agree that Hart will reduce the price of the house by 3 percent, because he will sell it directly and thus will not have to pay Boller's commission. In this situation, if Boller learns of Hart's actions, she can terminate the agency relationship and sue Hart for damages—including the 6 percent commission she should have earned on the sale of the house.

An agent can also withhold further performance and demand that the principal give an accounting. For example, a sales agent may demand an accounting if the agent and principal disagree on the amount of commissions the agent should have received for sales made during a specific period of time.

When the principal-agent relationship is not contractual, an agent has no right to specific performance. An agent can recover for past services and future damages but cannot force the principal to allow him or her to continue acting as an agent.

PRINCIPAL'S RIGHTS AND REMEDIES AGAINST AGENT

In general, a principal has contract remedies for an agent's breach of fiduciary duties. The principal also has tort remedies for misrepresentation, negligence, fraud, deceit, libel, slander, and trespass committed by the agent. In addition, any breach of a fiduciary duty by an agent may justify the principal's termination of the agency. The main actions available to the principal are constructive trust, avoidance, and indemnification.

Constructive Trust. Anything an agent obtains by virtue of the employment or agency relationship belongs to the principal. It is a breach of an agent's fiduciary duty to retain secretly benefits or profits that, by right, belong to the principal. For example, Andrews, a purchasing agent, gets cash rebates from a customer. If Andrews keeps the rebates, he violates his fiduciary duty to his principal, Metcalf. On finding out about the cash rebates, Metcalf can sue Andrews and recover them.

An agent is also prohibited from taking advantage of the agency relationship to obtain goods or property that the principal wants to purchase. For example, Peterson (the principal) wants to purchase property in the suburbs. Cox, Peterson's agent, learns that a valuable tract of land has just become available. Cox cannot buy the land for herself. Peterson gets the right of first refusal. If Cox purchases the land for her own benefit, the courts will impose a constructive trust on the land; that is, the land will be held for, and on behalf of, the principal despite the fact that the agent attempted to buy it in her own name.

Avoidance. When an agent breaches the agency agreement or agency duties under a contract, the principal has a right to avoid any contract entered into with the agent. This right of avoidance is at the election of the principal.

Indemnification. In certain situations, when a principal is sued by a third party for an agent's negligent conduct, the principal can sue the agent for an equal amount of damages. This is called *indemnification*. The same holds true if the agent violates the principal's instructions. For example, Lewis (the principal) tells his agent Moore, who is a used-car salesperson, to make no warranties for the used cars. Moore is eager to make a sale to Walters, a third party, and makes a warranty for the car's engine. Lewis is not absolved from liability to Walters for engine failure, but if Walters sues Lewis, Lewis normally can then sue Moore for indemnification for violating his instructions.

Sometimes it is difficult to distinguish between instructions of the principal that limit an agent's authority and those that are merely advice. For example, Willis (the principal) owns an office supply company;

Jones (the agent) is the manager. Willis tells Jones, "Don't order any more inventory this month." Willis goes on vacation. A large order comes in from a local business, and the present inventory is insufficient to meet it. What is Jones to do? In this situation, Jones probably has the inherent authority to order more inventory despite Willis's command. It is unlikely that Jones would be required to indemnify Willis in the event that the local business subsequently canceled the order.

TERMS AND CONCEPTS TO REVIEW

agency 572	fiduciary 572	independent contractor 573

QUESTIONS AND CASE PROBLEMS

31–1. AGENCY FORMATION. Paul Gett is a well-known, wealthy financier living in the city of Torris. Adam Wade, Gett's friend, tells Timothy Brown that he is Gett's agent for the purchase of rare coins. Wade even shows Brown a local newspaper clipping mentioning Gett's interest in coin collecting. Brown, knowing of Wade's friendship with Gett, contracts with Wade to sell a rare coin valued at $25,000 to Gett. Wade takes the coin and disappears with it. On the date of contract payment, Brown seeks to collect from Gett, claiming that Wade's agency made Gett liable. Gett does not deny that Wade was a friend, but he claims that Wade was never his agent. Discuss fully whether an agency was in existence at the time the contract for the rare coin was made.

31–2. AGENT'S DUTY TO PRINCIPAL. Peter hires Alice as an agent to sell a piece of property he owns. The price is to be at least $30,000. Alice discovers that because a shopping mall is planned for the area in which Peter's property is located, the fair market value of the property will be at least $45,000 and could be higher. Alice forms a real estate partnership with her cousin Carl, and she prepares for Peter's signature a contract for sale of the property to Carl for $32,000. Peter signs the contract. Just before closing and passage of title, Peter learns about the shopping mall and the increased fair market value of his property. Peter refuses to deed the property to Carl. Carl claims that Alice, as agent, solicited a price above that agreed on in the creation of the agency and that the contract is therefore binding and enforceable. Discuss fully whether Peter is bound to this contract.

31–3. AGENCY FORMATION. John Paul Corp. made the following contracts:

(a) A contract with Able Construction to build an addition to the corporate office building.

(b) A contract with a certified public accountant (CPA), a recent college graduate, to head the cost accounting section.

(c) A contract with a salesperson to travel a designated area to solicit orders (contracts) for the corporation.

Able contracts with Apex for materials for the addition; the CPA hires an experienced accountant to advise her on certain accounting procedures; and the salesperson contracts to sell a large order to Green, agreeing to deliver the goods in person within twenty days. Later, Able refuses to pick up the materials, the CPA is in default in paying the hired consultant, and the salesperson does not deliver on time. Apex, the accountant, and Green claim John Paul Corp. is liable under agency law. Discuss fully whether an agency relationship was created by John Paul with Able, the CPA, or the salesperson.

31–4. AGENT'S DUTIES TO PRINCIPAL. Ankir is hired by Peters as a traveling salesperson. Ankir not only solicits orders but also delivers the goods and collects payments from his customers. Ankir places all payments in his private checking account and at the end of each month draws sufficient cash from his bank to cover the payments made. Peters is totally unaware of this procedure. Because of a slowdown in the economy, Peters tells all his salespeople to offer 20 percent discounts on orders. Ankir solicits orders, but he offers only 15 percent discounts, pocketing the extra 5 percent paid by customers. Ankir has not lost any orders by this practice, and he is rated one of Peters's top salespersons. Peters learns of Ankir's actions. Discuss fully Peters's rights in this matter.

31–5. EMPLOYEE VERSUS INDEPENDENT CONTRACTOR. L.M.T. Steel Products, Inc., contracted with a school to install numerous room partitions. To accomplish this work, L.M.T. hired a man named Webster. Webster was not a regular employee of L.M.T., and it was stipulated that he was to be paid by the number of feet of partitions installed. Webster did not have a contractor's license. He hired other workers to do the installing, and these workers were paid by L.M.T. Webster was given blueprints by

L.M.T., but he was not otherwise at any time actively supervised by L.M.T. on the job. Needing to place a telephone call to L.M.T., Webster drove his own personal vehicle to a public telephone. On the way, he negligently collided with another car, and an occupant of that car, Peirson, was injured. Peirson sued L.M.T., claiming that Webster was an employee. L.M.T. claimed that Webster was an independent contractor. Who was correct? Explain. [*L.M.T. Steel Products, Inc. v. Peirson*, 47 Md.App. 633, 425 A.2d 242 (1981)]

31–6. PRINCIPAL'S DUTIES TO AGENT. Douglas agreed to buy oil and gas leases for Aztec Petroleum Corp. In return for his services, Douglas was to receive an initial $5,000 plus a royalty interest in the leases he obtained. Douglas obtained a number of leases for Aztec but represented to Aztec that the prices paid for the leases were higher than they actually were. By sending Aztec photocopies of checks altered as to both payee and amount, along with forged receipts, Douglas was able to keep for himself a substantial amount of the money that Aztec had entrusted to him for payment of the leases. This money was used by Douglas for personal purchases, including two new cars, a boat, and other personal items. When Aztec refused to grant Douglas the promised royalty interest in the leases, Douglas brought suit to obtain it. The trial court held for Aztec, and Douglas appealed. In view of Douglas's deceptive activities, is Aztec required to grant the royalty interest? Discuss fully. [*Douglas v. Aztec Petroleum Corp.*, 695 S.W.2d 312 (Tex.App. 1985)]

31–7. EMPLOYEE VERSUS INDEPENDENT CONTRACTOR. Stephen Hemmerling was a driver for the Happy Cab Co. Hemmerling paid certain fixed expenses and abided by a variety of rules relating to the use of the cab, the hours that could be worked, the solicitation of fares, and so on. Rates were set by the state. Happy Cab did not withhold taxes from Hemmerling's pay. While driving a cab, Hemmerling was injured in an accident and filed a claim against Happy Cab in a Nebraska state court for workers' compensation benefits. Such benefits are not available to independent contractors. On what basis might the court hold that Hemmerling is an employee? Explain. [*Hemmerling v. Happy Cab Co.*, 247 Neb. 919, 530 N.W.2d 916 (1995)]

31–8. AGENT'S DUTIES TO PRINCIPAL. Ana Barreto and Flavia Gugliuzzi asked Ruth Bennett, a real estate salesperson who worked for Smith Bell Real Estate, to list for sale their house in the Pleasant Valley area of Underhill, Vermont. Diana Carter, a California resident, visited the house as a potential buyer. Bennett worked under the supervision of David Crane, an officer of Smith Bell. Crane knew, but did not disclose to Bennett or Carter, that the house was subject to frequent and severe winds, that a window had blown in years earlier, and that other houses in the area had suffered wind damage. Crane knew of this because he lived in the Pleasant Valley area, had sold a number of nearby properties, and had been Underhill's zoning officer. Many valley residents, including Crane, had wind gauges on their homes to measure and compare wind speeds with their neighbors. Carter bought the house, and several months later, high winds blew in a number of windows and otherwise damaged the property. Carter filed a suit in a Vermont state court against Smith Bell and others, alleging fraud. She argued in part that Crane's knowledge of the winds was imputable to Smith Bell. Smith Bell responded that Crane's knowledge was obtained outside the scope of employment. What is the rule regarding how much of an agent's knowledge a principal is assumed to know? How should the court rule in this case? Why? [*Carter v. Gugliuzzi*, 716 A.2d 17 (Vt. 1998)]

31–9. IN YOUR COURT

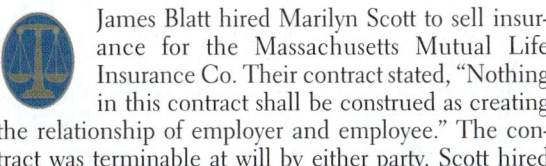

James Blatt hired Marilyn Scott to sell insurance for the Massachusetts Mutual Life Insurance Co. Their contract stated, "Nothing in this contract shall be construed as creating the relationship of employer and employee." The contract was terminable at will by either party. Scott hired and trained other agents according to Massachusetts Mutual's guidelines, but she financed her own office and staff, was paid according to performance, had no taxes withheld from her checks, and could sell products of Massachusetts Mutual's competitors. When Blatt terminated their contract, Scott filed a suit in a New York state court against him and Massachusetts Mutual. Scott claimed that she had been discriminated against on the basis of her gender, age, and marital status in violation of a state law prohibiting employment discrimination. The defendants filed a motion for summary judgment on the ground that the law applied only to employees and Scott was an independent contractor. Assume that you are the judge in the trial court hearing this case and answer the following questions:

(a) Your decision on whether to grant the defendants' motion for summary judgment in this case hinges on whether Scott was an independent contractor or an employee. What factors will you consider in deciding this issue?

(b) Based on your evaluation of these factors, what will your ruling be? Explain your reasoning.

(c) Compare this case to Case 31.1 (*Graham v. James*). Summarize the similarities and differences between these two cases.

31–10. A QUESTION OF ETHICS

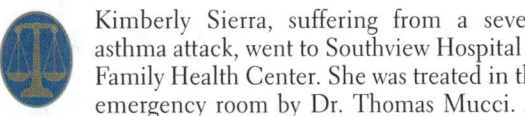

Kimberly Sierra, suffering from a severe asthma attack, went to Southview Hospital & Family Health Center. She was treated in the emergency room by Dr. Thomas Mucci. At the time, as a result of statements by Southview administrators, brochures, and ads, Sierra believed that the physicians at Southview were "hospital doctors." In fact, Mucci's contract with Southview stated, "The relationship between [Southview and Mucci] shall be that of independent contractor." Within a few hours, Sierra was pronounced dead. Sierra's mother, Edna Clark, sued Southview and others, alleging, in part, negligent medical care. Southview argued that it was not responsible for the acts of its independent contractors. The Supreme Court of Ohio heard the case and held that Southview was liable under the doctrine of agency by estoppel, based primarily on its "hold[ing] itself out to the public as a provider of medical services." [*Clark v. Southview Hospital & Family Health Center*, 68 Ohio St.3d 435, 628 N.E.2d 46 (1994)]

(a) Could Southview have avoided liability if Sierra had known that Mucci was an independent contractor? Is it ethical for a hospital to attempt to avoid such responsibility?

(b) Some department stores rent space in their stores to vendors of individual lines of products, such as cosmetics. In doing so, does a department store hold itself out to the public as a "provider" of cosmetics, subjecting itself to liability for the negligent acts of the independent contractors on its premises? Should the holding in the *Southview* case be applied in such contexts?

LAW ON THE WEB

For updated links to resources available on the Web, as well as a variety of other materials, visit this text's Web site at http://wbl.westbuslaw.com.

An excellent source for information on agency law, including court cases involving agency concepts, is the Legal Information Institute (LII) at Cornell University. You can access the LII's Web page on this topic at

http://www.law.cornell.edu/topics/agency.html

For a discussion of significant cases on fiduciary duties decided by the New York Court of Appeals (that state's highest court), go to the Web site of the *New York Law Journal* at

http://www.nylj.com/links/150sterk.html

and scroll down the page to "Fiduciary Duties."

LEGAL RESEARCH EXERCISES ON THE WEB

Go to http://wbl.westbuslaw.com, the Web site that accompanies this text. Select "Internet Applications," and then click on "Chapter 31." There you will find the following Internet research exercise that you can perform to learn more about the distinction between employees and independent contractors:

Activity 31–1: Employees or Independent Contractors?

CHAPTER 32

Liability to Third Parties and Termination

A S DISCUSSED IN THE PREVIOUS CHAPTER, the law of agency focuses on the special relationship that exists between a principal and an agent—how the relationship is formed and the duties the principal and agent assume once the relationship is established. This chapter deals with another important aspect of agency law—the liability of principals and agents to third parties.

We first look at the rights of third parties who enter into contracts with agents. Such a contract will make an agent's principal liable to the third party only if the agent had authority to make the contract or if the principal ratified, or was estopped from denying, the agent's acts. The second part of the chapter will deal with an agent's liability to third parties in contract and tort and the principal's liability to third parties because of an agent's torts. The chapter concludes with a discussion of how agency relationships are terminated.

SECTION 1

Scope of Agent's Authority

A principal's liability in a contract with a third party arises from the authority given the agent to enter legally binding contracts on the principal's behalf. An agent's authority can be either *actual* (express or implied) or *apparent*.

EXPRESS AUTHORITY

Express authority is embodied in that which the principal has engaged the agent to do. Express authority can be given orally or in writing. The **equal dignity rule** in most states requires that if the contract being executed is or must be in writing, then the agent's authority must also be in writing. Failure to comply with the equal dignity rule can make a contract voidable *at the option of the principal*. The law regards the contract at that point as a mere offer. If the principal decides to accept the offer, acceptance must be ratified, or affirmed, in writing. Assume that Pattberg (the principal) orally asks Austin (the agent) to sell a ranch that Pattberg owns. Austin finds a buyer and signs a sales contract (a contract for an interest in realty must be in writing) on behalf of Pattberg to sell the ranch. The buyer cannot enforce the contract unless Pattberg subsequently ratifies Austin's agency status in writing. Once the contract is ratified, either party can enforce rights under the contract.

An exception to the equal dignity rule exists in modern business practice. An executive officer of a corporation, when acting for the corporation in an ordinary business situation, is not required to obtain written authority from the corporation. In addition, the equal dignity rule does not apply when an agent acts in the presence of a principal or when the agent's act of signing is merely perfunctory. Thus, if Healy (the principal) negotiates a contract but is called out of town the day it is to be signed and orally authorizes Scougall to sign, the oral authorization is sufficient.

Giving an agent a **power of attorney** confers express authority.[1] The power of attorney is a written document and is usually notarized. (A document is notarized when a **notary public**—a public official authorized to attest to the authenticity of signatures—signs and dates the document and imprints it with his or her seal of authority.) A power of attorney can be special (permitting the agent to perform specified acts only), or it can be general (permitting the agent to transact all business for the principal). Because of the extensive authority granted to an agent by the latter (see Exhibit 32–1 on page 590), a general power of attorney should be used with great caution and usually only in exceptional circumstances.

An ordinary power of attorney terminates on the incapacity or death of the person giving the power. A *durable* power of attorney, however, provides an agent with very broad authority to act and make decisions for the principal and specifies that it is not affected by the principal's incapacity. An elderly person, for example, might grant a durable power of attorney to provide for the handling of property and investments or specific health-care needs should he or she become incompetent.

---

1. An agent who holds the power of attorney is called an attorney-in-fact for the principal. The holder does not have to be an attorney-at-law (and often is not).

IMPLIED AUTHORITY

Implied authority is conferred by custom, can be inferred from the position the agent occupies, or is implied by virtue of being reasonably necessary to carry out express authority. For example, Carlson is employed by Packard Grocery to manage one of its stores. Packard has not specified (expressly stated) Carlson's authority to contract with third persons. In this situation, though, authority to manage a business implies authority to do what is reasonably required (as is customary or can be inferred from a manager's position) to operate the business. This includes making contracts for obtaining employee help, for buying merchandise and equipment, and even for advertising the products sold in the store.

Because implied authority is conferred on the basis of custom, it is important for third persons to be familiar with the custom of the trade. The list of rules that have developed to determine what authority is implied based on custom or on the agent's position is extensive. In general, implied authority is authority customarily associated with the position occupied by the agent or authority that can be inferred from the express authority given to the agent to perform fully his or her duties.

For example, an agent who has authority to solicit orders for goods sold by the principal has no authority to collect payments for the goods unless the agent possesses the goods. The test is whether it was reasonable for the agent to believe that he or she had the authority to enter into the contract in question. The issue in the following case was whether it was reasonable for an attorney to believe that he had the authority to settle a case without the client's consent.

Gravens v. Auto-Owners Insurance Co.

Court of Appeals of
Indiana, 1996.
666 N.E.2d 964.

BACKGROUND AND FACTS   *James Gravens bought an insurance policy from Auto-Owners Insurance Company to cover his business, Pappy's Sunoco Service Station. The policy included a $20,000 limit on coverage of the contents of Pappy's, but when a burglary occurred on the premises, the loss exceeded the limit. Gravens hired an attorney to pursue a claim against Auto-Owners. He did not discuss with the attorney the amount for which he was willing to settle, and he did not give the attorney the authority to settle the claim without his consent. When the attorney agreed with Auto-Owners to settle the claim for $18,000, Gravens repudiated the agreement, hired a different attorney, and filed a suit in an Indiana state court against Auto-Owners. The court granted Auto-Owners a summary judgment. Gravens appealed.*

<table>
<tr><td>IN THE LANGUAGE
OF THE COURT</td><td>ROBERTSON, Judge.
*   *   *   *</td></tr>
</table>

IN THE LANGUAGE
OF THE COURT

ROBERTSON, Judge.

*   *   *   *

In Indiana, the attorney-client relationship is governed by the Model Rules of Professional Conduct. *   *   *

Professional Conduct Rule 1.2(a) reads, in pertinent part, as follows:

> A lawyer shall abide by a client's decision concerning the objectives of representation, *   *   *, and shall consult with the client as to the means by which they are to be pursued. A lawyer shall abide by a client's decision whether to accept an offer of settlement of a matter.

*   *   *

In *Klebes v. Forest Lake Corporation* [a previous case], we noted that under Prof.Cond.R. 1.2, a client has full authority over the decision whether or not to settle his case or proceed to trial. We noted that attorneys could enter into enforceable settlement agreements on their client's behalf if they first secure their client's consent to do so. The insurance company points out, correctly, that *Klebes* does not necessarily stand for the proposition that the client's authorization or consent is required before his attorney can bind him in a settlement agreement as the clients in *Klebes* had, in fact, approved the terms of settlement agreed to by their attorney.

Nevertheless, we hold that the requirement that an attorney must obtain his client's authority or consent to settle a case is implicit in the client's right to exercise ultimate authority over the settlement of a case as guaranteed by Prof.Cond.R. 1.2(a). Moreover, *the rule that an attorney does not have authority to compromise an action merely by virtue of the attorney-client relationship is essentially universal.* [Emphasis added.]

In this case, as in most insurance settlements, both parties understood that there would be no settlement without a release signed by the claimant, not by his attorney. This understanding was implicit when the draft and the release were tendered together. The insurance company had no enforceable expectation that the claim had, in fact, been settled until Gravens himself had signed the release, which he declined to do.

Gravens did not authorize his original attorney to settle the case and immediately repudiated the settlement agreement purported to have been reached by that attorney. Under these circumstances, Gravens was not bound by his attorney's agreement and the trial court's entry of summary judgment on this basis was erroneous.

**DECISION
AND REMEDY**

The intermediate state appellate court reversed the lower court's decision and remanded the case. Because Gravens did not authorize his attorney to settle the case, Gravens was not bound by the settlement.

APPARENT AUTHORITY AND ESTOPPEL

Actual authority (express or implied) arises from what the principal manifests *to the agent*. An agent has **apparent authority** when the principal, by either word or action, causes a *third party* reasonably to believe that the agent has authority to act, even though the agent has no express or implied authority. If the third party changes his or her position in reliance on the principal's representations, the principal may be *estopped* from denying that the agent had authority.

For example, assume that Adam is a traveling sales agent for a pesticide company. Adam neither possesses the goods ordered nor delivers them, and he has no express or implied authority to collect payments from customers. Now assume that a customer, Ling, pays Adam for a solicited order. Adam then takes the payment to the principal's accounting department. An accountant accepts payment and sends Ling a receipt. This procedure is thereafter followed for other orders solicited by Adam and paid for by Ling. Later, Adam solicits an order, and Ling pays Adam as before. This time, however, Adam absconds with the money.

Can Ling claim that the payment to Adam was authorized and thus, in effect, a payment to the principal? The answer is yes, because the principal's *repeated* acts of accepting Ling's payments through Adam led Ling reasonably to believe that Adam had authority to receive payments for goods solicited. Although Adam did

EXHIBIT 32–1   A SAMPLE GENERAL POWER OF ATTORNEY

POWER OF ATTORNEY
GENERAL

Know All Men by These Presents: That I, _____

_____

the undersigned (jointly and severally, if more than one) hereby make, constitute and appoint _____

_____

as a true and lawful Attorney for me and in my name, place and stead and for my use and benefit:

(a)   To ask, demand, sue for, recover, collect and receive each and every sum of money, debt, account, legacy, bequest, interest, dividend, annuity and demand (which now is or hereafter shall become due, owing or payable) belonging to or claimed by me, and to use and take any lawful means for the recovery thereof by legal process or otherwise, and to execute and deliver a satisfaction or release therefore, together with the right and power to compromise or compound any claim or demand;

(b) To exercise any or all of the following powers as to real property, any interest therein and/or any building thereon: To contract for, purchase, receive and take possession thereof and or evidence of title thereto; to lease the same for any term or purpose, including leases for business, residence, and oil and/or mineral development; to sell, exchange, grant or convey the same with or without warranty; and to mortgage, transfer in trust, or otherwise encumber or hypothecate the same to secure payment of a negotiable or non-negotiable note or performance of any obligation or agreement;

(c)   To exercise any or all of the following powers as to all kinds of personal property and goods, wares and merchandise, choses in action and other property in possession or in action: To contract for, buy, sell, exchange, transfer and in any legal manner deal in and with the same; and to mortgage, transfer in trust, or otherwise encumber or hypothecate the same to secure payment of a negotiable or non-negotiable note or performance of any obligation or agreement;

(d) To borrow money and to execute and deliver negotiable or non-negotiable notes therefore with or without security; and to loan money and receive negotiable or non-negotiable notes therefore with such security as he shall deem proper;

(e) To create, amend, supplement and terminate any trust and to instruct and advise the trustee of any trust wherein I am or may be trustor or beneficiary; to represent and vote stock, exercise stock rights, accept and deal with any dividend, distribution or bonus, join in any corporate financing, reorganization, merger, liquidation, consolidation or other action and the extension, compromise, conversion, adjustment, enforcement or foreclosure, singly or in conjunction with others, of any corporate stock, bond, note, debenture or other security; to compound, compromise, adjust, settle and satisfy any obligation, secured or unsecured, owing by or to me and to give or accept any property and/or money whether or not equal to or less in value than the amount owing in payment, settlement or satisfaction thereof;

(f) To transact business of any kind or class and as my act and deed to sign, execute, acknowledge and deliver any deed, lease, assignment of lease, covenant, indenture, indemnity, agreement, mortgage, deed of trust, assignment of mortgage or of the beneficial interest under deed of trust, extension or renewal of any obligation, subordination or waiver of priority, hypothecation, bottomry, charter-party, bill of lading, bill of sale, bill, bond, note, whether negotiable or non-negotiable, receipt, evidence of debt, full or partial release or satisfaction of mortgage, judgment and other debt, request for partial or full reconveyance of deed of trust and such other instruments in writing of any kind or class as may be necessary or proper in the premises.

Giving and Granting unto my said Attorney full power and authority to do so and perform all and every act and thing whatsoever requisite, necessary or appropriate to be done in and about the premises as fully to all intents and purposes as I might or could do if personally present, hereby ratifying all that my said Attorney shall lawfully do or cause to be done by virtue of these presents. The powers and authority hereby conferred upon my said Attorney shall be applicable to all real and personal property or interests therein now owned or hereafter acquired by me and wherever situated.

My said Attorney is empowered hereby to determine in his sole discretion the time when, purpose for and manner in which any power herein conferred upon him shall be exercised, and the conditions, provisions and covenants of any instrument or document which may be executed by him pursuant hereto; and in the acquisition or disposition of real or personal property, my said Attorney shall have exclusive power to fix the terms thereof for cash, credit and/or property, and if on credit with or without security.

The undersigned, if a married woman, hereby further authorizes and empowers my said Attorney, as my duly authorized agent, to join in my behalf, in the execution of any instrument by which any community real property or any interest therein, now owned or hereafter acquired by my spouse and myself, or either of us, is sold, leased, encumbered, or conveyed.

When the context so requires, the masculine gender includes the feminine and/or neuter, and the singular number includes the plural.

WITNESS my hand this _____ day of _____ , 20 ____

_____   _____

_____   _____

State of California
    County of _____   } SS.

On _____ , before me, the undersigned, a Notary Public in and for said
State, personally appeared _____

known to me to be the person _____ whose name _____ subscribed
to the within instrument and acknowledged that _____ executed the same.

Witness my hand and official seal.   (Seal) _____

Notary Public in and for said State.

not have express or implied authority, the principal's conduct gave Adam apparent authority to collect.

There are other ways in which agency by estoppel may arise based on apparent authority. If, for example, the principal has "clothed the agent" with both possession and apparent ownership of the principal's property, the agent has very broad powers and can deal with the property as if he or she were the true owner. For example, to deceive certain creditors, Sikora (the principal) and Hunter (the agent) agree verbally that Hunter will hold certain stock certificates for Sikora. Because the certificates are bearer paper (that is, they do not require indorsement to be transferred), Hunter's possession and apparent ownership of the stock certificates are such strong indications of ownership that a reasonable person would conclude that Hunter was the actual owner. If Hunter negotiates the stock certificates to a third person, Sikora will be estopped from denying Hunter's authority to transfer the stock.

When land is involved, courts have held that possession alone is not a sufficient indication of ownership (see Chapter 47 for details). If, however, the agent also possesses the deed to the property and sells the property against the principal's wishes to an unsuspecting buyer, the principal normally cannot cancel the sale or assert the claim to title.

The following case illustrates a situation dealing with apparent authority.

CASE 32.2   Cargill, Inc. v. Mountain Cement Co.

Supreme Court of
Wyoming, 1995.
891 P.2d 57.

**IN THE LANGUAGE
OF THE COURT**

BACKGROUND AND FACTS   *Cargill, Inc., hired Charlie Mandry to work as a sales representative. Cargill provided Mandry with an office, a telephone, and an expense account. Through Mandry, Salt Creek Welding ordered steel from Cargill to build a silo for Mountain Cement Company. Mandry arranged to have some of the steel supplied by another company. The other firm's product was defective, which caused the silo to collapse. Mountain Cement filed a suit in a Wyoming state court against Cargill and others. The court ruled in favor of Mountain Cement. On appeal, one of the issues was whether Mandry acted as Cargill's agent in arranging the sale of the defective steel to Salt Creek.*

TAYLOR, Justice.
*   *   *   *

Apparent authority is created when the principal holds the agent out as possessing the authority to bind the principal or when the principal allows the agent to claim such authority. *   *   * To recover on this theory [apparent authority] the third party must establish two facts: (1) the principal was responsible for the appearance of authority in the agent to conduct the transaction in question, and (2) the third party reasonably relied on the representations of the agent. *   *   *
*   *   *   *

*   *   * Cargill provided Mandry with a telephone, an expense account and office space. These facts indicate that Cargill intended to hold Mandry out as an agent who possessed the authority to bind Cargill. Further, Salt Creek reasonably relied on that apparent authority when it ordered steel from Cargill. Thus, both prongs of the apparent authority test are satisfied.

**DECISION
AND REMEDY**

The Supreme Court of Wyoming affirmed the lower court's decision on this issue and upheld the ruling in favor of Mountain Cement. Cargill held Mandry out as its agent, and Salt Creek reasonably relied on that apparent authority.

EMERGENCY POWERS

When an unforeseen emergency demands action by the agent to protect or preserve the property and rights of the principal, but the agent is unable to communicate with the principal, the agent has emergency power.

For example, Fulsom is an engineer for Pacific Railroad. While Fulsom is acting within the scope of his employment, he falls under the train many miles from home and is severely injured. Dusky, the conductor, directs Thompson, a doctor, to give medical aid to Fulsom and to charge Pacific for the medical services. Dusky, an agent, has no express or implied authority to bind the principal, Pacific Railroad, for the services of Thompson. Because of the emergency situation, however, the law recognizes Dusky as having authority to act appropriately under the circumstances.

RATIFICATION

Ratification occurs when the principal affirms an agent's unauthorized act. Ratification binds the principal to the agent's act and creates a situation in which the act is treated as if it had been authorized by the principal *from the outset.* Ratification can be either express or implied.

With respect to a contract, if the principal does not ratify, the principal is not bound, and the third party's agreement with the agent is merely an unaccepted offer. Because the third party's agreement is an unaccepted offer, the third party can revoke it any time before the principal ratifies, without liability. The agent, however, may be liable to the third party for misrepresenting his or her authority.

To be effective, a ratification must meet certain requirements. These include the following:

1. The agent must act on behalf of an identified principal who subsequently ratifies the action.
2. The principal must affirm the agent's act in its entirety.
3. The principal's affirmance must occur before the third party withdraws from the transaction.
4. The principal must have the legal capacity to authorize the transaction at the time the agent engages in the act and at the time the principal ratifies. The third party must also have the legal capacity to engage in the transaction.
5. The principal must know all of the material facts involved in the transaction.

Regarding this last requirement, if a principal ratifies a contract *without knowing* all of the facts, the principal can rescind (cancel) the ratification. If the third party has changed his or her position in reliance on the apparent contract, however, the principal can rescind but must reimburse the third party for his or her costs.

For example, suppose that an agent, without authority, contracts with a third person on behalf of a principal

for repair work to the principal's office building. The principal learns of the contract and agrees to "some repair work," thinking that it will involve only patching and painting the exterior of the building. In fact, the contract includes resurfacing the parking lot, which the principal does not want done. On learning of the additional provision, the principal rescinds the contract. If the third party has made preparations to do the work (such as purchasing materials, hiring additional workers, or renting equipment), in reliance on the principal's apparent ratification, the principal must reimburse the third party for the cost of those preparations.

SECTION 2

Liability for Contracts

Liability for contracts formed by an agent depends on how the principal is classified and on whether the actions of the agent were authorized or unauthorized.

Principals are classified as disclosed, partially disclosed, or undisclosed.[2] A **disclosed principal** is a principal whose identity is known by the third party at the time the contract is made by the agent. A **partially disclosed principal** is a principal whose identity is not known by the third party, but the third party knows that the agent is or may be acting for a principal at the time that the contract is made. An **undisclosed principal** is a principal whose identity is totally unknown by the third party, and the third party has no knowledge that the agent is acting in an agency capacity at the time the contract is made.

AUTHORIZED ACTS

If an agent acts within the scope of his or her authority, a disclosed or partially disclosed principal is liable to a third party for a contract made by the agent. If the principal is disclosed, an agent has no contractual liability for the nonperformance of the principal or the third party. If the principal is partially disclosed, in most states the agent is also treated as a party to the contract, and the third party can hold the agent liable for contractual nonperformance.[3]

When neither the fact of agency nor the identity of the principal is disclosed, the undisclosed principal is fully bound to perform just as if the principal had been fully disclosed at the time the contract was made. Exceptions to this rule are made in the following circumstances:

---

2. *Restatement (Second) of Agency*, Section 4.
3. *Restatement (Second) of Agency*, Section 321.

1. The undisclosed principal was expressly excluded as a party in the contract. For example, an agent contracts with a landlord for the lease of a building. The landlord does not know of the agency, and the lease specifically lists the agent as tenant, with no right of assignment without the landlord's consent. The undisclosed principal cannot enforce the lease.

2. The contract is a negotiable instrument. Here, the UCC provides that only the agent is liable if the instrument neither names the principal nor shows that the agent signed in a representative capacity.[4]

3. The performance of the agent is personal to the contract, allowing the third party to refuse the principal's performance. Typical examples involve extensions of credit and highly personal services, such as surgery.

4. The third party would not have entered into a contract with the principal had the third party known the principal's identity, the agent or the principal knew this, and the third party rescinds the contract.

When a principal's identity is undisclosed and the agent is forced to pay the third party, the agent is entitled to indemnification by the principal. It was the principal's duty to perform, even though his or her identity was undisclosed,[5] and failure to do so will make the principal ultimately liable. Once the undisclosed principal's identity is revealed, the third party generally can elect to hold either the principal or the agent liable on the contract. (One of the issues raised by online commerce has to do with the liability of principals for the actions of electronic agents. For a discussion of this topic, see this chapter's *Emerging Trends in Technology* on pages 596 and 597.)

UNAUTHORIZED ACTS

If an agent has no authority but nevertheless contracts with a third party, the principal cannot be held liable to the contract. It does not matter whether the principal was disclosed, partially disclosed, or undisclosed. The agent is liable, however. For example, Scammon signs a contract for the purchase of a truck, purportedly acting as an agent under authority granted by Johnson. In fact, Johnson has not given Scammon any such authority. Johnson refuses to pay for the truck, claiming that Scammon had no authority to purchase it. The seller of the truck is entitled to hold Scammon liable for payment.

If the principal is disclosed or partially disclosed, the agent's liability to the third party is based on the theory of breach of implied warranty of authority, not on breach of the contract itself.[6] The agent's implied warranty of authority can be breached intentionally or by a good faith mistake.[7] The agent is liable, as long as the third party relied on the agency status. Conversely, if the third party knows at the time the contract is made that the agent is mistaken about the extent of his or her authority, or the agent indicates to the third party *uncertainty* about the extent of authority, the agent is not personally liable for breach of warranty.

---

4. UCC 3–402(b)(2).
5. If the agent is a gratuitous agent, and the principal accepts the benefits of the agent's contract with a third party, then the principal will be liable to the agent on the theory of quasi contract (see Chapter 10).

6. The agent is not liable on the contract because the agent was never intended personally to be a party to the contract.
7. If the agent intentionally misrepresents his or her authority, then the agent can also be liable in tort for fraud.

CONCEPT SUMMARY 32.1   AUTHORITY OF AGENT TO BIND PRINCIPAL AND THIRD PARTY

AUTHORITY OF AGENT	DEFINITION	EFFECT ON PRINCIPAL AND THIRD PARTY
Express Authority	Authority expressly given by the principal to the agent.	Principal and third party are bound in contract.
Implied Authority	Authority implied (1) by custom, (2) from the position in which the principal has placed the agent, or (3) because such authority is necessary if the agent is to carry out expressly authorized duties and responsibilities.	Principal and third party are bound in contract.

CONCEPT SUMMARY 32.1 — AUTHORITY OF AGENT TO BIND PRINCIPAL AND THIRD PARTY (*continued*)

AUTHORITY OF AGENT	DEFINITION	EFFECT ON PRINCIPAL AND THIRD PARTY
Apparent Authority	Authority created when the conduct of the principal leads a third party to believe that the principal's agent has authority.	Principal and third party are bound in contract.
Unauthorized Acts	Acts committed by an agent that are outside the scope of his or her express, implied, or apparent authority.	Principal and third party are not bound in contract—*unless* the principal ratifies prior to the third party's withdrawal.

SECTION 3

Liability for Agent's Torts

Obviously, an agent is liable for his or her own torts. A principal may also be liable for an agent's torts if they result from one of the following:

1. The principal's own tortious conduct.
2. The principal's authorization of a tortious act.
3. The agent's unauthorized but tortious misrepresentation made within the scope of the agency.

If the agent is an employee, whose conduct the principal-employer controls, the employer may also be liable for torts committed by the employee in the course of employment under the doctrine of *respondeat superior,* as discussed below.

PRINCIPAL'S TORTIOUS CONDUCT

A principal conducting an activity through an agent may be liable for harm resulting from the principal's own negligence or recklessness, which may include giving improper instructions; authorizing the use of improper materials, tools, or the like; establishing improper rules; or failing to prevent others' tortious conduct while they are on the principal's property or using the principal's equipment, materials, or tools. For instance, if Jack knows that Kathy cannot drive but nevertheless authorizes her to use the company truck to deliver some equipment to a customer, he will be liable for his own negligence to anyone injured by her negligent driving.

PRINCIPAL'S AUTHORIZATION OF AGENT'S TORTIOUS CONDUCT

Similarly, a principal who authorizes an agent to commit a tortious act may be liable to persons or property injured thereby, because the act is considered to be the principal's. For example, Selkow directs Warren—an agent Selkow retained to oversee the harvest of crops he bought—to cut the corn on specific acreage, which neither of them has the right to do. The harvest is therefore a trespass, and Selkow is liable to whoever owns the corn.

In the same vein, assume that Victoria instructs Guthrie, her real estate agent, to tell prospective purchasers that there is oil beneath her property, when she knows there is not. Victoria will be liable to anyone who buys the property in reliance on the statements.

MISREPRESENTATION

A principal is exposed to tort liability whenever a third person sustains a loss due to the agent's misrepresentation. The principal's liability depends on whether the agent was actually or apparently authorized to make representations and whether such representations were made within the scope of the agency.

Fraudulent Misrepresentation. Assume that Bassett is a demonstrator for Moore's products. Moore sends Bassett to a home show to demonstrate the products and to answer questions from consumers. Moore has given Bassett authority to make statements about the products. If Bassett makes only true representations, all is fine; but if he makes false claims, Moore will be liable for any injuries or damages sustained by third parties in reliance on Bassett's false representations.

An interesting series of cases has arisen on the theory that when a principal has placed an agent in a position to defraud a third party, the principal is liable for the agent's fraudulent acts. For example, Frendak is a loan officer at First Security Bank. In the ordinary course of the job, Frendak approves and services loans and has access to the credit records of all customers. Frendak falsely represents to a borrower, McMillan, that the bank feels insecure about McMillan's loan and intends to call it in unless McMillan provides additional collateral, such as stocks and bonds. McMillan gives Frendak numerous stock certificates, which Frendak keeps in her own possession and later uses to make personal investments. The bank is liable to McMillan for losses sustained on the stocks even though the bank had no direct role in or knowledge of the fraudulent scheme.

The legal theory used here is that the agent's position conveys to third persons the impression that the agent has the authority to make statements and perform acts consistent with the ordinary duties that are within the scope of the position. When an agent appears to be acting within the scope of the authority that the position of agency confers but is actually taking advantage of a third party, the principal who placed the agent in that position is liable. In the example above, if a bank teller had told McMillan that the bank required additional security for the loan, McMillan would not have been justified in relying on the person's authority to make that representation. McMillan, however, could reasonably expect that the loan officer was telling the truth.

Innocent Misrepresentation. Tort liability based on fraud requires proof that a material misstatement was made knowingly and with the intent to deceive. An agent's innocent mistakes occurring in a contract transaction or involving a warranty contained in the contract can provide grounds for the third party's rescission of the contract and the award of damages. Moreover, justice dictates that when a principal knows that an agent is not accurately advised of facts but does not correct either the agent's or the third party's impressions, the principal is directly responsible to the third party for resulting damages. The point is that the principal is always directly responsible for an agent's misrepresentation made within the scope of authority.

THE DOCTRINE OF *RESPONDEAT SUPERIOR*

Under the doctrine of *respondeat superior*,[8] the principal-employer is liable for any harm caused to a third party by an agent-employee within the scope of employment. This doctrine imposes **vicarious liability** on the employer—that is, liability without regard to the personal fault of the employer for torts committed by an employee in the course or scope of employment.[9] Third persons injured through the negligence of an employee can sue either the employee who was negligent or the employer, if the employee's negligent conduct occurred while the employee was acting within the scope of employment.

At early common law, a servant (employee) was viewed as the master's (employer's) property. The master was deemed to have absolute control over the servant's acts and was held strictly liable for them no matter how carefully the master supervised the servant. The rationale for the doctrine of *respondeat superior* is based on the principle of social duty that requires every person to manage his or her affairs, whether accomplished by the person or through agents, so as not to injure another. Liability is imposed on employers because they are deemed to be in a better financial position to bear the loss. The superior financial position carries with it the duty to be responsible for damages.

Today the doctrine continues, but employers carry liability insurance and spread the cost of risk over the entire business enterprise. Public policy requires that an injured person be afforded effective relief, and recovery from a business enterprise provides far more effective relief than recovery from an individual employee. Liability rights exist under law because of public-policy protections of third parties. Thus, a master (employer) cannot contract with a servant (employee) to disclaim responsibilities for injuries resulting from the servant's acts, because such disclaimers are against public policy.

Liability for Employee's Negligence. For the employer to be liable for an employee's negligence, the employee's injury-causing act must have occurred within the course and scope of the employee's employment.

---

8. Pronounced ree-*spahn*-dee-uht soo-*peer*-ee-your. The doctrine of *respondeat superior* applies not only to employer-employee relationships but also to other principal-agent relationships in which the principal has the right of control over the agent.
9. The theory of *respondeat superior* is similar to the theory of strict liability covered in Chapter 6.

EMERGING TRENDS IN TECHNOLOGY

The Use of Intelligent Agents

"Intelligent agents," or electronic agents, are semiautonomous Internet computer programs that are capable of executing specific tasks. For example, intelligent agents on the World Wide Web can search through many databases and retrieve only relevant information for the user. Some intelligent agents are used to make purchases on the Internet. A user might use BargainFinder (PriceScan), for example, to search the many Internet Web sites that offer compact discs (CDs) and seek out the lowest price for a particular album. Once the lowest price is found, the intelligent agent usually offers links to the appropriate Web sites. Different shopping agents locate other

specific products in online catalogues and actually negotiate product acquisition, as well as delivery.

WHAT AGENCY LAW APPLIES?

Intelligent agents may be just that, but standard agency principles have applied only to *human* agents, who have express or implied authority to enter into specific contracts. Many questions in agency law revolve around whether the human agent acted within the scope of his or her authority. What does this concept mean when dealing with an electronic intelligent agent?

Consider a not-unusual example. Software that an intelligent agent might find for its user will undoubtedly involve a "click-on" agreement (see the discussion of electronic sales contracts in the *Emerging Trends in Technology* presented in Chapter 19). Intelligent agents searching

the Internet may run into a wide variety of such "click-on" agreements, which by necessity, contain many different terms and conditions. If the intelligent agent ignores the terms and conditions of a licensing agreement outlined in the "click-on" setting, is the user of the agent nonetheless bound by the agreement? Conversely, many "click-on" agreements exempt third parties from any liability resulting from the underlying product or service. Is the user of the intelligent agent bound by this particular term? With respect to human agents, the courts occasionally have found that an agent could not agree to such a term without explicit authority.[a]

To avoid problems created by the use of intelligent agents, some online stores have blocked intelligent agents from accessing pricing information. Other online

---

a. *Bernstein v. Seacliff Beach Club, Inc.*, 35 Misc.2d 153, 228 N.Y.S.2d 567 (1962).

Scope of Employment. The *Restatement (Second) of Agency*, Section 229, indicates the following general factors that courts will consider in determining whether or not a particular act occurred within the course and scope of employment:

1. Whether the employee's act was authorized by the employer.
2. The time, place, and purpose of the act.
3. Whether the act was one commonly performed by employees on behalf of their employers.
4. The extent to which the employer's interest was advanced by the act.
5. The extent to which the private interests of the employee were involved.

6. Whether the employer furnished the means or instrumentality (for example, a truck or a machine) by which an injury was inflicted.
7. Whether the employer had reason to know that the employee would perform the act in question and whether the employee had done it before.
8. Whether the act involved the commission of a serious crime.

Consider an example. Mandel (the employee) is a delivery driver for Schwartz (the employer). Schwartz provides Mandel with a vehicle and instructs him to use it for making company deliveries. One day, while he is making deliveries, Mandel negligently runs into Chan, a pedestrian, causing Chan to be seriously in-

EMERGING TRENDS IN TECHNOLOGY

The Use of Intelligent Agents, continued

stores are developing click-on agreements that can be understood by a computer and that are therefore more conspicuous for intelligent agents.

THE UNIFORM COMPUTER INFORMATION TRANSACTIONS ACT

The Uniform Computer Information Transactions Act (UCITA), which was proposed for adoption by the states in 1999, specifically addresses the issue of intelligent agents. Section 107(d) of the act provides that any individual or company that uses an electronic agent "is bound by the operations of the electronic agent, even if no individual was aware of or reviewed

the agent's operations or the results of the operations." The liability of individuals and companies for the acts of electronic agents, however, is qualified by Section 206(a) of the UCITA, which states that "a court may grant appropriate relief if the operations resulted from fraud, electronic mistake, or the like." As discussed in Chapter 9, the UCITA's provisions have generated substantial controversy, and it is not yet clear whether the act will be adopted by the states or, if it is, how it may be modified on adoption.

IMPLICATIONS FOR THE BUSINESSPERSON

1. Any businessperson who is contemplating the use of an electronic agent must proceed with caution. Time may be saved, but users of such agents must consider the possibility that they might be bound to contract terms of which they are unaware.

2. Although intelligent agents are becoming increasingly sophisticated, there is still the possibility that they may have more contracting authority than any businessperson wants them to have. The message for businesspersons is "user beware."

FOR CRITICAL ANALYSIS

1. What are the costs and benefits of using an intelligent shopping agent?
2. How might online shopping-site owners develop standardized click-on agreements that can be understood by electronic agents?

RELEVANT WEB SITES

For information on PriceScan, go to http://www.pricescan.com. Go to SelectSurf at http://www.selectsurf.com/shopping/compare, where you will find hot links to many intelligent shopping agents.

---

jured. Because the negligence occurred as part of Mandel's regular duties of employment (making deliveries), Schwartz is liable to Chan for the injuries caused by Mandel's negligence.

An employee going to and from work or to and from meals is usually considered outside the scope of employment. All travel time of traveling salespersons or others whose jobs require them to travel is normally considered within the scope of employment for the duration of the business trip, including the return trip home, unless there is a significant departure from the employer's business.

Departures from the Employer's Business. When an employee goes off on his or her own—that is, de-

parts from the employer's business to take care of personal affairs—is the employer liable? The answer depends on whether the employee's activity is a minor departure from the employer's business or a substantial departure akin to an utter abandonment of the employer's business. For example, a traveling salesperson, while driving the employer's vehicle to call on a customer, decides to stop at the post office—which is one block off his route—to mail a personal letter. As the employee approaches the post office, he negligently runs into a parked vehicle owned by Inga. In this situation, because the employee's detour from the employer's business is not substantial, the employee is still within the scope of employment, and the employer is liable.

The result would be different if the employee had decided to pick up a few friends for cocktails in another city and in the process had negligently run his vehicle into Inga's. In this situation, the departure from the employer's business would be substantial, to the point of abandoning the employer's business, and the employer normally would not be liable to Inga for damages. The employee would be considered to be on a "frolic" of his own, and only the employee could be held liable to Inga.

Courts often refer to the "detour-frolic" distinction when deciding whether a given action was within the course and scope of employment. The distinction was first drawn in the following classic case on "master-servant" (employer-employee) law.

CASE 32.3   Joel v. Morison

Court of Exchequer, England, 1834.
172 Eng.Rep. 1338.

BACKGROUND AND FACTS   *The plaintiff was walking across Bishopsgate Street when he was knocked down by a cart driven negligently by a servant of the defendant. The plaintiff suffered a fractured leg and multiple injuries. The plaintiff took the position that the defendant was liable for his injuries because the defendant's servant was driving the cart that caused the injuries. The defendant argued that his cart was never driven in the neighborhood in which the plaintiff was injured. Moreover, it was suggested that the defendant's servant had gone out of his way for his own purposes and might have taken the cart at a time when it was not wanted for business purposes to pay a visit to some friends.*

IN THE LANGUAGE OF THE COURT   PARKE, Judge.

*   *   *   *

*   *   * This is an action to recover damages for an injury sustained by the plaintiff, in consequence of the negligence of the defendant's servant. *   *   * If the servants, being on their master's business, took a detour to call upon a friend, the master will be responsible. If *   *   * the servants lent the cart to a person who was driving without the defendant's knowledge, he will not be responsible. Or, if *   *   * the young man who was driving took the cart surreptitiously, and was not at the time employed on his master's business, the defendant will not be liable. The master is only liable where the servant is acting in the course of his employment. If he was going out of his way, against his master's implied commands, when driving on his master's business, he will make his master liable; *but if he was going on a frolic of his own, without being at all on his master's business, the master will not be liable.* As to the damages, the master *   *   * [although not himself] guilty of any offence, *   *   * is only responsible in law, therefore the amount should be reasonable. [Emphasis added.]

DECISION AND REMEDY   *The verdict was for the plaintiff, and he was awarded damages of £30. In this case, the master was held liable for the acts of his servant.*

INTERNATIONAL CONSIDERATIONS   **Respondeat Superior *in Islamic Countries***   *The doctrine of respondeat superior is well established in the legal systems of the United States and most Western countries. Middle Eastern countries, however, do not employ the principle. Islamic law holds to a strict principle that responsibility for human actions lies with the individual and cannot be vicariously extended to others.*

Borrowed Servants.   Employers can lend the services of their employees to other employers. Suppose that an employer leases ground-moving equipment to another employer and sends along an employee to operate the machinery. Who is liable for injuries caused by the employee's negligent actions on the job site? Liability turns on *which employer had the primary right to control* the employee at the time the injuries occurred

Generally, the employer who rents out the equipment is presumed to retain control over his or her employee. If the rental is for a relatively long period of time, however, control may be deemed to pass to the employer who is renting the equipment and presumably controlling and directing the employee.

Notice of Dangerous Conditions.

The employer is charged with knowledge of any dangerous conditions discovered by an employee and pertinent to the employment situation. To illustrate: A maintenance employee in Martin's apartment building notices a lead pipe protruding from the ground in the building's courtyard. The employee neglects either to fix it or to inform the employer of the danger. John falls on the pipe and is injured. The employer is charged with knowledge of the dangerous condition regardless of whether or not the employee actually informed the employer. That knowledge is imputed to the employer by virtue of the employment relationship.

Liability for Employee's Intentional Torts.

Most intentional torts that employees commit have no relation to their employment; thus, their employers will not be held liable. Under the doctrine of *respondeat superior*, however, the employer is liable for intentional torts of the employee that are committed within the course and scope of employment, just as the employer is liable for negligence. For example, an employer is liable when an employee (such as a "bouncer" at a nightclub or a security guard at a department store) commits assault and battery or false imprisonment while acting within the scope of employment.

An employee acting at the employer's direction can be liable as a *tortfeasor* (one who commits a wrong, or tort), along with the employer, for committing the tortious act even if the employee was unaware of the wrongfulness of the act. For example, an employer directs an employee to burn out a field of crops. The employee does so, assuming that the field belongs to the employer, which it does not. Both can be found liable to the owner of the field for damages.

An employer who knows or should know that an employee has a propensity for committing tortious acts is liable for the employee's acts even if they would not ordinarily be considered within the scope of employment. For example, the Blue Moon employs Arnold Munn as a bouncer, knowing that he has a history of arrests for assault and battery. While he is working one night, and within the scope of his employment, he viciously attacks a patron who "looks at him funny." The Blue Moon will bear the responsibility for Munn's misdeeds, because it knew that he had a propensity for committing tortious acts.

An employer is also liable for permitting an employee to engage in reckless actions that can injure others. For example, an employer observes an employee smoking while filling containerized trucks with highly flammable liquids. Failure to stop the employee will cause the employer to be liable for any injuries that result if a truck explodes.

To reduce the likelihood of liability losses, employers set up stringent work rules. For example, employees who drive company vehicles may be prohibited from giving rides to other passengers. Employees who violate these rules by being careless or committing unlawful or tortious acts may be subject to discipline, including discharge. Almost without exception, employers purchase liability insurance to cover the actions of certain employees.

SECTION 4

Liability for Independent Contractor's Torts

The general rule concerning liability for the acts of independent contractors is that the employer is not liable for physical harm caused to a third person by the negligent act of an independent contractor in the performance of the contract. An employer who has no legal power to control the details of the physical performance of a contract cannot be held liable. Here again, the test is the *right to control*. Because an employer bargains with an independent contractor only for results and retains no control over the manner in which those results are achieved, the employer is generally not expected to bear the responsibility for torts committed by an independent contractor. A collection agency is a typical example of an independent contractor. The creditor is generally not liable for the acts of the collection agency, because collection is a distinct business occupation.

Generally, an exception to this doctrine prevails when unusually hazardous activities are involved. Typical examples of such activities include blasting operations, the transportation of highly volatile chemicals, and the use of poisonous gases. In these cases, an employer cannot be shielded from liability merely by using an independent contractor. Strict liability is imposed on the employer-principal as a matter of law.

Also, in some states, strict liability may be imposed by statute.

In the following case, one of the issues before the court was whether the negligence of an independent contractor, who was acting as an agent, could be imputed to the principal.

CASE 32.4   Haag v. Bongers

Supreme Court of
Nebraska, 1999.
256 Neb. 170,
589 N.W.2d 318.
http://www.findlaw.
com/11stategov/ne/
neca.html[a]

BACKGROUND AND FACTS   *When Leo Bongers died, his nephew, Alfred Bongers, was appointed one of the personal representatives of his estate, which included more than 120 antique cars, trucks, and motorcycles. The estate hired Bauer-Moravec Auctioneers and Clerks, and Dolan Realty and Auction Company to jointly conduct an auction of the vehicles. The auctioneers suggested that the auction be held in the summer, with the vehicles lined up outside, but the estate insisted on holding the auction as soon as possible, in the winter. The auction was heavily advertised at the estate's insistence, and was held on a farm owned by the estate, in a building open at both ends. With the estate's agreement, tents were set up at either end to enlarge the "bid barn," and each attendee was charged $25. Bongers was there. Assistants paid by the estate moved the vehicles through the members of the crowd, who were standing shoulder to shoulder in the barn. The estate had failed in its responsibility to put all of the vehicles in running order, so many of the vehicles were towed into the building using tractors, which the estate had approved, with hitch balls. As the assistants attempted to tow an antique Studebaker truck out of the barn, the hitch ball became detached, flew off the tractor, and hit Joseph Haag, who suffered serious head injuries. Haag filed a suit in a Nebraska state court against the estate and others, alleging, among other things, negligence on the part of the auctioneers. Haag argued that as agents for the estate, the auctioneers' negligence should be imputed to the estate. The estate responded in part that it was not liable for the acts of the auctioneers because they were independent contractors. The court entered a judgment in favor of Haag. The estate appealed to the Nebraska Supreme Court.*

**IN THE LANGUAGE
OF THE COURT**

MILLER-LEHRMAN, J. [Justice]

*   *   *   *

Generally, the employer of an independent contractor is not liable for physical harm caused to another by the acts or omissions of the contractor or his servants. *   *   * *The employer of an independent contractor may be vicariously liable to a third party* *   *   * *if the employer retains control over the contractor's work* *   *   * . [Emphasis added.]

*   *   *   *

Based on the facts of this case, we conclude that the auctioneers served as independent contractors. However, the Estate exercised sufficient control over the auction to subject it to liability, notwithstanding the participation of the auctioneers as independent contractors. The factors which demonstrate the Estate's control include, but are not limited to, the following facts: The auction was held on the Estate's property, and the Estate insisted that the auction be conducted in winter rather than in summer in a more expansive setting. The Estate was responsible for putting the vehicles in running order but failed to do so, resulting in the necessity of towing the vehicles at the auction. The Estate approved the use of tractors to tow the vehicles at the auction. The Estate approved the use of assistants. The Estate paid the assistants. The Estate insisted that the auction be heavily advertised, resulting in a shoulder-to-shoulder crowd through which the vehicles were to be towed. The Estate and the auctioneers decided to extend the bid barn and charge a $25 fee. Bongers was present at the auction at the time of the accident.

---

a. In the "Supreme Court Opinions" section, click on "1999." In that row, click on "February." On that page, scroll down the list of cases to the name of the case (the decision was issued on "02/12/1999") and click on the docket number to access the opinion.

Although actual performance of the task of towing the vehicles was to be performed by the independent contractor auctioneers, the facts in this case as to the Estate's active and considerable control over the activities that led to the accident are sufficient to subject the Estate to liability. In this regard, we note that the *Restatement (Second) of Torts*, Section 414 provides:

> One who entrusts work to an independent contractor, but who retains the control of any part of the work, is subject to liability for physical harm to others for whose safety the employer owes a duty to exercise reasonable care, which is caused by his failure to exercise his control with reasonable care.

We conclude that because the Estate retained considerable control over the relevant work, it is therefore liable for a failure to exercise reasonable care in the use of that control. Accordingly, imputing the negligence of the assistants to the Estate was justified by the facts *   *   * .

DECISION AND REMEDY   *The Nebraska Supreme Court affirmed the judgment of the trial court. The negligence of the assistants, who worked for the independent contractors (who acted as the agents of the estate and were paid by the estate) could be imputed to the estate because of the control exercised by the principal over the independent contractors.*

SECTION 5

Liability for Agent's Crimes

Obviously, an agent is liable for his or her own crimes. A principal or employer is not liable for an agent's or employee's crime simply because the agent or employee committed the crime while otherwise acting within the scope of authority or employment, unless the principal or employer participated by conspiracy or other action. In some jurisdictions, under specific statutes, a principal may be liable for an agent's violating, in the course and scope of employment, such regulations as those governing sanitation, prices, weights, and the sale of liquor.

SECTION 6

Liability for Subagent's Acts

In three instances, an agent can hire a subagent:

1. To perform simple, definite duties.
2. When it is the business custom.
3. For unforeseen emergencies.

If an agent is authorized to hire subagents for the principal under any one of these circumstances, then the principal is liable for the acts of the subagents.

The result is slightly different if the agent hires subagents for an undisclosed principal. In that situation, the agent is responsible for the subagent in contract law for such things as wages. The undisclosed principal, however, is generally held to be liable for tort injuries. An agent's unauthorized hiring of a subagent generally does not create any legal relationship between the principal and the subagent.

SECTION 7

Termination of an Agency

Agency law is similar to contract law in that both an agency and a contract may be terminated by an act of the parties or by operation of law. Once the relationship between the principal and the agent has ended, the agent no longer has *actual* authority to bind the principal—that is, he or she lacks the principal's consent to act in the principal's behalf. Generally, if the agency is terminated by an act of the parties, the principal can still be bound by the agent's acts if the agent has acted within the scope of his or her *apparent* authority, however. To terminate the agent's apparent authority, third parties must be notified of the agency termination—as will be discussed later.

TERMINATION BY ACT OF THE PARTIES

An agency relationship may be terminated by act of the parties in a number of ways, including those discussed here.

Lapse of Time. An agency agreement may specify the time period during which the agency relationship will exist. If so, the agency ends when that time expires. For example, Akers signs an agreement of agency with Jefferson "beginning January 1, 1998, and ending December 31, 1999." The agency is automatically terminated on December 31, 1999. Of course, the parties can agree to continue the relationship, in which case the same terms will apply.

If no definite time is stated, then the agency continues for a reasonable time and can be terminated at will by either party. What constitutes a reasonable time depends on the circumstances and the nature of the agency relationship. For example, Jefferson asks Akers to sell her car. If after two years Akers has not sold Jefferson's car and there has been no communication between Jefferson and Akers, it is safe to assume that the agency relationship has terminated. Akers no longer has the authority to sell Jefferson's car.

Purpose Achieved. An agent can be employed to accomplish a particular objective, such as the purchase of stock for a cattle rancher. In that situation, the agency automatically ends after the cattle have been purchased. If more than one agent is employed to accomplish the same purpose, such as the sale of real estate, the first agent to complete the sale automatically terminates the agency relationship for all the others.

Occurrence of a Specific Event. An agency can be created to terminate on the happening of a certain event. For example, Jefferson appoints Akers to handle her business affairs while she is away. When Jefferson returns, the agency automatically terminates.

Sometimes one aspect of the agent's authority terminates on the occurrence of a particular event, but the agency relationship itself does not terminate. For example, Jefferson, a banker, permits Akers, the credit manager, to grant a credit line of $5,000 to certain depositors who maintain a balance of $5,000 in a savings account. If any customer's savings account balance falls below $5,000, Akers can no longer make the credit line available to that customer. Akers, however, continues to have the right to extend credit to the other customers maintaining the minimum balance.

Mutual Agreement. Recall from basic contract law that parties can rescind (cancel) a contract by mutually agreeing to terminate the contractual relationship. The same holds true in agency law regardless of whether the agency contract is in writing or whether it is for a specific duration. For example, Jefferson no longer wishes Akers to be her agent, and Akers does not want to work for Jefferson anymore. Either party can communicate to the other the intent to terminate the relationship. Agreement to terminate effectively relieves each of the rights, duties, and powers inherent in the relationship.

Termination by One Party. As a *general* rule, either party can terminate the agency relationship. The agent's act is said to be a renunciation of authority. The principal's act is a revocation of authority. Although both parties may have the *power* to terminate—because agency is a consensual relationship, and thus neither party can be compelled to continue in the relationship—they may not possess the *right* to terminate and may therefore be liable for breach of contract. Wrongful termination can subject the canceling party to a suit for damages. For example, Akers has a one-year employment contract with Jefferson to act as Jefferson's agent for $25,000. Jefferson can discharge Akers before the contract period expires (Jefferson has the *power* to breach the contract); however, Jefferson will be liable to Akers for money damages, because Jefferson has no *right* to breach the contract.

Even in an agency at will (that is, an agency that either party may terminate at any time), the principal who wishes to terminate must give the agent a reasonable notice—that is, at least sufficient notice to allow the agent to recoup his or her expenses and, in some cases, to make a normal profit.

A special rule applies in an *agency coupled with an interest.* This type of agency is not an agency in the usual sense, because it is created for the agent's benefit instead of for the principal's benefit. For example, suppose that Julie borrows $5,000 from Rob, giving Rob some of her jewelry and signing a letter authorizing Rob to sell the jewelry as her agent if she fails to repay the loan. Julie, after she has received the $5,000 from Rob, then attempts to revoke Rob's authority to sell the jewelry. Julie will not succeed in this attempt, because a principal cannot revoke an agency created for the agent's benefit.

An agency coupled with an interest should not be confused with a situation in which the agent merely derives proceeds or profits from the sale of the subject matter. For example, an agent who merely receives a commission from the sale of real property does not have a beneficial interest in the property itself. Likewise, an attorney whose fee is a percentage of the recovery (a *contingency fee*—see Chapter 3) merely has an interest in the proceeds. These agency relationships are revocable by the principal, subject to any express contractual arrangements between the principal and the agent.

Notice of Termination.

When an agency has been terminated by act of the parties, it is the principal's duty to inform any third parties who know of the existence of the agency that it has been terminated (although notice of the termination may be given by others).

An agent's authority continues until the agent receives some notice of termination. As previously mentioned, notice to third parties follows the general rule that an agent's *apparent authority* continues until the third person receives notice (from any source of information) that the authority has been terminated. The principal is expected to notify *directly* any third person who the principal knows has dealt with the agent. For third persons who have heard about the agency but have not dealt with the agent, *constructive notice* is sufficient.[10]

No particular form is required for notice of termination of the principal-agent relationship to be effective. The principal can actually notify the agent, or the agent can learn of the termination through some other means. For example, Manning bids on a shipment of steel, and Stone is hired as an agent to arrange transportation of the shipment. When Stone learns that Manning has lost the bid, Stone's authority to make the transportation arrangement terminates.

If the agent's authority is written, it must be revoked in writing, and the writing must be shown to all people who saw the original writing that established the agency relationship. Sometimes, a written authorization (such as a power of attorney) contains an expiration date. The passage of the expiration date is sufficient notice of termination.

TERMINATION BY OPERATION OF LAW

Certain events will terminate agency authority automatically, because their occurrence makes it impossible for the agent to perform or improbable that the principal would continue to want performance. We look at these events here. Note that when an agency terminates by operation of law, there is no duty to notify third persons—unless the agent's authority is coupled with an interest.[11]

Death or Insanity.

The general rule is that the death or insanity of either the principal or the agent automatically and immediately terminates the ordinary agency relationship. Knowledge of the death is not required. For example, Jefferson sends Akers to the Far East to purchase a rare book. Before Akers makes the purchase, Jefferson dies. Akers's agent status is terminated at the moment of death, even though Akers does not know that Jefferson has died. (Some states, however, have changed the common law by statute to make knowledge of the principal's death a requirement for agency termination.)

An agent's transactions that occur after the death of the principal are not binding on the principal's estate. Assume that Akers is hired by Jefferson to collect a debt from Cochran (a third party). Jefferson dies, but Akers still collects the money from Cochran, not knowing of Jefferson's death. Cochran's payment to Akers is no longer legally sufficient to discharge Cochran's debt to Jefferson, because Akers no longer has Jefferson's authority to collect the money. If Akers absconds with the money, Cochran must pay the debt again, to Jefferson's estate.

Impossibility.

When the specific subject matter of an agency is destroyed or lost, the agency terminates. For example, Jefferson employs Akers to sell Jefferson's house. Prior to any sale, the house is destroyed by fire. Akers's agency and authority to sell the house terminate. Similarly, when it is impossible for the agent to perform the agency lawfully because of war or because of a change in the law, the agency terminates.

Changed Circumstances.

When an event occurs that has such an unusual effect on the subject matter of the agency that the agent can reasonably infer that the principal will not want the agency to continue, the agency terminates. Suppose that Jefferson hires Akers

---

10. With *constructive notice* of a fact, knowledge of the fact is imputed by law to a person if he or she could have discovered the fact by proper diligence. Constructive notice is often accomplished by publication in a newspaper.

11. There is an exception to this rule in banking. UCC 4–405 provides that the bank, as agent, can continue to exercise specific types of authority even after the customer's death or insanity unless it has knowledge of the death or insanity. When the bank has knowledge of the customer's death, it has authority for ten days after the death to pay checks (but not notes or drafts) drawn by the customer unless it receives a stop-payment order from someone who has an interest in the account, such as an heir.

to sell a tract of land for $10,000. Subsequently, Akers learns that there is oil under the land and that the land is therefore worth $1 million. The agency and Akers's authority to sell the land for $10,000 are terminated.

Bankruptcy.   If either the principal or the agent petition for bankruptcy, the agency is *usually* terminated. In certain circumstances, as when the agent's financial status is irrelevant to the purpose of the agency, the agency relationship may continue. Insolvency (defined as the

inability to pay debts when they become due or when liabilities exceed assets), as distinguished from bankruptcy, does not necessarily terminate the relationship.

War.   When the principal's country and the agent's country are at war with each other, the agency is terminated. In this situation, the agency is automatically suspended or terminated because there is no way to enforce the legal rights and obligations of the parties.

CONCEPT SUMMARY 32.2

TERMINATION OF AN AGENCY

METHOD OF TERMINATION	RULES	TERMINATION OF AGENT'S AUTHORITY
Act of the Parties 1. Lapse of time 2. Purpose achieved 3. Mutual agreement 4. Occurrence of a specific event 5. Termination by one party (revocation, if by principal; renunciation, if by agent)	Automatic at end of stated time. Automatic on completion of purpose. Mutual consent required. Normally automatic on the happening of the event. At-will agencies—generally no breach; cannot revoke an agency coupled with an interest. Specified-time agencies—breach unless there is legal cause.	**Notice to Third Persons Required—** 1. Direct to those who have dealt with agency. 2. Constructive to all others.
Operation of Law 1. Death or insanity 2. Impossibility—destruction of the specific subject matter 3. Changed circumstances 4. Bankruptcy 5. War between principal's country and agent's country	Automatic on death or insanity of either principal or agent (except when agency is coupled with an interest). Applies any time agency cannot be performed because of event beyond parties' control. Events so unusual, it would be inequitable to allow agency to continue to exist. Bankruptcy decree—not mere insolvency—usually terminates agency. Automatically suspends or terminates agency—no way to enforce legal rights.	**No Notice Required—** Automatic on the happening of the event.

TERMS AND CONCEPTS TO REVIEW

ratification 592   undisclosed principal 592   vicarious liability 595

respondeat superior 595

QUESTIONS AND CASE PROBLEMS

32–1. LIABILITY FOR AGENT'S CONTRACTS. Adam is a traveling salesperson for Peter Petri Plumbing Supply Corp. Adam has express authority to solicit orders from customers and to offer a 5 percent discount if payment is made within thirty days of delivery. Petri has said nothing to Adam about extending credit. Adam calls on a new prospective customer, John's Plumbing Firm. John tells Adam that he will place a large order for Petri products if Adam will give him a 10 percent discount with payment due in equal installments thirty, sixty, and ninety days from delivery. Adam says he has authority to make such a contract. John calls Petri and asks if Adam is authorized to make contracts giving a discount. No mention is made of payment terms. Petri replies that Adam has authority to make discounts on purchase orders. On the basis of this information, John orders $10,000 worth of plumbing supplies and fixtures. The goods are delivered and are being sold. One week later John receives a bill for $9,500, due in thirty days. John insists he owes only $9,000 and can pay it in three equal installments, at thirty, sixty, and ninety days from delivery. Discuss the liability of Petri and John only.

32–2. LIABILITY FOR AGENT'S CONTRACTS. Alice Adams is a purchasing agent-employee for the A & B Coal Supply partnership. Adams has authority to purchase the coal needed by A & B to satisfy the needs of its customers. While Adams is leaving a coal mine from which she has just purchased a large quantity of coal, her car breaks down. She walks into a small roadside grocery store for help. While there, she runs into Will Wilson. Wilson owns 360 acres back in the mountains with all mineral rights. Wilson, in need of money, offers to sell Adams the property at $1,500 per acre. On inspection of the property, Adams forms the opinion that the subsurface contains valuable coal deposits. Adams contracts to purchase the property for A & B Coal Supply, signing the contract "A & B Coal Supply, Alice Adams, agent." The closing date is August 1. Adams takes the contract to the partnership. The managing partner is furious, as A & B is not in the property business. Later, just before closing, both Wilson and the partnership learn that the value of the land is at least $15,000 per acre. Discuss the rights of A & B and Wilson concerning the land contract.

32–3. UNDISCLOSED PRINCIPAL. Paula Enterprises hires Able to act as its agent to purchase a one-thousand-acre tract of land from Thompson for $1,000 per acre. Paula Enterprises does not wish Thompson to know that it is the principal or that Able is its agent. Paula wants the land for a new country housing development, and Thompson may not sell the land for that purpose or may demand a premium price. Able makes the contract for the purchase, signing only his name as purchaser and not disclosing to Thompson the agency relationship. The closing and transfer of deed are to take place on September 1.

(a) If Thompson learns of Paula's identity on August 1, can Thompson legally refuse to deed the property on September 1? Explain.

(b) Paula gives Able the money for the closing, but Able absconds with the money, causing a breach of Able's contract at the date of closing. Thompson then learns of Paula's identity and wants to enforce the contract. Discuss fully Thompson's rights under these circumstances.

32–4. PRINCIPAL'S LIABILITY FOR AGENT'S TORTS. Able is hired as a traveling salesperson for the ABC Tire Corp. Able has a designated geographic area and time schedule within which to solicit orders and service customers. Able is given a company car to use in covering the territory. One day, Able decides to take his personal car to cover part of his territory. It is 11:00 A.M., and Able has just finished calling on all customers in the city of Tarrytown. Able's next appointment is in the city of Austex, twenty miles down the road, at 2:00 P.M. Able starts out for Austex, but halfway there he decides to visit a former college roommate who runs a farm ten miles off the main highway. Able is enjoying his visit with his former roommate when he realizes that it is 1:45 P.M. and that he will be late for the appointment in Austex. Driving at a high speed down the country road to reach the main highway, Able crashes his car into Thomas's tractor, severely injuring Thomas, a farmer. Thomas claims he can hold the ABC Tire Corp. liable for his injuries. Discuss fully ABC's liability in this situation.

32–5. RATIFICATION BY PRINCIPAL. Fred Hash worked for Van Stavern Construction Co. as a field supervisor in charge of constructing a new plant facility. Hash entered into a contract with Sutton's Steel & Supply, Inc., to provide steel to the construction site in several installments. Hash gave the name of B. D. Van Stavern, the president and owner of the construction firm, instead of the firm name as the party for whom he was acting. The contract and the subsequent invoices all had B. D. Van Stavern's name on them. Several loads were delivered by Sutton. All of the invoices were signed by Van Stavern employees, and corporate checks were made out to Sutton. When Sutton Steel later sued Van Stavern personally for unpaid debts totaling $40,437, it claimed that Van Stavern had ratified the acts of his employee, Hash, by allowing payment on previous invoices. Although Van Stavern had had no knowledge of the unauthorized arrangement, had he legally ratified the agreement by his silence? Explain. [*Sutton's Steel & Supply, Inc. v. Van Stavern*, 496 So.2d 1360 (La.App. 3d Cir. 1986)]

32–6. RESPONDEAT SUPERIOR. Justin Jones suffered from genital herpes and sought treatment from Dr. Steven Baisch of Region West Pediatric Services. A nurse's assistant, Jeni Hallgren, who was a Region West employee, told her friends and some of Jones's friends about Jones's condition. This was a violation of the Region West employee handbook, which required employees to maintain the confidentiality of patients' records. Jones filed a suit in a federal district court against Region West, among others, alleging that Region West should be held liable for its employee's actions on the basis of *respondeat superior*. On what basis might the court hold that Region West was not liable for Hallgren's acts? Discuss fully. [*Jones v. Baisch, M.D.*, 40 F.3d 252 (8th Cir. 1994)]

32–7. UNDISCLOSED PRINCIPAL. John Dunning was the sole officer of the R. B. Dunning Co. and was responsible for the management and operation of the business. When the company rented a warehouse from Samuel and Ruth Saliba, Dunning did not say that he was acting for the firm. The parties did not have a written lease. Business faltered, and the firm stopped paying rent. Eventually, it went bankrupt and vacated the property. The Salibas filed a suit in a Maine state court against Dunning personally, seeking to recover the unpaid rent. Dunning claimed the debt belonged to the company because he had only been acting as its agent. Who is liable for the rent, and why? [*Estate of Saliba v. Dunning*, 682 A.2d 224 (Me. 1996)]

32–8. LIABILITY FOR EMPLOYEE'S ACTS. Federated Financial Reserve Corp. leases consumer and business equipment. As part of its credit approval and debt-collection practices, Federated hires credit collectors, whom it authorizes to obtain credit reports on its customers. Janice Caylor, a Federated collector, used this authority to obtain a report on Karen Jones, who was not a Federated customer but who was the former wife of Caylor's roommate, Randy Lind. When Jones discovered that Lind had her address and how he had obtained it, she filed a suit in a federal district court against Federated and the others. Jones claimed in part that they had violated the Fair Credit Reporting Act, the goal of which is to protect consumers from the improper use of credit reports. Under what theory might an employer be held liable for an employee's violation of a statute? Does that theory apply in this case? Explain. [*Jones v. Federated Financial Reserve Corp.*, 144 F.3d 961 (6th Cir. 1998)]

32–9. IMPLIED AUTHORITY. Juanita Miller filed a complaint in an Indiana state court against Red Arrow Ventures, Ltd., Thomas Hayes, and Claudia Langman, alleging that they breached their promise to make payments on a promissory note issued to Miller. The defendants denied this allegation and asserted a counterclaim against Miller. After a trial, the judge announced that, although he would be ruling against the defendants, he had not yet determined what amount of damages would be awarded to Miller. Over the next three days, the parties' attorneys talked and agreed that the defendants would pay Miller $21,000. The attorneys exchanged correspondence acknowledging this settlement. When the defendants balked at paying this amount, the trial judge issued an order to enforce the settlement agreement. The defendants appealed to a state intermediate appellate court, arguing that they had not consented to the settlement agreement. What is the rule regarding the authority of an agent—in this case, the defendants' attorney—to agree to a settlement? How should the court apply the rule in this case? Why? [*Red Arrow Ventures, Ltd. v. Miller*, 692 N.E.2d 939 (Ind.App. 1998)]

32–10. IN YOUR COURT

 Richard Lanno worked for the Thermal Equipment Corp. as a project engineer. Lanno was allowed to keep a company van and tools at his home because he routinely drove to work sites directly from his home and because he was often needed for unanticipated trips during his off-hours. The arrangement had been made for the convenience of Thermal Equipment, even though Lanno's managers permitted him to make personal use of the van. Lanno was involved in a collision with Adams while driving the van home from work. At the time of the accident, Lanno had taken a detour to stop at a store—he had intended to purchase a few items and then go home. Adams sued Thermal Equipment, claiming that Lanno had acted within the scope of his employment. Assume that you are the judge in the trial court hearing this case and answer the following questions:

(a) How does the principle of law enunciated in Case 32.3 (*Joel v. Morison*) relate to the case now before your court?

(b) What will your ruling be with respect to Adams's claim? How will you justify your decision?

LAW ON THE WEB

For updated links to resources available on the Web, as well as a variety of other materials, visit this text's Web site at http://wbl.westbuslaw.com.

An excellent source for information on agency law, including court cases involving agency concepts, is the Legal Information Institute (LII) at Cornell University. You can access the LII's Web page on this topic at http://www.law.cornell.edu/topics/agency.html

The 'Lectric Law Library's Lawcopedia contains a summary of agency laws at

http://www.lectlaw.com/d-a.htm

Scroll down through the A's and select the link to Agent for useful information on this area of the law.

LEGAL RESEARCH EXERCISES ON THE WEB

Go to http://wbl.westbuslaw.com, the Web site that accompanies this text. Select "Internet Applications," and then click on "Chapter 32." There you will find the following Internet research exercise that you can perform to learn more about agency law:

Activity 32–1: Liability in Agency Relationships

UNIT SIX — CUMULATIVE BUSINESS HYPOTHETICAL

Sam Best is the sole owner of Best Buy Auto Center, Inc., a used-car business. Sam's hired assistants at Best Buy include three sales representatives, a mechanic, and a receptionist who also helps with the bookkeeping. In addition, Sam has engaged the services of a janitorial maintenance company that sends its employees to Best Buy two evenings a week to clean the premises.

1. Best Buy exercises considerable control over the details of the work and the day-to-day activities of the sales representatives, the mechanic, and the person who serves as the firm's receptionist-bookkeeper. These workers are paid hourly wages, accumulated in paychecks issued on the first of every month. Federal and state taxes are withheld from the paychecks. Best Buy also pays unemployment taxes and the employer's share of Social Security taxes at the end of every three months for these workers. The janitorial company provides its own supplies, performs its tasks as it sees fit, and sends Best Buy an invoice each month for the services rendered during that month. The bookkeeper at Best Buy pays the bill; no taxes are withheld from the payment to the janitorial firm. Which of these workers—the sales representatives, the mechanic, the receptionist, and the janitors—are employees, and which are independent contractors, if any? What factors would a court or an administrative agency, such as the IRS, consider in determining whether a worker should be classified as an employee or an independent contractor? How would this classification affect the responsibilities of the employer?

2. One day, Barry, one of the salespersons, anxious to make a sale, intentionally quotes a price to a customer that is $500 lower than Sam Best has authorized for that particular car. The customer purchases the car at the quoted price and pays for it with a cashier's check. When Sam learns of the deal, he claims that he is not legally bound to the sales contract because he did not authorize Barry to sell the car at that price. Is Sam bound by the contract? Discuss fully.

3. Suppose that Sam tells Barry and another sales representative, Jeff, to deliver a car that has just been sold to the purchaser's home. Jeff is told to drive the customer's car, and Barry is to drive another car (from the lot), follow Jeff, and give him a ride back to Best Buy. Jeff and Barry decide to stop for lunch at a deli located on the route to the customer's house. When Barry turns into the deli's parking lot, he negligently crashes into a car pulling out of the lot. Is Barry liable to the owner of the other car for damages? Can Best Buy be held liable for the damages?

4. Sam's good friend Walter learns that one of his colleagues plans to sell a 1955 Chevrolet that is in mint condition. Walter wants to buy the car but, because he has always chided the colleague about the old "junk heap," does not want the colleague to know that he is the buyer. Walter and Sam agree that Sam will buy the car from the colleague and then sell it immediately to Walter. Sam purchases the car, paying for it with a personal check, and drives the car to Walter's home. Walter has a change of heart and decides not to go through with the deal. Sam calls Walter's colleague, explains that he was really purchasing the car for someone else, and stops payment on his check. The colleague then sues Sam for the purchase price. Will the colleague succeed in this suit? Discuss the rights and obligations of the parties in these circumstances.

FOCUS ON LEGAL REASONING
Soberay Machine & Equipment Co. v. MRF Limited, Inc.

INTRODUCTION

The liability for contracts formed by agents is discussed in Chapter 32. In this *Focus on Legal Reasoning*, we examine *Soberay Machine & Equipment Co. v. MRF Limited, Inc.*,[1] a decision in which the issue involved an exception to the rule that an agent cannot be held liable for a contract entered into on behalf of a disclosed principal. The exception is that an agent can be held liable if he or she intended to be bound to the contract.

CASE BACKGROUND

Soberay Machine & Equipment Company sells used machinery and equipment from its office in Ohio.

---
1. 101 F.3d 759 (6th Cir. 1999).

MRF Limited, Inc., a corporation based in India, asked Soberay about the availability of a secondhand calender, a piece of machinery used in the production of rubber products. MRF also asked other equipment suppliers, including International Polymer Equipment Corporation (IPEC) about calenders. Chris Dias, MRF's director of engineering, was in charge of the calender purchase. Through Dias, MRF bought a used calender from IPEC. The invoices and bills of lading between IPEC and MRF indicated that IPEC was the seller. The invoices did not state that IPEC was MRF's agent.

IPEC had bought the calender from Soberay, and Soberay billed IPEC for it. Soberay's invoices stated "Sold to IPEC." MRF paid IPEC in full, but IPEC was in financial difficulty and did not pay Soberay in full. Soberay filed a suit against IPEC in an Ohio state court. Soberay also filed a suit against IPEC and MRF in a federal district court. IPEC filed a petition for bankruptcy under Chapter 7 (bankruptcy is discussed in Chapter 30), listing its debt to Soberay without including MRF as a co-debtor. Soberay filed a creditor's claim with the bankruptcy court and dropped IPEC from its suit in federal court. MRF argued in part that IPEC was an indispensable party to this suit and without IPEC, the case should be dismissed. When the federal court entered a judgment in favor of MRF, Soberay appealed to the U.S. Court of Appeals for the Sixth Circuit.

MAJORITY OPINION

CLAY, Circuit Judge.
* * * *

[The] general rule [is] that an agent who acts for a disclosed principal and who acts within the scope of his authority and in the name of the principal is ordinarily not liable on the contracts he makes because the third party intended to deal with the principal, not the agent * * * ; however, * * * there are several exceptions to this general rule of an agent's nonliability in relation to a disclosed principal: *First, an agent may be held personally liable when he has manifested an intention to bind or contract for himself.* See *WUPW TV-36 v. Direct Results Marketing, Inc.* (1990), 70 Ohio App.3d 710, 591 N.E.2d 1345. * * * [Emphasis added.]
* * * [W]e find that IPEC could be held liable under the first exception to the general rule inasmuch as the record indicates that IPEC intended to be bound and to be held liable on the contract with Plaintiff. It is undisputed that when IPEC filed a voluntary petition for bankruptcy under [C]hapter [S]even, it listed the balance owed to Plaintiff on the price of the calender as a debt; that IPEC did not list Defendant as a co-debtor on the debt owed to Plaintiff on the bankruptcy petition because IPEC did not consider Defendant a co-debtor; and that Plaintiff filed a claim against IPEC in bankruptcy court. These undisputed facts clearly indicate IPEC's intention to be held liable to the contract with Plaintiff. Furthermore, the fact Plaintiff filed suit against IPEC in state court seeking payment of the balance owed on the calender, after Plaintiff unsuccessfully attempted to collect the balance due from IPEC, plainly indicates that the parties (Plaintiff and IPEC) intended that IPEC be held liable on the contract for the sale of the calender.

Thus, even assuming that IPEC was acting as Defendant's agent in this case, and that Defendant was a disclosed principal, the undisputed facts indicate that IPEC falls squarely within Ohio's first exception to its general rule that agents who contract for a disclosed principal cannot be held liable on the contract, because IPEC intended to be held liable to Plaintiff for the price of the calender. See * * * *WUPW TV-36 v. Direct Results Mktg., Inc.,* * * * .

Accordingly, because the purchase orders between IPEC and Plaintiff indicate that IPEC was purchasing the calender from Plaintiff, and subsequent * * * invoices from IPEC to Defendant indicate that IPEC then sold the calender to Defendant; because Defendant was known to Plaintiff; and because Plaintiff originally sought legal action against IPEC in both state and federal courts for the balance owed on the calender, as well as filing a claim against IPEC in bankruptcy court after IPEC listed the balance of the purchase price of the calender as a debt owed to Plaintiff on IPEC's [C]hapter [S]even bankruptcy petition, Plaintiff intended IPEC to be held liable on the contract for the calender, not Defendant. The record indicates that it was only after IPEC filed [C]hapter [S]even bankruptcy that Plaintiff pursued legal action against Defendant alone. Therefore, IPEC is the real party in interest here, and the parties were prejudiced by IPEC's absence.

DISSENTING OPINION

BOGGS, Circuit Judge, dissenting.
* * * *

* * * An agent who acts for a disclosed principal and who acts within the scope of his authority and in the name of the principal is ordinarily not liable on the contracts he makes. The rationale for this rule is that, in this situation, the third party intends to deal with the principal, not his agent. The only possible qualification in this language is the phrase "and in the name of the principal." Here, IPEC is the name on the invoices * * * but * * * Soberay knew that IPEC was acting for MRF.

In fact, there is no situation such as is contended here, where only the agent and not the principal is liable. This could only be the case if the purported agent was not in fact truly an agent, but was acting for its own account, and [that is not what happened in this case]. * * * [J]udgment should have been rendered for Soberay as a matter of law.

LEGAL REASONING AND ANALYSIS

1. Legal Reasoning. Contrast the conclusions of the majority and the dissent. What reasons did each provide to justify its position? Which do you think is the better reasoned opinion? Why?

2. Legal Analysis. The majority cites, in its opinion, *WUPW TV-36 v. Direct Results Marketing, Inc.,* 70 Ohio App.3d 710, 591 N.E.2d 1345 (1990) (see the *Law on the Web* feature at the end of Chapter 2 for instructions on how to access state court opinions). How do the facts and issues in that case compare to the facts and issues of the *Soberay* case? How do the holdings in the two cases compare?

3. International Consideration. When conducting business with a company whose principal office is located in another country, what are the advantages of dealing through a third party whose principal office is in the same state as your own? What are the disadvantages?

4. Implications for Principals and Agents. What does the decision in this case indicate to those who buy or sell goods to, through, or for third parties?

5. Case Briefing Assignment. Using the guidelines for briefing cases given in Appendix A of this text, brief the *Soberay* case.

GOING ONLINE

This text's Web site, at http://wbl.westbuslaw.com, offers links to court cases, as well as to other online research sources. You can also locate court cases at the Web sites listed in the *Law on the Web* feature at the end of Chapter 2. Catalaw is a metaindex that provides links to Web pages within more than one hundred legal indexes. On Catalaw's page at http://www.catalaw.com/topics/Commerce.shtml, you can find links to legal resources on agency law and related business and commercial law topics. Catalaw is maintained by Catalaw, Inc.

FOCUS ON ETHICS
Agency

When one person agrees to act on behalf of another, as an agent does in an agency relationship, that person assumes certain ethical responsibilities. An agent acting on *behalf of* a principal implicitly promises to place the principal's interests above his or her own interests. Similarly, a principal in an agency relationship assumes certain ethical duties. If an agent incurs expenses or liability while acting on the principal's behalf, for example, it is only fair that the principal should assume responsibility for those expenses or that liability. In essence, agency law gives legal force to the ethical duties arising in an agency relationship. Although agency law also focuses on the rights of agents and principals, those rights are framed by the concept of duty—that is, an agent's duty becomes a right for the principal and vice versa.

Significantly, most of the duties of the principal and agent described below are negotiable at law. In forming a contract, the principal and the agent can extend or abridge many of the ordinary duties owed in such a relationship. Legal rules generally come into play when the contract is silent or ambiguous on an issue. Allowing the parties to negotiate their relative duties seems ethically fair, as long as the parties are able to understand their rights and make informed decisions.

THE AGENT'S DUTY TO THE PRINCIPAL

The very nature of the principal-agent relationship is one of trust, which we call a fiduciary relationship. Because of this, it is expected that an agent owes certain duties to the principal. These duties include being loyal and obedient, informing the principal of important facts concerning the agency, accounting to the principal for property or money received, and performing with reasonable diligence and skill.

Thus, ethical conduct would prevent an agent from representing two principals in the same transaction, making a secret profit from the agency relationship, or failing to disclose the interest of the agent in property the principal was purchasing. The expected ethical conduct of the agent has evolved into rules that, if breached, cause the agent to be held legally liable.

What about looking beyond the duty to the principal and thinking about one's duty to society? Consider, for example, the situation faced by an employee who knows that the employer is engaging in an unethical—or even illegal—practice, such as marketing an unsafe product. Does the employee's duty to the principal include keeping silent about this practice, which may harm users of the product? Does the employee have a duty to protect consumers by disclosing this information to the public, even if the employee loses his or her job as a result? Some scholars have argued that many of the greatest evils in the past twenty-five years have been accomplished in the name of duty to the principal.

THE PRINCIPAL'S DUTY TO THE AGENT

Just as agents owe certain fiduciary duties to their principals, so do principals owe ethical duties to their agents. Under agency law, principals have certain defined duties, such as compensating or reimbursing their agents for expenses incurred in the course of performing their duties as agents.

Principals also owe their agents a duty of cooperation. One might expect most principals to cooperate with their agents out of self-interest, but this is not universally the case. Suppose that a principal hires an agent on commission to sell a building, and the agent puts considerable time and expense into the process. If the principal changes his or her mind and decides to retain the building, he or she might want to prevent the agent from completing a sale. Is such action ethical? Does it violate a principal's duty of cooperation? What alternatives would such a principal have?

Another duty of principals is to provide safe working conditions. The principal therefore should not expose agents to unreasonable hazards as they go about their work. The definition of *safe* remains a difficult one, however, as every job probably entails some degree of unavoidable risk. Suppose, for example, that an employer hires a sales representative and supplies the representative with a car. Must the car contain air bags to ensure safe working conditions? Or would a car with seat belts be "safe enough"?

Although a principal is legally obligated to fulfill certain duties to the agent, these duties do not include any specific duty of loyalty. Some argue that the lack of employer loyalty to employees leads to a reduction of employee loyalty to employers. After all, they maintain, why should an employee be loyal to an employer's interests over the years when the employee knows that there is no corresponding legal duty on the part of the employer to be loyal to the employee's interests? Employers who do show a sense of loyalty to employees—for example, by not laying off long-time, faithful employees when business is slow or when those employees could be replaced by younger workers at lower cost—base that sense of loyalty primarily on ethical, not legal, considerations.

APPARENT AUTHORITY AND AGENCY BY ESTOPPEL

Agency law is designed to enforce the ethical or fiduciary duties that arise once an agency relationship is established. If the agent or the principal breaches his or her duties, the law will come to the aid of the innocent party. To perhaps an even greater extent, agency law is designed to protect third parties—people outside the agency relationship. The doctrines of apparent authority and agency by estoppel stem primarily from ethical considerations that arise when third parties suffer a loss from an apparent agency relationship.

Sometimes, for example, a third person may be led by the actions of the principal to believe that an individual is acting in the capacity of an agent, when in fact the individual is not an agent at all. For

instance, a patient treated by a doctor in a hospital's emergency room (ER) may assume that the doctor is an agent of the hospital, even though the doctor is an independent contractor and has no agency relationship with the hospital. If the patient suffers harm because of the doctor's negligence and the patient sues the hospital, a court may hold the hospital liable under an apparent agency theory. Certainly, many courts have held hospitals liable in similar circumstances. The reasoning is that it is logical for patients to assume that ER physicians are hospital employees.

Some hospitals have avoided such liability by posting signs in their emergency rooms informing patients that the ER physicians are independent contractors and disclaiming liability for the physicians' actions. In one case, though, even such disclaimers did not allow a Texas hospital to escape liability for one of its ER physicians' negligence in treating a patient. A Texas appellate court held that a hospital is *always* liable for an ER physician's negligence, regardless of the physician's employment status. The court, stressing that an injured party must rely on a hospital's emergency room because "there is no other place to go," concluded that public policy, and not traditional agency rules or tort law, "should underlie the decision to hold hospitals liable for malpractice which occurs in their emergency rooms."[1]

RESPONDEAT SUPERIOR

Another legal concept that addresses the effect of agency relationships on third parties is the doctrine of *respondeat superior.* The doctrine raises a significant ethical question: Why should

---

1. *Sampson v. Baptist Memorial Hospital System,* 940 S.W.2d.128 (Tex.App.—San Antonio 1996).

innocent employers be required to assume responsibility for the tortious actions of their agent-employees? Again, the answer has to do with the courts' perception that when one of two innocent parties must suffer a loss, the party in the best position to prevent that loss should bear the burden. In an employment relationship, for example, the employer has more control over the employee's behavior than a third party to the relationship does.

Another reason for retaining the doctrine of *respondeat superior* in our laws is based on the employer's assumed ability to pay. Our collection of shared beliefs suggests that an injured party should be afforded the most effective relief possible. Thus, even though an employer may be absolutely innocent, the employer has "deeper pockets" than the employee and will be more likely to have the funds necessary to make the injured party whole.

LIABILITY FOR THE TORTS OF INDEPENDENT CONTRACTORS

While employers may be liable for the torts of their employees under the doctrine of *respondeat superior,* as a general rule employers are not liable for torts committed by independent contractors. In the interests of fairness and justice, however, the courts often make exceptions to this rule. In fact, as one court pointed out, the general rule is so riddled with exceptions that the "exceptions . . . have practically subsumed the rule."[2] The *Restatement (Second) of Torts,* in Comment b to Section 409, also emphasizes the numerous exceptions to the rule, stating that it "can now be said to be 'general'

---

2. *Rowley v. City of Baltimore,* 305 Md. 456, 505 A.2d 494 (1986).

only in the sense that it is applied where no good reason is found for departing from it."

Exceptions to the general rule come in many forms. In a number of cases, courts make exceptions on the ground that certain duties are nondelegable. For example, in one case a woman sued a shopping mall owner to recover for injuries she sustained when she fell on a snow-covered entryway to the mall. The mall owner asserted that it was not liable for the injuries because the entryway was maintained by an independent contractor. The court, however, held that possessors of business premises have a duty to business invitees (those whom they invite onto their premises—see Chapter 5), and this duty simply cannot be delegated to others.[3]

In a number of other cases, courts have held that secured creditors have a nondelegable statutory duty not to breach the peace when resorting to the "self-help" provision of Article 9 of the Uniform Commercial Code (see Chapter 28). Therefore, if an independent contractor hired by a secured party to repossess collateral, such as an automobile, wrongfully or unlawfully breaches the peace when doing so, the secured party may be held liable for the independent contractor's actions.[4]

As discussed in Chapter 32, another exception is made when the employer exercises a significant degree of control over the independent contractor's work performance. This exception came into play in a case brought by a woman against the Kirby Company after she had been raped by a door-to-door seller of Kirby vacuum cleaners. Even though the door-to-door seller, Mickey Carter, operated as an independent contractor, the court held that the Kirby Company was liable. The court emphasized that by retaining control over where its independent contractors did their selling— specifically, Kirby required its salespersons to sell the vacuums in the homes of customers—Kirby also retained a legal duty to choose carefully the persons it hired to go into those homes. In this case, Kirby representatives had not bothered to check Carter's background when he applied for work. If they had, they would have found that Carter had pleaded guilty to a charge of indecency with a child. Also, had his employment references been checked, it would have been discovered that a number of women with whom he had worked had complained of his inappropriate sexual behavior.[5]

WORKS FOR HIRE

Whether a worker is classified as an employee or an independent contractor has important implications when works are done "for hire." Recall from Case 31.1 (*Graham v. James*) in Chapter 31 that under the Copyright Act of 1976, any copyrighted work created by an *employee* within the scope of his or her employment at the request of the employer is called a "work for hire." The employer owns and holds the copyright to such a work. If a freelancer, or independent contractor, creates the copyrighted work for the employer, however, the independent contractor will own the copyright in the work *unless* the parties have a written agreement stating that the work is "for hire."

As might be expected, when disputes arise between employers and freelancers over copyright ownership, employers often argue that the freelancers are not really independent contractors but employees. It is not always easy, though, for a court to make this determination. Consider a case that came before the U.S. Court of Appeals for the Sixth Circuit in 1995. The case involved a claim of copyright infringement brought by Hi-Tech Video Productions, Inc., against Capital Cities/ABC, Inc. (ABC). Hi-Tech, which had produced a travel video entitled *Mackinac Island: The Mackinac Video,* claimed that ABC had infringed Hi-Tech's copyright in the video when ABC featured parts of the video on ABC's television program *Good Morning America* without Hi-Tech's permission. ABC claimed that Hi-Tech had no valid copyright in the video, because the video had been created by independent contractors hired by Hi-Tech and with whom Hi-Tech had no written agreement stating that the video was a "work for hire."

The issue thus turned on whether Hi-Tech's hired workers (two videographers and a scriptwriter/narrator) were employees or independent contractors. The federal district court determined that the workers were employees; thus, Hi-Tech had a valid copyright in the video. In arriving at its conclusion, the district court gave considerable weight to the fact that Hi-Tech exercised substantial control over the workers' activities. On appeal, however, the federal appellate court stressed other factors, including the parties' perception of their relationship. The appellate court concluded that the workers were not employees; thus, the video was not a "work for hire," and Hi-Tech had no copyright in the work.[6]

It is clear that the courts can and do disagree on whether a

---

3. *Valenti v. Net Properties Management, Inc.,* 142 N.H. 633, 710 A.2d 399 (1998).

4. See, for example, *Sanchez v. Mbank of El Paso,* 792 S.W.2d 530 (Tex.App.— El Paso 1990); and *Williamson v. Fowler Toyota, Inc.,* 956 P.2d 858 (Okla. 1998).

5. *Read v. Scott Fetzer Co.,* 990 S.W.2d 732 (Tex. 1998).

6. *Hi-Tech Video Productions, Inc. v. Capital Cities/ABC, Inc.,* 58 F.3d 1093 (6th Cir. 1995).

worker should be classified as an employee or an independent contractor. It is equally clear that how a court decides the issue can have significant consequences for the parties involved. Although the outcome in the case just described may seem unfair to Hi-Tech, in fact, Hi-Tech could have guarded against the problem by simply making sure that it had a written agreement with the freelancers specifying that the work was "for hire."

DISCUSSION QUESTIONS

1. How much obedience and loyalty does an agent-employee owe an employer? What if the employer engages in an activity— or requests the employee to engage in an activity—that violates the employee's ethical standards but does not necessarily violate any public policy or law? In such a situation, does an employee's duty to abide by his or her own ethical standards override the employee's duty of loyalty to the employer?

2. Agency by estoppel occurs when the presumed principal's actions create the appearance of authority in a presumed agent and a third party reasonably relies, to his or her detriment, on the presumed agent's apparent authority. In what ways are the ethical considerations underlying the doctrine of agency by estoppel similar to those underlying the doctrine of *respondeat superior*? In what ways are the ethical considerations different?

3. If an agent injures a third party during the course of employment, under the doctrine of *respondeat superior,* the employer may be held liable for the agent's actions even though the employer did not authorize the action and was not even aware of it. Do you think that it is fair to hold employers liable in such situations? Do you think that it would be more equitable to hold that the employee alone should bear responsibility for his or her tortious actions to third parties, even when the actions are committed within the scope of employment?

4. Why do the courts make so many exceptions to the general rule that employers are not liable for the torts of their independent contractors?

5. What policy is served by the law that employers do not have copyright ownership in works created by independent contractors (unless there is a written "work for hire" agreement)?

UNIT SEVEN

Business Organizations

CONTENTS

CHAPTER 33

Sole Proprietorships and Partnerships

A BASIC QUESTION FACING ANYONE who wishes to start up a business is which of the several forms of business organization will be most appropriate for the business endeavor. In deciding this question, the **entrepreneur** (one who initiates and assumes the financial risk of a new enterprise) needs to consider a number of factors. Four important factors are (1) ease of creation, (2) the liability of the owners, (3) tax considerations, and (4) the need for capital. In studying this unit on business organizations, keep these factors in mind as you read about the various business organizational forms available to entrepreneurs.

Traditionally, entrepreneurs have used three major forms to structure their business enterprises—the sole proprietorship, the partnership, and the corporation. In this chapter, we examine the first two of these forms. The third major traditional form—the corporation—will be discussed in detail in Chapters 34 through 37. Two relatively new forms of business enterprise—limited liability companies (LLCs) and limited liability partnerships (LLPs)—offer special advantages to businesspersons, particularly with respect to taxation and liability. We will look at these business forms, which are coming into widespread use, in Chapter 38. In Chapter 39, we will describe a number of other forms of business organization as well as private franchises.

SECTION 1

Sole Proprietorships

The simplest form of business is a **sole proprietorship.** In this form, the owner is the business; thus, anyone who does business without creating a separate business organization has a sole proprietorship. Sole proprietorships constitute over two-thirds of all American businesses. They are also usually small enterprises—about 99 percent of the sole proprietorships existing in the United States have revenues of less than $1 million per year. Sole proprietors can own and manage any type of business from an informal, home-office undertaking to a large restaurant or construction firm.

A major advantage of the sole proprietorship is that the proprietor receives all of the profits (because he or she assumes all of the risk). In addition, it is often easier and less costly to start a sole proprietorship than to start any other kind of business, as few legal forms are involved. This type of business organization also provides more flexibility than does a partnership or a corporation. The sole proprietor is free to make any decision he or she wishes to concerning the business—whom to hire, when to take a vacation, what kind of business to pursue, and so on. A sole proprietor pays only personal income taxes on the business's profits, which are reported as personal income on the proprietor's personal income tax return. Sole proprietors are also allowed to establish tax-exempt retirement accounts in the form of Keogh plans.[1]

The major disadvantage of the sole proprietorship is that, as sole owner, the proprietor alone bears the burden of any losses or liabilities incurred by the business enterprise. In other words, the sole proprietor has unlimited liability, or legal responsibility, for all obligations that arise in doing business. This unlimited liability is a major factor to be considered in choosing a business form. The sole proprietorship also has the disadvantage of lacking continuity on the death of the proprietor. When the owner dies, so does the business—it is automatically dissolved. If the business is transferred to family members or other heirs, a new proprietorship is created.

Another disadvantage is that the proprietor's opportunity to raise capital is limited to personal funds and the funds of those who are willing to make loans to him or her. If the owner wishes to expand the business significantly, one way to raise more capital to finance the expansion is to join forces with another entrepreneur and establish a partnership or form a corporation.

Section 2

The Law Governing Partnerships

A **partnership** arises from an agreement, express or implied, between two or more persons to carry on a business for a profit. Partners are co-owners of a business and have joint control over its operation and the right to share in its profits. Note that in this chapter's discussion of partnership law and the rights and duties of partners, we are referring to ordinary partnerships, or *general partnerships*. In Chapter 38, we will examine some special forms of partnerships known as *limited partnerships* and *limited liability partnerships*, which receive different treatment under the law.

AGENCY CONCEPTS AND PARTNERSHIP LAW

When two or more persons agree to do business as partners, they enter into a special relationship with

one another. To an extent, their relationship is similar to an agency relationship, because each partner is deemed the agent of the other partners and of the partnership. The agency concepts that were discussed in Chapters 31 and 32 thus apply—specifically, the imputation of knowledge of, and responsibility for, acts carried out within the scope of the partnership relationship. In their relationship to one another, partners are also bound by the fiduciary ties that bind an agent and principal under agency law.

Partnership law is distinct from agency law in one significant way, however. A partnership is based on a voluntary contract between two or more competent persons who agree to place some or all of their money or other assets, labor, and skills in a business with the understanding that profits and losses will be shared. In a nonpartnership agency relationship, the agent usually does not have an ownership interest in the business, nor is he or she obligated to bear a portion of the ordinary business losses.

THE UNIFORM PARTNERSHIP ACT

The Uniform Partnership Act (UPA) governs the operation of partnerships *in the absence of express agreement* and has done much to reduce controversies in the law relating to partnerships. The UPA has been adopted in all of the states except Louisiana, as well as in the District of Columbia. The entire text of the UPA is presented in Appendix E at the end of this text. A revised version of the UPA, known as the Revised Uniform Partnership Act (RUPA), has been adopted by several states, and others are considering its adoption. Throughout our discussion of partnership law in this chapter, we indicate in footnotes the most significant changes made by the RUPA. Appendix F contains excerpts from the RUPA.

Section 3

Definition of Partnership

Parties commonly find themselves in conflict over whether their business enterprise is a legal partnership, especially in the absence of a formal, written partnership agreement. The UPA defines the term *partnership* as "an association of two or more persons to carry on as co-owners a business for profit" [UPA 6(1)]. The *intent* to associate is a key element of a partnership, and one cannot join a partnership unless all other partners consent [UPA 18(g)]. In resolving

---

1. A *Keogh plan* is a retirement program designed for self-employed persons by which a certain percentage of their income can be contributed to the plan, and interest earnings will not be taxed until funds are withdrawn from the plan.

disputes over whether partnership status exists, courts will usually look for the following three essential elements of partnership implicit in the UPA's definition:

1. A sharing of profits or losses.
2. A joint ownership of the business.
3. An equal right in the management of the business.

In the event that the evidence is insufficient to establish all three factors, the UPA provides a set of guidelines to be used. For example, the existence of a partnership will be inferred if profits and losses from a business are shared. No such inference is made, however, if the profits were received as payment of the following:

1. A debt by installments or interest on a loan.
2. Wages of an employee.
3. Rent to a landlord.
4. An annuity to a widow or representative of a deceased partner.
5. A sale of the goodwill of a business or property [UPA 7(4)].

To illustrate: Suppose that a debtor owes a creditor $5,000 on an unsecured debt. To repay the debt, the debtor agrees to pay (and the creditor, to accept) 10 percent of the debtor's monthly business profits until the loan with interest has been paid. Although the creditor is sharing profits from the business, the debtor and creditor are not presumed to be partners.

Joint ownership of property, obviously, does not in and of itself create a partnership. Therefore, the fact that, say, MacPherson and Bunker own real property as joint tenants or as tenants in common (a form of joint ownership) does not establish a partnership. In fact, the sharing of gross returns and even profits from such ownership is usually not enough to create a partnership [UPA 7(2), (3)]. Thus, if MacPherson and Bunker jointly owned a piece of rural property and leased the land to a farmer, the sharing of the profits from the farming operation by the farmer in lieu of set rental payments would ordinarily not make MacPherson, Bunker, and the farmer partners.

In the following case, two brothers and their mother bought a ranch that for many years, the brothers operated together. After the mother disclaimed her interest and one brother stopped participating in ranch activities, a question arose as to whether the brothers were ever partners.

CASE 33.1   Tarnavsky v. Tarnavsky

United States
Court of Appeals,
Eighth Circuit, 1998.
147 F.3d 674.
http://ls.wustl.edu/
cgi-bin/8th_byname.pl[a]

HISTORICAL AND SOCIAL SETTING   *In the 1700s, 90 percent of the U.S. work force was in agriculture. Today, that figure is less than 3 percent, but operating a farm or ranch has become far more of an exact science. To run a successful agribusiness today, a farmer or rancher must have knowledge of computers, economics, financial management, government regulation, human resources, marketing, and risk management. A farmer or rancher must be—or have access to—an accountant, an insurance agent, a lawyer, and a stockbroker and have a connection to his or her representative in Congress. Despite this situation, which would seem to favor agriconglomerates, about 90 percent of U.S. farms are individual or family operations, which account for about two-thirds of total agricultural production.*

BACKGROUND AND FACTS   *In 1967, Mary Tarnavsky and her sons Morris and Thomas (who was called T.R.) bought a ranch known as the Christ place. T.R. and Morris opened a bank account into which they deposited their shares of the ranch's proceeds, which were used to make payments on the property, to pay property taxes, and to buy cattle, equipment, supplies, and services. For the ranch, the brothers took out joint loans and jointly purchased cattle and machinery. They reported their activities on state and federal partnership income tax returns. Morris handled the livestock; T.R. handled the*

---

a. This database is maintained by Washington University School of Law. From this page, a search can be launched, based on a party's name, for a recent opinion of the U.S. Court of Appeals for the Eighth Circuit. In the "Search String" box, type "Tarnavsky" and then click on "Begin Search." From the search results, click on the appropriate link to access the case.

bookkeeping. In 1980, Mary disclaimed her interest in proceeds from the ranch. Eight years later, T.R. stopped doing the bookkeeping and began spending little time on ranch activities. Morris sent T.R. a "Notice of Dissolution of Partnership." After unsuccessful attempts to arrive at a settlement, T.R. filed a suit in a federal district court, requesting payment for his share of the partnership assets. The court ordered a payment of $220,000. Morris appealed, arguing in part that there was no partnership.

IN THE LANGUAGE OF THE COURT

JOHN R. GIBSON, Circuit Judge.

* * * *

* * * [C]ertain elements are critical to the existence of a partnership. These elements are: (1) an intention to be partners; (2) co-ownership of the business; and (3) profit motive.

* * * *

* * * T.R. and Morris reported their farming activities on state and federal partnership income tax returns * * * . Morris and T.R. opened a joint bank account * * * . From this account, they made the Christ place property payments, purchased cattle, seed, and related supplies. * * * These actions by Morris and T.R. evidence their intent to be partners.

Co-ownership, the second element necessary for a partnership, includes the sharing of profits and losses as well as the power of control in the management of the business. * * * [A]fter completing a sale of cattle or grain, the brothers would deposit their share of the income in their joint account. From this account, the brothers jointly paid expenses * * * . [J]ointly purchasing land and machinery with profits is a form of profit sharing. * * * [A]t the end of each year, Morris and T.R. would allocate the year's profits on the partnership income tax return equally between themselves * * * . This sharing of profits is further evidence that Morris and T.R. were partners.

* * * *

* * * [B]oth T.R. and Morris handled "marketing the cattle" and performed various administrative functions, such as the discussion of rations. * * * Morris was "in charge" of livestock production and "administered" equipment purchases, and * * * T.R. was "in charge" of paperwork and finances. This is strong evidence that T.R. and Morris both had the power of control over management of the business. * * * Control, when combined with profit sharing, strongly suggests the existence of a partnership.

The final critical element of a partnership is profit motive, and there is no dispute that the farming business was operated with such motive.

DECISION AND REMEDY

The U.S. Court of Appeals for the Eighth Circuit affirmed the lower court's order. Morris and T.R. were partners.

SECTION 4

The Nature of Partnerships

A partnership is sometimes called a *company* or a *firm*, terms that suggest that the partnership is an entity separate and apart from its aggregate members. Sometimes the law of partnership recognizes the independent entity for some purposes but may treat the partnership as a composite of individual partners for other purposes.

PARTNERSHIP AS AN ENTITY

At common law, a partnership was never treated as a separate legal entity. Thus, a common law suit could never be brought by or against the firm in its own name; each individual partner had to sue or be sued. Many states today provide specifically that the partnership can be treated as an entity for certain purposes. These usually include the capacity to sue or be sued, to collect judgments, and to have all accounting procedures in the name of the partnership. In addition, the

UPA recognizes that partnership property may be held in the name of the partnership rather than in the names of the individual partners. Finally, federal procedural laws frequently permit the partnership to be treated as an entity in such matters as lawsuits in federal courts, bankruptcy proceedings, and the filing of federal information tax returns. These matters are discussed here in some detail.

Legal Capacity. States vary on how a partnership is viewed as a party in a legal suit. Some permit a partnership to sue and be sued in the firm name; others allow a partnership to be sued as an entity but do not allow the partnership, as a plaintiff, to sue others in its firm name (that is, the partnership must use the names of the individual partners). Federal courts recognize the partnership as an entity that can sue or be sued when a federal question is involved. Otherwise, federal courts follow the practice adopted by the state in which the federal court is located.

Judgments. When a judgment is rendered *against the firm name*, partnership liability is first paid out of partnership assets. In a general partnership, the personal assets of the individual members are subject to liability if the partnership's assets are inadequate. Even in limited partnerships, at least one of the partners—the general partner—subjects his or her personal assets to liability for the partnership's obligations. Good legal practice dictates that when state law permits a firm to be sued, the individual partners should also be sued. This ensures that a wide range of assets will be available for paying the judgment.

Marshaling Assets. The general rule is that a judgment creditor of a partnership (a creditor in whose favor a money judgment has been entered by a court) can execute the judgment against the partners either jointly or severally (joint and several liability is discussed later in this chapter). In some states, however, the judgment creditor must exhaust the remedies against partnership property before proceeding to execute against the individual property of the partners. This is in accordance with the doctrine of **marshaling assets.** Marshaling assets is a common law equitable doctrine; it is not statutory.

In marshaling assets, assets are arranged, or ranked, in a certain order toward the payment of debts outstanding. In some situations, there are two classes of assets, and some creditors can enforce their claims against both, whereas others can enforce their claims against only one. When this occurs, the creditors of

the former class are compelled to exhaust the assets against which they alone have a claim before they can have recourse to other assets. This provides for the settlement of as many claims as possible.

As applied to a partnership, the doctrine of marshaling assets requires that partnership creditors have first priority to the partnership's assets and that personal creditors of the individual partners have first priority to the individual assets of those partners. When the partnership's assets are insufficient to satisfy a partnership creditor, that creditor does not have access to the assets of any individual partner until the personal creditors of that partner have been satisfied from those assets. This doctrine does not apply to partnerships that are in liquidation proceedings under Chapter 7 of the Bankruptcy Code (see Chapter 30).

Bankruptcy. In federal court, an adjudication of bankruptcy *in the firm name* applies only to the partnership entity. It does not constitute personal bankruptcy for the partners. Similarly, the personal bankruptcy of an individual partner does not bring the partnership entity or its assets into bankruptcy.

The doctrine of marshaling assets is modified when a partnership is granted an order of relief in bankruptcy. In such situations, if partnership assets are insufficient to cover debts owed to partnership creditors, each general partner becomes *personally* liable to the bankruptcy trustee for the amount of the deficiency.

Conveyance of Property. The title to real or personal property can be held in the partnership's firm name. In other words, the partnership as an entity can own property apart from that owned by its individual members [UPA 8(3)]. Thus, the property held in the firm name can be conveyed (transferred) without each of the individual partners joining in the transaction.

At common law, title to real estate could not be held in a partnership's firm name. Each partner had to join in all conveyances (transfers of rights in the real estate), because each partner was regarded as a co-owner, known in legal terminology as a *tenant in partnership.*[2] Tenancy in partnership is discussed later in this chapter. Although the modern rule of partnership property ownership does not require aggregate action (action by

2. The UPA retained this concept in UPA 25(1). Although property may be held in the name of the partnership, as tenants in partnership, partners are still regarded as co-owners. The RUPA, however, discards the concept of tenancy in partnership, stating simply that "[a] partner is not a co-owner of partnership property" [RUPA 501]. Further, "[p]roperty transferred to or otherwise acquired by a partnership is property of the partnership and not of the partners individually" [RUPA 203].

all the partners jointly) to convey property, there are some practical difficulties to consider.

Most states do not require that public records list the members of partnerships. Hence, in determining the validity of a conveyance in a partnership's name, it may be impossible to tell whether the person executing the deed is actually a partner and has authority to convey. Some states, however, have passed laws requiring firms to file a statement of partnership. This statement lists the members of the partnership who are authorized to execute conveyances on behalf of the firm.

AGGREGATE THEORY OF PARTNERSHIP

When the partnership is not regarded as a separate legal entity, it is treated as an *aggregate* of the individual partners. For example, for federal income tax purposes, a partnership is not a tax-paying entity. The profits or losses incurred by a partnership are "passed through" the partnership framework and attributed to the partners on their individual tax returns. The partnership as an entity has no tax liability. It is an entity only for the filing of an **information return** with the Internal Revenue Service, indicating the profit or loss that each partner will report on his or her individual tax return.

SECTION 5

Partnership Formation

As a general rule, agreements to form a partnership can be *oral, written,* or *implied by conduct.* Some partnership agreements, however, must be in writing to be legally enforceable within the Statute of Frauds (see Chapter 15 for details). For example, a partnership agreement that, by its terms, is to continue for more than one year or a partnership agreement that authorizes the partners to deal in transfers of real property must be evidenced by a sufficient writing. Generally, a partnership agreement, called **articles of partnership,** can include virtually any terms that the partners wish, unless they are illegal or contrary to public policy. A sample partnership agreement is shown in Exhibit 33–1 on pages 622 and 623.[3] Practically speaking, it is

___

3. The RUPA provides for the voluntary filing of a partnership statement, containing such information as the agency authority of the partners, with the secretary of state. The statement must be executed by at least two partners, a copy must be sent to all partners, and a certified copy must be filed in the office in which transfers of real property are recorded (in most states, in the county in which the property is located).

better if the provisions of any partnership agreement are in writing.

DURATION OF THE PARTNERSHIP

The partnership agreement can specify the duration of the partnership by designating a date or the completion of a particular project. This is called a *partnership for a term.* A dissolution of the partnership (how dissolution may occur will be discussed later in the chapter) without the consent of all the partners prior to the expiration of the partnership term constitutes a breach of the agreement, and the partner responsible for the breach can be liable for any losses resulting from it.

If no fixed duration is specified, the partnership is a *partnership at will.* Any partner can dissolve this type of partnership at any time without violating the agreement and without incurring liability for losses to other partners that result from the termination.

CAPACITY

Any person having the capacity to enter into a contract can become a partner. A partnership contract entered into with a minor as a partner is voidable and can be disaffirmed by the minor (see Chapter 13 for details). Lack of legal capacity due to insanity at the time of the agreement likewise allows the purported partner either to avoid the agreement or to enforce it. If a partner is adjudicated mentally incompetent during the course of the partnership, the partnership is not automatically dissolved, but dissolution can be decreed by a court on petition.

THE CORPORATION AS PARTNER

The Revised Model Business Corporation Act (see Appendix H) allows corporations generally to make contracts and incur liabilities. The UPA specifically permits a corporation to be a partner. By definition, "a partnership is an association of two or more persons," and the UPA defines a person as including corporations [UPA 2].

Although some states restrict the ability of corporations to become partners, such restrictions have become less common over the years. Many decisions in jurisdictions that do not permit corporate partners nevertheless validate the arrangements by characterizing them as joint ventures (see Chapter 39) rather than as partnerships.

EXHIBIT 33–1   A SAMPLE PARTNERSHIP AGREEMENT

PARTNERSHIP AGREEMENT

This agreement, made and entered into as of the _____, by and among _____ _____ (hereinafter collectively sometimes referred to as "Partners").

WITNESSETH:

Whereas, the Parties hereto desire to form a General Partnership (hereinafter referred to as the "Partnership"), for the term and upon the conditions hereinafter set forth;

Now, therefore, in consideration of the mutual covenants hereinafter contained, it is agreed by and among the Parties hereto as follows:

Article I
BASIC STRUCTURE

Form. The Parties hereby form a General Partnership pursuant to the Laws of _____ _____.

Name. The business of the Partnership shall be conducted under the name of _____ _____.

Place of Business. The principal office and place of business of the Partnership shall be located at _____, or such other place as the Partners may from time to time designate.

Term. The Partnership shall commence on _____, and shall continue for _____ years, unless earlier terminated in the following manner: (a) By the completion of the purpose intended, or (b) Pursuant to this Agreement, or (c) By applicable _____ law, or (d) By death, insanity, bankruptcy, retirement, withdrawal, resignation, expulsion, or disability of all of the then Partners.

Purpose—General. The purpose for which the Partnership is organized is _____ _____

Article II
FINANCIAL ARRANGEMENTS

Each Partner has contributed to the initial capital of the Partnership property in the amount and form indicated on Schedule A attached hereto and made a part hereof. Capital contributions to the Partnership shall not earn interest. An individual capital account shall be maintained for each Partner. If at any time during the existence of the Partnership it shall become necessary to increase the capital with which the said Partnership is doing business, then (upon the vote of the Managing Partner[s]): each party to this Agreement shall contribute to the capital of this Partnership within _____ days notice of such need in an amount according to his then Percentage Share of Capital as called for by the Managing Partner(s).

The Percentage Share of Profits and Capital of each Partner shall be (unless otherwise modified by the terms of this Agreement) as follows:

Names	Initial Percentage Share of Profits and Capital
_____	_____
_____	_____
_____	_____

No interest shall be paid on any contribution to the capital of the Partnership. No Partner shall have the right to demand the return of his capital contributions except as herein provided. Except as herein provided, the individual Partners shall have no right to any priority over each other as to the return of capital contributions.

Distributions to the Partners of net operating profits of the Partnership, as hereinafter defined, shall be made at _____. Such distributions shall be made to the Partners simultaneously.

For the purpose of this Agreement, net operating profit for any accounting period shall mean the gross receipts of the Partnership for such period, less the sum of all cash expenses of operation of the Partnership, and such sums as may be necessary to establish a reserve for operating expenses. In determining net operating profit, deductions for depreciation, amortization, or other similar charges not requiring actual current expenditures of cash shall *not* be taken into account in accordance with generally accepted accounting principles.

EXHIBIT 33–1 A SAMPLE PARTNERSHIP AGREEMENT (CONTINUED)

No Partner shall be entitled to receive any compensation from the Partnership, nor shall any Partner receive any drawing account from the Partnership.

Article III
MANAGEMENT

The Managing Partner(s) shall be _____.

The Managing Partner(s) shall have the right to vote as to the management and conduct of the business of the Partnership as follows:

Names	Vote
_____	_____
_____	_____
_____	_____

Article IV
DISSOLUTION

In the event that the Partnership shall hereafter be dissolved for any reason whatsoever, a full and general account of its assets, liabilities, and transactions shall at once be taken. Such assets may be sold and turned into cash as soon as possible and all debts and other amounts due the Partnership collected. The proceeds thereof shall thereupon be applied as follows:

(a) To discharge the debts and liabilities of the Partnership and the expenses of liquidation.

(b) To pay each Partner or his legal representative any unpaid salary, drawing account, interest, or profits to which he shall then be entitled and in addition, to repay to any Partner his capital contributions in excess of his original capital contribution.

(c) To divide the surplus, if any, among the Partners or their representatives as follows: (1) First (to the extent of each Partner's then capital account) in proportion to their then capital accounts. (2) Then according to each Partner's then Percentage Share of [*Capital/Income*].

No Partner shall have the right to demand and receive property in kind for his distribution.

Article V
MISCELLANEOUS

The Partnership's fiscal year shall commence on January 1st of each year and shall end on December 31st of each year. Full and accurate books of account shall be kept at such place as the Managing Partner(s) may from time to time designate, showing the condition of the business and finances of the Partnership; and each Partner shall have access to such books of account and shall be entitled to examine them at any time during ordinary business hours. At the end of each year, the Managing Partner(s) shall cause the Partnership's accountant to prepare a balance sheet setting forth the financial position of the Partnership as of the end of that year and a statement of operations (income and expenses) for that year. A copy of the balance sheet and statement of operations shall be delivered to each Partner as soon as it is available.

Each Partner shall be deemed to have waived all objections to any transaction or other facts about the operation of the Partnership disclosed in such balance sheet and/or statement of operations unless he shall have notified the Managing Partner(s) in writing of his objectives within thirty (30) days of the date on which such statement is mailed.

The Partnership shall maintain a bank account or bank accounts in the Partnership's name in a national or state bank in the State of _____. Checks and drafts shall be drawn on the Partnership's bank account for Partnership purposes only and shall be signed by the Managing Partner(s) or their designated agent.

Any controversy or claim arising out of or relating to this Agreement shall only be settled by arbitration in accordance with the rules of the American Arbitration Association, one Arbitrator, and shall be enforceable in any court having competent jurisdiction.

Witnesses	Partners
_____	_____
_____	_____

Dated: _____

PARTNERSHIP BY ESTOPPEL

Parties who are not partners can hold themselves out as partners and make representations that third persons rely on in dealing with them. In such a situation, a court may conclude that a **partnership by estoppel** exists, in which case liability is imposed on the alleged partner or partners (although partnership *rights* are not conferred on these persons).

There are two aspects of such liability. The person representing himself or herself to be a partner in an actual or alleged partnership is liable to any third person who extends credit in good faith reliance on such representations. Similarly, a person who expressly or impliedly consents to misrepresentation of an alleged partnership relationship is also liable to third persons who extend credit in good faith reliance [UPA 16].

For example, Moreno owns a small shop. Knowing that the Midland Bank will not make a loan on his credit alone, Moreno represents that Lukas, a financially secure businessperson, is a partner in Moreno's business. Lukas knows of Moreno's misrepresentation but fails to correct the bank's information. Midland Bank, relying on the strength of Lukas's reputation and credit, extends a loan to Moreno. Moreno will be liable to the bank for the loan repayment. In many states, Lukas would also be held liable to the bank. Lukas has impliedly consented to the misrepresentation and will normally be estopped from denying that she is a partner of Moreno. She will be regarded as if she were in fact a partner in Moreno's business insofar as this loan is concerned.

When a real partnership exists and a partner represents that a nonpartner is a member of the firm, the nonpartner is regarded as an agent whose acts are binding on the partner (but normally not on the partnership). For example, Middle Earth Movers has three partners—Jansen, Mathews, and Harran. Mathews represents to the business community that Tully is also a partner. If Tully negotiates a contract in the name of Middle Earth Movers, the contract will be binding on Mathews but normally not on Jansen and Harran (unless, of course, Jansen and Harran knew about, and consented to, Mathews's representation about Tully). Again, partnership by estoppel requires that a third person reasonably and detrimentally rely on the representation that a person was part of the partnership.

SECTION 6

Partnership Operation

The rights and duties of partners are governed largely by the specific terms of their partnership agreement. In the absence of provisions to the contrary in the partnership agreement, the law imposes the rights and duties discussed in the following subsections. The character and nature of the partnership business generally influence the application of these rights and duties.

RIGHTS AMONG PARTNERS

The rights held by partners in a partnership relate to the following areas: management, interest in the partnership, compensation, inspection of books, accounting, and property.

Management.   In a general partnership, "All partners have equal rights in the management and conduct of partnership business" [UPA 18(e)]. Unless the partners agree otherwise, each partner has one vote in management matters *regardless of the proportional size of his or her interest in the firm.* Often, in a large partnership partners will agree to delegate daily management responsibilities to a management committee made up of one or more of the partners.

The majority rule controls decisions in ordinary matters connected with partnership business, unless otherwise specified in the agreement. Unanimous consent of the partners is required, however, to bind the firm in any of the following actions, which significantly affect the nature of the partnership:

1. To alter the essential nature of the firm's business as expressed in the partnership agreement or to alter the capital structure of the partnership.
2. To admit new partners or to enter a wholly new business [UPA 18(g), (h)].
3. To assign partnership property into a trust for the benefit of creditors [UPA 9(3)(a)].
4. To dispose of the partnership's goodwill [UPA 9(3)(b)].
5. To confess judgment against the partnership or submit partnership claims to arbitration [UPA 9(3)(d), (e)]. (A **confession of judgment** is the act of a debtor in permitting a judgment to be entered

against him or her by a creditor, for an agreed sum, without the institution of legal proceedings.)

6. To undertake any act that would make further conduct of partnership business impossible [UPA 9(3)(c)].

7. To amend the articles of the partnership.

Interest in the Partnership. Each partner is entitled to the proportion of business profits and losses that is designated in the partnership agreement. If the agreement does not apportion profits or losses, the UPA provides that profits are to be shared equally and losses are to be shared in the same ratio as profits [UPA 18(a)].

Compensation. Devoting time, skill, and energy to partnership business is a partner's duty and generally not a compensable service. Partners can, of course, agree otherwise. For example, the managing partner of a law firm often receives a salary in addition to his or her share of profits for performing special administrative duties in office and personnel management. UPA 18(f) provides that on the death of a partner, a surviving partner is entitled to compensation for services in winding up partnership affairs (and reimbursement for expenses incurred in the process) above and apart from his or her share in the partnership profits.

Inspection of Books. Partnership books and records must be kept accessible to all partners. Each partner has the right to receive (and the corresponding duty to produce) full and complete information concerning the conduct of all aspects of partnership business [UPA 20]. Each firm retains books in which to record and secure such information. Partners contribute the information, and a bookkeeper typically has the duty to preserve it. The books must be kept at the firm's principal business office unless the partners agree otherwise [UPA 19]. Every partner, whether active or inactive, is entitled to inspect all books and records on demand and can make copies of the materials. The personal representative of a deceased partner's estate has the same right of access to partnership books and records that the decedent would have had.

Accounting. An accounting of partnership assets or profits is done to determine the value of each partner's proportionate share in the partnership. An accounting

can be called for voluntarily, or it can be compelled by the order of a court in equity.[4] Formal accounting occurs by right in connection with dissolution proceedings, but under UPA 22, a partner also has the right to a formal accounting in the following situations:

1. When the partnership agreement provides for a formal accounting.

2. When a partner is wrongfully excluded from the business, from access to the books, or from both.

3. When any partner is withholding profits or benefits belonging to the partnership in breach of the partner's fiduciary duty.

4. When circumstances render a formal accounting "just and reasonable."

Property Rights. A partner has the following three basic property rights:

1. An interest in the partnership.

2. A right in specific partnership property.

3. A right to participate in the management of the partnership, as previously discussed [UPA 24].

There is an important legal distinction between a partner's rights in specific property belonging to the firm to be used for business purposes and a partner's right to share in the firm's earned profits to the extent of his or her interest in the firm. A partner is co-owner with his or her partners of specific partnership property, holding the property as a tenant in partnership. A specific asset may constitute partnership property even when title to it is in an individual partner's name.

The rights of creditors in regard to partnerships were discussed earlier in this chapter. A judgment creditor of an individual partner has no right to execute or attach specific partnership property, but he or she can obtain the partner's share of profits. A creditor of the firm, however, can levy directly on partnership property.

Partner's Interest in the Firm. A partner's interest in the firm is a personal asset consisting of a proportionate

---

4. The principal remedy of a partner against co-partners is an equity suit for dissolution, an accounting, or both. With minor exceptions, a partner cannot maintain an action against other firm members for damages until partnership affairs are settled and an accounting is done. This rule is necessary because legal disputes among partners invariably involve conflicting claims to shares in the partnership. Logically, the value of each partner's share must first be determined by an accounting.

share of the profits earned [UPA 26] and a return of capital on the partnership's termination. A partner's interest is subject to assignment or to a judgment creditor's lien. Judgment creditors can attach a partner's interest by petitioning the court that entered the judgment to grant the creditors a **charging order.** This order entitles the creditors to the profits of the partner and to any assets available to the partner on dissolution [UPA 28]. Neither an assignment nor a court's charging order entitling a creditor to receive a share of the partner's money will cause dissolution of the firm [UPA 27].

Partnership Property. UPA 8(1) provides that "all property originally brought into the partnership's stock or subsequently acquired, by purchase or otherwise, *on account of the partnership,* is partnership property" (emphasis added). Evidence that an asset was acquired with the intention that it be a partnership asset is at the heart of the phrase *on account of the partnership.* Thus, the more closely an asset is associated with the business operations of the partnership, the more likely it is to be a partnership asset.[5] Moreover, when such an asset is purchased with partnership funds, it will belong to the partnership unless a contrary intention is shown. If, for example, a piece of property is purchased with partnership funds, it is presumed to be partnership property even if title is taken in the name of one of the partners.

As mentioned, partners are tenants in partnership of all firm property [UPA 25(1)]. Tenancy in partnership has several important effects. If a partner dies, the surviving partners, not the heirs of the deceased partner, have the right of survivorship to the specific property. Although surviving partners are entitled to possession, they have a duty to account to the decedent's estate for the value of the deceased partner's interest in that property [UPA 25(2)(d), (e)].

A partner has no right to sell, assign, or in any way deal with a particular item of partnership property other than for partnership purposes [UPA 25(2)(a), (b)]. Nor is a partner's personal credit related to partnership property; his or her creditors cannot use partnership property to satisfy the personal debts of the partner. Partnership property is available only to satisfy partnership debts, to enhance the firm's credit, or to achieve other business purposes.

Every partner is a co-owner with all other partners of specific partnership property, such as office equipment, office supplies, and vehicles. Each partner has an equal right to possess partnership property for business purposes or in satisfaction of firm debts, but not for any other purpose without the consent of all the other partners.

DUTIES, POWERS, AND LIABILITIES OF PARTNERS

The duties and powers of partners consist of a fiduciary duty of each partner to the others and general agency powers.

Fiduciary Duties. Partners stand in a fiduciary relationship to one another just as principals and agents do (see Chapter 31). It is a relationship of extraordinary trust and loyalty. This fiduciary duty imposes a responsibility on each partner to act in utmost good faith for the benefit of the partnership. It requires that each partner subordinate his or her personal interests to the mutual welfare of the partners.[6] Thus, a partner cannot engage in any independent competitive activities without the other partners' consent.

This fiduciary duty underlies the entire body of law pertaining to partnership and to agency. From it, certain other duties are commonly implied. Thus, a partner must account to the partnership for any personal profits or benefits derived without the consent of all the partners in any partnership transactions.[7] These include transactions among partners; transactions with third parties connected with the formation, conduct, or liquidation of the partnership; and transactions involving any use of partnership property [UPA 21].

A partner's fiduciary duty requires the highest degree of good faith and fair dealing. This is particularly true when a partner makes a partnership decision that

---

5. Under the RUPA, property that is not acquired in the name of the partnership is nonetheless partnership property if the instrument transferring title refers to (1) the person taking title as a partner or (2) the existence of the partnership [RUPA 204(a)(2)]. If the instrument refers to neither of these, the property is still presumed to be partnership property if it is acquired with partnership funds [RUPA 204(c)]. In all other circumstances, the property is presumed to be the property of an individual partner or partners, even if it is used in the partnership business [RUPA 204(d)].

---

6. The RUPA states that partners may pursue their own interests without automatically violating their fiduciary duties [RUPA 404(e)].
7. In this sense, to account to the partnership means not only to divulge the information but also to determine the value of any benefits or profits derived and to hold that money or property in trust on behalf of the partnership.

affects him or her personally, such as a division of the firm's profits. In that situation, how the profits are divided has a direct effect on the partner's own share of the profits, and thus the decision must be fair and reasonable. This aspect of a partner's fiduciary duty was at issue in the following case.

CASE 33.2   Starr v. Fordham

Supreme Judicial Court
of Massachusetts, 1995.
420 Mass. 178,
648 N.E.2d 1261.

BACKGROUND AND FACTS *Ian Starr was a partner in the law firm of Fordham & Starrett.[a] Under the partnership agreement, Laurence Fordham and Loyd Starrett (the founding partners) determined each partner's share of the firm's profits. The first year, the two divided the profits equally among all of the partners. Starr quit the firm on the last day of the second year. Fordham came up with a list of negative factors for determining Starr's share of the second year's profits and paid him less than half an equal share. Starr filed a suit in a Massachusetts state court against the partners, alleging, among other things, breach of fiduciary duty. The court awarded Starr an additional share of the profits. The partners appealed this award to the state's highest court, the Supreme Judicial Court of Massachusetts.*

IN THE LANGUAGE OF THE COURT

NOLAN, Justice.

* * * * *

* * * The judge found that the plaintiff had produced [business] that constituted * * * 15% * * * of the total * * * dollar amounts for all of the partners as a group. The judge noted, however, that the founding partners distributed only 6.3% of the firm's * * * profits to the plaintiff. * * * The judge determined that this * * * was unfair * * * . The judge also noted that Fordham had fabricated a list of negative factors that the founding partners had used in determining the plaintiff's share of the firm's profits. As a result, the judge concluded that the founding partners had violated their respective fiduciary duties to the plaintiff * * * .

Having examined the record, all 127 exhibits, and the judge's own findings of fact and rulings of law, we * * * cannot conclude that the judge committed a mistake in finding that the founding partners had violated * * * their fiduciary duties to the plaintiff * * * .

DECISION AND REMEDY

The Supreme Judicial Court of Massachusetts affirmed the judgment of the lower court. The partners violated their fiduciary duty by dividing the firm's profits unfairly.

a. Note that a firm may have more partners than its name implies, as in this case.

General Agency Powers. Each partner is an *agent* of every other partner and acts as both a principal and an agent in any business transaction within the scope of the partnership agreement. Each partner is a general agent of the partnership in carrying out the usual business of the firm.[8] Thus, every act of a partner concerning partnership business and every contract signed in the partnership name bind the firm [UPA 9(1)].

Authority of Partners. The UPA affirms general principles of agency law that pertain to the authority of a partner to bind a partnership in contract. Under the same principles, a partner may subject a partnership to liability in tort. When a partner is apparently carrying on partnership business with third persons in the usual way, both the partner and the firm share liability. It is only when third persons know that the partner has no such authority that the partnership is

8. The RUPA adds "or business of the kind carried on by the partnership" [RUPA 301(1)]. Basically, this addition gives added protection to third parties that deal with a partnership that is not familiar to them.

not liable. For example, Patricia, a partner in the partnership of Heise, Green, and Stevens, applies for a loan on behalf of the partnership without authorization from the other partners. The bank manager knows that Patricia has no authority. If the bank manager grants the loan, Patricia will be personally bound, but the firm will not be liable.

The agency concepts relating to apparent authority, actual authority, and ratification that were discussed in Chapter 32 also apply to partnerships. The extent of *implied authority* is generally broader for partners than for ordinary agents, however.

The Scope of Implied Powers.
The character and scope of the partnership business and the customary nature of the particular business operation determine the implied powers of partners. For example, each partner in a trading partnership—essentially, any partnership business that has goods in inventory and makes profits buying and selling those goods—has a wide range of implied powers to borrow money in the firm name and to extend the firm's credit in issuing or indorsing instruments.

In an ordinary partnership, firm members can exercise all implied powers reasonably necessary and customary to carry on that particular business. Some customarily implied powers include the authority to make warranties on goods in the sales business, the power to convey real property in the firm name when such conveyances are part of the ordinary course of partnership business, the power to enter into contracts consistent with the firm's regular course of business, and the power to make admissions and representations concerning partnership affairs [UPA 11].

If a partner acts within the scope of authority, the partnership is bound to third parties. For example, a partner's authority to sell partnership products carries with it the implied authority to transfer title and to make usual warranties. Hence, in a partnership that operates a retail tire store, any partner negotiating a contract with a customer for the sale of a set of tires can warrant that "each tire will be warranted for normal wear for 40,000 miles."

This same partner, however, does not have the authority to sell office equipment, fixtures, or the partnership office building without the consent of all the other partners. In addition, because partnerships are formed for profit, a partner does not generally have the authority to make charitable contributions without the consent of the other partners. No such action

is binding on the partnership unless it is ratified by all of the other partners.

Joint Liability.
In most states, partners are subject to joint liability on partnership debts and contracts [UPA 15(b)]. **Joint liability** means that if a third party sues a partner on, for example, a partnership debt, the partner has the right to insist that the other partners be sued with him or her. In fact, if the third party does not sue all of the partners, those partners sued cannot be required to pay a judgment, and the assets of the partnership cannot be used to satisfy the judgment. (Similarly, the third party's release of one partner releases all partners.) In other words, to bring a successful claim against the partnership on a debt or contract, a plaintiff must name all the partners as defendants. To simplify this rule, some states have enacted statutes providing that a partnership may be sued in its own name, and a judgment will be binding on the partnership and the individual partners even though not all the partners are named in the complaint.[9]

If the third party is successful, he or she may collect on the judgment against the assets of one or more of the partners. In other words, each partner is liable and may be required to pay the entire amount of the judgment. When one partner pays the entire amount, the partnership is required to indemnify (reimburse) that partner [UPA 18(b)]. If the partnership cannot do so, the obligation falls on the other partners.

Joint and Several Liability.
In a few states, partners are jointly and severally liable for partnership debts and contracts. In all states, partners are jointly and severally liable for torts and breaches of trust [UPA 15(a)].[10]

Joint and several liability means a third party may sue one or more of the partners separately (severally) or all of them together (jointly), at his or her option.[11] This is true even when a partner did not participate in, ratify, or know about whatever it was that gave rise to the cause of action.[12]

---

9. California is such a state.
10. Under the RUPA, partners' liability is joint and several for all debts [RUPA 306].
11. The term *several* stems from the medieval English term *severall*, which meant "separately," or "severed from" one another. As used here, *several* liability means *separate* liability.
12. The RUPA prevents creditors from bringing an action to collect debts from the partners of a nonbankrupt partnership without first having attempted unsuccessfully to collect from the partnership (or having convinced a court that the attempt would be unsuccessful) [RUPA 307(d)].

A judgment against one partner on his or her several (separate) liability does not extinguish the others' liability. (Similarly, a release of one partner discharges the partners' joint, but not several, liability.) Thus, those not sued in the first action may be sued subsequently. The first action, however, may have been conclusive on the question of liability. If, for example, in an action against one partner, the court held that the partnership was in no way liable, the third party cannot bring an action against another partner and succeed on the issue of the partnership's liability.

If the third party is successful, he or she may collect on the judgment only against the assets of those partners named as defendants. The partner who committed the tort, though, is required to indemnify the partnership for any damages it pays.

Liability of Incoming Partner. A partner newly admitted to an existing partnership has limited liability for whatever debts and obligations the partnership incurred *prior* to the new partner's admission. UPA 17 provides that the new partner's liability can be satisfied only from partnership assets. This means that the new partner has no personal liability for these debts and obligations, but the new partner's capital contribution may be used to satisfy the debts and obligations.

In cases involving old debts and new partners, two dates are of great significance: the date on which the debt arose and the date on which the partner joined the firm. The court in the following case had to determine the date on which a partnership debt arose.

CASE 33.3

Citizens Bank of Massachusetts v. Parham-Woodman Medical Associates

United States District Court, Eastern District of Virginia, Richmond Division, 1995. 874 F.Supp. 705.

BACKGROUND AND FACTS *Citizens Bank of Massachusetts agreed to lend Parham-Woodman Medical Associates, a partnership, $2 million to construct a new office building. Their agreement, which was signed on April 30, 1985, provided for the money to be disbursed in installments. Most of the funds had been disbursed before Richard Hunley, Nada Tas, and Joseph Tas joined the firm. When the partnership failed to repay the loan, the bank sold the building and obtained a deficiency judgment for more than $1.2 million. The bank filed a suit in a federal district court against the firm and the partners to recover this amount. Hunley and the Tases acknowledged that they had joined the firm before all of the money was disbursed. They argued, however, that because they had joined the firm after the loan agreement was made, they were not liable for the debt beyond the amount of their interest in partnership assets.*

IN THE LANGUAGE OF THE COURT

PAYNE, District Judge.

* * * *

[UPA] Section 17 makes an incoming partner liable for "all the obligations of the partnership arising before his admission," but provides that "this liability shall be satisfied only out of partnership property." * * * [A] partnership obligation arises, within the meaning of Section 17, when the creditor extends the credit to the partnership. In this instance, that occurred on April 30, 1985 and not on the occasion when the bank disbursed each advance.

* * * *

Here the documents were executed long before Dr. Hunley and the Tases joined Parham-Woodman and, upon execution, they were binding obligations on both Citizens Bank and the partnership. That is not changed merely because the passage of part of the consideration was delayed pursuant to a schedule which also was set before Dr. Hunley and the Tases became partners.

DECISION AND REMEDY *The federal district court held that Hunley and the Tases were liable only to the extent of their interests in partnership property.*

SECTION 7

Partnership Termination

Partnerships can be terminated for a variety of reasons. The partnership may be dissolved by agreement among the parties. For example, the partners may stipulate in their partnership agreement that the partnership will end on a certain date or after a particular business objective has been achieved. Alternatively, the partners may simply agree among themselves to terminate the business. A partner's withdrawal may automatically dissolve the partnership. The partnership may also end for other reasons, such as when a partner dies or becomes incapacitated or when a court orders the partnership to be dissolved because of special circumstances.

Generally, any change in the relations of the partners that demonstrates unwillingness or inability to carry on partnership business dissolves the partnership, resulting in termination [UPA 29]. If any partner wishes to continue the business, he or she is free to reorganize into a new partnership with the remaining partners.

The termination of a partnership has two stages—dissolution and winding up. Both stages must take place before termination is complete. **Dissolution** occurs when any partner ceases to be associated with the carrying on of partnership business. **Winding up** is the actual process of collecting and distributing the partnership's assets. Dissolution terminates the right of a partnership to endure as an ongoing concern, but the partnership continues to exist long enough to wind up its affairs. When winding up is complete, the partnership's *legal* existence is terminated.

DISSOLUTION

Dissolution, the first stage in the termination of a partnership, can be brought about by acts of the partners, by operation of law, or by judicial decree.

Dissolution by Acts of the Partners.   The following acts of the partners can bring about dissolution: agreement, the withdrawal of a partner,[13] the addition of a partner, and the transfer of a partner's interest.

---

13. The RUPA distinguishes the withdrawal of a partner that causes a breakup of a partnership from a withdrawal that causes only the end of a partner's participation in the business (and results in a buyout of that partner's interest) [RUPA 601, 701, 801]. Dissolution results only if the partnership must be liquidated [RUPA 801].

Dissolution by Agreement.   A partnership can be dissolved when certain events stipulated in the partnership agreement occur. For example, when a partnership agreement expresses a fixed time or a particular business objective to be accomplished, the passing of the date or the accomplishment of the project dissolves the partnership. Partners do not have to abide by the stipulations in the agreement, however. They can mutually agree to dissolve the partnership early or to extend it. If they agree to continue in the partnership, they become *partners at will*—meaning that any partner can dissolve the partnership at any time by withdrawing from the firm.

Partner's Power to Withdraw.   A partnership is a personal legal relationship among co-owners. No person can be compelled either to become a partner or to remain one. Implicit in a partnership is each partner's *power* to dissociate from the partnership at any time and thus dissolve the partnership. Note that although a partner always has the *power* to withdraw from the partnership, he or she may not always have the *right* to do so. In a partnership for a specified term or for a specified purpose, a partner does not have the right to withdraw until the term has lapsed or the purpose has been fulfilled. If a partner withdraws in violation of the partnership agreement, he or she will be liable to the other partners for damages resulting from wrongful dissolution of the partnership.

Admission of a New Partner.   A change in the composition of the partnership due to the admission of a new partner (without the consent of the other partners) results in dissolution. The new partnership carries the debts of the dissolved partnership. Creditors of the prior partnership become creditors of the partnership that is continuing the business [UPA 41].

Transfer of a Partner's Interest.   The UPA provides that neither a voluntary transfer of a partner's interest[14] nor an involuntary sale of a partner's interest for the benefit of creditors [UPA 28] by itself dissolves the partnership. (A transferee—the one to whom the interest is transferred—acquires the right to the transferring partner's profits but does not become a partner; thus, a transferee has no say in the management or administration of partnership affairs and no right to inspect partnership books.) Either occurrence, however,

---

14. A single partner cannot make another person a partner in a partnership merely by transferring his or her interest to that person [UPA 27].

can ultimately lead to judicial dissolution of the partnership, as will be discussed.

Dissolution by Operation of Law.
A partnership is dissolved by operation of law in the event of death, bankruptcy, or illegality.

Death.   A partnership is dissolved on the death of any partner, even if the partnership agreement provides for carrying on the business with the executor of the decedent's estate.[15] Any change in the composition of the partnership results in a new partnership.

Bankruptcy.   The bankruptcy of a partner will dissolve a partnership. Insolvency alone will not result in dissolution. Naturally, bankruptcy of the firm itself will result in dissolution of the partnership.

Illegality.   Any event that makes it unlawful for the partnership to continue its business or for any partner to carry on in the partnership will result in dissolution. If the illegality of the partnership business is a cause for dissolution, however, the partners can decide to change the nature of their business and continue in the partnership. When the illegality applies to an individual partner, the dissolution must occur. For example, suppose that the state legislature passes a law making it illegal for magistrates to engage in the practice of law. If an attorney in a law firm is appointed a magistrate, the partnership must be dissolved.

Dissolution by Judicial Decree.
Dissolution of a partnership can result from judicial decree. For dissolution to occur, an application or petition must be made in an appropriate court. The court then either denies the petition or grants a decree of dissolution. Under UPA 32, a court can dissolve a partnership for the reasons discussed below or whenever circumstances render it equitable to do so.

Insanity.   A partnership can obtain a judicial declaration of dissolution when a partner is adjudicated insane or is shown to be of unsound mind. This action often involves a series of complex tests and standards.

Incapacity.   When it appears that a partner has become incapable of performing his or her duties

under the partnership agreement, a decree of dissolution may be required. It must appear that the incapacity is permanent and will substantially affect the partner's ability to discharge his or her duties to the firm.

Business Impracticality.   When it becomes obvious that the firm's business can be operated only at a loss, judicial dissolution may be ordered.

Improper Conduct.   A partner's impropriety involving partnership business (for example, fraud perpetrated on the other partners) or improper behavior reflecting unfavorably on the firm (for instance, habitual drunkenness resulting in gross neglect of the partnership's business) will provide grounds for a judicial decree of dissolution.

Other Circumstances.   Dissolution may also be granted in other circumstances when the court finds it equitable to do so. For example, a court might order dissolution when personal dissension between partners becomes so persistent and harmful as to undermine the confidence and cooperation necessary to carry on the firm's business.

Notice of Dissolution.
A partner must communicate his or her intent to dissolve or to withdraw from a firm to each of the other partners. This notice of intent can come from the words of the partner (actual notice) or from the actions of the partner (constructive notice). All partners will share liability for the acts of any partner who continues to conduct business for the firm without knowing that the partnership has been dissolved.

For example, suppose that Alzor, Jennifer, and Carla have a partnership. Alzor tells Jennifer of her intent to withdraw. Before Carla learns of Alzor's intentions, she enters into a contract with a third party. The contract is equally binding on Alzor, Jennifer, and Carla. Unless the other partners have notice, the withdrawing partner will continue to be bound as a partner to all contracts created for the firm.

To avoid liability for obligations a partner incurs after dissolution of a partnership, the firm must give notice to all affected third persons. The manner of giving notice depends on the third person's relationship to the firm. Any third person who has extended credit to the partnership must receive actual notice. For all others, a newspaper announcement or similar public notice is sufficient.

---

15. Under the RUPA, the death of a partner represents that partner's "dissociation" from the partnership, but it is not an automatic ground for the partnership's dissolution [RUPA 601].

WINDING UP

Once dissolution has occurred and partners have been notified, they cannot create new obligations on behalf of the partnership. Their only authority is to complete transactions begun but not finished at the time of dissolution and to wind up the business of the partnership. Winding up includes collecting and preserving partnership assets, discharging liabilities (paying debts), and accounting to each partner for the value of his or her interest in the partnership.

When dissolution is caused by a partner's act that violates the partnership agreement, the innocent partners may have rights to damages resulting from the dissolution. Also, the innocent partners have the right to buy out the offending partner and to continue the business instead of winding up the partnership. A partner who has committed a wrongful act is barred from participating in the winding up of partnership business.

Dissolution resulting from the death of a partner vests all partnership assets in the surviving partners. The surviving partners act as fiduciaries in settling partnership affairs in a quick, practicable manner and in accounting to the estate of the deceased partner for the value of the decedent's interest in the partnership. The surviving partners are entitled to payment for their services in winding up the partnership, as well as to reimbursement for any costs incurred in the process [UPA 18(f)].

Does winding up require that all of the assets of a partnership be liquidated? Or is it enough if, on the death of a partner, the surviving partners take an inventory, provide an accounting to the dead partner's estate for the value of the business as of the date of dissolution, and pay the estate its proportionate share of the value of the partnership? Can the surviving partners then continue in business as a new partnership? Those were the questions in the following case.

CASE 33.4   Creel v. Lilly

Court of Appeals of
Maryland, 1999.
354 Md. 77,
725 A.2d 385.

BACKGROUND AND FACTS   *Joseph Creel, Arnold Lilly, and Roy Altizer formed a general partnership called "Joe's Racing" to sell NASCAR racing memorabilia. Their written agreement stated, in paragraph 7(a), that "at the termination of this partnership a full and accurate inventory shall be prepared, and the assets, liabilities, and income * * * shall be ascertained." Paragraph 7(d) added, "Upon the death or illness of a partner, his share will go to his estate. If his estate wishes to sell his interest, they must offer it to the remaining partners first." Nine months later, Creel died, and Joe's Racing dissolved. Creel's spouse, Anne Creel, was appointed personal representative of his estate.[a] Lilly and Altizer asked Mrs. Creel to release funds in a partnership account to which only Creel had had access. When she refused, Lilly and Altizer filed a suit in a Maryland state court against her. Meanwhile, Lilly and Altizer took an inventory of the merchandise, had an accountant compute the value of the business, and offered Mrs. Creel payment for Creel's share. Lilly and Altizer then ceased doing business as Joe's Racing and used the assets to begin doing business as "Good Ole Boys Racing." The court held, among other things, that Lilly and Altizer did not breach any fiduciary duty to Creel's estate. Mrs. Creel appealed, arguing in part that they should have liquidated the assets of Joe's Racing. The state intermediate appellate court affirmed the lower court's judgment. Mrs. Creel appealed to the Maryland Court of Appeals, the state's highest court.*

IN THE LANGUAGE
OF THE COURT

CHASANOW, Judge.
    *   *   *   *

    Even though the [Joe's Racing] partnership agreement uses the word "termination," paragraph 7(a) is really discussing the dissolution of the partnership and the attendant winding-up process that ultimately led to termination. Paragraph 7(a) requires that the

---

a. A *personal representative* administers a deceased person's estate. This administration includes taking an inventory of the deceased's assets and managing them to preserve their value. See Chapter 50.

assets, liabilities, and income be "ascertained," but it in no way mandates that this must be accomplished by a forced sale of the partnership assets. Indeed, a liquidation or sale of assets is not mentioned anywhere in 7(a).

In this case, the winding-up method outlined in 7(a) was followed exactly by the surviving partners: a full and accurate inventory was prepared * * * ; this information was given to an accountant, who ascertained the assets, liabilities, and income of the partnership; and finally, the remaining debt or profit was distributed * * * .

Mrs. Creel argues that the partnership agreement does not address the winding-up process and that we should look to UPA's default rules to fill in this gap. Her contention is incorrect. We only turn to UPA and its liquidation rule if there is no other option, and such is clearly not the case here. * * *

Assuming *arguendo* [for the sake of argument] that the Joe's Racing partnership agreement cannot be interpreted as outlining an alternative to liquidation in winding up the partnership in the event of a dissolution caused by a partner's death, we still find that a sale of all partnership assets is not required under either UPA or RUPA in order to ascertain the true value of the business. Support for this is found in Maryland's recent adoption of RUPA, which encourages businesses to continue in either their original or successor form, and also the holdings of out-of-state cases where other options besides a "fire sale" have been chosen when a partnership is dissolved under UPA.

* * * *

We find it is sound public policy to permit a partnership to continue either under the same name or as a successor partnership without all of the assets being liquidated. Liquidation can be a harmful and destructive measure, especially to a small business like Joe's Racing, and is often unnecessary to determining the true value of the partnership.

DECISION AND REMEDY *The Maryland Court of Appeals affirmed the decision of the lower court. Winding up does not require a forced sale of all partnership assets to determine the value of the business. On the death of a partner, it is acceptable to pay the deceased partner's estate its proportionate share of the value of the partnership, derived from an accurate accounting, without having to fully liquidate the business.*

DISTRIBUTION OF ASSETS

Creditors of the partnership, as well as creditors of the individual partners, can make claims on the partnership's assets when the partnership is terminated. Creditors of the partnership have priority over creditors of individual partners in the distribution of partnership assets; the converse priority is followed in the distribution of individual partner assets—except under bankruptcy law, which provides that a partner's individual assets may be utilized to pay claims against a partnership involved in bankruptcy proceedings.[16] (Bankruptcy law in general was discussed in Chapter 30.)

The priorities in the distribution of a partnership's assets are as follows [UPA 40(b)]:[17]

1. Payment of third party debts.
2. Refund of advances (loans) made to or for the firm by a partner.
3. Return of capital contribution to a partner.
4. Distribution of the balance, if any, to partners in accordance with the relative proportions of their respective shares in the profits.

The distribution of partnership assets begins with the subtraction of the partnership's total liabilities

---

16. 11 U.S.C. Section 723.

17. Under the RUPA, partner creditors are included among creditors who take first priority [RUPA 808]. Capital contributions and profits or losses are then calculated together to determine the amounts that the partners receive or the amounts that they pay.

from its total assets. Liabilities include amounts owed to creditors, to partners for other than capital contributions and profit, and to partners for their capital contributions. Amounts that remain after payment of the liabilities are distributed to the partners according to the profit-sharing ratio.

If the partnership's liabilities are greater than its assets, the partners bear the losses—in the absence of a contrary agreement—in the same proportion in which they shared the profits (rather than, for example, in proportion to their contributions to the partnership's capital). If the partnership is insolvent, the partners must still contribute their respective shares. If one of the partners does not contribute, the other or others must provide the additional amounts necessary to pay the liabilities; but he, she, or they have a **right of contribution** against (that is, a right to be reimbursed by) whoever has not paid his or her share.[18]

PARTNERSHIP BUY-SELL AGREEMENTS

Usually, when people enter into partnerships, they are getting along with one another. To prepare for the possibility that the situation may change and they

---

18. If an individual partner is insolvent and for that reason cannot pay his or her share of the loss, however, the solvent partner or partners will be unable to recover their additional contributions from the insolvent partner.

may become unable to work together amicably, the partners should make express arrangements during the formation of the partnership to provide for its smooth dissolution. An agreement may be made for one or more partners to buy out the other or others, should the situation warrant. Such an agreement is called a **buy-sell agreement,** or simply a buyout agreement. To agree beforehand on who buys what, under what circumstances, and, if possible, at what price may eliminate costly negotiations or litigation later. Alternatively, it may be agreed that one or more partners will determine the value of the interest being sold, and the other or others can decide whether to buy or sell.

A similar agreement can be formed for the transfer of a partner's interest on his or her death to the surviving partners. The partners can agree that the survivors will pay the value of the deceased partner's interest in the partnership to his or her representative. To fund the payment of the value of each partner's interest on his or her death, partnership funds can be used to purchase insurance.[19]

---

19. Under the RUPA, if a partner's dissociation does not result in a dissolution of the partnership, a buyout of the partner's interest is mandatory [RUPA 701(a)]. The RUPA contains an extensive set of buyout rules. Basically, a departing partner gets the same amount through a buyout that he or she would get if the business were winding up [RUPA 701(b)].

TERMS AND CONCEPTS TO REVIEW

articles of partnership 621	entrepreneur 616	partnership 617
buy-sell agreement 634	information return 621	partnership by estoppel 624
charging order 626	joint and several liability 628	right of contribution 634
confession of judgment 624	joint liability 628	sole proprietorship 616
dissolution 630	marshaling assets 620	winding up 630

QUESTIONS AND CASE PROBLEMS

33–1. INDICATIONS OF PARTNERSHIP. Daniel is the owner of a chain of shoe stores. He hires Rubya as the manager of a new store, which is to open in Grand Rapids, Michigan. Daniel, by written contract, agrees to pay Rubya a monthly salary. Also, Daniel agrees to pay Rubya 20 percent of the profits. Without Daniel's knowledge, Rubya represents himself to Classen as Daniel's partner, showing Classen the agreement to share profits. Classen extends credit to Rubya. Rubya defaults. Discuss whether Classen can hold Daniel liable as a partner.

33–2. THE NATURE OF PARTNERSHIPS. Aretha wishes to purchase some real property owned by Tropical Gardens. She learns that Tropical Gardens is a partnership owned by Waldheim, Berry, and Lamont. She also learns that the partnership needs capital and that the need for capital is one of the major reasons the partners are selling their real property. Because Tropical Gardens is a partnership, Aretha has the following concerns:

(a) Can the partnership convey the land in the name of Tropical Gardens?

(b) If there is a breach of contract, against whom must Aretha file a lawsuit?

(c) If Aretha obtains a judgment against Tropical Gardens, against whom can she execute it?

Discuss fully each of Aretha's concerns.

33–3. RIGHTS OF PARTNERS. Meyer, Knapp, and Cavanna establish a partnership to operate a window-washing service. Meyer contributes $10,000 to the partnership, and Knapp and Cavanna contribute $1,000 each. The partnership agreement is silent on how profits and losses will be shared. One month after the partnership has begun operation, Knapp and Cavanna vote, over Meyer's objection, to purchase another truck for the firm's operation. Meyer believes that because he contributed $10,000, no major commitment to purchase by the partnership can be made over his objection. In addition, Meyer claims that, in the absence of agreement, profits must be divided in the same ratio as capital contributions. Discuss Meyer's contentions.

33–4. COMPENSATION. Tandoori, Beth, and Nadia form a partnership to operate a hair-styling salon. After one year's operation, the salon has become very busy and profitable. Most customers have a preference as to which partner's services they use. Tandoori becomes ill, and Beth and Nadia start working sixty-hour weeks. It appears that Tandoori will not return to work for at least two months. Beth and Nadia want to bring in Dana as a new partner. Tandoori objects to Dana and refuses to consent to Dana's admission into the partnership. Beth and Nadia insist that they be paid extra compensation for having to work additional hours because of Tandoori's illness. Discuss whether Beth and Nadia are entitled to the extra compensation and whether Dana can be admitted as a new partner by majority vote.

33–5. DISTRIBUTION OF PARTNERSHIP ASSETS. Susan and Dominic formed a partnership. At the time of formation, Susan's capital contribution was $10,000, and Dominic's was $15,000. Later, Susan made a $10,000 loan to the partnership when it needed working capital. The partnership agreement provided that profits were to be shared, with 40 percent for Susan and 60 percent for Dominic. The partnership was dissolved by Dominic's death. At the end of the dissolution and the winding up of the partnership, the partnership's assets were $50,000, and the partnership's debts were $8,000. Discuss fully how the assets should be distributed.

33–6. PARTNERSHIP DISSOLUTION. Carola and Grogan were partners in a law firm. The partnership was created by an oral agreement and began doing business in 1974. On September 6, 1976, Carola withdrew from the partnership some of its files, furniture, and books, along with various other items of office equipment. The next day, Carola informed Grogan he had withdrawn from the partnership. Discuss whether Carola's actions on September 6, 1976, constituted effective notice of dissolution to Grogan. [*Carola v. Grogan*, 102 A.D.2d 934, 477 N.Y.S.2d 525 (1984)]

33–7. RIGHTS AMONG PARTNERS. B&R Communications was a general partner in Amarillo CellTelco. Under the partnership agreement, each partner had the right to inspect partnership records "at reasonable times during business hours," as long as the inspection did not "unreasonably interfere with the operation of the partnership." B&R believed that the managers of the firm were using partnership money to engage in lawsuits that were too costly. B&R and other general partners filed a suit in a Texas state court against the managers. B&R wanted to inspect the firm's records to discover information about the lawsuits, but the court denied B&R's request. B&R asked a state appellate court to order the trial judge to grant the request. On what ground did the appellate court issue the order? [*B&R Communications v. Lopez*, 890 S.W.2d 224 (Tex.App.—Amarillo 1994)]

33–8. LIABILITY OF PARTNERS. Frank Kolk was the manager of Triples American Grill, a sports bar and restaurant. Kolk and John Baines opened bank accounts in the name of the bar, each signing the account signature cards as "owner." Baines was often at the bar and had free access to its office. Baines told others that he was "an owner" and "a partner." Kolk told Steve Mager, the president of Cheesecake Factory, Inc., that Baines was a member of a partnership that owned Triples. On this basis, Cheesecake delivered its goods to Triples on credit. In fact, the bar was owned by a corporation. When the unpaid account totaled more than $20,000, Cheesecake filed a suit in a New Mexico state court against Baines to collect. On what basis might Baines be liable to Cheesecake? What does Cheesecake have to show to win its case? [*Cheesecake Factory, Inc. v. Baines*, 964 P.2d 183 (N.M.App. 1998)]

33–9. INDICATIONS OF PARTNERSHIP. Sandra Lerner was one of the original founders of Cisco Systems. When she sold her interest in Cisco, she received a substantial amount of money, which she invested, and she became extremely wealthy. Patricia Holmes met Lerner at Holmes's horse training facility, and they became friends. One evening in Lerner's mansion, while applying nail polish, Holmes layered a raspberry color over black to produce a new color, which Lerner liked. Later, the two created other colors with names like "Bruise," "Smog," and "Oil Slick," and titled their concept "Urban Decay." Lerner and Holmes started a firm to produce and market the polishes but never discussed the sharing of profits and losses. They agreed to build the business and then sell it. Together, they did market research, experimented with colors, worked on a logo and advertising, obtained capital from an investment firm, and hired employees. Then Lerner began working to edge Holmes out of the firm. Several months later, when Holmes was told not to attend meetings of the firm's officers, she filed a suit in a California state court against Lerner, claiming, among other things, a breach of their partnership agreement. Lerner responded in part that there was no partnership agreement because there was no agreement to divide profits. Was Lerner right? Why or why not? How should the court rule? [*Holmes v. Lerner*, 74 Cal.App.4th 442, 88 Cal.Rptr.2d 130 (1 Dist. 1999)]

33–10. IN YOUR COURT

Hal Frye sold some land to Aspen Estates, a general partnership, to build condominiums. Aspen gave a promissory note to Frye for $8 million as payment. A few years later, Jan Morry joined Aspen as a general partner. Morry left the firm before the note came due, but while she was a partner, interest accrued on the balance. The condominium project failed, and Aspen went out of business. Frye sued Morry to recover some of the interest on the note. Frye acknowledged that Morry was not liable for debts incurred before she joined the firm but argued that the interest that accrued while she was a partner was a "new" debt for which she was personally liable. Assume that you are the judge in the trial court hearing this case and answer the following questions:

(a) Review Case 33.3 (*Citizens Bank of Massachusetts v. Parham-Woodman Medical Associates*), which also concerned the liability of an incoming partner. To what extent, if any, do the principles relied on by the court in that case apply to the case now before your court?

(b) How will you rule in this case, and why?

LAW ON THE WEB

For updated links to resources available on the Web, as well as a variety of other materials, visit this text's Web site at http://wbl.westbuslaw.com.

For information on the taxation of partnerships, see the article on this topic by Dennis D'Annunzio at

http://www.sunbeltnetwork.com/Journal/Current/D970804dsd.html

For some of the advantages and disadvantages of doing business as a partnership, go to the following page, which is part of the Small Business Administration's Web site:

http://www.sba.gov/starting/indexfaqs.html

LEGAL RESEARCH EXERCISES ON THE WEB

Go to http://wbl.westbuslaw.com, the Web site that accompanies this text. Select "Internet Applications," and then click on "Chapter 33." There you will find the following Internet research exercise that you can perform to learn more about partnerships:

Activity 33–1: Partnerships

CHAPTER 34

CORPORATIONS—
Formation and Financing

THE CORPORATION IS A CREATURE OF STATUTE. A corporation is an artificial being, existing in law only and neither tangible nor visible. Its existence depends generally on state law, although some corporations, especially public organizations, can be created under federal law. Each state has its own body of corporate law, and these laws are not entirely uniform.

The Model Business Corporation Act (MBCA) is a codification of modern corporation law that has been influential in the codification of state corporation statutes. Today, the majority of state statutes are guided by the most recent version of the MBCA, often referred to as the Revised Model Business Corporation Act (RMBCA). Excerpts from the latter are included in Appendix H of this text. You should keep in mind, however, that there is considerable variation among the regulations of the states that have used the MBCA or the RMBCA as a basis for their statutes, and several states do not follow either act. Because of this, individual state corporation laws should be relied on to determine corporate law rather than the MBCA or RMBCA.

In this chapter, we examine the nature of the corporate form of business enterprise and the various classifications of corporations. We then discuss the formation and financing of today's corporation.

SECTION 1

The Nature of the Corporation

A corporation can consist of one or more *natural* persons (as opposed to the artificial "person" of the corporation) identified under a common name. The corporation substitutes itself for its shareholders in conducting corporate business and in incurring liability, yet its authority to act and the liability for its actions are separate and apart from the individuals who own it. (In certain limited situations, the "corporate veil" can be pierced; that is, liability for the corporation's obligations can be extended to shareholders, a topic to be discussed later in this chapter.)

CORPORATE PERSONNEL

Responsibility for the overall management of the corporation is entrusted to a board of directors, which is elected by the shareholders. The board of directors hires corporate officers and other employees to run the daily business operations of the corporation.

When an individual purchases a share of stock in a corporation, that person becomes a shareholder and an owner of the corporation. Unlike the members in a partnership, the body of shareholders can change constantly without affecting the continued existence of the corporation. A shareholder can sue the corporation, and the corporation can sue a shareholder. Additionally, under certain circumstances, a shareholder can sue on behalf of a corporation. The rights and duties of all corporate personnel will be examined in Chapter 35.

CORPORATE TAXATION

Corporate profits are taxed by state and federal governments. Corporations can do one of two things with corporate profits—retain them or pass them on to shareholders in the form of dividends. The corporation receives no tax deduction for dividends distributed to shareholders. Dividends are again taxable (except when they represent distributions of capital) as ordinary income to the shareholder receiving them. This double-taxation feature of the corporation is one of its major disadvantages.

Profits that are not distributed are retained by the corporation. These **retained earnings**, if invested properly, will yield higher corporate profits in the future and thus cause the price of the company's stock to rise. Individual shareholders can then reap the benefits of the retained earnings in the capital gains they receive when they sell their shares.

The consequences of a failure to pay taxes can be severe. As will be discussed in Chapter 36, the state may dissolve a corporation for this reason. Alternatively, corporate status may be suspended until the taxes are paid.

CONSTITUTIONAL RIGHTS OF CORPORATIONS

A corporation is recognized under state and federal law as a "person," and it enjoys many of the same rights and privileges that natural persons who are U.S. citizens enjoy. The Bill of Rights guarantees a person, as a citizen, certain protections, and corporations are considered persons in most instances. Accordingly, a corporation has the same right of access to the courts as an entity that can sue or be sued. It also has the right of due process before denial of life, liberty, or property, as well as freedom from unreasonable searches and seizures and from double jeopardy.

Under the First Amendment, corporations are entitled to freedom of speech. As we pointed out in Chapter 4, however, commercial speech (such as advertising) and political speech (such as contributions to political causes or candidates) receive significantly less protection than noncommercial speech.

Only the corporation's individual officers and employees possess the Fifth Amendment right against self-incrimination.[1] Additionally, the privileges and immunities clause of the Constitution (Article IV, Section 2) does not protect corporations, nor does it protect an unincorporated association.[2] This clause requires each state to treat citizens of other states equally with respect to access to courts, travel rights, and so forth.

TORTS AND CRIMINAL ACTS

A corporation is liable for the torts committed by its agents or officers within the course and scope of their employment. This principle applies to a corporation exactly as it applies to the ordinary agency relationships discussed in Chapter 32. It follows the doctrine of *respondeat superior*.

Under modern criminal law a corporation may also be held liable for the criminal acts of its agents and employees, provided the punishment is one that can be applied to the corporation. Obviously, corporations cannot be imprisoned, but they can be fined. (Of course, corporate directors and officers can be imprisoned, and in recent years, many have faced criminal penalties for their own actions or for the actions of employees under their supervision. The criminal liability of corporate directors and officers was examined in Chapter 8.)

CORPORATE SENTENCING GUIDELINES

Recall from Chapter 8 that the U.S. Sentencing Commission created standardized sentencing guidelines for federal crimes. These guidelines went into effect in 1987. The commission subsequently created the Federal Organizational Corporate Sentencing Guidelines, which consist of specific sentencing guidelines for crimes committed by corporate employees (white-collar crimes). The net effect of the guidelines has been a fivefold to tenfold increase in criminal penalties for crimes committed by corporate personnel.

The corporate sentencing guidelines cover thirty-two levels of offenses. The punishment for each of-

---

1. *In re Grand Jury No. 86-3 (Will Roberts Corp.)*, 816 F.2d 569 (11th Cir. 1987).
2. *W. C. M. Window Co. v. Bernardi*, 730 F.2d 486 (7th Cir. 1984).

fense depends on such things as the seriousness of the charge, the amount of money involved, and the extent to which top company executives are involved. Under the sentencing guidelines, corporate lawbreakers face sanctions and fines that can be as high as hundreds of millions of dollars. The guidelines allow judges to ease up on penalties, however, when companies have taken substantial steps to prevent, investigate, and punish wrongdoing. Additionally, if companies cooperate with government investigators, the penalties may be less severe.

The guidelines present judges with a complicated formula for determining penalties for businesses based on the seriousness of the offense and the degree of the company's guilt. The so-called *culpability score* of a company depends on what role senior management had in the alleged wrongdoing as well as the company's history of past violations and the extent of management's cooperation with federal investigators. Additionally, the effectiveness of the company's compliance program is important. Firms can establish "credits" against potential penalties if they undertake the following measures:

1. The firm must establish and put in writing crime prevention standards and procedures for all employees and agents, and these standards must be communicated to all employees and agents in writing, training programs, or both.
2. The standards must be enforced by high-level employees.
3. When an employee has demonstrated an apparent propensity to engage in criminal activities, the company must prevent that employee from exercising discretionary authority.
4. All anticrime standards of the company must include methods of detecting as well as preventing crimes.
5. Whistleblowers must be protected from reprisals.

SECTION 2

Corporate Powers

Under modern law, except as limited by charters, statutes, or constitutions, *a corporation can engage in any act and enter into any contract available to a natural person in order to accomplish the purposes for which it was created.* When a corporation is created, the express and implied powers necessary to achieve its purpose also come into existence.

EXPRESS AND IMPLIED POWERS

The express powers of a corporation are found in its **articles of incorporation** (a document containing information about the corporation, including the corporation's organization and functions), in the law of the state of incorporation, and in the state and federal constitutions. Corporate **bylaws** (rules of management adopted by the corporation at its first organizational meeting) and the resolutions of the corporation's board of directors also grant or restrict certain powers. The following order of priority is used when conflicts arise among documents involving corporations:

1. U.S. Constitution.
2. State constitutions.
3. State statutes.
4. Articles of incorporation.
5. Bylaws.
6. Resolutions of the board of directors.

Certain implied powers arise when a corporation is created. Barring express constitutional, statutory, or charter prohibitions, the corporation has the implied power to perform all acts reasonably appropriate and necessary to accomplish its corporate purposes. For this reason, a corporation has the implied power to borrow money within certain limits, to lend money, and to extend credit to those with whom it has a legal or contractual relationship.

To borrow money, the corporation acts through its board of directors to authorize the loan. Most often, the president or chief executive officer of the corporation will execute the necessary papers on behalf of the corporation. Corporate officers such as these have the implied power to bind the corporation in matters directly connected with the *ordinary* business affairs of the enterprise. A corporate officer does not have the authority to bind the corporation in matters of great significance to the corporate purpose or undertaking, such as the sale of substantial corporate assets, however.

ULTRA VIRES DOCTRINE

The term **ultra vires** means "beyond the powers." In corporate law, acts of a corporation that are beyond its express or implied powers are *ultra vires* acts. A majority of cases dealing with *ultra vires* acts have involved contracts made for unauthorized purposes. For example, it is difficult to see how a contract made by a plumbing company for the purchase of six thousand cases of brandy is reasonably related to the conduct and furtherance of the corporation's stated purpose of providing plumbing installation and services. Hence, such a contract would probably be held *ultra vires*.

In some states, when a contract is entirely executory (not yet performed by either party), a defense of *ultra vires* can be used by either party to prevent enforcement of the contract. In cases in which an *ultra vires* contract is partially or fully executed at the time of challenge, courts may enforce, or uphold, the contract if the circumstances are such that it would be inequitable to allow a party to assert the defense of *ultra vires*.

Under Section 3.04 of the RMBCA, the following remedies are available for *ultra vires* acts:

1. The shareholders may sue on behalf of the corporation to obtain an injunction (to prohibit the corporation from engaging in the *ultra vires* transactions) or to obtain damages for the harm caused by the transactions.
2. The corporation itself can sue the officers and directors who were responsible for the *ultra vires* transactions to recover damages.
3. The attorney general of the state may institute a proceeding to obtain an injunction against the *ultra vires* transactions or to institute dissolution proceedings against the corporation for *ultra vires* acts.

In the following case, the court had to decide whether the board of directors of a cooperative housing corporation had exceeded its authority when it set minimum prices for the cooperative's housing units.

CASE 34.1   Oakley v. Longview Owners, Inc.

Supreme Court
of New York,
Westchester County,
1995.
165 Misc.2d 192,
628 N.Y.S.2d 468.

HISTORICAL AND ECONOMIC SETTING   *Cooperative housing corporations are a special form of ownership of real property. A cooperative takes out a mortgage on, for example, an entire apartment building. Residents buy shares in the corporation representing their apartments (or units) and make payments to the cooperative to cover their proportionate shares of the cooperative's mortgage payment. The board of directors of a cooperative housing corporation often has the power to disapprove sales of units to protect other residents' stake in the building. In the early 1990s, the prices for units in some New York cooperatives were dropping.*

BACKGROUND AND FACTS   *Dorothy Oakley owned shares in Longview Owners, Inc., a cooperative housing corporation in New York. When she tried to sell her shares—that is, her apartment—the Longview board of directors refused to approve the sale, in part because the price was less than a minimum price for the apartments set by the board two months earlier. The board had set the minimum in a resolution without notifying the shareholder-owners or giving them the opportunity to vote on it. Neither the Longview bylaws nor the certificate of incorporation gave the board the authority to set prices. Oakley filed a suit in a New York state court against the board, alleging that it had exceeded its authority in refusing to approve the sale. The board filed a motion to dismiss.*

**IN THE LANGUAGE
OF THE COURT**

DONALD N. SILVERMAN, Justice.
       *   *   *   *
       *   *   * A cooperative board of directors may only act upon the authority which they are given. That authority may be found by looking to the by-laws of the corporation *   *   * and the certificate of incorporation.

Here, defendants are not granted by language expressed, or implied, authority to impose these restraints. In addition, there is no evidence that the shareholders of the corporation were ever given prior notice of this resolution and an opportunity to vote on this significant restriction affecting the stock of the corporation.

**DECISION
AND REMEDY**

The New York trial court denied the board's motion to dismiss and set the case for trial. Neither the certificate of incorporation nor the corporate bylaws gave the board authority to set minimum prices, and the shareholders had not been given the opportunity to vote on the issue.

SECTION 3

Classification of Corporations

The classification of a corporation normally depends on its location, purpose, and ownership characteristics.

DOMESTIC, FOREIGN, AND ALIEN CORPORATIONS

A corporation is known as a **domestic corporation** in its home state (the state in which it incorporates). A corporation that is formed in one state but is doing business in another is referred to in that other state as a **foreign corporation.** A corporation formed in another country (say, Mexico) but doing business in the United States is referred to in the United States as an **alien corporation.**

A corporation does not have an automatic right to do business in a state other than its state of incorporation. A corporation normally is required to obtain a *certificate of authority* in any state in which it plans to do business. Once the certificate has been issued, the powers conferred on the corporation by its home state generally can be exercised in the other state. Should a foreign corporation do business without obtaining a certificate of authority, the state can fine the corporation; deny it the privilege of using state courts; and even hold its officers, directors, or agents personally liable for corporate obligations, including contractual obligations, incurred in that state.[3]

PUBLIC AND PRIVATE CORPORATIONS

A public corporation is one formed by the government to meet some political or governmental purpose. Cities and towns that incorporate are common examples. In addition, many federal government organizations, such as the U.S. Postal Service, the Tennessee Valley Authority, and AMTRAK, are public corporations.

Private corporations, in contrast, are created either wholly or in part for private benefit. Most corporations are private. Although they may serve a public purpose, as a public utility does, they are owned by private persons rather than by the government.

NONPROFIT CORPORATIONS

Corporations formed for purposes other than making a profit are called *nonprofit* or *not-for-profit* corporations. Nonprofit corporations are usually (although not necessarily) private corporations. Private hospitals, educational institutions, charities, religious organizations, and the like are frequently organized as nonprofit corporations. The nonprofit corporation is a convenient form of organization that allows various groups to own property and to form contracts without the individual members' being personally exposed to liability.

CLOSE CORPORATIONS

A **close corporation** is one whose shares are held by members of a family or by relatively few persons. Close corporations are also referred to as *closely held, family,* or *privately held* corporations. Usually, the members of the small group constituting a close corporation are personally known to one another. Because the number of shareholders is so small, there is no trading market for the shares. In practice, a close corporation is often operated like a partnership. Some states recognize this similarity and have enacted special statutory provisions that cover close corporations. These provisions expressly permit close corporations to depart significantly from certain formalities required by traditional corporation law.[4]

Additionally, Section 7.32 of the RMBCA—a provision added to the RMBCA in 1991 and adopted in several states—gives close corporations a substantial amount of flexibility in determining the rules by which they will operate. Under Section 7.32, if all of the shareholders of a corporation agree in writing, the corporation can operate without directors, bylaws, annual or special shareholders' or directors' meetings, stock certificates, or formal records of shareholders' or directors' decisions.[5]

Management of Close Corporations. The close corporation has a single shareholder or a closely knit group of shareholders, who usually hold the positions of directors and officers. Management of a close corporation resembles that of a sole proprietorship or a partnership. As a corporation, however, the firm must meet whatever specific legal requirements are set forth in state statutes.

---

3. *Robertson v. Levy,* 197 A.2d 443 (D.C.App. 1964).

4. For example, in some states (such as Maryland), the close corporation need not have a board of directors.
5. Shareholders cannot agree, however, to eliminate certain rights of shareholders, such as the right to inspect corporate books and records or the right to bring derivative actions (lawsuits on behalf of the corporation—see Chapter 35).

To prevent a majority shareholder from dominating a close corporation, the corporation may specify that action can be taken by the board only on approval of more than a simple majority of the directors. Typically, this would not be required for ordinary business decisions but only for extraordinary actions, such as changing the amount of dividends or dismissing an employee-shareholder. Additionally, in some cases, courts have held that majority shareholders owe a fiduciary duty to minority shareholders (see Chapter 35 for a further discussion of the duties of majority shareholders).

Transfer of Shares in Close Corporations. By definition, a close corporation has a small number of shareholders. The transfer of one shareholder's shares to someone else can thus cause serious management problems. The other shareholders may find themselves required to share control with someone they do not know or like.

Consider an example. Three brothers, Terry, Damon, and Henry Johnson, are the only shareholders of Johnson's Car Wash, Inc. Henry wants to sell his shares to an unknown third person. Terry and Damon object to Henry's idea, and a dispute ensues. What could they have done to avoid this situation? The articles of incorporation could have restricted the transferability of shares to outside persons by stipulating that shareholders offer their shares to the corporation or other shareholders before selling them to an outside purchaser. In fact, a few states have statutes under which close corporation shares cannot be transferred unless certain persons—including shareholders, family members, and the corporation—are first given the opportunity to purchase the shares for the same price.

Another way that control of a close corporation can be stabilized is through the use of a shareholder agreement. A shareholder agreement can provide that when one of the original shareholders dies, his or her shares of stock in the corporation will be divided in such a way that the proportionate holdings of the survivors, and thus their proportionate control, will be maintained.

Key employees may be among those who are allowed to buy shares in the close corporation for which they work. A shareholder agreement may provide that if a key employee is discharged, the employee must offer to sell his or her shares to the corporation, which may be required to buy them. In such circumstances, a question may arise as to whether the corporation discharged its employees merely to buy their shares. That was one of the questions raised in the following case.

CASE 34.2   Crowder Construction Co. v. Kiser

Court of Appeals of
North Carolina, 1999.
517 S.E.2d 178.
http://www.aoc.state.
nc.us/www/public/html/
opinions.htm[a]

BACKGROUND AND FACTS *Crowder Construction Company allowed only members of the Crowder family and key employees to buy company stock. Under a shareholders' agreement, if a key employee was terminated, the employee was obligated to sell his or her shares to the company. Under a "buyout" provision, the company was required to buy the shares at a price based on their book value.[b] If those shares had been held for less than seven years, the price was less. In 1981, the firm hired Eugene Kiser, a certified public accountant who became the firm's chief financial officer. As a key employee, he bought Crowder stock at a substantial discount. By the end of 1994, Kiser had begun to openly question the competence of Otis Crowder, the firm's president, to make decisions. In January 1995, Kiser was discharged and told to sell his stock to the company. Had Kiser worked until August, he would have held all of his shares for more than seven years, which would have entitled him to an extra $180,000. When he refused to sell the shares that he had held for less than seven years, the firm filed a suit in a North Carolina state court against him to enforce the shareholders' agreement. Kiser argued, among other things, that the shareholders' agreement was unconscionable. In support of this argument,*

---

a. This Web site is maintained by the North Carolina Administrative Office of the Courts. In the "Court of Appeals Opinions" section, click on the "1999" box. When that page opens, scroll to "20 July 99" and click on the case name to access the opinion.

b. The *book value* of a corporation is generally understood to mean the value of the corporation's total assets less its total liabilities.

he claimed in part that he had been discharged so the company would not have to pay the full price for his stock. The court granted a summary judgment in favor of Crowder, and Kiser appealed to a state intermediate appellate court.

IN THE LANGUAGE OF THE COURT

HORTON, Judge.

* * * *

* * * In family owned corporations, or other corporations in which all shares of stock are held by a relatively small number of shareholders, it is not unusual for all shareholders to agree that the corporation, or the other shareholders, will be given the first opportunity to purchase the shares of a terminated or retiring shareholder. This agreement is valid under the North Carolina Corporations Act provided it is "reasonable" and is not "unconscionable under the circumstances." * * *

Since such restrictions make it even more difficult to dispose of minority stock interests in a closely held corporation, *these agreements often contain some version of mandatory "buy-out" provisions to ensure shareholders a ready market for their shares where there otherwise might not be one.* * * * [Emphasis added.]

* * * *

* * * Defendant [Kiser] contends that by prematurely terminating him, plaintiff saved $180,000.00 which defendant would have been due, and that defendant's termination * * * raises a reasonable inference * * * that the termination was motivated by plaintiff's desire to avoid paying defendant full value for his shares of stock. We disagree.

* * * Plaintiff's evidence tends to show that defendant was discharged for openly questioning the ability and competence of Company management to guide the affairs of the Company, resulting in an adversarial relationship between Kiser and other members of management. * * *

* * * *

* * * Even assuming, for the sake of argument, that enforcement of the stock purchase agreement would be inequitable if plaintiff had terminated defendant's employment solely to prevent his stock options from fully vesting, defendant comes forward with no evidence to support his bare assertion that he was discharged for an improper purpose. * * * Other than defendant's argument that an inference of wrongful purpose arises from his termination, defendant does not offer any evidence * * * . Plaintiff having offered competent evidence of a justifiable business purpose motivating defendant's termination, and defendant having failed to offer evidence on this issue in opposition to the motion for summary judgment, the trial court properly entered summary judgment on this issue.

DECISION AND REMEDY

The state intermediate appellate court affirmed the judgment of the lower court. There was no evidence that Kiser had been discharged so that Crowder could avoid paying him a higher price for his shares in the company. In the absence of such proof, neither the shareholder agreement nor Kiser's termination was unreasonable.

S CORPORATIONS

A close corporation that meets the qualifying requirements specified in Subchapter S of the Internal Revenue Code can operate as an **S corporation.** If a corporation has S corporation status, it can avoid the imposition of income taxes at the corporate level while retaining many of the advantages of a corporation, particularly limited liability.

Qualification Requirements for S Corporations. Among the numerous requirements for S corporation status, the following are the most important:

1. The corporation must be a domestic corporation.
2. The corporation must not be a member of an affiliated group of corporations.
3. The shareholders of the corporation must be individuals, estates, or certain trusts. Nonqualifying trusts

and partnerships cannot be shareholders. Corporations can be shareholders under certain circumstances.

4. The corporation must have seventy-five or fewer shareholders.

5. The corporation must have only one class of stock, although not all shareholders need have the same voting rights.

6. No shareholder of the corporation may be a non-resident alien.

Benefits of S Corporations. At times, it is beneficial for a regular corporation to elect S corporation status. Benefits include the following:

1. When the corporation has losses, the S election allows the shareholders to use the losses to offset other income.

2. When the stockholder's tax bracket is lower than the tax bracket for regular corporations, the S election causes the corporation's entire income to be taxed in the shareholder's bracket (because it is taxed as personal income), whether or not it is distributed. This is particularly attractive when the corporation wants to accumulate earnings for some future business purpose.

Because of these tax benefits, many close corporations opted for S corporation status in the past. Today, however, the S corporation is losing some of its significance—because the limited liability company and the limited liability partnership (discussed in Chapter 38) offer similar advantages plus additional benefits, including more flexibility in forming and operating the business.

PROFESSIONAL CORPORATIONS

Professional persons such as physicians, lawyers, dentists, and accountants can incorporate. Their corporations may be identified by such letters as *S.C.* (service corporation), *P.C.* (professional corporation), or *P.A.* (professional association). In general, the laws governing professional corporations are similar to those governing ordinary business corporations, but three basic areas of liability deserve brief attention.

First, a court might, for liability purposes, regard the professional corporation as a partnership in which each partner can be held liable for whatever malpractice liability is incurred by the others within the scope of the partnership. Second, a shareholder in a professional corporation is protected from the liability imposed because of torts (unrelated to malpractice) committed by other members. Third, many professional corporation statutes impose personal liability on professional persons not only for their acts but also for the professional acts performed under their supervision.

In some cases, shareholders of a professional corporation have not been shielded from personal liability by the corporate form because, in fact, they conduct the business more as a partnership than as a corporation. For example, suppose that a partnership, to obtain certain tax benefits or to limit the personal liability of partners, decides to incorporate. After incorporation, however, the members continue to conduct the business as a partnership. In a suit against the firm, a court may hold that partnership law, not corporate law, should govern the issue.

CONCEPT SUMMARY 34.1   CLASSIFICATION OF CORPORATIONS

CLASSIFICATION	DESCRIPTION
Domestic, Foreign, and Alien Corporations	A corporation is referred to as a *domestic corporation* in its home state (the state in which it incorporates). A corporation formed in one state but doing business in another is referred to in that other state as a *foreign corporation*. A corporation formed in another country but doing business in the United States is referred to in the United States as an *alien corporation*.
Public and Private Corporations	A *public corporation* is one formed by government (for example, a city or town that incorporates). A *private corporation* is one formed wholly or in part for private benefit. Most corporations are private corporations.
Nonprofit Corporation	A corporation formed for purposes other than profit (for example, charitable, educational, and religious organizations and hospitals).

CONCEPT SUMMARY 34.1

CLASSIFICATION OF CORPORATIONS (*continued*)

CLASSIFICATION	DESCRIPTION
Close Corporation	A corporation owned by a family or a relatively small number of individuals; transfer of shares is usually restricted, and the corporation cannot make a public offering of its securities.
S Corporation	A small domestic corporation (must have seventy-five or fewer shareholders) that, under Subchapter S of the Internal Revenue Code, is given special tax treatment. S corporations allow shareholders to enjoy the limited legal liability of the corporate form but avoid its double-taxation feature (a single tax is imposed at individual income tax rates at the shareholder level, and the S corporation is not taxed separately).
Professional Corporation	A corporation formed by professionals (for example, doctors or lawyers) to obtain the advantages of incorporation (such as tax benefits and limited liability). In most situations, the professional corporation is treated like other corporations, but sometimes the courts disregard the corporate form and treat the shareholders as partners.

SECTION 4

Corporate Formation

Corporations generally come into existence through two steps: (1) preliminary organizational and promotional undertakings (particularly, obtaining capital for the future corporation) and (2) the legal process of incorporation.

PROMOTIONAL ACTIVITIES

Before a corporation becomes a reality, people invest in the proposed corporation as subscribers, and contracts are frequently made by promoters on behalf of the future corporation. **Promoters** are those who, for themselves or others, take the preliminary steps in organizing a corporation. One of the tasks of the promoter is to issue a **prospectus,** which is a document required by federal or state securities laws (see Chapter 37) that describes the financial operations of the corporation, thus allowing an investor to make an informed decision. The promoter also secures the corporate charter.

Promoter's Liability. A promoter may purchase or lease property with a view toward selling it to the corporation when the corporation is formed. In addition, a promoter may enter into contracts with attorneys, accountants, architects, and other professionals whose services will be needed in planning for the proposed corporation. Finally, a promoter induces people to purchase stock in the corporation.

As a general rule, a promoter is held personally liable on preincorporation contracts. Courts simply hold that promoters are not agents when a corporation has yet to come into existence. If, however, the promoter secures the contracting party's agreement to hold only the corporation (not the promoter) liable on the contract, the promoter will not be liable in the event of any breach of contract.

Once the corporation is formed (the charter issued), the promoter remains personally liable until the corporation assumes the preincorporation contract by *novation* (see Chapter 17). Novation releases the promoter and makes the corporation liable for performing the contractual obligations. In some cases, the corporation adopts the promoter's contract by undertaking to perform it. Most courts hold that adoption in and of itself does not discharge the promoter from contractual liability. A corporation normally cannot ratify a preincorporation contract, as no principal was in existence at the time the contract was made.

Subscribers and Subscriptions. Prior to the actual formation of the corporation, the promoter can contact potential individual investors, and they can agree to purchase capital stock in the future corporation. This agreement is often referred to as a *subscription agreement*, and the potential investor is called a *subscriber*. Depending on state law, subscribers become shareholders as soon as the corporation is formed or as soon as the corporation accepts the agreement. This way, if corporation X becomes insolvent, the trustee in bankruptcy (see Chapter 30) can collect the consideration for any unpaid stock from a preincorporation subscriber.

Most courts view preincorporation subscriptions as continuing offers to purchase corporate stock. On or after its formation, the corporation can choose to accept the offer to purchase stock. Many courts also treat a subscription as a contract between the subscribers, making it irrevocable except with the consent of all of the subscribers. Under the RMBCA, a subscription is irrevocable for a period of six months unless otherwise provided in the subscription agreement or unless all the subscribers agree to the revocation of the subscription [RMBCA 6.20]. In other jurisdictions, the preincorporation subscriber can revoke the offer to purchase before acceptance without liability, however.

INCORPORATION PROCEDURES

Exact procedures for incorporation differ among the states, but the basic requirements are similar.

State Chartering. The first step in the incorporation procedure is to select a state in which to incorporate. Because state incorporation laws differ, individuals have found some advantage in looking for the states that offer the most advantageous tax or incorporation provisions. Delaware has historically had the least restrictive laws. Consequently, many corporations, including a number of the largest, have incorporated there. Delaware's statutes permit firms to incorporate in Delaware and carry out business and locate operating headquarters elsewhere. (Most other states now permit this as well.) Closely held corporations, however, particularly those of a professional nature, generally incorporate in the state in which their principal stockholders live and work.

Articles of Incorporation. The primary document needed to begin the incorporation process is called the *articles of incorporation* (see Exhibit 34–1). The articles include basic information about the corporation and serve as a primary source of authority for its future organization and business functions. The person or persons who execute the articles are called *incorporators* and will be discussed shortly. Generally, the information indicated below should be included in the articles of incorporation.

Corporate Name. The choice of a corporate name is subject to state approval to ensure against duplication or deception. State statutes usually require that the secretary of state run a check on the proposed name in the state of incorporation. Some states require that the incorporators, at their own expense, run a check on the proposed name for the newly formed corporation. Once cleared, a name can be reserved for a short time, for a fee, pending the completion of the articles of incorporation. All corporate statutes require the corporation name to include the word *Corporation, Incorporated, Company*, or *Limited* or an abbreviation of one of these terms [RMBCA 4.01, 4.02].

The new corporation's name may not be the same as, or deceptively similar to, the name of an existing corporation doing business within the state. For example, if an existing corporation is named General Dynamics, Inc., the state will not allow another corporation to be called General Dynamic, Inc., because that name is deceptively similar to the first, and it would impliedly transfer a part of the goodwill established by the first corporate user to the second corporation. (See Chapter 7 for a fuller discussion of trade names.)

Nature and Purpose. The intended business activities of the corporation must be specified in the articles, and naturally, they must be lawful. Stating a general corporate purpose is usually sufficient to give rise to all of the powers necessary or convenient to the purpose of the organization. The corporate charter can state, for example, that the corporation is organized "to engage in the production and sale of agricultural products." There is a trend toward allowing corporate charters to state that the corporation is organized for "any legal business." A broadly stated purpose creates greater flexibility and avoids unnecessary future amendments to the corporate charter should the corporation change or modify its line of business [RMBCA 2.02(b)(2)(i), 3.01].

Some states prohibit the incorporation of certain professionals, such as doctors or lawyers, except pursuant to a professional incorporation statute. Also, in some states, certain industries—such as banks, insur-

EXHIBIT 34–1   ARTICLES OF INCORPORATION

ARTICLE ONE

The name of the corporation is _____ .

ARTICLE TWO

The period of its duration is _____ (may be "perpetual," a number of years, or until a certain date).

ARTICLE THREE

The purpose (or purposes) for which the corporation is organized is (are) _____
_____ .

ARTICLE FOUR

The aggregate number of shares that the corporation shall have authority to issue is _____ of the par value
of _____ dollar(s) each (or "without par value").

ARTICLE FIVE

The corporation will not commence business until it has received for the issuance of its shares consideration
of the value of _____ (can be any sum not less than $1,000).

ARTICLE SIX

The address of the corporation's registered office is _____ ,
and the name of its registered agent at such address is _____
_____ .

(Use the street or building or rural address of the registered office, not a post office box number.)

ARTICLE SEVEN

The number of initial directors is _____ , and the names and addresses of the directors are
_____
_____ .

ARTICLE EIGHT

The name and address of the incorporator is _____
_____ .

(signed) _____

Incorporator

Sworn to on _____ by the above-named incorporator.
          (date)

_____
Notary Public

(Notary Seal)

ance companies, or public utilities—cannot be operated in the general corporate form and are governed by special incorporation statutes.

Duration.   A corporation can have perpetual existence under the corporate statutes of most states. A few states, however, prescribe a maximum duration, after which the corporation must formally renew its existence.

Capital Structure.   The capital structure of the corporation is generally set forth in the articles. A few state statutes require a very small capital investment for ordinary business corporations but a greater capital investment for those engaged in insurance or banking. The articles must also indicate the number of shares of stock the corporation is authorized to issue and may include other information, such as the valuation of the shares and the types or classes of stock authorized for issuance [RMBCA 2.02(a)].

Internal Organization. The articles should describe the internal management structure of the corporation, although this can be included in bylaws adopted after the corporation is formed [RMBCA 2.02]. The articles of incorporation commence the corporation; the bylaws are formed after commencement by the board of directors. Bylaws are subject to, and cannot conflict with, the incorporation statute or the corporation's charter [RMBCA 2.06].

Under the RMBCA, shareholders may amend or repeal bylaws. The board of directors may also amend or repeal bylaws unless the articles of incorporation or provisions of the incorporation statute reserve that power to shareholders exclusively [RMBCA 10.20]. Typical bylaw provisions describe voting procedures and requirements for shareholders, the election of the board of directors, the methods of replacing directors, and the manner and time of scheduling shareholders' meetings and board meetings (these procedures will be discussed in Chapter 35).

Registered Office and Agent. The corporation must indicate the location and address of its registered office within the state [RMBCA 2.02(a)(3)]. Usually, the registered office is also the principal office of the corporation. The corporation must give the name and address of a specific person who has been designated as an agent and who can receive legal documents on behalf of the corporation. These legal documents include service of process (the delivery of a court order requiring an appearance in court).

Incorporators. Each incorporator must be listed by name and must also indicate an address [RMBCA 2.02(a)(4)]. An incorporator is a person—often, the corporate promoter—who applies to the state on behalf of the corporation to obtain its corporate charter. The incorporator need not be a subscriber and need not have any interest at all in the corporation. Many states do not impose residency or age requirements for incorporators. States vary as to the required number of incorporators; it can be as few as one or as many as three. Incorporators are required to sign the articles of incorporation when they are submitted to the state; often, this is their only duty. In some states, they participate at the first organizational meeting of the corporation.

Certificate of Incorporation. Once the articles of incorporation have been prepared, signed, and authenticated by the incorporators, they are sent to the appropriate state official, usually the secretary of state, along with the appropriate filing fee. In many states, the secretary of state will then issue a **certificate of incorporation** representing the state's authorization for the corporation to conduct business. (This may be called the **corporate charter.**) The certificate and a copy of the articles are returned to the incorporators. The incorporators then hold the initial organizational meeting, which completes the details of incorporation [RMBCA 2.03].

Today, it is possible to incorporate—and receive a certificate of incorporation—via online incorporation services. For further information on this topic, see this chapter's *Emerging Trends in Technology.*

First Organizational Meeting. The first organizational meeting is often provided for in the articles of incorporation but is held after the charter is actually granted. At this meeting, the incorporators elect the first board of directors and complete the routine business of incorporation (pass bylaws, issue stock, and so forth). Sometimes, the meeting is held after the election of the board of directors, and the business to be transacted depends on the requirements of the state's incorporation statute, the nature of the business, the provisions made in the articles, and the desires of the promoters [RMBCA 2.05].

Adoption of bylaws—the internal rules of management for the corporation—is probably the most important function of the first organizational meeting. The shareholders, directors, and officers must abide by the bylaws in conducting corporate business. Corporate employees and third persons dealing with the corporation are not bound by them, however, unless they have reason to be familiar with them.

SECTION 5

Improper Incorporation

The procedures for incorporation are very specific. If they are not followed precisely, others may be able to challenge the existence of the corporation.

EMERGING TRENDS IN TECHNOLOGY

Online Incorporation

Today, just about anybody can form a corporation for any lawful purpose in any state. The requirements differ from state to state. You do not have to form your corporation in the state in which you live or the state in which you are doing business, however. In fact, many individuals obtain their corporate charters from the state of Delaware, because it has the fewest legal restrictions on corporate formation and operation. Traditionally, Delaware has also been the state most often chosen for "mail-order incorporation." Today, instead of incorporating by mail, entrepreneurs have the option of incorporating in the states of their choice via online companies that offer incorporation services.

FINDING INFORMATION ON INCORPORATION REQUIREMENTS

Most of the over one hundred companies that offer incorporation services are now online, and you can obtain information about incorporation at their Web sites. For example, at the Web site of The Company Corporation (TCC) of Delaware (at **http://www.incorporate.com**), you can read about the advantages and disadvantages of incorporating your business, the cost of

incorporating in your state (or in any other state), and the pros and cons of the various types of corporate entities that are available.

You can find similar information at other sites, including the Web site of Harvard Business Services, Inc. (at **http://www.delawareinc.com**). Here you can find guidelines that will help you choose the type of corporation that best suits your needs, a list of frequently asked questions about incorporation, telephone numbers for each state's corporations division, the annual legal costs of maintaining a corporation, and so on.

INCORPORATING ONLINE

If you wish to incorporate via an online incorporation service, all you need to do is fill out a form. For example, if you fill out the incorporation forms at the TCC Web site, TCC will then file the forms with the appropriate state office and obtain a certificate of incorporation (corporate charter) for you. Optional TCC services include making arrangements for a registered agent for your corporation, mail-forwarding services, obtaining a tax ID number, and obtaining a domain name registration for your business.

IMPLICATIONS FOR THE BUSINESSPERSON

1. "Do-it-yourself" incorporation via online incorporation services

may be sufficient for those who are interested in starting small businesses but who have no serious aspirations that their companies will grow much larger.
2. If you believe that the business in which you are going to engage has growth potential and may require significant financing in the future, you are best advised to contact a local lawyer to take you through the necessary steps in incorporating your business.

FOR CRITICAL ANALYSIS

1. Before incorporating (online or otherwise), what factors should you consider when deciding which form of business organization best suits your needs?
2. How can you determine whether an online incorporation service is accurately representing the law governing corporations in the state in which you wish to incorporate?

RELEVANT WEB SITES

For further information on incorporation, as well as how you can incorporate online, visit the Web sites of NCCF, Inc. (at **http://www.nccf.com**) and American Incorporators, Ltd. (at **www.ailcorp.com**). (You can also find providers of online incorporation services simply by searching the term *incorporation* using a search engine such as Yahoo.)

Errors in incorporation procedures can become important when, for example, a third person who is attempting to enforce a contract or bring suit for a tort injury fortuitously learns of them. On the basis of improper incorporation, the plaintiff could seek to make the would-be shareholders personally liable. Also, when the corporation attempts to enforce a contract against a defaulting party, if the defaulting party learns of a defect in the incorporation procedures, he or she may be able to avoid liability on that ground.

To prevent injustice, courts will sometimes attribute corporate existence to an improperly formed corporation by holding it to be a *de jure* corporation or a *de facto* corporation, as discussed below. In some cases, corporation by estoppel may also occur.

DE JURE AND
DE FACTO CORPORATIONS

In the event of substantial compliance with all conditions precedent to incorporation, a corporation is said to have *de jure* existence in law. In most states and under RMBCA 2.03(b), the certificate of incorporation is viewed as conclusive evidence that all mandatory statutory provisions have been met. This means that the corporation is properly formed, and only the state, not a third party, can attack its existence. If, for example, an incorporator's address was incorrectly listed, this would mean that the corporation was improperly formed. The law, however, does not regard such inconsequential procedural defects as detracting from substantial compliance, and courts will uphold the *de jure* status of the corporate entity.

Sometimes there is a defect in complying with statutory mandates—for example, the corporation charter may have expired. Under these circumstances, the corporation may have *de facto* status, meaning that its existence cannot be challenged by third parties except the state. The following elements are required for *de facto* status:

1. There must be a state statute under which the corporation can be validly incorporated.
2. The parties must have made a good faith attempt to comply with the statute.
3. The enterprise must already have undertaken to do business as a corporation.

CORPORATION BY ESTOPPEL

If an association that is neither an actual corporation nor a *de facto* or *de jure* corporation holds itself out as being a corporation, it will be estopped from denying corporate status in a lawsuit by a third party. This usually occurs when a third party contracts with an association that claims to be a corporation but does not hold a certificate of incorporation. When the third party brings suit naming the so-called corporation as the defendant, the association may not escape from

liability on the ground that no corporation exists. When justice requires, the courts treat an alleged corporation as if it were an actual corporation for the purpose of determining the rights and liabilities involved in a particular situation. Corporation by estoppel is thus determined by the circumstances. It does not extend recognition of corporate status beyond the resolution of the problem at hand.

SECTION 6

Disregarding the Corporate Entity

In some unusual situations, a corporate entity is used by its owners to perpetrate a fraud, circumvent the law, or in some other way accomplish an illegitimate objective. In these cases, the court will ignore the corporate structure by "piercing the corporate veil," exposing the shareholders to personal liability [RMBCA 2.04].

The following are some of the factors that may cause the courts to pierce the corporate veil:

1. A party is tricked or misled into dealing with the corporation rather than the individual.
2. The corporation is set up never to make a profit or always to be insolvent, or it is too "thinly" capitalized—that is, it has insufficient capital at the time it is formed to meet its prospective debts or potential liabilities.
3. Statutory corporate formalities, such as holding required corporation meetings, are not followed.
4. Personal and corporate interests are mixed together, or **commingled,** to the extent that the corporation has no separate identity.

To elaborate on the fourth factor in the preceding list, consider a close corporation that is formed according to law by a single person or by a few family members. In such a situation, the corporate entity and the sole stockholder (or family-member stockholders) must carefully preserve the separate status of the corporation and its owners. Certain practices invite trouble for the one-person or family-owned corporation: the commingling of corporate and personal funds; the failure to remit taxes, including payroll and sales taxes; and the shareholders' continuous personal use of corporate property (for example, vehicles).

Corporation laws usually do not specifically prohibit a stockholder from lawfully lending money to his or her corporation. When an officer, director, or majority shareholder lends the corporation money and takes back security in the form of corporate assets, however, the courts will scrutinize the transaction closely. Any such transaction must be made in good faith and for fair value.

When the corporate privilege is abused for personal benefit and the corporate business is treated in such a careless manner that the corporation and the shareholder in control are no longer separate entities, the court usually will require the shareholder to assume personal liability to creditors for the corporation's debts. In short, when the facts show that great injustice would result from the use of a corporation to avoid individual responsibility, a court of equity will look behind the corporate structure to the individual stockholder.

The following case illustrates a situation in which a corporation did business under an assumed name that was not registered with the state. At issue in the case was whether the president of the corporation could be held personally liable for corporate debts incurred under the assumed name.

CASE 34.3   Hoskins Chevrolet, Inc. v. Hochberg

Appellate Court of Illinois, First District, First Division, 1998. 294 Ill.App.3d 550, 691 N.E.2d 28, 229 Ill.Dec. 92.
http://www.state.il.us/court/ap1_98ix.html[a]

IN THE LANGUAGE OF THE COURT

BACKGROUND AND FACTS   *Ronald Hochberg is the president of Diamond Auto Body & Repair, Inc. Under the name "Diamond Auto Construction," Hochberg ordered and received auto parts from Hoskins Chevrolet, Inc. Hoskins Chevrolet sent invoices to "Diamond Auto Construction." Hochberg paid some of the invoices with checks drawn on the bank account of "Diamond Auto Construction." When the unpaid invoices totaled more than $40,000, Hoskins Chevrolet filed a suit in an Illinois state court to collect from Hochberg individually. Hochberg asserted that he did business with Hoskins Chevrolet only as the president of a corporation. Hoskins Chevrolet responded that "Diamond Auto Construction" was not registered with the state as the name of a corporation. The court granted a summary judgment in favor of Hoskins Chevrolet. Hochberg appealed.*

Presiding Justice BUCKLEY delivered the opinion of the court:
*   *   *   *

The [Illinois] Business Corporations Act (the Act) permits a corporation to elect to adopt an assumed name provided that certain procedures are followed. Where those procedures are not followed, the corporation is required to conduct business under its corporate name. *   *   *

*   *   * Diamond Auto Body & Repair, Inc., used the assumed name of Diamond Auto Construction without complying with *   *   * the Act. Further, the record contains no evidence that while using the assumed name in his dealings with plaintiff, defendant also disclosed the corporate name *   *   * . Accordingly, we find no error in the trial court's determination that under the Act, Diamond Auto Construction was neither a corporation nor the assumed name of a corporation for purposes of establishing contract liability in anyone other than defendant.

DECISION AND REMEDY   *The state intermediate appellate court affirmed the lower court's judgment. A person who incurs corporate debts under an unregistered corporate name is personally liable for those debts.*

a. This Web site is maintained by the state of Illinois. In the "Appellate Court" section, in the "First District Opinions" row, click on "1998." When that page opens, scroll down the list to the name of the case and click on it to read the opinion.

SECTION 7

Corporate Financing

Corporations are financed by the issuance and sale of corporate securities—that is, bonds and stock.

Securities evidence the obligation to pay money or the right to participate in earnings and the distribution of corporate assets. **Stocks,** or *equity securities*, represent the purchase of ownership in the business firm. **Bonds** (debentures), or *debt securities*, represent the borrowing of money by firms (and governments).

Of course, not all debt is in the form of debt securities. For example, some debt is in the form of accounts payable and notes payable. Accounts and notes payable are typically short-term debts. Bonds are simply a way for a corporation to split up its long-term debt so that it can market the debt more easily.

BONDS

Bonds are issued by business firms and by governments at all levels as evidence of the funds they are borrowing from investors. Bonds almost always have a designated *maturity date*—the date when the principal, or face amount, of the bond (or loan) is returned to the investor—and are sometimes referred to as *fixed-income securities*, because their owners receive fixed-dollar interest payments during the period of time prior to maturity.

The characteristics of corporate bonds vary widely, in part because corporations differ in their ability to generate the earnings and cash flow necessary to make interest payments and to repay the principal amount of the bonds at maturity. Furthermore, corporate bonds are only a part of the total debt and the overall financial structure of corporate business. The various types of corporate bonds are described in Exhibit 34–2.

EXHIBIT 34–2   TYPES OF CORPORATE BONDS

TYPE	DEFINITION
Debenture Bonds	Bonds for which no specific assets of the corporation are pledged as backing. Rather, they are backed by the general credit rating of the corporation, plus any assets that can be seized if the corporation allows the debentures to go into default.
Mortgage Bonds	Bonds that pledge specific property. If the corporation defaults on the bonds, the bondholders can foreclose on the property.
Convertible Bonds	Bonds that can be exchanged for a specified number of shares of stock under certain conditions.
Callable Bonds	Bonds that may be called in and the principal repaid at specified times or under conditions stipulated in the bond when it is issued.

STOCKS

Issuing stocks is another way for corporations to obtain financing [RMBCA 6.01]. The ways in which stocks differ from bonds are summarized in Exhibit 34–3. Basically, stocks represent ownership in a business firm, whereas bonds represent borrowing by the firm.

Exhibit 34–4 offers a summary of the types of stocks issued by corporations. The two major types are *common stock* and *preferred stock*.

Common Stock.   **Common stock** represents the true ownership of a corporation. It provides a proportionate interest in the corporation with regard to (1) control, (2) earnings, and (3) net assets. A shareholder's interest is generally in proportion to the number of shares owned out of the total number of shares issued.

Any person who purchases shares acquires voting rights—one vote per share held. Voting rights in a corporation apply to the election of the firm's board of directors and to any proposed changes in the ownership structure of the firm.[6] For example, a holder of common stock generally has the right to vote in a decision on a proposed merger, as mergers can change the proportion of ownership.

Holders of common stock are a group of investors who assume a *residual* position in the overall financial structure of a business. In terms of receiving returns on their investments, they are last in line. Their earnings depend on the corporation's paying all the other groups—suppliers, employees, managers, bankers, governments, bondholders, and holders of preferred stock—what is due them first. Once those groups are paid, the owners of common stock may be entitled to *all* the remaining earnings. But the board of directors normally is not under any duty to declare the remaining earnings as dividends.

Preferred Stock.   **Preferred stock** is stock with *preferences*. Usually, this means that holders of preferred stock have priority over holders of common stock as to dividends and to payment on dissolution of the corporation. Preferred stockholders may or may not have the right to vote (the trend is toward giving preferred stockholders the right to vote).

From an investment standpoint, preferred stock is more similar to bonds than to common stock.

---

6. State corporation law specifies the types of actions for which shareholder approval must be obtained.

EXHIBIT 34–3   HOW DO STOCKS AND BONDS DIFFER?

STOCKS	BONDS
1. Stocks represent ownership.	1. Bonds represent debt.
2. Stocks (common) do not have a fixed dividend rate.	2. Interest on bonds must always be paid, whether or not any profit is earned.
3. Stockholders can elect a board of directors, which controls the corporation.	3. Bondholders usually have no voice in or control over management of the corporation.
4. Stocks do not have a maturity date; the corporation does not usually repay the stockholder.	4. Bonds have a maturity date, when the corporation is to repay the bondholder the face value of the bond.
5. All corporations issue or offer to sell stocks. This is the usual definition of a corporation.	5. Corporations do not necessarily issue bonds.
6. Stockholders have a claim against the property and income of a corporation after all creditors' claims have been met.	6. Bondholders have a claim against the property and income of a corporation that must be met before the claims of stockholders.

Preferred shareholders receive periodic dividend payments, usually established as a fixed percentage of the face amount of each preferred share. A share of 6 percent preferred stock with a face amount of $100 per share would pay its owner a $6 dividend each year. Payment of these dividends is not a legal obligation on the part of the firm. Preferred stock is not included among the liabilities of a business, because it is technically equity. Like other equity securities, preferred shares have no fixed maturity date on which they must be retired by the firm. Although occasionally firms retire preferred stock, they are not legally obligated to do so. A sample cumulative convertible preferred-stock certificate is shown in Exhibit 34–5.

EXHIBIT 34–4   TYPES OF STOCKS

TYPE	DEFINITION
Common Stock	Voting shares that represent ownership interest in a corporation. Common stock has the lowest priority with respect to payment of dividends and distribution of assets on the corporation's dissolution.
Preferred Stock	Shares of stock that have priority over common-stock shares as to payment of dividends and distribution of assets on dissolution. Dividend payments are usually a fixed percentage of the face value of the share. Preferred shares may or may not be nonvoting shares.
Cumulative Preferred Stock	Preferred shares for which required dividends not paid in a given year must be paid in a subsequent year before any common-stock dividends can be paid.
Participating Preferred Stock	Preferred shares entitling the owner to receive (1) the preferred-stock dividend and (2) additional dividends after the corporation has paid dividends on common stock.
Convertible Preferred Stock	Preferred shares entitling the owner to convert his or her shares into a specified number of common shares either in the issuing corporation or, sometimes, in another corporation.
Redeemable, or Callable, Preferred Stock	Preferred shares issued with the express condition that the issuing corporation has the right to repurchase the shares as specified.

EXHIBIT 34–5   CUMULATIVE CONVERTIBLE PREFERRED-STOCK CERTIFICATE

TERMS AND CONCEPTS TO REVIEW

alien corporation 641	common stock 652	retained earnings 638
articles of incorporation 639	corporate charter 648	S corporation 643
bond 651	domestic corporation 641	securities 651
bylaw 639	foreign corporation 641	stock 651
certificate of incorporation 648	preferred stock 652	*ultra vires* 639
close corporation 641	promoter 645	
commingle 650	prospectus 645	

QUESTIONS AND CASE PROBLEMS

34–1. NATURE OF CORPORATIONS. Jonathan, Gary, and Rob are active members of a partnership called Swim City. The partnership manufactures, sells, and installs outdoor swimming pools in the states of Texas and Arkansas. The partners want to continue to be active in management and to expand the business into other states as well. They are concerned about rather large recent judgments entered against swimming pool companies throughout the United States. Based on these facts only, discuss whether the partnership should incorporate.

34–2. LIABILITY FOR PREINCORPORATION CONTRACTS. Cummings, Marvin, and Taft are recent college graduates who want to form a corporation to manufacture and sell personal computers. Peterson tells them he will set in motion the formation of their corporation. First, Peterson makes a contract for the purchase of a piece of land for $20,000 with Owens. Owens does not know of the prospective corporate formation at the time of the signing of the contract. Second, Peterson makes a contract with Babcock to build a small plant on the property being purchased. Babcock's contract is conditional on the corporation's formation. Peterson secures all necessary subscription agreements and capitalization, and he files the articles of incorporation. A charter is issued.

   (a) Discuss whether the newly formed corporation, Peterson, or both are liable on the contracts with Owens and Babcock.
   (b) Discuss whether the corporation is automatically liable to Babcock on formation.

34–3. SUBSCRIPTION AGREEMENTS. As a promoter forming a new corporation, Peterson enters into three preincorporation subscription agreements with Mary, Anne, and Harry. The three subscribers each agree to purchase one thousand shares of stock of the future corporation for $2,000. Two months later, just prior to the issuance of the corporate charter, Mary tells Peterson she is withdrawing from the agreement. The charter is issued the next week. Just before the first organizational meeting of the corporation, Harry also withdraws from the agreement. Discuss fully whether Mary, Harry, or both can withdraw from the subscription agreements without liability.

34–4. CORPORATE STATUS. Three brothers inherited a small paper-supply business from their father, who had operated the business as a sole proprietorship. The brothers decided to incorporate under the name of Miwa Corp. and retained an attorney to draw up the necessary documents. The attorney drew up the papers and had the brothers sign them but neglected to send the application for a corporate charter to the secretary of state's office. The brothers assumed that all necessary legal work had been taken care of, and they proceeded to do business as Miwa Corp. One day, a Miwa Corp. employee was delivering a carton of paper supplies to one of Miwa's customers. On the way to the customer's office, the employee negligently ran a red light and caused a car accident. Harman, the driver of the other vehicle, was injured as a result and sued Miwa Corp. for damages. Harman then learned that no state charter had ever been issued to Miwa Corp., so he sued each of the brothers personally for damages. Can the brothers avoid personal liability for the tort of their employee? Explain.

34–5. CORPORATE POWERS. Oya Paka and two business associates formed a corporation called Paka Corp. for the purpose of selling computer services. Oya, who owned 50 percent of the corporate shares, served as the corporation's president. Oya wished to obtain a personal loan from her bank for $250,000, but the bank required the note to be cosigned by a third party. Oya cosigned the note in the name of the corporation. Later, Oya defaulted on the note, and the bank sued the corporation for payment. The corporation asserted, as a defense, that Oya had exceeded her authority when she cosigned the note on behalf of the corporation. Had she? Explain.

34–6. LIABILITY OF SHAREHOLDERS. Moseley Group Management Co. (MGM) provided management services to apartment complexes. MGM's only assets were equipment worth $500 and a bank account with an average balance of $1,500. Richard Moseley ran the company and owned half of the stock. MGM contracted with Property Tax Research Co. (PTR) to obtain a lower property tax assessment on one of its complexes. PTR performed, but MGM refused to pay and transferred its assets and employees to Terrace Management, Inc., a corporation controlled by Moseley. PTR filed a suit in a Missouri state court against Moseley and others to recover the unpaid fees. Should the court pierce the corporate veil and hold Moseley personally liable for the debt? If so, on what basis? [*Sansone v. Moseley*, 912 S.W.2d 666 (Mo.App.W.D. 1995)]

34–7. CORPORATE POWERS. Soda Dispensing Systems, Inc., was owned by two shareholders, each of whom owned half of the stock. One shareholder was president of the corporation, and the other was vice president. Their shareholder agreement stated that neither shareholder could "encumber any corporate property . . . without the written consent of the other." When Soda Dispensing went out of business, the two shareholders agreed to sell the assets, split the proceeds, and pay $9,900 to their accountants, Cooper, Selvin & Strassberg. Later, the president committed Soda Dispensing to pay Cooper, Selvin more than $24,000, claiming that he had the authority, as president, to make that commitment. When the accountants tried to collect, the vice president objected, asserting that the president had exceeded his authority. Will the court order Soda Dispensing to pay? Explain. [*Cooper, Selvin & Strassberg v. Soda Dispensing Systems, Inc.*, 212 A.D.2d 498, 622 N.Y.S.2d 312 (1995)]

34–8. CORPORATE STATUS. Cecil Hill was in the construction trade. He did business as "C&M Builders, Inc.," although there was no such corporation. County Concrete Co. supplied "C&M Builders, Inc." with over $50,000 worth of concrete for which it was not paid. The supplier filed a suit in a Maryland state court against Hill personally. Hill argued that because the supplier thought it was doing business with a corporate entity, C&M was a *de facto* corporation, and thus Hill was not personally liable. Should Hill be allowed to avoid liability on this basis? Why or why not? [*Hill v. County Concrete Co.*, 108 Md.App. 527, 672 A.2d 667 (1996)]

34–9. DISREGARDING THE CORPORATE ENTITY. Steven and Janis Gimbert leased a warehouse to a manufacturing business owned by Manzar Zuberi. Zuberi signed the lease as the purported representative of "ATM Manufacturing, Inc.," which was a nonexistent corporation. Zuberi was actually the president of two existing corporations, ATM Enterprises, Inc., and Ameri-Pak International. Under the Ameri-Pak name, Zuberi manufactured a household cleaning product in the Gimberts' warehouse. The use of hydrochloric acid in the operations severely damaged the premises, and the Gimberts filed a suit in a Georgia state court against Zuberi personally to collect for the damage. On what basis might Zuberi be held personally liable? Discuss fully. [*Zuberi v. Gimbert*, 230 Ga.App. 471, 496 S.E.2d 741 (1998)]

34–10. S CORPORATIONS. James, Randolph, and Judith Agley, and Michael and Nancy Timmis were shareholders in F & M Distributors, Inc., Venture Packaging, Inc., and Diamond Automations, Inc. James Agley was also a shareholder in Middletown Aerospace. All of the firms were S corporations organized and located in Michigan and doing business in Ohio. None of the shareholders was a resident of Ohio, and none of them personally did business in Ohio. Between 1988 and 1992, the Agleys and the Timmises included their prorated share of the S corporations' income on Ohio personal income tax returns. They believed, however, that an out-of-state shareholder should not be taxed in Ohio on the income that he or she receives from an S corporation doing business in Ohio. They contended it is the S corporation that earns the income, not the shareholder. They also emphasized that none of them personally did business in the state. Finally, they asked the Ohio Tax Commissioner for refunds for those years. Should the state grant their request? Why or why not? [*Agley v. Tracy*, 87 Ohio St.3d 265, 719 N.E.2d 951 (1999)]

34–11. IN YOUR COURT

Jim Halter, the sole shareholder of J-Mart Jewelry Outlets, Inc., knew that as a result of financial difficulties, J-Mart would soon go out of business. Eight days before the firm stopped doing business, it paid the balance due on Halter's personal credit card. At the same time, Halter paid J-Mart $1 for a Cadillac that the firm had bought new for his personal use and on which it had made three payments. Four of J-Mart's creditors, including Standard Design, sued Halter to recover for J-Mart's unpaid debts. Assume that you are the judge in the trial court hearing this case and answer the following questions:

(a) Should you "pierce the corporate veil" and hold Halter personally liable to J-Mart's creditors in this case? Explain your reasoning.

(b) Compare this case to Case 34.3 (*Hoskins Chevrolet, Inc. v. Hochberg*). Why did the court in that case hold Hochberg personally liable for ostensibly corporate obligations? Does the court's ruling in that case shed any light on the issue in the case before your court? Why or why not?

LAW ON THE WEB

For updated links to resources available on the Web, as well as a variety of other materials, visit this text's Web site at http://wbl.westbuslaw.com.

Cornell University's Legal Information Institute has links to state corporation statutes at

http://fatty.law.cornell.edu/topics/state_statutes.html

For an example of one state's (Florida's) statute governing corporations, go to

http://www.ilrg.com/whatsnews/statute.html

and scroll down the page to "Corporations."

The Center for Corporate Law at the University of Cincinnati College of Law is a good source of information on corporate law. Go to

http://www.law.uc.edu/CCL

For information on incorporation, including a list of "frequently asked questions" on this topic, go to

http://www.bizfilings.com

LEGAL RESEARCH EXERCISES ON THE WEB

Go to http://wbl.westbuslaw.com, the Web site that accompanies this text. Select "Internet Applications," and then click on "Chapter 34." There you will find the following Internet research exercise that you can perform to learn more about the law governing corporations:

Activity 34–1: Corporate Law

CHAPTER 35

CORPORATIONS—Directors, Officers, and Shareholders

CORPORATE DIRECTORS, OFFICERS, and shareholders all play different roles within the corporate entity. Sometimes, actions that may benefit the corporation as a whole do not coincide with the separate interests of the individuals making up the corporation. In such situations, it is important to know the rights and duties of all participants in the corporate enterprise. This chapter focuses on these rights and duties and the ways in which conflicts among corporate participants are resolved.

SECTION 1

Role of Directors

Every corporation is governed by a board of directors. A director occupies a position of responsibility unlike that of other corporate personnel. Directors are sometimes inappropriately characterized as *agents* because they act on behalf of the corporation. No individual director, however, can act as an agent to bind the corporation; and as a group, directors collectively control the corporation in a way that no agent is able to control a principal. Directors are sometimes incorrectly characterized as *trustees* because they occupy positions of trust and control over the corporation. Unlike trustees, however, they do not own or hold title to property for the use and benefit of others.

Few legal requirements exist concerning directors' qualifications. Only a handful of states impose minimum age and residency requirements. A director is sometimes a shareholder, but this is not a necessary qualification—unless, of course, statutory provisions or corporate articles or bylaws require ownership.

ELECTION OF DIRECTORS

Subject to statutory limitations, the number of directors is set forth in the corporation's articles or bylaws. Historically, the minimum number of directors has been three, but today many states permit fewer. Indeed, the Revised Model Business Corporation Act (RMBCA), in Section 8.01, permits corporations with fewer than fifty shareholders to eliminate the board of directors.

The first board of directors is normally appointed by the incorporators on the creation of the corporation, or directors are named by the corporation itself in the articles. The initial board serves until the first annual shareholders' meeting. Subsequent directors are elected by a majority vote of the shareholders.

The term of office for a director is usually one year—from annual meeting to annual meeting. Longer and staggered terms are permissible under most state statutes. A common practice is to elect one-third of the board members each year for a three-year term. In this way, there is greater management continuity.

A director can be removed *for cause* (that is, for failing to perform a required duty), either as specified in the articles or bylaws or by shareholder action. Even the board of directors itself may be given power to remove a director for cause, subject to shareholder review. In most states, unless the shareholders have reserved the right at the time of election, a director cannot be removed without cause.

Vacancies can occur on the board of directors because of death or resignation or when a new position is created through amendment of the articles or bylaws. In these situations, either the shareholders or the board itself can fill the position, depending on state law or on the provisions of the bylaws.

BOARD OF DIRECTORS' MEETINGS

The board of directors conducts business by holding formal meetings with recorded minutes. The date on which regular meetings are held is usually established in the articles or bylaws or by board resolution, and no further notice is customarily required. Special meetings can be called, with notice sent to all directors.

Quorum requirements can vary among jurisdictions. (A **quorum** is the minimum number of members of a body of officials or other group that must be present in order for business to be validly transacted.) Many states leave the decision as to quorum requirements to the corporate articles or bylaws. In the absence of specific state statutes, most states provide that a quorum is a majority of the number of directors authorized in the articles or bylaws. Voting is done in person (unlike voting at shareholders' meetings, which can be done by proxy, as discussed later in this chapter).[1] The rule is

one vote per director. Ordinary matters generally require a simple majority vote; certain extraordinary issues may require a greater-than-majority vote.

RIGHTS OF DIRECTORS

A director of a corporation has a number of rights, including the rights of participation, inspection, compensation, and indemnification.

Participation and Inspection. A corporate director must have certain rights to function properly in that position. The main right is one of participation—meaning that the director must be notified of board of directors' meetings so as to participate in them. As pointed out earlier in this chapter, regular board meetings are usually established by the bylaws or by board resolution, and no notice of these meetings is required. If special meetings are called, however, notice is required unless waived by the director.

A director must have access to all of the corporate books and records to make decisions and to exercise the necessary supervision over corporate officers and employees. This right of inspection is virtually absolute and cannot be restricted.

Compensation and Indemnification. Nominal sums are often paid as honorariums to directors. In many corporations, directors are also chief corporate officers (president or chief executive officer, for example) and receive compensation in their managerial positions. Most directors also gain through indirect benefits, such as business contacts, prestige, and other rewards. There is a trend toward providing more than nominal compensation for directors, especially in large corporations in which directorships can be burdensome in terms of time, work, effort, and risk. Many states permit the corporate articles or bylaws to authorize compensation for directors, and in some cases the board can set its own compensation unless the articles or bylaws provide otherwise.

Corporate directors may become involved in lawsuits by virtue of their positions and their actions as directors. Most states (and RMBCA 8.51) permit a corporation to indemnify (guarantee reimbursement to) a director for legal costs, fees, and judgments involved in defending corporation-related suits. Many states specifically permit a corporation to purchase liability insurance for the directors and officers to cover indemnification. When the statutes are silent on this matter, the

---

1. Except in Louisiana, which allows a director to vote by proxy under certain circumstances. Most states, including California, Delaware, and New York, expressly permit companies to hold board meetings by conference call or similar means, as long as all participants can hear one another. To date, only one state—California—permits a board of directors to conduct meetings via electronic video screens.

authority to purchase such insurance is usually considered to be part of the corporation's implied power.

DIRECTORS' MANAGEMENT RESPONSIBILITIES

Directors have responsibility for all policymaking decisions necessary to the management of all corporate affairs. Just as shareholders cannot act individually to bind the corporation, the directors must act as a body in carrying out routine corporate business. One director has one vote, and customarily the majority rules. The general areas of responsibility of the board of directors include the following:

1. Authorization for major corporate policy decisions—for example, the initiation of proceedings for the sale or lease of corporate assets outside the regular course of business, the determination of new product lines, and the overseeing of major contract negotiations and major management-labor negotiations.
2. Appointment, supervision, and removal of corporate officers and other managerial employees and determination of their compensation.
3. Financial decisions, such as the declaration and payment of dividends to shareholders and the issuance of authorized shares and bonds.

Most states permit the board of directors to elect an executive committee from among the directors to handle the interim management decisions between board of directors' meetings, as provided in the bylaws. The executive committee is limited to making management decisions about ordinary business matters.

The board of directors can delegate some of its functions to an executive committee or to corporate officers. In doing so, the board is not relieved of its overall responsibility for directing the affairs of the corporation, but corporate officers and managerial personnel are empowered to make decisions relating to ordinary, daily corporate affairs within well-defined guidelines.

SECTION 2

Role of Corporate Officers and Executives

Officers and other executive employees are hired by the board of directors or, in rare instances, by the shareholders. In addition to carrying out the duties articulated in the bylaws, corporate and managerial officers act as agents of the corporation, and the ordinary rules of agency (discussed in Chapters 31 and 32) normally apply to their employment. The qualifications required of officers and executive employees are determined at the discretion of the corporation and are included in the articles or bylaws. In most states, a person can hold more than one office and can be both an officer and a director of the corporation.

The rights of corporate officers and other high-level managers are defined by employment contracts, because these persons are employees of the company. Corporate officers, though, can normally be removed by the board of directors at any time with or without cause and regardless of the terms of the employment contracts—although in so doing, the corporation may be liable for breach of contract. The duties of corporate officers are the same as those of directors, because both groups are involved in decision making and are in similar positions of control. Hence, officers and directors are viewed as having the same fiduciary duties of care and loyalty in their conduct of corporate affairs, a subject to which we now turn.

SECTION 3

Fiduciary Duties of Directors and Officers

Directors and officers are deemed fiduciaries of the corporation, because their relationship with the corporation and its shareholders is one of trust and confidence. As fiduciaries, directors and officers owe ethical—and legal—duties to the corporation and the shareholders. These fiduciary duties include the duty of care and the duty of loyalty.

DUTY OF CARE

Directors and officers must exercise due care in performing their duties. The standard of *due care* has been variously described in judicial decisions and codified in many corporation codes. Generally, a director or officer is expected to act in good faith, to exercise the care that an ordinarily prudent person would exercise in similar circumstances, and to act in what he or she considers to be the best interests of the corporation [RMBCA 8.30(a)]. Directors and officers who have not exercised the required duty of care can be held liable for the harms suffered by the corporation as a result of their negligence.

Duty to Make Informed and Reasonable Decisions. Directors and officers are expected to be informed on corporate matters. To be informed, a director or officer must do what is necessary to become informed: attend presentations, ask for information from those who have it, read reports, review other written materials such as contracts—in other words, carefully study a situation and its alternatives. Depending on the nature of the business, directors and officers are often expected to act in accordance with their own knowledge and training. Most states and Section 8.30(b) of the RMBCA, however, allow a director to make decisions in reliance on information furnished by competent officers or employees, professionals such as attorneys and accountants, or even an executive committee of the board without being accused of acting in bad faith or failing to exercise due care if such information turns out to be faulty.

Directors are also expected to make reasonable decisions. For example, a director should not accept a tender offer (an offer to purchase shares in the company that is made by another company directly to the shareholders) with only a moment's consideration based solely on the market price of the corporation's shares.

Duty to Exercise Reasonable Supervision. Directors are also expected to exercise a reasonable amount of supervision when they delegate work to corporate officers and employees. For example, suppose that a corporate bank director fails to attend any board of directors' meetings for five years, never inspects any of the corporate books or records, and generally neglects to supervise the efforts of the bank president and the loan committee. Meanwhile, a corporate officer, the bank president, makes various improper loans and permits large overdrafts. In this situation, the corporate director may be held liable to the corporation for losses resulting from the unsupervised actions of the bank president and the loan committee.

Dissenting Directors. Directors are expected to attend board of directors' meetings, and their votes should be entered into the minutes of corporate meetings. Unless a dissent is entered, the director is presumed to have assented. Directors who dissent are rarely held individually liable for mismanagement of the corporation. For this reason, a director who is absent from a given meeting sometimes registers with the secretary of the board a dissent to actions taken at the meeting.

DUTY OF LOYALTY

Loyalty can be defined as faithfulness to one's obligations and duties. In the corporate context, the duty of loyalty requires directors and officers to subordinate their personal interests to the welfare of the corporation.

For example, directors may not use corporate funds or confidential corporate information for personal advantage. Similarly, they must refrain from putting their personal interests above those of the corporation. For instance, a director should not oppose a transaction that is in the corporation's best interest simply because its acceptance may cost the director her or his position. Cases dealing with fiduciary duty typically involve one or more of the following:

1. Competing with the corporation.
2. Usurping (taking personal advantage of) a corporate opportunity.
3. Having an interest that conflicts with the interest of the corporation.
4. Engaging in insider trading (using information that is not public to make a profit trading securities, as discussed in Chapter 37).
5. Authorizing a corporate transaction that is detrimental to minority shareholders.
6. Selling control over the corporation.

Whether buying certain corporate property constituted a violation of two directors' fiduciary duties to their corporation was at issue in the following case.

CASE 35.1   Stokes v. Bruno

Court of Appeal of Louisiana,
Third Circuit, 1998.
720 So.2d 388.

HISTORICAL AND SOCIAL SETTING *A nonstock corporation is a corporation whose ownership is not recognized by stock but by a membership charter or agreement. Membership might be created according to a particular attribute, such as the ownership of land within the corporation's geographic reach. A corporation organized for other than a profit-making purpose is a nonprofit corporation. No part of the income of a nonprofit corporation is distributable to the directors, officers, or members. An example of a nonstock, nonprofit corporation might be a homeowners' association that is organized in a corporate form.*

BACKGROUND AND FACTS   *Point Cotile Parks Association, Inc. (PCPA), is a non-stock, nonprofit corporation whose members are limited to owners of lots or building sites within the Point Cotile Subdivision. The board of directors, including Gerald Bruno and Michael Wright, adopted resolutions that effectively granted Bruno and Wright the authority to sell certain "common ground" on PCPA's behalf. The board designated lots and set prices, based on professional appraisals. Six years later, when some of the lots had not sold for their original prices, Bruno and Wright sold to themselves, and to Bruno's wife, 5.45 acres of the "common ground." The sale included lots with timber that had not been previously offered for sale. On their own appraisal, Bruno and Wright set the price for the acreage lower than the board had set for the individual lots. When the board learned of the sale, Craig Stokes and other PCPA members filed a suit in a Louisiana state court against Bruno and Wright. The court declared the sale* ultra vires *and void. Bruno appealed.*

IN THE LANGUAGE OF THE COURT

DECUIR, Judge.

*   *   *   *

*   *   * This apparently was a clear case of self dealing. *   *   * [Bruno has] a duty to disclose to the Corporation several items. First that the sale consummated was the whole tract, not just the first lots as had been offered in prior sales. *   *   * Next he had a duty to disclose to the Corporation the potential for sales of timber, as well as the fact that the revised values he was negotiating with himself on behalf of the Corporation were based on his own determinations and no outside source. Once he took the position of evaluator of the land, he would be barred by fiduciary duty from consummating the sale without disclosing the reduction in price, offering an opportunity for other [PCPA] members to purchase, or make an effort to market the entire tract of land, as opposed to just the front lots.

*   *   * Mr. Bruno and Mr. Wright owed a fiduciary [duty] to the Corporation to maximize the return and the mere fact that a portion of the property had not sold at the original requested prices did not give [them] the unilateral authorization to add more land, reduce the price and then purchase themselves without disclosure.

DECISION AND REMEDY

The state intermediate appellate court affirmed the lower court's judgment. The sale of PCPA property under these circumstances was a breach of Bruno and Wright's fiduciary duty to the corporation. The appellate court ordered a rescission of the sale.

CONFLICTS OF INTEREST

Corporate directors often have many business affiliations, and a director can sit on the board of more than one corporation. Of course, directors are precluded from entering into or supporting businesses that operate in direct competition with corporations on whose boards they serve. Their fiduciary duty requires them to make a full disclosure of any potential conflicts of interest that might arise in any corporate transaction [RMBCA 8.60].

Sometimes a corporation enters into a contract or engages in a transaction in which an officer or director has a personal interest. The director or officer must make a *full disclosure* of that interest and must abstain from voting on the proposed transaction. For example, Ballo Corporation needs office space. Stephan Colson, one of its five directors, owns the building adjoining the corporation's headquarters. He negotiates a lease with Ballo for the space, making a full disclosure to Ballo and the other four board directors. The lease arrangement is fair and reasonable, and it is unanimously approved by the other members of the corporation's board of directors. In such a case, the contract is valid. The rule is one of reason; otherwise, directors would be prevented from ever giving financial assistance to the corporations they serve.

State statutes contain different standards, but a contract will generally not be voidable if it was fair and reasonable to the corporation at the time it was made, if there was a full disclosure of the interest of the officers or directors involved in the transaction, and if the contract was approved by a majority of the disinterested directors or shareholders [RMBCA 8.62].

Often, contracts are negotiated between corporations having one or more directors who are members of both boards. Such transactions require great care, as they are closely scrutinized by the courts. (As will be discussed in Chapter 45, in certain circumstances—if two large corporations are competing with each other, for example—it may constitute a violation of antitrust laws for a director to sit on the boards of both companies.)

SECTION 4

Liability of Directors and Officers

Directors and officers are exposed to liability on many fronts. Corporate directors and officers may be held liable for the crimes and torts committed by themselves or by corporate employees under their supervision, as discussed in Chapters 8 and 34. Additionally, shareholders may perceive that the corporate directors are not acting in the best interests of the corporation and may sue the directors, in what is called a *shareholder's derivative suit*, on behalf of the corporation. (This type of action is discussed later in this chapter, in the context of shareholders' rights.) Directors and officers are expected to exercise due care and to use their best judgment in guiding corporate management; if they do not, they may be held liable to the corporation for any resulting damages.

Under the so-called **business judgment rule**, however, a corporate director or officer may be able to avoid liability to the corporation or to its shareholders for exercising poor business judgment. After all, directors and officers are not insurers of business success, and honest mistakes of judgment and poor business decisions on their part do not automatically make them liable to the corporation. The business judgment rule generally immunizes directors and officers from liability for the consequences of a decision that is within managerial authority, as long as the decision complies with management's fiduciary duties and as long as acting on the decision is within the powers of the corporation. Consequently, if there is a reasonable basis for a business decision, it is unlikely that the court will interfere with that decision, even if the corporation suffers as a result.

To benefit from the rule, directors and officers must act in good faith, in what they consider to be the best interests of the corporation, and with the care that an ordinarily prudent person in a similar position would exercise in like circumstances. This requires an informed decision, with a rational basis, and with no conflict between the decision maker's personal interest and the interest of the corporation. (The importance of good faith also comes into play when making document-retention decisions—see this chapter's *Emerging Trends in Technology* on pages 666 and 667.)

At issue in the following case was whether the business judgment rule immunizes directors from liability for purely negligent acts.

CASE 35.2   Federal Deposit Insurance Corp. v. Castetter

United States Court of Appeals, Ninth Circuit, 1999. 184 F.3d 1040. http://www.ce9. uscourts.gov[a]

BACKGROUND AND FACTS   *Edward Peterson, a banker with twenty-six years of experience, opened Balboa National Bank in California in February 1983. Peterson was president, chief executive officer, and a member of the board of directors. None of the other directors, including Robert Castetter, had any significant banking experience. Peterson decided that the bank would focus on lending money to auto buyers. Frances Cragen, an experienced, high-level employee in Bank of America's auto loan department, came to work for Balboa. Peterson died unexpectedly in May 1984. The federal Office of the Comptroller of the Currency (OCC) examined the bank and found many problems. The board hired a new president and told him to implement better procedures for lending and collecting. The board also hired outside consultants for advice. In December, the*

a. In the "Info Links" column, click on the "Appeals Court Decisions" icon. On that page, click on "1999" to open the menu. Click on "July" and scroll down the list to the name of the case (released "07/21/99") and click on it to access the opinion.

directors fired Cragen and hired a national accounting firm to look more closely at the bank's lending practices. Problems continued, however, and the accounting firm's reports were found to be invalid. In 1987, the OCC found the board's supervision to be "inexcusable" and the bank's condition to be critical. Meanwhile, directors personally contributed over $2.8 million to the bank in an attempt to save it. In 1988, the OCC ordered the bank to close. The Federal Deposit Insurance Corporation (FDIC)ᵇ filed a suit in a federal district court against Castetter and the other directors, contending that they were negligent and personally liable for the bank's losses. The court applied California's business judgment rule in favor of the directors. The FDIC appealed to the U.S. Court of Appeals for the Ninth Circuit.

IN THE LANGUAGE OF THE COURT

THOMAS, Circuit Judge.

* * * *

* * * The California business judgment rule is intended to protect a director from liability for a mistake in business judgment which is made in good faith and in what he or she believes to be the best interest of the corporation, where no conflict of interest exists. It requires directors to act in good faith and with the prudence that an ordinary person would under like circumstances. However, it also entitles a director to rely on information supplied by others. *If directors meet the requirements of the business judgment rule, they are entitled to immunity from personal liability for acts of ordinary negligence* under California law. [Emphasis added.]

* * * *

* * * Under California law, a *prima facie* showing of good faith and reasonable investigation is established when a majority of the board is comprised of outside directors and the board has received the advice of independent consultants.

* * * *

Here, the defendant directors established a *prima facie* showing of a reasonable investigation. A majority of the board consisted of outside directors and it is undisputed that the board sought and obtained the advice of a number of outside expert consultants.

* * * *

This is not to say that directors of California corporations may immunize themselves simply by acquiring information. It is clear that the rule does not protect a director in certain situations, such as where there is a conflict of interest, fraud, oppression, or corruption. Neither does the business judgment rule protect a director who has wholly abdicated his corporate responsibility, closing his or her eyes to corporate affairs. But the rule does protect well-meaning directors who are misinformed, misguided, and honestly mistaken. * * *

* * * *

In this case, there is no dispute that the directors acted in good faith and with the belief that their actions were in the best interests of the corporation. The directors were initially misguided by the analysis of former President Peterson, who had over a quarter century of experience as a bank regulator. They were further misguided by an analysis of a national accounting firm. They attempted to follow the advice of several consultants, and invested—and lost—substantial sums of their own money. Despite these efforts, they were unable to avert the bank's collapse. The undisputed record indicates that the directors were entitled to the protection of the business judgment rule.

DECISION AND REMEDY

The U.S. Court of Appeals for the Ninth Circuit affirmed the judgment of the lower court. The business judgment rule insulated the bank's directors from individual liability for the bank's losses.

---

b. The Federal Deposit Insurance Corporation is a federal agency that insures, up to $100,000, the deposits in banks and savings associations.

CONCEPT SUMMARY 35.1 — ROLE OF DIRECTORS AND OFFICERS

Election of Directors	The first board of directors is usually appointed by the incorporators; thereafter, directors are elected by the shareholders. Directors usually serve a one-year term, although the term can be longer. Few qualifications are required; a director can be a shareholder but is not required to be. Compensation is usually specified in the corporate articles or bylaws.
Board of Directors' Meetings	The board of directors conducts business by holding formal meetings with recorded minutes. The date of regular meetings is usually established in the corporate articles or bylaws; special meetings can be called, with notice sent to all directors. Quorum requirements vary from state to state; usually, a quorum is the majority of the corporate directors. Voting must usually be done in person, and in ordinary matters only a majority vote is required.
Rights of Directors	Directors' rights include the rights of participation, inspection, compensation, and indemnification.
Directors' Management Responsibilities	Directors are responsible for authorizing major corporate decisions; appointing, supervising, and removing corporate officers and other managerial employees; determining employees' compensation; making financial decisions necessary to the management of corporate affairs; and issuing authorized shares and bonds. Directors may delegate some of their responsibilities to executive committees and corporate officers and executives.
Role of Corporate Officers and Executives	Corporate officers and other executive employees are normally hired by the board of directors. In most states, a person can hold more than one office and can be both an officer and a director of a corporation. The rights of corporate officers and executives are defined by employment contracts.
Duties of Directors and Officers	1. *Duty of care*—Directors and officers are obligated to act in good faith, to use prudent business judgment in the conduct of corporate affairs, and to act in the corporation's best interests. If a director or officer fails to exercise this duty of care, he or she may be answerable to the corporation and to the shareholders for breaching the duty. 2. *Duty of loyalty*—Directors and officers have a fiduciary duty to subordinate their own interests to those of the corporation in matters relating to the corporation. 3. *Conflicts of interest*—To fulfill their duty of loyalty, directors and officers must make a full disclosure of any potential conflicts between their personal interests and those of the corporation.
Liability of Directors and Officers	Corporate directors and officers are personally liable for their own torts and crimes; additionally, they may be held personally liable for the torts and crimes committed by corporate personnel under their direct supervision (see Chapters 8 and 34). The *business judgment rule* immunizes a director from liability for a corporate decision as long as the decision was within the powers of the corporation and the authority of the director to make and was an informed, reasonable, and loyal decision.

SECTION 5

The Role of Shareholders

The acquisition of a share of stock makes a person an owner and shareholder in a corporation. Shareholders thus own the corporation. Although they have no legal title to corporate property vested in the corporation, such as buildings and equipment, they do have an *equitable* (ownership) interest in the firm.

As a general rule, shareholders have no responsibility for the daily management of the corporation,

EMERGING TRENDS IN TECHNOLOGY

Retention Policies for E-Documents

Recall from Chapter 3 that if a corporation becomes the target of a civil lawsuit or criminal investigation, the company may be required to turn over any documents in its files relating to the matter being litigated. These documents may consist of legal documents, contracts, e-mails, faxes, letters, interoffice memorandums, notebooks, diaries, and other materials, even if they are kept in personal files in the homes of directors or officers. If a company refuses to comply with a request for documents—or destroys the documents—it may be subject to severe court sanctions[a] or even a criminal charge of obstruction of justice.

At one time, document-retention policies referred only to paper documents. Today, a document-retention policy must also take into consideration electronic documents and data, including e-mail. Because of its speed, relatively low cost, and ease of use, e-mail has virtually replaced hard copy as a means of communication within and between business firms. For all its benefits, however, e-mail can also lead to significant problems when e-mailed documents are requested during the discovery stage of a lawsuit. For this reason and others, today's firms are learning that policies on e-document management—particularly with respect to e-mail—are becoming imperative.

E-MAIL MANAGEMENT POLICIES

Creating an effective e-mail management policy has now become a priority for most firms due to the sheer volume of their e-mail exchanges. In many companies, employees exchange over a million e-mail messages per week. If the company were to keep all e-mail on back-up storage devices, in the event of a lawsuit it could face a time-consuming and costly problem: sorting through millions of messages to locate relevant documents. In one case, for example, the court ordered a defendant to review and produce about 30 million pages of e-mail stored on back-up tapes (at a cost of between $50,000 and $70,000).[b]

Companies are also creating e-mail management policies for another, obvious reason: to avoid having to produce e-mailed "smoking guns" (telling evidence) during litigation. The government's widely publicized antitrust lawsuit against Microsoft Corporation[c] sent a clear message to all businesses—that an electronic document, such as an e-mail memo, can turn out to be a star witness in litigation. In the case against Microsoft, the U.S. Department of Justice claimed that e-mail messages exchanged years ago by Microsoft executives tended to show that the company deliberately tried to monopolize access to the Internet.

WHICH E-DOCUMENTS SHOULD BE RETAINED?

To curb potential litigation problems stemming from the use of e-mail, some firms simply delete

a. See, for example, *Procter & Gamble Co. v. Haugen,* 179 F.R.D. [Federal Rules Decisions] 622 (D.Utah 1998), in which the court held that a business's failure to preserve e-mail communications was a sanctionable breach of discovery duties.

b. *In re Brand Name Prescription Drugs Antitrust Litigation,* 1995 WL 360526 (N.D.Ill. 1995).
c. See the *Emerging Trends in Technology* in Chapter 45 for a discussion of this case.

although they are ultimately responsible for choosing the board of directors, which does have such control. Ordinarily, corporate officers and other employees owe no direct duty to individual stockholders. Their duty is to the corporation as a whole. A director, however, is in a fiduciary relationship to the corporation and therefore serves the interests of the shareholders in general. Ordinarily, there is no legal relationship between shareholders and creditors of the corporation. Shareholders can, in fact, be creditors of the corporation and have the same rights of recovery against the corporation as any other creditor.

In this section, we look at the powers, rights, and liabilities of shareholders, which may be established in the articles of incorporation and under the state's general incorporation law.

EMERGING TRENDS IN TECHNOLOGY

Retention Policies for E-Documents, continued

e-mail after a specified period, such as two weeks or thirty days, and do not include e-mail on their routine back-ups. (Indeed, software by Disappearing, Inc., in San Francisco, and QV Tech, Inc., of Colorado Springs, Colorado, automatically deletes e-mail at a specified time, such as within one day or one week.) Other businesses keep back-up copies of their e-mail forever, in the event that they may need access to those messages at some future time (to defend against a lawsuit, for example). Still other companies print out or make back-up copies of important e-mail and trash the rest, just as they do with paper documents.

How does a company decide which electronic documents should be retained and which should be destroyed? Generally, e-documents are subject to the same requirements as any of the other records of an organization.

By law, corporations are required to keep certain types of documents, such as those specified in the *Code of Federal Regulations* and in regulations issued by government agencies, such as the Occupational Safety and Health Administration.

As a rule, any records that the company is not legally required to keep or that the company is sure it will have no legal need for should be removed from the files and destroyed. A joint-venture agreement, for example, should be kept. An e-mail message about last year's company picnic, however, should be removed from the electronic files and destroyed; obviously, it is just taking up storage space.

If a company becomes the target of an investigation, it usually must modify its document-retention policy until the investigation has been completed. Company officers, after receiving a subpoena to produce specific types of documents, should instruct the appropriate employees not to destroy relevant e-documents that would otherwise be disposed of as part of the company's normal document-retention program. Generally, company officials must always exercise good faith in deciding what documents should

or should not be destroyed when attempting to comply with a subpoena.

IMPLICATIONS FOR THE BUSINESSPERSON

1. Any business owner or manager should consider developing an e-document retention policy to ward off potential litigation nightmares.
2. Employers should let employees know not only which e-documents should be retained and deleted but also which types of documents should not be created in the first place.

FOR CRITICAL ANALYSIS

1. Would it ever be advantageous to a firm to retain all e-mail on back-up tapes indefinitely?
2. Is there any significant difference between a printout of an e-mail message and the computerized version of the message on a computer's hard drive or a back-up storage device?

RELEVANT WEB SITES

For a list of the types of corporate documents that should be retained, go to **http://www.hefcpa.com/ docret.html**.

SHAREHOLDERS' POWERS

Shareholders must approve fundamental changes affecting the corporation before the changes can be implemented. Hence, shareholders are empowered to amend the articles of incorporation (charter) and by-laws, approve a merger or the dissolution of the corporation, and approve the sale of all or substantially

all of the corporation's assets. Some of these powers are subject to prior board approval.

Election and removal of the board of directors are accomplished by a vote of the shareholders. The first board of directors is either named in the articles of incorporation or chosen by the incorporators to serve until the first shareholders' meeting. From that time on, selection and retention of directors are exclusively shareholder functions.

Directors usually serve their full terms; if they are not satisfactory, they are simply not reelected. Shareholders have the inherent power, however, to remove a director from office *for cause* (breach of duty or misconduct) by a majority vote.[2] Some state statutes even permit removal of directors without cause by the vote of a majority of the holders of outstanding shares entitled to vote.[3] Some corporate charters also expressly provide that shareholders, by majority vote, can remove a director at any time without cause.

SHAREHOLDERS' MEETINGS

Shareholders' meetings must occur at least annually, and in addition, special meetings can be called to take care of urgent matters.

Notice of Meetings. Shareholders are notified of the date and hour of a shareholders' meeting in a written announcement that is sent a reasonable length of time prior to the date of the meeting.[4] Notices of special meetings must include a statement of the purpose of the meeting; business transacted at a special meeting is limited to that purpose.

Proxies. Because it usually is not practical for owners of only a few shares of stock of publicly traded corporations to attend a shareholders' meeting, such stockholders normally give third parties written authorization to vote their shares at the meeting. This authorization is called a **proxy** (from the Latin *procurare*, "to manage, take care of"). Proxies are often solicited by management, but any person can solicit proxies to concentrate voting power. Proxies

have been used by a group of shareholders as a device for taking over a corporation (corporate takeovers are discussed in Chapter 36). Proxies are normally revocable (that is, they can be withdrawn), unless they are specifically designated as irrevocable. Under RMBCA 7.22(c), proxies last for eleven months.

Proxy Materials and Shareholder Proposals. When shareholders want to change a company policy, they can put their ideas up for a shareholder vote. They can do this by submitting a shareholder proposal to the board of directors and asking the board to include the proposal in the proxy materials that are sent to all shareholders before meetings.

The Securities and Exchange Commission (SEC), which regulates the purchase and sale of securities (see Chapter 37), has special provisions relating to proxies and shareholder proposals. SEC Rule 14a-8 requires that when a company sends proxy materials to its shareholders, the company must also include whatever proposals will be considered at the meeting and provide shareholders with the opportunity to vote on the proposals by marking and returning their proxy cards. SEC Rule 14a-8 provides that all shareholders who own stock worth at least $1,000 are eligible to submit proposals for inclusion in corporate proxy materials.

A corporation is not required to include in proxy materials proposals that relate to "ordinary business operations." Normally, only those proposals that relate to significant policy considerations must be included. Often, however, it is difficult to determine whether a proposal relates to ordinary business activities or significant policy issues. For example, in a 1976 ruling, the SEC stated that shareholder proposals concerning equal opportunity and affirmative action relate to significant policy issues on which shareholders should be allowed to vote.[5] In 1992, however, the SEC reversed its position and ruled that all employment-related shareholder proposals would be automatically omittable under the "ordinary business" exclusion, even if they raised social policy concerns. In the wake of substantial criticism of its 1992 rule, the SEC again changed its stance. In 1998, the SEC issued a rule that essentially allows such decisions to be made on a case-by-case basis.

---

2. A director can often demand court review of removal for cause.
3. Most states allow *cumulative voting* (which will be discussed shortly) for directors. If cumulative voting is authorized, a director may not be removed if the number of votes sufficient to elect him or her under cumulative voting is voted against his or her removal. See, for example, California Corporate Code Section 303A. Also see Section 8.08(c) of the RMBCA.
4. The shareholder can waive the requirement of written notice by signing a waiver form [RMBCA 7.06]. A shareholder who does not receive written notice but who learns of the meeting and attends without protesting the lack of notice is said to have waived notice by such conduct. State statutes and corporate bylaws typically set forth the time within which notice must be sent, what methods can be used, and what the notice must contain.

---

5. *Adoption of Amendments Relating to Proposals by Security Holders,* Exchange Act Release No. 12999, 41 Fed.Reg. 52,994 (December 3, 1976).

SHAREHOLDER VOTING

Shareholders exercise ownership control through the power of their votes. Each common shareholder is entitled to one vote per share, although the voting techniques discussed below all enhance the power of the shareholder's vote. The articles of incorporation can exclude or limit voting rights, particularly to certain classes of shares. For example, owners of preferred shares are usually denied the right to vote [RMBCA 7.21].

Quorum Requirements. For shareholders to act during a meeting, a quorum must be present. Generally, this condition is met when shareholders holding more than 50 percent of the outstanding shares are present. Corporate business matters are presented in the form of resolutions, which shareholders vote to approve or disapprove. If a state statute sets forth specific voting requirements, the corporation's articles or bylaws must be consistent with these statutory limitations. Some states provide that obtaining the unanimous written consent of shareholders is a permissible alternative to holding a shareholders' meeting [RMBCA 7.25].

Once a quorum is present, voting can proceed. A majority vote of the shares represented at the meeting is usually required to pass resolutions. Assume that Novo Pictures, Inc., has 10,000 outstanding shares of voting stock. Its articles of incorporation set the quorum at more than 50 percent of outstanding shares and provide that a majority vote of the shares present is necessary to pass on ordinary matters. Therefore, for this firm, at the shareholders' meeting, a quorum of stockholders representing 5,000 outstanding shares must be present to conduct business, and a vote of at least 2,501 of those shares is needed to pass ordinary resolutions. If 6,000 shares are represented, a vote of 3,001 will be necessary, and so on.

At times, more than a simple majority vote will be required either by statute or by corporate charter. Extraordinary corporate matters, such as a merger, a consolidation, or the dissolution of the corporation (see Chapter 36), require approval by a higher percentage of the representatives of all corporate shares entitled to vote, not just a majority of those present at that particular meeting [RMBCA 7.27].

Voting Lists. A voting list is prepared by the corporation prior to each shareholders' meeting. Persons whose names appear on the corporation's stockholder records as owners are the ones ordinarily entitled to vote.[6] The voting list contains the name and address of each shareholder as shown on the corporate records on a given cutoff date, or record date. (Under RMBCA 7.07, the record date may be as much as seventy days before the meeting.) The voting list also includes the number of voting shares held by each owner. The list is usually kept at the corporate headquarters and is available for shareholder inspection [RMBCA 7.20].

Cumulative Voting. Most states permit or require shareholders to elect directors by *cumulative voting*, a method of voting designed to allow minority shareholders representation on the board of directors.[7] When cumulative voting is allowed or required, the number of members of the board to be elected is multiplied by the total number of voting shares. The result equals the number of votes a shareholder has, and this total can be cast for one or more nominees for director. All nominees stand for election at the same time. When cumulative voting is not required either by statute or under the articles, the entire board can be elected by a majority of shares at a shareholders' meeting.

Suppose, for example, that a corporation has 10,000 shares issued and outstanding. The minority shareholders hold only 3,000 shares, and the majority shareholders hold the other 7,000 shares. Three members of the board are to be elected. The majority shareholders' nominees are Alomon, Beasley, and Caravel. The minority shareholders' nominee is Dovrik. Can Dovrik be elected to the board by the minority shareholders?

If cumulative voting is allowed, the answer is yes. The minority shareholders have 9,000 votes among them (the number of directors to be elected times the number of shares equals 3 times 3,000, which equals 9,000 votes). All of these votes can be cast to elect Dovrik. The majority shareholders have 21,000 votes (3 times 7,000 equals 21,000 votes), but these votes have to be distributed among their three nominees. The principle of cumulative voting is that no matter how the majority shareholders cast their 21,000 votes,

---

6. When the legal owner is deceased, bankrupt, incompetent, or in some other way under a legal disability, his or her vote can be cast by a person designated by law to control and manage the owner's property.

7. See, for example, California Corporate Code Section 708. Under RMBCA 7.28, however, no cumulative voting rights exist unless the articles of incorporation so provide.

they will not be able to elect all three directors if the minority shareholders cast all of their 9,000 votes for Dovrik, as illustrated in Exhibit 35–1.

Other Voting Techniques. A group of shareholders can agree in writing prior to a shareholders' meeting, in a *shareholder voting agreement,* to vote their shares together in a specified manner. Such agreements usually are held to be valid and enforceable. A shareholder can also appoint a voting agent and vote by proxy. As mentioned previously, a proxy is a written authorization to cast the shareholder's vote, and a person can solicit proxies from a number of shareholders in an attempt to concentrate voting power [RMBCA 7.22, 7.31].

Another technique is for shareholders to enter into a **voting trust,** which is an agreement (a trust contract) under which legal title (recorded ownership on the corporate books) is transferred to a trustee who is responsible for voting the shares. The agreement can specify how the trustee is to vote, or it can allow the trustee to use his or her discretion. The trustee takes physical possession of the stock certificate and in return gives the shareholder a *voting trust certificate.* The shareholder retains all of the rights of ownership (for example, the right to receive dividend payments) except for the power to vote the shares [RMBCA 7.30].

SECTION 6

Rights of Shareholders

Shareholders possess numerous rights. A significant right—the right to vote their shares—has already been discussed. In addition to voting rights, a shareholder has the rights, based on ownership of stock, to receive stock certificates (depending on the jurisdiction), to purchase newly issued stock, to receive divi-dends, to inspect corporate records, to transfer shares (with some exceptions), to receive a proportionate share of corporate assets on corporate dissolution, and to file suit on behalf of the corporation. These rights are discussed in the following subsections.

STOCK CERTIFICATES

A **stock certificate** is a certificate issued by a corporation that evidences ownership of a specified number of shares in the corporation. In jurisdictions that require the issuance of stock certificates, shareholders have the right to demand that the corporation issue certificates and record their names and addresses in the corporate stock record books. In most states (and under RMBCA 6.26), boards of directors may provide that shares of stock be uncertificated (that is, that no actual, physical stock certificates need be issued). In that circumstance, the corporation may be required to send the holders of uncertificated shares letters or some other form of notice containing the same information required to be included on the face of stock certificates.

Stock is intangible personal property, and the ownership right exists independently of the certificate itself. A stock certificate may be lost or destroyed, but ownership is not destroyed with it. A new certificate can be issued to replace one that has been lost or destroyed.[8] Notice of shareholders' meetings, dividends, and operational and financial reports are all distributed according to the recorded ownership listed in the corporation's books, not on the basis of possession of the certificate.

---

8. For a lost or destroyed certificate to be reissued, a shareholder normally must furnish an indemnity bond (a guaranty of payment) to protect the corporation against potential loss should the original certificate reappear at some future time in the hands of a bona fide purchaser [UCC 8–302, 8–405(2)].

EXHIBIT 35–1   RESULTS OF CUMULATIVE VOTING

BALLOT	MAJORITY SHAREHOLDER VOTES			MINORITY SHAREHOLDER VOTES	DIRECTORS ELECTED
	Alomon	*Beasley*	*Caravel*	*Dovrik*	
1	10,000	10,000	1,000	9,000	Alomon, Beasley, Dovrik
2	9,001	9,000	2,999	9,000	Alomon, Beasley, Dovrik
3	6,000	7,000	8,000	9,000	Beasley, Caravel, Dovrik

PREEMPTIVE RIGHTS

A **preemptive right** is a common law concept under which a preference is given to a shareholder over all other purchasers to subscribe to or purchase a prorated share of a new issue of stock. This right does not apply to **treasury shares**—shares that are authorized but that have not been issued. This allows the shareholder to maintain his or her portion of control, voting power, or financial interest in the corporation. Most statutes either (1) grant preemptive rights but allow them to be negated in the corporation's articles or (2) deny preemptive rights except to the extent that they are granted in the articles [RMBCA 6.30]. The result is that the articles of incorporation determine the existence and scope of preemptive rights. Generally, preemptive rights apply only to additional, newly issued stock sold for cash and must be exercised within a specified time period (such as thirty days).

For example, Tron Corporation authorizes and issues 1,000 shares of stock, and Omar Loren purchases 100 shares, making him the owner of 10 percent of the company's stock. Subsequently, Tron, by vote of its shareholders, authorizes the issuance of another 1,000 shares (amending the articles of incorporation). This increases its capital stock to a total of 2,000 shares. If preemptive rights have been provided, Loren can purchase one additional share of the new stock being issued for each share currently owned—or 100 additional shares. Thus, he can own 200 of the 2,000 shares outstanding, and his relative position as a shareholder will be maintained. If preemptive rights are not reserved, his proportionate control and voting power will be diluted from that of a 10 percent shareholder to that of a 5 percent shareholder because of the issuance of the additional 1,000 shares.

Preemptive rights can be very important for shareholders in close corporations. This is because of the relatively small number of shares and the substantial interest that each shareholder controls in a close corporation. Without preemptive rights, it would be possible for a shareholder to lose his or her proportionate control over the firm.

STOCK WARRANTS

Usually, when preemptive rights exist and a corporation is issuing additional shares, each shareholder is given **stock warrants,** which are transferable options to acquire a given number of shares from the corporation at a stated price. Warrants are often publicly traded on securities exchanges. When the warrant option is for a short period of time, the stock warrants are usually referred to as *rights*.

DIVIDENDS

A **dividend** is a distribution of corporate profits or income *ordered by the directors* and paid to the shareholders in proportion to their respective shares in the corporation. Dividends can be paid in cash, property, stock of the corporation that is paying the dividends, or stock of other corporations.[9]

State laws vary, but every state determines the general circumstances and legal requirements under which dividends are paid. State laws also control the sources of revenue to be used; only certain funds are legally available for paying dividends. Once declared, a cash dividend becomes a corporate debt enforceable at law like any other debt. Depending on state law, dividends may be paid from the following sources:

1. *Retained earnings.* All state statutes allow dividends to be paid from the undistributed net profits earned by the corporation, including capital gains from the sale of fixed assets. The undistributed net profits are called retained earnings.
2. *Net profits.* A few state statutes allow dividends to be issued from current net profits without regard to deficits in prior years.
3. *Surplus.* A number of state statutes allow dividends to be paid out of any kind of surplus.

Illegal Dividends. Sometimes dividends are improperly paid from an unauthorized account, or their payment causes the corporation to become insolvent. Generally, in such cases, shareholders must return illegal dividends only if they knew that the dividends were illegal when they received them. A dividend paid while the corporation is insolvent is automatically an illegal dividend, and shareholders may be liable for returning the payment to the corporation or its creditors. In all cases of illegal and improper dividends, the board of directors can be held personally liable for the amount of the payment. When directors can show that a shareholder knew a dividend was illegal when it was received, however, the directors are entitled to reimbursement from the shareholder.

---

9. Technically, dividends paid in stock are not dividends. They maintain each shareholder's proportional interest in the corporation. On one occasion, a distillery declared and paid a "dividend" in bonded whiskey.

Directors' Failure to Declare a Dividend. When directors fail to declare a dividend, shareholders can ask a court of equity for an injunction to compel the directors to meet and to declare a dividend. For the injunction to be granted, it must be shown that the directors have acted so unreasonably in withholding the dividend that their conduct is an abuse of their discretion.

Often, large money reserves are accumulated for a bona fide purpose, such as expansion, research, or some other legitimate corporate use. The mere fact that sufficient corporate earnings or surplus is available to pay a dividend is not enough to compel directors to distribute funds that, in the board's opinion, should not be distributed.[10] The courts are hesitant to interfere with corporate operations and will not compel directors to declare dividends unless abuse of discretion is clearly shown.

INSPECTION RIGHTS

Shareholders in a corporation enjoy both common law and statutory inspection rights. The shareholder's right of inspection is limited, however, to the inspection and copying of corporate books and records for a *proper purpose*, provided the request is made in advance. Either the shareholder can inspect in person, or an attorney, accountant, or other type of assistant can do so as the shareholder's agent. The RMBCA requires the corporation to maintain an alphabetical voting list of shareholders with addresses and number of shares owned; this list must be kept open at the annual meeting for inspection by any shareholder of record [RMBCA 7.20].

The power of inspection is fraught with potential abuses, and the corporation is allowed to protect itself from them. For example, a shareholder can properly be denied access to corporate records to prevent harassment or to protect trade secrets or other confidential corporate information. Some states require that a shareholder must have held his or her shares for a minimum period of time immediately preceding the demand to inspect or must hold a minimum number of outstanding shares. The RMBCA provides that every shareholder is entitled to examine specified corporate records [RMBCA 16.02]. A shareholder who is denied the right of inspection can seek a court order to compel the inspection.

TRANSFER OF SHARES

Corporate stock represents an ownership right in intangible personal property. The law generally recognizes the right of an owner to transfer property to another person unless there are valid restrictions on its transferability. Although stock certificates are negotiable and freely transferable by indorsement and delivery, transfer of stock in closely held corporations is generally restricted by the bylaws, by a restriction stamped on the stock certificate, or by a shareholder agreement (see Chapter 34). The existence of any restrictions on transferability must always be noted on the face of the stock certificate, and these restrictions must be reasonable.

Sometimes, corporations or their shareholders restrict transferability by reserving the option to purchase any shares offered for resale by a shareholder. This **right of first refusal** remains with the corporation or the shareholders for only a specified time or a reasonable period of time. Variations on the purchase option are possible. For example, a shareholder might be required to offer the shares to other shareholders or to the corporation first.

When shares are transferred, a new entry is made in the corporate stock book to indicate the new owner. Until the corporation is notified and the entry is complete, voting rights, notice of shareholders' meetings, dividend distribution, and so forth are all held by the current record owner.

RIGHTS ON DISSOLUTION

When a corporation is dissolved and its outstanding debts and the claims of its creditors have been satisfied, the remaining assets are distributed on a pro rata basis among the shareholders. If no preferences in distribution of assets on liquidation are given to any class of stock, then all of the stockholders share the remaining assets.

Shareholders also have the right to petition the court to dissolve the corporation. Suppose that a minority shareholder knows that the board of directors is mishandling corporate assets or is permitting a deadlock to threaten or irreparably injure the corporation's finances. The minority shareholder is not powerless to intervene. He or she can petition a court to appoint

---

10. A striking exception to this rule was made in *Dodge v. Ford Motor Co.*, 204 Mich. 459, 170 N.W. 668 (1919), when Henry Ford, the president and major stockholder of Ford Motor Company, refused to declare a dividend notwithstanding the firm's large capital surplus. The court, holding that Ford had abused his discretion, ordered the company to declare a dividend.

a receiver and to liquidate the business assets of the corporation.

The RMBCA permits any shareholder to initiate such an action in any of the following circumstances [RMBCA 14.30]:

1. The directors are deadlocked in the management of corporate affairs, shareholders are unable to break that deadlock, and irreparable injury to the corporation is being suffered or threatened.

2. The acts of the directors or those in control of the corporation are illegal, oppressive, or fraudulent.

3. Corporate assets are being misapplied or wasted.

4. The shareholders are deadlocked in voting power and have failed, for a specified period (usually two annual meetings), to elect successors to directors whose terms have expired or would have expired with the election of successors.

In the following case, one of a corporation's only two shareholders petitioned a court to dissolve the corporation because the shareholders could not agree on how to run the corporation.

CASE 35.3   Black v. Graham

Supreme Court of
Georgia, 1996.
464 S.E.2d 814.

BACKGROUND AND FACTS *Black and Graham each owned 50 percent of the stock of a building supplies corporation; they also served as the corporation's directors. When the two shareholder-directors deadlocked over differences of opinion on how to run their business, Graham filed a petition in a Georgia state court to dissolve the corporation. The parties agreed to the appointment of a custodian to run their firm while the court considered Graham's petition. Ultimately, the court ordered each shareholder to offer to buy the other out. This attempt to resolve the matter failed. The court then converted the custodian into a receiver, directed him to wind up the affairs of the business, and told him to liquidate the corporation. Both parties appealed to the Supreme Court of Georgia.*

IN THE LANGUAGE OF THE COURT

HINES, Justice.

*   *   *   *

*   *   * A deadlock occurs [w]here stock of [a] corporation is owned in equal shares by two contending parties, which condition threatens to result in destruction of [the] business, and it appears that [the] parties cannot agree upon management of [the] business, and under existing circumstances neither one is authorized to impose its views upon the other *   *   * . The evidence in this case portrays a classic situation of deadlock. Black and Graham as sole and equal shareholders functioned as *de facto* directors who were wholly unable to agree on the management of the business. Neither had the authority to prevail in his view and the hostile and static situation threatened irreparable injury to the corporation. Under these circumstances, the appointment of a receiver and dissolution was warranted.

DECISION AND REMEDY *The Supreme Court of Georgia affirmed the orders of the lower court. The corporation would be dissolved because the shareholders could not agree on how to run the firm.*

SHAREHOLDER'S DERIVATIVE SUITS

When those in control of a corporation—the corporate directors—fail to sue in the corporate name to redress a wrong suffered by the corporation, shareholders are permitted to do so "derivatively" in what is known as a **shareholder's derivative suit.** Some wrong must have been done to the corporation, and

before a derivative suit can be brought, the shareholders must first state their complaint to the board of directors. Only if the directors fail to solve the problem or to take appropriate action can the derivative suit go forward.

The right of shareholders to bring a derivative action is especially important when the wrong suffered by the corporation results from the actions of corporate directors. This is because the directors and officers would probably be unwilling to take any action against themselves.[11]

The shareholder's derivative suit is singular in that those suing are not pursuing rights or benefits for themselves personally but are acting as guardians of the corporate entity. Therefore, any damages recovered by the suit normally go into the corporation's treasury, not to the shareholders personally.

SECTION 7

Liability of Shareholders

One of the hallmarks of the corporate organization is that shareholders are not personally liable for the debts of the corporation. If the corporation fails, shareholders can lose their investments, but that is generally the limit of their liability. As discussed in Chapter 34, in certain instances of fraud, undercapitalization, or careless observance of corporate formalities, a court will pierce the corporate veil (disregard the corporate entity) and hold the shareholders individually liable. But these situations are the exception, not the rule.

Although rare, there are certain other instances in which a shareholder can be personally liable. One relates to illegal dividends, which were discussed previously. Two others relate to *stock subscriptions* and *watered stock.*

STOCK-SUBSCRIPTION AGREEMENTS

Sometimes, stock-subscription agreements—written contracts by which one agrees to buy capital stock of a corporation—exist prior to incorporation. Normally, these agreements are treated as continuing offers and are irrevocable (for up to six months under RMBCA 6.20). Once the corporation has been formed, it can sell shares to investors. In either case, once the subscription agreement or stock offer is accepted, a binding contract is formed. Any refusal to pay constitutes a breach resulting in the personal liability of the shareholder.

WATERED STOCK

Shares of stock can be paid for with property or services rendered instead of cash. (Shares cannot be purchased with promissory notes, however.) The general rule is that for **par-value shares** (that is, shares that have a specific face value, or formal cash-in value,

11. See RMBCA 7.40–7.47.

written on them, such as one penny or one dollar), the corporation must receive a value at least equal to the par-value amount. For **no-par shares** (that is, shares without a par value), the corporation must receive the value of the shares as determined by the board or the shareholders.

For either par-value or no-par shares, the setting of the value is based on the same factors: tax rates, whether the corporation needs capital surplus, and what the corporation will receive for the shares (money, property, or services). When shares are issued by the corporation for less than these stated values, the shares are referred to as **watered stock.**[12] In most cases, the shareholder who receives watered stock must pay the difference to the corporation (the shareholder is personally liable). In some states, the shareholder who receives watered stock may be liable to creditors of the corporation for unpaid corporate debts.

To illustrate the concept of watered stock: Suppose that during the formation of a corporation, Gomez, as one of the incorporators, transfers his property, Sunset Beach, to the corporation for 10,000 shares of stock at a par value of $100 per share for a total price of $1 million. After the property is transferred and the shares are issued, Sunset Beach is carried on the corporate books at a value of $1 million. On appraisal, it is discovered that the market value of the property at the time of transfer was only $500,000. The shares issued to Gomez are therefore watered stock, and he is liable to the corporation for the difference between the value of the shares and the value of the property.

SECTION 8

Duties of Majority Shareholders

In some cases, a majority shareholder is regarded as having a fiduciary duty to the corporation and to the minority shareholders. This occurs when a single shareholder (or a few shareholders acting in concert) owns a sufficient number of shares to exercise *de facto* (actual) control over the corporation. In these situations, majority shareholders owe a fiduciary duty to minority shareholders.

Consider an example. Three brothers, Alfred, Carl, and Eugene, each own a one-third interest in a corporation and had worked for the corporation for

12. The phrase *watered stock* was originally used to describe cattle that—kept thirsty during a long drive—were allowed to drink large quantities of water just prior to their sale. The increased weight of the "watered stock" allowed the seller to reap a higher profit.

most of their adult lives. When a dispute arose concerning discrepancies in the corporation's accounting records, Carl and Eugene fired Alfred and told the company's employees that Alfred had had a nervous breakdown, which was not true. Alfred sued Carl and Eugene, alleging, among other things, that they had breached their fiduciary duties. The brothers argued that because there was no diminution in the value of the corporation or the value of Alfred's shares in the company, they had not breached their fiduciary duties. The court, however, held that the brothers' conduct, which was unfairly prejudicial toward Alfred, supported a finding of breach of fiduciary duty.[13]

---

13. *Pedro v. Pedro,* 489 N.W.2d 798 (Minn.App. 1992).

CONCEPT SUMMARY 35.2

ROLE OF SHAREHOLDERS

Shareholders' Powers	Shareholders' powers include approval of all fundamental changes affecting the corporation and election of the board of directors.
Shareholders' Meetings	Shareholders' meetings must occur at least annually; special meetings can be called when necessary. Notice of the time and place of a meeting (and its purpose, if the meeting is specially called) must be sent to shareholders. Voting requirements and procedures are as follows: 1. A minimum number of shareholders (a quorum—generally, shareholders representing more than 50 percent of shares held) must be present at a meeting; resolutions are normally passed by majority vote. 2. A voting list of shareholders on record must be prepared by the corporation prior to each shareholders' meeting. 3. Cumulative voting may or may not be required or permitted so as to give minority shareholders a better chance to be represented on the board of directors. 4. Shareholders' voting agreements to vote their shares together are usually held to be valid and enforceable. 5. A shareholder may appoint a proxy (substitute) to vote his or her shares. 6. A shareholder may enter into a voting trust agreement by which title (record ownership) of his or her shares is given to a trustee, and the trustee votes the shares in accordance with the trust agreement.
Shareholders' Rights	Shareholders have numerous rights, which may include the following: 1. Voting rights. 2. The right to receive stock certificates (depending on the jurisdiction). 3. Preemptive rights (depending on the corporate charter). 4. The right to receive dividends (at the discretion of the directors). 5. The right to inspect the corporate records. 6. The right to transfer shares (this right may be restricted in close corporations). 7. The right to receive a share of corporate assets when the corporation is dissolved. 8. The right to sue on behalf of the corporation (bring a shareholder's derivative suit) when the directors fail to do so.
Shareholders' Liability	Shareholders may be liable for the retention of illegal dividends, for breach of a stock-subscription agreement, and for watered stock. In certain situations, majority shareholders may be regarded as having a fiduciary duty to minority shareholders and will be liable if that duty is breached.

TERMS AND CONCEPTS TO REVIEW

business judgment rule 663

dividend 671

no-par share 674

par-value share 674

preemptive rights 671

proxy 668

quorum 659

right of first refusal 672

shareholder's derivative suit 673

stock certificate 670

stock warrant 671

treasury share 671

voting trust 670

watered stock 674

QUESTIONS AND CASE PROBLEMS

35–1. DUTIES OF DIRECTORS. Otts Corp. is negotiating with the Wick Construction Co. for the renovation of the Otts corporate headquarters. Wick, owner of the Wick Construction Co., is also one of the five members of the board of directors of Otts. The contract terms are standard for this type of contract. Wick has previously informed two of the other directors of his interest in the construction company. The contract is approved by Otts's board on a three-to-two vote, with Wick voting with the majority. Discuss whether this contract is binding on the corporation.

35–2. DUTIES OF DIRECTORS. AstroStar, Inc., has a board of directors consisting of three members (Eckhart, Golum, and Macero) and has approximately five hundred shareholders. At a regular meeting of the board, the board selects Galiard as president of the corporation by a two-to-one vote, with Eckhart dissenting. The minutes of the meeting do not register Eckhart's dissenting vote. Later, on an audit, it is discovered that Galiard is a former convict and has openly embezzled $500,000 from AstroStar, Inc. This loss is not covered by insurance. The corporation wants to hold directors Eckhart, Golum, and Macero liable. Eckhart claims no liability. Discuss the personal liability of the directors to the corporation.

35–3. RIGHTS OF SHAREHOLDERS. Superal Corp. authorized 100,000 shares and issued all of them during its first six months in operation. Avril purchased 10,000 of the shares (10 percent). Later, Superal reacquired 10,000 of the shares it originally issued. With shareholder approval, Superal has now amended its articles so as to authorize and issue another 100,000 shares. It has also, by a resolution of the board of directors, made plans to reissue the 10,000 shares of treasury stock (the shares reacquired by the corporation). There is no provision in the corporate articles dealing with shareholders' preemptive rights. Because of her ownership of 10 percent of Superal, Avril claims that she has the preemptive right to purchase 10,000 shares of the new issue and 1,000 shares of the stock being reissued. Discuss her claims.

35–4. RIGHTS OF SHAREHOLDERS. Lucia has acquired one share of common stock of a multimillion-dollar corporation with over 500,000 shareholders. Lucia wants to know whether this one share entitles her to (1) attend and vote at shareholders' meetings, (2) inspect the corporate books, and (3) receive yearly dividends. Discuss Lucia's rights in these three matters.

35–5. LIABILITY OF SHAREHOLDERS. Riddle has made a preincorporation subscription agreement to purchase 500 shares of a newly formed corporation. The shares have a par value of $100 per share. The corporation is formed, and Riddle's subscription is accepted by the corporation. Riddle transfers a piece of land he owns to the corporation, and the corporation issues 250 shares for it. One year later, with the corporation in serious financial difficulty, the board declares and pays a dividend of $5 per share. It is now learned that the land transferred by Riddle had a market value of $18,000 at the time of transfer. Discuss any liability that shareholder Riddle has to the corporation or to creditors of the corporation.

35–6. RIGHTS OF SHAREHOLDERS. Jacob Schachter and Herbert Kulik, the founders of Ketek Electric Corp., each owned 50 percent of the corporation's shares, and they served as the corporation's only officers. Arnold Glenn, as trustee, and Kulik brought a shareholder's derivative suit in a New York state court against Schachter, alleging that Schachter had diverted Ketek assets and opportunities to Hoteltron Systems, Inc., a corporation wholly owned by Schachter. The trial court held for Glenn and Kulik, and it awarded damages to Kulik, not to Ketek. On appeal, the appellate court ruled that the damages should be awarded to the injured corporation, Ketek, rather than to the innocent shareholder, Kulik. Kulik appealed to the state supreme court, arguing that awarding damages to the corporation was inequitable because Schachter, as a shareholder of Ketek, would ultimately share in the proceeds of the award. How should the state supreme court rule, and why? [*Glenn v. Hoteltron Systems, Inc.*, 74 N.Y.2d 386, 547 N.E.2d 71, 547 N.Y.S.2d 816 (1989)]

35–7. DUTY OF LOYALTY. Mackinac Cellular Corp. offered to sell Robert Broz a license to operate a cellular phone system in Michigan. Broz was a director of Cellular Information Systems, Inc. (CIS). CIS, as a result of bankruptcy proceedings, was in the process of selling its cellular holdings. Broz did not formally present the opportunity to the CIS board, but he told some of the firm's officers and directors, who replied that CIS was not interested. At the time, PriCellular, Inc., a firm that wanted the Michigan license, was attempting to buy CIS. Without telling PriCellular, Broz bought the license himself. After PriCellular took over CIS, the company sued Broz, alleging that he had usurped a corporate opportunity. Has Broz done anything wrong? Discuss. [*Broz v. Cellular Information Systems, Inc.*, 673 A.2d 148 (Del. 1996)]

35–8. BUSINESS JUDGMENT RULE. The board of directors of Baltimore Gas and Electric Company (BGE) recommended a merger with Potomac Electric Power Company (PEPCO). After full disclosure, the BGE shareholders approved the merger. On the ground that each BGE director stood a chance of being named to the new company's board, Janice Wittman, a BGE shareholder, sued the directors, alleging, among other things, that they were prohibited from deciding whether to recommend the merger. Did the directors breach their duty of care by voting in favor of the merger? Discuss. [*Wittman v. Crooke*, 120 Md.App. 369, 707 A.2d 422 (1998)]

35–9. BUSINESS JUDGMENT RULE. Charles Pace and Maria Fuentez were shareholders of Houston Industries, Inc. (HII), and employees of Houston Lighting & Power, a subsidiary of HII, when they lost their jobs because of a company-wide reduction in its work force. Pace, as a shareholder, three times wrote to HII, demanding that the board of directors terminate certain HII directors and officers, and file a suit to recover damages for breach of fiduciary duty. Three times, the directors referred the charges to board committees and an outside law firm, which found that the facts did not support the charges. The board also received input from federal regulatory authorities about the facts behind some of the charges. The board notified Pace that it would refuse his demands. In response, Pace and Fuentez filed a shareholder's derivative suit against Don Jordan and the other HII directors, contending that the board's investigation was inadequate. The defendants moved for summary judgment, arguing that the suit was barred by the business judgment rule. How should the court rule? Why? [*Pace v. Jordan*, 999 S.W.2d 615 (Tex.App.—Houston [1 Dist.] 1999)]

35–10. IN YOUR COURT

Melissa and Gary Callicoat each owned 50 percent of Callicoat, Inc. They were also Callicoat's only directors. They could not agree on the day-to-day management of the firm. Neither could they agree on whether a debt owed to Arthur Baz was a personal or a corporate debt. Melissa suggested that they dissolve the corporation. Gary refused and shut her out from the operations of the firm. Melissa petitioned a court to dissolve the corporation. Assume that you are the judge in the trial court hearing this case and answer the following questions:

(a) On what basis might you order the dissolution of the firm?

(b) Review Case 35.3 (*Black v. Graham*). How does the law applied in that case apply to the case now before your court?

LAW ON THE WEB

For updated links to resources available on the Web, as well as a variety of other materials, visit this text's Web site at http://wbl.westbuslaw.com.

One of the best sources on the Web for information on corporations, including their directors, is the EDGAR database of the Securities and Exchange Commission (SEC) at

http://www.sec.gov/edgarhp.htm

LEGAL RESEARCH EXERCISES ON THE WEB

Go to http://wbl.westbuslaw.com, the Web site that accompanies this text. Select "Internet Applications," and then click on "Chapter 35." There you will find the following Internet research exercise that you can perform to learn more about the liability of corporate directors and officers:

Activity 35–1: Liability of Directors and Officers

CHAPTER 36

Corporations—Merger, Consolidation, and Termination

A CORPORATION TYPICALLY EXTENDS its operations by combining with another corporation through a merger, a consolidation, a purchase of assets, or a purchase of a controlling interest in the other corporation. This chapter examines these four types of corporate expansion. Dissolution and liquidation are the combined processes by which a corporation terminates its existence. The last part of this chapter discusses some of the typical reasons for terminating a corporation's existence and the methods used in the termination process.

SECTION 1

Merger and Consolidation

The terms *merger* and *consolidation* are often used interchangeably, but they refer to two legally distinct proceedings. Whether a combination is in fact a merger or a consolidation, however, the rights and liabilities of shareholders, the corporation, and the corporation's creditors are the same.

MERGER

A **merger** involves the legal combination of two or more corporations. After a merger, only one of the corporations continues to exist. For example, Corporation A and Corporation B decide to merge. It is agreed that A will absorb B; so on merger, B ceases to exist as a separate entity, and A continues as the **surviving corporation.** This process is illustrated in Exhibit 36–1.

After the merger, A is recognized as a single corporation possessing all the rights, privileges, and powers of itself and B. A automatically acquires all of B's property and assets without the necessity of formal transfer. A becomes liable for all of B's debts and obligations.[1] Finally, A's articles of incorporation are deemed amended to include any changes that are stated in the *articles of merger.*

In a merger, the surviving corporation is vested with the disappearing corporation's preexisting legal rights and obligations. For example, if the disappearing corporation had a right of action against a third party, the surviving corporation could bring suit after the merger to recover the disappearing corporation's damages.

---

1. A corporation that is subject to suit in some jurisdictions cannot avoid liability by merging with a corporation that could not otherwise have been sued in those jurisdictions. See, for example, *In re Silicone Gel Breast Implants Product Liability Litigation,* 837 F.Supp. 1123 (N.D. Ala. 1993).

CONSOLIDATION

In a **consolidation,** two or more corporations combine so that each corporation ceases to exist and a new one emerges. Corporation A and Corporation B consolidate to form an entirely new organization, Corporation C. In the process, A and B both terminate. C comes into existence as an entirely new entity. This process is illustrated in Exhibit 36–2.

The results of a consolidation are essentially the same as the results of a merger. C is recognized as a new corporation and a single entity; A and B cease to exist. C accedes to all the rights, privileges, and powers previously held by A and B. Title to any property and assets owned by A and B passes to C without formal transfer. C assumes liability for all debts and obligations owed by A and B. The *articles of consolidation* take the place of A's and B's original corporate articles and are thereafter regarded as C's corporate articles.

When a merger or a consolidation takes place, the surviving corporation or newly formed corporation will issue shares or pay some fair consideration to the shareholders of the corporation that ceases to exist.

MERGER AND CONSOLIDATION PROCEDURES

All states have statutes authorizing mergers and consolidations for domestic (in-state) corporations, and most states allow the combination of domestic and foreign (out-of-state) corporations. Although the procedures vary somewhat among jurisdictions, the basic requirements are as outlined below [RMBCA 11.01–11.07].

1. The board of directors of *each* corporation involved must approve a merger or consolidation plan.[2]

---

2. When a corporation undertakes a transaction that will cause a change in corporate control or that will break up the corporate entity, the directors have an obligation "to seek the best value reasonably available to the stockholders." See, for example, *Paramount Communications, Inc., v. QVC Network, Inc.,* 637 A.2d 34 (Del. 1994).

EXHIBIT 36–1   MERGER

In this illustration, Corporations A and B decide to merge. They agree that A will absorb B; so on merging, B ceases to exist as a separate entity, and A continues as the surviving corporation.

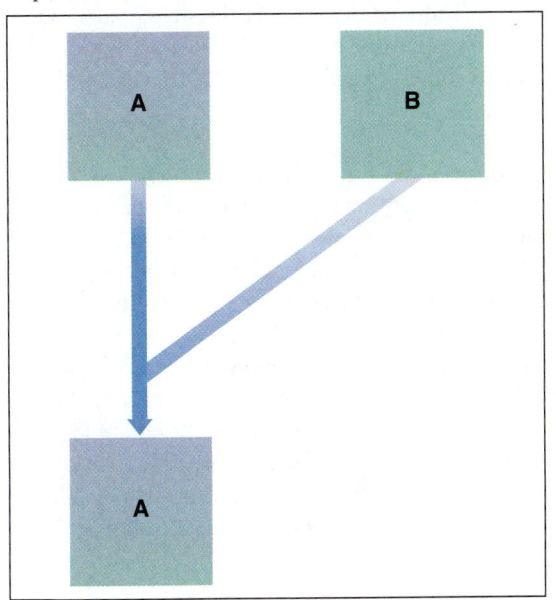

EXHIBIT 36–2   CONSOLIDATION

In this illustration, Corporations A and B consolidate to form an entirely new organization, Corporation C. In the process, A and B terminate, and C comes into existence as an entirely new entity.

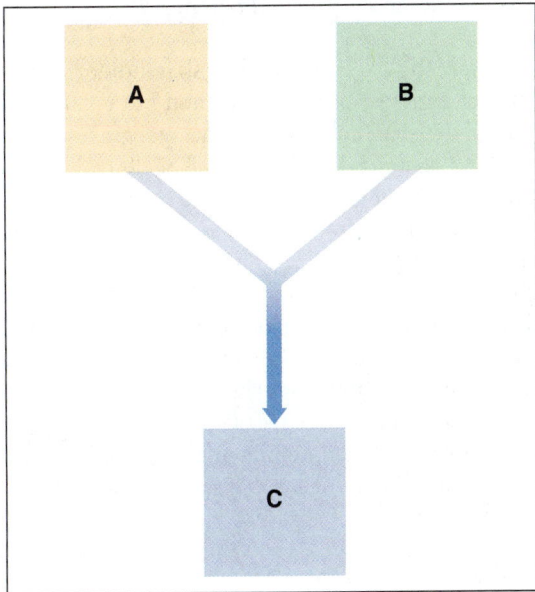

2. The shareholders of *each* corporation must vote approval of the plan at a shareholders' meeting. Most state statutes require the approval of two-thirds of the outstanding shares of voting stock, although some states require only a simple majority, and others require a four-fifths vote. Frequently, statutes require that each class of stock approve the merger; thus, the holders of nonvoting stock must also approve. A corporation's bylaws can dictate a stricter requirement.

3. Once approved by the directors and the shareholders of both corporations, the plan (articles of merger or consolidation) is filed, usually with the secretary of state.

4. When state formalities are satisfied, the state issues a certificate of merger to the surviving corporation or a certificate of consolidation to the newly consolidated corporation.

Short-Form Mergers.   RMBCA 11.04 provides a simplified procedure for the merger of a substantially owned subsidiary corporation into its parent corporation. Under these provisions, a **short-form merger**—also referred to as a **parent-subsidiary merger**—can be accomplished *without* the approval of the shareholders of either corporation. The short-form merger can be used only when the parent corporation owns at least 90 percent of the outstanding shares of each class of stock of the subsidiary corporation. The simplified procedure requires that a plan for the merger be approved by the board of directors of the parent corporation before it is filed with the state. A copy of the merger plan must be sent to each shareholder of record of the subsidiary corporation.

Appraisal Rights.   What if a shareholder disapproves of a merger or a consolidation but is outvoted by the other shareholders? The law recognizes that a dissenting shareholder should not be forced to become an unwilling shareholder in a corporation that is new or different from the one in which the shareholder originally invested. The shareholder has the right to dissent and may be entitled to be paid the fair value for the number of shares held on the date of the merger or consolidation. This right is referred to as the shareholder's **appraisal right.** If a shareholder is dissatisfied with the price received for the stock, he or she cannot sue the corporation on the ground of fraud or other illegal conduct; appraisal rights are the exclusive remedy.

Appraisal rights are available only when a state statute specifically provides for them. Appraisal rights normally extend to regular mergers, consolidations, short-form mergers, and sales of substantially all of the corporate assets not in the ordinary course of business.

Shareholders may lose their appraisal rights if they do not follow precisely the elaborate procedures prescribed by statute. When they lose the right to an appraisal, dissenting shareholders must go along with the transaction despite their objections. One of the usual requirements is that the dissenting shareholders file a written notice of dissent prior to the shareholders' vote on the proposed transaction. This notice of dissent is also basically a notice to all shareholders of the costs that dissenting shareholders may impose should the merger or consolidation be approved. In addition, after approval, the dissenting shareholders must make a written demand for payment and for the fair value of their shares.

Appraisal Rights and Shareholder Status.   Once a dissenting shareholder elects appraisal rights under a statute, in some jurisdictions the shareholder loses his or her shareholder status. Without that status, a shareholder cannot vote, receive dividends, or sue to enjoin whatever action prompted the dissent. In some of those jurisdictions, statutes provide or courts have held that shareholder status may be reinstated during the appraisal process (for example, if the shareholder decides to withdraw from the process and the corporation approves). In other jurisdictions, shareholder status may not be reinstated until the appraisal is concluded. Even if an individual loses his or her shareholder status, courts may allow the individual to sue on the ground of fraud or other illegal conduct associated with the merger.

Valuation of Shares.   Valuation of shares is often a point of contention between the dissenting shareholder and the corporation. RMBCA 13.01 provides that the "fair value of shares" normally is the value on the day prior to the date on which the vote was taken. The corporation must make a written offer to purchase a dissenting shareholder's stock, accompanying the offer with a current balance sheet and income statement for the corporation. If the shareholder and the corporation do not agree on the fair value, a court will determine it. How the fair value of shares should be determined was at issue in the following case.

CASE 36.1   Chokel v. First National Supermarkets, Inc.

Supreme Judicial Court
of Massachusetts,
Suffolk, 1996.
421 Mass. 631,
660 N.E.2d 644.

HISTORICAL AND SOCIAL SETTING   *Over the past fifty years, the number of small grocery stores has declined steadily. At the same time, the number of huge supermarkets has increased to more than 30,000. Although these supermarkets make up less than 20 percent of the total number of stores, their share of the market is more than 75 percent. The top ten supermarket chains make almost half of all grocery sales.*

BACKGROUND AND FACTS   *The management of First National Supermarkets, Inc., wanted to buy the company and offered the shareholders $24.45 per share. Most of the shareholders voted to accept the offer, but Jeffrey Chokel voted against it. Chokel later filed a suit in a Massachusetts state court to obtain an appraisal of his shares. The judge appraised the value at $29.78 per share, based in part on a price-earnings ratio of twenty.*[a] *First National appealed to the Supreme Judicial Court of Massachusetts, the state's highest court, arguing in part that the price-earnings ratio was too high.*

**IN THE LANGUAGE
OF THE COURT**

ABRAMS, Justice.
     *   *   *   *

     *   *   * The price-earnings ratio reflects the prospective financial condition of the corporation and the risk factor inherent in the corporation and the industry. It is usually selected by looking to the price-earnings ratios of comparable corporations.
     *   *   *   *

     *   *   * [On the date for determining the price of Chokel's shares, the] average for the supermarket industry was 12.75. The trial judge, rather than relying on the average *   *   * , chose to compare First National with the four comparable companies with the highest percentage growth in five-year projected earnings. With a projected 249% growth in five-year projected earnings, First National would have ranked second. The comparable companies with available price-earnings ratios all had *   *   * price-earnings ratios near twenty. *   *   *

     Given First National's projections and the price-earnings ratios of the most directly comparable companies, we believe the trial judge's choice of twenty as the price-earnings ratio to be within the range of reason.

**DECISION
AND REMEDY**

The Supreme Judicial Court of Massachusetts affirmed the decision of the lower court. The trial judge's appraisal of the value of the shares was reasonable.

a. A price-earnings ratio is calculated by dividing a stock's market price (per share) by its annual income (per share). The income may be based on past earnings, projected earnings, or a combination of the two.

SECTION 2

Purchase of Assets

When a corporation acquires all or substantially all of the assets of another corporation by direct purchase, the corporation purchasing the assets, or *acquiring corporation*, simply extends its ownership and control over more physical assets. Because no change in the legal entity occurs, the acquiring corporation is not required to obtain shareholder approval for the purchase.[3]

---

3. If the acquiring corporation plans to pay for the assets with its own corporate stock and not enough authorized unissued shares are available, the shareholders must vote to approve issuance of additional shares by amendment of the corporate articles. Also, acquiring corporations whose stock is traded on a national stock exchange can be required to obtain their own shareholders' approval if they plan to issue a significant number of shares, such as a number equal to 20 percent or more of the outstanding shares.

Although the acquiring corporation may not be required to obtain the shareholders' approval, the U.S. Department of Justice has issued guidelines that significantly constrain and often prohibit mergers that could result from a purchase of assets. These guidelines are part of the federal antitrust laws to enforce Section 7 of the Clayton Act (discussed in Chapter 45).

Note that the corporation that is *selling* all its assets is substantially changing its business position and perhaps its ability to carry out its corporate purposes. For that reason, the corporation whose assets are *acquired* must obtain approval from both its board of directors and its shareholders. In most states and under the RMBCA, a dissenting shareholder of the selling corporation can demand appraisal rights.

Generally, a corporation that purchases the assets of another corporation is not responsible for the liabilities of the selling corporation. Exceptions to this rule are made in the following circumstances:

1. When the purchasing corporation impliedly or expressly assumes the seller's liabilities.
2. When the sale amounts to what in fact is a merger or a consolidation.
3. When the purchaser continues the seller's business and retains the same personnel (same shareholders, directors, and officers).
4. When the sale is fraudulently executed to escape liability.

In any of these situations, the acquiring corporation will be held to have assumed both the assets and the liabilities of the selling corporation.

In the following case, the court was asked to determine whether a transfer of assets between two corporations was for the fraudulent purpose of escaping liability.

CASE 36.2

Eagle Pacific Insurance Co. v. Christensen Motor Yacht Corp.

Supreme Court of
Washington, 1998.
135 Wash.2d 894,
959 P.2d 1052.

BACKGROUND AND FACTS   *Christensen Motor Yacht Corporation (CMYC) was organized to build yachts. Eagle Pacific Insurance Company issued workers' compensation policies to CMYC but canceled the policies when CMYC failed to pay the premiums. CMYC had several contracts with buyers, but the yachts had not been completed, and CMYC lacked the ability to pay its debts. David Christensen, the chief executive officer and sole shareholder of CMYC, created a new corporation, Christensen Shipyards, Limited (CSL), to complete the boats. CMYC transferred its employees, facilities, and contracts to CSL. Meanwhile, claims had been filed against the Eagle policies, and Eagle filed a suit in a Washington state court against CMYC to collect the unpaid premiums. The court awarded Eagle $268,443. Because CMYC was insolvent, Eagle sought to recover the debt from others, including CSL as a successor corporation to CMYC. Christensen testified that he had effected the transfer between CMYC and CSL to avoid creditors and "save the business." The court ruled that CSL was liable for CMYC's debt to Eagle as a successor corporation. A state intermediate appellate court upheld the ruling. CSL appealed to the Washington Supreme Court.*

IN THE LANGUAGE OF THE COURT

DOLLIVER, Justice.
*   *   *   *

*   *   * CMYC's principal business purpose was the construction of yachts. In the course of the construction of the three yachts, CMYC incurred debts which it could not pay. With the transfer of the three yacht contracts to CSL, and CMYC's surrender of its employees and facilities to CSL, CMYC was stripped of its main potential source for future revenues. Christensen admits the yacht contracts were transferred to CSL to allow the continuation of construction on the yachts unhampered by creditors' efforts to collect unpaid bills.

Christensen's admitted reason for the transfer of assets from CMYC to CSL fits the definition of a fraudulent transfer. *   *   *

*   *   *   *

*   *   * *Transferring assets to another corporation to hinder or delay creditors is by definition a fraudulent transfer.* *   *   * In the course of conducting business and building yachts, CMYC incurred debts which Christensen sought to avoid by transferring the business to CSL. Because the assets were transferred to CSL to avoid the reach of the creditors, the transaction is fraudulent and successor liability attaches to CSL. The fact that the transaction was designed to "save the business" does not defeat imposition of successor liability. [Emphasis added.]

DECISION AND REMEDY *The Washington Supreme Court affirmed the lower court's judgment. The state supreme court held that the transfer of assets from CMYC to CSL fit the definition of a fraudulent transfer.*

SECTION 3

Purchase of Stock

An alternative to the purchase of another corporation's assets is the purchase of a substantial number of the voting shares of its stock. This enables the acquiring corporation to control the acquired corporation, or **target corporation.** The process of acquiring control over a corporation in this way is commonly referred to as a corporate **takeover.** The acquiring corporation deals directly with the shareholders in seeking to purchase the shares they hold.

When the acquiring corporation makes a public offer to all shareholders of the target corporation, it is called a **tender offer.** The price offered is generally higher than the market price of the target stock prior to the announcement of the tender offer. The higher price induces shareholders to tender (offer to sell) their shares to the acquiring firm. The tender offer can be conditioned on the receipt of a specified number of outstanding shares by a certain date. The offering corporation can make an *exchange* tender offer in which it offers target stockholders its own securities in exchange for their target stock. In a cash tender offer, the offering corporation offers cash in exchange for the target stock.

Federal securities laws strictly control the terms, duration, and circumstances under which most tender offers are made. In addition, a majority of states have passed takeover statutes that impose additional regulations on tender offers.

A firm may respond to a tender offer in numerous ways. Sometimes, a target firm's board of directors will see a tender offer as favorable and will recommend to the shareholders that they accept it. In contrast, to resist a takeover, a target company may make a *self-tender*, which is an offer to acquire stock from its own shareholders and thereby retain corporate control. Alternatively, a target corporation might resort to one of several other tactics to resist a takeover (see Exhibit 36–3). One commonly used tactic is known

EXHIBIT 36–3 THE TERMINOLOGY OF TAKEOVER DEFENSES

TERM	DEFINITION
Crown Jewel	When threatened with a takeover, management makes the company less attractive to the raider by selling to a third party the company's most valuable asset (the "crown jewel").
Golden Parachute	When a takeover is successful, top management is usually changed. With this in mind, a company may establish special termination or retirement benefits that must be paid to top managers if they are "retired." In other words, a departing high-level manager's parachute will be "golden" when he or she is forced to "bail out" of the company.
Greenmail	To regain control, a target company may pay a higher-than-market price to repurchase the stock that the acquiring corporation bought. When a takeover is attempted through a gradual accumulation of target stock rather than a tender offer, the intent may be to get the target company to buy back the shares at a premium price—a concept similar to blackmail.

EXHIBIT 36–3   THE TERMINOLOGY OF TAKEOVER DEFENSES (CONTINUED)

TERM	DEFINITION
Lobster Trap	Lobster traps are designed to catch large lobsters but to allow small lobsters to escape. In the "lobster trap" defense, holders of convertible securities (corporate bonds or stock that can be converted into common shares) are prohibited from converting the securities into common shares if the holders already own, or would own after conversion, 10 percent or more of the voting shares of stock.
Pac-Man	Named after the Atari video game, this is an aggressive defense by which the target corporation attempts its own takeover of the acquiring corporation.
Poison Pill	The target corporation issues to its stockholders rights to purchase additional shares at low prices when there is a takeover attempt. This makes the takeover undesirably or even prohibitively expensive for the acquiring corporation.
Scorched Earth	The target corporation sells off assets or divisions or takes out loans that it agrees to repay in the event of a takeover, thus making itself less financially attractive to the acquiring company.
Shark Repellent	To make a takeover more difficult, a target company may change its articles of incorporation or bylaws. For example, the bylaws may be amended to require that a large number of shareholders approve the firm's combination. This tactic casts the acquiring corporation in the role of a shark that must be repelled.
White Knight	The target corporation solicits a merger with a third party, which then makes a better (often simply a higher) tender offer to the target's shareholders. The third party that "rescues" the target is the "white knight."

as the "poison pill"—a target company gives its shareholders rights to purchase additional shares at low prices when there is a takeover attempt. The use of poison pills prevents takeovers by making them prohibitively expensive.

CONCEPT SUMMARY 36.1

METHODS OF EXPANDING CORPORATE OPERATIONS AND INTERESTS

Merger and Consolidation

1. *Merger*—The legal combination of two or more corporations, the result of which is that the surviving corporation acquires all the assets and obligations of the other corporation, which then ceases to exist.
2. *Consolidation*—The legal combination of two or more corporations, the result of which is that each corporation ceases to exist and a new one emerges. The new corporation assumes all the assets and obligations of the former corporations.
3. *Procedure*—Determined by state statutes. Basic requirements are the following:
   a. The board of directors of each corporation involved must approve the merger or consolidation plan.
   b. The shareholders of each corporation must approve the merger or consolidation plan at a shareholders' meeting.
   c. Articles of merger or consolidation (the plan) must be filed, usually with the secretary of state.
   d. The state issues a certificate of merger (or consolidation) to the surviving (or newly consolidated) corporation.
4. *Short-form merger (parent-subsidiary merger)*—Possible when the parent corporation owns at least 90 percent of the outstanding shares of each class of stock of the subsidiary corporation.

CONCEPT SUMMARY 36.1

METHODS OF EXPANDING CORPORATE OPERATIONS AND INTERESTS (*continued*)

Merger and Consolidation (continued)	a. Shareholder approval is not required. b. The merger must be approved only by the board of directors of the parent corporation. c. A copy of the merger plan must be sent to each shareholder of record. d. The merger plan must be filed with the state. 5. *Appraisal rights*—Rights of shareholders (given by state statute) to receive the *fair value* for their shares when a merger or consolidation takes place. If the shareholder and the corporation do not agree on the fair value, a court will determine it.
Purchase of Assets	A purchase of assets occurs when one corporation acquires all or substantially all of the assets of another corporation. 1. *Acquiring corporation*—The acquiring (purchasing) corporation is not required to obtain shareholder approval; the corporation is merely increasing its assets, and no fundamental business change occurs. 2. *Acquired corporation*—The acquired (purchased) corporation is required to obtain the approval of both its directors and its shareholders for the sale of its assets, because this creates a substantial change in the corporation's business position.
Purchase of Stock	A purchase of stock occurs when one corporation acquires a substantial number of the voting shares of the stock of another (target) corporation. 1. *Tender offer*—A public offer to all shareholders of the target corporation to purchase its stock at a price generally higher than the market price of the target stock prior to the announcement of the tender offer. Federal and state securities laws strictly control the terms, duration, and circumstances under which most tender offers are made. 2. *Target responses*—Ways in which target corporations respond to takeover bids. These include self-tender (the target firm's offer to acquire its own shareholders' stock) and numerous other strategies (see Exhibit 36–3).

SECTION 4

Termination

Termination of a corporate life, like termination of a partnership, has two phases—dissolution and liquidation. **Dissolution** is the legal death of the artificial "person" of the corporation. **Liquidation** is the process by which corporate assets are converted into cash and distributed among creditors and shareholders according to specific rules of preference.[4]

DISSOLUTION

Dissolution can be brought about voluntarily by the directors and shareholders or involuntarily by the state or through a court's order. Once a corporation is dissolved, either voluntarily or involuntarily, its corporate existence is ended except for the process of winding up corporate affairs and distributing corporate assets.

Voluntary Dissolution. There are basically two ways in which a corporation can be voluntarily dissolved once it has issued shares and commenced business operations.[5] First, the shareholders can initiate

---

4. On dissolution, the liquidated assets are first used to pay creditors. Any remaining assets are distributed to shareholders according to their respective stock rights; preferred stock has priority over common stock, generally by charter.

5. If the corporation was formed but has not yet undertaken any business or issued any shares, a majority of the incorporators can dissolve the corporation relatively simply—by filing articles of dissolution with the secretary of state's office, which will then issue a certificate of dissolution.

corporate dissolution proceedings by a unanimous vote to dissolve the corporation.[6] Second, the directors can propose that the corporation be dissolved and submit the proposal to the shareholders for a vote at a shareholders' annual meeting or a specially called shareholders' meeting.

Under RMBCA 14.03, once a decision is reached to dissolve the corporation, the corporation must file *articles of dissolution* with the secretary of state. These articles must include the name of the corporation, the date on which the dissolution was authorized, and how the dissolution was authorized. The effective date of dissolution will be the date of the articles of dissolution. The corporation must also notify the creditors of the dissolution and establish a date (at least 120 days following the date of dissolution) by which all claims against the corporation must be received [RMBCA 14.06].

Involuntary Dissolution. Corporations are creatures of statute, as stated earlier. Just as the state can allow a corporation to come into existence, so can it end that existence. The state, in an action brought by the secretary of state or the state attorney general, can dissolve a corporation for any of the following reasons [RMBCA 14.20]:

1. Failure of the corporation to comply with administrative requirements (such as failure to pay annual taxes, submit an annual report, or have a designated registered agent).

2. Procurement of a corporate charter through fraud or misrepresentation on the state.
3. Abuse of corporate powers (*ultra vires* acts).
4. Violation of the state criminal code after a demand to discontinue the violation has been made by the secretary of state.
5. Failure to commence business operations.
6. Abandonment of operations before starting up.

Corporate statutory provisions in some states provide that the articles of incorporation of a close corporation can empower any shareholder to dissolve the corporation at will or on the occurrence of a specified event—such as the death of another shareholder. This provides a shareholder in a close corporation with the same power to dissolve his or her business organization as a partner in a partnership.

Sometimes, an involuntary dissolution of a corporation is necessary—for example, when a board of directors is deadlocked. Courts hesitate to order involuntary dissolution in such circumstances unless there is specific statutory authorization to do so, but if the deadlock cannot be resolved by the shareholders and if it will irreparably injure the corporation, the court will proceed with an involuntary dissolution. Courts can also dissolve a corporation for mismanagement [RMBCA 14.30].

In the following case, a shareholder sued to have a corporation dissolved, because he and the other shareholders could not suspend their disputes in order to elect directors or even to choose a neutral third party to, in effect, arbitrate and select directors for them.

---

6. Delaware Code Section 275(c).

CASE 36.3   Chance v. Norwalk Fast Oil, Inc.

Appellate Court of
Connecticut, 1999.
55 Conn.App. 272,
739 A.2d 1275.

BACKGROUND AND FACTS   *Norwalk Fast Oil, Inc., was incorporated in Connecticut. Albert Chance owned 40 percent of the stock and 50 percent of the voting rights. Richard Kosminoff also held 40 percent of the stock with 50 percent of the voting rights. Seymour and Morris Epstein each owned 10 percent of the stock but gave their voting rights to Chance and Kosminoff in equal shares. A shareholders' agreement provided that "in the event that a stalemate is reached after tallying the votes on any substantive issue affecting the Corporation, then it is hereby agreed that the stalemate shall be broken by Chance and Kosminoff each selecting the same third person to whom the proposed question shall be submitted, and his decision on the matter shall be binding upon the Corporation and all of its shareholders." In 1990, disputes, which led to litigation, arose between the shareholders, and they stopped holding annual meetings. In 1997, Chance called a special shareholders' meeting to elect directors. Chance and Kosminoff could not agree on whom to elect, nor could they agree, according to the stalemate provision, to whom they should submit the issue. When they were no longer on speaking terms,*

Chance filed a suit in a Connecticut state court against Norwalk, Kosminoff, and the Epsteins, asking for the dissolution of Norwalk. The defendants filed a motion to dismiss on the basis of the stalemate provision. The court ordered Norwalk dissolved. The defendants appealed to a state intermediate appellate court.

IN THE LANGUAGE OF THE COURT

LAVERY, J. [Judge]

* * * *

It is fundamental to the concept of a corporation that its affairs are to be controlled by a board of directors elected by a majority of the stockholders * * * . In the instant case [the case before the court], there is no such board and no such board can be elected. Consequently, there has not been and cannot be any deliberative control of the company by a board of directors. The corporation is a mere shell inhabited by a business * * * . A receiver is properly appointed when there are such dissensions in the governing body of a corporation, or between sets of stockholders, each owning an equal amount of stock, that the corporation ceases to function in the manner provided for by its own by-laws and in accordance with the statutes relating to corporations. * * * For more than five years since the last annual meeting, the parties have failed to hold an annual meeting and to elect successor directors. Chance's effort to hold a special meeting of the corporation to elect successor directors is irrelevant. Furthermore, the parties created the stalemate themselves when they invited its possibility by entering into an agreement whereby control of the corporation was divided equally among them. [Emphasis added.]

The trial court, therefore, properly concluded that there is no more chance of breaking the deadlock between the parties in the future than there has been in the past and ordered the winding-up of the corporation.

* * * *

The [defendants claim] that the trial court improperly denied their motion to dismiss Chance's cause of action because it was barred by the stalemate provision of the shareholder agreement. We do not agree.

* * * *

The language of the stalemate provision clearly states that any stalemate shall be broken by Chance's and Kosminoff's each selecting the same third person to whom the proposed question shall be submitted. Given the five years of litigation among and between the parties, their failure to speak or to hold an annual meeting of the corporation and the equal voting power created by the parties, it is likely that the parties will never be able to break their deadlock. The trial court properly found the interaction between Chance and Kosminoff to be a perpetual power struggle * * * . The conflict was the result of the parties' own making and the trial court properly stepped in to break the stalemate by dissolving the corporation.

DECISION AND REMEDY

The state intermediate appellate court affirmed the judgment of the lower court. Norwalk could not function with control equally divided between shareholders who could not agree on a board of directors, could not hold annual shareholders' meetings, were involved in litigation against each other, and were not on speaking terms.

LIQUIDATION

When dissolution takes place by voluntary action, the members of the board of directors act as trustees of the corporate assets. As trustees, they are responsible for winding up the affairs of the corporation for the benefit of corporate creditors and shareholders. This makes the board members personally liable for any breach of their fiduciary trustee duties.

Liquidation can be accomplished without court supervision unless the members of the board do not wish to act in this capacity or unless shareholders or creditors can show cause to the court why the board should not be permitted to assume the trustee function. In either case, the court will appoint a **receiver** to wind up the corporate affairs and liquidate corporate assets. A receiver is always appointed by the court if the dissolution is involuntary.

TERMS AND CONCEPTS TO REVIEW

appraisal right 680	merger 678	surviving corporation 678
consolidation 679	parent-subsidiary merger 680	takeover 683
dissolution 685	receiver 687	target corporation 683
liquidation 685	short-form merger 680	tender offer 683

QUESTIONS AND CASE PROBLEMS

36–1. CORPORATE COMBINATIONS. Gretz is chairperson of the board of directors of Faraday, Inc., and Williams is chairperson of the board of directors of Firebrand, Inc. Faraday is a manufacturing corporation, and Firebrand is a transportation corporation. Gretz and Williams meet to consider the possibility of combining their corporations and activities into a single corporate entity. They consider two alternative courses of action: (1) acquisition by Faraday of all the stock and assets of Firebrand and (2) combination of the two corporations to form a new corporation, Farabrand, Inc. Both chairpersons are concerned about the necessity of formal transfer of property, liability for existing debts, and the problem of amending articles of incorporation. Discuss what the two proposed combinations are called and what legal effect each has on the transfer of property, the liabilities of the combined corporations, and the need to amend the articles of incorporation.

36–2. SHAREHOLDERS' RIGHTS. Alir owns 10,000 shares of Ajax Corp. Her shares represent a 10 percent ownership in Ajax. Zeta Corp. is interested in acquiring Ajax in a merger, and the board of directors of each corporation has approved the merger. The shareholders of Zeta have already approved the acquisition, and Ajax has called for a shareholders' meeting to approve the merger. Alir disapproves of the merger and does not want to accept Zeta shares for the Ajax shares she holds. The market price of Ajax shares is $20 per share the day before the shareholder vote and drops to $16 on the day the shareholders of Ajax approve the merger. Discuss Alir's rights in this matter, beginning with the notice of the proposed merger.

36–3. PURCHASE OF ASSETS. Green Corp. wants to acquire all the assets of Red Dot Corp. Green plans to pay for the assets by issuing its own corporate stock. Green's board of directors has already approved the merger. Discuss whether shareholder approval is required for this merger.

36–4. CORPORATE EXPANSION. Alitech Corp. is a small midwestern business that owns a valuable patent. Alitech has approximately 1,000 shareholders with 100,000 authorized and outstanding shares. Block Corp. would like to have use of the patent, but Alitech refuses to give Block a license. Block has tried to acquire Alitech by purchasing Alitech's assets, but Alitech's board of directors has refused to approve the acquisition. Alitech's shares are presently selling for $5 per share. Discuss how Block Corp. might proceed to gain the control and use of Alitech's patent.

36–5. TERMINATION. Saunders Corp. has been losing money for several years but still has valuable fixed assets. The shareholders see little hope that the corporation will ever make a profit. Another corporation, Topway Corp., has failed to pay state taxes for several years or to file annual reports as required by statute. In addition, Topway is accused of being guilty of gross and persistent *ultra vires* acts. Discuss whether these corporations will be terminated and how the assets of each would be handled on dissolution.

36–6. PURCHASE OF ASSETS. MRS Manufacturing, Inc., manufactured tractors, which it sold to Glades Equipment, Inc. Glades Equipment sold one of the tractors to the U.S. Sugar Corp. Later, Glade and Grove Supply, Inc., bought the Glades Equipment dealership under a contract that stated the sale covered only such property "as [Glades Equipment] has on hand at the time of the . . . sale." Daniel Brown, an employee of the U.S. Sugar Corp., was operating an MRS tractor when it rolled over and killed him. His wife, Patricia, filed a product-liability suit against Glade and Grove, among others. What factors will the court consider in determining whether Glade and Grove is liable? [*Brown v. Glade and Grove Supply, Inc.*, 647 So.2d 1033 (Fla.App. 1994)]

36–7. APPRAISAL RIGHTS. Travelers Corp. announced that it would merge with Primerica Corp. At a special shareholders' meeting, a vote of the Travelers shareholders revealed that 95 percent approved of the merger. Robert Brandt and other shareholders who did not approve of the merger sued Travelers and others, complaining that the defendants had not obtained "the highest possible price for shareholders." Travelers asked the court to dismiss the suit, contending that Brandt and the others had, as a remedy for their complaint, their statutory appraisal rights. On what basis might the court dismiss the suit? Discuss. [*Brandt v. Travelers Corp.*, 44 Conn.Supp. 12, 665 A.2d 616 (1995)]

36–8. CORPORATE DISSOLUTION. Jerry Yarmouth incorporated J&R Interiors, Inc., and was its president, secretary, and sole shareholder. J&R failed to file annual reports and pay annual fees, however, and was involuntarily dissolved by the state. More than a year later, Yarmouth bought a workbench in J&R's name from Equipto Division of Aurora Equipment Co. When the price was not paid, Equipto filed a suit in a Washington state court against Yarmouth, claiming that he was personally liable for payment. Yarmouth argued that he was not personally liable because he had acted as an agent for J&R. Does a corporation continue to exist after it is dissolved? If so, can it continue to conduct business? In whose favor should the court rule in this case, and why? [*Equipto Division Aurora Equipment Co. v. Yarmouth,* 83 Wash.App. 817, 924 P.2d 405 (1996)]

36–9. DISSOLUTION. In 1988, Farad Mohammed and Syed Parveen formed Hina Pharmacy, Health & Beauty Aids, Inc., to operate a pharmacy in New York. Parveen, an experienced pharmacist, contributed his expertise and $7,000. Mohammed contributed $120,000. Each took 50 percent of the Hina stock. Mohammed assigned his shares to his brother Azam, and Syed assigned his to his wife Aisha. A dispute soon arose over the disparity in capital contributions. The parties held only one shareholders' meeting, and they never attempted to elect directors. Syed later claimed that Azam, who exercised sole control over the daily management of Hina, kept 80 percent of the profits. Azam argued that Syed had agreed to work for 20 percent of the profits plus a salary. Syed stopped working at the pharmacy in 1994. Aisha filed a petition in a New York state court to dissolve Hina.

Could the court grant the petition? If so, on what basis? If not, why not? [*In re Parveen,* 259 A.D.2d 389, 687 N.Y.S.2d 90 (1 Dept. 1999)]

36–10. IN YOUR COURT

When EG&G, Inc., took over E. Van Noorden Co., the manufacturer of Vanco brand skylights, Van Noorden shareholders traded their stock for EG&G stock. Van Noorden ceased to exist. EG&G assumed its customer and supplier relationships and acquired all of its assets. EG&G continued to make Vanco skylights, using the same factory and employees, as well as at least two key Van Noorden officers. EG&G also assumed all of the obligations of Van Noorden necessary for uninterrupted operations. Clarence Sedbrook fell through a Vanco skylight on a hospital roof and suffered permanent injuries. Sedbrook and his family filed a suit in a Wisconsin state court against Zimmerman Design Group, Ltd. (the firm that designed the roof), EG&G, and others. EG&G asked to be dismissed from the suit on the ground that Van Noorden had manufactured the skylight before EG&G purchased Van Noorden's assets. Assume that you are the judge in the trial court hearing this case and answer the following questions:

(a) What factors will you consider in determining whether EG&G should be liable for Sedbrook's injury?

(b) What will your ruling be, and how will you justify your decision?

LAW ON THE WEB

For updated links to resources available on the Web, as well as a variety of other materials, visit this text's Web site at http://wbl.westbuslaw.com.

You may be able to find your state's statutory requirements for merger and consolidation procedures at

http://wwwsecure.law.cornell.edu/topics/state_statutes.html

The court opinions of Delaware's Court of Chancery, which is widely considered to be the nation's premier trial court for corporate law, are now available on the Web in a searchable database offered by the Delaware Corporate Law Clearinghouse. The site also offers valuable links to other sites dealing with corporate law and litigation. Go to

http://corporate-law.widener.edu

LEGAL RESEARCH EXERCISES ON THE WEB

Go to http://wbl.westbuslaw.com, the Web site that accompanies this text. Select "Internet Applications," and then click on "Chapter 36." There you will find the following Internet research exercise that you can perform to learn more about mergers:

Activity 36–1: Mergers

CHAPTER 37

Corporations— Securities Regulation and Investor Protection

THE STOCK MARKET CRASH OF OCTOBER 29, 1929, and the ensuing economic depression caused the public to focus on the importance of securities markets for the economic well-being of the nation. Congress was pressured to regulate securities trading, and the result was the Securities Act of 1933[1] and the Securities Exchange Act of 1934.[2] Both acts were designed to provide investors with more information to help them make buying and selling decisions about *securities*—generally defined as any documents evidencing corporate ownership (stock) or debts (bonds)—and to prohibit deceptive, unfair, and manipulative practices in the purchase and sale of securities. Basically, the 1933 act regulates the initial sales of corporate securities by businesses, and the 1934 act regulates subsequent purchases and sales of securities once they have been issued.

This chapter discusses the nature of federal securities regulation and its effect on the business world. We begin by looking at the federal administrative agency that regulates securities transactions, the Securities and Exchange Commission. The liability of accountants and attorneys for violations of the securities laws is discussed in more detail in Chapter 51.

SECTION 1

The Securities and Exchange Commission

The 1934 act created the Securities and Exchange Commission (SEC) as an independent regulatory agency whose function was to administer the 1933 and 1934 acts. The SEC plays a key role in interpreting the provisions of these acts (and their amendments) and in creating regulations governing the purchase and sale of securities.

THE BASIC FUNCTIONS OF THE SEC

The SEC regulates the securities industry by undertaking the following activities:

---

1. 15 U.S.C. Sections 77a–77aa.
2. 15 U.S.C. Sections 78a–78mm.

1. Requiring disclosure of facts concerning offerings of securities listed on national securities exchanges and offerings of certain securities traded over the counter (OTC).

2. Regulating the trade in securities on the national and regional securities exchanges and in the OTC markets.

3. Investigating securities fraud.

4. Requiring the registration of securities brokers, dealers, and investment advisers and regulating their activities.

5. Supervising activities conducted by mutual funds companies.

6. Recommending administrative sanctions, injunctive remedies, and criminal prosecution in cases involving violations of securities laws. (The Fraud Section of the Criminal Division of the Department of Justice prosecutes violations of federal securities laws.)

THE REGULATORY POWERS OF THE SEC

From the time of its creation until the present, the SEC's regulatory functions have gradually been increased by legislation granting it authority in different areas. During the 1990s, for example, Congress passed several acts that have significantly expanded the SEC's powers.

To further curb securities fraud, the Securities Enforcement Remedies and Penny Stock Reform Act of 1990[3] amended existing securities laws to expand greatly the types of securities violation cases that SEC administrative law judges can hear and the SEC's enforcement options. The act also provides that courts can bar persons who have engaged in securities fraud from serving as officers and directors of publicly held corporations.

The Securities Acts Amendments of 1990 authorized the SEC to seek sanctions against those who violate foreign securities laws.[4] These amendments increase the ability of the SEC to cooperate in international enforcement of securities laws. Under the Market Reform Act of 1990, the SEC can suspend trading in securities in the event that prices rise and fall excessively in a short period of time.[5]

The National Securities Markets Improvement Act of 1996 expanded the power of the SEC to exempt persons, securities, and transactions from the requirements of the securities laws.[6] (This part of the act is also known as the Capital Markets Efficiency Act.) The act also limited the authority of the states to regulate certain securities transactions, as well as particular investment advisory firms.[7]

Over the years, as more and more SEC rules were issued, the body of regulations governing securities transactions became increasingly cumbersome and complex. Congress and the SEC are now in the process of eliminating some rules, revising others, and generally attempting to streamline the regulatory process to make it more efficient and more relevant to today's securities trading practices.

SECTION 2

The Securities Act of 1933

As mentioned, the Securities Act of 1933 governs initial sales of stock by businesses. The act was designed to prohibit various forms of fraud and to stabilize the securities industry by requiring that all essential information concerning the issuance of securities be made available to the investing public.

Basically, the courts have interpreted the act's definition of what constitutes a security[8] to mean that a security exists in any transaction in which a person (1) invests (2) in a common enterprise (3) reasonably expecting profits (4) derived *primarily* or *substantially* from others' managerial or entrepreneurial efforts.[9]

For our purposes, it is probably most convenient to think of securities in their most common form—stocks and bonds issued by corporations. Bear in mind, though, that securities can take many forms and have been held to include whiskey, cosmetics, worms, beavers, boats, vacuum cleaners, muskrats, and cemetery lots, as well as investment contracts in condominiums, franchises, limited partnerships, oil or gas or other mineral rights, and farm animals accompanied by care agreements.

REGISTRATION STATEMENT

Section 5 of the Securities Act of 1933 broadly provides that if a security does not qualify for an exemption, that

---

3. 15 U.S.C. Section 77g.
4. See, for example, 15 U.S.C. Section 78o(b)(4)(B).
5. 15 U.S.C. Section 78i(h).

6. 15 U.S.C. Sections 77z-3, 78mm.
7. 15 U.S.C. Section 80b-3a.
8. See 15 U.S.C. Section 77b(a)(1).
9. *SEC v. W. J. Howey Co.*, 328 U.S. 293, 66 S.Ct. 1100, 90 L.Ed. 1244 (1946).

security must be *registered* before it is offered to the public either through the mails or through any facility of interstate commerce, including securities exchanges. Issuing corporations must file a *registration statement* with the SEC. Investors must be provided with a prospectus that describes the security being sold, the issuing corporation, and the risk attaching to the security. In principle, the registration statement and the prospectus supply sufficient information to enable unsophisticated investors to evaluate the financial risk involved.

Contents of the Registration Statement.   The registration statement must include the following:

1. A description of the significant provisions of the security offered for sale, including the relationship between that security and the other capital securities of the registrant. Also, the corporation must disclose how it intends to use the proceeds of the sale.
2. A description of the registrant's properties and business.
3. A description of the management of the registrant; its security holdings; and its remuneration and other benefits, including pensions and stock options. Any interests of directors or officers in any material transactions with the corporation must be disclosed.
4. A financial statement certified by an independent public accounting firm.
5. A description of pending lawsuits.

Other Requirements.   Before filing the registration statement and the prospectus with the SEC, the corporation is allowed to obtain an underwriter who will monitor the distribution of the new issue. There is a twenty-day waiting period (which can be accelerated by the SEC) after registration before the sale can take place. During this period, oral offers between interested investors and the issuing corporation concerning the purchase and sale of the proposed securities may take place, and very limited written advertising is allowed. At this time, what is known as a **red herring** prospectus may be distributed. It gets its name from the red legend printed across it stating that the registration has been filed but has not yet become effective.

After the waiting period, the registered securities can be legally bought and sold. Written advertising is allowed in the form of a so-called **tombstone ad,** so named because historically the format resembled a tombstone. Such ads simply tell the investor where and how to obtain a prospectus. Normally, any other type of advertising is prohibited.

EXEMPT SECURITIES

A number of specific securities are exempt from the registration requirements of the Securities Act of 1933. These securities—which can also generally be resold without being registered—include the following:[10]

1. All bank securities sold prior to July 27, 1933.
2. Commercial paper, if the maturity date does not exceed nine months.
3. Securities of charitable organizations.
4. Securities resulting from a corporate reorganization issued for exchange with the issuer's existing security holders and certificates issued by trustees, receivers, or debtors in possession under the bankruptcy laws (bankruptcy was discussed in Chapter 30).
5. Securities issued exclusively for exchange with the issuer's existing security holders, provided no commission is paid (for example, stock dividends and stock splits).
6. Securities issued to finance the acquisition of railroad equipment.
7. Any insurance, endowment, or annuity contract issued by a state-regulated insurance company.
8. Government-issued securities.
9. Securities issued by banks, savings and loan associations, farmers' cooperatives, and similar institutions subject to supervision by governmental authorities.
10. In consideration of the "small amount involved,"[11] an issuer's offer of up to $5 million in securities in any twelve-month period.

For the last exemption, under Regulation A,[12] the issuer must file with the SEC a notice of the issue and an offering circular, which must also be provided to investors before the sale. This is a much simpler and less expensive process than the procedures associated with full registration. Companies are allowed to "test the waters" for potential interest before preparing the offering circular. (To *test the waters* means to determine potential interest without actually selling any securities or requiring any commitment on the part of those who are interested.) Small-business issuers (companies with less than $25 million in annual revenues and less than $25 million in outstanding voting stock) can also utilize an integrated registration and reporting system that uses simpler forms than the full registration system.

10. 15 U.S.C. Section 77c.
11. 15 U.S.C. Section 77c(b).
12. 17 C.F.R. Sections 230.251–230.263.

Exhibit 37–1 summarizes the securities and transactions (discussed next) that are exempt from the registration requirements under the Securities Act of 1933 and SEC regulations.

EXEMPT TRANSACTIONS

An issuer of securities that are not exempt under any of the categories listed above can avoid the high cost and complicated procedures associated with registration by taking advantage of certain *exempt transactions*. These exemptions are very broad, and thus many sales occur without registration. Because there is some overlap in the coverage of the exemptions, an offering may qualify for more than one.

Small Offerings—Regulation D. The SEC's Regulation D contains four separate exemptions from

registration requirements for limited offers (offers that either involve a small amount of money or are made in a limited manner). Regulation D provides that any of these offerings made during any twelve-month period are exempt from the registration requirements.

Rule 504. Noninvestment company offerings up to $1 million in any twelve-month period are exempt.[13] In contrast to investment companies (discussed later in this chapter), noninvestment companies are firms that are not engaged primarily in the business of investing or trading in securities.

---

13. 17 C.F.R. Section 230.504. Rule 504 is the exemption used by most small businesses, but that could change under new SEC Rule 1001. This rule permits, under certain circumstances, "testing the waters" for offerings of up to $5 million *per transaction*. These offerings, however, can be made only to "qualified purchasers" (knowledgeable, sophisticated investors).

EXHIBIT 37–1   EXEMPTIONS UNDER THE 1933 ACT FOR SECURITIES OFFERINGS BY BUSINESSES

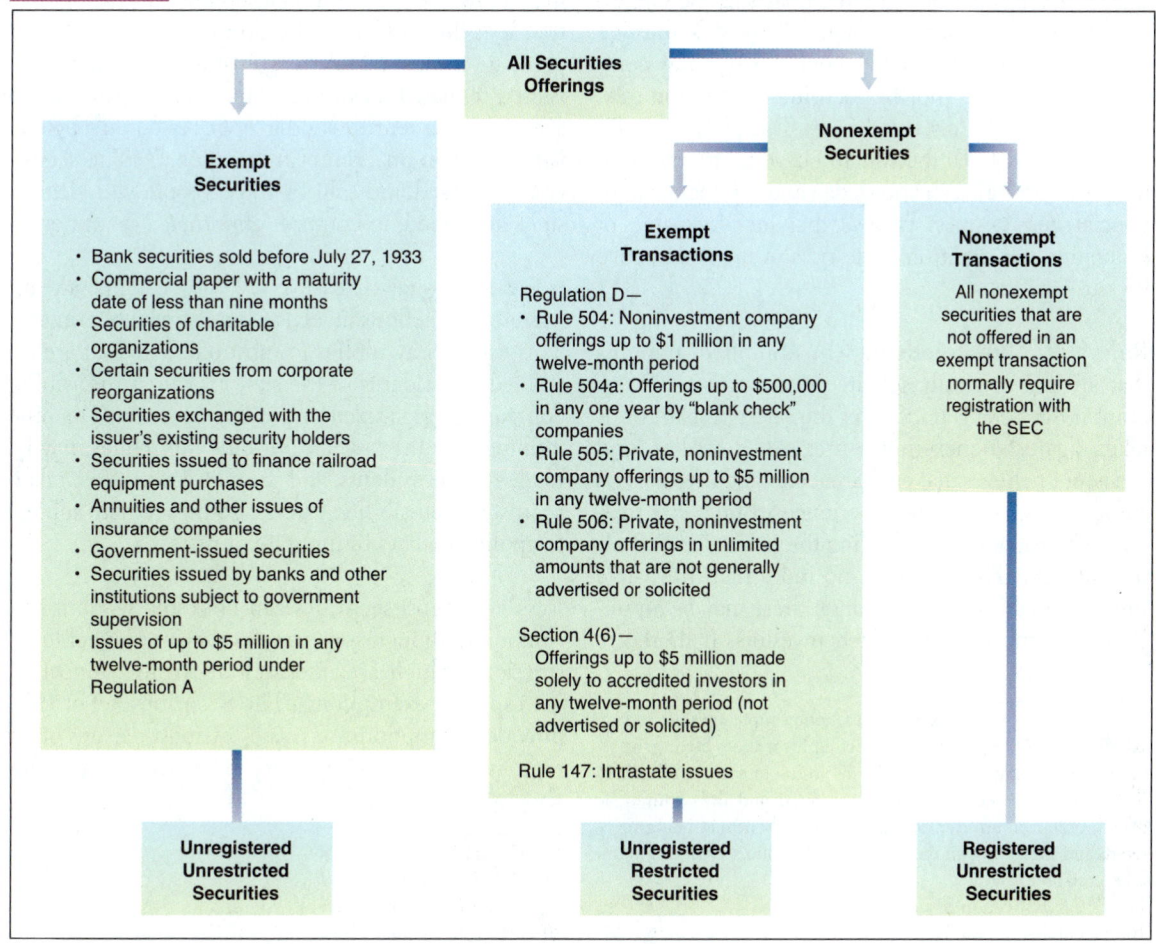

All Securities Offerings

Exempt Securities

- Bank securities sold before July 27, 1933
- Commercial paper with a maturity date of less than nine months
- Securities of charitable organizations
- Certain securities from corporate reorganizations
- Securities exchanged with the issuer's existing security holders
- Securities issued to finance railroad equipment purchases
- Annuities and other issues of insurance companies
- Government-issued securities
- Securities issued by banks and other institutions subject to government supervision
- Issues of up to $5 million in any twelve-month period under Regulation A

Unregistered Unrestricted Securities

Nonexempt Securities

Exempt Transactions

Regulation D—
- Rule 504: Noninvestment company offerings up to $1 million in any twelve-month period
- Rule 504a: Offerings up to $500,000 in any one year by "blank check" companies
- Rule 505: Private, noninvestment company offerings up to $5 million in any twelve-month period
- Rule 506: Private, noninvestment company offerings in unlimited amounts that are not generally advertised or solicited

Section 4(6)—
Offerings up to $5 million made solely to accredited investors in any twelve-month period (not advertised or solicited)

Rule 147: Intrastate issues

Unregistered Restricted Securities

Nonexempt Transactions

All nonexempt securities that are not offered in an exempt transaction normally require registration with the SEC

Registered Unrestricted Securities

Rule 504a. Offerings up to $500,000 in any one year by so-called blank check companies—companies with no specific business plans except to locate and acquire presently unknown businesses or opportunities—are exempt if no general solicitation or advertising is used; the SEC is notified of the sales; and precaution is taken against nonexempt, unregistered resales.[14] The limits on advertising and unregistered resales do not apply if the offering is made solely in states that provide for registration and disclosure and the securities are sold in compliance with those provisions.[15]

Rule 505. Private, noninvestment company offerings up to $5 million in any twelve-month period are exempt, regardless of the number of **accredited investors** (banks, insurance companies, investment companies, the issuer's executive officers and directors, and persons whose income or net worth exceeds certain limits), so long as there are no more than thirty-five unaccredited investors; no general solicitation or advertising is used; the SEC is notified of the sales; and precaution is taken against nonexempt, unregistered resales. If the sale involves *any* unaccredited investors, *all* investors must be given material information about the offering company, its business, and the securities before the sale. Unlike Rule 506 (discussed next), Rule 505 includes no requirement that the issuer believe each unaccredited investor "has such knowledge and experience in financial and business matters that he is capable of evaluating the merits and the risks of the prospective investment."[16]

Rule 506. Private offerings in unlimited amounts that are not generally solicited or advertised are exempt if the SEC is notified of the sales; precaution is taken against nonexempt, unregistered resales; and the issuer believes that each unaccredited investor has sufficient knowledge or experience in financial matters to be capable of evaluating the investment's merits and risks. There may be no more than thirty-five unaccredited investors, although there may be an unlimited number of accredited investors. If there are

any unaccredited investors, the issuer must provide to all purchasers material information about itself, its business, and the securities before the sale.[17]

This exemption is perhaps most important to those firms that want to raise funds through the sale of securities without registering them. It is often referred to as the *private placement* exemption, because it exempts "transactions not involving any public offering."[18] This provision applies to private offerings to a limited number of persons who are sufficiently sophisticated and in a sufficiently strong bargaining position to be able to assume the risk of the investment (and who thus have no need for federal registration protection), as well as to private offerings to similarly situated institutional investors.

Small Offerings—Section 4(6). Under Section 4(6) of the Securities Act of 1933, an offer made *solely* to accredited investors is exempt if its amount is not more than $5 million. Any number of accredited investors may participate, but no unaccredited investors may do so. No general solicitation or advertising may be used; the SEC must be notified of all sales; and precaution must be taken against nonexempt, unregistered resales. Precaution is necessary because these are *restricted* securities and may be resold only by registration or in an exempt transaction.[19] (The securities purchased and sold by most people who deal in stock are called, in contrast, *unrestricted* securities.)

Intrastate Issues—Rule 147. Also exempt are intrastate transactions involving purely local offerings.[20] This exemption applies to most offerings that are restricted to residents of the state in which the issuing company is organized and doing business. For nine months after the last sale, virtually no resales may be made to nonresidents, and precautions must be taken against this possibility. These offerings remain subject to applicable laws in the state of issue.

Resales. Most securities can be resold without registration (although some resales may be subject to restrictions, which are discussed above in connection with specific exemptions). The Securities Act of 1933 provides exemptions for resales by most persons other than issuers or underwriters. The average investor

---

14. Precautions to be taken against nonexempt, unregistered resales include asking the investor whether he or she is buying the securities for others; before the sale, disclosing to each purchaser in writing that the securities are unregistered and thus cannot be resold, except in an exempt transaction, without first being registered; and indicating on the certificates that the securities are unregistered and restricted.
15. 17 C.F.R. Section 230.504a.
16. 17 C.F.R. Section 230.505.

17. 17 C.F.R. Section 230.506.
18. 15 U.S.C. Section 77d(2).
19. 15 U.S.C. Section 77d(6).
20. 15 U.S.C. Section 77c(a)(11); 17 C.F.R. Section 230.147.

who sells shares of stock does not have to file a registration statement with the SEC. Resales of restricted securities acquired under Rule 504a, Rule 505, Rule 506, or Section 4(6), however, trigger the registration requirements unless the party selling them complies with Rule 144 or Rule 144A. These rules are sometimes referred to as "safe harbors."

Rule 144. Rule 144 exempts restricted securities from registration on resale if there is adequate current public information about the issuer, the person selling the securities has owned them for at least one year, they are sold in certain limited amounts in unsolicited brokers' transactions, and the SEC is given notice of the resale.[21] "Adequate current public information" consists of the reports that certain companies are required to file under the Securities Exchange Act of 1934. A person who has owned the securities for at least two years is subject to none of these requirements, unless the person is an affiliate. An *affiliate* is one who controls, is controlled by, or is in common control with the issuer. Sales of *nonrestricted* securities by an affiliate are also subject to the requirements for an exemption under Rule 144 (except that the affiliate need not have owned the securities for at least two years).

Rule 144A. Securities that at the time of issue are not of the same class as securities listed on a national securities exchange or quoted in a U.S. automated interdealer quotation system may be resold under Rule 144A.[22] They may be sold only to a qualified institutional buyer (an institution, such as an insurance company, an investment company, or a bank, that owns and invests at least $100 million in securities). The seller must take reasonable steps to ensure that the buyer knows that the seller is relying on the exemption under Rule 144A. A sample restricted stock certificate is shown in Exhibit 37–2 on page 696.

VIOLATIONS OF THE 1933 ACT

It is a violation of the Securities Act of 1933 to intentionally defraud investors by misrepresenting or omitting facts in a registration statement or prospectus. Liability is also imposed on those who are negligent for not discovering the fraud. Selling securities before the effective date of the registration statement or

under an exemption for which the securities do not qualify results in liability.

Defenses. There are three basic defenses to charges of violations under the 1933 act. A defendant can avoid liability if he or she can prove that, even if a statement was not true or a fact was left out, the statement or omission was not material. A defendant can also avoid liability by proving that the plaintiff knew about the misrepresentation and bought the stock anyway.

Any defendant, except the issuer of the stock, can also assert what is called the *due diligence* defense. To make this defense, a person must prove that he or she reasonably believed, at the time the registration statement became effective, that the statements in it were true and there were no omissions of material facts. (This defense is discussed in further detail in Chapter 51, in the context of the liability of accountants.)

Criminal Penalties. The U.S. Department of Justice brings criminal actions against those who willfully violate the 1933 act. Violators may be penalized by fines up to $10,000, imprisonment up to five years, or both.

Civil Sanctions. The SEC is authorized to seek, against those who willfully violate the 1933 act, an injunction against further sales of the securities involved. The SEC can also ask the court to grant other relief, such as an order to a violator to refund profits.

Those who purchase the securities and suffer harm as a result of the false or omitted statements, or other violation, may bring a suit in a federal court to recover their losses and other damages. If a registration statement or a prospectus contains material false statements or material omissions, for example, damages may be imposed on those who signed the statement or those who provided information used in preparing the statement (such as accountants and other experts—see Chapter 51).

SECTION 3

The Securities Exchange Act of 1934

The Securities Exchange Act of 1934 provides for the regulation and registration of securities exchanges, brokers, dealers, and national securities associations, such as the National Association of Securities Dealers (NASD). The SEC regulates the markets in which securities are traded by maintaining a continuous

---

21. 17 C.F.R. Section 230.144.
22. 17 C.F.R. Section 230.144A.

EXHIBIT 37–2   A SAMPLE RESTRICTED STOCK CERTIFICATE

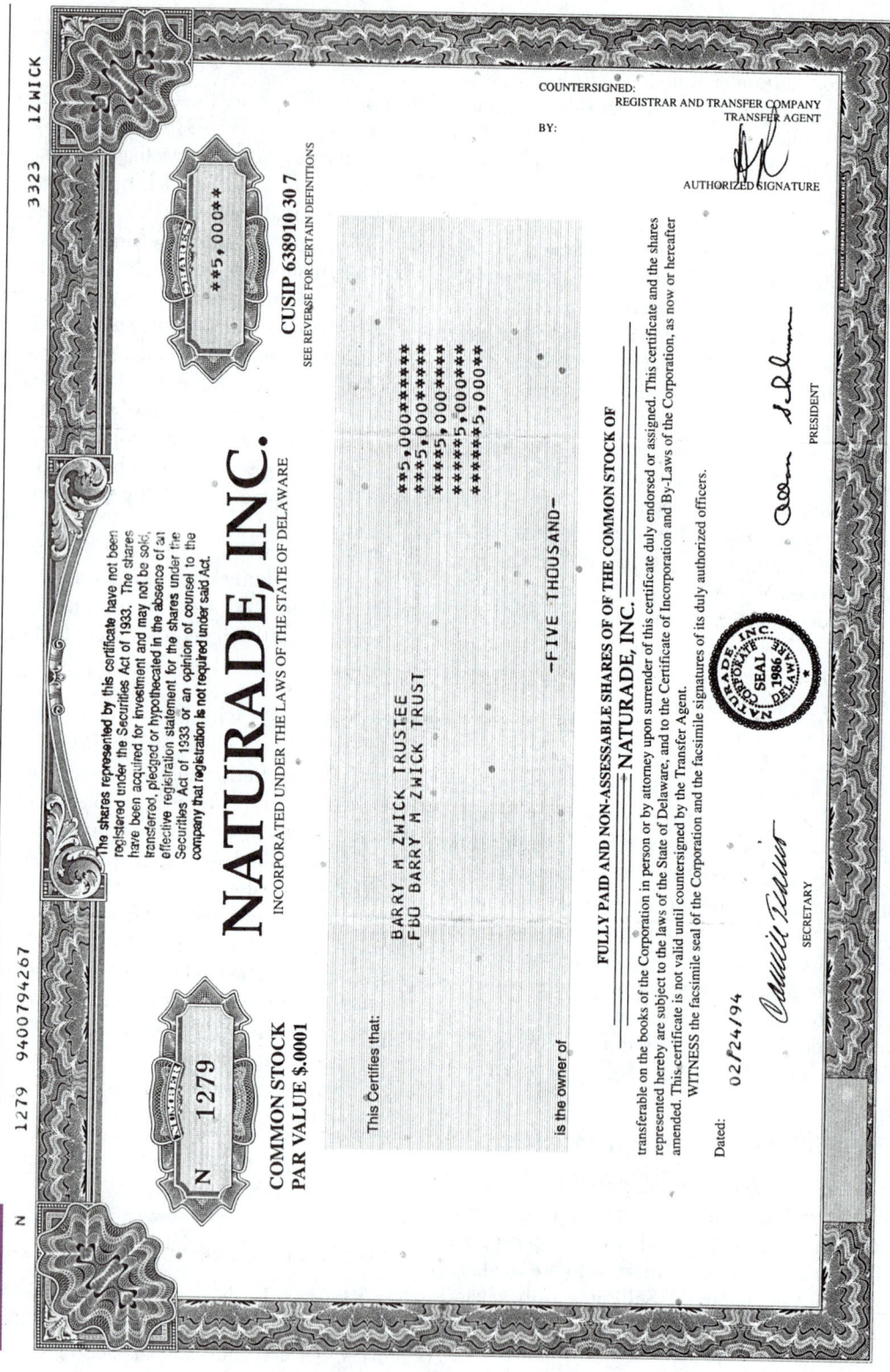

disclosure system for all corporations with securities on the securities exchanges and for those companies that have assets in excess of $10 million and five hundred or more shareholders. These corporations are referred to as Section 12 companies, as they are required to register their securities under Section 12 of the 1934 act.

The act regulates proxy solicitation for voting (see Chapter 35), and it allows the SEC to engage in market surveillance to regulate undesirable market practices such as fraud, market manipulation, misrepresentation, and stabilization. (*Stabilization* is a market-manipulating technique by which securities underwriters bid for securities to stabilize their prices during their issuance.)

SECTION 10(b) AND SEC RULE 10b-5

Section 10(b) is one of the most important sections of the Securities Exchange Act of 1934. This section prohibits the use of any manipulative or deceptive device in violation of SEC rules and regulations. Among the rules that the SEC has prescribed is **SEC Rule 10b-5,** which prohibits the commission of fraud in connection with the purchase or sale of any security. Rule 10b-5 states as follows:

> It shall be unlawful for any person, directly or indirectly, by the use of any means or instrumentality of interstate commerce, or of the mails or of any facility of any national securities exchange,
>
> (a) To employ any device, scheme, or artifice to defraud,
>
> (b) To make any untrue statement of a material fact or to omit to state a material fact necessary in order to make the statements made, in the light of the circumstances under which they were made, not misleading, or
>
> (c) To engage in any act, practice, or course of business which operates or would operate as a fraud or deceit upon any person, in connection with the purchase or sale of any security.[23]

One of the most important purposes of Section 10(b) and SEC Rule 10b-5 relates to what is called **insider trading.** Because of their positions, corporate directors and officers often obtain advance inside information that can affect the future market value of the corporate stock. Obviously, their positions can give them a trading advantage over the general public and shareholders. The 1934 Securities Exchange Act defines inside information and extends liability to officers and directors in their personal transactions for taking advantage of such information when they know that it is unavailable to the person with whom they are dealing.

Section 10(b) of the 1934 act and SEC Rule 10b-5 cover not only corporate officers, directors, and majority shareholders but also any persons having access to or receiving information of a nonpublic nature on which trading is based.

In the following classic case, a shareholder alleged that a corporate officer and a corporate director had breached their fiduciary duties by trading corporate shares on the basis of nonpublic information.

---

23. 17 C.F.R. Section 240.10b-5.

CASE 37.1   Diamond v. Oreamuno

Court of Appeals of
New York, 1969.
24 N.Y.2d 494,
248 N.E.2d 910,
301 N.Y.S.2d 78.

BACKGROUND AND FACTS   *The defendants in this case were the chairman of the board (Oreamuno) and president (Gonzalez) of Management Assistance, Inc. (MAI), a corporation that bought and leased computers, with maintenance services being provided by IBM. The defendants learned that IBM was going to increase its maintenance prices dramatically, to such an extent that MAI's profits would be cut by 75 percent per month. Just before the IBM maintenance price increase was announced, the defendants sold their MAI stock for $28 per share. After IBM publicly announced its price increase, MAI stock fell to $11 per share. The plaintiff (Diamond) brought a shareholder's derivative lawsuit on behalf of MAI to recover the profits the defendants had made by selling their shares at the higher price. The trial court granted the defendants' motion to dismiss, and the plaintiff appealed.*

IN THE LANGUAGE OF THE COURT

FULD, Chief Judge.
*   *   *   *

Accepting the truth of the complaint's allegations, there is no question but that the defendants were guilty of withholding material information from the purchasers of the shares and, indeed, the defendants acknowledge that the facts asserted constitute a violation of rule 10b-5. *   *   * Of course, any individual purchaser who could prove an injury as a result of a rule 10b-5 violation can bring his own action for rescission but we have not been referred to a single case in which such an action has been successfully prosecuted where the public sale of securities is involved. The reason for this is that sales of securities, whether through a stock exchange or over-the-counter, are characteristically anonymous transactions, usually handled through brokers, and the matching of the ultimate buyer with the ultimate seller presents virtually insurmountable obstacles.
*   *   *

*   *   * There is ample room in a situation such as is here presented for a "private Attorney General" to come forward and enforce proper behavior on the part of corporate officials through the medium of the derivative action brought in the name of the corporation. Only by sanctioning such a cause of action will there be any effective method to prevent the type of abuse of corporate office complained of in this case.

DECISION AND REMEDY

The court of appeals held that when corporate fiduciaries have breached their duty to the corporation by the use of nonpublic information, a shareholder may bring a derivative action for any profit resulting from the breach of duty.

Disclosure Requirements under SEC Rule 10b-5. Any material omission or misrepresentation of material facts in connection with the purchase or sale of a security may violate Section 10(b) and SEC Rule 10b-5. The key to liability (which can be civil or criminal) under this rule is whether the insider's information is *material*. The following are some examples of material facts calling for disclosure under the rule:

1. Fraudulent trading in the company stock by a broker-dealer.
2. A dividend change (whether up or down).
3. A contract for the sale of corporate assets.
4. A new discovery, a new process, or a new product.
5. A significant change in the financial condition of the firm.
6. Potential litigation against the company.

Ironically, one of the effects of SEC Rule 10b-5 was to deter disclosure. To understand why, consider an example. A company announces that its projected earnings in a certain time period will be X amount. It turns out that the forecast is wrong. The earnings are in fact much lower, and the price of the company's stock is affected—negatively. The shareholders then bring a class-action suit against the company, alleging

that the directors violated SEC Rule 10b-5 by disclosing misleading financial information.

In an attempt to rectify this problem and promote disclosure, Congress passed the Private Securities Litigation Reform Act of 1995. Among other things, the act provides a "safe harbor" for publicly held companies that make forward-looking statements, such as financial forecasts. Those who make such statements are protected against federal liability for securities fraud as long as the statements are accompanied by "meaningful cautionary statements identifying important factors that could cause actual results to differ materially from those in the forward-looking statement."[24]

The following is a landmark case interpreting SEC Rule 10b-5. The SEC sued several of Texas Gulf Sulphur Company's directors, officers, and employees under SEC Rule 10b-5 after these persons had purchased large amounts of the corporate stock prior to the announcement of a rich ore discovery by the corporation. At issue was whether the ore discovery was a material fact that had to be disclosed under Rule 10b-5.

---

24. 15 U.S.C. Sections 77z-2, 78u-5.

CASE 37.2   SEC v. Texas Gulf Sulphur Co.

United States
Court of Appeals,
Second Circuit, 1968.
401 F.2d 833.

BACKGROUND AND FACTS   *Texas Gulf Sulphur Company (TGS) conducted aerial geophysical surveys over more than 15,000 square miles of eastern Canada. The operations indicated concentrations of commercially exploitable minerals. At one site near Timmins, Ontario, TGS drilled a hole that appeared to yield a core with an exceedingly high mineral content. TGS kept secret the results of the core sample. Officers and employees of the company made substantial purchases of TGS's stock or accepted stock options after learning of the ore discovery, even though further drilling was necessary to establish whether there was enough ore to be mined commercially. Several months later, TGS announced that the strike was expected to yield at least 25 million tons of ore, substantially driving up the price of TGS stock. The SEC brought suit against the officers and employees of TGS for violating SEC Rule 10b-5. The officers and employees argued that the information on which they had traded had not been material at the time of their trades because the mine had not then been commercially proved. The trial court held that most of the defendants had not violated SEC Rule 10b-5, and the SEC appealed.*

**IN THE LANGUAGE
OF THE COURT**

WATERMAN, Circuit Judge.

*   *   *   *

*   *   * [W]hether facts are material within Rule 10b-5 when the facts relate to a particular event and are undisclosed by those persons who are knowledgeable thereof will depend at any given time upon a balancing of both the indicated probability that the event will occur and the anticipated magnitude of the event in light of the totality of the company activity. Here, *   *   * knowledge of the possibility, which surely was more than marginal, of the existence of a mine of the vast magnitude indicated by the remarkably rich drill core located rather close to the surface (suggesting mineability by the less expensive openpit method) within the confines of a large anomaly (suggesting an extensive region of mineralization) might well have affected the price of TGS stock and would certainly have been an important fact to a reasonable, if speculative, investor in deciding whether he should buy, sell, or hold.

*   *   *   *

*   *   * [A] major factor in determining whether the *   *   * discovery was a material fact is the importance attached to the drilling results by those who knew about it. *   *   * [T]he timing by those who knew of it of their stock purchases *   *   *—purchases in some cases by individuals who had never before purchased *   *   * TGS stock— virtually compels the inference that the insiders were influenced by the drilling results.

**DECISION
AND REMEDY**

The appellate court ruled in favor of the SEC. All of the trading by insiders who knew of the mineral find before its true extent had been publicly announced violated SEC Rule 10b-5.

Applicability of SEC Rule 10b-5.   SEC Rule 10b-5 applies in virtually all cases concerning the trading of securities, whether on organized exchanges, in over-the-counter markets, or in private transactions. The rule covers notes, bonds, certificates of interest and participation in any profit-sharing agreement, agreements to form a corporation, and joint-venture agreements; in short, the rule covers just about any form of security. It is immaterial whether a firm has securities registered under the 1933 act for the 1934 act to apply.

SEC Rule 10b-5 is applicable only when the requisites of federal jurisdiction (such as the use of the mails, of stock exchange facilities, or of any instrumentality of interstate commerce) are present. Virtually no commercial transaction, however, can be completed without such contact. In addition, the states have corporate securities laws, many of which include provisions similar to SEC Rule 10b-5.

SEC Rule 10b-5 and state securities laws also apply to online securities offerings and disclosures. See this chapter's *Emerging Trends in Technology* for a further discussion of this topic.

EMERGING TRENDS IN TECHNOLOGY

Online Securities Offerings and Disclosures

We have emphasized elsewhere how technological advances have affected business practices, as well as the law governing those practices. Not surprisingly, technology is also affecting practices in the securities industry—and securities law. Corporations are using the Internet to communicate information to the Securities and Exchange Commission (SEC), shareholders, potential investors, and others. Indeed, the SEC has changed or modified a number of its rules to encourage online filings of securities documents, including prospectuses.

Investors, in turn, can now use the Internet to access information that can help them make informed decisions. At the SEC's Web site (at **http://www.sec.gov**), for example, investors and others can view new SEC rules, recent announcements, enforcement actions, and the EDGAR (Electronic Data Gathering, Analysis, and Retrieval) database. This database includes initial public offerings, proxy statements, annual corporate reports, registration statements, and other

documents that have been filed with the SEC. EDGAR also provides public access to information regarding securities trading suspensions and current class-action suits for securities fraud.

These developments have brought about, according to one scholar, a "near-revolution" in the way in which securities are issued and traded.[a] Of course, the Internet has also been used to commit fraud, and the SEC has stepped up its monitoring of the Internet to detect fraudulent securities offerings and other activities.

SECURITIES OFFERINGS

In 1996, when the SEC allowed Spring Street Brewing Company to trade its shares via its Web site without registering as a broker-dealer, many people looked to the Internet as the stock market of tomorrow. It appears, however, that we are going to have to wait a few more years for that to take place. Although many other companies have taken advantage of the SEC's "green light" and offered stock directly to the public over the Internet, there have been no great success stories so far. No doubt, this will soon change as more and more established firms begin to

a. Robert A. Prentice, "The Future of Corporate Disclosure: The Internet, Securities Fraud, and Rule 10b-5," *Emory Law Journal*, Vol. 47, No. 1 (Winter 1998), p. 1.

use the Internet to publish prospectuses.

To date, offerings by small, nonpublic companies have been limited in scope, mainly because of regulatory restraints. To a large extent, any company wishing to make an initial public offering (IPO) of securities over the Internet has to comply with filing requirements dictated by federal and state law. Such filings are costly and time consuming. Typically, only those companies that are exempt from registration requirements have gone to the Internet to raise capital. Another problem relates to the lack of secondary markets for IPO shares sold directly on the Internet.

One of the questions raised by Internet transactions has to do with securities offerings by foreign companies. Today, anybody in the world can offer shares of stock worldwide via the Web without any additional cost. Traditionally, foreign companies have not been able to offer new shares to the U.S. public without first registering them with the SEC. How can these requirements be enforced for offerings made using the Internet?

In 1998, the SEC issued an interpretive release to address this question and similar concerns. The SEC stated that foreign issuers must implement measures to avoid targeting U.S. investors. For example, a foreign company offering shares of stock on the Internet must add a disclaimer on its Web site stating that it has not gone through the registration

Outsiders and SEC Rule 10b-5. The traditional insider-trading case involves true insiders—corporate officers, directors, and majority shareholders who have access to (and trade on) inside information.

Increasingly, liability under Section 10(b) of the 1934 act and SEC Rule 10b-5 has been extended to include certain "outsiders"—those who trade on inside information acquired indirectly. Two theories have

EMERGING TRENDS IN TECHNOLOGY

Online Securities Offerings and Disclosures,

continued

procedure in the United States. If the SEC believes that a Web site's offering of foreign securities has been targeted at U.S. residents, it will pursue that company in an attempt to require it to register in the United States.[b] Given that some Web site prospectuses for new security offerings have full audio and downloadable video, the investing public will probably become more interested in such Web sites. This means that the SEC's job of policing these Web sites will become increasingly difficult.

ONLINE DISCLOSURES

Virtually all major companies today have Web sites on which they post a variety of information, including forward-looking statements, press releases, and the like. If any of this information is misleading, a firm may face liability under securities

---
b. International Series Release #1125, March 23, 1998.

laws for violating the SEC's disclosure requirements.

For example, suppose that a company posts a press release on its Web site stating that its earnings for 2000 were $300 million and that the company expects to double those earnings in 2001. In June of 2001, the company learns that its 2000 earnings were, in fact, only $200 million and that the earnings could not possibly climb to $600 million in 2001. Further suppose that the company does not remove the former statement, which is now misleading, from its Web site. In this situation, the company would face potential liability for violating the disclosure requirements of the Securities Exchange Act of 1934.

A company also may face potential liability for misleading reports by securities analysts and magazine articles that are hyperlinked to the company's Web site. Even though the information may have been accurate when it was published, a viewer might reasonably rely on the information after it becomes outdated—and the company, by hyperlinking the materials to its Web page, could be held liable for violating SEC disclosure requirements.

IMPLICATIONS FOR THE BUSINESSPERSON

1. The message for businesspersons is clear. All forward-looking statements and other documents that investors

could reasonably rely on should be removed from Web sites after a reasonable time, such as three months.
2. Hyperlinked materials should also be examined frequently; if they become dated, the link should be deleted from the Web site.
3. Businesspersons should consider including disclaimers on their Web sites, indicating that certain information may be outdated.

FOR CRITICAL ANALYSIS

1. The SEC has initiated enforcement actions against issuers of securities, holding them responsible for false or misleading information disseminated online through third party analyst reports, even though the issuer did not participate in preparing the information. Is this fair?
2. Can fraudulent securities offerings via the Internet be policed effectively by the SEC?

RELEVANT WEB SITES

The SEC has issued an alert to help investors evaluate investments on the Internet at **http://www.sec. gov/consumer/cyberfr.htm**. A Web interface called EdgarScan allows users to locate key financial information on the SEC's EDGAR database and compare the information across companies. Go to **http://edgarscan.tc.pw.com**.

---

been developed under which outsiders may be held liable for insider trading: the *tipper/tippee theory* and the *misappropriation theory*.

Tipper/Tippee Theory. Anyone who acquires inside information as a result of a corporate insider's breach of his or her fiduciary duty can be liable under

SEC Rule 10b-5. This liability extends to **tippees** (those who receive "tips" from insiders) and even remote tippees (tippees of tippees).

The key to liability under this theory is that the inside information be obtained as a result of someone's breach of a fiduciary duty to the corporation whose shares are involved in the trading. Unless there is a breach of a duty not to disclose inside information, the disclosure is made in exchange for personal benefit, and the tippee knows of this breach (or should know

of it) and benefits from it, there is no liability under this theory.[25] Is the offering of a tip as a gift of profits to someone with whom the insider has a close relationship enough to infer that the insider realized a personal benefit? That was at issue in the following case.

---

25. See, for example, *Chiarella v. United States*, 445 U.S. 222, 100 S.Ct. 1108, 63 L.Ed.2d 348 (1980); and *Dirks v. SEC*, 463 U.S. 646, 103 S.Ct. 3255, 77 L.Ed.2d 911 (1983).

CASE 37.3   SEC v. Warde

United States
Court of Appeals,
Second Circuit, 1998.
151 F.3d 42.
**http://www.tourolaw.
edu/2ndcircuit/July98**[a]

BACKGROUND AND FACTS   *Edward Downe was a close friend of Fred Sullivan, chairman of Kidde, Inc. At Sullivan's request, Downe became a director of Kidde. Thomas Warde was a good friend of Downe. In June 1987, Sullivan learned that Kidde was the target of a takeover attempt by Hanson Trust PLC, a British firm. After negotiations, the Kidde board announced in August that it would merge with Hanson. The price of Kidde stock increased, and warrants for the shares, which had been priced at $1 in June, went to $26.50.[b] Between learning about the takeover attempt in June and the merger in August, Downe and Warde bought and sold warrants several times, earning very large profits. The SEC filed a suit in a federal district court against Warde and others, alleging insider trading in violation, in part, of Section 10(b). Warde contended that his purchases were based on market savvy, rumor, and public information. The jury found him liable. The court ordered him to pay more than $3 million in penalties and interest. Warde appealed to the U.S. Court of Appeals for the Second Circuit.*

**IN THE LANGUAGE
OF THE COURT**

LEVAL, Circuit Judge:
*   *   *   *

To affirm Warde's liability as a tippee *   *   * , we must find sufficient evidence to permit a reasonable finding that *   *   * Downe benefitted by the disclosure to Warde.
*   *   *

     *   *   *   *

    *   *   * [In *Dirks v. SEC*, 463 U.S. 646, 103 S.Ct. 3255, 77 L.Ed.2d 911 (1983), the United States] Supreme Court *   *   * made plain that to prove a Section 10(b) violation, the SEC need not show that the tipper expected or received a specific or tangible benefit in exchange for the tip. Rather, the "benefit" element of Section 10(b) is satisfied when the tipper "intend[s] to benefit the *   *   * recipient" or "makes a gift of confidential information to a trading relative or friend."

Under this standard, Downe clearly benefitted from Warde's inside trades. Warde's trades "resemble[d] trading by the insider himself followed by a gift of the profits to the recipient." The close friendship between Downe and Warde suggests that Downe's tip was "inten[ded] to benefit" Warde, and therefore allows a jury finding that Downe's tip breached a duty under Section 10(b).

---

a. This page provides access to opinions of the U.S. Court of Appeals for the Second Circuit decided in July 1998. Scroll down the list of cases to the *Warde* case and click on the link to access the opinion.
b. A warrant is an agreement to buy stock at a certain price before a certain date. If, before the warrant is exercised, the price goes up, the buyer profits. If the price never exceeds the level in the warrant, the warrant is worthless.

DECISION AND REMEDY	*The U.S. Court of Appeals for the Second Circuit affirmed the lower court's decision, concluding that the SEC presented sufficient evidence to support every element necessary to hold Warde liable. Warde was ordered to pay the fines, with interest.*

Misappropriation Theory. Liability for insider trading may also be established under the misappropriation theory. This theory holds that if an individual wrongfully obtains (misappropriates) inside information and trades on it for his or her personal gain, then the individual should be held liable because, in essence, the individual stole information rightfully belonging to another.

The misappropriation theory has been controversial because it significantly extends the reach of SEC Rule 10b-5 to outsiders who would not ordinarily be deemed fiduciaries of the corporations in whose stock they trade. At issue in the following case was whether the misappropriation theory can be applied under Rule 10b-5.

CASE 37.4   United States v. O'Hagan

Supreme Court of the United States, 1997.
521 U.S. 642,
117 S.Ct. 2199,
138 L.Ed.2d 724.
http://supct.law.
cornell.edu/supct[a]

COMPANY PROFILE *The law firm of Dorsey & Whitney LLP (Limited Liability Partnership) (http://www.dorseylaw.com) was founded in 1912. Today, Dorsey & Whitney is one of the forty largest law firms in the United States, with more than five hundred lawyers and seven hundred support staff. The firm is based in Minneapolis, Minnesota, with offices in a dozen other U.S. cities and in London, Brussels, and Hong Kong. The firm's attorneys have included the late Harry Blackmun, a former United States Supreme Court justice, and Walter Mondale, a former vice president of the United States and ambassador to Japan. The firm is organized into two large groups, each of which is broken down into smaller "practice" groups. These smaller groups include "Mergers & Acquisitions," the members of which, according to the firm's Web site, "have extensive experience in all types of mergers and acquisitions work."*

BACKGROUND AND FACTS *James O'Hagan was a partner in the law firm of Dorsey & Whitney. Grand Metropolitan PLC (Grand Met) hired Dorsey & Whitney to assist in a takeover of the Pillsbury Company. Before Grand Met made its tender offer, O'Hagan bought shares of Pillsbury stock. When the tender offer was announced, the price of Pillsbury stock increased more than 35 percent. O'Hagan sold his shares for a profit of more than $4 million. The Securities and Exchange Commission (SEC) prosecuted O'Hagan for, among other things, securities fraud in violation of Rule 10b-5 under the misappropriation theory. The SEC contended that O'Hagan breached fiduciary duties he owed to his law firm and Grand Met. When O'Hagan was convicted, he appealed to the U.S. Court of Appeals for the Eighth Circuit, which reversed the convictions. The SEC appealed to the United States Supreme Court.*

IN THE LANGUAGE OF THE COURT

Justice GINSBURG delivered the opinion of the Court.

*   *   *   *

---

a. This page provides access to some of the published opinions of the United States Supreme Court. In the right-hand column, in the "Arrayed by party name" section, in the "1997" row, click on "2nd party." When that page opens, find the *O'Hagan* case name and click on the link. From that page, click on the appropriate link to access the Court's opinion.

*   *   * [M]isappropriation   *   *   * satisfies [Section] 10(b)'s requirement that chargeable conduct involve a "deceptive device or contrivance" used "in connection with" the purchase or sale of securities. *   *   * [M]isappropriators   *   * deal in deception. A fiduciary who pretends loyalty to the principal while secretly converting the principal's information for personal gain dupes or defrauds the principal.

*   *   *   *

*   *   * [T]he fiduciary's fraud is consummated *   *   * when, without disclosure to his principal, he uses the information to purchase or sell securities. *   *   *

*   *   *   *

*   *   * An investor's informational disadvantage vis-à-vis a misappropriator with material, nonpublic information stems from contrivance, not luck; it is a disadvantage that cannot be overcome with research or skill.

DECISION AND REMEDY   *The United States Supreme Court held that liability under Rule 10b-5 can be based on the misappropriation theory, reversed the judgment, and remanded the case.*

INSIDER REPORTING AND TRADING — SECTION 16(b)

Officers, directors, and certain large stockholders[26] of Section 12 corporations are required to file reports with the SEC concerning their ownership and trading of the corporation's securities.[27] To discourage such insiders from using nonpublic information about their companies to their personal benefit in the stock market, Section 16(b) of the 1934 act provides for the recapture by the corporation of all profits realized by the insider on any purchase and sale or sale and purchase of the corporation's stock within any six-month period. It is irrelevant whether the insider actually uses inside information; *all such short-swing profits must be returned to the corporation.*

Section 16(b) applies not only to stock but to warrants, options, and securities convertible into stock. In addition, the courts have fashioned complex rules for determining profits. The SEC exempts a number of transactions under Rule 16b-3.[28] For all of these reasons, corporate insiders are wise to seek competent counsel prior to trading in the corporation's stock. Exhibit 37–3 on page 706 compares the effects of SEC Rule 10b-5 and Section 16(b).

Shareholders owning 10 percent or more of the stock of a Section 12 corporation may be held liable under Section 16(b). Determining whether a shareholder owns 10 percent is not always easy, however, as illustrated by the following case.

---

26. Those stockholders owning 10 percent of the class of equity securities registered under Section 12 of the 1934 act.
27. 15 U.S.C. Section 78l.

28. 17 C.F.R. Section 240.16b-3.

CASE 37.5   Medtox Scientific, Inc. v. Morgan Capital, L.L.C.[a]

United States District Court, District of Minnesota, 1999.
50 F.Supp.2d 896.

BACKGROUND AND FACTS   *On February 1, 1996, Editek, Inc.,[b] issued shares of convertible preferred stock.[c] Each share could be converted to Editek common stock at a price equal to the average price of the common stock for the five days preceding the date that a notice of conversion was given to Editek. In other words, the number of shares of common stock that the preferred stock would buy depended on the average price of*

---

a. L.L.C. is an abbreviation for "limited liability company." An LLC is a hybrid form of business enterprise that offers the limited liability of the corporation and the tax advantages of a partnership. See Chapter 38.
b. Editek later changed its name to Medtox Scientific, Inc.
c. *Convertible preferred stock* is preferred stock entitling the owner to convert the preferred shares into a specified number of common shares. See Exhibits 34–4 and 34–5 in Chapter 34.

the common shares. If this price declined, the number of shares that the preferred stock would buy increased, and vice versa. Morgan Capital, L.L.C., bought some of the preferred stock. At the time, the number of common shares that Morgan Capital could have received on conversion would have been less than 10 percent of the outstanding stock. The price of Editek's common shares decreased, however, and at any time after April 9, Morgan Capital could have converted its preferred shares for more than 10 percent of the common stock. On May 1, Morgan Capital converted all of its preferred stock and received more than 18 percent of the common stock. Before the end of June, Morgan Capital sold some of the common stock, realizing a profit of $551,456.84. Editek filed a suit in a federal district court against Morgan Capital, alleging that the firm had violated Section 16(b). Morgan Capital responded in part that before it converted its preferred shares, it could not have been a 10 percent owner of Editek stock, as required to violate Section 16(b), because the amount of common stock that it could acquire changed every day. Editek filed a motion for summary judgment.

IN THE LANGUAGE OF THE COURT

MONTGOMERY, District Judge.

* * * *

* * * [I]f Morgan Capital could have converted its Preferred Stock into more than ten percent of the outstanding shares of Editek's Common Stock on any given day, then the presumption arises under Section 16(b) that Morgan Capital's holdings afforded it the potential for access to corporate information not available to a smaller shareholder on that day. At the same time, however, due to the floating conversion rate of the Preferred Stock, Morgan Capital's standing as a "ten percent beneficial owner" was potentially subject to change daily. Thus, to establish liability under Section 16(b), Plaintiff [would] not simply have to show that Morgan Capital could have obtained more than ten percent of Editek's Common Stock on any given day prior to May 1, 1996, but that Morgan Capital could have obtained more than ten percent of Editek's Common Stock on the day before it actually made the illicit purchase—April 30, 1996. Otherwise, Morgan Capital presumably would not have had access to inside information when it actually purchased Editek Common Stock and, therefore, would not be subject to the strictures of Section 16(b).

* * * *

The price of Editek's Common Stock steadily declined throughout March and April 1996. As a result, on any day between April 9 and April 30, 1996, the price was sufficiently low that had Morgan Capital elected to convert its Preferred Stock, it would have received more than ten percent of the outstanding shares of Editek's Common Stock. * * *

* * * *

Morgan Capital became a "ten percent beneficial owner" of Editek Common Stock on April 9, 1996 * * *. By exercising the option to convert its Preferred Stock into Common Stock on May 1, 1996, Morgan Capital fixed the conversion price and thereby engaged in a matchable purchase of Editek's Common Stock for Section 16(b) liability purposes. Over the next two months, Morgan Capital sold a portion of the stock it purchased on May 1, 1996, for a total profit of $551,456.84. Because these transactions constitute "short-swing" insider trading in violation of Section 16(b), Editek is entitled to recover the full profit realized by Morgan Capital. Plaintiff's motion is therefore granted.

DECISION AND REMEDY

The court granted Editek's motion for summary judgment. Morgan Capital was a 10 percent shareholder of Editek for purposes of Section 16(b) liability, because for at least one day before Morgan Capital converted its preferred shares, those shares could have been converted to obtain more than 10 percent of the common stock.

PROXY STATEMENTS

Section 14(a) of the Securities Exchange Act of 1934 regulates the solicitation of proxies (see Chapter 35) from shareholders of Section 12 companies. The SEC regulates the content of proxy statements, which are statements sent to shareholders by corporate managers who are requesting authority to vote on behalf of the

EXHIBIT 37–3   COMPARISON OF COVERAGE, APPLICATION, AND LIABILITY UNDER SEC RULE 10b-5 AND SECTION 16(b)

	RULE 10b-5	SECTION 16(b)
Subject matter of transaction	Any security (does not have to be registered).	Any security (does not have to be registered).
Transactions covered	Purchase or sale.	Short-swing purchase and sale or short-swing sale and purchase.
Who is subject to liability?	Virtually anyone with inside information under a duty to disclose—including officers, directors, controlling stockholders, and tippees.	Officers, directors, and certain holders of large amounts of stock.
Is omission or misrepresentation necessary for liability?	Yes.	No.
Any exempt transactions?	No.	Yes, a variety of exemptions.
Is direct dealing with the party necessary?	No.	No.
Who may bring an action?	A person transacting with an insider, the SEC, or a purchaser or seller damaged by a wrongful act.	Corporation and shareholder by derivative action.

shareholders in a particular election on specified issues. Whoever solicits a proxy must fully and accurately disclose in the proxy statement all of the facts that are pertinent to the matter on which the shareholders are to vote. SEC Rule 14a-9 is similar to the antifraud provisions of SEC Rule 10b-5. Remedies for violations are extensive, ranging from injunctions to prevent a vote from being taken to monetary damages.

VIOLATIONS OF THE 1934 ACT

Violations of Section 10(b) and Rule 10b-5 of the Securities Exchange Act of 1934 include insider trading. This is a criminal offense, with criminal penalties. Violators of these laws may also be subject to civil liability. For any sanctions to be imposed, however, there must be *scienter*—the violator must have had an intent to defraud or knowledge of his or her misconduct (see Chapter 14). *Scienter* can be proved by showing a defendant made false statements or wrongfully failed to disclose material facts.

Violations of Section 16(b) include the sale by insiders of stock acquired less than six months before the sale. These violations are subject to civil sanctions. Liability under Section 16(b) is strict liability. *Scienter* is not required.

Criminal Penalties. For violations of Section 10(b) and Rule 10b-5, an individual may be fined up to $1 million, imprisoned up to ten years, or both. A partnership or a corporation may be fined up to $2.5 million.

Civil Sanctions. Both the SEC and private parties can bring actions to seek civil sanctions against violators of the 1934 act.

The Insider Trading Sanctions Act of 1984 permits the SEC to bring suit in a federal district court against anyone violating or aiding in a violation of the 1934 act or SEC rules by purchasing or selling a security while in the possession of material nonpublic information.[29] The violation must occur on or through the facilities of a national securities exchange or from or through a broker or dealer. Transactions pursuant to a public offering by an issuer of securities are excepted. The court may assess as a penalty as much as triple the profits gained or the loss avoided by the guilty party. Profit or loss is defined as "the difference between the purchase or sale price of the security and the value of that security as measured by the trading price of the

---

29. 15 U.S.C. Section 78u(d)(2)(A).

security at a reasonable period of time after public dissemination of the nonpublic information."[30]

The Insider Trading and Securities Fraud Enforcement Act of 1988 enlarged the class of persons who may be subject to civil liability for insider-trading violations. This act also gave the SEC authority to award **bounty payments** (rewards given by government officials for acts beneficial to the state) to persons providing information leading to the prosecution of insider-trading violations.[31]

Private parties may also sue violators of Section 10(b) and Rule 10b-5. A private party may obtain rescission of a contract to buy securities or damages to the extent of the violator's illegal profits. Those found liable have a right to seek contribution from those who share responsibility for the violations, including accountants, attorneys, and corporations.[32] (The liability of accountants and attorneys for violations of the securities laws is discussed in more detail in Chapter 51.) For violations of Section 16(b), a corporation can bring an action to recover the short-swing profits.

SECTION 4

Regulation of Investment Companies

Investment companies, and mutual funds in particular, grew rapidly after World War II. **Investment companies** act on behalf of many smaller shareholders/owners by buying a large portfolio of securities and managing that portfolio professionally. A **mutual fund** is a specific type of investment company that continually buys or sells to investors shares of ownership in a portfolio. Such companies are regulated by the Investment Company Act of 1940,[33] which provides for SEC regulation of their activities. The 1940 act was expanded by the Investment Company Act Amendments of 1970. Further minor changes were made in the Securities Acts Amendments of 1975. The National Securities Markets Improvement Act of 1996 increased the SEC's authority to regulate investment companies by limiting virtually all of the authority of the states to regulate these enterprises.

The 1940 act requires that every investment company register with the SEC and imposes restrictions on the activities of such companies and persons connected with them. For the purposes of the act, an investment company is defined as any entity that (1) "is . . . engaged primarily . . . in the business of investing, reinvesting, or trading in securities" or (2) is engaged in such business and more than 40 percent of the company's assets consist of investment securities. Excluded from coverage by the act are banks, insurance companies, savings and loan associations, finance companies, oil and gas drilling firms, charitable foundations, tax-exempt pension funds, and other special types of institutions, such as closely held corporations.

All investment companies must register with the SEC by filing a notification of registration. Each year, registered investment companies must file reports with the SEC. To safeguard company assets, all securities must be held in the custody of a bank or stock exchange member, and that bank or stock exchange member must follow strict procedures established by the SEC.

No dividends may be paid from any source other than accumulated, undistributed net income. Furthermore, there are some restrictions on investment activities. For example, investment companies are not allowed to purchase securities on the margin (pay only part of the total price, borrowing the rest), sell short (sell shares not yet owned), or participate in joint trading accounts.

SECTION 5

State Securities Laws

Today, all states have their own corporate securities laws, or **blue sky laws,** that regulate the offer and sale of securities within individual state borders. (The phrase *blue sky laws* dates to a 1917 United States Supreme Court decision in which the Court declared that the purpose of such laws was to prevent "speculative schemes which have no more basis than so many feet of 'blue sky.'"[34]) Article 8 of the Uniform Commercial Code, which has been adopted by all of the states, also imposes various requirements relating to the purchase and sale of securities. State securities laws apply only to intrastate transactions. Since the adoption of the 1933 and 1934 federal securities acts, the state and federal

---

30. 15 U.S.C. Section 78u(d)(2)(C).

31. 15 U.S.C. Section 78u-1.

32. Note that a private cause of action under Section 10(b) and SEC Rule 10b-5 cannot be brought against accountants, attorneys, and others who "aid and abet" violations of the act. Only the SEC can bring actions against so-called aiders and abettors. See *SEC v. Fehn*, 97 F.3d 1276 (9th Cir. 1996).

33. 15 U.S.C. Sections 80a-1 to 80a-64.

---

34. *Hall v. Geiger-Jones Co.*, 242 U.S. 539, 37 S.Ct. 217, 61 L.Ed. 480 (1917).

governments have regulated securities concurrently. Issuers must comply with both federal and state securities laws, and exemptions from federal law are not exemptions from state laws.

There are differences in philosophy among state statutes, but certain features are common to all state blue sky laws. Typically, state laws have disclosure requirements and antifraud provisions, many of which are patterned after Section 10(b) of the Securities Exchange Act of 1934 and SEC Rule 10b-5. State laws also provide for the registration or qualification of securities offered or issued for sale within the state and impose disclosure requirements. Unless an applicable exemption from registration is found, issuers must register or qualify their stock with the appropriate state

official, often called a *corporations commissioner.* Additionally, most state securities laws regulate securities brokers and dealers. The Uniform Securities Act, which has been adopted in part by several states, was drafted to be acceptable to states with differing regulatory philosophies.

The dual federal and state system has not always worked well, particularly during the early 1990s, when there was considerable expansion of the securities markets. The National Securities Markets Improvement Act of 1996 eliminated some of the duplicate regulations. While the states still regulate local and regional matters, the SEC exclusively regulates most of the national securities activities.

TERMS AND CONCEPTS TO REVIEW

accredited investor 694	investment company 707	tippee 702
blue sky law 707	mutual fund 707	tombstone ad 692
bounty payment 707	red herring 692	
insider trading 697	SEC Rule 10b-5 697	

QUESTIONS AND CASE PROBLEMS

37–1. REGISTRATION REQUIREMENTS. A corporation incorporated and doing business in Florida, Estrada Hermanos, Inc., decides to sell $1 million worth of its no-par-value common stock to the public. The stock will be sold only within the state of Florida. Jose Estrada, the chairman of the board, says the offering need not be registered with the Securities and Exchange Commission. His brother, Gustavo, disagrees. Who is right? Explain.

37–2. REGISTRATION REQUIREMENTS. Huron Corp. has 300,000 common shares outstanding. The owners of these outstanding shares live in several different states. Huron has decided to split the 300,000 shares two for one. Will Huron Corp. have to file a registration statement and prospectus on the 300,000 new shares to be issued as a result of the split? Explain.

37–3. SEC RULE 10b-5. Danny Cherif was employed by the First National Bank of Chicago in its International Financial Institutions Department from 1979 until 1987, when Cherif's position was eliminated because of an

internal reorganization. Cherif, using a forged memo to the bank's security department, caused his magnetic identification (ID) card—which he had received as an employee to allow him to enter the bank building—to remain activated after his employment was terminated. Cherif used his ID card to enter the building at night to obtain confidential financial information from the bank's Specialized Finance Department regarding extraordinary business transactions, such as tender offers. During 1988 and 1989, Cherif made substantial profits through securities trading based on this information. Eventually, Cherif's activities were investigated by the Securities and Exchange Commission (SEC), and Cherif was charged with violating Section 10(b) and SEC Rule 10b-5 by misappropriating and trading on inside information in violation of his fiduciary duties to his former employer. Cherif argued that the SEC had wrongfully applied the misappropriation theory to his activities, because as a former employee, he no longer had a fiduciary duty to the bank.

Explain whether Cherif is liable under SEC Rule 10b-5. [*SEC v. Cherif*, 933 F.2d 403 (7th Cir. 1991)]

37–4. SEC Rule 10b-5. Susan Waldbaum was a niece of the president and controlling shareholder of Waldbaum, Inc. Susan's mother (the president's sister) told Susan that the company was going to be sold at a favorable price and that a tender offer was soon to be made. She told Susan not to tell anyone except her husband, Keith Loeb, about the sale. The next day, Susan told her husband of the sale and cautioned him not to tell anyone, because "it could possibly ruin the sale." The day after he learned of the sale, Loeb called Robert Chestman, his broker, and told him that he "had some accurate information" that the company was about to be sold at a price "substantially higher" than the market value of its stock. That day, Chestman purchased shares of the company for himself, as well as for Loeb. Chestman was later convicted by a jury of, among other things, trading on misappropriated inside information in violation of SEC Rule 10b-5. On appeal, the central question in regard to liability under the misappropriation theory was whether Chestman had acquired the inside information about the Waldbaum company as a result of an insider's breach of a fiduciary duty. Essentially, the inquiry focused on whether Loeb owed a fiduciary duty to his wife's family or to his wife to keep the information confidential. How should the court rule? [*United States v. Chestman*, 947 F.2d 551 (2d Cir. 1991)]

37–5. Investor Protection. U.S. News & World Report, Inc., set up a profit-sharing plan in 1962 that allotted to certain employees specially issued stock known as bonus or anniversary stock. The stock was given to the employees for past services and could not be traded or sold to anyone other than the corporate issuer, U.S. News. This special stock was issued only to employees and for no other purpose than as bonuses. Because there was no market for the stock, U.S. News hired an independent appraiser to estimate the fair value of the stock so that the employees could redeem the shares. Charles Foltz and several other employees held stock through this plan and sought to redeem the shares with U.S. News, but Foltz disputed the value set by the appraisers. Foltz sued U.S. News for violation of securities regulations. What defense would allow U.S. News to resist Foltz's claim successfully? [*Foltz v. U.S. News & World Report, Inc.*, 627 F.Supp. 1143 (D.D.C. 1986)]

37–6. SEC Rule 10b-5. Louis Ferraro was the chairman and president of Anacomp, Inc. In June 1988, Ferraro told his good friend Michael Maio that Anacomp was negotiating a tender offer for stock in Xidex Corp. Maio passed on the information to Patricia Ladavac, a friend of both Ferraro and Maio. Maio and Ladavac immediately purchased shares in Xidex stock. On the day that the tender offer was announced—an announcement that caused the price of Xidex shares to increase—Maio and Ladavac sold their Xidex stock and made substantial profits (Maio made $211,000 from the transactions, and Ladavac gained $78,750). The SEC brought an action against the three individuals, alleging that they had violated, among other laws, SEC Rule 10b-5. Maio and Ladavac claimed that they had done nothing illegal. They argued that they had no fiduciary duty either to Anacomp or to Xidex, and therefore they had no duty to disclose or abstain from trading in the stock of those corporations. Had Maio and Ladavac violated SEC Rule 10b-5? Discuss fully. [*SEC v. Maio*, 51 F.3d 623 (7th Cir. 1995)]

37–7. Section 10(b). Joseph Jett worked for Kidder, Peabody & Co., a financial services firm owned by General Electric Co. (GE). Over a three-year period, Jett allegedly engaged in a scheme to generate false profits at Kidder, Peabody to increase his performance-based bonuses. When the scheme was discovered, Daniel Chill and other GE shareholders who had bought stock in the previous year filed a suit in a federal district court against GE. The shareholders alleged that GE had engaged in securities fraud in violation of Section 10(b). They claimed that GE's interest in justifying its investment in Kidder, Peabody gave GE "a motive to willfully blind itself to facts casting doubt on Kidder's purported profitability." On what basis might the court dismiss the shareholders' complaint? Discuss fully. [*Chill v. General Electric Co.*, 101 F.3d 263 (2d Cir. 1996)]

37–8. SEC Rule 10b-5. Grand Metropolitan PLC (Grand Met) planned to make a tender offer as part of an attempted takeover of the Pillsbury Company. Grand Met hired Robert Falbo, an independent contractor, to complete electrical work as part of security renovations to its offices to prevent leaks of information concerning the planned tender offer. Falbo was given a master key to access the executive offices. When an executive secretary told Falbo that a takeover was brewing, he used his key to access the offices and eavesdrop on conversations to learn that Pillsbury was the target. Falbo bought thousands of shares of Pillsbury stock for less than $40 per share. Within two months, Grand Met made an offer for all outstanding Pillsbury stock at $60 per share and ultimately paid up to $66 per share. Falbo made over $165,000 in profit. The Securities and Exchange Commission (SEC) filed a suit in a federal district court against Falbo and others for alleged violations of, among other things, SEC Rule 10b-5. Under what theory might Falbo be liable? Do the circumstances of this case meet all of the requirements for liability under that theory? Explain. [*SEC v. Falbo*, 14 F.Supp.2d 508 (S.D.N.Y. 1998)]

37–9. Definition of a Security. In 1997, Scott and Sabrina Levine formed Friendly Power Co. (FPC) and Friendly Power Franchise Co. (FPC-Franchise). FPC obtained a license to operate as a utility company in California. FPC granted FPC-Franchise the right to pay commissions to "operators" who converted residential customers to FPC. Each operator paid for a "franchise"—a geographic area, determined by such factors as the number of households and competition from other utilities. In exchange for 50 percent of FPC's net profits on sales to residential customers in its territory, each franchise was required to maintain a 5 percent market share of power customers in that territory. Franchises were sold to tele-marketing firms, which solicited customers. The telemarketers sold interests in each franchise to between fifty and ninety-four "partners," each of whom invested money. FPC began supplying electricity to its customers in May 1998. Less than three months later, the Securities and Exchange Commission (SEC) filed a suit in a federal district court against the Levines and others, alleging that the "franchises" were unregistered securities offered for sale to the public in violation of the Securities Act of 1933. What is the definition of a security? Should the court rule in favor of the SEC? Why or why not? [*SEC v. Friendly Power Co., LLC*, 49 F.Supp.2d 1363 (S.D.Fla. 1999)]

37–10. IN YOUR COURT

Emerson Electric Co. purchased 13.2 percent of Dodge Manufacturing Co.'s stock. Less than six months later, when Dodge merged with Reliance Electric Co., Emerson decided to sell its shares. To avoid being subject to the short-swing profit restrictions of Section 16(b) of the Securities Exchange Act of 1934, which pertain to any purchase and sale by any owner of 10 percent or more of a corporation's stock, Emerson decided on a two-step selling plan. First, it sold off sufficient shares to reduce its holdings to 9.96 percent, and then it sold the remaining stock—all within a six-month period. Reliance demanded that Emerson return the profits made on both sales. Emerson sought a declaratory judgment from the court that it was not liable, arguing that because at the time of the second sale it had not owned 10 percent of Dodge stock, Section 16 did not apply. Assume that you are the judge in the trial court hearing this case and answer the following questions:

(a) Does Section 16(b) of the Securities Exchange Act of 1934 apply to Emerson's transactions? Is Emerson liable to Reliance for its profits? How will you rule on these issues? Why?

(b) Does the court's opinion in Case 37.5 (*Medtox Scientific, Inc. v. Morgan Capital, L.L.C.*), which also involved an alleged violation of Section 16(b), shed any light on the issues now before your court? If so, in what way?

(c) Should Emerson's deliberate attempt to avoid the restrictions of Section 16(b) influence your decision? Why or why not?

LAW ON THE WEB

For updated links to resources available on the Web, as well as a variety of other materials, visit this text's Web site at http://wbl.westbuslaw.com.

To access the SEC's EDGAR database, go to

http://www.sec.gov/edgarhp.htm

The Center for Corporate Law at the University of Cincinnati College of Law examines all of the acts discussed in this chapter. Go to

http://www.law.uc.edu/CCL

To find the Securities Act of 1933, go to

http://www.law.uc.edu/CCL/33Act/index.html

To examine the Securities Exchange Act of 1934, go to

http://www.law.uc.edu/CCL/34Act/index.html

For information on investor protection and securities fraud, including answers to frequently asked questions on the topic of securities fraud, go to

http://www.securitieslaw.com

LEGAL RESEARCH EXERCISES ON THE WEB

Go to http://wbl.westbuslaw.com, the Web site that accompanies this text. Select "Internet Applications," and then click on "Chapter 37." There you will find the following Internet research exercise that you can perform to learn more about the SEC:

Activity 37–1: The SEC's Role

CHAPTER 38

Limited Liability Companies and Limited Partnerships

THE TWO MOST COMMON FORMS of business organization selected by two or more persons entering into business together are the partnership and the corporation. As explained in previous chapters, each form has distinct advantages and disadvantages. For partnerships, the advantage is that partnership income is taxed only once (all income is "passed through" the partnership entity to the partners themselves, who are taxed only as individuals); the disadvantage is the personal liability of the partners. For corporations, the advantage is the limited liability of shareholders; the disadvantage is the double taxation of corporate income. For many entrepreneurs and investors, the ideal business form would combine the tax advantages of the partnership form of business with the limited liability of the corporate enterprise.

A relatively new form of business organization called the **limited liability company (LLC)** is a hybrid form of business enterprise that meets these needs by offering the limited liability of the corporation and the tax advantages of a partnership. Increasingly, LLCs are becoming an organizational form of choice among businesspersons, a trend encouraged by state statutes permitting their use.

In this chapter, we begin by examining the LLC. We then look at a similar type of entity that is also relatively new—the limited liability partnership (LLP). The chapter concludes with a discussion of the limited partnership, a special type of partnership in which some of the partners have limited liability, and the limited liability limited partnership (LLLP).

SECTION 1

Limited Liability Companies

In 1977, Wyoming became the first state to pass legislation authorizing the creation of a limited liability company (LLC). Although LLCs emerged in the United States only in 1977, they have been in existence for over a century in other areas, including several European and South American nations. For example, the South American *limitada* is a form of business organization that operates more or less as a partnership but provides limited liability for the owners.

In the United States, after Wyoming's adoption of an LLC statute, it still was not known how the Internal Revenue Service (IRS) would treat the LLC for tax purposes. In 1988, however, the IRS ruled that Wyoming LLCs would be taxed as partnerships instead of as corporations, providing that certain requirements were met. Prior to this ruling, only one other state—Florida, in 1982—had authorized LLCs. The 1988 ruling encouraged other states to enact LLC statutes, and in less than a decade, all states had done so.

IRS rules that went into effect on January 1, 1997, encouraged even more widespread use of LLCs in the business world. These rules provide that any unincorporated business will automatically be taxed as a partnership unless it indicates otherwise on the tax form. The exceptions involve publicly traded companies, companies formed under a state incorporation statute, and certain foreign-owned companies. If a business chooses to be taxed as a corporation, it can indicate this choice by checking a box on the IRS form.

Part of the impetus behind creating LLCs in this country is that foreign investors are allowed to become LLC members. Generally, in an era increasingly characterized by global business efforts and investments, the LLC offers U.S. firms and potential investors from other countries flexibility and opportunities greater than those available through partnerships or corporations.

LLC FORMATION

Like the corporation, an LLC must be formed and operated in compliance with state law. About one-fourth of the states specifically require LLCs to have at least two owners, called **members.** In the rest of the states, although some LLC statutes are silent on this issue, one-member LLCs are usually permitted.

To form an LLC, **articles of organization** must be filed with a central state agency—usually the secretary of state's office. Typically, the articles are required to set forth such information as the name of the business, its principal address, the name and address of a registered agent, the names of the owners, and information on how the LLC will be managed. The business's name must include the words "Limited Liability Company" or the initials "LLC." In addition to filing the articles of organization, a few states require that a notice of the intention to form an LLC be published in a local newspaper.

Note that although the LLC, like the corporation, is a legal entity apart from its owners, for federal jurisdictional purposes an LLC is treated differently than a corporation. The federal jurisdiction statute provides that a corporation is deemed to be a citizen of the state in which it is incorporated and in which it maintains its principal place of business. The statute does not mention the citizenship of partnerships and other unincorporated associations, but courts have tended to regard these entities as citizens of every state in which their members are citizens.

The citizenship of LLCs may come into play when a party sues an LLC based on diversity of citizenship. Remember from Chapter 2 that in some circumstances, such as when parties to a lawsuit are from different states, a federal court can exercise diversity jurisdiction in cases in which the amount in controversy exceeds $75,000. *Complete* diversity of citizenship must exist, however. For example, a citizen of New York will not be able to bring a suit in federal court—on the basis of diversity jurisdiction—against multiple defendants if one of the defendants is also a citizen of New York.

One of the issues in the following case concerned the state citizenship of a limited liability company. Was there diversity of citizenship between the parties so that a federal court could exercise jurisdiction?

CASE 38.1   Cosgrove v. Bartolotta

United States
Court of Appeals,
Seventh Circuit, 1998.
150 F.3d 729.
http://www.findlaw.
com/casecode/courts/
7th.html[a]

BACKGROUND AND FACTS   *Joseph Bartolotta wanted to open a restaurant. He asked Barry Cosgrove, his friend and an experienced corporate attorney, for a $100,000 loan, plus Cosgrove's business and legal advice. Bartolotta promised, among other things, to give Cosgrove a 19 percent ownership interest in the restaurant. In reliance on this promise, Cosgrove helped Bartolotta negotiate a lease for the restaurant premises and advised Bartolotta to organize the venture as a limited liability company (LLC). Bartolotta formed Mary-Bart, LLC, and with Cosgrove's help, obtained other financing. Then, before Cosgrove made his loan, Bartolotta cut him out of the deal. The restaurant,*

a. This is a page, within the FindLaw Web site, that provides access to recent opinions of the U.S. Court of Appeals for the Seventh Circuit. In the "1998" row, click on the "July" link. When that page opens, scroll down the list of cases to the *Cosgrove* case. Click on the case name to access the opinion.

"Bartolotta's Lake Park Bistro," proved to be a success. Cosgrove filed a suit in a federal district court against Bartolotta and Mary-Bart, based in part on diversity of citizenship (Cosgrove and Bartolotta were residents of different states). The jury awarded Cosgrove $135,000, but the judge reduced the award, and both sides appealed.

IN THE LANGUAGE OF THE COURT

POSNER, Chief Judge.

* * * *

The principal defendant is Joseph Bartolotta, but his company—Mary-Bart, LLC—is also named as a defendant; and in a diversity case, whenever there is an unconventional party (that is, someone or something other than either a natural person suing in his own rather than a representative capacity, or a business corporation) a jurisdictional warning flag should go up. In the case of a regular corporation, the owners' state of citizenship is irrelevant to whether there is the required complete diversity; but in the case of a partnership, it is crucial. *The citizenship of a partnership is the citizenship of the partners, even if they are limited partners,* so that if even one of the partners (general or limited) is a citizen of the same state as the plaintiff, the suit cannot be maintained as a diversity suit. [Emphasis added.]

Mary-Bart is neither a partnership nor a corporation, but a "limited liability company." This animal is like a limited partnership;[b] the principal difference is that it need have no equivalent to a general partner, that is, an owner who has unlimited personal liability for the debts of the firm. Given the resemblance between an LLC and a limited partnership, and what seems to have crystallized as a principle that members of associations are citizens for diversity purposes unless Congress provides otherwise (as it has with respect to corporations), we conclude that the citizenship of an LLC for purposes of the diversity jurisdiction is the citizenship of its members. That does not defeat jurisdiction in this case, however, because Mary-Bart, LLC has only one member—Mr. Bartolotta, who is not a citizen of the same state as the plaintiff.

DECISION AND REMEDY

The U.S. Court of Appeals for the Seventh Circuit ruled that a federal court could exercise jurisdiction in this case. For purposes of federal court jurisdiction, the citizenship of an LLC is the citizenship of its members. The court also remanded the case with orders to reinstate the award to Cosgrove.

---

b. As will be discussed later in this chapter, the limited partnership is a special form of partnership in which some partners (called *limited partners*) have limited liability and some partners (called *general partners*) assume personal liability for the firm's debts and obligations. There must be at least one general partner in a limited partnership.

ADVANTAGES AND DISADVANTAGES OF LLCs

A key advantage of the LLC is that the liability of members is limited to the amount of their investments. Another significant advantage is that an LLC with two or more members can choose whether to be taxed as a partnership or a corporation.

LLCs that want to distribute profits to the members may prefer to be taxed as a partnership, to avoid the "double taxation" characteristic of the corporate entity. Remember that in the corporate form of business, the corporation as an entity pays income taxes on its profits, and the shareholders pay personal income taxes on profits distributed as dividends. Unless the LLC indicates that it wishes to be taxed as a corporation, it is automatically taxed as a partnership by the IRS. This means that the LLC as an entity pays no taxes; rather, as in a partnership, profits are "passed through" the LLC and paid personally by the members. If LLC members want to reinvest profits in the business, however, rather than distribute the profits to members, they may prefer to be taxed as a corporation if corporate income tax rates are lower than personal tax rates. Part of the attractiveness of the LLC for businesspersons is this flexibility with respect to taxation options.

For federal income tax purposes, one-member LLCs are automatically taxed as sole proprietorships unless they indicate that they wish to be taxed as corporations. With respect to state taxes, most states follow the IRS rules. Still another advantage of the LLC for businesspersons is the flexibility it offers in terms of business operations and management—as will be discussed shortly.

The disadvantages of the LLC are relatively few. Some of the initial disadvantages with respect to uncertainties over how LLCs would be taxed no longer exist. The only remaining disadvantage of the LLC is that state statutes are not yet uniform. In an attempt to promote some uniformity among the states in respect to LLC statutes, the National Conference of Commissioners on Uniform State Laws drafted a Uniform Limited Liability Company Act for submission to the states to consider for adoption. Until all of the states have adopted the uniform law, however, an LLC in one state will have to check the rules in the other states in which the firm does business to ensure that it retains its limited liability.

THE LLC OPERATING AGREEMENT

In an LLC, the members themselves can decide how to operate the various aspects of the business by forming an **operating agreement.** Operating agreements typically contain provisions relating to management, how profits will be divided, the transfer of member-

ship interests, whether the LLC will be dissolved on the death or departure of a member, and other important issues.

Operating agreements need not be in writing, and indeed they need not even be formed for an LLC to exist. Generally, though, LLC members should protect their interests by forming a written operating agreement.[1] As with any business arrangement, disputes may arise over any number of issues. If there is no agreement covering the topic being disputed, such as how profits will be divided, the state LLC statute will govern the outcome. For example, most LLC statutes provide that if the members have not specified how profits will be divided among the members, they will be divided equally.

Generally, with respect to issues not covered by an operating agreement or by an LLC statute, the principles of partnership law are applied. At issue in the following case was whether partnership law should apply to a dispute between LLC members as to how business receipts were to be divided on the firm's dissolution.

---

1. Some experts suggest that even a one-member LLC should have an operating agreement. An operating agreement provides evidence that the LLC is a separate entity and thus strengthens the member-owner's protection against being held personally liable for a business obligation.

CASE 38.2   **Hurwitz v. Padden**

Court of Appeals of
Minnesota, 1998.
581 N.W.2d 359.
http://www.courts.
state.mn.us/library/
archive/capgi.html[a]

BACKGROUND AND FACTS   *Thomas Hurwitz and Michael Padden formed a two-person law firm as a partnership without a written agreement. They shared all proceeds on a fifty-fifty basis and reported all income as partnership income. Less than eighteen months later, Hurwitz filed articles of organization with the state of Minnesota to establish the firm as an LLC. More than three years later, Padden told Hurwitz that he wanted to dissolve their professional relationship. They resolved all business issues between them, except for a division of fees from several of the firm's cases. Hurwitz filed a suit in a Minnesota state court against Padden, seeking, among other things, a distribution of the fees on a fifty-fifty basis. The court applied the principles of partnership law, ruled that the fees should be divided equally, and entered a judgment in favor of Hurwitz for $101,750. Padden appealed, arguing in part that these principles of partnership law should not apply to an LLC.*

**IN THE LANGUAGE
OF THE COURT**

SHORT, Judge.
        *   *   *   *

---

a. This page includes a partial list of Minnesota Court of Appeals opinions available in the Minnesota State Law Library online database. The last name of the parties in these cases begins with the letter G, H, or I. Scroll down the list to the *Hurwitz* name and click on the link to read the case.

*   *   * [T]he Minnesota Limited Liability Company Act specifically incorporates the definition and use of the term "dissolution" from the Uniform Partnership Act [UPA]. Under both statutes, the entity is not terminated upon dissolution, but continues until all business issues are resolved. Thus, the UPA provides guidance when examining the end stages of either entity's life. *   *   *

It is undisputed: (1) the firm had no written or oral agreement regarding the division of *   *   * fees upon dissolution; (2) the firm existed for approximately five-and-a-half years before Padden requested dissolution; (3) a little over five months elapsed between the date of dissolution and the date the parties [filed a suit] to settle the firm's remaining issues; (4) the firm's [disputed] fee cases were acquired before the firm's dissolution; (5) prior to its dissolution, the firm divided fees equally between the parties; and (6) at the time the parties filed suit, the firm was in a winding-up phase. Under these circumstances, partnership principles *   *   * govern the division of fees obtained from pre-dissolution *   *   * files. Thus, the *   *   * fees obtained from pre-dissolution case files must be divided equally between the parties, which is consistent with the pre-dissolution method of allocation.

DECISION AND REMEDY   *The state intermediate appellate court affirmed the decision of the lower court. The state intermediate appellate court concluded that the disputed fees should be divided equally, as the receipts were divided before the dissolution.*

LLC MANAGEMENT

Basically, there are two options with respect to the management of an LLC. The members may decide in their operating agreement to be either a "member-managed" or a "manager-managed" LLC.

In a *member-managed* LLC, all of the members participate in management. In a *manager-managed* LLC, the members designate a group of persons to manage the firm. The management group may consist of only members, both members and nonmembers, or only nonmembers. Most LLC statutes provide that unless the members agree otherwise, all members of the LLC will participate in management.

The members of an LLC can also set forth in their operating agreement provisions governing decision-making procedures. For example, the agreement can indicate what procedures are to be followed for choosing or removing managers, an issue on which most LLC statutes are silent. The members are also free to include in the agreement provisions designating when and for what purposes formal members' meetings will be held. In contrast to state laws governing corporations, LLC statutes in most states have no provisions regarding members' meetings. Members may also specify in their agreement how voting rights will be apportioned. If they do not, LLC statutes in most states provide that voting rights are apportioned according to the capital contributions made by each member. Some states provide that, in the absence of an agreement to the contrary, each member has one vote.

SECTION 2

Limited Liability Partnerships

The **limited liability partnership (LLP)** is similar to the LLC. The difference between an LLP and an LLC is that the LLP is designed more for professionals who normally do business as partners in a partnership. The major advantage of the LLP is that it allows a partnership to continue as a pass-through entity for tax purposes but limits the personal liability of the partners.

The first state to enact an LLP statute was Texas, in 1991. Other states quickly followed suit, and by 1997, virtually all of the states had enacted LLP statutes. Like LLCs, LLPs must be formed and operated in compliance with state statutes. The appropriate form must be filed with a central state agency, usually the secretary of state's office, and the business's name must include either "Limited Liability Partnership" or "LLP."

In most states, it is relatively easy to convert a traditional partnership into an LLP because the firm's basic organizational structure remains the same. Additionally, all of the statutory and common law rules governing partnerships still apply (apart from those modified by the LLP statute). Normally, LLP statutes are simply amendments to a state's already existing partnership law.

The LLP is especially attractive for two categories of businesses: professional services and family businesses. Professional service companies include law firms and accounting firms. Family limited liability partnerships are basically business organizations in which all of the partners are related (see the discussion later in this chapter).

Liability in an LLP

Many professionals, such as attorneys and accountants, work together using the business form of the partnership. Remember from Chapter 33 that a major disadvantage of the partnership is the unlimited personal liability of its owner-partners. Partners are also subject to joint and several (individual) liability for partnership obligations. For example, suppose that a group of lawyers is operating as a partnership. A client sues one of the attorneys for malpractice and wins a large judgment, and the firm's malpractice insurance is insufficient to cover the obligation. When the attorney's personal assets are exhausted, the personal assets of the other, innocent partners can be used to satisfy the judgment.

The LLP allows professionals to avoid personal liability for the malpractice of other partners. Although LLP statutes vary from state to state, generally each state statute limits in some way the liability of partners. For example, Delaware law protects each innocent partner from the "debts and obligations of the partnership arising from negligence, wrongful acts, or misconduct." In North Carolina, Texas, and Washington, D.C., the statutes protect innocent partners from obligations arising from "errors, omissions, negligence, incompetence, or malfeasance." Although the language of these statutes may seem to apply specifically to attorneys, virtually any group of professionals can use the LLP.

Questions remain, however, regarding the exact limits of this exemption from liability. One question concerns limits on liability outside the state in which the LLP was formed. Another question involves whether liability should be imposed to some extent on a negligent partner's supervising partner.

Liability outside the State of Formation. Because state LLP statutes are not uniform, a question arises when an LLP formed in one state does business in another state. If the LLP statutes in the two states provide different liability protection, which law applies? Most states apply the law of the state in which the LLP was formed, even when the firm does business in another state. Some states, though, do not expressly recognize foreign LLPs (that is, LLPs formed in another state), and others do not require foreign LLPs to register before doing business.[2] In these states, there

have been no cases to date, but disputes will likely arise over which law to apply.

Supervising Partner's Liability. A partner who commits a wrongful act, such as negligence, is liable for the results of the act. Also liable is the partner who supervises the party who commits a wrongful act. This is generally true for all types of partners and partnerships, including LLPs.

When the partners are members of an LLP and more than one member is negligent, there is a question as to how liability is to be shared. Is each partner jointly and severally liable for the entire result, as a general partner would be in most states? Some states provide for proportionate liability—that is, for separate determinations of the negligence of the partners.[3]

For example, suppose that accountants Don and Jane are partners in an LLP, with Don supervising Jane. Jane negligently fails to file tax returns for their client, Centaur Tools. Centaur files a suit against Don and Jane. In a state that does not allow for proportionate liability, Don can be held liable for the entire loss. Under a proportionate liability statute, Don will be liable for no more than his portion of the responsibility for the missed tax deadline. (Even if Jane settles the case quickly, Don will still be liable for his portion.)

Family Limited Liability Partnerships

A **family limited liability partnership (FLLP)** is a limited liability partnership in which the majority of the partners are persons related to each other, essentially as spouses, parents, grandparents, siblings, cousins, nephews, or nieces. A person acting in a fiduciary capacity for persons so related can also be a partner. All of the partners must be natural persons or persons acting in a fiduciary capacity for the benefit of natural persons.

Probably the most significant use of the FLLP form of business organization is in agriculture. Family-owned farms sometimes find this form to their benefit. The FLLP has the same advantages as other LLPs with some additional advantages, such as, in Iowa, an exemption from real estate transfer taxes when partnership real estate is transferred among partners.[4]

---

2. For example, Delaware and Texas do not expressly recognize foreign LLPs, and Utah does not require the registration of foreign LLPs.

3. See, for example, Colorado Revised Statutes Annotated Section 13-21-111.5(1) and Utah Code Annotated Section 78-27-39. The American Institute of Certified Public Accountants also supports the enactment of proportionate liability statutes.
4. Iowa Statutes Section 428A.

SECTION 3

Limited Partnerships

To this point, we have been discussing relatively new forms of limited liability business organizations. We now look at a far older business organizational form that limits the liability of some of its owners—the **limited partnership.** Limited partnerships originated in medieval Europe and have been existence in the United States since the early 1800s. In many ways, limited partnerships are like the general partnerships discussed in Chapter 33, but they also differ from general partnerships in several ways. Because of this, they are sometimes referred to as *special partnerships.*

Limited partnerships consist of at least one **general partner** and one or more **limited partners.** A general partner assumes management responsibility for the partnership and so has full responsibility for the partnership and for all debts of the partnership. A limited partner contributes cash or other property and owns an interest in the firm but does not undertake any management duties and is not personally liable for partnership debts beyond the amount of his or her investment.

A limited partner can forfeit limited liability by taking part in the management of the business. A comparison of the basic characteristics of general partnerships and limited partnerships appears in Exhibit 38–1.[5]

Until 1976, the law governing limited partnerships in all states except Louisiana was the Uniform Limited Partnership Act (ULPA). Since 1976, most states and the District of Columbia have adopted the revised version of the ULPA, known as the Revised Uniform Limited Partnership Act (RULPA). Because the RULPA is the dominant law governing limited partnerships in the United States, we will refer to the RULPA in the following discussion of limited partnerships.

FORMATION OF A LIMITED PARTNERSHIP

Compared with the informal, private, and voluntary agreement that usually suffices for a general partnership

---

5. Under the Revised Uniform Partnership Act (RUPA), which was discussed in Chapter 33, a general partnership can be converted into a limited partnership and vice versa [RUPA 902, 903]. The RUPA also provides for the merger of a general partnership with one or more general or limited partnerships under rules that are similar to those governing corporate mergers [RUPA 905].

EXHIBIT 38–1   A COMPARISON OF GENERAL PARTNERSHIPS AND LIMITED PARTNERSHIPS

CHARACTERISTIC	GENERAL PARTNERSHIP (UPA)	LIMITED PARTNERSHIP (RULPA)
Creation	By agreement of two or more persons to carry on a business as co-owners for profit.	By agreement of two or more persons to carry on a business as co-owners for profit. Must include one or more general partners and one or more limited partners. Filing of a certificate with the secretary of state is required.
Sharing of Profits and Losses	By agreement; or, in the absence of agreement, profits are shared equally by the partners, and losses are shared in the same ratio as profits.	Profits are shared as required in the certificate agreement, and losses are shared likewise, up to the amount of the limited partners' capital contributions. In the absence of a provision in the certificate agreement, profits and losses are shared on the basis of percentages of capital contributions.
Liability	Unlimited personal liability of all partners.	Unlimited personal liability of all general partners; limited partners liable only to the extent of their capital contributions.
Capital Contribution	No minimum or mandatory amount; set by agreement.	Set by agreement.
Management	By agreement, or in the absence of agreement, all partners have an equal voice.	General partners by agreement, or else each has an equal voice. Limited partners have no voice or else are subject to liability as general partners (but *only* if a third party has reason to believe that the limited partner is a general partner). A limited partner may act as an agent or employee

EXHIBIT 38–1   A COMPARISON OF GENERAL PARTNERSHIPS AND LIMITED PARTNERSHIPS (CONTINUED)

CHARACTERISTIC	GENERAL PARTNERSHIP (UPA)	LIMITED PARTNERSHIP (RULPA)
Management (continued)		of the partnership and vote on amending the certificate or on the sale or dissolution of the partnership.
Duration	By agreement, or can be dissolved by action of the partners (withdrawal), operation of law (death or bankruptcy), or court decree.	By agreement in the certificate or by withdrawal, death, or mental incompetence of a general partner in the absence of the right of the other general partners to continue the partnership. Death of a limited partner, unless he or she is the only remaining limited partner, does not terminate the partnership.
Distribution of Assets on Liquidation— Order of Priorities	1. Outside creditors. 2. Partner creditors. 3. Partners, according to capital contributions. 4. Partners, according to profits.	1. Outside creditors and partner creditors. 2. Partners and former partners entitled to distributions before withdrawal under the agreement or the RULPA. 3. Partners, according to capital contributions. 4. Partners, according to profits.

(see Chapter 33), the formation of a limited partnership is a public and formal proceeding that must follow statutory requirements. A limited partnership must have at least one general partner and one limited partner, as mentioned previously. Additionally, the partners must sign a **certificate of limited partnership,** which requires information similar to that found in a corporate charter (see Chapter 34). The certificate must be filed with the designated state official—under the RULPA, the secretary of state. The certificate is usually open to public inspection.

The following case illustrates the importance of complying carefully with the formal statutory requirements imposed on limited partnerships.

CASE 38.3   Miller v. Department of Revenue, State of Oregon

Supreme Court of
Oregon, 1998.
327 Or. 129,
958 P.2d 833.
http://www.ejsimmons.
com/advanced.html[a]

HISTORICAL AND ECONOMIC SETTING   *Oregon statutes provide that "[i]t is the intent of the [Oregon] Legislative Assembly * * * to make the Oregon personal income tax law identical in effect to the provisions of the federal Internal Revenue Code relating to the measurement of taxable income of individuals." Oregon applies federal tax laws and federal court interpretations of those laws in resolving the issues raised by taxpayers. Under federal law, taxes are to be based on the "objective economic realities of a transaction rather than * * * the particular form [that] the parties employed."[b] Under state law, a taxpayer has the burden of proving by a preponderance of the evidence that a claimed deduction is allowable.[c]*

BACKGROUND AND FACTS   *Robert Loverin and Paul Miller bought a low-income housing project and retained Rockwood Development Corporation to manage it. For the project, Loverin and Miller formed a limited partnership. The certificate and articles of limited partnership identified Loverin and Miller as general partners and Rockwood as the only limited partner. It allocated 2 percent of the profits and losses to the general partners and 98 percent to the limited partner. Eventually, twenty-one investors became limited*

---

a. This page provides access to opinions of the Oregon Supreme Court decided between July 1997 and December 3, 1998. In the "Query" box, type "Loverin" and click on "Submit Query." When the results appear, click on the "full" link to access the opinion. This site is maintained by attorney E. J. Simmons.
b. *Frank Lyon Co. v. United States,* 435 U.S. 561, 98 S.Ct. 1291, 55 L.Ed.2d 550 (1978).
c. *Reed v. Department of Revenue,* 310 Or. 260, 798 P.2d 235 (1990).

partners, but none of them signed the articles or the certificate. When American Properties Corporation (APC) replaced Rockwood as a limited partner, Loverin, Miller, and the president of APC signed a document that purported to amend the articles. The document provided in part that the partners could reallocate profits and losses as they "may agree." On their income tax returns, Loverin and Miller allocated 99.9 percent of the losses to themselves. The Oregon Department of Revenue reallocated the losses according to the provisions in the original articles—2 percent to general partners and 98 percent to limited partners. Miller and others appealed to the Oregon state tax court. The court upheld the assessment, and the plaintiffs appealed to the Oregon Supreme Court.

IN THE LANGUAGE OF THE COURT

LEESON, Justice.

 *   *   *   *

 *   *   * [Oregon Revised Statute (ORS)] 69.180(1) describes the procedure required for forming a limited partnership *   *   * . It provides, in part, that when two or more persons desire to form a limited partnership they shall "[s]ign and verify a certificate" and shall "[f]ile one copy of such certificate in the office of the Corporation Commissioner." Taxpayers followed that procedure with respect to the [original] articles *   *   * . ORS 69.410(1) describes the procedure required to amend a certificate of limited partnership to change a limited partnership's composition. That statute provides that the writing to amend a certificate of limited partnership shall: "Be signed and verified by all partners. *   *   * "

The only evidence regarding the amended articles that taxpayers submitted to the Tax Court was a document signed by taxpayers and the president of APC. There is no evidence in this record that the amended articles were signed by the 21 [other] limited partners *   *   * . Thus, the amended articles were not properly executed. Consequently, taxpayers were not entitled to rely on *   *   * the amended articles for the purposes of allocating profits and losses *   *   * . The only document that conforms to the statutory requirements and that is binding is the [original] articles. *   *   * [Those] articles unambiguously allocate 2 percent of the losses to the general partners and 98 percent of the losses to the limited partners.

DECISION AND REMEDY

The Oregon Supreme Court affirmed the lower court's decision, concluding that Loverin and Miller were not entitled to allocate 99.9 percent of the losses to themselves. The fact that none of the investing limited partners signed the purported amendments rendered them invalid.

RIGHTS AND LIABILITIES OF PARTNERS

General partners, unlike limited partners, are personally liable to the partnership's creditors; thus, at least one general partner is necessary in a limited partnership so that someone has personal liability. This policy can be circumvented in states that allow a corporation to be the general partner in a partnership. Because the corporation has limited liability by virtue of corporate laws, if a corporation is the general partner, no one in the limited partnership has personal liability.

Rights of Limited Partners. Subject to the limitations that will be discussed here, limited partners have essentially the same rights as general partners, including the right of access to partnership books and the right to other information regarding partnership business. On dissolution of the partnership, limited partners are entitled to a return of their contributions in accordance with the partnership certificate [RULPA 201(a)(10)]. They can also assign their interests subject to the certificate [RULPA 702, 704].

The RULPA provides a limited partner with the right to sue an outside party on behalf of the firm if the general partners with authority to do so have refused to file suit [RULPA 1001]. In addition, investor protection legislation, such as securities laws (discussed in Chapter 37), may give some protection to limited partners.

Liabilities of Limited Partners. In contrast to the personal liability of general partners, the liability of a limited partner is limited to the capital that he or she contributes or agrees to contribute to the partnership [RULPA 502].

A limited partnership is formed by good faith compliance with the requirements for signing and filing the certificate, even if it is incomplete or defective. When a limited partner discovers a defect in the formation of the limited partnership, he or she can avoid future liability by causing an appropriate amendment or certificate to be filed or by renouncing an interest in the profits of the partnership [RULPA 304]. If the limited partner takes neither of these actions on the discovery of the defect, however, the partner can be held personally liable by the firm's creditors. Liability for false statements in a partnership certificate runs in favor of persons relying on the false statements and against members who know of the falsity but still sign the certificate [RULPA 207].

Limited Partners and Management. Limited partners enjoy limited liability so long as they do not participate in management [RULPA 303]. A limited partner who participates in management will be just as liable as a general partner to any creditor who transacts business with the limited partnership and believes, based on a limited partner's conduct, that the limited partner is a general partner [RULPA 303]. How much actual review and advisement a limited partner can engage in before being exposed to liability is an unsettled question.[6] A limited partner who knowingly permits his or her name to be used in the name of the limited partnership is liable to creditors who extend credit to the limited partnership without knowledge that the limited partner is not a general partner [RULPA 102, 303(d)].

Although limited partners cannot participate in management, this does not mean that the general partners are totally free of restrictions in running the business. The general partners in a limited partnership have fiduciary obligations to the partnership and to the limited partners, as the following case illustrates.

---

6. It is an unsettled question partly because there are differences among the laws in different states. Factors to be considered under RULPA are listed in RULPA 303(b), (c).

CASE 38.4

BT-I v. Equitable Life Assurance Society of the United States

California Court
of Appeal,
Fourth District, 1999.
75 Cal.App.4th 1406,
76 Cal.App.4th 684E,
89 Cal.Rptr.2d 811.

BACKGROUND AND FACTS   *BT-I, a general partnership, entered into a general partnership with Equitable Life Assurance Society of the United States to develop and operate an office building and retail complex in California. Banque Paribas lent the firm $62.5 million for the project. Six years later, BT-I and Equitable dissolved their general partnership and entered into a limited partnership, with Equitable as general partner and BT-I as limited partner. Equitable was given title to the retail complex and the sole right to manage the partnership. Paragraph 5.1(c) of the limited partnership agreement gave Equitable broad powers, "provided, however, . . . that in no event shall the General Partner be required to take any action . . . to prevent Banque Paribas or any other lender from exercising any remedies in connection with any loan made to the Partnership." Later, when Banque Paribas solicited bids to "sell" its loan, Equitable (in its capacity as a corporate entity) bought it for $38.5 million. On the due date, Equitable demanded full payment from the partnership, but none was made. A month later, Equitable offered to sell the loan to the partnership, but the offer was not accepted. Equitable scheduled a foreclosure sale. Three days before the sale, BT-I offered $39 million for the project but Equitable turned it down. At the sale, Equitable bought the partnership's office building. BT-I filed a suit in a California state court against Equitable, alleging in part breach of fiduciary duty. Equitable argued that the partnership agreement allowed it to buy the loans and foreclose the same as any other lender. The court entered a judgment in Equitable's favor. BT-I appealed to a state intermediate appellate court.*

IN THE LANGUAGE OF THE COURT   *BEDSWORTH, J.* [Judge]
                                         *   *   *   *

In general, under the California Revised Limited Partnership Act, partners may determine by agreement many aspects of their relationship. But there are limitations. A general partner of a limited partnership is subject to the same restrictions, and has the same liabilities to the partnership and other partners, as in a general partnership. *   *   *

* * * *

We do not believe the partnership agreement can be read as permitting Equitable to purchase the loans for its own account and foreclose. Certainly, it does not expressly allow such conduct. Even if the language were broad enough to justify such an interpretation, we hold *a partnership agreement cannot relieve a general partner of its fiduciary duties to a limited partner and the partnership where the purchase and foreclosure of partnership debt is involved.* [Emphasis added.]

Paragraph 5.1(c) provides Equitable did not have to contribute any more money to the partnership or otherwise take any action to prevent foreclosure by any lender. Fairly read, this absolves Equitable of the duty to act affirmatively to bail out the partnership from the consequences of default. But Equitable's conduct in buying and foreclosing the loans went far beyond whatever safe harbor might be found in the partnership agreement. It is one thing simply to do nothing and suffer the consequences equally with all other partners. It is another to step out of the role of partner and into that of an aggressive (and apparently greedy) lender in the marketplace. * * * Equitable was BT-I's partner, not its lender, and it lost sight of this most basic distinction in its haste to pounce upon the loan.

Nor can we agree with Equitable that the Revised Uniform Limited Partnership Act * * * [justifies] what it did. It is true the act permits the parties to vary its effect * * * . But the fact that the act allows the parties to structure many aspects of their relationship is not a license to freely engage in self-dealing—it remains our responsibility to delimit the outer boundaries of permissible conduct by a fiduciary. In view of the rule against waiving fundamental fiduciary duties, we cannot stretch these general provisions to include giving Equitable a free hand to act for its own self-interest. Equitable was still a fiduciary, and its conduct must be measured by fiduciary standards.

DECISION AND REMEDY   *The state intermediate appellate court reversed the judgment of the lower court. A general partner in a limited partnership has the same fiduciary obligation as a general partner in a general partnership, and this duty cannot be contracted away.*

DISSOLUTION OF THE LIMITED PARTNERSHIP

A limited partnership is dissolved in much the same way as an ordinary partnership (see Chapter 33). The retirement, death, or mental incompetence of a general partner can dissolve the partnership, but not if the business can be continued by one or more of the other general partners in accordance with their certificate or by the consent of all of the members [RULPA 801]. The death or assignment of interest of a limited partner does not dissolve the limited partnership [RULPA 702, 704, 705]. A limited partnership can be dissolved by court decree [RULPA 802].

Bankruptcy or the withdrawal of a general partner dissolves a limited partnership. Bankruptcy of a limited partner, however, does not dissolve the partnership unless it causes the bankruptcy of the limited partnership. The retirement of a general partner causes a dissolution unless the members consent to a continuation by the remaining general partners or unless this contingency is provided for in the certificate.

On dissolution, creditors' rights, including those of partners who are creditors, take first priority. Then partners and former partners receive unpaid distributions of partnership assets and, except as otherwise agreed, amounts representing returns on their contributions and amounts proportionate to their shares of the distributions [RULPA 804].

SECTION 4

Limited Liability Limited Partnerships

A **limited liability limited partnership (LLLP)** is a type of limited partnership. The difference between a limited partnership and an LLLP is that the liability of a general partner in an LLLP is the same as the liability of a limited partner. That is, the liability of all partners is limited to the amount of their investments in the firm.

EXHIBIT 38–2   MAJOR FORMS OF BUSINESS COMPARED

CHARACTERISTIC	SOLE PROPRIETORSHIP	PARTNERSHIP	CORPORATION
Method of Creation	Created at will by owner.	Created by agreement of the parties.	Charter issued by state—created by statutory authorization.
Legal Position	Not a separate entity; owner is the business.	Not a separate legal entity in many states.	Always a legal entity separate and distinct from its owners—a legal fiction for the purposes of owning property and being a party to litigation.
Liability	Unlimited liability.	Unlimited liability.	Limited liability of shareholders—shareholders are not liable for the debts of the corporation.
Duration	Determined by owner; automatically dissolved on owner's death.	Terminated by agreement of the partners, by the death of one or more of the partners, by withdrawal of a partner, by bankruptcy, and so on.	Can have perpetual existence.
Transferability of Interest	Interest can be transferred, but individual's proprietorship then ends.	Although partnership interest can be assigned, assignee does not have full rights of a partner.	Shares of stock can be transferred.
Management	Completely at owner's discretion.	Each general partner has a direct and equal voice in management unless expressly agreed otherwise in the partnership agreement.	Shareholders elect directors, who set policy and appoint officers.
Taxation	Owner pays personal taxes on business income.	Each partner pays pro rata share of income taxes on net profits, whether or not they are distributed.	Double taxation—corporation pays income tax on net profits, with no deduction for dividends, and shareholders pay income tax on disbursed dividends they receive.
Organizational Fees, Annual License Fees, and Annual Reports	None.	None.	All required.
Transaction of Business in Other States	Generally no limitation.	Generally no limitation.[a]	Normally must qualify to do business and obtain certificate of authority.

a. A few states have enacted statutes requiring that foreign partnerships qualify to do business there.

EXHIBIT 38–2 MAJOR FORMS OF BUSINESS COMPARED (CONTINUED)

CHARACTERISTIC	LIMITED PARTNERSHIP	LIMITED LIABILITY COMPANY	LIMITED LIABILITY PARTNERSHIP
Method of Creation	Created by agreement to carry on a business for a profit. At least one party must be a general partner and the other(s) limited partner(s). Certificate of limited partnership is filed. Charter must be issued by the state.	Created by an agreement of the owner-members of the company. Articles of organization are filed. Charter must be issued by the state.	Created by agreement of the partners. Certificate of a limited liability partnership is filed. Charter must be issued by state.
Legal Position	Treated as a legal entity.	Treated as a legal entity.	Generally, treated same as a general partnership.
Liability	Unlimited liability of all general partners; limited partners are liable only to the extent of capital contributions.	Member-owners' liability is limited to the amount of capital contributions or investments.	Varies from state to state but usually limits liability of a partner for certain acts committed by other partners.
Duration	By agreement in certificate, or by termination of the last general partner (withdrawal, death, and so on) or last limited partner.	Unless a single-member LLC, can have perpetual existence (same as a corporation).	Terminated by agreement of partners, by death or withdrawal of a partner, or by law (such as bankruptcy).
Transferability of Interest	Interest can be assigned (same as general partnership), but if assignee becomes a member with consent of other partners, certificate must be amended.	Member interests are freely transferable.	Interest can be assigned same as in a general partnership.
Management	General partners have equal voice or by agreement. Limited partners may not retain limited liability if they actively participate in management.	Member-owners can fully participate in management, or member-owners can select managers to manage the firm on behalf of the members.	Same as a general partnership.
Taxation	Generally taxed as a partnership.	LLC is not taxed, and members are taxed personally on profits "passed through" the LLC.	Same as a general partnership.
Organizational Fees, Annual License Fees, and Annual Reports	Organizational fee required; usually not others.	Organizational fee required; others vary with states.	Organizational fee required (such as a set amount per partner); usually not others.
Transaction of Business in Other States	Generally, no limitation.	Generally, no limitation but may vary depending on state.	Generally, no limitation, but state laws vary as to formation and limitation of liability.

A few states provide expressly for LLLPs.[7] In states that do not provide for LLLPs but do allow for limited partnerships and limited liability partnerships, a limited partnership should probably still be able to register with the state as an LLLP.

SECTION 5

Major Business Forms Compared

When deciding which form of business organization would be most appropriate, businesspersons normally take several factors into consideration. As mentioned earlier, these factors include ease of creation, the liability of the owners, tax considerations, and the need for capital. Each major form of business organization

---

7. See, for example, Colorado Revised Statutes Annotated Section 7-62-109. Other states that provide expressly for limited liability limited partnerships include Delaware, Florida, Missouri, Pennsylvania, Texas, and Virginia.

offers distinct advantages and disadvantages with respect to these and other factors.

For example, the sole proprietorship has the advantage of being easily and inexpensively established, but the owner faces personal liability for business obligations as well as restrictions on obtaining capital for additional financing. The partnership is relatively easy to establish and provides a way for the business to obtain capital (from partners' contributions). It enjoys tax benefits as well. The partnership also has a major disadvantage: the personal liability of the partners. One of the advantages of the corporate form is that capital for expansion can be obtained by the issuance of shares of stock. Another advantage is the limited liability of the shareholder-owners. The limited liability company and the limited liability partnership increasingly are becoming forms of choice because of the many advantages they offer with respect to both the liability of the owners and taxation.

Exhibit 38–2 on pages 722 and 723 summarizes the essential advantages and disadvantages of each of the forms of business organization discussed in Chapters 33 through 37, as well as in this chapter.

TERMS AND CONCEPTS TO REVIEW

articles of organization 712

certificate of limited
    partnership 718

family limited liability
    partnership (FLLP) 716

general partner 717

limited liability company
    (LLC) 711

limited liability limited
    partnership (LLLP) 721

limited liability partnership
    (LLP) 715

limited partner 717

limited partnership 717

member 712

operating agreement 714

QUESTIONS AND CASE PROBLEMS

38–1. LIMITED LIABILITY COMPANIES. John, Lesa, and Trevor form an LLC. John contributes 60 percent of the capital, and Lesa and Trevor each contribute 20 percent. Nothing is decided about how profits will be divided. John assumes that he will be entitled to 60 percent of the profits, in accordance with his contribution. Lesa and Trevor, however, assume that the profits will be divided equally. A dispute over the issue arises,

and ultimately a court has to decide the issue. What law will the court apply? In most states, what will result? How could this dispute have been avoided in the first place? Discuss fully.

38–2. LIABILITY OF LIMITED PARTNERS. Asher and Breem form a limited partnership with Asher as the general partner and Breem as the limited partner. Breem puts up $15,000, and Asher contributes some office equipment that he owns. A certificate of limited partnership is properly filed, and business is begun. One month later, Asher becomes ill. Instead of hiring someone to manage the business, Breem takes over complete management himself. While Breem is in control, he makes a contract with Thaler involving a large sum of money. Asher returns to work. Because of other commitments, Asher and Breem breach the Thaler contract. Thaler contends that Asher and Breem will be personally liable for damages caused by the breach if the damages cannot be satisfied out of the assets of the limited partnership. Discuss this contention.

38–3. LIMITED PARTNERSHIPS. Dorinda, Lois, and Elizabeth form a limited partnership. Dorinda is a general partner, and Lois and Elizabeth are limited partners. Consider each of the separate events below, and discuss fully which event(s) constitute(s) a dissolution of the limited partnership.

    (a) Lois assigns her partnership interest to Ashley.

    (b) Elizabeth is petitioned into involuntary bankruptcy.

    (c) Dorinda dies.

38–4. LIABILITY OF LIMITED PARTNERS. Combat Associates was formed as a limited partnership to promote an exhibition boxing match between Lyle Alzado (a professional football player) and Muhammad Ali. Alzado and others had formed Combat Promotions; this organization was to be the general partner and Blinder, Robinson & Co. (Blinder), the limited partner in Combat Associates. The general partner's contribution consisted of assigning all contracts pertaining to the match, and the limited partner's contribution was a $250,000 letter of credit to ensure Ali's compensation. Alzado personally guaranteed to repay Blinder for any amount of loss if the proceeds of the match were less than $250,000. In preparation for the match, at Alzado's request, Blinder's president participated in interviews and a promotional rally, and the company sponsored parties and allowed its local office to be used as a ticket sales outlet. The proceeds of the match were insufficient, and Blinder sued Alzado on his guaranty. Alzado counterclaimed by asserting that Blinder had taken an active role in the control and management of Combat Associates and should be held liable as a general partner. How did the court rule on Alzado's counterclaim? Discuss. [*Blinder, Robinson & Co. v. Alzado,* 713 P.2d 1314 (Colo.App. 1985)]

38–5. LIABILITY OF GENERAL PARTNERS. Val Somers, Pat McGowan, and Brent Roberson were general partners in Vermont Place, a limited partnership formed to construct duplexes on a tract of land in Fort Smith, Arkansas. In 1984, the partnership mortgaged the property so that it could build there. McGowan owned a separate company, Advance Development Corp., which was hired by the partnership to develop the project. On September 3, 1984, Somers and Roberson discovered that McGowan had not been paying the suppliers to the project, including National Lumber Co., and had not been making the mortgage payments. The suppliers and

the bank sued the partnership and the general partners individually. Discuss whether Somers and Roberson could be held individually liable for the debts incurred by McGowan. [*National Lumber Co. v. Advance Development Corp.,* 293 Ark. 1, 732 S.W.2d 840 (1987)]

38–6. FOREIGN LIMITED LIABILITY COMPANIES. Page, Scrantom, Sprouse, Tucker & Ford, a Georgia law firm, entered into a lease of office equipment in Georgia. The lessor assigned the lease to Danka Funding Co. (DFC), a New York limited liability company (LLC) with its principal place of business in New Jersey. DFC was registered as a foreign LLC in New Jersey for almost two years before the registration lapsed or was withdrawn. Under the applicable statute, a foreign LLC "may not maintain any action . . . in this State until it has registered." When Page defaulted on the lease, DFC filed a complaint in a New Jersey state court against Page for more than $100,000. In its response, Page pointed out that DFC was not registered as a foreign LLC. DFC reregistered. Asserting that DFC had not been registered when it filed its suit, Page asked a federal district court to dismiss it. Should the court grant this request? Why or why not? [*Danka Funding, L.L.C. v. Page, Scrantom, Sprouse, Tucker & Ford, P.C.,* 21 F.Supp.2d 465 (D.N.J. 1998)]

38–7. LIMITED LIABILITY PARTNERSHIPS. Mudge Rose Guthrie Alexander & Ferdon, a law firm, was organized as a general partnership but converted into a limited liability partnership (LLP). Mudge's principal place of business was New York, where it was organized, but some of its members were citizens of Maryland. The firm filed a suit in a federal district court to recover unpaid legal fees from Robert Pickett and other citizens of Maryland. The defendants filed a motion to dismiss on the ground that there was not complete diversity of citizenship, because some of the LLC members were Maryland citizens also. Mudge argued that an LLP was like a corporation, and therefore the citizenship of the firm's members was irrelevant. How should the court rule? Explain. [*Mudge Rose Guthrie Alexander & Ferdon v. Pickett,* 11 F.Supp.2d 449 (S.D.N.Y. 1998)]

38–8. LIMITED LIABILITY COMPANIES. Gloria Duchin, a Rhode Island resident, was the sole shareholder and chief executive officer of Gloria Duchin, Inc. (Duchin, Inc.), which manufactured metallic Christmas ornaments and other novelty items. The firm was incorporated in Rhode Island. Duchin Realty, Inc., also incorporated in Rhode Island, leased real estate to Duchin, Inc. The Duchin entities hired Gottesman Co. to sell Duchin, Inc., and to sign with the buyer a consulting agreement for Gloria Duchin and a lease for Duchin Realty's property. Gottesman negotiated a sale, a consulting agreement, and a lease with Somerset Capital Corp. James Mitchell, a resident of Massachusetts, was the chairman and president of Somerset, and Mary Mitchell, also a resident of Massachusetts, was the senior vice president. The parties agreed that to buy Duchin, Inc., Somerset would create a new limited liability company, JMTR Enterprises, L.L.C., in Rhode Island, with the Mitchells as its members. When the deal fell apart, JMTR filed a suit in a Massachusetts state court against the Duchin entities, alleging, among other things, breach of contract. When the defendants tried to remove the case to a federal district court, JMTR argued that the court did not have jurisdiction because there was no diversity of citizenship between the parties: all of the plaintiffs and defendants were citizens of Rhode Island. Is JMTR correct? Why or why not? [*JMTR Enterprises, L.L.C. v. Duchin,* 42 F.Supp.2d 87 (D.Mass. 1999)]

38–9. IN YOUR COURT

Caton Avenue Associates was a limited partnership that owned rental property. Caton paid Theodore Dalmazio, one of the general partners, a management fee to manage the property. Dalmazio paid his employees with Caton's money. Dalmazio billed Caton for services that are normally performed by other property management firms at no cost and also billed Caton at an hourly rate for work that is normally billed to the rental unit. Alfred Friedman and the other limited partners filed a suit on Caton's behalf against Dalmazio and the other general partner to recover the improper billings as damages. Assume that you are the judge in the trial court hearing this case and answer the following questions:

(a) What is the basic issue in this case? Is it similar to the issue involved in Case 38.4 (*BT-I v. Equitable Life Assurance Society of the United States*)?

(b) On what basis might you rule in favor of the limited partners? What reasoning would you use to justify your decision?

LAW ON THE WEB

For updated links to resources available on the Web, as well as a variety of other materials, visit this text's Web site at http://wbl.westbuslaw.com.

You can find information on how to form an LLC, including the fees charged in each state for filing LLC articles of organization, at the Web site of BIZCORP International, Inc. Go to

http://www.bizcorp.com

Nolo Press provides information on LLCs and how they are operated at

http://www.nolo.com/chapter/RUNS/RUNS_toc.html

For an example of a state law (that of Florida) governing LLPs, go to the Internet Legal Resource Guide's Web page at

http://www.ilrg.com/whatsnews/statute.html

and scroll down the page to "Registered Limited Liability Partnerships."

The law firm of Wordes, Wilshin, Goren & Conner offers a comparison of the advantages and disadvantages of major business forms with respect to various factors, including ease of formation, management, and ability to raise capital. The firm's Web site can be accessed at

http://www.wwgc.com/wwgc-be1.htm

LEGAL RESEARCH EXERCISES ON THE WEB

Go to http://wbl.westbuslaw.com, the Web site that accompanies this text. Select "Internet Applications," and then click on "Chapter 38." There you will find the following Internet research exercise that you can perform to learn more about limited liability companies:

Activity 38–1: Limited Liability Companies

CHAPTER 39

Special Business Forms and Private Franchises

WE HAVE EXAMINED IN THE preceding chapters some of the most significant business forms—including sole proprietorships, partnerships, corporations, and limited liability companies and partnerships. In this chapter, after first describing a number of forms that can be used for special types of business ventures, we look in detail at private franchises. Although the franchise is not really a business organizational form, the franchising arrangement is widely used today by those seeking to make profits.

SECTION 1

Special Business Forms

Besides the business forms already discussed, several other forms can be used to organize a business. For the most part, these other business forms are hybrid organizations—that is, they have characteristics similar to those of partnerships or corporations, or combine features of both.

JOINT VENTURE

A **joint venture,** which is sometimes referred to as a joint adventure, is a relationship in which two or more persons or business entities combine their efforts or their property for a single transaction or project or a related series of transactions or projects. Unless otherwise agreed, joint venturers share profits and losses equally. For example, when several contractors combine their resources to build and sell houses in a single development, their relationship is a joint venture.

Joint ventures range in size from very small activities to huge, multimillion-dollar joint actions undertaken by some of the world's largest corporations. Large organizations often investigate new markets or new ideas by forming joint ventures with other enterprises. For instance, General Motors Corporation and Volvo Truck Corporation were involved in a joint venture—Volvo GM—to manufacture heavy-duty trucks and market them in the United States.

Characteristics of Joint Ventures. A joint venture resembles a partnership and is taxed like a partnership. The essential difference is that a joint venture typically involves the pursuit of a single project or series of transactions, and a partnership usually concerns an ongoing business. Of course, a partnership may be created to conduct a single transaction. For this reason, most courts apply the same principles to joint ventures as they apply to partnerships. Exceptions include the following:

1. The members of a joint venture have less implied and apparent authority than the partners in a partnership (under partnership law, each partner is an agent of the other partners), because the activities of a joint venture are more limited than the business of a partnership.
2. Although the death of a partner terminates a partnership, the death of a joint venturer ordinarily does not terminate a joint venture.

Duration. The members of a joint venture can specify its duration. If the members do not stipulate a duration, a joint venture normally terminates when the project or the transaction for which it was formed has been completed. Thus, the joint venture to build and sell houses in a single development would terminate once all the houses had been built and sold. If the members of a joint venture do not specify a particular duration and the joint venture does not clearly relate to the achievement of a certain goal, the joint venture is terminable at the will of any of its members.

Duties, Rights, and Liabilities among Joint Venturers. The duties that joint venturers owe to each other are the same as the duties that partners owe to each other (discussed in Chapter 33). Thus, joint venturers owe each other fiduciary duties, including a duty of loyalty. If one of the venturers secretly buys land that was to be acquired by the joint venture, the other joint venturers may be awarded damages for the breach of loyalty.

When the members of a joint venture are separately engaged in business operations that are similar to the activity of the joint venture, conflicts may develop in two areas of the law. First, when the members of a joint venture are competitors, each member may face a choice between disclosing trade secrets to a competitor and breaching the duty to disclose. Second, in those circumstances, there is also a potential for a violation of the antitrust laws (see Chapter 45). For both reasons, joint venturers should specify exactly the information that each will be required to disclose.

The joint venturers have equal rights to manage the activities of the enterprise. Control of the operation may be given to one of the members, however, without affecting the status of the relationship. Each joint venturer is liable to third parties for the actions of the other members of the joint venture in pursuit of the enterprise's goal.

At issue in the following case was the use that a joint venturer could make of the joint venture's property. The "property" consisted of what one party had learned in fulfilling its part of the deal. Although the joint venturers were not competitors, they had agreed to keep confidential what they disclosed to each other as part of the joint venture. The dispute, however, concerned knowledge that had been developed by one party alone.

CASE 39.1   Ultralite Container Corp. v. American President Lines, Ltd.

United States
Court of Appeals,
Seventh Circuit, 1999.
170 F.3d 784.
http://www.ca7.
uscourts.gov[a]

BACKGROUND AND FACTS *American President Lines, Limited (APL), and Stoughton Composites, Limited Liability Company, formed a joint venture, Ultralite Container Corporation, to manufacture intermodal shipping containers with thin walls.[b] APL contributed its knowledge of shipping requirements, plus about $4 million. Stoughton contributed its expertise in the design and manufacture of containers, plus manufacturing facilities. Stoughton was to design and make the containers. APL was to buy and sell some of them. The parties signed confidentiality agreements that prohibited each from using in its own business, or transferring to others, information disclosed by the other*

---

a. This Web site is maintained by the U.S. Court of Appeals for the Seventh Circuit. In the left-hand column, click on "Judicial Opinions." On that page, in the "Last Name or Corporation" section, click on "Begins," enter "Ultralite" in the box, and click on "Search for Person." When the result appears, click on the docket number to access the opinion.

b. Intermodal containers can be hauled by ship, rail, or truck, and commonly use a combination of these to reach their destinations.

party as part of the joint venture. Ultralite produced and delivered the first containers, but APL believed that they were prone to delamination (separation of the foam insulation from the wall) and refused to pay. Meanwhile, Stoughton began using what it had learned in developing the intermodal containers to make and market over-the-road containers for its own business. Stoughton and Ultralite filed a suit in a federal district court against APL, alleging breach of contract. APL counterclaimed, asking the court to order Stoughton not to use what APL argued was confidential information—the know-how to produce thin-walled shipping containers. The court ordered APL to pay damages to Stoughton and Stoughton to stop making thin-walled over-the-road containers. Stoughton appealed to the U.S. Court of Appeals for the Seventh Circuit, arguing that it could use information, in its own business, that it had developed. APL asserted that any information generated by either party as part of the joint venture could not be used for any other purpose.

IN THE LANGUAGE OF THE COURT

EASTERBROOK, Circuit Judge.

* * * * *

* * * Having put up development capital, APL wants to control (or profit from) all uses of the technology. Why would it finance Stoughton's engineering for a separate business, APL asks? But things are not so simple * * * . Stoughton invested too, contributing its personnel and manufacturing facilities. Stoughton's total outlay exceeded APL's. Ultralite was more likely to make progress if Stoughton committed the engineers most familiar with [the] technology. If the contracts mean what APL says they mean, however, by putting its staff to work on the Ultralite project even for a day Stoughton disabled everyone, perhaps forever, from working on the over-the-road part of its business. It would have had to erect a Chinese Wall to separate the knowledge, and the only practical way to do this would have been to have separate staffs for intermodal containers and over-the-road containers. That would have forfeited any economies of scope from investigating [the] technology that has applications to different kinds of containers—in other words, it would have required Stoughton to perform the same work twice, perhaps by sending Ultralite a cadre of inexperienced engineers, so that it would not poison the well for its core business.

Sometimes partners to a joint venture agree to a Chinese Wall around the information. Such agreements are most common when the parties otherwise are competitors, for neither wants to give the other a leg up, but APL and Stoughton are not rivals. Their businesses are complementary. (APL has conceded that Stoughton's over-the-road containers do not compete with it, and that it had no lost profits.) This joint venture was designed to jump off from intellectual property Stoughton already possessed; that could not be achieved if Stoughton had to segregate the bodies of knowledge rigidly, on pain of forfeiting the opportunity to make any technical advances in its original product base. Nothing in the [confidentiality] agreements demonstrates that the parties were this self-destructive. * * * Thus we conclude that the contracts permit Stoughton to use information from the Ultralite project in Stoughton's original business.

DECISION AND REMEDY

The U.S. Court of Appeals for the Seventh Circuit reversed the lower court's order. The parties' confidentiality agreements did not prevent Stoughton from using the joint venture's intellectual property, which it had developed from knowledge and expertise that it already possessed.

SYNDICATE

A group of individuals getting together to finance a particular project, such as the building of a shopping center or the purchase of a professional basketball franchise, is called a **syndicate**, or an *investment group*. The form of such groups varies considerably. A syndicate may exist as a corporation or as a general or limited partnership. In some cases, the members merely own property jointly and have no legally recognized business arrangement.

JOINT STOCK COMPANY

A **joint stock company** is a true hybrid of a partnership and a corporation. It has many characteristics of a corporation in that (1) its ownership is represented by transferable shares of stock, (2) it is usually managed by directors and officers of the company or association, and (3) it can have a perpetual existence. Most of its other features, however, are more characteristic of a partnership, and it is usually treated like a partnership. As with a partnership, it is formed by agreement (not statute), property is usually held in the names of the members, shareholders have personal liability, and generally the company is not treated as a legal entity for purposes of a lawsuit. In a joint stock company, however, shareholders are not considered to be agents of each other, as would be the case if the company were a true partnership (see Chapter 33).

BUSINESS TRUST

A **business trust** is created by a written trust agreement that sets forth the interests of the beneficiaries and the obligations and powers of the trustees. With a business trust, legal ownership and management of the property of the business stay with one or more of the trustees, and the profits are distributed to the beneficiaries.

The business trust was started in Massachusetts in an attempt to obtain the limited liability advantage of corporate status while avoiding certain restrictions on a corporation's ownership and development of real property. The business trust resembles a corporation in many respects. Beneficiaries of the trust, for example, are not personally responsible for the trust's debts or obligations. In fact, in a number of states, business trusts must pay corporate taxes.

COOPERATIVE

A **cooperative** is an association, either incorporated or not, that is organized to provide an economic service, without profit, to its members (or shareholders). An incorporated cooperative is subject to state laws governing nonprofit corporations. It makes distributions of dividends, or profits, to its owners on the basis of their transactions with the cooperative rather than on the basis of the amount of capital they contribute. Cooperatives that are unincorporated are often treated like partnerships. The members have joint liability for the cooperative's acts.

The cooperative form of business is generally adopted by groups of individuals who wish to pool their resources to gain some advantage in the marketplace. Consumer purchasing co-ops are formed to obtain lower prices through quantity discounts. Seller marketing co-ops are formed to control the market and thereby obtain higher sales prices from consumers. Often, because of their special status, cooperatives are exempt from certain federal laws, such as antitrust laws (laws prohibiting anticompetitive practices—see Chapter 45).

SECTION 2

Private Franchises

A **franchise** is defined as any arrangement in which the owner of a trademark, a trade name, or a copyright licenses others to use the trademark, trade name, or copyright in the selling of goods or services. A **franchisee** (a purchaser of a franchise) is generally legally independent of the **franchisor** (the seller of the franchise). At the same time, the franchise is economically dependent on the franchisor's integrated business system. In other words, a franchisee can operate as an independent businessperson but still obtain the advantages of a regional or national organization. Well-known franchises include McDonald's, KFC, and Burger King.

TYPES OF FRANCHISES

Because the franchising industry is so extensive and so many different types of businesses sell franchises, it is difficult to summarize the many types of franchises that now exist. Generally, though, franchises fall into one of the following three classifications: distributorships, chain-style business operations, and manufacturing or processing-plant arrangements.

Distributorship. A *distributorship* arises when a manufacturing concern (franchisor) licenses a dealer (franchisee) to sell its product. Often, a distributorship covers an exclusive territory. An example is an automobile dealership.

Chain-Style Business Operation. A *chain-style business operation* exists when a franchise operates under a franchisor's trade name and is identified as a member of a select group of dealers that engage in the franchisor's business. The franchisee is generally required to follow standardized or prescribed methods of operation. Often, the franchisor demands that the franchisee maintain certain standards of operation. In addition, sometimes the franchisee is obligated to deal exclusively with the franchisor to obtain materials and supplies. Examples of this type of franchise are McDonald's and most other fast-food chains.

Manufacturing or Processing-Plant Arrangement.

A *manufacturing* or *processing-plant arrangement* exists when the franchisor transmits to the franchisee the essential ingredients or formula to make a particular product. The franchisee then markets it either at wholesale or at retail in accordance with the franchisor's standards. Examples of this type of franchise are Coca-Cola and other soft-drink bottling companies.

Laws Governing Franchising

Because a franchise relationship is primarily a contractual relationship, it is governed by contract law. If the franchise exists primarily for the sale of products manufactured by the franchisor, the law governing sales contracts as expressed in Article 2 of the Uniform Commercial Code applies (see Chapters 19 through 23). Additionally, the federal government and most states have enacted laws governing certain aspects of franchising. Generally, these laws are designed to protect prospective franchisees from dishonest franchisors and to prohibit franchisors from terminating franchises without good cause.

Federal Protection for Franchisees. Automobile

dealership franchisees are protected from automobile manufacturers' bad faith termination of their franchises by the Automobile Dealers' Franchise Act[1]— also known as the Automobile Dealers' Day in Court Act—of 1965. If a manufacturer-franchisor terminates a franchise because of a dealer-franchisee's failure to comply with unreasonable demands (for example, failure to attain an unrealistically high sales quota), the manufacturer may be liable for damages.

Another federal statute is the Petroleum Marketing Practices Act (PMPA)[2] of 1979, which prescribes the grounds and conditions under which a franchisor may terminate or decline to renew a gasoline station franchise. Federal antitrust laws (discussed in Chapter 45), which prohibit certain types of anticompetitive agreements, may also apply in certain circumstances.

Additionally, the Federal Trade Commission (FTC) has issued regulations that require franchisors to disclose material facts necessary to a prospective

franchisee's making an informed decision concerning the purchase of a franchise.

State Protection for Franchisees. State legislation

tends to be similar to federal statutes and the FTC regulations. For example, to protect franchisees, a state law might require the disclosure of information that is material to making an informed decision regarding the purchase of a franchise. This could include such information as the actual costs of operation, recurring expenses, and profits earned, along with facts substantiating these figures. State deceptive trade practices acts may also prohibit certain types of actions on the part of franchisors.

In response to the need for a uniform franchise law, the National Conference of Commissioners on Uniform State Laws drafted a model law that standardizes the various state franchise regulations. Because the uniform law represents a compromise of so many diverse interests, it has met with little success in being adopted as law by the various states.

The Franchise Contract

The franchise relationship is defined by a contract between the franchisor and the franchisee. The franchise contract specifies the terms and conditions of the franchise and spells out the rights and duties of the franchisor and the franchisee. If either party fails to perform its contractual duties, that party may be subject to a lawsuit for breach of contract. Furthermore, if a franchisee is induced to enter into a franchise contract by the franchisor's fraudulent misrepresentation, the franchisor may be liable for damages. Generally, the statutory and case law governing franchising tend to emphasize the importance of good faith and fair dealing in franchise relationships.

Because each type of franchise relationship has its own characteristics, it is difficult to describe the broad range of details a franchising contract may include. In the remaining pages of this chapter, we look at some of the major issues that typically are addressed in a franchise contract.

Payment for the Franchise. The franchisee ordi-

narily pays an initial fee or lump-sum price for the franchise license (the privilege of being granted a franchise). This fee is separate from the various products that the franchisee purchases from or through the franchisor. In some industries, the franchisor relies heavily on the initial sale of the franchise for

1. 15 U.S.C. Sections 1221 *et seq.*
2. 15 U.S.C. Sections 2801 *et seq.*

realizing a profit. In other industries, the continued dealing between the parties brings profit to both. In most situations, the franchisor will receive a stated percentage of the annual sales or annual volume of business done by the franchisee. The franchise agreement may also require the franchisee to pay a percentage of the franchisor's advertising costs and certain administrative expenses.

Business Premises.   The franchise agreement may specify whether the premises for the business must be leased or purchased outright. In some cases, construction of a building is necessary to meet the terms of the agreement. Certainly, the agreement will specify whether the franchisor supplies equipment and furnishings for the premises or whether this is the responsibility of the franchisee.

Location of the Franchise.   Typically, the franchisor will determine the territory to be served. Some

franchise contracts will give the franchisee exclusive rights, or "territorial rights," to a certain geographic area. Other franchise contracts, while they define the territory allotted to a particular franchise, either specifically state that the franchise is nonexclusive or are silent on the issue of territorial rights.

Many franchise lawsuits involve disputes over territorial rights, and this is one area of franchising in which the implied covenant of good faith and fair dealing often comes into play. For example, suppose that a franchisee is not given exclusive territorial rights in the franchise contract, or the contract is silent on the issue. If the franchisor allows a competing franchise to be established nearby, the franchisee may suffer a significant loss in profits. In this situation, a court may hold that the franchisor's actions breached an implied covenant of good faith and fair dealing. At issue in the following case was whether a franchisor had breached this implied covenant.

CASE 39.2

Camp Creek Hospitality Inns, Inc. v. Sheraton Franchise Corp.

United States
Court of Appeals,
Eleventh Circuit, 1998.
139 F.3d 1396.
http://www.findlaw.
com/casecode/courts/
11th.html[a]

BACKGROUND AND FACTS   *In 1990, Camp Creek Hospitality Inns, Inc., entered into a contract with Sheraton Franchise Corporation (a subsidiary of ITT Sheraton Corporation) to operate a Sheraton Inn franchise west of the Atlanta airport. Because another franchisee, the Sheraton Hotel Atlanta Airport, already served that market, Sheraton named Camp Creek's facility "Sheraton Inn Hartsfield-West, Atlanta Airport." Three years later, ITT Sheraton bought a Hyatt hotel in the vicinity of the Atlanta airport and gave it the name "Sheraton Gateway Hotel, Atlanta Airport." The presence of three Sheraton properties in the same market caused some customer confusion. Also, the Inn and the Gateway competed for the same customers, which caused the Inn to suffer a decrease in the growth of its business. Camp Creek filed a suit in a federal district court against Sheraton and others, alleging in part that by establishing the Gateway, ITT Sheraton denied Camp Creek the fruits of its contract in breach of the implied covenant of good faith and fair dealing. The court issued a summary judgment in favor of the defendants. Camp Creek appealed to the U.S. Court of Appeals for the Eleventh Circuit.*

IN THE LANGUAGE OF THE COURT

BIRCH, Circuit Judge:

*   *   *   *

*   *   * [T]he contract, as executed, says nothing about whether or where Sheraton could establish a competing hotel. *   *   * Camp Creek had no contractual right to expect the Sheraton Franchise to refrain from licensing the Sheraton name to additional franchises beyond the site of the Inn. By the express terms of the contract, therefore, Sheraton could have authorized a competing franchise directly across the street from the Inn, and Camp Creek would have little recourse.

Sheraton, however, did not establish such a franchise in this case; instead, it purchased and operated the Gateway on its own behalf. *   *   *

---

a. This page contains links to recent opinions of the U.S. Court of Appeals for the Eleventh Circuit. In the "1998" row, click on the "April" link. When the results appear, click on the *Camp Creek* case name to access the opinion. This Web site is maintained by FindLaw.

As a result, we must determine whether the implied covenant of good faith and fair dealing permits the Sheraton to establish its own hotel in the same vicinity as the Inn.
*   *   *

*   *   * Sheraton emphasizes that the Inn has been more profitable every year since the Gateway opened. Camp Creek, however, *   *   * describe[d] a number of trends present in the market for hotel rooms in the Atlanta area, both before and after Sheraton began operating the Gateway, and present[ed] credible theories and measures of damages attributable to the additional intra-brand competition associated with the Gateway's entry to the market. We hold that Camp Creek's evidence is sufficient to withstand Sheraton's motion for summary judgment on this claim.

DECISION AND REMEDY   *The U.S. Court of Appeals for the Eleventh Circuit held that unless a franchise contract expressly provides otherwise, it could violate the implied covenant of good faith and fair dealing for a franchisor to compete against a franchisee in the same market for the same customers. The court reversed the judgment of the lower court and remanded the case for trial.*

Business Organization.   The business organization of the franchisee is of great concern to the franchisor. Depending on the terms of the franchise agreement, the franchisor may specify particular requirements for the form and capital structure of the business. The franchise agreement may also provide that standards of operation—relating to such aspects of the business as sales quotas, quality, and record keeping—be met by the franchisee. Furthermore, a franchisor may wish to retain stringent control over the training of personnel involved in the operation and over administrative aspects of the business.

Quality Control.   Although the day-to-day operation of the franchise business is normally left up to the franchisee, the franchise agreement may provide for the amount of supervision and control agreed on by the parties. When the franchise is a service operation, such as a motel, the contract often provides that the franchisor will establish certain standards for the facility in order to protect the franchise's name and reputation. Typically, the contract will state that the franchisor is permitted to make periodic inspections to ensure that the standards are being maintained.

As a general rule, the validity of a provision permitting the franchisor to establish and enforce certain quality standards is unquestioned. Because the franchisor has a legitimate interest in maintaining the quality of the product or service to protect its name and reputation, it can exercise greater control in this area than would otherwise be tolerated. Increasingly, however, franchisors are finding that if they exercise too much control over the operations of their franchisees, they may incur liability under agency theory for the acts of their franchisees' employees—as the following case illustrates. (A court may also find that a franchisee is, in fact, an employee, if the franchisor exercises a significant degree of control over the franchisee's work schedule and activities.)[3]

---

3. See, for example, *West Sanitation Services, Inc. v. Francis*, 1998 WL 11023 (N.Y.Sup.Ct.App.Div. 1998).

CASE 39.3   Miller v. D. F. Zee's, Inc.

United States District Court, District of Oregon, 1998. 31 F.Supp.2d 792.

COMPANY PROFILE   *Based in South Carolina, Flagstar Corporation franchised or owned Denny's restaurants, as well as the Carrows, Coco's, El Pollo Loco, Hardee's, and Quincy's Family Steakhouse chains. In the early 1990s, Denny's was the defendant in two civil rights class-action suits brought by African American customers who claimed that some restaurants refused to seat or serve them. Denny's paid more than $54 million to settle those suits and responded "quickly, decisively, and sincerely" to, among other things, hire and promote more minorities.*[a] *In the mid-1990s, Flagstar declared bankruptcy, sold the Hardee's and Quincy's chains, and renamed itself Advantica Restaurant*

---

a. Anne Faircloth, "Guess Who's Coming to Denny's," *Fortune*, August 3, 1998.

*Group, Inc. (**http://www.advantica-dine.com**). By the late 1990s, Advantica's annual sales approached $3 billion, with about 2 percent annual growth.*

BACKGROUND AND FACTS   *D. F. Zee's, Inc., owns a Denny's restaurant in Tualatin, Oregon. Under the franchise agreement, Zee's agreed to train and supervise employees in accordance with Denny's Operations and Food Service Standards Manuals. Denny's regularly sent inspectors to assess compliance and reserved the right to terminate the franchise for noncompliance. Denny's logo was displayed throughout the restaurant, and there was no indication that its owners were other than "Denny's." Christine Miller worked as a server at the restaurant. After several incidents of sexually inappropriate comments and conduct, Miller complained to Stanley Templeton, the manager. When her complaints were unavailing, Miller contacted the manager of another Denny's restaurant, who referred her to the district franchise manager for Denny's, who referred the complaint to Zee's. Templeton resigned, but the harassment continued. Finally, Miller and three other employees filed a suit in a federal district court against Zee's, Denny's, and others. Denny's filed a motion for summary judgment, contending in part that a franchisor cannot be held liable for harassment by franchise employees.*

IN THE LANGUAGE OF THE COURT   AIKEN, J.
＊　　＊　　＊　　＊

Here, Denny's is responsible for acts of harassment by employees at the Tualatin Denny's because employees of the Tualatin Denny's are agents of [Denny's].

＊　　＊　　＊ [A]n agency results from the manifestation of consent by one person to another so that the other will act on his or her behalf and "subject" to his or her control, and consent by the other to so act. An agency relationship may be evidenced by an express agreement between the parties, or it may be implied from the circumstances and conduct of the parties. The principal's consent and "right to control" are the essential elements of an agency relationship. ＊　　＊　　＊
＊　　＊　　＊　　＊

Here, ＊　　＊　　＊ the franchise agreement requires adherence to comprehensive, detailed [Franchise Operations and Food Service Standards] manuals for the operation of the restaurant. ＊　　＊　　＊

Here, ＊　　＊　　＊ defendants enforce the use of these methods by regularly sending inspectors into the restaurant to assess compliance and by its retained power to cancel the agreement.

Further, the Franchise Operations Manual provides that the defendants had the right to control their franchisees in the precise parts of the franchisee's business that allegedly resulted in plaintiffs' injuries—training and discipline of employees.

DECISION AND REMEDY   *The court denied Denny's motion for summary judgment. The court held that a franchisor may be held vicariously liable under an agency theory for the intentional acts of discrimination by the employees of a franchisee.*

Pricing Arrangements.   Franchises provide the franchisor with an outlet for the firm's goods and services. Depending on the nature of the business, the franchisor may require the franchisee to purchase certain supplies from the franchisor at an established price.[4] A franchisor cannot, however, set the prices at which the franchisee will resell the goods, because this may be a violation of state or federal antitrust laws, or both. A franchisor can suggest retail prices but cannot mandate them.

Termination of the Franchise.   The duration of the franchise is a matter to be determined between the

---

4. Although a franchisor can require franchisees to purchase supplies from it, requiring a franchisee to purchase exclusively from the franchisor may violate federal antitrust laws (see Chapter 45). For two landmark cases in these areas, see *United States v. Arnold,* *Schwinn & Co.,* 388 U.S. 365, 87 S.Ct. 1956, 18 L.Ed.2d 1249 (1967), and *Fortner Enterprises, Inc. v. U.S. Steel Corp.,* 394 U.S. 495, 89 S.Ct. 1252, 22 L.Ed.2d 495 (1969).

parties. Generally, a franchise relationship starts with a short trial period, such as a year, so that the franchisee and the franchisor can determine whether they want to stay in business with one another. Usually, the franchise agreement specifies that termination must be "for cause," such as death or disability of the franchisee, insolvency of the franchisee, breach of the franchise agreement, or failure to meet specified sales quotas. Most franchise contracts provide that notice of termination must be given. If no set time for termination is specified, then a reasonable time, with notice, is implied. A franchisee must be given reasonable time to wind up the business—that is, to do the accounting and return the copyright or trademark or any other property of the franchisor.

Because a franchisor's termination of a franchise often has adverse consequences for the franchisee, much franchise litigation involves claims of wrongful termination. Generally, the termination provisions of contracts are more favorable to the franchisor than the franchisee. This means that the franchisee, who normally invests a substantial amount of time and money in the franchise operation to make it successful, may receive little or nothing for the business on termination. The franchisor owns the trademark and hence the business.

It is in this area that statutory and case law become important. The federal and state laws discussed earlier attempt, among other things, to protect franchisees from the arbitrary or unfair termination of their franchises by the franchisors. Generally, both statutory and case law emphasize the importance of good faith and fair dealing in terminating a franchise relationship.

In determining whether a franchisor has acted in good faith when terminating a franchise agreement, the courts generally try to balance the rights of both parties. If a court perceives that a franchisor has arbitrarily or unfairly terminated a franchise, the franchisee will be provided with a remedy for wrongful termination. If a franchisor's decision to terminate a franchise was made in the normal course of the franchisor's business operations, however, and reasonable notice of termination was given to the franchisee, normally a court would not consider the termination wrongful.

TERMS AND CONCEPTS TO REVIEW

business trust 730	franchisee 730	joint venture 727
cooperative 730	franchisor 730	syndicate 729
franchise 730	joint stock company 730	

QUESTIONS AND CASE PROBLEMS

39–1. BUSINESS ORGANIZATIONS. Alan, Jane, and Kyle organize a nonprofit business—AJK Markets, Inc.—to buy groceries from wholesalers and sell them to consumers who buy a membership in AJK. Because the firm is a nonprofit entity, it is able to sell the groceries for less than a commercial grocer could. What form of business organization is AJK Markets? Is it significant that AJK is incorporated?

39–2. BUSINESS FORMS AND LIABILITY. Assume that Bateson Corp. is considering entering into two contracts—one with a joint stock company that distributes home products east of the Mississippi River and the other with a business trust formed by a number of sole proprietors who are sellers of home products on the West Coast. Both contracts involve large capital outlays for Bateson to supply the businesses with restaurant equipment. In both business organizations, at least two shareholders or beneficiaries are personally wealthy, but both business organizations have limited financial resources. The owner-managers of Bateson are not familiar with either form of business organization. Because each form resembles a corporation, they are concerned with potential limits on liability in the event that either business organization breaches the contract by failing to pay for the equipment. Discuss fully Bateson's concern.

39–3. FRANCHISE AGREEMENTS. Otmar has been interested in securing a particular high-quality ice cream franchise. The franchisor is willing to give him a franchise. A franchise agreement is made that calls for Otmar to sell the ice cream only at a specific location; to buy all the ice cream from the franchisor; to order and sell all the flavors produced by the franchisor; and to refrain from selling any ice cream stored for more than two weeks after delivery by the franchisor, as this ice cream decreases in quality after that period. After two months of operation, Otmar believes that he can increase his profits by moving the store to another part of the city. He refuses to order even a limited quantity of the "fruit delight" flavor because of its higher cost, and he has sold ice cream that has been stored longer than two weeks without customer complaint. Otmar claims that the franchisor has no right to restrict him in these practices. Discuss his claims.

39–4. FRANCHISE TERMINATION. In 1953, Atlantic Richfield Co. (Arco) and Razumic signed a printed form titled a "Dealer Lease." The agreement referred to the parties as lessor and lessee. It authorized Razumic to operate an Arco service station and provided, among other things, for Arco's signs and trade name to be prominently displayed at the service station and for gasoline and other related products to be sold. The agreement detailed other aspects of the parties' business relationship, including Razumic's obligation to operate the service station in such a manner as to reflect favorably on Arco's goodwill. These basic terms were in all renewal agreements made by the parties over the years. In 1973, Arco notified Razumic that the agreement was being terminated and gave him thirty days to vacate the premises. Razumic refused, and Arco filed suit to force termination of the agreement. Did the "Dealer Lease" constitute a franchise agreement? If so—in view of the fact that the Petroleum Marketing Practices Act had not yet been passed when this case was decided—on what grounds might the court hold that Arco could not terminate the franchise at will? Discuss. [*Atlantic Richfield Co. v. Razumic*, 480 Pa. 366, 390 A.2d 736 (1978)]

39–5. JOINT VENTURES. Frank Hartman, Jr., and Robert Wiesner visited the site of a derailment of a Burlington Northern (BN) train to bid on lumber carried on the train. Hartman was to provide the salvage expertise, and Wiesner was to provide the expertise to sell the lumber. They submitted a bid of $113,663, which BN accepted. To make the payment, Hartman and Wiesner contacted Dave Anderson, who contacted Doug Feller, the managing partner of BBD Partnership. Hartman, Wiesner, Anderson, and Feller agreed to share profits from the sale of the lumber. BBD then borrowed the money to pay BN. BBD, through Feller, had promised to get involved only if it could own the lumber, however. Thus, on the bill of sale, BN entered the names "Hartman Construction" and "Feller Associates," a sole proprietorship owned by Feller. BBD later sold its interest in the deal to another party. Two years later, Hartman, Wiesner, BBD, and Feller became involved in a lawsuit over the funds that BBD had borrowed. Was the deal between the parties a joint venture or simply a loan from BBD to Hartman and the others? Discuss fully. [*Wiesner v. BBD Partnership*, 845 P.2d 120 (Mont. 1993)]

39–6. FRANCHISE TERMINATION. Ormsby Motors, Inc. (OMI), was a General Motors Corp. (GM) dealership.

Their agreement provided for termination if OMI submitted "false . . . claims for any payment." Larry Kain was in charge of OMI's warranty claims. After several years of excessive claims, GM complained to OMI. When nothing changed, GM conducted a dealer audit. The audit uncovered, among other things, over eighty claims in one ten-day period for paint repair work that was never done. OMI denied knowledge of Kain's activities. GM terminated its dealership agreement with OMI. OMI asked a federal district court to stop the termination, arguing in part that GM did not have good cause. Did GM have good cause? Explain. [*Ormsby Motors, Inc. v. General Motors Corp.*, 842 F.Supp. 344 (N.D.Ill. 1994)]

39–7. GOOD FAITH IN FRANCHISE RELATIONS. Barn-Chestnut, Inc. (BCI), entered into a franchise agreement with Grocers Development Corp. (GDC) for a Convenient Food Mart "for as long as [BCI] . . . shall have a good and valid lease" to the property. GDC sold its interest in the franchise and the property to CFM Development Corp. When the lease was about to expire, CFM offered to enter into a new lease and franchise agreement with BCI at a significantly higher price. BCI declined. When CFM refused to make another deal, BCI filed a suit against CFM in a West Virginia state court on the ground that CFM had to offer BCI a lease because the franchise was contingent on a lease. The court did not agree. BCI then argued that the implied obligation of good faith required CFM to offer to renew the lease. Essentially, the question on appeal was whether the franchisor had an obligation to renew the franchise even though there was no clause in the contract requiring that the lease/franchise be renewed. Was BCI correct in contending that the franchisor did have such an obligation? Explain. [*Barn-Chestnut, Inc. v. CFM Development Corp.*, 193 W.Va. 565, 457 S.E.2d 502 (1995)]

39–8. FRANCHISE TERMINATION. C. B. Management Co. operated McDonald's restaurants in Cleveland, Ohio, under a franchise agreement with McDonald's Corp. The agreement required C. B. to make monthly payments of, among other things, certain percentages of the gross sales to McDonald's. If any payment was more than thirty days late, McDonald's had the right to terminate the franchise. The agreement stated, "No waiver by [McDonald's] of any breach . . . shall constitute a waiver of any subsequent breach." McDonald's sometimes accepted C. B.'s late payments, but when C. B. defaulted on the payments in July 1997 McDonald's gave notice of thirty days to comply or surrender possession of the restaurants. C. B. missed the deadline. McDonald's demanded that C. B. vacate the restaurants. C. B. refused. McDonald's filed a suit in a federal district court against C. B., alleging violations of the franchise agreement. C. B. counterclaimed in part that McDonald's had breached the implied covenant of good faith and fair dealing. McDonald's filed a motion to dismiss C. B.'s counterclaim. On what did C. B. base its claim? Will the court agree? Why or why not? [*McDonald's Corp. v. C. B. Management Co.*, 13 F.Supp.2d 705 (N.D.Ill. 1998)]

39–9. FRANCHISE TERMINATION. Heating and Air Specialists, Inc., doing business as A/C Service Co., marketed heating and air conditioning products. A/C contracted with Lennox Industries, Inc., to be a franchised dealer of Lennox products. The parties signed a standard franchise contract drafted by Lennox. The contract provided that either party could terminate the agreement with or without cause on thirty days' notice and that the agreement would terminate immediately if A/C opened another facility at a different location. At the time, A/C operated only one location in Arkansas. A few months later, A/C opened a second location in Tulsa, Oklahoma. Lennox's district sales manager gave A/C oral authorization to sell Lennox products in Tulsa, at least on a temporary basis, but nothing was put in writing. Several of Lennox's other dealers in Tulsa complained to Lennox about A/C's presence. Lennox gave A/C notice that it was terminating A/C's Tulsa franchise. Meanwhile, A/C had failed to keep its Lennox account current and owed the franchisor more than $200,000. Citing this delinquency, Lennox notified A/C that unless it paid its account within ten days, Lennox would terminate both franchises. A/C did not pay. Lennox terminated the franchises. A/C filed a suit in a federal district court against Lennox, alleging in part breach of the franchise agreement for terminating the Tulsa franchise. Is A/C right? Explain. [*Heating & Air Specialists, Inc. v. Jones*, 180 F.3d 923 (8th Cir. 1999)]

39–10. IN YOUR COURT

As a franchise, Entre Computer Associates sold, among other products, computer systems marketed by Kruger Systems, Inc. Entre's agreement with Kruger included a forum-selection clause that provided that any suit between the parties had to be filed in a California court. When Kruger terminated its relationship with Entre, Entre brought a suit against Kruger in a New Jersey state court. Kruger argued that the suit should be dismissed on the basis of the forum-selection clause. Entre argued that the clause violated California state franchise law, which invalidated forum-selection clauses in auto dealership franchises. Assume that you are the judge in the New Jersey court hearing this case and answer the following questions:

(a) The first issue you need to address in this case is whether a forum-selection clause in a franchise contract is fundamentally unfair to the franchisee.

(b) If you conclude that such a clause is unfair to the franchisee, what legal reasoning would you use to justify a decision to extend the California law governing auto dealership franchises to cover other types of franchises?

LAW ON THE WEB

For updated links to resources available on the Web, as well as a variety of other materials, visit this text's Web site at http://wbl.westbuslaw.com.

The Web site of the law firm of Reinhart et al. provides extensive information about business organizations. The URL for this site is

http://www.rbvdnr.com

To learn how the U.S. Small Business Administration assists in forming, financing, and operating businesses, go to

http://www.sbaonline.sba.gov

For information on the FTC regulations on franchising, as well as state laws regulating franchising, go to

http://www.ftc.gov/bcp/franchise/netfran.htm

A good source of information on the purchase and sale of franchises is Franchising.org, which is online at

http://www.franchising.org

LEGAL RESEARCH EXERCISES ON THE WEB

Go to http://wbl.westbuslaw.com, the Web site that accompanies this text. Select "Internet Applications," and then click on "Chapter 39." There you will find the following Internet research exercise that you can perform to learn more about franchising:

Activity 39–1: Franchises

CHAPTER 40

Ethics and
Business Decision Making

THE PURPOSE OF ORGANIZING a business, no matter what business form is chosen for the enterprise, normally is to make a profit. Generally, profit-making activities are encouraged by the laws, because the flourishing of trade and commerce confers benefits on society as a whole. At the same time, businesspersons should not let their profit-making activities exceed the ethical boundaries established by society. In the past, these boundaries were often regarded as being coterminous with the law—that is, if something was legal, it was ethical. In today's rights-conscious world, however, a business firm that decides it has no duties other than those prescribed by law may find it difficult to survive. If a firm's behavior is perceived as unethical—even though it may be legal—that firm may suffer negative publicity, lost profits, and even government sanctions.

In this chapter, we first examine the nature of business ethics and some commonly used approaches to ethical reasoning. We then look at the ethical component of business decision making in some detail. Throughout the chapter, we include specific examples of ethical issues that commonly arise in the business world.

SECTION 1

The Nature of Business Ethics

Before we examine the nature of business ethics, we need to discuss what is meant by ethics generally. **Ethics** can be defined as the study of what constitutes right or wrong behavior. It is the branch of philosophy that focuses on morality and the way in which moral principles are derived or the way in which a given set of moral principles applies to one's conduct in daily life. Ethics has to do with questions relating to the fairness, justness, rightness, or wrongness of an action. What is fair? What is just? What is the right thing to do in this situation? These are essentially ethical questions.

Often, moral principles serve as the guiding force in an individual's personal ethical system. Although the terms *ethical* and *moral* often are used interchangeably, these terms refer to slightly different concepts. Whereas ethics has to do with the philosophical, rational basis for conduct, morals are often defined as *universal* rules or guidelines (such as those rooted in religious precepts) that determine our actions and character. Morals generally are "revealed" truths—that is, they are revealed to us by our family, influential mentors, or religious sources, such as the Bible (for Christians) or the Koran (for Muslims). Ethics, in contrast, is a reasoned set of principles of conduct. These principles may be based either on moral truths or on premises derived through logic and reasoning.

DEFINING BUSINESS ETHICS

Business ethics focuses on what constitutes right or wrong behavior in the business world and on how moral and ethical principles are applied by businesspersons to situations that arise in their daily activities in the workplace. Note that business ethics is not a separate *kind* of ethics. The ethical standards that guide our behavior as, say, mothers, fathers, or students apply equally well to our activities as businesspersons. Business decision makers, though, often must address more complex ethical issues and conflicts in the workplace than they do in their personal lives.

CONFLICTING DUTIES

One of the reasons that ethical decision making is more complex in the business context than in our personal lives is because business firms are perceived to owe duties to a number of groups. Recall from the *Focus on Ethics* following Chapter 9 that these groups include the firm's owners (in a corporation, the shareholders), its employees, its suppliers, those who use its products or services (consumers), the community in which it operates, and, according to many, society at large. When these duties come into conflict, difficult choices must be made.

For example, suppose that Jemico, Inc., decides to reduce its costs by downsizing and restructuring its operations. Among other things, this would allow the company to cut back on its overhead by consolidating various supervisory and managerial positions. The question for Jemico is, which employees should be retained and which should be let go? Should the firm retain highly paid employees who have worked for—and received annual raises from—the firm for years? Alternatively, in the interests of cutting costs, should it retain (or hire) younger, less experienced persons at lower salaries?

Jemico would not necessarily be acting illegally if it pursued the second option. Unless a fired employee can prove that the employer has breached an employment contract or violated the Age Discrimination in Employment Act (ADEA) of 1967, he or she will not have a cause of action against the employer. As you will learn in Chapter 42, the ADEA prohibits discrimination against workers forty years of age and older on the basis of their age.

In deciding this issue, remember that Jemico must keep its eye on its profit margin. If it does not, the firm may fail, and the shareholders will lose their investments. Furthermore, why should the firm retain highly paid employees if it can obtain essentially the same work output for a lower cost from less highly paid employees? Does Jemico owe an ethical duty to employees who have served the firm loyally over a long period of time? Most people would say yes. Should this duty take precedence over Jemico's duty to the firm's owners to maintain or increase the profitability of the firm? What if the firm faced imminent bankruptcy if it could not lower its operational costs? What if longtime employees were willing to take a slight reduction in pay to help the firm through its financial difficulties? What if they were not?

In the following case, an employer was confronted with a dwindling market and decreasing sales. The employer decided to reduce its costs of doing business by eliminating some of its obligations to its employees.

CASE 40.1   Varity Corp. v. Howe

Supreme Court of the United States, 1996. 516 U.S. 489, 116 S.Ct. 1065, 134 L.Ed.2d 130.

BACKGROUND AND FACTS   *Varity Corporation manufactures and sells farm implements. In 1986, Varity set up a subsidiary, Massey Combines Corporation (MCC), to market its self-propelled combines and four-wheel-drive tractors. The sales of both products were at an all-time low. Varity convinced current and former employees who were, or had been, involved with the products to accept a transfer to MCC of their jobs and retirement benefit plans. Varity did not tell those employees that it expected MCC to fail. Within two years, MCC did fail. Among other consequences, some retirees stopped receiving benefits. The retirees and other former employees sued Varity in a federal district court under the Employee Retirement Income Security Act of 1974 (ERISA), a federal act regulating employer-provided pension plans (see Chapter 41). They claimed that Varity owed them a fiduciary duty, which it had breached. The court ruled in their* *favor, the U.S. Court of Appeals for the Eighth Circuit affirmed, and Varity appealed the case to the United States Supreme Court.*

IN THE LANGUAGE
OF THE COURT

Justice *BREYER* delivered the opinion of the Court.

*   *   *   *

*   *   * ERISA requires a "fiduciary" to "discharge his duties with respect to a [retirement benefit] plan solely in the interest of the participants and beneficiaries." To participate knowingly and significantly in deceiving a plan's beneficiaries in order to save the employer money at the beneficiaries' expense, is not to act "solely in the interest of the participants and beneficiaries." As other courts have held, "[l]ying is inconsistent with the duty of loyalty owed by all fiduciaries *   *   * ."

DECISION
AND REMEDY

The United States Supreme Court affirmed the decision of the lower court. Varity had violated its fiduciary duty to its employees with respect to their retirement benefits.

PUBLIC OPINION AND BUSINESS ETHICS

Another factor complicating business ethics is the increasingly important role played by public opinion in determining what is or is not ethical business behavior. In the last two decades, and particularly since the advent of the Internet, the actions of business firms have been much more closely scrutinized by the media and various interest groups (groups supporting human rights, animal rights, the environment, consumers, employees, and so on) than they ever were in the past. What this means is that if a corporation undertakes or continues an action deemed to be unethical by one or more of these groups, the firm's "unethical" behavior will probably become widely known. In the interests of preserving their good reputations, business firms thus pay attention to public opinion. If they do not, they may lose customers, be boycotted by investors concerned about ethical issues, and, ultimately, lose profits.

Business ethics thus has a practical element. As a manager, you might personally be convinced that there is nothing unethical about a certain business action. If a highly vocal interest group believes otherwise, though, you might want to reassess your decision with a view toward preserving the firm's goodwill and reputation in the community. If you decide to pursue the action regardless of public opinion, you may violate your ethical (and legal) duty to act in the firm's best interests. You should keep this practical concern with public opinion in mind as you read through the remaining pages in this chapter.

SECTION 2

Approaches to Ethical Reasoning

Each individual, when faced with a particular ethical dilemma, engages in **ethical reasoning**—that is, a reasoning process in which the individual links his or her moral convictions or ethical standards to the particular situation at hand. Businesspersons do likewise when making decisions with ethical implications.

How do business decision makers decide whether a given action is the "right" one for their firms? What ethical standards should be applied? Broadly speaking, ethical reasoning relating to business traditionally has been characterized by two fundamental approaches. One approach defines ethical behavior in terms of duty, which also implies certain rights. The other approach determines what is ethical in terms of the consequences, or outcome, of any given action. We examine each of these approaches here.

DUTY-BASED ETHICS

Duty-based ethical standards often are derived from revealed truths, such as religious precepts. They can also be derived through philosophical reasoning.

Religious Ethical Standards. In the Judeo-Christian tradition, which is the dominant religious tradition in the United States, the Ten Commandments of the Old Testament establish fundamental rules for moral action. Other religions have their own sources of revealed truth. Religious rules generally are absolute with respect to the behavior of their adherents. For example, the commandment "Thou shalt not steal" is an absolute mandate for a person, such as a Jew or a Christian, who believes that the Ten Commandments reflect revealed truth. Even a benevolent motive for stealing (such as Robin Hood's) cannot justify the act, because the act itself is inherently immoral and thus wrong.

Ethical standards based on religious teachings also involve an element of *compassion*. Therefore, for example, even though it might be profitable for a firm to lay off a less productive employee, if that employee would find it difficult to find employment elsewhere and his or her family would suffer as a result, this potential suffering would be given substantial weight by the decision makers. Compassionate treatment of others is also mandated—to a certain extent, at least—by the Golden Rule of the ancients ("Do unto others as you would have them do unto you"), which has been adopted by most religions.

Kantian Ethics. Duty-based ethical standards may also be derived solely from philosophical reasoning. The German philosopher Immanuel Kant (1724–1804), for example, identified some general guiding principles for moral behavior based on what he believed to be the fundamental nature of human beings. Kant held that it is rational to assume that human beings are qualitatively different from other physical objects occupying space. Persons are endowed with moral integrity and the capacity to reason and conduct their affairs rationally. Therefore, their thoughts and actions should be respected. When human beings are treated merely as a means to an end, they are being treated as the equivalent of objects and are being denied their basic humanity.

A central postulate in Kantian ethics is that individuals should evaluate their actions in light of the consequences that would follow if *everyone* in society acted in the same way. This **categorical imperative** can be applied to any action. For example, say that you are deciding whether to cheat on an examination. If you have adopted Kant's categorical imperative, you will decide not to cheat, because if everyone cheated, the examination would be meaningless.

The Principle of Rights. Duty-based ethical standards imply that human beings have basic rights, because a duty cannot exist without a corresponding right. For example, the commandment "Thou shalt

not kill" implies that individuals have a right to live. Additionally, religious ethics may involve a rights component because of the belief—characteristic of many religions—that an individual is "made in the image of God" or "Allah." This belief confers on the individual great dignity as a person. For one who holds this belief, not to respect that dignity—and the rights and status that flow from it—would be morally wrong. Kantian ethics also implies fundamental rights based on the personal dignity of each individual. Just as individuals have a duty not to treat others as means to an end, so individuals have a right to have their status and moral integrity as human beings treated with respect.

The principle that human beings have certain fundamental rights (to life, freedom, and the pursuit of happiness, for example) is deeply embedded in Western culture. As discussed in Chapter 1, the natural law tradition embraces the concept that certain actions (such as killing another person) are morally wrong because they are contrary to nature (the natural desire to continue living). Those who adhere to this **principle of rights,** or "rights theory," believe that a key factor in determining whether a business decision is ethical is how that decision affects the rights of others. These others include the firm's owners, its employees, the consumers of its products or services, its suppliers, the community in which it does business, and society as a whole.

OUTCOME-BASED ETHICS: UTILITARIANISM

"Thou shalt act so as to generate the greatest good for the greatest number." This is a paraphrase of the major premise of the utilitarian approach to ethics. **Utilitarianism** is a philosophical theory developed by Jeremy Bentham (1748–1832) and then advanced, with some modifications, by John Stuart Mill (1806–1873)—both British philosophers. In contrast to duty-based ethics, utilitarianism is outcome oriented. It focuses on the consequences of an action, not on the nature of the action itself or on any set of preestablished moral values or religious beliefs.

Under a utilitarian model of ethics, an action is morally correct, or "right," when, among the people it affects, it produces the greatest amount of good for the greatest number. When an action affects the majority adversely, it is morally wrong. Applying the utilitarian theory thus requires (1) a determination of which individuals will be affected by the action in question; (2) a **cost-benefit analysis**—an assessment of the negative and positive effects of alternative actions on these individuals; and (3) a choice among alternative actions that will produce maximum societal utility (the greatest positive net benefits for the greatest number of individuals).

The utilitarian approach to decision making commonly is employed by businesses, as well as by individuals. Weighing the consequences of a decision in terms of its costs and benefits for everyone affected by it is a useful analytical tool in the decision-making process. At the same time, utilitarianism is often criticized because its objective, calculated approach to problems tends to reduce the welfare of human beings to plus and minus signs on a cost-benefit worksheet and to "justify" human costs that many find totally unacceptable.

For example, from a utilitarian standpoint it might be ethically acceptable to test drugs or medicines on human beings because presumably a majority of the population would benefit from the experiments. If, however, one accepts the principle that each individual has basic human rights, then an action that deprives an individual or group of individuals of these rights—even for the greater good of society—is ethically unacceptable.

Section 3

Ethical Decision Making

Most major companies today ask three questions about any action before it is undertaken: Is the action profitable? Is it legal? Is it ethical? The first prong of this test for business decision making—determining whether a given course of action will be profitable—is foremost. After all, for-profit firms remain in business only if they make a profit. If the action would not be profitable, it probably will not be undertaken. If the action would be profitable, then the decision makers need to evaluate whether it also would be legal and ethical.

Is the Contemplated Action Legal?

In today's business world, legal compliance usually is regarded as the **moral minimum.** In other words, the

minimal acceptable standard for ethical business behavior is compliance with the law.

It may seem that answering a question concerning the legality of a given action should be simple. Either something is legal or it is not. In fact, one of the major challenges businesspersons face is that the legality of a particular action is not always clear. In part, this is because there are so many laws regulating business that it is possible to violate one of them without realizing it. There are also numerous "gray areas" in the law, making it difficult to predict with certainty how a court may apply a given law to a particular action.

Laws Regulating Business. Today's business firms are subject to extensive government regulation. As mentioned in Chapter 1, virtually every action a firm undertakes—from the initial act of going into business to hiring and firing personnel to selling products in the marketplace—is subject to statutory law and to numerous rules and regulations issued by administrative agencies. Furthermore, these rules and regulations are changed or supplemented frequently.

Determining whether a planned action is legal thus requires the decision makers to keep abreast of the law. Normally, large business firms have attorneys on their staffs to assist them in making key decisions. Small firms must also seek legal advice before making important business decisions—because the consequences of just one violation of a regulatory rule may be costly.

Ignorance of the law will not excuse a business owner or manager from liability for violating a statute or regulation. Recall from Chapter 8 that in one case, the court imposed criminal fines, as well as imprisonment, on a company's supervisory employee for violating a federal environmental act—even though the employee was totally unaware of what was required under the provisions of that act.[1]

In the following case, a company was alleged to have infringed on another's service mark "willfully or in bad faith." (Service marks, which are used in the sale or advertising of services, were discussed in Chapter 7.) In its defense, the company offered what it called a "credible, innocent explanation" for its continued use of the mark.

1. *United States v. Hanousek,* 176 F.3d 1116 (9th Cir. 1999). This case was presented as Case 8.1 in Chapter 8.

CASE 40.2

New York State Society of Certified Public Accountants v. Eric Louis Associates, Inc.

United States
District Court,
Southern District of
New York, 1999.
79 F.Supp.2d 331.

BACKGROUND AND FACTS   *The New York State Society of Certified Public Accountants (the Society) has more than 30,000 members. The Society sets standards for certified public accountants (CPAs) and protects the interests of its members and the public with respect to the practice of accountancy. Since 1984, the Society has used the service mark "NYSSCPA" on its business cards and other promotional material. In 1994, the Society registered the domain name "nysscpa.org." and, since 1997, has operated a Web site at this Internet address. Eric Louis Associates, Inc. (ELA), is a small firm engaged in the job placement of accountants and other professionals. Brian Elias was ELA's founder and president. In January 1999, ELA registered the domain name "nysscpa.com" and began operating a Web site at that address, using "NYSSCPA" as a meta tag.[a] ELA's home page stated that it was "not affiliated with" the Society, but clicking on a hyperlink from that page to the Society's site framed that site within ELA's site. On March 25, the Society wrote a letter to ELA, demanding that ELA stop using the "nysscpa.com" domain name and stop framing the Society's Web site. ELA agreed to do so if the Society would pay it $20,000 or provide, free of charge, an exhibitor's booth at the annual NYSSCPA conference for the next five years. On April 6, the Society sent a second letter, refusing ELA's offer and repeating its demands. When ELA did nothing, the Society filed a suit against ELA in a federal district court, which held that ELA had infringed the Society's mark. The next question was whether the infringement was willful or in bad faith, which would entitle the Society to collect its attorneys' fees from ELA.*

**IN THE LANGUAGE
OF THE COURT**

SAND, J. [Judge]
*   *   *   *

Our *   *   * determination that Defendant intentionally copied Plaintiff's mark takes us a considerable way toward determining that this copying was tinged with bad faith. *   *   * [T]he "nysscpa.com" domain name clearly was not selected because it reflected some characteristic of ELA. Rather, it appears that ELA adopted it with the intention of capitalizing on plaintiff's reputation and goodwill. As Mr. Elias [testified], ELA was a small, young company in the business of placing CPA's and other financial professionals. It was thus presented with the challenge of making such professionals aware of its services. The web site was presumably created for this purpose. What better way to attract CPA's to this site than to give it the "nysscpa.com" domain name, and embed the "NYSSCPA" meta-tag in the site's [source] code. *   *   *
*   *   *   *

This brings us, finally, to the question of whether Defendant has offered a credible innocent explanation of its adoption of Plaintiff's mark. *   *   *
*   *   *   *

Consider first Mr. Elias's response to the Society's March 25th cease and desist demand. Even if Mr. Elias genuinely believed that ELA had done nothing wrong prior to this date, this demand put him on notice that ELA's use of the "nysscpa.com" domain name and the "NYSSCPA" meta-tag was potentially illegal. If Mr. Elias had then consulted an attorney and been advised that ELA's actions were arguably legal, ELA could plausibly maintain that its continued infringement *   *   * of the Society's mark subsequent to the cease and desist demand was not willful. But Mr.

---

a. A *meta tag* is a key word in the source code used to create Web pages. A meta tag prompts a search engine to include the meta tag's Web site in the search engine's results. Meta tags and the lawfulness of their use were discussed in Chapter 9.

Elias chose a quite different course of conduct. Not only did he fail to seek the advice of counsel, but he proceeded to act on his uninformed belief that registration of the "nysscpa.com" domain name had given him certain rights by attempting to sell the name to the Society.

*   *   *   *

Even if we assume, however, that Mr. Elias had not crossed this line on March 26, with his offer to sell the domain name to Plaintiff, he surely crossed it by April 6, 1999: the date Defendant received Plaintiff's second cease and desist demand. *   *   * Defendant responded to this second cease and desist demand by continuing its two-pronged strategy of neither ceasing and desisting nor seeking the advice of counsel. On this date, therefore—at the latest—Mr. Elias's belief that ELA's actions were not violative of Plaintiff's trademark rights ceased being reasonable. As such, on this date—at the latest—Defendant's conduct commenced being willful and tinged with bad faith.

DECISION AND REMEDY *The court held that the Society was entitled to collect from ELA the attorneys' fees the Society owed for work done after April 6. ELA's conduct was willful and in bad faith after that date because, on learning that it may not have had any rights to the Society's service mark, ELA did not stop its use of the mark or seek the advice of counsel.*

"Gray Areas" in the Law. In many situations, business firms can predict with a fair amount of certainty whether a given action would be legal. For example, firing an employee solely because of that person's race or gender would clearly violate federal laws prohibiting employment discrimination. In some situations, though, the legality of a particular action may be less clear.

For example, suppose that a firm decides to launch a new advertising campaign. How far can the firm go in making claims for its product or services? Federal and state laws prohibit firms from engaging in "deceptive advertising." At the federal level, the test for deceptive advertising normally used by the Federal Trade Commission is whether an advertising claim would deceive a "reasonable consumer."[2] At what point, though, would a reasonable consumer be deceived by a particular ad?

Another gray area in the law has to do with product misuse. Recall from Chapter 6 that product-liability laws require manufacturers and sellers to warn consumers of

the kinds of injuries that might result from the foreseeable misuse of their products. An exception to this rule is made when a risk associated with a product is "open and obvious." Sharp knives, for example, can obviously injure their users. Sometimes, a business has no way of predicting how a court might rule in deciding whether a particular risk is open and obvious or whether consumers should be warned of the risk.

In short, whether a given action will be deemed legal or illegal often depends on how an administrative agency or a court in a particular jurisdiction decides to interpret and apply the law to the facts and issues of a particular case. Business decision makers thus need to proceed with caution and evaluate the action and its consequences from an ethical perspective. Generally, if a company can demonstrate that it acted in good faith and responsibly in the circumstances, it has a better chance of successfully defending its action in court or before an administrative law judge.

Even courts often disagree on certain issues. In the following case, for example, the trial court and the appellate court arrived at different conclusions on whether a warning on an aerosol can of butane adequately warned consumers of the danger of inhaling the contents of the can.

_____
2. See Chapter 44 for a discussion of the Federal Trade Commission's role in regulating deceptive trade practices, including misleading advertising.

CASE 40.3   Pavlik v. Lane Ltd./Tobacco Exporters International

United States
Court of Appeals,
Third Circuit, 1998.
135 F.3d 876.
http://www.findlaw.
com/casecode/courts/
3rd.html[a]

HISTORICAL AND ETHICAL SETTING   *It is human nature to play Monday morning quarterback—to second-guess the choices that others make after the consequences of those choices become fact. Sometimes, such hindsight consists of superimposing what one person believes is common knowledge onto another's set of beliefs and knowledge. This can occur when adults assume that children know what adults know—that an oven is hot, for example. A child has to be warned that an oven is hot, and even then he or she may not appreciate the danger, or the seriousness of the danger, depending on the context of the warning. Judges, in particular, have to avoid the temptation to impose their own assumptions about what is common knowledge onto the parties in the cases that come before them.*

BACKGROUND AND FACTS   *Butane is a fuel for cigarette lighters. Zeus brand butane is distributed in small aerosol cans by Lane Limited/Tobacco Exporters International (Lane). On each can is the warning "DO NOT BREATHE SPRAY." Twenty-year-old Stephen Pavlik died from intentionally inhaling the contents of one of the cans. His father, George Pavlik, filed a suit in a federal district court against Lane and others, claiming in part that the statement on the can did not adequately warn users of the hazards of butane inhalation. The court issued a summary judgment in the defendants' favor, reasoning in part that Stephen must have been aware of the dangers of inhaling butane and that a more specific warning would not have affected his conduct. George Pavlik appealed to the U.S. Court of Appeals for the Third Circuit.*

IN THE LANGUAGE OF THE COURT   BECKER, Chief Judge.

*   *   *   *

*   *   * [A]n otherwise properly designed product may still be unreasonably dangerous (and therefore "defective") for strict liability purposes if the product is distributed without sufficient warnings to apprise the ultimate user of the latent dangers in the product.

*   *   *   *

*   *   * [W]e have serious doubts that the Zeus warning sufficiently warns users of the potentially fatal consequences of butane inhalation, and we are not convinced of its adequacy *   *   * . More specifically, the "DO NOT BREATHE SPRAY" warning appears to give the user no notice of the serious nature of the danger posed by inhalation, intentional or otherwise, and no other language on the Zeus can does so. Yet, we similarly cannot find that such a directive is inadequate as a matter of law, and so we must leave the question for the jury.

DECISION AND REMEDY   *The U.S. Court of Appeals for the Third Circuit held that it was not clear that Stephen was fully aware of the dangers of inhaling butane, based on the label on the Zeus cans. The court reversed the judgment of the lower court and remanded the case for trial.*

---

a. In the "Browsing" section, in the "1998" row, click on "Feb." When that page opens, scroll down the list to the *Pavlik* case name and click on it to access the opinion.

IS THE CONTEMPLATED ACTION ETHICAL?

Even if a company is certain of the legality of a particular action, that does not necessarily mean that the action is ethical. For example, suppose that a corporation that markets baby formula in developing countries has learned that mothers in those countries often mix the formula with impure water, to make the formula go further. As a result, babies there are suffering from malnutrition, diarrhea, and even death. Although the corporation is not violating any law, many would contend that it should suspend sales of the formula in those countries.[3]

Typically, in deciding whether a given action would be ethical, a firm's decision makers are guided not only by their own ethical principles and reasoning processes but also by their company's ethical policies and code of conduct.

Ethical Codes and Corporate Compliance Programs.

Virtually all large corporations today have established ethical policies or codes of conduct to help guide their executives and managers (and all company personnel) in making decisions. Typically, an ethical code, or code of conduct, will indicate the company's commitment to legal compliance, as well as to the welfare of its employees, suppliers, consumers, and others who may be affected by the company's decisions and practices.

For example, look at the fold-out exhibit in this chapter showing Costco's Code of Ethics. This code clearly indicates Costco's commitment to legal compliance, as well as to the welfare of its members (those who belong to its clubs and purchase its products), its employees, and its vendors (suppliers). The code also details some specific ways in which the interests and welfare of these groups will be protected. If you look closely at the exhibit, you will also see that Costco acknowledges that by protecting these groups' interests, it will realize its "ultimate goal"—which is to reward its shareholders (those who own the company). Costco's code can guide management and supervisory personnel as they make decisions involving the ethical rights and obligations of each group.

In a large corporation, an ethical code usually is just one part of a comprehensive corporate compliance program. Other components of such a program may include a corporate ethics committee, ethical training programs, and internal audits (to monitor compliance with applicable laws and the company's standards of conduct). Some companies also have a special office to which employees can report—in person or perhaps anonymously via an 800 number—suspected improper conduct, including any legal, ethical, or policy violations that may occur.

By making ethical and legal conduct a top priority, ethical codes and compliance programs help business managers to conduct their firms' affairs responsibly. Still, questions often arise for which there are no clear-cut answers, particularly when they involve conflicting goals. For example, suppose that a company's employees are pressuring management for a wage increase. If the company agrees to increase employees' wages, this will cut into the firm's profits and thus adversely affect the shareholder-owners' interests. The decision to be made here involves not a choice between an ethical and an unethical action but rather a choice between two conflicting goals.

Determining Ethical Priorities.

An ethical issue involving conflicting duties can only be resolved by establishing which duties should take priority over others. For example, suppose that the Wellsen Company, a glue-manufacturing firm, learns that thousands of children in several Latin American countries have been inhaling its glue. As a result, many of the children may suffer severe health consequences in the future, including kidney disease and brain damage. Consumer activists have launched a media campaign against Wellsen, accusing it of being unethical by marketing its glue in those countries. What is the right thing to do in this situation? Should Wellsen cease selling its glue in the countries in question even though selling it is legal and profitable?

Assume that Wellsen decides to pull out of those markets. Whose interests would be adversely affected? First of all, the interests of the company's shareholder-owners would be—because the decision probably would result in lower profits. The interests of employees, particularly those with jobs at stake, would also be adversely affected by the decision. Additionally, those firms that supply Wellsen with the materials it needs in the glue-manufacturing process would see decreased profits, at least temporarily, because Wellsen would need fewer materials. Finally, what about the interests of the majority of the consumers in the Latin American countries, who do not misuse the glue? These consumers would also be adversely affected, because they could no longer purchase the glue for home or business purposes.

Clearly, if equal ethical weight were attached to the interests of each group, the right decision would be to continue marketing the product in Latin American countries. Indeed, from a utilitarian perspective, this action might be deemed the most

---

3. This situation faced the Nestlé Company in the 1970s. That company had concluded, on the basis of a cost-benefit analysis, that it was ethically justified in continuing to market its baby formula in developing countries. Nestlé was severely criticized for its behavior.

ethical, because the action would benefit the majority of those affected by the decision. From a duty-based (or rights-based) perspective, however, it would be difficult to justify a decision to continue selling a product that was harming some human beings, regardless of the fact that the harm was caused by product misuse.

SECTION 4

Maximum versus Optimum Profits

Today's corporate decision makers are, in a sense, poised on a fulcrum between profitability and ethical responsibility. If they emphasize profits at the expense of perceived ethical responsibilities to other groups, they may become the target of negative media exposure and even lawsuits. If they go too far in the other direction (keep an unprofitable plant open so that the employees do not lose their jobs, invest too heavily in charitable works or social causes, and so on), their profits will suffer and they may have to go out of business.

Striking the right balance on this fulcrum is difficult, and usually some profits must be sacrificed in the process. Instead of maximum profits, many firms today aim for **optimum profits**—the maximum profits a firm can realize while staying within legal *and* ethical limits. In the Wellsen Company's situation, if the decision makers base their reasoning on duty/rights-based ethical standards, they may conclude that they have an ethical duty to pull out of the Latin American markets. In other words, they may decide to settle for optimum profits rather than maximum profits.

Even from a utilitarian perspective, it might be wise to discontinue sales in the Latin American countries in question. Although utilitarian reasoning may lead to the conclusion that there is nothing unethical about continuing sales in those areas—because it would benefit the majority of persons affected by such a decision—Wellsen's reputation could suffer irreparable damage if it did so. In the long run, a decision to continue the sales thus could be an unprofitable one.

Note that in a utilitarian cost-benefit analysis of the ethical issue facing the Wellsen Company, the "cost" of potentially decreased profits in the long run was acknowledged primarily because of the media campaign against Wellsen. In other words, if consumer activists had not created widespread public awareness of Wellsen's actions, the outcome of the

utilitarian analysis of the issue would probably be a decision to continue marketing the glue in the Latin American countries.

SECTION 5

The Ever-Changing Ethical Landscape

Society's determination of what constitutes ethical business behavior changes over time. Consider the ethical landscape of business as it existed seventy-five years ago. At that time, a corporation was perceived to have one major duty: to serve the interests of its shareholders (basically, make profitable decisions) and to act within legal limits when doing so. In other words, in the corporate decision-making process, only two questions normally were asked: Is it profitable? Is it legal? The third question (Is it ethical?) was largely answered by the first two.

Indeed, most of the ethical and social issues discussed in this chapter and elsewhere in this text either did not exist or were of little public concern at that time. Technological innovations, the communications revolution, pressing environmental problems, and social movements resulting in greater rights for minorities, women, and consumers have all dramatically changed the society in which we live and, consequently, the business and ethical landscape of the United States. Today, society expects business leaders to acknowledge and fulfill ethical duties to all persons and groups that are affected by the decisions and activities of their firms.

Moreover, the global dimension of business activity today has led to ethical issues that were of little concern to American firms—or to the American public—in the past. We look next at some of these issues.

MONITORING THE EMPLOYMENT PRACTICES OF FOREIGN SUPPLIERS

Many U.S. businesses now contract with companies in developing nations to produce goods, such as shoes and clothing, because the wage rates in those nations are significantly lower than in the United States. Yet what if a foreign company exploits its workers—by hiring women and children at below-minimum-wage rates, for example, or by requiring its employees to work long hours in a workplace full of health hazards? What if the company's supervisors routinely engage in workplace conduct that is offensive to women?

Given today's global communications network, few companies can assume that their actions in other nations will go unnoticed by "corporate watch" groups that discover and publicize unethical corporate behavior. As a result, American businesses today usually take steps to avoid such adverse publicity—either by refusing to deal with certain suppliers or by making arrangements to monitor their suppliers' workplaces to make sure that the workers are not being mistreated.

THE FOREIGN CORRUPT PRACTICES ACT

Another ethical problem in international business dealings has to do with the legitimacy of certain side payments to government officials. In the United States, the majority of contracts are formed within the private sector. In many foreign countries, however, decisions on most major construction and manufacturing contracts are made by government officials because of extensive government regulation and control over trade and industry. Side payments to government officials in exchange for favorable business contracts are not unusual in such countries, nor are they considered to be unethical. In the past, U.S. corporations doing business in developing countries largely followed the dictum, "When in Rome, do as the Romans do."

In the 1970s, however, the U.S. press, and government officials as well, uncovered a number of business scandals involving large side payments by U.S. corporations—such as Lockheed Aircraft—to foreign representatives for the purpose of securing advantageous international trade contracts. In response to this unethical behavior, in 1977 Congress passed the Foreign Corrupt Practices Act (FCPA), which prohibits U.S. businesspersons from bribing foreign officials to secure advantageous contracts.

Prohibition against the Bribery of Foreign Officials.
The first part of the FCPA applies to all U.S. companies and their directors, officers, shareholders, employees, and agents. This part prohibits the bribery of most officials of foreign governments if the purpose of the payment is to get the official to act in his or her official capacity to provide business opportunities.

The FCPA does not prohibit payment of substantial sums to minor officials whose duties are ministerial. These payments are often referred to as "grease," or facilitating payments. They are meant to ensure that administrative services that might otherwise be performed at a slow pace are sped up. Thus, for example, if a firm makes a payment to a minor official to speed up an import licensing process, the firm has not violated the FCPA. Generally, the act, as amended, permits payments to foreign officials if such payments are lawful within the foreign country. The act also does not prohibit payments to private foreign companies or other third parties unless the U.S. firm knows that the payments will be passed on to a foreign government in violation of the FCPA.

Accounting Requirements.
The second part of the FCPA is directed toward accountants, because in the past bribes were often concealed in corporate financial records. All companies must keep detailed records that "accurately and fairly" reflect the company's financial activities. In addition, all companies must have an accounting system that provides "reasonable assurance" that all transactions entered into by the company are accounted for and legal. These requirements assist in detecting illegal bribes. The FCPA further prohibits any person from making false statements to accountants or false entries in any record or account.

Penalties for Violations.
In 1988, the FCPA was amended to provide that business firms that violate the act may be fined up to $2 million. Individual officers or directors who violate the FCPA may be fined up to $100,000 (the fine cannot be paid by the company) and may be imprisoned for up to five years.

OTHER NATIONS DENOUNCE BRIBERY

For twenty years, the FCPA was the only law of its kind in the world, despite attempts by U.S. political leaders to convince other nations to pass similar legislation. That situation is now changing. In 1997, the Organization for Economic Cooperation and Development, to which twenty-six of the world's leading industrialized nations belong, signed a convention (treaty) that made the bribery of foreign public officials a serious crime. Each signatory is obligated to enact legislation within its nation in accordance with the treaty. The agreement will not only improve the ethical climate in international trade but also level the playing field for U.S businesspersons.

TERMS AND CONCEPTS TO REVIEW

business ethics 739	ethical reasoning 740	optimum profits 747
categorical imperative 741	ethics 738	principle of rights 741
cost-benefit analysis 742	moral minimum 742	utilitarianism 741

QUESTIONS AND CASE PROBLEMS

40–1. BUSINESS ETHICS. Some business ethicists maintain that whereas personal ethics has to do with "right" or "wrong" behavior, business ethics is concerned with "appropriate" behavior. In other words, ethical behavior in business has less to do with moral principles than with what society deems to be appropriate behavior in the business context. Do you agree with this distinction? Do personal and business ethics ever overlap? Should personal ethics play any role in business ethical decision making?

40–2. BUSINESS ETHICS. If a firm engages in "ethical" behavior solely for the purpose of gaining profits from the goodwill it generates, the "ethical" behavior is essentially a means toward a self-serving end (profits and the accumulation of wealth). In this situation, is the firm acting unethically in any way? Which should carry greater weight on the ethical scales in this situation: motive or conduct?

40–3. ETHICAL REASONING. Susan Whitehead serves on the city planning commission. The city is planning to build a new subway system, and Susan's brother-in-law, Jerry, who owns the Custom Transportation Co., has submitted the lowest bid for the system. Susan knows that Jerry could complete the job for the estimated amount, but she also knows that once Jerry completes this job, he will probably sell his company and quit working. Susan is concerned that Custom Transportation's subsequent management might not be as easy to work with if revisions need to be made on the subway system after its completion. She is torn as to whether she should tell the city about the potential changes in Custom Transportation's management. If the city knew about the instability of Custom Transportation, it might prefer to give the contract to one of Jerry's competitors, whose bid was only slightly higher than Jerry's. Does Susan have an ethical obligation to disclose the information about Jerry to the city planning commission? How would you apply duty-based ethical standards to this question? What might be the outcome of a utilitarian analysis? Discuss fully.

40–4. ETHICAL DECISION MAKING. Assume that you are a high-level manager for a shoe manufacturer. You know that your firm could increase its profit margin by producing shoes in Indonesia, where you could hire women for $40 a month to assemble them. You also know, however, that a competing shoe manufacturer recently was accused by human rights advocates of engaging in exploitative labor practices because the manufacturer sold shoes made by Indonesian women working for similarly low wages. You personally do not believe that paying $40 a month to Indonesian women is unethical, because you know that in that impoverished country, $40 a month is a better-than-average wage rate. Assuming that the decision is yours to make, should you have the shoes manufactured in Indonesia and make higher profits for your company? Or should you avoid the risk of negative publicity and the consequences of that publicity for the firm's reputation and subsequent profits? Are there other alternatives? Discuss fully.

40–5. ETHICAL DECISION MAKING. Shokun Steel Co. owns many steel plants. One of its plants is much older than the others. Equipment at the old plant is outdated and inefficient, and the costs of production at that plant are now twice what they are at any of Shokun's other plants. The price of steel cannot be increased because of competition, both domestic and international. The plant is located in Twin Firs, Pennsylvania, which has a population of about forty-five thousand, and currently employs over a thousand workers. Shokun is contemplating whether to close the plant. What factors should the firm consider in making its decision? Will the firm violate any ethical duties if it closes the plant? Analyze these questions from the two basic perspectives on ethical reasoning discussed in this chapter.

40–6. EMPLOYMENT RELATIONSHIPS. Matt Theurer, an eighteen-year-old high school senior, worked part-time at a McDonald's restaurant in Oregon. Theurer volunteered to work an extra shift one day, in addition to his regular shifts (one preceding and one following the extra shift). After working about twelve hours during a twenty-four-hour period, Theurer told the manager that he was tired and asked to be excused from his next regularly scheduled shift so that he could rest. The manager agreed. While driving home from work, Theurer fell asleep at the wheel and crashed into a van driven by Frederic Faverty. Theurer died, and Faverty was severely injured. Faverty sued McDonald's, alleging, among other things, that McDonald's had been negligent in permitting Theurer to drive a car when it should have known that he was too tired to drive safely. Do employers have a duty to prevent fatigued employees from driving home from work? Should such a duty be imposed on them? How should the court decide this issue? How would you decide the issue if you were the judge? [*Faverty v. McDonald's Restaurants of Oregon, Inc.*, 133 Or.App. 514, 892 P.2d 703 (1994)]

40–7. LAWS REGULATING BUSINESS. Valdak Corp. operated a car wash that used an industrial dryer to spin-dry towels. The dryer was equipped with a device that was supposed to keep it locked while it spun, but the device often did not work. An employee reached into the dryer while it was spinning, and his arm was cut off above the elbow. The Occupational Safety and Health Administration (OSHA) cited Valdak for, among other things, a willful violation of a machine-guarding regulation and assessed a $28,000 penalty. Valdak appealed the decision, and ultimately the case was reviewed by a federal appellate court. On appeal, Valdak argued, in part, that it did not know about the specific regulation and thus could not be cited for a "willful" violation of it. What will the court decide, and why? [*Valdak Corp. v. Occupational Safety and Health Review Commission*, 73 F.3d 1466 (8th Cir. 1966)]

40–8. CONSUMER WELFARE. Isuzu Motors America, Inc., does not warn its customers of the danger of riding unrestrained in the cargo beds of its pickup trucks. Seventeen-year-old Donald Josue was riding unrestrained in the bed of an Isuzu truck driven by Iaone Frias. When Frias lost control of the truck, it struck a concrete center divider. Josue was ejected, and his consequent injuries rendered him a paraplegic. Josue filed a suit in a Hawaii state court against Isuzu, asserting a variety of legal claims based on its failure to warn of the danger of riding in the bed of the truck. Should Isuzu be held liable for Josue's injuries? Why or why not? [*Josue v. Isuzu Motors America, Inc.*, 87 Haw. 413, 958 P.2d 535 (1998)]

40–9. ETHICAL CONDUCT. Richard and Suzanne Weinstein owned Elm City Cheese Co. Elm City sold its products to three major customers that used the cheese as a "filler" to blend into their cheeses. In 1982, Mark Federico, a certified public accountant, became Elm City's accountant and the Weinsteins' personal accountant. The Weinsteins had known Federico since he was seven years old, and even before he became their accountant he knew the details of Elm City's business. Federico's duties went beyond typical accounting work, and when the Weinsteins were absent, Federico was put

in charge of operations. In 1992, Federico was made a vice president of the company, and a year later he was placed in charge of day-to-day operations. He also continued to serve as Elm City's accountant. The relationship between Federico and the Weinsteins deteriorated, and in 1995, he resigned as Elm City's employee and as its accountant. Less than two years later, Federico opened Lomar Foods, Inc., to make the same products as Elm City by the same process and to sell the products to the same customers. Federico located Lomar closer to Elm City's suppliers. Elm City filed a suit in a Connecticut state court against Federico and Lomar, alleging, among other things, misappropriation of trade secrets. Elm City argued that it was entitled to punitive damages because Federico's conduct was "willful and malicious." Federico responded in part that he did not act willfully and maliciously because he did not know that Elm City's business details were trade secrets. Were Federico's actions "willful and malicious"? Were they ethical? Explain. [*Elm City Cheese Co. v. Federico*, 251 Conn. 59, ___ A.2d ___ (1999)]

40–10. IN YOUR COURT

Francis Rogowski fell asleep at the wheel of his Mazda pickup truck and collided head-on with a large tree. To recover for the cost of his injuries, Rogowski sued the manufacturer of the pickup, Mazda Motor of America, Inc. Rogowski claimed, among other things, that Mazda should have warned him that the seat belts would not protect him from all injuries if he were in an accident. Assume that you are the judge in the trial court hearing this case and answer the following questions:

(a) The major issue before your court is whether the danger not warned of by Mazda (that the seat belts would not protect Rogowski from all injuries if he were in an accident) was open and obvious. If the danger was open and obvious, then Mazda had no duty to warn consumers of this danger under product-liability laws. How will you rule on this issue? Why?

(b) Compare this case to Case 40.3 (*Pavlik v. Lane Ltd./Tobacco Exporters International*), which involved a similar issue. What did the court decide in that case, and for what reasons? Does the court's decision in that case differ from your conclusion regarding Rogowski's claim? Explain.

40–11. A QUESTION OF ETHICS

Three-year-old Randy Welch climbed up to a shelf and picked up a disposable butane cigarette lighter. Randy then used the lighter to ignite a flame, which set fire to his pajama top. Welch and his parents brought a product-liability suit against the lighter's manufacturer, Scripto-Tokai Corp., for damages. One of the questions raised in this case was whether the risks attending the lighter were sufficiently "open and obvious" that the manufacturer did not need to warn of those risks. [*Welch v. Scripto-Tokai Corp.*, 651 N.E.2d 810 (Ind.App. 1995)]

(a) If you were the judge, how would you decide this issue? Explain your reasoning.

(b) Generally, how can a court decide what kinds of risks should be open and obvious for the ordinary consumer? How can a business decision maker decide such questions?

LAW ON THE WEB

For updated links to resources available on the Web, as well as a variety of other materials, visit this text's Web site at http://wbl.westbuslaw.com.

The Web site of DePaul University's Institute for Business and Professional Ethics includes several examples of the types of ethical issues that can arise in the business context. Go to

http://condor.depaul.edu/ethics/biz17.html

You can find articles on issues relating to shareholders and corporate accountability at the Corporate Governance Web site. Go to

http://www.corpgov.net

Numerous online groups focus on the activities of various corporations from an ethical perspective. A good starting point for locating these kinds of Web sites is Baobab's Corporate Power Information Center at

http://www.baobabcomputing.com/corporatepower

LEGAL RESEARCH EXERCISES ON THE WEB

Go to http://wbl.westbuslaw.com, the Web site that accompanies this text. Select "Internet Applications," and then click on "Chapter 40." There you will find the following Internet research exercises that you can perform to learn more about ethics and business decision making:

Activity 40–1: Ethics in Business

Activity 40–2: Environmental Self-Audits

UNIT SEVEN—CUMULATIVE BUSINESS HYPOTHETICAL

John leases an office and buys computer equipment. Initially, to pay for the lease and the equipment, he goes into the business of designing Web pages. He has an idea for a new software product, however, on which he works whenever he has time and which he hopes will be more profitable than designing Web pages.

1. After six months, Mary and Paul come to work in the office to help develop John's idea. John continues to pay the rent and other expenses, including salaries for Mary and Paul. John does not expect to make a profit at least until the software is developed, which could be months, and there may be very little profit if the product is not marketed successfully. John believes that if the product is successful, however, the company will be able to follow up with other products. In choosing a form of business organization for this firm, what are the important considerations? What are the advantages and disadvantages of each basic option?

2. It is decided that an organizational form for this firm should include limited liability for its owners. The owners will include John, Mary, Paul, and some members of their respective families. One of the features of the corporate form is limited liability. Ordinarily, however, corporate income is taxed at the corporate level and at the shareholder level. Which corporate form could the firm use to avoid this double taxation? Which other forms of business organization feature limited liability? What factors, other than liability and taxation, influence a firm's choice among these forms?

3. The firm is incorporated as Digital Software, Inc. (DSI). The software is developed and marketed successfully, and DSI prospers. John, Mary, and Paul become directors of DSI. For the marketing of DSI's next product, Paul makes a proposal that John and Mary approve at a board meeting. Implementing the proposal causes a drop in profits for DSI. If the shareholders accuse Paul of breaching his fiduciary duty to DSI, what is Paul's most likely defense? If the shareholders accuse John and Mary of the same breach, what is their best defense? In either case, if the shareholders file a suit, how is a court likely to rule?

4. International Investments, Inc., makes a public offer to buy the stock of DSI. The price of the offer is higher than the market price of the stock, but DSI's board believes that the offer should not be accepted and that International's attempt to take over DSI should be resisted. What steps can DSI take to resist the attempt?

5. Mary and Paul withdraw from DSI to set up their own firm. To obtain operating capital, they solicit investors who agree to become "general partners." Mary and Paul designate themselves "managing partners." The investors are spread over a wide geographic area and do not know anything about Mary and Paul's business until they are contacted. Are Mary and Paul truly soliciting partners, or are they selling securities? What are the criteria for determining whether an investment is a security? What are the advantages and disadvantages of selling securities compared to soliciting partners?

FOCUS ON LEGAL REASONING
Longman v. Food Lion, Inc.

INTRODUCTION

Section 10(b) and Rule 10b-5 of the Securities Exchange Act of 1934 are discussed in Chapter 37. In this *Focus on Legal Reasoning*, we examine *Longman v. Food Lion, Inc.*,[1] a recent decision in a suit filed under those laws. Omission or misrepresentation of material information is necessary to succeed in a suit based on Section 10(b) and Rule 10b-5. The focus of the opinion in the *Longman* case was whether certain information had been omitted or misrepresented to the securities market and whether that information was material to the purchasers of securities.

CASE BACKGROUND

In the early 1990s, Food Lion, Inc., operated a chain of approximately 1,000 retail grocery stores, employing about 60,000 persons. Its

---

1. 197 F.3d 675 (4th Cir. 1999).

annual earnings were about $200 million. As a management tool, Food Lion used "Effective Scheduling," under which employees were required to perform certain duties within specified times or risk losing their jobs. Food Lion issued optimistic statements about its relationship with its employees, the cleanliness of its stores, and its future.

At the same time, Food Lion was resisting the efforts of the United Food and Commercial Workers Union (UFCW) to unionize Food Lion workers. The UFCW filed a complaint with the U.S. Department of Labor, accusing Food Lion of encouraging its employees to work "off the clock" without pay. The UFCW publicized its complaint. Food Lion publicly denied the charge but agreed to pay $13.2 million in back wages and a $3 million penalty. This amount was equal to 1.67 cents per share of stock for each of two years.

Meanwhile, in 1992, ABC broadcast a *PrimeTime Live* episode about three Food Lion stores, alleging, among other things, unsanitary food handling practices. *PrimeTime Live* interviewed seventy current and former Food Lion employees and attributed the practices to Food Lion's "Effective Scheduling." After the broadcast, the price of Food Lion's stock fell.

David Longman and other shareholders who had recently bought the stock filed a suit in a federal district court against Food Lion, alleging securities fraud under Section 10(b) of the Securities Exchange Act of 1934 and Rule 10b-5. The plaintiffs claimed in part that Food Lion affirmatively misled the market about its violations of labor laws and its unsanitary practices. The court granted Food Lion's motion for summary judgment. The plaintiffs appealed to the U.S. Court of Appeals for the Fourth Circuit.

MAJORITY OPINION

NIEMEYER, Circuit Judge.
    *   *   *   *

Plaintiffs' securities fraud claim cannot succeed because, despite the fact that Food Lion denied the charges, the nature of the off-the-clock claims and the claims' risk to earnings were in fact well known to the market before the PrimeTime Live broadcast, and therefore Food Lion's omissions were not material. See *Hillson Partners Ltd. Partnership v. Adage, Inc.,* 42 F.3d 204 (4th Cir.1994) *   *   *.

Because the market was thus informed of the union's charges before PrimeTime Live aired, what PrimeTime Live disclosed was not material. Indeed, even the much larger problem alleged more than a year earlier by the

union was not material. Food Lion settled all of the claims made by the union with the Department of Labor for $16.2 million *   *   *. During the same period, Food Lion's earnings exceeded $200 million per year. Experts on both sides agree that this settlement, reflecting a charge of less than two cents per share for each year, was not material to Food Lion's stock price. *   *   *

In short, the off-the-clock violations disclosed during PrimeTime Live were already publicly available and, therefore, were not material either to Food Lion's earnings or the price of its stock.
    *   *   *   *

We turn now to the second category of alleged misstatements and omissions by Food Lion—those which related to unsanitary practices. *   *   *

* * * *

* * * [C]onsidering the entire PrimeTime Live broadcast, the district court stated it " * * * does not present evidence of widespread unsanitary conditions of which Defendants knew." * * * The court pointed out that the broadcast was filmed at only 3 of Food Lion's almost 1,000 stores and that out of 60,000 active employees and 40,000 former employees, PrimeTime Live interviewed a total of 70 current and former employees * * *. The district court concluded:

[T]o the extent that there are any isolated instances of workplace errors, * * * there is not a substantial likelihood that the reasonable investor would consider the limited instances of workplace errors important in deciding whether to purchase Food Lion securities * * *.

We agree with the district court * * *.

Dissenting Opinion

MURNAGHAN, Circuit Judge, dissenting:

* * * *

In *Hillson Partners* * * *, the corporation-defendants made misleading statements to the market about their economic situations. In [that case], however, the defendants admitted their financial problems through additional public disclosures. Because the market had access to the defendants'

financial problems, we held that the misleading statements were not material to the plaintiffs' decisions to purchase stock.

Hillson Partners * * * [does] not control the case at bar. The majority incorrectly suggests that any public information contradicting Food Lion's misleading statements forecloses the possibility of finding that those statements were material. However, the controlling principle is that in a fraud on the market case, Food Lion's failure to disclose material information may be excused where that information has been made credibly available to the market by other sources. * * *

* * * *

The information available to the public when the plaintiffs purchased Food Lion stock came from an admitted adversary of Food Lion [the UFCW]. Given the history of antagonism between the parties and Food Lion's vehement denials, the information about Food Lion's policies did not come from a credible source. A dispute of fact, therefore, exists as to whether Food Lion's representations were material to the plaintiffs' decisions to purchase Food Lion stock.

Because a dispute of fact exists as to whether Food Lion's representations were material, the district court's grant of summary judgment to Food Lion was inappropriate.

Legal Reasoning and Analysis

1. **Legal Analysis.** The majority and the dissent both cite, in their opinions, *Hillson Partners Ltd. Partnership v. Adage, Inc.,* 42 F.3d 204 (4th Cir.1994) (see the *Law on the Web* feature at the end of Chapter 2 for instructions on how to access federal court opinions). How do the facts and issues in that case compare to the facts and issues of the *Longman* case? How do the holdings in the two cases compare? Is the majority correct in applying the *Hillson* case to this case,

or is the dissent correct in asserting that *Hillson* does "not control the case at bar"?

2. **Legal Reasoning.** What reasons does the majority provide to justify its conclusion? Do you agree? Why or why not?

3. **Ethical Considerations.** What ethical obligation does a business firm such as Food Lion have to disclose the details behind ongoing litigation and administrative

investigations and to respond to negative media exposure? To whom, if anyone, does it owe this obligation?

4. **Implications for Investors.** What are the implications of the decision in this case for those who buy and sell securities?

5. **Case Briefing Assignment.** Using the guidelines for briefing cases given in Appendix A of this text, brief the *Hillson* case.

Going Online

This text's Web site, at http://wbl.westbuslaw.com, offers links to court cases, as well as to other online research sources. You can also locate court cases at the Web sites listed in the *Law on the Web* feature at the end of Chapter 2. Sec Law.com, a Web site at http://www.seclaw.com, is "an online guide to securities law." The site provides links to a variety of securities law resources, including its own monthly "Securities Law Letter," which covers some of the recent developments in securities law. This Web site is maintained by New York securities attorney Mark Astarita.

FOCUS ON ETHICS
Business Organizations

In Chapter 40, we examined a number of ethical issues that arise in the business context generally. Here, we examine selected areas in which ethical problems have to do with the relationships within specific business organizational forms.

FIDUCIARY DUTIES REVISITED

The law of agency, as outlined in Chapters 31 and 32, permeates virtually all relationships within any partnership or corporation. An important duty that arises in the law of agency, and that applies to all partners and corporate directors, officers, and management personnel, is the duty of loyalty. As caretakers of the shareholders' wealth, corporate directors and officers also have a fiduciary duty to exercise care when making decisions affecting the corporate enterprise.

The Duty of Loyalty

Every individual has his or her own personal interests, which may at times conflict with the interests of the partnership or corporation with which he or she is affiliated. In particular, a partner or a corporate director may face a conflict between personal interests and the interests of the business entity. Corporate officers may find themselves in a position to acquire assets that would also benefit the corporation if acquired in the corporation's name.

In one landmark case, *Guth v. Loft, Inc.,*[1] Charles G. Guth, the president and a director of Loft, Inc., a soft-drink bottling company,

negotiated with the Coca-Cola Company for a discount on its syrups. When negotiations with Coca-Cola failed to result in a discount for Loft, Guth decided to see what Pepsi Cola could offer. During his investigation of this possibility, Guth set up a new corporation to acquire the secret formula and trademark for the manufacture of Pepsi Cola. He did so without offering the opportunity to Loft. A shareholder brought a suit against Guth, arguing that the shares of the new corporation should belong to Loft, and not to Guth personally. The shareholder prevailed. The court ruled that Guth had *usurped* a corporate opportunity in violation of his duty of loyalty to the corporation.

The Duty of Care

In addition to the duty of loyalty, every corporate director or officer has a duty of care, which involves a duty to be informed and to make informed decisions. Traditionally, though, the duty of care did not include a duty to monitor the behavior of corporate employees to detect and prevent wrongdoing unless the directors had some reason to suspect that wrongful acts were in fact occurring. For example, in a leading case on the issue, the Delaware Supreme Court held in 1963 that corporate directors did not have a duty "to install and operate a corporate system of espionage to ferret out wrongdoing which they have no reason to suspect exists."[2]

Enter the corporate sentencing guidelines in 1991. Under these guidelines, the courts may impose—and have been imposing fairly regularly—substantial penalties on corporations and corporate directors for criminal wrongdoing. The guidelines, though, allow these penalties to be mitigated if a company can show that it has a compliance program in place—an effective program to detect and prevent wrongdoing by corporate personnel. The question here is, do the guidelines imply that directors have a *duty* to have such a program in place?

In 1996, a Delaware chancery (trial) court suggested that corporate directors do have such a duty. The case involved criminal behavior on the part of a company's middle-level and lower-level employees, and the question was whether the directors, who were apparently unaware of the actions, had breached their oversight duties. Under the traditional rule, as mentioned, directors had no duty to detect and "ferret out" wrongdoing. According to the court in this case, though, the corporate sentencing guidelines have changed this standard. The court stated that "a director's obligation includes a duty to attempt in good faith to assure that a corporation information and reporting system, which the board concludes is adequate, exists." The court also noted that in view of the potential impact of the sentencing guidelines on any business organization, "[a]ny rational person attempting in good faith to meet an organizational governance responsibility would be

---

1. 5 A.2d 503 (Del. 1939).

2. *Graham v. Allis-Chalmers Manufacturing Co.,* 188 A.2d 125 (Del. 1963).

bound to take into account this development and the enhanced penalties and the opportunities for reduced sanctions that it offers."[3]

Clearly, the corporate sentencing guidelines are altering the business and legal environment in which directors operate. In the case just discussed, the directors were able to avoid liability because there was a compliance program in place—which the company agreed to modify so that it would be more effective in the future.

Fiduciary Duties and Departing Partners

An ongoing problem faced by partnerships is that of departing partners who take their clients with them. There is nothing in the model ethical rules governing attorney conduct that expressly prohibits departing attorneys from soliciting business from clients with whom they have had an ongoing relationship. Yet the courts have placed some limits on what attorneys may or may not do when leaving their firms. Consider a case that came before the Illinois Supreme Court.

The case arose after two partners in a law firm left the firm to set up their own partnership. They took with them a major client of the firm, an insurance company whose business accounted for 58 percent of the firm's income, or approximately $6 million a year. The departing partners also took with them some of the firm's best paralegals and secretaries. Additionally, before they notified the firm that they were leaving, they had obtained a business loan, leased office space, furnished it, and arranged for telephone

service. The law firm sued the partners, claiming that they had breached their fiduciary duties to the other partners by secretly undertaking these actions before they had notified the other partners that they were leaving.

When the case reached the Illinois Supreme Court, the court remanded the case for fact finding on whether the departing partners had solicited the major client's business before or after they announced that they were leaving—the parties disputed this issue. The court also set forth some broad guidelines on what kind of behavior might constitute a breach of a law partner's fiduciary duties.

The court noted that departing attorneys are involved in a delicate venture. On the one hand, common sense dictates that an attorney who is dissatisfied with the existing association should take steps to locate alternative office space and associations—and do so confidentially. The court also noted that it is permissible for departing partners "to inform clients with whom they have a prior professional relationship about their impending withdrawal and new practice, and to remind the client of its freedom to retain counsel of its choice." On the other hand, departing partners must take care not to breach their fiduciary obligations to the other partners. The court stated that "secretly attempting to lure firm clients . . . to the new association . . . and abandoning the firm on short notice (taking clients and files) would not be consistent with a partner's fiduciary duties."[4]

According to the court, then, departing partners have fairly wide latitude in making preparations for departure, even in secret. The one thing they may not do is solicit the

firm's clients before leaving—or at least before notifying the partners of their intention to withdraw from the partnership.

INSIDER TRADING

Rule 10b-5 of the Securities and Exchange Commission (SEC) prohibits, among other things, insider trading—trading in securities by corporate insiders based on information that has not yet been made public. The ethical assumption underlying the prohibition against insider trading is that corporate insiders should not have advantages in the securities trading arena that the general public does not have. Nonetheless, some have questioned the fairness of the rule and its application.

One issue with obvious ethical implications has to do with the *scienter* requirement for insider-trading liability. As discussed elsewhere in this text, *scienter* requires an intent to defraud or to deceive another. The question is this: Does the mere possession of inside information while trading in securities establish an intent to defraud, or must the trader actually use the inside information for intent to be established?

The government and the SEC have adopted the position that the intent to defraud can be inferred when a person trades in securities while in the possession of inside information.[5] Others, however, maintain that people should not be held liable for insider trading unless the government can show that the trading was, in fact, based on the information. In *United States v. Smith*,[6] one of the few court decisions to squarely address this issue, the U.S. Court of Appeals for the Ninth Circuit came down firmly

---

3. *In re Caremark International, Inc. Derivative Litigation* (Del.Ch. 1996) [1996 WL 549894]. This decision, which has not yet been published in a reporter, can be accessed by use of the WESTLAW (WL) citation.

4. *Dowd & Dowd v. Gleason*, 181 Ill.2d 460, 693 N.E.2d 358, 230 Ill.Dec. 229 (1998).

5. This position was bolstered by the decision in *United States v. Teicher*, 987 F.2d 112 (2d Cir. 1993).
6. 155 F.3d 1051 (9th Cir. 1998).

on the "use" side of the debate. The court stated that the SEC's "possession" standard was too broad because it extended beyond situations involving actual fraud. "For instance," said the court, "an investor who has a preexisting plan to trade, and who carries through with that plan after coming into possession of material nonpublic information, does not intend to defraud or deceive; he simply intends to implement his pre-possession financial strategy."

The Ninth Circuit stated that it did "not take lightly" the SEC's argument that a "use" requirement poses difficulties of proof. The court, however, concluded that the difficulties were not insurmountable and that various types of circumstantial evidence might be employed to demonstrate use. "Suppose, for instance, that an individual who has never before invested comes into possession of material nonpublic information and the very next day invests a significant sum of money." The court was "confident that the government would have little trouble demonstrating 'use' in such a situation, or in other situations in which unique trading patterns or unusually large trading quantities suggest that an investor had used inside information."

THE PLIGHT OF MINORITY SHAREHOLDERS

Minority shareholders, particularly those in close corporations, often have little recourse when they suffer what they perceive to be unfair treatment by the majority shareholders. For example, assume that a corporation has four shareholders. Each shareholder owns 25 percent of the corporate shares, serves on the board of directors, and is employed by the corporation as an officer. Further assume that one of the shareholders has a falling-out, for

whatever reason, with the other three shareholders.

In these circumstances, the minority shareholder will have little recourse against certain coercive policies of the majority shareholders. For example, the majority shareholders may vote to fire the minority shareholder from his job with the firm. Further, they may decide to reinvest company profits in the business rather than issue dividends. In effect, the minority shareholder is locked out of the corporation. The shareholder is not only without a job but also without income in any form from the corporate enterprise. Of course, the minority shareholder could succeed in a derivative suit against the corporation if it can be shown that the majority shareholders are abusing their discretion or mismanaging corporate assets. But litigation is costly, and even if the minority shareholder wins such a suit, any damages obtained will go into the corporate coffers instead of to the plaintiff shareholder.

To protect the interests of minority shareholders, courts have shown an increasing willingness to allow minority shareholders to sue majority shareholders directly for breach of fiduciary duties. Some courts have also ordered close corporations to purchase minority shareholders' shares at fair value to resolve shareholder disputes. A few states have enacted statutes that provide for such buyouts.

FRANCHISE RELATIONSHIPS

A significant issue in franchise relationships has to do with quality control over the franchisee's activities. On the one hand, if the franchisor ignores the problem of quality control, the reputation of the franchisor's business may suffer. On the other hand, if a franchisor's control over the operations of the franchisee is too extensive, the franchisor may be liable for the

torts of the franchisee's employees.[7] Even though an independent business entity may purchase a franchise and even though the franchise agreement specifies that no agency relationship exists, the courts may find otherwise.

In a series of cases in the late 1990s, courts have even held franchisees to be employees of the franchisor, notwithstanding their franchise contracts. For example, in one case a franchisee of a commercial sanitation company was deemed to be an employee of the company even though he was designated as a franchisee in a franchise contract with the company.[8] In another case, the National Labor Relations Board ruled that some five hundred drivers for a New York company that provided limousine services should be considered as employees for labor law purposes, despite their franchise contracts with the company.[9] In these and other cases, the decisions were based on the extensive control exercised by the companies over the activities of the franchisees.

DISCUSSION QUESTIONS

1. Three decades ago, prosecution of corporations and corporate directors for crimes was a rare event, and penalties for corporate crime were relatively light. Today, this is no longer true. According to

---

7. See, for example, *Parker v. Domino's Pizza, Inc.,* 629 So.2d 1026 (Fla.App. 1993). As a result of several lawsuits brought by plaintiffs who had been injured by Domino's Pizza delivery drivers, Domino's changed some of its policies in regard to its franchisees. Particularly, it stopped requiring its franchisees to abide by the "thirty-minute delivery" requirement.
8. *West Sanitation Services, Inc. v. Francis,* 1998 WL 11023 (N.Y.Sup.Ct.App.Div. 1998).
9. *In re Elite Limousine Plus, Inc.,* 324 NLRB No. 182 (November 6, 1997).

the U.S. Sentencing Commission, companies are being sentenced under the corporate sentencing guidelines at a rate of more than two a week, and corporate fines reaching hundreds of millions of dollars are not especially uncommon. Does this development mean that corporations are committing more crimes today than in the past? Or is the government just getting tougher on corporate crime? How can a company avoid liability for crimes committed by its employees?

2. Investigating and prosecuting violations of SEC Rule 10b-5 is costly, both for the government and for those accused of insider trading. Some people contend that the rule's applicability is too broad, particularly its applicability to "outsiders"—those who are not corporate insiders but trade securities based on tips from insiders or misappropriated information. Others go so far as to argue that insider trading should be made legal. Does liability under SEC Rule 10b-5 extend too far? Would there be any benefit from the legalization of insider trading?

3. Shareholders in close corporations often rely on their corporate salaries, rather than on dividends, for income. In such situations, is it fair that majority shareholders should be able to "freeze out" or "squeeze out" a minority shareholder from corporate operations by firing the shareholder? Assuming that the fired employee-shareholder has no cause of action against the firm for discriminatory treatment, what recourse does the fired employee have against the firm and the other shareholders? Should the law intervene to protect a minority shareholder's job in these circumstances?

4. Understandably, a franchisor is concerned about quality control in its franchises because how its franchises are run can affect the reputation of the franchised product or service. Yet if a franchisor exercises too much control over a franchisee's business operations, a court may deem the franchisor to be liable as an employer for the torts committed by the franchisee's employees. How can holding franchisors liable in such circumstances be squared with the doctrine of freedom of contract?

UNIT EIGHT

Labor and
Employment Relations

CONTENTS

CHAPTER 41

Labor and Employment Law

A T ONE TIME IN THE UNITED STATES, employment relationships were governed primarily by the common law. Under the common law doctrine of **employment at will,** normally either party can terminate the employment relationship at any time and for any reason, unless an employment contract provides to the contrary. Other common law concepts governing employment relationships include those of contract, agency, and tort law.

Today, in contrast, the workplace is regulated extensively by federal and state statutes. Recall from Chapter 1 that common law doctrines only apply to areas *not* covered by statutory law. The common law employment-at-will doctrine has thus been displaced to a significant extent by statutory law. Additionally, even when the at-will doctrine is applicable, courts make a number of exceptions to the doctrine—as you will read later in this chapter.

In this chapter, we look at the most significant laws regulating employment relationships. We examine other important laws regulating the workplace—those prohibiting employment discrimination—in the next chapter.

SECTION 1

Wage-Hour Laws

In the 1930s, to protect employees against some of the adverse effects of the employment-at-will doctrine,

Congress enacted several laws regulating the wages and working hours of employees. In 1931, Congress passed the Davis-Bacon Act,[1] which requires the payment of "prevailing wages" to employees of contractors and subcontractors working on government construction projects. In 1936, the Walsh-Healey Act[2] was passed. This act requires that a minimum wage, as well as overtime pay of time and a half, be paid to employees of manufacturers or suppliers entering into contracts with agencies of the federal government.

In 1938, with the passage of the Fair Labor Standards Act[3] (FLSA), Congress extended wage-hour requirements to cover all employers engaged in interstate commerce or engaged in the production of goods for interstate commerce. We examine here the FLSA's provisions in regard to child labor, maximum hours, and minimum wages.

CHILD LABOR

The FLSA prohibits oppressive child labor. Children under fourteen years of age are allowed to do certain types of work, such as deliver newspapers, work for their parents, and be employed in the entertainment and (with some exceptions) agricultural areas. Children who are fourteen or fifteen years of age are allowed to

---

1. 40 U.S.C. Sections 276a–276a-5.
2. 41 U.S.C. Sections 35–45.
3. 29 U.S.C. Sections 201–260.

work, but not in hazardous occupations. There are also numerous restrictions on how many hours per day and per week they can work. For example, they cannot work during school hours, for more than three hours on a school day (or eight hours on a nonschool day), for more than eighteen hours during a school week (or forty hours during a nonschool week), or before 7 A.M. or after 7 P.M. (9 P.M. during the summer). Most states require persons under sixteen years of age to obtain work permits.

Persons between the ages of sixteen and eighteen do not face such restrictions on working times and hours, but they cannot be employed in hazardous jobs or in jobs detrimental to their health and well-being. Persons over the age of eighteen are not affected by any of the above-mentioned restrictions.

HOURS AND WAGES

Under the FLSA, any employee who agrees to work more than forty hours per week must be paid no less than one and a half times his or her regular pay for all hours over forty. Certain employees are exempt from the overtime provisions of the act. Exempt employees fall into four categories: executives, administrative employees, professional employees, and outside salespersons. Generally, to fall into one of these categories, an employee must earn more than a specified amount of income per week and devote a certain percentage of work time to the performance of specific types of duties, as determined by the FLSA. To qualify as an outside salesperson, the employee must regularly engage in sales work away from the office and spend no more than 20 percent of work time per week performing duties other than sales.

The FLSA provides that a **minimum wage** of a specified amount (currently, $5.15 per hour) must be paid to employees in covered industries. Congress periodically revises the amount of the minimum wage. Under the FLSA, the term *wages* includes the reasonable costs of the employer in furnishing employees with board, lodging, and other facilities if they are customarily furnished by that employer.

SECTION 2

Labor Unions

In the 1930s, in addition to wage-hour laws, the government enacted several other laws. These laws protect employees' rights to join labor unions, to bargain

with management over the terms and conditions of employment, and to conduct strikes.

FEDERAL LABOR LAWS

Federal labor laws governing union-employer relations have developed considerably since the first law was enacted in 1932. Initially, the laws were concerned with protecting the rights and interests of workers. Subsequent legislation placed some restraints on unions and granted rights to employers. We look here at four major federal statutes regulating union-employer relations.

Norris-LaGuardia Act. Congress protected peaceful strikes, picketing, and boycotts in 1932 in the Norris-LaGuardia Act.[4] The statute restricted the power of federal courts to issue injunctions against unions engaged in peaceful strikes. In effect, this act declared a national policy permitting employees to organize.

National Labor Relations Act. One of the foremost statutes regulating labor is the National Labor Relations Act (NLRA) of 1935.[5] This act established the rights of employees to engage in collective bargaining and to strike. The act also specifically defined a number of employer practices as unfair to labor:

1. Interference with the efforts of employees to form, join, or assist labor organizations or to engage in concerted activities for their mutual aid or protection.
2. An employer's domination of a labor organization or contribution of financial or other support to it.
3. Discrimination in the hiring of or the awarding of tenure to employees for reason of union affiliation.
4. Discrimination against employees for filing charges under the act or giving testimony under the act.
5. Refusal to bargain collectively with the duly designated representative of the employees.

The act also created the National Labor Relations Board (NLRB) to oversee union elections and to prevent employers from engaging in unfair and illegal union-related activities and unfair labor practices. The purpose of the NLRA was to secure for employees the rights to organize; to bargain collectively through representatives of their own choosing; and to engage in concerted activities for organizing, collective bargaining, and other purposes.

---

4. 29 U.S.C. Sections 101–110, 113–115.
5. 20 U.S.C. Sections 151–169.

The NLRB has the authority to investigate employees' charges of unfair labor practices and to serve complaints against employers in response to these charges. The NLRB may also issue **cease-and-desist orders**—orders compelling employers to cease engaging in the unfair practices—when violations are found. Cease-and-desist orders can be enforced by a circuit court of appeals if necessary. Arguments over alleged unfair labor practices are first decided by the NLRB and may then be appealed to a federal court.

To be protected under the NLRA, an individual must be an *employee,* as that term is defined in the statute. Courts have long held that job applicants fall within the definition (otherwise, the NLRA's ban on "discrimination in regard to hire" would mean nothing). In the following case, the United States Supreme Court considered whether an individual may be a company's employee if, at the same time, a union pays the individual to organize the company.

CASE 41.1   National Labor Relations Board v. Town & Country Electric, Inc.

Supreme Court of the United States, 1995.
516 U.S. 85,
116 S.Ct. 450,
133 L.Ed.2d 371.

BACKGROUND AND FACTS   *Town & Country Electric, Inc., advertised for job applicants but refused to interview ten of eleven applicants who were members of a union, the International Brotherhood of Electrical Workers. The applicants were union "salts"—persons paid by the union to apply for a job with a company and then, when hired, to unionize the company (in this case, Town & Country's work force). The applicants filed a complaint with the National Labor Relations Board (NLRB), alleging that the company had committed an unfair labor practice by discriminating against the applicants on the basis of union membership. The issue turned on whether job applicants paid by a union to organize a company could be considered employees under the National Labor Relations Act (NLRA). The NLRB determined that the applicants were employees and ruled in their favor. Town & Country appealed, and the U.S. Court of Appeals for the Eighth Circuit reversed. The applicants appealed to the United States Supreme Court.*

IN THE LANGUAGE OF THE COURT

Justice *BREYER* delivered the opinion of the Court.

*   *   *   *

*   *   * [T]he Board's decision is consistent with the broad language of the [NLRA] *   *   *. The ordinary dictionary definition of "employee" includes any "person who works for another in return for financial or other compensation." The phrasing of the [NLRA] seems to reiterate the breadth of the ordinary dictionary definition, for it says "[t]he term 'employee' shall include any employee." *   *   *

For another thing, the Board's broad, literal interpretation of the word "employee" is consistent with several of the [NLRA's] purposes, such as protecting "the right of employees to organize for mutual aid without employer interference" *   *   *.

DECISION AND REMEDY

The United States Supreme Court reversed the decision of the appellate court and remanded the case. The job applicants were "employees" for purposes of the NLRA.

Labor-Management Relations Act. The Labor-Management Relations Act (LMRA) of 1947[6] was passed to proscribe certain unfair union practices, such as the *closed shop.* A **closed shop** is a firm that

requires union membership of its workers as a condition of employment. Although the act made the closed shop illegal, it preserved the legality of the union shop. A **union shop** does not require membership as a prerequisite for employment but can, and usually does, require that workers join the union after a specified amount of time on the job.

---

6. 29 U.S.C. Sections 141 *et seq.*

The act also prohibited unions from refusing to bargain with employers, engaging in certain types of picketing, and featherbedding (causing employers to hire more employees than necessary). In addition, the act allowed individual states to pass their own **right-to-work laws**—laws making it illegal for union membership to be required for *continued* employment in any establishment. Thus, union shops are technically illegal in states with right-to-work laws.

Labor-Management Reporting and Disclosure Act.

The Labor-Management Reporting and Disclosure Act (LMRDA) of 1959[7] established an employee bill of rights and reporting requirements for union activities. The act strictly regulates internal union business procedures. Union elections, for example, are regulated by the LMRDA, which requires that regularly scheduled elections of officers occur and that secret ballots be used. Former convicts and Communists are prohibited from holding union office. Moreover, union officials are accountable for union property and funds. Members have the right to attend and to participate in union meetings, to nominate officers, and to vote in most union proceedings.

The act also outlawed **hot-cargo agreements**—agreements in which employers voluntarily agree with unions not to handle, use, or deal in goods of other employers produced by nonunion employees. The act made all such boycotts (called **secondary boycotts**) illegal.

Union Organization

Suppose that the workers of a particular firm want to join a union. How is a union formed? Typically, the first step in the process is to have the workers sign authorization cards. An authorization card usually states that the worker desires to have a certain union, such as the American Federation of Labor and Congress of Industrial Organizations (AFL–CIO), represent the work force. If those in favor of the union can obtain authorization cards from a majority of the workers, they may present the cards to the employer and ask the employer to recognize the union formally. If the employer refuses to do so, the unionizers can petition the NLRB for an election.

Union Elections.

For an election to be held, the unionizers must demonstrate that at least 30 percent of the workers to be represented support a union or an election on unionization. The NLRB supervises the election and ensures that the voting is secret and that the voters are eligible. If the election is a fair one and if the proposed union receives majority support, the NLRB certifies the union as the bargaining representative for the employees.

Union Election Campaigns.

Many disputes between labor and management arise during union election campaigns. Generally, the employer has control over unionizing activities that take place on company property and during working hours. Employers may thus limit the campaign activities of union supporters. For example, an employer may prohibit all solicitations and pamphlets on company property as long as the employer has a legitimate business reason for doing so. Suppose that a union sought to organize clerks at a department store. Courts have found that an employer can prohibit all solicitation in areas of the store open to the public. Union campaign activities in these circumstances could seriously interfere with the store's business. The employer may not, however, discriminate in its prohibition against solicitation in the workplace. For example, the employer could not prohibit union solicitation but allow solicitation for charitable causes.

An employer may also campaign among its workers against the union, but the NLRB carefully monitors and regulates the campaign tactics of management. Otherwise, management might use its economic power to coerce the workers to vote not to unionize. For example, an employer might tell its workers, "If the union wins, you'll all be fired." The NLRB prohibits employers from making such threats. If the employer issues threats or engages in other unfair labor practices, the NLRB may certify the union even though it lost the election. Alternatively, the NLRB may ask a court to order a new election.

Collective Bargaining

If a fair election is held and the union wins, the NLRB will certify the union as the *exclusive bargaining representative* of the workers. The central legal right of a union is to engage in collective bargaining on the members' behalf. **Collective bargaining** can be defined as the process by which labor and management negotiate the terms and conditions of employment, including wages, benefits, working conditions, and other matters. Through collective bargaining, union

7. 29 U.S.C. Sections 401 *et seq.*

representatives elected by union members speak on behalf of the members at the bargaining table.

When a union is officially recognized, it may demand to bargain with the employer and negotiate new terms or conditions of employment. In collective bargaining, as in most other business negotiations, each side uses its economic power to pressure or persuade the other side to grant concessions.

Bargaining is a somewhat vague term. Bargaining does not mean that one side must give in to the other or that compromises must be made. It does mean that a demand to bargain with the employer must be taken seriously and that both sides must bargain in "good faith." Good faith bargaining requires that management, for example, must be willing to meet with union representatives and consider the union's wishes when negotiating a contract. Examples of bad faith bargaining on the part of management include engaging in a campaign among workers to undermine the union, constantly shifting positions on disputed contract terms, and sending bargainers who lack authority to commit the company to a contract. If an employer (or a union) refuses to bargain in good faith without justification, it has committed an unfair labor practice, and the other party may petition the NLRB for an order requiring good faith bargaining.

STRIKES

Even when labor and management have bargained in good faith, they may be unable to reach a final agreement. When extensive collective bargaining has been conducted and an impasse results, the union may call a strike against the employer to pressure it into making concessions. A **strike** occurs when the unionized employees leave their jobs and refuse to work. The workers also typically picket the plant, standing outside the facility with signs that complain of management's unfairness.

A strike is an extreme action. Striking workers lose their right to be paid, and management loses production and may lose customers, whose orders cannot be filled. Labor law regulates the circumstances and conduct of strikes. Most strikes are "economic strikes," which are initiated because the union wants a better contract. A union may also strike when the employer has engaged in unfair labor practices.

The right to strike is guaranteed by the NLRA, within limits, and strike activities, such as picketing, are protected by the free speech guarantee of the First Amendment to the Constitution. Nonworkers have a

right to participate in picketing an employer. The NLRA also gives workers the right to refuse to cross a picket line of fellow workers who are engaged in a lawful strike. Employers are permitted to hire replacement workers to substitute for the workers who are on strike.

An important issue concerns the rights of strikers after a strike ends. In a typical economic strike over working conditions, the strikers have no right to return to their jobs. If satisfactory replacement workers have been found, the strikers may find themselves out of work. The law does prohibit the employer from discriminating against former strikers, however. Employers must give former strikers preferential rights to any new vacancies that arise and also allow them to retain their seniority rights. Different rules apply when a union strikes because the employer has engaged in unfair labor practices. In this situation, the employer may still hire replacements but must give the strikers back their jobs once the strike is over.

SECTION 3

Worker Health and Safety

Under the common law, employees injured on the job had to rely on tort law or contract law theories in suits they brought against their employers. Additionally, workers had some recourse under the common law governing agency relationships (discussed in Chapters 31 and 32), which imposes a duty on a principal-employer to provide a safe workplace for his or her agent-employee. Today, numerous state and federal statutes protect employees from the risk of accidental injury, death, or disease resulting from their employment. This section discusses the primary federal statute governing health and safety in the workplace, along with state workers' compensation acts.

THE OCCUPATIONAL SAFETY AND HEALTH ACT

At the federal level, the primary legislation for employee health and safety protection is the Occupational Safety and Health Act of 1970.[8] Congress passed this act in an attempt to ensure safe and healthful working conditions for practically every employee in the country. The act provides for specific standards that

---

8. 29 U.S.C. Sections 553, 651–678.

employers must meet, plus a general duty to keep workplaces safe.

Enforcement Agencies.

Three federal agencies develop and enforce the standards set by the Occupational Safety and Health Act. The Occupational Safety and Health Administration (OSHA) is part of the Department of Labor and has the authority to promulgate standards, make inspections, and enforce the act. OSHA has safety standards governing many workplace details, such as the structural stability of ladders and the requirements for railings. OSHA also establishes standards that protect employees against exposure to substances that may be harmful to their health.

The National Institute for Occupational Safety and Health is part of the Department of Health and Human Services. Its main duty is to conduct research on safety and health problems and to recommend standards for OSHA to adopt. Finally, the Occupational Safety and Health Review Commission is an independent agency set up to handle appeals from actions taken by OSHA administrators.

Procedures and Violations.

OSHA compliance officers may enter and inspect facilities of any establishment covered by the Occupational Safety and Health Act.[9] Employees may also file complaints of violations. Under the act, an employer cannot discharge an employee who files a complaint or who, in good faith, refuses to work in a high-risk area if bodily harm or death might result.

Employers with eleven or more employees are required to keep occupational injury and illness records for each employee. Each record must be made available for inspection when requested by an OSHA inspector. Whenever a work-related injury or disease occurs, employers must make reports directly to OSHA. Whenever an employee is killed in a work-related accident or when five or more employees are hospitalized in one accident, the employer must notify the Department of Labor within forty-eight hours. If the company fails to do so, it will be fined. Following the accident, a complete inspection of the premises is mandatory.

Criminal penalties for willful violation of the Occupational Safety and Health Act are limited.

Employers may be prosecuted under state laws, however. In other words, the act does not preempt state and local criminal laws.[10]

STATE WORKERS' COMPENSATION LAWS

State **workers' compensation laws** establish an administrative procedure for compensating workers injured on the job. Instead of suing, an injured worker files a claim with the administrative agency or board that administers the local workers' compensation claims.

Most workers' compensation statutes are similar. No state covers all employees. Typically excluded are domestic workers, agricultural workers, temporary employees, and employees of common carriers (companies that provide transportation services to the public). Generally, the statutes cover minors. Usually, the statutes allow employers to purchase insurance from a private insurer or a state fund to pay workers' compensation benefits in the event of a claim. Most states also allow employers to be *self-insured*—that is, employers who show an ability to pay claims do not need to buy insurance.

In general, the right to recover benefits is predicated wholly on the existence of an employment relationship and the fact that the worker's injury was *accidental* and *occurred on the job or in the course of employment*, regardless of fault. Intentionally inflicted self-injury, for example, would not be considered accidental and hence would not be covered. If an injury occurred while an employee was commuting to or from work, it usually would not be considered to have occurred on the job or in the course of employment and hence would not be covered.

An employee must notify his or her employer of an injury promptly (usually within thirty days of the injury's occurrence). Generally, an employee also must file a workers' compensation claim with the appropriate state agency or board within a certain period (sixty days to two years) from the time the injury is first noticed, rather than from the time of the accident.

An employee's acceptance of workers' compensation benefits bars the employee from suing for injuries caused by the employer's negligence. By barring lawsuits for negligence, workers' compensation laws also bar employers from raising common law defenses to

---

9. In the past, warrantless inspections were conducted. In 1978, however, the United States Supreme Court held that warrantless inspections violated the warrant clause of the Fourth Amendment to the Constitution. See *Marshall v. Barlow's, Inc.*, 436 U.S. 307, 98 S.Ct. 1816, 56 L.Ed.2d 305 (1978).

10. *Pedraza v. Shell Oil Co.*, 942 F.2d 48 (1st Cir. 1991); cert. denied, *Shell Oil Co. v. Pedraza*, 502 U.S. 1082, 112 S.Ct. 993, 117 L.Ed.2d 154 (1992).

negligence, such as contributory negligence. For example, an employer can no longer raise such defenses as contributory negligence or assumption of risk to avoid liability for negligence. A worker may sue an employer who *intentionally* injures the worker, however.

The court in the following case considered whether an employee's injury in an automobile accident arose out of and in the course of employment for purposes of workers' compensation.

CASE 41.2   Rogers v. Pacesetter Corp.

Missouri Court of Appeals, Eastern District, Division 4, 1998. 972 S.W.2d 540. http://www.osca.state. mo.us/courts/ pubopinions.nsf[a]

COMPANY PROFILE *Pacesetter Corporation (http://www.pacesettercorp.com), which has been in the home improvement business since 1962, calls itself "America's Leading Home Improvement Company!" Pacesetter sells a range of building supplies, including cabinet refacing, doors, siding, windows, and patio awnings and covers. The company designs, manufactures, finances the purchase of, installs, guarantees, and services its products, which are advertised as durable and energy efficient.*

BACKGROUND AND FACTS *Sean Rogers was a manager for Pacesetter Corporation. He worked at the Pacesetter offices from 9:00 A.M. to 9:00 P.M. Mondays through Fridays and 10:00 A.M. to 4:00 P.M. Saturdays. He also worked at home, drafting ads and conducting performance reviews, because he did not have enough time to do all of his work at the office. At the invitation of Rogers's supervisor, Rogers and the supervisor met at the River Port Club, a bar, to discuss a promotion. It was a Monday, when Rogers normally conducted performance reviews at home, which he planned to do after leaving the bar. While driving home, Rogers was injured in an automobile accident. He filed a claim for workers' compensation with the Missouri Division of Workers' Compensation. After a hearing, the administrative law judge awarded Rogers temporary compensation for a permanent partial disability. Pacesetter appealed to the Missouri Labor and Industrial Relations Commission, which reversed the award. Rogers appealed to a Missouri state court.*

IN THE LANGUAGE OF THE COURT

ROBERT G. DOWD, JR., Presiding Judge.
    *   *   *   *   *

An employee's injuries arise out of his employment if they are a natural and reasonable incident thereof, and they are in the course of employment if the accident occurs within the period of employment at a place where the employee may reasonably be fulfilling the duties of employment. *   *   *
    *   *   *   *

*   *   * [C]ompensation for injuries while traveling home may be proper *   *   * *when it can genuinely *   *   * be said that the home has become part of the employment premises.* *   *   * [A]n employee demonstrates this by showing a clear business use of the home at the end of the specific journey during which the accident occurred. [Emphasis added.]
    *   *   *   *

*   *   * Here, Claimant [Rogers] regularly worked twelve hours, Monday through Friday, and six hours each Saturday. Claimant also regularly did work for his employer at home *   *   *. The night of the accident was a Monday and it was Claimant's practice to do performance reviews *   *   * on Monday evenings in order that on Tuesday mornings he could discuss [the employees'] performance with them. Claimant testified it was necessary to conduct these performance reviews at home because *   *   * "there was insufficient time to perform [his duties] during regular office hours." Moreover, *   *   *

---

a. This page contains links to some of the opinions of the Missouri state courts. Click on "Eastern District." Click on "Eastern Appellate District." When that page opens, in the "Search for the following word(s)" box, type "Pacesetter" and click on "Search."

the work performed at home by Claimant was an integral part of the conduct of his employer's business, and not only a convenience to Claimant. Clearly a benefit accrued to employer by Claimant conducting these performance reviews at home. We conclude that * * * Claimant demonstrated that the demands of his employment created the expectation that work needed to be done at home for the benefit of his employer.

DECISION AND REMEDY   *The court reversed the decision of the commission and remanded the case for the entry of an award of compensation. The court held that Rogers's injury arose out of and in the course of employment for purposes of workers' compensation.*

SECTION 4

Income Security

Federal and state governments participate in insurance programs designed to protect employees and their families by covering the financial impact of retirement, disability, death, hospitalization, and unemployment. The key federal law on this subject is the Social Security Act of 1935.[11]

SOCIAL SECURITY AND MEDICARE

The Social Security Act of 1935 provides for old age (retirement), survivors, and disability insurance. The act is therefore often referred to as OASDI. Both employers and employees must "contribute" under the Federal Insurance Contributions Act (FICA)[12] to help pay for the employees' loss of income on retirement. The basis for the employee's and the employer's contribution is the employee's annual wage base—the maximum amount of the employee's wages that are subject to the tax. The employer withholds the employee's FICA contribution from the employee's wages and then matches this contribution. (In 2000, employers were required to withhold 6.2 percent of each employee's wages, up to a maximum amount of $76,200, and to match this contribution.)

Retired workers are eligible to receive monthly payments from the Social Security Administration, which administers the Social Security Act. Social Security benefits are fixed by statute but increase automatically with increases in the cost of living.

Medicare, a health-insurance program, is administered by the Social Security Administration for people sixty-five years of age and older and for some under age sixty-five who are disabled. It has two parts, one pertaining to hospital costs and the other to nonhospital medical costs, such as visits to doctors' offices. People who have Medicare hospital insurance can obtain additional federal medical insurance if they pay small monthly premiums, which increase as the cost of medical care increases. As with Social Security contributions, both the employer and the employee contribute to Medicare. Currently, 1.45 percent of the amount of all wages and salaries paid to employees, plus a matching amount paid by the employer, go toward financing Medicare. There is no cap on the amount of wages subject to the Medicare tax.

PRIVATE PENSION PLANS

There has been significant legislation to regulate employee retirement plans set up by employers to supplement Social Security benefits. The major federal act covering these retirement plans is the Employee Retirement Income Security Act (ERISA) of 1974.[13] This statute empowers the Labor Management Services Administration of the Department of Labor to enforce its provisions governing employers who have private pension funds for their employees. ERISA does not require an employer to establish a pension plan. When a plan exists, however, ERISA establishes standards for its management.

A key provision of ERISA concerns vesting. **Vesting** gives an employee a legal right to receive pension benefits at some future date when he or she stops working. Before ERISA was enacted, some employees who had worked for companies for as long as thirty years received no pension benefits when their employment terminated, because those benefits had

---

11. 42 U.S.C. Sections 301–1397e.
12. 26 U.S.C. Sections 3101–3125.
13. 29 U.S.C. Sections 1001 *et seq.*

not vested. ERISA establishes complex vesting rules. Generally, however, all employee contributions to pension plans vest immediately, and employee rights to employer pension-plan contributions vest after five years of employment.

In an attempt to prevent mismanagement of pension funds, ERISA has established rules on how they must be invested. Pension managers must be cautious in their investments and refrain from investing more than 10 percent of the fund in securities of the employer. ERISA also contains detailed record-keeping and reporting requirements.

UNEMPLOYMENT COMPENSATION

The United States has a system of unemployment insurance in which employers pay into a fund, the proceeds of which are paid out to qualified unemployed workers. The Federal Unemployment Tax Act of 1935[14] created a state-administered system that provides unemployment compensation to eligible individuals. The FUTA and state laws require employers that fall under the provisions of the act to pay unemployment taxes at regular intervals.

SECTION 5

COBRA

Federal legislation also addresses the issue of health insurance for workers whose jobs have been terminated and who are thus no longer eligible for group health-insurance plans. The Consolidated Omnibus Budget Reconciliation Act (COBRA) of 1985[15] prohibits the elimination of a worker's medical, optical, or dental insurance coverage on the voluntary or involuntary termination of the worker's employment. The act applies to most workers who have either lost their jobs or had their hours decreased so that they are no longer eligible for coverage under the employer's health plan. Only workers fired for gross misconduct are excluded from protection.

APPLICATION OF COBRA

The worker has sixty days (beginning with the date that the group coverage would stop) to decide

whether to continue with the employer's group insurance plan or not. If the worker chooses to discontinue the coverage, then the employer has no further obligation. If the worker chooses to continue coverage, however, the employer is obligated to keep the policy active for up to eighteen months. If the worker is disabled, the employer must extend coverage up to twenty-nine months. The coverage provided must be the same as that enjoyed by the worker prior to the termination or reduction of employment. If family members were originally included, for example, COBRA would prohibit their exclusion. This is not a free ride for the worker, however. To receive continued benefits, he or she may be required to pay all of the premium, as well as a 2 percent administrative charge.

EMPLOYERS' OBLIGATIONS UNDER COBRA

Employers, with some exceptions, must comply with COBRA if they employ twenty or more workers and provide a benefit plan to those workers. An employer must inform an employee of COBRA's provisions when that worker faces termination or a reduction of hours that would affect his or her eligibility for coverage under the plan.

An employer is relieved of the responsibility to provide benefit coverage if it completely eliminates its group benefit plan. An employer is also relieved of responsibility when the worker becomes eligible for Medicare, falls under a spouse's health plan, becomes insured under a different plan (with a new employer, for example), or fails to pay the premium.

An employer that fails to comply with COBRA risks substantial penalties. These penalties include a tax of up to 10 percent of the annual cost of the group plan or $500,000, whichever is less.

SECTION 6

Family and Medical Leave

In 1993, Congress passed the Family and Medical Leave Act (FMLA)[16] to protect employees who need time off work for family or medical reasons. A majority of the states also have legislation allowing for a leave from employment for family or medical reasons,

---

14. 26 U.S.C. Sections 3301–3310.
15. 29 U.S.C. Sections 1161–1169.

16. 29 U.S.C. Sections 2601, 2611–2619, 2651–2654.

and many employers maintain private family-leave plans for their workers.

COVERAGE AND APPLICATION OF THE FMLA

The FMLA requires employers who have fifty or more employees to provide employees with up to twelve weeks of family or medical leave during any twelve-month period. During the employee's leave, the employer must continue the worker's health-care coverage and guarantee employment in the same or a comparable position when the employee returns to work. An important exception to the FMLA, however, allows the employer to avoid reinstatement of a *key employee*—defined as an employee whose pay falls within the top 10 percent of the firm's work force. Additionally, the act does not apply to employees who have worked less than one year or less than twenty-five hours a week during the previous twelve months.

Generally, an employee may take family leave when he or she wishes to care for a newborn baby, a newly adopted child, or a foster child just placed in the employee's care.[17] An employee may take medical leave when the employee or the employee's spouse, child, or parent has a "serious health condition" requiring care. For most absences, the employee must demonstrate that the health condition requires continued treatment by a health-care provider and includes a period of incapacity of more than three days.

Under regulations issued by the Department of Labor (DOL) in 1995, employees suffering from certain chronic health conditions may take FMLA leave for their own incapacities that require absences of less than three days. For example, an employee who has asthma or diabetes may have periodic occurrences of illness, rather than episodes continuing over an extended period of time. Similarly, pregnancy may involve periodic visits to a health-care provider and bouts of morning sickness. According to the DOL's regulations, employees with such conditions are covered by the FMLA.

REMEDIES FOR VIOLATIONS OF THE FMLA

Remedies for violations of the FMLA include (1) damages for unpaid wages (or salary), lost benefits, denied compensation, and actual monetary losses (such as the cost of providing for care) up to an amount equivalent to the employee's wages for twelve weeks; (2) job reinstatement; and (3) promotion. The successful plaintiff is entitled to court costs, attorneys' fees, and—in cases involving bad faith on the part of the employer—double damages.

SECTION 7

Employee Privacy Rights

Recall from Chapter 4 that there is no provision in the U.S. Constitution that guarantees a right to privacy. A personal right to privacy, however, has been inferred from other constitutional guarantees provided by the First, Third, Fourth, Fifth, and Ninth Amendments to the Constitution. Additionally, state laws providing for privacy rights may apply in the employment context. Finally, remember from Chapter 5 that the invasion of another's privacy may constitute a tort.

In the last two decades, concerns about the privacy rights of employees have arisen in response to the sometimes invasive tactics used by employers in their efforts to monitor and screen workers. Lie-detector tests, drug tests, and other practices have increasingly been subject to challenge as violations of employee privacy rights. A particularly troublesome issue today has to do with electronic monitoring in the workplace. For a discussion of this issue, see this chapter's *Emerging Trends in Technology*.

LIE-DETECTOR TESTS

At one time, many employers required employees or job applicants to take polygraph examinations (lie-detector tests) in connection with their employment. To protect the privacy interests of employees and job applicants, in 1988 Congress passed the Employee Polygraph Protection Act.[18] The statute prohibits employers from (1) requiring or causing employees or job applicants to take lie-detector tests or suggesting or requesting that they do so; (2) using, accepting, referring to, or asking about the results of lie-detector tests taken by employees or applicants; and (3) taking or threatening negative employment-related action against employees or applicants based on results of lie-detector tests or on their refusal to take the tests.

---

17. The foster care must be state sanctioned for such an arrangement to fall within the coverage of the FMLA.

18. 29 U.S.C. Sections 2001 *et seq.*

EMERGING TRENDS IN TECHNOLOGY

Electronic Monitoring in the Workplace

In today's workplace, employees' use of electronic communications systems may subject employers to liability on many fronts. One risk is that e-mail could be used to harass employees. Another risk is that employees could reproduce, without authorization, copyright-protected materials on the Internet. Still another risk is that confidential information contained in e-mail or voice mail messages could fall into the hands of an outside party. Finally, personal use of the Internet by employees cuts into their work time. In an attempt to shield themselves from liability and to increase worker productivity, some companies monitor their employees' electronic communications.

ELECTRONIC MONITORING PRACTICES

According to the American Management Association, more than 45 percent of U.S. corporations engage in some intrusive employee monitoring practices. These practices may include monitoring employees' e-mail, voice mail, and telephone exchanges; recording employees' computer keystrokes; tracking employees' Internet use; and video-recording employees' job performance.[a]

Tracking employees' Internet use is made easier by a variety of specially designed software products. For example, software such as SurfWatch Professional Edition and LittleBrother allows employers to track virtually every move made by a worker using the Internet, including the specific Web sites visited by the worker and the time spent surfing the Internet. Other software, such as that created by Content Technologies, matches taboo key words in employees' e-mail messages against a stored list. Once alerted, the message is examined to see if it violates company policy. AT&T Corporation has gone even further: it has developed software that will "understand" taboo phrases, not just words, in e-mail messages.

Clearly, employers need to protect themselves from liability for their employees' online activities. At the same time, employees expect to have a certain zone of privacy in the workplace, and some claim that employers have gone too far in their monitoring practices.

----
a. "Don't Expect Privacy in the Workplace," *International Herald Tribune*, January 16–17, 1999, p. 4.

LAWS GOVERNING ELECTRONIC MONITORING

Generally, there is little specific government regulation of monitoring activities, although electronic monitoring by employers may violate the Electronic Communications Privacy Act (ECPA) of 1986.[b] This act amended existing federal wiretapping law to cover electronic forms of communications, such as communications via cellular telephones or e-mail. The ECPA prohibits the intentional interception of any wire or electronic communication or the intentional disclosure or use of the information obtained by the interception.

The act excludes from coverage, however, any electronic communications through devices that are "furnished to the subscriber or user by a provider of wire or electronic communication service" and that are being used by the subscriber or user, or by the provider of the service, "in the ordinary course of its business." Another exception to the ECPA allows employers to avoid liability under the act if employees *consent* to having their electronic communications intercepted by the employer. Thus, an employer may be able to avoid what laws do exist by simply informing employees that

----
b. 18 U.S.C. Sections 2510–2521.

Employers excepted from these prohibitions include federal, state, and local government employers; certain security service firms; and companies manufacturing and distributing controlled substances. Other employers may use polygraph tests when investigating losses attributable to theft, including embezzlement and the theft of trade secrets.

DRUG TESTING

In the interests of public safety and to reduce unnecessary costs, many of today's employers, including the government, require their employees to submit to drug testing. Laws relating to the privacy rights of private-sector employees vary from state to state. Some state

EMERGING TRENDS IN TECHNOLOGY

Electronic Monitoring in the Workplace, continued

they are subject to monitoring. Then, if employees challenge the monitoring practice, the employer can raise the defense of consent by claiming that the employees consented to the monitoring.[c] Generally, in cases challenging employee monitoring practices, the courts have sided with the employers, concluding that the employers' actions are based on legitimate concerns.

ALTERNATIVE APPROACHES

Many companies are finding that the benefits of electronic monitoring may not be worth the costs—a major cost being employee resentment of monitoring practices. An alternative being pursued by a growing number of

---

c. In some cases, even a verbal announcement to employees that their electronic communications would be monitored was sufficient to justify the use of the consent defense. See, for example, *Griffin v. City of Milwaukee,* 74 F.3d 824 (7th Cir. 1996).

companies, particularly in the high-tech industry, is to allow their employees to use their own discretion with respect to Internet use. Hewlett-Packard, for example, does not monitor employees' Internet use or block access to any Web sites.

Some observers claim that this "hands-off" approach with respect to employee use of the Internet is a sensible one. For one thing, some highly qualified job candidates may not want to work for a company that monitors their Internet use. For another, there is no evidence that Internet monitoring has increased worker productivity. Finally, how can an employer monitor Internet use while its employees are traveling or working at home—as more and more employees are doing?

Another alternative adopted by some companies is to use filtering software (discussed in Chapter 9). Instead of monitoring Internet use, these companies utilize filtering software to block access to certain Web sites, such as pornographic sites.

IMPLICATIONS FOR THE BUSINESSPERSON

1. Employers should carefully weigh the pros and cons of electronic monitoring in their workplaces to make sure that the monitoring practices are, in fact,

effective in increasing worker productivity and decreasing certain risks—of theft, for example, or liability for employee actions.
2. Employers who want to hire "the brightest and the best" employees may find it difficult to do so if they engage in overly intrusive monitoring practices.

FOR CRITICAL ANALYSIS

1. Why might an employer allow employees to make personal telephone calls using office telephones but prohibit them from using the Internet for personal reasons?
2. Should an employee have a reasonable expectation of privacy when using his or her employer's computer system to send personal e-mail messages? Why or why not?

RELEVANT WEB SITES

You can find a summary of the monitoring capabilities of LittleBrother at **http://www. kansmen.com/products/lb/index. htm**. To view the results of the latest American Management Association survey on electronic monitoring in the workplace, go to **http://www.amanet.org/research/ specials/monit.htm**.

---

constitutions prohibit private employers from testing for drugs, and state statutes may restrict drug testing by private employers in any number of ways. A collective bargaining agreement may also provide protection against drug testing. In some instances, employees have brought actions against their employers for the tort of invasion of privacy.

Constitutional limitations apply to the testing of government employees. The Fourth Amendment provides that individuals have the right to be "secure in their persons" against "unreasonable searches and seizures" conducted by government agents. Drug tests have been held to be constitutional, however, when there was a reasonable basis for suspecting government employees of using drugs. Additionally, when drug use in a particular government job could threaten public safety, testing has been upheld. For example, a U.S. Department of Transportation rule that requires employees engaged in oil and gas pipeline operations to submit to random drug testing was upheld, even though the rule did not require that before being tested the individual must have been suspected of drug use.[19] The court held that the government's interest in promoting public safety in the pipeline industry outweighed the employees' privacy interests.

An ongoing problem with respect to drug testing is that such tests are not foolproof. Suppose that a job applicant is not hired because of a positive drug test. If the results of the test are false, does the applicant have any legal recourse? In one case, for example, after a drug-testing laboratory mistakenly reported to an employer that a job applicant had failed a drug test, the applicant filed a suit against the laboratory. The court granted the employer's request for summary judgment, holding—as have a number of other courts— that while a laboratory may owe a duty of care to the employer for whom it conducts the drug tests, it owes no such duty to the employee being tested.[20]

In another case, a worker who had been fired because of a positive drug test sued the employer, alleging that the real reason he had been fired was racial animus. The fired employee claimed that his job had been classified as a "safety-sensitive position" even though it should not have been and that he had not ingested any drugs that would account for the positive drug-testing results. In short, claimed the worker, he had been "set up" by the employer. The court, however, granted summary judgment for the employer, largely because the employee did not follow the proper procedures for contesting drug-test results. (The procedures require the employee to mail a request in writing, along with $125, to the laboratory that performed the test. Moreover, the request had to arrive within twenty-four hours, and the laboratory would only re-test the same sample, not a new one.)[21]

AIDS TESTING

An increasing number of employers are testing their workers for acquired immune deficiency syndrome (AIDS). Few public issues involve more controversy than this practice. Some state laws restrict AIDS testing, and federal statutes offer some protection to employees and job applicants who have AIDS or have tested positive for the AIDS virus. The federal Americans with Disabilities Act of 1990[22] (discussed in Chapter 42), for example, prohibits discrimination against individuals with disabilities, and the term *disability* has been broadly defined to include those individuals with diseases such as AIDS. The law also requires employers to reasonably accommodate the needs of persons with disabilities. Generally, although the law may not prohibit AIDS testing, it may prohibit the discharge of employees based on the results of those tests.

SCREENING PROCEDURES

An area of concern to potential employees has to do with preemployment screening procedures. What kinds of questions on an employment application or a preemployment test are permissible? What kinds of questions go too far in terms of invading the potential employee's privacy? Is it an invasion of the potential employee's privacy, for example, to ask questions about his or her sexual orientation or religious convictions? Although an employer may believe that such information is relevant to the job for which the individual has applied, the applicant may feel differently about the matter. Generally, questions on an employment application must have a reasonable nexus, or connection, with the job for which an applicant is applying.[23]

SECTION 8

Employment-Related Immigration Laws

The most important immigration laws governing employment relationships are the Immigration Reform and Control Act (IRCA) of 1986[24] and the Immigration Act of 1990.[25] The IRCA, which is administered by the

19. *Electrical Workers Local 1245 v. Skinner*, 913 F.2d 1454 (9th Cir. 1990).
20. *Ney v. Axelrod*, 723 A.2d 719 (Pa.Super. 1999).
21. *Brown v. Allied Printing Ink Co.*, 241 Ga.App. 310, ___S.E.2d___ (1999).
22. 42 U.S.C. Sections 12102–12118.
23. See, for example, *Soroka v. Dayton Hudson Corp.*, 7 Cal.App.4th 203, 1 Cal.Rptr.2d 77 (1991).
24. 29 U.S.C. Section 1802.
25. This act amended various provisions of the Immigration and Nationality Act of 1952, 8 U.S.C. Sections 1101 *et seq.*

U.S. Immigration and Naturalization Service (INS), prohibits employers from hiring illegal immigrants. Employers must complete a special form—called INS Form I-9—for each employee and indicate on it that the employer has verified that the employee is either a U.S. citizen or is otherwise entitled to work in this country.

The Immigration Act of 1990 limits the number of legal immigrants entering the United States by capping the number of visas (entry permits) that are issued each year. Under the act, employers recruiting employees from other countries must complete a certification process and satisfy the Department of Labor that there is a shortage of qualified U.S. workers capable of performing the work. The employer must also establish that bringing immigrants into this country will not adversely affect the existing labor market in that particular area. In this way, the act attempts to serve two purposes: encouraging skilled workers to enter this country and at the same time restricting competition for American jobs.

SECTION 9

Wrongful Discharge

Whenever an employer discharges an employee in violation of an employment contract or a statutory law protecting employees, the employee may bring an action for **wrongful discharge.** If an employer's actions do not violate any express employment contract or statute, then the question is whether the employer has violated a common law doctrine. Because of the harsh effects of the employment-at-will doctrine for employees, courts have carved out various exceptions to the doctrine. These exceptions are based on contract theory, tort theory, and public policy.

EXCEPTIONS BASED ON CONTRACT THEORY

Some courts have held that an *implied* employment contract exists between the employer and the employee. If the employee is fired outside the terms of the implied contract, he or she may succeed in an action for breach of contract even though no written employment contract exists.

For example, an employer's manual or personnel bulletin may state that, as a matter of policy, workers will be dismissed only for good cause. If the employee

is aware of this policy and continues to work for the employer, a court may find that there is an implied contract based on the terms stated in the manual or bulletin. Promises that an employer makes to employees regarding discharge policy may also be considered part of an implied contract. If the employer fires a worker in a manner contrary to the procedure promised, a court may hold that the employer has violated the implied contract and is liable for damages. Most state courts will consider this claim and judge it by traditional contract standards.

A few states have gone further and held that all employment contracts contain an implied covenant of good faith. This means that both sides promise to abide by the contract in good faith. If an employer fires an employee for an arbitrary or unjustified reason, the employee can claim that the covenant of good faith was breached and the contract violated.

EXCEPTIONS BASED ON TORT THEORY

In a few cases, the discharge of an employee may give rise to an action for wrongful discharge under tort theories. Abusive discharge procedures may result in intentional infliction of emotional distress or defamation. In one case, a restaurant had suffered some thefts of supplies, and the manager announced that he would start firing waitresses alphabetically until the thief was identified. The first waitress fired said that she suffered great emotional distress as a result. The state's highest court upheld her claim as stating a valid cause of action.[26]

Some courts have permitted workers to sue their employers under the tort theory of fraud. Under this theory, an employer may be held liable for making false promises to a prospective employee if the employee detrimentally relies on the employer's representations by taking the job. For example, suppose that an employer induces a prospective employee to leave a lucrative job and move to another state by offering "a long-term job with a thriving business." In fact, the employer is having significant financial problems. Furthermore, the employer is planning a merger that will involve the elimination of the position offered to the prospective employee. If the employee takes the job in reliance on the employer's representations and is fired shortly thereafter, the

---

26. *Agis v. Howard Johnson Co.,* 371 Mass. 140, 355 N.E.2d 315 (1976).

employee may be able to bring an action against the employer for fraud.[27]

EXCEPTIONS BASED ON PUBLIC POLICY

The most widespread common law exception to the employment-at-will doctrine is an exception made on the basis of public policy. Courts may apply this exception when an employer fires a worker for reasons that violate a fundamental public policy of the jurisdiction.

Generally, the courts require that the public policy involved must be expressed clearly in the statutory law governing the jurisdiction. The public policy against employment discrimination, for example, is expressed clearly in federal and state statutes. Thus, if a worker is fired for discriminatory reasons but has no cause of action under statutory law (for example, if the workplace has too few employees to be covered by the statute), that worker may succeed in a suit against the employer for wrongful discharge in violation of public policy.[28]

Sometimes, an employer will direct an employee to perform an illegal act. If the employee refuses to perform the act, the employer may decide to fire the worker. Similarly, employees who "blow the whistle" on the wrongdoing of their employers often find themselves disciplined or even out of a job. **Whistleblowing** occurs when an employee tells a government official, upper-management authorities, or the press that his or her employer is engaged in some unsafe or illegal activity. Whistleblowers on occasion have been protected from wrongful discharge for reasons of public policy. For example, a bank was held to have wrongfully discharged an employee who pressured the employer to comply with state and federal consumer credit laws.[29]

The following case involved an employee who was discharged for refusing to perform an illegal act. The employee sued the company, alleging that her discharge violated public policy.

---

27. See, for example, *Lazar v. Superior Court of Los Angeles Co.*, 12 Cal.4th 631, 909 P.2d 981, 49 Cal.Rptr.2d 377 (1996).

28. See, for example, *Molesworth v. Brandon*, 341 Md. 621, 672 A.2d 608 (1996).

29. *Harless v. First National Bank in Fairmont*, 162 W.Va. 116, 246 S.E.2d 270 (1978).

CASE 41.3   Lins v. Children's Discovery Centers of America, Inc.

Court of Appeals of Washington, Division 2, 1999. 95 Wash.App. 486, 976 P.2d 168. http://www.findlaw. com/11stategov/wa/ waca.html[a]

BACKGROUND AND FACTS *Children's Discovery Centers of America, Inc. (CDC), operates child-care centers. Diane Lins was a regional director in charge of six centers in the Pacific Northwest, including the state of Washington. During her tenure, CDC promoted her and gave her good performance ratings. In March 1995, Pam French was hired to be CDC's West Coast operations director, Lins's supervisor. Less than ten days later, Lins and five of her subordinates were injured in an auto accident that occurred within the course and scope of their employment. Each employee filed a workers' compensation claim. Within two weeks of the accident, French ordered Lins to fire the other five employees. French had heard that two of them were consulting attorneys and she "didn't trust either of them not to sue the company, and she was not going to allow that to happen." She harbored similar feelings about the remaining three, even though they had not seen attorneys. A Washington state statute provides that "no employer may discharge or in any manner discriminate against any employee because such employee has filed or communicated to the employer an intent to file a claim for compensation or exercise any [related] rights." Realizing that she could not lawfully perform French's order, Lins refused to do so. On May 5, French gave Lins a poor performance rating and put her on probation. On June 22, French fired Lins for "Neglect of Duties/Poor Performance." Lins filed a suit in a Washington state court against CDC, alleging that she had been wrongfully discharged in violation of the state's public policy. CDC filed a motion for*

---

a. In the "Court of Appeals: Published" section, click on "1999." When the list appears, in the group of decisions released on "May 07, 1999," find the case name (it begins "IIDiane Lins") and click on the docket number ("22424-1") to access the opinion.

summary judgment, which the court granted. Lins appealed to a state intermediate appellate court.

IN THE LANGUAGE OF THE COURT

MORGAN, J. [Judge]

* * * *

Public policy * * * prohibits an employer from considering certain activities when deciding whether to discharge an employee. * * * [This principle is] often summarized by saying that *it is unlawful for an employer to retaliate against an employee for protected activity.* [Emphasis added.]

The problem, of course, is defining the "activity" that public policy "protects." Either the legislature or the judiciary may address that problem, the legislature through statutes and the judiciary through decisional law. When the judiciary addresses the problem, it inquires (1) whether a clear public policy exists; (2) whether that policy will be jeopardized unless the activity in issue is protected; (3) whether employers in general have overriding justification for wanting to use the activity in issue as a factor affecting the decision to discharge; and (4) whether the particular employee's activity in the case at bar was a substantial factor in (i.e., a cause of) the particular employer's decision to discharge. * * *

Turning to the first of the four elements * * *, we hold that Washington has a clear public policy against firing an employee because he or she has filed a worker's compensation claim. * * * [T]he legislature declared that "no employer may discharge or in any manner discriminate against any employee because such employee has filed or communicated to the employer an intent to file a claim for compensation or exercises any [related] rights * * * ."

Turning to the second element, we hold that the policy just described will be jeopardized if, without incurring liability, an employer can fire an employee for refusing to carry out a clearly unlawful order. If the employee's refusal is not protected from retaliation, the employee will likely perform the order to save his or her job; the employer will have a readily available means by which to implement its unlawful order; and the policy * * * will be impaired or destroyed. But if the employee's refusal is protected, the employee will be likely to refuse the order; the employer will be denied a readily available means by which to implement the order; and the policy * * * will be served.

Turning to the third element, we hold that employers do not have any overriding justification for wanting to consider an employee's refusal to perform an unlawful order when deciding whether to fire the employee. By virtue of the order being unlawful in the first instance, the employer should not have given it, and the employer has no legitimate interest in having it carried out.

Finally, on the fourth element, a jury could reasonably infer from the evidence in this record that Lins' refusal to carry out French's unlawful order was a substantial factor in Lins' being fired.

DECISION AND REMEDY

The Court of Appeals of Washington concluded that Lins's refusal to carry out French's order was conduct protected by public policy and that French's retaliation was thus unlawful. Public policy prevents an employer from discharging an employee in retaliation for the employee's refusal to carry out the employer's unlawful order. The court reversed the decision of the lower court and remanded the case for trial.

SECTION 10

Statutory Protection for Whistleblowers

To encourage workers to report employers' wrongdoing, such as fraud, most states have enacted so-called whistleblower statutes. These statutes protect whistleblowers from subsequent retaliation on the part of employers. On the federal level, the Whistleblower Protection Act of 1989[30] protects federal employees who blow the whistle on their employers from their

---

30. 5 U.S.C. Section 1201.

employers' retaliatory actions. Whistleblower statutes may also provide an incentive to disclose information by providing the whistleblower with a monetary reward. For example, the federal False Claims Reform Act of 1986[31] requires that a whistleblower who has

disclosed information relating to a fraud perpetrated against the U.S. government receive between 15 and 25 percent of the proceeds if the government brings suit against the wrongdoer.

---

31. 31 U.S.C. Sections 3729–3733. This act amended the False Claims Act of 1863.

TERMS AND CONCEPTS TO REVIEW

cease-and-desist order 762

closed shop 762

collective bargaining 763

employment at will 760

hot-cargo agreement 763

minimum wage 761

right-to-work law 763

secondary boycott 763

strike 764

union shop 762

vesting 767

whistleblowing 774

workers' compensation laws 765

wrongful discharge 773

QUESTIONS AND CASE PROBLEMS

41–1. LABOR LAWS. Calzoni Boating Co. is an interstate business engaged in manufacturing and selling boats. The company has five hundred nonunion employees. Representatives of these employees are requesting a four-day, ten-hours-per-day workweek, and Calzoni is concerned that this would require paying time and a half after eight hours per day. Which federal act is Calzoni thinking of that might require this? Will the act in fact require paying time and a half for all hours worked over eight hours per day if the employees' proposal is accepted? Explain.

41–2. HEALTH AND SAFETY REGULATIONS. Denton and Carlo were employed at an appliance plant. Their job required them to do occasional maintenance work while standing on a wire mesh twenty feet above the plant floor. Other employees had fallen through the mesh, and one of them had been killed by the fall. When Denton and Carlo were asked by their supervisor to do work that would likely require them to walk on the mesh, they refused because of their fear of bodily harm or death. Because of their refusal to do the requested work, the two employees were fired from their jobs. Was their discharge wrongful? If so, under what federal employment law? To what federal agency or department should they turn for assistance?

41–3. UNFAIR LABOR PRACTICES. Suppose that Consolidated Stores is undergoing a unionization campaign.

Prior to the union election, management says that the union is unnecessary to protect workers. Management also provides bonuses and wage increases to the workers during this period. The employees reject the union. Union organizers protest that the wage increases during the election campaign unfairly prejudiced the vote. Should these wage increases be regarded as an unfair labor practice? Discuss.

41–4. WORKERS' COMPENSATION. Galvin Strang worked for a tractor company in one of its factories. Near his work station was a conveyor belt that ran through a large industrial oven. Sometimes, the workers would use the oven to heat their meals. Thirty-inch-high flasks containing molds were fixed at regular intervals on the conveyor and were transported into the oven. Strang had to walk between the flasks to get to his work station. One day, the conveyor was not moving, and Strang used the oven to cook a frozen pot pie. As he was removing the pot pie from the oven, the conveyor came on. One of the flasks struck Strang and seriously injured him. Strang sought recovery under the state workers' compensation law. Should he recover? Why or why not?

41–5. EMPLOYMENT AT WILL. Robert Adams worked as a delivery truck driver for George W. Cochran & Co. Adams persistently refused to drive a truck that lacked a required inspection sticker and was subsequently fired as a result of his refusal. Adams was an at-will employee, and Cochran contended that because there was no written employment contract stating otherwise, Cochran was entitled to discharge Adams at will—that is, for cause or no cause. Adams sought to recover $7,094 in lost wages and $200,000 in damages for the "humiliation, mental anguish and emotional distress" that he had suffered as a result of being fired from his job. Under what legal doctrines discussed in this chapter—or exceptions to those doctrines—might Adams be able to recover damages from Cochran? Discuss fully. [*Adams v. George W. Cochran & Co.*, 597 A.2d 28 (D.C.App. 1991)]

41–6. WORKERS' COMPENSATION. Linda Burnett Kidwell, employed as a state traffic officer by the California Highway Patrol (CHP), suffered an injury at home, off duty, while practicing the standing long jump. The jump is a required component of the CHP's annual physical performance program fitness test. Kidwell filed a claim for workers' compensation benefits. The CHP and the California workers' compensation appeals board denied her claim. Kidwell appealed to a state appellate court. What is the requirement for granting a workers' compensation claim? Should Kidwell's claim be granted? [*Kidwell v. Workers' Compensation Appeals Board*, 33 Cal.App.4th 1130, 39 Cal.Rptr.2d 540 (1995)]

41–7. WHISTLEBLOWING. Gabor Nagy was a car salesperson for Whittlesey Automotive Group. Whittlesey asked Nagy to allow some of his phone conversations with "customers" to be recorded. The "customers" were actually employees of a company Whittlesey had hired to conduct a sales training program. Nagy refused to consent. He was eventually fired for his "negative attitude." Nagy filed a suit in a California state court against Whittlesey. He cited a state statute that makes eavesdropping a crime and alleged in part that he was wrongfully terminated in violation of public policy. Will the court agree? Discuss fully. [*Nagy v. Whittlesey Automotive Group*, 40 Cal.App.4th 1328, 47 Cal.Rptr.2d 395 (1995)]

41–8. WRONGFUL DISCHARGE. Stephen Fredrick, a pilot for Simmons Airlines, Inc., criticized the safety of the aircraft that Simmons used on many of its flights and warned the airline about possible safety problems. Simmons took no action. After one of the planes crashed, Fredrick appeared on the television program *Good Morning America* to discuss his safety concerns. The same day, Fredrick refused to allow employees of Simmons to search his personal bags before a flight that he was scheduled to work. Claiming insubordination, the airline terminated Fredrick. Fredrick filed a suit in a federal district court against Simmons, claiming, among other things, retaliatory discharge for his public criticism of the safety of Simmons's aircraft and that this discharge violated the public policy of providing for safe air travel. Simmons responded that an employee who "goes public" with his or her concerns should not be protected by the law. Will the court agree with Simmons? Explain. [*Fredrick v. Simmons Airlines Corp.*, 144 F.3d 500 (7th Cir. 1998)]

41–9. HOURS AND WAGES. Richard Ackerman was an advance sales representative and account manager for Coca-Cola Enterprises, Inc. His primary responsibility was to sell Coca-Cola products to grocery stores, convenience stores, and other sales outlets. Coca-Cola also employed merchandisers, who did not sell Coca-Cola products but performed tasks associated with their distribution and promotion, including restocking shelves, filling vending machines, and setting up displays. The account managers, who serviced the smaller accounts themselves, regularly worked between fifty-five and seventy-two hours each week. Coca-Cola paid them a salary, bonuses, and commissions, but it did not pay them—unlike the merchandisers—additional compensation for the overtime. Ackerman and the other account managers filed a suit in a federal district court against Coca-Cola, alleging that they were entitled to overtime compensation. Coca-Cola responded that because of an exemption under the Fair Labor Standards Act, it was not required to pay them overtime. Is Coca-Cola correct? Explain. [*Ackerman v. Coca-Cola Enterprises, Inc.*, 179 F.3d 1260 (10th Cir. 1999)]

41–10. IN YOUR COURT

Loomis Armored, Inc., has a company rule forbidding its armored truck drivers from leaving their trucks unattended. The employee handbook states, "Violations of this rule will be grounds for termination." Kevin Gardner worked for Loomis as a driver. During a scheduled stop at a bank, Gardner left the truck to aid a woman who was being threatened by a man with a knife. Gardner was discharged for violating Loomis's rule. Gardner subsequently sued Loomis, claiming that his employment termination in these circumstances violated public policy. Assume that you are the judge in the trial court hearing this case and answer the following questions:

(a) The court opinion in Case 41.3 (*Lins v. Children's Discovery Centers of America, Inc.*) lists four factors that courts consider when determining whether a certain type of activity is "protected." How would you apply each of these factors to the case now before your court?

(b) What public policy, if any, has Loomis violated? How will you rule on this issue, and why?

41–11. A QUESTION OF ETHICS

Keith Cline worked for Wal-Mart Stores, Inc., as a night maintenance supervisor. When he suffered a recurrence of a brain tumor, he took a leave from work, which was covered by the Family Medical and Leave Act of 1993 and authorized by his employer. When he returned to work, his employer refused to allow him to continue his supervisory job and demoted him to the status of a regular maintenance worker. A few weeks later, the company fired him, ostensibly because he "stole" company time by clocking in thirteen minutes early for a company meeting. Cline sued Wal-Mart, alleging, among other things, that Wal-Mart had violated the FMLA by refusing to return him to his prior position when he returned to work. In view of these facts, answer the following questions. [*Cline v. Wal-Mart Stores, Inc.*, 144 F.3d 294 (4th Cir. 1998)]

   (a) Did Wal-Mart violate the FMLA by refusing to return Cline to his prior position when he returned to work?

   (b) From an ethical perspective, the FMLA has been viewed as a choice on the part of society to shift to the employer family burdens caused by changing economic and social needs. What "changing" needs does the act meet? In other words, why did Congress feel that workers should have the right to family and medical leave in 1993, but not in 1983, or 1973, or earlier?

   (c) "Congress should amend the FMLA, which currently applies to employers with fifty or more employees, so that it applies to employers with twenty-five or more employees." Do you agree with this statement? Why or why not?

LAW ON THE WEB

For updated links to resources available on the Web, as well as a variety of other materials, visit this text's Web site at http://wbl.westbuslaw.com.

An excellent Web site for information on employee benefits, including the full text of the FMLA, COBRA, other relevant statutes and case law, and current articles, is BenefitsLink. Go to

http://www.benefitslink.com/columns.shtml

The American Federation of Labor–Congress of Industrial Organizations (AFL–CIO) provides links to a broad variety of labor-related resources at

http://www.aflcio.org

The Occupational Safety and Health Administration (OSHA) offers information related to workplace health and safety at

http://www.osha.gov

The Bureau of Labor Statistics provides a wide variety of data on employment, including data on employment compensation, working conditions, and productivity. Go to

http://stats.bls.gov/blshome.html

The National Labor Relations Board is online at the following URL:

http://www.nlrb.gov

LEGAL RESEARCH EXERCISES ON THE WEB

Go to http://wbl.westbuslaw.com, the Web site that accompanies this text. Select "Internet Applications," and then click on "Chapter 41." There you will find the following Internet research exercises that you can perform to learn more about employment laws and issues:

Activity 41–1: Workers' Compensation

Activity 41–2: Workplace Monitoring and Surveillance

CHAPTER 42

Employment Discrimination

OUT OF THE 1960s CIVIL RIGHTS movement to end racial and other forms of discrimination grew a body of law protecting employees against discrimination in the workplace. This protective legislation further eroded the employment-at-will doctrine, which was discussed in Chapter 41. In the past several decades, judicial decisions, administrative agency actions, and legislation have restricted the ability of employers, as well as unions, to discriminate against workers on the basis of race, color, religion, national origin, gender, age, or disability. A class of persons defined by one or more of these criteria is known as a **protected class.**

Several federal statutes prohibit **employment discrimination** against members of protected classes. The most important statute is Title VII of the Civil Rights Act of 1964.[1] Title VII prohibits employment discrimination on the basis of race, color, religion, national origin, and gender. Discrimination on the basis of age and disability are prohibited by the Age Discrimination in Employment Act of 1967[2] and the Americans with Disabilities Act of 1990,[3] respectively. The protections afforded under these laws extend to U.S. citizens who are working abroad for U.S. firms or for companies that are controlled by U.S. firms— *unless* to do so would violate the laws of the countries

in which their workplaces are located. This "foreign laws exception" allows employers to avoid being subjected to conflicting laws.

This chapter focuses on the kinds of discrimination prohibited by these federal statutes. Note, however, that discrimination against employees on the basis of any of the above-mentioned criteria may also violate state human rights statutes or other state laws prohibiting discrimination.

SECTION 1

Title VII of the Civil Rights Act of 1964

Title VII of the Civil Rights Act of 1964 and its amendments prohibit job discrimination against employees, applicants, and union members on the basis of race, color, national origin, religion, and gender at any stage of employment. Title VII applies to employers affecting interstate commerce with fifteen or more employees, labor unions with fifteen or more members, labor unions that operate hiring halls (to which members go regularly to be rationed jobs as they become available), employment agencies, and state and local governing units or agencies. A special section of the act prohibits discrimination in most federal government employment.

1. 42 U.S.C. Sections 2000e–2000e-17.
2. 29 U.S.C. Sections 621–634.
3. 42 U.S.C. Sections 12102–12118.

Title VII applies to any employer that "has fifteen or more employees for each working day in each of twenty or more calendar weeks in the current or preceding calendar year." One of the problems that courts have faced in applying Title VII is how to interpret the phrase "has fifteen or more employees." Does an employer "have" an employee on any working day on which the employer maintains an employment relationship with the employee, or only on working days on which the employee is actually receiving compensation from the employer?

In 1997, the United States Supreme Court resolved this issue by holding that the test for when an employer "has" an employee is whether the employer has an employment relationship with the individual on the day in question. This test is generally called the "payroll method," because the employment relationship is most readily demonstrated by the individual's appearance on the employer's payroll as a full-time or part-time worker.[4]

PROCEDURES UNDER TITLE VII

Compliance with Title VII is monitored by the Equal Employment Opportunity Commission (EEOC). A victim of alleged discrimination, before bringing a suit against the employer, must first file a claim with the EEOC. The EEOC may investigate the dispute and attempt to obtain the parties' voluntary consent to an out-of-court settlement. If voluntary agreement cannot be reached, the EEOC may then file a suit against the employer on the employee's behalf. If the EEOC decides not to investigate the claim, the victim may bring his or her own lawsuit against the employer.

The EEOC does not investigate every claim of employment discrimination; rather, it investigates only "priority cases." Generally, priority cases are cases that affect many workers, cases involving retaliatory discharge (firing an employee in retaliation for submitting a claim with the EEOC), and cases involving types of discrimination that are of particular concern to the EEOC.

INTENTIONAL AND UNINTENTIONAL DISCRIMINATION

Title VII of the Civil Rights Act of 1964 prohibits both intentional and unintentional discrimination.

4. *Walters v. Metropolitan Educational Enterprises, Inc.*, 519 U.S. 202, 117 S.Ct. 660, 136 L.Ed.2d 644 (1997).

Intentional Discrimination. Intentional discrimination by an employer against an employee is known as **disparate-treatment discrimination.** Because intent may sometimes be difficult to prove, courts have established certain procedures for resolving disparate-treatment cases. Suppose that a woman applies for employment with a construction firm and is rejected. If she sues on the basis of disparate-treatment discrimination in hiring, she must show that (1) she is a member of a protected class, (2) she applied and was qualified for the job in question, (3) she was rejected by the employer, and (4) the employer continued to seek applicants for the position or filled the position with a person not in a protected class.

If the woman can meet these relatively easy requirements, she makes out a *prima facie* case of illegal discrimination. Making out a *prima facie* case of discrimination means that the plaintiff has met her initial burden of proof and will win in the absence of a legally acceptable employer defense (defenses to claims of employment discrimination will be discussed later in this chapter). The burden then shifts to the employer-defendant, who must articulate a legal reason for not hiring the plaintiff. For example, the employer might say that the plaintiff was not hired because she lacked sufficient experience or training. To prevail, the plaintiff must then show that the employer's reason is a *pretext* (not the true reason) and that discriminatory intent actually motivated the employer's decision.

Disparate-Impact Discrimination. Employers often find it necessary to use interviews and testing procedures to choose from among a large number of applicants for job openings. Minimum educational requirements are also common. Employer practices, such as those involving educational requirements, may have an unintended discriminatory impact on a protected class. **Disparate-impact discrimination** occurs when, as a result of educational or other job requirements or hiring procedures, an employer's work force does not reflect the percentage of nonwhites, women, or members of other protected classes that characterizes the pool of qualified individuals in the local labor market. If a person challenging an employment practice having a discriminatory effect can show a connection between the practice and the disparity, he or she makes out a *prima facie* case, and no evidence of discriminatory intent needs to be shown.

Disparate-impact discrimination can also occur when an educational or other job requirement or hiring procedure excludes members of a protected class from an employer's work force at a substantially higher rate than nonmembers, regardless of the racial balance in the employer's work force. The EEOC has devised a test, called the "four-fifths rule," to determine whether an employment examination is discriminatory on its face. Under this rule, a selection rate for protected classes that is less than four-fifths, or 80 percent, of the rate for the group with the highest rate will generally be regarded as evidence of disparate impact. To illustrate: One hundred majority applicants take an employment test, and fifty pass the test and are hired. One hundred minority applicants take the test, and twenty pass the test and are hired. Because twenty is less than four-fifths (80 percent) of fifty, the test would be considered discriminatory under the EEOC guidelines.

DISCRIMINATION BASED ON RACE, COLOR, AND NATIONAL ORIGIN

Title VII prohibits employers from discriminating against employees or job applicants on the basis of race, color, or national origin. This prohibition extends to both intentional (disparate-treatment) and unintentional (disparate-impact) discrimination. If a company's standards or policies for selecting or promoting employees have the effect of discriminating

against employees or job applicants on the basis of race, color, or national origin, they are illegal—unless (except for race) they have a substantial, demonstrable relationship to realistic qualifications for the job in question. Discrimination against these protected classes in regard to employment conditions and benefits is also illegal.

Note that victims of racial or ethnic discrimination also may have a cause of action under 42 U.S.C. Section 1981. This section, which was enacted as part of the Civil Rights Act of 1866, prohibits discrimination on the basis of race or ethnicity in the formation or enforcement of contracts. Although Section 1981 remained a "dead letter" on the books for over a century, since the 1970s many plaintiffs have succeeded in Section 1981 cases against their employers. Unlike Title VII, Section 1981 does not place a cap on damages (see the discussion of Title VII remedies later in this chapter). Thus, if an employee can prove that he or she was discriminated against in the formation or enforcement of a contract, the employee may be able to obtain a greater amount in damages under Section 1981 than under Title VII.

In the following case, the court had to decide whether an employer's decision to promote one employee over another constituted discrimination based on race.

CASE 42.1   McCullough v. Real Foods, Inc.

United States
Court of Appeals,
Eighth Circuit, 1998.
140 F.3d 1123.
http://ls.wustl.edu/8th.
cir/opinions.html[a]

BACKGROUND AND FACTS *In 1992, Cynthia McCullough, an African American woman with a college degree in urban affairs, began working at a deli in Chubb's Finer Foods (Real Foods, Inc.), a grocery store owned and managed by Ron Meredith. More than a year later, Meredith hired Kathy Craven, a white woman, to work at the deli. Craven had no prior deli experience, only a sixth-grade education, and poor reading and math skills. For example, Craven could not calculate prices or read recipes. McCullough and Craven were the only deli employees. Three months after Craven's arrival, Meredith appointed her "deli manager." Meredith later said that he did not promote McCullough because he "understood" that she would not work past 3:00 P.M., that she felt she was overeducated for the position, that she spoke of quitting, and that she would not accept a managerial job for the salary he was willing to pay. Denying all of what Meredith "understood," McCullough filed a suit in a federal district court against Real Foods, alleging discrimination on the basis of race. The court granted a summary judgment in*

---

a. This page contains links to opinions of the U.S. Court of Appeals for the Eighth Circuit. Click on the "Party Name" link. In the "Search string" box, type "Real Foods" and click "Begin Search." When the results appear, click on the case number to access the opinion. This Web site is maintained by Washington University School of Law in St. Louis, Missouri.

favor of Real Foods, and McCullough appealed to the U.S. Court of Appeals for the Eighth Circuit.

IN THE LANGUAGE
OF THE COURT

HANSEN, Circuit Judge.

*   *   *   *

*   *   * McCullough had 15 months more hands-on experience working in the deli than did Craven, *   *   * [and] McCullough's objective educational qualifications greatly exceeded those of Craven. *   *   * [W]hen McCullough's education and experience are contrasted with Craven's poor reading, writing, and math skills—as evidenced by her inability to read recipes or calculate prices—a reasonable inference arises that Meredith promoted a substantially less qualified white woman over a substantially better qualified black woman. *We believe it is common business practice to pick the best qualified candidate for promotion. When that is not done, a reasonable inference arises that the employment decision was based on something other than the relative qualifications of the applicants.* [Emphasis added.]

Critical to our analysis in this case is the extremely subjective nature of the employer's stated promotion criteria. *   *   * [S]ubjective criteria for promotions are particularly easy for an employer to invent in an effort to sabotage a plaintiff's *prima facie* case and mask discrimination. *   *   *

*   *   * [W]hen the employer's asserted nondiscriminatory reasons are essentially checkmated by McCullough's denials that she ever made the statements the employer advances as its nondiscriminatory reasons, the failure to promote the objectively better qualified black woman raises a reasonable, nonspeculative inference that the decision to promote the less qualified white woman was based on an impermissible consideration—in this case race.

DECISION
AND REMEDY

The U.S. Court of Appeals for the Eighth Circuit reversed the lower court's judgment and remanded the case for trial. The court held that McCullough raised an inference that Real Foods's articulated reasons for promoting Craven were a pretext and that the real reason was illegal discriminatory intent.

DISCRIMINATION BASED ON RELIGION

Title VII of the Civil Rights Act of 1964 also prohibits government employers, private employers, and unions from discriminating against persons because of their religion. An employer must "reasonably accommodate" the religious practices of its employees, unless to do so would cause undue hardship to the employer's business. For example, if an employee's religion prohibits him or her from working on a certain day of the week or at a certain type of job, the employer must make a reasonable attempt to accommodate these religious requirements. Employers must reasonably accommodate an employee's religious belief even if the belief is not based on the tenets or dogma of a particular church, sect, or denomination. The only requirement is that the belief be sincerely held by the employee.[5]

DISCRIMINATION BASED ON GENDER

Under Title VII, as well as other federal acts, employers are forbidden to discriminate against employees on the basis of gender. Employers are prohibited from classifying jobs as male or female and from advertising in help-wanted columns that are designated male or female unless the employer can prove that the gender of the applicant is essential to the job. Furthermore, employers cannot have separate male and female seniority lists. Generally, to succeed in a suit for gender discrimination, a plaintiff must demonstrate that gender was a determining factor in the employer's decision to hire, fire, or promote him or her. Typically, this involves looking at all of the surrounding circumstances.

The Pregnancy Discrimination Act of 1978,[6] which amended Title VII, expanded the definition of

---

5. *Frazee v. Illinois Department of Employment Security*, 489 U.S. 829, 109 S.Ct. 1514, 103 L.Ed.2d 914 (1989).

6. 42 U.S.C. Section 2000e(k).

gender discrimination to include discrimination based on pregnancy. Women affected by pregnancy, childbirth, or related medical conditions must be treated—for all employment-related purposes, including the conferring of benefits under employee benefit programs—the same as other persons not so affected but similar in ability to work.

In the following case, the plaintiff (a male) charged the defendant (a female) with gender discrimination. The plaintiff made out a *prima facie* case, and the defendant presented a nondiscriminatory reason as a defense. Was the defendant's reason a pretext covering a discriminatory motive? That was the question before the court.

CASE 42.2   Carey v. Mount Desert Island Hospital

United States
Court of Appeals,
First Circuit, 1998.
156 F.3d 31.
http://www.law.emory.
edu/1circuit/aug98[a]

COMPANY PROFILE   *Mount Desert Island Hospital (MDI) (http://www.mdihospital.org) is a forty-nine-bed facility in Bar Harbor, Maine, with a medical staff that specializes in family practice, general surgery, internal medicine, ophthalmology, pathology, and radiology. A consulting staff includes practitioners of other medical specialties. MDI also operates an occupational health service, community health education, and affiliated health centers: Community Health Center in Southwest Harbor; Family Health Center, Women's Health Center, Breast Center, and High Street Health Center in Bar Harbor; and Northeast Harbor Clinic, open seasonally in Northeast Harbor. MDI is licensed by the state of Maine and fully accredited by the Joint Commission on Accreditation of Healthcare Organizations.*

BACKGROUND AND FACTS   *Michael Carey was a vice president in charge of the finance department for Mount Desert Island Hospital (MDI). When the position of chief executive officer (CEO) opened up, Carey applied, and his application was endorsed by Dan Hobbs, the acting CEO. At the time, an audit of the finance department revealed some deficiencies, but the auditor concluded that the department was "already attacking the problem." MDI's board offered the CEO post to Leslie Hawkins, a woman, who accepted. Less than a year later, Hawkins terminated Carey, giving as reasons the problems cited in the audit and "lack of confidence" in Carey. Carey filed a suit in a federal district court against MDI for gender discrimination in violation of Title VII and other laws. Evidence introduced during the trial included a statement by one female executive that "we have different standards for men and women," with regard to discipline and termination; and a statement by another female executive that "it's about time that we get a woman for this [CEO] position." The court awarded Carey more than $300,000 in damages. MDI appealed to the U.S. Court of Appeals for the First Circuit.*

IN THE LANGUAGE OF THE COURT   COFFIN, Senior Circuit Judge.

*   *   *   *

*   *   * [T]his was a case with much to say on either side, involving the always difficult question of probing the wellsprings of human motivation. *   *   *

*   *   *   *

In a case such as this, where a plaintiff must rely on circumstantial as opposed to direct evidence of gender discrimination, the evidence will necessarily be composed of bits and pieces, which may or may not point to an atmosphere of gender discrimination. While an employer should not find itself in jeopardy by reason of occasional stray remarks by ordinary employees, *circumstantial evidence of a discriminatory atmosphere at a plaintiff's place of employment is relevant to the question of motive in considering a discrimination claim* *   *   * . [Emphasis added.]

---

a. This page contains links to opinions of the U.S. Court of Appeals for the First Circuit decided in August 1998. Click on the *Carey* case name to access the opinion. This Web site is maintained by Emory University School of Law in Atlanta, Georgia.

*   *   *   *

*   *   * [Based on the record, we] hold that there was sufficient evidence to support a finding that deficiencies in Carey's handling of financial controls were not the real reason for his discharge but instead covered an action stemming from gender discrimination.

DECISION AND REMEDY   *The U.S. Court of Appeals for the First Circuit affirmed the lower court's judgment. The court held that that there was sufficient evidence to support a finding that the reason for Carey's discharge was gender discrimination.*

SEXUAL HARASSMENT

Title VII also protects employees against **sexual harassment** in the workplace. Sexual harassment can take two forms: *quid pro quo* harassment and hostile-environment harassment. *Quid pro quo* is a Latin phrase that is often translated to mean "something in exchange for something else." *Quid pro quo* harassment occurs when job opportunities, promotions, salary increases, and so on are given in return for sexual favors. According to the United States Supreme Court, hostile-environment harassment occurs when "the workplace is permeated with discriminatory intimidation, ridicule, and insult, that is sufficiently severe or pervasive to alter the conditions of the victim's employment and create an abusive working environment."[7]

Generally, the courts apply this Supreme Court guideline on a case-by-case basis. Some courts have held that just one incident of sexually offensive conduct—such as a sexist remark by a co-worker or a photo on an employer's desk of his bikini-clad wife—can create a hostile environment.[8] At least one court has held that a worker may recover damages under Title VII because *other* persons were harassed sexually in the workplace.[9] According to some employment specialists, employers should assume that hostile-environment harassment has occurred if an employee claims that it has.

Harassment by Supervisors. What if an employee is harassed by a manager or supervisor of a large firm,

and the firm itself (the "employer") is not aware of the harassment? Should the employer be held liable for the harassment nonetheless? For some time, the courts were in disagreement on this issue. Typically, employers were held liable for Title VII violations by the firm's managerial or supervisory personnel in *quid pro quo* harassment cases regardless of whether the employer knew about the harassment. In hostile-environment cases, in contrast, the majority of courts tended to hold employers liable only if the employer knew or should have known of the harassment and failed to take prompt remedial action.

In 1998, in two separate cases, the United States Supreme Court issued some significant guidelines relating to the liability of employers for their supervisors' harassment of employees in the workplace. In *Faragher v. City of Boca Raton,*[10] the Court held that an employer (a city) could be held liable for a supervisor's harassment of employees even though the employer was unaware of the behavior. The Court reached this conclusion primarily because, although the city had a written policy against sexual harassment, the policy had not been distributed to city employees. Additionally, the city had not established any procedures that could be followed by employees who felt that they were victims of sexual harassment. In *Burlington Industries, Inc. v. Ellerth,*[11] the Court ruled that a company could be held liable for the harassment of an employee by one of its vice presidents even though the employee suffered no adverse job consequences.

In these two cases, the Court set forth some common-sense guidelines on liability for harassment in the workplace that will be helpful to employers and

7. *Harris v. Forklift Systems,* 510 U.S. 17, 114 S.Ct. 367, 126 L.Ed.2d 295 (1993).

8. For other examples, see *Radtke v. Everett,* 442 Mich. 368, 501 N.W.2d 155 (1993); and *Nadeau v. Rainbow Rugs, Inc.,* 675 A.2d 973 (Me. 1996).

9. *Leibovitz v. New York City Transit Authority,* 4 F.Supp.2d 144 (E.D.N.Y. 1998).

10. 524 U.S. 725, 118 S.Ct. 2275, 141 L.Ed.2d 662 (1998).

11. 524 U.S. 742, 118 S.Ct. 2257, 141 L.Ed.2d 633 (1998).

employees alike. On the one hand, employees benefit by the ruling that employers may be held liable for their supervisors' harassment even though they were unaware of the actions and even though the employees suffered no adverse job consequences. On the other hand, the Court made it clear in both decisions that employers have an affirmative defense against liability for their supervisors' harassment of employees if they can show that (1) they have taken "reasonable care to prevent and correct promptly any sexually harassing behavior" (by establishing effective harassment policies and complaint procedures, for example), and (2) the employee suing for harassment failed to follow these policies and procedures.

Harassment by Co-Workers and Nonemployees. Often, employees alleging harassment complain that the actions of co-workers, not supervisors, are responsible for creating a hostile working environment. In such cases, the employee still has a cause of action against the employer. Generally, though, the employer will be held liable only if it knew or should have known about the harassment and failed to take immediate remedial action.

Employers may also be liable for harassment by *nonemployees* under certain conditions. For example, if a restaurant owner or manager knows that a certain customer repeatedly harasses a waitress and permits the harassment to continue, the restaurant owner may be liable under Title VII even though the customer is not an employee of the restaurant. The issue turns on the control that the employer exerts over a nonemployee. In one case, the owner of a Pizza Hut franchise was held liable for the harassment of a waitress by two male customers because no steps were taken to prevent the harassment.[12]

Same-Gender Harassment. The courts have also had to address the issue of whether men who are harassed by other men, or women who are harassed by other women, are also protected by laws that prohibit gender-based discrimination in the workplace. For example, what if the male president of a firm demands sexual favors from a male employee? Does this action qualify as sexual harassment? For some time, the courts were widely split on this question. In 1998, in *Oncale v. Sundowner Offshore Services, Inc.,*[13] the Supreme

Court resolved the issue by holding that Title VII protection extends to situations in which individuals are harassed by members of the same gender.

REMEDIES UNDER TITLE VII

Employer liability under Title VII may be extensive. If the plaintiff successfully proves that unlawful discrimination occurred, he or she may be awarded reinstatement, back pay, retroactive promotions, and damages.[14] Compensatory damages are available only in cases of intentional discrimination. Punitive damages may be recovered against a private employer only if the employer acted with malice or reckless indifference to an individual's rights. The sum of the amount of compensatory and punitive damages is limited by the statute to specific amounts against specific employers—ranging from $50,000 against employers with one hundred or fewer employees to $300,000 against employers with more than five hundred employees.

SECTION 2

Equal Pay Act of 1963

The Equal Pay Act of 1963 was enacted as an amendment to the Fair Labor Standards Act of 1938. Basically, the act prohibits gender-based discrimination in the wages paid for similar work. For the equal pay requirements to apply, the male and female employees must be employed at the same establishment.

A person alleging wage discrimination in violation of the Equal Pay Act may sue his or her employer. To determine whether the act has been violated, a court will look to the primary duties of the two jobs—it is job content rather than job description that controls in all cases. The jobs of a barber and a beautician, for example, are considered essentially equal. So, too, are those of a tailor and a seamstress. Small differences in job content do not justify higher pay for one gender. An employer will not be found liable for violating the act if it can be shown that the wage differential for equal work was based on (1) a seniority system, (2) a merit system, (3) a system that pays according to quality or quantity of production, or (4) any factor other than gender.

---

12. *Lockard v. Pizza Hut, Inc.,* 162 F.3d 1062 (10th Cir. 1998).
13. 523 U.S. 75, 118 S.Ct. 998, 140 L.Ed.2d 207 (1998).

14. Damages were not available under Title VII until 1991. The Civil Rights Act of that year amended Title VII to provide for both compensatory and punitive damages, as well as jury trials.

Section 3

Discrimination Based on Age

Age discrimination is potentially the most widespread form of discrimination, because anyone—regardless of race, color, national origin, or gender—could be a victim at some point in life. The Age Discrimination in Employment Act (ADEA) of 1967, as amended, prohibits employment discrimination on the basis of age against individuals forty years of age or older. The act also prohibits mandatory retirement for nonmanagerial workers. For the act to apply, an employer must have twenty or more employees, and the employer's business activities must affect interstate commerce. The EEOC administers the ADEA, but the act also permits private causes of action against employers for age discrimination.

Procedures under the ADEA

The burden-shifting procedure under the ADEA is similar to that under Title VII. If a plaintiff can establish that he or she (1) was a member of the protected age group, (2) was qualified for the position from which he or she was discharged, and (3) was discharged under circumstances that give rise to an inference of discrimination, the plaintiff has established a *prima facie* case of unlawful age discrimination. The burden then shifts to the employer, who must articulate a legitimate reason for the discrimination. If the plaintiff can prove that the employer's reason is only a pretext and that the plaintiff's age was a determining factor in the employer's decision, the employer will be held liable under the ADEA.

Numerous cases of alleged age discrimination have been brought against employers who, to cut costs, replaced older, higher-salaried employees with younger, lower-salaried workers. Whether a firing is discriminatory or simply part of a rational business decision to prune the company's ranks is not always clear. Companies generally defend a decision to discharge a worker by asserting that the worker could no longer perform his or her duties or that the worker's skills were no longer needed. The employee must prove that the discharge was motivated, at least in part, by age bias. Proof that qualified older employees are generally discharged before employees who are younger or that co-workers continually made unflat-

tering age-related comments about the discharged worker may be enough.

In the past, courts sometimes held that to establish a *prima facie* case of age discrimination, the plaintiff had to prove that he or she had been replaced by a person outside the protected class—that is, by a person under the age of forty years. In 1996, however, in *O'Connor v. Consolidated Coin Caterers Corp.*,[15] the United States Supreme Court held that a cause of action for age discrimination under the ADEA does not require the replacement worker to be outside the protected class. Rather, the issue in all ADEA cases turns on whether age discrimination has in fact occurred, regardless of the age of the replacement worker.

A Special Case—State Employees

Under the Eleventh Amendment to the Constitution, as that amendment has been interpreted by the Supreme Court, states are immune from lawsuits brought by private individuals in federal court, unless a state consents to the suit. In a number of age-discrimination cases brought in the late 1990s, state agencies that were sued by state employees for age discrimination sought to have the suits dismissed on this ground.

For example, in two Florida cases, professors and librarians contended that their employers—two Florida state universities—denied them salary increases and other benefits because they were getting old and their successors could be hired at lower cost. The universities claimed that as agencies of a sovereign state, they could not be sued without the state's consent. Because the courts were rendering conflicting opinions in these cases, the United States Supreme Court agreed to address the issue. In *Kimel v. Florida Board of Regents*,[16] decided in early 2000, the Court held that the sovereign immunity granted the states by the Eleventh Amendment precluded suits against them by private parties alleging violations of the ADEA. According to the Court, Congress had exceeded its constitutional authority when it included in the ADEA a provision stating that "all employers," including state employers, were subject to the act.

---

15. 517 U.S. 308, 116 S.Ct. 1307, 134 L.Ed.2d 433 (1996).
16. ___U.S.___, 120 S.Ct. 631, ___L.Ed.2d ___ (2000).

Understandably, the *Kimel* decision has been controversial, and it may become more so as state employees face the consequences of this decision. Even the Court was strongly divided on the issue (the vote was five to four). Shortly after the Court rendered its decision in *Kimel*, it agreed to decide another question with serious implications for state employees—whether a state employer can be sued for disability discrimination under the Americans with Disabilities Act.[17]

SECTION 4

Discrimination Based on Disability

The Americans with Disabilities Act (ADA) of 1990 is designed to eliminate discriminatory employment practices that prevent otherwise qualified workers with disabilities from fully participating in the national labor force. Prior to 1990, the major federal law providing protection to those with disabilities was the Rehabilitation Act of 1973. That act covered only federal government employees and those employed under federally funded programs. The ADA extends federal protection against disability-based discrimination to all workplaces with fifteen or more workers. Basically, the ADA requires that employers "reasonably accommodate" the needs of persons with disabilities unless to do so would cause the employer to suffer an "undue hardship."

To prevail on a claim under the ADA, a plaintiff must show that he or she (1) has a disability, (2) is otherwise qualified for the employment in question, and (3) was excluded from the employment solely because of the disability. As in Title VII cases, a claim alleging violation of the ADA may be commenced only after the plaintiff has pursued the claim through the EEOC, which administers the provisions of the act relating to disability-based discrimination in the employment context. Plaintiffs may sue for many of the same remedies available under Title VII. They may seek reinstatement, back pay, a limited amount of compensatory and punitive damages (for intentional discrimination), and certain other forms of relief. Repeat violators may be ordered to pay fines of up to $100,000.

WHAT IS A DISABILITY?

The ADA is broadly drafted to define persons with disabilities as persons with physical or mental impairments that "substantially limit" their everyday activities. More specifically, the ADA defines *disability* as "(1) a physical or mental impairment that substantially limits one or more of the major life activities of such individuals; (2) a record of such impairment; or (3) being regarded as having such an impairment."

Generally, the determination of whether an individual has a disability as defined by the ADA is made on a case-by-case basis. Unlike plaintiffs in cases brought under Title VII or the ADEA, who clearly are or are not members of the classes protected by those acts, a plaintiff suing under the ADA must *prove* that he or she has a disability and thus falls under the protection of the ADA. Meeting this first requirement for a case of disability-based discrimination may be difficult.

Health conditions that have been considered disabilities under federal law include blindness, alcoholism, heart disease, cancer, muscular dystrophy, cerebral palsy, paraplegia, diabetes, acquired immune deficiency syndrome (AIDS), and morbid obesity (defined as existing when an individual's weight is two times that of a normal person).[18] The ADA excludes from coverage certain conditions, such as kleptomania.

For some time, the courts were divided on the issue of whether a person who is infected with the human immunodeficiency virus (HIV) but who has no symptoms of AIDS should come under the protection of the ADA as a person with a disability. In 1998, the Supreme Court resolved this issue by holding that an HIV infection is a disability even if the infection has not yet progressed to the symptomatic phase.[19]

One issue that frequently arises in ADA cases is whether a person whose impairment is mitigated by medication or a corrective device qualifies for protection under the ADA. That issue arose in the following case, which was appealed to the United States Supreme Court by two pilots whose severe myopia could be corrected with glasses or contact lenses.

---

17. The Court will review a decision by the Court of Appeals for the Eleventh Circuit in which that court held that a state can be sued for disability discrimination. See *Florida Department of Corrections v. Dickson*, 139 F.3d 1326 (11th Cir. 1998).

18. *Cook v. Rhode Island Department of Mental Health*, 10 F.3d 17 (1st Cir. 1993).

19. *Bragdon v. Abbott*, 524 U.S. 624, 118 S.Ct. 2196, 141 L.Ed.2d 540 (1998).

CASE 42.3   Sutton v. United Airlines, Inc.

Supreme Court of the
United States, 1999.
527 U.S. 471,
119 S.Ct. 2139,
144 L.Ed.2d 450.
http://supct.law.
cornell.edu/supct/
supct.1999a.html[a]

BACKGROUND AND FACTS   *Karen and Kimberly Sutton are twin sisters, both of whom have severe myopia. Each woman's uncorrected visual acuity is 20/200 or worse in her right eye and 20/400 or worse in her left eye, but with the use of corrective lenses, such as glasses or contact lenses, each has vision that is 20/20 or better. In other words, without corrective lenses, neither individual can see well enough to do such things as drive a vehicle, watch television, or shop, but with corrective measures, each functions identically to individuals without a similar impairment. In 1992, the Suttons applied to United Airlines, Inc. (UA), for employment as commercial airline pilots. They met UA's age, education, experience, and Federal Aviation Administration certification qualifications, and were invited to flight simulator tests and interviews. Because the Suttons did not meet UA's minimum vision requirement, which was uncorrected visual acuity of 20/100 or better, the interviews were terminated, and neither pilot was offered a position. The Suttons filed a suit in a federal district court against UA, alleging discrimination under the Americans with Disabilities Act (ADA). The Suttons asserted in part that due to their severe myopia, they have a substantially limiting impairment and are thus disabled. The court disagreed and dismissed their complaint, and the U.S. Court of Appeals for the Tenth Circuit affirmed this judgment. The Suttons appealed to the United States Supreme Court.*

**IN THE LANGUAGE
OF THE COURT**

Justice O'CONNOR delivered the opinion of the Court.

*   *   *   *

*   *   * The Act defines a "disability" as "a physical or mental impairment that substantially limits one or more of the major life activities" of an individual. Because the phrase "substantially limits" appears in the Act in the present indicative verb form, we think the language is properly read as requiring that a person be presently—not potentially or hypothetically—substantially limited in order to demonstrate a disability. A "disability" exists only where an impairment "substantially limits" a major life activity, not where it "might," "could," or "would" be substantially limiting if mitigating measures were not taken. A person whose physical or mental impairment is corrected by medication or other measures does not have an impairment that presently "substantially limits" a major life activity. To be sure, a *person whose physical or mental impairment is corrected by mitigating measures still has an impairment, but if the impairment is corrected it does not "substantially limi[t]" a major life activity.* [Emphasis added.]

*   *   *   *

*   *   * The use of a corrective device does not, by itself, relieve one's disability. Rather, one has a disability under [the Act] if, notwithstanding the use of a corrective device, that individual is substantially limited in a major life activity. For example, individuals who use prosthetic limbs or wheelchairs may be mobile and capable of functioning in society but still be disabled because of a substantial limitation on their ability to walk or run. The same may be true of individuals who take medicine to lessen the symptoms of an impairment so that they can function but nevertheless remain substantially limited. *   *   * The use or nonuse of a corrective device does not determine whether an individual is disabled; that determination depends on whether the limitations an individual with an impairment actually faces are in fact substantially limiting.

Applying this reading of the Act to the case at hand, we conclude that the Court of Appeals correctly resolved the issue of disability in respondent's favor. *   *   * [P]etitioners allege that with corrective measures, their visual acuity is 20/20, and that they "function identically to individuals without a similar impairment." In addition, petitioners concede that they "do not argue that the use of corrective lenses in itself demonstrates a substantially limiting impairment." Accordingly, because we decide that

---

a. This page includes an alphabetical list of the 1999 decisions of the United States Supreme Court. Scroll down the list of cases to the *Sutton* case, and click on the name to access the opinion.

disability under the Act is to be determined with reference to corrective measures, we agree with the courts below that petitioners have not stated a claim that they are substantially limited in any major life activity. [Emphasis added.]

DECISION AND REMEDY   *The United States Supreme Court affirmed the decision of the lower court. The Supreme Court held that a person is not disabled (substantially limited in any major life activity) under the ADA if he or she has a condition that can be corrected with medication, or one, such as poor vision, that can be rectified with corrective devices, such as glasses.*

REASONABLE ACCOMMODATION

If a job applicant or an employee with a disability can perform essential job functions with reasonable accommodation, the employer must make the accommodation. Required modifications may include installing ramps for a wheelchair, establishing flexible working hours, creating or modifying job assignments, and creating or improving training materials and procedures.

Generally, employers should give primary consideration to employees' preferences in deciding what accommodations should be made. If an applicant or employee fails to let the employer know how his or her disability can be accommodated, the employer may avoid liability for failing to hire or retain the individual on the ground that the individual has failed to meet the "otherwise qualified" requirement.[20] Employers should be cautious in making this assumption in cases involving mental illness, though. For example, in one case, an employee was held to have a cause of action against his employer under the ADA even though the employee never explicitly told the employer how his disability could be accommodated.[21]

Employers who do not accommodate the needs of persons with disabilities must demonstrate that the accommodations would cause *undue hardship.* Generally, the law offers no uniform standards for identifying what is an undue hardship other than the imposition of a "significant difficulty or expense" on the employer.

Usually, the courts decide whether an accommodation constitutes an undue hardship on a case-by-case basis. In one case, the court decided that paying for a parking space near the office for an employee with a disability was not an undue hardship.[22] In another case, the court held that accommodating the request of an employee with diabetes for indefinite leave until his disease was under control would create an undue hardship for the employer, because the employer would not know when the employee was returning to work. The court stated that reasonable accommodation under the ADA means accommodation so that the employee can perform the job now or "in the immediate future" rather than at some unspecified distant time.[23]

Job Applications and Preemployment Physical Exams. Employers must modify their job-application process so that those with disabilities can compete for jobs with those who do not have disabilities. A job announcement that has only a phone number, for example, would discriminate against potential job applicants with hearing impairments. Thus, the job announcement must also provide an address.

Employers are restricted in the kinds of questions they may ask on job-application forms and during preemployment interviews. Furthermore, employers cannot require persons with disabilities to submit to preemployment physicals unless such exams are required of all other applicants. Employers can condition an offer of employment on the employee's successfully passing a medical examination, but disqualifications must result from the discovery of problems that render the applicant unable to perform the job for which he or she is to be hired.

Dangerous Workers. Employers are not required to hire or retain workers who, because of their disabilities, pose a "direct threat to the health or safety" of

---

20. See, for example, *Beck v. University of Wisconsin Board of Regents,* 75 F.3d 1130 (7th Cir. 1996); and *White v. York International Corp.,* 45 F.3d 357 (10th Cir. 1995).
21. *Bultemeyer v. Fort Wayne Community Schools,* 100 F.3d 1281 (7th Cir. 1996).

22. See *Lyons v. Legal Aid Society,* 68 F.3d 1512 (2d Cir. 1995).
23. *Myers v. Hase,* 50 F.3d 278 (4th Cir. 1995).

their co-workers. In the wake of the AIDS epidemic, many employers are concerned about hiring or continuing to employ a worker who has AIDS under the assumption that he or she might pose a direct threat to the health or safety of others in the workplace. Courts have generally held, however, that AIDS is not so contagious as to disqualify employees from most jobs. Therefore, employers must reasonably accommodate job applicants or employees who have AIDS or who test positive for HIV, the virus that causes AIDS.

The ADA prohibits employers from refusing to hire or retain persons with disabilities who are otherwise qualified for a particular position. The ADA does not require that *unqualified* disabled applicants be hired or retained, however.

Substance Abusers. Drug addiction is a disability under the ADA, because drug addiction is a substantially limiting impairment. Those who are currently using illegal drugs are not protected by the act. The ADA only protects persons with *former* drug addictions—those who have completed a supervised drug-rehabilitation program or who are currently in a supervised rehabilitation program. Individuals who have used drugs casually in the past are not protected under the act. They are not considered addicts and therefore do not have a disability (addiction).

People suffering from alcoholism are protected by the ADA. Employers cannot legally discriminate against employees simply because they are living with alcoholism and must treat them in the same way as they treat other employees. For example, an employee with alcoholism who comes to work late because he or she was drinking the night before cannot be disciplined any differently than an employee who comes to work late for another reason. Of course, employers have the right to prohibit the use of alcohol in the workplace and can require that employees not be under the influence of alcohol while working. Employers can also fire or refuse to hire a person with alcoholism if he or she poses a substantial risk of harm either to himself or herself or to others and the risk cannot be reduced by reasonable accommodation.

Health-Insurance Plans. Workers with disabilities must be given equal access to any health insurance provided to other employees. Employers can exclude from coverage preexisting health conditions and certain types of diagnostic or surgical procedures, however. An employer can also put a limit, or cap, on health-care payments in its particular group-health policy—as long as such caps are "applied equally to all insured employees" and do not "discriminate on the basis of disability." Whenever a group health-care plan makes a disability-based distinction in its benefits, the plan violates the ADA. The employer must then be able to justify the distinction by proving one of the following:

1. That limiting coverage of certain ailments is required to keep the plan financially sound.
2. That coverage of certain ailments would cause a significant increase in premium payments or their equivalent, making the plan unappealing to a significant number of employees.
3. That the disparate treatment is justified by the risks and costs associated with a particular disability.

SECTION 5

Defenses to Employment Discrimination

The first line of defense for an employer charged with employment discrimination is, of course, to assert that the plaintiff has failed to meet his or her initial burden of proof—proving that discrimination in fact occurred. As noted, plaintiffs bringing cases under the ADA may find it difficult to meet this initial burden, because they must prove that their alleged disabilities are disabilities covered by the ADA. Furthermore, plaintiffs in ADA cases must prove that they were otherwise qualified for the job.

Once a plaintiff succeeds in proving that discrimination occurred, then the burden shifts to the employer to justify the discriminatory practice. Often, employers attempt to justify the discrimination by claiming that it was the result of a business necessity, a bona fide occupational qualification, a seniority system, or employee misconduct.

BUSINESS NECESSITY

An employer may defend against a claim of discrimination by asserting that a practice that has a discriminatory effect is a **business necessity.** If requiring a high school diploma, for example, is shown to have a discriminatory effect, an employer might argue that a high school education is required for workers to perform the job at a required level of competence. If the employer can demonstrate to the court's satisfaction that a definite connection exists between a high school education and job performance, then the employer will succeed in this business necessity defense.

BONA FIDE OCCUPATIONAL QUALIFICATION

Another defense applies when discrimination against a protected class is essential to a job—that is, when a particular trait is a **bona fide occupational qualification (BFOQ)**. For example, a women's clothing boutique might legitimately hire only female attendants if part of an attendant's job involves assisting clients in the boutique's dressing rooms. Similarly, the Federal Aviation Administration can legitimately impose age limits for airline pilots. Race, however, can never be a BFOQ. Generally, courts have restricted the BFOQ defense to instances in which the employee's gender or religion is essential to the job.

SENIORITY SYSTEMS

An employer with a history of discrimination may have no members of protected classes in upper-level positions. Even if the employer now seeks to be unbiased, it may face a lawsuit seeking an order that minorities be promoted ahead of schedule to compensate for past discrimination. If no present intent to discriminate is shown, however, and if promotions or other job benefits are distributed according to a fair **seniority system** (in which workers with more years of service are promoted first or laid off last), the employer has a good defense against the suit.

AFTER-ACQUIRED EVIDENCE OF EMPLOYEE MISCONDUCT

In some situations, employers have attempted to avoid liability for employment discrimination on the basis of "after-acquired evidence" of an employee's misconduct. For example, suppose that an employer fires a worker, and the employee sues the employer for employment discrimination. During pretrial investigation, the employer learns that the employee made material misrepresentations on his or her employment application—misrepresentations that, had the employer known about them, would have served

as a ground to fire the individual. Can this after-acquired evidence be used as a defense?

According to the United States Supreme Court, after-acquired evidence of wrongdoing should not operate, "in every instance, to bar all relief for an earlier violation" of a federal law prohibiting discrimination.[24] Since this decision, the courts have generally held that after-acquired evidence, at best, can only serve to limit liability. While such evidence cannot be used to shield an employer entirely from liability for employment discrimination, it may be used to limit the amount of damages for which the employer is liable.

SECTION 6

Affirmative Action

Federal statutes and regulations providing for equal opportunity in the workplace were designed to reduce or eliminate discriminatory practices with respect to hiring, retaining, and promoting employees. **Affirmative action** programs go a step further and attempt to "make up" for past patterns of discrimination by giving members of protected classes preferential treatment in hiring or promotion.

Affirmative action programs have caused much controversy, particularly when they result in what is frequently called "reverse discrimination"—discrimination against "majority" workers, such as white males (or discrimination against other minority groups that are not given preferential treatment under a particular affirmative action program). At issue is whether affirmative action programs, because of their inherently discriminatory nature, violate the equal protection clause of the Fourteenth Amendment to the Constitution.

THE BAKKE CASE

An early nonemployment-related case addressing this issue, *Regents of the University of California v. Bakke,*[25] involved an affirmative action program implemented by the University of California at Davis. Allan Bakke, who had been turned down for medical school at the Davis campus, sued the university for reverse discrimination after he discovered that his academic record was

---

24. *McKennon v. Nashville Banner Publishing Co.,* 513 U.S. 352, 115 S.Ct. 879, 130 L.Ed.2d 852 (1995).
25. 438 U.S. 265, 98 S.Ct. 2733, 57 L.Ed.2d 750 (1978).

better than those of some of the minority applicants who had been admitted to the program.

The United States Supreme Court held that affirmative action programs were subject to intermediate scrutiny. Recall from the discussion of the equal protection clause in Chapter 4 that any law or action evaluated under a standard of intermediate scrutiny, to be constitutionally valid, must be substantially related to important government objectives. Applying this standard, the Court held that the university could give favorable weight to minority applicants as part of a plan to increase minority enrollment so as to achieve a more culturally diverse student body. The Court stated, however, that the use of a quota system, in which a certain number of places are explicitly reserved for minority applicants, violated the equal protection clause of the Fourteenth Amendment.

THE ADARAND CASE AND SUBSEQUENT DEVELOPMENTS

Although the *Bakke* case and later court decisions alleviated the harshness of the quota system, today's courts are going even further in questioning the constitutional validity of affirmative action programs. In 1995, in its landmark decision in *Adarand Constructors, Inc. v. Peña*,[26] the United States Supreme Court held that any federal, state, or local affirmative action program that uses racial or ethnic classifications as the basis for making decisions is subject to strict scrutiny by the courts.

In effect, the Court's opinion in *Adarand* means that an affirmative action program is constitutional only if it attempts to remedy past discrimination and does not make use of quotas or preferences. Furthermore, once such a program has succeeded in the goal of remedying past discrimination, it must be changed or dropped. Since then, other federal courts have followed the Supreme Court's lead by declaring affirmative action programs invalid unless they attempt to remedy past or current discrimination.[27]

The Court of Appeals for the Fifth Circuit went even further than the Supreme Court in its 1996 decision in *Hopwood v. State of Texas*.[28] In that case,

two white law school applicants sued the University of Texas School of Law in Austin, alleging that they were denied admission because of the school's affirmative action program. The program allowed admitting officials to take racial and other factors into consideration when determining which students would be admitted. The Court of Appeals for the Fifth Circuit held that the program violated the equal protection clause because it discriminated in favor of minority applicants. In its decision, the court directly challenged the *Bakke* decision by stating that the use of race even as a means of achieving diversity on college campuses "undercuts the Fourteenth Amendment." The United States Supreme Court declined to hear the case, thus letting the lower court's decision stand.

Additionally, California and Washington, by voter initiatives in 1996 and 1998, respectively, ended state-sponsored affirmative action in those states. Similar movements are currently under way in other states as well, such as Florida.

SECTION 7

State Laws Prohibiting Discrimination

Although the focus of this chapter is on federal legislation, most states also have statutes that prohibit employment discrimination. Generally, the kinds of discrimination prohibited under federal legislation are also prohibited by state laws. In addition, state statutes often provide protection for certain individuals who are not protected under federal laws. For example, a New Jersey appellate court has held that anyone over the age of eighteen was entitled to sue for age discrimination under the state law, which specified no threshold age limit.[29] Furthermore, state laws prohibiting discrimination may apply to firms with fewer employees than the threshold number required under federal statutes, thus offering protection to a greater number of workers. Finally, state laws may provide for additional damages, such as damages for emotional distress, that are not provided for under federal statutes.

26. 575 U.S. 200, 115 S.Ct. 2097, 132 L.Ed.2d 158 (1995).
27. See, for example, *Taxman v. Board of Education of the Township of Piscataway*, 91 F.3d 1547 (3d Cir. 1996); and *Schurr v. Resorts International Hotel, Inc.*, 196 F.3d 486 (3d Cir. 1999).
28. 84 F.3d 720 (5th Cir. 1996).

29. *Bergen Commercial Bank v. Sisler*, 307 N.J.Super. 333, 704 A.2d 1017 (1998).

TERMS AND CONCEPTS TO REVIEW

affirmative action 791

bona fide occupational
    qualification (BFOQ) 791

business necessity 790

disparate-impact
    discrimination 780

disparate-treatment
    discrimination 780

employment discrimination 779

prima facie case 780

protected class 779

seniority system 791

sexual harassment 784

QUESTIONS AND CASE PROBLEMS

42–1. TITLE VII VIOLATIONS. Discuss fully whether any of the following actions would constitute a violation of Title VII of the 1964 Civil Rights Act, as amended.

    (a) Tennington, Inc., is a consulting firm and has ten employees. These employees travel on consulting jobs in seven states. Tennington has an employment record of hiring only white males.

    (b) Novo Films is making a movie about Africa and needs to employ approximately one hundred extras for this picture. Novo advertises in all major newspapers in southern California for the hiring of these extras. The ad states that only African Americans need apply.

42–2. DISCRIMINATION BASED ON AGE. Tavo Jones had worked since 1974 for Westshore Resort, where he maintained golf carts. During the first decade, he received positive job evaluations and numerous merit pay raises. He was promoted to the position of supervisor of golf-cart maintenance at three courses. Then a new employee, Ben Olery, was placed in charge of the golf courses. He demoted Jones, who was over the age of forty, to running one of the three cart facilities, and he froze Jones's salary indefinitely. Olery also demoted five other men over the age of forty. Another cart facility was placed under the supervision of Blake Blair. Later, the cart facilities for the three courses were again consolidated, but Blair—not Jones—was put in charge. At the time, Blair was in his twenties. Jones overheard Blair say that "we are going to have to do away with these . . . old and senile" men. Jones quit and sued Westshore for employment discrimination. Should he prevail? Explain.

42–3. DISCRIMINATION BASED ON DISABILITY. Ananda is a hearing-impaired repairperson currently employed with the Southwestern Telephone Co. Her job requires her to drive the company truck to remote rural areas in all kinds of weather, to climb telephone poles, to make general repairs to telephone lines, and so on. She has held this position for five years, a full year longer than any other employee, and she is quite competent. Ananda recently applied for a promotion to the position of repair crew coordinator, a position that would require her to be in constant communication with all repairpersons in the field. Southwestern rejected Ananda's application, stating that the company "needs someone in this critical position who can speak and hear clearly, someone who does not suffer from any hearing disability." Ananda says she could easily perform the essentials of the job if Southwestern would provide her with a sign interpreter. Although Southwestern agrees that Ananda is otherwise qualified for the coordinator position, the company has concluded that the cost of hiring an interpreter would be prohibitive, and therefore it should not be required to accommodate her disability under the Americans with Disabilities Act. Who is correct? Discuss.

42–4. DEFENSES TO EMPLOYMENT DISCRIMINATION. Dorothea O'Driscoll had worked as a quality control inspector for Hercules, Inc., for six years when her employment was terminated in 1986. O'Driscoll, who was over forty years of age, sued Hercules for age discrimination in violation of the Age Discrimination in Employment Act of 1967. While preparing for trial, Hercules learned that O'Driscoll had made several misrepresentations when she applied for the job. Among other things, she misrepresented her age, did not disclose a previous employer, falsely represented that she had never applied for work with Hercules before, and untruthfully stated that she had completed two quarters of study at a technical college. Additionally, on her application for group insurance coverage, she misrepresented the age of her son, who would otherwise have been ineligible for coverage as her dependent. Hercules defended against O'Driscoll's claim of age discrimination by stating that had it known of this misconduct, it would have terminated her employment anyway. What should the court decide? Discuss fully. [*O'Driscoll v. Hercules, Inc.*, 12 F.3d 176 (10th Cir. 1994)]

42–5. DISCRIMINATION BASED ON NATIONAL ORIGIN. Phanna Xieng was sent by the Cambodian government to the United States in 1974 for "advanced military training." When the Cambodian government fell in 1975, Xieng remained in the United States and in 1979 was employed by Peoples National Bank of Washington. In performance appraisals from 1980 through 1985, Xieng was rated by his supervisors as "capable of dealing effectively with customers" and qualified for promotion, although in each appraisal it was noted that Xieng might improve his communication skills to maximize his possibilities for future advancement. Xieng sought job promotions on numerous occasions but was never promoted. In 1986, he filed a complaint against the bank, alleging employment discrimination based on national origin. The employer argued that its refusal to promote Xieng because of his accent or communication skills did not amount to discrimination based on national origin. Is it possible to separate discrimination based on an employee's accent and communication skills from discrimination based on national origin? How should the court rule on this issue? [*Xieng v. Peoples National Bank of Washington*, 120 Wash.2d 512, 844 P.2d 389 (1993)]

42–6. DISCRIMINATION BASED ON DISABILITY. When the University of Maryland Medical System Corp. learned that one of its surgeons was HIV positive, the university offered him transfers to positions that did not involve surgery. The surgeon refused, and the university terminated him. The surgeon filed a suit in a federal district court against the university, alleging in part a violation of the Americans with Disabilities Act. The surgeon claimed that he was "otherwise qualified" for his former position. What does he have to prove to win his case? Should he be reinstated? [*Doe v. University of Maryland Medical System Corp.*, 50 F.3d 1261 (4th Cir. 1995)]

42–7. DISCRIMINATION BASED ON RACE. Theodore Rosenblatt, a white attorney, worked for the law firm of Bivona & Cohen, P.C. When Bivona & Cohen terminated Rosenblatt's employment, he filed a suit in a federal district court against the firm. Rosenblatt claimed that he had been discharged because he was married to an African American and that a discharge for such a reason violated Title VII and other laws. The firm filed a motion for summary judgment, arguing that he was alleging discrimination against his wife, not himself, and thus did not have standing to sue under Title VII for racial discrimination. Should the court grant or deny the motion? Explain. [*Rosenblatt v. Bivona & Cohen, P.C.*, 946 F.Supp. 298 (S.D.N.Y. 1996)]

42–8. RELIGIOUS DISCRIMINATION. Mary Tiano, a devout Roman Catholic, worked for Dillard Department Stores, Inc. (Dillard's), in Phoenix, Arizona. Dillard's considered Tiano a productive employee because her sales exceeded $200,000 a year. At the time, the store gave its managers the discretion to grant unpaid leave to employees but prohibited vacations or leave during the holiday season—October through December. Tiano felt that she had a "calling" to go on a "pilgrimage" in October 1988 to Medjugorje, Yugoslavia, where some persons claimed to have had visions of the Virgin Mary. The Catholic Church had not designated the site an official pilgrimage site, the visions were not expected to be stronger in October, and tours were available at other times. The store managers denied Tiano's request for leave, but she had a nonrefundable ticket and left anyway. Dillard's terminated her employment. For a year, Tiano searched for a new job and did not attain the level of her Dillard's salary for four years. She filed a suit in a federal district court against Dillard's, alleging religious discrimination in violation of Title VII. Can Tiano establish a *prima facie* case of religious discrimination? Explain. [*Tiano v. Dillard Department Stores, Inc.*, 139 F.3d 679 (9th Cir. 1998)]

42–9. DISCRIMINATION BASED ON DISABILITY. Vaughn Murphy was first diagnosed with hypertension (high blood pressure) when he was ten years old. Unmedicated, his blood pressure is approximately 250/160. With medication, however, he can function normally and engage in the same activities as anyone else. In 1994, United Parcel Service, Inc. (UPS), hired Murphy to be a mechanic, a position that required him to drive commercial motor vehicles. To get the job, Murphy had to meet a U.S. Department of Transportation (DOT) regulation that a driver have "no current clinical diagnosis of high blood pressure likely to interfere with his/her ability to operate a commercial vehicle safely." At the time, Murphy's blood pressure was measured at 186/124, but he was erroneously certified and started work. Within a month, the error was discovered and he was fired. Murphy obtained another mechanic's job—one that did not require DOT certification—and filed a suit in a federal district court against UPS, claiming discrimination under the Americans with Disabilities Act. UPS filed a motion for summary judgment. Should the court grant UPS's motion? Explain. [*Murphy v. United Parcel Service, Inc.*, 527 U.S. 516, 119 S.Ct. 2133, 144 L.Ed.2d 484 (1999)]

42–10. IN YOUR COURT

Calvin Rhodes sold oil-field equipment for Anson Oil Tools. When he was discharged in 1986 at age fifty-six, he was told that the discharge was part of a reduction in the work force (RIF), and that he would be considered for reemployment. Within six weeks, Anson hired a forty-two-year-old person to do the same job. Rhodes brought a suit against Anson in a federal district court, claiming that the real reason he was discharged was age discrimination. At the trial, Anson offered as a defense Rhodes's "poor work performance" but did not present any company sales records or goals. Rhodes countered with customers' testimony about his expertise and diligence. The jury found that Rhodes was discharged because of his age. Anson appealed the decision. Assume that you are a judge on the federal appellate court reviewing this case and answer the following questions:

(a) Remember that as an appellate court judge, you should defer to the trial court's findings of fact—unless you conclude that there is no justification for the trial court's findings. The question you need to decide is therefore whether a reasonable jury could have found that Rhodes was a victim of age discrimination in violation of the ADEA. How will you answer this question? Why?

(b) Does it matter that Rhodes's replacement was also a member of the class of persons protected by the ADEA? Will your answer to this question affect your answer to question (a) above?

LAW ON THE WEB

For updated links to resources available on the Web, as well as a variety of other materials, visit this text's Web site at http://wbl.westbuslaw.com.

The law firm of Arent Fox posts articles on current issues in the area of employment law, including sexual harassment, on its Web site at

http://www.arentfox.com

An abundance of helpful information on disability-based discrimination, including the text of the Americans with Disabilities Act of 1990, can be found at the following Web site:

http://janweb.icdi.wvu.edu/kinder

An excellent source for information on various forms of employment discrimination is the Equal Employment Opportunity Commission's Web site at

http://www.eeoc.gov

LEGAL RESEARCH EXERCISES ON THE WEB

Go to http://wbl.westbuslaw.com, the Web site that accompanies this text. Select "Internet Applications," and then click on "Chapter 42." There you will find the following Internet research exercises that you can perform to learn more about laws prohibiting employment discrimination:

Activity 42–1: Americans with Disabilities

Activity 42–2: Equal Employment Opportunity

UNIT EIGHT—CUMULATIVE BUSINESS HYPOTHETICAL

Falwell Motors, Inc., is a large corporation that manufactures automobile batteries.

1. One of Falwell's salespersons, Loren, puts in long hours every week. He spends most of his time away from the office generating sales. Less than 10 percent of his work time is devoted to other duties. Usually, he receives a substantial bonus at the end of each year from his employer, and Loren has come to rely on this supplement to his annual salary and commission. One year, the employer does not give any of its employees year-end bonuses. Loren calculates the amount of hours he had worked during the year beyond the required forty hours a week. Then he tells Falwell's president that if he is not paid for these overtime hours, he will sue the company for the overtime pay he has "earned." Falwell's president tells Loren that Falwell is not obligated to pay Loren overtime because Loren is a salesperson. What federal statute governs this dispute? Under this statute, is Falwell required to pay Loren for the "overtime hours"? Why or why not?

2. One day Gina, a Falwell employee, suffered a serious burn when she accidentally spilled some acid on her hand. The accident occurred because another employee, who was suspected of using illegal drugs, carelessly bumped into her. The hand required a series of skin-grafting operations before it healed sufficiently to allow Gina to return to work. Gina wants to obtain compensation for her lost wages and medical expenses. Can she do so? If so, how?

3. After Gina's injury, Falwell decides to conduct random drug tests on all of its employees. Several employees claim that the testing violates their privacy rights. If the dispute is litigated, what factors will the court consider in deciding whether the random drug testing is legally permissible?

4. One of Falwell's company rules states that, without exception, anyone who appears for work under the influence of alcohol will be discharged. Jeff, one of Falwell's employees, is an alcoholic. For the first several months that he worked for Falwell, he did not touch alcohol. Then, one day, he came to work in an intoxicated condition. Jeff's supervisor fires Jeff on the spot. Jeff sues Falwell, contending that he suffers from a disability—alcoholism—and therefore his discharge violates the Americans with Disabilities Act of 1990. Is Jeff correct? Why or why not?

5. Aretha, a Falwell employee, is disgusted by the sexually offensive behavior of several male employees. She has complained to her supervisor on several occasions about the offensive behavior, but the supervisor merely laughs at her concerns. Aretha decides to bring a legal action against the company for sexual harassment. Does Aretha's complaint concern *quid pro quo* harassment or hostile-environment harassment? What federal statute protects employees from sexual harassment? What remedies are available under that statute? What procedures must Aretha follow in pursuing her legal action?

FOCUS ON LEGAL REASONING
Babick v. Oregon Arena Corp.

INTRODUCTION

Wrongful discharge and the legal bases supporting it are discussed in Chapter 41. In this *Focus on Legal Reasoning*, we examine *Babick v. Oregon Arena Corp.*,[1] a recent decision in a suit focused on that topic. Under the employment-at-will doctrine, an employer may discharge an employee at any time for any reason without consequences. Courts have created some exceptions to this doctrine, however. The opinion in the *Babick* case centered on the most common exception: the discharge of a worker for reasons that violate a public policy of the jurisdiction.

CASE BACKGROUND

Oregon Arena Corporation (OAC)

---

1. 160 Or.App. 140, 980 P.2d 1147 (1999).

owns the Memorial Coliseum, a large entertainment forum in Portland, Oregon. OAC hired Kenneth Babick and others to provide security and medical assistance at music concerts and other entertainment events held there. As part of their employment, Babick and the others received training from OAC to carry out their functions as security officers. That training included instruction on defensive tactics, the use of force, actions to be taken in cases of suspected drug possession and the possession of alcohol by minors, and arrest procedures.

One night, at a Phish concert, some of the security officers attempted to arrest some members of the audience for assaulting others and illegal drug and alcohol possession. The officers' actions were consistent with the training that they

had received from OAC and were otherwise lawful under Oregon state law. Other members of the audience, as well as some Phish employees, attacked the officers. OAC representatives publicly berated the officers and then forced them to release the audience members who had been arrested.

After the concert, OAC fired its entire security staff, including those who were not involved in the arrests, in retaliation for those enforcement actions. Babick and others filed a suit in an Oregon state court against OAC, claiming, among other things, wrongful discharge. When the court dismissed their claim, they appealed to an intermediate state appellate court, arguing that although they had been at-will employees, their discharge fell within the public-policy exception to the at-will employment rule.

MAJORITY OPINION

De MUNIZ, P.J. [Presiding Judge].
    *   *   *   *

    *   *   * Peace officers are statutorily authorized to enforce the criminal laws, and generally are the persons who make arrests. However, the [Oregon] legislature also has extended explicit arrest authority to private citizens, including authority for the use of justifiable force. *In empowering private citizens to make arrests, the public has tacitly recognized that peace officers may not be present in every situation where criminal laws are broken and has demonstrated a common concern for law enforcement in such situations.* [Emphasis added.]

Other statutes, as they relate to the circumstances here, further define the public policy involved. As pleaded by plaintiffs, defendant hired and trained plaintiffs solely to maintain order at a large, public music concert and, if necessary, to make arrests to effectuate that purpose. In such large public gatherings, the

potential for public disorder is increased. Further, it is reasonable to infer from defendant's hiring of plaintiffs that [peace] officers would not be present or not be present in sufficient numbers at the concert to ensure the preservation of public order. In those circumstances, Oregonians have expressed a common concern for reliable and effective private law enforcement, as demonstrated by ORS [Oregon Revised Statute] 181.870 through ORS 181.991, which regulate the licensing and training of persons who provide security services at such "public activities."

It is apparent from the above laws that Oregonians value an orderly and safe community. * * * Thus, we hold that, because plaintiffs were discharged for taking steps to maintain order at a large, public event, plaintiffs' discharge thwarted the important public policy of preserving order at such an event, where social disorder might occur and where police officers might not be present or not be present in sufficient numbers to ensure public order on their own.

Notwithstanding, defendant * * * [relies] on the substance of this employment relationship—i.e., that plaintiffs were hired as security officers—in arguing that the "public duty" exception to the employment-at-will doctrine does not apply here. Defendant argues that, at its core, this case turns on whether "an employer may decide against having its own employees perform [law enforcement] services on its property" * * * .

Underlying those arguments is the premise that defendant's discharge decision was based on plaintiffs' unsatisfactory job performance, not on the exercise of a public duty, and therefore was within the at-will employment rule. We disagree with that premise for the following [reason].

* * * There is no fact pleaded, nor is there any favorable inference that reasonably may be drawn from those facts, to suggest that plaintiffs performed their job duties unsatisfactorily. * * * Defendant fired plaintiffs solely in retaliation for preserving public safety and order at a large, public music concert where police officers might not be present or not be present in sufficient numbers to maintain public order. That factual assertion squarely implicates the public policy identified above.

DISSENTING OPINION

LINDER, J. [Judge], * * * dissenting * * * .
* * * *

* * * [P]laintiffs are not the police. They were people who were hired to perform services for defendant that, in some particulars, might resemble the law enforcement and public safety functions that the police provide. Significantly, the only authority that plaintiffs had at defendant's premises and over the persons on the premises stemmed from the fact that defendant hired them to be there. That is, plaintiffs were there, doing what they were doing, pursuant to their private contract of employment. Defendant terminated plaintiffs' employment, in effect, because plaintiffs were providing more "law enforcement" than defendant or defendant's patrons wanted. In other words, defendant regarded plaintiffs' performance of the parties' private agreement to be unsatisfactory.
* * * *

The majority's holding creates a significant dilemma for private employers. An employer is liable for the torts of its employees committed in the course and scope of the employment relationship. Law enforcement-type activities can be a source of substantial tort exposure, involving, as they do, an often delicate balance between maintaining public order and respecting individual civil liberties. An employee who overzealously or otherwise crosses the line between permissible law enforcement and an infringement of civil rights can create significant liability—even punitive in nature—for an employer. See, e.g., *Blume v. Fred Meyer, Inc.,* 155 Or.App. 102, 963 P.2d 700 (1998). For that and other legitimate reasons, an employer may decide to limit the authorization for employees to respond to suspected violations of the law (which can encompass potential acts of theft, trespass, harassment, and underage alcohol use, to identify only a few).

LEGAL REASONING AND ANALYSIS

1. Legal Analysis. The dissent cites, in its opinion, *Blume v. Fred Meyer, Inc.,* 155 Or.App. 102, 963 P.2d 700 (1998) (see the *Law on the Web* feature at the end of Chapter 2 for instructions on how to access state court opinions). Do the facts and issues in that case compare to the facts and issues of the *Babick* case? How do the holdings in the two cases compare? Is the dissent correct in its use of the *Blume* case, or is it unrelated to the circumstances in the *Babick* case?

2. Legal Reasoning. What reasons does the majority provide to justify its conclusion? How do those reasons contrast with the dissent's reasoning? With whom do you agree? Why?

3. Social Considerations. Do employees owe to the customers of their employers any obligations besides a public duty to obey the law? If so, what is the nature of those obligations? Do employers owe to their employees any obligations that go beyond the satisfaction of the employers' customers? If so, what is the nature of those obligations?

4. Implications for Employers. What do the reasoning and the outcome in this case indicate to those employers who expect their employees to obey the law?

5. Case Briefing Assignment. Using the guidelines for briefing cases given in Appendix A of this text, brief the *Blume* case.

GOING ONLINE

The Legal Information Institute (LII) offers links to federal, state, and private employment law resources at http://www.law.cornell.edu/topics/employment.html, a page within the LII Web site. LII is affiliated with Cornell Law School in Ithaca, New York.

FOCUS ON ETHICS
Labor and Employment Relations

Traditionally, employment decisions were largely in the hands of employers. Employers were free to hire and fire their employees "at will"—for any reason (or no reason) and at any time. Today, many employers face just the opposite situation. Statutes providing for employee safety, equal employment opportunity, and, to a more limited extent, privacy rights have significantly restricted the rights of employers to control their workplaces as they will. In effect, the legal pendulum has swung from employer protection to employee protection.

Statutes and court decisions affecting employment relationships rest ultimately on society's ethical convictions of what is right or wrong behavior in the employment context. In the following pages, we focus on the ethical dimensions of selected issues relating to employment relationships.

FAMILY AND MEDICAL LEAVE

The Family Medical and Leave Act (FMLA) of 1993 provides a clear example of a law that was necessitated by changing practices and values in our society. By 1993, nearly two-thirds of women with children worked outside the home, by choice or necessity. Additionally, about a fourth of all adults provided care for elderly relatives or anticipated the need to provide this care within the next five years. With so many women working, there was often no caretaker available to attend to medical emergencies or other family needs in the home. By

allowing employees to take a leave from work for family or medical reasons, the FMLA recognized the changing face of the United States.

The FMLA has now been in effect for some years, and both employers and employees have claimed that they have benefited from the act. Indeed, many have concluded that the act does not go far enough. As it is, the act applies only to employers with fifty or more employees. This means that more than half of the work force in the private sector does not fall under the act's protection. Should the government drop this threshold number to twenty-five, or even fifteen? Many believe that it should. Indeed, Congress is currently considering legislation that would broaden the scope of the law to cover employers with twenty-five or more employees and to provide leave for education-related purposes.

ARBITRATION CLAUSES IN EMPLOYMENT CONTRACTS

An ongoing issue in employment relationships concerns arbitration clauses in employment contracts. Recall from Chapter 2 that public policy, as expressed in the Federal Arbitration Act of 1925 and various state statutes, favors arbitration or some other method of alternative dispute resolution in the settlement of employment disputes. The Supreme Court, in its landmark decision in *Gilmer v. Interstate Johnson/Lane Corp.,*[1] held that arbitration agreements will be enforced even though an employee

claims protection under a specific federal statute governing employees. In *Gilmer,* the relevant statute was the Age Discrimination in Employment Act of 1967.

Critics of this policy (and of the Supreme Court's decision in *Gilmer*) claim that all employees, even those who sign contracts containing arbitration clauses, should be allowed to pursue remedies for employment discrimination provided by Title VII, the ADEA, and the ADA. Some recent court decisions indicate a similar concern. In a case reviewed by the Ninth Circuit Court of Appeals, for example, the court concluded that Congress intended to exempt Title VII claims from the Federal Arbitration Act.[2] A California appellate court went even further. It refused to enforce an arbitration agreement on the ground that it was unconscionable. The court pointed out that the plaintiff did not have the ability to bargain over the terms of the agreement, that the agreement limited each side's depositions to one witness and one expert, and that it otherwise generally gave the employer more rights and remedies than the employee.[3]

Even more significantly, the United States Supreme Court recently held, in *Wright v. Universal*

---

1. 500 U.S. 20, 111 S.Ct. 1647, 114 L.Ed.2d 26 (1991).

2. *Duffield v. Robertson Stephens & Co.,* 144 F.3d 1182 (9th Cir. 1998).
3. *Gonzalez v. Hughes Aircraft Employees Federal Credit Union,* 70 Cal.App.4th 468, 82 Cal.Rptr.2d 526 (1999). This case is currently on appeal to the California Supreme Court.

Maritime Services Corp.,[4] that an arbitration clause in a union contract was not binding because it did not "contain a clear and unmistakable waiver" of the right of union members to sue. According to Justice Scalia, "The right to a federal judicial forum is of sufficient importance" that it cannot be casually waived.

Some claim that these decisions mean that the "tide is turning" in favor of employees who want their day in court when their claims involve employment discrimination. Others suggest that the likely effect of such decisions will be that employers will take more care in drafting arbitration clauses—to ensure that they are fair. Notably, since the Supreme Court's *Gilmer* decision, the majority of the federal appellate courts have followed the Supreme Court's lead and upheld arbitration provisions in employment contracts.[5]

DISABILITY-BASED DISCRIMINATION

In providing protection for disabled persons in the employment context through the Americans with Disabilities Act (ADA), Congress expressed society's concern that persons with disabilities should be given a fair opportunity to compete in the workplace. Yet who should decide when a person with disabilities is "otherwise qualified" for a particular job? This is a thorny issue in the employment context, and the decisions of employers in this respect are often at odds with the law.

Consider an example: Should a freight company or airline be required to hire job candidates with monocular vision—persons who are blind in one eye? According to some federal courts, the answer to this question is yes. For instance, in one case, a federal appellate court held that a truck driver who was blind in one eye was "disabled" and thus could sue an employer who refused to hire him under the ADA.[6]

Another challenging problem for employers has to do with employees who have a history of alcohol abuse. Consider, for example, the problem faced by Exxon Corporation. When its supertanker, the *Exxon Valdez,* hit a reef in Prince William Sound, Alaska, in 1989, it caused one of the worst oil spills in history. Because it was widely believed that the captain of the tanker was intoxicated at the time of the accident, Exxon established a policy of not allowing anyone with a history of alcohol abuse to be a tanker captain or to work in certain other safety-sensitive positions.

It turned out that Exxon's policy, designed to minimize accidents and shield the company from liability under environmental laws, violated the ADA. In a suit against Exxon, the Equal Employment Opportunity Commission (EEOC) claimed that Exxon had violated the ADA by discriminating against some fifty employeees who were "rehabilitated substance abusers." The federal court agreed and held that Exxon could not discriminate against such employees unless it could show that they posed a direct threat to the health or safety of others.[7]

AT-WILL EMPLOYMENT

Because of the extensive array of statutory protections for workers, it is easy to lose sight of the fact that approximately 85 percent of American workers have the legal status of "employees at will." In all states but Montana, an employer may fire employees for any reason or no reason if they do not have employment contracts—unless, of course, the employees fall under the protection of a state or federal statute.[8]

A problem faced by many at-will employees is that not all employers are covered by federal and state statutes regulating the workplace. For example, as already mentioned, the Family Medical and Leave Act applies only to employers that have fifty or more workers. Additionally, the major federal law prohibiting employment discrimination applies only to firms with twenty-five or more employees that are engaged in interstate commerce. Similarly, state laws apply only to firms with over a certain number of employees, such as eight or ten employees. Even if an employer is subject to such statutes, these laws do not apply to many types of employment disputes, such as whether or not an employment contract was formed.

This means that the only hope for plaintiffs in many employment disputes is that a court will make an exception to the at-will doctrine—on the basis of public policy, for example. The public-policy exception, though, remains just that—an exception. Often, courts are reluctant to make such an exception unless it can be justified by a clearly expressed public policy.

4. 525 U.S. 70, 119 S.Ct. 391, 142 L.Ed.2d 361 (1998). This case was presented in Chapter 2 as Case 2.3.
5. For an example of a recent decision supporting the Supreme Court's interpretation of the law in *Gilmer,* see *Desiderio v. National Association of Securities Dealers, Inc.,* 191 F.3d 198 (1999).

6. *Kirkingburg v. Albertson's, Inc.,* 143 F.3d 1228 (9th Cir. 1998).
7. *EEOC v. Exxon Corp.,* 1 F.Supp.2d 635 (N.D.Tex. 1998).

8. Pauline Kim of Washington University's School of Law, as cited in Matt Seigel, "Yes, They Can Fire You," *Fortune,* October 26, 1998, p. 301.

Consider, for example, the situation faced by Lewis Kurtzman when he was terminated from his job with Applied Analytical Industries, Inc. (AAI). Kurtzman had worked in the pharmaceutical industry for over twenty years when he was contacted by AAI and offered a job as director of sales for the company, which was located in Wilmington, North Carolina. AAI representatives allegedly made such statements as "If you do your job, you'll have a job"; "This is a long-term growth opportunity for you"; "This is a secure position"; and "We're offering you a career position." Relying on these assurances, Kurtzman and his family sold their home in Massachusetts and moved to Wilmington. Seven months after he began working for AAI, he was fired "without cause."

Kurtzman sued AAI in a North Carolina court, claiming, among other things, that AAI had breached an implied employment contract under which his employment could not be terminated without some showing of cause. The trial jury found in favor of Kurtzman and awarded him $350,000 in damages, and a state appellate court upheld the verdict. The Supreme Court of North Carolina, however, reversed the lower courts' rulings. The state's highest court stated that "[t]he employment-at-will doctrine has prevailed in this state for a century. The narrow exceptions to it have been grounded in considerations of public policy." According to the court, the facts in this case did not "present policy concerns of this nature. Rather, they are representative of negotiations and circumstances characteristically associated with traditional at-will employment situations."[9]

ENGLISH-ONLY POLICIES

As the U.S. population becomes more and more multilingual, so does the work force. In response to this development, many employers have instituted English-only policies in their workplaces. Are such policies fair to workers who do not speak English? Do they violate Title VII of the Civil Rights Act of 1964, which, among other things, prohibits discrimination on the basis of race and national origin?

Employers seem to be caught between the proverbial "rock and a hard place" with respect to this issue. In one case, for example, an employee sued her employer, claiming that the employer's *failure* to institute an English-only policy violated her rights under Title VII. The federal court declined to dismiss the suit.[10] In several other cases, however, employers who have adopted English-only policies have been sued for violating Title VII's prohibition against discrimination based on national origin.

For example, when a Texas communications company prohibited employees from speaking any language but English at work except to customers who did not speak English, a number of workers complained about the policy and were fired as a result. The Equal Employment Opportunity Commission, on behalf of the fired workers, brought an action against the company, alleging that the work rule violated Title VII. The employer argued that the rule had a legitimate business basis—improvement of customer service and better employee oversight. Nonetheless, the court refused to dismiss the case, in part because the rule applied to employees even while they were on breaks.[11]

Generally, though, the courts have shown a fair degree of tolerance with respect to English-only rules. In *Garcia v. Spun Steak Co.,*[12] for example, several African American and Chinese American employees complained that the company's Spanish-speaking employees were making racist comments about them. Hoping to resolve the problem, the employer adopted an English-only policy—only to be faced with a lawsuit brought by the Spanish-speaking employees. They claimed that they had been denied their "right" to express their cultural heritage on the job. Additionally, they contended that they had been denied a privilege held by English-speaking employees: the opportunity to speak their native language in the workplace. They also argued that the policy intimidated them and made them feel isolated and inferior.

The Court of Appeals for the Ninth Circuit held for the defendant company, however. The court concluded that Title VII does not protect an employee's right to express his or her cultural heritage on the job. Furthermore, in the court's eyes, the employees had not been denied any privilege enjoyed by the English-speaking employees, because, as bilingual persons, they could elect to speak in English and therefore had the capability to converse in the workplace. Finally, in regard to the claim of "intimidation," which the court regarded as a type of hostile-environment claim, the court stated that it was unwilling to adopt a blanket rule that English-only policies create a hostile work environment.

DISCUSSION QUESTIONS

1. How would you support the argument that victims of employment discrimination should

---

9. *Kurtzman v. Applied Analytical Industries, Inc.,* 347 N.C. 329, 493 S.E.2d 420 (1997).

10. *McNeil v. Aguilos,* 831 F.Supp. 1079 (S.D.N.Y. 1993).

11. *EEOC v. Premier Operator Services, Inc.,* 75 F.Supp.2d 550 (N.D.Tex 1999).

12. 998 F.2d 1480 (9th Cir. 1993).

be entitled to a judicial forum rather than be forced to have their disputes resolved through arbitration? Would one of these forms of dispute settlement be fairer to employees than the other? How would you support the counterargument—that employees who sign arbitration clauses should be forced to arbitrate *all* employment disputes?

2. Do you think that the Americans with Disabilities Act goes too far in protecting the rights of employees with disabilities (or perceived disabilities)? Does it go far enough?

3. Should the courts be more willing to grant public-policy exceptions to the employment-at-will doctrine? Should the doctrine be abandoned entirely in favor of a doctrine under which all

employment arrangements constitute implied-in-fact contracts under which employees can only be discharged for cause?

4. Do you see any need for English-only policies in the workplace? Can such policies ever reduce tensions between different ethnic groups, some of which are caused by the use of different languages?

UNIT NINE

Government Regulation

CONTENTS

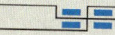

CHAPTER 43

Administrative Law

GOVERNMENT AGENCIES ESTABLISHED to administer the law have a tremendous impact on the day-to-day operation of the government and the economy. In the early years of our nation, the United States had a relatively simple, nonindustrial economy that required little regulation. Because often the purpose of administrative agencies is to create and enforce such regulations, there were relatively few such agencies. Today, however, there are rules covering virtually every aspect of a business's operation. Consequently, agencies have multiplied.

At the federal level, the Securities and Exchange Commission regulates the firm's capital structure and financing, as well as its financial reporting. The National Labor Relations Board oversees relations between the firm and any unions with which it may deal. The Equal Employment Opportunity Commission also regulates employer-employee relationships. The Environmental Protection Agency and the Occupational Safety and Health Administration affect the way the firm manufactures its products. The Federal Trade Commission influences the way it markets these products.

Added to this layer of federal regulation is a second layer of state regulation that, when not preempted by federal legislation, may cover many of the same activities or regulate independently those activities not covered by federal regulation. Finally, agency regulations at the county or municipal level also affect certain types of business activities.

Administrative agencies issue rules, orders, and decisions. These regulations make up the body of *administrative law.* You were introduced briefly to some of the main principles of administrative law in Chapter 1. In the following pages, we look at these principles in much greater detail.

SECTION 1

Agency Creation and Powers

Because Congress cannot possibly oversee the actual implementation of all the laws it enacts, it must delegate such tasks to others, particularly when the issues relate to highly technical areas, such as air and water pollution. By delegating some of its authority to make and implement laws to administrative agencies, Congress can monitor indirectly a particular area in which it has passed legislation without becoming bogged down in the details relating to enforcement—details that are often best left to specialists.

ENABLING LEGISLATION

To create an administrative agency, Congress passes **enabling legislation,** which specifies the name, purposes, functions, and powers of the agency being created. The enabling legislation for the Federal Trade Commission (FTC), for example, is the Federal Trade

Commission Act of 1914.[1] The act prohibits unfair methods of competition and deceptive trade practices. It also describes the procedures that the FTC must follow to charge persons or organizations with violations of the act, and it provides for judicial review of agency orders. The act grants the FTC the power to do the following:

1. Create "rules and regulations for the purpose of carrying out the Act."
2. Conduct investigations of business practices.
3. Obtain reports from interstate corporations concerning their business practices.
4. Investigate possible violations of federal antitrust statutes.[2]
5. Publish findings of its investigations.
6. Recommend new legislation.
7. Hold trial-like hearings to resolve certain kinds of trade disputes that involve FTC regulations or federal antitrust laws.

The commission that heads the FTC is composed of five members, each of whom the president appoints, with the advice and consent of the Senate, for a term of seven years. The president designates one of the commissioners to be chairperson. Various offices and bureaus within the FTC undertake different administrative activities for the agency. Exhibit 43–1 illustrates the organization of the FTC.

_____
1. 15 U.S.C. Sections 41–58.
2. The FTC shares enforcement of the Clayton Act with the Antitrust Division of the U.S. Department of Justice.

Federal administrative agencies may exercise only those powers that Congress has delegated to them in enabling legislation. Through similar enabling acts, state legislatures create state administrative agencies.

TYPES OF AGENCIES

As discussed in Chapter 1, there are two basic types of administrative agencies: executive agencies and independent regulatory agencies. Federal *executive agencies* include the cabinet departments of the executive branch, which were formed to assist the president in carrying out executive functions, and the subagencies within the cabinet departments. The Occupational Safety and Health Administration, for example, is a subagency within the Department of Labor. Exhibit 43–2 on the next page lists the cabinet departments and their most important subagencies.

All administrative agencies are part of the executive branch of government, but *independent regulatory agencies* are outside the major executive departments. The Federal Trade Commission and the Securities and Exchange Commission are examples of independent regulatory agencies. These and other selected independent regulatory agencies, as well as their principal functions, are listed in Exhibit 43–3 on page 807.

The significant difference between the two types of agencies lies in the accountability of the regulators. Agencies that are considered part of the executive branch are subject to the authority of the president, who has the power to appoint and remove federal officers. In theory, this power is less pronounced in

EXHIBIT 43–1   ORGANIZATION OF THE FEDERAL TRADE COMMISSION

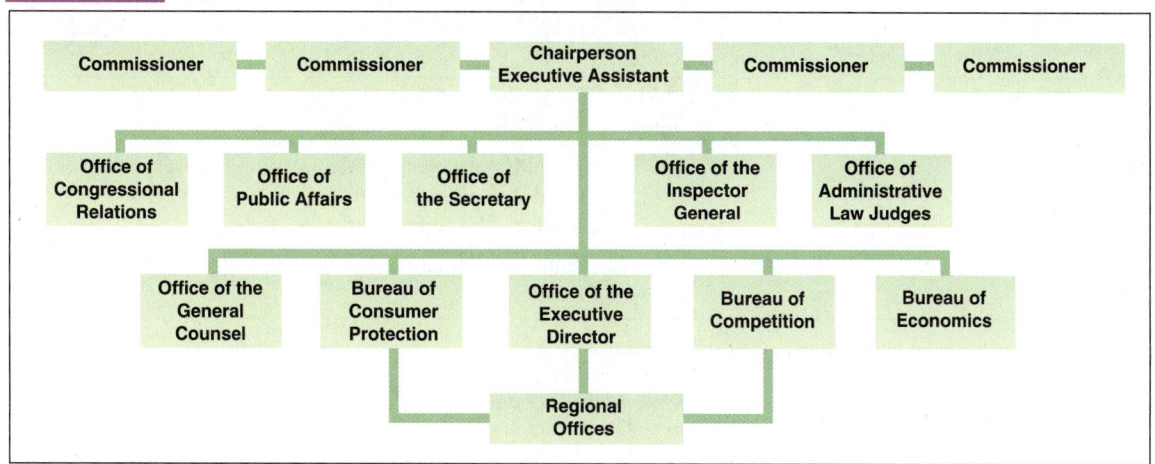

EXHIBIT 43–2   EXECUTIVE DEPARTMENTS AND IMPORTANT SUBAGENCIES

DEPARTMENT	DATE FORMED	IMPORTANT SUBAGENCIES
State	1789	Passport Office; Bureau of Diplomatic Security; Foreign Service; Bureau of Human Rights and Humanitarian Affairs; Bureau of Consular Affairs; Bureau of Intelligence and Research
Treasury	1789	Internal Revenue Service; Bureau of Alcohol, Tobacco, and Firearms; U.S. Secret Service; U.S. Mint; Customs Service
Interior	1849	U.S. Fish and Wildlife Service; National Park Service; Bureau of Indian Affairs; Bureau of Land Management
Justice	1870[a]	Federal Bureau of Investigation; Drug Enforcement Administration; Bureau of Prisons; U.S. Marshals Service; Immigration and Naturalization Service
Agriculture	1889	Soil Conservation Service; Agricultural Research Service; Food Safety and Inspection Service; Federal Crop Insurance Corporation; Farmers Home Administration
Commerce	1913[b]	Bureau of the Census; Bureau of Economic Analysis; Minority Business Development Agency; Patent and Trademark Office; National Oceanic and Atmospheric Administration; U.S. Travel and Tourism Administration
Labor	1913[b]	Occupational Safety and Health Administration; Bureau of Labor Statistics; Employment Standards Administration; Office of Labor-Management Standards; Employment and Training Administration
Defense	1949[c]	National Guard; Defense Investigative Service; National Security Agency; Joint Chiefs of Staff; Departments of the Air Force, Navy, Army
Housing and Urban Development	1965	Assistant Secretary for Community Planning and Development; Government National Mortgage Association; Assistant Secretary for Housing—Federal Housing Commissioner; Assistant Secretary for Fair Housing and Equal Opportunity
Transportation	1967	Federal Aviation Administration; Federal Highway Administration; National Highway Traffic Safety Administration; U.S. Coast Guard; Federal Transit Administration
Energy	1977	Office of Civilian Radioactive Waste Management; Bonneville Power Administration; Office of Nuclear Energy; Energy Information Administration; Office of Conservation and Renewable Energy
Health and Human Services	1980[d]	Food and Drug Administration; Health Care Financing Administration; Public Health Service
Education	1980[e]	Office of Special Education and Rehabilitation Services; Office of Elementary and Secondary Education; Office of Postsecondary Education; Office of Vocational and Adult Education
Veterans' Affairs	1989	Veterans Health Administration; Veterans Benefits Administration; National Cemetery System

a. Formed from the Office of the Attorney General (created in 1789).
b. Formed from the Department of Commerce and Labor (created in 1903).
c. Formed from the Department of War (created in 1789) and the Department of the Navy (created in 1798).
d. Formed from the Department of Health, Education, and Welfare (created in 1953).
e. Formed from the Department of Health, Education, and Welfare (created in 1953).

EXHIBIT 43–3 SELECTED INDEPENDENT REGULATORY AGENCIES

NAME	DATE FORMED	PRINCIPAL DUTIES
Federal Reserve System Board of Governors (Fed)	1913	Determines policy with respect to interest rates, credit availability, and the money supply.
Federal Trade Commission (FTC)	1914	Prevents businesses from engaging in unfair trade practices; stops the formation of monopolies in the business sector; protects consumer rights.
Securities and Exchange Commission (SEC)	1934	Regulates the nation's stock exchanges, in which shares of stock are bought and sold; enforces the securities laws, which require full disclosure of the financial profiles of companies that wish to sell stock and bonds to the public.
Federal Communications Commission (FCC)	1934	Regulates all communications by telegraph, cable, telephone, radio, satellite, and television.
National Labor Relations Board (NLRB)	1935	Protects employees' rights to join unions and bargain collectively with employers; attempts to prevent unfair labor practices by both employers and unions.
Equal Employment Opportunity Commission (EEOC)	1964	Works to eliminate discrimination in employment based on religion, gender, race, color, disability, national origin, or age; investigates claims of discrimination.
Environmental Protection Agency (EPA)	1970	Undertakes programs aimed at reducing air and water pollution; works with state and local agencies to help fight environmental hazards. (It has been suggested recently that its status be elevated to that of a department.)
Nuclear Regulatory Commission (NRC)	1975	Ensures that electricity-generating nuclear reactors in the United States are built and operated safely; regularly inspects operations of such reactors.

regard to independent agencies, whose officers serve for fixed terms and cannot be removed without just cause. In practice, however, the president's ability to exert influence over independent agencies is often considerable.

AGENCY POWERS AND THE CONSTITUTION

Administrative agencies occupy an unusual niche in the American legal scheme, because they exercise powers that are normally divided among the three branches of government. Notice that in the FTC's enabling legislation, discussed above, the FTC's grant of power incorporates functions associated with the legislative branch (rulemaking), the executive branch (enforcement of the rules), and the courts (**adjudication,** or the formal resolution of disputes).

The constitutional principle of checks and balances allows each branch of government to act as a check on the actions of the other two branches. Furthermore, the Constitution authorizes only the legislative branch to create laws. Yet administrative agencies, to which the Constitution does not specifically refer, make **legislative rules,** or *substantive rules*, that are as legally binding as laws that Congress passes.

Courts generally hold that Article I of the U.S. Constitution authorizes delegating such powers to administrative agencies. In fact, courts generally hold that Article I is the basis for all administrative law. Section 1 of that article grants all legislative powers to Congress and requires Congress to oversee the implementation of all laws. Article I, Section 8, gives Congress the power to make all laws necessary for executing its specified powers. The courts interpret these passages, under what is referred to as the **delegation doctrine,** as granting Congress the power to establish administrative agencies that can create rules for implementing those laws.

The three branches of government exercise certain controls over agency powers and functions, as will be discussed later in this chapter, but in many ways administrative agencies function independently. For this reason, administrative agencies, which constitute the **bureaucracy,** are sometimes referred to as the "fourth branch" of the U.S. government.

SECTION 2

Administrative Process

The three functions mentioned previously—rulemaking, enforcement, and adjudication—make up what is known as the **administrative process.** Administrative process involves the administration of law by administrative agencies, in contrast to **judicial process,** which comprises the administration of law by the courts.

All federal agencies must follow specific procedural requirements in their rulemaking, adjudication, and other functions. Sometimes, Congress specifies certain procedural requirements in an agency's enabling legislation. In the absence of any directives from Congress concerning a particular agency procedure, the Administrative Procedure Act (APA) of 1946[3] applies. The APA is such an integral part of the administrative process that its application will be examined as we go through the basic functions carried out by administrative agencies. In addition, agency procedures are guided indirectly by the courts' interpretation of APA requirements.

RULEMAKING

A major function of an administrative agency is **rulemaking**—the formulation of new regulations. In an agency's enabling legislation, Congress confers the agency's power to make rules. For example, the Occupational Safety and Health Act of 1970 authorized the Occupational Safety and Health Administration (OSHA) to develop and issue rules governing safety in the workplace. In formulating any new legislative rule, OSHA has to follow specific rulemaking procedures required under the APA.

Note that administrative agencies also make *interpretive rules.* These rules are not legally binding on the public but simply indicate how an agency plans to interpret and enforce its statutory authority. For example, the Equal Employment Opportunity Commission periodically issues interpretive rules, usually referred to as enforcement guidelines, indicating how it plans to interpret and apply a provision of a certain statute, such as the Americans with Disabilities Act. When making interpretive rules, an agency need not follow the requirements of the APA.

The most commonly used rulemaking procedure is called **notice-and-comment rulemaking.** This procedure involves three basic steps: notice of the proposed rulemaking, a comment period, and the final rule.

Notice of the Proposed Rulemaking. When a federal agency decides to create a new rule, the agency publishes a notice of the proposed rulemaking proceedings in the *Federal Register,* a daily publication of the executive branch that prints government orders, rules, and regulations. The notice states where and when the proceedings will be held, the agency's legal authority for making the rule (usually its enabling legislation), and the terms or subject matter of the proposed rule.

Comment Period. Following the publication of the notice of the proposed rulemaking proceedings, the agency must allow ample time for persons to comment in writing on the proposed rule. The purpose of this comment period is to give interested parties the opportunity to express their views on the proposed rule in an effort to influence agency policy. The comments may be in writing or, if a hearing is held, may be given orally. The agency need not respond to all comments, but it must respond to any significant comments that bear directly on the proposed rule. The agency responds by either modifying its final rule or explaining, in a statement accompanying the final rule, why it did not make any changes. In some circumstances, particularly when the procedure being used in a specific instance is less formal, an agency may accept comments after the comment period is closed. The agency should summarize these *ex parte* (private, "off-the-record") comments in the record for possible review.

The Final Rule. After the agency reviews the comments, it drafts the final rule and publishes it in the *Federal Register.* The final rule is later compiled with

---

3. 5 U.S.C. Sections 551–706.

the rules and regulations of other federal administrative agencies in the *Code of Federal Regulations* (C.F.R.). Final rules have binding legal effect unless the courts later overturn them.

In the following case, AT&T Corporation and other established local telephone service providers asked the United States Supreme Court to overturn a Federal Communications Commission (FCC) rule issued to implement part of the Telecommunications Act of 1996. The Court considered how the FCC interpreted certain terms in the act when it formulated its rule. This illustrates the interpretation and application of statutory terms that any agency must make in its rulemaking.

CASE 43.1   AT&T Corp. v. Iowa Utilities Board

Supreme Court of the United States, 1999.
525 U.S. 366,
119 S.Ct. 721,
142 L.Ed.2d 835.
http://supct.law.
cornell.edu/supct/
supct.January.1999.
html[a]

HISTORICAL AND TECHNOLOGICAL SETTING *Until the 1990s, local telephone service was thought to be a natural monopoly. States typically granted an exclusive franchise in each local service area to a local exchange carrier (LEC), which owns, among other things, the local loops (wires connecting telephones to switches), the switches (equipment directing calls to their destinations), and the transport trunks (wires carrying calls between switches) that constitute a local exchange network. When technological advances made competition among multiple providers of local service seem possible, however, Congress enacted the Telecommunications Act of 1996 to end the state-sanctioned monopolies.*

BACKGROUND AND FACTS *The Telecommunications Act required existing LECs to, among other things, share elements of their networks (loops, switches, and trunks) with their new competitors. The act ordered the Federal Communications Commission (FCC) to issue rules to implement this requirement. In deciding which elements to make available, the FCC was directed to consider whether access to each element was "necessary" and whether a lack of access would "impair" a competitor's ability to provide service. The FCC concluded that access was "necessary" even if a competitor could substitute an element from another source, and that "impairment" occurred if access was denied and a competitor had any increase in cost or decrease in quality. The FCC issued Rule 319, requiring the LECs to give their new competitors access to seven specific network elements.[b] The LECs, including AT&T Corporation, and others filed suits in courts across the United States to challenge the FCC's new rules, including Rule 319. The suits were combined into a single case in the U.S. Court of Appeals for the Eighth Circuit, which held, among other things, that the FCC's interpretations of "necessary" and "impair" were reasonable. The LECs appealed to the United States Supreme Court.*

IN THE LANGUAGE OF THE COURT

Justice SCALIA delivered the opinion of the Court.

*   *   *   *

*   *   * [T]he [Telecommunications] Act requires the FCC to apply some limiting standard, rationally related to the goals of the Act, which it has simply failed to do. *   *   * [I]t is hard to imagine when [an LEC's] failure to give access to the element[s] would not constitute an "impairment" under [the FCC's] standard. *   *   * [T]hat judgment allows [competitors], rather than the [FCC], to determine whether access to [the] elements is necessary, and whether the failure to obtain access to [the] elements would impair the ability to provide services. The [FCC] cannot, consistent with the statute, [ignore] the availability of elements outside the [LEC's] network. That failing alone

---

a. This page is part of the database of United States Supreme Court opinions maintained by the Legal Information Institute of Cornell Law School. On this page, click on the case title to access the opinion.
b. 47 C.F.R. Section 51.319. The seven elements included "the local loop, the network interface device, switching capability, interoffice transmission facilities, signaling networks and call-related databases, operations support systems functions, and operator services and directory assistance."

would require [Rule 319] to be set aside. In addition, however, the [FCC's] assumption that any increase in cost (or decrease in quality) imposed by denial of a network element renders access to that element "necessary," and causes the failure to provide that element to "impair" the [competitor's] ability to furnish its desired services, is simply not in accord with the ordinary and fair meaning of those terms. [A competitor] whose anticipated annual profits from the proposed service are reduced [by only 1 percent] of [its] investment has perhaps been "impaired" in its ability to amass earnings, but has not * * * been "impair[ed] * * * in its ability to provide the services it seeks to offer"; and it cannot realistically be said that the network element enabling it to [increase] its profits [by 1 percent] is "necessary." In a world of perfect competition, in which all carriers are providing their service at marginal [incremental] cost, the [FCC's] total equating of increased cost (or decreased quality) with "necessity" and "impairment" might be reasonable; but it has not established the existence of such an ideal world.

DECISION AND REMEDY   *The United States Supreme Court concluded that the FCC did not interpret the terms of the Telecommunications Act in a "reasonable fashion" and vacated Rule 319. The Court indicated that the FCC should consider the availability, to competitors, of elements outside the LECs' networks.*

INVESTIGATION

Administrative agencies conduct investigations of the entities that they regulate. One type of agency investigation occurs during the rulemaking process to obtain information about a certain individual, firm, or industry. The purpose of such an investigation is to ensure that the rule issued is based on a consideration of relevant factors rather than being arbitrary and capricious. After final rules are issued, agencies conduct investigations to monitor compliance with those rules. A typical agency investigation of this kind might begin when a citizen reports a possible violation.

Inspections.   Many agencies gather information through on-site inspections. Sometimes, inspecting an office, a factory, or some other business facility is the only way to obtain the evidence needed to prove a regulatory violation. Administrative inspections and tests cover a wide range of activities, including safety inspections of underground coal mines, safety tests of commercial equipment and automobiles, and environmental monitoring of factory emissions. An agency may also ask a firm or individual to submit certain documents or records to the agency for examination.

Normally, business firms comply with agency requests to inspect facilities or business records, because it is in any firm's interest to maintain a good relationship with regulatory bodies. In some instances, however, such as when a firm thinks an agency's request is unreasonable and may be detrimental to the firm's interest, the firm may refuse to comply with the

request. In such situations, an agency may resort to the use of a subpoena or a search warrant.

Subpoenas.   There are two basic types of subpoenas. The subpoena *ad testificandum* ("to testify") is an ordinary subpoena. It is a writ, or order, compelling a witness to appear at an agency hearing. The subpoena *duces tecum*[4] ("bring it with you") compels an individual or organization to hand over books, papers, records, or documents to the agency. An administrative agency may use either type of subpoena to obtain testimony or documents.

There are limits on what an agency can demand. To determine whether an agency is abusing its discretion in its pursuit of information as part of an investigation, a court may consider such factors as the following:

1. The purpose of the investigation. An investigation must have a legitimate purpose. An improper purpose is, for example, harassment.
2. The relevance of the information being sought. Information is relevant if it reveals that the law is being violated or if it assures the agency that the law is not being violated.
3. The specificity of the demand for testimony or documents. A subpoena must, for example, adequately describe the material being sought.
4. The burden of the demand on the party from whom the information is sought. In responding to a

---

4. Pronounced *doo*-cheez *tee*-kum.

request for information, a party must bear the costs of, for example, copying the documents that must be handed over; a business is generally protected from revealing such information as trade secrets, however.

In the following case, former bank directors challenged the right of an administrative agency to subpoena their personal financial records. The court considered the extent of the agency's investigative powers.

CASE 43.2   Federal Deposit Insurance Corp. v. Wentz

United States
Court of Appeals,
Third Circuit, 1995.
55 F.3d 905.
http://www.findlaw.
com/casecode/courts/
3rd.html[a]

HISTORICAL AND ECONOMIC SETTING   *Congress created the Federal Deposit Insurance Corporation (FDIC) in 1933 to help prevent commercial bank failures and to protect bank customers' accounts. In 1992, nearly five hundred banks failed. More than half of all bank failures can be attributed to agricultural loans, when the failure of farms leads to default on the loans. Fraud also often plays a role. When a bank fails, the FDIC covers each depositor's loss up to $100,000 and then sells the bank's assets, or takes other steps, to regain some of those funds.*

BACKGROUND AND FACTS   *Sidney Wentz and Natalie Koether were directors of Howard Savings Bank of Livingston, New Jersey, when it was declared insolvent in October 1992. The Federal Deposit Insurance Corporation (FDIC) was appointed receiver. In April 1993, the FDIC issued subpoenas* duces tecum *to Wentz, Koether, and others, seeking, among other things, their personal financial records. The directors refused to comply. The FDIC asked a federal district court to enforce the subpoenas, arguing that the records were needed to assess whether any bank losses might be due to breach of the directors' fiduciary duties. The court ordered the directors to produce only those records showing additions to or reductions in their assets. The directors appealed, contending that this order intruded on their privacy.*

**IN THE LANGUAGE
OF THE COURT**

WEIS, Circuit Judge.
*   *   *   *

When personal documents of individuals, as contrasted with business records of corporations, are the subject of an administrative subpoena, privacy concerns must be considered. *   *   * [R]elevant factors [include] such matters as the type of record requested, the information that it might contain, the potential for harm and subsequent nonconsensual disclosure, the adequacy of safeguards to prevent unauthorized disclosure, the degree of need for access, *   *   * and the presence of recognizable public interests justifying access.
*   *   *   *

The FDIC has shown a reasonable need for gaining access to the directors' records in order to determine whether they reveal breaches of fiduciary duties through the improper channeling of bank funds for personal benefit. Moreover, the directors have not produced any evidence to show that the information contained in their personal financial records is of such a high degree of sensitivity that the intrusion could be considered severe or that the [directors] are likely to suffer any adverse effects from disclosure to [FDIC] personnel. Finally, we observe that regulatory provisions have been promulgated to guard against subsequent unauthorized disclosure of the subpoenaed information.

**DECISION
AND REMEDY**

The U.S. Court of Appeals for the Third Circuit affirmed the district court's order. The directors were required to produce their records.

---

a. In the "Browsing" section, in the "1995" row, click on "June." When that page opens, scroll down the list to "FDIC v WENTZ" and click on it to access the opinion.

Search Warrants. The Fourth Amendment protects against unreasonable searches and seizures by requiring that in most instances a physical search for evidence must be conducted under the authority of a search warrant. An agency's search warrant is an order directing law enforcement officials to search a specific place for a specific item and present it to the agency. Although it was once thought that administrative inspections were exempt from the warrant requirement, the United States Supreme Court held in *Marshall v. Barlow's, Inc.*,[5] that the requirement does apply to the administrative process.

Agencies can conduct warrantless searches in several situations. Warrants are not required to conduct searches in highly regulated industries. Firms that sell firearms or liquor, for example, are automatically subject to inspections without warrants. Sometimes, a statute permits warrantless searches of certain types of hazardous operations, such as coal mines. Also, a warrantless inspection in an emergency situation is normally considered reasonable.

ADJUDICATION

After conducting an investigation of a suspected rule violation, an agency may begin to take administrative action against an individual or organization. Most administrative actions are resolved through negotiated settlements at their initial stages, without the need for formal adjudication.

Negotiated Settlements. Depending on the agency, negotiations may take the form of a simple conversation or a series of informal conferences. Whatever form the negotiations take, their purpose is to rectify the problem to the agency's satisfaction and eliminate the need for additional proceedings.

Settlement is an appealing option to firms for two reasons: to avoid appearing uncooperative and to avoid the expense involved in formal adjudication proceedings and in possible later appeals. Settlement is also an attractive option for agencies. To conserve their own resources and avoid formal actions, administrative agencies devote a great deal of effort to giving advice and negotiating solutions to problems.

Formal Complaints. If a settlement cannot be reached, the agency may issue a formal complaint

against the suspected violator. If the Environmental Protection Agency (EPA), for example, finds that a factory is polluting groundwater in violation of federal pollution laws, the EPA will issue a complaint against the violator in an effort to bring the plant into compliance with federal regulations. This complaint is a public document, and a press release may accompany it. The factory charged in the complaint will respond by filing an answer to the EPA's allegations. If the factory and the EPA cannot agree on a settlement, the case is heard in a trial-like setting before an **administrative law judge (ALJ)**. The adjudication process is described below and illustrated graphically in Exhibit 43–4.

The Role of the Administrative Law Judge. The ALJ presides over the hearing and has the power to administer oaths, take testimony, rule on questions of

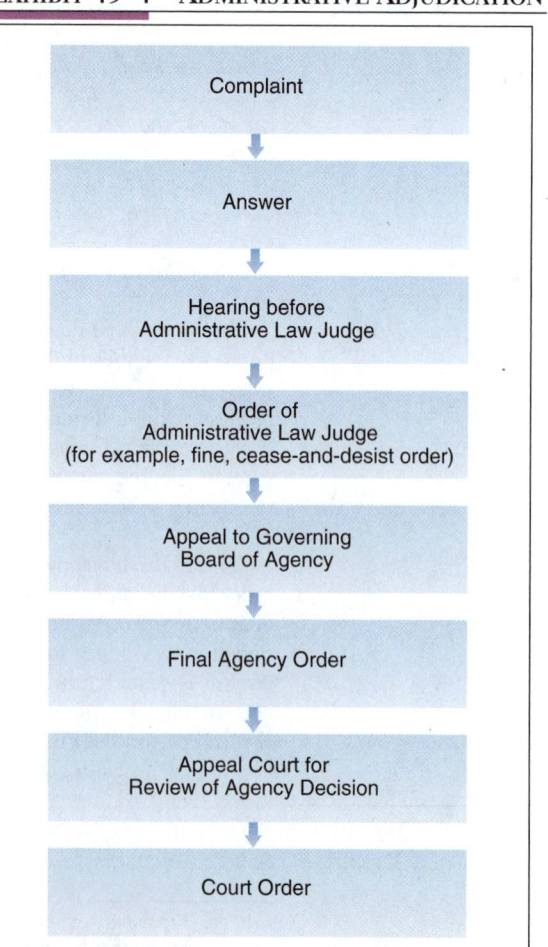

EXHIBIT 43–4 THE PROCESS OF FORMAL ADMINISTRATIVE ADJUDICATION

5. 436 U.S. 307, 98 S.Ct. 1816, 56 L.Ed.2d 305 (1978).

evidence, and make determinations of fact. Although formally, the ALJ works for the agency prosecuting the case (in our example, the EPA), the law requires an ALJ to be an unbiased adjudicator (judge).

Certain safeguards prevent bias on the part of the ALJ and promote fairness in the proceedings. For example, the APA requires that the ALJ be separate from an agency's investigative and prosecutorial staff. The APA also prohibits *ex parte* (private) communications between the ALJ and any party to an agency proceeding, such as the EPA or the factory. Finally, provisions of the APA protect the ALJ from agency disciplinary actions unless the agency can show good cause for such an action.

Hearing Procedures. Hearing procedures vary widely from agency to agency. Administrative agencies generally exercise substantial discretion over the type of hearing procedure that will be used. Frequently, disputes are resolved through informal adjudication proceedings. For example, the parties, their counsel, and the ALJ may simply meet at a table in a conference room for the dispute-settlement proceedings.

A formal adjudicatory hearing, in contrast, resembles a trial in many respects. Prior to the hearing, the parties are permitted to undertake extensive discovery (involving depositions, interrogatories, and requests for documents or other information, as described in Chapter 3). During the hearing, the parties may give testimony, present other evidence, and cross-examine adverse witnesses. A significant difference between a trial and an administrative agency hearing, though, is that normally much more information, including hearsay (secondhand information) can be introduced as evidence during an administrative hearing.

Agency Orders. Following a hearing, the ALJ renders an **initial order,** or decision, on the case. Either party can appeal the ALJ's decision to the board or commission that governs the agency. If the factory is dissatisfied with the ALJ's decision, for example, it can appeal the decision to the commission that governs the EPA. If the factory is dissatisfied with the commission's decision, it can appeal the decision to a federal court of appeals. If no party appeals the case, the ALJ's decision becomes the **final order** of the agency. The ALJ's decision also becomes final if a party appeals and the commission and the court decline to review the case. If a party appeals the case and the case is reviewed, the final order comes from the commission's decision or (if that decision is appealed to a federal appellate court) that of the court.

In the following case, an ALJ fined a company $2,000 for violating federal regulations governing mine safety. The company eventually asked a federal appellate court to review the order.

CASE 43.3   Buck Creek Coal, Inc. v. Federal Mine Safety and Health Administration

United States
Court of Appeals,
Seventh Circuit, 1995.
52 F.3d 133.
http://www.ca7.
uscourts.gov[a]

**IN THE LANGUAGE
OF THE COURT**

BACKGROUND AND FACTS *Buck Creek Coal, Inc., operates a coal mine in Sullivan County, Indiana. When James Holland, an inspector for the Mine Safety and Health Administration (MSHA), inspected the mine, he noted an accumulation of loose coal and coal dust in the feeder area, where mined coal is transferred from mine shuttle cars to conveyor belts. Holland issued a citation, charging Buck Creek with violations of federal regulations that require mine operators to keep feeder areas clean. After hearing evidence from both sides, an ALJ found that the evidence supported Holland's conclusions and fined Buck Creek $2,000. Buck Creek asked the Federal Mine Safety and Health Review Commission to review the ALJ's conclusions. When the commission declined, Buck Creek sought review in the courts.*

ILANA DIAMOND ROVNER, Circuit Judge.

*   *   *   *

*   *   *   [The ALJ] made these findings, based primarily on the testimony of Inspector Holland: "[T]here were substantial accumulations of loose coal, coal fines and

---

a. In the left column, click on "Judicial Opinions." On that page, in the "Case Numbers:" section, type "94" in the "Year" box and "2084" in the "Number" box, and click "Request Opinion" to access the case.

float coal dust, in the feeder area *   *   * . A heated roller turning in that combustible material could easily be an ignition source which could in turn cause a fire. *   *   * [I]n the event of a fire, smoke and gas inhalation by miners in the area would cause a reasonably serious injury requiring medical attention." *   *   * [N]o further evidence was necessary to support the ALJ's conclusion. First, *   *   * Inspector Holland [is] a federal mine inspector with 32 years of mining experience who specializes in mine ventilation. Nor was anything more than Inspector Holland's opinion necessary to support the common sense conclusion that a fire burning in an underground coal mine would present a serious risk of smoke and gas inhalation to miners who are present. *   *   * [F]ire is one of the primary safety concerns that has motivated federal regulation of the coal mining industry.

Nor has Buck Creek identified any evidence that tends to undermine the ALJ's conclusion. *   *   * Buck Creek has relied mainly on *   *   * testimony [that] pertained to Buck Creek's fire safety systems. *   *   * The fact that Buck Creek has safety measures in place *   *   * does not mean that fires do not pose a serious safety risk to miners. Indeed, the precautions are *   *   * in place *   *   * precisely because of the significant dangers associated with coal mine fires.

DECISION AND REMEDY *The U.S. Court of Appeals for the Seventh Circuit denied Buck Creek's petition for review. The ALJ's conclusions became the final order of the agency. Buck Creek was ordered to pay the fine.*

SECTION 3

Limitations on Agency Powers

Combining the functions normally divided among the three branches of government into an administrative agency concentrates considerable power in a single organization. Because of this concentration of authority, one of the major policy objectives of the government is to control the risks of arbitrariness and overreaching by administrative agencies without hindering the effective use of agency power to deal with particular problem areas, as Congress intends.

The judicial branch of the government exercises control over agency powers through the courts' review of agency actions. The executive and legislative branches of government also exercise control over agency authority.

JUDICIAL CONTROLS

The APA provides for judicial review of most agency decisions, as described above. Agency actions are not automatically subject to judicial review, however. Parties seeking review must demonstrate that they meet certain requirements. The party bringing the action must have *standing to sue* the agency (the party must have a direct stake in the outcome of the judicial

proceeding), and there must be an *actual controversy* at issue. These are basic judicial requirements that must be met before a court will hear a case, as discussed in Chapter 2. Furthermore, the party must have *exhausted all possible administrative remedies*. Each agency has its "chain of review," and the party must follow agency appeal procedures before a court will deem that administrative remedies have been exhausted.

Recall from Chapter 2 that appellate courts normally defer to the decisions of trial courts on questions of fact. In reviewing administrative actions, the courts are similarly reluctant to question the factual findings of agencies. In reviewing an administrative agency's decision, a court normally will consider the following types of issues:

1. Whether the agency has exceeded its authority under its enabling legislation.
2. Whether the agency has properly interpreted laws applicable to the agency action under review.
3. Whether the agency has violated any constitutional provisions.
4. Whether the agency has acted in accordance with procedural requirements of the law.
5. Whether the agency's actions were arbitrary, capricious, or an abuse of discretion.
6. Whether any conclusions drawn by the agency are not supported by substantial evidence.

EXECUTIVE CONTROLS

The executive branch of government exercises control over agencies both through the president's power to appoint federal officers and through the president's veto power. The president may veto enabling legislation presented by Congress or congressional attempts to modify an existing agency's authority.

LEGISLATIVE CONTROLS

Congress also exercises authority over agency powers. Through enabling legislation, Congress gives power to an agency. Of course, an agency may not exceed the power that Congress has delegated to it. Through subsequent legislation, Congress can take away that power or even abolish an agency altogether. Legislative authority is required to fund an agency, and enabling legislation usually sets certain time and monetary limits on the funding of particular programs. Congress can always revise these limits.

In addition to its power to create and fund agencies, Congress has the authority to investigate the implementation of its laws and the agencies that it has created. Individual legislators may also affect agency policy through their "casework" activities, which involve attempts to help their constituents deal with agencies.

Congress also has the power to "freeze" the enforcement of most federal regulations before the regulations take effect. Under the Small Business Regulatory Enforcement Fairness Act of 1996,[6] all federal agencies must submit final rules to Congress before the rules become effective. If, within sixty days, Congress passes a joint resolution of disapproval concerning a rule, enforcement of the regulation is frozen while the rule is reviewed by congressional committees.

Another legislative check on agency actions is the Administrative Procedure Act, discussed earlier in this chapter. Additionally, the laws discussed in the next section provide certain checks on the actions of administrative agencies.

SECTION 4

Public Accountability

As a result of growing public concern over the powers exercised by administrative agencies, Congress passed several laws to make agencies more accountable through public scrutiny. We discuss here the most significant of these laws.

FREEDOM OF INFORMATION ACT

Enacted in 1966, the Freedom of Information Act (FOIA)[7] requires the federal government to disclose certain "records" to "any person" on request, even if no reason is given for the request. The FOIA exempts certain types of records. For other records, though, a request that complies with the FOIA procedures need only contain a reasonable description of the information sought (see Exhibit 43–5 on the next page). An agency's failure to comply with a request may be challenged in a federal district court. The media, industry trade associations, public-interest groups, and even companies seeking information about competitors rely on these FOIA provisions to obtain information from government agencies.

Under a 1996 amendment to the FOIA, all federal government agencies now have to make their records available electronically—on the Internet, on computer disks, and in other electronic formats. As of November 1, 1996, any document created by an agency must be available on computer within a year after its creation. Agencies must also provide a clear index to all of their documents.

GOVERNMENT-IN-THE-SUNSHINE ACT

Congress passed the Government-in-the-Sunshine Act,[8] or open meeting law, in 1976. It requires that "every portion of every meeting of an agency" be open to "public observation." The act also requires the establishment of procedures to ensure that the public is provided with adequate advance notice of scheduled meetings and agendas. Like the FOIA, the sunshine act contains certain exceptions. Closed meetings are permitted when (1) the subject of the meeting concerns accusing any person of a crime, (2) an open meeting would frustrate implementation of agency actions, or (3) the subject of the meeting involves matters relating to future litigation or rulemaking. Courts interpret these exceptions to allow open access whenever possible.

---

6. 5 U.S.C. Sections 801–808.

7. 5 U.S.C. Section 552.
8. 5 U.S.C. Section 552b.

EXHIBIT 43–5   **SAMPLE LETTER REQUESTING INFORMATION FROM AN EXECUTIVE DEPARTMENT OR AGENCY**

Date

Agency Head or FOIA Officer
Title
Name of Agency
Address of Agency
City, State, Zip

Re: Freedom of Information Act Request.

Dear _____ :

  Under the provisions of the Freedom of Information Act, 5 U.S.C. Section 552, I am requesting access to
_____
[identify the records as clearly as possible].
  [Optional] I am requesting this information because _____
_____
[state the reason for your request if you think it will assist you in obtaining the information].
  If there are any fees for searching for, or copying, the records I have requested, please inform me before you fill the request [or:] please supply the records without informing me if the fees do not exceed $ _____ .
  [or:] As you know, the act permits you to reduce or waive fees when the release of the information is considered as "primarily benefiting the public." I believe that this request fits that category, and I therefore ask that you waive any fees.
  If all or any part of this request is denied, please cite the specific exemption(s) that you think justifies your refusal to release the information, and inform me of the appeal procedures available to me under the law.
  I would appreciate your handling this request as quickly as possible, and I look forward to hearing from you within 10 days, as the law stipulates.

                                        Sincerely,
                                        [Signature]
                                        Name
                                        Address
                                        City, State, Zip

SOURCE: U.S. Congress, House Committee on Government Operations, *A Citizen's Guide on How to Use the Freedom of Information Act and the Privacy Act Requesting Government Documents*, 95th Congress, 1st session, 1977.

REGULATORY FLEXIBILITY ACT

Concern over the effects of regulation on the efficiency of businesses, particularly smaller ones, led Congress to pass the Regulatory Flexibility Act in 1980.[9] Under this act, whenever a new regulation will have a "significant impact upon a substantial number of small entities," the agency must conduct a regulatory flexibility analysis. The analysis must measure the cost that the rule would impose on small businesses and must consider less burdensome alternatives. The act also contains provisions to alert small businesses—

through advertising in trade journals, for example—about forthcoming regulations. The act reduces some record-keeping burdens for small businesses, especially with regard to hazardous waste management.

SMALL BUSINESS REGULATORY ENFORCEMENT FAIRNESS ACT

As mentioned above, the Small Business Regulatory Enforcement Fairness Act (SBREFA) of 1996 allows Congress to review new federal regulations for at least sixty days before they take effect. This period gives opponents of the rules time to present their arguments to Congress.

9. 5 U.S.C. Sections 601–612.

The SBREFA also authorizes the courts to enforce the Regulatory Flexibility Act. This helps to ensure that federal agencies, such as the Internal Revenue Service, will consider ways to reduce the economic impact of new regulations on small businesses. Federal agencies are required to prepare guides that explain in "plain English" how small businesses can comply with federal regulations.

At the Small Business Administration, the SBREFA set up the National Enforcement Ombudsman to receive comments from small businesses about their dealings with federal agencies. Based on these comments, Regional Small Business Fairness Boards rate the agencies and publicize their findings.

Finally, the SBREFA allows small businesses to recover their expenses and legal fees from the government when an agency makes demands for fines or penalties that a court considers excessive.

Section 5

State Administrative Agencies

Although most of this chapter deals with federal administrative agencies, state agencies play a significant role in regulating activities within the states. Many of the factors that encouraged the proliferation of federal agencies also fostered the expanding presence of state agencies. For example, one reason for the growth of administrative agencies at all levels of government is the inability of Congress and state legislatures to oversee the implementation of their laws. Another is the greater technical competence of the agencies.

Parallel Agencies

Commonly, a state creates an agency as a parallel to a federal agency to provide similar services on a more localized basis. Such parallel agencies include the federal Social Security Administration and the state welfare agency, the Internal Revenue Service and the state revenue department, and the Environmental Protection Agency and the state pollution-control agency. Not all federal agencies have parallel state agencies, however. For example, the Federal Bureau of Investigation and the Nuclear Regulatory Commission have no parallel agencies at the state level.

Conflicts between Parallel Agencies

If the actions of parallel state and federal agencies conflict, the actions of the federal agency will prevail. For example, if the Federal Aviation Administration specifies the hours during which airplanes may land at and depart from airports, a state or local government cannot issue inconsistent laws or regulations governing the same activities. The priority of federal laws over conflicting state laws is based on the supremacy clause of the U.S. Constitution. Remember from Chapter 4 that this clause, which is found in Article VI of the Constitution, states that the Constitution and "the Laws of the United States which shall be made in Pursuance thereof . . . shall be the supreme Law of the Land."

Terms and Concepts to Review

adjudication 807

administrative law judge (ALJ) 812

administrative process 808

bureaucracy 808

delegation doctrine 808

enabling legislation 804

final order 813

initial order 813

judicial process 808

legislative rule 807

notice-and-comment rulemaking 808

rulemaking 808

QUESTIONS AND CASE PROBLEMS

43–1. RULEMAKING PROCEDURES. Assume that the Food and Drug Administration (FDA), using proper procedures, adopts a rule describing its future investigations. This new rule covers all future cases in which the FDA wants to regulate food additives. Under the new rule, the FDA is not to regulate food additives without giving food companies an opportunity to cross-examine witnesses. Some time later, the FDA wants to regulate methylisocyanate, a food additive. The FDA undertakes an informal rulemaking procedure, without cross-examination, and regulates methylisocyanate. Producers protest, saying that the FDA promised them the opportunity for cross-examination. The FDA responds that the Administrative Procedure Act does not require such cross-examination and that it is free to withdraw the promise made in its new rule. If the producers challenge the FDA in a court, on what basis would the court rule in their favor?

43–2. RULEMAKING AND ADJUDICATION POWERS. For decades, the Federal Trade Commission (FTC) resolved fair trade and advertising disputes through individual adjudications. In the 1960s, the FTC began promulgating rules that defined fair and unfair trade practices. In cases involving violations of these rules, the due process rights of participants were more limited and did not include cross-examination. Although anyone found violating a rule would receive a full adjudication, the legitimacy of the rule itself could not be challenged in the adjudication. Any party charged with violating a rule was almost certain to lose the adjudication. Affected parties complained to a court, arguing that their rights before the FTC were unduly limited by the new rules. What will the court examine to determine whether to uphold the new rules?

43–3. RULEMAKING PROCEDURES. The Department of Commerce issued a flammability standard that required all mattresses, including crib mattresses, to pass a test that involved contact with a burning cigarette. The manufacturers of crib mattresses petitioned the department to exempt their product from the test procedure, but the department refused to do so. The crib manufacturers sued the department and argued that applying such a rule to crib mattresses was arbitrary and capricious because infants do not smoke. On what basis might the court hold that the rule is not arbitrary and capricious? [*Bunny Bear, Inc. v. Peterson*, 473 F.2d 1002 (1st Cir. 1973)]

43–4. RULEMAKING PROCEDURES. The Atomic Energy Commission (AEC) was engaged in rulemaking proceedings for nuclear reactor safety. An environmental group sued the commission, arguing that its proceedings were inadequate. The commission had carefully complied with all requirements of the Administrative Procedure Act. The environmentalists argued, however, that the very haz-ardous and technical nature of the reactor safety issue required elaborate procedures above and beyond those set forth in the act. A federal court of appeals agreed and overturned the AEC rules. The commission appealed the case to the United States Supreme Court. How should the Court rule? Discuss. [*Vermont Yankee Nuclear Power Corp. v. Natural Resources Defense Council, Inc.*, 435 U.S. 519, 98 S.Ct. 1197, 55 L.Ed.2d 460 (1978)]

43–5. EXECUTIVE CONTROLS. In 1982, the president of the United States appointed Matthew Chabal, Jr., to the position of U.S. marshal. U.S. marshals are assigned to the federal courts. In the fall of 1985, Chabal received an unsatisfactory annual performance rating, and he was fired shortly thereafter by the president. Given that U.S. marshals are assigned to the federal courts, are these appointees members of the executive branch? Did the president have the right to fire Chabal without consulting Congress about the decision? [*Chabal v. Reagan*, 841 F.2d 1216 (3d Cir. 1988)]

43–6. ARBITRARY AND CAPRICIOUS TEST. In 1977, the Department of Transportation (DOT) adopted a passive-restraint standard (known as Standard 208) that required new cars to have either air bags or automatic seat belts. By 1981, it had become clear that all of the major auto manufacturers would install automatic seat belts to comply with this rule. The DOT determined that most purchasers of cars would detach their automatic seat belts, thus making them ineffective. Consequently, the department repealed the regulation. State Farm Mutual Automobile Insurance Co. and other insurance companies sued in the District of Columbia Circuit Court of Appeals for a review of the DOT's repeal of the regulation. That court held that the repeal was arbitrary and capricious because the DOT had reversed its rule without sufficient support. The motor vehicle manufacturers, who initially had wanted to avoid the costs associated with implementing Standard 208, then appealed this decision to the United States Supreme Court. What will result? Discuss fully. [*Motor Vehicle Manufacturers Association v. State Farm Mutual Automobile Insurance Co.*, 463 U.S. 29, 103 S.Ct. 2856, 77 L.Ed.2d 443 (1983)]

43–7. JUDICIAL REVIEW. American Message Centers (AMC) provides answering services to retailers. Calls to a retailer are automatically forwarded to AMC, which pays for the calls. AMC obtains telephone service at a discount from major carriers, including Sprint. Sprint's tariff (a public document setting out rates and rules relating to Sprint's services) states that the "subscriber shall be responsible for the payment of all charges for service." When AMC learned that computer hackers had obtained the access code for AMC's lines and had made nearly $160,000 in long-distance calls, it asked Sprint to absorb the cost. Sprint refused. AMC filed a complaint with the Federal Communications Commission (FCC), claiming in part that Sprint's tariff was vague and ambiguous, in violation of the Communications Act of 1934 and FCC rules. These laws require that a carrier's tariff "clearly and definitely" specify any "exceptions or conditions which in any way affect the rates named in the tariff." The FCC rejected AMC's complaint. AMC appealed the FCC's decision to a federal appellate court, claiming that the FCC's decision to reject AMC's complaint was arbitrary and capricious. What should the court decide? Discuss fully. [*American Message Centers v. Federal Communications Commission*, 50 F.3d 35 (D.C.Cir. 1995)]

43–8. RULEMAKING. The Occupational Safety and Health Administration (OSHA) is part of the U.S. Department of Labor. OSHA issued a "Directive" under which each employer in selected industries was to be inspected unless it adopted a "Comprehensive Compliance Program (CCP)"—a safety and health program designed to meet standards that in some respects exceeded those otherwise required by law. The Chamber of Commerce of the United States objected to the Directive and filed a petition for review with the U.S. Court of Appeals for the District of Columbia Circuit. The Chamber claimed, in part, that OSHA did not use proper rulemaking procedures in issuing the Directive. OSHA argued that it was not required to follow those procedures because the Directive itself was a "rule of procedure." OSHA claimed that the rule did not "alter the rights or interests of parties, although it may alter the manner in which the parties present themselves or their viewpoints to the agency."

What are the steps of the most commonly used rulemaking procedure? Which steps are missing in this case? In whose favor should the court rule? Why? [*Chamber of Commerce of the United States v. U.S. Department of Labor*, 74 F.3d 206 (D.C.Cir. 1999)]

43–9. IN YOUR COURT

Assume that the Securities and Exchange Commission (SEC) has a rule that it will enforce statutory provisions prohibiting insider trading only when the insiders make monetary profits for themselves. Then the SEC makes a new rule, declaring that it has the statutory authority to bring an enforcement action against an individual even if he or she does not personally profit from the insider trading. In making the new rule, the SEC does not conduct a rulemaking proceeding but simply announces its new decision. A securities organization objects and says that the new rule was unlawfully developed without opportunity for public comment. The organization challenges the rule in an action that ultimately is reviewed by a federal appellate court. Assume that you are a judge on the appellate court reviewing this case and answer the following questions:

(a) Should the SEC's new rule be invalidated under the Administrative Procedure Act? Why or why not?

(b) Is the SEC's new rule a legislative rule or an interpretive rule? Why is this distinction important to the outcome of this case?

LAW ON THE WEB

For updated links to resources available on the Web, as well as a variety of other materials, visit this text's Web site at http://wbl.westbuslaw.com.

The Federal Web Locator permits searches for the names of federal administrative agencies and provides links to agency-related information. Go to

http://www.infoctr.edu/fwl

The Web site of the U.S. Government Printing Office, called GPO Access, offers free online access to all of its databases, including the *Federal Register*, at

http://www.access.gpo.gov/su_docs

LEGAL RESEARCH EXERCISES ON THE WEB

Go to http://wbl.westbuslaw.com, the Web site that accompanies this text. Select "Internet Applications," and then click on "Chapter 43." There you will find the following Internet research exercise that you can perform to learn more about how to obtain information from government agencies:

Activity 43–1: The Freedom of Information Act

CHAPTER 44

Consumer and Environmental Law

ALL STATUTES, AGENCY RULES, AND COMMON law judicial decisions that serve to protect the interests of consumers are classified as **consumer law.** Traditionally, in disputes involving consumers, it was assumed that the freedom to contract carried with it the obligation to live by the deal made. Over time, this attitude has changed considerably. Today, myriad federal and state laws protect consumers from unfair trade practices, unsafe products, discriminatory or unreasonable credit requirements, and other problems related to consumer transactions. Nearly every agency and department of the federal government has an office of consumer affairs, and most states have one or more such offices to help consumers. Also, typically the attorney general's office assists consumers at the state level.

In the first part of this chapter, we examine some of the major laws and regulations protecting consumers. We then turn to a discussion of **environmental law**—which consists of all of the laws and regulations designed to protect and preserve our environmental resources.

SECTION 1

Consumer Law

Consumer transactions take a variety of forms, but they generally include those that involve an exchange of value for the purpose of acquiring goods, services, land, or credit for personal or family use. Because of the wide variation among state consumer protection laws, our primary focus in this chapter is on federal legislation. Exhibit 44–1 indicates some of the types of consumer transactions that are regulated by federal laws.

DECEPTIVE ADVERTISING

One of the earliest federal consumer protection laws—and still one of the most important—was the Federal Trade Commission Act of 1914.[1] As mentioned in the preceding chapter, the act created the Federal Trade Commission (FTC) to carry out the broadly stated goal of preventing unfair and deceptive trade practices, including deceptive advertising.[2]

Deceptive Advertising Defined. Advertising will be deemed deceptive if a consumer would be misled by the advertising claim. Vague generalities and obvious exaggerations are permissible. These claims are known as *puffing*. When a claim takes on the appearance of literal authenticity, however, it may create problems. Advertising that *appears* to be based on factual evidence

---

1. 15 U.S.C. Sections 41–58.
2. 15 U.S.C. Section 45.

EXHIBIT 44–1   AREAS OF CONSUMER LAW REGULATED BY STATUTES

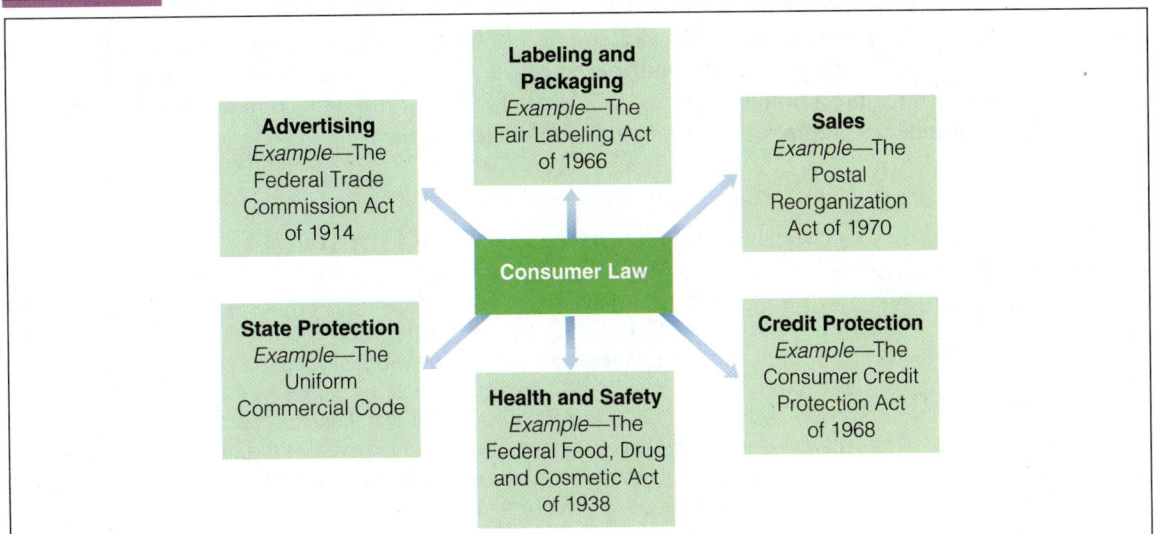

but that in fact is not will be deemed deceptive. A classic example is provided by a 1944 case in which the claim that a skin cream would restore youthful qualities to aged skin was deemed deceptive.[3]

Some advertisements contain "half-truths," meaning that the presented information is true but incomplete, and it leads consumers to a false conclusion. For example, the makers of Campbell's soups advertised that "most" Campbell's soups were low in fat and cholesterol and thus were helpful in fighting heart disease. What the ad did not say was that Campbell's soups are high in sodium, and high-sodium diets may increase the risk of heart disease. The FTC ruled that Campbell's claims were thus deceptive. Advertising that contains an endorsement by a celebrity may be deemed deceptive if the celebrity actually makes no use of the product.

Bait-and-Switch Advertising.   The FTC has promulgated specific rules to govern advertising techniques. One of the most important rules is contained in the FTC's "Guides Against Bait Advertising,"[4] issued in 1968. The rule seeks to prevent **bait-and-switch advertising**—that is, advertising a very low price for a particular item that will likely be unavailable to the

consumer, who will then be encouraged to purchase a more expensive item. The low price is the "bait" to lure the consumer into the store. The salesperson is instructed to "switch" the consumer to a different, more expensive item. Under the FTC guidelines, bait-and-switch advertising occurs if the seller refuses to show the advertised item, fails to have in stock a reasonable quantity of the item, fails to promise to deliver the advertised item within a reasonable time, or discourages employees from selling the item.

FTC Actions against Deceptive Advertising.   The FTC receives complaints from many sources, including competitors of alleged violators, consumers, consumer organizations, trade associations, Better Business Bureaus, government organizations, and state and local officials. If enough consumers complain and the complaints are widespread, the FTC will investigate the problem. If the FTC concludes that a given advertisement is unfair or deceptive, it drafts a formal complaint, which is sent to the alleged offender. The company may agree to settle the complaint without further proceedings, or the FTC can conduct a hearing in which the company can present its defense (see Chapter 43).

If the FTC succeeds in proving that an advertisement is unfair or deceptive, it usually issues a **cease-and-desist order** requiring that the challenged advertising be stopped. It might also impose a sanction

---

3. *Charles of the Ritz Distributing Corp. v. Federal Trade Commission*, 143 F.2d 676 (2d Cir. 1944).

4. 16 C.F.R. Part 238.

known as **counteradvertising** by requiring the company to advertise anew—in print, on radio, and on television—to inform the public about the earlier misinformation. The FTC may institute **multiple product orders,** which require a firm to cease and desist from false advertising not only in regard to the prod-

uct that was the subject of the action but also in regard to all of the firm's other products.

Is it false or misleading to advertise a product as effective when its effectiveness results only from users' belief that it works? The court addressed this issue in the following case.

CASE 44.1　　　　　**Federal Trade Commission v. Pantron I Corp.**

United States
Court of Appeals,
Ninth Circuit, 1994.
33 F.3d 1088.

**IN THE LANGUAGE
OF THE COURT**

BACKGROUND AND FACTS　*Pantron I Corporation sold the Helsinki Formula as a "cure" for baldness. Pantron claimed that the product reduced hair loss and promoted hair growth. The Federal Trade Commission filed a suit in a federal district court against Pantron and its owner, Hal Lederman, alleging that these claims constituted an unfair or deceptive trade practice. The court concluded in part that the product had a "placebo effect"—that is, that it worked when its users believed it would. The court issued an order that, among other things, allowed Pantron to continue claiming its product "works some of the time for a lot of people." The FTC appealed this order.*

REINHARDT, Circuit Judge:

*　*　*　*

*　*　*　Where, as here, a product's effectiveness arises solely as a result of the placebo effect, a representation that the product is effective constitutes a false advertisement even though some consumers may experience positive results. In such circumstances, the efficacy claim is misleading because the [product] is not inherently effective, its results being attributable to the psychosomatic effect produced by *　*　* advertising *　*　*.

*　*　*　Under the evidence in the record before us, it appears that massaging vegetable oil on one's head would likely produce the same positive results as using the Helsinki Formula. *　*　*　[A] court should not allow a seller to rely on such a placebo effect in supporting a claim of effectiveness *　*　*. [W]ere we to hold otherwise, advertisers would be encouraged to foist unsubstantiated claims on an unsuspecting public in the hope that consumers would believe the ads and the claims would be self-fulfilling.

**DECISION
AND REMEDY**

The U.S. Court of Appeals for the Ninth Circuit reversed this part of the lower court's order and remanded the case. Pantron could not continue to claim that its product "works some of the time for a lot of people."

Telemarketing and Electronic Advertising. The pervasive use of the telephone to market goods and services to homes and businesses led to the passage in 1991 of the Telephone Consumer Protection Act (TCPA).[5] The act prohibits telephone solicitation using an automatic telephone dialing system or a prerecorded voice. Most states also have laws regulating

telephone solicitation. The TCPA also makes it illegal to transmit ads via fax without first obtaining the recipient's permission. (Similar issues have arisen with respect to junk e-mail, called "spam"—see Chapter 9 for a discussion of this topic.)

The act is enforced by the Federal Communications Commission and also provides for a private right of action. Consumers can recover any actual monetary loss resulting from a violation of the act or receive $500 in

---

5. 47 U.S.C. Sections 227 *et seq.*

damages for each violation, whichever is greater. If a court finds that a defendant willfully or knowingly violated the act, the court has the discretion to treble the damages awarded.

The Telemarketing and Consumer Fraud and Abuse Prevention Act[6] of 1994 directed the FTC to establish rules governing telemarketing and to bring actions against fraudulent telemarketers. The FTC's Telemarketing Sales Rule[7] of 1995 requires a telemarketer, before making a sales pitch, to inform the recipient that the call is a sales call and to identify the seller's name and the product being sold. The rule makes it illegal for telemarketers to misrepresent information (including facts about their goods or services, earnings potential, profitability, the risk attending an investment, or the nature of a prize). Additionally, telemarketers must inform the people they call of the total cost of the goods being sold, any restrictions on obtaining or using the goods, and whether a sale will be considered to be final and nonrefundable. A telemarketer must also remove a consumer's name from its list of potential contacts if the customer so requests.

A major challenge in today's legal environment has to do with the advertising of products and services via the Internet. See this chapter's *Emerging Trends in Technology* on page 824 for a discussion of this issue.

LABELING AND PACKAGING LAWS

A number of federal and state laws deal specifically with the information given on labels and packages. In general, labels must be accurate, and they must use words that are easily understood by the ordinary consumer. For example, a box of cereal cannot be labeled "giant" if that would exaggerate the amount of cereal contained in the box. In some instances, labels must specify the raw materials used in the product, such as the percentage of cotton, nylon, or other fiber used in a garment. In other instances, the product must carry a warning. Cigarette packages and advertising, for example, must include one of several warnings about the health hazards associated with smoking.[8]

Federal laws regulating the labeling and packaging of products include the Wool Products Labeling Act of 1939,[9] the Fur Products Labeling Act of 1951,[10]

the Flammable Fabrics Act of 1953,[11] the Fair Packaging and Labeling Act of 1966,[12] the Smokeless Tobacco Health Education Act of 1986,[13] and the Nutrition Labeling and Education Act of 1990.[14] The Smokeless Tobacco Health Education Act, for example, requires that producers, packagers, and importers of smokeless tobacco label their product with one of several warnings about the health hazards associated with the use of smokeless tobacco; the warnings are similar to those contained on other tobacco product packages.

The Fair Packaging and Labeling Act requires that products carry labels that identify the product; the net quantity of the contents, as well as the quantity of servings, if the number of servings is stated; the manufacturer; and the packager or distributor. The act also authorizes requirements concerning words used to describe packages, terms that are associated with savings claims, information disclosures for ingredients in nonfood products, and standards for the partial filling of packages. Food products must bear labels detailing nutritional content, including how much fat the food contains and what kind of fat it is. These restrictions are enforced by the Department of Health and Human Services, as well as the FTC. The Nutrition Labeling and Education Act of 1990 requires standard nutrition facts (including fat content) on food labels; regulates the use of such terms as *fresh* and *low fat*; and, subject to the federal Food and Drug Administration's approval, authorizes certain health claims.

SALES

Many of the laws that protect consumers concern the disclosure of certain terms in sales transactions and provide rules governing the various forms of sales, such as door-to-door sales, mail-order sales, referral sales, and the unsolicited receipt of merchandise. Much of the federal regulation of sales is conducted by the FTC under its regulatory authority to curb unfair trade practices. Other federal agencies, however, are involved to various degrees. For example, the Federal Reserve Board of Governors has issued **Regulation Z**,[15] which governs credit provisions associated with sales contracts. Many states have also enacted laws governing

---

6. 15 U.S.C. Sections 6101–6108.
7. 16 C.F.R. Sections 310.1–310.8.
8. 15 U.S.C. Sections 1331–1341.
9. 15 U.S.C. Section 68.
10. 15 U.S.C. Section 69.

11. 15 U.S.C. Section 1191.
12. 15 U.S.C. Sections 1451 *et seq.*
13. 15 U.S.C. Sections 4401–4408.
14. 21 U.S.C. Section 343-1.
15. 12 C.F.R. Sections 226.1–226.30.

EMERGING TRENDS IN TECHNOLOGY

Protection against Internet Fraud

For years, the Federal Trade Commission (FTC) has fought deceptive advertising in printed materials and in radio and television broadcasts. Since the 1990s, it has spent a considerable portion of its resources on fighting deceptive advertising on the Internet. The FTC has moved particularly quickly on commercial Internet fraud schemes. It has even provided "hot links" on Web sites that it has targeted. A hot link takes the user to the FTC's own Web site, on which the complaint, restraining order, and other documents in the case can be read and downloaded.

Other agencies are also fighting online fraud and false advertising. For example, the Securities and Exchange Commission (SEC) has initiated actions against dozens of entities that have perpetrated online investment scams. One fraudulent scheme involved twenty thousand investors, who lost in all more than $3 million. Some cases have involved false claims about the earnings potential of home-

business programs, such as the claim that one could "earn $4,000 or more each month." Others have concerned claims for "guaranteed credit repair."

The Department of Transportation (DOT) has also brought actions against purported online violators of advertising and disclosure laws. In one case, the DOT fined Virgin Airlines for failing to disclose the true price of a flight that it advertised on the Web. Also, the Consumer Product Safety Commission (CPSC) has created what it calls a one-stop Web site at which it provides information that allows consumers to avoid the most obvious fraud problems on the Web and elsewhere.

Consumers themselves have also taken action to curb online fraud. For example, the National Consumers League has developed Web pages to help consumers learn about the most common types of Internet fraud. Various states are also setting up information sites to help consumers protect themselves.

IMPLICATIONS FOR THE BUSINESSPERSON

1. All business entities must be aware that the laws and government regulations controlling standard "paper" commerce and

advertising apply equally to the Internet.

2. Businesspersons should realize that even though Internet sites are seemingly infinite in number, the vastness of this number will not prevent federal and state agency "watchdogs" from discovering fraud and false advertising. An increasing number of government regulatory dollars are going into policing the Internet.

FOR CRITICAL ANALYSIS

1. Can there be more consumer fraud on the Internet than there has been with the use of mail-order catalogues? Explain.

2. How can a set of guidelines for online advertising be developed, given that the technology is changing so rapidly?

RELEVANT WEB SITES

For a list of the ten most common scams perpetrated online, go to the National Consumers League Web site at **http://www.fraud. org/ifw.htm**. You can access the CPSC's consumer law Web site at **http://www.consumer.gov**. For an example of a well-designed state Web site to help consumers, go to **http://www.state.nh.us/nhdoj/ Consumer/cpb.html**.

consumer sales transactions. Moreover, states have provided a number of consumer protection provisions through the adoption of the Uniform Commercial Code and, in those states that have adopted it, the Uniform Consumer Credit Code.

Door-to-Door Sales. Door-to-door sales are singled out for special treatment in the laws of most states, in part because of the nature of the sales transaction. Repeat purchases are not as likely as they are in stores, and thus the seller has less incentive to cultivate the goodwill of the purchaser. Furthermore, the seller is unlikely to present alternative products and their prices. Thus, a number of states have passed "cooling-off" laws that permit the buyers of goods sold door-to-door to cancel their contracts within a specified period of time, usually two to three days after the sale.

An FTC regulation also requires sellers to give consumers three days to cancel any door-to-door sale. Because this rule applies in addition to the relevant state statutes, consumers are given the most favorable benefits of the FTC rule and their own state statutes. In addition, the FTC rule requires that consumers be notified in Spanish of this right if the oral negotiations for the sale were in that language.

Telephone and Mail-Order Sales.
Sales made by either telephone or mail order are the greatest source of complaints to the nation's Better Business Bureaus. Many mail-order firms are far removed from most of their buyers, thus making it burdensome for buyers to bring complaints against them. To a certain extent, consumers are protected under federal laws prohibiting mail fraud, which were discussed in Chapter 8, and under state consumer protection laws that parallel and supplement the federal laws.

The FTC Mail or Telephone Order Merchandise Rule of 1993, which amended the FTC Mail-Order Rule of 1975,[16] provides specific protections for consumers who purchase goods via phone lines or through the mails. The 1993 rule extended the 1975 rule to include sales in which orders are transmitted by computer, fax machine, or some similar means involving telephone lines. Among other things, the rule requires mail-order merchants to ship orders within the time promised in their catalogues or advertisements, to notify consumers when orders cannot be shipped on time, and to issue a refund within a specified period of time when a consumer cancels an order.

In addition, the Postal Reorganization Act of 1970[17] provides that *unsolicited* merchandise sent by U.S. mail may be retained, used, discarded, or disposed of in any manner deemed appropriate, without the recipient's incurring any obligation to the sender.

CREDIT PROTECTION

Because of the extensive use of credit by American consumers, credit protection has become an especially important area regulated by consumer protection legislation. One of the most significant statutes regulating the credit and credit-card industry is Title I of the Consumer Credit Protection Act (CCPA),[18] which was passed by Congress in 1968 and is commonly referred to as the Truth-in-Lending Act (TILA).

The Truth-in-Lending Act.
The TILA is basically a *disclosure law*. It is administered by the Federal Reserve Board and requires sellers and lenders to disclose credit terms or loan terms so that individuals can shop around for the best financing arrangements. TILA requirements apply only to persons who, in the ordinary course of business, lend money, sell on credit, or arrange for the extension of credit. Thus, sales or loans made between two consumers do not come under the protection of the act. Additionally, only debtors who are natural persons (as opposed to the artificial "person" of the corporation) are protected by this law; other legal entities are not.

The disclosure requirements are contained in Regulation Z, which, as mentioned earlier in this chapter, was promulgated by the Federal Reserve Board. If the contracting parties are subject to the TILA, the requirements of Regulation Z apply to any transaction involving an installment sales contract in which payment is to be made in more than four installments. Transactions subject to Regulation Z typically include installment loans, retail and installment sales, car loans, home-improvement loans, and certain real estate loans if the amount of financing is less than $25,000.

Under the provisions of the TILA, all of the terms of a credit instrument must be clearly and conspicuously disclosed. The TILA provides for contract rescission (cancellation) if a creditor fails to follow *exactly* the procedures required by the act.[19] TILA requirements are strictly enforced.

Equal Credit Opportunity.
In 1974, the Equal Credit Opportunity Act (ECOA)[20] was enacted as an amendment to the TILA. The ECOA prohibits the denial of credit solely on the basis of race, religion, national origin, color, gender, marital status, or age. The act also prohibits credit discrimination on the basis of

---

16. 16 C.F.R. Sections 435.1–435.2.
17. 39 U.S.C. Section 3009.
18. 15 U.S.C. Sections 1601–1693r.
19. Note, however, that amendments to the TILA enacted in 1995 prevent borrowers from rescinding loans for minor clerical errors in closing documents [15 U.S.C. Sections 1605, 1631, 1635, 1640, and 1641].
20. 15 U.S.C. Sections 1691–1691f.

whether an individual receives certain forms of income, such as public-assistance benefits. Under the ECOA, a creditor may not require the signature of an applicant's spouse, other than as a joint applicant, on a credit instrument if the applicant qualifies under the creditor's standards of creditworthiness for the amount and terms of the credit request. Creditors are permitted to ask for any information from a credit applicant except that which could be used for the type of discrimination covered in the act or its amendments.

Credit-Card Rules. The TILA also contains provisions regarding credit cards. One provision limits the liability of a cardholder to $50 per card for unauthorized charges made before the creditor is notified that the card has been lost. Another provision prohibits a credit-card company from billing a consumer for any unauthorized charges if the credit card was improperly issued by the company; for example, if a consumer receives an unsolicited credit card in the mail and the card is later stolen and used by the thief to make purchases, the consumer to whom the card was sent will not be liable for the unauthorized charges.

Further provisions of the act concern billing disputes related to credit-card purchases. If a debtor thinks that an error has occurred in billing or wishes to withhold payment for a faulty product purchased by credit card, the act outlines specific procedures for both the consumer and the credit-card company to follow in settling the dispute.

Consumer Leases. The Consumer Leasing Act (CLA) of 1988[21] amended the TILA to provide protection for consumers who lease automobiles and other goods. The CLA applies to those who lease or arrange to lease consumer goods in the ordinary course of their business. The act applies only if the goods are priced at $25,000 or less and if the lease term exceeds four months. The CLA and its implementing regulation, Regulation M,[22] require lessors to disclose in writing all of the material terms of the lease.

The Fair Credit Reporting Act. In 1970, to protect consumers against inaccurate credit reporting, Congress enacted the Fair Credit Reporting Act (FCRA).[23] The act provides that consumer credit reporting agencies may issue credit reports to users only for specified purposes, including the extension of credit, the issuance of insurance policies, compliance with a court order, and in response to a consumer's request for a copy of his or her own credit report. The act further provides that any time a consumer is denied credit or insurance on the basis of the consumer's credit report, or is charged more than others ordinarily would be for credit or insurance, the consumer must be notified of that fact and of the name and address of the credit reporting agency that issued the credit report.

Under the act, consumers may request the source of any information being given out by a credit agency, as well as the identity of anyone who has received an agency's report. Consumers are also permitted to have access to the information contained about them in a credit reporting agency's files. If a consumer discovers that a credit reporting agency's files contain inaccurate information about the consumer's credit standing, the agency, on the consumer's written request, must investigate the matter and delete any unverifiable or erroneous information within a reasonable period of time.

An agency that fails to comply with the act is liable for actual damages, plus additional damages not to exceed $1,000 and attorneys' fees.[24] Damages are also available against anyone who uses a credit report for an improper purpose, as well as banks, credit-card companies, and other businesses that report information to credit agencies and do not respond adequately to customer complaints.

The Fair Debt Collection Practices Act. In 1977, Congress enacted the Fair Debt Collection Practices Act (FDCPA)[25] in an attempt to curb what were perceived to be abuses by collection agencies. The act applies only to specialized debt-collection agencies that regularly attempt to collect debts on behalf of someone else, usually for a percentage of the amount owed. Creditors attempting to collect debts are not covered by the act unless, by misrepresenting themselves, they cause debtors to believe they are collection agencies. The act explicitly prohibits a collection agency from using any of the following tactics:

1. Contacting the debtor at the debtor's place of employment if the debtor's employer objects.
2. Contacting the debtor during inconvenient or unusual times (for example, calling the debtor at three

---

21. 15 U.S.C. Sections 1667–1667e.
22. 12 C.F.R. Part 213.
23. 15 U.S.C. Sections 1681–1681t.

24. 15 U.S.C. Section 1681n.
25. 15 U.S.C. Section 1692.

o'clock in the morning) or at any time if the debtor is being represented by an attorney.

3. Contacting third parties other than the debtor's parents, spouse, or financial adviser about payment of a debt unless a court authorizes such action.

4. Using harassment or intimidation (for example, using abusive language or threatening violence) or employing false or misleading information (for example, posing as a police officer).

5. Communicating with the debtor at any time after receiving notice that the debtor is refusing to pay the debt, except to advise the debtor of further action to be taken by the collection agency.

The FDCPA also requires a collection agency to include a **validation notice** whenever it initially contacts a debtor for payment of a debt or within five days of that initial contact. The notice must state that the debtor has thirty days within which to dispute the debt and to request a written verification of the debt from the collection agency. The debtor's request for debt validation must be in writing.

The enforcement of the FDCPA is primarily the responsibility of the Federal Trade Commission. The act provides that a debt collector that fails to comply with

the act is liable for actual damages, plus additional damages not to exceed $1,000[26] and attorneys' fees.

Cases brought under the FDCPA often raise questions as to who qualifies as a debt collector or debt-collection agency subject to the act. For example, for several years it was not clear whether attorneys who attempted to collect debts owed to their clients were subject to the FDCPA's provisions. In 1995, the United States Supreme Court addressed this issue to resolve conflicting opinions in the lower courts. The Court held that an attorney who regularly tries to obtain payment of consumer debts through legal proceedings meets the FDCPA's definition of "debt collector."[27]

Another question that sometimes arises in the context of FDCPA litigation has to do with what, exactly, constitutes a "debt." In the following case, the court considered whether a dishonored check constituted a "debt" within the meaning of the FDCPA.

---

26. According to the U.S. Court of Appeals for the Sixth Circuit, the $1,000 limit on damages applies to each lawsuit, not to each violation. See *Wright v. Finance Service of Norwalk, Inc.*, 22 F.3d 647 (6th Cir. 1994).

27. *Heintz v. Jenkins*, 514 U.S. 291, 115 S.Ct. 1489, 131 L.Ed.2d 395 (1995).

CASE 44.2   Snow v. Jesse L. Riddle, P.C.

United States
Court of Appeals,
Tenth Circuit, 1998.
143 F.3d 1350.
http://www.kscourts.
org/ca10[a]

HISTORICAL AND SOCIAL SETTING   *The FDCPA defines debt as "any obligatory or alleged obligation of a consumer to pay money arising out of a transaction in which the money, property, insurance, or services which are the subject of the transaction are primarily for personal, family, or household purposes, whether or not such obligation has been reduced to judgment."[b] At one time, it was generally held that the type of transaction giving rise to a debt, within this definition, is the same type of transaction that is dealt with in all other parts of the Consumer Credit Protection Act: a transaction that involves an offer or extension of credit to a consumer. By the time the U.S. Court of Appeals for the Tenth Circuit decided this case, however, this view had changed.*

BACKGROUND AND FACTS   *At a Circle-K store, Alan Snow paid for merchandise with his personal check in the amount of $23.12. Circle-K deposited the check at its bank, but the check was dishonored because of insufficient funds. Circle-K sent the returned check to its attorney, Jesse L. Riddle, P.C., for collection. In a letter to Snow, Riddle wrote that "the check amount, along with a service fee of $15, must be paid within seven (7) days of this notice. If it is not paid, * * * [a] suit [will] be filed." Snow paid the check and then filed a suit in a federal district court against Riddle. Snow alleged in part that Riddle's letter violated the FDCPA because it did not contain a "validation notice." Riddle*

---

a. Washburn University School of Law maintains this Web site. Click on "Finding lists by plaintiff/defendant case name." After the page loads, scroll to the case name and click on it to access the opinion.
b. 15 U.S.C. Section 1692a(5).

filed a motion to dismiss on the ground that the FDCPA does not cover a dishonored check because it is not an "offer or extension of credit." The court granted the motion, and Snow appealed to the U.S. Court of Appeals for the Tenth Circuit.

IN THE LANGUAGE OF THE COURT

McWILLIAMS, Senior Circuit Judge.

* * * *

[The FDCPA] provides as follows:

* * * Abusive debt collection practices contribute to the number of personal bankruptcies, to marital instability, to the loss of jobs, and to invasions of individual privacy. * * * It is the purpose of [the FDCPA] to eliminate abusive debt collection practices by debt collectors * * * .

* * * *

* * * [A] payment obligation arising from a dishonored check create[s] a "debt" triggering the protections of the [FDCPA]. * * * [A]n offer or extension of credit is not required for a payment obligation to constitute a "debt" under the [FDCPA]. * * *

* * * *

* * * Under the "plain meaning" test, it would seem to us that a "debt" is created where one obtains goods and gives a dishonored check in return therefor.

DECISION AND REMEDY

The U.S. Court of Appeals for the Tenth Circuit reversed the decision of the lower court and remanded the case. The appellate court held that a dishonored check constitutes a debt within the meaning of the FDCPA.

Garnishment of Wages. Despite the increasing number of protections afforded debtors, creditors are not without means of securing payment on debts. One of these is the right to garnish a debtor's wages after the debt has gone uncollected for a prolonged period. Recall from Chapter 29 that *garnishment* is the legal procedure by which a creditor may collect on a debt by directly attaching, or seizing, a portion of the debtor's assets (such as wages) that are in the possession of a third party (such as an employer).

State law provides the basis for a process of garnishment, but the law varies among the states as to how easily garnishment can be obtained. Indeed, a few states, such as Texas, prohibit garnishment of wages altogether except for child support. In addition, constitutional due process and federal legislation under the TILA provide further protections against abuse.[28] In general, the debtor is entitled to notice and an opportunity to be heard in a process of garnishment. Moreover, wages cannot be garnished beyond 25 percent of the debtor's after-tax earnings, and the garnishment must leave the debtor with at least a specified minimum income.

CONSUMER HEALTH AND SAFETY

Laws discussed earlier regarding the labeling and packaging of products go a long way toward promoting consumer health and safety. But there is a significant distinction between regulating the information dispensed about a product and regulating the content of the product. The classic example is tobacco products. Tobacco products have not been altered by regulation or banned outright despite their obvious hazards. What has been regulated are the warnings that producers are required to give consumers about the hazards of tobacco.[29] This section focuses on laws that regulate the actual products made available to consumers.

The Federal Food, Drug and Cosmetic Act. The first federal legislation regulating food and drugs was enacted in 1906 as the Pure Food and Drugs Act. That law, as amended in 1938, exists presently as the Federal Food, Drug and Cosmetic Act (FFDCA).[30]

---

29. We are ignoring recent civil litigation concerning the liability of tobacco product manufacturers for injuries that arise from the use of tobacco.

30. 21 U.S.C. Sections 301–393.

28. 15 U.S.C. Sections 1671–1677.

The act protects consumers against adulterated and misbranded foods and drugs. More recent amendments have added substantive and procedural requirements to the act. In its present form, the act establishes food standards, specifies safe levels of potentially hazardous food additives, and sets classifications of food and food advertising.

Most of these statutory requirements are monitored and enforced by the Food and Drug Administration (FDA). Under an extensive set of procedures established by the FDA, drugs must be shown to be effective as well as safe before they may be marketed to the public, and the use of some food additives suspected of being carcinogenic is prohibited. A 1976 amendment to the FFDCA[31] authorizes the FDA to regulate medical devices, such as pacemakers and other health devices and equipment, and to withdraw from the market any such device that is mislabeled.

The Consumer Product Safety Act. Consumer product-safety legislation began in 1953 with the passage of the Flammable Fabrics Act, which prohibits the sale of highly flammable clothing or materials. Over the next two decades, Congress enacted legislation regarding the design or composition of specific classes of products. Then, in 1972, Congress, by enacting the Consumer Product Safety Act,[32] created a comprehensive scheme of regulation over matters of consumer safety. The act also established far-reaching authority over consumer safety under the Consumer Product Safety Commission (CPSC).

The CPSC conducts research on the safety of individual products, and it maintains a clearinghouse of information on the risks associated with various consumer products. The Consumer Product Safety Act authorizes the CPSC to set standards for consumer products and to ban the manufacture and sale of any product that it deems to be potentially hazardous to consumers. The CPSC also has authority to remove from the market any products it believes to be imminently hazardous and to require manufacturers to report on any products already sold or intended for sale if the products have proved to be dangerous. The CPSC also has authority to administer other product-safety legislation, such as the Child Protection and Toy Safety Act of 1969[33] and the Federal Hazardous Substances Act of 1960.[34]

The CPSC's authority is sufficiently broad to allow it to ban any product that it believes poses an "unreasonable risk" to consumers. Some of the products that the CPSC has banned include various types of fireworks, cribs, and toys, as well as many products containing asbestos or vinyl chloride.

STATE CONSUMER PROTECTION LAWS

Thus far, our primary focus has been on federal legislation. State laws, however, often provide more sweeping and significant protections for the consumer than do federal laws. The warranty and unconscionability provisions of the Uniform Commercial Code (discussed in Chapters 19 through 23) offer important protections for consumers against unfair practices on the part of sellers and lessors. The Magnuson-Moss Warranty Act, which was discussed in Chapter 23, supplements the UCC provisions in cases involving both a consumer transaction of at least $10 and an express written warranty.

Far less widely adopted than the UCC is the Uniform Consumer Credit Code (UCCC). The UCCC has provisions concerning truth in lending, maximum credit ceilings, door-to-door sales, fine-print clauses, and other practices affecting consumer transactions.

Virtually all states have specific consumer protection acts, often titled "deceptive trade practices acts." Although state consumer protection statutes vary widely in their provisions, a common thread runs through most of them. Typically, state consumer protection laws are directed at deceptive trade practices, such as a seller's providing false or misleading information to consumers. As just mentioned, some of the legislation provides broad protection for consumers. A prime example is the Texas Deceptive Trade Practices Act of 1973, which forbids a seller from selling to a buyer anything that the buyer does not need or cannot afford.

SECTION 2

Environmental Law

We now turn to a discussion of the various ways in which businesses are regulated by the government in

---

31. 21 U.S.C. Sections 352(o), 360(j), 360(k), and 360c–360k.
32. 15 U.S.C. Sections 2051–2083.
33. This act consists of amendments to 15 U.S.C. Sections 1261, 1262, and 1274.
34. 15 U.S.C. Sections 1261–1277.

the interest of protecting the environment. To a great extent, environmental law consists of statutes passed by federal, state, or local governments and regulations issued by administrative agencies. Before examining statutory and regulatory environmental laws, however, we look at the remedies against environmental pollution available under the common law.

COMMON LAW ACTIONS

Common law remedies against environmental pollution originated centuries ago in England. Those responsible for operations that created dirt, smoke, noxious odors, noise, or toxic substances were sometimes held liable under common law theories of nuisance or negligence. Today, injured individuals continue to rely on the common law to obtain damages and injunctions against business polluters. (Statutory remedies are also available, a topic that we treat later.)

Nuisance.   Under the common law doctrine of **nuisance,** persons may be held liable if they use their property in a manner that unreasonably interferes with others' rights to use or enjoy their own property. In these situations, it is common for courts to balance the equities between the harm caused by the pollution and the costs of stopping it.

Courts have often denied injunctive relief on the ground that the hardships to be imposed on the polluter and on the community are greater than the hardships to be suffered by the plaintiff. For example, a factory that causes neighboring landowners to suffer from smoke, dirt, and vibrations may be left in operation if it is the core of a local economy. The injured parties may be awarded only money damages. These damages may include compensation for the decreased value of their property that results from the factory's operation.

A property owner may be given relief from pollution in situations in which he or she can identify a distinct harm separate from that affecting the general public. This harm is referred to as a "private" nuisance. Under the common law, citizens were denied standing (access to the courts—see Chapter 2) unless they suffered a harm distinct from the harm suffered by the public at large. Some states still require this. Therefore, a group of citizens who wished to stop a new development that would cause significant water pollution was denied access to the courts on the ground that the harm to them did not differ from the

harm to the general public.[35] A public authority (such as a state's attorney general) can sue to abate a "public" nuisance.

Negligence and Strict Liability.   An injured party may sue a business polluter in tort under the negligence and strict liability theories discussed in Chapters 5 and 6. The basis for a negligence action is a business's alleged failure to use reasonable care toward a party whose injury was foreseeable and, of course, caused by the lack of reasonable care. For example, employees might sue an employer whose failure to use proper pollution controls contaminated the air, causing the employees to suffer respiratory illnesses. A developing area of tort law involves **toxic torts**—actions against toxic polluters.

Businesses that engage in ultrahazardous activities—such as the transportation of radioactive materials—are strictly liable for whatever injuries the activities cause. In a strict liability action, the injured party does not need to prove that the business failed to exercise reasonable care.

STATE AND LOCAL REGULATION

Many states regulate the degree to which the environment may be polluted. Thus, for example, even when state zoning laws permit a business's proposed development, the proposal may have to be altered to change the development's impact on the environment. State laws may restrict a business's discharge of chemicals into the air or water or regulate its disposal of toxic wastes. States may also regulate the disposal or recycling of other wastes, including glass, metal, and plastic containers and paper. Additionally, states may restrict the emissions from motor vehicles.

City, county, and other local governments control some aspects of the environment. For instance, local zoning laws control some land use. These laws may be designed to inhibit or direct the growth of cities and suburbs or to protect the natural environment. Other aspects of the environment may be subject to local regulation for other reasons. Methods of waste and garbage removal and disposal, for example, can have a substantial impact on a community. The appearance of buildings and other structures, including advertising signs and billboards, may affect traffic safety, property values, or local aesthetics. Noise generated by a

---

35. *Save the Bay Committee, Inc. v. Mayor of City of Savannah,* 227 Ga. 436, 181 S.E.2d 351 (1971).

business or its customers may be annoying, disruptive, or damaging to its neighbors. The location and condition of parks, streets, and other public uses of land subject to local control affect the environment and can also affect business.

FEDERAL REGULATION

Congress has passed a number of statutes to control the impact of human activities on the environment. Exhibit 44–2 on the next page lists and summarizes the major federal environmental statutes discussed in this chapter. Some of these statutes were passed in an attempt to improve air and water quality. Others specifically regulate toxic chemicals—including pesticides, herbicides, and hazardous wastes.

The most well known of the agencies regulating environmental law is the Environmental Protection Agency (EPA), which was created in 1970 to coordinate federal environmental responsibilities. Other federal agencies with authority for regulating specific environmental matters include the Department of the Interior, the Department of Defense, the Department of Labor, the Food and Drug Administration, and the Nuclear Regulatory Commission. These regulatory agencies—and all other agencies of the federal government—must take environmental factors into consideration when making significant decisions.

The National Environmental Policy Act (NEPA) of 1969[36] requires that for every major federal action that significantly affects the quality of the environment, an **environmental impact statement (EIS)** must be prepared. An EIS must analyze (1) the impact on the environment that the action will have, (2) any adverse effects on the environment and alternative actions that might be taken, and (3) irreversible effects the action might generate. EISs have become instruments for private citizens, consumer interest groups, businesses, and others to challenge federal agency actions on the basis that the actions improperly threaten the environment.

Other federal laws also require that environmental values be considered in agency decision making. Among the most important of these laws are those that have been enacted to protect fish and wildlife. Under the Fish and Wildlife Coordination Act of 1958,[37] federal agencies proposing to approve the impounding or diversion of a stream's waters must consult with the Fish and Wildlife Service with a view to preventing the loss of fish and wildlife resources. Also important is the Endangered Species Act of 1973.[38] Under this act, all federal agencies are required to take steps to ensure that their actions "do not jeopardize the continued existence of endangered species" or the habitat of an endangered species. An action may jeopardize the continued existence of a species if it sets in motion a chain of events that reduces the chances that the species will survive.

AIR POLLUTION

Federal involvement with air pollution goes back to the 1950s, when Congress authorized funds for air-pollution research. In 1963, the federal government passed the Clean Air Act,[39] which focused on multistate air pollution and provided assistance to states. Various amendments, particularly in 1970, 1977, and 1990, strengthened the government's authority to regulate air quality. These laws provide the basis for issuing regulations to control pollution coming primarily from mobile sources (such as automobiles) and stationary sources (such as electric utilities and industrial plants).

Mobile Sources. Regulations governing air pollution from automobiles and other mobile sources specify pollution standards and time schedules for meeting these standards. For example, under the 1990 amendments to the Clean Air Act, automobile manufacturers must cut new automobiles' exhaust emission of nitrogen oxide by 60 percent and emission of other pollutants by 35 percent. By 1998, all new automobiles had to meet this standard. Regulations that will go into effect beginning with 2004 model cars call for cutting nitrogen oxide tailpipe emissions by nearly 10 percent by 2007. For the first time, sport utility vehicles and light trucks were also required to meet the same emission standards as automobiles.

Service stations are also subject to environmental regulations. The 1990 amendments require service stations to sell gasoline with a higher oxygen content in forty-one cities that experience carbon monoxide pollution in the winter. Service stations are required to sell even cleaner burning gasoline in Los Angeles and another eight of the most polluted urban areas.

The EPA attempts to update pollution-control standards when new scientific information becomes

---

36. 42 U.S.C. Sections 4321–4370d.
37. 16 U.S.C. Sections 661–666c.

38. 16 U.S.C. Sections 1531–1544.
39. 42 U.S.C. Sections 7401–7671q.

EXHIBIT 44–2   FEDERAL ENVIRONMENTAL STATUTES

POPULAR NAME	PURPOSE	STATUTE REFERENCE
Rivers and Harbors Appropriations Act (1899)	To prohibit ships and manufacturers from discharging and depositing refuse in navigable waterways.	33 U.S.C. Sections 401–418.
Federal Insecticide, Fungicide, and Rodenticide Act (FIFRA) (1947)	To control the use of pesticides and herbicides.	7 U.S.C. Sections 136–136y.
Federal Water Pollution Control Act (FWPCA) (1948)	To eliminate the discharge of pollutants from major sources into navigable waters.	33 U.S.C. Sections 1251–1387.
Atomic Energy Act (1954)	To limit environmental harm from the private nuclear industry.	42 U.S.C. Sections 2011 to 2297g-4.
Clean Air Act (1963)	To control air pollution from mobile and stationary sources.	42 U.S.C. Sections 7401–7671q.
National Environmental Policy Act (NEPA) (1969)	To limit environmental harm from federal government activities.	42 U.S.C. Sections 4321–4370d.
Marine Protection, Research, and Sanctuaries Act (Ocean Dumping Act) of 1972	To regulate the transporting and dumping of material into ocean waters.	16 U.S.C. Sections 1401–1445.
Noise Control Act (1972)	To regulate noise pollution from transportation and nontransportation sources.	42 U.S.C. Sections 4901–4918.
Endangered Species Act (1973)	To protect species that are threatened with extinction.	16 U.S.C. Sections 1531–1544.
Safe Drinking Water Act (1974)	To regulate pollutants in public drinking water systems.	42 U.S.C. Sections 300f to 300j-25.
Resource Conservation and Recovery Act (RCRA) (1976)	To establish standards for hazardous waste disposal.	42 U.S.C. Sections 6901–6986.
Toxic Substances Control Act (1976)	To regulate toxic chemicals and chemical compounds.	15 U.S.C. Sections 2601–2692.
Comprehensive Environmental Response, Compensation, and Liability Act (CERCLA) (Superfund) (1980)	To regulate the clean-up of hazardous waste-disposal sites.	42 U.S.C. Sections 9601–9675.
Low Level Radioactive Waste Policy Act (1980)	To assign to the states responsibility for nuclear power plants' low-level radioactive waste.	42 U.S.C. Sections 2021b–2021j.
Nuclear Waste Policy Act (1982)	To provide for the designation of a permanent radioactive waste-disposal site.	42 U.S.C. Sections 10101–10270.
Oil Pollution Act (1990)	To establish liability for the clean-up of navigable waters after oil-spill disasters.	33 U.S.C. Sections 2701–2761.

available. In light of evidence that very small particles (2.5 microns, or millionths of a meter) of soot affect our health as significantly as larger particles, the EPA issued new particulate standards for motor vehicle exhaust systems and other sources of pollution. The EPA also increased the acceptable standard for ozone, which is formed when sunlight combines with pollutants from cars and other sources. Ozone is the basic ingredient of smog. The EPA's particulate standards and the acceptable standard for ozone are being challenged in the courts.[40] Meanwhile, the old standards are in force.

Stationary Sources.

The Clean Air Act authorizes the EPA to establish air-quality standards for stationary sources (such as manufacturing plants) but recognizes that the primary responsibility for preventing and controlling air pollution rests with state and local governments. The EPA sets primary and secondary levels of ambient standards—that is, the maximum levels of certain pollutants—and the states formulate plans to achieve those standards. The plans are to provide for the attainment of primary standards within three years and secondary standards within a reasonable time. For economic, political, and technological reasons, however, the deadlines are often subject to change.

Different standards apply to sources of pollution in clean areas and those in polluted areas. Different standards also apply to existing sources of pollution and major new sources. Major new sources include existing sources modified by a change in a method of operation that increases emissions. Performance standards for major sources require use of the *maximum achievable control technology*, or MACT, to reduce emissions from the combustion of fossil fuels (coal and oil). As mentioned, the EPA issues guidelines as to what equipment meets this standard.

Under the 1990 amendments to the Clean Air Act, 110 of the oldest coal-burning power plants in the United States must cut their emissions by 40 percent by the year 2001 to reduce acid rain. Utilities were granted "credits" to emit certain amounts of sulfur dioxide, and those that emit less than the allowed amounts can sell their credits to other polluters. Controls on other factories and businesses are intended to reduce ground-level ozone pollution in ninety-six cities to healthful levels by 2005 (except Los Angeles, which has until 2010). Industrial emissions of 189 hazardous air pollutants must be reduced by 90 percent by 2000. By 2002, the production of chlorofluorocarbons (such as Freon),

carbon tetrachloride, and methyl chloroform—used in air conditioning, refrigeration, and insulation and linked to depletion of the ozone layer—must stop.

Hazardous Air Pollutants.

Hazardous air pollutants are those likely to cause an increase in mortality or in serious irreversible or incapacitating illness. As noted, there are 189 of these pollutants, including asbestos, benzene, beryllium, cadmium, mercury, and vinyl chloride. These pollutants may cause cancer as well as neurological and reproductive damage. They are emitted from stationary sources by a variety of business activities, including smelting, dry cleaning, house painting, and commercial baking. Instead of establishing specific emissions standards for each hazardous air pollutant, the 1990 amendments to the Clean Air Act require industry to use pollution-control equipment that represents the maximum achievable control technology, or MACT, to limit emissions. As mentioned, the EPA issues guidelines as to what equipment meets this standard.

In 1996, the EPA issued a rule to regulate hazardous air pollutants emitted by landfills. The rule requires landfills constructed after May 30, 1991, that emit more than a specified amount of pollutants to install landfill gas collection and control systems. The rule also requires the states to impose the same requirements on landfills constructed before May 30, 1991, if they accepted waste after November 8, 1987.[41]

Violations of the Clean Air Act.

For violations of emission limits under the Clean Air Act, the EPA can assess civil penalties of up to $25,000 per day. Additional fines of up to $5,000 per day can be assessed for other violations, such as failing to maintain the required records. To penalize those for whom it is more cost effective to violate the act than to comply with it, the EPA is authorized to obtain a penalty equal to the violator's economic benefits from noncompliance. Persons who provide information about violators may be paid up to $10,000. Private citizens can also sue violators.

Those who knowingly violate the act may be subject to criminal penalties, including fines of up to $1 million and imprisonment for up to two years (for false statements or failures to report violations). Corporate officers are among those who may be subject to these penalties.

---

40. See, for example, *American Trucking Associations v. Environmental Protection Agency*, 175 F.3d 1027 (D.C.Cir. 1999), modified on rehearing, 195 F.3d 4 (D.C.Cir. 1999); and *American Petroleum Institute v. U.S. Environmental Protection Agency*, 198 F.3d 275 (D.C.Cir. 2000).

41. 40 C.F.R. Sections 60.750–759.

WATER POLLUTION

Federal regulations governing water pollution can be traced back to the Rivers and Harbors Appropriations Act of 1899.[42] These regulations prohibited ships and manufacturers from discharging or depositing refuse in navigable waterways.

Navigable Waters.   Once limited to waters actually used for navigation, the term *navigable waters* is today interpreted to include intrastate lakes and streams used by interstate travelers and industries, as well as coastal and freshwater wetlands. (The EPA defines **wetlands** as "those areas that are inundated or saturated by surface or ground water at a frequency and duration sufficient to support, and that under normal circumstances do support, a prevalence of vegetation typically adapted for life in saturated soil conditions.") In 1948, Congress passed the Federal Water Pollution Control Act (FWPCA),[43] but its regulatory system and enforcement proved inadequate. In 1972, amendments to the FWPCA—known as the Clean Water Act—established the following goals: (1) make waters safe for swimming, (2) protect fish and wildlife, and (3) eliminate the discharge of pollutants into the water. The amendments required that municipal and industrial polluters apply for permits before discharging wastes into navigable waters.

They also set forth specific time schedules, which were extended by amendment in 1977 and by the Water Quality Act of 1987.[44] Under these schedules, the EPA establishes limitations for discharges of types of pollutants based on the technology available for controlling them. Regulations, for the most part, specify that the *best available control technology*, or BACT, be installed. The EPA issues guidelines as to what equipment meets this standard, which essentially requires the most effective pollution-control equipment available. New sources must install BACT equipment before beginning operations. Existing sources are subject to timetables for installation of BACT equipment. These sources must immediately install equipment that utilizes the *best practical control technology*, or BPCT. The EPA also issues guidelines as to what equipment meets this standard.

Under the Clean Water Act, violators are subject to a variety of civil and criminal penalties. Depending on the violation, civil penalties range from a maximum of $10,000 per day, and not more than $25,000 per violation, to as much as $25,000 per day. Criminal penalties range from a fine of $2,500 per day and imprisonment for up to one year to a fine of $1 million and fifteen years' imprisonment. Injunctive relief and damages can also be imposed. The polluting party can be required to clean up the pollution or pay for the cost of doing so. Criminal penalties apply only if a violation was intentional.

Drinking Water.   Another statute governing water pollution is the Safe Drinking Water Act.[45] Passed in 1974, this act requires the EPA to set maximum levels for pollutants in public water systems. Operators of public water supply systems must come as close as possible to meeting the EPA's standards by using the best available technology that is economically and technologically feasible. The EPA is particularly concerned with contamination from underground sources. Pesticides and wastes leaked from landfills or disposed of in underground injection wells are among the more than two hundred pollutants known to exist in groundwater used for drinking in at least thirty-four states. Many of these substances are associated with cancer and damage to the central nervous system, liver, and kidneys.

The act was amended in 1996 to give the EPA greater flexibility in setting regulatory standards governing drinking water. Prior to the 1996 amendments, the EPA had to set standards for twenty-five different drinking water contaminants every three years, which it had largely failed to do. Under the 1996 amendments, the EPA can move at whatever rate it deems necessary to control contaminants that are of greatest concern to the public health. The 1996 amendments also imposed new requirements on suppliers of drinking water. Each supplier must send to every household it supplies with water an annual statement describing the source of its water, the level of any contaminants contained in the water, and any possible health concerns associated with the contaminants.

Ocean Dumping.   The Marine Protection, Research, and Sanctuaries Act of 1972[46] (known popularly as the Ocean Dumping Act) regulates the transportation and dumping of material into ocean waters. (The term *material* is synonymous with the

---

42. 33 U.S.C. Sections 401–418.
43. 33 U.S.C. Sections 1251–1387.
44. This act amended 33 U.S.C. Section 1251.

45. 42 U.S.C. Sections 300f to 300j-25.
46. 16 U.S.C. Sections 1401–1445.

term *pollutant* as used in the Federal Water Pollution Control Act.) The Ocean Dumping Act prohibits entirely the ocean-dumping of radiological, chemical, and biological warfare agents and high-level radioactive waste. The act establishes a permit program for transporting and dumping other materials. There are specific exemptions—materials subject to the permit provisions of other pollution legislation, wastes from structures regulated by other laws (for example, offshore oil exploration and drilling platforms), sewage, and other wastes. The Ocean Dumping Act also authorizes the designation of marine sanctuaries for "preserving or restoring such areas for their conservation, recreational, ecological, or esthetic values."

Each violation of any provision or permit may result in a civil penalty of not more than $50,000 or revocation or suspension of the permit. A knowing violation is a criminal offense that may result in a $50,000 fine, imprisonment for not more than a year, or both. An injunction may also be imposed.

Oil Pollution. The Oil Pollution Act of 1990[47] provides that any onshore or offshore oil facility, oil shipper, vessel owner, or vessel operator that discharges oil into navigable waters or onto an adjoining shore may be liable for clean-up costs, as well as damages. The act created a $1 billion oil clean-up and economic compensation fund and decreed that by the year 2011, oil tankers using U.S. ports must be double hulled to limit the severity of accidental spills.

Under the act, damage to natural resources, private property, and the local economy, including the increased cost of providing public services, is compensable. The act provides for civil penalties of $1,000 per barrel spilled or $25,000 for each day of the violation. The party held responsible for the clean-up costs can bring a civil suit for contribution from other potentially liable parties.

NOISE POLLUTION

Regulations concerning noise pollution include the Noise Control Act of 1972.[48] This act requires the EPA to establish noise emission standards (maximum noise levels below which no harmful effects occur from interference with speech or other activity)—for example, for railroad noise emissions. The standards must be achievable by the best available technology, and they must be economically within reason.

The act prohibits, among other things, distributing products manufactured in violation of the noise emission standards and tampering with noise control devices. Either of these activities can result in an injunction or whatever other remedy "is necessary to protect the public health and welfare." Illegal product distribution can also result in a fine and imprisonment. Violations of provisions of the Noise Control Act can result in penalties of not more than $50,000 per day and imprisonment for not more than two years.

TOXIC CHEMICALS

Originally, most environmental clean-up efforts were directed toward reducing smog and making water safe for fishing and swimming. Over time, however, control of toxic chemicals has become an important part of environmental law.

Pesticides and Herbicides. The federal statute regulating pesticides and herbicides is the Federal Insecticide, Fungicide, and Rodenticide Act (FIFRA) of 1947.[49] Under FIFRA, pesticides and herbicides must be (1) registered before they can be sold, (2) certified and used only for approved applications, and (3) used in limited quantities when applied to food crops. If a substance is identified as harmful, the EPA can cancel its registration after a hearing. If the harm is imminent, the EPA can suspend registration pending the hearing. The EPA, or state officers or employees, may also inspect factories in which these chemicals are manufactured.

Under 1996 amendments to the Federal Food, Drug and Cosmetic Act, for a pesticide to remain on the market, there must be a "reasonable certainty of no harm" to people from exposure to the pesticide.[50] This means that there must be no more than a one-in-a-million risk to people of developing cancer from exposure in any way, including eating food that contains residues from the pesticide. Pesticide residues are in nearly all fruits and vegetables and processed foods. Under the 1996 amendments, the EPA must distribute to grocery stores brochures on high-risk pesticides that are in food, and the stores must display these brochures for consumers.

---

47. 33 U.S.C. Sections 2701–2761.
48. 42 U.S.C. Sections 4901–4918.

49. 7 U.S.C. Sections 136–136y.
50. 21 U.S.C. Section 346a.

It is a violation of FIFRA to sell a pesticide or herbicide that is unregistered, a pesticide or herbicide with a registration that has been canceled or suspended, or a pesticide or herbicide with a false or misleading label. For example, it is an offense to sell a substance that is adulterated (that has a chemical strength different from the concentration declared on the label). It is also an offense to destroy or deface any labeling required under the act. The act's labeling requirements include directions for the use of the pesticide or herbicide, warnings to protect human health and the environment, a statement of treatment in the case of poisoning, and a list of the ingredients.

A private party can petition the EPA to suspend or cancel the registration of a pesticide or herbicide. If the EPA fails to act, the private party can petition a federal court to review the EPA's failure. Penalties for registrants and producers for violating FIFRA include imprisonment for up to one year and a fine of no more than $50,000. Penalties for commercial dealers include imprisonment for up to one year and a fine of no more than $25,000. Farmers and other private users of pesticides or herbicides who violate the act are subject to a $1,000 fine and imprisonment for up to thirty days.

Toxic Substances. The first comprehensive law covering toxic substances was the Toxic Substances Control Act of 1976.[51] The act was passed to regulate chemicals and chemical compounds that are known to be toxic—such as asbestos and polychlorinated biphenyls, popularly known as PCBs—and to institute investigation of any possible harmful effects from new chemical compounds. The regulations authorize the EPA to require that manufacturers, processors, and other organizations planning to use chemicals first determine their effects on human health and the environment. The EPA can regulate substances that may pose an imminent hazard or an unreasonable risk of injury to health or the environment. The EPA may require special labeling, limit the use of a substance, set production quotas, or prohibit the use of a substance altogether.

HAZARDOUS WASTES

Some industrial, agricultural, and household wastes pose more serious threats than others. If not properly disposed of, these toxic chemicals may present a substantial danger to human health and the environment. If released into the environment, they may contaminate public drinking water resources.

Resource Conservation and Recovery Act. In 1976, Congress passed the Resource Conservation and Recovery Act (RCRA)[52] in reaction to an ever-increasing concern with the effects of hazardous waste materials on the environment. The RCRA required the EPA to establish regulations to monitor and control hazardous waste disposal and to determine which forms of solid waste should be considered hazardous and thus subject to regulation. The act authorized the EPA to promulgate various technical requirements for some types of facilities for storage and treatment of hazardous waste. The act also requires all producers of hazardous waste materials to label and package properly any hazardous waste to be transported.

The RCRA was amended in 1984 and 1986 to decrease the use of land containment in the disposal of hazardous waste and to require compliance with the act by some generators of hazardous waste—such as those generating less than 1,000 kilograms (2,200 pounds) a month—that had previously been excluded from regulation under the RCRA.

Under the RCRA, a company may be assessed a civil penalty based on the seriousness of the violation, the probability of harm, and the extent to which the violation deviates from RCRA requirements. The assessment may be up to $25,000 for each violation. Criminal penalties include fines up to $50,000 for each day of violation, imprisonment for up to two years (in most instances), or both. Criminal fines and the time of imprisonment can be doubled for certain repeat offenders.

Superfund. In 1980, the U.S. Congress passed the Comprehensive Environmental Response, Compensation, and Liability Act (CERCLA),[53] commonly known as Superfund. The basic purpose of Superfund is to regulate the clean-up of disposal sites in which hazardous waste is leaking into the environment. A special federal fund was created for that purpose.

Superfund provides that when a release or a threatened release of hazardous chemicals from a site occurs, the EPA can clean up the site and recover the cost of the clean-up from the following persons: (1) the

---

51. 15 U.S.C. Sections 2601–2692.

52. 42 U.S.C. Sections 6901–6986.
53. 42 U.S.C. Sections 9601–9675.

person who generated the wastes disposed of at the site, (2) the person who transported the wastes to the site, (3) the person who owned or operated the site at the time of the disposal, or (4) the current owner or operator. A person falling within one of these categories is referred to as a **potentially responsible party (PRP)**.

Liability under Superfund is usually joint and several—that is, a PRP who generated only a fraction of the hazardous waste disposed of at the site may nevertheless be liable for all of the clean-up costs. CERCLA authorizes a party who has incurred clean-up costs to bring a "contribution action" against any other person who is liable or potentially liable for a percentage of the costs. The following case involved a challenge to a court's allocation of clean-up costs among PRPs.

CASE 44.3   ### Browning-Ferris Industries of Illinois, Inc. v. Ter Maat

United States
Court of Appeals,
Seventh Circuit, 1999.
195 F.3d 953.
http://www.ca7.
uscourts.gov[a]

BACKGROUND AND FACTS   *In 1971, the owners of a landfill leased it to a company that later became Browning-Ferris Industries of Illinois, Inc., which operated it until the fall of 1975. During that time, the operator illegally dumped at the site a large quantity of particularly toxic wastes from an auto plant run by Chrysler Corporation. Between the fall of 1975 and 1988, M.I.G. Investments, Inc., and AAA Disposal Systems, Inc., operated the landfill. Richard Ter Maat was the president and principal shareholder of M.I.G. and AAA. In June 1988, after AAA was sold and Ter Maat moved to Florida, M.I.G. abandoned the landfill without covering it properly. Two years later, the EPA ordered that the site be cleaned up. Browning-Ferris, and other companies that shared responsibility for the pollution at the site, agreed to clean it up. Browning-Ferris and the others then filed a suit in a federal district court against Ter Maat, M.I.G., and AAA under CERCLA to recover the costs. The court ruled, among other things, that 45 percent of the costs was allocable to the owners of the landfill and the generators of the toxic wastes dumped in it, 22 percent was the responsibility of Browning-Ferris, and the other 33 percent was the responsibility of M.I.G. and AAA. The plaintiffs appealed to the U.S. Court of Appeals for the Seventh Circuit. Browning-Ferris claimed in part that too much of the liability for the pollution at the site had been allocated to it relative to M.I.G. and AAA. Browning-Ferris argued that the costs should be allocated according to the volume of wastes for which each party was responsible.*

IN THE LANGUAGE OF THE COURT   POSNER, Chief Judge.
*   *   *   *

The *   *   * question *   *   * is whether the court must find a causal relation between a party's pollution and the actual cost of cleaning up the site. To answer this question we have to distinguish between a necessary condition (or "but-for cause") and a sufficient condition. If event A is a necessary condition of event B, this means that, without A, B will not occur. If A is a sufficient condition of B, this means that, if A occurs, B will occur. If A is that the murder weapon was loaded and B is the murder, then A is a necessary condition. If A is shooting a person through the heart and B is the death of the shooting victim, then A is a sufficient condition of B but not a necessary condition, because a wound to another part of the victim's body might have been fatal as well.

This distinction may sometimes be important in the pollution context. It is easy to imagine a case in which, had X not polluted a site, no clean-up costs would have been incurred; X's pollution would be a necessary condition of those costs and it would be natural to think that he should pay at least a part of them. But suppose that even if X had not polluted the site, it would have to be cleaned up—and at the same cost—because of the amount of pollution by Y. *   *   * Then X's pollution would not be a necessary

---

a. In the left-hand column, click on "Judicial Opinions." On that page, in the "Last Name or Corporation" section, click on "Begins," enter "Browning-Ferris" in the box, and click on "Search for Person." When the result appears, click on the docket number for the case to access the opinion.

condition of the clean up, or of any of the costs incurred in the clean up. But that should not necessarily let X off the hook. For suppose that though if X had not polluted the site at all there still would have been enough pollution from Y to require a clean up, if Y had not polluted the site X's pollution would have been sufficient to require the clean up. In that case, the conduct of X and the conduct of Y would each be a sufficient but not a necessary condition of the clean up, and it would be entirely arbitrary to let either (or, even worse, both) off the hook on this basis. So far as appears, this is such a case; Browning-Ferris's pollution was serious enough (if indeed it dumped a large quantity of Chrysler's particularly toxic wastes) to require that the site be cleaned up, but the other pollution at the site was also enough. If Browning-Ferris's conduct was thus a sufficient though not a necessary condition of the clean up, it is not inequitable to make it contribute substantially to the cost.

       *   *   *   [N]o principle of law, logic, or common sense required the court to allocate [the] total costs among the polluters on the basis of the volume of wastes alone. Not only do wastes differ in their toxicity, harm to the environment, and costs of cleaning up, and so relative volume is not a reliable guide to the marginal costs imposed by each polluter; but polluters differ in the blameworthiness of the decisions or omissions that led to the pollution, and blameworthiness is relevant to an equitable allocation of joint costs.

DECISION AND REMEDY   *The U.S. Court of Appeals for the Seventh Circuit held that the allocation of 22 percent of the clean-up costs to Browning-Ferris had been fair. There were a number of factors to consider, and the lower court had not abused its discretion in deciding that those factors warranted this allocation. The court remanded the case for the determination of other issues.*

TERMS AND CONCEPTS TO REVIEW

bait-and-switch advertising 821	environmental law 820	toxic tort 830
cease-and-desist order 821	multiple product orders 822	validation notice 827
consumer law 820	nuisance 830	wetland 834
counteradvertising 822	potentially responsible party (PRP) 837	
environmental impact statement (EIS) 831	Regulation Z 823	

QUESTIONS AND CASE PROBLEMS

44–1. UNSOLICITED MERCHANDISE. Andrew, a resident of California, received a flyer in the U.S. mail announcing a new line of regional cookbooks distributed by the Every-Kind Cookbook Co. Andrew was not interested and threw the flyer away. Two days later, Andrew received in the mail an introductory cookbook entitled *Lower Mongolian Regional Cookbook*, as announced in the flyer, on a "trial basis" from Every-Kind. Andrew was not interested but did not go to the trouble to return the

cookbook. Every-Kind demanded payment of $20.95 for the *Lower Mongolian Regional Cookbook*. Discuss whether Andrew can be required to pay for the cookbook.

44–2. CLEAN AIR ACT. Some scientific knowledge indicates that there is no safe level of exposure to a cancer-causing agent. In theory, even one molecule of such a substance has the potential for causing cancer. Section 112 of the Clean Air Act requires that all cancer-causing substances be regulated to ensure a margin of safety.

Some environmental groups have argued that all emissions of such substances must be eliminated in order for such a margin of safety to be reached. A total elimination would likely shut down many major U.S. industries. Should the Environmental Protection Agency totally eliminate all emissions of cancer-causing chemicals? Discuss.

44–3. Door-to-Door Sales. On June 28, a sales representative for Renowned Books called on the Gonchars at their home. After a very persuasive sales pitch on the part of the sales agent, the Gonchars agreed in writing to purchase a twenty-volume set of historical encyclopedias from Renowned Books for a total of $299. An initial down payment of $35 was required, with the remainder of the price to be paid in monthly payments over a one-year period. Two days later the Gonchars, having second thoughts, contacted the book company and stated that they had decided to rescind the contract. Renowned Books said this would be impossible. Has Renowned Books violated any consumer law by not allowing the Gonchars to rescind their contract? Explain.

44–4. Environmental Laws. Fruitade, Inc., is a processor of a soft drink called Freshen Up. Fruitade uses returnable bottles, as well as a special acid to clean its bottles for further beverage processing. The acid is diluted by water and then allowed to pass into a navigable stream. Fruitade crushes its broken bottles and throws the crushed glass into the stream. Discuss fully any environmental laws that Fruitade has violated.

44–5. Deceptive Advertising. Thompson Medical Co. marketed a new cream called Aspercreme that was supposed to help arthritis victims and others suffering from minor aches. Aspercreme contained no aspirin. Thompson's television advertisements stated that the product provided "the strong relief of aspirin right where you hurt" and showed the announcer holding up aspirin tablets as well as a tube of Aspercreme. The Federal Trade Commission held that the advertisements were misleading, because they led consumers to believe that Aspercreme contained aspirin. Thompson Medical Co. appealed this decision and argued that the advertisements never actually stated that the product contained aspirin. How should the court rule? Discuss. [*Thompson Medical Co. v. Federal Trade Commission*, 791 F.2d 189 (D.C.Cir. 1986)]

44–6. Truth in Lending. Renee Purtle bought a 1986 Chevrolet Blazer from Eldridge Auto Sales, Inc. To finance the purchase through Eldridge, Purtle filled out a credit application on which she misrepresented her employment status. Based on the misrepresentation, Eldridge extended credit. In the credit contract, Eldridge did not disclose the finance charge, the annual percentage rate, or the total sales price or use the term "amount financed," as the TILA and its regulations require. Purtle defaulted on the loan, and Eldridge repossessed the vehicle. Purtle filed a suit in a federal district court against Eldridge, alleging violations of the TILA. The court awarded Purtle $1,000 in damages,

plus attorneys' fees and costs. Eldridge appealed, arguing in part that Purtle was not entitled to damages because she had committed fraud on her credit application. What will the court decide on appeal? Why? [*Purtle v. Eldridge Auto Sales, Inc.*, 91 F.3d 797 (6th Cir. 1996)]

44–7. Clean Water Act. Attique Ahmad owned the Spin-N-Market, a convenience store and gas station. The gas pumps were fed by underground tanks, one of which had a leak at its top that allowed water to enter. Ahmad emptied the tank by pumping its contents into a storm drain and a sewer system. Through the storm drain, gasoline flowed into a creek, forcing the city to clean the water. Through the sewer system, gasoline flowed into a sewage treatment plant, forcing the city to evacuate the plant and two nearby schools. Ahmad was charged with discharging a pollutant without a permit, which is a criminal violation of the Clean Water Act. The act provides that a person who "knowingly violates" the act commits a felony. Ahmad claimed that he had believed he was discharging only water. Did Ahmad commit a felony? Why or why not? Discuss fully. [*U.S. v. Ahmad*, 101 F.3d 386 (5th Cir. 1996)]

44–8. Fair Debt Collection. A condominium association, Rancho Santa Margarita Recreation and Landscape Corp., attempted unsuccessfully to collect an assessment fee from Andrew Ladick. The association referred the matter to the Law Offices of Gerald J. Van Gemert. Van Gemert sent Ladick a letter demanding payment of the fee. The letter did not include a "validation notice," as required by the Fair Debt Collection Practices Act (FDCPA), nor did it disclose that Van Gemert was attempting to collect a debt and that any information obtained would be used for that purpose. Ladick filed a suit in a federal district court against Van Gemert and his office, alleging violations of the FDCPA. Van Gemert filed a motion for summary judgment on the ground that the assessment was not a "debt," as defined by the FDCPA, in part because there was no "transaction," as required by the FDCPA definition, out of which Ladick's obligation arose. Will the court agree with Van Gemert? Why or why not? [*Ladick v. Van Gemert*, 146 F.3d 1205 (10th Cir. 1998)]

44–9. Fair Debt Collection. Gloria Mahon incurred a bill of $279.70 for medical services rendered by Dr. Larry Bowen. For more than two years, Bowen sent monthly billing statements to the Mahons at their home address (where they had lived for forty-five years). Getting no response, Bowen assigned the collection of their account to Credit Bureau of Placer County, Inc. Credit Bureau uses computerized collection tracking and filing software, known as Columbia Ultimate Business Systems (CUBS). CUBS automatically generates standardized collection notices and acts as an electronic filing system for each account, recording all collection activities, including which notices are sent to whom and on what date. Credit Bureau employees monitor the activity, routinely noting whether an envelope is returned undelivered. Credit Bureau mailed three CUBS—generated notices to the Mahons. According to Credit Bureau's records, the notices were not returned and the Mahons did not respond. Credit Bureau reported the Mahons' account as delinquent. The Mahons filed a suit in a federal district court against Credit Bureau, alleging in part that the agency had failed to send a validation notice, as required by the Fair Debt Collection Practices Act. Credit Bureau filed a motion for summary judgment. Should a notice be considered sent only if a debtor acknowledges its receipt? Why or why not? [*Mahon v. Credit Bureau of Placer County, Inc.*, 171 F.3d 1197 (9th Cir. 1999)]

44–10. In Your Court

Kimberly Sage saw an advertisement in a newspaper for a Kimball spinet piano on sale for $899 at a local piano store. Because the style of the piano drawn in the advertisement matched her furniture, Sage was particularly interested in the Kimball. When she went to the piano store, however, she learned that the drawing closely resembled another, more expensive Crest piano and that the Kimball spinet looked quite different from the piano sketched in the drawing. The salesperson told Sage that he was unable to order a spinet piano of the style Sage requested. When Sage asked for the names of other customers who had purchased the advertised piano, the salesperson became extremely upset and said that he would not, under any circumstances, sell Sage a piano. Sage then brought suit against the piano store in a state court, alleging that the store had engaged in deceptive advertising in violation of state law. Assume that you are the judge in the trial court hearing this case and answer the following questions:

(a) Assume that bait-and-switch advertising is illegal under your state's deceptive practices act. Did the piano store's actions constitute bait-and-switch advertising? Why or why not?

(b) What federal law prohibits bait-and-switch advertising? Could Sage sue the piano store under that law? Explain.

LAW ON THE WEB

For updated links to resources available on the Web, as well as a variety of other materials, visit this text's Web site at http://wbl.westbuslaw.com.

For current articles concerning consumer issues, go to the Alexander Law Firm's "Consumer Law Page," which is online at

http://consumerlawpage.com/intro.html

The law firm of Arent Fox offers extensive information relating to advertising law at

http://www.advertisinglaw.com

The Virtual Law Library of the Indiana University School of Law provides numerous links to online environmental law sources. Go to

http://www.law.indiana.edu

LEGAL RESEARCH EXERCISES ON THE WEB

Go to http://wbl.westbuslaw.com, the Web site that accompanies this text. Select "Internet Applications," and then click on "Chapter 44." There you will find the following Internet research exercises that you can perform to learn more about consumer and environmental law:

Activity 44–1: Consumer Law

Activity 44–2: Nuisance Law

CHAPTER 45

Antitrust Law

TODAY'S ANTITRUST LAWS ARE the direct descendants of common law actions intended to limit **restraints on trade** (agreements between firms that have the effect of reducing competition in the marketplace). Concern over monopolistic practices arose following the Civil War with the growth of large corporate enterprises and their attempts to reduce or eliminate competition. They did this by legally tying themselves together in a *business trust*, a type of business entity described in Chapter 39. The participants in the most famous trust—the Standard Oil trust in the late 1800s—transferred their stock to a trustee and received trust certificates in exchange. The trustee then made decisions fixing prices, controlling production, and determining the control of exclusive geographic markets for all of the oil companies that were in the Standard Oil trust. It became apparent that the trust wielded so much economic power that corporations outside the trust could not compete effectively.

Many states attempted to control such monopolistic behavior by enacting statutes outlawing the use of trusts. That is why all of the laws that regulate economic competition today are referred to as **antitrust laws.** At the national level, the government recognized the problem in 1887 and passed the Interstate Commerce Act,[1] followed by the Sherman Antitrust Act in 1890.[2] In 1914, Congress passed the Clayton

Act[3] and the Federal Trade Commission Act[4] to further curb anticompetitive or unfair business practices. Since their passage, the 1914 acts have been amended by Congress to broaden and strengthen their coverage, and they continue to be an important element in the legal environment in which businesses operate.

This chapter examines these major antitrust statutes, focusing particularly on the Sherman Act and the Clayton Act, as amended, and the types of activities prohibited by those acts. Remember in reading this chapter that the basis of antitrust legislation is the desire to foster competition. Antitrust legislation was initially created—and continues to be enforced—because of our belief that competition leads to lower prices, more product information, and a better distribution of wealth between consumers and producers.

SECTION 1

The Sherman Antitrust Act

The author of the Sherman Antitrust Act of 1890, Senator John Sherman, was the brother of the famed Civil War general and a recognized financial authority. He had been concerned for years about the diminishing competition within American industry. He

---

1. 49 U.S.C. Sections 501–526.
2. 15 U.S.C. Sections 1–7.

3. 15 U.S.C. Sections 12–26a.
4. 15 U.S.C. Sections 45–48.

told Congress that the Sherman Act "does not announce a new principle of law, but applies old and well-recognized principles of the common law."[5]

The common law regarding trade regulation was not always consistent. Certainly, it was not very familiar to the legislators of the Fifty-first Congress of the United States in 1890. The public concern over large business integrations and trusts was familiar, however, and in 1890 Congress passed "An Act to Protect Trade and Commerce against Unlawful Restraints and Monopolies"—more commonly referred to as the Sherman Antitrust Act, or simply the Sherman Act.

MAJOR PROVISIONS OF THE SHERMAN ACT

Sections 1 and 2 contain the main provisions of the Sherman Act:

1: Every contract, combination in the form of trust or otherwise, or conspiracy, in restraint of trade or commerce among the several States, or with foreign nations, is hereby declared to be illegal [and is a felony punishable by fine and/or imprisonment].

2: Every person who shall monopolize, or attempt to monopolize, or combine or conspire with any other person or persons, to monopolize any part of the trade or commerce among the several States, or with foreign nations, shall be deemed guilty of a felony [and is similarly punishable].

These two sections of the Sherman Act are quite different. Section 1 requires two or more persons, as a person cannot contract, combine, or conspire alone. Thus, the essence of the illegal activity is *the act of joining together.* Section 2 applies both to an individual person and to several people, because it refers to "[e]very person." Thus, unilateral conduct can result in a violation of Section 2.

The cases brought to the courts under Section 1 of the Sherman Act differ from those brought under Section 2. Section 1 cases are often concerned with finding an agreement (written or oral) that leads to a restraint of trade. Section 2 cases deal with the structure of a **monopoly** that exists in the marketplace. The term *monopoly* is generally used to describe a market in which there is a single seller. Whereas Section 1 focuses on agreements that are restrictive—that is, agreements that have a wrongful purpose—Section 2 looks at the so-called misuse of **monopoly power** in the marketplace. Monopoly power exists when a firm has an extreme amount of **market power**—the power

to affect the market price of its product. Both Section 1 and Section 2 seek to curtail market industrial practices that result in undesired monopoly pricing and output behavior. Any case brought under Section 2, however, must be one in which the "threshold" or "necessary" amount of monopoly power already exists. We will return to a discussion of these two sections of the Sherman Act after we look at the act's jurisdictional requirements.

JURISDICTIONAL REQUIREMENTS

The Sherman Act applies only to restraints that have a significant impact on interstate commerce. As will be discussed later in this chapter, the Sherman Act also extends to U.S. nationals abroad who are engaged in activities that have an effect on U.S. foreign commerce. State regulation of anticompetitive practices addresses purely local restraints on competition. Courts have generally held that any activity that substantially affects interstate commerce falls within the ambit of the Sherman Act. As discussed in Chapter 4, courts have construed the meaning of *interstate commerce* more and more broadly over the years, bringing even local activities within the regulatory power of the national government.

SECTION 2

Section 1 of the Sherman Act

The underlying assumption of Section 1 of the Sherman Act is that society's welfare is harmed if rival firms are permitted to join in an agreement that consolidates their market power or otherwise restrains competition. Not all agreements between rivals, however, result in enhanced market power or *unreasonably* restrain trade. Under what is called the **rule of reason,** anticompetitive agreements that allegedly violate Section 1 of the Sherman Act are analyzed with the view that they may, in fact, constitute reasonable restraints on trade. When applying this rule, the court considers the purpose of the arrangement, the powers of the parties, and the effect of their actions in restraining trade. If the court deems that legitimate competitive benefits outweigh the anticompetitive effects of the agreement, it will be held lawful.

The need for a rule-of-reason analysis of some agreements in restraint of trade is obvious—if the rule of reason had not been developed, virtually any business agreement could conceivably violate the Sherman Act.

---
5. 21 Congressional Record 2456 (1890).

Justice Louis D. Brandeis effectively phrased this sentiment in *Chicago Board of Trade v. United States*,[6] a case decided in 1918:

> Every agreement concerning trade, every regulation of trade, restrains. To bind, to restrain, is of their very essence. The true test of legality is whether the restraint imposed is such as merely regulates and perhaps thereby promotes competition or whether it is such as may suppress or even destroy competition.

When analyzing an alleged Section 1 violation under the rule of reason, a court will consider several factors, including the purpose of the agreement, the parties' power to implement the agreement to achieve that purpose, and the effect or potential effect of the agreement on competition. Another factor that might be considered is whether the parties could have relied on less restrictive means to achieve their purpose.

Some agreements, however, are so blatantly and substantially anticompetitive that they are deemed illegal *per se* (on their faces, or inherently) under Section 1. If an agreement is found to be of a type that is deemed a ***per se* violation,** a court is precluded from determining whether the agreement's benefits outweigh its anticompetitive effects.

The dividing line between agreements that constitute *per se* violations and agreements that should be judged under a rule of reason is seldom clear. Moreover, in some cases, the United States Supreme Court has stated that it is applying a *per se* rule, and yet a careful reading of the Court's analysis suggests that the Court is weighing benefits against harms under a rule of reason. Perhaps the most that can be said with certainty is that although the distinction between the two rules seems clear in theory, in the actual application of antitrust laws, the distinction has not always been so obvious.

We turn now to the types of trade restraints prohibited by Section 1 of the Sherman Act. Generally, these restraints fall into two broad categories: *horizontal restraints* and *vertical restraints*. Some restraints are *per se* violations of Section 1, but others may be permissible; those that are not *per se* violations are tested under the rule of reason.

HORIZONTAL RESTRAINTS

The term **horizontal restraint** is encountered frequently in antitrust law. A horizontal restraint is any agreement that in some way restrains competition between rival firms competing in the same market.

Price Fixing. Any agreement among competitors to fix prices, or **price-fixing agreement,** constitutes a *per se* violation of Section 1 of the Sherman Act. Perhaps the definitive case regarding price-fixing agreements remains the 1940 case of *United States v. Socony-Vacuum Oil Co.*[7] In that case, a group of independent oil producers in Texas and Louisiana were caught between falling demand due to the Great Depression of the 1930s and increasing supply from newly discovered oil fields in the region. In response to these conditions, a group of the major refining companies agreed to buy "distress" gasoline (excess supplies) from the independents so as to dispose of it in an "orderly manner."

Although there was no explicit agreement as to price, it was clear that the purpose of the agreement was to limit the supply of gasoline on the market and thereby raise prices. There may have been good reasons for the agreement. Nonetheless, the United States Supreme Court recognized the dangerous effects that such an agreement could have on open and free competition. The Court held that the reasonableness of a price-fixing agreement is never a defense; any agreement that restricts output or artificially fixes price is a *per se* violation of Section 1. The rationale of the *per se* rule was best stated in what is now the most famous portion of the Court's opinion. In footnote 59, Justice William O. Douglas compared a freely functioning price system to a body's central nervous system, condemning price-fixing agreements as threats to "the central nervous system of the economy."

Group Boycotts. A **group boycott** is an agreement by two or more sellers to refuse to deal with (boycott) a particular person or firm. Such group boycotts have been held to constitute *per se* violations of Section 1 of the Sherman Act. Section 1 has been violated if it can be demonstrated that the boycott or joint refusal to deal was undertaken with the intention of eliminating competition or preventing entry into a given market. Some boycotts, such as group boycotts against a supplier for political reasons, may be protected under the First Amendment right to freedom of expression.

The issue in the following case was whether a *single* buyer's decision to buy from one supplier rather than another should be considered a group boycott.

---

6. 246 U.S. 231, 38 S.Ct. 242, 62 L.Ed. 683 (1918).

7. 310 U.S. 150, 60 S.Ct. 811, 84 L.E.2d 1129 (1940).

CASE 45.1   NYNEX Corp. v. Discon, Inc.

Supreme Court of the
United States, 1998.
525 U.S. 128,
119 S.Ct. 493,
142 L.Ed.2d 510.
http://supct.law.
cornell.edu/supct[a]

BACKGROUND AND FACTS   *NYNEX Corporation owns New York Telephone Company (NYTel), which provides telephone service to most of New York. NYTel has a monopoly on phone service in the areas that it serves. NYNEX also owns NYNEX Material Enterprises. Material Enterprises obtains removal services for NYTel. These services consist of salvaging and disposing of obsolete equipment. Material Enterprises, which had been using the services of Discon, Inc., switched its business to AT&T Technologies, Inc., which supplied the removal services at inflated prices. Material Enterprises charged the inflated prices to NYTel, which passed the charges on to its customers. Material Enterprises later received secret rebates of the excessive charges from AT&T. (Essentially, Material Enterprises and NYNEX used NYTel's monopoly to obtain increased revenues.) When the scheme was uncovered, NYTel agreed to refund over $35 million to its customers. Discon, Inc., filed a suit in a federal district court against NYNEX and others, alleging, among other things, that as part of their scheme, the defendants had conspired to eliminate Discon from the market in favor of AT&T, because Discon had refused to participate in the rebate scheme. Discon contended that this was an illegal group boycott. The defendants filed a motion to dismiss, which the court granted. Discon appealed to the U.S. Court of Appeals for the Second Circuit, which reversed the lower court's judgment and held that the treatment of Discon could be an illegal group boycott. The defendants appealed to the United States Supreme Court.*

IN THE LANGUAGE
OF THE COURT

Justice BREYER delivered the opinion of the Court.

*   *   *   *

*   *   * [T]he specific legal question before us is whether an antitrust court considering an agreement by a buyer to purchase goods or services from one supplier rather than another should (after examining the buyer's reasons or justifications) apply the *per se* rule if it finds no legitimate business reason for that purchasing decision. We conclude no boycott-related *per se* rule applies and that the plaintiff here must allege and prove harm, not just to a single competitor, but to the competitive process, i.e., to competition itself.

Our conclusion rests in large part upon precedent, for precedent limits the *per se* rule in the boycott context to cases involving horizontal agreements among direct competitors. *   *   *

*   *   * [In a previous case] this Court *   *   * held that a "vertical restraint is not illegal *per se* unless it includes some agreement on price or price levels." This precedent makes the *per se* rule inapplicable, for the case before us concerns only a vertical agreement and a vertical restraint, a restraint that takes the form of depriving a supplier of a potential customer.

Nor have we found any special feature of this case that could distinguish it from the precedent *   *   * . We concede Discon's claim that the petitioners' behavior hurt consumers by raising telephone service rates. But that consumer injury naturally flowed not so much from a less competitive market for removal services, as from the exercise of market power that is lawfully in the hands of a monopolist, namely, New York Telephone, combined with a deception worked upon the regulatory agency that prevented the agency from controlling New York Telephone's exercise of its monopoly power.

To apply the *per se* rule here—where the buyer's decision, though not made for competitive reasons, composes part of a regulatory fraud—would transform cases involving business behavior that is improper for various reasons, say, cases involving nepotism or

a. In the right column, in the "Arrayed by party name:" section, in the "1998" row, click on "1st party." On the page that opens, scroll to the case name and click on it. When that page opens, choose the format in which you want to view the opinion and click on its link to access it.

personal pique, into treble-damages antitrust cases. And that *per se* rule would discourage firms from changing suppliers—even where the competitive process itself does not suffer harm.

The freedom to switch suppliers lies close to the heart of the competitive process that the antitrust laws seek to encourage. At the same time, other laws, for example, "unfair competition" laws, business tort laws, or regulatory laws, provide remedies for various competitive practices thought to be offensive to proper standards of business morality. Thus, this Court has refused to apply *per se* reasoning in cases involving that kind of activity. [Emphasis added.]

DECISION AND REMEDY   *The Supreme Court vacated the decision of the U.S. Court of Appeals for the Second Circuit and remanded the case for further proceedings. A choice by a single buyer to buy from one supplier rather than another is not subject to the* per se *group boycott rule, even if there is no legitimate business reason for that buyer's purchasing decision.*

Horizontal Market Division.   It is a *per se* violation of Section 1 of the Sherman Act for competitors to divide up territories or customers. For example, manufacturers A, B, and C compete against one another in the states of Kansas, Nebraska, and Iowa. By agreement, A sells products only in Kansas; B sells only in Nebraska; and C sells only in Iowa. This concerted action reduces costs and allows each of the three (assuming there is no other competition) to raise the price of the goods sold in its own state. The same violation would take place if A, B, and C simply agreed that A would sell only to institutional purchasers (school districts, universities, state agencies and departments, cities, and so on) in the three states, B only to wholesalers, and C only to retailers.

Trade Associations.   Businesses in the same general industry or profession frequently organize trade associations to pursue common interests. Their joint activities may provide for exchanges of information, representation of the members' business interests before governmental bodies, advertising campaigns, and the setting of regulatory standards to govern their industry or profession. Generally, the rule of reason is applied to many of these horizontal actions. For example, if a court finds that a trade association practice or agreement that restrains trade is nonetheless sufficiently beneficial both to the association and to the public, it may deem the restraint reasonable.

Other trade association agreements may have such substantially anticompetitive effects that the court will consider them to be in violation of Section 1 of the Sherman Act. In *National Society of Professional Engineers v. United States*,[8] for example, it was held that the society's code of ethics—which prohibited discussion of prices with a potential customer until after the customer had chosen an engineer—was a Section 1 violation. The United States Supreme Court found that this ban on competitive bidding was "nothing less than a frontal assault on the basic policy of the Sherman Act."

Joint Ventures.   Joint ventures undertaken by competitors are also subject to antitrust laws. As discussed in Chapter 39, a *joint venture* is an undertaking by two or more individuals or firms for a specific purpose. If a joint venture does not involve price fixing or market divisions, the agreement will be analyzed under the rule of reason. Whether the venture will then be upheld under Section 1 depends on an overall assessment of the purposes of the venture, a strict analysis of the potential benefits relative to the likely harms, and in some cases, an assessment of whether there are less restrictive alternatives for achieving the same goals.[9]

VERTICAL RESTRAINTS

A **vertical restraint** of trade is one that results from an agreement between firms at different levels in the manufacturing and distribution process. In contrast to horizontal relationships, which occur at the same level

---

8. 453 U.S. 679, 98 S.Ct. 1355, 55 L.Ed.2d 637 (1978).
9. See, for example, *United States v. Morgan*, 118 F.Supp. 621 (S.D.N.Y. 1953). This case is often cited as a classic example of how to judge joint ventures under the rule of reason.

of operation, vertical relationships encompass the entire chain of production: the purchase of inputs, basic manufacturing, distribution to wholesalers, and eventual sale of a product at the retail level. For some products, these distinct phases are carried on by different firms. In other instances, a single firm carries out two or more of the separate functional phases. Such enterprises are considered to be **vertically integrated firms.**

Even though firms operating at different functional levels are not in direct competition with one another, they are in competition with other firms operating at their own respective levels of operation. Thus, agreements between firms standing in a vertical relationship do significantly affect competition. Some vertical restraints are *per se* violations of Section 1; others are judged under the rule of reason.

Territorial or Customer Restrictions.   In arranging for the distribution of its products, a manufacturer often wishes to insulate dealers from direct competition with other dealers selling its products. In this endeavor, the manufacturer may institute territorial restrictions or may attempt to prohibit wholesalers or retailers from reselling the products to certain classes of buyers, such as competing retailers. There may be legitimate, procompetitive reasons for imposing such territorial or customer restrictions. For example, a

manufacturer may wish to prevent a dealer from reducing costs and undercutting rivals by providing the product without promotion or customer service, while relying on a nearby dealer to provide these services. In this situation, the cost-cutting dealer reaps the benefits (sales of the product) paid for by other dealers who undertake promotion and arrange for customer service. This is an example of the "free rider" problem.[10] The cost-cutting dealer, by not providing customer service, may also harm the manufacturer's reputation.

Territorial and customer restrictions are judged under a rule of reason. In the following case, *Continental T.V., Inc. v. GTE Sylvania, Inc.,* the United States Supreme Court overturned its earlier stance, which had been set out in *United States v. Arnold, Schwinn & Co.*[11] In *Schwinn,* the Court had held territorial and customer restrictions to be *per se* violations of Section 1 of the Sherman Act. The *Continental* case has been heralded as one of the most important antitrust cases since the 1940s. It marked a definite shift from rigid characterization of these kinds of vertical restraints to a more flexible, economic analysis of the restraints under the rule of reason.

---

10. For a discussion of the free rider problem in the context of sports telecasting, see *Chicago Professional Sports Limited Partnership v. National Basketball Association,* 961 F.2d 667 (7th Cir. 1993).
11. 388 U.S. 365, 87 S.Ct. 1856, 18 L.Ed.2d 1249 (1967).

CASE 45.2   ## Continental T.V., Inc. v. GTE Sylvania, Inc.

Supreme Court of the United States, 1977.
433 U.S. 36,
97 S.Ct. 2549,
53 L.Ed.2d 568.
**http://www.findlaw.
com/casecode/
supreme.html[a]**

HISTORICAL AND ECONOMIC SETTING   *In determining what is or is not permitted under the antitrust laws, the trend has been to establish a flexible standard, rather than a rigid one, particularly in regard to conduct that is considered to have procompetitive benefits. Under a flexible standard, a business practice that is considered a criminal offense in one decade may be judged a corporate virtue in the next. In the mid-1970s, for example, the United States Supreme Court began to qualify or overrule many of its previous decisions that prohibited certain business practices as* per se *violations of the antitrust laws. The Court appeared to be focusing on economic considerations, such as consumer welfare,[b] economic efficiency,[c] and interbrand versus intrabrand competition.*

BACKGROUND AND FACTS   *GTE Sylvania, Inc., a manufacturer of television sets, adopted a franchise plan that limited the number of franchises granted in any given geographic area and that required each franchise to sell only Sylvania products from the location or locations at which it was franchised. Sylvania retained sole discretion to increase the number of retailers in an area, depending on the success or failure of existing retailers in developing their markets. Continental T.V., Inc., was a retailer under*

---

a. In the "Citation Search" section, type "433" in the first box, type "36" in the second box, and click on "Get It" to access the case.
b. *Reiter v. Sonotone Corp.,* 442 U.S. 330, 99 S.Ct. 2326, 60 L.Ed.2d 931 (1979).
c. *Broadcast Music, Inc. v. Columbia Broadcasting System, Inc.,* 441 U.S. 1, 99 S.Ct. 1551, 60 L.Ed.2d 1 (1979).

Sylvania's franchise plan. Shortly after Sylvania proposed a new franchise that would compete with Continental, Sylvania terminated Continental's franchise, and a suit was brought in a federal district court for money owed. Continental claimed that Sylvania's vertically restrictive franchise system violated Section 1 of the Sherman Act. The district court held for Continental, and Sylvania appealed. The appellate court reversed the trial court's decision. Continental appealed to the United States Supreme Court.

IN THE LANGUAGE OF THE COURT

Mr. Justice POWELL delivered the opinion of the Court.

*   *   *   *

Vertical restrictions reduce intrabrand competition by limiting the number of sellers of a particular product competing for the business of a given group of buyers. *   *   *

Vertical restrictions promote interbrand competition by allowing the manufacturer to achieve certain efficiencies in the distribution of his products. *   *   * Established manufacturers can use them to induce retailers to engage in promotional activities or to provide service and repair facilities necessary to the efficient marketing of their products. *   *   * The availability and quality of such services affect a manufacturer's goodwill and the competitiveness of his product. *   *   * [Emphasis added.]

*   *   *   *

*   *   * When anticompetitive effects are shown to result from particular vertical restrictions they can be adequately policed under the rule of reason *   *   *.

DECISION AND REMEDY

The United States Supreme Court upheld the appellate court's reversal of the district court's decision. Sylvania's vertical system, which was not price restrictive, did not constitute a per se *violation of Section 1 of the Sherman Act.*

Resale Price Maintenance Agreements. An agreement between a manufacturer and a distributor or retailer in which the manufacturer specifies what the retail prices of its products must be is known as a **resale price maintenance agreement.** This type of agreement may violate Section 1 of the Sherman Act.

In a 1968 case, *Albrecht v. Herald Co.,*[12] the United States Supreme Court held that these vertical price-fixing agreements constituted *per se* violations of Section 1 of the Sherman Act. In the following case, which involved an agreement that set a maximum price for the resale of products supplied by a wholesaler to a dealer, the Supreme Court reevaluated its approach in *Albrecht.* At issue was whether such price-fixing arrangements should continue to be deemed *per se* violations of Section 1 of the Sherman Act or whether the rule of reason should be applied.

---

12. 390 U.S. 145, 88 S.Ct. 869, 19 L.Ed.2d 998 (1968).

CASE 45.3   **State Oil Co. v. Khan**

Supreme Court of the United States, 1997.
522 U.S. 3,
118 S.Ct. 275,
139 L.Ed.2d 199.
http://www.findlaw. com/casecode/ supreme.html[a]

BACKGROUND AND FACTS   *Barkat Khan leased a gas station under a contract with State Oil Company, which also agreed to supply gas to Khan for resale. Under the contract, State Oil would set a suggested retail price and sell gas to Khan for 3.25 cents per gallon less than that price. Khan could sell the gas at a higher price, but he would then be required to pay State Oil the difference (which would equal the entire profit Khan realized from raising the price). Khan failed to pay some of the rent due under the lease, and State Oil terminated the contract. Khan filed a suit in a federal district court against State Oil, alleging, among other things, price fixing in violation of the Sherman Act. The court granted summary judgment for State Oil. Khan appealed. The U.S. Court of*

---

a. This page, which is part of a Web site maintained by FindLaw, contains links to opinions of the United States Supreme Court. In the "Party Name Search" box, type "Khan" and click on "Search." When the results appear, click on the case name to access the opinion.

Appeals for the Seventh Circuit reversed this judgment, and State Oil appealed to the United States Supreme Court.

IN THE LANGUAGE OF THE COURT

Justice O'CONNOR delivered the opinion of the Court.

*   *   *   *

*   *   * Our analysis is *   *   * guided by our general view that the primary purpose of the antitrust laws is to protect interbrand competition. *   *   * [C]ondemnation of practices resulting in lower prices to consumers is especially costly because cutting prices in order to increase business often is the very essence of competition.

*   *   * [W]e find it difficult to maintain that vertically-imposed maximum prices could harm consumers or competition to the extent necessary to justify their *per se* invalidation. *   *   *

*   *   *   *

*   *   * [T]he *per se* rule *   *   * could in fact exacerbate problems related to the unrestrained exercise of market power by monopolist-dealers. Indeed, *both courts and antitrust scholars have noted that [the* per se*] rule may actually harm consumers and manufacturers.* *   *   * [Emphasis added.]

*   *   *   *

*   *   *[V]ertical maximum price fixing, like the majority of commercial arrangements subject to the antitrust laws, should be evaluated under the rule of reason. In our view, rule-of-reason analysis can effectively identify those situations in which vertical maximum price fixing amounts to anticompetitive conduct.

DECISION AND REMEDY

The United States Supreme Court vacated the decision of the appellate court and remanded the case. The Supreme Court held that vertical price fixing is not a per se *violation of the Sherman Act but should be evaluated under the rule of reason.*

Refusals to Deal. As discussed previously, joint refusals to deal (group boycotts) are subject to close scrutiny under Section 1 of the Sherman Act. A single manufacturer acting unilaterally, however, is generally free to deal, or not to deal, with whomever it wishes. In vertical arrangements, however, a manufacturer can refuse to deal with retailers or dealers that cut prices to levels substantially below the manufacturer's suggested retail prices. In *United States v. Colgate & Co.,*[13] for example, the United States Supreme Court held that a manufacturer's advance announcement that it would not sell to price cutters was not a violation of the Sherman Act.

There are instances, however, in which a unilateral refusal to deal violates antitrust laws. These instances involve offenses proscribed under Section 2 of the Sherman Act and occur only if (1) the firm refusing to deal has—or is likely to acquire—monopoly power and (2) the refusal is likely to have an anticompetitive effect on a particular market.

SECTION 3

Section 2 of the Sherman Act

Section 1 of the Sherman Act proscribes certain concerted, or joint, activities that restrain trade. In contrast, Section 2 condemns "every person who shall monopolize, or attempt to monopolize." Thus, two distinct types of behavior are subject to sanction under Section 2: *monopolization* and *attempts to monopolize*. A tactic that may be involved in either offense is **predatory pricing**. Predatory pricing involves an attempt by one firm to drive its competitors from the market by selling its product at prices substantially *below* the normal costs of production; once the competitors are eliminated, the firm will attempt to recapture its losses and go on to earn very high profits by driving prices up far above their competitive levels.

MONOPOLIZATION

In *United States v. Grinnell Corp.,*[14] the United States Supreme Court defined **monopolization** as involving

---

13. 250 U.S. 300, 39 S.Ct. 465, 63 L.Ed. 992 (1919).

14. 384 U.S. 563, 86 S.Ct. 1698, 16 L.Ed.2d 778 (1966).

the following two elements: "(1) the possession of monopoly power in the relevant market and (2) the willful acquisition or maintenance of the power as distinguished from growth or development as a consequence of a superior product, business acumen, or historic accident." A violation of Section 2 requires that both these elements—monopoly power and an intent to monopolize—be established.

Monopoly Power.

The Sherman Act does not define *monopoly*. In economic parlance, monopoly refers to control by a single entity. It is well established in antitrust law, however, that a firm may be a monopolist even though it is not the sole seller in a market. Additionally, size alone does not determine whether a firm is a monopoly. For example, a "mom and pop" grocery located in an isolated desert town is a monopolist if it is the only grocery serving that particular market. Size in relation to the market is what matters, because monopoly involves the power to affect prices and output. *Monopoly power*, as mentioned earlier in this chapter, exists when a firm has sufficient market power to control prices and exclude competition.

As difficult as it is to define market power precisely, it is even more difficult to measure it. Courts often use the so-called **market-share test**[15]—a firm's percentage share of the "relevant market"—in determining the extent of the firm's market power. A firm generally is considered to have monopoly power if its share of the relevant market is 70 percent or more. This is merely a rule of thumb, however; it is not a binding principle of law. In some cases, a smaller share may be held to constitute monopoly power.[16]

The relevant market consists of two elements: (1) a relevant product market and (2) a relevant geographic market. What should the relevant product market include? No doubt, it must include all products that, although produced by different firms, have identical attributes, such as sugar. Products that are not identical, however, may sometimes be substituted for one another. Coffee may be substituted for tea, for example.

In defining the relevant product market, the key issue is the degree of interchangeability between products. If one product is a sufficient substitute for another, the two products are considered to be part of the same product market.

The second component of the relevant market is the geographic boundaries of the market. For products that are sold nationwide, the geographic boundaries of the market encompass the entire United States. If a producer and its competitors sell in only a limited area (one in which customers have no access to other sources of the product), then the geographic market is limited to that area. A national firm may thus compete in several distinct areas and have monopoly power in one area but not in another.

The Intent Requirement.

Monopoly power, in and of itself, does not constitute the offense of monopolization under Section 2 of the Sherman Act. The offense also requires an *intent* to monopolize. A dominant market share may be the result of business acumen or the development of a superior product. It may simply be the result of historical accident. In these situations, the acquisition of monopoly power is not an antitrust violation. Indeed, it would be counter to society's interest to condemn every firm that acquired a position of power because it was well managed, was efficient, and marketed a product desired by consumers. If, however, a firm possesses market power as a result of carrying out some purposeful act to acquire or maintain that power through anticompetitive means, then it is in violation of Section 2. In most monopolization cases, intent may be inferred from evidence that the firm had monopoly power and engaged in anticompetitive behavior.

ATTEMPTS TO MONOPOLIZE

Section 2 also prohibits **attempted monopolization** of a market. Any action challenged as an attempt to monopolize must have been specifically intended to exclude competitors and garner monopoly power. In addition, the attempt must have had a "dangerous" probability of success—only *serious* threats of monopolization are condemned as violations. The probability cannot be dangerous unless the alleged offender possesses some degree of market power. (See this chapter's *Emerging Trends in Technology* on the next page for a discussion of the widely publicized case brought against Microsoft Corporation for alleged violations of antitrust laws, including monopolization and attempted monopolization.)

---

15. Other measures of market power have been devised, but the market-share test is the most widely used.

16. This standard was first articulated by Judge Learned Hand in *United States v. Aluminum Co. of America*, 148 F.2d 416 (2d Cir. 1945). A 90 percent share was held to be clear evidence of monopoly power. Anything less than 64 percent, said Judge Hand, made monopoly power doubtful, and anything less than 30 percent was clearly not monopoly power.

EMERGING TRENDS IN TECHNOLOGY

Protecting Competition in Cyberspace

In the United States, competition between businesses is seen as a primary factor for the success of our economy. It is believed that those who violate laws protecting competition—antitrust laws—cause us to pay higher prices for products of lesser quality. Violations of antitrust laws can also block new advances in technology.

To date, there are very few cases involving the application of antitrust law in cyberspace. One court has held that it likely was not a violation of antitrust law for an Internet service provider, America Online, Inc. (AOL), to refuse to transmit free e-mail ads to its subscribers.[a]

THE CASE AGAINST MICROSOFT

Currently, the most well-known instance involving cyberspace technology and antitrust law is the case brought by the U.S. Department of Justice and twenty states' attorneys general against Microsoft Corporation. The plaintiffs charged, in part, that Microsoft committed the following violations of antitrust law:

■ Unreasonably restrained competition by "tying" its Internet browser to Windows 98, by entering into "exclusive-dealing" arrangements with various Internet providers, and by

imposing start-up screen restrictions on computer manufacturers. (The elements of these and other violations of antitrust law are discussed in more detail in this chapter.)
■ Illegally maintained a monopoly in its operating system software.
■ Attempted to monopolize the market for Internet browsers.
■ Unlawfully used its operating system monopoly to obtain a competitive advantage in the browser market.

In "findings of fact" issued in late 1999, U.S. district court judge Thomas Jackson declared that Microsoft held monopoly power in the relevant market and that it has used its dominant position in the operating-system and browser markets to thwart competition from other companies.[b] The judge then referred the case for mediation. When mediation attempts failed, Judge Jackson issued his "findings of law" (his verdict in the case) in April 2000, ruling that Microsoft was a monopoly and that it had "maintained its monopoly by anticompetitive means and attempted to monopolize the Web browser market." Microsoft had illegally used its power to keep an "oppressive thumb" on competitors and stifle innovation, hurting consumers in the process. Not every allegation was proved by the government, however. According to Judge Jackson, the government had failed to prove that Microsoft's exclusive marketing arrangements with other firms constituted unlawful exclusive dealing under federal antitrust laws.[c]

a. *Cyber Promotions, Inc. v. America Online, Inc.,* 948 F.Supp. 456 (E.D.Pa. 1996).

b. *United States v. Microsoft Corp.,* 65 F.Supp.2d 1 (D.D.C. 1999).
c. *United States v. Microsoft,* __F.Supp.__ [2000 WL 340768] (D.D.C. 2000).

AFTER THE VERDICT, THEN WHAT?

Microsoft has stated that it will appeal the decision, and the case is likely to be tied up in the appellate court for some time. Even if Microsoft loses on appeal, what sanctions against Microsoft would be appropriate? Should the company be broken up into component parts? Should it—and all other software producers—be regulated by the government?

IMPLICATIONS FOR THE BUSINESSPERSON

1. Companies that provide Internet-related software should think twice about asking the government to intervene. The end result may include government regulation where it never existed before.

FOR CRITICAL ANALYSIS

1. How is it possible to define the relevant market with respect to Internet products?
2. Some argue that breaking up Microsoft into component parts would generate so much confusion in the marketplace that consumers would inevitably suffer as a result. Do you agree?

RELEVANT WEB SITES

Judge Jackson's findings of facts, as well as other trial proceedings (including testimony and deposition transcripts) are posted on the U.S. Department of Justice's Web site at **http://www.usdoj.gov/atr/cases/ms_index.htm**. For Microsoft's response to the findings, go to **http://www.mercurycenter.com/business/microsoft/trial/content.html**.

SECTION 4

The Clayton Act

In 1914, Congress attempted to strengthen federal antitrust laws by enacting the Clayton Act. The Clayton Act was aimed at specific anticompetitive or monopolistic practices that the Sherman Act did not cover. The substantive provisions of the act deal with four distinct forms of business behavior, which are declared illegal but not criminal. With regard to each of the four provisions, the act's prohibitions are qualified by the general condition that the behavior is illegal only if it tends to substantially lessen competition or to create monopoly power. The major offenses under the Clayton Act are set out in Sections 2, 3, 7, and 8 of the act.

PRICE DISCRIMINATION

Price discrimination, which occurs when a seller charges different prices to competing buyers for identical goods, is prohibited by Section 2 of the Clayton Act. Because businesses frequently circumvented Section 2 of the act, Congress strengthened this section by amending it with the passage of the Robinson-Patman Act in 1936.

As amended, Section 2 prohibits price discrimination that cannot be justified by differences in production costs, transportation costs, or cost differences due to other reasons. To violate Section 2, the seller must be engaged in interstate commerce, and the effect of the price discrimination must be to substantially lessen competition or create a competitive injury.

In other words, a seller is prohibited from reducing a price to one buyer below the price charged to that buyer's competitor. An exception is made if the seller can justify the price reduction by demonstrating (1) that he or she charged the lower price temporarily and in good faith to meet another seller's equally low price to the buyer's competitor or (2) that a particular buyer's purchases saved the seller costs in producing and selling the goods (called *cost justification*). To violate the Clayton Act, a seller's pricing policies must also include a reasonable prospect of the seller's recouping its losses.[17]

EXCLUSIONARY PRACTICES

Under Section 3 of the Clayton Act, sellers or lessors cannot sell or lease goods "on the condition, agreement or understanding that the . . . purchaser or lessee thereof shall not use or deal in the goods . . . of a competitor or competitors of the seller." In effect, this section prohibits two types of vertical agreements involving exclusionary practices—exclusive-dealing contracts and tying arrangements.

Exclusive-Dealing Contracts. A contract under which a seller forbids a buyer to purchase products from the seller's competitors is called an **exclusive-dealing contract.** A seller is prohibited from making an exclusive-dealing contract under Section 3 if the effect of the contract is "to substantially lessen competition or tend to create a monopoly."

The leading exclusive-dealing decision was made by the Supreme Court in the case of *Standard Oil Co. of California v. United States.*[18] In this case, the then-largest gasoline seller in the nation made exclusive-dealing contracts with independent stations in seven western states. The contracts involved 16 percent of all retail outlets, whose sales were approximately 7 percent of all retail sales in that market. The Court noted that the market was substantially concentrated because the seven largest gasoline suppliers all used exclusive-dealing contracts with their independent retailers and together controlled 65 percent of the market. Looking at market conditions after the arrangements were instituted, the Court found that market shares were extremely stable, and entry into the market was apparently restricted. Thus, the Court held that Section 3 of the Clayton Act had been violated, because competition was "foreclosed in a substantial share" of the relevant market.

Tying Arrangements. When a seller conditions the sale of a product (the tying product) on the buyer's agreement to purchase another product (the tied product) produced or distributed by the same seller, a **tying arrangement,** or *tie-in sales agreement*, results. The legality of a tie-in agreement depends on many factors, particularly the purpose of the agreement and the agreement's likely effect on competition in the relevant markets (the market for the tying product and the market for the tied product). In 1936, for example, the United States Supreme Court held that International Business Machines and Remington

---

17. See, for example, *Brooke Group, Ltd. v. Brown & Williamson Tobacco Corp.*, 509 U.S. 209, 113 S.Ct. 2578, 125 L.Ed.2d 168 (1993), in which the Supreme Court held that a seller's price-cutting policies could not be predatory "[g]iven the market's realities"—the size of the seller's market share, expanding output by other sellers, and other factors.

18. 37 U.S. 293, 69 S.Ct. 1051, 93 L.Ed. 1371 (1949).

Rand had violated Section 3 of the Clayton Act by requiring the purchase of their own machine cards (the tied product) as a condition to the leasing of their tabulation machines (the tying product). Because only these two firms sold completely automated tabulation machines, the Court concluded that each possessed market power sufficient to "substantially lessen competition" through the tying arrangements.[19]

Section 3 of the Clayton Act has been held to apply only to commodities, not to services. Tying arrangements, however, also can be considered agreements that restrain trade in violation of Section 1 of the Sherman Act. Thus, cases involving tying arrangements of services have been brought under Section 1 of the Sherman Act. Traditionally, the courts have held tying arrangements brought under the Sherman Act to be illegal *per se*. In recent years, however, courts have shown a willingness to look at factors that are important in a rule-of-reason analysis.

MERGERS

Under Section 7 of the Clayton Act, a person or business organization cannot hold stock or assets in more than one business where "the effect . . . may be to substantially lessen competition." Section 7 is the statutory authority for preventing mergers that could result in monopoly power or a substantial lessening of competition in the marketplace. Section 7 applies to three types of mergers: horizontal mergers, vertical mergers, and conglomerate mergers. We discuss each type of merger in the following subsections.

A crucial consideration in most merger cases is **market concentration.** Determining market concentration involves allocating percentage market shares among the various companies in the relevant market. When a small number of companies share a large part of the market, the market is concentrated. For example, if the four largest grocery stores in Chicago accounted for 80 percent of all retail food sales, the market clearly would be concentrated in those four firms. Competition, however, is not necessarily diminished solely as a result of market concentration, and other factors must be considered in determining whether a merger will violate Section 7. Another concept of particular importance in evaluating the effects of a merger is whether the merger will make it more

difficult for potential competitors to enter the relevant market.

Horizontal Mergers. Mergers between firms that compete with each other in the same market are called **horizontal mergers.** If a horizontal merger creates an entity with anything other than a small-percentage market share, the merger will be presumed illegal. This is because of the United States Supreme Court's interpretation that Congress, in amending Section 7 of the Clayton Act in 1950, intended to prevent mergers that increase market concentration.[20] Three other factors that the courts also consider in analyzing the legality of a horizontal merger are the overall concentration of the relevant market, the relevant market's history of tending toward concentration, and whether the merger is apparently designed to establish market power or restrict competition.

The Federal Trade Commission (FTC) and the U.S. Department of Justice (DOJ) have established guidelines indicating which mergers will be challenged. Under the guidelines, the first factor to be considered in determining whether a merger will be challenged is the degree of concentration in the relevant market. This is done by comparing the pre-merger market concentration with the anticipated postmerger market concentration.

In determining market concentration, the FTC and the DOJ employ what is known as the **Herfindahl-Hirschman Index (HHI).** The HHI is computed by summing the squares of each of the percentage market shares of firms in the relevant market. For example, if there are four firms with shares of 30 percent, 30 percent, 20 percent, and 20 percent, respectively, then the pre-merger HHI equals 2,600 ($30^2 + 30^2 + 20^2 + 20^2 = 2,600$).

If the pre-merger HHI is less than 1,000, then the market is unconcentrated, and the merger will not likely be challenged. If the pre-merger HHI is between 1,000 and 1,800, the industry is moderately concentrated, and the merger will be challenged only if it increases the HHI by 100 points or more. If the pre-merger HHI is greater than 1,800, the market is highly concentrated. In a highly concentrated market, a merger that produces an increase in the HHI between 50 and 100 points raises significant competitive concerns. Mergers that produce an increase in the

19. *International Business Machines Corp. v. United States*, 298 U.S. 131, 56 S.Ct. 701, 80 L.Ed. 1085 (1936).

20. *Brown Shoe v. United States*, 370 U.S. 294, 82 S.Ct. 1502, 8 L.Ed.2d 510 (1962).

HHI of more than 100 points in a highly concentrated market are deemed likely to enhance market power.

The guidelines stress that the determination of market share and market concentration is only the starting point in analyzing the potential anticompetitive effects of a merger. Before deciding to challenge a merger, the FTC and the DOJ will look at a number of other factors, including the ease of entry into the relevant market, economic efficiency, the financial condition of the merging firms, the nature and price of the product or products involved, and so on. In the case of a leading firm—one having a market share that is at least 35 percent and is twice that of the next leading firm—any merger with a firm having as little as a 1 percent share will be challenged.

Vertical Mergers.   A **vertical merger** occurs when a company at one stage of production acquires a company at a higher or lower stage of production. An example of a vertical merger is a company merging with one of its suppliers or retailers. Courts in the past have almost exclusively focused on "foreclosure" in assessing vertical mergers. Foreclosure occurs when competitors of the merging firms lose opportunities either to sell products to or buy products from the merging firms.

For example, in *United States v. E. I. du Pont de Nemours & Co.,*[21] du Pont was challenged for acquiring a considerable amount of General Motors (GM) stock. In holding that the transaction was illegal, the United States Supreme Court noted that stock acquisition would enable du Pont to foreclose other sellers of fabrics and finishes from selling to GM, which then accounted for 50 percent of all auto fabric and finishes purchases.

Today, whether a vertical merger will be deemed illegal generally depends on several factors, including market concentration, barriers to entry into the market, and the apparent intent of the merging parties. Mergers that do not prevent competitors of either of the merging firms from competing in a segment of the market will not be condemned as foreclosing competition and are legal.

Conglomerate Mergers.   There are three general types of **conglomerate mergers**: market-extension, product-extension, and diversification mergers. A market-extension merger occurs when a firm seeks to sell its product in a new market by merging with a firm already established in that market. A product-extension merger occurs when a firm seeks to add a closely related product to its existing line by merging with a firm already producing that product. For example, a manufacturer might seek to extend its line of household products to include floor wax by acquiring a leading manufacturer of floor wax. Diversification occurs when a firm merges with another firm that offers a product or service wholly unrelated to the first firm's existing activities. An example of a diversification merger is an automobile manufacturer's acquisition of a motel chain.

INTERLOCKING DIRECTORATES

Section 8 of the Clayton Act deals with *interlocking directorates*—that is, the practice of having individuals serve as directors on the boards of two or more competing companies simultaneously. Specifically, no person may be a director in two or more competing corporations at the same time if either of the corporations has capital, surplus, or undivided profits aggregating more than $16,732,000 or competitive sales of $1,673,200 or more. The threshold amounts are adjusted each year by the Federal Trade Commission (FTC). (The amounts given here are those announced by the FTC in 2000.)

SECTION 5

The Federal Trade Commission Act

The Federal Trade Commission Act was enacted in 1914, the same year the Clayton Act was written into law. Section 5 is the sole substantive provision of the act. It provides, in part, as follows: "Unfair methods of competition in or affecting commerce, and unfair or deceptive acts or practices in or affecting commerce are hereby declared illegal." Section 5 condemns all forms of anticompetitive behavior that are not covered under other federal antitrust laws. The act also created the Federal Trade Commission to implement the act's provisions.

SECTION 6

Enforcement of Antitrust Laws

The federal agencies that enforce the federal antitrust laws are the U.S. Department of Justice (DOJ) and

---

21. 353 U.S. 586, 77 S.Ct. 872, 1 L.Ed.2d 1057 (1957).

the Federal Trade Commission (FTC). Only the DOJ can prosecute violations of the Sherman Act as either criminal or civil violations. Violations of the Clayton Act are not crimes, and the DOJ or the FTC can enforce that statute through civil proceedings. The various remedies that the DOJ or the FTC has asked the courts to impose include **divestiture** (making a company give up one or more of its operating functions) and dissolution. The DOJ or the FTC might force a group of meat packers, for example, to divest itself of control or ownership of butcher shops.

The FTC has sole authority to enforce violations of Section 5 of the Federal Trade Commission Act. FTC actions are effected through administrative orders, but if a firm violates an FTC order, the FTC can seek court sanctions for the violation.

A private party can sue for treble damages and attorneys' fees if the party is injured as a result of a violation of the Sherman Act or the Clayton Act. In some instances, private parties may also seek injunctive relief to prevent antitrust violations. The courts have determined that the ability to sue depends on the directness of the injury suffered by the would-be plaintiff. Thus, a person wishing to sue under the Sherman Act must prove (1) that the antitrust violation either caused or was a substantial factor in causing the injury that was suffered and (2) that the unlawful actions of the accused party affected business activities of the plaintiff that were protected by the antitrust laws.

In recent years, more than 90 percent of all antitrust actions have been brought by private plaintiffs. One reason for this is, of course, that successful plaintiffs may recover three times the damages that they have suffered as a result of the violation. Such recoveries by private plaintiffs for antitrust violations have been rationalized as encouraging people to act as "private attorneys general" who will vigorously pursue antitrust violators on their own initiative.

SECTION 7

U.S. Antitrust Laws in the Global Context

U.S. antitrust laws have a broad application. They may subject persons in foreign nations to their provisions as well as protect foreign consumers and competitors

from violations committed by U.S. business firms. Consequently, *foreign persons*, a term that by definition includes foreign governments, may sue under U.S. antitrust laws in U.S. courts.

Section 1 of the Sherman Act of 1890 provides for the extraterritorial effect of the U.S. antitrust laws. The United States is a major proponent of free competition in the global economy, and thus any conspiracy that has a substantial effect on U.S. commerce is within the reach of the Sherman Act. The violation may even occur outside the United States, and foreign governments as well as persons can be sued for violation of U.S. antitrust laws. Before U.S. courts will exercise jurisdiction and apply antitrust laws, it must be shown that the alleged violation had a *substantial effect* on U.S. commerce. U.S. jurisdiction is automatically invoked, however, when a *per se* violation occurs.

If a domestic firm, for example, joins a foreign cartel to control the production, price, or distribution of goods, and this cartel has a *substantial effect* on U.S. commerce, a *per se* violation may exist. Hence, both the domestic firm and the foreign cartel could be sued for violation of the U.S. antitrust laws. Likewise, if a foreign firm doing business in the United States enters into a price-fixing or other anticompetitive agreement to control a portion of U.S. markets, a *per se* violation may exist.

In 1982, Congress amended the Sherman Act and the Federal Trade Commission Act of 1914 to limit their application when unfair methods of competition are involved in U.S. export trade or commerce with foreign nations. The acts are not limited, however, when there is a "direct, substantial, and reasonably foreseeable effect" on U.S. domestic commerce that results in a claim for damages.

SECTION 8

Exemptions from Antitrust Law

There are many legislative and constitutional limitations on antitrust enforcement. Most statutory and judicially created exemptions to the antitrust laws apply to the following areas or activities:

1. *Labor.* Section 6 of the Clayton Act generally permits labor unions to organize and bargain without violating antitrust laws. Section 20 of the Clayton Act specifies that strikes and other labor activities are not

violations of any law of the United States. A union can lose its exemption, however, if it combines with a nonlabor group rather than acting simply in its own self-interest.

2. *Agricultural associations and fisheries.* Section 6 of the Clayton Act (along with the Cooperative Marketing Associations Act of 1922[22]) exempts agricultural cooperatives from the antitrust laws. The Fisheries Cooperative Marketing Act of 1976 exempts from antitrust legislation individuals in the fishing industry who collectively catch, produce, and prepare their products for market. Both exemptions allow members of such co-ops to combine and set prices for a particular product, but they do not allow them to engage in exclusionary practices or restraints of trade directed at competitors.

3. *Insurance.* The McCarran-Ferguson Act[23] of 1945 exempts the insurance business from the antitrust laws whenever state regulation exists. This exemption does not cover boycotts, coercion, or intimidation on the part of insurance companies.

4. *Foreign trade.* Under the provisions of the 1918 Webb-Pomerene Act,[24] American exporters may engage in cooperative activity to compete with similar foreign associations. This type of cooperative activity may not, however, restrain trade within the United States or injure other American exporters. The Export Trading Company Act[25] of 1982 broadened the Webb-Pomerene Act by permitting the Department of Justice to certify properly qualified export trading companies. Any activity within the scope described by the certificate is exempt from public prosecution under the antitrust laws.

5. *Professional baseball.* In 1922, the United States Supreme Court held that professional baseball was not within the reach of federal antitrust laws because it did not involve "interstate commerce."[26] Some of the effects of this decision, however, were modified by the Curt Flood Act of 1998. Essentially, the act allows players the option of suing team owners for anticompetitive practices if, for example, the owners collude

to "blacklist" players, hold down players' salaries, or force players to play for specific teams.

6. *Oil marketing.* The 1935 Interstate Oil Compact allows states to determine quotas on oil that will be marketed in interstate commerce.

7. *Cooperative research and production.* Cooperative research among small business firms is exempt under the Small Business Act[27] of 1958. Research or production of a product, process, or service by joint ventures consisting of competitors is exempt under special federal legislation, including the National Cooperative Research Act[28] of 1984, as amended by the National Cooperative Research and Production Act of 1993.

8. *Joint efforts by businesspersons to obtain legislative or executive action.* This is often referred to as the Noerr-Pennington doctrine.[29] For example, video producers might jointly lobby Congress to change the copyright laws without being held liable for attempting to restrain trade. Though selfish rather than purely public-minded conduct is permitted, there is an exception: an action will not be protected if it is clear that the action is "objectively baseless in the sense that no reasonable [person] could reasonably expect success on the merits" and it is an attempt to make anticompetitive use of government processes.[30]

9. *Other exemptions.* Other activities exempt from antitrust laws include activities approved by the president in furtherance of the defense of our nation (under the Defense Production Act[31] of 1950); state actions, when the state policy is clearly articulated and the policy is actively supervised by the state;[32] and activities of regulated industries (such as the transportation, communication, and banking industries) when federal agencies (such as the Federal Communications Commission) have primary regulatory authority.

22. 7 U.S.C. Sections 291–292.

23. 15 U.S.C. Sections 1011–1015.

24. 15 U.S.C. Sections 61–66.

25. 15 U.S.C. Sections 4001–4003.

26. *Federal Baseball Club of Baltimore, Inc. v. National League of Professional Baseball Clubs,* 259 U.S. 200, 42 S.Ct. 465, 66 L.Ed. 898 (1922).

27. 15 U.S.C. Sections 631–657.

28. 15 U.S.C. Sections 4301–4306.

29. See *United Mine Workers of America v. Pennington,* 381 U.S. 657, 89 S.Ct. 1585, 14 L.Ed.2d 626 (1965); and *Eastern Railroad Presidents Conference v. Noerr Motor Freight, Inc.,* 365 U.S. 127, 81 S.Ct. 523, 5 L.Ed.2d 464 (1961).

30. *Professional Real Estate Investors, Inc. v. Columbia Pictures Industries, Inc.,* 508 U.S. 49, 113 S.Ct. 1920, 123 L.Ed.2d 611 (1993).

31. 50 App.U.S.C. 2061–2171.

32. See *Parker v. Brown,* 347 U.S. 341, 63 S.Ct. 307, 87 L.Ed. 315 (1943).

TERMS AND CONCEPTS TO REVIEW

antitrust law 841

attempted monopolization 849

conglomerate merger 853

divestiture 854

exclusive-dealing contract 851

group boycott 843

Herfindahl-Hirschman Index
   (HHI) 852

horizontal merger 852

horizontal restraint 843

market concentration 852

market power 842

market-share test 849

monopolization 848

monopoly 842

monopoly power 842

per se violation 843

predatory pricing 848

price discrimination 851

price-fixing agreement 843

resale price maintenance
   agreement 847

restraint on trade 841

rule of reason 842

tying arrangement 851

vertical merger 853

vertical restraint 845

vertically integrated firm 846

QUESTIONS AND CASE PROBLEMS

45–1. ANTITRUST LAWS. Allitron, Inc., and Donovan, Ltd., are interstate competitors selling similar appliances, principally in the states of Indiana, Kentucky, Illinois, and Ohio. Allitron and Donovan agree that Allitron will no longer sell in Ohio and Indiana and that Donovan will no longer sell in Kentucky and Illinois. Have Allitron and Donovan violated any antitrust law? If so, which law? Explain.

45–2. ANTITRUST LAWS. The partnership of Alvaredo and Parish is engaged in the oil-wellhead service industry in the states of New Mexico and Colorado. The firm presently has about 40 percent of the market for this service. Webb Corp. competes with the Alvaredo-Parish partnership in the same state area. Webb has approximately 35 percent of the market. Alvaredo and Parish acquire the stock and assets of Webb Corp. Do the antitrust laws prohibit the type of action undertaken by Alvaredo and Parish? Discuss fully.

45–3. HORIZONTAL RESTRAINTS. Jorge's Appliance Corp. was a new retail seller of appliances in Sunrise City. Because of its innovative sales techniques and financing, Jorge's caused a substantial loss of sales from the appliance department of No-Glow Department Store, a large chain store with a great deal of buying power. No-Glow told a number of appliance manufacturers from whom it made large-volume purchases that if they continued to sell to Jorge's, No-Glow would discontinue purchasing from them. The manufacturers immediately stopped selling appliances to Jorge's. Jorge's filed suit against No-Glow and the manufacturers, claiming that their actions constituted an antitrust viola-

tion. No-Glow and the manufacturers were able to prove that Jorge's was a small retailer with a small market share. They claimed that because the relevant market was not substantially affected, they were not guilty of restraint of trade. Discuss fully whether there was an antitrust violation.

45–4. EXCLUSIONARY PRACTICES. Instant Foto Corp. is a manufacturer of photography film. At the present time, Instant Foto has approximately 50 percent of the market. Instant Foto advertises that the purchase price for Instant Foto film includes photo processing by Instant Foto Corp. Instant Foto claims that its film processing is specially designed to improve the quality of photos taken with Instant Foto film. Is Instant Foto's combination of film purchase and film processing an antitrust violation? Explain.

45–5. TYING ARRANGEMENTS. Eastman Kodak Co. has about a 20 percent share of the highly competitive market for high-volume photocopiers and microfilm equipment and controls nearly the entire market for replacement parts for its equipment (which are not interchangeable with parts for other manufacturers' equipment). Prior to 1985, Kodak sold replacement parts for its equipment without significant restrictions. As a result, a number of independent service organizations (ISOs) purchased Kodak parts to use when repairing and servicing Kodak copiers. In 1985, Kodak changed its policy to prevent the ISOs from competing with Kodak's own service organizations. It ceased selling parts to ISOs and refused to sell replacement parts to its customers unless they agreed not to have their equipment serviced by ISOs. In 1987, Image

Technical Services, Inc., and seventeen other ISOs sued Kodak, alleging that Kodak's policy was a tying arrangement in violation of Section 1 of the Sherman Act. Assuming that Kodak does not have market power in the market for photocopying and microfilm equipment, does Kodak's restrictive policy constitute an illegal tying arrangement? Does it violate antitrust laws in any way? Discuss fully. [*Eastman Kodak Co. v. Image Technical Services, Inc.*, 504 U.S. 451, 112 S.Ct. 2072, 119 L.Ed.2d 265 (1992)]

45–6. ROBINSON-PATMAN ACT. Stelwagon Manufacturing Co. agreed with Tarmac Roofing Systems, Inc., to promote and develop a market for Tarmac's products in the Philadelphia area. In return, Tarmac promised not to sell its products to other area distributors. In 1991, Stelwagon learned that Tarmac had been selling its products to Stelwagon's competitors—the Standard Roofing Co. and the Celotex Corp.—at substantially lower prices. Stelwagon filed a suit against Tarmac in a federal district court. What is the principal factor in determining whether Tarmac violated the Robinson-Patman Act? Did Tarmac violate the act? [*Stelwagon Manufacturing Co. v. Tarmac Roofing Systems, Inc.*, 63 F.3d 1267 (3d Cir. 1995)]

45–7. ANTITRUST LAWS. Great Western Directories, Inc. (GW), is an independent publisher of telephone directory Yellow Pages. GW buys information for its listings from Southwestern Bell Telephone Co. (SBT). Southwestern Bell Corp. owns SBT, as well as Southwestern Bell Yellow Pages (SBYP), which publishes a directory in competition with GW. In June 1988, in some markets, SBT raised the price for its listing information, and SBYP lowered the price for advertising in its Yellow Pages. GW feared that these companies would do the same thing in other local markets, and it would then be too expensive to compete in those markets. Because of this fear, GW left one market and declined to compete in another. Consequently, SBYP had a monopoly in those markets. GW and another independent publisher filed a suit in a federal district court against Southwestern Bell Corp. What antitrust law, if any, did Southwestern Bell Corp. violate? Should the independent companies be entitled to damages? [*Great Western Directories, Inc. v. Southwestern Bell Telephone Co.*, 74 F.3d 613 (5th Cir. 1996)]

45–8. RESTRAINT OF TRADE. The National Collegiate Athletic Association (NCAA) coordinates the intercollegiate athletic programs of its members by issuing rules and setting standards governing, among other things, the coaching staffs. The NCAA set up a "Cost Reduction Committee" to consider ways to cut the costs of intercollegiate athletics while maintaining competition. The committee included financial aid personnel, intercollegiate athletic administrators, college presidents, university faculty members, and a university chancellor. It was felt that "only a collaborative effort could reduce costs while maintaining a level playing field." The committee proposed a rule to restrict the annual compensation of certain coaches to $16,000. The NCAA adopted the rule. Basketball coaches affected by the rule filed a suit in a federal district court against the NCAA, alleging a violation of Section 1 of the Sherman Antitrust Act. Is the rule a *per se* violation of the Sherman Act, or should it be evaluated under the rule of reason? If it is subject to the rule of reason, is it an illegal restraint of trade? Discuss fully. [*Law v. National Collegiate Athletic Association*, 134 F.3d 1010 (10th Cir. 1998)]

45–9. TYING ARRANGEMENT. Public Interest Corp. (PIC) owned and operated television station WTMV-TV in Lakeland, Florida. MCA Television, Ltd., owns and licenses syndicated television programs. The parties entered into a licensing contract with respect to several television shows. MCA conditioned the license on PIC's agreeing to take another show, *Harry and the Hendersons*. PIC agreed to this arrangement, although it would not have chosen to license *Harry* if it did not have to do so to secure the licenses for the other shows. More than two years into the contract, a dispute arose over PIC's payments, and negotiations failed to resolve the dispute. In a letter, MCA suspended PIC's broadcast rights for all of its shows and stated that "[a]ny telecasts of MCA programming by WTMV-TV . . . will be deemed unauthorized and shall constitute an infringement of MCA's copyrights." PIC nonetheless continued broadcasting MCA's programs, with the exception of *Harry*. MCA filed a suit in a federal district court against PIC, alleging breach of contract and copyright infringement. PIC filed a counterclaim, contending in part that MCA's deal was an illegal tying arrangement. Is PIC correct? Explain. [*MCA Television, Ltd. v. Public Interest Corp.*, 171 F.3d 1265 (11th Cir. 1999)]

45–10. IN YOUR COURT

Timothy Lane purchased feed from Fur Breeders Agricultural Cooperative (the co-op) for use in his fur-breeding business. All members of the co-op, including Lane, were charged the same price for the feed. The co-op, however, offered free delivery services to all of its members except Lane, who had to pick up the feed. Lane sued the co-op, alleging that the co-op's actions constituted price discrimination in violation of Section 2 of the Clayton Act, as amended. Lane argued that the added cost he had to incur in picking up the feed (about $16,000 per year) effectively raised the "price" he paid for the feed relative to the other members. As a result, contended Lane, it was difficult for him to make significant profits in this highly competitive industry. The co-op moved to dismiss the case on the ground that all members were charged the same "price," and thus there could be no "price" discrimination. Assume that you are the judge in the trial court hearing this case and answer the following questions:

(a) Should the cost of picking up the feed be included in the "price" Lane paid for the feed? How will you answer this question?

(b) Generally, what factors should you consider in determining whether to grant a motion to dismiss a case? In the case now before your court, should you grant the defendant's motion to dismiss? Why or why not?

45–11. A Question of Ethics

A group of lawyers in the District of Columbia regularly acted as court-appointed attorneys for indigent defendants in District of Columbia criminal cases. At a meeting of the Superior Court Trial Lawyers Association (SCTLA), the attorneys agreed to stop providing this representation until the district increased their compensation. Their subsequent boycott had a severe impact on the district's criminal justice system, and the District of Columbia gave in to the lawyers' demands for higher pay. After the lawyers had returned to work, the Federal Trade Commission filed a complaint against the SCTLA and four of its officers and, after an investigation, ruled that the SCTLA's activities constituted an illegal group boycott in violation of antitrust laws. [*Federal Trade Commission v. Superior Court Trial Lawyers Association*, 493 U.S. 411, 110 S.Ct. 768, 107 L.Ed.2d 851 (1990)]

(a) The SCTLA obviously was aware of the negative impact its decision would have on the district's criminal justice system. Given this fact, do you think the lawyers behaved ethically?

(b) On appeal, the SCTLA claimed that its boycott was undertaken to publicize the fact that the attorneys were underpaid and that the boycott thus constituted an expression protected by the First Amendment. Do you agree with this argument?

(c) Labor unions have the right to strike when negotiations between labor and management fail. The SCTLA is prohibited from striking. Is it fair to prohibit members of the SCTLA from "striking" against their employer, the District of Columbia, simply because the SCTLA is a professional organization and not a labor union?

LAW ON THE WEB

For updated links to resources available on the Web, as well as a variety of other materials, visit this text's Web site at http://wbl.westbuslaw.com.

You can access the Antitrust Division of the U.S. Department of Justice online at

http://www.usdoj.gov

To see the American Bar Association's Web page on antitrust law, go to

http://www.abanet.org/antitrust

The Federal Trade Commission offers an abundance of information on antitrust law, including "A Plain English Guide to Antitrust Laws," at

http://www.ftc.gov/ftc/antitrust.htm

LEGAL RESEARCH EXERCISES ON THE WEB

Go to http://wbl.westbuslaw.com, the Web site that accompanies this text. Select "Internet Applications," and then click on "Chapter 45." There you will find the following Internet research exercises that you can perform to learn more about the application of antitrust laws to vertical restraints:

Activity 45–1: Vertical Restraints and the Rule of Reason

Activity 45–2: Microsoft and Monopolization

UNIT NINE—CUMULATIVE BUSINESS HYPOTHETICAL

Falwell Motors, Inc., is a large corporation that manufactures automobile batteries.

1. The Occupational Safety and Health Administration (OSHA) has proposed a new safety rule governing the handling of certain acids in the workplace, including those used by Falwell in its manufacturing operations. Falwell concludes that the rule, which will involve substantial compliance costs, will not significantly increase workplace safety. Falwell sends a letter to OSHA indicating its objections to the proposed rule and enclosing research reports and other data supporting those objections. Does OSHA have any obligation to consider these objections? What procedures must OSHA follow when it makes new rules, such as this one?

2. The Federal Trade Commission (FTC) learns that one of the retail stores that sells Falwell's batteries engages in deceptive advertising practices. What actions can the FTC take against the retailer?

3. For years, Falwell has shipped the toxic waste created by its manufacturing process to a waste-disposal site in the next county. The waste site has become contaminated by leakage from toxic waste containers delivered to the site by other manufacturers. Can Falwell be held liable for clean-up costs, even though its containers were not the ones that leaked? If so, what is the extent of its liability?

4. Falwell faces stiff competition from Alchem, Inc., another battery manufacturer. To acquire control over Alchem, Falwell makes a tender offer to Alchem's shareholders. If Falwell succeeds in its attempt and Alchem is merged into Falwell, will the merger violate any antitrust laws? Suppose the merger falls through. The vice president of Falwell's battery division and the president of Alchem agree to divide up the market between them, so they will not have to compete for customers. Is this agreement legal? Explain.

FOCUS ON LEGAL REASONING
California Dental Association
v. Federal Trade Commission

INTRODUCTION

The application of Section 5 of the Federal Trade Commission Act in the context of antitrust law is discussed in Chapter 45. In this *Focus on Legal Reasoning*, we examine *California Dental Association v. Federal Trade Commission*,[1] a recent decision by the United States Supreme Court concerning that statute. The case involved a trade association. Generally, the rule of reason is applied to assess the anticompetitive or procompetitive nature of such an association's activities when those activities are challenged under the antitrust laws, including sections of the Federal Trade Commision Act.

1. 526 U.S. 756, 119 S.Ct. 1604, 143 L.Ed.2d 935 (1999).

CASE BACKGROUND

The California Dental Association (CDA) is a nonprofit association of local dentists' organizations to which about 75 percent of California's dentists belong. The CDA provides preferential insurance arrangements and other benefits for its members, and engages in lobbying, litigation, marketing, and public relations on the members' behalf.

The CDA's members agree to abide by the association's Code of Ethics, which, among other things, prohibits false or misleading advertising. The CDA has issued interpretive advisory opinions and guidelines relating to advertising. These guidelines included restrictions on two types of truthful, nondeceptive advertising: price

advertising, particularly discounted fees, and advertising relating to the quality of dental services.

The Federal Trade Commission (FTC) filed a complaint with an administrative law judge (ALJ), alleging that the CDA violated Section 5 of the Federal Trade Commission Act in applying its guidelines to restrict the price and quality advertising. The ALJ found that the CDA violated Section 5. On appeal, the FTC upheld this finding, as did the U.S. Court of Appeals for the Ninth Circuit. The CDA appealed to the United States Supreme Court. One issue was the "sufficiency of the analysis of the anticompetitive effects" by the lower court.

MAJORITY OPINION

Justice *SOUTER* delivered the opinion of the Court.
* * * *

The case before us * * * fails to present a situation in which the likelihood of anticompetitive effects is * * * obvious. Even on [the] view that bars [prohibitions] on truthful and verifiable price and quality advertising are *prima facie* anticompetitive and place the burden of procompetitive justification on those who agree to adopt them, the very issue at the threshold of this case is whether professional price and quality advertising is sufficiently verifiable in theory and in fact to fall within such a general rule. * * * [I]t seems to us that the CDA's advertising restrictions might plausibly be thought to have a net procompetitive effect, or possibly no effect at all on competition. The restrictions on * * * advertising are, at least on their face, designed to avoid false or deceptive advertising in a market characterized by striking disparities between

the information available to the professional and the patient. In a market for professional services, in which advertising is relatively rare and the comparability of service packages not easily established, the difficulty for customers or potential competitors to get and verify information about the price and availability of services magnifies the dangers to competition associated with misleading advertising. What is more, the quality of professional services tends to resist either calibration or monitoring by individual patients or clients, partly because of the specialized knowledge required to evaluate the services, and partly because of the difficulty in determining whether, and the degree to which, an outcome is attributable to the quality of services (like a poor job of tooth-filling) or to something else (like a very tough walnut). Patients' attachments to particular professionals, the rationality of which is difficult to assess, complicate the picture even further. The existence of such significant challenges to informed decisionmaking by the customer for professional services immediately suggests that advertising restrictions arguably protecting patients from misleading or irrelevant advertising call for more than cursory treatment as obviously comparable to classic horizontal agreements to limit output or price competition.

* * * *

* * * Because the Court of Appeals did not scrutinize the assumption of relative anticompetitive tendencies, we vacate the judgment and remand the case for a fuller consideration of the issue.

DISSENTING OPINION

Justice *BREYER,* * * * dissenting * * * .

* * * *

In the Court's view, the legal analysis conducted by the Court of Appeals was insufficient, and the Court remands the case for a more thorough application of the rule of reason. But in what way did the Court of Appeals fail? * * *

* * * *

The upshot, in my view, is that the Court of Appeals, applying ordinary antitrust principles, reached an unexceptional conclusion. It is the same legal conclusion that this Court itself reached in *FTC v. Indiana Federation of Dentists,* 476 U.S. 447, 106 S.Ct. 2009, 90 L.Ed.2d 445 (1986)—a much closer case than this one. There the Court found that an agreement by dentists not to submit dental X rays to insurers violated the rule of reason. The anticompetitive tendency of that agreement was to reduce competition among dentists in respect to their willingness to submit X rays to insurers—a matter in respect to which consumers are relatively indifferent, as compared to advertising of price discounts and service quality, the matters at issue here. The redeeming virtue in *Indiana Federation* was the alleged undesirability of having insurers consider a range of matters when deciding whether treatment was justified—a virtue no less plausible, and no less proved, than the virtue offered here. The "power" of the dentists to enforce their agreement was no greater than that at issue here (control of 75% to 90% of the relevant markets). It is difficult to see how the two cases can be reconciled.

LEGAL REASONING AND ANALYSIS

1. Legal Reasoning. What reasons does the majority provide to justify its conclusion? How do those reasons contrast with the dissent's analysis? What seems to be the issue of contention in this case? With whom do you agree? Why?

2. Legal Analysis. The dissent cites, in its opinion, *Federal Trade Commission v. Indiana Federation of Dentists,* 476 U.S. 447, 106 S.Ct. 2009, 90 L.Ed.2d 445 (1986) (see the *Law on the Web* feature at the end of Chapter 2 for instructions on how to access state court opinions). Do the facts and issues in that case compare to the facts and issues of the *California Dental* case? How do the holdings in the cases compare? Do the reasoning and the law of the *Indiana Federation* case support the position of the majority or the dissent in the *California Dental* case?

3. Economic Considerations. Under what circumstances might a court conclude that a trade association's restraint of trade is reasonable?

4. Implications for Associations. What do the reasoning and the outcome in this case suggest to those nonprofit associations that expect their members to follow the associations' marketing guidelines?

5. Case Briefing Assignment. Using the guidelines for briefing cases given in Appendix A of this text, brief the *Indiana Federation* case.

GOING ONLINE

Within the Web site of the Federal Trade Commission (FTC), the page at http://www.ftc.gov/ftc/antitrust.htm includes links to complaints, orders, and final actions by the FTC in the area of antitrust law.

FOCUS ON ETHICS
Government Regulation

If this text had been written a hundred years ago, it would have had little to say about federal government regulation. To be sure, by the 1890s, the beginnings of federal antitrust law had been manifested in the form of the Interstate Commerce Act and the Sherman Act, but there was little or no legislation designed to protect consumers or the environment. Today, in contrast, virtually every area of economic activity is regulated by the government.

From a very broad perspective, ethical issues in government regulation arise because regulation, by its very nature, means that some traditional rights and freedoms have to be given up to ensure that other rights and freedoms are protected. Essentially, government regulation brings two ethical principles into conflict. On the one hand, deeply embedded in American culture is the idea that the government should play a limited role in directing our lives. Indeed, this nation was founded so that Americans could be free from the "heavy hand of government" experienced by the colonists under English rule. On the other hand, one of the basic functions of government is to protect the welfare of individuals and the environment in which they live.

Ultimately, virtually every law or rule regulating business represents a decision to give up certain rights in order to protect other perceived rights. In this *Focus on Ethics,* we look at some of the ethical aspects of government regulation.

ENVIRONMENTAL LAW

Questions of fairness inevitably arise in regard to environmental law. Has the government gone too far in regulating businesses in the interest of protecting the environment? Has the government gone far enough? At what point do the costs of environmental regulations become too burdensome for society to bear? These are broad questions, but they are ethical in nature, because they ultimately relate to society's notions of what is right, just, or good.

If manufacturers ceased all production and Americans returned to the rural life of earlier times, the environment would certainly benefit. Obviously, Americans do not want to pay that high a cost. Certainly, we want to enjoy the fruits of our advanced economy, and economic productivity has always been a policy goal of the American government. But environmental protection means that some sacrifices will have to be made. How much are we willing to sacrifice today to ensure that future generations will continue to have a healthful world in which to live?

Economic Productivity versus Environmental Protection

This tension between the two goals of economic productivity and environmental protection was highlighted in a case brought by two Oregon ranchers—Brad Bennett and Mario Giordano—and two Oregon irrigation districts (collectively, the Bennett group) against the Fish and Wildlife Service (FSW) and the secretary of the Department of the Interior. The case originated after the FWS proposed that the minimum water levels in two reservoirs be increased to protect two endangered species of fish. If the proposal were implemented, less water could be drawn from the reservoirs for irrigation and other purposes, which would have a serious economic impact on the ranchers' businesses.

In a citizens' suit against the FWS, the Bennett group claimed that the agency neglected to use the best available scientific and commercial data in making its decision, as required under the Endangered Species Act (ESA) of 1973; nor did the FWS take into account the economic impact of its water-level recommendations. At issue in the case, which ultimately reached the United States Supreme Court, was whether the ranchers had standing to sue under the ESA. The question was significant because the Bennett group was not seeking to protect the environment but to safeguard their economic interests.

Both a federal district court and a federal appellate court held that the group did not have standing to sue because its claim did not fall within the "zone of interests" watched over by the ESA, which was to protect species. The zone-of-interests test has long been applied by the federal courts in determining whether a party has standing to sue under a specific law. Basically, to have standing under this test, a plaintiff must show that the interest that he or she seeks to protect is the kind of interest protected by that specific law.

The Supreme Court, however, unanimously reversed the appellate court's decision. In applying the zone-of-interests test, the Court looked to the citizen-suit language of the ESA, which gives "any person" the right to sue. According to the Court, this language was expansive enough to include the economic interests of the Bennett group.

Moreover, the Court held that in determining whether a party has standing, the courts must look not to the overall purpose of an act but to the particular provision of an act on which the party based his or her complaint. In this case, the Bennett group alleged that the FWS failed to abide by a specific ESA provision that requires an agency to use the "best scientific and commercial data available." The Court noted that while this provision "no doubt serves to advance the ESA's overall goal of species preservation, we think it readily apparent that another objective (if not indeed the primary one) is to avoid needless economic dislocation produced by agency officials zealously but unintelligently pursuing their environmental objectives."[1]

Superfund and Toxic Waste

Although everybody is in favor of cleaning up America's toxic waste dumps, nobody has the slightest idea what this task will ultimately cost. Much of the problem in determining the eventual costs of the Superfund program (CERCLA—see Chapter 44) stems from the difficulty of estimating the costs of cleaning up a site. Until the clean-up is actually undertaken, it is often difficult to assess the extent of contamination. Moreover, there is no agreed-on standard as to how clean these sites need to be before they no

longer pose any threat of harm to life. Do you have to remove *all* of the contamination, or would removal of some lesser amount achieve a reasonable degree of environmental quality? On the cost side of the picture, another question exists: If, say, 90 percent of the waste at a given site could be removed for $50,000, but the removal of the other 10 percent would cost $2 million, is it reasonable to remove that remaining 10 percent?

Another aspect of Superfund that raises questions of fairness is the joint and several liability imposed by the act. This means that a party may be liable for the total costs of cleaning up a hazardous waste site, even though that party was responsible for only a small fraction of the toxic waste dumped at the site.

For some time, Congress has been under pressure to overhaul the Superfund legislation for these and other reasons. Proposed changes to the law would, among other things, allow the Environmental Protection Agency to consider what the land is likely to be used for in the future when determining how clean a site has to be. Another proposed change would eliminate joint and several liability at most sites and exempt certain small businesses from liability.

FAIR DEBT COLLECTION

By passing the Fair Debt Collection Practices Act (FDCPA), Congress expressed society's concern with unfair debt-collection practices. The act prohibits those that collect debts for other parties, such as collection agencies, from engaging in certain abusive tactics, as discussed in Chapter 44. Some have argued that the act did not go far enough in the direction of protecting consumer-debtors, because the act does not cover creditors that collect their own

debts rather than have a third party, such as a collection agency, do so.

Consider, for example, the situation in *Sterling Mirror of Maryland, Inc. v. Gordon.*[2] Sterling Mirror of Maryland, Inc., had installed mirrors in the home of John and Daisy Gordon. Only John signed the contract. Because one of the mirrors was chipped while it was being installed, John Gordon refused to pay the balance due to Sterling Mirror. Sterling Mirror tried to pressure the Gordons into paying for the mirrors by making numerous calls to Daisy at her place of employment. When Sterling Mirror sued the Gordons for the balance due, Daisy counterclaimed for damages under the FDCPA, asserting, among other things, that Sterling Mirror had violated the provisions of that act by contacting her at work. Had Sterling Mirror violated the FDCPA? No, it had not, because Sterling Mirror was not a collection agency, and thus the FDCPA did not apply. Had it been a collection agency, however, it would have violated the FDCPA, because under the act, collection agencies are allowed to contact only the debtor (not the debtor's spouse) at the debtor's place of employment, and then only if the employer does not object.

ANTITRUST LAW AND CONSUMER PROTECTION

From its beginnings in the nineteenth century, antitrust law has sought to maintain a freely competitive business environment so that consumers would not be victimized by monopoly pricing tactics. Consumer welfare has thus from the outset been a touchstone issue in antitrust cases. Sometimes, though, this aspect of antitrust law, which is rooted in ethical notions of fairness, becomes lost in the thicket

---

1. *Bennett v. Spear,* 520 U.S. 154, 117 S.Ct. 1154, 137 L.Ed.2d 281 (1997).

2. 619 A.2d 64 (D.C.App. 1993).

of antitrust lawsuits among competitors.

The Court of Appeals for the Eighth Circuit emphasized the importance of the consumer perspective in antitrust law in a case involving alleged predatory pricing. The case was brought by Gilbert Bathke and other gasoline retailers (the plaintiffs) located in small Iowa communities against Casey's General Stores, Inc. During the 1980s, Casey's, a multistate retailer of gasoline and other goods, had begun to lose profits to its competitors. In an attempt to increase its sales, Casey's had directed its stores that were losing sales to reduce gas prices. The plaintiffs claimed that Casey's price reductions amounted to predatory pricing in violation of, among other laws, Section 2 of the Sherman Act.

One of the central issues in the case concerned Casey's share of the relevant geographic market. The plaintiffs contended that the relevant geographic market consisted of the small towns in which Casey's operated its stores. After all, contended the plaintiffs, consumers preferred to buy their gasoline in the towns in which they lived, and gasoline retailers' trade came mostly from in-town customers. The court, however, stated that a geographic market is determined not by where consumers actually go for their gasoline but where they *could* go. Evidence of consumers' actual habits is not enough, said the court, to establish the relevant geographic market. To demonstrate the "logic and necessity of applying such a requirement in this case," the court illustrated the difference between a "trade area" and a "relevant market."

"Consider the following illustration," stated the court. "Fifteen miles outside of City A is a small town, Town B, which contains a single shoe store, Smith's Clothing. The only people who ever shop in Smith's Clothing are residents of Town B. When Smith's is accused of monopolization, the plaintiffs argue that Town B defines the relevant geographic market, since all of the store's customers come from there. In that case, Smith's market share is 100%. But further inquiry shows the following. Last year 800 residents of Town B purchased shoes. 400 of them purchased from Smith's Clothing, and the other 400 purchased from the numerous shoe stores in City A. Note that this conclusion is absolutely consistent with the proposition that Smith's 'trade area' is Town B. . . . In sum, 'trade area' considers the extent to which customers will travel in order to do business at Smith's. 'Relevant market' considers the extent to which customers will travel in order to avoid doing business at Smith's."

The court concluded that the plaintiffs' evidence, at best, demonstrated only the "trade area" of Casey's stores. The plaintiffs looked at the issue "only from the perspective of Casey's rivals, not from the perspective of the consumer. This is not the correct approach to use in antitrust cases."[3]

DISCUSSION QUESTIONS

1. In the discussion of Superfund in this *Focus on Ethics,* the following question was raised: "If,

---

3. *Bathke v. Casey's General Stores, Inc.,* 64 F.3d 340 (8th Cir. 1995).

say, 90 percent of the waste at a given site could be removed for $50,000, but the removal of the other 10 percent would cost $2 million, is it reasonable to remove that remaining 10 percent?" How would you answer this question?

2. Both environmental and occupational safety laws strive to protect the public health from hazardous substances. Should standards in these two contexts be the same? Or should employees be allowed to voluntarily accept some greater risk in return for a higher wage scale?

3. Assume that removing all asbestos from all public buildings in the nation would save perhaps ten lives per year. If the cost of the asbestos removal were $250 billion, in effect, Americans would be paying $250 million per life saved. Is this too high a price to pay? Should cost ever be a consideration when human lives are at stake?

4. Creditors must comply strictly with the requirements of such consumer protection laws as the Truth-in-Lending Act, the Equal Credit Opportunity Act, and the Fair Debt Collection Practices Act. Even a minor, unintended violation may permit a consumer to sue a creditor for damages. In some cases, consumers have sought damages for violations when the creditor has abided by the "spirit" of the law but not the "letter." Should courts make exceptions when consumers are clearly abusing these protective laws for their own gain? Or should the courts hold creditors liable even when the result is unfair to the creditor?

UNIT TEN

Property

Contents

CHAPTER 46

Personal Property and Bailments

PROPERTY CONSISTS OF THE LEGALLY protected rights and interests a person has in anything with an ascertainable value that is subject to ownership. Property would have little value if the law did not define the right to use it, to sell or dispose of it, and to prevent trespassing on it.

In the beginning of this chapter, we examine the basic attributes of personal and real property, the ways in which ownership rights in both of these forms of property can be held, and issues relating to various types of property. The remainder of the chapter focuses on bailment relationships. A *bailment* is created when property is temporarily delivered into the care of another without a transfer of title. This is the distinguishing characteristic of a bailment compared with a sale or a gift—there is no passage of title and no intent to transfer title.

SECTION 1

Property Classification

Property may be divided into real property and personal property. **Real property** (sometimes called *realty* or *real estate*) means the land and everything permanently attached to it. When structures are permanently attached to the land, then everything attached permanently to the structures is also realty. Everything else is **personal property,** or *personalty*. Attorneys sometimes refer to personal property as **chattel,** a term used under the common law to denote all forms of personal property.

Personal property can be tangible or intangible. Tangible personal property, such as a television set, heavy construction equipment, or a car, has physical substance. Intangible personal property represents some set of rights and interests, but it has no real physical existence. Stocks and bonds are intangible personal property. So, too, are patents, trademarks, and copyrights, as discussed in Chapter 7.

SECTION 2

Fixtures

Certain personal property can become so closely associated with the real property to which it is attached that the law views it as real property. Such property is known as a **fixture**—a thing affixed to realty. A thing is affixed to realty when it is attached to it by roots; embedded in it; or permanently attached by means of cement, plaster, bolts, nails, or screws. The fixture can be physically attached to real property, or attached to another fixture; it can even be an item, such as a statue, that is not physically attached to the land, as long as the owner *intends* the property to be a fixture.

Fixtures are included in the sale of land if the sales contract does not provide otherwise. The sale of a house includes the land and the house and garage on it, as well as the cabinets, plumbing, and windows. Because these are permanently affixed to the property, they are considered to be a part of it. Unless otherwise agreed, however, the curtains and throw rugs are not included. Items such as drapes and window-unit air conditioners are difficult to classify. Thus, a contract for the sale of a house or commercial property should indicate which items of this sort are included in the sale.

The Role of Intent

To determine whether a certain item is a fixture, the *intention* of the party who placed the object must be examined. If the facts indicate that the person intended the item to be a fixture, then it will be a fixture. When the intent of the party who placed the

fixture on the realty is in dispute, the courts usually determine the intent based on either or both of the following factors:

1. If the property attached cannot be removed without causing substantial damage to the remaining realty, it is usually deemed a fixture.
2. If the property attached is so adapted to the rest of the realty as to become a part of it, the property is usually deemed a fixture.

Certain items can only be attached to property permanently; such items are fixtures. It is assumed that the owner intended them to be fixtures, because they had to be permanently attached to the property. A tile floor, cabinets, and carpeting are examples. Also, when an item of property is custom-made for installation on real property, as storm windows are, the item is usually classified as a fixture. The courts assume that owners, in making such installations, intend the objects to become part of their real property. At issue in the following case was whether telephone poles, wires, and other communications equipment qualified as fixtures.

CASE 46.1

New England Telephone and Telegraph Co. v. City of Franklin

Supreme Court of New Hampshire, 1996.
685 A.2d 913.
http:www.state.nh.us/
courts/supreme/
opinions/9611/
netel.htm[a]

IN THE LANGUAGE OF THE COURT

BACKGROUND AND FACTS *To obtain revenue, cities and towns tax the owners of real property within their jurisdictions. The tax is based on an assessment of the value of the property. New England Telephone and Telegraph Company (NETT) and other telephone companies filed a lawsuit in a New Hampshire state court against the City of Franklin and other municipalities, challenging the cities' property assessments. NETT and the other plaintiffs objected to the inclusion in their assessments of communications equipment, including telephone poles, wires, and central office equipment. They argued that the equipment was personal property and therefore should not have been taxed. The court granted the telephone companies' motion for summary judgment, and the cities appealed.*

HORTON, Justice.
* * * *

* * * [W]hether an item of property is properly classified as either personalty or a fixture turns on several factors, including: the item's nature and use; the intent of the party making the annexation; the degree and extent to which the item is specially adapted to the realty; the degree and extent of the item's annexation to the realty; and the relationship between the realty's owner and the person claiming the item. The central factors are the nature of the article and its use, as connected with the use of the

---

a. This page contains the opinion in this case. This opinion is part of a database on a Web site maintained by the New Hampshire state library for the New Hampshire state government.

underlying land, because these factors provide the basis for ascertaining the intent of the party who affixes or annexes the item in question.

In this case, the items of communications equipment did not constitute fixtures. * * * The poles, wires, and central office equipment, though placed in the ground or bolted to the buildings, were readily removable and transportable without affecting the utility of the underlying land, the buildings, or the equipment itself. * * * In addition, the very nature of telephone poles and wires, as well as their use by the [telephone companies] in connection with integrated telecommunications systems, belies the proposition that the equipment became a permanent and essential part of the underlying realty so as to pass by conveyance with it.

DECISION AND REMEDY   *The Supreme Court of New Hampshire affirmed the trial court's decision. The telephone poles, wires, and central equipment were not fixtures and thus not subject to taxation by the cities as real property.*

TRADE FIXTURES

An exception to the rule that fixtures are a part of the real property involves **trade fixtures**. A trade fixture is personal property that is installed for a commercial purpose by the tenant (one who rents real property from the owner, or landlord). Trade fixtures remain the property of the tenant, unless removal would irreparably damage the building or realty. A walk-in cooler, for example, purchased and installed by a tenant who uses the premises for a restaurant, is a trade fixture. The tenant can remove the cooler from the premises when the lease terminates but ordinarily must repair any damage that the removal causes or compensate the landlord for the damage.

SECTION 3

Property Ownership

Property ownership can be viewed as a bundle of rights. These rights include the right to possess the property and the right to dispose of the property—by sale, gift, rental, lease, and so on.

FEE SIMPLE

A person who holds the entire bundle of rights is said to be the owner in **fee simple.** The owner in fee simple is entitled to use, possess, and dispose of the property as he or she chooses during his or her lifetime; and on death, the owner's interest in the property descends to his or her heirs. We will look further at ownership in fee simple in Chapter 47, in the context of real property ownership.

CONCURRENT OWNERSHIP

Persons who share ownership rights simultaneously in particular property are said to be concurrent owners. There are two principal types of **concurrent ownership:** *tenancy in common* and *joint tenancy.* Concurrent ownership rights can also be held in a tenancy by the entirety or as community property, although these latter two types of concurrent ownership are less common.

Tenancy in Common. The term **tenancy in common** refers to a form of co-ownership in which each of two or more persons owns an undivided interest in the property. The interest is undivided because each tenant has rights in the *whole* property. For example, Rosa and Chad own a rare stamp collection as tenants in common. This does not mean that Rosa owns some particular stamps and Chad others. Rather, it means that Rosa and Chad each have rights in the entire collection. (If each person had rights in specific items of property, then the interest would be divided.)

On the death of a tenant in common, that tenant's interest in the property passes to his or her heirs. For example, should Rosa die before Chad, a one-half interest in the stamp collection would become the property of Rosa's heirs. If Rosa sold her interest to Fred before she died, Fred and Chad would be co-owners as tenants in common. If Fred died, his interest in the personal property would pass to his heirs, and they in turn would own the property with Chad as tenants in common.

Joint Tenancy.   In a **joint tenancy**, each of two or more persons owns an undivided interest in the property, and a deceased joint tenant's interest passes to the surviving joint tenant or tenants. The rights of a surviving joint tenant to inherit a deceased joint tenant's ownership interest, which are referred to as *survivorship rights*, distinguish the joint tenancy from the tenancy in common. A joint tenancy can be terminated before a joint tenant's death by gift or by sale, in which situation the person who receives the property as a gift or who purchases the property becomes a tenant in common, not a joint tenant.

To illustrate: In the preceding example, if Rosa and Chad held their stamp collection in a joint tenancy and if Rosa died before Chad, the entire collection would become Chad's property; Rosa's heirs would receive absolutely no interest in the collection. If Rosa, while living, sold her interest to Fred, however, the sale would terminate the joint tenancy, and Fred and Chad would become owners as tenants in common.

Additionally, a joint tenancy can be transferred by *partition*; that is, the tenants can physically divide the property into equal parts. Because a joint tenant's interest is capable of being conveyed without the consent of the other joint tenants, it can be levied against (seized by court order) to satisfy the tenant's judgment creditors. This characteristic is also a feature of the tenancy in common.

Generally, it is presumed that a co-tenancy is a tenancy in common unless there is a clear intention to establish a joint tenancy. Thus, language such as "to Jerrold and Eva as joint tenants with right of survivorship, and not as tenants in common" would be necessary to create a joint tenancy.

Tenancy by the Entirety.   A **tenancy by the entirety** typically is created by a conveyance (transfer) of real property to a husband and wife. It is distinguished from a joint tenancy by the inability of either spouse to transfer separately his or her interest during his or her lifetime without the consent of the other spouse. In some states where statutes give the wife the right to convey her property, this form of concurrent ownership has been effectively abolished. A divorce, either spouse's death, or mutual agreement will terminate a tenancy by the entirety. A tenancy by the entirety is less common today than it once was.

Community Property.   Only a limited number of states[1] allow property to be owned by a married couple as **community property.** If property is held as community property, each spouse technically owns an undivided one-half interest in the property. This type of ownership applies to most property acquired by the husband or the wife during the course of the marriage. It generally does not apply to property acquired prior to the marriage or to property acquired by gift or inheritance during the marriage. After a divorce, community property is divided equally in some states and according to the discretion of the court in other states.

SECTION 4

Acquiring Ownership of Personal Property

Ownership of personal property can be acquired through purchase, possession, production, gift, will or inheritance, accession, and confusion. Purchasing personal property, which was discussed in Chapters 19 through 23, is one of the most common ways of acquiring or transferring personalty. The other forms of acquisition are discussed below.

POSSESSION

One example of acquiring ownership through possession is the capture of wild animals. Wild animals belong to no one in their natural state, and the first person to take possession of a wild animal normally owns it. The killing of a wild animal amounts to assuming ownership of it. Merely being in hot pursuit does not give title, however. There are two exceptions to this basic rule. First, any wild animals captured by a trespasser are the property of the landowner, not the trespasser. The fish in a pond on a farmer's land, for example, are the farmer's property, not the property of a trespasser who fishes for and catches them. Second, if wild animals are captured or killed in violation of wild game statutes, the capturer does not obtain title to the animals; rather, the state does.

Those who find lost or abandoned property also can acquire ownership rights through mere possession of the property, as will be discussed later in this

---

1. These states include Alaska, Arizona, California, Idaho, Louisiana, Nevada, New Mexico, Texas, Washington, and Wisconsin. Puerto Rico allows property to be owned as community property as well.

chapter. (Real property can also be acquired through possession—see the discussion of adverse possession in the next chapter.)

PRODUCTION

Production is another means of acquiring ownership of personal property. As discussed in Chapter 7, writers, inventors, manufacturers, and others who produce personal property may thereby acquire title to it. (In some situations, though, as when a researcher is hired to invent a new product or technique, the researcher may not own what is produced—see Chapter 31.)

GIFT

A **gift** is another fairly common means of acquiring or transferring ownership of property. A gift is essentially a *voluntary* transfer of property ownership. It is not supported by legally sufficient consideration (see Chapter 12), because the very essence of a gift is giving without consideration. Gifts can be made during a person's lifetime, or they can be made in a last will and testament. A gift made by will is called a *testamentary* gift.

There are three requirements for an effective gift—delivery, donative intent on the part of the *donor* (the one giving the gift), and acceptance by the *donee* (the one receiving the gift). Each of these requirements is discussed below. Until these three requirements are met, no effective gift has been made. For example, suppose that your aunt tells you that she is going to give you a new Mercedes-Benz for your next birthday. This is simply a promise to make a gift. It is not considered a gift until the Mercedes-Benz is delivered.

Delivery. Delivery is obvious in most cases, but some objects cannot be relinquished physically. Then the question of delivery depends on the surrounding circumstances. When the physical object itself cannot be delivered, a symbolic delivery, or **constructive delivery,** will be sufficient.

Constructive delivery does not confer actual possession of the object in question. It is a general term for all those acts that the law holds to be equivalent to acts of real delivery. Suppose that you want to make a gift of various old rare coins that you have stored in a safe-deposit box at your bank. You certainly cannot deliver the box itself to the donee, and you do not want to take the coins out of the bank. Instead, you can simply deliver the key to the box to the donee and

authorize the donee's access to the box and its contents. This constitutes symbolic, or constructive, delivery of the contents of the box. Delivery of intangible personal property, such as stock-ownership rights, must be accomplished by symbolic or constructive delivery, such as by the delivery of a stock certificate.

An effective delivery also requires giving up *complete dominion*[2] *and control* over the subject matter of the gift. The outcome of disputes often turns on the retaining or relinquishing of control. The Internal Revenue Service scrutinizes transactions between relatives when one has given income-producing property to the other. A relative who does not relinquish complete control over a piece of property will have to pay taxes on the income from that property.

Delivery can be accomplished by means of a third person. The third person may be the agent of the donor or of the donee. If the person is the agent of the donor, the gift is effective when the agent delivers the property to the donee. If, in contrast, the third person is the agent of the donee, the gift is effective when the donor delivers the property to the donee's agent.[3] When there is doubt as to whose agent the third party is, he or she is generally presumed to be the agent of the donor. Naturally, no delivery is necessary if the gift is already in the hands of the donee. All that is necessary to complete the gift in such a case is the required intent and acceptance by the donee.

Donative Intent. Donative intent (the intent to make a gift) is determined from the language of the donor and the surrounding circumstances. When a gift is challenged in court, for example, the court may look at the relationship between the parties and the size of the gift in relation to the donor's other assets. Donative intent might be questioned by a court if the gift was made to an archenemy. Similarly, when a person has given away a large portion of his or her assets, the court will scrutinize the transactions to determine whether the donor was mentally competent or whether fraud or duress was involved. In the following case, the court looked at the intent of the donor and the question of delivery.

---

2. The term *dominion* in this sense refers to absolute ownership rights in, and control over, property. One who has dominion over property both possesses and has title to the property.
3. *Bickford v. Mattocks,* 95 Me. 547, 50 A.894 (1901).

CASE 46.2   In re Estate of Piper[a]

Missouri Court of
Appeals, 1984.
676 S.W.2d 897.

BACKGROUND AND FACTS   *Gladys Piper died intestate (without a will). At the time of her death, she owned personal property consisting of household goods, two old automobiles, farm machinery, and "miscellaneous" items totaling $5,150. This did not include jewelry or cash. When Piper died, she had $206.75 in cash and her two diamond rings, known as the "Andy Piper" rings, in her purse. The contents of Piper's purse were taken by her niece Wanda Brown on Piper's death, allegedly to preserve them for the estate. Clara Kauffman, a friend of Gladys Piper, filed a claim against the estate for $4,800. For several years before Piper's death, Kauffman had taken Piper to the doctor, beauty salon, and grocery store; written her checks to pay her bills; and helped her care for her home. Kauffman maintained that Piper had promised to pay her for these services and that Piper had intended the diamond rings to be a gift to her. The trial court denied Kauffman's request for payment of $4,800 on the basis that the services had been voluntary. Kauffman then filed a petition for delivery of personal property (the rings), which was granted by the trial court. The defendants—Piper's heirs and the administrator of Piper's estate—appealed.*

IN THE LANGUAGE OF THE COURT

GREENE, Judge.
*   *   *   *

While no particular form is necessary to effect a delivery, and while the delivery may be actual, constructive, or symbolical, there must be some evidence to support a delivery theory. What we have here, at best, *   *   * was an intention on the part of Gladys, at some future time, to make a gift of the rings to Clara. Such an intention, no matter how clearly expressed, which has not been carried into effect, confers no ownership rights in the property in the intended donee. *Language written or spoken, expressing an intention to give, does not constitute a gift, unless the intention is executed by a complete and unconditional delivery of the subject matter, or delivery of a proper written instrument evidencing the gift.* There is no evidence in this case to prove delivery, and, for such reason, the trial court's judgment is erroneous. [Emphasis added.]

DECISION AND REMEDY   *The judgment of the trial court was reversed. No effective gift of the rings had been made, because Piper had never delivered the rings to Kauffman.*

---

a. Recall that *in re* means "in the matter of," "concerning," or "regarding." Case titles that begin with *in re* indicate that the matter before the court did not involve adversarial parties but rather called for some judicial action to be taken—in this case, a determination of who had ownership rights in Gladys Piper's rings.

Acceptance.   The final requirement of a valid gift is acceptance by the donee. This rarely presents any problems, because most donees readily accept their gifts. The courts generally assume acceptance unless shown otherwise.

Gifts *Inter Vivos* and Gifts *Causa Mortis*.   A gift made during the donor's lifetime is called a **gift *inter vivos*.** A **gift *causa mortis*** is made in contemplation of imminent death. To be effective, a gift *causa mortis* must meet the three requirements of delivery, intent, and acceptance. Gifts *causa mortis* do not become

absolute until the donor dies from the contemplated illness or disease. A gift *causa mortis* is revocable at any time up to the death of the donor and is automatically revoked if the donor recovers.

Suppose that Steck is to be operated on for a cancerous tumor. Before the operation, he delivers an envelope to a close business associate. The envelope contains a letter saying, "I realize my days are numbered, and I want to give you this check for $1 million in the event of my death from this operation." The business associate cashes the check. The surgeon performs the operation and removes the tumor. Steck recovers fully. Several months later, Steck dies from a heart attack that is totally unrelated to the operation. If Steck's personal representative (the party charged with administering Steck's estate) tries to recover the $1 million, normally she will succeed. The gift *causa mortis* is automatically revoked if the donor recovers. The *specific event* that was contemplated in making the gift was death from a particular operation. Because Steck's death was not the result of this event, the gift is revoked, and the $1 million passes to Steck's estate.[4]

WILL OR INHERITANCE

Ownership of property may be transferred by will or by inheritance under state statutes. These types of transfers are dealt with at length in Chapter 50.

ACCESSION

Accession means "something added." It occurs when someone adds value to a piece of personal property by use of either labor or materials. Generally, there is no dispute about who owns the property after accession has occurred, especially when the accession is accomplished with the owner's consent. For example, a Corvette-customizing specialist comes to Hoshi's house. Hoshi has all the materials necessary. The customizing specialist uses them to add a unique bumper to Hoshi's Corvette. Hoshi simply pays the customizer for the value of the labor, obviously retaining title to the property.

Ownership can be at issue after the occurrence of an accession if (1) a party has wrongfully caused the accession or (2) the materials added or labor expended greatly increases the value of the property or changes the identity of the property. Some general rules can be applied in these situations.

When accession occurs without the owner's consent, the courts will tend to favor the owner over the improver—the one who improves the property—provided the accession is done in bad faith. This is true even if the value of the property is increased substantially. In addition, many courts will deny the improver (wrongdoer) any compensation for the value added; for example, a car thief who puts new tires on the stolen car will obviously not be compensated for the value of the new tires.

If the accession is performed in good faith, however, even without the owner's consent, ownership of the improved item most often depends on whether the accession has increased the value of the property or changed its identity. The greater the increase, the more likely that ownership will pass to the improver. Obviously, when this occurs, the improver must compensate the original owner for the value the property had prior to the accession. If the increase in value is not sufficient for ownership to be passed to the improver, most courts require the owner to compensate the improver for the value added.

CONFUSION

Confusion is defined as the commingling of goods so that one person's personal property cannot be distinguished from another's. It frequently involves goods that are fungible.[5] *Fungible goods* are goods consisting of identical particles, such as grain or oil. For example, if two farmers put their number 2 grade winter wheat into the same silo, confusion will occur. When goods are confused due to a wrongful and willful act and the wrongdoer is unable to prove what percentage of the confused goods belongs to him or her, then the innocent party ordinarily acquires title to the whole.

This rule does not apply when confusion occurs by agreement, honest mistake, or the act of some third party. When any of these three events occurs, the owners all share ownership as tenants in common. Suppose that you enter into a cooperative arrangement with five other farmers in your local community of Midway, Iowa. Each fall, everyone harvests the same amount of number 2 yellow corn. The corn is stored in silos that are held by the cooperative. Each of you owns one-sixth of the total corn in the silos. If anything happens to the corn, you will bear the loss in equal proportions of one-sixth.

Now suppose you share ownership in some other proportion. Often, owners do not have equal interests. In such cases, the owners must keep careful records of their respective proportions. If a dispute over ownership or loss arises, the courts will presume that everyone has an equal interest in the goods. Therefore, you must be prepared to prove that you own more or less than an equal part.

Suppose that you own two-thirds of the corn in the Midway co-op silos. Further assume that the silos are damaged by a tornado and thunderstorm. How much

---

4. *Brind v. International Trust Co.*, 66 Colo. 60, 179 P. 148 (1919).

5. See UCC 1–201(17).

have you lost if one-half of the corn is blown away by the storm? You have lost one-half of your two-thirds, or one-third of the total. When corn is stored by several owners, each owning a different proportion of the total, loss is shared proportionally.

SECTION 5

Mislaid, Lost, or Abandoned Property

As already noted, one of the methods of acquiring ownership of property is to possess it. Simply finding something and holding onto it, however, does not *necessarily* entitle the finder to it. Different rules apply, depending on whether the property was mislaid, lost, or abandoned.

MISLAID PROPERTY

Property that has been voluntarily placed somewhere by the owner and then inadvertently forgotten is **mislaid property.** Suppose that you go to the theater and leave your opera glasses at the concession stand. The glasses are mislaid property, and the theater owner is entrusted with the duty of reasonable care for the goods. When mislaid property is found, the finder does not obtain title to the goods.[6] Instead, the owner of the place where the property was mislaid becomes the caretaker of the property, because it is highly likely that the true owner will return.[7]

LOST PROPERTY

Property that is *involuntarily* left is **lost property.** A finder of lost property can claim title to the property against the whole world, *except the true owner*. If the true owner demands that the lost property be returned, the finder must return it. If a third party attempts to take possession of lost property from a finder, the third party cannot assert a better title than the finder.

When a finder knows who the true owner of property is and fails to return the property to that person, the finder is guilty of a tort known as *conversion* (see Chapter 5). Finally, many states require the finder to make a reasonably diligent search to locate the true owner of lost property.

Suppose Kamal works in a large library at night. After work, as he is walking through the courtyard of the library, he finds a piece of gold jewelry that contains several apparently precious stones. Kamal decides to take it to a jewelry store to have it appraised. While pretending to weigh the jewelry, an employee of the jeweler removes several of the stones. If Kamal brings an action to recover the stones from the jeweler, he will win, because he found lost property and holds valid title against everyone except the true owner. Because the property was lost and not mislaid, the owner of the library is not the caretaker of the jewelry. Instead, Kamal acquires title good against the whole world (except the true owner).[8]

Many states have **estray statutes** to encourage and facilitate the return of property to its true owner and to reward the finder for honesty if the property remains unclaimed. Such statutes provide an incentive for finders to report their discoveries by making it possible for them, after passage of a specified period of time, to acquire legal title to the property they have found if the property remains unclaimed. The statutes usually require the county clerk to advertise the property in an attempt to help the owner recover what has been lost. Some preliminary questions must always be resolved before the estray statute can be employed. The item must be lost property, not mislaid or abandoned property. When the situation indicates that the property was probably lost and not mislaid or abandoned, as a matter of public policy, loss is presumed, and the estray statute applies.

ABANDONED PROPERTY

Property that has been *discarded* by the true owner, who has *no intention* of claiming title to it, is referred to as abandoned property. Someone who finds **abandoned property** acquires title to it, and such title is good against the whole world, *including the original owner*. The owner of lost property who eventually gives up any further attempt to find it is frequently held to have abandoned the property.

For example, assume that Aleka is driving with the windows down in her car. Somewhere along her route, a valuable scarf blows out the window. She

---

6. The finder is an involuntary bailee—see the discussion of bailments later in this chapter.

7. The owner of the place where property is mislaid is a bailee with right of possession against all except the true owner.

8. See *Armory v. Delamirie*, 93 Eng. Rep. 664 (K.B. [King's Bench] 1722). If Kamal had found the jewelry during the course of his employment, however, his employer would be the involuntary bailee. Further, many courts now say that when lost property is recovered in a private place, the owner of the place, not the finder, becomes the bailee (even if the finder is not a trespasser).

retraces her route and searches for the scarf but cannot find it. She finally decides that further search is futile and proceeds to her destination five hundred miles away. Six months later, Frye, a hitchhiker, finds the scarf. Frye has acquired title, which is good even against Aleka. By completely giving up her search, Aleka abandoned the scarf just as effectively as if she had intentionally discarded it.

A trespasser who finds an item of abandoned personal property does not acquire title to it, however. The owner of the real property on which it was found does. The same rule applies if the property was lost. Similarly, if a landowner employs a crew to install an underground septic tank, for example, and the crew digs up a cache of pioneer relics, the landowner has first claim to the relics, because they were buried in his or her ground.

In contrast, if the crew unearths money, gold, silver, or bullion (instead of pewter dishes, tin cups, brass buttons, and old muskets), the find may be classified as **treasure trove** (treasure that is found), and the crew may be able to keep it. In the United States, in the absence of a statute, a finder has title to treasure trove against all but the true owner. (In Great Britain, the Crown gets it.) Generally, to constitute treasure trove, property need not have been buried— it can have been hidden in some other private place, such as behind loose bricks in an old chimney—but its owner must be unknown, and its finders must not have been trespassing.

CONCEPT SUMMARY 46.1  PERSONAL PROPERTY

CONCEPT	DESCRIPTION
Personal Property	Personal property (personalty) is considered to include all property not classified as real property (realty). Personal property can be tangible (such as a TV set or a car) or intangible (such as stocks or bonds). Personal property may be referred to legally as *chattel*—a term used under the common law to denote all forms of personal property.
Fixtures	Personal property that is so affixed to real property that it is considered a part of the real property is called a fixture. The cabinets, plumbing, and windows in a house are examples of fixtures. In determining whether personal property should be classified as a fixture, the intention of the owner, when installing the property, is the most important factor.

Common Types of Property Ownership	1. *Fee simple*—Ownership in which individuals have the right to use, possess, or dispose of the property as they choose during their lifetimes and to pass on the property to their heirs at death.
	2. *Concurrent ownership*—
	  a. Tenancy in common—Co-ownership in which two or more persons own an undivided interest in property; on one tenant's death, the property interest passes to his or her heirs.
	  b. Joint tenancy—Co-ownership in which two or more persons own an undivided interest in property; on the death of a joint tenant, the property interest transfers to the remaining tenant(s), not to the heirs of the deceased.
	  c. Tenancy by the entirety—A form of co-ownership between a husband and wife that is similar to a joint tenancy, except that a spouse cannot transfer separately his or her interest during his or her lifetime.
	  d. Community property—A form of co-ownership between a husband and wife in which each spouse technically owns an undivided one-half interest in property acquired during the marriage. This type of ownership occurs in only a few states.

CONCEPT SUMMARY 46.1

PERSONAL PROPERTY (*continued*)

CONCEPT	DESCRIPTION

Acquisition of Personal Property	The most common means of acquiring ownership in personal property is by purchasing it (see Chapters 19 through 23). Another way in which personal property is often acquired is by will or inheritance (see Chapter 50). The following are additional methods of acquiring personal property:
	1. *Possession*—Ownership may be acquired by possession if no other person has ownership title (for example, capturing wild animals or finding abandoned property).
	2. *Production*—Any product or item produced by an individual (with minor exceptions) becomes the property of that individual.
	3. *Gift*—An effective gift is made when the following conditions exist:
	   a. There is evidence of *intent* to make a gift of the property in question.
	   b. The gift is delivered (physically or constructively) to the donee or the donee's agent.
	   c. The gift is accepted by the donee or the donee's agent.
	4. *Accession*—When someone adds value to a piece of property by use of labor or materials, the added value generally becomes the property of the owner of the original property (when accessions are made in bad faith or wrongfully). Good faith accessions that substantially increase the property's value or change the identity of the property may cause title to pass to the improver.
	5. *Confusion*—In the case of fungible goods, if a person wrongfully and willfully commingles goods with those of another in order to render them indistinguishable, the innocent party acquires title to the whole. Otherwise, the owners become tenants in common of the commingled goods.

Mislaid, Lost, and Abandoned Property	1. *Mislaid property*—Property that is placed somewhere voluntarily by the owner and then inadvertently forgotten. A finder of mislaid property will not acquire title to the goods, and the owner of the place where the property was mislaid becomes a caretaker of the mislaid property. 2. *Lost property*—Property that is involuntarily left and forgotten. A finder of lost property can claim title to the property against the whole world *except the true owner.* 3. *Abandoned property*—Property that has been discarded by the true owner, who has no intention of claiming title to the property in the future. A finder of abandoned property can claim title to it against the whole world, *including the original owner.*

SECTION 6

Bailments

A **bailment** is formed by the delivery of personal property, without transfer of title, by one person (called a **bailor**) to another (called a **bailee**), usually under an agreement for a particular purpose—for example, to loan, store, repair, or transport the property. On completion of the purpose, the bailee is obligated to return the bailed property in the same or better condition to the bailor or a third person or to dispose of it as directed.

Most bailments are created by agreement, but not necessarily by contract, because in many bailments not all of the elements of a contract (such as mutual assent and consideration) are present. For example, if you loan your business law text to a friend, a bailment is created, but not by contract, because there is no consideration. Most commercial bailments, such as the delivery of your suit to the cleaners for dry cleaning, are based on contract, however. A bailment is distinguished from a sale or a gift in that possession is transferred without passage of title or intent to transfer title. In a sale or a gift, title is transferred from the seller or donor to the buyer or donee.

The law of bailments applies to many routine personal and business transactions. When individuals deal with bailments, whether they realize it or not, they are subject to the obligations and duties that arise from the bailment relationship. The number, scope, and importance of bailments created daily in the business community and in everyday life make it desirable to understand the elements necessary for the creation of a bailment and to know what rights, duties, and liabilities flow from bailments.

ELEMENTS OF A BAILMENT

Not all transactions involving the delivery of property from one person to another create a bailment. For such a transfer to become a bailment, the following three elements must be present:

1. Personal property.
2. Delivery of possession (without title).
3. Agreement that the property be returned to the bailor or otherwise disposed of according to its owner's directions.

Personal Property Requirement.   Only personal property is bailable; there can be no bailment of persons. Although a bailment of your luggage is created when it is transported by an airline, as a passenger you are not the subject of a bailment. Also, you cannot bail realty; thus, leasing your house to a tenant is not a bailment. Bailments commonly involve *tangible* items—jewelry, cattle, automobiles, and the like. *Intangible* personal property, such as promissory notes and shares of corporate stock, may also be bailed.

Delivery of Possession.   *Delivery of possession* means transfer of possession of property to the bailee. Two requirements must be met for delivery of possession to occur:

1. The bailee must be given exclusive possession and control over the property.

2. The bailee must *knowingly* accept the personal property.[9] In other words, the bailee must *intend* to exercise control over it.

If either delivery of possession or knowing acceptance is lacking, there is no bailment relationship. For example, suppose that Sudi is in a hurry to catch his plane. He has a package he wants to check at the airport. He arrives at the airport check-in station, but the person in charge has gone on a coffee break. Sudi decides to leave the package on the counter. Even though there has clearly been physical transfer of the package, the person in charge of the check-in station has not knowingly accepted the personal property. Therefore, there has been no effective delivery. The result is the same in the following example: Delacroix checks her coat at a restaurant. In the coat pocket is a $20,000 diamond necklace. In accepting the coat, the bailee does not *knowingly* also accept the necklace.

Two types of delivery—*physical* and *constructive*—will result in the bailee's exclusive possession of and control over the property. Physical delivery, as the phrase implies, occurs when the property is actually, physically transferred to the bailee. For example, if a restaurant patron checks a coat with an attendant, the property has been physically delivered to the bailee. As discussed earlier, in the context of gifts, constructive delivery is a substitute, or symbolic, delivery. What is delivered to the bailee is not the actual property bailed (such as a car) but something so related to the property (such as the car keys) that the requirement of delivery is satisfied.

In certain unique situations, a bailment is found despite the apparent lack of the requisite elements of control and knowledge. One example of such a situation occurs when the bailee acquires the property accidentally or by mistake—as in finding someone else's lost or mislaid property. A bailment is created even though the bailor did not voluntarily deliver the property to the bailee. Such bailments are referred to as *constructive* or *involuntary* bailments.

---

9. We are dealing here with *voluntary bailments*. Under some circumstances, regardless of whether a person intentionally accepts possession of someone else's personal property, the law imposes on him or her the obligation to redeliver it. For example, if property is accidentally left in another's possession without negligence on the part of its owner, the person in whose possession it has been left may be responsible for its return. This is referred to as an *involuntary bailment*.

THE BAILMENT AGREEMENT

A bailment agreement can be *express* or *implied*. Although no written agreement is required for bailments of less than one year (that is, the Statute of Frauds does not apply—see Chapter 15), it is a good idea to have a written agreement, especially when valuable property is involved.

The bailment agreement expressly or impliedly provides for the return of the bailed property to the bailor or to a third person, or provides for disposal by the bailee. The agreement presupposes that the bailee will return the identical goods originally given by the bailor. In certain types of bailments, however, such as bailments of fungible goods,[10] only equivalent property must be returned. For example, if Hobson stores his grain (fungible goods) in Kwam's grain elevator, a bailment is created. But at the end of the storage period, the grain elevator company is not obligated to return to Hobson exactly the same grain that was stored. As long as the company returns goods of the same type, grade, and quantity, the company— the bailee—has performed its obligation.

SECTION 7

Ordinary Bailments

Bailments are either *ordinary* or *special (extraordinary)*. There are three types of ordinary bailments. The distinguishing feature among them is which party receives a benefit from the bailment. Ultimately, the courts may use this factor to determine the standard of care required of the bailee while in possession of the personal property, and this factor will dictate the rights and liabilities of the parties. The three types of ordinary bailments are as follows:

1. *Bailment for the sole benefit of the bailor.* This is a type of gratuitous bailment (one that involves no consideration) for the convenience and benefit of the bailor. The bailee is liable only for gross negligence. (Negligence is discussed in Chapter 5.)
2. *Bailment for the sole benefit of the bailee.* This is typically a loan of an article to a person (the bailee) solely for that person's convenience and benefit. The bailee is liable for even slight negligence.

3. *Bailment for the mutual benefit of the bailee and the bailor.* This is the most common kind of bailment and involves some form of compensation for storing items or holding property. It is a contractual bailment and is often referred to as a bailment for hire. The bailee is liable for ordinary negligence, or the failure to observe ordinary care, which is the care that a reasonably prudent person would use under the circumstances.

RIGHTS OF THE BAILEE

In a bailment situation, both the bailee and the bailor have rights and duties. Implicit in the bailment agreement is the right of the bailee to take possession, to utilize the property for accomplishing the purpose of the bailment, to receive some form of compensation (unless the bailment is intended to be gratuitous), and to limit his or her liability for the bailed goods. Depending on the nature of the bailment and the terms of the bailment agreement, these rights of the bailee are present (with some limitations) in varying degrees in all bailment transactions.

Rights of Possession. A hallmark of the bailment agreement is that the bailee acquires the *right to control and possess the property temporarily.* The meaning of *temporary* depends on the terms of the bailment agreement. If a specified period is expressed in the bailment agreement, then the bailment is continuous for that time period. Earlier termination by the bailor is a breach of contract (if the bailment involves consideration), and the bailee can recover damages from the bailor. If no duration is specified, the bailment ends when either the bailor or the bailee so demands and possession of bailed property is returned to the bailor.

A bailee's right of possession, even though temporary, permits the bailee to recover damages from any third persons for damage or loss to the property. For example, No-Spot Dry Cleaners sends all suede leather garments to Cleanall Company for special processing. If Cleanall loses or damages any leather goods, No-Spot has the right to recover against Cleanall.

If the personal property is stolen from the bailee during the bailment, the bailee has a legal right to regain possession of (to recapture) the goods or to obtain damages from any third person who has wrongfully interfered with the bailee's possessory rights.

Right to Use Bailed Property. Naturally, the extent to which bailees can use the personal property entrusted to them depends on the terms of the bailment

---

10. As mentioned earlier, *fungible goods* are goods that consist of identical particles, such as wheat. Fungible goods are defined in UCC 1–201(17).

contract. When no provision is made, the extent of use depends on how necessary it is for the goods to be at the bailee's disposal for the ordinary purpose of the bailment to be carried out. When leasing drilling machinery, for example, the bailee is expected to use the equipment to drill. In contrast, when providing long-term storage for a car, the bailee is not expected to use the car, because the ordinary purpose of a storage bailment does not include use of the property (unless an emergency dictates such use to protect the car).

Right of Compensation.

A bailee has a right to be compensated as provided for in the bailment agreement, to be reimbursed for costs and services rendered in the keeping of the bailed property, or both. In mutual-benefit bailments, the amount of compensation is often expressed in the bailment contract. For example, in the rental (bailment) of a car, the contract provides for charges on the basis of time, mileage, or a combination of the two, plus other possible charges. In nonrental bailments, such as when a car is left at a service station for an oil change, the bailee makes a service charge for the work performed.

Even in a gratuitous bailment, a bailee has a right to be reimbursed or compensated for costs incurred in the keeping of the bailed property. For example, Hetta loses her pet dog, which is found by Jesse. Jesse takes Hetta's dog to his home and feeds it. Even though he takes good care of the dog, it becomes ill, and a veterinarian is called. Jesse pays the bill for the veterinarian's services and the medicine. He is normally entitled to be reimbursed by Hetta for these reasonable costs incurred in the keeping of her dog.

To enforce the right of compensation, the bailee has a right to place a *possessory* lien (claim) on the specific bailed property until he or she has been fully compensated. This lien on specific bailed property is sometimes referred to as a **bailee's lien,** or artisan's lien. The lien is effective only so long as the bailee has not agreed to extend credit to the bailor and the bailee retains possession over the bailed property.

If the bailor refuses to pay or cannot pay the charges (compensation), the bailee is entitled in most states to foreclose on the lien. This means that the bailee can sell the property and be paid out of the proceeds for the amount owed from the bailment, returning any excess to the bailor.

For example, Sarito takes his car to the garage and enters into an agreement for repairs. The repairs are to be paid for in cash. On completion of the repairs, the garage tenders Sarito his car, but because of unexpected bills, he cannot pay the garage. The garage has a right to retain possession of Sarito's car, exercising a bailee's lien. Unless Sarito can make arrangements for payment, the garage will normally be entitled to sell the car to be compensated for the repairs.

Right to Limit Liability.

In ordinary bailments, bailees have the right to limit their liability by type of risk, by monetary amount, or both, as long as (1) the limitations are called to the attention of the bailor and (2) the limitations are not against public policy.

Any enforceable limitation on liability imposed by the ordinary bailee must be brought to the bailor's attention. Although the bailee is not required to read orally or interpret the limitation for the bailor, the bailor must in some way know of the limitation. Thus, a sign in Nikolai's garage stating that Nikolai will not be responsible "for loss due to theft, fire, or vandalism" may or may not be held to be notice to the bailor. Whether the notice will be effective will depend on the size of the sign, its location, and any other circumstances affecting the likelihood of its being noticed by Nikolai's patrons. The same holds true with limitations placed on the back of identification receipts (stubs) for parked cars, checked coats, or stored bailed goods. Most courts require additional notice, because the bailor rarely reads the receipt and usually treats it merely as an identification number to be used when reclaiming the bailed goods.

Even if the bailor has received notice, certain types of disclaimers of liability are considered to be against public policy and therefore illegal. Clauses that limit a person's liability for his or her own wrongful acts, called *exculpatory clauses,* are carefully scrutinized by the courts, and in bailments they are often held to be illegal. The classic illustration of an exculpatory clause is found on parking receipts: "We assume no risk for damage to or loss of automobile or its contents regardless of cause. It is agreed that the vehicle owner assumes all such risks." Even though the language may vary, if the bailee attempts to exclude liability for the bailee's own negligence, the result is the same—the clause is unenforceable because it is against public policy. This is especially true in the case of bailees providing quasi-public services, such as warehousers (discussed later in this chapter).

DUTIES OF THE BAILEE

The bailee has two basic responsibilities: (1) to take appropriate care of the property and (2) to surrender or dispose of the property at the end of the bailment. The bailee's duties are based on a mixture of tort law and contract law.

The Duty of Care. The bailee must exercise reasonable care in preserving the bailed property. The duty of care involves the standards and principles of tort law discussed in Chapter 5. What constitutes reasonable care in a bailment situation normally depends on the nature and specific circumstances of the bailment. Traditionally, courts have determined the appropriate standard of care on the basis of the type of bailments involved. In a bailment for the sole benefit of the bailor, for example, the bailee need exercise only a slight degree of care. In a bailment for the sole benefit of the bailee, however, the bailee must exercise great care. In a mutual-benefit bailment, courts normally will impose a reasonable standard of care—that is, the bailee must exercise the degree of care that a reasonable and prudent person would exercise in the same circumstances. Exhibit 46–1 on page 882 illustrates these concepts.

Determining whether a bailee exercised an appropriate degree of care is usually a question of fact. This means that the trier of fact (a judge or a jury) weighs the facts of a particular situation and concludes that the bailee did or did not exercise the requisite degree of care at the time the loss or damage occurred. A bailee's failure to exercise appropriate care in handling the bailor's property results in tort liability.

Duty to Return Bailed Property. At the end of the bailment, the bailee normally must relinquish the identical undamaged property (unless it is fungible) to either the bailor or someone the bailor designates or must otherwise dispose of it as directed. This is usually a *contractual* duty arising from the bailment agreement (contract). Failure to give up possession at the time the bailment ends is a breach of contract and could result in the tort of conversion.

Generally, the bailee has a duty to return the bailed goods to the bailor. A bailee may be liable if the goods being held or delivered are given to the wrong person. Hence, a bailee must be satisfied that a person (other than the bailor) to whom the goods are being delivered is the actual owner or has authority from the owner to take possession of the goods. Should the bailee deliver in error, then the bailee may be liable for conversion or misdelivery.

The court in the following case weighed the duty of a bailee to return bailed property to the bailor against charges that giving car keys to an intoxicated person constituted negligent entrustment.

CASE 46.3   Umble v. Sandy McKie and Sons, Inc.

Appellate Court of
Illinois,
Second District, 1998.
294 Ill.App.3d 449,
690 N.E.2d 157,
228 Ill.Dec. 848.

HISTORICAL AND SOCIAL SETTING *Sometimes, the question arises as to whether individuals have a duty to prevent an intoxicated driver from driving his or her vehicle. Consider an example. Edward Hoag went to the beach with several friends, including Ronald Niemeyer. After Hoag became intoxicated, Niemeyer drove Hoag's car to Niemeyer's house. Hoag then attempted to drive home but was involved in an accident in which Keith Lombardo was injured. Lombardo sued Hoag and Niemeyer, and one of the questions in the suit was whether Niemeyer had a duty to prevent Hoag from driving Hoag's car while intoxicated. The court refused to impose such a duty on Niemeyer. The court explained that "[o]ne problem with * * * that particular form of a duty is that the standard is so broad that it would conceivably apply to gas station attendants, toll booth collectors, parking lot attendants, repair services, and onlookers who may have observed the participants get into a vehicle driven by an intoxicated person."[a] Most courts would agree.*

BACKGROUND AND FACTS *Jerome Butzen brought his car to Sandy McKie & Sons, Inc., to fix a leaking tire and replace a burned-out headlight. Butzen was intoxicated, which was apparent to the McKie employees. The car was repaired, Butzen paid for the repairs, and McKie returned the car. Shortly afterwards, Butzen's car collided with one driven by Phillip Umble, who died in the collision. Mary Ellen Umble filed a suit in an Illinois state court against McKie, alleging in part that McKie was negligent in giving car keys to an obviously intoxicated driver. The court dismissed the suit, and Umble appealed.*

---

a. *Lombardo v. Hoag*, 269 N.J.Super. 36, 634 A.2d 550 (1993).

IN THE LANGUAGE
OF THE COURT

Justice *McLAREN* delivered the opinion of the court:

* * * *

* * * Negligent entrustment occurs where one entrusts to another something under the actor's control if the actor knows that the third person will use the thing to create an unreasonable risk of harm to others. Thus, *an essential element of a negligent entrustment cause of action is that the person charged with liability have a superior right to control the property.* * * * [Emphasis added.]

* * * [A] majority of courts * * * have held that a bailee for hire is not liable for returning the property to the bailor. * * *

* * * *

In light of these precedents, defendant [McKie] was clearly a bailee for hire. Once Butzen paid for the repairs and demanded the return of his keys, defendant had no discretion to refuse without being found liable for conversion. Because Butzen already owned the car, defendant cannot be liable for negligently "entrusting" it to him.

DECISION
AND REMEDY

The state intermediate appellate court affirmed the lower court's judgment. A bailee is not liable for returning bailed property to an intoxicated bailor.

Presumption of Negligence.   Sometimes, the duty of care and the duty to return bailed property are combined to determine the bailee's liability. At the end of the bailment, a bailee has the duty to return the bailor's property in the condition in which it was received (allowing for ordinary wear and aging). In some cases, the bailor can sue the bailee in tort for damage to or loss of goods on the theory of negligence or conversion. There are times, though, when it is not possible for the bailor to discover and prove what specific acts of negligence or conversion committed by the bailee caused damage or loss to the property.[11]

Thus, the law of bailments recognizes a rule whereby a *presumption* that the bailee is guilty of negligence or conversion will be made if the bailee fails to return the property or dispose of it in accordance with the bailor's instructions or if the bailee returns the property in a damaged condition. Once this is shown, the bailee must prove that he or she was not at fault. A bailee who is able to *rebut* (contradict) the presumption is not liable to the bailor.

When damage to goods is of the type that normally results only from someone's negligence, and when the bailee had full control of the goods, it is more likely than not that the damage was caused by the bailee's negligence. Therefore, the bailee's negligence is presumed. How the presumption applies is illustrated by the following case.

---

11. The basic formula for finding negligence requires proof that (1) a duty exists, (2) a breach of that duty occurred, (3) the breach is the proximate cause of damage or loss, and (4) actual loss or damage resulted.

CASE 46.4

Lembaga Enterprises, Inc. v. Cace Trucking & Warehouse, Inc.

Superior Court
of New Jersey,
Appellate Division, 1999.
320 N.J.Super. 501,
727 A.2d 1026.

BACKGROUND AND FACTS   *Lembaga Enterprises, Inc., is an importer and distributor of toiletries and cosmetics. Cace Trucking & Warehouse, Inc., is a common carrier and warehouser. Lembaga and Cace had a business relationship for several years. For Lembaga, Cace would pick up shipment containers, store them in its warehouse, and deliver them. An eight-foot high, barbed-wire fence bordered Cace's warehouse. The two gates were locked at night. There were no security guards, but the truck trailers were locked at all times with pin locks. The interior of the warehouse had an alarm system. One afternoon, Cace picked up two containers of perfume for Lembaga. When the containers arrived at the warehouse, Cace's vice president of operations, George Cunningham, phoned Lembaga's president, Nathan Kumar, who told Cunningham not to unload the* *containers until the next day. The next day, the first container was brought into the warehouse and unloaded. When a driver went to retrieve the second container, it had disappeared. Part of a broken pin lock was on the ground where the container had been. Lembaga filed a suit in a New Jersey state court against Cace for the loss of its cargo valued at $366,879.53, alleging, among other things, negligence and conversion. Lembaga filed a motion for a directed verdict, arguing that Cace was presumed to have converted the container because it disappeared mysteriously from Cace's truck. According to Lembaga, to rebut this presumption Cace had to prove exactly what happened to the goods, which it could not do because no one knew what had happened. The court denied the motion, the jury found in Cace's favor, and Lembaga appealed to a state intermediate appellate court.*

IN THE LANGUAGE OF THE COURT

RODRIGUEZ, A. A., J.A.D. [Judge, Appellate Division]
 * * * [W]e hold that proof of damage to or loss of goods while in the custody of a bailee gives rise to a presumption of conversion by the bailee. The bailee may rebut the presumption by proof that the bailee did not intentionally or negligently convert the goods and that it was not negligent in preventing third parties from causing the loss or damage. However, the burden of proof that the bailee converted the goods rests with the bailor at all times.

Therefore, in a conversion action, the bailor has the burden to prove that the bailee has unlawfully converted the goods. When goods are delivered to a bailee in good condition and then are lost or damaged, the law presumes a conversion and casts upon the bailee the burden of going forward with the evidence to show that the loss did not occur through his negligence or if he cannot affirmatively do this, that he exercised a degree of care sufficient to rebut the presumption of it. * * *
 * * * *

Here, the thrust of Cace's defense was that it had adequate security to prevent a theft of the container by third parties. It did not present evidence to rebut the presumption that Cace, its agents or employees had converted the container. Thus, a jury question was presented on the conversion cause of action. * * * [C]onversion is a broader concept than theft. *A conversion can occur even when a bailee has not stolen the merchandise but has acted negligently in permitting the loss of the merchandise from its premises.* [Emphasis added.]

Therefore, here, the judge should have instructed the jury that if Lembaga established that the container had disappeared while in the care of Cace, there is a rebuttable presumption [an assumption that may be disproved by evidence] of conversion based either on Cace's negligent conduct in permitting third parties to steal the container, or by the negligent or intentional conduct of Cace's employees or agents. The burden to prove conversion, however, rests at all times with Lembaga.

Accordingly, we reverse and remand to the [lower court] for a new trial. At that trial, the judge should instruct the jury that if Lembaga establishes that the container disappeared while in Cace's care, there is a rebuttable presumption that Cace is liable for the loss. In that instance, Cace has the burden of rebutting the presumption. The jury should then be asked to determine whether Lembaga met its burden to prove that the loss was caused by: (a) the intentioned conversion of the goods by Cace; or (b) negligent conversion by Cace or theft by third parties.

DECISION AND REMEDY

The state intermediate appellate court reversed the judgment of the lower court and remanded the case for a new trial. Proof of loss of or injury to the goods while in the custody of the bailee establishes a prima facie *case against the bailee, who must then rebut the presumption.*

RIGHTS AND DUTIES OF THE BAILOR

A bailee's duties and a bailor's rights are complementary. In other words, the rights of the bailor are essentially the same as the duties of a bailee, and vice versa.

Rights of the Bailor. A bailor has the right to expect the following:

1. The property will be protected with reasonable care while in the possession of the bailee.

EXHIBIT 46–1   DEGREE OF CARE REQUIRED OF A BAILEE

Bailment for the Sole Benefit of the Bailor	Mutual-Benefit Bailment	Bailment for the Sole Benefit of the Bailee
	DEGREE OF CARE	
SLIGHT	REASONABLE	GREAT

2. The bailee will utilize the property as agreed in the bailment agreement (or not at all).

3. The property will be relinquished at the conclusion of the bailment according to directions given by the bailor.

4. The bailee will not convert (alter) the goods except as agreed.

5. The bailor will not be bound by any limitations on the bailee's liability unless these limitations are known and are enforceable by law.

6. Repairs or service on the property will be completed without defective workmanship.

Duties of the Bailor.   Obviously, a bailor has a duty to compensate the bailee either as agreed or as reimbursement for costs incurred by the bailee in keeping the bailed property. A bailor also has an all-encompassing duty to provide the bailee with goods or chattel that are free from hidden defects that could injure the bailee. This duty translates into two rules:

1. In a *mutual-benefit bailment*, the bailor must notify the bailee of all known defects and any hidden defects that the bailor knew of or could have discovered with reasonable diligence and proper inspection.

2. In a *bailment for the sole benefit of the bailee*, the bailor must notify the bailee of any known defects.

The bailor's duty to reveal defects is based on a negligence theory of tort law. A bailor who fails to give the appropriate notice is liable to the bailee and to any other person who might reasonably be expected to come into contact with the defective article.

For example, assume that Rentco (the bailor) leases four tractors to Hal Iverson. Unknown to Rentco (but discoverable by reasonable inspection), the brake mechanism on one of the tractors is defective at the time the bailment is made. Iverson uses the defective tractor without knowledge of the brake problem and is injured along with two other field workers when the tractor rolls out of control. Rentco is liable on a negligence theory for injuries sustained by Iverson and the two others.

This is the analysis: Rentco has a mutual-benefit bailment and a *duty* to notify Iverson of the discoverable brake defect. Rentco's failure to notify is the *proximate cause* of injuries to farm workers who might be expected to use, or have contact with, the tractor. Therefore, Rentco is liable for the resulting injuries.

A bailor can also incur warranty liability based on contract law (see Chapter 23) for injuries resulting from bailment of defective articles. Property leased by a bailor must be *fit for the intended purpose of the bailment.* The bailor's knowledge of or ability to discover any defects is immaterial. Warranties of fitness arise by law in sales contracts and have been applied by judicial interpretation in cases involving bailments "for hire." Article 2A of the UCC extends implied warranties of merchantability and fitness for a particular purpose to bailments whenever those bailments include rights to use the bailed goods.[12]

TERMINATION OF BAILMENTS

Bailments for a specific term end when the stated period lapses. When no duration is specified, the bailment can be terminated at any time by the following events:

1. The mutual agreement of both parties.
2. A demand by either party.
3. The completion of the purpose of the bailment.
4. An act by the bailee that is inconsistent with the terms of the bailment.
5. The operation of law.

SECTION 8

Special Types of Bailments

Most of this discussion of bailments has concerned ordinary bailments, or bailments in which bailees are expected to exercise ordinary care in the handling of

---

12. UCC 2A–212, 2A–213.

bailed property. Some bailment transactions warrant special consideration. These include bailments in which the bailee's duty of care is extraordinary—that is, his or her liability for loss or damage to the property is absolute—as is generally true in cases involving common carriers and innkeepers. Warehouse companies have the same duty of care as ordinary bailees; but like carriers, they are subject to extensive coverage of federal and state laws, including the UCC's Article 7.

DOCUMENTS OF TITLE AND ARTICLE 7

A shipment or storage of goods may be covered by a *bill of lading*, a *warehouse receipt*, or a *delivery order*. These documents of title are subject to Article 7 of the UCC.[13] To be a **document of title**, a document "must purport to be issued by or addressed to a bailee and purport to cover goods in the bailee's possession which are either identified or are fungible portions of an identified mass."[14]

A **bill of lading** is a document verifying the receipt of goods for shipment issued by a person engaged in the business of transporting or forwarding goods.[15] A **warehouse receipt** is a receipt issued by a person engaged in the business of storing goods for hire.[16] A **delivery order** is a written order to deliver goods directed to a warehouser, carrier, or other person who, in the ordinary course of business, issues warehouse receipts or bills of lading.[17]

Simply put, a document of title is a receipt for goods in the charge of a bailee-carrier or a bailee-warehouser and a contract for the shipment or storage of identified goods.

NEGOTIABILITY OF DOCUMENTS OF TITLE

Negotiability is a concept that applies to documents of title when they contain the words "bearer" or "to

the order of."[18] If a document of title is negotiable—that is, if it specifies that the goods are to be delivered to bearer or to the order of a named person—the following are also possible:

1. The possessor of the document of title is entitled to receive, hold, and dispose of the document and the goods it covers.
2. A good faith purchaser of the document may acquire greater rights to the document and the goods it covers than the transferor had or had the authority to convey (that is, a good faith purchaser may take free of the claims and defenses of prior parties).

If a document of title is nonnegotiable—that is, if it is not made payable to the order of any named person or to bearer—it may be transferred by assignment but not negotiation.[19]

The concept of negotiability under Articles 3 and 7 of the UCC are similar. There are important distinctions between them, however. For example, Article 7 refers to the negotiation process as due negotiation. **Due negotiation** requires that the purchaser of a document of title take it in good faith, for value, without notice of a defense against or a claim to it, in the regular course of business or financing, and not in the settlement or payment of a money obligation.[20] In other words, even if all other requirements are met, transfer of a negotiable document of title to a nonbusinessperson is not due negotiation. In such situations, the transferee acquires only those rights the transferor had or had the authority to convey.[21]

On due negotiation, however, a transferee can acquire greater rights in a document of title than the transferor had. The transferee obtains title to the document and to the goods, including rights to goods delivered to the bailee after the document was issued, and takes free of all prior claims and defenses of which he or she had no notice. The document's issuer remains obligated to store or deliver the goods according to the document's terms.[22] Under this provision, businesspersons can extend credit on documents of title without concern for adverse claims of third parties.

---

13. Of course, when applicable, federal law takes priority [see UCC 7–103]. For example, the Federal Bills of Lading Act [49 U.S.C. Sections 81–124], enacted in 1916, applies to bills of lading issued by common carriers for goods shipped in interstate or foreign commerce, and the United States Warehouse Act [7 U.S.C. Sections 241–243], also enacted in 1916, applies to receipts covering agricultural products stored for interstate or foreign commerce.
14. UCC 1–201(15), 7–102(1)(e); see also UCC 7–401.
15. UCC 1–201(6).
16. UCC 1–201(45); see also UCC 7–201 and 7–202. UCC 7–102(h) defines the person engaged in the storing of goods for hire as a *warehouseman*.
17. UCC 7–102(1)(d).

18. UCC 7–104(1). Negotiability is a concept that also applies in situations involving negotiable instruments.
19. UCC 7–104(2).
20. UCC 7–501(4).
21. UCC 7–504. Until the bailee is notified of the transfer, the transferee's rights may be defeated by certain creditors of the transferor; by a buyer from the transferor in the ordinary course of business, if the bailee has delivered the goods to the buyer; or by the bailee who has dealt with the transferor in good faith.
22. UCC 7–502.

To prevent a thief or a finder of goods from defeating the rights of the true owner (by, for example, taking them to a warehouse and subsequently negotiating the warehouse receipt to a third party who would otherwise take the goods free of the claims of others), the goods must be delivered to the issuer of the document of title by their owner or the owner's agent.[23] Otherwise, the document does not represent title to the goods. Even if the document does not represent title, however, the bailee will not be liable if he or she acts in good faith and observes reasonable commercial standards in receiving and delivering the goods.[24]

In other words, a carrier or warehouser who receives goods from a thief or finder and delivers them according to that individual's instructions is not liable to the goods' true owner. The reason for this rule is that carriers and warehousers are not links in the chain of title and do not represent the owner in transactions affecting title but simply furnish a service necessary to trade and commerce.

COMMON CARRIERS

Common carriers are publicly licensed to provide transportation services to the general public. They are distinguished from private carriers, which operate transportation facilities for a select clientele. A private carrier is not bound to provide service to every person or company making a request. The common carrier, however, must arrange carriage for all who apply, within certain limitations.[25]

The common-carrier contract of transportation creates a *mutual-benefit bailment*. Unlike the bailee in ordinary mutual-benefit bailments, however, the common carrier is held to a standard of care based on *strict liability*, rather than a standard of reasonable care, in protecting the bailed personal property. This means that the common carrier is absolutely liable, regardless of negligence, for all loss or damage to goods except loss or damage caused by one of the five common law exceptions:

1. An act of God.
2. An act of a public enemy.

3. An order of a public authority.
4. An act of the shipper.
5. The inherent nature of the goods.

The UCC retained the common law liability of common carriers in UCC 7–309. Common carriers are treated as if they were absolute insurers for the safe delivery of goods to the destination, even though they are not. They cannot contract away this liability for damaged goods; subject to government regulations, however, they are permitted to limit their dollar liability to an amount stated on the shipment contract.[26]

Except for the five exceptions mentioned, the common carrier is liable for any damage to goods in shipment, even that caused by the willful acts of third persons or by sheer accident. Thus, a common-carrier trucking company moving cargo is liable for acts of vandalism, mechanical defects in refrigeration units, or a dam bursting, if any of these acts results in damage to the cargo. But damage caused by acts of God—an earthquake or lightning, for example—is the shipper's loss.

Shipper's Loss. The shipper bears any loss occurring through its own faulty or improper crating or packaging procedures. For example, if a bird dies because its crate was poorly ventilated, the shipper, not the carrier, bears the loss.

Connecting Carriers. A bill of lading that specifies one or more connecting carriers is called a *through bill of lading*. When connecting carriers are involved in transporting goods under a through bill of lading, the shipper can recover from the original carrier or any connecting carrier.[27] Normally, the *last* carrier is presumed to have received the goods in satisfactory condition.

WAREHOUSE COMPANIES

Warehousing is the business of providing storage of property for compensation. Like ordinary bailees, warehouse companies are liable for loss or damage to property resulting from *negligence*. A warehouser must "exercise such care . . . as a reasonably careful [person] would exercise under like circumstances but unless otherwise agreed he is not liable for damages which could not have been avoided by the exercise of

---

23. UCC 7–503(1).
24. UCC 7–404.
25. A common carrier is not required to take any and all property anywhere in all instances. Public regulatory agencies govern common carriers, and carriers may be restricted to geographic areas. They may also be limited to carrying certain kinds of goods or to providing only special types of transportation equipment.

---

26. Federal laws require common carriers to offer shippers the opportunity to obtain higher dollar limits for loss by paying a higher fee for the transport.
27. UCC 7–302.

such care."[28] A warehouse company can limit the dollar amount of liability, but the bailor must be given the option of paying an increased storage rate for an increase in the liability limit.[29]

INNKEEPERS

At common law, innkeepers, hotel owners, and similar operators were held to the same strict liability as common carriers with respect to property brought into the rooms by guests. Today, only those who provide lodging to the public for compensation as *regular* business are covered under this rule of strict liability. Moreover, the rule applies only to those who are *guests*, as opposed to *lodgers*. A lodger is a permanent resident of the hotel or inn, whereas a guest is a traveler.

In many states, innkeepers can avoid strict liability for loss of guests' valuables and money by providing a safe in which to keep them. Each guest must be clearly notified of the availability of such a safe. Statutes often limit the liability of innkeepers with regard to articles that are not kept in the safe or that are of such a nature that they are not ordinarily kept in a safe. These statutes may limit the amount of monetary damages or even provide that the innkeeper incurs no liability in the absence of negligence. Commonly, hotels notify guests of the state laws governing the liability of innkeepers by posting a notice on the inside of the door of the hotel room or in some other prominent place within the room.

Normally, the innkeeper assumes no responsibility for the safety of a guest's automobile, because the guest usually retains possession and control. If, however, the innkeeper provides parking facilities, and the guest's car is entrusted to the innkeeper or to an employee, the rules governing ordinary bailments will apply.

---

28. UCC 7–204(1).
29. UCC 7–204(2).

CONCEPT SUMMARY 46.2

RIGHTS AND DUTIES OF THE BAILEE AND THE BAILOR

CONCEPT	DESCRIPTION
Rights of a Bailee (Duties of a Bailor)	1. The right of possession allows actions against third persons who damage or convert the bailed property and allows actions against the bailor for wrongful breach of the bailment.
	2. A bailee has the right to be compensated or reimbursed for keeping bailed property. This right is based in contract or quasi contract.
	3. Unpaid compensation or reimbursement entitles the bailee to a possessory lien on the bailed property and the right of foreclosure.
	4. A bailee has the right to limit his or her liability. An ordinary bailee can limit the types of risk, monetary amount, or both, provided proper notice is given and the limitation is not against public policy. In special bailments, limitations on the types of risk are usually not allowed, but limitations on the monetary amount of loss are permitted by regulation.
Duties of a Bailee (Rights of a Bailor)	1. A bailee must exercise reasonable care over property entrusted to him or her. A common carrier (special bailee) is held to a standard of care based on strict liability unless the bailed property is lost or destroyed due to (a) an act of God, (b) an act of a public enemy, (c) an act of a government authority, (d) an act of a shipper, or (e) the inherent nature of the goods.
	2. Bailed goods in a bailee's possession must be returned to the bailor or be disposed of according to the bailor's directions. Failure to return the property gives rise to a presumption of negligence.
	3. A bailee cannot use or profit from bailed goods except by agreement or in situations in which the use is implied to further the bailment purpose.

TERMS AND CONCEPTS TO REVIEW

abandoned property 873	constructive delivery 870	lost property 873
accession 872	delivery order 883	mislaid property 873
bailee 875	document of title 883	personal property 866
bailee's lien 878	due negotiation 883	property 866
bailment 875	estray statute 873	real property 866
bailor 875	fee simple 868	tenancy by the entirety 869
bill of lading 883	fixture 866	tenancy in common 868
chattel 866	gift 870	trade fixture 868
community property 869	gift *causa mortis* 871	treasure trove 874
concurrent ownership 868	gift *inter vivos* 871	warehouse receipt 883
confusion 872	joint tenancy 869	

QUESTIONS AND CASE PROBLEMS

46–1. GIFTS. Jaspal has a severe heart attack and is taken to the hospital. He is not expected to live, and he knows it. Because he is a bachelor with no close relatives nearby, Jaspal gives his car keys to his close friend, Friedrich, telling Friedrich that he is expected to die and that the car is Friedrich's. Jaspal survives the heart attack, but two months later he dies from pneumonia. Jaspal's uncle, Sam, the executor of Jaspal's estate, wants Friedrich to return the car. Friedrich refuses, claiming that the car was given to him by Jaspal as a gift. Discuss whether Friedrich will be required to return the car to Jaspal's estate.

46–2. REQUIREMENTS OF A BAILMENT. Curtis is an executive on a business trip to the West Coast. He has driven his car on this trip and checks into the Hotel Ritz. The hotel has a guarded underground parking lot. Curtis gives his car keys to the parking lot attendant but fails to notify the attendant that his wife's $10,000 fur coat is in a box in the trunk. The next day, on checking out, he discovers that his car has been stolen. Curtis wants to hold the hotel liable for both the car and the coat. Discuss the probable success of his claim.

46–3. FOUND PROPERTY. Bill Heise is a janitor for the First Mercantile Department Store. While walking to work, Bill discovers an expensive watch lying on the curb. Bill gives the watch to his son, Otto. Two weeks later, Martin Avery, the true owner of the watch, discovers that Bill found the watch and demands it back from Otto. Discuss who is entitled to the watch and why.

46–4. LIABILITY OF THE BAILOR. Orlando borrows from his neighbor, Max, a gasoline-driven lawn edger.

Max has not used the lawn edger for two years. Orlando is not familiar with using a lawn edger, because he has never owned one. Max previously used this edger often, and if he had made a reasonable inspection, he would have discovered that the blade was loose. Orlando is injured when the blade becomes detached while he is edging his yard.

(a) Can Orlando hold Max liable for his injuries?

(b) Would your answer be any different if Orlando had rented the edger from Max and paid a fee? Explain.

46–5. LIABILITY OF THE BAILEE. Gerald Stavely entrusted a valuable painting to the care of Patricia Bolger. Bolger put the painting in the trunk of her husband's Cadillac. Her husband left the car at his country club in the care of a parking attendant who worked for Jack Boles Services, Inc. The car and painting were stolen. Bolger's car was eventually returned to him, but the painting was missing. Stavely filed a suit in a Texas state court against Boles, arguing that the bailee was responsible for the theft. The court agreed. Boles appealed. What will the appellate court decide? Why? [*Jack Boles Services, Inc. v. Stavely*, 906 S.W.2d 185 (Tex.App.— Austin 1995)]

46–6. FOUND PROPERTY. Using a metal detector, Billy Ray Shivers found metal tokens at the site of an abandoned sawmill that once belonged to Aldridge Lumber Company. The tokens were used fifty to a hundred years ago by the mill as payment for its workers. Because the site was in Angelina National Forest, the federal government claimed ownership of the tokens and seized them. Shivers filed a motion in a federal district court against the government, seeking to have the tokens returned. Should the court grant the motion? Why or why not? [*United States v. Shivers*, 96 F.3d 120 (5th Cir. 1996)]

46–7. GIFTS. Hugh Chalmers issued a promissory note to his father in the amount of $50,000, plus interest. The note was secured by a deed of trust on certain real estate and was payable on demand or within sixty days of the father's death. More than seventeen years later, the father assigned the deed of trust to his wife, Nina. The existence of the note was mentioned in the assignment, which was recorded in the appropriate state office with the deed of trust. After the father died, Nina found the note in a safe-deposit box. On the back of the note, the father had indorsed the note to Nina. When Chalmers refused to pay the amount due, Nina filed a lawsuit in an Arkansas state court against him. Chalmers argued that the note had not been effectively delivered. What should the court hold? Discuss. [*Chalmers v. Chalmers*, 937 S.W.2d 171 (Ark. 1997)]

46–8. GIFTS *INTER VIVOS*. Thomas Stafford owned four promissory notes. Payments on the notes were deposited into a bank account in the names of Stafford and his daughter, June Zink, "as joint tenants with right of survivorship." Stafford kept control of the notes and would not allow Zink to spend any of the proceeds. He also kept the interest on the account. On one note, Stafford endorsed "Pay to the order of Thomas J. Stafford or June S. Zink, or the survivor." The payee on each of the other notes was "Thomas J. Stafford and June S. Zink, or the survivor." When Stafford died, Zink took possession of the notes, claiming that she had been

a joint tenant of the notes with her father. Stafford's son, also Thomas, filed a suit in a Virginia state court against Zink, claiming that the notes were partly his. Thomas argued that their father had not made a valid gift *inter vivos* of the notes to Zink. In whose favor will the court rule? Why? [*Zink v. Stafford*, 509 S.E.2d 833 (Va. 1999)]

46–9 IN YOUR COURT

Jim and Sonja were lovers for nearly twenty years. They often lived together; they held themselves out as husband and wife; and Jim even gave Sonja a wedding band, which she wore. Two days before his death, Jim told Sonja that he felt "terribly bad," that he had a "heaviness" in his chest, and that he believed he would die. That night, he gave Sonja a check for $100,000 and told her that if he died, he wanted her "to be taken care of." After Jim's death, the administrator of Jim's estate petitioned the court to declare that Sonja was not entitled to the money represented by the check. Assume that you are the judge in the court hearing this case and answer the following questions:

(a) To be effective, a gift—whether it be a gift *inter vivos* or a gift *causa mortis*—must meet three requirements. What are these requirements?

(b) Was each of the requirements met in this case? [Hint: Had Jim really given up "complete dominion and control" over the $100,000 in his bank account at the time the gift was made?]

(c) Even if the gift was not effective, should you make an exception in this case and allow Sonja to have the $100,000? Why or why not?

LAW ON THE WEB

For updated links to resources available on the Web, as well as a variety of other materials, visit this text's Web site at http://wbl.westbuslaw.com.

To learn about whether a married person has ownership rights in a gift received by his or her spouse, go to Scott Law Firm's Web page at

http://www.scottlawfirm.com/property.htm

For a discussion of the origins of the term *bailment* and how bailment relationships have been defined, go to

http://www.lectlaw.com/def/b005.htm

LEGAL RESEARCH EXERCISES ON THE WEB

Go to http://wbl.westbuslaw.com, the Web site that accompanies this text. Select "Internet Applications," and then click on "Chapter 46." There you will find the following Internet research exercise that you can perform to learn more about bailment relationships:

Activity 46–1: Bailments

CHAPTER 47

Real Property

F ROM THE EARLIEST TIMES, PROPERTY has provided a means for survival. Primitive peoples lived off the fruits of the land, eating the vegetation and wildlife. Later, as the wildlife was domesticated and the vegetation cultivated, property provided pasturage and farmland. In the twelfth and thirteenth centuries, the power of feudal lords was exemplified by the amount of land that they held. After the age of feudalism passed, property continued to be an indicator of family wealth and social position. In the Western world, the protection of an individual's right to his or her property has become one of the most important features of citizenship.

In this chapter, we first look at the nature of ownership rights in real property. We then examine the legal requirements involved in the transfer of real property, including the kinds of rights that are transferred by various types of deeds; the procedures used in the sale of real estate; and a way in which real property can, under certain conditions, be transferred merely by possession.

Realize that real property rights are never absolute. There is a higher right—that of the government to take, for compensation, private land for public use. The concluding section in this chapter discusses this right, called *eminent domain*, as well as zoning laws and other restrictions on the ownership of property.

S E C T I O N 1

The Nature of Real Property

As discussed in Chapter 46, *real property* consists of land and the buildings, plants, and trees that it contains. Personal property is movable; real property is immovable. Real property usually means land, but it also includes subsurface and air rights, plant life and vegetation, and fixtures.

LAND

Land includes the soil on the surface of the earth and the natural products or artificial structures that are attached to it. Land further includes all the waters contained on or under its surface and the air space above it (subject, of course, to the legal use by pilots). In other words, unless a statute or case law holds otherwise, a landowner has the right to everything existing permanently below the surface of his or her property to the center of the earth and above it to the heavens.

AIR SPACE AND SUBSURFACE RIGHTS

The owner of real property has relatively exclusive rights to the air space above the land as well as the soil and minerals underneath it. Significant limitations on either air rights or subsurface rights normally have to be indicated on the document transferring title at the time of purchase. When no such limitations, or *encumbrances*, are noted, a purchaser can expect to have an unfettered right to possession of the property. The ways in which ownership rights in real property can be limited are examined in detail later in this chapter.

Air Rights.   Until seventy-five years ago, the right to use the air space over an owner's property was not too significant. Early cases involving air rights dealt with matters such as whether a telephone wire could be run across a person's property when the wire did not touch any of the property[1] and whether a bullet shot over a person's land constituted trespass.[2]

Today, cases involving air rights present questions such as the right of commercial and private planes to fly over property and the right of individuals and governments to seed clouds and produce artificial rain. Flights over private land normally do not violate the property owners' rights unless the flights are low and frequent, causing a direct interference with the enjoyment and use of the land.[3]

Subsurface Rights.   Ownership of the surface of land can be separated from ownership of its subsurface. Subsurface rights can be extremely valuable when minerals, oil, or natural gas is located beneath the surface. But a subsurface owner's rights would be of little value if he or she could not use the surface to exercise those rights. Hence, a subsurface owner will have a right (called a *profit*, discussed later in this chapter) to go onto the surface of the land to, for example, find and remove minerals.

Of course, conflicts may arise between surface and subsurface owners when attempts are made to excavate below the surface. At common law, a landowner has the right to have the land supported in its natural condition by the owners of the interests under the surface. If the owners of the subsurface rights excavate, they are absolutely liable if their excavation causes the surface to collapse. Depending on the circumstances,

the excavators may also be liable for any damage to structures on the land. Many states have statutes that extend excavators' liability to include damage to structures on the property. Typically, these statutes provide exact guidelines as to the requirements for excavations of various depths.

PLANT LIFE AND VEGETATION

Plant life, both natural and cultivated, is also considered to be real property. In many instances, natural vegetation, such as trees, adds greatly to the value of realty. When a parcel of land is sold and the land has growing crops on it, the sale includes the crops, unless otherwise specified in the sales contract. When crops are sold by themselves, however, they are considered to be personal property or goods. Consequently, the sale of crops is a sale of goods, and it is governed by the Uniform Commercial Code rather than by real property law.[4]

SECTION 2

Ownership Interests in Real Property

Ownership of property is an abstract concept that cannot exist independently of the legal system. No one can actually possess, or *hold*, a piece of land, the air above, the earth below, and all the water contained on it. One can only possess *rights* in real property. Numerous rights are involved in real property ownership. As discussed in Chapter 46, one who holds the entire bundle of rights owns the property in *fee simple*. Here we look first at the fee simple and then at some common examples of how an owner in fee simple can part with some, but not all, of his or her rights in real property.

FEE SIMPLE

In a **fee simple absolute,** the owner has the greatest aggregation of rights, privileges, and power possible. The owner can give the property away, sell the property for a price, or transfer the property by will to another. The fee simple absolute is limited to a person and his or her heirs and is assigned forever without limitation or condition. The rights that accompany a fee simple absolute include the right to use the land

1. *Butler v. Frontier Telephone Co.*, 186 N.Y. 486, 79 N.E. 716 (1906). Stringing a wire across someone's property violates the air rights of that person. Leaning walls and projecting eave spouts and roofs also violate the air rights of the property owner.
2. *Herrin v. Sutherland*, 74 Mont. 587, 241 P. 328 (1925). Shooting over a person's land normally constitutes trespass.
3. *United States v. Causby*, 328 U.S. 256, 66 S.Ct. 1062, 90 L.Ed. 1206 (1946).

4. See UCC 2–107(2).

for whatever purpose the owner sees fit, subject to laws that prevent the owner from unreasonably interfering with another person's land and subject to applicable zoning laws. Furthermore, the owner has the right of *exclusive* possession of the property. A fee simple is potentially infinite in duration and can be disposed of by deed or by will (by selling or giving it to another). When there is no will, the fee simple passes to the owner's legal heirs.

LIFE ESTATES

A **life estate** is an estate that lasts for the life of some specified individual. A **conveyance,** or transfer of real property, "to A for his life" creates a life estate.[5] In a life estate, the life tenant's ownership rights cease to exist on the life tenant's death. The life tenant has the right to use the land, provided no waste (injury to the land) is committed. In other words, the life tenant cannot injure the land in a manner that would adversely affect its value. The life tenant can use the land to harvest crops or, if mines and oil wells are already on the land, can extract minerals and oil from it, but the life tenant cannot exploit the land by creating new wells or mines.

The life tenant has the right to mortgage the life estate and create liens, easements, and leases; but none can extend beyond the life of the tenant. In addition, with few exceptions, the owner of a life estate has an exclusive right to possession during his or her lifetime.

Along with these rights, the life tenant also has some duties—to keep the property in repair and to pay property taxes. In sum, the owner of the life estate has the same rights as a fee simple owner except that he or she must maintain the value of the property during his or her tenancy, less the decrease in value resulting from the normal use of the property allowed by the life tenancy.

LEASEHOLD ESTATES

A **leasehold estate** is created when a real property owner or lessor (landlord) agrees to convey the right to possess and use the property to a lessee (tenant) for a certain period of time. In every leasehold estate, the tenant has a *qualified* right to exclusive possession

(qualified by the right of the landlord to enter on the premises to assure that waste is not being committed). The tenant can use the land—for example, by harvesting crops—but cannot injure the land by such activities as cutting down timber for sale or extracting oil. The respective rights and duties of the landlord and tenant that arise under a lease agreement will be discussed in greater detail in Chapter 48. Here, we look at the types of leasehold estates, or tenancies, that can be created when real property is leased.

Tenancy for Years. A **tenancy for years** is created by an express contract (which can sometimes be oral) by which property is leased for a specified period of time, such as a month, a year, or a period of years. For example, signing a one-year lease to occupy an apartment creates a tenancy for years. At the end of the period specified in the lease, the lease ends (without notice), and possession of the apartment returns to the lessor. If the tenant dies during the period of the lease, the lease interest passes to the tenant's heirs as personal property. Often, leases include renewal or extension provisions.

Periodic Tenancy. A **periodic tenancy** is created by a lease that does not specify how long it is to last but does specify that rent is to be paid at certain intervals. This type of tenancy is automatically renewed for another rental period unless properly terminated. For example, a periodic tenancy is created by a lease that states, "Rent is due on the tenth day of every month." This provision creates a tenancy from month to month. A week-to-week or year-to-year tenancy can also be created. A periodic tenancy sometimes arises when a landlord allows a tenant under a tenancy for years to hold over (retain possession after the lease term ends) and continue paying monthly or weekly rent.

At common law, to terminate a periodic tenancy, the landlord or tenant must give one period's notice to the other party. If the tenancy is month to month, for example, one month's notice must be given. State statutes often require a different period for notice of termination in a periodic tenancy, however.

Tenancy at Will. Suppose that a landlord rents an apartment to a tenant "for as long as both agree." In such a case, the tenant receives a leasehold estate known as a **tenancy at will.** At common law, either party can terminate the tenancy without notice (that is, "at will"). This type of estate usually arises when a tenant who has been under a tenancy for years retains

---

5. A less common type of life estate is created by the conveyance "to A for the life of B." This is known as an estate *pur autre vie,* or an estate for the duration of the life of another.

possession after the termination date of that tenancy with the landlord's consent. Before the tenancy has been converted into a periodic tenancy (by the periodic payment of rent), it is a tenancy at will, terminable by either party without notice. Once the tenancy is treated as a periodic tenancy, termination notice must conform to the requirements already discussed. The death of either party or the voluntary commission of waste by the tenant will terminate a tenancy at will.

Tenancy at Sufferance.

The possession of land without right is called a **tenancy at sufferance.** A tenancy at sufferance is created when a tenant *wrongfully* retains possession of property. It is not a true tenancy for that reason. For example, when a tenancy for years or a periodic tenancy ends and the tenant continues to retain possession of the premises without the owner's permission, a tenancy at sufferance is created.

NONPOSSESSORY INTERESTS

Some interests in land do not include any rights of possession. These interests, known as nonpossessory interests, include *easements, profits,* and *licenses.* Because easements and profits are similar, and the same rules apply to both, we discuss them together.

Easements and Profits.

An **easement** is the right of a person to make limited use of another person's real property without taking anything from the property. An easement, for example, can be the right to walk across another's property. In contrast, a **profit** is the right to go onto land in possession of another and take away some part of the land itself or some product of the land. For example, Mack, the owner of Sandy View, gives Ann the right to go there and remove all the sand and gravel that she needs for her cement business. Ann has a profit. Easements and profits can be classified as either appurtenant or in gross.

An easement or profit *appurtenant* arises when the owner of one piece of land has a right to go onto (or remove things from) an adjacent piece of land owned by another. Suppose Owen has a right to drive his car across Green's land, which is adjacent to Owen's property. This right-of-way over Green's property is an easement appurtenant to Owen's land and can be used only by Owen. Owen can convey the easement when he conveys his property.

With an easement or profit *in gross,* the right to use or take things from another's land does not depend on the owner of the easement or profit's owning an adjacent tract of land. When a utility company is granted an easement to run its power lines across another's property, it obtains an easement in gross. An easement or profit in gross requires the existence of only one parcel of land, which must be owned by someone other than the owner of the easement or profit in gross.

Creation of an Easement or Profit.

Profits and easements can be created by deed or will, contract, implication, necessity, or prescription. Creation by deed or will simply involves the delivery of a *deed* or a transfer by *will* by the owner of an easement stating that the grantee (the person receiving the profit or easement) is granted the rights that the grantor had in the easement or profit. Easements or profits can also be created by *contract,* with the contract terms defining the extent and length of time of use.

An easement or profit may arise by *implication* when the circumstances surrounding the division of a parcel of property imply its creation. If Barrow divides a parcel of land that has only one well for drinking water and conveys the half without a well to Dan, a profit by implication arises, because Dan needs drinking water.

An easement may also be created by necessity. An easement by *necessity* does not require division of property for its existence. A person who rents an apartment, for example, has an easement by necessity in the private road leading up to the dwelling.

An easement arises by *prescription* when one person exercises an easement, such as a right-of-way, on another person's land without the landowner's consent, and the use is apparent and continues for a period of time equal to the applicable statute of limitations. In much the same way, title to property may be obtained by adverse possession, discussed later in this chapter.

Effect of a Sale of Property.

When a parcel of land that is *benefited* by an easement or profit appurtenant is sold, the property carries the easement or profit along with it. Thus, if Owen sells his property to Thomas and includes the appurtenant right-of-way across Green's property in the deed to Thomas, Thomas will own both the property and the easement that benefits it.

When a parcel of land that has the *burden* of an easement or profit appurtenant is sold, the new owner must recognize its existence only if he or she knew or should have known of it or if it was recorded in the appropriate office of the county. Thus, if Owen records his easement across Green's property in the appropriate county office before Green conveys the land, the new owner of Green's property will have to allow Owen, or any subsequent owner of Owen's property, to continue to use the path across the land formerly owned by Green.

Termination of an Easement or Profit.   An easement or profit can be terminated or extinguished in several ways. The simplest way is to deed it back to the owner of the land that is burdened by it. Also, if the owner of an easement or profit becomes the owner of the property burdened by it, then it is merged into the property. Another way is to abandon it with the intent to relinquish the right to use it.

Licenses.   A **license** is the revocable right of a person to come onto another person's land. It is a personal privilege that arises from the consent of the owner of the land and that can be revoked by the owner. A ticket to attend a movie at a theater is an example of a license. Assume that a Broadway theater owner issues to Roxanna a ticket to see a play. If Roxanna is refused entry into the theater because she is improperly dressed, she has no right to force her way into the theater. The ticket is only a revocable license, not a conveyance of an interest in property.

CONCEPT SUMMARY 47.1   INTERESTS IN REAL PROPERTY

TYPE OF INTEREST	DESCRIPTION
Ownership Interests	1. *Fee simple absolute*—The most complete form of ownership. 2. *Life estate*—An estate that lasts for the life of a specified individual; ownership rights in a life estate are subject to the rights of the future-interest holder. 3. *Concurrent interests*—Exist when title to property is held by two or more persons. Co-ownership can take the form of a tenancy in common, a joint tenancy, a tenancy by the entirety, or community property (see Chapter 46 for a description of concurrent ownership).
Leasehold Interests	A leasehold interest, or estate, is an interest in real property that is held only for a limited period of time, as specified in the lease agreement. Types of tenancies relating to leased property include the following: 1. *Tenancy for years*—Tenancy for a period of time stated by express contract. 2. *Periodic tenancy*—Tenancy for a period determined by the frequency of rent payments; automatically renewed unless proper notice is given. 3. *Tenancy at will*—Tenancy for as long as both parties agree; no notice of termination is required. 4. *Tenancy at sufferance*—Possession of land without legal right.
Nonpossessory Interests	Interests that involve the right to use real property but not to possess it. Easements, profits, and licenses are nonpossessory interests.

SECTION 3

Transfer of Ownership

Ownership of real property can pass from one person to another in a number of ways. Ownership rights in real property are commonly transferred through sale of the property or by will or inheritance. Real property ownership can also be transferred by gift, by possession, or (as will be discussed later in the chapter) by eminent domain. When ownership rights in real property are transferred, the type of interest being transferred and the conditions of the transfer normally are set forth in a *deed* executed by the one who is conveying the property.

DEEDS

Possession and title to land are passed from person to person by means of a **deed**—the instrument of conveyance of real property. A deed is a writing signed by an owner of real property by which title to it is transferred to another. Deeds must meet certain requirements. Unlike a contract, a deed does not have to be supported by legally sufficient consideration. Gifts of real property are common, and they require deeds even though there is no consideration for the gift. The necessary components of a valid deed are the following:

1. The names of the *grantor* (the giver or seller) and the *grantee* (the donee or buyer).
2. Words evidencing an intent to convey (for example, "I hereby bargain," "I hereby sell," "I hereby grant," or "I hereby give").
3. A legally sufficient description of the land.
4. The grantor's (and usually his or her spouse's) signature.
5. Delivery of the deed.

Warranty Deed.   The **warranty deed** makes the greatest number of warranties and thus provides the most extensive protection against defects of title. A sample warranty deed is illustrated in Exhibit 47–1. In most states, special language is required to make a warranty deed. If a contract calls for a "warranty deed" without specifying the covenants to be included in the deed, or if a deed states that the seller is providing the "usual covenants," most courts will infer from this language that the following covenants are being made: a covenant that the grantor has the title to, and the power to convey, the property; a covenant that the buyer will not be disturbed in his or her possession of the land; and a covenant that transfer of the property is made without knowledge of adverse claims of third parties.

Special Warranty Deed.   In contrast to the warranty deed, the **special warranty deed** warrants only that the grantor or seller has not previously done anything to lessen the value of the real estate. If the special warranty deed discloses all liens or other encumbrances, the seller will not be liable to the buyer if a third person subsequently interferes with the buyer's ownership. If the third person's claim arises out of, or is related to, some act of the seller, however, the seller will be liable to the buyer for damages.

Quitclaim Deed.   A **quitclaim deed** warrants less than any other deed. Essentially, it simply conveys to the grantee whatever interest the grantor had. In other words, if the grantor had nothing, then the grantee receives nothing. Naturally, if the grantor had a defective title or no title at all, a conveyance by warranty deed or special warranty deed would not cure the defects. Such deeds, however, will give the buyer a cause of action to sue the seller.

A quitclaim deed can and often does serve as a release of the grantor's interest in a particular parcel of property. For instance, suppose Sandor owns a strip of waterfront property on which he wants to build condominiums. Lanz has an interest in a section of the property, which he might assert either to prevent the development or to insist on a share of its earnings. Sandor can negotiate with Lanz for a release of the claim. Lanz's signing of a quitclaim deed would constitute such a release.

Grant Deed.   With a **grant deed,** the grantor simply states, "I grant the property to you" or "I convey, or bargain and sell, the property to you." By state statute, grant deeds may carry with them an implied warranty that the grantor owns the property being transferred and has not previously encumbered it or conveyed it to someone else.

Sheriff's Deed.   A **sheriff's deed** is a document giving ownership rights to a buyer at a sheriff's sale, which is a sale held by a sheriff to pay a court judgment against the owner of the property. Typically, the property was subject to a mortgage or tax payments and the owner defaulted on the payments. A deed is given to the buyer at the sale as part of the foreclosure process on the mortgage or tax lien. The giving of the deed begins the running of the period of time during which the defaulting owner can redeem the property (see Chapter 29).

Recording Statutes.   Every jurisdiction has **recording statutes,** which allow deeds to be recorded. Recording a deed gives notice to the public that a certain person is now the owner of a particular parcel of real estate. Thus, prospective buyers can check the public records for transactions creating interests or rights in specific parcels of real property. Placing everyone on notice as to the true owner is intended to prevent the previous owners from fraudulently conveying the land to other purchasers. Deeds are generally recorded in the county in which the property is located. Many state statutes require that the grantor sign the deed in the presence of two witnesses before it can be recorded. There are three basic types of recording statutes:

EXHIBIT 47–1   A SAMPLE WARRANTY DEED

Date: May 31, 2001

Grantor: GAYLORD A. JENTZ AND WIFE, JOANN H. JENTZ

Grantor's Mailing Address (including county):
        4106 North Loop Drive
        Austin, Travis County, Texas

Grantee: DAVID F. FRIEND AND WIFE, JOAN E. FRIEND AS JOINT TENANTS
          WITH RIGHT OF SURVIVORSHIP
Grantee's Mailing Address (including county):
        5929 Fuller Drive
        Austin, Travis County, Texas

Consideration:
For and in consideration of the sum of Ten and No/100 Dollars ($10.00) and other
valuable consideration to the undersigned paid by the grantees herein named, the
receipt of which is hereby acknowledged, and for which no lien is retained, either
express or implied.

Property (including any improvements):
Lot 23, Block "A", Northwest Hills, Green Acres Addition, Phase 4, Travis County,
Texas, according to the map or plat of record in volume 22, pages 331-336 of the
Plat Records of Travis County, Texas.

Reservations from and Exceptions to Conveyance and Warranty:

This conveyance with its warranty is expressly made subject to the following:

Easements and restrictions of record in Volume 7863, Page 53, Volume 8430,
Page 35, Volume 8133, Page 152 of the Real Property Record of Travis County,
Texas, Volume 22, Pages 335-339, of the Plat Records of Travis County, Texas;
and to any other restrictions and easements affecting said property which are
of record in Travis County, Texas.

   Grantor, for the consideration and subject to the reservations from and exceptions to conveyance and warranty, grants, sells,
and conveys to Grantee the property, together with all and singular the rights and appurtenances thereto in any wise belonging,
to have and hold it to Grantee, Grantee's heirs, executors, administrators, successors, or assigns forever. Grantor binds
Grantor and Grantor's heirs, executors, administrators, and successors to warrant and forever defend all and singular the
property to Grantee and Grantee's heirs, executors, administrators, successors, and assigns against every person whomsoever
lawfully claiming or to claim the same or any part thereof, except as to the reservations from and exceptions to conveyance
and warranty.

   When the context requires, singular nouns and pronouns include the plural.

                                         BY: _____
                                             Gaylord A. Jentz

                                         BY: _____
                                             JoAnn H. Jentz

                              (Acknowledgment)

STATE OF TEXAS
COUNTY OF TRAVIS

      This instrument was acknowledged before me on the   31st day of May   , 2001
by Gaylord A. and JoAnn H. Jentz

                                    _____
                                    Notary Public, State of Texas
                                    Notary's name (printed): Rosemary Potter

            Notary Seal
                                    Notary's commission expires: 1/31/2005

1. A *race statute* provides that the first purchaser to record a deed has superior rights to the property, regardless of whether he or she knew that someone else had already bought the property but had failed to record the deed.[6] Under these statutes, recording is a "race," and whoever files first "wins."

2. A *pure notice statute* provides that, regardless of who files first, a person who knows that someone else has already bought the property cannot claim priority. In contrast, a subsequent good faith purchaser who, at the time he or she acquires a deed, has no notice of a previous deed—because, for example, it has not been recorded—may successfully assert a superior claim to the property. (A *good faith purchaser* is one who purchases for value, in good faith, and without notice.)

3. A *notice-race statute* protects a purchaser who does not know that someone else has already bought the property and who records his or her deed first.

Recording a deed involves a fee. The grantee typically pays this fee, because he or she is the one who will be protected by recording the deed.

CONTRACTS FOR THE SALE OF REAL ESTATE

Transfers of ownership interests in real property are frequently accomplished by means of a sale. The sale of real estate is similar to the sale of goods, because it involves a transfer of ownership, often with specific warranties. In the sale of real estate, however, certain formalities are observed that are not required in the sale of goods. For example, to meet the requirements of law, a deed must be signed and delivered.[7]

Exhibit 47–2 summarizes the steps involved in any sale of real property. The first step is the formation of the land sales contract. A title search (to verify that the seller has good title to the property and that no other claims to the property exist) follows, along with, usually, negotiations to obtain financing for the purchase. The final step is the closing. We examine some of the legal considerations involved in these steps below, as well as other requirements relating to the sale of real property. First, however, we look at the important role played by real estate agents, or brokers, in the sale of real property.

Brokers. Buyers and sellers of real property frequently enlist the services of a *real estate agent*, or broker. Real estate agents are information brokers. They provide buyers and sellers of real estate with information and specialize in matching the wants of buyers with the property being offered for sale by sellers.

Normally, the broker is retained by the seller and acts as the seller's agent in the sale of the property. In compensation for their services, brokers usually receive a commission (which can range from 1 to 10 percent of the purchase price) from the seller when the sale is concluded. A broker can also act as an agent of the buyer, in which case a dual agency exists. Generally, a broker may not act as an agent for more than one party without the consent of all parties involved, and state laws often place further restrictions on dual agencies. Most states require real estate brokers to be licensed, and in some states, brokers may be required to meet continuing-education or other requirements.

Formation of the Sales Contract. If someone decides to purchase real estate, normally he or she makes a written offer to purchase the property and puts up *earnest money* to show that an earnest, or serious, offer is being made. (If the buyer decides to withdraw the offer, the earnest money will often be forfeited, as liquidated damages, to the seller.) The offer states in some detail the exact offering price for the property and lists any other conditions that may be appropriate. The offer may be conditioned on the offeror's ability to obtain financing, for example. Within a specified time period, the seller of the property either accepts or rejects the offer—or, as is often the case, makes a counteroffer. The seller then becomes the offeror and the buyer the offeree.

Once the offer (or counteroffer) is accepted, then a contract of sale is drawn up. Because an oral agreement for a sale of land is not enforceable under the Statute of Frauds, the agreement should be put in writing. The written agreement should include at least the names and addresses of the parties, a description of the property, the time for the closing, the type of deed that will be delivered, and the price. The contract might also state which party bears the risk of loss if, after the contract is formed, the property is destroyed (for example, if the house burns down).[8] Usually, the signing of the sales contract is accompanied by a deposit, which,

---

6. Only two states (Delaware and North Carolina) use race statutes. Usage in the rest of the states is split about evenly between the pure notice statute and the notice-race statute.

7. The phrase *signed, sealed, and delivered* once referred to the requirements for transferring title to real property by deed. The seal has fallen from use, but signature and delivery are still required.

8. Unless the contract states otherwise, the buyer will suffer any loss (assuming that the loss is not the seller's fault). Either party can take out an insurance policy against the risk, however.

EXHIBIT 47–2   STEPS INVOLVED IN THE SALE OF REAL ESTATE

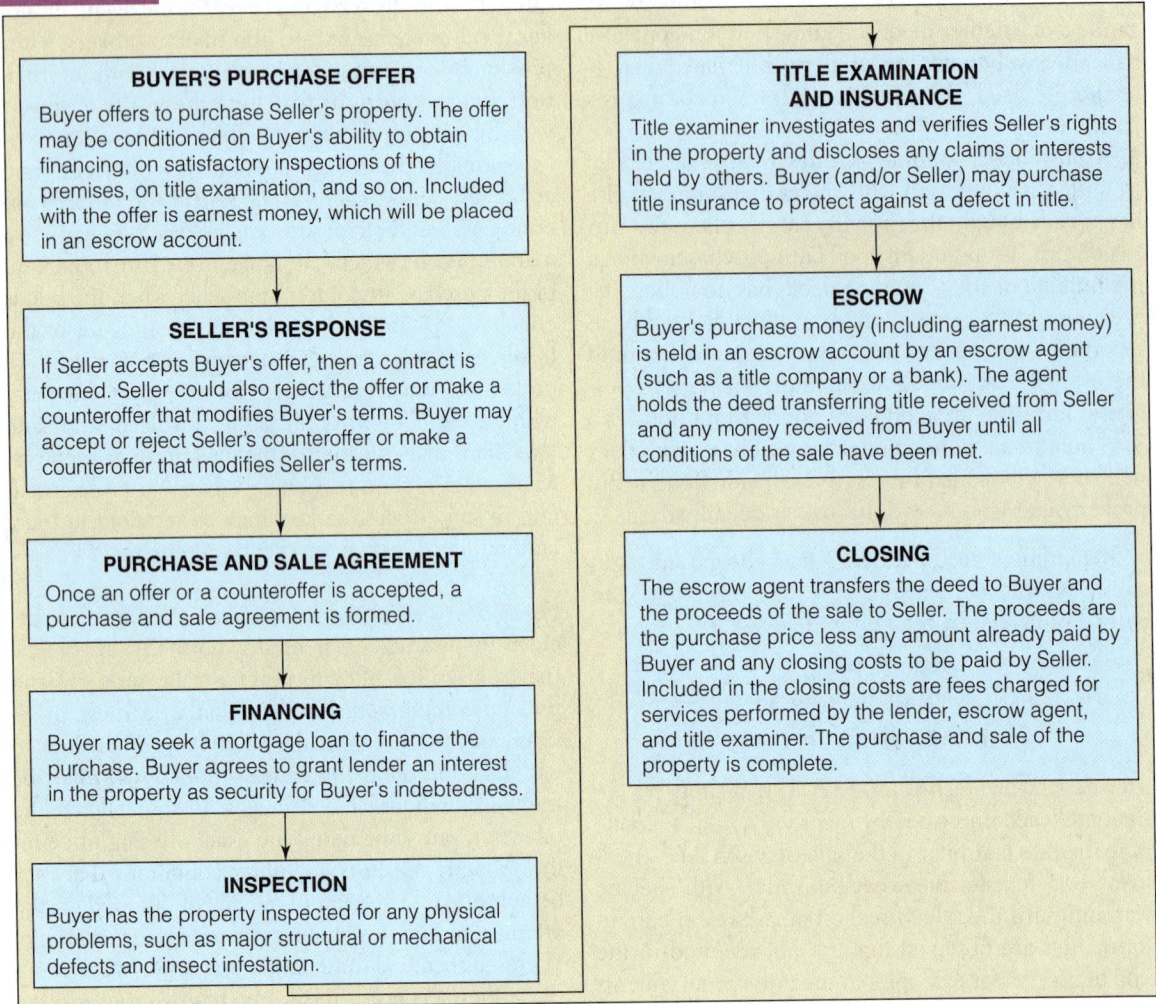

combined with the earnest money, may total 10 percent of the purchase price paid to the seller.

Deposits toward the purchase price normally are held in a special account, called an **escrow account,** until all of the conditions of sale have been met and the closing takes place, at which time the money is transferred to the seller. The *escrow agent,* which may be a title company, bank, or special escrow company, acts as a neutral party in the sales transaction and facilitates the sale by allowing the buyer and seller to close the transaction without having to exchange documents and funds.

Title Examination. After the sales contract has been negotiated, the buyer or the buyer's attorney (or the escrow agent, title insurance company, or lending institution from which the purchase price is borrowed) performs a *title examination.* This entails examining at the county recording office the history of all past transfers of, liens on, and sales of the property in question.

A contract for the sale of land includes the seller's implied obligation to transfer marketable title. **Marketable title** is title that is free from encumbrances (such as mortgages and restrictive covenants, both of which are discussed below), defects in the chain of title (such as a previous sale of the property by the seller), and other events that affect title (such as adverse possession and eminent domain, both of which are discussed below). Title is considered marketable even if the property is subject to zoning restrictions or public easements, such as sidewalks and sewers. If a title examination uncovers a material defect that has not been disclosed in the contract, the seller is considered to have breached the contract, and the buyer may seek any appropriate remedies (damages, rescission, or specific performance with a price adjustment).

Title examinations are not foolproof, and buyers of real property generally purchase **title insurance** to protect their interests in the event that some defect in the title was not discovered during the examination. A title insurance policy insures against loss resulting from any defects in the title and guarantees that if any defects do arise, the title company issuing the policy will defend the owner's interests and pay all legal expenses involved.

Financing. Unless a buyer pays cash for the property, the buyer must obtain financing for the purchase with a mortgage loan. A **mortgage** is a loan made by an individual or institution, such as a banking institution or trust company, for which the property is given as security. In some states, the *mortgagor* (the borrower) holds title to the property; in others, the *mortgagee* (the lender) holds title until the loan is completely repaid. In several states, a trustee—a third party—holds title on behalf of the lender. The trustee then deeds the property to the borrower when the loan is repaid. If the payments are not made, the trustee can deed the property to the lender or dispose of it by foreclosure, depending on state law.

Closing. The final step in the sale of real estate is the **closing**—also called *settlement* or *closing of escrow.* The escrow agent coordinates the closing with the recording of deeds, the obtaining of title insurance, and other concurrent closing activities. Several costs must be paid, in cash, at the time of closing. These costs include fees for services, including those performed by the lender, escrow agent, and title company, and they can range from several hundred to several thousand dollars, depending on the amount of the mortgage loan and other conditions of sale. The 1976 amendments to the Real Estate Settlement Procedures Act of 1974[9] require lending institutions to notify—within a specified time period—each applicant for a mortgage loan of the specific costs that must be paid at the closing.

Warranty of Habitability. The common law rule of *caveat emptor* ("let the buyer beware") held that the

---

9. 12 U.S.C. Sections 2601–2617.

seller of a home made no warranties with respect to its soundness or fitness unless such a warranty was specifically included in the deed or contract of sale. There is currently a strong trend against this rule and in favor of an **implied warranty of habitability.** Under this approach, which is the law in the majority of states, the seller of a new house warrants that it will be fit for human habitation regardless of whether any such warranty is included in the deed or contract of sale. This warranty is similar to the UCC's implied warranty of merchantability for sales of personal property.

Essentially, under an implied warranty of habitability, the seller warrants that the house is in reasonable working order and is of reasonably sound construction. To recover damages for breach of the implied warranty of habitability, the purchaser is required to prove only that the home he or she purchased was somehow defective and to prove that the damages were caused by the defect. Thus, under the warranty of habitability theory, the seller of a new home is in effect a guarantor of the home's fitness. In some states, the warranty protects not only the first purchaser but any subsequent purchaser as well.

Seller's Duty to Disclose. Traditionally, under the rule of *caveat emptor*, a seller had no duty to disclose to the buyer defects in the property, even if the seller knew about the defects and the buyer had no reasonable way to discover them. Currently, in most jurisdictions, courts have placed on sellers a duty to disclose any known defect that materially affects the value of the property and that the buyer could not reasonably discover. Under these circumstances, nondisclosure is similar to representing that the defect does not exist, and the buyer may have grounds for a successful lawsuit based on fraud or misrepresentation.

For example, Nick sells Nora a five-year-old house that he knows has roof problems. Nick does not tell Nora about these problems. During the first rain after the sale, water gushes from the house's ceilings and light fixtures. Nora contacts a roofing contractor, who tells her that repair would be a temporary solution and only a new roof would be watertight. Nora might sue Nick for breach of contract, fraud, and misrepresentation, seeking rescission of their contract and a return of whatever amount she paid Nick toward the purchase price of the house.

At issue in the following case was whether a seller was required to disclose a defect that was evident, at least in part, from a visual inspection.

CASE 47.1   Smith v. Levine

Court of
Appeals of Texas,
San Antonio, 1995.
911 S.W.2d 427.

BACKGROUND AND FACTS   *Donald and Pat Smith put their house on the market. Monte Grissom considered buying it and hired Jim Bradley, an engineer, to inspect it. Bradley's inspection report stated that the foundation was defective. Grissom did not buy the house, but he told the Smiths about the foundation. Subsequently, Ronald and Serena Levine considered buying the house but noticed cracks in the walls and a slope in the floor. The Smiths said that these were "superficial" and "routine" and did not mention Bradley's report. The Levines then bought the house. For part of the purchase price, they signed a promissory note payable to the Smiths. Two years later, when the Levines learned of Bradley's report, they hired an attorney and confronted the Smiths with a demand for damages. The Smiths then filed a suit against the Levines in a Texas state court to collect on the note. A jury found that the Smiths had committed fraud and awarded the Levines more than $80,000 in damages. The Smiths appealed this part of the judgment.*

**IN THE LANGUAGE
OF THE COURT**

DUNCAN, Justice.
    *   *   *   *

        *   *   * [T]he Smiths argue that *   *   * they cannot be held liable for knowingly failing to disclose information of which the Levines were or should have been equally aware. We cannot agree that the record supports the Smiths' factual premise.

        By virtue of their awareness of Bradley's report, and Grissom's resulting refusal to purchase, the jury was entitled to find that the Smiths knew the foundation was defective by the time of the Smith-Levine transaction. This foundation problem was not simply a matter of "superficial" and "routine" cracks in interior walls or the slope in the floor—defects of which the Levines were made aware by their own visual inspection *   *   *. Rather, the foundation problem arose out of a perimeter grade beam that had become so deflected as to damage the superstructure of the house. That is the information contained in Bradley's report, and that is the information the jury could reasonably have found the Smiths should have but did not disclose to the Levines.

**DECISION
AND REMEDY**

The intermediate state appellate court affirmed the jury's award to the Levines. The Smiths' failure to disclose to the Levines the problems with the house's foundation constituted fraud.

TRANSFER BY INHERITANCE

Property that is transferred on an owner's death is passed either by will or by inheritance laws. If the owner of land dies with a will, that land passes according to the terms of the will. If the owner dies without a will, state statutes prescribe how and to whom the property will pass. The transfer of property by inheritance will be discussed in Chapter 50.

ADVERSE POSSESSION

Adverse possession is a means of obtaining title to land without delivery of a deed. Essentially, when one person possesses the property of another for a certain statutory period of time (three to thirty years, with ten years being most common), that person, called the adverse possessor, acquires title to the land and cannot be removed from it by the original owner. The

adverse possessor may ultimately be vested with good title just as if there had been a conveyance by deed.

For property to be held adversely, four elements must be satisfied:

1. Possession must be actual and exclusive; that is, the possessor must take sole physical occupancy of the property.
2. The possession must be open, visible, and notorious, not secret or clandestine. The possessor must occupy the land for all the world to see.
3. Possession must be continuous and peaceable for the required period of time. This requirement means that the possessor must not be interrupted in the occupancy by the true owner or by the courts.
4. Possession must be hostile and adverse. In other words, the possessor must claim the property as against the whole world. He or she cannot be living on the property with the permission of the owner.

There are a number of public-policy reasons for the adverse possession doctrine. These include society's interest in resolving boundary disputes, in quieting (determining) title when title to property is in question, and in assuring that real property remains in the stream of commerce. More fundamentally, policies behind the doctrine include punishing owners who sit on their rights too long and rewarding possessors for putting land to productive use.

In the following case, the question before the court was whether a couple had obtained title to a certain piece of land by adverse possession.

CASE 47.2   Klos v. Molenda

Superior Court of
Pennsylvania, 1986.
355 Pa.Super. 399,
513 A.2d 490.

HISTORICAL AND CULTURAL SETTING *After World War II ended in 1945, members of the armed forces returned to their families or began families, and the birthrate increased dramatically each year. Many of the former servicepeople went to college, but even those who did not go back to school needed relatively low-cost housing. In 1947, a builder, Abraham Levitt, and his sons developed Levittown—a community on Long Island consisting of inexpensive houses and a playground, shops, and other amenities. Over the next few years, other builders began to imitate Levitt's idea, and by 1950, suburban developments were sprawling across the American landscape.*

BACKGROUND AND FACTS *In September 1950, Michael and Albina Klos purchased part of some property owned by John and Anne Molenda. The Kloses' lot was 50 feet wide and 135 feet deep. Rather than surveying the property, the seller and buyer paced off the lot and placed stakes in the ground as boundary markers. The Kloses built a house on the lot in 1952 and put in a sidewalk along the full front. They also put in a driveway thirty inches from the stake line. They planted grass and a hedge in that thirty inches and maintained it until 1984. In 1983, Mr. Molenda died, and his widow hired a surveyor to inventory the landholdings. The survey located the rightful property line between the Molendas' and Kloses' land as being thirty inches closer to the Kloses' house than it currently was. This placed the property line right along the Kloses' driveway, instead of thirty inches to the side of the driveway. On learning this, Mrs. Molenda dug up the grass strip and the hedgerow and erected a fence right along the Kloses' driveway, marking the property line. The Kloses brought this action challenging Mrs. Molenda's conduct, claiming that they held title to the land by adverse possession. The trial court held that the Kloses had title to the land. Mrs. Molenda appealed.*

**IN THE LANGUAGE
OF THE COURT**

WIEAND, Judge.

*   *   *   *

It is well settled that he who asserts title by adverse possession must prove it affirmatively. One who claims title by adverse possession must prove that he had *actual, continuous, exclusive, visible, notorious, distinct, and hostile possession of the land* for twenty-one years. *   *   * Each of these elements must exist, otherwise the possession will not confer title. An adverse possessor must intend to hold the land for himself, and that intention must be made manifest by his acts. *   *   * He must keep his flag flying and present a hostile front to all adverse pretensions. [Emphasis added.]

On appeal, Mrs. Molenda's principal contentions are that the Klos possession was (1) sporadic rather than continuous, and (2) permissive and neither hostile nor adverse. We reject these arguments. The evidence disclosed that appellees had continuously maintained the strip of land in lawn between 1952 and 1984, when their maintenance of the lawn was prevented by the fence which Anne Molenda had erected. The use of land for lawn purposes and the continuous maintenance thereof in connection with a residence, it has been held, are sufficient to establish adverse possession.

The hostile nature of the Klos possession was not destroyed because the stake line may have been placed along a property line mistakenly located by the adjoining landowners. This fact did not render Klos' possession permissive. The parties intended that the Kloses should have title to that line, and thereafter the Kloses kept their flag flying continuously on the thirty (30) inch strip of land. Their possession, open, notorious and exclusive for more than twenty-one years, presented a hostile front to any person or persons intending to make a conflicting pretension of ownership.

DECISION AND REMEDY   *The appellate court affirmed the trial court's decision. The Kloses held rightful title to the land by adverse possession.*

SECTION 4

Limitations on the Rights of Property Owners

No ownership rights in real property can ever really be absolute. That is, an owner of real property cannot always do whatever he or she wishes on or with the property. Nuisance and environmental laws, for example, restrict certain types of activities. Holding the property is also conditional on the payment of property taxes. If these taxes are not paid, ownership of the property will be forfeited to the state. In addition, if a property owner fails to pay debts, the property may be seized to satisfy judgment creditors. In short, the rights of every property owner are subject to certain conditions and limitations. In this final section of the chapter, we look at some of the important ways in which owners' rights in real property can be limited.

EMINENT DOMAIN

Even if ownership in real property is in fee simple absolute, there is still a superior ownership that limits the fee simple absolute. Just as in medieval England, the king was the ultimate landowner, so in the United States, the government has ultimate ownership rights in all land. This right is called **eminent domain,** and it is sometimes referred to as the *condemnation power* of the government to take land for public use. It gives a right to the government to acquire possession of real property in the manner directed by the Constitution and the laws of the state whenever the public interest requires it. Property may not be taken for private benefit, but only for public use.

For example, when a new public highway is to be built, the government must decide where to build it and how much land to condemn. The power of eminent domain is generally invoked through condemnation proceedings. After the government determines that a particular parcel of land is necessary for public use, it brings a judicial proceeding to obtain title to the land. Then, in another proceeding, the court determines the *fair value* of the land, which is usually approximately equal to its market value. When the government takes land owned by a private party for public use, it is referred to as a **taking,** and the government must compensate the private party. Under the so-called *takings clause* of the Fifth Amendment, the government may not take private property for public use without "just compensation." State constitutions contain similar provisions. The following case involved a challenge to a state statute on this basis.

CASE 47.3   ## Purdie v. Attorney General

Supreme Court of New Hampshire, 1999.
732 A.2d 442.
http://www.state.nh.us/
courts/supreme/
opinions/9906.html[a]

BACKGROUND AND FACTS   *In 1995, the New Hampshire state legislature enacted a statute that recognized the state's public trust rights[b] in "all shorelands subject to the ebb and flow of the tide to the high water mark and subject to those littoral rights recognized at common law." (Littoral rights concern property that abuts an ocean, a sea, or a lake, rather than a river or a stream.) The statute defined "high water mark" in part as "the furthest landward limit reached by the highest tidal flow" over the nineteen-year tidal cycle, excluding "abnormal" storms. William Purdie and forty other beach-front property owners*

---

a. The "Judicial Branch of the New Hampshire State Government" maintains this Web site. In the "June 24, 1999" section, click on the case name to access the opinion.
b. *Public trust rights* are the public's rights to the use of land under water for navigation, fishing, and recreation. A state has a responsibility to act as the public's trustee to protect and preserve those rights.

filed a suit in a New Hampshire state court against the state, asserting that the statute effected a taking of their property without just compensation in violation of the state constitution and the Fifth Amendment of the U.S. Constitution. The state filed a motion for summary judgment. In ruling for the plaintiffs, the court concluded that common law defines the phrase "high water mark" as the "mean high tide line," and therefore, the legislature's action in setting the boundary line at the highest elevation of tidal action was an unconstitutional extension of public property rights and a taking of the plaintiffs' property. The state appealed to the New Hampshire Supreme Court.

IN THE LANGUAGE OF THE COURT

BRODERICK, J. [Justice]

*   *   *   *

After an extensive review, we conclude that New Hampshire common law establishes the high water mark at the level of mean high tide. In 1862, this court referred to the public-private shoreland boundary line as the "ordinary high water mark." Over one hundred years later [in 1969, in *Sibson v. State*] we held that public "[t]idewaters are those in which the tide ordinarily ebbs and flows."

The context of the *Sibson* case makes clear that the common law public-private boundary line or "ordinary high water mark" was at the level of mean high tide. *   *   * [T]he United States Supreme Court [has] held that the shoreland boundary for purposes of federal grants was the "ordinary high water mark," which it defined as the "mean high tide line," that is, "the average height of all the high waters" over a complete tidal cycle. *   *   *

*   *   *   *

Finally, New Hampshire common law regarding other public waters indicates that the mean high tide mark was intended as the public-private shoreland boundary. [In other cases, we] have held that large ponds are owned by the State in trust for public use up to their "natural mean high water mark." Moreover, we have noted that "[t]he law of public waters is presumably uniform, and on many questions it is not material whether an authority relates to tide-water or to large ponds." Accordingly, we conclude that the mean high tide is the high water mark or common law coastal boundary between public and private shorelands.

*   *   *   *

Having determined that New Hampshire common law limits public ownership of the shorelands to the mean high water mark, we conclude that the legislature went beyond these common law limits by extending public trust rights to the highest high water mark. Although the legislature has the power to change or redefine the common law to conform to current standards and public needs, *property rights created by the common law may not be taken away legislatively without due process of law.* Because [the statute in question] unilaterally authorizes the taking of private shoreland for public use and provides no compensation for landowners whose property has been appropriated, it violates the prohibition in the State Constitution and the Fifth Amendment of the Federal Constitution against the taking of property for public use without just compensation. Although it may be desirable for the State to expand public beaches to cope with increasing crowds, the State may not do so without compensating the affected landowners. [Emphasis added.]

DECISION AND REMEDY

The New Hampshire Supreme Court affirmed the ruling of the lower court and remanded the case for a decision regarding the actual location of the mean high water mark and a determination as to which, if any, of the plaintiffs were entitled to damages. The statute was unconstitutional because it constituted a taking of private property without just compensation.

ZONING

The state's power to control the use of land through legislation is derived from two sources: eminent domain and police power. Through eminent domain, the government can take land for public use, but it must pay just compensation. Consequently, eminent domain is an expensive method of land-use control. Under its police power, however, the state can pass laws aimed at protecting public health, safety, morals, and general welfare. These laws include *zoning laws*, by which the state can regulate uses of land without having to compensate the landowner. If, however, a state law restricts a landowner's property rights too much, the state's regulation will be deemed a *confiscation*, or a taking, and may be subject to the eminent domain requirement that just compensation be paid.

Suppose that Perez owns a large tract of land, which she purchased with the intent to subdivide it and develop it into residential properties. At the time of the purchase, there were no zoning regulations restricting use of the land. If the government attempts to zone Perez's entire tract of land as "public parkland only" and thus to prohibit her from developing any part of it, the action will be deemed confiscatory; this is because the government will be denying her the ability to use her property for any reasonable income-producing or private purpose for which it is suited and because she had reasonable, investment-backed expectations in her development plans. The zoning regulation normally will be held unconstitutional and void, or the government will have to compensate Perez, because it has effectively confiscated her land.

The state's power to regulate the use of land is limited in two other ways, both of which arise from the Fourteenth Amendment. First, the state cannot regulate the use of land arbitrarily or unreasonably, because this would be taking property without due process. There must be a *rational basis* for the classifications that the state imposes on property. Any act that is reasonably related to the health or general welfare of the public is deemed to have a rational basis. Second, a state's regulation of land use cannot be discriminatory. A zoning ordinance is considered discriminatory if it affects one parcel of land in a way in which it does not affect surrounding parcels and if there is no rational basis for the difference.

Variances.   A landowner whose land has been limited by a zoning ordinance to a particular use cannot make an alternative use of the land unless he or she first obtains a zoning variance. A landowner must meet three criteria to be entitled to a variance:

1. The landowner must find it impossible to realize a reasonable return on the land as zoned.
2. The zoning ordinance must have an adverse effect that is particular to the person seeking the variance rather than being similar for all the landowners within the same zone.

3. Granting of the variance must not substantially alter the essential character of the zoned area.

Courts tend to be rather lenient about the first two requirements. By far the most important criterion in granting a variance is whether it will substantially alter the character of the neighborhood.

Building Permits.   As part of its power to control the use of land through legislation, the state can regulate such things as the overall appearance of a community. For example, local ordinances may prohibit a property owner's tearing down or remodeling a historic landmark. The state may also require property owners to make concessions for such public needs as transportation. Typically, these goals are accomplished in part by requiring that an owner obtain a building permit from a local review board before undertaking a building project. In issuing a permit, the board may impose certain restrictions. Builder-developers are routinely required, for example, to include sidewalks and access roads in their developments.

The United States Supreme Court has held that such restrictions do not constitute a taking of an owner's property if they "substantially advance legitimate state interests" and do not "den[y] an owner economically viable use of his land."[10] It is not clear, however, exactly what constitutes a "legitimate state interest" or when particular restrictions "substantially advance" that interest. Furthermore, the phrase "economically viable use" is not yet clearly defined. (For a recent Supreme Court case concerning this issue, see the *Focus on Legal Reasoning* following Chapter 48.)

RESTRICTIVE COVENANTS

A private restriction on the use of land is known as a **restrictive covenant.** If the restriction is binding on the party who purchases the property originally and on subsequent purchasers as well—in other words, if its benefit or obligation passes with the land's ownership—it is said to "run with the land."

Covenants Running with the Land.   A restrictive covenant that runs with the land goes with the land and cannot be separated from it. Consider an example. Owen is the owner of Grasslands, a twenty-acre estate whose northern half contains a small reservoir. Owen wishes to convey the northern half to Arid City, but

---

10. *Agins v. Tiburon,* 447 U.S. 255, 100 S.Ct. 2138, 65 L.Ed.2d 106 (1980).

before he does, he digs an irrigation ditch connecting the reservoir with the lower ten acres, which he uses as farmland. When Owen conveys the northern ten acres to Arid City, he enters into an agreement with the city. The agreement, which is contained in the deed, states, "Arid City, its heirs and assigns, promises not to remove more than five thousand gallons of water per day from the Grasslands reservoir." Owen has created a restrictive covenant running with the land. Under this covenant, Arid City and all future owners of the northern ten acres of Grasslands are limited as to the amount of water they can draw from its reservoir.

Four requirements must be met for a covenant running with the land to be enforceable. If they are not met, the covenant will apply to the two original parties to a contract only and will not run with the land to future owners. The requirements are as follows:

1. The covenant running with the land must be created in a written agreement (covenant). It is usually contained in the document that conveys the land.
2. The parties must intend that the covenant run with the land. In other words, the instrument that contains the covenant must state not only that the promisor is bound by the terms of the covenant but that all the promisor's "successors, heirs, or assigns" will be bound.
3. The covenant must *touch and concern* the land. That is, the limitations on the activities of the owner of the burdened land must have some connection with the land. For example, a purchaser of land cannot be bound by a covenant requiring him or her to drive only Ford pickups, because such a restriction has no relation to the land purchased.
4. The successors to the original parties to the covenant must have notice of the covenant.

To satisfy the last requirement, the notice may be actual or constructive. For example, in the course of developing a fifty-lot suburban subdivision, Levitt records a declaration of restrictions that effectively limits construction on each lot to one single-family house. In each lot's deed is a reference to the declaration with a provision that the purchaser and his or her successors are bound to those restrictions. Thus, each purchaser assumes ownership with notice of the restrictions. If an owner attempts to build a duplex (or any structure that does not comply with the restrictions) on a lot, the other owners may obtain a court order enjoining the construction.

In fact, Levitt might simply have included the restrictions on the subdivision's map, filed the map in the appropriate public office, and included a reference to the map in each deed. In this way, each owner would also have been held to have constructive notice of the restrictions.

Illegal Restrictive Covenants. Restrictive covenants have sometimes been used to perpetuate neighborhood segregation, and in these cases they have been invalidated by the courts. In the United States Supreme Court case of *Shelley v. Kraemer*,[11] restrictive covenants proscribing resale to members of minority groups were declared unconstitutional. In addition, the Civil Rights Act of 1968 (also known as the Fair Housing Act) prohibits all discrimination based on race, color, religion, or national origin in the sale and leasing of housing.

---

11. 334 U.S. 1, 68 S.Ct. 836, 92 L.Ed. 1161 (1948).

TERMS AND CONCEPTS TO REVIEW

adverse possession 898	fee simple absolute 889	marketable title 896
closing 897	grant deed 893	mortgage 897
conveyance 890	implied warranty of habitability 897	periodic tenancy 890
deed 893		profit 891
easement 891	leasehold estate 890	quitclaim deed 893
eminent domain 900	license 892	recording statute 893
escrow account 896	life estate 890	restrictive covenant 902

QUESTIONS AND CASE PROBLEMS

47–1. DEEDS. Madison owned a tract of land, but he was not sure that he had full title to the property. When Rafael expressed an interest in buying the property, Madison sold Rafael the land and executed a quitclaim deed. Rafael properly recorded the deed immediately. Several months later, Madison learned that he had had full title to the tract of land. He then sold the land to Linda by warranty deed. Linda knew of the earlier purchase by Rafael but took the deed anyway and later sued to have Rafael evicted from the land. Linda claimed that because she had a warranty deed, her title to the land was better than that conferred by Rafael's quitclaim deed. Will Linda succeed in claiming title to the land? Explain.

47–2. DEEDS. Wilfredo and Patricia are neighbors. Wilfredo's lot is extremely large, and his present and future use of it will not involve the entire area. Patricia wants to build a single-car garage and driveway along the present lot boundary. Because of ordinances requiring buildings to be set back fifteen feet from an owner's property line, and because of the placement of her existing structures, Patricia cannot build the garage. Patricia contracts to purchase ten feet of Wilfredo's property along their boundary line for $3,000. Wilfredo is willing to sell but will give Patricia only a quitclaim deed, whereas Patricia wants a warranty deed. Discuss the differences between these deeds as they would affect the rights of the parties if the title to this ten feet of land later proved to be defective.

47–3. OWNERSHIP OF REAL PROPERTY. Glenn is the owner of a lakeside house and lot. He deeds the house and lot "to my wife, Livia, for life, then to my daughter, Sarina." Given these facts, answer the following questions. What is Livia's interest called? Is there any limitation on her rights to use the property as she wishes? Discuss.

47–4. EMINENT DOMAIN. The Minneapolis Police Department, in trying to apprehend a suspect who had entered and hidden himself in Harriet Wegner's house, severely damaged the house. The police and a SWAT team called in to assist the police were unable to persuade the suspect to come out, so they fired twenty-five rounds of tear gas into the house, as well as three concussion ("flash-bang") grenades. The police finally apprehended the suspect as he crawled out of a basement window. Wegner alleged that these events caused damages of $71,000 to her home. Her insurance carrier, Milwaukee Mutual Insurance Company, paid her about $28,000 but refused to pay for the rest of the damage. Wegner and Milwaukee Mutual both sued the city of Minneapolis, alleging that the police department's ac- tions constituted a compensable taking under the Minnesota constitution. (The insurance company sought reimbursement for the money it had paid to Wegner and for possible future liability on her claim.) The trial court granted summary judgment for the city on the taking issue, holding that "[e]minent domain is not intended as a limitation on [the] police power" of the state. The appellate court affirmed. Wegner and the insurance company appealed to the Minnesota Supreme Court. How should the court rule? Explain. [*Wegner v. Milwaukee Mutual Insurance Co.*, 479 N.W.2d 38 (Minn. 1991)]

47–5. COVENANT RUNNING WITH THE LAND. In 1961, Mary Schaefers divided her real property and conveyed it to her children, William, Elfreda, Julienne, and Rosemary. The deed from Mary Schaefers to her daughter Rosemary contained the following language: "It is further mutually agreed by and between the grantor and the grantee that as part of the consideration set out above, the grantee agrees to provide a permanent home for my daughter, Elfreda, should she desire or request one, and for my son, William Schaefers, should he desire or request one. Failure to perform the above will be considered a material breach of the consideration set out herein." In 1974, Rosemary conveyed her portion of her mother's property to Edward and Arthur Apel. Subsequently, William Schaefers attempted to prevent the sale to the Apels from taking place by telling them that the house was encumbered by a covenant running with the land and that if they purchased the house, they would be bound to provide a home for William and Elfreda Schaefers. Is Rosemary's promise to provide a home for William and Elfreda (should they demand one) a covenant running with the land? Explain. [*Schaefers v. Apel*, 295 Ala. 277, 328 So.2d 274 (1976)]

47–6. EASEMENTS. Moses Webster owned a parcel of land that extended down to the Atlantic Ocean. He conveyed the strip of the property fronting the ocean to another party. The deed included the following statement: "Reserve being had for said Moses Webster the right of way by land or water." The strip of property is now owned by Margaret Williams, and the portion retained by Webster now belongs to Thomas O'Neill. Williams is denying O'Neill access to the ocean. O'Neill has brought an action to establish his title to an easement over Williams's property. What should the court decide? Discuss fully. [*O'Neill v. Williams*, 527 A.2d 322 (Me. 1987)]

47–7. ZONING AND LAND-USE RESTRICTIONS. Florence Dolan owned the A-Boy West Hardware store in downtown Tigard, Oregon. Wanting to expand the store and its parking lot, Dolan applied to the city for a permit. Under the Tigard Community Development Code (the local zoning regulations), the city could attach conditions to downtown development to provide for projected transportation and public-facility needs. The city told Dolan that she could expand if she would dedicate a portion of her property for the improvement of a storm drainage system, including a public greenway along a creek, and dedicate an additional strip of land as a pedestrian/bicycle pathway. The dedication would represent about 10 percent of Dolan's property. Dolan sought a variance, which the city denied, and Dolan appealed. The city claimed that there was a sufficient connection between the expansion of the store and the dedication requirements, because the expansion would increase traffic to the area and would also increase storm runoff. Dolan conceded that there would be increases but contended that the increases would not be enough to justify taking 10 percent of her property. Dolan claimed that the city's restriction was an uncompensated taking of her property in violation of the Fifth Amendment. How should the court rule? Discuss fully. [*Dolan v. City of Tigard*, 512 U.S. 374, 114 S.Ct. 2309, 129 L.Ed.2d 304 (1994)]

47–8. TAKING. Richard and Jaquelyn Jackson owned property in a residential subdivision near an airport operated by the Metropolitan Knoxville Airport Authority in Blount County, Tennessee. The Airport Authority considered extending a runway near the subdivision and undertook a study that found that the noise, vibration, and pollution from aircraft using the extension would render the Jacksons' property incompatible with residential use. The airport built the extension, bringing about the predicted results, and the Jacksons filed a suit against the Airport Authority, alleging a taking of their property. The Airport Authority responded that there was no taking because there were no direct flights over the Jacksons' property. In whose favor will the court rule, and why? [*Jackson v. Metropolitan Knoxville Airport Authority*, 922 S.W.2d 860 (Tenn. 1996)]

47–9. ADVERSE POSSESSION. In 1972, Ted Pafundi bought a quarry in West Pawlet, Vermont, from his neighbor, Marguerite Scott. The deed vaguely described the eastern boundary of the quarry as "the westerly boundary of the lands of" the neighboring property owners. Pafundi quarried green slate from the west wall until his death in 1979, when his son Gary began to work the east wall until *his* death in 1989. Gary's daughter Connie took over operations. All of the Pafundis used the floor of the quarry as their base of operations. In 1992, N.A.S. Holdings, Inc., bought the neighboring property. A survey revealed that virtually the entire quarry was within the boundaries of N.A.S.'s property and that twenty years earlier, Ted had actually bought only a small strip of land on the west side. When N.A.S. attempted to begin quarrying, Connie blocked the access. N.A.S. filed a suit in a Vermont state court against Connie, seeking to establish title. Connie argued that she had title to the quarry through adverse possession under a state statute with a possessory period of fifteen years. What are the elements to acquire title by adverse possession? Are they satisfied in this case? In whose favor should the court rule, and why? [*N.A.S. Holdings, Inc. v. Pafundi*, 736 A.2d 280 (Vt. 1999)]

47–10. IN YOUR COURT

For over forty years, Jake Fox assumed that a fence located at the southern end of his property marked the southern boundary of the property. Fox had always maintained and generally exercised control over the property up to the fence line. Allen Jackson purchased the property to the south of Fox and had a survey taken. The survey showed that the true boundary was approximately eleven feet north of the existing fence. Jackson asked Fox to remove the fence, but Fox refused to do so, asserting that he held title to the disputed portion of the property by adverse possession. Jackson then brought an action to compel Fox to remove the fence. Assume that you are the judge in the trial court hearing this case and answer the following questions:

(a) What requirements must be satisfied for property to be acquired by adverse possession? According to the court in Case 47.2 (*Klos v. Molenda*), which party has the burden of proving that these requirements have been met?

(b) In the case now before your court, will you rule that Fox acquired ownership, by adverse possession, of the disputed strip of land? Why or why not?

LAW ON THE WEB

For updated links to resources available on the Web, as well as a variety of other materials, visit this text's Web site at http://wbl.westbuslaw.com.

Homes and Communities is a Web site offered by the U.S. Department of Housing and Urban Development. Information of interest to both consumers and businesses is available at this site, which can be accessed at

http://www.hud.gov

Information on the buying and financing of homes, as well as the full text of the Real Estate Settlement Procedures Act, is online at http://www.hud.gov/fha/fhahome.html

For answers to frequently asked questions on Veterans Administration home loans, go to

http://www.va.gov/vas/loan/index.htm

LEGAL RESEARCH EXERCISES ON THE WEB

Go to http://wbl.westbuslaw.com, the Web site that accompanies this text. Select "Internet Applications," and then click on "Chapter 47." There you will find the following Internet research exercises that you can perform to learn more about laws governing real property:

Activity 47–1: Real Estate Law

Activity 47–2: Fair Housing

CHAPTER 48

Landlord-Tenant Relationships

ANYONE WHO RENTS HOUSING OR rents space for commercial purposes becomes subject to the laws governing landlord-tenant relationships. The owner of the property is the landlord, or **lessor;** the party assuming temporary possession is the tenant, or **lessee;** and their rental agreement is the lease contract, or, more simply, the **lease.** The property interest involved in a landlord-tenant relationship is known as a *leasehold estate*, as discussed in the previous chapter. The *temporary* nature of possession, under a lease, is what distinguishes a tenant from a purchaser, who acquires title to the property. The *exclusivity* of possession distinguishes a tenant from a licensee, who acquires the temporary right to a *nonexclusive* use, such as sitting in a theater seat.

In the past century—and particularly in the past three decades—landlord-tenant relationships have become much more complex than they once were, as have the laws governing them. Generally, the law has come to apply contract doctrines, such as those providing for implied warranties and unconscionability, to the landlord-tenant relationship. Increasingly, landlord-tenant relationships have become subject to specific state and local statutes and ordinances as well. In 1972, in an effort to create more uniformity in the law governing landlord-tenant relationships, the National Conference of Commissioners on Uniform State Laws approved the Uniform Residential Landlord and Tenant Act (URLTA) for adoption by the states. Over one-fourth of the states have adopted variations of the URLTA.

SECTION 1

Creation of the Landlord-Tenant Relationship

A landlord-tenant relationship is established by a lease contract, which may be oral or written. As is the case with most oral agreements, however, a party who seeks to enforce an oral lease may have difficulty proving its existence. In all states, statutes mandate that leases be in writing for some tenancies (such as those exceeding one year).

FORM OF THE LEASE

To create a landlord-tenant relationship, a contract must do the following:

1. Express an intent to establish the relationship.
2. Provide for transfer of the property's possession to the tenant at the beginning of the term.
3. Provide for the landlord's *reversionary* (future) interest, which entitles the property owner to retake possession at the end of the term.

4. Describe the property—for example, give its street address.

5. Indicate the length of the term, the amount of the rent, and how and when it is to be paid.

In the drafting of commercial leases, sound business practice dictates that the leases be written carefully and that the parties' rights and obligations be clearly defined in the lease agreements.

ILLEGALITY

State or local law often dictates permissible lease terms. The URLTA, for example, prohibits the inclusion in a lease agreement of a clause under which the tenant agrees to pay the landlord's attorneys' fees in a suit to enforce the lease. A statute or ordinance may prohibit leasing a structure that is in disrepair or is not in compliance with local building codes. Similarly, a statute may prohibit the leasing of property for a particular purpose, such as gambling. In this case, if a landlord and tenant intend that the leased premises be used only to house an illegal betting operation, their lease is unenforceable.

A property owner cannot legally discriminate against prospective tenants on the basis of race, color, religion, national origin, or gender.[1] Similarly, a tenant cannot legally promise to do something counter to laws prohibiting discrimination. A tenant, for example, cannot legally promise to do business only with members of a particular race. The public policy underlying these prohibitions is to treat all people equally.

UNCONSCIONABILITY

The unconscionability concept is one of the most important of the contract doctrines applied to leases. Basically, in some jurisdictions (and under URLTA 1.303), the concept follows the provision of Section 2–302 of the Uniform Commercial Code. As discussed in Chapter 19, under this provision, a court may declare an entire contract or any of its clauses unconscionable and thus illegal, depending on the circumstances surrounding the transaction and the parties' relative bargaining positions. In a residential lease, for example, a clause claiming to absolve a landlord from responsibility for interruptions in such essential services as central heating

and air conditioning will not shield a landlord from liability if the systems break down when they are needed the most.

SECTION 2

Parties' Rights and Duties

At common law, the parties to a lease had relative freedom to include whatever terms they chose in the lease. Currently, the trend is to base the rights and duties of the parties on the principles of real estate law and contract law. These rights and duties generally pertain to the four broad areas of concern for landlords and tenants—the possession, use, maintenance, and, of course, rent of the leased property.

POSSESSION

A landlord is obligated to give a tenant possession of the property that the tenant has agreed to lease. The "English" rule, followed in many states and by the URLTA, requires the landlord to provide actual *physical possession* to the tenant—unless the parties agree otherwise. If, for example, a previous tenant is still living on the premises on the date the new tenant is entitled to possession, the landlord must remove the previous tenant or breach the obligation to the new tenant. The "American" rule, followed in other states, requires the landlord to transfer only the legal right to possession. Under this rule, the new tenant in the preceding example would have been responsible for removing the previous tenant, who no longer had the *legal right to possession.*

After obtaining possession, the tenant retains it exclusively until the lease expires, unless the lease provides otherwise or the tenant defaults under the terms of the lease. Most leases expressly give the landlord the right to come onto the property for the purpose of inspecting it, making necessary repairs, or showing the property to prospective purchasers or (toward the end of an expiring term) to possible future tenants.

COVENANT OF QUIET ENJOYMENT

Under the *covenant of quiet enjoyment,* the landlord promises that during the lease term neither the landlord nor anyone having a superior title to the property will disturb the tenant's use and enjoyment of the property. This covenant forms the essence of the landlord-

---

1. See, for example, *Osborn v. Kellogg,* 4 Neb.App. 594, 547 N.W.2d 504 (1996).

tenant relationship. If the covenant is breached, the tenant can terminate the lease and sue for damages.

EVICTION

If the landlord deprives the tenant of the tenant's possession of the leased property or interferes with his or her use or enjoyment of the property, an **eviction** occurs. This is the case, for example, when the landlord changes the lock and refuses to give the tenant a new key. A *partial eviction* occurs if the landlord deprives the tenant of the use of a part—one room, for example—of the leased premises. Assuming that the tenant has a legal right to possession of the property, he or she may either (1) sue for damages or possession or (2) consider the eviction a breach of the lease contract and cease paying rent or terminate the lease.

Constructive eviction occurs whenever the landlord wrongfully performs, or fails to perform, any of the duties the lease requires, thereby making the tenant's further use and enjoyment of the property exceedingly difficult or virtually impossible. Examples of constructive eviction include a landlord's failure to provide heat in the winter, light, or other essential utilities. To claim that a constructive eviction has occurred, the tenant must first notify the landlord of the problem. If the landlord fails to remedy the situation within a reasonable period of time, the tenant must then abandon the premises. On vacating the premises, the tenant's obligation to pay further rent ceases. As in cases of wrongful eviction, the tenant may sue to move back onto the property or terminate the lease and seek damages.

When a landlord evicts a tenant for complaining to a government agency about the improper condition of the leased premises, it is termed a **retaliatory eviction.** Under some statutes, a retaliatory motive is presumed when eviction proceedings are begun within a certain time after a tenant has complained. Regardless of the time elapsed, if a tenant can prove that a landlord's primary purpose in evicting or attempting to evict the tenant is retaliation for reporting violations—of a housing or sanitation code, for example—the tenant may be entitled to stop the eviction proceedings or collect damages.

USE OF THE PREMISES

If the parties do not limit by agreement the uses to which the property may be put, the tenant may make any use of it, so long as the use is legal, reasonably relates to the purpose for which the property is adapted

or ordinarily used, and does not injure the landlord's interest.

Also, the tenant is not entitled to create a *nuisance* by substantially interfering with others' quiet enjoyment of their property rights. To constitute a nuisance, conduct must be more than simply aggravating. Arguing with the neighbors may be annoying behavior, for example, but it would probably not qualify as a nuisance, unless it constituted harassment. Consistently playing drums in the middle of the night in an apartment complex, however, probably would be considered a nuisance.

Tenant's Duty Not to Commit Waste. The tenant has no right to remove or otherwise damage leased property without the landlord's consent. The duty of a tenant not to damage the premises is a duty not to commit **waste,** which is the abuse or destructive use of property by one in rightful possession. A tenant cannot knock out an inside wall in a leased house to enlarge a living room, for example, or remove a fence or a grove of trees to accommodate grazing livestock unless he or she first obtains the landlord's permission to do so.

The tenant is responsible for all damage he or she causes, intentionally or negligently, and the tenant may be held liable for the cost of returning the property to the physical condition it was in at the lease's inception. Unless the parties have agreed otherwise, however, the tenant is not responsible for ordinary wear and tear and the property's consequent depreciation in value.

If, at some time during the lease term, the tenant decides to stop using the property but to continue paying the rent, the lease may require the tenant to give the landlord notice of the nonuse. There is always a greater chance of vandalism, fire, or some other cause of damage to property when it is not being used, and the nonuse may affect insurance coverage.

Altering the Premises. In most states, the tenant may make no alterations to the leased premises without the landlord's consent. In other jurisdictions, the tenant may make alterations, without being liable for the expense of their removal, if they were necessary for the tenant's use of the property and did not reduce its value. **Alterations** include improvements or changes that materially affect the condition of the property. Thus, for example, erecting additional structures probably would be considered making alterations, whereas painting interior walls would not.

Unless the parties have agreed otherwise, neither the landlord nor the tenant is required to make specific alterations or otherwise improve the property.

Once a residential tenant affixes an item of personal property—such as a storage cabinet—to real property, it becomes a *fixture* (see Chapter 46). In some jurisdictions, fixtures become the landlord's property and may not be removed at the end of the lease term. In other jurisdictions, fixtures can be removed at the end of the lease period if they can be taken without damage to the landlord's property.

MAINTAINING THE PREMISES

At common law, a tenant took the property "as is." Today, this common law rule has generally been replaced with statutes requiring landowners to comply with certain safety, health, and fire-protection standards. Also, in most states, statutes or judicial decisions impose a duty on a landlord who leases residential property to furnish premises that are *habitable*—that is, in a condition fit for human occupancy—and to make repairs for damages not caused by the tenant's actions. Nevertheless, under a long-term commercial lease, a tenant may still assume the responsibility of making all necessary repairs, including, for example, rebuilding a structure after its destruction in a fire.

Statutory Requirements. Usually, the landlord must comply with state statutes and city ordinances that delineate specific standards for the construction and maintenance of buildings. Typically, these codes contain structural requirements common to the construction, wiring, and plumbing of residential and commercial buildings. In some jurisdictions, land-lords of residential property are required by statute to maintain the premises in good repair.

The landlord is also responsible for maintaining **common areas**—areas such as halls, stairways, elevators, and so on that are used by all tenants. This duty relates not only to defects of which the landlord has actual knowledge but also to those about which the landlord should reasonably know. A landlord, for example, cannot avoid responsibility for repairing a dilapidated but little-used back stairway by asserting that he or she never used it and did not know it needed to be fixed.

Obligations under the Lease. In a long-term lease for the use of commercial property, the parties may choose to designate in the lease which of them has the responsibility to maintain the leased premises and to what extent. Generally, an express promise to repair is legally binding.

Under most circumstances, a residential tenant is not required to make major repairs, such as replacing an old roof or laying a new foundation. Additionally, without a lease provision under which the tenant assumes a duty to maintain the leased property, the tenant is under no obligation to do so. The tenant is liable for repairs required as a result of his or her intentional or negligent actions, however.

The following case involved a commercial tenant's rights under a lease that required the landlord to maintain the parking area. The issue was as follows: When the landlord did not repair potholes in the parking area, did the tenant need to show that this failure undercut its profits before it could terminate the lease?

CASE 48.1   Decade 80-1, Ltd. v. PDQ Food Stores, Inc., of Madison

Court of Appeals of
Wisconsin, 1999.
226 Wis.2d 42,
593 N.W.2d 94.
http://www.findlaw.
com/11stategov/wi/
wica.html[a]

BACKGROUND AND FACTS   *In October 1978, PDQ Food Stores, Inc., of Madison and Nash-Finch Company (PDQ) entered into a lease with Decade 80-I, Limited. PDQ agreed to lease a retail store. The parties provided in the lease that PDQ would pay an additional sum over and above the amount of the rent for the premises in return for a well-maintained parking lot. A default provision read, "Tenant shall give Landlord written notice of any default by Landlord . . . and if such default continues for a period of thirty (30) days . . . Tenant at its election may declare this Lease terminated." In October 1992, PDQ gave Decade a written notice of default, stating that "the driveways, walkways and parking lots of the Shopping*

---

a. In the "Court of Appeals" section, in the "1999" row, click on "March." When that page opens, scroll down the list of cases to the name of the case (the decision was released on "03/24/1999") and click on the docket number to access the opinion.

Center have not been maintained and at present contain numerous potholes." Three weeks later, Decade responded that it would repair the potholes when construction of a nearby McDonald's was complete. On December 2, PDQ notified Decade that because the default had not been cured within thirty days, PDQ was terminating the lease. PDQ moved out later that month. Decade filed a suit in a Wisconsin state court against PDQ, seeking the amount of the rent for the rest of the original term of the lease. The court found that Decade had breached the lease. Decade appealed to a state intermediate appellate court. Decade argued in part that PDQ failed to show the condition of the parking lot justified terminating the lease because it did not prove the potholes caused PDQ any lost profits.

IN THE LANGUAGE OF THE COURT

BROWN, J. [Judge]

* * * *

* * * Decade maintains that PDQ had to show the existence of one or more of the following: lost profits, loss of use of the building for a substantial period of time, an inability of suppliers or customers to get to the store, or a loss of goodwill. * * *

* * * *

* * * PDQ claims that Decade made an agreement to do something, to do it within a certain time period, and then did not do it. * * *

The covenant at issue in this case is a specific provision requiring maintenance of the parking lot * * * . It makes sense that a commercial retail lease would contain a specific covenant for parking lot maintenance for aesthetics and the convenience of customers, if nothing else. For these reasons, a well-maintained parking lot is very important to a retailer, as the testimony in this case and common sense show. The inclusion of the maintenance provision in the lease was part of the bargain struck between PDQ and Decade just as much as the rent was. PDQ is entitled to the benefit of that bargain. Nothing in the covenant envisions that the tenant must prove the infliction of actual economic loss before invoking the remedies provided. Furthermore, to read in such a requirement would be an unfaithful interpretation of the lease. *In construing the lease, we must apply its unambiguous language*—here, a specific promise to maintain a parking lot * * * . [Emphasis added.]

To rule otherwise would render largely illusory any specific agreement that the owner of commercial property keep the parking lot well maintained. In a commercial setting, it will almost always be difficult for a tenant to prove a connection between large potholes in a parking lot and loss of profits. Knowing this, the landlord could simply ignore its agreement to maintain the parking lot, understanding that its failure to act would rarely result in any significant consequences. We refuse to offer a free pass to landlords to ignore contractual agreements. If the owner of commercial property agrees to keep a parking lot maintained, and rent is paid partly in consideration for that promise, then a breach of that promise is grounds for terminating the lease, whether the breach causes lost profits or not. The tenant, after all, is paying for parking lot maintenance and expects the lot to be kept in good condition. The tenant should be allowed to obtain the full measure of its expectations without having to prove a dent in profits.

DECISION AND REMEDY

The state intermediate appellate court affirmed the decision of the lower court. Because the parking area maintenance provision in the lease was part of the bargain between the parties, the landlord's failure to repair gave the tenant the right to get out of the lease without proving that the failure substantially damaged the tenant's business interests.

Implied Warranty of Habitability. The implied warranty of habitability requires that a landlord who leases residential property furnish the premises in a habitable condition at the beginning of a lease term and maintain them in that condition for the lease's duration. Some state legislatures have enacted this warranty into law. In other jurisdictions, courts have based this warranty on the existence of a landlord's statutory duty to repair or simply have applied it as a matter of public policy.

Generally, this warranty applies only to major—or substantial—physical defects that the landlord knows or should know about and has had a reasonable time to repair (for example, a big hole in the roof). In deciding whether a defect is sufficiently substantial to be in violation of the warranty, courts may consider the following factors:

1. Whether the tenant caused the defect or is otherwise responsible for it.
2. How long the defect has existed.
3. The age of the building, because a newer dwelling is expected to have fewer problems.
4. The defect's impact—potential or real—on the tenant's health, safety, and activities such as sleeping and eating.
5. Whether the defect contravenes applicable housing, building, or sanitation statutes.

An unattractive or annoying feature, such as a crack in the wall, may be unpleasant, but unless the crack is evidence of a structural defect or affects the residence's capacity to be heated, it is probably not sufficiently substantial to make the structure uninhabitable. A leak that causes the carpet in a portion of the leased structure to become soaked periodically, however, may be enough to make the premises uninhabitable.[2] A malfunctioning air conditioner, the presence of rodents and pests on the premises, and the periodic lack of hot water and electricity—if the landlord promised to maintain the premises and provide utilities—is enough to render the premises uninhabitable.[3] At issue in the following case was whether the lack of a smoke detector constituted a violation of a statutory requirement that rental property be "in reasonable repair and fit for human habitation."

---

2. *Weingarden v. Eagle Ridge Condominiums*, 71 Ohio Misc.2d 7, 653 N.E.2d 759 (1995).

3. *Davidow v. Inwood North Professional Group—Phase I*, 747 S.W.2d 373 (Tex. 1988).

CASE 48.2   Schiernbeck v. Davis

United States
Court of Appeals,
Eighth Circuit, 1998.
143 F.3d 434.
http://www.findlaw.
com/casecode/courts/
8th.html[a]

**IN THE LANGUAGE
OF THE COURT**

BACKGROUND AND FACTS   *Linda Schiernbeck rented a house from Clark and Rosa Davis. A month after moving into the house, Schiernbeck noticed a discolored circular area where, she determined, a smoke detector had previously been attached to the wall. Schiernbeck later claimed that she told Clark Davis about the missing detector. Davis did not remember the conversation. He stated, however, that he gave Schiernbeck a detector, which she denied. At any rate, when a fire in the house severely injured Schiernbeck, she filed a suit in a federal district court against the Davises, alleging negligence and breach of contract for failing to provide a detector. The Davises filed a motion for summary judgment, arguing that they had no duty to install a detector in a rental house. The court ruled in the Davises' favor, and Schiernbeck appealed to the U.S. Court of Appeals for the Eighth Circuit.*

WATERS, District Judge.

*   *   *   *

*   *   * South Dakota Codified Laws Section 43-32-8 requires that the lessor keep the leased premises "in reasonable repair and fit for human habitation *   *   * ." We do not believe that equipping the leased premises with a smoke detector constitutes keeping the premises in "reasonable repair." *   *   * [T]he accepted dictionary definition [of "repair" is:] "To restore to a sound or good state after decay, injury, dilapidation, or partial destruction." Schiernbeck cites an additional part of the dictionary's definition which states *   *   * "to supply *   *   * that which is lost or destroyed" to include

---

a. This page provides access to some of the opinions of the U.S. Court of Appeals for the Eighth Circuit. In the "Docket Number Search" box, type "97-3431" and click on "Get It" to access the *Schiernbeck* opinion. This Web site is maintained by FindLaw.

replacing a missing smoke detector in the definition of repair. We conclude, however, that when reading the entire definition, the term "repair" does not encompass replacing a missing smoke detector.

    *   *   *   *

In addition, we do not believe that the Davises were required to replace the smoke detector in order to make the rental house "fit for human habitation." *   *   * Clearly, unstable stairs create a place that is unfit for human habitation, as does a lack of running water, heat, or electricity. We do not believe, however, that a lessor *   *   * is required to equip his or her residential premises with smoke detectors, fire extinguishers, carbon monoxide detectors, etc. in order to make the leased premises "fit for human habitation."

DECISION AND REMEDY
The U.S. Court of Appeals for the Eighth Circuit held that a landlord's statutory duty to keep rental premises "in reasonable repair and fit for human habitation" does not include installing a smoke detector. The court affirmed the lower court's judgment.

INTERNATIONAL CONSIDERATIONS
The Warranty of Habitability in England   *English law traditionally adhered to the principle of* caveat tenant *("let the tenant beware"). The Landlord and Tenant Act of 1985, however, requires that leased premises be fit for human habitation, although the act applies mainly to dwellings rented for very low rates. The act also sets forth details relating to the landlord's obligations to maintain and repair leased premises. Unlike U.S. law governing landlord-tenant relationships, much of which evolved under the common law, English landlord-tenant law has been created, to a great extent, by statute.*

Remedies for Landlord's Failure to Maintain Leased Property.
The tenant's remedies for the landlord's failure to maintain the leased premises vary with the circumstances and with state laws.

Withholding Rent.   Rent withholding is a remedy that is generally associated with the landlord's breach of the warranty of habitability. When rent withholding is authorized under a statute (sometimes referred to as a "rent strike" statute), the tenant must usually put the amount withheld into an *escrow account.* This account is held in the name of the depositor (in this case, the tenant) and an *escrow agent* (in this case, usually the court or a government agency), and the funds are returnable to the depositor if the third person (in this case, the landlord) fails to fulfill the escrow condition.

Generally, the tenant may withhold an amount equal to the amount by which the defect rendering the premises unlivable reduces the property's rental value. How much that is may be determined in different ways, and the tenant who withholds more than is legally permissible is liable to the landlord for the excessive amount withheld.

Repairing and Deducting.   Under **repair-and-deduct statutes** or judicial recognition of a right to repair and deduct, the tenant pays for the repairs and deducts their cost from the rent. As in the case of rent withholding, this remedy is usually associated with the landlord's breach of the warranty of habitability.

Before a tenant can use this remedy, the problem—which in some states must concern a basic service, such as heat or water—must be the landlord's responsibility, and the landlord must be notified and fail to do anything about the situation within a reasonable time. Under some statutes, the deductible amount is restricted to a month's rent or some other fixed sum.

Canceling the Lease.   Terminating the lease is a remedy normally available to the tenant only when the landlord's failure to repair constitutes either constructive eviction or a breach of the warranty of habitability.

Suing for Damages.   Although a lawsuit for damages is always a possible course of action, it is not necessarily economical. The amount a tenant can negotiate or be awarded may be based on the cost of a defect's repair or on the difference between the rental values of the defective property and the repaired property.

RENT

Rent is the tenant's payment to the landlord for the tenant's occupancy or use of the landlord's real property. Generally, the tenant must pay the rent even if he or she refuses to occupy the property or moves out, as long as the refusal or the move is unjustifiable and the lease is in force. Rent is payable according to an applicable statute, custom, or what the parties decide. The amount may be subject to a legislated ceiling—as in New York City—or it may be as much or as little as the market will bear. Usually, rent is payable in advance or periodically throughout the lease term, but rent payable in crops may not be due until the end of a term.

Some states provide that the landlord must wait for as many as ten days after the rent's due date before initiating proceedings to terminate the lease for failure on the part of the tenant to pay rent. Notice may be required before a suit can be filed. Also, the landlord may impliedly waive the right to prompt payment if in the past he or she has accepted late payments.

Security Deposits.
At the lease's inception, the landlord may require a deposit to secure the tenant's obligation to fulfill the lease. If the tenant fails to pay the rent or damages the property, the landlord may retain the deposit.

Under the URLTA (for residential leases only), the amount of the deposit is limited to one month's rent. After the end of the lease term, the deposit must be returned—less any amounts owed for damages or unpaid rent—within fourteen days of the tenant's request for its return. Some states permit larger deposits and longer periods before their return. Under the URLTA and some state laws, if the landlord withholds any amount from the deposit to cover damages, the tenant must be given an itemized list of the damages. In some states, the landlord must also pay interest on the deposit, less an appropriate sum as compensation for the effort involved in meeting this obligation. If the landlord fails to comply with these requirements, the tenant may recover at least the amount due. In some states, the tenant may recover triple the amount due and attorneys' fees.

Late Charges.
Legally, late charges can be imposed if a tenant does not pay rent when it is due. In general, the amount of a late charge may not be excessive, and it must bear some logical relation to the amount of the rent or to how long the payment has been overdue.

Rent Escalation.
Unless there is a clause in the lease providing otherwise, the amount of the rent cannot be increased during the lease term. If there is a clause allowing for the rent to be increased in the future—a **rent escalation clause**—the amount may be linked to the landlord's operating costs, indexed to increases in the cost of living or increases in property taxes, or subject to a real or anticipated increase in a commercial tenant's business activity.

Property Taxes.
In most jurisdictions, the tenant is not obligated to pay assessments and taxes on leased property. The responsibility for paying those charges may be transferred from the landlord to the tenant in the lease, however, or the lease may provide that the rent will be raised if the taxes increase. The tenant may be liable for the amount of the increase if it is due to improvements (such as the installation of trade fixtures in commercial premises) made by the tenant.

Landlord's Remedies for Tenant's Failure to Pay Rent.
Depending on the jurisdiction, if a tenant fails to pay rent or refuses to give up possession of leased property, the landlord can resort to one of three actions: a landlord's lien, a lawsuit, or recovery of possession.

Landlord's Lien. At common law, when a tenant did not pay the rent, the landlord could simply take and keep or sell whatever of the defaulting tenant's personal property was on the leased premises. Today, the landlord does not have this alternative unless the parties have contracted for it or it is permitted under a statute.

Among states that by statute preserve this remedy, known as a **landlord's lien,** some states grant the landlord a lien on all of the tenant's personal property but require the landlord to initiate court proceedings to exercise the lien. Typically, the court will authorize a sheriff to seize the tenant's property. Other states allow the landlord to seize specific items of the tenant's property and hold them as *security* for unpaid rent (that is, as protection or assurance that the landlord will recoup something on the tenant's obligation), but the landlord must obtain a court order to sell the tenant's property.

Lawsuit. Just as the landlord may sue a tenant responsible for damaging leased property, so the landlord may sue a defaulting tenant to collect unpaid rent.

Recovery of Possession. At common law, on the tenant's breach of the lease, the landlord could—with force, if necessary—evict the tenant and recover possession of the leased property without legal proceedings. Today, the landlord must use legal process, even if the parties have stipulated in the lease that the landlord has, and may exercise without legal proceedings, a **right of entry** (a right to retake possession peaceably).

There are two procedures to which the landlord may resort to evict the tenant. One is the common law remedy of **ejectment,** which requires the landlord to appear in court and show that the defaulting tenant is in wrongful possession. An action in ejectment does not take priority over other proceedings and, consequently, may be delayed for a long time. During the delay, the tenant can remain in possession. Thus, this action is used infrequently.

The remedy of ejectment has been modified under statutes that provide for a summary judicial procedure, generally referred to as an **unlawful detainer.** During the unlawful detainer proceeding, the landlord attempts to prove that the tenant breached the lease or that the lease expired and the tenant refused to leave. The court makes its decision quickly, or summarily. If the landlord prevails, the court orders the sheriff to remove the tenant.

Landlord's Duty to Mitigate Damages. At common law and in many states, when a tenant vacates leased property unjustifiably (not as a result of constructive eviction or the landlord's breach of the warranty of habitability), the tenant remains obligated to pay the rent for the remainder of the lease term—however long that might be. The landlord may refuse to lease the premises to an acceptable new tenant and let the property stand vacant.

In a growing number of jurisdictions, however, the landlord is required to *mitigate* his or her damages—that is, the landlord is required to make a reasonable attempt to lease the property to another party. In those jurisdictions, the tenant's liability for unpaid rent is restricted to the period of time that it would reasonably take for the landlord to lease the property to another tenant. Damages may also be allowed for the landlord's costs in re-letting the property.[4]

What is considered a reasonable period of time with respect to re-letting the property varies with the type of lease and the location of the leased premises.

Under a long-term residential lease, for example, this period might be three months. In some jurisdictions, if reasonable—but unsuccessful—attempts are made to re-let, the tenant remains liable for the rent for the remainder of the lease.

SECTION 3

Liability for Injuries on the Premises

At common law, whether a party in possession of property was liable to an individual who was injured on the property depended in part on that individual's classification as an invitee, a licensee, or a trespasser. Recall from Chapter 5 that an invitee is one whom the party in possession invites onto the premises for the possessing party's benefit, such as a business customer or a dinner-party guest. A *licensee* is one whom the party in possession invites or allows onto the premises for the licensee's benefit, such as a salesperson. A *trespasser* is one whom the party in possession does not invite and who has no other right to be on the premises. Each classification might require a different standard of care on the part of the person in possession of the property. Under certain circumstances—if the injured trespasser was a very young child, who might be expected to be attracted to a dangerous condition on the property, such as an unfenced swimming pool—the **attractive nuisance doctrine** could apply, requiring yet a different standard of care.

These distinctions are still made. Today, however, liability is more likely to depend on who controls the area where the injury occurred, and the governing standard is one of *reasonable care* under all circumstances. Applying the standard of reasonable care requires taking into consideration the predictability of a particular event (that is, applying the principle of *foreseeable risk*). The person who has responsibility for a particular part of the premises must take the same precautions regarding the area's safety as would a person of ordinary prudence in the same circumstances.[5]

LANDLORD'S LIABILITY

Traditionally, when the landlord surrendered possession of his or her property to the tenant, the landlord

---

4. For a fuller discussion of mitigation of damages, see Chapter 18.

5. Essentially, this standard of care is the same as that applied in cases of negligence (discussed in Chapter 5).

also relinquished responsibility for injuries occurring on the property. This was true regardless of whether the injury was caused by a condition that existed at the time the property was leased or a condition that developed later. Today, however, in recognition of the policies underlying the warranty of habitability, the landlord bears greater responsibility for the conditions of the premises and for injuries resulting from those conditions.

Currently, the landlord is generally liable for injuries occurring on the part of the property within the landlord's control—that is, common areas such as basements, hallways, and elevators. Also, when the landlord assumes an obligation to repair, the landlord's liability may extend to injuries attributable either to failure to make repairs or to negligently made repairs. Thus, the landlord may be responsible for injuries that occur on the part of the premises subject to the tenant's control—that is, the apartment, the house, or the store that the tenant leased from the landlord—when that responsibility is based on the landlord's duty to repair.

Injuries Caused by Defects on the Premises.   The landlord's liability extends to injuries resulting from a dangerous condition about which the landlord knew or should have known, when the landlord fails to tell the tenant about it or actually conceals it. The landlord need not believe that the condition is unsafe; the situation need only be one that would lead a reasonable person to conclude that there is an unreasonable risk of harm. The landlord may be liable if he or she knows that the mortar is very loose in a brick wall, for example, and a brick subsequently falls and injures a tenant.

In most states, the landlord is not under a duty to inspect residential premises before leasing them, unless there is reason to suspect that a potentially harmful defect exists. Also, the landlord is under no obligation to disclose to the tenant conditions about which the tenant knows when he or she signs the lease or conditions that are obvious, such as a lumpy carpet in the hall.

Commercial Property.   When property is leased for public purposes, including commercial activities, the landlord does have an obligation to inspect the property and make repairs before the tenant takes possession. This obligation is imposed to protect the public from unreasonable risks. Unreasonable risks do not include obvious conditions, which people can be expected to avoid.

The landlord's liability covers only that part of the leased premises that is open to the public. If, for example, a customer disregards a sign reading "Employees Only," goes through the door, and is somehow injured on the other side, the landlord normally will not be held liable. Similarly, the landlord is normally not liable for the tenant's negligence in maintaining the premises, assuming that they were in good condition when the tenant moved in. The liability of a landlord of leased commercial property was at issue in the following case.

CASE 48.3   ## Johnson County Sheriff's Posse, Inc. v. Endsley

Supreme Court
of Texas, 1996.
926 S.W.2d 284.

BACKGROUND AND FACTS   *The Johnson County Sheriff's Posse (the Posse) owns an enclosed arena that it rents to sponsors of functions such as rodeos. The Posse rented the arena to Teresa McClendon and Cynthia Skinner for a one-day barrel racing competition. During the competition, Tim Endsley, a spectator, suffered a serious eye injury when he was struck by a rock that was kicked into the air by a horse. Endsley filed a suit in a Texas state court against the Posse, alleging that the existence of rocks on the arena's dirt floor created an unreasonably dangerous condition and that the Posse was negligent in failing to maintain a rock-free dirt floor. The court entered a summary judgment in favor of the Posse, and Endsley appealed. An intermediate state appellate court reversed, and the Posse appealed to the Texas Supreme Court.*

IN THE LANGUAGE OF THE COURT   Justice GONZALEZ delivered the opinion for a unanimous Court.
*   *   *   *

A lessor generally has no duty to tenants or their invitees for dangerous conditions on the leased premises. This general rule stems from the notion that a lessor relinquishes possession or occupancy of the premises to the lessee. We have, however, recognized several exceptions to the general rule. For example, a lessor who makes repairs may be liable for injuries resulting from the lessor's negligence in making the repairs. A lessor who conceals defects on the leased premises of which the lessor is aware may also be liable. In addition, a lessor may be liable for injuries caused by a defect on a portion of premises that remain under the lessor's control. [Emphasis added.]

*   *   *   *

*   *   * The uncontradicted evidence shows that the Posse had a policy requiring the tenants to maintain and prepare the arena grounds for their particular event. The Posse had a water truck, a tractor, a harrow, and other equipment available, but did not instruct the tenants on the preparation of the arena grounds. On occasion, a Posse member helped with the water truck or helped start the tractor, but did not otherwise help with the preparation of the arena. [Posse member Tom] Jones testified that the same dirt was in the arena as when it was built several years before. *   *   *

*   *   *   *

*   *   * Endsley presented the affidavit of Clem McSpadden, a general manager, producer, and announcer for rodeos, who testified that anyone furnishing a rodeo arena with any rocks in the dirt is "derelict in his duty" because a rock can be propelled at great speed, causing injury to contestants, animals, and spectators. Endsley testified that he was "pretty certain" he was hit by a rock, and saw some rocks underneath the bleachers where he was sitting. Posse member Jones testified that he had seen rocks in the arena dirt "thumbnail" size or smaller.

*   *   * Endsley's theory is that the Posse should have made the dirt "rock free," or in other words, safer than ordinary dirt. The natural state of dirt, that it may be slippery when wet or may contain small rocks, can present a hazard under the right conditions, but not unreasonably so. Otherwise, a landlord would be an insurer against all injury to a tenant's lessees. Under the facts of this case, dirt containing small rocks is not an unreasonably dangerous condition for which a landlord may be held liable as a matter of law.

DECISION AND REMEDY   *The Texas Supreme Court reversed the decision of the intermediate state appellate court and issued a judgment in favor of the Posse.*

Common Areas.   The landlord is responsible for—and liable for any injuries resulting from—the condition of common areas, as long as the areas are under his or her control. This responsibility includes a duty to inspect and repair such conditions as peeling lead-based paint, rotting stair railings, burned-out or dim lighting, and defective water heaters. It also includes a duty to correct such conditions as wet steps or a loose mat placed over the slippery surface of a polished floor.

When the landlord retains control over part of the premises leased to the tenant—for example, an apartment's walls—the landlord may be liable for injuries caused by that part's disrepair. The landlord is not, however, liable for injuries occurring on parts of his or her residential property where people could not be reasonably expected to go—for example, a roof or a closed basement.

Repairs.   In many jurisdictions, under building, housing, or sanitation codes or the warranty of habit-ability, the landlord is required to put or keep premises for lease in good repair. Breach of this duty may constitute negligence and establish the landlord's liability for any injuries caused by this negligence.

The landlord's express agreement to repair may be a basis for the landlord's liability if an injury is caused by the landlord's failure to fulfill the agreement. Ordinarily, the landlord has a reasonable time, after discovering or being told that a condition requires repair, within which to do the repair work or see that it is done. Regardless of whether the landlord has agreed to make repairs, once the landlord undertakes them, he or she is liable for injuries attributable to negligence in the repair work.

Injuries Caused by Crimes of Third Persons.   The landlord normally is not required to set up an elaborate security system to protect tenants from criminals. But when crimes are reasonably foreseeable and the landlord takes no steps to prevent them, he or she may be liable for negligence—failure to provide adequate security—if an injury results.

Courts consider several factors in determining whether a crime is foreseeable and preventable. It is logical to assume that some prior criminal activity in the geographic area in which the property is located is required to make future crimes reasonably predictable. Similarly, it is reasonable to base an expectation of future crime on how recently the previous crime occurred.

Also, courts may consider the type of crime that occurred previously. In this area, the courts are divided. Some follow the *prior similar incidents* rule, under which establishing foreseeability requires showing the existence of earlier, similar crimes. Others follow what is known as the *totality of the circumstances* rule. Under the latter rule, foreseeability is determined in light of all of the circumstances, and what must be foreseeable is the general character of the event or harm, not its precise nature or manner of occurrence.

Exculpatory Clauses.   A lease may contain a clause that claims to relieve the landlord from any liability for injuries or other damages, including those caused by the landlord's own negligence. Known as *exculpatory clauses* (see Chapter 13), these provisions are unenforceable if injury or damage results from the landlord's failure to fulfill a statutory duty, such as compliance with a state's building code. When included in a lease for residential property, an exculpatory clause releasing a landlord from liability for his or her negligence is unenforceable.

TENANT'S LIABILITY

A tenant has a duty to maintain in a reasonably safe condition those areas under his or her control. When commercial property is involved, this duty extends to all parts of the premises onto which a customer or other member of the public might be expected to go—such as the aisles in a grocery store. The grocer's duty includes using care in displaying his or her wares so that they present no threat to customers' safety. The goods should not be stacked, for example, so as to block an aisle or to fall onto a customer taking an item for purchase. Similarly, the grocer may be liable if a customer slips on the spilled contents of a broken jar and is injured.

In some situations—particularly when property is leased for commercial purposes—the tenant's duty may coincide with the landlord's duty. When this

happens, both the landlord and the tenant may be liable for a third party's injuries.

SECTION 4

Transferring Rights to Leased Property

Either the landlord or the tenant may wish to transfer his or her rights to the leased property during the term of the lease.

TRANSFERRING THE LANDLORD'S INTEREST

Just as any other real property owner can sell, give away, or otherwise transfer his or her real property (see Chapter 47), so can a landlord—who is, of course, the leased property's owner. Furthermore, the landlord may make a deal involving only the lease, only the landlord's interest in the property after the lease has been terminated, only the rent accruable under the lease, or any of these property rights in combination.

If complete title—that is, the landlord's reversionary interest—to the leased property is transferred, the tenant becomes the tenant of the new owner. The new owner may collect subsequent rent but must then abide by the terms of the existing lease agreement.

TRANSFERRING THE TENANT'S INTEREST

The tenant's transfer of his or her entire interest in the leased property to a third person is an assignment of the lease. The tenant's transfer of all or part of the premises for a period shorter than the lease term is a **sublease.** Under neither an assignment nor a sublease can the assignee's or sublessee's rights against the landlord be *greater* than those of the original tenant.

Assignments.   A controlling statute or a clause in the lease may require the landlord's consent to the tenant's assignment of his or her interest in the lease. It may also require that the landlord not unreasonably withhold such consent, however. If the statute does not contain the latter condition, some courts will impose it nonetheless. Typically, clauses that require the landlord's consent to assignment are written as *forfeiture restraints*—that is, they provide that the landlord may terminate the tenancy if the tenant attempts to assign the lease without consent. This restriction is meant to protect the landlord from an assignee-tenant who might damage the property, fail to pay the rent, or otherwise be irresponsible. The landlord's knowing acceptance of rent from an assignee, however, may constitute a waiver of the consent requirement.

When an assignment is valid, the assignee acquires all of the tenant's rights under the lease. But an assignment does not release the assigning tenant from the obligation to pay rent should the assignee default. Also, if the assignee exercises an option under the original lease to extend the term, the assigning tenant remains liable for the rent during the extension, unless the landlord agrees otherwise.

Subleases. The restrictions that apply to an assignment of the tenant's interest in the leased premises also apply to a sublease. For example, if the landlord's consent is required, a sublease without such permission is ineffective. Also, a sublease does not release the tenant from his or her obligations under the lease any more than an assignment does.

To illustrate: A student, Adya, leases an apartment for a two-year period. Adya has been planning to attend summer school, but she is offered a job in Europe for the summer months, and she accepts. To avoid paying three months' rent for an unoccupied apartment, she can sublease the apartment to another student. (Adya may have to obtain her landlord's consent for this sublease if the lease requires it.) The sublessee will take the apartment under the same lease terms as Adya. The landlord can hold Adya liable should the sublessee violate those terms.

SECTION 5

Termination or Renewal of the Lease

Usually, a lease terminates when its term ends. The tenant surrenders the property to the landlord, who retakes possession. If the lease does not contain an option for renewal and the parties have not agreed that the tenant may stay on, the tenant has no right to remain. If the lease is renewable and the tenant decides to exercise the option, the tenant must comply with any conditions requiring notice to the landlord of the tenant's decision.

TERMINATION

In addition to the expiration of the lease term, a lease can be terminated in several other ways.

Termination by Notice. If the lease states the time it will end, the landlord is not required to give the tenant notice—that is, to remind the tenant that the lease is going to expire—even as the time approaches. The lease terminates automatically. The lease may require that notice be given, however, or notice may be required under a statute. The procedures and time periods vary, but usually one or two months' notice is enough to end a tenancy for a year, and a week will suffice to end a tenancy for a shorter period.

In contrast, a *periodic tenancy* will renew automatically unless one of the parties gives timely notice (usually, one rental period) of termination. A periodic tenancy is a tenancy from week to week, month to month, or year to year. (Periodic tenancies were discussed in Chapter 47.)

Release and Merger. A lease may also give the tenant the opportunity to purchase the leased property during the term or at its end. Regardless of whether the lease provides this option, the landlord can convey his or her interest in the property to the tenant. This transfer is a **release,** and the tenant's interest in the property merges into the title to the property, which he or she now holds. Of course, a release effectively relieves the tenant of his or her obligations under the lease while bestowing on him or her title to the property, as well as all of the former landlord's responsibilities regarding the property. Because a release is a transfer of real property, it is subject to the Statute of Frauds (discussed in Chapter 15) and thus must be in writing.

Surrender by Agreement. The parties may agree to end a tenancy before it would otherwise terminate. If the lease was subject to the Statute of Frauds, surrender of the property by agreement must be in writing, because technically, the tenant is conveying his or her possessory interest in the property to the landlord. Surrender of the property by operation of law, however, does not require a writing. A surrender by operation of law is sometimes held to occur when the tenant abandons the property (as discussed below).

Abandonment. A landlord may treat a tenant's **abandonment** of the property—that is, the tenant's moving off the premises completely with no intention of returning—before the end of the term as an offer of surrender. The landlord's retaking of possession of the property will relieve the tenant of the obligation to pay rent. Sometimes, actions that the landlord takes to mitigate his or her damages—for example, refinishing an abandoned apartment's floors when preparing to lease it to another party—may be interpreted as accepting the tenant's offer of surrender, thereby absolving the tenant of responsibility for future rent payment.

Forfeiture.   The termination of a lease, according to its terms or the terms of a statute, when one of the parties fails to fulfill a condition under the lease and thereby breaches it, is referred to as a **forfeiture.** If, for instance, the lease provides that the tenant will forfeit his or her interest in the leased property on failing to pay rent when it is due, the tenant's late payment of rent could prompt forfeiture. Generally, the courts do not favor forfeiture, and when neither the lease nor a statute provides for it, the landlord may only claim damages.

Destruction of the Property.   Under statutes in most states, destruction of the leased property brought about by a fire, flood, or other cause beyond the landlord's control can terminate a residential lease. Usually, the landlord is under no obligation to restore the premises.

Similarly, the destruction of an entire building leased for business purposes may release the commercial tenant from any responsibility for continued payment of rent. (Terms vary among leases. If there is,

for example, a fire, a commercial tenant's rent may only be reduced proportionally, according to how much property has been destroyed. The responsibility for restoring the property may rest on the tenant.)

RENEWAL

The lease may provide for renewal, or the landlord and the tenant may simply agree to renew it. When the lease includes an option to renew, it typically also includes a requirement that the tenant notify the landlord within a specific period of time—usually days or months—before the lease expires as to whether the tenant will exercise the option. The tenant must comply with any particulars regarding the notice's form (for example, that it be in writing), or the renewal will be invalid, even if the tenant stays on the property. The tenant's attempt to alter other terms to which the renewal is subject can be interpreted as a choice not to exercise the option to renew.

If a tenant neither renews a lease in accordance with its terms nor moves off the leased premises, but stays on without the landlord's consent, he or she can be treated as a trespasser. The tenant may be held liable to the landlord for damages.

TERMS AND CONCEPTS TO REVIEW

abandonment 919	forfeiture 920	rent escalation clause 914
alteration 909	landlord's lien 914	repair-and-deduct statute 913
attractive nuisance doctrine 915	lease 907	retaliatory eviction 909
common area 910	lessee 907	right of entry 915
constructive eviction 909	lessor 907	sublease 918
ejectment 915	release 919	unlawful detainer 915
eviction 909	rent 914	waste 909

QUESTIONS AND CASE PROBLEMS

48–1. LEASE VERSUS LICENSE.   Turner owns an apartment building. She contracts with Alvarez for one year to place coin-operated washing machines and dryers in laundry rooms in the building complex. The contract requires Alvarez to service the washers and dryers within twenty-four hours after notice is given that service is necessary. Some of the apartment leaseholders complain to Turner that Alvarez's service is poor and that Alvarez does not promptly refund money lost in the machines. After an argument, Turner orders Alvarez to remove all the machines within one week and not to come on the property again. Alvarez claims that he has a lease of the laundry rooms for one year. Turner claims that Alvarez has a revocable license (see Chapter 47). Discuss fully the property rights of the parties in this matter.

48–2. CONSTRUCTIVE EVICTION. James owns a three-story building. He leases the ground floor to Juan's Mexican restaurant. The lease is to run for a five-year period and contains an express covenant of quiet enjoyment. One year later, James leases the top two stories to the Upbeat Club, a discotheque. The club's hours run from 5:00 P.M. to 11:00 P.M. The noise from the Upbeat Club is so loud that it is driving customers away from Juan's restaurant. Juan has notified the landlord of the interference and has called the police on a number of occasions. The landlord refuses to talk to the owners of the Upbeat Club or to do anything to remedy the situation. Juan abandons the premises. James files suit for breach of the lease agreement and for the rental payments still due under the lease. Juan claims that he was constructively evicted and files a countersuit for damages. Discuss who will be held liable.

48–3. TENANT'S RIGHTS. Thomas has been a tenant of the Crestview Apartments for more than ten years. His tenancy is a month-to-month tenancy. During the ten years of his tenancy, the building's condition has steadily deteriorated. Indeed, the deterioration has reached the point at which the premises are in violation of city health and housing ordinances. Thomas has repeatedly complained to the landlord, but no repairs have been made. Thomas helps to organize a tenants' council, and the council reports numerous housing, building, and health violations to the authorities. The authorities bring actions against the landlord.

(a) Assume that immediately after the authorities bring their actions, Thomas is given notice of termination of his lease. Thomas wants to prevent his eviction. Discuss how successful he will be.

(b) Assume that Thomas and the other tenants want to withhold rent payments until the premises are repaired. Discuss whether the tenants may withhold the rent payments and, if so, to what extent and on what grounds.

48–4. LANDLORD'S RESPONSIBILITIES. Sarah has rented a house from Franks. The house is only two years old. Sarah's roof leaks every time it rains. The water that has accumulated in the attic has caused plaster to fall off ceilings in the upstairs bedrooms, and one ceiling has started to sag. Sarah has complained to Franks and asked him to have the roof repaired. Franks says he has caulked the roof, but the roof still leaks. Franks claims that because Sarah has sole control of the leased premises, she has the duty to repair the roof. Sarah insists that the repair of the roof is Franks's responsibility. Discuss fully who is responsible for repairing the roof and, if the responsibility belongs to Franks, what remedies are available to Sarah.

48–5. TENANT'S RIGHTS AND RESPONSIBILITIES. You are a student in college and plan to attend classes for nine months. You sign a twelve-month lease for an apartment and pay a security deposit of $150. Discuss fully each of the following situations:

(a) You have a summer job in your hometown and wish to assign the balance of your lease (three months) to a fellow student who will be attending summer school. Can you do so?

(b) You are graduating in May. The lease will have three months remaining. Can you terminate the lease without liability by giving a thirty-day notice to the landlord?

(c) The lease period has expired. Are you entitled to the return of your $150 security deposit?

48–6. LEASE RENEWAL. MCM Ventures, II, Inc., leased premises from Rushing Construction Co. on which to operate a restaurant. The lease term was for two years: January 1, 1987, to December 31, 1988. The lease agreement stated in part that MCM "shall have a continuing option for a period of eight (8) consecutive years to renew this lease." MCM did nothing to renew the lease before it expired but, after it expired on December 31, 1988, made monthly rent payments in the same amount as before in January and February 1989. Then, on February 28, 1989, MCM notified Rushing by mail that it wanted to exercise its option to renew the lease. Rushing refused to renew the lease, contending that MCM had forfeited the option by not exercising it prior to the expiration of the lease agreement in which the option had been given. Discuss fully whether MCM still had a right to exercise the lease renewal option as late as February 28, 1989. [*Rushing Construction Co. v. MCM Ventures, II, Inc.*, 100 N.C.App. 259, 395 S.E.2d 130 (1990)]

48–7. LIABILITY FOR INJURIES ON LEASED PREMISES. Commerce Properties, Inc. (CPI), owned an apartment complex in which Jonathan Linthicum, who was four years old, and his parents lived as tenants. There were no warning signs in the parking area adjacent to the rental units to notify automobile drivers that they should reduce driving speed because children might be playing there. There were no speed bumps to slow the automobile traffic, nor was any other traffic warning or safety device in place. Jonathan was playing in the parking lot when he was struck by a car driven by a neighbor and seriously injured. Jonathan sued CPI for negligent maintenance of the parking lot. How should the court decide this case? If Jonathan's parents knew or should have known of the risk, will CPI escape liability? Discuss fully. [*Commerce Properties, Inc. v. Linthicum*, 209 Ga.App. 853, 434 S.E.2d 769 (1993)]

48–8. WARRANTY OF HABITABILITY. Three-year-old Nkenge Lynch fell from the window of her third-floor apartment and suffered serious and permanent injuries. There were no window stops or guards on the window. The use of window stops, even if installed, is at the tenant's option. Stanley James owned the apartment building. Zsa Zsa Kinsey, Nkenge's mother, filed a suit on Nkenge's behalf in a Massachusetts state court against James, alleging in part a breach of an implied warranty of habitability. The plaintiff did not argue that the absence of stops or guards made the apartment unfit for human habitation but that their absence "endangered and materially impaired her health and safety," and therefore the failure to install them was a breach of warranty. Should the court rule that the absence of window stops breached a warranty of habitability? Should the court mandate that landlords provide window guards? Why or why not? [*Lynch v. James*, 44 Mass.App.Ct. 448, 692 N.E.2d 81 (1998)]

48–9. SECURITY DEPOSITS. Jennifer Tribble leased an apartment from Spring Isle II, a limited partnership. The written lease agreement provided that if Tribble was forced to move because of a job transfer or because she accepted a new job, she could vacate on sixty days' notice and owe only an extra two months' rent plus no more than a $650 re-renting fee. The initial term was for one year, and the parties renewed the lease for a second one-year term. The security deposit was $900. State law allowed a landlord to withhold a security deposit for the nonpayment of rent but required timely notice stating valid reasons for the withholding or the tenant would be entitled to twice the amount of the deposit as damages. One month into the second term, Tribble notified Spring Isle in writing that she had accepted a new job and would move out within a week. She paid the extra rent required by the lease, but not the re-rental fee, and vacated the apartment. Spring Isle wrote her a letter, stating that it was keeping the entire security deposit until the apartment was re-rented or the lease term ended, whichever came first. Spring Isle later filed a suit in a Wisconsin state court against Tribble, claiming that she owed, among other things, the rest of the rent until the apartment had been re-rented and the costs of re-renting. Tribble responded that withholding the security deposit was improper, and she was entitled to "any penalties." Does Tribble owe Spring Isle anything? Does Spring Isle owe Tribble anything? Explain. [*Spring Isle II v. Tribble*, __ N.W.2d __, 2000 WL 38918 (Wis.App. 2000)]

48–10. IN YOUR COURT

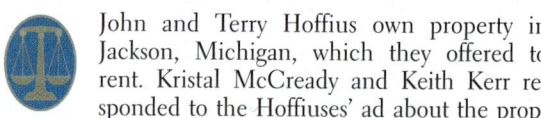

Janet Goss leased property in a shopping center from Central Properties, Inc. According to Goss, before signing the lease agreement she had told Central that she wanted to locate in an upscale shopping center that would attract a wealthy clientele, and Central had assured her that no discount stores would be allowed to lease space in the shopping center. The lease included a clause stipulating that Goss would not conduct any type of business commonly called a discount store, surplus store, or other similar enterprise. Goss later stated that she assumed that the other leases for shopping center space contained similar provisions. The lease agreement further stated that "[n]o representation, inducement, understanding or anything of any nature whatsoever made, stated or represented on Landlord's behalf, either orally or in writing (except this Lease), has induced Tenant to enter into this lease." When Central subsequently leased space to discount stores, Goss sued

Central for breach of the lease contract. Central moved for summary judgment in its favor, on the ground that the written lease contract represented the entire agreement of the parties, which Central had not breached. Goss argued that she was fraudulently induced to enter the contract by Central's oral promise. Assume that you are the judge in the trial court hearing this case and answer the following questions:

(a) What rules of contract law (discussed in Chapters 10 through 18) apply to contract interpretation? Under those rules, if a written contract states that it represents the entire agreement between the parties, can extraneous evidence (evidence outside the contract, such as evidence of the alleged oral promise made by Central to Goss) be considered when deciding the rights and duties of the parties under the contract?

(b) Under what circumstances is summary judgment appropriate? Is it appropriate in this case? Why or why not?

(c) If you decide that Goss was fraudulently induced to enter the lease contract, can you grant her a remedy in spite of the contract clause stating that it was the final agreement of the parties? If so, what remedy would be appropriate?

(d) After considering the above questions, how will you rule in this case? Fully explain your reasoning.

48–11. A QUESTION OF ETHICS

John and Terry Hoffius own property in Jackson, Michigan, which they offered to rent. Kristal McCready and Keith Kerr responded to the Hoffiuses' ad about the property. The Hoffiuses refused to rent to McCready and Kerr, however, when they learned that the two were single and intended to live together. John Hoffius told all prospective tenants that unmarried cohabitation violated his religious beliefs. McCready and others filed a suit in a Michigan state court against the Hoffiuses. They alleged in part that the Hoffiuses' actions violated the plaintiffs' civil rights under a state law that prohibits discrimination on the basis of "marital status." The Hoffiuses responded in part that forcing them to rent to unmarried couples in violation of the Hoffiuses' religious beliefs would be unconstitutional. [*McCready v. Hoffius*, 586 N.W.2d 723 (Mich. 1998)]

(a) Was it the plaintiffs' "marital status" or their conduct to which the defendants objected? Did the defendants violate the plaintiffs' civil rights? Explain.

(b) Should a court, in the interest of preventing discrimination in housing, compel a landlord to violate his or her conscience? In other words, whose rights should prevail in this case? Why?

(c) Is there an objective rule that determines when civil rights or religious freedom, or any two similarly important principles, should prevail? If so, what is it? If not, should there be?

LAW ON THE WEB

For updated links to resources available on the Web, as well as a variety of other materials, visit this text's Web site at http://wbl.westbuslaw.com.

You can find online links to most uniform laws, including the URLTA, at

http://www.lawsource.com

Many Web sites now provide information on laws and other information relating to landlord-tenant relaionships. One of them is TenantNet at

http://tenant.net

LEGAL RESEARCH EXERCISES ON THE WEB

Go to http://wbl.westbuslaw.com, the Web site that accompanies this text. Select "Internet Applications," and then click on "Chapter 48." There you will find the following Internet research exercise that you can perform to learn more about landlord-tenant relationships:

Activity 48–1: The Rights of Tenants

UNIT TEN—CUMULATIVE BUSINESS HYPOTHETICAL

Joel and Marsha Cummings operate a consulting business out of their home. Most of their work consists of creating and maintaining "home pages" on the Internet for various clients.

1. Joel and Marsha own both of their cars as joint tenants. If Joel dies and is survived by his wife (Marsha) and their two children, who will inherit the two cars?

2. One day, Marsha's computer malfunctions, and she takes it to a computer shop for repairs. The next day, the computer technician calls Marsha and tells her that her computer is missing. Marsha claims that the shop is liable for the value of the computer. The shop contends that it was not negligent in any way and therefore cannot be held liable. Will Marsha succeed in a suit against the shop? Explain.

3. Business is thriving, and Joel and Marsha need to expand their home-office area. To create more room for their office equipment, they decide to purchase a storage shed in which to store some of their household items and furniture. They buy a storage shed from their local Wal-Mart store and position the shed, which measures eight feet by ten feet, in their back yard. The shed is mounted on a cement foundation and secured to the foundation with heavy bolts. Some years later, when they sell their home, the buyers claim that the shed is a fixture and therefore part of the real property. Joel argues

that it is personal property, and therefore he and Marsha can remove the shed and take it with them to some new property in the country that they have purchased. Is the shed a fixture? What factors would a court consider in deciding this question?

4. Marsha and Joel's new country home is not adjacent to any public road. When they purchased the property, Joel and Marsha also acquired, by deed, the right to use a portion of land owned by a neighbor, Sam, as a driveway. What is this right called? What if Sam sells his property? Will Joel and Marsha lose this right?

5. Business is booming, and Marsha and Joel cannot keep up with all of the requests for their services. They decide to lease office space in a nearby town and hire some assistants. They form a lease contract with the owner of an office building, Dan Silver. The written lease contract, a brief-form contract, provides that the term of the lease is one year; that the monthly rent is $500, to be paid on the first of each month; and that Marsha and Joel will pay all utility bills. After they move to the new office space, Marsha and Joel learn that the electrical wiring is deficient, the roof leaks, and the furnace doesn't function properly. Silver refuses to make any repairs. What legal options do Marsha and Joel have in this situation? Can they break the lease without liability? Discuss fully.

FOCUS ON LEGAL REASONING
City of Monterey v.
Del Monte Dunes at Monterey, Ltd.

INTRODUCTION

The power of a state to regulate the use of land was discussed in Chapter 47. According to the United States Supreme Court, state and local restrictions on land use constitute an unconstitutional taking of an owner's property unless those restrictions "substantially advance legitimate state interests" and do not "den[y] an owner economically viable use of his land."[1] In this *Focus on Legal Reasoning*, we examine *City of Monterey v. Del Monte Dunes at Monterey, Ltd.*,[2] a recent decision by

1. *Agins v. Tiburon*, 447 U.S. 255, 100 S.Ct. 2138, 65 L.Ed.2d 106 (1980).
2. 526 U.S. 687, 119 S.Ct. 1624, 143 L.Ed.2d 882 (1999).

the United States Supreme Court that involved a challenge to local regulations on that basis.

CASE BACKGROUND

The owners of ocean-front property in the City of Monterey, California, applied to the city several times for a permit to build a residential development. Del Monte Dunes at Monterey, Limited, bought the property and continued to seek a permit. Each time, the city denied use of more of the property until no part remained available for a use inconsistent with leaving the property in its natural state. Del Monte sold the property to the state for $800,000 more than it paid and

filed a suit against the city in a federal district court. Del Monte claimed in part that the restrictions on use were an unconstitutional taking. The jury found in Del Monte's favor and awarded the plaintiff nearly $1.5 million in damages. The city appealed, arguing in part that Del Monte was not entitled to a jury trial on the legal issue involved in this case. The U.S. Court of Appeals for the Ninth Circuit upheld the award, and the city appealed to the United States Supreme Court.

MAJORITY OPINION

Justice *KENNEDY* delivered the opinion of the Court.
 * * * *

 * * * [I]n suits sounding in tort for money damages [suits brought not for the recovery of things, such as land or goods, but for damages only], questions of liability were [historically] decided by the jury, rather than the judge, in most cases. * * *
 * * * *

In *Williamson County Regional Planning Commission v. Hamilton Bank of Johnson City*, 473 U.S. 172, 105 S.Ct. 3108, 87 L.Ed.2d 126 (1985), we * * * review[ed] a regulatory takings case in which the plaintiff landowner sued a county planning commission in federal court for money damages * * * . Whether the commission had denied the plaintiff all economically viable use of the property had been submitted to the jury. Although the Court did not consider the point, it assumed the propriety of this procedure.
 * * * *

In actions at law predominantly factual issues are in most cases allocated to the jury. The allocation rests on a firm historical foundation and serves to preserve the right to a jury's resolution of the ultimate dispute. [Emphasis added.]

Almost from the inception of our regulatory takings doctrine, we have held that whether a regulation of property goes so far that there must be an exercise of eminent domain and compensation to sustain the act * * * depends upon the particular facts. Consistent with this understanding, we have described determinations of liability in regulatory takings cases as essentially * * * factual inquiries, requiring complex factual assessments of the purposes and economic effects of government actions.

In accordance with these pronouncements, we hold that the issue whether a landowner has been deprived of all economically viable use of his property is a predominantly factual question. As our implied acknowledgment of the procedure in *Williamson* suggests, in actions at law otherwise within the purview of the Seventh Amendment, this question is for the jury.

The jury's role in determining whether a land-use decision substantially advances legitimate public interests within the meaning of our regulatory takings doctrine presents a more difficult question. Although our cases make clear that this inquiry involves an essential factual component, it no doubt has a legal aspect as well, and is probably best understood as a mixed question of fact and law.

In this case, the narrow question submitted to the jury was whether, when viewed in light of the context and protracted history of the development application process, the city's decision to reject a particular development plan bore a reasonable relationship to its proffered justifications. As the [U.S. Court of Appeals for the Ninth Circuit] recognized, this question was "essentially fact-bound [in] nature." Under these circumstances, we hold that it was proper to submit this narrow, factbound question to the jury.

* * * *

* * * While juries are not customarily called upon to assume the subtleties of deferential review, courts apply this sort of limited scrutiny in all sorts of contexts and are routinely accorded institutional competence to do it. Scrutinizing the legal basis for governmental action is one of those things that judges often do and are likely to do better than juries unburdened by training in exegesis [critical interpretation]. It therefore should bring no surprise to find that in the taking cases a question whether regulatory action substantially advances a legitimate public aim has more often than not been treated by the federal courts as a legal issue. These practices point up the great gulf between the practical realities of taking litigation, and the Court's reliance on the assertion that "in suits sounding in tort for money damages, questions of liability were [historically] decided by the jury, rather than the judge, in most cases."

DISSENTING OPINION

Justice *SOUTER*, * * * dissenting * * * .

LEGAL REASONING AND ANALYSIS

1. Legal Reasoning. The opinions of the majority and the dissent in this case agree that in any case, there may be questions of fact, questions of law, and mixed questions of fact and law. On what point do they disagree? What conclusions do they reach, and what arguments do they use to support their conclusions? With whom do you agree and why?

2. Legal Analysis. The majority cites, in its opinion, *Williamson County Regional Planning Commission v. Hamilton Bank of Johnson City,* 473 U.S. 172, 105 S.Ct. 3108, 87 L.Ed.2d 126 (1985) (see the *Law on the Web* feature at

the end of Chapter 2 for instructions on how to access federal court opinions). How do the facts, issues, and holdings in that case contrast with the facts and issues of the *City of Monterey* case? Do the law and the reasoning of the *Williamson* case support the position of the majority in the *City of Monterey* case?

3. Political Considerations. The majority in the *City of Monterey* case limited its opinion to the narrow circumstances in the case rather than extending "its conceptual reach" to apply to many cases. Why would the Court restrict the application of its decision? What

would be the consequences if the reasoning in the majority's opinion were applied to other questions relating to "the respective provinces of judge and jury"?

4. Implications for Property Owners. How is the holding in this case of interest to property owners who are restricted by local governments in the use of their property?

5. Case Briefing Assignment. Using the guidelines for briefing cases given in Appendix A of this text, brief the *City of Monterey* case.

GOING ONLINE

The Web site for the Center on Environmental and Land Use Law at http://www.nyu.edu/pages/elc contains a "Program on Land Use Law" with a link to "Takings." Through this link, the "Online Resources on Takings" includes full text links to United States Supreme Court decisions on takings, state takings legislation, and other resources. This Web site is maintained by New York University School of Law in New York City.

FOCUS ON ETHICS
Property

Property rights have long been given extensive legal protection, under both English and American law. In the United States, the right to own property is closely associated with liberty, the pursuit of happiness, and other concepts that have played an integral role in American life. At the same time, conflicts often arise over who owns what and over how property should be used. In this *Focus on Ethics,* we explore some of the ethical dimensions of property laws and disputes over property ownership rights.

DEFINING RIGHTS IN PERSONAL PROPERTY

Who owns what many times becomes a serious question. One of these times, for a lot of people, is during divorce proceedings. Family law judges constantly have to decide which spouse is entitled to what assets after the dissolution of a marriage. In community property states, most property acquired after marriage is owned equally by the spouses. In many other states, on dissolution of the marriage, there is an "equitable" distribution of the couple's property.

The term *equitable,* of course, has no objective definition. And even if it did, numerous questions would remain about what actually is an asset that is subject to division during a divorce proceeding. Is the value of a professional license, say, to practice medicine, part of marital property to be divided? In a majority of states, no.[1] But a few

states, including California and New York, have held that professional licenses are marital property.[2]

What about an academic degree earned during marriage by one party with the financial assistance of the other? Is such a degree to be considered distributable marital property? Yes again, said the Appellate Division of the New York Supreme Court in *McGowan v. McGowan.*[3] If, in contrast, the property is a teaching certificate that a spouse earned shortly after marriage, this is not treated as marital property. Why not? Because the certificate is the result of educational achievements the person completed prior to marriage.

A challenging—if less significant—issue has to do with the ownership of engagement rings. Suppose that a couple becomes engaged to be married, and the man gives the woman an expensive engagement ring. If the marriage is called off, who "owns" the ring? The courts are widely split on this question. Some courts apply a fault-based principle: if the woman breaks the engagement, she should return the ring to the man, but if the man breaks the engagement, then the woman gets to keep the ring. Other courts follow a no-fault rule under which the ring should be returned to the donor, no matter who broke the engagement or for what reason. Still other judges have held that an

engagement ring is essentially a gift. If a donor intends to give the donee a ring, delivers the ring to the donee, and the donee accepts the ring, then all of the conditions for a valid gift exist.[4]

FINDERS' RIGHTS

The well-known children's adage "finders keepers, losers weepers" is actually written into law—provided that the loser (the rightful owner) cannot be found, that is. A finder may acquire good title to found personal property against everyone *except the true owner.* A number of landmark cases have made this principle clear.

An early English case, *Armory v. Delamirie,*[5] is considered to be a landmark in Anglo-American jurisprudence concerning so-called actions in *trover*—an early form of recovery of damages for the conversion of property. The plaintiff in this case was Armory, a chimney sweep who found a jewel in its setting during the course of his work. He took the jewel to a goldsmith to have it appraised. The goldsmith refused to return the jewel to Armory, claiming that Armory was not the rightful owner of the property. The court held that the finder, as prior possessor of the item, had rights to the jewel superior to those of all others except the rightful owner. The court said, "The finder of a jewel, though

---

1. See, for example, *Johnson v. Johnson,* 855 P.2d 250 (Utah App. 1993).

2. See, for example, *O'Brien v. O'Brien,* 66 N.Y.2d 576, 489 N.E.2d 712, 498 N.Y.S.2d 743 (1985).

3. 142 A.D.2d 355, 535 N.Y.S.2d 990 (1988).

4. For a summary of these and other approaches to determining ownership rights in engagement rings, see *Heiman v. Parrish,* 262 Kan. 926, 942 P.2d 6731 (1997).

5. 93 Eng.Rep.664 (K.B. [King's Bench] 1722).

he does not by such finding acquire an absolute property or ownership, yet . . . has such a property as will enable him to keep it against all but the rightful owner, and consequently maintain trover."

The *Armory* case illustrates the doctrine of the *relativity of title.* Under this doctrine, if two contestants, neither of whom can claim absolute title to the property, are before the court, the one who can claim prior possession will likely have established sufficient rights to the property to win the case.

A curious situation arises when goods wrongfully obtained by one person are in turn wrongfully obtained by another and the two parties contest their rights to possession. In such a case, does the *Armory* rule still apply—that is, does the first (illegal) possessor have more rights in the property than the second (illegal) possessor? In a case that came before the Minnesota Supreme Court, *Anderson v. Gouldberg,*[6] the court said yes. The plaintiffs had trespassed on another's land and wrongfully cut timber. The defendants later took the logs from the mill site, allegedly in the name of the owner of the property where the timber had been cut. The evidence at trial indicated that both parties had illegally acquired the property.

The court instructed the jury that even if the plaintiffs had been trespassers when they cut the logs, they were entitled to recover them from later possessors—except the true owner or an agent of the true owner. The jury found for the plaintiffs, a decision affirmed later by the Minnesota Supreme Court. The latter court held that the plaintiffs' possession, "though wrongfully obtained," justified an action to repossess against another who took it from them.

A case involving finder's rights, *Columbus-America Discovery*

Group, Inc. v. Atlantic Mutual Insurance Co.,[7] also raised issues of fairness. In that case, the finders of a sunken vessel that went down off the coast of South Carolina in 1857 expended time and substantial sums of money in locating the ship and raising its sunken treasure (gold being transported from Panama to New York) to the surface. When the ownership of the gold was disputed, however, the court held that the finders had no ownership interest in the treasure because the true owners had never abandoned the property. Rather, the insurers of the true owners, under policies executed over a century before, were entitled to the treasure. If not for the efforts of the treasure hunters, however, the insurance companies would have had nothing at all. Is it fair that the insurers had greater rights in the gold, when they did not assist in the search that located the treasure?

ETHICS AND BAILMENTS

The standard of care expected of a bailee clearly illustrates how the law reflects ethical principles. For example, suppose that a friend asks to borrow your business law text for the weekend. You agree to loan your friend the book. In this situation, which is a bailment for the sole benefit of the bailee (your friend), most people would agree that your friend has an ethical obligation to take great care of your book. After all, if your friend lost your book, you would incur damages. You would have to purchase another one, and if you could not, you might find it difficult to do well in your homework assignments, examinations, and so on.

It would be different if you had loaned your book to your friend totally for your own benefit. For

example, suppose that you are leaving town during the summer, and a friend offers to store several boxes of books for you until you return in the fall. In this situation, a benefit for the sole benefit of the bailor (you) exists. If your books are destroyed through the bailee's (your friend's) negligence and you sue the bailee for damages, a court will likely take into consideration the fact that the bailee was essentially doing you a favor by storing the books. Although bailees generally have a duty to exercise reasonable care over bailed property, what constitutes reasonable care in a specific situation normally depends on the surrounding circumstances—including the reason for the bailment and who stood to benefit from the arrangement.

PRIVATE VERSUS PUBLIC PROPERTY RIGHTS

Environmental regulations and other legislation to control land use are prevalent throughout the United States. Generally, these laws reflect the public's interest in preserving the beauty and natural resources of the land and in allowing the public to have access to and enjoy limited resources, such as coastal areas. Although few would disagree with the rationale underlying these laws, owners of the private property directly affected by the laws may feel that they should be compensated for the limitation imposed on their right to do as they wish with the land.

Several cases have been brought by private property owners who allege that regulations limiting their control over the land essentially constitute a taking of private property rights in the public interest. Therefore, the private property owners should receive the just compensation guaranteed under the Fifth Amendment. The ethical issue here involves who

6. 51 Minn. 294, 53 N.W. 636 (1892).

7. 974 F.2d 450 (4th Cir. 1992).

should have to bear the burden of environmental preservation, private property owners or the public.

Consider, for example, a case involving a New Jersey property developer, Loveladies Harbor, Inc. Loveladies Harbor owned fifty-one acres of land and planned to construct thirty-five single-family homes on fifty of the acres. A significant portion of the land (a little over twelve acres) consisted of wetlands that would need to be filled. Loveladies sought a permit from the Army Corps of Engineers to fill these wetlands, as required under the Clean Water Act (see Chapter 44). The Corps denied the permit, and ultimately Loveladies brought an action alleging that the refusal to allow it to develop the acres in question constituted a compensable taking under the Fifth Amendment.

The trial court held that when the Corps denied the permit to fill the wetlands, a taking had occurred. In affirming the trial court's decision, the federal appellate court phrased the essential question in the case as follows: "[W]hen the Government fulfills its obligation to preserve and protect the public interest, may the cost of obtaining that public benefit fall solely upon the affected property owner, or is it to be shared by the community at large[?]" The court, adopting the view of an increasing number of other courts, concluded that the expense should be borne by the public.[8]

For years, courts evaluating similar claims brought by private property owners alleging regulatory takings generally sided with the public authorities and held that no compensable takings had occurred. Beginning in the 1980s, however, the tide began to turn, and the courts now give more weight to the interests of private property owners. (See, for

example, the case discussed in the *Focus on Legal Reasoning* on the pages just preceding this *Focus on Ethics*.)

FAIR HOUSING VERSUS RELIGIOUS FREEDOM

Numerous restraints are imposed on landlords by federal and state antidiscrimination laws, but sometimes these laws conflict with other constitutional rights, such as the freedom of religion. For example, suppose that a landlord feels it would violate his or her religious principles to rent premises to an unmarried couple. Should the law, in the interest of preventing discrimination in housing, compel the landlord to violate his or her conscience? This issue brings into conflict two fundamental ethical principles— one promoting freedom from discrimination and the other promoting freedom of religion. It is simply not possible to develop an objective rule to determine which principle should prevail in all cases, and the courts have reached different conclusions.

Consider a Minnesota case, *Cooper v. French*.[9] Layle French owned a two-bedroom house in Marshall, Minnesota, which he put up for rent when he decided to move to the country. French advertised the house and agreed to rent it to Susan Parsons. He accepted a $250 check from her as a security deposit. French then realized that Parsons planned to share the house with her fiancé, Wesley Jenson, and that the two would likely engage in sexual relations before they were married while inhabiting French's house. French, a member of the Evangelical Free Church, told Parsons that he had changed his mind because the cohabitation of unmarried adults of opposite sexes violated his religious beliefs.

Parsons sued French, alleging that French was in violation of the Minnesota Human Rights Act, which prohibited discrimination on the basis of marital status. Minnesota's Department of Human Rights agreed with Parsons; so, too, did an administrative law judge, as well as an appellate court's panel of justices. The Supreme Court of Minnesota, however, did not agree. That court argued, among other things, that the landlord's right to exercise his religion under the Freedom of Conscience provision of the Minnesota constitution outweighed any interest of the tenant to cohabit with her fiancé in rented property prior to her marriage.

The California Supreme Court reached quite a different conclusion in a 1996 case involving similar facts, however. The court held that a landlord's refusal to rent commercial property to an unmarried couple for religious reasons violated a California statute that prohibited discrimination because of "marital status." The court stated that enforcing the law would not "substantially burden" the landlord's freedom of religion under either the federal Constitution or the California state constitution.[10]

DISCRIMINATION IN HOUSING

In the context of a home purchase, the Fair Housing Act prohibits mortgage lenders from refusing to lend money toward the purchase of homes in certain areas. Prohibiting this practice, known as *redlining*, severely restricts lenders' ability to choose freely where (or where not) to invest their money. Should lenders be coerced by law into lending money toward the

---

8. *Loveladies Harbor, Inc. v. United States,* 28 F.3d 1171 (Fed.Cir. 1994).

9. 460 N.W.2d 2 (Minn. 1990).

10. *Smith v. Fair Employment and Housing Commission,* 12 Cal.4th 1143, 913 P.2d 909, 51 Cal.Rptr.2d 700 (1996).

purchase of homes that are located in neighborhoods in which criminal activity is on the increase and property values are rapidly declining? The lender is in business to make money on its loan; it is not a charitable organization. The public policy expressed in the Fair Housing Act protects disadvantaged borrowers in this context, by making more housing available to them. Lenders, however, are forced to extend credit in areas that may increase their risk of loss.

DISCUSSION QUESTIONS

1. How might the decision in *Columbus-America Discovery Group, Inc. v. Atlantic Mutual Insurance Co.* affect future treasure hunting for lost ships?

2. Land-use control involves winners and losers. The losers are obviously those whose land decreases in value because of a new rule, regulation, or law that eliminates some of the possible uses of that land. Who are the winners? Should the winners compensate the losers? What does it mean to say that land-use control is in the "best interests of society"?

3. What limits can be placed on a person's use of private property? Consider an owner of ocean-front property who wants to develop a resort. What if such development would threaten the habitat of an endangered species? Should the individual defer to species protection? Should the government intervene to compel species protection?

4. Do you believe that the government has gone too far in protecting tenants' rights? Do you believe that tenants should have even greater protection? When tenants' rights, such as the right to be free of discrimination, conflict with a landlord's constitutionally protected rights, such as the free exercise of religion, which rights should prevail?

UNIT ELEVEN

Special Topics

CONTENTS

CHAPTER 49

Insurance

MANY PRECAUTIONS CAN BE TAKEN to protect against the hazards of life. For example, an individual can wear a seat belt to protect against automobile injuries or install smoke detectors to guard against the risk of injury from fire. Of course, no one can predict whether an accident or a fire will ever occur, but individuals and businesses must establish plans to protect their personal and financial interests should some event threaten to undermine their security.

Insurance is a contract by which the insurance company (the insurer) promises to pay a sum of money or give something of value to another (either the insured or the beneficiary) to compensate the other for a particular, stated loss. Insurance protection may provide for compensation for the injury or death of the insured or another, for damage to the insured's property, or for other types of losses, such as those resulting from lawsuits. Basically, insurance is an arrangement for *transferring and allocating risk*. In many cases, **risk** can be described as a prediction concerning potential loss based on known and unknown factors. Insurance, however, involves much more than a game of chance.

Risk management normally involves the transfer of certain risks from the individual to the insurance company by a contractual agreement. We examine the insurance contract and its provisions in this chapter. First, however, we look at some basic insurance terminology and concepts.

SECTION 1

Insurance Terminology and Concepts

Like other areas of law, insurance has its own special concepts and terminology, a knowledge of which is essential to an understanding of insurance law.

INSURANCE TERMINOLOGY

An insurance contract is called a **policy;** the consideration paid to the insurer is called a **premium;** and the insurance company is sometimes called an **underwriter.** The parties to an insurance policy are the *insurer* (the insurance company) and the *insured* (the person covered by its provisions).

Insurance contracts are usually obtained through an *agent,* who usually works for the insurance company, or through a *broker,* who is usually an independent contractor. When a broker deals with an applicant for insurance, the broker is, in effect, the applicant's agent. In contrast, an insurance agent is an agent of the insurance company, not an agent of the applicant. As a general rule, the insurance company is bound by the acts of its agents when they act within the scope of the agency relationship (see Chapters 31 and 32). In most situations, state law determines the status of all parties writing or obtaining insurance.

The Concept of Risk Pooling

All types of insurance companies use the principle of risk pooling; that is, they spread the risk among a large number of people—the pool—to make the premiums small compared with the coverage offered. Life insurance companies, for example, know that only a small proportion of the individuals in any particular age group will die in any one year. If a large percentage of people in this age group pay premiums to the company in exchange for a benefit payment in the event of death, there will be a sufficient amount of money to pay the beneficiaries of the policyholders who die. Through the extensive correlation of data over a period of time, insurers can estimate fairly accurately the total amount they will have to pay if they insure a particular group, as well as the rates that they will have to charge each member of the group so they can make the necessary payments and still show a profit.

Classifications of Insurance

Insurance is classified according to the nature of the risk involved. For example, fire insurance, casualty insurance, life insurance, and title insurance apply to different types of risk. Furthermore, policies of these types differ in the persons and interests that they protect. This is reasonable because the types of losses that are expected and the types that are foreseeable or unforeseeable vary with the nature of the activity. See Exhibit 49–1 on pages 935 and 936 for a list of various insurance classifications. (For a relatively new type of insurance coverage, see this chapter's *Emerging Trends in Technology* on page 937.)

Insurable Interest

A person can insure anything in which he or she has an **insurable interest.** Without this insurable interest, there is no enforceable contract, and a transaction to purchase insurance coverage would have to be treated as a wager. The existence of an insurable interest is a primary concern in determining liability under an insurance policy.

Life Insurance.   In regard to life insurance, one must have a reasonable expectation of benefit from the continued life of another to have an insurable interest in that person's life. The insurable interest must exist *at the time the policy is obtained.* The benefit may be pecuniary (related to money), or it may be founded on the relationship between the parties (by blood or affinity). Close family relationships give a person an insurable interest in the life of another. Generally, blood or marital relationships fit this category. A husband can take out an insurance policy on his wife and vice versa; parents can take out life insurance policies on their children; brothers and sisters, on each other; and grandparents, on grandchildren—as all these are close family relationships. A policy that a person takes out on his or her spouse remains valid even if they divorce, unless a specific provision in the policy calls for its termination on divorce.

Key-person insurance is insurance obtained by an organization on the life of a person who is important to that organization. Because the organization expects to receive some pecuniary gain from the continuation of the key person's life or some financial loss from the key person's death, the organization has an insurable interest. Typically, a partnership will insure the life of each partner, because the death of any one partner will cause some degree of loss to the partnership. Similarly, a corporation has an insurable interest in the life expectancy of a key executive whose death would result in financial loss to the company. If a firm insures a key person's life and then that person leaves the firm and dies, the firm can collect on the insurance policy, provided it continued to pay premiums.

Property Insurance.   In regard to real and personal property, an insurable interest exists when the insured derives a pecuniary benefit from the preservation and continued existence of the property. That is, one has an insurable interest in property when one would sustain a pecuniary loss from its destruction. Both a mortgagor and a mortgagee, for example, have an insurable interest in the mortgaged property. So do a landlord and a tenant in leased property, a secured party in the property in which he or she has a security interest, a partner in partnership property, and a stockholder in corporate property. John or Jane Doe, however, cannot obtain fire insurance on the White House.

The existence of an insurable interest is a primary concern in determining liability under an insurance policy. The insurable interest in property must exist when the loss occurs. Even if an insurable interest exists, however, the amount of that interest is often disputed. For example, even when a mortgagee has an insurable interest in property destroyed by fire, how much is the mortgagee entitled to recover from the property's insurer? The court in the following case addressed this question.

CASE 49.1   Sotelo v. Washington Mutual Insurance Co.

Superior Court of
Pennsylvania, 1999.
734 A.2d 421.

BACKGROUND AND FACTS *In November 1990, Carol Sotelo and Delhurst Corporation sold the Delhurst Country Inn in Erie County, Pennsylvania, to Patricia Cook and Brian and Cheryl Randall. The buyers subsequently formed Randco, Inc., and transferred the Inn to Randco. The Inn was mortgaged to Sotelo for $389,000 and insured by Washington Mutual Insurance Company under a policy with a $432,000 limit. A fire destroyed the Inn on October 27, 1992. At the time, Randco owed Sotelo $395,545.37, including $12,763.62 in late payment penalties, on two validly recorded mortgages. (Mortgages and recording statutes were discussed in Chapter 47.) Eight months after the fire, Washington Mutual sent Sotelo a check for $220,576.17. Claiming that this was not enough and asserting breach of contract, Sotelo filed a suit in a Pennsylvania state court against Washington Mutual. The court determined that the actual cash value (ACV) of the property was $485,000 and based its award to Sotelo on this ACV. The court subtracted the $220,576.17 already paid to Sotelo and $9,020.83 paid to local authorities for back taxes, and awarded Sotelo $255,403. Washington Mutual and Sotelo appealed to a state intermediate appellate court. The insurer claimed in part that Sotelo's insurable interest could not be more than the amount of the mortgage debt. Sotelo contended that back taxes should not have been deducted from her recovery.*

**IN THE LANGUAGE
OF THE COURT**

TAMILIA, J. [Judge]
*   *   *   *

*   *   * In order to have an insurable interest in property, a person must derive pecuniary advantage [an advantage consisting of, or relating to, money] from the continued existence of the property or suffer pecuniary loss from its destruction. The mortgagee's insurable interest is *prima facie* the value mortgaged, and extends only to the amount of the debt, not exceeding the value of the mortgaged property. Generally, the mortgagee's insurable interest is the amount of the mortgage debt since the debt represents its personal interest in the property. The mortgagee's insurable interest is initially presumed to be the value mortgaged, however, and a mortgagee's insurable interest cannot exceed the value of the property subject to the mortgage. Consequently, a mortgagee's ability to recover is limited to the extent of the debt secured by the property.

*   *   *   *

*   *   * [W]e *   *   * conclude the trial court erred by basing its award on the property's ACV, instead of the mortgage amount. As previously stated, *a mortgagee's insurable interest cannot exceed the value of the property subject to the mortgage.* If the mortgage amount exceeds the property's ACV, then the value of the property "subject to the mortgage" would obviously include the entire ACV of the property. However, in this case, the property's ACV exceeded the mortgage amount. [Emphasis added.]

A mortgagee's insured interest is limited to the outstanding mortgage debt, to the extent it is secured by the property. There is no dispute that the principal balance owed on the mortgages on October 27, 1992, the date of the loss, was $382,781.75. As previously noted, however, Randco also owed an additional $12,763.62 incurred as late payment penalties. This part of the debt was secured by both mortgage agreements. Thus, appellee's insurable interest was $395,545.37 or the total of the outstanding mortgage debt. *   *   *

*   *   *   *

*   *   * Sotelo contends the trial court erred by crediting appellants for their $9,020.83 payment to [local authorities for back taxes]. We agree. *   *   * Since the [authorities'] claims accrued after Sotelo's validly recorded mortgages, Sotelo could foreclose on the property, have her mortgages satisfied and never pay the [authorities'] claims.

**DECISION
AND REMEDY**

The state intermediate appellate court vacated the judgment of the lower court and remanded the case. Sotelo's recovery was to be based on the outstanding mortgage debt and late payment penalties totaling $395,545.37, minus what she had already been paid, plus interest. The amount owed by the mortgagors for back taxes was not to be deducted from Sotelo's recovery.

EXHIBIT 49–1 INSURANCE CLASSIFICATIONS

TYPE OF INSURANCE	COVERAGE
Accident	Covers expenses, losses, and suffering incurred by the insured because of accidents causing physical injury and any consequent disability; sometimes includes a specified payment to heirs of the insured if death results from an accident.
All-risk	Covers all losses that the insured may incur except those resulting from fraud on the part of the insured.
Automobile	May cover damage to automobiles resulting from specified hazards or occurrences (such as fire, vandalism, theft, or collision); normally provides protection against liability for personal injuries and property damage resulting from the operation of the vehicle.
Casualty	Protects against losses that may be incurred by the insured as a result of being held liable for personal injuries or property damage sustained by others.
Credit	Pays to a creditor the balance of a debt on the disability, death, insolvency, or bankruptcy of the debtor; often offered by lending institutions.
Decreasing-term life	Provides life insurance; requires uniform payments over the life (term) of the policy, but with a decreasing face value (amount of coverage).
Employer's liability	Insures employers against liability for injuries or losses sustained by employees during the course of their employment; covers claims not covered under workers' compensation insurance.
Fidelity or guaranty	Provides indemnity against losses in trade or losses caused by the dishonesty of employees, the insolvency of debtors, or breaches of contract.
Fire	Covers losses to the insured caused by fire.
Floater	Covers movable property, as long as the property is within the territorial boundaries specified in the contract.
Group	Provides individual life, medical, or disability insurance coverage but is obtainable through a group of persons, usually employees; the policy premium is paid either entirely by the employer or partially by the employer and partially by the employee.
Health	Covers expenses incurred by the insured resulting from physical injury or illness and other expenses relating to health and life maintenance.
Homeowners'	Protects homeowners against some or all risks of loss to their residences and the residences' contents or liability arising from the use of the property.
Key-person	Protects a business in the event of the death or disability of a key employee.
Liability	Protects against liability imposed on the insured resulting from injuries to the person or property of another.
Life	Covers the death of the policyholder. On the death of the insured, an amount specified in the policy is paid by the insurer to the insured's beneficiary.
Major medical	Protects the insured against major hospital, medical, or surgical expenses.
Malpractice	Protects professionals (doctors, lawyers, and others) against malpractice claims brought against them by their patients or clients; a form of liability insurance.
Marine	Covers movable property (including ships, freight, and cargo) against certain perils or navigation risks during a specific voyage or time period.
Mortgage	Covers a mortgage loan; the insurer pays the balance of the mortgage to the creditor on the death or disability of the debtor.
No-fault auto	Covers personal injury and (sometimes) property damage resulting from automobile accidents. The insured submits his or her claims to his or her own insurance company,

EXHIBIT 49–1   INSURANCE CLASSIFICATIONS (CONTINUED)

TYPE OF INSURANCE	COVERAGE
No-fault auto (continued)	regardless of who was at fault. A person may sue the party at fault or that party's insurer only in cases involving serious medical injury and consequent high medical costs. Governed by state "no-fault" statutes.
Term life	Provides life insurance for a specified period of time (term) with no cash surrender value; usually renewable.
Title	Protects against any defects in title to real property and any losses incurred as a result of existing claims against or liens on the property at the time of purchase.

SECTION 2

The Insurance Contract

An insurance contract is governed by the general principles of contract law, although the insurance industry is heavily regulated by the states.[1] Customarily, a party offers to purchase insurance by submitting an insurance application to the insurance company. The company can either accept or reject the offer. Sometimes, the insurance company's acceptance is conditional—on the results of a life insurance applicant's medical examination, for example. For the insurance contract to be binding, consideration (in the form of a premium) must be given, and the parties forming the contract must have the required contractual capacity to do so.

APPLICATION FOR INSURANCE

The filled-in application form for insurance is usually attached to the policy and made a part of the insurance contract. Thus, an insurance applicant is bound by any false statements that appear in the application (subject to certain exceptions). Because the insurance company evaluates the risk factors based on the information included in the insurance application, misstatements or misrepresentations can void a policy, especially if the insurance company can show

that it would not have extended insurance if it had known the facts.[2]

EFFECTIVE DATE

The effective date of an insurance contract—that is, the date on which the insurance coverage begins—is important. In some instances, the insurance applicant is not protected until a formal written policy is issued. In other situations, the applicant is protected between the time the application is received and the time the insurance company either accepts or rejects it. Four facts should be kept in mind:

1. A broker is the agent of an applicant. Therefore, if the broker fails to procure a policy, the applicant normally is not insured. According to general principles of agency law, if the broker fails to obtain policy coverage and the applicant is damaged as a result, then the broker is liable to the damaged applicant-principal for the loss.

2. A person who seeks insurance from an insurance company's agent is usually protected from the moment the application is made, provided—in the case of life insurance—that some form of premium has been paid. Between the time the application is received and the time it is either rejected or accepted, the applicant is covered (possibly subject to certain conditions, such as passing a physical examination). Usually, the agent will write a memorandum, or

---

1. The states were given authority to regulate the insurance industry by the McCarran-Ferguson Act of 1945, 15 U.S.C. Sections 1011–1015.

2. See, for example, *Berthiaume v. Minnesota Mutual Life Insurance Co.*, 388 N.W.2d 15 (Minn.App. 1986).

EMERGING TRENDS IN TECHNOLOGY

Risk Management in Cyberspace

Internet transactions pose special risks for businesspersons, risks that are not covered by traditional types of insurance. For example, suppose that the Celeste Company sells its products via its Web site. The buyers purchase the products using their credit cards. A hacker accesses the business's server containing the customers' credit-card numbers and then uses those numbers to purchase goods. Consumers, of course, are protected against unauthorized use of their cards under federal law (see Chapter 44). The Celeste Company, however, may be liable to the credit-card companies for negligence if it failed to maintain appropriate security measures to protect the data from unauthorized access.

Not surprisingly, a growing number of companies are now offering insurance policies that are designed to cover these and other Web-related risks. For example, consider the types of coverage offered by Net Secure, a venture undertaken by IBM, several insurance companies, and a New York broker. Net Secure provides insurance protection against losses resulting from programming errors; network and Web site disruptions; the theft of electronic data and assets, including intellectual property; Web-related defamation, copyright infringement, and false advertising; and the violation of users' privacy rights.

InsureTrust.com, an insurer affiliated with three leading insurance companies—American International Group, Lloyd's of London, and Reliance National—offers similar coverage. Insurance for Web-related perils is also being added to the offerings of existing insurers, such as Lloyd's of London, Hartford Insurance, and the Chubb Group of Insurance Companies. Clearly, the market for these new types of insurance coverage is rapidly evolving, and new policies will continue to appear.

Unlike traditional insurance policies, which are generally drafted by insurance companies and presented to insurance applicants on a "take-it-or-leave-it" basis, Internet-specific policies are usually customized to provide protection against particular risks faced by different types of businesses. For example, an Internet service provider will face different risks than an online merchant, and a banking institution will face different risks than a law firm. The specific business-related risks are taken into consideration when determining the policy premium.

IMPLICATIONS FOR THE BUSINESSPERSON

1. Because traditional insurance policies typically do not provide adequate protection against Internet-related risks, the new types of insurance discussed in this feature will greatly assist businesspersons in managing business hazards.

2. The proliferation of Web-related insurance offerings is beneficial to businesspersons because it allows them to shop around for the best price for a policy that meets their needs.

FOR CRITICAL ANALYSIS

1. How could an insurance company that sells Web site policies evaluate the extent of the risk posed by, say, computer viruses?

2. Why are Internet insurance policies usually customized, while traditional insurance policies are not?

RELEVANT WEB SITES

For an article from *Forbes* magazine on the "Risk e-Business" of e-commerce and the emergence of Internet insurance to address these risks, go to **http://www. forbes.com/tool/html/99/jun/0611/ feat.htm**. For another article on this topic, go to **http://cnn.com/TECH/ computing/9811/03/netinsure.idg**.

binder, indicating that a policy is pending and stating its essential terms.

3. If the parties agree that the policy will be issued and delivered at a later time, the contract is not effective until the policy is issued and delivered or sent to the applicant, depending on the agreement. Thus, any loss sustained between the time of application and the delivery of the policy is not covered.

4. Parties may agree that a life insurance policy will be binding at the time the insured pays the first premium, or the policy may be expressly contingent on the applicant's passing a physical examination. If the applicant pays the premium and passes the examination, then the policy coverage is continuously in effect. If the applicant pays the premium but dies before having the physical examination, then in order to collect, the applicant's estate normally must show that the applicant would have passed the examination had he or she not died. An insurance contract may also include a clause stating that the applicant must be "still insurable" on the effective date of the policy.[3]

In sum, coverage on an insurance policy can begin when a binder is written; when the policy is issued; or, depending on the terms of the contract, after a certain period of time has elapsed.

PROVISIONS AND CLAUSES

Some of the important provisions and clauses contained in insurance contracts are defined and discussed in the following subsections.

Provisions Mandated by Statute.   If a statute mandates that a certain provision be included in insurance contracts, a court will deem that an insurance policy contains the provision regardless of whether the parties actually included it in the language of their contract. If a statute requires that any limitations regarding coverage be stated in the contract, a court will not allow an insurer to avoid liability for a claim through reliance on an unexpressed restriction.

Incontestability Clauses.   Statutes commonly require that a life or health insurance policy provide that after the policy has been in force for a specified length of time—often two or three years—the insurer cannot contest statements made in the application. This is known as an *incontestability clause*. Once a policy becomes incontestable, the insurer cannot later avoid a claim on the basis of, for example, fraud on the part of the insured, unless the clause provides an exception for that circumstance. The clause does not prohibit an insurer's refusal or reduction of payment for a claim

due to nonpayment of premiums, failure to file proof of death within a certain period, or lack of an insurable interest.

Coinsurance Clauses.   Often, when taking out fire insurance policies, property owners insure their property for less than full value. Part of the reason for this is that most fires do not result in a total loss. To encourage owners to insure their property for an amount as close to full value as possible, a standard provision of fire insurance policies is a coinsurance clause. Typically, a *coinsurance clause* provides that if the owner insures the property up to a specified percentage—usually 80 percent—of its value, he or she will recover any loss up to the face amount of the policy. If the insurance is for less than the fixed percentage, the owner is responsible for a proportionate share of the loss.

Coinsurance applies only in instances of partial loss. For example, if the owner of property valued at $100,000 took out a policy in the amount of $40,000 and suffered a loss of $30,000, the recovery would be $15,000. The formula for calculating the recovery amount is as follows:

$$\frac{\text{amount of insurance}\ (\$40,000)}{\text{coinsurance percentage}\ (80\%) \times \text{property value}\ (\$100,000)} = \begin{array}{l}\text{recovery}\\ \text{percentage}\\ (50\%)\end{array}$$

recovery percentage (50%) × amount of loss ($30,000) = recovery amount ($15,000)

If the owner had taken out a policy in the amount of $80,000, then according to the same formula, the full loss would have been recovered.

Appraisal and Arbitration Clauses.   Most fire insurance policies provide that if the parties cannot agree on the amount of a loss covered under the policy or on the value of the property lost, an *appraisal* can be demanded. An appraisal is an estimate of the property's value determined by suitably qualified individuals who have no interest in the property. Typically, two appraisers are used, one being appointed by each party. A third party, or umpire, may be called on to resolve differences. Other types of insurance policies also contain provisions for appraisal and arbitration when the insured and insurer disagree as to the value of a loss.

---

3. See, for example, *Life Insurance Co. of North America v. Cichowlas*, 659 So.2d 1333 (Fla.App.4th 1995).

Multiple Insurance Coverage. If an insured has *multiple insurance coverage*—that is, policies with several companies covering the same insurance interest—and the amount of coverage exceeds the loss, the insured can collect from each insurer only the company's proportionate share of the liability, relative to the total amount of insurance. Many fire insurance policies include a pro rata clause, which requires that any loss be shared proportionately by all carriers. For example, if Grumbling insured $50,000 worth of property with two companies, each of whose policies had a liability limit of $40,000, then on the property's total destruction Grumbling could collect only $25,000 from each insurer.

Antilapse Clauses. A life insurance policy may provide, or a statute may require a policy to provide, that it will not automatically lapse if no payment is made on the date due. Ordinarily, under an *antilapse provision*, the insured has a *grace period* of thirty or thirty-one days within which to pay an overdue premium. If the insured fails to pay a premium altogether, there are alternatives to cancellation:

1. The insurer may be required to extend the insurance for a period of time.
2. The insurer may issue a policy with less coverage to reflect the amount of the payments made.
3. The insurer may pay to the insured the policy's **cash surrender value**—the amount the insurer has agreed to pay on the policy's cancellation before the insured's death. (In determining this value, the following factors are considered: the period that the policy has already run, the amount of the premium, the insured's age and life expectancy, and amounts to be repaid on any outstanding loans taken out against the policy.)

When the insurance contract states that the insurer cannot cancel the policy, these alternatives are important.

INTERPRETING PROVISIONS OF AN INSURANCE CONTRACT

The courts are increasingly cognizant of the fact that most people do not have the special training necessary to understand the intricate terminology used in insurance policies. The words used in an insurance contract have their ordinary meanings and are interpreted by courts in light of the nature of the coverage involved. When there is an ambiguity in the policy, the provision is interpreted against the insurance

company. When it is unclear whether an insurance contract actually exists because the written policy has not been delivered, the uncertainty is resolved against the insurance company. The court presumes that the policy is in effect unless the company can show otherwise. Similarly, an insurer must take care to make sure that the insured is adequately notified of any change in coverage under an existing policy.

CANCELLATION

The insured can cancel a policy at any time, and the insurer can cancel under certain circumstances. When an insurance company can cancel its insurance contract, the policy or a state statute usually requires that the insurer give advance written notice of the cancellation. Any premium paid in advance and not yet earned may be refundable. The insured may also be entitled to a life insurance policy's cash surrender value.

The insurer may cancel an insurance policy for various reasons, depending on the type of insurance. For example, automobile insurance can be canceled for nonpayment of premiums or suspension of the insured's driver's license. Property insurance can be canceled for nonpayment of premiums or for other reasons, including the insured's fraud or misrepresentation, gross negligence, or conviction for a crime that increases the hazard insured against. Life and health policies can be canceled because of false statements made by the insured in the application, but cancellation can only take place before the effective date of an incontestability clause. An insurer cannot cancel—or refuse to renew—a policy because of the national origin or race of an applicant or because the insured has appeared as a witness in a case brought against the company.

State laws normally impose a requirement that an insured must be notified in writing of an insurance policy cancellation.[4] The same requirement applies when only part of a policy is canceled. The exact form that this notice should take is not always specified, however, and the issue in the following case was what and how much notice are sufficient to effect a cancellation.

---

4. At issue in one case was whether a notification of cancellation included on a diskette sent to the insured constituted "written notice" of cancellation. The court held that the computerized document, which could be printed out as "hard copy," constituted written notice. See *Clyburn v. Allstate Insurance Co.*, 826 F.Supp. 955 (D.S.C. 1993).

CASE 49.2   Westfield Cos. v. Rovan, Inc.

Court of Appeals of
Indiana, 2000.
722 N.E.2d 851.
http://www.state.in.us/
judiciary/opinions/
search.html[a]

BACKGROUND AND FACTS   *Rovan, Inc., repairs and renovates automobiles and recreational vehicles in Indiana. Cheryl Robinson is the president of Rovan. In 1997, Westfield Companies issued an insurance policy to Rovan. The policy was more than one hundred pages long and contained forty-two "forms," which were listed by description, not by number. In January 1998, Rovan leased from Cheryl's son Brandon a 1995 Chevy pickup truck. As part of the lease, Rovan agreed to provide insurance for Brandon when he drove the truck. A copy of the lease was forwarded to Westfield, which added the Chevy to Rovan's policy. Westfield also added a clause (the "Lessor Endorsement") to cover Brandon when he drove a vehicle that he leased to Rovan. In March, Rovan replaced the lease of the Chevy with a lease of a 1998 Ford Mustang GT from Brandon under the same terms and conditions as the previous lease. Westfield was notified of the change and, in the policy, deleted the Chevy and added the Mustang. Westfield sent to Rovan an "Amended Common Policy Declaration" that noted the change in vehicles and stated, at the bottom, "DELETED FORM CA2001 07/97. This endorsement changes your policy. Please attach it to your original policy." FORM CA2001 07/97 was the Lessor Endorsement. In June, Cheryl agreed to replace the Mustang with Brandon's 1997 Dodge pickup truck. Within a few days, Brandon, while driving the Dodge, was involved in an accident that left three minors dead and two others seriously injured. Westfield filed a request with an Indiana state court for a declaratory judgment that its policy had not covered Brandon at the time of the accident. The court granted a summary judgment in favor of Rovan. Westfield appealed to a state intermediate appellate court.*

IN THE LANGUAGE OF THE COURT

MATTINGLY, Judge.

*   *   *   *

The question of what and how much notice of cancellation by the insurer is sufficient to effectively cancel an insurance policy is one of first impression for [never before decided by] this court. While generally in the absence of a specific statutory or policy provision, any form of notice of cancellation is sufficient, we hold *such notice must positively and unequivocally inform the insured of the insurer's intention that the policy cease to be binding.* *   *   * [Emphasis added.]

In this case, no form of notice of cancellation is required by either Policy provision or statute. Therefore, Westfield was required to send Rovan only such notice as would positively and unequivocally inform Rovan that Westfield was canceling the Lessor Endorsement. Westfield argues the Amended Common Policy Declaration was sufficient. *   *   * Westfield argues the statement at the bottom deleting Form CA2001 07/97 (the Lessor Endorsement) in conjunction with the sentences recognizing the Amended Common Policy Declaration as a change in the policy is sufficient to provide notice of cancellation. We disagree and find the phrase "DELETED FORM CA2001 07/97" decidedly cryptic and completely uninformative. All it expresses is that one out of some forty-two forms contained in the Policy had been deleted. It does not suggest the importance or practical consequences of this deletion by positively and unequivocally informing Rovan that the Lessor Endorsement would cease to be binding. In other words, it is not a clear expression of intent to cancel so as to be apparent to the ordinary person.

We are not persuaded by Westfield's suggesting that "[a]nyone who looked at the Policy could easily correlate the form number with the title of the form." The Policy is well over one hundred pages long and contains roughly forty-two separately numbered

_____

a. In the "Select one or more opinion groups to search" section, click on the box next to "Appeals Court." In the "Please enter the cause number, party name(s), key word or phrases, separated by commas" box, type "Rovan," and click on "SEARCH." When the results return, click on "converted file msm" to access the opinion.

"forms" of various page lengths. The several tables of contents list the parts of the Policy by description, not by form number. The only way for one to determine which form had been deleted would be to examine each and every page of the Policy. In this case, the search would have uncovered the Lessor Endorsement approximately three-quarters of the way through the Policy located immediately after the "Nuclear Energy Liability Exclusion Endorsement."

Westfield, by failing to provide notice of cancellation, did not effectively cancel coverage under the Lessor Endorsement. Accordingly, the Lessor Endorsement remained in effect on * * * the date of the accident.

DECISION AND REMEDY   *The state intermediate appellate court affirmed the summary judgment in Rovan's favor. Westfield had not provided sufficient notice of its cancellation of coverage because the notice did not "positively and unequivocally inform the insured of the insurer's intention."*

BASIC DUTIES AND RIGHTS

Essentially, the parties to an insurance contract are responsible for the obligations the contract imposes. These include the basic contractual duties discussed in Chapters 10 through 18 of this text, which cover contract law.

In applying for insurance, for example, the obligation to act in good faith means that a party must reveal everything necessary for the insurer to evaluate the risk. In other words, the applicant must disclose all material facts. These include all facts that would influence an insurer in determining whether to charge a higher premium or to refuse to issue a policy altogether.

Once the insurer has accepted the risk, and on the occurrence of an event giving rise to a claim, the insurer has a duty to investigate to determine the facts. When a policy provides insurance against third party claims, the insurer is obligated to make reasonable efforts to settle such a claim. If a settlement cannot be reached, then regardless of the claim's merit, the insurer must defend any suit against the insured. Usually, a policy provides that in this situation the insured must cooperate. A policy provision may expressly require the insured to attend hearings and trials, to help in obtaining evidence and witnesses, and to assist in reaching a settlement.

DEFENSES AGAINST PAYMENT

An insurance company can raise any of the defenses that would be valid in any ordinary action on a contract, as well as some defenses that do not apply in ordinary contract actions. If the insurance company can show that the policy was procured through fraud or misrepresentation, for example, it may have a valid defense for not paying on a claim. (The insurance company may also have the right to disaffirm or rescind an insurance contract.) An absolute defense exists if the insurer can show that the insured lacked an insurable interest—thus rendering the policy void from the beginning. Improper actions, such as those that are against public policy or that are otherwise illegal, can also give the insurance company a defense against the payment of a claim or allow it to rescind the contract.

The insurance company can be prevented, or estopped, from asserting some defenses that are normally available. For example, if a company tells an insured that information requested on a form is optional and the insured provides it anyway, the company cannot use the information to avoid its contractual obligation under the insurance contract. Similarly, incorrect statements as to the age of the insured normally do not provide the insurance company with a way to escape payment on the death of the insured. Also, incontestability clauses prevent the insurer from asserting certain defenses. Some states follow the *concurrent causation doctrine*, which requires that the insurer pay on a claim when the accident was due to more than one cause, at least one of which was covered under the policy.[5]

In the following case, an insurance company attempted to avoid payment under a policy for life and disability insurance by claiming that the policy owner did not have an insurable interest, thus rendering the policy void from the outset.

---

5. This doctrine was enunciated by the California Supreme Court in *State Farm Mutual Automobile Insurance Co. v. Partridge*, 10 Cal.3d 94, 514 P.2d 123, 109 Cal.Rptr. 811 (1973). Subsequently, a number of other states, particularly in the Midwest, adopted the doctrine. But see *Vanguard Insurance Co. v. Clarke*, 438 Mich. 463, 475 N.W.2d 48 (1991), in which the Michigan Supreme Court rejected the doctrine.

CASE 49.3   Paul Revere Life Insurance Co. v. Fima

United States
Court of Appeals,
Ninth Circuit, 1997.
105 F.3d 490.
http://www.ce9.
uscourts.gov[a]

**IN THE LANGUAGE
OF THE COURT**

BACKGROUND AND FACTS   *Raoul Fima applied to Paul Revere Life Insurance
Company for a disability policy. On the application, Fima stated his income as $105,000
for the previous year and $85,000 for the current year. Fima's actual income for those
years was $21,603 and $6,320, respectively. The policy included the following incontestability clause: "After your policy has been in force for two years, . . . we cannot contest the statements in the application." Three years later, when Fima filed a claim under
the policy, Revere discovered the truth regarding Fima's income. Revere filed a suit in a
federal district court against Fima, seeking to have the policy declared void* ab initio *(from
the beginning) on the ground that he lacked an insurable interest. The court denied the
request. Revere appealed.*

BRUNETTI, Circuit Judge:
          *   *   *   *

   Fima had an insurable interest under California Insurance Code [S]ection 10110 as
a matter of law. Section 10110 states that "[e]very person has an insurable interest in the
life and health of *   *   * [h]imself." Because Fima had an insurable interest under
[S]ection 10110, his disability insurance policy was not void *ab initio.*
          *   *   *   *

   *   *   * Because that policy is not void *ab initio* and because the period for contesting the policy has passed under the incontestability clause, Revere may not now
challenge the terms of the policy or the extent of Fima's insurable interest.

**DECISION
AND REMEDY**

*The U.S. Court of Appeals for the Ninth Circuit affirmed the judgment of the lower court.
Every person has an insurable interest in his or her own life and health.*

**INTERNATIONAL
CONSIDERATIONS**

False Statements on Insurance Applications in the United Kingdom *The United
Kingdom has stricter rules than most states in the United States in regard to false statements made on insurance applications. In the United Kingdom, insurance applicants are
held to a standard of* uberrima fides *(Latin for "the most abundant good faith"). Even an
innocent (unintentional) misrepresentation on an insurance application makes the contract voidable at the option of the insurer.*

----

a. In the "Info Links" column, click on the "Appeals Court Decisions" icon. On that page, click on
"1997" to open the menu. Click on "January," then scroll down the list to the name of the case, and click
on it to access the opinion.

SECTION 3

Types of Insurance

There are four general types of insurance coverage:
life insurance, fire and homeowners' insurance, automobile insurance, and business liability insurance.
We now examine briefly the coverage available under
each of these types of insurance. In the course of our
discussion, we point out certain features and provisions as they relate to the law, with special emphasis
on life and fire insurance policies.

LIFE INSURANCE

There are five basic types of life insurance:

1. **Whole life** is sometimes referred to as straight life,
ordinary life, or cash-value insurance. This type of insurance provides protection with a cumulated cash
surrender value that can be used as collateral for a
loan. Premiums are paid by the insured during the insured's entire lifetime, with a fixed payment to the
beneficiary on death.

2. **Limited-payment life** might be a twenty-payment
life policy. Premiums are paid for a stated number of

years, after which the policy is paid up and fully effective during the insured's life. Naturally, premiums are higher than for whole life. This insurance has a cash surrender value.

3. **Term insurance** is a type of policy for which premiums are paid for a specified term. Payment on the policy is due only if death occurs within the term period. Premiums are less expensive than for whole life or limited-payment life, and there is usually no cash surrender value. Frequently, this type of insurance can be converted to another type of life insurance.

4. **Endowment insurance** involves fixed premium payments that are made for a definite term. At the end of the term, a fixed amount is to be paid to the insured or, on the death of the insured during the specified period, to a beneficiary. Thus, this type of insurance represents both term insurance and a form of **annuity** (the right to receive fixed, periodic payments for life or—as in this case—for a term of years). Endowment insurance has a rapidly increasing cash surrender value, but premiums are high, as payment is required at the end of the term even if the insured is still living.

5. **Universal life** is a type of insurance that combines some aspects of term insurance and some of whole life insurance. Every payment, usually called a "contribution," involves two deductions made by the issuing life insurance company. The first one is a charge for term insurance protection; the second is for company expenses and profit. The money that remains after these deductions earns interest for the policyholder at a rate determined by the company. The interest-earning money in the policy is called the policy's cash value, but that term does not mean the same thing as it does for a traditional whole life insurance policy. With a universal life policy, the cash value grows at a variable interest rate rather than at a predetermined rate.

The rights and liabilities of the parties in life insurance are basically dependent on the insurance contract. A few features deserve special attention.

Liability. The life insurance contract determines not only the extent of the insurer's liability but, generally, whether the insurer is liable on the death of the insured. Most life insurance contracts exclude liability for death caused by suicide, military action during war, execution by a state or federal government, and even a mishap that occurs while the insured is a passenger in a commercial vehicle. In the absence of ex-

clusion, most courts today construe any cause of death to be one of the insurer's risks.

Adjustment Due to Misstatement of Age. The insurance policy constitutes the agreement between the parties. The application for insurance is part of the policy and is usually attached to the policy. When the insured misstates his or her age in the application, an error is introduced, particularly as to the amount of premiums paid. Misstatement of age is not a material error sufficient to allow the insurer to void the policy. Instead, on discovery of the error, the insurer will adjust the premium payments and/or benefits accordingly.

Assignment. Most life insurance policies permit the insured to change beneficiaries. When this is the case, in the absence of any prohibition or notice requirement, the insured can assign the rights to the policy (for example, as security for a loan) without the consent of the insurer or the beneficiary. If the beneficiary's right is *vested*—that is, has become absolute, entitling the beneficiary to payment of the proceeds—the policy cannot be assigned without the consent of the beneficiary. For the most part, life insurance contracts permit assignment and require notice only to the insurer to be effective.

Creditors' Rights. Unless insurance proceeds are exempt under state law, the insured's interest in life insurance is an asset that is subject to the rights of judgment creditors. These creditors generally can reach insurance proceeds payable to the insured's estate, proceeds payable to anyone if the payment of premiums constituted a fraud on creditors, and proceeds payable to a named beneficiary unless the beneficiary's rights have vested. Creditors, however, cannot compel the insured to make available the cash surrender value of the policy or to change the named beneficiary to that of the creditor. Almost all states exempt at least a part of the proceeds of life insurance from creditors' claims.

Termination. Although the insured can cancel and terminate the policy, the insurer generally cannot do so. Therefore, termination usually takes place only on the occurrence of the following:

1. Default in premium payments that causes the policy to lapse.
2. Death and payment of benefits.
3. Expiration of the term of the policy.
4. Cancellation by the insured.

FIRE AND HOMEOWNERS' INSURANCE

There are basically two types of insurance policies for a home—standard fire insurance policies and homeowners' policies.

Standard Fire Insurance Policies. The standard fire insurance policy protects the homeowner against fire and lightning, as well as damage from smoke and water caused by the fire or the fire department. Most fire insurance policies are classified according to the type of property covered and the extent (amount) of the issuer's liability. Exhibit 49–2 lists typical fire insurance policies.

As with life insurance, certain features and provisions of fire insurance deserve special mention. In reading the following, it is important to note some basic differences in the treatment of life and fire policies.

Liability. The insurer's liability is determined from the terms of the policy. Most policies, however, limit recovery to losses resulting from *hostile* fires—basically, those that break out or begin in places where no fire was intended to burn. A *friendly* fire—one burning in a place where it was intended to burn—is not covered. Therefore, smoke from a fireplace is not covered, but smoke from a fire caused by a defective electrical outlet is covered. Sometimes, owners add "extended coverage" to the fire policy to cover losses from "friendly" fires.

If the policy is a *valued* policy (see Exhibit 49–2) and the subject matter is completely destroyed, the insurer is liable for the amount specified in the policy. If it is an *open* policy, then the extent of actual loss must be determined, and the insurer is liable only for the amount of the loss or for the maximum amount specified in the policy, whichever is less. For partial losses, actual loss must always be determined, and the insurer's liability is limited to that amount. Most insurance policies permit the insurer either to restore or replace the property destroyed or to pay for the loss.

Proof of Loss. Fire insurance policies require the insured to file with the insurer, within a specified period or immediately (within a reasonable time), a proof of loss as a condition for recovery. Failure to comply *could* allow the insurance carrier to avoid liability. Courts vary somewhat on the enforcement of such clauses.

Occupancy Clause. Most standard policies require that the premises be occupied at the time of loss. The relevant clause states that if the premises become vacant or unoccupied for a given period, unless consent by the insurer is given, the coverage is suspended until the premises are reoccupied. Persons going on extended vacations should check their policies regarding this point.

Assignment. Before a loss has occurred, a fire insurance policy is not assignable without the consent of the insurer. The theory is that the fire insurance policy is a personal contract between the insured and the insurer. The nonassignability of the policy is extremely

EXHIBIT 49–2   TYPICAL FIRE INSURANCE POLICIES

TYPE OF POLICY	COVERAGE
Blanket	Covers a class of property rather than specific property, because the property is expected to shift or vary in nature. A policy covering the inventory of a business is an example.
Floater	Usually supplements a specific policy. It is intended to cover property that may change in either location or quantity. To illustrate, if the painting mentioned below under "specific policy" were to be exhibited during the year at numerous locations throughout the state, a floater policy would be desirable.
Open	A policy in which the value of the property insured is not agreed on. The policy usually provides for a maximum liability of the insurer, but payment for loss is restricted to the fair market value of the property at the time of loss or to the insurer's limit, whichever is less.
Specific	Covers a specific item of property at a specific location. An example is a particular painting located in a residence or a piece of machinery located in a factory or business.
Valued	A policy in which, by agreement, a specific value is placed on the subject to be insured to cover the eventuality of its total loss.

important in the purchase of a house. The purchaser must procure his or her own insurance. If the purchaser wishes to assume the remaining insurance coverage period of the seller, consent of the insurer is essential.

To illustrate: Ann is selling her home and lot to Jeff. Ann has a one-year fire policy with Ajax Insurance Company, with six months of coverage remaining at the date on which the sale is to close. Ann agrees to assign the balance of her policy, but Ajax has not given its consent. One day after passage of the deed, a fire totally destroys the house. Can Jeff recover from Ajax?

The answer is no, as the policy is actually voided on the closing of the transaction and the deeding of the property. The reason the policy is voided is that Ann no longer has an insurable interest at the time of loss, and Jeff has no rights in a nonassignable policy.

Homeowners' Policies. A homeowners' policy provides protection against a number of risks under a single policy, allowing the policyholder to avoid the cost of buying each protection separately. There are two basic types of homeowners' coverage:

1. *Property coverage* includes the garage, house, and other private buildings on the policyholder's lot. It also includes the personal possessions and property of the policyholder at home, in travel, or at work. It pays additional expenses for living away from home because of a fire or some other covered peril.
2. *Liability coverage* is for personal liability in case someone is injured on the insured's property, the insured damages someone else's property, or the insured injures someone else who is not in an automobile.

Perils insured under property coverage often include fire, lightning, wind, hail, vandalism, and theft (of personal property). Personal property that is typically not included under property coverage, in the absence of a specific provision, includes such items as motor vehicles, farm equipment, airplanes, and boats. Coverage for other property, such as jewelry and securities, is usually limited to a specified dollar amount.

Liability coverage under a homeowners' policy applies when others are injured or property is damaged because of the unsafe condition of the policyholder's premises. It also applies when the policyholder is negligent. It does not normally apply, however, if the liability arises from business or professional activities or from the operation of a motor vehicle. These are subjects for separate policies. Also excluded is liability arising from intentional misconduct. Similar to liability coverage is coverage for the medical payments of others who are injured on the policyholder's property and coverage for property of others that is damaged by a member of the policyholder's family.

Renters, too, take out insurance policies to protect against losses to personal property. Renters' insurance covers personal possessions against various perils and includes coverage for additional living expenses and liability.

AUTOMOBILE INSURANCE

There are two basic kinds of automobile insurance: liability insurance and collision and comprehensive insurance.

Liability Insurance. Automobile liability insurance covers bodily injury and property damage liability. Liability limits are usually described by a series of three numbers, such as 100/300/50. This means that the policy, for one accident, will pay a maximum of $100,000 for bodily injury to one person, a maximum of $300,000 for bodily injury to more than one person, and a maximum of $50,000 for property damage. Many insurance companies offer liability up to $500,000 and sometimes higher.

Individuals who are dissatisfied with the maximum liability limits offered by regular automobile insurance coverage can purchase separate coverage under an *umbrella policy*. Umbrella limits sometimes go as high as $5 million. Umbrella policies also cover personal liability in excess of the liability limits of a homeowners' policy.

Collision and Comprehensive Insurance. Collision insurance covers damage to the insured's car in any type of collision. Usually, it is not advisable to purchase full collision coverage (otherwise known as zero deductible). The price per year is relatively high, because it is likely that some small repair jobs will be required each year. Most people prefer to take out coverage with a deductible of $100, $250, or $500, which costs substantially less than zero-deductible coverage.

Comprehensive insurance covers loss, damage, and destruction due to fire, hurricane, hail, vandalism, and theft. It can be obtained separately from collision insurance.

Other Automobile Insurance. Other types of automobile insurance coverage include the following:

1. *Uninsured motorist coverage.* Uninsured motorist coverage insures the driver and passengers against injury caused by any driver without insurance or by a hit-and-run driver. Certain states require that it be included in all insurance policies sold to drivers.

2. *Accidental death benefits.* Sometimes referred to as *double indemnity*, accidental death benefits provide a lump sum to named beneficiaries if the policyholder dies in an automobile accident. This coverage generally costs very little, but it may not be necessary if the insured has a sufficient amount of life insurance.

3. *Medical payment coverage.* Medical payment coverage provided by an auto insurance policy pays hospital and other medical bills and sometimes funeral expenses. This type of insurance protects all the passengers in the insured's car when the insured is driving.

4. *Other-driver coverage.* An **omnibus clause,** or an *other-driver clause,* protects the vehicle owner who has taken out the insurance and anyone who drives the vehicle with the owner's permission. This coverage may be held to extend to a third party who drives the vehicle with the permission of the person to whom the owner gave permission.

5. *No-fault insurance.* Under no-fault statutes, claims arising from an accident are made against the claimant's own insurer, regardless of whose fault the accident was. In some cases—for example, when injuries involve expensive medical treatment—an injured party may seek recovery from another party or insurer. In those instances, the injured party may collect the maximum amount of no-fault insurance and still sue for total damages from the party at fault, although usually, on winning an award, the injured party must reimburse the insurer for its no-fault payments.

Business Liability Insurance

A business may be vulnerable to all sorts of risks. A key employee may die or become disabled; a customer may be injured when using a manufacturer's product; the patron of an establishment selling liquor may leave the premises and injure a third party in an automobile accident; or a professional may overlook some important detail, causing liability for malpractice. Should the first situation arise (for instance, if the company president dies), the firm may have some protection under a key-person insurance policy, discussed

previously. In the other circumstances, other types of insurance may apply.

General Liability.   Comprehensive general liability insurance can cover virtually as many risks as the insurer agrees to cover. For example, among the types of coverage that a business might wish to acquire is protection from liability for injuries arising from on-premises events not otherwise covered, such as company social functions. Some specialized establishments, such as taverns, may be subject to liability in individualized circumstances, and policies can be drafted to meet their needs. In many jurisdictions, for example, statutes impose liability on a seller of liquor when a buyer of the liquor, intoxicated as a result of the sale, injures a third party. Legal protection may extend not only to immediately consequent injuries, such as quadriplegia resulting from an automobile accident, but also to the loss of financial support suffered by a family because of the injuries. Insurance can provide coverage for these injuries and financial losses.

Product Liability.   Manufacturers may be subject to liability for injuries that their products cause, and product-liability insurance can be written to match specific products' risks. Coverage can be procured under a comprehensive general liability policy or under a separate policy. The coverage may include payment for expenses involved in recalling and replacing a product that has proved to be defective. (For a comprehensive discussion of product liability, see Chapter 6.)

Professional Malpractice.   In recent years, professionals—attorneys, physicians, architects, and engineers, for example—have increasingly become the targets of negligence suits. Professionals may purchase malpractice insurance to protect themselves against such claims. The large judgments in some malpractice suits have received considerable publicity and are sometimes cited in what has been termed "the insurance crisis," because they have contributed to a significant increase in malpractice insurance premiums.

Workers' Compensation.   Workers' compensation insurance covers payments to employees who are injured in accidents arising out of and in the course of employment (that is, on the job). Workers' compensation, which was discussed in detail in Chapter 41, is governed by state statutes.

TERMS AND CONCEPTS TO REVIEW

annuity 943

binder 937

cash surrender value 939

endowment insurance 943

insurable interest 933

insurance 932

limited-payment life 942

omnibus clause 946

policy 932

premium 932

risk 932

risk management 932

term insurance 943

underwriter 932

universal life 943

whole life 942

QUESTIONS AND CASE PROBLEMS

49–1. INSURABLE INTEREST. Adia owns a house and has an elderly third cousin living with her. Adia decides she needs fire insurance on the house and a life insurance policy on her third cousin to cover funeral and other expenses that will result from her cousin's death. Adia takes out a fire insurance policy from Ajax Insurance Co. and a $10,000 life insurance policy from Beta Insurance Co. on her third cousin. Six months later, Adia sells the house to John and transfers title to him. Adia and her cousin move into an apartment. With two months remaining on the Ajax policy, a fire totally destroys the house; at the same time, Adia's third cousin dies. Both insurance companies tender back premiums but claim they have no liability under the insurance contracts, as Adia did not have an insurable interest. Discuss their claims.

49–2. INSURER'S DEFENSES. Patrick contracts with an Ajax Insurance Co. agent for a $50,000 ordinary life insurance policy. The application form is filled in to show Patrick's age as thirty-two. In addition, the application form asks whether Patrick has ever had any heart ailments or problems. Patrick answers no, forgetting that as a young child he was diagnosed as having a slight heart murmur. A policy is issued. Three years later, Patrick becomes seriously ill. A review of the policy discloses that Patrick was actually thirty-three at the time of application and issuance of the policy and that he erred in answering the question about a history of heart ailments. Discuss whether Ajax can void the policy and escape liability on Patrick's death.

49–3. ASSIGNMENT OF INSURANCE. Sapata has an ordinary life insurance policy on her life and a fire insurance policy on her house. Both policies have been in force for a number of years. Sapata's life insurance names her son, Rory, as beneficiary. Sapata has specifi-

cally removed her right to change beneficiaries, and the life policy is silent on right of assignment. Sapata is going on a one-year European vacation and borrows money from Leonard to finance the trip. Leonard takes an assignment of the life insurance policy as security for the loan, as the policy has accumulated a substantial cash surrender value. Sapata also rents out her house to Leonard and assigns to him her fire insurance policy. Discuss fully whether Sapata's assignment of these policies is valid.

49–4. COINSURANCE CLAUSES. Fritz has an open fire insurance policy on his home for a maximum liability of $60,000. The policy has a number of standard clauses, including the right of the insurer to restore or rebuild the property in lieu of a monetary payment, and it has a standard coinsurance clause. A fire in Fritz's house virtually destroys a utility room and part of the kitchen. The fire was caused by the overheating of an electric water heater. The total damage to the property is $10,000. The property at the time of loss is valued at $100,000. Fritz files a proof-of-loss claim for $10,000. Discuss the insurer's liability in this situation.

49–5. MULTIPLE INSURANCE COVERAGE. Lori has a large house. She secures two open fire insurance policies on the house. Her policy with the Ajax Insurance Co. is for a maximum of $100,000, and her policy with the Beta Insurance Co. is for a maximum of $50,000. Lori's house burns to the ground. The value of the house at the time of the loss is $120,000. Discuss the liability of Ajax and Beta to Lori.

49–6. EFFECTIVE DATE OF COVERAGE. Robert Gladney applied for disability insurance from Paul Revere Life Insurance Co., enclosing with the application a check for $3,100, which represented the first semi-annual premium. The issuance of the policy was conditional on the insurance company's receipt of a medical form that was to be completed by Gladney's doctor following a physical examination. Gladney was a busy man and kept putting off the physical examination. Over a month later, Gladney submitted a second application, because the first one was too old. The insurance agent advised Gladney to leave the application undated so that if Gladney failed to have the physical examination within a month, he would not have to submit yet a third application. Gladney told the agent that he would notify him when the examination was completed. Soon thereafter, Gladney fell ill. His doctor examined him but did not conduct all the tests normally required by Paul Revere for disability insurance. A month later, Gladney was hospitalized and underwent heart surgery. Gladney never told the insurance agent about his visit to the doctor and the fact that the doctor had examined him. Gladney now claims that he is entitled to disability benefits under the policy because he paid the premium and would have been approved for insurance had he notified the insurance company of his examination. Will the court agree? Discuss fully. [*Gladney v. Paul Revere Life Insurance Co.*, 895 F.2d 238 (5th Cir. 1990)]

49–7. INSURER'S DEFENSES. Kirk Johnson applied for life insurance with New York Life Insurance Co. on October 7, 1986. In answer to a question about smoking habits, Johnson stated that he had not smoked in the past twelve months and that he had never smoked cigarettes. In fact, Johnson had smoked for thirteen years, and during the month prior to the insurance application, he was smoking approximately ten cigarettes per day. Johnson died on July 17, 1988, for reasons unrelated to smoking. Johnson's father, Lawrence Johnson, who was the beneficiary of the policy, filed a claim for the insurance proceeds. While investigating the claim, New York Life discovered Kirk Johnson's misrepresentation and denied the claim. The company canceled the policy and sent Lawrence Johnson a check for the premiums that had been paid. Lawrence Johnson refused to accept the check, and New York Life brought an action for a declaratory judgment (a court determination of a plaintiff's rights). What should the court decide? Discuss fully. [*New York Life Insurance Co. v. Johnson*, 923 F.2d 279 (3d Cir. 1991)]

49–8. INSURER'S DEFENSES. Jeffrey Duke purchased a life insurance policy on his own life from New England Mutual Life Insurance Co. Duke listed as his beneficiary his lover and business adviser, William Remmelink. On his insurance application, however, Duke described his beneficiary as merely his business partner. After Duke died of acquired immune deficiency syndrome (AIDS), New England Mutual brought an action against William Johnson, the executor of Duke's estate, to rescind (cancel) the insurance contract on the ground that Duke had "materially misrepresented his relationship with his beneficiary." Johnson claimed that New England Mutual's attempt to rescind the contract was in bad faith and asked for

both punitive damages and attorneys' fees. During the trial, an underwriter with twenty-four years of experience testified that New England Mutual had never before rescinded a policy because of a misrepresentation regarding the relationship between the beneficiary and the insured. Did Duke mischaracterize his relationship with his beneficiary? If so, was such a misrepresentation material? How should the court decide? [*New England Mutual Life Insurance Co. v. Johnson*, 155 Misc.2d 680, 589 N.Y.S.2d 736 (1992)]

49–9. INSURER'S DEFENSES. The City of Worcester, Massachusetts, adopted an ordinance in 1990 that required rooming houses to be equipped with automatic sprinkler systems no later than September 25, 1995. In Worcester, James and Mark Duffy owned a forty-eight-room lodging house with two retail stores on the first floor. In 1994, the Duffys applied with General Star Indemnity Co. for an insurance policy to cover the premises. The application indicated that the premises had sprinkler systems. General issued a policy that required, among other safety features, a sprinkler system. Within a month, the premises were inspected on behalf of General. On the inspection form forwarded to the insurer, in the list of safety systems, next to the word "sprinkler" the inspector had inserted only a hyphen. In July 1995, when the premises sustained over $100,000 in fire damage, General learned that there was no sprinkler system. The insurer filed a suit in a federal district court against the Duffys to rescind the policy, alleging misrepresentation in their insurance application about the presence of sprinklers. How should the court rule, and why? [*General Star Indemnity Co. v. Duffy*, 191 F.3d 55 (1st Cir. 1999)]

49–10. IN YOUR COURT

Metro Insurance Co. issued an insurance policy to Kevin Moore to cover his aircraft. One provision of the policy excluded coverage for a "resident spouse." A different provision included coverage for "any passenger." Kevin was piloting the aircraft, with his wife, Sheila, as a passenger, when it crashed. Kevin was killed, and Sheila was injured. At the time, Sheila and Kevin had been living together. Sheila filed a suit in a federal district court to collect under the policy for her injuries. Metro claimed that the policy clearly excluded Sheila. Sheila argued that the policy was ambiguous. Assume that you are the judge in the trial court hearing this case and answer the following questions:

(a) In your opinion, is the Metro policy ambiguous as to who would or would not be covered under the policy?

(b) Generally, when a contract includes ambiguous terms, which party is held responsible for the ambiguity? Does this principle of contract law apply to insurance contracts as well?

(c) In the case now before your court, how will you rule? Explain your reasoning.

LAW ON THE WEB

For updated links to resources available on the Web, as well as a variety of other materials, visit this text's Web site at http://wbl.westbuslaw.com.

For a summary of the law governing insurance contracts in the United States, including rules of interpretation, go to

http://www.consumerlawpage.com/article/insureds.shtml

The law firm of Anderson Kill & Olick usually includes a number of articles relating to insurance on its Web site. Go to the following URL and click on "What's New":

http://www.andersonkill.com/home2.cgi

LEGAL RESEARCH EXERCISES ON THE WEB

Go to http://wbl.westbuslaw.com, the Web site that accompanies this text. Select "Internet Applications," and then click on "Chapter 49." There you will find the following Internet research exercises that you can perform to learn more about new types of insurance coverage and some of the consequences of settlements in insurance cases:

Activity 49–1: Technoinsurance

Activity 49–2: Disappearing Decisions

CHAPTER 50

Wills, Trusts, and Elder Law

As the old adage states, "You can't take it with you." All of the real and personal property that you own will be transferred on your death to others. A person can direct the passage of his or her property after death by *will*, subject to certain limitations imposed by the state. If no valid will has been executed, the decedent is said to have died **intestate,** and state **intestacy laws** prescribe the distribution of the property among heirs or next of kin. If no heirs or kin can be found, the property will **escheat**[1] (title will be transferred to the state). In addition, a person can transfer property through a *trust.* In a trust arrangement, the owner (who may be called the grantor or the settlor) of the property transfers legal title to a trustee, who has a duty imposed by law to hold the property for the use or benefit of another (the beneficiary).

Wills and trusts are two basic devices used in the process of **estate planning**—planning in advance how one's property and obligations should be transferred on death. In this chapter, we examine wills and trusts in some detail. Other estate-planning devices include life insurance (discussed in Chapter 49) and joint-tenancy arrangements (described in Chapter 46). Typically, estate planning involves consultations with professionals, including attorneys, accountants, and financial planners.

For many people, a major estate-planning consideration is the possibility of becoming incapacitated,

through accident or illness, at some future time or of needing long-term health care. In the final section of this chapter, we look at a relatively new legal specialty, *elder law,* which addresses these and other needs of older persons.

Section 1

Wills

A **will** is the final declaration of how a person desires to have his or her property disposed of after death. One who makes a will is known as a **testator** (from the Latin *testari,* "to make a will"). A will is referred to as a *testamentary disposition* of property, and one who dies after having made a valid will is said to have died **testate.**

A will can serve other purposes besides the distribution of property. It can appoint a guardian for minor children or incapacitated adults. It can also appoint a personal representative to settle the affairs of the deceased. An **executor** is a personal representative named in a will. An **administrator** is a personal representative appointed by the court for a decedent who dies without a will, who fails to name an executor in the will, who names an executor lacking the capacity to serve, or who writes a will that the court refuses to admit to probate. Exhibit 50–1 presents a copy of the will written by John Lennon, the musician and former member of the "Beatles" musical group.

---

1. Pronounced ush-*cheet.*

EXHIBIT 50–1   A SAMPLE WILL

LAST WILL AND TESTAMENT
OF
JOHN WINSTON ONO LENNON

I, JOHN WINSTON ONO LENNON, a resident of the County of New York, State of New York, which I declare to be my domicile do hereby make, publish and declare this to be my Last Will and Testament, hereby revoking all other Wills, Codicils and Testamentary dispositions by me at any time heretofore made.

FIRST: The expenses of my funeral and the administration of my estate, and all inheritance, estate or successions taxes, including interest and penalties, payable by reason of my death shall be paid out of and charged generally against the principal of my residuary estate without apportionment or proration. My Executor shall not seek contribution or reimbursement for any such payments.

SECOND: Should my wife survive me, I give, devise and bequeath to her absolutely, an amount equal to that portion of my residuary estate, the numerator and denominator of which shall be determined as follows:

1. The numerator shall be an amount equal to one-half ($\frac{1}{2}$) of my adjusted gross estate less the value of all other property included in my gross estate for Federal Estate Tax purposes and which pass or shall have passed to my wife either under any other provision of this Will or in any manner outside of this Will in such manner as to qualify for and be allowed as a marital deduction. The words "pass," "have passed," "marital deduction" and "adjusted gross estate" shall have the same meaning as said words have under those provisions of the United States Internal Revenue Code applicable to my estate.

2. The denominator shall be an amount representing the value of my residuary estate.

THIRD: I give, devise and bequeath all the rest, residue and remainder of my estate, wheresoever situated, to the Trustees under a Trust Agreement dated November 12, 1979, which I signed with my wife YOKO ONO, and ELI GARBER as Trustees, to be added to the trust property and held and distributed in accordance with the terms of that agreement and any amendments made pursuant to its terms before my death.

FOURTH: In the event that my wife and I die under such circumstances that there is not sufficient evidence to determine which of us has predeceased the other, I hereby declare it to be my will that it shall be deemed that I shall have predeceased her and that this, my Will, and any and all of its provisions shall be construed based upon that assumption.

FIFTH: I hereby nominate, constitute and appoint my beloved wife, YOKO ONO, to act as the Executor of this my Last Will and Testament. In the event that my beloved wife YOKO ONO shall predecease me or chooses not to act for any reason, I nominate and appoint ELI GARBER, DAVID WARMFLASH and CHARLES PETTIT, in the order named, to act in her place and stead.

SIXTH: I nominate, constitute and appoint my wife YOKO ONO, as the Guardian of the person and property of any children of the marriage who may survive me. In the event that she predeceases me, or for any reason she chooses not to act in that capacity, I nominate, constitute and appoint SAM GREEN to act in her place and stead.

SEVENTH: No person named herein to serve in any fiduciary capacity shall be required to file or post any bond for the faithful performance of his or her duties, in that capacity in this or in any other jurisdiction, any law to the contrary notwithstanding.

EIGHTH: If any legatee or beneficiary under this will or the trust agreement between myself as Grantor and YOKO ONO LENNON and ELI GARBER as Trustees, dated November 12, 1979 shall interpose objections to the probate of this Will, or institute or prosecute or be in any way interested or instrumental in the institution or prosecution of any action or proceeding for the purpose of setting aside or invalidating this Will, then and in each such case, I direct that such legatee or beneficiary shall receive nothing whatsoever under this Will or the aforementioned Trust.

IN WITNESS WHEREOF, I have subscribed and sealed and do publish and declare these presents as and for my Last Will and Testament, this 12th day of November, 1979.

/s/

John Winston Ono Lennon

THE FOREGOING INSTRUMENT consisting of four (4) typewritten pages, including this page, was on the 12th day of November, 1979, signed, sealed, published and declared by JOHN WINSTON ONO LENNON, the Testator therein named as and for his Last Will and Testament, in the presence of us, who at his request, and in his presence, and in the presence of each other, have hereunto set our names as witnesses.

(The names of the three witnesses are illegible.)

LAWS GOVERNING WILLS

Laws governing wills come into play when a will is probated. To **probate** (prove) a will means to establish its validity and carry the administration of the estate through a process supervised by a probate court. Probate laws vary from state to state. In 1969, however, the American Bar Association and the National Conference of Commissioners on Uniform State Laws approved the Uniform Probate Code (UPC).

The UPC, which was significantly revised in 1990, codifies general principles and procedures for the resolution of conflicts in settling estates and relaxes some of the requirements for a valid will contained in earlier state laws. Nearly all of the states have enacted some part of the UPC and incorporated it into their own probate codes. For this reason, references to its provisions will be included in this chapter. Nonetheless, succession and inheritance laws vary widely among states, and one should always check the particular laws of the state involved.[2]

GIFTS BY WILL

A gift of real estate by will is generally called a **devise,** and a gift of personal property under a will is called a **bequest,** or **legacy.** The recipient of a gift by will is a *devisee* or a *legatee,* depending on whether the gift was a devise or a legacy.

Types of Gifts.   Gifts by will can be specific, general, or residuary. A *specific* devise or bequest (legacy) describes particular property (such as "Eastwood Estate" or "my gold pocket watch") that can be distinguished from the rest of the testator's property. A *general* devise or bequest (legacy) uses less restrictive terminology. For example, "I devise all my lands" is a general devise. A general bequest often specifies a sum of money instead of a particular item of property, such as a watch or an automobile. For example, "I give to my nephew, Carleton, $30,000" is a general bequest.

Sometimes a will provides that any assets remaining after specific gifts have been made and debts have been paid—called the *residuary* (or *residuum*) of the estate—are to be given to the testator's spouse, distributed to the testator's descendants, or disposed of in some other way. If the testator has not indicated what party or parties should receive the residuary of the estate, the residuary passes according to state laws of intestacy.

Abatement.   If the assets of an estate are insufficient to pay in full all general bequests provided for in the will, an *abatement* takes place, meaning that the legatees receive reduced benefits. For example, Julie's will leaves "$15,000 each to my children, Tamara and Lynn." On Julie's death, only $10,000 is available to honor these bequests. By abatement, each child will receive $5,000. If bequests are more complicated, abatement may be more complex. The testator's intent, as expressed in the will, controls.

Lapsed Legacies.   If a legatee dies prior to the death of the testator or before the legacy is payable, a lapsed legacy results. At common law, the legacy failed. Today, the legacy may not lapse if the legatee is in a certain blood relationship to the testator (such as a child, grandchild, brother, or sister) and has left a child or other surviving descendant.

REQUIREMENTS FOR A VALID WILL

A will must comply with statutory formalities designed to ensure that the testator understood his or her actions at the time the will was made. These formalities are intended to help prevent fraud. Unless they are followed, the will is declared void, and the decedent's property is distributed according to the laws of intestacy of that state. The requirements are not uniform among the jurisdictions. Most states, however, uphold certain basic requirements for executing a will. We now look at these requirements.

Testamentary Capacity and Intent.   For a will to be valid, the testator must have testamentary capacity—that is, the testator must be of legal age and sound mind *at the time the will is made.* The legal age for executing a will varies, but in most states and under the UPC the minimum age is eighteen years [UPC 2–501]. Thus, the will of a twenty-one-year-old decedent written when the person was sixteen is invalid if, under state law, the legal age for executing a will is eighteen.

The concept of "being of sound mind" refers to the testator's ability to formulate and to comprehend a personal plan for the disposition of property. Generally, a testator must (1) intend the document to be his or her last will and testament, (2) comprehend the kind and character of the property being distributed, and (3) comprehend and remember the "natural objects of his or her bounty" (usually, family members and persons for whom the testator has affection).

---

2. For example, California law differs substantially from the UPC.

A valid will is one that represents the maker's intention to transfer and distribute his or her property. When it can be shown that the decedent's plan of distribution was the result of fraud or of undue influence, the will is declared invalid. Undue influence may be inferred by the court if the testator ignored blood relatives and named as beneficiary a nonrelative who was in constant close contact with the testator and in a position to influence the making of the will. For example, if a nurse or friend caring for the testator at the time of death was named as beneficiary to the exclusion of all family members, the validity of the will might well be challenged on the basis of undue influence.

In the following case, the issue before the court was whether the testator intended his estate to be distributed to his relatives and friends in sixteen equal shares or in fourteen equal shares. The court looked first at the words used by the testator in his will to determine his intent.

CASE 50.1   Estate of Klauzer

Supreme Court of
South Dakota, 2000.
604 N.W.2d 474.
http://www.sdbar.org/
opinions/sdindex.htm[a]

BACKGROUND AND FACTS   *John Klauzer executed a will in 1990 and passed away in 1996. His estate was valued at $1.4 million. The will appointed his brother Frank as personal representative of the estate. The will disposed of the majority of his estate in a residuary clause:*

> *I hereby give, devise and bequeath unto my brother, Thomas Klauzer, my sister, Agnes Blake, my sister, Anna Malenovsky Baker, my brother, Raymond Klauzer, my niece, Jenny Culver, my niece, Judy Klauzer, my niece, Bernice Cunningham, my nephew, Wade Klauzer, my nephew, Jim Klauzer, my niece, Debra Klauzer, friends, Douglas Olson and Fern Olson, and my friends, William Hollister and Shirley Hollister, my brother, Frank Klauzer, and my sister-in-law, Patricia Klauzer, all of my property of every kind and character and wheresoever situated, in equal shares, share and share alike. That should any of the individuals above named predecease me, then their share of my estate shall go to their [descendants] surviving.*

Klauzer's nephew Wade asked a South Dakota state court to supervise the administration of the estate. The court ordered in part that, under the residuary clause, the estate should be distributed in sixteen equal shares. Frank objected and appealed to the South Dakota Supreme Court. Frank argued that the twelve Klauzer relatives named in the clause should take one share each while friends, Doug and Fern Olson and William and Shirley Hollister, should receive one share per couple, resulting in a division of the estate into fourteen equal shares.

**IN THE LANGUAGE
OF THE COURT**

SABERS, Justice.

*   *   *   *

Our goal in interpreting a will is to discern the testator's intent. If the intent is clear from the language used, that intent controls. However, if *   *   * doubt remains as to [the] decedent's intent, the language used and the circumstances surrounding the execution of the writing will again be examined in light of pertinent rules of construction. Our inquiry is limited to what the testator meant by what he said, not what we think the testator meant to say.

*   *   * Language is ambiguous when it is reasonably capable of being understood in more than one sense. An ambiguity is not of itself created simply because the parties differ as to the interpretation of the will. *   *   * *All the words and provisions appearing in a will must be given effect as far as possible, and none should be cast aside as meaningless.* [Emphasis added.]

---

a. This Web site is maintained by the State Bar of South Dakota. In the left column, click on "2000 Opinions." On that page, scroll down the list to the case and click on the name to access the opinion.

The [residuary] clause in John's will * * * names each individual followed by their relationship to John. Olsons and Hollisters are referenced as follows: "friends, Douglas Olson and Fern Olson, and my friends, William Hollister and Shirley Hollister * * * ." Each spouse is named as an individual. They are not referred to as "Mr. and Mrs. Olson" nor as "William and Shirley Hollister."

The clause contains other language to support the position that John intended that his estate be divided sixteen ways versus fourteen ways. After naming all sixteen individuals, the clause provides that they should receive his property "in equal shares, share and share alike. That should any of the individuals above named predecease me, then their share of my estate shall go to their [descendants] surviving."

First, John refers to his friends as individuals. Second, he requests that they receive his property "in equal shares, share and share alike." Third, he states that if one individual predeceases him, his or her share "shall go to their [descendants] surviving." In this regard, it is important to point out that married couples may have different descendants.

We determine that the testator's intent is clearly expressed within the four corners of the document [within the document itself]. We are bound by the unambiguous language of the will. Therefore, extrinsic evidence [evidence external to the will] is not needed. * * *

* * * *

The structure and language of the clause itself * * * convince us that John intended to leave one share to Douglas Olson, one share to Fern Olson, one share to William Hollister and one share to Shirley Hollister. Therefore, we affirm the trial court's order to distribute the estate in sixteen equal shares.

DECISION AND REMEDY   *The South Dakota Supreme Court affirmed the decision of the lower court. The language of the will evidenced the testator's intent regarding the distribution of his property in sixteen equal shares.*

Writing Requirements. Generally, a will must be in writing. The writing itself can be informal as long as it substantially complies with the statutory requirements. In some states, a will can be handwritten in crayon or ink. It can be written on a sheet or scrap of paper, on a paper bag, or on a piece of cloth. A will that is completely in the handwriting of the testator is called a **holographic will** (sometimes referred to as an *olographic will*).

A **nuncupative will** is an oral will made before witnesses. It is not permitted in most states. Where authorized by statute, such wills are generally valid only if made during the last illness of the testator and are therefore sometimes referred to as *deathbed wills*. Normally, only personal property can be transferred by a nuncupative will. Statutes frequently permit soldiers and sailors to make nuncupative wills when on active duty.

Signature Requirements. A fundamental requirement for a valid will is that the testator's signature appear on the will, generally at the end of the document. Each jurisdiction dictates by statute and court decision what constitutes a signature. Initials, an X or other mark, and words such as "Mom" have all been upheld as valid when it was shown that the testators *intended* them to be signatures.

Witness Requirements. A will normally must be attested (sworn to) by two, and sometimes three, witnesses. The number of witnesses, their qualifications, and the manner in which the witnessing must be done are generally set out in a statute. A witness may be required to be disinterested—that is, not a beneficiary under the will. The UPC, however, provides that a will is valid even if it is attested by an interested witness [UPC 2–505]. There are no age requirements for witnesses, but witnesses must be mentally competent.

The purpose of witnesses is to verify that the testator actually executed (signed) the will and had the requisite intent and capacity at the time. A witness does not have to read the contents of the will. Usually, the testator and all witnesses must sign in the sight or the presence of one another, but the UPC deems it sufficient if the testator acknowledges his or her signature to the witnesses [UPC 2–502]. The UPC does not require all parties to sign in the presence of one another.

Publication Requirements.

The maker of a will *publishes* the will by orally declaring to the witnesses that the document they are about to sign is his or her "last will and testament." Publication is becoming an unnecessary formality in most states, and it is not required under the UPC.

REVOCATION OF WILLS

An executed will is revocable by the maker at any time during the maker's lifetime. The maker may revoke a will by a physical act, such as tearing up the will, or by a subsequent writing. Wills can also be revoked by operation of law. Revocation can be partial or complete, and it must follow certain strict formalities.

Revocation by a Physical Act of the Maker.

The testator may revoke a will by intentionally burning, tearing, canceling, obliterating, or destroying it or by having someone else do so in the presence of the maker and at the maker's direction.[3] In some states, partial revocation by physical act of the maker is recognized. Thus, those portions of a will lined out or torn away are dropped, and the remaining parts of the will are valid. In no case, however, can a provision be crossed out and an additional or substitute provision written in. Such altered portions require reexecution (re-signing) and reattestation (rewitnessing).

To revoke a will by physical act, it is necessary to follow the mandates of a state statute exactly. When a state statute prescribes the specific methods for revoking a will by physical act, those are the only methods that will revoke the will.

Revocation by a Subsequent Writing.

A will may also be wholly or partially revoked by a **codicil**, a written instrument separate from the will that amends or revokes provisions in the will. A codicil

eliminates the necessity of redrafting an entire will merely to add to it or amend it. It can also be used to revoke an entire will. The codicil must be executed with the same formalities required for a will, and it must refer expressly to the will. In effect, it updates a will, because the will is "incorporated by reference" into the codicil.

A new will (second will) can be executed that may or may not revoke the first or a prior will, depending on the language used. To revoke a prior will, the second will must use language specifically revoking other wills, such as, "This will hereby revokes all prior wills." If the second will is otherwise valid and properly executed, it will revoke all prior wills. If the express *declaration of revocation* is missing, then both wills are read together. If any of the dispositions made in the second will are inconsistent with the prior will, the second will controls.

Revocation by Operation of Law.

Revocation by operation of law occurs when marriage, divorce or annulment, or the birth of a child takes place after a will has been executed. In most states, when a testator marries after executing a will that does not include the new spouse, on the testator's death the spouse can still receive the amount he or she would have taken had the testator died intestate (how an intestate's property is distributed under state laws will be discussed shortly). In effect, this revokes the will to the point of providing the spouse with an intestate share. The rest of the estate is passed under the will [UPC 2–301, 2–508]. If, however, the new spouse is otherwise provided for in the will (or by transfer of property outside the will), the new spouse will not be given an intestate amount.

At common law and under the UPC, divorce does not necessarily revoke the entire will. A divorce or an annulment occurring after a will has been executed will revoke those dispositions of property made under the will to the former spouse [UPC 2–508].

If a child is born after a will has been executed and if it appears that the deceased parent would have made a provision for the child, then the child is entitled to receive whatever portion of the estate he or she is allowed under state laws providing for the distribution of an intestate's property. Most state laws allow a child to receive some portion of a parent's estate if no provision is made in the parent's will, unless it appears from the terms of the will that the testator intended to disinherit the child. Under the UPC, the rule is the same.

---

3. The destruction cannot be inadvertent. The maker's intent to revoke must be shown. When a will has been burned or torn accidentally, it is normally recommended that the maker have a new document created so that it will not falsely appear that the maker intended to revoke the will.

RIGHTS UNDER A WILL

The law imposes certain limitations on the way a person can dispose of property in a will. For example, a married person who makes a will generally cannot avoid leaving a certain portion of the estate to the surviving spouse. In most states, this is called an elective share, a forced share, or a widow's (or widower's) share, and it is often one-third of the estate or an amount equal to a spouse's share under intestacy laws.

Beneficiaries under a will have rights as well. A beneficiary can renounce (disclaim) his or her share of the property given under a will. Further, a surviving spouse can renounce the amount given under a will and elect to take the forced share when the forced share is larger than the amount of the gift—this is the widow's (or widower's) election, or right of election. State statutes provide the methods by which a surviving spouse accomplishes renunciation. The purpose of these statutes is to allow the spouse to obtain whichever distribution would be most advantageous. The revised UPC gives the surviving spouse an elective right to take a percentage of the total estate determined by the length of time that the spouse and the decedent were married to each other [UPC 2–201].

PROBATE PROCEDURES

Typically, probate procedures vary, depending on the size of the decedent's estate.

Informal Probate Proceedings. For smaller estates, most state statutes provide for the distribution of assets without formal probate proceedings. Faster and less expensive methods are then used. For example, property can be transferred by affidavit (a written statement taken in the presence of a person who has authority to affirm it), and problems or questions can be handled during an administrative hearing. In addition, some state statutes provide that title to cars, savings and checking accounts, and certain other property can be passed merely by filling out forms.

A majority of states also provide for family settlement agreements, which are private agreements among the beneficiaries. Once a will is admitted to probate, the family members can agree to settle among themselves the distribution of the decedent's assets. Although a family settlement agreement speeds the settlement process, a court order is still needed to protect the estate from future creditors and to clear title to the assets

involved. The use of these and other types of summary procedures in estate administration can save time and money.

Formal Probate Proceedings. For larger estates, formal probate proceedings are normally undertaken, and the probate court supervises every aspect of the settlement of the decedent's estate. Additionally, in some situations—such as when a guardian for minor children or for an incompetent person must be appointed and a trust has been created to protect the minor or the incompetent person—more formal probate procedures cannot be avoided. Formal probate proceedings may take several months to complete, and as a result, a sizable portion of the decedent's assets (up to perhaps 10 percent) may have to go toward payment of fees charged by attorneys and personal representatives, as well as court costs.

PROPERTY TRANSFERS OUTSIDE THE PROBATE PROCESS

Commonly, beneficiaries under a will must wait until the probate process is complete—which can take several months if formal probate proceedings are undertaken—to have access to money or other assets received under the will. For this and other reasons, some persons arrange to have property transferred in ways other than by will and outside the probate process.

One method of accomplishing this is by establishing a living trust, as discussed later in this chapter. Another method is through the joint ownership of property. For example, a person can arrange to hold title to certain real or personal property as a joint tenant with a spouse or other person. Recall from Chapter 46 that in a joint tenancy, when one joint tenant dies, the other joint tenant or tenants automatically inherit the deceased tenant's share of the property. This is true even if the deceased tenant has provided otherwise in his or her will.

Yet another way of transferring property outside the probate process is by making gifts to children or others while one is still living. Additionally, to make sure that a spouse, children, or some other dependent is provided for, many people take out life insurance policies. On the death of the policyholder, the proceeds of the policy go directly to the beneficiary and are not involved in the probate process. The balance in an Individual Retirement Account (IRA) may also pass to a named beneficiary without being involved in the probate process.

CONCEPT SUMMARY 50.1

WILLS

CONCEPT	DESCRIPTION
Terminology	1. *Intestate*—Describes one who dies without a valid will. 2. *Testator*—A person who makes out a will. 3. *Personal representative*—A person appointed in a will or by a court to settle the affairs of a decedent. A personal representative named in the will is an *executor*; a personal representative appointed by the court for an intestate decedent is an *administrator*. 4. *Devise*—A gift of real estate by will; may be general or specific. The recipient of a devise is a *devisee*. 5. *Bequest, or legacy*—A gift of personal property by will; may be general or specific. The recipient of a bequest (legacy) is a *legatee*.
Requirements for a Valid Will	1. The testator must have testamentary capacity (be of legal age and sound mind at the time the will is made). 2. A will must be in writing (except for nuncupative wills). 3. A will must be signed by the testator; what constitutes a signature varies from jurisdiction to jurisdiction. 4. A nonholographic will normally must be witnessed in the manner prescribed by state statute. 5. A will may have to be *published*—that is, the testator may be required to announce to witnesses that this is his or her "last will and testament." Not required under the UPC.

Revocation of Wills	1. *By physical act of the maker*—Tearing up, canceling, obliterating, or deliberately destroying part or all of a will.
	2. *By subsequent writing*—
	  a. Codicil—A formal, separate document that amends or revokes an existing will.
	  b. Second will, or new will—A new, properly executed will expressly revoking the existing will.
	3. *By operation of law*—
	  a. Marriage—Generally revokes a will written before the marriage to the extent of providing for the spouse.
	  b. Divorce or annulment—Revokes dispositions of property made to the former spouse under a will made before the divorce or annulment.
	  c. Subsequently born child—It is inferred that the child is entitled to receive the portion of the estate granted under intestacy distribution laws.

Probate Procedures	To *probate* a will means to establish its validity and to carry the administration of the estate through a court process. Probate laws vary from state to state. Probate procedures may be informal or formal, depending on the size of the estate and other factors, such as whether a guardian for minor children must be appointed.

In all of these situations, the person who sets up the living trust, arranges for the joint tenancy, takes out the insurance policy, or names a beneficiary for an IRA should pay careful attention as to whom the arrangement benefits. A court will not apply the same principles in reviewing a transfer outside probate as it would apply to a testamentary transfer, as indicated in the following case.

CASE 50.2   Bielat v. Bielat

Supreme Court
of Ohio, 2000.
87 Ohio St.3d 350,
721 N.E.2d 28.
http://www.
lawyersweekly.com/
ohsc.htm[a]

BACKGROUND AND FACTS   *In 1983, Chester Bielat opened an Individual Retirement Account (IRA) with Merrill Lynch, Pierce, Fenner & Smith, Inc. In the "Adoption Agreement" that he signed to open the account, Chester named his sister, Stella, as the beneficiary of the account on his death. Later, Chester executed a will that gave all of his property to his wife, Dorothy, on his death. In 1993, Ohio enacted its version of the Uniform Transfer-on-Death Security Registration Act, which provided that "[a]ny transfer-on-death resulting from a registration in beneficiary form . . . is not testamentary." This exempted such transfers from the formalities that apply to testamentary dispositions. The act applied to registrations in beneficiary forms made "prior to, on, or after the effective date of this section." After Chester's death in 1996, Dorothy discovered that Stella was the beneficiary of the IRA. Dorothy filed a complaint in an Ohio state court against Stella, claiming that she was entitled to the IRA. She argued in part that because the state constitution prohibited the legislature from passing retroactive laws and protected "vested rights" from "new legislative encroachments," the act did not apply to Chester's IRA beneficiary clause. Dorothy asserted that the court should apply the law in effect when Chester executed his will, which, according to Dorothy, would void the designation of Stella as the beneficiary of the IRA. Stella responded with a motion to dismiss, which the court granted. Dorothy appealed to a state intermediate appellate court, which affirmed the lower court's judgment. Dorothy appealed to the Ohio Supreme Court.*

**IN THE LANGUAGE
OF THE COURT**

COOK, J. [Justice]
    *   *   *   *

Dorothy cannot claim a vested right to the proceeds of the IRA under the law of contracts, for she was in no way connected to the IRA Adoption Agreement that Mr. Bielat executed with Merrill Lynch. *   *   * The Adoption Agreement signed by Mr. Bielat and Merrill Lynch placed valid contractual obligations upon them, with Merrill Lynch bound to pay the IRA balance to the beneficiary that Chester designated. The IRA Adoption Agreement created no rights or obligations for Dorothy. Dorothy thus had no vested contractual right impaired by the retroactive application of the disputed statutes; she had no contractual rights to impair.

Likewise, at the time of the [Uniform Transfer-on-Death Security Registration] Act's effective date, Dorothy had no vested right to the IRA proceeds as the sole beneficiary under Chester's will. *   *   * *Until a will has been probated, the legatee under such will has no rights whatever. A mere expectation of property in the future is not a vested right.* *   *   * If Dorothy had no vested rights in the contract that Mr. Bielat executed with Merrill Lynch, and no vested rights in Chester's probate estate until his death, then the Act did not impair any vested rights of hers when it applied retrospectively to validate the pay-on-death beneficiary clause in Chester's preexisting contract with Merrill Lynch. [Emphasis added.]
    *   *   *   *

*   *   * Dorothy [also] submits that to resolve this dispute, we should apply the law in effect at the time Mr. Bielat executed his will, since that is the law that frames the intent of the testator. Dorothy argues that since Chester executed his will prior to the existence of the Act, he must have done so with the expectation that the designation of Stella as the transfer-on-death beneficiary of his IRA was void, since the Act was not yet in place to explicitly validate it. *   *   * [This argument] represents a correct statement of the law of interpreting wills, but we are not interpreting Chester's will in this case. This is not a will contest action, where the true intent of the testator may be at the heart

a. This Web site is maintained by Lawyers Weekly, Inc., a publisher of legal newspapers for practicing attorneys. In the "2000 Opinions" section, click on "January." When the page opens, scroll to the name of the case and click on it to access the opinion.

of the dispute, nor is it a situation where an unclear testamentary provision requires construction by the court. Rather, we are faced with two equally unambiguous acts by Mr. Bielat: (1) the designation of his sister Stella as the beneficiary of his IRA in his contract with Merrill Lynch, and (2) the clause in his will leaving all of his property to Dorothy.

DECISION AND REMEDY *The Ohio Supreme Court affirmed the judgment of the state intermediate appellate court. The state supreme court reasoned that Dorothy's rights were not impaired by the state's version of the Uniform Transfer-on-Death Security Registration Act because she had no right to the IRA proceeds or to Chester's estate before he died. The court also explained that because the case did not involve the interpretation of a will, the principles that govern interpretation of wills did not apply.*

SECTION 2

Intestacy Laws

Each state regulates by statute how property will be distributed when a person dies intestate (without a valid will). These statutes are called statutes of descent and distribution—or, more simply, intestacy laws, as mentioned in this chapter's introduction. Intestacy laws attempt to carry out the likely intent and wishes of the decedent. These laws assume that deceased persons would have intended that their natural heirs (spouses, children, grandchildren, or other family members) inherit their property. Therefore, intestacy statutes set out rules and priorities under which these heirs inherit the property. If no heirs exist, the state will assume ownership of the property.

The rules of descent vary widely from state to state. It is thus extremely important to refer to the exact terms of the applicable state statutes when addressing any problem of intestacy distribution.

SURVIVING SPOUSE AND CHILDREN

Usually, state statutes provide for the rights of the surviving spouse and children. In addition, the law provides that first the debts of the decedent must be satisfied out of his or her estate, and then the remaining assets can pass to the surviving spouse and the children. A surviving spouse usually receives only a share of the estate—one-half if there is also a surviving child and one-third if there are two or more children. Only if no children or grandchildren survive the decedent will a surviving spouse receive the entire estate.

Assume that Allen dies intestate and is survived by his wife, Della, and his children, Duane and Tara.

Allen's property passes according to intestacy laws. After Allen's outstanding debts are paid, Della will receive the homestead (either in fee simple or as a life estate) and ordinarily a one-third to one-half interest in all other property. The remaining real and personal property will pass to Duane and Tara in equal portions. Under most state intestacy laws and under the UPC, in-laws do not share in an estate. If a child dies before his or her parents, the child's spouse will not receive an inheritance on the parents' death. For example, if Duane died before his father (Allen), Duane's spouse would not inherit Duane's share of Allen's estate.

When there is no surviving spouse or child, the order of inheritance is grandchildren, then parents of the decedent. These relatives are usually called *lineal descendants*. If there are no lineal descendants, then *collateral heirs*—brothers, sisters, nieces, nephews, aunts, and uncles of the decedent—make up the next group to share. If there are no survivors in any of these groups, most statutes provide for the property to be distributed among the next of kin of the collateral heirs.

STEPCHILDREN, ADOPTED CHILDREN, AND ILLEGITIMATE CHILDREN

Under intestacy laws, stepchildren are not considered kin. Legally adopted children, however, are recognized as lawful heirs of their adoptive parents. Whether an illegitimate child inherits depends on state statutes. In some states, intestate succession between the father and the child can occur only when the child has been "legitimized" by ceremony or "acknowledged" by the father. Under the revised UPC, the same rule applies to intestate succession between the child and the mother [UPC 2–114]. The

United States Supreme Court has allowed state illegitimacy statutes to stand, concluding that they serve legitimate state purposes.[4]

DISTRIBUTION TO GRANDCHILDREN

When a person who dies is survived by descendants of deceased children, a question arises as to what share the grandchildren of the decedent will receive. *Per stirpes* is a method of dividing an intestate share by which a class or group of distributees (for example, grandchildren) take the share that their deceased parent would have been entitled to inherit had that parent lived.

Assume that Moss, a widower, has two children, Scott and Jules. Scott has two children (Bonita and Holly), and Jules has one child (Paul). At the time of Moss's death, Scott and Jules have already died. If Moss's estate is distributed *per stirpes*, the following distribution will take place:

1. Bonita and Holly: one-fourth each, taking Scott's share.
2. Paul: one-half, taking Jules's share.

Exhibit 50–2 illustrates the *per stirpes* method of distribution.

An estate may also be distributed on a *per capita* basis. This means that each person takes an equal share of the estate. If Moss's estate is distributed *per capita*, Bonita, Holly, and Paul will each receive a one-third share. Exhibit 50–3 illustrates the *per capita* method of distribution.

SECTION 3

Trusts

A **trust** involves any arrangement by which legal title to property is transferred from one person to be administered by a trustee for another's benefit. It can also be defined as a right of property (real or personal) held by one party for the benefit of another. A trust can be created for any purpose that is not illegal or against public policy. As mentioned, trusts are important estate-planning devices for several reasons. These reasons will become clear as you read through this section.

---

4. *Labine v. Vincent*, 401 U.S. 532, 91 S.Ct. 1017, 28 L.Ed.2d 288 (1971). In *Trimble v. Gordon*, 430 U.S. 762, 97 S.Ct. 1459, 52 L.Ed.2d 31 (1977), however, the United States Supreme Court ruled that an Illinois illegitimacy statute was unconstitutional because it did not bear a rational relationship to a legitimate state purpose.

EXHIBIT 50–2 PER STIRPES DISTRIBUTION

Under this method of distribution, an heir takes the share that his or her deceased parent would have been entitled to inherit, had the parent lived. This may mean that a class of distributees—the grandchildren, in this example—will not inherit in equal portions. (Note that Bonita and Holly receive only one-fourth of Moss's estate, whereas Paul inherits one-half.)

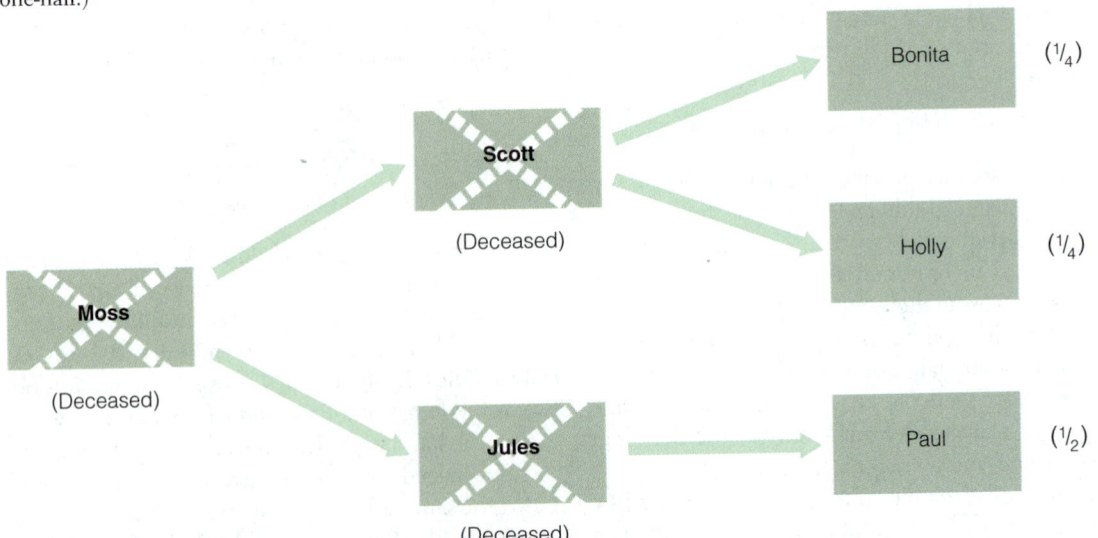

Exhibit 50–3   Per Capita Distribution

Under this method of distribution, all heirs in a certain class—in this case, the grandchildren—inherit equally. Note that Bonita and Holly in this situation each inherit one-third of Moss's estate (not one-fourth, as they do under the *per stirpes* method of distribution).

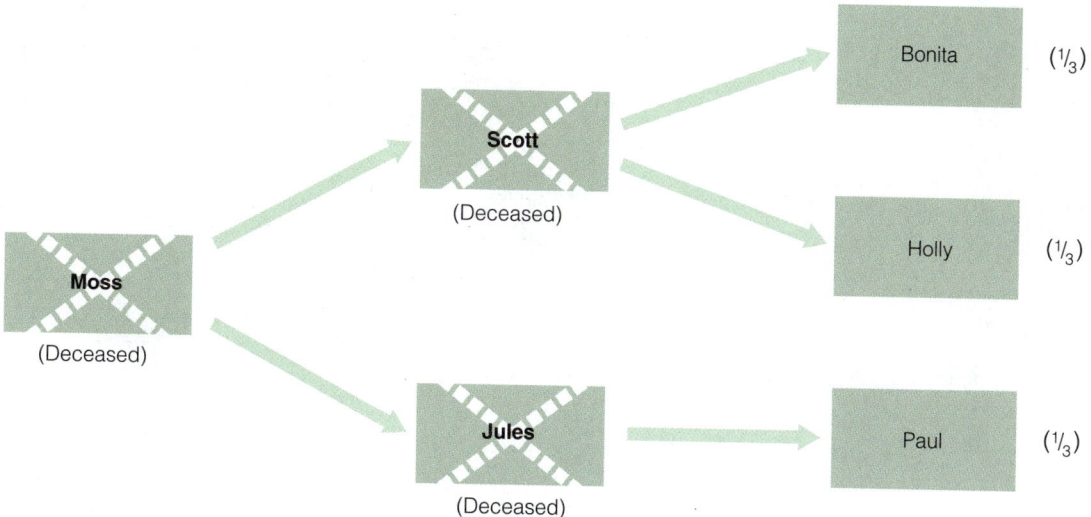

Essential Elements of a Trust

The essential elements of a trust are as follows:

1. A designated beneficiary.
2. A designated trustee.
3. A fund sufficiently identified to enable title to pass to the trustee.
4. Actual delivery to the trustee with the intention of passing title.

If Shanahan conveys his farm to First Bank of Minnesota to be held for the benefit of his daughters, Shanahan has created a trust. Shanahan is the settlor, or grantor (the one creating the trust), First Bank of Minnesota is the trustee, and Shanahan's daughters are the beneficiaries. This arrangement is illustrated in Exhibit 50–4 on page 962.

Express Trusts

An express trust is one that is created or declared in explicit terms, usually in writing. There are numerous types of express trusts, each with its own special characteristics.

Living Trust.   A living trust—or **inter vivos trust** (*inter vivos* is Latin for "between or among the living")—is a trust executed by a grantor during his or her lifetime. A living trust may be an attractive estate-planning option

because living trusts are not included in the property of a decedent's estate that is probated.

Living trusts can be irrevocable or revocable. The distinction between these two types of trusts is an important one for estate planners. In an *irrevocable* living trust, the grantor permanently gives up control over the property. In a *revocable* living trust, in contrast, the grantor retains control over the trust property during his or her lifetime.

To establish an irrevocable living trust, the grantor executes a trust deed, and legal title to the trust property passes to the named trustee. The trustee has a duty to administer the property as directed by the grantor for the benefit and in the interest of the beneficiaries. The trustee must preserve the trust property; make it productive; and, if required by the terms of the trust agreement, pay income to the beneficiaries, all in accordance with the terms of the trust. Once an irrevocable *inter vivos* trust has been created, the grantor has, in effect, given over the property for the benefit of the beneficiaries.

To establish a revocable living trust, the grantor deeds the property to the trust but retains the power to amend, alter, or revoke the trust during his or her lifetime. The grantor may also arrange to receive income earned by the trust assets during his or her lifetime. Unless the trust is revoked, the principal of the trust is transferred to the trust beneficiary on the grantor's death.

EXHIBIT 50–4   TRUST ARRANGEMENT

In a trust, there is a separation of interests in the trust property. The trustee takes *legal* title, which appears to be complete ownership and possession but which does not include the right to receive any benefits from the property. The beneficiary takes *equitable* title, which is the right to receive all benefits from the property.

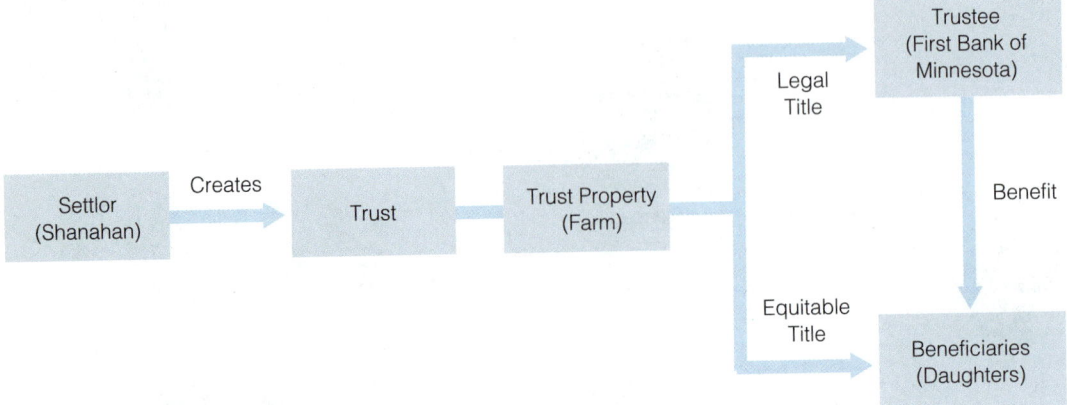

Testamentary Trusts.   A trust created by will to come into existence on the settlor's death is called a **testamentary trust.** Although a testamentary trust has a trustee who maintains legal title to the trust property, actions of the trustee are subject to judicial approval. This trustee can be named in the will or appointed by the court. Thus, a testamentary trust does not fail because a trustee has not been named in the will. The legal responsibilities of the trustee are the same as in an *inter vivos* trust.

If the will setting up a testamentary trust is invalid, then the trust will also be invalid. The property that was supposed to be in the trust will then pass according to intestacy laws, not according to the terms of the trust.

Charitable Trusts.   A trust designed for the benefit of a segment of the public or the public in general is a **charitable trust.** It differs from other types of trusts in that the identities of the beneficiaries are uncertain. Usually, to be deemed a charitable trust, a trust must be created for charitable, educational, religious, or scientific purposes.

Spendthrift Trusts.   As a general rule, a trust beneficiary may assign his or her rights to receive the principal or income of a trust to a third party (assignments are discussed in Chapter 16). Additionally, distributions of trust funds to beneficiaries normally are subject to creditors' claims. In a **spendthrift trust,** however, the beneficiary is not permitted to transfer his or her right

to the trust's principal or to future payments of income from the trust. To qualify as a spendthrift trust, the trust must explicitly place restraints on the alienation—transfer to others—of the trust funds.

The majority of states enforce spendthrift trust provisions that prohibit creditors from attaching the beneficiary's interest in future distributions from the trust. State laws provide for some exceptions, however. For example, a divorced spouse or a minor child of the beneficiary may be permitted to obtain alimony or child-support payments. Additionally, creditors that have provided *necessaries* (see Chapter 13) to spendthrift trust recipients normally can compel payment from the trust income or principal.

Totten Trusts.   A special type of trust created when one person deposits money in his or her own name as a trustee for another is a **Totten trust,**[5] or tentative trust. This trust is tentative in that it is revocable at will until the depositor dies or completes the gift in his or her lifetime by some unequivocal act or declaration (for example, delivery of the funds to the intended beneficiary). If the depositor dies before the beneficiary dies and if the depositor has not revoked the trust expressly or impliedly, a presumption arises that an absolute (a binding, irrevocable) trust has been created for the benefit of the beneficiary. At the

5. This type of trust derives its unusual name from *In the Matter of Totten,* 179 N.Y. 112, 71 N.E. 748 (1904).

death of the depositor, the beneficiary obtains property rights to the balance on hand.

IMPLIED TRUSTS

Sometimes a trust is imposed by law, even in the absence of an express trust. Customarily, these implied trusts are characterized as either constructive trusts or resulting trusts.

Constructive Trusts. A **constructive trust** arises by operation of law in the interests of equity and fairness. A constructive trust enables plaintiffs to recover property (and sometimes damages) from defendants who would otherwise be unjustly enriched. In a constructive trust, the legal owner is declared to be a trustee for the parties who are, in equity, actually entitled to the beneficial enjoyment that flows from the trust.

One source of a constructive trust is a wrongful action, such as the violation of a fiduciary relationship. To illustrate: Arturo and Spring are partners in buying, developing, and selling real estate. Arturo learns through the staff of the partnership that two hundred acres of land will soon come on the market and that the staff will recommend that the partnership purchase the land. Arturo purchases the property secretly in his own name, thus violating his fiduciary relationship. When these facts are discovered, a court will determine that Arturo must hold the property in trust for the partnership.

Constructive trusts may be imposed for other reasons as well. In the following case, the issue concerns whether a constructive trust should be imposed to counter the effects of an insurance company's failure to change the beneficiary on a life insurance policy after the insured had requested the change.

CASE 50.3   Zeigler v. Cardona

United States District Court, Middle District of Alabama, 1993. 830 F.Supp. 1395.

COMPANY PROFILE *Liberty National Life Insurance Company markets its policies for life, accident, and health insurance in rural regions to lower-income customers. Liberty National life insurance costs three times more than other insurers' life insurance and ten times more than others' group coverage. But Liberty National sells policies without a physical examination and offers a personal, monthly premium-collection service. Liberty National is the ninth largest life insurer in the United States; in the early 1990s, its profit margin was twice as high as that of the average life insurance company. Liberty National is owned by Torchmark Corporation (**http://www.torchmarkcorp.com**), a diversified insurance and financial services company headquartered in Birmingham.*

BACKGROUND AND FACTS *Antonio Suarez, Sr., purchased a $50,000 insurance policy on his life from Liberty National. The only designated beneficiary was Suarez's mother, Guarina Cardona. At the time the policy was issued, Suarez was living with his aunt, Ruby Zeigler. Suarez, Winifred Hamilton (the insurance agent), and Zeigler met to change the beneficiary on the policy from Cardona to Zeigler. Suarez made clear that he wanted the proceeds of the policy used for the benefit of his two children, Antonio (aged nine) and Ebony (aged eight). Apparently owing to a clerical error, Liberty National never changed the name of the beneficiary on the policy. During the months that Suarez lived with Zeigler, Zeigler paid the insurance premiums. Following Suarez's death, a suit was brought to establish who had rights in the insurance proceeds. Because of Liberty National's error, Cardona was the only beneficiary of record. Antonio and Ebony sought to have the proceeds placed in a constructive trust on their behalf, as Suarez had intended.*

IN THE LANGUAGE OF THE COURT

De MENT, District Judge.
    *   *   *   *
    *   *   * As it relates to changing of beneficiaries, the law of equity regards as having been done that which ought to be done and the courts will give effect to the intention of the insured by holding that a change of beneficiary has been accomplished where he or she has done all that he or she could do in order to comply with the provisions of the policy. *   *   *

*   *   * [It] is the court's opinion that Mr. Suarez did all that he could do in order to effectuate [bring about] the change to name Ruby Zeigler as his primary beneficiary. Having found that Mrs. Zeigler is the proper beneficiary on the policy, the court now directs its attention to the issue of constructive trust.

*   *   *   *

*   *   * The evidence is undisputed that Mr. Suarez wanted the proceeds of his life insurance policy to go to the benefit of the children. *   *   * There was no discussion with Mr. Suarez as to the exact manner [in] which the money should be divided between Mrs. Zeigler and the children. The children clearly have an equitable interest in the proceeds of the policy since it was their father's intent that the policy proceeds be used for them. A constructive trust may be imposed on life insurance proceeds even though the designated beneficiary is not guilty of fraud or wrongdoing.

DECISION AND REMEDY   *The court held that Zeigler was entitled to $10,000. A constructive trust on the remainder of the proceeds was imposed for the benefit of Antonio and Ebony. Cardona received nothing.*

Resulting Trusts. A **resulting trust** arises from the conduct of the parties. Here, the trust results, or is created, when circumstances raise an inference that the party holding legal title to the property does so for the benefit of another, unless the inference is refuted or the beneficial interest is otherwise disposed of.

To illustrate: Glenda wants to put one acre of land she owns on the market for sale. Because she is going out of the country for two years and will not be available to deed the property to a buyer during that period, she conveys the property to her good friend Oscar. Oscar can then sell and deed the property, with the proceeds to be turned over to Glenda. Because Glenda's intent in deeding the property to Oscar is neither a sale nor a gift, the property will be held in a resulting trust by Oscar (as trustee) for the benefit of Glenda. Therefore, on Glenda's return, Oscar will be required either to deed back the property to Glenda or, if the property has been sold, to turn over the proceeds (held in trust) to her.

THE TRUSTEE

The trustee is the person holding the trust property. Anyone legally capable of holding title to, and dealing in, property can be a trustee. If the settlor of a trust fails to name a trustee, or if a named trustee cannot or will not serve, the trust does not fail—an appropriate court can appoint a trustee.

Trustee's Duties. A trustee must act with honesty, good faith, and prudence in administering the trust and must exercise a high degree of loyalty toward the trust

beneficiary. The general standard of care is the degree of care a prudent person would exercise in his or her personal affairs.[6] The duty of loyalty requires that the trustee act in the exclusive interest of the beneficiary.

Among specific duties, a trustee must keep clear and accurate accounts of the trust's administration and furnish complete and correct information to the beneficiary. A trustee must keep trust assets separate from his or her own assets. A trustee has a duty to pay to an income beneficiary the net income of the trust assets at reasonable intervals. A trustee has a duty to distribute the risk of loss from investments by reasonable diversification and a duty to dispose of assets that do not represent prudent investments. Investments in federal, state, or municipal bonds; corporate bonds; and shares of preferred or common stock may be prudent investments under particular circumstances.

Trustee's Powers. When a settlor creates a trust, he or she may prescribe the trustee's powers and performance. Generally, state law[7] applies in the absence

---

6. Revised Uniform Principal and Income Act Section 2(a)(3); *Restatement (Third) of Trusts*, Section 227. This rule is in force in the majority of states by statute and in a small number of states under the common law. See also *O'Neill v. Commissioner of Internal Revenue*, 994 F.2d 302 (6th Cir. 1993).

7. In eight states, the law consists, in part, of the Uniform Principal and Income Act, published in 1931. The Revised Uniform Principal and Income Act, issued in 1962, has been adopted in thirty-four states. There are other uniform acts that may apply—for instance, about a third of the states have enacted the Uniform Trustees' Powers Act, promulgated in 1964. In addition, most states have their own statutes covering particular procedures and practices.

of specific terms in the trust.[8] When state law does apply, it is most likely to restrict the trustee's investment of trust funds. Typically, statutes confine trustees to investments in conservative debt securities such as government, utility, and railroad bonds and first-mortgage loans on realty. It is common, however, for a settlor to grant a trustee discretionary investment power. In that circumstance, any statute may be considered only advisory, with the trustee's decisions subject in most states to the prudent person rule.

A difficult question concerns the extent of a trustee's discretion to "invade" the principal and distribute it to an income beneficiary, if the income is found to be insufficient to provide for the beneficiary in an appropriate manner. A similar question concerns the extent of a trustee's discretion to retain trust income and add it to the principal, if the income is found to be more than sufficient to provide for the beneficiary in an appropriate manner. Generally, the answer to both questions is that the income beneficiary should be provided with a somewhat predictable annual income, but with a view to the safety of the principal. Thus, a trustee may make individualized adjustments in annual distributions.

Of course, a trustee is responsible for carrying out the purposes of the trust. If the trustee fails to comply with the terms of the trust or the controlling statute, he or she is personally liable for any loss.

Allocations between Principal and Income.
Frequently, a settlor will provide one beneficiary with a life estate and another beneficiary with the remainder interest in a trust. A farmer, for example, may create a testamentary trust providing that the farm's income be paid to his or her surviving spouse and that on the surviving spouse's death, the farm be given to their children. Among the income and principal beneficiaries, questions may arise concerning the apportionment of receipts and expenses for the farm's management, as well as the trust's administration between income and principal. Even when income and principal beneficiaries are the same, these questions may arise.

To the extent that a trust instrument does not provide instructions, a trustee must refer to applicable state law. The general rule is that ordinary receipts and expenses are chargeable to the income beneficiary, whereas extraordinary receipts and expenses are allocated to the principal beneficiaries.[9] To illustrate: The receipt of rent from trust realty would be ordinary, as would the expense of paying the property's taxes. The cost of long-term improvements and proceeds from the property's sale, however, would be extraordinary.

TRUST TERMINATION

The terms of a trust should expressly state the event on which the settlor wishes it to terminate—for example, the beneficiary's or the trustee's death. If the trust instrument does not provide for termination on the beneficiary's death, the beneficiary's death will not end it. Similarly, without an express provision, a trust will not terminate on the trustee's death.

Typically, a trust instrument specifies a termination date. For example, a trust created to educate the settlor's child may provide that the trust ends when the beneficiary reaches the age of twenty-five. If the trust's purpose is fulfilled before that date, a court may order the trust's termination. If no date is specified, a trust will terminate when its purpose has been fulfilled. Of course, if a trust's purpose becomes impossible or illegal, the trust will terminate.

---

8. Revised Uniform Principal and Income Act Section 2(a)(1); *Restatement (Second) of Trusts*, Section 164.

9. Revised Uniform Principal and Income Act, Sections 3, 6, 8, 13; *Restatement (Second) of Trusts*, Section 233.

CONCEPT SUMMARY 50.2   TRUSTS

CONCEPT	DESCRIPTION
Definition and Essential Elements	A trust is any arrangement by which property is transferred from one person to be administered by a trustee for another's benefit. The essential elements of a trust are (1) a designated beneficiary, (2) a designated trustee, (3) a fund sufficiently identified to enable title to pass to the trustee, and (4) actual delivery to the trustee with the intention of passing title.

CONCEPT SUMMARY 50.2  TRUSTS *(continued)*

Types of Trusts	1. *Living* (inter vivos) *trust*—A trust executed by a grantor during his or her lifetime. A living trust may be revocable or irrevocable. 2. *Testamentary trust*—A trust created by will and coming into existence on the death of the grantor. 3. *Charitable trust*—A trust designed for the benefit of a public group or the public in general. 4. *Spendthrift trust*—A trust created to provide for the maintenance of a beneficiary by allowing only a certain portion of the total amount to be received by the beneficiary at any one time. 5. *Totten trust*—A trust created when one person deposits money in his or her own name as a trustee for another.
Implied Trusts	Implied trusts, which are imposed by law in the interests of fairness and justice, include the following: 1. *Constructive trust*—Arises by operation of law whenever a transaction takes place in which the person who takes title to property is, in equity, not entitled to enjoy the beneficial interest therein. 2. *Resulting trust*—Arises from the conduct of the parties when an apparent *intention* to create a trust is present.

SECTION 4

Estate Administration

The orderly procedure used to collect assets, settle debts, and distribute the remaining assets when a person dies is the subject matter of estate administration. The rules and procedures for managing the estate of a deceased are controlled by statute. Thus, they vary from state to state. In every state, there is a special court, often called a probate court, that oversees the management of estates of decedents.

LOCATING THE WILL

The first step after a person dies is usually to determine whether the decedent left a will. In most cases, the decedent's attorney will have that information. If there is uncertainty as to whether a valid will exists, the personal papers of the deceased must be reviewed. If a will exists, it probably names a personal representative (executor) to administer the estate. If there is no will, or if the will fails to name a personal representative, then the court must appoint an administrator. Under the UPC, the term *personal representative* refers to either an

executor (a person named in the will) or an administrator (a person appointed by the court) [UPC 1–201(30)].

DUTIES OF THE PERSONAL REPRESENTATIVE

The personal representative has a number of duties. The first is to inventory and collect the assets of the decedent. If necessary, the assets are appraised to determine their value. Both the rights of creditors and the rights of beneficiaries must be protected during the estate-administration proceedings. In addition, the personal representative is responsible for managing the assets of the estate during the administration period and for preventing them from being wasted or unnecessarily depleted.

The personal representative receives and pays valid claims of creditors and arranges for the estate to pay federal and state income taxes and estate taxes (or inheritance taxes, depending on the state). A personal representative is required to post a bond to ensure honest and faithful performance. Usually, the bond exceeds the estimated value of the personal estate of the decedent. Under most state statutes, the will can specify that the personal representative need not post a bond.

ESTATE AND INHERITANCE TAXES

The death of an individual may result in tax liabilities at both the federal and state levels. At the federal level, a tax is levied on the total value of the estate after debts and expenses for administration have been deducted and after various exemptions have been allowed. The tax is on the estate itself rather than on the beneficiaries.

The majority of states assess a death tax in the form of an inheritance tax imposed on the recipient of a bequest rather than the estate. Some states also have a state estate tax similar to the federal estate tax. In general, inheritance tax rates are graduated according to the type of relationship between the beneficiary and the decedent. The lowest rates and largest exemptions are applied to a surviving spouse and the children of the decedent.

DISTRIBUTION OF ASSETS

When the ultimate distribution of assets to the beneficiaries is determined, the personal representative is responsible for distributing the estate pursuant to the court order. Once the assets have been distributed, an accounting is rendered to the court, the estate is closed, and the personal representative is relieved of any further responsibility or liability for the estate.

SECTION 5

Elder Law

In the past, elderly people sought legal assistance primarily for estate-planning purposes, in preparation for their deaths. Today, an increasing percentage of Americans are reaching retirement age, and elderly persons are facing the need to prepare for other possibilities—that they will become incapacitated, for example, or will have to depend on others for their health care and basic needs.

The aging of the U.S. population, a trend that will continue for decades to come, has led to a new legal specialty—elder law. Basically, **elder law** is a legal practice area in which attorneys assist older persons in dealing with such problems as disability, long-term health care, age discrimination, grandparents' visitation rights, and other problems relating to age. Here we look at just two aspects of elder law—planning for disability and Medicaid planning.

PLANNING FOR DISABILITY

With an increasingly large number of individuals living into their eighties and nineties, one important issue in elder law relates to power of attorney. Adult children need to seek power of attorney from their aging parents, particularly if the parents are becoming mentally incompetent or afflicted by Alzheimer's disease. An elder law attorney might help in arranging for the aging parent to sign a power of attorney and other documents, such as a durable power of attorney or a living will, that will enable the adult children to take over the parent's affairs if the parent becomes mentally and perhaps physically incapacitated.

Durable Power of Attorney. One technique that is often used to provide for future disability involves the durable power of attorney. A **durable power of attorney** authorizes a person to act on behalf of an incompetent person—write checks, collect insurance proceeds, and otherwise manage the disabled person's affairs, including health care—when he or she becomes incapacitated. A person who is advanced in age may give such a power of attorney to an adult child. Although becoming incapacitated is of particular concern to older persons, younger spouses often give each other durable power of attorney as well—in the event they are incapacitated due to an accident, for example.

Health-Care Power of Attorney. A **health-care power of attorney** designates a person who will have the power to choose what type of and how much medical treatment a person who is unable to make such a choice will receive. The health-care power of attorney is growing in importance as medical technology allows doctors and hospitals to keep people technically alive but in a so-called vegetative state for ever-increasing periods of time.

Living Will. A similar power is created by what is referred to as a **living will.** A living will is not a will in the usual sense—that is, it does not appoint an estate representative, dispose of property, establish trusts, and so on. Rather, it allows a person to control what medical treatment may be used after a serious accident or illness. Through a living will, a person can designate whether he or she wants certain lifesaving procedures to be undertaken in situations in which the treatment will not result in a reasonable quality of life. Most states have enacted statutes permitting living wills, and it is important that the requirements of state law be followed exactly in creating such wills. Typically, under state statutes, physicians are obligated to abide by the terms of living wills, and living wills often are included with a patient's medical records.

MEDICAID PLANNING

A serious problem facing older persons is the cost of long-term care—in a nursing home, for example. Suppose that a person can no longer look after his or her own needs and either cannot or does not wish to rely on family or friends to provide full-time care. In all likelihood, this person will end up in an assisted-living facility or a nursing home, and such arrangements are costly. Even those who can afford to spend $60,000 or more per year for nursing-home care might prefer to transfer their assets to others, such as their children, and "go on Medicaid" so that the government will pay for the care. One area of elder law addresses Medicaid planning.

Medicaid versus Medicare. Medicaid is not the same as Medicare. As you read in Chapter 41, Medicare is a federal program that is financed through the Social Security system and primarily addresses the needs of the elderly. Medicaid, in contrast, is a cooperative federal-state program that provides health-care services to the poor of all ages. Because the program is administered by state agencies, regulations governing Medicaid vary from state to state. At the federal level, Medicaid is administered by the Health Care Financing Administration.

Medicaid Planning. When Medicaid pays for long-term care, all of the person's income must be paid to the state. There are exceptions, though, and this is where Medicaid planning becomes important. One home, one automobile, and other assets up to a total value of $75,000 are exempt from Medicaid accounting. Thus, one strategy is for the elderly person to bring down the total value of all of his or her other assets to less than $75,000 by spending assets in excess of that amount to fix up his or her house or to buy an expensive new car.

Assets might also be transferred to others, such as children and friends, prior to applying for Medicaid. A person who makes uncompensated transfers within three years (or five years, if a trust transfer is involved) prior to applying for Medicaid, however, faces a "penalty period" during which he or she will not qualify for Medicaid.[10] This waiting period is derived by

dividing the value of uncompensated transfers made during the "look back" period of three (or five) years by the average monthly cost of nursing-home care in the region. For example, suppose that Joanne transfers stock worth $60,000 to her daughter so as to reduce her assets to a value of less than $75,000. A year later, Joanne applies for Medicaid to cover nursing-home costs. If the average nursing home in her area charges $6,000, Joanne will not be eligible to receive Medicaid for ten months ($60,000 divided by $6,000).

Criminalizing Medicaid Planning. In 1996, Congress passed a law[11] that made it a crime for elderly Americans to transfer their assets to others, including trusts, before going into a nursing home if state Medicaid officials concluded that the transfer triggered a "penalty period." A person who violated the act was subject to a fine of up to $25,000, imprisonment for up to five years, or both. The law, which became effective on January 1, 1997, outraged elder-care professionals and others and was immediately dubbed the "Granny Goes to Jail" law.

The law was short lived. In August 1997, Congress amended the law to strike the language in Section 217 and add a provision making it a crime for attorneys to advise elderly clients to give away assets to get Medicaid coverage of nursing-home costs.[12] Attorneys who violated the act were subject to a fine of up to $10,000, imprisonment for up to one year, or both. This provision, popularly called the "Granny's Lawyer Goes to Jail" law, has also been under attack. Attorneys claim that it poses an ethical dilemma for them because it forces them to choose between committing a crime by giving advice and committing malpractice by not doing so. In 1998, U.S. attorney general Janet Reno stated that the Justice Department would not defend the constitutionality of the act, and a federal district court granted a preliminary injunction against the law's enforcement on constitutional grounds.[13] Until the law is repealed by Congress, though, attorneys have no guarantees that the Justice Department will continue its policy of nonenforcement.

---

10. 42 U.S.C. Section 1396p(c)(1)(B).

11. Section 217 of the Health Insurance Portability and Accountability Act of 1996 [42 U.S.C. Section 1320a-7b(a)].
12. Section 4734 of the Balanced Budget Act of 1997 [42 U.S.C. Section 1320a-7b(a)].
13. *New York State Bar Association v. Reno*, 999 F.Supp. 710 (N.D.N.Y. 1998).

TERMS AND CONCEPTS TO REVIEW

administrator 950

bequest 952

charitable trust 962

codicil 955

constructive trust 963

devise 952

durable power of attorney 967

elder law 967

escheat 950

estate planning 950

executor 950

health-care power of attorney 967

holographic will 954

inter vivos trust 961

intestacy laws 950

intestate 950

legacy 952

living will 967

nuncupative will 954

per capita 960

per stirpes 960

probate 952

resulting trust 964

spendthrift trust 962

testamentary trust 962

testate 950

testator 950

Totten trust 962

trust 960

will 950

QUESTIONS AND CASE PROBLEMS

50–1. ESTATE DISTRIBUTION. Flint is a widower who has two married children, Janek and Abrial. Abrial has two children, Phil and Paula. Janek has no children. Flint dies, leaving a typewritten will that gives all his property equally to his children, Janek and Abrial. The will also provides that should a child predecease him, leaving grandchildren, the grandchildren are to take *per stirpes*. The will was witnessed by Abrial and Flint's lawyer and signed by Flint in their presence. Abrial has predeceased Flint. Janek claims the will is invalid.

   (a) Discuss whether the will is valid.

   (b) Discuss the distribution of Flint's estate if the will is invalid.

   (c) Discuss the distribution of Flint's estate if the will is valid.

50–2. WILLS AND SUBSEQUENT MARRIAGES OR CHILDREN. While single, James made out a will naming his mother, Carol, as sole beneficiary. Later, James married Lisa.

   (a) If James died while married to Lisa without changing his will, would the estate go to his mother, Carol? Explain.

   (b) Assume that James made out a new will on his marriage to Lisa, leaving his entire estate to Lisa. Later he divorced Lisa and married Mandis, but he did not change his will. Discuss the rights of Lisa and Mandis to his estate after his death.

   (c) Assume that James divorced Lisa, married Mandis, and changed his will, leaving his estate to Mandis. Later, a daughter, Claire, was born. James died without having included Claire in his will. Discuss fully whether Claire has any rights in the estate.

50–3. VALIDITY OF WILLS. Merlin Winters had three sons. Merlin and his youngest son, Abraham, had a falling out in 1994 and stopped speaking to each other. Merlin made a formal will in 1996, leaving all his property to the two older children and deliberately excluding Abraham. Merlin's health began to deteriorate, and by 1997, he was under the full-time care of a nurse, Julia. In 1998, he made a new will expressly revoking the 1996 will and leaving all his property to Julia. On Merlin's death, the two older children contested the 1998 will, claiming that Julia had exercised undue influence over their father. Abraham claimed that both wills were invalid, because the first will had been revoked by the second will, and the second will was invalid on the ground of undue influence. Is Abraham's contention correct? Explain.

50–4. UNDUE INFLUENCE OVER TESTATOR. Rohan, an eighty-three-year-old invalid, employs a nurse, Sarah, to care for him. Prior to Sarah's employment, Rohan executed a will leaving his entire estate to his only living relative—his great-grandson, Leon. Sarah convinces Rohan that Leon is dead and gets Rohan to change his will, naming Sarah as his sole beneficiary. After Rohan's death, Leon appears and contests the will. Discuss the probable success of Leon's action.

50–5. RESULTING TRUSTS. Robert and Everett Kling, two brothers, purchased rental property in Fenton, Missouri. Robert contributed $5,544 and Everett, $5,624 toward the purchase price of $19,005. Title to the property was taken in the name of Everett's wife, Nancy. The brothers maintained an account in which they made deposits and from which they paid expenses related to the rental property. Although each brother had agreed to contribute $20 per month toward the remaining purchase price, Robert never did do so, and Everett consequently increased his contribution to $40 per month. When Robert died, Everett and Nancy claimed 100 percent ownership of the Fenton property. Robert's children, John and Janet, filed suit, claiming that Everett and Nancy held the property as a resulting trust and that they (John and Janet) were entitled to half of the property. Discuss whether a resulting trust had been created and, if so, what the distribution should be. [*Estate of Kling*, 736 S.W.2d 65 (Mo.App. 1987)]

50–6. REVOCATION OF A WILL. Myrtle Courziel executed a valid will that provided for the establishment of a scholarship fund designed to encourage the study of corrosion as it affects metallurgical engineering. The recipients were to be students in the upper half of their classes at the University of Alabama. Subsequently, Courziel died. John Calhoun, the eventual administrator of her estate, obtained access to Courziel's safe-deposit box to search for her will. He found the will intact, except that the last page of the will, which had contained Courziel's signature and the signatures of the witnesses, had been removed from the document and was not in the safe-deposit box or anywhere else to be found. Because Courziel had had sole control over the will, should it be presumed that by removing the last page of the will (or allowing it to be removed), she effectively revoked the will? [*Board of Trustees of University of Alabama v. Calhoun*, 514 So.2d 895 (Ala. 1987)]

50–7. ADOPTED CHILDREN. Gail MacCallum was the daughter of Anita Seymour. After the death of Gail's father, Anita married Richard Seymour, who adopted Gail the next year, when she was seven years old. The same year, Janet Seymour was born to Richard and Anita. Almost forty years later, when Richard's brother Philip died, both Gail and Janet sought to share in the estate. A Vermont state court concluded that Gail could not share in the estate because a state statute prohibited "inheritance between the person adopted . . . and collateral kin of the person or persons making the adoption." Gail appealed, arguing that the statute was unconstitutional. Will the court agree? Discuss fully. [*MacCallum v. Seymour*, 686 A.2d 935 (Vt. 1996)]

50–8. REVOCATION OF A WILL. William Laneer urged his son, also William, to join the family business. The son, who was made partner, became suspicious of the handling of the business's finances. He filed a suit against the business and reported it to the Internal Revenue Service. Laneer then executed a will that disinherited his son, giving him one dollar and leaving the balance of the estate equally to Laneer's four daughters, including Bellinda Barrera. Until his death more than twenty years later, Laneer harbored ill feelings toward his son. After Laneer's death, his original copy of the will could not be found. A photocopy was found in his safe-deposit box, however, and his lawyer's original copy was entered for probate in an Arkansas state court. Barrera, who wanted her brother William to share an equal portion of the inheritance, filed a petition to contest the will. Barrera claimed, among other things, that Laneer

had revoked the will, and that was why his original copy of the will could not be found. Was the will revoked? If so, to whom would the estate be distributed? [*Barrera v. Vanpelt*, 332 Ark. 482, 965 S.W.2d 780 (1998)]

50–9. ESTATE ADMINISTRATION. Rose Martin died in 1995. At the time, she owned thirty-five of the eighty outstanding shares in Refrigeration Supplies Distributors, Inc. (RSD), a family business that had existed for ninety years. Rose's daughter Alice Karlebach, an RSD officer and director, owned five RSD shares. Karlebach was appointed executor of Rose's estate. Karlebach hired Cronkite & Roda (C&R), an independent professional appraiser, to determine the value of the shares. C&R determined that Rose's RSD shares were worth $9.7 million, or approximately $277,142.86 per share, on the date of Rose's death. To pay the estate's taxes, Karlebach sold 22.5 of the estate's RSD shares to RSD for $6.235 million. Patrick Martin was Rose's grandson, Alice's nephew, and a beneficiary of one-sixth of the residuary estate. Martin filed a petition with the California state probate court that was overseeing the administration of the estate to void the sale of the shares. Martin contended that Karlebach had breached her fiduciary duty to act in the best interests of the estate. How should the court rule? Why? [*Estate of Martin*, 72 Cal.App.4th 148, 86 Cal.Rptr.2d 37 (2 Dist. 1999)]

50–10. IN YOUR COURT

In the last fourteen years of Eva Thompson's life, Kenneth Lindell, the pastor of her church, became her spiritual adviser and close personal friend. Lindell—and no one else—actively participated in helping Thompson draft her will. He gave Thompson a church-sponsored booklet on will drafting, recommended an attorney (a church member) to do the drafting, and reviewed the terms of the will with Thompson. When Thompson died, she left most of her estate to Lindell's church. Lindell personally received nothing under the will. Thompson's nephew and only heir, Richard Park, contested the validity of the will, arguing that Lindell had unduly influenced Thompson. Assume that you are the judge in the court hearing this case and answer the following questions:

(a) In what circumstances may a court infer that undue influence has been exercised over a testator? Do such circumstances exist with respect to Thompson's will?

(b) Although Lindell's church benefited economically from Thompson's will, Lindell received no *personal* advantage. Can a party who receives no personal benefit under a will be regarded as having exercised undue influence over the testator?

(c) Will you decide that Lindell exercised undue influence over Thompson? Why or why not? Would your answer be different if Thompson had consulted with independent counsel (an attorney who was not affiliated with her church in any way) before signing her will? Explain.

50–11. A QUESTION OF ETHICS

Heber Burke and his wife Evelyn spent most of their lives in Ohio and jointly accumulated a substantial amount of property there. When Evelyn died in February 1985, the Burkes had been married for fifty-three years and had two children, four grandchildren, and four great-grandchildren. Heber had originally hailed from Pike County, Kentucky, and in June 1985, he returned to Pike County and bought a house there. In the same month, he told his children that he was going to marry Lexie Damron, a widow who attended his church. Lexie and Heber were married on July 20. On July 27, Heber executed a will, which was drawn up by Lexie's attorney, in which he left all of his property to Lexie. Heber died three weeks later. Heber's children, Donald Burke and Beatrice Bates, contested the will, alleging that Heber had lacked testamentary capacity and that Heber's will had resulted from Lexie's undue influence over him. Friends and relatives of Heber in Pike County testified that they had never known Heber to drink and that, although he seemed saddened by his first wife's death, he was not incapacitated by it. According to the children's witnesses, however, after Evelyn's death, Heber allegedly drank heavily and constantly; had frequent crying spells; repeatedly visited his wife's grave; tried to dig her up so that he could talk to her; and had hallucinations, talking to people who were not present and claiming that Evelyn visited him regularly at night, which frightened him into sleeping in the attic. The jury found the will to be invalid on the grounds of undue influence, and Lexie appealed. [*Burke v. Burke*, 801 S.W.2d 691 (Ken.App. 1990)]

(a) The appellate court had to weigh two conflicting policies in deciding this issue. What two policies are in conflict here, and what criteria should be used in resolving the issue?

(b) Given the circumstances described above, would you infer undue influence on the part of Lexie if you were the judge? Would you conclude that Heber lacked testamentary capacity? What would be the fairest solution, in your opinion?

(c) Heber's first wife, Evelyn, contributed substantially to the acquisition of the property subject to Heber's will. A natural assumption is that Evelyn would have wanted their children to inherit the jointly acquired property. Yet if the court found that Heber was of sound mind and not the victim of any undue influence, it would let stand a will that totally disregarded the children. Is this fair to Evelyn's presumed intentions? To the children? Is there any solution to the possible unfairness that can result from giving people the right to disregard natural heirs in their wills?

LAW ON THE WEB

For updated links to resources available on the Web, as well as a variety of other materials, visit this text's Web site at http://wbl.westbuslaw.com.

The wills of various historical figures and celebrities, including Elvis Presley, Jacqueline Kennedy Onassis, and Richard Nixon, are online at

http://www.ca-probate.com/wills.htm

The Senior Law Web site offers information on a variety of topics, including elder law, estate planning, and trusts. The URL for this site is

http://www.seniorlaw.com

You can find the Uniform Probate Code, as well as links to various state probate statutes, at Cornell Law University's Legal Information Institute. Go to

http://www.law.cornell.edu/uniform/probate.html

LEGAL RESEARCH EXERCISES ON THE WEB

Go to http://wbl.westbuslaw.com, the Web site that accompanies this text. Select "Internet Applications," and then click on "Chapter 50." There you will find the following Internet research exercises that you can perform to learn more about wills, trusts, and elder law:

Activity 50–1: Wills and Trusts

Activity 50–2: Elder Law

CHAPTER 51

Liability of Accountants and Other Professionals

PROFESSIONALS SUCH AS ACCOUNTANTS, attorneys, physicians, architects, and others are increasingly faced with the threat of liability. Perhaps the reason is a greater public awareness of the fact that professionals are required to deliver competent services and are obligated to adhere to standards of performance commonly accepted within their professions.

Considering the many potential sources of legal liability that may be imposed on them, accountants, attorneys, and other professionals should be well aware of their legal obligations. In the first part of this chapter, we look at the potential liability of professionals under the common law and then examine the potential liability of accountants under securities laws and the Internal Revenue Code. The chapter concludes with a brief examination of other topics of concern for professionals, including rights to working papers, professional-client privilege, and the increasing use of the limited liability partnership by accountants and other professionals to limit their tort liability.

SECTION 1

Common Law Liability to Clients

Under the common law, professionals may be liable to clients for breach of contract, negligence, or fraud.

LIABILITY FOR BREACH OF CONTRACT

Accountants and other professionals face liability for any breach of contract under the common law. A professional owes a duty to his or her client to honor the terms of the contract and to perform the contract within the stated time period. If the professional fails to perform as agreed in the contract, then he or she has breached the contract, and the client has the right to recover damages from the professional. A professional may be held liable for expenses incurred by his or her client in securing another professional to provide the contracted-for services, for penalties imposed on the client for failure to meet time deadlines, and for any other reasonable and foreseeable monetary losses that arise from the professional's breach.

LIABILITY FOR NEGLIGENCE

Accountants and other professionals may also be held liable under the common law for negligence in the performance of their services. As with any negligence claim, the elements that must be proved to establish negligence on the part of a professional are as follows:

1. A duty of care existed.
2. That duty of care was breached.
3. The plaintiff suffered an injury.

4. The injury was proximately caused by the defendant's breach of the duty of care.

All professionals are subject to standards of conduct established by codes of professional standards and ethics, by state statutes, and by judicial decisions. They are also governed by the contracts into which they enter with their clients. In their performance of contracts, professionals must exercise the established standard of care, knowledge, and judgment generally accepted by members of their professional group. We look below at the duty of care owed by two groups of professionals that frequently perform services for business firms: accountants and attorneys.

Accountant's Duty of Care. Accountants play a major role in a business's financial system. Accountants have the necessary expertise and experience in establishing and maintaining accurate financial records to design, control, and audit record-keeping systems; to prepare reliable statements that reflect an individual's or a business's financial status; and to give tax advice and prepare tax returns.

An *audit* is a systematic inspection, by analyses and tests, of a business's financial records. The purpose of an audit is to provide the auditor with evidence to support an opinion on the fairness of the business's financial statements. A normal audit is not intended to uncover fraud or other misconduct. An accountant may be liable for failing to detect misconduct, however, if a normal audit would have revealed it or the auditor agreed to examine the records for evidence of fraud or other misconduct.

After performing an audit, the auditor issues an opinion letter stating whether, in his or her opinion, the financial statements fairly present the business's financial position. The opinion letter is said to certify the financial statements. Normally, an auditor issues an *unqualified opinion*, which means that the audit and the financial statements comply with the principles and standards discussed in the next section.

Standard of Care. Generally, an accountant must possess the skills that an ordinarily prudent accountant would have and must exercise the degree of care that an ordinarily prudent accountant would exercise. The level of skill expected of accountants and the degree of care that they should exercise in performing their services are reflected in what are known as **generally accepted accounting principles (GAAP)** and **generally accepted auditing standards (GAAS).** The Financial Accounting Standards Board (FASB,

usually pronounced "faz-bee") determines what accounting conventions, rules, and procedures constitute GAAP at a given point in time. GAAS are standards concerning an auditor's professional qualities and the judgment that he or she exercises in auditing financial records. GAAS are established by the American Institute of Certified Public Accountants. GAAP and GAAS are also reflected in the rules established by the Securities and Exchange Commission (see Chapter 37).

As long as an accountant conforms to GAAP and acts in good faith, he or she normally will not be held liable to the client for incorrect judgment. As mentioned above, an accountant is not required to discover every impropriety, **defalcation**[1] (embezzlement), or fraud in a client's books. If, however, the impropriety, defalcation, or fraud has gone undiscovered because of an accountant's negligence or failure to perform an express or implied duty, the accountant will be liable for any resulting losses suffered by the client. Therefore, an accountant who uncovers suspicious financial transactions and fails to investigate the matter fully or to inform his or her client of the discovery can be held liable to the client for the resulting loss.

A violation of GAAP and GAAS will be considered *prima facie* evidence of negligence on the part of the accountant. Compliance with GAAP and GAAS, however, does not necessarily relieve an accountant from potential legal liability. An accountant may be held to a higher standard of conduct established by state statute and by judicial decisions. If an accountant is found to have been negligent in the performance of accounting services for a client, the client may collect damages for any losses that arose from the accountant's negligence.

Defenses to Negligence. Accountants have several defenses available. Possible defenses include the following allegations:

1. The accountant was not negligent.
2. If the accountant was negligent, this negligence was not the proximate cause of the client's losses.
3. The client was also negligent (depending on whether state law allows contributory negligence or comparative negligence as a defense—see Chapter 5).

---

1. This term, pronounced deh-ful-*kay*-shun, is derived from the Latin *de* ("off") and *falx* ("sickle"—a tool for cutting grain or tall grass). In law, the term refers to the act of a defaulter or of an embezzler. As used here, it means embezzlement.

Qualified Opinions and Disclaimers. In issuing an opinion letter, an auditor may qualify the opinion or include a disclaimer. An auditor will not be held liable for damages resulting from whatever is qualified or disclaimed. An opinion that disclaims any liability for false or misleading financial statements is too general, however. A qualified opinion or a disclaimer must be specific. For example, an auditor might qualify an opinion, in an audit of a corporation, by stating that there is uncertainty about how a lawsuit against the firm will be resolved. The auditor will not be liable if the result of the suit is bad for the firm. The auditor could still be liable, however, for failing to discover other problems that an audit in compliance with GAAS and GAAP would have revealed.

Unaudited Financial Statements. Sometimes accountants are hired to prepare unaudited financial statements. (A financial statement is considered unaudited if no auditing procedures have been used in its preparation or if insufficient procedures have been used to justify an opinion.) Accountants may be subject to liability for failing, in accordance with standard accounting procedures, to designate a balance sheet as "unaudited." An accountant will also be held liable for failure to disclose to a client facts or circumstances that give reason to believe that misstatements have been made or that a fraud has been committed.

Attorney's Duty of Care. The conduct of attorneys is governed by rules established by each state and by the American Bar Association's Model Rules of Professional Conduct. All attorneys owe a duty to provide competent and diligent representation. Attorneys are required to be familiar with well-settled principles of law applicable to a case and to discover law that can be found through a reasonable amount of research.

The lawyer also must investigate and discover facts that could materially affect the client's legal rights.

Standard of Care. In judging an attorney's performance, the standard used will normally be that of a reasonably competent general practitioner of ordinary skill, experience, and capacity. If an attorney holds himself or herself out as having expertise in a special area of law (for example, domestic relations), then the attorney's standard of care in that area is higher than for attorneys without such expertise.

Liability for Malpractice. When an attorney fails to exercise reasonable care and professional judgment, he or she breaches the duty of care and can be held liable for *malpractice* (professional negligence). In malpractice cases—as in all cases involving allegations of negligence—the plaintiff must prove that the attorney's breach of the duty of care actually caused the plaintiff to suffer some injury. For example, if the attorney allows the statute of limitations to lapse on a client's claim, he or she can be held liable for malpractice because the client can no longer file a cause of action in this case and has lost a potential award of damages.

Traditionally, to establish causation, the client normally had to show that "but for" the attorney's negligence, the client would not have suffered the injury. In recent years, however, several courts have held that plaintiffs in malpractice cases need only show that the defendant's negligence was a "substantial factor" in causing the plaintiff's injury. In the following case, the Supreme Court of New Jersey addressed the issue of what standard should be applied in determining whether an attorney's malpractice was the proximate cause of the plaintiffs' injuries.

CASE 51.1   Conklin v. Hannoch Weisman

Supreme Court
of New Jersey, 1996.
145 N.J. 395,
678 A.2d 1060.

BACKGROUND AND FACTS *The Conklins hired the law firm of Hannoch Weisman, Professional Corporation, to represent them in a sale of one hundred acres of their farm to Longview Estates. The purchase price of the land was $12 million. Longview made a $3 million down payment and gave the Conklins a mortgage for the balance. The mortgage, however, was subordinate (second in priority) to a mortgage held by another lender: if Longview defaulted on its payments, the other lender would be paid first. When Longview defaulted, the other lender took the land, and the Conklins got nothing. They filed a suit in a New Jersey state court against Hannoch Weisman, claiming that the firm had not explained completely the risks of a subordinate mortgage. The jury was charged (instructed) to hold the firm liable only if the Conklins proved that their loss would not have* occurred "but for" the firm's negligence. The jury issued a verdict in favor of the law firm, but the judge decided that the jury charge had been unclear and ordered a new trial. Hannoch Weisman appealed. The intermediate state appellate court affirmed the order of the trial judge (calling for a new trial), and the law firm appealed to the Supreme Court of New Jersey.

IN THE LANGUAGE OF THE COURT

O'HERN, [Justice].
     *   *   *   *

In reality, there is usually no such thing as a risk-free deal. The best that a lawyer can do is to control the risks to help the clients to achieve their financial objectives. *   *   * Through advice and negotiating the terms of the contract, the parties and their lawyers control the risks of the deal. The Conklins wanted a specific price—twelve million dollars. They made a poor deal and sustained a grave loss. The question is whether the lack of adequate advice was a substantial factor in causing the Conklins' exposure to an unwanted risk of harm.
     *   *   *   *

     *   *   * [T]he jury charge *   *   * could have confused the jury and led to an unjust result *   *   * . [T]he traditional jury charge [in which liability is subject to the "but for" test] *   *   * is inapt [inappropriate] for legal malpractice cases in which there are concurrent independent causes of harm and *   *   * a jury in such cases must be instructed to determine whether the negligence was a substantial factor in bringing about the ultimate harm.

DECISION AND REMEDY

The Supreme Court of New Jersey affirmed the judgment of the lower court. A new trial should be held because the jury was given erroneous instructions in the applicable law. The law in New Jersey (and other states) provides that to recover in a legal malpractice case, a plaintiff needs to show only that the lawyer's negligence was a "substantial factor" in causing the harm.

LIABILITY FOR FRAUD

Recall from Chapter 14 that fraud, or misrepresentation, consists of the following elements:

1. A misrepresentation of a material fact has occurred.
2. There exists an intent to deceive.
3. The innocent party has justifiably relied on the misrepresentation.
4. For damages, the innocent party must have been injured.

A professional may be held liable for *actual* fraud when he or she intentionally misstates a material fact to mislead his or her client and the client justifiably relies on the misstated fact to his or her injury. A material fact is one that a reasonable person would consider important in deciding whether to act.

In contrast, a professional may be held liable for *constructive* fraud whether or not he or she acted with fraudulent intent. For example, constructive fraud may be found when an accountant is grossly negligent in the performance of his or her duties. The intentional failure to perform a duty in reckless disregard of the consequences of such a failure would constitute gross negligence on the part of a professional.

SECTION 2

Liability to Third Parties

Traditionally, an accountant or other professional only owed a duty to those with whom he or she was in *privity of contract*. (Recall from Chapter 16 that privity of contract refers to the relationship that exists between the promisor and the promisee of a contract.) In other words, a professional owed no duty to a third party outside the contractual relationship—a professional's duty was only to his or her client. Violations of statutory laws, fraud, and other intentional or reckless acts of wrongdoing were the only exceptions to this general rule.

Today, numerous third parties—including investors, shareholders, creditors, corporate managers and directors, regulatory agencies, and others—rely on the opinions of auditors (accountants) when making decisions. In view of this extensive reliance, many courts have all but abandoned the privity requirement in regard to accountants' liability to third parties. Like accountants, attorneys may be held liable under the common law to third parties who rely on legal opinions to their detriment. Generally, however, an attorney is not liable to a nonclient unless there is fraud (or malicious conduct) by the attorney. The liability principles stated in Section 552 of the *Restatement (Second) of Torts* (these principles will be discussed shortly), however, may apply to attorneys just as they apply to accountants.

Understanding an auditor's common law liability to third parties is critical, because when a business fails, its independent auditor may be one of the few potentially solvent defendants. The majority of courts now hold that auditors can be held liable to third parties for negligence, but the standard for the imposition of this liability varies. There are generally three different views of accountants' liability to third parties:

1. Accountants should be liable only to those with whom they are in privity or "near privity" of contract (the *Ultramares* rule).
2. Accountants should be liable to foreseen, or known, users of their reports or financial statements (the *Restatement* rule).
3. Accounts should be liable to those whose use of their reports or financial statements is reasonably foreseeable.

We discuss each of these views here.

The Ultramares Rule

The traditional rule regarding an accountant's liability to third parties was enunciated by Chief Judge Benjamin Cardozo in *Ultramares Corp. v. Touche*,[2] a case decided in 1931. In *Ultramares*, Fred Stern & Company (Stern) hired the public accounting firm of Touche, Niven & Company (Touche) to review Stern's financial records and prepare a balance sheet for the year ending December 31, 1923.[3] Touche prepared the balance sheet and supplied Stern with thirty-two certified copies. According to the certified balance

sheet, Stern had a net worth (assets less liabilities) of $1,070,715.26. In reality, however, Stern was insolvent—the company's records had been falsified by insiders at Stern to reflect a positive net worth. In reliance on the certified balance sheets, a lender, Ultramares Corporation, loaned substantial amounts to Stern. After Stern was declared bankrupt, Ultramares brought an action against Touche for negligence in an attempt to recover damages.

The New York Court of Appeals (that state's highest court) refused to impose liability on the accountants and concluded that they owed a duty of care only to those persons for whose "primary benefit" the statements were intended. In this case, Stern was the only one for whose primary benefit the statements were intended. The court held that in the absence of privity or a relationship "so close as to approach that of privity," a party could not recover from an accountant.

The court's requirement of privity has since been referred to as the *Ultramares* rule, or the New York rule. The rule was restated and somewhat modified in a 1985 New York case, *Credit Alliance Corp. v. Arthur Andersen & Co.*[4] In that case, the court held that if a third party has a sufficiently close relationship or nexus (link or connection) with an accountant, then the *Ultramares* privity requirement may be satisfied without the establishment of an accountant-client relationship. The rule enunciated in *Credit Alliance* is often referred to as the "near privity" rule. Only a minority of states have adopted this rule of accountants' liability to third parties.

The Restatement Rule

Auditors perform much of their work for use by persons who are not parties to the contract; thus, it is asserted that they owe a duty to these third parties. Consequently, there has been an erosion of the *Ultramares* rule, and accountants have increasingly been exposed to potential liability to third parties.

The majority of courts have adopted the position taken by the *Restatement (Second) of Torts*, which states that accountants are subject to liability for negligence not only to their clients but also to foreseen, or *known*, users—or classes of users—of their reports or financial statements. Under Section 552(2) of the *Restatement (Second) of Torts*, an accountant's liability

---

2. 255 N.Y. 170, 174 N.E. 441 (1931).
3. Banks, creditors, stockholders, purchasers, and sellers often rely on balance sheets when making decisions relating to a company's business.

4. 65 N.Y.2d 536, 483 N.E.2d 110 (1985): A "relationship sufficiently intimate to be equated with privity" is sufficient for a third party to sue another's accountant for negligence.

extends to those persons for whose benefit and guidance the accountant "intends to supply the information or knows that the recipient intends to supply it" and to those persons whom the accountant "intends the information to influence or knows that the recipient so intends." In other words, if an accountant prepares a financial statement for a client and knows that the client will submit that statement to a bank to secure a loan, the accountant may be held liable to the bank for negligent misstatements or omissions—because the accountant knew that the bank would rely on the accountant's work product when deciding whether to make the loan.

In the following case, the court considered the question of the extent of an accountant's liability to a third party. Note how the court, in determining the issue, relied on the position taken in the *Restatement (Second) of Torts.*

CASE 51.2   Boykin v. Arthur Andersen & Co.

Supreme Court of
Alabama, 1994.
639 So.2d 504.

BACKGROUND AND FACTS   *Secor Bank hired Arthur Andersen & Company, independent certified public accountants, to certify the bank's annual reports. The reports did not mention losses resulting from millions of dollars of bad commercial loans. Samuel Boykin and Apon, Inc., were Secor shareholders. When they learned of the losses, they filed a suit in an Alabama state court against Andersen and others, alleging in part professional negligence. The court dismissed the suit, ruling in part that the claim did not satisfy the "near privity" rule enunciated in* Credit Alliance. *Boykin and Apon appealed to the Supreme Court of Alabama, which adopted the* Restatement *rule.*

**IN THE LANGUAGE
OF THE COURT**

SHORES, Justice.

　　*　　*　　*　　*

*　　*　　* [T]he *Restatement* clarifies any confusion as to the question of *　　*　　* privity *　　*　　*. The *Restatement* *　　*　　* allow[s] *　　*　　* a restricted group of third parties to recover for pecuniary losses attributable to inaccurate financial statements. *　　*　　* *The restricted group includes third parties whom the accountants intend to influence and those whom the accountants know their clients intend to influence.* *　　*　　* [Emphasis added.]

*　　*　　* Basic principles of justice require that an accounting firm be held liable for its intentional or negligent dissemination of inaccurate financial reports to specifically foreseen and limited groups of third parties for whose benefit and guidance the accounting firm supplied the information.

**DECISION
AND REMEDY**

The Supreme Court of Alabama held, under the Restatement *rule, that Boykin and Apon had stated a claim for professional negligence against Andersen. The court reversed the lower court's judgment and remanded the case for trial.*

**INTERNATIONAL
CONSIDERATIONS**

Liability of Accountants to Third Parties in England   *After a long history of requiring privity, English courts began permitting foreseeable third parties to sue accountants for negligence. This produced a backlash, and a 1990 decision restricted such third party liability. The court described the "frightening" extent of accountants' liability in the United States and stressed that English courts should "demonstrate a greater concern for equity."*

LIABILITY TO
REASONABLE FORESEEABLE USERS

A small minority of courts hold accountants liable to any users whose reliance on an accountant's state-ments or reports was *reasonably foreseeable.* This standard has been criticized as extending liability too far. In *Raritan River Steel Co. v. Cherry, Bekaert & Holland,* for example, the North Carolina Supreme Court stated that "in fairness accountants should not be liable in circumstances where they are unaware of the use to which their opinions will be put. Instead, their liability should be commensurate with those persons or classes of persons whom they know will rely on their work. With such knowledge the auditor can, through purchase of liability insurance, setting fees, and adopting other protective measures appropriate to the risk, prepare accordingly."[5]

The North Carolina court's statement echoes the view of the majority of the courts that the *Restatement's* approach is the more reasonable one because it allows accountants to control their exposure to liability. Liability is "fixed by the accountants' particular knowledge at the moment the audit is published," not by the foreseeability of the harm that might occur to a third party after the report is released.[6]

Even the California courts, which for years had relied on reasonable foreseeability as the standard for determining an auditor's liability to third parties, have changed their position. In a 1992 case, the California Supreme Court held that an accountant "owes no general duty of care regarding the conduct of an audit to persons other than the client." The court went on to say that if third parties rely on an auditor's opinion, "there is no liability even though the [auditor] should reasonably have foreseen such a possibility."[7]

SECTION 3

Liability of Accountants under Securities Laws

Both civil and criminal liability may be imposed on accountants under the Securities Act of 1933, the Securities Exchange Act of 1934, and the Private Securities Litigation Reform Act of 1995.[8]

LIABILITY UNDER THE SECURITIES ACT OF 1933

The Securities Act of 1933 requires registration statements to be filed with the Securities and Exchange

Commission (SEC) prior to an offering of securities (see Chapter 37).[9] Accountants frequently prepare and certify the issuer's financial statements that are included in the registration statement.

Liability under Section 11. Section 11 of the Securities Act of 1933 imposes civil liability on accountants for misstatements and omissions of material facts in registration statements. An accountant may be held liable if he or she prepared any financial statements included in the registration statement that "contained an untrue statement of a material fact or omitted to state a material fact required to be stated therein or necessary to make the statements therein not misleading."[10]

Liability to Purchasers of Securities. An accountant may be liable to anyone who acquires a security covered by the registration statement. A purchaser of a security need only demonstrate that he or she has suffered a loss on the security. Proof of reliance on the materially false statement or misleading omission is not ordinarily required, nor is there a requirement of privity between the accountant and the security purchaser.

The Due Diligence Standard. Section 11 imposes a duty on accountants to use **due diligence** in the preparation of financial statements included in the filed registration statements. After the purchaser has proved the loss on the security, the accountant bears the burden of showing that he or she exercised due diligence in the preparation of the financial statements. To avoid liability, the accountant must show that he or she had, "after reasonable investigation, reasonable grounds to believe and did believe, at the time such part of the registration statement became effective, that the statements therein were true and that there was no omission of a material fact required to be stated therein or necessary to make the statements therein not misleading."[11] Further, the failure to follow GAAP and GAAS is also proof of a lack of due diligence.

In particular, the due diligence standard places a burden on accountants to verify information furnished by a corporation's officers and directors. The burden of proving due diligence requires an accountant to

5. 322 N.C. 200, 367 S.E.2d 609 (1988).
6. *Bethlehem Steel Corp. v. Ernst & Whinney*, 822 S.W.2d 592 (Tenn. 1991).
7. *Bily v. Arthur Young & Co.*, 3 Cal.4th 370, 834 P.2d 745, 11 Cal.Rptr.2d 51 (1992).
8. Civil and criminal liability may be imposed on accountants and other professionals under other statutes, including the Racketeer Influenced and Corrupt Organizations Act (RICO). RICO is discussed in Chapter 8.

9. Many securities and transactions are expressly exempted from the 1933 act.
10. 15 U.S.C. Section 77k(a).
11. 15 U.S.C. Section 77k(b)(3).

demonstrate that he or she did not commit negligence or fraud. The accountants in *Escott v. BarChris Construction Corp.*,[12] for example, were held liable for a failure to detect danger signals in materials that, under GAAS, required further investigation under the circumstances. Merely asking questions is not always sufficient to satisfy the requirement of due diligence.

Defenses to Liability. Besides proving that he or she has acted with due diligence, an accountant may raise the following defenses to Section 11 liability:

1. There were no misstatements or omissions.
2. The misstatements or omissions were not of material facts.
3. The misstatements or omissions had no causal connection to the plaintiff's loss.
4. The plaintiff purchaser invested in the securities knowing of the misstatements or omissions.

Another defense is that an alleged misstatement or omission was not part of a financial statement that the accountant prepared or certified. Whether an accountant prepared or certified a particular statement is not always as obvious as it might seem, as illustrated by the following case.

---

12. 283 F.Supp. 643 (S.D.N.Y. 1968).

CASE 51.3   Endo v. Arthur Andersen & Co.

United States
Court of Appeals,
Seventh Circuit, 1999.
163 F.3d 463.
http://www.kentlaw.
edu/7circuit[a]

BACKGROUND AND FACTS *Arthur Andersen & Company audited the financial statements of Fruit of the Loom, Inc. (FOL), for 1985. The statements included a footnote that said FOL was contesting, in federal court, $105 million in deficiencies assessed by the Internal Revenue Service (IRS). The footnote warned that the ultimate payment to the IRS could, with interest, exceed $105 million. This warning did not appear in FOL's 1986 financial statements, which were audited by Ernst & Young. In 1987, FOL made a stock offering that required the firm to disclose its 1985 financial statements. FOL asked Andersen to consent to a republication of its 1985 report without the warning in the footnote. Andersen checked with Ernst & Young, which certified that nothing had been discovered to warrant changing the data in the 1985 statements. Andersen consented to the republication. Within a year, FOL was ordered to pay the IRS more than $105 million. The price of the FOL stock dropped by 33 percent. Investors who lost money filed a suit in a federal district court against Andersen and others, alleging in part that omitting the warning from the footnote in the republished report violated Section 11 of the Securities Act of 1933. The court granted a summary judgment in Andersen's favor. The plaintiffs appealed to the U.S. Court of Appeals for the Seventh Circuit.*

**IN THE LANGUAGE
OF THE COURT**

POSNER, Chief Judge.
    *   *   *   *

   *   *   * The investor who reads the documentation accompanying FOL's [stock offering] sees a column for the company's 1985 financial results, a column for its 1986 results, a set of footnotes dealing with contingent [potential] liabilities not reflected in the columns, and notations that Andersen audited the 1985 results and continues to stand by them and that Ernst & Young audited the 1986 results. *   *   *

   The footnotes are, it is true, a part of the financial statements. But remember that *an accountant's liability for misleading representations in a registration statement is limited to the portion of any financial statements which purports to have been prepared or certified by him.* Andersen did not purport to certify the footnotes to Fruit of the Loom's 1986

---

a. This Web site is maintained by the Center for Law and Computers at Chicago-Kent College of Law, Illinois Institute of Technology, in Chicago, Illinois. Click on "Browse the 7th Circuit Database." When that page opens, in the "1999 Decisions" section, click on "January." Scroll down the list to the case name and click on it to access the opinion.

financial statements *   *   * . Nor would any reasonable investor have thought otherwise. [Emphasis added.]

*   *   *   *

*   *   * The investor does not expect the same financial data and estimates to be audited by two separate audit companies. He expects the current data, including the current estimates of contingent liabilities, to be audited by the current auditor, and data for
periods prior to the hiring of this auditor to be audited by a former auditor. Ernst &
Young did not audit the 1985 financials; Andersen did. Andersen did not audit the 1986
predictions; Ernst & Young did.[b]

**DECISION
AND REMEDY**   *The U.S. Court of Appeals for the Seventh Circuit affirmed the judgment of the lower
court. The omitted warning was a past prediction about a future event as to which
Andersen's successor had more current information. A reasonable investor would expect
current data, including estimates of tax liability, to be audited by the current auditor.*

b. The investors also filed a suit against Ernst & Young, which was settled out of court.

Liability under Section 12(2). Section 12(2) of the
Securities Act of 1933 imposes civil liability for fraud
on anyone offering or selling a security to any purchaser of the security.[13] Liability is based on communication to an investor, whether orally or in the written
prospectus,[14] of an untrue statement or omission of a
material fact.

Penalties and Sanctions for Violations. Those who
purchase securities and suffer harm as a result of a false
or omitted statement, or some other violation, may
bring a suit in a federal court to recover their losses and
other damages. The U.S. Department of Justice brings
criminal actions against those who commit willful violations. The penalties include fines up to $10,000, im-
prisonment up to five years, or both. The SEC is
authorized to seek, against a willful violator, an injunction against further violations. The SEC can also ask a
court to grant other relief, such as an order to a violator
to refund profits derived from an illegal transaction.

LIABILITY UNDER THE
SECURITIES EXCHANGE ACT OF 1934

Under Sections 18 and 10(b) of the Securities Exchange
Act of 1934 and Rule 10b-5 of the Securities and

Exchange Commission, an accountant may be found
liable for fraud. A plaintiff has a substantially heavier
burden of proof under the 1934 act than under the 1933
act. Unlike the 1933 act, which provides that an accountant must prove due diligence to escape liability,
the 1934 act relieves an accountant from liability if the
accountant acted in "good faith."

Liability under Section 18. Section 18 of the 1934
act imposes civil liability on an accountant who makes
or causes to be made in any application, report, or document a statement that at the time and in light of the
circumstances was false or misleading with respect to
any material fact.[15]

Section 18 liability is narrow in that it applies only
to applications, reports, documents, and registration
statements filed with the SEC. This remedy is further
limited in that it applies only to sellers and purchasers. Under Section 18, a seller or purchaser must
prove one of the following:

1. That the false or misleading statement affected the
price of the security.
2. That the purchaser or seller relied on the false or
misleading statement in making the purchase or sale
and was not aware of the inaccuracy of the statement.

Even if a purchaser or seller proves these two elements, an accountant can be exonerated of liability by

---

13. 15 U.S.C. Section 77l.
14. As discussed in Chapter 34, a *prospectus* contains financial disclosures about the corporation for the benefit of potential investors.

15. 15 U.S.C. Section 78r(a).

proving good faith in the preparation of the financial statement. To demonstrate good faith, an accountant must show that he or she had no knowledge that the financial statement was false or misleading. Acting in good faith requires the total absence of an intention on the part of the accountant to seek an unfair advantage over, or to defraud, another party. Proving a lack of intent to deceive, manipulate, or defraud is frequently referred to as proving a lack of *scienter* (knowledge on the part of a misrepresenting party that material facts have been misrepresented or omitted with an intent to deceive).

The absence of good faith can be demonstrated not only by proof of *scienter* but also by the accountant's reckless conduct and gross negligence. (Note that "mere" negligence in the preparation of a financial statement does not constitute liability under the 1934 act. This differs from provisions of the 1933 act, under which an accountant is liable for all negligent actions.) In addition to the good faith defense, accountants have available as a defense the buyer's or seller's knowledge that the financial statement was false or misleading.

Under Section 18 of the 1934 act, a court also has the discretion to assess reasonable costs, including attorneys' fees, against accountants.[16] Sellers and purchasers may maintain a cause of action "within one year after the discovery of the facts constituting the cause of action and within three years after such cause of action accrued."[17]

Liability under Section 10(b) and SEC Rule 10b-5.

The Securities Exchange Act of 1934 further subjects accountants to potential legal liability in its antifraud provisions. Section 10(b) of the 1934 act and SEC Rule 10b-5 contain the antifraud provisions. As stated in *Herman & MacLean v. Huddleston*, "a private right of action under Section 10(b) of the 1934 act and Rule 10b-5 has been consistently recognized for more than 35 years."[18]

Section 10(b) makes it unlawful for any person, including accountants, to use, in connection with the purchase or sale of any security, any manipulative or deceptive device or contrivance in contravention of SEC rules and regulations.[19] Rule 10b-5 further makes it unlawful for any person, by use of any means or instrumentality of interstate commerce, to do the following:

1. Employ any device, scheme, or artifice to defraud.
2. Make any untrue statement of a material fact or omit to state a material fact necessary to make the statements made, in light of the circumstances, not misleading.
3. Engage in any act, practice, or course of business that operates or would operate as a fraud or deceit on any person, in connection with the purchase or sale of any security.[20]

Accountants may be held liable only to sellers or purchasers under Section 10(b) and Rule 10b-5.[21] The scope of these antifraud provisions is extremely wide. Privity is not necessary for a recovery. Under these provisions, an accountant may be found liable not only for fraudulent misstatements of material facts in written material filed with the SEC but also for any fraudulent oral statements or omissions made in connection with the purchase or sale of any security.

For a plaintiff to recover from an accountant under the antifraud provisions of the 1934 act, he or she must, in addition to establishing status as a purchaser or seller, prove *scienter*,[22] a fraudulent action or deception, reliance, materiality, and causation. A plaintiff who fails to establish these elements cannot recover damages from an accountant under Section 10(b) or Rule 10b-5.

THE PRIVATE SECURITIES LITIGATION REFORM ACT OF 1995

The Private Securities Litigation Reform Act of 1995 made some changes to the potential liability of accountants and other professionals in securities fraud cases. Among other things, the act imposed a new statutory obligation on accountants. An auditor must use adequate procedures in an audit to detect any illegal acts of the company being audited. If something illegal is detected, the auditor must disclose it to the

---

16. 15 U.S.C. Section 78r(a).
17. 15 U.S.C. Section 78r(c).
18. 459 U.S. 375, 103 S.Ct. 683, 74 L.Ed.2d 548 (1983).
19. 15 U.S.C. Section 78j(b).

20. 17 C.F.R. Section 240.10b-5.
21. See *Blue Chip Stamps v. Manor Drug Stores*, 421 U.S. 723, 95 S.Ct. 1917, 44 L.Ed.2d 539 (1975).
22. See *Ernst & Ernst v. Hochfelder*, 425 U.S. 185, 96 S.Ct. 1375, 47 L.Ed.2d 668 (1976).

EMERGING TRENDS IN TECHNOLOGY

The Confidentiality of E-Mail

The widespread use of the Internet by lawyers to communicate with their clients has raised a significant question: Does communicating with a client via e-mail violate the confidentiality rule (discussed on page 984)?

Although the courts have not yet addressed this question, bar associations in several states have rendered ethical opinions on the subject. Among the first to do so was South Carolina, which concluded in 1994 that lawyers should not use e-mail for sensitive client communications because it is possible for e-mail to be intercepted. For the next few years, there seemed to be a growing

consensus that only encrypted communications (encoded messages, using encryption software) with clients could be considered confidential.

Since 1997, however, several states have reached the opposite conclusion. For example, when the Vermont state bar's ethics panel considered the issue, it reasoned that since "(a) e-mail privacy is no less to be expected than in ordinary phone calls, and (b) unauthorized interception is illegal, a lawyer does not violate [the confidentiality rule] by communicating with a client by e-mail . . . without encryption." The panel went on to say that in various instances "of a very sensitive nature, encryption might be prudent, in which case ordinary phone calls would obviously be deemed inadequate." This reasoning is typical of state bar ethics committees in about two dozen other states, including Illinois, Arizona, and even South

Carolina—which reversed its earlier opinion when it revisited the issue later.

In 1999, the American Bar Association (ABA) issued an opinion on the matter. According to the ABA's Standing Committee on Ethics and Professional Responsibility, "a lawyer may transmit information relating to the representation of a client by unencrypted e-mail" without violating the ABA's rules governing attorney conduct. The committee went on to state that plain, unencrypted e-mail "affords a reasonable expectation of privacy from a technological and legal standpoint." According to one commentator, when this announcement was made, the "sigh of relief" among attorneys was "almost audible."[a]

---

a. Wendy R. Leibowitz, "E-Mail Ethics Evolving," *The National Law Journal,* May 17, 1999, p. A17.

company's board of directors, the audit committee, or the SEC, depending on the circumstances.[23]

In terms of liability, the 1995 act provides that in most situations, a party is liable only for that proportion of damages for which he or she is responsible.[24] For example, if an accountant actually participated in defrauding investors, he or she could be liable for the entire loss. If the accountant was not aware of the fraud, however, his or her liability could be proportionately less.

The act also stated that aiding and abetting a violation of the Securities Exchange Act of 1934 is a violation in itself. The SEC can enforce this provision

by seeking an injunction or money damages against any person who knowingly aids and abets primary violators of the securities law. An accountant aids and abets when he or she is generally aware that he or she is participating in an activity that is improper and knowingly assists the activity. Silence may constitute aiding.

For example, Smith & Jones, an accounting firm, performs an audit for ABC Sales Company that is so inadequate as to constitute gross negligence. ABC uses the materials provided by Smith & Jones as part of a scheme to defraud investors. When the scheme is uncovered, the SEC can bring an action against Smith & Jones for aiding and abetting on the ground that the firm knew or should have known of the material misrepresentations that were in its audit and on which investors were likely to rely.

---

23. 15 U.S.C. Section 78j-1.
24. 15 U.S.C. Section 78u-4(g).

EMERGING TRENDS IN TECHNOLOGY

The Confidentiality of E-Mail, continued

Nonetheless, attorneys remain concerned. Although the ABA's opinions wield considerable influence, it is entirely possible that a court may arrive at a different conclusion. For this reason, many attorneys remain cautious when communicating with clients over the Internet. Encrypting e-mail and files that are transmitted over the Internet is one way to avoid confidentiality problems. Another is to add disclaimers to e-mail indicating that the communications may not be secure. Finally, some legal ethicists suggest that lawyers should discuss the issue with their clients and let the clients decide on how sensitive information should be exchanged.

IMPLICATIONS FOR THE BUSINESSPERSON

1. An attorney who breaches his or her duty to preserve the confidentiality of client information may face serious consequences, including liability to the client for damages caused by the breach and the possibility of a disciplinary action by the state bar association. Because the law is not yet settled on the issue of e-mail as a confidential mode of communication, legal professionals should consider encrypting their e-mail messages to or about clients, using disclaimers, and discussing this issue with their clients.
2. Businesspersons who communicate with their attorneys via the Internet should bring up the issue of confidentiality if their attorneys do not. Otherwise, the attorney-client privilege may be jeopardized.

FOR CRITICAL ANALYSIS

1. In terms of privacy and confidentiality, what is the difference between cell phone conversations and e-mail communications?
2. Attorney-client confidentiality is one of the central tenets of the ethical rules governing attorneys. Why is this? Is the rule of confidentiality *always* beneficial to society?

RELEVANT WEB SITES

The ABA has posted its opinion on confidentiality and e-mail on its Web site at **http://www.abanet.org/cpr/fo99-413.html**. For further information on this topic, go to **http://www.legalethics.com/index.law**.

SECTION 4

Potential Criminal Liability of Accountants

An accountant may be found criminally liable for violations of the Securities Act of 1933, the Securities Exchange Act of 1934, the Internal Revenue Code, and both state and federal criminal codes. Under both the 1933 act and the 1934 act, accountants may be subject to criminal penalties for *willful* violations—imprisonment of up to five years and/or a fine of up to $10,000 under the 1933 act and up to ten years and $100,000 under the 1934 act.

The Internal Revenue Code, Section 7206(2),[25] makes aiding or assisting in the preparation of a false tax return a felony punishable by a fine of $100,000 ($500,000 in the case of a corporation) and imprisonment for up to three years. Those who prepare tax returns for others also may face liability under the Internal Revenue Code. Note that one does not have to be an accountant to be subject to liability for tax-preparer penalties. The Internal Revenue Code defines a tax preparer as any person who prepares for compensation, or who employs one or more persons

---

25. 26 U.S.C. Section 7206(2).

to prepare for compensation, all or a substantial portion of a tax return or a claim for a tax refund.[26]

Section 6694[27] of the Internal Revenue Code imposes on the tax preparer a penalty of $250 per return for negligent understatement of the client's tax liability and a penalty of $1,000 for willful understatement of tax liability or reckless or intentional disregard of rules or regulations. A tax preparer may also be subject to penalties under Section 6695[28] for failing to furnish the taxpayer with a copy of the return, failing to sign the return, or failing to furnish the appropriate tax identification numbers.

Section 6701[29] of the Internal Revenue Code imposes a penalty of $1,000 per document for aiding and abetting an individual's understatement of tax liability (the penalty is increased to $10,000 in corporate cases). The tax preparer's liability is limited to one penalty per taxpayer per tax year. If this penalty is imposed, no penalty can be imposed under Section 6694 with respect to the same document.

In most states, criminal penalties may be imposed for such actions as knowingly certifying false or fraudulent reports; falsifying, altering, or destroying books of account; and obtaining property or credit through the use of false financial statements.

SECTION 5

Working Papers

Performing an audit for a client involves an accumulation of **working papers**—the various documents used and developed during the audit. These include notes, computations, memoranda, copies, and other papers that make up the work product of an accountant's services to a client. Under the common law, which in this instance has been codified in a number of states, working papers remain the accountant's property. It is important for accountants to retain such records in the event that they need to defend against lawsuits for negligence or other actions in which their competence is challenged. But because an accountant's working papers reflect the client's financial situation, the client has a right of access to them. (An accountant must return to his or her client any of the client's records or journals on the client's request, and failure to do so may result in liability.)

The client must give permission before working papers can be transferred to another accountant. Without the client's permission or a valid court order, the contents of working papers are not to be disclosed. Disclosure would constitute a breach of the accountant's fiduciary duty to the client. On grounds of unauthorized disclosure, the client could initiate a malpractice suit. The accountant's best defense would be that the client gave permission for the papers' release.

SECTION 6

Confidentiality and Privilege

Professionals are restrained by the ethical tenets of their professions to keep all communications with their clients confidential. The confidentiality of attorney-client communications is also protected by law, which confers a *privilege* on such communications. This privilege is granted because of the need for full disclosure to the attorney of the facts of a client's case.

To encourage frankness, confidential attorney-client communications relating to representation are normally held in strictest confidence and protected by law. The attorney and his or her employees may not discuss the client's case with anyone—even under court order—without the client's permission. The client holds the privilege, and only the client may waive it—by disclosing privileged information to someone outside the privilege, for example. (One of the questions facing the legal profession in recent years is whether attorney-client communications transmitted via e-mail can be considered "confidential." See this chapter's *Emerging Trends in Technology* on pages 982 and 983 for a discussion of this issue.)

In a few states, accountant-client communications are privileged by state statute. In these states, accountant-client communications may not be revealed even in court or in court-sanctioned proceedings without the client's permission. The majority of states, however, abide by the common law, which provides that, if a court so orders, an accountant must disclose information about his or her client to the court. Physicians and other professionals may similarly be compelled to disclose in court information given to them in confidence by patients or clients.

---

26. 26 U.S.C. Section 7701(a)(36).
27. 26 U.S.C. Section 6694.
28. 26 U.S.C. Section 6695.
29. 26 U.S.C. Section 6701.

Communications between professionals and their clients—other than those between an attorney and his or her client—are not privileged under federal law. In cases involving federal law, state-provided rights to confidentiality of accountant-client communications are not recognized. Thus, in those cases, in response to a court order, an accountant must provide the information sought.

SECTION 7

Limiting Professionals' Liability

As mentioned earlier in this chapter, accountants (and other professionals) can limit their liability to some extent by disclaiming it. Depending on the circumstances, a disclaimer that does not meet certain requirements will not be effective, however; and in some situations, a disclaimer may not be effective at all.

Professionals may be able to limit their liability for the misconduct of other professionals with whom they work by organizing the business as a professional corporation (P.C.) or a limited liability partnership (LLP). In some states, a professional who is a member of a P.C. is not personally liable for a co-member's misconduct unless he or she participated in it or supervised the member who acted wrongly. The innocent professional is liable only to the extent of his or her interest in the assets of the firm. This is also true for professionals who are partners in an LLP. P.C.s were discussed in more detail in Chapter 34. LLPs were covered in Chapter 38.

CONCEPT SUMMARY 51.1

LIABILITY OF ACCOUNTANTS AND OTHER PROFESSIONALS

COMMON LAW LIABILITY

Liability to Client	1. *Breach of contract*—An accountant or other professional who fails to perform according to his or her contractual obligations can be held liable for breach of contract and resulting damages. 2. *Negligence*—An accountant or other professional, in performance of his or her duties, must use the care, knowledge, and judgment generally used by professionals in the same or similar circumstances. Failure to do so is negligence. An accountant's violation of generally accepted accounting principles and generally accepted auditing standards is *prima facie* evidence of negligence. An accountant who reveals confidential information or the contents of working papers without the client's permission or a court order can be held liable for malpractice. 3. *Fraud*—Actual intent to misrepresent a material fact to a client, when the client relies on the misrepresentation, is fraud. Gross negligence in performance of duties is constructive fraud.
Liability to Third Parties	An accountant may be liable for negligence to any third person the accountant knows or should have known will benefit from the accountant's work. The standard for imposing this liability varies, but generally courts follow one of the following three rules: 1. *Ultramares rule*—Liability will be imposed only if the accountant is in privity, or near privity, with the third party. 2. *Restatement rule*—Liability will be imposed only if the third party's reliance is foreseen or known or if the third party is among a class of foreseeable or known users. The majority of courts adopt this rule. 3. *"Reasonably foreseeable user" rule*—Liability will be imposed if the third party's use was reasonably foreseeable.

CONCEPT SUMMARY 51.1

LIABILITY OF ACCOUNTANTS AND OTHER PROFESSIONALS (*continued*)

STATUTORY LIABILITY

Securities Act of 1933, Sections 11 and 12(2)	Under Section 11 of the 1933 Securities Act, an accountant who makes a false statement or omits a material fact in audited financial statements required for registration of securities under the law may be liable to anyone who acquires securities covered by the registration statement. The accountant's defense is basically the use of due diligence and the reasonable belief that the work was complete and correct. The burden of proof is on the accountant. Willful violations of this act may be subject to criminal penalties. Section 12(2) of the 1933 act imposes civil liability for fraud on anyone offering or selling a security to any purchaser of the security.
Securities Exchange Act of 1934, Sections 10(b) and 18	Under Sections 10(b) and 18 of the 1934 Securities Exchange Act, accountants are held liable for false and misleading applications, reports, and documents required under the act. The burden is on the plaintiff, and the accountant has numerous defenses, including good faith and lack of knowledge that what was submitted was false. Willful violations of this act may be subject to criminal penalties.
Internal Revenue Code	1. Aiding or assisting in the preparation of a false tax return is a felony. Aiding and abetting an individual's understatement of tax liability is a separate crime. 2. Tax preparers who negligently or willfully understate a client's tax liability or who recklessly or intentionally disregard Internal Revenue rules or regulations are subject to criminal penalties. 3. Tax preparers who fail to provide a taxpayer with a copy of the return, fail to sign the return, or fail to furnish the appropriate tax identification numbers may also be subject to criminal penalties.

TERMS AND CONCEPTS TO REVIEW

defalcation 973

due diligence 978

generally accepted accounting
   principles (GAAP) 973

generally accepted auditing
   standards (GAAS) 973

working papers 984

QUESTIONS AND CASE PROBLEMS

51–1. *ULTRAMARES RULE.* Larkin, Inc., retains Howard Perkins to manage its books and prepare its financial statements. Perkins, a certified public accountant, lives in Indiana and practices there. After twenty years, Perkins has become a bit bored with the format of generally accepted accounting principles and has become creative in his accounting methods. Now, though, Perkins has a problem, as he is being sued by Molly Tucker, one of Larkin's creditors. Tucker alleges that Perkins either knew or should have known that Larkin's financial statements would be distributed to various individuals. Furthermore, she asserts that these financial statements were negligently prepared and seriously inaccurate. What are the consequences of Perkins's failure to adopt generally accepted accounting principles? Under the traditional *Ultramares* rule, can Tucker recover damages from Perkins? Explain.

51–2. ACCOUNTANT'S LIABILITY TO THIRD PARTIES AND PUBLIC POLICY. The accounting firm of Goldman, Walters, Johnson & Co. prepared financial statements for Lucy's Fashions, Inc. After reviewing the various financial statements, Happydays State Bank agreed to loan Lucy's Fashions $35,000 for expansion. When Lucy's Fashions declared bankruptcy under Chapter 11 six months later, Happydays State Bank promptly filed an action against Goldman, Walters, Johnson & Co., alleging negligent preparation of financial statements. Assuming that the court has abandoned the *Ultramares* approach, what is the result? What are the policy reasons for holding accountants liable to third parties with whom they are not in privity?

51–3. ACCOUNTANT'S LIABILITY UNDER RULE 10b-5. In early 1995, Bennett, Inc., offered a substantial number of new common shares to the public. Harvey Helms had a long-standing interest in Bennett because his grandfather had once been president of the company. On receiving a prospectus prepared and distributed by Bennett, Helms was dismayed by the pessimism it embodied. Helms decided to delay purchasing stock in the company. Later, Helms asserted that the prospectus prepared by the accountants was overly pessimistic and contained materially misleading statements. Discuss fully how successful Helms would be in bringing a cause of action under Rule 10b-5 against the accountants of Bennett, Inc.

51–4. AUDITOR'S LIABILITY TO THIRD PARTIES. The plaintiffs, Harry and Barry Rosenblum, brought an action against Touche Ross & Co., a prominent accounting firm. The plaintiffs alleged that they had relied on the correctness of audits performed by the firm in acquiring Giant common stock in conjunction with the sale of their business to Giant. The financial statements of Giant were found to be fraudulent, and the stock that the Rosenblums had acquired proved to be worthless. The plaintiffs alleged that Touche's negligence in conducting the audits was the proximate cause of their loss. There was no statement in the audits limiting to whom the company might disseminate the information. To which third parties should an auditor be liable? Explain. [*H. Rosenblum, Inc. v. Adler*, 93 N.J. 324, 461 A.2d 138 (1983)]

51–5. AUDITOR'S LIABILITY TO THIRD PARTIES. An accounting firm was engaged by two car rental companies to determine the net worth of those businesses by preparing an audited statement. At the request of their clients, the accountants did not audit the accounts receivable, made appropriate exceptions to the accounts receivable in the balance sheet, and qualified their opinion with a caveat stating that this had been done. After the audit had been performed and on the basis of the figures reflected in the balance sheet, Stephens Industries, Inc., purchased two-thirds of the car rental companies' stock. The car rental businesses thereafter failed, and

Stephens Industries brought an action against the accounting firm for allegedly having misrepresented the status of the accounts receivable in the audit. What was the result? [*Stephens Industries, Inc. v. Haskins & Sells*, 438 F.2d 357 (10th Cir. 1971)]

51–6. ACCOUNTANT'S LIABILITY UNDER RULE 10b-5. The plaintiffs were the purchasers of all the stock in companies owned by the defendant sellers. Alleging fraud under the federal securities laws and under the New York common law of fraud, the plaintiffs sued the defendant sellers and their accounting firm. What should be the result with respect to the accounting firm, assuming that the treatment of shipping costs, expenses, and other charges was not in accordance with generally accepted accounting principles and hence created an inaccurate financial picture in the financial statements? [*Berkowitz v. Baron*, 428 F.Supp. 1190 (S.D.N.Y. 1977)]

51–7. ACCOUNTANT'S LIABILITY TO THIRD PARTIES. Toro Co. was a major supplier of equipment and credit to Summit Power Equipment Distributors. Toro required audited reports from Summit to evaluate the distributor's financial condition. Summit supplied Toro with reports prepared by Krouse, Kern & Co., an accounting firm. The reports allegedly contained mistakes and omissions regarding Summit's financial condition. According to Toro, it extended and renewed large amounts of credit to Summit in reliance on the audited reports. Summit was unable to repay these amounts, and Toro brought a negligence action against the accounting firm and the individual accountants. Evidence produced at the trial showed that Krouse knew that the reports it furnished to Summit were to be used by Summit to induce Toro to extend credit, but no evidence was produced to show either a contractual relationship between Krouse and Toro or a link between these companies evidencing Krouse's understanding of Toro's actual reliance on the reports. The relevant state law follows the *Ultramares* rule. What was the result? [*Toro Co. v. Krouse, Kern & Co.*, 827 F.2d 155 (7th Cir. 1987)]

51–8. ATTORNEY'S DUTY OF CARE. Sheila Simpson and the other two shareholders in H. P. Enterprises Corp. decided to sell the corporation and turned to Ed Oliver, an attorney, for assistance. Oliver formed a corporation, Tide Creek, for a group of investors, and Tide Creek then purchased the assets of H. P. Enterprises for $500,000, of which $100,000 was paid at the time of the sale in November 1983. As security for the sellers, Oliver provided a lien on the stock of Tide Creek and personal guaranties of the buyers on the corporation's $400,000 note to the sellers. Oliver was the sole source of legal advice for both parties. About six months after the sale, a fire destroyed Tide Creek's inventory. In October 1984, Oliver left the law firm in which he had been a partner, and one of the other partners, David James, took over the Simpson and Tide Creek accounts. In January 1985, James advised Simpson that Tide Creek was having financial difficulties and suggested that the note be restructured; this was done. When Simpson asked James what he would do if her interests and those of Tide Creek diverged, James replied, "We would have to support you." Tide Creek later filed for bankruptcy, as did the individuals who had personally guaranteed the note, and Simpson and the others received nothing. Did the sellers succeed in a lawsuit against James for negligence? Discuss fully. [*Simpson v. James*, 903 F.2d 372 (5th Cir. 1990)]

51–9. ACCOUNTANT'S LIABILITY TO THIRD PARTIES. In June 1993, Sparkomatic Corp. agreed to negotiate a sale of its Kenco Engineering division to Williams Controls, Inc. At the end of July, Sparkomatic asked its accountants, Parente, Randolph, Orlando, Carey & Associates, to audit Kenco's financial statements for the previous three years and to certify interim and closing balance sheets to be included with the sale's closing documents. All of the parties knew that these documents would serve as a basis for setting the sale price. Within a few days, Williams signed an "Asset Purchase Agreement" that promised access to Parente's records with respect to Kenco. The sale closed in mid-August. In September, Williams was given the financial statements for Kenco's previous three years and the interim and closing balance sheets, all of which were certified by Parente. Williams's accountant found no errors in the closing balance sheet but did not review any of the other documents. The parties set a final purchase price. Later, however, Williams filed a suit in a federal district court against Parente, claiming negligent misrepresentation, among other things, in connection with Parente's preparation of the financial documents. Parente responded with a motion for summary judgment, asserting that the parties lacked privity. Under the *Restatement (Second) of Torts*, Section 552, how should the court rule? Explain. [*Williams Controls, Inc. v. Parente, Randolph, Orlando, Carey & Associates*, 39 F.Supp.2d 517 (M.D.Pa. 1999)]

51–10. IN YOUR COURT

Regal Furnishings, Inc., planned to purchase Gantry Furniture Co. and wished to determine its net worth. Regal hired an accounting firm, Coase & Banks, to review an audit prepared by certified public accountants for Gantry. Coase & Banks advised Regal that Gantry's accountants had performed a high-quality audit and that Gantry's inventory on the audit dates was fairly stated on the general ledger. As a result of these representations, Regal went forward with its purchase of Gantry. Later, Regal discovered that the review by Coase & Banks was materially inaccurate and misleading, primarily because the inventory was grossly overstated on the balance sheet. In the lawsuit that followed, Regal alleged that Coase & Banks had violated Section 10(b) of the Securities Exchange Act and SEC Rule 10b-5. Regal claimed that Coase & Banks had acted recklessly in failing to detect and disclose material omissions on the audit during its review. Assume that you are the judge in the trial court hearing this case and answer the following questions:

(a) Generally, what requirements must be met before a plaintiff can recover from an accountant under Section 10(b) of the Securities and Exchange Act of 1934 and SEC Rule 10b-5? Has Regal met these requirements?

(b) Specifically, has Regal established that its purchase of Gantry was a purchase of securities? Does "acting recklessly in failing to detect and disclose material omissions" on an audit equate to *scienter*?

(c) In view of your answers to the above two questions, what will your decision be in this case, and why?

LAW ON THE WEB

For updated links to resources available on the Web, as well as a variety of other materials, visit this text's Web site at http://wbl.westbuslaw.com.

The Web site for the Financial Accounting Standards Board can be found at

http://www.rutgers.edu/Accounting/raw/fasb

For information on the accounting profession, including articles from the *Journal of Accountancy*, go to the Web site for the American Institute of Certified Public Accountants (AICPA) at

http://www.aicpa.org/index.htm

LEGAL RESEARCH EXERCISES ON THE WEB

Go to http://wbl.westbuslaw.com, the Web site that accompanies this text. Select "Internet Applications," and then click on "Chapter 51." There you will find the following Internet research exercise that you can perform to learn more about some of the steps professionals can take to avoid liability:

Activity 51–1: Avoiding Legal Liability

CHAPTER 52

International and Comparative Law

INTERNATIONAL BUSINESS TRANSACTIONS are not unique to the modern world. Indeed, since ancient times independent peoples and nations have traded their goods and wares with one another. What is new in our day is the dramatic growth in world trade and the emergence of a global business community. Today, nearly every major business considers the potential of international markets for its products or services. It is no longer uncommon for a U.S. corporation to have investments or manufacturing plants in a foreign country or for a foreign corporation to have operations in the United States. Because the exchange of goods, services, and ideas on a worldwide level is now routine, students of business law should be familiar with the laws pertaining to international business transactions.

Laws affecting the international legal environment of business include both international law and national law. **International law** can be defined as a body of law—formed as a result of international customs, treaties, and organizations—that governs relations among or between nations. **National law** is the law of a particular nation, such as the United States, Japan, Germany, or Brazil. In this chapter, we examine how both international law and national law frame business operations in the international context.

SECTION 1

International Law

The major difference between international law and national law is the fact that government authorities can enforce national law. What government, however, can enforce international law? By definition, a *nation* is a sovereign entity—which means that there is no higher authority to which that nation must submit. If a nation violates an international law, the most that other countries or international organizations can do (when persuasive tactics fail) is resort to coercive actions—from severance of diplomatic relations and boycotts to, as a last resort, war—against the violating nation.

In essence, international law is the result of centuries-old attempts to reconcile the traditional need of each country to be the final authority over its own affairs with the desire of nations to benefit economically from trade and harmonious relations with one another. Sovereign nations can, and do, voluntarily agree to be governed in certain respects by international law for the purpose of facilitating international trade and commerce, as well as civilized discourse. As a result, a body of international law has evolved. In this section, we examine the primary sources and characteristics of that body of law, as well as some important legal principles and doctrines that have been developed over time to facilitate dealings among nations.

SOURCES OF INTERNATIONAL LAW

Basically, there are three sources of international law: international customs, treaties and international agreements, and international organizations and conferences. We look at each of these sources here.

International Customs.   One important source of international law consists of the international customs that have evolved among nations in their relations with one another. In Article 38(1) of the Statute of the International Court of Justice, an international custom is referred to as "evidence of a general practice accepted as law." The legal principles and doctrines that you will read about shortly are rooted in international customs and traditions that evolved over time in the international arena.

Treaties and International Agreements.   Treaties and other explicit agreements between or among foreign nations provide another important source of international law. A **treaty** is an agreement or contract between two or more nations that must be authorized and ratified by the supreme power of each nation. Under Article II, Section 2, of the U.S. Constitution, the president has the power "by and with the Advice and Consent of the Senate, to make Treaties, provided two-thirds of the Senators present concur."

A *bilateral* agreement, as the term implies, occurs when two nations form an agreement that will govern their commercial exchanges or other relations with one another. *Multilateral* agreements are those formed by several nations. For example, regional trade associations such as the European Union (EU) and the trading unit established by the North American Free Trade Agreement (NAFTA), both of which are discussed later in this chapter, are the result of multilateral trade agreements. Other regional trade associations that have been created through multilateral agreements include the Association of Southeast Asian Nations (ASEAN) and the Andean Common Market (ANCOM).

International Organizations and Conferences.   International organizations and conferences further contribute to international law. In international law, the term **international organization** generally refers to an organization composed mainly of nations and usually established by treaty.

The United States is a member of more than one hundred multilateral and bilateral organizations, including at least twenty through the United Nations (see Exhibit 52–1). These organizations adopt resolutions, declarations, and other types of standards that often require a particular behavior of nations. The General Assembly of the United Nations, for example, has adopted numerous nonbinding resolutions and declarations that embody principles of international law. Disputes with respect to these resolutions and declarations may be brought before the International Court of Justice. That court, however, normally has authority to settle legal disputes only when nations voluntarily submit to its jurisdiction.

The United Nations Commission on International Trade Law has made considerable progress in establishing uniformity in international law as it relates to trade and commerce. One of the commission's most significant creations to date is the 1980 Convention on Contracts for the International Sale of Goods (CISG). Recall from Chapters 19 through 23, which cover contracts for the sale of goods, that the CISG is similar to Article 2 of the Uniform Commercial Code in that it is designed to settle disputes between parties to sales contracts. It spells out the duties of international buyers and sellers that will apply if the parties have not agreed otherwise in their contracts. The CISG only governs sales contracts between trading partners in nations that have ratified the CISG, however.

LEGAL PRINCIPLES AND DOCTRINES

Over time, a number of legal principles and doctrines have evolved and have been employed—to a greater or lesser extent—by the courts of various nations to resolve or reduce conflicts that involve a foreign element. The three important legal principles discussed below are based primarily on courtesy and respect and are applied in the interests of maintaining harmonious relations among nations.

The Principle of Comity.   Under what is known as the principle of **comity**, one nation will defer and give effect to the laws and judicial decrees of another country, as long as those laws and judicial decrees are consistent with the law and public policy of the accommodating nation. For example, assume that a Swedish seller and an American buyer have formed a

EXHIBIT 52–1   MULTILATERAL INTERNATIONAL ORGANIZATIONS IN WHICH THE UNITED STATES PARTICIPATES

NAME	PURPOSE
Customs Cooperation Council	Established in 1950. Supervises the application and interpretation of an international code classifying goods and customs tariffs.
International Bank for Reconstruction and Development	Popularly known as the World Bank; a specialized agency of the United Nations since 1947. Promotes growth, trade, and balance of trade by facilitating and providing technical assistance, particularly in agriculture, energy, transportation, and telecommunications.
International Center for the Settlement of Investment Disputes	Established in 1966. Conciliates and arbitrates disputes between private investors and governments of other countries.
International Civil Aviation Organization	Established in 1947 and became a specialized agency of the United Nations seven months later. Develops international civil aviation by issuing rules and policies for safe and efficient airports and air navigation.
International Court of Justice (World Court)	Established in 1922 and became one of the principal organs of the United Nations in 1945. Jurisdiction comprises all cases that are referred to it. Decides disputes in accord with the rules of international law.
International Maritime Organization	Established in 1948. Promotes cooperation in the areas of government regulation, practices and technical matters of all kinds affecting shipping in international trade, the adoption of standards of maritime safety and efficiency, and the abolition of discrimination and unnecessary restrictions.
International Monetary Fund (IMF)	Created in 1944 at the United Nations Monetary and Financial Conference. Promotes economic stability by aiding the growth of international trade and the stability of currency exchange rates, as well as by providing for a system of international monetary assistance.
International Telecommunications Satellite Organization	Established in 1964. Operates an international public communications satellite system on a commercial, nondiscriminatory basis.
Permanent Court of Arbitration	Established in 1899 to facilitate the settlement of international disputes. The court has jurisdiction over all cases that it is requested to arbitrate.
United Nations (UN)	Established in 1945 to maintain international peace and security. Promotes international cooperation.
World Intellectual Property Organization	Established in 1967 and became a specialized agency of the United Nations in 1974. Promotes protection of intellectual property throughout the world.
World Trade Organization (WTO)	Established in 1994 during the final round of negotiations of the General Agreement on Tariffs and Trade (GATT). The GATT was created in 1947 and was the first global commercial agreement in history. It became the principal instrument for regulating international trade and limiting tariffs and other barriers to world trade on particular commodities and other items. GATT ceased to exist in 1995, when the WTO came into existence to regulate worldwide trade.

contract, which the buyer breaches. The seller sues the buyer in a Swedish court, which awards damages. The buyer's assets, however, are in the United States and cannot be reached unless the judgment is enforced by a U.S. court of law. In such a situation, if a U.S. court determined that the procedures and laws applied in the Swedish court were consistent with U.S. national law and policy, the U.S. court would likely defer to, and enforce, the foreign court's judgment.

The Act of State Doctrine. The **act of state doctrine** is a judicially created doctrine that provides that the judicial branch of one country will not examine the validity of public acts committed by a recognized foreign government within its own territory. This doctrine is premised on the theory that the judicial branch should not "pass upon the validity of foreign acts when to do so would vex the harmony of our international relations with that foreign nation."[1]

The act of state doctrine can have important consequences for individuals and firms doing business with, and investing in, other countries. For example, this doctrine is frequently employed in cases involving **expropriation,** which occurs when a government seizes a privately owned business or privately owned goods for a proper public purpose and awards just compensation. When a government seizes private property for an illegal purpose and without just compensation, the taking is referred to as a **confiscation.** The line between these two forms of taking is sometimes blurred because of differing interpretations of what is illegal and what constitutes just compensation. To illustrate: Tim Flaherty, an American businessperson, owns a mine in Brazil. The government of Brazil seizes the mine for public use and claims that the profits Tim has already realized from the mine constitute just compensation. Tim disagrees, but the act of state doctrine may prevent Tim's recovery in a U.S. court of law.

When applicable, both the act of state doctrine and the doctrine of *sovereign immunity*, which we discuss next, tend to shield foreign nations from the jurisdiction of U.S. courts. What this means is that, generally, firms or individuals who own property overseas have little legal protection against government actions in the countries in which they operate.

The Doctrine of Sovereign Immunity. When certain conditions are satisfied, the doctrine of **sovereign immunity** exempts foreign nations from the jurisdiction of the U.S. courts. In 1976, Congress codified this rule in the Foreign Sovereign Immunities Act (FSIA).[2] The FSIA also modified previous applications of the doctrine in certain respects by expanding the rights of plaintiff creditors against foreign nations.

The FSIA exclusively governs the circumstances in which an action may be brought in the United States against a foreign nation. Section 1605 of the FSIA sets forth the major exceptions to the jurisdictional immunity of a foreign state. A foreign state is not immune

from the jurisdiction of the courts of the United States when the state has "waived its immunity either explicitly or by implication" or when the state has engaged in actions that are taken "in connection with a commercial activity carried on in the United States by the foreign state" or that have "a direct effect in the United States."

Issues frequently arise as to whether particular entities fall within the category of foreign state. Under Section 1603 of the FSIA, a foreign state is defined to include both a political subdivision of a foreign state and an instrumentality of a foreign state (an agency or entity acting for the state). The question of what is a commercial activity has also been the subject of dispute, because the particulars of what constitutes a commercial activity are not defined in the act. Rather, it is left up to the courts to decide whether a particular activity is governmental or commercial in nature.

SECTION 2

Doing Business Internationally

A U.S. domestic firm can engage in international business transactions in a number of ways. Contracts for the international purchase and sale of goods were discussed earlier in this text, in Chapters 19 through 23. Here, we look at other aspects of international business transactions, including the ways in which businesspersons typically extend their business operations into the international arena, laws regulating international business activities, and dispute settlement in the international context.

TYPES OF INTERNATIONAL BUSINESS OPERATIONS

Most U.S. companies make the initial foray into international business through exporting. There are several other alternatives, however, including those discussed here.

Exporting. The simplest way of entering into international business operations is to seek out foreign markets for domestically produced products. In other words, U.S. firms can **export** their goods and services to foreign markets. Exporting can take two forms: direct exporting and indirect exporting. In *direct exporting*, a U.S. company signs a sales contract with a foreign purchaser that provides for the conditions of shipment and

---

1. *Libra Bank Ltd. v. Banco Nacional de Costa Rica, S.A.*, 570 F.Supp. 870 (S.D.N.Y. 1983).
2. 28 U.S.C. Sections 1602–1611.

payment for the goods. (How payments are made in international transactions through the use of letters of credit was discussed in Chapter 21.) If business develops sufficiently in foreign countries, a U.S. company may, through the appointment of a foreign agent or a foreign distributor, develop a specialized marketing organization in the foreign market. This is called *indirect exporting.*

When a U.S. firm desires a limited involvement in an international market, it will typically establish an agency relationship with a foreign firm. In an agency relationship, one person (the agent) agrees to act on behalf of, or instead of, another (the principal)—see Chapter 31. The foreign agent is thereby empowered to enter into contracts in the agent's country on behalf of the U.S. principal.

When a substantial market exists in a foreign country, a U.S. firm may wish to appoint a distributor located in that country. The U.S. firm and the distributor enter into a **distribution agreement,** which is a contract between the seller and the distributor setting out the terms and conditions of the distributorship—for example, price, currency of payment, guarantee of supply availability, and method of payment. The terms and conditions primarily involve contract law. Disputes concerning distribution agreements may involve jurisdictional or other issues, however.

Manufacturing Abroad. An alternative to direct or indirect exporting is the establishment of foreign manufacturing facilities. Typically, U.S. firms want to establish manufacturing plants abroad if they believe that by doing so they will reduce costs—particularly for labor, shipping, and raw materials—and thereby be able to compete more effectively in foreign markets. Apple Computer, IBM, General Motors, and Ford are some of the many U.S. companies that have established manufacturing facilities abroad. Foreign firms have done the same in the United States. Sony, Nissan, and other Japanese manufacturers have established U.S. plants to avoid import duties that the U.S. Congress may impose on Japanese products entering this country.

An American firm can conduct manufacturing operations in other countries in several ways. They include licensing and franchising, as well as investing in a wholly owned subsidiary or a joint venture.

Licensing. A U.S. firm can obtain business from abroad by licensing a foreign manufacturing company to use its copyrighted, patented, or trademarked intellectual property or trade secrets. Like any other licensing agreement (see Chapter 9), a licensing agreement with a foreign-based firm calls for a payment of royalties on some basis—such as so many cents per unit produced or a certain percentage of profits from units sold in a particular geographical territory. For example, the Coca-Cola Bottling Company licenses firms worldwide to use (and keep confidential) its secret formula for the syrup used in that soft drink, in return for a percentage of the income gained from the sale of Coca-Cola by those firms.

The licensing of intellectual property rights benefits all parties to the transaction: the firm that receives the license can take advantage of an established reputation for quality, and the firm that grants the license receives income from the foreign sales of its products, as well as establishing a global reputation. Also, once a firm's trademark is known worldwide, the demand for other products manufactured or sold by that firm may increase—obviously an important consideration.

Franchising. Franchising is a well-known form of licensing. Recall from Chapter 39 that a franchise can be defined as an arrangement in which the owner of a trademark, trade name, or copyright (the franchisor) licenses another (the franchisee) to use the trademark, trade name, or copyright, under certain conditions or limitations, in the selling of goods or services. In return, the franchisee pays a fee, which is usually based on a percentage of gross or net sales. Examples of international franchises include McDonald's, Holiday Inn, Avis, and Hertz.

Investing in a Wholly Owned Subsidiary or a Joint Venture. One way to expand into a foreign market is to establish a wholly owned subsidiary firm in a foreign country. The European subsidiary would likely take the form of a *société anonyme* (S.A.), which is similar to a U.S. corporation. In German-speaking nations, it would be called an *Aktiengesellschaft* (A.G.). When a wholly owned subsidiary is established, the parent company, which remains in the United States, retains complete ownership of all the facilities in the foreign country, as well as total authority and control over all phases of the operation.

The expansion of a U.S. firm into international markets can also take the form of a joint venture. In a joint venture, the U.S. company owns only part of the operation; the rest is owned either by local owners in the foreign country or by another foreign entity. In a joint venture, responsibilities, as well as profits and liabilities, are shared by all of the firms involved in the venture. (See Chapter 39 for a more detailed discussion of joint ventures.)

THE REGULATION OF INTERNATIONAL BUSINESS ACTIVITIES

Doing business abroad can affect the economies, foreign policy, domestic politics, and other national interests of the countries involved. For this reason, nations impose laws to restrict or facilitate international business. Controls may also be imposed by international agreements.

Investing. Investing in foreign nations involves a risk that the foreign government may expropriate the investment property. As mentioned earlier in this chapter, expropriation occurs when property is taken and the owner is paid just compensation for what is taken. This does not violate generally observed principles of international law. Such principles are normally violated, however, when property is confiscated by a government without compensation (or without adequate compensation).

Few remedies are available for confiscation of property by a foreign government. Claims are often resolved by lump-sum settlements after negotiations between the United States and the taking nation. For example, investors whose claims arose out of confiscations following the Russian Revolution in 1917 were offered a lump-sum settlement by the Union of Soviet Socialist Republics in 1974. Still outstanding are $2 billion in claims against Cuba for confiscations that occurred in 1959 and 1960.

To counter the deterrent effect that the possibility of confiscation may have on potential investors, many countries guarantee compensation to foreign investors if property is taken. A guarantee can be in the form of national constitutional or statutory laws or provisions in international treaties. As further protection for foreign investments, some countries provide insurance for their citizens' investments abroad.

Export Control. The U.S. Constitution provides in Article I, Section 9, that "No Tax or Duty shall be laid on Articles exported from any State." Thus, Congress cannot impose any export taxes. Congress can, however, use a variety of other devices to control exports. Congress may set export quotas on various items, such as grain being sold abroad. Under the

Export Administration Act of 1979,[3] restrictions can be imposed on the flow of technologically advanced products and technical data. A controversial control in recent years has been the U.S. Department of Commerce's attempt to restrict the export of encryption software (discussed in Chapter 9).

Devices to stimulate exports and thereby aid domestic businesses include export incentives and subsidies. The Revenue Act of 1971, for example, gave tax benefits to firms marketing their products overseas through certain foreign sales corporations, exempting income produced by the exports.[4] Under the Export Trading Company Act of 1982,[5] U.S. banks are encouraged to invest in export trading companies. An export trading company consists of exporting firms joined together to export a line of goods. The Export-Import Bank provides financial assistance, consisting primarily of credit guaranties given to commercial banks that in turn loan funds to U.S. exporting companies.

Import Control. All nations have restrictions on imports, and the United States is no exception. Restrictions include strict prohibitions, quotas, and tariffs. Under the Trading with the Enemy Act of 1917,[6] for example, no goods may be imported from nations that have been designated enemies of the United States. Other laws prohibit the importation of illegal drugs, books that urge insurrection against the United States, and agricultural products that pose dangers to domestic crops or animals.

Quotas are limits on the amounts of goods that can be imported. At one time, the United States had legal quotas on the numbers of automobiles that could be imported from Japan. Currently, Japan "voluntarily" restricts the numbers of automobiles exported to the United States. **Tariffs** are taxes on imports. A tariff is usually a percentage of the value of the import, but it can be a flat rate per unit (such as per barrel of oil). Tariffs raise the prices of goods, causing some consumers to purchase less expensive, domestically manufactured goods.

The United States has specific laws directed at what it sees as unfair international trade practices. **Dumping,** for example, is the sale of imported goods at "less than fair value." *Fair value* is usually determined by the price of those goods in the exporting

3. 50 U.S.C. App. Sections 2401–2420.
4. 26 U.S.C. Sections 991–994.
5. 15 U.S.C. Sections 4001, 4003.
6. 12 U.S.C. Section 95a.

country. Dumping is designed to undersell U.S. businesses and obtain a larger share of the U.S. market. To prevent this, an extra tariff—known as an *antidumping duty*—may be assessed on the imports.

The procedure for imposing antidumping duties involves two U.S. government agencies: the International Trade Commission (ITC) and the International Trade Administration (ITA). The ITC is an independent agency that makes recommendations to the president concerning temporary import restrictions. The ITC assesses the effects of dumping on domestic businesses.

The ITA is part of the Department of Commerce and decides whether imports were sold at less than fair value. The ITA determination establishes the amount of antidumping duties, which are set to equal the difference between the price charged in the United States and the price charged in the exporting country. A duty may be retroactive to cover past dumping.

In the following case, the United States Supreme Court considered a challenge to tariff classifications imposed on clothing assembled from U.S. components and then "permapressed" in Mexico.

CASE 52.1   United States v. Haggar Apparel Co.

Supreme Court of the
United States, 1999.
526 U.S. 380,
119 S.Ct. 1392,
143 L.Ed.2d 480.
http://www.supct.law.
cornell.edu/supct[a]

COMPANY PROFILE   *Haggar Apparel Company (http://www.haggar.com) is a leading maker of men's clothing. Haggar's products, including its "wrinkle-free" pants, are sold in more than seven thousand stores in the United States. These stores include seventy Haggar outlet stores. Haggar also makes lower-priced brands, private-label clothing, and women's wear, through Jerell, Inc., its Selena and Stonebridge brands, and Haggar Canada. Haggar's products are sold all over the world, with wholly owned subsidiaries in Canada, Great Britain, and Japan. Haggar has plants in the United States, the Dominican Republic, and Mexico.*

BACKGROUND AND FACTS   *Haggar Apparel Company buys fabric in the United States, has it treated it with a chemical resin, has it cut, and then ships it to Mexico with thread, buttons, and zippers to make pants. The trousers are then sewn, permapressed, and shipped back to the United States. Permapressing is designed to maintain a garment's crease in the desired place and to avoid other creases or wrinkles that detract from its appearance. Permapressing is a baking process that activates the chemical resin to impart the permapress quality. To obtain that quality, extra steps would be needed if the baking were delayed until the garments were shipped back to the United States. Under a federal agency regulation, goods with U.S. components that are assembled abroad and reshipped to the United States are exempt from a duty that is charged against other incoming goods. The U.S. Customs Service levied a duty on Haggar's pants, however, under a regulation that deems all permapressing operations to be an additional step in manufacture, not part of or incidental to the assembly process. Haggar filed a suit in the U.S. Court of International Trade against the federal government, seeking a refund of the duty. Haggar argued that its permapressing was part of the assembly process. The court ruled in Haggar's favor, and the U.S. Court of Appeals for the Federal Circuit affirmed this ruling. The government appealed to the United States Supreme Court.*

IN THE LANGUAGE
OF THE COURT

Justice *KENNEDY* delivered the opinion of the Court.

    ❖   ❖   ❖   ❖

    ❖   ❖   ❖   [Haggar] says the regulation binds Customs Service employees when they classify imported merchandise under the tariff schedules but does not bind the importers themselves. The statutory scheme does not support this limited view of the force

a. In the right column, in the "Arrayed by party name" section, in the "1999" row, click on "2nd party." Scroll down the list of cases to "Haggar Apparel Co., United States v." and click on it to access a syllabus of the case. On that page, click on the appropriate link to read the full opinion.

and effect of the regulation. The Customs Service (which is within the Treasury Department) is charged [by statute] with the classification of imported goods under the proper provision of the tariff schedules in the first instance. * * * In addition, the Secretary [of the Treasury] is directed by statute to "establish and promulgate such rules and regulations not inconsistent with the law * * * as may be necessary to secure a just, impartial and uniform appraisement of imported merchandise and the classification and assessment of duties thereon at the various ports of entry." The Secretary, in turn, has delegated to the Commissioner of Customs the authority to issue generally applicable regulations, subject to the Secretary's approval.

Respondent [Haggar] relies on the specific direction to the Secretary to make rules of classification for "the various ports of entry" to argue that the statute authorizes promulgation of regulations that do nothing more than ensure that customs officers in field offices around the country classify goods according to a similar and consistent scheme. The regulations issued under the statute have no bearing, says respondent, on the rights of the importer. We disagree. The phrase in question is explained by the simple fact that *classification decisions must be made at the port where goods enter.* We shall not assume Congress was concerned only to ensure that customs officials at the various ports of entry make uniform decisions but that it had no concern for uniformity once the goods entered the country and judicial proceedings commenced. *The tariffs do not mean one thing for customs officers and another for importers.* * * * [Emphasis added.]

* * * *

* * * Particularly in light of the fact that the agency utilized the notice-and-comment rulemaking process[b] before issuing the regulations, the argument that they were not intended to be entitled to judicial deference implies a sufficient departure from conventional contemporary administrative practice that we ought not to adopt it absent a different statutory structure and more express language to this effect in the regulations themselves.

DECISION AND REMEDY   *The Supreme Court vacated the judgment of the lower court and remanded the case for further proceedings. Congress authorized the Treasury Department and the Customs Service to administer the tariff regulations, which were the product of notice-and-comment rulemaking. The Court held that without language to the contrary in the enabling statutes or the regulations, the tariff classifications were entitled to "judicial deference."*

---

b. Notice-and-comment rulemaking was discussed in Chapter 43.

International Organizations and Agreements. Over the last decade, countries competing for international trade have become more evenly matched competitors than in earlier years. In part, this is due to the increased use and success of international and regional organizations, such as the World Trade Organization, the European Union, and the North American Free Trade Agreement.

The World Trade Organization. The origins of the World Trade Organization (WTO) date to 1947, when the General Agreement on Tariffs and Trade (GATT) was formed for the purpose of minimizing trade barriers among nations. In subsequent decades, the GATT became the principal instrument for regulating international trade and over time negotiated tariff reductions on a broad range of products.

In 1994, in a final round of GATT negotiations, called the "Uruguay Round," representatives from over one hundred nations signed agreements relating to investment policies, dispute resolution, and other topics. One of these agreements, the Trade-Related Aspects of Intellectual Property Rights Agreement (TRIPS), was discussed in Chapter 7. The Uruguay Round also established the World Trade Organization (WTO), which replaced the GATT beginning in 1995. Each member country of the WTO agreed to grant **most-favored-nation status** to other member countries. This means that each WTO member must treat other WTO members at least as well as it treats the country that receives its most favorable treatment with regard to imports or exports. (Excerpts from the agreements made during the Uruguay Round of the GATT are presented in Appendix P at the end of this text.)

The European Union (EU).   The European Union (EU) arose out of the 1957 Treaty of Rome, which created the Common Market, a free trade zone comprising the nations of Belgium, France, West Germany, Italy, the Netherlands, and Luxembourg. Since 1957, more nations have been added. In 1995, the EU became a single integrated European trading unit made up of fifteen European nations.

The EU has its own governing authorities. One is the Council of Ministers, which coordinates economic policies and includes one representative from each nation. The EU also has a commission that proposes regulations to the council and an elected assembly, which oversees the commission. The EU also has its own court, the European Court of Justice, which can review each nation's judicial decisions and is the ultimate authority on EU law.

The EU has gone far toward creating a new body of law to govern all of the member nations—although some of its efforts to create uniform laws have been confounded by nationalism. The council and the commission issue regulations, or directives, that define EU law in various areas, and these requirements normally are binding on all member countries. EU directives govern such issues as environmental law, product liability, anticompetitive practices, and laws governing corporations. The EU directive on product liability, for example, states that a "producer of an article shall be liable for damages caused by a defect in the article, whether or not he knew or could have known of the defect." Liability extends to anyone who puts a trademark or other identifying feature on an article, and liability may not be excluded, even by contract.

The North American Free Trade Agreement (NAFTA).   The North American Free Trade Agreement (NAFTA), which was signed in 1993 and became effective on January 1, 1994, created a regional trading unit consisting of Mexico, the United States, and Canada. The primary goal of NAFTA is to eliminate tariffs among these three nations on substantially all goods over a period of fifteen to twenty years.

NAFTA gives the three countries a competitive advantage by retaining tariffs on goods imported from countries outside the NAFTA trading unit. Additionally, NAFTA provides for the elimination of barriers that traditionally have prevented the cross-border movement of services, such as financial and transportation services. For example, NAFTA provides that, with some exceptions, U.S. firms do not have to relocate in Mexico or Canada to provide services in those countries. NAFTA also attempts to eliminate citizenship requirements for

the licensing of accountants, attorneys, physicians, and other professionals. Appendix Q at the end of this text presents excerpts from NAFTA.

DISPUTE SETTLEMENT IN THE INTERNATIONAL CONTEXT

Businesspersons who engage in international business transactions normally take special precautions to protect themselves in the event that a party with whom they are dealing in another country breaches an agreement. Recall from Chapter 2 that the arbitration of civil disputes is becoming an increasingly attractive alternative to costly litigation through the court system. This is true on the international level as well. For example, arbitration clauses are frequently found in contracts governing the international sale of goods. By means of such clauses, the parties agree in advance to be bound by the decision of a specified third party in the event of a dispute.

The third party may be a neutral entity (such as the International Chamber of Commerce), a panel of individuals representing both parties' interests, or some other group or organization. The United Nations Convention on the Recognition and Enforcement of Foreign Arbitral Awards[7]—which has been implemented in more than fifty countries, including the United States—assists in the enforcement of arbitration clauses, as do provisions in specific treaties among nations. The American Arbitration Association (discussed in Chapter 2) provides arbitration services for international as well as domestic disputes.

When no arbitration clause is contained in a sales contract, a contract dispute may end in litigation. If the contract includes forum-selection and choice-of-law clauses (discussed in Chapter 19), a court in the specified forum country will hear the lawsuit according to that country's law. If no forum or choice of law has been designated, however, legal proceedings will be more complex and attended by much more uncertainty. For example, litigation may take place in two or more countries, with each country applying its own choice-of-law rules to determine which substantive law will be applied to the particular transactions.

Furthermore, even if a plaintiff wins a favorable judgment in a lawsuit litigated in the plaintiff's country, there is no guarantee that the court's judgment will be enforced by judicial bodies in the defendant's country. As discussed earlier in this chapter, under

7. June 10, 1958, 21 U.S.T. 2517, T.I.A.S. No. 6997 (the "New York Convention").

the principle of comity, the judgment may be enforced in the defendant's country, particularly if the defendant's country is the United States and the foreign court's decision is consistent with U.S. national law and policy. Other nations, however, may not be as accommodating as the United States, and the plaintiff may be left empty-handed.

SECTION 3

Comparative Law

When doing business in a foreign nation, a company generally will be subject to the jurisdiction and laws of that nation. Therefore, businesspersons will find it helpful to become familiar with the legal systems and laws of foreign nations in which they conduct commercial transactions. We look at some similarities and differences in national legal systems, laws, and cultural and business traditions in this section on **comparative law,** which can be defined as the study and comparison of legal systems and laws across nations.

COMPARATIVE LEGAL SYSTEMS

The legal systems of foreign nations differ, in widely varying degrees, from that of the United States. Additionally, a number of nations have specialized commercial law courts to deal with business disputes (in the United States, some jurisdictions are establishing similar courts). France instituted such courts in 1807, and most nations with commercial codes have done likewise. The United Kingdom also has special commercial courts overseen by judges with expertise in business law.

Common Law and Civil Law Systems. Legal systems around the globe generally are divided into *common law* and *civil law* systems. As discussed in Chapter 1, in a common law system, the courts independently develop the rules governing certain areas of law, such as torts and contracts. These common law rules apply to all areas not covered by statutory law. Although the common law doctrine of *stare decisis* obligates judges to follow precedential decisions in their jurisdictions, courts may modify or even overturn precedents when deemed necessary. Additionally, if there is no case law to guide a court, the court may create a new rule of law. Common law systems exist today in countries that were once a part of the British Empire (such as Australia, India, and the United States).

In contrast to Great Britain and the other common law countries, most of the European nations base their legal systems on Roman civil law, or "code law." The term *civil law,* as used here, refers not to civil as opposed to criminal law but to *codified* law—an ordered grouping of legal principles enacted into law by a legislature or other governing body. In a **civil law system,** the only official source of law is a statutory code. Courts are required to interpret the code and apply the rules to individual cases, but courts may not depart from the code and develop their own laws. In theory, the law code will set forth all the principles needed for the legal system.

Today, civil law systems are followed in most of the continental European countries, as well as in the Latin American, African, and Asian countries that were once colonies of the continental European nations. Japan and South Africa also have civil law systems. Components of the civil law system are found in the Islamic courts of predominantly Muslim countries. In the United States, the state of Louisiana, because of its historical ties to France, has, in part, a civil law system. Exhibit 52–2 lists some of the nations that use common law systems and some that use civil law systems.

Legal Systems Compared. Common law and civil law systems are not wholly distinct. For example, although the United States has a common law system, crimes are defined by statute as in civil law systems. Civil law systems also may allow considerable room for judges to develop law. There is also some variation within common law and civil law systems. The judges of different common law nations have produced differing common law principles. Although the United States and India both derived their legal traditions from England, the common law principles governing contract law vary in some respects between the two countries.

Similarly, the laws of nations that have civil law systems differ considerably. For example, the French code tends to set forth general principles of law, while the German code is far more specific and runs to thousands of sections. In some Middle Eastern countries, codes are grounded in the religious law of Islam, called **sharia.** The religious basis of these codes makes them far more difficult to alter.

Foreign laws may apply to international transactions of U.S. companies, even in those cases heard in U.S. courts, as the following case illustrates.

CASE 52.2

Universe Sales Co., Ltd. v. Silver Castle, Ltd.

United States
Court of Appeals,
Ninth Circuit, 1999.
182 F.3d 1036.
http://www.ce9.
uscourts.gov[a]

BACKGROUND AND FACTS   *Universe Sales Company, Ltd., sold sportswear and had been paying royalties on products to Offshore Sportswear, Inc. (Sportswear). After a general dispute, Universe claimed to have discovered that Sportswear did not own the trademarks on the products under Japanese law, which applied to the contract. Universe sued to recover the royalties as unjust enrichment. The parties presented evidence to a federal district court. Sportswear presented as evidence the declaration of a Japanese attorney, Mitsuhiro Kamiya, who specialized in trademark and contract law. Kamiya declared that Universe owed royalties under Japanese contract law regardless of the trademark's ownership at the time the license agreement was executed. The district court did not give credit to the affidavit and granted summary judgment for Universe. Sportswear appealed.*

IN THE LANGUAGE OF THE COURT

BRUNETTI, Circuit Judge:

* * * *

* * * We agree with Sportswear's arguments regarding the district court's failure properly to take the Kamiya declaration into account.

The Kamiya declaration states that Japanese contract law, not Japanese trademark law, is controlling in this situation. Under Japanese contract law, explains the declaration, the License Agreement is both valid and enforceable, and as such requires that Universe make royalty payments to Sportswear. According to the declaration, under Japanese contract law a "licensee will be unable to cancel the license agreement or refuse to pay royalties strictly on the grounds that the licensor was not the registered owner of the licensed trademark when the license agreement was executed. In other words, only if the licensor cannot acquire proper title from the registered owner of the licensed trademark . . . will the license agreement be terminable." Here, the declaration states, Sportswear can and has obtained proper title of the two trademarks at issue, and therefore is entitled to collect royalty payments from Universe.

The Kamiya declaration is admissible pursuant to Federal Rule of Civil Procedure Rule 44.1, which provides, in relevant part: "The court, in determining foreign law, may consider any relevant material or source, including testimony, whether or not submitted by a party or admissible under the Federal Rules of Evidence." * * *

In this case, the expert testimony of Kamiya, in the form of a declaration with attached exhibits, was submitted by Sportswear. * * * [T]he declaration reasons that Japanese contract law applies, and under that body of law, Universe is obligated to pay royalties to Sportswear. Although Universe had numerous opportunities to present evidence that would rebut this portion of Kamiya's declaration regarding Japanese law, Universe introduced nothing. Also, the district court performed no independent research of Japanese law. The district court should have considered the fact that the Kamiya declaration states that Japanese contract law is controlling. The district court then could have instructed the parties to present further evidence regarding the interpretation of Japanese law on that point; or, the district court may have performed its own research. Because the Kamiya declaration stands as an unrebutted presentation and interpretation of Japanese law, the district court erred in granting summary judgment to Universe.

DECISION AND REMEDY   *The court reversed the grant of summary judgment for Universe, granted summary judgment for Offshore Sportswear, and remanded the case to the district court to consider any remaining issues.*

---

a. In the "Info Links" column, click on the "Appeals Court Decisions" icon. On that page, click on "1999" to open the menu. Click on "June," then scroll down the list to the name of the case, and click on it to access the opinion.

EXHIBIT 52–2   THE LEGAL
                SYSTEMS OF NATIONS

CIVIL LAW	COMMON LAW
Argentina	Australia
Austria	Bangladesh
Brazil	Canada
Chile	Ghana
China	India
Egypt	Israel
Finland	Jamaica
France	Kenya
Germany	Malaysia
Greece	New Zealand
Indonesia	Nigeria
Iran	Singapore
Italy	United Kingdom
Japan	United States
Mexico	Zambia
Poland	
South Korea	
Sweden	
Tunisia	
Venezuela	

Judges and Procedures. Judges play similar roles in virtually all countries: their primary function is the resolution of litigation. The characteristics and qualifications of judges, which are typically set forth in the nation's constitution, can vary widely, however. The U.S. judge normally does not actively participate in a trial, but many foreign judges involve themselves closely in the proceedings, such as by questioning witnesses.

The procedures employed in resolving cases also vary substantially from country to country. A knowledge of a nation's legal procedures is important for a person conducting business transactions in that nation. For example, an American businessperson was on trial in Saudi Arabia for assaulting and slandering a co-worker, an offense for which he might have been jailed or deported. He initially was required to present two witnesses to his version of events, but he had only one. Fortunately, he became aware that he could "demand the oath." In this procedure, he swore before God that he had neither kicked nor slandered the complainant. After taking the oath, he was promptly adjudged not guilty, as lying under oath is one of the most serious sins under Islamic law. Had he failed to demand the oath, he almost certainly would have been found guilty.

NATIONAL LAWS COMPARED

A businessperson engaging in business operations abroad would be wise to learn about the relevant national laws that may affect those operations. Virtually all nations have laws governing torts, contracts, employment, and other areas. Even when the basic principles are fundamentally similar (as in contract law), there are significant variations in the practical application and effect of these laws across countries. This section summarizes some of the similarities and differences among national laws relating to tort law, contracts, and employment relationships.

Tort Law. Tort law, which allows persons to recover damages for harms or injuries caused by the wrongful actions of others (see Chapters 5 and 6), may vary widely among nations. Common law nations have developed a body of judge-made law regarding what kinds of actions constitute negligence or some other tort that permits recovery. Civil law nations must authorize such recovery in their codes. Exhibit 52–3 shows how the civil law codes of several nations define what constitutes a tort.

Even when the statutory language is similar, the application of tort law varies among nations. For example, which party has the burden of proof in a tort lawsuit differs among countries. In the United States, the burden of proof is on the plaintiff. In Russia, the defendant has the burden of proving that he or she was not at fault. Statutes of limitations (deadlines for filing a lawsuit) in other countries also vary considerably. Generally, the limitations period is longer in other countries than it is in the United States. Additionally, national tort laws vary with respect to certain concepts, including failures to act and damages.

Failures to Act. National tort laws differ considerably with respect to liability for omissions, or failures to act. In some situations, a failure to act will not be regarded as a tort. For example, in the United States, tort law imposes no "duty to rescue," and a person normally is not liable for failing to rescue another person in distress. German law is basically similar. In some countries, though, the failure to rescue another in distress is regarded as negligence.

Damages. National tort laws also differ in the way in which damages in tort cases are calculated. For example, Swiss law and Turkish law permit a court to reduce damages if an award of full damages would

EXHIBIT 52–3   CIVIL CODE TORT DEFINITIONS

 **Brazil:** He who, by a voluntary act or omission, by negligence or carelessness, violates another's right, or causes him harm, is bound to compensate for the damage.

Egypt: Every culpable act that causes damage to another obliges the person who did it to compensate for it.

 The Netherlands: Every unlawful act by which damage is caused to another obliges the person by whose fault the damage occurred to compensate for it.

Spain: He who by act or omission causes damage to another, either by fault or negligence, is obliged to compensate for the damage caused.

Tunisia: Every act a person does without lawful justification that causes willful and voluntary damage—material or moral—to another obliges the person who did it to compensate for the aforesaid damage, when it is shown that the act is the direct cause.

Uruguay: Every unlawful act a person does which causes damage to another imposes on the person whose malice, fault, or negligence brought it about the obligation to compensate for it. When the unlawful act was done maliciously, i.e., with the intention of causing harm—it amounts to a delict [an intentional tort, discussed in Chapter 6, or a crime], when the intention to cause harm is not present, the unlawful act amounts to a quasi-delict [a tort or a crime caused by negligence]. In either case, the unlawful act can be negative or positive according to whether the breach of duty consists of an act or omission.

SOURCE: Andre Tunc, *International Encyclopedia of Comparative Law*, Vol. XI, Chapter 2, pp. 5–6.

cause undue hardship for a party who was found negligent. In some nations of northern Africa, different amounts of damages are awarded depending on the type of tortious action committed and the degree of intent involved. In the United States, the calculation of actual (compensatory) damages does not depend on whether the tort was negligent or intentional.

Contract Law. Because international business transactions typically involve contracts, businesspersons should familiarize themselves with the contract law of the countries in which they do business. To a

degree, the United Nations Convention on Contracts for the International Sale of Goods (CISG), which was described in detail in Chapter 19, has simplified matters for parties to international sales contracts.

For many transactions, however, the CISG may not be applicable. For one thing, the CISG applies only to transactions involving firms in countries that have signed the convention, or agreement, and parties (in nonsignatory nations) that have stipulated in their contracts that the CISG will govern any dispute. When transactions involve firms in countries that are not signatory to the CISG, the contract parties need to determine which nation's law will govern any disputes that may arise under the contract. Additionally, even when the CISG would apply, it does so only if the parties have not agreed otherwise in their contract. For example, parties may agree in their contract that German law or U.S. law or some other nation's law will govern any contract dispute that arises. For these reasons, the contract laws of individual nations remain important to businesspersons involved in international contracts.

Generally, the laws of other nations governing contracts are similar to those in the United States. Recall from Chapter 10 that for a valid contract to be formed, four requirements must be met—agreement, consideration, capacity, and legality. These requirements were discussed at length in Chapters 11 through 13. Additionally, a valid contract may be unenforceable if genuineness of assent was lacking or if the contract was not in the proper form—such as in writing when the law requires that type of contract to be in writing. Many of these requirements exist under other nations' laws as well, but there are some significant differences.

Agreement. The requirement of agreement (offer and acceptance) is common among countries, although what is considered an offer varies by jurisdiction. In the United States, an offer, once made, normally can be revoked (canceled, or taken back) by the offeror at any time prior to the offer's acceptance. Many nations, however, require that an offer must remain open for some minimum period of time. For example, the German Civil Code, which has detailed provisions governing offer and acceptance, requires that a written contractual offer must be held open for a reasonable time, unless the offer specifically states otherwise. Unlike those in the United States, oral contractual offers (those made in person or by telephone) in Germany must be accepted immediately, or they terminate.

Mexico has some special rules for offer and acceptance. If a time for acceptance is not stated in an offer, the offer is deemed to be held open for three days, plus whatever time is necessary for the offer and acceptance to be sent through the mails. If acceptance is desired sooner, the offeror must state the time for acceptance in the offer.

In the United States, a contract's terms must be sufficiently definite that the parties (and a court) can determine whether the contract has been formed (see Chapter 11). For contracts for the sale of goods, however, the Uniform Commercial Code (UCC) has substantially relaxed common law requirements in respect to definiteness of contract terms (see Chapter 19). Mexico also has adopted a commercial code, which, like the UCC, liberalizes the traditional requirements of definiteness in mercantile transactions. Under contract law in some countries, such as Saudi Arabia, however, there are strict requirements about the definiteness of a contract's terms. If the terms of an offer are too vague or indefinite, acceptance of that offer normally will not create a valid contract.

Consideration.   In contrast to contract law in the United States, contract law in most civil law countries does not require consideration in order for a contract to be legally binding on the parties. German law, for example, does not require the exchange of consideration. An agreement to make a gift may thus be enforceable by the donee (the gift's recipient). In the United States, because consideration is required for a valid contract, promises to make gifts normally are not enforceable (because the donee does not give consideration for the gift—see Chapter 12).

In other countries, such as Saudi Arabia, consideration is required. Similarly, in India, consideration normally is required, although some contracts may be lawful even when the consideration consists of "past consideration" (that is, consideration that consists of an action that occurred in the past). As noted in Chapter 12, in the United States past consideration is no consideration.

Remedies for Breach of Contract.   The types of remedies available for breach of contract vary widely throughout the world. In many countries, as in the United States, the normal remedy is damages—money given to the nonbreaching party to compensate that party for the losses incurred owing to the breach (see Chapter 18). The calculation of damages resulting from a breach of contract, however, may differ from one country to another, as does the calculation of damages under tort law.

National contract laws also differ as to whether and when equitable remedies, such as specific performance (discussed in Chapter 18), will be granted. Germany's typical remedy for a breach of contract is specific performance, which means that the party must go forward and perform the contract. Damages are available only after certain procedures have been employed to seek performance. In contrast, in the United States, the equitable remedy of specific performance will usually not be granted unless the remedy at law (money damages) is inadequate and the subject matter of the contract is unique.

Defenses.   As in the United States, contract law in most nations allows parties to defend against contractual liability by claiming that certain requirements for contract enforceability are lacking. For example, many nations, including the United States, have laws requiring that certain types of contracts must be in writing. If such contracts are not in writing, they will not be enforced. In Saudi Arabia, the law strongly encourages parties to put all contracts in writing, and any written contract should be formally witnessed by two males or a male and a female. In that country, it may be difficult to enforce an oral contract.

Another common defense is the assertion that a contract was entered into because of a mistake, fraud, or duress, and thus genuineness of assent to the contract's terms was lacking. In some countries, a party may claim that a contract was not formed because the consideration supporting the contract was inadequate—that is, not *enough* value or money was given in exchange for a contractual promise. Indian courts, for example, look to the adequacy of consideration when determining whether the parties' assent to the contract was truly genuine and therefore whether the contract should be enforced. In the United States, in contrast, courts rarely inquire into the adequacy of consideration. Normally, only in cases in which the consideration is so grossly inadequate as to "shock the conscience of the court" will a court refuse to enforce a contract on this basis.

Employment Law.   Employment law is particularly important in many foreign nations. The United States traditionally left the details of the employment relationship to a negotiation between the employer and the employee. Under the common law *employment-at-will doctrine* (discussed in Chapter 41), employers are free to hire and fire employees "at will," meaning that an employee can be fired for any reason or no reason at all. Today, this common law doctrine is less applicable in the United States, because the workplace is regulated extensively by federal and state statutory law. Employment relationships in other nations also are subject to government regulation.

Modifications to the At-Will Doctrine.
Many other countries, similar to the United States, have modified their traditional at-will employment rules. In France, for example, the concept of employment at will can be traced back to the original Napoleonic Code. Over the years, the French have modified this doctrine considerably. French courts developed the doctrine of **abus de droit** (abuse of rights), which prohibited employers from firing workers for illness, pregnancy, unionization, political beliefs, the exercise of certain rights, or even personal dislike. French courts also began requiring employers to follow customary procedures before terminating workers. French employee-discharge laws were codified in the Dismissal Law of 1973, which also established procedural requirements that employers must follow when discharging workers (to be discussed shortly).

Under the Polish labor code, employment continues to be predominantly "at will." Either party may terminate the employment relationship at any time. Advance notice is generally required, however, and notice requirements vary, depending on the length of the worker's tenure with the employer. An employer may terminate an employee immediately and without notice if the worker has committed a criminal offense, lost a license or other employment qualification, seriously breached his or her duties, or failed to appear regularly at the job site. An employer cannot immediately discharge an employee for the last reason if the employee's absence was due to child-care needs, infectious disease, or entitled sick leave.

Wages and Benefits.
One of the reasons U.S. businesspersons decide to establish business operations, such as factories, in other countries is to cut production costs by taking advantage of lower wage rates. Although workers' wages may be lower in some countries than in the United States, typically workers in other countries have many paid holidays, plus vacation time. In addition, employers in other countries may be subject to a variety of requirements not found in the United States.

In Mexico, for example, workers have a right to an annual bonus equal to fifteen days' salary and paid at the end of the year. Mexican law requires a minimum amount of paid vacation time (six days in the first year

of employment) and also requires that companies give workers a 25 percent bonus above their ordinary pay rates during those vacations. For example, if a worker's ordinary pay is $200 per week, the vacation pay is $250 per week. Mexican employers also must periodically give training courses to workers. In some countries, such as Egypt, fringe benefits for employees account for as much as 40 percent of an employer's payroll costs.

Equal Employment Opportunity.
National laws around the globe vary widely with respect to equal employment opportunity. In the United States, employers are prohibited from discriminating against employees or job applicants on the basis of race, color, national origin, gender, religion, age, or disability. U.S. laws prohibiting discrimination on these bases also apply to all U.S. employees working for U.S. employers abroad. Generally, a U.S. employer must abide by U.S. laws prohibiting employment discrimination *unless* to do so would violate the laws of the country in which the employer's workplace is located. This "foreign laws exception" usually allows U.S. employers abroad to avoid being subjected to conflicting laws.

Some other countries also prohibit discriminatory practices. For example, in Indonesia, the Ministry of Manpower, which implements employment laws and regulations, prohibits discrimination in the workplace. Mexican law forbids employers from discriminating against employees on the basis of race, religion, or gender. The Japanese constitution prohibits discrimination based on race, religion, nationality, or gender.

In contrast, some countries, such as Egypt and Turkey, have no laws requiring equal employment opportunity. In Argentina, racial, religious, or other discrimination is not a political issue or a practice prohibited by law. Similarly, in Brazil, equal opportunity is not a factor in employment relationships.

Generally, in those countries that do prohibit employment discrimination, employers retain some flexibility in hiring and firing managerial personnel. In Mexico, for example, employers traditionally have been allowed to hire and fire "confidential" employees—managerial employees—at their discretion. In Italy, workers classified as managers are also less protected by the law than rank-and-file employees are.

Employment Termination.
In many countries, employers find it difficult, and often quite costly, to discharge employees. Employment laws may prohibit

the firing of employees for discriminatory reasons, and other laws may also come into play. For example, in France, if an employment contract is for an indefinite term, the employer can fire the worker only for genuine and serious cause or for economic reasons. The law also establishes procedural requirements. Before terminating a worker for cause, the employer must undertake a conciliatory session with labor court mediators. The employer has the burden of proving to the labor court that the cause of the dismissal was serious.

In Egypt, employers commonly use fixed-period employment contracts, which are automatically terminated at the end of the contract period. If an employee continues to work after the end of the contract period and no new contract is created, the employment contract becomes indefinite. It is very difficult to discharge an employee with an indefinite contract. The employee must first commit a serious offense, whereupon the employer must submit a proposal for termination to a committee consisting of representatives of the union, the employer, and the government. Employees may appeal adverse decisions of this committee.

Taiwanese law places clear restrictions on the termination of employment. An employer must provide a reason for discharging an employee. An employer may discharge an employee with advance notice and severance pay for a number of economic reasons or if the worker is incapable of performing the assigned work. Employers may fire employees without notice or severance pay only for certain reasons, such as violence, imprisonment, or extensive absenteeism.

CULTURAL AND BUSINESS TRADITIONS

The ability to conduct business successfully in a foreign nation requires not only a knowledge of that nation's laws but also some familiarity with its cultural traditions, economy, and business climate. One obvious cultural difference among nations is language. For example, Rolls-Royce changed the name of its "Silver Mist" in Germany, because in that country, *mist* translates as "manure." In Japan, Esso had difficulty selling gasoline in part because *Esso* sounds like the Japanese word for stalled car. Pepsi's "Come Alive with Pepsi" campaign was translated in Taiwan as "Pepsi brings your ancestors back from the grave."

The meaning of nonverbal language (body movements, gestures, facial expressions, and the like) also varies from culture to culture. In the United States, for example, a nod of the head indicates "yes," while in some countries, such as Greece, the same gesture means "no."

There are also some important ethical differences. In Islamic countries, for example, the consumption of alcohol and certain foods is forbidden by the Koran (the sacred book of the Islamic religion). It would be thoughtless and imprudent to invite a Saudi Arabian business contact out for a drink. Additionally, in many foreign nations, gift giving is a common practice among contracting companies or between companies and government. To Americans, such gift giving may look suspiciously like an unethical (and possibly illegal) bribe. This has been an important source of friction in international business, particularly after the U.S. Congress passed the Foreign Corrupt Practices Act (FCPA) in 1977 (discussed in Chapter 40). The act prohibits American business firms from offering certain side payments to foreign officials to secure favorable contracts.

The role played by women in other countries may present some troublesome ethical problems for U.S. firms doing business internationally. Equal employment opportunity is a fundamental public policy in the United States, and Title VII of the Civil Rights Act of 1964 (discussed in Chapter 42) prohibits discrimination against women in the employment context. Some other countries, however, largely reject any professional role for women, which may cause difficulties for American women conducting business transactions in those countries. For example, when the World Bank sent a delegation including women to negotiate with the Central Bank of Korea, the Koreans were surprised and offended. They thought that the presence of women meant that the Koreans were not being taken seriously.

TERMS AND CONCEPTS TO REVIEW

abus de droit 1003   act of state doctrine 991   civil law system 998

comity 990

comparative law 998

confiscation 992

distribution agreement 993

dumping 994

export 992

expropriation 992

international law 989

international organization 990

most-favored-nation status 996

national law 989

quota 994

sharia 998

sovereign immunity 992

tariff 994

treaty 990

QUESTIONS AND CASE PROBLEMS

52–1. COMPARATIVE EMPLOYMENT LAWS. Assume that you are the president of a manufacturing company that intends to expand overseas. Shipping costs and tariffs for your product are uniformly low. Your manufacturing process, however, is highly labor intensive. How would the employment laws of various nations influence your decision on where to situate a new manufacturing plant?

52–2. WOMEN AND BUSINESS. Joe Henderson is the president of an Asian branch of a U.S. bank. His top vice president is a woman, Betty Carter. He would like to take her with him to an important meeting at which he will undertake loan negotiations with a huge overseas company. He has been advised, however, that he will lose respect in the eyes of the foreign company—and perhaps the company's business—if she accompanies him. He talks with her, and she informs him that she does not mind deferring to men at social activities, if local customs demand such deference, but that at the corporate meetings, she will expect business as usual and will not alter her behavior simply because she is a woman. What should Henderson do? Discuss.

52–3. INTERNATIONAL BUSINESS CONTRACTS. In 1995, France implemented a law making the use of the French language mandatory in certain legal documents. Documents relating to securities offerings, such as prospectuses, for example, must be written in French. So must instruction manuals and warranties for goods and services offered for sale in France. Additionally, all agreements entered into with French state or local authorities, with entities controlled by state or local authorities, and with private entities carrying out a public service (such as providing utilities) must be written in French. What kinds of problems might this law pose for U.S. businesspersons who wish to form contracts with French persons or business firms?

52–4. LEGAL SYSTEMS. As China and the formerly Communist nations move toward free enterprise, they must develop a new set of business laws. If you could start from scratch, what kind of business law system would you adopt, a civil law system or a common law system? What kind of business regulations would you impose?

52–5. ACT OF STATE DOCTRINE. W. S. Kirkpatrick & Co. learned that the Republic of Nigeria was interested in contracting for the construction and equipping of a medical center in Nigeria. Kirkpatrick, with the aid of a Nigerian citizen, secured the contract as a result of bribing Nigerian officials. Nigerian law prohibits both the payment and the receipt of bribes in connection with the awarding of government contracts, and the U.S. Foreign Corrupt Practices Act (FCPA) of 1977 expressly prohibits U.S. firms and their agents from bribing foreign officials to secure favorable contracts. Environmental Tectonics Corp., International (ETC), an unsuccessful bidder for the contract, learned of the bribery and sued Kirkpatrick in a federal district court for damages. The district court granted summary judgment for Kirkpatrick, because resolution of the case in favor of ETC would require imputing to foreign officials an unlawful motivation (the obtaining of bribes) and accordingly might embarrass the Nigerian government or interfere with the conduct of U.S. foreign policy. Was the district court correct in assuming that the act of state doctrine barred ETC's action against Kirkpatrick? What should happen on appeal? Discuss fully. [*W. S. Kirkpatrick & Co. v. Environmental Tectonics Corp., International*, 493 U.S. 400, 110 S.Ct. 701, 107 L.Ed.2d 816 (1990)]

52–6. SOVEREIGN IMMUNITY. George Janini and other former professors and employees of Kuwait University (the plaintiffs) were terminated from their positions following Iraq's invasion of Kuwait in August 1990. Following the invasion, the government of Kuwait issued a decree stating, among other things, that "contracts concluded between the Government and those non-Kuwaiti workers who worked for it . . . shall be considered automatically abrogated because of the impossibility of enforcement due to the Iraqi invasion." The plaintiffs sued Kuwait University in a U.S. court, alleging that their termination breached their employment contracts, which required nine months' notice before termination. The plaintiffs sought back pay and other benefits to which they were entitled under their contracts. The university claimed that, as a government-operated institution, it was immune from the jurisdiction of U.S. courts under the doctrine of sovereign immunity. What exceptions are made to this doctrine? Will an exception apply to the university's activities with respect to the plaintiffs? Discuss fully. [*Janini v. Kuwait University*, 43 F.3d 1534 (D.C. Cir. 1995)]

52–7. DISCRIMINATION CLAIMS. Radio Free Europe and Radio Liberty (RFE/RL), a U.S. corporation doing business in Germany, employs more than three hundred U.S. citizens at its principal place of business in Munich, Germany. The concept of mandatory retirement is deeply embedded in German labor policy, and a contract formed in 1982 between RFE/RL and a German labor union contained a clause that required workers to be retired when they reached the age of sixty-five. When William Mahoney and other American employees (the plaintiffs) reached the age of sixty-five, RFE/RL terminated their employment as required under its contract with the labor union. The plaintiffs sued RFE/RL for discriminating against them on the basis of age, in violation of the U.S. Age Discrimination in Employment Act of 1967. Will the plaintiffs succeed in their suit? Discuss fully. [*Mahoney v. RFE/RL, Inc.*, 47 F.3d 447 (D.C. Cir. 1995)]

52–8. SOVEREIGN IMMUNITY. Nuovo Pignone, Inc., is an Italian company that designs and manufactures turbine systems. Nuovo sold a turbine system to Cabinda Gulf Oil Co. (CABGOC). The system was manufactured, tested, and inspected in Italy, then sent to Louisiana for mounting on a platform by CABGOC's contractor. Nuovo sent a representative to consult on the mounting. The platform went to a CABGOC site off the coast of West Africa. Marcus Pere, an instrument technician at the site, was killed when a turbine within the system exploded. Pere's widow filed a suit in a federal district court against Nuovo and others. Nuovo claimed sovereign immunity on the ground that its majority shareholder at the time of the explosion was Ente Nazionale Idrocaburi, which was created by the government of Italy to lead its oil and gas exploration and development. Is Nuovo exempt from suit under the doctrine of sovereign immunity? Is it subject to suit under the "commercial activity" exception? Why or why not? [*Pere v. Nuovo Pignone, Inc.*, 150 F.3d 477 (5th Cir. 1998)]

52–9. DUMPING. In response to a petition filed on behalf of the U.S. pineapple industry, the U.S. Commerce Department initiated an investigation of canned pineapple fruit imported from Thailand. The investigation concerned Thai producers of the canned fruit, including The Thai Pineapple Public Co. The Thai producers also turned out products, such as pineapple juice and juice concentrate, outside the scope of the investigation. These products use separate parts of the same fresh pineapple, and so they share raw material costs. The Commerce Department had to calculate the Thai producers' cost of production, for the purpose of determining fair value and antidumping duties, and in so doing, had to allocate a portion of the shared fruit costs to the canned fruit. These allocations were based on the producers' own financial records, which were consistent with Thai generally accepted accounting principles. The result was a determination that more than 90 percent of the canned fruit sales were below the cost of production. The producers filed a suit in the U.S. Court of International Trade against the federal government, challenging this allocation. The producers argued that their records did not reflect actual production costs, which instead should be based on the weight of fresh fruit used to make the products. Did the Commerce Department act reasonably in determining the cost of production? Why or why not? [*The Thai Pineapple Public Co. v. United States*, 187 F.3d 1362 (Fed.Cir. 1999)]

52–10. IN YOUR COURT

Texas Trading & Milling Corp. and other companies brought an action for breach of contract against the Republic of Nigeria and its central bank. Nigeria, a rapidly developing and oil-rich nation, had contracted to purchase more cement from Texas Trading than it could use. Unable to accept delivery of the cement, Nigeria had repudiated the contract, alleging immunity under the Foreign Sovereign Immunities Act (FSIA) of 1976, because the buyer of the cement was the Nigerian government. Assume that you are the judge in the trial court hearing this case and answer the following questions:

(a) What section of the FSIA is particularly applicable to this dispute?

(b) Given the provisions of that section, should the doctrine of sovereign immunity remove the dispute from the jurisdiction of U.S. courts? Explain your reasoning.

LAW ON THE WEB

For updated links to resources available on the Web, as well as a variety of other materials, visit this text's Web site at http://wbl.westbuslaw.com.

An extensive collection of URLs offering access to various international organizations is offered by the Villanova University School of Law at

http://vill.law.edu/compass/international/index.htm

The University of Arizona College of Law has an online collection of various resources relating to international law, as well as to the national laws of some foreign countries. You can access this collection by going to

http://www.law.arizona.edu/library/intlinks.html

The Library of Congress's Global Legal Information Network has information on the national laws of more than thirty-five countries, as well as a comprehensive Guide to Law Online. You can access this site at

http://lcweb2.loc.gov/glin/lawhome.html

LEGAL RESEARCH EXERCISES ON THE WEB

Go to http://wbl.westbuslaw.com, the Web site that accompanies this text. Select "Internet Applications," and then click on "Chapter 52." There you will find the following Internet research exercises that you can perform to learn more about international organizations and trade:

Activity 52–1: The World Trade Organization

Activity 52–2: Overseas Business Opportunities

CHAPTER 53

Law for Entrepreneurs

ENTREPRENEURS ARE RESPONSIBLE for creating much of the wealth and many of the new jobs in the United States. While some new companies, such as Microsoft and Dell Computer Corporation, have become highly successful, most entrepreneurial ventures fail. A lack of understanding of legal issues and how to respond to them is one of the reasons for such failures.

For the most part, the underlying laws of interest to entrepreneurs are no different from the general business laws covered throughout this text. In the entrepreneurial context, however, these laws often take on special significance. Most entrepreneurs, for example, cannot afford to hire attorneys as paid employees of their firms. Nor can they afford to suffer large amount of damages in lawsuits brought against their firms—or themselves individually. Often, a small enterprise cannot even afford to pay the litigation costs involved in defending against a lawsuit. In other words, it is one thing for an officer or director of a large corporation to make a decision that entails the risk of being sued; it is quite another for a small-business owner to do so—because the consequences of even one legal action can be disastrous for the firm.

In this chapter, we discuss some of the options and legal requirements faced by entrepreneurs who wish to start up their own businesses. We also indicate how the general legal principles found throughout this book apply in the entrepreneurial context. Because of the importance of legal compliance in the success of any entrepreneurial venture, we begin the chapter with a discussion of the importance of obtaining legal counsel.

SECTION 1

The Importance of Legal Counsel

Nearly everyone who starts up a business enterprise faces the following question: "Do I need an attorney?" The answer to this question will likely be "Yes." Today, nonexperts find that it is virtually impossible to keep up with the myriad rules and regulations that govern the way in which business can be conducted in the United States. Indeed, businesspersons today sometimes incur penalties for violating laws or regulations of which they are totally unaware, as noted in Chapter 40. Obtaining competent legal counsel can help entrepreneurs avoid a number of pitfalls. Relevant questions for the entrepreneur thus include how to find the right attorney and how to hold down legal costs as much as possible.

Although attorneys may seem expensive—anywhere from $60 to $500 per hour—the cautious entrepreneur will make sure that he or she is not "penny wise and pound foolish." The consultation fee paid to an attorney may be a drop in the bucket compared with the potential liability facing a businessperson for violating a statutory law or regulation. Also, outside legal help may be essential for certain tasks associated with forming a new business, such as drafting and filing the documents necessary for incorporation. Failure to comply with specific state incorporation requirements may subject the owners of the new enterprise to personal liability for contracts or other obligations.

FINDING AN ATTORNEY

In selecting an attorney, most businesspersons rely on referrals from friends, business associates, and other local entrepreneurs. Business networks, such as chambers of commerce and bar organizations, may also help identify knowledgeable attorneys. Attorneys and their areas of specialty are also listed in the Yellow Pages of the telephone book. A good source of information is the *Martindale-Hubbell Law Directory*, which can be found at most law libraries. (It is also available at http://www.martindale.com on the Internet.) This directory lists the names, addresses, telephone numbers, areas of legal practice, and other data for more than 900,000 attorneys and law firms in the United States.

INTERVIEWING AND EVALUATING ATTORNEYS

After you have obtained a list of possibilities, conduct interviews with the attorneys you have selected and evaluate them. In evaluating a particular attorney, ask yourself the following questions: Did the attorney seem knowledgeable about what you need to do to start up your business? Did he or she seem willing to investigate the laws relevant to your business plans? Did you communicate well with each other? Did the attorney perceive what issues were of foremost concern to you and address those issues to your satisfaction? Did the attorney "speak your language" when explaining the legal implications of those issues?

RETAINING AN ATTORNEY

Retaining an experienced attorney will yield benefits beyond the resolution of legal problems. Many attorneys have valuable contacts, including potential investors in your enterprise. An attorney may also have valuable business expertise. Furthermore, because the law protects the confidentiality of attorney-client communications, an attorney provides a useful sounding board for business plans.

At the start-up stage, you may not have much money to pay attorneys, especially those charging a high hourly rate. Attorneys have responded to this situation with innovative fee arrangements, especially in such hotbeds of entrepreneurship as Silicon Valley. Most attorneys will not charge for your initial consultation, and some will provide a substantial amount of service for free in exchange for a promise of future legal business after the venture is established. Some attorneys may accept an equity stake in the new business in lieu of cash. As the client, you often have the opportunity to negotiate a compensation system suited to your needs.

Some small-business owners keep an attorney on retainer. This means that the client pays the attorney a fixed amount every month, and the attorney handles all necessary legal business that arises during the month. The amount of the retainer is negotiated with an eye toward expected legal needs, so this approach probably will not save money overall. A retainer arrangement, however, has the benefit of making your legal costs even and predictable over time.

RETAINING AN ACCOUNTANT

In a new business, the proper management of accounts receivable and costs is critical. There are software accounting programs to handle the job, but many small businesses hire a professional accountant to do their bookkeeping. While more expensive, having an accountant adds to your credibility with investors and lenders. Bookkeeping accuracy is also legally important, as errors often provoke litigation.

SECTION 2

Selecting an Appropriate Business Form

The various forms of business organization available to entrepreneurs were described in Chapters 33 through 39. In the earliest stages of the business, the entrepreneur may commence business as a sole proprietorship, which requires few legal formalities. The law considers all new, single-owner businesses to be sole proprietorships unless the owner affirmatively adopts some other form. Once business is under way, the sole proprietorship form may become untenable, however, if additional investors are needed and the personal financial risks of the business become too great. The entrepreneur may then want to establish a more formal organization, such as a limited partnership, a corporation, an S corporation, a limited liability company, or a limited liability partnership.

The different business forms have particular advantages and disadvantages. Factors to consider when choosing a business form include liability, taxation, continuity of life, and the legal formalities and costs associated with starting up the business.

LIMITATIONS ON LIABILITY

A key consideration in starting up a business is whether the business form chosen will limit one's personal liability for business debts and obligations. If you form a limited liability entity, such as a corporation, you can normally avoid personal liability if, say, a customer slips and breaks his ankle in your store, sues your store, and is awarded damages by a court. Although the business entity may be liable for damages, you and other owners generally will not be personally liable beyond the extent of your contribution to the firm.

All corporate business forms offer limited liability to the shareholder-owners. In a general partnership, however, there is no limited liability—each partner is personally liable for the debts and obligations of the partnership. In a limited partnership, the limited partners have limited liability. A limited partnership requires at least one general partner, however, who remains personally liable for the partnership's obligations.

All states now permit businesspersons to conduct their business operations as limited liability companies (LLCs), and a growing number of states permit single-owner LLCs. Also, many states now provide for limited liability partnerships (LLPs). These increasingly popular business forms also offer the advantage of limited personal liability for business debts and obligations (see Chapter 38 for a more detailed discussion of this aspect of LLCs and LLPs). LLCs often offer tax advantages for start-up companies.

Limited personal liability does not obviate the need to obtain insurance for significant business liability risks (see Chapter 49). Limited liability organizations only protect personal assets, and a substantial uninsured liability can bankrupt the business and cause the loss of everything the entrepreneur has invested in it.

TAX CONSIDERATIONS

Taxes are another critical factor to be considered in choosing a business form. A sole proprietorship is not a separate legal entity, and the owner pays taxes on business income as an individual. All revenues are taxable, but business expenses can be deducted, so the owner is taxed only once on the business's profits. Partnerships are taxed in the same fashion, with income and deductions apportioned among the partners. All corporations must pay certain state and local taxes (such as franchise taxes, property taxes, and the like), but the key consideration involves income taxes. A corporation involves what is known as double taxation. The company must pay a corporate income tax on its profits, and the shareholder-owners must also pay individual income tax on any distributions of remaining profits that they have received from the corporation. The double taxation is limited to distributions of profits, though, so corporations are taxed only once on retained earnings.

The S corporation was created to allow certain small businesses to take advantage of "pass through" taxation, where profits are taxed only once on the owners' individual return and business profits are not taxed. The government imposed a variety of restrictions on qualifying for S corporation status, which limited corporate flexibility. LLCs and LLPs allow entrepreneurs to avoid these restrictions and limitations on flexibility, while at the same time reaping the tax benefits of the S corporation.

CONTINUITY OF LIFE

Continuity of life is another concern in selecting a business form. Entrepreneurs may fail to consider the possibility that an owner can die, resign, be expelled, or become incapacitated. Corporations have continuity of life—that is, they survive their owners—except in the unusual event that the corporate documents provide otherwise. On the death of a corporate shareholder-owner, that shareholder's ownership interest simply passes to his or her heirs. In a partnership, the death or withdrawal of a partner causes the termination of the partnership, unless the partners have expressly provided otherwise. (In those states that have adopted the Revised Uniform Partnership Act, however, the death of a partner does not necessarily dissolve the partnership—see Chapter 33.) By definition, a sole proprietorship terminates with the death of the sole proprietor.

LEGAL FORMALITY AND EXPENSE

Another factor for entrepreneurs to consider has to do with the legal formalities and costs required to start up a business. The requirements and costs associated with forming and operating as a corporation can be considerable. Some additional costs are associated with qualifying as an S corporation. The costs of establishing a limited partnership may also be quite significant. For these reasons, some entrepreneurs initially undertake business operations as sole proprietorships or general partnerships—and run considerable financial risk because of the personal liability associated with each of these business forms. LLCs generally involve fewer requirements in terms of start-up formalities and costs than do corporations or limited partnerships.

Although sole proprietorships and general partnerships avoid the legal formalities associated with incorporating or creating a limited partnership, sole proprietors and partners still must comply with many laws. Any business, whatever its form, must meet a variety of legal requirements, which typically relate to the following:

1. Business name registration.
2. Occupational licensing.
3. State tax registration (for example, to obtain permits for sales taxes).
4. Health and environmental permits.
5. Zoning and building codes.
6. Import/export regulations.

If the business has employees, the owner must also comply with a host of laws governing the workplace. We look at many of these laws in the final section of this chapter.

The entrepreneur should not overlook the potential benefits that may be gained in return for establishing a business arrangement more formal than the sole proprietorship. Consider a family business that is owned and operated by a husband and wife. At the outset, the spouses should consider the possibility that they may have a falling out in the future. If they run their business as a sole proprietorship, it may be difficult to establish their respective ownership rights in the business should a dispute arise.

If they form a partnership, however, they can specify in a written partnership agreement how profits and losses will be shared, as well as the extent of each partner's ownership interest in the partnership. Alternatively, the spouses could incorporate and form a shareholder agreement providing for various eventualities (shareholder agreements are discussed later in this chapter) and permitting the company's continuation.

S E C T I O N 3

Creating the Business Entity

There are no special requirements for creating a sole proprietorship, and a general partnership requires

only an agreement between the partners. Forming a limited partnership is more complicated. The agreement of the limited partnership, often called a certificate of limited partnership, must be prepared and recorded with the appropriate governmental authority. State laws also regulate the names of limited partnerships, require certain record keeping, and govern other aspects of the business.

The process of incorporation may be complicated. Compliance with legal formalities, including those discussed in the following subsections, is essential to reap the benefits of incorporation. If a company is improperly incorporated, the benefits of corporate status may be lost, and the shareholder-owners may be subject to personal liability for corporate obligations. (See Chapter 34 for a more extensive discussion of the consequences of improper incorporation.) To ensure that all state incorporation requirements are met, entrepreneurs typically hire attorneys to create the documents necessary for incorporation and file those documents with the appropriate state official.

CHOOSING A CORPORATE NAME

To incorporate, you first must choose a corporate name and file that name with the appropriate state office, usually the office of the secretary of state. The name must be different from those used by existing businesses (even unincorporated businesses). While there are private databases to use in checking names, the secretary of state's office should have all the information necessary. The name of your new company also should include the word *Corporation, Company,* or *Incorporated* (abbreviated *Corp., Co.,* and *Inc.,* respectively).

Note that filing a name with the appropriate state official will protect the name as a trade name only within the state. Therefore, businesspersons who anticipate doing business nationally—via the Internet, for example—will want to make sure that their trade names will be protected under trademark law (to be discussed shortly).

ARTICLES OF INCORPORATION, BYLAWS, AND INITIAL MEETINGS

The second key step in incorporation is preparing and filing your articles of incorporation. Other steps involve drafting the corporate bylaws and holding the initial board of directors' meeting.

Articles of Incorporation.   As discussed in Chapter 34, state requirements vary with respect to what provisions must be included in the articles. For example, you may be required to have a minimum number of incorporators, a minimum number of directors, a minimum capital contribution, and so on. As mentioned, typically entrepreneurs enlist the services of an attorney to help them draft and file the documents necessary to incorporate, including the articles of incorporation.

If the incorporators want to obtain the tax benefits provided by S corporation status, the new company must qualify for that status under Subchapter S of the Internal Revenue Code. The new company must file additional forms with the Internal Revenue Service (IRS) and, in most states, with the appropriate state agency. When a company was late in filing its state form in Pennsylvania, the company lost the state tax benefits of S corporation status for that year.[1]

Drafting Corporate Bylaws. An important step in the incorporation process is drafting the corporation's bylaws, which become the company's governing rules. The bylaws include provisions for the dates on which annual meetings will be held, terms for voting quorums, and other rules. You do not want to include all of the corporate rules in your articles of incorporation, because the articles are relatively difficult to change. Bylaws are binding rules, but they are more easily modified. Usually, bylaws can be changed by a majority vote of the shareholders; in some states, the bylaws can be modified by the board of directors.

Holding the Initial Board of Directors' Meeting. The corporation should then hold its first board of directors' meeting. The initial corporate directors are designated in the articles of incorporation. The directors can adopt the agreed-on bylaws, appoint corporate officers and define their respective authority, issue stock, create a bank account, and take other necessary actions. The directors will continue to meet periodically and must stand for election at annual shareholders' meetings.

CREATING A
CORPORATE RECORDS BOOK

The next step is to establish a corporate records book that organizes your important documents. The book contains the articles of incorporation, minutes of directors' and shareholders' meetings, and other docu-

ments. You will need to create stock certificates for distribution to owners. A special corporate seal may be important, as banks and other institutions may require that documents have such a seal. Again, these are tasks that an attorney typically handles as part of the incorporation process.

SECTION 4

Intellectual Property

Protecting rights in intellectual property is the central concern for some new businesses, such as software companies. Such businesses depend on their copyrights and patents to protect their investments in the research and development required to create new programs. If there were no copyright or patent protection available for this type of intellectual property, a competitor or a customer could simply copy the software. Laws governing rights in intellectual property were discussed in detail in Chapter 7. Here, we examine some aspects of intellectual property law that entrepreneurs should consider at the outset of any business venture.

CHOOSING AND
PROTECTING YOUR TRADEMARK

Choosing a trademark and making sure that it can be protected under trademark law can be crucial to the success of a new business venture. One of the factors to consider in choosing a name for your business entity is whether you want to use your business name as a trademark. Assume that you plan to incorporate your business. When the firm is incorporated, the secretary of state (or other state agency with which the business name is filed) only approves your company's name as a trade name—the name that you can use on checks, invoices, and letterhead stationery. You have legal permission to own your trade name only in your state.

A trademark (or a service mark) is a word, phrase, slogan, design, or symbol that identifies a specific product brand and that is used to market products. If you decide to use your business (trade) name as a trademark, then you need to follow the principles of trademark law. The general rule is that you cannot use a trademark that is the same or quite similar to another's distinctive or famous mark or that might lead a customer to think that your product was produced by someone else.

Generally, the first business to use a trademark owns it. The way to qualify as a first user is to be the

---

1. *Chloe Eichelberger Textiles, Inc. v. Commonwealth of Pennsylvania*, 675 A.2d 1297 (Pa. 1996).

first company to actually use the trademark in the marketplace or to register the trademark with the U.S. Patent and Trademark Office (PTO) in Washington, D.C. First use takes precedence over federal registration. For example, suppose that you have used a particular trademark for two years but have not registered the mark with the PTO. If another company then registers the same mark with the PTO, you will probably have the traditional common law right to continue using that mark but only in the geographic region in which you have been selling. Outside that region, the federal registrant would own the mark.

Choosing Your Trademark. In deciding on a trademark, you need to make sure the mark is distinctive. Use of your name or a mere description of your product will probably receive, at most, only weak protection. If you have started a new online company, you cannot call it "Internet" and expect to receive protection. While it is tempting to make up a slight twist on the word, this may lead to confusion—over eight hundred Internet companies already have the word "net" as part of their names.[2] A made-up word (such as

Exxon or Kodak) may be a good choice. There are consulting companies that provide assistance in selecting marks, but the services of such firms may be too expensive for small-business entrepreneurs.

Undertaking a Trademark Search. Once you have chosen a mark, you should do a trademark search to ensure that the mark is not too similar to existing marks. You can examine the Yellow Pages in any area in which you do business and consult the *Gale Trade Names Directory* in your local library. You can look at the federal trademark register, as well as the trademark register in your state. (You can also go to http://www.uspto.gov to access the PTO's online federal trademark register.) You can access other trademark databases, such as TrademarkScan, on the Internet as well. Finally, you can hire a trademark search firm to do the search for you.

If you plan to use your trademark as an Internet domain name (see Chapter 9), you will want to make sure that someone else has not already registered that domain name. For information on domain-name availability and registration, you can check with your local Internet service provider. Can you use a competitor's trademark as a domain name if the competitor has not yet registered the mark as a domain name? This was the issue before the court in the following case.

---

2. Laurie Flynn, "High Tech Companies Are Forced to Play a Very Competitive Name Game," *The New York Times*, September 23, 1996, p. C5. When Lucent Technologies was starting up, the company had to rule out over five hundred possible names because they had already been taken.

CASE 53.1   # Cardservice International, Inc. v. McGee

United States District Court, Eastern District of Virginia, 1997. 950 F.Supp. 737.

IN THE LANGUAGE OF THE COURT

BACKGROUND AND FACTS *Cardservice International, Inc., which provides credit-card and debit-card processing services, registered the trademark "Cardservice" with the U.S. Patent and Trademark Office. Webster McGee, through his sole proprietorship WRM & Associates, provides similar services. Without the permission of Cardservice, McGee registered the domain name "cardservice.com" with Network Solutions, Inc.[a] At that address on the Internet, McGee advertised his "Card Service." Cardservice asked McGee to give up cardservice.com as a domain name, but he refused. The company then filed a suit in a federal district court against McGee, seeking an injunction on the ground of trademark infringement.*

CLARKE, District Judge.
   *   *   *   *

Because of McGee's use of "cardservice.com," Cardservice International has no access to an Internet domain name containing its registered mark * * * . Cardservice International's customers who wish to take advantage of its Internet services but do not know its domain name are likely to assume that "cardservice.com" belongs to

---

a. At the time this case was decided, Network Solutions, Inc., regulated the use of domain names on the Internet. See Chapter 9 for a discussion of domain-name registration.

Cardservice International. These customers would instead reach McGee and see a home page for "Card Service." They would find that McGee's Internet site offers advertisements for and provides access to the same services as Cardservice International * * * . Many would assume that they have reached Cardservice International or, even if they realize that is not who they have reached, take advantage of McGee's services because they do not otherwise know how to reach Cardservice International. * * *

Such a result is exactly what the trademark laws were designed to protect against. Cardservice International has obtained a trademark to ensure that the name "cardservice" will be associated by consumers only with Cardservice International. * * * The fact that Cardservice International has been awarded a trademark means that it should not be forced to compete with others who would also use the words "cardservice." * * * Unauthorized use of a domain name which includes a protected trademark to engage in commercial activity over the Internet * * * is in direct conflict with federal trademark law.

DECISION AND REMEDY   *The court ordered McGee and WRM & Associates to stop using the term "Card Service" and to give up any interest in the domain name "cardservice.com."*

Registering Your Trademark. After selecting a trademark that appears to be available and that is not confusingly similar to an existing mark, you should register the mark with both the state government and the federal government. Registration is not required for you to have a right to the mark. If you do not register, however, your protection may be limited to the area in which you do business. Federal registration gives your trademark nationwide protection, provided that the trademark is currently being used or will be used within six months.

To register your trademark, you must submit a form, the first page of which is shown in Exhibit 53–1. You must provide a specimen (picture) of your trademark, declare when you first used your trademark, and provide other information. You may want to register more than one mark. If your logo consists of a distinctive name as well as a graphic, you can register each item independently. For example, Apple Computer, Inc., uses a rainbow-colored apple as a registered logo and the name Apple as a trademark. The apple logo and the Apple name could be registered separately to get independent protection.

After applying for registration, you may hear nothing for several months. You may then receive an action letter from the PTO indicating that there is a problem with your application. The problem may be technical, such as a failure to fill in the form properly; or the PTO may consider your trademark too similar to an existing trademark or too general, in which case you will need to change it. The government thus gives you a chance to amend your application before sending you a final rejection or approval notice.

Protecting Your Trademark. After registering your trademark, you must take care of it. If your mark is federally registered, you may use the symbol ® along with your mark; this puts others on notice of your registration. Even if you are not registered, you can use the symbol ™ along with your mark. Five years after you initially register your mark, you should file the appropriate forms with the PTO to renew your registration. Thereafter, you can renew your registration at ten-year intervals. Filing for renewal informs the government that your mark is still in use and enhances its strength — others cannot contest the validity of your mark.

The trademark owner should also keep alert to possible infringement. If another company uses your trademark or a mark extremely similar to yours, you should take prompt action by sending that company a letter of complaint and considering the possibility of filing a lawsuit for trademark infringement. If you ignore the problem, you may lose rights in your trademark. If, for example, a media outlet improperly refers to your trademark as if it were a generic word, send it a letter of correction and keep a copy in your files. You may at some point need to demonstrate that you have consistently sought to enforce your rights in the mark.

Under certain circumstances, a trademark owner can be considered to have legally abandoned his or her exclusive right to use a mark. Once a mark is abandoned, it is available for another party's use.

EXHIBIT 53–1   TRADEMARK APPLICATION FORM

TRADEMARK/SERVICE MARK APPLICATION, PRINCIPAL REGISTER, WITH DECLARATION	MARK (Word(s) and/or Design)	CLASS NO. (If known)

TO THE ASSISTANT COMMISSIONER FOR TRADEMARKS:

APPLICANT'S NAME:

APPLICANTS BUSINESS ADDRESS:
(Display address exactly as it should appear on registration) _____

APPLICANT'S ENTITY TYPE: (Check one and supply requested information)

Individual—Citizen of (Country): _____
Partnership—State where organized (Country, if appropriate): _____
Names and Citizenship (Country) of General Partners: _____

Corporation—State (Country, if appropriate) of Incorporation: _____

Other (Specific Nature of Entity and Domicile): _____

GOODS AND/OR SERVICES:

Applicant requests registration of the trademark/service mark shown in the accompanying drawing in the United States Patent and Trademark Office on the Principal Register established by the Act of July 5, 1946 (15 U.S.C. 1051 et seq., as amended) for the following goods/services (SPECIFIC GOODS AND/OR SERVICES MUST BE INSERTED HERE):
_____
_____
_____
_____

BASIS FOR APPLICATION: (Check boxes which apply, but never both the first AND second boxes, and supply requested information related to each box checked.)

[ ] Applicant is using mark in commerce on or in connection with the above identified goods/services. (15 U.S.C. 1051(a), as amended.) Three specimens showing the mark as used in commerce are submitted with this application.
  • Date of first use of the mark in commerce which the U.S. Congress may regulate (for example, interstate or between the U.S. and a foreign country):
  • Specify the type of commerce: _____
      (for example, interstate or between the U.S. and a specified foreign country)
  • Date of first use anywhere (the same as or before use in commerce date): _____
  • Specify intended manner or mode of use of mark on or in connection with the goods/services: _____

  (for example, trademark is applied to labels, service mark is used in advertisements)

[ ] Applicant has a bona fide intention to use the mark in commerce on or in connection with the above identified goods/ services. (15 U.S.C. 1051(b), as amended.)
  • Specify manner or mode of use of mark on or in connection with the goods/services: _____

  (for example, trademark will be applied to labels, service mark will be used in advertisements)

[ ] Applicant has a bona fide intention to use the mark in commerce on or in connection with the above identified goods/ services and asserts a claim of priority based upon a foreign application in accordance with 15 U.S.C. 1126(d), as amended.
  • Country of foreign filing: _____   • Date of foreign filing: _____

[ ] Applicant has a bona fide intention to use the mark in commerce or in connection with the above identified goods/ services, and, accompanying this application, submits a certification or certified copy of a foreign registration in accordance with 15 U.S.C. 1126(e), as amended.
  • Country of registration: _____   • Registration number: _____

NOTE: Declaration, on Reverse Side, MUST be Signed

PTO Form 1478 (REV 10:94)
OMB No. 0651-2099 (Exp. 5-30-95)

U.S. DEPARTMENT OF COMMERCE Patent and Trademark Office

Abandonment occurs if the owner actually stops using the mark, with the intent to abandon it, or if the owner uses it in a way that causes it to lose its significance as an indication of the origin of the product. Abandonment is presumed if a mark registered with the PTO is not used for two or more years. (In other words, the owner of a mark must "use it or lose it.") Also, allowing others to use a mark without restrictions, or at least without protest, can constitute abandonment and make it difficult, if not impossible, to protect the mark later.

PROTECTING TRADE SECRETS

Much of the value of some new enterprises consists of trade secrets. As discussed in Chapter 7, trade secrets are anything that makes a company unique and that would have value to a competitor. Trade secrets may include information concerning product development, production processes and techniques, or customer lists.

Trade secrets must be divulged to key employees, and thus any business runs the risk that those employees might disclose the secrets to competitors—or even set up competing businesses themselves. Generally, protecting against the possibility that valuable trade secrets will fall into the hands of others, especially competitors, presents an ongoing challenge for businesses, including new enterprises.

To protect their trade secrets, companies may require employees that have access to these secrets to agree in their employment contracts never to divulge those secrets. A company may also include a covenant not to compete in an employment contract to protect against the possibility that a key employee may go to work for a competitor or set up a competing business, in which case the company's trade secrets will likely be disclosed. (Covenants not to compete are discussed later in the chapter.)

Trade secrets are protected under the common law, as discussed in Chapter 7,[3] and thus a company can sue an individual or firm that has misappropriated the company's trade secrets. In one case, for example, two engineers developed new software products for an established company. A new, small company then hired the engineers. After the engineers developed a similar product for their new employer, the established company sued for infringement of trade secrets and prevailed in court. The new company was prohibited

from selling any of the contested products for three years.[4]

SECTION 5

Raising Financial Capital

Raising financial capital is critical to entrepreneurial success. In the very early days of a business, sole proprietors or partners may be able to contribute only very limited amounts of capital. If the business becomes successful, the owner or owners may want to raise capital from external sources to expand the business. There are several ways to do this. One way is to borrow funds. Another is to exchange equity (ownership rights) in the company in return for financial capital, either through private arrangements or through public stock offerings.

LOANS

A business can raise capital through a bank loan, but this option may not be available for many entrepreneurs. Banks are usually reluctant to lend significant sums to unestablished businesses. Even if a bank is willing to make such a loan, the bank may require personal guaranty contracts from the entrepreneurs (see Chapter 29).

If a bank loan is available, the entrepreneur may find it beneficial to obtain one, because raising capital in this way leaves the entrepreneur in full ownership and control of the business (though the loan itself may place some restrictions on future business decisions). Loans with desirable terms may be available from the federal Small Business Administration (SBA). One special SBA program provides loans of up to $25,000 for women, low-income, and minority businesspersons. Some entrepreneurs have even used their credit cards to obtain initial capital.

VENTURE CAPITAL

Many new businesses raise needed capital by exchanging certain ownership rights (equity) in the firm for **venture capital.** In other words, an outsider contributes money in exchange for an ownership interest in the company. **Venture capitalists** are those who seek out promising entrepreneurial ventures and fund them in exchange for equity stakes. Akin to venture capitalists are individuals, known as "angels," who typically invest somewhat smaller sums in new businesses.

---

3. The theft of trade secrets is also a federal crime under the Economic Espionage Act of 1996 (see Chapter 8).

4. *Scully Signal Co. v. Joyal*, 881 F.Supp. 727 (D.R.I. 1995).

In 1998, venture capitalists invested $14.3 billion in over 2,500 new companies. The average investment was around $5 million.[5] Venture capitalists, in addition to making needed financing available, offer other advantages for entrepreneurs. Venture capitalists are often experienced managers who can provide invaluable assistance to entrepreneurs with respect to strategic business decisions, marketing, and making important business contacts. Obtaining this assistance may be crucial to a new company's success. The disadvantage is that the venture capitalist with a substantial equity stake will demand a corresponding degree of operational control over a company and proportion of future profits. (For information on how to locate potential investors, see this chapter's *Emerging Trends in Technology.*)

To attract outside venture capital, you will need a **business plan.** The plan should be relatively concise (less than fifty pages). It should describe the company, its products, and its anticipated future performance. You may present your plan to a venture capitalist, who may then carefully investigate your venture. This may require you to disclose trade secrets, and you should insist that the potential investor sign a confidentiality agreement. If all goes well, you will then negotiate the terms of financing. A key point to be negotiated is how much ownership and control the venture capitalist will receive in exchange for the capital contribution. Exhibit 53–2 on page 1019 summarizes some key issues involved in venture capital negotiations.

SECURITIES REGULATION

Securities regulation is an area of significant concern to those raising capital. Many entrepreneurs do not use venture capitalists but raise money from friends or business acquaintances. Whatever method is used, the investor exchanges capital for an interest in the enterprise. If this interest consists of shares of stock (or otherwise qualifies as a security under federal or state law), the entrepreneur may become subject to extraordinarily detailed regulatory requirements. It may be necessary to register the securities with the Securities and Exchange Commission (SEC) or with the state in which the offering is made, unless the offering falls within an exemption to securities laws.

Private Offering.   In certain circumstances, legal exemptions are available so that the entrepreneur need not worry about full registration or compli-

ance with all of the securities regulations. The securities regulations and exemptions were discussed in detail in Chapter 37. In short, the exemptions permit you to raise a certain limited amount of money from a certain limited number of investors in what is sometimes called a private offering. If your offering qualifies, you need not register your shares as securities with the SEC. States have separate regulatory schemes and different terms for their exemptions from registration. Raising capital in this manner is typically done through a private placement memorandum distributed to selected potential investors.

Public Offering.   A public offering may be made if your business proves especially successful. A public offering makes a certain number of your shares available for purchase by members of the public at a price that you have set. Public offerings are highly regulated, but they may allow you to raise very large amounts of capital. Securities issued through public offerings must be registered with the SEC and applicable state regulatory agencies.

Full registration is complex, but the states and the SEC have jointly created a simplified securities registration for small businesses. The Small Corporate Offering Registration (SCOR) involves a form with only fifty questions that can be used for small offerings. Forty-three states use the SCOR offering, but the states have varying laws relating to use of the form.

SECTION 6

Buy-Sell Agreements and Key-Person Insurance

In the excitement of forming a new business venture, it is easy to overlook the possibility that partners or shareholders may die or become disabled or that disputes among partners or shareholders may make business decision making impossible. At the outset of any enterprise involving two or more owners, provisions can and should be made, and put in writing, to establish how such problems will be resolved.

SHAREHOLDER AGREEMENTS

Even if only two individuals start up and finance a new company, they should have a shareholder agreement that defines their relative ownership rights and interests. Such agreements are vital for small, closely

---

5. *Time,* September 27, 1999, p. 70.

EMERGING TRENDS IN TECHNOLOGY

Locating Potential Investors

Technology via the Internet has allowed promoters and others to access, easily and inexpensively, a large number of potential investors. Today, there are several online "matching services." These services specialize in matching potential investors with companies or future companies that are seeking investors. A corporate promoter or a small company seeking capital investment could pay a fee to one of these service companies, which would then include a description of the company in a list that it makes available to investors—also for a fee.

For example, the American Venture Capital Exchange, or AVCE (at **www.avce.com**), lists hundreds of companies that seek financing. Some of these companies are just starting up, while others are existing firms that wish to expand their businesses. For each company listed, AVCE provides a summary of its business plan for potential investors to review. Potential investors can then contact the companies in which they are interested. A similar service is offered by the National Finance Company (at **http:// www.natlfinance.com/ company.htm**). The company's "Computer Capital Matching" service is designed to match those

seeking financing to expand or start up a business with potential investors. Garage.com (at **www.garage.com**) provides a list of start-up companies and summaries of their business plans in the "Garage" area of its site and a list of potential investors in the "Heaven" area. Potential investors who are interested in one of the listed start-up companies may contact those companies directly.

A number of companies specialize in matching entrepreneurs in specific industries with potential investors. For example, Capital Access Network (at **http://neturn.com/can/ finance4tek.html**) offers matching services for "techpreneurs"— persons seeking capital for high-tech ventures. Also, some companies include listings of companies or start-ups not only in the United States but in other countries as well. For example, AVCE's listings include companies or start-ups in Canada, Europe, Russia, Mexico, South America, Asia, and Australia. Other companies restrict their services to firms within a certain region, such as the Pacific Northwest in the United States.

Matching services are not new. For decades, several enterprises have provided such services by using computerized databases to match business firms' investment needs with potential investors. What is new is that a number of these service providers are now online, and many of them have significantly expanded the geographic scope of their operations.

IMPLICATIONS FOR THE BUSINESSPERSON

1. Online matching services allow entrepreneurs to reach a wide group of potential investors quickly and with relatively little effort. They also make it possible for a new or existing company to locate investors who are interested in the company's specific type of business ventures.
2. Several of these online matching services also offer other types of assistance, such as help with creating an effective business plan or tips on how to manage financial issues. Businesspersons, and especially entrepreneurs just starting up their businesses, can also benefit from this type of guidance.

FOR CRITICAL ANALYSIS

1. How can investors who use online matching services protect themselves against fraud?
2. What factors would a venture capitalist be likely to consider when deciding whether to invest in a start-up company?

RELEVANT WEB SITES

In addition to the Web sites listed in this feature, hundreds of Web sites offer useful information and contacts for entrepreneurs and venture capitalists. To begin a search for this type of information, go to any major search engine, such as Yahoo, and search for "venture capital."

held companies, in large part because shares in such entities cannot be readily sold. This means that an owner may be locked into the investment against his or her will. Additionally, a venture capitalist will normally contribute to a new venture only on the condition that a shareholder agreement be formed to

EXHIBIT 53–2   VENTURE CAPITAL ISSUES

Type and Quantity of Stock	The venture capitalists will negotiate the amount of stock (which will determine their ownership share of the enterprise) and the type of stock (which will usually be preferred stock).
Stock Preferences	If the venture capitalists receive preferred shares, the shares will generally (1) provide for an annual per-share dividend to be paid before common stockholders receive any dividends and (2) give the venture capitalists priority among shareholders in the event of the firm's liquidation.
Conversion and Antidilution Rights	The preferred shares will be convertible into common stock at the option of the venture capitalists, and the company will be restrained from issuing new stock in an amount that would materially dilute the venture capitalists' ownership interests.
Board of Directors	The venture capitalists will define their proportionate representation on the board of directors.
Registration Rights	Should the company conduct a public offering or register its shares at a later date, the venture capitalists will have the right to have their shares registered also ("piggy-backed"), making those shares more marketable.
Representations and Warranties	The entrepreneur will be required to make representations about the firm's capital structure, its possession of necessary government authorizations, its financial statements, and other material facts.

specify the rights and obligations of shareholders in specific circumstances.

One key term of the shareholder agreement is a *buy-sell agreement*. This type of agreement was discussed in Chapter 33 in the context of a partnership agreement. In a corporate shareholder agreement, a buy-sell agreement provides for the buyout of a shareholder and establishes criteria for the price to be paid for that shareholder's ownership interest. A buy-sell agreement might be triggered by the death of a shareholder, enabling that shareholder's heirs to cash out the investment. Other common triggering events include the bankruptcy of a shareholder, the divorce of a shareholder, and the legal attachment of a shareholder's shares for other reasons.

Buy-sell agreements can also resolve serious deadlocks that may develop between co-owners as the business grows. One owner may have a contract option to buy out the others in the event that such a deadlock occurs. Alternatively, all co-owners might submit sealed bids to buy out each other, with the highest bidder being allowed to buy out the others. Another provision that might be included in a buy-sell agreement is a right of first refusal. Such a provision will prevent an owner from selling to a third party without first giving the other owners a right to buy out his or her interest. An alternative to the right of first refusal is a provision for a "take-along right." This right allows an investor to participate in any sale

of shares to a third party. The right can protect relatively passive investors from the possibility that managing shareholders may "bail out" of the corporation by selling their shares to third parties.

KEY-PERSON INSURANCE

Much of the value of the new enterprise may rest in the skills of one or more employees (such as a software designer or a top management executive). To protect against the risk that these key persons may become disabled or die, business enterprises typically obtain key-person insurance (see Chapter 49). The proceeds of a key-person insurance policy can help cover the losses caused by the death or disability of essential employees. Venture capitalists or other investors may require that the company take out a key-person insurance policy as a condition of investing in the corporation.

SECTION 7

Contract Law and the Entrepreneur

Entrepreneurs are subject to the common law of contracts, which was covered in detail in Chapters 10 through 18. Any business venture will require that contracts be formed and signed. For example, if you lease business premises, you will need to sign a lease contract. Any equipment you purchase or sell will also involve contracts. A review of basic contract law principles can help to ensure that any contracts you form will be valid and enforceable. As a general rule, you should make sure that any contractual agreement is in writing. Then, should a dispute arise, there will be written evidence of the contract's terms. Additionally, as discussed in Chapter 15, some contracts—such as contracts for the sale of goods priced at $500 or more—fall under the Statute of Frauds, which means that they must be in writing to be enforceable.

Entrepreneurs often consult with their attorneys in creating contract forms for specific purposes. For example, a new business may wish to provide a warranty for its products but also limit the scope of that war-

ranty. This decision is best made through the mutual judgment of the entrepreneur and his or her attorney, so that both business and legal concerns are met.

Contract law contains traps of which the entrepreneur should be aware. If you incorporate, you will want to enter contracts as an agent of the corporation, not in your individual capacity. Otherwise, you may be personally liable on the contracts. This principle applies to negotiable instruments as well. For example, if you sign a promissory note on behalf of the corporation, you should indicate that you are signing in a representative capacity (see Chapter 26 for further details on signature liability with respect to negotiable instruments). The same advice applies to partners and partnerships. The following case is illustrative.

CASE 53.2

The Boston Globe Newspaper Co. v. The Folktree Concertmakers, Inc.

Massachusetts
Appellate Division,
Northern District, 1998.
1998 Mass.App.Div. 206.

COMPANY PROFILE   *The* Boston Globe (**http://www.boston.com/globe**) *is New England's leading daily newspaper and winner of fifteen Pulitzer Prizes. Based in Boston, Massachusetts, the* Globe *operates seven local, five national, and six foreign news bureaus. The New York Times Company* (**http://www.nyt.com**) *owns the* Globe, *which is the company's second largest revenue and earnings producer. The New York Times Company owns nineteen other daily newspapers, three weekly publications, half of the* International Herald Tribune, *eight television stations, and two radio stations, among other media operations.*

BACKGROUND AND FACTS   *Harry Lipson was the president of the Folktree Concertmakers, Inc. To obtain concert advertising in the* Boston Globe, *Lipson completed the newspaper's "Standard Application for Credit." He signed the application "Harry Lipson as President of Folktree Concertmakers, Inc." The application package also contained a form called a Guaranty, which he signed simply as "Harry Lipson." Between 1970 and 1995, Folktree placed about $67,000 in advertising with the paper but failed to pay bills totaling $8,556.55. The Boston Globe Newspaper Company sued both Folktree and Lipson, and the trial court granted summary judgment for the newspaper. Lipson appealed on the ground that he was not personally liable for the debt.*

IN THE LANGUAGE OF THE COURT

CURTIN, Justice.
          *   *   *   *

Although the guaranty in this case does not use the words "personally" or "personal," a fair reading of the terms of the contract renders it clear that Globe required a personal guaranty before it would permit the corporate defendant to purchase advertising on credit. The guaranty expressly and unambiguously states that "[i]n consideration for the Globe extending credit to the above-named applicant [that is, Folktree] the undersigned hereby unconditionally guarantees payment to the Globe of all amounts owed by the applicant to the Globe." The consistent use of the term "applicant" when referring to the corporate entity as distinguished from the "undersigned" throughout the guaranty indicates the parties' clear intent to have someone other than the corporation guarantee its debt. The ordinary meaning of the term "guaranty" is indeed that "someone else is primarily liable for a debt and that the guarantor will pay it if the primary debtor does not."

If, as Lipson contends, the "undersigned" is construed to mean Lipson in only his capacity as president of Folktree, the guaranty would be meaningless as Folktree would then be simply guaranteeing its own obligation to the Globe.

The guaranty in the credit application was set forth conspicuously in bold type. Lipson was on notice that the Globe would not extend credit to Folktree for the advertising necessary for the corporation's business unless Lipson assumed personal responsibility by executing the guaranty in his individual capacity.

DECISION AND REMEDY *The court dismissed Lipson's appeal and affirmed the entry of summary judgment for the Boston Globe Newspaper Company.*

SECTION 8

Credit and Payment

A common concern of entrepreneurs is positive cash flow, which requires that customers make their payments fairly promptly. Many businesses give their customers thirty to sixty days to pay or otherwise extend short-term credit. A number of customers will fail to pay during this extended period, however, and this can create a substantial problem for the new business.

To give customers an incentive to pay on time, companies may charge for late payments. A company may also charge interest on overdue balances, but such a policy entails some legal complications. For consumer sales, the Truth-in-Lending Act (TILA) requires that certain disclosures be made concerning how the interest will be calculated, and so on. TILA and other consumer protection laws were discussed in Chapter 44.

The entrepreneur has a variety of devices available to encourage prompt payment. For consumer sales, some businesses offer free shipping with prepayment. A company may choose to offer price discounts for prompt payment. The sales contract may also contain a provision making the buyer responsible for all costs involved in collecting overdue payments. Companies frequently run credit checks on consumers or other contract parties before extending credit to those parties.

If a problem with late payments persists, you will need to undertake collection efforts. In so doing, you must comply with laws that govern debt-collection practices. Federal law prohibits the use of abusive collection efforts, such as calling individuals frequently at home at inconvenient times, or at work. Typically, state laws also prohibit such practices. Certain threats and harassment are also commonly proscribed.

SECTION 9

Employment Issues

Start-up businesses are exempt from some employment laws. For example, businesses with fewer than fifteen employees are exempt from federal laws prohibiting employment discrimination and certain other federal acts, such as the Family and Medical Leave Act of 1993. Some state statutes have similar exemptions for small businesses. A knowledge of employment law is crucial for entrepreneurs starting up businesses, however, because even the smallest businesses are subject to many employment laws.

For example, the sometimes detailed regulations of the federal Occupational Safety and Health Administration have no small-business exemptions. It may be true that small businesses are less likely to be inspected for violations. If enforcement and penalties are applied, however, they can be far more disastrous for start-up companies than for larger, established companies that are in a better position to absorb these costs. Similarly, just one successful lawsuit against a small business firm can mean bankruptcy for the firm, as indicated earlier in this chapter.

HIRING EMPLOYEES

Hiring good employees can be crucial to business success. Several legal issues are important in this process.

1. Be sure that the person you hire will not be disclosing protected trade secrets of his or her former employer.
2. Do not make promises of job security unless you are sure you can keep them. If you promise an employee

that his or her job will be permanent and the employee relies on your assurances, you may find it difficult to fire the employee.

3. Determine what screening tests are appropriate for the job. In some circumstances, you may be able to require the applicant to take a drug test.

4. Comply with all requirements imposed by the Immigration and Naturalization Service with respect to verifying whether workers are U.S. citizens and whether employees who are not citizens are authorized to work in this country.

Generally, you should put all employment agreements in writing. An employment contract might specify that the contract is for at-will employment (see Chapter 41), meaning that you can fire the employee at any time for any reason, providing that no employment laws are violated. In new businesses, an employee might want stock or options in lieu of some salary. While this saves scarce cash, granting equity to an employee dilutes the other owners' interests. For high-level employees at least, you would be wise to consult with an attorney regarding what contractual provisions should be included.

It goes without saying that you should consult with former employers of job applicants and verify the applicants' credentials and job experience. You should also make sufficient inquiries to avoid a negligent-hiring lawsuit. Suppose that you hire a person who has been convicted twice for criminal assault. If that employee attacks a customer, the customer could sue your business for negligence in screening the worker's background during the hiring process. You therefore should check to see if a job applicant has a criminal history. You should also check a job applicant's driving record if the job involves driving a vehicle for business purposes. Additionally, actions of dishonest employees can cause a small business to suffer substantial economic losses. Thorough screening procedures will help you to avoid such problems.

EMPLOYEE COMPENSATION

Compensation for employees is governed by the Fair Labor Standards Act (FLSA). This law applies to all businesses that have $500,000 or more in sales or that are engaged in interstate commerce. The FLSA requires that employees be paid at least the minimum wage plus time and a half for overtime. The law also requires that employers keep detailed records of wages paid and hours worked. Executives and professionals are exempted from the minimum-pay and overtime requirements, as are independent contractors. State laws that govern the workplace may require meal breaks or rest breaks for employees.

WORKERS' COMPENSATION

Most states require that employers carry workers' compensation insurance. If one of your employees is injured in the course of employment, the employee will be compensated for the injury by the state workers' compensation fund. That employee generally cannot sue you for further damages. Workers' compensation insurance premiums may be high, and they may constitute one of the greatest expenses for small businesses. Premiums are initially based on the size of your payroll and the amount of risk involved in the business that you operate. After some time, your rates may be raised or lowered, depending on the safety record of your business. The fewer claims made against you, the lower your workers' compensation insurance costs will be.

UNEMPLOYMENT COMPENSATION

Unemployment compensation (see Chapter 41) is another cost that new businesses must consider. Unemployment compensation tax rates are based in part on the size of your payroll. Your liability is also affected by the number of claimants from your business. The fewer people you fire, the lower your required payments. Employees are not entitled to unemployment compensation if they voluntarily terminated their employment or if they were fired for misconduct or malfeasance, such as theft.

FIRING EMPLOYEES

Unfortunately, at one time or another, a small-business owner will probably find it necessary to fire a worker. Unless otherwise specified in employment contracts, your employees are presumptively at-will employees, whom you can fire without having to give any reason for doing so. It is nevertheless generally advisable to document good cause for terminating a worker—otherwise, he or she may succeed in a lawsuit against you for unlawful discrimination or some other legal violation.

Generally, you should keep a file on each employee in which you include the employee's application, performance reviews, and other relevant information. If you fire the employee, full documentation of why he or she was fired should also be added to the file.

Realize, however, that nearly half the states have laws that allow employees to have access to their personnel records. If you fire a worker, you are not required to give severance pay (unless you have previously promised to do so). Most states have laws governing when you must provide the employee with his or her final paycheck, however.

Some states recognize a legal action for wrongful discharge, but these actions are generally limited to terminations in bad faith. You must be aware of any promises you made to the employee in a written contract, in an employee handbook, or even orally. These promises may prevent you from firing the employee without due process, good cause, or whatever else you may have promised. Employers may also be liable for defamation if they make false statements to others about the reason for termination. You should also be cautious in what you say to a prospective employer who asks you for a job reference for a former employee. Do not be tempted to do your former employee a favor by giving

him or her an undeserved glowing reference. If the person or company to whom you give the reference hires your former employee and suffers harm as a result, you may be liable for misrepresentation.

Even though employers with fewer than fifteen employees are not covered by federal laws prohibiting discrimination, you should not regard this exemption for small businesses as a license to discriminate against employees. Small businesses that employ fewer than fifteen employees may be held liable for discriminatory treatment on the ground that such treatment violates a state law prohibiting employment discrimination, the equal protection clause of the U.S. Constitution, or some established public policy. For example, in the following case, a woman who worked in a small medical office with fewer than five employees contended that her employer's alleged discrimination against her on the basis of pregnancy violated the state's public policy against gender-based discrimination.

CASE 53.3   Badih v. Myers

California Court
of Appeal,
First District, Division 1,
1995.
36 Cal.App.4th 1289,
43 Cal.Rptr.2d 229.

BACKGROUND AND FACTS *Fatmeh Badih was a medical assistant for Dr. Leonard Myers. When Badih got married and became pregnant, Myers fired her. Badih filed a suit in a California state court against Myers, alleging in part discrimination on the basis of pregnancy in violation of public policy. The court awarded Badih damages. Myers appealed, asserting that he was not subject to any state law prohibiting discrimination in employment on the basis of pregnancy. Badih argued that pregnancy discrimination in employment is a form of sex (gender) discrimination prohibited by the California constitution, which states that "[a] person may not be disqualified from * * * employment because of sex."*

DOSSEE, Associate Justice.
  *   *   *   *

IN THE LANGUAGE OF THE COURT

  *   *   * [California c]ourts *   *   * may not declare public policy without a basis in either constitutional or statutory provisions.
  *   *   *

  *   *   * [Federal and state] statutes, regulations, and decisions *   *   * strongly support the notion that pregnancy discrimination in employment should be treated as a form of sex discrimination. *   *   * [T]here is no reason why a different definition of sex discrimination should be applied in the context of [the state constitution].

  *   *   * [W]e conclude that pregnancy discrimination is a form of sex discrimination under *   *   * the California Constitution. Since [the constitution] expresses a fundamental public policy against sex discrimination in employment, Badih was properly allowed to maintain her cause of action *   *   *.

DECISION AND REMEDY *The California appellate court affirmed the lower court's decision. Pregnancy discrimination constituted a violation of the public policy against gender discrimination in employment.*

COVENANTS NOT TO COMPETE

Covenants not to compete are very important in the entrepreneurial context. Many employers include such covenants, or clauses, in their employment contracts with workers. A typical covenant not to compete might require the worker to agree not to work for or establish a competing business within the same area of the state for six months or one year after his or her employment is terminated. You may want to require your workers to sign such an agreement in order to prevent them from leaving your business and setting up a competing operation. When hiring new workers, you also need to be alert to the possibility that they may be violating such a clause.

As discussed in Chapter 13, covenants not to compete in employment contracts are generally enforceable so long as they are not unreasonably restrictive in terms of the time period covered or the geographic area involved. A covenant not to compete that restricts an employee from working for a competitor for five years or "anywhere in the world" normally will not be enforced. There have been rare exceptions, however. In one case, when a consultant for a software company left to form a new company in a related area of business, her former employer brought a legal action to enforce a covenant not to compete to prevent her from taking on this work. The court enforced the covenant, even though it had worldwide scope and prevented her from working for a competitor anywhere on the globe.[6]

USING INDEPENDENT CONTRACTORS

Independent contractors are not considered to be employees. As stated in Chapter 31, according to the *Restatement (Second) of Agency*, an independent contractor is "a person who contracts with another to do something for him but who is not controlled by the other nor subject to the other's right to control with respect to his physical conduct in the performance of the undertaking."

Benefits of Using Independent Contractors. The use of independent contractors offers many advantages to small businesses. For one thing, you need not withhold income taxes and Social Security and Medicare taxes from payments made to independent contractors, as you are required to do when you pay wages to employees. Furthermore, you need not match the amount withheld for Social Security and Medicare taxes, which can be costly for an employer. Additionally, you need not pay premiums for workers' compensation insurance or unemployment insurance.

Another important benefit of hiring workers as independent contractors rather than employees is that you are not subject to laws governing employment relationships, including laws prohibiting discrimination. Normally, an independent contractor will not be permitted by a court to bring a suit against you for age discrimination, for example, or for any other type of discrimination prohibited by federal or state laws governing employment relationships—because these laws only protect *employees*, not independent contractors.

Liability for Misclassification of Workers. Of course, the trade-off in using independent contractors is that you cannot exercise a significant amount of control over how they perform their work. If you do, the IRS or another government agency may decide that they are not independent contractors but employees. Misclassification of an employee as an independent contractor can subject you to considerable tax liability, including penalties.

The potential seriousness of misclassification was felt recently by Microsoft. In a tax audit, the IRS concluded that Microsoft exercised significant control over workers designated by Microsoft as independent contractors and reclassified them as employees. The company accepted the ruling and paid overdue employment taxes. Then several hundred independent contractors sued the company to recover the benefits that Microsoft had made available to its employees but not to the independent contractors. The court held that the workers were entitled to participate in Microsoft's stock-purchase plan and other benefits available to the company's employees worth millions of dollars.[7]

6. *Business Intelligence Services, Inc. v. Hudson*, 580 F.Supp. 1068 (S.D.N.Y. 1984).

7. *Vizcaino v. Microsoft Corp.*, 173 F.3d 713 (9th Cir. 1999). See the *Emerging Trends in Business Law* in Chapter 31 for a further discussion of this case.

TERMS AND CONCEPTS TO REVIEW

business plan 1017   venture capital 1016   venture capitalist 1016

QUESTIONS AND CASE PROBLEMS

53–1. TAXES. George Costanza has plans for establishing a new business with Elaine Benes. They will both be managers, and each will take an annual salary of $50,000. The company will have other expenses of $175,000. They expect to take in $375,000 in the first year of operation and share the profits equally. George and Elaine have not yet decided whether to incorporate the new business or run it as a partnership. What are the tax differences between the two approaches?

53–2. SHAREHOLDER AGREEMENTS. Herman Fryar was a shareholder in a small company, Bryan-Barber Realty, Inc. Fryar's ownership was subject to a shareholder agreement stating that he could not sell or otherwise dispose of his stock without the permission of the other shareholders. In divorce proceedings, the court directed Herman to transfer the stock to his wife, Judith. Bryan-Barber subsequently obtained a judgment against Herman and sought to recover his shares. The company claimed that Harold was still the owner of the shares, because the shareholder agreement prohibited the transfer of Herman's shares to anyone else, including Judith, without the permission of the other shareholders. Discuss whether this claim should succeed. [*Bryan-Barber Realty, Inc. v. Fryar*, 461 S.E.2d 29 (N.C.App. 1995)]

53–3. CORPORATE FORMALITIES. Jerold Murphy and three others incorporated Country House, Inc. All four shareholders worked for the company. When the company had a surplus, it gave "bonuses" to the four individuals. Murphy initially contributed one-fourth of the capital to Country House, but he owned only one-ninth of the company at the time of the payments and was offered one-ninth of the surplus as his bonus. He claimed that he did one-fourth of the work and should receive one-fourth of the surplus as his bonus. Discuss the magnitude of the bonus to which Murphy is entitled. [*Murphy v. Country House, Inc.*, 349 N.W.2d 289 (Minn. App. 1984)]

53–4. TRADEMARKS. Ken McShea was the sole shareholder in a new entrepreneurial venture. His business was a bakery in upstate New York. He named the company McBagel's, Inc., and used the name on his store. McDonald's Corp., the national fast-food chain, sued for trademark infringement, and McShea argued that there was no likelihood of confusion. Discuss who should win

this case. [*McDonald's Corp. v. McBagel's, Inc.*, 649 F.Supp. 1268 (S.D.N.Y. 1986)]

53–5. HIRING AND FIRING. Lori McKenzie worked as a personnel director for Renberg's, Inc. She warned the company president that Renberg's was going to be sued for specific violations of the Fair Labor Standards Act. After this encounter, the president stopped speaking to her and fired her sixteen days later. She sued the company for wrongful discharge. The company claimed that she had been fired for improperly and negligently notarizing a "contract" between two other workers for sexual favors. The jury ruled that she had been improperly fired, but the trial court overruled this finding, holding that the company had had adequate legal grounds for firing her. McKenzie appealed. Discuss whether the trial court's ruling should be upheld. [*McKenzie v. Renberg's Inc.*, 94 F.3d 1478 (10th Cir. 1996)]

53–6. LIABILITY. Gregory and Dale Stires and Stanley Hall owned and operated the Elk Valley Game Ranch as partners. Hall bought thirty-eight head of elk from Martin Carelli and signed a promissory note agreeing to pay $36,000. Hall also signed a security agreement identifying the elk as collateral. Both the note and the security agreement referred to Hall but not to the Stireses. The elk were kept at the ranch. After Hall quit the partnership, the Stireses continued to operate the ranch. When the note was not paid, Carelli filed a suit in a Montana state court against Hall and the Stireses. The court ruled in Carelli's favor. The Stireses appealed, claiming that Hall was personally liable and they were not. What will the appellate court decide? Why? [*Carelli v. Hall*, 926 P.2d 756 (Mont. 1996)]

53–7. HIRING AND FIRING. Carol Anstett was a salaried, at-will employee of the Plastics Division of Eagle-Picher Industries, Inc. The Plastics Division had an express severance policy under which "[s]alaried employees terminated other than for cause or voluntary separation" were entitled to certain benefits. In July 1997, Eagle-Picher sold the Plastics Division to Cambridge Industries, Inc. Eagle-Picher notified the Plastics Division employees of what was happening to their health insurance and retirement benefits on "termination of service." Cambridge immediately reemployed nearly all of the Plastics Division personnel, including Anstett. The employees believed that the sale of the division triggered an application of the severance policy and asked Eagle-Picher to pay. The company refused, claiming that the employees had not been terminated. Anstett and others filed a suit in a federal district court against Eagle-Picher, seeking the separation benefits. Eagle-Picher responded that the policy was intended only to cover employees who suffered a loss of income, not to cover a corporate asset sale in which the purchaser immediately rehired the employees. How should the court rule? Explain. [*Anstett v. Eagle-Picher Industries, Inc.,* 203 F.3d 501 (7th Cir. 2000)]

53–8. In Your Court

Edward Lance is the president of Lance Equities, Inc. (Equities), a firm that owns and manages real estate. Equities had a corporate Visa account for which one credit card was issued in Lance's name. Lance personally reviewed all credit-card statements until he hired Susan Rush as his assistant. Rush's duties included reviewing the statements. Without Lance's consent, Rush obtained a second credit card for the Equities Visa account. Over the next twenty months, she made more than $400,000 in unauthorized charges. When the theft was discovered, Rush agreed to repay $250,000. Lance and his firm sued the credit-card company to recover their payments for the other charges. Lance argued that the credit-card company should be liable for these charges because they were fraudulent and unauthorized. The credit-card company submitted a motion for summary judgment in its favor. Assume that you are the judge in the trial court hearing this case and answer the following questions:

(a) Generally, in what circumstances will a court grant a party's motion for summary judgment? (You may wish to review the court procedures discussed in Chapter 3 before answering this question.)

(b) Will you grant summary judgment in favor of the credit-card company in this case? Why or why not?

Law on the Web

For updated links to resources available on the Web, as well as a variety of other materials, visit this text's Web site at http://wbl.westbuslaw.com.

Several commercial services on the Web help businesses get their names on the Web. Most of these services are free, at least for basic listings. Here are the names and URLs of a few of these services:

■ Postmaster:

http://www.netcreations.com/postmaster

■ Register It!:

http://www.register-it.com

■ Web Promote:

http://www.webpromote.com

To obtain tax information and forms, go to the Web site of the Internal Revenue Service at

http://www.irs.ustreas.gov

Legal Research Exercises on the Web

Go to http://wbl.westbuslaw.com, the Web site that accompanies this text. Select "Internet Applications," and then click on "Chapter 53." There you will find the following Internet research exercises that you can perform to learn more about starting and financing a business:

Activity 53–1: Starting a Business

Activity 53–2: Financing a Business

UNIT ELEVEN—CUMULATIVE BUSINESS HYPOTHETICAL

JB Mediquip, Inc., is in the business of manufacturing hospital equipment. The business was formed several years ago by Jerrold Botran, who remains the company's president and major shareholder. Jerrold's business acumen and managerial skills have caused the company to prosper. JB now does business throughout the world and has manufacturing plants in two other countries.

1. When he started up his business, Jerrold was concerned about the potential liability he would incur if a customer was injured while on his business premises. He was also concerned about the liability he could face if a user of his equipment brought a product-liability suit against his firm—which could happen if any equipment that he sold was defective and harmed a user as a result. Furthermore, he wanted to protect against the loss of income that the business and his family would suffer if he was disabled or died. What types of insurance policies would best meet each of these needs? Explain.

2. Jerrold is a widower with two children, Steve and Julie. Jerrold's will designates his daughter Julie as his sole heir and says nothing about Steve. If, on Jerrold's death, Steve contested the will, would he succeed in obtaining any of his father's property? Assume that Jerrold, before he dies, has a change of heart. He writes a new will in which he leaves everything he owns to both of his children in equal shares. In the new will, he says nothing about revoking his prior will. Who will inherit what in these circumstances?

3. Aaron Falkner, a certified public accountant, provides accounting services to JB Mediquip. The services include preparing JB's financial reports and issuing opinion letters based on those reports. One year, JB falls into serious financial trouble, but neither Falkner's reports nor his opinion letters indicate this situation. Relying on Falkner's portrayal of the company's financial health, JB borrows substantial sums of money to invest in the construction of a new manufacturing plant. The bank, in lending JB the money, relies on an opinion letter from Falkner. Falkner is aware of the bank's reliance on the letter. Assuming that Falkner did not engage in intentional fraud but was negligent, what is his potential liability in this situation? Discuss fully.

4. JB agrees to sell fifty hospital beds to a health-care facility operated on a military base in Zamboria, a foreign country. The health-care facility is owned and operated by the Zamborian government. JB ships the beds, but the health-care facility refuses to pay for them. To recover the price of the beds, JB sues the health-care facility in a U.S. district court. Zamboria moves to dismiss JB's action, contending that a U.S. court cannot exercise jurisdiction over the matter. On what ground might Zamboria base its assertion? Is Zamboria correct?

FOCUS ON LEGAL REASONING
Marcus Brothers Textiles, Inc. v. Price Waterhouse, LLP

INTRODUCTION

When making business decisions, many parties, including managers, investors, and creditors, rely on the opinions of accountants with whom they are not in privity of contract. Auditors' potential liability to these third parties is discussed in Chapter 51. In most jurisdictions, auditors may be liable for negligence to third parties whom they know will use the auditors' reports. In this *Focus on Legal Reasoning*, we examine *Marcus Brothers Textiles, Inc. v. Price Waterhouse, LLP*,[1] a recent decision that dealt with the issue of auditors' liability.

CASE BACKGROUND

Marcus Brothers Textiles, Inc., is a New York-based converter of textiles

1. 350 N.C. 214, 513 S.E.2d 320 (1999).

that buys unfinished woven material, has it finished by independent contractors, and sells it to apparel manufacturers or retailers of fabric for home sewing. Piece Goods Shops Company, L.P., was a North Carolina–based retailer of fabrics, patterns, sewing notions, needlecraft supplies, and sewing machines, and a frequent customer of Marcus Brothers. Price Waterhouse, LLP, is an independent certified public accounting firm with offices in North Carolina. Beginning in 1986, Price Waterhouse performed audits of Piece Goods's year-end financial statements. Based on the 1992 audited statement, Marcus Brothers extended credit to Piece Goods. The next year, Piece Goods filed a petition for bankruptcy. At the time, Piece Goods owed Marcus Brothers $288,848.14.

Marcus Brothers filed a suit in a North Carolina state court against

Price Waterhouse, alleging in part negligent misrepresentation. Marcus Brothers claimed the 1992 statement "included [Price Waterhouse's] unqualified opinion that the Financial Statement fairly and in all material respects accurately presented [Piece Goods'] financial position," but that it actually contained material misrepresentations and reflected departures from generally accepted accounting principles.

Price Waterhouse filed a motion for summary judgment, which the court granted, and Marcus Brothers appealed. The state intermediate appellate court reversed this judgment, and Price Waterhouse appealed to the North Carolina Supreme Court.

MAJORITY OPINION

WAINWRIGHT, Justice.

* * * *

The issue of the scope of an accountant's liability to persons other than the client for whom an audit report was prepared is relatively new in the annals of North Carolina jurisprudence. This Court first addressed the issue in [*Raritan River Steel Co. v. Cherry, Bekaert & Holland*, 322 N.C. 200, 367 S.E.2d 609 (1988)]. In *Raritan*, this Court stated that under certain circumstances, the tort of negligent misrepresentation set forth in section 552 of the *Restatement (Second) of Torts* could provide an appropriate remedy to plaintiffs who had been injured as a result of an accountant's negligence. * * * According to this Court in *Raritan*, the *Restatement* approach recognizes that liability should extend not only to those with whom the

accountant is in privity or near privity, but also to those persons, or classes of persons, whom he knows and intends will rely on his opinion, or whom he knows his client intends will so rely. * * *

* * * *

In support of its case, Marcus Brothers cites numerous circumstances which indicate genuine issues of material fact as to the knowledge [of Price Waterhouse]. First, there is unrefuted testimony that Piece Goods had been a client of Price Waterhouse since 1986. In addition, there is deposition testimony from James J. Quinn, Director of Corporate Credit for Marcus Brothers, indicating that Piece Goods has been sending its audited financial statements to Marcus Brothers since 1983, and that these financial statements were regularly used in determining whether to extend credit to Piece Goods. * * * There is further deposition testimony from Karen C. Frazier, an audit manager for Price Waterhouse who oversaw the audit of Piece Goods' 1992 financial statement, which indicates that audited financial statements are "used by the management of the company and possibly outsiders," and that such outsiders "could" include trade creditors such as Marcus Brothers. * * *

* * * *

At this stage of the proceedings, and after carefully reviewing the foregoing evidence in the light most favorable to Marcus Brothers, we conclude it can reasonably be inferred that Price Waterhouse knew Piece Goods regularly provided copies of its financial statements to a limited group of major trade creditors, of which group Marcus Brothers was a member.

* * * *

In summary, we conclude the Court of Appeals properly reversed the trial court's entry of summary judgment for Price Waterhouse on Marcus Brothers' claim for negligent misrepresentation.

DISSENTING OPINION

MITCHELL, Chief Justice, dissenting.

* * * *

The "actual knowledge" standard controlling an accountant's liability to a third party non-client for negligent misrepresentation of the financial statements of the accountant's client was established by this Court in [*Raritan*]. In adopting the actual knowledge standard, this Court expressly rejected the "reasonably foreseeable" standard, "because it would result in liability more expansive than an accountant should be expected to bear." Therefore, we have rejected the notion that an accountant's liability may be extended in cases such as the present case to all persons that the accountant could reasonably foresee might obtain and rely on his work. Thus, the proper standard is not what the accountant reasonably should have known, but what the accountant in fact knew.

* * * Here, no evidence whatsoever was forecast tending to show that Price Waterhouse itself intended to influence plaintiff Marcus Brothers. Therefore, the issue presented by this case is whether Price Waterhouse knew of Piece Goods' intent to provide Marcus Brothers with the 1992 financial statement for the purpose of influencing Marcus Brothers, or a limited group including Marcus Brothers, in the transactions at issue in this case or in substantially similar transactions. I find nothing in the evidence to support a reasonable fact finder in finding that defendant Price Waterhouse possessed such actual knowledge at the time it performed the work in question for Piece Goods.

LEGAL REASONING AND ANALYSIS

1. Legal Reasoning. The majority and the dissent in this case agree on the application of Section 552 of the *Restatement (Second) of Torts*. On what point do they disagree? With whom do you agree and why?

2. Legal Analysis. The majority and dissent both cite, in their opinions, *Raritan River Steel Co. v. Cherry, Bekaert & Holland*, 322 N.C. 200, 367 S.E.2d 609 (1988) (see the *Law on the Web* feature at the end of Chapter 2 for instructions on how to access state court opinions). How do the facts, issues, and holdings in that case compare to the facts and issues in the *Marcus Brothers* case? Do the principles for which the *Raritan* case is cited support the position of the majority or the dissent in the *Marcus Brothers* case?

3. Social Considerations. Why should liability in this case be extended to anyone beyond the creditor, who, in lending credit, presumably assumed the risk the money might not be repaid?

4. Implications for Accountants. What does the holding in this case say to accountants who audit businesses' financial statements?

5. Case Briefing Assignment. Using the guidelines for briefing cases given in Appendix A of this text, brief the *Marcus Brothers* case.

GOING ONLINE

The American Institute of Certified Public Accountants (AICPA) maintains a Web site that contains, at http://aicpa.org/yellow/index.htm, links to other sites related to auditing and accounting, including some of those by, and concerning, Federal Reserve banks, securities exchanges, state and federal governments, and state CPA associations.

FOCUS ON ETHICS
Special Topics

Unique situations present particular ethical problems. In this final *Focus on Ethics,* we consider some of the ethical dimensions of the special legal topics discussed in the chapters of this unit.

INSURANCE

A number of ethical issues arise in the area of insurance, some of which we examine here.

Incontestability Clauses

Issues of fairness often arise when insurance companies attempt to avoid payment on policies. Recall from Chapter 49 that policies for life or health insurance commonly include, by statutory requirement, incontestability clauses.

An incontestability clause provides that after the policy has been in force for a specified length of time—often two or three years— the insurer cannot contest statements made in the application. In other words, the insurer cannot later avoid paying on the policy on the basis of a material misrepresentation made by the insured on the policy application. A case recently decided by the California Supreme Court, *Amex Life Assurance Co. v. Superior Court,*[1] provides a good example of how questions of fairness can arise with respect to incontestability clauses.

The insured in this case died of AIDS (acquired immune deficiency syndrome) in 1983. Prior to his death, he had sold his insurance policy to Slome Capital

Corporation—one of approximately sixty companies in the United States that constitute the relatively new viatical industry. Businesses in this industry, including Slome, purchase life insurance policies from terminally ill patients at a discounted rate, continue to make the premium payments, and then collect the benefits under the policy. In this way, the initial policyholders obtain cash to pay for medical and other needs during their illnesses before they die.

The insurer in the case, Amex Life Assurance Company, refused to pay the $180,000 in death benefits to Slome on the ground that the insured had not disclosed on his insurance application the fact that he had AIDS. Moreover, the insured had arranged for an imposter to take the physical examination and blood test that were required as part of the application process. Slome sued Amex, and the question was whether the policy's incontestability clause precluded Amex's refusal to pay on the policy on the ground of fraud on the part of the applicant.

Ultimately, the case reached the California Supreme Court, which held in Slome's favor. The court noted that Amex had had plenty of time during the two-year period provided for in the incontestability clause to discover the fraud. Amex could have required identification from the imposter prior to the physical examination but did not. Furthermore, even a cursory examination would have revealed that the imposter's height, weight, and age did not correspond to the information provided by the insured on his application. Amex put forth

several arguments to avoid liability, but the court was not convinced. Amex had formed a contract with the insured. Because of the incontestability clause, it could not assert the "imposter defense" to avoid payment.

Notice Requirements

In disputes between insurance companies and policyholders, the courts tend to take a protective stance toward policyholders. For example, as mentioned in Chapter 49, if an insurance policy contains ambiguous terms, the courts generally decide in favor of the insured. This is in accordance with the general principles of contract law. Remember from Chapter 10 that one of the rules of contract interpretation applied by the court is that if a party that drafts an agreement uses ambiguous expressions, that party will be held responsible for the ambiguities. In other words, when the language used in a contract has more than one meaning, it will be interpreted against the party that drafted the contract.

Similarly, if an insurance company sends a notice of a change in coverage under a policy, the notice must clearly indicate what the change is. Consider the case of *Koski v. Allstate Insurance Co.*[2] This case arose when Allstate Insurance Company refused to pay a claim submitted by the insured, Thomas Koski, because the coverage had changed—and Allstate had notified Koski of the

1. 930 P.2d 1264, 60 Cal.Rptr.2d 898 (1997).

2. 213 Mich.App. 166, 539 N.W.2d 561 (1995).

change. The policy was a homeowners' policy, which Koski had initially purchased in 1976 and renewed each year since then.

In 1982, Allstate made some changes in its coverage under the policy. It sent a packet to Koski that included a cover letter, a brochure describing the changes in coverage, and a copy of the revised insurance policy that would be effective on receipt of Koski's 1982 premium payment. The cover letter invited the reader to "take a few minutes to read your new policy [and] the enclosed booklet," and it set forth several features of the new policy without mentioning any exclusions from coverage. The enclosed brochure contained the following language: "An exclusion has been added stating that we will not provide liability protection when members of the same household are engaged in a liability suit against each other." Koski renewed the policy without reading the brochure.

In 1984, Koski's daughter, Nikki, was seriously injured in an accident involving machinery being operated by Koski. In 1986, Nikki and her mother, Marsha, sued Koski for negligence, and a judgment was entered in their favor. Allstate refused to pay on Koski's claim because of the 1982 change in coverage. Koski sued Allstate for breach of contract, and the question before the court was whether Allstate had adequately notified Koski of the policy change in 1982.

The court acknowledged that an insured "is obligated to read the insurance policy and to raise questions concerning coverage within a reasonable time after issuance of the policy." The court stated, however, that an exception to this rule exists "where a policy is renewed without actual notice to the insured that the policy has been altered. Where a renewal policy is issued without calling the insured's attention to a reduction in

coverage, the insurer is bound to the greater coverage in the earlier policy." "In this case," stated the court, "the notice to plaintiff of the new exclusion consisted of a single unemphasized reference in a twelve-page booklet." The court concluded that the notice provided by Allstate "was inadequate as a matter of law."

Misstatements on Insurance Applications

A question with ethical implications also arises when an insurance applicant mistakenly makes a misstatement, or misrepresentation, on his or her application for insurance. For example, when Harold Green applied for a health-insurance policy, he answered "no" to a question asking whether, within the last five years, he had, or had been told that he had, "kidney failure." A year later, Green made a claim against the policy after he had been hospitalized for kidney failure, among other things. The insurance company, after learning from Green's medical records that he had suffered for several years from chronic kidney failure, canceled the policy and returned to Green all of the premiums that he had paid for the policy.

Green sued the company to obtain reimbursement for the cost of his hospitalization, contending that his physician had never told him that he had kidney failure and that he had answered the question truthfully on the application. Green's physician testified that it was his regular practice to use layperson's terms, rather than medical terms, when informing patients of their conditions. The physician stated that he probably told Green that he had "some sluggish kidneys" or "slow kidneys."

The insurance company countered by stating that even though Green may have innocently misled the company, a state statute

provided that an insurance company could deny recovery under a policy if the insured had made any material misrepresentation, innocently or otherwise, on the application that would alter the nature of the risk assumed by the insurer. Relying on this statutory authority, the trial court entered summary judgment in favor of the insurance company. On appeal, however, the state supreme court reversed that decision.

The state supreme court pointed to the following words in the application form, which appeared just above the signature line: "The answers given by me are full, true and complete to the best of my knowledge and belief." The court held that "truthful answers on an insurance application according to the best of the insured's 'knowledge and belief' do not constitute misstatements within the meaning of [the relevant statutory provision] and therefore cannot provide the grounds for the insurer's rescission of the insurance policy." The court emphasized that the insurance company, which drafted the application form, chose to include the words "to the best of my knowledge and belief." By doing so, the company elected to bypass the "rigid statutory standards." "In essence," stated the court, the insurer "now seeks to repudiate its own contract and, as a fall back position, claim refuge in the stricter statutory standard, a method that disadvantages a good faith insured."[3]

LIABILITY OF ACCOUNTANTS

A question with obvious ethical implications often faces the courts with respect to negligence suits brought against accountants by

---

3. *Green v. Life & Health of America*, 704 So.2d 1386 (Fla. 1998).

third parties: How far should an accountant's liability extend? As discussed in Chapter 51, courts in different jurisdictions have drawn different conclusions on this issue.

At one end of the spectrum are a minority of courts that hold that accountants are liable only to third parties who are in privity or "near privity" with the accountants. At the other end are a minority of courts that have ruled that accountants may be held liable to third parties whose reliance on the accountants' statements or reports was "reasonably foreseeable." In the eyes of many, accountants' liability to third parties is too restricted in the former jurisdictions and too extensive in the latter. For accountants, the courts' varying approaches to liability to third parties pose a significant problem: How can they predict, and control, the extent of their liability?

Further complicating this difficulty is the possibility that accountants may be liable to third parties under consumer protection statutes. Consider, for example, a decision by the Texas Supreme Court in which the court held that a third party, as a "consumer," could sue an accounting firm for violations of the state Deceptive Trade Practices Act (DTPA).[4] The Texas DTPA, which is similar to statutes in many other states, allows the successful plaintiff to recover treble damages as well as attorneys' fees. The burden of proof under the DTPA is relatively light for the plaintiff: the plaintiff need only show that there was a "knowing" violation of the statute to recover damages. The statute also imposes strict liability on defendants.

Society has obviously deemed it fair that accountants (and other professionals) should be held to a duty of care and that they should stand prepared to compensate

clients and others for violating that duty. Still, many consider it unfair that there are no uniform, well-defined limits to the potential liability of accountants.

ETHICS AND INTERNATIONAL LAW

Differences in the laws and customs of the various nations of the globe present unique ethical issues for firms engaged in international business transactions. Some of these issues were discussed in Chapter 40, in the context of ethics and business decision making. Here, we look at a few other problems, focusing particularly on some ethical issues relating to international doctrines and to U.S. laws as they apply to international transactions.

Sovereign Immunity

Sometimes, the application of the doctrine of sovereign immunity may lead to seemingly inequitable results. The economy of the United States is primarily controlled by private interests, whereas the economies of many foreign countries, particularly developing nations, are extensively controlled by government. When a U.S. firm does business with a foreign firm in a developing country, therefore, the chances are that the U.S. firm will work closely with foreign government officials. Should a dispute arise between the parties, the question then becomes whether the U.S. firm can bring a lawsuit against the foreign firm. If the foreign defendant raises the defense of sovereign immunity, alleging that it is a government-controlled operation, then it may be immune from liability. The ethical issue in these situations is whether it is fair that U.S. firms be left without any legal recourse when they suffer damages as a result of actions controlled by foreign governments.

Consider, for example, the situation that arose in *Antares Aircraft, L.P. v. Federal Republic of Nigeria.*[5] In that case, Antares Aircraft, a New York limited partnership, had one asset—a DC-8-55 aircraft registered in Nigeria. Antares was required by the Nigerian government to leave the plane at the airport in Lagos, Nigeria, until certain fees (which had been incurred by a previous owner of the plane) were paid. Antares paid the $100,000 in fees, but the Nigerian government did not release the plane until five months later. In the meantime, the plane had been damaged by exposure to the elements.

Antares filed suit against the Nigerian government for the tort of conversion, alleging that the Nigerian government had wrongfully detained the plane. Antares argued that the Nigerian government's actions fell within the commercial activity exception to the Foreign Sovereign Immunities Act (FSIA) and therefore the Nigerian government was not immune from the jurisdiction of U.S. courts.

Although the court agreed with Antares that the fees collected by the Nigerian government were connected with a commercial activity, it found that the activity did not have a "direct effect" in the United States—in which case the commercial activity exception to the FSIA did not apply. The court therefore held that the Nigerian government was immune from liability. The court stated that "the detention of Antares' sole asset affected the financial well-being of the American partnership. However, the fact that an American individual or firm suffers some financial loss from a foreign tort cannot, standing alone, suffice to trigger the [commercial activity] exception."

---

4. *Arthur Andersen & Co. v. Perry Equipment Corp.*, 945 S.W.2d 812 (Tex. 1997).

5. 999 F.2d 33 (2d Cir. 1993).

Because the FSIA does not define exactly what types of activities on the part of a foreign government fall under the commercial activity exception, the courts exercise considerable discretion in deciding such issues. Although the majority on the court hearing the *Antares* case concluded that the loss suffered by Antares was not sufficiently significant to constitute a "direct effect in the United States," other courts might have concluded differently.

Certainly, the dissenting judge in *Antares* believed that the detention of the plane did have a direct effect in the United States. The partners lived in the United States and lost money because of a foreign government's interference with their property. The dissent concluded that the partnership's loss should be sufficient to establish an exception to immunity under the FSIA.

Liability for Human Rights Violations

A significant ethical issue confronting U.S. businesspersons has to do with the rights of workers employed in other countries. Recall from Chapter 40 that U.S. firms increasingly are being held ethically accountable, by human rights groups and others, for how their suppliers in other countries treat their workers. In addition, a U.S. firm may face potential *legal* responsibility for employee mistreatment. For example, if a joint venturer located in another nation mistreats its workers, the

U.S. partner may be held liable for that mistreatment, even though the U.S. partner was unaware of it.

Consider the situation in which Unocal Corporation, an American corporation, found itself when its joint venturer in Burma (Myanmar) was accused of mistreating its workers. Unocal had entered into a joint venture with an agency of the Burmese government for the purpose of constructing a gas pipeline in Burma.

A group of Burmese workers sued the Burmese government and Unocal Corporation, alleging that these employers had committed human rights violations. The plaintiffs complained that they were the victims of rape, forced labor, involuntary relocation, and torture. A U.S. district court dismissed the claims against the Burmese government, holding that the claims against the Burmese government did not fall within the "commercial activities" exception to the Foreign Sovereign Immunities Act.[6] In essence, this left Unocal Corporation as the only defendant in the case. This decision, understandably, has led American companies to think twice about doing business with overseas partners.

DISCUSSION QUESTIONS

1. Suppose that an applicant for insurance knowingly makes a false statement concerning a material fact on the application form. Is it fair to the insurance company to make it pay out later on the policy

6. *John Doe I v. Unocal Corp.*, 963 F.Supp. 880 (C.D.Cal. 1997).

on the ground that, under the provisions of an incontestability clause, it cannot contest any statements made on the application?

2. Under viatical contracts, companies purchase the life insurance policies of terminally ill persons at discounted prices. Then, when those persons die, the companies profit by collecting the full death benefits of the policies. Is it ethical for companies to profit from the deaths of terminally ill persons? From an ethical perspective, can such contracts be justified? Explain.

3. At one time, most courts held that accountants could not be held liable to third parties in negligence lawsuits. On what contract doctrine was this rule based? Why do the majority of courts today hold that accountants can be held liable to third parties? Generally, what public policies must be balanced by the courts in determining whether third parties can recover from accountants for damages caused by accountants' negligence?

4. What are some of the implications of the doctrine of sovereign immunity for businesspersons doing business internationally? Should the courts make more exceptions to this doctrine?

5. Should U.S. business owners be held liable for human rights violations in the workplaces of overseas suppliers or business partners even if the U.S. owners are unaware of such violations?

APPENDICES

CONTENTS

How to Brief Cases and Analyze Case Problems

HOW TO BRIEF CASES

To fully understand the law with respect to business, you need to be able to read and understand court decisions. To make this task easier, you can use a method of case analysis that is called *briefing*. There is a fairly standard procedure that you can follow when you "brief" any court case. You must first read the case opinion carefully. When you feel you understand the case, you can prepare a brief of it.

Although the format of the brief may vary, typically it will present the essentials of the case under headings such as those listed below.

1. **Citation.** Give the full citation for the case, including the name of the case, the date it was decided, and the court that decided it.
2. **Facts.** Briefly indicate (a) the reasons for the lawsuit; (b) the identity and arguments of the plaintiff(s) and defendant(s), respectively; and (c) the lower court's decision—if appropriate.
3. **Issue.** Concisely phrase, in the form of a question, the essential issue before the court. (If more than one issue is involved, you may have two—or even more—questions here.)
4. **Decision.** Indicate here—with a "yes" or "no," if possible—the court's answer to the question (or questions) in the *Issue* section above.
5. **Reason.** Summarize as briefly as possible the reasons given by the court for its decision (or decisions) and the case

or statutory law relied on by the court in arriving at its decision.

BRIEFED SAMPLE COURT CASE

As an example of the format used in briefing cases, we present here a briefed version of the sample court case that was presented in Chapter 1 in Exhibit 1–5.

FEDERAL EXPRESS CORP. v. FEDERAL ESPRESSO, INC.
United States Court of Appeals,
Second Circuit, 2000.
201 F.3d 168.

FACTS In 1997, Federal Express sued a small company called Federal Espresso and its owners, John Dobbs, Anna Dobbs, and David J. Ruston (collectively, the defendants). The defendants operated two coffee shops called Federal Espresso in Syracuse, New York. Federal Express asserted that the defendants, by using the name Federal Espresso, had infringed on its trademark and diluted the distinctive quality of its famous mark. Federal Express sought a preliminary injunction against the defendants' continued use of the Federal Espresso name for their business. The district court denied the motion, concluding that Federal Express had failed to demonstrate any likelihood of confusion between the two products and hence did not show that it was likely to succeed on the merits of those claims. Federal Express appealed.

ISSUE   Was there a likelihood of confusion sufficient to allow Federal Express to succeed on the merits of its trademark claims, thus warranting a preliminary injunction?

DECISION   No. The appellate court affirmed the lower court's decision.

REASON   The appellate court stated that because coffee and overnight delivery service were dissimilar products, there would be little likelihood of confusion. The court also emphasized that while Federal Express is "a vast organization, operating in 210 countries, employing 140,000 persons, and grossing more than $11 billion annually," the defendants were merely three individuals who operated two stores in Syracuse, New York. Given the dissimilar products and the small extent of overlap among customers of Federal Express and Federal Espresso, Federal Express was unlikely to succeed on the merits of its trademark claims, and thus a preliminary injunction against Federal Espresso was not warranted.

REVIEW OF SAMPLE COURT CASE

Here we provide a review of the briefed version to indicate the kind of information that is contained in each section.

CITATION   The name of the case is *Federal Express Corp. v. Federal Espresso, Inc.* The plaintiff is Federal Express Corp., and the defendant is Federal Espresso, Inc. The case was decided by the United States Court of Appeals for the Second Circuit in 2000. The citation indicates that the case can be found in Volume 201 of West's *Federal Reporter, Third Series,* on page 168.

FACTS   The *Facts* section identifies the parties to the lawsuit—the plaintiff and the defendants—and describes the events leading up to the lawsuit and its appeal. Because this is an appeal to a federal appellate court—the United States Court of Appeals for the Second Circuit—the lower (district) court's opinion is included as part of the history of the case.

ISSUE   The *Issue* section presents the central issue (or issues) to be decided by the court. In this case, the issue before the United States Court of Appeals for the Second Circuit is whether the trial court erred in refusing to grant Federal Express's motion for a preliminary injunction against Federal Espresso's continued use of its business name. Because this question turns on whether Federal Express had a cause of action for trademark infringement, including dilution, the real question on appeal was whether there was a likelihood of confusion between the products of the two companies sufficient to allow Federal Express to succeed on the merits of its trademark claims, thus warranting a preliminary injunction.

DECISION   The *Decision* section, as the term indicates, contains the court's decision on the issue or issues before it. The decision reflects the opinion of the majority of the judges or justices hearing the case. Decisions by appellate courts are frequently phrased in reference to the lower court's decision. That is, the appellate court may "affirm" the lower court's decision or "reverse" it. In this particular case, the federal appellate court affirmed the lower (district) court's decision.

REASON   The *Reason* section indicates what relevant laws and judicial principles were applied in forming the particular conclusion arrived at in the case at bar (before the court). In this case, the relevant law consisted of judicial principles that have been established over time to indicate when a "likelihood of confusion" between trademarks may exist.

HOW TO ANALYZE CASE PROBLEMS

In addition to learning how to brief cases, students of business law also find it helpful to know how to analyze case problems. Part of the study of business law usually involves analyzing case problems, such as those included in this text at the end of each chapter.

For each case problem in this book, we provide the relevant background and facts of the lawsuit and the issue before the court. When you are assigned one of these problems, your job will be to determine how the court should decide the issue and why. In other words, you will need to engage in legal analysis and reasoning. Here we offer some suggestions on how to make this task less daunting. We begin by presenting a sample problem:

> While Janet Lawson, a famous pianist, was shopping in Quality Market, she slipped and fell on a wet floor in one of the aisles. The floor had recently been mopped by one of the store's employees, but there were no signs warning customers that the floor in that area was wet. As a result of the fall, Lawson injured her right arm and was unable to perform piano concerts for the next six months. Had she been able to perform the scheduled concerts, she would have earned approximately $60,000 over that period of time. Lawson sued Quality Market for this amount, plus another $10,000 in medical expenses. She claimed that the store's failure to warn customers of the wet floor constituted negligence and therefore the market was liable for her injuries. Will the court agree with Lawson? Discuss.

UNDERSTAND THE FACTS

This may sound obvious, but before you can analyze or apply the relevant law to a specific set of facts, you must clearly understand those facts. In other words, you should read through the case problem carefully and more than once, if necessary, to make sure you understand the identity of the plaintiff(s) and defendant(s) in the case and the progression of events that led to the lawsuit.

In the sample case just given, the identity of the parties is fairly obvious. Janet Lawson is the one bringing the suit; therefore, she is the plaintiff. Quality Market, against whom she is bringing the suit, is the defendant. Some of the case problems you work on may have multiple plaintiffs or defendants. Often, it is helpful to use abbreviations for the parties. To indicate a reference to a plaintiff, for example, the pi symbol—π—is often used, and a defendant is denoted by a delta—Δ—a triangle.

The events leading to the lawsuit are also fairly straightforward. Lawson slipped and fell on a wet floor, and she contends that Quality Market should be liable for her injuries because it was negligent in not posting a sign warning customers of the wet floor.

When you are working on case problems, realize that the facts should be accepted as they are given. For example, in our sample problem, it should be accepted that the floor was wet and that there was no sign. In other words, avoid making conjectures, such as "Maybe the floor wasn't too wet," or "Maybe an employee was getting a sign to put up," or "Maybe someone stole the sign." Questioning the facts as they are presented only adds confusion to your analysis.

LEGAL ANALYSIS AND REASONING

Once you understand the facts given in the case problem, you can begin to analyze the case. Recall from Chapter 1 that the IRAC method is a helpful tool to use in the legal analysis and reasoning process. IRAC is an acronym for Issue, Rule, Application, Conclusion. Applying this method to our sample problem would involve the following steps:

1. First, you need to decide what legal **issue** is involved in the case. In our sample case, the basic issue is whether Quality Market's failure to warn customers of the wet floor constituted negligence. As discussed in Chapter 5, negligence is a *tort*—a civil wrong. In a tort lawsuit, the plaintiff seeks to be compensated for another's wrongful act. A defendant will be deemed negligent if he or she breached a duty of care owed to the plaintiff and the breach of that duty caused the plaintiff to suffer harm.

2. Once you have identified the issue, the next step is to determine what **rule of law** applies to the issue. To make this determination, you will want to review carefully the text of the chapter in which the problem appears to find the relevant rule of law. Our sample case involves the tort of negli-

gence, covered in Chapter 5. The applicable rule of law is the tort law principle that business owners owe a duty to exercise reasonable care to protect their customers ("business invitees"). Reasonable care, in this context, includes either removing—or warning customers of—*foreseeable* risks about which the owner *knew* or *should have known*. Business owners need not warn customers of "open and obvious" risks, however. If a business owner breaches this duty of care (fails to exercise the appropriate degree of care toward customers), and the breach of duty causes a customer to be injured, the business owner will be liable to the customer for the customer's injuries.

3. The next—and usually the most difficult—step in analyzing case problems is the **application** of the relevant rule of law to the specific facts of the case you are studying. In our sample problem, applying the tort law principle just discussed presents few difficulties. An employee of the store had mopped the floor in the aisle where Lawson slipped and fell, but no sign was present indicating that the floor was wet. That a customer might fall on a wet floor is clearly a foreseeable risk. Therefore, the failure to warn customers about the wet floor was a breach of the duty of care owed by the business owner to the store's customers.

4. Once you have completed step 3 in the IRAC method, you should be ready to draw your **conclusion**. In our sample case, Quality Market is liable to Lawson for her injuries, because the market's breach of its duty of care caused Lawson's injuries.

The fact patterns in the case problems presented in this text are not always as simple as those presented in our sample problem. Often, for example, there may be more than one plaintiff or defendant. There also may be more than one issue involved in a case and more than one applicable rule of law. Furthermore, in some case problems the facts may indicate that the general rule of law should not apply. For example, suppose a store employee advised Lawson not to walk on the floor in the aisle because it was wet, but Lawson decided to walk on it anyway. This fact could alter the outcome of the case because the store could then raise the defense of assumption of risk (see Chapter 5). Nonetheless, a careful review of the chapter should always provide you with the knowledge you need to analyze the problem thoroughly and arrive at accurate conclusions.

The Constitution of the United States

PREAMBLE

We the People of the United States, in Order to form a more perfect Union, establish Justice, insure domestic Tranquility, provide for the common defence, promote the general Welfare, and secure the Blessings of Liberty to ourselves and our Posterity, do ordain and establish this Constitution for the United States of America.

ARTICLE I

Section 1. All legislative Powers herein granted shall be vested in a Congress of the United States, which shall consist of a Senate and House of Representatives.

Section 2. The House of Representatives shall be composed of Members chosen every second Year by the People of the several States, and the Electors in each State shall have the Qualifications requisite for Electors of the most numerous Branch of the State Legislature.

No Person shall be a Representative who shall not have attained to the Age of twenty five Years, and been seven Years a Citizen of the United States, and who shall not, when elected, be an Inhabitant of that State in which he shall be chosen.

Representatives and direct Taxes shall be apportioned among the several States which may be included within this Union, according to their respective Numbers, which shall be determined by adding to the whole Number of free Persons, including those bound to Service for a Term of Years, and excluding Indians not taxed, three fifths of all other Persons. The actual Enumeration shall be made within three Years after the first Meeting of the Congress of the United States, and within every subsequent Term of ten Years, in such Manner as they shall by Law direct. The Number of Representatives shall not exceed one for every thirty Thousand, but each State shall have at Least one Representative; and until such enumeration shall be made, the State of New Hampshire shall be entitled to chuse three, Massachusetts eight, Rhode Island and Providence Plantations one, Connecticut five, New York six, New Jersey four, Pennsylvania eight, Delaware one, Maryland six, Virginia ten, North Carolina five, South Carolina five, and Georgia three.

When vacancies happen in the Representation from any State, the Executive Authority thereof shall issue Writs of Election to fill such Vacancies.

The House of Representatives shall chuse their Speaker and other Officers; and shall have the sole Power of Impeachment.

Section 3. The Senate of the United States shall be composed of two Senators from each State, chosen by the Legislature thereof, for six Years; and each Senator shall have one Vote.

Immediately after they shall be assembled in Consequence of the first Election, they shall be divided as equally as may be into three Classes. The Seats of the Senators of the first Class shall be vacated at the Expiration of the second Year, of the second Class at the

Expiration of the fourth Year, and of the third Class at the Expiration of the sixth Year, so that one third may be chosen every second Year; and if Vacancies happen by Resignation, or otherwise, during the Recess of the Legislature of any State, the Executive thereof may make temporary Appointments until the next Meeting of the Legislature, which shall then fill such Vacancies.

No Person shall be a Senator who shall not have attained to the Age of thirty Years, and been nine Years a Citizen of the United States, and who shall not, when elected, be an Inhabitant of that State for which he shall be chosen.

The Vice President of the United States shall be President of the Senate, but shall have no Vote, unless they be equally divided.

The Senate shall chuse their other Officers, and also a President pro tempore, in the Absence of the Vice President, or when he shall exercise the Office of President of the United States.

The Senate shall have the sole Power to try all Impeachments. When sitting for that Purpose, they shall be on Oath or Affirmation. When the President of the United States is tried, the Chief Justice shall preside: And no Person shall be convicted without the Concurrence of two thirds of the Members present.

Judgment in Cases of Impeachment shall not extend further than to removal from Office, and disqualification to hold and enjoy any Office of honor, Trust, or Profit under the United States: but the Party convicted shall nevertheless be liable and subject to Indictment, Trial, Judgment, and Punishment, according to Law.

Section 4. The Times, Places and Manner of holding Elections for Senators and Representatives, shall be prescribed in each State by the Legislature thereof; but the Congress may at any time by Law make or alter such Regulations, except as to the Places of chusing Senators.

The Congress shall assemble at least once in every Year, and such Meeting shall be on the first Monday in December, unless they shall by Law appoint a different Day.

Section 5. Each House shall be the Judge of the Elections, Returns, and Qualifications of its own Members, and a Majority of each shall constitute a Quorum to do Business; but a smaller Number may adjourn from day to day, and may be authorized to compel the Attendance of absent Members, in such Manner, and under such Penalties as each House may provide.

Each House may determine the Rules of its Proceedings, punish its Members for disorderly Behavior, and, with the Concurrence of two thirds, expel a Member.

Each House shall keep a Journal of its Proceedings, and from time to time publish the same, excepting such Parts as may in their Judgment require Secrecy; and the Yeas and Nays of the Members of either House on any question shall, at the Desire of one fifth of those Present, be entered on the Journal.

Neither House, during the Session of Congress, shall, without the Consent of the other, adjourn for more than three days, nor to any other Place than that in which the two Houses shall be sitting.

Section 6. The Senators and Representatives shall receive a Compensation for their Services, to be ascertained by Law, and paid out of the Treasury of the United States. They shall in all Cases, except Treason, Felony and Breach of the Peace, be privileged from Arrest during their Attendance at the Session of their respective Houses, and in going to and returning from the same; and for any Speech or Debate in either House, they shall not be questioned in any other Place.

No Senator or Representative shall, during the Time for which he was elected, be appointed to any civil Office under the Authority of the United States, which shall have been created, or the Emoluments whereof shall have been increased during such time; and no Person holding any Office under the United States, shall be a Member of either House during his Continuance in Office.

Section 7. All Bills for raising Revenue shall originate in the House of Representatives; but the Senate may propose or concur with Amendments as on other Bills.

Every Bill which shall have passed the House of Representatives and the Senate, shall, before it become a Law, be presented to the President of the United States; If he approve he shall sign it, but if not he shall return it, with his Objections to the House in which it shall have originated, who shall enter the Objections at large on their Journal, and proceed to reconsider it. If after such Reconsideration two thirds of that House shall agree to pass the Bill, it shall be sent together with the Objections, to the other House, by which it shall likewise be reconsidered, and if approved by two thirds of that House, it shall become a Law. But in all such Cases the Votes of both Houses shall be determined by Yeas and Nays, and the Names of the Persons voting for and against the Bill shall be entered on the Journal of each House respectively. If any Bill shall not be returned by the President within ten Days (Sundays excepted) after it shall have been presented to him, the Same shall be a Law, in like Manner as if he had signed it, unless the Congress by their Adjournment prevent its Return in which Case it shall not be a Law.

Every Order, Resolution, or Vote, to which the Concurrence of the Senate and House of Representatives may be necessary (except on a question of Adjournment) shall be presented to the President of the United States; and before the Same shall take Effect, shall be approved by him, or being disapproved by him, shall be repassed by two thirds of the Senate and House of Representatives, according to the Rules and Limitations prescribed in the Case of a Bill.

Section 8. The Congress shall have Power To lay and collect Taxes, Duties, Imposts and Excises, to pay the Debts and provide for the common Defence and general Welfare of the United States; but all Duties, Imposts and Excises shall be uniform throughout the United States;

To borrow Money on the credit of the United States;

To regulate Commerce with foreign Nations, and among the several States, and with the Indian Tribes;

To establish an uniform Rule of Naturalization, and uniform Laws on the subject of Bankruptcies throughout the United States;

To coin Money, regulate the Value thereof, and of foreign Coin, and fix the Standard of Weights and Measures;

To provide for the Punishment of counterfeiting the Securities and current Coin of the United States;

To establish Post Offices and post Roads;

To promote the Progress of Science and useful Arts, by securing for limited Times to Authors and Inventors the exclusive Right to their respective Writings and Discoveries;

To constitute Tribunals inferior to the supreme Court;

To define and punish Piracies and Felonies committed on the high Seas, and Offenses against the Law of Nations;

To declare War, grant Letters of Marque and Reprisal, and make Rules concerning Captures on Land and Water;

To raise and support Armies, but no Appropriation of Money to that Use shall be for a longer Term than two Years;

To provide and maintain a Navy;

To make Rules for the Government and Regulation of the land and naval Forces;

To provide for calling forth the Militia to execute the Laws of the Union, suppress Insurrections and repel Invasions;

To provide for organizing, arming, and disciplining, the Militia, and for governing such Part of them as may be employed in the Service of the United States, reserving to the States respectively, the Appointment of the Officers, and the Authority of training the Militia according to the discipline prescribed by Congress;

To exercise exclusive Legislation in all Cases whatsoever, over such District (not exceeding ten Miles square) as may, by Cession of particular States, and the Acceptance of Congress, become the Seat of the Government of the United States, and to exercise like Authority over all Places purchased by the Consent of the Legislature of the State in which the Same shall be,

for the Erection of Forts, Magazines, Arsenals, dock-Yards, and other needful Buildings;—And

To make all Laws which shall be necessary and proper for carrying into Execution the foregoing Powers, and all other Powers vested by this Constitution in the Government of the United States, or in any Department or Officer thereof.

Section 9. The Migration or Importation of such Persons as any of the States now existing shall think proper to admit, shall not be prohibited by the Congress prior to the Year one thousand eight hundred and eight, but a Tax or duty may be imposed on such Importation, not exceeding ten dollars for each Person.

The privilege of the Writ of Habeas Corpus shall not be suspended, unless when in Cases of Rebellion or Invasion the public Safety may require it.

No Bill of Attainder or ex post facto Law shall be passed.

No Capitation, or other direct, Tax shall be laid, unless in Proportion to the Census or Enumeration herein before directed to be taken.

No Tax or Duty shall be laid on Articles exported from any State.

No Preference shall be given by any Regulation of Commerce or Revenue to the Ports of one State over those of another: nor shall Vessels bound to, or from, one State be obliged to enter, clear, or pay Duties in another.

No Money shall be drawn from the Treasury, but in Consequence of Appropriations made by Law; and a regular Statement and Account of the Receipts and Expenditures of all public Money shall be published from time to time.

No Title of Nobility shall be granted by the United States: And no Person holding any Office of Profit or Trust under them, shall, without the Consent of the Congress, accept of any present, Emolument, Office, or Title, of any kind whatever, from any King, Prince, or foreign State.

Section 10. No State shall enter into any Treaty, Alliance, or Confederation; grant Letters of Marque and Reprisal; coin Money; emit Bills of Credit; make any Thing but gold and silver Coin a Tender in Payment of Debts; pass any Bill of Attainder, ex post facto Law, or Law impairing the Obligation of Contracts, or grant any Title of Nobility.

No State shall, without the Consent of the Congress, lay any Imposts or Duties on Imports or Exports, except what may be absolutely necessary for executing its inspection Laws: and the net Produce of all Duties and Imposts, laid by any State on Imports or Exports, shall be for the Use of the Treasury of the United States; and all such Laws shall be subject to the Revision and Controul of the Congress.

No State shall, without the Consent of Congress, lay any Duty of Tonnage, keep Troops, or Ships of War in time of Peace, enter into any Agreement or Compact with another State, or with a foreign Power, or engage in War, unless actually invaded, or in such imminent Danger as will not admit of delay.

ARTICLE II

Section 1.   The executive Power shall be vested in a President of the United States of America. He shall hold his Office during the Term of four Years, and, together with the Vice President, chosen for the same Term, be elected, as follows:

Each State shall appoint, in such Manner as the Legislature thereof may direct, a Number of Electors, equal to the whole Number of Senators and Representatives to which the State may be entitled in the Congress; but no Senator or Representative, or Person holding an Office of Trust or Profit under the United States, shall be appointed an Elector.

The Electors shall meet in their respective States, and vote by Ballot for two Persons, of whom one at least shall not be an Inhabitant of the same State with themselves. And they shall make a List of all the Persons voted for, and of the Number of Votes for each; which List they shall sign and certify, and transmit sealed to the Seat of the Government of the United States, directed to the President of the Senate. The President of the Senate shall, in the Presence of the Senate and House of Representatives, open all the Certificates, and the Votes shall then be counted. The Person having the greatest Number of Votes shall be the President, if such Number be a Majority of the whole Number of Electors appointed; and if there be more than one who have such Majority, and have an equal Number of Votes, then the House of Representatives shall immediately chuse by Ballot one of them for President; and if no Person have a Majority, then from the five highest on the List the said House shall in like Manner chuse the President. But in chusing the President, the Votes shall be taken by States, the Representation from each State having one Vote; A quorum for this Purpose shall consist of a Member or Members from two thirds of the States, and a Majority of all the States shall be necessary to a Choice. In every Case, after the Choice of the President, the Person having the greater Number of Votes of the Electors shall be the Vice President. But if there should remain two or more who have equal Votes, the Senate shall chuse from them by Ballot the Vice President.

The Congress may determine the Time of chusing the Electors, and the Day on which they shall give their Votes; which Day shall be the same throughout the United States.

No person except a natural born Citizen, or a Citizen of the United States, at the time of the Adoption of this Constitution, shall be eligible to the Office of President; neither shall any Person be eligible to that Office who shall not have attained to the Age of thirty five Years, and been fourteen Years a Resident within the United States.

In Case of the Removal of the President from Office, or of his Death, Resignation or Inability to discharge the Powers and Duties of the said Office, the same shall devolve on the Vice President, and the Congress may by Law provide for the Case of Removal, Death, Resignation or Inability, both of the President and Vice President, declaring what Officer shall then act as President, and such Officer shall act accordingly, until the Disability be removed, or a President shall be elected.

The President shall, at stated Times, receive for his Services, a Compensation, which shall neither be increased nor diminished during the Period for which he shall have been elected, and he shall not receive within that Period any other Emolument from the United States, or any of them.

Before he enter on the Execution of his Office, he shall take the following Oath or Affirmation: "I do solemnly swear (or affirm) that I will faithfully execute the Office of President of the United States, and will to the best of my Ability, preserve, protect and defend the Constitution of the United States."

Section 2.   The President shall be Commander in Chief of the Army and Navy of the United States, and of the Militia of the several States, when called into the actual Service of the United States; he may require the Opinion, in writing, of the principal Officer in each of the executive Departments, upon any Subject relating to the Duties of their respective Offices, and he shall have Power to grant Reprieves and Pardons for Offenses against the United States, except in Cases of Impeachment.

He shall have Power, by and with the Advice and Consent of the Senate to make Treaties, provided two thirds of the Senators present concur; and he shall nominate, and by and with the Advice and Consent of the Senate, shall appoint Ambassadors, other public Ministers and Consuls, Judges of the supreme Court, and all other Officers of the United States, whose Appointments are not herein otherwise provided for, and which shall be established by Law; but the Congress may by Law vest the Appointment of such inferior Officers, as they think proper, in the President alone, in the Courts of Law, or in the Heads of Departments.

The President shall have Power to fill up all Vacancies that may happen during the Recess of the Senate, by granting Commissions which shall expire at the End of their next Session.

Section 3.   He shall from time to time give to the Congress Information of the State of the Union, and recommend to their Consideration such Measures as he shall judge necessary and expedient; he may, on extraordinary Occasions, convene both Houses, or either of them, and in Case of Disagreement between them, with Respect to the Time of Adjournment, he may adjourn them to such Time as he shall think proper; he shall receive Ambassadors and other public Ministers; he shall take Care that the Laws be faithfully executed, and shall Commission all the Officers of the United States.

Section 4. The President, Vice President and all civil Officers of the United States, shall be removed from Office on Impeachment for, and Conviction of, Treason, Bribery, or other high Crimes and Misdemeanors.

ARTICLE III

Section 1. The judicial Power of the United States, shall be vested in one supreme Court, and in such inferior Courts as the Congress may from time to time ordain and establish. The Judges, both of the supreme and inferior Courts, shall hold their Offices during good Behaviour, and shall, at stated Times, receive for their Services a Compensation, which shall not be diminished during their Continuance in Office.

Section 2. The judicial Power shall extend to all Cases, in Law and Equity, arising under this Constitution, the Laws of the United States, and Treaties made, or which shall be made, under their Authority;—to all Cases affecting Ambassadors, other public Ministers and Consuls;—to all Cases of admiralty and maritime Jurisdiction;—to Controversies to which the United States shall be a Party;—to Controversies between two or more States;—between a State and Citizens of another State;—between Citizens of different States;—between Citizens of the same State claiming Lands under Grants of different States, and between a State, or the Citizens thereof, and foreign States, Citizens or Subjects.

In all Cases affecting Ambassadors, other public Ministers and Consuls, and those in which a State shall be a Party, the supreme Court shall have original Jurisdiction. In all the other Cases before mentioned, the supreme Court shall have appellate Jurisdiction, both as to Law and Fact, with such Exceptions, and under such Regulations as the Congress shall make.

The Trial of all Crimes, except in Cases of Impeachment, shall be by Jury; and such Trial shall be held in the State where the said Crimes shall have been committed; but when not committed within any State, the Trial shall be at such Place or Places as the Congress may by Law have directed.

Section 3. Treason against the United States, shall consist only in levying War against them, or, in adhering to their Enemies, giving them Aid and Comfort. No Person shall be convicted of Treason unless on the Testimony of two Witnesses to the same overt Act, or on Confession in open Court.

The Congress shall have Power to declare the Punishment of Treason, but no Attainder of Treason shall work Corruption of Blood, or Forfeiture except during the Life of the Person attainted.

ARTICLE IV

Section 1. Full Faith and Credit shall be given in each State to the public Acts, Records, and judicial Proceedings of every other State. And the Congress may by general Laws prescribe the Manner in which such Acts, Records and Proceedings shall be proved, and the Effect thereof.

Section 2. The Citizens of each State shall be entitled to all Privileges and Immunities of Citizens in the several States.

A Person charged in any State with Treason, Felony, or other Crime, who shall flee from Justice, and be found in another State, shall on Demand of the executive Authority of the State from which he fled, be delivered up, to be removed to the State having Jurisdiction of the Crime.

No Person held to Service or Labour in one State, under the Laws thereof, escaping into another, shall, in Consequence of any Law or Regulation therein, be discharged from such Service or Labour, but shall be delivered up on Claim of the Party to whom such Service or Labour may be due.

Section 3. New States may be admitted by the Congress into this Union; but no new State shall be formed or erected within the Jurisdiction of any other State; nor any State be formed by the Junction of two or more States, or Parts of States, without the Consent of the Legislatures of the States concerned as well as of the Congress.

The Congress shall have Power to dispose of and make all needful Rules and Regulations respecting the Territory or other Property belonging to the United States; and nothing in this Constitution shall be so construed as to Prejudice any Claims of the United States, or of any particular State.

Section 4. The United States shall guarantee to every State in this Union a Republican Form of Government, and shall protect each of them against Invasion; and on Application of the Legislature, or of the Executive (when the Legislature cannot be convened) against domestic Violence.

ARTICLE V

The Congress, whenever two thirds of both Houses shall deem it necessary, shall propose Amendments to this Constitution, or, on the Application of the Legislatures of two thirds of the several States, shall call a Convention for proposing Amendments, which, in either Case, shall be valid to all Intents and Purposes, as part of this Constitution, when ratified by the Legislatures of three fourths of the several States, or by Conventions in three fourths thereof, as the one or the other Mode of Ratification may be proposed by the Congress; Provided that no Amendment which may be made prior to the Year One thousand eight hundred and eight shall in any Manner affect the first and fourth Clauses in the Ninth Section of the first Article; and that no State, without its Consent, shall be deprived of its equal Suffrage in the Senate.

ARTICLE VI

All Debts contracted and Engagements entered into, before the Adoption of this Constitution shall be as valid against the United States under this Constitution, as under the Confederation.

This Constitution, and the Laws of the United States which shall be made in Pursuance thereof; and all Treaties made, or which shall be made, under the Authority of the United States, shall be the supreme Law of the Land; and the Judges in every State shall be bound thereby, any Thing in the Constitution or Laws of any State to the Contrary notwithstanding.

The Senators and Representatives before mentioned, and the Members of the several State Legislatures, and all executive and judicial Officers, both of the United States and of the several States, shall be bound by Oath or Affirmation, to support this Constitution; but no religious Test shall ever be required as a Qualification to any Office or public Trust under the United States.

ARTICLE VII

The Ratification of the Conventions of nine States shall be sufficient for the Establishment of this Constitution between the States so ratifying the Same.

AMENDMENT I [1791]

Congress shall make no law respecting an establishment of religion, or prohibiting the free exercise thereof; or abridging the freedom of speech, or of the press; or the right of the people peaceably to assembly, and to petition the Government for a redress of grievances.

AMENDMENT II [1791]

A well regulated Militia, being necessary to the security of a free State, the right of the people to keep and bear Arms, shall not be infringed.

AMENDMENT III [1791]

No Soldier shall, in time of peace be quartered in any house, without the consent of the Owner, nor in time of war, but in a manner to be prescribed by law.

AMENDMENT IV [1791]

The right of the people to be secure in their persons, houses, papers, and effects, against unreasonable searches and seizures, shall not be violated, and no Warrants shall issue, but upon probable cause, supported by Oath or affirmation, and particularly describing the place to be searched, and the persons or things to be seized.

AMENDMENT V [1791]

No person shall be held to answer for a capital, or otherwise infamous crime, unless on a presentment or indictment of a Grand Jury, except in cases arising in the land or naval forces, or in the Militia, when in actual service in time of War or public danger; nor shall any person be subject for the same offence to be twice put in jeopardy of life or limb; nor shall be compelled in any criminal case to be a witness against himself, nor be deprived of life, liberty, or property, without due process of law; nor shall private property be taken for public use, without just compensation.

AMENDMENT VI [1791]

In all criminal prosecutions, the accused shall enjoy the right to a speedy and public trial, by an impartial jury of the State and district wherein the crime shall have been committed, which district shall have been previously ascertained by law, and to be informed of the nature and cause of the accusation; to be confronted with the witnesses against him; to have compulsory process for obtaining witnesses in his favor, and to have the Assistance of Counsel for his defence.

AMENDMENT VII [1791]

In Suits at common law, where the value in controversy shall exceed twenty dollars, the right of trial by jury shall be preserved, and no fact tried by jury, shall be otherwise re-examined in any Court of the United States, than according to the rules of the common law.

AMENDMENT VIII [1791]

Excessive bail shall not be required, nor excessive fines imposed, nor cruel and unusual punishments inflicted.

AMENDMENT IX [1791]

The enumeration in the Constitution, of certain rights, shall not be construed to deny or disparage others retained by the people.

AMENDMENT X [1791]

The powers not delegated to the United States by the Constitution, nor prohibited by it to the States, are reserved to the States respectively, or to the people.

AMENDMENT XI [1798]

The Judicial power of the United States shall not be construed to extend to any suit in law or equity, commenced or prosecuted against one of the United States by Citizens of another State, or by Citizens or Subjects of any Foreign State.

AMENDMENT XII [1804]

The Electors shall meet in their respective states, and vote by ballot for President and Vice-President, one of whom, at least, shall not be an inhabitant of the same state with themselves; they shall name in their ballots the person voted for as President, and in distinct ballots the person voted for as Vice-President, and they shall make distinct lists of all persons voted for as President, and of all persons voted for as Vice-President, and of the number of votes for each, which lists they shall sign and certify, and transmit sealed to the seat of the government of the United States, directed to the President of the Senate;—The President of the Senate shall, in the presence of the Senate and House of Representatives, open all the certificates and the votes shall then be counted;—The person having the greatest number of votes for President, shall be the President, if such number be a majority of the whole number of Electors appointed; and if no person have such majority, then from the persons having the highest numbers not exceeding three on the list of those voted for as President, the House of Representatives shall choose immediately, by ballot, the President. But in choosing the President, the votes shall be taken by states, the representation from each state having one vote; a quorum for this purpose shall consist of a member or members from two-thirds of the states, and a majority of all states shall be necessary to a choice. And if the House of Representatives shall not choose a President whenever the right of choice shall devolve upon them, before the fourth day of March next following, then the Vice-President shall act as President, as in the case of the death or other constitutional disability of the President.—The person having the greatest number of votes as Vice-President, shall be the Vice-President, if such number be a majority of the whole number of Electors appointed, and if no person have a majority, then from the two highest numbers on the list, the Senate shall choose the Vice-President; a quorum for the purpose shall consist of two-thirds of the whole number of Senators, and a majority of the whole number shall be necessary to a choice. But no person constitutionally ineligible to the office of President shall be eligible to that of Vice-President of the United States.

AMENDMENT XIII [1865]

Section 1. Neither slavery nor involuntary servitude, except as a punishment for crime whereof the party shall have been duly convicted, shall exist within the United States, or any place subject to their jurisdiction.

Section 2. Congress shall have power to enforce this article by appropriate legislation.

AMENDMENT XIV [1868]

Section 1. All persons born or naturalized in the United States, and subject to the jurisdiction thereof, are citizens of the United States and of the State wherein they reside. No State shall make or enforce any law which shall abridge the privileges or immunities of citizens of the United States; nor shall any State deprive any person of life, liberty, or property, without due process of law; nor deny to any person within its jurisdiction the equal protection of the laws.

Section 2. Representatives shall be apportioned among the several States according to their respective numbers, counting the whole number of persons in each State, excluding Indians not taxed. But when the right to vote at any election for the choice of electors for President and Vice President of the United States, Representatives in Congress, the Executive and Judicial officers of a State, or the members of the Legislature thereof, is denied to any of the male inhabitants of such State, being twenty-one years of age, and citizens of the United States, or in any way abridged, except for participation in rebellion, or other crime, the basis of representation therein shall be reduced in the proportion which the number of such male citizens shall bear to the whole number of male citizens twenty-one years of age in such State.

Section 3. No person shall be a Senator or Representative in Congress, or elector of President and Vice President, or hold any office, civil or military, under the United States, or under any State, who having previously taken an oath, as a member of Congress, or as an officer of the United States, or as a member of any State legislature, or as an executive or judicial officer of any State, to support the Constitution of the United States, shall have engaged in insurrection or rebellion against the same, or given aid or comfort to the enemies thereof. But Congress may by a vote of two-thirds of each House, remove such disability.

Section 4. The validity of the public debt of the United States, authorized by law, including debts incurred for payment of pensions and bounties for services in suppressing insurrection or rebellion, shall not be questioned. But neither the United States nor any State shall assume or pay any debt or obligation incurred in aid of insurrection or rebellion against the United States, or any claim for the loss or emancipation of any slave; but all such debts, obligations and claims shall be held illegal and void.

Section 5. The Congress shall have power to enforce, by appropriate legislation, the provisions of this article.

AMENDMENT XV [1870]

Section 1. The right of citizens of the United States to vote shall not be denied or abridged by the United States or by any State on account of race, color, or previous condition of servitude.

Section 2. The Congress shall have power to enforce this article by appropriate legislation.

AMENDMENT XVI [1913]

The Congress shall have power to lay and collect taxes on incomes, from whatever source derived, without apportionment among the several States, and without regard to any census or enumeration.

AMENDMENT XVII [1913]

Section 1. The Senate of the United States shall be composed of two Senators from each State, elected by the people thereof, for six years; and each Senator shall have one vote. The electors in each State shall have the qualifications requisite for electors of the most numerous branch of the State legislatures.

Section 2. When vacancies happen in the representation of any State in the Senate, the executive authority of such State shall issue writs of election to fill such vacancies: *Provided*, That the legislature of any State may empower the executive thereof to make temporary appointments until the people fill the vacancies by election as the legislature may direct.

Section 3. This amendment shall not be so construed as to affect the election or term of any Senator chosen before it becomes valid as part of the Constitution.

AMENDMENT XVIII [1919]

Section 1. After one year from the ratification of this article the manufacture, sale, or transportation of intoxicating liquors within, the importation thereof into, or the exportation thereof from the United States and all territory subject to the jurisdiction thereof for beverage purposes is hereby prohibited.

Section 2. The Congress and the several States shall have concurrent power to enforce this article by appropriate legislation.

Section 3. This article shall be inoperative unless it shall have been ratified as an amendment to the Constitution by the legislatures of the several States, as provided in the Constitution, within seven years from the date of the submission hereof to the States by the Congress.

AMENDMENT XIX [1920]

Section 1. The right of citizens of the United States to vote shall not be denied or abridged by the United States or by any State on account of sex.

Section 2. Congress shall have power to enforce this article by appropriate legislation.

AMENDMENT XX [1933]

Section 1. The terms of the President and Vice President shall end at noon on the 20th day of January, and the terms of Senators and Representatives at noon on the 3d day of January, of the years in which such terms would have ended if this article had not been ratified; and the terms of their successors shall then begin.

Section 2. The Congress shall assemble at least once in every year, and such meeting shall begin at noon on the 3d day of January, unless they shall by law appoint a different day.

Section 3. If, at the time fixed for the beginning of the term of the President, the President elect shall have died, the Vice President elect shall become President. If the President shall not have been chosen before the time fixed for the beginning of his term, or if the President elect shall have failed to qualify, then the Vice President elect shall act as President until a President shall have qualified; and the Congress may by law provide for the case wherein neither a President elect nor a Vice President elect shall have qualified, declaring who shall then act as President, or the manner in which one who is to act shall be selected, and such person shall act accordingly until a President or Vice President shall have qualified.

Section 4. The Congress may by law provide for the case of the death of any of the persons from whom the House of Representatives may choose a President whenever the right of choice shall have devolved upon them, and for the case of the death of any of the persons from whom the Senate may choose a Vice President whenever the right of choice shall have devolved upon them.

Section 5. Sections 1 and 2 shall take effect on the 15th day of October following the ratification of this article.

Section 6. This article shall be inoperative unless it shall have been ratified as an amendment to the Constitution by the legislatures of three-fourths of the several States within seven years from the date of its submission.

AMENDMENT XXI [1933]

Section 1. The eighteenth article of amendment to the Constitution of the United States is hereby repealed.

Section 2. The transportation or importation into any State, Territory, or possession of the United States for delivery or use therein of intoxicating liquors, in violation of the laws thereof, is hereby prohibited.

Section 3. This article shall be inoperative unless it shall have been ratified as an amendment to the Constitution by conventions in the several States, as provided in the Constitution, within seven years from the date of the submission hereof to the States by the Congress.

AMENDMENT XXII [1951]

Section 1. No person shall be elected to the office of the President more than twice, and no person who has held the office of President, or acted as President, for more than two years of a term to which some other person was elected President shall be elected to the office of President more than once. But this Article shall not apply to any person holding the office of President when this Article was proposed by the Congress, and shall not prevent any person who may be holding the office of President, or acting as President, during the term within which this Article becomes operative from holding the office of President or acting as President during the remainder of such term.

Section 2. This article shall be inoperative unless it shall have been ratified as an amendment to the Constitution by the legislatures of three-fourths of the several States within seven years from the date of its submission to the States by the Congress.

AMENDMENT XXIII [1961]

Section 1. The District constituting the seat of Government of the United States shall appoint in such manner as the Congress may direct:

A number of electors of President and Vice President equal to the whole number of Senators and Representatives in Congress to which the District would be entitled if it were a State, but in no event more than the least populous state; they shall be in addition to those appointed by the states, but they shall be considered, for the purposes of the election of President and Vice President, to be electors appointed by a state; and they shall meet in the District and perform such duties as provided by the twelfth article of amendment.

Section 2. The Congress shall have power to enforce this article by appropriate legislation.

AMENDMENT XXIV [1964]

Section 1. The right of citizens of the United States to vote in any primary or other election for President or Vice President, for electors for President or Vice President, or for Senator or Representative in Congress, shall not be denied or abridged by the United States, or any State by reason of failure to pay any poll tax or other tax.

Section 2. The Congress shall have power to enforce this article by appropriate legislation.

AMENDMENT XXV [1967]

Section 1. In case of the removal of the President from office or of his death or resignation, the Vice President shall become President.

Section 2. Whenever there is a vacancy in the office of the Vice President, the President shall nominate a Vice President who shall take office upon confirmation by a majority vote of both Houses of Congress.

Section 3. Whenever the President transmits to the President pro tempore of the Senate and the Speaker of the House of Representatives his written declaration that he is unable to discharge the powers and duties of his office, and until he transmits to them a written declaration to the contrary, such powers and duties shall be discharged by the Vice President as Acting President.

Section 4. Whenever the Vice President and a majority of either the principal officers of the executive departments or of such other body as Congress may by law provide, transmit to the President pro tempore of the Senate and the Speaker of the House of Representatives their written declaration that the President is unable to discharge the powers and duties of his office, the Vice President shall immediately assume the powers and duties of the office as Acting President.

Thereafter, when the President transmits to the President pro tempore of the Senate and the Speaker of the House of Representatives his written declaration that no inability exists, he shall resume the powers and duties of his office unless the Vice President and a majority of either the principal officers of the executive department or of such other body as Congress may by law provide, transmit within four days to the President pro tempore of the Senate and the Speaker of the House of Representatives their written declaration that the President is unable to discharge the powers and duties of his office. Thereupon Congress shall decide the issue, assembling within forty-eight hours for that purpose if not in session. If the Congress, within twenty-one days after receipt of the latter written declaration, or, if Congress is not in session, within twenty-one days after Congress is required to assemble, determines by two-thirds vote of both Houses that the President is unable to discharge the powers and duties of his office, the Vice President shall continue to discharge the same as Acting President; otherwise, the President shall resume the powers and duties of his office.

AMENDMENT XXVI [1971]

Section 1. The right of citizens of the United States, who are eighteen years of age or older, to vote shall not be denied or abridged by the United States or by any State on account of age.

Section 2. The Congress shall have power to enforce this article by appropriate legislation.

AMENDMENT XXVII [1992]

No law, varying the compensation for the services of the Senators and Representatives, shall take effect, until an election of Representatives shall have intervened.

The Uniform Commercial Code

(Adopted in fifty-two jurisdictions; all fifty States, although Louisiana has adopted only Articles 1, 3, 4, 7, 8, and 9; the District of Columbia; and the Virgin Islands.)

The Code consists of the following articles:

Art.

1. General Provisions
2. Sales
2A. Leases
3. Commercial Paper
4. Bank Deposits and Collections
4A. Funds Transfers
5. Letters of Credit
6. Bulk Transfers (including Alternative B)
7. Warehouse Receipts, Bills of Lading and Other Documents of Title
8. Investment Securities
9. Secured Transactions: Sales of Accounts and Chattel Paper
10. Effective Date and Repealer
11. Effective Date and Transition Provisions

Article 1
GENERAL PROVISIONS

Part 1 Short Title, Construction, Application and Subject Matter of the Act

§ 1—101. Short Title.

This Act shall be known and may be cited as Uniform Commercial Code.

§ 1—102. Purposes; Rules of Construction; Variation by Agreement.

(1) This Act shall be liberally construed and applied to promote its underlying purposes and policies.

(2) Underlying purposes and policies of this Act are

(a) to simplify, clarify and modernize the law governing commercial transactions;

(b) to permit the continued expansion of commercial practices through custom, usage and agreement of the parties;

(c) to make uniform the law among the various jurisdictions.

(3) The effect of provisions of this Act may be varied by agreement, except as otherwise provided in this Act and except that the obligations of good faith, diligence, reasonableness and care prescribed by this Act may not be disclaimed by agreement but the parties may by agreement determine the standards by which the performance of such

obligations is to be measured if such standards are not manifestly unreasonable.

(4) The presence in certain provisions of this Act of the words "unless otherwise agreed" or words of similar import does not imply that the effect of other provisions may not be varied by agreement under subsection (3).

(5) In this Act unless the context otherwise requires

(a) words in the singular number include the plural, and in the plural include the singular;

(b) words of the masculine gender include the feminine and the neuter, and when the sense so indicates words of the neuter gender may refer to any gender.

§ 1—103. Supplementary General Principles of Law Applicable.

Unless displaced by the particular provisions of this Act, the principles of law and equity, including the law merchant and the law relative to capacity to contract, principal and agent, estoppel, fraud, misrepresentation, duress, coercion, mistake, bankruptcy, or other validating or invalidating cause shall supplement its provisions.

§ 1—104. Construction Against Implicit Repeal.

This Act being a general act intended as a unified coverage of its subject matter, no part of it shall be deemed to be impliedly repealed by subsequent legislation if such construction can reasonably be avoided.

§ 1—105. Territorial Application of the Act; Parties' Power to Choose Applicable Law.

(1) Except as provided hereafter in this section, when a transaction bears a reasonable relation to this state and also to another state or nation the parties may agree that the law either of this state or of such other state or nation shall govern their rights and duties. Failing such agreement this Act applies to transactions bearing an appropriate relation to this state.

(2) Where one of the following provisions of this Act specifies the applicable law, that provision governs and a contrary agreement is effective only to the extent permitted by the law (including the conflict of laws rules) so specified:

Rights of creditors against sold goods. Section 2—402.

Applicability of the Article on Leases. Sections 2A—105 and 2A—106.

Applicability of the Article on Bank Deposits and Collections. Section 4—102.

Governing law in the Article on Funds Transfers. Section 4A—507.

Letters of Credit, Section 5—116.

Bulk sales subject to the Article on Bulk Sales. Section 6—103.

Applicability of the Article on Investment Securities. Section 8—106.

Perfection provisions of the Article on Secured Transactions. Section 9—103.

§ 1—106. Remedies to Be Liberally Administered.

(1) The remedies provided by this Act shall be liberally administered to the end that the aggrieved party may be put in as good a position as if the other party had fully performed but neither consequential or special nor penal damages may be had except as specifically provided in this Act or by other rule of law.

(2) Any right or obligation declared by this Act is enforceable by action unless the provision declaring it specifies a different and limited effect.

§ 1—107. Waiver or Renunciation of Claim or Right After Breach.

Any claim or right arising out of an alleged breach can be discharged in whole or in part without consideration by a written waiver or renunciation signed and delivered by the aggrieved party.

§ 1—108. Severability.

If any provision or clause of this Act or application thereof to any person or circumstances is held invalid, such invalidity shall not affect other provisions or applications of the Act which can be given effect without the invalid provision or application, and to this end the provisions of this Act are declared to be severable.

§ 1—109. Section Captions.

Section captions are parts of this Act.

Part 2 General Definitions and Principles of Interpretation

§ 1—201. General Definitions.

Subject to additional definitions contained in the subsequent Articles of this Act which are applicable to specific Articles or Parts thereof, and unless the context otherwise requires, in this Act:

(1) "Action" in the sense of a judicial proceeding includes recoupment, counterclaim, set-off, suit in equity and any other proceedings in which rights are determined.

(2) "Aggrieved party" means a party entitled to resort to a remedy.

(3) "Agreement" means the bargain of the parties in fact as found in their language or by implication from other circumstances including course of dealing or usage of trade or course of performance as provided in this Act (Sections 1—205 and 2—208). Whether an agreement has legal

consequences is determined by the provisions of this Act, if applicable; otherwise by the law of contracts (Section 1—103). (Compare "Contract".)

(4) "Bank" means any person engaged in the business of banking.

(5) "Bearer" means the person in possession of an instrument, document of title, or certificated security payable to bearer or indorsed in blank.

(6) "Bill of lading" means a document evidencing the receipt of goods for shipment issued by a person engaged in the business of transporting or forwarding goods, and includes an airbill. "Airbill" means a document serving for air transportation as a bill of lading does for marine or rail transportation, and includes an air consignment note or air waybill.

(7) "Branch" includes a separately incorporated foreign branch of a bank.

(8) "Burden of establishing" a fact means the burden of persuading the triers of fact that the existence of the fact is more probable than its non-existence.

(9) "Buyer in ordinary course of business" means a person who in good faith and without knowledge that the sale to him is in violation of the ownership rights or security interest of a third party in the goods buys in ordinary course from a person in the business of selling goods of that kind but does not include a pawnbroker. All persons who sell minerals or the like (including oil and gas) at wellhead or minehead shall be deemed to be persons in the business of selling goods of that kind. "Buying" may be for cash or by exchange of other property or on secured or unsecured credit and includes receiving goods or documents of title under a pre-existing contract for sale but does not include a transfer in bulk or as security for or in total or partial satisfaction of a money debt.

(10) "Conspicuous": A term or clause is conspicuous when it is so written that a reasonable person against whom it is to operate ought to have noticed it. A printed heading in capitals (as: NON-NEGOTIABLE BILL OF LADING) is conspicuous. Language in the body of a form is "conspicuous" if it is in larger or other contrasting type or color. But in a telegram any stated term is "conspicuous". Whether a term or clause is "conspicuous" or not is for decision by the court.

(11) "Contract" means the total legal obligation which results from the parties' agreement as affected by this Act and any other applicable rules of law. (Compare "Agreement".)

(12) "Creditor" includes a general creditor, a secured creditor, a lien creditor and any representative of creditors, including an assignee for the benefit of creditors, a trustee in bankruptcy, a receiver in equity and an executor or administrator of an insolvent debtor's or assignor's estate.

(13) "Defendant" includes a person in the position of defendant in a cross-action or counterclaim.

(14) "Delivery" with respect to instruments, documents of title, chattel paper, or certificated securities means voluntary transfer of possession.

(15) "Document of title" includes bill of lading, dock warrant, dock receipt, warehouse receipt or order for the delivery of goods, and also any other document which in the regular course of business or financing is treated as adequately evidencing that the person in possession of it is entitled to receive, hold and dispose of the document and the goods it covers. To be a document of title a document must purport to be issued by or addressed to a bailee and purport to cover goods in the bailee's possession which are either identified or are fungible portions of an identified mass.

(16) "Fault" means wrongful act, omission or breach.

(17) "Fungible" with respect to goods or securities means goods or securities of which any unit is, by nature or usage of trade, the equivalent of any other like unit. Goods which are not fungible shall be deemed fungible for the purposes of this Act to the extent that under a particular agreement or document unlike units are treated as equivalents.

(18) "Genuine" means free of forgery or counterfeiting.

(19) "Good faith" means honesty in fact in the conduct or transaction concerned.

(20) "Holder" with respect to a negotiable instrument, means the person in possession if the instrument is payable to bearer or, in the cases of an instrument payable to an identified person, if the identified person is in possession. "Holder" with respect to a document of title means the person in possession if the goods are deliverable to bearer or to the order of the person in possession.

(21) To "honor" is to pay or to accept and pay, or where a credit so engages to purchase or discount a draft complying with the terms of the credit.

(22) "Insolvency proceedings" includes any assignment for the benefit of creditors or other proceedings intended to liquidate or rehabilitate the estate of the person involved.

(23) A person is "insolvent" who either has ceased to pay his debts in the ordinary course of business or cannot pay his debts as they become due or is insolvent within the meaning of the federal bankruptcy law.

(24) "Money" means a medium of exchange authorized or adopted by a domestic or foreign government and includes a monetary unit of account established by an intergovernmental organization or by agreement between two or more nations.

(25) A person has "notice" of a fact when

   (a) he has actual knowledge of it; or

   (b) he has received a notice or notification of it; or

(c) from all the facts and circumstances known to him at the time in question he has reason to know that it exists.

A person "knows" or has "knowledge" of a fact when he has actual knowledge of it. "Discover" or "learn" or a word or phrase of similar import refers to knowledge rather than to reason to know. The time and circumstances under which a notice or notification may cease to be effective are not determined by this Act.

(26) A person "notifies" or "gives" a notice or notification to another by taking such steps as may be reasonably required to inform the other in ordinary course whether or not such other actually comes to know of it. A person "receives" a notice or notification when

(a) it comes to his attention; or

(b) it is duly delivered at the place of business through which the contract was made or at any other place held out by him as the place for receipt of such communications.

(27) Notice, knowledge or a notice or notification received by an organization is effective for a particular transaction from the time when it is brought to the attention of the individual conducting that transaction, and in any event from the time when it would have been brought to his attention if the organization had exercised due diligence. An organization exercises due diligence if it maintains reasonable routines for communicating significant information to the person conducting the transaction and there is reasonable compliance with the routines. Due diligence does not require an individual acting for the organization to communicate information unless such communication is part of his regular duties or unless he has reason to know of the transaction and that the transaction would be materially affected by the information.

(28) "Organization" includes a corporation, government or governmental subdivision or agency, business trust, estate, trust, partnership or association, two or more persons having a joint or common interest, or any other legal or commercial entity.

(29) "Party", as distinct from "third party", means a person who has engaged in a transaction or made an agreement within this Act.

(30) "Person" includes an individual or an organization (See Section 1—102).

(31) "Presumption" or "presumed" means that the trier of fact must find the existence of the fact presumed unless and until evidence is introduced which would support a finding of its non-existence.

(32) "Purchase" includes taking by sale, discount, negotiation, mortgage, pledge, lien, issue or re-issue, gift or any other voluntary transaction creating an interest in property.

(33) "Purchaser" means a person who takes by purchase.

(34) "Remedy" means any remedial right to which an aggrieved party is entitled with or without resort to a tribunal.

(35) "Representative" includes an agent, an officer of a corporation or association, and a trustee, executor or administrator of an estate, or any other person empowered to act for another.

(36) "Rights" includes remedies.

(37) "Security interest" means an interest in personal property or fixtures which secures payment or performance of an obligation. The retention or reservation of title by a seller of goods notwithstanding shipment or delivery to the buyer (Section 2—401) is limited in effect to a reservation of a "security interest". The term also includes any interest of a buyer of accounts or chattel paper which is subject to Article 9. The special property interest of a buyer of goods on identification of those goods to a contract for sale under Section 2—401 is not a "security interest", but a buyer may also acquire a "security interest" by complying with Article 9. Unless a consignment is intended as security, reservation of title thereunder is not a "security interest," but a consignment is in any event subject to the provisions on consignment sales (Section 2—326).

Whether a transaction creates a lease or security interest is determined by the facts of each case; however, a transaction creates a security interest if the consideration the lessee is to pay the lessor for the right to possession and use of the goods is an obligation for the term of the lease not subject to termination by the lessee, and

(a) the original term of the lease is equal to or greater than the remaining economic life of the goods,

(b) the lessee is bound to renew the lease for the remaining economic life of the goods or is bound to become the owner of the goods,

(c) the lessee has an option to renew the lease for the remaining economic life of the goods for no additional consideration or nominal additional consideration upon compliance with the lease agreement, or

(d) the lessee has an option to become the owner of the goods for no additional consideration or nominal additional consideration upon compliance with the lease agreement.

A transaction does not create a security interest merely because it provides that

(a) the present value of the consideration the lessee is obligated to pay the lessor for the right to possession and use of the goods is substantially equal to or is greater than the fair market value of the goods at the time the lease is entered into,

(b) the lessee assumes risk of loss of the goods, or agrees to pay taxes, insurance, filing, recording, or registration fees, or service or maintenance costs with respect to the goods,

(c) the lessee has an option to renew the lease or to become the owner of the goods,

(d) the lessee has an option to renew the lease for a fixed rent that is equal to or greater than the reasonably predictable fair market rent for the use of the goods for the term of the renewal at the time the option is to be performed, or

(e) the lessee has an option to become the owner of the goods for a fixed price that is equal to or greater than the reasonably predictable fair market value of the goods at the time the option is to be performed.

For purposes of this subsection (37):

(x) Additional consideration is not nominal if (i) when the option to renew the lease is granted to the lessee the rent is stated to be the fair market rent for the use of the goods for the term of the renewal determined at the time the option is to be performed, or (ii) when the option to become the owner of the goods is granted to the lessee the price is stated to be the fair market value of the goods determined at the time the option is to be performed. Additional consideration is nominal if it is less than the lessee's reasonably predictable cost of performing under the lease agreement if the option is not exercised;

(y) "Reasonably predictable" and "remaining economic life of the goods" are to be determined with reference to the facts and circumstances at the time the transaction is entered into; and

(z) "Present value" means the amount as of a date certain of one or more sums payable in the future, discounted to the date certain. The discount is determined by the interest rate specified by the parties if the rate is not manifestly unreasonable at the time the transaction is entered into; otherwise, the discount is determined by a commercially reasonable rate that takes into account the facts and circumstances of each case at the time the transaction was entered into.

(38) "Send" in connection with any writing or notice means to deposit in the mail or deliver for transmission by any other usual means of communication with postage or cost of transmission provided for and properly addressed and in the case of an instrument to an address specified thereon or otherwise agreed, or if there be none to any address reasonable under the circumstances. The receipt of any writing or notice within the time at which it would have arrived if properly sent has the effect of a proper sending.

(39) "Signed" includes any symbol executed or adopted by a party with present intention to authenticate a writing.

(40) "Surety" includes guarantor.

(41) "Telegram" includes a message transmitted by radio, teletype, cable, any mechanical method of transmission, or the like.

(42) "Term" means that portion of an agreement which relates to a particular matter.

(43) "Unauthorized" signature means one made without actual, implied or apparent authority and includes a forgery.

(44) "Value". Except as otherwise provided with respect to negotiable instruments and bank collections (Sections 3—303, 4—210 and 4—211) a person gives "value" for rights if he acquires them

(a) in return for a binding commitment to extend credit or for the extension of immediately available credit whether or not drawn upon and whether or not a chargeback is provided for in the event of difficulties in collection; or

(b) as security for or in total or partial satisfaction of a pre-existing claim; or

(c) by accepting delivery pursuant to a preexisting contract for purchase; or

(d) generally, in return for any consideration sufficient to support a simple contract.

(45) "Warehouse receipt" means a receipt issued by a person engaged in the business of storing goods for hire.

(46) "Written" or "writing" includes printing, typewriting or any other intentional reduction to tangible form.

§1—202. Prima Facie Evidence by Third Party Documents.

A document in due form purporting to be a bill of lading, policy or certificate of insurance, official weigher's or inspector's certificate, consular invoice, or any other document authorized or required by the contract to be issued by a third party shall be prima facie evidence of its own authenticity and genuineness and of the facts stated in the document by the third party.

§ 1—203. Obligation of Good Faith.

Every contract or duty within this Act imposes an obligation of good faith in its performance or enforcement.

§ 1—204. Time; Reasonable Time; "Seasonably".

(1) Whenever this Act requires any action to be taken within a reasonable time, any time which is not manifestly unreasonable may be fixed by agreement.

(2) What is a reasonable time for taking any action depends on the nature, purpose and circumstances of such action.

(3) An action is taken "seasonably" when it is taken at or within the time agreed or if no time is agreed at or within a reasonable time.

§ 1—205. Course of Dealing and Usage of Trade.

(1) A course of dealing is a sequence of previous conduct between the parties to a particular transaction which is fairly

to be regarded as establishing a common basis of understanding for interpreting their expressions and other conduct.

(2) A usage of trade is any practice or method of dealing having such regularity of observance in a place, vocation or trade as to justify an expectation that it will be observed with respect to the transaction in question. The existence and scope of such a usage are to be proved as facts. If it is established that such a usage is embodied in a written trade code or similar writing the interpretation of the writing is for the court.

(3) A course of dealing between parties and any usage of trade in the vocation or trade in which they are engaged or of which they are or should be aware give particular meaning to and supplement or qualify terms of an agreement.

(4) The express terms of an agreement and an applicable course of dealing or usage of trade shall be construed wherever reasonable as consistent with each other; but when such construction is unreasonable express terms control both course of dealing and usage of trade and course of dealing controls usage trade.

(5) An applicable usage of trade in the place where any part of performance is to occur shall be used in interpreting the agreement as to that part of the performance.

(6) Evidence of a relevant usage of trade offered by one party is not admissible unless and until he has given the other party such notice as the court finds sufficient to prevent unfair surprise to the latter.

§ 1—206. Statute of Frauds for Kinds of Personal Property Not Otherwise Covered.

(1) Except in the cases described in subsection (2) of this section a contract for the sale of personal property is not enforceable by way of action or defense beyond five thousand dollars in amount or value of remedy unless there is some writing which indicates that a contract for sale has been made between the parties at a defined or stated price, reasonably identifies the subject matter, and is signed by the party against whom enforcement is sought or by his authorized agent.

(2) Subsection (1) of this section does not apply to contracts for the sale of goods (Section 2—201) nor of securities (Section 8—113) nor to security agreements (Section 9—203).

§ 1—207. Performance or Acceptance Under Reservation of Rights.

(1) A party who with explicit reservation of rights performs or promises performance or assents to performance in a manner demanded or offered by the other party does not thereby prejudice the rights reserved. Such words as "without prejudice", "under protest" or the like are sufficient.

(2) Subsection (1) does not apply to an accord and satisfaction.

§ 1—208. Option to Accelerate at Will.

A term providing that one party or his successor in interest may accelerate payment or performance or require collateral or additional collateral "at will" or "when he deems himself insecure" or in words of similar import shall be construed to mean that he shall have power to do so only if he in good faith believes that the prospect of payment or performance is impaired. The burden of establishing lack of good faith is on the party against whom the power has been exercised.

§ 1—209. Subordinated Obligations.

An obligation may be issued as subordinated to payment of another obligation of the person obligated, or a creditor may subordinate his right to payment of an obligation by agreement with either the person obligated or another creditor of the person obligated. Such a subordination does not create a security interest as against either the common debtor or a subordinated creditor. This section shall be construed as declaring the law as it existed prior to the enactment of this section and not as modifying it. Added 1966.

Note: *This new section is proposed as an optional provision to make it clear that a subordination agreement does not create a security interest unless so intended.*

Article 2
SALES

Part 1 Short Title, General Construction and Subject Matter

§ 2—101. Short Title.

This Article shall be known and may be cited as Uniform Commercial Code—Sales.

§ 2—102. Scope; Certain Security and Other Transactions Excluded From This Article.

Unless the context otherwise requires, this Article applies to transactions in goods; it does not apply to any transaction which although in the form of an unconditional contract to sell or present sale is intended to operate only as a security transaction nor does this Article impair or repeal any statute regulating sales to consumers, farmers or other specified classes of buyers.

§ 2—103. Definitions and Index of Definitions.

(1) In this Article unless the context otherwise requires

(a) "Buyer" means a person who buys or contracts to buy goods.

(b) "Good faith" in the case of a merchant means honesty in fact and the observance of reasonable commercial standards of fair dealing in the trade.

(c) "Receipt" of goods means taking physical possession of them.

(d) "Seller" means a person who sells or contracts to sell goods.

(2) Other definitions applying to this Article or to specified Parts thereof, and the sections in which they appear are:

"Acceptance". Section 2—606.
"Banker's credit". Section 2—325.
"Between merchants". Section 2—104.
"Cancellation". Section 2—106(4).
"Commercial unit". Section 2—105.
"Confirmed credit". Section 2—325.
"Conforming to contract". Section 2—106.
"Contract for sale". Section 2—106.
"Cover". Section 2—712.
"Entrusting". Section 2—403.
"Financing agency". Section 2—104.
"Future goods". Section 2—105.
"Goods". Section 2—105.
"Identification". Section 2—501.
"Installment contract". Section 2—612.
"Letter of Credit". Section 2—325.
"Lot". Section 2—105.
"Merchant". Section 2—104.
"Overseas". Section 2—323.
"Person in position of seller". Section 2—707.
"Present sale". Section 2—106.
"Sale". Section 2—106.
"Sale on approval". Section 2—326.
"Sale or return". Section 2—326.
"Termination". Section 2—106.

(3) The following definitions in other Articles apply to this Article:

"Check". Section 3—104.
"Consignee". Section 7—102.
"Consignor". Section 7—102.
"Consumer goods". Section 9—109.
"Dishonor". Section 3—507.
"Draft". Section 3—104.

(4) In addition Article 1 contains general definitions and principles of construction and interpretation applicable throughout this Article.

§ 2—104. Definitions: "Merchant"; "Between Merchants"; "Financing Agency".

(1) "Merchant" means a person who deals in goods of the kind or otherwise by his occupation holds himself out as having knowledge or skill peculiar to the practices or goods involved in the transaction or to whom such knowledge or skill may be attributed by his employment of an agent or broker or other intermediary who by his occupation holds himself out as having such knowledge or skill.

(2) "Financing agency" means a bank, finance company or other person who in the ordinary course of business makes advances against goods or documents of title or who

by arrangement with either the seller or the buyer intervenes in ordinary course to make or collect payment due or claimed under the contract for sale, as by purchasing or paying the seller's draft or making advances against it or by merely taking it for collection whether or not documents of title accompany the draft. "Financing agency" includes also a bank or other person who similarly intervenes between persons who are in the position of seller and buyer in respect to the goods (Section 2—707).

(3) "Between merchants" means in any transaction with respect to which both parties are chargeable with the knowledge or skill of merchants.

§ 2—105. Definitions: Transferability; "Goods"; "Future" Goods; "Lot"; "Commercial Unit".

(1) "Goods" means all things (including specially manufactured goods) which are movable at the time of identification to the contract for sale other than the money in which the price is to be paid, investment securities (Article 8) and things in action. "Goods" also includes the unborn young of animals and growing crops and other identified things attached to realty as described in the section on goods to be severed from realty (Section 2—107).

(2) Goods must be both existing and identified before any interest in them can pass. Goods which are not both existing and identified are "future" goods. A purported present sale of future goods or of any interest therein operates as a contract to sell.

(3) There may be a sale of a part interest in existing identified goods.

(4) An undivided share in an identified bulk of fungible goods is sufficiently identified to be sold although the quantity of the bulk is not determined. Any agreed proportion of such a bulk or any quantity thereof agreed upon by number, weight or other measure may to the extent of the seller's interest in the bulk be sold to the buyer who then becomes an owner in common.

(5) "Lot" means a parcel or a single article which is the subject matter of a separate sale or delivery, whether or not it is sufficient to perform the contract.

(6) "Commercial unit" means such a unit of goods as by commercial usage is a single whole for purposes of sale and division of which materially impairs its character or value on the market or in use. A commercial unit may be a single article (as a machine) or a set of articles (as a suite of furniture or an assortment of sizes) or a quantity (as a bale, gross, or carload) or any other unit treated in use or in the relevant market as a single whole.

§ 2—106. Definitions: "Contract"; "Agreement"; "Contract for Sale"; "Sale"; "Present Sale"; "Conforming" to Contract; "Termination"; "Cancellation".

(1) In this Article unless the context otherwise requires "contract" and "agreement" are limited to those relating to

the present or future sale of goods. "Contract for sale" includes both a present sale of goods and a contract to sell goods at a future time. A "sale" consists in the passing of title from the seller to the buyer for a price (Section 2—401). A "present sale" means a sale which is accomplished by the making of the contract.

(2) Goods or conduct including any part of a performance are "conforming" or conform to the contract when they are in accordance with the obligations under the contract.

(3) "Termination" occurs when either party pursuant to a power created by agreement or law puts an end to the contract otherwise than for its breach. On "termination" all obligations which are still executory on both sides are discharged but any right based on prior breach or performance survives.

(4) "Cancellation" occurs when either party puts an end to the contract for breach by the other and its effect is the same as that of "termination" except that the cancelling party also retains any remedy for breach of the whole contract or any unperformed balance.

§ 2—107. Goods to Be Severed From Realty: Recording.

(1) A contract for the sale of minerals or the like (including oil and gas) or a structure or its materials to be removed from realty is a contract for the sale of goods within this Article if they are to be severed by the seller but until severance a purported present sale thereof which is not effective as a transfer of an interest in land is effective only as a contract to sell.

(2) A contract for the sale apart from the land of growing crops or other things attached to realty and capable of severance without material harm thereto but not described in subsection (1) or of timber to be cut is a contract for the sale of goods within this Article whether the subject matter is to be severed by the buyer or by the seller even though it forms part of the realty at the time of contracting, and the parties can by identification effect a present sale before severance.

(3) The provisions of this section are subject to any third party rights provided by the law relating to realty records, and the contract for sale may be executed and recorded as a document transferring an interest in land and shall then constitute notice to third parties of the buyer's rights under the contract for sale.

Part 2 Form, Formation and Readjustment of Contract

§ 2—201. Formal Requirements; Statute of Frauds.

(1) Except as otherwise provided in this section a contract for the sale of goods for the price of $500 or more is not enforceable by way of action or defense unless there is some writing sufficient to indicate that a contract for sale has been made between the parties and signed by the party against whom enforcement is sought or by his authorized agent or broker. A writing is not insufficient because it omits or incorrectly states a term agreed upon but the contract is not enforceable under this paragraph beyond the quantity of goods shown in such writing.

(2) Between merchants if within a reasonable time a writing in confirmation of the contract and sufficient against the sender is received and the party receiving it has reason to know its contents, its satisfies the requirements of subsection (1) against such party unless written notice of objection to its contents is given within ten days after it is received.

(3) A contract which does not satisfy the requirements of subsection (1) but which is valid in other respects is enforceable

(a) if the goods are to be specially manufactured for the buyer and are not suitable for sale to others in the ordinary course of the seller's business and the seller, before notice of repudiation is received and under circumstances which reasonably indicate that the goods are for the buyer, has made either a substantial beginning of their manufacture or commitments for their procurement; or

(b) if the party against whom enforcement is sought admits in his pleading, testimony or otherwise in court that a contract for sale was made, but the contract is not enforceable under this provision beyond the quantity of goods admitted; or

(c) with respect to goods for which payment has been made and accepted or which have been received and accepted (Sec. 2—606).

§ 2—202. Final Written Expression: Parol or Extrinsic Evidence.

Terms with respect to which the confirmatory memoranda of the parties agree or which are otherwise set forth in a writing intended by the parties as a final expression of their agreement with respect to such terms as are included therein may not be contradicted by evidence of any prior agreement or of a contemporaneous oral agreement but may be explained or supplemented

(a) by course of dealing or usage of trade (Section 1—205) or by course of performance (Section 2—208); and

(b) by evidence of consistent additional terms unless the court finds the writing to have been intended also as a complete and exclusive statement of the terms of the agreement.

§ 2—203. Seals Inoperative.

The affixing of a seal to a writing evidencing a contract for sale or an offer to buy or sell goods does not constitute the writing a sealed instrument and the law with respect to sealed instruments does not apply to such a contract or offer.

§ 2—204. Formation in General.

(1) A contract for sale of goods may be made in any manner sufficient to show agreement, including conduct by both parties which recognizes the existence of such a contract.

(2) An agreement sufficient to constitute a contract for sale may be found even though the moment of its making is undetermined.

(3) Even though one or more terms are left open a contract for sale does not fail for indefiniteness if the parties have intended to make a contract and there is a reasonably certain basis for giving an appropriate remedy.

§ 2—205. Firm Offers.

An offer by a merchant to buy or sell goods in a signed writing which by its terms gives assurance that it will be held open is not revocable, for lack of consideration, during the time stated or if no time is stated for a reasonable time, but in no event may such period of irrevocability exceed three months; but any such term of assurance on a form supplied by the offeree must be separately signed by the offeror.

§ 2—206. Offer and Acceptance in Formation of Contract.

(1) Unless other unambiguously indicated by the language or circumstances

   (a) an offer to make a contract shall be construed as inviting acceptance in any manner and by any medium reasonable in the circumstances;

   (b) an order or other offer to buy goods for prompt or current shipment shall be construed as inviting acceptance either by a prompt promise to ship or by the prompt or current shipment of conforming or non-conforming goods, but such a shipment of non-conforming goods does not constitute an acceptance if the seller seasonably notifies the buyer that the shipment is offered only as an accommodation to the buyer.

(2) Where the beginning of a requested performance is a reasonable mode of acceptance an offeror who is not notified of acceptance within a reasonable time may treat the offer as having lapsed before acceptance.

§ 2—207. Additional Terms in Acceptance or Confirmation.

(1) A definite and seasonable expression of acceptance or a written confirmation which is sent within a reasonable time operates as an acceptance even though it states terms additional to or different from those offered or agreed upon, unless acceptance is expressly made conditional on assent to the additional or different terms.

(2) The additional terms are to be construed as proposals for addition to the contract. Between merchants such terms become part of the contract unless:

   (a) the offer expressly limits acceptance to the terms of the offer;

   (b) they materially alter it; or

   (c) notification of objection to them has already been given or is given within a reasonable time after notice of them is received.

(3) Conduct by both parties which recognizes the existence of a contract is sufficient to establish a contract for sale although the writings of the parties do not otherwise establish a contract. In such case the terms of the particular contract consist of those terms on which the writings of the parties agree, together with any supplementary terms incorporated under any other provisions of this Act.

§ 2—208. Course of Performance or Practical Construction.

(1) Where the contract for sale involves repeated occasions for performance by either party with knowledge of the nature of the performance and opportunity for objection to it by the other, any course of performance accepted or acquiesced in without objection shall be relevant to determine the meaning of the agreement.

(2) The express terms of the agreement and any such course of performance, as well as any course of dealing and usage of trade, shall be construed whenever reasonable as consistent with each other; but when such construction is unreasonable, express terms shall control course of performance and course of performance shall control both course of dealing and usage of trade (Section 1—205).

(3) Subject to the provisions of the next section on modification and waiver, such course of performance shall be relevant to show a waiver or modification of any term inconsistent with such course of performance.

§ 2—209. Modification, Rescission and Waiver.

(1) An agreement modifying a contract within this Article needs no consideration to be binding.

(2) A signed agreement which excludes modification or rescission except by a signed writing cannot be otherwise modified or rescinded, but except as between merchants such a requirement on a form supplied by the merchant must be separately signed by the other party.

(3) The requirements of the statute of frauds section of this Article (Section 2—201) must be satisfied if the contract as modified is within its provisions.

(4) Although an attempt at modification or rescission does not satisfy the requirements of subsection (2) or (3) it can operate as a waiver.

(5) A party who has made a waiver affecting an executory portion of the contract may retract the waiver by reasonable notification received by the other party that strict performance will be required of any term waived, unless the retraction would be unjust in view of a material change of position in reliance on the waiver.

§ 2—210. Delegation of Performance; Assignment of Rights.

(1) A party may perform his duty through a delegate unless otherwise agreed or unless the other party has a substantial interest in having his original promisor perform or control the acts required by the contract. No delegation of performance relieves the party delegating of any duty to perform or any liability for breach.

(2) Unless otherwise agreed all rights of either seller or buyer can be assigned except where the assignment would materially change the duty of the other party, or increase materially the burden or risk imposed on him by his contract, or impair materially his chance of obtaining return performance. A right to damages for breach of the whole contract or a right arising out of the assignor's due performance of his entire obligation can be assigned despite agreement otherwise.

(3) Unless the circumstances indicate the contrary a prohibition of assignment of "the contract" is to be construed as barring only the delegation to the assignee of the assignor's performance.

(4) An assignment of "the contract" or of "all my rights under the contract" or an assignment in similar general terms is an assignment of rights and unless the language or the circumstances (as in an assignment for security) indicate the contrary, it is a delegation of performance of the duties of the assignor and its acceptance by the assignee constitutes a promise by him to perform those duties. This promise is enforceable by either the assignor or the other party to the original contract.

(5) The other party may treat any assignment which delegates performance as creating reasonable grounds for insecurity and may without prejudice to his rights against the assignor demand assurances from the assignee (Section 2—609).

Part 3 General Obligation and Construction of Contract

§ 2—301. General Obligations of Parties.

The obligation of the seller is to transfer and deliver and that of the buyer is to accept and pay in accordance with the contract.

§ 2—302. Unconscionable Contract or Clause.

(1) If the court as a matter of law finds the contract or any clause of the contract to have been unconscionable at the time it was made the court may refuse to enforce the contract, or it may enforce the remainder of the contract without the unconscionable clause, or it may so limit the application of any unconscionable clause as to avoid any unconscionable result.

(2) When it is claimed or appears to the court that the contract or any clause thereof may be unconscionable the parties shall be afforded a reasonable opportunity to present evidence as to its commercial setting, purpose and effect to aid the court in making the determination.

§ 2—303. Allocations or Division of Risks.

Where this Article allocates a risk or a burden as between the parties "unless otherwise agreed", the agreement may not only shift the allocation but may also divide the risk or burden.

§ 2—304. Price Payable in Money, Goods, Realty, or Otherwise.

(1) The price can be made payable in money or otherwise. If it is payable in whole or in part in goods each party is a seller of the goods which he is to transfer.

(2) Even though all or part of the price is payable in an interest in realty the transfer of the goods and the seller's obligations with reference to them are subject to this Article, but not the transfer of the interest in realty or the transferor's obligations in connection therewith.

§ 2—305. Open Price Term.

(1) The parties if they so intend can conclude a contract for sale even though the price is not settled. In such a case the price is a reasonable price at the time for delivery if

(a) nothing is said as to price; or

(b) the price is left to be agreed by the parties and they fail to agree; or

(c) the price is to be fixed in terms of some agreed market or other standard as set or recorded by a third person or agency and it is not so set or recorded.

(2) A price to be fixed by the seller or by the buyer means a price for him to fix in good faith.

(3) When a price left to be fixed otherwise than by agreement of the parties fails to be fixed through fault of one party the other may at his option treat the contract as cancelled or himself fix a reasonable price.

(4) Where, however, the parties intend not to be bound unless the price be fixed or agreed and it is not fixed or agreed there is no contract. In such a case the buyer must return any goods already received or if unable so to do must pay their reasonable value at the time of delivery and the seller must return any portion of the price paid on account.

§ 2—306. Output, Requirements and Exclusive Dealings.

(1) A term which measures the quantity by the output of the seller or the requirements of the buyer means such actual output or requirements as may occur in good faith, except that no quantity unreasonably disproportionate to any stated estimate or in the absence of a stated estimate to any normal or otherwise comparable prior output or requirements may be tendered or demanded.

(2) A lawful agreement by either the seller or the buyer for exclusive dealing in the kind of goods concerned imposes unless otherwise agreed an obligation by the seller to use best efforts to supply the goods and by the buyer to use best efforts to promote their sale.

§ 2—307. Delivery in Single Lot or Several Lots.

Unless otherwise agreed all goods called for by a contract for sale must be tendered in a single delivery and payment is due only on such tender but where the circumstances give either party the right to make or demand delivery in lots the price if it can be apportioned may be demanded for each lot.

§ 2—308. Absence of Specified Place for Delivery.

Unless otherwise agreed

(a) the place for delivery of goods is the seller's place of business or if he has none his residence; but

(b) in a contract for sale of identified goods which to the knowledge of the parties at the time of contracting are in some other place, that place is the place for their delivery; and

(c) documents of title may be delivered through customary banking channels.

§ 2—309. Absence of Specific Time Provisions; Notice of Termination.

(1) The time for shipment or delivery or any other action under a contract if not provided in this Article or agreed upon shall be a reasonable time.

(2) Where the contract provides for successive performances but is indefinite in duration it is valid for a reasonable time but unless otherwise agreed may be terminated at any time by either party.

(3) Termination of a contract by one party except on the happening of an agreed event requires that reasonable notification be received by the other party and an agreement dispensing with notification is invalid if its operation would be unconscionable.

§ 2—310. Open Time for Payment or Running of Credit; Authority to Ship Under Reservation.

Unless otherwise agreed

(a) payment is due at the time and place at which the buyer is to receive the goods even though the place of shipment is the place of delivery; and

(b) if the seller is authorized to send the goods he may ship them under reservation, and may tender the documents of title, but the buyer may inspect the goods after their arrival before payment is due unless such inspection is inconsistent with the terms of the contract (Section 2—513); and

(c) if delivery is authorized and made by way of documents of title otherwise than by subsection (b) then

payment is due at the time and place at which the buyer is to receive the documents regardless of where the goods are to be received; and

(d) where the seller is required or authorized to ship the goods on credit the credit period runs from the time of shipment but post-dating the invoice or delaying its dispatch will correspondingly delay the starting of the credit period.

§ 2—311. Options and Cooperation Respecting Performance.

(1) An agreement for sale which is otherwise sufficiently definite (subsection (3) of Section 2—204) to be a contract is not made invalid by the fact that it leaves particulars of performance to be specified by one of the parties. Any such specification must be made in good faith and within limits set by commercial reasonableness.

(2) Unless otherwise agreed specifications relating to assortment of the goods are at the buyer's option and except as otherwise provided in subsections (1)(c) and (3) of Section 2—319 specifications or arrangements relating to shipment are at the seller's option.

(3) Where such specification would materially affect the other party's performance but is not seasonably made or where one party's cooperation is necessary to the agreed performance of the other but is not seasonably forthcoming, the other party in addition to all other remedies

(a) is excused for any resulting delay in his own performance; and

(b) may also either proceed to perform in any reasonable manner or after the time for a material part of his own performance treat the failure to specify or to cooperate as a breach by failure to deliver or accept the goods.

§ 2—312. Warranty of Title and Against Infringement; Buyer's Obligation Against Infringement.

(1) Subject to subsection (2) there is in a contract for sale a warranty by the seller that

(a) the title conveyed shall be good, and its transfer rightful; and

(b) the goods shall be delivered free from any security interest or other lien or encumbrance of which the buyer at the time of contracting has no knowledge.

(2) A warranty under subsection (1) will be excluded or modified only by specific language or by circumstances which give the buyer reason to know that the person selling does not claim title in himself or that he is purporting to sell only such right or title as he or a third person may have.

(3) Unless otherwise agreed a seller who is a merchant regularly dealing in goods of the kind warrants that the goods shall be delivered free of the rightful claim of any third person by way of infringement or the like but a buyer who

furnishes specifications to the seller must hold the seller harmless against any such claim which arises out of compliance with the specifications.

§ 2—313. Express Warranties by Affirmation, Promise, Description, Sample.

(1) Express warranties by the seller are created as follows:

(a) Any affirmation of fact or promise made by the seller to the buyer which relates to the goods and becomes part of the basis of the bargain creates an express warranty that the goods shall conform to the affirmation or promise.

(b) Any description of the goods which is made part of the basis of the bargain creates an express warranty that the goods shall conform to the description.

(c) Any sample or model which is made part of the basis of the bargain creates an express warranty that the whole of the goods shall conform to the sample or model.

(2) It is not necessary to the creation of an express warranty that the seller use formal words such as "warrant" or "guarantee" or that he have a specific intention to make a warranty, but an affirmation merely of the value of the goods or a statement purporting to be merely the seller's opinion or commendation of the goods does not create a warranty.

§ 2—314. Implied Warranty: Merchantability; Usage of Trade.

(1) Unless excluded or modified (Section 2—316), a warranty that the goods shall be merchantable is implied in a contract for their sale if the seller is a merchant with respect to goods of that kind. Under this section the serving for value of food or drink to be consumed either on the premises or elsewhere is a sale.

(2) Goods to be merchantable must be at least such as

(a) pass without objection in the trade under the contract description; and

(b) in the case of fungible goods, are of fair average quality within the description; and

(c) are fit for the ordinary purposes for which such goods are used; and

(d) run, within the variations permitted by the agreement, of even kind, quality and quantity within each unit and among all units involved; and

(e) are adequately contained, packaged, and labeled as the agreement may require; and

(f) conform to the promises or affirmations of fact made on the container or label if any.

(3) Unless excluded or modified (Section 2—316) other implied warranties may arise from course of dealing or usage of trade.

§ 2—315. Implied Warranty: Fitness for Particular Purpose.

Where the seller at the time of contracting has reason to know any particular purpose for which the goods are required and that the buyer is relying on the seller's skill or judgment to select or furnish suitable goods, there is unless excluded or modified under the next section an implied warranty that the goods shall be fit for such purpose.

§ 2—316. Exclusion or Modification of Warranties.

(1) Words or conduct relevant to the creation of an express warranty and words or conduct tending to negate or limit warranty shall be construed wherever reasonable as consistent with each other; but subject to the provisions of this Article on parol or extrinsic evidence (Section 2—202) negation or limitation is inoperative to the extent that such construction is unreasonable.

(2) Subject to subsection (3), to exclude or modify the implied warranty of merchantability or any part of it the language must mention merchantability and in case of a writing must be conspicuous, and to exclude or modify any implied warranty of fitness the exclusion must be by a writing and conspicuous. Language to exclude all implied warranties of fitness is sufficient if it states, for example, that "There are no warranties which extend beyond the description on the face hereof."

(3) Notwithstanding subsection (2)

(a) unless the circumstances indicate otherwise, all implied warranties are excluded by expressions like "as is", "with all faults" or other language which in common understanding calls the buyer's attention to the exclusion of warranties and makes plain that there is no implied warranty; and

(b) when the buyer before entering into the contract has examined the goods or the sample or model as fully as he desired or has refused to examine the goods there is no implied warranty with regard to defects which an examination ought in the circumstances to have revealed to him; and

(c) an implied warranty can also be excluded or modified by course of dealing or course of performance or usage of trade.

(4) Remedies for breach of warranty can be limited in accordance with the provisions of this Article on liquidation or limitation of damages and on contractual modification of remedy (Sections 2—718 and 2—719).

§ 2—317. Cumulation and Conflict of Warranties Express or Implied.

Warranties whether express or implied shall be construed as consistent with each other and as cumulative, but if such construction is unreasonable the intention of the parties shall determine which warranty is dominant. In ascertaining that intention the following rules apply:

(a) Exact or technical specifications displace an inconsistent sample or model or general language of description.

(b) A sample from an existing bulk displaces inconsistent general language of description.

(c) Express warranties displace inconsistent implied warranties other than an implied warranty of fitness for a particular purpose.

§ 2—318. Third Party Beneficiaries of Warranties Express or Implied.

Note: If this Act is introduced in the Congress of the United States this section should be omitted. (States to select one alternative.)

Alternative A

A seller's warranty whether express or implied extends to any natural person who is in the family or household of his buyer or who is a guest in his home if it is reasonable to expect that such person may use, consume or be affected by the goods and who is injured in person by breach of the warranty. A seller may not exclude or limit the operation of this section.

Alternative B

A seller's warranty whether express or implied extends to any natural person who may reasonably be expected to use, consume or be affected by the goods and who is injured in person by breach of the warranty. A seller may not exclude or limit the operation of this section.

Alternative C

A seller's warranty whether express or implied extends to any person who may reasonably be expected to use, consume or be affected by the goods and who is injured by breach of the warranty. A seller may not exclude or limit the operation of this section with respect to injury to the person of an individual to whom the warranty extends. As amended 1966.

§ 2—319. F.O.B. and F.A.S. Terms.

(1) Unless otherwise agreed the term F.O.B. (which means "free on board") at a named place, even though used only in connection with the stated price, is a delivery term under which

(a) when the term is F.O.B. the place of shipment, the seller must at that place ship the goods in the manner provided in this Article (Section 2—504) and bear the expense and risk of putting them into the possession of the carrier; or

(b) when the term is F.O.B. the place of destination, the seller must at his own expense and risk transport the goods to that place and there tender delivery of them in the manner provided in this Article (Section 2—503);

(c) when under either (a) or (b) the term is also F.O.B. vessel, car or other vehicle, the seller must in addition at his own expense and risk load the goods on board. If the term is F.O.B. vessel the buyer must name the vessel and in an appropriate case the seller must comply with the provisions of this Article on the form of bill of lading (Section 2—323).

(2) Unless otherwise agreed the term F.A.S. vessel (which means "free alongside") at a named port, even though used only in connection with the stated price, is a delivery term under which the seller must

(a) at his own expense and risk deliver the goods alongside the vessel in the manner usual in that port or on a dock designated and provided by the buyer; and

(b) obtain and tender a receipt for the goods in exchange for which the carrier is under a duty to issue a bill of lading.

(3) Unless otherwise agreed in any case falling within subsection (1)(a) or (c) or subsection (2) the buyer must seasonably give any needed instructions for making delivery, including when the term is F.A.S. or F.O.B. the loading berth of the vessel and in an appropriate case its name and sailing date. The seller may treat the failure of needed instructions as a failure of cooperation under this Article (Section 2—311). He may also at his option move the goods in any reasonable manner preparatory to delivery or shipment.

(4) Under the term F.O.B. vessel or F.A.S. unless otherwise agreed the buyer must make payment against tender of the required documents and the seller may not tender nor the buyer demand delivery of the goods in substitution for the documents.

§ 2—320. C.I.F. and C. & F. Terms.

(1) The term C.I.F. means that the price includes in a lump sum the cost of the goods and the insurance and freight to the named destination. The term C. & F. or C.F. means that the price so includes cost and freight to the named destination.

(2) Unless otherwise agreed and even though used only in connection with the stated price and destination, the term C.I.F. destination or its equivalent requires the seller at his own expense and risk to

(a) put the goods into the possession of a carrier at the port for shipment and obtain a negotiable bill or bills of lading covering the entire transportation to the named destination; and

(b) load the goods and obtain a receipt from the carrier (which may be contained in the bill of lading) showing that the freight has been paid or provided for; and

(c) obtain a policy or certificate of insurance, including any war risk insurance, of a kind and on terms then current at the port of shipment in the usual amount, in the currency of the contract, shown to cover the same goods covered by the bill of lading and providing for payment of loss to the order of the buyer or for the account of whom it may concern; but the seller may add to the price the amount of the premium for any such war risk insurance; and

(d) prepare an invoice of the goods and procure any other documents required to effect shipment or to comply with the contract; and

(e) forward and tender with commercial promptness all the documents in due form and with any indorsement necessary to perfect the buyer's rights.

(3) Unless otherwise agreed the term C. & F. or its equivalent has the same effect and imposes upon the seller the same obligations and risks as a C.I.F. term except the obligation as to insurance.

(4) Under the term C.I.F. or C. & F. unless otherwise agreed the buyer must make payment against tender of the required documents and the seller may not tender nor the buyer demand delivery of the goods in substitution for the documents.

§ 2—321. C.I.F. or C. & F.: "Net Landed Weights"; "Payment on Arrival"; Warranty of Condition on Arrival.

Under a contract containing a term C.I.F. or C. & F.

(1) Where the price is based on or is to be adjusted according to "net landed weights", "delivered weights", "out turn" quantity or quality or the like, unless otherwise agreed the seller must reasonably estimate the price. The payment due on tender of the documents called for by the contract is the amount so estimated, but after final adjustment of the price a settlement must be made with commercial promptness.

(2) An agreement described in subsection (1) or any warranty of quality or condition of the goods on arrival places upon the seller the risk of ordinary deterioration, shrinkage and the like in transportation but has no effect on the place or time of identification to the contract for sale or delivery or on the passing of the risk of loss.

(3) Unless otherwise agreed where the contract provides for payment on or after arrival of the goods the seller must before payment allow such preliminary inspection as is feasible; but if the goods are lost delivery of the documents and payment are due when the goods should have arrived.

§ 2—322. Delivery "Ex-Ship".

(1) Unless otherwise agreed a term for delivery of goods "ex-ship" (which means from the carrying vessel) or in equivalent language is not restricted to a particular ship and requires delivery from a ship which has reached a place at the named port of destination where goods of the kind are usually discharged.

(2) Under such a term unless otherwise agreed

(a) the seller must discharge all liens arising out of the carriage and furnish the buyer with a direction which puts the carrier under a duty to deliver the goods; and

(b) the risk of loss does not pass to the buyer until the goods leave the ship's tackle or are otherwise properly unloaded.

§ 2—323. Form of Bill of Lading Required in Overseas Shipment; "Overseas".

(1) Where the contract contemplates overseas shipment and contains a term C.I.F. or C. & F. or F.O.B. vessel, the seller unless otherwise agreed must obtain a negotiable bill of lading stating that the goods have been loaded on board or, in the case of a term C.I.F. or C. & F., received for shipment.

(2) Where in a case within subsection (1) a bill of lading has been issued in a set of parts, unless otherwise agreed if the documents are not to be sent from abroad the buyer may demand tender of the full set; otherwise only one part of the bill of lading need be tendered. Even if the agreement expressly requires a full set

(a) due tender of a single part is acceptable within the provisions of this Article on cure of improper delivery (subsection (1) of Section 2—508); and

(b) even though the full set is demanded, if the documents are sent from abroad the person tendering an incomplete set may nevertheless require payment upon furnishing an indemnity which the buyer in good faith deems adequate.

(3) A shipment by water or by air or a contract contemplating such shipment is "overseas" insofar as by usage of trade or agreement it is subject to the commercial, financing or shipping practices characteristic of international deep water commerce.

§ 2—324. "No Arrival, No Sale" Term.

Under a term "no arrival, no sale" or terms of like meaning, unless otherwise agreed,

(a) the seller must properly ship conforming goods and if they arrive by any means he must tender them on arrival but he assumes no obligation that the goods will arrive unless he has caused the non-arrival; and

(b) where without fault of the seller the goods are in part lost or have so deteriorated as no longer to conform to the contract or arrive after the contract time, the buyer may proceed as if there had been casualty to identified goods (Section 2—613).

§ 2—325. "Letter of Credit" Term; "Confirmed Credit".

(1) Failure of the buyer seasonably to furnish an agreed letter of credit is a breach of the contract for sale.

(2) The delivery to seller of a proper letter of credit suspends

the buyer's obligation to pay. If the letter of credit is dishonored, the seller may on seasonable notification to the buyer require payment directly from him.

(3) Unless otherwise agreed the term "letter of credit" or "banker's credit" in a contract for sale means an irrevocable credit issued by a financing agency of good repute and, where the shipment is overseas, of good international repute. The term "confirmed credit" means that the credit must also carry the direct obligation of such an agency which does business in the seller's financial market.

§ 2—326. Sale on Approval and Sale or Return; Consignment Sales and Rights of Creditors.

(1) Unless otherwise agreed, if delivered goods may be returned by the buyer even though they conform to the contract, the transaction is

(a) a "sale on approval" if the goods are delivered primarily for use, and

(b) a "sale or return" if the goods are delivered primarily for resale.

(2) Except as provided in subsection (3), goods held on approval are not subject to the claims of the buyer's creditors until acceptance; goods held on sale or return are subject to such claims while in the buyer's possession.

(3) Where goods are delivered to a person for sale and such person maintains a place of business at which he deals in goods of the kind involved, under a name other than the name of the person making delivery, then with respect to claims of creditors of the person conducting the business the goods are deemed to be on sale or return. The provisions of this subsection are applicable even though an agreement purports to reserve title to the person making delivery until payment or resale or uses such words as "on consignment" or "on memorandum". However, this subsection is not applicable if the person making delivery

(a) complies with an applicable law providing for a consignor's interest or the like to be evidenced by a sign, or

(b) establishes that the person conducting the business is generally known by his creditors to be substantially engaged in selling the goods of others, or

(c) complies with the filing provisions of the Article on Secured Transactions (Article 9).

(4) Any "or return" term of a contract for sale is to be treated as a separate contract for sale within the statute of frauds section of this Article (Section 2—201) and as contradicting the sale aspect of the contract within the provisions of this Article on parol or extrinsic evidence (Section 2—202).

§ 2—327. Special Incidents of Sale on Approval and Sale or Return.

(1) Under a sale on approval unless otherwise agreed

(a) although the goods are identified to the contract the risk of loss and the title do not pass to the buyer until acceptance; and

(b) use of the goods consistent with the purpose of trial is not acceptance but failure seasonably to notify the seller of election to return the goods is acceptance, and if the goods conform to the contract acceptance of any part is acceptance of the whole; and

(c) after due notification of election to return, the return is at the seller's risk and expense but a merchant buyer must follow any reasonable instructions.

(2) Under a sale or return unless otherwise agreed

(a) the option to return extends to the whole or any commercial unit of the goods while in substantially their original condition, but must be exercised seasonably; and

(b) the return is at the buyer's risk and expense.

§ 2—328. Sale by Auction.

(1) In a sale by auction if goods are put up in lots each lot is the subject of a separate sale.

(2) A sale by auction is complete when the auctioneer so announces by the fall of the hammer or in other customary manner. Where a bid is made while the hammer is falling in acceptance of a prior bid the auctioneer may in his discretion reopen the bidding or declare the goods sold under the bid on which the hammer was falling.

(3) Such a sale is with reserve unless the goods are in explicit terms put up without reserve. In an auction with reserve the auctioneer may withdraw the goods at any time until he announces completion of the sale. In an auction without reserve, after the auctioneer calls for bids on an article or lot, that article or lot cannot be withdrawn unless no bid is made within a reasonable time. In either case a bidder may retract his bid until the auctioneer's announcement of completion of the sale, but a bidder's retraction does not revive any previous bid.

(4) If the auctioneer knowingly receives a bid on the seller's behalf or the seller makes or procures such as bid, and notice has not been given that liberty for such bidding is reserved, the buyer may at his option avoid the sale or take the goods at the price of the last good faith bid prior to the completion of the sale. This subsection shall not apply to any bid at a forced sale.

Part 4 Title, Creditors and Good Faith Purchasers

§ 2—401. Passing of Title; Reservation for Security; Limited Application of This Section.

Each provision of this Article with regard to the rights, obligations and remedies of the seller, the buyer, purchasers or other third parties applies irrespective of title to the goods except where the provision refers to such title. Insofar as situations are not covered by the other provisions of this Article and matters concerning title became material the following rules apply:

(1) Title to goods cannot pass under a contract for sale prior to their identification to the contract (Section 2—501), and unless otherwise explicitly agreed the buyer acquires by their identification a special property as limited by this Act. Any retention or reservation by the seller of the title (property) in goods shipped or delivered to the buyer is limited in effect to a reservation of a security interest. Subject to these provisions and to the provisions of the Article on Secured Transactions (Article 9), title to goods passes from the seller to the buyer in any manner and on any conditions explicitly agreed on by the parties.

(2) Unless otherwise explicitly agreed title passes to the buyer at the time and place at which the seller completes his performance with reference to the physical delivery of the goods, despite any reservation of a security interest and even though a document of title is to be delivered at a different time or place; and in particular and despite any reservation of a security interest by the bill of lading

(a) if the contract requires or authorizes the seller to send the goods to the buyer but does not require him to deliver them at destination, title passes to the buyer at the time and place of shipment; but

(b) if the contract requires delivery at destination, title passes on tender there.

(3) Unless otherwise explicitly agreed where delivery is to be made without moving the goods,

(a) if the seller is to deliver a document of title, title passes at the time when and the place where he delivers such documents; or

(b) if the goods are at the time of contracting already identified and no documents are to be delivered, title passes at the time and place of contracting.

(4) A rejection or other refusal by the buyer to receive or retain the goods, whether or not justified, or a justified revocation of acceptance revests title to the goods in the seller. Such revesting occurs by operation of law and is not a "sale".

§ 2—402. Rights of Seller's Creditors Against Sold Goods.

(1) Except as provided in subsections (2) and (3), rights of unsecured creditors of the seller with respect to goods which have been identified to a contract for sale are subject to the buyer's rights to recover the goods under this Article (Sections 2—502 and 2—716).

(2) A creditor of the seller may treat a sale or an identification of goods to a contract for sale as void if as against him a retention of possession by the seller is fraudulent under any rule of law of the state where the goods are situated, except that retention of possession in good faith and current course of trade by a merchant-seller for a commercially reasonable time after a sale or identification is not fraudulent.

(3) Nothing in this Article shall be deemed to impair the rights of creditors of the seller

(a) under the provisions of the Article on Secured Transactions (Article 9); or

(b) where identification to the contract or delivery is made not in current course of trade but in satisfaction of or as security for a pre-existing claim for money, security or the like and is made under circumstances which under any rule of law of the state where the goods are situated would apart from this Article constitute the transaction a fraudulent transfer or voidable preference.

§ 2—403. Power to Transfer; Good Faith Purchase of Goods; "Entrusting".

(1) A purchaser of goods acquires all title which his transferor had or had power to transfer except that a purchaser of a limited interest acquires rights only to the extent of the interest purchased. A person with voidable title has power to transfer a good title to a good faith purchaser for value. When goods have been delivered under a transaction of purchase the purchaser has such power even though

(a) the transferor was deceived as to the identity of the purchaser, or

(b) the delivery was in exchange for a check which is later dishonored, or

(c) it was agreed that the transaction was to be a "cash sale", or

(d) the delivery was procured through fraud punishable as larcenous under the criminal law.

(2) Any entrusting of possession of goods to a merchant who deals in goods of that kind gives him power to transfer all rights of the entruster to a buyer in ordinary course of business.

(3) "Entrusting" includes any delivery and any acquiescence in retention of possession regardless of any condition expressed between the parties to the delivery or acquiescence and regardless of whether the procurement of the entrusting or the possessor's disposition of the goods have been such as to be larcenous under the criminal law.

(4) The rights of other purchasers of goods and of lien creditors are governed by the Articles on Secured Transactions (Article 9), Bulk Transfers (Article 6) and Documents of Title (Article 7).

Part 5 Performance

§ 2—501. Insurable Interest in Goods; Manner of Identification of Goods.

(1) The buyer obtains a special property and an insurable interest in goods by identification of existing goods as goods

to which the contract refers even though the goods so identified are non-conforming and he has an option to return or reject them. Such identification can be made at any time and in any manner explicitly agreed to by the parties. In the absence of explicit agreement identification occurs

(a) when the contract is made if it is for the sale of goods already existing and identified;

(b) if the contract is for the sale of future goods other than those described in paragraph (c), when goods are shipped, marked or otherwise designated by the seller as goods to which the contract refers;

(c) when the crops are planted or otherwise become growing crops or the young are conceived if the contract is for the sale of unborn young to be born within twelve months after contracting or for the sale of crops to be harvested within twelve months or the next normal harvest season after contracting whichever is longer.

(2) The seller retains an insurable interest in goods so long as title to or any security interest in the goods remains in him and where the identification is by the seller alone he may until default or insolvency or notification to the buyer that the identification is final substitute other goods for those identified.

(3) Nothing in this section impairs any insurable interest recognized under any other statute or rule of law.

§ 2—502. Buyer's Right to Goods on Seller's Insolvency.

(1) Subject to subsection (2) and even though the goods have not been shipped a buyer who has paid a part or all of the price of goods in which he has a special property under the provisions of the immediately preceding section may on making and keeping good a tender of any unpaid portion of their price recover them from the seller if the seller becomes insolvent within ten days after receipt of the first installment on their price.

(2) If the identification creating his special property has been made by the buyer he acquires the right to recover the goods only if they conform to the contract for sale.

§ 2—503. Manner of Seller's Tender of Delivery.

(1) Tender of delivery requires that the seller put and hold conforming goods at the buyer's disposition and give the buyer any notification reasonably necessary to enable him to take delivery. The manner, time and place for tender are determined by the agreement and this Article, and in particular

(a) tender must be at a reasonable hour, and if it is of goods they must be kept available for the period reasonably necessary to enable the buyer to take possession; but

(b) unless otherwise agreed the buyer must furnish facilities reasonably suited to the receipt of the goods.

(2) Where the case is within the next section respecting shipment tender requires that the seller comply with its provisions.

(3) Where the seller is required to deliver at a particular destination tender requires that he comply with subsection (1) and also in any appropriate case tender documents as described in subsections (4) and (5) of this section.

(4) Where goods are in the possession of a bailee and are to be delivered without being moved

(a) tender requires that the seller either tender a negotiable document of title covering such goods or procure acknowledgment by the bailee of the buyer's right to possession of the goods; but

(b) tender to the buyer of a non-negotiable document of title or of a written direction to the bailee to deliver is sufficient tender unless the buyer seasonably objects, and receipt by the bailee of notification of the buyer's rights fixes those rights as against the bailee and all third persons; but risk of loss of the goods and of any failure by the bailee to honor the non-negotiable document of title or to obey the direction remains on the seller until the buyer has had a reasonable time to present the document or direction, and a refusal by the bailee to honor the document or to obey the direction defeats the tender.

(5) Where the contract requires the seller to deliver documents

(a) he must tender all such documents in correct form, except as provided in this Article with respect to bills of lading in a set (subsection (2) of Section 2—323); and

(b) tender through customary banking channels is sufficient and dishonor of a draft accompanying the documents constitutes non-acceptance or rejection.

§ 2—504. Shipment by Seller.

Where the seller is required or authorized to send the goods to the buyer and the contract does not require him to deliver them at a particular destination, then unless otherwise agreed he must

(a) put the goods in the possession of such a carrier and make such a contract for their transportation as may be reasonable having regard to the nature of the goods and other circumstances of the case; and

(b) obtain and promptly deliver or tender in due form any document necessary to enable the buyer to obtain possession of the goods or otherwise required by the agreement or by usage of trade; and

(c) promptly notify the buyer of the shipment.

Failure to notify the buyer under paragraph (c) or to make a proper contract under paragraph (a) is a ground for rejection only if material delay or loss ensues.

§ 2—505. Seller's Shipment under Reservation.

(1) Where the seller has identified goods to the contract by or before shipment:

(a) his procurement of a negotiable bill of lading to his own order or otherwise reserves in him a security interest in the goods. His procurement of the bill to the order of a financing agency or of the buyer indicates in addition only the seller's expectation of transferring that interest to the person named.

(b) a non-negotiable bill of lading to himself or his nominee reserves possession of the goods as security but except in a case of conditional delivery (subsection (2) of Section 2—507) a non-negotiable bill of lading naming the buyer as consignee reserves no security interest even though the seller retains possession of the bill of lading.

(2) When shipment by the seller with reservation of a security interest is in violation of the contract for sale it constitutes an improper contract for transportation within the preceding section but impairs neither the rights given to the buyer by shipment and identification of the goods to the contract nor the seller's powers as a holder of a negotiable document.

§ 2—506. Rights of Financing Agency.

(1) A financing agency by paying or purchasing for value a draft which relates to a shipment of goods acquires to the extent of the payment or purchase and in addition to its own rights under the draft and any document of title securing it any rights of the shipper in the goods including the right to stop delivery and the shipper's right to have the draft honored by the buyer.

(2) The right to reimbursement of a financing agency which has in good faith honored or purchased the draft under commitment to or authority from the buyer is not impaired by subsequent discovery of defects with reference to any relevant document which was apparently regular on its face.

§ 2—507. Effect of Seller's Tender; Delivery on Condition.

(1) Tender of delivery is a condition to the buyer's duty to accept the goods and, unless otherwise agreed, to his duty to pay for them. Tender entitles the seller to acceptance of the goods and to payment according to the contract.

(2) Where payment is due and demanded on the delivery to the buyer of goods or documents of title, his right as against the seller to retain or dispose of them is conditional upon his making the payment due.

§ 2—508. Cure by Seller of Improper Tender or Delivery; Replacement.

(1) Where any tender or delivery by the seller is rejected because non-conforming and the time for performance has not yet expired, the seller may seasonably notify the buyer of his intention to cure and may then within the contract time make a conforming delivery.

(2) Where the buyer rejects a non-conforming tender which the seller had reasonable grounds to believe would be acceptable with or without money allowance the seller may if he seasonably notifies the buyer have a further reasonable time to substitute a conforming tender.

§ 2—509. Risk of Loss in the Absence of Breach.

(1) Where the contract requires or authorizes the seller to ship the goods by carrier

(a) if it does not require him to deliver them at a particular destination, the risk of loss passes to the buyer when the goods are duly delivered to the carrier even though the shipment is under reservation (Section 2—505); but

(b) if it does require him to deliver them at a particular destination and the goods are there duly tendered while in the possession of the carrier, the risk of loss passes to the buyer when the goods are there duly so tendered as to enable the buyer to take delivery.

(2) Where the goods are held by a bailee to be delivered without being moved, the risk of loss passes to the buyer

(a) on his receipt of a negotiable document of title covering the goods; or

(b) on acknowledgment by the bailee of the buyer's right to possession of the goods; or

(c) after his receipt of a non-negotiable document of title or other written direction to deliver, as provided in subsection (4)(b) of Section 2—503.

(3) In any case not within subsection (1) or (2), the risk of loss passes to the buyer on his receipt of the goods if the seller is a merchant; otherwise the risk passes to the buyer on tender of delivery.

(4) The provisions of this section are subject to contrary agreement of the parties and to the provisions of this Article on sale on approval (Section 2—327) and on effect of breach on risk of loss (Section 2—510).

§ 2—510. Effect of Breach on Risk of Loss.

(1) Where a tender or delivery of goods so fails to conform to the contract as to give a right of rejection the risk of their loss remains on the seller until cure or acceptance.

(2) Where the buyer rightfully revokes acceptance he may to the extent of any deficiency in his effective insurance coverage treat the risk of loss as having rested on the seller from the beginning.

(3) Where the buyer as to conforming goods already identified to the contract for sale repudiates or is otherwise in breach before risk of their loss has passed to him, the seller may to the extent of any deficiency in his effective insurance coverage treat the risk of loss as resting on the buyer for a commercially reasonable time.

§ 2—511. Tender of Payment by Buyer; Payment by Check.

(1) Unless otherwise agreed tender of payment is a condition to the seller's duty to tender and complete any delivery.

(2) Tender of payment is sufficient when made by any means or in any manner current in the ordinary course of business unless the seller demands payment in legal

tender and gives any extension of time reasonably necessary to procure it.

(3) Subject to the provisions of this Act on the effect of an instrument on an obligation (Section 3—310), payment by check is conditional and is defeated as between the parties by dishonor of the check on due presentment.

§ 2—512. Payment by Buyer Before Inspection.

(1) Where the contract requires payment before inspection non-conformity of the goods does not excuse the buyer from so making payment unless

(a) the non-conformity appears without inspection; or

(b) despite tender of the required documents the circumstances would justify injunction against honor under the provisions of this Act (Section 5—114).

(2) Payment pursuant to subsection (1) does not constitute an acceptance of goods or impair the buyer's right to inspect or any of his remedies.

§ 2—513. Buyer's Right to Inspection of Goods.

(1) Unless otherwise agreed and subject to subsection (3), where goods are tendered or delivered or identified to the contract for sale, the buyer has a right before payment or acceptance to inspect them at any reasonable place and time and in any reasonable manner. When the seller is required or authorized to send the goods to the buyer, the inspection may be after their arrival.

(2) Expenses of inspection must be borne by the buyer but may be recovered from the seller if the goods do not conform and are rejected.

(3) Unless otherwise agreed and subject to the provisions of this Article on C.I.F. contracts (subsection (3) of Section 2—321), the buyer is not entitled to inspect the goods before payment of the price when the contract provides

(a) for delivery "C.O.D." or on other like terms; or

(b) for payment against documents of title, except where such payment is due only after the goods are to become available for inspection.

(4) A place or method of inspection fixed by the parties is presumed to be exclusive but unless otherwise expressly agreed it does not postpone identification or shift the place for delivery or for passing the risk of loss. If compliance becomes impossible, inspection shall be as provided in this section unless the place or method fixed was clearly intended as an indispensable condition failure of which avoids the contract.

§ 2—514. When Documents Deliverable on Acceptance; When on Payment.

Unless otherwise agreed documents against which a draft is drawn are to be delivered to the drawee on acceptance of the draft if it is payable more than three days after presentment; otherwise, only on payment.

§ 2—515. Preserving Evidence of Goods in Dispute.

In furtherance of the adjustment of any claim or dispute

(a) either party on reasonable notification to the other and for the purpose of ascertaining the facts and preserving evidence has the right to inspect, test and sample the goods including such of them as may be in the possession or control of the other; and

(b) the parties may agree to a third party inspection or survey to determine the conformity or condition of the goods and may agree that the findings shall be binding upon them in any subsequent litigation or adjustment.

Part 6 Breach, Repudiation and Excuse

§ 2—601. Buyer's Rights on Improper Delivery.

Subject to the provisions of this Article on breach in installment contracts (Section 2—612) and unless otherwise agreed under the sections on contractual limitations of remedy (Sections 2—718 and 2—719), if the goods or the tender of delivery fail in any respect to conform to the contract, the buyer may

(a) reject the whole; or

(b) accept the whole; or

(c) accept any commercial unit or units and reject the rest.

§ 2—602. Manner and Effect of Rightful Rejection.

(1) Rejection of goods must be within a reasonable time after their delivery or tender. It is ineffective unless the buyer seasonably notifies the seller.

(2) Subject to the provisions of the two following sections on rejected goods (Sections 2—603 and 2—604),

(a) after rejection any exercise of ownership by the buyer with respect to any commercial unit is wrongful as against the seller; and

(b) if the buyer has before rejection taken physical possession of goods in which he does not have a security interest under the provisions of this Article (subsection (3) of Section 2—711), he is under a duty after rejection to hold them with reasonable care at the seller's disposition for a time sufficient to permit the seller to remove them; but

(c) the buyer has no further obligations with regard to goods rightfully rejected.

(3) The seller's rights with respect to goods wrongfully rejected are governed by the provisions of this Article on Seller's remedies in general (Section 2—703).

§ 2—603. Merchant Buyer's Duties as to Rightfully Rejected Goods.

(1) Subject to any security interest in the buyer (subsection (3) of Section 2—711), when the seller has no agent or place of business at the market of rejection a merchant

buyer is under a duty after rejection of goods in his possession or control to follow any reasonable instructions received from the seller with respect to the goods and in the absence of such instructions to make reasonable efforts to sell them for the seller's account if they are perishable or threaten to decline in value speedily. Instructions are not reasonable if on demand indemnity for expenses is not forthcoming.

(2) When the buyer sells goods under subsection (1), he is entitled to reimbursement from the seller or out of the proceeds for reasonable expenses of caring for and selling them, and if the expenses include no selling commission then to such commission as is usual in the trade or if there is none to a reasonable sum not exceeding ten per cent on the gross proceeds.

(3) In complying with this section the buyer is held only to good faith and good faith conduct hereunder is neither acceptance nor conversion nor the basis of an action for damages.

§ 2—604. Buyer's Options as to Salvage of Rightfully Rejected Goods.

Subject to the provisions of the immediately preceding section on perishables if the seller gives no instructions within a reasonable time after notification of rejection the buyer may store the rejected goods for the seller's account or reship them to him or resell them for the seller's account with reimbursement as provided in the preceding section. Such action is not acceptance or conversion.

§ 2—605. Waiver of Buyer's Objections by Failure to Particularize.

(1) The buyer's failure to state in connection with rejection a particular defect which is ascertainable by reasonable inspection precludes him from relying on the unstated defect to justify rejection or to establish breach

(a) where the seller could have cured it if stated seasonably; or

(b) between merchants when the seller has after rejection made a request in writing for a full and final written statement of all defects on which the buyer proposes to rely.

(2) Payment against documents made without reservation of rights precludes recovery of the payment for defects apparent on the face of the documents.

§ 2—606. What Constitutes Acceptance of Goods.

(1) Acceptance of goods occurs when the buyer

(a) after a reasonable opportunity to inspect the goods signifies to the seller that the goods are conforming or that he will take or retain them in spite of their nonconformity; or

(b) fails to make an effective rejection (subsection (1) of Section 2—602), but such acceptance does not

occur until the buyer has had a reasonable opportunity to inspect them; or

(c) does any act inconsistent with the seller's ownership; but if such act is wrongful as against the seller it is an acceptance only if ratified by him.

(2) Acceptance of a part of any commercial unit is acceptance of that entire unit.

§ 2—607. Effect of Acceptance; Notice of Breach; Burden of Establishing Breach After Acceptance; Notice of Claim or Litigation to Person Answerable Over.

(1) The buyer must pay at the contract rate for any goods accepted.

(2) Acceptance of goods by the buyer precludes rejection of the goods accepted and if made with knowledge of a non-conformity cannot be revoked because of it unless the acceptance was on the reasonable assumption that the non-conformity would be seasonably cured but acceptance does not of itself impair any other remedy provided by this Article for non-conformity.

(3) Where a tender has been accepted

(a) the buyer must within a reasonable time after he discovers or should have discovered any breach notify the seller of breach or be barred from any remedy; and

(b) if the claim is one for infringement or the like (subsection (3) of Section 2—312) and the buyer is sued as a result of such a breach he must so notify the seller within a reasonable time after he receives notice of the litigation or be barred from any remedy over for liability established by the litigation.

(4) The burden is on the buyer to establish any breach with respect to the goods accepted.

(5) Where the buyer is sued for breach of a warranty or other obligation for which his seller is answerable over

(a) he may give his seller written notice of the litigation. If the notice states that the seller may come in and defend and that if the seller does not do so he will be bound in any action against him by his buyer by any determination of fact common to the two litigations, then unless the seller after seasonable receipt of the notice does come in and defend he is so bound.

(b) if the claim is one for infringement or the like (subsection (3) of Section 2—312) the original seller may demand in writing that his buyer turn over to him control of the litigation including settlement or else be barred from any remedy over and if he also agrees to bear all expense and to satisfy any adverse judgment, then unless the buyer after seasonable receipt of the demand does turn over control the buyer is so barred.

(6) The provisions of subsections (3), (4) and (5) apply to any obligation of a buyer to hold the seller harmless against infringement or the like (subsection (3) of Section 2—312).

§ 2—608. Revocation of Acceptance in Whole or in Part.

(1) The buyer may revoke his acceptance of a lot or commercial unit whose non-conformity substantially impairs its value to him if he has accepted it

(a) on the reasonable assumption that its nonconformity would be cured and it has not been seasonably cured; or

(b) without discovery of such non-conformity if his acceptance was reasonably induced either by the difficulty of discovery before acceptance or by the seller's assurances.

(2) Revocation of acceptance must occur within a reasonable time after the buyer discovers or should have discovered the ground for it and before any substantial change in condition of the goods which is not caused by their own defects. It is not effective until the buyer notifies the seller of it.

(3) A buyer who so revokes has the same rights and duties with regard to the goods involved as if he had rejected them.

§ 2—609. Right to Adequate Assurance of Performance.

(1) A contract for sale imposes an obligation on each party that the other's expectation of receiving due performance will not be impaired. When reasonable grounds for insecurity arise with respect to the performance of either party the other may in writing demand adequate assurance of due performance and until he receives such assurance may if commercially reasonable suspend any performance for which he has not already received the agreed return.

(2) Between merchants the reasonableness of grounds for insecurity and the adequacy of any assurance offered shall be determined according to commercial standards.

(3) Acceptance of any improper delivery or payment does not prejudice the party's right to demand adequate assurance of future performance.

(4) After receipt of a justified demand failure to provide within a reasonable time not exceeding thirty days such assurance of due performance as is adequate under the circumstances of the particular case is a repudiation of the contract.

§ 2—610. Anticipatory Repudiation.

When either party repudiates the contract with respect to a performance not yet due the loss of which will substantially impair the value of the contract to the other, the aggrieved party may

(a) for a commercially reasonable time await performance by the repudiating party; or

(b) resort to any remedy for breach (Section 2—703 or Section 2—711), even though he has notified the repudiating party that he would await the latter's performance and has urged retraction; and

(c) in either case suspend his own performance or proceed in accordance with the provisions of this Article on the seller's right to identify goods to the contract notwithstanding breach or to salvage unfinished goods (Section 2—704).

§ 2—611. Retraction of Anticipatory Repudiation.

(1) Until the repudiating party's next performance is due he can retract his repudiation unless the aggrieved party has since the repudiation cancelled or materially changed his position or otherwise indicated that he considers the repudiation final.

(2) Retraction may be by any method which clearly indicates to the aggrieved party that the repudiating party intends to perform, but must include any assurance justifiably demanded under the provisions of this Article (Section 2—609).

(3) Retraction reinstates the repudiating party's rights under the contract with due excuse and allowance to the aggrieved party for any delay occasioned by the repudiation.

§ 2—612. "Installment Contract"; Breach.

(1) An "installment contract" is one which requires or authorizes the delivery of goods in separate lots to be separately accepted, even though the contract contains a clause "each delivery is a separate contract" or its equivalent.

(2) The buyer may reject any installment which is non-conforming if the non-conformity substantially impairs the value of that installment and cannot be cured or if the non-conformity is a defect in the required documents; but if the non-conformity does not fall within subsection (3) and the seller gives adequate assurance of its cure the buyer must accept that installment.

(3) Whenever non-conformity or default with respect to one or more installments substantially impairs the value of the whole contract there is a breach of the whole. But the aggrieved party reinstates the contract if he accepts a non-conforming installment without seasonably notifying of cancellation or if he brings an action with respect only to past installments or demands performance as to future installments.

§ 2—613. Casualty to Identified Goods.

Where the contract requires for its performance goods identified when the contract is made, and the goods suffer casualty without fault of either party before the risk of loss passes to the buyer, or in a proper case under a "no arrival, no sale" term (Section 2—324) then

(a) if the loss is total the contract is avoided; and

(b) if the loss is partial or the goods have so deteriorated as no longer to conform to the contract the buyer may nevertheless demand inspection and at his option either treat the contract as voided or accept the goods with due allowance from the contract price for the deterioration or the deficiency in quantity but without further right against the seller.

§ 2—614. Substituted Performance.

(1) Where without fault of either party the agreed berthing, loading, or unloading facilities fail or an agreed type of carrier becomes unavailable or the agreed manner of delivery otherwise becomes commercially impracticable but a commercially reasonable substitute is available, such substitute performance must be tendered and accepted.

(2) If the agreed means or manner of payment fails because of domestic or foreign governmental regulation, the seller may withhold or stop delivery unless the buyer provides a means or manner of payment which is commercially a substantial equivalent. If delivery has already been taken, payment by the means or in the manner provided by the regulation discharges the buyer's obligation unless the regulation is discriminatory, oppressive or predatory.

§ 2—615. Excuse by Failure of Presupposed Conditions.

Except so far as a seller may have assumed a greater obligation and subject to the preceding section on substituted performance:

(a) Delay in delivery or non-delivery in whole or in part by a seller who complies with paragraphs (b) and (c) is not a breach of his duty under a contract for sale if performance as agreed has been made impracticable by the occurrence of a contingency the nonoccurrence of which was a basic assumption on which the contract was made or by compliance in good faith with any applicable foreign or domestic governmental regulation or order whether or not it later proves to be invalid.

(b) Where the causes mentioned in paragraph (a) affect only a part of the seller's capacity to perform, he must allocate production and deliveries among his customers but may at his option include regular customers not then under contract as well as his own requirements for further manufacture. He may so allocate in any manner which is fair and reasonable.

(c) The seller must notify the buyer seasonably that there will be delay or non-delivery and, when allocation is required under paragraph (b), of the estimated quota thus made available for the buyer.

§ 2—616. Procedure on Notice Claiming Excuse.

(1) Where the buyer receives notification of a material or indefinite delay or an allocation justified under the preceding section he may by written notification to the seller as to any delivery concerned, and where the prospective deficiency substantially impairs the value of the whole contract under the provisions of this Article relating to breach of installment contracts (Section 2—612), then also as to the whole,

(a) terminate and thereby discharge any unexecuted portion of the contract; or

(b) modify the contract by agreeing to take his available quota in substitution.

(2) If after receipt of such notification from the seller the buyer fails so to modify the contract within a reasonable time not exceeding thirty days the contract lapses with respect to any deliveries affected.

(3) The provisions of this section may not be negated by agreement except in so far as the seller has assumed a greater obligation under the preceding section.

Part 7 Remedies

§ 2—701. Remedies for Breach of Collateral Contracts Not Impaired.

Remedies for breach of any obligation or promise collateral or ancillary to a contract for sale are not impaired by the provisions of this Article.

§ 2—702. Seller's Remedies on Discovery of Buyer's Insolvency.

(1) Where the seller discovers the buyer to be insolvent he may refuse delivery except for cash including payment for all goods theretofore delivered under the contract, and stop delivery under this Article (Section 2—705).

(2) Where the seller discovers that the buyer has received goods on credit while insolvent he may reclaim the goods upon demand made within ten days after the receipt, but if misrepresentation of solvency has been made to the particular seller in writing within three months before delivery the ten day limitation does not apply. Except as provided in this subsection the seller may not base a right to reclaim goods on the buyer's fraudulent or innocent misrepresentation of solvency or of intent to pay.

(3) The seller's right to reclaim under subsection (2) is subject to the rights of a buyer in ordinary course or other good faith purchaser under this Article (Section 2—403). Successful reclamation of goods excludes all other remedies with respect to them.

§ 2—703. Seller's Remedies in General.

Where the buyer wrongfully rejects or revokes acceptance of goods or fails to make a payment due on or before delivery or repudiates with respect to a part or the whole, then with respect to any goods directly affected and, if the breach is of the whole contract (Section 2—612), then also with respect to the whole undelivered balance, the aggrieved seller may

(a) withhold delivery of such goods;

(b) stop delivery by any bailee as hereafter provided (Section 2—705);

(c) proceed under the next section respecting goods still unidentified to the contract;

(d) resell and recover damages as hereafter provided (Section 2—706);

(e) recover damages for non-acceptance (Section 2—708) or in a proper case the price (Section 2—709);

(f) cancel.

§ 2—704. Seller's Right to Identify Goods to the Contract Notwithstanding Breach or to Salvage Unfinished Goods.

(1) An aggrieved seller under the preceding section may

(a) identify to the contract conforming goods not already identified if at the time he learned of the breach they are in his possession or control;

(b) treat as the subject of resale goods which have demonstrably been intended for the particular contract even though those goods are unfinished.

(2) Where the goods are unfinished an aggrieved seller may in the exercise of reasonable commercial judgment for the purposes of avoiding loss and of effective realization either complete the manufacture and wholly identify the goods to the contract or cease manufacture and resell for scrap or salvage value or proceed in any other reasonable manner.

§ 2—705. Seller's Stoppage of Delivery in Transit or Otherwise.

(1) The seller may stop delivery of goods in the possession of a carrier or other bailee when he discovers the buyer to be insolvent (Section 2—702) and may stop delivery of carload, truckload, planeload or larger shipments of express or freight when the buyer repudiates or fails to make a payment due before delivery or if for any other reason the seller has a right to withhold or reclaim the goods.

(2) As against such buyer the seller may stop delivery until

(a) receipt of the goods by the buyer; or

(b) acknowledgment to the buyer by any bailee of the goods except a carrier that the bailee holds the goods for the buyer; or

(c) such acknowledgment to the buyer by a carrier by reshipment or as warehouseman; or

(d) negotiation to the buyer of any negotiable document of title covering the goods.

(3) (a) To stop delivery the seller must so notify as to enable the bailee by reasonable diligence to prevent delivery of the goods.

(b) After such notification the bailee must hold and deliver the goods according to the directions of the seller but the seller is liable to the bailee for any ensuing charges or damages.

(c) If a negotiable document of title has been issued for goods the bailee is not obliged to obey a notification to stop until surrender of the document.

(d) A carrier who has issued a non-negotiable bill of lading is not obliged to obey a notification to stop received from a person other than the consignor.

§ 2—706. Seller's Resale Including Contract for Resale.

(1) Under the conditions stated in Section 2—703 on seller's remedies, the seller may resell the goods concerned or the undelivered balance thereof. Where the resale is made in good faith and in a commercially reasonable manner the seller may recover the difference between the resale price and the contract price together with any incidental damages allowed under the provisions of this Article (Section 2—710), but less expenses saved in consequence of the buyer's breach.

(2) Except as otherwise provided in subsection (3) or unless otherwise agreed resale may be at public or private sale including sale by way of one or more contracts to sell or of identification to an existing contract of the seller. Sale may be as a unit or in parcels and at any time and place and on any terms but every aspect of the sale including the method, manner, time, place and terms must be commercially reasonable. The resale must be reasonably identified as referring to the broken contract, but it is not necessary that the goods be in existence or that any or all of them have been identified to the contract before the breach.

(3) Where the resale is at private sale the seller must give the buyer reasonable notification of his intention to resell.

(4) Where the resale is at public sale

(a) only identified goods can be sold except where there is a recognized market for a public sale of futures in goods of the kind; and

(b) it must be made at a usual place or market for public sale if one is reasonably available and except in the case of goods which are perishable or threaten to decline in value speedily the seller must give the buyer reasonable notice of the time and place of the resale; and

(c) if the goods are not to be within the view of those attending the sale the notification of sale must state the place where the goods are located and provide for their reasonable inspection by prospective bidders; and

(d) the seller may buy.

(5) A purchaser who buys in good faith at a resale takes the goods free of any rights of the original buyer even though the seller fails to comply with one or more of the requirements of this section.

(6) The seller is not accountable to the buyer for any profit made on any resale. A person in the position of a seller (Section 2—707) or a buyer who has rightfully rejected or justifiably revoked acceptance must account for any excess over the amount of his security interest, as hereinafter defined (subsection (3) of Section 2—711).

§ 2—707. "Person in the Position of a Seller".

(1) A "person in the position of a seller" includes as against a principal an agent who has paid or become responsible for the price of goods on behalf of his principal

or anyone who otherwise holds a security interest or other right in goods similar to that of a seller.

(2) A person in the position of a seller may as provided in this Article withhold or stop delivery (Section 2—705) and resell (Section 2—706) and recover incidental damages (Section 2—710).

§ 2—708. Seller's Damages for Non-Acceptance or Repudiation.

(1) Subject to subsection (2) and to the provisions of this Article with respect to proof of market price (Section 2—723), the measure of damages for non-acceptance or repudiation by the buyer is the difference between the market price at the time and place for tender and the unpaid contract price together with any incidental damages provided in this Article (Section 2—710), but less expenses saved in consequence of the buyer's breach.

(2) If the measure of damages provided in subsection (1) is inadequate to put the seller in as good a position as performance would have done then the measure of damages is the profit (including reasonable overhead) which the seller would have made from full performance by the buyer, together with any incidental damages provided in this Article (Section 2—710), due allowance for costs reasonably incurred and due credit for payments or proceeds of resale.

§ 2—709. Action for the Price.

(1) When the buyer fails to pay the price as it becomes due the seller may recover, together with any incidental damages under the next section, the price

(a) of goods accepted or of conforming goods lost or damaged within a commercially reasonable time after risk of their loss has passed to the buyer; and

(b) of goods identified to the contract if the seller is unable after reasonable effort to resell them at a reasonable price or the circumstances reasonably indicate that such effort will be unavailing.

(2) Where the seller sues for the price he must hold for the buyer any goods which have been identified to the contract and are still in his control except that if resale becomes possible he may resell them at any time prior to the collection of the judgment. The net proceeds of any such resale must be credited to the buyer and payment of the judgment entitles him to any goods not resold.

(3) After the buyer has wrongfully rejected or revoked acceptance of the goods or has failed to make a payment due or has repudiated (Section 2—610), a seller who is held not entitled to the price under this section shall nevertheless be awarded damages for non-acceptance under the preceding section.

§ 2—710. Seller's Incidental Damages.

Incidental damages to an aggrieved seller include any commercially reasonable charges, expenses or commis-

sions incurred in stopping delivery, in the transportation, care and custody of goods after the buyer's breach, in connection with return or resale of the goods or otherwise resulting from the breach.

§ 2—711. Buyer's Remedies in General; Buyer's Security Interest in Rejected Goods.

(1) Where the seller fails to make delivery or repudiates or the buyer rightfully rejects or justifiably revokes acceptance then with respect to any goods involved, and with respect to the whole if the breach goes to the whole contract (Section 2—612), the buyer may cancel and whether or not he has done so may in addition to recovering so much of the price as has been paid

(a) "cover" and have damages under the next section as to all the goods affected whether or not they have been identified to the contract; or

(b) recover damages for non-delivery as provided in this Article (Section 2—713).

(2) Where the seller fails to deliver or repudiates the buyer may also

(a) if the goods have been identified recover them as provided in this Article (Section 2—502); or

(b) in a proper case obtain specific performance or replevy the goods as provided in this Article (Section 2—716).

(3) On rightful rejection or justifiable revocation of acceptance a buyer has a security interest in goods in his possession or control for any payments made on their price and any expenses reasonably incurred in their inspection, receipt, transportation, care and custody and may hold such goods and resell them in like manner as an aggrieved seller (Section 2—706).

§ 2—712. "Cover"; Buyer's Procurement of Substitute Goods.

(1) After a breach within the preceding section the buyer may "cover" by making in good faith and without unreasonable delay any reasonable purchase of or contract to purchase goods in substitution for those due from the seller.

(2) The buyer may recover from the seller as damages the difference between the cost of cover and the contract price together with any incidental or consequential damages as hereinafter defined (Section 2—715), but less expenses saved in consequence of the seller's breach.

(3) Failure of the buyer to effect cover within this section does not bar him from any other remedy.

§ 2—713. Buyer's Damages for Non-Delivery or Repudiation.

(1) Subject to the provisions of this Article with respect to proof of market price (Section 2—723), the measure of

damages for non-delivery or repudiation by the seller is the difference between the market price at the time when the buyer learned of the breach and the contract price together with any incidental and consequential damages provided in this Article (Section 2—715), but less expenses saved in consequence of the seller's breach.

(2) Market price is to be determined as of the place for tender or, in cases of rejection after arrival or revocation of acceptance, as of the place of arrival.

§ 2—714. Buyer's Damages for Breach in Regard to Accepted Goods.

(1) Where the buyer has accepted goods and given notification (subsection (3) of Section 2—607) he may recover as damages for any non-conformity of tender the loss resulting in the ordinary course of events from the seller's breach as determined in any manner which is reasonable.

(2) The measure of damages for breach of warranty is the difference at the time and place of acceptance between the value of the goods accepted and the value they would have had if they had been as warranted, unless special circumstances show proximate damages of a different amount.

(3) In a proper case any incidental and consequential damages under the next section may also be recovered.

§ 2—715. Buyer's Incidental and Consequential Damages.

(1) Incidental damages resulting from the seller's breach include expenses reasonably incurred in inspection, receipt, transportation and care and custody of goods rightfully rejected, any commercially reasonable charges, expenses or commissions in connection with effecting cover and any other reasonable expense incident to the delay or other breach.

(2) Consequential damages resulting from the seller's breach include

(a) any loss resulting from general or particular requirements and needs of which the seller at the time of contracting had reason to know and which could not reasonably be prevented by cover or otherwise; and

(b) injury to person or property proximately resulting from any breach of warranty.

§ 2—716. Buyer's Right to Specific Performance or Replevin.

(1) Specific performance may be decreed where the goods are unique or in other proper circumstances.

(2) The decree for specific performance may include such terms and conditions as to payment of the price, damages, or other relief as the court may deem just.

(3) The buyer has a right of replevin for goods identified to the contract if after reasonable effort he is unable to effect cover for such goods or the circumstances reasonably indicate that such effort will be unavailing or if the goods have been shipped under reservation and satisfaction of the security interest in them has been made or tendered.

§ 2—717. Deduction of Damages From the Price.

The buyer on notifying the seller of his intention to do so may deduct all or any part of the damages resulting from any breach of the contract from any part of the price still due under the same contract.

§ 2—718. Liquidation or Limitation of Damages; Deposits.

(1) Damages for breach by either party may be liquidated in the agreement but only at an amount which is reasonable in the light of the anticipated or actual harm caused by the breach, the difficulties of proof of loss, and the inconvenience or nonfeasibility of otherwise obtaining an adequate remedy. A term fixing unreasonably large liquidated damages is void as a penalty.

(2) Where the seller justifiably withholds delivery of goods because of the buyer's breach, the buyer is entitled to restitution of any amount by which the sum of his payments exceeds

(a) the amount to which the seller is entitled by virtue of terms liquidating the seller's damages in accordance with subsection (1), or

(b) in the absence of such terms, twenty per cent of the value of the total performance for which the buyer is obligated under the contract or $500, whichever is smaller.

(3) The buyer's right to restitution under subsection (2) is subject to offset to the extent that the seller establishes

(a) a right to recover damages under the provisions of this Article other than subsection (1), and

(b) the amount or value of any benefits received by the buyer directly or indirectly by reason of the contract.

(4) Where a seller has received payment in goods their reasonable value or the proceeds of their resale shall be treated as payments for the purposes of subsection (2); but if the seller has notice of the buyer's breach before reselling goods received in part performance, his resale is subject to the conditions laid down in this Article on resale by an aggrieved seller (Section 2—706).

§ 2—719. Contractual Modification or Limitation of Remedy.

(1) Subject to the provisions of subsections (2) and (3) of this section and of the preceding section on liquidation and limitation of damages,

(a) the agreement may provide for remedies in addition to or in substitution for those provided in this Article and may limit or alter the measure of damages recoverable under this Article, as by limiting the buyer's remedies to return of the goods and repayment of the price or to repair and replacement of non-conforming goods or parts; and

(b) resort to a remedy as provided is optional unless the remedy is expressly agreed to be exclusive, in which case it is the sole remedy.

(2) Where circumstances cause an exclusive or limited remedy to fail of its essential purpose, remedy may be had as provided in this Act.

(3) Consequential damages may be limited or excluded unless the limitation or exclusion is unconscionable. Limitation of consequential damages for injury to the person in the case of consumer goods is prima facie unconscionable but limitation of damages where the loss is commercial is not.

§ 2—720. Effect of "Cancellation" or "Rescission" on Claims for Antecedent Breach.

Unless the contrary intention clearly appears, expressions of "cancellation" or "rescission" of the contract or the like shall not be construed as a renunciation or discharge of any claim in damages for an antecedent breach.

§ 2—721. Remedies for Fraud.

Remedies for material misrepresentation or fraud include all remedies available under this Article for non-fraudulent breach. Neither rescission or a claim for rescission of the contract for sale nor rejection or return of the goods shall bar or be deemed inconsistent with a claim for damages or other remedy.

§ 2—722. Who Can Sue Third Parties for Injury to Goods.

Where a third party so deals with goods which have been identified to a contract for sale as to cause actionable injury to a party to that contract

(a) a right of action against the third party is in either party to the contract for sale who has title to or a security interest or a special property or an insurable interest in the goods; and if the goods have been destroyed or converted a right of action is also in the party who either bore the risk of loss under the contract for sale or has since the injury assumed that risk as against the other;

(b) if at the time of the injury the party plaintiff did not bear the risk of loss as against the other party to the contract for sale and there is no arrangement between them for disposition of the recovery, his suit or settlement is, subject to his own interest, as a fiduciary for the other party to the contract;

(c) either party may with the consent of the other sue for the benefit of whom it may concern.

§ 2—723. Proof of Market Price: Time and Place.

(1) If an action based on anticipatory repudiation comes to trial before the time for performance with respect to some or all of the goods, any damages based on market price (Section 2—708 or Section 2—713) shall be determined according to the price of such goods prevailing at the time when the aggrieved party learned of the repudiation.

(2) If evidence of a price prevailing at the times or places described in this Article is not readily available the price prevailing within any reasonable time before or after the time described or at any other place which in commercial judgment or under usage of trade would serve as a reasonable substitute for the one described may be used, making any proper allowance for the cost of transporting the goods to or from such other place.

(3) Evidence of a relevant price prevailing at a time or place other than the one described in this Article offered by one party is not admissible unless and until he has given the other party such notice as the court finds sufficient to prevent unfair surprise.

§ 2—724. Admissibility of Market Quotations.

Whenever the prevailing price or value of any goods regularly bought and sold in any established commodity market is in issue, reports in official publications or trade journals or in newspapers or periodicals of general circulation published as the reports of such market shall be admissible in evidence. The circumstances of the preparation of such a report may be shown to affect its weight but not its admissibility.

§ 2—725. Statute of Limitations in Contracts for Sale.

(1) An action for breach of any contract for sale must be commenced within four years after the cause of action has accrued. By the original agreement the parties may reduce the period of limitation to not less than one year but may not extend it.

(2) A cause of action accrues when the breach occurs, regardless of the aggrieved party's lack of knowledge of the breach. A breach of warranty occurs when tender of delivery is made, except that where a warranty explicitly extends to future performance of the goods and discovery of the breach must await the time of such performance the cause of action accrues when the breach is or should have been discovered.

(3) Where an action commenced within the time limited by subsection (1) is so terminated as to leave available a remedy by another action for the same breach such other action may be commenced after the expiration of the time limited and within six months after the termination of the first action unless the termination resulted from voluntary discontinuance or from dismissal for failure or neglect to prosecute.

(4) This section does not alter the law on tolling of the statute of limitations nor does it apply to causes of action which have accrued before this Act becomes effective.

Article 2A
LEASES

Part 1 General Provisions

§ 2A—101. Short Title.

This Article shall be known and may be cited as the Uniform Commercial Code—Leases.

§ 2A—102. Scope.

This Article applies to any transaction, regardless of form, that creates a lease.

§ 2A—103. Definitions and Index of Definitions.

(1) In this Article unless the context otherwise requires:

(a) "Buyer in ordinary course of business" means a person who in good faith and without knowledge that the sale to him [or her] is in violation of the ownership rights or security interest or leasehold interest of a third party in the goods buys in ordinary course from a person in the business of selling goods of that kind but does not include a pawnbroker. "Buying" may be for cash or by exchange of other property or on secured or unsecured credit and includes receiving goods or documents of title under a pre-existing contract for sale but does not include a transfer in bulk or as security for or in total or partial satisfaction of a money debt.

(b) "Cancellation" occurs when either party puts an end to the lease contract for default by the other party.

(c) "Commercial unit" means such a unit of goods as by commercial usage is a single whole for purposes of lease and division of which materially impairs its character or value on the market or in use. A commercial unit may be a single article, as a machine, or a set of articles, as a suite of furniture or a line of machinery, or a quantity, as a gross or carload, or any other unit treated in use or in the relevant market as a single whole.

(d) "Conforming" goods or performance under a lease contract means goods or performance that are in accordance with the obligations under the lease contract.

(e) "Consumer lease" means a lease that a lessor regularly engaged in the business of leasing or selling makes to a lessee who is an individual and who takes under the lease primarily for a personal, family, or household "purpose [, if" the total payments to be made under the lease contract, excluding payments for options to renew or buy, do not exceed. . . .

(f) "Fault" means wrongful act, omission, breach, or default.

(g) "Finance lease" means a lease with respect to which:

(i) the lessor does not select, manufacture or supply the goods;

(ii) the lessor acquires the goods or the right to possession and use of the goods in connection with the lease; and

(iii) one of the following occurs:

(A) the lessee receives a copy of the contract by which the lessor acquired the goods or the right to possession and use of the goods before signing the lease contract;

(B) the lessee's approval of the contract by which the lessor acquired the goods or the right to possession and use of the goods is a condition to effectiveness of the lease contract;

(C) the lessee, before signing the lease contract, receives an accurate and complete statement designating the promises and warranties, and any disclaimers of warranties, limitations or modifications of remedies, or liquidated damages, including those of a third party, such as the manufacturer of the goods, provided to the lessor by the person supplying the goods in connection with or as part of the contract by which the lessor acquired the goods or the right to possession and use of the goods; or

(D) if the lease is not a consumer lease, the lessor, before the lessee signs the lease contract, informs the lessee in writing (a) of the identity of the person supplying the goods to the lessor, unless the lessee has selected that person and directed the lessor to acquire the goods or the right to possession and use of the goods from that person, (b) that the lessee is entitled under this Article to any promises and warranties, including those of any third party, provided to the lessor by the person supplying the goods in connection with or as part of the contract by which the lessor acquired the goods or the right to possession and use of the goods, and (c) that the lessee may communicate with the person supplying the goods to the lessor and receive an accurate and complete statement of those promises and warranties, including any disclaimers and limitations of them or of remedies.

(h) "Goods" means all things that are movable at the time of identification to the lease contract, or are fixtures (Section 2A—309), but the term does not include money, documents, instruments, accounts, chattel paper, general intangibles, or minerals or the like, including oil and gas, before extraction. The term also includes the unborn young of animals.

(i) "Installment lease contract" means a lease contract that authorizes or requires the delivery of goods in separate lots to be separately accepted, even though the lease contract contains a clause "each delivery is a eparate lease" or its equivalent.

(j) "Lease" means a transfer of the right to possession and use of goods for a term in return for consideration, but a sale, including a sale on approval or a sale or return, or retention or creation of a security interest is not a lease. Unless the context clearly indicates otherwise, the term includes a sublease.

(k) "Lease agreement" means the bargain, with respect to the lease, of the lessor and the lessee in fact as found in their language or by implication from other circumstances including course of dealing or usage of trade or course of performance as provided in this Article. Unless the context clearly indicates otherwise, the term includes a sublease agreement.

(l) "Lease contract" means the total legal obligation that results from the lease agreement as affected by this Article and any other applicable rules of law. Unless the context clearly indicates otherwise, the term includes a sublease contract.

(m) "Leasehold interest" means the interest of the lessor or the lessee under a lease contract.

(n) "Lessee" means a person who acquires the right to possession and use of goods under a lease. Unless the context clearly indicates otherwise, the term includes a sublessee.

(o) "Lessee in ordinary course of business" means a person who in good faith and without knowledge that the lease to him [or her] is in violation of the ownership rights or security interest or leasehold interest of a third party in the goods, leases in ordinary course from a person in the business of selling or leasing goods of that kind but does not include a pawnbroker. "Leasing" may be for cash or by exchange of other property or on secured or unsecured credit and includes receiving goods or documents of title under a pre-existing lease contract but does not include a transfer in bulk or as security for or in total or partial satisfaction of a money debt.

(p) "Lessor" means a person who transfers the right to possession and use of goods under a lease. Unless the context clearly indicates otherwise, the term includes a sublessor.

(q) "Lessor's residual interest" means the lessor's interest in the goods after expiration, termination, or cancellation of the lease contract.

(r) "Lien" means a charge against or interest in goods to secure payment of a debt or performance of an obligation, but the term does not include a security interest.

(s) "Lot" means a parcel or a single article that is the subject matter of a separate lease or delivery, whether or not it is sufficient to perform the lease contract.

(t) "Merchant lessee" means a lessee that is a merchant with respect to goods of the kind subject to the lease.

(u) "Present value" means the amount as of a date certain of one or more sums payable in the future, discounted to the date certain. The discount is determined by the interest rate specified by the parties if the rate was not manifestly unreasonable at the time the transaction was entered into; otherwise, the discount is determined by a commercially reasonable rate that takes into account the facts and circumstances of each case at the time the transaction was entered into.

(v) "Purchase" includes taking by sale, lease, mortgage, security interest, pledge, gift, or any other voluntary transaction creating an interest in goods.

(w) "Sublease" means a lease of goods the right to possession and use of which was acquired by the lessor as a lessee under an existing lease.

(x) "Supplier" means a person from whom a lessor buys or leases goods to be leased under a finance lease.

(y) "Supply contract" means a contract under which a lessor buys or leases goods to be leased.

(z) "Termination" occurs when either party pursuant to a power created by agreement or law puts an end to the lease contract otherwise than for default.

(2) Other definitions applying to this Article and the sections in which they appear are:

"Accessions". Section 2A—310(1).
"Construction mortgage". Section 2A—309(1)(d).
"Encumbrance". Section 2A—309(1)(e).
"Fixtures". Section 2A—309(1)(a).
"Fixture filing". Section 2A—309(1)(b).
"Purchase money lease". Section 2A—309(1)(c).

(3) The following definitions in other Articles apply to this Article:

"Accounts". Section 9—106.
"Between merchants". Section 2—104(3).
"Buyer". Section 2—103(1)(a).
"Chattel paper". Section 9—105(1)(b).
"Consumer goods". Section 9—109(1).
"Document". Section 9—105(1)(f).
"Entrusting". Section 2—403(3).
"General intangibles". Section 9—106.
"Good faith". Section 2—103(1)(b).
"Instrument". Section 9—105(1)(i).
"Merchant". Section 2—104(1).
"Mortgage". Section 9—105(1)(j).
"Pursuant to commitment". Section 9—105(1)(k).
"Receipt". Section 2—103(1)(c).
"Sale". Section 2—106(1).
"Sale on approval". Section 2—326.
"Sale or return". Section 2—326.
"Seller". Section 2—103(1)(d).

(4) In addition Article 1 contains general definitions and principles of construction and interpretation applicable throughout this Article.

As amended in 1990.

§ 2A—104. Leases Subject to Other Law.

(1) A lease, although subject to this Article, is also subject to any applicable:

(a) certificate of title statute of this State: (list any certificate of title statutes covering automobiles, trailers, mobile homes, boats, farm tractors, and the like);

(b) certificate of title statute of another jurisdiction (Section 2A—105); or

(c) consumer protection statute of this State, or final consumer protection decision of a court of this State existing on the effective date of this Article.

(2) In case of conflict between this Article, other than Sections 2A—105, 2A—304(3), and 2A—305(3), and a statute or decision referred to in subsection (1), the statute or decision controls.

(3) Failure to comply with an applicable law has only the effect specified therein.

As amended in 1990.

§ 2A—105. Territorial Application of Article to Goods Covered by Certificate of Title.

Subject to the provisions of Sections 2A—304(3) and 2A—305(3), with respect to goods covered by a certificate of title issued under a statute of this State or of another jurisdiction, compliance and the effect of compliance or non-compliance with a certificate of title statute are governed by the law (including the conflict of laws rules) of the jurisdiction issuing the certificate until the earlier of (a) surrender of the certificate, or (b) four months after the goods are removed from that jurisdiction and thereafter until a new certificate of title is issued by another jurisdiction.

§ 2A—106. Limitation on Power of Parties to Consumer Lease to Choose Applicable Law and Judicial Forum.

(1) If the law chosen by the parties to a consumer lease is that of a jurisdiction other than a jurisdiction in which the lessee resides at the time the lease agreement becomes enforceable or within 30 days thereafter or in which the goods are to be used, the choice is not enforceable.

(2) If the judicial forum chosen by the parties to a consumer lease is a forum that would not otherwise have jurisdiction over the lessee, the choice is not enforceable.

§ 2A—107. Waiver or Renunciation of Claim or Right After Default.

Any claim or right arising out of an alleged default or breach of warranty may be discharged in whole or in part without consideration by a written waiver or renunciation signed and delivered by the aggrieved party.

§ 2A—108. Unconscionability.

(1) If the court as a matter of law finds a lease contract or any clause of a lease contract to have been unconscionable at the time it was made the court may refuse to enforce the lease contract, or it may enforce the remainder of the lease contract without the unconscionable clause, or it may so limit the application of any unconscionable clause as to avoid any unconscionable result.

(2) With respect to a consumer lease, if the court as a matter of law finds that a lease contract or any clause of a lease contract has been induced by unconscionable conduct or that unconscionable conduct has occurred in the collection of a claim arising from a lease contract, the court may grant appropriate relief.

(3) Before making a finding of unconscionability under subsection (1) or (2), the court, on its own motion or that of a party, shall afford the parties a reasonable opportunity to present evidence as to the setting, purpose, and effect of the lease contract or clause thereof, or of the conduct.

(4) In an action in which the lessee claims unconscionability with respect to a consumer lease:

(a) If the court finds unconscionability under subsection (1) or (2), the court shall award reasonable attorney's fees to the lessee.

(b) If the court does not find unconscionability and the lessee claiming unconscionability has brought or maintained an action he [or she] knew to be groundless, the court shall award reasonable attorney's fees to the party against whom the claim is made.

(c) In determining attorney's fees, the amount of the recovery on behalf of the claimant under subsections (1) and (2) is not controlling.

§ 2A—109. Option to Accelerate at Will.

(1) A term providing that one party or his [or her] successor in interest may accelerate payment or performance or require collateral or additional collateral "at will" or "when he [or she] deems himself [or herself] insecure" or in words of similar import must be construed to mean that he [or she] has power to do so only if he [or she] in good faith believes that the prospect of payment or performance is impaired.

(2) With respect to a consumer lease, the burden of establishing good faith under subsection (1) is on the party who exercised the power; otherwise the burden of establishing lack of good faith is on the party against whom the power has been exercised.

Part 2 Formation and Construction of Lease Contract

§ 2A—201. Statute of Frauds.

(1) A lease contract is not enforceable by way of action or defense unless:

(a) the total payments to be made under the lease contract, excluding payments for options to renew or buy, are less than $1,000; or

(b) there is a writing, signed by the party against whom enforcement is sought or by that party's authorized agent, sufficient to indicate that a lease contract has been made between the parties and to describe the goods leased and the lease term.

(2) Any description of leased goods or of the lease term is sufficient and satisfies subsection (1)(b), whether or not it is specific, if it reasonably identifies what is described.

(3) A writing is not insufficient because it omits or incorrectly states a term agreed upon, but the lease contract is not enforceable under subsection (1)(b) beyond the lease term and the quantity of goods shown in the writing.

(4) A lease contract that does not satisfy the requirements of subsection (1), but which is valid in other respects, is enforceable:

(a) if the goods are to be specially manufactured or obtained for the lessee and are not suitable for lease or sale to others in the ordinary course of the lessor's business, and the lessor, before notice of repudiation is received and under circumstances that reasonably indicate that the goods are for the lessee, has made either a substantial beginning of their manufacture or commitments for their procurement;

(b) if the party against whom enforcement is sought admits in that party's pleading, testimony or otherwise in court that a lease contract was made, but the lease contract is not enforceable under this provision beyond the quantity of goods admitted; or

(c) with respect to goods that have been received and accepted by the lessee.

(5) The lease term under a lease contract referred to in subsection (4) is:

(a) if there is a writing signed by the party against whom enforcement is sought or by that party's authorized agent specifying the lease term, the term so specified;

(b) if the party against whom enforcement is sought admits in that party's pleading, testimony, or otherwise in court a lease term, the term so admitted; or

(c) a reasonable lease term.

§ 2A—202. Final Written Expression: Parol or Extrinsic Evidence.

Terms with respect to which the confirmatory memoranda of the parties agree or which are otherwise set forth in a writing intended by the parties as a final expression of their agreement with respect to such terms as are included therein may not be contradicted by evidence of any prior agreement or of a contemporaneous oral agreement but may be explained or supplemented:

(a) by course of dealing or usage of trade or by course of performance; and

(b) by evidence of consistent additional terms unless the court finds the writing to have been intended also as a complete and exclusive statement of the terms of the agreement.

§ 2A—203. Seals Inoperative.

The affixing of a seal to a writing evidencing a lease contract or an offer to enter into a lease contract does not render the writing a sealed instrument and the law with respect to sealed instruments does not apply to the lease contract or offer.

§ 2A—204. Formation in General.

(1) A lease contract may be made in any manner sufficient to show agreement, including conduct by both parties which recognizes the existence of a lease contract.

(2) An agreement sufficient to constitute a lease contract may be found although the moment of its making is undetermined.

(3) Although one or more terms are left open, a lease contract does not fail for indefiniteness if the parties have intended to make a lease contract and there is a reasonably certain basis for giving an appropriate remedy.

§ 2A—205. Firm Offers.

An offer by a merchant to lease goods to or from another person in a signed writing that by its terms gives assurance it will be held open is not revocable, for lack of consideration, during the time stated or, if no time is stated, for a reasonable time, but in no event may the period of irrevocability exceed 3 months. Any such term of assurance on a form supplied by the offeree must be separately signed by the offeror.

§ 2A—206. Offer and Acceptance in Formation of Lease Contract.

(1) Unless otherwise unambiguously indicated by the language or circumstances, an offer to make a lease contract must be construed as inviting acceptance in any manner and by any medium reasonable in the circumstances.

(2) If the beginning of a requested performance is a reasonable mode of acceptance, an offeror who is not notified of acceptance within a reasonable time may treat the offer as having lapsed before acceptance.

§ 2A—207. Course of Performance or Practical Construction.

(1) If a lease contract involves repeated occasions for performance by either party with knowledge of the nature of the performance and opportunity for objection to it by the other, any course of performance accepted or acquiesced in without objection is relevant to determine the meaning of the lease agreement.

(2) The express terms of a lease agreement and any course of performance, as well as any course of dealing and usage of trade, must be construed whenever reasonable as consistent with each other; but if that construction is unreasonable,

express terms control course of performance, course of performance controls both course of dealing and usage of trade, and course of dealing controls usage of trade.

(3) Subject to the provisions of Section 2A—208 on modification and waiver, course of performance is relevant to show a waiver or modification of any term inconsistent with the course of performance.

§ 2A—208. Modification, Rescission and Waiver.

(1) An agreement modifying a lease contract needs no consideration to be binding.

(2) A signed lease agreement that excludes modification or rescission except by a signed writing may not be otherwise modified or rescinded, but, except as between merchants, such a requirement on a form supplied by a merchant must be separately signed by the other party.

(3) Although an attempt at modification or rescission does not satisfy the requirements of subsection (2), it may operate as a waiver.

(4) A party who has made a waiver affecting an executory portion of a lease contract may retract the waiver by reasonable notification received by the other party that strict performance will be required of any term waived, unless the retraction would be unjust in view of a material change of position in reliance on the waiver.

§ 2A—209. Lessee under Finance Lease as Beneficiary of Supply Contract.

(1) The benefit of the supplier's promises to the lessor under the supply contract and of all warranties, whether express or implied, including those of any third party provided in connection with or as part of the supply contract, extends to the lessee to the extent of the lessee's leasehold interest under a finance lease related to the supply contract, but is subject to the terms warranty and of the supply contract and all defenses or claims arising therefrom.

(2) The extension of the benefit of supplier's promises and of warranties to the lessee (Section 2A–209(1)) does not: (i) modify the rights and obligations of the parties to the supply contract, whether arising therefrom or otherwise, or (ii) impose any duty or liability under the supply contract on the lessee.

(3) Any modification or rescission of the supply contract by the supplier and the lessor is effective between the supplier and the lessee unless, before the modification or rescission, the supplier has received notice that the lessee has entered into a finance lease related to the supply contract. If the modification or rescission is effective between the supplier and the lessee, the lessor is deemed to have assumed, in addition to the obligations of the lessor to the lessee under the lease contract, promises of the supplier to the lessor and warranties that were so modified or rescinded as they existed and were available to the lessee before modification or rescission.

(4) In addition to the extension of the benefit of the supplier's promises and of warranties to the lessee under subsection (1), the lessee retains all rights that the lessee may have against the supplier which arise from an agreement between the lessee and the supplier or under other law.

As amended in 1990.

§ 2A—210. Express Warranties.

(1) Express warranties by the lessor are created as follows:

(a) Any affirmation of fact or promise made by the lessor to the lessee which relates to the goods and becomes part of the basis of the bargain creates an express warranty that the goods will conform to the affirmation or promise.

(b) Any description of the goods which is made part of the basis of the bargain creates an express warranty that the goods will conform to the description.

(c) Any sample or model that is made part of the basis of the bargain creates an express warranty that the whole of the goods will conform to the sample or model.

(2) It is not necessary to the creation of an express warranty that the lessor use formal words, such as "warrant" or "guarantee," or that the lessor have a specific intention to make a warranty, but an affirmation merely of the value of the goods or a statement purporting to be merely the lessor's opinion or commendation of the goods does not create a warranty.

§ 2A—211. Warranties Against Interference and Against Infringement; Lessee's Obligation Against Infringement.

(1) There is in a lease contract a warranty that for the lease term no person holds a claim to or interest in the goods that arose from an act or omission of the lessor, other than a claim by way of infringement or the like, which will interfere with the lessee's enjoyment of its leasehold interest.

(2) Except in a finance lease there is in a lease contract by a lessor who is a merchant regularly dealing in goods of the kind a warranty that the goods are delivered free of the rightful claim of any person by way of infringement or the like.

(3) A lessee who furnishes specifications to a lessor or a supplier shall hold the lessor and the supplier harmless against any claim by way of infringement or the like that arises out of compliance with the specifications.

§ 2A—212. Implied Warranty of Merchantability.

(1) Except in a finance lease, a warranty that the goods will be merchantable is implied in a lease contract if the lessor is a merchant with respect to goods of that kind.

(2) Goods to be merchantable must be at least such as

(a) pass without objection in the trade under the description in the lease agreement;

(b) in the case of fungible goods, are of fair average quality within the description;

(c) are fit for the ordinary purposes for which goods of that type are used;

(d) run, within the variation permitted by the lease agreement, of even kind, quality, and quantity within each unit and among all units involved;

(e) are adequately contained, packaged, and labeled as the lease agreement may require; and

(f) conform to any promises or affirmations of fact made on the container or label.

(3) Other implied warranties may arise from course of dealing or usage of trade.

§ 2A—213. Implied Warranty of Fitness for Particular Purpose.

Except in a finance of lease, if the lessor at the time the lease contract is made has reason to know of any particular purpose for which the goods are required and that the lessee is relying on the lessor's skill or judgment to select or furnish suitable goods, there is in the lease contract an implied warranty that the goods will be fit for that purpose.

§ 2A—214. Exclusion or Modification of Warranties.

(1) Words or conduct relevant to the creation of an express warranty and words or conduct tending to negate or limit a warranty must be construed wherever reasonable as consistent with each other; but, subject to the provisions of Section 2A—202 on parol or extrinsic evidence, negation or limitation is inoperative to the extent that the construction is unreasonable.

(2) Subject to subsection (3), to exclude or modify the implied warranty of merchantability or any part of it the language must mention "merchantability", be by a writing, and be conspicuous. Subject to subsection (3), to exclude or modify any implied warranty of fitness the exclusion must be by a writing and be conspicuous. Language to exclude all implied warranties of fitness is sufficient if it is in writing, is conspicuous and states, for example, "There is no warranty that the goods will be fit for a particular purpose".

(3) Notwithstanding subsection (2), but subject to subsection (4),

(a) unless the circumstances indicate otherwise, all implied warranties are excluded by expressions like "as is" or "with all faults" or by other language that in common understanding calls the lessee's attention to the exclusion of warranties and makes plain that there is no implied warranty, if in writing and conspicuous;

(b) if the lessee before entering into the lease contract has examined the goods or the sample or model as fully as desired or has refused to examine the goods, there is no implied warranty with regard to defects that an examination ought in the circumstances to have revealed; and

(c) an implied warranty may also be excluded or modified by course of dealing, course of performance, or usage of trade.

(4) To exclude or modify a warranty against interference or against infringement (Section 2A—211) or any part of it, the language must be specific, be by a writing, and be conspicuous, unless the circumstances, including course of performance, course of dealing, or usage of trade, give the lessee reason to know that the goods are being leased subject to a claim or interest of any person.

§ 2A—215. Cumulation and Conflict of Warranties Express or Implied.

Warranties, whether express or implied, must be construed as consistent with each other and as cumulative, but if that construction is unreasonable, the intention of the parties determines which warranty is dominant. In ascertaining that intention the following rules apply:

(a) Exact or technical specifications displace an inconsistent sample or model or general language of description.

(b) A sample from an existing bulk displaces inconsistent general language of description.

(c) Express warranties displace inconsistent implied warranties other than an implied warranty of fitness for a particular purpose.

§ 2A—216. Third-Party Beneficiaries of Express and Implied Warranties.

Alternative A

A warranty to or for the benefit of a lessee under this Article, whether express or implied, extends to any natural person who is in the family or household of the lessee or who is a guest in the lessee's home if it is reasonable to expect that such person may use, consume, or be affected by the goods and who is injured in person by breach of the warranty. This section does not displace principles of law and equity that extend a warranty to or for the benefit of a lessee to other persons. The operation of this section may not be excluded, modified, or limited, but an exclusion, modification, or limitation of the warranty, including any with respect to rights and remedies, effective against the lessee is also effective against any beneficiary designated under this section.

Alternative B

A warranty to or for the benefit of a lessee under this Article, whether express or implied, extends to any natural person who may reasonably be expected to use, consume, or be affected by the goods and who is injured in person by breach of the warranty. This section does not displace principles of law and equity that extend a warranty to or for the benefit of a lessee to other persons. The operation of this section may not be excluded, modified, or limited, but an exclusion, modification, or limitation of the warranty, including any with respect to rights and remedies, effective against the lessee is also effective against the beneficiary designated under this section.

Alternative C

A warranty to or for the benefit of a lessee under this Article, whether express or implied, extends to any person who may reasonably be expected to use, consume, or be affected by the goods and who is injured by breach of the warranty. The operation of this section may not be excluded, modified, or limited with respect to injury to the person of an individual to whom the warranty extends, but an exclusion, modification, or limitation of the warranty, including any with respect to rights and remedies, effective against the lessee is also effective against the beneficiary designated under this section.

§ 2A—217. Identification.

Identification of goods as goods to which a lease contract refers may be made at any time and in any manner explicitly agreed to by the parties. In the absence of explicit agreement, identification occurs:

(a) when the lease contract is made if the lease contract is for a lease of goods that are existing and identified;

(b) when the goods are shipped, marked, or otherwise designated by the lessor as goods to which the lease contract refers, if the lease contract is for a lease of goods that are not existing and identified; or

(c) when the young are conceived, if the lease contract is for a lease of unborn young of animals.

§ 2A—218. Insurance and Proceeds.

(1) A lessee obtains an insurable interest when existing goods are identified to the lease contract even though the goods identified are nonconforming and the lessee has an option to reject them.

(2) If a lessee has an insurable interest only by reason of the lessor's identification of the goods, the lessor, until default or insolvency or notification to the lessee that identification is final, may substitute other goods for those identified.

(3) Notwithstanding a lessee's insurable interest under subsections (1) and (2), the lessor retains an insurable interest until an option to buy has been exercised by the lessee and risk of loss has passed to the lessee.

(4) Nothing in this section impairs any insurable interest recognized under any other statute or rule of law.

(5) The parties by agreement may determine that one or more parties have an obligation to obtain and pay for insurance covering the goods and by agreement may determine the beneficiary of the proceeds of the insurance.

§ 2A—219. Risk of Loss.

(1) Except in the case of a finance lease, risk of loss is retained by the lessor and does not pass to the lessee. In the case of a finance lease, risk of loss passes to the lessee.

(2) Subject to the provisions of this Article on the effect of default on risk of loss (Section 2A—220), if risk of loss is to pass to the lessee and the time of passage is not stated, the following rules apply:

(a) If the lease contract requires or authorizes the goods to be shipped by carrier

(i) and it does not require delivery at a particular destination, the risk of loss passes to the lessee when the goods are duly delivered to the carrier; but

(ii) if it does require delivery at a particular destination and the goods are there duly tendered while in the possession of the carrier, the risk of loss passes to the lessee when the goods are there duly so tendered as to enable the lessee to take delivery.

(b) If the goods are held by a bailee to be delivered without being moved, the risk of loss passes to the lessee on acknowledgment by the bailee of the lessee's right to possession of the goods.

(c) In any case not within subsection (a) or (b), the risk of loss passes to the lessee on the lessee's receipt of the goods if the lessor, or, in the case of a finance lease, the supplier, is a merchant; otherwise the risk passes to the lessee on tender of delivery.

§ 2A—220. Effect of Default on Risk of Loss.

(1) Where risk of loss is to pass to the lessee and the time of passage is not stated:

(a) If a tender or delivery of goods so fails to conform to the lease contract as to give a right of rejection, the risk of their loss remains with the lessor, or, in the case of a finance lease, the supplier, until cure or acceptance.

(b) If the lessee rightfully revokes acceptance, he [or she], to the extent of any deficiency in his [or her] effective insurance coverage, may treat the risk of loss as having remained with the lessor from the beginning.

(2) Whether or not risk of loss is to pass to the lessee, if the lessee as to conforming goods already identified to a lease contract repudiates or is otherwise in default under the lease contract, the lessor, or, in the case of a finance lease, the supplier, to the extent of any deficiency in his [or her] effective insurance coverage may treat the risk of loss as resting on the lessee for a commercially reasonable time.

§ 2A—221. Casualty to Identified Goods.

If a lease contract requires goods identified when the lease contract is made, and the goods suffer casualty without fault of the lessee, the lessor or the supplier before delivery, or the goods suffer casualty before risk of loss passes to the lessee pursuant to the lease agreement or Section 2A—219, then:

(a) if the loss is total, the lease contract is avoided; and

(b) if the loss is partial or the goods have so deteriorated as to no longer conform to the lease contract, the lessee may nevertheless demand inspection and at his [or her] option either treat the lease contract as avoided or, except in a finance lease that is not a consumer lease, accept the goods with due allowance from the rent payable for the balance of the lease term for the deterioration or the deficiency in quantity but without further right against the lessor.

Part 3 Effect Of Lease Contract

§ 2A—301. Enforceability of Lease Contract.

Except as otherwise provided in this Article, a lease contract is effective and enforceable according to its terms between the parties, against purchasers of the goods and against creditors of the parties.

§ 2A—302. Title to and Possession of Goods.

Except as otherwise provided in this Article, each provision of this Article applies whether the lessor or a third party has title to the goods, and whether the lessor, the lessee, or a third party has possession of the goods, notwithstanding any statute or rule of law that possession or the absence of possession is fraudulent.

§ 2A—303. Alienability of Party's Interest Under Lease Contract or of Lessor's Residual Interest in Goods; Delegation of Performance; Transfer of Rights.

(1) As used in this section, "creation of a security interest" includes the sale of a lease contract that is subject to Article 9, Secured Transactions, by reason of Section 9—102(1)(b).

(2) Except as provided in subsections (3) and (4), a provision in a lease agreement which (i) prohibits the voluntary or involuntary transfer, including a transfer by sale, sublease, creation or enforcement of a security interest, or attachment, levy, or other judicial process, of an interest of a party under the lease contract or of the lessor's residual interest in the goods, or (ii) makes such a transfer an event of default, gives rise to the rights and remedies provided in subsection (5), but a transfer that is prohibited or is an event of default under the lease agreement is otherwise effective.

(3) A provision in a lease agreement which (i) prohibits the creation or enforcement of a security interest in an interest of a party under the lease contract or in the lessor's residual interest in the goods, or (ii) makes such a transfer an event of default, is not enforceable unless, and then only to the extent that, there is an actual transfer by the lessee of the lessee's right of possession or use of the goods in violation of the provision or an actual delegation of a material performance of either party to the lease contract in violation of the provision. Neither the granting nor the enforcement of a security interest in (i) the lessor's interest under the lease contract or (ii) the lessor's residual interest in the goods is a transfer that materially impairs the prospect of obtaining return performance by, materially changes the duty of, or materially increases the burden or risk imposed on, the lessee within the purview of subsec-

tion (5) unless, and then only to the extent that, there is an actual delegation of a material performance of the lessor.

(4) A provision in a lease agreement which (i) prohibits a transfer of a right to damages for default with respect to the whole lease contract or of a right to payment arising out of the transferor's due performance of the transferor's entire obligation, or (ii) makes such a transfer an event of default, is not enforceable, and such a transfer is not a transfer that materially impairs the prospect of obtaining return performance by, materially changes the duty of, or materially increases the burden or risk imposed on, the other party to the lease contract within the purview of subsection (5).

(5) Subject to subsections (3) and (4):

(a) if a transfer is made which is made an event of default under a lease agreement, the party to the lease contract not making the transfer, unless that party waives the default or otherwise agrees, has the rights and remedies described in Section 2A—501(2);

(b) if paragraph (a) is not applicable and if a transfer is made that (i) is prohibited under a lease agreement or (ii) materially impairs the prospect of obtaining return performance by, materially changes the duty of, or materially increases the burden or risk imposed on, the other party to the lease contract, unless the party not making the transfer agrees at any time to the transfer in the lease contract or otherwise, then, except as limited by contract, (i) the transferor is liable to the party not making the transfer for damages caused by the transfer to the extent that the damages could not reasonably be prevented by the party not making the transfer and (ii) a court having jurisdiction may grant other appropriate relief, including cancellation of the lease contract or an injunction against the transfer.

(6) A transfer of "the lease" or of "all my rights under the lease," or a transfer in similar general terms, is a transfer of rights and, unless the language or the circumstances, as in a transfer for security, indicate the contrary, the transfer is a delegation of duties by the transferor to the transferee. Acceptance by the transferee constitutes a promise by the transferee to perform those duties. The promise is enforceable by either the transferor or the other party to the lease contract.

(7) Unless otherwise agreed by the lessor and the lessee, a delegation of performance does not relieve the transferor as against the other party of any duty to perform or of any liability for default.

(8) In a consumer lease, to prohibit the transfer of an interest of a party under the lease contract or to make a transfer an event of default, the language must be specific, by a writing, and conspicuous.

As amended in 1990.

§ 2A—304. Subsequent Lease of Goods by Lessor.

(1) Subject to Section 2A—303, a subsequent lessee from a lessor of goods under an existing lease contract obtains,

to the extent of the leasehold interest transferred, the leasehold interest in the goods that the lessor had or had power to transfer, and except as provided in subsection (2) and Section 2A—527(4), takes subject to the existing lease contract. A lessor with voidable title has power to transfer a good leasehold interest to a good faith subsequent lessee for value, but only to the extent set forth in the preceding sentence. If goods have been delivered under a transaction of purchase the lessor has that power even though:

(a) the lessor's transferor was deceived as to the identity of the lessor;

(b) the delivery was in exchange for a check which is later dishonored;

(c) it was agreed that the transaction was to be a "cash sale"; or

(d) the delivery was procured through fraud punishable as larcenous under the criminal law.

(2) A subsequent lessee in the ordinary course of business from a lessor who is a merchant dealing in goods of that kind to whom the goods were entrusted by the existing lessee of that lessor before the interest of the subsequent lessee became enforceable against that lessor obtains, to the extent of the leasehold interest transferred, all of that lessor's and the existing lessee's rights to the goods, and takes free of the existing lease contract.

(3) A subsequent lessee from the lessor of goods that are subject to an existing lease contract and are covered by a certificate of title issued under a statute of this State or of another jurisdiction takes no greater rights than those provided both by this section and by the certificate of title statute.

As amended in 1990.

§ 2A—305. Sale or Sublease of Goods by Lessee.

(1) Subject to the provisions of Section 2A—303, a buyer or sublessee from the lessee of goods under an existing lease contract obtains, to the extent of the interest transferred, the leasehold interest in the goods that the lessee had or had power to transfer, and except as provided in subsection (2) and Section 2A—511(4), takes subject to the existing lease contract. A lessee with a voidable leasehold interest has power to transfer a good leasehold interest to a good faith buyer for value or a good faith sublessee for value, but only to the extent set forth in the preceding sentence. When goods have been delivered under a transaction of lease the lessee has that power even though:

(a) the lessor was deceived as to the identity of the lessee;

(b) the delivery was in exchange for a check which is later dishonored; or

(c) the delivery was procured through fraud punishable as larcenous under the criminal law.

(2) A buyer in the ordinary course of business or a sublessee in the ordinary course of business from a lessee who is a merchant dealing in goods of that kind to whom the goods were entrusted by the lessor obtains, to the extent of the interest transferred, all of the lessor's and lessee's rights to the goods, and takes free of the existing lease contract.

(3) A buyer or sublessee from the lessee of goods that are subject to an existing lease contract and are covered by a certificate of title issued under a statute of this State or of another jurisdiction takes no greater rights than those provided both by this section and by the certificate of title statute.

§ 2A—306. Priority of Certain Liens Arising by Operation of Law.

If a person in the ordinary course of his [or her] business furnishes services or materials with respect to goods subject to a lease contract, a lien upon those goods in the possession of that person given by statute or rule of law for those materials or services takes priority over any interest of the lessor or lessee under the lease contract or this Article unless the lien is created by statute and the statute provides otherwise or unless the lien is created by rule of law and the rule of law provides otherwise.

§ 2A—307. Priority of Liens Arising by Attachment or Levy on, Security Interests in, and Other Claims to Goods.

(1) Except as otherwise provided in Section 2A—306, a creditor of a lessee takes subject to the lease contract.

(2) Except as otherwise provided in subsections (3) and (4) and in Sections 2A—306 and 2A—308, a creditor of a lessor takes subject to the lease contract unless:

(a) the creditor holds a lien that attached to the goods before the lease contract became enforceable,

(b) the creditor holds a security interest in the goods and the lessee did not give value and receive delivery of the goods without knowledge of the security interest; or

(c) the creditor holds a security interest in the goods which was perfected (Section 9—303) before the lease contract became enforceable.

(3) A lessee in the ordinary course of business takes the leasehold interest free of a security interest in the goods created by the lessor even though the security interest is perfected (Section 9—303) and the lessee knows of its existence.

(4) A lessee other than a lessee in the ordinary course of business takes the leasehold interest free of a security interest to the extent that it secures future advances made after the secured party acquires knowledge of the lease or more than 45 days after the lease contract becomes enforceable, whichever first occurs, unless the future advances are made pursuant to a commitment entered into without knowledge of the lease and before the expiration of the 45-day period.

§ 2A—308. Special Rights of Creditors.

(1) A creditor of a lessor in possession of goods subject to a lease contract may treat the lease contract as void if as against the creditor retention of possession by the lessor is

fraudulent under any statute or rule of law, but retention of possession in good faith and current course of trade by the lessor for a commercially reasonable time after the lease contract becomes enforceable is not fraudulent.

(2) Nothing in this Article impairs the rights of creditors of a lessor if the lease contract (a) becomes enforceable, not in current course of trade but in satisfaction of or as security for a pre-existing claim for money, security, or the like, and (b) is made under circumstances which under any statute or rule of law apart from this Article would constitute the transaction a fraudulent transfer or voidable preference.

(3) A creditor of a seller may treat a sale or an identification of goods to a contract for sale as void if as against the creditor retention of possession by the seller is fraudulent under any statute or rule of law, but retention of possession of the goods pursuant to a lease contract entered into by the seller as lessee and the buyer as lessor in connection with the sale or identification of the goods is not fraudulent if the buyer bought for value and in good faith.

§ 2A—309. Lessor's and Lessee's Rights When Goods Become Fixtures.

(1) In this section:

(a) goods are "fixtures" when they become so related to particular real estate that an interest in them arises under real estate law;

(b) a "fixture filing" is the filing, in the office where a mortgage on the real estate would be filed or recorded, of a financing statement covering goods that are or are to become fixtures and conforming to the requirements of Section 9—402(5);

(c) a lease is a "purchase money lease" unless the lessee has possession or use of the goods or the right to possession or use of the goods before the lease agreement is enforceable;

(d) a mortgage is a "construction mortgage" to the extent it secures an obligation incurred for the construction of an improvement on land including the acquisition cost of the land, if the recorded writing so indicates; and

(e) "encumbrance" includes real estate mortgages and other liens on real estate and all other rights in real estate that are not ownership interests.

(2) Under this Article a lease may be of goods that are fixtures or may continue in goods that become fixtures, but no lease exists under this Article of ordinary building materials incorporated into an improvement on land.

(3) This Article does not prevent creation of a lease of fixtures pursuant to real estate law.

(4) The perfected interest of a lessor of fixtures has priority over a conflicting interest of an encumbrancer or owner of the real estate if:

(a) the lease is a purchase money lease, the conflicting interest of the encumbrancer or owner arises before the goods become fixtures, the interest of the lessor is perfected by a fixture filing before the goods become fixtures or within ten days thereafter, and the lessee has an interest of record in the real estate or is in possession of the real estate; or

(b) the interest of the lessor is perfected by a fixture filing before the interest of the encumbrancer or owner is of record, the lessor's interest has priority over any conflicting interest of a predecessor in title of the encumbrancer or owner, and the lessee has an interest of record in the real estate or is in possession of the real estate.

(5) The interest of a lessor of fixtures, whether or not perfected, has priority over the conflicting interest of an encumbrancer or owner of the real estate if:

(a) the fixtures are readily removable factory or office machines, readily removable equipment that is not primarily used or leased for use in the operation of the real estate, or readily removable replacements of domestic appliances that are goods subject to a consumer lease, and before the goods become fixtures the lease contract is enforceable; or

(b) the conflicting interest is a lien on the real estate obtained by legal or equitable proceedings after the lease contract is enforceable; or

(c) the encumbrancer or owner has consented in writing to the lease or has disclaimed an interest in the goods as fixtures; or

(d) the lessee has a right to remove the goods as against the encumbrancer or owner. If the lessee's right to remove terminates, the priority of the interest of the lessor continues for a reasonable time.

(6) Notwithstanding paragraph (4)(a) but otherwise subject to subsections (4) and (5), the interest of a lessor of fixtures, including the lessor's residual interest, is subordinate to the conflicting interest of an encumbrancer of the real estate under a construction mortgage recorded before the goods become fixtures if the goods become fixtures before the completion of the construction. To the extent given to refinance a construction mortgage, the conflicting interest of an encumbrancer of the real estate under a mortgage has this priority to the same extent as the encumbrancer of the real estate under the construction mortgage.

(7) In cases not within the preceding subsections, priority between the interest of a lessor of fixtures, including the lessor's residual interest, and the conflicting interest of an encumbrancer or owner of the real estate who is not the lessee is determined by the priority rules governing conflicting interests in real estate.

(8) If the interest of a lessor of fixtures, including the lessor's residual interest, has priority over all conflicting interests of all owners and encumbrancers of the real

estate, the lessor or the lessee may (i) on default, expiration, termination, or cancellation of the lease agreement but subject to the agreement and this Article, or (ii) if necessary to enforce other rights and remedies of the lessor or lessee under this Article, remove the goods from the real estate, free and clear of all conflicting interests of all owners and encumbrancers of the real estate, but the lessor or lessee must reimburse any encumbrancer or owner of the real estate who is not the lessee and who has not otherwise agreed for the cost of repair of any physical injury, but not for any diminution in value of the real estate caused by the absence of the goods removed or by any necessity of replacing them. A person entitled to reimbursement may refuse permission to remove until the party seeking removal gives adequate security for the performance of this obligation.

(9) Even though the lease agreement does not create a security interest, the interest of a lessor of fixtures, including the lessor's residual interest, is perfected by filing a financing statement as a fixture filing for leased goods that are or are to become fixtures in accordance with the relevant provisions of the Article on Secured Transactions (Article 9).

As amended in 1990.

§ 2A—310. Lessor's and Lessee's Rights When Goods Become Accessions.

(1) Goods are "accessions" when they are installed in or affixed to other goods.

(2) The interest of a lessor or a lessee under a lease contract entered into before the goods became accessions is superior to all interests in the whole except as stated in subsection (4).

(3) The interest of a lessor or a lessee under a lease contract entered into at the time or after the goods became accessions is superior to all subsequently acquired interests in the whole except as stated in subsection (4) but is subordinate to interests in the whole existing at the time the lease contract was made unless the holders of such interests in the whole have in writing consented to the lease or disclaimed an interest in the goods as part of the whole.

(4) The interest of a lessor or a lessee under a lease contract described in subsection (2) or (3) is subordinate to the interest of

(a) a buyer in the ordinary course of business or a lessee in the ordinary course of business of any interest in the whole acquired after the goods became accessions; or

(b) a creditor with a security interest in the whole perfected before the lease contract was made to the extent that the creditor makes subsequent advances without knowledge of the lease contract.

(5) When under subsections (2) or (3) and (4) a lessor or a lessee of accessions holds an interest that is superior to all interests in the whole, the lessor or the lessee may (a) on

default, expiration, termination, or cancellation of the lease contract by the other party but subject to the provisions of the lease contract and this Article, or (b) if necessary to enforce his [or her] other rights and remedies under this Article, remove the goods from the whole, free and clear of all interests in the whole, but he [or she] must reimburse any holder of an interest in the whole who is not the lessee and who has not otherwise agreed for the cost of repair of any physical injury but not for any diminution in value of the whole caused by the absence of the goods removed or by any necessity for replacing them. A person entitled to reimbursement may refuse permission to remove until the party seeking removal gives adequate security for the performance of this obligation.

§ 2A—311. Priority Subject to Subordination.

Nothing in this Article prevents subordination by agreement by any person entitled to priority.

As added in 1990.

Part 4 Performance Of Lease Contract: Repudiated, Substituted And Excused

§ 2A—401. Insecurity: Adequate Assurance of Performance.

(1) A lease contract imposes an obligation on each party that the other's expectation of receiving due performance will not be impaired.

(2) If reasonable grounds for insecurity arise with respect to the performance of either party, the insecure party may demand in writing adequate assurance of due performance. Until the insecure party receives that assurance, if commercially reasonable the insecure party may suspend any performance for which he [or she] has not already received the agreed return.

(3) A repudiation of the lease contract occurs if assurance of due performance adequate under the circumstances of the particular case is not provided to the insecure party within a reasonable time, not to exceed 30 days after receipt of a demand by the other party.

(4) Between merchants, the reasonableness of grounds for insecurity and the adequacy of any assurance offered must be determined according to commercial standards.

(5) Acceptance of any nonconforming delivery or payment does not prejudice the aggrieved party's right to demand adequate assurance of future performance.

§ 2A—402. Anticipatory Repudiation.

If either party repudiates a lease contract with respect to a performance not yet due under the lease contract, the loss of which performance will substantially impair the value of the lease contract to the other, the aggrieved party may:

(a) for a commercially reasonable time, await retraction of repudiation and performance by the repudiating party;

(b) make demand pursuant to Section 2A—401 and await assurance of future performance adequate under the circumstances of the particular case; or

(c) resort to any right or remedy upon default under the lease contract or this Article, even though the aggrieved party has notified the repudiating party that the aggrieved party would await the repudiating party's performance and assurance and has urged retraction. In addition, whether or not the aggrieved party is pursuing one of the foregoing remedies, the aggrieved party may suspend performance or, if the aggrieved party is the lessor, proceed in accordance with the provisions of this Article on the lessor's right to identify goods to the lease contract notwithstanding default or to salvage unfinished goods (Section 2A—524).

§ 2A—403. Retraction of Anticipatory Repudiation.

(1) Until the repudiating party's next performance is due, the repudiating party can retract the repudiation unless, since the repudiation, the aggrieved party has cancelled the lease contract or materially changed the aggrieved party's position or otherwise indicated that the aggrieved party considers the repudiation final.

(2) Retraction may be by any method that clearly indicates to the aggrieved party that the repudiating party intends to perform under the lease contract and includes any assurance demanded under Section 2A—401.

(3) Retraction reinstates a repudiating party's rights under a lease contract with due excuse and allowance to the aggrieved party for any delay occasioned by the repudiation.

§ 2A—404. Substituted Performance.

(1) If without fault of the lessee, the lessor and the supplier, the agreed berthing, loading, or unloading facilities fail or the agreed type of carrier becomes unavailable or the agreed manner of delivery otherwise becomes commercially impracticable, but a commercially reasonable substitute is available, the substitute performance must be tendered and accepted.

(2) If the agreed means or manner of payment fails because of domestic or foreign governmental regulation:

(a) the lessor may withhold or stop delivery or cause the supplier to withhold or stop delivery unless the lessee provides a means or manner of payment that is commercially a substantial equivalent; and

(b) if delivery has already been taken, payment by the means or in the manner provided by the regulation discharges the lessee's obligation unless the regulation is discriminatory, oppressive, or predatory.

§ 2A—405. Excused Performance.

Subject to Section 2A—404 on substituted performance, the following rules apply:

(a) Delay in delivery or nondelivery in whole or in part by a lessor or a supplier who complies with paragraphs (b) and

(c) is not a default under the lease contract if performance as agreed has been made impracticable by the occurrence of a contingency the nonoccurrence of which was a basic assumption on which the lease contract was made or by compliance in good faith with any applicable foreign or domestic governmental regulation or order, whether or not the regulation or order later proves to be invalid.

(b) If the causes mentioned in paragraph (a) affect only part of the lessor's or the supplier's capacity to perform, he [or she] shall allocate production and deliveries among his [or her] customers but at his [or her] option may include regular customers not then under contract for sale or lease as well as his [or her] own requirements for further manufacture. He [or she] may so allocate in any manner that is fair and reasonable.

(c) The lessor seasonably shall notify the lessee and in the case of a finance lease the supplier seasonably shall notify the lessor and the lessee, if known, that there will be delay or nondelivery and, if allocation is required under paragraph (b), of the estimated quota thus made available for the lessee.

§ 2A—406. Procedure on Excused Performance.

(1) If the lessee receives notification of a material or indefinite delay or an allocation justified under Section 2A—405, the lessee may by written notification to the lessor as to any goods involved, and with respect to all of the goods if under an installment lease contract the value of the whole lease contract is substantially impaired (Section 2A—510):

(a) terminate the lease contract (Section 2A—505(2)); or

(b) except in a finance lease that is not a consumer lease, modify the lease contract by accepting the available quota in substitution, with due allowance from the rent payable for the balance of the lease term for the deficiency but without further right against the lessor.

(2) If, after receipt of a notification from the lessor under Section 2A—405, the lessee fails so to modify the lease agreement within a reasonable time not exceeding 30 days, the lease contract lapses with respect to any deliveries affected.

§ 2A—407. Irrevocable Promises: Finance Leases.

(1) In the case of a finance lease that is not a consumer lease the lessee's promises under the lease contract become irrevocable and independent upon the lessee's acceptance of the goods.

(2) A promise that has become irrevocable and independent under subsection (1):

(a) is effective and enforceable between the parties, and by or against third parties including assignees of the parties, and

(b) is not subject to cancellation, termination, modification, repudiation, excuse, or substitution without the consent of the party to whom the promise runs.

(3) This section does not affect the validity under any other law of a covenant in any lease contract making the lessee's promises irrevocable and independent upon the lessee's acceptance of the goods.

As amended in 1990.

Part 5 Default

A. In General

§ 2A—501. Default: Procedure.

(1) Whether the lessor or the lessee is in default under a lease contract is determined by the lease agreement and this Article.

(2) If the lessor or the lessee is in default under the lease contract, the party seeking enforcement has rights and remedies as provided in this Article and, except as limited by this Article, as provided in the lease agreement.

(3) If the lessor or the lessee is in default under the lease contract, the party seeking enforcement may reduce the party's claim to judgment, or otherwise enforce the lease contract by self-help or any available judicial procedure or nonjudicial procedure, including administrative proceeding, arbitration, or the like, in accordance with this Article.

(4) Except as otherwise provided in Section 1–106(1) or this Article or the lease agreement, the rights and remedies referred to in subsections (2) and (3) are cumulative.

(5) If the lease agreement covers both real property and goods, the party seeking enforcement may proceed under this Part as to the goods, or under other applicable law as to both the real property and the goods in accordance with that party's rights and remedies in respect of the real property, in which case this Part does not apply.

As amended in 1990.

§ 2A—502. Notice After Default.

Except as otherwise provided in this Article or the lease agreement, the lessor or lessee in default under the lease contract is not entitled to notice of default or notice of enforcement from the other party to the lease agreement.

§ 2A—503. Modification or Impairment of Rights and Remedies.

(1) Except as otherwise provided in this Article, the lease agreement may include rights and remedies for default in addition to or in substitution for those provided in this Article and may limit or alter the measure of damages recoverable under this Article.

(2) Resort to a remedy provided under this Article or in the lease agreement is optional unless the remedy is expressly agreed to be exclusive. If circumstances cause an exclusive or limited remedy to fail of its essential purpose, or provision for an exclusive remedy is unconscionable, remedy may be had as provided in this Article.

(3) Consequential damages may be liquidated under Section 2A—504, or may otherwise be limited, altered, or excluded unless the limitation, alteration, or exclusion is unconscionable. Limitation, alteration, or exclusion of consequential damages for injury to the person in the case of consumer goods is prima facie unconscionable but limitation, alteration, or exclusion of damages where the loss is commercial is not prima facie unconscionable.

(4) Rights and remedies on default by the lessor or the lessee with respect to any obligation or promise collateral or ancillary to the lease contract are not impaired by this Article.

As amended in 1990.

§ 2A—504. Liquidation of Damages.

(1) Damages payable by either party for default, or any other act or omission, including indemnity for loss or diminution of anticipated tax benefits or loss or damage to lessor's residual interest, may be liquidated in the lease agreement but only at an amount or by a formula that is reasonable in light of the then anticipated harm caused by the default or other act or omission.

(2) If the lease agreement provides for liquidation of damages, and such provision does not comply with subsection (1), or such provision is an exclusive or limited remedy that circumstances cause to fail of its essential purpose, remedy may be had as provided in this Article.

(3) If the lessor justifiably withholds or stops delivery of goods because of the lessee's default or insolvency (Section 2A—525 or 2A—526), the lessee is entitled to restitution of any amount by which the sum of his [or her] payments exceeds:

(a) the amount to which the lessor is entitled by virtue of terms liquidating the lessor's damages in accordance with subsection (1); or

(b) in the absence of those terms, 20 percent of the then present value of the total rent the lessee was obligated to pay for the balance of the lease term, or, in the case of a consumer lease, the lesser of such amount or $500.

(4) A lessee's right to restitution under subsection (3) is subject to offset to the extent the lessor establishes:

(a) a right to recover damages under the provisions of this Article other than subsection (1); and

(b) the amount or value of any benefits received by the lessee directly or indirectly by reason of the lease contract.

§ 2A—505. Cancellation and Termination and Effect of Cancellation, Termination, Rescission, or Fraud on Rights and Remedies.

(1) On cancellation of the lease contract, all obligations that are still executory on both sides are discharged, but

any right based on prior default or performance survives, and the cancelling party also retains any remedy for default of the whole lease contract or any unperformed balance.

(2) On termination of the lease contract, all obligations that are still executory on both sides are discharged but any right based on prior default or performance survives.

(3) Unless the contrary intention clearly appears, expressions of "cancellation," "rescission," or the like of the lease contract may not be construed as a renunciation or discharge of any claim in damages for an antecedent default.

(4) Rights and remedies for material misrepresentation or fraud include all rights and remedies available under this Article for default.

(5) Neither rescission nor a claim for rescission of the lease contract nor rejection or return of the goods may bar or be deemed inconsistent with a claim for damages or other right or remedy.

§ 2A—506. Statute of Limitations.

(1) An action for default under a lease contract, including breach of warranty or indemnity, must be commenced within 4 years after the cause of action accrued. By the original lease contract the parties may reduce the period of limitation to not less than one year.

(2) A cause of action for default accrues when the act or omission on which the default or breach of warranty is based is or should have been discovered by the aggrieved party, or when the default occurs, whichever is later. A cause of action for indemnity accrues when the act or omission on which the claim for indemnity is based is or should have been discovered by the indemnified party, whichever is later.

(3) If an action commenced within the time limited by subsection (1) is so terminated as to leave available a remedy by another action for the same default or breach of warranty or indemnity, the other action may be commenced after the expiration of the time limited and within 6 months after the termination of the first action unless the termination resulted from voluntary discontinuance or from dismissal for failure or neglect to prosecute.

(4) This section does not alter the law on tolling of the statute of limitations nor does it apply to causes of action that have accrued before this Article becomes effective.

§ 2A—507. Proof of Market Rent: Time and Place.

(1) Damages based on market rent (Section 2A—519 or 2A—528) are determined according to the rent for the use of the goods concerned for a lease term identical to the remaining lease term of the original lease agreement and prevailing at the times specified in Sections 2A–519 and 2A–528.

(2) If evidence of rent for the use of the goods concerned for a lease term identical to the remaining lease term of the original lease agreement and prevailing at the times or places described in this Article is not readily available, the rent prevailing within any reasonable time before or after the time described or at any other place or for a different lease term which in commercial judgment or under usage of trade would serve as a reasonable substitute for the one described may be used, making any proper allowance for the difference, including the cost of transporting the goods to or from the other place.

(3) Evidence of a relevant rent prevailing at a time or place or for a lease term other than the one described in this Article offered by one party is not admissible unless and until he [or she] has given the other party notice the court finds sufficient to prevent unfair surprise.

(4) If the prevailing rent or value of any goods regularly leased in any established market is in issue, reports in official publications or trade journals or in newspapers or periodicals of general circulation published as the reports of that market are admissible in evidence. The circumstances of the preparation of the report may be shown to affect its weight but not its admissibility.

As amended in 1990.

B. Default by Lessor

§ 2A—508. Lessee's Remedies.

(1) If a lessor fails to deliver the goods in conformity to the lease contract (Section 2A—509) or repudiates the lease contract (Section 2A—402), or a lessee rightfully rejects the goods (Section 2A—509) or justifiably revokes acceptance of the goods (Section 2A—517), then with respect to any goods involved, and with respect to all of the goods if under an installment lease contract the value of the whole lease contract is substantially impaired (Section 2A—510), the lessor is in default under the lease contract and the lessee may:

(a) cancel the lease contract (Section 2A—505(1));

(b) recover so much of the rent and security as has been paid and is just under the circumstances;

(c) cover and recover damages as to all goods affected whether or not they have been identified to the lease contract (Sections 2A—518 and 2A—520), or recover damages for nondelivery (Sections 2A—519 and 2A—520);

(d) exercise any other rights or pursue any other remedies provided in the lease contract..

(2) If a lessor fails to deliver the goods in conformity to the lease contract or repudiates the lease contract, the lessee may also:

(a) if the goods have been identified, recover them (Section 2A—522); or

(b) in a proper case, obtain specific performance or replevy the goods (Section 2A—521).

(3) If a lessor is otherwise in default under a lease contract, the lessee may exercise the rights and pursue the remedies

provided in the lease contract, which may include a right to cancel the lease, and in Section 2A–519(3).

(4) If a lessor has breached a warranty, whether express or implied, the lessee may recover damages (Section 2A–519(4)).

(5) On rightful rejection or justifiable revocation of acceptance, a lessee has a security interest in goods in the lessee's possession or control for any rent and security that has been paid and any expenses reasonably incurred in their inspection, receipt, transportation, and care and custody and may hold those goods and dispose of them in good faith and in a commercially reasonable manner, subject to Section 2A–527(5).

(6) Subject to the provisions of Section 2A–407, a lessee, on notifying the lessor of the lessee's intention to do so, may deduct all or any part of the damages resulting from any default under the lease contract from any part of the rent still due under the same lease contract.

As amended in 1990.

§ 2A–509. Lessee's Rights on Improper Delivery; Rightful Rejection.

(1) Subject to the provisions of Section 2A–510 on default in installment lease contracts, if the goods or the tender or delivery fail in any respect to conform to the lease contract, the lessee may reject or accept the goods or accept any commercial unit or units and reject the rest of the goods.

(2) Rejection of goods is ineffective unless it is within a reasonable time after tender or delivery of the goods and the lessee seasonably notifies the lessor.

§ 2A–510. Installment Lease Contracts: Rejection and Default.

(1) Under an installment lease contract a lessee may reject any delivery that is nonconforming if the nonconformity substantially impairs the value of that delivery and cannot be cured or the nonconformity is a defect in the required documents; but if the nonconformity does not fall within subsection (2) and the lessor or the supplier gives adequate assurance of its cure, the lessee must accept that delivery.

(2) Whenever nonconformity or default with respect to one or more deliveries substantially impairs the value of the installment lease contract as a whole there is a default with respect to the whole. But, the aggrieved party reinstates the installment lease contract as a whole if the aggrieved party accepts a nonconforming delivery without seasonably notifying of cancellation or brings an action with respect only to past deliveries or demands performance as to future deliveries.

§ 2A–511. Merchant Lessee's Duties as to Rightfully Rejected Goods.

(1) Subject to any security interest of a lessee (Section 2A–508(5)), if a lessor or a supplier has no agent or place of business at the market of rejection, a merchant lessee, after rejection of goods in his [or her] possession or control, shall follow any reasonable instructions received from the lessor or the supplier with respect to the goods. In the absence of those instructions, a merchant lessee shall make reasonable efforts to sell, lease, or otherwise dispose of the goods for the lessor's account if they threaten to decline in value speedily. Instructions are not reasonable if on demand indemnity for expenses is not forthcoming.

(2) If a merchant lessee (subsection (1)) or any other lessee (Section 2A–512) disposes of goods, he [or she] is entitled to reimbursement either from the lessor or the supplier or out of the proceeds for reasonable expenses of caring for and disposing of the goods and, if the expenses include no disposition commission, to such commission as is usual in the trade, or if there is none, to a reasonable sum not exceeding 10 percent of the gross proceeds.

(3) In complying with this section or Section 2A–512, the lessee is held only to good faith. Good faith conduct hereunder is neither acceptance or conversion nor the basis of an action for damages.

(4) A purchaser who purchases in good faith from a lessee pursuant to this section or Section 2A–512 takes the goods free of any rights of the lessor and the supplier even though the lessee fails to comply with one or more of the requirements of this Article.

§ 2A–512. Lessee's Duties as to Rightfully Rejected Goods.

(1) Except as otherwise provided with respect to goods that threaten to decline in value speedily (Section 2A–511) and subject to any security interest of a lessee (Section 2A–508(5)):

   (a) the lessee, after rejection of goods in the lessee's possession, shall hold them with reasonable care at the lessor's or the supplier's disposition for a reasonable time after the lessee's seasonable notification of rejection;

   (b) if the lessor or the supplier gives no instructions within a reasonable time after notification of rejection, the lessee may store the rejected goods for the lessor's or the supplier's account or ship them to the lessor or the supplier or dispose of them for the lessor's or the supplier's account with reimbursement in the manner provided in Section 2A–511; but

   (c) the lessee has no further obligations with regard to goods rightfully rejected.

(2) Action by the lessee pursuant to subsection (1) is not acceptance or conversion.

§ 2A–513. Cure by Lessor of Improper Tender or Delivery; Replacement.

(1) If any tender or delivery by the lessor or the supplier is rejected because nonconforming and the time for performance has not yet expired, the lessor or the supplier may

seasonably notify the lessee of the lessor's or the supplier's intention to cure and may then make a conforming delivery within the time provided in the lease contract.

(2) If the lessee rejects a nonconforming tender that the lessor or the supplier had reasonable grounds to believe would be acceptable with or without money allowance, the lessor or the supplier may have a further reasonable time to substitute a conforming tender if he [or she] seasonably notifies the lessee.

§ 2A—514. Waiver of Lessee's Objections.

(1) In rejecting goods, a lessee's failure to state a particular defect that is ascertainable by reasonable inspection precludes the lessee from relying on the defect to justify rejection or to establish default:

(a) if, stated seasonably, the lessor or the supplier could have cured it (Section 2A—513); or

(b) between merchants if the lessor or the supplier after rejection has made a request in writing for a full and final written statement of all defects on which the lessee proposes to rely.

(2) A lessee's failure to reserve rights when paying rent or other consideration against documents precludes recovery of the payment for defects apparent on the face of the documents.

§ 2A—515. Acceptance of Goods.

(1) Acceptance of goods occurs after the lessee has had a reasonable opportunity to inspect the goods and

(a) the lessee signifies or acts with respect to the goods in a manner that signifies to the lessor or the supplier that the goods are conforming or that the lessee will take or retain them in spite of their nonconformity; or

(b) the lessee fails to make an effective rejection of the goods (Section 2A—509(2)).

(2) Acceptance of a part of any commercial unit is acceptance of that entire unit.

§ 2A—516. Effect of Acceptance of Goods; Notice of Default; Burden of Establishing Default after Acceptance; Notice of Claim or Litigation to Person Answerable Over.

(1) A lessee must pay rent for any goods accepted in accordance with the lease contract, with due allowance for goods rightfully rejected or not delivered.

(2) A lessee's acceptance of goods precludes rejection of the goods accepted. In the case of a finance lease, if made with knowledge of a nonconformity, acceptance cannot be revoked because of it. In any other case, if made with knowledge of a nonconformity, acceptance cannot be revoked because of it unless the acceptance was on the reasonable assumption that the nonconformity would be seasonably cured. Acceptance does not of itself impair any other remedy provided by this Article or the lease agreement for nonconformity.

(3) If a tender has been accepted:

(a) within a reasonable time after the lessee discovers or should have discovered any default, the lessee shall notify the lessor and the supplier, if any, or be barred from any remedy against the party notified;

(b) except in the case of a consumer lease, within a reasonable time after the lessee receives notice of litigation for infringement or the like (Section 2A—211) the lessee shall notify the lessor or be barred from any remedy over for liability established by the litigation; and

(c) the burden is on the lessee to establish any default.

(4) If a lessee is sued for breach of a warranty or other obligation for which a lessor or a supplier is answerable over the following apply:

(a) The lessee may give the lessor or the supplier, or both, written notice of the litigation. If the notice states that the person notified may come in and defend and that if the person notified does not do so that person will be bound in any action against that person by the lessee by any determination of fact common to the two litigations, then unless the person notified after seasonable receipt of the notice does come in and defend that person is so bound.

(b) The lessor or the supplier may demand in writing that the lessee turn over control of the litigation including settlement if the claim is one for infringement or the like (Section 2A—211) or else be barred from any remedy over. If the demand states that the lessor or the supplier agrees to bear all expense and to satisfy any adverse judgment, then unless the lessee after seasonable receipt of the demand does turn over control the lessee is so barred.

(5) Subsections (3) and (4) apply to any obligation of a lessee to hold the lessor or the supplier harmless against infringement or the like (Section 2A—211).

As amended in 1990.

§ 2A—517. Revocation of Acceptance of Goods.

(1) A lessee may revoke acceptance of a lot or commercial unit whose nonconformity substantially impairs its value to the lessee if the lessee has accepted it:

(a) except in the case of a finance lease, on the reasonable assumption that its nonconformity would be cured and it has not been seasonably cured; or

(b) without discovery of the nonconformity if the lessee's acceptance was reasonably induced either by the lessor's assurances or, except in the case of a finance lease, by the difficulty of discovery before acceptance.

(2) Except in the case of a finance lease that is not a consumer lease, a lessee may revoke acceptance of a lot or

commercial unit if the lessor defaults under the lease contract and the default substantially impairs the value of that lot or commercial unit to the lessee.

(3) If the lease agreement so provides, the lessee may revoke acceptance of a lot or commercial unit because of other defaults by the lessor.

(4) Revocation of acceptance must occur within a reasonable time after the lessee discovers or should have discovered the ground for it and before any substantial change in condition of the goods which is not caused by the nonconformity. Revocation is not effective until the lessee notifies the lessor.

(5) A lessee who so revokes has the same rights and duties with regard to the goods involved as if the lessee had rejected them.

As amended in 1990.

§ 2A—518. Cover; Substitute Goods.

(1) After a default by a lessor under the lease contract of the type described in Section 2A—508(1), or, if agreed, after other default by the lessor, the lessee may cover by making any purchase or lease of or contract to purchase or lease goods in substitution for those due from the lessor.

(2) Except as otherwise provided with respect to damages liquidated in the lease agreement (Section 2A—504) or otherwise determined pursuant to agreement of the parties (Sections 1—102(3) and 2A—503), if a lessee's cover is by lease agreement substantially similar to the original lease agreement and the new lease agreement is made in good faith and in a commercially reasonable manner, the lessee may recover from the lessor as damages (i) the present value, as of the date of the commencement of the term of the new lease agreement, of the rent under the new lease agreement applicable to that period of the new lease term which is comparable to the then remaining term of the original lease agreement minus the present value as of the same date of the total rent for the then remaining lease term of the original lease agreement, and (ii) any incidental or consequential damages, less expenses saved in consequence of the lessor's default.

(3) If a lessee's cover is by lease agreement that for any reason does not qualify for treatment under subsection (2), or is by purchase or otherwise, the lessee may recover from the lessor as if the lessee had elected not to cover and Section 2A—519 governs.

As amended in 1990.

§ 2A—519. Lessee's Damages for Non-Delivery, Repudiation, Default, and Breach of Warranty in Regard to Accepted Goods.

(1) Except as otherwise provided with respect to damages liquidated in the lease agreement (Section 2A—504) or otherwise determined pursuant to agreement of the parties (Sections 1—102(3) and 2A—503), if a lessee elects not to

cover or a lessee elects to cover and the cover is by lease agreement that for any reason does not qualify for treatment under Section 2A—518(2), or is by purchase or otherwise, the measure of damages for non-delivery or repudiation by the lessor or for rejection or revocation of acceptance by the lessee is the present value, as of the date of the default, of the then market rent minus the present value as of the same date of the original rent, computed for the remaining lease term of the original lease agreement, together with incidental and consequential damages, less expenses saved in consequence of the lessor's default.

(2) Market rent is to be determined as of the place for tender or, in cases of rejection after arrival or revocation of acceptance, as of the place of arrival.

(3) Except as otherwise agreed, if the lessee has accepted goods and given notification (Section 2A—516(3)), the measure of damages for non-conforming tender or delivery or other default by a lessor is the loss resulting in the ordinary course of events from the lessor's default as determined in any manner that is reasonable together with incidental and consequential damages, less expenses saved in consequence of the lessor's default.

(4) Except as otherwise agreed, the measure of damages for breach of warranty is the present value at the time and place of acceptance of the difference between the value of the use of the goods accepted and the value if they had been as warranted for the lease term, unless special circumstances show proximate damages of a different amount, together with incidental and consequential damages, less expenses saved in consequence of the lessor's default or breach of warranty.

As amended in 1990.

§ 2A—520. Lessee's Incidental and Consequential Damages.

(1) Incidental damages resulting from a lessor's default include expenses reasonably incurred in inspection, receipt, transportation, and care and custody of goods rightfully rejected or goods the acceptance of which is justifiably revoked, any commercially reasonable charges, expenses or commissions in connection with effecting cover, and any other reasonable expense incident to the default.

(2) Consequential damages resulting from a lessor's default include:

(a) any loss resulting from general or particular requirements and needs of which the lessor at the time of contracting had reason to know and which could not reasonably be prevented by cover or otherwise; and

(b) injury to person or property proximately resulting from any breach of warranty.

§ 2A—521. Lessee's Right to Specific Performance or Replevin.

(1) Specific performance may be decreed if the goods are unique or in other proper circumstances.

(2) A decree for specific performance may include any terms and conditions as to payment of the rent, damages, or other relief that the court deems just.

(3) A lessee has a right of replevin, detinue, sequestration, claim and delivery, or the like for goods identified to the lease contract if after reasonable effort the lessee is unable to effect cover for those goods or the circumstances reasonably indicate that the effort will be unavailing.

§ 2A—522. Lessee's Right to Goods on Lessor's Insolvency.

(1) Subject to subsection (2) and even though the goods have not been shipped, a lessee who has paid a part or all of the rent and security for goods identified to a lease contract (Section 2A—217) on making and keeping good a tender of any unpaid portion of the rent and security due under the lease contract may recover the goods identified from the lessor if the lessor becomes insolvent within 10 days after receipt of the first installment of rent and security.

(2) A lessee acquires the right to recover goods identified to a lease contract only if they conform to the lease contract.

C. Default by Lessee

§ 2A—523. Lessor's Remedies.

(1) If a lessee wrongfully rejects or revokes acceptance of goods or fails to make a payment when due or repudiates with respect to a part or the whole, then, with respect to any goods involved, and with respect to all of the goods if under an installment lease contract the value of the whole lease contract is substantially impaired (Section 2A—510), the lessee is in default under the lease contract and the lessor may:

(a) cancel the lease contract (Section 2A—505(1));

(b) proceed respecting goods not identified to the lease contract (Section 2A—524);

(c) withhold delivery of the goods and take possession of goods previously delivered (Section 2A—525);

(d) stop delivery of the goods by any bailee (Section 2A—526);

(e) dispose of the goods and recover damages (Section 2A—527), or retain the goods and recover damages (Section 2A—528), or in a proper case recover rent (Section 2A—529)

(f) exercise any other rights or pursue any other remedies provided in the lease contract.

(2) If a lessor does not fully exercise a right or obtain a remedy to which the lessor is entitled under subsection (1), the lessor may recover the loss resulting in the ordinary course of events from the lessee's default as determined in any reasonable manner, together with incidental damages, less expenses saved in consequence of the lessee's default.

(3) If a lessee is otherwise in default under a lease contract, the lessor may exercise the rights and pursue the remedies provided in the lease contract, which may include a right to cancel the lease. In addition, unless otherwise provided in the lease contract:

(a) if the default substantially impairs the value of the lease contract to the lessor, the lessor may exercise the rights and pursue the remedies provided in subsections (1) or (2); or

(b) if the default does not substantially impair the value of the lease contract to the lessor, the lessor may recover as provided in subsection (2).

As amended in 1990.

§ 2A—524. Lessor's Right to Identify Goods to Lease Contract.

(1) After default by the lessee under the lease contract of the type described in Section 2A—523(1) or 2A—523(3)(a) or, if agreed, after other default by the lessee, the lessor may:

(a) identify to the lease contract conforming goods not already identified if at the time the lessor learned of the default they were in the lessor's or the supplier's possession or control; and

(b) dispose of goods (Section 2A—527(1)) that demonstrably have been intended for the particular lease contract even though those goods are unfinished.

(2) If the goods are unfinished, in the exercise of reasonable commercial judgment for the purposes of avoiding loss and of effective realization, an aggrieved lessor or the supplier may either complete manufacture and wholly identify the goods to the lease contract or cease manufacture and lease, sell, or otherwise dispose of the goods for scrap or salvage value or proceed in any other reasonable manner.

As amended in 1990.

§ 2A—525. Lessor's Right to Possession of Goods.

(1) If a lessor discovers the lessee to be insolvent, the lessor may refuse to deliver the goods.

(2) After a default by the lessee under the lease contract of the type described in Section 2A—523(1) or 2A—523(3)(a) or, if agreed, after other default by the lessee, the lessor has the right to take possession of the goods. If the lease contract so provides, the lessor may require the lessee to assemble the goods and make them available to the lessor at a place to be designated by the lessor which is reasonably convenient to both parties. Without removal, the lessor may render unusable any goods employed in trade or business, and may dispose of goods on the lessee's premises (Section 2A—527).

(3) The lessor may proceed under subsection (2) without judicial process if that can be done without breach of the peace or the lessor may proceed by action.

As amended in 1990.

§ 2A—526. Lessor's Stoppage of Delivery in Transit or Otherwise.

(1) A lessor may stop delivery of goods in the possession of a carrier or other bailee if the lessor discovers the lessee to be insolvent and may stop delivery of carload, truckload, planeload, or larger shipments of express or freight if the lessee repudiates or fails to make a payment due before delivery, whether for rent, security or otherwise under the lease contract, or for any other reason the lessor has a right to withhold or take possession of the goods.

(2) In pursuing its remedies under subsection (1), the lessor may stop delivery until

(a) receipt of the goods by the lessee;

(b) acknowledgment to the lessee by any bailee of the goods, except a carrier, that the bailee holds the goods for the lessee; or

(c) such an acknowledgment to the lessee by a carrier via reshipment or as warehouseman.

(3) (a) To stop delivery, a lessor shall so notify as to enable the bailee by reasonable diligence to prevent delivery of the goods.

(b) After notification, the bailee shall hold and deliver the goods according to the directions of the lessor, but the lessor is liable to the bailee for any ensuing charges or damages.

(c) A carrier who has issued a nonnegotiable bill of lading is not obliged to obey a notification to stop received from a person other than the consignor.

§ 2A—527. Lessor's Rights to Dispose of Goods.

(1) After a default by a lessee under the lease contract of the type described in Section 2A—523(1) or 2A–523(3)(a) or after the lessor refuses to deliver or takes possession of goods (Section 2A—525 or 2A—526), or, if agreed, after other default by a lessee, the lessor may dispose of the goods concerned or the undelivered balance thereof by lease, sale, or otherwise.

(2) Except as otherwise provided with respect to damages liquidated in the lease agreement (Section 2A—504) or otherwise determined pursuant to agreement of the parties (Sections 1—102(3) and 2A—503), if the disposition is by lease agreement substantially similar to the original lease agreement and the new lease agreement is made in good faith and in a commercially reasonable manner, the lessor may recover from the lessee as damages (i) accrued and unpaid rent as of the date of the commencement of the term of the new lease agreement, (ii) the present value, as of the same date, of the total rent for the then remaining lease term of the original lease agreement minus the present value, as of the same date, of the rent under the new lease agreement applicable to that period of the new lease term which is comparable to the then remaining term of

the original lease agreement, and (iii) any incidental damages allowed under Section 2A—530, less expenses saved in consequence of the lessee's default.

(3) If the lessor's disposition is by lease agreement that for any reason does not qualify for treatment under subsection (2), or is by sale or otherwise, the lessor may recover from the lessee as if the lessor had elected not to dispose of the goods and Section 2A—528 governs.

(4) A subsequent buyer or lessee who buys or leases from the lessor in good faith for value as a result of a disposition under this section takes the goods free of the original lease contract and any rights of the original lessee even though the lessor fails to comply with one or more of the requirements of this Article.

(5) The lessor is not accountable to the lessee for any profit made on any disposition. A lessee who has rightfully rejected or justifiably revoked acceptance shall account to the lessor for any excess over the amount of the lessee's security interest (Section 2A—508(5)).

As amended in 1990.

§ 2A—528. Lessor's Damages for Non-acceptance, Failure to Pay, Repudiation, or Other Default.

(1) Except as otherwise provided with respect to damages liquidated in the lease agreement (Section 2A—504) or otherwise determined pursuant to agreement of the parties (Section 1—102(3) and 2A—503), if a lessor elects to retain the goods or a lessor elects to dispose of the goods and the disposition is by lease agreement that for any reason does not qualify for treatment under Section 2A—527(2), or is by sale or otherwise, the lessor may recover from the lessee as damages for a default of the type described in Section 2A—523(1) or 2A—523(3)(a), or if agreed, for other default of the lessee, (i) accrued and unpaid rent as of the date of the default if the lessee has never taken possession of the goods, or, if the lessee has taken possession of the goods, as of the date the lessor repossesses the goods or an earlier date on which the lessee makes a tender of the goods to the lessor, (ii) the present value as of the date determined under clause (i) of the total rent for the then remaining lease term of the original lease agreement minus the present value as of the same date of the market rent as the place where the goods are located computed for the same lease term, and (iii) any incidental damages allowed under Section 2A—530, less expenses saved in consequence of the lessee's default.

(2) If the measure of damages provided in subsection (1) is inadequate to put a lessor in as good a position as performance would have, the measure of damages is the present value of the profit, including reasonable overhead, the lessor would have made from full performance by the lessee, together with any incidental damages allowed under Section 2A—530, due allowance for costs

reasonably incurred and due credit for payments or proceeds of disposition.

As amended in 1990.

§ 2A—529. Lessor's Action for the Rent.

(1) After default by the lessee under the lease contract of the type described in Section 2A—523(1) or 2A—523(3)(a) or, if agreed, after other default by the lessee, if the lessor complies with subsection (2), the lessor may recover from the lessee as damages:

    (a) for goods accepted by the lessee and not repossessed by or tendered to the lessor, and for conforming goods lost or damaged within a commercially reasonable time after risk of loss passes to the lessee (Section 2A—219), (i) accrued and unpaid rent as of the date of entry of judgment in favor of the lessor (ii) the present value as of the same date of the rent for the then remaining lease term of the lease agreement, and (iii) any incidental damages allowed under Section 2A—530, less expenses saved in consequence of the lessee's default; and

    (b) for goods identified to the lease contract if the lessor is unable after reasonable effort to dispose of them at a reasonable price or the circumstances reasonably indicate that effort will be unavailing, (i) accrued and unpaid rent as of the date of entry of judgment in favor of the lessor, (ii) the present value as of the same date of the rent for the then remaining lease term of the lease agreement, and (iii) any incidental damages allowed under Section 2A—530, less expenses saved in consequence of the lessee's default.

(2) Except as provided in subsection (3), the lessor shall hold for the lessee for the remaining lease term of the lease agreement any goods that have been identified to the lease contract and are in the lessor's control.

(3) The lessor may dispose of the goods at any time before collection of the judgment for damages obtained pursuant to subsection (1). If the disposition is before the end of the remaining lease term of the lease agreement, the lessor's recovery against the lessee for damages is governed by Section 2A—527 or Section 2A—528, and the lessor will cause an appropriate credit to be provided against a judgment for damages to the extent that the amount of the judgment exceeds the recovery available pursuant to Section 2A—527 or 2A—528.

(4) Payment of the judgment for damages obtained pursuant to subsection (1) entitles the lessee to the use and possession of the goods not then disposed of for the remaining lease term of and in accordance with the lease agreement.

(5) After default by the lessee under the lease contract of the type described in Section 2A—523(1) or Section 2A—523(3)(a) or, if agreed, after other default by the lessee, a lessor who is held not entitled to rent under this section must nevertheless be awarded damages for non-acceptance under Sections 2A—527 and 2A—528.

As amended in 1990.

§ 2A—530. Lessor's Incidental Damages.

Incidental damages to an aggrieved lessor include any commercially reasonable charges, expenses, or commissions incurred in stopping delivery, in the transportation, care and custody of goods after the lessee's default, in connection with return or disposition of the goods, or otherwise resulting from the default.

§ 2A—531. Standing to Sue Third Parties for Injury to Goods.

(1) If a third party so deals with goods that have been identified to a lease contract as to cause actionable injury to a party to the lease contract (a) the lessor has a right of action against the third party, and (b) the lessee also has a right of action against the third party if the lessee:

    (i) has a security interest in the goods;

    (ii) has an insurable interest in the goods; or

    (iii) bears the risk of loss under the lease contract or has since the injury assumed that risk as against the lessor and the goods have been converted or destroyed.

(2) If at the time of the injury the party plaintiff did not bear the risk of loss as against the other party to the lease contract and there is no arrangement between them for disposition of the recovery, his [or her] suit or settlement, subject to his [or her] own interest, is as a fiduciary for the other party to the lease contract.

(3) Either party with the consent of the other may sue for the benefit of whom it may concern.

§ 2A—532. Lessor's Rights to Residual Interest.

In addition to any other recovery permitted by this Article or other law, the lessor may recover from the lessee an amount that will fully compensate the lessor for any loss of or damage to the lessor's residual interest in the goods caused by the default of the lessee.

As added in 1990.

Revised Article 3
NEGOTIABLE INSTRUMENTS

Part 1 General Provisions and Definitions

§ 3—101. Short Title.

This Article may be cited as Uniform Commercial Code—Negotiable Instruments.

§ 3—102. Subject Matter.

(a) This Article applies to negotiable instruments. It does not apply to money, to payment orders governed by Article

4A, or to securities governed by Article 8.

(b) If there is conflict between this Article and Article 4 or 9, Articles 4 and 9 govern.

(c) Regulations of the Board of Governors of the Federal Reserve System and operating circulars of the Federal Reserve Banks supersede any inconsistent provision of this Article to the extent of the inconsistency.

§ 3—103. Definitions.

(a) In this Article:

(1) "Acceptor" means a drawee who has accepted a draft.

(2) "Drawee" means a person ordered in a draft to make payment.

(3) "Drawer" means a person who signs or is identified in a draft as a person ordering payment.

(4) "Good faith" means honesty in fact and the observance of reasonable commercial standards of fair dealing.

(5) "Maker" means a person who signs or is identified in a note as a person undertaking to pay.

(6) "Order" means a written instruction to pay money signed by the person giving the instruction. The instruction may be addressed to any person, including the person giving the instruction, or to one or more persons jointly or in the alternative but not in succession. An authorization to pay is not an order unless the person authorized to pay is also instructed to pay.

(7) "Ordinary care" in the case of a person engaged in business means observance of reasonable commercial standards, prevailing in the area in which the person is located, with respect to the business in which the person is engaged. In the case of a bank that takes an instrument for processing for collection or payment by automated means, reasonable commercial standards do not require the bank to examine the instrument if the failure to examine does not violate the bank's prescribed procedures and the bank's procedures do not vary unreasonably from general banking usage not disapproved by this Article or Article 4.

(8) "Party" means a party to an instrument.

(9) "Promise" means a written undertaking to pay money signed by the person undertaking to pay. An acknowledgment of an obligation by the obligor is not a promise unless the obligor also undertakes to pay the obligation.

(10) "Prove" with respect to a fact means to meet the burden of establishing the fact (Section 1—201(8)).

(11) "Remitter" means a person who purchases an instrument from its issuer if the instrument is payable to an identified person other than the purchaser.

(b);(c) [Other definitions' section references deleted.]

(d) In addition, Article 1 contains general definitions and principles of construction and interpretation applicable throughout this Article.

§ 3—104. Negotiable Instrument.

(a) Except as provided in subsections (c) and (d), "negotiable instrument" means an unconditional promise or order to pay a fixed amount of money, with or without interest or other charges described in the promise or order, if it:

(1) is payable to bearer or to order at the time it is issued or first comes into possession of a holder;

(2) is payable on demand or at a definite time; and

(3) does not state any other undertaking or instruction by the person promising or ordering payment to do any act in addition to the payment of money, but the promise or order may contain (i) an undertaking or power to give, maintain, or protect collateral to secure payment, (ii) an authorization or power to the holder to confess judgment or realize on or dispose of collateral, or (iii) a waiver of the benefit of any law intended for the advantage or protection of an obligor.

(b) "Instrument" means a negotiable instrument.

(c) An order that meets all of the requirements of subsection (a), except paragraph (1), and otherwise falls within the definition of "check" in subsection (f) is a negotiable instrument and a check.

(d) A promise or order other than a check is not an instrument if, at the time it is issued or first comes into possession of a holder, it contains a conspicuous statement, however expressed, to the effect that the promise or order is not negotiable or is not an instrument governed by this Article.

(e) An instrument is a "note" if it is a promise and is a "draft" if it is an order. If an instrument falls within the definition of both "note" and "draft," a person entitled to enforce the instrument may treat it as either.

(f) "Check" means (i) a draft, other than a documentary draft, payable on demand and drawn on a bank or (ii) a cashier's check or teller's check. An instrument may be a check even though it is described on its face by another term, such as "money order."

(g) "Cashier's check" means a draft with respect to which the drawer and drawee are the same bank or branches of the same bank.

(h) "Teller's check" means a draft drawn by a bank (i) on another bank, or (ii) payable at or through a bank.

(i) "Traveler's check" means an instrument that (i) is payable on demand, (ii) is drawn on or payable at or through a bank, (iii) is designated by the term "traveler's check" or by a substantially similar term, and

(iv) requires, as a condition to payment, a countersignature by a person whose specimen signature appears on the instrument.

(j) "Certificate of deposit" means an instrument containing an acknowledgment by a bank that a sum of money has been received by the bank and a promise by the bank to repay the sum of money. A certificate of deposit is a note of the bank.

§ 3—105. Issue of Instrument.

(a) "Issue" means the first delivery of an instrument by the maker or drawer, whether to a holder or nonholder, for the purpose of giving rights on the instrument to any person.

(b) An unissued instrument, or an unissued incomplete instrument that is completed, is binding on the maker or drawer, but nonissuance is a defense. An instrument that is conditionally issued or is issued for a special purpose is binding on the maker or drawer, but failure of the condition or special purpose to be fulfilled is a defense.

(c) "Issuer" applies to issued and unissued instruments and means a maker or drawer of an instrument.

§ 3—106. Unconditional Promise or Order.

(a) Except as provided in this section, for the purposes of Section 3—104(a), a promise or order is unconditional unless it states (i) an express condition to payment, (ii) that the promise or order is subject to or governed by another writing, or (iii) that rights or obligations with respect to the promise or order are stated in another writing. A reference to another writing does not of itself make the promise or order conditional.

(b) A promise or order is not made conditional (i) by a reference to another writing for a statement of rights with respect to collateral, prepayment, or acceleration, or (ii) because payment is limited to resort to a particular fund or source.

(c) If a promise or order requires, as a condition to payment, a countersignature by a person whose specimen signature appears on the promise or order, the condition does not make the promise or order conditional for the purposes of Section 3—104(a). If the person whose specimen signature appears on an instrument fails to countersign the instrument, the failure to countersign is a defense to the obligation of the issuer, but the failure does not prevent a transferee of the instrument from becoming a holder of the instrument.

(d) If a promise or order at the time it is issued or first comes into possession of a holder contains a statement, required by applicable statutory or administrative law, to the effect that the rights of a holder or transferee are subject to claims or defenses that the issuer could assert against the original payee, the promise or order is not thereby made conditional for the purposes of Section 3—104(a); but if the promise or order is an instrument, there cannot be a holder in due course of the instrument.

§ 3—107. Instrument Payable in Foreign Money.

Unless the instrument otherwise provides, an instrument that states the amount payable in foreign money may be paid in the foreign money or in an equivalent amount in dollars calculated by using the current bank-offered spot rate at the place of payment for the purchase of dollars on the day on which the instrument is paid.

§ 3—108. Payable on Demand or at Definite Time.

(a) A promise or order is "payable on demand" if it (i) states that it is payable on demand or at sight, or otherwise indicates that it is payable at the will of the holder, or (ii) does not state any time of payment.

(b) A promise or order is "payable at a definite time" if it is payable on elapse of a definite period of time after sight or acceptance or at a fixed date or dates or at a time or times readily ascertainable at the time the promise or order is issued, subject to rights of (i) prepayment, (ii) acceleration, (iii) extension at the option of the holder, or (iv) extension to a further definite time at the option of the maker or acceptor or automatically upon or after a specified act or event.

(c) If an instrument, payable at a fixed date, is also payable upon demand made before the fixed date, the instrument is payable on demand until the fixed date and, if demand for payment is not made before that date, becomes payable at a definite time on the fixed date.

§ 3—109. Payable to Bearer or to Order.

(a) A promise or order is payable to bearer if it:

(1) states that it is payable to bearer or to the order of bearer or otherwise indicates that the person in possession of the promise or order is entitled to payment;

(2) does not state a payee; or

(3) states that it is payable to or to the order of cash or otherwise indicates that it is not payable to an identified person.

(b) A promise or order that is not payable to bearer is payable to order if it is payable (i) to the order of an identified person or (ii) to an identified person or order. A promise or order that is payable to order is payable to the identified person.

(c) An instrument payable to bearer may become payable to an identified person if it is specially indorsed pursuant to Section 3—205(a). An instrument payable to an identified person may become payable to bearer if it is indorsed in blank pursuant to Section 3—205(b).

§ 3—110. Identification of Person to Whom Instrument Is Payable.

(a) The person to whom an instrument is initially payable is determined by the intent of the person, whether or not authorized, signing as, or in the name or behalf of, the issuer of the instrument. The instrument is payable to the person intended by the signer even if that person is identified in the instrument by a name or other identification that is not that of the intended person. If more than one person signs in the name or behalf of the issuer of an instrument and all the signers do not intend the same person as payee, the instrument is payable to any person intended by one or more of the signers.

(b) If the signature of the issuer of an instrument is made by automated means, such as a check-writing machine, the payee of the instrument is determined by the intent of the person who supplied the name or identification of the payee, whether or not authorized to do so.

(c) A person to whom an instrument is payable may be identified in any way, including by name, identifying number, office, or account number. For the purpose of determining the holder of an instrument, the following rules apply:

    (1) If an instrument is payable to an account and the account is identified only by number, the instrument is payable to the person to whom the account is payable. If an instrument is payable to an account identified by number and by the name of a person, the instrument is payable to the named person, whether or not that person is the owner of the account identified by number.

    (2) If an instrument is payable to:

        (i) a trust, an estate, or a person described as trustee or representative of a trust or estate, the instrument is payable to the trustee, the representative, or a successor of either, whether or not the beneficiary or estate is also named;

        (ii) a person described as agent or similar representative of a named or identified person, the instrument is payable to the represented person, the representative, or a successor of the representative;

        (iii) a fund or organization that is not a legal entity, the instrument is payable to a representative of the members of the fund or organization; or

        (iv) an office or to a person described as holding an office, the instrument is payable to the named person, the incumbent of the office, or a successor to the incumbent.

(d) If an instrument is payable to two or more persons alternatively, it is payable to any of them and may be negotiated, discharged, or enforced by any or all of them in possession of the instrument. If an instrument is payable to two or more persons not alternatively, it is payable to all of them and may be negotiated, discharged, or enforced only by all of them. If an instrument payable to two or more persons is ambiguous as to whether it is payable to the persons alternatively, the instrument is payable to the persons alternatively.

§ 3—111. Place of Payment.

Except as otherwise provided for items in Article 4, an instrument is payable at the place of payment stated in the instrument. If no place of payment is stated, an instrument is payable at the address of the drawee or maker stated in the instrument. If no address is stated, the place of payment is the place of business of the drawee or maker. If a drawee or maker has more than one place of business, the place of payment is any place of business of the drawee or maker chosen by the person entitled to enforce the instrument. If the drawee or maker has no place of business, the place of payment is the residence of the drawee or maker.

§ 3—112. Interest.

(a) Unless otherwise provided in the instrument, (i) an instrument is not payable with interest, and (ii) interest on an interest-bearing instrument is payable from the date of the instrument.

(b) Interest may be stated in an instrument as a fixed or variable amount of money or it may be expressed as a fixed or variable rate or rates. The amount or rate of interest may be stated or described in the instrument in any manner and may require reference to information not contained in the instrument. If an instrument provides for interest, but the amount of interest payable cannot be ascertained from the description, interest is payable at the judgment rate in effect at the place of payment of the instrument and at the time interest first accrues.

§ 3—113. Date of Instrument.

(a) An instrument may be antedated or postdated. The date stated determines the time of payment if the instrument is payable at a fixed period after date. Except as provided in Section 4—401(c), an instrument payable on demand is not payable before the date of the instrument.

(b) If an instrument is undated, its date is the date of its issue or, in the case of an unissued instrument, the date it first comes into possession of a holder.

§ 3—114. Contradictory Terms of Instrument.

If an instrument contains contradictory terms, typewritten terms prevail over printed terms, handwritten terms prevail over both, and words prevail over numbers.

§ 3—115. Incomplete Instrument.

(a) "Incomplete instrument" means a signed writing, whether or not issued by the signer, the contents of which show at the time of signing that it is incomplete but that the signer intended it to be completed by the addition of words or numbers.

(b) Subject to subsection (c), if an incomplete instrument is an instrument under Section 3—104, it may be enforced according to its terms if it is not completed, or according to its terms as augmented by completion. If an incomplete instrument is not an instrument under Section 3—104, but, after completion, the requirements of Section 3—104 are met, the instrument may be enforced according to its terms as augmented by completion.

(c) If words or numbers are added to an incomplete instrument without authority of the signer, there is an alteration of the incomplete instrument under Section 3—407.

(d) The burden of establishing that words or numbers were added to an incomplete instrument without authority of the signer is on the person asserting the lack of authority.

§ 3—116. Joint and Several Liability; Contribution.

(a) Except as otherwise provided in the instrument, two or more persons who have the same liability on an instrument as makers, drawers, acceptors, indorsers who indorse as joint payees, or anomalous indorsers are jointly and severally liable in the capacity in which they sign.

(b) Except as provided in Section 3—419(e) or by agreement of the affected parties, a party having joint and several liability who pays the instrument is entitled to receive from any party having the same joint and several liability contribution in accordance with applicable law.

(c) Discharge of one party having joint and several liability by a person entitled to enforce the instrument does not affect the right under subsection (b) of a party having the same joint and several liability to receive contribution from the party discharged.

§ 3—117. Other Agreements Affecting Instrument.

Subject to applicable law regarding exclusion of proof of contemporaneous or previous agreements, the obligation of a party to an instrument to pay the instrument may be modified, supplemented, or nullified by a separate agreement of the obligor and a person entitled to enforce the instrument, if the instrument is issued or the obligation is incurred in reliance on the agreement or as part of the same transaction giving rise to the agreement. To the extent an obligation is modified, supplemented, or nullified by an agreement under this section, the agreement is a defense to the obligation.

§ 3—118. Statute of Limitations.

(a) Except as provided in subsection (e), an action to enforce the obligation of a party to pay a note payable at a definite time must be commenced within six years after the due date or dates stated in the note or, if a due date is accelerated, within six years after the accelerated due date.

(b) Except as provided in subsection (d) or (e), if demand for payment is made to the maker of a note payable on demand, an action to enforce the obligation of a party to pay the note must be commenced within six years after the demand. If no demand for payment is made to the maker, an action to enforce the note is barred if neither principal nor interest on the note has been paid for a continuous period of 10 years.

(c) Except as provided in subsection (d), an action to enforce the obligation of a party to an unaccepted draft to pay the draft must be commenced within three years after dishonor of the draft or 10 years after the date of the draft, whichever period expires first.

(d) An action to enforce the obligation of the acceptor of a certified check or the issuer of a teller's check, cashier's check, or traveler's check must be commenced within three years after demand for payment is made to the acceptor or issuer, as the case may be.

(e) An action to enforce the obligation of a party to a certificate of deposit to pay the instrument must be commenced within six years after demand for payment is made to the maker, but if the instrument states a due date and the maker is not required to pay before that date, the six-year period begins when a demand for payment is in effect and the due date has passed.

(f) An action to enforce the obligation of a party to pay an accepted draft, other than a certified check, must be commenced (i) within six years after the due date or dates stated in the draft or acceptance if the obligation of the acceptor is payable at a definite time, or (ii) within six years after the date of the acceptance if the obligation of the acceptor is payable on demand.

(g) Unless governed by other law regarding claims for indemnity or contribution, an action (i) for conversion of an instrument, for money had and received, or like action based on conversion, (ii) for breach of warranty, or (iii) to enforce an obligation, duty, or right arising under this Article and not governed by this section must be commenced within three years after the [cause of action] accrues.

§ 3—119. Notice of Right to Defend Action.

In an action for breach of an obligation for which a third person is answerable over pursuant to this Article or Article 4, the defendant may give the third person written notice of the litigation, and the person notified may then give similar notice to any other person who is answerable over. If the notice states (i) that the person notified may come in and defend and (ii) that failure to do so will bind the person notified in an action later brought by the person giving the notice as to any determination of fact common to the two litigations, the person notified is so bound unless after seasonable receipt of the notice the person notified does come in and defend.

Part 2 Negotiation, Transfer, and Indorsement

§ 3—201. Negotiation.

(a) "Negotiation" means a transfer of possession, whether voluntary or involuntary, of an instrument by a person other than the issuer to a person who thereby becomes its holder.

(b) Except for negotiation by a remitter, if an instrument is payable to an identified person, negotiation requires transfer of possession of the instrument and its indorsement by the holder. If an instrument is payable to bearer, it may be negotiated by transfer of possession alone.

§ 3—202. Negotiation Subject to Rescission.

(a) Negotiation is effective even if obtained (i) from an infant, a corporation exceeding its powers, or a person without capacity, (ii) by fraud, duress, or mistake, or (iii) in breach of duty or as part of an illegal transaction.

(b) To the extent permitted by other law, negotiation may be rescinded or may be subject to other remedies, but those remedies may not be asserted against a subsequent holder in due course or a person paying the instrument in good faith and without knowledge of facts that are a basis for rescission or other remedy.

§ 3—203. Transfer of Instrument; Rights Acquired by Transfer.

(a) An instrument is transferred when it is delivered by a person other than its issuer for the purpose of giving to the person receiving delivery the right to enforce the instrument.

(b) Transfer of an instrument, whether or not the transfer is a negotiation, vests in the transferee any right of the transferor to enforce the instrument, including any right as a holder in due course, but the transferee cannot acquire rights of a holder in due course by a transfer, directly or indirectly, from a holder in due course if the transferee engaged in fraud or illegality affecting the instrument.

(c) Unless otherwise agreed, if an instrument is transferred for value and the transferee does not become a holder because of lack of indorsement by the transferor, the transferee has a specifically enforceable right to the unqualified indorsement of the transferor, but negotiation of the instrument does not occur until the indorsement is made.

(d) If a transferor purports to transfer less than the entire instrument, negotiation of the instrument does not occur. The transferee obtains no rights under this Article and has only the rights of a partial assignee.

§ 3—204. Indorsement.

(a) "Indorsement" means a signature, other than that of a signer as maker, drawer, or acceptor, that alone or accompanied by other words is made on an instrument for the purpose of (i) negotiating the instrument, (ii) restricting payment of the instrument, or (iii) incurring indorser's liability on the instrument, but regardless of the intent of the signer, a signature and its accompanying words is an indorsement unless the accompanying words, terms of the instrument, place of the signature, or other circumstances unambiguously indicate that the signature was made for a purpose other than indorsement. For the purpose of determining whether a signature is made on an instrument, a paper affixed to the instrument is a part of the instrument.

(b) "Indorser" means a person who makes an indorsement.

(c) For the purpose of determining whether the transferee

of an instrument is a holder, an indorsement that transfers a security interest in the instrument is effective as an unqualified indorsement of the instrument.

(d) If an instrument is payable to a holder under a name that is not the name of the holder, indorsement may be made by the holder in the name stated in the instrument or in the holder's name or both, but signature in both names may be required by a person paying or taking the instrument for value or collection.

§ 3—205. Special Indorsement; Blank Indorsement; Anomalous Indorsement.

(a) If an indorsement is made by the holder of an instrument, whether payable to an identified person or payable to bearer, and the indorsement identifies a person to whom it makes the instrument payable, it is a "special indorsement." When specially indorsed, an instrument becomes payable to the identified person and may be negotiated only by the indorsement of that person. The principles stated in Section 3—110 apply to special indorsements.

(b) If an indorsement is made by the holder of an instrument and it is not a special indorsement, it is a "blank indorsement." When indorsed in blank, an instrument becomes payable to bearer and may be negotiated by transfer of possession alone until specially indorsed.

(c) The holder may convert a blank indorsement that consists only of a signature into a special indorsement by writing, above the signature of the indorser, words identifying the person to whom the instrument is made payable.

(d) "Anomalous indorsement" means an indorsement made by a person who is not the holder of the instrument. An anomalous indorsement does not affect the manner in which the instrument may be negotiated.

§ 3—206. Restrictive Indorsement.

(a) An indorsement limiting payment to a particular person or otherwise prohibiting further transfer or negotiation of the instrument is not effective to prevent further transfer or negotiation of the instrument.

(b) An indorsement stating a condition to the right of the indorsee to receive payment does not affect the right of the indorsee to enforce the instrument. A person paying the instrument or taking it for value or collection may disregard the condition, and the rights and liabilities of that person are not affected by whether the condition has been fulfilled.

(c) If an instrument bears an indorsement (i) described in Section 4—201(b), or (ii) in blank or to a particular bank using the words "for deposit," "for collection," or other words indicating a purpose of having the instrument collected by a bank for the indorser or for a particular account, the following rules apply:

(1) A person, other than a bank, who purchases the instrument when so indorsed converts the instrument unless the amount paid for the instrument is received

by the indorser or applied consistently with the indorsement.

(2) A depository bank that purchases the instrument or takes it for collection when so indorsed converts the instrument unless the amount paid by the bank with respect to the instrument is received by the indorser or applied consistently with the indorsement.

(3) A payor bank that is also the depository bank or that takes the instrument for immediate payment over the counter from a person other than a collecting bank converts the instrument unless the proceeds of the instrument are received by the indorser or applied consistently with the indorsement.

(4) Except as otherwise provided in paragraph (3), a payor bank or intermediary bank may disregard the indorsement and is not liable if the proceeds of the instrument are not received by the indorser or applied consistently with the indorsement.

(d) Except for an indorsement covered by subsection (c), if an instrument bears an indorsement using words to the effect that payment is to be made to the indorsee as agent, trustee, or other fiduciary for the benefit of the indorser or another person, the following rules apply:

(1) Unless there is notice of breach of fiduciary duty as provided in Section 3—307, a person who purchases the instrument from the indorsee or takes the instrument from the indorsee for collection or payment may pay the proceeds of payment or the value given for the instrument to the indorsee without regard to whether the indorsee violates a fiduciary duty to the indorser.

(2) A subsequent transferee of the instrument or person who pays the instrument is neither given notice nor otherwise affected by the restriction in the indorsement unless the transferee or payor knows that the fiduciary dealt with the instrument or its proceeds in breach of fiduciary duty.

(e) The presence on an instrument of an indorsement to which this section applies does not prevent a purchaser of the instrument from becoming a holder in due course of the instrument unless the purchaser is a converter under subsection (c) or has notice or knowledge of breach of fiduciary duty as stated in subsection (d).

(f) In an action to enforce the obligation of a party to pay the instrument, the obligor has a defense if payment would violate an indorsement to which this section applies and the payment is not permitted by this section.

§ 3—207. Reacquisition.

Reacquisition of an instrument occurs if it is transferred to a former holder, by negotiation or otherwise. A former holder who reacquires the instrument may cancel indorsements made after the reacquirer first became a holder of the instrument. If the cancellation causes the instrument to be payable to the reacquirer or to bearer, the reacquirer

may negotiate the instrument. An indorser whose indorsement is canceled is discharged, and the discharge is effective against any subsequent holder.

Part 3 Enforcement of Instruments

§ 3—301. Person Entitled to Enforce Instrument.

"Person entitled to enforce" an instrument means (i) the holder of the instrument, (ii) a nonholder in possession of the instrument who has the rights of a holder, or (iii) a person not in possession of the instrument who is entitled to enforce the instrument pursuant to Section 3—309 or 3—418(d). A person may be a person entitled to enforce the instrument even though the person is not the owner of the instrument or is in wrongful possession of the instrument.

§ 3—302. Holder in Due Course.

(a) Subject to subsection (c) and Section 3—106(d), "holder in due course" means the holder of an instrument if:

(1) the instrument when issued or negotiated to the holder does not bear such apparent evidence of forgery or alteration or is not otherwise so irregular or incomplete as to call into question its authenticity; and

(2) the holder took the instrument (i) for value, (ii) in good faith, (iii) without notice that the instrument is overdue or has been dishonored or that there is an uncured default with respect to payment of another instrument issued as part of the same series, (iv) without notice that the instrument contains an unauthorized signature or has been altered, (v) without notice of any claim to the instrument described in Section 3—306, and (vi) without notice that any party has a defense or claim in recoupment described in Section 3—305(a).

(b) Notice of discharge of a party, other than discharge in an insolvency proceeding, is not notice of a defense under subsection (a), but discharge is effective against a person who became a holder in due course with notice of the discharge. Public filing or recording of a document does not of itself constitute notice of a defense, claim in recoupment, or claim to the instrument.

(c) Except to the extent a transferor or predecessor in interest has rights as a holder in due course, a person does not acquire rights of a holder in due course of an instrument taken (i) by legal process or by purchase in an execution, bankruptcy, or creditor's sale or similar proceeding, (ii) by purchase as part of a bulk transaction not in ordinary course of business of the transferor, or (iii) as the successor in interest to an estate or other organization.

(d) If, under Section 3—303(a)(1), the promise of performance that is the consideration for an instrument has been partially performed, the holder may assert rights as a holder in due course of the instrument only to the fraction of the amount payable under the instrument equal to the value of the partial performance divided by the value of the promised performance.

(e) If (i) the person entitled to enforce an instrument has only a security interest in the instrument and (ii) the person obliged to pay the instrument has a defense, claim in recoupment, or claim to the instrument that may be asserted against the person who granted the security interest, the person entitled to enforce the instrument may assert rights as a holder in due course only to an amount payable under the instrument which, at the time of enforcement of the instrument, does not exceed the amount of the unpaid obligation secured.

(f) To be effective, notice must be received at a time and in a manner that gives a reasonable opportunity to act on it.

(g) This section is subject to any law limiting status as a holder in due course in particular classes of transactions.

§ 3—303. Value and Consideration.

(a) An instrument is issued or transferred for value if:

(1) the instrument is issued or transferred for a promise of performance, to the extent the promise has been performed;

(2) the transferee acquires a security interest or other lien in the instrument other than a lien obtained by judicial proceeding;

(3) the instrument is issued or transferred as payment of, or as security for, an antecedent claim against any person, whether or not the claim is due;

(4) the instrument is issued or transferred in exchange for a negotiable instrument; or

(5) the instrument is issued or transferred in exchange for the incurring of an irrevocable obligation to a third party by the person taking the instrument.

(b) "Consideration" means any consideration sufficient to support a simple contract. The drawer or maker of an instrument has a defense if the instrument is issued without consideration. If an instrument is issued for a promise of performance, the issuer has a defense to the extent performance of the promise is due and the promise has not been performed. If an instrument is issued for value as stated in subsection (a), the instrument is also issued for consideration.

§ 3—304. Overdue Instrument.

(a) An instrument payable on demand becomes overdue at the earliest of the following times:

(1) on the day after the day demand for payment is duly made;

(2) if the instrument is a check, 90 days after its date; or

(3) if the instrument is not a check, when the instrument has been outstanding for a period of time after its date which is unreasonably long under the circumstances of the particular case in light of the nature of the instrument and usage of the trade.

(b) With respect to an instrument payable at a definite time the following rules apply:

(1) If the principal is payable in installments and a due date has not been accelerated, the instrument becomes overdue upon default under the instrument for nonpayment of an installment, and the instrument remains overdue until the default is cured.

(2) If the principal is not payable in installments and the due date has not been accelerated, the instrument becomes overdue on the day after the due date.

(3) If a due date with respect to principal has been accelerated, the instrument becomes overdue on the day after the accelerated due date.

(c) Unless the due date of principal has been accelerated, an instrument does not become overdue if there is default in payment of interest but no default in payment of principal.

§ 3—305. Defenses and Claims in Recoupment.

(a) Except as stated in subsection (b), the right to enforce the obligation of a party to pay an instrument is subject to the following:

(1) a defense of the obligor based on (i) infancy of the obligor to the extent it is a defense to a simple contract, (ii) duress, lack of legal capacity, or illegality of the transaction which, under other law, nullifies the obligation of the obligor, (iii) fraud that induced the obligor to sign the instrument with neither knowledge nor reasonable opportunity to learn of its character or its essential terms, or (iv) discharge of the obligor in insolvency proceedings;

(2) a defense of the obligor stated in another section of this Article or a defense of the obligor that would be available if the person entitled to enforce the instrument were enforcing a right to payment under a simple contract; and

(3) a claim in recoupment of the obligor against the original payee of the instrument if the claim arose from the transaction that gave rise to the instrument; but the claim of the obligor may be asserted against a transferee of the instrument only to reduce the amount owing on the instrument at the time the action is brought.

(b) The right of a holder in due course to enforce the obligation of a party to pay the instrument is subject to defenses of the obligor stated in subsection (a)(1), but is not subject to defenses of the obligor stated in subsection (a)(2) or claims in recoupment stated in subsection (a)(3) against a person other than the holder.

(c) Except as stated in subsection (d), in an action to enforce the obligation of a party to pay the instrument, the obligor may not assert against the person entitled to enforce the instrument a defense, claim in recoupment, or claim to the instrument (Section 3—306) of another person, but the other person's claim to the instrument may be asserted by the obligor if the other person is joined in the action and personally asserts the claim against the person entitled to enforce the instrument. An obligor is not obliged to pay the instrument if the person seeking enforcement of the instrument does not have rights of a holder in due course and the obligor proves that the instrument is a lost or stolen instrument.

(d) In an action to enforce the obligation of an accommodation party to pay an instrument, the accommodation party may assert against the person entitled to enforce the instrument any defense or claim in recoupment under subsection (a) that the accommodated party could assert against the person entitled to enforce the instrument, except the defenses of discharge in insolvency proceedings, infancy, and lack of legal capacity.

§ 3—306. **Claims to an Instrument.**

A person taking an instrument, other than a person having rights of a holder in due course, is subject to a claim of a property or possessory right in the instrument or its proceeds, including a claim to rescind a negotiation and to recover the instrument or its proceeds. A person having rights of a holder in due course takes free of the claim to the instrument.

§ 3—307. **Notice of Breach of Fiduciary Duty.**

(a) In this section:

(1) "Fiduciary" means an agent, trustee, partner, corporate officer or director, or other representative owing a fiduciary duty with respect to an instrument.

(2) "Represented person" means the principal, beneficiary, partnership, corporation, or other person to whom the duty stated in paragraph (1) is owed.

(b) If (i) an instrument is taken from a fiduciary for payment or collection or for value, (ii) the taker has knowledge of the fiduciary status of the fiduciary, and (iii) the represented person makes a claim to the instrument or its proceeds on the basis that the transaction of the fiduciary is a breach of fiduciary duty, the following rules apply:

(1) Notice of breach of fiduciary duty by the fiduciary is notice of the claim of the represented person.

(2) In the case of an instrument payable to the represented person or the fiduciary as such, the taker has notice of the breach of fiduciary duty if the instrument is (i) taken in payment of or as security for a debt known by the taker to be the personal debt of the fiduciary, (ii) taken in a transaction known by the taker to be for the personal benefit of the fiduciary, or (iii) deposited to an account other than an account of the fiduciary, as such, or an account of the represented person.

(3) If an instrument is issued by the represented person or the fiduciary as such, and made payable to the fiduciary personally, the taker does not have notice of the breach of fiduciary duty unless the taker knows of the breach of fiduciary duty.

(4) If an instrument is issued by the represented person or the fiduciary as such, to the taker as payee, the taker has notice of the breach of fiduciary duty if the instrument is (i) taken in payment of or as security for a debt known by the taker to be the personal debt of the fiduciary, (ii) taken in a transaction known by the taker to be for the personal benefit of the fiduciary, or (iii) deposited to an account other than an account of the fiduciary, as such, or an account of the represented person.

§ 3—308. **Proof of Signatures and Status as Holder in Due Course.**

(a) In an action with respect to an instrument, the authenticity of, and authority to make, each signature on the instrument is admitted unless specifically denied in the pleadings. If the validity of a signature is denied in the pleadings, the burden of establishing validity is on the person claiming validity, but the signature is presumed to be authentic and authorized unless the action is to enforce the liability of the purported signer and the signer is dead or incompetent at the time of trial of the issue of validity of the signature. If an action to enforce the instrument is brought against a person as the undisclosed principal of a person who signed the instrument as a party to the instrument, the plaintiff has the burden of establishing that the defendant is liable on the instrument as a represented person under Section 3—402(a).

(b) If the validity of signatures is admitted or proved and there is compliance with subsection (a), a plaintiff producing the instrument is entitled to payment if the plaintiff proves entitlement to enforce the instrument under Section 3—301, unless the defendant proves a defense or claim in recoupment. If a defense or claim in recoupment is proved, the right to payment of the plaintiff is subject to the defense or claim, except to the extent the plaintiff proves that the plaintiff has rights of a holder in due course which are not subject to the defense or claim.

§ 3—309. **Enforcement of Lost, Destroyed, or Stolen Instrument.**

(a) A person not in possession of an instrument is entitled to enforce the instrument if (i) the person was in possession of the instrument and entitled to enforce it when loss of possession occurred, (ii) the loss of possession was not the result of a transfer by the person or a lawful seizure, and (iii) the person cannot reasonably obtain possession of the instrument because the instrument was destroyed, its whereabouts cannot be determined, or it is in the wrongful possession of an unknown person or a person that cannot be found or is not amenable to service of process.

(b) A person seeking enforcement of an instrument under subsection (a) must prove the terms of the instrument and the person's right to enforce the instrument. If that proof is made, Section 3—308 applies to the case as if the person seeking enforcement had produced the instrument. The court may not enter judgment in favor of the person seeking enforcement unless it finds that the person required to pay the instrument is adequately protected against loss that might occur by reason of a claim by another person to enforce the instrument. Adequate protection may be provided by any reasonable means.

§ 3—310. Effect of Instrument on Obligation for Which Taken.

(a) Unless otherwise agreed, if a certified check, cashier's check, or teller's check is taken for an obligation, the obligation is discharged to the same extent discharge would result if an amount of money equal to the amount of the instrument were taken in payment of the obligation. Discharge of the obligation does not affect any liability that the obligor may have as an indorser of the instrument.

(b) Unless otherwise agreed and except as provided in subsection (a), if a note or an uncertified check is taken for an obligation, the obligation is suspended to the same extent the obligation would be discharged if an amount of money equal to the amount of the instrument were taken, and the following rules apply:

(1) In the case of an uncertified check, suspension of the obligation continues until dishonor of the check or until it is paid or certified. Payment or certification of the check results in discharge of the obligation to the extent of the amount of the check.

(2) In the case of a note, suspension of the obligation continues until dishonor of the note or until it is paid. Payment of the note results in discharge of the obligation to the extent of the payment.

(3) Except as provided in paragraph (4), if the check or note is dishonored and the obligee of the obligation for which the instrument was taken is the person entitled to enforce the instrument, the obligee may enforce either the instrument or the obligation. In the case of an instrument of a third person which is negotiated to the obligee by the obligor, discharge of the obligor on the instrument also discharges the obligation.

(4) If the person entitled to enforce the instrument taken for an obligation is a person other than the obligee, the obligee may not enforce the obligation to the extent the obligation is suspended. If the obligee is the person entitled to enforce the instrument but no longer has possession of it because it was lost, stolen, or destroyed, the obligation may not be enforced to the extent of the amount payable on the instrument, and to that extent the obligee's rights against the obligor are limited to enforcement of the instrument.

(c) If an instrument other than one described in subsection (a) or (b) is taken for an obligation, the effect is (i) that stated in subsection (a) if the instrument is one on which a bank is liable as maker or acceptor, or (ii) that stated in subsection (b) in any other case.

§ 3—311. Accord and Satisfaction by Use of Instrument.

(a) If a person against whom a claim is asserted proves that (i) that person in good faith tendered an instrument to the claimant as full satisfaction of the claim, (ii) the amount of the claim was unliquidated or subject to a bona fide dispute, and (iii) the claimant obtained payment of the instrument, the following subsections apply.

(b) Unless subsection (c) applies, the claim is discharged if the person against whom the claim is asserted proves that the instrument or an accompanying written communication contained a conspicuous statement to the effect that the instrument was tendered as full satisfaction of the claim.

(c) Subject to subsection (d), a claim is not discharged under subsection (b) if either of the following applies:

(1) The claimant, if an organization, proves that (i) within a reasonable time before the tender, the claimant sent a conspicuous statement to the person against whom the claim is asserted that communications concerning disputed debts, including an instrument tendered as full satisfaction of a debt, are to be sent to a designated person, office, or place, and (ii) the instrument or accompanying communication was not received by that designated person, office, or place.

(2) The claimant, whether or not an organization, proves that within 90 days after payment of the instrument, the claimant tendered repayment of the amount of the instrument to the person against whom the claim is asserted. This paragraph does not apply if the claimant is an organization that sent a statement complying with paragraph (1)(i).

(d) A claim is discharged if the person against whom the claim is asserted proves that within a reasonable time before collection of the instrument was initiated, the claimant, or an agent of the claimant having direct responsibility with respect to the disputed obligation, knew that the instrument was tendered in full satisfaction of the claim.

§ 3—312. Lost, Destroyed, or Stolen Cashier's Check, Teller's Check, or Certified Check.

(a) In this section:

(1) "Check" means a cashier's check, teller's check, or certified check.

(2) "Claimant" means a person who claims the right to receive the amount of a cashier's check, teller's check, or certified check that was lost, destroyed, or stolen.

(3) "Declaration of loss" means a written statement, made under penalty of perjury, to the effect that (i) the declarer lost possession of a check, (ii) the declarer is the drawer or payee of the check, in the case of a certified check, or the remitter or payee of the check, in the case of a cashier's check or teller's check, (iii) the loss of possession was not the result of a transfer by the declarer or a lawful seizure, and (iv) the declarer cannot reasonably obtain possession of the check because the check was destroyed, its whereabouts cannot be determined, or it is in the wrongful possession of an unknown person or a person that cannot be found or is not amenable to service of process.

(4) "Obligated bank" means the issuer of a cashier's check or teller's check or the acceptor of a certified check.

(b) A claimant may assert a claim to the amount of a check by a communication to the obligated bank describing the check with reasonable certainty and requesting payment of the amount of the check, if (i) the claimant is the drawer or payee of a certified check or the remitter or payee of a cashier's check or teller's check, (ii) the communication contains or is accompanied by a declaration of loss of the claimant with respect to the check, (iii) the communication is received at a time and in a manner affording the bank a reasonable time to act on it before the check is paid, and (iv) the claimant provides reasonable identification if requested by the obligated bank. Delivery of a declaration of loss is a warranty of the truth of the statements made in the declaration. If a claim is asserted in compliance with this subsection, the following rules apply:

(1) The claim becomes enforceable at the later of (i) the time the claim is asserted, or (ii) the 90th day following the date of the check, in the case of a cashier's check or teller's check, or the 90th day following the date of the acceptance, in the case of a certified check.

(2) Until the claim becomes enforceable, it has no legal effect and the obligated bank may pay the check or, in the case of a teller's check, may permit the drawee to pay the check. Payment to a person entitled to enforce the check discharges all liability of the obligated bank with respect to the check.

(3) If the claim becomes enforceable before the check is presented for payment, the obligated bank is not obliged to pay the check.

(4) When the claim becomes enforceable, the obligated bank becomes obliged to pay the amount of the check to the claimant if payment of the check has not been made to a person entitled to enforce the check. Subject to Section 4—302(a)(1), payment to the claimant discharges all liability of the obligated bank with respect to the check.

(c) If the obligated bank pays the amount of a check to a claimant under subsection (b)(4) and the check is pre-sented for payment by a person having rights of a holder in due course, the claimant is obliged to (i) refund the payment to the obligated bank if the check is paid, or (ii) pay the amount of the check to the person having rights of a holder in due course if the check is dishonored.

(d) If a claimant has the right to assert a claim under subsection (b) and is also a person entitled to enforce a cashier's check, teller's check, or certified check which is lost, destroyed, or stolen, the claimant may assert rights with respect to the check either under this section or Section 3—309.

Part 4 Liability of Parties

§ 3—401. Signature.

(a) A person is not liable on an instrument unless (i) the person signed the instrument, or (ii) the person is represented by an agent or representative who signed the instrument and the signature is binding on the represented person under Section 3—402.

(b) A signature may be made (i) manually or by means of a device or machine, and (ii) by the use of any name, including a trade or assumed name, or by a word, mark, or symbol executed or adopted by a person with present intention to authenticate a writing.

§ 3—402. Signature by Representative.

(a) If a person acting, or purporting to act, as a representative signs an instrument by signing either the name of the represented person or the name of the signer, the represented person is bound by the signature to the same extent the represented person would be bound if the signature were on a simple contract. If the represented person is bound, the signature of the representative is the "authorized signature of the represented person" and the represented person is liable on the instrument, whether or not identified in the instrument.

(b) If a representative signs the name of the representative to an instrument and the signature is an authorized signature of the represented person, the following rules apply:

(1) If the form of the signature shows unambiguously that the signature is made on behalf of the represented person who is identified in the instrument, the representative is not liable on the instrument.

(2) Subject to subsection (c), if (i) the form of the signature does not show unambiguously that the signature is made in a representative capacity or (ii) the represented person is not identified in the instrument, the representative is liable on the instrument to a holder in due course that took the instrument without notice that the representative was not intended to be liable on the instrument. With respect to any other person, the representative is liable on the instrument unless the representative proves that the original par-

ties did not intend the representative to be liable on the instrument.

(c) If a representative signs the name of the representative as drawer of a check without indication of the representative status and the check is payable from an account of the represented person who is identified on the check, the signer is not liable on the check if the signature is an authorized signature of the represented person.

§ 3—403. Unauthorized Signature.

(a) Unless otherwise provided in this Article or Article 4, an unauthorized signature is ineffective except as the signature of the unauthorized signer in favor of a person who in good faith pays the instrument or takes it for value. An unauthorized signature may be ratified for all purposes of this Article.

(b) If the signature of more than one person is required to constitute the authorized signature of an organization, the signature of the organization is unauthorized if one of the required signatures is lacking.

(c) The civil or criminal liability of a person who makes an unauthorized signature is not affected by any provision of this Article which makes the unauthorized signature effective for the purposes of this Article.

§ 3—404. Impostors; Fictitious Payees.

(a) If an impostor, by use of the mails or otherwise, induces the issuer of an instrument to issue the instrument to the impostor, or to a person acting in concert with the impostor, by impersonating the payee of the instrument or a person authorized to act for the payee, an indorsement of the instrument by any person in the name of the payee is effective as the indorsement of the payee in favor of a person who, in good faith, pays the instrument or takes it for value or for collection.

(b) If (i) a person whose intent determines to whom an instrument is payable (Section 3—110(a) or (b)) does not intend the person identified as payee to have any interest in the instrument, or (ii) the person identified as payee of an instrument is a fictitious person, the following rules apply until the instrument is negotiated by special indorsement:

    (1) Any person in possession of the instrument is its holder.

    (2) An indorsement by any person in the name of the payee stated in the instrument is effective as the indorsement of the payee in favor of a person who, in good faith, pays the instrument or takes it for value or for collection.

(c) Under subsection (a) or (b), an indorsement is made in the name of a payee if (i) it is made in a name substantially similar to that of the payee or (ii) the instrument, whether or not indorsed, is deposited in a depositary bank to an account in a name substantially similar to that of the payee.

(d) With respect to an instrument to which subsection (a) or (b) applies, if a person paying the instrument or taking it for value or for collection fails to exercise ordinary care in paying or taking the instrument and that failure substantially contributes to loss resulting from payment of the instrument, the person bearing the loss may recover from the person failing to exercise ordinary care to the extent the failure to exercise ordinary care contributed to the loss.

§ 3—405. Employer's Responsibility for Fraudulent Indorsement by Employee.

(a) In this section:

    (1) "Employee" includes an independent contractor and employee of an independent contractor retained by the employer.

    (2) "Fraudulent indorsement" means (i) in the case of an instrument payable to the employer, a forged indorsement purporting to be that of the employer, or (ii) in the case of an instrument with respect to which the employer is the issuer, a forged indorsement purporting to be that of the person identified as payee.

    (3) "Responsibility" with respect to instruments means authority (i) to sign or indorse instruments on behalf of the employer, (ii) to process instruments received by the employer for bookkeeping purposes, for deposit to an account, or for other disposition, (iii) to prepare or process instruments for issue in the name of the employer, (iv) to supply information determining the names or addresses of payees of instruments to be issued in the name of the employer, (v) to control the disposition of instruments to be issued in the name of the employer, or (vi) to act otherwise with respect to instruments in a responsible capacity. "Responsibility" does not include authority that merely allows an employee to have access to instruments or blank or incomplete instrument forms that are being stored or transported or are part of incoming or outgoing mail, or similar access.

(b) For the purpose of determining the rights and liabilities of a person who, in good faith, pays an instrument or takes it for value or for collection, if an employer entrusted an employee with responsibility with respect to the instrument and the employee or a person acting in concert with the employee makes a fraudulent indorsement of the instrument, the indorsement is effective as the indorsement of the person to whom the instrument is payable if it is made in the name of that person. If the person paying the instrument or taking it for value or for collection fails to exercise ordinary care in paying or taking the instrument and that failure substantially contributes to loss resulting from the fraud, the person bearing the loss may recover from the person failing to exercise ordinary care to the extent the failure to exercise ordinary care contributed to the loss.

(c) Under subsection (b), an indorsement is made in the name of the person to whom an instrument is payable if (i) it is made in a name substantially similar to the name of that person or (ii) the instrument, whether or not indorsed, is deposited in a depositary bank to an account in a name substantially similar to the name of that person.

§ 3—406. Negligence Contributing to Forged Signature or Alteration of Instrument.

(a) A person whose failure to exercise ordinary care substantially contributes to an alteration of an instrument or to the making of a forged signature on an instrument is precluded from asserting the alteration or the forgery against a person who, in good faith, pays the instrument or takes it for value or for collection.

(b) Under subsection (a), if the person asserting the preclusion fails to exercise ordinary care in paying or taking the instrument and that failure substantially contributes to loss, the loss is allocated between the person precluded and the person asserting the preclusion according to the extent to which the failure of each to exercise ordinary care contributed to the loss.

(c) Under subsection (a), the burden of proving failure to exercise ordinary care is on the person asserting the preclusion. Under subsection (b), the burden of proving failure to exercise ordinary care is on the person precluded.

§ 3—407. Alteration.

(a) "Alteration" means (i) an unauthorized change in an instrument that purports to modify in any respect the obligation of a party, or (ii) an unauthorized addition of words or numbers or other change to an incomplete instrument relating to the obligation of a party.

(b) Except as provided in subsection (c), an alteration fraudulently made discharges a party whose obligation is affected by the alteration unless that party assents or is precluded from asserting the alteration. No other alteration discharges a party, and the instrument may be enforced according to its original terms.

(c) A payor bank or drawee paying a fraudulently altered instrument or a person taking it for value, in good faith and without notice of the alteration, may enforce rights with respect to the instrument (i) according to its original terms, or (ii) in the case of an incomplete instrument altered by unauthorized completion, according to its terms as completed.

§ 3—408. Drawee Not Liable on Unaccepted Draft.

A check or other draft does not of itself operate as an assignment of funds in the hands of the drawee available for its payment, and the drawee is not liable on the instrument until the drawee accepts it.

§ 3—409. Acceptance of Draft; Certified Check.

(a) "Acceptance" means the drawee's signed agreement to pay a draft as presented. It must be written on the draft and may consist of the drawee's signature alone. Acceptance may be made at any time and becomes effective when notification pursuant to instructions is given or the accepted draft is delivered for the purpose of giving rights on the acceptance to any person.

(b) A draft may be accepted although it has not been signed by the drawer, is otherwise incomplete, is overdue, or has been dishonored.

(c) If a draft is payable at a fixed period after sight and the acceptor fails to date the acceptance, the holder may complete the acceptance by supplying a date in good faith.

(d) "Certified check" means a check accepted by the bank on which it is drawn. Acceptance may be made as stated in subsection (a) or by a writing on the check which indicates that the check is certified. The drawee of a check has no obligation to certify the check, and refusal to certify is not dishonor of the check.

§ 3—410. Acceptance Varying Draft.

(a) If the terms of a drawee's acceptance vary from the terms of the draft as presented, the holder may refuse the acceptance and treat the draft as dishonored. In that case, the drawee may cancel the acceptance.

(b) The terms of a draft are not varied by an acceptance to pay at a particular bank or place in the United States, unless the acceptance states that the draft is to be paid only at that bank or place.

(c) If the holder assents to an acceptance varying the terms of a draft, the obligation of each drawer and indorser that does not expressly assent to the acceptance is discharged.

§ 3—411. Refusal to Pay Cashier's Checks, Teller's Checks, and Certified Checks.

(a) In this section, "obligated bank" means the acceptor of a certified check or the issuer of a cashier's check or teller's check bought from the issuer.

(b) If the obligated bank wrongfully (i) refuses to pay a cashier's check or certified check, (ii) stops payment of a teller's check, or (iii) refuses to pay a dishonored teller's check, the person asserting the right to enforce the check is entitled to compensation for expenses and loss of interest resulting from the nonpayment and may recover consequential damages if the obligated bank refuses to pay after receiving notice of particular circumstances giving rise to the damages.

(c) Expenses or consequential damages under subsection (b) are not recoverable if the refusal of the obligated bank to pay occurs because (i) the bank suspends payments, (ii) the obligated bank asserts a claim or defense of the bank that it has reasonable grounds to believe is available against the person entitled to enforce the instrument, (iii) the obligated bank has a reasonable doubt whether the person demanding payment is the person entitled to enforce the instrument, or (iv) payment is prohibited by law.

§ 3—412. Obligation of Issuer of Note or Cashier's Check.

The issuer of a note or cashier's check or other draft drawn on the drawer is obliged to pay the instrument (i) according to its terms at the time it was issued or, if not issued, at the time it first came into possession of a holder, or (ii) if the issuer signed an incomplete instrument, according to its terms when completed, to the extent stated in Sections 3—115 and 3—407. The obligation is owed to a person entitled to enforce the instrument or to an indorser who paid the instrument under Section 3—415.

§ 3—413. Obligation of Acceptor.

(a) The acceptor of a draft is obliged to pay the draft (i) according to its terms at the time it was accepted, even though the acceptance states that the draft is payable "as originally drawn" or equivalent terms, (ii) if the acceptance varies the terms of the draft, according to the terms of the draft as varied, or (iii) if the acceptance is of a draft that is an incomplete instrument, according to its terms when completed, to the extent stated in Sections 3—115 and 3—407. The obligation is owed to a person entitled to enforce the draft or to the drawer or an indorser who paid the draft under Section 3—414 or 3—415.

(b) If the certification of a check or other acceptance of a draft states the amount certified or accepted, the obligation of the acceptor is that amount. If (i) the certification or acceptance does not state an amount, (ii) the amount of the instrument is subsequently raised, and (iii) the instrument is then negotiated to a holder in due course, the obligation of the acceptor is the amount of the instrument at the time it was taken by the holder in due course.

§ 3—414. Obligation of Drawer.

(a) This section does not apply to cashier's checks or other drafts drawn on the drawer.

(b) If an unaccepted draft is dishonored, the drawer is obliged to pay the draft (i) according to its terms at the time it was issued or, if not issued, at the time it first came into possession of a holder, or (ii) if the drawer signed an incomplete instrument, according to its terms when completed, to the extent stated in Sections 3—115 and 3—407. The obligation is owed to a person entitled to enforce the draft or to an indorser who paid the draft under Section 3—415.

(c) If a draft is accepted by a bank, the drawer is discharged, regardless of when or by whom acceptance was obtained.

(d) If a draft is accepted and the acceptor is not a bank, the obligation of the drawer to pay the draft if the draft is dishonored by the acceptor is the same as the obligation of an indorser under Section 3—415(a) and (c).

(e) If a draft states that it is drawn "without recourse" or otherwise disclaims liability of the drawer to pay the draft, the drawer is not liable under subsection (b) to pay the draft if the draft is not a check. A disclaimer of the liability stated in subsection (b) is not effective if the draft is a check.

(f) If (i) a check is not presented for payment or given to a depositary bank for collection within 30 days after its date, (ii) the drawee suspends payments after expiration of the 30-day period without paying the check, and (iii) because of the suspension of payments, the drawer is deprived of funds maintained with the drawee to cover payment of the check, the drawer to the extent deprived of funds may discharge its obligation to pay the check by assigning to the person entitled to enforce the check the rights of the drawer against the drawee with respect to the funds.

§ 3—415. Obligation of Indorser.

(a) Subject to subsections (b), (c), and (d) and to Section 3—419(d), if an instrument is dishonored, an indorser is obliged to pay the amount due on the instrument (i) according to the terms of the instrument at the time it was indorsed, or (ii) if the indorser indorsed an incomplete instrument, according to its terms when completed, to the extent stated in Sections 3—115 and 3—407. The obligation of the indorser is owed to a person entitled to enforce the instrument or to a subsequent indorser who paid the instrument under this section.

(b) If an indorsement states that it is made "without recourse" or otherwise disclaims liability of the indorser, the indorser is not liable under subsection (a) to pay the instrument.

(c) If notice of dishonor of an instrument is required by Section 3—503 and notice of dishonor complying with that section is not given to an indorser, the liability of the indorser under subsection (a) is discharged.

(d) If a draft is accepted by a bank after an indorsement is made, the liability of the indorser under subsection (a) is discharged.

(e) If an indorser of a check is liable under subsection (a) and the check is not presented for payment, or given to a depositary bank for collection, within 30 days after the day the indorsement was made, the liability of the indorser under subsection (a) is discharged.

§ 3—416. Transfer Warranties.

(a) A person who transfers an instrument for consideration warrants to the transferee and, if the transfer is by indorsement, to any subsequent transferee that:

(1) the warrantor is a person entitled to enforce the instrument;

(2) all signatures on the instrument are authentic and authorized;

(3) the instrument has not been altered;

(4) the instrument is not subject to a defense or claim in recoupment of any party which can be asserted against the warrantor; and

(5) the warrantor has no knowledge of any insolvency proceeding commenced with respect to the maker or acceptor or, in the case of an unaccepted draft, the drawer.

(b) A person to whom the warranties under subsection (a) are made and who took the instrument in good faith may recover from the warrantor as damages for breach of warranty an amount equal to the loss suffered as a result of the breach, but not more than the amount of the instrument plus expenses and loss of interest incurred as a result of the breach.

(c) The warranties stated in subsection (a) cannot be disclaimed with respect to checks. Unless notice of a claim for breach of warranty is given to the warrantor within 30 days after the claimant has reason to know of the breach and the identity of the warrantor, the liability of the warrantor under subsection (b) is discharged to the extent of any loss caused by the delay in giving notice of the claim.

(d) A [cause of action] for breach of warranty under this section accrues when the claimant has reason to know of the breach.

§ 3—417. Presentment Warranties.

(a) If an unaccepted draft is presented to the drawee for payment or acceptance and the drawee pays or accepts the draft, (i) the person obtaining payment or acceptance, at the time of presentment, and (ii) a previous transferor of the draft, at the time of transfer, warrant to the drawee making payment or accepting the draft in good faith that:

(1) the warrantor is, or was, at the time the warrantor transferred the draft, a person entitled to enforce the draft or authorized to obtain payment or acceptance of the draft on behalf of a person entitled to enforce the draft;

(2) the draft has not been altered; and

(3) the warrantor has no knowledge that the signature of the drawer of the draft is unauthorized.

(b) A drawee making payment may recover from any warrantor damages for breach of warranty equal to the amount paid by the drawee less the amount the drawee received or is entitled to receive from the drawer because of the payment. In addition, the drawee is entitled to compensation for expenses and loss of interest resulting from the breach. The right of the drawee to recover damages under this subsection is not affected by any failure of the drawee to exercise ordinary care in making payment. If the drawee accepts the draft, breach of warranty is a defense to the obligation of the acceptor. If the acceptor makes payment with respect to the draft, the acceptor is entitled to recover from any warrantor for breach of warranty the amounts stated in this subsection.

(c) If a drawee asserts a claim for breach of warranty under subsection (a) based on an unauthorized indorsement of the draft or an alteration of the draft, the warrantor may defend by proving that the indorsement is effective under Section 3—404 or 3—405 or the drawer is precluded under Section 3—406 or 4—406 from asserting against the drawee the unauthorized indorsement or alteration.

(d) If (i) a dishonored draft is presented for payment to the drawer or an indorser or (ii) any other instrument is presented for payment to a party obliged to pay the instrument, and (iii) payment is received, the following rules apply:

(1) The person obtaining payment and a prior transferor of the instrument warrant to the person making payment in good faith that the warrantor is, or was, at the time the warrantor transferred the instrument, a person entitled to enforce the instrument or authorized to obtain payment on behalf of a person entitled to enforce the instrument.

(2) The person making payment may recover from any warrantor for breach of warranty an amount equal to the amount paid plus expenses and loss of interest resulting from the breach.

(e) The warranties stated in subsections (a) and (d) cannot be disclaimed with respect to checks. Unless notice of a claim for breach of warranty is given to the warrantor within 30 days after the claimant has reason to know of the breach and the identity of the warrantor, the liability of the warrantor under subsection (b) or (d) is discharged to the extent of any loss caused by the delay in giving notice of the claim.

(f) A [cause of action] for breach of warranty under this section accrues when the claimant has reason to know of the breach.

§ 3—418. Payment or Acceptance by Mistake.

(a) Except as provided in subsection (c), if the drawee of a draft pays or accepts the draft and the drawee acted on the mistaken belief that (i) payment of the draft had not been stopped pursuant to Section 4—403 or (ii) the signature of the drawer of the draft was authorized, the drawee may recover the amount of the draft from the person to whom or for whose benefit payment was made or, in the case of acceptance, may revoke the acceptance. Rights of the drawee under this subsection are not affected by failure of the drawee to exercise ordinary care in paying or accepting the draft.

(b) Except as provided in subsection (c), if an instrument has been paid or accepted by mistake and the case is not covered by subsection (a), the person paying or accepting may, to the extent permitted by the law governing mistake and restitution, (i) recover the payment from the person to whom or for whose benefit payment was made or (ii) in the case of acceptance, may revoke the acceptance.

(c) The remedies provided by subsection (a) or (b) may not be asserted against a person who took the instrument in good faith and for value or who in good faith changed position in reliance on the payment or acceptance. This subsection does not limit remedies provided by Section 3—417 or 4—407.

(d) Notwithstanding Section 4—215, if an instrument is paid or accepted by mistake and the payor or acceptor recovers payment or revokes acceptance under subsection (a) or (b), the instrument is deemed not to have been paid or accepted and is treated as dishonored, and the person from whom payment is recovered has rights as a person entitled to enforce the dishonored instrument.

§ 3—419. Instruments Signed for Accommodation.

(a) If an instrument is issued for value given for the benefit of a party to the instrument ("accommodated party") and another party to the instrument ("accommodation party") signs the instrument for the purpose of incurring liability on the instrument without being a direct beneficiary of the value given for the instrument, the instrument is signed by the accommodation party "for accommodation."

(b) An accommodation party may sign the instrument as maker, drawer, acceptor, or indorser and, subject to subsection (d), is obliged to pay the instrument in the capacity in which the accommodation party signs. The obligation of an accommodation party may be enforced notwithstanding any statute of frauds and whether or not the accommodation party receives consideration for the accommodation.

(c) A person signing an instrument is presumed to be an accommodation party and there is notice that the instrument is signed for accommodation if the signature is an anomalous indorsement or is accompanied by words indicating that the signer is acting as surety or guarantor with respect to the obligation of another party to the instrument. Except as provided in Section 3—605, the obligation of an accommodation party to pay the instrument is not affected by the fact that the person enforcing the obligation had notice when the instrument was taken by that person that the accommodation party signed the instrument for accommodation.

(d) If the signature of a party to an instrument is accompanied by words indicating unambiguously that the party is guaranteeing collection rather than payment of the obligation of another party to the instrument, the signer is obliged to pay the amount due on the instrument to a person entitled to enforce the instrument only if (i) execution of judgment against the other party has been returned unsatisfied, (ii) the other party is insolvent or in an insolvency proceeding, (iii) the other party cannot be served with process, or (iv) it is otherwise apparent that payment cannot be obtained from the other party.

(e) An accommodation party who pays the instrument is entitled to reimbursement from the accommodated party and is entitled to enforce the instrument against the accommodated party. An accommodated party who pays the instrument has no right of recourse against, and is not entitled to contribution from, an accommodation party.

§ 3—420. Conversion of Instrument.

(a) The law applicable to conversion of personal property applies to instruments. An instrument is also converted if it is taken by transfer, other than a negotiation, from a person not entitled to enforce the instrument or a bank makes or obtains payment with respect to the instrument for a person not entitled to enforce the instrument or receive payment. An action for conversion of an instrument may not be brought by (i) the issuer or acceptor of the instrument or (ii) a payee or indorsee who did not receive delivery of the instrument either directly or through delivery to an agent or a co-payee.

(b) In an action under subsection (a), the measure of liability is presumed to be the amount payable on the instrument, but recovery may not exceed the amount of the plaintiff's interest in the instrument.

(c) A representative, other than a depositary bank, who has in good faith dealt with an instrument or its proceeds on behalf of one who was not the person entitled to enforce the instrument is not liable in conversion to that person beyond the amount of any proceeds that it has not paid out.

Part 5 Dishonor

§ 3—501. Presentment.

(a) "Presentment" means a demand made by or on behalf of a person entitled to enforce an instrument (i) to pay the instrument made to the drawee or a party obliged to pay the instrument or, in the case of a note or accepted draft payable at a bank, to the bank, or (ii) to accept a draft made to the drawee.

(b) The following rules are subject to Article 4, agreement of the parties, and clearing-house rules and the like:

(1) Presentment may be made at the place of payment of the instrument and must be made at the place of payment if the instrument is payable at a bank in the United States; may be made by any commercially reasonable means, including an oral, written, or electronic communication; is effective when the demand for payment or acceptance is received by the person to whom presentment is made; and is effective if made to any one of two or more makers, acceptors, drawees, or other payors.

(2) Upon demand of the person to whom presentment is made, the person making presentment must (i) exhibit the instrument, (ii) give reasonable identification and, if presentment is made on behalf of another person, reasonable evidence of authority to do so, and (. . .) sign a receipt on the instrument for

any payment made or surrender the instrument if full payment is made.

(3) Without dishonoring the instrument, the party to whom presentment is made may (i) return the instrument for lack of a necessary indorsement, or (ii) refuse payment or acceptance for failure of the presentment to comply with the terms of the instrument, an agreement of the parties, or other applicable law or rule.

(4) The party to whom presentment is made may treat presentment as occurring on the next business day after the day of presentment if the party to whom presentment is made has established a cut-off hour not earlier than 2 P.M. for the receipt and processing of instruments presented for payment or acceptance and presentment is made after the cut-off hour.

§ 3—502. Dishonor.

(a) Dishonor of a note is governed by the following rules:

(1) If the note is payable on demand, the note is dishonored if presentment is duly made to the maker and the note is not paid on the day of presentment.

(2) If the note is not payable on demand and is payable at or through a bank or the terms of the note require presentment, the note is dishonored if presentment is duly made and the note is not paid on the day it becomes payable or the day of presentment, whichever is later.

(3) If the note is not payable on demand and paragraph (2) does not apply, the note is dishonored if it is not paid on the day it becomes payable.

(b) Dishonor of an unaccepted draft other than a documentary draft is governed by the following rules:

(1) If a check is duly presented for payment to the payor bank otherwise than for immediate payment over the counter, the check is dishonored if the payor bank makes timely return of the check or sends timely notice of dishonor or nonpayment under Section 4—301 or 4—302, or becomes accountable for the amount of the check under Section 4—302.

(2) If a draft is payable on demand and paragraph (1) does not apply, the draft is dishonored if presentment for payment is duly made to the drawee and the draft is not paid on the day of presentment.

(3) If a draft is payable on a date stated in the draft, the draft is dishonored if (i) presentment for payment is duly made to the drawee and payment is not made on the day the draft becomes payable or the day of presentment, whichever is later, or (ii) presentment for acceptance is duly made before the day the draft becomes payable and the draft is not accepted on the day of presentment.

(4) If a draft is payable on elapse of a period of time after sight or acceptance, the draft is dishonored if presentment for acceptance is duly made and the draft is not accepted on the day of presentment.

(c) Dishonor of an unaccepted documentary draft occurs according to the rules stated in subsection (b)(2), (3), and (4), except that payment or acceptance may be delayed without dishonor until no later than the close of the third business day of the drawee following the day on which payment or acceptance is required by those paragraphs.

(d) Dishonor of an accepted draft is governed by the following rules:

(1) If the draft is payable on demand, the draft is dishonored if presentment for payment is duly made to the acceptor and the draft is not paid on the day of presentment.

(2) If the draft is not payable on demand, the draft is dishonored if presentment for payment is duly made to the acceptor and payment is not made on the day it becomes payable or the day of presentment, whichever is later.

(e) In any case in which presentment is otherwise required for dishonor under this section and presentment is excused under Section 3—504, dishonor occurs without presentment if the instrument is not duly accepted or paid.

(f) If a draft is dishonored because timely acceptance of the draft was not made and the person entitled to demand acceptance consents to a late acceptance, from the time of acceptance the draft is treated as never having been dishonored.

§ 3—503. Notice of Dishonor.

(a) The obligation of an indorser stated in Section 3—415(a) and the obligation of a drawer stated in Section 3—414(d) may not be enforced unless (i) the indorser or drawer is given notice of dishonor of the instrument complying with this section or (ii) notice of dishonor is excused under Section 3—504(b).

(b) Notice of dishonor may be given by any person; may be given by any commercially reasonable means, including an oral, written, or electronic communication; and is sufficient if it reasonably identifies the instrument and indicates that the instrument has been dishonored or has not been paid or accepted. Return of an instrument given to a bank for collection is sufficient notice of dishonor.

(c) Subject to Section 3—504(c), with respect to an instrument taken for collection by a collecting bank, notice of dishonor must be given (i) by the bank before midnight of the next banking day following the banking day on which the bank receives notice of dishonor of the instrument, or (ii) by any other person within 30 days following the day on which the person receives notice of dishonor. With respect to any other instrument, notice of dishonor must be given within 30 days following the day on which dishonor occurs.

§ 3—504. Excused Presentment and Notice of Dishonor.

(a) Presentment for payment or acceptance of an instrument is excused if (i) the person entitled to present the instrument cannot with reasonable diligence make presentment, (ii) the maker or acceptor has repudiated an obligation to pay the instrument or is dead or in insolvency proceedings, (iii) by the terms of the instrument presentment is not necessary to enforce the obligation of indorsers or the drawer, (iv) the drawer or indorser whose obligation is being enforced has waived presentment or otherwise has no reason to expect or right to require that the instrument be paid or accepted, or (v) the drawer instructed the drawee not to pay or accept the draft or the drawee was not obligated to the drawer to pay the draft.

(b) Notice of dishonor is excused if (i) by the terms of the instrument notice of dishonor is not necessary to enforce the obligation of a party to pay the instrument, or (ii) the party whose obligation is being enforced waived notice of dishonor. A waiver of presentment is also a waiver of notice of dishonor.

(c) Delay in giving notice of dishonor is excused if the delay was caused by circumstances beyond the control of the person giving the notice and the person giving the notice exercised reasonable diligence after the cause of the delay ceased to operate.

§ 3—505. Evidence of Dishonor.

(a) The following are admissible as evidence and create a presumption of dishonor and of any notice of dishonor stated:

(1) a document regular in form as provided in subsection (b) which purports to be a protest;

(2) a purported stamp or writing of the drawee, payor bank, or presenting bank on or accompanying the instrument stating that acceptance or payment has been refused unless reasons for the refusal are stated and the reasons are not consistent with dishonor;

(3) a book or record of the drawee, payor bank, or collecting bank, kept in the usual course of business which shows dishonor, even if there is no evidence of who made the entry.

(b) A protest is a certificate of dishonor made by a United States consul or vice consul, or a notary public or other person authorized to administer oaths by the law of the place where dishonor occurs. It may be made upon information satisfactory to that person. The protest must identify the instrument and certify either that presentment has been made or, if not made, the reason why it was not made, and that the instrument has been dishonored by nonacceptance or nonpayment. The protest may also certify that notice of dishonor has been given to some or all parties.

Part 6 Discharge and Payment

§ 3—601. Discharge and Effect of Discharge.

(a) The obligation of a party to pay the instrument is discharged as stated in this Article or by an act or agreement with the party which would discharge an obligation to pay money under a simple contract.

(b) Discharge of the obligation of a party is not effective against a person acquiring rights of a holder in due course of the instrument without notice of the discharge.

§ 3—602. Payment.

(a) Subject to subsection (b), an instrument is paid to the extent payment is made (i) by or on behalf of a party obliged to pay the instrument, and (ii) to a person entitled to enforce the instrument. To the extent of the payment, the obligation of the party obliged to pay the instrument is discharged even though payment is made with knowledge of a claim to the instrument under Section 3—306 by another person.

(b) The obligation of a party to pay the instrument is not discharged under subsection (a) if:

(1) a claim to the instrument under Section 3—306 is enforceable against the party receiving payment and (i) payment is made with knowledge by the payor that payment is prohibited by injunction or similar process of a court of competent jurisdiction, or (ii) in the case of an instrument other than a cashier's check, teller's check, or certified check, the party making payment accepted, from the person having a claim to the instrument, indemnity against loss resulting from refusal to pay the person entitled to enforce the instrument; or

(2) the person making payment knows that the instrument is a stolen instrument and pays a person it knows is in wrongful possession of the instrument.

§ 3—603. Tender of Payment.

(a) If tender of payment of an obligation to pay an instrument is made to a person entitled to enforce the instrument, the effect of tender is governed by principles of law applicable to tender of payment under a simple contract.

(b) If tender of payment of an obligation to pay an instrument is made to a person entitled to enforce the instrument and the tender is refused, there is discharge, to the extent of the amount of the tender, of the obligation of an indorser or accommodation party having a right of recourse with respect to the obligation to which the tender relates.

(c) If tender of payment of an amount due on an instrument is made to a person entitled to enforce the instrument, the obligation of the obligor to pay interest after the due date on the amount tendered is discharged. If presentment is required with respect to an instrument and the obligor is able and ready to pay on the due date at every place of payment stated in the instrument, the obligor is deemed to have made tender of payment on the due date to the person entitled to enforce the instrument.

§ 3—604. Discharge by Cancellation or Renunciation.

(a) A person entitled to enforce an instrument, with or without consideration, may discharge the obligation of a party to pay the instrument (i) by an intentional voluntary act, such as surrender of the instrument to the party, destruction, mutilation, or cancellation of the instrument, cancellation or striking out of the party's signature, or the addition of words to the instrument indicating discharge, or (ii) by agreeing not to sue or otherwise renouncing rights against the party by a signed writing.

(b) Cancellation or striking out of an indorsement pursuant to subsection (a) does not affect the status and rights of a party derived from the indorsement.

§ 3—605. Discharge of Indorsers and Accommodation Parties.

(a) In this section, the term "indorser" includes a drawer having the obligation described in Section 3—414(d).

(b) Discharge, under Section 3—604, of the obligation of a party to pay an instrument does not discharge the obligation of an indorser or accommodation party having a right of recourse against the discharged party.

(c) If a person entitled to enforce an instrument agrees, with or without consideration, to an extension of the due date of the obligation of a party to pay the instrument, the extension discharges an indorser or accommodation party having a right of recourse against the party whose obligation is extended to the extent the indorser or accommodation party proves that the extension caused loss to the indorser or accommodation party with respect to the right of recourse.

(d) If a person entitled to enforce an instrument agrees, with or without consideration, to a material modification of the obligation of a party other than an extension of the due date, the modification discharges the obligation of an indorser or accommodation party having a right of recourse against the person whose obligation is modified to the extent the modification causes loss to the indorser or accommodation party with respect to the right of recourse. The loss suffered by the indorser or accommodation party as a result of the modification is equal to the amount of the right of recourse unless the person enforcing the instrument proves that no loss was caused by the modification or that the loss caused by the modification was an amount less than the amount of the right of recourse.

(e) If the obligation of a party to pay an instrument is secured by an interest in collateral and a person entitled to enforce the instrument impairs the value of the interest in collateral, the obligation of an indorser or accommodation party having a right of recourse against the obligor is discharged to the extent of the impairment. The value of an interest in collateral is impaired to the extent (i) the value of the interest is reduced to an amount less than the amount of the right of recourse of the party asserting discharge, or (ii) the reduction in value of the interest causes an increase in the amount by which the amount of the right of recourse exceeds the value of the interest. The burden of proving impairment is on the party asserting discharge.

(f) If the obligation of a party is secured by an interest in collateral not provided by an accommodation party and a person entitled to enforce the instrument impairs the value of the interest in collateral, the obligation of any party who is jointly and severally liable with respect to the secured obligation is discharged to the extent the impairment causes the party asserting discharge to pay more than that party would have been obliged to pay, taking into account rights of contribution, if impairment had not occurred. If the party asserting discharge is an accommodation party not entitled to discharge under subsection (e), the party is deemed to have a right to contribution based on joint and several liability rather than a right to reimbursement. The burden of proving impairment is on the party asserting discharge.

(g) Under subsection (e) or (f), impairing value of an interest in collateral includes (i) failure to obtain or maintain perfection or recordation of the interest in collateral, (ii) release of collateral without substitution of collateral of equal value, (iii) failure to perform a duty to preserve the value of collateral owed, under Article 9 or other law, to a debtor or surety or other person secondarily liable, or (iv) failure to comply with applicable law in disposing of collateral.

(h) An accommodation party is not discharged under subsection (c), (d), or (e) unless the person entitled to enforce the instrument knows of the accommodation or has notice under Section 3—419(c) that the instrument was signed for accommodation.

(i) A party is not discharged under this section if (i) the party asserting discharge consents to the event or conduct that is the basis of the discharge, or (ii) the instrument or a separate agreement of the party provides for waiver of discharge under this section either specifically or by general language indicating that parties waive defenses based on suretyship or impairment of collateral.

ADDENDUM TO REVISED ARTICLE 3

Notes to Legislative Counsel

1. If revised Article 3 is adopted in your state, the reference in Section 2—511 to Section 3—802 should be changed to Section 3—310.

2. If revised Article 3 is adopted in your state and the Uniform Fiduciaries Act is also in effect in your state, you may want to consider amending Uniform Fiduciaries Act § 9 to conform to Section 3—307(b)(2)(iii) and (4)(iii). See Official Comment 3 to Section 3—307.

Revised Article 4
BANK DEPOSITS AND COLLECTIONS

Part 1 General Provisions and Definitions

§ 4—101. Short Title.

This Article may be cited as Uniform Commercial Code—Bank Deposits and Collections.

§ 4—102. Applicability.

(a) To the extent that items within this Article are also within Articles 3 and 8, they are subject to those Articles. If there is conflict, this Article governs Article 3, but Article 8 governs this Article.

(b) The liability of a bank for action or non-action with respect to an item handled by it for purposes of presentment, payment, or collection is governed by the law of the place where the bank is located. In the case of action or non-action by or at a branch or separate office of a bank, its liability is governed by the law of the place where the branch or separate office is located.

§ 4—103. Variation by Agreement; Measure of Damages; Action Constituting Ordinary Care.

(a) The effect of the provisions of this Article may be varied by agreement, but the parties to the agreement cannot disclaim a bank's responsibility for its lack of good faith or failure to exercise ordinary care or limit the measure of damages for the lack or failure. However, the parties may determine by agreement the standards by which the bank's responsibility is to be measured if those standards are not manifestly unreasonable.

(b) Federal Reserve regulations and operating circulars, clearing-house rules, and the like have the effect of agreements under subsection (a), whether or not specifically assented to by all parties interested in items handled.

(c) Action or non-action approved by this Article or pursuant to Federal Reserve regulations or operating circulars is the exercise of ordinary care and, in the absence of special instructions, action or non-action consistent with clearing-house rules and the like or with a general banking usage not disapproved by this Article, is prima facie the exercise of ordinary care.

(d) The specification or approval of certain procedures by this Article is not disapproval of other procedures that may be reasonable under the circumstances.

(e) The measure of damages for failure to exercise ordinary care in handling an item is the amount of the item reduced by an amount that could not have been realized by the exercise of ordinary care. If there is also bad faith it includes any other damages the party suffered as a proximate consequence.

§ 4—104. Definitions and Index of Definitions.

(a) In this Article, unless the context otherwise requires:

(1) "Account" means any deposit or credit account with a bank, including a demand, time, savings, passbook, share draft, or like account, other than an account evidenced by a certificate of deposit;

(2) "Afternoon" means the period of a day between noon and midnight;

(3) "Banking day" means the part of a day on which a bank is open to the public for carrying on substantially all of its banking functions;

(4) "Clearing house" means an association of banks or other payors regularly clearing items;

(5) "Customer" means a person having an account with a bank or for whom a bank has agreed to collect items, including a bank that maintains an account at another bank;

(6) "Documentary draft" means a draft to be presented for acceptance or payment if specified documents, certificated securities (Section 8—102) or instructions for uncertificated securities (Section 8—102), or other certificates, statements, or the like are to be received by the drawee or other payor before acceptance or payment of the draft;

(7) "Draft" means a draft as defined in Section 3—104 or an item, other than an instrument, that is an order;

(8) "Drawee" means a person ordered in a draft to make payment;

(9) "Item" means an instrument or a promise or order to pay money handled by a bank for collection or payment. The term does not include a payment order governed by Article 4A or a credit or debit card slip;

(10) "Midnight deadline" with respect to a bank is midnight on its next banking day following the banking day on which it receives the relevant item or notice or from which the time for taking action commences to run, whichever is later;

(11) "Settle" means to pay in cash, by clearing-house settlement, in a charge or credit or by remittance, or otherwise as agreed. A settlement may be either provisional or final;

(12) "Suspends payments" with respect to a bank means that it has been closed by order of the supervisory authorities, that a public officer has been appointed to take it over, or that it ceases or refuses to make payments in the ordinary course of business.

(b);(c) [Other definitions' section references deleted.]

(d) In addition, Article 1 contains general definitions and principles of construction and interpretation applicable throughout this Article.

§ 4—105. "Bank"; "Depository Bank"; "Payor Bank"; "Intermediary Bank"; "Collecting Bank"; "Presenting Bank".

In this Article:

(1) "Bank" means a person engaged in the business of banking, including a savings bank, savings and loan association, credit union, or trust company;

(2) "Depository bank" means the first bank to take an item even though it is also the payor bank, unless the item is presented for immediate payment over the counter;

(3) "Payor bank" means a bank that is the drawee of a draft;

(4) "Intermediary bank" means a bank to which an item is transferred in course of collection except the depositary or payor bank;

(5) "Collecting bank" means a bank handling an item for collection except the payor bank;

(6) "Presenting bank" means a bank presenting an item except a payor bank.

§ 4—106. Payable Through or Payable at Bank: Collecting Bank.

(a) If an item states that it is "payable through" a bank identified in the item, (i) the item designates the bank as a collecting bank and does not by itself authorize the bank to pay the item, and (ii) the item may be presented for payment only by or through the bank.

Alternative A

(b) If an item states that it is "payable at" a bank identified in the item, the item is equivalent to a draft drawn on the bank.

Alternative B

(b) If an item states that it is "payable at" a bank identified in the item, (i) the item designates the bank as a collecting bank and does not by itself authorize the bank to pay the item, and (ii) the item may be presented for payment only by or through the bank.

(c) If a draft names a nonbank drawee and it is unclear whether a bank named in the draft is a co-drawee or a collecting bank, the bank is a collecting bank.

§ 4—107. Separate Office of Bank.

A branch or separate office of a bank is a separate bank for the purpose of computing the time within which and determining the place at or to which action may be taken or notices or orders shall be given under this Article and under Article 3.

§ 4—108. Time of Receipt of Items.

(a) For the purpose of allowing time to process items, prove balances, and make the necessary entries on its books to determine its position for the day, a bank may fix an afternoon hour of 2 P.M. or later as a cutoff hour for the handling of money and items and the making of entries on its books.

(b) An item or deposit of money received on any day after a cutoff hour so fixed or after the close of the banking day may be treated as being received at the opening of the next banking day.

§ 4—109. Delays.

(a) Unless otherwise instructed, a collecting bank in a good faith effort to secure payment of a specific item drawn on a payor other than a bank, and with or without the approval of any person involved, may waive, modify, or extend time limits imposed or permitted by this [act] for a period not exceeding two additional banking days without discharge of drawers or indorsers or liability to its transferor or a prior party.

(b) Delay by a collecting bank or payor bank beyond time limits prescribed or permitted by this [act] or by instructions is excused if (i) the delay is caused by interruption of communication or computer facilities, suspension of payments by another bank, war, emergency conditions, failure of equipment, or other circumstances beyond the control of the bank, and (ii) the bank exercises such diligence as the circumstances require.

§ 4—110. Electronic Presentment.

(a) "Agreement for electronic presentment" means an agreement, clearing-house rule, or Federal Reserve regulation or operating circular, providing that presentment of an item may be made by transmission of an image of an item or information describing the item ("presentment notice") rather than delivery of the item itself. The agreement may provide for procedures governing retention, presentment, payment, dishonor, and other matters concerning items subject to the agreement.

(b) Presentment of an item pursuant to an agreement for presentment is made when the presentment notice is received.

(c) If presentment is made by presentment notice, a reference to "item" or "check" in this Article means the presentment notice unless the context otherwise indicates.

§ 4—111. Statute of Limitations.

An action to enforce an obligation, duty, or right arising under this Article must be commenced within three years after the [cause of action] accrues.

Part 2 Collection of Items: Depositary and Collecting Banks

§ 4—201. Status of Collecting Bank As Agent and Provisional Status of Credits; Applicability of Article; Item Indorsed "Pay Any Bank".

(a) Unless a contrary intent clearly appears and before the time that a settlement given by a collecting bank for an item is or becomes final, the bank, with respect to an item, is an agent or sub-agent of the owner of the item and any settlement given for the item is provisional. This provision applies regardless of the form of indorsement or lack of indorsement and even though credit given for the item is subject to immediate withdrawal as of right or is in fact withdrawn; but the continuance of ownership of an item by its owner and any rights of the owner to proceeds of the item are subject to rights of a collecting bank, such as those resulting from outstanding advances on the item and rights of recoupment or setoff. If an item is handled by banks for purposes of presentment, payment, collection, or return, the relevant provisions of this Article apply even though action of the parties clearly establishes that a particular bank has purchased the item and is the owner of it.

(b) After an item has been indorsed with the words "pay any bank" or the like, only a bank may acquire the rights of a holder until the item has been:

(1) returned to the customer initiating collection; or

(2) specially indorsed by a bank to a person who is not a bank.

§ 4—202. Responsibility for Collection or Return; When Action Timely.

(a) A collecting bank must exercise ordinary care in:

(1) presenting an item or sending it for presentment;

(2) sending notice of dishonor or nonpayment or returning an item other than a documentary draft to the bank's transferor after learning that the item has not been paid or accepted, as the case may be;

(3) settling for an item when the bank receives final settlement; and

(4) notifying its transferor of any loss or delay in transit within a reasonable time after discovery thereof.

(b) A collecting bank exercises ordinary care under subsection (a) by taking proper action before its midnight deadline following receipt of an item, notice, or settlement. Taking proper action within a reasonably longer time may constitute the exercise of ordinary care, but the bank has the burden of establishing timeliness.

(c) Subject to subsection (a)(1), a bank is not liable for the insolvency, neglect, misconduct, mistake, or default of another bank or person or for loss or destruction of an item in the possession of others or in transit.

§ 4—203. Effect of Instructions.

Subject to Article 3 concerning conversion of instruments (Section 3—420) and restrictive indorsements (Section 3—206), only a collecting bank's transferor can give instructions that affect the bank or constitute notice to it, and a collecting bank is not liable to prior parties for any action taken pursuant to the instructions or in accordance with any agreement with its transferor.

§ 4—204. Methods of Sending and Presenting; Sending Directly to Payor Bank.

(a) A collecting bank shall send items by a reasonably prompt method, taking into consideration relevant instructions, the nature of the item, the number of those items on hand, the cost of collection involved, and the method generally used by it or others to present those items.

(b) A collecting bank may send:

(1) an item directly to the payor bank;

(2) an item to a nonbank payor if authorized by its transferor; and

(3) an item other than documentary drafts to a nonbank payor, if authorized by Federal Reserve regulation or operating circular, clearing-house rule, or the like.

(c) Presentment may be made by a presenting bank at a place where the payor bank or other payor has requested that presentment be made.

§ 4—205. Depositary Bank Holder of Unindorsed Item.

If a customer delivers an item to a depositary bank for collection:

(1) the depositary bank becomes a holder of the item at the time it receives the item for collection if the customer at the time of delivery was a holder of the item, whether or not the customer indorses the item, and, if the bank satisfies the other requirements of Section 3—302, it is a holder in due course; and

(2) the depositary bank warrants to collecting banks, the payor bank or other payor, and the drawer that the amount of the item was paid to the customer or deposited to the customer's account.

§ 4—206. Transfer Between Banks.

Any agreed method that identifies the transferor bank is sufficient for the item's further transfer to another bank.

§ 4—207. Transfer Warranties.

(a) A customer or collecting bank that transfers an item and receives a settlement or other consideration warrants to the transferee and to any subsequent collecting bank that:

(1) the warrantor is a person entitled to enforce the item;

(2) all signatures on the item are authentic and authorized;

(3) the item has not been altered;

(4) the item is not subject to a defense or claim in recoupment (Section 3—305(a)) of any party that can be asserted against the warrantor; and

(5) the warrantor has no knowledge of any insolvency proceeding commenced with respect to the maker or

acceptor or, in the case of an unaccepted draft, the drawer.

(b) If an item is dishonored, a customer or collecting bank transferring the item and receiving settlement or other consideration is obliged to pay the amount due on the item (i) according to the terms of the item at the time it was transferred, or (ii) if the transfer was of an incomplete item, according to its terms when completed as stated in Sections 3—115 and 3—407. The obligation of a transferor is owed to the transferee and to any subsequent collecting bank that takes the item in good faith. A transferor cannot disclaim its obligation under this subsection by an indorsement stating that it is made "without recourse" or otherwise disclaiming liability.

(c) A person to whom the warranties under subsection (a) are made and who took the item in good faith may recover from the warrantor as damages for breach of warranty an amount equal to the loss suffered as a result of the breach, but not more than the amount of the item plus expenses and loss of interest incurred as a result of the breach.

(d) The warranties stated in subsection (a) cannot be disclaimed with respect to checks. Unless notice of a claim for breach of warranty is given to the warrantor within 30 days after the claimant has reason to know of the breach and the identity of the warrantor, the warrantor is discharged to the extent of any loss caused by the delay in giving notice of the claim.

(e) A cause of action for breach of warranty under this section accrues when the claimant has reason to know of the breach.

§ 4—208. Presentment Warranties.

(a) If an unaccepted draft is presented to the drawee for payment or acceptance and the drawee pays or accepts the draft, (i) the person obtaining payment or acceptance, at the time of presentment, and (ii) a previous transferor of the draft, at the time of transfer, warrant to the drawee that pays or accepts the draft in good faith that:

(1) the warrantor is, or was, at the time the warrantor transferred the draft, a person entitled to enforce the draft or authorized to obtain payment or acceptance of the draft on behalf of a person entitled to enforce the draft;

(2) the draft has not been altered; and

(3) the warrantor has no knowledge that the signature of the purported drawer of the draft is unauthorized.

(b) A drawee making payment may recover from a warrantor damages for breach of warranty equal to the amount paid by the drawee less the amount the drawee received or is entitled to receive from the drawer because of the payment. In addition, the drawee is entitled to compensation for expenses and loss of interest resulting from the breach. The right of the drawee to recover damages under this subsection is not affected by any failure of the drawee to exer-

cise ordinary care in making payment. If the drawee accepts the draft (i) breach of warranty is a defense to the obligation of the acceptor, and (ii) if the acceptor makes payment with respect to the draft, the acceptor is entitled to recover from a warrantor for breach of warranty the amounts stated in this subsection.

(c) If a drawee asserts a claim for breach of warranty under subsection (a) based on an unauthorized indorsement of the draft or an alteration of the draft, the warrantor may defend by proving that the indorsement is effective under Section 3—404 or 3—405 or the drawer is precluded under Section 3—406 or 4—406 from asserting against the drawee the unauthorized indorsement or alteration.

(d) If (i) a dishonored draft is presented for payment to the drawer or an indorser or (ii) any other item is presented for payment to a party obliged to pay the item, and the item is paid, the person obtaining payment and a prior transferor of the item warrant to the person making payment in good faith that the warrantor is, or was, at the time the warrantor transferred the item, a person entitled to enforce the item or authorized to obtain payment on behalf of a person entitled to enforce the item. The person making payment may recover from any warrantor for breach of warranty an amount equal to the amount paid plus expenses and loss of interest resulting from the breach.

(e) The warranties stated in subsections (a) and (d) cannot be disclaimed with respect to checks. Unless notice of a claim for breach of warranty is given to the warrantor within 30 days after the claimant has reason to know of the breach and the identity of the warrantor, the warrantor is discharged to the extent of any loss caused by the delay in giving notice of the claim.

(f) A cause of action for breach of warranty under this section accrues when the claimant has reason to know of the breach.

§ 4—209. Encoding and Retention Warranties.

(a) A person who encodes information on or with respect to an item after issue warrants to any subsequent collecting bank and to the payor bank or other payor that the information is correctly encoded. If the customer of a depositary bank encodes, that bank also makes the warranty.

(b) A person who undertakes to retain an item pursuant to an agreement for electronic presentment warrants to any subsequent collecting bank and to the payor bank or other payor that retention and presentment of the item comply with the agreement. If a customer of a depositary bank undertakes to retain an item, that bank also makes this warranty.

(c) A person to whom warranties are made under this section and who took the item in good faith may recover from the warrantor as damages for breach of warranty an amount equal to the loss suffered as a result of the breach, plus expenses and loss of interest incurred as a result of the breach.

§ 4—210. Security Interest of Collecting Bank in Items, Accompanying Documents and Proceeds.

(a) A collecting bank has a security interest in an item and any accompanying documents or the proceeds of either:

(1) in case of an item deposited in an account, to the extent to which credit given for the item has been withdrawn or applied;

(2) in case of an item for which it has given credit available for withdrawal as of right, to the extent of the credit given, whether or not the credit is drawn upon or there is a right of charge-back; or

(3) if it makes an advance on or against the item.

(b) If credit given for several items received at one time or pursuant to a single agreement is withdrawn or applied in part, the security interest remains upon all the items, any accompanying documents or the proceeds of either. For the purpose of this section, credits first given are first withdrawn.

(c) Receipt by a collecting bank of a final settlement for an item is a realization on its security interest in the item, accompanying documents, and proceeds. So long as the bank does not receive final settlement for the item or give up possession of the item or accompanying documents for purposes other than collection, the security interest continues to that extent and is subject to Article 9, but:

(1) no security agreement is necessary to make the security interest enforceable (Section 9—203(1)(a));

(2) no filing is required to perfect the security interest; and

(3) the security interest has priority over conflicting perfected security interests in the item, accompanying documents, or proceeds.

§ 4—211. When Bank Gives Value for Purposes of Holder in Due Course.

For purposes of determining its status as a holder in due course, a bank has given value to the extent it has a security interest in an item, if the bank otherwise complies with the requirements of Section 3—302 on what constitutes a holder in due course.

§ 4—212. Presentment by Notice of Item Not Payable by, Through, or at Bank; Liability of Drawer or Indorser.

(a) Unless otherwise instructed, a collecting bank may present an item not payable by, through, or at a bank by sending to the party to accept or pay a written notice that the bank holds the item for acceptance or payment. The notice must be sent in time to be received on or before the day when presentment is due and the bank must meet any requirement of the party to accept or pay under Section 3—501 by the close of the bank's next banking day after it knows of the requirement.

(b) If presentment is made by notice and payment, acceptance, or request for compliance with a requirement under Section 3—501 is not received by the close of business on the day after maturity or, in the case of demand items, by the close of business on the third banking day after notice was sent, the presenting bank may treat the item as dishonored and charge any drawer or indorser by sending it notice of the facts.

§ 4—213. Medium and Time of Settlement by Bank.

(a) With respect to settlement by a bank, the medium and time of settlement may be prescribed by Federal Reserve regulations or circulars, clearing-house rules, and the like, or agreement. In the absence of such prescription:

(1) the medium of settlement is cash or credit to an account in a Federal Reserve bank of or specified by the person to receive settlement; and

(2) the time of settlement is:

(i) with respect to tender of settlement by cash, a cashier's check, or teller's check, when the cash or check is sent or delivered;

(ii) with respect to tender of settlement by credit in an account in a Federal Reserve Bank, when the credit is made;

(iii) with respect to tender of settlement by a credit or debit to an account in a bank, when the credit or debit is made or, in the case of tender of settlement by authority to charge an account, when the authority is sent or delivered; or

(iv) with respect to tender of settlement by a funds transfer, when payment is made pursuant to Section 4A—406(a) to the person receiving settlement.

(b) If the tender of settlement is not by a medium authorized by subsection (a) or the time of settlement is not fixed by subsection (a), no settlement occurs until the tender of settlement is accepted by the person receiving settlement.

(c) If settlement for an item is made by cashier's check or teller's check and the person receiving settlement, before its midnight deadline:

(1) presents or forwards the check for collection, settlement is final when the check is finally paid; or

(2) fails to present or forward the check for collection, settlement is final at the midnight deadline of the person receiving settlement.

(d) If settlement for an item is made by giving authority to charge the account of the bank giving settlement in the bank receiving settlement, settlement is final when the charge is made by the bank receiving settlement if there are funds available in the account for the amount of the item.

§ 4—214. Right of Charge-Back or Refund; Liability of Collecting Bank: Return of Item.

(a) If a collecting bank has made provisional settlement with its customer for an item and fails by reason of dishonor, suspension of payments by a bank, or otherwise to receive settlement for the item which is or becomes final, the bank may revoke the settlement given by it, charge back the amount of any credit given for the item to its customer's account, or obtain refund from its customer, whether or not it is able to return the item, if by its midnight deadline or within a longer reasonable time after it learns the facts it returns the item or sends notification of the facts. If the return or notice is delayed beyond the bank's midnight deadline or a longer reasonable time after it learns the facts, the bank may revoke the settlement, charge back the credit, or obtain refund from its customer, but it is liable for any loss resulting from the delay. These rights to revoke, charge back, and obtain refund terminate if and when a settlement for the item received by the bank is or becomes final.

(b) A collecting bank returns an item when it is sent or delivered to the bank's customer or transferor or pursuant to its instructions.

(c) A depositary bank that is also the payor may charge back the amount of an item to its customer's account or obtain refund in accordance with the section governing return of an item received by a payor bank for credit on its books (Section 4—301).

(d) The right to charge back is not affected by:

(1) previous use of a credit given for the item; or

(2) failure by any bank to exercise ordinary care with respect to the item, but a bank so failing remains liable.

(e) A failure to charge back or claim refund does not affect other rights of the bank against the customer or any other party.

(f) If credit is given in dollars as the equivalent of the value of an item payable in foreign money, the dollar amount of any charge-back or refund must be calculated on the basis of the bank-offered spot rate for the foreign money prevailing on the day when the person entitled to the charge-back or refund learns that it will not receive payment in ordinary course.

§ 4—215. Final Payment of Item by Payor Bank; When Provisional Debits and Credits Become Final; When Certain Credits Become Available for Withdrawal.

(a) An item is finally paid by a payor bank when the bank has first done any of the following:

(1) paid the item in cash;

(2) settled for the item without having a right to revoke the settlement under statute, clearing-house rule, or agreement; or

(3) made a provisional settlement for the item and failed to revoke the settlement in the time and manner permitted by statute, clearing-house rule, or agreement.

(b) If provisional settlement for an item does not become final, the item is not finally paid.

(c) If provisional settlement for an item between the presenting and payor banks is made through a clearing house or by debits or credits in an account between them, then to the extent that provisional debits or credits for the item are entered in accounts between the presenting and payor banks or between the presenting and successive prior collecting banks seriatim, they become final upon final payment of the item by the payor bank.

(d) If a collecting bank receives a settlement for an item which is or becomes final, the bank is accountable to its customer for the amount of the item and any provisional credit given for the item in an account with its customer becomes final.

(e) Subject to (i) applicable law stating a time for availability of funds and (ii) any right of the bank to apply the credit to an obligation of the customer, credit given by a bank for an item in a customer's account becomes available for withdrawal as of right:

(1) if the bank has received a provisional settlement for the item, when the settlement becomes final and the bank has had a reasonable time to receive return of the item and the item has not been received within that time;

(2) if the bank is both the depositary bank and the payor bank, and the item is finally paid, at the opening of the bank's second banking day following receipt of the item.

(f) Subject to applicable law stating a time for availability of funds and any right of a bank to apply a deposit to an obligation of the depositor, a deposit of money becomes available for withdrawal as of right at the opening of the bank's next banking day after receipt of the deposit.

§ 4—216. Insolvency and Preference.

(a) If an item is in or comes into the possession of a payor or collecting bank that suspends payment and the item has not been finally paid, the item must be returned by the receiver, trustee, or agent in charge of the closed bank to the presenting bank or the closed bank's customer.

(b) If a payor bank finally pays an item and suspends payments without making a settlement for the item with its customer or the presenting bank which settlement is or becomes final, the owner of the item has a preferred claim against the payor bank.

(c) If a payor bank gives or a collecting bank gives or receives a provisional settlement for an item and thereafter suspends payments, the suspension does not prevent or interfere with the settlement's becoming final if the finality occurs automatically upon the lapse of certain time or the happening of certain events.

(d) If a collecting bank receives from subsequent parties settlement for an item, which settlement is or becomes final and the bank suspends payments without making a settlement for the item with its customer which settlement is or becomes final, the owner of the item has a preferred claim against the collecting bank.

Part 3　Collection of Items: Payor Banks

§ 4—301. Deferred Posting; Recovery of Payment by Return of Items; Time of Dishonor; Return of Items by Payor Bank.

(a) If a payor bank settles for a demand item other than a documentary draft presented otherwise than for immediate payment over the counter before midnight of the banking day of receipt, the payor bank may revoke the settlement and recover the settlement if, before it has made final payment and before its midnight deadline, it

(1) returns the item; or

(2) sends written notice of dishonor or nonpayment if the item is unavailable for return.

(b) If a demand item is received by a payor bank for credit on its books, it may return the item or send notice of dishonor and may revoke any credit given or recover the amount thereof withdrawn by its customer, if it acts within the time limit and in the manner specified in subsection (a).

(c) Unless previous notice of dishonor has been sent, an item is dishonored at the time when for purposes of dishonor it is returned or notice sent in accordance with this section.

(d) An item is returned:

(1) as to an item presented through a clearing house, when it is delivered to the presenting or last collecting bank or to the clearing house or is sent or delivered in accordance with clearing-house rules; or

(2) in all other cases, when it is sent or delivered to the bank's customer or transferor or pursuant to instructions.

§ 4—302. Payor Bank's Responsibility for Late Return of Item.

(a) If an item is presented to and received by a payor bank, the bank is accountable for the amount of:

(1) a demand item, other than a documentary draft, whether properly payable or not, if the bank, in any case in which it is not also the depositary bank, retains the item beyond midnight of the banking day of receipt without settling for it or, whether or not it is also the depositary bank, does not pay or return the item or send notice of dishonor until after its midnight deadline; or

(2) any other properly payable item unless, within the time allowed for acceptance or payment of that item,

the bank either accepts or pays the item or returns it and accompanying documents.

(b) The liability of a payor bank to pay an item pursuant to subsection (a) is subject to defenses based on breach of a presentment warranty (Section 4—208) or proof that the person seeking enforcement of the liability presented or transferred the item for the purpose of defrauding the payor bank.

§ 4—303. When Items Subject to Notice, Stop-Payment Order, Legal Process, or Setoff; Order in Which Items May Be Charged or Certified.

(a) Any knowledge, notice, or stop-payment order received by, legal process served upon, or setoff exercised by a payor bank comes too late to terminate, suspend, or modify the bank's right or duty to pay an item or to charge its customer's account for the item if the knowledge, notice, stop-payment order, or legal process is received or served and a reasonable time for the bank to act thereon expires or the setoff is exercised after the earliest of the following:

(1) the bank accepts or certifies the item;

(2) the bank pays the item in cash;

(3) the bank settles for the item without having a right to revoke the settlement under statute, clearing-house rule, or agreement;

(4) the bank becomes accountable for the amount of the item under Section 4—302 dealing with the payor bank's responsibility for late return of items; or

(5) with respect to checks, a cutoff hour no earlier than one hour after the opening of the next banking day after the banking day on which the bank received the check and no later than the close of that next banking day or, if no cutoff hour is fixed, the close of the next banking day after the banking day on which the bank received the check.

(b) Subject to subsection (a), items may be accepted, paid, certified, or charged to the indicated account of its customer in any order.

Part 4　Relationship Between Payor Bank and its Customer

§ 4—401. When Bank May Charge Customer's Account.

(a) A bank may charge against the account of a customer an item that is properly payable from the account even though the charge creates an overdraft. An item is properly payable if it is authorized by the customer and is in accordance with any agreement between the customer and bank.

(b) A customer is not liable for the amount of an overdraft if the customer neither signed the item nor benefited from the proceeds of the item.

(c) A bank may charge against the account of a customer

a check that is otherwise properly payable from the account, even though payment was made before the date of the check, unless the customer has given notice to the bank of the postdating describing the check with reasonable certainty. The notice is effective for the period stated in Section 4—403(b) for stop-payment orders, and must be received at such time and in such manner as to afford the bank a reasonable opportunity to act on it before the bank takes any action with respect to the check described in Section 4—303. If a bank charges against the account of a customer a check before the date stated in the notice of postdating, the bank is liable for damages for the loss resulting from its act. The loss may include damages for dishonor of subsequent items under Section 4—402.

(d) A bank that in good faith makes payment to a holder may charge the indicated account of its customer according to:

(1) the original terms of the altered item; or

(2) the terms of the completed item, even though the bank knows the item has been completed unless the bank has notice that the completion was improper.

§ 4—402. Bank's Liability to Customer for Wrongful Dishonor; Time of Determining Insufficiency of Account.

(a) Except as otherwise provided in this Article, a payor bank wrongfully dishonors an item if it dishonors an item that is properly payable, but a bank may dishonor an item that would create an overdraft unless it has agreed to pay the overdraft.

(b) A payor bank is liable to its customer for damages proximately caused by the wrongful dishonor of an item. Liability is limited to actual damages proved and may include damages for an arrest or prosecution of the customer or other consequential damages. Whether any consequential damages are proximately caused by the wrongful dishonor is a question of fact to be determined in each case.

(c) A payor bank's determination of the customer's account balance on which a decision to dishonor for insufficiency of available funds is based may be made at any time between the time the item is received by the payor bank and the time that the payor bank returns the item or gives notice in lieu of return, and no more than one determination need be made. If, at the election of the payor bank, a subsequent balance determination is made for the purpose of reevaluating the bank's decision to dishonor the item, the account balance at that time is determinative of whether a dishonor for insufficiency of available funds is wrongful.

§ 4—403. Customer's Right to Stop Payment; Burden of Proof of Loss.

(a) A customer or any person authorized to draw on the account if there is more than one person may stop payment of any item drawn on the customer's account or close

the account by an order to the bank describing the item or account with reasonable certainty received at a time and in a manner that affords the bank a reasonable opportunity to act on it before any action by the bank with respect to the item described in Section 4—303. If the signature of more than one person is required to draw on an account, any of these persons may stop payment or close the account.

(b) A stop-payment order is effective for six months, but it lapses after 14 calendar days if the original order was oral and was not confirmed in writing within that period. A stop-payment order may be renewed for additional six-month periods by a writing given to the bank within a period during which the stop-payment order is effective.

(c) The burden of establishing the fact and amount of loss resulting from the payment of an item contrary to a stop-payment order or order to close an account is on the customer. The loss from payment of an item contrary to a stop-payment order may include damages for dishonor of subsequent items under Section 4—402.

§ 4—404. Bank Not Obliged to Pay Check More Than Six Months Old.

A bank is under no obligation to a customer having a checking account to pay a check, other than a certified check, which is presented more than six months after its date, but it may charge its customer's account for a payment made thereafter in good faith.

§ 4—405. Death or Incompetence of Customer.

(a) A payor or collecting bank's authority to accept, pay, or collect an item or to account for proceeds of its collection, if otherwise effective, is not rendered ineffective by incompetence of a customer of either bank existing at the time the item is issued or its collection is undertaken if the bank does not know of an adjudication of incompetence. Neither death nor incompetence of a customer revokes the authority to accept, pay, collect, or account until the bank knows of the fact of death or of an adjudication of incompetence and has reasonable opportunity to act on it.

(b) Even with knowledge, a bank may for 10 days after the date of death pay or certify checks drawn on or before the date unless ordered to stop payment by a person claiming an interest in the account.

§ 4—406. Customer's Duty to Discover and Report Unauthorized Signature or Alteration.

(a) A bank that sends or makes available to a customer a statement of account showing payment of items for the account shall either return or make available to the customer the items paid or provide information in the statement of account sufficient to allow the customer reasonably to identify the items paid. The statement of account provides sufficient information if the item is described by item number, amount, and date of payment.

(b) If the items are not returned to the customer, the person retaining the items shall either retain the items or, if the items are destroyed, maintain the capacity to furnish legible copies of the items until the expiration of seven years after receipt of the items. A customer may request an item from the bank that paid the item, and that bank must provide in a reasonable time either the item or, if the item has been destroyed or is not otherwise obtainable, a legible copy of the item.

(c) If a bank sends or makes available a statement of account or items pursuant to subsection (a), the customer must exercise reasonable promptness in examining the statement or the items to determine whether any payment was not authorized because of an alteration of an item or because a purported signature by or on behalf of the customer was not authorized. If, based on the statement or items provided, the customer should reasonably have discovered the unauthorized payment, the customer must promptly notify the bank of the relevant facts.

(d) If the bank proves that the customer failed, with respect to an item, to comply with the duties imposed on the customer by subsection (c), the customer is precluded from asserting against the bank:

(1) the customer's unauthorized signature or any alteration on the item, if the bank also proves that it suffered a loss by reason of the failure; and

(2) the customer's unauthorized signature or alteration by the same wrongdoer on any other item paid in good faith by the bank if the payment was made before the bank received notice from the customer of the unauthorized signature or alteration and after the customer had been afforded a reasonable period of time, not exceeding 30 days, in which to examine the item or statement of account and notify the bank.

(e) If subsection (d) applies and the customer proves that the bank failed to exercise ordinary care in paying the item and that the failure substantially contributed to loss, the loss is allocated between the customer precluded and the bank asserting the preclusion according to the extent to which the failure of the customer to comply with subsection (c) and the failure of the bank to exercise ordinary care contributed to the loss. If the customer proves that the bank did not pay the item in good faith, the preclusion under subsection (d) does not apply.

(f) Without regard to care or lack of care of either the customer or the bank, a customer who does not within one year after the statement or items are made available to the customer (subsection (a)) discover and report the customer's unauthorized signature on or any alteration on the item is precluded from asserting against the bank the unauthorized signature or alteration. If there is a preclusion under this subsection, the payor bank may not recover for breach or warranty under Section 4-208 with respect to the unauthorized signature or alteration to which the preclusion applies.

§ 4-407. Payor Bank's Right to Subrogation on Improper Payment.

If a payor has paid an item over the order of the drawer or maker to stop payment, or after an account has been closed, or otherwise under circumstances giving a basis for objection by the drawer or maker, to prevent unjust enrichment and only to the extent necessary to prevent loss to the bank by reason of its payment of the item, the payor bank is subrogated to the rights

(1) of any holder in due course on the item against the drawer or maker;

(2) of the payee or any other holder of the item against the drawer or maker either on the item or under the transaction out of which the item arose; and

(3) of the drawer or maker against the payee or any other holder of the item with respect to the transaction out of which the item arose.

Part 5 Collection of Documentary Drafts

§ 4-501. Handling of Documentary Drafts; Duty to Send for Presentment and to Notify Customer of Dishonor.

A bank that takes a documentary draft for collection shall present or send the draft and accompanying documents for presentment and, upon learning that the draft has not been paid or accepted in due course, shall seasonably notify its customer of the fact even though it may have discounted or bought the draft or extended credit available for withdrawal as of right.

§ 4-502. Presentment of "On Arrival" Drafts.

If a draft or the relevant instructions require presentment "on arrival", "when goods arrive" or the like, the collecting bank need not present until in its judgment a reasonable time for arrival of the goods has expired. Refusal to pay or accept because the goods have not arrived is not dishonor; the bank must notify its transferor of the refusal but need not present the draft again until it is instructed to do so or learns of the arrival of the goods.

§ 4-503. Responsibility of Presenting Bank for Documents and Goods; Report of Reasons for Dishonor; Referee in Case of Need.

Unless otherwise instructed and except as provided in Article 5, a bank presenting a documentary draft:

(1) must deliver the documents to the drawee on acceptance of the draft if it is payable more than three days after presentment, otherwise, only on payment; and

(2) upon dishonor, either in the case of presentment for acceptance or presentment for payment, may seek and follow instructions from any referee in case of need designated in the draft or, if the presenting bank does not choose to utilize the referee's services, it must use

diligence and good faith to ascertain the reason for dishonor, must notify its transferor of the dishonor and of the results of its effort to ascertain the reasons therefor, and must request instructions.

However, the presenting bank is under no obligation with respect to goods represented by the documents except to follow any reasonable instructions seasonably received; it has a right to reimbursement for any expense incurred in following instructions and to prepayment of or indemnity for those expenses.

§ 4—504. Privilege of Presenting Bank to Deal With Goods; Security Interest for Expenses.

(a) A presenting bank that, following the dishonor of a documentary draft, has seasonably requested instructions but does not receive them within a reasonable time may store, sell, or otherwise deal with the goods in any reasonable manner.

(b) For its reasonable expenses incurred by action under subsection (a) the presenting bank has a lien upon the goods or their proceeds, which may be foreclosed in the same manner as an unpaid seller's lien.

Article 4A
FUNDS TRANSFERS

Part 1 Subject Matter and Definitions

§ 4A—101. Short Title.
This Article may be cited as Uniform Commercial Code—Funds Transfers.

§ 4A—102. Subject Matter.
Except as otherwise provided in Section 4A—108, this Article applies to funds transfers defined in Section 4A—104.

§ 4A—103. Payment Order—Definitions.
(a) In this Article:

(1) "Payment order" means an instruction of a sender to a receiving bank, transmitted orally, electronically, or in writing, to pay, or to cause another bank to pay, a fixed or determinable amount of money to a beneficiary if:

(i) the instruction does not state a condition to payment to the beneficiary other than time of payment,

(ii) the receiving bank is to be reimbursed by debiting an account of, or otherwise receiving payment from, the sender, and

(iii) the instruction is transmitted by the sender directly to the receiving bank or to an agent, funds-transfer system, or communication system for transmittal to the receiving bank.

(2) "Beneficiary" means the person to be paid by the beneficiary's bank.

(3) "Beneficiary's bank" means the bank identified in a payment order in which an account of the beneficiary is to be credited pursuant to the order or which otherwise is to make payment to the beneficiary if the order does not provide for payment to an account.

(4) "Receiving bank" means the bank to which the sender's instruction is addressed.

(5) "Sender" means the person giving the instruction to the receiving bank.

(b) If an instruction complying with subsection (a)(1) is to make more than one payment to a beneficiary, the instruction is a separate payment order with respect to each payment.

(c) A payment order is issued when it is sent to the receiving bank.

§ 4A—104. Funds Transfer—Definitions.

In this Article:

(a) "Funds transfer" means the series of transactions, beginning with the originator's payment order, made for the purpose of making payment to the beneficiary of the order. The term includes any payment order issued by the originator's bank or an intermediary bank intended to carry out the originator's payment order. A funds transfer is completed by acceptance by the beneficiary's bank of a payment order for the benefit of the beneficiary of the originator's payment order.

(b) "Intermediary bank" means a receiving bank other than the originator's bank or the beneficiary's bank.

(c) "Originator" means the sender of the first payment order in a funds transfer.

(d) "Originator's bank" means (i) the receiving bank to which the payment order of the originator is issued if the originator is not a bank, or (ii) the originator if the originator is a bank.

§ 4A—105. Other Definitions.

(a) In this Article:

(1) "Authorized account" means a deposit account of a customer in a bank designated by the customer as a source of payment of payment orders issued by the customer to the bank. If a customer does not so designate an account, any account of the customer is an authorized account if payment of a payment order from that account is not inconsistent with a restriction on the use of that account.

(2) "Bank" means a person engaged in the business of banking and includes a savings bank, savings and loan association, credit union, and trust company. A branch or separate office of a bank is a separate bank for purposes of this Article.

(3) "Customer" means a person, including a bank, having an account with a bank or from whom a bank has agreed to receive payment orders.

(4) "Funds-transfer business day" of a receiving bank means the part of a day during which the receiving bank is open for the receipt, processing, and transmittal of payment orders and cancellations and amendments of payment orders.

(5) "Funds-transfer system" means a wire transfer network, automated clearing house, or other communication system of a clearing house or other association of banks through which a payment order by a bank may be transmitted to the bank to which the order is addressed.

(6) "Good faith" means honesty in fact and the observance of reasonable commercial standards of fair dealing.

(7) "Prove" with respect to a fact means to meet the burden of establishing the fact (Section 1—201(8)).

(b) Other definitions applying to this Article and the sections in which they appear are:

"Acceptance"	Section 4A—209
"Beneficiary"	Section 4A—103
"Beneficiary's bank"	Section 4A—103
"Executed"	Section 4A—301
"Execution date"	Section 4A—301
"Funds transfer"	Section 4A—104
"Funds-transfer system rule"	Section 4A—501
"Intermediary bank"	Section 4A—104
"Originator"	Section 4A—104
"Originator's bank"	Section 4A—104
"Payment by beneficiary's bank to beneficiary"	Section 4A—405
"Payment by originator to beneficiary"	Section 4A—406
"Payment by sender to receiving bank"	Section 4A—403
"Payment date"	Section 4A—401
"Payment order"	Section 4A—103
"Receiving bank"	Section 4A—103
"Security procedure"	Section 4A—201
"Sender"	Section 4A—103

(c) The following definitions in Article 4 apply to this Article:

"Clearing house"	Section 4—104
"Item"	Section 4—104
"Suspends payments"	Section 4—104

(d) In addition, Article 1 contains general definitions and principles of construction and interpretation applicable throughout this Article.

§ 4A—106. Time Payment Order Is Received.

(a) The time of receipt of a payment order or communication cancelling or amending a payment order is determined by the rules applicable to receipt of a notice stated in Section 1—201(27). A receiving bank may fix a cut-off time or times on a funds-transfer business day for the receipt and processing of payment orders and communications cancelling or amending payment orders. Different cut-off times may apply to payment orders, cancellations, or amendments, or to different categories of payment orders, cancellations, or amendments. A cut-off time may apply to senders generally or different cut-off times may apply to different senders or categories of payment orders. If a payment order or communication cancelling or amending a payment order is received after the close of a funds-transfer business day or after the appropriate cut-off time on a funds-transfer business day, the receiving bank may treat the payment order or communication as received at the opening of the next funds-transfer business day.

(b) If this Article refers to an execution date or payment date or states a day on which a receiving bank is required to take action, and the date or day does not fall on a funds-transfer business day, the next day that is a funds-transfer business day is treated as the date or day stated, unless the contrary is stated in this Article.

§ 4A—107. Federal Reserve Regulations and Operating Circulars.

Regulations of the Board of Governors of the Federal Reserve System and operating circulars of the Federal Reserve Banks supersede any inconsistent provision of this Article to the extent of the inconsistency.

§ 4A—108. Exclusion of Consumer Transactions Governed by Federal Law.

This Article does not apply to a funds transfer any part of which is governed by the Electronic Fund Transfer Act of 1978 (Title XX, Public Law 95—630, 92 Stat. 3728, 15 U.S.C. § 1693 et seq.) as amended from time to time.

Part 2 Issue and Acceptance of Payment Order

§ 4A—201. Security Procedure.

"Security procedure" means a procedure established by agreement of a customer and a receiving bank for the purpose of (i) verifying that a payment order or communication amending or cancelling a payment order is that of the customer, or (ii) detecting error in the transmission or the content of the payment order or communication. A security procedure may require the use of algorithms or other codes, identifying words or numbers, encryption, callback procedures, or similar security devices. Comparison of a signature on a payment order or communication with an authorized specimen signature of the customer is not by itself a security procedure.

§ 4A—202. Authorized and Verified Payment Orders.

(a) A payment order received by the receiving bank is the authorized order of the person identified as sender if that person authorized the order or is otherwise bound by it under the law of agency.

(b) If a bank and its customer have agreed that the authenticity of payment orders issued to the bank in the name of the customer as sender will be verified pursuant to a security procedure, a payment order received by the receiving bank is effective as the order of the customer, whether or not authorized, if (i) the security procedure is a commercially reasonable method of providing security against unauthorized payment orders, and (ii) the bank proves that it accepted the payment order in good faith and in compliance with the security procedure and any written agreement or instruction of the customer restricting acceptance of payment orders issued in the name of the customer. The bank is not required to follow an instruction that violates a written agreement with the customer or notice of which is not received at a time and in a manner affording the bank a reasonable opportunity to act on it before the payment order is accepted.

(c) Commercial reasonableness of a security procedure is a question of law to be determined by considering the wishes of the customer expressed to the bank, the circumstances of the customer known to the bank, including the size, type, and frequency of payment orders normally issued by the customer to the bank, alternative security procedures offered to the customer, and security procedures in general use by customers and receiving banks similarly situated. A security procedure is deemed to be commercially reasonable if (i) the security procedure was chosen by the customer after the bank offered, and the customer refused, a security procedure that was commercially reasonable for that customer, and (ii) the customer expressly agreed in writing to be bound by any payment order, whether or not authorized, issued in its name and accepted by the bank in compliance with the security procedure chosen by the customer.

(d) The term "sender" in this Article includes the customer in whose name a payment order is issued if the order is the authorized order of the customer under subsection (a), or it is effective as the order of the customer under subsection (b).

(e) This section applies to amendments and cancellations of payment orders to the same extent it applies to payment orders.

(f) Except as provided in this section and in Section 4A—203(a)(1), rights and obligations arising under this section or Section 4A—203 may not be varied by agreement.

§ 4A—203. Unenforceability of Certain Verified Payment Orders.

(a) If an accepted payment order is not, under Section 4A—202(a), an authorized order of a customer identified as sender, but is effective as an order of the customer pursuant to Section 4A—202(b), the following rules apply:

(1) By express written agreement, the receiving bank may limit the extent to which it is entitled to enforce or retain payment of the payment order.

(2) The receiving bank is not entitled to enforce or retain payment of the payment order if the customer proves that the order was not caused, directly or indirectly, by a person (i) entrusted at any time with duties to act for the customer with respect to payment orders or the security procedure, or (ii) who obtained access to transmitting facilities of the customer or who obtained, from a source controlled by the customer and without authority of the receiving bank, information facilitating breach of the security procedure, regardless of how the information was obtained or whether the customer was at fault. Information includes any access device, computer software, or the like.

(b) This section applies to amendments of payment orders to the same extent it applies to payment orders.

§ 4A—204. Refund of Payment and Duty of Customer to Report with Respect to Unauthorized Payment Order.

(a) If a receiving bank accepts a payment order issued in the name of its customer as sender which is (i) not authorized and not effective as the order of the customer under Section 4A—202, or (ii) not enforceable, in whole or in part, against the customer under Section 4A—203, the bank shall refund any payment of the payment order received from the customer to the extent the bank is not entitled to enforce payment and shall pay interest on the refundable amount calculated from the date the bank received payment to the date of the refund. However, the customer is not entitled to interest from the bank on the amount to be refunded if the customer fails to exercise ordinary care to determine that the order was not authorized by the customer and to notify the bank of the relevant facts within a reasonable time not exceeding 90 days after the date the customer received notification from the bank that the order was accepted or that the customer's account was debited with respect to the order. The bank is not entitled to any recovery from the customer on account of a failure by the customer to give notification as stated in this section.

(b) Reasonable time under subsection (a) may be fixed by agreement as stated in Section 1—204(1), but the obligation of a receiving bank to refund payment as stated in subsection (a) may not otherwise be varied by agreement.

§ 4A—205. Erroneous Payment Orders.

(a) If an accepted payment order was transmitted pursuant

to a security procedure for the detection of error and the payment order (i) erroneously instructed payment to a beneficiary not intended by the sender, (ii) erroneously instructed payment in an amount greater than the amount intended by the sender, or (iii) was an erroneously transmitted duplicate of a payment order previously sent by the sender, the following rules apply:

(1) If the sender proves that the sender or a person acting on behalf of the sender pursuant to Section 4A—206 complied with the security procedure and that the error would have been detected if the receiving bank had also complied, the sender is not obliged to pay the order to the extent stated in paragraphs (2) and (3).

(2) If the funds transfer is completed on the basis of an erroneous payment order described in clause (i) or (iii) of subsection (a), the sender is not obliged to pay the order and the receiving bank is entitled to recover from the beneficiary any amount paid to the beneficiary to the extent allowed by the law governing mistake and restitution.

(3) If the funds transfer is completed on the basis of a payment order described in clause (ii) of subsection (a), the sender is not obliged to pay the order to the extent the amount received by the beneficiary is greater than the amount intended by the sender. In that case, the receiving bank is entitled to recover from the beneficiary the excess amount received to the extent allowed by the law governing mistake and restitution.

(b) If (i) the sender of an erroneous payment order described in subsection (a) is not obliged to pay all or part of the order, and (ii) the sender receives notification from the receiving bank that the order was accepted by the bank or that the sender's account was debited with respect to the order, the sender has a duty to exercise ordinary care, on the basis of information available to the sender, to discover the error with respect to the order and to advise the bank of the relevant facts within a reasonable time, not exceeding 90 days, after the bank's notification was received by the sender. If the bank proves that the sender failed to perform that duty, the sender is liable to the bank for the loss the bank proves it incurred as a result of the failure, but the liability of the sender may not exceed the amount of the sender's order.

(c) This section applies to amendments to payment orders to the same extent it applies to payment orders.

§ 4A—206. Transmission of Payment Order through Funds-Transfer or Other Communication System.

(a) If a payment order addressed to a receiving bank is transmitted to a funds-transfer system or other third party communication system for transmittal to the bank, the system is deemed to be an agent of the sender for the purpose of transmitting the payment order to the bank. If there is a discrepancy between the terms of the payment order transmitted to the system and the terms of the payment order transmitted by the system to the bank, the terms of the payment order of the sender are those transmitted by the system. This section does not apply to a funds-transfer system of the Federal Reserve Banks.

(b) This section applies to cancellations and amendments to payment orders to the same extent it applies to payment orders.

§ 4A—207. Misdescription of Beneficiary.

(a) Subject to subsection (b), if, in a payment order received by the beneficiary's bank, the name, bank account number, or other identification of the beneficiary refers to a nonexistent or unidentifiable person or account, no person has rights as a beneficiary of the order and acceptance of the order cannot occur.

(b) If a payment order received by the beneficiary's bank identifies the beneficiary both by name and by an identifying or bank account number and the name and number identify different persons, the following rules apply:

(1) Except as otherwise provided in subsection (c), if the beneficiary's bank does not know that the name and number refer to different persons, it may rely on the number as the proper identification of the beneficiary of the order. The beneficiary's bank need not determine whether the name and number refer to the same person.

(2) If the beneficiary's bank pays the person identified by name or knows that the name and number identify different persons, no person has rights as beneficiary except the person paid by the beneficiary's bank if that person was entitled to receive payment from the originator of the funds transfer. If no person has rights as beneficiary, acceptance of the order cannot occur.

(c) If (i) a payment order described in subsection (b) is accepted, (ii) the originator's payment order described the beneficiary inconsistently by name and number, and (iii) the beneficiary's bank pays the person identified by number as permitted by subsection (b)(1), the following rules apply:

(1) If the originator is a bank, the originator is obliged to pay its order.

(2) If the originator is not a bank and proves that the person identified by number was not entitled to receive payment from the originator, the originator is not obliged to pay its order unless the originator's bank proves that the originator, before acceptance of the originator's order, had notice that payment of a payment order issued by the originator might be made by the beneficiary's bank on the basis of an identifying or bank account number even if it identifies a person different from the named beneficiary. Proof of notice may be made by any admissible evidence. The originator's bank satisfies the burden of proof if it proves that the originator, before the payment order was

accepted, signed a writing stating the information to which the notice relates.

(d) In a case governed by subsection (b)(1), if the beneficiary's bank rightfully pays the person identified by number and that person was not entitled to receive payment from the originator, the amount paid may be recovered from that person to the extent allowed by the law governing mistake and restitution as follows:

(1) If the originator is obliged to pay its payment order as stated in subsection (c), the originator has the right to recover.

(2) If the originator is not a bank and is not obliged to pay its payment order, the originator's bank has the right to recover.

§ 4A—208. Misdescription of Intermediary Bank or Beneficiary's Bank.

(a) This subsection applies to a payment order identifying an intermediary bank or the beneficiary's bank only by an identifying number.

(1) The receiving bank may rely on the number as the proper identification of the intermediary or beneficiary's bank and need not determine whether the number identifies a bank.

(2) The sender is obliged to compensate the receiving bank for any loss and expenses incurred by the receiving bank as a result of its reliance on the number in executing or attempting to execute the order.

(b) This subsection applies to a payment order identifying an intermediary bank or the beneficiary's bank both by name and an identifying number if the name and number identify different persons.

(1) If the sender is a bank, the receiving bank may rely on the number as the proper identification of the intermediary or beneficiary's bank if the receiving bank, when it executes the sender's order, does not know that the name and number identify different persons. The receiving bank need not determine whether the name and number refer to the same person or whether the number refers to a bank. The sender is obliged to compensate the receiving bank for any loss and expenses incurred by the receiving bank as a result of its reliance on the number in executing or attempting to execute the order.

(2) If the sender is not a bank and the receiving bank proves that the sender, before the payment order was accepted, had notice that the receiving bank might rely on the number as the proper identification of the intermediary or beneficiary's bank even if it identifies a person different from the bank identified by name, the rights and obligations of the sender and the receiving bank are governed by subsection (b)(1), as though the sender were a bank. Proof of notice may be made by any admissible evidence. The receiving bank satis-

fies the burden of proof if it proves that the sender, before the payment order was accepted, signed a writing stating the information to which the notice relates.

(3) Regardless of whether the sender is a bank, the receiving bank may rely on the name as the proper identification of the intermediary or beneficiary's bank if the receiving bank, at the time it executes the sender's order, does not know that the name and number identify different persons. The receiving bank need not determine whether the name and number refer to the same person.

(4) If the receiving bank knows that the name and number identify different persons, reliance on either the name or the number in executing the sender's payment order is a breach of the obligation stated in Section 4A—302(a)(1).

§ 4A—209. Acceptance of Payment Order.

(a) Subject to subsection (d), a receiving bank other than the beneficiary's bank accepts a payment order when it executes the order.

(b) Subject to subsections (c) and (d), a beneficiary's bank accepts a payment order at the earliest of the following times:

(1) When the bank (i) pays the beneficiary as stated in Section 4A—405(a) or 4A—405(b), or (ii) notifies the beneficiary of receipt of the order or that the account of the beneficiary has been credited with respect to the order unless the notice indicates that the bank is rejecting the order or that funds with respect to the order may not be withdrawn or used until receipt of payment from the sender of the order;

(2) When the bank receives payment of the entire amount of the sender's order pursuant to Section 4A—403(a)(1) or 4A—403(a)(2); or

(3) The opening of the next funds-transfer business day of the bank following the payment date of the order if, at that time, the amount of the sender's order is fully covered by a withdrawable credit balance in an authorized account of the sender or the bank has otherwise received full payment from the sender, unless the order was rejected before that time or is rejected within (i) one hour after that time, or (ii) one hour after the opening of the next business day of the sender following the payment date if that time is later. If notice of rejection is received by the sender after the payment date and the authorized account of the sender does not bear interest, the bank is obliged to pay interest to the sender on the amount of the order for the number of days elapsing after the payment date to the day the sender receives notice or learns that the order was not accepted, counting that day as an elapsed day. If the withdrawable credit balance during that period falls below the

amount of the order, the amount of interest payable is reduced accordingly.

(c) Acceptance of a payment order cannot occur before the order is received by the receiving bank. Acceptance does not occur under subsection (b)(2) or (b)(3) if the beneficiary of the payment order does not have an account with the receiving bank, the account has been closed, or the receiving bank is not permitted by law to receive credits for the beneficiary's account.

(d) A payment order issued to the originator's bank cannot be accepted until the payment date if the bank is the beneficiary's bank, or the execution date if the bank is not the beneficiary's bank. If the originator's bank executes the originator's payment order before the execution date or pays the beneficiary of the originator's payment order before the payment date and the payment order is subsequently cancelled pursuant to Section 4A—211(b), the bank may recover from the beneficiary any payment received to the extent allowed by the law governing mistake and restitution.

§ 4A—210. Rejection of Payment Order.

(a) A payment order is rejected by the receiving bank by a notice of rejection transmitted to the sender orally, electronically, or in writing. A notice of rejection need not use any particular words and is sufficient if it indicates that the receiving bank is rejecting the order or will not execute or pay the order. Rejection is effective when the notice is given if transmission is by a means that is reasonable in the circumstances. If notice of rejection is given by a means that is not reasonable, rejection is effective when the notice is received. If an agreement of the sender and receiving bank establishes the means to be used to reject a payment order, (i) any means complying with the agreement is reasonable and (ii) any means not complying is not reasonable unless no significant delay in receipt of the notice resulted from the use of the noncomplying means.

(b) This subsection applies if a receiving bank other than the beneficiary's bank fails to execute a payment order despite the existence on the execution date of a withdrawable credit balance in an authorized account of the sender sufficient to cover the order. If the sender does not receive notice of rejection of the order on the execution date and the authorized account of the sender does not bear interest, the bank is obliged to pay interest to the sender on the amount of the order for the number of days elapsing after the execution date to the earlier of the day the order is cancelled pursuant to Section 4A—211(d) or the day the sender receives notice or learns that the order was not executed, counting the final day of the period as an elapsed day. If the withdrawable credit balance during that period falls below the amount of the order, the amount of interest is reduced accordingly.

(c) If a receiving bank suspends payments, all unaccepted payment orders issued to it are are deemed rejected at the time the bank suspends payments.

(d) Acceptance of a payment order precludes a later rejection of the order. Rejection of a payment order precludes a later acceptance of the order.

§ 4A—211. Cancellation and Amendment of Payment Order.

(a) A communication of the sender of a payment order cancelling or amending the order may be transmitted to the receiving bank orally, electronically, or in writing. If a security procedure is in effect between the sender and the receiving bank, the communication is not effective to cancel or amend the order unless the communication is verified pursuant to the security procedure or the bank agrees to the cancellation or amendment.

(b) Subject to subsection (a), a communication by the sender cancelling or amending a payment order is effective to cancel or amend the order if notice of the communication is received at a time and in a manner affording the receiving bank a reasonable opportunity to act on the communication before the bank accepts the payment order.

(c) After a payment order has been accepted, cancellation or amendment of the order is not effective unless the receiving bank agrees or a funds-transfer system rule allows cancellation or amendment without agreement of the bank.

(1) With respect to a payment order accepted by a receiving bank other than the beneficiary's bank, cancellation or amendment is not effective unless a conforming cancellation or amendment of the payment order issued by the receiving bank is also made.

(2) With respect to a payment order accepted by the beneficiary's bank, cancellation or amendment is not effective unless the order was issued in execution of an unauthorized payment order, or because of a mistake by a sender in the funds transfer which resulted in the issuance of a payment order (i) that is a duplicate of a payment order previously issued by the sender, (ii) that orders payment to a beneficiary not entitled to receive payment from the originator, or (iii) that orders payment in an amount greater than the amount the beneficiary was entitled to receive from the originator. If the payment order is cancelled or amended, the beneficiary's bank is entitled to recover from the beneficiary any amount paid to the beneficiary to the extent allowed by the law governing mistake and restitution.

(d) An unaccepted payment order is cancelled by operation of law at the close of the fifth funds-transfer business day of the receiving bank after the execution date or payment date of the order.

(e) A cancelled payment order cannot be accepted. If an accepted payment order is cancelled, the acceptance is nullified and no person has any right or obligation based on the acceptance. Amendment of a payment order is deemed to be cancellation of the original order at the time of amendment and issue of a new payment order in the amended form at the same time.

(f) Unless otherwise provided in an agreement of the parties or in a funds-transfer system rule, if the receiving bank, after accepting a payment order, agrees to cancellation or amendment of the order by the sender or is bound by a funds-transfer system rule allowing cancellation or amendment without the bank's agreement, the sender, whether or not cancellation or amendment is effective, is liable to the bank for any loss and expenses, including reasonable attorney's fees, incurred by the bank as a result of the cancellation or amendment or attempted cancellation or amendment.

(g) A payment order is not revoked by the death or legal incapacity of the sender unless the receiving bank knows of the death or of an adjudication of incapacity by a court of competent jurisdiction and has reasonable opportunity to act before acceptance of the order.

(h) A funds-transfer system rule is not effective to the extent it conflicts with subsection (c)(2).

§ 4A—212. Liability and Duty of Receiving Bank Regarding Unaccepted Payment Order.

If a receiving bank fails to accept a payment order that it is obliged by express agreement to accept, the bank is liable for breach of the agreement to the extent provided in the agreement or in this Article, but does not otherwise have any duty to accept a payment order or, before acceptance, to take any action, or refrain from taking action, with respect to the order except as provided in this Article or by express agreement. Liability based on acceptance arises only when acceptance occurs as stated in Section 4A—209, and liability is limited to that provided in this Article. A receiving bank is not the agent of the sender or beneficiary of the payment order it accepts, or of any other party to the funds transfer, and the bank owes no duty to any party to the funds transfer except as provided in this Article or by express agreement.

Part 3 Execution of Sender's Payment Order by Receiving Bank

§ 4A—301. Execution and Execution Date.

(a) A payment order is "executed" by the receiving bank when it issues a payment order intended to carry out the payment order received by the bank. A payment order received by the beneficiary's bank can be accepted but cannot be executed.

(b) "Execution date" of a payment order means the day on which the receiving bank may properly issue a payment order in execution of the sender's order. The execution date may be determined by instruction of the sender but cannot be earlier than the day the order is received and, unless otherwise determined, is the day the order is received. If the sender's instruction states a payment date, the execution date is the payment date or an earlier date on which execution is reasonably necessary to allow payment to the beneficiary on the payment date.

§ 4A—302. Obligations of Receiving Bank in Execution of Payment Order.

(a) Except as provided in subsections (b) through (d), if the receiving bank accepts a payment order pursuant to Section 4A—209(a), the bank has the following obligations in executing the order:

(1) The receiving bank is obliged to issue, on the execution date, a payment order complying with the sender's order and to follow the sender's instructions concerning (i) any intermediary bank or funds-transfer system to be used in carrying out the funds transfer, or (ii) the means by which payment orders are to be transmitted in the funds transfer. If the originator's bank issues a payment order to an intermediary bank, the originator's bank is obliged to instruct the intermediary bank according to the instruction of the originator. An intermediary bank in the funds transfer is similarly bound by an instruction given to it by the sender of the payment order it accepts.

(2) If the sender's instruction states that the funds transfer is to be carried out telephonically or by wire transfer or otherwise indicates that the funds transfer is to be carried out by the most expeditious means, the receiving bank is obliged to transmit its payment order by the most expeditious available means, and to instruct any intermediary bank accordingly. If a sender's instruction states a payment date, the receiving bank is obliged to transmit its payment order at a time and by means reasonably necessary to allow payment to the beneficiary on the payment date or as soon thereafter as is feasible.

(b) Unless otherwise instructed, a receiving bank executing a payment order may (i) use any funds-transfer system if use of that system is reasonable in the circumstances, and (ii) issue a payment order to the beneficiary's bank or to an intermediary bank through which a payment order conforming to the sender's order can expeditiously be issued to the beneficiary's bank if the receiving bank exercises ordinary care in the selection of the intermediary bank. A receiving bank is not required to follow an instruction of the sender designating a funds-transfer system to be used in carrying out the funds transfer if the receiving bank, in good faith, determines that it is not feasible to follow the instruction or that following the instruction would unduly delay completion of the funds transfer.

(c) Unless subsection (a)(2) applies or the receiving bank is otherwise instructed, the bank may execute a payment order by transmitting its payment order by first class mail or by any means reasonable in the circumstances. If the receiving bank is instructed to execute the sender's order by transmitting its payment order by a particular means, the receiving bank may issue its payment order by the means stated or by any means as expeditious as the means stated.

(d) Unless instructed by the sender, (i) the receiving bank may not obtain payment of its charges for services and expenses in connection with the execution of the sender's order by issuing a payment order in an amount equal to the amount of the sender's order less the amount of the charges, and (ii) may not instruct a subsequent receiving bank to obtain payment of its charges in the same manner.

§ 4A—303. Erroneous Execution of Payment Order.

(a) A receiving bank that (i) executes the payment order of the sender by issuing a payment order in an amount greater than the amount of the sender's order, or (ii) issues a payment order in execution of the sender's order and then issues a duplicate order, is entitled to payment of the amount of the sender's order under Section 4A—402(c) if that subsection is otherwise satisfied. The bank is entitled to recover from the beneficiary of the erroneous order the excess payment received to the extent allowed by the law governing mistake and restitution.

(b) A receiving bank that executes the payment order of the sender by issuing a payment order in an amount less than the amount of the sender's order is entitled to payment of the amount of the sender's order under Section 4A—402(c) if (i) that subsection is otherwise satisfied and (ii) the bank corrects its mistake by issuing an additional payment order for the benefit of the beneficiary of the sender's order. If the error is not corrected, the issuer of the erroneous order is entitled to receive or retain payment from the sender of the order it accepted only to the extent of the amount of the erroneous order. This subsection does not apply if the receiving bank executes the sender's payment order by issuing a payment order in an amount less than the amount of the sender's order for the purpose of obtaining payment of its charges for services and expenses pursuant to instruction of the sender.

(c) If a receiving bank executes the payment order of the sender by issuing a payment order to a beneficiary different from the beneficiary of the sender's order and the funds transfer is completed on the basis of that error, the sender of the payment order that was erroneously executed and all previous senders in the funds transfer are not obliged to pay the payment orders they issued. The issuer of the erroneous order is entitled to recover from the beneficiary of the order the payment received to the extent allowed by the law governing mistake and restitution.

§ 4A—304. Duty of Sender to Report Erroneously Executed Payment Order.

If the sender of a payment order that is erroneously executed as stated in Section 4A—303 receives notification from the receiving bank that the order was executed or that the sender's account was debited with respect to the order, the sender has a duty to exercise ordinary care to determine, on the basis of information available to the sender, that the order was erroneously executed and to notify the bank of the relevant facts within a reasonable time not exceeding 90 days after the notification from the bank was received by the sender. If the sender fails to perform that duty, the bank is not obliged to pay interest on any amount refundable to the sender under Section 4A—402(d) for the period before the bank learns of the execution error. The bank is not entitled to any recovery from the sender on account of a failure by the sender to perform the duty stated in this section.

§ 4A—305. Liability for Late or Improper Execution or Failure to Execute Payment Order.

(a) If a funds transfer is completed but execution of a payment order by the receiving bank in breach of Section 4A—302 results in delay in payment to the beneficiary, the bank is obliged to pay interest to either the originator or the beneficiary of the funds transfer for the period of delay caused by the improper execution. Except as provided in subsection (c), additional damages are not recoverable.

(b) If execution of a payment order by a receiving bank in breach of Section 4A—302 results in (i) noncompletion of the funds transfer, (ii) failure to use an intermediary bank designated by the originator, or (iii) issuance of a payment order that does not comply with the terms of the payment order of the originator, the bank is liable to the originator for its expenses in the funds transfer and for incidental expenses and interest losses, to the extent not covered by subsection (a), resulting from the improper execution. Except as provided in subsection (c), additional damages are not recoverable.

(c) In addition to the amounts payable under subsections (a) and (b), damages, including consequential damages, are recoverable to the extent provided in an express written agreement of the receiving bank.

(d) If a receiving bank fails to execute a payment order it was obliged by express agreement to execute, the receiving bank is liable to the sender for its expenses in the transaction and for incidental expenses and interest losses resulting from the failure to execute. Additional damages, including consequential damages, are recoverable to the extent provided in an express written agreement of the receiving bank, but are not otherwise recoverable.

(e) Reasonable attorney's fees are recoverable if demand for compensation under subsection (a) or (b) is made and refused before an action is brought on the claim. If a claim is made for breach of an agreement under subsection (d) and the agreement does not provide for damages, reasonable attorney's fees are recoverable if demand for compensation under subsection (d) is made and refused before an action is brought on the claim.

(f) Except as stated in this section, the liability of a receiving bank under subsections (a) and (b) may not be varied by agreement.

Part 4 Payment

§ 4A—401. Payment Date.

"Payment date" of a payment order means the day on which the amount of the order is payable to the beneficiary by the beneficiary's bank. The payment date may be determined by instruction of the sender but cannot be earlier than the day the order is received by the beneficiary's bank and, unless otherwise determined, is the day the order is received by the beneficiary's bank.

§ 4A—402. Obligation of Sender to Pay Receiving Bank.

(a) This section is subject to Sections 4A—205 and 4A—207.

(b) With respect to a payment order issued to the beneficiary's bank, acceptance of the order by the bank obliges the sender to pay the bank the amount of the order, but payment is not due until the payment date of the order.

(c) This subsection is subject to subsection (e) and to Section 4A—303. With respect to a payment order issued to a receiving bank other than the beneficiary's bank, acceptance of the order by the receiving bank obliges the sender to pay the bank the amount of the sender's order. Payment by the sender is not due until the execution date of the sender's order. The obligation of that sender to pay its payment order is excused if the funds transfer is not completed by acceptance by the beneficiary's bank of a payment order instructing payment to the beneficiary of that sender's payment order.

(d) If the sender of a payment order pays the order and was not obliged to pay all or part of the amount paid, the bank receiving payment is obliged to refund payment to the extent the sender was not obliged to pay. Except as provided in Sections 4A—204 and 4A—304, interest is payable on the refundable amount from the date of payment.

(e) If a funds transfer is not completed as stated in subsection (c) and an intermediary bank is obliged to refund payment as stated in subsection (d) but is unable to do so because not permitted by applicable law or because the bank suspends payments, a sender in the funds transfer that executed a payment order in compliance with an instruction, as stated in Section 4A—302(a)(1), to route the funds transfer through that intermediary bank is entitled to receive or retain payment from the sender of the payment order that it accepted. The first sender in the funds transfer that issued an instruction requiring routing through that intermediary bank is subrogated to the right of the bank that paid the intermediary bank to refund as stated in subsection (d).

(f) The right of the sender of a payment order to be excused from the obligation to pay the order as stated in subsection (c) or to receive refund under subsection (d) may not be varied by agreement.

§ 4A—403. Payment by Sender to Receiving Bank.

(a) Payment of the sender's obligation under Section 4A—402 to pay the receiving bank occurs as follows:

(1) If the sender is a bank, payment occurs when the receiving bank receives final settlement of the obligation through a Federal Reserve Bank or through a funds-transfer system.

(2) If the sender is a bank and the sender (i) credited an account of the receiving bank with the sender, or (ii) caused an account of the receiving bank in another bank to be credited, payment occurs when the credit is withdrawn or, if not withdrawn, at midnight of the day on which the credit is withdrawable and the receiving bank learns of that fact.

(3) If the receiving bank debits an account of the sender with the receiving bank, payment occurs when the debit is made to the extent the debit is covered by a withdrawable credit balance in the account.

(b) If the sender and receiving bank are members of a funds-transfer system that nets obligations multilaterally among participants, the receiving bank receives final settlement when settlement is complete in accordance with the rules of the system. The obligation of the sender to pay the amount of a payment order transmitted through the funds-transfer system may be satisfied, to the extent permitted by the rules of the system, by setting off and applying against the sender's obligation the right of the sender to receive payment from the receiving bank of the amount of any other payment order transmitted to the sender by the receiving bank through the funds-transfer system. The aggregate balance of obligations owed by each sender to each receiving bank in the funds-transfer system may be satisfied, to the extent permitted by the rules of the system, by setting off and applying against that balance the aggregate balance of obligations owed to the sender by other members of the system. The aggregate balance is determined after the right of setoff stated in the second sentence of this subsection has been exercised.

(c) If two banks transmit payment orders to each other under an agreement that settlement of the obligations of each bank to the other under Section 4A—402 will be made at the end of the day or other period, the total amount owed with respect to all orders transmitted by one bank shall be set off against the total amount owed with respect to all orders transmitted by the other bank. To the extent of the setoff, each bank has made payment to the other.

(d) In a case not covered by subsection (a), the time when payment of the sender's obligation under Section 4A—402(b) or 4A—402(c) occurs is governed by applicable principles of law that determine when an obligation is satisfied.

§ 4A—404. Obligation of Beneficiary's Bank to Pay and Give Notice to Beneficiary.

(a) Subject to Sections 4A—211(e), 4A—405(d), and 4A—405(e), if a beneficiary's bank accepts a payment order, the bank is obliged to pay the amount of the order to the beneficiary of the order. Payment is due on the payment date of the order, but if acceptance occurs on the payment date after the close of the funds-transfer business day of the bank, payment is due on the next funds-transfer business day. If the bank refuses to pay after demand by the beneficiary and receipt of notice of particular circumstances that will give rise to consequential damages as a result of nonpayment, the beneficiary may recover damages resulting from the refusal to pay to the extent the bank had notice of the damages, unless the bank proves that it did not pay because of a reasonable doubt concerning the right of the beneficiary to payment.

(b) If a payment order accepted by the beneficiary's bank instructs payment to an account of the beneficiary, the bank is obliged to notify the beneficiary of receipt of the order before midnight of the next funds-transfer business day following the payment date. If the payment order does not instruct payment to an account of the beneficiary, the bank is required to notify the beneficiary only if notice is required by the order. Notice may be given by first class mail or any other means reasonable in the circumstances. If the bank fails to give the required notice, the bank is obliged to pay interest to the beneficiary on the amount of the payment order from the day notice should have been given until the day the beneficiary learned of receipt of the payment order by the bank. No other damages are recoverable. Reasonable attorney's fees are also recoverable if demand for interest is made and refused before an action is brought on the claim.

(c) The right of a beneficiary to receive payment and damages as stated in subsection (a) may not be varied by agreement or a funds-transfer system rule. The right of a beneficiary to be notified as stated in subsection (b) may be varied by agreement of the beneficiary or by a funds-transfer system rule if the beneficiary is notified of the rule before initiation of the funds transfer.

§ 4A—405. Payment by Beneficiary's Bank to Beneficiary.

(a) If the beneficiary's bank credits an account of the beneficiary of a payment order, payment of the bank's obligation under Section 4A—404(a) occurs when and to the extent (i) the beneficiary is notified of the right to withdraw the credit, (ii) the bank lawfully applies the credit to a debt of the beneficiary, or (iii) funds with respect to the order are otherwise made available to the beneficiary by the bank.

(b) If the beneficiary's bank does not credit an account of the beneficiary of a payment order, the time when payment of the bank's obligation under Section 4A—404(a) occurs is governed by principles of law that determine when an obligation is satisfied.

(c) Except as stated in subsections (d) and (e), if the beneficiary's bank pays the beneficiary of a payment order under a condition to payment or agreement of the beneficiary giving the bank the right to recover payment from the beneficiary if the bank does not receive payment of the order, the condition to payment or agreement is not enforceable.

(d) A funds-transfer system rule may provide that payments made to beneficiaries of funds transfers made through the system are provisional until receipt of payment by the beneficiary's bank of the payment order it accepted. A beneficiary's bank that makes a payment that is provisional under the rule is entitled to refund from the beneficiary if (i) the rule requires that both the beneficiary and the originator be given notice of the provisional nature of the payment before the funds transfer is initiated, (ii) the beneficiary, the beneficiary's bank, and the originator's bank agreed to be bound by the rule, and (iii) the beneficiary's bank did not receive payment of the payment order that it accepted. If the beneficiary is obliged to refund payment to the beneficiary's bank, acceptance of the payment order by the beneficiary's bank is nullified and no payment by the originator of the funds transfer to the beneficiary occurs under Section 4A—406.

(e) This subsection applies to a funds transfer that includes a payment order transmitted over a funds-transfer system that (i) nets obligations multilaterally among participants, and (ii) has in effect a loss-sharing agreement among participants for the purpose of providing funds necessary to complete settlement of the obligations of one or more participants that do not meet their settlement obligations. If the beneficiary's bank in the funds transfer accepts a payment order and the system fails to complete settlement pursuant to its rules with respect to any payment order in the funds transfer, (i) the acceptance by the beneficiary's bank is nullified and no person has any right or obligation based on the acceptance, (ii) the beneficiary's bank is entitled to recover payment from the beneficiary, (iii) no payment by the originator to the beneficiary occurs under Section 4A—406, and (iv) subject to Section 4A—402(e), each sender in the funds transfer is excused from its obligation to pay its payment order under Section 4A—402(c) because the funds transfer has not been completed.

§ 4A—406. Payment by Originator to Beneficiary; Discharge of Underlying Obligation.

(a) Subject to Sections 4A—211(e), 4A—405(d), and 4A—405(e), the originator of a funds transfer pays the beneficiary of the originator's payment order (i) at the time a payment order for the benefit of the beneficiary is accepted by the beneficiary's bank in the funds transfer and (ii) in an amount equal to the amount of the order accepted by the beneficiary's bank, but not more than the amount of the originator's order.

(b) If payment under subsection (a) is made to satisfy an obligation, the obligation is discharged to the same extent discharge would result from payment to the beneficiary of the same amount in money, unless (i) the payment under subsection (a) was made by a means prohibited by the contract of the beneficiary with respect to the obligation, (ii) the beneficiary, within a reasonable time after receiving notice of receipt of the order by the beneficiary's bank, notified the originator of the beneficiary's refusal of the payment, (iii) funds with respect to the order were not withdrawn by the beneficiary or applied to a debt of the beneficiary, and (iv) the beneficiary would suffer a loss that could reasonably have been avoided if payment had been made by a means complying with the contract. If payment by the originator does not result in discharge under this section, the originator is subrogated to the rights of the beneficiary to receive payment from the beneficiary's bank under Section 4A—404(a).

(c) For the purpose of determining whether discharge of an obligation occurs under subsection (b), if the beneficiary's bank accepts a payment order in an amount equal to the amount of the originator's payment order less charges of one or more receiving banks in the funds transfer, payment to the beneficiary is deemed to be in the amount of the originator's order unless upon demand by the beneficiary the originator does not pay the beneficiary the amount of the deducted charges.

(d) Rights of the originator or of the beneficiary of a funds transfer under this section may be varied only by agreement of the originator and the beneficiary.

Part 5 Miscellaneous Provisions

§ 4A—501. Variation by Agreement and Effect of Funds-Transfer System Rule.

(a) Except as otherwise provided in this Article, the rights and obligations of a party to a funds transfer may be varied by agreement of the affected party.

(b) "Funds-transfer system rule" means a rule of an association of banks (i) governing transmission of payment orders by means of a funds-transfer system of the association or rights and obligations with respect to those orders, or (ii) to the extent the rule governs rights and obligations between banks that are parties to a funds transfer in which a Federal Reserve Bank, acting as an intermediary bank, sends a payment order to the beneficiary's bank. Except as otherwise provided in this Article, a funds-transfer system rule governing rights and obligations between participating banks using the system may be effective even if the rule conflicts with this Article and indirectly affects another party to the

funds transfer who does not consent to the rule. A funds-transfer system rule may also govern rights and obligations of parties other than participating banks using the system to the extent stated in Sections 4A—404(c), 4A—405(d), and 4A—507(c).

§ 4A—502. Creditor Process Served on Receiving Bank; Setoff by Beneficiary's Bank.

(a) As used in this section, "creditor process" means levy, attachment, garnishment, notice of lien, sequestration, or similar process issued by or on behalf of a creditor or other claimant with respect to an account.

(b) This subsection applies to creditor process with respect to an authorized account of the sender of a payment order if the creditor process is served on the receiving bank. For the purpose of determining rights with respect to the creditor process, if the receiving bank accepts the payment order the balance in the authorized account is deemed to be reduced by the amount of the payment order to the extent the bank did not otherwise receive payment of the order, unless the creditor process is served at a time and in a manner affording the bank a reasonable opportunity to act on it before the bank accepts the payment order.

(c) If a beneficiary's bank has received a payment order for payment to the beneficiary's account in the bank, the following rules apply:

(1) The bank may credit the beneficiary's account. The amount credited may be set off against an obligation owed by the beneficiary to the bank or may be applied to satisfy creditor process served on the bank with respect to the account.

(2) The bank may credit the beneficiary's account and allow withdrawal of the amount credited unless creditor process with respect to the account is served at a time and in a manner affording the bank a reasonable opportunity to act to prevent withdrawal.

(3) If creditor process with respect to the beneficiary's account has been served and the bank has had a reasonable opportunity to act on it, the bank may not reject the payment order except for a reason unrelated to the service of process.

(d) Creditor process with respect to a payment by the originator to the beneficiary pursuant to a funds transfer may be served only on the beneficiary's bank with respect to the debt owed by that bank to the beneficiary. Any other bank served with the creditor process is not obliged to act with respect to the process.

§ 4A—503. Injunction or Restraining Order with Respect to Funds Transfer.

For proper cause and in compliance with applicable law, a court may restrain (i) a person from issuing a payment order to initiate a funds transfer, (ii) an originator's bank from executing the payment order of the originator, or

(iii) the beneficiary's bank from releasing funds to the beneficiary or the beneficiary from withdrawing the funds. A court may not otherwise restrain a person from issuing a payment order, paying or receiving payment of a payment order, or otherwise acting with respect to a funds transfer.

§ 4A—504. Order in Which Items and Payment Orders May Be Charged to Account; Order of Withdrawals from Account.

(a) If a receiving bank has received more than one payment order of the sender or one or more payment orders and other items that are payable from the sender's account, the bank may charge the sender's account with respect to the various orders and items in any sequence.

(b) In determining whether a credit to an account has been withdrawn by the holder of the account or applied to a debt of the holder of the account, credits first made to the account are first withdrawn or applied.

§ 4A—505. Preclusion of Objection to Debit of Customer's Account.

If a receiving bank has received payment from its customer with respect to a payment order issued in the name of the customer as sender and accepted by the bank, and the customer received notification reasonably identifying the order, the customer is precluded from asserting that the bank is not entitled to retain the payment unless the customer notifies the bank of the customer's objection to the payment within one year after the notification was received by the customer.

§ 4A—506. Rate of Interest.

(a) If, under this Article, a receiving bank is obliged to pay interest with respect to a payment order issued to the bank, the amount payable may be determined (i) by agreement of the sender and receiving bank, or (ii) by a funds-transfer system rule if the payment order is transmitted through a funds-transfer system.

(b) If the amount of interest is not determined by an agreement or rule as stated in subsection (a), the amount is calculated by multiplying the applicable Federal Funds rate by the amount on which interest is payable, and then multiplying the product by the number of days for which interest is payable. The applicable Federal Funds rate is the average of the Federal Funds rates published by the Federal Reserve Bank of New York for each of the days for which interest is payable divided by 360. The Federal Funds rate for any day on which a published rate is not available is the same as the published rate for the next preceding day for which there is a published rate. If a receiving bank that accepted a payment order is required to refund payment to the sender of the order because the funds transfer was not completed, but the failure to complete was not due to any fault by the bank, the interest payable is reduced by a percentage equal to the reserve requirement on deposits of the receiving bank.

§ 4A—507. Choice of Law.

(a) The following rules apply unless the affected parties otherwise agree or subsection (c) applies:

(1) The rights and obligations between the sender of a payment order and the receiving bank are governed by the law of the jurisdiction in which the receiving bank is located.

(2) The rights and obligations between the beneficiary's bank and the beneficiary are governed by the law of the jurisdiction in which the beneficiary's bank is located.

(3) The issue of when payment is made pursuant to a funds transfer by the originator to the beneficiary is governed by the law of the jurisdiction in which the beneficiary's bank is located.

(b) If the parties described in each paragraph of subsection (a) have made an agreement selecting the law of a particular jurisdiction to govern rights and obligations between each other, the law of that jurisdiction governs those rights and obligations, whether or not the payment order or the funds transfer bears a reasonable relation to that jurisdiction.

(c) A funds-transfer system rule may select the law of a particular jurisdiction to govern (i) rights and obligations between participating banks with respect to payment orders transmitted or processed through the system, or (ii) the rights and obligations of some or all parties to a funds transfer any part of which is carried out by means of the system. A choice of law made pursuant to clause (i) is binding on participating banks. A choice of law made pursuant to clause (ii) is binding on the originator, other sender, or a receiving bank having notice that the funds-transfer system might be used in the funds transfer and of the choice of law by the system when the originator, other sender, or receiving bank issued or accepted a payment order. The beneficiary of a funds transfer is bound by the choice of law if, when the funds transfer is initiated, the beneficiary has notice that the funds-transfer system might be used in the funds transfer and of the choice of law by the system. The law of a jurisdiction selected pursuant to this subsection may govern, whether or not that law bears a reasonable relation to the matter in issue.

(d) In the event of inconsistency between an agreement under subsection (b) and a choice-of-law rule under subsection (c), the agreement under subsection (b) prevails.

(e) If a funds transfer is made by use of more than one funds-transfer system and there is inconsistency between choice-of-law rules of the systems, the matter in issue is governed by the law of the selected jurisdiction that has the most significant relationship to the matter in issue.

Revised (1995) Article 5
LETTERS OF CREDIT

§ 5—101. Short Title.

This article may be cited as Uniform Commercial Code— Letters of Credit.

§ 5—102. Definitions.

(a) In this article:

(1) "Adviser" means a person who, at the request of the issuer, a confirmer, or another adviser, notifies or requests another adviser to notify the beneficiary that a letter of credit has been issued, confirmed, or amended.

(2) "Applicant" means a person at whose request or for whose account a letter of credit is issued. The term includes a person who requests an issuer to issue a letter of credit on behalf of another if the person making the request undertakes an obligation to reimburse the issuer.

(3) "Beneficiary" means a person who under the terms of a letter of credit is entitled to have its complying presentation honored. The term includes a person to whom drawing rights have been transferred under a transferable letter of credit.

(4) "Confirmer" means a nominated person who undertakes, at the request or with the consent of the issuer, to honor a presentation under a letter of credit issued by another.

(5) "Dishonor" of a letter of credit means failure timely to honor or to take an interim action, such as acceptance of a draft, that may be required by the letter of credit.

(6) "Document" means a draft or other demand, document of title, investment security, certificate, invoice, or other record, statement, or representation of fact, law, right, or opinion (i) which is presented in a written or other medium permitted by the letter of credit or, unless prohibited by the letter of credit, by the standard practice referred to in Section 5—108(e) and (ii) which is capable of being examined for compliance with the terms and conditions of the letter of credit. A document may not be oral.

(7) "Good faith" means honesty in fact in the conduct or transaction concerned.

(8) "Honor" of a letter of credit means performance of the issuer's undertaking in the letter of credit to pay or deliver an item of value. Unless the letter of credit otherwise provides, "honor" occurs

(i) upon payment,

(ii) if the letter of credit provides for acceptance, upon acceptance of a draft and, at maturity, its payment, or

(iii) if the letter of credit provides for incurring a deferred obligation, upon incurring the obligation and, at maturity, its performance.

(9) "Issuer" means a bank or other person that issues a letter of credit, but does not include an individual who makes an engagement for personal, family, or household purposes.

(10) "Letter of credit" means a definite undertaking that satisfies the requirements of Section 5—104 by an issuer to a beneficiary at the request or for the account of an applicant or, in the case of a financial institution, to itself or for its own account, to honor a documentary presentation by payment or delivery of an item of value.

(11) "Nominated person" means a person whom the issuer (i) designates or authorizes to pay, accept, negotiate, or otherwise give value under a letter of credit and (ii) undertakes by agreement or custom and practice to reimburse.

(12) "Presentation" means delivery of a document to an issuer or nominated person for honor or giving of value under a letter of credit.

(13) "Presenter" means a person making a presentation as or on behalf of a beneficiary or nominated person.

(14) "Record" means information that is inscribed on a tangible medium, or that is stored in an electronic or other medium and is retrievable in perceivable form.

(15) "Successor of a beneficiary" means a person who succeeds to substantially all of the rights of a beneficiary by operation of law, including a corporation with or into which the beneficiary has been merged or consolidated, an administrator, executor, personal representative, trustee in bankruptcy, debtor in possession, liquidator, and receiver.

(b) Definitions in other Articles applying to this article and the sections in which they appear are:

"Accept" or "Acceptance" Section 3—409

"Value" Sections 3—303, 4—211

(c) Article 1 contains certain additional general definitions and principles of construction and interpretation applicable throughout this article.

§ 5—103. Scope.

(a) This article applies to letters of credit and to certain rights and obligations arising out of transactions involving letters of credit.

(b) The statement of a rule in this article does not by itself require, imply, or negate application of the same or a different rule to a situation not provided for, or to a person not specified, in this article.

(c) With the exception of this subsection, subsections (a) and (d), Sections 5—102(a)(9) and (10), 5—106(d), and

5—114(d), and except to the extent prohibited in Sections 1—102(3) and 5—117(d), the effect of this article may be varied by agreement or by a provision stated or incorporated by reference in an undertaking. A term in an agreement or undertaking generally excusing liability or generally limiting remedies for failure to perform obligations is not sufficient to vary obligations prescribed by this article.

(d) Rights and obligations of an issuer to a beneficiary or a nominated person under a letter of credit are independent of the existence, performance, or nonperformance of a contract or arrangement out of which the letter of credit arises or which underlies it, including contracts or arrangements between the issuer and the applicant and between the applicant and the beneficiary.

§ 5—104. Formal Requirements.

A letter of credit, confirmation, advice, transfer, amendment, or cancellation may be issued in any form that is a record and is authenticated (i) by a signature or (ii) in accordance with the agreement of the parties or the standard practice referred to in Section 5—108(e).

§ 5—105. Consideration.

Consideration is not required to issue, amend, transfer, or cancel a letter of credit, advice, or confirmation.

§ 5—106. Issuance, Amendment, Cancellation, and Duration.

(a) A letter of credit is issued and becomes enforceable according to its terms against the issuer when the issuer sends or otherwise transmits it to the person requested to advise or to the beneficiary. A letter of credit is revocable only if it so provides.

(b) After a letter of credit is issued, rights and obligations of a beneficiary, applicant, confirmer, and issuer are not affected by an amendment or cancellation to which that person has not consented except to the extent the letter of credit provides that it is revocable or that the issuer may amend or cancel the letter of credit without that consent.

(c) If there is no stated expiration date or other provision that determines its duration, a letter of credit expires one year after its stated date of issuance or, if none is stated, after the date on which it is issued.

(d) A letter of credit that states that it is perpetual expires five years after its stated date of issuance, or if none is stated, after the date on which it is issued.

§ 5—107. Confirmer, Nominated Person, and Adviser.

(a) A confirmer is directly obligated on a letter of credit and has the rights and obligations of an issuer to the extent of its confirmation. The confirmer also has rights against and obligations to the issuer as if the issuer were an applicant and the confirmer had issued the letter of credit at the request and for the account of the issuer.

(b) A nominated person who is not a confirmer is not obligated to honor or otherwise give value for a presentation.

(c) A person requested to advise may decline to act as an adviser. An adviser that is not a confirmer is not obligated to honor or give value for a presentation. An adviser undertakes to the issuer and to the beneficiary accurately to advise the terms of the letter of credit, confirmation, amendment, or advice received by that person and undertakes to the beneficiary to check the apparent authenticity of the request to advise. Even if the advice is inaccurate, the letter of credit, confirmation, or amendment is enforceable as issued.

(d) A person who notifies a transferee beneficiary of the terms of a letter of credit, confirmation, amendment, or advice has the rights and obligations of an adviser under subsection (c). The terms in the notice to the transferee beneficiary may differ from the terms in any notice to the transferor beneficiary to the extent permitted by the letter of credit, confirmation, amendment, or advice received by the person who so notifies.

§ 5—108. Issuer's Rights and Obligations.

(a) Except as otherwise provided in Section 5—109, an issuer shall honor a presentation that, as determined by the standard practice referred to in subsection (e), appears on its face strictly to comply with the terms and conditions of the letter of credit. Except as otherwise provided in Section 5—113 and unless otherwise agreed with the applicant, an issuer shall dishonor a presentation that does not appear so to comply.

(b) An issuer has a reasonable time after presentation, but not beyond the end of the seventh business day of the issuer after the day of its receipt of documents:

(1) to honor,

(2) if the letter of credit provides for honor to be completed more than seven business days after presentation, to accept a draft or incur a deferred obligation, or

(3) to give notice to the presenter of discrepancies in the presentation.

(c) Except as otherwise provided in subsection (d), an issuer is precluded from asserting as a basis for dishonor any discrepancy if timely notice is not given, or any discrepancy not stated in the notice if timely notice is given.

(d) Failure to give the notice specified in subsection (b) or to mention fraud, forgery, or expiration in the notice does not preclude the issuer from asserting as a basis for dishonor fraud or forgery as described in Section 5—109(a) or expiration of the letter of credit before presentation.

(e) An issuer shall observe standard practice of financial institutions that regularly issue letters of credit.

Determination of the issuer's observance of the standard practice is a matter of interpretation for the court. The court shall offer the parties a reasonable opportunity to present evidence of the standard practice.

(f) An issuer is not responsible for:

(1) the performance or nonperformance of the underlying contract, arrangement, or transaction,

(2) an act or omission of others, or

(3) observance or knowledge of the usage of a particular trade other than the standard practice referred to in subsection (e).

(g) If an undertaking constituting a letter of credit under Section 5—102(a)(10) contains nondocumentary conditions, an issuer shall disregard the nondocumentary conditions and treat them as if they were not stated.

(h) An issuer that has dishonored a presentation shall return the documents or hold them at the disposal of, and send advice to that effect to, the presenter.

(i) An issuer that has honored a presentation as permitted or required by this article:

(1) is entitled to be reimbursed by the applicant in immediately available funds not later than the date of its payment of funds;

(2) takes the documents free of claims of the beneficiary or presenter;

(3) is precluded from asserting a right of recourse on a draft under Sections 3—414 and 3—415;

(4) except as otherwise provided in Sections 5—110 and 5—117, is precluded from restitution of money paid or other value given by mistake to the extent the mistake concerns discrepancies in the documents or tender which are apparent on the face of the presentation; and

(5) is discharged to the extent of its performance under the letter of credit unless the issuer honored a presentation in which a required signature of a beneficiary was forged.

§ 5—109. Fraud and Forgery.

(a) If a presentation is made that appears on its face strictly to comply with the terms and conditions of the letter of credit, but a required document is forged or materially fraudulent, or honor of the presentation would facilitate a material fraud by the beneficiary on the issuer or applicant:

(1) the issuer shall honor the presentation, if honor is demanded by (i) a nominated person who has given value in good faith and without notice of forgery or material fraud, (ii) a confirmer who has honored its confirmation in good faith, (iii) a holder in due course of a draft drawn under the letter of credit which was taken after acceptance by the issuer or nominated per-

son, or (iv) an assignee of the issuer's or nominated person's deferred obligation that was taken for value and without notice of forgery or material fraud after the obligation was incurred by the issuer or nominated person; and

(2) the issuer, acting in good faith, may honor or dishonor the presentation in any other case.

(b) If an applicant claims that a required document is forged or materially fraudulent or that honor of the presentation would facilitate a material fraud by the beneficiary on the issuer or applicant, a court of competent jurisdiction may temporarily or permanently enjoin the issuer from honoring a presentation or grant similar relief against the issuer or other persons only if the court finds that:

(1) the relief is not prohibited under the law applicable to an accepted draft or deferred obligation incurred by the issuer;

(2) a beneficiary, issuer, or nominated person who may be adversely affected is adequately protected against loss that it may suffer because the relief is granted;

(3) all of the conditions to entitle a person to the relief under the law of this State have been met; and

(4) on the basis of the information submitted to the court, the applicant is more likely than not to succeed under its claim of forgery or material fraud and the person demanding honor does not qualify for protection under subsection (a)(1).

§ 5—110. Warranties.

(a) If its presentation is honored, the beneficiary warrants:

(1) to the issuer, any other person to whom presentation is made, and the applicant that there is no fraud or forgery of the kind described in Section 5—109(a); and

(2) to the applicant that the drawing does not violate any agreement between the applicant and beneficiary or any other agreement intended by them to be augmented by the letter of credit.

(b) The warranties in subsection (a) are in addition to warranties arising under Article 3, 4, 7, and 8 because of the presentation or transfer of documents covered by any of those articles.

§ 5—111. Remedies.

(a) If an issuer wrongfully dishonors or repudiates its obligation to pay money under a letter of credit before presentation, the beneficiary, successor, or nominated person presenting on its own behalf may recover from the issuer the amount that is the subject of the dishonor or repudiation. If the issuer's obligation under the letter of credit is not for the payment of money, the claimant may obtain specific performance or, at the claimant's election, recover an amount equal to the value of performance from the issuer. In either case, the claimant may also recover incidental but not consequential damages. The claimant is not obligated to take action to avoid damages that might be due from the issuer under this subsection. If, although not obligated to do so, the claimant avoids damages, the claimant's recovery from the issuer must be reduced by the amount of damages avoided. The issuer has the burden of proving the amount of damages avoided. In the case of repudiation the claimant need not present any document.

(b) If an issuer wrongfully dishonors a draft or demand presented under a letter of credit or honors a draft or demand in breach of its obligation to the applicant, the applicant may recover damages resulting from the breach, including incidental but not consequential damages, less any amount saved as a result of the breach.

(c) If an adviser or nominated person other than a confirmer breaches an obligation under this article or an issuer breaches an obligation not covered in subsection (a) or (b), a person to whom the obligation is owed may recover damages resulting from the breach, including incidental but not consequential damages, less any amount saved as a result of the breach. To the extent of the confirmation, a confirmer has the liability of an issuer specified in this subsection and subsections (a) and (b).

(d) An issuer, nominated person, or adviser who is found liable under subsection (a), (b), or (c) shall pay interest on the amount owed thereunder from the date of wrongful dishonor or other appropriate date.

(e) Reasonable attorney's fees and other expenses of litigation must be awarded to the prevailing party in an action in which a remedy is sought under this article.

(f) Damages that would otherwise be payable by a party for breach of an obligation under this article may be liquidated by agreement or undertaking, but only in an amount or by a formula that is reasonable in light of the harm anticipated.

§ 5—112. Transfer of Letter of Credit.

(a) Except as otherwise provided in Section 5–113, unless a letter of credit provides that it is transferable, the right of a beneficiary to draw or otherwise demand performance under a letter of credit may not be transferred.

(b) Even if a letter of credit provides that it is transferable, the issuer may refuse to recognize or carry out a transfer if:

(1) the transfer would violate applicable law; or

(2) the transferor or transferee has failed to comply with any requirement stated in the letter of credit or any other requirement relating to transfer imposed by the issuer which is within the standard practice referred to in Section 5–108(e) or is otherwise reasonable under the circumstances.

§ 5—113. Transfer by Operation of Law.

(a) A successor of a beneficiary may consent to amendments, sign and present documents, and receive payment or other items of value in the name of the beneficiary without disclosing its status as a successor.

(b) A successor of a beneficiary may consent to amendments, sign and present documents, and receive payment or other items of value in its own name as the disclosed successor of the beneficiary. Except as otherwise provided in subsection (e), an issuer shall recognize a disclosed successor of a beneficiary as beneficiary in full substitution for its predecessor upon compliance with the requirements for recognition by the issuer of a transfer of drawing rights by operation of law under the standard practice referred to in Section 5—108(e) or, in the absence of such a practice, compliance with other reasonable procedures sufficient to protect the issuer.

(c) An issuer is not obliged to determine whether a purported successor is a successor of a beneficiary or whether the signature of a purported successor is genuine or authorized.

(d) Honor of a purported successor's apparently complying presentation under subsection (a) or (b) has the consequences specified in Section 5—108(i) even if the purported successor is not the successor of a beneficiary. Documents signed in the name of the beneficiary or of a disclosed successor by a person who is neither the beneficiary nor the successor of the beneficiary are forged documents for the purposes of Section 5—109.

(e) An issuer whose rights of reimbursement are not covered by subsection (d) or substantially similar law and any confirmer or nominated person may decline to recognize a presentation under subsection (b).

(f) A beneficiary whose name is changed after the issuance of a letter of credit has the same rights and obligations as a successor of a beneficiary under this section.

§ 5—114. Assignment of Proceeds.

(a) In this section, "proceeds of a letter of credit" means the cash, check, accepted draft, or other item of value paid or delivered upon honor or giving of value by the issuer or any nominated person under the letter of credit. The term does not include a beneficiary's drawing rights or documents presented by the beneficiary.

(b) A beneficiary may assign its right to part or all of the proceeds of a letter of credit. The beneficiary may do so before presentation as a present assignment of its right to receive proceeds contingent upon its compliance with the terms and conditions of the letter of credit.

(c) An issuer or nominated person need not recognize an assignment of proceeds of a letter of credit until it consents to the assignment.

(d) An issuer or nominated person has no obligation to give or withhold its consent to an assignment of proceeds of a letter of credit, but consent may not be unreasonably withheld if the assignee possesses and exhibits the letter of credit and presentation of the letter of credit is a condition to honor.

(e) Rights of a transferee beneficiary or nominated person are independent of the beneficiary's assignment of the proceeds of a letter of credit and are superior to the assignee's right to the proceeds.

(f) Neither the rights recognized by this section between an assignee and an issuer, transferee beneficiary, or nominated person nor the issuer's or nominated person's payment of proceeds to an assignee or a third person affect the rights between the assignee and any person other than the issuer, transferee beneficiary, or nominated person. The mode of creating and perfecting a security interest in or granting an assignment of a beneficiary's rights to proceeds is governed by Article 9 or other law. Against persons other than the issuer, transferee beneficiary, or nominated person, the rights and obligations arising upon the creation of a security interest or other assignment of a beneficiary's right to proceeds and its perfection are governed by Article 9 or other law.

§ 5—115. Statute of Limitations.

An action to enforce a right or obligation arising under this article must be commenced within one year after the expiration date of the relevant letter of credit or one year after the [claim for relief] [cause of action] accrues, whichever occurs later. A [claim for relief] [cause of action] accrues when the breach occurs, regardless of the aggrieved party's lack of knowledge of the breach.

§ 5—116. Choice of Law and Forum.

(a) The liability of an issuer, nominated person, or adviser for action or omission is governed by the law of the jurisdiction chosen by an agreement in the form of a record signed or otherwise authenticated by the affected parties in the manner provided in Section 5—104 or by a provision in the person's letter of credit, confirmation, or other undertaking. The jurisdiction whose law is chosen need not bear any relation to the transaction.

(b) Unless subsection (a) applies, the liability of an issuer, nominated person, or adviser for action or omission is governed by the law of the jurisdiction in which the person is located. The person is considered to be located at the address indicated in the person's undertaking. If more than one address is indicated, the person is considered to be located at the address from which the person's undertaking was issued. For the purpose of jurisdiction, choice of law, and recognition of interbranch letters of credit, but not enforcement of a judgment, all branches of a bank are considered separate juridical entities and a bank is considered to be located at the place where its relevant branch is considered to be located under this subsection.

(c) Except as otherwise provided in this subsection, the liability of an issuer, nominated person, or adviser is governed by any rules of custom or practice, such as the Uniform Customs and Practice for Documentary Credits, to which the letter of credit, confirmation, or other undertaking is expressly made subject. If (i) this article would govern the liability of an issuer, nominated person, or adviser under subsection (a) or (b), (ii) the relevant undertaking incorporates rules of custom or practice, and (iii) there is conflict between this article and those rules as applied to that undertaking, those rules govern except to the extent of any conflict with the nonvariable provisions specified in Section 5—103(c).

(d) If there is conflict between this article and Article 3, 4, 4A, or 9, this article governs.

(e) The forum for settling disputes arising out of an undertaking within this article may be chosen in the manner and with the binding effect that governing law may be chosen in accordance with subsection (a).

§ 5—117. Subrogation of Issuer, Applicant, and Nominated Person.

(a) An issuer that honors a beneficiary's presentation is subrogated to the rights of the beneficiary to the same extent as if the issuer were a secondary obligor of the underlying obligation owed to the beneficiary and of the applicant to the same extent as if the issuer were the secondary obligor of the underlying obligation owed to the applicant.

(b) An applicant that reimburses an issuer is subrogated to the rights of the issuer against any beneficiary, presenter, or nominated person to the same extent as if the applicant were the secondary obligor of the obligations owed to the issuer and has the rights of subrogation of the issuer to the rights of the beneficiary stated in subsection (a).

(c) A nominated person who pays or gives value against a draft or demand presented under a letter of credit is subrogated to the rights of:

(1) the issuer against the applicant to the same extent as if the nominated person were a secondary obligor of the obligation owed to the issuer by the applicant;

(2) the beneficiary to the same extent as if the nominated person were a secondary obligor of the underlying obligation owed to the beneficiary; and

(3) the applicant to same extent as if the nominated person were a secondary obligor of the underlying obligation owed to the applicant.

(d) Notwithstanding any agreement or term to the contrary, the rights of subrogation stated in subsections (a) and

(b) do not arise until the issuer honors the letter of credit or otherwise pays and the rights in subsection (c) do not arise until the nominated person pays or otherwise gives value. Until then, the issuer, nominated person, and the applicant do not derive under this section present or prospective rights forming the basis of a claim, defense, or excuse.

Transition Provisions

§ [ ]. Effective Date.

This [Act] shall become effective on _____, 199___.

§ [ ]. Repeal.

This [Act] [repeals] [amends] [insert citation to existing Article 5].

§ [ ]. Applicability.

This [Act] applies to a letter of credit that is issued on or after the effective date of this [Act]. This [Act] does not apply to a transaction, event, obligation, or duty arising out of or associated with a letter of credit that was issued before the effective date of this [Act].

§ [ ]. Savings Clause.

A transaction arising out of or associated with a letter of credit that was issued before the effective date of this [Act] and the rights, obligations, and interests flowing from that transaction are governed by any statute or other law amended or repealed by this [Act] as if repeal or amendment had not occurred and may be terminated, completed, consummated, or enforced under that statute or other law.

Article 6
BULK TRANSFERS

§ 6—101. Short Title.

This Article shall be known and may be cited as Uniform Commercial Code—Bulk Transfers.

§ 6—102. "Bulk Transfers"; Transfers of Equipment; Enterprises Subject to This Article; Bulk Transfers Subject to This Article.

(1) A "bulk transfer" is any transfer in bulk and not in the ordinary course of the transferor's business of a major part of the materials, supplies, merchandise or other inventory (Section 9—109) of an enterprise subject to this Article.

(2) A transfer of a substantial part of the equipment (Section 9—109) of such an enterprise is a bulk transfer if it is made in connection with a bulk transfer of inventory, but not otherwise.

(3) The enterprises subject to this Article are all those whose principal business is the sale of merchandise from stock, including those who manufacture what they sell.

(4) Except as limited by the following section all bulk transfers of goods located within this state are subject to this Article.

§ 6—103. Transfers Excepted From This Article.

The following transfers are not subject to this Article:

(1) Those made to give security for the performance of an obligation;

(2) General assignments for the benefit of all the creditors of the transferor, and subsequent transfers by the assignee thereunder;

(3) Transfers in settlement or realization of a lien or other security interests;

(4) Sales by executors, administrators, receivers, trustees in bankruptcy, or any public officer under judicial process;

(5) Sales made in the course of judicial or administrative proceedings for the dissolution or reorganization of a corporation and of which notice is sent to the creditors of the corporation pursuant to order of the court or administrative agency;

(6) Transfers to a person maintaining a known place of business in this State who becomes bound to pay the debts of the transferor in full and gives public notice of that fact, and who is solvent after becoming so bound;

(7) A transfer to a new business enterprise organized to take over and continue the business, if public notice of the transaction is given and the new enterprise assumes the debts of the transferor and he receives nothing from the transaction except an interest in the new enterprise junior to the claims of creditors;

(8) Transfers of property which is exempt from execution.

Public notice under subsection (6) or subsection (7) may be given by publishing once a week for two consecutive weeks in a newspaper of general circulation where the transferor had its principal place of business in this state an advertisement including the names and addresses of the transferor and transferee and the effective date of the transfer.

§ 6—104. Schedule of Property, List of Creditors.

(1) Except as provided with respect to auction sales (Section 6—108), a bulk transfer subject to this Article is ineffective against any creditor of the transferor unless:

(a) The transferee requires the transferor to furnish a list of his existing creditors prepared as stated in this section; and

(b) The parties prepare a schedule of the property transferred sufficient to identify it; and

(c) The transferee preserves the list and schedule for six months next following the transfer and permits inspection of either or both and copying therefrom at all reasonable hours by any creditor of the transferor, or files the list and schedule in (a public office to be here identified).

(2) The list of creditors must be signed and sworn to or affirmed by the transferor or his agent. It must contain the names and business addresses of all creditors of the transferor, with the amounts when known, and also the names of all persons who are known to the transferor to assert claims against him even though such claims are disputed. If the transferor is the obligor of an outstanding issue of bonds, debentures or the like as to which there is an indenture trustee, the list of creditors need include only the name and address of the indenture trustee and the aggregate outstanding principal amount of the issue.

(3) Responsibility for the completeness and accuracy of the list of creditors rests on the transferor, and the transfer is not rendered ineffective by errors or omissions therein unless the transferee is shown to have had knowledge.

§ 6—105. Notice to Creditors.

In addition to the requirements of the preceding section, any bulk transfer subject to this Article except one made by auction sale (Section 6—108) is ineffective against any creditor of the transferor unless at least ten days before he takes possession of the goods or pays for them, whichever happens first, the transferee gives notice of the transfer in the manner and to the persons hereafter provided (Section 6—107).

§ 6—106. Application of the Proceeds.

In addition to the requirements of the two preceding sections:

(1) Upon every bulk transfer subject to this Article for which new consideration becomes payable except those made by sale at auction it is the duty of the transferee to assure that such consideration is applied so far as necessary to pay those debts of the transferor which are either shown on the list furnished by the transferor (Section 6—104) or filed in writing in the place stated in the notice (Section 6—107) within thirty days after the mailing of such notice. This duty of the transferee runs to all the holders of such debts, and may be enforced by any of them for the benefit of all.

(2) If any of said debts are in dispute the necessary sum may be withheld from distribution until the dispute is settled or adjudicated.

(3) If the consideration payable is not enough to pay all of the said debts in full distribution shall be made pro rata.]

Note: *This section is bracketed to indicate division of opinion as to whether or not it is a wise provision, and to suggest that this is a point on which State enactments may differ without serious damage to the principle of uniformity. In any State where this section is omitted, the following parts of sections, also bracketed in the text, should also be omitted, namely:*
Section 6—107(2)(e).
    6—108(3)(c).
    6—109(2).
   In any State where this section is enacted, these other provisions should be also.

Optional Subsection (4)

[(4) The transferee may within ten days after he takes possession of the goods pay the consideration into the (specify court) in the county where the transferor had its principal place of business in this state and thereafter may discharge his duty under this section by giving notice by registered or certified mail to all the persons to whom the duty runs that the consideration has been paid into that court and that they should file their claims there. On motion of any interested party, the court may order the distribution of the consideration to the persons entitled to it.]

Note: *Optional subsection (4) is recommended for those states which do not have a general statute providing for payment of money into court.*

§ 6—107. The Notice.

(1) The notice to creditors (Section 6—105) shall state:

   (a) that a bulk transfer is about to be made; and

   (b) the names and business addresses of the transferor and transferee, and all other business names and addresses used by the transferor within three years last past so far as known to the transferee; and

   (c) whether or not all the debts of the transferor are to be paid in full as they fall due as a result of the transaction, and if so, the address to which creditors should send their bills.

(2) If the debts of the transferor are not to be paid in full as they fall due or if the transferee is in doubt on that point then the notice shall state further:

   (a) the location and general description of the property to be transferred and the estimated total of the transferor's debts;

   (b) the address where the schedule of property and list of creditors (Section 6—104) may be inspected;

   (c) whether the transfer is to pay existing debts and if so the amount of such debts and to whom owing;

   (d) whether the transfer is for new consideration and if so the amount of such consideration and the time and place of payment; [and]

   [(e) if for new consideration the time and place where creditors of the transferor are to file their claims.]

(3) The notice in any case shall be delivered personally or sent by registered or certified mail to all the persons shown on the list of creditors furnished by the transferor (Section 6—104) and to all other persons who are known to the transferee to hold or assert claims against the transferor.

§ 6—108. Auction Sales; "Auctioneer".

(1) A bulk transfer is subject to this Article even though it is by sale at auction, but only in the manner and with the results stated in this section.

(2) The transferor shall furnish a list of his creditors and assist in the preparation of a schedule of the property to be sold, both prepared as before stated (Section 6—104).

(3) The person or persons other than the transferor who direct, control or are responsible for the auction are collectively called the "auctioneer". The auctioneer shall:

(a) receive and retain the list of creditors and prepare and retain the schedule of property for the period stated in this Article (Section 6—104);

(b) give notice of the auction personally or by registered or certified mail at least ten days before it occurs to all persons shown on the list of creditors and to all other persons who are known to him to hold or assert claims against the transferor; [and]

[(c) assure that the net proceeds of the auction are applied as provided in this Article (Section 6—106).]

(4) Failure of the auctioneer to perform any of these duties does not affect the validity of the sale or the title of the purchasers, but if the auctioneer knows that the auction constitutes a bulk transfer such failure renders the auctioneer liable to the creditors of the transferor as a class for the sums owing to them from the transferor up to but not exceeding the net proceeds of the auction. If the auctioneer consists of several persons their liability is joint and several.

§ 6—109. What Creditors Protected; [Credit for Payment to Particular Creditors].

(1) The creditors of the transferor mentioned in this Article are those holding claims based on transactions or events occurring before the bulk transfer, but creditors who become such after notice to creditors is given (Sections 6—105 and 6—107) are not entitled to notice.

[(2) Against the aggregate obligation imposed by the provisions of this Article concerning the application of the proceeds (Section 6—106 and subsection (3)(c) of 6—108) the transferee or auctioneer is entitled to credit for sums paid to particular creditors of the transferor, not exceeding the sums believed in good faith at the time of the payment to be properly payable to such creditors.]

§ 6—110. Subsequent Transfers.

When the title of a transferee to property is subject to a defect by reason of his noncompliance with the requirements of this Article, then:

(1) a purchaser of any of such property from such transferee who pays no value or who takes with notice of such noncompliance takes subject to such defect, but

(2) a purchaser for value in good faith and without such notice takes free of such defect.

§ 6—111. Limitation of Actions and Levies.

No action under this Article shall be brought nor levy made more than six months after the date on which the transferee took possession of the goods unless the transfer has been concealed. If the transfer has been concealed, actions may be brought or levies made within six months after its discovery.

Note to Article 6: *Section 6—106 is bracketed to indicate division of opinion as to whether or not it is a wise provision, and to suggest that this is a point on which State enactments may differ without serious damage to the principle of uniformity.*

In any State where Section 6—106 is not enacted, the following parts of sections, also bracketed in the text, should also be omitted, namely:
Sec. 6—107(2)(e).
   6—108(3)(c).
   6—109(2).
In any State where Section 6—106 is enacted, these other provisions should be also.

Article 6
Alternative B*

§ 6—101. Short Title.

This Article shall be known and may be cited as Uniform Commercial Code—Bulk Sales.

§ 6—102. Definitions and Index of Definitions.

(1) In this Article, unless the context otherwise requires:

(a) "Assets" means the inventory that is the subject of a bulk sale and any tangible and intangible personal property used or held for use primarily in, or arising from, the seller's business and sold in connection with that inventory, but the term does not include:

(i) fixtures (Section 9—313(1)(a)) other than readily removable factory and office machines;

(ii) the lessee's interest in a lease of real property; or

(iii) property to the extent it is generally exempt from creditor process under nonbankruptcy law.

(b) "Auctioneer" means a person whom the seller engages to direct, conduct, control, or be responsible for a sale by auction.

(c) "Bulk sale" means:

(i) in the case of a sale by auction or a sale or series of sales conducted by a liquidator on the seller's behalf, a sale or series of sales not in the ordinary course of the seller's business of more than half of the seller's inventory, as measured by value on the date of the bulk-sale agreement, if on that date the auctioneer or liquidator has notice, or after reasonable inquiry would have had notice, that the seller will not continue to operate the

---

*Approved in substance by the National Conference of Commissioners on Uniform State Laws and The American Law Institute. States have the choice of adopting this alternative to the existing Article 6 or repealing Article 6 entirely (Alternative A).

same or a similar kind of business after the sale or series of sales; and

(ii) in all other cases, a sale not in the ordinary course of the seller's business of more than half the seller's inventory, as measured by value on the date of the bulk-sale agreement, if on that date the buyer has notice, or after reasonable inquiry would have had notice, that the seller will not continue to operate the same or a similar kind of business after the sale.

(d) "Claim" means a right to payment from the seller, whether or not the right is reduced to judgment, liquidated, fixed, matured, disputed, secured, legal, or equitable. The term includes costs of collection and attorney's fees only to the extent that the laws of this state permit the holder of the claim to recover them in an action against the obligor.

(e) "Claimant" means a person holding a claim incurred in the seller's business other than:

(i) an unsecured and unmatured claim for employment compensation and benefits, including commissions and vacation, severance, and sick-leave pay;

(ii) a claim for injury to an individual or to property, or for breach of warranty, unless:

(A) a right of action for the claim has accrued;

(B) the claim has been asserted against the seller; and

(C) the seller knows the identity of the person asserting the claim and the basis upon which the person has asserted it; and

(States to Select One Alternative)

Alternative A

[(iii) a claim for taxes owing to a governmental unit.]

Alternative B

[(iii) a claim for taxes owing to a governmental unit, if:

(A) a statute governing the enforcement of the claim permits or requires notice of the bulk sale to be given to the governmental unit in a manner other than by compliance with the requirements of this Article; and

(B) notice is given in accordance with the statute.]

(f) "Creditor" means a claimant or other person holding a claim.

(g)(i) "Date of the bulk sale" means:

(A) if the sale is by auction or is conducted by a liquidator on the seller's behalf, the date on

which more than ten percent of the net proceeds is paid to or for the benefit of the seller; and

(B) in all other cases, the later of the date on which:

(I) more than ten percent of the net contract price is paid to or for the benefit of the seller; or

(II) more than ten percent of the assets, as measured by value, are transferred to the buyer.

(ii) For purposes of this subsection:

(A) delivery of a negotiable instrument (Section 3−104(1)) to or for the benefit of the seller in exchange for assets constitutes payment of the contract price pro tanto;

(B) to the extent that the contract price is deposited in an escrow, the contract price is paid to or for the benefit of the seller when the seller acquires the unconditional right to receive the deposit or when the deposit is delivered to the seller or for the benefit of the seller, whichever is earlier; and

(C) an asset is transferred when a person holding an unsecured claim can no longer obtain through judicial proceedings rights to the asset that are superior to those of the buyer arising as a result of the bulk sale. A person holding an unsecured claim can obtain those superior rights to a tangible asset at least until the buyer has an unconditional right, under the bulk-sale agreement, to possess the asset, and a person holding an unsecured claim can obtain those superior rights to an intangible asset at least until the buyer has an unconditional right, under the bulk-sale agreement, to use the asset.

(h) "Date of the bulk-sale agreement" means:

(i) in the case of a sale by auction or conducted by a liquidator (subsection (c)(i)), the date on which the seller engages the auctioneer or liquidator; and

(ii) in all other cases, the date on which a bulk-sale agreement becomes enforceable between the buyer and the seller.

(i) "Debt" means liability on a claim.

(j) "Liquidator" means a person who is regularly engaged in the business of disposing of assets for businesses contemplating liquidation or dissolution.

(k) "Net contract price" means the new consideration the buyer is obligated to pay for the assets less:

(i) the amount of any proceeds of the sale of an asset, to the extent the proceeds are applied in partial or total satisfaction of a debt secured by the asset; and

(ii) the amount of any debt to the extent it is secured by a security interest or lien that is enforceable against the asset before and after it has been sold to a buyer. If a debt is secured by an asset and other property of the seller, the amount of the debt secured by a security interest or lien that is enforceable against the asset is determined by multiplying the debt by a fraction, the numerator of which is the value of the new consideration for the asset on the date of the bulk sale and the denominator of which is the value of all property securing the debt on the date of the bulk sale.

(l) "Net proceeds" means the new consideration received for assets sold at a sale by auction or a sale conducted by a liquidator on the seller's behalf less:

(i) commissions and reasonable expenses of the sale;

(ii) the amount of any proceeds of the sale of an asset, to the extent the proceeds are applied in partial or total satisfaction of a debt secured by the asset; and

(iii) the amount of any debt to the extent it is secured by a security interest or lien that is enforceable against the asset before and after it has been sold to a buyer. If a debt is secured by an asset and other property of the seller, the amount of the debt secured by a security interest or lien that is enforceable against the asset is determined by multiplying the debt by a fraction, the numerator of which is the value of the new consideration for the asset on the date of the bulk sale and the denominator of which is the value of all property securing the debt on the date of the bulk sale.

(m) A sale is "in the ordinary course of the seller's business" if the sale comports with usual or customary practices in the kind of business in which the seller is engaged or with the seller's own usual or customary practices.

(n) "United States" includes its territories and possessions and the Commonwealth of Puerto Rico.

(o) "Value" means fair market value.

(p) "Verified" means signed and sworn to or affirmed.

(2) The following definitions in other Articles apply to this Article:

(a) "Buyer."	Section 2—103(1)(a).
(b) "Equipment."	Section 9—109(2).
(c) "Inventory."	Section 9—109(4).
(d) "Sale."	Section 2—106(1).
(e) "Seller."	Section 2—103(1)(d).

(3) In addition, Article 1 contains general definitions and principles of construction and interpretation applicable throughout this Article.

§ 6—103. Applicability of Article.

(1) Except as otherwise provided in subsection (3), this Article applies to a bulk sale if:

(a) the seller's principal business is the sale of inventory from stock; and

(b) on the date of the bulk-sale agreement the seller is located in this state or, if the seller is located in a jurisdiction that is not a part of the United States, the seller's major executive office in the United States is in this state.

(2) A seller is deemed to be located at his [or her] place of business. If a seller has more than one place of business, the seller is deemed located at his [or her] chief executive office.

(3) This Article does not apply to:

(a) a transfer made to secure payment or performance of an obligation;

(b) a transfer of collateral to a secured party pursuant to Section 9—503;

(c) a sale of collateral pursuant to Section 9—504;

(d) retention of collateral pursuant to Section 9—505;

(e) a sale of an asset encumbered by a security interest or lien if (i) all the proceeds of the sale are applied in partial or total satisfaction of the debt secured by the security interest or lien or (ii) the security interest or lien is enforceable against the asset after it has been sold to the buyer and the net contract price is zero;

(f) a general assignment for the benefit of creditors or to a subsequent transfer by the assignee;

(g) a sale by an executor, administrator, receiver, trustee in bankruptcy, or any public officer under judicial process;

(h) a sale made in the course of judicial or administrative proceedings for the dissolution or reorganization of an organization;

(i) a sale to a buyer whose principal place of business is in the United States and who:

(i) not earlier than 21 days before the date of the bulk sale, (A) obtains from the seller a verified and dated list of claimants of whom the seller has notice three days before the seller sends or delivers the list to the buyer or (B) conducts a reasonable inquiry to discover the claimants;

(ii) assumes in full the debts owed to claimants of whom the buyer has knowledge on the date the buyer receives the list of claimants from the seller or on the date the buyer completes the reasonable inquiry, as the case may be;

(iii) is not insolvent after the assumption; and

(iv) gives written notice of the assumption not later than 30 days after the date of the bulk sale by sending or delivering a notice to the claimants identified in subparagraph (ii) or by filing a notice in the office of the [Secretary of State];

(j) a sale to a buyer whose principal place of business is in the United States and who:

(i) assumes in full the debts that were incurred in the seller's business before the date of the bulk sale;

(ii) is not insolvent after the assumption; and

(iii) gives written notice of the assumption not later than 30 days after the date of the bulk sale by sending or delivering a notice to each creditor whose debt is assumed or by filing a notice in the office of the [Secretary of State];

(k) a sale to a new organization that is organized to take over and continue the business of the seller and that has its principal place of business in the United States if:

(i) the buyer assumes in full the debts that were incurred in the seller's business before the date of the bulk sale;

(ii) the seller receives nothing from the sale except an interest in the new organization that is subordinate to the claims against the organization arising from the assumption; and

(iii) the buyer gives written notice of the assumption not later than 30 days after the date of the bulk sale by sending or delivering a notice to each creditor whose debt is assumed or by filing a notice in the office of the [Secretary of State];

(l) a sale of assets having:

(i) a value, net of liens and security interests, of less than $10,000. If a debt is secured by assets and other property of the seller, the net value of the assets is determined by subtracting from their value an amount equal to the product of the debt multiplied by a fraction, the numerator of which is the value of the assets on the date of the bulk sale and the denominator of which is the value of all property securing the debt on the date of the bulk sale; or

(ii) a value of more than $25,000,000 on the date of the bulk-sale agreement; or

(m) a sale required by, and made pursuant to, statute.

(4) The notice under subsection (3)(i)(iv) must state: (i) that a sale that may constitute a bulk sale has been or will be made; (ii) the date or prospective date of the bulk sale; (iii) the individual, partnership, or corporate names and the addresses of the seller and buyer; (iv) the address

to which inquiries about the sale may be made, if different from the seller's address; and (v) that the buyer has assumed or will assume in full the debts owed to claimants of whom the buyer has knowledge on the date the buyer receives the list of claimants from the seller or completes a reasonable inquiry to discover the claimants.

(5) The notice under subsections (3)(j)(iii) and (3)(k)(iii) must state: (i) that a sale that may constitute a bulk sale has been or will be made; (ii) the date or prospective date of the bulk sale; (iii) the individual, partnership, or corporate names and the addresses of the seller and buyer; (iv) the address to which inquiries about the sale may be made, if different from the seller's address; and (v) that the buyer has assumed or will assume the debts that were incurred in the seller's business before the date of the bulk sale.

(6) For purposes of subsection (3)(l), the value of assets is presumed to be equal to the price the buyer agrees to pay for the assets. However, in a sale by auction or a sale conducted by a liquidator on the seller's behalf, the value of assets is presumed to be the amount the auctioneer or liquidator reasonably estimates the assets will bring at auction or upon liquidation.

§ 6—104. Obligations of Buyer.

(1) In a bulk sale as defined in Section 6—102(1)(c)(ii) the buyer shall:

(a) obtain from the seller a list of all business names and addresses used by the seller within three years before the date the list is sent or delivered to the buyer;

(b) unless excused under subsection (2), obtain from the seller a verified and dated list of claimants of whom the seller has notice three days before the seller sends or delivers the list to the buyer and including, to the extent known by the seller, the address of and the amount claimed by each claimant;

(c) obtain from the seller or prepare a schedule of distribution (Section 6—106(1));

(d) give notice of the bulk sale in accordance with Section 6—105;

(e) unless excused under Section 6—106(4), distribute the net contract price in accordance with the undertakings of the buyer in the schedule of distribution; and

(f) unless excused under subsection (2), make available the list of claimants (subsection (1)(b)) by:

(i) promptly sending or delivering a copy of the list without charge to any claimant whose written request is received by the buyer no later than six months after the date of the bulk sale;

(ii) permitting any claimant to inspect and copy the list at any reasonable hour upon request received by the buyer no later than six months after the date of the bulk sale; or

(iii) filing a copy of the list in the office of the [Secretary of State] no later than the time for giving a notice of the bulk sale (Section 6—105(5)). A list filed in accordance with this subparagraph must state the individual, partnership, or corporate name and a mailing address of the seller.

(2) A buyer who gives notice in accordance with Section 6—105(2) is excused from complying with the requirements of subsections (1)(b) and (1)(f).

§ 6—105. **Notice to Claimants.**

(1) Except as otherwise provided in subsection (2), to comply with Section 6—104(1)(d) the buyer shall send or deliver a written notice of the bulk sale to each claimant on the list of claimants (Section 6—104(1)(b)) and to any other claimant of which the buyer has knowledge at the time the notice of the bulk sale is sent or delivered.

(2) A buyer may comply with Section 6—104(1)(d) by filing a written notice of the bulk sale in the office of the [Secretary of State] if:

(a) on the date of the bulk-sale agreement the seller has 200 or more claimants, exclusive of claimants holding secured or matured claims for employment compensation and benefits, including commissions and vacation, severance, and sick-leave pay; or

(b) the buyer has received a verified statement from the seller stating that, as of the date of the bulk-sale agreement, the number of claimants, exclusive of claimants holding secured or matured claims for employment compensation and benefits, including commissions and vacation, severance, and sick-leave pay, is 200 or more.

(3) The written notice of the bulk sale must be accompanied by a copy of the schedule of distribution (Section 6—106(1)) and state at least:

(a) that the seller and buyer have entered into an agreement for a sale that may constitute a bulk sale under the laws of the State of _____ ;

(b) the date of the agreement;

(c) the date on or after which more than ten percent of the assets were or will be transferred;

(d) the date on or after which more than ten percent of the net contract price was or will be paid, if the date is not stated in the schedule of distribution;

(e) the name and a mailing address of the seller;

(f) any other business name and address listed by the seller pursuant to Section 6—104(1)(a);

(g) the name of the buyer and an address of the buyer from which information concerning the sale can be obtained;

(h) a statement indicating the type of assets or describing the assets item by item;

(i) the manner in which the buyer will make available the list of claimants (Section 6—104(1)(f)), if applicable; and

(j) if the sale is in total or partial satisfaction of an antecedent debt owed by the seller, the amount of the debt to be satisfied and the name of the person to whom it is owed.

(4) For purposes of subsections (3)(e) and (3)(g), the name of a person is the person's individual, partnership, or corporate name.

(5) The buyer shall give notice of the bulk sale not less than 45 days before the date of the bulk sale and, if the buyer gives notice in accordance with subsection (1), not more than 30 days after obtaining the list of claimants.

(6) A written notice substantially complying with the requirements of subsection (3) is effective even though it contains minor errors that are not seriously misleading.

(7) A form substantially as follows is sufficient to comply with subsection (3):

Notice of Sale

(1) _____ , whose address is _____ , is described in this notice as the "seller."

(2) _____ , whose address is _____ , is described in this notice as the "buyer."

(3) The seller has disclosed to the buyer that within the past three years the seller has used other business names, operated at other addresses, or both, as follows:

_____ .

(4) The seller and the buyer have entered into an agreement dated _____ , for a sale that may constitute a bulk sale under the laws of the State of _____ .

(5) The date on or after which more than ten percent of the assets that are the subject of the sale were or will be transferred is _____ , and [if not stated in the schedule of distribution] the date on or after which more than ten percent of the net contract price was or will be paid is _____ .

(6) The following assets are the subject of the sale: _____ .

(7) [If applicable] The buyer will make available to claimants of the seller a list of the seller's claimants in the following manner: _____ .

(8) [If applicable] The sale is to satisfy $ _____ of an antecedent debt owed by the seller to _____ .

(9) A copy of the schedule of distribution of the net contract price accompanies this notice.

[End of Notice]

§ 6—106. **Schedule of Distribution.**

(1) The seller and buyer shall agree on how the net contract price is to be distributed and set forth their agreement in a written schedule of distribution.

(2) The schedule of distribution may provide for distribution to any person at any time, including distribution of the entire net contract price to the seller.

(3) The buyer's undertakings in the schedule of distribution run only to the seller. However, a buyer who fails to distribute the net contract price in accordance with the buyer's undertakings in the schedule of distribution is liable to a creditor only as provided in Section 6—107(1).

(4) If the buyer undertakes in the schedule of distribution to distribute any part of the net contract price to a person other than the seller, and, after the buyer has given notice in accordance with Section 6—105, some or all of the anticipated net contract price is or becomes unavailable for distribution as a consequence of the buyer's or seller's having complied with an order of court, legal process, statute, or rule of law, the buyer is excused from any obligation arising under this Article or under any contract with the seller to distribute the net contract price in accordance with the buyer's undertakings in the schedule if the buyer:

(a) distributes the net contract price remaining available in accordance with any priorities for payment stated in the schedule of distribution and, to the extent that the price is insufficient to pay all the debts having a given priority, distributes the price pro rata among those debts shown in the schedule as having the same priority;

(b) distributes the net contract price remaining available in accordance with an order of court;

(c) commences a proceeding for interpleader in a court of competent jurisdiction and is discharged from the proceeding; or

(d) reaches a new agreement with the seller for the distribution of the net contract price remaining available, sets forth the new agreement in an amended schedule of distribution, gives notice of the amended schedule, and distributes the net contract price remaining available in accordance with the buyer's undertakings in the amended schedule.

(5) The notice under subsection (4)(d) must identify the buyer and the seller, state the filing number, if any, of the original notice, set forth the amended schedule, and be given in accordance with subsection (1) or (2) of Section 6—105, whichever is applicable, at least 14 days before the buyer distributes any part of the net contract price remaining available.

(6) If the seller undertakes in the schedule of distribution to distribute any part of the net contract price, and, after the buyer has given notice in accordance with Section 6—105, some or all of the anticipated net contract price is or becomes unavailable for distribution as a consequence of the buyer's or seller's having complied with an order of court, legal process, statute, or rule of law, the seller and any person in control of the seller are excused from any obligation arising under this Article or under any agreement with the buyer to distribute the net contract price in accordance with the seller's undertakings in the schedule if the seller:

(a) distributes the net contract price remaining available in accordance with any priorities for payment stated in the schedule of distribution and, to the extent that the price is insufficient to pay all the debts having a given priority, distributes the price pro rata among those debts shown in the schedule as having the same priority;

(b) distributes the net contract price remaining available in accordance with an order of court;

(c) commences a proceeding for interpleader in a court of competent jurisdiction and is discharged from the proceeding; or

(d) prepares a written amended schedule of distribution of the net contract price remaining available for distribution, gives notice of the amended schedule, and distributes the net contract price remaining available in accordance with the amended schedule.

(7) The notice under subsection (6)(d) must identify the buyer and the seller, state the filing number, if any, of the original notice, set forth the amended schedule, and be given in accordance with subsection (1) or (2) of Section 6—105, whichever is applicable, at least 14 days before the seller distributes any part of the net contract price remaining available.

§ 6—107. Liability for Noncompliance.

(1) Except as provided in subsection (3), and subject to the limitation in subsection (4):

(a) a buyer who fails to comply with the requirements of Section 6—104(1)(e) with respect to a creditor is liable to the creditor for damages in the amount of the claim, reduced by any amount that the creditor would not have realized if the buyer had complied; and

(b) a buyer who fails to comply with the requirements of any other subsection of Section 6—104 with respect to a claimant is liable to the claimant for damages in the amount of the claim, reduced by any amount that the claimant would not have realized if the buyer had complied.

(2) In an action under subsection (1), the creditor has the burden of establishing the validity and amount of the claim, and the buyer has the burden of establishing the amount that the creditor would not have realized if the buyer had complied.

(3) A buyer who:

(a) made a good faith and commercially reasonable effort to comply with the requirements of Section 6—104(1) or to exclude the sale from the application of this Article under Section 6—103(3); or

(b) on or after the date of the bulk-sale agreement, but before the date of the bulk sale, held a good faith and commercially reasonable belief that this Article does not apply to the particular sale

is not liable to creditors for failure to comply with the requirements of Section 6—104. The buyer has the burden of establishing the good faith and commercial reasonableness of the effort or belief.

(4) In a single bulk sale the cumulative liability of the buyer for failure to comply with the requirements of Section 6—104(1) may not exceed an amount equal to:

(a) if the assets consist only of inventory and equipment, twice the net contract price, less the amount of any part of the net contract price paid to or applied for the benefit of the seller or a creditor; or

(b) if the assets include property other than inventory and equipment, twice the net value of the inventory and equipment less the amount of the portion of any part of the net contract price paid to or applied for the benefit of the seller or a creditor which is allocable to the inventory and equipment.

(5) For the purposes of subsection (4)(b), the "net value" of an asset is the value of the asset less (i) the amount of any proceeds of the sale of an asset, to the extent the proceeds are applied in partial or total satisfaction of a debt secured by the asset and (ii) the amount of any debt to the extent it is secured by a security interest or lien that is enforceable against the asset before and after it has been sold to a buyer. If a debt is secured by an asset and other property of the seller, the amount of the debt secured by a security interest or lien that is enforceable against the asset is determined by multiplying the debt by a fraction, the numerator of which is the value of the asset on the date of the bulk sale and the denominator of which is the value of all property securing the debt on the date of the bulk sale. The portion of a part of the net contract price paid to or applied for the benefit of the seller or a creditor that is "allocable to the inventory and equipment" is the portion that bears the same ratio to that part of the net contract price as the net value of the inventory and equipment bears to the net value of all of the assets.

(6) A payment made by the buyer to a person to whom the buyer is, or believes he [or she] is, liable under subsection (1) reduces pro tanto the buyer's cumulative liability under subsection (4).

(7) No action may be brought under subsection (1)(b) by or on behalf of a claimant whose claim is unliquidated or contingent.

(8) A buyer's failure to comply with the requirements of Section 6—104(1) does not (i) impair the buyer's rights in or title to the assets, (ii) render the sale ineffective, void, or voidable, (iii) entitle a creditor to more than a single satisfaction of his [or her] claim, or (iv) create liability other than as provided in this Article.

(9) Payment of the buyer's liability under subsection (1) discharges pro tanto the seller's debt to the creditor.

(10) Unless otherwise agreed, a buyer has an immediate right of reimbursement from the seller for any amount paid to a creditor in partial or total satisfaction of the buyer's liability under subsection (1).

(11) If the seller is an organization, a person who is in direct or indirect control of the seller, and who knowingly, intentionally, and without legal justification fails, or causes the seller to fail, to distribute the net contract price in accordance with the schedule of distribution is liable to any creditor to whom the seller undertook to make payment under the schedule for damages caused by the failure.

§ 6—108. Bulk Sales by Auction; Bulk Sales Conducted by Liquidator.

(1) Sections 6—104, 6—105, 6—106, and 6—107 apply to a bulk sale by auction and a bulk sale conducted by a liquidator on the seller's behalf with the following modifications:

(a) "buyer" refers to auctioneer or liquidator, as the case may be;

(b) "net contract price" refers to net proceeds of the auction or net proceeds of the sale, as the case may be;

(c) the written notice required under Section 6—105(3) must be accompanied by a copy of the schedule of distribution (Section 6—106(1)) and state at least:

(i) that the seller and the auctioneer or liquidator have entered into an agreement for auction or liquidation services that may constitute an agreement to make a bulk sale under the laws of the State of _____;

(ii) the date of the agreement;

(iii) the date on or after which the auction began or will begin or the date on or after which the liquidator began or will begin to sell assets on the seller's behalf;

(iv) the date on or after which more than ten percent of the net proceeds of the sale were or will be paid, if the date is not stated in the schedule of distribution;

(v) the name and a mailing address of the seller;

(vi) any other business name and address listed by the seller pursuant to Section 6—104(1)(a);

(vii) the name of the auctioneer or liquidator and an address of the auctioneer or liquidator from which information concerning the sale can be obtained;

(viii) a statement indicating the type of assets or describing the assets item by item;

(ix) the manner in which the auctioneer or liquidator will make available the list of claimants (Section 6—104(1)(f)), if applicable; and

(x) if the sale is in total or partial satisfaction of an antecedent debt owed by the seller, the amount of the debt to be satisfied and the name of the person to whom it is owed; and

(d) in a single bulk sale the cumulative liability of the auctioneer or liquidator for failure to comply with the requirements of this section may not exceed the amount of the net proceeds of the sale allocable to inventory and equipment sold less the amount of the portion of any part of the net proceeds paid to or applied for the benefit of a creditor which is allocable to the inventory and equipment.

(2) A payment made by the auctioneer or liquidator to a person to whom the auctioneer or liquidator is, or believes he [or she] is, liable under this section reduces pro tanto the auctioneer's or liquidator's cumulative liability under subsection (1)(d).

(3) A form substantially as follows is sufficient to comply with subsection (1)(c):

Notice of Sale

(1) _____ , whose address is _____ , is described in this notice as the "seller."

(2) _____ , whose address is _____ , is described in this notice as the "auctioneer" or "liquidator."

(3) The seller has disclosed to the auctioneer or liquidator that within the past three years the seller has used other business names, operated at other addresses, or both, as follows: _____ .

(4) The seller and the auctioneer or liquidator have entered into an agreement dated _____ for auction or liquidation services that may constitute an agreement to make a bulk sale under the laws of the State of _____ .

(5) The date on or after which the auction began or will begin or the date on or after which the liquidator began or will begin to sell assets on the seller's behalf is _____ , and [if not stated in the schedule of distribution] the date on or after which more than ten percent of the net proceeds of the sale were or will be paid is _____ .

(6) The following assets are the subject of the sale: _____ .

(7) [If applicable] The auctioneer or liquidator will make available to claimants of the seller a list of the seller's claimants in the following manner: _____ .

(8) [If applicable] The sale is to satisfy $ _____ of an antecedent debt owed by the seller to _____ .

(9) A copy of the schedule of distribution of the net proceeds accompanies this notice.

[End of Notice]

(4) A person who buys at a bulk sale by auction or conducted by a liquidator need not comply with the requirements of Section 6—104(1) and is not liable for the failure of an auctioneer or liquidator to comply with the requirements of this section.

§ 6—109. What Constitutes Filing; Duties of Filing Officer; Information from Filing Officer.

(1) Presentation of a notice or list of claimants for filing and tender of the filing fee or acceptance of the notice or list by the filing officer constitutes filing under this Article.

(2) The filing officer shall:

(a) mark each notice or list with a file number and with the date and hour of filing;

(b) hold the notice or list or a copy for public inspection;

(c) index the notice or list according to each name given for the seller and for the buyer; and

(d) note in the index the file number and the addresses of the seller and buyer given in the notice or list.

(3) If the person filing a notice or list furnishes the filing officer with a copy, the filing officer upon request shall note upon the copy the file number and date and hour of the filing of the original and send or deliver the copy to the person.

(4) The fee for filing and indexing and for stamping a copy furnished by the person filing to show the date and place of filing is $ _____ for the first page and $ _____ for each additional page. The fee for indexing each name beyond the first two is $ _____ .

(5) Upon request of any person, the filing officer shall issue a certificate showing whether any notice or list with respect to a particular seller or buyer is on file on the date and hour stated in the certificate. If a notice or list is on file, the certificate must give the date and hour of filing of each notice or list and the name and address of each seller, buyer, auctioneer, or liquidator. The fee for the certificate is $ _____ if the request for the certificate is in the standard form prescribed by the [Secretary of State] and otherwise is $ _____ . Upon request of any person, the filing officer shall furnish a copy of any filed notice or list for a fee of $ _____ .

(6) The filing officer shall keep each notice or list for two years after it is filed.

§ 6—110. Limitation of Actions.

(1) Except as provided in subsection (2), an action under this Article against a buyer, auctioneer, or liquidator must be commenced within one year after the date of the bulk sale.

(2) If the buyer, auctioneer, or liquidator conceals the fact that the sale has occurred, the limitation is tolled and an action under this Article may be commenced within the earlier of (i) one year after the person bringing the action

discovers that the sale has occurred or (ii) one year after the person bringing the action should have discovered that the sale has occurred, but no later than two years after the date of the bulk sale. Complete noncompliance with the requirements of this Article does not of itself constitute concealment.

(3) An action under Section 6—107(11) must be commenced within one year after the alleged violation occurs.

Article 7
Warehouse Receipts, Bills of Lading and Other Documents of Title

Part 1　General

§ 7—101.　Short Title.

This Article shall be known and may be cited as Uniform Commercial Code—Documents of Title.

§ 7—102.　Definitions and Index of Definitions.

(1) In this Article, unless the context otherwise requires:

(a) "Bailee" means the person who by a warehouse receipt, bill of lading or other document of title acknowledges possession of goods and contracts to deliver them.

(b) "Consignee" means the person named in a bill to whom or to whose order the bill promises delivery.

(c) "Consignor" means the person named in a bill as the person from whom the goods have been received for shipment.

(d) "Delivery order" means a written order to deliver goods directed to a warehouseman, carrier or other person who in the ordinary course of business issues warehouse receipts or bills of lading.

(e) "Document" means document of title as defined in the general definitions in Article 1 (Section 1—201).

(f) "Goods" means all things which are treated as movable for the purposes of a contract of storage or transportation.

(g) "Issuer" means a bailee who issues a document except that in relation to an unaccepted delivery order it means the person who orders the possessor of goods to deliver. Issuer includes any person for whom an agent or employee purports to act in issuing a document if the agent or employee has real or apparent authority to issue documents, notwithstanding that the issuer received no goods or that the goods were misdescribed or that in any other respect the agent or employee violated his instructions.

(h) "Warehouseman" is a person engaged in the business of storing goods for hire.

(2) Other definitions applying to this Article or to specified Parts thereof, and the sections in which they appear are:

"Duly negotiate". Section 7—501.

"Person entitled under the document". Section 7—403(4).

(3) Definitions in other Articles applying to this Article and the sections in which they appear are:

"Contract for sale". Section 2—106.

"Overseas". Section 2—323.

"Receipt" of goods. Section 2—103.

(4) In addition Article 1 contains general definitions and principles of construction and interpretation applicable throughout this Article.

§ 7—103.　Relation of Article to Treaty, Statute, Tariff, Classification or Regulation.

To the extent that any treaty or statute of the United States, regulatory statute of this State or tariff, classification or regulation filed or issued pursuant thereto is applicable, the provisions of this Article are subject thereto.

§ 7—104.　Negotiable and Nonnegotiable Warehouse Receipt, Bill of Lading or Other Document of Title.

(1) A warehouse receipt, bill of lading or other document of title is negotiable

(a) if by its terms the goods are to be delivered to bearer or to the order of a named person; or

(b) where recognized in overseas trade, if it runs to a named person or assigns.

(2) Any other document is nonnegotiable. A bill of lading in which it is stated that the goods are consigned to a named person is not made negotiable by a provision that the goods are to be delivered only against a written order signed by the same or another named person.

§ 7—105.　Construction Against Negative Implication.

The omission from either Part 2 or Part 3 of this Article of a provision corresponding to a provision made in the other Part does not imply that a corresponding rule of law is not applicable.

Part 2　Warehouse Receipts: Special Provisions

§ 7—201.　Who May Issue a Warehouse Receipt; Storage Under Government Bond.

(1) A warehouse receipt may be issued by any warehouseman.

(2) Where goods including distilled spirits and agricultural commodities are stored under a statute requiring a bond against withdrawal or a license for the issuance of receipts in the nature of warehouse receipts, a receipt issued for the goods has like effect as a warehouse receipt even though issued by a person who is the owner of the goods and is not a warehouseman.

§ 7—202. Form of Warehouse Receipt; Essential Terms; Optional Terms.

(1) A warehouse receipt need not be in any particular form.

(2) Unless a warehouse receipt embodies within its written or printed terms each of the following, the warehouseman is liable for damages caused by the omission to a person injured thereby:

(a) the location of the warehouse where the goods are stored;

(b) the date of issue of the receipt;

(c) the consecutive number of the receipt;

(d) a statement whether the goods received will be delivered to the bearer, to a specified person, or to a specified person or his order;

(e) the rate of storage and handling charges, except that where goods are stored under a field warehousing arrangement a statement of that fact is sufficient on a nonnegotiable receipt;

(f) a description of the goods or of the packages containing them;

(g) the signature of the warehouseman, which may be made by his authorized agent;

(h) if the receipt is issued for goods of which the warehouseman is owner, either solely or jointly or in common with others, the fact of such ownership; and

(i) a statement of the amount of advances made and of liabilities incurred for which the warehouseman claims a lien or security interest (Section 7—209). If the precise amount of such advances made or of such liabilities incurred is, at the time of the issue of the receipt, unknown to the warehouseman or to his agent who issues it, a statement of the fact that advances have been made or liabilities incurred and the purpose thereof is sufficient.

(3) A warehouseman may insert in his receipt any other terms which are not contrary to the provisions of this Act and do not impair his obligation of delivery (Section 7—403) or his duty of care (Section 7—204). Any contrary provisions shall be ineffective.

§ 7—203. Liability for Nonreceipt or Misdescription.

A party to or purchaser for value in good faith of a document of title other than a bill of lading relying in either case upon the description therein of the goods may recover from the issuer damages caused by the nonreceipt or misdescription of the goods, except to the extent that the document conspicuously indicates that the issuer does not know whether any part or all of the goods in fact were received or conform to the description, as where the description is in terms of marks or labels or kind, quantity or condition, or the receipt or description is qualified by "contents, condition and quality unknown", "said to con-

tain" or the like, if such indication be true, or the party or purchaser otherwise has notice.

§ 7—204. Duty of Care; Contractual Limitation of Warehouseman's Liability.

(1) A warehouseman is liable for damages for loss of or injury to the goods caused by his failure to exercise such care in regard to them as a reasonably careful man would exercise under like circumstances but unless otherwise agreed he is not liable for damages which could not have been avoided by the exercise of such care.

(2) Damages may be limited by a term in the warehouse receipt or storage agreement limiting the amount of liability in case of loss or damage, and setting forth a specific liability per article or item, or value per unit of weight, beyond which the warehouseman shall not be liable; provided, however, that such liability may on written request of the bailor at the time of signing such storage agreement or within a reasonable time after receipt of the warehouse receipt be increased on part or all of the goods thereunder, in which event increased rates may be charged based on such increased valuation, but that no such increase shall be permitted contrary to a lawful limitation of liability contained in the warehouseman's tariff, if any. No such limitation is effective with respect to the warehouseman's liability for conversion to his own use.

(3) Reasonable provisions as to the time and manner of presenting claims and instituting actions based on the bailment may be included in the warehouse receipt or tariff.

(4) This section does not impair or repeal ...

Note: *Insert in subsection (4) a reference to any statute which imposes a higher responsibility upon the warehouseman or invalidates contractual limitations which would be permissible under this Article.*

§ 7—205. Title Under Warehouse Receipt Defeated in Certain Cases.

A buyer in the ordinary course of business of fungible goods sold and delivered by a warehouseman who is also in the business of buying and selling such goods takes free of any claim under a warehouse receipt even though it has been duly negotiated.

§ 7—206. Termination of Storage at Warehouseman's Option.

(1) A warehouseman may on notifying the person on whose account the goods are held and any other person known to claim an interest in the goods require payment of any charges and removal of the goods from the warehouse at the termination of the period of storage fixed by the document, or, if no period is fixed, within a stated period not less than thirty days after the notification. If the goods are not removed before the date specified in the notification, the warehouseman may sell them in accordance with the provisions of the section on enforcement of a warehouseman's lien (Section 7—210).

(2) If a warehouseman in good faith believes that the goods are about to deteriorate or decline in value to less than the amount of his lien within the time prescribed in subsection (1) for notification, advertisement and sale, the warehouseman may specify in the notification any reasonable shorter time for removal of the goods and in case the goods are not removed, may sell them at public sale held not less than one week after a single advertisement or posting.

(3) If as a result of a quality or condition of the goods of which the warehouseman had no notice at the time of deposit the goods are a hazard to other property or to the warehouse or to persons, the warehouseman may sell the goods at public or private sale without advertisement on reasonable notification to all persons known to claim an interest in the goods. If the warehouseman after a reasonable effort is unable to sell the goods he may dispose of them in any lawful manner and shall incur no liability by reason of such disposition.

(4) The warehouseman must deliver the goods to any person entitled to them under this Article upon due demand made at any time prior to sale or other disposition under this section.

(5) The warehouseman may satisfy his lien from the proceeds of any sale or disposition under this section but must hold the balance for delivery on the demand of any person to whom he would have been bound to deliver the goods.

§ 7—207. Goods Must Be Kept Separate; Fungible Goods.

(1) Unless the warehouse receipt otherwise provides, a warehouseman must keep separate the goods covered by each receipt so as to permit at all times identification and delivery of those goods except that different lots of fungible goods may be commingled.

(2) Fungible goods so commingled are owned in common by the persons entitled thereto and the warehouseman is severally liable to each owner for that owner's share. Where because of overissue a mass of fungible goods is insufficient to meet all the receipts which the warehouseman has issued against it, the persons entitled include all holders to whom overissued receipts have been duly negotiated.

§ 7—208. Altered Warehouse Receipts.

Where a blank in a negotiable warehouse receipt has been filled in without authority, a purchaser for value and without notice of the want of authority may treat the insertion as authorized. Any other unauthorized alteration leaves any receipt enforceable against the issuer according to its original tenor.

§ 7—209. Lien of Warehouseman.

(1) A warehouseman has a lien against the bailor on the goods covered by a warehouse receipt or on the proceeds thereof in his possession for charges for storage or transportation (including demurrage and terminal charges),

insurance, labor, or charges present or future in relation to the goods, and for expenses necessary for preservation of the goods or reasonably incurred in their sale pursuant to law. If the person on whose account the goods are held is liable for like charges or expenses in relation to other goods whenever deposited and it is stated in the receipt that a lien is claimed for charges and expenses in relation to other goods, the warehouseman also has a lien against him for such charges and expenses whether or not the other goods have been delivered by the warehouseman. But against a person to whom a negotiable warehouse receipt is duly negotiated a warehouseman's lien is limited to charges in an amount or at a rate specified on the receipt or if no charges are so specified then to a reasonable charge for storage of the goods covered by the receipt subsequent to the date of the receipt.

(2) The warehouseman may also reserve a security interest against the bailor for a maximum amount specified on the receipt for charges other than those specified in subsection (1), such as for money advanced and interest. Such a security interest is governed by the Article on Secured Transactions (Article 9).

(3)(a) A warehouseman's lien for charges and expenses under subsection (1) or a security interest under subsection (2) is also effective against any person who so entrusted the bailor with possession of the goods that a pledge of them by him to a good faith purchaser for value would have been valid but is not effective against a person as to whom the document confers no right in the goods covered by it under Section 7—503.

   (b) A warehouseman's lien on household goods for charges and expenses in relation to the goods under subsection (1) is also effective against all persons if the depositor was the legal possessor of the goods at the time of deposit. "Household goods" means furniture, furnishings and personal effects used by the depositor in a dwelling.

(4) A warehouseman loses his lien on any goods which he voluntarily delivers or which he unjustifiably refuses to deliver.

§ 7—210. Enforcement of Warehouseman's Lien.

(1) Except as provided in subsection (2), a warehouseman's lien may be enforced by public or private sale of the goods in bloc or in parcels, at any time or place and on any terms which are commercially reasonable, after notifying all persons known to claim an interest in the goods. Such notification must include a statement of the amount due, the nature of the proposed sale and the time and place of any public sale. The fact that a better price could have been obtained by a sale at a different time or in a different method from that selected by the warehouseman is not of itself sufficient to establish that the sale was not made in a commercially reasonable manner. If the warehouseman

either sells the goods in the usual manner in any recognized market therefor, or if he sells at the price current in such market at the time of his sale, or if he has otherwise sold in conformity with commercially reasonable practices among dealers in the type of goods sold, he has sold in a commercially reasonable manner. A sale of more goods than apparently necessary to be offered to ensure satisfaction of the obligation is not commercially reasonable except in cases covered by the preceding sentence.

(2) A warehouseman's lien on goods other than goods stored by a merchant in the course of his business may be enforced only as follows:

(a) All persons known to claim an interest in the goods must be notified.

(b) The notification must be delivered in person or sent by registered or certified letter to the last known address of any person to be notified.

(c) The notification must include an itemized statement of the claim, a description of the goods subject to the lien, a demand for payment within a specified time not less than ten days after receipt of the notification, and a conspicuous statement that unless the claim is paid within the time the goods will be advertised for sale and sold by auction at a specified time and place.

(d) The sale must conform to the terms of the notification.

(e) The sale must be held at the nearest suitable place to that where the goods are held or stored.

(f) After the expiration of the time given in the notification, an advertisement of the sale must be published once a week for two weeks consecutively in a newspaper of general circulation where the sale is to be held. The advertisement must include a description of the goods, the name of the person on whose account they are being held, and the time and place of the sale. The sale must take place at least fifteen days after the first publication. If there is no newspaper of general circulation where the sale is to be held, the advertisement must be posted at least ten days before the sale in not less than six conspicuous places in the neighborhood of the proposed sale.

(3) Before any sale pursuant to this section any person claiming a right in the goods may pay the amount necessary to satisfy the lien and the reasonable expenses incurred under this section. In that event the goods must not be sold, but must be retained by the warehouseman subject to the terms of the receipt and this Article.

(4) The warehouseman may buy at any public sale pursuant to this section.

(5) A purchaser in good faith of goods sold to enforce a warehouseman's lien takes the goods free of any rights of persons against whom the lien was valid, despite noncompliance by the warehouseman with the requirements of this section.

(6) The warehouseman may satisfy his lien from the proceeds of any sale pursuant to this section but must hold the balance, if any, for delivery on demand to any person to whom he would have been bound to deliver the goods.

(7) The rights provided by this section shall be in addition to all other rights allowed by law to a creditor against his debtor.

(8) Where a lien is on goods stored by a merchant in the course of his business the lien may be enforced in accordance with either subsection (1) or (2).

(9) The warehouseman is liable for damages caused by failure to comply with the requirements for sale under this section and in case of willful violation is liable for conversion.

Part 3 Bills of Lading: Special Provisions

§ 7—301. Liability for Nonreceipt or Misdescription; "Said to Contain"; "Shipper's Load and Count"; Improper Handling.

(1) A consignee of a nonnegotiable bill who has given value in good faith or a holder to whom a negotiable bill has been duly negotiated relying in either case upon the description therein of the goods, or upon the date therein shown, may recover from the issuer damages caused by the misdating of the bill or the nonreceipt or misdescription of the goods, except to the extent that the document indicates that the issuer does not know whether any part of all of the goods in fact were received or conform to the description, as where the description is in terms of marks or labels or kind, quantity, or condition or the receipt or description is qualified by "contents or condition of contents of packages unknown", "said to contain", "shipper's weight, load and count" or the like, if such indication be true.

(2) When goods are loaded by an issuer who is a common carrier, the issuer must count the packages of goods if package freight and ascertain the kind and quantity if bulk freight. In such cases "shipper's weight, load and count" or other words indicating that the description was made by the shipper are ineffective except as to freight concealed by packages.

(3) When bulk freight is loaded by a shipper who makes available to the issuer adequate facilities for weighing such freight, an issuer who is a common carrier must ascertain the kind and quantity within a reasonable time after receiving the written request of the shipper to do so. In such cases "shipper's weight" or other words of like purport are ineffective.

(4) The issuer may by inserting in the bill the words "shipper's weight, load and count" or other words of like purport indicate that the goods were loaded by the shipper; and if such statement be true the issuer shall not be liable for damages caused by the improper loading. But their omission does not imply liability for such damages.

(5) The shipper shall be deemed to have guaranteed to the issuer the accuracy at the time of shipment of the description, marks, labels, number, kind, quantity, condition and weight, as furnished by him; and the shipper shall indemnify the issuer against damage caused by inaccuracies in such particulars. The right of the issuer to such indemnity shall in no way limit his responsibility and liability under the contract of carriage to any person other than the shipper.

§ 7—302. Through Bills of Lading and Similar Documents.

(1) The issuer of a through bill of lading or other document embodying an undertaking to be performed in part by persons acting as its agents or by connecting carriers is liable to anyone entitled to recover on the document for any breach by such other persons or by a connecting carrier of its obligation under the document but to the extent that the bill covers an undertaking to be performed overseas or in territory not contiguous to the continental United States or an undertaking including matters other than transportation this liability may be varied by agreement of the parties.

(2) Where goods covered by a through bill of lading or other document embodying an undertaking to be performed in part by persons other than the issuer are received by any such person, he is subject with respect to his own performance while the goods are in his possession to the obligation of the issuer. His obligation is discharged by delivery of the goods to another such person pursuant to the document, and does not include liability for breach by any other such persons or by the issuer.

(3) The issuer of such through bill of lading or other document shall be entitled to recover from the connecting carrier or such other person in possession of the goods when the breach of the obligation under the document occurred, the amount it may be required to pay to anyone entitled to recover on the document therefor, as may be evidenced by any receipt, judgment, or transcript thereof, and the amount of any expense reasonably incurred by it in defending any action brought by anyone entitled to recover on the document therefor.

§ 7—303. Diversion; Reconsignment; Change of Instructions.

(1) Unless the bill of lading otherwise provides, the carrier may deliver the goods to a person or destination other than that stated in the bill or may otherwise dispose of the goods on instructions from

    (a) the holder of a negotiable bill; or

    (b) the consignor on a nonnegotiable bill notwithstanding contrary instructions from the consignee; or

    (c) the consignee on a nonnegotiable bill in the absence of contrary instructions from the consignor, if the goods have arrived at the billed destination or if the consignee is in possession of the bill; or

    (d) the consignee on a nonnegotiable bill if he is entitled as against the consignor to dispose of them.

(2) Unless such instructions are noted on a negotiable bill of lading, a person to whom the bill is duly negotiated can hold the bailee according to the original terms.

§ 7—304. Bills of Lading in a Set.

(1) Except where customary in overseas transportation, a bill of lading must not be issued in a set of parts. The issuer is liable for damages caused by violation of this subsection.

(2) Where a bill of lading is lawfully drawn in a set of parts, each of which is numbered and expressed to be valid only if the goods have not been delivered against any other part, the whole of the parts constitute one bill.

(3) Where a bill of lading is lawfully issued in a set of parts and different parts are negotiated to different persons, the title of the holder to whom the first due negotiation is made prevails as to both the document and the goods even though any later holder may have received the goods from the carrier in good faith and discharged the carrier's obligation by surrender of his part.

(4) Any person who negotiates or transfers a single part of a bill of lading drawn in a set is liable to holders of that part as if it were the whole set.

(5) The bailee is obliged to deliver in accordance with Part 4 of this Article against the first presented part of a bill of lading lawfully drawn in a set. Such delivery discharges the bailee's obligation on the whole bill.

§ 7—305. Destination Bills.

(1) Instead of issuing a bill of lading to the consignor at the place of shipment a carrier may at the request of the consignor procure the bill to be issued at destination or at any other place designated in the request.

(2) Upon request of anyone entitled as against the carrier to control the goods while in transit and on surrender of any outstanding bill of lading or other receipt covering such goods, the issuer may procure a substitute bill to be issued at any place designated in the request.

§ 7—306. Altered Bills of Lading.

An unauthorized alteration or filling in of a blank in a bill of lading leaves the bill enforceable according to its original tenor.

§ 7—307. Lien of Carrier.

(1) A carrier has a lien on the goods covered by a bill of lading for charges subsequent to the date of its receipt of the goods for storage or transportation (including demurrage and terminal charges) and for expenses necessary for preservation of the goods incident to their transportation or reasonably incurred in their sale pursuant to law. But against a purchaser for value of a negotiable bill of lading a carrier's lien is limited to charges stated in the bill or the

applicable tariffs, or if no charges are stated then to a reasonable charge.

(2) A lien for charges and expenses under subsection (1) on goods which the carrier was required by law to receive for transportation is effective against the consignor or any person entitled to the goods unless the carrier had notice that the consignor lacked authority to subject the goods to such charges and expenses. Any other lien under subsection (1) is effective against the consignor and any person who permitted the bailor to have control or possession of the goods unless the carrier had notice that the bailor lacked such authority.

(3) A carrier loses his lien on any goods which he voluntarily delivers or which he unjustifiably refuses to deliver.

§ 7—308. Enforcement of Carrier's Lien.

(1) A carrier's lien may be enforced by public or private sale of the goods, in bloc or in parcels, at any time or place and on any terms which are commercially reasonable, after notifying all persons known to claim an interest in the goods. Such notification must include a statement of the amount due, the nature of the proposed sale and the time and place of any public sale. The fact that a better price could have been obtained by a sale at a different time or in a different method from that selected by the carrier is not of itself sufficient to establish that the sale was not made in a commercially reasonable manner. If the carrier either sells the goods in the usual manner in any recognized market therefor or if he sells at the price current in such market at the time of his sale or if he has otherwise sold in conformity with commercially reasonable practices among dealers in the type of goods sold he has sold in a commercially reasonable manner. A sale of more goods than apparently necessary to be offered to ensure satisfaction of the obligation is not commercially reasonable except in cases covered by the preceding sentence.

(2) Before any sale pursuant to this section any person claiming a right in the goods may pay the amount necessary to satisfy the lien and the reasonable expenses incurred under this section. In that event the goods must not be sold, but must be retained by the carrier subject to the terms of the bill and this Article.

(3) The carrier may buy at any public sale pursuant to this section.

(4) A purchaser in good faith of goods sold to enforce a carrier's lien takes the goods free of any rights of persons against whom the lien was valid, despite noncompliance by the carrier with the requirements of this section.

(5) The carrier may satisfy his lien from the proceeds of any sale pursuant to this section but must hold the balance, if any, for delivery on demand to any person to whom he would have been bound to deliver the goods.

(6) The rights provided by this section shall be in addition to all other rights allowed by law to a creditor against his debtor.

(7) A carrier's lien may be enforced in accordance with either subsection (1) or the procedure set forth in subsection (2) of Section 7—210.

(8) The carrier is liable for damages caused by failure to comply with the requirements for sale under this section and in case of willful violation is liable for conversion.

§ 7—309. Duty of Care; Contractual Limitation of Carrier's Liability.

(1) A carrier who issues a bill of lading whether negotiable or nonnegotiable must exercise the degree of care in relation to the goods which a reasonably careful man would exercise under like circumstances. This subsection does not repeal or change any law or rule of law which imposes liability upon a common carrier for damages not caused by its negligence.

(2) Damages may be limited by a provision that the carrier's liability shall not exceed a value stated in the document if the carrier's rates are dependent upon value and the consignor by the carrier's tariff is afforded an opportunity to declare a higher value or a value as lawfully provided in the tariff, or where no tariff is filed he is otherwise advised of such opportunity; but no such limitation is effective with respect to the carrier's liability for conversion to its own use.

(3) Reasonable provisions as to the time and manner of presenting claims and instituting actions based on the shipment may be included in a bill of lading or tariff.

Part 4 Warehouse Receipts and Bills of Lading: General Obligations

§ 7—401. Irregularities in Issue of Receipt or Bill or Conduct of Issuer.

The obligations imposed by this Article on an issuer apply to a document of title regardless of the fact that

(a) the document may not comply with the requirements of this Article or of any other law or regulation regarding its issue, form or content; or

(b) the issuer may have violated laws regulating the conduct of his business; or

(c) the goods covered by the document were owned by the bailee at the time the document was issued; or

(d) the person issuing the document does not come within the definition of warehouseman if it purports to be a warehouse receipt.

§ 7—402. Duplicate Receipt or Bill; Overissue.

Neither a duplicate nor any other document of title purporting to cover goods already represented by an outstanding document of the same issuer confers any right in the goods, except as provided in the case of bills in a set, overissue of documents for fungible goods and substitutes for lost, stolen or destroyed documents. But the issuer is liable for damages caused by his overissue or failure to identify a duplicate document as such by conspicuous notation on its face.

§ 7—403. Obligation of Warehouseman or Carrier to Deliver; Excuse.

(1) The bailee must deliver the goods to a person entitled under the document who complies with subsections (2) and (3), unless and to the extent that the bailee establishes any of the following:

    (a) delivery of the goods to a person whose receipt was rightful as against the claimant;

    (b) damage to or delay, loss or destruction of the goods for which the bailee is not liable [, but the burden of establishing negligence in such cases is on the person entitled under the document];

Note: *The brackets in (1)(b) indicate that State enactments may differ on this point without serious damage to the principle of uniformity.*

    (c) previous sale or other disposition of the goods in lawful enforcement of a lien or on warehouseman's lawful termination of storage;

    (d) the exercise by a seller of his right to stop delivery pursuant to the provisions of the Article on Sales (Section 2—705);

    (e) a diversion, reconsignment or other disposition pursuant to the provisions of this Article (Section 7—303) or tariff regulating such right;

    (f) release, satisfaction or any other fact affording a personal defense against the claimant;

    (g) any other lawful excuse.

(2) A person claiming goods covered by a document of title must satisfy the bailee's lien where the bailee so requests or where the bailee is prohibited by law from delivering the goods until the charges are paid.

(3) Unless the person claiming is one against whom the document confers no right under Sec. 7—503(1), he must surrender for cancellation or notation of partial deliveries any outstanding negotiable document covering the goods, and the bailee must cancel the document or conspicuously note the partial delivery thereon or be liable to any person to whom the document is duly negotiated.

(4) "Person entitled under the document" means holder in the case of a negotiable document, or the person to whom delivery is to be made by the terms of or pursuant to written instructions under a nonnegotiable document.

§ 7—404. No Liability for Good Faith Delivery Pursuant to Receipt or Bill.

A bailee who in good faith including observance of reasonable commercial standards has received goods and delivered or otherwise disposed of them according to the terms of the document of title or pursuant to this Article is not liable therefor. This rule applies even though the person from whom he received the goods had no authority to procure the document or to dispose of the goods and even though the person to whom he delivered the goods had no authority to receive them.

Part 5 Warehouse Receipts and Bills of Lading: Negotiation and Transfer

§ 7—501. Form of Negotiation and Requirements of "Due Negotiation".

(1) A negotiable document of title running to the order of a named person is negotiated by his indorsement and delivery. After his indorsement in blank or to bearer any person can negotiate it by delivery alone.

(2)(a) A negotiable document of title is also negotiated by delivery alone when by its original terms it runs to bearer.

    (b) When a document running to the order of a named person is delivered to him the effect is the same as if the document had been negotiated.

(3) Negotiation of a negotiable document of title after it has been indorsed to a specified person requires indorsement by the special indorsee as well as delivery.

(4) A negotiable document of title is "duly negotiated" when it is negotiated in the manner stated in this section to a holder who purchases it in good faith without notice of any defense against or claim to it on the part of any person and for value, unless it is established that the negotiation is not in the regular course of business or financing or involves receiving the document in settlement or payment of a money obligation.

(5) Indorsement of a nonnegotiable document neither makes it negotiable nor adds to the transferee's rights.

(6) The naming in a negotiable bill of a person to be notified of the arrival of the goods does not limit the negotiability of the bill nor constitute notice to a purchaser thereof of any interest of such person in the goods.

§ 7—502. Rights Acquired by Due Negotiation.

(1) Subject to the following section and to the provisions of Section 7—205 on fungible goods, a holder to whom a negotiable document of title has been duly negotiated acquires thereby:

    (a) title to the document;

    (b) title to the goods;

    (c) all rights accruing under the law of agency or estoppel, including rights to goods delivered to the bailee after the document was issued; and

    (d) the direct obligation of the issuer to hold or deliver the goods according to the terms of the document free of any defense or claim by him except those arising under the terms of the document or under this Article. In the case of a delivery order the bailee's obligation accrues only upon acceptance and the obligation acquired by the holder is that the issuer and any indorser will procure the acceptance of the bailee.

(2) Subject to the following section, title and rights so acquired are not defeated by any stoppage of the goods represented by the document or by surrender of such goods by the bailee, and are not impaired even though the negotiation or any prior negotiation constituted a breach of duty or even though any person has been deprived of possession of the document by misrepresentation, fraud, accident, mistake, duress, loss, theft or conversion, or even though a previous sale or other transfer of the goods or document has been made to a third person.

§ 7—503. Document of Title to Goods Defeated in Certain Cases.

(1) A document of title confers no right in goods against a person who before issuance of the document had a legal interest or a perfected security interest in them and who neither

>   (a) delivered or entrusted them or any document of title covering them to the bailor or his nominee with actual or apparent authority to ship, store or sell or with power to obtain delivery under this Article (Section 7—403) or with power of disposition under this Act (Sections 2—403 and 9—307) or other statute or rule of law; nor

>   (b) acquiesced in the procurement by the bailor or his nominee of any document of title.

(2) Title to goods based upon an unaccepted delivery order is subject to the rights of anyone to whom a negotiable warehouse receipt or bill of lading covering the goods has been duly negotiated. Such a title may be defeated under the next section to the same extent as the rights of the issuer or a transferee from the issuer.

(3) Title to goods based upon a bill of lading issued to a freight forwarder is subject to the rights of anyone to whom a bill issued by the freight forwarder is duly negotiated; but delivery by the carrier in accordance with Part 4 of this Article pursuant to its own bill of lading discharges the carrier's obligation to deliver.

§ 7—504. Rights Acquired in the Absence of Due Negotiation; Effect of Diversion; Seller's Stoppage of Delivery.

(1) A transferee of a document, whether negotiable or nonnegotiable, to whom the document has been delivered but not duly negotiated, acquires the title and rights which his transferor had or had actual authority to convey.

(2) In the case of a nonnegotiable document, until but not after the bailee receives notification of the transfer, the rights of the transferee may be defeated

>   (a) by those creditors of the transferor who could treat the sale as void under Section 2—402; or

>   (b) by a buyer from the transferor in ordinary course of business if the bailee has delivered the goods to the buyer or received notification of his rights; or

>   (c) as against the bailee by good faith dealings of the bailee with the transferor.

(3) A diversion or other change of shipping instructions by the consignor in a nonnegotiable bill of lading which causes the bailee not to deliver to the consignee defeats the consignee's title to the goods if they have been delivered to a buyer in ordinary course of business and in any event defeats the consignee's rights against the bailee.

(4) Delivery pursuant to a nonnegotiable document may be stopped by a seller under Section 2—705, and subject to the requirement of due notification there provided. A bailee honoring the seller's instructions is entitled to be indemnified by the seller against any resulting loss or expense.

§ 7—505. Indorser Not a Guarantor for Other Parties.

The indorsement of a document of title issued by a bailee does not make the indorser liable for any default by the bailee or by previous indorsers.

§ 7—506. Delivery Without Indorsement: Right to Compel Indorsement.

The transferee of a negotiable document of title has a specifically enforceable right to have his transferor supply any necessary indorsement but the transfer becomes a negotiation only as of the time the indorsement is supplied.

§ 7—507. Warranties on Negotiation or Transfer of Receipt or Bill.

Where a person negotiates or transfers a document of title for value otherwise than as a mere intermediary under the next following section, then unless otherwise agreed he warrants to his immediate purchaser only in addition to any warranty made in selling the goods

(a) that the document is genuine; and

(b) that he has no knowledge of any fact which would impair its validity or worth; and

(c) that his negotiation or transfer is rightful and fully effective with respect to the title to the document and the goods it represents.

§ 7—508. Warranties of Collecting Bank as to Documents.

A collecting bank or other intermediary known to be entrusted with documents on behalf of another or with collection of a draft or other claim against delivery of documents warrants by such delivery of the documents only its own good faith and authority. This rule applies even though the intermediary has purchased or made advances against the claim or draft to be collected.

§ 7—509. Receipt or Bill: When Adequate Compliance With Commercial Contract.

The question whether a document is adequate to fulfill the obligations of a contract for sale or the conditions of a credit is governed by the Articles on Sales (Article 2) and on Letters of Credit (Article 5).

Part 6 Warehouse Receipts and Bills of Lading: Miscellaneous Provisions

§ 7—601. Lost and Missing Documents.

(1) If a document has been lost, stolen or destroyed, a court may order delivery of the goods or issuance of a substitute document and the bailee may without liability to any person comply with such order. If the document was negotiable the claimant must post security approved by the court to indemnify any person who may suffer loss as a result of non-surrender of the document. If the document was not negotiable, such security may be required at the discretion of the court. The court may also in its discretion order payment of the bailee's reasonable costs and counsel fees.

(2) A bailee who without court order delivers goods to a person claiming under a missing negotiable document is liable to any person injured thereby, and if the delivery is not in good faith becomes liable for conversion. Delivery in good faith is not conversion if made in accordance with a filed classification or tariff or, where no classification or tariff is filed, if the claimant posts security with the bailee in an amount at least double the value of the goods at the time of posting to indemnify any person injured by the delivery who files a notice of claim within one year after the delivery.

§ 7—602. Attachment of Goods Covered by a Negotiable Document.

Except where the document was originally issued upon delivery of the goods by a person who had no power to dispose of them, no lien attaches by virtue of any judicial process to goods in the possession of a bailee for which a negotiable document of title is outstanding unless the document be first surrendered to the bailee or its negotiation enjoined, and the bailee shall not be compelled to deliver the goods pursuant to process until the document is surrendered to him or impounded by the court. One who purchases the document for value without notice of the process or injunction takes free of the lien imposed by judicial process.

§ 7—603. Conflicting Claims; Interpleader.

If more than one person claims title or possession of the goods, the bailee is excused from delivery until he has had a reasonable time to ascertain the validity of the adverse claims or to bring an action to compel all claimants to interplead and may compel such interpleader, either in defending an action for nondelivery of the goods, or by original action, whichever is appropriate.

Revised (1994) Article 8
INVESTMENT SECURITIES

Part 1 Short Title and General Matters

§ 8—101. Short Title.

This Article may be cited as Uniform Commercial Code—Investment Securities.

§ 8—102. Definitions.

(a) In this Article:

(1) "Adverse claim" means a claim that a claimant has a property interest in a financial asset and that it is a violation of the rights of the claimant for another person to hold, transfer, or deal with the financial asset.

(2) "Bearer form," as applied to a certificated security, means a form in which the security is payable to the bearer of the security certificate according to its terms but not by reason of an indorsement.

(3) "Broker" means a person defined as a broker or dealer under the federal securities laws, but without excluding a bank acting in that capacity.

(4) "Certificated security" means a security that is represented by a certificate.

(5) "Clearing corporation" means:

(i) a person that is registered as a "clearing agency" under the federal securities laws;

(ii) a federal reserve bank; or

(iii) any other person that provides clearance or settlement services with respect to financial assets that would require it to register as a clearing agency under the federal securities laws but for an exclusion or exemption from the registration requirement, if its activities as a clearing corporation, including promulgation of rules, are subject to regulation by a federal or state governmental authority.

(6) "Communicate" means to:

(i) send a signed writing; or

(ii) transmit information by any mechanism agreed upon by the persons transmitting and receiving the information.

(7) "Entitlement holder" means a person identified in the records of a securities intermediary as the person having a security entitlement against the securities intermediary. If a person acquires a security entitlement by virtue of Section 8—501(b)(2) or (3), that person is the entitlement holder.

(8) "Entitlement order" means a notification communicated to a securities intermediary directing transfer or redemption of a financial asset to which the entitlement holder has a security entitlement.

(9) "Financial asset," except as otherwise provided in Section 8—103, means:

(i) a security;

(ii) an obligation of a person or a share, participation, or other interest in a person or in property or an enterprise of a person, which is, or is of a type, dealt in or traded on financial markets, or which is recognized in any area in which it is issued or dealt in as a medium for investment; or

(iii) any property that is held by a securities intermediary for another person in a securities account if the securities intermediary has expressly agreed with the other person that the property is to be treated as a financial asset under this Article.

As context requires, the term means either the interest itself or the means by which a person's claim to it is evidenced, including a certificated or uncertificated security, a security certificate, or a security entitlement.

(10) "Good faith," for purposes of the obligation of good faith in the performance or enforcement of contracts or duties within this Article, means honesty in fact and the observance of reasonable commercial standards of fair dealing.

(11) "Indorsement" means a signature that alone or accompanied by other words is made on a security certificate in registered form or on a separate document for the purpose of assigning, transferring, or redeeming the security or granting a power to assign, transfer, or redeem it.

(12) "Instruction" means a notification communicated to the issuer of an uncertificated security which directs that the transfer of the security be registered or that the security be redeemed.

(13) "Registered form," as applied to a certificated security, means a form in which:

(i) the security certificate specifies a person entitled to the security; and

(ii) a transfer of the security may be registered upon books maintained for that purpose by or on behalf of the issuer, or the security certificate so states.

(14) "Securities intermediary" means:

(i) a clearing corporation; or

(ii) a person, including a bank or broker, that in the ordinary course of its business maintains securities accounts for others and is acting in that capacity.

(15) "Security," except as otherwise provided in Section 8—103, means an obligation of an issuer or a share, participation, or other interest in an issuer or in property or an enterprise of an issuer:

(i) which is represented by a security certificate in bearer or registered form, or the transfer of which may be registered upon books maintained for that purpose by or on behalf of the issuer;

(ii) which is one of a class or series or by its terms is divisible into a class or series of shares, participations, interests, or obligations; and

(iii) which:

(A) is, or is of a type, dealt in or traded on securities exchanges or securities markets; or

(B) is a medium for investment and by its terms expressly provides that it is a security governed by this Article.

(16) "Security certificate" means a certificate representing a security.

(17) "Security entitlement" means the rights and property interest of an entitlement holder with respect to a financial asset specified in Part 5.

(18) "Uncertificated security" means a security that is not represented by a certificate.

(b) Other definitions applying to this Article and the sections in which they appear are:

Appropriate person	Section 8—107
Control	Section 8—106
Delivery	Section 8—301
Investment company security	Section 8—103
Issuer	Section 8—201
Overissue	Section 8—210
Protected purchaser	Section 8—303
Securities account	Section 8—501

(c) In addition, Article 1 contains general definitions and principles of construction and interpretation applicable throughout this Article.

(d) The characterization of a person, business, or transaction for purposes of this Article does not determine the characterization of the person, business, or transaction for purposes of any other law, regulation, or rule.

§ 8—103. Rules for Determining Whether Certain Obligations and Interests Are Securities or Financial Assets.

(a) A share or similar equity interest issued by a corporation, business trust, joint stock company, or similar entity is a security.

(b) An "investment company security" is a security. "Investment company security" means a share or similar equity interest issued by an entity that is registered as an investment company under the federal investment company laws, an interest in a unit investment trust that is so registered, or a face-amount certificate issued by a face-amount certificate company that is so registered. Investment company security does not include an insurance policy or endowment policy or annuity contract issued by an insurance company.

(c) An interest in a partnership or limited liability company is not a security unless it is dealt in or traded on securities exchanges or in securities markets, its terms expressly provide that it is a security governed by this Article, or it is an investment company security. However, an interest in a partnership or limited liability company is a financial asset if it is held in a securities account.

(d) A writing that is a security certificate is governed by this Article and not by Article 3, even though it also meets the requirements of that Article. However, a negotiable instrument governed by Article 3 is a financial asset if it is held in a securities account.

(e) An option or similar obligation issued by a clearing corporation to its participants is not a security, but is a financial asset.

(f) A commodity contract, as defined in Section 9—115, is not a security or a financial asset.

§ 8—104. Acquisition of Security or Financial Asset or Interest Therein.

(a) A person acquires a security or an interest therein, under this Article, if:

    (1) the person is a purchaser to whom a security is delivered pursuant to Section 8—301; or

    (2) the person acquires a security entitlement to the security pursuant to Section 8—501.

(b) A person acquires a financial asset, other than a security, or an interest therein, under this Article, if the person acquires a security entitlement to the financial asset.

(c) A person who acquires a security entitlement to a security or other financial asset has the rights specified in Part 5, but is a purchaser of any security, security entitlement, or other financial asset held by the securities intermediary only to the extent provided in Section 8—503.

(d) Unless the context shows that a different meaning is intended, a person who is required by other law, regulation, rule, or agreement to transfer, deliver, present, surrender, exchange, or otherwise put in the possession of another person a security or financial asset satisfies that requirement by causing the other person to acquire an interest in the security or financial asset pursuant to subsection (a) or (b).

§ 8—105. Notice of Adverse Claim.

(a) A person has notice of an adverse claim if:

    (1) the person knows of the adverse claim;

    (2) the person is aware of facts sufficient to indicate that there is a significant probability that the adverse claim exists and deliberately avoids information that would establish the existence of the adverse claim; or

    (3) the person has a duty, imposed by statute or regulation, to investigate whether an adverse claim exists, and the investigation so required would establish the existence of the adverse claim.

(b) Having knowledge that a financial asset or interest therein is or has been transferred by a representative imposes no duty of inquiry into the rightfulness of a transaction and is not notice of an adverse claim. However, a person who knows that a representative has transferred a financial asset or interest therein in a transaction that is, or whose proceeds are being used, for the individual benefit of the representative or otherwise in breach of duty has notice of an adverse claim.

(c) An act or event that creates a right to immediate performance of the principal obligation represented by a security certificate or sets a date on or after which the certificate is to be presented or surrendered for redemption or exchange does not itself constitute notice of an adverse claim except in the case of a transfer more than:

    (1) one year after a date set for presentment or surrender for redemption or exchange; or

    (2) six months after a date set for payment of money against presentation or surrender of the certificate, if money was available for payment on that date.

(d) A purchaser of a certificated security has notice of an adverse claim if the security certificate:

    (1) whether in bearer or registered form, has been indorsed "for collection" or "for surrender" or for some other purpose not involving transfer; or

    (2) is in bearer form and has on it an unambiguous statement that it is the property of a person other than the transferor, but the mere writing of a name on the certificate is not such a statement.

(e) Filing of a financing statement under Article 9 is not notice of an adverse claim to a financial asset.

§ 8—106. Control.

(a) A purchaser has "control" of a certificated security in bearer form if the certificated security is delivered to the purchaser.

(b) A purchaser has "control" of a certificated security in registered form if the certificated security is delivered to the purchaser, and:

    (1) the certificate is indorsed to the purchaser or in blank by an effective indorsement; or

    (2) the certificate is registered in the name of the purchaser, upon original issue or registration of transfer by the issuer.

(c) A purchaser has "control" of an uncertificated security if:

(1) the uncertificated security is delivered to the purchaser; or

(2) the issuer has agreed that it will comply with instructions originated by the purchaser without further consent by the registered owner.

(d) A purchaser has "control" of a security entitlement if:

(1) the purchaser becomes the entitlement holder; or

(2) the securities intermediary has agreed that it will comply with entitlement orders originated by the purchaser without further consent by the entitlement holder.

(e) If an interest in a security entitlement is granted by the entitlement holder to the entitlement holder's own securities intermediary, the securities intermediary has control.

(f) A purchaser who has satisfied the requirements of subsection (c)(2) or (d)(2) has control even if the registered owner in the case of subsection (c)(2) or the entitlement holder in the case of subsection (d)(2) retains the right to make substitutions for the uncertificated security or security entitlement, to originate instructions or entitlement orders to the issuer or securities intermediary, or otherwise to deal with the uncertificated security or security entitlement.

(g) An issuer or a securities intermediary may not enter into an agreement of the kind described in subsection (c)(2) or (d)(2) without the consent of the registered owner or entitlement holder, but an issuer or a securities intermediary is not required to enter into such an agreement even though the registered owner or entitlement holder so directs. An issuer or securities intermediary that has entered into such an agreement is not required to confirm the existence of the agreement to another party unless requested to do so by the registered owner or entitlement holder.

§ 8—107. Whether Indorsement, Instruction, or Entitlement Order Is Effective.

(a) "Appropriate person" means:

(1) with respect to an indorsement, the person specified by a security certificate or by an effective special indorsement to be entitled to the security;

(2) with respect to an instruction, the registered owner of an uncertificated security;

(3) with respect to an entitlement order, the entitlement holder;

(4) if the person designated in paragraph (1), (2), or (3) is deceased, the designated person's successor taking under other law or the designated person's personal representative acting for the estate of the decedent; or

(5) if the person designated in paragraph (1), (2), or (3) lacks capacity, the designated person's guardian,

conservator, or other similar representative who has power under other law to transfer the security or financial asset.

(b) An indorsement, instruction, or entitlement order is effective if:

(1) it is made by the appropriate person;

(2) it is made by a person who has power under the law of agency to transfer the security or financial asset on behalf of the appropriate person, including, in the case of an instruction or entitlement order, a person who has control under Section 8—106(c)(2) or (d)(2); or

(3) the appropriate person has ratified it or is otherwise precluded from asserting its ineffectiveness.

(c) An indorsement, instruction, or entitlement order made by a representative is effective even if:

(1) the representative has failed to comply with a controlling instrument or with the law of the State having jurisdiction of the representative relationship, including any law requiring the representative to obtain court approval of the transaction; or

(2) the representative's action in making the indorsement, instruction, or entitlement order or using the proceeds of the transaction is otherwise a breach of duty.

(d) If a security is registered in the name of or specially indorsed to a person described as a representative, or if a securities account is maintained in the name of a person described as a representative, an indorsement, instruction, or entitlement order made by the person is effective even though the person is no longer serving in the described capacity.

(e) Effectiveness of an indorsement, instruction, or entitlement order is determined as of the date the indorsement, instruction, or entitlement order is made, and an indorsement, instruction, or entitlement order does not become ineffective by reason of any later change of circumstances.

§ 8—108. Warranties in Direct Holding.

(a) A person who transfers a certificated security to a purchaser for value warrants to the purchaser, and an indorser, if the transfer is by indorsement, warrants to any subsequent purchaser, that:

(1) the certificate is genuine and has not been materially altered;

(2) the transferor or indorser does not know of any fact that might impair the validity of the security;

(3) there is no adverse claim to the security;

(4) the transfer does not violate any restriction on transfer;

(5) if the transfer is by indorsement, the indorsement is made by an appropriate person, or if the indorsement is by an agent, the agent has actual authority to act on behalf of the appropriate person; and

(6) the transfer is otherwise effective and rightful.

(b) A person who originates an instruction for registration of transfer of an uncertificated security to a purchaser for value warrants to the purchaser that:

(1) the instruction is made by an appropriate person, or if the instruction is by an agent, the agent has actual authority to act on behalf of the appropriate person;

(2) the security is valid;

(3) there is no adverse claim to the security; and

(4) at the time the instruction is presented to the issuer:

(i) the purchaser will be entitled to the registration of transfer;

(ii) the transfer will be registered by the issuer free from all liens, security interests, restrictions, and claims other than those specified in the instruction;

(iii) the transfer will not violate any restriction on transfer; and

(iv) the requested transfer will otherwise be effective and rightful.

(c) A person who transfers an uncertificated security to a purchaser for value and does not originate an instruction in connection with the transfer warrants that:

(1) the uncertificated security is valid;

(2) there is no adverse claim to the security;

(3) the transfer does not violate any restriction on transfer; and

(4) the transfer is otherwise effective and rightful.

(d) A person who indorses a security certificate warrants to the issuer that:

(1) there is no adverse claim to the security; and

(2) the indorsement is effective.

(e) A person who originates an instruction for registration of transfer of an uncertificated security warrants to the issuer that:

(1) the instruction is effective; and

(2) at the time the instruction is presented to the issuer the purchaser will be entitled to the registration of transfer.

(f) A person who presents a certificated security for registration of transfer or for payment or exchange warrants to the issuer that the person is entitled to the registration, payment, or exchange, but a purchaser for value and without notice of adverse claims to whom transfer is registered war-

rants only that the person has no knowledge of any unauthorized signature in a necessary indorsement.

(g) If a person acts as agent of another in delivering a certificated security to a purchaser, the identity of the principal was known to the person to whom the certificate was delivered, and the certificate delivered by the agent was received by the agent from the principal or received by the agent from another person at the direction of the principal, the person delivering the security certificate warrants only that the delivering person has authority to act for the principal and does not know of any adverse claim to the certificated security.

(h) A secured party who redelivers a security certificate received, or after payment and on order of the debtor delivers the security certificate to another person, makes only the warranties of an agent under subsection (g).

(i) Except as otherwise provided in subsection (g), a broker acting for a customer makes to the issuer and a purchaser the warranties provided in subsections (a) through (f). A broker that delivers a security certificate to its customer, or causes its customer to be registered as the owner of an uncertificated security, makes to the customer the warranties provided in subsection (a) or (b), and has the rights and privileges of a purchaser under this section. The warranties of and in favor of the broker acting as an agent are in addition to applicable warranties given by and in favor of the customer.

§ 8—109. Warranties in Indirect Holding.

(a) A person who originates an entitlement order to a securities intermediary warrants to the securities intermediary that:

(1) the entitlement order is made by an appropriate person, or if the entitlement order is by an agent, the agent has actual authority to act on behalf of the appropriate person; and

(2) there is no adverse claim to the security entitlement.

(b) A person who delivers a security certificate to a securities intermediary for credit to a securities account or originates an instruction with respect to an uncertificated security directing that the uncertificated security be credited to a securities account makes to the securities intermediary the warranties specified in Section 8—108(a) or (b).

(c) If a securities intermediary delivers a security certificate to its entitlement holder or causes its entitlement holder to be registered as the owner of an uncertificated security, the securities intermediary makes to the entitlement holder the warranties specified in Section 8—108(a) or (b).

§ 8—110. Applicability; Choice of Law.

(a) The local law of the issuer's jurisdiction, as specified in subsection (d), governs:

(1) the validity of a security;

(2) the rights and duties of the issuer with respect to registration of transfer;

(3) the effectiveness of registration of transfer by the issuer;

(4) whether the issuer owes any duties to an adverse claimant to a security; and

(5) whether an adverse claim can be asserted against a person to whom transfer of a certificated or uncertificated security is registered or a person who obtains control of an uncertificated security.

(b) The local law of the securities intermediary's jurisdiction, as specified in subsection (e), governs:

(1) acquisition of a security entitlement from the securities intermediary;

(2) the rights and duties of the securities intermediary and entitlement holder arising out of a security entitlement;

(3) whether the securities intermediary owes any duties to an adverse claimant to a security entitlement; and

(4) whether an adverse claim can be asserted against a person who acquires a security entitlement from the securities intermediary or a person who purchases a security entitlement or interest therein from an entitlement holder.

(c) The local law of the jurisdiction in which a security certificate is located at the time of delivery governs whether an adverse claim can be asserted against a person to whom the security certificate is delivered.

(d) "Issuer's jurisdiction" means the jurisdiction under which the issuer of the security is organized or, if permitted by the law of that jurisdiction, the law of another jurisdiction specified by the issuer. An issuer organized under the law of this State may specify the law of another jurisdiction as the law governing the matters specified in subsection (a)(2) through (5).

(e) The following rules determine a "securities intermediary's jurisdiction" for purposes of this section:

(1) If an agreement between the securities intermediary and its entitlement holder specifies that it is governed by the law of a particular jurisdiction, that jurisdiction is the securities intermediary's jurisdiction.

(2) If an agreement between the securities intermediary and its entitlement holder does not specify the governing law as provided in paragraph (1), but expressly specifies that the securities account is maintained at an office in a particular jurisdiction, that jurisdiction is the securities intermediary's jurisdiction.

(3) If an agreement between the securities intermediary and its entitlement holder does not specify a jurisdiction

as provided in paragraph (1) or (2), the securities intermediary's jurisdiction is the jurisdiction in which is located the office identified in an account statement as the office serving the entitlement holder's account.

(4) If an agreement between the securities intermediary and its entitlement holder does not specify a jurisdiction as provided in paragraph (1) or (2) and an account statement does not identify an office serving the entitlement holder's account as provided in paragraph (3), the securities intermediary's jurisdiction is the jurisdiction in which is located the chief executive office of the securities intermediary.

(f) A securities intermediary's jurisdiction is not determined by the physical location of certificates representing financial assets, or by the jurisdiction in which is organized the issuer of the financial asset with respect to which an entitlement holder has a security entitlement, or by the location of facilities for data processing or other record keeping concerning the account.

§ 8–111. Clearing Corporation Rules.

A rule adopted by a clearing corporation governing rights and obligations among the clearing corporation and its participants in the clearing corporation is effective even if the rule conflicts with this [Act] and affects another party who does not consent to the rule.

§ 8–112. Creditor's Legal Process.

(a) The interest of a debtor in a certificated security may be reached by a creditor only by actual seizure of the security certificate by the officer making the attachment or levy, except as otherwise provided in subsection (d). However, a certificated security for which the certificate has been surrendered to the issuer may be reached by a creditor by legal process upon the issuer.

(b) The interest of a debtor in an uncertificated security may be reached by a creditor only by legal process upon the issuer at its chief executive office in the United States, except as otherwise provided in subsection (d).

(c) The interest of a debtor in a security entitlement may be reached by a creditor only by legal process upon the securities intermediary with whom the debtor's securities account is maintained, except as otherwise provided in subsection (d).

(d) The interest of a debtor in a certificated security for which the certificate is in the possession of a secured party, or in an uncertificated security registered in the name of a secured party, or a security entitlement maintained in the name of a secured party, may be reached by a creditor by legal process upon the secured party.

(e) A creditor whose debtor is the owner of a certificated security, uncertificated security, or security entitlement is entitled to aid from a court of competent jurisdiction, by injunction or otherwise, in reaching the certificated security, uncertificated security, or security entitlement or in satisfying the claim by means allowed at law or in equity in regard to property that cannot readily be reached by other legal process.

§ 8—113. Statute of Frauds Inapplicable.

A contract or modification of a contract for the sale or purchase of a security is enforceable whether or not there is a writing signed or record authenticated by a party against whom enforcement is sought, even if the contract or modification is not capable of performance within one year of its making.

§ 8—114. Evidentiary Rules Concerning Certificated Securities.

The following rules apply in an action on a certificated security against the issuer:

(1) Unless specifically denied in the pleadings, each signature on a security certificate or in a necessary indorsement is admitted.

(2) If the effectiveness of a signature is put in issue, the burden of establishing effectiveness is on the party claiming under the signature, but the signature is presumed to be genuine or authorized.

(3) If signatures on a security certificate are admitted or established, production of the certificate entitles a holder to recover on it unless the defendant establishes a defense or a defect going to the validity of the security.

(4) If it is shown that a defense or defect exists, the plaintiff has the burden of establishing that the plaintiff or some person under whom the plaintiff claims is a person against whom the defense or defect cannot be asserted.

§ 8—115. Securities Intermediary and Others Not Liable to Adverse Claimant.

A securities intermediary that has transferred a financial asset pursuant to an effective entitlement order, or a broker or other agent or bailee that has dealt with a financial asset at the direction of its customer or principal, is not liable to a person having an adverse claim to the financial asset, unless the securities intermediary, or broker or other agent or bailee:

(1) took the action after it had been served with an injunction, restraining order, or other legal process enjoining it from doing so, issued by a court of competent jurisdiction, and had a reasonable opportunity to act on the injunction, restraining order, or other legal process; or

(2) acted in collusion with the wrongdoer in violating the rights of the adverse claimant; or

(3) in the case of a security certificate that has been stolen, acted with notice of the adverse claim.

§ 8—116. Securities Intermediary as Purchaser for Value.

A securities intermediary that receives a financial asset and establishes a security entitlement to the financial asset in favor of an entitlement holder is a purchaser for value of the financial asset. A securities intermediary that acquires a security entitlement to a financial asset from another securities intermediary acquires the security entitlement for value if the securities intermediary acquiring the security entitlement establishes a security entitlement to the financial asset in favor of an entitlement holder.

Part 2   Issue and Issuer

§ 8—201. Issuer.

(a) With respect to an obligation on or a defense to a security, an "issuer" includes a person that:

(1) places or authorizes the placing of its name on a security certificate, other than as authenticating trustee, registrar, transfer agent, or the like, to evidence a share, participation, or other interest in its property or in an enterprise, or to evidence its duty to perform an obligation represented by the certificate;

(2) creates a share, participation, or other interest in its property or in an enterprise, or undertakes an obligation, that is an uncertificated security;

(3) directly or indirectly creates a fractional interest in its rights or property, if the fractional interest is represented by a security certificate; or

(4) becomes responsible for, or in place of, another person described as an issuer in this section.

(b) With respect to an obligation on or defense to a security, a guarantor is an issuer to the extent of its guaranty, whether or not its obligation is noted on a security certificate.

(c) With respect to a registration of a transfer, issuer means a person on whose behalf transfer books are maintained.

§ 8—202. Issuer's Responsibility and Defenses; Notice of Defect or Defense.

(a) Even against a purchaser for value and without notice, the terms of a certificated security include terms stated on the certificate and terms made part of the security by reference on the certificate to another instrument, indenture, or document or to a constitution, statute, ordinance, rule, regulation, order, or the like, to the extent the terms referred to do not conflict with terms stated on the certificate. A reference under this subsection does not of itself charge a purchaser for value with notice of a defect going to the validity of the security, even if the certificate expressly states that a person accepting it admits notice. The terms of an uncertificated security include those stated in any instrument, indenture, or document or in a constitution, statute, ordinance, rule, regulation, order, or the like, pursuant to which the security is issued.

(b) The following rules apply if an issuer asserts that a security is not valid:

(1) A security other than one issued by a government or governmental subdivision, agency, or instrumentality, even though issued with a defect going to its validity, is valid in the hands of a purchaser for value and without notice of the particular defect unless the defect involves a violation of a constitutional provision. In that case, the security is valid in the hands of a purchaser for value and without notice of the defect, other than one who takes by original issue.

(2) Paragraph (1) applies to an issuer that is a government or governmental subdivision, agency, or instrumentality only if there has been substantial compliance with the legal requirements governing the issue or the issuer has received a substantial consideration for the issue as a whole or for the particular security and a stated purpose of the issue is one for which the issuer has power to borrow money or issue the security.

(c) Except as otherwise provided in Section 8—205, lack of genuineness of a certificated security is a complete defense, even against a purchaser for value and without notice.

(d) All other defenses of the issuer of a security, including nondelivery and conditional delivery of a certificated security, are ineffective against a purchaser for value who has taken the certificated security without notice of the particular defense.

(e) This section does not affect the right of a party to cancel a contract for a security "when, as and if issued" or "when distributed" in the event of a material change in the character of the security that is the subject of the contract or in the plan or arrangement pursuant to which the security is to be issued or distributed.

(f) If a security is held by a securities intermediary against whom an entitlement holder has a security entitlement with respect to the security, the issuer may not assert any defense that the issuer could not assert if the entitlement holder held the security directly.

§ 8—203. Staleness as Notice of Defect or Defense.

After an act or event, other than a call that has been revoked, creating a right to immediate performance of the principal obligation represented by a certificated security or setting a date on or after which the security is to be presented or surrendered for redemption or exchange, a purchaser is charged with notice of any defect in its issue or defense of the issuer, if the act or event:

(1) requires the payment of money, the delivery of a certificated security, the registration of transfer of an uncertificated security, or any of them on presentation

or surrender of the security certificate, the money or security is available on the date set for payment or exchange, and the purchaser takes the security more than one year after that date; or

(2) is not covered by paragraph (1) and the purchaser takes the security more than two years after the date set for surrender or presentation or the date on which performance became due.

§ 8—204. Effect of Issuer's Restriction on Transfer.

A restriction on transfer of a security imposed by the issuer, even if otherwise lawful, is ineffective against a person without knowledge of the restriction unless:

(1) the security is certificated and the restriction is noted conspicuously on the security certificate; or

(2) the security is uncertificated and the registered owner has been notified of the restriction.

§ 8—205. Effect of Unauthorized Signature on Security Certificate.

An unauthorized signature placed on a security certificate before or in the course of issue is ineffective, but the signature is effective in favor of a purchaser for value of the certificated security if the purchaser is without notice of the lack of authority and the signing has been done by:

(1) an authenticating trustee, registrar, transfer agent, or other person entrusted by the issuer with the signing of the security certificate or of similar security certificates, or the immediate preparation for signing of any of them; or

(2) an employee of the issuer, or of any of the persons listed in paragraph (1), entrusted with responsible handling of the security certificate.

§ 8—206. Completion of Alteration of Security Certificate.

(a) If a security certificate contains the signatures necessary to its issue or transfer but is incomplete in any other respect:

(1) any person may complete it by filling in the blanks as authorized; and

(2) even if the blanks are incorrectly filled in, the security certificate as completed is enforceable by a purchaser who took it for value and without notice of the incorrectness.

(b) A complete security certificate that has been improperly altered, even if fraudulently, remains enforceable, but only according to its original terms.

§ 8—207. Rights and Duties of Issuer with Respect to Registered Owners.

(a) Before due presentment for registration of transfer of a certificated security in registered form or of an instruction requesting registration of transfer of an uncertificated security, the issuer or indenture trustee may treat the registered owner as the person exclusively entitled to vote, receive notifications, and otherwise exercise all the rights and powers of an owner.

(b) This Article does not affect the liability of the registered owner of a security for a call, assessment, or the like.

§ 8—208. Effect of Signature of Authenticating Trustee, Registrar, or Transfer Agent.

(a) A person signing a security certificate as authenticating trustee, registrar, transfer agent, or the like, warrants to a purchaser for value of the certificated security, if the purchaser is without notice of a particular defect, that:

(1) the certificate is genuine;

(2) the person's own participation in the issue of the security is within the person's capacity and within the scope of the authority received by the person from the issuer; and

(3) the person has reasonable grounds to believe that the certificated security is in the form and within the amount the issuer is authorized to issue.

(b) Unless otherwise agreed, a person signing under subsection (a) does not assume responsibility for the validity of the security in other respects.

§ 8—209. Issuer's Lien.

A lien in favor of an issuer upon a certificated security is valid against a purchaser only if the right of the issuer to the lien is noted conspicuously on the security certificate.

§ 8—210. Overissue.

(a) In this section, "overissue" means the issue of securities in excess of the amount the issuer has corporate power to issue, but an overissue does not occur if appropriate action has cured the overissue.

(b) Except as otherwise provided in subsections (c) and (d), the provisions of this Article which validate a security or compel its issue or reissue do not apply to the extent that validation, issue, or reissue would result in overissue.

(c) If an identical security not constituting an overissue is reasonably available for purchase, a person entitled to issue or validation may compel the issuer to purchase the security and deliver it if certificated or register its transfer if uncertificated, against surrender of any security certificate the person holds.

(d) If a security is not reasonably available for purchase, a person entitled to issue or validation may recover from the issuer the price the person or the last purchaser for value paid for it with interest from the date of the person's demand.

Part 3 Transfer of Certificated and Uncertificated Securities

§ 8—301. Delivery.

(a) Delivery of a certificated security to a purchaser occurs when:

(1) the purchaser acquires possession of the security certificate;

(2) another person, other than a securities intermediary, either acquires possession of the security certificate on behalf of the purchaser or, having previously acquired possession of the certificate, acknowledges that it holds for the purchaser; or

(3) a securities intermediary acting on behalf of the purchaser acquires possession of the security certificate, only if the certificate is in registered form and has been specially indorsed to the purchaser by an effective indorsement.

(b) Delivery of an uncertificated security to a purchaser occurs when:

(1) the issuer registers the purchaser as the registered owner, upon original issue or registration of transfer; or

(2) another person, other than a securities intermediary, either becomes the registered owner of the uncertificated security on behalf of the purchaser or, having previously become the registered owner, acknowledges that it holds for the purchaser.

§ 8—302. Rights of Purchaser.

(a) Except as otherwise provided in subsections (b) and (c), upon delivery of a certificated or uncertificated security to a purchaser, the purchaser acquires all rights in the security that the transferor had or had power to transfer.

(b) A purchaser of a limited interest acquires rights only to the extent of the interest purchased.

(c) A purchaser of a certificated security who as a previous holder had notice of an adverse claim does not improve its position by taking from a protected purchaser.

§ 8—303. Protected Purchaser.

(a) "Protected purchaser" means a purchaser of a certificated or uncertificated security, or of an interest therein, who:

(1) gives value;

(2) does not have notice of any adverse claim to the security; and

(3) obtains control of the certificated or uncertificated security.

(b) In addition to acquiring the rights of a purchaser, a protected purchaser also acquires its interest in the security free of any adverse claim.

§ 8—304. Indorsement.

(a) An indorsement may be in blank or special. An indorsement in blank includes an indorsement to bearer. A special indorsement specifies to whom a security is to be transferred or who has power to transfer it. A holder may convert a blank indorsement to a special indorsement.

(b) An indorsement purporting to be only of part of a security certificate representing units intended by the issuer to be separately transferable is effective to the extent of the indorsement.

(c) An indorsement, whether special or in blank, does not constitute a transfer until delivery of the certificate on which it appears or, if the indorsement is on a separate document, until delivery of both the document and the certificate.

(d) If a security certificate in registered form has been delivered to a purchaser without a necessary indorsement, the purchaser may become a protected purchaser only when the indorsement is supplied. However, against a transferor, a transfer is complete upon delivery and the purchaser has a specifically enforceable right to have any necessary indorsement supplied.

(e) An indorsement of a security certificate in bearer form may give notice of an adverse claim to the certificate, but it does not otherwise affect a right to registration that the holder possesses.

(f) Unless otherwise agreed, a person making an indorsement assumes only the obligations provided in Section 8—108 and not an obligation that the security will be honored by the issuer.

§ 8—305. Instruction.

(a) If an instruction has been originated by an appropriate person but is incomplete in any other respect, any person may complete it as authorized and the issuer may rely on it as completed, even though it has been completed incorrectly.

(b) Unless otherwise agreed, a person initiating an instruction assumes only the obligations imposed by Section 8—108 and not an obligation that the security will be honored by the issuer.

§ 8—306. Effect of Guaranteeing Signature, Indorsement, or Instruction.

(a) A person who guarantees a signature of an indorser of a security certificate warrants that at the time of signing:

(1) the signature was genuine;

(2) the signer was an appropriate person to indorse, or if the signature is by an agent, the agent had actual authority to act on behalf of the appropriate person; and

(3) the signer had legal capacity to sign.

(b) A person who guarantees a signature of the originator of an instruction warrants that at the time of signing:

(1) the signature was genuine;

(2) the signer was an appropriate person to originate the instruction, or if the signature is by an agent, the agent had actual authority to act on behalf of the appropriate person, if the person specified in the instruction as the registered owner was, in fact, the registered owner, as to which fact the signature guarantor does not make a warranty; and

(3) the signer had legal capacity to sign.

(c) A person who specially guarantees the signature of an originator of an instruction makes the warranties of a signature guarantor under subsection (b) and also warrants that at the time the instruction is presented to the issuer:

(1) the person specified in the instruction as the registered owner of the uncertificated security will be the registered owner; and

(2) the transfer of the uncertificated security requested in the instruction will be registered by the issuer free from all liens, security interests, restrictions, and claims other than those specified in the instruction.

(d) A guarantor under subsections (a) and (b) or a special guarantor under subsection (c) does not otherwise warrant the rightfulness of the transfer.

(e) A person who guarantees an indorsement of a security certificate makes the warranties of a signature guarantor under subsection (a) and also warrants the rightfulness of the transfer in all respects.

(f) A person who guarantees an instruction requesting the transfer of an uncertificated security makes the warranties of a special signature guarantor under subsection (c) and also warrants the rightfulness of the transfer in all respects.

(g) An issuer may not require a special guaranty of signature, a guaranty of indorsement, or a guaranty of instruction as a condition to registration of transfer.

(h) The warranties under this section are made to a person taking or dealing with the security in reliance on the guaranty, and the guarantor is liable to the person for loss resulting from their breach. An indorser or originator of an instruction whose signature, indorsement, or instruction has been guaranteed is liable to a guarantor for any loss suffered by the guarantor as a result of breach of the warranties of the guarantor.

§ 8—307. Purchaser's Right to Requisites for Registration of Transfer.

Unless otherwise agreed, the transferor of a security on due demand shall supply the purchaser with proof of authority to transfer or with any other requisite necessary to obtain registration of the transfer of the security, but if the transfer is not for value, a transferor need not comply unless the purchaser pays the necessary expenses. If the transferor fails within a reasonable time to comply with the demand, the purchaser may reject or rescind the transfer.

Part 4   Registration

§ 8—401. Duty of Issuer to Register Transfer.

(a) If a certificated security in registered form is presented to an issuer with a request to register transfer or an instruction is presented to an issuer with a request to register transfer of an uncertificated security, the issuer shall register the transfer as requested if:

(1) under the terms of the security the person seeking registration of transfer is eligible to have the security registered in its name;

(2) the indorsement or instruction is made by the appropriate person or by an agent who has actual authority to act on behalf of the appropriate person;

(3) reasonable assurance is given that the indorsement or instruction is genuine and authorized (Section 8—402);

(4) any applicable law relating to the collection of taxes has been complied with;

(5) the transfer does not violate any restriction on transfer imposed by the issuer in accordance with Section 8—204;

(6) a demand that the issuer not register transfer has not become effective under Section 8—403, or the issuer has complied with Section 8—403(b) but no legal process or indemnity bond is obtained as provided in Section 8—403(d); and

(7) the transfer is in fact rightful or is to a protected purchaser.

(b) If an issuer is under a duty to register a transfer of a security, the issuer is liable to a person presenting a certificated security or an instruction for registration or to the person's principal for loss resulting from unreasonable delay in registration or failure or refusal to register the transfer.

§ 8—402. Assurance That Indorsement or Instruction Is Effective.

(a) An issuer may require the following assurance that each necessary indorsement or each instruction is genuine and authorized:

(1) in all cases, a guaranty of the signature of the person making an indorsement or originating an instruction including, in the case of an instruction, reasonable assurance of identity;

(2) if the indorsement is made or the instruction is originated by an agent, appropriate assurance of actual authority to sign;

(3) if the indorsement is made or the instruction is originated by a fiduciary pursuant to Section 8—107(a)(4) or (a)(5), appropriate evidence of appointment or incumbency;

(4) if there is more than one fiduciary, reasonable assurance that all who are required to sign have done so; and

(5) if the indorsement is made or the instruction is originated by a person not covered by another provision of this subsection, assurance appropriate to the case corresponding as nearly as may be to the provisions of this subsection.

(b) An issuer may elect to require reasonable assurance beyond that specified in this section.

(c) In this section:

(1) "Guaranty of the signature" means a guaranty signed by or on behalf of a person reasonably believed by the issuer to be responsible. An issuer may adopt standards with respect to responsibility if they are not manifestly unreasonable.

(2) "Appropriate evidence of appointment or incumbency" means:

(i) in the case of a fiduciary appointed or qualified by a court, a certificate issued by or under the direction or supervision of the court or an officer thereof and dated within 60 days before the date of presentation for transfer; or

(ii) in any other case, a copy of a document showing the appointment or a certificate issued by or on behalf of a person reasonably believed by an issuer to be responsible or, in the absence of that document or certificate, other evidence the issuer reasonably considers appropriate.

§ 8—403. Demand That Issuer Not Register Transfer.

(a) A person who is an appropriate person to make an indorsement or originate an instruction may demand that the issuer not register transfer of a security by communicating to the issuer a notification that identifies the registered owner and the issue of which the security is a part and provides an address for communications directed to the person making the demand. The demand is effective only if it is received by the issuer at a time and in a manner affording the issuer reasonable opportunity to act on it.

(b) If a certificated security in registered form is presented to an issuer with a request to register transfer or an instruction is presented to an issuer with a request to register transfer of an uncertificated security after a demand that the issuer not register transfer has become effective, the issuer shall promptly communicate to (i) the person who initiated the demand at the address provided in the demand and (ii) the person who presented the security for registration of transfer or initiated the instruction requesting registration of transfer a notification stating that:

(1) the certificated security has been presented for registration of transfer or the instruction for registration of transfer of the uncertificated security has been received;

(2) a demand that the issuer not register transfer had previously been received; and

(3) the issuer will withhold registration of transfer for a period of time stated in the notification in order to provide the person who initiated the demand an opportunity to obtain legal process or an indemnity bond.

(c) The period described in subsection (b)(3) may not exceed 30 days after the date of communication of the notification. A shorter period may be specified by the issuer if it is not manifestly unreasonable.

(d) An issuer is not liable to a person who initiated a demand that the issuer not register transfer for any loss the person suffers as a result of registration of a transfer pursuant to an effective indorsement or instruction if the person who initiated the demand does not, within the time stated in the issuer's communication, either:

(1) obtain an appropriate restraining order, injunction, or other process from a court of competent jurisdiction enjoining the issuer from registering the transfer; or

(2) file with the issuer an indemnity bond, sufficient in the issuer's judgment to protect the issuer and any transfer agent, registrar, or other agent of the issuer involved from any loss it or they may suffer by refusing to register the transfer.

(e) This section does not relieve an issuer from liability for registering transfer pursuant to an indorsement or instruction that was not effective.

§ 8—404. Wrongful Registration.

(a) Except as otherwise provided in Section 8—406, an issuer is liable for wrongful registration of transfer if the issuer has registered a transfer of a security to a person not entitled to it, and the transfer was registered:

(1) pursuant to an ineffective indorsement or instruction;

(2) after a demand that the issuer not register transfer became effective under Section 8—403(a) and the issuer did not comply with Section 8—403(b);

(3) after the issuer had been served with an injunction, restraining order, or other legal process enjoining

it from registering the transfer, issued by a court of competent jurisdiction, and the issuer had a reasonable opportunity to act on the injunction, restraining order, or other legal process; or

(4) by an issuer acting in collusion with the wrongdoer.

(b) An issuer that is liable for wrongful registration of transfer under subsection (a) on demand shall provide the person entitled to the security with a like certificated or uncertificated security, and any payments or distributions that the person did not receive as a result of the wrongful registration. If an overissue would result, the issuer's liability to provide the person with a like security is governed by Section 8—210.

(c) Except as otherwise provided in subsection (a) or in a law relating to the collection of taxes, an issuer is not liable to an owner or other person suffering loss as a result of the registration of a transfer of a security if registration was made pursuant to an effective indorsement or instruction.

§ 8—405. Replacement of Lost, Destroyed, or Wrongfully Taken Security Certificate.

(a) If an owner of a certificated security, whether in registered or bearer form, claims that the certificate has been lost, destroyed, or wrongfully taken, the issuer shall issue a new certificate if the owner:

(1) so requests before the issuer has notice that the certificate has been acquired by a protected purchaser;

(2) files with the issuer a sufficient indemnity bond; and

(3) satisfies other reasonable requirements imposed by the issuer.

(b) If, after the issue of a new security certificate, a protected purchaser of the original certificate presents it for registration of transfer, the issuer shall register the transfer unless an overissue would result. In that case, the issuer's liability is governed by Section 8—210. In addition to any rights on the indemnity bond, an issuer may recover the new certificate from a person to whom it was issued or any person taking under that person, except a protected purchaser.

§ 8—406. Obligation to Notify Issuer of Lost, Destroyed, or Wrongfully Taken Security Certificate.

If a security certificate has been lost, apparently destroyed, or wrongfully taken, and the owner fails to notify the issuer of that fact within a reasonable time after the owner has notice of it and the issuer registers a transfer of the security before receiving notification, the owner may not assert against the issuer a claim for registering the transfer under Section 8-404 or a claim to a new security certificate under Section 8-405.

§ 8—407. Authenticating Trustee, Transfer Agent, and Registrar.

A person acting as authenticating trustee, transfer agent, registrar, or other agent for an issuer in the registration of a transfer of its securities, in the issue of new security certificates or uncertificated securities, or in the cancellation of surrendered security certificates has the same obligation to the holder or owner of a certificated or uncertificated security with regard to the particular functions performed as the issuer has in regard to those functions.

Part 5 Security Entitlements

§ 8—501. Securities Account; Acquisition of Security Entitlement from Securities Intermediary.

(a) "Securities account" means an account to which a financial asset is or may be credited in accordance with an agreement under which the person maintaining the account undertakes to treat the person for whom the account is maintained as entitled to exercise the rights that comprise the financial asset.

(b) Except as otherwise provided in subsections (d) and (e), a person acquires a security entitlement if a securities intermediary:

(1) indicates by book entry that a financial asset has been credited to the person's securities account;

(2) receives a financial asset from the person or acquires a financial asset for the person and, in either case, accepts it for credit to the person's securities account; or

(3) becomes obligated under other law, regulation, or rule to credit a financial asset to the person's securities account.

(c) If a condition of subsection (b) has been met, a person has a security entitlement even though the securities intermediary does not itself hold the financial asset.

(d) If a securities intermediary holds a financial asset for another person, and the financial asset is registered in the name of, payable to the order of, or specially indorsed to the other person, and has not been indorsed to the securities intermediary or in blank, the other person is treated as holding the financial asset directly rather than as having a security entitlement with respect to the financial asset.

(e) Issuance of a security is not establishment of a security entitlement.

§ 8—502. Assertion of Adverse Claim against Entitlement Holder.

An action based on an adverse claim to a financial asset, whether framed in conversion, replevin, constructive trust, equitable lien, or other theory, may not be asserted against a person who acquires a security entitlement under Section 8—501 for value and without notice of the adverse claim.

§ 8—503. Property Interest of Entitlement Holder in Financial Asset Held by Securities Intermediary.

(a) To the extent necessary for a securities intermediary to satisfy all security entitlements with respect to a particular financial asset, all interests in that financial asset held by the securities intermediary are held by the securities intermediary for the entitlement holders, are not property of the securities intermediary, and are not subject to claims of creditors of the securities intermediary, except as otherwise provided in Section 8—511.

(b) An entitlement holder's property interest with respect to a particular financial asset under subsection (a) is a pro rata property interest in all interests in that financial asset held by the securities intermediary, without regard to the time the entitlement holder acquired the security entitlement or the time the securities intermediary acquired the interest in that financial asset.

(c) An entitlement holder's property interest with respect to a particular financial asset under subsection (a) may be enforced against the securities intermediary only by exercise of the entitlement holder's rights under Sections 8—505 through 8—508.

(d) An entitlement holder's property interest with respect to a particular financial asset under subsection (a) may be enforced against a purchaser of the financial asset or interest therein only if:

(1) insolvency proceedings have been initiated by or against the securities intermediary;

(2) the securities intermediary does not have sufficient interests in the financial asset to satisfy the security entitlements of all of its entitlement holders to that financial asset;

(3) the securities intermediary violated its obligations under Section 8—504 by transferring the financial asset or interest therein to the purchaser; and

(4) the purchaser is not protected under subsection (e).

The trustee or other liquidator, acting on behalf of all entitlement holders having security entitlements with respect to a particular financial asset, may recover the financial asset, or interest therein, from the purchaser. If the trustee or other liquidator elects not to pursue that right, an entitlement holder whose security entitlement remains unsatisfied has the right to recover its interest in the financial asset from the purchaser.

(e) An action based on the entitlement holder's property interest with respect to a particular financial asset under subsection (a), whether framed in conversion, replevin, constructive trust, equitable lien, or other theory, may not be asserted against any purchaser of a financial asset or interest therein who gives value, obtains control, and does not act in collusion with the securities intermediary in violating the securities intermediary's obligations under Section 8—504.

§ 8—504. Duty of Securities Intermediary to Maintain Financial Asset.

(a) A securities intermediary shall promptly obtain and thereafter maintain a financial asset in a quantity corresponding to the aggregate of all security entitlements it has established in favor of its entitlement holders with respect to that financial asset. The securities intermediary may maintain those financial assets directly or through one or more other securities intermediaries.

(b) Except to the extent otherwise agreed by its entitlement holder, a securities intermediary may not grant any security interests in a financial asset it is obligated to maintain pursuant to subsection (a).

(c) A securities intermediary satisfies the duty in subsection (a) if:

(1) the securities intermediary acts with respect to the duty as agreed upon by the entitlement holder and the securities intermediary; or

(2) in the absence of agreement, the securities intermediary exercises due care in accordance with reasonable commercial standards to obtain and maintain the financial asset.

(d) This section does not apply to a clearing corporation that is itself the obligor of an option or similar obligation to which its entitlement holders have security entitlements.

§ 8—505. Duty of Securities Intermediary with Respect to Payments and Distributions.

(a) A securities intermediary shall take action to obtain a payment or distribution made by the issuer of a financial asset. A securities intermediary satisfies the duty if:

(1) the securities intermediary acts with respect to the duty as agreed upon by the entitlement holder and the securities intermediary; or

(2) in the absence of agreement, the securities intermediary exercises due care in accordance with reasonable commercial standards to attempt to obtain the payment or distribution.

(b) A securities intermediary is obligated to its entitlement holder for a payment or distribution made by the issuer of a financial asset if the payment or distribution is received by the securities intermediary.

§ 8—506. Duty of Securities Intermediary to Exercise Rights as Directed by Entitlement Holder.

A securities intermediary shall exercise rights with respect to a financial asset if directed to do so by an entitlement holder. A securities intermediary satisfies the duty if:

(1) the securities intermediary acts with respect to the duty as agreed upon by the entitlement holder and the securities intermediary; or

(2) in the absence of agreement, the securities intermediary either places the entitlement holder in a position to exercise the rights directly or exercises due care in accordance with reasonable commercial standards to follow the direction of the entitlement holder.

§ 8—507. Duty of Securities Intermediary to Comply with Entitlement Order.

(a) A securities intermediary shall comply with an entitlement order if the entitlement order is originated by the appropriate person, the securities intermediary has had reasonable opportunity to assure itself that the entitlement order is genuine and authorized, and the securities intermediary has had reasonable opportunity to comply with the entitlement order. A securities intermediary satisfies the duty if:

(1) the securities intermediary acts with respect to the duty as agreed upon by the entitlement holder and the securities intermediary; or

(2) in the absence of agreement, the securities intermediary exercises due care in accordance with reasonable commercial standards to comply with the entitlement order.

(b) If a securities intermediary transfers a financial asset pursuant to an ineffective entitlement order, the securities intermediary shall reestablish a security entitlement in favor of the person entitled to it, and pay or credit any payments or distributions that the person did not receive as a result of the wrongful transfer. If the securities intermediary does not reestablish a security entitlement, the securities intermediary is liable to the entitlement holder for damages.

§ 8—508. Duty of Securities Intermediary to Change Entitlement Holder's Position to Other Form of Security Holding.

A securities intermediary shall act at the direction of an entitlement holder to change a security entitlement into another available form of holding for which the entitlement holder is eligible, or to cause the financial asset to be transferred to a securities account of the entitlement holder with another securities intermediary. A securities intermediary satisfies the duty if:

(1) the securities intermediary acts as agreed upon by the entitlement holder and the securities intermediary; or

(2) in the absence of agreement, the securities intermediary exercises due care in accordance with reasonable commercial standards to follow the direction of the entitlement holder.

§ 8—509. Specification of Duties of Securities Intermediary by Other Statute or Regulation; Manner of Performance of Duties of Securities Intermediary and Exercise of Rights of Entitlement Holder.

(a) If the substance of a duty imposed upon a securities intermediary by Sections 8—504 through 8—508 is the subject of other statute, regulation, or rule, compliance with that statute, regulation, or rule satisfies the duty.

(b) To the extent that specific standards for the performance of the duties of a securities intermediary or the exercise of the rights of an entitlement holder are not specified by other statute, regulation, or rule or by agreement between the securities intermediary and entitlement holder, the securities intermediary shall perform its duties and the entitlement holder shall exercise its rights in a commercially reasonable manner.

(c) The obligation of a securities intermediary to perform the duties imposed by Sections 8—504 through 8—508 is subject to:

(1) rights of the securities intermediary arising out of a security interest under a security agreement with the entitlement holder or otherwise; and

(2) rights of the securities intermediary under other law, regulation, rule, or agreement to withhold performance of its duties as a result of unfulfilled obligations of the entitlement holder to the securities intermediary.

(d) Sections 8—504 through 8—508 do not require a securities intermediary to take any action that is prohibited by other statute, regulation, or rule.

§ 8—510. Rights of Purchaser of Security Entitlement from Entitlement Holder.

(a) An action based on an adverse claim to a financial asset or security entitlement, whether framed in conversion, replevin, constructive trust, equitable lien, or other theory, may not be asserted against a person who purchases a security entitlement, or an interest therein, from an entitlement holder if the purchaser gives value, does not have notice of the adverse claim, and obtains control.

(b) If an adverse claim could not have been asserted against an entitlement holder under Section 8—502, the adverse claim cannot be asserted against a person who purchases a security entitlement, or an interest therein, from the entitlement holder.

(c) In a case not covered by the priority rules in Article 9, a purchaser for value of a security entitlement, or an interest therein, who obtains control has priority over a purchaser of a security entitlement, or an interest therein, who does not obtain control. Purchasers who have control rank equally, except that a securities intermediary as purchaser has priority over a conflicting purchaser who has control unless otherwise agreed by the securities intermediary.

§ 8—511. Priority among Security Interests and Entitlement Holders.

(a) Except as otherwise provided in subsections (b) and (c), if a securities intermediary does not have sufficient interests in a particular financial asset to satisfy both its obligations to entitlement holders who have security entitlements to that financial asset and its obligation to a creditor of the securities intermediary who has a security interest in that financial asset, the claims of entitlement holders, other than the creditor, have priority over the claim of the creditor.

(b) A claim of a creditor of a securities intermediary who has a security interest in a financial asset held by a securities intermediary has priority over claims of the securities intermediary's entitlement holders who have security entitlements with respect to that financial asset if the creditor has control over the financial asset.

(c) If a clearing corporation does not have sufficient financial assets to satisfy both its obligations to entitlement holders who have security entitlements with respect to a financial asset and its obligation to a creditor of the clearing corporation who has a security interest in that financial asset, the claim of the creditor has priority over the claims of entitlement holders.

Part 6 Transition Provisions for Revised Article 8

§ 8—601. Effective Date.

This [Act] takes effect....

§ 8—602. Repeals.

This [Act] repeals....

§ 8—603. Savings Clause.

(a) This [Act] does not affect an action or proceeding commenced before this [Act] takes effect.

(b) If a security interest in a security is perfected at the date this [Act] takes effect, and the action by which the security interest was perfected would suffice to perfect a security interest under this [Act], no further action is required to continue perfection. If a security interest in a security is perfected at the date this [Act] takes effect but the action by which the security interest was perfected would not suffice to perfect a security interest under this [Act], the security interest remains perfected for a period of four months after the effective date and continues perfected thereafter if appropriate action to perfect under this [Act] is taken within that period. If a security interest is perfected at the date this [Act] takes effect and the security interest can be perfected by filing under this [Act], a financing statement signed by the secured party instead of the debtor may be filed within that period to continue perfection or thereafter to perfect.

Article 9

SECURED TRANSACTIONS; SALES OF ACCOUNTS AND CHATTEL PAPER

Note: *The adoption of this Article should be accompanied by the repeal of existing statutes dealing with conditional sales, trust receipts, factor's liens where the factor is given a nonpossessory lien, chattel mortgages, crop mortgages, mortgages on railroad equipment, assignment of accounts and generally statutes regulating security interests in personal property.*

Where the state has a retail installment selling act or small loan act, that legislation should be carefully examined to determine what changes in those acts are needed to conform them to this Article. This Article primarily sets out rules defining rights of a secured party against persons dealing with the debtor; it does not prescribe regulations and controls which may be necessary to curb abuses arising in the small loan business or in the financing of consumer purchases on credit. Accordingly there is no intention to repeal existing regulatory acts in those fields by enactment or re-enactment of Article 9. See Section 9—203(4) and the Note thereto.

Part 1 Short Title, Applicability and Definitions

§ 9—101. Short Title.

This Article shall be known and may be cited as Uniform Commercial Code—Secured Transactions.

§ 9—102. Policy and Subject Matter of Article.

(1) Except as otherwise provided in Section 9—104 on excluded transactions, this Article applies

    (a) to any transaction (regardless of its form) which is intended to create a security interest in personal property or fixtures including goods, documents, instruments, general intangibles, chattel paper or accounts; and also

    (b) to any sale of accounts or chattel paper.

(2) This Article applies to security interests created by contract including pledge, assignment, chattel mortgage, chattel trust, trust deed, factor's lien, equipment trust, conditional sale, trust receipt, other lien or title retention contract and lease or consignment intended as security. This Article does not apply to statutory liens except as provided in Section 9—310.

(3) The application of this Article to a security interest in a secured obligation is not affected by the fact that the obligation is itself secured by a transaction or interest to which this Article does not apply.

§ 9—103. Perfection of Security Interest in Multiple State Transactions.

(1) Documents, instruments and ordinary goods.

    (a) This subsection applies to documents, instruments, rights to proceeds of written letters of credit, and goods other than those covered by a certificate of title described in subsection (2), mobile goods described in subsection (3), and minerals described in subsection (5).

    (b) Except as otherwise provided in this subsection, perfection and the effect of perfection or non-perfection of a security interest in collateral are governed by the law of the jurisdiction where the collateral is when the last event occurs on which is based the assertion that the security interest is perfected or unperfected.

    (c) If the parties to a transaction creating a purchase money security interest in goods in one jurisdiction understand at the time that the security interest attaches that the goods will be kept in another jurisdiction, then the law of the other jurisdiction governs the perfection and the effect of perfection or non-perfection of the security interest from the time it attaches until thirty days after the debtor receives possession of the goods and thereafter if the goods are taken to the other jurisdiction before the end of the thirty-day period.

    (d) When collateral is brought into and kept in this state while subject to a security interest perfected under the law of the jurisdiction from which the collateral was removed, the security interest remains perfected, but if action is required by Part 3 of this Article to perfect the security interest,

        (i) if the action is not taken before the expiration of the period of perfection in the other jurisdiction or the end of four months after the collateral is brought into this state, whichever period first expires, the security interest becomes unperfected at the end of that period and is thereafter deemed to have been unperfected as against a person who became a purchaser after removal;

        (ii) if the action is taken before the expiration of the period specified in subparagraph (i), the security interest continues perfected thereafter;

        (iii) for the purpose of priority over a buyer of consumer goods (subsection (2) of Section 9—307), the period of the effectiveness of a filing in the jurisdiction from which the collateral is removed is governed by the rules with respect to perfection in subparagraphs (i) and (ii).

(2) Certificate of title.

    (a) This subsection applies to goods covered by a certificate of title issued under a statute of this state or of another jurisdiction under the law of which indication of a security interest on the certificate is required as a condition of perfection.

    (b) Except as otherwise provided in this subsection, perfection and the effect of perfection or non-perfection of the security interest are governed by the law (including the conflict of laws rules) of the jurisdiction issuing the certificate until four months after the goods are removed from that jurisdiction and thereafter until the goods are registered in another jurisdiction, but in any event not beyond surrender of the certificate. After the expiration of that period, the goods are not covered by the certificate of title within the meaning of this section.

(c) Except with respect to the rights of a buyer described in the next paragraph, a security interest, perfected in another jurisdiction otherwise than by notation on a certificate of title, in goods brought into this state and thereafter covered by a certificate of title issued by this state is subject to the rules stated in paragraph (d) of subsection (1).

(d) If goods are brought into this state while a security interest therein is perfected in any manner under the law of the jurisdiction from which the goods are removed and a certificate of title is issued by this state and the certificate does not show that the goods are subject to the security interest or that they may be subject to security interests not shown on the certificate, the security interest is subordinate to the rights of a buyer of the goods who is not in the business of selling goods of that kind to the extent that he gives value and receives delivery of the goods after issuance of the certificate and without knowledge of the security interest.

(3) Accounts, general intangibles and mobile goods.

(a) This subsection applies to accounts (other than an account described in subsection (5) on minerals) and general intangibles (other than uncertificated securities) and to goods which are mobile and which are of a type normally used in more than one jurisdiction, such as motor vehicles, trailers, rolling stock, airplanes, shipping containers, road building and construction machinery and commercial harvesting machinery and the like, if the goods are equipment or are inventory leased or held for lease by the debtor to others, and are not covered by a certificate of title described in subsection (2).

(b) The law (including the conflict of laws rules) of the jurisdiction in which the debtor is located governs the perfection and the effect of perfection or non-perfection of the security interest.

(c) If, however, the debtor is located in a jurisdiction which is not a part of the United States, and which does not provide for perfection of the security interest by filing or recording in that jurisdiction, the law of the jurisdiction in the United States in which the debtor has its major executive office in the United States governs the perfection and the effect of perfection or non-perfection of the security interest through filing. In the alternative, if the debtor is located in a jurisdiction which is not a part of the United States or Canada and the collateral is accounts or general intangibles for money due or to become due, the security interest may be perfected by notification to the account debtor. As used in this paragraph, "United States" includes its territories and possessions and the Commonwealth of Puerto Rico.

(d) A debtor shall be deemed located at his place of business if he has one, at his chief executive office if he has more than one place of business, otherwise at his residence. If, however, the debtor is a foreign air carrier under the Federal Aviation Act of 1958, as amended, it shall be deemed located at the designated office of the agent upon whom service of process may be made on behalf of the foreign air carrier.

(e) A security interest perfected under the law of the jurisdiction of the location of the debtor is perfected until the expiration of four months after a change of the debtor's location to another jurisdiction, or until perfection would have ceased by the law of the first jurisdiction, whichever period first expires. Unless perfected in the new jurisdiction before the end of that period, it becomes unperfected thereafter and is deemed to have been unperfected as against a person who became a purchaser after the change.

(4) Chattel paper.

The rules stated for goods in subsection (1) apply to a possessory security interest in chattel paper. The rules stated for accounts in subsection (3) apply to a nonpossessory security interest in chattel paper, but the security interest may not be perfected by notification to the account debtor.

(5) Minerals.

Perfection and the effect of perfection or non-perfection of a security interest which is created by a debtor who has an interest in minerals or the like (including oil and gas) before extraction and which attaches thereto as extracted, or which attaches to an account resulting from the sale thereof at the wellhead or minehead are governed by the law (including the conflict of laws rules) of the jurisdiction wherein the wellhead or minehead is located.

(6) Investment property.

(a) This subsection applies to investment property.

(b) Except as otherwise provided in paragraph (f), during the time that a security certificate is located in a jurisdiction, perfection of a security interest, the effect of perfection or non-perfection, and the priority of a security interest in the certificated security represented thereby are governed by the local law of that jurisdiction.

(c) Except as otherwise provided in paragraph (f), perfection of a security interest, the effect of perfection or non-perfection, and the priority of a security interest in an uncertificated security are governed by the local law of the issuer's jurisdiction as specified in Section 8—110(d).

(d) Except as otherwise provided in paragraph (f), perfection of a security interest, the effect of perfection or non-perfection, and the priority of a security interest in a security entitlement or securities account are governed by the local law of the securities intermediary's jurisdiction as specified in Section 8—110(e).

(e) Except as otherwise provided in paragraph (f), perfection of a security interest, the effect of perfection or non-perfection, and the priority of a security interest in a commodity contract or commodity account are governed by the local law of the commodity intermediary's jurisdiction. The following rules determine a "commodity intermediary's jurisdiction" for purposes of this paragraph:

(i) If an agreement between the commodity intermediary and commodity customer specifies that it is governed by the law of a particular jurisdiction, that jurisdiction is the commodity intermediary's jurisdiction.

(ii) If an agreement between the commodity intermediary and commodity customer does not specify the governing law as provided in subparagraph (i), but expressly specifies that the commodity account is maintained at an office in a particular jurisdiction, that jurisdiction is the commodity intermediary's jurisdiction.

(iii) If an agreement between the commodity intermediary and commodity customer does not specify a jurisdiction as provided in subparagraphs (i) or (ii), the commodity intermediary's jurisdiction is the jurisdiction in which is located the office identified in an account statement as the office serving the commodity customer's account.

(iv) If an agreement between the commodity intermediary and commodity customer does not specify a jurisdiction as provided in subparagraphs (i) or (ii) and an account statement does not identify an office serving the commodity customer's account as provided in subparagraph (iii), the commodity intermediary's jurisdiction is the jurisdiction in which is located the chief executive office of the commodity intermediary.

(f) Perfection of a security interest by filing, automatic perfection of a security interest in investment property granted by a broker or securities intermediary, and automatic perfection of a security interest in a commodity contract or commodity account granted by a commodity intermediary are governed by the local law of the jurisdiction in which the debtor is located.

§ 9—104. Transactions Excluded From Article.

This Article does not apply

(a) to a security interest subject to any statute of the United States, to the extent that such statute governs the rights of parties to and third parties affected by transactions in particular types of property; or

(b) to a landlord's lien; or

(c) to a lien given by statute or other rule of law for services or materials except as provided in Section 9—310 on priority of such liens; or

(d) to a transfer of a claim for wages, salary or other compensation of an employee; or

(e) to a transfer by a government or governmental subdivision or agency; or

(f) to a sale of accounts or chattel paper as part of a sale of the business out of which they arose, or an assignment of accounts or chattel paper which is for the purpose of collection only, or a transfer of a right to payment under a contract to an assignee who is also to do the performance under the contract or a transfer of a single account to an assignee in whole or partial satisfaction of a preexisting indebtedness; or

(g) to a transfer of an interest in or claim in or under any policy of insurance, except as provided with respect to proceeds (Section 9—306) and priorities in proceeds (Section 9—312); or

(h) to a right represented by a judgment (other than a judgment taken on a right to payment which was collateral); or

(i) to any right of set-off; or

(j) except to the extent that provision is made for fixtures in Section 9—313, to the creation or transfer of an interest in or lien on real estate, including a lease or rents thereunder; or

(k) to a transfer in whole or in part of any claim arising out of tort; or

(l) to a transfer of an interest in any deposit account (subsection (1) of Section 9—105), except as provided with respect to proceeds (Section 9—306) and priorities in proceeds (Section 9—312).

(m) to a transfer of an interest in a letter of credit other than the rights to proceeds of a written letter of credit.

§ 9—105. Definitions and Index of Definitions.

(1) In this Article unless the context otherwise requires:

(a) "Account debtor" means the person who is obligated on an account, chattel paper or general intangible;

(b) "Chattel paper" means a writing or writings which evidence both a monetary obligation and a security interest in or a lease of specific goods, but a charter or other contract involving the use or hire of a vessel is not chattel paper. When a transaction is evidenced both by such a security agreement or a lease and by an instrument or a series of instruments, the group of writings taken together constitutes chattel paper;

(c) "Collateral" means the property subject to a security interest, and includes accounts and chattel paper which have been sold;

(d) "Debtor" means the person who owes payment or other performance of the obligation secured, whether or not he owns or has rights in the collateral, and includes the seller of accounts or chattel paper. Where the debtor and the owner of the collateral are not the same person, the term "debtor" means the owner of the collateral in any provision of the Article dealing with the collateral, the obligor in any provision dealing with the obligation, and may include both where the context so requires;

(e) "Deposit account" means a demand, time, savings, passbook or like account maintained with a bank, savings and loan association, credit union or like organization, other than an account evidenced by a certificate of deposit;

(f) "Document" means document of title as defined in the general definitions of Article 1 (Section 1—201), and a receipt of the kind described in subsection (2) of Section 7—201;

(g) "Encumbrance" includes real estate mortgages and other liens on real estate and all other rights in real estate that are not ownership interests;

(h) "Goods" includes all things which are movable at the time the security interest attaches or which are fixtures (Section 9—313), but does not include money, documents, instruments, investment property, commodity contracts accounts, chattel paper, general intangibles, or minerals or the like (including oil and gas) before extraction. "Goods" also includes standing timber which is to be cut and removed under a conveyance or contract for sale, the unborn young of animals, and growing crops;

(i) "Instrument" means a negotiable instrument (defined in Section 3—104), or any other writing which evidences a right to the payment of money and is not itself a security agreement or lease and is of a type which is in ordinary course of business transferred by delivery with any necessary indorsement or assignment. The term does not include investment property.

(j) "Mortgage" means a consensual interest created by a real estate mortgage, a trust deed on real estate, or the like;

(k) An advance is made "pursuant to commitment" if the secured party has bound himself to make it, whether or not a subsequent event of default or other event not within his control has relieved or may relieve him from his obligation;

(l) "Security agreement" means an agreement which creates or provides for a security interest;

(m) "Secured party" means a lender, seller or other person in whose favor there is a security interest, including a person to whom accounts or chattel paper have been sold. When the holders of obligations issued under an indenture of trust, equipment trust agreement or the like are represented by a trustee or other person, the representative is the secured party;

(n) "Transmitting utility" means any person primarily engaged in the railroad, street railway or trolley bus business, the electric or electronics communications transmission business, the transmission of goods by pipeline, or the transmission or the production and transmission of electricity, steam, gas or water, or the provision of sewer service.

(2) Other definitions applying to this Article and the sections in which they appear are:

"Account". Section 9—106.

"Attach". Section 9—203.

"Commodity contract". Section 9—115.

"Commodity customer". Section 9—115.

"Commodity intermediary". Section 9—115.

"Construction mortgage". Section 9—313(1).

"Consumer goods". Section 9—109(1).

"Control". Section 9—115.

"Equipment". Section 9—109(2).

"Farm products". Section 9—109(3).

"Fixture". Section 9—313(1).

"Fixture filing". Section 9—313(1).

"General intangibles". Section 9—106.

"Inventory". Section 9—109(4).

"Investment property". Section 9—115.

"Lien creditor". Section 9—301(3).

"Proceeds". Section 9—306(1).

"Purchase money security interest". Section 9—107.

"United States". Section 9—103.

(3) The following definitions in other Articles apply to this Article:

"Broker". Section. 8—102.

"Certified security". Section 8—102.

"Check". Section 3—104.

"Clearing corporation". Section 8—102.

"Contract for sale". Section 2—106.

"Control". Section 8—106.

"Delivery". Section 8—301.

"Entitlement holder". Section 8—102.

"Financial asset". Section 8—102.

"Holder in due course". Section 3—302.

"Letter of credit". Section 5—102.

"Note". Section 3—104.

"Proceeds of a letter of credit". Section 5—114(a).

"Sale". Section 2—106.

"Securities intermediary". Section 8—102.

"Security". Section 8—102.

"Security certificate". Section 8—102.

"Security entitlement". Section 8—102.

"Uncertertificated security". Section 8—102.

(4) In addition Article 1 contains general definitions and principles of construction and interpretation applicable throughout this Article.

§ 9—106. Definitions: "Account"; "General Intangibles".

"Account" means any right to payment for goods sold or leased or for services rendered which is not evidenced by an instrument or chattel paper, whether or not it has been earned by performance. "General intangibles" means any personal property (including things in action) other than goods, accounts, chattel paper, documents, instruments, investment property, rights to proceeds of written letters of credit, and money. All rights to payment earned or unearned under a charter or other contract involving the use or hire of a vessel and all rights incident to the charter or contract are accounts.

§ 9—107. Definitions: "Purchase Money Security Interest".

A security interest is a "purchase money security interest" to the extent that it is

(a) taken or retained by the seller of the collateral to secure all or part of its price; or

(b) taken by a person who by making advances or incurring an obligation gives value to enable the debtor to acquire rights in or the use of collateral if such value is in fact so used.

§ 9—108. When After-Acquired Collateral Not Security for Antecedent Debt.

Where a secured party makes an advance, incurs an obligation, releases a perfected security interest, or otherwise gives new value which is to be secured in whole or in part by after-acquired property his security interest in the after-acquired collateral shall be deemed to be taken for new value and not as security for an antecedent debt if the debtor acquires his rights in such collateral either in the ordinary course of his business or under a contract of purchase made pursuant to the security agreement within a reasonable time after new value is given.

§ 9—109. Classification of Goods; "Consumer Goods"; "Equipment"; "Farm Products"; "Inventory".

Goods are

(1) "consumer goods" if they are used or bought for use primarily for personal, family or household purposes;

(2) "equipment" if they are used or bought for use primarily in business (including farming or a profession) or by a debtor who is a non-profit organization or a governmental subdivision or agency or if the goods are not included in the definitions of inventory, farm products or consumer goods;

(3) "farm products" if they are crops or livestock or supplies used or produced in farming operations or if they are products of crops or livestock in their unmanufactured states (such as ginned cotton, wool-clip, maple syrup, milk and eggs), and if they are in the possession of a debtor engaged in raising, fattening, grazing or other farming operations. If goods are farm products they are neither equipment nor inventory;

(4) "inventory" if they are held by a person who holds them for sale or lease or to be furnished under contracts of service or if he has so furnished them, or if they are raw materials, work in process or materials used or consumed in a business. Inventory of a person is not to be classified as his equipment.

§ 9—110. Sufficiency of Description.

For purposes of this Article any description of personal property or real estate is sufficient whether or not it is specific if it reasonably identifies what is described.

§ 9—111. Applicability of Bulk Transfer Laws.

The creation of a security interest is not a bulk transfer under Article 6 (see Section 6—103).

§ 9—112. Where Collateral Is Not Owned by Debtor.

Unless otherwise agreed, when a secured party knows that collateral is owned by a person who is not the debtor, the owner of the collateral is entitled to receive from the secured party any surplus under Section 9—502(2) or under Section 9—504(1), and is not liable for the debt or for any deficiency after resale, and he has the same right as the debtor

(a) to receive statements under Section 9—208;

(b) to receive notice of and to object to a secured party's proposal to retain the collateral in satisfaction of the indebtedness under Section 9—505;

(c) to redeem the collateral under Section 9—506;

(d) to obtain injunctive or other relief under Section 9—507(1); and

(e) to recover losses caused to him under Section 9—208(2).

§ 9—113. Security Interests Arising Under Article on Sales or Under Article on Leases.

A security interest arising solely under the Article on Sales (Article 2) or the Article on Leases is subject to the provisions of this Article except that to the extent that and so long as the debtor does not have or does not lawfully obtain possession of the goods

(a) no security agreement is necessary to make the security interest enforceable; and

(b) no filing is required to perfect the security interest; and

(c) the rights of the secured party on default by the debtor are governed (i) by the Article on Sales (Article 2) in the case of a security interest arising solely under such Article or (ii) by the Article on Leases (Article 2A) in the case of a security interest arising solely under such Article.

§ 9—114. Consignment.

(1) A person who delivers goods under a consignment which is not a security interest and who would be required to file under this Article by paragraph (3)(c) of Section 2—326 has priority over a secured party who is or becomes a creditor of the consignee and who would have a perfected security interest in the goods if they were the property of the consignee, and also has priority with respect to identifiable cash proceeds received on or before delivery of the goods to a buyer, if

(a) the consignor complies with the filing provision of the Article on Sales with respect to consignments (paragraph (3)(c) of Section 2—326) before the consignee receives possession of the goods; and

(b) the consignor gives notification in writing to the holder of the security interest if the holder has filed a financing statement covering the same types of goods before the date of the filing made by the consignor; and

(c) the holder of the security interest receives the notification within five years before the consignee receives possession of the goods; and

(d) the notification states that the consignor expects to deliver goods on consignment to the consignee, describing the goods by item or type.

(2) In the case of a consignment which is not a security interest and in which the requirements of the preceding subsection have not been met, a person who delivers goods to another is subordinate to a person who would have a perfected security interest in the goods if they were the property of the debtor.

§ 9—115. Investment Property.

(1) In this Article:

(a) "Commodity account" means an account maintained by a commodity intermediary in which a commodity contract is carried for a commodity customer.

(b) "Commodity contract" means a commodity futures contract, an option on a commodity futures contract, a commodity option, or other contract that, in each case, is:

(i) traded on or subject to the rules of a board of trade that has been designated as a contract market for such a contract pursuant to the federal commodities laws; or

(ii) traded on a foreign commodity board of trade, exchange, or market, and is carried on the books of a commodity intermediary for a commodity customer.

(c) "Commodity customer" means a person for whom a commodity intermediary carries a commodity contract on its books.

(d) "Commodity intermediary" means:

(i) a person who is registered as a futures commission merchant under the federal commodities laws; or

(ii) a person who in the ordinary course of its business provides clearance or settlement services for a board of trade that has been designated as a contract market pursuant to the federal commodities laws.

(e) "Control" with respect to a certificated security, uncertificated security, or security entitlement has the meaning specified in Section 8—106. A secured party has control over a commodity contract if by agreement among the commodity customer, the commodity intermediary, and the secured party, the commodity intermediary has agreed that it will apply any value distributed on account of the commodity contract as directed by the secured party without further consent by the commodity customer. If a commodity customer grants a security interest in a commodity contract to its own commodity intermediary, the commodity intermediary as secured party has control. A secured party has control over a securities account or commodity account if the secured party has control over all security entitlements or commodity contracts carried in the securities account or commodity account.

(f) "Investment property" means:

(i) a security, whether certificated or uncertificated;

(ii) a security entitlement;

(iii) a securities account;

(iv) a commodity contract; or

(v) a commodity account.

(2) Attachment or perfection of a security interest in a securities account is also attachment or perfection of a security interest in all security entitlements carried in the securities account. Attachment or perfection of a security interest in a commodity account is also attachment or perfection of a security interest in all commodity contracts carried in the commodity account.

(3) A description of collateral in a security agreement or financing statement is sufficient to create or perfect a security interest in a certificated security, uncertificated security, security entitlement, securities account, commodity contract, or commodity account whether it describes the collateral by those terms, or as investment property, or by description of the underlying security, financial asset, or commodity contract. A description of investment property collateral in a security agreement or financing statement is sufficient if it identifies the collateral by specific listing, by category, by quantity, by a computational or allocational

formula or procedure, or by any other method, if the identity of the collateral is objectively determinable.

(4) Perfection of a security interest in investment property is governed by the following rules:

(a) A security interest in investment property may be perfected by control.

(b) Except as otherwise provided in paragraphs (c) and (d), a security interest in investment property may be perfected by filing.

(c) If the debtor is a broker or securities intermediary a security interest in investment property is perfected when it attaches. The filing of a financing statement with respect to a security interest in investment property granted by a broker or securities intermediary has no effect for purposes of perfection or priority with respect to that security interest.

(d) If a debtor is a commodity, intermediary, a security interest in a commodity contract or a commodity account is perfected when it attaches. The filing of a financing statement with respect to a security interest in a commodity contract or a commodity account granted by a commodity intermediary has no effect for purposes of perfection or priority with respect to that security interest.

(5) Priority between conflicting security interests in the same investment property is governed by the following rules:

(a) A security interest of a secured party who has control over investment property has priority over a security interest of a secured party who does not have control over the investment property.

(b) Except as otherwise provided in paragraphs (c) and (d), conflicting security interests of secured parties each of whom has control rank equally.

(c) Except as otherwise agreed by the securities intermediary, a security interest in a security entitlement or a securities account granted to the debtor's own securities intermediary has priority over any security interest granted by the debtor to another secured party.

(d) Except as otherwise agreed by the commodity intermediary, a security interest in a commodity contract or a commodity account granted to the debtor's own commodity intermediary has priority over any security interest granted by the debtor to another secured party.

(e) Conflicting security interests granted by a broker, a securities intermediary, or a commodity intermediary which are perfected without control rank equally.

(f) In all other cases, priority between conflicting security interests in investment property is governed by Section 9—312(5), (6), and (7). Section 9—312(4) does not apply to investment property.

(6) If a security certificate in registered form is delivered to a secured party pursuant to agreement, a written security agreement is not required for attachment or enforceability of the security interest, delivery suffices for perfection of the security interest, and the security interest has priority over a conflicting security interest perfected by means other than control, even if a necessary indorsement is lacking.

§ 9—116. Security Interest Arising in Purchase or Delivery of Financial Asset.

(1) If a person buys a financial asset through a securities intermediary in a transaction in which the buyer is obligated to pay the purchase price to the securities intermediary at the time of the purchase, and the securities intermediary credits the financial asset to the buyer's securities account before the buyer pays the securities intermediary, the securities intermediary has a security interest in the buyer's security entitlement securing the buyer's obligation to pay. A security agreement is not required for attachment or enforceability of the security interest, and the security interest is automatically perfected.

(2) If a certificated security, or other financial asset represented by a writing which in the ordinary course of business is transferred by delivery with any necessary indorsement or assignment is delivered pursuant to an agreement between persons in the business of dealing with such securities or financial assets and the agreement calls for delivery versus payment, the person delivering the certificate or other financial asset has a security interest in the certificated security or other financial asset securing the seller's right to receive payment. A security agreement is not required for attachment or enforceability of the security interest, and the security interest is automatically perfected.

Part 2 Validity of Security Agreement and Rights of Parties Thereto

§ 9—201. General Validity of Security Agreement.

Except as otherwise provided by this Act a security agreement is effective according to its terms between the parties, against purchasers of the collateral and against creditors. Nothing in this Article validates any charge or practice illegal under any statute or regulation thereunder governing usury, small loans, retail installment sales, or the like, or extends the application of any such statute or regulation to any transaction not otherwise subject thereto.

§ 9—202. Title to Collateral Immaterial.

Each provision of this Article with regard to rights, obligations and remedies applies whether title to collateral is in the secured party or in the debtor.

§ 9—203. Attachment and Enforceability of Security Interest; Proceeds; Formal Requisites.

(1) Subject to the provisions of Section 4—210 on the security interest of a collecting bank, Sections 9—115 and 9—116 on security interests in investment property, and Section 9—113 on a security interest arising under the

Articles on Sales and Leases, a security interest is not enforceable against the debtor or third parties with respect to the collateral and does not attach unless:

(a) the collateral is in the possession of the secured party pursuant to agreement, the collateral is investment property and the secured party has control pursuant to agreement, or the debtor has signed a security agreement which contains a description of the collateral and in addition, when the security interest covers crops growing or to be grown or timber to be cut, a description of the land concerned;

(b) value has been given; and

(c) the debtor has rights in the collateral.

(2) A security interest attaches when it becomes enforceable against the debtor with respect to the collateral. Attachment occurs as soon as all of the events specified in subsection (1) have taken place unless explicit agreement postpones the time of attaching.

(3) Unless otherwise agreed a security agreement gives the secured party the rights to proceeds provided by Section 9—306.

(4) A transaction, although subject to this Article, is also subject to . . . .*, and in the case of conflict between the provisions of this Article and any such statute, the provisions of such statute control. Failure to comply with any applicable statute has only the effect which is specified therein.

Note: At * in subsection (4) insert reference to any local statute regulating small loans, retail installment sales and the like.

The foregoing subsection (4) is designed to make it clear that certain transactions, although subject to this Article, must also comply with other applicable legislation.

This Article is designed to regulate all the "security" aspects of transactions within its scope. There is, however, much regulatory legislation, particularly in the consumer field, which supplements this Article and should not be repealed by its enactment. Examples are small loan acts, retail installment selling acts and the like. Such acts may provide for licensing and rate regulation and may prescribe particular forms of contract. Such provisions should remain in force despite the enactment of this Article. On the other hand if a retail installment selling act contains provisions on filing, rights on default, etc., such provisions should be repealed as inconsistent with this Article except that inconsistent provisions as to deficiencies, penalties, etc., in the Uniform Consumer Credit Code and other recent related legislation should remain because those statutes were drafted after the substantial enactment of the Article and with the intention of modifying certain provisions of this Article as to consumer credit.

§ 9—204. After-Acquired Property; Future Advances.

(1) Except as provided in subsection (2), a security agreement may provide that any or all obligations covered by the security agreement are to be secured by after-acquired collateral.

(2) No security interest attaches under an after-acquired property clause to consumer goods other than accessions (Section 9—314) when given as additional security unless the debtor acquires rights in them within ten days after the secured party gives value.

(3) Obligations covered by a security agreement may include future advances or other value whether or not the advances or value are given pursuant to commitment (subsection (1) of Section 9—105).

§ 9—205. Use or Disposition of Collateral Without Accounting Permissible.

A security interest is not invalid or fraudulent against creditors by reason of liberty in the debtor to use, commingle or dispose of all or part of the collateral (including returned or repossessed goods) or to collect or compromise accounts or chattel paper, or to accept the return of goods or make repossessions, or to use, commingle or dispose of proceeds, or by reason of the failure of the secured party to require the debtor to account for proceeds or replace collateral. This section does not relax the requirements of possession where perfection of a security interest depends upon possession of the collateral by the secured party or by a bailee.

§ 9—206. Agreement Not to Assert Defenses Against Assignee; Modification of Sales Warranties Where Security Agreement Exists.

(1) Subject to any statute or decision which establishes a different rule for buyers or lessees of consumer goods, an agreement by a buyer or lessee that he will not assert against an assignee any claim or defense which he may have against the seller or lessor is enforceable by an assignee who takes his assignment for value, in good faith and without notice of a claim or defense, except as to defenses of a type which may be asserted against a holder in due course of a negotiable instrument under the Article on Negotiable Instruments (Article 3). A buyer who as part of one transaction signs both a negotiable instrument and a security agreement makes such an agreement.

(2) When a seller retains a purchase money security interest in goods the Article on Sales (Article 2) governs the sale and any disclaimer, limitation or modification of the seller's warranties.

§ 9—207. Rights and Duties When Collateral is in Secured Party's Possession

(1) A secured party must use reasonable care in the custody and preservation of collateral in his possession. In the case of an instrument or chattel paper reasonable care includes taking necessary steps to preserve rights against prior parties unless otherwise agreed.

(2) Unless otherwise agreed, when collateral is in the secured party's possession

(a) reasonable expenses (including the cost of any insurance and payment of taxes or other charges) incurred in the custody, preservation, use or operation of the collateral are chargeable to the debtor and are secured by the collateral;

(b) the risk of accidental loss or damage is on the debtor to the extent of any deficiency in any effective insurance coverage;

(c) the secured party may hold as additional security any increase or profits (except money) received from the collateral, but money so received, unless remitted to the debtor, shall be applied in reduction of the secured obligation;

(d) the secured party must keep the collateral identifiable but fungible collateral may be commingled;

(e) the secured party may repledge the collateral upon terms which do not impair the debtor's right to redeem it.

(3) A secured party is liable for any loss caused by his failure to meet any obligation imposed by the preceding subsections but does not lose his security interest.

(4) A secured party may use or operate the collateral for the purpose of preserving the collateral or its value or pursuant to the order of a court of appropriate jurisdiction or, except in the case of consumer goods, in the manner and to the extent provided in the security agreement.

§ 9—208. Request for Statement of Account or List of Collateral.

(1) A debtor may sign a statement indicating what he believes to be the aggregate amount of unpaid indebtedness as of a specified date and may send it to the secured party with a request that the statement be approved or corrected and returned to the debtor. When the security agreement or any other record kept by the secured party identifies the collateral a debtor may similarly request the secured party to approve or correct a list of the collateral.

(2) The secured party must comply with such a request within two weeks after receipt by sending a written correction or approval. If the secured party claims a security interest in all of a particular type of collateral owned by the debtor he may indicate that fact in his reply and need not approve or correct an itemized list of such collateral. If the secured party without reasonable excuse fails to comply he is liable for any loss caused to the debtor thereby; and if the debtor has properly included in his request a good faith statement of the obligation or a list of the collateral or both the secured party may claim a security interest only as shown in the statement against persons misled by his failure to comply. If he no longer has an interest in the obligation or collateral at the time the request is received he must disclose the name and address of any successor in interest known to him and he is liable for any loss caused to the debtor as a result of failure to disclose. A successor in interest is not subject to this section until a request is received by him.

(3) A debtor is entitled to such a statement once every six months without charge. The secured party may require payment of a charge not exceeding $10 for each additional statement furnished.

Part 3 Rights of Third Parties; Perfected and Unperfected Security Interests; Rules of Priority

§ 9—301. Persons Who Take Priority Over Unperfected Security Interests; Rights of "Lien Creditor".

(1) Except as otherwise provided in subsection (2), an unperfected security interest is subordinate to the rights of

(a) persons entitled to priority under Section 9—312;

(b) a person who becomes a lien creditor before the security interest is perfected;

(c) in the case of goods, instruments, documents, and chattel paper, a person who is not a secured party and who is a transferee in bulk or other buyer not in ordinary course of business or is a buyer of farm products in ordinary course of business, to the extent that he gives value and receives delivery of the collateral without knowledge of the security interest and before it is perfected;

(d) in the case of accounts, general intangibles, and investment property a person who is not a secured party and who is a transferee to the extent that he gives value without knowledge of the security interest and before it is perfected.

(2) If the secured party files with respect to a purchase money security interest before or within ten days after the debtor receives possession of the collateral, he takes priority over the rights of a transferee in bulk or of a lien creditor which arise between the time the security interest attaches and the time of filing.

(3) A "lien creditor" means a creditor who has acquired a lien on the property involved by attachment, levy or the like and includes an assignee for benefit of creditors from the time of assignment, and a trustee in bankruptcy from the date of the filing of the petition or a receiver in equity from the time of appointment.

(4) A person who becomes a lien creditor while a security interest is perfected takes subject to the security interest only to the extent that it secures advances made before he becomes a lien creditor or within 45 days thereafter or made without knowledge of the lien or pursuant to a commitment entered into without knowledge of the lien.

§ 9—302. When Filing Is Required to Perfect Security Interest; Security Interests to Which Filing Provisions of This Article Do Not Apply.

(1) A financing statement must be filed to perfect all security interests except the following:

(a) a security interest in collateral in possession of the secured party under Section 9—305;

(b) a security interest temporarily perfected in instruments, certificated securities, or documents without delivery under Section 9—304 or in proceeds for a 10 day period under Section 9—306;

(c) a security interest created by an assignment of a beneficial interest in a trust or a decedent's estate;

(d) a purchase money security interest in consumer goods; but filing is required for a motor vehicle required to be registered; and fixture filing is required for priority over conflicting interests in fixtures to the extent provided in Section 9—313;

(e) an assignment of accounts which does not alone or in conjunction with other assignments to the same assignee transfer a significant part of the outstanding accounts of the assignor;

(f) a security interest of a collecting bank (Section 4—210) or arising under the Articles on Sales and Leases (see Section 9—113) or covered in subsection (3) of this section;

(g) an assignment for the benefit of all the creditors of the transferor, and subsequent transfers by the assignee thereunder.

(h) a security interest in investment property which is perfected without filing under Section 9—115 or Section 9—116.

(2) If a secured party assigns a perfected security interest, no filing under this Article is required in order to continue the perfected status of the security interest against creditors of and transferees from the original debtor.

(3) The filing of a financing statement otherwise required by this Article is not necessary or effective to perfect a security interest in property subject to

(a) a statute or treaty of the United States which provides for a national or international registration or a national or international certificate of title or which specifies a place of filing different from that specified in this Article for filing of the security interest; or

(b) the following statutes of this state; [list any certificate of title statute covering automobiles, trailers, mobile homes, boats, farm tractors, or the like, and any central filing statute.]; but during any period in which collateral is inventory held for sale by a person who is in the business of selling goods of that kind, the filing provisions of this Article (Part 4) apply to a security interest in that collateral created by him as debtor; or

(c) a certificate of title statute of another jurisdiction under the law of which indication of a security interest on the certificate is required as a condition of perfection (subsection (2) of Section 9—103).

(4) Compliance with a statute or treaty described in subsection (3) is equivalent to the filing of a financing statement under this Article, and a security interest in property subject to the statute or treaty can be perfected only by compliance therewith except as provided in Section 9—103 on multiple state transactions. Duration and renewal of perfection of a security interest perfected by compliance with the statute or treaty are governed by the provisions of the statute or treaty; in other respects the security interest is subject to this Article.

§ 9—303. When Security Interest Is Perfected; Continuity of Perfection.

(1) A security interest is perfected when it has attached and when all of the applicable steps required for perfection have been taken. Such steps are specified in Sections 9—115, 9—302, 9—304, 9—305 and 9—306. If such steps are taken before the security interest attaches, it is perfected at the time when it attaches.

(2) If a security interest is originally perfected in any way permitted under this Article and is subsequently perfected in some other way under this Article, without an intermediate period when it was unperfected, the security interest shall be deemed to be perfected continuously for the purposes of this Article.

§ 9—304. Perfection of Security Interest in Instruments, Documents, Proceeds of a Written Letter of Credit, and Goods Covered by Documents; Perfection by Permissive Filing; Temporary Perfection Without Filing or Transfer of Possession.

(1) A security interest in chattel paper or negotiable documents may be perfected by filing. A security interest in the rights to proceeds of a written letter of credit can be perfected only by the secured party's taking possession of the letter of credit. A security interest in money or instruments (other than instruments which constitute part of chattel paper) can be perfected only by the secured party's taking possession, except as provided in subsections (4) and (5) of this section and subsections (2) and (3) of Section 9—306 on proceeds.

(2) During the period that goods are in the possession of the issuer of a negotiable document therefor, a security interest in the goods is perfected by perfecting a security interest in the document, and any security interest in the goods otherwise perfected during such period is subject thereto.

(3) A security interest in goods in the possession of a bailee other than one who has issued a negotiable document therefor is perfected by issuance of a document in the name of the secured party or by the bailee's receipt of notification of the secured party's interest or by filing as to the goods.

(4) A security interest in instruments, certificated securities, or negotiable documents is perfected without filing or the taking of possession for a period of 21 days from the time it attaches to the extent that it arises for new value given under a written security agreement.

(5) A security interest remains perfected for a period of 21 days without filing where a secured party having a perfected

security interest in an instrument, a certificated security, a negotiable document or goods in possession of a bailee other than one who has issued a negotiable document therefor

(a) makes available to the debtor the goods or documents representing the goods for the purpose of ultimate sale or exchange or for the purpose of loading, unloading, storing, shipping, transshipping, manufacturing, processing or otherwise dealing with them in a manner preliminary to their sale or exchange, but priority between conflicting security interests in the goods is subject to subsection (3) of Section 9—312; or

(b) delivers the instrument or certificated security to the debtor for the purpose of ultimate sale or exchange or of presentation, collection, renewal or registration of transfer.

(6) After the 21 day period in subsections (4) and (5) perfection depends upon compliance with applicable provisions of this Article.

§ 9—305. When Possession by Secured Party Perfects Security Interest Without Filing.

A security interest in goods, instruments, money, negotiable documents, or chattel paper may be perfected by the secured party's taking possession of the collateral. A security interest in the right to proceeds of a written letter of credit may be perfected by the secured party's taking possession of the letter of credit. If such collateral other than goods covered by a negotiable document is held by a bailee, the secured party is deemed to have possession from the time the bailee receives notification of the secured party's interest. A security interest is perfected by possession from the time possession is taken without a relation back and continues only so long as possession is retained, unless otherwise specified in this Article. The security interest may be otherwise perfected as provided in this Article before or after the period of possession by the secured party.

§ 9—306. "Proceeds"; Secured Party's Rights on Disposition of Collateral.

(1) "Proceeds" includes whatever is received upon the sale, exchange, collection or other disposition of collateral or proceeds. Insurance payable by reason of loss or damage to the collateral is proceeds, except to the extent that it is payable to a person other than a party to the security agreement. Any payments or distributions made with respect to investment property collateral are proceeds. Money, checks, deposit accounts, and the like are "cash proceeds". All other proceeds are "noncash proceeds".

(2) Except where this Article otherwise provides, a security interest continues in collateral notwithstanding sale, exchange or other disposition thereof unless the disposition was authorized by the secured party in the security agreement or otherwise, and also continues in any identifiable proceeds including collections received by the debtor.

(3) The security interest in proceeds is a continuously perfected security interest if the interest in the original collateral was perfected but it ceases to be a perfected security interest and becomes unperfected ten days after receipt of the proceeds by the debtor unless

(a) a filed financing statement covers the original collateral and the proceeds are collateral in which a security interest may be perfected by filing in the office or offices where the financing statement has been filed and, if the proceeds are acquired with cash proceeds, the description of collateral in the financing statement indicates the types of property constituting the proceeds; or

(b) a filed financing statement covers the original collateral and the proceeds are identifiable cash proceeds; or

(c) the original collateral was investment property and the proceeds are identifiable cash proceeds; or

(d) the security interest in the proceeds is perfected before the expiration of the ten day period.

Except as provided in this section, a security interest in proceeds can be perfected only by the methods or under the circumstances permitted in this Article for original collateral of the same type.

(4) In the event of insolvency proceedings instituted by or against a debtor, a secured party with a perfected security interest in proceeds has a perfected security interest only in the following proceeds:

(a) in identifiable noncash proceeds and in separate deposit accounts containing only proceeds;

(b) in identifiable cash proceeds in the form of money which is neither commingled with other money nor deposited in a deposit account prior to the insolvency proceedings;

(c) in identifiable cash proceeds in the form of checks and the like which are not deposited in a deposit account prior to the insolvency proceedings; and

(d) in all cash and deposit accounts of the debtor in which proceeds have been commingled with other funds, but the perfected security interest under this paragraph (d) is

(i) subject to any right to set-off; and

(ii) limited to an amount not greater than the amount of any cash proceeds received by the debtor within ten days before the institution of the insolvency proceedings less the sum of (I) the payments to the secured party on account of cash proceeds received by the debtor during such period and (II) the cash proceeds received by the debtor during such period to which the secured party is entitled under paragraphs (a) through (c) of this subsection (4).

(5) If a sale of goods results in an account or chattel paper which is transferred by the seller to a secured party, and if

the goods are returned to or are repossessed by the seller or the secured party, the following rules determine priorities:

(a) If the goods were collateral at the time of sale, for an indebtedness of the seller which is still unpaid, the original security interest attaches again to the goods and continues as a perfected security interest if it was perfected at the time when the goods were sold. If the security interest was originally perfected by a filing which is still effective, nothing further is required to continue the perfected status; in any other case, the secured party must take possession of the returned or repossessed goods or must file.

(b) An unpaid transferee of the chattel paper has a security interest in the goods against the transferor. Such security interest is prior to a security interest asserted under paragraph (a) to the extent that the transferee of the chattel paper was entitled to priority under Section 9—308.

(c) An unpaid transferee of the account has a security interest in the goods against the transferor. Such security interest is subordinate to a security interest asserted under paragraph (a).

(d) A security interest of an unpaid transferee asserted under paragraph (b) or (c) must be perfected for protection against creditors of the transferor and purchasers of the returned or repossessed goods.

§ 9—307. Protection of Buyers of Goods.

(1) A buyer in ordinary course of business (subsection (9) of Section 1—201) other than a person buying farm products from a person engaged in farming operations takes free of a security interest created by his seller even though the security interest is perfected and even though the buyer knows of its existence [subject to the Food Security Act of 1985 (7 U.S.C. Section 1631)].

(2) In the case of consumer goods, a buyer takes free of a security interest even though perfected if he buys without knowledge of the security interest, for value and for his own personal, family or household purposes unless prior to the purchase the secured party has filed a financing statement covering such goods.

(3) A buyer other than a buyer in ordinary course of business (subsection (1) of this section) takes free of a security interest to the extent that it secures future advances made after the secured party acquires knowledge of the purchase, or more than 45 days after the purchase, whichever first occurs, unless made pursuant to a commitment entered into without knowledge of the purchase and before the expiration of the 45 day period.

§ 9—308. Purchase of Chattel Paper and Instruments.

A purchaser of chattel paper or an instrument who gives new value and takes possession of it in the ordinary course of his business has priority over a security interest in the chattel paper or instrument

(a) which is perfected under Section 9—304 (permissive filing and temporary perfection) or under Section 9—306 (perfection as to proceeds) if he acts without knowledge that the specific paper or instrument is subject to a security interest; or

(b) which is claimed merely as proceeds of inventory subject to a security interest (Section 9—306) even though he knows that the specific paper or instrument is subject to the security interest.

§ 9—309. Protection of Purchasers of Instruments, Documents and Securities.

Nothing in this Article limits the rights of a holder in due course of a negotiable instrument (Section 3—302) or a holder to whom a negotiable document of title has been duly negotiated (Section 7—501) or a bona fide purchaser of a security (Section 8—302) and the holders or purchasers take priority over an earlier security interest even though perfected. Filing under this Article does not constitute notice of the security interest to such holders or purchasers.

§ 9—310. Priority of Certain Liens Arising by Operation of Law.

When a person in the ordinary course of his business furnishes services or materials with respect to goods subject to a security interest, a lien upon goods in the possession of such person given by statute or rule of law for such materials or services takes priority over a perfected security interest unless the lien is statutory and the statute expressly provides otherwise.

§ 9—311. Alienability of Debtor's Rights: Judicial Process.

The debtor's rights in collateral may be voluntarily or involuntarily transferred (by way of sale, creation of a security interest, attachment, levy, garnishment or other judicial process) notwithstanding a provision in the security agreement prohibiting any transfer or making the transfer constitute a default.

§ 9—312. Priorities Among Conflicting Security Interests in the Same Collateral.

(1) The rules of priority stated in other sections of this Part and in the following sections shall govern when applicable: Section 4—208 with respect to the security interests of collecting banks in items being collected, accompanying documents and proceeds; Section 9—103 on security interests related to other jurisdictions; Section 9—114 on consignments.

(2) A perfected security interest in crops for new value given to enable the debtor to produce the crops during the production season and given not more than three months before the crops become growing crops by planting or otherwise takes priority over an earlier perfected security interest to the extent that such earlier interest secures obligations due more than six months before the crops become growing crops by planting or otherwise, even

though the person giving new value had knowledge of the earlier security interest.

(3) A perfected purchase money security interest in inventory has priority over a conflicting security interest in the same inventory and also has priority in identifiable cash proceeds received on or before the delivery of the inventory to a buyer if

(a) the purchase money security interest is perfected at the time the debtor receives possession of the inventory; and

(b) the purchase money secured party gives notification in writing to the holder of the conflicting security interest if the holder had filed a financing statement covering the same types of inventory (i) before the date of the filing made by the purchase money secured party, or (ii) before the beginning of the 21 day period where the purchase money security interest is temporarily perfected without filing or possession (subsection (5) of Section 9—304); and

(c) the holder of the conflicting security interest receives the notification within five years before the debtor receives possession of the inventory; and

(d) the notification states that the person giving the notice has or expects to acquire a purchase money security interest in inventory of the debtor, describing such inventory by item or type.

(4) A purchase money security interest in collateral other than inventory has priority over a conflicting security interest in the same collateral or its proceeds if the purchase money security interest is perfected at the time the debtor receives possession of the collateral or within ten days thereafter.

(5) In all cases not governed by other rules stated in this section (including cases of purchase money security interests which do not qualify for the special priorities set forth in subsections (3) and (4) of this section), priority between conflicting security interests in the same collateral shall be determined according to the following rules:

(a) Conflicting security interests rank according to priority in time of filing or perfection. Priority dates from the time a filing is first made covering the collateral or the time the security interest is first perfected, whichever is earlier, provided that there is no period thereafter when there is neither filing nor perfection.

(b) So long as conflicting security interests are unperfected, the first to attach has priority.

(6) For the purposes of subsection (5) a date of filing or perfection as to collateral is also a date of filing or perfection as to proceeds.

(7) If future advances are made while a security interest is perfected by filing, the taking of possession, or under Section 8—321 on securities, the security interest has the same priority for the purposes of subsection (5) with respect to the future advances as it does with respect to the first advance. If a commitment is made before or while the security interest is so perfected, the security interest has the same priority with respect to advances made pursuant thereto. In other cases a perfected security interest has priority from the date the advance is made.

§ 9—313. **Priority of Security Interests in Fixtures.**

(1) In this section and in the provisions of Part 4 of this Article referring to fixture filing, unless the context otherwise requires

(a) goods are "fixtures" when they become so related to particular real estate that an interest in them arises under real estate law

(b) a "fixture filing" is the filing in the office where a mortgage on the real estate would be filed or recorded of a financing statement covering goods which are or are to become fixtures and conforming to the requirements of subsection (5) of Section 9—402

(c) a mortgage is a "construction mortgage" to the extent that it secures an obligation incurred for the construction of an improvement on land including the acquisition cost of the land, if the recorded writing so indicates.

(2) A security interest under this Article may be created in goods which are fixtures or may continue in goods which become fixtures, but no security interest exists under this Article in ordinary building materials incorporated into an improvement on land.

(3) This Article does not prevent creation of an encumbrance upon fixtures pursuant to real estate law.

(4) A perfected security interest in fixtures has priority over the conflicting interest of an encumbrancer or owner of the real estate where

(a) the security interest is a purchase money security interest, the interest of the encumbrancer or owner arises before the goods become fixtures, the security interest is perfected by a fixture filing before the goods become fixtures or within ten days thereafter, and the debtor has an interest of record in the real estate or is in possession of the real estate; or

(b) the security interest is perfected by a fixture filing before the interest of the encumbrancer or owner is of record, the security interest has priority over any conflicting interest of a predecessor in title of the encumbrancer or owner, and the debtor has an interest of record in the real estate or is in possession of the real estate; or

(c) the fixtures are readily removable factory or office machines or readily removable replacements of domestic appliances which are consumer goods, and before the goods become fixtures the security interest is perfected by any method permitted by this Article; or

(d) the conflicting interest is a lien on the real estate obtained by legal or equitable proceedings after the security interest was perfected by any method permitted by this Article.

(5) A security interest in fixtures, whether or not perfected, has priority over the conflicting interest of an encumbrancer or owner of the real estate where

    (a) the encumbrancer or owner has consented in writing to the security interest or has disclaimed an interest in the goods as fixtures; or

    (b) the debtor has a right to remove the goods as against the encumbrancer or owner. If the debtor's right terminates, the priority of the security interest continues for a reasonable time.

(6) Notwithstanding paragraph (a) of subsection (4) but otherwise subject to subsections (4) and (5), a security interest in fixtures is subordinate to a construction mortgage recorded before the goods become fixtures if the goods become fixtures before the completion of the construction. To the extent that it is given to refinance a construction mortgage, a mortgage has this priority to the same extent as the construction mortgage.

(7) In cases not within the preceding subsections, a security interest in fixtures is subordinate to the conflicting interest of an encumbrancer or owner of the related real estate who is not the debtor.

(8) When the secured party has priority over all owners and encumbrancers of the real estate, he may, on default, subject to the provisions of Part 5, remove his collateral from the real estate but he must reimburse any encumbrancer or owner of the real estate who is not the debtor and who has not otherwise agreed for the cost of repair of any physical injury, but not for any diminution in value of the real estate caused by the absence of the goods removed or by any necessity of replacing them. A person entitled to reimbursement may refuse permission to remove until the secured party gives adequate security for the performance of this obligation.

§ 9—314. Accessions.

(1) A security interest in goods which attaches before they are installed in or affixed to other goods takes priority as to the goods installed or affixed (called in this section "accessions") over the claims of all persons to the whole except as stated in subsection (3) and subject to Section 9—315(1).

(2) A security interest which attaches to goods after they become part of a whole is valid against all persons subsequently acquiring interests in the whole except as stated in subsection (3) but is invalid against any person with an interest in the whole at the time the security interest attaches to the goods who has not in writing consented to the security interest or disclaimed an interest in the goods as part of the whole.

(3) The security interests described in subsections (1) and (2) do not take priority over

    (a) a subsequent purchaser for value of any interest in the whole; or

    (b) a creditor with a lien on the whole subsequently obtained by judicial proceedings; or

    (c) a creditor with a prior perfected security interest in the whole to the extent that he makes subsequent advances

if the subsequent purchase is made, the lien by judicial proceedings obtained or the subsequent advance under the prior perfected security interest is made or contracted for without knowledge of the security interest and before it is perfected. A purchaser of the whole at a foreclosure sale other than the holder of a perfected security interest purchasing at his own foreclosure sale is a subsequent purchaser within this section.

(4) When under subsections (1) or (2) and (3) a secured party has an interest in accessions which has priority over the claims of all persons who have interests in the whole, he may on default subject to the provisions of Part 5 remove his collateral from the whole but he must reimburse any encumbrancer or owner of the whole who is not the debtor and who has not otherwise agreed for the cost of repair of any physical injury but not for any diminution in value of the whole caused by the absence of the goods removed or by any necessity for replacing them. A person entitled to reimbursement may refuse permission to remove until the secured party gives adequate security for the performance of this obligation.

§ 9—315. Priority When Goods Are Commingled or Processed.

(1) If a security interest in goods was perfected and subsequently the goods or a part thereof have become part of a product or mass, the security interest continues in the product or mass if

    (a) the goods are so manufactured, processed, assembled or commingled that their identity is lost in the product or mass; or

    (b) a financing statement covering the original goods also covers the product into which the goods have been manufactured, processed or assembled.

In a case to which paragraph (b) applies, no separate security interest in that part of the original goods which has been manufactured, processed or assembled into the product may be claimed under Section 9—314.

(2) When under subsection (1) more than one security interest attaches to the product or mass, they rank equally according to the ratio that the cost of the goods to which each interest originally attached bears to the cost of the total product or mass.

§ 9—316. Priority Subject to Subordination.

Nothing in this Article prevents subordination by agreement by any person entitled to priority.

§ 9—317. Secured Party Not Obligated on Contract of Debtor.

The mere existence of a security interest or authority given to the debtor to dispose of or use collateral does not impose contract or tort liability upon the secured party for the debtor's acts or omissions.

§ 9—318. Defenses Against Assignee; Modification of Contract After Notification of Assignment; Term Prohibiting Assignment Ineffective; Identification and Proof of Assignment.

(1) Unless an account debtor has made an enforceable agreement not to assert defenses or claims arising out of a sale as provided in Section 9—206 the rights of an assignee are subject to

(a) all the terms of the contract between the account debtor and assignor and any defense or claim arising therefrom; and

(b) any other defense or claim of the account debtor against the assignor which accrues before the account debtor receives notification of the assignment.

(2) So far as the right to payment or a part thereof under an assigned contract has not been fully earned by performance, and notwithstanding notification of the assignment, any modification of or substitution for the contract made in good faith and in accordance with reasonable commercial standards is effective against an assignee unless the account debtor has otherwise agreed but the assignee acquires corresponding rights under the modified or substituted contract. The assignment may provide that such modification or substitution is a breach by the assignor.

(3) The account debtor is authorized to pay the assignor until the account debtor receives notification that the amount due or to become due has been assigned and that payment is to be made to the assignee. A notification which does not reasonably identify the rights assigned is ineffective. If requested by the account debtor, the assignee must seasonably furnish reasonable proof that the assignment has been made and unless he does so the account debtor may pay the assignor.

(4) A term in any contract between an account debtor and an assignor is ineffective if it prohibits assignment of an account or prohibits creation of a security interest in a general intangible for money due or to become due or requires the account debtor's consent to such assignment or security interest.

Part 4 Filing

§ 9—401. Place of Filing; Erroneous Filing; Removal of Collateral.

First Alternative Subsection (1)

(1) The proper place to file in order to perfect a security interest is as follows:

(a) when the collateral is timber to be cut or is minerals or the like (including oil and gas) or accounts subject to subsection (5) of Section 9—103, or when the financing statement is filed as a fixture filing (Section 9—313) and the collateral is goods which are or are to become fixtures, then in the office where a mortgage on the real estate would be filed or recorded;

(b) in all other cases, in the office of the [Secretary of State].

Second Alternative Subsection (1)

(1) The proper place to file in order to perfect a security interest is as follows:

(a) when the collateral is equipment used in farming operations, or farm products, or accounts or general intangibles arising from or relating to the sale of farm products by a farmer, or consumer goods, then in the office of the . . . . in the county of the debtor's residence or if the debtor is not a resident of this state then in the office of the . . . . in the county where the goods are kept, and in addition when the collateral is crops growing or to be grown in the office of the . . . . in the county where the land is located;

(b) when the collateral is timber to be cut or is minerals or the like (including oil and gas) or accounts subject to subsection (5) of Section 9—103, or when the financing statement is filed as a fixture filing (Section 9—313) and the collateral is goods which are or are to become fixtures, then in the office where a mortgage on the real estate would be filed or recorded;

(c) in all other cases, in the office of the [Secretary of State].

Third Alternative Subsection (1)

(1) The proper place to file in order to perfect a security interest is as follows:

(a) when the collateral is equipment used in farming operations, or farm products, or accounts or general intangibles arising from or relating to the sale of farm products by a farmer, or consumer goods, then in the office of the . . . . in the county of the debtor's residence or if the debtor is not a resident of this state then in the office of the . . . . in the county where the goods are kept, and in addition when the collateral is crops growing or to be grown in the office of the . . . . in the county where the land is located;

(b) when the collateral is timber to be cut or is minerals or the like (including oil and gas) or accounts subject to subsection (5) of Section 9—103, or when the financing statement is filed as a fixture filing (Section 9—313) and the collateral is goods which are or are to become fixtures, then in the office where a mortgage on the real estate would be filed or recorded;

(c) in all other cases, in the office of the [Secretary of State] and in addition, if the debtor has a place of business in only one county of this state, also in the office of . . . . of such county, or, if the debtor has no place of business in this state, but resides in the state, also in the office of . . . . of the county in which he resides.

Note: *One of the three alternatives should be selected as subsection (1).*

(2) A filing which is made in good faith in an improper place or not in all of the places required by this section is nevertheless effective with regard to any collateral as to which the filing complied with the requirements of this Article and is also effective with regard to collateral coered by the financing statement against any person who has knowledge of the contents of such financing statement.

(3) A filing which is made in the proper place in this state continues effective even though the debtor's residence or place of business or the location of the collateral or its use, whichever controlled the original filing, is thereafter changed.

Alternative Subsection (3)

[(3) A filing which is made in the proper county continues effective for four months after a change to another county of the debtor's residence or place of business or the location of the collateral, whichever controlled the original filing. It becomes ineffective thereafter unless a copy of the financing statement signed by the secured party is filed in the new county within said period. The security interest may also be perfected in the new county after the expiration of the four-month period; in such case perfection dates from the time of perfection in the new county. A change in the use of the collateral does not impair the effectiveness of the original filing.]

(4) The rules stated in Section 9—103 determine whether filing is necessary in this state.

(5) Notwithstanding the preceding subsections, and subject to subsection (3) of Section 9—302, the proper place to file in order to perfect a security interest in collateral, including fixtures, of a transmitting utility is the office of the [Secretary of State]. This filing constitutes a fixture filing (Section 9—313) as to the collateral described therein which is or is to become fixtures.

(6) For the purposes of this section, the residence of an organization is its place of business if it has one or its chief executive office if it has more than one place of business.

Note: *Subsection (6) should be used only if the state chooses the Second or Third Alternative Subsection (1).*

§ 9—402. Formal Requisites of Financing Statement; Amendments; Mortgage as Financing Statement.

(1) A financing statement is sufficient if it gives the names of the debtor and the secured party, is signed by the debtor, gives an address of the secured party from which information concerning the security interest may be obtained, gives a mailing address of the debtor and contains a statement indicating the types, or describing the items, of collateral. A financing statement may be filed before a security agreement is made or a security interest otherwise attaches. When the financing statement covers crops growing or to be grown, the statement must also contain a description of the real estate concerned. When the financing statement covers timber to be cut or covers minerals or the like (including oil and gas) or accounts subject to subsection (5) of Section 9—103, or when the financing statement is filed as a fixture filing (Section 9—313) and the collateral is goods which are or are to become fixtures, the statement must also comply with subsection (5). A copy of the security agreement is sufficient as a financing statement if it contains the above information and is signed by the debtor. A carbon, photographic or other reproduction of a security agreement or a financing statement is sufficient as a financing statement if the security agreement so provides or if the original has been filed in this state.

(2) A financing statement which otherwise complies with subsection (1) is sufficient when it is signed by the secured party instead of the debtor if it is filed to perfect a security interest in

(a) collateral already subject to a security interest in another jurisdiction when it is brought into this state, or when the debtor's location is changed to this state. Such a financing statement must state that the collateral was brought into this state or that the debtor's location was changed to this state under such circumstances; or

(b) proceeds under Section 9—306 if the security interest in the original collateral was perfected. Such a financing statement must describe the original collateral; or

(c) collateral as to which the filing has lapsed; or

(d) collateral acquired after a change of name, identity or corporate structure of the debtor (subsection (7)).

(3) A form substantially as follows is sufficient to comply with subsection (1):

Name of debtor (or assignor) . . . .
Address . . . .
Name of secured party (or assignee) . . . .
Address . . . .
1. This financing statement covers the following types (or items) of property:
    (Describe) . . . .
2. (If collateral is crops) The above described crops are growing or are to be grown on:
    (Describe Real Estate) . . . .
3. (If applicable) The above goods are to become fixtures on *
*Where appropriate substitute either "The above timber is standing on . . . ." or "The above minerals or the

like (including oil and gas) or accounts will be financed at the wellhead or minehead of the well or mine located on . . . ."

(Describe Real Estate) . . . . and this financing statement is to be filed [for record] in the real estate records. (If the debtor does not have an interest of record) The name of a record owner is

. . . .

4. (If products of collateral are claimed) Products of the collateral are also covered.

(use . . . .
whichever   Signature of Debtor (or Assignor)

is   . . . .
applicable)   Signature of Secured Party
                          (or Assignee)

(4) A financing statement may be amended by filing a writing signed by both the debtor and the secured party. An amendment does not extend the period of effectiveness of a financing statement. If any amendment adds collateral, it is effective as to the added collateral only from the filing date of the amendment. In this Article, unless the context otherwise requires, the term "financing statement" means the original financing statement and any amendments.

(5) A financing statement covering timber to be cut or covering minerals or the like (including oil and gas) or accounts subject to subsection (5) of Section 9—103, or a financing statement filed as a fixture filing (Section 9—313) where the debtor is not a transmitting utility, must show that it covers this type of collateral, must recite that it is to be filed [for record] in the real estate records, and the financing statement must contain a description of the real estate [sufficient if it were contained in a mortgage of the real estate to give constructive notice of the mortgage under the law of this state]. If the debtor does not have an interest of record in the real estate, the financing statement must show the name of a record owner.

(6) A mortgage is effective as a financing statement filed as a fixture filing from the date of its recording if

(a) the goods are described in the mortgage by item or type; and

(b) the goods are or are to become fixtures related to the real estate described in the mortgage; and

(c) the mortgage complies with the requirements for a financing statement in this section other than a recital that it is to be filed in the real estate records; and

(d) the mortgage is duly recorded.

No fee with reference to the financing statement is required other than the regular recording and satisfaction fees with respect to the mortgage.

(7) A financing statement sufficiently shows the name of the debtor if it gives the individual, partnership or corpo-

rate name of the debtor, whether or not it adds other trade names or names of partners. Where the debtor so changes his name or in the case of an organization its name, identity or corporate structure that a filed financing statement becomes seriously misleading, the filing is not effective to perfect a security interest in collateral acquired by the debtor more than four months after the change, unless a new appropriate financing statement is filed before the expiration of that time. A filed financing statement remains effective with respect to collateral transferred by the debtor even though the secured party knows of or consents to the transfer.

(8) A financing statement substantially complying with the requirements of this section is effective even though it contains minor errors which are not seriously misleading.

Note: *Language in brackets is optional.*

Note: *Where the state has any special recording system for real estate other than the usual grantor-grantee index (as, for instance, a tract system or a title registration or Torrens system) local adaptations of subsection (5) and Section 9—403(7) may be necessary. See Mass.Gen.Laws Chapter 106, Section 9—409.*

§ 9—403. What Constitutes Filing; Duration of Filing; Effect of Lapsed Filing; Duties of Filing Officer.

(1) Presentation for filing of a financing statement and tender of the filing fee or acceptance of the statement by the filing officer constitutes filing under this Article.

(2) Except as provided in subsection (6) a filed financing statement is effective for a period of five years from the date of filing. The effectiveness of a filed financing statement lapses on the expiration of the five year period unless a continuation statement is filed prior to the lapse. If a security interest perfected by filing exists at the time insolvency proceedings are commenced by or against the debtor, the security interest remains perfected until termination of the insolvency proceedings and thereafter for a period of sixty days or until expiration of the five year period, whichever occurs later. Upon lapse the security interest becomes unperfected, unless it is perfected without filing. If the security interest becomes unperfected upon lapse, it is deemed to have been unperfected as against a person who became a purchaser or lien creditor before lapse.

(3) A continuation statement may be filed by the secured party within six months prior to the expiration of the five year period specified in subsection (2). Any such continuation statement must be signed by the secured party, identify the original statement by file number and state that the original statement is still effective. A continuation statement signed by a person other than the secured party of record must be accompanied by a separate written statement of assignment signed by the secured party of record and complying with subsection (2) of Section 9—405, including payment of the required fee. Upon timely filing of the continuation statement, the effectiveness of the original statement is continued for five years after the last date

to which the filing was effective whereupon it lapses in the same manner as provided in subsection (2) unless another continuation statement is filed prior to such lapse. Succeeding continuation statements may be filed in the same manner to continue the effectiveness of the original statement. Unless a statute on disposition of public records provides otherwise, the filing officer may remove a lapsed statement from the files and destroy it immediately if he has retained a microfilm or other photographic record, or in other cases after one year after the lapse. The filing officer shall so arrange matters by physical annexation of financing statements to continuation statements or other related filings, or by other means, that if he physically destroys the financing statements of a period more than five years past, those which have been continued by a continuation statement or which are still effective under subsection (6) shall be retained.

(4) Except as provided in subsection (7) a filing officer shall mark each statement with a file number and with the date and hour of filing and shall hold the statement or a microfilm or other photographic copy thereof for public inspection. In addition the filing officer shall index the statement according to the name of the debtor and shall note in the index the file number and the address of the debtor given in the statement.

(5) The uniform fee for filing and indexing and for stamping a copy furnished by the secured party to show the date and place of filing for an original financing statement or for a continuation statement shall be $. . . . . . . if the statement is in the standard form prescribed by the [Secretary of State] and otherwise shall be $. . . . . . ., plus in each case, if the financing statement is subject to subsection (5) of Section 9—402, $. . . . . . . The uniform fee for each name more than one required to be indexed shall be $. . . . . . . The secured party may at his option show a trade name for any person and an extra uniform indexing fee of $. . . . . . . shall be paid with respect thereto.

(6) If the debtor is a transmitting utility (subsection (5) of Section 9—401) and a filed financing statement so states, it is effective until a termination statement is filed. A real estate mortgage which is effective as a fixture filing under subsection (6) of Section 9—402 remains effective as a fixture filing until the mortgage is released or satisfied of record or its effectiveness otherwise terminates as to the real estate.

(7) When a financing statement covers timber to be cut or covers minerals or the like (including oil and gas) or accounts subject to subsection (5) of Section 9—103, or is filed as a fixture filing, [it shall be filed for record and] the filing officer shall index it under the names of the debtor and any owner of record shown on the financing statement in the same fashion as if they were the mortgagors in a mortgage of the real estate described, and, to the extent that the law of this state provides for indexing of mortgages under the name of the mortgagee, under the name of the secured party as if he were the mortgagee thereunder, or where indexing is by description in the same fashion as if the financing statement were a mortgage of the real estate described.

Note: *In states in which writings will not appear in the real estate records and indices unless actually recorded the bracketed language in subsection (7) should be used.*

§ 9—404. Termination Statement.

(1) If a financing statement covering consumer goods is filed on or after . . . ., then within one month or within ten days following written demand by the debtor after there is no outstanding secured obligation and no commitment to make advances, incur obligations or otherwise give value, the secured party must file with each filing officer with whom the financing statement was filed, a termination statement to the effect that he no longer claims a security interest under the financing statement, which shall be identified by file number. In other cases whenever there is no outstanding secured obligation and no commitment to make advances, incur obligations or otherwise give value, the secured party must on written demand by the debtor send the debtor, for each filing officer with whom the financing statement was filed, a termination statement to the effect that he no longer claims a security interest under the financing statement, which shall be identified by file number. A termination statement signed by a person other than the secured party of record must be accompanied by a separate written statement of assignment signed by the secured party of record complying with subsection (2) of Section 9—405, including payment of the required fee. If the affected secured party fails to file such a termination statement as required by this subsection, or to send such a termination statement within ten days after proper demand therefor, he shall be liable to the debtor for one hundred dollars, and in addition for any loss caused to the debtor by such failure.

(2) On presentation to the filing officer of such a termination statement he must note it in the index. If he has received the termination statement in duplicate, he shall return one copy of the termination statement to the secured party stamped to show the time of receipt thereof. If the filing officer has a microfilm or other photographic record of the financing statement, and of any related continuation statement, statement of assignment and statement of release, he may remove the originals from the files at any time after receipt of the termination statement, or if he has no such record, he may remove them from the files at any time after one year after receipt of the termination statement.

(3) If the termination statement is in the standard form prescribed by the [Secretary of State], the uniform fee for filing and indexing the termination statement shall be $. . . . . . ., and otherwise shall be $. . . . . . ., plus in each case an additional fee of $. . . . . . . for each name more than one against which the termination statement is required to be indexed.

Note: *The date to be inserted should be the effective date of the revised Article 9.*

§ 9—405. Assignment of Security Interest; Duties of Filing Officer; Fees.

(1) A financing statement may disclose an assignment of a security interest in the collateral described in the financing statement by indication in the financing statement of the name and address of the assignee or by an assignment itself or a copy thereof on the face or back of the statement. On presentation to the filing officer of such a financing statement the filing officer shall mark the same as provided in Section 9—403(4). The uniform fee for filing, indexing and furnishing filing data for a financing statement so indicating an assignment shall be $. . . . . . . if the statement is in the standard form prescribed by the [Secretary of State] and otherwise shall be $. . . . . . ., plus in each case an additional fee of $. . . . . . . for each name more than one against which the financing statement is required to be indexed.

(2) A secured party may assign of record all or part of his rights under a financing statement by the filing in the place where the original financing statement was filed of a separate written statement of assignment signed by the secured party of record and setting forth the name of the secured party of record and the debtor, the file number and the date of filing of the financing statement and the name and address of the assignee and containing a description of the collateral assigned. A copy of the assignment is sufficient as a separate statement if it complies with the preceding sentence. On presentation to the filing officer of such a separate statement, the filing officer shall mark such separate statement with the date and hour of the filing. He shall note the assignment on the index of the financing statement, or in the case of a fixture filing, or a filing covering timber to be cut, or covering minerals or the like (including oil and gas) or accounts subject to subsection (5) of Section 9—103, he shall index the assignment under the name of the assignor as grantor and, to the extent that the law of this state provides for indexing the assignment of a mortgage under the name of the assignee, he shall index the assignment of the financing statement under the name of the assignee. The uniform fee for filing, indexing and furnishing filing data about such a separate statement of assignment shall be $. . . . . if the statement is in the standard form prescribed by the [Secretary of State] and otherwise shall be $. . . . ., plus in each case an additional fee of $. . . . . for each name more than one against which the statement of assignment is required to be indexed. Notwithstanding the provisions of this subsection, an assignment of record of a security interest in a fixture contained in a mortgage effective as a fixture filing (subsection (6) of Section 9—402) may be made only by an assignment of the mortgage in the manner provided by the law of this state other than this Act.

(3) After the disclosure or filing of an assignment under this section, the assignee is the secured party of record.

§ 9—406. Release of Collateral; Duties of Filing Officer; Fees.

A secured party of record may by his signed statement release all or a part of any collateral described in a filed financing statement. The statement of release is sufficient if it contains a description of the collateral being released, the name and address of the debtor, the name and address of the secured party, and the file number of the financing statement. A statement of release signed by a person other than the secured party of record must be accompanied by a separate written statement of assignment signed by the secured party of record and complying with subsection (2) of Section 9—405, including payment of the required fee. Upon presentation of such a statement of release to the filing officer he shall mark the statement with the hour and date of filing and shall note the same upon the margin of the index of the filing of the financing statement. The uniform fee for filing and noting such a statement of release shall be $. . . . . if the statement is in the standard form prescribed by the [Secretary of State] and otherwise shall be $. . . . ., plus in each case an additional fee of $. . . . . for each name more than one against which the statement of release is required to be indexed.

§ 9—407. Information From Filing Officer.

[(1) If the person filing any financing statement, termination statement, statement of assignment, or statement of release, furnishes the filing officer a copy thereof, the filing officer shall upon request note upon the copy the file number and date and hour of the filing of the original and deliver or send the copy to such person.]

[(2) Upon request of any person, the filing officer shall issue his certificate showing whether there is on file on the date and hour stated therein, any presently effective financing statement naming a particular debtor and any statement of assignment thereof and if there is, giving the date and hour of filing of each such statement and the names and addresses of each secured party therein. The uniform fee for such a certificate shall be $. . . . . if the request for the certificate is in the standard form prescribed by the [Secretary of State] and otherwise shall be $. . . . . . Upon request the filing officer shall furnish a copy of any filed financing statement or statement of assignment for a uniform fee of $. . . . . per page.]

Note: *This section is proposed as an optional provision to require filing officers to furnish certificates. Local law and practices should be consulted with regard to the advisability of adoption.*

§ 9—408. Financing Statements Covering Consigned or Leased Goods.

A consignor or lessor of goods may file a financing statement using the terms "consignor," "consignee," "lessor," "lessee" or the like instead of the terms specified in Section 9—402. The provisions of this Part shall apply as appropriate to such a financing statement but its filing shall not of itself be a factor in determining whether or not the consignment or lease is intended as security (Section 1—201(37)). However, if it is determined for other reasons that the consignment or lease is so intended, a security interest of the consignor or lessor which attaches to the consigned or leased goods is perfected by such filing.

Part 5 Default

§ 9—501. Default; Procedure When Security Agreement Covers Both Real and Personal Property.

(1) When a debtor is in default under a security agreement, a secured party has the rights and remedies provided in this Part and except as limited by subsection (3) those provided in the security agreement. He may reduce his claim to judgment, foreclose or otherwise enforce the security interest by any available judicial procedure. If the collateral is documents the secured party may proceed either as to the documents or as to the goods covered thereby. A secured party in possession has the rights, remedies and duties provided in Section 9—207. The rights and remedies referred to in this subsection are cumulative.

(2) After default, the debtor has the rights and remedies provided in this Part, those provided in the security agreement and those provided in Section 9—207.

(3) To the extent that they give rights to the debtor and impose duties on the secured party, the rules stated in the subsections referred to below may not be waived or varied except as provided with respect to compulsory disposition of collateral (subsection (3) of Section 9—504 and Section 9—505) and with respect to redemption of collateral (Section 9—506) but the parties may by agreement determine the standards by which the fulfillment of these rights and duties is to be measured if such standards are not manifestly unreasonable:

  (a) subsection (2) of Section 9—502 and subsection (2) of Section 9—504 insofar as they require accounting for surplus proceeds of collateral;

  (b) subsection (3) of Section 9—504 and subsection (1) of Section 9—505 which deal with disposition of collateral;

  (c) subsection (2) of Section 9—505 which deals with acceptance of collateral as discharge of obligation;

  (d) Section 9—506 which deals with redemption of collateral; and

  (e) subsection (1) of Section 9—507 which deals with the secured party's liability for failure to comply with this Part.

(4) If the security agreement covers both real and personal property, the secured party may proceed under this Part as to the personal property or he may proceed as to both the real and the personal property in accordance with his rights and remedies in respect of the real property in which case the provisions of this Part do not apply.

(5) When a secured party has reduced his claim to judgment the lien of any levy which may be made upon his collateral by virtue of any execution based upon the judgment shall relate back to the date of the perfection of the security interest in such collateral. A judicial sale, pursuant to such execution, is a foreclosure of the security interest by judicial procedure within the meaning of this section, and the secured party may purchase at the sale and thereafter hold the collateral free of any other requirements of this Article.

§ 9—502. Collection Rights of Secured Party.

(1) When so agreed and in any event on default the secured party is entitled to notify an account debtor or the obligor on an instrument to make payment to him whether or not the assignor was theretofore making collections on the collateral, and also to take control of any proceeds to which he is entitled under Section 9—306.

(2) A secured party who by agreement is entitled to charge back uncollected collateral or otherwise to full or limited recourse against the debtor and who undertakes to collect from the account debtors or obligors must proceed in a commercially reasonable manner and may deduct his reasonable expenses of realization from the collections. If the security agreement secures an indebtedness, the secured party must account to the debtor for any surplus, and unless otherwise agreed, the debtor is liable for any deficiency. But, if the underlying transaction was a sale of accounts or chattel paper, the debtor is entitled to any surplus or is liable for any deficiency only if the security agreement so provides.

§ 9—503. Secured Party's Right to Take Possession After Default.

Unless otherwise agreed a secured party has on default the right to take possession of the collateral. In taking possession a secured party may proceed without judicial process if this can be done without breach of the peace or may proceed by action. If the security agreement so provides the secured party may require the debtor to assemble the collateral and make it available to the secured party at a place to be designated by the secured party which is reasonably convenient to both parties. Without removal a secured party may render equipment unusable, and may dispose of collateral on the debtor's premises under Section 9—504.

§ 9—504. Secured Party's Right to Dispose of Collateral After Default; Effect of Disposition.

(1) A secured party after default may sell, lease or otherwise dispose of any or all of the collateral in its then condition or following any commercially reasonable

preparation or processing. Any sale of goods is subject to the Article on Sales (Article 2). The proceeds of disposition shall be applied in the order following to

(a) the reasonable expenses of retaking, holding, preparing for sale or lease, selling, leasing and the like and, to the extent provided for in the agreement and not prohibited by law, the reasonable attorneys' fees and legal expenses incurred by the secured party;

(b) the satisfaction of indebtedness secured by the security interest under which the disposition is made;

(c) the satisfaction of indebtedness secured by any subordinate security interest in the collateral if written notification of demand therefor is received before distribution of the proceeds is completed. If requested by the secured party, the holder of a subordinate security interest must seasonably furnish reasonable proof of his interest, and unless he does so, the secured party need not comply with his demand.

(2) If the security interest secures an indebtedness, the secured party must account to the debtor for any surplus, and, unless otherwise agreed, the debtor is liable for any deficiency. But if the underlying transaction was a sale of accounts or chattel paper, the debtor is entitled to any surplus or is liable for any deficiency only if the security agreement so provides.

(3) Disposition of the collateral may be by public or private proceedings and may be made by way of one or more contracts. Sale or other disposition may be as a unit or in parcels and at any time and place and on any terms but every aspect of the disposition including the method, manner, time, place and terms must be commercially reasonable. Unless collateral is perishable or threatens to decline speedily in value or is of a type customarily sold on a recognized market, reasonable notification of the time and place of any public sale or reasonable notification of the time after which any private sale or other intended disposition is to be made shall be sent by the secured party to the debtor, if he has not signed after default a statement renouncing or modifying his right to notification of sale. In the case of consumer goods no other notification need be sent. In other cases notification shall be sent to any other secured party from whom the secured party has received (before sending his notification to the debtor or before the debtor's renunciation of his rights) written notice of a claim of an interest in the collateral. The secured party may buy at any public sale and if the collateral is of a type customarily sold in a recognized market or is of a type which is the subject of widely distributed standard price quotations he may buy at private sale.

(4) When collateral is disposed of by a secured party after default, the disposition transfers to a purchaser for value all of the debtor's rights therein, discharges the security interest under which it is made and any security interest or lien subordinate thereto. The purchaser takes free of all such rights and interests even though the secured party fails to

comply with the requirements of this Part or of any judicial proceedings

(a) in the case of a public sale, if the purchaser has no knowledge of any defects in the sale and if he does not buy in collusion with the secured party, other bidders or the person conducting the sale; or

(b) in any other case, if the purchaser acts in good faith.

(5) A person who is liable to a secured party under a guaranty, indorsement, repurchase agreement or the like and who receives a transfer of collateral from the secured party or is subrogated to his rights has thereafter the rights and duties of the secured party. Such a transfer of collateral is not a sale or disposition of the collateral under this Article.

§ 9—505. Compulsory Disposition of Collateral; Acceptance of the Collateral as Discharge of Obligation.

(1) If the debtor has paid sixty per cent of the cash price in the case of a purchase money security interest in consumer goods or sixty per cent of the loan in the case of another security interest in consumer goods, and has not signed after default a statement renouncing or modifying his rights under this Part a secured party who has taken possession of collateral must dispose of it under Section 9—504 and if he fails to do so within ninety days after he takes possession the debtor at his option may recover in conversion or under Section 9—507(1) on secured party's liability.

(2) In any other case involving consumer goods or any other collateral a secured party in possession may, after default, propose to retain the collateral in satisfaction of the obligation. Written notice of such proposal shall be sent to the debtor if he has not signed after default a statement renouncing or modifying his rights under this subsection. In the case of consumer goods no other notice need be given. In other cases notice shall be sent to any other secured party from whom the secured party has received (before sending his notice to the debtor or before the debtor's renunciation of his rights) written notice of a claim of an interest in the collateral. If the secured party receives objection in writing from a person entitled to receive notification within twenty-one days after the notice was sent, the secured party must dispose of the collateral under Section 9—504. In the absence of such written objection the secured party may retain the collateral in satisfaction of the debtor's obligation. Amended in 1972.

§ 9—506. Debtor's Right to Redeem Collateral.

At any time before the secured party has disposed of collateral or entered into a contract for its disposition under Section 9—504 or before the obligation has been discharged under Section 9—505(2) the debtor or any other secured party may unless otherwise agreed in writing after default redeem the collateral by tendering fulfillment of all obligations secured by the collateral as well as the expenses reasonably incurred by the secured party in retaking, holding and preparing the collateral for disposition, in arranging for the sale, and to the extent provided in the agreement and not prohibited by law, his reasonable attorneys' fees and legal expenses.

§ 9—507. Secured Party's Liability for Failure to Comply With This Part.

(1) If it is established that the secured party is not proceeding in accordance with the provisions of this Part disposition may be ordered or restrained on appropriate terms and conditions. If the disposition has occurred the debtor or any person entitled to notification or whose security interest has been made known to the secured party prior to the disposition has a right to recover from the secured party any loss caused by a failure to comply with the provisions of this Part. If the collateral is consumer goods, the debtor has a right to recover in any event an amount not less than the credit service charge plus ten per cent of the principal amount of the debt or the time price differential plus 10 per cent of the cash price.

(2) The fact that a better price could have been obtained by a sale at a different time or in a different method from that selected by the secured party is not of itself sufficient to establish that the sale was not made in a commercially reasonable manner. If the secured party either sells the collateral in the usual manner in any recognized market therefor or if he sells at the price current in such market at the time of his sale or if he has otherwise sold in conformity with reasonable commercial practices among dealers in the type of property sold he has sold in a commercially reasonable manner. The principles stated in the two preceding sentences with respect to sales also apply as may be appropriate to other types of disposition. A disposition which has been approved in any judicial proceeding or by any bona fide creditors' committee or representative of creditors shall conclusively be deemed to be commercially reasonable, but this sentence does not indicate that any such approval must be obtained in any case nor does it indicate that any disposition not so approved is not commercially reasonable.

Revised (1999) Article 9
SECURED TRANSACTIONS

Part 1 General Provisions

[Subpart 1. Short Title, Definitions, and General Concepts]

§ 9—101. Short Title.

This article may be cited as Uniform Commercial Code—Secured Transactions.

§ 9—102. Definitions and Index of Definitions.

(a) In this article:

(1) "Accession" means goods that are physically united with other goods in such a manner that the identity of the original goods is not lost.

(2) "Account", except as used in "account for", means a right to payment of a monetary obligation, whether or not earned by performance, (i) for property that has been or is to be sold, leased, licensed, assigned, or otherwise disposed of, (ii) for services rendered or to be rendered, (iii) for a policy of insurance issued or to be issued, (iv) for a secondary obligation incurred or to be incurred, (v) for energy provided or to be provided, (vi) for the use or hire of a vessel under a charter or other contract, (vii) arising out of the use of a credit or charge card or information contained on or for use with the card, or (viii) as winnings in a lottery or other game of chance operated or sponsored by a State, governmental unit of a State, or person licensed or authorized to operate the game by a State or governmental unit of a State. The term includes health-care insurance receivables. The term does not include (i) rights to payment evidenced by chattel paper or an instrument, (ii) commercial tort claims, (iii) deposit accounts, (iv) investment property, (v) letter-of-credit rights or letters of credit, or (vi) rights to payment for money or funds advanced or sold, other than rights arising out of the use of a credit or charge card or information contained on or for use with the card.

(3) "Account debtor" means a person obligated on an account, chattel paper, or general intangible. The term does not include persons obligated to pay a negotiable instrument, even if the instrument constitutes part of chattel paper.

(4) "Accounting", except as used in "accounting for", means a record:

    (A) authenticated by a secured party;

    (B) indicating the aggregate unpaid secured obligations as of a date not more than 35 days earlier or 35 days later than the date of the record; and

    (C) identifying the components of the obligations in reasonable detail.

(5) "Agricultural lien" means an interest, other than a security interest, in farm products:

    (A) which secures payment or performance of an obligation for:

        (i) goods or services furnished in connection with a debtor's farming operation; or

        (ii) rent on real property leased by a debtor in connection with its farming operation;

    (B) which is created by statute in favor of a person that:

(i) in the ordinary course of its business furnished goods or services to a debtor in connection with a debtor's farming operation; or

(ii) leased real property to a debtor in connection with the debtor's farming operation; and

(C) whose effectiveness does not depend on the person's possession of the personal property.

(6) "As-extracted collateral" means:

(A) oil, gas, or other minerals that are subject to a security interest that:

(i) is created by a debtor having an interest in the minerals before extraction; and

(ii) attaches to the minerals as extracted; or

(B) accounts arising out of the sale at the wellhead or minehead of oil, gas, or other minerals in which the debtor had an interest before extraction.

(7) "Authenticate" means:

(A) to sign; or

(B) to execute or otherwise adopt a symbol, or encrypt or similarly process a record in whole or in part, with the present intent of the authenticating person to identify the person and adopt or accept a record.

(8) "Bank" means an organization that is engaged in the business of banking. The term includes savings banks, savings and loan associations, credit unions, and trust companies.

(9) "Cash proceeds" means proceeds that are money, checks, deposit accounts, or the like.

(10) "Certificate of title" means a certificate of title with respect to which a statute provides for the security interest in question to be indicated on the certificate as a condition or result of the security interest's obtaining priority over the rights of a lien creditor with respect to the collateral.

(11) "Chattel paper" means a record or records that evidence both a monetary obligation and a security interest in specific goods, a security interest in specific goods and software used in the goods, a security interest in specific goods and license of software used in the goods, a lease of specific goods, or a lease of specific goods and license of software used in the goods. In this paragraph, "monetary obligation" means a monetary obligation secured by the goods or owed under a lease of the goods and includes a monetary obligation with respect to software used in the goods. The term does not include (i) charters or other contracts involving the use or hire of a vessel or (ii) records that evidence a right to payment arising out of the use of a credit or charge card or information contained on or for use with the card. If a transaction is evidenced by records that include an instrument or series of instruments, the group of records taken together constitutes chattel paper.

(12) "Collateral" means the property subject to a security interest or agricultural lien. The term includes:

(A) proceeds to which a security interest attaches;

(B) accounts, chattel paper, payment intangibles, and promissory notes that have been sold; and

(C) goods that are the subject of a consignment.

(13) "Commercial tort claim" means a claim arising in tort with respect to which:

(A) the claimant is an organization; or

(B) the claimant is an individual and the claim:

(i) arose in the course of the claimant's business or profession; and

(ii) does not include damages arising out of personal injury to or the death of an individual.

(14) "Commodity account" means an account maintained by a commodity intermediary in which a commodity contract is carried for a commodity customer.

(15) "Commodity contract" means a commodity futures contract, an option on a commodity futures contract, a commodity option, or another contract if the contract or option is:

(A) traded on or subject to the rules of a board of trade that has been designated as a contract market for such a contract pursuant to federal commodities laws; or

(B) traded on a foreign commodity board of trade, exchange, or market, and is carried on the books of a commodity intermediary for a commodity customer.

(16) "Commodity customer" means a person for which a commodity intermediary carries a commodity contract on its books.

(17) "Commodity intermediary" means a person that:

(A) is registered as a futures commission merchant under federal commodities law; or

(B) in the ordinary course of its business provides clearance or settlement services for a board of trade that has been designated as a contract market pursuant to federal commodities law.

(18) "Communicate" means:

(A) to send a written or other tangible record;

(B) to transmit a record by any means agreed upon by the persons sending and receiving the record; or

(C) in the case of transmission of a record to or by a filing office, to transmit a record by any means prescribed by filing-office rule.

(19) "Consignee" means a merchant to which goods are delivered in a consignment.

(20) "Consignment" means a transaction, regardless of its form, in which a person delivers goods to a merchant for the purpose of sale and:

(A) the merchant:

(i) deals in goods of that kind under a name other than the name of the person making delivery;

(ii) is not an auctioneer; and

(iii) is not generally known by its creditors to be substantially engaged in selling the goods of others;

(B) with respect to each delivery, the aggregate value of the goods is $1,000 or more at the time of delivery;

(C) the goods are not consumer goods immediately before delivery; and

(D) the transaction does not create a security interest that secures an obligation.

(21) "Consignor" means a person that delivers goods to a consignee in a consignment.

(22) "Consumer debtor" means a debtor in a consumer transaction.

(23) "Consumer goods" means goods that are used or bought for use primarily for personal, family, or household purposes.

(24) "Consumer-goods transaction" means a consumer transaction in which:

(A) an individual incurs an obligation primarily for personal, family, or household purposes; and

(B) a security interest in consumer goods secures the obligation.

(25) "Consumer obligor" means an obligor who is an individual and who incurred the obligation as part of a transaction entered into primarily for personal, family, or household purposes.

(26) "Consumer transaction" means a transaction in which (i) an individual incurs an obligation primarily for personal, family, or household purposes, (ii) a security interest secures the obligation, and (iii) the collateral is held or acquired primarily for personal, family, or household purposes. The term includes consumer-goods transactions.

(27) "Continuation statement" means an amendment of a financing statement which:

(A) identifies, by its file number, the initial financing statement to which it relates; and

(B) indicates that it is a continuation statement for, or that it is filed to continue the effectiveness of, the identified financing statement.

(28) "Debtor" means:

(A) a person having an interest, other than a security interest or other lien, in the collateral, whether or not the person is an obligor;

(B) a seller of accounts, chattel paper, payment intangibles, or promissory notes; or

(C) a consignee.

(29) "Deposit account" means a demand, time, savings, passbook, or similar account maintained with a bank. The term does not include investment property or accounts evidenced by an instrument.

(30) "Document" means a document of title or a receipt of the type described in Section 7—201(2).

(31) "Electronic chattel paper" means chattel paper evidenced by a record or records consisting of information stored in an electronic medium.

(32) "Encumbrance" means a right, other than an ownership interest, in real property. The term includes mortgages and other liens on real property.

(33) "Equipment" means goods other than inventory, farm products, or consumer goods.

(34) "Farm products" means goods, other than standing timber, with respect to which the debtor is engaged in a farming operation and which are:

(A) crops grown, growing, or to be grown, including:

(i) crops produced on trees, vines, and bushes; and

(ii) aquatic goods produced in aquacultural operations;

(B) livestock, born or unborn, including aquatic goods produced in aquacultural operations;

(C) supplies used or produced in a farming operation; or

(D) products of crops or livestock in their unmanufactured states.

(35) "Farming operation" means raising, cultivating, propagating, fattening, grazing, or any other farming, livestock, or aquacultural operation.

(36) "File number" means the number assigned to an initial financing statement pursuant to Section 9—519(a).

(37) "Filing office" means an office designated in Section 9—501 as the place to file a financing statement.

(38) "Filing-office rule" means a rule adopted pursuant to Section 9—526.

(39) "Financing statement" means a record or records composed of an initial financing statement and any filed record relating to the initial financing statement.

(40) "Fixture filing" means the filing of a financing statement covering goods that are or are to become fix-

tures and satisfying Section 9—502(a) and (b). The term includes the filing of a financing statement covering goods of a transmitting utility which are or are to become fixtures.

(41) "Fixtures" means goods that have become so related to particular real property that an interest in them arises under real property law.

(42) "General intangible" means any personal property, including things in action, other than accounts, chattel paper, commercial tort claims, deposit accounts, documents, goods, instruments, investment property, letter-of-credit rights, letters of credit, money, and oil, gas, or other minerals before extraction. The term includes payment intangibles and software.

(43) "Good faith" means honesty in fact and the observance of reasonable commercial standards of fair dealing.

(44) "Goods" means all things that are movable when a security interest attaches. The term includes (i) fixtures, (ii) standing timber that is to be cut and removed under a conveyance or contract for sale, (iii) the unborn young of animals, (iv) crops grown, growing, or to be grown, even if the crops are produced on trees, vines, or bushes, and (v) manufactured homes. The term also includes a computer program embedded in goods and any supporting information provided in connection with a transaction relating to the program if (i) the program is associated with the goods in such a manner that it customarily is considered part of the goods, or (ii) by becoming the owner of the goods, a person acquires a right to use the program in connection with the goods. The term does not include a computer program embedded in goods that consist solely of the medium in which the program is embedded. The term also does not include accounts, chattel paper, commercial tort claims, deposit accounts, documents, general intangibles, instruments, investment property, letter-of-credit rights, letters of credit, money, or oil, gas, or other minerals before extraction.

(45) "Governmental unit" means a subdivision, agency, department, county, parish, municipality, or other unit of the government of the United States, a State, or a foreign country. The term includes an organization having a separate corporate existence if the organization is eligible to issue debt on which interest is exempt from income taxation under the laws of the United States.

(46) "Health-care-insurance receivable" means an interest in or claim under a policy of insurance which is a right to payment of a monetary obligation for health-care goods or services provided.

(47) "Instrument" means a negotiable instrument or any other writing that evidences a right to the payment of a monetary obligation, is not itself a security agree-

ment or lease, and is of a type that in ordinary course of business is transferred by delivery with any necessary indorsement or assignment. The term does not include (i) investment property, (ii) letters of credit, or (iii) writings that evidence a right to payment arising out of the use of a credit or charge card or information contained on or for use with the card.

(48) "Inventory" means goods, other than farm products, which:

(A) are leased by a person as lessor;

(B) are held by a person for sale or lease or to be furnished under a contract of service;

(C) are furnished by a person under a contract of service; or

(D) consist of raw materials, work in process, or materials used or consumed in a business.

(49) "Investment property" means a security, whether certificated or uncertificated, security entitlement, securities account, commodity contract, or commodity account.

(50) "Jurisdiction of organization", with respect to a registered organization, means the jurisdiction under whose law the organization is organized.

(51) "Letter-of-credit right" means a right to payment or performance under a letter of credit, whether or not the beneficiary has demanded or is at the time entitled to demand payment or performance. The term does not include the right of a beneficiary to demand payment or performance under a letter of credit.

(52) "Lien creditor" means:

(A) a creditor that has acquired a lien on the property involved by attachment, levy, or the like;

(B) an assignee for benefit of creditors from the time of assignment;

(C) a trustee in bankruptcy from the date of the filing of the petition; or

(D) a receiver in equity from the time of appointment.

(53) "Manufactured home" means a structure, transportable in one or more sections, which, in the traveling mode, is eight body feet or more in width or 40 body feet or more in length, or, when erected on site, is 320 or more square feet, and which is built on a permanent chassis and designed to be used as a dwelling with or without a permanent foundation when connected to the required utilities, and includes the plumbing, heating, air-conditioning, and electrical systems contained therein. The term includes any structure that meets all of the requirements of this paragraph except the size requirements and with respect to which the manufacturer voluntarily files a certification required by the United States Secretary of Housing and

Urban Development and complies with the standards established under Title 42 of the United States Code.

(54) "Manufactured-home transaction" means a secured transaction:

(A) that creates a purchase-money security interest in a manufactured home, other than a manufactured home held as inventory; or

(B) in which a manufactured home, other than a manufactured home held as inventory, is the primary collateral.

(55) "Mortgage" means a consensual interest in real property, including fixtures, which secures payment or performance of an obligation.

(56) "New debtor" means a person that becomes bound as debtor under Section 9—203(d) by a security agreement previously entered into by another person.

(57) "New value" means (i) money, (ii) money's worth in property, services, or new credit, or (iii) release by a transferee of an interest in property previously transferred to the transferee. The term does not include an obligation substituted for another obligation.

(58) "Noncash proceeds" means proceeds other than cash proceeds.

(59) "Obligor" means a person that, with respect to an obligation secured by a security interest in or an agricultural lien on the collateral, (i) owes payment or other performance of the obligation, (ii) has provided property other than the collateral to secure payment or other performance of the obligation, or (iii) is otherwise accountable in whole or in part for payment or other performance of the obligation. The term does not include issuers or nominated persons under a letter of credit.

(60) "Original debtor", except as used in Section 9—310(c), means a person that, as debtor, entered into a security agreement to which a new debtor has become bound under Section 9—203(d).

(61) "Payment intangible" means a general intangible under which the account debtor's principal obligation is a monetary obligation.

(62) "Person related to", with respect to an individual, means:

(A) the spouse of the individual;

(B) a brother, brother-in-law, sister, or sister-in-law of the individual;

(C) an ancestor or lineal descendant of the individual or the individual's spouse; or

(D) any other relative, by blood or marriage, of the individual or the individual's spouse who shares the same home with the individual.

(63) "Person related to", with respect to an organization, means:

(A) a person directly or indirectly controlling, controlled by, or under common control with the organization; ·

(B) an officer or director of, or a person performing similar functions with respect to, the organization;

(C) an officer or director of, or a person performing similar functions with respect to, a person described in subparagraph (A);

(D) the spouse of an individual described in subparagraph (A), (B), or (C); or

(E) an individual who is related by blood or marriage to an individual described in subparagraph (A), (B), (C), or (D) and shares the same home with the individual.

(64) "Proceeds", except as used in Section 9—609(b), means the following property:

(A) whatever is acquired upon the sale, lease, license, exchange, or other disposition of collateral;

(B) whatever is collected on, or distributed on account of, collateral;

(C) rights arising out of collateral;

(D) to the extent of the value of collateral, claims arising out of the loss, nonconformity, or interference with the use of, defects or infringement of rights in, or damage to, the collateral; or

(E) to the extent of the value of collateral and to the extent payable to the debtor or the secured party, insurance payable by reason of the loss or nonconformity of, defects or infringement of rights in, or damage to, the collateral.

(65) "Promissory note" means an instrument that evidences a promise to pay a monetary obligation, does not evidence an order to pay, and does not contain an acknowledgment by a bank that the bank has received for deposit a sum of money or funds.

(66) "Proposal" means a record authenticated by a secured party which includes the terms on which the secured party is willing to accept collateral in full or partial satisfaction of the obligation it secures pursuant to Sections 9—620, 9—621, and 9—622.

(67) "Public-finance transaction" means a secured transaction in connection with which:

(A) debt securities are issued;

(B) all or a portion of the securities issued have an initial stated maturity of at least 20 years; and

(C) the debtor, obligor, secured party, account debtor or other person obligated on collateral, assignor or assignee of a secured obligation, or assignor or assignee of a security interest is a State or a governmental unit of a State.

(68) "Pursuant to commitment", with respect to an advance made or other value given by a secured party, means pursuant to the secured party's obligation, whether or not a subsequent event of default or other event not within the secured party's control has relieved or may relieve the secured party from its obligation.

(69) "Record", except as used in "for record", "of record", "record or legal title", and "record owner", means information that is inscribed on a tangible medium or which is stored in an electronic or other medium and is retrievable in perceivable form.

(70) "Registered organization" means an organization organized solely under the law of a single State or the United States and as to which the State or the United States must maintain a public record showing the organization to have been organized.

(71) "Secondary obligor" means an obligor to the extent that:

(A) the obligor's obligation is secondary; or

(B) the obligor has a right of recourse with respect to an obligation secured by collateral against the debtor, another obligor, or property of either.

(72) "Secured party" means:

(A) a person in whose favor a security interest is created or provided for under a security agreement, whether or not any obligation to be secured is outstanding;

(B) a person that holds an agricultural lien;

(C) a consignor;

(D) a person to which accounts, chattel paper, payment intangibles, or promissory notes have been sold;

(E) a trustee, indenture trustee, agent, collateral agent, or other representative in whose favor a security interest or agricultural lien is created or provided for; or

(F) a person that holds a security interest arising under Section 2−401, 2−505, 2−711(3), 2A−508(5), 4−210, or 5−118.

(73) "Security agreement" means an agreement that creates or provides for a security interest.

(74) "Send", in connection with a record or notification, means:

(A) to deposit in the mail, deliver for transmission, or transmit by any other usual means of communication, with postage or cost of transmission provided for, addressed to any address reasonable under the circumstances; or

(B) to cause the record or notification to be received within the time that it would have been received if properly sent under subparagraph (A).

(75) "Software" means a computer program and any supporting information provided in connection with a transaction relating to the program. The term does not include a computer program that is included in the definition of goods.

(76) "State" means a State of the United States, the District of Columbia, Puerto Rico, the United States Virgin Islands, or any territory or insular possession subject to the jurisdiction of the United States.

(77) "Supporting obligation" means a letter-of-credit right or secondary obligation that supports the payment or performance of an account, chattel paper, a document, a general intangible, an instrument, or investment property.

(78) "Tangible chattel paper" means chattel paper evidenced by a record or records consisting of information that is inscribed on a tangible medium.

(79) "Termination statement" means an amendment of a financing statement which:

(A) identifies, by its file number, the initial financing statement to which it relates; and

(B) indicates either that it is a termination statement or that the identified financing statement is no longer effective.

(80) "Transmitting utility" means a person primarily engaged in the business of:

(A) operating a railroad, subway, street railway, or trolley bus;

(B) transmitting communications electrically, electromagnetically, or by light;

(C) transmitting goods by pipeline or sewer; or

(D) transmitting or producing and transmitting electricity, steam, gas, or water.

(b) The following definitions in other articles apply to this article:

"Applicant"	Section 5−102
"Beneficiary"	Section 5−102
"Broker"	Section 8−102
"Certificated security"	Section 8−102
"Check"	Section 3−104
"Clearing corporation"	Section 8−102
"Contract for sale"	Section 2−106
"Customer"	Section 4−104
"Entitlement holder"	Section 8−102
"Financial asset"	Section 8−102
"Holder in due course"	Section 3−302
"Issuer" (with respect to a letter of credit or letter-of-credit right)	Section 5−102

"Issuer" (with respect to a security)	Section 8—201
"Lease"	Section 2A—103
"Lease agreement"	Section 2A—103
"Lease contract"	Section 2A—103
"Leasehold interest"	Section 2A—103
"Lessee"	Section 2A—103
"Lessee in ordinary course of business"	Section 2A—103
"Lessor"	Section 2A—103
"Lessor's residual interest"	Section 2A—103
"Letter of credit"	Section 5—102
"Merchant"	Section 2—104
"Negotiable instrument"	Section 3—104
"Nominated person"	Section 5—102
"Note"	Section 3—104
"Proceeds of a letter of credit"	Section 5—114
"Prove"	Section 3—103
"Sale"	Section 2—106
"Securities account"	Section 8—501
"Securities intermediary"	Section 8—102
"Security"	Section 8—102
"Security certificate"	Section 8—102
"Security entitlement"	Section 8—102
"Uncertificated security"	Section 8—102

(c) Article 1 contains general definitions and principles of construction and interpretation applicable throughout this article.

§ 9—103. Purchase-Money Security Interest; Application of Payments; Burden of Establishing.

(a) In this section:

(1) "purchase-money collateral" means goods or software that secures a purchase-money obligation incurred with respect to that collateral; and

(2) "purchase-money obligation" means an obligation of an obligor incurred as all or part of the price of the collateral or for value given to enable the debtor to acquire rights in or the use of the collateral if the value is in fact so used.

(b) A security interest in goods is a purchase-money security interest:

(1) to the extent that the goods are purchase-money collateral with respect to that security interest;

(2) if the security interest is in inventory that is or was purchase-money collateral, also to the extent that the security interest secures a purchase-money obligation incurred with respect to other inventory in which the secured party holds or held a purchase-money security interest; and

(3) also to the extent that the security interest secures a purchase-money obligation incurred with respect to software in which the secured party holds or held a purchase-money security interest.

(c) A security interest in software is a purchase-money security interest to the extent that the security interest also secures a purchase-money obligation incurred with respect to goods in which the secured party holds or held a purchase-money security interest if:

(1) the debtor acquired its interest in the software in an integrated transaction in which it acquired an interest in the goods; and

(2) the debtor acquired its interest in the software for the principal purpose of using the software in the goods.

(d) The security interest of a consignor in goods that are the subject of a consignment is a purchase-money security interest in inventory.

(e) In a transaction other than a consumer-goods transaction, if the extent to which a security interest is a purchase-money security interest depends on the application of a payment to a particular obligation, the payment must be applied:

(1) in accordance with any reasonable method of application to which the parties agree;

(2) in the absence of the parties' agreement to a reasonable method, in accordance with any intention of the obligor manifested at or before the time of payment; or

(3) in the absence of an agreement to a reasonable method and a timely manifestation of the obligor's intention, in the following order:

(A) to obligations that are not secured; and

(B) if more than one obligation is secured, to obligations secured by purchase-money security interests in the order in which those obligations were incurred.

(f) In a transaction other than a consumer-goods transaction, a purchase-money security interest does not lose its status as such, even if:

(1) the purchase-money collateral also secures an obligation that is not a purchase-money obligation;

(2) collateral that is not purchase-money collateral also secures the purchase-money obligation; or

(3) the purchase-money obligation has been renewed, refinanced, consolidated, or restructured.

(g) In a transaction other than a consumer-goods transaction, a secured party claiming a purchase-money security interest has the burden of establishing the extent to which the security interest is a purchase-money security interest.

(h) The limitation of the rules in subsections (e), (f), and (g) to transactions other than consumer-goods transactions is intended to leave to the court the determination of the proper rules in consumer-goods transactions. The court may not infer from that limitation the nature of the proper rule in consumer-goods transactions and may continue to apply established approaches.

§ 9—104. Control of Deposit Account.

(a) A secured party has control of a deposit account if:

(1) the secured party is the bank with which the deposit account is maintained;

(2) the debtor, secured party, and bank have agreed in an authenticated record that the bank will comply with instructions originated by the secured party directing disposition of the funds in the deposit account without further consent by the debtor; or

(3) the secured party becomes the bank's customer with respect to the deposit account.

(b) A secured party that has satisfied subsection (a) has control, even if the debtor retains the right to direct the disposition of funds from the deposit account.

§ 9—105. Control of Electronic Chattel Paper.

A secured party has control of electronic chattel paper if the record or records comprising the chattel paper are created, stored, and assigned in such a manner that:

(1) a single authoritative copy of the record or records exists which is unique, identifiable and, except as otherwise provided in paragraphs (4), (5), and (6), unalterable;

(2) the authoritative copy identifies the secured party as the assignee of the record or records;

(3) the authoritative copy is communicated to and maintained by the secured party or its designated custodian;

(4) copies or revisions that add or change an identified assignee of the authoritative copy can be made only with the participation of the secured party;

(5) each copy of the authoritative copy and any copy of a copy is readily identifiable as a copy that is not the authoritative copy; and

(6) any revision of the authoritative copy is readily identifiable as an authorized or unauthorized revision.

§ 9—106. Control of Investment Property.

(a) A person has control of a certificated security, uncertificated security, or security entitlement as provided in Section 8—106.

(b) A secured party has control of a commodity contract if:

(1) the secured party is the commodity intermediary with which the commodity contract is carried; or

(2) the commodity customer, secured party, and commodity intermediary have agreed that the commodity intermediary will apply any value distributed on account of the commodity contract as directed by the secured party without further consent by the commodity customer.

(c) A secured party having control of all security entitlements or commodity contracts carried in a securities account or commodity account has control over the securities account or commodity account.

§ 9—107. Control of Letter-of-Credit Right.

A secured party has control of a letter-of-credit right to the extent of any right to payment or performance by the issuer or any nominated person if the issuer or nominated person has consented to an assignment of proceeds of the letter of credit under Section 5—114(c) or otherwise applicable law or practice.

§ 9—108. Sufficiency of Description.

(a) Except as otherwise provided in subsections (c), (d), and (e), a description of personal or real property is sufficient, whether or not it is specific, if it reasonably identifies what is described.

(b) Except as otherwise provided in subsection (d), a description of collateral reasonably identifies the collateral if it identifies the collateral by:

(1) specific listing;

(2) category;

(3) except as otherwise provided in subsection (e), a type of collateral defined in [the Uniform Commercial Code];

(4) quantity;

(5) computational or allocational formula or procedure; or

(6) except as otherwise provided in subsection (c), any other method, if the identity of the collateral is objectively determinable.

(c) A description of collateral as "all the debtor's assets" or "all the debtor's personal property" or using words of similar import does not reasonably identify the collateral.

(d) Except as otherwise provided in subsection (e), a description of a security entitlement, securities account, or commodity account is sufficient if it describes:

(1) the collateral by those terms or as investment property; or

(2) the underlying financial asset or commodity contract.

(e) A description only by type of collateral defined in [the Uniform Commercial Code] is an insufficient description of:

    (1) a commercial tort claim; or

    (2) in a consumer transaction, consumer goods, a security entitlement, a securities account, or a commodity account.

[Subpart 2. Applicability of Article]

§ 9—109. Scope.

(a) Except as otherwise provided in subsections (c) and (d), this article applies to:

    (1) a transaction, regardless of its form, that creates a security interest in personal property or fixtures by contract;

    (2) an agricultural lien;

    (3) a sale of accounts, chattel paper, payment intangibles, or promissory notes;

    (4) a consignment;

    (5) a security interest arising under Section 2—401, 2—505, 2—711(3), or 2A—508(5), as provided in Section 9—110; and

    (6) a security interest arising under Section 4—210 or 5—118.

(b) The application of this article to a security interest in a secured obligation is not affected by the fact that the obligation is itself secured by a transaction or interest to which this article does not apply.

(c) This article does not apply to the extent that:

    (1) a statute, regulation, or treaty of the United States preempts this article;

    (2) another statute of this State expressly governs the creation, perfection, priority, or enforcement of a security interest created by this State or a governmental unit of this State;

    (3) a statute of another State, a foreign country, or a governmental unit of another State or a foreign country, other than a statute generally applicable to security interests, expressly governs creation, perfection, priority, or enforcement of a security interest created by the State, country, or governmental unit; or

    (4) the rights of a transferee beneficiary or nominated person under a letter of credit are independent and superior under Section 5—114.

(d) This article does not apply to:

    (1) a landlord's lien, other than an agricultural lien;

    (2) a lien, other than an agricultural lien, given by statute or other rule of law for services or materials, but Section 9—333 applies with respect to priority of the lien;

    (3) an assignment of a claim for wages, salary, or other compensation of an employee;

    (4) a sale of accounts, chattel paper, payment intangibles, or promissory notes as part of a sale of the business out of which they arose;

    (5) an assignment of accounts, chattel paper, payment intangibles, or promissory notes which is for the purpose of collection only;

    (6) an assignment of a right to payment under a contract to an assignee that is also obligated to perform under the contract;

    (7) an assignment of a single account, payment intangible, or promissory note to an assignee in full or partial satisfaction of a preexisting indebtedness;

    (8) a transfer of an interest in or an assignment of a claim under a policy of insurance, other than an assignment by or to a health-care provider of a health-care-insurance receivable and any subsequent assignment of the right to payment, but Sections 9—315 and 9—322 apply with respect to proceeds and priorities in proceeds;

    (9) an assignment of a right represented by a judgment, other than a judgment taken on a right to payment that was collateral;

    (10) a right of recoupment or set-off, but:

        (A) Section 9—340 applies with respect to the effectiveness of rights of recoupment or set-off against deposit accounts; and

        (B) Section 9—404 applies with respect to defenses or claims of an account debtor;

    (11) the creation or transfer of an interest in or lien on real property, including a lease or rents thereunder, except to the extent that provision is made for:

        (A) liens on real property in Sections 9—203 and 9—308;

        (B) fixtures in Section 9—334;

        (C) fixture filings in Sections 9—501, 9—502, 9—512, 9—516, and 9—519; and

        (D) security agreements covering personal and real property in Section 9—604;

    (12) an assignment of a claim arising in tort, other than a commercial tort claim, but Sections 9—315 and 9—322 apply with respect to proceeds and priorities in proceeds; or

    (13) an assignment of a deposit account in a consumer transaction, but Sections 9—315 and 9—322 apply with respect to proceeds and priorities in proceeds.

§ 9—110. Security Interests Arising under Article 2 or 2A.

A security interest arising under Section 2—401, 2—505, 2—711(3), or 2A—508(5) is subject to this article. However, until the debtor obtains possession of the goods:

(1) the security interest is enforceable, even if Section 9—203(b)(3) has not been satisfied;

(2) filing is not required to perfect the security interest;

(3) the rights of the secured party after default by the debtor are governed by Article 2 or 2A; and

(4) the security interest has priority over a conflicting security interest created by the debtor.

Part 2 Effectiveness of Security Agreement; Attachment of Security Interest; Rights of Parties to Security Agreement

[Subpart 1. Effectiveness and Attachment]

§ 9—201. General Effectiveness of Security Agreement.

(a) Except as otherwise provided in [the Uniform Commercial Code], a security agreement is effective according to its terms between the parties, against purchasers of the collateral, and against creditors.

(b) A transaction subject to this article is subject to any applicable rule of law which establishes a different rule for consumers and [insert reference to (i) any other statute or regulation that regulates the rates, charges, agreements, and practices for loans, credit sales, or other extensions of credit and (ii) any consumer-protection statute or regulation].

(c) In case of conflict between this article and a rule of law, statute, or regulation described in subsection (b), the rule of law, statute, or regulation controls. Failure to comply with a statute or regulation described in subsection (b) has only the effect the statute or regulation specifies.

(d) This article does not:

(1) validate any rate, charge, agreement, or practice that violates a rule of law, statute, or regulation described in subsection (b); or

(2) extend the application of the rule of law, statute, or regulation to a transaction not otherwise subject to it.

§ 9—202. Title to Collateral Immaterial.

Except as otherwise provided with respect to consignments or sales of accounts, chattel paper, payment intangibles, or promissory notes, the provisions of this article with regard to rights and obligations apply whether title to collateral is in the secured party or the debtor.

§ 9—203. Attachment and Enforceability of Security Interest; Proceeds; Supporting Obligations; Formal Requisites.

(a) A security interest attaches to collateral when it becomes enforceable against the debtor with respect to the collateral, unless an agreement expressly postpones the time of attachment.

(b) Except as otherwise provided in subsections (c) through (i), a security interest is enforceable against the debtor and third parties with respect to the collateral only if:

(1) value has been given;

(2) the debtor has rights in the collateral or the power to transfer rights in the collateral to a secured party; and

(3) one of the following conditions is met:

(A) the debtor has authenticated a security agreement that provides a description of the collateral and, if the security interest covers timber to be cut, a description of the land concerned;

(B) the collateral is not a certificated security and is in the possession of the secured party under Section 9—313 pursuant to the debtor's security agreement;

(C) the collateral is a certificated security in registered form and the security certificate has been delivered to the secured party under Section 8—301 pursuant to the debtor's security agreement; or

(D) the collateral is deposit accounts, electronic chattel paper, investment property, or letter-of-credit rights, and the secured party has control under Section 9—104, 9—105, 9—106, or 9—107 pursuant to the debtor's security agreement.

(c) Subsection (b) is subject to Section 4—210 on the security interest of a collecting bank, Section 5—118 on the security interest of a letter-of-credit issuer or nominated person, Section 9—110 on a security interest arising under Article 2 or 2A, and Section 9—206 on security interests in investment property.

(d) A person becomes bound as debtor by a security agreement entered into by another person if, by operation of law other than this article or by contract:

(1) the security agreement becomes effective to create a security interest in the person's property; or

(2) the person becomes generally obligated for the obligations of the other person, including the obligation secured under the security agreement, and acquires or succeeds to all or substantially all of the assets of the other person.

(e) If a new debtor becomes bound as debtor by a security agreement entered into by another person:

(1) the agreement satisfies subsection (b)(3) with respect to existing or after-acquired property of the new debtor to the extent the property is described in the agreement; and

(2) another agreement is not necessary to make a security interest in the property enforceable.

(f) The attachment of a security interest in collateral gives the secured party the rights to proceeds provided by Section 9—315 and is also attachment of a security interest in a supporting obligation for the collateral.

(g) The attachment of a security interest in a right to payment or performance secured by a security interest or other lien on personal or real property is also attachment of a security interest in the security interest, mortgage, or other lien.

(h) The attachment of a security interest in a securities account is also attachment of a security interest in the security entitlements carried in the securities account.

(i) The attachment of a security interest in a commodity account is also attachment of a security interest in the commodity contracts carried in the commodity account.

§ 9—204. After-Acquired Property; Future Advances.

(a) Except as otherwise provided in subsection (b), a security agreement may create or provide for a security interest in after-acquired collateral.

(b) A security interest does not attach under a term constituting an after-acquired property clause to:

(1) consumer goods, other than an accession when given as additional security, unless the debtor acquires rights in them within 10 days after the secured party gives value; or

(2) a commercial tort claim.

(c) A security agreement may provide that collateral secures, or that accounts, chattel paper, payment intangibles, or promissory notes are sold in connection with, future advances or other value, whether or not the advances or value are given pursuant to commitment.

§ 9—205. Use or Disposition of Collateral Permissible.

(a) A security interest is not invalid or fraudulent against creditors solely because:

(1) the debtor has the right or ability to:

(A) use, commingle, or dispose of all or part of the collateral, including returned or repossessed goods;

(B) collect, compromise, enforce, or otherwise deal with collateral;

(C) accept the return of collateral or make repossessions; or

(D) use, commingle, or dispose of proceeds; or

(2) the secured party fails to require the debtor to account for proceeds or replace collateral.

(b) This section does not relax the requirements of possession if attachment, perfection, or enforcement of a security interest depends upon possession of the collateral by the secured party.

§ 9—206. Security Interest Arising in Purchase or Delivery of Financial Asset.

(a) A security interest in favor of a securities intermediary attaches to a person's security entitlement if:

(1) the person buys a financial asset through the securities intermediary in a transaction in which the person is obligated to pay the purchase price to the securities intermediary at the time of the purchase; and

(2) the securities intermediary credits the financial asset to the buyer's securities account before the buyer pays the securities intermediary.

(b) The security interest described in subsection (a) secures the person's obligation to pay for the financial asset.

(c) A security interest in favor of a person that delivers a certificated security or other financial asset represented by a writing attaches to the security or other financial asset if:

(1) the security or other financial asset:

(A) in the ordinary course of business is transferred by delivery with any necessary indorsement or assignment; and

(B) is delivered under an agreement between persons in the business of dealing with such securities or financial assets; and

(2) the agreement calls for delivery against payment.

(d) The security interest described in subsection (c) secures the obligation to make payment for the delivery.

[Subpart 2. Rights and Duties]

§ 9—207. Rights and Duties of Secured Party Having Possession or Control of Collateral.

(a) Except as otherwise provided in subsection (d), a secured party shall use reasonable care in the custody and preservation of collateral in the secured party's possession. In the case of chattel paper or an instrument, reasonable care includes taking necessary steps to preserve rights against prior parties unless otherwise agreed.

(b) Except as otherwise provided in subsection (d), if a secured party has possession of collateral:

(1) reasonable expenses, including the cost of insurance and payment of taxes or other charges, incurred in the custody, preservation, use, or operation of the collateral are chargeable to the debtor and are secured by the collateral;

(2) the risk of accidental loss or damage is on the debtor to the extent of a deficiency in any effective insurance coverage;

(3) the secured party shall keep the collateral identifiable, but fungible collateral may be commingled; and

(4) the secured party may use or operate the collateral:

(A) for the purpose of preserving the collateral or its value;

(B) as permitted by an order of a court having competent jurisdiction; or

(C) except in the case of consumer goods, in the manner and to the extent agreed by the debtor.

(c) Except as otherwise provided in subsection (d), a secured party having possession of collateral or control of collateral under Section 9—104, 9—105, 9—106, or 9—107:

(1) may hold as additional security any proceeds, except money or funds, received from the collateral;

(2) shall apply money or funds received from the collateral to reduce the secured obligation, unless remitted to the debtor; and

(3) may create a security interest in the collateral.

(d) If the secured party is a buyer of accounts, chattel paper, payment intangibles, or promissory notes or a consignor:

(1) subsection (a) does not apply unless the secured party is entitled under an agreement:

(A) to charge back uncollected collateral; or

(B) otherwise to full or limited recourse against the debtor or a secondary obligor based on the nonpayment or other default of an account debtor or other obligor on the collateral; and

(2) subsections (b) and (c) do not apply.

§ 9—208. Additional Duties of Secured Party Having Control of Collateral.

(a) This section applies to cases in which there is no outstanding secured obligation and the secured party is not committed to make advances, incur obligations, or otherwise give value.

(b) Within 10 days after receiving an authenticated demand by the debtor:

(1) a secured party having control of a deposit account under Section 9—104(a)(2) shall send to the bank with which the deposit account is maintained an authenticated statement that releases the bank from any further obligation to comply with instructions originated by the secured party;

(2) a secured party having control of a deposit account under Section 9—104(a)(3) shall:

(A) pay the debtor the balance on deposit in the deposit account; or

(B) transfer the balance on deposit into a deposit account in the debtor's name;

(3) a secured party, other than a buyer, having control of electronic chattel paper under Section 9—105 shall:

(A) communicate the authoritative copy of the electronic chattel paper to the debtor or its designated custodian;

(B) if the debtor designates a custodian that is the designated custodian with which the authoritative copy of the electronic chattel paper is maintained for the secured party, communicate to the custodian an authenticated record releasing the designated custodian from any further obligation to comply with instructions originated by the secured party and instructing the custodian to comply with instructions originated by the debtor; and

(C) take appropriate action to enable the debtor or its designated custodian to make copies of or revisions to the authoritative copy which add or change an identified assignee of the authoritative copy without the consent of the secured party;

(4) a secured party having control of investment property under Section 8—106(d)(2) or 9—106(b) shall send to the securities intermediary or commodity intermediary with which the security entitlement or commodity contract is maintained an authenticated record that releases the securities intermediary or commodity intermediary from any further obligation to comply with entitlement orders or directions originated by the secured party; and

(5) a secured party having control of a letter-of-credit right under Section 9—107 shall send to each person having an unfulfilled obligation to pay or deliver proceeds of the letter of credit to the secured party an authenticated release from any further obligation to pay or deliver proceeds of the letter of credit to the secured party.

§ 9—209. Duties of Secured Party If Account Debtor Has Been Notified of Assignment.

(a) Except as otherwise provided in subsection (c), this section applies if:

(1) there is no outstanding secured obligation; and

(2) the secured party is not committed to make advances, incur obligations, or otherwise give value.

(b) Within 10 days after receiving an authenticated demand by the debtor, a secured party shall send to an account debtor that has received notification of an assignment to the secured party as assignee under Section 9—406(a) an authenticated record that releases the account debtor from any further obligation to the secured party.

(c) This section does not apply to an assignment constituting the sale of an account, chattel paper, or payment intangible.

§ 9—210. Request for Accounting; Request Regarding List of Collateral or Statement of Account.

(a) In this section:

(1) "Request" means a record of a type described in paragraph (2), (3), or (4).

(2) "Request for an accounting" means a record authenticated by a debtor requesting that the recipient provide an accounting of the unpaid obligations secured by collateral and reasonably identifying the transaction or relationship that is the subject of the request.

(3) "Request regarding a list of collateral" means a record authenticated by a debtor requesting that the recipient approve or correct a list of what the debtor believes to be the collateral securing an obligation and reasonably identifying the transaction or relationship that is the subject of the request.

(4) "Request regarding a statement of account" means a record authenticated by a debtor requesting that the recipient approve or correct a statement indicating what the debtor believes to be the aggregate amount of unpaid obligations secured by collateral as of a specified date and reasonably identifying the transaction or relationship that is the subject of the request.

(b) Subject to subsections (c), (d), (e), and (f), a secured party, other than a buyer of accounts, chattel paper, payment intangibles, or promissory notes or a consignor, shall comply with a request within 14 days after receipt:

(1) in the case of a request for an accounting, by authenticating and sending to the debtor an accounting; and

(2) in the case of a request regarding a list of collateral or a request regarding a statement of account, by authenticating and sending to the debtor an approval or correction.

(c) A secured party that claims a security interest in all of a particular type of collateral owned by the debtor may comply with a request regarding a list of collateral by sending to the debtor an authenticated record including a statement to that effect within 14 days after receipt.

(d) A person that receives a request regarding a list of collateral, claims no interest in the collateral when it receives the request, and claimed an interest in the collateral at an earlier time shall comply with the request within 14 days after receipt by sending to the debtor an authenticated record:

(1) disclaiming any interest in the collateral; and

(2) if known to the recipient, providing the name and mailing address of any assignee of or successor to the recipient's interest in the collateral.

(e) A person that receives a request for an accounting or a request regarding a statement of account, claims no interest in the obligations when it receives the request, and claimed an interest in the obligations at an earlier time shall comply with the request within 14 days after receipt by sending to the debtor an authenticated record:

(1) disclaiming any interest in the obligations; and

(2) if known to the recipient, providing the name and mailing address of any assignee of or successor to the recipient's interest in the obligations.

(f) A debtor is entitled without charge to one response to a request under this section during any six-month period. The secured party may require payment of a charge not exceeding $25 for each additional response.

Part 3 Perfection and Priority

[Subpart 1. Law Governing Perfection and Priority]

§ 9—301. Law Governing Perfection and Priority of Security Interests.

Except as otherwise provided in Sections 9—303 through 9—306, the following rules determine the law governing perfection, the effect of perfection or nonperfection, and the priority of a security interest in collateral:

(1) Except as otherwise provided in this section, while a debtor is located in a jurisdiction, the local law of that jurisdiction governs perfection, the effect of perfection or nonperfection, and the priority of a security interest in collateral.

(2) While collateral is located in a jurisdiction, the local law of that jurisdiction governs perfection, the effect of perfection or nonperfection, and the priority of a possessory security interest in that collateral.

(3) Except as otherwise provided in paragraph (4), while negotiable documents, goods, instruments, money, or tangible chattel paper is located in a jurisdiction, the local law of that jurisdiction governs:

(A) perfection of a security interest in the goods by filing a fixture filing;

(B) perfection of a security interest in timber to be cut; and

(C) the effect of perfection or nonperfection and the priority of a nonpossessory security interest in the collateral.

(4) The local law of the jurisdiction in which the wellhead or minehead is located governs perfection, the effect of perfection or nonperfection, and the priority of a security interest in as-extracted collateral.

§ 9—302. Law Governing Perfection and Priority of Agricultural Liens.

While farm products are located in a jurisdiction, the local law of that jurisdiction governs perfection, the effect of perfection or nonperfection, and the priority of an agricultural lien on the farm products.

§ 9—303. Law Governing Perfection and Priority of Security Interests in Goods Covered by a Certificate of Title.

(a) This section applies to goods covered by a certificate of title, even if there is no other relationship between the jurisdiction under whose certificate of title. the goods are covered and the goods or the debtor.

(b) Goods become covered by a certificate of title when a valid application for the certificate of title and the applicable fee are delivered to the appropriate authority. Goods cease to be covered by a certificate of title at the earlier of the time the certificate of title ceases to be effective under the law of the issuing jurisdiction or the time the goods become covered subsequently by a certificate of title issued by another jurisdiction.

(c) The local law of the jurisdiction under whose certificate of title the goods are covered governs perfection, the effect of perfection or nonperfection, and the priority of a security interest in goods covered by a certificate of title from the time the goods become covered by the certificate of title until the goods cease to be covered by the certificate of title.

§ 9—304. Law Governing Perfection and Priority of Security Interests in Deposit Accounts.

(a) The local law of a bank's jurisdiction governs perfection, the effect of perfection or nonperfection, and the priority of a security interest in a deposit account maintained with that bank.

(b) The following rules determine a bank's jurisdiction for purposes of this part:

(1) If an agreement between the bank and the debtor governing the deposit account expressly provides that a particular jurisdiction is the bank's jurisdiction for purposes of this part, this article, or [the Uniform Commercial Code], that jurisdiction is the bank's jurisdiction.

(2) If paragraph (1) does not apply and an agreement between the bank and its customer governing the deposit account expressly provides that the agreement is governed by the law of a particular jurisdiction, that jurisdiction is the bank's jurisdiction.

(3) If neither paragraph (1) nor paragraph (2) applies and an agreement between the bank and its customer governing the deposit account expressly provides that the deposit account is maintained at an office in a particular jurisdiction, that jurisdiction is the bank's jurisdiction.

(4) If none of the preceding paragraphs applies, the bank's jurisdiction is the jurisdiction in which the office identified in an account statement as the office serving the customer's account is located.

(5) If none of the preceding paragraphs applies, the bank's jurisdiction is the jurisdiction in which the chief executive office of the bank is located.

§ 9—305. Law Governing Perfection and Priority of Security Interests in Investment Property.

(a) Except as otherwise provided in subsection (c), the following rules apply:

(1) While a security certificate is located in a jurisdiction, the local law of that jurisdiction governs perfection, the effect of perfection or nonperfection, and the priority of a security interest in the certificated security represented thereby.

(2) The local law of the issuer's jurisdiction as specified in Section 8—110(d) governs perfection, the effect of perfection or nonperfection, and the priority of a security interest in an uncertificated security.

(3) The local law of the securities intermediary's jurisdiction as specified in Section 8—110(e) governs perfection, the effect of perfection or nonperfection, and the priority of a security interest in a security entitlement or securities account.

(4) The local law of the commodity intermediary's jurisdiction governs perfection, the effect of perfection or nonperfection, and the priority of a security interest in a commodity contract or commodity account.

(b) The following rules determine a commodity intermediary's jurisdiction for purposes of this part:

(1) If an agreement between the commodity intermediary and commodity customer governing the commodity account expressly provides that a particular jurisdiction is the commodity intermediary's jurisdiction for purposes of this part, this article, or [the Uniform Commercial Code], that jurisdiction is the commodity intermediary's jurisdiction.

(2) If paragraph (1) does not apply and an agreement between the commodity intermediary and commodity customer governing the commodity account expressly provides that the agreement is governed by the law of a particular jurisdiction, that jurisdiction is the commodity intermediary's jurisdiction.

(3) If neither paragraph (1) nor paragraph (2) applies and an agreement between the commodity intermediary and commodity customer governing the commodity account expressly provides that the commodity account is maintained at an office in a particular jurisdiction, that jurisdiction is the commodity intermediary's jurisdiction.

(4) If none of the preceding paragraphs applies, the commodity intermediary's jurisdiction is the jurisdiction in which the office identified in an account statement as the office serving the commodity customer's account is located.

(5) If none of the preceding paragraphs applies, the commodity intermediary's jurisdiction is the jurisdiction in which the chief executive office of the commodity intermediary is located.

(c) The local law of the jurisdiction in which the debtor is located governs:

(1) perfection of a security interest in investment property by filing;

(2) automatic perfection of a security interest in investment property created by a broker or securities intermediary; and

(3) automatic perfection of a security interest in a commodity contract or commodity account created by a commodity intermediary.

§ 9—306. Law Governing Perfection and Priority of Security Interests in Letter-of-Credit Rights.

(a) Subject to subsection (c), the local law of the issuer's jurisdiction or a nominated person's jurisdiction governs perfection, the effect of perfection or nonperfection, and the priority of a security interest in a letter-of-credit right if the issuer's jurisdiction or nominated person's jurisdiction is a State.

(b) For purposes of this part, an issuer's jurisdiction or nominated person's jurisdiction is the jurisdiction whose law governs the liability of the issuer or nominated person with respect to the letter-of-credit right as provided in Section 5—116.

(c) This section does not apply to a security interest that is perfected only under Section 9—308(d).

§ 9—307. Location of Debtor.

(a) In this section, "place of business" means a place where a debtor conducts its affairs.

(b) Except as otherwise provided in this section, the following rules determine a debtor's location:

(1) A debtor who is an individual is located at the individual's principal residence.

(2) A debtor that is an organization and has only one place of business is located at its place of business.

(3) A debtor that is an organization and has more than one place of business is located at its chief executive office.

(c) Subsection (b) applies only if a debtor's residence, place of business, or chief executive office, as applicable, is located in a jurisdiction whose law generally requires information concerning the existence of a nonpossessory security interest to be made generally available in a filing, recording, or registration system as a condition or result of the security interest's obtaining priority over the rights of a lien creditor with respect to the collateral. If subsection (b) does not apply, the debtor is located in the District of Columbia.

(d) A person that ceases to exist, have a residence, or have a place of business continues to be located in the jurisdiction specified by subsections (b) and (c).

(e) A registered organization that is organized under the law of a State is located in that State.

(f) Except as otherwise provided in subsection (i), a registered organization that is organized under the law of the United States and a branch or agency of a bank that is not organized under the law of the United States or a State are located:

(1) in the State that the law of the United States designates, if the law designates a State of location;

(2) in the State that the registered organization, branch, or agency designates, if the law of the United States authorizes the registered organization, branch, or agency to designate its State of location; or

(3) in the District of Columbia, if neither paragraph (1) nor paragraph (2) applies.

(g) A registered organization continues to be located in the jurisdiction specified by subsection (e) or (f) notwithstanding:

(1) the suspension, revocation, forfeiture, or lapse of the registered organization's status as such in its jurisdiction of organization; or

(2) the dissolution, winding up, or cancellation of the existence of the registered organization.

(h) The United States is located in the District of Columbia.

(i) A branch or agency of a bank that is not organized under the law of the United States or a State is located in the State in which the branch or agency is licensed, if all branches and agencies of the bank are licensed in only one State.

(j) A foreign air carrier under the Federal Aviation Act of 1958, as amended, is located at the designated office of the agent upon which service of process may be made on behalf of the carrier.

(k) This section applies only for purposes of this part.

[Subpart 2. Perfection]

§ 9—308. When Security Interest or Agricultural Lien Is Perfected; Continuity of Perfection.

(a) Except as otherwise provided in this section and Section 9—309, a security interest is perfected if it has attached and all of the applicable requirements for perfection in Sections 9—310 through 9—316 have been satisfied. A security interest is perfected when it attaches if the applicable requirements are satisfied before the security interest attaches.

(b) An agricultural lien is perfected if it has become effective and all of the applicable requirements for perfection in Section 9—310 have been satisfied. An agricultural lien is perfected when it becomes effective if the applicable requirements are satisfied before the agricultural lien becomes effective.

(c) A security interest or agricultural lien is perfected continuously if it is originally perfected by one method under this article and is later perfected by another method under this article, without an intermediate period when it was unperfected.

(d) Perfection of a security interest in collateral also perfects a security interest in a supporting obligation for the collateral.

(e) Perfection of a security interest in a right to payment or performance also perfects a security interest in a security interest, mortgage, or other lien on personal or real property securing the right.

(f) Perfection of a security interest in a securities account also perfects a security interest in the security entitlements carried in the securities account.

(g) Perfection of a security interest in a commodity account also perfects a security interest in the commodity contracts carried in the commodity account.

Legislative Note: Any statute conflicting with subsection (e) must be made expressly subject to that subsection.

§ 9—309. Security Interest Perfected upon Attachment.

The following security interests are perfected when they attach:

(1) a purchase-money security interest in consumer goods, except as otherwise provided in Section 9—311(b) with respect to consumer goods that are subject to a statute or treaty described in Section 9—311(a);

(2) an assignment of accounts or payment intangibles which does not by itself or in conjunction with other assignments to the same assignee transfer a significant part of the assignor's outstanding accounts or payment intangibles;

(3) a sale of a payment intangible;

(4) a sale of a promissory note;

(5) a security interest created by the assignment of a health-care-insurance receivable to the provider of the health-care goods or services;

(6) a security interest arising under Section 2—401, 2—505, 2—711(3), or 2A—508(5), until the debtor obtains possession of the collateral;

(7) a security interest of a collecting bank arising under Section 4—210;

(8) a security interest of an issuer or nominated person arising under Section 5—118;

(9) a security interest arising in the delivery of a financial asset under Section 9—206(c);

(10) a security interest in investment property created by a broker or securities intermediary;

(11) a security interest in a commodity contract or a commodity account created by a commodity intermediary;

(12) an assignment for the benefit of all creditors of the transferor and subsequent transfers by the assignee thereunder; and

(13) a security interest created by an assignment of a beneficial interest in a decedent's estate.

§ 9—310. When Filing Required to Perfect Security Interest or Agricultural Lien; Security Interests and Agricultural Liens to Which Filing Provisions Do Not Apply.

(a) Except as otherwise provided in subsection (b) and Section 9—312(b), a financing statement must be filed to perfect all security interests and agricultural liens.

(b) The filing of a financing statement is not necessary to perfect a security interest:

(1) that is perfected under Section 9—308(d), (e), (f), or (g);

(2) that is perfected under Section 9—309 when it attaches;

(3) in property subject to a statute, regulation, or treaty described in Section 9—311(a);

(4) in goods in possession of a bailee which is perfected under Section 9—312(d)(1) or (2);

(5) in certificated securities, documents, goods, or instruments which is perfected without filing or possession under Section 9—312(e), (f), or (g);

(6) in collateral in the secured party's possession under Section 9—313;

(7) in a certificated security which is perfected by delivery of the security certificate to the secured party under Section 9—313;

(8) in deposit accounts, electronic chattel paper, investment property, or letter-of-credit rights which is perfected by control under Section 9—314;

(9) in proceeds which is perfected under Section 9—315; or

(10) that is perfected under Section 9—316.

(c) If a secured party assigns a perfected security interest or agricultural lien, a filing under this article is not required to continue the perfected status of the security interest against creditors of and transferees from the original debtor.

§ 9—311. Perfection of Security Interests in Property Subject to Certain Statutes, Regulations, and Treaties.

(a) Except as otherwise provided in subsection (d), the filing of a financing statement is not necessary or effective to perfect a security interest in property subject to:

(1) a statute, regulation, or treaty of the United States whose requirements for a security interest's obtaining priority over the rights of a lien creditor with respect to the property preempt Section 9—310(a);

(2) [list any certificate-of-title statute covering automobiles, trailers, mobile homes, boats, farm tractors, or the like, which provides for a security interest to be indicated on the certificate as a condition or result of perfection, and any non-Uniform Commercial Code central filing statute]; or

(3) a certificate-of-title statute of another jurisdiction which provides for a security interest to be indicated on the certificate as a condition or result of the security interest's obtaining priority over the rights of a lien creditor with respect to the property.

(b) Compliance with the requirements of a statute, regulation, or treaty described in subsection (a) for obtaining priority over the rights of a lien creditor is equivalent to the filing of a financing statement under this article. Except as otherwise provided in subsection (d) and Sections 9—313 and 9—316(d) and (e) for goods covered by a certificate of title, a security interest in property subject to a statute, regulation, or treaty described in subsection (a) may be perfected only by compliance with those requirements, and a security interest so perfected remains perfected notwithstanding a change in the use or transfer of possession of the collateral.

(c) Except as otherwise provided in subsection (d) and Section 9—316(d) and (e), duration and renewal of perfection of a security interest perfected by compliance with the requirements prescribed by a statute, regulation, or treaty described in subsection (a) are governed by the statute, regulation, or treaty. In other respects, the security interest is subject to this article.

(d) During any period in which collateral subject to a statute specified in subsection (a)(2) is inventory held for sale or lease by a person or leased by that person as lessor and that person is in the business of selling goods of that kind, this section does not apply to a security interest in that collateral created by that person.

Legislative Note: This Article contemplates that perfection of a security interest in goods covered by a certificate of title occurs upon receipt by appropriate State officials of a properly tendered application for a certificate of title on which the security interest is to be indicated, without a relation back to an earlier time. States whose certificate-of-title statutes provide for perfection at a different time or contain a relation-back provision should amend the statutes accordingly.

§ 9—312. **Perfection of Security Interests in Chattel Paper, Deposit Accounts, Documents, Goods Covered by Documents, Instruments, Investment Property, Letter-of-Credit Rights, and Money; Perfection by Permissive Filing; Temporary Perfection without Filing or Transfer of Possession.**

(a) A security interest in chattel paper, negotiable documents, instruments, or investment property may be perfected by filing.

(b) Except as otherwise provided in Section 9—315(c) and (d) for proceeds:

(1) a security interest in a deposit account may be perfected only by control under Section 9—314;

(2) and except as otherwise provided in Section 9—308(d), a security interest in a letter-of-credit right may be perfected only by control under Section 9—314; and

(3) a security interest in money may be perfected only by the secured party's taking possession under Section 9—313.

(c) While goods are in the possession of a bailee that has issued a negotiable document covering the goods:

(1) a security interest in the goods may be perfected by perfecting a security interest in the document; and

(2) a security interest perfected in the document has priority over any security interest that becomes perfected in the goods by another method during that time.

(d) While goods are in the possession of a bailee that has issued a nonnegotiable document covering the goods, a security interest in the goods may be perfected by:

(1) issuance of a document in the name of the secured party;

(2) the bailee's receipt of notification of the secured party's interest; or

(3) filing as to the goods.

(e) A security interest in certificated securities, negotiable documents, or instruments is perfected without filing or the taking of possession for a period of 20 days from the time it attaches to the extent that it arises for new value given under an authenticated security agreement.

(f) A perfected security interest in a negotiable document or goods in possession of a bailee, other than one that has issued a negotiable document for the goods, remains perfected for 20 days without filing if the secured party makes available to the debtor the goods or documents representing the goods for the purpose of:

(1) ultimate sale or exchange; or

(2) loading, unloading, storing, shipping, transshipping, manufacturing, processing, or otherwise dealing with them in a manner preliminary to their sale or exchange.

(g) A perfected security interest in a certificated security or instrument remains perfected for 20 days without filing if the secured party delivers the security certificate or instrument to the debtor for the purpose of:

(1) ultimate sale or exchange; or

(2) presentation, collection, enforcement, renewal, or registration of transfer.

(h) After the 20-day period specified in subsection (e), (f), or (g) expires, perfection depends upon compliance with this article.

§ 9—313. When Possession by or Delivery to Secured Party Perfects Security Interest without Filing.

(a) Except as otherwise provided in subsection (b), a secured party may perfect a security interest in negotiable documents, goods, instruments, money, or tangible chattel paper by taking possession of the collateral. A secured party may perfect a security interest in certificated securities by taking delivery of the certificated securities under Section 8—301.

(b) With respect to goods covered by a certificate of title issued by this State, a secured party may perfect a security interest in the goods by taking possession of the goods only in the circumstances described in Section 9—316(d).

(c) With respect to collateral other than certificated securities and goods covered by a document, a secured party takes possession of collateral in the possession of a person other than the debtor, the secured party, or a lessee of the collateral from the debtor in the ordinary course of the debtor's business, when:

> (1) the person in possession authenticates a record acknowledging that it holds possession of the collateral for the secured party's benefit; or

> (2) the person takes possession of the collateral after having authenticated a record acknowledging that it will hold possession of collateral for the secured party's benefit.

(d) If perfection of a security interest depends upon possession of the collateral by a secured party, perfection occurs no earlier than the time the secured party takes possession and continues only while the secured party retains possession.

(e) A security interest in a certificated security in registered form is perfected by delivery when delivery of the certificated security occurs under Section 8—301 and remains perfected by delivery until the debtor obtains possession of the security certificate.

(f) A person in possession of collateral is not required to acknowledge that it holds possession for a secured party's benefit.

(g) If a person acknowledges that it holds possession for the secured party's benefit:

> (1) the acknowledgment is effective under subsection (c) or Section 8—301(a), even if the acknowledgment violates the rights of a debtor; and

> (2) unless the person otherwise agrees or law other than this article otherwise provides, the person does not owe any duty to the secured party and is not required to confirm the acknowledgment to another person.

(h) A secured party having possession of collateral does not relinquish possession by delivering the collateral to a person other than the debtor or a lessee of the collateral from the debtor in the ordinary course of the debtor's business if the person was instructed before the delivery or is instructed contemporaneously with the delivery:

> (1) to hold possession of the collateral for the secured party's benefit; or

> (2) to redeliver the collateral to the secured party.

(i) A secured party does not relinquish possession, even if a delivery under subsection (h) violates the rights of a debtor. A person to which collateral is delivered under subsection (h) does not owe any duty to the secured party and is not required to confirm the delivery to another person unless the person otherwise agrees or law other than this article otherwise provides.

§ 9—314. Perfection by Control.

(a) A security interest in investment property, deposit accounts, letter-of-credit rights, or electronic chattel paper may be perfected by control of the collateral under Section 9—104, 9—105, 9—106, or 9—107.

(b) A security interest in deposit accounts, electronic chattel paper, or letter-of-credit rights is perfected by control under Section 9—104, 9—105, or 9—107 when the secured party obtains control and remains perfected by control only while the secured party retains control.

(c) A security interest in investment property is perfected by control under Section 9—106 from the time the secured party obtains control and remains perfected by control until:

> (1) the secured party does not have control; and

> (2) one of the following occurs:

>> (A) if the collateral is a certificated security, the debtor has or acquires possession of the security certificate;

>> (B) if the collateral is an uncertificated security, the issuer has registered or registers the debtor as the registered owner; or

>> (C) if the collateral is a security entitlement, the debtor is or becomes the entitlement holder.

§ 9—315. Secured Party's Rights on Disposition of Collateral and in Proceeds.

(a) Except as otherwise provided in this article and in Section 2—403(2):

> (1) a security interest or agricultural lien continues in collateral notwithstanding sale, lease, license, exchange, or other disposition thereof unless the secured party authorized the disposition free of the security interest or agricultural lien; and

(2) a security interest attaches to any identifiable proceeds of collateral.

(b) Proceeds that are commingled with other property are identifiable proceeds:

(1) if the proceeds are goods, to the extent provided by Section 9—336; and

(2) if the proceeds are not goods, to the extent that the secured party identifies the proceeds by a method of tracing, including application of equitable principles, that is permitted under law other than this article with respect to commingled property of the type involved.

(c) A security interest in proceeds is a perfected security interest if the security interest in the original collateral was perfected.

(d) A perfected security interest in proceeds becomes unperfected on the 21st day after the security interest attaches to the proceeds unless:

(1) the following conditions are satisfied:

(A) a filed financing statement covers the original collateral;

(B) the proceeds are collateral in which a security interest may be perfected by filing in the office in which the financing statement has been filed; and

(C) the proceeds are not acquired with cash proceeds;

(2) the proceeds are identifiable cash proceeds; or

(3) the security interest in the proceeds is perfected other than under subsection (c) when the security interest attaches to the proceeds or within 20 days thereafter.

(e) If a filed financing statement covers the original collateral, a security interest in proceeds which remains perfected under subsection (d)(1) becomes unperfected at the later of:

(1) when the effectiveness of the filed financing statement lapses under Section 9—515 or is terminated under Section 9—513; or

(2) the 21st day after the security interest attaches to the proceeds.

§ 9—316. Continued Perfection of Security Interest Following Change in Governing Law.

(a) A security interest perfected pursuant to the law of the jurisdiction designated in Section 9—301(1) or 9—305(c) remains perfected until the earliest of:

(1) the time perfection would have ceased under the law of that jurisdiction;

(2) the expiration of four months after a change of the debtor's location to another jurisdiction; or

(3) the expiration of one year after a transfer of collateral to a person that thereby becomes a debtor and is located in another jurisdiction.

(b) If a security interest described in subsection (a) becomes perfected under the law of the other jurisdiction before the earliest time or event described in that subsection, it remains perfected thereafter. If the security interest does not become perfected under the law of the other jurisdiction before the earliest time or event, it becomes unperfected and is deemed never to have been perfected as against a purchaser of the collateral for value.

(c) A possessory security interest in collateral, other than goods covered by a certificate of title and as-extracted collateral consisting of goods, remains continuously perfected if:

(1) the collateral is located in one jurisdiction and subject to a security interest perfected under the law of that jurisdiction;

(2) thereafter the collateral is brought into another jurisdiction; and

(3) upon entry into the other jurisdiction, the security interest is perfected under the law of the other jurisdiction.

(d) Except as otherwise provided in subsection (e), a security interest in goods covered by a certificate of title which is perfected by any method under the law of another jurisdiction when the goods become covered by a certificate of title from this State remains perfected until the security interest would have become unperfected under the law of the other jurisdiction had the goods not become so covered.

(e) A security interest described in subsection (d) becomes unperfected as against a purchaser of the goods for value and is deemed never to have been perfected as against a purchaser of the goods for value if the applicable requirements for perfection under Section 9—311(b) or 9—313 are not satisfied before the earlier of:

(1) the time the security interest would have become unperfected under the law of the other jurisdiction had the goods not become covered by a certificate of title from this State; or

(2) the expiration of four months after the goods had become so covered.

(f) A security interest in deposit accounts, letter-of-credit rights, or investment property which is perfected under the law of the bank's jurisdiction, the issuer's jurisdiction, a nominated person's jurisdiction, the securities intermediary's jurisdiction, or the commodity intermediary's jurisdiction, as applicable, remains perfected until the earlier of:

(1) the time the security interest would have become unperfected under the law of that jurisdiction; or

(2) the expiration of four months after a change of the applicable jurisdiction to another jurisdiction.

(g) If a security interest described in subsection (f) becomes perfected under the law of the other jurisdiction before the earlier of the time or the end of the period described in that subsection, it remains perfected thereafter. If the security interest does not become perfected under the law of the other jurisdiction before the earlier of that time or the end of that period, it becomes unperfected and is deemed never to have been perfected as against a purchaser of the collateral for value.

[Subpart 3. Priority]

§ 9—317. Interests That Take Priority over or Take Free of Security Interest or Agricultural Lien.

(a) A security interest or agricultural lien is subordinate to the rights of:

(1) a person entitled to priority under Section 9—322; and

(2) except as otherwise provided in subsection (e), a person that becomes a lien creditor before the earlier of the time:

(A) the security interest or agricultural lien is perfected; or

(B) one of the conditions specified in Section 9—203(b)(3) is met and a financing statement covering the collateral is filed.

(b) Except as otherwise provided in subsection (e), a buyer, other than a secured party, of tangible chattel paper, documents, goods, instruments, or a security certificate takes free of a security interest or agricultural lien if the buyer gives value and receives delivery of the collateral without knowledge of the security interest or agricultural lien and before it is perfected.

(c) Except as otherwise provided in subsection (e), a lessee of goods takes free of a security interest or agricultural lien if the lessee gives value and receives delivery of the collateral without knowledge of the security interest or agricultural lien and before it is perfected.

(d) A licensee of a general intangible or a buyer, other than a secured party, of accounts, electronic chattel paper, general intangibles, or investment property other than a certificated security takes free of a security interest if the licensee or buyer gives value without knowledge of the security interest and before it is perfected.

(e) Except as otherwise provided in Sections 9—320 and 9—321, if a person files a financing statement with respect to a purchase-money security interest before or within 20 days after the debtor receives delivery of the collateral, the security interest takes priority over the rights of a buyer, lessee, or lien creditor which arise between the time the security interest attaches and the time of filing.

§ 9—318. No Interest Retained in Right to Payment That Is Sold; Rights and Title of Seller of Account or Chattel Paper with Respect to Creditors and Purchasers.

(a) A debtor that has sold an account, chattel paper, payment intangible, or promissory note does not retain a legal or equitable interest in the collateral sold.

(b) For purposes of determining the rights of creditors of, and purchasers for value of an account or chattel paper from, a debtor that has sold an account or chattel paper, while the buyer's security interest is unperfected, the debtor is deemed to have rights and title to the account or chattel paper identical to those the debtor sold.

§ 9—319. Rights and Title of Consignee with Respect to Creditors and Purchasers.

(a) Except as otherwise provided in subsection (b), for purposes of determining the rights of creditors of, and purchasers for value of goods from, a consignee, while the goods are in the possession of the consignee, the consignee is deemed to have rights and title to the goods identical to those the consignor had or had power to transfer.

(b) For purposes of determining the rights of a creditor of a consignee, law other than this article determines the rights and title of a consignee while goods are in the consignee's possession if, under this part, a perfected security interest held by the consignor would have priority over the rights of the creditor.

§ 9—320. Buyer of Goods.

(a) Except as otherwise provided in subsection (e), a buyer in ordinary course of business, other than a person buying farm products from a person engaged in farming operations, takes free of a security interest created by the buyer's seller, even if the security interest is perfected and the buyer knows of its existence.

(b) Except as otherwise provided in subsection (e), a buyer of goods from a person who used or bought the goods for use primarily for personal, family, or household purposes takes free of a security interest, even if perfected, if the buyer buys:

(1) without knowledge of the security interest;

(2) for value;

(3) primarily for the buyer's personal, family, or household purposes; and

(4) before the filing of a financing statement covering the goods.

(c) To the extent that it affects the priority of a security interest over a buyer of goods under subsection (b), the period of effectiveness of a filing made in the jurisdiction in which the seller is located is governed by Section 9—316(a) and (b).

(d) A buyer in ordinary course of business buying oil, gas, or other minerals at the wellhead or minehead or after extraction takes free of an interest arising out of an encumbrance.

(e) Subsections (a) and (b) do not affect a security interest in goods in the possession of the secured party under Section 9—313.

§ 9—321. Licensee of General Intangible and Lessee of Goods in Ordinary Course of Business.

(a) In this section, "licensee in ordinary course of business" means a person that becomes a licensee of a general intangible in good faith, without knowledge that the license violates the rights of another person in the general intangible, and in the ordinary course from a person in the business of licensing general intangibles of that kind. A person becomes a licensee in the ordinary course if the license to the person comports with the usual or customary practices in the kind of business in which the licensor is engaged or with the licensor's own usual or customary practices.

(b) A licensee in ordinary course of business takes its rights under a nonexclusive license free of a security interest in the general intangible created by the licensor, even if the security interest is perfected and the licensee knows of its existence.

(c) A lessee in ordinary course of business takes its leasehold interest free of a security interest in the goods created by the lessor, even if the security interest is perfected and the lessee knows of its existence.

§ 9—322. Priorities among Conflicting Security Interests in and Agricultural Liens on Same Collateral.

(a) Except as otherwise provided in this section, priority among conflicting security interests and agricultural liens in the same collateral is determined according to the following rules:

(1) Conflicting perfected security interests and agricultural liens rank according to priority in time of filing or perfection. Priority dates from the earlier of the time a filing covering the collateral is first made or the security interest or agricultural lien is first perfected, if there is no period thereafter when there is neither filing nor perfection.

(2) A perfected security interest or agricultural lien has priority over a conflicting unperfected security interest or agricultural lien.

(3) The first security interest or agricultural lien to attach or become effective has priority if conflicting security interests and agricultural liens are unperfected.

(b) For the purposes of subsection (a)(1):

(1) the time of filing or perfection as to a security interest in collateral is also the time of filing or perfection as to a security interest in proceeds; and

(2) the time of filing or perfection as to a security interest in collateral supported by a supporting obligation is also the time of filing or perfection as to a security interest in the supporting obligation.

(c) Except as otherwise provided in subsection (f), a security interest in collateral which qualifies for priority over a conflicting security interest under Section 9—327, 9—328, 9—329, 9—330, or 9—331 also has priority over a conflicting security interest in:

(1) any supporting obligation for the collateral; and

(2) proceeds of the collateral if:

(A) the security interest in proceeds is perfected;

(B) the proceeds are cash proceeds or of the same type as the collateral; and

(C) in the case of proceeds that are proceeds of proceeds, all intervening proceeds are cash proceeds, proceeds of the same type as the collateral, or an account relating to the collateral.

(d) Subject to subsection (e) and except as otherwise provided in subsection (f), if a security interest in chattel paper, deposit accounts, negotiable documents, instruments, investment property, or letter-of-credit rights is perfected by a method other than filing, conflicting perfected security interests in proceeds of the collateral rank according to priority in time of filing.

(e) Subsection (d) applies only if the proceeds of the collateral are not cash proceeds, chattel paper, negotiable documents, instruments, investment property, or letter-of-credit rights.

(f) Subsections (a) through (e) are subject to:

(1) subsection (g) and the other provisions of this part;

(2) Section 4—210 with respect to a security interest of a collecting bank;

(3) Section 5—118 with respect to a security interest of an issuer or nominated person; and

(4) Section 9—110 with respect to a security interest arising under Article 2 or 2A.

(g) A perfected agricultural lien on collateral has priority over a conflicting security interest in or agricultural lien on the same collateral if the statute creating the agricultural lien so provides.

§ 9—323. Future Advances.

(a) Except as otherwise provided in subsection (c), for purposes of determining the priority of a perfected security interest under Section 9—322(a)(1), perfection of the security interest dates from the time an advance is made to the extent that the security interest secures an advance that:

(1) is made while the security interest is perfected only:

(A) under Section 9—309 when it attaches; or

(B) temporarily under Section 9—312(e), (f), or (g); and

(2) is not made pursuant to a commitment entered into before or while the security interest is perfected by a method other than under Section 9—309 or 9—312(e), (f), or (g).

(b) Except as otherwise provided in subsection (c), a security interest is subordinate to the rights of a person that becomes a lien creditor to the extent that the security interest secures an advance made more than 45 days after the person becomes a lien creditor unless the advance is made:

(1) without knowledge of the lien; or

(2) pursuant to a commitment entered into without knowledge of the lien.

(c) Subsections (a) and (b) do not apply to a security interest held by a secured party that is a buyer of accounts, chattel paper, payment intangibles, or promissory notes or a consignor.

(d) Except as otherwise provided in subsection (e), a buyer of goods other than a buyer in ordinary course of business takes free of a security interest to the extent that it secures advances made after the earlier of:

(1) the time the secured party acquires knowledge of the buyer's purchase; or

(2) 45 days after the purchase.

(e) Subsection (d) does not apply if the advance is made pursuant to a commitment entered into without knowledge of the buyer's purchase and before the expiration of the 45-day period.

(f) Except as otherwise provided in subsection (g), a lessee of goods, other than a lessee in ordinary course of business, takes the leasehold interest free of a security interest to the extent that it secures advances made after the earlier of:

(1) the time the secured party acquires knowledge of the lease; or

(2) 45 days after the lease contract becomes enforceable.

(g) Subsection (f) does not apply if the advance is made pursuant to a commitment entered into without knowledge of the lease and before the expiration of the 45-day period.

§ 9—324. Priority of Purchase-Money Security Interests.

(a) Except as otherwise provided in subsection (g), a perfected purchase-money security interest in goods other than inventory or livestock has priority over a conflicting security interest in the same goods, and, except as otherwise provided in Section 9—327, a perfected security interest in its identifiable proceeds also has priority, if the purchase-money security interest is perfected when the debtor receives possession of the collateral or within 20 days thereafter.

(b) Subject to subsection (c) and except as otherwise provided in subsection (g), a perfected purchase-money security interest in inventory has priority over a conflicting security interest in the same inventory, has priority over a conflicting security interest in chattel paper or an instrument constituting proceeds of the inventory and in proceeds of the chattel paper, if so provided in Section 9—330, and, except as otherwise provided in Section 9—327, also has priority in identifiable cash proceeds of the inventory to the extent the identifiable cash proceeds are received on or before the delivery of the inventory to a buyer, if:

(1) the purchase-money security interest is perfected when the debtor receives possession of the inventory;

(2) the purchase-money secured party sends an authenticated notification to the holder of the conflicting security interest;

(3) the holder of the conflicting security interest receives the notification within five years before the debtor receives possession of the inventory; and

(4) the notification states that the person sending the notification has or expects to acquire a purchase-money security interest in inventory of the debtor and describes the inventory.

(c) Subsections (b)(2) through (4) apply only if the holder of the conflicting security interest had filed a financing statement covering the same types of inventory:

(1) if the purchase-money security interest is perfected by filing, before the date of the filing; or

(2) if the purchase-money security interest is temporarily perfected without filing or possession under Section 9—312(f), before the beginning of the 20-day period thereunder.

(d) Subject to subsection (e) and except as otherwise provided in subsection (g), a perfected purchase-money security interest in livestock that are farm products has priority over a conflicting security interest in the same livestock, and, except as otherwise provided in Section 9—327, a perfected security interest in their identifiable proceeds and identifiable products in their unmanufactured states also has priority, if:

(1) the purchase-money security interest is perfected when the debtor receives possession of the livestock;

(2) the purchase-money secured party sends an authenticated notification to the holder of the conflicting security interest;

(3) the holder of the conflicting security interest receives the notification within six months before the debtor receives possession of the livestock; and

(4) the notification states that the person sending the notification has or expects to acquire a purchase-money security interest in livestock of the debtor and describes the livestock.

(e) Subsections (d)(2) through (4) apply only if the holder of the conflicting security interest had filed a financing statement covering the same types of livestock:

    (1) if the purchase-money security interest is perfected by filing, before the date of the filing; or

    (2) if the purchase-money security interest is temporarily perfected without filing or possession under Section 9—312(f), before the beginning of the 20-day period thereunder.

(f) Except as otherwise provided in subsection (g), a perfected purchase-money security interest in software has priority over a conflicting security interest in the same collateral, and, except as otherwise provided in Section 9—327, a perfected security interest in its identifiable proceeds also has priority, to the extent that the purchase-money security interest in the goods in which the software was acquired for use has priority in the goods and proceeds of the goods under this section.

(g) If more than one security interest qualifies for priority in the same collateral under subsection (a), (b), (d), or (f):

    (1) a security interest securing an obligation incurred as all or part of the price of the collateral has priority over a security interest securing an obligation incurred for value given to enable the debtor to acquire rights in or the use of collateral; and

    (2) in all other cases, Section 9—322(a) applies to the qualifying security interests.

§ 9—325. Priority of Security Interests in Transferred Collateral.

(a) Except as otherwise provided in subsection (b), a security interest created by a debtor is subordinate to a security interest in the same collateral created by another person if:

    (1) the debtor acquired the collateral subject to the security interest created by the other person;

    (2) the security interest created by the other person was perfected when the debtor acquired the collateral; and

    (3) there is no period thereafter when the security interest is unperfected.

(b) Subsection (a) subordinates a security interest only if the security interest:

    (1) otherwise would have priority solely under Section 9—322(a) or 9—324; or

    (2) arose solely under Section 2—711(3) or 2A—508(5).

§ 9—326. Priority of Security Interests Created by New Debtor.

(a) Subject to subsection (b), a security interest created by a new debtor which is perfected by a filed financing statement that is effective solely under Section 9—508 in collateral in which a new debtor has or acquires rights is subordinate to a security interest in the same collateral which is perfected other than by a filed financing statement that is effective solely under Section 9—508.

(b) The other provisions of this part determine the priority among conflicting security interests in the same collateral perfected by filed financing statements that are effective solely under Section 9—508. However, if the security agreements to which a new debtor became bound as debtor were not entered into by the same original debtor, the conflicting security interests rank according to priority in time of the new debtor's having become bound.

§ 9—327. Priority of Security Interests in Deposit Account.

The following rules govern priority among conflicting security interests in the same deposit account:

(1) A security interest held by a secured party having control of the deposit account under Section 9—104 has priority over a conflicting security interest held by a secured party that does not have control.

(2) Except as otherwise provided in paragraphs (3) and (4), security interests perfected by control under Section 9—314 rank according to priority in time of obtaining control.

(3) Except as otherwise provided in paragraph (4), a security interest held by the bank with which the deposit account is maintained has priority over a conflicting security interest held by another secured party.

(4) A security interest perfected by control under Section 9—104(a)(3) has priority over a security interest held by the bank with which the deposit account is maintained.

§ 9—328. Priority of Security Interests in Investment Property.

The following rules govern priority among conflicting security interests in the same investment property:

(1) A security interest held by a secured party having control of investment property under Section 9—106 has priority over a security interest held by a secured party that does not have control of the investment property.

(2) Except as otherwise provided in paragraphs (3) and (4), conflicting security interests held by secured parties each of which has control under Section 9—106 rank according to priority in time of:

    (A) if the collateral is a security, obtaining control;

    (B) if the collateral is a security entitlement carried in a securities account and:

        (i) if the secured party obtained control under Section 8—106(d)(1), the secured party's becoming the person for which the securities account is maintained;

(ii) if the secured party obtained control under Section 8—106(d)(2), the securities intermediary's agreement to comply with the secured party's entitlement orders with respect to security entitlements carried or to be carried in the securities account; or

(iii) if the secured party obtained control through another person under Section 8—106(d)(3), the time on which priority would be based under this paragraph if the other person were the secured party; or

(C) if the collateral is a commodity contract carried with a commodity intermediary, the satisfaction of the requirement for control specified in Section 9—106(b)(2) with respect to commodity contracts carried or to be carried with the commodity intermediary.

(3) A security interest held by a securities intermediary in a security entitlement or a securities account maintained with the securities intermediary has priority over a conflicting security interest held by another secured party.

(4) A security interest held by a commodity intermediary in a commodity contract or a commodity account maintained with the commodity intermediary has priority over a conflicting security interest held by another secured party.

(5) A security interest in a certificated security in registered form which is perfected by taking delivery under Section 9—313(a) and not by control under Section 9—314 has priority over a conflicting security interest perfected by a method other than control.

(6) Conflicting security interests created by a broker, securities intermediary, or commodity intermediary which are perfected without control under Section 9—106 rank equally.

(7) In all other cases, priority among conflicting security interests in investment property is governed by Sections 9—322 and 9—323.

§ 9—329. Priority of Security Interests in Letter-of-Credit Right.

The following rules govern priority among conflicting security interests in the same letter-of-credit right:

(1) A security interest held by a secured party having control of the letter-of-credit right under Section 9—107 has priority to the extent of its control over a conflicting security interest held by a secured party that does not have control.

(2) Security interests perfected by control under Section 9—314 rank according to priority in time of obtaining control.

§ 9—330. Priority of Purchaser of Chattel Paper or Instrument.

(a) A purchaser of chattel paper has priority over a security interest in the chattel paper which is claimed merely as proceeds of inventory subject to a security interest if:

(1) in good faith and in the ordinary course of the purchaser's business, the purchaser gives new value and takes possession of the chattel paper or obtains control of the chattel paper under Section 9—105; and

(2) the chattel paper does not indicate that it has been assigned to an identified assignee other than the purchaser.

(b) A purchaser of chattel paper has priority over a security interest in the chattel paper which is claimed other than merely as proceeds of inventory subject to a security interest if the purchaser gives new value and takes possession of the chattel paper or obtains control of the chattel paper under Section 9—105 in good faith, in the ordinary course of the purchaser's business, and without knowledge that the purchase violates the rights of the secured party.

(c) Except as otherwise provided in Section 9—327, a purchaser having priority in chattel paper under subsection (a) or (b) also has priority in proceeds of the chattel paper to the extent that:

(1) Section 9—322 provides for priority in the proceeds; or

(2) the proceeds consist of the specific goods covered by the chattel paper or cash proceeds of the specific goods, even if the purchaser's security interest in the proceeds is unperfected.

(d) Except as otherwise provided in Section 9—331(a), a purchaser of an instrument has priority over a security interest in the instrument perfected by a method other than possession if the purchaser gives value and takes possession of the instrument in good faith and without knowledge that the purchase violates the rights of the secured party.

(e) For purposes of subsections (a) and (b), the holder of a purchase-money security interest in inventory gives new value for chattel paper constituting proceeds of the inventory.

(f) For purposes of subsections (b) and (d), if chattel paper or an instrument indicates that it has been assigned to an identified secured party other than the purchaser, a purchaser of the chattel paper or instrument has knowledge that the purchase violates the rights of the secured party.

§ 9—331. Priority of Rights of Purchasers of Instruments, Documents, and Securities under Other Articles; Priority of Interests in Financial Assets and Security Entitlements under Article 8.

(a) This article does not limit the rights of a holder in due course of a negotiable instrument, a holder to which a negotiable document of title has been duly negotiated, or a protected purchaser of a security. These holders or purchasers take priority over an earlier security interest, even if perfected, to the extent provided in Articles 3, 7, and 8.

(b) This article does not limit the rights of or impose liability on a person to the extent that the person is protected against the assertion of a claim under Article 8.

(c) Filing under this article does not constitute notice of a claim or defense to the holders, or purchasers, or persons described in subsections (a) and (b).

§ 9—332. **Transfer of Money; Transfer of Funds from Deposit Account.**

(a) A transferee of money takes the money free of a security interest unless the transferee acts in collusion with the debtor in violating the rights of the secured party.

(b) A transferee of funds from a deposit account takes the funds free of a security interest in the deposit account unless the transferee acts in collusion with the debtor in violating the rights of the secured party.

§ 9—333. **Priority of Certain Liens Arising by Operation of Law.**

(a) In this section, "possessory lien" means an interest, other than a security interest or an agricultural lien:

(1) which secures payment or performance of an obligation for services or materials furnished with respect to goods by a person in the ordinary course of the person's business;

(2) which is created by statute or rule of law in favor of the person; and

(3) whose effectiveness depends on the person's possession of the goods.

(b) A possessory lien on goods has priority over a security interest in the goods unless the lien is created by a statute that expressly provides otherwise.

§ 9—334. **Priority of Security Interests in Fixtures and Crops.**

(a) A security interest under this article may be created in goods that are fixtures or may continue in goods that become fixtures. A security interest does not exist under this article in ordinary building materials incorporated into an improvement on land.

(b) This article does not prevent creation of an encumbrance upon fixtures under real property law.

(c) In cases not governed by subsections (d) through (h), a security interest in fixtures is subordinate to a conflicting interest of an encumbrancer or owner of the related real property other than the debtor.

(d) Except as otherwise provided in subsection (h), a perfected security interest in fixtures has priority over a conflicting interest of an encumbrancer or owner of the real property if the debtor has an interest of record in or is in possession of the real property and:

(1) the security interest is a purchase-money security interest;

(2) the interest of the encumbrancer or owner arises before the goods become fixtures; and

(3) the security interest is perfected by a fixture filing before the goods become fixtures or within 20 days thereafter.

(e) A perfected security interest in fixtures has priority over a conflicting interest of an encumbrancer or owner of the real property if:

(1) the debtor has an interest of record in the real property or is in possession of the real property and the security interest:

(A) is perfected by a fixture filing before the interest of the encumbrancer or owner is of record; and

(B) has priority over any conflicting interest of a predecessor in title of the encumbrancer or owner;

(2) before the goods become fixtures, the security interest is perfected by any method permitted by this article and the fixtures are readily removable:

(A) factory or office machines;

(B) equipment that is not primarily used or leased for use in the operation of the real property; or

(C) replacements of domestic appliances that are consumer goods;

(3) the conflicting interest is a lien on the real property obtained by legal or equitable proceedings after the security interest was perfected by any method permitted by this article; or

(4) the security interest is:

(A) created in a manufactured home in a manufactured-home transaction; and

(B) perfected pursuant to a statute described in Section 9—311(a)(2).

(f) A security interest in fixtures, whether or not perfected, has priority over a conflicting interest of an encumbrancer or owner of the real property if:

(1) the encumbrancer or owner has, in an authenticated record, consented to the security interest or disclaimed an interest in the goods as fixtures; or

(2) the debtor has a right to remove the goods as against the encumbrancer or owner.

(g) The priority of the security interest under paragraph (f)(2) continues for a reasonable time if the debtor's right to remove the goods as against the encumbrancer or owner terminates.

(h) A mortgage is a construction mortgage to the extent that it secures an obligation incurred for the construction of an improvement on land, including the acquisition cost of the land, if a recorded record of the mortgage so indicates. Except as otherwise provided in subsections (e) and (f), a security interest in fixtures is subordinate to a construction mortgage if a record of the mortgage is recorded before the goods become fixtures and the goods become fixtures before the completion of the construction. A mortgage has this priority to the same extent as a construction mortgage to the extent that it is given to refinance a construction mortgage.

(i) A perfected security interest in crops growing on real property has priority over a conflicting interest of an encumbrancer or owner of the real property if the debtor has an interest of record in or is in possession of the real property.

(j) Subsection (i) prevails over any inconsistent provisions of the following statutes:

[List here any statutes containing provisions inconsistent with subsection (i).]

Legislative Note: States that amend statutes to remove provisions inconsistent with subsection (i) need not enact subsection (j).

§ 9—335. Accessions.

(a) A security interest may be created in an accession and continues in collateral that becomes an accession.

(b) If a security interest is perfected when the collateral becomes an accession, the security interest remains perfected in the collateral.

(c) Except as otherwise provided in subsection (d), the other provisions of this part determine the priority of a security interest in an accession.

(d) A security interest in an accession is subordinate to a security interest in the whole which is perfected by compliance with the requirements of a certificate-of-title statute under Section 9—311(b).

(e) After default, subject to Part 6, a secured party may remove an accession from other goods if the security interest in the accession has priority over the claims of every person having an interest in the whole.

(f) A secured party that removes an accession from other goods under subsection (e) shall promptly reimburse any holder of a security interest or other lien on, or owner of, the whole or of the other goods, other than the debtor, for the cost of repair of any physical injury to the whole or the other goods. The secured party need not reimburse the holder or owner for any diminution in value of the whole or the other goods caused by the absence of the accession removed or by any necessity for replacing it. A person entitled to reimbursement may refuse permission to remove until the secured party gives adequate assurance for the performance of the obligation to reimburse.

§ 9—336. Commingled Goods.

(a) In this section, "commingled goods" means goods that are physically united with other goods in such a manner that their identity is lost in a product or mass.

(b) A security interest does not exist in commingled goods as such. However, a security interest may attach to a product or mass that results when goods become commingled goods.

(c) If collateral becomes commingled goods, a security interest attaches to the product or mass.

(d) If a security interest in collateral is perfected before the collateral becomes commingled goods, the security interest that attaches to the product or mass under subsection (c) is perfected.

(e) Except as otherwise provided in subsection (f), the other provisions of this part determine the priority of a security interest that attaches to the product or mass under subsection (c).

(f) If more than one security interest attaches to the product or mass under subsection (c), the following rules determine priority:

(1) A security interest that is perfected under subsection (d) has priority over a security interest that is unperfected at the time the collateral becomes commingled goods.

(2) If more than one security interest is perfected under subsection (d), the security interests rank equally in proportion to the value of the collateral at the time it became commingled goods.

§ 9—337. Priority of Security Interests in Goods Covered by Certificate of Title.

If, while a security interest in goods is perfected by any method under the law of another jurisdiction, this State issues a certificate of title that does not show that the goods are subject to the security interest or contain a statement that they may be subject to security interests not shown on the certificate:

(1) a buyer of the goods, other than a person in the business of selling goods of that kind, takes free of the security interest if the buyer gives value and receives delivery of the goods after issuance of the certificate and without knowledge of the security interest; and

(2) the security interest is subordinate to a conflicting security interest in the goods that attaches, and is perfected under Section 9—311(b), after issuance of the certificate and without the conflicting secured party's knowledge of the security interest.

§ 9—338. Priority of Security Interest or Agricultural Lien Perfected by Filed Financing Statement Providing Certain Incorrect Information.

If a security interest or agricultural lien is perfected by a filed financing statement providing information described in Section 9—516(b)(5) which is incorrect at the time the financing statement is filed:

(1) the security interest or agricultural lien is subordinate to a conflicting perfected security interest in the collateral to the extent that the holder of the conflicting security interest gives value in reasonable reliance upon the incorrect information; and

(2) a purchaser, other than a secured party, of the collateral takes free of the security interest or agricultural lien to the extent that, in reasonable reliance upon the incorrect information, the purchaser gives value and, in the case of chattel paper, documents, goods, instruments, or a security certificate, receives delivery of the collateral.

§ 9—339. Priority Subject to Subordination.

This article does not preclude subordination by agreement by a person entitled to priority.

[Subpart 4. Rights of Bank]

§ 9—340. Effectiveness of Right of Recoupment or Set-Off against Deposit Account.

(a) Except as otherwise provided in subsection (c), a bank with which a deposit account is maintained may exercise any right of recoupment or set-off against a secured party that holds a security interest in the deposit account.

(b) Except as otherwise provided in subsection (c), the application of this article to a security interest in a deposit account does not affect a right of recoupment or set-off of the secured party as to a deposit account maintained with the secured party.

(c) The exercise by a bank of a set-off against a deposit account is ineffective against a secured party that holds a security interest in the deposit account which is perfected by control under Section 9—104(a)(3), if the set-off is based on a claim against the debtor.

§ 9—341. Bank's Rights and Duties with Respect to Deposit Account.

Except as otherwise provided in Section 9—340(c), and unless the bank otherwise agrees in an authenticated record, a bank's rights and duties with respect to a deposit account maintained with the bank are not terminated, suspended, or modified by:

(1) the creation, attachment, or perfection of a security interest in the deposit account;

(2) the bank's knowledge of the security interest; or

(3) the bank's receipt of instructions from the secured party.

§ 9—342. Bank's Right to Refuse to Enter into or Disclose Existence of Control Agreement.

This article does not require a bank to enter into an agreement of the kind described in Section 9—104(a)(2), even if its customer so requests or directs. A bank that has entered into such an agreement is not required to confirm the existence of the agreement to another person unless requested to do so by its customer.

Part 4 Rights of Third Parties

§ 9—401. Alienability of Debtor's Rights.

(a) as otherwise provided in subsection (b) and Sections 9—406, 9—407, 9—408, and 9—409, whether a debtor's rights in collateral may be voluntarily or involuntarily transferred is governed by law other than this article.

(b) An agreement between the debtor and secured party which prohibits a transfer of the debtor's rights in collateral or makes the transfer a default does not prevent the transfer from taking effect.

§ 9—402. Secured Party Not Obligated on Contract of Debtor or in Tort.

The existence of a security interest, agricultural lien, or authority given to a debtor to dispose of or use collateral, without more, does not subject a secured party to liability in contract or tort for the debtor's acts or omissions.

§ 9—403. Agreement Not to Assert Defenses against Assignee.

(a) In this section, "value" has the meaning provided in Section 3—303(a).

(b) Except as otherwise provided in this section, an agreement between an account debtor and an assignor not to assert against an assignee any claim or defense that the account debtor may have against the assignor is enforceable by an assignee that takes an assignment:

(1) for value;

(2) in good faith;

(3) without notice of a claim of a property or possessory right to the property assigned; and

(4) without notice of a defense or claim in recoupment of the type that may be asserted against a person entitled to enforce a negotiable instrument under Section 3—305(a).

(c) Subsection (b) does not apply to defenses of a type that may be asserted against a holder in due course of a negotiable instrument under Section 3—305(b).

(d) In a consumer transaction, if a record evidences the account debtor's obligation, law other than this article requires that the record include a statement to the effect that the rights of an assignee are subject to claims or defenses that the account debtor could assert against the original obligee, and the record does not include such a statement:

(1) the record has the same effect as if the record included such a statement; and

(2) the account debtor may assert against an assignee those claims and defenses that would have been available if the record included such a statement.

(e) This section is subject to law other than this article which establishes a different rule for an account debtor who is an individual and who incurred the obligation primarily for personal, family, or household purposes.

(f) Except as otherwise provided in subsection (d), this section does not displace law other than this article which gives effect to an agreement by an account debtor not to assert a claim or defense against an assignee.

§ 9—404. Rights Acquired by Assignee; Claims and Defenses against Assignee.

(a) Unless an account debtor has made an enforceable agreement not to assert defenses or claims, and subject to subsections (b) through (e), the rights of an assignee are subject to:

(1) all terms of the agreement between the account debtor and assignor and any defense or claim in recoupment arising from the transaction that gave rise to the contract; and

(2) any other defense or claim of the account debtor against the assignor which accrues before the account debtor receives a notification of the assignment authenticated by the assignor or the assignee.

(b) Subject to subsection (c) and except as otherwise provided in subsection (d), the claim of an account debtor against an assignor may be asserted against an assignee under subsection (a) only to reduce the amount the account debtor owes.

(c) This section is subject to law other than this article which establishes a different rule for an account debtor who is an individual and who incurred the obligation primarily for personal, family, or household purposes.

(d) In a consumer transaction, if a record evidences the account debtor's obligation, law other than this article requires that the record include a statement to the effect that the account debtor's recovery against an assignee with respect to claims and defenses against the assignor may not exceed amounts paid by the account debtor under the record, and the record does not include such a statement, the extent to which a claim of an account debtor against the assignor may be asserted against an assignee is determined as if the record included such a statement.

(e) This section does not apply to an assignment of a health-care-insurance receivable.

§ 9—405. Modification of Assigned Contract.

(a) A modification of or substitution for an assigned contract is effective against an assignee if made in good faith.

The assignee acquires corresponding rights under the modified or substituted contract. The assignment may provide that the modification or substitution is a breach of contract by the assignor. This subsection is subject to subsections (b) through (d).

(b) Subsection (a) applies to the extent that:

(1) the right to payment or a part thereof under an assigned contract has not been fully earned by performance; or

(2) the right to payment or a part thereof has been fully earned by performance and the account debtor has not received notification of the assignment under Section 9—406(a).

(c) This section is subject to law other than this article which establishes a different rule for an account debtor who is an individual and who incurred the obligation primarily for personal, family, or household purposes.

(d) This section does not apply to an assignment of a health-care-insurance receivable.

§ 9—406. Discharge of Account Debtor; Notification of Assignment; Identification and Proof of Assignment; Restrictions on Assignment of Accounts, Chattel Paper, Payment Intangibles, and Promissory Notes Ineffective.

(a) Subject to subsections (b) through (i), an account debtor on an account, chattel paper, or a payment intangible may discharge its obligation by paying the assignor until, but not after, the account debtor receives a notification, authenticated by the assignor or the assignee, that the amount due or to become due has been assigned and that payment is to be made to the assignee. After receipt of the notification, the account debtor may discharge its obligation by paying the assignee and may not discharge the obligation by paying the assignor.

(b) Subject to subsection (h), notification is ineffective under subsection (a):

(1) if it does not reasonably identify the rights assigned;

(2) to the extent that an agreement between an account debtor and a seller of a payment intangible limits the account debtor's duty to pay a person other than the seller and the limitation is effective under law other than this article; or

(3) at the option of an account debtor, if the notification notifies the account debtor to make less than the full amount of any installment or other periodic payment to the assignee, even if:

(A) only a portion of the account, chattel paper, or payment intangible has been assigned to that assignee;

(B) a portion has been assigned to another assignee; or

(C) the account debtor knows that the assignment to that assignee is limited.

(c) Subject to subsection (h), if requested by the account debtor, an assignee shall seasonably furnish reasonable proof that the assignment has been made. Unless the assignee complies, the account debtor may discharge its obligation by paying the assignor, even if the account debtor has received a notification under subsection (a).

(d) Except as otherwise provided in subsection (e) and Sections 2A—303 and 9—407, and subject to subsection (h), a term in an agreement between an account debtor and an assignor or in a promissory note is ineffective to the extent that it:

(1) prohibits, restricts, or requires the consent of the account debtor or person obligated on the promissory note to the assignment or transfer of, or the creation, attachment, perfection, or enforcement of a security interest in, the account, chattel paper, payment intangible, or promissory note; or

(2) provides that the assignment or transfer or the creation, attachment, perfection, or enforcement of the security interest may give rise to a default, breach, right of recoupment, claim, defense, termination, right of termination, or remedy under the account, chattel paper, payment intangible, or promissory note.

(e) Subsection (d) does not apply to the sale of a payment intangible or promissory note.

(f) Except as otherwise provided in Sections 2A—303 and 9—407 and subject to subsections (h) and (i), a rule of law, statute, or regulation that prohibits, restricts, or requires the consent of a government, governmental body or official, or account debtor to the assignment or transfer of, or creation of a security interest in, an account or chattel paper is ineffective to the extent that the rule of law, statute, or regulation:

(1) prohibits, restricts, or requires the consent of the government, governmental body or official, or account debtor to the assignment or transfer of, or the creation, attachment, perfection, or enforcement of a security interest in the account or chattel paper; or

(2) provides that the assignment or transfer or the creation, attachment, perfection, or enforcement of the security interest may give rise to a default, breach, right of recoupment, claim, defense, termination, right of termination, or remedy under the account or chattel paper.

(g) Subject to subsection (h), an account debtor may not waive or vary its option under subsection (b)(3).

(h) This section is subject to law other than this article which establishes a different rule for an account debtor who is an individual and who incurred the obligation primarily for personal, family, or household purposes.

(i) This section does not apply to an assignment of a health-care-insurance receivable.

(j) This section prevails over any inconsistent provisions of the following statutes, rules, and regulations:

[List here any statutes, rules, and regulations containing provisions inconsistent with this section.]

Legislative Note: States that amend statutes, rules, and regulations to remove provisions inconsistent with this section need not enact subsection (j).

§ 9—407. Restrictions on Creation or Enforcement of Security Interest in Leasehold Interest or in Lessor's Residual Interest.

(a) Except as otherwise provided in subsection (b), a term in a lease agreement is ineffective to the extent that it:

(1) prohibits, restricts, or requires the consent of a party to the lease to the assignment or transfer of, or the creation, attachment, perfection, or enforcement of a security interest in an interest of a party under the lease contract or in the lessor's residual interest in the goods; or

(2) provides that the assignment or transfer or the creation, attachment, perfection, or enforcement of the security interest may give rise to a default, breach, right of recoupment, claim, defense, termination, right of termination, or remedy under the lease.

(b) Except as otherwise provided in Section 2A—303(7), a term described in subsection (a)(2) is effective to the extent that there is:

(1) a transfer by the lessee of the lessee's right of possession or use of the goods in violation of the term; or

(2) a delegation of a material performance of either party to the lease contract in violation of the term.

(c) The creation, attachment, perfection, or enforcement of a security interest in the lessor's interest under the lease contract or the lessor's residual interest in the goods is not a transfer that materially impairs the lessee's prospect of obtaining return performance or materially changes the duty of or materially increases the burden or risk imposed on the lessee within the purview of Section 2A—303(4) unless, and then only to the extent that, enforcement actually results in a delegation of material performance of the lessor.

§ 9—408. Restrictions on Assignment of Promissory Notes, Health-Care-Insurance Receivables, and Certain General Intangibles Ineffective.

(a) Except as otherwise provided in subsection (b), a term in a promissory note or in an agreement between an account debtor and a debtor which relates to a health-care-insurance receivable or a general intangible, including a contract, permit, license, or franchise, and which term prohibits, restricts, or requires the consent of the person obligated on the promissory note or the account debtor to, the assignment or transfer of, or creation, attachment, or perfection of a security interest in, the promissory note, health-care-insurance receivable, or general intangible, is ineffective to the extent that the term:

(1) would impair the creation, attachment, or perfection of a security interest; or

(2) provides that the assignment or transfer or the creation, attachment, or perfection of the security interest may give rise to a default, breach, right of recoupment, claim, defense, termination, right of termination, or remedy under the promissory note, health-care-insurance receivable, or general intangible.

(b) Subsection (a) applies to a security interest in a payment intangible or promissory note only if the security interest arises out of a sale of the payment intangible or promissory note.

(c) A rule of law, statute, or regulation that prohibits, restricts, or requires the consent of a government, governmental body or official, person obligated on a promissory note, or account debtor to the assignment or transfer of, or creation of a security interest in, a promissory note, health-care-insurance receivable, or general intangible, including a contract, permit, license, or franchise between an account debtor and a debtor, is ineffective to the extent that the rule of law, statute, or regulation:

(1) would impair the creation, attachment, or perfection of a security interest; or

(2) provides that the assignment or transfer or the creation, attachment, or perfection of the security interest may give rise to a default, breach, right of recoupment, claim, defense, termination, right of termination, or remedy under the promissory note, health-care-insurance receivable, or general intangible.

(d) To the extent that a term in a promissory note or in an agreement between an account debtor and a debtor which relates to a health-care-insurance receivable or general intangible or a rule of law, statute, or regulation described in subsection (c) would be effective under law other than this article but is ineffective under subsection (a) or (c), the creation, attachment, or perfection of a security interest in the promissory note, health-care-insurance receivable, or general intangible:

(1) is not enforceable against the person obligated on the promissory note or the account debtor;

(2) does not impose a duty or obligation on the person obligated on the promissory note or the account debtor;

(3) does not require the person obligated on the promissory note or the account debtor to recognize the security interest, pay or render performance to the secured party, or accept payment or performance from the secured party;

(4) does not entitle the secured party to use or assign the debtor's rights under the promissory note, health-care-insurance receivable, or general intangible, including any related information or materials furnished to the debtor in the transaction giving rise to the promissory note, health-care-insurance receivable, or general intangible;

(5) does not entitle the secured party to use, assign, possess, or have access to any trade secrets or confidential information of the person obligated on the promissory note or the account debtor; and

(6) does not entitle the secured party to enforce the security interest in the promissory note, health-care-insurance receivable, or general intangible.

(e) This section prevails over any inconsistent provisions of the following statutes, rules, and regulations:

[List here any statutes, rules, and regulations containing provisions inconsistent with this section.]

Legislative Note: States that amend statutes, rules, and regulations to remove provisions inconsistent with this section need not enact subsection (e).

§ 9—409. Restrictions on Assignment of Letter-of-Credit Rights Ineffective.

(a) A term in a letter of credit or a rule of law, statute, regulation, custom, or practice applicable to the letter of credit which prohibits, restricts, or requires the consent of an applicant, issuer, or nominated person to a beneficiary's assignment of or creation of a security interest in a letter-of-credit right is ineffective to the extent that the term or rule of law, statute, regulation, custom, or practice:

(1) would impair the creation, attachment, or perfection of a security interest in the letter-of-credit right; or

(2) provides that the assignment or the creation, attachment, or perfection of the security interest may give rise to a default, breach, right of recoupment, claim, defense, termination, right of termination, or remedy under the letter-of-credit right.

(b) To the extent that a term in a letter of credit is ineffective under subsection (a) but would be effective under law other than this article or a custom or practice applicable to the letter of credit, to the transfer of a right to draw or otherwise demand performance under the letter of credit, or to the assignment of a right to proceeds of the letter of credit, the creation, attachment, or perfection of a security interest in the letter-of-credit right:

(1) is not enforceable against the applicant, issuer, nominated person, or transferee beneficiary;

(2) imposes no duties or obligations on the applicant, issuer, nominated person, or transferee beneficiary; and

(3) does not require the applicant, issuer, nominated person, or transferee beneficiary to recognize the security interest, pay or render performance to the secured party, or accept payment or other performance from the secured party.

Part 5 Filing

[Subpart 1. Filing Office; Contents and Effectiveness of Financing Statement]

§ 9—501. Filing Office.

(a) Except as otherwise provided in subsection (b), if the local law of this State governs perfection of a security interest or agricultural lien, the office in which to file a financing statement to perfect the security interest or agricultural lien is:

> (1) the office designated for the filing or recording of a record of a mortgage on the related real property, if:
>
>> (A) the collateral is as-extracted collateral or timber to be cut; or
>>
>> (B) the financing statement is filed as a fixture filing and the collateral is goods that are or are to become fixtures; or
>
> (2) the office of [ ] [or any office duly authorized by [ ]], in all other cases, including a case in which the collateral is goods that are or are to become fixtures and the financing statement is not filed as a fixture filing.

(b) The office in which to file a financing statement to perfect a security interest in collateral, including fixtures, of a transmitting utility is the office of [ ]. The financing statement also constitutes a fixture filing as to the collateral indicated in the financing statement which is or is to become fixtures.

Legislative Note: The State should designate the filing office where the brackets appear. The filing office may be that of a governmental official (e.g., the Secretary of State) or a private party that maintains the State's filing system.

§ 9—502 Contents of Financing Statement; Record of Mortgage as Financing Statement; Time of Filing Financing Statement.

(a) Subject to subsection (b), a financing statement is sufficient only if it:

> (1) provides the name of the debtor;
>
> (2) provides the name of the secured party or a representative of the secured party; and
>
> (3) indicates the collateral covered by the financing statement.

(b) Except as otherwise provided in Section 9—501(b), to be sufficient, a financing statement that covers as-extracted collateral or timber to be cut, or which is filed as a fixture

filing and covers goods that are or are to become fixtures, must satisfy subsection (a) and also:

> (1) indicate that it covers this type of collateral;
>
> (2) indicate that it is to be filed [for record] in the real property records;
>
> (3) provide a description of the real property to which the collateral is related [sufficient to give constructive notice of a mortgage under the law of this State if the description were contained in a record of the mortgage of the real property]; and
>
> (4) if the debtor does not have an interest of record in the real property, provide the name of a record owner.

(c) A record of a mortgage is effective, from the date of recording, as a financing statement filed as a fixture filing or as a financing statement covering as-extracted collateral or timber to be cut only if:

> (1) the record indicates the goods or accounts that it covers;
>
> (2) the goods are or are to become fixtures related to the real property described in the record or the collateral is related to the real property described in the record and is as-extracted collateral or timber to be cut;
>
> (3) the record satisfies the requirements for a financing statement in this section other than an indication that it is to be filed in the real property records; and
>
> (4) the record is [duly] recorded.

(d) A financing statement may be filed before a security agreement is made or a security interest otherwise attaches.

Legislative Note: Language in brackets is optional. Where the State has any special recording system for real property other than the usual grantor-grantee index (as, for instance, a tract system or a title registration or Torrens system) local adaptations of subsection (b) and Section 9—519(d) and (e) may be necessary. See, e.g., Mass. Gen. Laws Chapter 106, Section 9—410.

§ 9—503. Name of Debtor and Secured Party.

(a) A financing statement sufficiently provides the name of the debtor:

> (1) if the debtor is a registered organization, only if the financing statement provides the name of the debtor indicated on the public record of the debtor's jurisdiction of organization which shows the debtor to have been organized;
>
> (2) if the debtor is a decedent's estate, only if the financing statement provides the name of the decedent and indicates that the debtor is an estate;
>
> (3) if the debtor is a trust or a trustee acting with respect to property held in trust, only if the financing statement:

(A) provides the name specified for the trust in its organic documents or, if no name is specified, provides the name of the settlor and additional information sufficient to distinguish the debtor from other trusts having one or more of the same settlors; and

(B) indicates, in the debtor's name or otherwise, that the debtor is a trust or is a trustee acting with respect to property held in trust; and

(4) in other cases:

(A) if the debtor has a name, only if it provides the individual or organizational name of the debtor; and

(B) if the debtor does not have a name, only if it provides the names of the partners, members, associates, or other persons comprising the debtor.

(b) A financing statement that provides the name of the debtor in accordance with subsection (a) is not rendered ineffective by the absence of:

(1) a trade name or other name of the debtor; or

(2) unless required under subsection (a)(4)(B), names of partners, members, associates, or other persons comprising the debtor.

(c) A financing statement that provides only the debtor's trade name does not sufficiently provide the name of the debtor.

(d) Failure to indicate the representative capacity of a secured party or representative of a secured party does not affect the sufficiency of a financing statement.

(e) A financing statement may provide the name of more than one debtor and the name of more than one secured party.

§ 9—504. Indication of Collateral.

A financing statement sufficiently indicates the collateral that it covers if the financing statement provides:

(1) a description of the collateral pursuant to Section 9—108; or

(2) an indication that the financing statement covers all assets or all personal property.

§ 9—505. Filing and Compliance with Other Statutes and Treaties for Consignments, Leases, Other Bailments, and Other Transactions.

(a) A consignor, lessor, or other bailor of goods, a licensor, or a buyer of a payment intangible or promissory note may file a financing statement, or may comply with a statute or treaty described in Section 9—311(a), using the terms "consignor", "consignee", "lessor", "lessee", "bailor", "bailee", "licensor", "licensee", "owner", "registered owner", "buyer", "seller", or words of similar import, instead of the terms "secured party" and "debtor".

(b) This part applies to the filing of a financing statement under subsection (a) and, as appropriate, to compliance that is equivalent to filing a financing statement under Section 9—311(b), but the filing or compliance is not of itself a factor in determining whether the collateral secures an obligation. If it is determined for another reason that the collateral secures an obligation, a security interest held by the consignor, lessor, bailor, licensor, owner, or buyer which attaches to the collateral is perfected by the filing or compliance.

§ 9—506. Effect of Errors or Omissions.

(a) A financing statement substantially satisfying the requirements of this part is effective, even if it has minor errors or omissions, unless the errors or omissions make the financing statement seriously misleading.

(b) Except as otherwise provided in subsection (c), a financing statement that fails sufficiently to provide the name of the debtor in accordance with Section 9—503(a) is seriously misleading.

(c) If a search of the records of the filing office under the debtor's correct name, using the filing office's standard search logic, if any, would disclose a financing statement that fails sufficiently to provide the name of the debtor in accordance with Section 9—503(a), the name provided does not make the financing statement seriously misleading.

(d) For purposes of Section 9—508(b), the "debtor's correct name" in subsection (c) means the correct name of the new debtor.

§ 9—507. Effect of Certain Events on Effectiveness of Financing Statement.

(a) A filed financing statement remains effective with respect to collateral that is sold, exchanged, leased, licensed, or otherwise disposed of and in which a security interest or agricultural lien continues, even if the secured party knows of or consents to the disposition.

(b) Except as otherwise provided in subsection (c) and Section 9—508, a financing statement is not rendered ineffective if, after the financing statement is filed, the information provided in the financing statement becomes seriously misleading under Section 9—506.

(c) If a debtor so changes its name that a filed financing statement becomes seriously misleading under Section 9—506:

(1) the financing statement is effective to perfect a security interest in collateral acquired by the debtor before, or within four months after, the change; and

(2) the financing statement is not effective to perfect a security interest in collateral acquired by the debtor more than four months after the change, unless an

amendment to the financing statement which renders the financing statement not seriously misleading is filed within four months after the change.

§ 9–508. Effectiveness of Financing Statement If New Debtor Becomes Bound by Security Agreement.

(a) Except as otherwise provided in this section, a filed financing statement naming an original debtor is effective to perfect a security interest in collateral in which a new debtor has or acquires rights to the extent that the financing statement would have been effective had the original debtor acquired rights in the collateral.

(b) If the difference between the name of the original debtor and that of the new debtor causes a filed financing statement that is effective under subsection (a) to be seriously misleading under Section 9–506:

(1) the financing statement is effective to perfect a security interest in collateral acquired by the new debtor before, and within four months after, the new debtor becomes bound under Section 9B–203(d); and

(2) the financing statement is not effective to perfect a security interest in collateral acquired by the new debtor more than four months after the new debtor becomes bound under Section 9–203(d) unless an initial financing statement providing the name of the new debtor is filed before the expiration of that time.

(c) This section does not apply to collateral as to which a filed financing statement remains effective against the new debtor under Section 9–507(a).

§ 9–509. Persons Entitled to File a Record.

(a) A person may file an initial financing statement, amendment that adds collateral covered by a financing statement, or amendment that adds a debtor to a financing statement only if:

(1) the debtor authorizes the filing in an authenticated record or pursuant to subsection (b) or (c); or

(2) the person holds an agricultural lien that has become effective at the time of filing and the financing statement covers only collateral in which the person holds an agricultural lien.

(b) By authenticating or becoming bound as debtor by a security agreement, a debtor or new debtor authorizes the filing of an initial financing statement, and an amendment, covering:

(1) the collateral described in the security agreement; and

(2) property that becomes collateral under Section 9–315(a)(2), whether or not the security agreement expressly covers proceeds.

(c) By acquiring collateral in which a security interest or agricultural lien continues under Section 9–315(a)(1), a

debtor authorizes the filing of an initial financing statement, and an amendment, covering the collateral and property that becomes collateral under Section 9–315(a)(2).

(d) A person may file an amendment other than an amendment that adds collateral covered by a financing statement or an amendment that adds a debtor to a financing statement only if:

(1) the secured party of record authorizes the filing; or

(2) the amendment is a termination statement for a financing statement as to which the secured party of record has failed to file or send a termination statement as required by Section 9–513(a) or (c), the debtor authorizes the filing, and the termination statement indicates that the debtor authorized it to be filed.

(e) If there is more than one secured party of record for a financing statement, each secured party of record may authorize the filing of an amendment under subsection (d).

§ 9–510. Effectiveness of Filed Record.

(a) A filed record is effective only to the extent that it was filed by a person that may file it under Section 9–509.

(b) A record authorized by one secured party of record does not affect the financing statement with respect to another secured party of record.

(c) A continuation statement that is not filed within the six-month period prescribed by Section 9–515(d) is ineffective.

§ 9–511. Secured Party of Record.

(a) A secured party of record with respect to a financing statement is a person whose name is provided as the name of the secured party or a representative of the secured party in an initial financing statement that has been filed. If an initial financing statement is filed under Section 9–514(a), the assignee named in the initial financing statement is the secured party of record with respect to the financing statement.

(b) If an amendment of a financing statement which provides the name of a person as a secured party or a representative of a secured party is filed, the person named in the amendment is a secured party of record. If an amendment is filed under Section 9–514(b), the assignee named in the amendment is a secured party of record.

(c) A person remains a secured party of record until the filing of an amendment of the financing statement which deletes the person.

§ 9–512. Amendment of Financing Statement.

[Alternative A]

(a) Subject to Section 9–509, a person may add or delete collateral covered by, continue or terminate the effectiveness of, or, subject to subsection (e), otherwise amend the information provided in, a financing statement by filing an amendment that:

(1) identifies, by its file number, the initial financing statement to which the amendment relates; and

(2) if the amendment relates to an initial financing statement filed [or recorded] in a filing office described in Section 9—501(a)(1), provides the information specified in Section 9—502(b).

[Alternative B]

(a) Subject to Section 9—509, a person may add or delete collateral covered by, continue or terminate the effectiveness of, or, subject to subsection (e), otherwise amend the information provided in, a financing statement by filing an amendment that:

(1) identifies, by its file number, the initial financing statement to which the amendment relates; and

(2) if the amendment relates to an initial financing statement filed [or recorded] in a filing office described in Section 9—501(a)(1), provides the date [and time] that the initial financing statement was filed [or recorded] and the information specified in Section 9—502(b).

[End of Alternatives]

(b) Except as otherwise provided in Section 9—515, the filing of an amendment does not extend the period of effectiveness of the financing statement.

(c) A financing statement that is amended by an amendment that adds collateral is effective as to the added collateral only from the date of the filing of the amendment.

(d) A financing statement that is amended by an amendment that adds a debtor is effective as to the added debtor only from the date of the filing of the amendment.

(e) An amendment is ineffective to the extent it:

(1) purports to delete all debtors and fails to provide the name of a debtor to be covered by the financing statement; or

(2) purports to delete all secured parties of record and fails to provide the name of a new secured party of record.

Legislative Note: States whose real-estate filing offices require additional information in amendments and cannot search their records by both the name of the debtor and the file number should enact Alternative B to Sections 9—512(a), 9—518(b), 9—519(f), and 9—522(a).

§ 9—513. Termination Statement.

(a) A secured party shall cause the secured party of record for a financing statement to file a termination statement for the financing statement if the financing statement covers consumer goods and:

(1) there is no obligation secured by the collateral covered by the financing statement and no commitment to make an advance, incur an obligation, or otherwise give value; or

(2) the debtor did not authorize the filing of the initial financing statement.

(b) To comply with subsection (a), a secured party shall cause the secured party of record to file the termination statement:

(1) within one month after there is no obligation secured by the collateral covered by the financing statement and no commitment to make an advance, incur an obligation, or otherwise give value; or

(2) if earlier, within 20 days after the secured party receives an authenticated demand from a debtor.

(c) In cases not governed by subsection (a), within 20 days after a secured party receives an authenticated demand from a debtor, the secured party shall cause the secured party of record for a financing statement to send to the debtor a termination statement for the financing statement or file the termination statement in the filing office if:

(1) except in the case of a financing statement covering accounts or chattel paper that has been sold or goods that are the subject of a consignment, there is no obligation secured by the collateral covered by the financing statement and no commitment to make an advance, incur an obligation, or otherwise give value;

(2) the financing statement covers accounts or chattel paper that has been sold but as to which the account debtor or other person obligated has discharged its obligation;

(3) the financing statement covers goods that were the subject of a consignment to the debtor but are not in the debtor's possession; or

(4) the debtor did not authorize the filing of the initial financing statement.

(d) Except as otherwise provided in Section 9—510, upon the filing of a termination statement with the filing office, the financing statement to which the termination statement relates ceases to be effective. Except as otherwise provided in Section 9—510, for purposes of Sections 9—519(g), 9—522(a), and 9—523(c), the filing with the filing office of a termination statement relating to a financing statement that indicates that the debtor is a transmitting utility also causes the effectiveness of the financing statement to lapse.

§ 9—514. Assignment of Powers of Secured Party of Record.

(a) Except as otherwise provided in subsection (c), an initial financing statement may reflect an assignment of all of the secured party's power to authorize an amendment to the financing statement by providing the name and mailing address of the assignee as the name and address of the secured party.

(b) Except as otherwise provided in subsection (c), a secured party of record may assign of record all or part of its power to authorize an amendment to a financing statement by filing in the filing office an amendment of the financing statement which:

(1) identifies, by its file number, the initial financing statement to which it relates;

(2) provides the name of the assignor; and

(3) provides the name and mailing address of the assignee.

(c) An assignment of record of a security interest in a fixture covered by a record of a mortgage which is effective as a financing statement filed as a fixture filing under Section 9—502(c) may be made only by an assignment of record of the mortgage in the manner provided by law of this State other than [the Uniform Commercial Code].

§ 9—515. Duration and Effectiveness of Financing Statement; Effect of Lapsed Financing Statement.

(a) Except as otherwise provided in subsections (b), (e), (f), and (g), a filed financing statement is effective for a period of five years after the date of filing.

(b) Except as otherwise provided in subsections (e), (f), and (g), an initial financing statement filed in connection with a public-finance transaction or manufactured-home transaction is effective for a period of 30 years after the date of filing if it indicates that it is filed in connection with a public-finance transaction or manufactured-home transaction.

(c) The effectiveness of a filed financing statement lapses on the expiration of the period of its effectiveness unless before the lapse a continuation statement is filed pursuant to subsection (d). Upon lapse, a financing statement ceases to be effective and any security interest or agricultural lien that was perfected by the financing statement becomes unperfected, unless the security interest is perfected otherwise. If the security interest or agricultural lien becomes unperfected upon lapse, it is deemed never to have been perfected as against a purchaser of the collateral for value.

(d) A continuation statement may be filed only within six months before the expiration of the five-year period specified in subsection (a) or the 30-year period specified in subsection (b), whichever is applicable.

(e) Except as otherwise provided in Section 9—510, upon timely filing of a continuation statement, the effectiveness of the initial financing statement continues for a period of five years commencing on the day on which the financing statement would have become ineffective in the absence of the filing. Upon the expiration of the five-year period, the

financing statement lapses in the same manner as provided in subsection (c), unless, before the lapse, another continuation statement is filed pursuant to subsection (d). Succeeding continuation statements may be filed in the same manner to continue the effectiveness of the initial financing statement.

(f) If a debtor is a transmitting utility and a filed financing statement so indicates, the financing statement is effective until a termination statement is filed.

(g) A record of a mortgage that is effective as a financing statement filed as a fixture filing under Section 9—502(c) remains effective as a financing statement filed as a fixture filing until the mortgage is released or satisfied of record or its effectiveness otherwise terminates as to the real property.

§ 9—516. What Constitutes Filing; Effectiveness of Filing.

(a) Except as otherwise provided in subsection (b), communication of a record to a filing office and tender of the filing fee or acceptance of the record by the filing office constitutes filing.

(b) Filing does not occur with respect to a record that a filing office refuses to accept because:

(1) the record is not communicated by a method or medium of communication authorized by the filing office;

(2) an amount equal to or greater than the applicable filing fee is not tendered;

(3) the filing office is unable to index the record because:

(A) in the case of an initial financing statement, the record does not provide a name for the debtor;

(B) in the case of an amendment or correction statement, the record:

(i) does not identify the initial financing statement as required by Section 9—512 or 9—518, as applicable; or

(ii) identifies an initial financing statement whose effectiveness has lapsed under Section 9—515;

(C) in the case of an initial financing statement that provides the name of a debtor identified as an individual or an amendment that provides a name of a debtor identified as an individual which was not previously provided in the financing statement to which the record relates, the record does not identify the debtor's last name; or

(D) in the case of a record filed [or recorded] in the filing office described in Section 9—501(a)(1), the record does not provide a sufficient description of the real property to which it relates;

(4) in the case of an initial financing statement or an amendment that adds a secured party of record, the record does not provide a name and mailing address for the secured party of record;

(5) in the case of an initial financing statement or an amendment that provides a name of a debtor which was not previously provided in the financing statement to which the amendment relates, the record does not:

(A) provide a mailing address for the debtor;

(B) indicate whether the debtor is an individual or an organization; or

(C) if the financing statement indicates that the debtor is an organization, provide:

(i) a type of organization for the debtor;

(ii) a jurisdiction of organization for the debtor; or

(iii) an organizational identification number for the debtor or indicate that the debtor has none;

(6) in the case of an assignment reflected in an initial financing statement under Section 9—514(a) or an amendment filed under Section 9—514(b), the record does not provide a name and mailing address for the assignee; or

(7) in the case of a continuation statement, the record is not filed within the six-month period prescribed by Section 9—515(d).

(c) For purposes of subsection (b):

(1) a record does not provide information if the filing office is unable to read or decipher the information; and

(2) a record that does not indicate that it is an amendment or identify an initial financing statement to which it relates, as required by Section 9—512, 9—514, or 9—518, is an initial financing statement.

(d) A record that is communicated to the filing office with tender of the filing fee, but which the filing office refuses to accept for a reason other than one set forth in subsection (b), is effective as a filed record except as against a purchaser of the collateral which gives value in reasonable reliance upon the absence of the record from the files.

§ 9—517. Effect of Indexing Errors.

The failure of the filing office to index a record correctly does not affect the effectiveness of the filed record.

§ 9—518. Claim Concerning Inaccurate or Wrongfully Filed Record.

(a) A person may file in the filing office a correction statement with respect to a record indexed there under the person's name if the person believes that the record is inaccurate or was wrongfully filed.

[**Alternative A**]

(b) A correction statement must:

(1) identify the record to which it relates by the file number assigned to the initial financing statement to which the record relates;

(2) indicate that it is a correction statement; and

(3) provide the basis for the person's belief that the record is inaccurate and indicate the manner in which the person believes the record should be amended to cure any inaccuracy or provide the basis for the person's belief that the record was wrongfully filed.

[**Alternative B**]

(b) A correction statement must:

(1) identify the record to which it relates by:

(A) the file number assigned to the initial financing statement to which the record relates; and

(B) if the correction statement relates to a record filed [or recorded] in a filing office described in Section 9—501(a)(1), the date [and time] that the initial financing statement was filed [or recorded] and the information specified in Section 9—502(b);

(2) indicate that it is a correction statement; and

(3) provide the basis for the person's belief that the record is inaccurate and indicate the manner in which the person believes the record should be amended to cure any inaccuracy or provide the basis for the person's belief that the record was wrongfully filed.

[**End of Alternatives**]

(c) The filing of a correction statement does not affect the effectiveness of an initial financing statement or other filed record.

Legislative Note: States whose real-estate filing offices require additional information in amendments and cannot search their records by both the name of the debtor and the file number should enact Alternative B to Sections 9–512(a), 9–518(b), 9–519(f), and 9–522(a).

[**Subpart 2. Duties and Operation of Filing Office**]

§ 9—519. Numbering, Maintaining, and Indexing Records; Communicating Information Provided in Records.

(a) For each record filed in a filing office, the filing office shall:

(1) assign a unique number to the filed record;

(2) create a record that bears the number assigned to the filed record and the date and time of filing;

(3) maintain the filed record for public inspection; and

(4) index the filed record in accordance with subsections (c), (d), and (e).

(b) A file number [assigned after January 1, 2002,] must include a digit that:

(1) is mathematically derived from or related to the other digits of the file number; and

(2) aids the filing office in determining whether a number communicated as the file number includes a single-digit or transpositional error.

(c) Except as otherwise provided in subsections (d) and (e), the filing office shall:

(1) index an initial financing statement according to the name of the debtor and index all filed records relating to the initial financing statement in a manner that associates with one another an initial financing statement and all filed records relating to the initial financing statement; and

(2) index a record that provides a name of a debtor which was not previously provided in the financing statement to which the record relates also according to the name that was not previously provided.

(d) If a financing statement is filed as a fixture filing or covers as-extracted collateral or timber to be cut, [it must be filed for record and] the filing office shall index it:

(1) under the names of the debtor and of each owner of record shown on the financing statement as if they were the mortgagors under a mortgage of the real property described; and

(2) to the extent that the law of this State provides for indexing of records of mortgages under the name of the mortgagee, under the name of the secured party as if the secured party were the mortgagee thereunder, or, if indexing is by description, as if the financing statement were a record of a mortgage of the real property described.

(e) If a financing statement is filed as a fixture filing or covers as-extracted collateral or timber to be cut, the filing office shall index an assignment filed under Section 9—514(a) or an amendment filed under Section 9—514(b):

(1) under the name of the assignor as grantor; and

(2) to the extent that the law of this State provides for indexing a record of the assignment of a mortgage under the name of the assignee, under the name of the assignee.

[Alternative A]

(f) The filing office shall maintain a capability:

(1) to retrieve a record by the name of the debtor and by the file number assigned to the initial financing statement to which the record relates; and

(2) to associate and retrieve with one another an initial financing statement and each filed record relating to the initial financing statement.

[Alternative B]

(f) The filing office shall maintain a capability:

(1) to retrieve a record by the name of the debtor and:

(A) if the filing office is described in Section 9—501(a)(1), by the file number assigned to the initial financing statement to which the record relates and the date [and time] that the record was filed [or recorded]; or

(B) if the filing office is described in Section 9—501(a)(2), by the file number assigned to the initial financing statement to which the record relates; and

(2) to associate and retrieve with one another an initial financing statement and each filed record relating to the initial financing statement.

[End of Alternatives]

(g) The filing office may not remove a debtor's name from the index until one year after the effectiveness of a financing statement naming the debtor lapses under Section 9—515 with respect to all secured parties of record.

(h) The filing office shall perform the acts required by subsections (a) through (e) at the time and in the manner prescribed by filing-office rule, but not later than two business days after the filing office receives the record in question.

[(i) Subsection[s] [(b)] [and] [(h)] do[es] not apply to a filing office described in Section 9—501(a)(1).]

Legislative Notes:

1. States whose filing offices currently assign file numbers that include a verification number, commonly known as a "check digit," or can implement this requirement before the effective date of this Article should omit the bracketed language in subsection (b).

2. In States in which writings will not appear in the real property records and indices unless actually recorded the bracketed language in subsection (d) should be used.

3. States whose real-estate filing offices require additional information in amendments and cannot search their records by both the name of the debtor and the file number should enact Alternative B to Sections 9—512(a), 9—518(b), 9—519(f), and 9—522(a).

4. A State that elects not to require real-estate filing offices to comply with either or both of subsections (b) and (h) may adopt an applicable variation of subsection (i) and add "Except as otherwise provided in subsection (i)," to the appropriate subsection or subsections.

§ 9—520. Acceptance and Refusal to Accept Record.

(a) filing office shall refuse to accept a record for filing for a reason set forth in Section 9—516(b) and may refuse to accept a record for filing only for a reason set forth in Section 9—516(b).

(b) If a filing office refuses to accept a record for filing, it shall communicate to the person that presented the record the fact of and reason for the refusal and the date and time the record would have been filed had the filing office accepted it. The communication must be made at the time and in the manner prescribed by filing-office rule but [, in the case of a filing office described in Section 9—501(a)(2),] in no event more than two business days after the filing office receives the record.

(c) A filed financing statement satisfying Section 9–502(a) and (b) is effective, even if the filing office is required to refuse to accept it for filing under subsection (a). However, Section 9—338 applies to a filed financing statement providing information described in Section 9—516(b)(5) which is incorrect at the time the financing statement is filed.

(d) If a record communicated to a filing office provides information that relates to more than one debtor, this part applies as to each debtor separately.

Legislative Note: A State that elects not to require real-property filing offices to comply with subsection (b) should include the bracketed language.

§ 9—521. Uniform Form of Written Financing Statement and Amendment.

(a) A filing office that accepts written records may not refuse to accept a written initial financing statement in the following form and format except for a reason set forth in Section 9—516(b):

[NATIONAL UCC FINANCING STATEMENT (FORM UCC)(REV. 7/29/98)]

[NATIONAL UCC FINANCING STATEMENT ADDENDUM (FORM UCC 1Ad)(REV. 07/29/98)]

(b) A filing office that accepts written records may not refuse to accept a written record in the following form and format except for a reason set forth in Section 9—516(b):

[NATIONAL UCC FINANCING STATEMENT AMENDMENT (FORM UCC)(REV. 07/29/98)]

[NATIONAL UCC FINANCING STATEMENT AMENDMENT ADDENDUM (FORM UCC3Ad)(REV. 07/29/98)]

§ 9—522. Maintenance and Destruction of Records.

[Alternative A]

(a) The filing office shall maintain a record of the information provided in a filed financing statement for at least one year after the effectiveness of the financing statement has lapsed under Section 9—515 with respect to all secured parties of record. The record must be retrievable by using the name of the debtor and by using the file number assigned to the initial financing statement to which the record relates.

[Alternative B]

(a) The filing office shall maintain a record of the information provided in a filed financing statement for at least one year after the effectiveness of the financing statement has lapsed under Section 9—515 with respect to all secured parties of record. The record must be retrievable by using the name of the debtor and:

(1) if the record was filed [or recorded] in the filing office described in Section 9—501(a)(1), by using the file number assigned to the initial financing statement to which the record relates and the date [and time] that the record was filed [or recorded]; or

(2) if the record was filed in the filing office described in Section 9—501(a)(2), by using the file number assigned to the initial financing statement to which the record relates.

[End of Alternatives]

(b) Except to the extent that a statute governing disposition of public records provides otherwise, the filing office immediately may destroy any written record evidencing a financing statement. However, if the filing office destroys a written record, it shall maintain another record of the financing statement which complies with subsection (a).

Legislative Note: States whose real-estate filing offices require additional information in amendments and cannot search their records by both the name of the debtor and the file number should enact Alternative B to Sections 9—512(a), 9—518(b), 9—519(f), and 9—522(a).

§ 9—523. Information from Filing Office; Sale or License of Records.

(a) If a person that files a written record requests an acknowledgment of the filing, the filing office shall send to the person an image of the record showing the number assigned to the record pursuant to Section 9—519(a)(1) and the date and time of the filing of the record. However, if the person furnishes a copy of the record to the filing office, the filing office may instead:

(1) note upon the copy the number assigned to the record pursuant to Section 9—519(a)(1) and the date and time of the filing of the record; and

(2) send the copy to the person.

(b) If a person files a record other than a written record, the filing office shall communicate to the person an acknowledgment that provides:

(1) the information in the record;

(2) the number assigned to the record pursuant to Section 9—519(a)(1); and

(3) the date and time of the filing of the record.

(c) The filing office shall communicate or otherwise make available in a record the following information to any person that requests it:

(1) whether there is on file on a date and time specified by the filing office, but not a date earlier than three business days before the filing office receives the request, any financing statement that:

(A) designates a particular debtor [or, if the request so states, designates a particular debtor at the address specified in the request];

(B) has not lapsed under Section 9—515 with respect to all secured parties of record; and

(C) if the request so states, has lapsed under Section 9—515 and a record of which is maintained by the filing office under Section 9—522(a);

(2) the date and time of filing of each financing statement; and

(3) the information provided in each financing statement.

(d) In complying with its duty under subsection (c), the filing office may communicate information in any medium. However, if requested, the filing office shall communicate information by issuing [its written certificate] [a record that can be admitted into evidence in the courts of this State without extrinsic evidence of its authenticity].

(e) The filing office shall perform the acts required by subsections (a) through (d) at the time and in the manner prescribed by filing-office rule, but not later than two business days after the filing office receives the request.

(f) At least weekly, the [insert appropriate official or governmental agency] [filing office] shall offer to sell or license to the public on a nonexclusive basis, in bulk, copies of all records filed in it under this part, in every medium from time to time available to the filing office.

Legislative Notes:

1. States whose filing office does not offer the additional service of responding to search requests limited to a particular address should omit the bracketed language in subsection (c)(1)(A).

2. A State that elects not to require real-estate filing offices to comply with either or both of subsections (e) and (f) should specify in the appropriate subsection(s) only the filing office described in Section 9—501(a)(2).

§ 9—524. Delay by Filing Office.

Delay by the filing office beyond a time limit prescribed by this part is excused if:

(1) the delay is caused by interruption of communication or computer facilities, war, emergency conditions, failure of equipment, or other circumstances beyond control of the filing office; and

(2) the filing office exercises reasonable diligence under the circumstances.

§ 9—525. Fees.

(a) Except as otherwise provided in subsection (e), the fee for filing and indexing a record under this part, other than an initial financing statement of the kind described in subsection (b), is [the amount specified in subsection (c), if applicable, plus]:

(1) $[X] if the record is communicated in writing and consists of one or two pages;

(2) $[2X] if the record is communicated in writing and consists of more than two pages; and

(3) $[½X] if the record is communicated by another medium authorized by filing-office rule.

(b) Except as otherwise provided in subsection (e), the fee for filing and indexing an initial financing statement of the following kind is [the amount specified in subsection (c), if applicable, plus]:

(1) $_____ if the financing statement indicates that it is filed in connection with a public-finance transaction;

(2) $_____ if the financing statement indicates that it is filed in connection with a manufactured-home transaction.

[Alternative A]

(c) The number of names required to be indexed does not affect the amount of the fee in subsections (a) and (b).

[Alternative B]

(c) Except as otherwise provided in subsection (e), if a record is communicated in writing, the fee for each name more than two required to be indexed is $_____.

[End of Alternatives]

(d) The fee for responding to a request for information from the filing office, including for [issuing a certificate showing] [communicating] whether there is on file any financing statement naming a particular debtor, is:

(1) $_____ if the request is communicated in writing; and

(2) $_____ if the request is communicated by another medium authorized by filing-office rule.

(e) This section does not require a fee with respect to a record of a mortgage which is effective as a financing statement filed as a fixture filing or as a financing statement covering as-extracted collateral or timber to be cut under Section 9—502(c). However, the recording and satisfaction fees that otherwise would be applicable to the record of the mortgage apply.

Legislative Notes:

1. To preserve uniformity, a State that places the provisions of this section together with statutes setting fees for other services should do so without modification.

2. A State should enact subsection (c), Alternative A, and omit the bracketed language in subsections (a) and (b) unless its indexing system entails a substantial additional cost when indexing additional names.

§ 9—526. Filing-Office Rules.

(a) The [insert appropriate governmental official or agency] shall adopt and publish rules to implement this article. The filing-office rules must be:

(1)] consistent with this article[; and

(2) adopted and published in accordance with the [insert any applicable state administrative procedure act]].

(b) To keep the filing-office rules and practices of the filing office in harmony with the rules and practices of filing offices in other jurisdictions that enact substantially this part, and to keep the technology used by the filing office compatible with the technology used by filing offices in other jurisdictions that enact substantially this part, the [insert appropriate governmental official or agency], so far as is consistent with the purposes, policies, and provisions of this article, in adopting, amending, and repealing filing-office rules, shall:

(1) consult with filing offices in other jurisdictions that enact substantially this part; and

(2) consult the most recent version of the Model Rules promulgated by the International Association of Corporate Administrators or any successor organization; and

(3) take into consideration the rules and practices of, and the technology used by, filing offices in other jurisdictions that enact substantially this part.

§ 9—527. Duty to Report.

The [insert appropriate governmental official or agency] shall report [annually on or before _____] to the [Governor and Legislature] on the operation of the filing office. The report must contain a statement of the extent to which:

(1) the filing-office rules are not in harmony with the rules of filing offices in other jurisdictions that enact substantially this part and the reasons for these variations; and

(2) the filing-office rules are not in harmony with the most recent version of the Model Rules promulgated by the International Association of Corporate Administrators, or any successor organization, and the reasons for these variations.

Part 6 Default

[Subpart 1. Default and Enforcement of Security Interest]

§ 9—601. Rights after Default; Judicial Enforcement; Consignor or Buyer of Accounts, Chattel Paper, Payment Intangibles, or Promissory Notes.

(a) After default, a secured party has the rights provided in this part and, except as otherwise provided in Section 9—602, those provided by agreement of the parties. A secured party:

(1) may reduce a claim to judgment, foreclose, or otherwise enforce the claim, security interest, or agricultural lien by any available judicial procedure; and

(2) if the collateral is documents, may proceed either as to the documents or as to the goods they cover.

(b) A secured party in possession of collateral or control of collateral under Section 9—104, 9—105, 9—106, or 9—107 has the rights and duties provided in Section 9—207.

(c) The rights under subsections (a) and (b) are cumulative and may be exercised simultaneously.

(d) Except as otherwise provided in subsection (g) and Section 9—605, after default, a debtor and an obligor have the rights provided in this part and by agreement of the parties.

(e) If a secured party has reduced its claim to judgment, the lien of any levy that may be made upon the collateral by virtue of an execution based upon the judgment relates back to the earliest of:

(1) the date of perfection of the security interest or agricultural lien in the collateral;

(2) the date of filing a financing statement covering the collateral; or

(3) any date specified in a statute under which the agricultural lien was created.

(f) A sale pursuant to an execution is a foreclosure of the security interest or agricultural lien by judicial procedure within the meaning of this section. A secured party may purchase at the sale and thereafter hold the collateral free of any other requirements of this article.

(g) Except as otherwise provided in Section 9—607(c), this part imposes no duties upon a secured party that is a consignor or is a buyer of accounts, chattel paper, payment intangibles, or promissory notes.

§ 9—602. Waiver and Variance of Rights and Duties.

Except as otherwise provided in Section 9—624, to the extent that they give rights to a debtor or obligor and impose duties on a secured party, the debtor or obligor may not waive or vary the rules stated in the following listed sections:

(1) Section 9—207(b)(4)(C), which deals with use and operation of the collateral by the secured party;

(2) Section 9—210, which deals with requests for an accounting and requests concerning a list of collateral and statement of account;

(3) Section 9—607(c), which deals with collection and enforcement of collateral;

(4) Sections 9—608(a) and 9—615(c) to the extent that they deal with application or payment of noncash proceeds of collection, enforcement, or disposition;

(5) Sections 9—608(a) and 9—615(d) to the extent that they require accounting for or payment of surplus proceeds of collateral;

(6) Section 9–609 to the extent that it imposes upon a secured party that takes possession of collateral without judicial process the duty to do so without breach of the peace;

(7) Sections 9—610(b), 9—611, 9—613, and 9—614, which deal with disposition of collateral;

(8) Section 9—615(f), which deals with calculation of a deficiency or surplus when a disposition is made to the secured party, a person related to the secured party, or a secondary obligor;

(9) Section 9—616, which deals with explanation of the calculation of a surplus or deficiency;

(10) Sections 9—620, 9—621, and 9—622, which deal with acceptance of collateral in satisfaction of obligation;

(11) Section 9—623, which deals with redemption of collateral;

(12) Section 9—624, which deals with permissible waivers; and

(13) Sections 9—625 and 9—626, which deal with the secured party's liability for failure to comply with this article.

§ 9—603. Agreement on Standards Concerning Rights and Duties.

(a) The parties may determine by agreement the standards measuring the fulfillment of the rights of a debtor or obligor and the duties of a secured party under a rule stated in Section 9—602 if the standards are not manifestly unreasonable.

(b) Subsection (a) does not apply to the duty under Section 9—609 to refrain from breaching the peace.

§ 9—604. Procedure If Security Agreement Covers Real Property or Fixtures.

(a) If a security agreement covers both personal and real property, a secured party may proceed:

(1) under this part as to the personal property without prejudicing any rights with respect to the real property; or

(2) as to both the personal property and the real property in accordance with the rights with respect to the real property, in which case the other provisions of this part do not apply.

(b) Subject to subsection (c), if a security agreement covers goods that are or become fixtures, a secured party may proceed:

(1) under this part; or

(2) in accordance with the rights with respect to real property, in which case the other provisions of this part do not apply.

(c) Subject to the other provisions of this part, if a secured party holding a security interest in fixtures has priority over all owners and encumbrancers of the real property, the secured party, after default, may remove the collateral from the real property.

(d) A secured party that removes collateral shall promptly reimburse any encumbrancer or owner of the real property, other than the debtor, for the cost of repair of any physical injury caused by the removal. The secured party need not reimburse the encumbrancer or owner for any diminution in value of the real property caused by the absence of the goods removed or by any necessity of replacing them. A person entitled to reimbursement may refuse permission to remove until the secured party gives adequate assurance for the performance of the obligation to reimburse.

§ 9—605. Unknown Debtor or Secondary Obligor.

A secured party does not owe a duty based on its status as secured party:

(1) to a person that is a debtor or obligor, unless the secured party knows:

(A) that the person is a debtor or obligor;

(B) the identity of the person; and

(C) how to communicate with the person; or

(2) to a secured party or lienholder that has filed a financing statement against a person, unless the secured party knows:

(A) that the person is a debtor; and

(B) the identity of the person.

§ 9—606. Time of Default for Agricultural Lien.

For purposes of this part, a default occurs in connection with an agricultural lien at the time the secured party becomes entitled to enforce the lien in accordance with the statute under which it was created.

§ 9—607. Collection and Enforcement by Secured Party.

(a) If so agreed, and in any event after default, a secured party:

(1) may notify an account debtor or other person obligated on collateral to make payment or otherwise render performance to or for the benefit of the secured party;

(2) may take any proceeds to which the secured party is entitled under Section 9—315;

(3) may enforce the obligations of an account debtor or other person obligated on collateral and exercise the rights of the debtor with respect to the obligation of the account debtor or other person obligated on collateral to make payment or otherwise render performance to the debtor, and with respect to any property that secures the obligations of the account debtor or other person obligated on the collateral;

(4) if it holds a security interest in a deposit account perfected by control under Section 9—104(a)(1), may apply the balance of the deposit account to the obligation secured by the deposit account; and

(5) if it holds a security interest in a deposit account perfected by control under Section 9—104(a)(2) or (3), may instruct the bank to pay the balance of the deposit account to or for the benefit of the secured party.

(b) If necessary to enable a secured party to exercise under subsection (a)(3) the right of a debtor to enforce a mortgage nonjudicially, the secured party may record in the office in which a record of the mortgage is recorded:

(1) a copy of the security agreement that creates or provides for a security interest in the obligation secured by the mortgage; and

(2) the secured party's sworn affidavit in recordable form stating that:

(A) a default has occurred; and

(B) the secured party is entitled to enforce the mortgage nonjudicially.

(c) A secured party shall proceed in a commercially reasonable manner if the secured party:

(1) undertakes to collect from or enforce an obligation of an account debtor or other person obligated on collateral; and

(2) is entitled to charge back uncollected collateral or otherwise to full or limited recourse against the debtor or a secondary obligor.

(d) A secured party may deduct from the collections made pursuant to subsection (c) reasonable expenses of collection and enforcement, including reasonable attorney's fees and legal expenses incurred by the secured party.

(e) This section does not determine whether an account debtor, bank, or other person obligated on collateral owes a duty to a secured party.

§ 9—608. Application of Proceeds of Collection or Enforcement; Liability for Deficiency and Right to Surplus.

(a) If a security interest or agricultural lien secures payment or performance of an obligation, the following rules apply:

(1) A secured party shall apply or pay over for application the cash proceeds of collection or enforcement under Section 9—607 in the following order to:

(A) the reasonable expenses of collection and enforcement and, to the extent provided for by agreement and not prohibited by law, reasonable attorney's fees and legal expenses incurred by the secured party;

(B) the satisfaction of obligations secured by the security interest or agricultural lien under which the collection or enforcement is made; and

(C) the satisfaction of obligations secured by any subordinate security interest in or other lien on the collateral subject to the security interest or agricultural lien under which the collection or enforcement is made if the secured party receives an authenticated demand for proceeds before distribution of the proceeds is completed.

(2) If requested by a secured party, a holder of a subordinate security interest or other lien shall furnish reasonable proof of the interest or lien within a reasonable time. Unless the holder complies, the secured party need not comply with the holder's demand under paragraph (1)(C).

(3) A secured party need not apply or pay over for application noncash proceeds of collection and enforcement under Section 9—607 unless the failure to do so would be commercially unreasonable. A secured party that applies or pays over for application noncash proceeds shall do so in a commercially reasonable manner.

(4) A secured party shall account to and pay a debtor for any surplus, and the obligor is liable for any deficiency.

(b) If the underlying transaction is a sale of accounts, chattel paper, payment intangibles, or promissory notes, the debtor is not entitled to any surplus, and the obligor is not liable for any deficiency.

§ 9—609. Secured Party's Right to Take Possession after Default.

(a) After default, a secured party:

(1) may take possession of the collateral; and

(2) without removal, may render equipment unusable and dispose of collateral on a debtor's premises under Section 9—610.

(b) A secured party may proceed under subsection (a):

(1) pursuant to judicial process; or

(2) without judicial process, if it proceeds without breach of the peace.

(c) If so agreed, and in any event after default, a secured party may require the debtor to assemble the collateral and make it available to the secured party at a place to be designated by the secured party which is reasonably convenient to both parties.

§ 9—610. Disposition of Collateral after Default.

(a) After default, a secured party may sell, lease, license, or otherwise dispose of any or all of the collateral in its present condition or following any commercially reasonable preparation or processing.

(b) Every aspect of a disposition of collateral, including the method, manner, time, place, and other terms, must be commercially reasonable. If commercially reasonable, a secured party may dispose of collateral by public or private proceedings, by one or more contracts, as a unit or in parcels, and at any time and place and on any terms.

(c) A secured party may purchase collateral:

(1) at a public disposition; or

(2) at a private disposition only if the collateral is of a kind that is customarily sold on a recognized market or the subject of widely distributed standard price quotations.

(d) A contract for sale, lease, license, or other disposition includes the warranties relating to title, possession, quiet enjoyment, and the like which by operation of law accompany a voluntary disposition of property of the kind subject to the contract.

(e) A secured party may disclaim or modify warranties under subsection (d):

(1) in a manner that would be effective to disclaim or modify the warranties in a voluntary disposition of property of the kind subject to the contract of disposition; or

(2) by communicating to the purchaser a record evidencing the contract for disposition and including an express disclaimer or modification of the warranties.

(f) A record is sufficient to disclaim warranties under subsection (e) if it indicates "There is no warranty relating to title, possession, quiet enjoyment, or the like in this disposition" or uses words of similar import.

§ 9—611. Notification before Disposition of Collateral.

(a) In this section, "notification date" means the earlier of the date on which:

(1) a secured party sends to the debtor and any secondary obligor an authenticated notification of disposition; or

(2) the debtor and any secondary obligor waive the right to notification.

(b) Except as otherwise provided in subsection (d), a secured party that disposes of collateral under Section 9—610 shall send to the persons specified in subsection (c) a reasonable authenticated notification of disposition.

(c) To comply with subsection (b), the secured party shall send an authenticated notification of disposition to:

(1) the debtor;

(2) any secondary obligor; and

(3) if the collateral is other than consumer goods:

(A) any other person from which the secured party has received, before the notification date, an authenticated notification of a claim of an interest in the collateral;

(B) any other secured party or lienholder that, 10 days before the notification date, held a security interest in or other lien on the collateral perfected by the filing of a financing statement that:

(i) identified the collateral;

(ii) was indexed under the debtor's name as of that date; and

(iii) was filed in the office in which to file a financing statement against the debtor covering the collateral as of that date; and

(C) any other secured party that, 10 days before the notification date, held a security interest in the collateral perfected by compliance with a statute, regulation, or treaty described in Section 9—311(a).

(d) Subsection (b) does not apply if the collateral is perishable or threatens to decline speedily in value or is of a type customarily sold on a recognized market.

(e) A secured party complies with the requirement for notification prescribed by subsection (c)(3)(B) if:

(1) not later than 20 days or earlier than 30 days before the notification date, the secured party requests, in a commercially reasonable manner, information concerning financing statements indexed under the debtor's name in the office indicated in subsection (c)(3)(B); and

(2) before the notification date, the secured party:

(A) did not receive a response to the request for information; or

(B) received a response to the request for information and sent an authenticated notification of disposition to each secured party or other lienholder named in that response whose financing statement covered the collateral.

§ 9—612. Timeliness of Notification before Disposition of Collateral.

(a) Except as otherwise provided in subsection (b), whether a notification is sent within a reasonable time is a question of fact.

(b) In a transaction other than a consumer transaction, a notification of disposition sent after default and 10 days or more before the earliest time of disposition set forth in the notification is sent within a reasonable time before the disposition.

§ 9—613. Contents and Form of Notification before Disposition of Collateral: General.

Except in a consumer-goods transaction, the following rules apply:

(1) The contents of a notification of disposition are sufficient if the notification:

(A) describes the debtor and the secured party;

(B) describes the collateral that is the subject of the intended disposition;

(C) states the method of intended disposition;

(D) states that the debtor is entitled to an accounting of the unpaid indebtedness and states the charge, if any, for an accounting; and

(E) states the time and place of a public disposition or the time after which any other disposition is to be made.

(2) Whether the contents of a notification that lacks any of the information specified in paragraph (1) are nevertheless sufficient is a question of fact.

(3) The contents of a notification providing substantially the information specified in paragraph (1) are sufficient, even if the notification includes:

(A) information not specified by that paragraph; or

(B) minor errors that are not seriously misleading.

(4) A particular phrasing of the notification is not required.

(5) The following form of notification and the form appearing in Section 9—614(3), when completed, each provides sufficient information:

NOTIFICATION OF DISPOSITION OF COLLATERAL

To: [Name of debtor, obligor, or other person to which the notification is sent]

From: [Name, address, and telephone number of secured party]

Name of Debtor(s): [Include only if debtor(s) are not an addressee]

[For a public disposition:]

We will sell [or lease or license, as applicable] the [describe collateral] [to the highest qualified bidder] in public as follows:

Day and Date: _____

Time: _____

Place: _____

[For a private disposition:]

We will sell [or lease or license, as applicable] the [describe collateral] privately sometime after [day and date].

You are entitled to an accounting of the unpaid indebtedness secured by the property that we intend to sell [or lease or license, as applicable] [for a charge of $_____]. You may request an accounting by calling us at [telephone number].

[End of Form]

§ 9—614. Contents and Form of Notification before Disposition of Collateral: Consumer-Goods Transaction.

In a consumer-goods transaction, the following rules apply:

(1) A notification of disposition must provide the following information:

(A) the information specified in Section 9—613(1);

(B) a description of any liability for a deficiency of the person to which the notification is sent;

(C) a telephone number from which the amount that must be paid to the secured party to redeem the collateral under Section 9—623 is available; and

(D) a telephone number or mailing address from which additional information concerning the disposition and the obligation secured is available.

(2) A particular phrasing of the notification is not required.

(3) The following form of notification, when completed, provides sufficient information:

[Name and address of secured party]

[Date]

NOTICE OF OUR PLAN TO SELL PROPERTY

[Name and address of any obligor who is also a debtor]

Subject: [Identification of Transaction]

We have your [describe collateral], because you broke promises in our agreement.

[For a public disposition:]

We will sell [describe collateral] at public sale. A sale could include a lease or license. The sale will be held as follows:

Date: _____

Time: _____

Place: _____

You may attend the sale and bring bidders if you want.

[For a private disposition:]

We will sell [describe collateral] at private sale sometime after [date]. A sale could include a lease or license.

The money that we get from the sale (after paying our costs) will reduce the amount you owe. If we get less money than you owe, you [will or will not, as applicable] still owe us the difference. If we get more money than you owe, you will get the extra money, unless we must pay it to someone else.

You can get the property back at any time before we sell it by paying us the full amount you owe (not just the past due payments), including our expenses. To learn the exact amount you must pay, call us at [telephone number].

If you want us to explain to you in writing how we have figured the amount that you owe us, you may call us at [telephone number] [or write us at [secured party's address]] and request a written explanation. [We will charge you $_____ for the explanation if we sent you another written explanation of the amount you owe us within the last six months.]

If you need more information about the sale call us at [telephone number] [or write us at [secured party's address]].

We are sending this notice to the following other people who have an interest in [describe collateral] or who owe money under your agreement:

[Names of all other debtors and obligors, if any]

[End of Form]

(4) A notification in the form of paragraph (3) is sufficient, even if additional information appears at the end of the form.

(5) A notification in the form of paragraph (3) is sufficient, even if it includes errors in information not required by paragraph (1), unless the error is misleading with respect to rights arising under this article.

(6) If a notification under this section is not in the form of paragraph (3), law other than this article determines the effect of including information not required by paragraph (1).

§ 9—615. Application of Proceeds of Disposition; Liability for Deficiency and Right to Surplus.

(a) A secured party shall apply or pay over for application the cash proceeds of disposition under Section 9—610 in the following order to:

    (1) the reasonable expenses of retaking, holding, preparing for disposition, processing, and disposing,

and, to the extent provided for by agreement and not prohibited by law, reasonable attorney's fees and legal expenses incurred by the secured party;

(2) the satisfaction of obligations secured by the security interest or agricultural lien under which the disposition is made;

(3) the satisfaction of obligations secured by any subordinate security interest in or other subordinate lien on the collateral if:

    (A) the secured party receives from the holder of the subordinate security interest or other lien an authenticated demand for proceeds before distribution of the proceeds is completed; and

    (B) in a case in which a consignor has an interest in the collateral, the subordinate security interest or other lien is senior to the interest of the consignor; and

(4) a secured party that is a consignor of the collateral if the secured party receives from the consignor an authenticated demand for proceeds before distribution of the proceeds is completed.

(b) If requested by a secured party, a holder of a subordinate security interest or other lien shall furnish reasonable proof of the interest or lien within a reasonable time. Unless the holder does so, the secured party need not comply with the holder's demand under subsection (a)(3).

(c) A secured party need not apply or pay over for application noncash proceeds of disposition under Section 9—610 unless the failure to do so would be commercially unreasonable. A secured party that applies or pays over for application noncash proceeds shall do so in a commercially reasonable manner.

(d) If the security interest under which a disposition is made secures payment or performance of an obligation, after making the payments and applications required by subsection (a) and permitted by subsection (c):

    (1) unless subsection (a)(4) requires the secured party to apply or pay over cash proceeds to a consignor, the secured party shall account to and pay a debtor for any surplus; and

    (2) the obligor is liable for any deficiency.

(e) If the underlying transaction is a sale of accounts, chattel paper, payment intangibles, or promissory notes:

    (1) the debtor is not entitled to any surplus; and

    (2) the obligor is not liable for any deficiency.

(f) The surplus or deficiency following a disposition is calculated based on the amount of proceeds that would have been realized in a disposition complying with this part to a transferee other than the secured party, a person related to the secured party, or a secondary obligor if:

(1) the transferee in the disposition is the secured party, a person related to the secured party, or a secondary obligor; and

(2) the amount of proceeds of the disposition is significantly below the range of proceeds that a complying disposition to a person other than the secured party, a person related to the secured party, or a secondary obligor would have brought.

(g) A secured party that receives cash proceeds of a disposition in good faith and without knowledge that the receipt violates the rights of the holder of a security interest or other lien that is not subordinate to the security interest or agricultural lien under which the disposition is made:

(1) takes the cash proceeds free of the security interest or other lien;

(2) is not obligated to apply the proceeds of the disposition to the satisfaction of obligations secured by the security interest or other lien; and

(3) is not obligated to account to or pay the holder of the security interest or other lien for any surplus.

§ 9—616. **Explanation of Calculation of Surplus or Deficiency.**

(a) In this section:

(1) "Explanation" means a writing that:

(A) states the amount of the surplus or deficiency;

(B) provides an explanation in accordance with subsection (c) of how the secured party calculated the surplus or deficiency;

(C) states, if applicable, that future debits, credits, charges, including additional credit service charges or interest, rebates, and expenses may affect the amount of the surplus or deficiency; and

(D) provides a telephone number or mailing address from which additional information concerning the transaction is available.

(2) "Request" means a record:

(A) authenticated by a debtor or consumer obligor;

(B) requesting that the recipient provide an explanation; and

(C) sent after disposition of the collateral under Section 9—610.

(b) In a consumer-goods transaction in which the debtor is entitled to a surplus or a consumer obligor is liable for a deficiency under Section 9—615, the secured party shall:

(1) send an explanation to the debtor or consumer obligor, as applicable, after the disposition and:

(A) before or when the secured party accounts to the debtor and pays any surplus or first makes writ-

ten demand on the consumer obligor after the disposition for payment of the deficiency; and

(B) within 14 days after receipt of a request; or

(2) in the case of a consumer obligor who is liable for a deficiency, within 14 days after receipt of a request, send to the consumer obligor a record waiving the secured party's right to a deficiency.

(c) To comply with subsection (a)(1)(B), a writing must provide the following information in the following order:

(1) the aggregate amount of obligations secured by the security interest under which the disposition was made, and, if the amount reflects a rebate of unearned interest or credit service charge, an indication of that fact, calculated as of a specified date:

(A) if the secured party takes or receives possession of the collateral after default, not more than 35 days before the secured party takes or receives possession; or

(B) if the secured party takes or receives possession of the collateral before default or does not take possession of the collateral, not more than 35 days before the disposition;

(2) the amount of proceeds of the disposition;

(3) the aggregate amount of the obligations after deducting the amount of proceeds;

(4) the amount, in the aggregate or by type, and types of expenses, including expenses of retaking, holding, preparing for disposition, processing, and disposing of the collateral, and attorney's fees secured by the collateral which are known to the secured party and relate to the current disposition;

(5) the amount, in the aggregate or by type, and types of credits, including rebates of interest or credit service charges, to which the obligor is known to be entitled and which are not reflected in the amount in paragraph (1); and

(6) the amount of the surplus or deficiency.

(d) A particular phrasing of the explanation is not required. An explanation complying substantially with the requirements of subsection (a) is sufficient, even if it includes minor errors that are not seriously misleading.

(e) A debtor or consumer obligor is entitled without charge to one response to a request under this section during any six-month period in which the secured party did not send to the debtor or consumer obligor an explanation pursuant to subsection (b)(1). The secured party may require payment of a charge not exceeding $25 for each additional response.

§ 9—617. **Rights of Transferee of Collateral.**

(a) A secured party's disposition of collateral after default:

(1) transfers to a transferee for value all of the debtor's rights in the collateral;

(2) discharges the security interest under which the disposition is made; and

(3) discharges any subordinate security interest or other subordinate lien [other than liens created under [cite acts or statutes providing for liens, if any, that are not to be discharged]].

(b) A transferee that acts in good faith takes free of the rights and interests described in subsection (a), even if the secured party fails to comply with this article or the requirements of any judicial proceeding.

(c) If a transferee does not take free of the rights and interests described in subsection (a), the transferee takes the collateral subject to:

(1) the debtor's rights in the collateral;

(2) the security interest or agricultural lien under which the disposition is made; and

(3) any other security interest or other lien.

§ 9—618. Rights and Duties of Certain Secondary Obligors.

(a) A secondary obligor acquires the rights and becomes obligated to perform the duties of the secured party after the secondary obligor:

(1) receives an assignment of a secured obligation from the secured party;

(2) receives a transfer of collateral from the secured party and agrees to accept the rights and assume the duties of the secured party; or

(3) is subrogated to the rights of a secured party with respect to collateral.

(b) An assignment, transfer, or subrogation described in subsection (a):

(1) is not a disposition of collateral under Section 9—610; and

(2) relieves the secured party of further duties under this article.

§ 9—619. Transfer of Record or Legal Title.

(a) In this section, "transfer statement" means a record authenticated by a secured party stating:

(1) that the debtor has defaulted in connection with an obligation secured by specified collateral;

(2) that the secured party has exercised its post-default remedies with respect to the collateral;

(3) that, by reason of the exercise, a transferee has acquired the rights of the debtor in the collateral; and

(4) the name and mailing address of the secured party, debtor, and transferee.

(b) A transfer statement entitles the transferee to the transfer of record of all rights of the debtor in the collateral specified in the statement in any official filing, recording, registration, or certificate-of-title system covering the collateral. If a transfer statement is presented with the applicable fee and request form to the official or office responsible for maintaining the system, the official or office shall:

(1) accept the transfer statement;

(2) promptly amend its records to reflect the transfer; and

(3) if applicable, issue a new appropriate certificate of title in the name of the transferee.

(c) A transfer of the record or legal title to collateral to a secured party under subsection (b) or otherwise is not of itself a disposition of collateral under this article and does not of itself relieve the secured party of its duties under this article.

§ 9—620. Acceptance of Collateral in Full or Partial Satisfaction of Obligation; Compulsory Disposition of Collateral.

(a) Except as otherwise provided in subsection (g), a secured party may accept collateral in full or partial satisfaction of the obligation it secures only if:

(1) the debtor consents to the acceptance under subsection (c);

(2) the secured party does not receive, within the time set forth in subsection (d), a notification of objection to the proposal authenticated by:

(A) a person to which the secured party was required to send a proposal under Section 9—621; or

(B) any other person, other than the debtor, holding an interest in the collateral subordinate to the security interest that is the subject of the proposal;

(3) if the collateral is consumer goods, the collateral is not in the possession of the debtor when the debtor consents to the acceptance; and

(4) subsection (e) does not require the secured party to dispose of the collateral or the debtor waives the requirement pursuant to Section 9—624.

(b) A purported or apparent acceptance of collateral under this section is ineffective unless:

(1) the secured party consents to the acceptance in an authenticated record or sends a proposal to the debtor; and

(2) the conditions of subsection (a) are met.

(c) For purposes of this section:

(1) a debtor consents to an acceptance of collateral in partial satisfaction of the obligation it secures only if the debtor agrees to the terms of the acceptance in a record authenticated after default; and

(2) a debtor consents to an acceptance of collateral in full satisfaction of the obligation it secures only if the debtor agrees to the terms of the acceptance in a record authenticated after default or the secured party:

> (A) sends to the debtor after default a proposal that is unconditional or subject only to a condition that collateral not in the possession of the secured party be preserved or maintained;

> (B) in the proposal, proposes to accept collateral in full satisfaction of the obligation it secures; and

> (C) does not receive a notification of objection authenticated by the debtor within 20 days after the proposal is sent.

(d) To be effective under subsection (a)(2), a notification of objection must be received by the secured party:

> (1) in the case of a person to which the proposal was sent pursuant to Section 9—621, within 20 days after notification was sent to that person; and

> (2) in other cases:

>> (A) within 20 days after the last notification was sent pursuant to Section 9—621; or

>> (B) if a notification was not sent, before the debtor consents to the acceptance under subsection (c).

(e) A secured party that has taken possession of collateral shall dispose of the collateral pursuant to Section 9—610 within the time specified in subsection (f) if:

> (1) 60 percent of the cash price has been paid in the case of a purchase-money security interest in consumer goods; or

> (2) 60 percent of the principal amount of the obligation secured has been paid in the case of a non-purchase-money security interest in consumer goods.

(f) To comply with subsection (e), the secured party shall dispose of the collateral:

> (1) within 90 days after taking possession; or

> (2) within any longer period to which the debtor and all secondary obligors have agreed in an agreement to that effect entered into and authenticated after default.

(g) In a consumer transaction, a secured party may not accept collateral in partial satisfaction of the obligation it secures.

§ 9—621. Notification of Proposal to Accept Collateral.

(a) A secured party that desires to accept collateral in full or partial satisfaction of the obligation it secures shall send its proposal to:

> (1) any person from which the secured party has received, before the debtor consented to the acceptance, an authenticated notification of a claim of an interest in the collateral;

> (2) any other secured party or lienholder that, 10 days before the debtor consented to the acceptance, held a security interest in or other lien on the collateral perfected by the filing of a financing statement that:

>> (A) identified the collateral;

>> (B) was indexed under the debtor's name as of that date; and

>> (C) was filed in the office or offices in which to file a financing statement against the debtor covering the collateral as of that date; and

> (3) any other secured party that, 10 days before the debtor consented to the acceptance, held a security interest in the collateral perfected by compliance with a statute, regulation, or treaty described in Section 9—311(a).

(b) A secured party that desires to accept collateral in partial satisfaction of the obligation it secures shall send its proposal to any secondary obligor in addition to the persons described in subsection (a).

§ 9—622. Effect of Acceptance of Collateral.

(a) A secured party's acceptance of collateral in full or partial satisfaction of the obligation it secures:

> (1) discharges the obligation to the extent consented to by the debtor;

> (2) transfers to the secured party all of a debtor's rights in the collateral;

> (3) discharges the security interest or agricultural lien that is the subject of the debtor's consent and any subordinate security interest or other subordinate lien; and

> (4) terminates any other subordinate interest.

(b) A subordinate interest is discharged or terminated under subsection (a), even if the secured party fails to comply with this article.

§ 9—623. Right to Redeem Collateral.

(a) A debtor, any secondary obligor, or any other secured party or lienholder may redeem collateral.

(b) To redeem collateral, a person shall tender:

> (1) fulfillment of all obligations secured by the collateral; and

> (2) the reasonable expenses and attorney's fees described in Section 9—615(a)(1).

(c) A redemption may occur at any time before a secured party:

(1) has collected collateral under Section 9—607;

(2) has disposed of collateral or entered into a contract for its disposition under Section 9—610; or

(3) has accepted collateral in full or partial satisfaction of the obligation it secures under Section 9—622.

§ 9—624. Waiver.

(a) A debtor or secondary obligor may waive the right to notification of disposition of collateral under Section 9—611 only by an agreement to that effect entered into and authenticated after default.

(b) A debtor may waive the right to require disposition of collateral under Section 9—620(e) only by an agreement to that effect entered into and authenticated after default.

(c) Except in a consumer-goods transaction, a debtor or secondary obligor may waive the right to redeem collateral under Section 9—623 only by an agreement to that effect entered into and authenticated after default.

[Subpart 2. Noncompliance with Article]

§ 9—625. Remedies for Secured Party's Failure to Comply with Article.

(a) If it is established that a secured party is not proceeding in accordance with this article, a court may order or restrain collection, enforcement, or disposition of collateral on appropriate terms and conditions.

(b) Subject to subsections (c), (d), and (f), a person is liable for damages in the amount of any loss caused by a failure to comply with this article. Loss caused by a failure to comply may include loss resulting from the debtor's inability to obtain, or increased costs of, alternative financing.

(c) Except as otherwise provided in Section 9—628:

(1) a person that, at the time of the failure, was a debtor, was an obligor, or held a security interest in or other lien on the collateral may recover damages under subsection (b) for its loss; and

(2) if the collateral is consumer goods, a person that was a debtor or a secondary obligor at the time a secured party failed to comply with this part may recover for that failure in any event an amount not less than the credit service charge plus 10 percent of the principal amount of the obligation or the time-price differential plus 10 percent of the cash price.

(d) A debtor whose deficiency is eliminated under Section 9—626 may recover damages for the loss of any surplus. However, a debtor or secondary obligor whose deficiency is eliminated or reduced under Section 9—626 may not otherwise recover under subsection (b) for noncompliance with the provisions of this part relating to collection, enforcement, disposition, or acceptance.

(e) In addition to any damages recoverable under subsection (b), the debtor, consumer obligor, or person named as a debtor in a filed record, as applicable, may recover $500 in each case from a person that:

(1) fails to comply with Section 9—208;

(2) fails to comply with Section 9—209;

(3) files a record that the person is not entitled to file under Section 9—509(a);

(4) fails to cause the secured party of record to file or send a termination statement as required by Section 9—513(a) or (c);

(5) fails to comply with Section 9—616(b)(1) and whose failure is part of a pattern, or consistent with a practice, of noncompliance; or

(6) fails to comply with Section 9—616(b)(2).

(f) A debtor or consumer obligor may recover damages under subsection (b) and, in addition, $500 in each case from a person that, without reasonable cause, fails to comply with a request under Section 9—210. A recipient of a request under Section 9—210 which never claimed an interest in the collateral or obligations that are the subject of a request under that section has a reasonable excuse for failure to comply with the request within the meaning of this subsection.

(g) If a secured party fails to comply with a request regarding a list of collateral or a statement of account under Section 9—210, the secured party may claim a security interest only as shown in the list or statement included in the request as against a person that is reasonably misled by the failure.

§ 9—626. Action in Which Deficiency or Surplus Is in Issue.

(a) In an action arising from a transaction, other than a consumer transaction, in which the amount of a deficiency or surplus is in issue, the following rules apply:

(1) A secured party need not prove compliance with the provisions of this part relating to collection, enforcement, disposition, or acceptance unless the debtor or a secondary obligor places the secured party's compliance in issue.

(2) If the secured party's compliance is placed in issue, the secured party has the burden of establishing that the collection, enforcement, disposition, or acceptance was conducted in accordance with this part.

(3) Except as otherwise provided in Section 9—628, if a secured party fails to prove that the collection, enforcement, disposition, or acceptance was conducted in accordance with the provisions of this part relating to collection, enforcement, disposition, or acceptance, the liability of a debtor or a secondary obligor for a defi-

ciency is limited to an amount by which the sum of the secured obligation, expenses, and attorney's fees exceeds the greater of:

(A) the proceeds of the collection, enforcement, disposition, or acceptance; or

(B) the amount of proceeds that would have been realized had the noncomplying secured party proceeded in accordance with the provisions of this part relating to collection, enforcement, disposition, or acceptance.

(4) For purposes of paragraph (3)(B), the amount of proceeds that would have been realized is equal to the sum of the secured obligation, expenses, and attorney's fees unless the secured party proves that the amount is less than that sum.

(5) If a deficiency or surplus is calculated under Section 9—615(f), the debtor or obligor has the burden of establishing that the amount of proceeds of the disposition is significantly below the range of prices that a complying disposition to a person other than the secured party, a person related to the secured party, or a secondary obligor would have brought.

(b) The limitation of the rules in subsection (a) to transactions other than consumer transactions is intended to leave to the court the determination of the proper rules in consumer transactions. The court may not infer from that limitation the nature of the proper rule in consumer transactions and may continue to apply established approaches.

§ 9—627. **Determination of Whether Conduct Was Commercially Reasonable.**

(a) The fact that a greater amount could have been obtained by a collection, enforcement, disposition, or acceptance at a different time or in a different method from that selected by the secured party is not of itself sufficient to preclude the secured party from establishing that the collection, enforcement, disposition, or acceptance was made in a commercially reasonable manner.

(b) A disposition of collateral is made in a commercially reasonable manner if the disposition is made:

(1) in the usual manner on any recognized market;

(2) at the price current in any recognized market at the time of the disposition; or

(3) otherwise in conformity with reasonable commercial practices among dealers in the type of property that was the subject of the disposition.

(c) A collection, enforcement, disposition, or acceptance is commercially reasonable if it has been approved:

(1) in a judicial proceeding;

(2) by a bona fide creditors' committee;

(3) by a representative of creditors; or

(4) by an assignee for the benefit of creditors.

(d) Approval under subsection (c) need not be obtained, and lack of approval does not mean that the collection, enforcement, disposition, or acceptance is not commercially reasonable.

§ 9—628. **Nonliability and Limitation on Liability of Secured Party; Liability of Secondary Obligor.**

(a) Unless a secured party knows that a person is a debtor or obligor, knows the identity of the person, and knows how to communicate with the person:

(1) the secured party is not liable to the person, or to a secured party or lienholder that has filed a financing statement against the person, for failure to comply with this article; and

(2) the secured party's failure to comply with this article does not affect the liability of the person for a deficiency.

(b) A secured party is not liable because of its status as secured party:

(1) to a person that is a debtor or obligor, unless the secured party knows:

(A) that the person is a debtor or obligor;

(B) the identity of the person; and

(C) how to communicate with the person; or

(2) to a secured party or lienholder that has filed a financing statement against a person, unless the secured party knows:

(A) that the person is a debtor; and

(B) the identity of the person.

(c) A secured party is not liable to any person, and a person's liability for a deficiency is not affected, because of any act or omission arising out of the secured party's reasonable belief that a transaction is not a consumer-goods transaction or a consumer transaction or that goods are not consumer goods, if the secured party's belief is based on its reasonable reliance on:

(1) a debtor's representation concerning the purpose for which collateral was to be used, acquired, or held; or

(2) an obligor's representation concerning the purpose for which a secured obligation was incurred.

(d) A secured party is not liable to any person under Section 9—625(c)(2) for its failure to comply with Section 9—616.

(e) A secured party is not liable under Section 9—625(c)(2) more than once with respect to any one secured obligation.

Part 7   Transition

§ 9—701.   Effective Date.

This [Act] takes effect on July 1, 2001.

§ 9—702.   Savings Clause.

(a) Except as otherwise provided in this part, this [Act] applies to a transaction or lien within its scope, even if the transaction or lien was entered into or created before this [Act] takes effect.

(b) Except as otherwise provided in subsection (c) and Sections 9—703 through 9—709:

(1) transactions and liens that were not governed by [former Article 9], were validly entered into or created before this [Act] takes effect, and would be subject to this [Act] if they had been entered into or created after this [Act] takes effect, and the rights, duties, and interests flowing from those transactions and liens remain valid after this [Act] takes effect; and

(2) the transactions and liens may be terminated, completed, consummated, and enforced as required or permitted by this [Act] or by the law that otherwise would apply if this [Act] had not taken effect.

(c) This [Act] does not affect an action, case, or proceeding commenced before this [Act] takes effect.

§ 9—703.   Security Interest Perfected before Effective Date.

(a) A security interest that is enforceable immediately before this [Act] takes effect and would have priority over the rights of a person that becomes a lien creditor at that time is a perfected security interest under this [Act] if, when this [Act] takes effect, the applicable requirements for enforceability and perfection under this [Act] are satisfied without further action.

(b) Except as otherwise provided in Section 9—705, if, immediately before this [Act] takes effect, a security interest is enforceable and would have priority over the rights of a person that becomes a lien creditor at that time, but the applicable requirements for enforceability or perfection under this [Act] are not satisfied when this [Act] takes effect, the security interest:

(1) is a perfected security interest for one year after this [Act] takes effect;

(2) remains enforceable thereafter only if the security interest becomes enforceable under Section 9—203 before the year expires; and

(3) remains perfected thereafter only if the applicable requirements for perfection under this [Act] are satisfied before the year expires.

§ 9—704.   Security Interest Unperfected before Effective Date.

A security interest that is enforceable immediately before this [Act] takes effect but which would be subordinate to the rights of a person that becomes a lien creditor at that time:

(1) remains an enforceable security interest for one year after this [Act] takes effect;

(2) remains enforceable thereafter if the security interest becomes enforceable under Section 9—203 when this [Act] takes effect or within one year thereafter; and

(3) becomes perfected:

(A) without further action, when this [Act] takes effect if the applicable requirements for perfection under this [Act] are satisfied before or at that time; or

(B) when the applicable requirements for perfection are satisfied if the requirements are satisfied after that time.

§ 9—705.   Effectiveness of Action Taken before Effective Date.

(a) If action, other than the filing of a financing statement, is taken before this [Act] takes effect and the action would have resulted in priority of a security interest over the rights of a person that becomes a lien creditor had the security interest become enforceable before this [Act] takes effect, the action is effective to perfect a security interest that attaches under this [Act] within one year after this [Act] takes effect. An attached security interest becomes unperfected one year after this [Act] takes effect unless the security interest becomes a perfected security interest under this [Act] before the expiration of that period.

(b) The filing of a financing statement before this [Act] takes effect is effective to perfect a security interest to the extent the filing would satisfy the applicable requirements for perfection under this [Act].

(c) This [Act] does not render ineffective an effective financing statement that, before this [Act] takes effect, is filed and satisfies the applicable requirements for perfection under the law of the jurisdiction governing perfection as provided in [former Section 9—103]. However, except as otherwise provided in subsections (d) and (e) and Section 9—706, the financing statement ceases to be effective at the earlier of:

(1) the time the financing statement would have ceased to be effective under the law of the jurisdiction in which it is filed; or

(2) June 30, 2006.

(d) The filing of a continuation statement after this [Act] takes effect does not continue the effectiveness of the financing statement filed before this [Act] takes effect. However, upon the timely filing of a continuation statement after this [Act] takes effect and in accordance with the law of the jurisdiction governing perfection as provided in Part 3, the effectiveness of a financing statement filed in the same office in that jurisdiction before this [Act] takes effect continues for the period provided by the law of that jurisdiction.

(e) Subsection (c)(2) applies to a financing statement that, before this [Act] takes effect, is filed against a transmitting utility and satisfies the applicable requirements for perfection under the law of the jurisdiction governing perfection as provided in [former Section 9—103] only to the extent that Part 3 provides that the law of a jurisdiction other than the jurisdiction in which the financing statement is filed governs perfection of a security interest in collateral covered by the financing statement.

(f) A financing statement that includes a financing statement filed before this [Act] takes effect and a continuation statement filed after this [Act] takes effect is effective only to the extent that it satisfies the requirements of Part 5 for an initial financing statement.

§ 9—706. When Initial Financing Statement Suffices to Continue Effectiveness of Financing Statement.

(a) The filing of an initial financing statement in the office specified in Section 9—501 continues the effectiveness of a financing statement filed before this [Act] takes effect if:

(1) the filing of an initial financing statement in that office would be effective to perfect a security interest under this [Act];

(2) the pre-effective-date financing statement was filed in an office in another State or another office in this State; and

(3) the initial financing statement satisfies subsection (c).

(b) The filing of an initial financing statement under subsection (a) continues the effectiveness of the pre-effective-date financing statement:

(1) if the initial financing statement is filed before this [Act] takes effect, for the period provided in [former Section 9—403] with respect to a financing statement; and

(2) if the initial financing statement is filed after this [Act] takes effect, for the period provided in Section 9—515 with respect to an initial financing statement.

(c) To be effective for purposes of subsection (a), an initial financing statement must:

(1) satisfy the requirements of Part 5 for an initial financing statement;

(2) identify the pre-effective-date financing statement by indicating the office in which the financing statement was filed and providing the dates of filing and file numbers, if any, of the financing statement and of the most recent continuation statement filed with respect to the financing statement; and

(3) indicate that the pre-effective-date financing statement remains effective.

§ 9—707. Amendment of Pre-Effective-Date Financing Statement.

(a) In this section, "Pre-effective-date financing statement" means a financing statement filed before this [Act] takes effect.

(b) After this [Act] takes effect, a person may add or delete collateral covered by, continue or terminate the effectiveness of, or otherwise amend the information provided in, a pre-effective-date financing statement only in accordance with the law of the jurisdiction governing perfection as provided in Part 3. However, the effectiveness of a pre-effective-date financing statement also may be terminated in accordance with the law of the jurisdiction in which the financing statement is filed.

(c) Except as otherwise provided in subsection (d), if the law of this State governs perfection of a security interest, the information in a pre-effective-date financing statement may be amended after this [Act] takes effect only if:

(1) the pre-effective-date financing statement and an amendment are filed in the office specified in Section 9—501;

(2) an amendment is filed in the office specified in Section 9—501 concurrently with, or after the filing in that office of, an initial financing statement that satisfies Section 9—706(c); or

(3) an initial financing statement that provides the information as amended and satisfies Section 9—706(c) is filed in the office specified in Section 9—501.

(d) If the law of this State governs perfection of a security interest, the effectiveness of a pre-effective-date financing statement may be continued only under Section 9—705(d) and (f) or 9—706.

(e) Whether or not the law of this State governs perfection of a security interest, the effectiveness of a pre-effective-date financing statement filed in this State may be terminated after this [Act] takes effect by filing a termination statement in the office in which the pre-effective-date financing statement is filed, unless an initial financing statement that satisfies Section 9—706(c) has been filed in the office specified by the law of the jurisdiction governing perfection as provided in Part 3 as the office in which to file a financing statement.

§ 9—708. Persons Entitled to File Initial Financing Statement or Continuation Statement.

A person may file an initial financing statement or a continuation statement under this part if:

(1) the secured party of record authorizes the filing; and

(2) the filing is necessary under this part:

(A) to continue the effectiveness of a financing statement filed before this [Act] takes effect; or

(B) to perfect or continue the perfection of a security interest.

§ 9—709. Priority.

(a) This [Act] determines the priority of conflicting claims to collateral. However, if the relative priorities of the claims were established before this [Act] takes effect, [former Article 9] determines priority.

(b) For purposes of Section 9—322(a), the priority of a security interest that becomes enforceable under Section 9—203 of this [Act] dates from the time this [Act] takes effect if the security interest is perfected under this [Act] by the filing of a financing statement before this [Act] takes effect which would not have been effective to perfect the security interest under [former Article 9]. This subsection does not apply to conflicting security interests each of which is perfected by the filing of such a financing statement.

The United Nations Convention on Contracts for the International Sale of Goods (Excerpts)

Part I. SPHERE OF APPLICATION AND GENERAL PROVISIONS

*   *   *   *

Chapter II—General Provisions

*   *   *   *

Article 8

(1) For the purposes of this Convention statements made by and other conduct of a party are to be interpreted according to his intent where the other party knew or could not have been unaware what that intent was.

(2) If the preceding paragraph is not applicable, statements made by and other conduct of a party are to be interpreted according to the understanding that a reasonable person of the same kind as the other party would have had in the same circumstances.

(3) In determining the intent of a party or the understanding a reasonable person would have had, due consideration is to be given to all relevant circumstances of the case including the negotiations, any practices which the parties have established between themselves, usages and any subsequent conduct of the parties.

Article 9

(1) The parties are bound by any usage to which they have agreed and by any practices which they have established between themselves.

(2) The parties are considered, unless otherwise agreed, to have impliedly made applicable to their contract or its formation a usage of which the parties knew or ought to have known and which in international trade is widely known to, and regularly observed by, parties to contracts of the type involved in the particular trade concerned.

*   *   *   *

Article 11

A contract of sale need not be concluded in or evidenced by writing and is not subject to any other requirement as to form. It may be proved by any means, including witnesses.

*   *   *   *

Part II.   FORMATION OF THE CONTRACT

Article 14

(1) A proposal for concluding a contract addressed to one or more specific persons constitutes an offer if it is sufficiently definite and indicates the intention of the offeror to be bound in case of acceptance. A proposal is sufficiently definite if it indicates the goods and expressly or implicitly fixes or makes provision for determining the quantity and the price.

(2) A proposal other than one addressed to one or more specific persons is to be considered merely as an invitation to make offers, unless the contrary is clearly indicated by the person making the proposal.

Article 15

(1) An offer becomes effective when it reaches the offeree.

(2) An offer, even if it is irrevocable, may be withdrawn if the withdrawal reaches the offeree before or at the same time as the offer.

Article 16

(1) Until a contract is concluded an offer may be revoked if the revocation reaches the offeree before he has dispatched an acceptance.

(2) However, an offer cannot be revoked:

(a) If it indicates, whether by stating a fixed time for acceptance or otherwise, that it is irrevocable; or

(b) If it was reasonable for the offeree to rely on the offer as being irrevocable and the offeree has acted in reliance on the offer.

Article 17

An offer, even if it is irrevocable, is terminated when a rejection reaches the offeror.

Article 18

(1) A statement made by or other conduct of the offeree indicating assent to an offer is an acceptance. Silence or inactivity does not in itself amount to acceptance.

(2) An acceptance of an offer becomes effective at the moment the indication of assent reaches the offeror. An acceptance is not effective if the indication of assent does not reach the offeror within the time he has fixed or, if no time is fixed, within a reasonable time, due account being taken of the circumstances of the transaction, including the rapidity of the means of communication employed by the offeror. An oral offer must be accepted immediately unless the circumstances indicate otherwise.

(3) However, if, by virtue of the offer or as a result of practices which the parties have established between themselves or of usage, the offeree may indicate assent by performing an act, such as one relating to the dispatch of the goods or payment of the price, without notice to the offeror, the acceptance is effective at the moment the act

is performed, provided that the act is performed within the period of time laid down in the preceding paragraph.

Article 19

(1) A reply to an offer which purports to be an acceptance but contains additions, limitations or other modifications is a rejection of the offer and constitutes a counter-offer.

(2) However, a reply to an offer which purports to be an acceptance but contains additional or different terms which do not materially alter the terms of the offer constitutes an acceptance, unless the offeror, without undue delay, objects orally to the discrepancy or dispatches a notice to that effect. If he does not so object, the terms of the contract are the terms of the offer with the modifications contained in the acceptance.

(3) Additional or different terms relating, among other things, to the price, payment, quality and quantity of the goods, place and time of delivery, extent of one party's liability to the other or the settlement of disputes are considered to alter the terms of the offer materially.

*   *   *   *

Article 22

An acceptance may be withdrawn if the withdrawal reaches the offeror before or at the same time as the acceptance would have become effective.

*   *   *   *

Part III.   SALE OF GOODS

Chapter I—General Provisions

Article 25

A breach of contract committed by one of the parties is fundamental if it results in such detriment to the other party as substantially to deprive him of what he is entitled to expect under the contract, unless the party in breach did not foresee and a reasonable person of the same kind in the same circumstances would not have foreseen such a result.

*   *   *   *

Article 28

If, in accordance with the provisions of this Convention, one party is entitled to require performance of any obligation by the other party, a court is not bound to enter a judgment for specific performance unless the court would do so under its own law in respect of similar contracts of sale not governed by this Convention.

Article 29

(1) A contract may be modified or terminated by the mere agreement of the parties.

(2) A contract in writing which contains a provision requiring any modification or termination by agreement to be in writing may not be otherwise modified or terminated by agreement. However, a party may be precluded by his

conduct from asserting such a provision to the extent that the other party has relied on that conduct.

❋   ❋   ❋   ❋

Chapter II—Obligations of the Seller

❋   ❋   ❋   ❋

Section II. Conformity of the Goods and Third Party Claims

Article 35

(1) The seller must deliver goods which are of the quantity, quality and description required by the contract and which are contained or packaged in the manner required by the contract.

(2) Except where the parties have agreed otherwise, the goods do not conform with the contract unless they:

(a) Are fit for the purposes for which goods of the same description would ordinarily be used;

(b) Are fit for any particular purpose expressly or impliedly made known to the seller at the time of the conclusion of the contract, except where the circumstances show that the buyer did not rely, or that it was unreasonable for him to rely, on the seller's skill and judgment;

(c) Possess the qualities of goods which the seller has held out to the buyer as a sample or model;

(d) Are contained or packaged in the manner usual for such goods or, where there is no such manner, in a manner adequate to preserve and protect the goods.

(3) The seller is not liable under subparagraphs (a) to (d) of the preceding paragraph for any lack of conformity of the goods if at the time of the conclusion of the contract the buyer knew or could not have been unaware of such lack of conformity.

❋   ❋   ❋   ❋

Article 64

(1) The seller may declare the contract avoided:

(a) If the failure by the buyer to perform any of his obligations under the contract or this Convention amounts to a fundamental breach of contract; or

(b) If the buyer does not, within the additional period of time fixed by the seller in accordance with paragraph (1) of article 63, perform his obligation to pay the price or take delivery of the goods, or if he declares that he will not do so within the period so fixed.

(2) However, in cases where the buyer has paid the price, the seller loses the right to declare the contract avoided unless he does so:

(a) In respect of late performance by the buyer, before the seller has become aware that performance has been rendered; or

(b) In respect of any breach other than late perform-

ance by the buyer, within a reasonable time:

(i) After the seller knew or ought to have known of the breach; or

(ii) After the expiration of any additional period of time fixed by the seller in accordance with paragraph (1) of article 63, or after the buyer has declared that he will not perform his obligations within such an additional period.

❋   ❋   ❋   ❋

Chapter IV—Passing of Risk

❋   ❋   ❋   ❋

Article 67

(1) If the contract of sale involves carriage of the goods and the seller is not bound to hand them over at a particular place, the risk passes to the buyer when the goods are handed over to the first carrier for transmission to the buyer in accordance with the contract of sale. If the seller is bound to hand the goods over to a carrier at a particular place, the risk does not pass to the buyer until the goods are handed over to the carrier at that place. The fact that the seller is authorized to retain documents controlling the disposition of the goods does not affect the passage of the risk.

(2) Nevertheless, the risk does not pass to the buyer until the goods are clearly identified to the contract, whether by markings on the goods, by shipping documents, by notice given to the buyer or otherwise.

❋   ❋   ❋   ❋

Chapter V—Provisions Common to the Obligations of the Seller and of the Buyer

Section I. Anticipatory Breach and Instalment Contracts

Article 71

(1) A party may suspend the performance of his obligations if, after the conclusion of the contract, it becomes apparent that the other party will not perform a substantial part of his obligations as a result of:

(a) A serious deficiency in his ability to perform or in his creditworthiness; or

(b) His conduct in preparing to perform or in performing the contract.

(2) If the seller has already dispatched the goods before the grounds described in the preceding paragraph become evident, he may prevent the handing over of the goods to the buyer even though the buyer holds a document which entitles him to obtain them. The present paragraph relates only to the rights in the goods as between the buyer and the seller.

(3) A party suspending performance, whether before or after dispatch of the goods, must immediately give notice of the suspension to the other party and must continue with performance if the other party provides adequate assurance of his performance.

Article 72

(1) If prior to the date for performance of the contract it is clear that one of the parties will commit a fundamental breach of contract, the other party may declare the contract avoided.

(2) If time allows, the party intending to declare the contract avoided must give reasonable notice to the other party in order to permit him to provide adequate assurance of his performance.

(3) The requirements of the preceding paragraph do not apply if the other party has declared that he will not perform his obligations.

Article 73

(1) In the case of a contract for delivery of goods by instalments, if the failure of one party to perform any of his obligations in respect of any instalment constitutes a fundamental breach of contract with respect to that instalment, the other party may declare the contract avoided with respect to that instalment.

(2) If one party's failure to perform any of his obligations in respect of any instalment gives the other party good grounds to conclude that a fundamental breach of contract will occur with respect to future instalments, he may declare the contract avoided for the future, provided that he does so within a reasonable time.

(3) A buyer who declares the contract avoided in respect of any delivery may, at the same time, declare it avoided in respect of deliveries already made or of future deliveries if, by reason of their interdependence, those deliveries could not be used for the purpose contemplated by the parties at the time of the conclusion of the contract.

Section II. Damages

Article 74

Damages for breach of contract by one party consist of a sum equal to the loss, including loss of profit, suffered by the other party as a consequence of the breach. Such damages may not exceed the loss which the party in breach foresaw or ought to have foreseen at the time of the conclusion of the contract, in the light of the facts and matters of which he then knew or ought to have known, as a possible consequence of the breach of contract.

Article 75

If the contract is avoided and if, in a reasonable manner and within a reasonable time after avoidance, the buyer has bought goods in replacement or the seller has resold the goods, the party claiming damages may recover the difference between the contract price and the price in the substitute transaction as well as any further damages recoverable under article 74.

Article 76

(1) If the contract is avoided and there is a current price for the goods, the party claiming damages may, if he has not made a purchase or resale under article 75, recover the difference between the price fixed by the contract and the current price at the time of avoidance as well as any further damages recoverable under article 74. If, however, the party claiming damages has avoided the contract after taking over the goods, the current price at the time of such taking over shall be applied instead of the current price at the time of avoidance.

(2) For the purposes of the preceding paragraph, the current price is the price prevailing at the place where delivery of the goods should have been made or, if there is no current price at that place, the price at such other place as serves as a reasonable substitute, making due allowance for differences in the cost of transporting the goods.

Article 77

A party who relies on a breach of contract must take such measures as are reasonable in the circumstances to mitigate the loss, including loss of profit, resulting from the breach. If he fails to take such measures, the party in breach may claim a reduction in the damages in the amount by which the loss should have been mitigated.

The Uniform Partnership Act

(Adopted in forty-nine states [all of the states except Louisiana], the District of Columbia, the Virgin Islands, and Guam. The adoptions by Alabama and Nebraska do not follow the official text in every respect, but are substantially similar, with local variations.)

The Act consists of 7 Parts as follows:

I. Preliminary Provisions

II. Nature of Partnership

III. Relations of Partners to Persons Dealing with the Partnership

IV. Relations of Partners to One Another

V. Property Rights of a Partner

VI. Dissolution and Winding Up

VII. Miscellaneous Provisions

An Act to make uniform the Law of Partnerships

Be it enacted, etc.:

Part I   Preliminary Provisions

Sec. 1. Name of Act

This act may be cited as Uniform Partnership Act.

Sec. 2. Definition of Terms

In this act, "Court" includes every court and judge having jurisdiction in the case.

"Business" includes every trade, occupation, or profession.

"Person" includes individuals, partnerships, corporations, and other associations.

"Bankrupt" includes bankrupt under the Federal Bankruptcy Act or insolvent under any state insolvent act.

"Conveyance" includes every assignment, lease, mortgage, or encumbrance.

"Real property" includes land and any interest or estate in land.

Sec. 3. Interpretation of Knowledge and Notice

(1) A person has "knowledge" of a fact within the meaning of this act not only when he has actual knowledge thereof, but also when he has knowledge of such other facts as in the circumstances shows bad faith.

(2) A person has "notice" of a fact within the meaning of this act when the person who claims the benefit of the notice:

(a) States the fact to such person, or

(b) Delivers through the mail, or by other means of communication, a written statement of the fact to such person or to a proper person at his place of business or residence.

Sec. 4. Rules of Construction

(1) The rule that statutes in derogation of the common law are to be strictly construed shall have no application to this act.

(2) The law of estoppel shall apply under this act.

(3) The law of agency shall apply under this act.

(4) This act shall be so interpreted and construed as to effect its general purpose to make uniform the law of those states which enact it.

(5) This act shall not be construed so as to impair the obligations of any contract existing when the act goes into effect, nor to affect any action or proceedings begun or right accrued before this act takes effect.

Sec. 5. Rules for Cases Not Provided for in This Act.

In any case not provided for in this act the rules of law and equity, including the law merchant, shall govern.

Part II   Nature of Partnership

Sec. 6. Partnership Defined

(1) A partnership is an association of two or more persons to carry on as co-owners a business for profit.

(2) But any association formed under any other statute of this state, or any statute adopted by authority, other than the authority of this state, is not a partnership under this act, unless such association would have been a partnership in this state prior to the adoption of this act; but this act shall apply to limited partnerships except in so far as the statutes relating to such partnerships are inconsistent herewith.

Sec. 7. Rules for Determining the Existence of a Partnership

In determining whether a partnership exists, these rules shall apply:

(1) Except as provided by Section 16 persons who are not partners as to each other are not partners as to third persons.

(2) Joint tenancy, tenancy in common, tenancy by the entireties, joint property, common property, or part ownership does not of itself establish a partnership, whether such co-owners do or do not share any profits made by the use of the property.

(3) The sharing of gross returns does not of itself establish a partnership, whether or not the persons sharing them have a joint or common right or interest in any property from which the returns are derived.

(4) The receipt by a person of a share of the profits of a business is prima facie evidence that he is a partner in the business, but no such inference shall be drawn if such profits were received in payment:

   (a) As a debt by installments or otherwise,

   (b) As wages of an employee or rent to a landlord,

   (c) As an annuity to a widow or representative of a deceased partner,

   (d) As interest on a loan, though the amount of pay-ment vary with the profits of the business,

   (e) As the consideration for the sale of a good-will of a business or other property by installments or otherwise.

Sec. 8. Partnership Property

(1) All property originally brought into the partnership stock or subsequently acquired by purchase or otherwise, on account of the partnership, is partnership property.

(2) Unless the contrary intention appears, property acquired with partnership funds is partnership property.

(3) Any estate in real property may be acquired in the partnership name. Title so acquired can be conveyed only in the partnership name.

(4) A conveyance to a partnership in the partnership name, though without words of inheritance, passes the entire estate of the grantor unless a contrary intent appears.

Part III   Relations of Partners to Persons Dealing with the Partnership

Sec. 9. Partner Agent of Partnership as to Partnership Business

(1) Every partner is an agent of the partnership for the purpose of its business, and the act of every partner, including the execution in the partnership name of any instrument, for apparently carrying on in the usual way the business of the partnership of which he is a member binds the partnership, unless the partner so acting has in fact no authority to act for the partnership in the particular matter, and the person with whom he is dealing has knowledge of the fact that he has no such authority.

(2) An act of a partner which is not apparently for the carrying on of the business of the partnership in the usual way does not bind the partnership unless authorized by the other partners.

(3) Unless authorized by the other partners or unless they have abandoned the business, one or more but less than all the partners have no authority to:

   (a) Assign the partnership property in trust for creditors or on the assignee's promise to pay the debts of the partnership,

   (b) Dispose of the good-will of the business,

   (c) Do any other act which would make it impossible to carry on the ordinary business of a partnership,

   (d) Confess a judgment,

   (e) Submit a partnership claim or liability to arbitration or reference.

(4) No act of a partner in contravention of a restriction on authority shall bind the partnership to persons having knowledge of the restriction.

Sec. 10. Conveyance of Real Property of the Partnership

(1) Where title to real property is in the partnership name, any partner may convey title to such property by a conveyance executed in the partnership name; but the partnership may recover such property unless the partner's act binds the partnership under the provisions of paragraph (1) of section 9, or unless such property has been conveyed by the grantee or a person claiming through such grantee to a holder for value without knowledge that the partner, in making the conveyance, has exceeded his authority.

(2) Where title to real property is in the name of the partnership, a conveyance executed by a partner, in his own name, passes the equitable interest of the partnership, provided the act is one within the authority of the partner under the provisions of paragraph (1) of section 9.

(3) Where title to real property is in the name of one or more but not all the partners, and the record does not disclose the right of the partnership, the partners in whose name the title stands may convey title to such property, but the partnership may recover such property if the partners' act does not bind the partnership under the provisions of paragraph (1) of section 9, unless the purchaser or his assignee, is a holder for value, without knowledge.

(4) Where the title to real property is in the name of one or more or all the partners, or in a third person in trust for the partnership, a conveyance executed by a partner in the partnership name, or in his own name, passes the equitable interest of the partnership, provided the act is one within the authority of the partner under the provisions of paragraph (1) of section 9.

(5) Where the title to real property is in the names of all the partners a conveyance executed by all the partners passes all their rights in such property.

Sec. 11. Partnership Bound by Admission of Partner

An admission or representation made by any partner concerning partnership affairs within the scope of his authority as conferred by this act is evidence against the partnership.

Sec. 12. Partnership Charged with Knowledge of or Notice to Partner

Notice to any partner of any matter relating to partnership affairs, and the knowledge of the partner acting in the particular matter, acquired while a partner or then present to his mind, and the knowledge of any other partner who reasonably could and should have communicated it to the acting partner, operate as notice to or knowledge of the partnership, except in the case of a fraud on the partnership committed by or with the consent of that partner.

Sec. 13. Partnership Bound by Partner's Wrongful Act

Where, by any wrongful act or omission of any partner acting in the ordinary course of the business of the partnership or with the authority of his co-partners, loss or injury is caused to any person, not being a partner in the partnership, or any penalty is incurred, the partnership is liable therefor to the same extent as the partner so acting or omitting to act.

Sec. 14. Partnership Bound by Partner's Breach of Trust

The partnership is bound to make good the loss:

(a) Where one partner acting within the scope of his apparent authority receives money or property of a third person and misapplies it; and

(b) Where the partnership in the course of its business receives money or property of a third person and the money or property so received is misapplied by any partner while it is in the custody of the partnership.

Sec. 15. Nature of Partner's Liability

All partners are liable

(a) Jointly and severally for everything chargeable to the partnership under sections 13 and 14.

(b) Jointly for all other debts and obligations of the partnership; but any partner may enter into a separate obligation to perform a partnership contract.

Sec. 16. Partner by Estoppel

(1) When a person, by words spoken or written or by conduct, represents himself, or consents to another representing him to any one, as a partner in an existing partnership or with one or more persons not actual partners, he is liable to any such person to whom such representation has been made, who has, on the faith of such representation, given credit to the actual or apparent partnership, and if he has made such representation or consented to its being made in a public manner he is liable to such person, whether the representation has or has not been made or communicated to such person so giving credit by or with the knowledge of the apparent partner making the representation or consenting to its being made.

(a) When a partnership liability results, he is liable as though he were an actual member of the partnership.

(b) When no partnership liability results, he is liable jointly with the other persons, if any, so consenting to the contract or representation as to incur liability, otherwise separately.

(2) When a person has been thus represented to be a partner in an existing partnership, or with one or more persons not actual partners, he is an agent of the persons consenting to such representation to bind them to the same extent and in the same manner as though he were a partner in fact, with respect to persons who rely upon the representation. Where all the members of the existing partnership consent to the representation, a partnership act or obligation results; but in all other cases it is the joint act or

obligation of the person acting and the persons consenting to the representation.

Sec. 17. Liability of Incoming Partner

A person admitted as a partner into an existing partnership is liable for all the obligations of the partnership arising before his admission as though he had been a partner when such obligations were incurred, except that this liability shall be satisfied only out of partnership property.

Part IV   Relations of Partners to One Another

Sec. 18. Rules Determining Rights and Duties of Partners

The rights and duties of the partners in relation to the partnership shall be determined, subject to any agreement between them, by the following rules:

(a) Each partner shall be repaid his contributions, whether by way of capital or advances to the partnership property and share equally in the profits and surplus remaining after all liabilities, including those to partners, are satisfied; and must contribute towards the losses, whether of capital or otherwise, sustained by the partnership according to his share in the profits.

(b) The partnership must indemnify every partner in respect of payments made and personal liabilities reasonably incurred by him in the ordinary and proper conduct of its business, or for the preservation of its business or property.

(c) A partner, who in aid of the partnership makes any payment or advance beyond the amount of capital which he agreed to contribute, shall be paid interest from the date of the payment or advance.

(d) A partner shall receive interest on the capital contributed by him only from the date when repayment should be made.

(e) All partners have equal rights in the management and conduct of the partnership business.

(f) No partner is entitled to remuneration for acting in the partnership business, except that a surviving partner is entitled to reasonable compensation for his services in winding up the partnership affairs.

(g) No person can become a member of a partnership without the consent of all the partners.

(h) Any difference arising as to ordinary matters connected with the partnership business may be decided by a majority of the partners; but no act in contravention of any agreement between the partners may be done rightfully without the consent of all the partners.

Sec. 19. Partnership Books

The partnership books shall be kept, subject to any agreement between the partners, at the principal place of business of the partnership, and every partner shall at all times have access to and may inspect and copy any of them.

Sec. 20. Duty of Partners to Render Information

Partners shall render on demand true and full information of all things affecting the partnership to any partner or the legal representative of any deceased partner or partner under legal disability.

Sec. 21. Partner Accountable as a Fiduciary

(1) Every partner must account to the partnership for any benefit, and hold as trustee for it any profits derived by him without the consent of the other partners from any transaction connected with the formation, conduct, or liquidation of the partnership or from any use by him of its property.

(2) This section applies also to the representatives of a deceased partner engaged in the liquidation of the affairs of the partnership as the personal representatives of the last surviving partner.

Sec. 22. Right to an Account

Any partner shall have the right to a formal account as to partnership affairs:

(a) If he is wrongfully excluded from the partnership business or possession of its property by his co-partners,

(b) If the right exists under the terms of any agreement,

(c) As provided by section 21,

(d) Whenever other circumstances render it just and reasonable.

Sec. 23. Continuation of Partnership beyond Fixed Term

(1) When a partnership for a fixed term or particular undertaking is continued after the termination of such term or particular undertaking without any express agreement, the rights and duties of the partners remain the same as they were at such termination, so far as is consistent with a partnership at will.

(2) A continuation of the business by the partners or such of them as habitually acted therein during the term, without any settlement or liquidation of the partnership affairs, is prima facie evidence of a continuation of the partnership.

Part V   Property Rights of a Partner

Sec. 24. Extent of Property Rights of a Partner

The property rights of a partner are (1) his rights in specific partnership property, (2) his interest in the partnership, and (3) his right to participate in the management.

Sec. 25. Nature of a Partner's Right in Specific Partnership Property

(1) A partner is co-owner with his partners of specific partnership property holding as a tenant in partnership.

(2) The incidents of this tenancy are such that:

(a) A partner, subject to the provisions of this act and

to any agreement between the partners, has an equal right with his partners to possess specific partnership property for partnership purposes; but he has no right to possess such property for any other purpose without the consent of his partners.

(b) A partner's right in specific partnership property is not assignable except in connection with the assignment of rights of all the partners in the same property.

(c) A partner's right in specific partnership property is not subject to attachment or execution, except on a claim against the partnership. When partnership property is attached for a partnership debt the partners, or any of them, or the representatives of a deceased partner, cannot claim any right under the homestead or exemption laws.

(d) On the death of a partner his right in specific partnership property vests in the surviving partner or partners, except where the deceased was the last surviving partner, when his right in such property vests in his legal representative. Such surviving partner or partners, or the legal representative of the last surviving partner, has no right to possess the partnership property for any but a partnership purpose.

(e) A partner's right in specific partnership property is not subject to dower, curtesy, or allowances to widows, heirs, or next of kin.

Sec. 26. Nature of Partner's Interest in the Partnership

A partner's interest in the partnership is his share of the profits and surplus, and the same is personal property.

Sec. 27. Assignment of Partner's Interest

(1) A conveyance by a partner of his interest in the partnership does not of itself dissolve the partnership, nor, as against the other partners in the absence of agreement, entitle the assignee, during the continuance of the partnership, to interfere in the management or administration of the partnership business or affairs, or to require any information or account of partnership transactions, or to inspect the partnership books; but it merely entitles the assignee to receive in accordance with his contract the profits to which the assigning partner would otherwise be entitled.

(2) In case of a dissolution of the partnership, the assignee is entitled to receive his assignor's interest and may require an account from the date only of the last account agreed to by all the partners.

Sec. 28. Partner's Interest Subject to Charging Order

(1) On due application to a competent court by any judgment creditor of a partner, the court which entered the judgment, order, or decree, or any other court, may charge the interest of the debtor partner with payment of the unsatisfied amount of such judgment debt with interest thereon; and may then or later appoint a receiver of his

share of the profits, and of any other money due or to fall due to him in respect of the partnership, and make all other orders, directions, accounts and inquiries which the debtor partner might have made, or which the circumstances of the case may require.

(2) The interest charged may be redeemed at any time before foreclosure, or in case of a sale being directed by the court may be purchased without thereby causing a dissolution:

(a) With separate property, by any one or more of the partners, or

(b) With partnership property, by any one or more of the partners with the consent of all the partners whose interests are not so charged or sold.

(3) Nothing in this act shall be held to deprive a partner of his right, if any, under the exemption laws, as regards his interest in the partnership.

Part VI   Dissolution and Winding up

Sec. 29. Dissolution Defined

The dissolution of a partnership is the change in the relation of the partners caused by any partner ceasing to be associated in the carrying on as distinguished from the winding up of the business.

Sec. 30. Partnership not Terminated by Dissolution

On dissolution the partnership is not terminated, but continues until the winding up of partnership affairs is completed.

Sec. 31. Causes of Dissolution

Dissolution is caused:

(1) Without violation of the agreement between the partners,

(a) By the termination of the definite term or particular undertaking specified in the agreement,

(b) By the express will of any partner when no definite term or particular undertaking is specified,

(c) By the express will of all the partners who have not assigned their interests or suffered them to be charged for their separate debts, either before or after the termination of any specified term or particular undertaking,

(d) By the expulsion of any partner from the business bona fide in accordance with such a power conferred by the agreement between the partners;

(2) In contravention of the agreement between the partners, where the circumstances do not permit a dissolution under any other provision of this section, by the express will of any partner at any time;

(3) By any event which makes it unlawful for the business of the partnership to be carried on or for the members to carry it on in partnership;

(4) By the death of any partner;

(5) By the bankruptcy of any partner or the partnership;

(6) By decree of court under section 32.

Sec. 32. Dissolution by Decree of Court

(1) On application by or for a partner the court shall decree a dissolution whenever:

    (a) A partner has been declared a lunatic in any judicial proceeding or is shown to be of unsound mind,

    (b) A partner becomes in any other way incapable of performing his part of the partnership contract,

    (c) A partner has been guilty of such conduct as tends to affect prejudicially the carrying on of the business,

    (d) A partner wilfully or persistently commits a breach of the partnership agreement, or otherwise so conducts himself in matters relating to the partnership business that it is not reasonably practicable to carry on the business in partnership with him,

    (e) The business of the partnership can only be carried on at a loss,

    (f) Other circumstances render a dissolution equitable.

(2) On the application of the purchaser of a partner's interest under sections 28 or 29 [should read 27 or 28];

    (a) After the termination of the specified term or particular undertaking,

    (b) At any time if the partnership was a partnership at will when the interest was assigned or when the charging order was issued.

Sec. 33. General Effect of Dissolution on Authority of Partner

Except so far as may be necessary to wind up partnership affairs or to complete transactions begun but not then finished, dissolution terminates all authority of any partner to act for the partnership,

(1) With respect to the partners,

    (a) When the dissolution is not by the act, bankruptcy or death of a partner; or

    (b) When the dissolution is by such act, bankruptcy or death of a partner, in cases where section 34 so requires.

(2) With respect to persons not partners, as declared in section 35.

Sec. 34. Rights of Partner to Contribution from Copartners after Dissolution

Where the dissolution is caused by the act, death or bankruptcy of a partner, each partner is liable to his copartners for his share of any liability created by any partner acting for the partnership as if the partnership had not been dissolved unless

    (a) The dissolution being by act of any partner, the partner acting for the partnership had knowledge of the dissolution, or

    (b) The dissolution being by the death or bankruptcy of a partner, the partner acting for the partnership had knowledge or notice of the death or bankruptcy.

Sec. 35. Power of Partner to Bind Partnership to Third Persons after Dissolution

(1) After dissolution a partner can bind the partnership except as provided in Paragraph (3).

    (a) By any act appropriate for winding up partnership affairs or completing transactions unfinished at dissolution;

    (b) By any transaction which would bind the partnership if dissolution had not taken place, provided the other party to the transaction

        (I) Had extended credit to the partnership prior to dissolution and had no knowledge or notice of the dissolution; or

        (II) Though he had not so extended credit, had nevertheless known of the partnership prior to dissolution, and, having no knowledge or notice of dissolution, the fact of dissolution had not been advertised in a newspaper of general circulation in the place (or in each place if more than one) at which the partnership business was regularly carried on.

(2) The liability of a partner under paragraph (1b) shall be satisfied out of partnership assets alone when such partner had been prior to dissolution

    (a) Unknown as a partner to the person with whom the contract is made; and

    (b) So far unknown and inactive in partnership affairs that the business reputation of the partnership could not be said to have been in any degree due to his connection with it.

(3) The partnership is in no case bound by any act of a partner after dissolution

    (a) Where the partnership is dissolved because it is unlawful to carry on the business, unless the act is appropriate for winding up partnership affairs; or

    (b) Where the partner has become bankrupt; or

    (c) Where the partner has no authority to wind up partnership affairs; except by a transaction with one who

        (I) Had extended credit to the partnership prior to dissolution and had no knowledge or notice of his want of authority; or

        (II) Had not extended credit to the partnership prior to dissolution, and, having no knowledge or notice of his want of authority, the fact of his want of authority has not been advertised in the manner provided for advertising the fact of dissolution in paragraph (1bII).

(4) Nothing in this section shall affect the liability under Section 16 of any person who after dissolution represents himself or consents to another representing him as a partner in a partnership engaged in carrying on business.

Sec. 36. Effect of Dissolution on Partner's Existing Liability

(1) The dissolution of the partnership does not of itself discharge the existing liability of any partner.

(2) A partner is discharged from any existing liability upon dissolution of the partnership by an agreement to that effect between himself, the partnership creditor and the person or partnership continuing the business; and such agreement may be inferred from the course of dealing between the creditor having knowledge of the dissolution and the person or partnership continuing the business.

(3) Where a person agrees to assume the existing obligations of a dissolved partnership, the partners whose obligations have been assumed shall be discharged from any liability to any creditor of the partnership who, knowing of the agreement, consents to a material alteration in the nature or time of payment of such obligations.

(4) The individual property of a deceased partner shall be liable for all obligations of the partnership incurred while he was a partner but subject to the prior payment of his separate debts.

Sec. 37. Right to Wind Up

Unless otherwise agreed the partners who have not wrongfully dissolved the partnership or the legal representative of the last surviving partner, not bankrupt, has the right to wind up the partnership affairs; provided, however, that any partner, his legal representative or his assignee, upon cause shown, may obtain winding up by the court.

Sec. 38. Rights of Partners to Application of Partnership Property

(1) When dissolution is caused in any way, except in contravention of the partnership agreement, each partner, as against his co-partners and all persons claiming through them in respect of their interests in the partnership, unless otherwise agreed, may have the partnership property applied to discharge its liabilities, and the surplus applied to pay in cash the net amount owing to the respective partners. But if dissolution is caused by expulsion of a partner, bona fide under the partnership agreement and if the expelled partner is discharged from all partnership liabilities, either by payment or agreement under section 36(2), he shall receive in cash only the net amount due him from the partnership.

(2) When dissolution is caused in contravention of the partnership agreement the rights of the partners shall be as follows:

(a) Each partner who has not caused dissolution wrongfully shall have,

   (I) All the rights specified in paragraph (1) of this section, and

   (II) The right, as against each partner who has caused the dissolution wrongfully, to damages for breach of the agreement.

(b) The partners who have not caused the dissolution wrongfully, if they all desire to continue the business in the same name, either by themselves or jointly with others, may do so, during the agreed term for the partnership and for that purpose may possess the partnership property, provided they secure the payment by bond approved by the court, or pay to any partner who has caused the dissolution wrongfully, the value of his interest in the partnership at the dissolution, less any damages recoverable under clause (2a II) of the section, and in like manner indemnify him against all present or future partnership liabilities.

(c) A partner who has caused the dissolution wrongfully shall have:

   (I) If the business is not continued under the provisions of paragraph (2b) all the rights of a partner under paragraph (1), subject to clause (2a II), of this section,

   (II) If the business is continued under paragraph (2b) of this section the right as against his co-partners and all claiming through them in respect of their interests in the partnership, to have the value of his interest in the partnership, less any damages caused to his co-partners by the dissolution, ascertained and paid to him in cash, or the payment secured by bond approved by the court, and to be released from all existing liabilities of the partnership; but in ascertaining the value of the partner's interest the value of the good-will of the business shall not be considered.

Sec. 39. Rights Where Partnership Is Dissolved for Fraud or Misrepresentation

Where a partnership contract is rescinded on the ground of the fraud or misrepresentation of one of the parties thereto, the party entitled to rescind is, without prejudice to any other right, entitled,

(a) To a lien on, or right of retention of, the surplus of the partnership property after satisfying the partnership liabilities to third persons for any sum of money paid by him for the purchase of an interest in the partnership and for any capital or advances contributed by him; and

(b) To stand, after all liabilities to third persons have been satisfied, in the place of the creditors of the partnership for any payments made by him in respect of the partnership liabilities; and

(c) To be indemnified by the person guilty of the fraud or making the representation against all debts and liabilities of the partnership.

Sec. 40. Rules for Distribution

In settling accounts between the partners after dissolution, the following rules shall be observed, subject to any agreement to the contrary:

(a) The assets of the partnership are:

    (I) The partnership property,

    (II) The contributions of the partners necessary for the payment of all the liabilities specified in clause (b) of this paragraph.

(b) The liabilities of the partnership shall rank in order of payment, as follows:

    (I) Those owing to creditors other than partners,

    (II) Those owing to partners other than for capital and profits,

    (III) Those owing to partners in respect of capital,

    (IV) Those owing to partners in respect of profits.

(c) The assets shall be applied in the order of their declaration in clause (a) of this paragraph to the satisfaction of the liabilities.

(d) The partners shall contribute, as provided by section 18(a) the amount necessary to satisfy the liabilities; but if any, but not all, of the partners are insolvent, or, not being subject to process, refuse to contribute, the other partners shall contribute their share of the liabilities, and, in the relative proportions in which they share the profits, the additional amount necessary to pay the liabilities.

(e) An assignee for the benefit of creditors or any person appointed by the court shall have the right to enforce the contributions specified in clause (d) of this paragraph.

(f) Any partner or his legal representative shall have the right to enforce the contributions specified in clause (d) of this paragraph, to the extent of the amount which he has paid in excess of his share of the liability.

(g) The individual property of a deceased partner shall be liable for the contributions specified in clause (d) of this paragraph.

(h) When partnership property and the individual properties of the partners are in possession of a court for distribution, partnership creditors shall have priority on partnership property and separate creditors on individual property, saving the rights of lien or secured creditors as heretofore.

(i) Where a partner has become bankrupt or his estate is insolvent the claims against his separate property shall rank in the following order:

    (I) Those owing to separate creditors,

    (II) Those owing to partnership creditors,

    (III) Those owing to partners by way of contribution.

Sec. 41. Liability of Persons Continuing the Business in Certain Cases

(1) When any new partner is admitted into an existing partnership, or when any partner retires and assigns (or the representative of the deceased partner assigns) his rights in partnership property to two or more of the partners, or to one or more of the partners and one or more third persons, if the business is continued without liquidation of the partnership affairs, creditors of the first or dissolved partnership are also creditors of the partnership so continuing the business.

(2) When all but one partner retire and assign (or the representative of a deceased partner assigns) their rights in partnership property to the remaining partner, who continues the business without liquidation of partnership affairs, either alone or with others, creditors of the dissolved partnership are also creditors of the person or partnership so continuing the business.

(3) When any partner retires or dies and the business of the dissolved partnership is continued as set forth in paragraphs (1) and (2) of this section, with the consent of the retired partners or the representative of the deceased partner, but without any assignment of his right in partnership property, rights of creditors of the dissolved partnership and of the creditors of the person or partnership continuing the business shall be as if such assignment had been made.

(4) When all the partners or their representatives assign their rights in partnership property to one or more third persons who promise to pay the debts and who continue the business of the dissolved partnership, creditors of the dissolved partnership are also creditors of the person or partnership continuing the business.

(5) When any partner wrongfully causes a dissolution and the remaining partners continue the business under the provisions of section 38(2b), either alone or with others, and without liquidation of the partnership affairs, creditors of the dissolved partnership are also creditors of the person or partnership continuing the business.

(6) When a partner is expelled and the remaining partners continue the business either alone or with others, without liquidation of the partnership affairs, creditors of the dissolved partnership are also creditors of the person or partnership continuing the business.

(7) The liability of a third person becoming a partner in the partnership continuing the business, under this section, to the creditors of the dissolved partnership shall be satisfied out of partnership property only.

(8) When the business of a partnership after dissolution is continued under any conditions set forth in this section the creditors of the dissolved partnership, as against the separate creditors of the retiring or deceased partner or the representative of the deceased partner, have a prior right to any claim of the retired partner or the representative of the

deceased partner against the person or partnership continuing the business, on account of the retired or deceased partner's interest in the dissolved partnership or on account of any consideration promised for such interest or for his right in partnership property.

(9) Nothing in this section shall be held to modify any right of creditors to set aside any assignment on the ground of fraud.

(10) The use by the person or partnership continuing the business of the partnership name, or the name of a deceased partner as part thereof, shall not of itself make the individual property of the deceased partner liable for any debts contracted by such person or partnership.

Sec. 42. Rights of Retiring or Estate of Deceased Partner When the Business Is Continued

When any partner retires or dies, and the business is continued under any of the conditions set forth in section 41 (1, 2, 3, 5, 6), or section 38(2b) without any settlement of accounts as between him or his estate and the person or partnership continuing the business, unless otherwise agreed, he or his legal representative as against such persons or partnership may have the value of his interest at the date of dissolution ascertained, and shall receive as an ordinary creditor an amount equal to the value of his interest in the dissolved partnership with interest, or, at his option

or at the option of his legal representative, in lieu of interest, the profits attributable to the use of his right in the property of the dissolved partnership; provided that the creditors of the dissolved partnership as against the separate creditors, or the representative of the retired or deceased partner, shall have priority on any claim arising under this section, as provided by section 41(8) of this act.

Sec. 43. Accrual of Actions

The right to an account of his interest shall accrue to any partner, or his legal representative, as against the winding up partners or the surviving partners or the person or partnership continuing the business, at the date of dissolution, in the absence of any agreement to the contrary.

Part VII   Miscellaneous Provisions

Sec. 44. When Act Takes Effect

This act shall take effect on the ___ day of ___ one thousand nine hundred and ___ .

Sec. 45. Legislation Repealed

All acts or parts of acts inconsistent with this act are hereby repealed.

The Revised Uniform Partnership Act (Excerpts)

Article 2.
GENERAL PROVISIONS

✳   ✳   ✳   ✳

§ 201. Partnership as Entity.

A partnership is an entity.

✳   ✳   ✳   ✳

§ 203. Partnership Property.

Property transferred to or otherwise acquired by a partnership is property of the partnership and not of the partners individually.

§ 204. When Property is Partnership Property.

(a) Property is partnership property if acquired in the name of:

(1) the partnership; or

(2) one or more partners with an indication in the instrument transferring title to the property of the person's capacity as a partner or of the existence of a partnership but without an indication of the name of the partnership.

(b) Property is acquired in the name of the partnership by a transfer to:

(1) the partnership in its name; or

(2) one or more partners in their capacity as partners in the partnership, if the name of the partnership is indicated in the instrument transferring title to the property.

(c) Property is presumed to be partnership property if purchased with partnership assets, even if not acquired in the name of the partnership or of one or more partners with an indication in the instrument transferring title to the property of the person's capacity as a partner or of the existence of a partnership.

(d) Property acquired in the name of one or more of the partners, without an indication in the instrument transferring title to the property of the person's capacity as a partner or of the existence of a partnership and without use of partnership assets, is presumed to be separate property, even if used for partnership purposes.

Article 3.
RELATIONS OF PARTNERS TO PERSONS DEALING WITH PARTNERSHIP

✳   ✳   ✳   ✳

§ 302. Transfer of Partnership Property.

(a) Subject to the effect of a statement of partnership authority under Section 303:

(1) Partnership property held in the name of the partnership may be transferred by an instrument of transfer executed by a partner in the partnership name.

(2) Partnership property held in the name of one or more partners with an indication in the instrument transferring the property to them of their capacity as partners or of the existence of a partnership, but without an indication of the name of the partnership, may be transferred by an instrument of transfer executed by the persons in whose name the property is held.

(3) A partnership may recover property transferred under this subsection if it proves that execution of the instrument of transfer did not bind the partnership under Section 301, unless the property was transferred by the initial transferee or a person claiming through the initial transferee to a subsequent transferee who gave value without having notice that the person who executed the instrument of initial transfer lacked authority to bind the partnership.

(b) Partnership property held in the name of one or more persons other than the partnership, without an indication in the instrument transferring the property to them of their capacity as partners or of the existence of a partnership, may be transferred free of claims of the partnership or the partners by the persons in whose name the property is held to a transferee who gives value without having notice that it is partnership property.

(c) If a person holds all of the partners' interests in the partnership, all of the partnership property vests in that person. The person may execute a document in the name of the partnership to evidence vesting of the property in that person and may file or record the document.

* * * *

§ 306. Partner's Liability.

All partners are liable jointly and severally for all obligations of the partnership unless otherwise agreed by the claimant or provided by law.

§ 307. Actions by and Against Partnership and Partners.

(a) A partnership may sue and be sued in the name of the partnership.

(b) An action may be brought against the partnership and any or all of the partners in the same action or in separate actions.

(c) A judgment against a partnership is not by itself a judgment against a partner. A judgment against a partnership may not be satisfied from a partner's assets unless there is also a judgment against the partner.

(d) A judgment creditor of a partner may not levy execu-

tion against the assets of the partner to satisfy a judgment based on a claim against the partnership unless:

(1) a judgment based on the same claim has been obtained against the partnership and a writ of execution on the judgment has been returned unsatisfied in whole or in part;

(2) an involuntary case under Title 11 of the United States Code has been commenced against the partnership and has not been dismissed within 60 days after commencement, or the partnership has commenced a voluntary case under Title 11 of the United States Code and the case has not been dismissed;

(3) the partner has agreed that the creditor need not exhaust partnership assets;

(4) a court grants permission to the judgment creditor to levy execution against the assets of a partner based on a finding that partnership assets subject to execution are clearly insufficient to satisfy the judgment, that exhaustion of partnership assets is excessively burdensome, or that the grant of permission is an appropriate exercise of the court's equitable powers; or

(5) liability is imposed on the partner by law or contract independent of the existence of the partnership.

(e) This section applies to any partnership liability or obligation resulting from a representation by a partner or purported partner under Section 308.

* * * *

Article 5.
TRANSFEREES AND CREDITORS OF PARTNER

§ 501. Partner's Interest in Partnership Property not Transferable.

A partner is not a co-owner of partnership property and has no interest in partnership property which can be transferred, either voluntarily or involuntarily.

* * * *

Article 6.
PARTNER'S DISSOCIATION

§ 601. Events Causing Partner's Dissociation.

A partner is dissociated from a partnership upon:

(1) receipt by the partnership of notice of the partner's express will to withdraw as a partner or upon any later date specified in the notice;

(2) an event agreed to in the partnership agreement as causing the partner's dissociation;

(3) the partner's expulsion pursuant to the partnership agreement;

(4) the partner's expulsion by the unanimous vote of the other partners if:

(i) it is unlawful to carry on the partnership business with that partner;

(ii) there has been a transfer of all or substantially all of that partner's transferable interest in the partnership, other than a transfer for security purposes, or a court order charging the partner's interest, which has not been foreclosed;

(iii) within 90 days after the partnership notifies a corporate partner that it will be expelled because it has filed a certificate of dissolution or the equivalent, its charter has been revoked, or its right to conduct business has been suspended by the jurisdiction of its incorporation, there is no revocation of the certificate of dissolution or no reinstatement of its charter or its right to conduct business; or

(iv) a partnership that is a partner has been dissolved and its business is being wound up;

(5) on application by the partnership or another partner, the partner's expulsion by judicial determination because:

(i) the partner engaged in wrongful conduct that adversely and materially affected the partnership business;

(ii) the partner willfully or persistently committed a material breach of the partnership agreement or of a duty owed to the partnership or the other partners under Section 404; or

(iii) the partner engaged in conduct relating to the partnership business which makes it not reasonably practicable to carry on the business in partnership with the partner;

(6) the partner's:

(i) becoming a debtor in bankruptcy;

(ii) executing an assignment for the benefit of creditors;

(iii) seeking, consenting to, or acquiescing in the appointment of a trustee, receiver, or liquidator of that partner or of all or substantially all of that partner's property; or

(iv) failing, within 90 days after the appointment, to have vacated or stayed the appointment of a trustee, receiver, or liquidator of the partner or of all or substantially all of the partner's property obtained without the partner's consent or acquiescence, or failing within 90 days after the expiration of a stay to have the appointment vacated;

(7) in the case of a partner who is an individual:

(i) the partner's death;

(ii) the appointment of a guardian or general conservator for the partner; or

(iii) a judicial determination that the partner has otherwise become incapable of performing the partner's duties under the partnership agreement;

(8) in the case of a partner that is a trust or is acting as a partner by virtue of being a trustee of a trust, distribution of the trust's entire transferable interest in the partnership, but not merely by reason of the substitution of a successor trustee;

(9) in the case of a partner that is an estate or is acting as a partner by virtue of being a personal representative of an estate, distribution of the estate's entire transferable interest in the partnership, but not merely by reason of the substitution of a successor personal representative; or

(10) termination of a partner who is not an individual, partnership, corporation, trust, or estate.

* * * *

Article 7.
PARTNER'S DISSOCIATION WHEN BUSINESS NOT WOUND UP

§ 701. Purchase of Dissociated Partner's Interest.

(a) If a partner is dissociated from a partnership without resulting in a dissolution and winding up of the partnership business under Section 801, the partnership shall cause the dissociated partner's interest in the partnership to be purchased for a buyout price determined pursuant to subsection (b).

(b) The buyout price of a dissociated partner's interest is the amount that would have been distributable to the dissociating partner under Section 808(b) if, on the date of dissociation, the assets of the partnership were sold at a price equal to the greater of the liquidation value or the value based on a sale of the entire business as a going concern without the dissociated partner and the partnership were wound up as of that date. In either case, the selling price of the partnership assets must be determined on the basis of the amount that would be paid by a willing buyer to a willing seller, neither being under any compulsion to buy or sell, and with knowledge of all relevant facts. Interest must be paid from the date of dissociation to the date of payment.

(c) Damages for wrongful dissociation under Section 602(b), and all other amounts owing, whether or not presently due, from the dissociated partner to the partnership, must be offset against the buyout price. Interest must be paid from the date the amount owed becomes due to the date of payment.

(d) A partnership shall indemnify a dissociated partner against all partnership liabilities incurred before the dissociation, except liabilities then unknown to the partnership, and against all partnership liabilities incurred after the dissociation, except liabilities incurred by an act of the dissociated partner under Section 702. For purposes of this subsection, a liability not known to a partner other than the dissociated partner is not known to the partnership.

(e) If no agreement for the purchase of a dissociated partner's interest is reached within 120 days after a written demand for payment, the partnership shall pay, or cause to be paid, in cash to the dissociated partner the amount the partnership estimates to be the buyout price and accrued interest, reduced by any offsets and accrued interest under subsection (c).

(f) If a deferred payment is authorized under subsection (h), the partnership may tender a written offer to pay the amount it estimates to be the buyout price and accrued interest, reduced by any offsets under subsection (c), stating the time of payment, the amount and type of security for payment, and the other terms and conditions of the obligation.

(g) The payment or tender required by subsection (e) or (f) must be accompanied by the following:

(1) a statement of partnership assets and liabilities as of the date of dissociation;

(2) the latest available partnership balance sheet and income statement, if any;

(3) an explanation of how the estimated amount of the payment was calculated; and

(4) written notice that the payment is in full satisfaction of the obligation to purchase unless, within 120 days after the written notice, the dissociated partner commences an action to determine the buyout price, any offsets under subsection (c), or other terms of the obligation to purchase.

(h) A partner who wrongfully dissociates before the expiration of a definite term or the completion of a particular undertaking is not entitled to payment of any portion of the buyout price until the expiration of the term or completion of the undertaking, unless the partner establishes to the satisfaction of the court that earlier payment will not cause undue hardship to the business of the partnership. A deferred payment must be adequately secured and bear interest.

(i) A dissociated partner may maintain an action against the partnership, pursuant to Section 406(b)(2)(ii), to determine the buyout price of that partner's interest, any offsets under subsection (c), or other terms of the obligation to purchase. The action must be commenced within 120 days after the partnership has tendered payment or an offer to pay or within one year after written demand for payment if no payment or offer to pay is tendered. The court shall determine the buyout price of the dissociated partner's interest, any offset due under subsection (c), and accrued interest, and enter judgment for any additional payment or refund. If deferred payment is authorized under subsection (h), the court shall also determine the security for payment and other terms of the obligation to purchase. The court may assess reasonable attorney's fees and the fees and expenses of appraisers or other experts for a party to the action, in amounts the court finds equitable, against a party that the court finds acted arbitrarily, vexatiously, or not in good faith. The finding may be based on the partnership's failure to tender payment or an offer to pay or to comply with subsection (g).

The Revised Uniform Limited Partnership Act

Article 1
GENERAL PROVISIONS

Section 101. Definitions.

As used in this [Act], unless the context otherwise requires:

(1) "Certificate of limited partnership" means the certificate referred to in Section 201, and the certificate as amended or restated.

(2) "Contribution" means any cash, property, services rendered, or a promissory note or other binding obligation to contribute cash or property or to perform services, which a partner contributes to a limited partnership in his capacity as a partner.

(3) "Event of withdrawal of a general partner" means an event that causes a person to cease to be a general partner as provided in Section 402.

(4) "Foreign limited partnership" means a partnership formed under the laws of any state other than this State and having as partners one or more general partners and one or more limited partners.

(5) "General partner" means a person who has been admitted to a limited partnership as a general partner in accordance with the partnership agreement and named in the certificate of limited partnership as a general partner.

(6) "Limited partner" means a person who has been admitted to a limited partnership as a limited partner in accordance with the partnership agreement.

(7) "Limited partnership" and "domestic limited partnership" mean a partnership formed by two or more persons under the laws of this State and having one or more general partners and one or more limited partners.

(8) "Partner" means a limited or general partner.

(9) "Partnership agreement" means any valid agreement, written or oral, of the partners as to the affairs of a limited partnership and the conduct of its business.

(10) "Partnership interest" means a partner's share of the profits and losses of a limited partnership and the right to receive distributions of partnership assets.

(11) "Person" means a natural person, partnership, limited partnership (domestic or foreign), trust, estate, association, or corporation.

(12) "State" means a state, territory, or possession of the United States, the District of Columbia, or the Commonwealth of Puerto Rico.

Section 102. Name.

The name of each limited partnership as set forth in its certificate of limited partnership:

(1) shall contain without abbreviation the words "limited partnership";

(2) may not contain the name of a limited partner unless (i) it is also the name of a general partner or the corporate name of a corporate general partner, or (ii) the business of the limited partnership had been carried on under that name before the admission of that limited partner;

(3) may not be the same as, or deceptively similar to, the name of any corporation or limited partnership organized under the laws of this State or licensed or registered as a foreign corporation or limited partnership in this State; and

(4) may not contain the following words [here insert prohibited words].

Section 103. Reservation of Name.

(a) The exclusive right to the use of a name may be reserved by:

(1) any person intending to organize a limited partnership under this [Act] and to adopt that name;

(2) any domestic limited partnership or any foreign limited partnership registered in this State which, in either case, intends to adopt that name;

(3) any foreign limited partnership intending to register in this State and adopt that name; and

(4) any person intending to organize a foreign limited partnership and intending to have it register in this State and adopt that name.

(b) The reservation shall be made by filing with the Secretary of State an application, executed by the applicant, to reserve a specified name. If the Secretary of State finds that the name is available for use by a domestic or foreign limited partnership, he [or she] shall reserve the name for the exclusive use of the applicant for a period of 120 days. Once having so reserved a name, the same applicant may not again reserve the same name until more than 60 days after the expiration of the last 120-day period for which that applicant reserved that name. The right to the exclusive use of a reserved name may be transferred to any other person by filing in the office of the Secretary of State a notice of the transfer, executed by the applicant for whom the name was reserved and specifying the name and address of the transferee.

Section 104. Specified Office and Agent.

Each limited partnership shall continuously maintain in this State:

(1) an office, which may but need not be a place of its business in this State, at which shall be kept the records required by Section 105 to be maintained; and

(2) an agent for service of process on the limited partnership, which agent must be an individual resident of this State, a domestic corporation, or a foreign corporation authorized to do business in this State.

Section 105. Records to Be Kept.

(a) Each limited partnership shall keep at the office referred to in Section 104(1) the following:

(1) a current list of the full name and last known business address of each partner, separately identifying the general partners (in alphabetical order) and the limited partners (in alphabetical order);

(2) a copy of the certificate of limited partnership and all certificates of amendment thereto, together with executed copies of any powers of attorney pursuant to which any certificate has been executed;

(3) copies of the limited partnership's federal, state and local income tax returns and reports, if any, for the three most recent years;

(4) copies of any then effective written partnership agreements and of any financial statements of the limited partnership for the three most recent years; and

(5) unless contained in a written partnership agreement, a writing setting out:

(i) the amount of cash and a description and statement of the agreed value of the other property or services contributed by each partner and which each partner has agreed to contribute;

(ii) the times at which or events on the happening of which any additional contributions agreed to be made by each partner are to be made;

(iii) any right of a partner to receive, or of a general partner to make, distributions to a partner which include a return of all or any part of the partner's contribution; and

(iv) any events upon the happening of which the limited partnership is to be dissolved and its affairs wound up.

(b) Records kept under this section are subject to inspection and copying at the reasonable request and at the expense of any partner during ordinary business hours.

Section 106. Nature of Business.

A limited partnership may carry on any business that a partnership without limited partners may carry on except [here designate prohibited activities].

Section 107. Business Transactions of Partners with Partnership.

Except as provided in the partnership agreement, a partner may lend money to and transact other business with the limited partnership and, subject to other applicable law, has the same rights and obligations with respect thereto as a person who is not a partner.

Article 2
FORMATION; CERTIFICATE OF LIMITED PARTNERSHIP

Section 201. Certificate of Limited Partnership.

(a) In order to form a limited partnership, a certificate of limited partnership must be executed and filed in the office of the Secretary of State. The certificate shall set forth:

(1) the name of the limited partnership;

(2) the address of the office and the name and address of the agent for service of process required to be maintained by Section 104;

(3) the name and the business address of each general partner;

(4) the latest date upon which the limited partnership is to dissolve; and

(5) any other matters the general partners determine to include therein.

(b) A limited partnership is formed at the time of the filing of the certificate of limited partnership in the office of the Secretary of State or at any later time specified in the certificate of limited partnership if, in either case, there has been substantial compliance with the requirements of this section.

Section 202. Amendment to Certificate.

(a) A certificate of limited partnership is amended by filing a certificate of amendment thereto in the office of the Secretary of State. The certificate shall set forth:

(1) the name of the limited partnership;

(2) the date of filing the certificate; and

(3) the amendment to the certificate.

(b) Within 30 days after the happening of any of the following events, an amendment to a certificate of limited partnership reflecting the occurrence of the event or events shall be filed:

(1) the admission of a new general partner;

(2) the withdrawal of a general partner; or

(3) the continuation of the business under Section 801 after an event of withdrawal of a general partner.

(c) A general partner who becomes aware that any statement in a certificate of limited partnership was false when made or that any arrangements or other facts described have changed, making the certificate inaccurate in any respect, shall promptly amend the certificate.

(d) A certificate of limited partnership may be amended at any time for any other proper purpose the general partners determine.

(e) No person has any liability because an amendment to a certificate of limited partnership has not been filed to reflect the occurrence of any event referred to in subsection (b) of this section if the amendment is filed within the 30-day period specified in subsection (b).

(f) A restated certificate of limited partnership may be executed and filed in the same manner as a certificate of amendment.

Section 203. Cancellation of Certificate.

A certificate of limited partnership shall be cancelled upon the dissolution and the commencement of winding up of the partnership or at any other time there are no limited partners. A certificate of cancellation shall be filed in the office of the Secretary of State and set forth:

(1) the name of the limited partnership;

(2) the date of filing of its certificate of limited partnership;

(3) the reason for filing the certificate of cancellation;

(4) the effective date (which shall be a date certain) of cancellation if it is not to be effective upon the filing of the certificate; and

(5) any other information the general partners filing the certificate determine.

Section 204. Execution of Certificates.

(a) Each certificate required by this Article to be filed in the office of the Secretary of State shall be executed in the following manner:

(1) an original certificate of limited partnership must be signed by all general partners;

(2) a certificate of amendment must be signed by at least one general partner and by each other general partner designated in the certificate as a new general partner; and

(3) a certificate of cancellation must be signed by all general partners.

(b) Any person may sign a certificate by an attorney-in-fact, but a power of attorney to sign a certificate relating to the admission of a general partner must specifically describe the admission.

(c) The execution of a certificate by a general partner constitutes an affirmation under the penalties of perjury that the facts stated therein are true.

Section 205. Execution by Judicial Act.

If a person required by Section 204 to execute any certificate fails or refuses to do so, any other person who is adversely affected by the failure or refusal may petition the [designate the appropriate court] to direct the execution of the certificate. If the court finds that it is proper for the certificate to be executed and that any person so designated has failed or refused to execute the certificate, it shall order the Secretary of State to record an appropriate certificate.

Section 206. Filing in Office of Secretary of State.

(a) Two signed copies of the certificate of limited partnership and of any certificates of amendment or cancellation (or of any judicial decree of amendment or cancellation) shall be delivered to the Secretary of State. A person who executes a certificate as an agent or fiduciary need not exhibit evidence of his [or her] authority as a prerequisite to filing. Unless the Secretary of State finds that any certificate does not conform to law, upon receipt of all filing fees required by law he [or she] shall:

(1) endorse on each duplicate original the word "Filed" and the day, month, and year of the filing thereof;

(2) file one duplicate original in his [or her] office; and

(3) return the other duplicate original to the person who filed it or his [or her] representative.

(b) Upon the filing of a certificate of amendment (or judicial decree of amendment) in the office of the Secretary of State, the certificate of limited partnership shall be amended as set forth therein, and upon the effective date of a certificate of cancellation (or a judicial decree thereof), the certificate of limited partnership is cancelled.

Section 207. Liability for False Statement in Certificate.

If any certificate of limited partnership or certificate of amendment or cancellation contains a false statement, one who suffers loss by reliance on the statement may recover damages for the loss from:

(1) any person who executes the certificate, or causes another to execute it on his behalf, and knew, and any general partner who knew or should have known, the statement to be false at the time the certificate was executed; and

(2) any general partner who thereafter knows or should have known that any arrangement or other fact described in the certificate has changed, making the statement inaccurate in any respect within a sufficient time before the statement was relied upon reasonably to have enabled that general partner to cancel or amend the certificate, or to file a petition for its cancellation or amendment under Section 205.

Section 208. Scope of Notice.

The fact that a certificate of limited partnership is on file in the office of the Secretary of State is notice that the partnership is a limited partnership and the persons designated therein as general partners are general partners, but it is not notice of any other fact.

Section 209. Delivery of Certificates to Limited Partners.

Upon the return by the Secretary of State pursuant to Section 206 of a certificate marked "Filed," the general partners shall promptly deliver or mail a copy of the certificate of limited partnership and each certificate of amendment or cancellation to each limited partner unless the partnership agreement provides otherwise.

Article 3
LIMITED PARTNERS

Section 301. Admission of Additional Limited Partners.

(a) A person becomes a limited partner on the later of:

(1) the date the original certificate of limited partnership is filed; or

(2) the date stated in the records of the limited partnership as the date that person becomes a limited partner.

(b) After the filing of a limited partnership's original certificate of limited partnership, a person may be admitted as an additional limited partner:

(1) in the case of a person acquiring a partnership interest directly from the limited partnership, upon compliance with the partnership agreement or, if the partnership agreement does not so provide, upon the written consent of all partners; and

(2) in the case of an assignee of a partnership interest of a partner who has the power, as provided in Section 704, to grant the assignee the right to become a limited partner, upon the exercise of that power and compliance with any conditions limiting the grant or exercise of the power.

Section 302. Voting.

Subject to Section 303, the partnership agreement may grant to all or a specified group of the limited partners the right to vote (on a per capita or other basis) upon any matter.

Section 303. Liability to Third Parties.

(a) Except as provided in subsection (d), a limited partner is not liable for the obligations of a limited partnership unless he [or she] is also a general partner or, in addition to the exercise of his [or her] rights and powers as a limited partner, he [or she] participates in the control of the business. However, if the limited partner participates in the control of the business, he [or she] is liable only to persons who transact business with the limited partnership reasonably believing, based upon the limited partner's conduct, that the limited partner is a general partner.

(b) A limited partner does not participate in the control of the business within the meaning of subsection (a) solely by doing one or more of the following:

(1) being a contractor for or an agent or employee of the limited partnership or of a general partner or being an officer, director, or shareholder of a general partner that is a corporation;

(2) consulting with and advising a general partner with respect to the business of the limited partnership;

(3) acting as surety for the limited partnership or guaranteeing or assuming one or more specific obligations of the limited partnership;

(4) taking any action required or permitted by law to bring or pursue a derivative action in the right of the limited partnership;

(5) requesting or attending a meeting of partners;

(6) proposing, approving, or disapproving, by voting or otherwise, one or more of the following matters:

(i) the dissolution and winding up of the limited partnership;

(ii) the sale, exchange, lease, mortgage, pledge, or other transfer of all or substantially all of the assets of the limited partnership;

(iii) the incurrence of indebtedness by the limited partnership other than in the ordinary course of its business;

(iv) a change in the nature of the business;

(v) the admission or removal of a general partner;

(vi) the admission or removal of a limited partner;

(vii) a transaction involving an actual or potential conflict of interest between a general partner and the limited partnership or the limited partners;

(viii) an amendment to the partnership agreement or certificate of limited partnership; or

(ix) matters related to the business of the limited partnership not otherwise enumerated in this subsection (b), which the partnership agreement states in writing may be subject to the approval or disapproval of limited partners;

(7) winding up the limited partnership pursuant to Section 803; or

(8) exercising any right or power permitted to limited partners under this [Act] and not specifically enumerated in this subsection (b).

(c) The enumeration in subsection (b) does not mean that the possession or exercise of any other powers by a limited partner constitutes participation by him [or her] in the business of the limited partnership.

(d) A limited partner who knowingly permits his [or her] name to be used in the name of the limited partnership, except under circumstances permitted by Section 102(2), is liable to creditors who extend credit to the limited partnership without actual knowledge that the limited partner is not a general partner.

Section 304. Person Erroneously Believing Himself [or Herself] Limited Partner.

(a) Except as provided in subsection (b), a person who makes a contribution to a business enterprise and erroneously but in good faith believes that he [or she] has become a limited partner in the enterprise is not a general partner in the enterprise and is not bound by its obligations by reason of making the contribution, receiving distributions from the enterprise, or exercising any rights of a limited partner, if, on ascertaining the mistake, he [or she]:

(1) causes an appropriate certificate of limited partnership or a certificate of amendment to be executed and filed; or

(2) withdraws from future equity participation in the enterprise by executing and filing in the office of the Secretary of State a certificate declaring withdrawal under this section.

(b) A person who makes a contribution of the kind described in subsection (a) is liable as a general partner to any third party who transacts business with the enterprise (i) before the person withdraws and an appropriate certificate is filed to show withdrawal, or (ii) before an appropriate certificate is filed to show that he [or she] is not a general partner, but in either case only if the third party actually believed in good faith that the person was a general partner at the time of the transaction.

Section 305. Information.

Each limited partner has the right to:

(1) inspect and copy any of the partnership records required to be maintained by Section 105; and

(2) obtain from the general partners from time to time upon reasonable demand (i) true and full information regarding the state of the business and financial condition of the limited partnership, (ii) promptly after becoming available, a copy of the limited partnership's federal, state, and local income tax returns for each year, and (iii) other information regarding the affairs of the limited partnership as is just and reasonable.

Article 4
GENERAL PARTNERS

Section 401. Admission of Additional General Partners.

After the filing of a limited partnership's original certificate of limited partnership, additional general partners may be admitted as provided in writing in the partnership agreement or, if the partnership agreement does not provide in writing for the admission of additional general partners, with the written consent of all partners.

Section 402. Events of Withdrawal.

Except as approved by the specific written consent of all partners at the time, a person ceases to be a general partner of a limited partnership upon the happening of any of the following events:

(1) the general partner withdraws from the limited partnership as provided in Section 602;

(2) the general partner ceases to be a member of the limited partnership as provided in Section 702;

(3) the general partner is removed as a general partner in accordance with the partnership agreement;

(4) unless otherwise provided in writing in the partnership agreement, the general partner: (i) makes an assignment for the benefit of creditors; (ii) files a voluntary petition in bankruptcy; (iii) is adjudicated a bankrupt or insolvent; (iv) files a petition or answer seeking for himself [or herself] any reorganization, arrangement, composition, readjustment, liquidation, dissolution, or similar relief under any statute, law, or regulation; (v) files an answer or other pleading admitting or failing to contest the material allegations of a petition filed against him [or her] in any proceeding of this nature; or (vi) seeks, consents to, or acquiesces in the appointment of a trustee, receiver, or liquidator of the general partner or of all or any substantial part of his [or her] properties;

(5) unless otherwise provided in writing in the partnership agreement, [120] days after the commencement of any proceeding against the general partner seeking reorganization, arrangement, composition, readjustment, liquidation, dissolution, or similar relief under any statute, law, or regulation, the proceeding has not been dismissed, or if within [90] days after the appointment without his [or her] consent or acquiescence of a trustee, receiver, or liquidator of the general partner or of all or any substantial part of his [or her] properties, the appointment is not vacated or stayed or within [90] days after the expiration of any such stay, the appointment is not vacated;

(6) in the case of a general partner who is a natural person,

(i) his [or her] death; or

(ii) the entry of an order by a court of competent jurisdiction adjudicating him [or her] incompetent to manage his [or her] person or his [or her] estate;

(7) in the case of a general partner who is acting as a general partner by virtue of being a trustee of a trust, the termination of the trust (but not merely the substitution of a new trustee);

(8) in the case of a general partner that is a separate partnership, the dissolution and commencement of winding up of the separate partnership;

(9) in the case of a general partner that is a corporation, the filing of a certificate of dissolution, or its equivalent, for the corporation or the revocation of its charter; or

(10) in the case of an estate, the distribution by the fiduciary of the estate's entire interest in the partnership.

Section 403. General Powers and Liabilities.

(a) Except as provided in this [Act] or in the partnership agreement, a general partner of a limited partnership has the rights and powers and is subject to the restrictions of a partner in a partnership without limited partners.

(b) Except as provided in this [Act], a general partner of a limited partnership has the liabilities of a partner in a partnership without limited partners to persons other than the partnership and the other partners. Except as provided in this [Act] or in the partnership agreement, a general partner of a limited partnership has the liabilities of a partner in a partnership without limited partners to the partnership and to the other partners.

Section 404. Contributions by General Partner.

A general partner of a limited partnership may make contributions to the partnership and share in the profits and losses of, and in distributions from, the limited partnership as a general partner. A general partner also may make contributions to and share in profits, losses, and distributions as a limited partner. A person who is both a general partner and a limited partner has the rights and powers, and is subject to the restrictions and liabilities, of a general partner and, except as provided in the partnership agreement, also has the powers, and is subject to the restrictions, of a limited partner to the extent of his [or her] participation in the partnership as a limited partner.

Section 405. Voting.

The partnership agreement may grant to all or certain identified general partners the right to vote (on a per capita or any other basis), separately or with all or any class of the limited partners, on any matter.

Article 5
FINANCE

Section 501. Form of Contribution.

The contribution of a partner may be in cash, property, or services rendered, or a promissory note or other obligation to contribute cash or property or to perform services.

Section 502. Liability for Contribution.

(a) A promise by a limited partner to contribute to the limited partnership is not enforceable unless set out in a writing signed by the limited partner.

(b) Except as provided in the partnership agreement, a partner is obligated to the limited partnership to perform any enforceable promise to contribute cash or property or to perform services, even if he [or she] is unable to perform because of death, disability, or any other reason. If a partner does not make the required contribution of property or services, he [or she] is obligated at the option of the limited partnership to contribute cash equal to that portion of the value, as stated in the partnership records required to be kept pursuant to Section 105, of the stated contribution which has not been made.

(c) Unless otherwise provided in the partnership agreement, the obligation of a partner to make a contribution or return money or other property paid or distributed in violation of this [Act] may be compromised only by consent of all partners. Notwithstanding the compromise, a creditor of a limited partnership who extends credit, or, otherwise acts in reliance on that obligation after the partner signs a writing which reflects the obligation and before the amendment or cancellation thereof to reflect the compromise may enforce the original obligation.

Section 503. Sharing of Profits and Losses.

The profits and losses of a limited partnership shall be allocated among the partners, and among classes of partners, in the manner provided in writing in the partnership agreement. If the partnership agreement does not so provide in writing, profits and losses shall be allocated on the basis of the value, as stated in the partnership records required to be kept pursuant to Section 105, of the contributions made by each partner to the extent they have been received by the partnership and have not been returned.

Section 504. Sharing of Distributions.

Distributions of cash or other assets of a limited partnership shall be allocated among the partners and among classes of partners in the manner provided in writing in the partnership agreement. If the partnership agreement does not so provide in writing, distributions shall be made on the basis of the value, as stated in the partnership records required to be kept pursuant to Section 105, of the contributions made by each partner to the extent they have been received by the partnership and have not been returned.

Article 6
DISTRIBUTIONS
AND WITHDRAWAL

Section 601. Interim Distributions.

Except as provided in this Article, a partner is entitled to receive distributions from a limited partnership before his [or her] withdrawal from the limited partnership and before the dissolution and winding up thereof to the extent and at the times or upon the happening of the events specified in the partnership agreement.

Section 602. Withdrawal of General Partner.

A general partner may withdraw from a limited partnership at any time by giving written notice to the other partners, but if the withdrawal violates the partnership agreement, the limited partnership may recover from the withdrawing general partner damages for breach of the partnership agreement and offset the damages against the amount otherwise distributable to him [or her].

Section 603. Withdrawal of Limited Partner.

A limited partner may withdraw from a limited partnership at the time or upon the happening of events specified in writing in the partnership agreement. If the agreement does not specify in writing the time or the events upon the happening of which a limited partner may withdraw or a definite time for the dissolution and winding up of the limited partnership, a limited partner may withdraw upon not less than six months' prior written notice to each general partner at his [or her] address on the books of the limited partnership at its office in this State.

Section 604. Distribution Upon Withdrawal.

Except as provided in this Article, upon withdrawal any withdrawing partner is entitled to receive any distribution to which he [or she] is entitled under the partnership agreement and, if not otherwise provided in the agreement, he [or she] is entitled to receive, within a reasonable time after withdrawal, the fair value of his [or her] interest in the limited partnership as of the date of withdrawal based upon his [or her] right to share in distributions from the limited partnership.

Section 605. Distribution in Kind.

Except as provided in writing in the partnership agreement, a partner, regardless of the nature of his [or her] contribution, has no right to demand and receive any distribution from a limited partnership in any form other than cash. Except as provided in writing in the partnership agreement, a partner may not be compelled to accept a distribution of any asset in kind from a limited partnership to the extent that the percentage of the asset distributed to him [or her] exceeds a percentage of that asset which is equal to the percentage in which he [or she] shares in distributions from the limited partnership.

Section 606. Right to Distribution.

At the time a partner becomes entitled to receive a distribution, he [or she] has the status of, and is entitled to all remedies available to, a creditor of the limited partnership with respect to the distribution.

Section 607. Limitations on Distribution.

A partner may not receive a distribution from a limited partnership to the extent that, after giving effect to the distribution, all liabilities of the limited partnership, other than liabilities to partners on account of their partnership interests, exceed the fair value of the partnership assets.

Section 608. Liability Upon Return of Contribution.

(a) If a partner has received the return of any part of his [or her] contribution without violation of the partnership agreement or this [Act], he [or she] is liable to the limited partnership for a period of one year thereafter for the amount of the returned contribution, but only to the extent necessary to discharge the limited partnership's liabilities to creditors who extended credit to the limited partnership during the period the contribution was held by the partnership.

(b) If a partner has received the return of any part of his [or her] contribution in violation of the partnership agreement or this [Act], he [or she] is liable to the limited partnership for a period of six years thereafter for the amount of the contribution wrongfully returned.

(c) A partner receives a return of his [or her] contribution to the extent that a distribution to him [or her] reduces his [or her] share of the fair value of the net assets of the limited partnership below the value, as set forth in the partnership records required to be kept pursuant to Section 105, of his [or her] contribution which has not been distributed to him [or her].

Article 7
ASSIGNMENT OF PARTNERSHIP INTERESTS

Section 701. Nature of Partnership Interest.

A partnership interest is personal property.

Section 702. Assignment of Partnership Interest.

Except as provided in the partnership agreement, a partnership interest is assignable in whole or in part. An assignment of a partnership interest does not dissolve a limited partnership or entitle the assignee to become or to exercise any rights of a partner. An assignment entitles the assignee to receive, to the extent assigned, only the distribution to which the assignor would be entitled. Except as provided in the partnership agreement, a partner ceases to be a partner upon assignment of all his [or her] partnership interest.

Section 703. Rights of Creditor.

On application to a court of competent jurisdiction by any judgment creditor of a partner, the court may charge the partnership interest of the partner with payment of the unsatisfied amount of the judgment with interest. To the extent so charged, the judgment creditor has only the rights of an assignee of the partnership interest. This [Act] does not deprive any partner of the benefit of any exemption laws applicable to his [or her] partnership interest.

Section 704. Right of Assignee to Become Limited Partner.

(a) An assignee of a partnership interest, including an assignee of a general partner, may become a limited partner if and to the extent that (i) the assignor gives the assignee that right in accordance with authority described in the partnership agreement, or (ii) all other partners consent.

(b) An assignee who has become a limited partner has, to the extent assigned, the rights and powers, and is subject to the restrictions and liabilities, of a limited partner under the partnership agreement and this [Act]. An assignee who becomes a limited partner also is liable for the obligations of his [or her] assignor to make and return contributions as provided in Articles 5 and 6. However, the assignee is not obligated for liabilities unknown to the assignee at the time he [or she] became a limited partner.

(c) If an assignee of a partnership interest becomes a limited partner, the assignor is not released from his [or her] liability to the limited partnership under Sections 207 and 502.

Section 705. Power of Estate of Deceased or Incompetent Partner.

If a partner who is an individual dies or a court of competent jurisdiction adjudges him [or her] to be incompetent to manage his [or her] person or his [or her] property, the partner's executor, administrator, guardian, conservator, or other legal representative may exercise all of the partner's rights for the purpose of settling his [or her] estate or administering his [or her] property, including any power the partner had to give an assignee the right to become a limited partner. If a partner is a corporation, trust, or other entity and is dissolved or terminated, the powers of that partner may be exercised by its legal representative or successor.

Article 8
DISSOLUTION

Section 801. Nonjudicial Dissolution.

A limited partnership is dissolved and its affairs shall be wound up upon the happening of the first to occur of the following:

(1) at the time specified in the certificate of limited partnership;

(2) upon the happening of events specified in writing in the partnership agreement;

(3) written consent of all partners;

(4) an event of withdrawal of a general partner unless at the time there is at least one other general partner and the written provisions of the partnership agreement permit the business of the limited partnership to be carried on by the remaining general partner and that partner does so, but the limited partnership is not dissolved and is not required to be wound up by reason of any event of withdrawal if, within 90 days after the withdrawal, all partners agree in writing to continue the business of the limited partnership and to the appointment of one or more additional general partners if necessary or desired; or

(5) entry of a decree of judicial dissolution under Section 802.

Section 802. Judicial Dissolution.

On application by or for a partner the [designate the appropriate court] court may decree dissolution of a limited partnership whenever it is not reasonably practicable to carry on the business in conformity with the partnership agreement.

Section 803. Winding Up.

Except as provided in the partnership agreement, the general partners who have not wrongfully dissolved a limited partnership or, if none, the limited partners, may wind up the limited partnership's affairs; but the [designate the appropriate court] court may wind up the limited partnership's affairs upon application of any partner, his [or her] legal representative, or assignee.

Section 804. Distribution of Assets.

Upon the winding up of a limited partnership, the assets shall be distributed as follows:

(1) to creditors, including partners who are creditors, to the extent permitted by law, in satisfaction of liabilities of the limited partnership other than liabilities for distributions to partners under Section 601 or 604;

(2) except as provided in the partnership agreement, to partners and former partners in satisfaction of liabilities for distributions under Section 601 or 604; and

(3) except as provided in the partnership agreement, to partners first for the return of their contributions and secondly respecting their partnership interests, in the proportions in which the partners share in distributions.

Article 9
FOREIGN LIMITED PARTNERSHIPS

Section 901. Law Governing.

Subject to the Constitution of this State, (i) the laws of the state under which a foreign limited partnership is organized govern its organization and internal affairs and the liability of its limited partners, and (ii) a foreign limited partnership may not be denied registration by reason of any difference between those laws and the laws of this State.

Section 902. Registration.

Before transacting business in this State, a foreign limited partnership shall register with the Secretary of State. In order to register, a foreign limited partnership shall submit to the Secretary of State, in duplicate, an application for registration as a foreign limited partnership, signed and sworn to by a general partner and setting forth:

(1) the name of the foreign limited partnership and, if different, the name under which it proposes to register and transact business in this State;

(2) the State and date of its formation;

(3) the name and address of any agent for service of process on the foreign limited partnership whom the for-

eign limited partnership elects to appoint; the agent must be an individual resident of this State, a domestic corporation, or a foreign corporation having a place of business in, and authorized to do business in, this State;

(4) a statement that the Secretary of State is appointed the agent of the foreign limited partnership for service of process if no agent has been appointed under paragraph (3) or, if appointed, the agent's authority has been revoked or if the agent cannot be found or served with the exercise of reasonable diligence;

(5) the address of the office required to be maintained in the state of its organization by the laws of that state or, if not so required, of the principal office of the foreign limited partnership;

(6) the name and business address of each general partner; and

(7) the address of the office at which is kept a list of the names and addresses of the limited partners and their capital contributions, together with an undertaking by the foreign limited partnership to keep those records until the foreign limited partnership's registration in this State is cancelled or withdrawn.

Section 903. Issuance of Registration.

(a) If the Secretary of State finds that an application for registration conforms to law and all requisite fees have been paid, he [or she] shall:

(1) endorse on the application the word "Filed", and the month, day, and year of the filing thereof;

(2) file in his [or her] office a duplicate original of the application; and

(3) issue a certificate of registration to transact business in this State.

(b) The certificate of registration, together with a duplicate original of the application, shall be returned to the person who filed the application or his [or her] representative.

Section 904. Name.

A foreign limited partnership may register with the Secretary of State under any name, whether or not it is the name under which it is registered in its state of organization, that includes without abbreviation the words "limited partnership" and that could be registered by a domestic limited partnership.

Section 905. Changes and Amendments.

If any statement in the application for registration of a foreign limited partnership was false when made or any arrangements or other facts described have changed, making the application inaccurate in any respect, the foreign limited partnership shall promptly file in the office of the Secretary of State a certificate, signed and sworn to by a general partner, correcting such statement.

Section 906. Cancellation of Registration.

A foreign limited partnership may cancel its registration by filing with the Secretary of State a certificate of cancellation signed and sworn to by a general partner. A cancellation does not terminate the authority of the Secretary of State to accept service of process on the foreign limited partnership with respect to [claims for relief] [causes of action] arising out of the transactions of business in this State.

Section 907. Transaction of Business Without Registration.

(a) A foreign limited partnership transacting business in this State may not maintain any action, suit, or proceeding in any court of this State until it has registered in this State.

(b) The failure of a foreign limited partnership to register in this State does not impair the validity of any contract or act of the foreign limited partnership or prevent the foreign limited partnership from defending any action, suit, or proceeding in any court of this State.

(c) A limited partner of a foreign limited partnership is not liable as a general partner of the foreign limited partnership solely by reason of having transacted business in this State without registration.

(d) A foreign limited partnership, by transacting business in this State without registration, appoints the Secretary of State as its agent for service of process with respect to [claims for relief] [causes of action] arising out of the transaction of business in this State.

Section 908. Action by [Appropriate Official].

The [designate the appropriate official] may bring an action to restrain a foreign limited partnership from transacting business in this State in violation of this Article.

Article 10
DERIVATIVE ACTIONS

Section 1001. Right of Action.

A limited partner may bring an action in the right of a limited partnership to recover a judgment in its favor if general partners with authority to do so have refused to bring the action or if an effort to cause those general partners to bring the action is not likely to succeed.

Section 1002. Proper Plaintiff.

In a derivative action, the plaintiff must be a partner at the time of bringing the action and (i) must have been a partner at the time of the transaction of which he [or she] complains or (ii) his [or her] status as a partner must have devolved upon him by operation of law or pursuant to the terms of the partnership agreement from a person who was a partner at the time of the transaction.

Section 1003. Pleading.

In a derivative action, the complaint shall set forth with particularity the effort of the plaintiff to secure initiation of the action by a general partner or the reasons for not making the effort.

Section 1004. Expenses.

If a derivative action is successful, in whole or in part, or if anything is received by the plaintiff as a result of a judgment, compromise, or settlement of an action or claim, the court may award the plaintiff reasonable expenses, including reasonable attorney's fees, and shall direct him [or her] to remit to the limited partnership the remainder of those proceeds received by him [or her].

Article 11
MISCELLANEOUS

Section 1101. Construction and Application.

This [Act] shall be so applied and construed to effectuate its general purpose to make uniform the law with respect to the subject of this [Act] among states enacting it.

Section 1102. Short Title.

This [Act] may be cited as the Uniform Limited Partnership Act.

Section 1103. Severability.

If any provision of this [Act] or its application to any person or circumstance is held invalid, the invalidity does not affect other provisions or applications of the [Act] which can be given effect without the invalid provision or application, and to this end the provisions of this [Act] are severable.

Section 1104. Effective Date, Extended Effective Date, and Repeal.

Except as set forth below, the effective date of this [Act] is _____ and the following acts [list existing limited partnership acts] are hereby repealed:

(1) The existing provisions for execution and filing of certificates of limited partnerships and amendments thereunder and cancellations thereof continue in effect until [specify time required to create central filing system], the extended effective date, and Sections 102, 103, 104, 105, 201, 202, 203, 204 and 206 are not effective until the extended effective date.

(2) Section 402, specifying the conditions under which a general partner ceases to be a member of a limited partnership, is not effective until the extended effective date, and the applicable provisions of existing law continue to govern until the extended effective date.

(3) Sections 501, 502 and 608 apply only to contributions

and distributions made after the effective date of this [Act].

(4) Section 704 applies only to assignments made after the effective date of this [Act].

(5) Article 9, dealing with registration of foreign limited partnerships, is not effective until the extended effective date.

(6) Unless otherwise agreed by the partners, the applicable provisions of existing law governing allocation of profits and losses (rather than the provisions of Section 503), distributions to a withdrawing partner (rather than the provisions of Section 604), and distributions of assets upon the winding up of a limited partnership (rather than the provisions of Section 804) govern limited partnerships formed before the effective date of this [Act].

Section 1105. Rules for Cases Not Provided For in This [Act].

In any case not provided for in this [Act] the provisions of the Uniform Partnership Act govern.

Section 1106. Savings Clause.

The repeal of any statutory provision by this [Act] does not impair, or otherwise affect, the organization or the continued existence of a limited partnership existing at the effective date of this [Act], nor does the repeal of any existing statutory provision by this [Act] impair any contract or affect any right accrued before the effective date of this [Act].

APPENDIX H

The Revised Model Business Corporation Act (Excerpts)

Chapter 2.
INCORPORATION

§ 2.01 Incorporators

One or more persons may act as the incorporator or incorporators of a corporation by delivering articles of incorporation to the secretary of state for filing.

§ 2.02 Articles of Incorporation

(a) The articles of incorporation must set forth:

(1) a corporate name *   *   * ;

(2) the number of shares the corporation is authorized to issue;

(3) the street address of the corporation's initial registered office and the name of its initial registered agent at that office; and

(4) the name and address of each incorporator.

(b) The articles of incorporation may set forth:

(1) the names and addresses of the individuals who are to serve as the initial directors;

(2) provisions not inconsistent with law regarding:

(i) the purpose or purposes for which the corporation is organized;

(ii) managing the business and regulating the affairs of the corporation;

(iii) defining, limiting, and regulating the powers of the corporation, its board of directors, and shareholders;

(iv) a par value for authorized shares or classes of shares;

(v) the imposition of personal liability on shareholders for the debts of the corporation to a specified extent and upon specified conditions;

(3) any provision that under this Act is required or permitted to be set forth in the bylaws; and

(4) a provision eliminating or limiting the liability of a director to the corporation or its shareholders for money damages for any action taken, or any failure to take any action, as a director, except liability for (A) the amount of a financial benefit received by a director to which he is not entitled; (B) an intentional infliction of harm on the corporation or the shareholders; (C) [unlawful distributions]; or (D) an intentional violation of criminal law.

(c) The articles of incorporation need not set forth any of the corporate powers enumerated in this Act.

§ 2.03 Incorporation

(a) Unless a delayed effective date is specified, the corporate existence begins when the articles of incorporation are filed.

(b) The secretary of state's filing of the articles of incorporation is conclusive proof that the incorporators satisfied all conditions precedent to incorporation except in a proceeding by the state to cancel or revoke the incorporation or involuntarily dissolve the corporation.

§ 2.04 Liability for Preincorporation Transactions

All persons purporting to act as or on behalf of a corporation, knowing there was no incorporation under this Act, are jointly and severally liable for all liabilities created while so acting.

§ 2.05 Organization of Corporation

(a) After incorporation:

(1) if initial directors are named in the articles of incorporation, the initial directors shall hold an organizational meeting, at the call of a majority of the directors, to complete the organization of the corporation by appointing officers, adopting bylaws, and carrying on any other business brought before the meeting;

(2) if initial directors are not named in the articles, the incorporator or incorporators shall hold an organizational meeting at the call of a majority of the incorporators:

(i) to elect directors and complete the organization of the corporation; or

(ii) to elect a board of directors who shall complete the organization of the corporation.

(b) Action required or permitted by this Act to be taken by incorporators at an organizational meeting may be taken without a meeting if the action taken is evidenced by one or more written consents describing the action taken and signed by each incorporator.

(c) An organizational meeting may be held in or out of this state.

*   *   *   *

Chapter 3.
PURPOSES AND POWERS

§ 3.01 Purposes

(a) Every corporation incorporated under this Act has the purpose of engaging in any lawful business unless a more limited purpose is set forth in the articles of incorporation.

(b) A corporation engaging in a business that is subject to regulation under another statute of this state may incorporate under this Act only if permitted by, and subject to all limitations of, the other statute.

§ 3.02 General Powers

Unless its articles of incorporation provide otherwise, every corporation has perpetual duration and succession in its corporate name and has the same powers as an individual to do all things necessary or convenient to carry out its business and affairs, including without limitation power:

(1) to sue and be sued, complain and defend in its corporate name;

(2) to have a corporate seal, which may be altered at will, and to use it, or a facsimile of it, by impressing or affixing it or in any other manner reproducing it;

(3) to make and amend bylaws, not inconsistent with its articles of incorporation or with the laws of this state, for managing the business and regulating the affairs of the corporation;

(4) to purchase, receive, lease, or otherwise acquire, and own, hold, improve, use, and otherwise deal with, real or personal property, or any legal or equitable interest in property, wherever located;

(5) to sell, convey, mortgage, pledge, lease, exchange, and otherwise dispose of all or any part of its property;

(6) to purchase, receive, subscribe for, or otherwise acquire; own, hold, vote, use, sell, mortgage, lend, pledge, or otherwise dispose of; and deal in and with shares or other interests in, or obligations of, any other entity;

(7) to make contracts and guarantees, incur liabilities, borrow money, issue its notes, bonds, and other obligations (which may be convertible into or include the option to purchase other securities of the corporation), and secure any of its obligations by mortgage or pledge of any of its property, franchises, or income;

(8) to lend money, invest and reinvest its funds, and receive and hold real and personal property as security for repayment;

(9) to be a promoter, partner, member, associate, or manager of any partnership, joint venture, trust, or other entity;

(10) to conduct its business, locate offices, and exercise the powers granted by this Act within or without this state;

(11) to elect directors and appoint officers, employees, and agents of the corporation, define their duties, fix their compensation, and lend them money and credit;

(12) to pay pensions and establish pension plans, pension trusts, profit sharing plans, share bonus plans, share option plans, and benefit or incentive plans for any or all of its current or former directors, officers, employees, and agents;

(13) to make donations for the public welfare or for charitable, scientific, or educational purposes;

(14) to transact any lawful business that will aid governmental policy;

(15) to make payments or donations, or do any other act, not inconsistent with law, that furthers the business and affairs of the corporation.

* * * *

Chapter 5.
OFFICE AND AGENT

§ 5.01 Registered Office and Registered Agent

Each corporation must continuously maintain in this state:

(1) a registered office that may be the same as any of its places of business; and

(2) a registered agent, who may be:

(i) an individual who resides in this state and whose business office is identical with the registered office;

(ii) a domestic corporation or not-for-profit domestic corporation whose business office is identical with the registered office; or

(iii) a foreign corporation or not-for-profit foreign corporation authorized to transact business in this state whose business office is identical with the registered office.

* * * *

§ 5.04 Service on Corporation

(a) A corporation's registered agent is the corporation's agent for service of process, notice, or demand required or permitted by law to be served on the corporation.

(b) If a corporation has no registered agent, or the agent cannot with reasonable diligence be served, the corporation may be served by registered or certified mail, return receipt requested, addressed to the secretary of the corporation at its principal office. Service is perfected under this subsection at the earliest of:

(1) the date the corporation receives the mail;

(2) the date shown on the return receipt, if signed on behalf of the corporation; or

(3) five days after its deposit in the United States Mail, if mailed postpaid and correctly addressed.

(c) This section does not prescribe the only means, or necessarily the required means, of serving a corporation.

Chapter 6.
SHARES AND DISTRIBUTIONS

* * * *

Subchapter B. Issuance of Shares

* * * *

§ 6.21 Issuance of Shares

(a) The powers granted in this section to the board of directors may be reserved to the shareholders by the articles of incorporation.

(b) The board of directors may authorize shares to be issued for consideration consisting of any tangible or intangible property or benefit to the corporation, including cash, promissory notes, services performed, contracts for services to be performed, or other securities of the corporation.

(c) Before the corporation issues shares, the board of directors must determine that the consideration received or to be received for shares to be issued is adequate. That determination by the board of directors is conclusive insofar as the adequacy of consideration for the issuance of shares relates to whether the shares are validly issued, fully paid, and nonassessable.

(d) When the corporation receives the consideration for which the board of directors authorized the issuance of shares, the shares issued therefor are fully paid and nonassessable.

(e) The corporation may place in escrow shares issued for a contract for future services or benefits or a promissory note, or make other arrangements to restrict the transfer of the shares, and may credit distributions in respect of the shares against their purchase price, until the services are performed, the note is paid, or the benefits received. If the services are not performed, the note is not paid, or the benefits are not received, the shares escrowed or restricted and the distributions credited may be cancelled in whole or part.

* * * *

§ 6.27 Restriction on Transfer or Registration of Shares and Other Securities

(a) The articles of incorporation, bylaws, an agreement among shareholders, or an agreement between shareholders and the corporation may impose restrictions on the transfer or registration of transfer of shares of the corporation. A restriction does not affect shares issued before the restriction was adopted unless the holders of the shares are parties to the restriction agreement or voted in favor of the restriction.

(b) A restriction on the transfer or registration of transfer of shares is valid and enforceable against the holder or a transferee of the holder if the restriction is authorized by this section and its existence is noted conspicuously on the front or back of the certificate or is contained in the information statement [sent to the shareholder]. Unless so noted, a restriction is not enforceable against a person without knowledge of the restriction.

(c) A restriction on the transfer or registration of transfer of shares is authorized:

(1) to maintain the corporation's status when it is dependent on the number or identity of its shareholders;

(2) to preserve exemptions under federal or state securities law;

(3) for any other reasonable purpose.

(d) A restriction on the transfer or registration of transfer of shares may:

(1) obligate the shareholder first to offer the corporation or other persons (separately, consecutively, or simultaneously) an opportunity to acquire the restricted shares;

(2) obligate the corporate or other persons (separately, consecutively, or simultaneously) to acquire the restricted shares;

(3) require the corporation, the holders of any class of its shares, or another person to approve the transfer of the restricted shares, if the requirement is not manifestly unreasonable;

(4) prohibit the transfer of the restricted shares to designated persons or classes of persons, if the prohibition is not manifestly unreasonable.

(e) For purposes of this section, "shares" includes a security convertible into or carrying a right to subscribe for or acquire shares.

*   *   *   *

Chapter 7.
SHAREHOLDERS

Subchapter A. Meetings

§ 7.01 Annual Meeting

(a) A corporation shall hold annually at a time stated in or fixed in accordance with the bylaws a meeting of shareholders.

(b) Annual shareholders' meetings may be held in or out of this state at the place stated in or fixed in accordance with the bylaws. If no place is stated in or fixed in accordance with the bylaws, annual meetings shall be held at the corporation's principal office.

(c) The failure to hold an annual meeting at the time stated in or fixed in accordance with a corporation's bylaws does not affect the validity of any corporate action.

*   *   *   *

§ 7.05 Notice of Meeting

(a) A corporation shall notify shareholders of the date, time, and place of each annual and special shareholders' meeting no fewer than 10 nor more than 60 days before the meeting date. Unless this Act or the articles of incorporation require otherwise, the corporation is required to give notice only to shareholders entitled to vote at the meeting.

(b) Unless this Act or the articles of incorporation require otherwise, notice of an annual meeting need not include a description of the purpose or purposes for which the meeting is called.

(c) Notice of a special meeting must include a description of the purpose or purposes for which the meeting is called.

(d) If not otherwise fixed *   *   *, the record date for determining shareholders entitled to notice of and to vote at an annual or special shareholders' meeting is the day before the first notice is delivered to shareholders.

(e) Unless the bylaws require otherwise, if an annual or special shareholders' meeting is adjourned to a different date, time, or place, notice need not be given of the new date, time, or place if the new date, time, or place is announced at the meeting before adjournment. *   *   *

*   *   *   *

§ 7.07 Record Date

(a) The bylaws may fix or provide the manner of fixing the record date for one or more voting groups in order to determine the shareholders entitled to notice of a shareholders' meeting, to demand a special meeting, to vote, or to take any other action. If the bylaws do not fix or provide for fixing a record date, the board of directors of the corporation may fix a future date as the record date.

(b) A record date fixed under this section may not be more than 70 days before the meeting or action requiring a determination of shareholders.

(c) A determination of shareholders entitled to notice of or to vote at a shareholders' meeting is effective for any adjournment of the meeting unless the board of directors fixes a new record date, which it must do if the meeting is adjourned to a date more than 120 days after the date fixed for the original meeting.

(d) If a court orders a meeting adjourned to a date more than 120 days after the date fixed for the original meeting, it may provide that the original record date continues in effect or it may fix a new record date.

Subchapter B. Voting

§ 7.20 Shareholders' List for Meeting

(a) After fixing a record date for a meeting, a corporation shall prepare an alphabetical list of the names of all its shareholders who are entitled to notice of a shareholders' meeting. The list must be arranged by voting group (and within each voting group by class or series of shares) and show the address of and number of shares held by each shareholder.

(b) The shareholders' list must be available for inspection by any shareholder, beginning two business days after notice of the meeting is given for which the list was prepared and continuing through the meeting, at the corporation's principal office or at a place identified in the meeting notice in the city where the meeting will be held. A shareholder, his agent, or attorney is entitled on written demand to inspect and, subject to the requirements of section 16.02(c), to copy the list, during regular business hours and at his expense, during the period it is available for inspection.

(c) The corporation shall make the shareholders' list available at the meeting, and any shareholder, his agent, or attorney is entitled to inspect the list at any time during the meeting or any adjournment.

(d) If the corporation refuses to allow a shareholder, his agent, or attorney to inspect the shareholders' list before or at the meeting (or copy the list as permitted by subsection (b)), the [name or describe] court of the county where a corporation's principal office (or, if none in this state, its registered office) is located, on application of the shareholder, may summarily order the inspection or copying at the corporation's expense and may postpone the meeting for which the list was prepared until the inspection or copying is complete.

(e) Refusal or failure to prepare or make available the shareholders' list does not affect the validity of action taken at the meeting.

*   *   *   *

§ 7.22 Proxies

(a) A shareholder may vote his shares in person or by proxy.

(b) A shareholder may appoint a proxy to vote or otherwise act for him by signing an appointment form, either personally or by his attorney-in-fact.

(c) An appointment of a proxy is effective when received by the secretary or other officer or agent authorized to tabulate votes. An appointment is valid for 11 months unless a longer period is expressly provided in the appointment form.

*   *   *   *

§ 7.28 Voting for Directors; Cumulative Voting

(a) Unless otherwise provided in the articles of incorporation, directors are elected by a plurality of the votes cast by the shares entitled to vote in the election at a meeting at which a quorum is present.

(b) Shareholders do not have a right to cumulate their votes for directors unless the articles of incorporation so provide.

(c) A statement included in the articles of incorporation that "[all] [a designated voting group of] shareholders are entitled to cumulate their votes for directors" (or words of similar import) means that the shareholders designated are entitled to multiply the number of votes they are entitled to cast by the number of directors for whom they are entitled to vote and cast the product for a single candidate or distribute the product among two or more candidates.

(d) Shares otherwise entitled to vote cumulatively may not be voted cumulatively at a particular meeting unless:

(1) the meeting notice or proxy statement accompanying the notice states conspicuously that cumulative voting is authorized; or

(2) a shareholder who has the right to cumulate his votes gives notice to the corporation not less than 48

hours before the time set for the meeting of his intent to cumulate his votes during the meeting, and if one shareholder gives this notice all other shareholders in the same voting group participating in the election are entitled to cumulate their votes without giving further notice.

*   *   *   *

Subchapter D. Derivative Proceedings
*   *   *   *

§ 7.41 Standing

A shareholder may not commence or maintain a derivative proceeding unless the shareholder:

(1) was a shareholder of the corporation at the time of the act or omission complained of or became a shareholder through transfer by operation of law from one who was a shareholder at that time; and

(2) fairly and adequately represents the interests of the corporation in enforcing the right of the corporation.

§ 7.42 Demand

No shareholder may commence a derivative proceeding until:

(1) a written demand has been made upon the corporation to take suitable action; and

(2) 90 days have expired from the date the demand was made unless the shareholder has earlier been notified that the demand has been rejected by the corporation or unless irreparable injury to the corporation would result by waiting for the expiration of the 90 day period.

*   *   *   *

Chapter 8.
DIRECTORS AND OFFICERS
Subchapter A. Board of Directors
*   *   *   *

§ 8.02 Qualifications of Directors

The articles of incorporation or bylaws may prescribe qualifications for directors. A director need not be a resident of this state or a shareholder of the corporation unless the articles of incorporation or bylaws so prescribe.

§ 8.03 Number and Election of Directors

(a) A board of directors must consist of one or more individuals, with the number specified in or fixed in accordance with the articles of incorporation or bylaws.

(b) If a board of directors has power to fix or change the number of directors, the board may increase or decrease by 30 percent or less the number of directors last approved by the shareholders, but only the shareholders may increase or decrease by more than 30 percent the number of directors last approved by the shareholders.

(c) The articles of incorporation or bylaws may establish a variable range for the size of the board of directors by fixing a minimum and maximum number of directors. If a variable range is established, the number of directors may be fixed or changed from time to time, within the minimum and maximum, by the shareholders or the board of directors. After shares are issued, only the shareholders may change the range for the size of the board or change from a fixed to a variable-range size board or vice versa.

(d) Directors are elected at the first annual shareholders' meeting and at each annual meeting thereafter unless their terms are staggered under section 8.06.

* * * *

§ 8.08 Removal of Directors by Shareholders

(a) The shareholders may remove one or more directors with or without cause unless the articles of incorporation provide that directors may be removed only for cause.

(b) If a director is elected by a voting group of shareholders, only the shareholders of that voting group may participate in the vote to remove him.

(c) If cumulative voting is authorized, a director may not be removed if the number of votes sufficient to elect him under cumulative voting is voted against his removal. If cumulative voting is not authorized, a director may be removed only if the number of votes cast to remove him exceeds the number of votes cast not to remove him.

(d) A director may be removed by the shareholders only at a meeting called for the purpose of removing him and the meeting notice must state that the purpose, or one of the purposes, of the meeting is removal of the director.

* * * *

Subchapter B. Meetings and Action of the Board

§ 8.20 Meetings

(a) The board of directors may hold regular or special meetings in or out of this state.

(b) Unless the articles of incorporation or bylaws provide otherwise, the board of directors may permit any or all directors to participate in a regular or special meeting by, or conduct the meeting through the use of, any means of communication by which all directors participating may simultaneously hear each other during the meeting. A director participating in a meeting by this means is deemed to be present in person at the meeting.

* * * *

§ 8.22 Notice of Meeting

(a) Unless the articles of incorporation or bylaws provide otherwise, regular meetings of the board of directors may be held without notice of the date, time, place, or purpose of the meeting.

(b) Unless the articles of incorporation or bylaws provide for a longer or shorter period, special meetings of the board of directors must be preceded by at least two days' notice of the date, time, and place of the meeting. The notice need not describe the purpose of the special meeting unless required by the articles of incorporation or bylaws.

* * * *

§ 8.24 Quorum and Voting

(a) Unless the articles of incorporation or bylaws require a greater number, a quorum of a board of directors consists of:

(1) a majority of the fixed number of directors if the corporation has a fixed board size; or

(2) a majority of the number of directors prescribed, or if no number is prescribed the number in office immediately before the meeting begins, if the corporation has a variable-range size board.

(b) The articles of incorporation or bylaws may authorize a quorum of a board of directors to consist of no fewer than one-third of the fixed or prescribed number of directors determined under subsection (a).

(c) If a quorum is present when a vote is taken, the affirmative vote of a majority of directors present is the act of the board of directors unless the articles of incorporation or bylaws require the vote of a greater number of directors.

(d) A director who is present at a meeting of the board of directors or a committee of the board of directors when corporate action is taken is deemed to have assented to the action taken unless: (1) he objects at the beginning of the meeting (or promptly upon his arrival) to holding it or transacting business at the meeting; (2) his dissent or abstention from the action taken is entered in the minutes of the meeting; or (3) he delivers written notice of his dissent or abstention to the presiding officer of the meeting before its adjournment or to the corporation immediately after adjournment of the meeting. The right of dissent or abstention is not available to a director who votes in favor of the action taken.

* * * *

Subchapter C. Standards of Conduct

§ 8.30 General Standards for Directors

(a) A director shall discharge his duties as a director, including his duties as a member of a committee:

(1) in good faith;

(2) with the care an ordinarily prudent person in a like position would exercise under similar circumstances; and

(3) in a manner he reasonably believes to be in the best interests of the corporation.

(b) In discharging his duties a director is entitled to rely on information, opinions, reports, or statements, including financial statements and other financial data, if prepared or presented by:

(1) one or more officers or employees of the corporation whom the director reasonably believes to be reliable and competent in the matters presented;

(2) legal counsel, public accountants, or other persons as to matters the director reasonably believes are within the person's professional or expert competence; or

(3) a committee of the board of directors of which he is not a member if the director reasonably believes the committee merits confidence.

(c) A director is not acting in good faith if he has knowledge concerning the matter in question that makes reliance otherwise permitted by subsection (b) unwarranted.

(d) A director is not liable for any action taken as a director, or any failure to take any action, if he performed the duties of his office in compliance with this section.

* * * *

Subchapter D. Officers
* * * *

§ 8.41 Duties of Officers

Each officer has the authority and shall perform the duties set forth in the bylaws or, to the extent consistent with the bylaws, the duties prescribed by the board of directors or by direction of an officer authorized by the board of directors to prescribe the duties of other officers.

§ 8.42 Standards of Conduct for Officers

(a) An officer with discretionary authority shall discharge his duties under that authority:

(1) in good faith;

(2) with the care an ordinarily prudent person in a like position would exercise under similar circumstances; and

(3) in a manner he reasonably believes to be in the best interests of the corporation.

(b) In discharging his duties an officer is entitled to rely on information, opinions, reports, or statements, including financial statements and other financial data, if prepared or presented by:

(1) one or more officers or employees of the corporation whom the officer reasonably believes to be reliable and competent in the matters presented; or

(2) legal counsel, public accountants, or other persons as to matters the officer reasonably believes are within the person's professional or expert competence.

(c) An officer is not acting in good faith if he has knowledge concerning the matter in question that makes reliance otherwise permitted by subsection (b) unwarranted.

(d) An officer is not liable for any action taken as an officer, or any failure to take any action, if he performed the duties of his office in compliance with this section.

* * * *

Chapter 11.
MERGER AND SHARE EXCHANGE

§ 11.01 Merger

(a) One or more corporations may merge into another corporation if the board of directors of each corporation adopts and its shareholders (if required * * *) approve a plan of merger.

(b) The plan of merger must set forth:

(1) the name of each corporation planning to merge and the name of the surviving corporation into which each other corporation plans to merge;

(2) the terms and conditions of the merger; and

(3) the manner and basis of converting the shares of each corporation into shares, obligations, or other securities of the surviving or any other corporation or into cash or other property in whole or part.

(c) The plan of merger may set forth:

(1) amendments to the articles of incorporation of the surviving corporation; and

(2) other provisions relating to the merger.

* * * *

§ 11.04 Merger of Subsidiary

(a) A parent corporation owning at least 90 percent of the outstanding shares of each class of a subsidiary corporation may merge the subsidiary into itself without approval of the shareholders of the parent or subsidiary.

(b) The board of directors of the parent shall adopt a plan of merger that sets forth:

(1) the names of the parent and subsidiary; and

(2) the manner and basis of converting the shares of the subsidiary into shares, obligations, or other securities of the parent or any other corporation or into cash or other property in whole or part.

(c) The parent shall mail a copy or summary of the plan of merger to each shareholder of the subsidiary who does not waive the mailing requirement in writing.

(d) The parent may not deliver articles of merger to the secretary of state for filing until at least 30 days after the date it mailed a copy of the plan of merger to each shareholder of the subsidiary who did not waive the mailing requirement.

(e) Articles of merger under this section may not contain amendments to the articles of incorporation of the parent corporation (except for amendments enumerated in section 10.02).

* * * *

§ 11.06 Effect of Merger or Share Exchange

(a) When a merger takes effect:

(1) every other corporation party to the merger merges into the surviving corporation and the separate existence of every corporation except the surviving corporation ceases;

(2) the title to all real estate and other property owned by each corporation party to the merger is vested in the surviving corporation without reversion or impairment;

(3) the surviving corporation has all liabilities of each corporation party to the merger;

(4) a proceeding pending against any corporation party to the merger may be continued as if the merger did not occur or the surviving corporation may be substituted in the proceeding for the corporation whose existence ceased;

(5) the articles of incorporation of the surviving corporation are amended to the extent provided in the plan of merger; and

(6) the shares of each corporation party to the merger that are to be converted into shares, obligations, or other securities of the surviving or any other corporation or into cash or other property are converted and the former holders of the shares are entitled only to the rights provided in the articles of merger or to their rights under chapter 13.

(b) When a share exchange takes effect, the shares of each acquired corporation are exchanged as provided in the plan, and the former holders of the shares are entitled only to the exchange rights provided in the articles of share exchange or to their rights under chapter 13.

* * * *

Chapter 13.
DISSENTERS' RIGHTS

Subchapter A. Right to Dissent and Obtain Payment for Shares

* * * *

§ 13.02 Right to Dissent

(a) A shareholder is entitled to dissent from, and obtain payment of the fair value of his shares in the event of, any of the following corporate actions:

(1) consummation of a plan of merger to which the corporation is a party (i) if shareholder approval is required for the merger by [statute] or the articles of incorporation and the shareholder is entitled to vote on the merger or (ii) if the corporation is a subsidiary that is merged with its parent under section 11.04;

(2) consummation of a plan of share exchange to which the corporation is a party as the corporation

whose shares will be acquired, if the shareholder is entitled to vote on the plan;

(3) consummation of a sale or exchange of all, or substantially all, of the property of the corporation other than in the usual and regular course of business, if the shareholder is entitled to vote on the sale or exchange, including a sale in dissolution, but not including a sale pursuant to court order or a sale for cash pursuant to a plan by which all or substantially all of the net proceeds of the sale will be distributed to the shareholders within one year after the date of sale;

(4) an amendment of the articles of incorporation that materially and adversely affects rights in respect of a dissenter's shares because it:

(i) alters or abolishes a preferential right of the shares;

(ii) creates, alters, or abolishes a right in respect of redemption, including a provision respecting a sinking fund for the redemption or repurchase, of the shares;

(iii) alters or abolishes a preemptive right of the holder of the shares to acquire shares or other securities;

(iv) excludes or limits the right of the shares to vote on any matter, or to cumulate votes, other than a limitation by dilution through issuance of shares or other securities with similar voting rights; or

(v) reduces the number of shares owned by the shareholder to a fraction of a share if the fractional share so created is to be acquired for cash * * *; or

(5) any corporate action taken pursuant to a shareholder vote to the extent the articles of incorporation, bylaws, or a resolution of the board of directors provides that voting or nonvoting shareholders are entitled to dissent and obtain payment for their shares.

(b) A shareholder entitled to dissent and obtain payment for his shares under this chapter may not challenge the corporate action creating his entitlement unless the action is unlawful or fraudulent with respect to the shareholder or the corporation.

* * * *

Subchapter B. Procedure for Exercise of Dissenters' Rights

* * * *

§ 13.21 Notice of Intent to Demand Payment

(a) If proposed corporate action creating dissenters' rights under section 13.02 is submitted to a vote at a shareholders' meeting, a shareholder who wishes to assert dissenters' rights (1) must deliver to the corporation before the vote is taken written notice of his intent to demand payment for his shares if the proposed action is effectuated and (2) must not vote his shares in favor of the proposed action.

(b) A shareholder who does not satisfy the requirements of subsection (a) is not entitled to payment for his shares under this chapter.

* * * *

§ 13.25 **Payment**

(a) * * * [A]s soon as the proposed corporate action is taken, or upon receipt of a payment demand, the corporation shall pay each dissenter * * * the amount the corporation estimates to be the fair value of his shares, plus accrued interest.

* * * *

§ 13.28 **Procedure If Shareholder Dissatisfied with Payment or Offer**

(a) A dissenter may notify the corporation in writing of his own estimate of the fair value of his shares and amount of interest due, and demand payment of his estimate (less any payment under section 13.25) * * * if:

(1) the dissenter believes that the amount paid under section 13.25 * * * is less than the fair value of his shares or that the interest due is incorrectly calculated;

(2) the corporation fails to make payment under section 13.25 within 60 days after the date set for demanding payment; or

(3) the corporation, having failed to take the proposed action, does not return the deposited certificates or release the transfer restrictions imposed on uncertificated shares within 60 days after the date set for demanding payment.

(b) A dissenter waives his right to demand payment under this section unless he notifies the corporation of his demand in writing under subsection (a) within 30 days after the corporation made or offered payment for his shares.

* * * *

Chapter 14.
DISSOLUTION

Subchapter A. Voluntary Dissolution

* * * *

§ 14.02 **Dissolution by Board of Directors and Shareholders**

(a) A corporation's board of directors may propose dissolution for submission to the shareholders.

(b) For a proposal to dissolve to be adopted:

(1) the board of directors must recommend dissolution to the shareholders unless the board of directors determines that because of conflict of interest or other special circumstances it should make no recommendation and communicates the basis for its determination to the shareholders; and

(2) the shareholders entitled to vote must approve the proposal to dissolve as provided in subsection (e).

(c) The board of directors may condition its submission of the proposal for dissolution on any basis.

(d) The corporation shall notify each shareholder, whether or not entitled to vote, of the proposed shareholders' meeting in accordance with section 7.05. The notice must also state that the purpose, or one of the purposes, of the meeting is to consider dissolving the corporation.

(e) Unless the articles of incorporation or the board of directors (acting pursuant to subsection (c)) require a greater vote or a vote by voting groups, the proposal to dissolve to be adopted must be approved by a majority of all the votes entitled to be cast on that proposal.

* * * *

§ 14.05 **Effect of Dissolution**

(a) A dissolved corporation continues its corporate existence but may not carry on any business except that appropriate to wind up and liquidate its business and affairs, including:

(1) collecting its assets;

(2) disposing of its properties that will not be distributed in kind to its shareholders;

(3) discharging or making provision for discharging its liabilities;

(4) distributing its remaining property among its shareholders according to their interests; and

(5) doing every other act necessary to wind up and liquidate its business and affairs.

(b) Dissolution of a corporation does not:

(1) transfer title to the corporation's property;

(2) prevent transfer of its shares or securities, although the authorization to dissolve may provide for closing the corporation's share transfer records;

(3) subject its directors or officers to standards of conduct different from those prescribed in chapter 8;

(4) change quorum or voting requirements for its board of directors or shareholders; change provisions for selection, resignation, or removal of its directors or officers or both; or change provisions for amending its bylaws;

(5) prevent commencement of a proceeding by or against the corporation in its corporate name;

(6) abate or suspend a proceeding pending by or against the corporation on the effective date of dissolution; or

(7) terminate the authority of the registered agent of the corporation.

*   *   *   *

Subchapter C. Judicial Dissolution

§ 14.30 Grounds for Judicial Dissolution

The [name or describe court or courts] may dissolve a corporation:

(1) in a proceeding by the attorney general if it is established that:

(i) the corporation obtained its articles of incorporation through fraud; or

(ii) the corporation has continued to exceed or abuse the authority conferred upon it by law;

(2) in a proceeding by a shareholder if it is established that:

(i) the directors are deadlocked in the management of the corporate affairs, the shareholders are unable to break the deadlock, and irreparable injury to the corporation is threatened or being suffered, or the business and affairs of the corporation can no longer be conducted to the advantage of the shareholders generally, because of the deadlock;

(ii) the directors or those in control of the corporation have acted, are acting, or will act in a manner that is illegal, oppressive, or fraudulent;

(iii) the shareholders are deadlocked in voting power and have failed, for a period that includes at least two consecutive annual meeting dates, to elect successors to directors whose terms have expired; or

(iv) the corporate assets are being misapplied or wasted;

(3) in a proceeding by a creditor if it is established that:

(i) the creditor's claim has been reduced to judgment, the execution on the judgment returned unsatisfied, and the corporation is insolvent; or

(ii) the corporation has admitted in writing that the creditor's claim is due and owing and the corporation is insolvent; or

(4) in a proceeding by the corporation to have its voluntary dissolution continued under court supervision.

*   *   *   *

Chapter 16.
RECORDS AND REPORTS

Subchapter A. Records

§ 16.01 Corporate Records

(a) A corporation shall keep as permanent records minutes of all meetings of its shareholders and board of directors, a record of all actions taken by the shareholders or board of directors without a meeting, and a record of all actions taken by a committee of the board of directors in place of the board of directors on behalf of the corporation.

(b) A corporation shall maintain appropriate accounting records.

(c) A corporation or its agent shall maintain a record of its shareholders, in a form that permits preparation of a list of the names and addresses of all shareholders, in alphabetical order by class of shares showing the number and class of shares held by each.

(d) A corporation shall maintain its records in written form or in another form capable of conversion into written form within a reasonable time.

(e) A corporation shall keep a copy of the following records at its principal office:

(1) its articles or restated articles of incorporation and all amendments to them currently in effect;

(2) its bylaws or restated bylaws and all amendments to them currently in effect;

(3) resolutions adopted by its board of directors creating one or more classes or series of shares, and fixing their relative rights, preferences, and limitations, if shares issued pursuant to those resolutions are outstanding;

(4) the minutes of all shareholders' meetings, and records of all action taken by shareholders without a meeting, for the past three years;

(5) all written communications to shareholders generally within the past three years, including the financial statements furnished for the past three years *   *   *;

(6) a list of the names and business addresses of its current directors and officers; and

(7) its most recent annual report delivered to the secretary of state *   *   *.

§ 16.02 Inspection of Records by Shareholders

(a) Subject to section 16.03(c), a shareholder of a corporation is entitled to inspect and copy, during regular business hours at the corporation's principal office, any of the records of the corporation described in section 16.01(e) if he gives the corporation written notice of his demand at least five business days before the date on which he wishes to inspect and copy.

(b) A shareholder of a corporation is entitled to inspect and copy, during regular business hours at a reasonable location specified by the corporation, any of the following records of the corporation if the shareholder meets the requirements of subsection (c) and gives the corporation written notice of his demand at least five business days before the date on which he wishes to inspect and copy:

(1) excerpts from minutes of any meeting of the board of directors, records of any action of a committee of the

board of directors while acting in place of the board of directors on behalf of the corporation, minutes of any meeting of the shareholders, and records of action taken by the shareholders or board of directors without a meeting, to the extent not subject to inspection under section 16.02(a);

(2) accounting records of the corporation; and

(3) the record of shareholders.

(c) A shareholder may inspect and copy the records identified in subsection (b) only if:

(1) his demand is made in good faith and for a proper purpose;

(2) he describes with reasonable particularity his purpose and the records he desires to inspect; and

(3) the records are directly connected with his purpose.

(d) The right of inspection granted by this section may not be abolished or limited by a corporation's articles of incorporation or bylaws.

(e) This section does not affect:

(1) the right of a shareholder to inspect records under section 7.20 or, if the shareholder is in litigation with the corporation, to the same extent as any other litigant;

(2) the power of a court, independently of this Act, to compel the production of corporate records for examination.

(f) For purposes of this section, "shareholder" includes a beneficial owner whose shares are held in a voting trust or by a nominee on his behalf.

The Uniform Limited Liability Company Act (Excerpts)

[ARTICLE] 2.
ORGANIZATION

Section 201. Limited liability company as legal entity.

A limited liability company is a legal entity distinct from its members.

Section 202. Organization.

(a) One or more persons may organize a limited liability company, consisting of one or more members, by delivering articles of organization to the office of the [Secretary of State] for filing.

(b) Unless a delayed effective date is specified, the existence of a limited liability company begins when the articles of organization are filed.

(c) The filing of the articles of organization by the [Secretary of State] is conclusive proof that the organizers satisfied all conditions precedent to the creation of a limited liability company.

Section 203. Articles of organization.

(a) Articles of organization of a limited liability company must set forth:

(1) the name of the company;

(2) the address of the initial designated office;

(3) the name and street address of the initial agent for service of process;

(4) the name and address of each organizer;

(5) whether the company is to be a term company and, if so, the term specified;

(6) whether the company is to be manager-managed, and, if so, the name and address of each initial manager; and

(7) whether one or more of the members of the company are to be liable for its debts and obligations under Section 303(c).

(b) Articles of organization of a limited liability company may set forth:

(1) provisions permitted to be set forth in an operating agreement; or

(2) other matters not inconsistent with law.

(c) Articles of organization of a limited liability company may not vary the nonwaivable provisions of Section 103(b). As to all other matters, if any provision of an operating agreement is inconsistent with the articles of organization:

(1) the operating agreement controls as to managers, members, and members' transferees; and

(2) the articles of organization control as to persons, other than managers, members and their transferees, who reasonably rely on the articles to their detriment.

* * * *

Section 208. Certificate of existence or authorization.

(a) A person may request the [Secretary of State] to furnish a certificate of existence for a limited liability company or a certificate of authorization for a foreign limited liability company.

(b) A certificate of existence for a limited liability company must set forth:

(1) the company's name;

(2) that it is duly organized under the laws of this State, the date of organization, whether its duration is at-will or for a specified term, and, if the latter, the period specified;

(3) if payment is reflected in the records of the [Secretary of State] and if nonpayment affects the existence of the company, that all fees, taxes, and penalties owed to this State have been paid;

(4) whether its most recent annual report required by Section 211 has been filed with the [Secretary of State];

(5) that articles of termination have not been filed; and

(6) other facts of record in the office of the [Secretary of State] which may be requested by the applicant.

(c) A certificate of authorization for a foreign limited liability company must set forth:

(1) the company's name used in this State;

(2) that it is authorized to transact business in this State;

(3) if payment is reflected in the records of the [Secretary of State] and if nonpayment affects the authorization of the company, that all fees, taxes, and penalties owed to this State have been paid;

(4) whether its most recent annual report required by Section 211 has been filed with the [Secretary of State];

(5) that a certificate of cancellation has not been filed; and

(6) other facts of record in the office of the [Secretary of State] which may be requested by the applicant.

(d) Subject to any qualification stated in the certificate, a certificate of existence or authorization issued by the [Secretary of State] may be relied upon as conclusive evidence that the domestic or foreign limited liability company is in existence or is authorized to transact business in this State.

* * * *

[ARTICLE] 3.
RELATIONS OF MEMBERS AND MANAGERS TO PERSONS DEALING WITH LIMITED LIABILITY COMPANY

* * * *

Section 303. Liability of members and managers.

(a) Except as otherwise provided in subsection (c), the debts, obligations, and liabilities of a limited liability company, whether arising in contract, tort, or otherwise, are solely the debts, obligations, and liabilities of the company. A member or manager is not personally liable for a debt, obligation, or liability of the company solely by reason of being or acting as a member or manager.

(b) The failure of a limited liability company to observe the usual company formalities or requirements relating to the exercise of its company powers or management of its business is not a ground for imposing personal liability on the members or managers for liabilities of the company.

(c) All or specified members of a limited liability company are liable in their capacity as members for all or specified debts, obligations, or liabilities of the company if:

(1) a provision to that effect is contained in the articles of organization; and

(2) a member so liable has consented in writing to the adoption of the provision or to be bound by the provision.

* * * *

[ARTICLE] 4.
RELATIONS OF MEMBERS TO EACH OTHER AND TO LIMITED LIABILITY COMPANY

* * * *

Section 404. Management of limited liability company.

(a) In a member-managed company:

(1) each member has equal rights in the management and conduct of the company's business; and

(2) except as otherwise provided in subsection (c) or in Section 801(b)(3)(i), any matter relating to the business of the company may be decided by a majority of the members.

(b) In a manager-managed company:

(1) each manager has equal rights in the management and conduct of the company's business;

(2) except as otherwise provided in subsection (c) or in Section 801(b)(3)(i), any matter relating to the

business of the company may be exclusively decided by the manager or, if there is more than one manager, by a majority of the managers; and

(3) a manager:

(i) must be designated, appointed, elected, removed, or replaced by a vote, approval, or consent of a majority of the members; and

(ii) holds office until a successor has been elected and qualified, unless the manager sooner resigns or is removed.

(c) The only matters of a member or manager-managed company's business requiring the consent of all of the members are:

(1) the amendment of the operating agreement under Section 103;

(2) the authorization or ratification of acts or transactions under Section 103(b)(2)(ii) which would otherwise violate the duty of loyalty;

(3) an amendment to the articles of organization under Section 204;

(4) the compromise of an obligation to make a contribution under Section 402(b);

(5) the compromise, as among members, of an obligation of a member to make a contribution or return money or other property paid or distributed in violation of this [Act];

(6) the making of interim distributions under Section 405(a), including the redemption of an interest;

(7) the admission of a new member;

(8) the use of the company's property to redeem an interest subject to a charging order;

(9) the consent to dissolve the company under Section 801(b)(2);

(10) a waiver of the right to have the company's business wound up and the company terminated under Section 802(b);

(11) the consent of members to merge with another entity under Section 904(c)(1); and

(12) the sale, lease, exchange, or other disposal of all, or substantially all, of the company's property with or without goodwill.

(d) Action requiring the consent of members or managers under this [Act] may be taken without a meeting.

(e) A member or manager may appoint a proxy to vote or otherwise act for the member or manager by signing an appointment instrument, either personally or by the member's or manager's attorney-in-fact.

*   *   *   *

APPENDIX J

The Securities Act of 1933 (Excerpts)

Definitions

Section 2. When used in this title, unless the context requires—

(1) The term "security" means any note, stock, treasury stock, bond, debenture, evidence of indebtedness, certificate of interest or participation in any profit-sharing agreement, collateral-trust certificate, preorganization certificate or subscription, transferable share, investment contract, voting-trust certificate, certificate of deposit for a security, fractional undivided interest in oil, gas, or other mineral rights, any put, call, straddle, option, or privilege on any security, certificate of deposit, or group or index of securities (including any interest therein or based on the value thereof), or any put, call, straddle, option, or privilege entered into on a national securities exchange relating to foreign currency, or, in general, any interest or participation in, temporary or interim certificate for, receipt for, guarantee of, or warrant or right to subscribe to or purchase, any of the foregoing.

Exempted Securities

Section 3. (a) Except as hereinafter expressly provided the provisions of this title shall not apply to any of the following classes of securities:

* * * *

(2) Any security issued or guaranteed by the United States or any territory thereof, or by the District of Columbia, or by any State of the United States, or by any political subdivision of a State or Territory, or by any public instrumentality of one or more States or Territories, or by any person controlled or supervised by and acting as an instrumentality of the Government of the United States pursuant to authority granted by the Congress of the United States; or any certificate of deposit for any of the foregoing; or any security issued or guaranteed by any bank; or any security issued by or representing an interest in or a direct obligation of a Federal Reserve Bank. * * *

(3) Any note, draft, bill of exchange, or banker's acceptance which arises out of a current transaction or the proceeds of which have been or are to be used for current transactions, and which has a maturity at the time of issuance of not exceeding nine months, exclusive of days of grace, or any renewal thereof the maturity of which is likewise limited;

(4) Any security issued by a person organized and operated exclusively for religious, educational, benevolent, fraternal, charitable, or reformatory purposes and not for pecuniary profit, and no part of the net earnings of which inures to the benefit of any person, private stockholder, or individual;

* * * *

(11) Any security which is a part of an issue offered and sold only to persons resident within a single State or Territory, where the issuer of such security is a person resident and doing business within, or, if a corporation,

incorporated by and doing business within, such State or Territory.

(b) The Commission may from time to time by its rules and regulations and subject to such terms and conditions as may be described therein, add any class of securities to the securities exempted as provided in this section, if it finds that the enforcement of this title with respect to such securities is not necessary in the public interest and for the protection of investors by reason of the small amount involved or the limited character of the public offering; but no issue of securities shall be exempted under this subsection where the aggregate amount at which such issue is offered to the public exceeds $5,000,000.

Exempted Transactions

Section 4. The provisions of section 5 shall not apply to—

(1) transactions by any person other than an issuer, underwriter, or dealer.

(2) transactions by an issuer not involving any public offering.

(3) transactions by a dealer (including an underwriter no longer acting as an underwriter in respect of the security involved in such transactions), except—

(A) transactions taking place prior to the expiration of forty days after the first date upon which the security was bona fide offered to the public by the issuer or by or through an underwriter.

(B) transactions in a security as to which a registration statement has been filed taking place prior to the expiration of forty days after the effective date of such registration statement or prior to the expiration of forty days after the first date upon which the security was bona fide offered to the public by the issuer or by or through an underwriter after such effective date, whichever is later (excluding in the computation of such forty days any time during which a stop order issued under section 8 is in effect as to the security), or such shorter period as the Commission may specify by rules and regulations or order, and

(C) transactions as to the securities constituting the whole or a part of an unsold allotment to or subscription by such dealer as a participant in the distribution of such securities by the issuer or by or through an underwriter.

With respect to transactions referred to in clause (B), if securities of the issuer have not previously been sold pursuant to an earlier effective registration statement the applicable period, instead of forty days, shall be ninety days, or such shorter period as the Commission may specify by rules and regulations or order.

(4) brokers' transactions, executed upon customers' orders on any exchange or in the over-the-counter market but not the solicitation of such orders.

*   *   *   *

(6) transactions involving offers or sales by an issuer solely to one or more accredited investors, if the aggregate offering price of an issue of securities offered in reliance on this paragraph does not exceed the amount allowed under Section 3(b) of this title, if there is no advertising or public solicitation in connection with the transaction by the issuer or anyone acting on the issuer's behalf, and if the issuer files such notice with the Commission as the Commission shall prescribe.

Prohibitions Relating to Interstate Commerce and the Mails

Section 5. (a) Unless a registration statement is in effect as to a security, it shall be unlawful for any person, directly or indirectly—

(1) to make use of any means or instruments of transportation or communication in interstate commerce or of the mails to sell such security through the use or medium of any prospectus or otherwise; or

(2) to carry or cause to be carried through the mails or in interstate commerce, by any means or instruments of transportation, any such security for the purpose of sale or for delivery after sale.

(b) It shall be unlawful for any person, directly or indirectly—

(1) to make use of any means or instruments of transportation or communication in interstate commerce or of the mails to carry or transmit any prospectus relating to any security with respect to which a registration statement has been filed under this title, unless such prospectus meets the requirements of section 10, or

(2) to carry or to cause to be carried through the mails or in interstate commerce any such security for the purpose of sale or for delivery after sale, unless accompanied or preceded by a prospectus that meets the requirements of subsection (a) of section 10.

(c) It shall be unlawful for any person, directly, or indirectly, to make use of any means or instruments of transportation or communication in interstate commerce or of the mails to offer to sell or offer to buy through the use or medium of any prospectus or otherwise any security, unless a registration statement has been filed as to such security, or while the registration statement is the subject of a refusal order or stop order or (prior to the effective date of the registration statement) any public proceeding of examination under section 8.

The Securities Exchange Act of 1934 (Excerpts)

Definitions and Application of Title

Section 3. (a) When used in this title, unless the context otherwise requires—

* * * *

(4) The term "broker" means any person engaged in the business of effecting transactions in securities for the account of others, but does not include a bank.

(5) The term "dealer" means any person engaged in the business of buying and selling securities for his own account, through a broker or otherwise, but does not include a bank, or any person insofar as he buys or sells securities for his own account, either individually or in some fiduciary capacity, but not as part of a regular business.

* * * *

(7) The term "director" means any director of a corporation or any person performing similar functions with respect to any organization, whether incorporated or unincorporated.

(8) The term "issuer" means any person who issues or proposes to issue any security; except that with respect to certificates of deposit for securities, voting-trust certificates, or collateral-trust certificates, or with respect to certificates of interest or shares in an unincorporated investment trust not having a board of directors or the fixed, restricted management, or unit type, the term "issuer" means the person or persons performing the acts and assuming the duties of depositor or manager pursuant to the provisions of the trust or other agreement or instrument under which such securities are issued; and except that with respect to equipment-trust certificates or like securities, the term "issuer" means the person by whom the equipment or property is, or is to be, used.

(9) The term "person" means a natural person, company, government, or political subdivision, agency, or instrumentality of a government.

Regulation of the Use of Manipulative and Deceptive Devices

Section 10. It shall be unlawful for any person, directly or indirectly, by the use of any means or instrumentality of interstate commerce or of the mails, or of any facility of any national securities exchange—

(a) To effect a short sale, or to use or employ any stop-loss order in connection with the purchase or sale, of any security registered on a national securities exchange, in contravention of such rules and regulations as the Commission may prescribe as necessary or appropriate in the public interest or for the protection of investors.

(b) To use or employ, in connection with the purchase or sale of any security registered on a national securities exchange or any security not so registered, any manipulative or deceptive device or contrivance in contravention of such rules and regulations as the Commission may prescribe as necessary or appropriate in the public interest or for the protection of investors.

Title VII of the Civil Rights Act of 1964 (Excerpts)

Section 703. Unlawful Employment Practices. (a) It shall be an unlawful employment practice for an employer—

(1) to fail or refuse to hire or to discharge any individual, or otherwise to discriminate against any individual with respect to his compensation, terms, conditions, or privileges of employment, because of such individual's race, color, religion, sex, or national origin; or

(2) to limit, segregate, or classify his employees or applicants for employment in any way which would deprive or tend to deprive any individual of employment opportunities or otherwise adversely affect his status as an employee, because of such individual's race, color, religion, sex, or national origin.

(b) It shall be an unlawful employment practice for an employment agency to fail or refuse to refer for employment, or otherwise to discriminate against, any individual because of his race, color, religion, sex, or national origin, or to classify or refer for employment any individual on the basis or his race, color, religion, sex, or national origin.

(c) It shall be an unlawful employment practice for a labor organization—

(1) to exclude or to expel from its membership, or otherwise to discriminate against, any individual because of his race, color, religion, sex, or national origin;

(2) to limit, segregate, or classify its membership or applicants for membership, or to classify or fail or refuse to refer for employment any individual, in any way which would deprive or tend to deprive any individual of employment opportunities, or would limit such employment opportunities or otherwise adversely affect his status as an employee or as an applicant for employment, because of such individual's race, color, religion, sex, or national origin; or

(3) to cause or attempt to cause an employer to discriminate against an individual in violation of this section.

(d) It shall be an unlawful employment practice for any employer, labor organization, or joint labor-management committee controlling apprenticeship or other training or retraining, including on-the-job training programs to discriminate against any individual because of his race, color, religion, sex, or national origin in admission to, or employment in, any program established to provide apprenticeship or other training.

(e) Notwithstanding any other provision of this subchapter—

(1) it shall not be an unlawful employment practice for an employer to hire and employ employees, for an employment agency to classify, or refer for employment any individual, for a labor organization to classify its membership or to classify or refer for employment any individual, or for an employer, labor organization, or joint labor-management committee controlling apprenticeship or other training or retraining programs to admit or employ any individual in any such program, on the basis of his religion, sex, or

national origin in those certain instances where religion, sex, or national origin is a bona fide occupational qualification reasonably necessary to the normal operation of that particular business or enterprise, and

(2) it shall not be an unlawful employment practice for a school, college, university, or other educational institution or institution of learning to hire and employ employees of a particular religion if such school, college, university, or other educational institution or institution of learning is, in whole or in substantial part, owned, supported, controlled, or managed by a particular religion or by a particular religious corporation, association, or society, or if the curriculum of such school, college, university, or other educational institution or institution of learning is directed toward the propagation of a particular religion.

(f) As used in this subchapter, the phrase "unlawful employment practice" shall not be deemed to include any action or measure taken by an employer, labor organization, joint labor-management committee, or employment agency with respect to an individual who is a member of the Communist Party of the United States or of any other organization required to register as a Communist-action or Communist-front organization. * * *

(g) Notwithstanding any other provision of this subchapter, it shall not be an unlawful employment practice for an employer to fail or refuse to hire and employ any individual for any position, for an employer to discharge any individual from any position, or for an employment agency to fail or refuse to refer any individual for employment in any position, or for a labor organization to fail or refuse to refer any individual for employment in any position, if—

(1) the occupancy of such position, or access to the premises in or upon which any part of the duties of such position is performed or is to be performed, is subject to any requirement imposed in the interest of the national security of the United States * * * and

(2) such individual has not fulfilled or has ceased to fulfill that requirement.

(h) Notwithstanding any other provision of this subchapter, it shall not be an unlawful employment practice for an employer to apply different standards of compensation, or different terms, conditions, or privileges of employment pursuant to a bona fide seniority or merit system, or a system which measures earnings by quantity or quality of production or to employees who work in different locations, provided that such differences are not the result of an intention to discriminate because of race, color, religion, sex, or national origin, nor shall it be an unlawful employment practice for an employer to give and act upon the results of any professionally developed ability test provided that such test, its administration or action upon the results is not designed, intended or used to discriminate because of race, color, religion, sex, or national origin. * * *

(j) Nothing contained in this subchapter shall be interpreted to require any employer, employment agency, labor organization, or joint labor-management committee subject to this subchapter to grant preferential treatment to any individual or to any group because of the race, color, religion, sex, or national origin of such individual or group on account of an imbalance which may exist with respect to the total number or percentage of persons of any race, color, religion, sex, or national origin employed by any employer, referred or classified for employment by any employment agency or labor organization, or admitted to, or employed in, any apprenticeship or other training program, in comparison with the total number or percentage of persons of such race, color, religion, sex, or national origin in any community, State, section, or other area, or in the available work force in any community, State, section, or other area.

* * * *

Section 704. Other Unlawful Employment Practices.

(a) It shall be an unlawful employment practice for an employer to discriminate against any of his employees or applicants for employment, for an employment agency, or joint labor-management committee controlling apprenticeship or other training or retraining, including on-the-job training programs, to discriminate against any individual, or for a labor organization to discriminate against any member thereof or applicant for membership, because he has opposed any practice made an unlawful employment practice by this subchapter, or because he has made a charge, testified, assisted, or participated in any manner in an investigation, proceeding, or hearing under this subchapter.

(b) It shall be an unlawful employment practice for an employer, labor organization, employment agency, or joint labor-management committee controlling apprenticeship or other training or retraining, including on-the-job training programs, to print or publish or cause to be printed or published any notice or advertisement relating to employment by such an employer or membership or any classification or referral for employment by such a labor organization, or relating to any classification or referral for employment by such an employment agency, or relating to admission to, or employment in, any program established to provide apprenticeship or other training by such a joint-labor-management committee, indicating any preference, limitation, specification, or discrimination, based on race, color, religion, sex, or national origin, except that such a notice or advertisement may indicate a preference, limitation, specification, or discrimination based on religion, sex or national origin when religion, sex, or national origin is a bona fide occupational qualification for employment.

APPENDIX M

The Americans with Disabilities Act of 1990 (Excerpts)

Title I—EMPLOYMENT

Sec. 101. Definitions.

As used in this title: * * *

(8) **Qualified individual with a disability.**—The term "qualified individual with a disability" means an individual with a disability who, with or without reasonable accommodation, can perform the essential functions of the employment position that such individual holds or desires. For the purposes of this title, consideration shall be given to the employer's judgment as to what functions of a job are essential, and if an employer has prepared a written description before advertising or interviewing applicants for the job, this description shall be considered evidence of the essential functions of the job.

(9) **Reasonable accommodation.**—The term "reasonable accommodation" may include—

(A) making existing facilities used by employees readily accessible to and usable by individuals with disabilities; and

(B) job restructuring, part-time or modified work schedules, reassignment to a vacant position, acquisition or modification of equipment or devices, appropriate adjustment or modifications of examinations, training materials or policies, the provision of qualified readers or interpreters, and other similar accommodations for individuals with disabilities.

(10) **Undue Hardship.**—

(A) **In general.**—The term "undue hardship" means an action requiring significant difficulty or expense, when con-

sidered in light of the factors set forth in subparagraph (B).

(B) **Factors to be considered.**—In determining whether an accommodation would impose an undue hardship on a covered entity, factors to be considered include—

(i) the nature and cost of accommodation needed under this Act;

(ii) the overall financial resources of the facility or facilities involved in the provision of the reasonable accommodation; the number of persons employed at such facility; the effect on expenses and resources, or the impact otherwise of such accommodation upon the operation of the facility;

(iii) the overall financial resources of the covered entity; the overall size of the business of a covered entity with respect to the number of its employees; the number, type, and location of its facilities; and

(iv) the type of operation or operations of the covered entity, including the composition, structure, and functions of the workforce of such entity; the geographic separateness, administrative, or fiscal relationship of the facility or facilities in question to the covered entity.

Sec. 102. Discrimination.

(a) **General Rule.**—No covered entity shall discriminate against a qualified individual with a disability because of the disability of such individual in regard to job application procedures, the hiring, advancement, or discharge of employees, employee compensation, job training, and other terms, conditions, and privileges of employment.

(b) **Construction.**—As used in subsection (a), the term "discriminate" includes—

(1) limiting, segregating, or classifying a job applicant or employee in a way that adversely affects the opportunities or status of such applicant or employee because of the disability of such applicant or employee;

(2) participating in a contractual or other arrangement or relationship that has the effect of subjecting a covered entity's qualified applicant or employee with a disability to the discrimination prohibited by this title (such relationship includes a relationship with an employment or referral agency, labor union, an organization providing fringe benefits to an employee of the covered entity, or an organization providing training and apprenticeship programs);

(3) utilizing standards, criteria, or methods of administration—

(A) that have the effect of discrimination on the basis of disability; or

(B) that perpetuate the discrimination of others who are subject to common administrative control;

(4) excluding or otherwise denying equal jobs or benefits to a qualified individual because of the known disability of an individual with whom the qualified individual is known to have a relationship or association;

(5)

(A) not making reasonable accommodations to the known physical or mental limitations of an otherwise qualified individual with a disability who is an applicant or employee, unless such covered entity can demonstrate that the accommodation would impose an undue hardship on the operation of the business of such covered entity; or

(B) denying employment opportunities to a job applicant or employee who is an otherwise qualified individual with a disability, if such denial is based on the need of such covered entity to make reasonable accommodation to the physical or mental impairments of the employee or applicant;

(6) using qualification standards, employment tests or other selection criteria that screen out or tend to screen out an individual with a disability or a class of individuals with disabilities unless the standard, test or other selection criteria, as used by the covered entity, is shown to be job-related for the position in question and is consistent with business necessity; and

(7) failing to select and administer tests concerning employment in the most effective manner to ensure that, when such test is administered to a job applicant or employee who has a disability that impairs sensory, manual, or speaking skills, such test results accurately reflect the skills, aptitude, or whatever other factor of such applicant or employee that such test purports to measure, rather than reflecting the impaired sensory, manual, or speaking skills of such employee or applicant (except where such skills are the factors that the test purports to measure). *   *   *

Sec. 104. Illegal Use of Drugs and Alcohol. *   *   *

(b) **Rules of Construction.**—Nothing in subsection (a) shall be construed to exclude as a qualified individual with a disability an individual who—

(1) has successfully completed a supervised drug rehabilitation program and is no longer engaging in the illegal use of drugs, or has otherwise been rehabilitated successfully and is no longer engaging in such use;

(2) is participating in a supervised rehabilitation program and is no longer engaging in such use; or

(3) is erroneously regarded as engaging in such use, but is not engaging in such use; except that it shall not be a violation of this Act for a covered entity to adopt or administer reasonable policies or procedures, including but not limited to drug testing, designed to ensure that an individual described in paragraph (1) or (2) is no longer engaging in the illegal use of drugs. *   *   *

Sec. 107. Enforcement.

(a) **Powers, Remedies, and Procedures.**—The powers, remedies, and procedures set forth in sections 705, 706, 707, 709, and 710 of the Civil Rights Act of 1964 (42 U.S.C. 2000e-4, 2000e-5, 2000e-6, 2000e-8, and 2000e-9) shall be the powers, remedies, and procedures this title provides to the Commission, to the Attorney General, or to any person alleging discrimination on the basis of disability in violation of any provision of this Act, or regulations promulgated under section 106, concerning employment.

(b) **Coordination.**—The agencies with enforcement authority for actions which allege employment discrimination under this title and under the Rehabilitation Act of 1973 shall develop procedures to ensure that administrative complaints filed under this title and under the Rehabilitation Act of 1973 are dealt with in a manner that avoids duplication of effort and prevents imposition of inconsistent or conflicting standards for the same requirements under this title and the Rehabilitation Act of 1973. The Commission, the Attorney General, and the Office of Federal Contract Compliance Programs shall establish such coordinating mechanisms (similar to provisions contained in the joint regulations promulgated by the Commission and the Attorney General at part 42 of title 28 and part 1691 of title 29, Code of Federal Regulations, and the Memorandum of Understanding between the Commission and the Office of Federal Contract Compliance Programs dated January 16, 1981 (46 Fed. Reg. 7435, January 23, 1981)) in regulations implementing this title and Rehabilitation Act of 1973 not later than 18 months after the date of enactment of this Act.

Sec. 108. Effective Date.

This title shall become effective 24 months after the date of enactment.

The Civil Rights Act of 1991 (Excerpts)

Section 3. Purposes.

The purposes of this Act are—

(1) to provide appropriate remedies for intentional discrimination and unlawful harassment in the workplace;

(2) to codify the concepts of "business necessity" and "job related" enunciated by the Supreme Court in *Griggs v. Duke Power Co.*, 401 U.S. 424 (1971), and in the other Supreme Court decisions prior to *Wards Cove Packing Co. v. Atonio*, 490 U.S. 642 (1989);

(3) to confirm statutory authority and provide statutory guidelines for the adjudication of disparate impact suits under title VII of the Civil Rights Act of 1964 (42 U.S.C. 2000e *et seq.*); and

(4) to respond to recent decisions of the Supreme Court by expanding the scope of relevant civil rights statutes in order to provide adequate protection to victims of discrimination.

Section 101. Prohibition against All Racial Discrimination in the Making and Enforcement of Contracts.

Section 1977 of the Revised Statutes (42 U.S.C. 1981) is amended * * * by adding at the end the following new subsections:

(b) For purposes of this section, the term "make and enforce contracts" includes the making, performance, modification, and termination of contracts, and the enjoyment of all benefits, privileges, terms, and conditions of the contractual relationship.

(c) The rights protected by this section are protected against impairment by nongovernmental discrimination and impairment under color of State law.

Section 102. Damages in Cases of Intentional Discrimination.

The Revised Statutes are amended by inserting after section 1977 (42 U.S.C.1981) the following new section:

Section 1977A. Damages in Cases of Intentional Discrimination in Employment.

(a) Right of Recovery.—

(1) Civil Rights.—In an action brought by a complaining party under section 706 or 717 of the Civil Rights Act of 1964 (42 U.S.C. 2000e-5) against a respondent who engaged in unlawful intentional discrimination (not an employment practice that is unlawful because of its disparate impact) prohibited under section 703, 704, or 717 of the Act (42 U.S.C. 2000e-2 or 2000e-3), and provided that the complaining party cannot recover under section 1977 of the Revised Statutes (42 U.S.C.1981), the complaining party may recover compensatory and punitive damages as allowed in subsection (b), in addition to any relief authorized by section 706(g) of the Civil Rights Act of 1964, from the respondent.

* * * *

(b) Compensatory and Punitive Damages.—

(1) Determination of Punitive Damages.—A complaining party may recover punitive damages under this section against a respondent (other than a government, government agency or political subdivision) if the complaining party demonstrates that the respondent engaged in a discriminatory practice or discriminatory practices with malice or with reckless indifference to the federally protected rights of an aggrieved individual.

(2) Exclusions from Compensatory Damages.—Compensatory damages awarded under this section shall not include backpay, interest on backpay, or any other type of relief authorized under section 706(g) of the Civil Rights Act of 1964.

(3) Limitations.—The sum of the amount of compensatory damages awarded under this section for future pecuniary losses, emotional pain, suffering, inconvenience, mental anguish, loss of enjoyment of life, and other nonpecuniary losses, and the amount of punitive damages awarded under this section, shall not exceed, for each complaining party—

(A) in the case of a respondent who has more than 14 and fewer than 101 employees in each of 20 or more calendar weeks in the current or preceding calendar year, $50,000;

(B) in the case of a respondent who has more than 100 and fewer than 201 employees in each of 20 or more calendar weeks in the current or preceding calendar year, $100,000; and

(C) in the case of a respondent who has more than 200 and fewer than 501 employees in each of 20 or more calendar weeks in the current or preceding calendar year, $200,000; and

(D) in the case of a respondent who has more than 500 employees in each of 20 or more calendar weeks in the current or preceding calendar year, $300,000.

*   *   *   *

Section 105. Burden of Proof in Disparate Impact Cases.

(a) Section 703 of the Civil Rights Act of 1964 (42 U.S.C. 2000e-2) is amended by adding at the end the following new [subsections to 703(k)(1)]—

(A) An unlawful employment practice based on disparate impact is established under this title only if—

(i) a complaining party demonstrates that a respondent uses a particular employment practice that causes a disparate impact on the basis of race, color, religion, sex, or national origin and the respondent fails to demonstrate that the challenged practice is job related for the position in question and consistent with business necessity; or

(ii) the complaining party makes the demonstration described in subparagraph (C) with respect to an alternative employment practice and the respondent refuses to adopt such alternative employment practice.

*   *   *   *

(C) The demonstration referred to by subparagraph (A)(ii) shall be in accordance with the law as it existed on June 4, 1989, with respect to the concept of "alternative employment practice."

*   *   *   *

Section 107. Clarifying Prohibition against Impermissible Consideration of Race, Color, Religion, Sex, or National Origin in Employment Practices.

(a) In General.—Section 703 of the Civil Rights Act of 1964 (42 U.S.C. 2000e-2) (as amended by sections 105 and 106) is further amended by adding at the end the following new subsection:

(m) Except as otherwise provided in this title, an unlawful employment practice is established when the complaining party demonstrates that race, color, religion, sex, or national origin was a motivating factor for any employment practice, even though other factors also motivated the practice.

*   *   *   *

Section 109. Protection of Extraterritorial Employment.

(a) Definition of Employee.—Section 701(f) of the Civil Rights Act of 1964 (42 U.S.C. 2000e(f)) and section 101(4) of the Americans with Disabilities Act of 1990 (42 U.S.C. 12111(4)) are each amended by adding at the end the following: "With respect to employment in a foreign country, such term includes an individual who is a citizen of the United States."

The Administrative Procedure Act of 1946 (Excerpts)

Section 551. Definitions

For the purpose of this subchapter—

* * * *

(4) "rule" means the whole or a part of an agency state-ment of general or particular applicability and future effect designed to implement, interpret, or prescribe law or policy or describing the organization, procedure, or practice requirements of an agency and includes the approval or prescription for the future of rates, wages, corporate or financial structures or reorganizations thereof, prices, facilities, appliances, services or allowances therefor or of valuations, costs, or account-ing, or practices bearing on any of the foregoing[.]

* * * *

Section 552. Public Information; Agency Rules, Opinions, Orders, Records, and Proceedings

(a) Each agency shall make available to the public infor-mation as follows:

(1) Each agency shall separately state and currently publish in the Federal Register for the guidance of the public—

(A) descriptions of its central and field organiza-tion and the established places at which, the employees * * * from whom, and the methods whereby, the public may obtain information, make submittals or requests, or obtain decisions;

* * * *

(C) rules of procedure, descriptions of forms avail-able or the places at which forms may be obtained, and instructions as to the scope and contents of all papers, reports, or examinations;

(D) substantive rules of general applicability adopted as authorized by law, and statements of gen-eral policy or interpretations of general applicability formulated and adopted by the agency[.] * * *

* * * *

Section 552b. Open Meetings

* * * *

(j) Each agency subject to the requirements of this section shall annually report to Congress regarding its compliance with such requirements, including a tabulation of the total number of agency meetings open to the public, the total number of meetings closed to the public, the reasons for closing such meetings, and a description of any litigation brought against the agency under this section, including any costs assessed against the agency in such litigation * * *.

* * * *

Section 553. Rule Making

* * * *

(b) General notice of proposed rule making shall be pub-lished in the Federal Register, unless persons subject thereto are named and either personally served or otherwise have actual notice thereof in accordance with law. * * *

(c) After notice required by this section, the agency shall give interested persons an opportunity to participate in the rule making through submission of written data, views, or arguments with or without opportunity for oral presentation. *   *   *

*   *   *   *

Section 554. Adjudications

*   *   *   *

(b) Persons entitled to notice of an agency hearing shall be timely informed of—

(1) the time, place, and nature of the hearing;

(2) the legal authority and jurisdiction under which the hearing is to be held; and

(3) the matters of fact and law asserted.

*   *   *   *

(c) The agency shall give all interested parties opportunity for—

(1) the submission and consideration of facts, arguments, offers of settlement, or proposals of adjustment when time, the nature of the proceeding, and the public interest permit; and

(2) to the extent that the parties are unable so to determine a controversy by consent, hearing and decision on notice *   *   * .

*   *   *   *

Section 555. Ancillary Matters

*   *   *   *

(c) Process, requirement of a report, inspection, or other investigative act or demand may not be issued, made, or enforced except as authorized by law. A person compelled to submit data or evidence is entitled to retain or, on payment of lawfully prescribed costs, procure a copy or transcript thereof, except that in a nonpublic investigatory proceeding the witness may for good cause be limited to inspection of the official transcript of his testimony.

*   *   *   *

(e) Prompt notice shall be given of the denial in whole or in part of a written application, petition, or other request of an interested person made in connection with any agency proceeding. *   *   *

Section 556. Hearings; Presiding Employees; Powers and Duties; Burden of Proof; Evidence; Record as Basis of Decision

*   *   *   *

(b) There shall preside at the taking of evidence—

(1) the agency;

(2) one or more members of the body which comprises the agency; or

(3) one or more administrative law judges *   *   * .

*   *   *   *

(c) Subject to published rules of the agency and within its powers, employees presiding at hearings may—

(1) administer oaths and affirmations;

(2) issue subpoenas authorized by law;

(3) rule on offers of proof and receive relevant evidence;

(4) take depositions or have depositions taken when the ends of justice would be served;

(5) regulate the course of the hearing;

(6) hold conferences for the settlement or simplification of the issues by consent of the parties or by the use of alternative means of dispute resolution as provided in subchapter IV of this chapter;

(7) inform the parties as to the availability of one or more alternative means of dispute resolution, and encourage use of such methods;

*   *   *   *

(9) dispose of procedural requests or similar matters;

(10) make or recommend decisions in accordance with *   *   * this title; and

(11) take other action authorized by agency rule consistent with this subchapter.

*   *   *   *

Section 702. Right of Review

A person suffering legal wrong because of agency action *   *   * is entitled to judicial review thereof. An action in a court of the United States seeking relief other than money damages and stating a claim that an agency or an officer or employee thereof acted or failed to act in an official capacity or under color of legal authority shall not be dismissed nor relief therein be denied on the ground that it is against the United States or that the United States is an indispensable party. The United States may be named as a defendant in any such action, and a judgment or decree may be entered against the United States: Provided, [t]hat any mandatory or injunctive decree shall specify the [f]ederal officer or officers (by name or by title), and their successors in office, personally responsible for compliance. *   *   *

*   *   *   *

Section 704. Actions Reviewable

Agency action made reviewable by statute and final agency action for which there is no other adequate remedy in a court are subject to judicial review. A preliminary, procedural, or intermediate agency action or ruling not directly reviewable is subject to review on the review of the final agency action.

The General Agreement on Tariffs and Trade of 1994 (Excerpts)

Part I

FINAL ACT EMBODYING THE RESULTS OF THE URUGUAY ROUND OF MULTILATERAL TRADE NEGOTIATIONS

1. Having met in order to conclude the Uruguay Round of Multilateral Trade Negotiations, the representatives of the Governments and of the European Communities, members of the Trade Negotiations Committee * * *, *agree* that the Agreement Establishing the Multilateral Trade Organization and the Ministerial Decisions and Declarations * * * embody the results of their negotiations and form an integral part of this Final Act.

* * * *

Part II

AGREEMENT ESTABLISHING THE MULTILATERAL TRADE ORGANIZATION

The *Parties* to this Agreement,

Recognizing that their relations in the field of trade and economic endeavour should be conducted with a view to raising standards of living, ensuring full employment and a large and steadily growing volume of real income and effective demand, and expanding the production and trade in good and services, while allowing for the optimal use of the world's resources in accordance with the objective of sustainable development, seeking both to protect and preserve the environment and enhance the means for doing so in a manner consistent with their respective needs and concerns at different levels of economic development,

Recognizing further that there is need for positive efforts designed to ensure that developing countries * * * secure a share in the growth in international trade commensurate with the needs of their economic development,

Being desirous of contributing to these objectives by entering into reciprocal and mutually advantageous arrangements directed to the substantial reduction of tariffs and other barriers to trade and to the elimination of discriminatory treatment in international trade relations,

Resolved, therefore, to develop an integrated, more viable and durable multilateral trading system encompassing the General Agreement on Tariffs and Trade, the results of the past trade liberalization efforts, and all of the results of the Uruguay Round of multilateral trade negotiations,

Determined to preserve the basic principles and to further the objectives underlying this multilateral trading system,

Agree as follows:

*   *   *   *

The Multilateral Trade Organization [MTO] *   *   * is hereby established.

*   *   *   *

[The] MTO shall facilitate the implementation, administration, operation, and further the objectives, of this Agreement and of the Multilateral Trade Agreements, and shall also provide the framework for the implementation, administration and operation of the Plurilateral Trade Agreements.

*   *   *   *

[Except] as otherwise provided for under this Agreement or the Multilateral Trade Agreements, the MTO shall be guided by the decisions, procedures and customary practices followed by the contracting parties of the GATT 1947 and the bodies established in the framework of the GATT 1947.

*   *   *   *

AGREEMENT ON AGRICULTURE

*   *   *   *

2. In accordance with the Mid-Term Review Agreement that government measures of assistance, whether direct or indirect, to encourage agricultural and rural development are an integral part of the development programmes of developing countries, investment subsidies which are generally available to agriculture in developing country Members and agricultural input subsidies generally available to low-income or resource poor producers in developing country Members shall be exempt from domestic support reduction commitments that would otherwise be applicable to such measures, as shall domestic support to producers in developing country Members to encourage diversification from growing illicit narcotic crops. *   *   *

*   *   *   *

AGREEMENT ON TEXTILES AND CLOTHING

*   *   *

1. Members agree that circumvention by transshipment, rerouting, false declaration concerning country or place of origin, and falsification of official documents, frustrates the implementation of this Agreement to integrate the textiles and clothing sector into the GATT 1994. Accordingly, Members should establish the necessary legal provisions and/or administrative procedures to address and take action against such circumvention. Members further agree that, consistent with their domestic laws and procedures,

they will cooperate fully to address problems arising from circumvention.

*   *   *   *

2. Safeguard action may be taken *   *   * when, on the basis of a determination by a Member, it is demonstrated that a particular product is being imported into its territory in such increased quantities as to cause serious damage, or actual threat thereof, to the domestic industry producing like and/or directly competitive products. Serious damage or actual threat thereof must demonstrably be caused by such increased quantities in total imports of that product and not by such other factors as technological changes or changes in consumer preference.

*   *   *   *

AGREEMENT ON TECHNICAL BARRIERS TO TRADE

*   *   *   *

2.2 Members shall ensure that technical regulations are not prepared, adopted or applied with a view to or with the effect of creating unnecessary obstacles to international trade. For this purpose, technical regulations shall not be more trade-restrictive than necessary to fulfil a legitimate objective, taking account of the risks non-fulfilment would create. Such legitimate objectives [include] national security requirements; the prevention of deceptive practices; protection of human health or safety, animal or plant life or health, or the environment. In assessing such risks, relevant elements of consideration [include] *   *   * available scientific and technical information, related processing technology or intended end uses of products.

*   *   *   *

AGREEMENT ON IMPLEMENTATION OF ARTICLE VI OF GATT 1994

*   *   *   *

2.1 For the purpose of this Agreement a product is to be considered as being dumped, i.e., introduced into the commerce of another country at less than its normal value, if the export price of the product exported from one country to another is less than the comparable price, in the ordinary course of trade, for the like product when destined for consumption in the exporting country.

*   *   *   *

3.5 It must be demonstrated that the dumped imports are *   *   * causing injury within the meaning of this Agreement. The demonstration of a causal relationship between the dumped imports and the injury to the domestic industry shall be based on an examination of all relevant evidence before the authorities. The authorities shall also examine any known factors other than the dumped imports which at the same time are injuring the domestic industry, and the injuries caused by these other factors must not be attributed to the dumped imports. Factors which may be relevant in this respect include *   *   * the volume and prices of imports not sold at dumping prices, contraction in demand or changes in the patterns of consumption, trade restrictive practices of and competition between the foreign and domestic producers, developments in technology and the export performance and productivity of the domestic industry.

*   *   *   *

9.2 When an anti-dumping duty is imposed in respect of any product, such anti-dumping duty shall be collected in the appropriate amounts in each case, on a non-discriminatory basis on imports of such product from all sources found to be dumped and causing injury, except as to imports from those sources from which price undertakings under the terms of this Agreement have been accepted. The authorities shall name the supplier or suppliers of the product concerned. If, however, several suppliers from the same country are involved, and it is impracticable to name all of these suppliers, the authorities may name the supplying country concerned. If several suppliers from more than one country are involved, the authorities may name either all the suppliers involved, or, if this is impracticable, all the supplying countries involved.

*   *   *   *

AGREEMENT ON
PRESHIPMENT INSPECTION

*   *   *   *

12. User Members shall ensure that preshipment inspection entities do not request exporters to provide information regarding:

(a) manufacturing data related to patented, licensed or undisclosed processes, or to processes for which a patent is pending;

(b) unpublished technical data other than necessary to demonstrate compliance with technical regulations or standards;

(c) internal pricing, including manufacturing costs;

(d) profit levels;

(e) the terms of contracts between exporters and their suppliers unless it is not otherwise possible for the entity to conduct the inspection in question. In such cases, the entity shall only request the information necessary for this purpose.

*   *   *   *

AGREEMENT ON SUBSIDIES
AND COUNTERVAILING MEASURES

*   *   *   *

3.1 Except as provided in the Agreement on Agriculture, the following subsidies *   *   * shall be prohibited:

(a) subsidies contingent, in law or in fact, whether solely or as one of several other conditions, upon export performance *   *   * ;

(b) subsidies contingent, whether solely or as one of several other conditions, upon the use of domestic over imported goods.

*   *   *   *

AGREEMENT ON SAFEGUARDS

*   *   *   *

2. A Member may apply a safeguard measure to a product only if that Member has determined *   *   * that such product is being imported into its territory in such increased quantities, absolute or relative to domestic production, and under such conditions as to cause or threaten to cause serious injury to the domestic industry that produces like or directly competitive products.

*   *   *   *

8. Safeguard measures shall be applied only to the extent as may be necessary to prevent or remedy serious injury and to facilitate adjustment. *   *   *

*   *   *   *

12. The total period of application of a safeguard measure including the period of application of any provisional measure, the period of initial application and any extension thereof, shall not exceed eight years.

*   *   *   *

19. Safeguard measures shall not be applied against a product originating in a developing country Member as long as its share of imports of the product concerned in the importing Member does not exceed 3 [percent], provided that, developing country Members with less than 3 [percent] import share collectively account for not more than 9 [percent] of total imports of the product concerned.

*   *   *   *

GENERAL AGREEMENT
ON TRADE IN SERVICES

*   *   *   *

1. With respect to any measure covered by this Agreement, each Member shall accord immediately and unconditionally to services and service suppliers of any other Member, treatment no less favourable than that it

accords to like services and service suppliers of any other country.

*   *   *   *

AGREEMENT ON TRADE-RELATED ASPECTS OF INTELLECTUAL PROPERTY RIGHTS, INCLUDING TRADE IN COUNTERFEIT GOODS

*   *   *   *

1. Members shall ensure that enforcement procedures *   *   * are available under their national laws so as to permit effective action against any act of infringement of intellectual property rights covered by this Agreement, including expeditious remedies to prevent infringements and remedies which constitute a deterrent to further infringements. These procedures shall be applied in such a manner as to avoid the creation of barriers to legitimate trade and to provide for safeguards against their abuse.

2. Procedures concerning the enforcement of intellectual property rights shall be fair and equitable. They shall not be unnecessarily complicated or costly, or entail unreasonable time-limits or unwarranted delays.

*   *   *   *

UNDERSTANDING ON RULES AND PROCEDURES GOVERNING THE SETTLEMENT OF DISPUTES

*   *   *   *

2.1 The Dispute Settlement Body (DSB) *   *   * shall administer these rules and procedures and *   *   * the consultation and dispute settlement provisions of the covered agreements. *   *   *

APPENDIX Q

The North American Free Trade Agreement of 1993 (Excerpts)

Part One: GENERAL PART

Chapter One: Objectives

Article 101: Establishment of the Free Trade Area

The Parties to this Agreement * * * hereby establish a free trade area.

Article 102: Objectives

1. The objectives of this Agreement * * * are to: (a) eliminate barriers to trade in, and facilitate the cross-border movement of, goods and services between the territories of the Parties; (b) promote conditions of fair competition in the free trade area; (c) increase substantially investment opportunities in the territories of the Parties; (d) provide adequate and effective protection and enforcement of intellectual property rights in each Party's territory; (e) create effective procedures for the implementation and application of this Agreement, for its joint administration and for the resolution of disputes; and (f) establish a framework for further trilateral, regional and multilateral cooperation to expand and enhance the benefits of this Agreement.

* * * *

Part Two: TRADE IN GOODS

Chapter Three: National Treatment and Market Access for Goods

* * * *

Article 301: National Treatment

1. Each Party shall accord national treatment to the goods of another Party in accordance with Article III of the General Agreement on Tariffs and Trade (GATT) * * * .

2. [N]ational treatment shall mean, with respect to a state or province, treatment no less favorable than the most favorable treatment accorded by such state or province to any like, directly competitive or substitutable goods, as the case may be, of the Party of which it forms a part.

* * * *

Article 302: Tariff Elimination

1. Except as otherwise provided in this Agreement, no Party may increase any existing customs duty, or adopt any customs duty, on an originating good.

2. [E]ach Party shall progressively eliminate its customs duties on originating goods in accordance with its Schedule * * * .

* * * *

Article 316: Consultations and Committee on Trade in Goods

1. The Parties hereby establish a Committee on Trade in Goods, comprising representatives of each Party.

* * * *

3. The Parties shall convene at least once each year a meeting of their officials responsible for customs, immigration, inspection of food and agricultural products, border inspection facilities, and regulation of transportation for the purpose of addressing issues related to movement of goods through the Parties' ports of entry.

* * * *

Part Three: TECHNICAL BARRIERS TO TRADE
Chapter Nine: Standards-Related Measures

* * * *

Article 904: Basic Rights and Obligations

Right to Take Standards-Related Measures

1. Each Party may * * * adopt, maintain or apply any standards-related measure, including any such measure relating to safety, the protection of human, animal or plant life or health, the environment or consumers, and any measure to ensure its enforcement or implementation. Such measures include those to prohibit the importation of a good of another Party or the provision of a service by a service provider of another Party that fails to comply with the applicable requirements of those measures or to complete the Party's approval procedures.

* * * *

Unnecessary Obstacles

4. No Party may prepare, adopt, maintain or apply any standards-related measure with a view to or with the effect of creating an unnecessary obstacle to trade between the Parties. An unnecessary obstacle to trade shall not be deemed to be created where: (a) the demonstrable purpose of the measure is to achieve a legitimate objective; and (b) the measure does not operate to exclude goods of another Party that meet that legitimate objective.

* * * *

Article 913: Committee on Standards-Related Measures

1. The Parties hereby establish a Committee on Standards-Related Measures, comprising representatives of each Party.

2. The Committee's functions shall include: (a) monitoring the implementation and administration of this Chapter

* * * ; (b) facilitating the process by which the Parties make compatible their standards-related measures; (c) providing a forum for the Parties to consult on issues relating to standards-related measures * * * ; (d) enhancing cooperation on the development, application and enforcement of standards-related measures; and (e) considering non-governmental, regional and multilateral developments regarding standards-related measures, including under the GATT.

* * * *

Part Five: INVESTMENT, SERVICES AND RELATED MATTERS
Chapter Eleven: Investment
SECTION A—INVESTMENT

* * * *

Article 1102: National Treatment

* * * *

2. Each Party shall accord to investments of investors of another Party treatment no less favorable than that it accords, in like circumstances, to investments of its own investors with respect to the establishment, acquisition, expansion, management, conduct, operation, and sale or other disposition of investments.

* * * *

4. For greater certainty, no Party may: (a) impose on an investor of another Party a requirement that a minimum level of equity in an enterprise in the territory of the Party be held by its nationals, other than nominal qualifying shares for directors or incorporators of corporations; or (b) require an investor of another Party, by reason of its nationality, to sell or otherwise dispose of an investment in the territory of the Party.

* * * *

Part Six: INTELLECTUAL PROPERTY
Chapter Seventeen: Intellectual Property
Article 1701: Nature and Scope of Obligations

1. Each Party shall provide in its territory to the nationals of another Party adequate and effective protection and enforcement of intellectual property rights, while ensuring that measures to enforce intellectual property rights do not themselves become barriers to legitimate trade.

* * * *

Article 1705: Copyright

* * * *

2. Each Party shall provide to authors and their successors

in interest those rights enumerated in the Berne Convention in respect of works covered by paragraph 1, including the right to authorize or prohibit: (a) the importation into the Party's territory of copies of the work made without the right holder's authorization; (b) the first public distribution of the original and each copy of the work by sale, rental or otherwise; (c) the communication of a work to the public; and (d) the commercial rental of the original or a copy of a computer program. Subparagraph (d) shall not apply where the copy of the computer program is not itself an essential object of the rental. Each Party shall provide that putting the original or a copy of a computer program on the market with the right holder's consent shall not exhaust the rental right.

*   *   *   *

4. Each Party shall provide that, where the term of protection of a work, other than a photographic work or a work of applied art, is to be calculated on a basis other than the life of a natural person, the term shall be not less than 50 years from the end of the calendar year of the first authorized publication of the work or, failing such authorized publication within 50 years from the making of the work, 50 years from the end of the calendar year of making.

5. Each Party shall confine limitations or exceptions to the rights provided for in this Article to certain special cases that do not conflict with a normal exploitation of the work and do not unreasonably prejudice the legitimate interests of the right holder.

*   *   *   *

Article 1706: Sound Recordings

1. Each Party shall provide to the producer of a sound recording the right to authorize or prohibit: (a) the direct or indirect reproduction of the sound recording; (b) the importation into the Party's territory of copies of the sound recording made without the producer's authorization; (c) the first public distribution of the original and each copy of the sound recording by sale, rental or otherwise; and (d) the commercial rental of the original or a copy of the sound recording, except where expressly otherwise provided in a contract between the producer of the sound recording and the authors of the works fixed therein. Each Party shall provide that putting the original or a copy of a sound recording on the market with the right holder's consent shall not exhaust the rental right.

*   *   *   *

Article 1708: Trademarks

*   *   *   *

4. Each Party shall provide a system for the registration of trademarks, which shall include: (a) examination of applications; (b) notice to be given to an applicant of the reasons for the refusal to register a trademark; (c) a reasonable

opportunity for the applicant to respond to the notice; (d) publication of each trademark either before or promptly after it is registered; and (e) a reasonable opportunity for interested persons to petition to cancel the registration of a trademark. A Party may provide for a reasonable opportunity for interested persons to oppose the registration of a trademark.

*   *   *   *

7. Each Party shall provide that the initial registration of a trademark be for a term of at least 10 years and that the registration be indefinitely renewable for terms of not less than 10 years when conditions for renewal have been met.

*   *   *   *

Article 1709: Patents

1. Subject to paragraphs 2 and 3, each Party shall make patents available for any inventions, whether products or processes, in all fields of technology, provided that such inventions are new, result from an inventive step and are capable of industrial application. For purposes of this Article, a Party may deem the terms "inventive step" and "capable of industrial application" to be synonymous with the terms "non-obvious" and "useful," respectively.

*   *   *   *

Article 1711: Trade Secrets

1. Each Party shall provide the legal means for any person to prevent trade secrets from being disclosed to, acquired by, or used by others without the consent of the person lawfully in control of the information in a manner contrary to honest commercial practices, in so far as: (a) the information is secret in the sense that it is not, as a body or in the precise configuration and assembly of its components, generally known among or readily accessible to persons that normally deal with the kind of information in question; (b) the information has actual or potential commercial value because it is secret; and (c) the person lawfully in control of the information has taken reasonable steps under the circumstances to keep it secret.

*   *   *   *

Article 1714: Enforcement of Intellectual Property Rights: General Provisions

*   *   *   *

3. Each Party shall provide that decisions on the merits of a case in judicial and administrative enforcement proceedings shall: (a) preferably be in writing and preferably state the reasons on which the decisions are based; (b) be made available at least to the parties in a proceeding without undue delay; and (c) be based only on evidence in respect of which such parties were offered the opportunity to be heard.

4. Each Party shall ensure that parties in a proceeding have an opportunity to have final administrative decisions

reviewed by a judicial authority of that Party and, subject to jurisdictional provisions in its domestic laws concerning the importance of a case, to have reviewed at least the legal aspects of initial judicial decisions on the merits of a case. Notwithstanding the above, no Party shall be required to provide for judicial review of acquittals in criminal cases.

* * * *

Article 1717: Criminal Procedures and Penalties

1. Each Party shall provide criminal procedures and penalties to be applied at least in cases of willful trademark counterfeiting or copyright piracy on a commercial scale. Each Party shall provide that penalties available include imprisonment or monetary fines, or both, sufficient to provide a deterrent, consistent with the level of penalties applied for crimes of a corresponding gravity.

2. Each Party shall provide that, in appropriate cases, its judicial authorities may order the seizure, forfeiture and destruction of infringing goods and of any materials and implements the predominant use of which has been in the commission of the offense.

Spanish Equivalents for Important Legal Terms in English

Abandoned property: bienes abandonados

Acceptance: aceptación; consentimiento; acuerdo

Acceptor: aceptante

Accession: toma de posesión; aumento; accesión

Accommodation indorser: avalista de favor

Accommodation party: firmante de favor

Accord: acuerdo; convenio; arregio

Accord and satisfaction: transacción ejecutada

Act of state doctrine: doctrina de acto de gobierno

Administrative law: derecho administrativo

Administrative process: procedimiento o metódo administrativo

Administrator: administrador (-a)

Adverse possession: posesión de hecho susceptible de proscripción adquisitiva

Affirmative action: acción afirmativa

Affirmative defense: defensa afirmativa

After-acquired property: bienes adquiridos con posterioridad a un hecho dado

Agency: mandato; agencia

Agent: mandatorio; agente; representante

Agreement: convenio; acuerdo; contrato

Alien corporation: empresa extranjera

Allonge: hojas adicionales de endosos

Answer: contestación de la demande; alegato

Anticipatory repudiation: anuncio previo de las partes de su imposibilidad de cumplir con el contrato

Appeal: apelación; recurso de apelación

Appellate jurisdiction: jurisdicción de apelaciones

Appraisal right: derecho de valuación

Arbitration: arbitraje

Arson: incendio intencional

Articles of partnership: contrato social

Artisan's lien: derecho de retención que ejerce al artesano

Assault: asalto; ataque; agresión

Assignment of rights: transmisión; transferencia; cesión

Assumption of risk: no resarcimiento por exposición voluntaria al peligro

Attachment: auto judicial que autoriza el embargo; embargo

Bailee: depositario

Bailment: depósito; constitución en depósito

Bailor: depositante

Bankruptcy trustee: síndico de la quiebra

Battery: agresión; física

Bearer: portador; tenedor

Bearer instrument: documento al portador

Bequest or legacy: legado (de bienes

muebles)

Bilateral contract: contrato bilateral

Bill of lading: conocimiento de embarque; carta de porte

Bill of Rights: declaración de derechos

Binder: póliza de seguro provisoria; recibo de pago a cuenta del precio

Blank indorsement: endoso en blanco

Blue sky laws: leyes reguladoras del comercio bursátil

Bond: título de crédito; garantía; caución

Bond indenture: contrato de emisión de bonos; contrato del ampréstito

Breach of contract: incumplimiento de contrato

Brief: escrito; resumen; informe

Burglary: violación de domicilio

Business judgment rule: regla de juicio comercial

Business tort: agravio comercial

Case law: ley de casos; derecho casuístico

Cashier's check: cheque de caja

Causation in fact: causalidad en realidad

Cease-and-desist order: orden para cesar y desistir

Certificate of deposit: certificado de depósito

Certified check: cheque certificado

Charitable trust: fideicomiso para fines benéficos

Chattel: bien mueble

Check: cheque

Chose in action: derecho inmaterial; derecho de acción

Civil law: derecho civil

Close corporation: sociedad de un solo accionista o de un grupo restringido de accionistas

Closed shop: taller agremiado (emplea solamente a miembros de un gremio)

Closing argument: argumento al final

Codicil: codicilo

Collateral: garantía; bien objeto de la guarantía real

Comity: cortesía; cortesía entre naciones

Commercial paper: instrumentos negociables; documentos a valores commerciales

Common law: derecho consuetudinario; derecho común; ley común

Common stock: acción ordinaria

Comparative negligence: negligencia comparada

Compensatory damages: daños y perjuicios reales o compensatorios

Concurrent conditions: condiciones concurrentes

Concurrent jurisdiction: competencia concurrente de varios tribunales para entender en una misma causa

Concurring opinion: opinión concurrente

Condition: condición

Condition precedent: condición suspensiva

Condition subsequent: condición resolutoria

Confiscation: confiscación

Confusion: confusión; fusión

Conglomerate merger: fusión de firmas que operan en distintos mercados

Consent decree: acuerdo entre las partes aprobado por un tribunal

Consequential damages: daños y perjuicios indirectos

Consideration: consideración; motivo; contraprestación

Consolidation: consolidación

Constructive delivery: entrega simbólica

Constructive trust: fideicomiso creado por aplicación de la ley

Consumer protection law: ley para proteger el consumidor

Contract: contrato

Contract under seal: contrato formal o sellado

Contributory negligence: negligencia de la parte actora

Conversion: usurpación; conversión de valores

Copyright: derecho de autor

Corporation: sociedad anónima; corporación; persona juridica

Co-sureties: cogarantes

Counterclaim: reconvención; contrademanda

Counteroffer: contraoferta

Course of dealing: curso de transacciones

Course of performance: curso de cumplimiento

Covenant: pacto; garantía; contrato

Covenant not to sue: pacto or contrato a no demandar

Covenant of quiet enjoyment: garantía del uso y goce pacífico del inmueble

Creditors' composition agreement: concordato preventivo

Crime: crimen; delito; contravención

Criminal law: derecho penal

Cross-examination: contrainterrogatorio

Cure: cura; cuidado; derecho de remediar un vicio contractual

Customs receipts: recibos de derechos aduaneros

Damages: daños; indemnización por daños y perjuicios

Debit card: tarjeta de dé bito

Debtor: deudor

Debt securities: seguridades de deuda

Deceptive advertising: publicidad engañosa

Deed: escritura; título; acta translativa de domino

Defamation: difamación

Delegation of duties: delegación de obligaciones

Demand deposit: depósito a la vista

Depositions: declaración de un testigo fuera del tribunal

Devise: legado; deposición testamentaria (bienes inmuebles)

Directed verdict: veredicto según orden del juez y sin participación activa del jurado

Direct examination: interrogatorio directo; primer interrogatorio

Disaffirmance: repudiación; renuncia; anulación

Discharge: descargo; liberación; cumplimiento

Disclosed principal: mandante revelado

Discovery: descubrimiento; producción de la prueba

Dissenting opinion: opinión disidente

Dissolution: disolución; terminación

Diversity of citizenship: competencia de los tribunales federales para entender en causas cuyas partes intervinientes son cuidadanos de distintos estados

Divestiture: extinción premature de derechos reales

Dividend: dividendo

Docket: orden del día; lista de causas pendientes

Domestic corporation: sociedad local

Draft: orden de pago; letrade cambio

Drawee: girado; beneficiario

Drawer: librador

Duress: coacción; violencia

Easement: servidumbre

Embezzlement: desfalco; malversación

Eminent domain: poder de expropiación

Employment discrimination: discriminación en el empleo

Entrepreneur: empresario

Environmental law: ley ambiental

Equal dignity rule: regla de dignidad egual

Equity security: tipo de participación en una sociedad

Estate: propiedad; patrimonio; derecho

Estop: impedir; prevenir

Ethical issue: cuestión ética

Exclusive jurisdiction: competencia exclusiva

Exculpatory clause: cláusula eximente

Executed contract: contrato ejecutado

Execution: ejecución; cumplimiento

Executor: albacea

Executory contract: contrato aún no completamente consumado

Executory interest: derecho futuro

Express contract: contrato expreso

Expropriation: expropriación

Federal question: caso federal

Fee simple: pleno dominio; dominio absoluto

Fee simple absolute: dominio absoluto

Fee simple defeasible: dominio sujeta a una condición resolutoria

Felony: crimen; delito grave

Fictitious payee: beneficiario ficticio

Fiduciary: fiduciario

Firm offer: oferta en firme

Fixture: inmueble por destino, incorporación a anexación

Floating lien: gravamen continuado

Foreign corporation: sociedad extranjera; U.S. sociedad constituída en otro estado

Forgery: falso; falsificación

Formal contract: contrato formal

Franchise: privilegio; franquicia; concesión

Franchisee: persona que recibe una concesión

Franchisor: persona que vende una concesión

Fraud: fraude; dolo; engaño

Future interest: bien futuro

Garnishment: embargo de derechos

General partner: socio comanditario

General warranty deed: escritura translativa de domino con garantía de título

Gift: donación

Gift *causa mortis:* donación por causa de muerte

Gift *inter vivos:* donación entre vivos

Good faith: buena fe

Good faith purchaser: comprador de buena fe

Holder: tenedor por contraprestación

Holder in due course: tenedor legítimo

Holographic will: testamento ológrafico

Homestead exemption laws: leyes que exceptúan las casas de familia de ejecución por duedas generales

Horizontal merger: fusión horizontal

Identification: identificación

Implied-in-fact contract: contrato implícito en realidad

Implied warranty: guarantía implícita

Implied warranty of merchantability: garantía implícita de vendibilidad

Impossibility of performance: imposibilidad de cumplir un contrato

Imposter: imposter

Incidental beneficiary: beneficiario incidental; beneficiario secundario

Incidental damages: daños incidentales

Indictment: auto de acusación; acusación

Indorsee: endosatario

Indorsement: endoso

Indorser: endosante

Informal contract: contrato no formal; contrato verbal

Information: acusación hecha por el ministerio público

Injunction: mandamiento; orden de no innovar

Innkeeper's lien: derecho de retención que ejerce el posadero

Installment contract: contrato de pago en cuotas

Insurable interest: interés asegurable

Intended beneficiary: beneficiario destinado

Intentional tort: agravio; cuasi-delito intenciónal

International law: derecho internaciónal

Interrogatories: preguntas escritas sometidas por una parte a la otra o a un testigo

Inter vivos trust: fideicomiso entre vivos

Intestacy laws: leyes de la condición de morir intestado

Intestate: intestado

Investment company: compañia de inversiones

Issue: emisión

Joint tenancy: derechos conjuntos en un bien inmueble en favor del beneficiario sobreviviente

Judgment *n.o.v.:* juicio no obstante veredicto

Judgment rate of interest: interés de juicio

Judicial process: acto de procedimiento; proceso jurídico

Judicial review: revisión judicial

Jurisdiction: jurisdicción

Larceny: robo; hurto

Law: derecho; ley; jurisprudencia

Lease: contrato de locación; contrato de alquiler

Leasehold estate: bienes forales

Legal rate of interest: interés legal
Legatee: legatario
Letter of credit: carta de crédito
Levy: embargo; comiso
Libel: libelo; difamación escrita
Life estate: usufructo
Limited partner: comanditario
Limited partnership: sociedad en comandita
Liquidation: liquidación; realización
Lost property: objetos perdidos

Majority opinion: opinión de la mayoría
Maker: persona que realiza u ordena; librador
Mechanic's lien: gravamen de constructor
Mediation: mediación; intervención
Merger: fusión
Mirror image rule: fallo de reflejo
Misdemeanor: infracción; contravención
Mislaid property: bienes extraviados
Mitigation of damages: reducción de daños
Mortgage: hypoteca
Motion to dismiss: excepción parentoria
Mutual fund: fondo mutual

Negotiable instrument: instrumento negociable
Negotiation: negociación
Nominal damages: daños y perjuicios nominales
Novation: novación
Nuncupative will: testamento nuncupativo

Objective theory of contracts: teoria objetiva de contratos
Offer: oferta
Offeree: persona que recibe una oferta
Offeror: oferente
Order instrument: instrumento o documento a la orden
Original jurisdiction: jurisdicción de primera instancia
Output contract: contrato de producción

Parol evidence rule: regla relativa a la prueba oral

Partially disclosed principal: mandante revelado en parte
Partnership: sociedad colectiva; asociación; asociación de participación
Past consideration: causa o contraprestación anterior
Patent: patente; privilegio
Pattern or practice: muestra o práctica
Payee: beneficiario de un pago
Penalty: pena; penalidad
Per capita: por cabeza
Perfection: perfeción
Performance: cumplimiento; ejecución
Personal defenses: excepciones personales
Personal property: bienes muebles
Per stirpes: por estirpe
Plea bargaining: regateo por un alegato
Pleadings: alegatos
Pledge: prenda
Police powers: poders de policia y de prevención del crimen
Policy: póliza
Positive law: derecho positivo; ley positiva
Possibility of reverter: posibilidad de reversión
Precedent: precedente
Preemptive right: derecho de prelación
Preferred stock: acciones preferidas
Premium: recompensa; prima
Presentment warranty: garantía de presentación
Price discrimination: discriminación en los precios
Principal: mandante; principal
Privity: nexo jurídico
Privity of contract: relación contractual
Probable cause: causa probable
Probate: verificación; verificación del testamento
Probate court: tribunal de sucesiones y tutelas
Proceeds: resultados; ingresos
Profit: beneficio; utilidad; lucro
Promise: promesa
Promisee: beneficiario de una promesa
Promisor: promtente
Promissory estoppel: impedimento

promisorio
Promissory note: pagaré; nota de pago
Promoter: promotor; fundador
Proximate cause: causa inmediata o próxima
Proxy: apoderado; poder
Punitive, or exemplary, damages: daños y perjuicios punitivos o ejemplares

Qualified indorsement: endoso con reservas
Quasi contract: contrato tácito o implícito
Quitclaim deed: acto de transferencia de una propiedad por finiquito, pero sin ninguna garantía sobre la validez del título transferido

Ratification: ratificación
Real property: bienes inmuebles
Reasonable doubt: duda razonable
Rebuttal: refutación
Recognizance: promesa; compromiso; reconocimiento
Recording statutes: leyes estatales sobre registros oficiales
Redress: reporacíon
Reformation: rectificación; reforma; corrección
Rejoinder: dúplica; contrarréplica
Release: liberación; renuncia a un derecho
Remainder: substitución; reversión
Remedy: recurso; remedio; reparación
Replevin: acción reivindicatoria; reivindicación
Reply: réplica
Requirements contract: contrato de suministro
Rescission: rescisión
Res judicata: cosa juzgada; res judicata
Respondeat superior: responsabilidad del mandante o del maestro
Restitution: restitución
Restrictive indorsement: endoso restrictivo
Resulting trust: fideicomiso implícito
Reversion: reversión; sustitución
Revocation: revocación; derogación
Right of contribution: derecho de contribución

Right of reimbursement: derecho de reembolso

Right of subrogation: derecho de subrogación

Right-to-work law: ley de libertad de trabajo

Robbery: robo

Rule 10b-5: Regla 10b-5

Sale: venta; contrato de compreventa

Sale on approval: venta a ensayo; venta sujeta a la aprobación del comprador

Sale or return: venta con derecho de devolución

Sales contract: contrato de compraventa; boleto de compraventa

Satisfaction: satisfacción; pago

Scienter: a sabiendas

S corporation: S corporación

Secured party: acreedor garantizado

Secured transaction: transacción garantizada

Securities: volares; titulos; seguridades

Security agreement: convenio de seguridad

Security interest: interés en un bien dado en garantía que permite a quien lo detenta venderlo en caso de incumplimiento

Service mark: marca de identificación de servicios

Shareholder's derivative suit: acción judicial entablada por un accionista en nombre de la sociedad

Signature: firma; rúbrica

Slander: difamación oral; calumnia

Sovereign immunity: immunidad soberana

Special indorsement: endoso especial; endoso a la orden de una person en particular

Specific performance: ejecución precisa, según los términos del contrato

Spendthrift trust: fideicomiso para pródigos

Stale check: cheque vencido

Stare decisis: acatar las decisiones, observar los precedentes

Statutory law: derecho estatutario; derecho legislado; derecho escrito

Stock: acciones

Stock warrant: certificado para la compra de acciones

Stop-payment order: orden de suspensión del pago de un cheque dada por el librador del mismo

Strict liability: responsabilidad unconditional

Summary judgment: fallo sumario

Tangible property: bienes corpóreos

Tenancy at will: inguilino por tiempo indeterminado (según la voluntad del propietario)

Tenancy by sufferance: posesión por tolerancia

Tenancy by the entirety: locación conyugal conjunta

Tenancy for years: inguilino por un término fijo

Tenancy in common: specie de copropiedad indivisa

Tender: oferta de pago; oferta de ejecución

Testamentary trust: fideicomiso testamentario

Testator: testador (-a)

Third party beneficiary contract: contrato para el beneficio del tercero-beneficiario

Tort: agravio; cuasi-delito

Totten trust: fideicomiso creado por un depósito bancario

Trade acceptance: letra de cambio aceptada

Trademark: marca registrada

Trade name: nombre comercial; razón social

Traveler's check: cheque del viajero

Trespass to land: ingreso no authorizado a las tierras de otro

Trespass to personal property: violación de los derechos posesorios de un tercero con respecto a bienes muebles

Trust: fideicomiso; trust

Ultra vires: ultra vires; fuera de la facultad (de una sociedad anónima)

Unanimous opinion: opinión unámine

Unconscionable contract or clause: contrato leonino; cláusula leonino

Underwriter: subscriptor; asegurador

Unenforceable contract: contrato que no se puede hacer cumplir

Unilateral contract: contrato unilateral

Union shop: taller agremiado; empresa en la que todos los empleados son miembros del gremio o sindicato

Universal defenses: defensas legitimas o legales

Usage of trade: uso comercial

Usury: usura

Valid contract: contrato válido

Venue: lugar; sede del proceso

Vertical merger: fusión vertical de empresas

Voidable contract: contrato anulable

Void contract: contrato nulo; contrato inválido, sin fuerza legal

Voir dire: examen preliminar de un testigo a jurado por el tribunal para determinar su competencia

Voting trust: fideicomiso para ejercer el derecho de voto

Waiver: renuncia; abandono

Warranty of habitability: garantía de habitabilidad

Watered stock: acciones diluídos; capital inflado

White-collar crime: crimen administrativo

Writ of attachment: mandamiento de ejecución; mandamiento de embargo

Writ of *certiorari*: auto de avocación; auto de certiorari

Writ of execution: auto ejecutivo; mandamiento de ejecutión

Writ of mandamus: auto de mandamus; mandamiento; orden judicial

GLOSSARY

A

Abandoned property   Property with which the owner has voluntarily parted, with no intention of recovering it.

Abandonment   In landlord-tenant law, a tenant's departure from leased premises completely, with no intention of returning before the end of the lease term.

Abatement   A process by which legatees receive reduced benefits if the assets of an estate are insufficient to pay in full all general bequests provided for in the will.

Abus de droit   A doctrine developed in the French courts. The doctrine modified employment at will and protected workers exercising their rights from wrongful discharge and other employer abuses.

Acceleration clause   A clause in an installment contract that provides for all future payments to become due immediately on the failure to tender timely payments or on the occurrence of a specified event.

Acceptance   (1) In contract law, the offeree's notification to the offeror that the offeree agrees to be bound by the terms of the offeror's proposal. Although historically the terms of acceptance had to be the mirror image of the terms of the offer, the Uniform Commercial Code provides that even modified terms of the offer in a definite expression of acceptance constitute a contract. (2) In negotiable instruments law, the drawee's signed agreement to pay a draft when presented.

Acceptor   The person (the drawee) who accepts a draft and who agrees to be primarily responsible for its payment.

Accession   Occurs when an individual adds value to personal property by either labor or materials. In some situations, a person may acquire ownership rights in another's property through accession.

Accommodation party   A person who signs an instrument for the purpose of lending his or her name as credit to another party on the instrument.

Accord and satisfaction   An agreement for payment (or other performance) between two parties, one of whom has a right of action against the other. After the payment has been accepted or other performance has been made, the "accord and satisfaction" is complete and the obligation is discharged.

Accredited investors   In the context of securities offerings, "sophisticated" investors, such as banks, insurance companies, investment companies, the issuer's executive officers and directors, and persons whose income or net worth exceeds certain limits.

Acquittal   A certification or declaration following a trial that the individual accused of a crime is innocent, or free from guilt, and is thus absolved of the charges.

Act of state doctrine   A doctrine that provides that the judicial branch of one country will not examine the validity of public acts committed by a recognized foreign government within its own territory.

Actionable   Capable of serving as the basis of a lawsuit.

Actual authority   Authority of an agent that is express or implied.

Actual malice   Real and demonstrable evil intent. In a defamation suit, a statement made about a public figure normally must be made with actual malice (with either knowledge of its falsity or a reckless disregard of the truth) for liability to be incurred.

Actus reus   (pronounced *ak*-tus *ray*-uhs)   A guilty (prohibited) act. The commission of a prohibited act is one of the two essential elements required for criminal liability, the other element being the intent to commit a crime.

Adequate protection doctrine   In bankruptcy law, a doctrine that protects secured creditors from losing their security as a result of an automatic stay on legal proceedings by creditors against the debtor once the debtor petitions for bankruptcy relief. In certain circumstances, the bankruptcy court may provide adequate protection by requiring the debtor or trustee to pay the creditor or provide additional guaranties to protect the creditor against the losses suffered by the creditor as a result of the stay.

Adhesion contract   A "standard-form" contract, such as that between a large retailer and a consumer, in which the stronger party dictates the terms.

Adjudicate   To render a judicial decision. In the administrative process, the proceeding in which an administrative law judge hears and decides on issues that arise when an administrative agency charges a person or a firm with violating a law or regulation enforced by the agency.

Adjudication   The process of adjudicating. *See* Adjudicate

Administrative agency   A federal or state government agency established to perform a specific function. Administrative agencies are authorized by legislative acts to make and enforce rules to administer and enforce the acts.

Administrative law   The body of law created by administrative agencies (in the form of rules, regulations, orders, and decisions) in order to carry out their duties and responsibilities.

Administrative law judge (ALJ)   One who presides over an administrative agency hearing and who has the power to administer oaths, take testimony, rule on questions of evidence, and make determinations of fact.

Administrative process   The procedure used by administrative agencies in the administration of law.

Administrator One who is appointed by a court to handle the probate (disposition) of a person's estate if that person dies intestate (without a valid will) or if the executor named in the will cannot serve.

Adverse possession The acquisition of title to real property by occupying it openly, without the consent of the owner, for a period of time specified by a state statute. The occupation must be actual, open, notorious, exclusive, and in opposition to all others, including the owner.

Affidavit A written or printed voluntary statement of facts, confirmed by the oath or affirmation of the party making it and made before a person having the authority to administer the oath or affirmation.

Affirm To validate; to give legal force to. *See also* Ratification

Affirmative action Job-hiring policies that give special consideration to members of protected classes in an effort to overcome present effects of past discrimination.

Affirmative defense A response to a plaintiff's claim that does not deny the plaintiff's facts but attacks the plaintiff's legal right to bring an action. An example is the running of the statute of limitations.

After-acquired evidence A type of evidence submitted in support of an affirmative defense in employment discrimination cases. Evidence that, prior to the employer's discriminatory act, the employee engaged in misconduct sufficient to warrant dismissal had the employer known of it earlier.

After-acquired property Property of the debtor that is acquired after the execution of a security agreement.

Age of majority The age at which an individual is considered legally capable of conducting himself or herself responsibly. A person of this age is entitled to the full rights of citizenship, including the right to vote in elections. In contract law, one who is no longer an infant and can no longer disaffirm a contract.

Agency A relationship between two parties in which one party (the agent) agrees to represent or act for the other (the principal).

Agency by estoppel Arises when a principal negligently allows an agent to exercise powers not granted to the agent, thus justifying others in believing that the agent possesses the requisite agency authority. *See also* Promissory estoppel

Agent A person who agrees to represent or act for another, called the principal.

Aggressor The acquiring corporation in a takeover attempt.

Agreement A meeting of two or more minds in regard to the terms of a contract; usually broken down into two events—an offer by one party to form a contract, and an acceptance of the offer by the person to whom the offer is made.

Alien corporation A designation in the United States for a corporation formed in another country but doing business in the United States.

Alienation In real property law, the voluntary transfer of property from one person to another (as opposed to a transfer by operation of law).

Allegation A statement, claim, or assertion.

Allege To state, recite, assert, or charge.

Allonge (pronounced uh-*lohnj*) A piece of paper firmly attached to a negotiable instrument, on which transferees can make indorsements if there is no room left on the instrument itself.

Alteration In the context of leaseholds, an improvement or change made that materially affects the condition of the property. Thus, for example, erecting an additional structure probably would (and painting interior walls would not) be considered making an alteration.

Alternative dispute resolution (ADR) The resolution of disputes in ways other than those involved in the traditional judicial process. Negotiation, mediation, and arbitration are forms of ADR.

Amend To change and improve through a formal procedure.

American Arbitration Association (AAA) The major organization offering arbitration services in the United States.

Analogy In logical reasoning, an assumption that if two things are similar in some respects, they will be similar in other respects also. Often used in legal reasoning to infer the appropriate application of legal principles in a case being decided by referring to previous cases involving different facts but considered to come within the policy underlying the rule.

Annuity An insurance policy that pays the insured fixed, periodic payments for life or for a term of years, as stipulated in the policy, after the insured reaches a specified age.

Annul To cancel; to make void.

Answer Procedurally, a defendant's response to the plaintiff's complaint.

Antecedent claim A preexisting claim. In negotiable instruments law, taking an instrument in satisfaction of an antecedent claim is taking the instrument for value — that is, for valid consideration.

Anticipatory repudiation An assertion or action by a party indicating that he or she will not perform an obligation that the party is contractually obligated to perform at a future time.

Antitrust law The body of federal and state laws and statutes protecting trade and commerce from unlawful restraints, price discrimination, price fixing, and monopolies. The principal federal antitrust statues are the Sherman Act of 1890, the Clayton Act of 1914, and the Federal Trade Commission Act of 1914.

Apparent authority Authority that is only apparent, not real. In agency law, a person may be deemed to have had the power to act as an agent for another party if the other party's manifestations to a third party led the third party to believe that an agency existed when, in fact, it did not.

Appeal Resort to a superior court, such as an appellate court, to review the decision of an inferior court, such as a trial court or an administrative agency.

Appellant The party who takes an appeal from one court to another.

Appellate court A court having appellate jurisdiction. Each state court system has at least one level of appellate courts. In the federal court system, the appellate courts are the circuit courts of appeals (intermediate appellate courts) and the United States Supreme Court (the highest appellate court in the federal system).

Appellate jurisdiction Courts having appellate jurisdiction act as reviewing courts, or appellate courts. Generally, cases can be brought before appellate courts only on appeal from an order or a judgment of a trial court or other lower court.

Appellee The party against whom an appeal is taken—that is, the party who opposes setting aside or reversing the judgment.

Appraisal right The right of a dissenting shareholder, if he or she objects to an extraordinary transaction of the corporation (such as a merger or consolidation), to have his or her shares appraised and to be paid the fair value of his or her shares by the corporation.

Appropriation In tort law, the use by one person of another person's name, likeness, or other identifying characteristic without permission and for the benefit of the user.

Arbitrary and capricious test The court reviewing an informal administrative agency action applies this test to determine whether or not that action was in clear error. The court gives wide discretion to the expertise of the agency and decides if the agency had sufficient factual information on which to base its action. If no clear error was made, then the agency's action stands.

Arbitration The settling of a dispute by submitting it to a disinterested third party (other than a court), who renders a decision. The decision may or may not be legally binding.

Arbitration clause A clause in a contract that provides that, in the event of a dispute, the parties will submit the dispute to arbitration rather than litigate the dispute in court.

Arraignment A procedure in which an accused person is brought before the court to plead to the criminal charge in the indictment or information. The charge is read to the person, and he or she is asked to enter a plea—such as "guilty" or "not guilty."

Arson The malicious burning of another's dwelling. Some statutes have expanded this to include any real property regardless of ownership and the destruction of property by other means—for example, by explosion.

Articles of incorporation The document filed with the appropriate governmental agency, usually the secretary of state, when a business is incorporated; state statutes usually prescribe what kind of information must be contained in the articles of incorporation.

Articles of organization The document filed with a designated state official by which a limited liability company is formed.

Articles of partnership A written agreement that sets forth each partner's rights and obligations with respect to the partnership.

Artisan's lien A possessory lien given to a person who has made improvements and added value to another person's personal property as security for payment for services performed.

Assault Any word or action intended to make another person fearful of immediate physical harm; a reasonably believable threat.

Assignee The person to whom contract rights are assigned.

Assignment The act of transferring to another all or part of one's rights arising under a contract.

Assignor The person who assigns contract rights.

Assumption of risk A defense against negligence that can be used when the plaintiff is aware of a danger and voluntarily assumes the risk of injury from that danger.

Attachment (1) In the context of secured transactions, the process by which a security interest in the property of another becomes enforceable. (2) In the context of judicial liens, a court-ordered seizure and taking into custody of property prior to the securing of a judgment for a past-due debt.

Attempted monopolization Any actions by a firm to eliminate competition and gain monopoly power.

Attractive nuisance doctrine A common law doctrine under which a landowner or landlord may be held liable for injuries incurred by children who are lured onto the property by something dangerous and enticing thereon.

Authority In agency law, the agent's permission to act on behalf of the principal. An agent's authority may be actual (express or implied) or apparent. *See also* Actual authority; Apparent authority

Authorized means In contract law, the means of acceptance authorized by the offeror.

Automatic stay In bankruptcy proceedings, the suspension of virtually all litigation and other action by creditors against the debtor or the debtor's property; the stay is effective the moment the debtor files a petition in bankruptcy.

Award In the context of litigation, the amount of money awarded to a plaintiff in a civil lawsuit as damages. In the context of arbitration, the arbitrator's decision.

B

Bail An amount of money set by the court that must be paid by a criminal defendant to the court before the defendant will be released from custody. Bail is set to assure that an individual accused of a crime will appear for further criminal proceedings. If the accused provides bail, whether in cash or in a surety bond, then he or she is released from jail.

Bailee One to whom goods are entrusted by a bailor. Under the Uniform Commercial Code, a party who, by a bill of lading, warehouse receipt, or other document of title, acknowledges possession of goods and contracts.

Bailee's lien A possessory lien, or claim, that a bailee entitled to compensation can place on the bailed property to ensure that he or she will be paid for the services provided. The lien is effective as long as the bailee retains possession of the bailed goods and has not agreed to extend credit to the bailor. Sometimes referred to as an artisan's lien.

Bailment A situation in which the personal property of one person (a bailor) is entrusted to another (a bailee), who is obligated to return the bailed property to the bailor or dispose of it as directed.

Bailor One who entrusts goods to a bailee.

Bait-and-switch advertising Advertising a product at a very attractive price (the "bait") and then informing the consumer, once he or she is in the store, that the advertised product is either not available or is of poor quality; the customer is then urged to purchase ("switched" to) a more expensive item.

Banker's acceptance A negotiable instrument that is commonly used in international trade. A banker's acceptance is drawn by a creditor against the debtor, who pays the draft at maturity. The drawer creates a draft without designating a payee. The draft can pass through many parties' hands before a bank (drawee) accepts it, transforming the draft into a banker's acceptance. Acceptances can be purchased and sold in a way similar to securities.

Bankruptcy court A federal court of limited jurisdiction that handles only bankruptcy proceedings. Bankruptcy proceedings are governed by federal bankruptcy law.

Bargain A mutual undertaking, contract, or agreement between two parties; to negotiate over the terms of a purchase or contract.

Basis of the bargain In contract law, the affirmation of fact or promise on which the sale of goods is predicated, creating an express warranty.

Battery The unprivileged, intentional touching of another.

Beachhead acquistion The gradual accumulation of a bloc of a target corporation's shares by an aggressor during an attempt to obtain control of the corporation.

Bearer A person in the possession of an instrument payable to bearer or indorsed in blank.

Bearer instrument Any instrument that is not payable to a specific person, including instruments payable to the bearer or to "cash."

Beneficiary One to whom life insurance proceeds are payable or for whose benefit a trust has been established or property under a will has been transferred.

Bequest A gift by will of personal property (from the verb—to bequeath).

Beyond a reasonable doubt The standard used to determine the guilt or innocence of a person criminally charged. To be guilty of a crime, one must be proved guilty "beyond and to the exclusion of every reasonable doubt." A reasonable doubt is one that would cause a prudent person to hesitate before acting in matters important to him or her.

Bilateral contract A type of contract that arises when a promise is given in exchange for a return promise.

Bill of lading A document that serves both as evidence of the receipt of goods for shipment and as documentary evidence of title to the goods.

Bill of Rights The first ten amendments to the U.S. Constitution.

Binder A written, temporary insurance policy.

Binding authority Any source of law that a court must follow when deciding a case. Binding authorities include constitutions, statutes, and regulations that govern the issue being decided, as well as court decisions that are controlling precedents within the jurisdiction.

Blank indorsement An indorsement that specifies no particular indorsee and that can consist of a mere signature. An order instrument that is indorsed in blank becomes a bearer instrument.

Blue laws State or local laws that prohibit the performance of certain types of commercial activities on Sunday.

Blue sky laws State laws that regulate the offer and sale of securities.

Bona fide Good faith. A bona fide obligation is one made in good faith—that is, sincerely and honestly.

Bona fide occupational qualification (BFOQ) Identifiable characteristics reasonably necessary to the normal operation of a particular business. These characteristics can include gender, national origin, and religion, but not race.

Bond A certificate that evidences a corporate (or government) debt. It is a security that involves no ownership interest in the issuing entity.

Bond indenture A contract between the issuer of a bond and the bondholder.

Bounty payment A reward (payment) given to a person or persons who perform a certain service—such as informing legal authorities of illegal actions.

Boycott A concerted refusal to do business with a particular person or entity in order to obtain concessions or to express displeasure with certain acts or practices of that person or business. *See also* Secondary boycott

Breach To violate a law, by an act or an omission, or to break a legal obligation that one owes to another person or to society.

Breach of contract The failure, without legal excuse, of a promisor to perform the obligations of a contract.

Bribery The offering, giving, receiving, or soliciting of anything of value with the aim of influencing an official action or an official's discharge of a legal or public duty or (with respect to commercial bribery) a business decision.

Brief A formal legal document submitted by the attorney for the appellant—or the appellee (in answer to the appellant's brief)—to an appellate court when a case is appealed. The appellant's brief outlines the facts and issues of the case, the judge's rulings or jury's findings that should be reversed or modified, the applicable law, and the arguments on the client's behalf.

Bulk transfer A bulk sale or transfer, not made in the ordinary course of business, of a major part of the materials, supplies, merchandise, or other inventory of an enterprise.

Bureaucracy A large organization that is structured hierarchically to carry out specific functions.

Burglary The unlawful entry into a building with the intent to commit a felony. (Some state statutes expand this to include the intent to commit any crime.)

Business ethics Ethics in a business context; a consensus of what constitutes right or wrong behavior in the world of business and the application of moral principles to situations that arise in a business setting.

Business invitees Those people, such as customers or clients, who are invited onto business premises by the owner of those premises for business purposes.

Business judgment rule A rule that immunizes corporate management from liability for actions that result in corporate losses or damages if the actions are undertaken in good faith and are within both the power of the corporation and the authority of management to make.

Business necessity A defense to allegations of employment discrimination in which the employer demonstrates that an employment practice that discriminates against members of a protected class is related to job performance.

Business plan A document describing a company, its products, and its anticipated future performance. Creating a business plan is normally the first step in obtaining loans or venture-capital funds for a new business enterprise.

Business tort The wrongful interference with the business rights of another.

Business trust A voluntary form of business organization in which investors (trust beneficiaries) transfer cash or property to trustees in exchange for trust certificates that represent their investment shares. Management of the business and trust property is handled by the trustees for the use and benefit of the investors. The certificate holders have limited liability (are not responsible for the debts and obligations incurred by the trust) and share in the trust's profits.

Buyer in the ordinary course of business A buyer who, in good faith and without knowledge that the sale to him or her is in violation of the ownership rights or security interest of a third party in the goods, purchases goods in the ordinary course of business from a person in the business of selling goods of that kind.

Buy-sell agreement In the context of partnerships, an express agreement made at the time of partnership formation for one or more of the partners to buy out the other or others should the situation warrant—and thus provide for the smooth dissolution of the partnership.

Bylaws A set of governing rules adopted by a corporation or other association.

Bystander A spectator, witness, or person standing nearby when an event occurred and who did not engage in the business or act leading to the event.

C

C.I.F. or C.&F. Cost, insurance, and freight—or just cost and freight. A pricing term in a contract for the sale of goods requiring, among other things, that the seller place the goods in the possession of a carrier before risk passes to the buyer.

C.O.D. Cash on delivery. In sales transactions, a term meaning that the buyer will pay for the goods on delivery and before inspecting the goods.

Callable bond A bond that may be called in and the principal repaid at specified times or under conditions specified in the bond when it is issued.

Cancellation The act of nullifying, or making void. *See also* Rescission

Capital Accumulated goods, possessions, and assets used for the production of profits and wealth; the equity of owners in a business.

Carrier An individual or organization engaged in transporting passengers or goods for hire. *See also* Common carrier

Case law The rules of law announced in court decisions. Case law includes the aggregate of reported cases that interpret judicial precedents, statutes, regulations, and constitutional provisions.

Case on point A previous case involving factual circumstances and issues that are similar to the case before the court.

Cash surrender value The amount that the insurer has agreed to pay to the insured if a life insurance policy is canceled before the insured's death.

Cashier's check A check drawn by a bank on itself.

Categorical imperative A concept developed by the philosopher Immanuel Kant as an ethical guideline for behavior. In deciding whether an action is right or wrong, or desirable or undesirable, a person should evaluate the action in terms of what would happen if everybody else in the same situation, or category, acted the same way.

Causation in fact An act or omission without ("but for") which an event would not have occurred.

Cause of action A situation or state of facts that would entitle a party to sustain a legal action and give the party a right to seek a judicial remedy.

Cease-and-desist order An administrative or judicial order prohibiting a person or business firm from conducting activities that an agency or court has deemed illegal.

Certificate of deposit (CD) A note of a bank in which a bank acknowledges a receipt of money from a party and promises to repay the money, with interest, to the party on a certain date.

Certificate of incorporation The primary document that evidences corporate existence (referred to as articles of incorporation in some states).

Certificate of limited partnership The basic document filed with a designated state official by which a limited partnership is formed.

Certification In negotiable instruments law, the act of certifying a check. *See* Certified check

Certification mark A mark used by one or more persons, other than the owner, to certify the region, materials, mode of manufacture, quality, or accuracy of the owner's goods or services. When used by members of a cooperative, association, or other organization, such a mark is referred to as a collective mark. Examples of certification marks include the "Good Housekeeping Seal of Approval" and "UL Tested."

Certified check A check that has been accepted by the bank on which it is drawn. Essentially, the bank, by certifying (accepting) the check, promises to pay the check at the time the check is presented.

Certiorari *See* Writ of *certiorari*

Chain-style business franchise A franchise that operates under a franchisor's trade name and that is identified as a member of a select group of dealers that engage in the franchisor's business. The franchisee is generally required to follow standardized or prescribed methods of operation. Examples of this type of franchise are McDonald's and most other fast-food chains.

Chancellor An adviser to the king at the time of the early king's courts of England. Individuals petitioned the king for relief when they could not obtain an adequate remedy in a court of law, and these petitions were decided by the chancellor.

Charging order In partnership law, an order granted by a court to a judgment creditor that entitles the creditor to attach profits or assets of a partner on dissolution of the partnership.

Charitable trust A trust in which the property held by a trustee must be used for a charitable purpose, such as the advancement of health, education, or religion.

Charter *See* Corporate charter

Chattel All forms of personal property.

Chattel paper Any writing or writings that show both a debt and the fact that the debt is secured by personal property. In many instances, chattel paper consists of a negotiable instrument coupled with a security agreement.

Check A draft drawn by a drawer ordering the drawee bank or financial institution to pay a certain amount of money to the holder on demand.

Checks and balances The national government is composed of three separate branches: the executive, the legislative, and the judicial branches. Each branch of the government exercises a check on the actions of the others.

Choice-of-language clause A clause in a contract designating the official language by which the contract will be interpreted in the event of a future disagreement over the contract's terms.

Choice-of-law clause A clause in a contract designating the law (such as the law of a particular state or nation) that will govern the contract.

Citation A reference to a publication in which a legal authority—such as a statute or a court decision—or other source can be found.

Civil law The branch of law dealing with the definition and enforcement of all private or public rights, as opposed to criminal matters.

Civil law system A system of law derived from that of the Roman Empire and based on a code rather than case law; the predominant system of law in the nations of continental Europe and the nations that were once their colonies. In the United States, Louisiana is the only state that has a civil law system.

Claim As a verb, to assert or demand. As a noun, a right to payment.

Clearinghouse A system or place where banks exchange checks and drafts drawn on each other and settle daily balances.

Close corporation A corporation whose shareholders are limited to a small group of persons, often including only family members. The rights of shareholders of a close corporation usually are restricted regarding transfer of shares to others.

Closed shop A firm that requires union membership by its workers as a condition of employment. The closed shop was made illegal by the Labor-Management Relations Act of 1947.

Closing The final step in the sale of real estate—also called settlement or closing escrow. The escrow agent coordinates the closing with the recording of deeds, the obtaining of title insurance, and other concurrent closing activities. A number of costs must be paid, in cash, at the time of closing, and they can range from several hundred to several thousand dollars, depending on the amount of the mortgage loan and other conditions of the sale.

Closing argument An argument made after the plaintiff and defendant have rested their cases. Closing arguments are made prior to the jury charges.

Codicil A written supplement or modification to a will. A codicil must be executed with the same formalities as a will.

Collateral Under Article 9 of the Uniform Commercial Code, the property subject to a security interest, including accounts and chattel paper that have been sold.

Collateral promise A secondary promise that is ancillary (subsidiary) to a principal transaction or primary contractual relationship, such as a promise made by one person to pay the debts of another if the latter fails to perform. A collateral promise normally must be in writing to be enforceable.

Collecting bank Any bank handling an item for collection, except the payor bank.

Collective bargaining The process by which labor and management negotiate the terms and conditions of employment, including working hours and workplace conditions.

Collective mark A mark used by members of a cooperative, association, or other organization to certify the region, materials, mode of manufacture, quality, or accuracy of the specific goods or services. Examples of collective marks include the labor union marks found on tags of certain products and the credits of movies, which indicate the various associations and organizations that participated in the making of the movies.

Comity A deference by which one nation gives effect to the laws and judicial decrees of another nation. This recognition is based primarily on respect.

Comment period A period of time following an administrative agency's publication or a notice of a proposed rule during which private parties may comment in writing on the agency proposal in an effort to influence agency policy. The agency takes any comments received into consideration when drafting the final version of the regulation.

Commerce clause The provision in Article I, Section 8, of the U.S. Constitution that gives Congress the power to regulate interstate commerce.

Commercial impracticability A doctrine under which a seller may be excused from performing a contract when (1) a contingency occurs, (2) the contingency's occurrence makes performance impracticable, and (3) the nonoccurrence of the contingency was a basic assumption on which the contract was made. Despite the fact that UCC 2–615 expressly frees only sellers under this doctrine, courts have not distinguished between buyers and sellers in applying it.

Commercial paper *See* Negotiable instrument

Commingle To mix together. To put funds or goods together into one mass so that the funds or goods are so mixed that they no longer have separate identities. In corporate law, if personal and corporate interests are commingled to the extent that the corporation has no separate identity, a court may "pierce the corporate veil" and expose the shareholders to personal liability.

Common area In landlord-tenant law, a portion of the premises over which the landlord retains control and maintenance responsibilities. Common areas may include stairs, lobbies, garages, hallways, and other areas in common use.

Common carrier A carrier that holds itself out or undertakes to carry persons or goods of all persons indifferently, or of all who choose to employ it.

Common law That body of law developed from custom or judicial decisions in English and U.S. courts, not attributable to a legislature.

Common stock Shares of ownership in a corporation that give the owner of the stock a proportionate interest in the corporation with regard to control, earnings, and net assets; shares of common stock are lowest in priority with respect to payment of dividends and distribution of the corporation's assets on dissolution.

Community property A form of concurrent ownership of property in which each spouse technically owns an undivided one-half interest in property acquired during the marriage. This form of joint ownership occurs in only nine states and Puerto Rico.

Comparative law The study and comparison of legal systems and laws across nations.

Comparative negligence A theory in tort law under which the liability for injuries resulting from negligent acts is shared by all parties who were negligent (including the injured party), on the basis of each person's proportionate negligence.

Compensatory damages A money award equivalent to the actual value of injuries or damages sustained by the aggrieved party.

Complaint The pleading made by a plaintiff alleging wrongdoing on the part of the defendant; the document that, when filed with a court, initiates a lawsuit.

Complete performance Performance of a contract strictly in accordance with the contract's terms.

Composition agreement *See* Creditors' composition agreement

Computer crime Any wrongful act that is directed against computers and computer parties, or wrongful use or abuse of computers or software.

Concentrated industry An industry in which a large percentage of market sales is controlled by either a single firm or a small number of firms.

Conciliation A form of alternative dispute resolution in which the parties reach an agreement themselves with the help of a neutral third party, called a conciliator, who facilitates the negotiations.

Concurrent conditions Conditions in a contract that must occur or be performed at the same time; they are mutually dependent. No obligations arise until these conditions are simultaneously performed.

Concurrent jurisdiction Jurisdiction that exists when two different courts have the power to hear a case. For example, some cases can be heard in either a federal or a state court.

Concurrent ownership Joint ownership.

Concurring opinion A written opinion outlining the views of a judge or justice to make or emphasize a point that was not made or emphasized in the majority opinion.

Condition A qualification, provision, or clause in a contractual agreement, the occurrence of which creates, suspends, or terminates the obligations of the contracting parties.

Condition precedent A condition in a contract that must be met before a party's promise becomes absolute.

Condition subsequent A condition in a contract that operates to terminate a party's absolute promise to perform.

Conditional contract A contract subject to a condition that must be met for the contract to be enforceable. *See* Condition precedent

Confession of judgment The act of a debtor in permitting a judgment to be entered against him or her by a creditor, for an agreed sum, without the institution of legal proceedings.

Confiscation A government's taking of privately owned business or personal property without a proper public purpose or an award of just compensation.

Conforming goods Goods that conform to contract specifications.

Confusion The mixing together of goods belonging to two or more owners so that the separately owned goods cannot be identified.

Conglomerate merger A merger between firms that do not compete with each other because they are in different markets (as opposed to horizontal and vertical mergers).

Consent Voluntary agreement to a proposition or an act of another. A concurrence of wills.

Consequential damages   Special damages that compensate for a loss that is not direct or immediate (for example, lost profits). The special damages must have been reasonably foreseeable at the time the breach or injury occurred in order for the plaintiff to collect them.

Consideration   Generally, the value given in return for a promise. The consideration, which must be present to make the contract legally binding, must be something of legally sufficient value and bargained for and must result in a detriment to the promisee or a benefit to the promisor.

Consignee   One to whom goods are delivered on consignment. *See also* Consignment

Consignment   A transaction in which an owner of goods (the consignor) delivers the goods to another (the consignee) for the consignee to sell. The consignee pays the consignor for the goods when they are sold by the consignee.

Consignor   One who consigns goods to another. *See also* Consignment

Consolidation   A contractual and statutory process in which two or more corporations join to become a completely new corporation. The original corporations cease to exist, and the new corporation acquires all their assets and liabilities.

Constitutional law   Law that is based on the U.S. Constitution and the constitutions of the various states.

Constructive condition   A condition in a contract that is neither expressed nor implied by the contract but rather is imposed by law for reasons of justice.

Constructive delivery   An act equivalent to the actual, physical delivery of property that cannot be physically delivered because of difficulty or impossibility; for example, the transfer of a key to a safe constructively delivers the contents of the safe.

Constructive eviction   A form of eviction that occurs when a landlord fails to perform adequately any of the undertakings (such as providing heat in the winter) required by the lease, thereby making the tenant's further use and enjoyment of the property exceedingly difficult or impossible.

Constructive trust   An equitable trust that is imposed in the interests of fairness and justice when someone wrongfully holds legal title to property. A court may require the owner to hold the property in trust for the person or persons who rightfully should own the property.

Consumer credit   Credit extended primarily for personal or household use.

Consumer-debtor   An individual whose debts are primarily consumer debts (debts for purchases made primarily for personal or household use).

Consumer goods   Goods that are primarily for personal or household use.

Consumer law   The body of statutes, agency rules, and judicial decisions protecting consumers of goods and services from dangerous manufacturing techniques, mislabeling, unfair credit practices, deceptive advertising, and so on. Consumer laws provide remedies and protec-

tions that are not ordinarily available to merchants or to businesses.

Contingency fee   An attorney's fee that is based on a percentage of the final award received by his or her client as a result of litigation.

Continuation statement   A statement that, if filed within six months prior to the expiration date of the original financing statement, continues the perfection of the original security interest for another five years. The perfection of a security interest can be continued in the same manner indefinitely.

Contract   An agreement that can be enforced in court; formed by two or more parties, each of whom agrees to perform or to refrain from performing some act now or in the future.

Contract implied in law   *See* Quasi contract

Contract under seal   A formal agreement in which the seal is a substitute for consideration. A court will not invalidate a contract under seal for lack of consideration.

Contractual agreement   *See* Contract

Contractual capacity   The threshold mental capacity required by the law for a party who enters into a contract to be bound by that contract.

Contribution   *See* Right of contribution

Contributory negligence   A theory in tort law under which a complaining party's own negligence contributed to or caused his or her injuries. Contributory negligence is an absolute bar to recovery in a minority of jurisdictions.

Conversion   The wrongful taking, using, or retaining possession of personal property that belongs to another.

Convertible bond   A bond that can be exchanged for a specified number of shares of common stock under certain conditions.

Conveyance   The transfer of a title to land from one person to another by deed; a document (such as a deed) by which an interest in land is transferred from one person to another.

Conviction   The outcome of a criminal trial in which the defendant has been found guilty of the crime with which he or she was charged and on which sentencing, or punishment, is based.

Cooperative   An association that is organized to provide an economic service to its members (or shareholders). An incorporated cooperative is a nonprofit corporation. It will make distributions of dividends, or profits, to its owners on the basis of their transactions with the cooperative rather than on the basis of the amount of capital they contributed. Examples of cooperatives are consumer purchasing cooperatives, credit cooperatives, and farmers' cooperatives.

Co-ownership   Joint ownership.

Copyright   The exclusive right of authors to publish, print, or sell an intellectual production for a statutory period of time. A copyright has the same monopolistic nature as a patent or trademark, but it differs in that it applies exclusively to works of art, literature, and other works of authorship, including computer programs.

Corporate charter The document issued by a state agency or authority (usually the secretary of state) that grants a corporation legal existence and the right to function.

Corporate social responsibility The concept that corporations can and should act ethically and be accountable to society for their actions.

Corporation A legal entity formed in compliance with statutory requirements. The entity is distinct from its shareholders-owners.

Cosign The act of signing a document (such as a note promising to pay another in return for a loan or other benefit) jointly with another person and thereby assuming liability for performing what was promised in the document.

Cost-benefit analysis A decision-making technique that involves weighing the costs of a given action against the benefits of the action.

Co-surety A joint surety. One who assumes liability jointly with another surety for the payment of an obligation.

Counteradvertising New advertising that is undertaken pursuant to a Federal Trade Commission order for the purpose of correcting earlier false claims that were made about a product.

Counterclaim A claim made by a defendant in a civil lawsuit that in effect sues the plaintiff.

Counteroffer An offeree's response to an offer in which the offeree rejects the original offer and at the same time makes a new offer.

Course of dealing Prior conduct between parties to a contract that establishes a common basis for their understanding.

Course of performance The conduct that occurs under the terms of a particular agreement; such conduct indicates what the parties to an agreement intended it to mean.

Court of equity A court that decides controversies and administers justice according to the rules, principles, and precedents of equity.

Court of law A court in which the only remedies that could be granted were things of value, such as money damages. In the early English king's courts, courts of law were distinct from courts of equity.

Covenant against encumbrances A grantor's assurance that on land conveyed there are no encumbrances—that is, that no third parties have rights to or interests in the land that would diminish its value to the grantee.

Covenant not to compete A contractual promise to refrain from competing with another party for a certain period of time (not excessive in duration) and within a reasonable geographic area. Although covenants not to compete restrain trade, they are commonly found in partnership agreements, business sale agreements, and employment contracts. If they are ancillary to such agreements, covenants not to compete will normally be enforced by the courts unless the time period or geographic area is deemed unreasonable.

Covenant not to sue An agreement to substitute a contractual obligation for some other type of legal action based on a valid claim.

Covenant of quiet enjoyment A promise by a grantor (or landlord) that the grantee (or tenant) will not be evicted or disturbed by the grantor or a person having a lien or superior title.

Covenant of the right to convey A grantor's assurance that he or she has sufficient capacity and title to convey the estate that he or she undertakes to convey by deed.

Covenant running with the land An executory promise made between a grantor and a grantee to which they and subsequent owners of the land are bound.

Cover Under the Uniform Commercial Code, a remedy of the buyer or lessee that allows the buyer or lessee, on the seller's or lessor's breach, to purchase the goods from another seller or lessor and substitute them for the goods due under the contract. If the cost of cover exceeds the cost of the contract goods, the breaching seller or lessor will be liable to the buyer or lessee for the difference. In obtaining cover, the buyer or lessee must act in good faith and without unreasonable delay.

Cram-down provision A provision of the Bankruptcy Code that allows a court to confirm a debtor's Chapter 11 reorganization plan even though only one class of creditors has accepted it. To exercise the court's right under this provision, the court must demonstrate that the plan does not discriminate unfairly against any creditors and is fair and equitable.

Crashworthiness doctrine A doctrine that imposes liability for defects in the design or construction of motor vehicles that increase the extent of injuries to passengers if an accident occurs. The doctrine holds even when the defects do not actually cause the accident.

Creditor A person to whom a debt is owed by another person (the debtor).

Creditor beneficiary A third party beneficiary who has rights in a contract made by the debtor and a third person. The terms of the contract obligate the third person to pay the debt owed to the creditor. The creditor beneficiary can enforce the debt against either party.

Creditors' composition agreement An agreement formed between a debtor and his or her creditors in which the creditors agree to accept a lesser sum than that owed by the debtor in full satisfaction of the debt.

Crime A wrong against society proclaimed in a statute and, if committed, punishable by society through fines and/or imprisonment—and, in some cases, death.

Criminal act *See Actus reus*

Criminal intent *See Mens rea*

Criminal law Law that defines and governs actions that constitute crimes. Generally, criminal law has to do with wrongful actions committed against society for which society demands redress.

Cross-examination The questioning of an opposing witness during the trial.

Cumulative voting A method of shareholder voting designed to allow minority shareholders to be represented on the board of directors. With cumulative voting, the number of members of the board to be elected is multiplied by the total number of voting shares held.

The result equals the number of votes a shareholder has, and this total can be cast for one or more nominees for director.

Cure Under the Uniform Commercial Code, the right of a party who tenders nonconforming performance to correct his or her performance within the contract period.

Cyber crime A crime that occurs online, in the virtual community of the Internet, as opposed to the physical world.

Cyber hate speech Extreme hate speech on the Internet. Racist materials and Holocaust denials disseminated on the Web are examples.

Cyber mark A trademark in cyberspace.

Cyber stalker A person who commits the crime of stalking in cyberspace. Generally, stalking consists of harassing a person and putting that person in reasonable fear for his or her safety or the safety of the person's immediate family.

Cyber terrorist A hacker whose purpose is to exploit a target computer for a serious impact, such as the corruption of a program to sabotage a business.

Cyber tort A tort committed in cyberspace.

D

Damages Money sought as a remedy for a breach of contract or for a tortious act.

Debenture bond A bond for which no specific assets of the corporation are pledged as backing; rather, the bond is backed by the general credit rating of the corporation, plus any assets that can be seized if the corporation allows the debentures to go into default.

Debtor Under Article 9 of the Uniform Commercial Code, a debtor is any party who owes payment or performance of a secured obligation, whether or not the party actually owns or has rights in the collateral.

Debtor in possession (DIP) In Chapter 11 bankruptcy proceedings, a debtor who is allowed to continue in possession of the estate in property (the business) and to continue business operations.

Declaratory judgment A court's judgment on a justiciable controversy when the plaintiff is in doubt as to his or her legal rights; a binding adjudication of the rights and status of litigants even though no consequential relief is awarded.

Decree The judgment of a court of equity.

Deed A document by which title to property (usually real property) is passed.

Defalcation The misuse of funds.

Defamation Any published or publicly spoken false statement that causes injury to another's good name, reputation, or character.

Default The failure to observe a promise or discharge an obligation. The term is commonly used to mean the failure to pay a debt when it is due.

Default judgment A judgment entered by a court against a defendant who has failed to appear in court to answer or defend against the plaintiff's claim.

Defendant One against whom a lawsuit is brought; the accused person in a criminal proceeding.

Defense That which a defendant offers and alleges in an action or suit as a reason why the plaintiff should not recover or establish what he or she seeks.

Deficiency judgment A judgment against a debtor for the amount of a debt remaining unpaid after collateral has been repossessed and sold.

Delegatee One to whom contract duties are delegated by another, called the delegator.

Delegation The transfer of a contractual duty to a third party. The party delegating the duty (the delegator) to the third party (the delegatee) is still obliged to perform on the contract should the delegatee fail to perform.

Delegation doctrine A doctrine based on Article I, Section 8, of the U.S. Constitution, which has been construed to allow Congress to delegate some of its power to make and implement laws to administrative agencies. The delegation is considered to be proper as long as Congress sets standards outlining the scope of the agency's authority.

Delegator One who delegates his or her duties under a contract to another, called the delegatee.

Delivery In contract law, the one party's act of placing the subject matter of the contract within the other party's possession or control.

Delivery ex ship Delivery from the carrying ship. A contract term indicating that risk of loss will not pass to the buyer until the goods leave the ship or are otherwise properly unloaded.

Delivery order A written order to deliver goods directed to a warehouser, carrier, or other person who, in the ordinary course of business, issues warehouse receipts or bills of lading [UCC 7–102(1)(d)].

Demand deposit Funds (accepted by a bank) subject to immediate withdrawal, in contrast to a time deposit, which requires that a depositor wait a specific time before withdrawing or pay a penalty for early withdrawal.

Demurrer *See* Motion to dismiss

De novo Anew; afresh; a second time. In a hearing *de novo*, an appellate court hears the case as a court of original jurisidction—that is, as if the case had not previously been tried and a decision rendered.

Depositary bank The first bank to receive a check for payment.

Deposition The testimony of a party to a lawsuit or a witness taken under oath before a trial.

Destination contract A contract for the sale of goods in which the seller is required or authorized to ship the goods by carrier and deliver them at a particular destination. The seller assumes liability for any losses or damage to the goods until they are tendered at the destination specified in the contract.

Devise To make a gift of real property by will.

Dilution With respect to trademarks, a doctrine under which distinctive or famous trademarks are protected from certain unauthorized uses of the marks regardless of a showing of competition or a likelihood of confusion. Congress created a federal cause of action for dilution in 1995 with the passage of the Federal Trademark Dilution Act.

Direct examination The examination of a witness by the attorney who calls the witness to the stand to testify on behalf of the attorney's client.

Directed verdict *See* Motion for a directed verdict

Disaffirmance The legal avoidance, or setting aside, of a contractual obligation.

Discharge The termination of an obligation. (1) In contract law, discharge occurs when the parties have fully performed their contractual obligations or when events, conduct of the parties, or operation of the law releases the parties from performance. (2) In bankruptcy proceedings, the extinction of the debtor's dischargeable debts.

Discharge in bankruptcy The release of a debtor from all debts that are provable, except those specifically excepted from discharge by statute.

Disclosed principal A principal whose identity is known to a third party at the time the agent makes a contract with the third party.

Discovery A phase in the litigation process during which the opposing parties may obtain information from each other and from third parties prior to trial.

Dishonor To refuse to accept or pay a draft or a promissory note when it is properly presented. An instrument is dishonored when presentment is properly made and acceptance or payment is refused or cannot be obtained within the prescribed time.

Disparagement of property An economically injurious falsehood made about another's product or property. A general term for torts that are more specifically referred to as slander of quality or slander of title.

Disparate-impact discrimination A form of employment discrimination that results from certain employer practices or procedures that, although not discriminatory on their face, have a discriminatory effect.

Disparate-treatment discrimination A form of employment discrimination that results when an employer intentionally discriminates against employees who are members of protected classes.

Dissenting opinion A written opinion by a judge or justice who disagrees with the majority opinion.

Dissolution The formal disbanding of a partnership or a corporation. It can take place by (1) acts of the partners or, in a corporation, of the shareholders and board of directors; (2) the death of a partner; (3) the expiration of a time period stated in a partnership agreement or a certificate of incorporation; or (4) judicial decree.

Distribution agreement A contract between a seller and a distributor of the seller's products setting out the terms and conditions of the distributorship.

Distributorship A business arrangement that is established when a manufacturer licenses a dealer to sell its product. An example of a distributorship is an automobile dealership.

Diversity of citizenship Under Article III, Section 2, of the Constitution, a basis for federal court jurisdiction over a lawsuit between (1) citizens of different states, (2) a foreign country and citizens of a state or of different states, or (3) citizens of a state and citizens or subjects of a foreign country. The amount in controversy must be more than $75,000 before a federal court can take jurisdiction in such cases.

Divestiture The act of selling one or more of a company's parts, such as a subsidiary or plant; often mandated by the courts in merger or monopolization cases.

Dividend A distribution to corporate shareholders of corporate profits or income, disbursed in proportion to the number of shares held.

Docket The list of cases entered on a court's calendar and thus scheduled to be heard by the court.

Document of title Paper exchanged in the regular course of business that evidences the right to possession of goods (for example, a bill of lading or a warehouse receipt).

Domain name The series of letters and symbols used to identify site operators on the Internet; Internet "addresses."

Domestic corporation In a given state, a corporation that does business in, and is organized under the law of, that state.

Domestic relations court A court that deals with domestic (household) relationships, such as adoption, divorce, support payments, child custody, and the like.

Donee beneficiary A third party beneficiary who has rights under a contract as a direct result of the intention of the contract parties to make a gift to the third party.

Double jeopardy A situation occurring when a person is tried twice for the same criminal offense; prohibited by the Fifth Amendment to the Constitution.

Double taxation A feature (and disadvantage) of the corporate form of business. Because a corporation is a separate legal entity, corporate profits are taxed by state and federal governments. Dividends are again taxable as ordinary income to the shareholders receiving them.

Draft Any instrument drawn on a drawee (such as a bank) that orders the drawee to pay a certain sum of money, usually to a third party (the payee), on demand or at a definite future time.

Dram shop act A state statute that imposes liability on the owners of bars and taverns, as well as those who serve alcoholic drinks to the public, for injuries resulting from accidents caused by intoxicated persons when the sellers or servers of alcoholic drinks contributed to the intoxication.

Drawee The party that is ordered to pay a draft or check. With a check, a financial institution is always the drawee.

Drawer The party that initiates a draft (such as a check), thereby ordering the drawee to pay.

Due diligence A required standard of care that certain professionals, such as accountants, must meet to avoid liability for securities violations. Under securities law, an accountant will be deemed to have exercised due diligence if he or she followed generally accepted accounting principles and generally accepted auditing standards and had, "after reasonable investigation, reasonable grounds to believe and did believe, at the time such part of the registration statement became effective, that the statements therein were true and that there was no omission of a material fact required to be stated therein or necessary to make the statements therein not misleading."

Due negotiation The transfer of a document of title in such form that the transferee becomes a holder [UCC 7–501].

Due process clause The provisions of the Fifth and Fourteenth Amendments to the Constitution that guarantee that no person shall be deprived of life, liberty, or property without due process of law. Similar clauses are found in most state constitutions.

Dumping The selling of goods in a foreign country at a price below the price charged for the same goods in the domestic market.

Durable power of attorney A document that authorizes a person to act on behalf of an incompetent person—write checks, collect insurance proceeds, and otherwise manage the disabled person's affairs, including health care—when he or she becomes incapacitated. Spouses often give each other durable power of attorney and, if they are advanced in age, may give a second such power of attorney to an older child.

Duress Unlawful pressure brought to bear on a person, causing the person to perform an act that he or she would not otherwise perform.

Duty of care The duty of all persons, as established by tort law, to exercise a reasonable amount of care in their dealings with others. Failure to exercise due care, which is normally determined by the "reasonable person standard," constitutes the tort of negligence.

E

E-commerce Business transacted in cyberspace.

E-contract A contract that is entered into in cyberspace and is evidenced only by electronic impulses (such as those that make up a computer's memory), rather than, for example, a typewritten form.

E-money Prepaid funds recorded on a computer or a card (such as a *smart card*).

Early neutral case evaluation A form of alternative dispute resolution in which a neutral third party evaluates the strengths and weakness of the disputing parties' positions; the evaluator's opinion forms the basis for negotiating a settlement.

Easement A nonpossessory right to use another's property in a manner established by either express or implied agreement.

Ejectment The eviction of a tenant from leased premises. A remedy at common law to which the landlord can resort when a tenant fails to pay rent for leased premises. To obtain possession of the premises, the landlord must appear in court and show that the defaulting tenant is in wrongful possession.

Elder law A relatively new area of legal practice in which attorneys assist older persons in dealing with such problems as disability, long-term health care, age discrimination, grandparents' visitation rights, and other problems relating to age.

Electronic fund transfer (EFT) A transfer of funds with the use of an electronic terminal, a telephone, a computer, or magnetic tape.

Emancipation In regard to minors, the act of being freed from parental control; occurs when a child's parent or legal guardian relinquishes the legal right to exercise control over the child. Normally, a minor who leaves home to support himself or herself is considered emancipated.

Embezzlement The fraudulent appropriation of money or other property by a person to whom the money or property has been entrusted.

Eminent domain The power of a government to take land for public use from private citizens for just compensation.

Employee A person who works for an employer for a salary or for wages.

Employer An individual or business entity that hires employees, pays them salaries or wages, and exercises control over their work.

Employment at will A common law doctrine under which either party may terminate an employment relationship at any time for any reason, unless a contract specifies otherwise.

Employment discrimination Treating employees or job applicants unequally on the basis of race, color, national origin, religion, gender, age, or disability; prohibited by federal statutes.

Enabling legislation A statute enacted by Congress that authorizes the creation of an administrative agency and specifies the name, composition, purpose, and powers of the agency being created.

Encryption The process by which a message (plaintext) is transformed into something (ciphertext) that the sender and receiver intend third parties not to understand.

Endowment insurance A type of insurance that combines life insurance with an investment so that if the insured outlives the policy, the face value is paid to him or her; if the insured does not outlive the policy, the face value is paid to his or her beneficiary.

Entrapment In criminal law, a defense in which the defendant claims that he or she was induced by a public official—usually an undercover agent or police officer—to commit a crime that he or she would otherwise not have committed.

Entrepreneur One who initiates and assumes the financial risks of a new enterprise and who undertakes to provide or control its management.

Entrustment The transfer of goods to a merchant who deals in goods of that kind and who may transfer those goods and all rights to them to a buyer in the ordinary course of business [UCC 2–403(2)].

Environmental impact statement (EIS) A statement required by the National Environmental Policy Act for any major federal action that will significantly affect the quality of the environment. The statement must analyze the action's impact on the environment and explore alternative actions that might be taken.

Environmental law The body of statutory, regulatory, and common law relating to the protection of the environment.

Equal dignity rule In most states, a rule stating that express authority given to an agent must be in writing if the contract to be made on behalf of the principal is required to be in writing.

Equal protection clause The provision in the Fourteenth Amendment to the Constitution that guarantees that no state will "deny to any person within its jurisdiction the equal protection of the laws." This clause mandates that state governments treat similarly situated individuals in a similar manner.

Equitable maxims General propositions or principles of law that have to do with fairness (equity).

Equity of redemption The right of a mortgagor who has breached the mortgage agreement to redeem or purchase the property prior to foreclosure proceedings.

Escheat The transfer of property to the state when the owner of the property dies without heirs.

Escrow account An account that is generally held in the name of the depositor and escrow agent; the funds in the account are paid to a third person only on fulfillment of the escrow condition.

Establishment clause The provision in the First Amendment to the U.S. Constitution that prohibits Congress from creating any law "respecting an establishment of religion."

Estate The interest that a person has in real and personal property.

Estate planning Planning in advance how one's property and obligations should be transferred on one's death. Wills and trusts are two basic devices used in the process of estate planning.

Estop To bar, impede, or preclude.

Estoppel The principle that a party's own acts prevent him or her from claiming a right to the detriment of another who was entitled to and did rely on those acts. *See also* Agency by estoppel; Promissory estoppel

Estray statute A statute defining finders' rights in property when the true owners are unknown.

Ethical reasoning A reasoning process in which an individual links his or her moral convictions or ethical standards to the particular situation at hand.

Ethics Moral principles and values applied to social behavior.

Evidence Proof offered at trial—in the form of testimony, documents, records, exhibits, objects, and so on—for the purpose of convincing the court or jury of the truth of a contention.

Eviction A landlord's act of depriving a tenant of possession of the leased premises.

Ex *parte* contact Communications with an administrative agency that are not placed in the record.

Ex ship *See* Delivery ex ship

Exclusionary rule In criminal procedure, a rule under which any evidence that is obtained in violation of the accused's constitutional rights guaranteed by the Fourth, Fifth, and Sixth Amendments, as well as any evidence derived from illegally obtained evidence, will not be admissible in court.

Exclusive distributorship A distributorship in which the seller and the distributor of the seller's products agree that the distributor has the exclusive right to distribute the seller's products in a certain geographic area.

Exclusive jurisdiction Jurisdiction that exists when a case can be heard only in a particular court or type of court, such as a federal court or a state court.

Exclusive-dealing contract An agreement under which a seller forbids a buyer to purchase products from the seller's competitors.

Exculpatory clause A clause that releases a contractual party from liability in the event of monetary or physical injury, no matter who is at fault.

Executed contract A contract that has been completely performed by both parties.

Execution An action to carry into effect the directions in a court decree or judgment.

Executive agency An administrative agency within the executive branch of government. At the federal level, executive agencies are those within the cabinet departments.

Executor A person appointed by a testator to see that his or her will is administered appropriately.

Executory contract A contract that has not as yet been fully performed.

Export To sell products to buyers located in other countries.

Express authority Authority expressly given by one party to another. In agency law, an agent has express authority to act for a principal if both parties agree, orally or in writing, that an agency relationship exists in which the agent had the power (authority) to act in the place of, and on behalf of, the principal.

Express contract A contract in which the terms of the agreement are fully and explicitly stated in words, oral or written.

Express warranty A seller's or lessor's oral or written promise, ancillary to an underlying sales or lease agreement, as to the quality, description, or performance of the goods being sold or leased.

Expropriation The seizure by a government of privately owned business or personal property for a proper public purpose and with just compensation.

Extension clause A clause in a time instrument that allows the instrument's date of maturity to be extended into the future.

F

F.A.S. Free alongside. A contract term that requires the seller, at his or her own expense and risk, to deliver the goods alongside the ship before risk passes to the buyer.

F.O.B. Free on board. A contract term that indicates that the selling price of the goods includes transportation costs (and that the seller carries the risk of loss) to the specific F.O.B. place named in the contract. The place can be either the place of initial shipment (for example, the seller's city or place of business) or the place of destination (for example, the buyer's city or place of business).

Family limited liability partnership (FLLP) A limited liability partnership (LLP) in which the majority of the partners are persons related to each other, essentially as spouses, parents, grandparents, siblings, cousins, nephews, or nieces. A person acting in a fiduciary capacity for persons so related could also be a partner. All of the partners must be natural persons or persons acting in a fiduciary capacity for the benefit of natural persons.

Federal form of government A system of government in which the states form a union and the sovereign power is divided between a central government and the member states.

Federal question A question that pertains to the U.S. Constitution, acts of Congress, or treaties. A federal question provides a basis for federal jurisdiction.

Federal Reserve System A network of twelve central banks, located around the country and headed by the Federal Reserve Board of Governors. Most banks in the United States have Federal Reserve accounts.

Federal Rules of Civil Procedure (FRCP) The rules controlling procedural matters in civil trials brought before the federal district courts.

Federal system A system of government in which power is divided by a written constitution between a central government and regional, or subdivisional, governments. Each level must have some domain in which its policies are dominant and some genuine political or constitutional guarantee of its authority.

Fee simple An absolute form of property ownership entitling the property owner to use, possess, or dispose of the property as he or she chooses during his or her lifetime. On death, the interest in the property descends to the owner's heirs; a fee simple absolute.

Fee simple absolute An ownership interest in land in which the owner has the greatest possible aggregation of rights, privileges, and power. Ownership in fee simple absolute is limited absolutely to a person and his or her heirs.

Fellow-servant doctrine A doctrine that bars an employee from suing his or her employer for injuries caused by a fellow employee.

Felony A crime—such as arson, murder, rape, or robbery—that carries the most severe sanctions, usually ranging from one year in a state or federal prison to the forfeiture of one's life.

Fictitious payee A payee on a negotiable instrument whom the maker or drawer does not intend to have an interest in the instrument. Indorsements by fictitious payees are not treated as unauthorized under Article 3 of the Uniform Commercial Code.

Fiduciary As a noun, a person having a duty created by his or her undertaking to act primarily for another's ben-

efit in matters connected with the undertaking. As an adjective, a relationship founded on trust and confidence.

Fiduciary duty The duty, imposed on a fiduciary by virtue of his or her position, to act primarily for another's benefit.

Filtering software A computer program that includes a pattern through which data are passed. When designed to block access to certain Web sites, the pattern blocks the retrieval of a site whose URL or key words are on a list within the program.

Final order The final decision of an administrative agency on an issue. If no appeal is taken, or if the case is not reviewed or considered anew by the agency commission, the administrative law judge's initial order becomes the final order of the agency.

Financial institution An organization authorized to do business under state or federal laws relating to financial institutions. For example, under the Electronic Fund Transfer Act, financial institutions include banks, savings and loan associations, credit unions, and other business entities that directly or indirectly hold accounts belonging to consumers.

Financing statement A document prepared by a secured creditor and filed with the appropriate state or local official to give notice to the public that the creditor claims an interest in collateral belonging to the debtor named in the statement. The financing statement must be signed by the debtor, contain the addresses of both the debtor and the creditor, and describe the collateral by type or item.

Firm offer An offer (by a merchant) that is irrevocable without consideration for a period of time (not longer than three months). A firm offer by a merchant must be in writing and must be signed by the offeror.

Fitness for a particular purpose *See* Implied warranty of fitness for a particular purpose

Fixture A thing that was once personal property but that has become attached to real property in such a way that it takes on the characteristics of real property and becomes part of that real property.

Flame An online message in which one party attacks another in harsh, often personal, terms.

Floating lien A security interest in proceeds, after-acquired property, or property purchased under a line of credit (or all three); a security interest in collateral that is retained even when the collateral changes in character, classification, or location.

Force majeure (pronounced mah-*zhure*) **clause** A provision in a contract stipulating that certain unforeseen events—such as war, political upheavals, acts of God, or other events—will excuse a party from liability for non-performance of contractual obligations.

Foreclosure A proceeding in which a mortgagee either takes title to or forces the sale of the mortgagor's property in satisfaction of a debt.

Foreign corporation In a given state, a corporation that does business in the state without being incorporated therein.

Foreseeable risk In negligence law, the risk of harm or injury to another that a person of ordinary intelligence and prudence should have reasonably anticipated or foreseen when undertaking an action or refraining from undertaking an action.

Forfeiture The termination of a lease, according to its terms or the terms of a statute, when one of the parties fails to fulfill a condition under the lease and thereby breaches it.

Forgery The fraudulent making or altering of any writing in a way that changes the legal rights and liabilities of another.

Formal contract A contract that by law requires for its validity a specific form, such as executed under seal.

Forum A jurisdiction, court, or place in which disputes are litigated and legal remedies are sought.

Forum-selection clause A provision in a contract designating the court, jurisdiction, or tribunal that will decide any disputes arising under the contract.

Franchise Any arrangement in which the owner of a trademark, trade name, or copyright licenses another to use that trademark, trade name, or copyright, under specified conditions or limitations, in the selling of goods and services.

Franchisee One receiving a license to use another's (the franchisor's) trademark, trade name, or copyright in the sale of goods and services.

Franchisor One licensing another (the franchisee) to use his or her trademark, trade name, or copyright in the sale of goods or services.

Fraud Any misrepresentation, either by misstatement or omission of a material fact, knowingly made with the intention of deceiving another and on which a reasonable person would and does rely to his or her detriment.

Fraud in the execution In the law of negotiable instruments, a type of fraud that occurs when a person is deceived into signing a negotiable instrument, believing that he or she is signing something else (such as a receipt); also called fraud in the inception. Fraud in the execution is a universal defense to payment on a negotiable instrument.

Fraud in the inducement Ordinary fraud. In the law of negotiable instruments, fraud in the inducement occurs when a person issues a negotiable instrument based on false statements by the other party. The issuing party will be able to avoid payment on that instrument unless the holder is a holder in due course; in other words, fraud in the inducement is a personal defense to payment on a negotiable instrument.

Fraudulent misrepresentation (fraud) Any misrepresentation, either by misstatement or omission of a material fact, knowingly made with the intention of deceiving another and on which a reasonable person would and does rely to his or her detriment.

Free exercise clause The provision in the First Amendment to the U.S. Constitution that prohibits Congress from making any law "prohibiting the free exercise" of religion.

Frustration of purpose A court-created doctrine under which a party to a contract will be relieved of his or her duty to perform when the objective purpose for performance no longer exists (due to reasons beyond that party's control).

Full faith and credit clause A clause in Article IV, Section 1, of the Constitution that provides that "Full Faith and Credit shall be given in each State to the public Acts, Records, and Judicial Proceedings of every other States." The clause ensures that rights established under deeds, wills, contracts, and the like in one state will be honored by the other states and that any judicial decision with respect to such property rights will be honored and enforced in all states.

Full warranty A warranty as to full performance covering generally both labor and materials.

Fungible goods Goods that are alike by physical nature, by agreement, or by trade usage. Examples of fungible goods are wheat, oil, and wine that are identical in type and quality.

G

Garnishment A legal process used by a creditor to collect a debt by seizing property of the debtor (such as wages) that is being held by a third party (such as the debtor's employer).

General jurisdiction Exists when a court's subject-matter jurisdiction is not restricted. A court of general jurisdiction normally can hear any type of case.

General partner In a limited partnership, a partner who assumes responsibility for the management of the partnership and liability for all partnership debts.

General partnership *See* Partnership

Generally accepted accounting principles (GAAP) The conventions, rules, and procedures necessary to define accepted accounting practices at a particular time. The source of the principles is the Federal Accounting Standards Board.

Generally accepted auditing standards (GAAS) Standards concerning an auditor's professional qualities and the judgment exercised by him or her in the performance of an examination and report. The source of the standards is the American Institute of Certified Public Accountants.

Genuineness of assent Knowing and voluntary assent to the terms of a contract. If a contract is formed as a result of a mistake, misrepresentation, undue influence, or duress, genuineness of assent is lacking, and the contract will be voidable.

Gift Any voluntary transfer of property made without consideration, past or present.

Gift *causa mortis* A gift made in contemplation of death. If the donor does not die of that ailment, the gift is revoked.

Gift *inter vivos* A gift made during one's lifetime and not in contemplation of imminent death, in contrast to a gift *causa mortis*.

Good faith Under the Uniform Commercial Code good faith means honesty in fact; with regard to merchants, good faith means honesty in fact *and* the observance of reasonable commercial standards of fair dealing in the trade.

Good faith purchaser A purchaser who buys without notice of any circumstance that would put a person of ordinary prudence on inquiry as to whether the seller has valid title to the goods being sold.

Good Samaritan statute A state statute that provides that persons who rescue or provide emergency services to others in peril—unless they do so recklessly, thus causing further harm—cannot be sued for negligence.

Grand jury A group of citizens called to decide, after hearing the state's evidence, whether a reasonable basis (probable cause) exists for believing that a crime has been committed and whether a trial ought to be held.

Grant deed A deed that simply recites words of consideration and conveyance. Under statute, a grant deed may impliedly warrant that at least the grantor has not conveyed the property's title to someone else.

Grantee One to whom a grant (of land or property, for example) is made.

Grantor A person who makes a grant, such as a transferor of property or the creator of a trust.

Group boycott The refusal to deal with a particular person or firm by a group of competitors; prohibited by the Sherman Act.

Guarantor A person who agrees to satisfy the debt of another (the debtor) only after the principal debtor defaults; a guarantor's liability is thus secondary.

H

Habitability *See* Implied warranty of habitability

Hacker A person who uses one computer to break into another. Professional computer programmers refer to such persons as "crackers."

Health-care power of attorney A document that designates a person who will have the power to choose what type of and how much medical treatment a person who is unable to make such a choice will receive.

Hearsay An oral or written statement made out of court that is later offered in court by a witness (not the person who made the statement) to prove the truth of the matter asserted in the statement. Hearsay is generally inadmissible as evidence.

Hirfindahl-Hirschman Index (HHI) An index of market power used to calculate whether a merger of two businesses will result in sufficient monopoly power to violate antitrust laws.

Historical school A school of legal thought that emphasizes the evolutionary process of law and that looks to the past to discover what the principles of contemporary law should be.

Holder Any person in the possession of an instrument drawn, issued, or indorsed to him or her, to his or her order, to bearer, or in blank.

Holder in due course (HDC) A holder who acquires a negotiable instrument for value; in good faith; and without notice that the instrument is overdue, that it has been dishonored, that any person has a defense against it or a claim to it, or that the instrument contains unauthorized signatures, alterations, or is so irregular or incomplete as to call into question its authenticity.

Holographic will A will written entirely in the signer's handwriting and usually not witnessed.

Homestead exemption A law permitting a debtor to retain the family home, either in its entirety or up to a specified dollar amount, free from the claims of unsecured creditors or trustees in bankruptcy.

Horizontal merger A merger between two firms that are competing in the same market.

Horizontal restraint Any agreement that in some way restrains competition between rival firms competing in the same market.

Hot-cargo agreement An agreement in which employers voluntarily agree with unions not to handle, use, or deal in nonunion-produced goods of other employers; a type of secondary boycott explicitly prohibited by the Labor-Management Reporting and Disclosure Act of 1959.

Hung jury A jury whose members are so irreconcilably divided in their opinions that they cannot come to a verdict by the requisite number of jurors. The judge in this situation may order a new trial.

I

Identification In a sale of goods, the express designation of the goods provided for in the contract.

Illusory promise A promise made without consideration, which renders the promise unenforceable.

Immunity A status of being exempt, or free, from certain duties or requirements. In criminal law, the state may grant an accused person immunity from prosecution—or agree to prosecute for a lesser offense—if the accused person agrees to give the state information that would assist the state in prosecuting other individuals for crimes. In tort law, freedom from liability for defamatory speech. *See also* Privilege

Implied authority Authority that is created not by an explicit oral or written agreement but by implication. In agency law, implied authority (of the agent) can be conferred by custom, inferred from the position the agent occupies, or implied by virtue of being reasonably necessary to carry out express authority.

Implied warranty A warranty that the law derives by implication or inference from the nature of the transaction or the relative situation or circumstances of the parties.

Implied warranty of fitness for a particular purpose A warranty that goods sold or leased are fit for a particular purpose. The warranty arises when any seller or lessor knows the particular purpose for which a buyer or lessee will use the goods and knows that the buyer or lessee is relying on the skill and judgment of the seller or lessor to select suitable goods.

Implied warranty of habitability An implied promise by a landlord that rented residential premises are fit for human habitation—that is, in a condition that is safe and suitable for people to live in.

Implied warranty of merchantability A warranty that goods being sold or leased are reasonably fit for the general purpose for which they are sold or leased, are properly packaged and labeled, and are of proper quality. The warranty automatically arises in every sale or lease of goods made by a merchant who deals in goods of the kind sold or leased.

Implied-in-fact contract A contract formed in whole or in part from the conduct of the parties (as opposed to an express contract).

Impossibility of performance A doctrine under which a party to a contract is relieved of his or her duty to perform when performance becomes impossible or totally impracticable (through no fault of either party).

Imposter One who, by use of the mails, telephone, or personal appearance, induces a maker or drawer to issue an instrument in the name of an impersonated payee. Indorsements by imposters are not treated as unauthorized under Article 3 of the Uniform Commercial Code.

In pari delicto At equal fault.

In personam **jurisdiction** Court jurisdiction over the "person" involved in a legal action; personal jurisdiction.

In rem **jurisdiction** Court jurisdiction over a defendant's property.

Incidental beneficiary A third party who incidentally benefits from a contract but whose benefit was not the reason the contract was formed; an incidental beneficiary has no rights in a contract and cannot sue to have the contract enforced.

Incidental damages Damages resulting from a breach of contract, including all reasonable expenses incurred because of the breach.

Indemnify To compensate or reimburse another for losses or expenses incurred.

Independent contractor One who works for, and receives payment from, an employer but whose working conditions and methods are not controlled by the employer. An independent contractor is not an employee but may be an agent.

Independent regulatory agency An administrative agency that is not considered part of the government's executive branch and is not subject to the authority of the president. Independent agency officials cannot be removed without cause.

Indictment (pronounced in-*dyte*-ment) A charge by a grand jury that a named person has committed a crime.

Indorsee The person to whom a negotiable instrument is transferred by indorsement.

Indorsement A signature placed on an instrument for the purpose of transferring one's ownership rights in the instrument.

Indorser A person who transfers an instrument by signing (indorsing) it and delivering it to another person.

Industry-wide liability Product liability that is imposed on an entire industry when it is unclear which of several sellers within the industry manufactured a particular product. *See also* Market-share liability

Informal contract A contract that does not require a specified form or formality in order to be valid.

Information A formal accusation or complaint (without an indictment) issued in certain types of actions (usually criminal actions involving lesser crimes) by a law officer, such as a magistrate.

Information return A tax return submitted by a partnership that only reports the income earned by the business. The partnership as an entity does not pay taxes on the income received by the partnership. A partner's profit from the partnership (whether distributed or not) is taxed as individual income to the individual partner.

Infringement A violation of another's legally recognized right. The term is commonly used with reference to the invasion by one party of another party's rights in a patent, trademark, or copyright.

Initial order In the context of administrative law, an agency's disposition in a matter other than a rulemaking. An administrative law judge's initial order becomes final unless it is appealed.

Injunction A court decree ordering a person to do or refrain from doing a certain act or activity.

Innkeeper An owner of an inn, hotel, motel, or other lodgings.

Innkeeper's lien A possessory or statutory lien allowing the innkeeper to take the personal property of a guest, brought into the hotel, as security for nonpayment of the guest's bill (debt).

Innocent misrepresentation A false statement of fact or an act made in good faith that deceives and causes harm or injury to another.

Insider A corporate director or officer, or other employee or agent, with access to confidential information and a duty not to disclose that information in violation of insider-trading laws.

Insider trading The purchase or sale of securities on the basis of "inside information" (information that has not been made available to the public) in violation of a duty owed to the company whose stock is being traded.

Insolvent Under the Uniform Commercial Code, a term describing a person who ceases to pay "his debts in the ordinary course of business or cannot pay his debts as they become due or is insolvent within the meaning of federal bankruptcy law" [UCC 1–201(23)].

Installment contract Under the Uniform Commercial Code, a contract that requires or authorizes delivery in two or more separate lots to be accepted and paid for separately.

Instrument *See* Negotiable instrument

Insurable interest An interest either in a person's life or well-being or in property that is sufficiently substantial that insuring against injury to (or the death of) the person or against damage to the property does not amount to a mere wagering (betting) contract.

Insurance A contract in which, for a stipulated consideration, one party agrees to compensate the other for loss on a specific subject by a specified peril.

Intangible property Property that is incapable of being apprehended by the senses (such as by sight or touch); intellectual property is an example of intangible property.

Integrated contract A written contract that constitutes the final expression of the parties' agreement. If a contract is integrated, evidence extraneous to the contract that contradicts or alters the meaning of the contract in any way is inadmissible.

Intellectual property Property resulting from intellectual, creative processes. Patents, trademarks, and copyrights are examples of intellectual property.

Intended beneficiary A third party for whose benefit a contract is formed; an intended beneficiary can sue the promisor if such a contract is breached.

Intentional tort A wrongful act knowingly committed.

Inter vivos **gift** *See* Gift *inter vivos*

Inter vivos **trust** A trust created by the grantor (settlor) and effective during the grantor's lifetime (that is, a trust not established by a will).

Intermediary bank Any bank to which an item is transferred in the course of collection, except the depositary or payor bank.

International law The law that governs relations among nations. International customs and treaties are generally considered to be two of the most important sources of international law.

International organization In international law, a term that generally refers to an organization composed mainly of nations and usually established by treaty. The United States is a member of more than one hundred multilateral and bilateral organizations, including at least twenty through the United Nations.

Interpretive rule An administrative agency rule that is simply a statement or opinion issued by the agency explaining how it interprets and intends to apply the statutes it enforces. Such rules are not automatically binding on private individuals or organizations.

Interrogatories A series of written questions for which written answers are prepared and then signed under oath by a party to a lawsuit, usually with the assistance of the party's attorney.

Intestacy laws State statutes that specify how property will be distributed when a person dies intestate (without a valid will); statutes of descent and distribution.

Intestate As a noun, one who has died without having created a valid will; as an adjective, the state of having died without a will.

Investment company A company that acts on behalf of many smaller shareholder-owners by buying a large portfolio of securities and professionally managing that portfolio.

Invitee A person who, either expressly or impliedly, is privileged to enter onto another's land. The inviter owes the invitee (for example, a customer in a store) the duty to exercise reasonable care to protect the invitee from harm.

Irrevocable offer An offer that cannot be revoked or recalled by the offeror without liability. A merchant's firm offer is an example of an irrevocable offer.

Issue The first transfer, or delivery, of an instrument to a holder.

J

Joint and several liability In partnership law, a doctrine under which a plaintiff may sue, and collect a judgment from, one or more of the partners separately (severally, or individually) or all of the partners together (jointly). This is true even if one of the partners sued did not participate in, ratify, or know about whatever it was that gave rise to the cause of action.

Joint liability Shared liability. In partnership law, partners incur joint liability for partnership obligations and debts. For example, if a third party sues a partner on a partnership debt, the partner has the right to insist that the other partners be sued with him or her.

Joint stock company A hybrid form of business organization that combines characteristics of a corporation (shareholder-owners, management by directors and officers of the company, and perpetual existence) and a partnership (it is formed by agreement, not statute; property is usually held in the names of the members; and the shareholders have personal liability for business debts). Usually, the joint stock company is regarded as a partnership for tax and other legally related purposes.

Joint tenancy The joint ownership of property by two or more co-owners in which each co-owner owns an undivided portion of the property. On the death of one of the joint tenants, his or her interest automatically passes to the surviving joint tenants.

Joint venture A joint undertaking of a specific commercial enterprise by an association of persons. A joint venture is normally not a legal entity and is treated like a partnership for federal income tax purposes.

Judgment The final order or decision resulting from a legal action.

Judgment *n.o.v.* *See* Motion for judgment *n.o.v.*

Judgment rate of interest A rate of interest fixed by statute that is applied to a monetary judgment from the moment the judgment is awarded by a court until the judgment is paid or terminated.

Judicial lien A lien on property created by a court order.

Judicial process The procedures relating to, or connected with, the administration of justice through the judicial system.

Judicial review The process by which courts decide on the constitutionality of legislative enactments and actions of the executive branch.

Jurisdiction The authority of a court to hear and decide a specific action.

Jurisprudence The science or philosophy of law.

Justiciable (pronounced jus-*tish*-a-bul) **controversy** A controversy that is not hypothetical or academic but real and substantial; a requirement that must be satisfied before a court will hear a case.

K

King's court A medieval English court. The king's courts, or *curiae regis*, were established by the Norman conquerors of England. The body of law that developed in these courts was common to the entire English realm and thus became known as the common law.

L

Laches The equitable doctrine that bars a party's right to legal action if the party has neglected for an unreasonable length of time to act on his or her rights.

Landlord An owner of land or rental property who leases it to another person, called the tenant.

Landlord's lien A landlord's remedy for a tenant's failure to pay rent. When permitted under a statute or the lease agreement, the landlord may take and keep or sell whatever of the defaulting tenant's property is on the leased premises.

Larceny The wrongful taking and carrying away of another person's personal property with the intent to permanently deprive the owner of the property. Some states classify larceny as either grand or petit, depending on the property's value.

Last clear chance A doctrine under which a plaintiff may recover from a defendant for injuries or damages suffered, notwithstanding the plaintiff's own negligence, when the defendant had the opportunity—a last clear chance—to avoid harming the plaintiff through the exercise of reasonable care but failed to do so.

Law A body of enforceable rules governing relationships among individuals and between individuals and their society.

Lawsuit The litigation process. *See* Litigation

Lease In real property law, a contract by which the owner of real property (the landlord, or lessor) grants to a person (the tenant, or lessee) an exclusive right to use and possess the property, usually for a specified period of time, in return for rent or some other form of payment.

Lease agreement In regard to the lease of goods, an agreement in which one person (the lessor) agrees to transfer the right to the possession and use of property to another person (the lessee) in exchange for rental payments.

Leasehold estate An estate in realty held by a tenant under a lease. In every leasehold estate, the tenant has a qualified right to possess and/or use the land.

Legacy A gift of personal property under a will.

Legal positivists Adherents to the positivist school of legal thought. This school holds that there can be no higher law than a nation's positive law—law created by a particular society at a particular point in time. In contrast to the natural law school, the positivist school maintains that there are no "natural" rights; rights come into existence only when there is a sovereign power (government) to confer and enforce those rights.

Legal rate of interest A rate of interest fixed by statute as either the maximum rate of interest allowed by law or a rate of interest applied when the parties to a contract intend, but do not fix, an interest rate in the contract. In the latter case, the rate is frequently the same as the statutory maximum rate permitted.

Legal realism A school of legal thought that was popular in the 1920s and 1930s and that challenged many existing jurisprudential assumptions, particularly the assumption that subjective elements play no part in judicial reasoning. Legal realists generally advocated a less abstract and more realistic approach to the law, an approach that would take into account customary practices and the circumstances in which transactions take place. The school left a lasting imprint on American jurisprudence.

Legal reasoning The process of reasoning by which a judge harmonizes his or her decision with the judicial decisions of previous cases.

Legatee One designated in a will to receive a gift of personal property.

Legislative rule An administrative agency rule that carries the same weight as a congressionally enacted statute.

Lessee A person who acquires the right to the possession and use of another's property in exchange for rental payments.

Lessor A person who sells the right to the possession and use of property to another in exchange for rental payments.

Letter of credit A written instrument, usually issued by a bank on behalf of a customer or other person, in which the issuer promises to honor drafts or other demands for payment by third persons in accordance with the terms of the instrument.

Leveraged buyout (LBO) A corporate takeover financed by loans secured by the acquired corporation's assets or by the issuance of corporate bonds, resulting in a high debt load for the corporation.

Levy The obtaining of money by legal process through the seizure and sale of property, usually done after a writ of execution has been issued.

Liability Any actual or potential legal obligation, duty, debt, or responsibility.

Libel Defamation in writing or other form (such as in a videotape) having the quality of permanence.

License A revocable right or privilege of a person to come on another person's land.

Licensee One who receives a license to use, or enter onto, another's property.

Lien (pronounced leen) An encumbrance on a property to satisfy a debt or protect a claim for payment of a debt.

Lien creditor One whose claim is secured by a lien on particular property, as distinguished from a general creditor, who has no such security.

Life estate An interest in land that exists only for the duration of the life of some person, usually the holder of the estate.

Limited jurisdiction Exists when a court's subject-matter jurisdiction is limited. Bankruptcy courts and probate courts are examples of courts with limited jurisdiction.

Limited liability Exists when the liability of the owners of a business is limited to the amount of their investments in the firm.

Limited liability company (LLC) A hybrid form of business enterprise that offers the limited liability of the corporation but the tax advantages of a partnership.

Limited liability limited partnership (LLLP) A type of limited partnership. The difference between a limited partnership and an LLLP is that the liability of the general partner in an LLLP is the same as the liability of the limited partner. That is, the liability of all partners is limited to the amount of their investments in the firm.

Limited liability partnership (LLP) A form of partnership that allows professionals to enjoy the tax benefits of a partnership while limiting their personal liability for the malpractice of other partners.

Limited partner In a limited partnership, a partner who contributes capital to the partnership but has no right to participate in the management and operation of the business. The limited partner assumes no liability for partnership debts beyond the capital contributed.

Limited partnership A partnership consisting of one or more general partners (who manage the business and are liable to the full extent of their personal assets for debts of the partnership) and one or more limited partners (who contribute only assets and are liable only to the extent of their contributions).

Limited-payment life A type of life insurance for which premiums are payable for a definite period, after which the policy is fully paid.

Limited warranty A written warranty that fails to meet one or more of the minimum standards for a full warranty.

Liquidated damages An amount, stipulated in the contract, that the parties to a contract believe to be a reasonable estimation of the damages that will occur in the event of a breach.

Liquidated debt A debt that is due and certain in amount.

Liquidation (1) In regard to bankruptcy, the sale of all of the nonexempt assets of a debtor and the distribution of the proceeds to the debtor's creditors. Chapter 7 of the Bankruptcy Code provides for liquidation bankruptcy proceedings. (2) In regard to corporations, the process by which corporate assets are converted into cash and distributed among creditors and shareholders according to specific rules of preference.

Litigant A party to a lawsuit.

Litigation The process of resolving a dispute through the court system.

Living will A document that allows a person to control the methods of medical treatment that may be used after a serious accident or illness.

Loan workout *See* Workout

Long arm statute A state statute that permits a state to obtain personal jurisdiction over nonresident defendants. A defendant must have "minimum contacts" with that state for the statute to apply.

Lost property Property with which the owner has involuntarily parted and then cannot find or recover.

M

Magistrate's court A court of limited jurisdiction that is presided over by a public official (magistrate) with certain judicial authority, such as the power to set bail.

Mailbox rule A rule providing that an acceptance of an offer becomes effective on dispatch (on being placed in a mailbox), if mail is, expressly or impliedly, an authorized means of communication of acceptance to the offeror.

Main purpose rule A rule of contract law under which an exception to the Statute of Frauds is made if the main purpose in accepting secondary liability under a contract is to secure a personal benefit. If this situation exists, the contract need not be in writing to be enforceable.

Majority *See* Age of majority

Majority opinion A court's written opinion, outlining the views of the majority of the judges or justices deciding the case.

Maker One who promises to pay a certain sum to the holder of a promissory note or certificate of deposit (CD).

Malpractice Professional misconduct or the failure to exercise the requisite degree of skill as a professional. Negligence—the failure to exercise due care—on the part of a professional, such as a physician or an attorney, is commonly referred to as malpractice.

Manufacturing or processing-plant franchise A franchise that is created when the franchisor transmits to the franchisee the essential ingredients or formula to make a particular product. The franchisee then markets the product either at wholesale or at retail in accordance with the franchisor's standards. Examples of this type of franchise are Coca-Cola and other soft-drink bottling companies.

Marine insurance Insurance protecting shippers and vessel owners from losses or damages sustained by a vessel or its cargo during the transport of goods or materials by water.

Mark *See* Trademark

Market concentration A situation that exists when a small number of firms share the market for a particular good or service. For example, if the four largest grocery stores in Chicago accounted for 80 percent of all retail food sales, the market clearly would be concentrated in those four firms.

Market power The power of a firm to control the market price of its product. A monopoly has the greatest degree of market power.

Marketable title Title to real estate that is reasonably free from encumbrances, defects in the chain of title, and other events that affect title, such as adverse possession.

Market-share liability A method of sharing liability among several firms that manufactured or marketed a particular product that may have caused a plaintiff's injury. This form of liability sharing is used when the true source of the product is unidentifiable. Each firm's liability is proportionate to its respective share of the relevant market for the product. Market-share liability applies only if the injuring product is fungible, the true manufacturer is unidentifiable, and the unknown character of the manufacturer is not the plaintiff's fault.

Market-share test The primary measure of monopoly power. A firm's market share is the percentage of a market that the firm controls.

Marshalling assets The arrangement or ranking of assets in a certain order toward the payment of debts. In equity, when two creditors have recourse to the same property of the debtor, but one has recourse to other property of the debtor, that creditor must resort first to those assets of the debtor that are not available to the other creditor.

Material alteration *See* Alteration

Material fact A fact to which a reasonable person would attach importance in determining his or her course of action. In regard to tender offers, for example, a fact is material if there is a substantial likelihood that a reasonable shareholder would consider it important in deciding how to vote.

Mechanic's lien A statutory lien on the real property of another, created to ensure payment for work performed and materials furnished in the repair or improvement of real property, such as a building.

Mediation A method of settling disputes outside of court by using the services of a neutral third party, called a mediator. The mediator acts as a communicating agent between the parties and suggests ways in which the parties can resolve their dispute.

Member The term used to designate a person who has an ownership interest in a limited liability company.

Mens rea (pronounced *mehns ray*-uh) Mental state, or intent. A wrongful mental state is as necessary as a wrongful act to establish criminal liability. What constitutes a mental state varies according to the wrongful action. Thus, for murder, the *mens rea* is the intent to take a life; for theft, the *mens rea* must involve both the knowledge that the property belongs to another and the intent to deprive the owner of it.

Merchant A person who is engaged in the purchase and sale of goods. Under the Uniform Commercial Code, a person who deals in goods of the kind involved in the sales contract; for further definitions, see UCC 2–104.

Merger A contractual and statutory process in which one corporation (the surviving corporation) acquires all of the assets and liabilities of another corporation (the merged corporation). The shareholders of the merged corporation receive either payment for their shares or shares in the surviving corporation.

Meta tags Words inserted into a Web site's key words field to increase the site's appearance in search engine results.

Minimum-contacts requirement The requirement that before a state court can exercise jurisdiction over a foreign corporation, the foreign corporation must have sufficient contacts with the state. A foreign corporation that has its home office in the state or that has manufacturing plants in the state meets this requirement.

Minimum wage The lowest wage, either by government regulation or union contract, that an employer may pay an hourly worker.

Mini-trial A private proceeding in which each party to a dispute argues its position before the other side and vice versa. A neutral third party may be present and act as an adviser if the parties fail to reach an agreement.

Mirror image rule A common law rule that requires, for a valid contractual agreement, that the terms of the offeree's acceptance adhere exactly to the terms of the offeror's offer.

Misdemeanor A lesser crime than a felony, punishable by a fine or imprisonment for up to one year in other than a state or federal penitentiary.

Mislaid property Property with which the owner has voluntarily parted and then cannot find or recover.

Misrepresentation A false statement of fact or an action that deceives and causes harm or injury to another. *See also* Fraudulent misrepresentation (fraud); Innocent misrepresentation

Mitigation of damages A rule requiring a plaintiff to have done whatever was reasonable to minimize the damages caused by the defendant.

Money laundering Falsely reporting income that has been obtained through criminal activity as income obtained through a legitimate business enterprise—in effect, "laundering" the "dirty money."

Monopolization The possession of monopoly power in the relevant market and the willful acquisition or maintenance of the power, as distinguished from growth or development as a consequence of a superior product, business acumen, or historic accident.

Monopoly A term generally used to describe a market in which there is a single seller or a limited number of sellers.

Monopoly power The ability of a monopoly to dictate what takes place in a given market.

Moral minimum The minimum degree of ethical behavior expected of a business firm, which is usually defined as compliance with the law.

Mortgage A written instrument giving a creditor (the mortgagee) an interest in (a lien on) the debtor's (mortgagor's) property as security for a debt.

Mortgage bond A bond that pledges specific property. If the corporation defaults on the bond, the bondholder can take the property.

Mortgagee Under a mortgage agreement, the creditor who takes a security interest in the debtor's property.

Mortgagor   Under a mortgage agreement, the debtor who gives the creditor a security interest in the debtor's property in return for a mortgage loan.

Most-favored-nation status   A status granted in an international treaty by a provision stating that the citizens of the contracting nations may enjoy the privileges accorded by either party to citizens of the most favored nations. Generally, most-favored-nation clauses are designed to establish equality of international treatment.

Motion   A procedural request or application presented by an attorney to the court on behalf of a client.

Motion for a directed verdict   In a jury trial, a motion for the judge to take the decision out of the hands of the jury and direct a verdict for the moving party on the ground that the other party has not produced sufficient evidence to support his or her claim; referred to as a motion for judgment as a matter of law in the federal courts.

Motion for a new trial   A motion asserting that the trial was so fundamentally flawed (because of error, newly discovered evidence, prejudice, or other reason) that a new trial is necessary to prevent a miscarriage of justice.

Motion for judgment *n.o.v.*   A motion requesting the court to grant judgment in favor of the party making the motion on the ground that the jury verdict against him or her was unreasonable and erroneous.

Motion for judgment on the pleadings   A motion by either party to a lawsuit at the close of the pleadings requesting the court to decide the issue solely on the pleadings without proceeding to trial. The motion will be granted only if no facts are in dispute.

Motion for summary judgment   A motion requesting the court to enter a judgment without proceeding to trial. The motion can be based on evidence outside the pleadings and will be granted only if no facts are in dispute.

Motion to dismiss   A pleading in which a defendant asserts that the plaintiff's claim fails to state a cause of action (that is, has no basis in law) or that there are other grounds on which a suit should be dismissed.

Multiple product order   An order issued by the Federal Trade Commission to a firm that has engaged in deceptive advertising by which the firm is required to cease and desist from false advertising not only in regard to the product that was the subject of the action but also in regard to all the firm's other products.

Municipal court   A city or community court with criminal jurisdiction over traffic violations and, less frequently, with civil jurisdiction over other minor matters.

Mutual assent   The element of agreement in the formation of a contract. The manifestation of contract parties' mutual assent to the same bargain is required to establish a contract.

Mutual fund   A specific type of investment company that continually buys or sells to investors shares of ownership in a portfolio.

Mutual rescission   An agreement between the parties to cancel their contract, releasing the parties from further obligations under the contract. The object of the agreement is to restore the parties to the positions they would have occupied had no contract ever been formed. *See also* Rescission

N

National law   Law that pertains to a particular nation (as opposed to international law).

Natural law   The belief that government and the legal system should reflect universal moral and ethical principles that are inherent in human nature. The natural law school is the oldest and one of the most significant schools of legal thought.

Necessaries   Necessities required for life, such as food, shelter, clothing, and medical attention; may include whatever is believed to be necessary to maintain a person's standard of living or financial and social status.

Necessity   In criminal law, a defense against liability; under Section 3.02 of the Model Penal Code, this defense is justifiable if "the harm or evil sought to be avoided" by a given action "is greater than that sought to be prevented by the law defining the offense charged."

Negligence   The failure to exercise the standard of care that a reasonable person would exercise in similar circumstances.

Negligence *per se*   An act (or failure to act) in violation of a statutory requirement.

Negligent misrepresentation   Any manifestation through words or conduct that amounts to an untrue statement of fact made in circumstances in which a reasonable and prudent person would not have done (or failed to do) that which led to the misrepresentation. A representation made with an honest belief in its truth may still be negligent due to (1) a lack of reasonable care in ascertaining the facts, (2) the manner of expression, or (3) the absence of the skill or competence required by a particular business or profession.

Negotiable instrument   A signed writing that contains an unconditional promise or order to pay an exact sum of money, on demand or at an exact future time, to a specific person or order, or to bearer.

Negotiation   (1) In regard to dispute settlement, a process in which parties attempt to settle their dispute without going to court, with or without attorneys to represent them. (2) In regard to instruments, the transfer of an instrument in such a way that the transferee (the person to whom the instrument is transferred) becomes a holder.

Nominal damages   A small monetary award (often one dollar) granted to a plaintiff when no actual damage was suffered.

Nonconforming goods   Goods that do not conform to contract specifications.

No-par shares   Corporate shares that have no face value—that is, no specific dollar amount is printed on their face.

Notary public   A public official authorized to attest to the authenticity of signatures.

Note A written instrument signed by a maker unconditionally promising to pay a fixed amount of money to a payee or a holder on demand or on a specific date.

Notice-and-comment rulemaking An administrative rulemaking procedure that involves the publication of a notice of a proposed rulemaking in the *Federal Register*, a comment period for interested parties to express their views on the proposed rule, and the publication of the agency's final rule in the *Federal Register*.

Notice of Proposed Rulemaking A notice published (in the *Federal Register*) by an administrative agency describing a proposed rule. The notice must give the time and place for which agency proceedings on the proposed rule will be held, a description of the nature of the proceedings, the legal authority for the proceedings (which is usually the agency's enabling legislation), and the terms of the proposed rule or the subject matter of the proposed rule.

Novation The substitution, by agreement, of a new contract for an old one, with the rights under the old one being terminated. Typically, there is a substitution of a new person who is responsible for the contract and the removal of an original party's rights and duties under the contract.

Nuisance A common law doctrine under which persons may be held liable for using their property in a manner that unreasonably interferes with others' rights to use or enjoy their own property.

Nuncupative will An oral will (often called a deathbed will) made before witnesses; usually limited to transfers of personal property.

O

Objective theory of contracts A theory under which the intent to form a contract will be judged by outward, objective facts (what the party said when entering into the contract, how the party acted or appeared, and the circumstances surrounding the transaction) as interpreted by a reasonable person, rather than by the party's own secret, subjective intentions.

Obligee One to whom an obligation is owed.

Obligor One that owes an obligation to another.

Offer A promise or commitment to perform or refrain from performing some specified act in the future.

Offeree A person to whom an offer is made.

Offeror A person who makes an offer.

Omnibus clause A provision in an automobile insurance policy that protects the vehicle owner who has taken out the insurance policy and anyone who drives the vehicle with the owner's permission.

Opening statement A statement made to the jury at the beginning of a trial by a party's attorney, prior to the presentation of evidence. The attorney briefly outlines the evidence that will be offered and the legal theory that will be pursued.

Operating agreement In a limited liability company, an agreement in which the members set forth the details of how the business will be managed and operated.

Operation of law A term expressing the manner in which certain rights or liabilities may be imposed on a person by the application of established rules of law to the particular transaction, without regard to the actions or cooperation of the party himself or herself.

Opinion A statement by the court expressing the reasons for its decision in a case.

Optimum profits The amount of profits that a business can make and still act ethically, as opposed to maximum profits, defined as the amount of profits a firm can make if it is willing to disregard ethical concerns.

Option contract A contract under which the offeror cannot revoke his or her offer for a stipulated time period, and the offeree can accept or reject the offer during this period without fear that the offer will be made to another person. The offeree must give consideration for the option (the irrevocable offer) to be enforceable.

Order for relief A court's grant of assistance to a complainant. In bankruptcy proceedings, the order relieves the debtor of the immediate obligation to pay the debts listed in the bankruptcy petition.

Order instrument A negotiable instrument that is payable "to the order of an identified person" or "to an identified person or order."

Ordinance A law passed by a local governing unit, such as a municipality or a county.

Original jurisdiction Courts having original jurisdiction are courts of the first instance, or trial courts—that is, courts in which lawsuits begin, trials take place, and evidence is presented.

Output contract An agreement in which a seller agrees to sell and a buyer agrees to buy all or up to a stated amount of what the seller produces.

Overdraft A check written on a checking account in which there are insufficient funds to cover the amount of the check.

P

Parent-subsidiary merger A merger of companies in which one company (the parent corporation) owns most of the stock of the other (the subsidiary corporation). A parent-subsidiary merger (short-form merger) can use a simplified procedure when the parent corporation owns at least 90 percent of the outstanding shares of each class of stock of the subsidiary corporation.

Parol evidence A term that originally meant "oral evidence," but which has come to refer to any negotiations or agreements made prior to a contract or any contemporaneous oral agreements made by the parties.

Parol evidence rule A substantive rule of contracts under which a court will not receive into evidence the parties' prior negotiations, prior agreements, or contemporaneous oral agreements if that evidence contradicts or varies the terms of the parties' written contract.

Partially disclosed principal A principal whose identity is unknown by a third person, but the third person knows that the agent is or may be acting for a principal at the time the agent and the third person form a contract.

Partner A co-owner of a partnership.

Partnership An agreement by two or more persons to carry on, as co-owners, a business for profit.

Partnership by estoppel A judicially created partnership that may, at the court's discretion, be imposed for purposes of fairness. The court can prevent those who present themselves as partners (but who are not) from escaping liability if a third person relies on an alleged partnership in good faith and is harmed as a result.

Par-value shares Corporate shares that have a specific face value, or formal cash-in value, written on them, such as one dollar.

Past consideration An act done before the contract is made, which ordinarily, by itself, cannot be consideration for a later promise to pay for the act.

Patent A government grant that gives an inventor the exclusive right or privilege to make, use, or sell his or her invention for a limited time period. The word *patent* usually refers to some invention and designates either the instrument by which patent rights are evidenced or the patent itself.

Payee A person to whom an instrument is made payable.

Payor bank The bank on which a check is drawn (the drawee bank).

Penalty A sum inserted into a contract, not as a measure of compensation for its breach but rather as punishment for a default. The agreement as to the amount will not be enforced, and recovery will be limited to actual damages.

Per capita A Latin term meaning "per person." In the law governing estate distribution, a method of distributing the property of an intestate's estate in which each heir in a certain class (such as grandchildren) receives an equal share.

Per curiam By the whole court; a court opinion written by the court as a whole instead of being authored by a judge or justice.

Per se A Latin term meaning "in itself" or "by itself."

Per se violation A type of anticompetitive agreement—such as a horizontal price-fixing agreement—that is considered to be so injurious to the public that there is no need to determine whether it actually injures market competition; rather, it is in itself (*per se*) a violation of the Sherman Act.

Per stirpes A Latin term meaning "by the roots." In the law governing estate distribution, a method of distributing an intestate's estate in which each heir in a certain class (such as grandchildren) takes the share to which his or her deceased ancestor (such as a mother or father) would have been entitled.

Perfect tender rule A common law rule under which a seller was required to deliver to the buyer goods that conformed perfectly to the requirements stipulated in the sales contract. A tender of nonconforming goods would automatically constitute a breach of contract. Under the Uniform Commercial Code, the rule has been greatly modified.

Perfection The legal process by which secured parties protect themselves against the claims of third parties who may wish to have their debts satisfied out of the same collateral; usually accomplished by the filing of a financing statement with the appropriate government official.

Performance In contract law, the fulfillment of one's duties arising under a contract with another; the normal way of discharging one's contractual obligations.

Periodic tenancy A lease interest in land for an indefinite period involving payment of rent at fixed intervals, such as week to week, month to month, or year to year.

Personal defense A defense that can be used to avoid payment to an ordinary holder of a negotiable instrument but not a holder in due course (HDC) or a holder with the rights of an HDC.

Personal identification number (PIN) A number given to the holder of an access card (debit card, credit card, ATM card, or the like) that is used to conduct financial transactions electronically. Typically, the card will not provide access to a system without the number, which is meant to be kept secret to inhibit unauthorized use of the card.

Personal jurisdiction *See In personam* jurisdiction

Personal property Property that is movable; any property that is not real property.

Personalty Personal property.

Petition in bankruptcy The document that is filed with a bankruptcy court to initiate bankruptcy proceedings. The official forms required for a petition in bankruptcy must be completed accurately, sworn to under oath, and signed by the debtor.

Petitioner In equity practice, a party that initiates a lawsuit.

Petty offense In criminal law, the least serious kind of criminal offense, such as a traffic or building-code violation.

Pierce the corporate veil To disregard the corporate entity, which limits the liability of shareholders, and hold the shareholders personally liable for a corporate obligation.

Plaintiff One who initiates a lawsuit.

Plea In criminal law, a defendant's allegation, in response to the charges brought against him or her, of guilt or innocence.

Plea bargaining The process by which a criminal defendant and the prosecutor in a criminal case work out a mutually satisfactory disposition of the case, subject to court approval; usually involves the defendant's pleading guilty to a lesser offense in return for a lighter sentence.

Pleadings Statements made by the plaintiff and the defendant in a lawsuit that detail the facts, charges, and defenses involved in the litigation; the complaint and answer are part of the pleadings.

Pledge A common law security device (retained in Article 9 of the Uniform Commercial Code) in which personal property is turned over to the creditor as security for the payment of a debt and retained by the creditor until the debt is paid.

Police powers Powers possessed by states as part of their inherent sovereignty. These powers may be exercised to protect or promote the public order, health, safety, morals, and general welfare.

Policy In insurance law, a contract between the insurer and the insured in which, for a stipulated consideration, the insurer agrees to compensate the insured for loss on a specific subject by a specified peril.

Positive law The body of conventional, or written, law of a particular society at a particular point in time.

Positivist school A school of legal thought whose adherents believe that there can be no higher law than a nation's positive law—the body of conventional, or written, law of a particular society at a particular time.

Possessory lien A lien that allows one person to retain possession of another's property as security for a debt or obligation owed by the owner of the property to the lienholder. An example of a possessory lien is an artisan's lien.

Potential competition doctrine A doctrine under which a conglomerate merger may be prohibited by law because it would be injurious to potential competition.

Potentially responsible party (PRP) A potentially liable party under the Comprehensive Environmental Response, Compensation and Liability Act (CERCLA). Any person who generated the hazardous waste, transported the hazardous waste, owned or operated a waste site at the time of disposal, or currently owns or operates a site may be responsible for some or all of the clean-up costs involved in removing the hazardous chemicals.

Power of attorney A written document, which is usually notarized, authorizing another to act as one's agent; can be special (permitting the agent to do specified acts only) or general (permitting the agent to transact all business for the principal).

Preauthorized transfer A transaction authorized in advance to recur at substantially regular intervals. The terms and procedures for preauthorized electronic fund transfers through certain financial institutions are subject to the Electronic Fund Transfer Act.

Precedent A court decision that furnishes an example or authority for deciding subsequent cases involving identical or similar facts.

Predatory pricing The pricing of a product below cost with the intent to drive competitors out of the market.

Preemption A doctrine under which certain federal laws preempt, or take precedence over, conflicting state or local laws.

Preemptive rights Rights held by shareholders that entitle them to purchase newly issued shares of a corporation's stock, equal in percentage to shares presently held, before the stock is offered to any outside buyers. Preemptive rights enable shareholders to maintain their proportionate ownership and voice in the corporation.

Preference In bankruptcy proceedings, property transfers or payments made by the debtor that favor (give pref-erence to) one creditor over others. The bankruptcy trustee is allowed to recover payments made both voluntarily and involuntarily to one creditor in preference over another.

Preferred stock Classes of stock that have priority over common stock both as to payment of dividends and distribution of assets on the corporation's dissolution.

Prejudgment interest Interest that accrues on the amount of a court judgment from the time of the filing of a lawsuit to the court's issuance of a judgment.

Preliminary hearing An initial hearing used in many felony cases to establish whether or not it is proper to detain the defendant. A magistrate reviews the evidence and decides if there is probable cause to believe that the defendant committed the crime with which he or she has been charged.

Premium In insurance law, the price paid by the insured for insurance protection for a specified period of time.

Prenuptial agreement An agreement made before marriage that defines each partner's ownership rights in the other partner's property. Prenuptial agreements must be in writing to be enforceable.

Preponderance of the evidence A standard in civil law cases under which the plaintiff must convince the court that, based on the evidence presented by both parties, it is more likely than not that the plaintiff's allegation is true.

Presentment The act of presenting an instrument to the party liable on the instrument to collect payment; presentment also occurs when a person presents an instrument to a drawee for acceptance.

Presentment warranties Implied warranties, made by any person who presents an instrument for payment or acceptance, that (1) the person obtaining payment or acceptance is entitled to enforce the instrument or is authorized to obtain payment or acceptance on behalf of a person who is entitled to enforce the instrument, (2) the instrument has not been altered, and (3) the person obtaining payment or acceptance has no knowledge that the signature of the drawer of the instrument is unauthorized.

Pretrial conference A conference, scheduled before the trial begins, between the judge and the attorneys litigating the suit. The parties may settle the dispute, clarify the issues, schedule discovery, and so on during the conference.

Pretrial motion A written or oral application to a court for a ruling or order, made before trial.

Price discrimination Setting prices in such a way that two competing buyers pay two different prices for an identical product or service.

Price-fixing agreement An agreement between competitors in which the competitors agree to fix the prices of products or services at a certain level; prohibited by the Sherman Act.

Prima facie **case** A case in which the plaintiff has produced sufficient evidence of his or her conclusion that the case can go to to a jury; a case in which the evidence compels the plaintiff's conclusion if the defendant produces no evidence to disprove it.

Primary liability In negotiable instruments law, absolute responsibility for paying a negotiable instrument. Makers and acceptors are primarily liable.

Principal In agency law, a person who agrees to have another, called the agent, act on his or her behalf.

Principle of rights The principle that human beings have certain fundamental rights (to life, freedom, and the pursuit of happiness, for example). Those who adhere to this "rights theory" believe that a key factor in determining whether a business decision is ethical is how that decision affects the rights of others. These others include the firm's owners, its employees, the consumers of its products or services, its suppliers, the community in which it does business, and society as a whole.

Privatization The replacement of government-provided products and services by private firms.

Privilege In tort law, the ability to act contrary to another person's right without that person's having legal redress for such acts. Privilege may be raised as a defense to defamation.

Privileges and immunities clause Special rights and exceptions provided by law. Article IV, Section 2, of the Constitution requires states not to discriminate against one another's citizens. A resident of one state cannot be treated as an alien when in another state; he or she may not be denied such privileges and immunities as legal protection, access to courts, travel rights, or property rights.

Privity of contract The relationship that exists between the promisor and the promisee of a contract.

Pro rata Proportionately; in proportion.

Probable cause Reasonable grounds to believe the existence of facts warranting certain actions, such as the search or arrest of a person.

Probate The process of proving and validating a will and the settling of all matters pertaining to administration, guardianship, and the like.

Probate court A state court of limited jurisdiction that conducts proceedings relating to the settlement of a deceased person's estate.

Procedural due process The requirement that any government decision to take life, liberty, or property must be made fairly. For example, fair procedures must be used in determining whether a person will be subjected to punishment or have some burden imposed on him or her.

Procedural law Rules that define the manner in which the rights and duties of individuals may be enforced.

Procedural unconscionability Occurs when, due to one contractual party's vastly superior bargaining power, the other party lacks a knowledge or understanding of the contract terms due to inconspicuous print or the lack of an opportunity to read the contract or to ask questions about its meaning. Procedural unconscionability often involves an *adhesion contract*, which is a contract drafted

by the dominant party and then presented to the other—the adhering party—on a take-it-or-leave-it basis.

Proceeds Under Article 9 of the Uniform Commercial Code, whatever is received when the collateral is sold or otherwise disposed of, such as by exchange.

Product liability The legal liability of manufacturers, sellers, and lessors of goods to consumers, users, and bystanders for injuries or damages that are caused by the goods.

Product misuse A defense against product liability that may be raised when the plaintiff used a product in a manner not intended by the manufacturer. If the misuse is reasonably foreseeable, the seller will not escape liability unless measures were taken to guard against the harm that could result from the misuse.

Professional corporation A corporation formed by professional persons, such as physicians, lawyers, dentists, and accountants, to gain tax benefits. Subject to certain exceptions (when a court may treat a professional corporation as a partnership for liability purposes), the shareholders of a professional corporation have the limited liability characteristic of the corporate form of business.

Profit In real property law, the right to enter onto and remove things from the property of another (for example, the right to enter onto a person's land and remove sand and gravel therefrom).

Promise A declaration that something either will or will not happen in the future.

Promisee A person to whom a promise is made.

Promisor A person who makes a promise.

Promissory estoppel A doctrine that applies when a promisor makes a clear and definite promise on which the promisee justifiably relies; such a promise is binding if justice will be better served by the enforcement of the promise. *See also* Estoppel

Promissory note A written promise made by one person (the maker) to pay a fixed sum of money to another person (the payee or a subsequent holder) on demand or on a specified date.

Promoter A person who takes the preliminary steps in organizing a corporation, including (usually) issuing a prospectus, procuring stock subscriptions, making contract purchases, securing a corporate charter, and the like.

Property Legally protected rights and interests in anything with an ascertainable value that is subject to ownership.

Prospectus A document required by federal or state securities laws that describes the financial operations of the corporation, thus allowing investors to make informed decisions.

Protected class A class of persons with identifiable characteristics who historically have been victimized by discriminatory treatment for certain purposes. Depending on the context, these characteristics include age, color, gender, national origin, race, and religion.

Proximate cause   Legal cause; exists when the connection between an act and an injury is strong enough to justify imposing liability.

Proxy   In corporation law, a written agreement between a stockholder and another under which the stockholder authorizes the other to vote the stockholder's shares in a certain manner.

Proxy fight   A conflict between an individual, group, or firm attempting to take control of a corporation and the corporation's management for the votes of the shareholders.

Public figures   Individuals who are thrust into the public limelight. Public figures include government officials and politicians, movie stars, well-known businesspersons, and generally anybody who becomes known to the public because of his or her position or activities.

Public policy   A government policy based on widely held societal values and (usually) expressed or implied in laws or regulations.

Public prosecutor   An individual, acting as a trial lawyer, who initiates and conducts criminal cases in the government's name and on behalf of the people.

Puffery   A salesperson's often exaggerated claims concerning the quality of property offered for sale. Such claims involve opinions rather than facts and are not considered to be legally binding promises or warranties.

Punitive damages   Money damages that may be awarded to a plaintiff to punish the defendant and deter future similar conduct.

Purchase-money security interest (PMSI)   A security interest that arises when a seller or lender extends credit for part or all of the purchase price of goods purchased by a buyer.

Q

Qualified indorsement   An indorsement on a negotiable instrument in which the indorser disclaims any contract liability on the instrument; the notation "without recourse" is commonly used to create a qualified indorsement.

Quantum meruit   (pronounced *kwahn*-tuhm *mehr*-oo-wuht)   Literally, "as much as he deserves"—an expression describing the extent of liability on a contract implied in law (quasi contract). An equitable doctrine based on the concept that one who benefits from another's labor and materials should not be unjustly enriched thereby but should be required to pay a reasonable amount for the benefits received, even absent a contract.

Quasi contract   A fictional contract imposed on parties by a court in the interests of fairness and justice; usually, quasi contracts are imposed to avoid the unjust enrichment of one party at the expense of another.

Question of fact   In a lawsuit, an issue involving a factual dispute that can only be decided by a judge (or, in a jury trial, a jury).

Question of law   In a lawsuit, an issue involving the application or interpretation of a law; therefore, the judge, and not the jury, decides the issue.

Quiet enjoyment.   *See* Covenant of quiet enjoyment

Quitclaim deed   A deed intended to pass any title, interest, or claim that the grantor may have in the property but not warranting that such title is valid. A quitclaim deed offers the least amount of protection against defects in the title.

Quorum   The number of members of a decision-making body that must be present before business may be transacted.

Quota   An assigned import limit on goods.

R

Ratification   The act of accepting and giving legal force to an obligation that previously was not enforceable.

Reaffirmation agreement   An agreement between a debtor and a creditor in which the debtor reaffirms, or promises to pay, a debt dischargeable in bankruptcy. To be enforceable, the agreement must be made prior to the discharge of the debt by the bankruptcy court.

Real defense   *See* Universal defense

Real property   Land and everything attached to it, such as foliage and buildings.

Reasonable care   The degree of care that a person of ordinary prudence would exercise in the same or similar circumstances.

Reasonable doubt   *See* Beyond a reasonable doubt

Reasonable person standard   The standard of behavior expected of a hypothetical "reasonable person." The standard against which negligence is measured and that must be observed to avoid liability for negligence.

Rebuttal   The refutation of evidence introduced by an adverse party's attorney.

Receiver   In a corporate dissolution, a court-appointed person who winds up corporate affairs and liquidates corporate assets.

Recording statutes   Statutes that allow deeds, mortgages, and other real property transactions to be recorded so as to provide notice to future purchasers or creditors of an existing claim on the property.

Red herring   A preliminary prospectus that can be distributed to potential investors after the registration statement (for a securities offering) has been filed with the Securities and Exchange Commission. The name derives from the red legend printed across the prospectus stating that the registration has been filed but has not become effective.

Redemption   A repurchase, or buying back. In secured transactions law, a debtor's repurchase of collateral securing a debt after a creditor has taken title to the collateral due to the debtor's default but before the secured party disposes of the collateral.

Reformation   A court-ordered correction of a written contract so that it reflects the true intentions of the parties.

Regulation E   A set of rules issued by the Federal Reserve System's board of governors under the authority of the Electronic Fund Transfer Act to protect users of electronic fund transfer systems.

Regulation Z A set of rules promulgated by the Federal Reserve Board to implement the provisions of the Truth-in-Lending Act.

Reimbursement *See* Right of reimbursement

Rejection In contract law, an offeree's express or implied manifestation not to accept an offer. In the law governing contracts for the sale of goods, a buyer's manifest refusal to accept goods on the ground that they do not conform to contract specifications.

Rejoinder The defendant's answer to the plaintiff's rebuttal.

Release A contract in which one party forfeits the right to pursue a legal claim against the other party.

Relevant evidence Evidence tending to make a fact at issue in the case more or less probable than it would be without the evidence. Only relevant evidence is admissible in court.

Remainder A future interest in property held by a person other than the original owner.

Remanded Sent back. If an appellate court disagrees with a lower court's judgment, the case may be remanded to the lower court for further proceedings in which the lower court's decision should be consistent with the appellate court's opinion on the matter.

Remedy The relief given to an innocent party to enforce a right or compensate for the violation of a right.

Remedy at law A remedy available in a court of law. Money damages are awarded as a remedy at law.

Remedy in equity A remedy allowed by courts in situations where remedies at law are not appropriate. Remedies in equity are based on settled rules of fairness, justice, and honesty, and include injunction, specific performance, rescission and restitution, and reformation.

Remitter A person who sends money, or remits payment.

Rent The consideration paid for the use or enjoyment of another's property. In landlord-tenant relationships, the payment made by the tenant to the landlord for the right to possess the premises.

Rent escalation clause A clause providing for an increase in rent during a lease term. .

Repair-and-deduct statutes Statutes providing that a tenant may pay for repairs and deduct the cost of the repairs from the rent, as a remedy for a landlord's failure to maintain leased premises.

Replevin (pronounced ruh-*pleh*-vin) An action to recover specific goods in the hands of a party who is wrongfully withholding them from the other party.

Reply Procedurally, a plaintiff's response to a defendant's answer.

Reporter A publication in which court cases are published, or reported.

Repudiation The renunciation of a right or duty; the act of a buyer or seller in rejecting a contract either partially or totally. *See also* Anticipatory repudiation

Requirements contract An agreement in which a buyer agrees to purchase and the seller agrees to sell all or up to a stated amount of what the buyer needs or requires.

Res ipsa loquitur (pronounced *rehs ehp*-suh *low*-quuh-duhr) A doctrine under which negligence may be inferred simply because an event occurred, if it is the type of event that would not occur in the absence of negligence. Literally, the term means "the facts speak for themselves."

Resale price maintenance agreement An agreement between a manufacturer and a retailer in which the manufacturer specifies the minimum retail price of its products. Resale price maintenance agreements are illegal *per se* under the Sherman Act.

Rescind (pronounced reh-*sihnd*) To cancel. *See also* Rescission

Rescission (pronounced reh-*sih*-zhen) A remedy whereby a contract is canceled and the parties are returned to the positions they occupied before the contract was made; may be effected through the mutual consent of the parties, by their conduct, or by court decree.

Residuary The surplus of a testator's estate remaining after all of the debts and particular legacies have been discharged.

Respondeat superior (pronounced ree-*spahn*-dee-uht soo-*peer*-ee-your) In Latin, "Let the master respond." A doctrine under which a principal or an employer is held liable for the wrongful acts committed by agents or employees while acting within the course and scope of their agency or employment.

Respondent In equity practice, the party who answers a bill or other proceeding.

Restitution An equitable remedy under which a person is restored to his or her original position prior to loss or injury, or placed in the position he or she would have been in had the breach not occurred.

Restraint on trade Any contract or combination that tends to eliminate or reduce competition, effect a monopoly, artificially maintain prices, or otherwise hamper the course of trade and commerce as it would be carried on if left to the control of natural economic forces.

Restrictive covenant A private restriction on the use of land that is binding on the party that purchases the property originally as well as on subsequent purchasers. If its benefit or obligation passes with the land's ownership, it is said to "run with the land."

Restrictive indorsement Any indorsement on a negotiable instrument that requires the indorsee to comply with certain instructions regarding the funds involved. A restrictive indorsement does not prohibit the further negotiation of the instrument.

Resulting trust An implied trust arising from the conduct of the parties. A trust in which a party holds the actual legal title to another's property but only for that person's benefit.

Retained earnings The portion of a corporation's profits that has not been paid out as dividends to shareholders.

Retaliatory eviction   The eviction of a tenant because of the tenant's complaints, participation in a tenant's union, or similar activity with which the landlord does not agree.

Reverse   To reject or overrule a court's judgment. An appellate court, for example, might reverse a lower court's judgment on an issue if it feels that the lower court committed an error during the trial or that the jury was improperly instructed.

Reverse discrimination   Discrimination against majority groups, such as white males, that results from affirmative action programs, in which preferences are given to minority members and women.

Reversible error   An error by a lower court that is sufficiently substantial to justify an appellate court's reversal of the lower court's decision.

Reversionary interest   A future interest in property retained by the original owner.

Revocation   In contract law, the withdrawal of an offer by an offeror. Unless an offer is irrevocable, it can be revoked at any time prior to acceptance without liability.

Right of contribution   The right of a co-surety who pays more than his or her proportionate share on a debtor's default to recover the excess paid from other co-sureties.

Right of entry   The right to peaceably take or resume possession of real property.

Right of first refusal   The right to purchase personal or real property—such as corporate shares or real estate—before the property is offered for sale to others.

Right of redemption   *See* Equity of redemption; Redemption

Right of reimbursement   The legal right of a person to be restored, repaid, or indemnified for costs, expenses, or losses incurred or expended on behalf of another.

Right of subrogation   The right of a person to stand in the place of (be substituted for) another, giving the substituted party the same legal rights that the original party had.

Right-to-work law   A state law providing that employees are not to be required to join a union as a condition of obtaining or retaining employment.

Risk   A prediction concerning potential loss based on known and unknown factors.

Risk management   Planning that is undertaken to protect one's interest should some event threaten to undermine its security. In the context of insurance, risk management involves transferring certain risks from the insured to the insurance company.

Robbery   The act of forcefully and unlawfully taking personal property of any value from another; force or intimidation is usually necessary for an act of theft to be considered a robbery.

Rule of four   A rule of the United States Supreme Court under which the Court will not issue a writ of *certiorari* unless at least four justices approve of the decision to issue the writ.

Rule of reason   A test by which a court balances the positive effects (such as economic efficiency) of an agreement against its potentially anticompetitive effects.

In antitrust litigation, many practices are analyzed under the rule of reason.

Rule 10b-5   *See* SEC Rule 10b-5

Rulemaking   The process undertaken by an administrative agency when formally adopting a new regulation or amending an old one. Rulemaking involves notifying the public of a proposed rule or change and receiving and considering the public's comments.

Rules of evidence   Rules governing the admissibility of evidence in trial courts.

S

S corporation   A close business corporation that has met certain requirements as set out by the Internal Revenue Code and thus qualifies for special income tax treatment. Essentially, an S corporation is taxed the same as a partnership, but its owners enjoy the privilege of limited liability.

Sale   The passing of title from the seller to the buyer for a price.

Sale on approval   A type of conditional sale in which the buyer may take the goods on a trial basis. The sale becomes absolute only when the buyer approves of (or is satisfied with) the goods being sold.

Sale or return   A type of conditional sale in which title and possession pass from the seller to the buyer; however, the buyer retains the option to return the goods during a specified period even though the goods conform to the contract.

Sales contract   A contract for the sale of goods under which the ownership of goods is transferred from a seller to a buyer for a price.

Satisfaction   *See* Accord and satisfaction

Scienter   (pronounced *sy-en-*ter)   Knowledge by the misrepresenting party that material facts have been falsely represented or omitted with an intent to deceive.

Search warrant   An order granted by a public authority, such as a judge, that authorizes law enforcement personnel to search particular premises or property.

Seasonably   Within a specified time period, or, if no period is specified, within a reasonable time.

SEC Rule 10b-5   A rule of the Securities and Exchange Commission that makes it unlawful, in connection with the purchase or sale of any security, to make any untrue statement of a material fact or to omit a material fact if such omission causes the statement to be misleading.

Secondary boycott   A union's refusal to work for, purchase from, or handle the products of a secondary employer, with whom the union has no dispute, for the purpose of forcing that employer to stop doing business with the primary employer, with whom the union has a labor dispute.

Secondary liability   In negotiable instruments law, the contingent liability of drawers and indorsers. A secondarily liable party becomes liable on an instrument only if the party that is primarily liable on the instrument dishonors it or, in regard to drafts and checks, the drawee fails to pay or to accept the instrument, whichever is required.

Secured party   A lender, seller, or any other person in whose favor there is a security interest, including a person to whom accounts or chattel paper has been sold.

Secured transaction   Any transaction in which the payment of a debt is guaranteed, or secured, by personal property owned by the debtor or in which the debtor has a legal interest.

Securities   Generally, corporate stocks and bonds. A security may also be a note, debenture, stock warrant, or any document given as evidence of an ownership interest in a corporation or as a promise of repayment by a corporation.

Security agreement   An agreement that creates or provides for a security interest between the debtor and a secured party.

Security interest   Any interest "in personal property or fixtures which secures payment or performance of an obligation" [UCC 1–201(37)].

Self-defense   The legally recognized privilege to protect one's self or property against injury by another. The privilege of self-defense protects only acts that are reasonably necessary to protect one's self or property.

Seniority system   In regard to employment relationships, a system in which those who have worked longest for the company are first in line for promotions, salary increases, and other benefits; they are also the last to be laid off if the work force must be reduced.

Service mark   A mark used in the sale or the advertising of services, such as to distinguish the services of one person from the services of others. Titles, character names, and other distinctive features of radio and television programs may be registered as service marks.

Service of process   The delivery of the complaint and summons to a defendant.

Settlor   One creating a trust.

Sexual harassment   In the employment context, the granting of job promotions or other benefits in return for sexual favors or language or conduct that is so sexually offensive that it creates a hostile working environment.

Sham transaction   A false transaction without substance that is undertaken with the intent to defraud a creditor or the government. An example of a sham transaction is the sale of assets to a friend or relative for the purpose of concealing assets from creditors or a bankruptcy court.

Share   A unit of stock. *See also* Stock

Shareholder   One who purchases shares of a corporation's stock, thus acquiring an equity interest in the corporation.

Shareholder's derivative suit   A suit brought by a shareholder to enforce a corporate cause of action against a third person.

Sharia   Civil law principles of some Middle Eastern countries that are based on the Islamic directives that follow the teachings of the prophet Mohammed.

Shelter principle   The principle that the holder of a negotiable instrument who cannot qualify as a holder in due course (HDC), but who derives his or her title through an HDC, acquires the rights of an HDC.

Sheriff's deed   The deed given to the purchaser of property at a sheriff's sale as part of the foreclosure process against the owner of the property.

Shipment contract   A contract for the sale of goods in which the seller is required or authorized to ship the goods by carrier. The buyer assumes liability for any losses or damage to the goods after they are delivered to the carrier.

Short-form merger   A merger between a subsidiary corporation and a parent corporation that owns at least 90 percent of the outstanding shares of each class of stock issued by the subsidiary corporation. Short-form mergers can be accomplished without the approval of the shareholders of either corporation.

Short-swing profits   Profits made by officers, directors, and certain large stockholders resulting from the use of nonpublic (inside) information about their companies; prohibited by Section 12 of the 1934 Securities Exchange Act.

Sight draft   In negotiable instruments law, a draft payable on sight—that is, when it is presented for payment.

Signature   Under the Uniform Commercial Code, "any symbol executed or adopted by a party with a present intention to authenticate a writing."

Slander   Defamation in oral form.

Slander of quality (trade libel)   The publication of false information about another's product, alleging that it is not what its seller claims.

Slander of title   The publication of a statement that denies or casts doubt on another's legal ownership of any property, causing financial loss to that property's owner.

Small claims courts   Special courts in which parties may litigate small claims (usually, claims involving $2,500 or less). Attorneys are not required in small claims courts, and in many states attorneys are not allowed to represent the parties.

Smart card   Prepaid funds recorded on a microprocessor chip embedded on a card. One type of *e-money*.

Sociological school   A school of legal thought that views the law as a tool for promoting justice in society.

Sole proprietorship   The simplest form of business, in which the owner is the business; the owner reports business income on his or her personal income tax return and is legally responsible for all debts and obligations incurred by the business.

Sovereign immunity   A doctrine that immunizes foreign nations from the jurisdiction of U.S. courts when certain conditions are satisfied.

Spam   Bulk, unsolicited ("junk") e-mail.

Special indorsement   An indorsement on an instrument that indicates the specific person to whom the indorser intends to make the instrument payable; that is, it names the indorsee.

Special warranty deed   A deed in which the grantor only covenants to warrant and defend the title against claims and demands of the grantor and all persons claiming by, through, and under the grantor.

Specific performance An equitable remedy requiring exactly the performance that was specified in a contract; usually granted only when money damages would be an inadequate remedy and the subject matter of the contract is unique (for example, real property).

Spendthrift trust A trust created to prevent the beneficiary from spending all the money to which he or she is entitled. Only a certain portion of the total amount is given to the beneficiary at any one time, and most states prohibit creditors from attaching assets of the trust.

Spot zoning Granting a zoning classification to a parcel of land that is different from the classification given to other land in the immediate area.

Stale check A check, other than a certified check, that is presented for payment more than six months after its date.

Standing to sue The requirement that an individual must have a sufficient stake in a controversy before he or she can bring a lawsuit. The plaintiff must demonstrate that he or she either has been injured or threatened with injury.

Stare decisis (pronounced *ster*-ay dih-*si*-ses) A common law doctrine under which judges are obligated to follow the precedents established in prior decisions.

Statute of Frauds A state statute under which certain types of contracts must be in writing to be enforceable.

Statute of limitations A federal or state statute setting the maximum time period during which a certain action can be brought or certain rights enforced.

Statute of repose Basically, a statute of limitations that is not dependent on the happening of a cause of action. Statutes of repose generally begin to run at an earlier date and run for a longer period of time than statutes of limitations.

Statutory law The body of law enacted by legislative bodies (as opposed to constitutional law, administrative law, or case law).

Statutory lien A lien created by statute.

Statutory period of redemption A time period (usually set by state statute) during which the property subject to a defaulted mortgage, land contract, or other contract can be redeemed by the debtor after foreclosure or judicial sale.

Stock An equity (ownership) interest in a corporation, measured in units of shares.

Stock certificate A certificate issued by a corporation evidencing the ownership of a specified number of shares in the corporation.

Stock option *See* Stock warrant

Stock warrant A certificate that grants the owner the option to buy a given number of shares of stock, usually within a set time period.

Stockholder *See* Shareholder

Stop-payment order An order by a bank customer to his or her bank not to pay or certify a certain check.

Strict liability Liability regardless of fault. In tort law, strict liability may be imposed on defendants in cases involving abnormally dangerous activities, dangerous animals, or defective products.

Strike An extreme action undertaken by unionized workers when collective bargaining fails; the workers leave their jobs, refuse to work, and (typically) picket the employer's workplace.

Subject-matter jurisdiction Jurisdiction over the subject matter of a lawsuit.

Sublease A lease executed by the lessee of real estate to a third person, conveying the same interest that the lessee enjoys but for a shorter term than that held by the lessee.

Subpoena A document commanding a person to appear at a certain time and place or give testimony concerning a certain matter.

Subrogation *See* Right of subrogation

Subscriber An investor who agrees, in a subscription agreement, to purchase capital stock in a corporation.

Substantial evidence test The test applied by a court reviewing an administrative agency's informal action. The court determines whether the agency acted unreasonably and overturns the agency's findings only if unsupported by a substantial body of evidence.

Substantial performance Performance that does not vary greatly from the performance promised in a contract; the performance must create substantially the same benefits as those promised in the contract.

Substantive due process A requirement that focuses on the content, or substance, of legislation. If a law or other governmental action limits a fundamental right, such as the right to travel or to vote, it will be held to violate substantive due process unless it promotes a compelling or overriding state interest.

Substantive law Law that defines the rights and duties of individuals with respect to each other, as opposed to procedural law, which defines the manner in which these rights and duties may be enforced.

Substantive unconscionability Results from contracts, or portions of contracts, that are oppressive or overly harsh. Courts generally focus on provisions that deprive one party of the benefits of the agreement or leave that party without remedy for nonperformance by the other. An example of substantive unconscionability is the agreement by a welfare recipient with a fourth-grade education to purchase a refrigerator for $2,000 under an installment contract.

Suit *See* Lawsuit; Litigation

Summary judgment *See* Motion for summary judgment

Summary jury trial (SJT) A method of settling disputes in which a trial is held, but the jury's verdict is not binding. The verdict acts only as a guide to both sides in reaching an agreement during the mandatory negotiations that immediately follow the summary jury trial.

Summons A document informing a defendant that a legal action has been commenced against him or her and that the defendant must appear in court on a certain date to answer the plaintiff's complaint. The document is delivered by a sheriff or any other person so authorized.

Superseding cause An intervening force or event that breaks the connection between a wrongful act and an injury to another; in negligence law, a defense to liability.

Supremacy clause The provision in Article VI of the Constitution that provides that the Constitution, laws, and treaties of the United States are "the supreme Law of the Land." Under this clause, state and local laws that directly conflict with federal law will be rendered invalid.

Surety A person, such as a cosigner on a note, who agrees to be primarily responsible for the debt of another.

Suretyship An express contract in which a third party to a debtor-creditor relationship (the surety) promises to be primarily responsible for the debtor's obligation.

Surviving corporation The remaining, or continuing, corporation following a merger. The surviving corporation is vested with the merged corporation's legal rights and obligations.

Syllogism A form of deductive reasoning consisting of a major premise, a minor premise, and a conclusion.

Symbolic speech Nonverbal conduct that expresses opinions or thoughts about a subject. Symbolic speech is protected under the First Amendment's guarantee of freedom of speech.

Syndicate An investment group of persons or firms brought together for the purpose of financing a project that they would not or could not undertake independently.

T

Tag A key word in a document that can serve as an index reference to the document. On the Web, search engines return results based, in part, on the tags in Web documents.

Takeover The acquisition of control over a corporation through the purchase of a substantial number of the voting shares of the corporation.

Taking The taking of private property by the government for public use. Under the Fifth Amendment to the Constitution, the government may not take private property for public use without "just compensation."

Tangible property Property that has physical existence and can be distinguished by the senses of touch, sight, and so on. A car is tangible property; a patent right is intangible property.

Target corporation The corporation to be acquired in a corporate takeover; a corporation to whose shareholders a tender offer is submitted.

Tariff An tax on imported goods.

Technology licensing Allowing another to use and profit from intellectual property (patents, copyrights, trademarks, innovative products or processes, and so on) for consideration. In the context of international business transactions, technology licensing is sometimes an attractive alternative to the establishment of foreign production facilities.

Teller's check A negotiable instrument drawn by a bank on another bank or drawn by a bank and payable at or payable through a bank.

Tenancy at sufferance A type of tenancy under which one who, after rightfully being in possession of leased premises, continues (wrongfully) to occupy the property after the lease has been terminated. The tenant has no rights to possess the property and occupies it only because the person entitled to evict the tenant has not done so.

Tenancy at will A type of tenancy under which either party can terminate the tenancy without notice; usually arises when a tenant who has been under a tenancy for years retains possession, with the landlord's consent, after the tenancy for years has terminated.

Tenancy by the entirety The joint ownership of property by a husband and wife. Neither party can transfer his or her interest in the property without the consent of the other.

Tenancy for years A type of tenancy under which property is leased for a specified period of time, such as a month, a year, or a period of years.

Tenancy in common Co-ownership of property in which each party owns an undivided interest that passes to his or her heirs at death.

Tenancy in partnership Co-ownership of partnership property.

Tenant One who has the temporary use and occupation of real property owned by another person, called the landlord; the duration and terms of the tenancy are usually established by a lease.

Tender An unconditional offer to perform an obligation by a person who is ready, willing, and able to do so.

Tender of delivery Under the Uniform Commercial Code, a seller's or lessor's act of placing conforming goods at the disposal of the buyer or lessee and giving the buyer or lessee whatever notification is reasonably necessary to enable the buyer or lessee to take delivery.

Tender offer An offer to purchase made by one company directly to the shareholders of another (target) company; often referred to as a "takeover bid."

Term insurance A type of life insurance policy for which premiums are paid for a specified term. Payment on the policy is due only if death occurs within the term period. Premiums are less expensive than for whole life or limited-payment life, and there is usually no cash surrender value.

Testamentary trust A trust that is created by will and therefore does not take effect until the death of the testator.

Testate The condition of having died with a valid will.

Testator One who makes and executes a will.

Third party beneficiary One for whose benefit a promise is made in a contract but who is not a party to the contract.

Time draft A draft that is payable at a definite future time.

Tippee A person who receives inside information.

Title insurance Insurance commonly purchased by a purchaser of real property to protect against loss in the event that the title to the property is not free from liens or superior ownership claims.

Tombstone ad   An advertisement, historically in a format resembling a tombstone, of a securities offering. The ad informs potential investors of where and how they may obtain a prospectus.

Tort   A civil wrong not arising from a breach of contract. A breach of a legal duty that proximately causes harm or injury to another.

Tortfeasor   One who commits a tort.

Totten trust   A trust created by the deposit of a person's own money in his or her own name as a trustee for another. It is a tentative trust, revocable at will until the depositor dies or completes the gift in his or her lifetime by some unequivocal act or declaration.

Toxic tort   Failure to use or to clean up properly toxic chemicals that cause harm to a person or society.

Trade acceptance   A draft that is drawn by a seller of goods ordering the buyer to pay a specified sum of money to the seller, usually at a stated time in the future. The buyer accepts the draft by signing the face of the draft, thus creating an enforceable obligation to pay the draft when it comes due. On a trade acceptance, the seller is both the drawer and the payee.

Trade dress   The image and overall appearance of a product—for example, the distinctive decor, menu, layout, and style of service of a particular restaurant. Basically, trade dress is subject to the same protection as trademarks.

Trade fixture   The personal property of a commercial tenant that has been installed or affixed to real property for a business purpose. When the lease ends, the tenant can remove the fixture but must repair any damage to the real property caused by the fixture's removal.

Trade libel   The publication of false information about another's product, alleging it is not what its seller claims; also referred to as slander of quality.

Trade name   A term that is used to indicate part or all of a business's name and that is directly related to the business's reputation and goodwill. Trade names are protected under the common law (and under trademark law, if the name is the same as the firm's trademarked property).

Trade secret   Information or a process that gives a business an advantage over competitors who do not know the information or process.

Trademark   A distinctive mark, motto, device, or implement that a manufacturer stamps, prints, or otherwise affixes to the goods it produces so that they may be identified on the market and their origins made known. Once a trademark is established (under the common law or through registration), the owner is entitled to its exclusive use.

Transfer warranties   Implied warranties, made by any person who transfers an instrument for consideration to subsequent transferees and holders who take the instrument in good faith, that (1) the transferor is entitled to enforce the instrument, (2) all signatures are authentic and authorized, (3) the instrument has not been altered,

(4) the instrument is not subject to a defense or claim of any party that can be asserted against the transferor, and (5) the transferor has no knowledge of any insolvency proceedings against the maker, the acceptor, or the drawer of the instrument.

Transferee   In negotiable instruments law, one to whom a negotiable instrument is transferred (delivered).

Transferor   In negotiable instruments law, one who transfers (delivers) a negotiable instrument to another.

Traveler's check   A check that is payable on demand, drawn on or payable through a bank, and designated as a traveler's check.

Treasure trove   Money or coin, gold, silver, or bullion found hidden in the earth or other private place, the owner of which is unknown; literally, treasure found.

Treasury shares   Corporate shares that are authorized by the corporation but that have not been issued.

Treaty   An agreement formed between two or more independent nations.

Treble damages   Damages consisting of single damages determined by a jury and tripled in amount in certain cases as required by statute.

Trespass to land   The entry onto, above, or below the surface of land owned by another without the owner's permission or legal authorization.

Trespass to personal property   The unlawful taking or harming of another's personal property; interference with another's right to the exclusive possession of his or her personal property.

Trespasser   One who commits the tort of trespass in one of its forms.

Trial court   A court in which trials are held and testimony taken.

Trust   An arrangement in which title to property is held by one person (a trustee) for the benefit of another (a beneficiary).

Trust indorsement   An indorsement for the benefit of the indorser or a third person; also known as an agency indorsement. The indorsement results in legal title vesting in the original indorsee.

Trustee   One who holds title to property for the use or benefit of another (the beneficiary).

Tying arrangement   An agreement between a buyer and a seller in which the buyer of a specific product or service becomes obligated to purchase additional products or services from the seller.

U

U.S. trustee   A government official who performs certain administrative tasks that a bankruptcy judge would otherwise have to perform.

Ultra vires (pronounced *uhl*-trah *vye*-reez)   A Latin term meaning "beyond the powers"; in corporate law, acts of a corporation that are beyond its express and implied powers to undertake.

Unanimous opinion A court opinion in which all of the judges or justices of the court agree to the court's decision.

Unconscionable (pronounced un-*kon*-shun-uh-bul) **contract or clause** A contract or clause that is void on the basis of public policy because one party, as a result of his or her disproportionate bargaining power, is forced to accept terms that are unfairly burdensome and that unfairly benefit the dominating party. *See also* Procedural unconscionability; Substantive unconscionability

Underwriter In insurance law, the insurer, or the one assuming a risk in return for the payment of a premium.

Undisclosed principal A principal whose identity is unknown by a third person, and the third person has no knowledge that the agent is acting for a principal at the time the agent and the third person form a contract.

Unenforceable contract A valid contract rendered unenforceable by some statute or law.

Uniform law A model law created by the National Conference of Commissioners (NCC) on Uniform State Laws and/or the American Law Institute for the states to consider adopting. If the state adopts the law, it becomes statutory law in that state. Each state has the option of adopting or rejecting all or part of a uniform law.

Unilateral contract A contract that results when an offer can only be accepted by the offeree's performance.

Union shop A place of employment in which all workers, once employed, must become union members within a specified period of time as a condition of their continued employment.

Unitary system A centralized governmental system in which local or subdivisional governments exercise only those powers given to them by the central government.

Universal defense A defense that is valid against all holders of a negotiable instrument, including holders in due course (HDCs) and holders with the rights of HDCs. Universal defenses are also called real defenses.

Universal life A type of insurance that combines some aspects of term insurance with some aspects of whole life insurance.

Unlawful detainer The unjustifiable retention of the possession of real property by one whose right to possession has terminated—as when a tenant holds over after the end of the lease term in spite of the landlord's demand for possession.

Unliquidated debt A debt that is uncertain in amount.

Unreasonably dangerous product In product liability, a product that is defective to the point of threatening a consumer's health and safety. A product will be considered unreasonably dangerous if it is dangerous beyond the expectation of the ordinary consumer or if a less dangerous alternative was economically feasible for the manufacturer, but the manufacturer failed to produce it.

Usage of trade Any practice or method of dealing having such regularity of observance in a place, vocation, or trade as to justify an expectation that it will be observed with respect to the transaction in question.

Usurpation In corporation law, the taking advantage of a corporate opportunity by a corporate officer or director for his or her personal gain and in violation of his or her fiduciary duties.

Usury Charging an illegal rate of interest.

Utilitarianism An approach to ethical reasoning in which ethically correct behavior is not related to any absolute ethical or moral values but to an evaluation of the consequences of a given action on those who will be affected by it. In utilitarian reasoning, a "good" decision is one that results in the greatest good for the greatest number of people affected by the decision.

V

Valid contract A contract that results when elements necessary for contract formation (agreement, consideration, legal purpose, and contractual capacity) are present.

Validation notice An initial notice to a debtor from a collection agency informing the debtor that he or she has thirty days to challenge the debt and request verification.

Vendee One who purchases property from another, called the vendor.

Vendor One who sells property to another, called the vendee.

Venture capital Funds that are invested in, or that are available for investment in, a new corporate enterprise.

Venture capitalist A person or entity that seeks out promising entrepreneurial ventures and funds them in exchange for equity stakes.

Venue (pronounced *ven*-yoo) The geographical district in which an action is tried and from which the jury is selected.

Verdict A formal decision made by a jury.

Vertical merger The acquisition by a company at one stage of production of a company at a higher or lower stage of production (such as a company merging with one of its suppliers or retailers).

Vertical restraint Any restraint on trade created by agreements between firms at different levels in the manufacturing and distribution process.

Vertically integrated firm A firm that carries out two or more functional phases (manufacture, distribution, retailing, and so on) of a product.

Vesting The creation of an absolute or unconditional right or power.

Vicarious liability Legal responsibility placed on one person for the acts of another.

Virtual courtroom A courtroom that is conceptual and not physical. In the context of cyberspace, a virtual courtroom could be a location on the Internet at which judicial proceedings take place.

Virtual property Property that, in the context of cyberspace, is conceptual, as opposed to physical. Intellectual property that exists on the Internet is virtual property.

Void contract A contract having no legal force or binding effect.

Voidable contract A contract that may be legally avoided (canceled, or annulled) at the option of one of the parties.

Voidable preference   In bankruptcy law, a preference that may be avoided, or set aside, by the trustee.

Voir dire (pronounced *vwahr deehr*)   A French phrase meaning, literally, "to see, to speak." In jury trials, the phrase refers to the process in which the attorneys question prospective jurors to determine whether they are biased or have any connection with a party to the action or with a prospective witness.

Voting trust   An agreement (trust contract) under which legal title to shares of corporate stock is transferred to a trustee who is authorized by the shareholders to vote the shares on their behalf.

W

Waiver   An intentional, knowing relinquishment of a legal right.

Warehouse receipt   A document of title issued by a bailee-warehouser to cover the goods stored in the warehouse.

Warehouser   One in the business of operating a warehouse.

Warranty   A promise that certain facts are truly as they are represented to be.

Warranty deed   A deed in which the grantor guarantees to the grantee that the grantor has title to the property conveyed in the deed, that there are no encumbrances on the property other than what the grantor has represented, and that the grantee will enjoy quiet possession of the property; a deed that provides the greatest amount of protection for the grantee.

Warranty disclaimer   A seller's or lessor's negation or qualification of a warranty.

Warranty of fitness   *See* Implied warranty of fitness for a particular purpose

Warranty of merchantability   *See* Implied warranty of merchantability

Warranty of title   An implied warranty made by a seller that the seller has good and valid title to the goods sold and that the transfer of the title is rightful.

Waste   The abuse or destructive use of real property by one who is in rightful possession of the property but who does not have title to it. Waste does not include ordinary depreciation due to age and normal use.

Watered stock   Shares of stock issued by a corporation for which the corporation receives, as payment, less than the stated value of the shares.

Wetlands   Areas of land designated by government agencies (such as the Army Corps of Engineers or the Environmental Protection Agency) as protected areas that support wildlife and that therefore cannot be filled in or dredged by private contractors or parties.

Whistleblowing   An employee's disclosure to government, the press, or upper-management authorities that the employer is engaged in unsafe or illegal activities.

White-collar crime   Nonviolent crime committed by individuals or corporations to obtain a personal or business advantage.

Whole life   A life insurance policy in which the insured pays a level premium for his or her entire life and in which there is a constantly accumulating cash value that can be withdrawn or borrowed against by the borrower. Sometimes referred to as straight life insurance.

Will   An instrument directing what is to be done with the testator's property on his or her death, made by the testator and revocable during his or her lifetime. No interests in the testator's property pass until the testator dies.

Willful   Intentional.

Winding up   The second of two stages involved in the termination of a partnership or corporation. Once the firm is dissolved, it continues to exist legally until the process of winding up all business affairs (collecting and distributing the firm's assets) is complete.

Workers' compensation laws   State statutes establishing an administrative procedure for compensating workers' injuries that arise out of—or in the course of—their employment, regardless of fault.

Working papers   The various documents used and developed by an accountant during an audit. Working papers include notes, computations, memoranda, copies, and other papers that make up the work product of an accountant's services to a client.

Workout   An out-of-court agreement between a debtor and his or her creditors in which the parties work out a payment plan or schedule under which the debtor's debts can be discharged.

Writ of attachment   A court's order, prior to a trial to collect a debt, directing the sheriff or other officer to seize nonexempt property of the debtor; if the creditor prevails at trial, the seized property can be sold to satisfy the judgment.

Writ of *certiorari* (pronounced sur-shee-uh-*rah*-ree)   A writ from a higher court asking the lower court for the record of a case.

Writ of execution   A court's order, after a judgment has been entered against the debtor, directing the sheriff to seize (levy) and sell any of the debtor's nonexempt real or personal property. The proceeds of the sale are used to pay off the judgment, accrued interest, and costs of the sale; any surplus is paid to the debtor.

Wrongful discharge   An employer's termination of an employee's employment in violation of an employment contract or laws that protect employees.

Z

Zoning   The division of a city by legislative regulation into districts and the application in each district of regulations having to do with structural and architectural designs of buildings and prescribing the use to which buildings within designated districts may be put.

Table of Cases

X

Y

Z

Index

settlement, 300
shareholder, 1017–1019
stock-subscription, 646, 674
surrender by, 919
tie-in sales, 851–852
Agricultural associations, exemption of, from antitrust laws, 855
Ahalt, Arthur, 50
AIDS (acquired immune deficiency syndrome)
as disability, 772, 787
failure to disclose, on insurance application, 1030
reasonable accommodations and, 790
testing for, 772
Air pollution, 831–833
Air rights, 888–889
Aktiengesellschaft (A.G.), 993
Alcohol. *See also* Drug(s)
intoxication and, 154, 242–243, 800. *See also* Intoxication
use of
age for, 240n
employees and, 790
Islamic law and, 1004
ALI (American Law Institute), 10, 11, 17, 115–116, 144n, 198n
Alien corporation, 641
Alienation, restraints against, 285
ALJ (administrative law judge), 812–814
Allegation, 7
Allocation
of risk, 932
between trust principal and income, 965
Allstate Insurance Co., 1030–1031
Alteration(s)
of checks, 482–484
of contract, 301
defined, 909–910
material, 464
of premises, 909–910
Alternative dispute resolution (ADR), 35, 37–43. *See also* Arbitration; Mediation
defined, 35
online, 38–39
Amendment(s)
of Articles of Confederation, 68
defined, 68
of financing statement, 520
to United States Constitution. *See* Bill of Rights; *individual amendments*
America Online (AOL), 850

American Arbitration Association (AAA), 38, 39, 42, 997
American Bar Association (ABA), 152, 952
Model Rules of, of Professional Conduct, 974
Standing Committee of, on Ethics and Professional Responsibility, 982–983
American Digest System (West), 19
American Federation of Labor and Congress of Industrial Organizations (AFL-CIO), 763
American Institute of Certified Public Accountants, 716n
American International Group, 937
American Jurisprudence, Second Edition (West), 19
American law, sources of, 9–12
American Law Institute (ALI), 10, 11, 17, 115–116, 144n, 198n
American Management Association, 770
American Venture Capital Exchange, 1018
Americans with Disabilities Act (ADA)(1990), 772, 779, 787–790, 800, 808
Amex Life Assurance Company, 1030
AMTRAK, 641
Analogy, reasoning by, 8
Analysis, cost-benefit, 742, 746n
ANCOM (Andean Common Market), 990
Andean Common Market (ANCOM), 990
Animals, dangerous, 111
Antares Aircraft, L.P., 1032–1033
Antecedent claim, 443
Anticipatory breach, 299, 378–380
Antidumping duty, 995
Antilapse clauses, 939
Antitrust law(s), 841–859, 862. *See also* Clayton Act; Sherman Antitrust Act
customer restrictions and, 846–847
defined, 841
enforcement of, 805n, 853–854
ethics and, 863–864
exclusionary practices and, 851–852
exclusive-dealing contracts and, 851
exemptions from, 854–855
in global context, 854
group boycotts and, 843–845
horizontal market division and, 845

interlocking directorates and, 853
market concentration and, 852
mergers and, 852–853
monopolization and, 848–849
per se violations of, 843, 845, 846, 847–848, 852, 854
predatory pricing and, 848, 864
price discrimination and, 851
price-fixing agreements and, 843
refusals to deal and, 848
resale price maintenance agreements and, 847–848
rule of reason and, 842–843
territorial restrictions and, 846–847
trade associations and, 845
trade restraints and. *See* Restraint(s) on trade
tying arrangements and, 851–852
vertically integrated firms and, 846
AOL (America Online), 850
APA (Administrative Procedure Act)(1946), 808, 813, 814, 815
Apparent authority, 587, 589, 591, 601, 603
Appeal(s)
filing of, 63
notice of, 63
record on, 63
Appellant, 19, 63
Appellate courts
appellate review and, 63
decisions of, 6, 14, 16–17, 19–20
defined, 13
federal. *See* Federal court system, appellate courts of
higher, 63–64
judicial review and, 27, 69n
opinions of, 13, 19–20
state. *See* State court system(s), appellate courts of
Appellate jurisdiction, 29
Appellate review, 63
Appellee, 19, 63
Apple Computer, 993, 1014
Application
for insurance, 936, 942, 1030, 1031
for job, 789
for trademark, form for, illustrated, 1015
Applied Analytical Industries, Inc., 801
Appraisal clauses, 938
Appraisal rights, 680–681
Appropriation, 91
Approval, sale on, 363–364
Arbitration
automobile lemon laws and, 394

General Legal Resources

ABA Section on Business Law	http://www.abanet.org/buslaw/home.html
Academy of Legal Studies in Business	http://www.alsb.org/
Counsel Quest	http://www.CounselQuest.com/
Court TV Online	http://www.courttv.com/
FindLaw	http://www.findlaw.com/
Hieros Gamos	http://www.hg.org/
Law News Network	http://www.lawnewsnetwork.com/
Legal Information Institute (LII)	http://www.law.cornell.edu/

Legal Terms

Everybody's Law Dictionary (Nolo Press)	http://www.nolo.com/dictionary/wordindex.cfm

Court Cases

Bankruptcy Court Opinions (FindLaw)	http://www.findlaw.com/casecode/bankruptcy.html
Federal Circuit Court Opinions (FindLaw)	http://www.findlaw.com/casecode/courts/index.html
Federal District Court Opinions (FindLaw)	http://www.findlaw.com/casecode/district.html
State Court Opinions (FindLaw)	http://www.findlaw.com/casecode/state.html
Supreme Court Cases (1893-Present) (FindLaw)	http://www.findlaw.com/casecode/supreme.html
Supreme Court Cases (1937-1975) (Fedworld)	http://www.fedworld.gov/supcourt/index.htm
Supreme Court Cases (1990-Present) (LII)	http://supct.law.cornell.edu/supct/
The Oyez Project Audio recordings of key Supreme Court cases (Northwestern University)	http://oyez.nwu.edu/
West's Case Updates	http://www.westbuslaw.com/topic_index.html

Acts, Codes, Treaties, and the Constitution

Code of Federal Regulations (LII)	http://www4.law.cornell.edu/cfr/
GATT (The Trading Floor)	http://trading.wmw.com/gatt/
NAFTA (Wiretap)	gopher://wiretap.spies.com/11/Gov/NAFTA
Securities Acts (University of Cincinnati)	http://www.law.uc.edu/CCL/sldtoc.html
State Codes (FindLaw)	http://www.findlaw.com/casecode/state.html
U.S. Code (LII)	http://www4.law.cornell.edu/uscode/
U.S. Constitution (USConstitution.net)	http://www.usconstitution.net/
Uniform Commercial Code (LII)	http://www.law.cornell.edu/ucc/ucc.table.html

Alternate Dispute Resolution

ABA Section on Dispute Resolution	http://www.abanet.org/dispute/home.html
American Arbitration Association	http://www.adr.org/
Guide to ADR (Hieros Gamos)	http://hg.org/adr.html

Ethics

Institute for Global Ethics	http://www.globalethics.org/
Institute for Business and Professional Ethics (DePaul University)	http://condor.depaul.edu/ethics/
Legalethics.com	http://www.legalethics.com/